1933 — Inez Beverly Prosser becomes the first African-American woman to receive a doctoral degree in psychology from a U.S. institution (Ph.D., University of Cincinnati).

1935 — Christiana Morgan and Henry Murray introduce the Thematic Apperception Test to elicit fantasies from people undergoing psychoanalysis.

1936 — Egas Moniz, Portuguese physician, publishes work on the first frontal lobotomies performed on humans.

1938 — B. F. Skinner publishes *The Behavior of Organisms*, which describes operant conditioning of animals.

— In *Primary Mental Abilities*, Louis L. Thurstone proposes seven such abilities.

— Ugo Cerletti and Lucino Bini use electroshock treatment with a human patient.

1939 — David Wechsler publishes the Wechsler-Bellevue intelligence test, forerunner of the Wechsler Intelligence Scale for Children (WISC) and the Wechsler Adult Intelligence Scale (WAIS).

— Mamie Phipps Clark (pictured) receives a master's degree from Howard University. In collaboration with Kenneth B. Clark, she later extends her thesis, "The Development of Consciousness of Self in Negro Preschool Children," providing joint research cited in the U.S. Supreme Court's **1954** decision to end racial segregation in public schools.

— Edward Alexander Bott helps found the Canadian Psychological Association. He becomes its first president in **1940.**

— World War II provides many opportunities for psychologists to enhance the popularity and influence of psychology, especially in applied areas.

1943 — Psychologist Starke Hathaway and physician J. Charnley McKinley publish the Minnesota Multiphasic Personality Inventory (MMPI).

1945 — Karen Horney, who criticized Freud's theory of female sexual development, publishes *Our Inner Conflicts.*

1946 — Benjamin Spock's first edition of *The Commonsense Book of Baby and Child Care* appears; the book will influence child-rearing in North America for several decades.

1948 — Alfred Kinsey and his colleagues publish *Sexual Behavior in the Human Male,* and they publish *Sexual Behavior in the Human Female* in **1953.**

— B. F. Skinner's novel, *Walden Two,* describes a U nity based on positive reinforcement, which bec call for applying psychological principles in eve especially communal living.

— Ernest R. Hilgard publishes *Theories of Learning,* required reading for several generations of psych in North America.

1949 — Raymond B. Cattell publishes the Sixteen Perso Questionnaire (16PF).

Continued on in.

1869 — Francis Galton, Charles Darwin's cousin, publishes *Hereditary Genius*, in which he claims that intelligence is inher ted. In **1876** he coins the expression "nature and nurture" to correspond with "heredity and environment."

1874 — Carl Wernicke, a German neurologist and psychiatrist, shows that damage to a specific area in the left temporal lobe (now called Wernicke's area) disrupts ability to comprehend or produce spoken or written language.

1878 — G. Stanley Hall receives from Harvard University's Department of Philosophy the first U.S. Ph.D. degree based on psychological research.

1879 — Wilhelm Wundt establishes at the University of Leipzig, Germany, the first psychology laboratory, which becomes a Mecca for psychology students from all over the world.

1883 — G. Stanley Hall, student of Wilhelm Wundt, establishes the first formal U.S. psychology laboratory at Johns Hopkins University.

1885 — Hermann Ebbinghaus publishes *On Memory*, summarizing his extensive research on learning and memory, including the "forgetting curve."

1886 — Joseph Jastrow receives from Johns Hopkins University the first Ph.D. degree in psychology awarded by a Department of Psychology in the United States.

1889 — Alfred Binet and Henri Beaunis establish the first psychology laboratory in France at the Sorbonne, and the first International Congress of Psychology meets in Paris.

1890 — William James, Harvard University philosopher and psychologist, publishes *The Principles of Psychology,* describing psychology as "the science of mental life."

1891 — James Mark Baldwin establishes the first psychology laboratory in the British Commonwealth at the University of Toronto.

1892 — G. Stanley Hall spearheads the founding of the American Psychological Association (APA) and becomes its first president.

1893 — Mary Whiton Calkins (pictured) and Christine Ladd-Franklin are the first women elected to membership in the APA.

1894 — Margaret Floy Washburn is the first woman to receive a Ph.D. degree in psychology (Cornell University).

— Harvard University denies Mary Whiton Calkins admission to doctoral candidacy because of her gender, despite Hugo Münsterberg's claim that she was the best student he had ever had there.

1896 — John Dewey publishes "The Reflex Arc Concept in Psychology," helping to formalize the school of psychology called functionalism.

1898 — In "Animal Intelligence," Edward L. Thorndike, Columbia University, describes his learning experiments with cats in "puzzle boxes." In **1905,** he proposes the "law of effect."

1900 — Sigmund Freud publishes *The Interpretation of Dreams,* his major theoretical work on psychoanalysis.

MYERS' PSYCHOLOGY FOR AP*

TEACHER'S EDITION

*AP is a trademark registered
and/or owned by the College
Board, which was not involved
in the production of, and does
not endorse, this product.

MYERS' PSYCHOLOGY FOR AP*

TEACHER'S EDITION

AMY C. FINEBURG
Oak Mountain High School, Alabama

David G. Myers
Hope College, Holland, Michigan

WORTH PUBLISHERS/BFW

Credits for timeline photos, inside front and back covers (by date): 1637, Corbis-Bettmann; 1808, Hulton Archive/Getty Images; 1859, Granger Collection; 1878, 1879, 1890, Brown Brothers; 1893, 1894, Wellesley College Archives; 1898, Yale University Library; 1905, Sovfoto; 1913, 1920, 1933, 1939, Archives of the History of American Psychology, University of Akron; 1924, Larsen/Watson Papers, Archives of the History of American Psychology, University of Akron; 1938, Bettmann/ Corbis; 1945, Corbis; 1951, Courtesy of Carl Rogers Memorial Library; 1954, Ted Polumbaum/Life magazine, © 1968 TimeWarner, Inc.; 1959, Chris Felver/Archive Images; 1963, Courtesy of CUNY Graduate School and University Center; 1966 (Johnson), Bettmann/Corbis; 1966, Courtesy of John Garcia; 1969, Courtesy of Albert Bandura, Stanford University; 1974, Russell Fernald, Courtesy of the Stanford University News Service; 1979, Courtesy of Elizabeth Loftus, University of California, Irvine; 1981, Courtesy of the Archives, California Institute of Technology; 1987, Courtesy of Laurel Furumoto; 1993, Chet Snedden/American Airlines Corporate Communications.

Grateful acknowledgment is given for permission to reprint the following photos: p. xxxii: Ant Strack/ Corbis; p. 18: Gerhard Westrich/laif/Redux; p. 50: Image Source/Corbis; p. 114: Bloomimage/ Corbis; p. 174: Anthony-Masterson/Getty Images; p. 214: David Young-Wolff/Photo Edit; p. 254: Janine Wiedel Photolibrary/Alamy; p. 326: Chris Hyde/Getty Images; p. 410: Todd Wright/ Jupiterimages; p. 478: Howard Pyle/zefa/Corbis; p. 522: Jeremy Woodhouse/Getty Images; p. 560: Corbis; p. 604 Olivier Voisin/Photo Researchers, Inc.; p. 642: Rolf Bruderer/Corbis.

Senior Publisher: Catherine Woods

Senior Acquisitions Editor: Kevin Feyen

Development Editor: Christine Brune

Executive Marketing Manager: Cindi Weiss

Marketing Manager: Nicole Sheppard

Executive Editor: Ann Heath

Media and Supplements Editor: Peter Twickler

Associate Managing Editor: Tracey Kuehn

Production Manager: Sarah Segal

Photo Editor: Bianca Moscatelli

Photo Researchers: Jacqui Wong and Donna Ranieri

Art Director: Babs Reingold

Interior Designer: GLC (General Learning Communications)

Cover Designer: Lyndall Culbertson

Illustration Coordinator: Bill Page

Illustrations: TSI Graphics, Keith Kasnot

Composition: GLC (General Learning Communications)—Elissa Chamberlain, Kristen Naffah, and Gregory Ledger

Printing and Binding: RR Donnelley

Cover Illustration: Rafael Lopez

ISBN-13: 978-1-4292-5251-5

ISBN-10: 1-4292-5251-0

Printed in the United States of America

First printing 2010

All royalties from the sale of this book are assigned to the David and Carol Myers Foundation, which exists to receive and distribute funds to other charitable organizations.

Worth Publishers/BFW

41 Madison Avenue

New York, NY 10010

www.bfwpub.com/highschool

About the Author

Amy C. Fineburg, Oak Mountain High School (AL)

Fineburg has taught for 14 years and holds a doctorate in educational psychology from the University of Alabama. Her career passion is to use psychological principles to improve teaching and learning. She has chaired the Teachers of Psychology in Secondary Schools (TOPSS) committee, served as a Reader and then Table Leader at the AP Reading, contributed articles to AP Central, provided a national syllabus sample for the AP Psychology Audit, and written the 2003 edition of the *Teacher's Guide for AP Psychology*. She received the Moffett Memorial Teaching Award, given to the nation's most outstanding high school psychology teacher by the Society for the Teaching of Psychology (STP—APA Division 2). She is chair of the APA's Working Group to revise the National Standards for the teaching of high school psychology. She has helped coordinate and has presented at the National Institute for the Teaching of Biopsychology and the TOPSS Clark University workshops. Fineburg is a frequent presenter at the National Council for the Social Studies (NCSS) annual conference, through which she is a member of the Psychology Community and winner of the 2009 Alabama Outstanding Secondary Social Studies Teacher of the Year. She serves on the Advisory Council for the Social Studies Council of Alabama and as Assistant Chair of the Teaching Awards Committee for STP. Fineburg has written several book chapters promoting the teaching of positive psychology in high schools, the teaching of diversity issues, and using the National Standards in all high school psychology classes. She served as a managing editor for the *Encyclopedia of Positive Psychology*, contributing entries on academic achievement and learned optimism. In addition to authoring this Teacher's Edition, Fineburg also created the Teacher's Edition for Charlie Blair-Broeker and Randy Ernst's *Thinking About Psychology* text.

Why Should I Use *Myers' Psychology for AP**?

If you are trying to decide on a text for your Advanced Placement (AP) Psychology course, you cannot do better than the book you're holding right now. David Myers designed this new, college-level text specifically for the AP course! Its organization perfectly matches the College Board's 14-unit outline; it is full of high school–specific examples and photos, and extended Exam-related content; there are AP practice questions at the end of each unit; and it has a marvelous AP-specific supplements package that includes this Teacher's Edition, an AP-format Test Bank, an AP-specific Teacher's Resource Binder, the online Faculty Lounge for all teachers, and an AP-specific Study Guide.

Myers is well-known for his bestselling college texts. This new text incorporates trademark features from his college texts, including the accessible narrative, clear explanations of difficult concepts, evenhanded treatment of unresolved issues, the use of humor, and the engaging examples and quotations used to illustrate content.

From my perspective as a teacher, I could not hope for a better partner to help prepare students for the challenge of the AP Exam. The comprehensive coverage in this text, with its emphasis on up-to-date research findings, will prepare your students to excel on Exam day. Whether you are a veteran with vast files of supplementary materials or a rookie just beginning the adventure of teaching AP Psychology, you will appreciate the support of this text and its extensive package. (See page xxii for more details.)

Why Is Psychology the Perfect AP Class?

If you've taught AP courses, you know that it takes extra effort to prepare for an AP class and extra enthusiasm to teach it. There is more stress involved as we work to make sure our students are ready for the AP Exam in May.

Yet there is something particularly satisfying about leading students to new levels of commitment and academic achievement. The rewards of watching them grow in confidence and ability more than compensate for the additional demands of teaching AP.

Although all AP courses are special in these ways, the topic of psychology lends a unique freshness to the AP teaching experience. How can a student *not* be interested in behavior and mental processes? Our subject has a relevance that no other course can match. Our discipline has a breadth that leads students on a fantastic journey from the impact of neurotransmitters at the synapse to the dynamics of decision making on a jury; from the psychophysics of depth perception to the stability of babies' temperaments in their developing personalities. Even if students happen to not be interested in the topic of this week's lessons, by next week we will have moved on to something new and different.

*AP is a trademark registered and/or owned by the College Board, which was not involved in the production of, and does not endorse, this product.

The content, of course, is only part of the story. The *process* of psychology also serves students well as they chart their courses toward the future. The scientific nature of psychology allows us to teach the critical thinking skills that are so important for personal and society-level decision making. While most of our students will not end up as researchers, all of them need to have enough scientific literacy to understand what they hear in the media. Psychology shares methods with chemistry, astronomy, and other sciences, but students tend to be more interested in psychological research because it's more directly relevant to their lives. Through our classes, they learn the tools that allow them to evaluate claims effectively and make rational decisions. In a world where noncritical thinking and pseudoscience have powerful footholds, students need all the help they can get to distinguish supported statements from individuals' opinions.

AP Psychology is a course that works well with all types of students—from those who are taking their seventh AP course to those who have never set foot in an advanced class. The content is accessible enough that it engages student interest, but challenging enough to push even the most academically savvy student. AP Psychology is not only a fun course to teach, it is a course that can help support your school's efforts to increase equity and access to the AP curricula.

How Is the AP Psychology Exam Formatted and Administered?

The AP Psychology Exam has been administered annually in May since 1992. Except for the difficulty level (it's harder now than it used to be), little has changed since that first year. Every Exam consists of two sections.

1. 100 multiple-choice items

2. 2 free-response prompts (often called "essay questions")

Let's take a closer look at each section in the order students will encounter them on Exam day.

Multiple Choice Students have 70 minutes to complete this part of the test. Rigorously pretested, the questions (each with five options) are arranged by difficulty level, with the easier questions at the beginning of the Exam. Correct answers are worth 1 point, but incorrect answers cost students only ¼ point. The point total earned on this section is 66.7 percent of the final score. Most students finish this section ahead of the time limit, but they must wait the full 70 minutes before starting the second section of the test.

Free Response Students have 50 minutes to address both free-response prompts. The integrated nature of the prompts challenges students to apply their knowledge of several content areas (for example, scientific methods, biological foundations, and motivation) in the same answer. While potential point totals for each prompt may vary, the two answers are weighted equally and together contribute 33.3 percent of the final score.

How Should I Set Up My AP Psychology Course for Optimal Effectiveness?

It is hard to beat a well-planned, well-taught course when preparing students for the AP Psychology Exam. Charlie Blair-Broeker (Cedar Falls High School, IA) and Randy Ernst (Lincoln Public Schools, NE) generated the following tips from personal experience and from discussions with dozens of AP teachers.

1. ***Establish a schedule and stick to it.*** Assemblies, weather, and illness can derail progress, but do all you can to stay on track. This Teacher's Edition offers a Pacing Guide to help you plan how much time to devote to each unit according to the AP Course Description. (See **FIGURE 1**.) The Guide includes suggestions for those who teach traditional, year-round courses as well as those teaching within semester or block schedules. Note that the percentages in the College Board's *Course Description,* which are indicated in this Pacing Guide, represent the proportion of the AP Exam that is dedicated to those concepts. This does not necessarily map directly onto the number of text pages or class days to spend on the concepts, because different concepts require different lengths of time to be effectively absorbed by students.

2. ***Incorporate active learning in your classroom.*** Your students will retain more of the knowledge you are imparting if your teaching includes demonstrations, experiments, writing exercises, and other active learning resources, such as those found in this Teacher's Edition (**FIGURE 2**, next page).

3. ***Require textbook reading.*** You can't cover everything in class. Use quizzes, assignments, and exams to hold students accountable for text material you don't cover. Teach students how to take effective reading notes.

4. ***Give tests resembling the AP Exam format.*** If you're on a block schedule, 50 multiple-choice questions and one free-response prompt will easily fit into a class period. Cut down on the number of multiple-choice questions for more traditional-length class periods.

5. ***Teach writing.*** If writing is not your strength, ask a trusted English teacher to give you a hand. Students need to be able to convey information clearly in high-pressure testing situations. Writing for the AP Psychology Exam is more straightforward than writing for AP U.S. History or AP English Literature. Remember that parroting the prompt in a long introduction is unnecessary and never earns points. (Below you will find more tips on teaching writing, and on using grading rubrics.)

6. ***Use grading rubrics to score exams.*** Every summer at the AP Exam Reading, a rubric is developed to score the free-response answers. Rubrics add grading speed and reliability to test scoring and allow you to explain why a particular answer did or did not earn points. This Teacher's Edition provides free-response prompts with grading rubrics for each unit.

7. ***Give cumulative or review tests regularly.*** Unit tests are fine, but cumulative tests more closely resemble the AP Exam, help students keep previously learned material in mind, and allow students to make connections among all the concepts that they are learning.

8. ***Obtain and administer actual AP Exams.*** Every free-response question is released 48 hours after the test is given in May. Rubrics for each Exam are also

➤ **FIGURE 1**

Pacing Guide The Pacing Guide at the beginning of each unit will help you cover all the important concepts for the AP Exam without losing sight of the fun of the course, and the importance of incorporating interesting demonstrations and activities.

UNIT 3A

Pacing Guide

Use the following guide to determine how many instructional days to devote to this portion of the unit depending on the type of course you teach:

Year-long course: 3 days
Block schedule/Semester-long course: 1–2 days

This entire unit (Parts A, B, & C) encompasses 8–10 percent of the AP Exam. Spending an appropriate amount of time on this unit will help students do well on the AP Exam.

CRITICAL THINKING

Delayed gratification is a skill many parents want their children to have. People who can delay gratification are able to achieve more in life. Have students consider the following questions:

- What types of "real world" rewards occur on a delayed schedule?

- Did you learn to wait for rewards? Why or why not?

- Does the media encourage people to delay gratification? Why or why not?

At this time, you may want to use **Classroom Exercise: *Consideration of Future Consequences Scale*** (p. 12) from Bolt's Teacher's Resource Binder.

RESEARCH

Students can experience what it is like to train Pavlov's dogs with this interactive Pavlov game found via the Nobel Prize Organization: http://nobelprize.org/educational_games/medicine/pavlov/index.html
    This Web site showcases the work of faculty and students at Nebraska Wesleyan University. Annually, NWU hosts the Xtreme Rat Challenge, which challenges students to train their rats to do amazing feats using classical conditioning techniques: http://rats.nebrwesleyan.edu/index.php

DEMO

Have students take the sleep deprivation quiz in Table 5.1. Have them evaluate whether the quiz indicates sleep deprivation. Then have them reflect on why they may be sleep deprived. Challenge them to consider ways in which lack of sleep has adversely affected their lives and what they can realistically do to add more sleep to their daily schedules.
    At this point, you may want to use **Classroom Exercise: *The Sleep IQ Test*** (p. 4) from Bolt's Teacher's Resource Binder.

INTERCONNECTING

Alcohol has been shown to affect the hippocampus, the area of the brain that is responsible for forming new memories. This effect helps explain why people who drink heavily lose their memories of the time they were intoxicated.

TEACHING TIP

Be sure to point out the name for the hallucinations people experience when they are in the early stages of sleep—hypnagogic sensations. This term may show up on the AP Exam.
    At this point, you may want to use **Student Project: *Catching the Hypnagogic State*** (p. 7) from Bolt's Teacher's Resource Binder.

TECHNOLOGY RESOURCES

These resources will be helpful for teaching the concepts in this portion of the unit:

- *Videos: The Brain,* 2nd ed., *Module 13: Sleep and Circadian Rhythms; Module 14: Sleep: Brain Functions; Module 15: REM Sleep and Dreaming**

- *Video: Psychology: The Human Experience, Module 9: Circadian Rhythms*

- *Psychology Video Tool Kit: Sleep and Sleeplessness; Sleep Terror Disorder; Hypnosis: Medical and Psychological Applications; Hypnosis: An Altered Mental State?; The Nature and Abuse of Ecstasy (MDMA); The Medical Use of Marijuana; The Effects of Sleep Deprivation: Three Brave Souls*

- *Videos: Scientific American Frontiers,* 2nd ed., *Segment 13: Catching Catnaps; Segment 15: Can You Beat Jet Lag?; Segment 14: What's in a Dream?*

- *PsychSim 5: EEG and Sleep Stages; Your Mind on Drugs*

- *ActivePsych: Digital Media Archive,* 2nd ed.: *Narcoleptic Dogs; The Brain's Reward Center*

- *Videos: The Mind,* 2nd ed., *Module 2: Hypnotic Dissociation and Pain Relief; Module 30: Treating Drug Addiction: A Behavioral Approach; Module 22: Depressants and Their Addictive Effect on the Brain; Module 29: Alcohol Addiction: Hereditary Factors*

➤ **FIGURE 2**

Active Learning This Teacher's Edition contains a wealth of active learning resources.

available either from the College Board or from seasoned AP teachers who keep good files. Four of the actual multiple-choice tests have also been released, and the College Board offers an official practice exam online via AP Central. The released Exams may be purchased online from the College Board (http://apcentral.collegeboard.com/).

What Professional Development Is Available for AP Psychology Teachers?

Especially if you are new to teaching the AP course, you should consider attending an all-day AP Psychology teaching workshop. Dozens of these workshops take place across North America each year. AP Psychology teachers also benefit tremendously when they participate in a five-day AP summer institute. The AP coordinator in your school will receive information on the workshops and institutes nearest you, and you can find AP workshops and institutes online via AP Central.

Networking with other AP teachers is also invaluable. You may achieve this by joining Worth Publishers' free online Faculty Lounge (www.bfwpub.com/highschool/psychologyfacultylounge), by attending a workshop or institute, or by joining a listserv dedicated to teaching AP Psychology. The College Board AP Psychology listserv is a good place to start (http://apcentral.collegeboard.com/). Joining organizations such as APA's Teachers of Psychology in Secondary Schools (TOPSS: www.apa.org/ed/topss/), the Society for the Teaching of Psychology (http://teachpsych.org), and the National Council for Social Studies (NCSS) Psychology Community (www.ncss.org)

will also help you network while providing access to excellent content and pedagogical resources.

How Can I Train Writers to Become Readers? Teaching Free-Response Writing for AP Psychology

Writing for the two free-response prompts for AP Psychology is different from writing in English or history class. Good writing basics still apply—students should write in complete sentences and use good grammar—but writing for AP Psychology is more like writing in other sciences. Students need to be direct, concise, and to-the-point. Students may find this type of writing challenging if they are used to incorporating stylistic elements into their writing. The goal of the AP Psychology free-response prompts is to test whether students can synthesize concepts and apply them to particular situations. Doing well on the multiple-choice portion is essential, but successfully addressing the free-response prompts is also important for earning a good overall score.

The best way to teach students how to *write* effective free-response answers is to teach them how to *grade* effective free-response answers. Each summer, high school and college psychology faculty come together to read the free-response answers for the AP Psychology Exam. They work for one week to grade what is now approaching 200,000 student responses! This process of preparing, training, and applying the rubric to these responses is easy to simulate with your students. Not only will they learn the way to write a response, but they will also learn how they will be assessed, helping them interpret the prompts and write their responses better.

Note: Charlie Blair-Broeker and Randy Ernst have written free-response prompts and rubrics for each unit in this book (see **FIGURE 3**). Blair-Broeker and Ernst are uniquely qualified to write AP Psychology-style prompts: both have worked on the AP Psychology Test Development Committee, and both have participated in the AP Reading as Question Leaders, directing the development of the actual rubrics used at the Readings. The procedure in this lesson can be applicable to any essay-writing lesson.

➤ **FIGURE 3**

Sample of the Free-Response Questions with Grading Rubrics Found in *Myers' Psychology for AP**

Free-Response Question

You have been hired to write and direct short, educational films covering a variety of different brain injuries. In five short paragraphs, explain five ideas you have for scripts. In each case, create a character who has suffered a brain injury. Include the name of the brain part injured and a description of the loss of function that occurs as a result of that injury.

Rubric for Grading the Free-Response Question

This is a 10-point question. Scoring depends on the scenarios created by the student. Each of the five paragraphs is worth two points— one point for mentioning a brain part and one point for connecting damage to that part to the appropriate loss of function. For example, it would be worth two points if a student described a condition that damaged a person's hippocampus and indicated that there would be a loss of memory as a result.

Procedure

Step 1 Train yourself to grade your students' essays with a rubric. To accomplish this, use any of the free-response prompts and rubrics from any of the units in this book, or a free-response prompt and rubric from a released AP Exam (which may be purchased on the AP Central Web site).

The AP Psychology Reading uses the following procedure to train Readers:

- Read over the entire rubric first, highlighting which phrasing will score a point and which will not.

- Using the rubric, grade a few sample responses. You are not grading these for a final score. Rather, you are grading the responses to see if the rubric is capturing the different ways students are correctly responding to the prompt. You want to be sure your rubric is loose enough to allow for creative responses but tight enough to reward only correct responses.

- If you are using prompts and rubrics from released AP Exams, check your accuracy in applying the rubric by reviewing the Scoring Commentary (also found on AP Central), which gives a point-by-point explanation of how the essay was graded by actual AP Readers.

Step 2 When you have familiarized yourself with the prompts and rubrics you want to use with students, simulate actual testing conditions for the AP Psychology Exam by assigning two essay prompts for students to complete during a 50-minute period of time.

Before they begin writing, teach students the following helpful hints for essay writing:

- Identify the verbs in the question. Verbs indicate what type of answers students should give.
    - The verbs "identify," "describe," and "define" require definitions or examples that define the concepts.
    - The words "explain," "analyze," and "discuss" require application of the concepts to the situations within the question.
- Students should not parrot the question's language in their response. They should extend the wording of the question to demonstrate their knowledge of the material.
- Use line spacing or a separate paragraph for each concept listed in the question. Readers will appreciate the effort.
- Lengthy or parroted introductions and conclusions are not necessary. Students should only provide introductions and conclusions if these provide responses to the prompt.
- Outlines, graphics, or bulleted lists will not be graded. Students should write in complete sentences. **Note:** Students may use bullets to differentiate each concept, but the writing after the bullet should be in complete sentences, not phrases.

Step 3 Grade your own students' essays using the rubric. Depending on your style, use either of the following methods:

- Mark the points you awarded on the responses, highlighting the phrasing they used to earn the points. You may want to cross out any superfluous phrasing that does not earn points. This will help your students learn how to be concise with their responses. Point out any misinformation the students may have included. While they do not lose points for wrong information (unless they are contradicting correct information), use their misconceptions as a teachable moment.

- Make a grading grid that shows which points were awarded. The grid should have a column or row for each scored point so students can see which points they earned and which points they did not.

Step 4 Train your students to grade with the rubric, using a procedure similar to the one you used to learn the rubric. This time, you are the leader, reviewing the rubric and answering questions from students about what phrasing scores points.

- First have students read through the rubric, noting which phrases score points and which do not.
- After reviewing the rubric, have students grade a sample essay individually. If you are using a prompt from a released Exam, sample essays are available on AP Central. If you are using a prompt from this text, you may want to create a few sample essays of your own (showing responses that score all of the points, a few of the points, and none of the points), or you may want to use actual student responses that are stripped of any identifying information. If you do use student responses, get permission from those students before you do so.
- Once they have graded the samples, have students discuss their grading with a partner. Then, bring students together as a class and read the sample essay aloud, having students indicate when they hear phrasing that earns a point. Discuss why or why not to award a point. If you are using prompts from a released Exam, use the Scoring Commentary (also found on AP Central) to help them keep to both the letter and spirit of the rubric. You may want to have students grade three or four responses in order to ensure they are applying the rubric appropriately.
- Once the class feels comfortable with the rubric, distribute the students' own graded responses to them.
  - If you marked the responses, students can review your grading to see how it corresponds to the rubric they are now familiar with. Students can see how crossed-out sections can help them be more concise in the future.
  - If you did not mark on the essays, students can grade their own responses according to the rubric. Then you can distribute the grading sheets you used, discussing any discrepancies and highlighting any superfluous or erroneous information.

Potential Pitfalls to Watch for in Teaching Writing for AP Psychology

Pitfall #1 The free-response prompts and rubrics are designed to assess the knowledge of the nearly 200,000 students who now take the AP Psychology Exam in a given year. It is difficult to create a prompt that challenges students from a broad range of AP Psychology experiences. Help students prepare for the prompts they may see with the following advice:

- In the last several years, the prompts have followed a trend. One question challenges students to cover a wide range of psychological content, asking them to make connections among multiple topic areas. They may need to show how six to eight concepts relate to a common theme. I call this type of question the "general" question. The other question is more narrowly focused, asking students to relate concepts from two to four related content areas to a particular context. I call this type of question the "specific" question. Using released prompts, have students identify which questions are general or specific.
- Students are likely to encounter concepts on at least one free-response prompt that they have forgotten they ever heard. Prepare students to focus on concepts they know rather than dwell on concepts they don't know.

- Students need to respond in the best way as prescribed by the prompt. If the prompt asks them to give examples, they should give examples. If it calls on them to create an experimental design, they should create an experimental design, not a correlational or descriptive design. Students who know the concepts can fail to earn points if they do not answer the prompt in context.

Pitfall #2 Students will probably want to argue that their own particular phrasing is acceptable when the rubric does not allow it. Here is advice given during the AP Reading for these types of situations:

- Readers cannot infer answers. If a student seems to know an answer but does not use the proper phrasing or give a complete answer, a point will not be awarded.

- Readers seek counsel from other Readers if they are unsure of whether a student has answered effectively. Readers are teachers just like you, and they are instructed to treat every response as if it were written by their own students. They do everything they can to award points when earned. But Readers can't dwell too long on a single point on a single response. Sometimes a judgment call must be made.

How Can I Help Students Review for the AP Exam?

Reviewing for the AP Exam is critical to helping students do well. Whether you teach a year-long or semester course, leaving adequate time for review is important to helping students remember and integrate all they have learned. Here are some tips you can use to review effectively:

- Schedule your course to finish a few days or weeks early to allow time for in-class review. This will give you and the students some breathing room to reflect on the totality of the course.

- Don't limit yourself to class time. Many effective review sessions can occur after school or on weekends. Work with students' schedules to come up with times outside of the school day to review. Make it fun by having food—ordering a pizza or having a potluck.

- Apply psychological concepts while reviewing:
  - Don't cram the entire course into one review session. Chunk units that interconnect well into different review sessions so students can see how the concepts bridge from one unit to the next.
  - Encourage students to develop their own mnemonics for more efficient recall. Remember, the more personal or unique the mnemonic, the easier it is to recall the information.
  - Focus on concepts that are most often confused. Concepts that are opposites (e.g., proactive and retroactive interference) need special attention. I have highlighted these concepts in the "Troubleshooting" notes throughout this Teacher's Edition. (See **FIGURE 4**.)

➤ **FIGURE 4**
Examples of Troubleshooting Feature

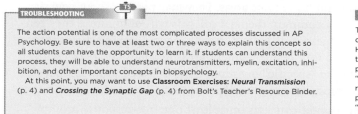

TROUBLESHOOTING

The action potential is one of the most complicated processes discussed in AP Psychology. Be sure to have at least two or three ways to explain this concept so all students can have the opportunity to learn it. If students can understand this process, they will be able to understand neurotransmitters, myelin, excitation, inhibition, and other important concepts in biopsychology.

At this point, you may want to use **Classroom Exercises: *Neural Transmission*** (p. 4) and ***Crossing the Synaptic Gap*** (p. 4) from Bolt's Teacher's Resource Binder.

TROUBLESHOOTING

Table 6.3 describes a concept called "positive punishment." Help students understand that this is not a desirable type of punishment. Rather, the words "positive" and "negative" when referring to reinforcement and punishment mean "adding" and "subtracting" respectively. When we add a punishing stimulus for a behavior, then it is considered positive punishment.

- Review good test-taking skills as well as content:
  - Have students cover up the answer choices on the multiple-choice section so familiar-looking answer choices won't confuse them.
  - Remind students that if they can eliminate at least one item from the multiple-choice list, they should guess.
  - Students should focus on what they know rather than dwell on what they don't know.
- Use games! Any game-show format is conducive to review in psychology. You can create the questions or have students create their own games to review certain units.
- Have students create "concept webs" that show how different concepts are interconnected. This type of exercise can help students prepare for the general free-response prompts. You can do this a couple of different ways:
  - Give students a concept (such as dopamine or fundamental attribution error) and have them connect as many other concepts to it as they can. This will show you how well they can apply the concept for the free-response prompt.
  - Give students two or three concepts and have them connect those concepts using a "six degrees of separation" type of game. For instance, you may give students the concepts "dopamine" and "fundamental attribution error." Students now have to connect these two in as few steps as possible. They may say that dopamine is linked as a possible cause of schizophrenia, and the ways in which people with schizophrenia behave may cause people to make the fundamental attribution error about their behavior. Students can justify their links before the class, spurring debates about which links are valid and which are not.
  - *Note:* The "Interconnecting" feature in this Teacher's Edition provides some ideas for concepts to use for this type of activity.
- Have students be responsible for reviewing the units about which they feel the most uncomfortable. This will help them focus on content that is more challenging for them.

What Can We Do in Class AFTER the AP Exam?

For many schools, the College Board's AP Exam schedule does not fit nicely into their academic year. The AP Exams are typically given in early May, and many schools are still in session through late June. This scheduling can leave several weeks of time teachers have to spend with students with no content or test as motivation, which can be challenging to manage. Here are some suggestions for what to do if you have time after the Exam:

- *Myers' Psychology for AP** offers four appendices full of optional content that is generally not tested for on the AP Exam. These are good topics nonetheless that can engage students as you wind down the year.
- For many teachers, there is not enough time before the Exam to show movies that apply psychological concepts. The Teacher's Resource Binder suggests several assignments featuring full-length movies that showcase psychological content. You can use the time after the Exam to show these movies and use these assignments.
- The time after the Exam would be excellent for putting together a psychology fair. Assign students in groups to create a booth for the psychology fair that showcases their favorite psychological concepts. They can set up demonstrations for fair-goers

to participate in, helping to educate the community at large about psychology and recruiting students for your classes for next year.

- Students could also use this time to conduct psychological research. Students may be interested in investigating how the concepts they learned about might apply to students in their school or people in their community. Have students propose research to conduct, set up a review board of adult leaders to review the proposals, and facilitate selection of participants as they conduct their research. You could have students present their research at a psychology fair.

- Invite guest speakers from the community or local colleges or universities to speak to your students about their areas of research or special interest.

- Visit a local mental health facility, planning activities for the clients and their families. Students can see how mental health care is conducted in their community and perhaps meet people who have mental illness. This type of activity can build tolerance and understanding in students.

- Consider planning a community service project devoted to mental health issues. Students could plan a community-wide fundraiser for mental health causes or collect supplies for a school for students with special needs.

- You can hold a psychology career fair to help students see the different careers available for psychologists.

* * *

Teaching AP Psychology has been a great joy of my life. I love interacting with students about a course they find interesting and challenging, and I love watching them try to apply psychology to their own lives. Not only have I gotten to share my love of psychology with students, but I have also been able to share psychology with a vast network of fellow AP Psychology teachers, whom I have met through workshops, institutes, committees, and online, and at the AP Psychology Reading. Too often, psychology teachers are alone in their buildings, teaching a course no one else teaches or understands. Connecting with other psychology teachers helps end that isolation, providing colleagues with whom to share ideas and new teaching techniques. You can be a part of something special by teaching AP Psychology. I hope that the tips you find in this book will help you feel more comfortable teaching psychology and more confident in sharing your own ideas with others. If we don't share our love of psychology with our students and colleagues, we miss out on giving psychology away. It's too good to keep to ourselves.

Amy C. Fineburg, Oak Mountain High School (AL)

MYERS' PSYCHOLOGY FOR AP*

David G. Myers

Hope College
Holland, Michigan

*AP is a trademark registered and/or owned by the College Board, which was not involved in the production of, and does not endorse, this product.

WORTH PUBLISHERS

Credits for timeline photos, inside front and back covers (by date): 1637, Corbis-Bettmann; 1808, Hulton Archive/Getty Images; 1859, Granger Collection; 1878, 1879, 1890, Brown Brothers; 1893, 1894, Wellesley College Archives; 1898, Yale University Library; 1905, Sovfoto; 1913, 1920, 1933, 1939, Archives of the History of American Psychology, University of Akron; 1924, Larsen/Watson Papers, Archives of the History of American Psychology, University of Akron; 1938, Bettmann/ Corbis; 1945, Corbis; 1951, Courtesy of Carl Rogers Memorial Library; 1954, Ted Polumbaum/Life magazine, © 1968 TimeWarner, Inc.; 1959, Chris Felver/Archive Images; 1963, Courtesy of CUNY Graduate School and University Center; 1966 (Johnson), Bettmann/Corbis; 1966, Courtesy of John Garcia; 1969, Courtesy of Albert Bandura, Stanford University; 1974, Russell Fernald, Courtesy of the Stanford University News Service; 1979, Courtesy of Elizabeth Loftus, University of California, Irvine; 1981, Courtesy of the Archives, California Institute of Technology; 1987: Courtesy of Laurel Furumoto; 1993, Chet Snedden/American Airlines Corporate Communications.

Grateful acknowledgment is given for permission to reprint the following photos: p. xxxii: Ant Strack/ Corbis; p. 18: Gerhard Westrich/laif/Redux; p. 50: Image Source/Corbis; p. 114: Bloomimage/ Corbis; p. 174: Anthony-Masterson/Getty Images; p. 214: David Young-Wolff/Photo Edit; p. 254: Janine Wiedel Photolibrary/Alamy; p. 326: Chris Hyde/Getty Images; p. 410: Todd Wright/ Jupiterimages; p. 478: Howard Pyle/zefa/Corbis; p. 522: Jeremy Woodhouse/Getty Images; p. 560: Corbis; p. 604 Olivier Voisin/Photo Researchers, Inc.; p. 642: Rolf Bruderer/Corbis.

Senior Publisher: Catherine Woods

Senior Acquisitions Editor: Kevin Feyen

Development Editors: Christine Brune, Trish Morgan

Executive Marketing Manager: Cindi Weiss

Marketing Manager: Nicole Sheppard

Executive Editor: Ann Heath

Media and Supplements Editor: Peter Twickler

Associate Managing Editor: Tracey Kuehn

Production Manager: Sarah Segal

Photo Editor: Bianca Moscatelli

Photo Researchers: Jacqui Wong and Donna Ranieri

Art Director: Babs Reingold

Interior Designers: Lissi Sigillo and Lyndall Culbertson

Cover Designer: Lyndall Culbertson

Illustration Coordinator: Bill Page

Illustrations: TSI Graphics, Keith Kasnot

Composition: GLC (General Learning Communications)—Elissa Chamberlain, Gregory Ledger, Kristen Naffah

Printing and Binding: RR Donnelley

Cover Illustration: Rafael Lopez

Library of Congress Control Number: 2010921793

ISBN-13: 978-1-4292-4436-7

ISBN-10: 1-4292-4436-4

Printed in the United States of America

First printing 2010

All royalties from the sale of this book are assigned to the David and Carol Myers Foundation, which exists to receive and distribute funds to other charitable organizations.

Worth Publishers
41 Madison Avenue
New York, NY 10010
www.worthpublishers.com

TO MY BFW HIGH SCHOOL TEAM FRIENDS

with gratitude for their wonderful support

About the Author

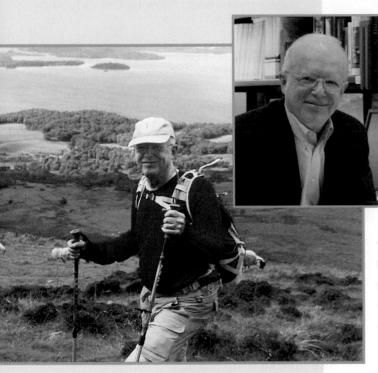

David Myers received his psychology Ph.D. from the University of Iowa. He has spent his career at Hope College, Michigan, where he has taught dozens of introductory psychology sections. Hope College students have invited him to be their commencement speaker and voted him "outstanding professor."

Myers' scientific articles have, with support from National Science Foundation grants, appeared in more than two dozen scientific periodicals, including *Science, American Scientist, Psychological Science,* and the *American Psychologist*. In addition to his scholarly writing and his textbooks for introductory and social psychology, he also digests psychological science for the general public. His writings have appeared in three dozen magazines, from *Today's Education* to *Scientific American*. He also has authored five general audience books, including *The Pursuit of Happiness* and *Intuition: Its Powers and Perils*. Drawing on his experience, Myers has written articles and a book *(A Quiet World)* about hearing loss, and he is advocating a transformation in American assistive listening technology (see www.hearingloop.org).

David Myers has chaired his city's Human Relations Commission, helped found a thriving assistance center for families in poverty, and spoken to hundreds of college, community, and high school groups (including a recent AP Psychology Reading). He also served on the American Psychological Association's working group that created the 2010 revision of the *National Standards for High School Psychology Curricula*.

He bikes to work year-round and plays pickup basketball daily. David and Carol Myers have raised two sons and a daughter. In 2009, Dave and three of his family hiked Scotland's 95-mile West Highland Way.

v

Brief Contents

Contents

478
UNIT 10
Personality

522
UNIT 11
Testing and Individual Differences

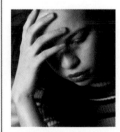

560
UNIT 12
Abnormal Psychology

The Advanced Placement (AP) Psychology course represents a wonderful opportunity for high school students to be challenged by the rigor of a college-level course, while learning life-relevant, mind-expanding concepts from the humanly significant discipline of psychology. It has been exciting to watch the explosive growth of the AP Psychology course! From its modest beginning in 1992, AP Psychology course enrollments have soared, and continue to soar. In 2009, 151,006 students from 4,989 high schools took the AP Exam (**FIGURE 1**).

➤ **FIGURE 1** **Number of AP Psychology Exam-Takers**

Many AP Psychology teachers and their students have used my regular college text for this course (complete with its references to dorm life, professors, and memories from the "old days" in high school). As a result, I've been fortunate to have heard lots of helpful feedback, some of which has pertained to the special demands of the AP course and Exam, and some to the high school environment (where students won't connect with examples that assume college surroundings). And thus was born the vision for this new *Psychology for AP**. This college-level, AP-focused, and high school–appropriate text offers

- an ***organization*** that precisely matches the 14-unit College Board course outline.
- ***high school–specific examples and photos.***
- ***extended exam-related content*** as advised by a ***stellar panel of leaders in the teaching of high school psychology,*** including our focus group participants (listed later in this Preface) and our Editorial Advisory Board members (see next page).
- ***AP-style questions*** (15 multiple-choice practice questions and one free-response question—all in AP Exam format— for the end of each unit).
- a wraparound ***Teacher's Edition,*** created by Amy Fineburg (Oak Mountain High School, AL), with annotated teaching tips and resources.

*AP is a trademark registered and/or owned by the College Board, which was not involved in the production of, and does not endorse, this product.

xv

- an *AP-format Test Bank,* created by John Brink (Calvin College), Robert McEntarffer (Lincoln Public Schools, NE), Kristin Whitlock (Viewmont High School, UT), and Alan Feldman (Glen Rock High School, NJ).

For this edition, I was fortunate to have **Charlie Blair-Broeker** (Cedar Falls High School, IA) and **Randy Ernst** (Lincoln Public Schools, NE) as special consultants throughout the development process—from conception of the idea to completion of the final project. They each offered numerous suggestions for making examples even more relevant and appropriate to the AP Psychology classroom, for illustrating concepts with photos and art that would be more appealing to the high school audience, and for elaborating on key concepts that often appear on the AP Exam. In addition, Blair-Broeker and Ernst created the end-of-unit, AP-specific practice tests. We also had a superb **Editorial Advisory Board of renowned educators** that provided sage guidance during the book's development process on key content, organizational, pedagogical, and supplements issues. I extend gratitude and admiration to each of them for their enduring contributions to the teaching of psychology:

- Alan Feldman, Glen Rock High School (NJ)
- Amy Fineburg, Oak Mountain High School (AL)
- Kent A. Korek, Germantown High School (WI)
- Robert McEntarffer, Lincoln Public Schools (NE)
- Debra Park, West Deptford High School (NJ)
- Hilary Rosenthal, Glenbrook South High School (IL)
- Marissa M. Sarabando, Lamar Academy (TX)

What Makes *Psychology for AP** So Special?

Psychology for AP* is a college-level text written with the needs of AP teachers and students in mind.

A Perfect Match to the College Board Outline
for the AP Psychology Course

With help from my sharp-eyed editors, I have worked to create an organization that matches up with the College Board's 2010–2011 outline for the AP Psychology course, so that teachers can be sure they are providing their students with the best possible preparation for the AP Exam. This means my text offers the same 14 units, in order, and the same distribution of content coverage among those 14 units, as the new College Board outline released in 2009. Where the outline has recommended coverage within specific units, you can be sure that you will find that coverage (sometimes with references to more, related coverage elsewhere). For example, the College Board outline recommends the following for Unit 4, Sensation and Perception: "Discuss the role of attention in behavior." In Unit 4, you will find nearly three text pages covering the subject of Selective Attention. (In some of my other texts, I have covered this topic in the States of Consciousness material, though it works just as well here in Sensation and Perception.) Here's another example: The College Board outline recommends, for Unit 7, Cognition: "List the characteristics of creative thought and creative thinkers." I have included two pages on creativity in Unit 7B. (In my other texts, this coverage may be found in the Intelligence material.)

---

*AP is a trademark registered and/or owned by the College Board, which was not involved in the production of, and does not endorse, this product.

Although the College Board outline is not intended to be an exhaustive list of topics, it represents an excellent starting point—to which I have added coverage based on my own knowledge of what is needed to succeed in other college courses, what's new and important in the world of psychology research, and, perhaps most important, what an educated person needs to know.

Amy Fineburg has created tables correlating each of the College Board's AP Psychology learning objectives with corresponding content in this text (**FIGURE 2**). *We will be updating these tables every two years—each time the College Board comes out with its biennial update to their AP Psychology course description.*

➤ FIGURE 2

Example From Unit 1 of the Online Correlation Guide to the College Board Learning Objectives, to be updated every two years.

UNIT 1

Myers' Section	AP Learning Objective
What Is Psychology?: Psychology's Roots	Recognize how philosophical perspectives shaped the development of psychological thought.
	Identify the major historical figures in psychology (e.g., Mary Whiton Calkins, Charles Darwin, Dorothea Dix, Sigmund Freud, G. Stanley Hall, William James, Ivan Pavlov, Jean Piaget, Carl Rogers, B. F. Skinner, Margaret Floy Washburn, John B. Watson, Wilhelm Wundt).
What Is Psychology?: Psychological Science Develops	Describe and compare different theoretical approaches in explaining behavior: • structuralism, functionalism, and behaviorism in the early years; • Gestalt, psychoanalytic/psychodynamic, and humanism emerging later
	Identify the major historical figures in psychology (e.g., Mary Whiton Calkins, Charles Darwin, Dorothea Dix, Sigmund Freud, G. Stanley Hall, William James, Ivan Pavlov, Jean Piaget, Carl Rogers, B. F. Skinner, Margaret Floy Washburn, John B. Watson, Wilhelm Wundt).
Contemporary Psychology: Psychology's Biggest Question	Recognize the strengths and limitations of applying theories to explain behavior. Describe and compare different theoretical approaches in explaining behavior: • evolutionary, biological, and cognitive as more contemporary approaches.
Contemporary Psychology: Psychology's Three Main Levels of Analysis	Describe and compare different theoretical approaches in explaining behavior: • evolutionary, biological, and cognitive as more contemporary approaches.
Contemporary Psychology: Psychology's Subfields	Describe and compare different theoretical approaches in explaining behavior: • evolutionary, biological, and cognitive as more contemporary approaches. Distinguish the different domains of psychology: • biological, clinical, cognitive, counseling, developmental, educational, experimental, human factors, industrial–organizational, personality, psychometric, and social.
Close-Up: Tips for Studying Psychology	The AP Psychology Exam includes a 70-minute multiple-choice section that accounts for two-thirds of the exam grade, and a 50-minute free-response section made up of two questions that accounts for one-third of the exam grade.

Extended Exam-Related Content

Under the guidance of Charlie Blair-Broeker, Randy Ernst, and the rest of our Editorial Advisory Board, and in careful consultation with the College Board outline, I have included additional coverage in this text of topics and people that often appear on the AP Exam. For example, I have, as the College Board outline recommends, added

- coverage of "how philosophical perspectives shaped the development of psychological thought" to Unit 1, Psychology's History and Approaches.
- the key term "confounding variable" to Unit 2, Research Methods.
- more on "how ethical and legal guidelines (e.g., those provided by the American Psychological Association, federal regulations, local institutional review boards) protect research participants and promote sound ethical practice" in Unit 2.

- mentions of Gustav Fechner in Unit 4, Sensation and Perception, and Edward Tolman in Unit 6, Learning.
- a discussion of learned helplessness in Unit 6 (moved here from the Personality coverage).
- sections addressing culture and child-rearing, and the nature and nurture of gender in Unit 9, Developmental Psychology, to help "discuss the interaction of nature and nurture (including cultural variations) in the determination of behavior."
- a discussion of Culture and the Self in Unit 10, Personality, to help students "speculate how cultural context can facilitate or constrain personality development, especially as it relates to self-concept (e.g., collectivistic versus individualistic cultures)."
- explanations in Unit 13, Treatment of Psychological Disorders, that will help students "describe prevention strategies that build resilience and promote competence," with "resilience" as a key term.
- the key term "self-fulfilling prophecy" to Unit 14, Social Psychology, to help students "anticipate the impact of behavior on a self-fulfilling prophecy."
- a lengthy discussion of cultural influences to Unit 14, so that students may "articulate the impact of social and cultural categories (e.g., gender, race, ethnicity) on self-concept and relations with others."

High School–Specific Examples and Illustrations

Again, with the helpful guidance of Charlie Blair-Broeker, Randy Ernst, and the rest of our Editorial Advisory Board, I have added a number of new examples and illustrations that will be more relevant to high school students. Here are a few examples:

- Unit 1, Psychology's History and Approaches, has a new photo of graduating senior twins to illustrate the nature-nurture debate discussion.
- The limits of interviewer intuition in Unit 2, Research Methods, is now illustrated with a high school student interviewing for a summer job (replacing a photo of a young professional).
- The signal detection discussion in Unit 4, Sensation and Perception, offers a narrative example of teachers detecting student cheating, and also a new visual of a high school student detecting a text message (replacing a military photo of a man watching a radar screen).
- In Unit 8, Motivation and Emotion, the James-Lange theory illustration now shows shared joy in a girls' high school basketball team celebrating victory (replacing a men's college basketball team).
- The adolescence coverage in Unit 9, Developmental Psychology, is now in the present rather than past tense.
- The Unit 10, Personality, "extraversion" photo now shows a high school boy dancing (rather than a young professional woman goofing around in the office).
- Unit 12, Abnormal Psychology, offers a new photo example of teen volunteers rebuilding bikes after Hurricane Katrina's devastation—modeling strengths related to love and justice.
- Unit 13, Treatment of Psychological Disorders, includes new research that extends to depressed teens the benefits of disputing negative thoughts.
- A fraternity club example in Unit 14, Social Psychology, has been changed to a student government example.

- A new football coach example illustrates "categorization" in Unit 14.
- Throughout the text, examples have become high school–appropriate, for example by using "bedroom" instead of "dorm room," "teacher" instead of "professor," "school cafeteria" instead of "dining hall," and "As teenagers, you . . ." instead of "As adults, we . . ."

Thoughtful Study Aids Include AP-Specific Guidance

In order to be optimally prepared for the AP Exam, students need as much practice as they can get with the format of the questions they will see on the Exam, and they need to review to test their knowledge throughout the course.

Psychology for AP* includes the following study aids:

- *Numbered Questions* establish learning objectives for each significant section of text and direct student reading.
- *"Before You Move On" Features,* found at the end of each major section of text, include *Ask Yourself questions,* which encourage students to apply new concepts to their own experiences, and *Test Yourself questions* (with answers in an appendix) that assess student mastery and encourage big-picture thinking.
- *Unit-Ending Review Sections* repeat the numbered objective questions and address them with a narrative summary followed by page-referenced Terms and Concepts to Remember.
- *AP* Practice Test Questions* provide a chance for students to test the depth of their knowledge. Answers may be found in the *Teacher's Edition* for the 15 multiple-choice questions that appear at the end of each unit. Students will also encounter a *free-response question* at the end of each unit that is designed to prepare them specifically for the AP Exam, for example, by asking about concepts that cross unit topics rather than cover just the topics in that specific unit of the text. **Grading rubrics** for the free-response questions may be found in the *Teacher's Edition.* (Note that the *Teacher's Edition* also has an "Interconnecting" feature to help your students get comfortable connecting topics in the way the AP Exam will demand.)

Cultural and Gender Diversity Coverage

Psychology for AP* presents a thoroughly cross-cultural perspective on psychology (**TABLE 1**, next page)—reflected in research findings, and text and photo examples. Coverage of the psychology of women and men is also thoroughly integrated (turn the page for **TABLE 2**). Discussion of the relevance of cultural and gender diversity begins on the first page of the first unit and continues throughout the text.

Strong Critical Thinking Coverage and Research Emphasis

I aim to introduce students to critical thinking throughout the book. Learning objective questions at the beginning of main sections, and Review sections at the end of each unit, encourage critical reading to glean an understanding of important concepts. *Psychology for AP** also includes the following opportunities for students to learn or practice their critical thinking skills and to work toward a better understanding of research design principles—both of which are essential to AP Exam success.

---

*AP is a trademark registered and/or owned by the College Board, which was not involved in the production of, and does not endorse, this product.

Table 1 Culture and Multicultural Experience

In Units 1–14, and in the appendices, coverage of culture and multicultural experience can be found on the following pages:

Aggression, pp. 673–674

Aging population, p. 457

AIDS, pp. 311, 405

Anger, p. 387

Animal research ethics, pp. 44–45

Attraction:
love and marriage, p. 684
speed-dating, p. 679

Attractiveness, pp. 106, 678–679, 680–682

Attribution, political effects of, p. 645

Behavioral effects of culture, pp. 101–102

Body ideal, p. 338

Categorization, p. 299

Complementary/alternative medicine, p. C-9

Conformity, pp. 651, 654

Corporal punishment practices, p. 234

Cultural norms, pp. 108, 439–440, 662

Culture:
context effects, p. 164
definition, pp. 661–662
and the self, pp. 516–518
shock, pp. 400–401, 506, 662–663

Deaf culture, pp. 82–83, 87, 138–140, 315, 317, 318, D-3, D-5

Development:
adolescence, p. 445
attachment, pp. 429, 432
child-rearing, pp. 434–435
cognitive development, p. 423
moral development, p. 449
social development, p. 429

Drugs:
psychological effects of, pp. 197, 200

use of, pp. 209–210

Eating disorders: Western culture and, p. 338

Emotion:
emotion-detecting ability, pp. 377–378
experiencing, pp. 385, 387
expressing, pp. 379, 380–382

Enemy perceptions, p. 689

Fear, p. 309

Flow, pp. B-1–B-2

Flynn effect, pp. 537–538

Fundamental attribution error, p. 644

Gender:
roles, pp. 439–440
social power, p. 436

Grief, expressing, pp. 470–471

Happiness, p. 394–395

Hindsight bias, p. 20

History of psychology, pp. 2–7

Human diversity/kinship, pp. 43, 661–662

Identity, forming a social, p. 451

Individualism/collectivism, pp. 516–518

Intelligence, pp. 524, 532, 534, 537–538, 549–550, 531–533
bias, pp. 554–555
nutrition and, pp. 552–553

Language, pp. 313–316, 317, 318–321, 661–662
monolingual/bilingual, p. 321

Leaving the nest, p. 454

Life satisfaction, pp. 392–393

Life expectancy, p. 457

Life span and well-being, p. 469

Loop systems, p. B-15

Management styles, pp. B-12–B-13

Marriage, p. 467

Mating preferences, pp. 106–107

Meditation, p. C-10

Memory, encoding, pp. 264, 280

Menopause, p. 456

Mental illness rate, pp. 599–600

Molecular genetics: "missing women," pp. 102–103

Motivation: hierarchy of needs, p. 330

Need to belong, pp. 359–361

Neurotransmitters: curare, p. 58

Obesity, pp. 340, 344–345

Obesity guidance/counseling, p. 341

Observational learning:
attachment and television viewing, p. 431
television and aggression, p. 247

Optimism and health, p. C-3

Organ donation, p. 312

Pace of life, pp. 29, 662

Pain, perception of, p. 145

Parapsychology, p. 166

Parent and peer relationships, pp. 452–453

Participative management, pp. B-12–B-15

Peacemaking:
conciliation, p. 692
contact, pp. 689–690
cooperation, p. 691

Peer influence, p. 444

Personal space, p. 662

Personality, p. 504

Prejudice, pp. 35–36, 46, 664–670

Prejudice prototypes, pp. 299–300

Psychoanalysis, p. 608

Psychological disorders:

antisocial personality disorder, p. 598

cultural norms, p. 562

depression, pp. 580, 582, 583, 588

dissociative identity disorder, p. 578

eating disorders, pp. 338, 564–565

rates of, pp. 561–562, 599

schizophrenia, pp. 565, 593

somatoform, p. 576

suicide, p. 584–585

susto, p. 564

taijin-kyofusho, p. 565

Psychotherapy:
culture and values in, pp. 626–627

EMDR training, p. 624

Puberty and adult independence, p. 454

Self-esteem, p. 396

Self-serving bias, pp. 513, 514

Sex drive, pp. 105–106

Similarities, pp. 104–105

Social clock, pp. 465–466

Social loafing, p. 658

Social-cultural perspective, p. 10

Spirituality: Israeli kibbutz communities, pp. C-11–C-12

Stress:
adjusting to a new culture, p. 400
racism and, p. 401

Taste preferences, pp. 335–336

Teen sexuality, pp. 352–354

Testing bias, pp. 555–556

Theory of mind: internalizing language, pp. 422–423

Weight control, p. 336

- *Unit 2, Research Methods: Thinking Critically With Psychological Science,* introduces students to psychology's research methods, emphasizing the fallacies of our everyday intuition and common sense and, thus, the need for psychological science. Critical thinking is introduced as a key term in this unit (p. 24). The Statistical Reasoning discussion encourages students to "focus on thinking smarter by applying simple statistical principles to everyday reasoning" (pp. 37–41).

- Throughout the text, additional opportunities may be found for students to test their understanding of *research design,* with narrative and marginal self-test review questions (with answers following in the narrative, or upside down

TABLE 2 The Psychology of Men and Women

Coverage of the psychology of men and women can be found on the following pages:

ADHD, p. 563

Adulthood: physical changes, p. 456

Aggression, pp. 671–676
  pornography, pp. 674–675
  rape, pp. 673, 674–676

Alcohol:
  addiction and, p. 200
  use, pp. 199–200
  sexual aggression and, p. 200

Altruism: help-receiving, p. 686

Antisocial personality disorder, p. 597

Attraction, pp. 679–681

Autism, p. 424

Behavioral effects of gender, p. 43

Biological predispositions, and the color red, pp. 224–225

Biological sex/gender, pp. 438–439

Bipolar disorder, p. 581

Body image, pp. 338–339

Classical conditioning and trauma/rape, p. 228

Color vision, p. 132

Conformity: obedience, p. 654

Dating, p. 680

Depression, pp. 580, 582, 587

Dream content, p. 188

Drug use:
  biological influences, p. 209

methamphetamines, p. 201
  psychological/social-cultural influences, pp. 209–210

Eating disorders, pp. 337–339

Emotion-detecting ability, pp. 379–380, 549

Empty nest, p. 468

Father care, pp. 354, 429

Freud's views:
  evaluating, p. 487
  identification/gender identity, p. 482
  Oedipus/Electra complexes, p. 482
  penis envy, pp. 484–485

Gender:
  and anxiety, p. 570
  and child-rearing, pp. 337, 440
  development, pp. 435–440
  prejudice, pp. 664–666
  roles, pp. 439–440
  similarities/differences, pp. 435–438

Gendered brain, pp. 352, 357, 359, 438

Generic pronoun "he," p. 320

Grief, p. 470

Group polarization, p. 659

Happiness, p. 396

Hormones and:
  aggression, pp. 671–672
  sexual behavior, pp. 350–351

sexual development, pp. 438–439, 445–448
  testosterone-replacement therapy, pp. 350–351

Intelligence, pp. 549–551
  bias, p. 555
  low extreme, p. 542

Leadership: transformational, p. B-12

Life expectancy, p. 457

Losing weight, p. 346

Marriage, pp. 466–468, C-4

Maturation, pp. 445–448

Menarche, p. 447

Menopause, p. 456

Midlife crisis, p. 465

Molecular genetics: "missing women," p. 665, 667

Obesity:
  genetic factors, p. 344
  guidance/counseling, p. 341
  health risks, pp. 340–341
  ingested calories, pp. 344–345
  weight discrimination, pp. 341–342

Observational learning: sexually violent media, p. 249

TV's influence, pp. 247–248

Pornography, pp. 351–352

Post-traumatic stress disorder: development of, pp. 572–573

Prejudice, pp. 300, 664–667

Psychological disorders, rates of, pp. 599–600

Rape, p. 670

Religiosity and: life expectancy, p. C-11

REM sleep, arousal in, p. 180

Romantic love, pp. 683–685

Savant syndrome, p. 525

Schizophrenia, pp. 591–592

Sense of smell, pp. 149–150

Sexual attraction, pp. 105–106

Sexual fantasies, p. 352

Sexuality, pp. 349–354
  adolescent, pp. 352–354
  evolutionary explanation, pp. 105–107
  external stimuli, pp. 351–352

Sleep, p. 182

Stereotyping, pp. 163–164

Stress:
  and depression, p. 403
  and health and sexual abuse, pp. C-5–C-6
  and heart disease, pp. 402–403
  and HIV, p. 405
  and the immune system, pp. 403–405
  response, p. 399

Suicide, pp. 584–585

Women in psychology, pp. 5–6

in a nearby margin), and in some of the free-response questions at the ends of the units.

- **"Thinking Critically About . . ." boxes** are found throughout the book, modeling for students a critical approach to some key issues in psychology. For example, see "Thinking Critically About: The Fear Factor—Do We Fear the Right Things?" (pp. 308–309).

- **Detective-style stories** throughout the narrative get students thinking critically about psychology's key research questions. (See, for example, the story of language in the brain on pp. 80–82.)

- **"Apply this" and "Think about it"**-style discussions keep students active in their study of each unit. Experience, for example, the sleep lab on pp. 178–181; or apply to your own life the therapeutic life-style change tips on pp. 636–637.)

- **Critical examinations of pop psychology** sprinkled throughout the narrative spark interest and provide important lessons in thinking critically about everyday topics. (Consider, for example, the critical analysis of ESP on pp. 166–169.)

See **TABLE 3**, next page, for a summary of this text's coverage of critical thinking and research-related topics, and for a list of the Thinking Critically About boxes.

TABLE 3 Critical Thinking and Research Emphasis

Critical thinking coverage, and in-depth stories of psychology's scientific research process, can be found on the following pages:

Thinking Critically About . . . boxes:

The Fear Factor—Do We Fear the Right Things?, pp. 308–309

Lie Detection, pp. 372–373

How to Be a "Successful" Astrologer or Palm Reader, pp. 498–499

ADHD—Normal High Energy or Genuine Disorder?, p. 563

Insanity and Responsibility, p. 569

"Regressing" from Unusual to Usual, p. 621

Complementary and Alternative Medicine, p. C-9

Critical Examinations of Pop Psychology:

The need for psychological science, p. 19

Perceiving order in random events, pp. 32–33

Do we use only 10 percent of our brains?, p. 79

Critiquing the evolutionary perspective, p. 107

Is there extrasensory perception?, pp. 166–169

Can hypnosis enhance recall? Coerce action? Be therapeutic? Alleviate pain?, pp. 193–194

Has the concept of "addiction" been stretched too far?, pp. 197–198

Near-death experiences, p. 206

How much credit (or blame) do parents deserve?, p. 443–444

How valid is the Rorschach test?, p. 486

Is repression a myth?, pp. 487–488

Is Freud credible?, pp. 487–490

Is psychotherapy effective?, pp. 619–623

Evaluating alternative therapies, pp. 623–625

Do video games teach or release violence?, pp. 676–677

Thinking Critically With Psychological Science:

The limits of intuition and common sense, pp. 19–22

The scientific attitude, pp. 22–24

"Critical thinking" introduced as a key term, p. 24

The scientific method, pp. 25–26

Correlation and causation, pp. 31–32

Illusory correlation, p. 32

Exploring cause and effect, p. 34

Random assignment, pp. 34–35

Independent and dependent variables, pp. 35–36

Statistical reasoning, pp. 37–41

Describing data, pp. 37–40

Making inferences, pp. 40–41

Scientific Detective Stories:

Is breast milk better than formula?, pp. 34–36

Our divided brains, pp. 83–86

Twin and adoption studies, pp. 96–100

Parallel processing, pp. 130–132

How do we see in color?, pp. 132–133

Why do we sleep?, pp. 181–185

Why do we dream?, pp. 189–191

Is hypnosis an extension of normal consciousness or an altered state?, pp. 194–196

How do we store memories in our brains?, pp. 268–274

How are memories constructed?, pp. 285–293

Why do we feel hunger?, pp. 331–335

The pursuit of happiness: Who is happy, and why?, pp. 389–396

Why—and in whom—does stress contribute to heart disease?, pp. 401–403

How a child's mind develops, pp. 417–426

Aging and intelligence, pp. 462–465

Self-esteem versus self-serving bias, pp. 513–516

What causes mood disorders?, pp. 582–589

Do prenatal viral infections increase risk of schizophrenia?, pp. 593–594

Is psychotherapy effective?, pp. 619–622

Why do people fail to help in emergencies?, pp. 685–687

How and why is social support linked with health?, pp. C-4–C-6

Do animals exhibit language?, pp. D-3–D-6

Innovative Multimedia Supplements Package

We know that the AP Psychology course requires extra preparation. Like the text, our ancillary materials are here to support teacher planning and student learning. *Psychology for AP** boasts impressive electronic and print supplements designed specifically for the AP classroom. For more information about any of these titles, visit Worth Publishers' online catalog at www.bfwpub.com/highschool.

Teacher's Edition

Drawing on her own many years of successfully teaching the AP course, Amy Fineburg's (Oak Mountain High School, AL) *Teacher's Edition* includes a pacing guide for many different-length courses (semester, block, full-year) so that teachers will be able to cover all the important concepts for the AP Exam without losing sight of the fun of the course, and the importance of incorporating interesting demonstrations and activities. Our *Teacher's Edition* also offers an abundance of teaching tips and resources for every unit, with a guide to the materials available from Worth Publishers and where they would fit best in the course. Additional resources within the *Teacher's Edition* include "How to Teach Essay Writing for Doing Well on the AP Exam," "How to Use Grading Rubrics Effectively," "How to Review for the AP Exam," and "What to do AFTER the AP Exam" (including ideas for covering some of the fun and abundant material in this text's appendices).

*AP is a trademark registered and/or owned by the College Board, which was not involved in the production of, and does not endorse, this product.

AP-Specific Test Bank

Working with John Brink's (Calvin College) Test Bank, Robert McEntarffer (Lincoln Public Schools, NE), with assistance from Kristin Whitlock (Viewmont High School, UT) and Alan Feldman (Glen Rock High School, NJ), created a thoroughly comprehensive set of questions that will help prepare students effectively for the AP Exam. Brink has authored every edition of the extremely well-received Test Bank for my texts. McEntarffer, with his years of experience as a Question Leader at the AP Psychology Readings, has ensured that the rigor and style of each question is in keeping with the demands of the AP Exam. This AP-specific Test Bank includes a number of additional questions, five distracters for each question (matching the AP Exam format), and a guide to creating unit tests that offers the same percentage of questions on key topics that students will encounter on the AP Exam. McEntarffer has also created a guide to how the Test Bank questions match up with the learning objectives from the College Board outline. This guide is available online (see www.bfwhighschool.com) and will be updated biennially—each time the College Board updates its outline for the course.

Teacher's Resource Binder

Expert teacher and longtime classroom resource provider Martin Bolt (Calvin College) created this Teacher's Resource Binder, with activities and handouts designed for this text and a guide to the videos and other resources available from Worth Publishers. This collection includes suggested lecture and discussion topics, demonstrations, in-class or homework projects, and fact/falsehood quizzes at the beginning of each unit to entice student interest in the subjects of discussion. Handouts offer opportunities for students to take what they are learning outside of the classroom to share with family and friends, or to work individually or with small groups in the classroom on topics that generate discussion.

Faculty Lounge for High School Psychology
www.bfwpub.com/highschool/psychologyfacultylounge

The Faculty Lounge for High School Psychology is an online community, with a repository of resources, where teachers may exchange ideas, share teaching tips, and develop professionally. The Faculty Lounge allows all teachers of General and AP Psychology easy searching for demonstrations, videos, or other materials uploaded by teaching colleagues across the country. Download resources to complement your teaching of a particular concept. Upload your own helpful content ideas. Link up with teaching colleagues in other parts of the country. Or participate in periodic online sessions with various experts, commissioned by Worth Publishers to talk or host discussions on teaching and research topics. Teachers using Worth texts will have special access to search through and download presentation and demonstration materials developed by Worth.

PsychPortal

Integrating the best online material that Worth Publishers has to offer, PsychPortal is an innovative learning space that combines a powerful quizzing engine with unparalleled media resources (see **FIGURE 3**, next page). PsychPortal conveniently offers all the functionality you need to support an online course, yet it is flexible, customizable, and simple enough to enhance your traditional course. The following interactive learning materials contained within PsychPortal make it truly unique:

- *An interactive eBook* allows students to highlight, bookmark, and make their own notes just as they would with a printed textbook.
- Thomas Ludwig's (Hope College) suite of interactive media—*PsychSim 5.0, PsychInquiry,* and the new *Concepts in Action*—bring key concepts to life.

➤ **FIGURE 3**
PsychPortal opening page

- *The Online Study Center* combines PsychPortal's powerful assessment engine with Worth's unparalleled collection of interactive study resources. Based on their quiz results, students receive Personalized Study Plans that direct them to sections in the book and also to simulations, animations, links, and tutorials that will help them succeed in mastering the concepts. Teachers can access reports indicating their students' strengths and weaknesses (based on class quiz results) and browse suggestions for helpful presentation materials (from Worth's renowned videos and demonstrations) to focus their teaching efforts accordingly.

- *The Psychology Video Tool Kit* includes 52 engaging video modules that teachers can easily assign, assess, and customize for their students **(FIGURE 4)**. Videos cover classic experiments, current news footage, and cutting-edge research, all of which are sure to spark discussion and encourage critical thinking.

- *Scientific American News Feed* highlights current behavioral research.

Additional Student Media

- Book Companion Site
- Worth eBook for *Psychology for AP**
- The Online Study Center
- Psych2Go (audio downloads for study and review)
- PsychSim 5.0 (on CD-ROM)
- Psychology Video Tool Kit (online and on CD-ROM)

*AP is a trademark registered and/or owned by the College Board, which was not involved in the production of, and does not endorse, this product.

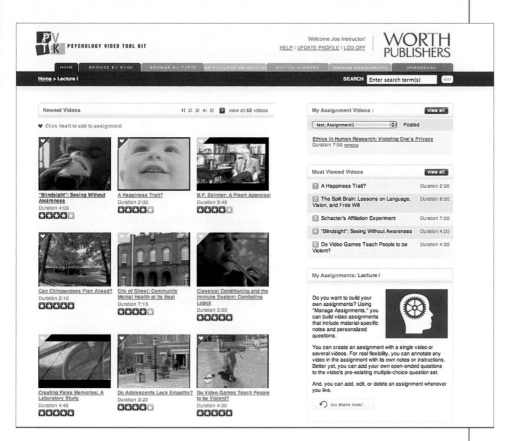

➤ FIGURE 4
Sample from our Psychology Video Tool Kit

Course Management

- Enhanced Course Management Solutions

Assessment

- Printed Test Bank
- Diploma Computerized Test Bank
- i•Clicker Radio Frequency Classroom Response System

Presentation

- ActivePsych: Classroom Activities Project and Video Teaching Modules (including Worth's Digital Media Archive, Second Edition, and *Scientific American* Frontiers Video Collection, Third Edition)
- Teacher's Resource CD-ROM
- Worth's Image and Lecture Gallery at www.worthpublishers.com/ilg

Video and DVD

- Psychology Video Tool Kit
- Digital Media Archive, Second Edition (available within ActivePsych and on closed-captioned DVD)
- *Scientific American* Frontiers Video Collection, Third Edition (available within ActivePsych and on closed-captioned DVD)

- Worth Digital Media Archive
- *Scientific American* Frontiers Video Collection, Second Edition
- The Mind Video Teaching Modules, Second Edition
- The Brain Video Teaching Modules, Second Edition
- Psychology: The Human Experience Teaching Modules
- The Many Faces of Psychology Video

Print Resources

- Teacher's Resource Binder and Lecture Guides, by Martin Bolt (Calvin College)
- Instructor's Media Guide
- Study Guide, by Richard Straub (University of Michigan, Dearborn)
- *Psychology and the Real World: Essays Illustrating Fundamental Contributions to Society* edited by Morton Ann Gernsbacher (University of Wisconsin-Madison), Richard W. Pew (BBN Technologies), Leaetta M. Hough (The Dunnette Group), and James R. Pomerantz (Rice University), with a foreword by Malcolm Gladwell (*New Yorker* magazine) and original essays by 39 key psychology researchers
- *Pursuing Human Strengths: A Positive Psychology Guide,* by Martin Bolt (Calvin College)
- *Critical Thinking Companion,* Second Edition, by Jane Halonen (University of West Florida)

Scientific American Resources

- *Scientific American Mind*
- NEW *Scientific American Reader to Accompany Myers*
- *Improving the Mind and Brain: A Scientific American Special Issue*
- *Scientific American Explores the Hidden Mind: A Collector's Edition*

In Appreciation

If it is true that "whoever walks with the wise becomes wise" then I am wiser for all the wisdom and advice received from my colleagues. Aided by over a thousand consultants and reviewers over the last two decades, my texts have become better, more accurate books than one author alone (this author, at least) could write. As my editors and I keep reminding ourselves, all of us together are smarter than any one of us.

My indebtedness continues to each of the teacher-scholars whose influence I have benefited from in previous editions of my texts, to the innumerable researchers who have been so willing to share their time and talent to help me accurately report their research, and to the hundreds of high school teachers and college instructors who have taken the time over the years to respond to our information-gathering surveys and to questions from their Worth representatives. All of this input has greatly improved the words you are about to read.

My gratitude extends to the colleagues who contributed criticism, corrections, and creative ideas specifically related to the content, pedagogy, and format of this edition and its supplements package. This includes the reviewers of my regular college text (*Psychology,* Ninth Edition, listed on the next page), from which much of this text's content was drawn, as well as those who were involved specifically with *Psychology for AP**. For their expertise and encouragement, and the gifts of their time to the teaching of psychology, I thank the reviewers and consultants listed next.

Focus Group Participants

Laura Brandt,
Adlai Stevenson High School (IL)

William Elmhorst,
Marshfield Senior High School (WI)

Dori Franck,
Glenbrook North High School (IL)

Melissa Kennedy,
Holy Names Academy (WA)

Ryan Mahoney,
Lincoln Southwest High School (NE)

Peter Masciopinto,
Glenbrook South High School (IL)

Hilary Rosenthal,
Glenbrook South High School (IL)

John Seiple,
Lyons Township High School (IL)

Justin Singleton,
Aldine High School (TX)

Sejal Vaughn,
Glenbrook South High School (IL)

Virginia Welle,
Chippewa Falls Senior High School (WI)

Dorothy Wenzel,
Patuxent High School (MD)

Reviewers

Richard Alexander,
Muskegon Community College

Carol Anderson,
Bellevue Community College

Aaron Ashly,
Weber State University

John Baker,
University of Wisconsin, Stephens Point

Dave Baskind,
Delta College

Beth Lanes Battinelli,
Union County College

Alan Beauchamp,
Northern Michigan University

Brooke Bennett,
Florida State University

Sylvia Beyer,
University of Wisconsin, Parkside

Patricia Bishop,
Cleveland State Community College

James Bodle,
College of Mount Saint Joseph

Linda Bradford,
Community College of Aurora

Steve Brasel,
Moody Bible Institute

June Breninger,
Cascade College

Tom Brothen,
University of Minnesota

Eric L. Bruns,
Campbellsville University

David Campell,
Humboldt State University

LeeAnn Cardaciotto,
La Salle University

Jill Carlivati,
George Washington University

Kenneth Carter,
Oxford College

Lorelei Carvajal,
Triton College

Sarah Caverly,
George Mason University

Clara Cheng,
American University

Jennifer Cina,
Barnard College

Virgil Davis,
Ashland Community and Technical College

Joyce C. Day,
Naugatuck Valley Community College

Dawn Delaney,
Madison Area Technical College

G. William Domhoff,
University of California, Santa Cruz

Darlene Earley-Hereford,
Southern Union State Community College, Opelika

Kimberly Fairchild,
Rutgers University, Livingston

Pam Fergus,
Inver Hills Community College

Christopher J. Ferguson,
Texas A&M International University

Faith Florer,
New York University

Jocelyn Folk,
Kent State University

Patricia Foster,
Austin Community College, Northridge

Lauren Fowler,
Weber State University

Daniel J. Fox,
Sam Houston State University

Ron Friedman,
Rochester University

Stan Friedman,
Southwest Texas State University

Sandra Geer,
Northeastern University

*AP is a trademark registered and/or owned by the College Board, which was not involved in the production of, and does not endorse, this product.

David D. Simpson,
Carroll College

Jeff Skowronek,
University of Tampa

Todd Smith,
Lake Superior State University

Bettina Spencer,
Saint Mary's College

O'Ann Steere,
College of DuPage

Barry Stennett,
Gainesville State College

Bruce Stevenson,
North Island College

Colleen Stevenson,
Muskingum College

Jaine Strauss,
Macalester College

Cynthia Symons,
Houghton College

Rachelle Tannenbaum,
Anne Arundel Community College

Sarah Ting,
Cerritos College

Barbara Van Horn,
Indian River Community College

Michael Verro,
Champlain College

Craig Vickio,
Bowling Green State University

Denise Vinograde,
LaGuardia Community College, CUNY

Joan Warmbold,
Oakton Community College

Eric Weiser,
Curry College

Diane Wille,
Indiana University Southeast

Paul Young,
Houghton College

At Worth Publishers a host of people played key roles in creating this new edition.

Christine Brune, chief editor for many editions of my texts, is a wonder worker. She offers just the right mix of encouragement, gentle admonition, attention to detail, and passion for excellence. She worked tirelessly to guide the creation of *Psychology for AP**. An author could not ask for more.

Editor Trish Morgan has repeatedly amazed me with her wide-ranging knowledge, meticulous focus, and deft editing.

Senior Psychology Acquisitions Editor Kevin Feyen has become a valued team leader, thanks to his dedication, creativity, and sensitivity. Kevin coordinated input from teachers across the country—with support from our wonderful high school sales and marketing group—and worked to build the team that helped guide this text's creation.

Publisher Catherine Woods helped construct and execute the plan for this text and its supplements. Catherine was also a trusted sounding board as we faced a seemingly unending series of discrete decisions along the way. Peter Twickler coordinated production of the huge supplements package for this edition. Betty Probert efficiently edited and produced the print supplements and, in the process, also helped fine-tune the whole book. Adam Frese, with help from Emily Ernst, provided invaluable support in commissioning and organizing the multitude of reviews, mailing information to professors, and handling numerous other daily tasks related to the book's development and production. Bianca Moscatelli and Jacqui Wong worked together to locate the myriad photos.

Associate Managing Editor Tracey Kuehn displayed tireless tenacity, commitment, and impressive organization in leading Worth's gifted artistic production team and coordinating editorial input throughout the production process. Production Manager Sarah Segal masterfully kept the book to its tight schedule, and Babs Reingold skillfully directed creation of the beautiful design and art program. Supplements Production Manager Stacey Alexander, along with Supplements Production Editor Jenny Chiu, did their usual excellent work of producing the many supplements.

To achieve our goal of supporting the teaching of psychology, this teaching package not only must be authored, reviewed, edited, and produced, but also made available to teachers of psychology. For their exceptional success in doing that, our author team is grateful to Worth Publishers' professional sales and marketing team. We are espe-

*AP is a trademark registered and/or owned by the College Board, which was not involved in the production of, and does not endorse, this product.

cially grateful to Mike Saltzman, Director of High School Sales and Marketing; Cindi Weiss, Executive Marketing Manager; and Nicole Sheppard, Marketing Manager, for their determined efforts to inform our teaching colleagues of our efforts to assist their teaching, and for the joy of working with them.

At Hope College, the supporting team members for this text included Kathryn Brownson, who researched countless bits of information and proofed hundreds of pages. Kathryn has become a knowledgeable and sensitive adviser on many matters, and Sara Neevel has become our high-tech manuscript developer, par excellence.

Again, I gratefully acknowledge the influence and editing assistance of my writing coach, poet Jack Ridl, whose influence resides in the voice you will be hearing in the pages that follow. He, more than anyone, cultivated my delight in dancing with the language, and taught me to approach writing as a craft that shades into art.

After hearing countless dozens of people say that my books' supplements have taken their teaching to a new level, I reflect on how fortunate I am to be a part of a team in which everyone has produced work marked by the highest professional standards. For their remarkable talents, their long-term dedication, and their friendship, I thank my collaborators John Brink, Thomas Ludwig, and Richard Straub. Sadly, our friend and collaborator Martin Bolt died on Christmas Day 2009, after already completing the Teacher's Resource Binder materials used for this AP edition.

Finally, my gratitude extends to the many students and teachers who have written to offer suggestions or just an encouraging word. It is for them, and those about to begin their study of psychology, that I have done my best to introduce the field I love.

For all of us who are teachers, to be entrusted with discerning and communicating psychology's insights is both an exciting honor and a great responsibility. The day this book went to press was the day I started gathering information and ideas for the next edition. Your input will influence how this book continues to evolve. So, please, do share your thoughts.

David Myers

Hope College
Holland, Michigan 49422-9000
davidmyers.org

MYERS' PSYCHOLOGY FOR AP*

Pacing Guide

Use the following guide to determine how many instructional days to devote to this unit depending on the type of course you teach:

Year-long course: 3–5 days
Block schedule/Semester-long course: 1–2 days

This unit encompasses 2–4 percent of the AP Exam. Spending an appropriate amount of time on this unit will help students do well on the AP Exam.

INTERCONNECTING

History of psychology topics are addressed throughout the text. Where their theories and research are relevant, the psychologists from this unit will be mentioned. Make sure students connect the people and ideas they learned in this unit with those mentioned later.

TEACHING TIP

Students may leave this unit believing that psychologists still subscribe to defined perspectives. Modern psychologists are more eclectic, using ideas, theories, and research from multiple perspectives according to their needs.

Suggested Readings

Use the following books as teacher-preparation tools or as enrichment for eager students:

Guthrie, R. V. (2003). *Even the rat was white: A historical view of psychology.* New York: Allyn & Bacon.

Harris, J. R. (1998). *The nurture assumption.* New York: Free Press.

Hunt, M. (1993). *The story of psychology.* New York: Doubleday.

Kimble, G. A., & Wertheimer, M. (Eds.) (2000). *Portraits of pioneers in psychology,* vols. 1–4. Washington, D.C.: APA.

Pickren, W. E., & Dewsbury, D. A. (Eds.) (2002). *Evolving perspectives in the history of psychology.* Washington, D.C.: APA.

Pinker, S. (2002). *The blank slate: The modern denial of human nature.* New York: Viking.

Street, W. R. (1994). *A chronology of noteworthy events in American psychology.* Washington, D.C.: APA.

Psychology's History and Approaches

Harvard astronomer Owen Gingerich (2006) reports that there are more than 100 billion galaxies. Just one of these, our own relative speck of a galaxy, has some 200 billion stars, many of which, like our Sun-star, are circled by planets. On the scale of outer space, we are less than a single grain of sand on all the oceans' beaches, and our lifetime but a relative nanosecond.

Yet there is nothing more awe inspiring and absorbing than our own inner space. Our brain, adds Gingerich, "is by far the most complex physical object known to us in the entire cosmos" (p. 29). Our consciousness—mind somehow arising from matter—remains a profound mystery. Our thinking, emotions, and actions (and their interplay with others' thinking, emotions, and actions) fascinate us. Outer space staggers us with its enormity, but inner space enthralls us. Enter psychological science.

For people whose exposure to psychology comes from pop-culture Web sites, books, magazines, and TV, psychologists analyze personality, offer counseling, and dispense child-rearing advice. Do they? Yes, and much more. Consider some of psychology's questions that from time to time you may wonder about:

- Have you ever found yourself reacting to something as one of your biological parents would—perhaps in a way you vowed you never would—and then wondered how much of your personality you inherited? *To what extent are person-to-person differences in personality predisposed by our genes? To what extent by the home and community environments?*
- Have you ever worried about how to act among people of a different culture, race, or gender? *In what ways are we alike as members of the human family? How do we differ?*
- Have you ever awakened from a nightmare and, with a wave of relief, wondered why you had such a crazy dream? *How often, and why, do we dream?*
- Have you ever played peekaboo with a 6-month-old and wondered why the baby finds the game so delightful? The infant reacts as though, when you momentarily move behind a door, you actually disappear—only to reappear later out of thin air. *What do babies actually perceive and think?*
- Have you ever wondered what leads to school and work success? Are some people just born smarter? *Does sheer intelligence explain why some people get richer, think more creatively, or relate more sensitively?*

"I have made a ceaseless effort not to ridicule, not to bewail, not to scorn human actions, but to understand them."
Benedict Spinoza, *A Political Treatise*, 1677

Key Terms

What Is Psychology?
empiricism
structuralism
functionalism
experimental psychology
behaviorism
humanistic psychology
cognitive neuroscience
psychology

Contemporary Psychology
nature-nurture issue
natural selection
levels of analysis
biopsychosocial approach
biological psychology
evolutionary psychology
psychodynamic psychology
behavioral psychology
cognitive psychology
social-cultural psychology
psychometrics
basic research
developmental psychology
educational psychology
personality psychology
social psychology
applied research
industrial-organizational (I/O)
 psychology
human factors psychology
counseling psychology
clinical psychology
psychiatry
SQ3R

Key People

Aristotle
Francis Bacon
Mary Whiton Calkins
Charles Darwin
René Descartes
Dorothea Dix
Sigmund Freud
G. Stanley Hall

William James
John Locke
Abraham Maslow
Ivan Pavlov
Jean Piaget
Plato
Rosalie Rayner
Carl Rogers

B. F. Skinner
Socrates
E. B. Titchener
Margaret Floy Washburn
John B. Watson
Wilhelm Wundt

TEACHING TIP

Students need to expand their definitions of psychology beyond the therapist and her couch. Emphasize that psychology is a wide ranging discipline that can encompass any aspect of human and nonhuman behavior. All the questions Myers poses here represent only the tip of the iceberg when it comes to the range of topics studied in psychology.

At this time, you may want to use **Introductory Exercise: *Fact or Falsehood?*** (p. 2) from Bolt's Teacher's Resource Binder, which accompanies this text.

CRITICAL THINKING

Have students read some key philosophical texts to understand how philosophers tried to address basic questions in psychology. Students can report about Plato's "Allegory of the Cave" or Aristotle's "On Memory and Reminiscence" to compare how modern psychology has evolved from these early philosophical contemplations on behavior and mental processes.

At this time, you may want to use **Lecture/Discussion Topic: *Aristotle's Psychology*** (p. 2) from Bolt's Teacher's Resource Binder.

▼
A smile is a smile the world around Throughout this book, you will see examples not only of our cultural and gender diversity but also of the similarities that define our shared human nature. People in different cultures vary in when and how often they smile, but a naturally happy smile *means* the same thing anywhere in the world.

- Have you ever become depressed or anxious and wondered whether you'll ever feel "normal"? *What triggers our bad moods—and our good ones?*

Such questions provide grist for psychology's mill, because psychology is a science that seeks to answer all sorts of questions about us all—how and why we think, feel, and act as we do.

What Is Psychology?

Psychology's Roots

ONCE UPON A TIME, ON A PLANET IN this neighborhood of the universe, there came to be people. Soon thereafter, these creatures became intensely interested in themselves and in one another: *Who are we? What produces our thoughts? Our feelings? Our actions? And how are we to understand and manage those around us?*

Prescientific Psychology

1: How did psychology develop from its prescientific roots in early understandings of mind and body to the beginnings of modern science?

We can trace many of psychology's current questions back through human history. These early thinkers wondered: How do our minds work? How do our bodies relate to our minds? How much of what we know comes built in? How much is acquired through experience? In India, Buddha pondered how sensations and perceptions combine to form ideas. In China, Confucius stressed the power of ideas and of an educated mind. In ancient Israel, Hebrew scholars anticipated today's psychology by linking mind and emotion to the body; people were said to think with their heart and feel with their bowels.

In ancient Greece, the philosopher-teacher Socrates (469–399 B.C.E.) and his student Plato (428–348 B.C.E.) concluded that mind is separable from body and continues after the body dies—and that knowledge is innate—born within us. Unlike Socrates and Plato, who derived principles by logic, Plato's student Aristotle (384–322 B.C.E.) had a love of data. An intellectual ancestor of today's scientists, Aristotle

● To assist your active learning, I will periodically offer learning objectives. These will be framed as questions that you can answer as you read on. ●

CRITICAL THINKING

Have students examine how medieval thought and practices contributed to the development of science. Students can contemplate the role of religious and cultural mores in the development and hindrance of scientific thought and practice after the 1600s.

At this time, you may want to use **Lecture/Discussion Topics: *Psychology's First Experiments*** (p. 3) or ***History of Psychology*** (p. 3) from Bolt's Teacher's Resource Binder.

derived principles from careful observations. Moreover, he said knowledge is *not* preexisting (sorry, Socrates and Plato); instead it grows from the experiences stored in our memories.

The next 2000 years brought few enduring new insights into human nature, but that changed in the 1600s, when modern science began to flourish. With it came new theories of human behavior, and new versions of the ancient debates. A frail but brilliant Frenchman named René Descartes (1595–1650) agreed with Socrates and Plato about the existence of innate ideas and mind's being "entirely distinct from body" and able to survive its death. Descartes' concept of mind forced him to conjecture, as people have ever since, how the immaterial mind and physical body communicate. A scientist as well as a philosopher, Descartes dissected animals and concluded that the fluid in the brain's cavities contained "animal spirits." These spirits, he surmised, flowed from the brain through what we call the nerves (which he thought were hollow) to the muscles, provoking movement. Memories formed as experiences opened pores in the brain into which the animal spirits also flowed.

Descartes was right that nerve paths are important and that they enable reflexes. Yet, genius though he was, and standing upon the knowledge accumulated from 99+ percent of our human history, he hardly had a clue of what today's average 12-year-old knows. Indeed, most of the scientific story of our self-exploration—the story told in this book—has been written in but the last historical eyeblink of human time.

Meanwhile, across the English Channel in Britain, science was taking a more down-to-earth form, centered on experiment, experience, and common-sense judgment. Francis Bacon (1561–1626) became one of the founders of modern science, and his influence lingers in the experiments of today's psychological science. Bacon also was fascinated by the human mind and its failings. Anticipating what we have come to appreciate about our mind's hunger to perceive patterns even in random events, he wrote that "the human understanding, from its peculiar nature, easily supposes a greater degree of order and equality in things than it really finds" (*Novum Organuum*). He also foresaw research findings on our noticing and remembering events that confirm our beliefs: "All superstition is much the same whether it be that of astrology, dreams, omens . . . in all of which the deluded believers observe events which are fulfilled, but neglect and pass over their failure, though it be much more common."

Some 50 years after Bacon's death, John Locke (1632–1704), a British political philosopher, sat down to write a one-page essay on "our own abilities" for an upcoming discussion with friends. After 20 years and hundreds of pages, Locke had completed one of history's greatest late papers (*An Essay Concerning Human Understanding*), in which he famously argued that the mind at birth is a *tabula rasa*—a "blank slate"—on which experience writes. This idea, adding to Bacon's ideas, helped form modern **empiricism**, the view that knowledge originates in experience and that science should, therefore, rely on observation and experimentation.

A seventeenth-century view of nerves In his *Treatise of Man*, Descartes proposed the hydraulics of a simple reflex. ▲···

• Throughout the text, important concepts are boldfaced. As you study, you can find these terms with their definitions in a nearby margin and in the Glossary at the end of the book. •

::**empiricism** the view that knowledge originates in experience and that science should, therefore, rely on observation and experimentation.

CULTURAL CONNECTIONS

Most of the discussion here focuses on Western philosophical traditions. Have students examine Eastern cultural and philosophical traditions and compare these with the Western traditions described in the text.

TEACHING TIP

Descartes promoted a concept called "dualism," in which the mind and body were separate. Have students discuss whether they think Descartes' idea has merit in light of today's ideas in cognitive neuroscience.

CRITICAL THINKING

The idea of the *tabula rasa* has been influential in science and politics. Discuss with students how the idea of a "blank slate" might inform one's views about behavior.

WEB CONNECT

Have students find out what important events happened in psychology on their birthday. Warren Street maintains a Web site where students can search for important events in psychology according to a date. Have students create a poster detailing a few of the events that happened on their birthday.

Web site: Today in the History of Psychology: www.cwu.edu/~warren/today.html.

UNIT 1

Wilhelm Wundt Wundt (far left) established the first psychology laboratory at the University of Leipzig, Germany.

• Information sources are cited in parentheses, with name and date. Every citation can be found in the end-of-book References, with complete documentation that follows American Psychological Association style. •

"The rose is smooth-petaled, sweetly aromatic,..."

Edward Bradford Titchener Titchener used introspection to search for the mind's structural elements.

TEACHING TIP

The birth of modern psychology occurred in December 1879 in Leipzig, Germany. Wundt and two students—Max Friedrich, a German, and G. Stanley Hall, an American— set up an experiment on the third floor of a shabby building called Konvikt ("hostel" or "retreat"). The three men intended to collect data for Friedrich's dissertation on "the duration of apperception"—the time lag between the subject's recognition that he has heard the ball hit the platform and his pressing of the telegraph key.

Hunt, M. (1993). *The story of psychology*. New York: Doubleday.

Psychological Science Is Born

2: When and how did modern psychological science begin?

Philosophers' thinking about thinking continued until the birth of psychology as we know it, on a December day in 1879, in a small, third-floor room at Germany's University of Leipzig. There, two young men were helping an austere, middle-aged professor, Wilhelm Wundt, create an experimental apparatus. Their machine measured the time lag between people's hearing a ball hit a platform and their pressing a telegraph key (Hunt, 1993). Curiously, people responded in about one-tenth of a second when asked to press the key as soon as the sound occurred—and in about two-tenths of a second when asked to press the key as soon as they were consciously aware of perceiving the sound. (To be aware of one's awareness takes a little longer.) Wundt was seeking to measure "atoms of the mind"—the fastest and simplest mental processes. Thus began what many consider psychology's first experiment, launching the first psychological laboratory, staffed by Wundt and psychology's first graduate students.

Before long, this new science of psychology became organized into different branches, or schools of thought, each promoted by pioneering thinkers. These early schools included *structuralism, functionalism,* and *behaviorism,* described here (with more on behaviorism in Unit 6), and two schools described in later units: Gestalt psychology (Unit 4) and psychoanalysis (Unit 10).

Thinking About the Mind's Structure

Soon after receiving his Ph.D. in 1892, Wundt's student Edward Bradford Titchener joined the Cornell University faculty and introduced **structuralism**. As physicists and chemists discerned the structure of matter, so Titchener aimed to discover the structural elements of mind. His method was to engage people in self-reflective *introspection* (looking inward), training them to report elements of their experience as they looked at a rose, listened to a metronome, smelled a scent, or tasted a substance. What were their immediate sensations, their images, their feelings? And how did these relate to one another? Titchener shared with the English essayist C. S. Lewis the view that "there is one thing, and only one in the whole universe which we know more about than we could learn from external observation." That one thing, Lewis said, is ourselves. "We have, so to speak, inside information" (1960, pp. 18–19).

Alas, introspection required smart, verbal people. It also proved somewhat unreliable, its results varying from person to person and experience to experience. Moreover, we often just don't know why we feel what we feel and do what we do. Recent studies indicate that people's recollections frequently err. So do their self-reports about what, for example, has caused them to help or hurt another (Myers, 2002). As introspection waned, so did structuralism.

Thinking About the Mind's Functions

Unlike those hoping to assemble the structure of mind from simple elements—which was rather like trying to understand a car by examining its disconnected parts—philosopher-psychologist William James thought it more fruitful to consider the evolved *functions* of our thoughts and feelings. Smelling is what the nose does;

CRITICAL THINKING

Have students consider the contributions of the following people in psychology:

Dorothea Dix (1802-1887)—helped reform inhumane treatments for psychological disorders

Francis Cecil Sumner—the first African American male to receive a Ph.D. in psychology (Clark University, 1920)

Inez Beverly Prosser—the first African American female to receive a Ph.D. in psychology (The University of Cincinnati, 1933).

Kenneth Clark and Mamie Phipps Clark—Kenneth was the first African American president of the APA (1970), and he and Mamie Phipps Clark conducted research cited in the 1954 *Brown v. Board of Education* Supreme Court decision.

Ellen Langer—the first woman granted tenure in psychology at Harvard University in 1981.

Judith Rodin—the first female president of an Ivy League school (the University of Pennsylvania, 1993).

thinking is what the brain does. But why do the nose and brain do these things? Under the influence of evolutionary theorist Charles Darwin, James assumed that thinking, like smelling, developed because it was *adaptive*—it contributed to our ancestors' survival. Consciousness serves a function. It enables us to consider our past, adjust to our present circumstances, and plan our future. As a **functionalist**, James encouraged explorations of down-to-earth emotions, memories, willpower, habits, and moment-to-moment streams of consciousness.

James' greatest legacy, however, came less from his laboratory than from his Harvard teaching and his writing. When not plagued by ill health and depression, James was an impish, outgoing, and joyous man, who once recalled that "the first lecture on psychology I ever heard was the first I ever gave." During one of his wise-cracking lectures, a student interrupted and asked him to get serious (Hunt, 1993). He loved his students, his family, and the world of ideas, but he tired of painstaking chores such as proofreading. "Send me no proofs!" he once told an editor. "I will return them unopened and never speak to you again" (Hunt, 1993, p.145).

James displayed the same spunk in 1890, when—over the objections of Harvard's president—he admitted Mary Calkins into his graduate seminar (Scarborough & Furumoto, 1987). (In those years women lacked even the right to vote.) When Calkins joined, the other students (all men) dropped out. So James tutored her alone. Later, she finished all the requirements for a Harvard Ph.D., outscoring all the male students on the qualifying exams. Alas, Harvard denied her the degree she had earned, offering her instead a degree from Radcliffe College, its undergraduate sister school for women. Calkins resisted the unequal treatment and refused the degree. (More than a century later, psychologists and psychology students were lobbying Harvard to posthumously award Calkins the Ph.D. she earned [*Feminist Psychologist*, 2002].) Calkins nevertheless went on to become a distinguished memory researcher and the American Psychological Association's (APA's) first female president in 1905.

When Harvard denied Calkins the claim to being psychology's first female psychology Ph.D., that honor fell to Margaret Floy Washburn, who later wrote an influential book, *The Animal Mind*, and became the second female APA president in 1921. Although

::**structuralism** an early school of psychology that used introspection to explore the structural elements of the human mind.

::**functionalism** a school of psychology that focused on how our mental and behavioral processes function—how they enable us to adapt, survive, and flourish.

> "You don't know your own mind."
> Jonathan Swift
> *Polite Conversation*, 1738

William James and Mary Whiton Calkins James, legendary teacher-writer, mentored Calkins, who became a pioneering memory researcher and the first woman to be president of the American Psychological Association.
▲.................

Margaret Floy Washburn The first woman to receive a psychology Ph.D., Washburn synthesized animal behavior research in *The Animal Mind*.
▲.................

TROUBLESHOOTING

Structuralism and Functionalism, the two early schools of thought in psychology, are often confused by students. Because these two concepts are less relevant to students' later study of psychology, helping students to appreciate the differences between them will be useful at test time:

- Structuralism has its basis in Wundt's European perspective. Titchener established this school based on his work as Wundt's student in Germany.

- Functionalism is based on William James' ideas about psychology having practical applications to life.

- Structuralists sought to identify what the mind and consciousness were.

- Functionalists sought to identify how the mind and consciousness worked.

TROUBLESHOOTING

Students should leave AP Psychology with the strong idea that psychology is a science. Psychologists use scientific methodology to study behavior and mental processes, just as those who study chemistry, physics, and biology do.

At this time, you may want to use **Classroom Exercises:** *Psychologist as Scientist* (p. 6) or *Psychology as Science (PAS) Scale* (p. 7) from Bolt's Teacher's Resource Binder.

TEACHING TIP

Connect John Locke's idea of the *tabula rasa* with John B. Watson's ideas about behaviorism. Watson believed he could take any infant and raise the child in a chosen environment to create any type of person he might want. He believed environment was the main component of psychology, just as Locke believed.

TROUBLESHOOTING

Humanistic psychology is often referred to in history books as the "third force" in psychology. Students often don't understand why humanistic psychology has this nickname. At the time of its beginnings in the 1950s and 1960s, psychologists followed either the behaviorist or the psychoanalytic perspective. Humanistic psychology offered a third way of thinking about behavior:

- Humanistic psychologists believed people were essentially good, unlike psychoanalytic psychologists.

- Humanistic psychologists believed humans were unique and distinct from animals, unlike behaviorists.

::**experimental psychology** the study of behavior and thinking using the experimental method.

::**behaviorism** the view that psychology (1) should be an objective science that (2) studies behavior without reference to mental processes. Most research psychologists today agree with (1) but not with (2).

::**humanistic psychology** historically significant perspective that emphasized the growth potential of healthy people and the individual's potential for personal growth.

::**cognitive neuroscience** the interdisciplinary study of the brain activity linked with cognition (including perception, thinking, memory, and language).

::**psychology** the science of behavior and mental processes.

Sigmund Freud The controversial ideas of this famed personality theorist and therapist have influenced humanity's self-understanding. ▲

Washburn's thesis was the first foreign study Wundt published in his journal, her gender meant she was barred from joining the organization of **experimental psychologists** (who explore behavior and thinking with experiments), despite its being founded by Titchener, her own graduate adviser (Johnson, 1997). What a different world from the recent past—1996 to 2009—when women claimed two-thirds or more of new U.S. psychology Ph.D.s and were 6 of the 13 elected presidents of the science-oriented Association for Psychological Science. In Canada and Europe, too, most recent psychology doctorates have been earned by women.

James' influence reached even further through his dozens of well-received articles, which moved the publisher Henry Holt to offer a contract for a textbook of the new science of psychology. James agreed and began work in 1878, with an apology for requesting two years to finish his writing. The text proved an unexpected chore and actually took him 12 years. (Why am I not surprised?) More than a century later, people still read the resulting *Principles of Psychology* and marvel at the brilliance and elegance with which James introduced psychology to the educated public.

Psychological Science Develops

3: How did psychology continue to develop from the 1920s through today?

The young science of psychology developed from the more established fields of philosophy and biology. Wundt was both a philosopher and a physiologist. James was an American philosopher. Ivan Pavlov, who pioneered the study of learning, was a Russian physiologist. Sigmund Freud, who developed the influential *psychoanalytic* theory of personality, was an Austrian physician. Jean Piaget, the last century's most influential observer of children, was a Swiss biologist. This list of pioneering psychologists—"Magellans of the mind," as Morton Hunt (1993) has called them—illustrates psychology's origins in many disciplines and countries.

The rest of the story of psychology—the subject of this book—develops at many levels. With pursuits ranging from the study of nerve cell activity to the study of international conflicts, *psychology* is not easily defined.

In psychology's early days, Wundt and Titchener focused on inner sensations, images, and feelings. James, too, engaged in introspective examination of the stream of consciousness and of emotion. Freud emphasized the ways emotional responses to childhood experiences and our unconscious thought processes affect our behavior. Thus, until the 1920s, *psychology* was defined as "the science of mental life."

From the 1920s into the 1960s, American psychologists, initially led by flamboyant and provocative John B. Watson and later by the equally provocative B. F. Skinner, dismissed introspection and redefined *psychology* as "the scientific study of observable behavior." After all, said these **behaviorists**, science is rooted in observation. You cannot observe a sensation, a feeling, or a thought, but you *can* observe and record people's *behavior* as they respond to different situations. (More on these psychologists in Unit 6.)

During the 1960s and beyond, **humanistic psychology** rebelled against Freudian psychology and behaviorism. Pioneers Carl Rogers and Abraham Maslow found behaviorism's focus on learned behaviors too mechanistic. Rather than focusing on the meaning of early childhood memories, as a psychoanalyst might, the humanistic psychologists emphasized the importance of current environmental influences on our growth potential, and the importance of having our needs for love and acceptance satisfied. (More on this in Unit 10.)

In the 1960s, another movement emerged as psychology began to recapture its initial interest in mental processes. This *cognitive revolution* supported ideas developed by

CRITICAL THINKING

Carl Rogers, one of the founders of humanistic psychology, and B. F. Skinner, the prominent behaviorist, often engaged in lively debates about the relative strengths of their views on behavior. Set up a debate among your students pitting the humanistic view against the behaviorist view.

At this time, you may want to use **Student Project/Lecture/Discussion Topic:** *The Twentieth Century's Most Eminent Psychologists* (p. 6) from Bolt's Teacher's Resource Binder.

John B. Watson and Rosalie Rayner Working with Rayner, Watson championed psychology as the science of behavior and demonstrated conditioned responses in a baby who became famous as "Little Albert."

B. F. Skinner A leading behaviorist, Skinner rejected intro-spection and studied how consequences shape behavior.

earlier psychologists, such as the importance of how our mind processes and retains information. But cognitive psychology and more recently **cognitive neuroscience** (the study of brain activity linked with mental activity) have expanded upon those ideas to explore scientifically the ways we perceive, process, and remember information. This approach has been especially beneficial in helping to develop new ways to understand and treat disorders such as depression, as we shall see in Units 12 and 13.

To encompass psychology's concern with observable behavior *and* with inner thoughts and feelings, today we define **psychology** as the *science of behavior and mental processes*.

Let's unpack this definition. *Behavior* is anything an organism *does*—any action we can observe and record. Yelling, smiling, blinking, sweating, talking, and questionnaire marking are all observable behaviors. *Mental processes* are the internal, subjective experiences we infer from behavior—sensations, perceptions, dreams, thoughts, beliefs, and feelings.

The key word in psychology's definition is *science*. Psychology, as I will emphasize throughout this book, is less a set of findings than a way of asking and answering questions. My aim, then, is not merely to report results but also to show you how psychologists play their game. You will see how researchers evaluate conflicting opinions and ideas. And you will learn how all of us, whether scientists or simply curious people, can think smarter when describing and explaining the events of our lives.

BEFORE YOU MOVE ON . . .

➤ **ASK YOURSELF**

How do you think psychology might change as more people from non-Western countries contribute their ideas to the field?

➤ **TEST YOURSELF 1**

What event defined the founding of modern scientific psychology?

Answers to the Test Yourself questions can be found in Appendix E at the end of the book.

● These "Before you move on . . ." sections will appear at the end of each main section of text. The *Ask Yourself* questions will help you make the material more meaningful to your own life (and therefore more memorable). If you can answer the *Test Yourself* questions, which will provide a review of the key points of the previous section, you are, indeed, ready to move on! You can check your answers to the Test Yourself Questions in Appendix E at the end of the book. ●

INTERCONNECTING

Point out another school of thought in psychology that is mentioned elsewhere in the text:

Gestalt psychology—an early school of psychology from Germany that studied how people organized perceptual experiences in understandable ways. They are famous for developing rules for how we organize what we sense and perceive, and for the statement that "the whole is greater than the sum of its parts." Gestalt psychology is discussed in Unit 4.

INTERCONNECTING

Point out the different technologies that psychologists use to study how cognition and biology interact. These technologies—fMRI, CT scan, EEG, PET scan—are used to study the brain and diagnose mental and physical illness. These are discussed more thoroughly in Unit 3B.

TEACHING TIP

At this time, you may want to use **Student Project:** *Interviewing a Psychologist* (p. 6) from Bolt's Teacher's Resource Binder.

TEACHING TIP

Inspire critical thinking in your students by playing devil's advocate for both sides of the nature/nurture debate. The exercise might show students who lean toward a particular side the complexity of the interaction of both nature and nurture in determining human behavior. Set up debates among students focused on the questions Myers poses here in the text. Have students defend either the nature or nurture side of the debate. End the debates with a discussion of how nature and nurture are not opposed, but rather work together to influence behavior and mental processes.

TROUBLESHOOTING

Some students may be uncomfortable discussing Darwin's theory of evolution. They may feel that his theory conflicts with their religious beliefs. Have students focus on the key elements of evolution that are important to psychology: natural selection and adaptation within species. These ideas have a significant scientific basis in all species, including humans. Focus more on how one's present environment would necessitate physical and psychological adaptation for the success of future generations.

::**nature-nurture issue** the longstanding controversy over the relative contributions that genes and experience make to the development of psychological traits and behaviors. Today's science sees traits and behaviors arising from the interaction of nature and nurture.

::**natural selection** the principle that, among the range of inherited trait variations, those contributing to reproduction and survival will most likely be passed on to succeeding generations.

Contemporary Psychology

LIKE ITS PIONEERS, TODAY'S PSYCHOLOGISTS are citizens of many lands. The International Union of Psychological Science has 69 member nations, from Albania to Zimbabwe. Nearly everywhere, membership in psychological societies is mushrooming—from 4183 American Psychological Association members and affiliates in 1945 to nearly 150,000 today, with similarly rapid growth in the British Psychological Society (from 1100 to 45,000). In China, the first university psychology department began in 1978; by 2008 there were 200 (Tversky, 2008). Worldwide, some 500,000 people have been trained as psychologists, and 130,000 of them belong to European psychological organizations (Tikkanen, 2001). Moreover, thanks to international publications, joint meetings, and the Internet, collaboration and communication cross borders now more than ever. "We are moving rapidly toward a single world of psychological science," reports Robert Bjork (2000). Psychology is *growing* and it is *globalizing*.

Across the world, psychologists are debating enduring issues, viewing behavior from the differing perspectives offered by the subfields in which they teach, work, and do research.

Psychology's Biggest Question

4: What is psychology's historic big issue?

During its short history, psychology has wrestled with some issues that will reappear throughout this book. The biggest and most persistent is the **nature-nurture issue**—*the controversy over the relative contributions of biology and experience.* As we have seen, the origins of this debate are ancient. Do our human traits develop through experience, or are we born with them? The ancient Greeks debated this, with Plato assuming that character and intelligence are largely inherited and that certain ideas are also inborn, and Aristotle countering that there is nothing in the mind that does not first come in from the external world through the senses. In the 1600s, philosophers rekindled the debate. Locke rejected the notion of inborn ideas, suggesting that the mind is a blank slate on which experience writes. Descartes disagreed, believing that some ideas are innate.

Charles Darwin Darwin argued that natural selection shapes behaviors as well as bodies.

Two centuries later, Descartes' views gained support from a curious naturalist. In 1831, an indifferent student but ardent collector of beetles, mollusks, and shells set sail on what was to prove a historic round-the-world journey. The 22-year-old voyager was Charles Darwin, and for some time afterward, he pondered the incredible species variation he had encountered, including tortoises on one island that differed from those on other islands of the region. Darwin's 1859 *On the Origin of Species* explained this diversity of life by proposing the evolutionary process of **natural selection**: From among chance variations, nature selects the traits that best enable an organism to survive and

Monika Suteski

DEMO

Use these quick demonstrations to show that many traits and behaviors are inherited.

- Have students draw a straight horizontal line on a sheet of paper. When the tip of their ring finger is placed on the line, does the tip of the forefinger also reach the line? *(Research indicates that short forefingers are determined by a recessive trait in females, whereas in males it is dominant.)*

- When interlocking their fingers, do students place the left or right thumb on top? *(This particular characteristic is genetically controlled. Practice or experience has no effect.)*

reproduce in a particular environment. Darwin's principle of natural selection—"the single best idea anyone has ever had," says philosopher Daniel Dennett (1996)—is still with us 150 years later as an organizing principle of biology. Evolution also has become an important principle for twenty-first-century psychology. This would surely have pleased Darwin, for he believed his theory explained not only animal structures (such as a polar bear's white coat) but also animal behaviors (such as the emotional expressions associated with human lust and rage).

The nature-nurture debate weaves a thread from the ancient Greeks' time to our own. Today's psychologists explore the issue by asking, for example:

- How are we humans alike (because of our common biology and evolutionary history) and diverse (because of our differing environments)?
- Are gender differences biologically predisposed or socially constructed?
- Is children's grammar mostly innate or formed by experience?
- How are differences in intelligence and personality influenced by heredity and by environment?
- Are sexual behaviors more "pushed" by inner biology or "pulled" by external incentives?
- Should we treat psychological disorders—depression, for example—as disorders of the brain, disorders of thought, or both?

Such debates continue. Yet over and over again we will see that in contemporary science the nature-nurture tension dissolves: *Nurture works on what nature endows.* Our species is biologically endowed with an enormous capacity to learn and adapt. Moreover, every psychological event (every thought, every emotion) is simultaneously a biological event. Thus, depression can be *both* a brain disorder *and* a thought disorder.

A nature-made nature-nurture experiment Because identical twins have the same genes, they are ideal participants in studies designed to shed light on hereditary and environmental influences on intelligence, personality, and other traits. Studies of identical and fraternal twins provide a rich array of findings—described in later units—that underscore the importance of both nature and nurture.

Psychology's Three Main Levels of Analysis

5: What are psychology's levels of analysis and related perspectives?

Each of us is a complex system that is part of a larger social system. But each of us is also composed of smaller systems, such as our nervous system and body organs, which are composed of still smaller systems—cells, molecules, and atoms.

TROUBLESHOOTING

Address several misunderstandings about evolutionary psychology:

- Evolution does not imply genetic determinism.
- Behavior can be changed.
- Organisms do not have a conscious or unconscious goal of maximizing gene reproduction. Rather, the most adaptive traits will survive due to natural selection.

Buss, D. M. (1999). *Evolutionary psychology: The new science of the mind.* Needham Heights, MA: Allyn & Bacon.

TEACHING TIP

At this time, you may want to use **Classroom Exercises:** *Self-Assessment on Some of Psychology's Big Issues* (p. 8) or *Is Human Nature Fixed or Changeable?* (p. 8) from Bolt's Teacher's Resource Binder.

UNIT 1

CRITICAL THINKING

The biopsychosocial approach in psychology highlights how integrated psychology is as a discipline. Take a simple behavior—smiling at another person in the hallway—and have students brainstorm about the biological, psychological (cognitive), and social-cultural reasons why someone might perform this behavior. This will help students understand how even the simplest behavior is really rather complex.

INTERCONNECTING

Throughout the course, you may want to have students use this graphic in Figure 1.1 to analyze any behavior you will discuss. For instance, in Unit 14, Social Psychology, you could have students fill in the biological, psychological, and social-cultural reasons for the results of the Milgram obedience studies or the Asch conformity studies. This type of activity will help students remember these three levels of analysis.

TEACHING TIP

The psychodynamic perspective is less concerned with the sexual emphasis Freud advocated. Psychodynamic psychologists focus more on childhood relationships and how those affect normal adult behavior.

➤ **FIGURE 1.1**
Biopsychosocial approach This integrated viewpoint incorporates various levels of analysis and offers a more complete picture of any given behavior or mental process.

::**levels of analysis** the differing complementary views, from biological to psychological to social-cultural, for analyzing any given phenomenon.

::**biopsychosocial approach** an integrated approach that incorporates biological, psychological, and social-cultural levels of analysis.

::**biological psychology** a branch of psychology that studies the links between biological (including neuroscience and behavior genetics) and psychological processes.

::**evolutionary psychology** the study of the roots of behavior and mental processes using the principles of natural selection.

::**psychodynamic psychology** a branch of psychology that studies how unconscious drives and conflicts influence behavior, and uses that information to treat people with psychological disorders.

::**behavioral psychology** the scientific study of observable behavior, and its explanation by principles of learning.

::**cognitive psychology** the scientific study of all the mental activities associated with thinking, knowing, remembering, and communicating.

::**social-cultural psychology** the study of how situations and cultures affect our behavior and thinking.

These tiered systems suggest different **levels of analysis**, which offer complementary outlooks. It's like explaining why grizzly bears hibernate. Is it because hibernation helped their ancestors to survive and reproduce? Because their inner physiology drives them to do so? Because cold environments hinder food gathering during winter? Such perspectives are complementary because "everything is related to everything else" (Brewer, 1996). Together, different levels of analysis form an integrated **biopsychosocial approach**, which considers the influences of biological, psychological, and social-cultural factors (**FIGURE 1.1**).

Each level provides a valuable vantage point for looking at behavior, yet each by itself is incomplete. Like different academic disciplines, psychology's varied approaches, or perspectives, ask different questions and have their own limits. One perspective may stress the biological, psychological, or social-cultural level more than another, but the different perspectives described in **TABLE 1.1** complement one another. Consider, for example, how they shed light on anger.

- Someone working from a **biological** perspective might study brain circuits that cause us to be "red in the face" and "hot under the collar," or how heredity and experience influence our individual differences in temperament.

- Someone working from the **evolutionary** perspective might analyze how anger facilitated the survival of our ancestors' genes.

- Someone working from the **psychodynamic** perspective might view an outburst as an outlet for unconscious hostility.

- Someone working from the **behavioral** perspective might attempt to determine which external stimuli trigger angry responses or aggressive acts.

- Someone working from the **cognitive** perspective might study how our interpretation of a situation affects our anger and how our anger affects our thinking.

- Someone working from the *humanistic perspective* (a historically important approach) might have been interested in understanding how angry feelings affect a person's potential for growth and personal fulfillment.

- Someone working from the **social-cultural** perspective might explore how expressions of anger vary across cultural contexts.

TEACHING TIP

Point out to students that positive psychology is the modern evolution of humanistic psychology. Positive psychology holds many of the same ideals as humanistic psychology—discovering human potential and fulfillment—but relies more on scientific methodology rather than theorizing to explore ideas.

TABLE 1.1

PSYCHOLOGY'S APPROACHES

Approach	Focus	Sample Questions
Biological	How the body and brain enable emotions, memories, and sensory experiences; how genes combine with environment to influence individual differences	How are messages transmitted within the body? How is blood chemistry linked with moods and motives? To what extent are traits such as intelligence, personality, sexual orientation, and depression attributable to our genes? To our environment?
Evolutionary	How the natural selection of traits promoted the survival of genes	How does evolution influence behavior tendencies?
Psychodynamic	How behavior springs from unconscious drives and conflicts	How can someone's personality traits and disorders be explained in terms of sexual and aggressive drives or as the disguised effects of unfulfilled wishes and childhood traumas?
Behavioral	How we learn observable responses	How do we learn to fear particular objects or situations? What is the best way to alter our behavior, say, to lose weight or stop smoking?
Cognitive	How we encode, process, store, and retrieve information	How do we use information in remembering? Reasoning? Solving problems?
Humanistic	How we meet our needs for love and acceptance and achieve self-fulfillment	How can we work toward fulfilling our potential? How can we overcome barriers to our personal growth?
Social-cultural	How behavior and thinking vary across situations and cultures	How are we humans alike as members of one human family? As products of different environmental contexts, how do we differ?

The point to remember: Like two-dimensional views of a three-dimensional object, each of psychology's perspectives is helpful. But each by itself fails to reveal the whole picture.

So bear in mind psychology's limits. Don't expect it to answer the ultimate questions, such as those posed by Russian novelist Leo Tolstoy (1904): "Why should I live? Why should I do anything? Is there in life any purpose which the inevitable death that awaits me does not undo and destroy?" Instead, expect that psychology will help you understand why people think, feel, and act as they do. Then you should find the study of psychology fascinating and useful.

Views of anger How would each of psychology's levels of analysis explain what's going on here?

Radius Images/Alamy

TROUBLESHOOTING

This list of subfields in psychology is not exhaustive. You may want to supplement this list by referencing several sources, including the APA's list of divisions available on p. A-6 in Appendix A of this text. It is important that students recognize the great diversity of subfields in psychology that might show up on the AP Exam. There is more information available in Appendix A: Careers in Psychology.

At this time, you may want to use **Lecture/Discussion Topic: *Illustrating Psychology's Complementary Perspectives: The Case of Andrea Yates*** (p. 9) from Bolt's Teacher's Resource Binder.

TEACHING TIP

Consider inviting psychological professionals to your classroom to discuss the variety of career options available to students of psychology. You may also want to ask local research psychologists if they have any projects your students could help with as lab interns. Applying psychology in this way can help your students appreciate what psychologists do.

UNIT 1

::**psychometrics** the scientific study of the measurement of human abilities, attitudes, and traits.

::**basic research** pure science that aims to increase the scientific knowledge base.

::**developmental psychology** the scientific study of physical, cognitive, and social change throughout the life span.

::**educational psychology** the study of how psychological processes affect and can enhance teaching and learning.

::**personality psychology** the study of an individual's characteristic pattern of thinking, feeling, and acting.

::**social psychology** the scientific study of how we think about, influence, and relate to one another.

::**applied research** scientific study that aims to solve practical problems.

::**industrial-organizational (I/O) psychology** the application of psychological concepts and methods to optimizing human behavior in workplaces.

Students often overlook the difference between basic and applied research:

- Basic research is more concerned with discovering concepts or processes. It is less practical in nature.

- Applied research is more concerned with providing solutions to problems. It is more practical in nature.

Some psychologists from each of the subfields mentioned engage in basic research, while others engage in applied research. Some areas, like I/O or human factors psychology, are largely applied in nature while others, like developmental psychology, are more basic in nature.

Psychology's Subfields

6: What are psychology's main subfields?

Picturing a chemist at work, you probably envision a white-coated scientist surrounded by glassware and high-tech equipment. Picture a psychologist at work and you would be right to envision

- a white-coated scientist probing a rat's brain.

- an intelligence researcher measuring how quickly an infant shows boredom by looking away from a familiar picture.

- an executive evaluating a new "healthy life-styles" training program for employees.

"I'm a social scientist, Michael. That means I can't explain electricity or anything like that, but if you ever want to know about people, I'm your man."

- someone at a computer analyzing data on whether adopted teens' temperaments more closely resemble those of their adoptive parents or their biological parents.

- a therapist listening carefully to a client's depressed thoughts.

- a researcher visiting another culture and collecting data on variations in human values and behaviors.

- a teacher or writer sharing the joy of psychology with others.

The cluster of subfields we call psychology has less unity than most other sciences. But there is a payoff: Psychology is a meeting ground for different disciplines. "Psychology is a hub scientific discipline," said Association for Psychological Science president John Cacioppo (2007). Thus, it's a perfect home for those with wide-ranging interests. In their diverse activities, from biological experimentation to cultural comparisons, the tribe of psychology is united by a common quest: describing and explaining behavior and the mind underlying it. There is even a branch of psychology devoted to studying the measurement of our abilities, attitudes, and traits: **psychometrics**.

I see you! A biological psychologist might view this child's delighted response as evidence of brain maturation. A cognitive psychologist might see it as a demonstration of the baby's growing knowledge of his surroundings. For a cross-cultural psychologist, the role of grandparents in different societies might be the issue of interest. As you will see throughout this book, these and other perspectives offer complementary views of behavior.

Basic research is much like structuralism, whose adherents wanted to discover what the mind and consciousness were. Applied research is much like functionalism, whose practitioners wanted to discover how the mind and consciousness worked and how they helped people adapt to circumstances.

Some psychologists conduct **basic research** that builds psychology's knowledge base. In the pages that follow we will meet a wide variety of such researchers, including:

- *biological psychologists* exploring the links between brain and mind.
- **developmental psychologists** studying our changing abilities from womb to tomb.
- *cognitive psychologists* experimenting with how we perceive, think, and solve problems.
- **educational psychologists** studying influences on teaching and learning.
- **personality psychologists** investigating our persistent traits.
- **social psychologists** exploring how we view and affect one another.

(For a more complete list of the major subfields of psychology, see Appendix A at the end of this text.)

These psychologists also may conduct **applied research** that tackles practical problems. So do other psychologists, including **industrial-organizational psychologists**, who use psychology's concepts and methods in the workplace to help organizations and companies select and train employees, boost morale and productivity, design products, and implement systems. Within that domain, **human factors psychologists** focus on the interaction of people, machines, and physical environments. (More on this subject in Appendix B.)

Although most psychology textbooks focus on psychological science, psychology is also a helping profession devoted to such practical issues as how to have a happy marriage, how to overcome anxiety or depression, and how to raise thriving children. As a science, psychology at its best bases such interventions on evidence of effectiveness. **Counseling psychologists** help people to cope with challenges and crises (including academic, vocational, and marital issues) and to improve their personal and social functioning. **Clinical psychologists** assess and treat mental, emotional, and behavior disorders (APA, 2003). Both counseling and clinical psychologists administer and interpret tests, provide counseling and therapy, and sometimes conduct basic and applied research. By contrast, **psychiatrists**, who also often provide psychotherapy, are medical doctors licensed to prescribe drugs and otherwise treat physical causes of psychological disorders. Some clinical psychologists are lobbying for a similar right to prescribe mental-health–related drugs, and in 2002 and 2004 New Mexico and Louisiana became the first states to grant that right to specially trained and licensed psychologists.

::**human factors psychology** the study of how people and machines interact and the design of safe and easily used machines and environments.

::**counseling psychology** a branch of psychology that assists people with problems in living (often related to school, work, or marriage) and in achieving greater well-being.

::**clinical psychology** a branch of psychology that studies, assesses, and treats people with psychological disorders.

::**psychiatry** a branch of medicine dealing with psychological disorders; practiced by physicians who often provide medical (for example, drug) treatments as well as psychological therapy.

▼ **Psychology: A science and a profession** Psychologists experiment with, observe, test, and treat behavior. Here we see psychologists testing a child, measuring emotion-related physiology, and doing face-to-face therapy.

Michael Newman/Photo Edit

©2007 John Kish IV

Bob Daemmrich/The Image Works

UNIT 1

INTERCONNECTING

SQ3R is one of the most widely researched and validated study techniques around. This method incorporates many psychological concepts you will teach this year:

- Successful recall requires effort and deep processing.

- Distributed rehearsal, rather than cramming, is more effective for long-term recall.

- Chunking—breaking information into meaningful units—helps with recall.

- Active listening, which involves making mental connections among items to be recalled, is key to long-term recall.

- Overlearning leads not only to more effective recall, but also to more efficient recall.

With perspectives ranging from the biological to the social, and with settings from the laboratory to the clinic, psychology relates to many fields, ranging from mathematics to biology to sociology to philosophy. And more and more, psychology's methods and findings aid other disciplines. Psychologists teach in medical schools, law schools, and high schools, and they work in hospitals, factories, and corporate offices. They engage in interdisciplinary studies, such as psychohistory (the psychological analysis of historical characters), psycholinguistics (the study of language and thinking), and psychoceramics (the study of crackpots).[1]

Psychology also influences modern culture. Knowledge transforms us. Learning about the solar system and the germ theory of disease alters the way people think and act. Learning psychology's findings also changes people: They less often judge psychological disorders as moral failings, treatable by punishment and ostracism. They less often regard and treat women as men's mental inferiors. They less often view and rear children as ignorant, willful beasts in need of taming. "In each case," notes Morton Hunt (1990, p. 206), "knowledge has modified attitudes,

[1]Confession: I wrote the last part of this sentence on April Fools' Day.

CLOSE-UP

Tips for Studying Psychology

7: How can psychological principles help you as a student?

The investment you are making in studying psychology should enrich your life and enlarge your vision. Although many of life's significant questions are beyond psychology, some very important ones are illuminated by even a first psychology course. Through painstaking research, psychologists have gained insights into brain and mind, dreams and memories, depression and joy. Even the unanswered questions can enrich us, by renewing our sense of mystery about "things too wonderful" for us yet to understand. Your study of psychology can also help teach you *how to ask and answer important questions*—how to think critically as you evaluate competing ideas and claims.

Having your life enriched and your vision enlarged (and getting a decent grade) requires effective study. As you will see in Unit 7A, to master information you must *actively process it*. Your mind is not like your stomach, something to be filled passively; it is more like a muscle that grows stronger with exercise. Countless experiments reveal that people learn and remember best when they put material in their own words, rehearse it, and then review and rehearse it again.

The **SQ3R** study method incorporates these principles (Robinson, 1970). SQ3R is an acronym for its five steps: *Survey, Question, Read, Rehearse, Review.*

To study a unit in this text, first *survey*, taking a bird's-eye view. Scan the headings, and notice how the unit is organized.

As you prepare to read each section, use its heading or numbered objective question to form a *question* you should answer. For this section, you might have asked, "How can I most effectively and efficiently master the information in this book?"

Then *read*, actively searching for the answer. At each sitting, read only as much of the unit (usually a single main section) as you can absorb without tiring. Read actively and critically. Ask questions. Make notes. Consider implications: How does what you've read relate to your own life? Does it support or challenge your assumptions? How convincing is the evidence?

Having read a section, *rehearse* in your own words what you read. Test yourself by trying to answer your question, rehearsing what you can recall, then glancing back over what you can't recall.

Finally, *review*: Read over any notes you have taken, again with an eye on the unit's organization, and quickly review the whole unit.

Survey, question, read, rehearse, review. I have organized this book's units to facilitate your use of the SQ3R study system. Each unit begins with an outline that aids your *survey*. Headings and learning objective *questions* suggest issues and concepts you should consider as you *read*. The material is organized into sections of readable length. At the end of each section is a "Before you move on . . ." box with "Ask Yourself" and "Test Yourself" questions that help you *rehearse* what you know. The Unit *Review* provides answers to the learning objective questions, and the list of key terms helps you check your mastery of important concepts. Survey, question, read . . .

TEACHING TIP

At this time, you may want to use **Classroom Exercise: *Eliciting "Metaphors" for Learning and Teaching*** (p. 16) from Bolt's Teacher's Resource Binder.

and, through them, behavior." Once aware of psychology's well-researched ideas—about how body and mind connect, how a child's mind grows, how we construct our perceptions, how we remember (and mismember) our experiences, how people across the world differ (and are alike)—your mind may never again be quite the same.

> "Once expanded to the dimensions of a larger idea, [the mind] never returns to its original size."
> Oliver Wendell Holmes, 1809–1894

BEFORE YOU MOVE ON . . .

➤ **ASK YOURSELF**

When you signed up for this course, what did you think psychology would be all about?

➤ **TEST YOURSELF 2**

What are psychology's major levels of analysis?

Answers to the Test Yourself questions can be found in Appendix E at the end of the book.

● Want to learn more? See Appendix A, Careers in Psychology, at the end of this book for more information about psychology's subfields and to learn about the many interesting options available to those with bachelor's, master's, and doctoral degrees in psychology. ●

Five additional study tips may further boost your learning:

Distribute your study time. One of psychology's oldest findings is that *spaced practice* promotes better retention than *massed practice.* You'll remember material better if you space your work over several study periods—perhaps one hour a day, six days a week—rather than cram it into one long study blitz. For example, rather than trying to read an entire unit in a single sitting, read just one main section and then turn to something else.

Learn to think critically. Whether you are reading or in class, note people's assumptions and values. What perspective or bias underlies an argument? Evaluate evidence. Is it anecdotal, or is it supported by reliable science? Assess conclusions. Are there alternative explanations?

In class, listen actively. Listen for the main ideas and sub-ideas of a lesson. *Write them down.* Ask questions during and after class. In class, as with your homework, process the information actively and you will understand and retain it better. As psychologist William James urged a century ago, *"No reception without reaction, no impression without . . . expression."*

Overlearn. Psychology tells us that overlearning improves retention. We are prone to overestimating how much we know. You may understand a unit as you read it, but by devoting extra study time to testing yourself and reviewing what you think you know, you will retain your new knowledge long into the future.

Be a smart test-taker. If a test contains both multiple-choice questions and an essay question, turn first to the essay. Read the question carefully, noting exactly what the teacher is asking. On the back of a page, pencil in a list of points you'd like to make and then organize them. Before writing, put aside the essay and work through the multiple-choice questions. (As you do so, your mind may continue to mull over the essay question. Sometimes the multiple-choice questions will bring pertinent thoughts to mind.) Then reread the essay question, rethink your answer, and start writing. When you finish, proofread your answer to eliminate spelling and grammatical errors that make you look less competent than you are.

When reading multiple-choice questions, don't confuse yourself by trying to imagine how each choice might be the right one. Instead, try to answer each question as if it were a fill-in-the-blank question. First cover the answers and form a sentence in your mind, recalling what you know to complete the sentence. Then read the answers on the test and find the alternative that best matches your own answer.

While exploring psychology, you will learn much more than effective study techniques. Psychology deepens our appreciation for how we humans perceive, think, feel, and act. By so doing it can indeed enrich our lives and enlarge our vision. Through this book I hope to help guide you toward that end. As educator Charles Eliot said a century ago: "Books are the quietest and most constant of friends, and the most patient of teachers."

::SQ3R a study method incorporating five steps: *Survey, Question, Read, Rehearse, Review.*

TROUBLESHOOTING

Students may be hesitant to use SQ3R for their daily studying. Students—especially those taking their first AP course—typically have not developed methodical study habits in their other classes. They often rely on inefficient study techniques—using flashcards, rewriting their notes, glancing over the textbook right before the test. These habits, while at times effective in the short term, often don't lend themselves to long-term recall and understanding.

Encourage students to use SQ3R throughout the year. You will need to help them develop habits that utilize SQ3R by creating assignments that make them use the technique. You may want to create some type of formative assessment that will monitor and reward those who use SQ3R as their main study tool. Emphasize that while SQ3R may seem cumbersome at first, this type of studying makes future study sessions shorter and more efficient as knowledge builds throughout the year.

 TEACHING TIP

At this time, you may want to use **Classroom Exercise/Student Project:** *Applying Psychology's Specific Theoretical Perspectives* (p. 11) from Bolt's Teacher's Resource Binder.

ANSWERS to Multiple-Choice Questions

1. **b.** Psychodynamic
2. **d.** the nature-nurture issue.
3. **a.** Psychiatrist
4. **d.** review.
5. **c.** Social
6. **b.** observation.
7. **b.** Clinical
8. **c.** cognitive neuroscience.
9. **d.** Wilhelm Wundt.
10. **a.** Functionalist
11. **a.** Humanistic
12. **b.** Using psychological concepts to boost morale and productivity.
13. **c.** structuralists.
14. **b.** Cognitive
15. **e.** psychology.

UNIT REVIEW: Psychology's History and Approaches

What Is Psychology?

1: How did psychology develop from its prescientific roots in early understandings of mind and body to the beginnings of modern science?

Psychology traces its roots back through recorded history to India, China, the Middle East, and Europe. Buddha and Confucius focused on the powers and origin of ideas. The ancient Hebrews, Socrates, Plato, and Aristotle pondered whether mind and body are connected or distinct, and whether human ideas are innate or result from experience. Descartes and Locke reengaged those ancient debates, with Locke offering his famous description of the mind as a "blank slate" on which experience writes. The ideas of Bacon and Locke contributed to the development of modern *empiricism*.

2: When and how did modern psychological science begin?

Psychological science had its modern beginning with the first psychological laboratory, founded in 1879 by German philosopher and physiologist Wilhelm Wundt, and from the later work of other scholars from several disciplines and many countries.

3: How did psychology continue to develop from the 1920s through today?

Having begun as a "science of mental life," psychology evolved in the 1920s into the "scientific study of observable behavior." After rediscovering the mind, *psychology* since the 1960s has been widely defined as the *science of behavior and mental processes*.

Contemporary Psychology

4: What is psychology's historic big issue?

Psychology's biggest and most enduring issue concerns the relative contributions and interplay between the influences of *nature* (genes) and *nurture* (all other influences, from conception to death). Today's science emphasizes the interaction of genes and experiences in specific environments.

5: What are psychology's levels of analysis and related perspectives?

The *biopsychosocial approach* integrates information from the biological, psychological, and social-cultural *levels of analysis*. Psychologists study human behaviors and mental processes from many different perspectives (including the *biological, evolutionary, psychodynamic, behavioral, cognitive,* and *social-cultural perspectives*, and the historically influential *humanistic* approach).

6: What are psychology's main subfields?

Psychology's subfields encompass *basic research* (often done by biological, *developmental*, cognitive, *educational*, *personality*, and *social psychologists*), *applied research* (sometimes conducted by *industrial-organizational* and *human factors psychologists*), and clinical science and applications (the work of *counseling psychologists* and *clinical psychologists*). *Psychometric* psychologists study measurement methods. Clinical psychologists study, assess, and treat (with psychotherapy) people with psychological disorders. *Psychiatrists* also study, assess, and treat people with disorders, but as medical doctors, they may prescribe drugs in addition to psychotherapy.

7: How can psychological principles help you as a student?

Research has shown that learning and memory are enhanced by active study. The *SQ3R* study method—survey, question, read, rehearse, and review—applies the principles derived from this research.

Terms and Concepts to Remember

empiricism, p. 3
structuralism, p. 4
functionalism, p. 5
experimental psychology, p. 6
behaviorism, p. 6
humanistic psychology, p. 6
cognitive neuroscience, p. 7
psychology, p. 7
nature-nurture issue, p. 8
natural selection, p. 8
levels of analysis, p. 10

biopsychosocial approach, p. 10
biological psychology, p. 10
evolutionary psychology, p. 10
psychodynamic psychology, p. 10
behavioral psychology, p. 10
cognitive psychology, p. 10
social-cultural psychology, p. 10
psychometrics, p. 12
basic research, p. 13
developmental psychology, p. 13
educational psychology, p. 13

personality psychology, p. 13
social psychology, p. 13
applied research, p. 13
industrial-organizational (I/O) psychology, p. 13
human factors psychology, p. 13
counseling psychology, p. 13
clinical psychology, p. 13
psychiatry, p. 13
SQ3R, p. 14

TECHNOLOGY RESOURCES

You may want to use these video, computer, and multimedia resources to enhance your lessons:

- *PsychSim 5: Psychology's Timeline*
- *Psychology Video Tool Kit: Why Do People Help? Explaining Behavior; Postpartum Psychosis: The Case of Andrea Yates*
- *Video: Psychology: The Human Experience, Module 42: Psychological Principles in Everyday Life*

AP* Practice Test Questions ◄ ···

Multiple-Choice Questions

1. Which perspective would most likely explain anger as "an outlet for unconscious hostility"?
a. Social-cultural
b. Psychodynamic
c. Behavioral
d. Functionalist
e. Biological

2. The debate on the relative contributions of biology and experience to human development is most often referred to as
a. evolutionary analysis.
b. behaviorism.
c. the cognitive revolution.
d. the nature-nurture issue.
e. natural selection.

3. Which of the following professionals is also a medical doctor?
a. Psychiatrist
b. Psychologist
c. Clinician
d. Counselor
e. Biologist

4. SQ3R is an acronym for a study method that includes survey, question, read, rehearse, and
a. rigor.
b. recite.
c. response.
d. review.
e. reserve.

5. Which of the following psychologists would most likely explore how we view and affect each other?
a. Developmental
b. Biological
c. Social
d. Cognitive
e. Personality

6. For behaviorists, psychological science is rooted in
a. introspection.
b. observation.
c. cultural influences.
d. growth potential.
e. basic needs.

7. Which of the following psychologists would most likely conduct psychotherapy?
a. Biological
b. Clinical
c. Industrial-organizational
d. Cognitive
e. Evolutionary

8. The study of mental activity linked with brain activity best describes
a. humanistic psychology.
b. Gestalt psychology.
c. cognitive neuroscience.
d. the psychodynamic perspective.
e. the evolutionary perspective.

9. The first psychological laboratory, opened in 1879, belonged to
a. Charles Darwin.
b. Sigmund Freud.
c. René Descartes.
d. Wilhelm Wundt.
e. William James.

10. The _____ school of psychology focused on how mental and behavioral processes enable us to adapt and flourish.
a. Functionalist
b. Structuralist
c. Behavioral
d. Humanistic
e. Psychodynamic

11. The study of current environmental influences and the importance of satisfying the needs for love and acceptance best describe which school of psychology?
a. Humanistic
b. Behaviorial
c. Psychodynamic
d. Structuralist
e. Functionalist

12. Which of the following is the best example of applied research?
a. Investigating basic human traits.
b. Using psychological concepts to boost morale and productivity.
c. Experimenting with how we perceive stimuli.
d. Studying the changing abilities of a child from age 2 to age 5.
e. Exploring the mind-brain connections in adolescents.

13. Self-reflective introspection (looking inward) to discern the elements of experience best describes a technique used by
a. Darwinists.
b. empiricists.
c. structuralists.
d. behaviorists.
e. ancient Greek philosophers.

14. Which perspective would most look at how our *interpretation* of a situation affects how we react to it?
a. Psychodynamic
b. Cognitive
c. Biological
d. Social-cultural
e. Evolutionary

15. The science of behavior and mental processes best defines
a. philosophy.
b. cognitive neuroscience.
c. basic research.
d. applied research.
e. psychology.

Free-Response Question

Psychology has a variety of complementary yet incomplete perspectives that help us understand behavior. How might each of the following perspectives explain aggression?
- Biological
- Cognitive
- Evolutionary
- Social-cultural

 WEB

Multiple-choice self-tests and more may be found at www.worthpublishers.com/myers

Rubric for Grading the Free-Response Question

This is a 9-point question. Allow one point for an adequate discussion of each of the following concepts or terms from each perspective. Modify the rubric by adding or subtracting terms depending on what was emphasized in class.

Biological

Brain: Different parts of the brain (need not name the parts) are active when someone is acting aggressively. (1 point)

Heredity: Some could have a genetic predisposition to act aggressively. (1 point)

Temperament: Some are born with a more aggressive disposition than others. (1 point)

Cognitive

Thoughts: Acting aggressively affects one's thinking. (1 point)

Interpretation: Our interpretation of events could affect aggressive behavior. (1 point)

Evolutionary

Gene survival: Aggression might have facilitated survival and the subsequent passing of genes from one generation to the next. (1 point)

Natural selection of traits: From among chance variations, nature selects the traits that best enable an organism to survive and reproduce in a particular environment. (1 point)

Social-Cultural

Different Cultures: What is seen as aggressive in one culture might be seen as normal in another, depending on the cultural context. (1 point)

Situation: A situation might affect aggressive thinking and behavior. (1 point)

Pacing Guide

Use the following guide to determine how many instructional days to devote to this unit depending on the type of course you teach:

Year-long course: 10 days
Block schedule/Semester-long course: 4–6 days

This unit encompasses 8–10 percent of the AP Exam. Spending an appropriate amount of time on this unit will help students do well on the AP Exam.

TROUBLESHOOTING

Research methods is one of the more important topic areas for the AP Exam. Students, however, don't often find this information particularly interesting or important. Try some of these ways to make this content both interesting and relevant to students:

- Help students see that the scientific method in psychology is not different from other sciences.

- Create opportunities for your students to do active research. Students can conduct quick surveys, do observational research, do a case study, or even conduct experiments. These types of activities put the concepts into practice, which helps students remember them later.

- Refer back to concepts from this unit throughout the course. Have students identify the types of research used in psychology's famous studies or identify variables in experiments described in the text.

18

Suggested Readings

Gelman, A., & Nolen, D. (2002). *Teaching statistics: A bag of tricks.* New York: Oxford.

Good, P. I. (2006). *Common errors in statistics (and how to avoid them).* (2nd ed.). New York: Wiley-Interscience.

Huff, D., & Geis, I. (1993). *How to lie with statistics.* New York: Norton.

Smith, R. A. (1995). *Challenging your preconceptions: Thinking critically about psychology.* Pacific Grove, CA: Brooks/Cole.

Stanovich, K. (2006). *How to think straight about psychology* (8th ed.). Boston: Allyn & Bacon.

Research Methods:
Thinking Critically With Psychological Science

Hoping to satisfy their curiosity about people and to remedy their own woes, millions turn to "psychology." They listen to talk radio counseling, read articles on psychic powers, attend stop-smoking hypnosis seminars, and devote countless hours to Web pages on the meaning of dreams, the path to ecstatic love, and the roots of personal happiness.

Others, intrigued by claims of psychological truth, wonder: Do mothers and infants bond in the first hours after birth? Should we trust childhood sexual abuse memories that get "recovered" in adulthood—and prosecute the alleged predators? Are firstborn children more driven to achieve? Does psychotherapy heal?

In working with such questions, how can we separate uninformed opinions from examined conclusions? *How can we best use psychology to understand why people think, feel, and act as they do?*

The Need for Psychological Science

1: Why are the answers that flow from the scientific approach more reliable than those based on intuition and common sense?

SOME PEOPLE SUPPOSE that psychology merely documents and dresses in jargon what people already know: "So what else is new—you get paid for using fancy methods to prove what everyone knows?" Others place their faith in human intuition: "Buried deep within each and every one of us, there is an instinctive, heart-felt awareness that provides—if we allow it to—the most reliable guide," offered Prince Charles (2000). "I know there's no evidence that shows the death penalty has a deterrent effect," George W. Bush (1999) reportedly said as Texas governor, "but I just feel in my gut it must be true." "I'm a gut player. I rely on my instincts," said the former president in explaining to Bob Woodward (2002) his decision to launch the Iraq war.

Prince Charles and former President Bush have much company. A long list of pop psychology books encourage us toward "intuitive managing," "intuitive trading," "intuitive healing," and much more. Today's psychological science does document a vast intuitive mind. As we will see, our thinking, memory, and attitudes operate on two levels, conscious and unconscious, with the larger part operating automatically, offscreen. Like jumbo jets, we fly mostly on autopilot.

So, are we smart to listen to the whispers of our inner wisdom, to simply trust "the force within"? Or should we more often be subjecting our intuitive hunches to skeptical scrutiny?

This much seems certain. Intuition is important, but we often underestimate its perils. My geographical intuition tells me that

19

Key Terms

The Need for Psychological Science
hindsight bias
critical thinking

How Do Psychologists Ask and Answer Questions?
theory
hypothesis
operational definition
replication
case study
survey
population
random sample
naturalistic observation
correlation
correlation coefficient
scatterplot
illusory correlation
experiment
random assignment
double-blind procedure
placebo effect
experimental group
control group
independent variable
confounding variable
dependent variable

Statistical Reasoning in Everyday Life
mode
mean
median
range
standard deviation
normal curve
statistical significance

Frequently Asked Questions About Psychology
culture
informed consent
debriefing

Wilson, J. H. (2004). *Essential statistics.* Englewood Cliffs, NJ: Prentice Hall.

Key People
Kenneth Clark
Mamie Phipps Clark
Daniel Kahneman
James Randi
Amos Tversky

UNIT 2

TEACHING TIP

A great way to introduce this unit is to present common misconceptions about behavior that are persistent in popular culture. By pointing out misconceptions and the evidence against them, students can be more aware of other misconceptions they may have. Ask your students to consider whether each of the following are true or false before discussing each one:

- Most people suffer from unrealistically low self-esteem. (False)

- The opinions of 1500 randomly selected people can provide a fairly accurate picture of the opinions of an entire nation. (True)

- The scientific finding that depressed people tend to have low self-esteem proves that depression causes people to be down on themselves. (False)

At this point, you may also want to use **Introductory Exercise: *Fact or Falsehood?*** (p. 3) from Bolt's Teacher's Resource Binder, which accompanies this text.

The limits of intuition
Personnel interviewers tend to be overconfident of their gut feelings about job applicants. Their confidence stems partly from their recalling cases where their favorable impression proved right, and partly from their ignorance about rejected applicants who succeeded elsewhere.

> "He who trusts in his own heart is a fool."
> Proverbs 28:26

> "Life is lived forwards, but understood backwards."
> Philosopher Søren Kierkegaard, 1813–1855

> "Anything seems commonplace, once explained."
> Dr. Watson to Sherlock Holmes

::**hindsight bias** the tendency to believe, after learning an outcome, that one would have foreseen it. (Also known as the *I-knew-it-all-along phenomenon*.)

Reno is east of Los Angeles, that Rome is south of New York, that Atlanta is east of Detroit. But I am wrong, wrong, and wrong.

Units to come will show that experiments have found people greatly overestimating their lie detection accuracy, their eyewitness recollections, their interviewee assessments, their risk predictions, and their stock-picking talents. "The first principle," said Richard Feynman (1997), "is that you must not fool yourself—and you are the easiest person to fool."

Indeed, observed Madeleine L'Engle, "The naked intellect is an extraordinarily inaccurate instrument" (1973). Two phenomena—hindsight bias and judgmental overconfidence—illustrate why we cannot rely solely on intuition and common sense.

Did We Know It All Along? Hindsight Bias

How easy it is to seem astute when drawing the bull's eye after the arrow has struck. After the North Tower of New York's World Trade Center was hit on September 11, 2001, commentators said people in the South Tower *should* have immediately evacuated. (It became obvious only later that the strike was not an accident.) After the U.S. occupation of Iraq led to a bloody civil war rather than a peaceful democracy, commentators saw the result as inevitable. *Before* the invasion was launched, these results seemed anything but obvious: In voting to allow the Iraq invasion, most U.S. senators did not anticipate the chaos that would seem so predictable in hindsight. Finding that something has happened makes it seem inevitable, a tendency we call **hindsight bias** (also known as the *I-knew-it-all-along phenomenon*).

This phenomenon is easy to demonstrate: Give half the members of a group some purported psychological finding, and give the other half an opposite result. Tell the first group, "Psychologists have found that separation weakens romantic attraction. As the saying goes, 'Out of sight, out of mind.'" Ask them to imagine why this might be true. Most people can, and nearly all will then regard this true finding as unsurprising.

Tell the second group the opposite, "Psychologists have found that separation strengthens romantic attraction. As the saying goes, 'Absence makes the heart grow fonder.'" People given this untrue result can also easily imagine it, and they overwhelmingly see it as unsurprising common sense. Obviously, when both a supposed finding and its opposite seem like common sense, there is a problem.

Such errors in our recollections and explanations show why we need psychological research. Just asking people how and why they felt or acted as they did can sometimes be misleading—*not* because common sense is usually wrong, but because common sense more easily describes what *has* happened than what *will* happen. As physicist Neils Bohr reportedly said, "Prediction is very difficult, especially about the future."

Hindsight bias is widespread. Some 100 studies have observed it in various countries and among both children and adults (Blank et al., 2007). Nevertheless, our intuition is often right. As Yogi Berra once said, "You can observe a lot by watching." (We have Berra to thank for other gems, such as "Nobody ever comes here—it's too crowded," and "If the people don't want to come out to the ballpark, nobody's gonna stop 'em.") Because we're all behavior watchers, it would be surprising if many of psychology's

TEACHING TIP

Another example of errors in critical thinking occurred after the 1995 Oklahoma City bombings. Immediately after the bombings, alerts were issued to be on the lookout for suspicious-looking persons of Middle Eastern or Arabic descent. The prevailing notion was that Muslim extremists were at fault for the devastating act of terror. However, the perpetrator was a White male, Timothy McVay, who was disgruntled at the government's involvement with the events in Waco, Texas, five years earlier. Have students consider how criminal profiling can help officials be more efficient in making arrests, but can also lead to false accusations and missed opportunities.

findings had *not* been foreseen. Many people believe that love breeds happiness, and they are right (we have what Unit 8A calls a deep "need to belong"). Indeed, note Daniel Gilbert, Brett Pelham, and Douglas Krull (2003), "good ideas in psychology usually have an oddly familiar quality, and the moment we encounter them we feel certain that we once came close to thinking the same thing ourselves and simply failed to write it down." Good ideas are like good inventions; once created, they seem obvious.

But sometimes our intuition, informed by countless casual observations, has it wrong. In later units we will see how research has overturned popular ideas—that familiarity breeds contempt, that dreams predict the future, and that emotional reactions coincide with menstrual phase. (See also **TABLE 2.1**.) We will also see how it has surprised us with discoveries about how the brain's chemical messengers control our moods and memories, about other animals' abilities, and about the effects of stress on our capacity to fight disease.

Hindsight bias *After* the horror of 9/11, it seemed obvious that the U.S. intelligence analysts should have taken advance warnings more seriously, that airport security should have anticipated box-cutter–wielding terrorists, that occupants of the South Tower of the World Trade Center should have known to play it safe and leave. With 20/20 hindsight, everything seems obvious. Thus we now spend billions to protect ourselves against what the terrorists did last time.

AP Photo/The Roanoke Times, Matt Gentry

TABLE 2.1

TRUE OR FALSE?

Psychological research discussed in units to come will either confirm or refute each of these statements (adapted, in part, from Furnham et al., 2003). Can you predict which of these popular ideas have been confirmed and which refuted? (Check your answers at the bottom of this table.)

1. If you want to teach a habit that persists, reward the desired behavior every time, not just intermittently (see Unit 6).

2. Patients whose brains are surgically split down the middle survive and function much as they did before the surgery (see Unit 3B).

3. Traumatic experiences, such as sexual abuse or surviving the Holocaust, are typically "repressed" from memory (see Unit 7A).

4. Most abused children do *not* become abusive adults (see Unit 9).

5. Most infants recognize their own reflection in a mirror by the end of their first year (see Unit 9).

6. Adopted siblings usually do not develop similar personalities, even though they are reared by the same parents (see Unit 3C).

7. Fears of harmless objects, such as flowers, are just as easy to acquire as fears of potentially dangerous objects, such as snakes (see Unit 8A).

8. Lie detection tests often lie (see Unit 8B).

9. Most of us use only about 10 percent of our brains (see Unit 3B).

10. The brain remains active during sleep (see Unit 5).

Answers: 1. F, 2. T, 3. F, 4. T, 5. F, 6. T, 7. F, 8. T, 9. F, 10. T

Overconfidence

We humans tend to be overconfident. As Unit 7B explains, we tend to think we know more than we do. Asked how sure we are of our answers to factual questions (Is Boston north or south of Paris?), we tend to be more confident than correct.[1] Or consider these three anagrams, which Richard Goranson (1978) asked people to unscramble:

[1]Boston is south of Paris.

• Fun anagram solutions from Wordsmith.org:
Elvis = lives
Dormitory = dirty room
Slot machines = cash lost in 'em. •

CRITICAL THINKING

The Research Methods unit provides one of the best opportunities for teaching critical thinking. Have students predict what grade they will get on their next quiz or test. Have them also rate, on a scale of 1 to 10, how confident they are that their prediction will be correct. Then, after the quiz or test, have students compare their original predictions with their actual scores. How many students fell victim to overconfidence? Hindsight bias?

At this point, you may want to use **Classroom Exercises: *The Hindsight Bias and Predicting Research Outcomes*** (p. 5) or ***The Overconfidence Phenomenon*** (p. 5) from Bolt's Teacher's Resource Binder.

UNIT 2

CRITICAL THINKING

Most people, including students in our classes, do not think of psychologists as scientists. Create a list of questions that can be scientifically tested. Have students decide what type of scientist would be best at testing the question. You might consider some of these questions:

- What parts of our brain do we use to feel happy?

- How do we see color?

- What happens in the brain when we dream?

- In what ways does background noise affect our ability to pay attention?

While students may offer up many different types of scientists (physicists, biologists, neuroscientists, etc.) who would be interested in these questions, all of these questions can be addressed by psychologists. In fact, one could argue that a working knowledge of psychological science is key to understanding the answers to these questions.

> "We don't like their sound. Groups of guitars are on their way out."
> Decca Records, in turning down a recording contract with the Beatles in 1962

> "Computers in the future may weigh no more than 1.5 tons."
> *Popular Mechanics*, 1949

> "The telephone may be appropriate for our American cousins, but not here, because we have an adequate supply of messenger boys."
> British expert group evaluating the invention of the telephone

> "They couldn't hit an elephant at this distance."
> General John Sedgwick just before being killed during a U.S. Civil War battle, 1864

> "The scientist . . . must be free to ask any question, to doubt any assertion, to seek for any evidence, to correct any errors."
> Physicist J. Robert Oppenheimer, *Life*, October 10, 1949

WREAT → WATER
ETRYN → ENTRY
GRABE → BARGE

About how many seconds do you think it would have taken you to unscramble each of these?

Once people know the answer, hindsight makes it seem obvious—so much so that they become overconfident. They think they would have seen the solution in only 10 seconds or so, when in reality the average problem solver spends 3 minutes, as you also might, given a similar anagram without the solution: OCHSA. (See margin on opposite page to check your answer.)

Are we any better at predicting our social behavior? To find out, Robert Vallone and his associates (1990) had students predict at the beginning of the school year whether they would drop a course, vote in an upcoming election, call their parents more than twice a month, and so forth. On average, the students felt 84 percent confident in making these self-predictions. Later quizzes about their actual behavior showed their predictions were only 71 percent correct. Even when students were 100 percent sure of themselves, their self-predictions erred 15 percent of the time.

It's not just students. Ohio State University psychologist Philip Tetlock (1998, 2005) has collected more than 27,000 expert predictions of world events, such as the future of South Africa or whether Quebec would separate from Canada. His repeated finding: These predictions, which experts made with 80 percent confidence on average, were right less than 40 percent of the time. Nevertheless, even those who erred maintained their confidence by noting they were "almost right." "The Québécois separatists *almost* won the secessionist referendum."

The point to remember: Hindsight bias and overconfidence often lead us to overestimate our intuition. But scientific inquiry can help us sift reality from illusion.

The Scientific Attitude

2: What are three main components of the scientific attitude?

Underlying all science is, first, a hard-headed *curiosity*, a passion to explore and understand without misleading or being misled. Some questions (Is there life after death?) are beyond science. To answer them in any way requires a leap of faith. With many other ideas (Can some people demonstrate ESP?), the proof is in the pudding. No matter how sensible or crazy an idea sounds, the critical thinker's question is, *Does it work?* When put to the test, can its predictions be confirmed?

This scientific approach has a long history. As ancient a figure as Moses used such an approach. How do you evaluate a self-proclaimed prophet? His answer: Put the prophet to the test. If the predicted event "does not take place or prove true," then so much the worse for the prophet (Deuteronomy 18:22). By letting the facts speak for themselves, Moses was using what we now call an *empirical approach*. Magician James Randi uses this approach when testing those claiming to see auras around people's bodies:

> Randi: Do you see an aura around my head?
> Aura-seer: Yes, indeed.
> Randi: Can you still see the aura if I put this magazine in front of my face?
> Aura-seer: Of course.
> Randi: Then if I were to step behind a wall barely taller than I am, you could determine my location from the aura visible above my head, right?

Randi has told me that no aura-seer has agreed to take this simple test.

WEB CONNECT

James Randi, also known as the Amazing Randi, maintains a Web site devoted to critical thinking and skepticism about all manner of phenomena: www.randi.org/site/. Randi is famous for debunking the psychic claims of those who say they have paranormal powers, and he offers a $1 million prize for anyone who can demonstrate their "powers" in a scientifically controlled setting.

At this point, you may want to use **Classroom Exercise: *A Psychic Reading*** (p. 7) from Bolt's Teacher's Resource Binder.

When subjected to such scrutiny, crazy-sounding ideas sometimes find support. During the 1700s, scientists scoffed at the notion that meteorites had extraterrestrial origins. When two Yale scientists dared to deviate from the conventional opinion, Thomas Jefferson jeered, "Gentlemen, I would rather believe that those two Yankee Professors would lie than to believe that stones fell from heaven." Sometimes scientific inquiry turns jeers into cheers.

More often, science becomes society's garbage disposal by sending crazy-sounding ideas to the waste heap, atop previous claims of perpetual motion machines, miracle cancer cures, and out-of-body travels into centuries past. Today's "truths" sometimes become tomorrow's fallacies. To sift reality from fantasy, sense from nonsense, therefore requires a scientific attitude: being skeptical but not cynical, open but not gullible.

"To believe with certainty," says a Polish proverb, "we must begin by doubting." As scientists, psychologists approach the world of behavior with a *curious skepticism*, persistently asking two questions: *What do you mean? How do you know?*

When ideas compete, skeptical testing can reveal which ones best match the facts. Do parental behaviors determine children's sexual orientation? Can astrologers predict your future based on the position of the planets at your birth? As we will see, putting such claims to the test has led psychological scientists to doubt them.

Putting a scientific attitude into practice requires not only skepticism but also *humility*—an awareness of our own vulnerability to error and an openness to surprises and new perspectives. In the last analysis, what matters is not my opinion or yours, but the truths nature reveals in response to our questioning. If people or other animals don't behave as our ideas predict, then so much the worse for our ideas. This humble attitude was expressed in one of psychology's early mottos: "The rat is always right."

Historians of science tell us that these three attitudes—curiosity, skepticism, and humility—helped make modern science possible. Many of its founders, including Copernicus and Newton, were people whose religious convictions made them humble before nature and skeptical of mere human authority (Hooykaas, 1972; Merton, 1938). Some deeply religious people today may view science, including psychological science, as a threat. Yet, notes sociologist Rodney Stark (2003a,b), the scientific revolution was led mostly by deeply religious people acting on the idea that "in order to love and honor God, it is necessary to fully appreciate the wonders of his handiwork."

Of course, scientists, like anyone else, can have big egos and may cling to their preconceptions. We all view nature through the spectacles of our preconceived ideas. Nevertheless, the ideal that unifies psychologists with all scientists is the curious, skeptical, humble scrutiny of competing ideas. As a community, scientists check and recheck one another's findings and conclusions.

Non Sequitur

The Amazing Randi The magician James Randi exemplifies skepticism. He has tested and debunked a variety of psychic phenomena.
▲

> "A skeptic is one who is willing to question any truth claim, asking for clarity in definition, consistency in logic, and adequacy of evidence."
>
> Philosopher Paul Kurtz
> *The Skeptical Inquirer*, 1994

> "My deeply held belief is that if a god anything like the traditional sort exists, our curiosity and intelligence are provided by such a god. We would be unappreciative of those gifts . . . if we suppressed our passion to explore the universe and ourselves."
>
> Carl Sagan, *Broca's Brain*, 1979

Solution to anagram on previous page: CHAOS.

Courtesy of the James Randi Education Foundation

Reprinted by permission of Universal Press Syndicate. © 1997 Wiley.

TROUBLESHOOTING

This text does not use the term *generalizability*, which is often used on the AP Exam. Generalizability refers to what degree the results of a study can be applied to different types of populations.

CRITICAL THINKING ?

Testing magic tricks is a good way for students to see the scientific method in action. Consider performing some simple magic or card tricks in class and have students use the scientific method to test the "magic" of the trick. Students can also research some famous magicians or magicians' tricks to see how controlling variables and exhibiting healthy skepticism are important to scientific thinking.

At this point, you may want to use **Classroom Exercise: *A Psychic Reading*** (p. 7) from Bolt's Teacher's Resource Binder.

INTERCONNECTING

Notice again how research methods underlie the rest of the course. Myers lists several findings that are discussed further in later units. As you teach this unit, you can use findings such as these to spur interest in the course and help students see how interconnected psychological content is. A good working knowledge of the scientific method is important to understanding psychology.

::**critical thinking** thinking that does not blindly accept arguments and conclusions. Rather, it examines assumptions, discerns hidden values, evaluates evidence, and assesses conclusions.

> "The real purpose of the scientific method is to make sure Nature hasn't misled you into thinking you know something you don't actually know."
>
> Robert M. Pirsig, *Zen and the Art of Motorcycle Maintenance*, 1974

Critical Thinking

The scientific attitude prepares us to think smarter. Smart thinking, called **critical thinking**, examines assumptions, discerns hidden values, evaluates evidence, and assesses conclusions. Whether reading a news report or listening to a conversation, critical thinkers ask questions. Like scientists, they wonder, How do they know that? What is this person's agenda? Is the conclusion based on anecdote and gut feelings, or on evidence? Does the evidence justify a cause-effect conclusion? What alternative explanations are possible?

Has psychology's critical inquiry been open to surprising findings? The answer, as ensuing units illustrate, is plainly *yes*. Believe it or not . . .

- massive losses of brain tissue early in life may have minimal long-term effects (see Unit 3B).
- within days, newborns can recognize their mother's odor and voice (see Unit 9).
- brain damage can leave a person able to learn new skills yet unaware of such learning (see Unit 7B).
- diverse groups—men and women, old and young, rich and middle class, those with disabilities and those without—report roughly comparable levels of personal happiness (see Unit 8B).
- electroconvulsive therapy (delivering an electric shock to the brain) is often a very effective treatment for severe depression (see Unit 13).

And has critical inquiry convincingly debunked popular presumptions? The answer, as ensuing units also illustrate, is again *yes*. The evidence indicates that . . .

- sleepwalkers are *not* acting out their dreams (see Unit 5).
- our past experiences are *not* all recorded verbatim in our brains; with brain stimulation or hypnosis, one *cannot* simply "hit the replay button" and relive long-buried or repressed memories (see Unit 7A).
- most people do *not* suffer from unrealistically low self-esteem, and high self-esteem is not all good (see Unit 10).
- opposites do *not* generally attract (see Unit 14).

In each of these instances and more, what has been learned is not what is widely believed.

BEFORE YOU MOVE ON . . .

➤ **ASK YOURSELF**

How might critical thinking help us assess someone's interpretations of people's dreams or their claims to communicate with the dead?

➤ **TEST YOURSELF 1**

What is the scientific attitude, and why is it important for critical thinking?

Answers to the Test Yourself questions can be found in Appendix E at the end of the book.

How Do Psychologists Ask and Answer Questions?

PSYCHOLOGISTS ARM THEIR SCIENTIFIC attitude with the *scientific method*. Psychological science evaluates competing ideas with careful observation and rigorous analysis. In its attempt to describe and explain human nature, it welcomes hunches and plausible-sounding theories. And it puts them to the test. If a theory works—if the data support its predictions—so much the better for that theory. If the predictions fail, the theory will be revised or rejected.

The Scientific Method

3: How do theories advance psychological science?

In everyday conversation, we often use *theory* to mean "mere hunch." In science, how-ever, theory is linked with observation. A scientific **theory** *explains* through an inte-grated set of principles that *organizes* observations and *predicts* behaviors or events. By organizing isolated facts, a theory simplifies. There are too many facts about behavior to remember them all. By linking facts and bridging them to deeper principles, a theory offers a useful summary. As we connect the observed dots, a coherent picture emerges.

A good theory of depression, for example, helps us organize countless depression-related observations into a short list of principles. Imagine that we observe over and over that people with depression describe their past, present, and future in gloomy terms. We might therefore theorize that at the heart of depression lies low self-esteem. So far so good: Our self-esteem principle neatly summarizes a long list of facts about people with depression.

Yet no matter how reasonable a theory may sound—and low self-esteem seems a reasonable explanation of depression—we must put it to the test. A good theory pro-duces testable predictions, called **hypotheses**. By enabling us to test and to reject or revise the theory, such predictions give direction to research. They specify what results would support the theory and what results would disconfirm it. To test our self-esteem theory of depression, we might assess people's self-esteem by having them re-spond to statements such as "I have good ideas" and "I am fun to be with." Then we could see whether, as we hypothesized, people who report poorer self-images also score higher on a depression scale (**FIGURE 2.1**).

In testing our theory, we should be aware that it can bias subjective observa-tions. Having theorized that depression springs from low self-esteem, we may see

::**theory** an explanation using an inte-grated set of principles that organizes observations and predicts behaviors or events.

::**hypothesis** a testable prediction, often implied by a theory.

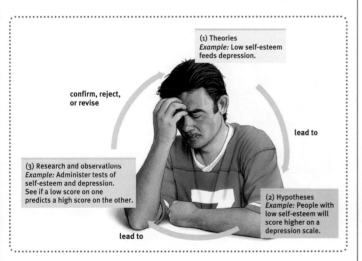

(1) **Theories**
Example: Low self-esteem feeds depression.

confirm, reject, or revise

lead to

(3) **Research and observations**
Example: Administer tests of self-esteem and depression. See if a low score on one predicts a high score on the other.

(2) **Hypotheses**
Example: People with low self-esteem will score higher on a depression scale.

lead to

➤ **FIGURE 2.1**
The scientific method A self-correcting process for asking questions and observing nature's answers.

UNIT 2

TROUBLESHOOTING

Operational definitions are often tough for students to understand. The operational definition is perhaps the most important part of the research study, because it defines what the researcher will be observing and manipulating. Students get hung up on the definition itself, however. They often want the definition to be "correct" or all-encompassing of the concept described. Help students realize that operational definitions need to be 1) measurable and 2) manageable. If they are not measurable and manageable, the research will be difficult to conduct.

DEMO

Have students generate operational definitions for the following variables:

- Happiness
- A smile
- Intelligence
- Popularity
- Good music

Students will find it difficult to generate a measurable and manageable definition for each of these variables, so help guide them toward those goals.

TEACHING TIP

Replication is the main goal of all good research. Replication allows researchers to test hypotheses with other samples from other populations so that results can be generalized. If results work for many different types of populations, then scientists can be reasonably comfortable that those results would apply to most people.

::**operational definition** a statement of the procedures (operations) used to define research variables. For example, *human intelligence* may be operationally defined as what an intelligence test measures.

::**replication** repeating the essence of a research study, usually with different participants in different situations, to see whether the basic finding extends to other participants and circumstances.

::**case study** an observation technique in which one person is studied in depth in the hope of revealing universal principles.

::**survey** a technique for ascertaining the self-reported attitudes or behaviors of a particular group, usually by questioning a representative, random sample of the group.

• Good theories explain by
(1) organizing and linking observed facts, and
(2) implying hypotheses that offer testable predictions and, sometimes, practical applications. •

---

what we expect. We may perceive depressed people's neutral comments as self-disparaging. The urge to see what we expect is an ever-present temptation, in the laboratory and outside of it. Perhaps you are aware of students who, because they have developed an excellent reputation, can now do no wrong in the eyes of teachers. If they're in the hall during class, nobody worries. Other students can do no good. Because they have behaved badly in the past, even their positive behaviors are viewed suspiciously.

As a check on their biases, psychologists report their research with precise **operational definitions** of procedures and concepts. Unlike dictionary definitions, operational definitions describe concepts with precise procedures or measures. *Hunger*, for example, might be defined as "hours without eating," *generosity* as "money contributed." Such carefully worded statements should allow others to **replicate** (repeat) the original observations. If other researchers re-create a study with different participants and materials and get similar results, then our confidence in the finding's reliability grows. The first study of hindsight bias aroused psychologists' curiosity. Now, after many successful replications with differing people and questions, we feel sure of the phenomenon's power.

In the end, our theory will be useful if it (1) effectively *organizes* a range of self-reports and observations, and (2) implies clear *predictions* that anyone can use to check the theory or to derive practical applications. (If we boost people's self-esteem, will their depression lift?) Eventually, our research will probably lead to a revised theory (such as the one in Unit 12) that better organizes and predicts what we know about depression.

As we will see next, we can test our hypotheses and refine our theories using *descriptive* methods (which describe behaviors, often using case studies, surveys, or naturalistic observations), *correlational* methods (which associate different factors), and *experimental* methods (which manipulate factors to discover their effects). To think critically about popular psychology claims, we need to recognize these methods and know what conclusions they allow.

Description

4: How do psychologists observe and describe behavior?

The starting point of any science is description. In everyday life, all of us observe and describe people, often drawing conclusions about why they behave as they do. Professional psychologists do much the same, though more objectively and systematically.

▼ **The case of the conversational chimpanzee** In case studies of chimpanzees, psychologists have asked whether language is uniquely human. Here Nim Chimpsky signs *hug* as his trainer, psychologist Herbert Terrace, shows him the puppet Ernie. But is Nim really using language? Psychologists debate that issue.

Susan Kuklin/Photo Researchers

The Case Study

Among the oldest research methods, the **case study** examines one individual in depth in hopes of revealing things true of us all. Some examples: Much of our early knowledge about the brain came from case studies of individuals who suffered a particular impairment after damage to a certain brain region. Jean Piaget taught us about children's thinking after carefully observing and questioning only a few children. Studies of only a few chimpanzees have revealed their capacity for understanding and language. Intensive case studies are sometimes very revealing.

TEACHING TIP

Some of the most famous psychological phenomena are based on case study research:

- **Psychoanalysis**: Sigmund Freud and Carl Jung developed much of their theories of human personality based on case studies.

- **Behaviorism**: John Watson and Rosalie Rayner conducted an intensive experiment known as the "Little Albert" study to demonstrate classically conditioned emotions. Little Albert was trained to fear white, furry objects by associating those objects with a loud noise.

- **Neuroscience**: Paul Broca had a patient who could only utter one syllable: "tan." Upon Tan's death, Broca studied the patient's brain, hypothesizing that the damaged area was where our ability to speak lies.

Case studies often suggest directions for further study, and they show us what *can* happen. But individual cases may mislead us if the individual being studied is atypical. Unrepresentative information can lead to mistaken judgments and false conclusions. Indeed, anytime a researcher mentions a finding ("Smokers die younger: 95 percent of men over 85 are nonsmokers") someone is sure to offer a contradictory anecdote ("Well, I have an uncle who smoked two packs a day and lived to be 89"). Dramatic stories and personal experiences (even psychological case examples) command our attention, and they are easily remembered. Which of the following do you find more memorable? (1) "In one study of 1300 dream reports concerning a kidnapped child, only 5 percent correctly envisioned the child as dead (Murray & Wheeler, 1937)." (2) "I know a man who dreamed his sister was in a car accident, and two days later she died in a head-on collision!" Numbers can be numbing, but the plural of *anecdote* is not *evidence*. As psychologist Gordon Allport (1954, p. 9) said, "Given a thimbleful of [dramatic] facts we rush to make generalizations as large as a tub."

The point to remember: Individual cases can suggest fruitful ideas. What's true of all of us can be glimpsed in any one of us. But to discern the general truths that cover individual cases, we must answer questions with other research methods.

The Survey

The **survey** method looks at many cases in less depth. Researchers do surveys when wanting to estimate, from a representative sample of people, the attitudes or reported behaviors of a whole population. Questions about everything from cell-phone use to political opinions are put to the public. Harris and Gallup polls have revealed that 72 percent of Americans think there is too much TV violence, 89 percent favor equal job opportunities for homosexual people, 89 percent are facing high stress, and 96 percent would like to change something about their appearance. In Britain, seven in ten 18- to 29-year-olds recently supported gay marriage; among those over 50, about the same ratio opposed it (a generation gap found in many Western countries). But asking questions is tricky, and the answers often depend on the ways questions are worded and respondents are chosen.

Wording Effects Even subtle changes in the order or wording of questions can have major effects. Should cigarette ads or pornography be allowed on television? People are much more likely to approve "not allowing" such things than "forbidding" or "censoring" them. In one national survey, only 27 percent of Americans approved of "government censorship" of media sex and violence, though 66 percent approved of "more restrictions on what is shown on television" (Lacayo, 1995). People are similarly much more approving of "aid to the needy" than of "welfare," of "affirmative action" than of "preferential treatment," and of "revenue enhancers" than of "taxes." Because wording is such a delicate matter, critical thinkers will reflect on how the phrasing of a question might affect people's expressed opinions.

Random Sampling We can describe human experience by drawing on memorable anecdotes and personal experience. But for an accurate picture of a whole population's attitudes and experience, there's only one game in town—the representative sample.

We can extend this point to everyday thinking, as we generalize from samples we observe, especially vivid cases. Given (a) a statistical summary of auto owners' evaluations of their car's make and (b) the vivid comments of two frustrated owners, one's impression may be influenced as much by the two unhappy owners as by the many more evaluations in the statistical summary. The temptation to generalize from a few vivid but unrepresentative cases is nearly irresistible.

> "'Well my dear,' said Miss Marple, 'human nature is very much the same everywhere, and of course, one has opportunities of observing it at closer quarters in a village.'"
>
> Agatha Christie,
> *The Tuesday Club Murders*, 1933

• With very large samples, estimates become quite reliable. *E* is estimated to represent 12.7 percent of the letters in written English. *E*, in fact, is 12.3 percent of the 925,141 letters in Melville's *Moby Dick*, 12.4 percent of the 586,747 letters in Dickens' *A Tale of Two Cities*, and 12.1 percent of the 3,901,021 letters in 12 of Mark Twain's works (Chance News, 1997). •

HEY BOB! ACCORDING TO THIS NEW POLL, NINETY-THREE PERCENT OF THE AMERICAN PEOPLE BELIEVE THAT POLLS HAVE NO STATISTICAL VALIDITY WHATSOEVER!

WELL, GOSH-- IF THAT'S WHAT EVERYONE THINKS, THEN IT *MUST* BE TRUE!

This Modern World by Tom Tomorrow © 1991

Students must understand the difference between random sampling and random assignment in order to do well on the AP Exam.

• Random sampling involves choosing at random participants from a larger population. Random samples are chosen for many types of research including surveys, interviews, and experiments.

• Random assignment involves taking a randomly chosen sample and assigning the participants at random to either the experimental or control group of an experiment. Random assignment only applies to experiments.

At this point, you may want to use **Lecture/Discussion Topic:** *Survey Research and Random Samples* (p. 16) from Bolt's Teacher's Resource Binder.

DEMO

Generate random samples from a population—your class. This demonstration helps students see that there are several ways to generate a random sample.

• Acquire a random number table, perhaps from a math textbook. Choose a number on the list at random, and use the last two digits of the number to choose 5–10 students from your class roll.

• Take a coin and flip it as you come to each student in the room. Choose heads for participants and tails for nonparticipants.

• Put all the students' names into a hat. Draw out half the names for your participants.

At this point, you may want to use **Classroom Exercise:** *Choosing a Random Sample* (p. 15) from Bolt's Teacher's Resource Binder.

TROUBLESHOOTING

A random sample typically generates a representative sample. These two terms are similar and often are referring to the same group of participants in a research study. Help students see how these two terms are related.

UNIT 2

::population all the cases in a group being studied, from which samples may be drawn. (*Note:* Except for national studies, this does *not* refer to a country's whole population.)

"*How would you like me to answer that question? As a member of my ethnic group, educational class, income group, or religious category?*"

CRITICAL THINKING

To evaluate research your class may be examining, have students discuss whether the samples generated are also representative. Representative samples represent the population, and students can see if the sample generated represents the population from which it came. Do the percentages of males and females match between sample and population? Do percentages of racial/ethnic identity match? Other demographics?

CRITICAL THINKING

Some disciplines, such as anthropology, sociology, and zoology, rely heavily on case studies and observational research. Have students contact working researchers in these fields to assess how they use these techniques to increase basic knowledge in their fields. Students may also explore the lives and work of some famous researchers such as primatologists Jane Goodall and Dian Fossey who used observational field research extensively.

At this point, you may want to use **Lecture/Discussion Topics:** *Case Studies* (p. 12) or *Surveys, Evaluation Apprehension and Naturalistic Observation* (p. 13) from Bolt's Teacher's Resource Binder.

The point to remember. The best basis for generalizing is from a representative sample of cases.

So how do you obtain a representative sample—say, of the students at your high school? How could you choose a group that would represent the total student **population**, the whole group you want to study and describe? Typically, you would choose a **random sample**, in which every person in the entire group has an equal chance of participating. This means you would not send each student a questionnaire. (The conscientious people who return it would not be a random sample.) Rather, you might number the names in the general student listing and then use a random number generator to pick the participants for your survey. Large representative samples are better than small ones, but a small representative sample of 100 is better than an unrepresentative sample of 500.

Political pollsters sample voters in national election surveys just this way. Using only 1500 randomly sampled people, drawn from all areas of a country, they can provide a remarkably accurate snapshot of the nation's opinions. Without random sampling, large samples—including call-in phone samples and TV or Web site polls (think of the voting on shows like *American Idol*)—often merely give misleading results.

The point to remember. Before accepting survey findings, think critically. Consider the sample. You cannot compensate for an unrepresentative sample by simply adding more people.

Naturalistic Observation

A third descriptive method records behavior in natural environments. These **naturalistic observations** range from watching chimpanzee societies in the jungle, to unobtrusively videotaping (and later systematically analyzing) parent-child interactions in different cultures, to recording racial differences in students' self-seating patterns in the school cafeteria.

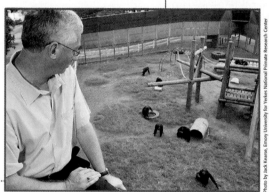

A natural observer Chimpanzee researcher Frans de Waal (2005) reports that "I am a born observer.... When picking a seat in a restaurant I want to face as many tables as possible. I enjoy following the social dynamics—love, tension, boredom, antipathy—around me based on body language, which I consider more informative than the spoken word. Since keeping track of others is something I do automatically, becoming a fly on the wall of an ape colony came naturally to me." ▲

Like the case study and survey methods, naturalistic observation does not *explain* behavior. It *describes* it. Nevertheless, descriptions can be revealing. We once thought, for example, that only humans use tools. Then naturalistic observation revealed that chimpanzees sometimes insert a stick in a termite mound and withdraw it, eating the stick's load of termites. Such unobtrusive naturalistic observations paved the way for later studies of animal thinking, language, and emotion, which further expanded our understanding of our fellow animals. "Observations, made in the natural habitat, helped to show that the societies and behavior of animals are far more complex than previously supposed," notes chimpanzee observer Jane Goodall (1998). For example, chimpanzees and baboons have been observed using deception. Psychologists Andrew Whiten and Richard Byrne (1988) repeatedly saw one young baboon pretending to have been attacked by another as a tactic to get its mother to drive the other baboon away from its food. Moreover, the more developed a primate species' brain, the more likely it is that the animals will display deceptive behaviors (Byrne & Corp, 2004).

Naturalistic observations also illuminate human behavior. Here are three findings you might enjoy.

- *A funny finding.* We humans laugh 30 times more often in social situations than in solitary situations. (Have you noticed how seldom you laugh when alone?) As we laugh, 17 muscles contort our mouth and squeeze our eyes, and we emit a series of 75-millisecond vowel-like sounds that are spaced about one-fifth of a second apart (Provine, 2001).

TEACHING TIP

Have students conduct their own naturalistic observation. Have students identify a behavior and a group of people to observe. They should work in pairs and count the number of times that a group exhibits the behavior. They can compare notes afterward to examine the idea of inter-rater reliability. NOTE: To protect student safety, you might consider limiting the venues in which they can conduct this project. This project can be conducted easily during school, perhaps in the cafeteria or other common areas.

At this point, you may want to use **Student Project/Classroom Exercise:** *Naturalistic Observation in the Cafeteria* (p. 17) from Bolt's Teacher's Resource Binder.

- *Sounding out students.* What, really, are introductory psychology students saying and doing during their everyday lives? To find out, Matthias Mehl and James Pennebaker (2003) equipped 52 such students from the University of Texas with electronically activated belt-worn tape recorders. For up to four days, the recorders captured 30 seconds of the students' waking hours every 12.5 minutes, thus enabling the researchers to eavesdrop on more than 10,000 half-minute life slices by the end of the study. On what percentage of the slices do you suppose they found the students talking with someone? What percentage captured the students at a computer? The answers: 28 and 9 percent. (What percentage of *your* waking hours are spent in these activities?)

An EAR for naturalistic observation Psychologists Matthias Mehl and James Pennebaker have used Electronically Activated Recorders (EAR) to sample naturally occurring slices of daily life.

Courtesy of Matthias Mehl

- *Culture, climate, and the pace of life.* Naturalistic observation also enabled Robert Levine and Ara Norenzayan (1999) to compare the pace of life in 31 countries. (Their operational definition of *pace of life* included walking speed, the speed with which postal clerks completed a simple request, and the accuracy of public clocks.) Their conclusion: Life is fastest paced in Japan and Western Europe, and slower paced in economically less-developed countries. People in colder climates also tend to live at a faster pace (and are more prone to die from heart disease).

Naturalistic observation offers interesting snapshots of everyday life, but it does so without controlling for all the factors that may influence behavior. It's one thing to observe the pace of life in various places, but another to understand what makes some people walk faster than others. Yet naturalistic observation, like surveys, can provide data for correlational research, which we consider next.

Correlation

5: What are positive and negative correlations, and why do they enable prediction but not cause-effect explanation?

Describing behavior is a first step toward predicting it. Surveys and naturalistic observations often show us that one trait or behavior is related to another. In such cases, we say the two **correlate**. A statistical measure (the **correlation coefficient**) helps us figure how closely two things vary together, and thus how well either one *predicts* the other. Knowing how much aptitude test scores *correlate* with school success tells us how well the scores *predict* school success.

Throughout this book we will often ask how strongly two sets of scores are related: For example, how closely related are the personality scores of identical twins? How well do intelligence test scores predict achievement? How closely is stress related to disease?

FIGURE 2.2, next page, contains three **scatterplots**, illustrating the range of possible correlations from a perfect positive to a perfect negative. (Perfect correlations rarely occur in the "real world.") Each dot in a scatterplot represents the scattered values of two variables. A correlation is positive if two sets of scores, such as height and weight, tend to rise or fall together. Saying that a correlation is "negative" says nothing about its strength or weakness. A correlation is negative if two sets of scores relate inversely, one set going up as the other goes down. Exercise and weight correlate negatively. As exercise goes up from zero, body weight has some tendency to go down. A weak correlation, indicating little relationship, has a coefficient near zero.

::**random sample** a sample that fairly represents a population because each member has an equal chance of inclusion.

::**naturalistic observation** observing and recording behavior in naturally occurring situations without trying to manipulate and control the situation.

::**correlation** a measure of the extent to which two factors vary together, and thus of how well either factor predicts the other.

::**correlation coefficient** a statistical index of the relationship between two things (from –1 to +1).

::**scatterplot** a graphed cluster of dots, each of which represents the values of two variables. The slope of the points suggests the direction of the relationship between the two variables. The amount of scatter suggests the strength of the correlation (little scatter indicates high correlation).

DEMO

Scatterplots are easy to demonstrate to students. Collect any two points of data—quiz scores and hours spent studying—and have students graph them on a scatterplot. Ask students to evaluate whether the data shows any tendency toward a positive or negative correlation.

At this point, you may want to use **Classroom Exercise:** *Correlating Test-Taking Time and Performance* (p. 18) from Bolt's Teacher's Resource Binder.

TEACHING TIP

Students should know the more technical terms for positive and negative correlations:

- Positive correlations are also known as **direct** correlations. These variables have a direct relationship between them—as one increases or decreases, so does the other in the same direction.

- Negative correlations are also known as **inverse** correlations. These variables have an inverse relationship—as one increases the other decreases.

At this point, you may want to use *PsychSim 5: Statistics: Correlation*, which can be found on the free Book Companion Site (www.worthpublishers.com/myers).

UNIT 2

➤ **FIGURE 2.2**
Scatterplots, showing patterns of correlation Correlations can range from +1.00 (scores on one measure increase in direct proportion to scores on another) to −1.00 (scores on one measure decrease precisely as scores rise on the other).

TROUBLESHOOTING

Note how the graphs in Figure 2.2 and Figure 2.3 differ. Rarely do positive and negative correlations look as nice as the graphs in Figure 2.2! Often, they look more scattered, like the graph in Figure 2.3.

CRITICAL THINKING

Psychological studies are reported in the popular press on an almost daily basis. Often these studies are reported as "experiments" when they actually are correlational. Have students collect reports of studies from newspapers and magazines and evaluate whether the reports represent the appropriate interpretations of the conclusions of the studies.

- Does the report represent a correlational study as an experimental study? Why or why not?

- What are the variables that are evaluated by the study? What outcome does the article suggest can be drawn from this study?

- Are the primary researchers interviewed for the story? If so, do they caution people to interpret a correlational study appropriately? Why or why not?

At this point, you may want to use **Classroom Exercise:** *Correlations and Predicting Test Performance* (p. 18) from Bolt's Teacher's Resource Binder.

Here are four recent news reports of correlational research, some derived from surveys or natural observations. Can you spot which are reporting positive correlations, which negative? (Answers below.)

TABLE 2.2		
HEIGHT AND TEMPERAMENT OF 20 MEN		
Person	**Height in Inches**	**Temperament**
1	80	75
2	63	66
3	61	60
4	79	90
5	74	60
6	69	42
7	62	42
8	75	60
9	77	81
10	60	39
11	64	48
12	76	69
13	71	72
14	66	57
15	73	63
16	70	75
17	63	30
18	71	57
19	68	84
20	70	39

1. The more young children watch TV, the less they read (Kaiser, 2003).

2. The more sexual content teens see on TV, the more likely they are to have sex (Collins et al., 2004).

3. The longer children are breast-fed, the greater their later academic achievement (Horwood & Fergusson, 1998).

4. The more often adolescents eat breakfast, the lower their body mass (Timlin et al., 2008).

Statistics can help us see what the naked eye sometimes misses. To demonstrate this for yourself, try an imaginary project. Wondering if tall men are more or less easygoing, you collect two sets of scores: men's heights and men's temperaments. You measure the height of 20 men, and you have someone else independently assess their temperaments (from zero for extremely calm to 100 for highly reactive).

With all the relevant data (**TABLE 2.2**) right in front of you, can you tell whether there is (1) a positive correlation between height and reactive temperament, (2) very little or no correlation, or (3) a negative correlation?

Comparing the columns in Table 2.2, most people detect very little relationship between height and temperament. In fact, the correlation in this imaginary example is moderately positive, +0.63, as we can see if we display the data as a scatterplot. In **FIGURE 2.3**, moving from left to right, the upward, oval-shaped slope of the cluster of points shows that our two imaginary sets of scores (height and reactivity) tend to rise together.

• Answers to correlation question: 1. negative, 2. positive, 3. positive, 4. negative. •

TEACHING TIP

One of the main ways correlational data is obtained is through survey research. Have students write and distribute a short survey (no more than 5 items). They can tabulate their results and even run correlations on data that is not categorical (such as Likert [Agree-Disagree] ratings or class test scores).

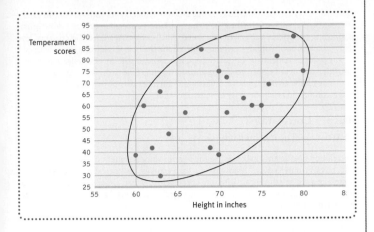

➤ FIGURE 2.3
Scatterplot for height and temperament
This display of data from 20 imagined men (each represented by a data point) reveals an upward slope, indicating a positive correlation. The considerable scatter of the data indicates the correlation is much lower than +1.0.

If we fail to see a relationship when data are presented as systematically as in Table 2.2, how much less likely are we to notice them in everyday life? To see what is right in front of us, we sometimes need statistical illumination. We can easily see evidence of gender discrimination when given statistically summarized information about job level, seniority, performance, gender, and salary. But we often see no discrimination when the same information dribbles in, case by case (Twiss et al., 1989).

The point to remember. A correlation coefficient, which can range from –1.0 to +1.0, reveals the extent to which two things relate.

Correlation and Causation

Correlations help us predict. Low self-esteem correlates with (and therefore predicts) depression. (This correlation might be indicated by a correlation coefficient, or just by a finding that people who score on the lower half of a self-esteem scale have an elevated depression rate.) So, does low self-esteem *cause* depression? If, based on the correlational evidence, you assume that it does, you have much company. A nearly irresistible thinking error is assuming that an association, sometimes presented as a correlation coefficient, proves causation. But no matter how strong the relationship, it does not *prove* anything!

As options 2 and 3 in FIGURE 2.4 show, we'd get the same negative correlation between low self-esteem and depression if depression caused people to be down on themselves, or if some third factor—such as heredity or brain chemistry—caused both low self-esteem and depression. Among men, for example, length of marriage correlates positively with hair loss—because both are associated with a third factor, age.

This point is so important—so basic to thinking smarter with psychology—that it merits one more example, from a survey of more than 12,000 adolescents. The study found that the more teens feel loved by their parents, the less likely they are to behave in unhealthy ways—having early sex, smoking, abusing alcohol and drugs, exhibiting violence (Resnick et al., 1997). "Adults have a powerful effect on their children's behavior right through the high school years," gushed an Associated

➤ FIGURE 2.4
Three possible cause-effect relationships
People low in self-esteem are more likely to report depression than are those high in self-esteem. One possible explanation of this negative correlation is that a bad self-image causes depressed feelings. But, as the diagram indicates, other cause-effect relationships are possible.

TROUBLESHOOTING

Emphasize to students that the term *correlation* does not mean *causation*. Remind them that a **correlation** tells you that certain variables are related but not why they are related. As students learn the details about the experimental method, their ability to distinguish correlation from causation becomes very important, in particular when they need to act as critical thinkers about research reports in the media.

At this point, you may want to use **Lecture/Discussion Topic: *Misinterpreting Correlations*** (p. 19) from Bolt's Teacher's Resource Binder.

TROUBLESHOOTING

Students often have trouble interpreting the correlation coefficient. They often think the sign tells them how strong the correlation is. They believe that negative correlations indicate weak relationships. The number represents the *strength* of the correlation. The sign represents the *direction* of the correlation. A correlation coefficient of –.70 indicates a stronger relationship than a coefficient of +.65. The relationship for –.70, however, is inverse rather than direct.

DEMO

Take a survey of your students, asking them questions about their birthday, shoe size, favorite color, favorite food, favorite soft drink, mother's first name, etc. Have students find another student in the room who has the most items the same as their own. You may find that you have two students who share the same birthday, cola preference, and mother's name! This seemingly spooky similarity is actually quite predictable.

At this point, you may want to use **Classroom Exercise: *Extraordinary Events and Chance: Your Birth Date in Pi?*** (p. 22) from Bolt's Teacher's Resource Binder.

UNIT 2

INTERCONNECTING

Point out that illusory correlations are often influenced by confirmation bias. We tend to look for evidence that confirms our beliefs and ignore evidence that disconfirms our beliefs. Figure 2.5 will help you demonstrate this to students.

TEACHING TIP

Ask your students whether they believe that the more you study, the lower the test grade you will get. This illusory correlation is flawed in a couple of ways:

- The operational definition of "study" is unclear. What exactly does it mean to "study"? Is the work you do while you are doing homework or listening in class "studying"? Or does it only refer to time dedicated outside of class for note and text review?

- The relationship is based on anecdotal evidence. Just because one person gets a high test score after minimal studying doesn't mean that all students who study minimally will get high scores. If you take all the evidence into account, the apparent correlation would probably be close to zero if not inversely related.

Students should remember that operational definitions and thorough investigations are crucial to interpreting correlations accurately.

At this point, you may want to use **Classroom Exercise: *Illusory Correlation*** (p. 21) from Bolt's Teacher's Resource Binder.

Correlation need not mean causation Length of marriage correlates with hair loss in men. Does this mean that marriage causes men to lose their hair (or that balding men make better husbands)? In this case, as in many others, a third factor obviously explains the correlation: Golden anniversaries and baldness both accompany aging.

• A study reported in the *British Medical Journal* found that youths who identify with the goth subculture attempt, more often than other young people, to harm or kill themselves (Young et al., 2006). Can you imagine multiple possible explanations for this association? •

➤ **FIGURE 2.5**
Illusory correlation in everyday life Many people believe infertile couples become more likely to conceive a child after adopting a baby. This belief arises from their attention being drawn to such cases. The many couples who adopt without conceiving or conceive without adopting grab less attention. To determine whether there actually is a correlation between adoption and conception, we need data from all four cells in this figure. (From Gilovich, 1991.)

Press (AP) story reporting the finding. But this correlation comes with no built-in cause-effect arrow. Said differently (turn the volume up here), *association does not prove causation.*[2] Thus, the AP could as well have reported, "Well-behaved teens feel their parents' love and approval; out-of-bounds teens more often think their parents are disapproving jerks."

The point to remember: Correlation indicates the *possibility* of a cause-effect relationship, *but it does not prove causation.* Knowing that two events are associated need not tell us anything about causation. Remember this principle and you will be wiser as you read and hear news of scientific studies.

Illusory Correlations

6: What are illusory correlations?

Correlation coefficients make visible the relationships we might otherwise miss. They also restrain our "seeing" relationships that actually do not exist. A perceived but nonexistent correlation is an **illusory correlation**. When we *believe* there is a relationship between two things, we are likely to *notice* and *recall* instances that confirm our belief (Trolier & Hamilton, 1986).

Because we are sensitive to dramatic or unusual events, we are especially likely to notice and remember the occurrence of two such events in sequence—say, a premonition of an unlikely phone call followed by the call. When the call does not follow the premonition, we are less likely to note and remember the nonevent. Illusory correlations help explain many superstitious beliefs, such as the presumption that infertile couples who adopt become more likely to conceive (Gilovich, 1991). Couples who conceive after adopting capture our attention. We're less likely to notice those who adopt and never conceive, or those who conceive without adopting. In other words, illusory correlations occur when we over-rely on the top left cell of **FIGURE 2.5**, ignoring equally essential information in the other cells.

Such illusory thinking helps explain why for so many years people believed (and many still do) that sugar makes children hyperactive, that getting chilled and wet causes people to catch a cold, and that changes in the weather trigger arthritis pain. We are, it seems, prone to perceiving patterns, whether they're there or not.

The point to remember: When we notice random coincidences, we may forget that they are random and instead see them as correlated. Thus, we can easily deceive ourselves by seeing what is not there.

Perceiving Order in Random Events

In our natural eagerness to make sense of our world—what poet Wallace Stevens called our "rage for order"—we look for order even in random data. And we usually find it, because—

	Conceive	Do not conceive
Adopt	confirming evidence	disconfirming evidence
Do not adopt	disconfirming evidence	confirming evidence

[2]Because many associations are stated as correlations, the famously worded principle is "Correlation does not prove causation." That's true, but it's also true of associations verified by other nonexperimental statistics (Hatfield et al., 2006).

here's a curious fact of life—*random sequences often don't look random*. Consider a random coin flip: If someone flipped a coin six times, which of the following sequences of heads (H) and tails (T) would be most likely: HHHTTT or HTTHTH or HHHHHH?

Daniel Kahneman and Amos Tversky (1972) found that most people believe HTTHTH would be the most likely random sequence. Actually, all three are equally likely (or, you might say, equally unlikely). A poker hand of 10 through ace, all of hearts, would seem extraordinary; actually, it would be no more or less likely than any other specific hand of cards (FIGURE 2.6).

In actual random sequences, patterns and streaks (such as repeating digits) occur more often than people expect. To demonstrate this phenomenon for myself (as you can do), I flipped a coin 51 times, with these results:

1. H	11. T	21. T	31. T	41. H	51. T
2. T	12. H	22. T	32. T	42. H	
3. T	13. H	23. H	33. T	43. H	
4. T	14. T	24. T	34. T	44. H	
5. H	15. T	25. T	35. T	45. T	
6. H	16. T	26. T	36. H	46. H	
7. H	17. T	27. T	37. T	47. H	
8. T	18. T	28. T	38. T	48. T	
9. T	19. H	29. H	39. H	49. T	
10. T	20. H	30. T	40. T	50. T	

Looking over the sequence, patterns jump out: Tosses 10 to 22 provided an almost perfect pattern of pairs of tails followed by pairs of heads. On tosses 30 to 38 I had a "cold hand," with only one head in eight tosses. But my fortunes immediately reversed with a "hot hand"—seven heads out of the next nine tosses. Similar streaks happen, about as often as one would expect in random sequences, in basketball shooting, baseball hitting, and mutual fund stock pickers' selections (Gilovich et al., 1985; Malkiel, 1989, 1995; Myers, 2002). These sequences often don't look random, and so get overinterpreted ("When you're hot, you're hot!").

What explains these streaky patterns? Was I exercising some sort of paranormal control over my coin? Did I snap out of my tails funk and get in a heads groove? No such explanations are needed, for these are the sorts of streaks found in any random data. Comparing each toss to the next, 24 of the 50 comparisons yielded a changed result—just the sort of near 50-50 result we expect from coin tossing. Despite seeming patterns, the outcome of one toss gives no clue to the outcome of the next.

However, some happenings seem so extraordinary that we struggle to conceive an ordinary, chance-related explanation (as applies to our coin tosses). In such cases, statisticians often are less mystified. When Evelyn Marie Adams won the New Jersey lottery *twice*, newspapers reported the odds of her feat as 1 in 17 trillion. Bizarre? Actually, 1 in 17 trillion are indeed the odds that a given person who buys a single ticket for two New Jersey lotteries will win both times. But statisticians Stephen Samuels and George McCabe (1989) reported that, given the millions of people who buy U.S. state lottery tickets, it was "practically a sure thing" that someday, somewhere, someone would hit a state jackpot twice. Indeed, said fellow statisticians Persi Diaconis and Frederick Mosteller (1989), "with a large enough sample, any outrageous thing is likely to happen." An event that happens to but 1 in 1 billion people every day occurs about six times a day, 2000 times a year.

::illusory correlation the perception of a relationship where none exists.

● A *New York Times* writer reported a massive survey showing that "adolescents whose parents smoked were 50 percent more likely than children of nonsmokers to report having had sex." He concluded (would you agree?) that the survey indicated a causal effect—that "to reduce the chances that their children will become sexually active at an early age" parents might "quit smoking" (O'Neil, 2002). ●

➤ FIGURE 2.6
Two random sequences Your chances of being dealt either of these hands are precisely the same: 1 in 2,598,960.

● On March 11, 1998, Utah's Ernie and Lynn Carey gained three new grandchildren when three of their daughters gave birth—on the same day (*Los Angeles Times*, 1998). ●

Bizarre-looking, perhaps. But actually no more unlikely than any other number sequence.

© 1990 by Sidney Harris/American Scientist magazine.

TEACHING TIP

Daniel Kahneman won the Nobel Prize in Economics for his work with Amos Tversky on how people make irrational decisions depending on how the decision is framed. Instead of making decisions based on all available evidence, we have a tendency to make judgments based on intuition or illusory correlations. Their work has helped economists make better predictions about how markets will work.

(Note: Unfortunately, Tversky died before the prize was awarded, so he did not share Kahneman's prize. The Nobel Prize committee does not award posthumous prizes.)

TEACHING TIP

Have students go to a news Web site and find reports about a psychological study. Have them evaluate the article using the following questions as guidelines:

● What was the hypothesis of the study?

● Who were the subjects for this study? Is this population representative of people in general?

● Is this study correlational? If so, what factors are being related? Does the article make it seem like the results are due to a cause-and-effect relationship?

UNIT 2

There are two main ways to group participants in a study:

- A *within-subjects design* involves comparing participants to themselves. Typically, the researcher will give the participants a pre-test. All of the participants will be exposed to the independent variable and then will take a post-test. In this design, the participants serve as their own control group.

- A *between-subjects design* involves comparing one group of participants to another. This is the most common experimental set up. Only one group in this design is exposed to the independent variable.

The between-subjects design is more efficient because you can usually conduct the research in one sitting. However, individual differences are more likely to influence the results since the difference in groups could be due to different people being in each group. The within-subjects design is less efficient, but more resistant to the effects of individual differences, because the participants are compared to themselves.

At this point, you may want to use the *Worth Publishers Video: Psychology: The Human Experience,* Module 3: Experimental Design.

The only type of study that can determine cause-and-effect is the experiment. Students often miss this key distinction.

::**experiment** a research method in which an investigator manipulates one or more factors (independent variables) to observe the effect on some behavior or mental process (the dependent variable). By *random assignment* of participants, the experimenter aims to control other relevant factors.

::**random assignment** assigning participants to experimental and control groups by chance, thus minimizing preexisting differences between those assigned to the different groups.

::**double-blind procedure** an experimental procedure in which both the research participants and the research staff are ignorant (blind) about whether the research participants have received the treatment or a placebo. Commonly used in drug-evaluation studies.

::**placebo** [pluh-SEE-bo; Latin for "I shall please"] **effect** experimental results caused by expectations alone; any effect on behavior caused by the administration of an inert substance or condition, which the recipient assumes is an active agent.

::**experimental group** in an experiment, the group that is exposed to the treatment, that is, to one version of the independent variable.

::**control group** in an experiment, the group that is *not* exposed to the treatment; contrasts with the experimental group and serves as a comparison for evaluating the effect of the treatment.

::**independent variable** the experimental factor that is manipulated; the variable whose effect is being studied.

::**confounding variable** a factor other than the independent variable that might produce an effect in an experiment.

::**dependent variable** the outcome factor; the variable that may change in response to manipulations of the independent variable.

Experimentation

7: How do experiments, powered by random assignment, clarify cause and effect?

Happy are they, remarked the Roman poet Virgil, "who have been able to perceive the causes of things." To isolate cause and effect, psychologists can statistically control for other factors. For example, researchers have found that breast-fed infants grow up with somewhat higher intelligence scores than do infants bottle-fed with cow's milk (Angelsen et al., 2001; Mortensen et al., 2002; Quinn et al., 2001). They have also found that breast-fed British babies have been more likely than their bottle-fed counterparts to eventually move into a higher social class (Martin et al., 2007). But the "breast is best" intelligence effect shrinks when researchers compare breast-fed and bottle-fed children from the same families (Der et al., 2006).

So, does this mean that smarter mothers (who in modern countries more often breast-feed) have smarter children? Or, as some researchers believe, do the nutrients of mother's milk contribute to brain development? To help answer this question, researchers have "controlled for" (statistically removed differences in) certain other factors, such as maternal age, education, and income. And they have found that in infant nutrition, mother's milk correlates modestly but positively with later intelligence.

Correlational research cannot control for all possible factors. But researchers can isolate cause and effect with an **experiment**. Experiments enable a researcher to focus on the possible effects of one or more factors by (1) *manipulating the factors of interest* and (2) *holding constant ("controlling") other factors*. With parental permission, a British research team *randomly assigned* 424 hospital preterm infants either to standard infant formula feedings or to donated breast milk feedings (Lucas et al., 1992). On intelligence tests taken at age 8, the children nourished with breast milk had significantly higher intelligence scores than their formula-fed counterparts. Earlier we mentioned the place of *random sampling* in a well-done survey. Consider now the equally important place of *random assignment* in a well-done experiment.

Random Assignment

No single experiment is conclusive, of course. But by **randomly assigning** infants to one feeding group or the other, researchers were able to hold constant all factors except nutrition. This eliminated alternative explanations and supported the conclusion that breast is indeed best for developing intelligence (at least for preterm infants).

If a behavior (such as test performance) changes when we vary an experimental factor (such as infant nutrition), then we infer the factor is having an effect. *The point to remember*: Unlike correlational studies, which uncover naturally occurring relationships, an experiment manipulates a factor to determine its effect.

Consider, too, how we might assess a therapeutic intervention. Our tendency to seek new remedies when we are ill or emotionally down can produce misleading testimonies. If three days into a cold we start taking vitamin C tablets and find our cold symptoms lessening, we may credit the pills rather than the cold naturally subsiding. If, after nearly failing the first test, we listen to a "peak learning" subliminal CD and then improve on the next test, we may credit the CD rather than conclude that our performance has returned to our average. In the 1700s, bloodletting *seemed* effective. Sometimes people improved after the treatment; when they didn't, the practitioner inferred the disease was just too advanced to be reversed. (We, of course, now know that usually bloodletting is a *bad* treatment.) So, whether or not a remedy is truly effective, enthusiastic users will probably endorse it. To find out whether it actually is effective, we must experiment.

The need for two sample groups can be overlooked. Richard Sprinthall cites that a common argument against capital punishment is that it has no deterrent effect. Support for this argument can be found in the fact that, years ago, pickpockets worked the very crowds observing the public hangings of other convicted pickpockets. The fallacy is that there is no comparison group. How about the number of pockets picked in crowds at a horse race or a carnival? If pocket picking was lower at the public hangings, then perhaps capital punishment did have a deterrent effect.

Sprinthall, R. (1997). *Basic statistical analysis* (5th ed.). Needham Heights, MA: Allyn & Bacon.

And that is precisely how investigators evaluate new drug treatments and new methods of psychological therapy (Unit 13). The participants in these studies are randomly assigned to the research groups and are often *blind* (uninformed) about what treatment, if any, they are receiving. One group receives a treatment (such as medication or other therapy). The other group receives a pseudotreatment—an inert *placebo* (perhaps a pill with no drug in it). If the study is using a **double-blind procedure**, neither the participants nor the research assistants collecting the data will know which group is receiving the treatment. In such studies, researchers can check a treatment's actual effects apart from the participants' belief in its healing powers and the staff's enthusiasm for its potential. Just *thinking* you are getting a treatment can boost your spirits, relax your body, and relieve your symptoms. This **placebo effect** is well documented in reducing pain, depression, and anxiety (Kirsch & Sapirstein, 1998). And the more expensive the placebo, the more "real" it seems to us—a fake pill that costs $2.50 works better than one costing 10 cents (Waber et al., 2008). To know how effective a therapy really is, researchers must control for a possible placebo effect.

The double-blind procedure is one way to create an **experimental group**, in which people receive the treatment, and a contrasting **control group** that does not receive the treatment. By randomly assigning people to these conditions, researchers can be fairly certain the two groups are otherwise identical. Random assignment roughly equalizes the two groups in age, attitudes, and every other characteristic. With random assignment, as occurred with the infants in the breast milk experiment, we also can conclude that any later differences between people in the experimental and control groups will usually be the result of the treatment.

Independent and Dependent Variables

Here is an even more potent example: The drug Viagra was approved for use after 21 clinical trials. One trial was an experiment in which researchers randomly assigned 329 men with erectile dysfunction to either an experimental group (Viagra takers) or a control group (placebo takers). It was a double-blind procedure—neither the men nor the person who gave them the pills knew which drug they were receiving. The result: At peak doses, 69 percent of Viagra-assisted attempts at intercourse were successful, compared with 22 percent for men receiving the placebo (Goldstein et al., 1998). Viagra worked.

This simple experiment manipulated just one factor: the drug dosage (none versus peak dose). We call this experimental factor the **independent variable** because we can vary it *independently* of other factors, such as the men's age, weight, and personality. These other factors, which can potentially influence the results of the experiment, are called **confounding variables.** Random assignment controls for possible confounding variables.

Experiments examine the effect of one or more independent variables on some measurable behavior, called the **dependent variable** because it can vary *depending* on what takes place during the experiment. Both variables are given precise *operational definitions*, which specify the procedures that manipulate the independent variable (the precise drug dosage and timing in this study) or measure the dependent variable (the questions that assessed the men's responses). These definitions answer the "What do you mean?" question with a level of precision that enables others to repeat the study. (See **FIGURE 2.7**, next page, for the breast milk experiment's design.)

Let's pause to check your understanding using a simple psychology experiment: To test the effect of perceived ethnicity on the availability of a rental house, Adrian Carpusor and William Loges (2006) sent identically worded e-mail inquiries to 1115 Los Angeles-area landlords. The researchers varied the ethnic connotation of the sender's name and tracked the percentage of positive replies (invitations to view the apartment in person). "Patrick McDougall," "Said Al-Rahman," and "Tyrell Jackson"

"If I don't think it's going to work, will it still work?"

• Note the distinction between random sampling in surveys (discussed earlier in relation to surveys) and random assignment in experiments (depicted in Figure 2.7). *Random sampling* helps us generalize to a larger population. *Random assignment* controls extraneous influences, which helps us infer cause and effect •

UNIT 2

TROUBLESHOOTING

Be sure to emphasize the differing goals of the different research methods. Case studies and naturalistic observations only *describe* behavior. Correlations can be used to *predict* future phenomena. Experiments *determine cause and effect.* Students should not try to assign causal conclusions to anything but experiments.

DEMO

Conduct a simple experiment testing the hypothesis, "Oreo cookies improve memory." Randomly assign students to either the experimental or control group. Give the experimental group one Oreo cookie each, and do not give the control group any cookies. Then, give students a quick test of memory by having them recall a list of random words. Compare how many words each group remembers.

You will find no real differences between the two groups. This demo provides wonderful opportunities for discussion of what went right and wrong with this experiment.

- Did random assignment help control for confounding variables like IQ or gender? *(Yes. Have students consider how different the results would have been if groups were divided by gender or GPA.)*

- Did knowing which group got the IV introduce more confounding variables? Why or why not? *(Typically, participants do not know what the IV is to keep them from responding the way they think the researcher is hoping for.)*

- In what ways could this experiment be conducted better? *(Putting each group in a different room, having a placebo, etc.)*

received, respectively, 89 percent, 66 percent, and 56 percent invitations. In this experiment, what was the independent variable? The dependent variable?[3]

Experiments can also help us evaluate social programs. Do early childhood education programs boost impoverished children's chances for success? What are the effects of different anti-smoking campaigns? Do school sex-education programs reduce teen pregnancies? To answer such questions, we can experiment: If an intervention is welcomed but resources are scarce, we could use a lottery to randomly assign some people (or regions) to experience the new program and others to a control condition. If later the two groups differ, the intervention's effect will be confirmed (Passell, 1993).

Let's recap. A *variable* is anything that can vary (infant nutrition, intelligence, TV exposure—anything within the bounds of what is feasible and ethical). Experiments aim to *manipulate* an *independent* variable, *measure* the *dependent* variable, and *control* confounding variables. An experiment has at least two different groups: an *experimental group* and a *comparison* or *control group. Random assignment* works to equate the groups before any treatment effects. In this way, an experiment tests the effect of at least one independent variable (what we manipulate) on at least one dependent variable (the outcome we measure).

TABLE 2.3 compares the features of psychology's research methods.

➤ **FIGURE 2.7**
Experimentation To discern causation, psychologists may randomly assign some participants to an experimental group, others to a control group. Measuring the dependent variable (intelligence score in later childhood) will determine the effect of the independent variable (type of milk).

TABLE 2.3

COMPARING RESEARCH METHODS

Research Method	Basic Purpose	How Conducted	What Is Manipulated	Strengths	Weaknesses
Descriptive	To observe and record behavior	Case studies, surveys, or naturalistic observations	Nothing	Case studies require only one participant; surveys may be done fairly quickly and inexpensively (compared to experiments); naturalistic observations may be done when it is not ethical to manipulate variables.	No control of variables; single cases may be misleading
Correlational	To detect naturally occurring relationships; to assess how well one variable predicts another	Compute statistical association, sometimes among survey responses	Nothing	Works with large groups of data, and may be used in situations where an experiment would not be ethical or possible	Does not specify cause and effect
Experimental	To explore cause and effect	Manipulate one or more factors; use random assignment	The independent variable(s)	Specifies cause and effect, and variables are controlled	Sometimes not feasible; results may not generalize to other contexts; not ethical to manipulate certain variables

[3]The independent variable, which the researchers manipulated, was the ethnicity-related names. The dependent variable, which they measured, was the positive response rate.

➤ **ASK YOURSELF**

If you were to become a research psychologist, what questions would you like to explore with experiments?

➤ **TEST YOURSELF 2**

Why, when testing a new drug to control blood pressure, would we learn more about its effectiveness from giving it to half of the participants in a group of 1000 than to all 1000 participants?

Answers to the Test Yourself questions can be found in Appendix E at the end of the book.

Statistical Reasoning in Everyday Life

IN DESCRIPTIVE, CORRELATIONAL, and experimental research, statistics are tools that help us see and interpret what the unaided eye might miss. But statistical understanding benefits more than just researchers. To be an educated person today is to be able to apply simple statistical principles to everyday reasoning. One needn't memorize complicated formulas to think more clearly and critically about data.

The-top-of-the-head estimates often misread reality and then mislead the public. Someone throws out a big, round number. Others echo it, and before long the big, round number becomes public misinformation. A few examples:

- *Ten percent of people are lesbians or gay men.* Or is it 2 to 3 percent, as suggested by various national surveys (Unit 8A)?
- *We ordinarily use but 10 percent of our brain.* Or is it closer to 100 percent (Unit 3B)?
- *The human brain has 100 billion nerve cells.* Or is it more like 40 billion, as suggested by extrapolation from sample counts (Unit 3A)?

The point to remember: Doubt big, round, undocumented numbers. Rather than swallowing top-of-the-head estimates, focus on thinking smarter by applying simple statistical principles to everyday reasoning.

Describing Data

8: How can we describe data with measures of central tendency and variation?

Once researchers have gathered their data, they must organize them in some meaningful way. One way to do this is to convert the data into a simple *bar graph*, as in **FIGURE 2.8**, next page, which displays a distribution of different brands of trucks still on the road after a decade. When reading statistical graphs such as this, take care. It's easy to design a graph to make a difference look big (Figure 2.8a) or small (Figure 2.8b). The secret lies in how you label the vertical scale (the Y-axis).

The point to remember: Think smart. When viewing figures in magazines and on television, read the scale labels and note their range.

Measures of Central Tendency

The next step is to summarize the data using some *measure of central tendency*, a single score that represents a whole set of scores. The simplest measure is the **mode**, the most

"Figures can be misleading—so I've written a song which I think expresses the real story of the firm's performance this quarter."

::**mode** the most frequently occurring score(s) in a distribution.

Help students understand that the type of statistics computed for a set of data depends on what type of data is collected.

- Gender is an example of *nominal data,* which is data that simply identifies categories. Other examples include Yes/No answers on surveys and class level in school (senior, junior, etc.).
- *Ordinal data* identifies the order in which data falls in a set. Any ranking of items, from one-hit wonders to class rank to home-run sluggers, is done as ordinal data.
- *Interval data* includes data that falls within a number line that has a zero point. Weight has a real zero point in that a weight of zero means no weight (of course, zero weight means something does not exist!). Height is another example of interval data.
- *Ratio data* includes data that falls in a number line where zero is just another number on the line. For instance, a temperature of zero degrees does not mean there is no temperature. Test scores can also be ratio data in that a score of zero usually doesn't mean "absence of knowledge."

Give students the test scores from a recent test given in your classroom (without names to protect privacy) and have them create a frequency distribution of the data. Also have them calculate the mode, median, and mean of the data. They can see how meaningful their own test scores are compared to the distribution and measures of central tendency.

At this point, you may want to use **Classroom Exercise:** *An M&M's Sampling Demonstration* (p. 28) from Bolt's Teacher's Resource Binder.

UNIT 2

Measures of central tendency are the simplest, yet most often confused, type of basic statistics:

- Central tendency refers to how the data measure the center of a set of data. The mode, median, and mean all point to where the middle of the data should be.

- If the mode, median, and mean are all the same number, the graph of the data will look like a normal curve. If the mode, median, and mean are different, the graph will be skewed, or off center, in some way.

- The mean is most susceptible to extremes in the data. The mean is the number that gets pulled up or down depending on how extreme the data points are.

At this point, you may want to use *PsychSim 5: Descriptive Statistics,* which can be found on the free Book Companion Site (www.worthpublishers.com/myers).

Students will likely get positive and negative skew confused. Point out that positive skew occurs when scores pull the mean toward the higher end of the scores. Hence, the mean is more "positive" or greater than the rest of the scores. Negative skew is the opposite, with the mean being pulled down toward the lower end of the scores.

At this point, you may want to use **Classroom Exercise/Student Project:** *Describing Data* (p. 28) from Bolt's Teacher's Resource Binder.

> **FIGURE 2.8**
Read the scale labels An American truck manufacturer offered graph (a)—with actual brand names included—to suggest the much greater durability of its trucks. Note, however, how the apparent difference shrinks as the vertical scale changes in graph (b).

> **FIGURE 2.9**
A skewed distribution This graphic representation of the distribution of a village's incomes illustrates the three measures of central tendency—mode, median, and mean. Note how just a few high incomes make the mean—the fulcrum point that balances the incomes above and below—deceptively high.

frequently occurring score or scores. The most commonly reported is the **mean**, or arithmetic average—the sum of all the scores divided by the number of scores. On a divided highway, the median is the middle. So, too, with data: The **median** is the midpoint—the 50th percentile. If you arrange all the scores in order from the highest to the lowest, half will be above the median and half will be below it. In a symmetrical bell-shaped distribution of scores, the mode, mean, and median scores may be the same or very similar.

Measures of central tendency neatly summarize data. But consider what happens to the mean when a distribution is lopsided or *skewed*. With income data, for example, the mode, median, and mean often tell very different stories (**FIGURE 2.9**). This happens because the mean is biased by a few extreme scores. When Microsoft co-founder Bill Gates sits down in an intimate café, its average (mean) customer instantly becomes a billionaire. But the customer's median wealth remains unchanged. Understanding this, you can see how a British newspaper could accurately run the headline "Income for 62% Is Below Average" (Waterhouse, 1993). Because the bottom *half* of British income earners receive only a *quarter* of the national income cake, most British people, like most people everywhere, make less than the mean. In the United States, Republicans

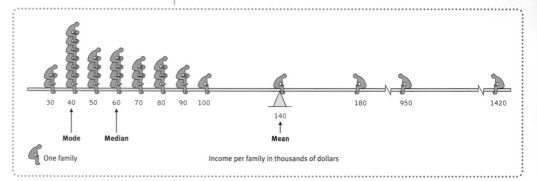

Have students take some data and create a frequency table and chart. You can use any kind of data, from test scores to heights of students in the class to shoe sizes.

- To create a table, have students put each different type of data (such as the various possible heights in inches) in one column and the data points for that level of data (how many students are of that specific height) in another column.

- To create a chart, have students plot the number of data for each point on a graph. Typically, a bar graph is best.

have tended to tout the economy's solid growth since 2000 using average income; Democrats have lamented the economy's lackluster growth using median income (Paulos, 2006). Mean and median tell different true stories.

The point to remember. Always note which measure of central tendency is reported. Then, if it is a mean, consider whether a few atypical scores could be distorting it.

Measures of Variation

Knowing the value of an appropriate measure of central tendency can tell us a great deal. But the single number omits other information. It helps to know something about the amount of *variation* in the data—how similar or diverse the scores are. Averages derived from scores with low variability are more reliable than averages based on scores with high variability. Consider a basketball player who scored between 13 and 17 points in each of her first 10 games in a season. Knowing this, we would be more confident that she would score near 15 points in her next game than if her scores had varied from 5 to 25 points.

The **range** of scores—the gap between the lowest and highest scores—provides only a crude estimate of variation because a couple of extreme scores in an otherwise uniform group, such as the $950,000 and $1,420,000 incomes in Figure 2.9, will create a deceptively large range.

The more useful standard for measuring how much scores deviate from one another is the **standard deviation**. It better gauges whether scores are packed together or dispersed, because it uses information from each score (**TABLE 2.4**). The computation assembles information about how much individual scores differ from the mean. If your high school serves a community where most families have similar incomes, family income data will have a relatively small standard deviation compared with a school in a more diverse community population.

 • The average person has one ovary and one testicle. •

::mean the arithmetic average of a distribution, obtained by adding the scores and then dividing by the number of scores.

::median the middle score in a distribution; half the scores are above it and half are below it.

::range the difference between the highest and lowest scores in a distribution.

::standard deviation a computed measure of how much scores vary around the mean score.

TABLE 2.4

STANDARD DEVIATION IS MUCH MORE INFORMATIVE THAN MEAN ALONE

Note that the test scores in Class A and Class B have the same mean (80), but very different standard deviations, which tell us more about how the students in each class are really faring.

Test Scores in Class A			Test Scores in Class B		
Score	Deviation from the Mean	Squared Deviation	Score	Deviation from the Mean	Squared Deviation
72	-8	64	60	-20	400
74	-6	36	60	-20	400
77	-3	9	70	-10	100
79	-1	1	70	-10	100
82	+2	4	90	+10	100
84	+4	16	90	+10	100
85	+5	25	100	+2-	400
87	+7	49	100	+20	400

Total = 640
Mean = 640 ÷ 8 = 80

Sum of (deviations)² = 204

Total = 640
Mean = 640 ÷ 8 = 80

Sum of (deviations)² = 2000

Standard deviation =

$$\sqrt{\frac{\text{Sum of (deviations)}^2}{\text{Number of scores}}} = \sqrt{\frac{204}{8}} = 5.0$$

Standard deviation =

$$\sqrt{\frac{\text{Sum of (deviations)}^2}{\text{Number of scores}}} = \sqrt{\frac{2000}{8}} = 15.8$$

 TEACHING TIP

It is unlikely that the AP Exam will have students conduct difficult calculations, such as standard deviation. The AP Exam in Psychology does not allow students to use calculators, and while it is certainly possible to calculate standard deviation without a calculator, it is not often done by students today. Students may be asked to interpret standard deviation, but they will probably not need to know how to calculate it.

TROUBLESHOOTING

Standard deviation is often misunderstood, but it is actually a highly valuable statistic. Knowing the standard deviation for a set of data can reveal how similar the scores are. The higher the standard deviation, the less similar the scores are.

- For example: if a set of test scores has a standard deviation of 5, then everyone who took the test scored similarly. If the scores have a standard deviation of 50, then the test-takers' scores were not very similar at all!

TEACHING TIP

Standard deviation tells us how different the scores are from each other. Notice how Myers points out that less variability is better than greater variability. Therefore, if a group of scores has a smaller standard deviation, then you can draw more stable conclusions from that data set. If the set of scores has a large standard deviation, the conclusions you can draw are less stable.

UNIT 2

Knowing the percentages of scores that fall one, two, and three standard deviations from the mean is important for the AP Exam (see Figure 2.10). Make sure students know these percentages well.

INTERCONNECTING

Reliability and validity of data will be discussed again in Unit 11 during the discussion of testing in psychology. Students often confuse these concepts, so introducing them here might help reinforce through repetition.

TEACHING TIP

Again, because students cannot use calculators during the AP Exam, they will probably not have to calculate statistical significance. Rather, they will need to interpret what statistical significance means. Focus more on conceptual knowledge rather than practical knowledge for this concept.

➤ **FIGURE 2.10**
The normal curve Scores on aptitude tests tend to form a normal, or bell-shaped, curve. For example, the Wechsler Adult Intelligence Scale calls the average score 100.

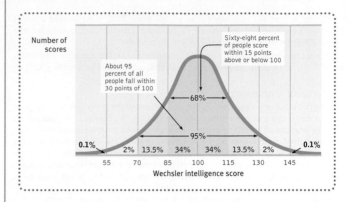

You can grasp the meaning of the standard deviation if you consider how scores tend to be distributed in nature. Large numbers of data—heights, weights, intelligence scores, grades (though not incomes)—often form a symmetrical, bell-shaped distribution. Most cases fall near the mean, and fewer cases fall near either extreme. This bell-shaped distribution is so typical that we call the curve it forms the **normal curve**.

As **FIGURE 2.10** shows, a useful property of the normal curve is that roughly 68 percent of the cases fall within one standard deviation on either side of the mean. About 95 percent of cases fall within two standard deviations. Thus, Unit 11 notes that about 68 percent of people taking an intelligence test will score within ±15 points of 100. About 95 percent will score within ±30 points.

Making Inferences

9: What principles can guide our making generalizations from samples and deciding whether differences are significant?

Data are "noisy." The average score in one group (breast-fed babies) could conceivably differ from the average score in another group (formula-fed babies) not because of any real difference but merely because of chance fluctuations in the people sampled. How confidently, then, can we infer that an observed difference accurately estimates the true difference? For guidance, we can ask how reliable and significant the differences are.

When Is an Observed Difference Reliable?

In deciding when it is safe to generalize from a sample, we should keep three principles in mind.

1. **Representative samples are better than biased samples.** The best basis for generalizing is not from the exceptional and memorable cases one finds at the extremes but from a representative sample of cases. Research never randomly samples the whole human population. Thus, it pays to keep in mind what population a study has sampled.

2. **Less-variable observations are more reliable than those that are more variable.** As we noted in the example of the basketball player whose game-to-game points were consistent, an average is more reliable when it comes from scores with low variability.

3. **More cases are better than fewer.** An eager high school senior visits two university campuses, each for a day. At the first, the student randomly attends two classes and discovers both instructors to be witty and engaging. At the next campus, the two sampled instructors seem dull and uninspiring. Returning home, the student (discounting the small sample size of only two teachers at each institution) tells friends about the "great teachers" at the first school, and the "bores" at the second. Again, we know it but we ignore it: *Averages based on many cases are more reliable* (less variable) than averages based on only a few cases.

The point to remember: Don't be overly impressed by a few anecdotes. Generalizations based on a few unrepresentative cases are unreliable.

When Is a Difference Significant?

Statistical tests also help us determine whether differences are meaningful. Here is the underlying logic: When averages from two samples are each reliable measures of their respective populations (as when each is based on many observations that have small variability), then their *difference* is likely to be reliable as well. (Example: The less the variability in women's and in men's aggression scores, the more confidence we would have that any observed gender difference is reliable.) And when the difference between the sample averages is *large*, we have even more confidence that the difference between them reflects a real difference in their populations.

In short, when the sample averages are reliable, and when the difference between them is relatively large, we say the difference has **statistical significance**. This means that the observed difference is probably not due to chance variation between the samples.

In judging statistical significance, psychologists are conservative. They are like juries who must presume innocence until guilt is proven. For most psychologists, proof beyond a reasonable doubt means not making much of a finding unless the odds of its occurring by chance are less than 5 percent (an arbitrary criterion).

Peanuts

When reading about research, you should remember that, given large enough or homogeneous enough samples, a difference between them may be "statistically significant" yet have little practical significance. For example, comparisons of intelligence test scores among hundreds of thousands of first-born and later-born individuals indicate a highly significant tendency for first-born individuals to have higher average scores than their later-born siblings (Kristensen & Bjerkedal, 2007; Zajonc & Markus, 1975). But because the scores differ by only one to three points, the difference has little practical importance. Such findings have caused some psychologists to advocate alternatives to significance testing (Hunter, 1997). Better, they say, to use other ways to express a finding's *effect size*—its magnitude and reliability.

The point to remember: Statistical significance indicates the *likelihood* that a result will happen by chance. But this does not say anything about the *importance* of the result.

::**normal curve** (normal distribution) a symmetrical, bell-shaped curve that describes the distribution of many types of data; most scores fall near the mean (68 percent fall within one standard deviation of it) and fewer and fewer near the extremes.

::**statistical significance** a statistical statement of how likely it is that an obtained result occurred by chance.

Help students understand *significance* in the following ways:

- Statistical significance refers to how two groups' means are different. If you graphed the data from two groups and the graphs did not overlap or only overlapped a little, then the difference would be significant. If the graphs overlapped a lot, then the difference would not be significant.

- Significance allows you to say how likely the difference in means is due to chance. The usual goal is to get a significance level of .05, which says that the results are only 5 percent due to chance (or 95 percent due to your independent variable!).

At this point, you may want to use **Lecture/Discussion Topic:** *Differences Between Groups* (p. 31) from Bolt's Teacher's Resource Binder.

TEACHING TIP

Effect size (the measure of the strength of a relationship between variables) is becoming the new way for researchers to report their results. When used along with tests of statistical significance, effect size tells more about the quality of the data collected than significance can alone.

At this point, you may want to use **Classroom Exercise/Student Project:** *When is a Difference Significant?* (p. 30) from Bolt's Teacher's Resource Binder.

UNIT 2

TEACHING TIP

Help students see that controlling for confounding, or extraneous, variables is the goal of the experimental method. The more controlled the environment, the more likely you will be able to tell whether the IV caused the DV. A highly-controlled experimental environment is not much like reality, but it does help simplify the complexity of the real world and helps provide a clearer picture of how variables in the real world work together.

At this point, you may want to use **Classroom Exercise: *Main Effects and Interactions or "It All Depends"*** (p. 26) from Bolt's Teacher's Resource Binder.

INTERCONNECTING

Emphasize to students that experiments are more likely to be replicated effectively if clear operational definitions are used. Operational definitions attempt to clearly define the behaviors that the researchers are looking for. If the operational definitions are clear enough, then others can more easily and accurately replicate the study.

At this point, you may want to use **Lecture/Discussion Topic: *Field and Laboratory Experiments*** (p. 32) from Bolt's Teacher's Resource Binder.

BEFORE YOU MOVE ON . . .

➤ **ASK YOURSELF**

Find a graph in a popular magazine ad. How does the advertiser use (or abuse) statistics to make a point?

➤ **TEST YOURSELF 3**

Consider a question posed by Christopher Jepson, David Krantz, and Richard Nisbett (1983) to University of Michigan introductory psychology students:

> The registrar's office at the University of Michigan has found that usually about 100 students in Arts and Sciences have perfect grades at the end of their first term at the University. However, only about 10 to 15 students graduate with perfect grades. What do you think is the most likely explanation for the fact that there are more perfect grades after one term than at graduation?

Answers to the Test Yourself questions can be found in Appendix E at the end of the book.

Frequently Asked Questions About Psychology

WE HAVE REFLECTED ON HOW A scientific approach can restrain biases. We have seen how case studies, surveys, and naturalistic observations help us describe behavior. We have also noted that correlational studies assess the association between two factors, which indicates how well one thing predicts another. We have examined the logic that underlies experiments, which use control conditions and random assignment of participants to isolate the effects of an independent variable on a dependent variable. And we have considered how statistical tools can help us see and interpret the world around us.

Yet, even knowing this much, you may still be approaching psychology with a mixture of curiosity and apprehension. So before we plunge in, let's entertain some frequently asked questions.

Psychology Applied

10: Can laboratory experiments illuminate everyday life?

When you see or hear about psychological research, do you ever wonder whether people's behavior in the lab will predict their behavior in real life? For example, does detecting the blink of a faint red light in a dark room have anything useful to say about flying a plane at night? After viewing a violent, sexually explicit film, does an aroused man's increased willingness to push buttons that he thinks will electrically shock a woman really say anything about whether violent pornography makes a man more likely to abuse a woman?

Before you answer, consider: The experimenter *intends* the laboratory environment to be a simplified reality—one that simulates and controls important features of everyday life. Just as a wind tunnel lets airplane designers re-create airflow forces under controlled conditions, a laboratory experiment lets psychologists re-create psychological forces under controlled conditions.

An experiment's purpose is not to re-create the exact behaviors of everyday life but to test *theoretical principles* (Mook, 1983). In aggression studies, deciding whether to push a button that delivers a shock may not be the same as slapping someone in the face, but the principle is the same. *It is the resulting principles—not the specific findings—that help explain everyday behaviors.*

TROUBLESHOOTING

One of the goals of research is to be able to generalize the findings to the public at large. A study has little value if the findings only apply to a specific group of people. The more a study is replicated, the more likely the findings can be applied to the general public. This generalizability of studies helps eventually make the findings applicable to the "real world."

When psychologists apply laboratory research on aggression to actual violence, they are applying theoretical principles of aggressive behavior, principles they have refined through many experiments. Similarly, it is the principles of the visual system, developed from experiments in artificial settings (such as looking at red lights in the dark), that we apply to more complex behaviors such as night flying. And many investigations show that principles derived in the laboratory do typically generalize to the everyday world (Anderson et al., 1999).

The point to remember: Psychologists' concerns lie less with unique behaviors than with discovering general principles that help explain many behaviors.

::culture the enduring behaviors, ideas, attitudes, and traditions shared by a group of people and transmitted from one generation to the next.

11: Does behavior depend on one's culture and gender?

What can psychological studies done in one time and place, often with White Europeans or North Americans, really tell us about people in general? As we will see time and again, **culture**—shared ideas and behaviors that one generation passes on to the next—matters. Our culture shapes our behavior. It influences our standards of promptness and frankness, our attitudes toward premarital sex and varying body shapes, our tendency to be casual or formal, our willingness to make eye contact, our conversational distance, and much, much more. Being aware of such differences, we can restrain our assumptions that others will think and act as we do. Given the growing mixing and clashing of cultures, our need for such awareness is urgent.

It is also true, however, that our shared biological heritage unites us as a universal human family. The same underlying processes guide people everywhere:

Soccer shoes? Because culture shapes social behavior, actions that seem ordinary to others may seem odd to us. Yet underlying these differences are powerful similarities. Children everywhere love to play sports such as soccer. But most U.S. children would play with athletic shoes on grass, not barefoot on the street, as with these Burkina Faso boys.

- People diagnosed with dyslexia, a reading disorder, exhibit the same brain malfunction whether they are Italian, French, or British (Paulesu et al., 2001).

- Variation in languages may impede communication across cultures. Yet all languages share deep principles of grammar, and people from opposite hemispheres can communicate with a smile or a frown.

- People in different cultures vary in feelings of loneliness. But across cultures, loneliness is magnified by shyness, low self-esteem, and being unmarried (Jones et al., 1985; Rokach et al., 2002).

The point to remember: We are each in certain respects like all others, like some others, and like no other. Studying people of all races and cultures helps us discern our similarities and our differences, our human kinship and our diversity.

You will see throughout this book that gender matters, too. Researchers report gender differences in what we dream, in how we express and detect emotions, and in our risk for alcohol dependence, depression, and eating disorders. Gender differences fascinate us, and studying them is potentially beneficial. For example, many researchers believe that women carry on conversations more readily to build relationships, while men talk more to give information and advice (Tannen, 1990). Knowing this difference can help us prevent conflicts and misunderstandings in everyday relationships.

But again, psychologically as well as biologically, women and men are overwhelmingly similar. Whether female or male, we learn to walk at about the same age. We experience the same sensations of light and sound. We feel the same pangs of hunger, desire, and fear. We exhibit similar overall intelligence and well-being.

The point to remember: Even when specific attitudes and behaviors vary by gender or across cultures, as they often do, the underlying processes are much the same.

"All people are the same; only their habits differ."

Confucius, 551–479 B.C.E.

INTERCONNECTING

Psychological studies have in the past often been criticized for using samples that are not representative of the general public—for example by not including multiple cultures or both genders. One famous researcher whose studies are often criticized for this is Lawrence Kohlberg. Kohlberg conducted several studies on moral development, but he only used White teenaged boys from Chicago. Some critics, like psychologist Carol Gilligan, believe his findings cannot be applied to girls or to people from non-White cultural backgrounds because of this limitation.

At this point, you may want to use **Lecture/Discussion Topic: *Gender Differences*** (p. 33) from Bolt's Teacher's Resource Binder.

TEACHING TIP

Have students discuss what other behaviors might be common to all people and what might be particular to a culture or gender. Emphasize to students that if a study is designed well, it can be conducted with multiple samples that will eventually represent people from all cultural and gender perspectives.

At this point, you may want to use **Lecture/Discussion Topic: *Differences in Cultural Norms*** (p. 32) from Bolt's Teacher's Resource Binder.

UNIT 2

DEMO

The APA Ethics Code requires that institutions that allow animal experimentation to take place establish an Animal Care and Use Committee to review whether the studies done on animals follow ethical standards. Divide students into groups and, using **Classroom Exercise:** *Animal Rights* (p. 34) (from Bolt's Teacher's Resource Binder), have them test their knowledge of the ethics of animal research by pretending to be on an Animal Care and Use Committee to determine whether a series of experiments should be allowed to go forward.

TEACHING TIP

Have students discuss any other ethical considerations that might be necessary for conducting experiments on human and nonhuman subjects. Challenge them to develop an ethics code for conducting their own experiments.

- What considerations might need to be enhanced?

- What additional ethical considerations must be followed when working with minors?

- How does the use of deception affect the ethics of a study?

At this point, you may want to use *Ethics in Animal Research: The Sad Case of Boee the Chimp* from the *Psychology Video Tool Kit*.

Ethics in Research

12: Why do psychologists study animals, and is it ethical to experiment on animals?

> "Rats are very similar to humans except that they are not stupid enough to purchase lottery tickets."
> Dave Barry, July 2, 2002

Many psychologists study animals because they find them fascinating. They want to understand how different species learn, think, and behave. Psychologists also study animals to learn about people, by doing experiments permissible only with animals. Human physiology resembles that of many other animals. We humans are not *like* animals; we *are* animals. Animal experiments have therefore led to treatments for human diseases—insulin for diabetes, vaccines to prevent polio and rabies, transplants to replace defective organs.

Likewise, the same processes by which humans see, exhibit emotion, and become obese are present in rats and monkeys. To discover more about the basics of human learning, researchers even study sea slugs. To understand how a combustion engine works, you would do better to study a lawn mower's engine than a Mercedes'. Like Mercedes engines, human nervous systems are complex. But the simplicity of the sea slug's nervous system is precisely what makes it so revealing of the neural mechanisms of learning.

> "I believe that to prevent, cripple, or needlessly complicate the research that can relieve animal and human suffering is profoundly inhuman, cruel, and immoral."
> Psychologist Neal Miller, 1983

If we share important similarities with other animals, then should we not respect them? "We cannot defend our scientific work with animals on the basis of the similarities between them and ourselves and then defend it morally on the basis of differences," noted Roger Ulrich (1991). The animal protection movement protests the use of animals in psychological, biological, and medical research. Researchers remind us that the animals used worldwide each year in research are but a fraction of 1 percent of the billions of animals killed annually for food. And yearly, for every dog or cat used in an experiment and cared for under humane regulations, 50 others are killed in humane animal shelters (Goodwin & Morrison, 1999).

Some animal protection organizations want to replace experiments on animals with naturalistic observation. Many animal researchers respond that this is not a question of good versus evil but of compassion for animals versus compassion for people. How many of us would have attacked Louis Pasteur's experiments with rabies, which caused some dogs to suffer but led to a vaccine that spared millions of people (and dogs) from agonizing death? And would we really wish to have deprived ourselves of the animal research that led to effective methods of training children with mental disorders; of understanding aging; and of relieving fears and depression? The answers to such questions vary by culture. In Gallup surveys in Canada and the United States, about 60 percent of adults deem medical testing on animals "morally acceptable." In Britain, only 37 percent do (Mason, 2003).

> "Please do not forget those of us who suffer from incurable diseases or disabilities who hope for a cure through research that requires the use of animals."
> Psychologist Dennis Feeney [1987]

Out of this heated debate, two issues emerge. The basic one is whether it is right to place the well-being of humans above that of animals. In experiments on stress and cancer, is it right that mice get tumors in the hope that people might not? Should some monkeys be exposed to an HIV-like virus in the search for an AIDS vaccine? Is our use and consumption of other animals as natural as the behavior of carnivorous hawks, cats, and whales? Defenders of research on animals argue that anyone who has eaten a hamburger, worn leather shoes, tolerated hunting and fishing, or supported the extermination of crop-destroying or plague-carrying pests has already agreed that, yes, it is sometimes permissible to sacrifice animals for the sake of human well-being.

> "The righteous know the needs of their animals."
> Proverbs 12:10

Scott Plous (1993) notes, however, that our compassion for animals varies, as does our compassion for people—based on their perceived similarity to us. As Unit 14 explains, we feel more attraction, give more help, and act less aggressively toward similar others. Likewise, we value animals according to their perceived kinship with us. Thus, primates and companion pets get top priority. (Western people raise or trap mink and foxes for their fur, but not dogs or cats.) Other mammals occupy the second rung on the privilege ladder, followed by birds, fish, and reptiles on the third rung, with insects at the bottom. In deciding which animals have rights, we each draw our own cut-off line somewhere across the animal kingdom.

INTERCONNECTING

Some famous studies in social psychology spurred a tightening of ethical standards. Stanley Milgram's obedience study and Philip Zimbardo's prison-guard study forced researchers to consider the long-term psychological effects on participants who may commit acts they didn't realize they were capable of. You may want to highlight these two studies and discuss how different they might look if conducted today.

At this point, you may want to use **Lecture/Discussion Topic:** *Interrogations and the Use of Torture* (p. 37) from Bolt's Teacher's Resource Binder.

If we give human life first priority, the second issue is the priority we give to the well-being of animals in research. What safeguards should protect them? Most researchers today feel ethically obligated to enhance the well-being of captive animals and protect them from needless suffering. In one survey of animal researchers, 98 percent or more supported government regulations protecting primates, dogs, and cats, and 74 percent supported regulations providing for the humane care of rats and mice (Plous & Herzog, 2000). Many professional associations and funding agencies already have such guidelines. For example, British Psychological Society guidelines call for housing animals under reasonably natural living conditions, with companions for social animals (Lea, 2000). American Psychological Association (2002) guidelines mandate ensuring the "comfort, health, and humane treatment" of animals, and of minimizing "infection, illness, and pain of animal subjects." Humane care also leads to more effective science, because pain and stress would distort the animals' behavior during experiments.

Animals have themselves benefited from animal research. One Ohio team of research psychologists measured stress hormone levels in samples of millions of dogs brought each year to animal shelters. They devised handling and stroking methods to reduce stress and ease the dogs' transition to adoptive homes (Tuber et al., 1999). In New York, formerly listless and idle Bronx Zoo animals now stave off boredom by working for their supper, as they would in the wild (Stewart, 2002). Other studies have helped improve care and management in animals' natural habitats. By revealing our behavioral kinship with animals and the remarkable intelligence of chimpanzees, gorillas, and other animals, experiments have also led to increased empathy and protection for them. At its best, a psychology concerned for humans and sensitive to animals serves the welfare of both.

13: Is it ethical to experiment on people?

If the image of researchers delivering supposed electric shocks troubles you, you may be relieved to know that in most psychological studies, especially those with human participants, blinking lights, flashing words, and pleasant social interactions are more common.

Occasionally, though, researchers do temporarily stress or deceive people—though more mildly than the stresses that people sometimes willingly undergo in network reality TV programs. But stress and deception are used sparingly—only when researchers believe it is essential to a justifiable end, such as understanding and controlling violent behavior or studying mood swings. Such experiments wouldn't work if the participants knew all there was to know about the experiment beforehand. Wanting to be helpful, the participants might try to confirm the researcher's predictions.

Ethical principles developed by the American Psychological Association (1992), by the British Psychological Society (1993), and by psychologists internationally (Pettifor, 2004), urge investigators to (1) obtain the **informed consent** of potential participants, (2) protect them from harm and discomfort, (3) treat information about individual participants confidentially, and (4) fully **debrief** people: explain the research afterward. Moreover, most universities (where a great deal of research is conducted) now screen research proposals through an ethics committee—an "Institutional Review Board"—that safeguards the well-being of every participant.

The ideal is for a researcher to be sufficiently informative *and* considerate so that participants will leave feeling at least as good about themselves as when they came in. Better yet, they should be repaid by having learned something. If treated respectfully, most participants enjoy or accept their engagement (Epley & Huff, 1998; Kimmel, 1998). Indeed, say psychology's defenders, teachers provoke much greater anxiety by giving and returning class tests than do researchers in a typical experiment.

Much research occurs outside of university laboratories, in places where there may be no ethics committees. For example, retail stores routinely survey people, photograph their purchasing behavior, track their buying patterns, and test the effectiveness of advertising. Curiously, such research attracts less attention than the scientific research done to advance human understanding.

Animal research benefiting animals
Thanks partly to research on the benefits of novelty, control, and stimulation, these gorillas are enjoying an improved quality of life in New York's Bronx Zoo.
▲

::**informed consent** an ethical principle that research participants be told enough to enable them to choose whether they wish to participate.

::**debriefing** the postexperimental explanation of a study, including its purpose and any deceptions, to its participants.

TEACHING TIP

Contact a nearby university or medical school to see what type of animal research is conducted at that particular institution.

- What are the goals of the research studies being conducted on animals? Are they trying to learn more about animal behavior or human behavior?

- How does the institution ensure that animals are treated ethically?

- Has the institution been a target for animal rights protesters? Why or why not?

At this point, you may want to use *Death of a Subject: The Ethics of Mental Health Research* from the *Psychology Video Tool Kit*.

TEACHING TIP

Have students explore the APA's Web site to see the APA Ethics Code in more detail. They can see what specific considerations researchers must follow when conducting experiments with both human and animal subjects. You can find the code at www.apa.org/ethics.

At this point, you may want to use **Lecture/Discussion Topic: Research Ethics** (p. 35) from Bolt's Teacher's Resource Binder.

TEACHING TIP

Discuss with students the additional ethics considerations of confidentiality and anonymity.

- Confidentiality refers to keeping participant information private. If a researcher collects identifying information, that information must not be released and the data must not be presented so that the individual participants can be identified through any kind of process of elimination.

- Anonymity refers to participating in a study without providing identifying information. Many studies do not require participants to identify themselves at all. For some research, the guarantee of anonymity might help participants respond more truthfully.

TEACHING TIP

Some people think science should be value-free. These people might believe psychology is not a science because it often reflects or examines "soft" topics such as values. The methodology of psychology defines it as a science, and using the scientific method to examine "soft" topics enhances our understanding of these types of topics. The method is value-free, but the conclusions are not.

At this point, you may want to use **Classroom Exercise: *Observing Versus Interpreting*** (p. 36) from Bolt's Teacher's Resource Binder.

> **FIGURE 2.11**
What do you see? People interpret ambiguous information to fit their preconceptions. Do you see a duck or a rabbit? Before showing some friends this image, ask them if they can see the duck lying on its back (or the bunny in the grass). (From Shepard, 1990.)

"It is doubtless impossible to approach any human problem with a mind free from bias."

Simone de Beauvoir,
The Second Sex, 1953

Psychology speaks In making its historic 1954 school desegregation decision, the U.S. Supreme Court cited the expert testimony and research of psychologists Kenneth Clark and Mamie Phipps Clark (1947). The Clarks reported that, when given a choice between Black and White dolls, most African-American children chose the White doll, which seemingly indicated internalized anti-Black prejudice. ·············· ▲

14: Is psychology free of value judgments?

Psychology is definitely not value-free. Values affect what we study, how we study it, and how we interpret results. Researchers' values influence their choice of topics. Should we study worker productivity or worker morale? Sex discrimination or gender differences? Conformity or independence? Values can also color "the facts." As we noted earlier, our preconceptions can bias our observations and interpretations; sometimes we see what we want or expect to see (**FIGURE 2.11**).

Even the words we use to describe something can reflect our values. Are the sex acts that an individual does not practice "perversions" or "sexual variations"? Both in and out of psychology, labels describe and labels evaluate: The same holds true in everyday speech. One person's "rigidity" is another's "consistency." One person's "faith" is another's "fanaticism." Our labeling someone as "firm" or "stubborn," "careful" or "picky," "discreet" or "secretive" reveals our feelings.

Popular applications of psychology also contain hidden values. If you defer to "professional" guidance about how to live—how to raise children, how to achieve self-fulfillment, what to do with sexual feelings, how to get ahead at work—you are accepting value-laden advice. A science of behavior and mental processes can certainly help us reach our goals, but it cannot decide what those goals should be.

If some people see psychology as merely common sense, others have a different concern—that it is becoming dangerously powerful. Is it an accident that astronomy is the oldest science and psychology the youngest? To some people, exploring the external universe seems far safer than exploring our own inner universe. Might psychology, they ask, be used to manipulate people?

Knowledge, like all power, can be used for good or evil. Nuclear power has been used to light up cities—and to demolish them. Persuasive power has been used to educate people—and to deceive them. Although psychology does indeed have the power to deceive, its purpose is to enlighten. Every day, psychologists are exploring ways to enhance learning, creativity, and compassion. Psychology speaks to many of our world's great problems—war, overpopulation, prejudice, family crises, crime—all of which involve attitudes and behaviors. Psychology also speaks to our deepest longings—for nourishment, for love, for happiness. Psychology cannot address all of life's great questions, but it speaks to some mighty important ones.

BEFORE YOU MOVE ON . . .

> **ASK YOURSELF**
Were any of the Frequently Asked Questions your questions? Do you have other questions or concerns about psychology?

> **TEST YOURSELF 4**
How are human and animal research subjects protected?

Answers to the Test Yourself questions can be found in Appendix E at the end of the book.

INTERCONNECTING

The picture of Kenneth Clark and Mamie Phipps Clark highlights the contributions of people of color to psychology. The Clarks conducted some of the most famous studies in psychology. Their work was the first psychological research to be cited in a Supreme Court decision. Their work highlighted the importance of examining controversial and societal issues with scientific methodology.

UNIT REVIEW: Research Methods: Thinking Critically With Psychological Science

The Need for Psychological Science

1: **Why are the answers that flow from the scientific approach more reliable than those based on intuition and common sense?**

Although common sense often serves us well, we are prone to *hindsight bias* (also called the "I-knew-it-all-along phenomenon"), the tendency to believe, after learning an outcome, that we would have foreseen it. We also are routinely overconfident of our judgments, thanks partly to our bias to seek information that confirms them. Although limited by the testable questions it can address, scientific inquiry can help us sift reality from illusion and restrain the biases of our unaided intuition.

2: **What are three main components of the scientific attitude?**

The three components of the scientific attitude are (1) a curious eagerness to (2) skeptically scrutinize competing ideas and (3) an open-minded humility before nature. This attitude carries into everyday life as *critical thinking*, which examines assumptions, discerns hidden values, evaluates evidence, and assesses outcomes. Putting ideas, even crazy-sounding ideas, to the test helps us winnow sense from nonsense.

How Do Psychologists Ask and Answer Questions?

3: **How do theories advance psychological science?**

Psychological *theories* organize observations and imply predictive *hypotheses*. After constructing precise *operational definitions* of their procedures, researchers test their hypotheses, validate and refine the theory, and, sometimes, suggest practical applications. If other researchers can *replicate* the study with similar results, we can then place greater confidence in the conclusion.

4: **How do psychologists observe and describe behavior?**

Psychologists observe and describe behavior using individual *case studies*, *surveys* among *random samples* of a *population*, and *naturalistic observations*. In generalizing from observations, remember: Representative samples are a better guide than vivid anecdotes.

5: **What are positive and negative correlations, and why do they enable prediction but not cause-effect explanation?**

Scatterplots help us to see *correlations*. A positive correlation (ranging from 0 to +1.00) indicates the extent to which two factors rise together. In a negative correlation (ranging from 0 to −1.00), one item rises as the other falls. An association (sometimes stated as a *correlation coefficient*) indicates the possibility of a cause-effect relationship, but it does not prove the direction of the influence, or whether an underlying third factor may explain the correlation.

6: **What are illusory correlations?**

Illusory correlations are random events that we notice and falsely assume are related. Patterns or sequences occur naturally in sets of random data, but we tend to interpret these patterns as meaningful connections, perhaps in an attempt to make sense of the world around us

7: **How do experiments, powered by random assignment, clarify cause and effect?**

To discover cause-effect relationships, psychologists conduct *experiments*, manipulating one or more factors of interest and controlling other *confounding variables*. *Random assignment* minimizes preexisting differences between the *experimental group* (exposed to the treatment) and the *control group* (given a placebo or different version of the treatment). The *independent variable* is the factor you manipulate to study its effect. The *dependent variable* is the factor you measure to discover any changes that occur in response to these manipulations. Studies may use a *double-blind procedure* to avoid the *placebo effect* and researcher's bias.

Statistical Reasoning in Everyday Life

8: **How can we describe data with measures of central tendency and variation?**

Three measures of central tendency are the *median* (the middle score in a group of data), the *mode* (the most frequently occurring score), and the *mean* (the arithmetic average). Measures of variation tell us how similar or diverse data are. A *range* describes the gap between the highest and lowest scores. The more useful measure, the *standard deviation*, states how much scores vary around the mean, or average, score. The *normal curve* is a bell-shaped curve that describes the distribution of many types of data.

9: **What principles can guide our making generalizations from samples and deciding whether differences are significant?**

Three principles are worth remembering: (1) Representative samples are better than biased samples. (2) Less-variable observations are more reliable than those that are more variable. (3) More cases are better than fewer.

When averages from two samples are each reliable measures of their own populations, and the difference between them is relatively large, we can assume that the result is *statistically significant* that it did not occur by chance alone.

Frequently Asked Questions About Psychology

10: **Can laboratory experiments illuminate everyday life?**

By intentionally creating a controlled, artificial environment in the lab, researchers aim to test theoretical principles. These general principles help explain everyday behaviors.

11: **Does behavior depend on one's culture and gender?**

Attitudes and behaviors vary across *cultures*, but the underlying principles vary much less because of our human kinship. Although gender differences tend to capture attention, it is important to remember our greater gender similarities.

ANSWERS to Multiple-Choice Questions

1. **d** Standard deviation
2. **c** humility
3. **b** Experiment
4. **d** median.
5. **b** The presence or absence of cookies.
6. **a** From a third-floor window, researchers watch how elementary school children interact on a playground.
7. **b** hindsight bias.
8. **a** there are more similarities than differences between the genders.
9. **b** The writer pulls the names of five students from a hat that contains all students' names. She interviews the five selected students.
10. **a** As study time decreases, students achieve lower grades.
11. **a** If the participants are randomly assigned, the researcher can assume that the people in each of the groups are pretty similar.
12. **c** Intuition and common sense are not always correct.
13. **c** They may be misleading because they don't fairly represent other cases.
14. **e** It is never acceptable for a researcher to deceive a participant during the research.
15. **a** We cannot conclude anything about cause and effect.

12: Why do psychologists study animals, and is it ethical to experiment on animals?
Some psychologists are primarily interested in animal behavior. Others study animals to better understand the physiological and psychological processes shared by humans. Under ethical and legal guidelines, animals used in experiments rarely experience pain. Nevertheless, animal rights groups raise an important issue: Even if it leads to the relief of human suffering, is an animal's temporary suffering justified?

13: Is it ethical to experiment on people?
Researchers may temporarily stress or deceive people in order to learn something important. However, animal protection legislation, laboratory regulation and inspection, and local ethics committees serve to protect human and animal welfare. At universities, Institutional Review Boards screen research proposals. Ethical principles developed by international psychological organizations urge researchers using human participants to obtain *informed consent*, to protect them from harm and discomfort, to treat their personal information confidentially, and to fully *debrief* all participants.

14: Is psychology free of value judgments?
Psychologists' values influence their choice of research topics, their theories and observations, their labels for behavior, and their professional advice. Applications of psychology's principles have been used mainly in the service of humanity.

Terms and Concepts to Remember

hindsight bias, p. 20
critical thinking, p. 24
theory, p. 25
hypothesis, p. 25
operational definition, p. 26
replication, p. 26
case study, p. 26
survey, p. 27
population, p. 28
random sample, p. 28
naturalistic observation, p. 28
correlation, p. 29

correlation coefficient, p. 29
scatterplot, p. 29
illusory correlation, p. 32
experiment, p. 34
random assignment, p. 34
double-blind procedure, p. 35
placebo effect, p. 35
experimental group, p. 35
control group, p. 35
independent variable, p. 35
confounding variable, p. 35
dependent variable, p. 35

mode, p. 37
mean, p. 38
median, p. 38
range, p. 39
standard deviation, p. 39
normal curve, p. 40
statistical significance, p. 41
culture, p. 43
informed consent, p. 45
debriefing, p. 45

 AP* Practice Test Questions

Multiple-Choice Questions

1. What statistical technique would be appropriate for a researcher to use in trying to determine how consistent intelligence scores are over time?
   a. Correlation coefficient
   b. Mean
   c. Median
   d. Standard deviation
   e. Range

2. A scientist's willingness to admit that she is wrong is an example of
   a. curiosity.
   b. intelligence.
   c. humility.
   d. skepticism.
   e. cynicism.

3. Let's say a psychology researcher is interested in testing whether a particular parenting technique would lead adolescents to feel more satisfied with their lives. What method should be used?
   a. Case study
   b. Experiment
   c. Survey
   d. Naturalistic observation
   e. Correlation

4. When a distribution of scores is skewed, the best representation of central tendency is the
   a. inference.
   b. standard deviation.
   c. mean.
   d. median.
   e. correlation coefficient.

5. A researcher wants to conduct an experiment to determine if eating a cookie before class each day improves students' grades. He uses two psychology classes for the experiment, providing daily cookies to one and nothing to the other. At the end of the semester, the researcher compares the final grades of students in the two classes. What is the independent variable for this experiment?
   a. The students in the class that received cookies.
   b. The presence or absence of cookies.
   c. The students in the class that didn't receive cookies.
   d. The period of the day that the two classes met.
   e. Semester grades.

*AP is a trademark registered and/or owned by the College Board, which was not involved in the production of, and does not endorse, this product.

Rubric for Grading the Free-Response Question

This is a 9-point question; one point for each of the bulleted concepts. For each point, the student must refer to the visualization technique experiment and demonstrate an understanding of the relevance of the bulleted concept.

Point 1: Population. The student must make clear that the population is the group of individuals that the participants are drawn from. In this case, the population is Olympic divers (or some subset of Olympic divers).

Point 2: Sample. The student must recognize that the sample is the group of Olympic divers that is selected for this experiment. The sample must be random so the results of the experiment can be generalized to the population.

6. Which of the following represents naturalistic observation?

a. From a third-floor window, researchers watch how elementary school children interact on a playground.

b. Researchers bring people into a laboratory to see how they respond when asked to solve a puzzle with no solution.

c. A principal sits in the back of a classroom to evaluate a teacher.

d. A social worker spends the afternoon in the home of a mother accused of neglecting her children.

e. Two grandparents sit in the front row to watch as their grandson performs his piano recital.

7. "Monday morning quarterbacks" rarely act surprised about the outcome of weekend football games. Their tendency to believe they knew how the game would turn out is explained by

a. overconfidence.

b. hindsight bias.

c. intuition.

d. illusory correlation.

e. random sampling.

8. Researchers studying gender have found that

a. there are more similarities than differences between the genders.

b. there are no significant cognitive differences between the genders.

c. there are no significant emotional differences between the genders.

d. research tools are not capable of determining if there are true differences or not.

e. differences between the genders are becoming more pronounced over time.

9. A student is writing an article for her school newspaper about the school's new cell-phone policy, and she'd like to include survey results from a random sample of students in her article. Which of the following constitutes a random sample?

a. The writer arrives at school early and interviews the first five students who come through the main entrance.

b. The writer pulls the names of five students from a hat that contains all students' names. She interviews the five selected students.

c. The writer asks her teacher if she can distribute a brief survey to the students in her AP Psychology class.

d. The writer passes out brief surveys to 50 students in the hall and uses the 18 surveys returned to her as the basis of her article.

e. The writer asks the principal for the names of 10 students who have had their cell phones confiscated for a day for violating the policy. She interviews these 10 students.

10. Which of the following is a positive correlation?

a. As study time decreases, students achieve lower grades.

b. As levels of self-esteem decline, levels of depression increase.

c. People who exercise regularly are less likely to be obese.

d. Gas mileage decreases as vehicle weight increases.

e. Repeatedly shooting free throws is associated with a smaller percentage of missed free throws.

11. Why is random assignment of participants to groups an important aspect of a properly designed experiment?

a. If the participants are randomly assigned, the researcher can assume that the people in each of the groups are pretty similar.

b. By randomly assigning, the researcher knows that whatever is learned from the experiment will also be true for the population from which the participants were selected.

c. Random assignment keeps expectations from influencing the results of the experiment.

d. If participants are not randomly assigned, it is impossible to replicate the experiment.

e. Statistical analysis cannot be performed on an experiment if random assignment is not used.

12. Which of the following demonstrates the need for psychological science?

a. Psychology's methods are unlike those of any other science.

b. Psychological experiments are less valuable without psychological science.

c. Intuition and common sense are not always correct.

d. Intuition can never be right unless applied scientifically.

e. Psychological science can be used to answer fundamental questions about religion.

13. Which of the following is a potential problem with case studies?

a. They provide too much detail and the researcher is likely to lose track of the most important facts.

b. They are generally too expensive to be economical.

c. They may be misleading because they don't fairly represent other cases.

d. They are technically difficult and most researchers don't have the skills to do them properly.

e. The dependent variable is difficult to operationally define in a case study.

14. Which of the following is *not* an ethical principle regarding research on humans?

a. Researchers must protect participants from needless harm and discomfort.

b. Participants must take part in the study on a voluntary basis.

c. Personal information about individual participants must be kept private.

d. The research must be fully explained to participants when the study is completed.

e. It is never acceptable for a researcher to deceive a participant during the research.

15. There is a negative correlation between TV watching and grades. What can we properly conclude from this discovery?

a. We cannot conclude anything about cause and effect.

b. We can conclude that TV watching leads to lower grades.

c. We can conclude that TV watching increases grades.

d. We can conclude that the grades students get have an effect on their TV watching habits.

e. We can conclude that this is an illusory correlation.

Free-Response Question

Imagine that you are a sports psychologist interested in the usefulness of a new visualization technique that has been developed for Olympic divers. You have decided to conduct an experiment to determine if the technique is effective. Discuss the importance of each of the following in regard to the experiment you are designing: population, sample, hypothesis, independent variable, dependent variable, operational definitions, control group, random assignment, and replication.

 WEB

Multiple-choice self-tests and more may be found at www.worthpublishers.com/myers

Point 3 Hypothesis. The student must explain that the hypothesis is the statement of expectation about the outcome of the experiment. In this case, the hypothesis is that the new visualization technique will produce better dives. The student may state the null hypothesis, such as: "There is no difference between groups of Olympic divers." Students must state the hypothesis for this particular experiment; a basic definition of "hypothesis" alone should not earn the point.

Point 4: Independent variable. The student must be aware that the independent variable is the variable manipulated by the experimenter. In this case, the IV is whether or not a diver is taught the new visualization technique. Students must state the independent variable for this particular experiment; a basic definition of "independent

 Rubric continued

variable" alone should not earn the point.

Point 5: Dependent variable. The student must be aware that the dependent variable shows the effect of the independent variable. In this case, the dependent variable is the quality of the dives. Again, students must state the dependent variable for this particular experiment to earn the point.

Point 6: Operational definitions. To earn this point, the student must explain exactly how the dependent variable will be measured. The clearest way to do this is with diving scores.

Point 7: Control group. The student must explain the need for a group to which results of the visualization group may be compared. In this case, the control group would be a similar group of divers that is not trained in the new technique.

Point 8: Random assignment. The student must understand the importance of randomly assigning participants to the visualization and control groups. This allows the experimenter to assume that the only difference between the divers in the two groups is whether or not they are taught the visualization technique.

Point 9: Replication. The student must explain that experimental results are not fully accepted until the experiment is repeated. If the experiment cannot be replicated, the results were probably caused by chance instead of by the independent variable.

Pacing Guide

Use the following guide to determine how many instructional days to devote to this portion of the unit depending on the type of course you teach:

Year-long course: 3 days
Block schedule/Semester-long
course: 1–2 days

   This entire unit (Parts A, B, & C) encompasses 8–10 percent of the AP Exam. Spending an appropriate amount of time on this unit will help students do well on the AP Exam.

 TEACHING TIP

Teach this unit early in the course so students can get the foundational knowledge offered in this unit. Understanding the concepts in this unit is important to mastering the entire course content. However, due to the amount of material covered in this unit, it has been broken down into three parts. Helping students chunk this information will help them learn a large amount of very important material more easily.

INTERCONNECTING

Keep in mind that the following units will also rely heavily on a thorough understanding of the biological bases of behavior:

Unit 4: Sensation and Perception
Unit 5: States of Consciousness
Unit 7: Part A: Memory
Unit 8: Part B: Emotions, Stress,
               and Health
Unit 12: Abnormal Psychology
Unit 13: Treatment of
               Psychological Disorders

50

Suggested Readings

Harris, J. R. (1998). *The nurture assumption.* New York: Free Press.

Horstman, J. (2009). The Scientific American *day in the life of your brain.* New York: Jossey-Bass.

Pinker, S. (2002). *The blank slate: The modern denial of human nature.* New York: Viking.

Ramachandran, V. S., & Blakeslee, S. (1998). *Phantoms in the brain: probing the mysteries of the human mind.* New York: William Morrow.

Sacks, O. (1973). *Awakenings.* New York: HarperCollins.

Sacks, O. (1985). *The man who mistook his wife for a hat.* New York: Summit Books.

Biological Bases of Behavior:
3A—Neural Processing and the Endocrine System

No principle is more central to today's psychology, or to this book, than this: *Everything psychological is simultaneously biological.* Your every idea, every mood, every urge is a biological happening. You love, laugh, and cry with your body. Without your body—your genes, your brain, your appearance—you are, indeed, nobody. Although we find it convenient to talk separately of biological and psychological influences on behavior, we need to remember: To think, feel, or act without a body would be like running without legs.

Today's science is riveted on our body's most amazing parts—the brain, its component neural systems, and their genetic instructions. The brain's ultimate challenge? To understand itself. How does the brain organize and communicate with itself? How do heredity and experience together wire the brain? How does the brain process the information we need to shoot a basketball? To delight in a guitarist's notes? To remember our first kiss?

Our understanding of how the brain gives birth to the mind has come a long way. The ancient Greek philosopher Plato correctly located the mind in the spherical head—his idea of the perfect form. His student, Aristotle, believed the mind was in the heart, which pumps warmth and vitality to the body. The heart remains our symbol for love, but science has long since overtaken philosophy on this issue. It's your brain, not your heart, that falls in love.

We have come far since the early 1800s, when the German physician Franz Gall invented *phrenology*, a popular but ill-fated theory that claimed bumps on the skull could reveal our mental abilities and our character traits (**FIGURE 3A.1**). At one point, Britain had 29 phrenological societies, and phrenologists traveled North America giving skull readings (Hunt, 1993). Using a false name, humorist Mark Twain put one famous phrenologist to the test. "He found a cavity [and] startled me by saying that that cavity represented the total absence of the sense of humor!" Three months later, Twain sat for a second reading, this time identifying himself. Now

➤ **FIGURE 3A.1**
A wrongheaded theory
Despite initial acceptance of Franz Gall's speculations, bumps on the skull tell us nothing about the brain's underlying functions. Nevertheless, some of Gall's assumptions have held true. Different parts of the brain do control different aspects of behavior, as you will see throughout this unit.

Key Terms
biological psychology

Neural Communication
neuron
sensory neurons
motor neurons
interneurons
dendrite
axon
myelin sheath
action potential
threshold
synapse
neurotransmitter
reuptake
endorphins

The Nervous System
nervous system
central nervous system (CNS)
peripheral nervous system (PNS)
nerves
somatic nervous system
autonomic nervous system
sympathetic nervous system
parasympathetic nervous system
reflex

The Endocrine System
endocrine system
hormones
adrenal glands
pituitary gland

Key People
While there are no prominent names featured in this unit, one key study students may want to be familiar with in order to appreciate the science of behavior and mental processes was conducted in 1972. Rosenzweig, Bennett, and Diamond conducted research with rats that showed that enriched environments contributed to more complex neuronal connections in the cortex. This study shows that neural complexity could be influenced by environmental factors, showing how nature and nurture interact.

UNIT 3A

Point out to students the organization of this unit's content—from a micro level to a macro level. Helping students organize this material will help them keep it straight when they take the test.

> "If I were a college student today, I don't think I could resist going into neuroscience."
>
> Novelist Tom Wolfe, 2004

::**biological psychology** a branch of psychology concerned with the links between biology and behavior. (Some biological psychologists call themselves *behavioral neuroscientists, neuropsychologists, behavior geneticists, physiological psychologists,* or *biopsychologists.*)

::**neuron** a nerve cell; the basic building block of the nervous system.

::**sensory neurons** neurons that carry incoming information from the sensory receptors to the brain and spinal cord.

::**motor neurons** neurons that carry outgoing information from the brain and spinal cord to the muscles and glands.

::**interneurons** neurons within the brain and spinal cord that communicate internally and intervene between the sensory inputs and motor outputs.

::**dendrite** the bushy, branching extensions of a neuron that receive messages and conduct impulses toward the cell body.

::**axon** the extension of a neuron, ending in branching terminal fibers, through which messages pass to other neurons or to muscles or glands.

"the cavity was gone, and in its place was . . . the loftiest bump of humor he had ever encountered in his life-long experience!" (Lopez, 2002). Phrenology did, however, correctly focus attention on the idea that various brain regions have particular functions.

You and I enjoy a privilege Gall did not have. We are living in a time when discoveries about the interplay of our biology and our behavior and mental processes are occurring at an exhilarating pace. Within little more than the last century, researchers seeking to understand the biology of the mind have discovered that

- the body is composed of cells.
- among these are nerve cells that conduct electricity and "talk" to one another by sending chemical messages across a tiny gap that separates them.
- specific brain systems serve specific functions (though not the functions Gall supposed).
- we integrate information processed in these different brain systems to construct our experience of sights and sounds, meanings and memories, pain and passion.
- our adaptive brain is wired by our experience.

By studying the links between biological activity and psychological events, **biological psychologists** continue to expand our understanding of sleep and dreams, depression and schizophrenia, hunger and sex, stress and disease.

We have also realized that we are each a system composed of subsystems that are in turn composed of even smaller subsystems. Tiny cells organize to form such body organs as the stomach, heart, and brain. These organs in turn form larger systems for digestion, circulation, and information processing. And those systems are part of an even larger system—the individual, who in turn is a part of a family, culture, and community. Thus, we are *biopsychosocial* systems, and to understand our behavior, we need to study how these biological, psychological, and social-cultural systems work and interact.

In this book we start small and build from the bottom up—from nerve cells up to the brain in Units 3A and 3B, and to the environmental and cultural influences that interact with our biology in Unit 3C and in later units. We will also work from the top down, as we consider how our thinking and emotions influence our brain and our health. At all levels, psychologists examine how we process information—how we take in information; how we organize, interpret, and store it; and how we use it.

The body's information system handling all these tasks is built from billions of interconnected cells called *neurons*. To fathom our thoughts and actions, memories and moods, we must first understand how neurons work and communicate.

Neural Communication

FOR SCIENTISTS, IT IS A HAPPY FACT OF nature that the information systems of humans and other animals operate similarly—so similarly, in fact, that you could not distinguish between small samples of brain tissue from a human and a monkey. This similarity allows researchers to study relatively simple animals, such as squids and sea slugs, to discover how our neural systems operate. It allows them to study other mammals' brains to understand the organization of our own. Cars differ, but all have engines, accelerators, steering wheels, and brakes. A Martian could study any one of them and grasp the operating principles. Likewise, animals differ, yet their nervous systems operate similarly. Though the human brain is more complex than a rat's, both follow the same principles.

Students often assume that all research discussed in this unit was done on humans. In fact, most of the research done in this unit was done on animals. Help students appreciate how similarities in biology contribute to our understanding of not only ourselves but of nonhuman animals as well.

Neurons

1: What are neurons, and how do they transmit information?

Our body's neural information system is complexity built from simplicity. Its building blocks are **neurons**, or nerve cells. **Sensory neurons** carry messages from the body's tissues and sensory organs inward to the brain and spinal cord, for processing. The brain and spinal cord then send instructions out to the body's tissues via the **motor neurons**. Between the sensory input and motor output, information is processed in the brain's internal communication system via its **interneurons.** Our complexity resides mostly in our interneuron systems. Our nervous system has a few million sensory neurons, a few million motor neurons, and billions and billions of interneurons. All are variations on the same theme (**FIGURE 3A.2**). Each consists of a cell body and its branching fibers. The bushy **dendrite** fibers receive information and conduct it toward the cell body. From there, the cell's **axon** passes the message along to other neurons or to muscles or glands. Axons speak. Dendrites listen.

Unlike the short dendrites, axons are sometimes very long, projecting several feet through the body. A motor neuron carrying orders to a leg muscle, for example, has a cell body and axon roughly on the scale of a basketball attached to a rope 4 miles long. Much as home electrical wire is insulated, so a layer of fatty tissue, called the **myelin sheath**, insulates the axons of some neurons and helps speed their impulses. As myelin is laid down up to about age 25, neural efficiency, judgment, and self-control grow (Fields, 2008). If the myelin sheath degenerates, *multiple sclerosis* results: Communication to muscles slows, with eventual loss of muscle control.

Depending on the type of fiber, a neural impulse travels at speeds ranging from a sluggish 2 miles per hour to a breakneck 200 or more miles per hour. But even this top speed is 3 million times slower than that of electricity through a wire. We measure brain activity in milliseconds (thousandths of a second) and computer activity in nanoseconds (billionths of a second). Thus, unlike the nearly instantaneous reactions of a high-speed computer, your reaction to a sudden event, such as a book slipping off your desk during class, may take a quarter-second or more. Your brain is vastly more complex than a computer, but slower at executing simple responses.

Neurons transmit messages when stimulated by signals from our senses or when triggered by chemical signals from neighboring neurons. At such times, a neuron fires an impulse, called the **action potential**—a brief electrical charge that travels down its axon.

Dendrites (receive messages from other cells)

Terminal branches of axon (form junctions with other cells)

Axon (passes messages away from the cell body to other neurons, muscles, or glands)

Cell body (the cell's life-support center)

Neural impulse (action potential) (electrical signal traveling down the axon)

Myelin sheath (covers the axon of some neurons and helps speed neural impulses)

::**myelin** [MY-uh-lin] **sheath** a layer of fatty tissue segmentally encasing the fibers of many neurons; enables vastly greater transmission speed of neural impulses as the impulse hops from one node to the next.

::**action potential** a neural impulse; a brief electrical charge that travels down an axon.

• To remember that dendrites bring information in and axons convey information out, just remember: "Axons away!" •

➤ **FIGURE 3A.2**
A motor neuron

UNIT 3A :: NEURAL PROCESSING AND THE ENDOCRINE SYSTEM 53

TEACHING TIP

Neuroglia are another category of neural cells that provide the support network of cells surrounding the neurons and blood vessels of the brain and nervous system. They are thought to outnumber typical neurons 10 to 1. There are three types of neuroglia in the body:

- *Oligodendroglia* (o-lig-o-den-drog-glia) are cells found in the central nervous system (CNS) that produce myelin, a protective covering of axons that speed neural transmissions.

- *Schwann cells* perform the same function as oligodendroglia, but are found in the peripheral nervous system (PNS). Aside from location, the main difference between Schwann cells and oligodendroglia is that only Schwann cells can help axons regenerate.

- *Astrocytes* are star-shaped and form most of the matrix in which neural cells are embedded and envelop blood vessels in the brain. They also absorb dead neural cells.

TROUBLESHOOTING

While studying neural communication, students often fail to appreciate the complexity of the neural network in the nervous system. The neural chain presented in the text is the simplest way neurons communicate. For the vast majority of the nervous system, multiple neurons connect with each other, creating a complex network capable of almost endless combinations of neurons communicating. Help students understand that this simple presentation does not capture the true complexity of neural communication.

At this point, you may want to use **Classroom Exercise:** *Modeling a Neuron and Using Dominoes to Illustrate the Action Potential* (p. 3) from Bolt's Teacher's Resource Binder, which accompanies this text.

UNIT 3A

An explanation of the following terms may help students better understand the concept of the action potential:

- **Ions** have a charge, either positive or negative. When these particles move, they create electricity, which is what the action potential is.

- The natural tendency for matter is to move from a more crowded situation to a less crowded situation. The neuron is packed with negatively charged ions, with the positively charged ions positioned on the outside of the cell.

- The neuron's membrane is normally **impermeable,** but neurotransmitters weaken it, allowing the ions to move according to the principle above.

DEMO

An interesting way to demonstrate how the action potential works is to compare the process to a flushing toilet. Here are some concepts to highlight:

- All-or-none law is similar to the strength of each flush. When you depress the lever, the flush is the same each time.

- Threshold: A softer push of the lever will not create a flush at all since it did not reach threshold.

- Refractory period: In order to flush, the tank must be full. You cannot have two flushes occur in a row if the tank has not had time to fill.

> "I sing the body electric."
> Walt Whitman, "Children of Adam" (1855)

> "What one neuron tells another neuron is simply how much it is excited."
> Francis Crick,
> *The Astonishing Hypothesis*, 1994

Neurons, like batteries, generate electricity from chemical events. The chemistry-to-electricity process involves the exchange of *ions,* electrically charged atoms. The fluid interior of a resting axon has an excess of negatively charged ions, while the fluid outside the axon membrane has more positively charged ions. This positive-outside/negative-inside state is called the *resting potential.* Like a tightly guarded facility, the axon's surface is very selective about what it allows in. We say the axon's surface is *selectively permeable.* For example, a resting axon has gates that block positive sodium ions.

When a neuron fires, however, the security parameters change: The first bit of the axon opens its gates, rather like sewer covers flipping open, and the positively charged sodium ions flood through the membrane (**FIGURE 3A.3**). This *depolarizes* that section of the axon, causing the axon's next channel to open, and then the next, like dominoes falling, each one tripping the next. During a resting pause (the *refractory period*), the neuron pumps the positively charged sodium ions back outside. Then it can fire again. (In myelinated neurons, as in Figure 3A.2, the action potential speeds up by hopping from one myelin "sausage" to the next.) The mind boggles when imagining this electrochemical process repeating up to 100 or even 1000 times a second. But this is just the first of many astonishments.

Each neuron is itself a miniature decision-making device performing complex calculations as it receives signals from hundreds, even thousands, of other neurons. Most of these signals are *excitatory,* somewhat like pushing a neuron's accelerator. Others are *inhibitory,* more like pushing its brake. If excitatory signals minus inhibitory signals exceed a minimum intensity, or **threshold,** the combined signals trigger an action potential. (Think of it as a class vote: If the excitatory people with their hands up outvote the inhibitory people with their hands down, then the vote passes.) The action potential then travels down the axon, which branches into

➤ **FIGURE 3A.3**
Action potential

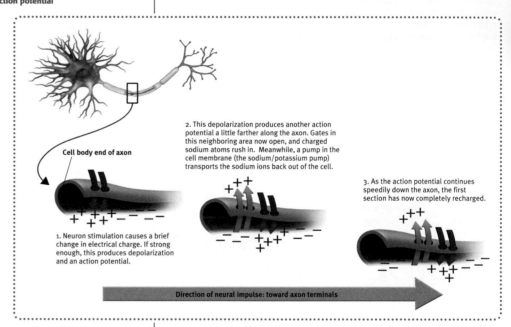

Cell body end of axon

1. Neuron stimulation causes a brief change in electrical charge. If strong enough, this produces depolarization and an action potential.

2. This depolarization produces another action potential a little farther along the axon. Gates in this neighboring area now open, and charged sodium atoms rush in. Meanwhile, a pump in the cell membrane (the sodium/potassium pump) transports the sodium ions back out of the cell.

3. As the action potential continues speedily down the axon, the first section has now completely recharged.

Direction of neural impulse: toward axon terminals

TROUBLESHOOTING

The action potential is one of the most complicated processes discussed in AP Psychology. Be sure to have at least two or three ways to explain this concept so all students can have the opportunity to learn it. If students can understand this process, they will be able to understand neurotransmitters, myelin, excitation, inhibition, and other important concepts in biopsychology.

At this point, you may want to use **Classroom Exercises:** *Neural Transmission* (p. 4) and *Crossing the Synaptic Gap* (p. 4) from Bolt's Teacher's Resource Binder.

junctions with hundreds or thousands of other neurons and with the body's muscles and glands.

Increasing the level of stimulation above the threshold, however, will not increase the neural impulse's intensity. The neuron's reaction is an *all-or-none response*: Like guns, neurons either fire or they don't. How then do we detect the intensity of a stimulus? How do we distinguish a gentle touch from a big hug? A strong stimulus—a slap rather than a tap—can trigger *more* neurons to fire, and to fire more often. But it does not affect the action potential's strength or speed. Squeezing a trigger harder won't make a bullet go faster.

How Neurons Communicate

2: How do nerve cells communicate with other nerve cells?

Neurons interweave so intricately that even with a microscope you would have trouble seeing where one neuron ends and another begins. Scientists once believed that the axon of one cell fused with the dendrites of another in an uninterrupted fabric. Then British physiologist Sir Charles Sherrington (1857–1952) noticed that neural impulses were taking an unexpectedly long time to travel a neural pathway. Inferring that there must be a brief interruption in the transmission, Sherrington called the meeting point between neurons a **synapse**.

We now know that the axon terminal of one neuron is in fact separated from the receiving neuron by a *synaptic gap* (or *synaptic cleft*) less than a millionth of an inch wide. Spanish anatomist Santiago Ramón y Cajal (1852–1934) marveled at these near-unions of neurons, calling them "protoplasmic kisses." "Like elegant ladies air-kissing so as not to muss their makeup, dendrites and axons don't quite touch," notes poet Diane Ackerman (2004). How do the neurons execute this protoplasmic kiss, sending information across the tiny synaptic gap? The answer is one of the important scientific discoveries of our age.

When an action potential reaches the knoblike terminals at an axon's end, it triggers the release of chemical messengers, called **neurotransmitters** (FIGURE 3A.4 on the next page). Within 1/10,000th of a second, the neurotransmitter molecules cross the synaptic gap and bind to receptor sites on the receiving neuron—as precisely as a key fits a lock. For an instant, the neurotransmitter unlocks tiny channels at the receiving site, and electrically charged atoms flow in, exciting or inhibiting the receiving neuron's readiness to fire. Then, in a process called **reuptake**, the sending neuron reabsorbs the excess neurotransmitters.

How Neurotransmitters Influence Us

3: How do neurotransmitters influence behavior, and how do drugs and other chemicals affect neurotransmission?

In their quest to understand neural communication, researchers have discovered dozens of different neurotransmitters and almost as many new questions: Are certain neurotransmitters found only in specific places? How do they affect our moods, memories, and mental abilities? Can we boost or diminish these effects through drugs or diet?

In later units we will examine neurotransmitter influences on depression and euphoria, hunger and thinking, addictions and therapy. For now, let's glimpse how neurotransmitters influence our motions and our emotions. A particular pathway in the brain may use only one or two neurotransmitters, and particular neurotransmitters

::**threshold** the level of stimulation required to trigger a neural impulse.

::**synapse** [SIN-aps] the junction between the axon tip of the sending neuron and the dendrite or cell body of the receiving neuron. The tiny gap at this junction is called the synaptic gap or synaptic cleft.

::**neurotransmitters** chemical messengers that cross the synaptic gaps between neurons. When released by the sending neuron, neurotransmitters travel across the synapse and bind to receptor sites on the receiving neuron, thereby influencing whether that neuron will generate a neural impulse.

::**reuptake** a neurotransmitter's reabsorption by the sending neuron.

"All information processing in the brain involves neurons 'talking to' each other at synapses."
Neuroscientist Solomon H. Snyder (1984)

"When it comes to the brain, if you want to see the action, follow the neurotransmitters."
Neuroscientist Floyd Bloom (1993)

INTERCONNECTING

Neurotransmitters are the key component for all behavior and mental processes. The neurotransmitters, or NTs for short, carry the messages for all that we do. NTs send messages to be happy or sad, to move or stay still. NTs can function differently depending on where they are located in the nervous system. Scientists are still discovering how these chemicals work, so students should be aware that the information in this unit in no way is comprehensive or definitive, only the tip of the iceberg.

TEACHING TIP

The sodium-potassium pump is the mechanism by which ions are allowed to pass through the membrane of the neural cell. Named for the two primary elements present in the ion exchange, this pump brings positively charged ions into the cell and then pumps them back out when the action potential is over. This term may show up on the AP Exam.

At this point, you may want to use *Video: Digital Media Archive*, 2nd ed.: *Neural Communication: Impulse Transmission Across the Synapse*.

TROUBLESHOOTING

The importance of the myelin sheath cannot be emphasized enough. Myelin, produced by glia cells, helps make neural communication more efficient. Without myelin, neurons would not communicate as quickly, making behavior and mental processes occur more slowly or perhaps not occur at all. Multiple sclerosis is a disorder in which myelin is attacked by the body's immune system, and people who have this disorder find movement increasingly difficult.

TEACHING TIP

The Nodes of Ranvier are the spaces in between the myelin cells that encircle the axon. These spaces are important to keeping the charge going through the relatively long axon. Without these spaces, the charge might lose its intensity before reaching the end of the cell.

UNIT 3A

TROUBLESHOOTING

From the diagram, it may seem to students that only one neuron and one neurotransmitter act on each synapse. However, some neurons can house more than one neurotransmitter, and usually more than one neuron is present at any given synapse. Help students to realize that this diagram is intentionally simplified to help communicate the basic idea of the process involved in neural communication, but that the reality is amazingly complex.

RESEARCH

Have students research **myasthenia gravis**, a neurological disorder resulting from the depletion of acetylcholine. Without ACh, the muscles do not move properly. People with this disorder experience extreme fatigue since it takes enormous effort to move muscles at all.

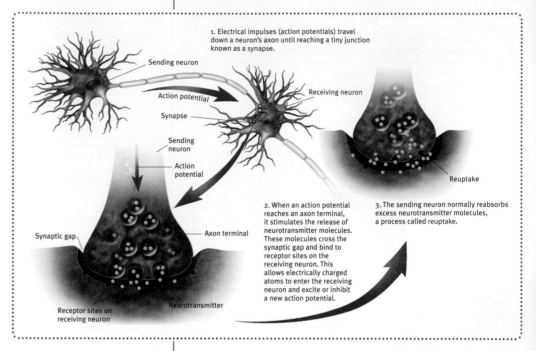

1. Electrical impulses (action potentials) travel down a neuron's axon until reaching a tiny junction known as a synapse.

Sending neuron

Action potential

Synapse

Sending neuron

Action potential

Synaptic gap

Receptor sites on receiving neuron

Neurotransmitter

Axon terminal

Receiving neuron

Reuptake

2. When an action potential reaches an axon terminal, it stimulates the release of neurotransmitter molecules. These molecules cross the synaptic gap and bind to receptor sites on the receiving neuron. This allows electrically charged atoms to enter the receiving neuron and excite or inhibit a new action potential.

3. The sending neuron normally reabsorbs excess neurotransmitter molecules, a process called reuptake.

➤ **FIGURE 3A.4**
How neurons communicate

may have particular effects on behavior and emotions. (See **FIGURE 3A.5** and **TABLE 3A.1** for examples.) *Acetylcholine (ACh)* is one of the best-understood neurotransmitters. In addition to its role in learning and memory, ACh is the messenger at every junction between a motor neuron and skeletal muscle. When ACh is released to our muscle cell receptors, the muscle contracts. If ACh transmission is blocked, as happens during some kinds of anesthesia, the muscles cannot contract and we are paralyzed.

Serotonin pathways

Dopamine pathways

Both photos from *Mapping the Mind*, Rita Carter, © 1989 University of California Press.

➤ **FIGURE 3A.5**
Neurotransmitter pathways Each of the brain's differing chemical messengers has designated pathways where it operates, as shown here for serotonin and dopamine (Carter, 1998).

TEACHING TIP

Figure 3A.5 shows pathways for serotonin and dopamine throughout the brain. Point out that the function of the neurotransmitter depends on which part of the brain it acts upon.

- If the NT is acting in the brainstem, it affects basic functions like breathing and heartbeat.
- If it acts on areas in the midbrain, it affects functions like memory and emotion.

- Finally, if it acts on areas in the cortex, higher functions like memory integration, problem solving, and perception are affected.

Helping students see this hierarchical organization of the brain and how NTs play a role in that will give them a better understanding of neuroanatomy.

TABLE 3A.1

SOME NEUROTRANSMTTERS AND THEIR FUNCTIONS

Neurotransmitter	Function	Examples of Malfunctions
Acetylcholine (ACh)	Enables muscle action, learning, and memory.	With Alzheimer's disease, ACh-producing neurons deteriorate.
Dopamine	Influences movement, learning, attention, and emotion.	Excess dopamine receptor activity is linked to schizophrenia. Starved of dopamine, the brain produces the tremors and decreased mobility of Parkinson's disease.
Serotonin	Affects mood, hunger, sleep, and arousal.	Undersupply linked to depression. Prozac and some other antidepressant drugs raise serotonin levels.
Norepinephrine	Helps control alertness and arousal.	Undersupply can depress mood.
GABA (gamma-aminobutyric acid)	A major inhibitory neurotransmitter.	Undersupply linked to seizures, tremors, and insomnia.
Glutamate	A major excitatory neurotransmitter; involved in memory.	Oversupply can overstimulate brain, producing migraines or seizures (which is why some people avoid MSG, monosodium glutamate, in food).

Candace Pert and Solomon Snyder (1973) made an exciting discovery about neurotransmitters when they attached a radioactive tracer to morphine, showing where it was taken up in an animal's brain. The morphine, an opiate drug that elevates mood and eases pain, bound to receptors in areas linked with mood and pain sensations. But why would the brain have these "opiate receptors"? Why would it have a chemical lock, unless it also had a natural key to open it?

Researchers soon confirmed that the brain does indeed produce its own naturally occurring opiates. Our body releases several types of neurotransmitter molecules similar to morphine in response to pain and vigorous exercise. These **endorphins** (short for *endo*genous [produced within] *morphine*), as we now call them, help explain good feelings such as the "runner's high," the painkilling effects of acupuncture, and the indifference to pain in some severely injured people. But once again, new knowledge led to new questions.

How Drugs and Other Chemicals Alter Neurotransmission

If indeed the endorphins lessen pain and boost mood, why not flood the brain with artificial opiates, thereby intensifying the brain's own "feel-good" chemistry? One problem is that when flooded with opiate drugs such as heroin and morphine, the brain may stop producing its own natural opiates. When the drug is withdrawn, the brain may then be deprived of any form of opiate, causing intense discomfort. For suppressing the body's own neurotransmitter production, nature charges a price.

Drugs and other chemicals affect brain chemistry at synapses, often by either amplifying or blocking a neurotransmitter's activity. An *agonist* molecule may be similar enough to a neurotransmitter to bind to its receptor and mimic its effects (**FIGURE 3A.6b** on the next page). Some opiate drugs are agonists and produce a temporary "high" by amplifying normal sensations of arousal or pleasure. Not so pleasant are the effects of black widow spider venom, which floods synapses with ACh. The result? Violent muscle contractions, convulsions, and possible death.

> Physician Lewis Thomas, on the endorphins: "There it is, a biologically universal act of mercy. I cannot explain it, except to say that I would have put it in had I been around at the very beginning, sitting as a member of a planning committee."
> *The Youngest Science*, 1983

::**endorphins** [en-DOR-fins] "morphine within"—natural, opiatelike neurotransmitters linked to pain control and to pleasure.

TEACHING TIP

Each of the neurotransmitters featured in Table 3A.1 is chemically similar to a drug or other chemical that affects behavior, cognition, and emotion. Here are some similarities the chart does not point out:

- Dopamine is similar to cocaine.
- Serotonin is similar to LSD and Ecstasy.

Just as our body produces its own painkillers, so, too, does it produce the chemicals necessary for energy, euphoria, and even hallucinations. In healthy people, these chemicals are balanced to produce normal experiences. Taking illegal or non-prescribed drugs disrupts this balance, causing abnormal levels of energy, emotion, and sensory experience.

TEACHING TIP

Another neurotransmitter not described in the table is Substance P, the body's pain NT. This NT works in opposition with endorphins to regulate pain. Substance P signals that the body is in pain, and endorphins are triggered to inhibit the pain signal.

TROUBLESHOOTING

Be sure students understand the difference between agonist and antagonist when these terms pertain to drugs. These terms are often confused, so knowing them will help students if these terms show up on the AP Exam.

UNIT 3A

TEACHING TIP

In order for drugs to have an effect on the body, there must be an accompanying receptor site on a neuron that matches the structure of that drug. So the body produces naturally chemical substances that are similar to many of the drugs that affect the body. When we introduce drugs into our bodies, we are either increasing the amount of these substances in the body or blocking substances that are supposed to work in a specific way.

But not all substances can pass through the body's **blood-brain barrier,** which protects the brain from pathogens and harmful substances. For example, Parkinson's patients cannot simply take dopamine to alleviate their symptoms. They must take a precursor of dopamine called L-dopa that will metabolize into dopamine once it reaches the brain.

At this point, you may want to use *Lecture/Discussion Topic/ Feature Film: Parkinson's Disease and Awakenings* (p. 6) from Bolt's Teacher's Resource Binder.

RESEARCH

Have students research how common prescription and recreational drugs are related to neurotransmitters. Discuss with students how our understanding of neurotransmitters can both help people with neurological disorders and help us see how those who abuse drugs harm themselves.

➤ **FIGURE 3A.6**
Agonists and antagonists

Antagonists also bind to receptors but their effect is instead to block a neurotransmitter's functioning. Botulin, a poison that can form in improperly canned food, causes paralysis by blocking ACh release. (Small injections of botulin—Botox—smooth wrinkles by paralyzing the underlying facial muscles.) Other antagonists are enough like the natural neurotransmitter to occupy its receptor site and block its effect, as in Figure 3A.6c, but are not similar enough to stimulate the receptor (rather like foreign coins that fit into, but won't operate, a soda or candy machine). Curare, a poison certain South American Indians have applied to hunting-dart tips, occupies and blocks ACh receptor sites, leaving the neurotransmitter unable to affect the muscles. Struck by one of these darts, an animal becomes paralyzed.

BEFORE YOU MOVE ON . . .

➤ **ASK YOURSELF**
Can you recall a time when the endorphin response may have protected you from feeling extreme pain?

➤ **TEST YOURSELF 1**
How do neurons communicate with one another?

Answers to the Test Yourself questions can be found in Appendix E at the end of the book.

The Nervous System

4: What are the functions of the nervous system's main divisions?

TO LIVE IS TO TAKE IN INFORMATION from the world and the body's tissues, to make decisions, and to send back information and orders to the body's tissues. All this happens thanks to our body's speedy electrochemical communications network, our **nervous system** (FIGURE 3A.7). The brain and spinal cord form the **central nervous system (CNS)**, which communicates with the body's sensory receptors, muscles, and glands via the **peripheral nervous system (PNS)**.

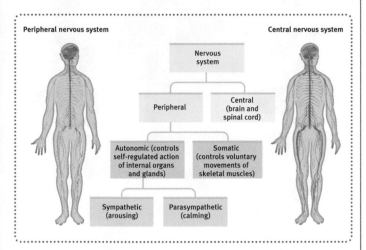

➤ FIGURE 3A.7
The functional divisions of the human nervous system

Neurons are the nervous system's building blocks. PNS information travels through axons that are bundled into the electrical cables we know as **nerves.** The optic nerve, for example, bundles a million axon fibers into a single cable carrying the messages each eye sends to the brain (Mason & Kandel, 1991). As noted earlier, information travels in the nervous system through sensory neurons, motor neurons, and interneurons.

The Peripheral Nervous System

Our peripheral nervous system has two components—somatic and autonomic. Our **somatic nervous system** enables voluntary control of our skeletal muscles. As the bell signals the end of class, your somatic nervous system reports to your brain the current state of your skeletal muscles and carries instructions back, triggering your body to rise from your seat.

Our **autonomic nervous system** controls our glands and the muscles of our internal organs, influencing such functions as glandular activity, heartbeat, and digestion. Like an automatic pilot, this system may be consciously overridden, but usually it operates on its own (autonomously).

The autonomic nervous system serves two important, basic functions. The **sympathetic nervous system** arouses and expends energy. If something alarms, enrages, or challenges you (such as taking the AP Psychology exam), your sympathetic

::**nervous system** the body's speedy, electrochemical communication network, consisting of all the nerve cells of the peripheral and central nervous systems.

::**central nervous system (CNS)** the brain and spinal cord.

::**peripheral nervous system (PNS)** the sensory and motor neurons that connect the central nervous system (CNS) to the rest of the body.

::**nerves** bundled axons that form neural "cables" connecting the central nervous system with muscles, glands, and sense organs.

::**somatic nervous system** the division of the peripheral nervous system that controls the body's skeletal muscles. Also called the *skeletal nervous system*.

::**autonomic** [aw-tuh-NAHM-ik] **nervous system** the part of the peripheral nervous system that controls the glands and the muscles of the internal organs (such as the heart). Its sympathetic division arouses; its parasympathetic division calms.

::**sympathetic nervous system** the division of the autonomic nervous system that arouses the body, mobilizing its energy in stressful situations.

::**parasympathetic nervous system** the division of the autonomic nervous system that calms the body, conserving its energy.

::**reflex** a simple, automatic response to a sensory stimulus, such as the knee-jerk response.

The sympathetic and parasympathetic nervous systems together make an **opponent process** system. Opponent processes work in opposition of each other, with one system performing one role and the other system performing the exact opposite role. In this case, the sympathetic nervous system causes the body to rise to the challenge it faces and the parasympathetic nervous system causes the body to calm after the challenge has been addressed. This opposition creates **homeostasis,** or balance, in the body.

Remember what the sympathetic nervous system does by thinking about what we do when we feel *sympathy*—we try to help actively by comforting and consoling others. We have to act to help others, so the sympathetic nervous system will kick in, giving us the energy we need to accomplish our goals.

➤ **FIGURE 3A.8**
The dual functions of the autonomic nervous system The autonomic nervous system controls the more autonomous (or self-regulating) internal functions. Its sympathetic division arouses and expends energy. Its parasympathetic division calms and conserves energy, allowing routine maintenance activity. For example, sympathetic stimulation accelerates heartbeat, whereas parasympathetic stimulation slows it.

"The body is made up of millions and millions of crumbs."

system will accelerate your heartbeat, raise your blood pressure, slow your digestion, raise your blood sugar, and cool you with perspiration, making you alert and ready for action (**FIGURE 3A.8**). When the stress subsides, your **parasympathetic nervous system** produces opposite effects. It conserves energy as it calms you by decreasing your heartbeat, lowering your blood sugar, and so forth. In everyday situations, the sympathetic and parasympathetic nervous systems work together to keep you in a steady internal state.

The Central Nervous System

From the simplicity of neurons "talking" to other neurons arises the complexity of the central nervous system's brain and spinal cord.

It is the brain that enables our humanity—our thinking, feeling, and acting. Tens of billions of neurons, each communicating with thousands of other neurons, yield an ever-changing wiring diagram that dwarfs a powerful computer. With some 40 billion neurons, each having roughly 10,000 contacts with other neurons, we end up with perhaps 400 trillion synapses—places where neurons meet and greet their neighbors (de Courten-Myers, 2005). A grain-of-sand–sized speck of your brain contains some 100,000 neurons and one billion "talking" synapses (Ramachandran & Blakeslee, 1998).

The brain's neurons cluster into work groups called *neural networks*. To understand why, Stephen Kosslyn and Olivier Koenig (1992, p. 12) invite us to "think about why cities exist; why don't people distribute themselves more evenly across the countryside?" Like people networking with people, neurons network with nearby neurons with which they can have short, fast connections. As in **FIGURE 3A.9**, the cells in each layer of a neural network connect with various cells in the next layer. Learning occurs as feedback strengthens connections. Learning to play the violin, for example, builds neural connections. Neurons that fire together wire together.

Stephen Colbert: "How does the brain work? Five words or less."
Steven Pinker: "Brain cells fire in patterns."
The Colbert Report, February 8, 2007

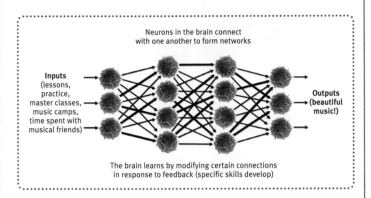

Inputs (lessons, practice, master classes, music camps, time spent with musical friends)

Neurons in the brain connect with one another to form networks

Outputs (beautiful music!)

The brain learns by modifying certain connections in response to feedback (specific skills develop)

➤ **FIGURE 3A.9**
A simplified neural network: learning to play the violin Neurons network with nearby neurons. Encoded in these networks of interrelating neurons is your own enduring identity (as a musician, an athlete, a devoted friend)—your sense of self that extends across the years.

The *spinal cord* is an information highway connecting the peripheral nervous system to the brain. Ascending neural fibers send up sensory information, and descending fibers send back motor-control information. The neural pathways governing our **reflexes**, our automatic responses to stimuli, illustrate the spinal cord's work. A simple spinal reflex pathway is composed of a single sensory neuron and a single motor neuron. These often communicate through an interneuron. The knee-jerk response, for example, involves one such simple pathway. A headless warm body could do it.

Another such pathway enables the pain reflex (**FIGURE 3A.10**, on the next page). When your finger touches a flame, neural activity excited by the heat travels via sensory neurons to interneurons in your spinal cord. These interneurons respond by activating motor neurons leading to the muscles in your arm. Because the simple pain reflex pathway runs through the spinal cord and right back out, your hand jerks from the candle's flame *before* your brain receives and responds to the information that causes you to feel pain. That's why it feels as if your hand jerks away not by your choice, but on its own.

Information travels to and from the brain by way of the spinal cord. Were the top of your spinal cord severed, you would not feel pain from your paralyzed body below. Nor would you feel pleasure. With your brain literally out of touch with your body, you would lose all sensation and voluntary movement in body regions with sensory and motor connections to the spinal cord below its point of injury. You would exhibit the knee-jerk without feeling the tap. To produce bodily pain or pleasure, the sensory information must reach the brain.

"If the nervous system be cut off between the brain and other parts, the experiences of those other parts are nonexistent for the mind. The eye is blind, the ear deaf, the hand insensible and motionless."
William James,
Principles of Psychology, 1890

TEACHING TIP

The dendrites of neurons contribute significantly to the complexity of the neural network. The more dendrites a neuron has, the greater the number of connections that one neuron can make with other neurons, increasing the likelihood that its message will get passed along the chain.

TEACHING TIP

Sensory neurons connect to the spinal cord dorsally, or in the back. Motor neurons connect in the anterior of the spinal cord, or in the front. Therefore, it is possible to lose feeling in lower portions of the body in a spinal cord injury but retain the ability to move if the spinal cord is not completely severed.

TEACHING TIP

Have you ever jerked away from a hot surface only to feel the burn after a delay? **Interneurons** make reflexes happen. These cells in the spinal cord process motor responses quickly to protect the body from harm. Without interneurons, you would experience severe burns if you left your hand on that hot surface long enough to process both the heat and the pain before jerking away!

TROUBLESHOOTING

The neural chain, also known as the **reflex arc,** can be described graphically:

The brain processes the sensory info and decides what to do

Sensory information enters the body through receptor cells.

Motor nerves receive commands from the brain and react.

UNIT 3A

➤ **FIGURE 3A.10**
A simple reflex

1. In this simple hand-withdrawal reflex, information is carried from skin receptors along a sensory neuron to the spinal cord (shown by the red arrow). From here it is passed via interneurons to motor neurons that lead to muscles in the hand and arm (blue arrow).

Brain

Sensory neuron (incoming information)

Interneuron

Muscle

Spinal cord

Skin receptors

Motor neuron (outgoing information)

2. Because this reflex involves only the spinal cord, the hand jerks away from the candle flame even before information about the event has reached the brain, causing the experience of pain.

TEACHING TIP

The movement for reflexes occurs before the brain has a chance to process the incoming sensory information. Reflexes enable us to respond to stimuli before they have a chance to do us harm. It's almost as if the spinal cord is a brain itself, having the ability to process danger before the brain has to do so.

DEMO

Show students how slowly the brain processes information by forming a human-sized neural chain. Have students stand in a circle, holding hands. Choose one student to be the start of the chain, with the student on his/her left being the end of the chain. Using a stopwatch, time how long it takes for students to squeeze each other's hand as they go around the circle. Then, have students stand with their backs to each other and have them put their hands on the shoulders of the person in front of them. This time, they should squeeze only one shoulder, but it should be the opposite shoulder than the one they felt being squeezed. The difference in times between the first and second trials should be significant, showing how processing (thinking) can slow our reactions.

At this point, you may want to use **Classroom Exercise: *Reaction-Time Measure of Neural Transmission and Mental Processes*** (p. 7) from Bolt's Teacher's Resource Binder.

BEFORE YOU MOVE ON . . .

➤ **ASK YOURSELF**
Does our nervous system's design—with its synaptic gaps that chemical messenger molecules cross in an imperceptibly brief instant—surprise you? Would you have designed yourself differently?

➤ **TEST YOURSELF 2**
How does information flow through your nervous system as you pick up a fork? Can you summarize this process?

Answers to the Test Yourself questions can be found in Appendix E at the end of the book.

::**endocrine** [EN-duh-krin] **system** the body's "slow" chemical communication system; a set of glands that secrete hormones into the bloodstream.

::**hormones** chemical messengers that are manufactured by the endocrine glands, travel through the bloodstream, and affect other tissues.

::**adrenal** [ah-DREEN-el] **glands** a pair of endocrine glands that sit just above the kidneys and secrete hormones (epinephrine and norepinephrine) that help arouse the body in times of stress.

::**pituitary gland** the endocrine system's most influential gland. Under the influence of the hypothalamus, the pituitary regulates growth and controls other endocrine glands.

The Endocrine System

5: How does the endocrine system—the body's slower information system—transmit its messages?

SO FAR WE HAVE FOCUSED ON THE BODY'S speedy electrochemical information system. Interconnected with your nervous system is a second communication system, the **endocrine system** (FIGURE 3A.11). The endocrine system's glands secrete another form of chemical messengers, **hormones**, which travel through the bloodstream and affect other tissues, including the brain. When they act on the brain, they influence our interest in sex, food, and aggression.

Some hormones are chemically identical to neurotransmitters (those chemical messengers that diffuse across a synapse and excite or inhibit an adjacent neuron). The endocrine system and nervous system are therefore close relatives: Both produce molecules that act on receptors elsewhere. Like many relatives, they also

---

RESEARCH

Have students research disorders of the endocrine system, including diabetes, abnormal growth, and hypo- and hyperthyroidism. Focus on the following questions:

- What physical problems do these disorders cause?
- What emotional problems do these disorders cause?
- What treatments are available for these disorders?

differ. The speedy nervous system zips messages from eyes to brain to hand in a fraction of a second. Endocrine messages trudge along in the bloodstream, taking several seconds or more to travel from the gland to the target tissue. If the nervous system's communication delivers messages rather like e-mail, the endocrine system is the body's postal mail. But slow and steady sometimes wins the race. Endocrine messages tend to outlast the effects of neural messages. That helps explain why upset feelings may linger, sometimes beyond our thinking about what upset us. It takes time for us to "simmer down." In a moment of danger, for example, the autonomic nervous system orders the **adrenal glands** on top of the kidneys to release *epinephrine* and *norepinephrine* (also called *adrenaline* and *noradrenaline* in our *fight-or-flight* response). These hormones increase heart rate, blood pressure, and blood sugar, providing us with a surge of energy. When the emergency passes, the hormones—and the feelings of excitement—linger a while. The endocrine system's hormones influence many aspects of our lives—growth, reproduction, metabolism, mood—working with our nervous system to keep everything in balance while we respond to stress, exertion, and our own thoughts.

The most influential endocrine gland is the **pituitary gland**, a pea-sized structure located in the core of the brain, where it is controlled by an adjacent brain area, the hypothalamus (which you will hear more about in Unit 3B). The pituitary releases hormones that influence growth, and its secretions also influence the release of hormones by other endocrine glands. The pituitary, then, is a sort of master gland (whose own master is the hypothalamus). For example, under the brain's influence, the pituitary triggers your sex glands to release sex hormones. These in turn influence your brain and behavior.

This feedback system (brain→pituitary→other glands→hormones→brain) reveals the intimate connection of the nervous and endocrine systems. The nervous system directs endocrine secretions, which then affect the nervous system. Conducting and coordinating this whole electrochemical orchestra is that maestro we call the brain.

Hypothalamus
(brain region controlling the pituitary gland)

Pituitary gland
(secretes many different hormones, some of which affect other glands)

Parathyroids
(help regulate the level of calcium in the blood)

Thyroid gland
(affects metabolism, among other things)

Adrenal glands
(inner part helps trigger the "fight-or-flight" response)

Pancreas
(regulates the level of sugar in the blood)

Testis
(secretes male sex hormones)

Ovary
(secretes female sex hormones)

▶ FIGURE 3A.11
The endocrine system

BEFORE YOU MOVE ON . . .

➤ **ASK YOURSELF**
Can you remember feeling an extended period of discomfort after some particularly stressful event? How long did those feelings last?

➤ **TEST YOURSELF 3**
Why is the pituitary gland called the "master gland"?

Answers to the Test Yourself questions can be found in Appendix E at the end of the book.

TROUBLESHOOTING

Students don't realize that hormones and neurotransmitters are the same. They are only different based on where they are manufactured and located in the body. Neurotransmitters are manufactured in neurons and other nervous system cells and located in the nervous system, while hormones are manufactured by glands and based in the body and bloodstream.

TEACHING TIP

Some important endocrine glands and the hormones they secrete are listed below:

- *Anterior pituitary gland* secretes growth hormone. Too little produces dwarfism; too much results in gigantism.

- *Posterior pituitary gland* secretes vasopressin (in addition to oxytocin), constricting blood vessels and raising blood pressure. *Oxytocin* in women sparks labor during pregnancy.

- *Thyroid* releases thyroxine and triiodothyronine, increasing metabolic rate, growth, and maturation.

- *Parathyroids* release parathyroid hormone, increasing blood calcium and decreasing potassium.

- *Pancreas* secretes insulin, regulating the level of sugar in the bloodstream.

- *Ovaries* secrete estrogen, promoting ovulation and female sexual characteristics.

- *Testes* release androgens, promoting sperm production and male sexual characteristics.

At this point, you may want to use **Lecture/Discussion Topic:** *Oxytocin: The Hormone of Love, Bonding, and Generosity?* (p. 8) from Bolt's Teacher's Resource Binder.

TEACHING TIP

Exocrine glands secrete substances outside the body. Examples include salivary glands, tear glands, and sweat glands. Endocrine means "within": endocrine glands secrete from within the body into the bloodstream.

UNIT 3A

ANSWERS to Multiple-Choice Questions

1. **c.** the same principles govern neural functioning in all species.
2. **a.** action potential.
3. **d.** neuron.
4. **b.** Hormones
5. **a.** Acetylcholine
6. **a.** pituitary.
7. **e.** speed the transmission of information within a neuron.
8. **e.** is the part of the nervous system that does not include the brain and the spinal cord.
9. **a.** interneurons.
10. **d.** agonists.
11. **b.** somatic nervous system.
12. **a.** all psychological processes depend upon it.
13. **a.** the bumps on the skull.
14. **c.** to understand people we must study how biological, psychological, and social-cultural systems work and interact.
15. **b.** agonists, because they mimic other neurotransmitters' pain-diminishing effects.

UNIT REVIEW: Neural Processing and the Endocrine System

Neural Communication

1: What are neurons, and how do they transmit information?

Neurons are the elementary components of the nervous system, the body's speedy electrochemical information system. *Sensory neurons* carry incoming information from sense receptors to the brain and spinal cord, and *motor neurons* carry information from the brain and spinal cord out to the muscles and glands. *Interneurons* communicate within the brain and spinal cord and between sensory and motor neurons. A neuron sends signals through its *axons,* and receives signals through its branching *dendrites.* If the combined signals are strong enough, the neuron fires, transmitting an electrical impulse (the *action potential*) down its axon by means of a chemistry-to-electricity process. The neuron's reaction is an all-or-none process.

2: How do nerve cells communicate with other nerve cells?

When action potentials reach the end of an axon (the axon terminals), they stimulate the release of *neurotransmitters.* These chemical messengers carry a message from the sending neuron across a *synapse* to receptor sites on a receiving neuron. The sending neuron, in a process called *reuptake,* then normally absorbs the excess neurotransmitter molecules in the synaptic gap. The receiving neuron, if the signals from that neuron and others are strong enough, generates its own action potential and relays the message to other cells.

3: How do neurotransmitters influence behavior, and how do drugs and other chemicals affect neurotransmission?

Each neurotransmitter travels a designated path in the brain and has a particular effect on behavior and emotions. Acetylcholine affects muscle action, learning, and memory. *En-*

dorphins are natural opiates released in response to pain and exercise. (See Table 3A.1 on p. 57 to review the key neurotransmitters.) Drugs and other chemicals affect communication at the synapse. Agonists bind to and activate receptors, thus mimicking particular neurotransmitters. Antagonists block receptors, thus blocking a neurotransmitter's natural effect.

The Nervous System

4: What are the functions of the nervous system's main divisions?

One major division of the *nervous system* is the *central nervous system (CNS),* the brain and spinal cord. The other is the *peripheral nervous system (PNS),* which connects the CNS to the rest of the body by means of *nerves.* The peripheral nervous system has two main divisions. The *somatic nervous system* enables voluntary control of the skeletal muscles. The *autonomic nervous system,* through its *sympathetic* and *parasympathetic* divisions, controls involuntary muscles and glands. Neurons cluster into working networks.

The Endocrine System

5: How does the endocrine system—the body's slower information system—transmit its messages?

The *endocrine system* is a set of glands that secrete *hormones* into the bloodstream, where they travel through the body and affect other tissues, including the brain. The endocrine system's master gland, the *pituitary,* influences hormone release by other glands. In an intricate feedback system, the brain's hypothalamus influences the pituitary gland, which influences other glands, which release hormones, which in turn influence the brain.

Terms and Concepts to Remember

biological psychology, p. 52
neuron, p. 53
sensory neurons, p. 53
motor neurons, p. 53
interneurons, p. 53
dendrite, p. 53
axon, p. 53
myelin [MY-uh-lin] sheath, p. 53
action potential, p. 53
threshold, p. 54

synapse [SIN-aps], p. 55
neurotransmitters, p. 55
reuptake, p. 55
endorphins [en-DOR-fins], p. 57
nervous system, p. 59
central nervous system (CNS), p. 59
peripheral nervous system (PNS), p. 59
nerves, p. 59
somatic nervous system, p. 59

autonomic [aw-tuh-NAHM-ik] nervous system, p. 59
sympathetic nervous system, p. 59
parasympathetic nervous system, p. 60
reflex, p. 61
endocrine [EN-duh-krin] system, p. 62
hormones, p. 62
adrenal [ah-DREEN-el] glands, p. 63
pituitary gland, p. 63

TECHNOLOGY RESOURCES

These resources will be helpful for teaching the concepts in this portion of the unit:

- *PsychSim 5: Neural Messages*
- *Video: Psychology: The Human Experience, Module 6: Neurological Disorder*
- *Video: Psychology: The Human Experience, Module 7: Brain Surgery for Neurological Disorder*
- *Video: Digital Media Archive: Psychology,* 2nd ed., *Video Clip 1: Neural Communication*
- *Video: The Brain,* 2nd ed., *Module 2: The Effects of Hormones and Environment on Brain Development*

AP* Practice Test Questions

Multiple-Choice Questions

1. Researchers study the brains of non-human animals because

a. it is not ethical to study human brains.
b. human brains are too complex to study meaningfully.
c. the same principles govern neural functioning in all species.
d. it is too expensive to study human brains.
e. the technology is still being developed for the study of human brains.

2. A brief electrical charge that travels down an axon is called a(n)

a. action potential.
b. resting potential.
c. all-or-none impulse.
d. refractory period.
e. myelination response.

3. The basic building block of the nervous system is the

a. neurotransmitter.
b. brain.
c. synapse.
d. neuron.
e. dendrite.

4. Which of the following does the endocrine system rely on to communicate?

a. Action potentials
b. Hormones
c. Agonists
d. Neurotransmitters
e. Reuptake

5. An individual is having trouble with cognitive tasks related to learning and memory. Which of the following neurotransmitters is most likely to be involved with the problem?

a. Acetylcholine
b. Dopamine
c. Serotonin
d. The endorphins
e. GABA

6. The most influential of the endocrine glands is (are) the

a. pituitary.
b. adrenal glands.
c. dendrites.
d. threshold glands.
e. parasympathetic.

7. The purpose of the myelin sheath is to

a. make the transfer of information across a synapse more efficient.
b. increase the amount of neurotransmitter available in the neuron.
c. reduce the antagonistic effect of certain drugs.
d. establish a resting potential in the axon.
e. speed the transmission of information within a neuron.

8. The peripheral nervous system

a. connects the brain to the spinal cord.
b. calms the body after an emergency.
c. is limited to the control of voluntary movement.
d. controls only the arms and the legs.
e. is the part of the nervous system that does not include the brain and the spinal cord.

9. The cells most important for processing information are

a. interneurons.
b. sensory neurons.
c. motor neurons.
d. endocrine cells.
e. sympathetic nervous system cells.

10. Drugs that amplify neurotransmitter activity are called

a. addictive.
b. excitatory.
c. antagonists.
d. agonists.
e. inhibitory.

11. To walk across a street, a person would rely most directly on his

a. central nervous system.
b. somatic nervous system.
c. peripheral nervous system.
d. autonomic nervous system.
e. parasympathetic nervous system.

12. The nervous system is of critical importance to psychology because

a. all psychological processes depend upon it.
b. it is the largest system in the human body.
c. it is a model for the functioning of other body systems.
d. it is the mechanism by which the endocrine system exerts its functions.
e. it is the most recent human system to have evolved.

13. Phrenology is the study of

a. the bumps on the skull.
b. the influence of neurotransmitters.
c. the function of the peripheral nervous system.
d. endocrine glands and their hormones.
e. heredity's influence on nervous system development.

14. Understanding people as biopsychosocial systems means that

a. biological factors have the largest influence on people, followed by psychological factors and finally social factors.
b. the nervous system is equal parts biological, psychological, and sociological.
c. to understand people we must study how biological, psychological, and social-cultural systems work and interact.
d. the nervous system is less important in the understanding of people than was believed a decade ago.
e. psychology is the central component in the understanding of human behavior.

15. Opiate drugs such as morphine are classified as

a. antagonists, because they block neurotransmitter receptors for pain.
b. agonists, because they mimic other neurotransmitters' pain-diminishing effects.
c. excitatory neurotransmitters, because they activate pain control mechanisms.
d. sympathetic nervous system agents, because they prepare the body for a challenge.
e. parasympathetic nervous system agents, because they calm the body,

Free-Response Question

Explain how information travels in the nervous system, both *within* neurons and *between* neurons.

WEB

Multiple-choice self-tests and more may be found at www.worthpublishers.com/myers

---

Rubric for Grading the Free-Response Question

This is a 10-point question. Allow one point for an adequate discussion of each of the following terms. The rubric can be modified by adding or subtracting terms depending on what you have emphasized in class.

Within neuron communication

- **Resting potential**—the condition of a neuron when it is "charged" and ready to fire

- **Action potential**—the brief electrical charge that travels down the axon when a neuron "fires"

- **Refractory period**—the recharging period that must occur to ready a neuron to generate another action potential

- **All-or-none response**—the principle that a neuron always generates action potentials of equal strength

- **Threshold**—the minimum energy required to generate an action potential

Between neuron communication

- **Synapse**—the small gap between neurons across which information must travel

- **Dendrites**—the fibers on a neuron that receive the neurotransmitters

- **Neurotransmitters**—the chemical messengers that carry information across the synapse between one neuron and the next

- **Excitation**—the process of making the neuron receiving neurotransmitters more likely to generate an action potential

- **Inhibition**—the process of making the neuron receiving neurotransmitters less likely to generate an action potential

---

- *Video: The Mind, 2nd ed., Module 5: Endorphins: The Brain's Natural Morphine*
- *Video: The Brain, 2nd ed., Module 30: Understanding the Brain Through Epilepsy*
- *Psychology Video Tool Kit: Chemically Induced Hallucinations: Studies of Anesthetic Drugs; The Runner's High; Parkinson's Disease: A Case Study; Treating Parkinson's Disease: Deep Brain Electrode Implantation*

Pacing Guide

Use the following guide to determine how many instructional days to devote to this portion of the unit depending on the type of course you teach:

Year-long course: 3–4 days
Block schedule/Semester-long course: 2–3 days

This entire unit (Parts A, B, & C) encompasses 8–10 percent of the AP Exam. Spending an appropriate amount of time on this unit will help students do well on the AP Exam.

TEACHING TIP

Teach this unit early in the course so students can get the foundational knowledge offered in this unit. Understanding the concepts in this unit is important to mastering the entire course content. However, due to the amount of material covered in this unit, it has been broken down into three parts. Helping students chunk this information will help them learn a large amount of very important material more easily.

INTERCONNECTING

Keep in mind that the following units will also rely heavily on a thorough understanding of the biological bases of behavior:

Unit 4: Sensation and Perception
Unit 5: States of Consciousness
Unit 7: Part A: Memory
Unit 8: Part B: Emotions, Stress, and Health
Unit 12: Abnormal Psychology
Unit 13: Treatment of Psychological Disorders

Biological Bases of Behavior:
3B—The Brain

In a jar on a display shelf in Cornell University's psychology department resides the well-preserved brain of Edward Bradford Titchener, a great turn-of-the-century experimental psychologist and proponent of the study of consciousness. Imagine yourself gazing at that wrinkled mass of grayish tissue, wondering if in any sense Titchener is still there.[1]

You might answer that, without the living whir of electrochemical activity, there could be nothing of Titchener in his preserved brain. Consider then an experiment about which the inquisitive Titchener himself might have daydreamed. Imagine that just moments before his death, someone removed Titchener's brain from his body and kept it alive by floating it in a tank of cerebral fluid while feeding it enriched blood. Would Titchener still be in there? Further imagine that someone then transplanted the still-living brain into the body of a person with severe brain damage. To whose home should the recovered patient return?

That we can imagine such questions illustrates how convinced we are that we live "somewhere north of the neck" (Fodor, 1999). And for good reason: The brain enables the mind—seeing, hearing, smelling, feeling, remembering, thinking, speaking, dreaming. The brain is what poet Diane Ackerman (2004, p. 3) calls "that shiny mound of being . . . that dream factory . . . that huddle of neurons calling all the plays . . . that fickle pleasuredrome."

Moreover, it is the brain that self-reflectively analyzes the brain. When we're thinking *about* our brain, we're thinking *with* our brain—by firing countless millions of synapses and releasing billions of neurotransmitter molecules. The effect of hormones on experiences such as love reminds us that we would not be of the same mind if we were a bodiless brain. Brain + body = mind. Nevertheless, say neuroscientists, the *brain enables the mind.* If all your organs were transplanted, you would still be much the same person, unless, as psychologist Jonathan Haidt has said, one of those organs was the brain. But precisely where and how are the mind's functions tied to the brain? Let's first see how scientists explore such questions.

[1]Carl Sagan's *Broca's Brain* (1979) inspired this question.

"You're certainly a lot less fun since the operation."

"I am a brain, Watson. The rest of me is a mere appendix."
  Sherlock Holmes, in Arthur Conan Doyle's "The Adventure of the Mazarin Stone"

Suggested Readings

Harris, J. R. (1998). *The nurture assumption.* New York: Free Press.

Horstman, J. (2009). *The* Scientific American *day in the life of your brain.* New York: Jossey-Bass.

Pinker, S. (2002). *The blank slate: The modern denial of human nature.* New York: Viking.

Ramachandran, V. S., & Blakeslee, S. (1998). *Phantoms in the brain: Probing the mysteries of the human mind.* New York: William Morrow.

Sacks, O. (1973). *Awakenings.* New York: HarperCollins.

Sacks, O. (1985). *The man who mistook his wife for a hat.* New York: Summit Books.

The Tools of Discovery: Having Our Head Examined

1: How do neuroscientists study the brain's connections to behavior and mind?

FOR CENTURIES, WE HAD NO TOOLS high-powered yet gentle enough to explore the living human brain. Clinical observations of patients revealed some brain-mind connections. Physicians noted, for example, that damage to one side of the brain often caused numbness or paralysis on the body's opposite side, suggesting that the body's right side is wired to the brain's left side, and vice versa. Others noticed that damage to the back of the brain disrupted vision, and that damage to the left-front part of the brain produced speech difficulties. Gradually, these early explorers were mapping the brain.

Now, within a lifetime, the whole brain-mapping process has changed. The known universe's most amazing organ is being probed and mapped by a new generation of neural cartographers. Whether in the interests of science or medicine, they can selectively **lesion** (destroy) tiny clusters of normal or defective brain cells, leaving the surrounding tissue unharmed. Such studies have revealed, for example, that damage to one area of the hypothalamus in a rat's brain reduces eating, causing the rat to starve unless force-fed. Damage in another area produces *overeating*.

Today's scientists can also electrically, chemically, or magnetically stimulate various parts of the brain and note the effects; snoop on the messages of individual neurons and eavesdrop on the chatter of billions of neurons; and see color representations of the brain's energy-consuming activity. These techniques for peering into the thinking, feeling brain are doing for psychology what the microscope did for biology and the telescope did for astronomy. Let's look at a few of them and see how neuroscientists study the working brain.

Banking brains Francine Benes, director of McLean Hospital's Brain Bank, sees the collection as a valuable database.

::**lesion** [LEE-zhuhn] tissue destruction; a brain lesion is a naturally or experimentally caused destruction of brain tissue.

::**electroencephalogram (EEG)** an amplified recording of the waves of electrical activity that sweep across the brain's surface. These waves are measured by electrodes placed on the scalp.

Recording the Brain's Electrical Activity

Right now, your mental activity is giving off telltale electrical, metabolic, and magnetic signals that would enable neuroscientists to observe your brain at work. The tips of modern microelectrodes are so small they can detect the electrical pulse in a single neuron. For example, we can now detect exactly where the information goes in a cat's brain when someone strokes its whisker.

Electrical activity in the brain's billions of neurons sweeps in regular waves across its surface. An **electroencephalogram (EEG)** is an amplified readout of such waves. Studying an EEG of the brain's activity is like studying a car engine by listening to its hum. By presenting a stimulus repeatedly and having a computer filter out brain activity unrelated to the stimulus, one can identify the electrical wave evoked by the stimulus (**FIGURE 3B.1**).

➤ **FIGURE 3B.1**
An electroencephalograph providing amplified tracings of waves of electrical activity in the brain Here it is displaying the brain activity of this 4-year-old who has epilepsy.

67

Key People

Paul Broca
Phineas Gage
Michael Gazzaniga
Roger Sperry
Karl Wernicke

UNIT 3B

TEACHING TIP

Many of the now-outdated ideas about the brain—the 10 percent myth, phrenology, brain size equaling intelligence, etc.—were debunked thanks to neuroimaging techniques. The ability to see the inner working of the brain in action has revolutionized the way we think about psychology.

TROUBLESHOOTING

The CT scan is the modern name for the CAT scan.

At this point, you may want to use **Lecture/Discussion Topic: *Neuroimaging Techniques*** (p. 7) from Bolt's Teacher's Resource Binder, which accompanies this text.

INTERCONNECTING

The scans discussed here are used to gain knowledge about most of the theories discussed throughout the book:

- Diagnosing psychological disorders
- Determining how drugs affect the brain and body
- Assessing the usefulness of hypnosis
- Examining whether unconscious processes affect behavior
- Exploring the interaction of sensation and perception

These are just a few of the ways that brain scans help psychologists understand behavior and mental processes better.

At this point, you may want to use **Lecture/Discussion Topic: *Assessing Awareness in Brain-Injured Patients*** (p. 8) from Bolt's Teacher's Resource Binder.

Neuroimaging Techniques

"You must look into people, as well as at them," advised Lord Chesterfield in a 1746 letter to his son. Newer windows into the brain give us that Supermanlike ability to see inside the living brain. For example, the **CT (computed tomography) scan** examines the brain by taking X-ray photographs that can reveal brain damage. Even more dramatic is the **PET (positron emission tomography) scan** (FIGURE 3B.2), which depicts brain activity by showing each brain area's consumption of its chemical fuel, the sugar glucose. Active neurons are glucose hogs. After a person receives temporarily radioactive glucose, the PET scan detects where this "food for thought" goes by locating the radioactivity. Rather like weather radar showing rain activity, PET scan "hot spots" show which brain areas are most active as the person performs mathematical calculations, looks at images of faces, or daydreams.

In **MRI (magnetic resonance imaging)** brain scans, the head is put in a strong magnetic field, which aligns the spinning atoms of brain molecules. Then a radio-wave pulse momentarily disorients the atoms. When the atoms return to their normal spin, they release signals that provide a detailed picture of the brain's soft tissues. (MRI scans are also used to scan other body parts.) MRI scans have revealed a larger-than-average neural area in the left hemisphere of musicians who display perfect pitch (Schlaug et al., 1995). They have also revealed enlarged, fluid-filled brain areas in some patients who have schizophrenia, a disabling psychological disorder (FIGURE 3B.3).

A special application of MRI—**fMRI (functional MRI)**—can reveal the brain's functioning as well as its structure. Where the brain is especially active, blood goes. By comparing MRI scans taken less than a second apart, researchers can watch the brain "light up" (with increased oxygen-laden bloodflow) as a person performs different mental functions. As the person looks at a scene, for example, the fMRI machine detects blood rushing to the back of the brain, which processes visual information (see Figure 3B.14). Such snapshots of the brain's changing activity provide new insights into how the brain divides its labor.

To be learning about the neurosciences now is like studying world geography while Magellan was exploring the seas. This truly is the golden age of brain science.

➤ **FIGURE 3B.2**

The PET scan To obtain a PET scan, researchers inject volunteers with a low and harmless dose of a short-lived radioactive sugar. Detectors around the person's head pick up the release of gamma rays from the sugar, which has concentrated in active brain areas. A computer then processes and translates these signals into a map of the brain at work.

Courtesy of Brookhaven National Laboratories

➤ **FIGURE 3B.3**

MRI scan of a healthy individual (left) and a person with schizophrenia (right) Note the enlarged, fluid-filled brain region in the image on the right.

Both photos from Daniel Weinberger, M.D., CBDB, NIMH

Older Brain Structures

2: What are the functions of important lower-level brain structures?

IF YOU COULD OPEN THE SKULL and look inside, the first thing you might note is the brain's size. In dinosaurs, the brain represents 1/100,000th of the body's weight; in whales, 1/10,000th; in elephants, 1/600th; in humans, 1/45th. It looks as though a principle is emerging. But read on. In mice, the brain is 1/40th of the body's weight, and in marmosets, 1/25th. So there are exceptions to the rule that the ratio of brain to body weight provides a clue to a species' intelligence.

Indicators about an animal's capacities come from its brain structures. In primitive animals, such as sharks, a not-so-complex brain primarily regulates basic survival functions: breathing, resting, and feeding. In lower mammals, such as rodents, a more complex brain enables emotion and greater memory. In advanced mammals, such as humans, a brain that processes more information enables foresight as well.

This increasing complexity arises from new brain systems built on top of the old, much as the Earth's landscape covers the old with the new. Digging down, one discovers the fossil remnants of the past—brainstem components performing for us much as they did for our distant ancestors. Let's start with the brain's basement and work up to the newer systems.

The Brainstem

The brain's oldest and innermost region is the **brainstem**. It begins where the spinal cord swells slightly after entering the skull. This slight swelling is the **medulla** (**FIGURE 3B.4**). Here lie the controls for your heartbeat and breathing. Just above the medulla sits the *pons*, which helps coordinate movements. If a cat's brainstem is severed from the rest of the brain above it, the animal will still breathe and live—and even run, climb, and groom (Klemm, 1990). But with its brainstem cut off from the brain's higher regions, the cat won't purposefully run or climb to get food.

::**CT (computed tomography) scan** a series of X-ray photographs taken from different angles and combined by computer into a composite representation of a slice through the body. *Also called CAT scan.*

::**PET (positron emission tomography) scan** a visual display of brain activity that detects where a radioactive form of glucose goes while the brain performs a given task.

::**MRI (magnetic resonance imaging)** a technique that uses magnetic fields and radio waves to produce computer-generated images of soft tissue. MRI scans show brain anatomy.

::**fMRI (functional MRI)** a technique for revealing bloodflow and, therefore, brain activity by comparing successive MRI scans. fMRI scans show brain function.

::**brainstem** the oldest part and central core of the brain, beginning where the spinal cord swells as it enters the skull; the brainstem is responsible for automatic survival functions.

::**medulla** [muh-DUL-uh] the base of the brainstem; controls heartbeat and breathing.

➤ **FIGURE 3B.4**
The brainstem and thalamus The brainstem, including the pons and medulla, is an extension of the spinal cord. The thalamus is attached to the top of the brainstem. The reticular formation passes through both structures.

Thalamus
Reticular formation
Pons
Brainstem
Medulla

CRITICAL THINKING

When Myers refers to "older" parts of the brain, he is highlighting the parts that are shared in common with other mammals and are therefore the earliest parts of the brain to evolve. Have students debate the following questions:

- If humans and other mammals share so many parts of the brain, what makes humans different from other mammals?

- Does explaining the brain from an evolutionary standpoint make you feel more or less different from other animals? Why?

TROUBLESHOOTING

Discussing the brain as having "older" structures points to the influence of evolution on the ways we think about the brain. Some students may feel that discussing evolution runs counter to religious or cultural beliefs. Focus this discussion on the ideas of how mammals share common parts of the nervous system. This commonality has allowed us to understand better both nonhuman animals and ourselves.

At this point, you may want to use **Classroom Exercise:** *Individual Differences in Physiological Functioning and Behavior* (p. 9) from Bolt's Teacher's Resource Binder.

TEACHING TIP

Identifying and labeling diagrams are a type of question that often shows up on the AP Exam. Give your students the opportunity to practice this type of question by having them label diagrams like the one in Figure 3B.4.

TROUBLESHOOTING

Make sure students know that the nerves from each side of the body cross over in the brainstem. The right side of the brain controls the left side of the body and vice versa. Students will need to know this later in the portion of the unit when they study hemisphere specialization.

 TEACHING TIP

The reticular formation is not very well understood in humans. If the studies with cats are any indication of similar functioning in humans, the reticular formation may be responsible for our ability to attend to new stimuli in the environment.

 INTERCONNECTING

Some research has indicated that the reticular formation may play a role in dreaming. The activation synthesis theory of dreams proposes that dream signals originate in the brainstem, and perhaps more specifically the reticular formation. The cortex then takes those signals and reorganizes them into the dream story as best it can.

 TEACHING TIP

All sensory information—except for smell—is routed through the thalamus, which sends the information to the appropriate cortex for processing. Smell, an "old" sense on the evolutionary scale, travels to the olfactory cortex and then to the thalamus for processing. It seems that our brains adapted other senses after smell, causing it them to be processed differently.

::**reticular formation** a nerve network in the brainstem that plays an important role in controlling arousal.

::**thalamus** [THAL-uh-muss] the brain's sensory switchboard, located on top of the brainstem; it directs messages to the sensory receiving areas in the cortex and transmits replies to the cerebellum and medulla.

::**cerebellum** [sehr-uh-BELL-um] the "little brain" at the rear of the brainstem; functions include processing sensory input and coordinating movement output and balance.

::**limbic system** doughnut-shaped neural system (including the *hippocampus, amygdala,* and *hypothalamus*) located below the cerebral hemispheres; associated with emotions and drives.

::**amygdala** [uh-MIG-duh-la] two lima bean–sized neural clusters in the limbic system; linked to emotion.

The brainstem is a crossover point, where most nerves to and from each side of the brain connect with the body's opposite side. This peculiar cross-wiring is but one of the brain's many surprises.

Inside the brainstem, between your ears, lies the **reticular** ("netlike") **formation**, a finger-shaped network of neurons that extends from the spinal cord right up to the thalamus. As the spinal cord's sensory input travels up to the thalamus, some of it travels through the reticular formation, which filters incoming stimuli and relays important information to other areas of the brain.

In 1949, Giuseppe Moruzzi and Horace Magoun discovered that electrically stimulating the reticular formation of a sleeping cat almost instantly produced an awake, alert animal. When Magoun *severed* a cat's reticular formation from higher brain regions, without damaging the nearby sensory pathways, the effect was equally dramatic: The cat lapsed into a coma from which it never awakened. Magoun could clap his hands by the cat's ear, even pinch it; still, no response. The conclusion? The reticular formation is involved in arousal.

The Thalamus

Sitting at the top of the brainstem is the **thalamus** (Figure 3B.4). This joined pair of egg-shaped structures acts as the brain's sensory switchboard. It receives information from all the senses except smell and routes it to the higher brain regions that deal with seeing, hearing, tasting, and touching. Think of the thalamus as being to sensory input what London is to England's trains: a hub through which traffic passes en route to various destinations. The thalamus also receives some of the higher brain's replies, which it then directs to the medulla and to the cerebellum.

The Cerebellum

Extending from the rear of the brainstem is the baseball-sized **cerebellum**, meaning "little brain," which is what its two wrinkled halves resemble (**FIGURE 3B.5**). As you will see in Unit 7A, the cerebellum enables one type of nonverbal learning and memory. It helps us judge time, modulate our emotions, and discriminate sounds and textures (Bower & Parsons, 2003). It also coordinates voluntary movement (with

➤ **FIGURE 3B.5**
The brain's organ of agility
Hanging at the back of the brain, the cerebellum coordinates our voluntary movements, as when David Beckham directs the ball precisely.

Cerebellum

Spinal cord

 TEACHING TIP

Research indicates that part of the cerebellum's function is to tell the brain what to expect from the body's own movements. S. Blakemore and her colleagues studied why people can't tickle themselves. Volunteers lay in a brain-scanning machine with their eyes closed. A plastic rod with a piece of soft foam tickled the participants' left palms. The volunteers were either tickling themselves or were being tickled. They concluded that the cerebellum tells the somatosensory cortex what sensation to expect and this dampens the tickling sensation.

Blakemore, S., Wolpert, D., & Frith, C. (1998). Central cancellation of self-produced tickle sensation. *Nature Neuroscience, 1,* 635-640.

assistance from the pons). When soccer great David Beckham fires the ball into the net with a perfectly timed kick, give his cerebellum some credit. If you injured your cerebellum, you would have difficulty walking, keeping your balance, or shaking hands. Your movements would be jerky and exaggerated. Under alcohol's influence on the cerebellum, walking may lack coordination, as many a driver has learned after being pulled over and given a roadside test.

Note: These older brain functions all occur without any conscious effort. This illustrates another of our recurring themes: *Our brain processes most information outside of our awareness.* We are aware of the *results* of our brain's labor (say, our current visual experience) but not of *how* we construct the visual image. Likewise, whether we are asleep or awake, our brainstem manages its life-sustaining functions, freeing our newer brain regions to think, talk, dream, or savor a memory.

The Limbic System

At the border ("limbus") between the brain's older parts and the *cerebral hemispheres*—the two halves of the brain—is the **limbic system** (FIGURE 3B.6). We will see in Unit 7A how one limbic system component, the *hippocampus*, processes memory. (If animals or humans lose their hippocampus to surgery or injury, they become unable to process new memories of facts and episodes.) For now, let's look at the limbic system's links to emotions (such as fear and anger) and to basic motives (such as those for food and sex).

The Amygdala

In the limbic system, two lima bean–sized neural clusters, the **amygdala**, influence aggression and fear (FIGURE 3B.7). In 1939, psychologist Heinrich Klüver and neurosurgeon Paul Bucy surgically lesioned the part of a rhesus monkey's brain that included the amygdala. The result? The normally ill-tempered monkey turned into the most mellow of creatures. Poke it, pinch it, do virtually anything that normally would trigger a ferocious response, and still the animal remained placid. In later studies with other wild animals, including the lynx, wolverine, and wild rat, researchers noted the same effect. What then might happen if we electrically stimulated the amygdala in a normally placid domestic animal, such as a cat? Do so in one spot and the cat prepares to attack, hissing with its back arched, its pupils dilated, its hair on end. Move the electrode only slightly within the amygdala, cage the cat with a small mouse, and now it cowers in terror.

These experiments confirm the amygdala's role in rage and fear, including the perception of these emotions and the processing of emotional memories (Anderson & Phelps, 2000; Poremba & Gabriel, 2001). Still, we must be careful. The brain is not neatly organized into structures that correspond to our categories of behavior. Aggressive and fearful

"Consciousness is a small part of what the brain does."
Neuroscientist Joseph LeDoux, in "Mastery of Emotions," 2006

➤ FIGURE 3B.6
The limbic system This neural system sits between the brain's older parts and its cerebral hemispheres. The limbic system's hypothalamus controls the nearby pituitary gland.

Hypothalamus
Pituitary gland
Amygdala
Hippocampus

➤ FIGURE 3B.7
The amygdala

Mtoonrunner Design Ltd, UK

Frank Siteman/Stock, Boston

Aggression as a brain state Back arched and fur fluffed, this fierce cat is ready to attack. Electrical stimulation of a cat's amygdala provokes reactions such as the one shown here, suggesting its role in emotions like rage. Which division of the autonomic nervous system is activated by such stimulation? (Answer below.)

▲ ... The cat would be aroused via its sympathetic nervous system.

TROUBLESHOOTING

Typically, the thalamus, cerebellum, and limbic system are a part of the midbrain rather than part of the brainstem. They are mainly divided this way due to the functions they govern. Brainstem sections govern basic functions like heartbeat and breathing. Midbrain sections govern hormones, memory processing, and sensory input. These functions are a little less vital, but no less important, than those governed by the brainstem.

INTERCONNECTING

Notice how Myers points out the further discussion of hippocampus function in Unit 7A. Be sure students know how the parts of the brain are connected to other content:

● Amygdala: Unit 8: Part B: Emotions, Stress, and Health

● Thalamus: Unit 4: Sensation and Perception

● Hypothalamus: Unit 8: Part A: Motivation

● Reticular Formation: Unit 5: States of Consciousness

 TEACHING TIP

The amygdala and the frontal lobes work together to regulate emotional responses. The amygdala supplies the emotional feelings while the frontal lobe makes the judgment regarding the appropriate expression of the emotion. Have students imagine what types of behaviors would occur if each of these components had to work alone instead of together.

 TEACHING TIP

At this point, you may want to use **Lecture/Discussion Topic and Video:** *The Case of Clive Wearing* (p. 9) from Bolt's Teacher's Resource Binder.

UNIT 3B

INTERCONNECTING

Studies in rats have shown that the hypothalamus can be divided into two sections: the lateral side (LH), which controls hunger, and the ventromedial side (VMH), which controls satiety. In these studies, stimulation to the LH produced behaviors that led to seeking out food while lesions to the VMH caused rats to overeat to the point of becoming obese. This function of the hypothalamus will be discussed in greater detail in Unit 8A: Motivation.

TEACHING TIP

Make sure students realize that the hypothalamus controls all aspects of behavior that are regulated by hormones—eating, the stress response, and sexual desire.

INTERCONNECTING

Help students remember the functioning of the hypothalamus by reminding them that it controls the function of the pituitary gland, studied in Unit 3A. The pituitary gland, being the "master gland," directs the hormonal system in its functioning. If our hormones regulate everything from hunger to stress reactions to sex, then the hypothalamus really does control the body!

---

behavior involves neural activity in many brain levels. Even within the limbic system, stimulating structures other than the amygdala can evoke such behavior. If you charge your cell phone's dead battery, you can activate the phone and make a call. Yet the battery is merely one link in an integrated system that makes a cell phone work.

The Hypothalamus

Just below (*hypo*) the thalamus is the **hypothalamus** (**FIGURE 3B.8**), an important link in the chain of command governing bodily maintenance. Some neural clusters in the hypothalamus influence hunger; others regulate thirst, body temperature, and sexual behavior.

➤ **FIGURE 3B.8**
The hypothalamus This small but important structure, colored yellow/orange in this MRI scan photograph, helps keep the body's internal environment in a steady state.

The hypothalamus both monitors blood chemistry and takes orders from other parts of the brain. For example, thinking about sex (in your brain's cerebral cortex) can stimulate your hypothalamus to secrete hormones. These hormones in turn trigger the adjacent "master gland," the pituitary (see Figure 3B.6), to influence hormones released by other glands. (As we saw in Unit 3A, we again see here the interplay between the nervous and endocrine systems: The brain influences the endocrine system, which in turn influences the brain.)

A remarkable discovery about the hypothalamus illustrates how progress in science often occurs—when curious, open-minded investigators make an unexpected observation. Two young McGill University neuropsychologists, James Olds and Peter Milner (1954), were trying to implant an electrode in a rat's reticular formation when they made a magnificent mistake: They incorrectly placed the electrode in what they later discovered was a region of the rat's hypothalamus (Olds, 1975). Curiously, as if seeking more stimulation, the rat kept returning to the location where it had been stimulated by this misplaced electrode. On discovering their mistake, Olds and Milner alertly realized they had stumbled upon a brain center that provides a pleasurable reward.

In a meticulous series of experiments, Olds (1958) went on to locate other "pleasure centers," as he called them. (What the rats actually experience only they know, and they aren't telling. Rather than attribute human feelings to rats, today's scientists refer to *reward centers*, not "pleasure centers.") When allowed to press pedals to trigger their own stimulation in these areas, rats would sometimes do so at a feverish pace—up to 7000 times per hour—until they dropped from exhaustion. Moreover, to get this stimulation, they would even cross an electrified floor that a starving rat would not cross to reach food (**FIGURE 3B.9**).

> "If you were designing a robot vehicle to walk into the future and survive, . . . you'd wire it up so that behavior that ensured the survival of the self or the species—like sex and eating—would be naturally reinforcing."
>
> Candace Pert (1986)

::**hypothalamus** [hi-po-THAL-uh-muss] a neural structure lying below (*hypo*) the thalamus; it directs several maintenance activities (eating, drinking, body temperature), helps govern the endocrine system via the pituitary gland, and is linked to emotion and reward.

➤ **FIGURE 3B.9**
Rat with an implanted electrode With an electrode implanted in a reward center of its hypothalamus, the rat readily crosses an electrified grid, accepting the painful shocks, to press a pedal that sends electrical impulses to that center.

Stimulation pedal   Electrified grid

TEACHING TIP

At this point, you may want to use **Student Project:** *The Human Brain Coloring Book* (p. 12) from Bolt's Teacher's Resource Binder.

Similar reward centers in or near the hypothalamus were later discovered in many other species, including goldfish, dolphins, and monkeys. In fact, animal research has revealed both a general reward system that triggers the release of the neurotransmitter dopamine, and specific centers associated with the pleasures of eating, drinking, and sex. Animals, it seems, come equipped with built-in systems that reward activities essential to survival.

Experimenters have found new ways of using limbic stimulation to control animals' actions. By using brain stimulation to reward rats for turning left or right, Sanjiv Talwar and his colleagues (2002) trained previously caged rats to navigate natural environments (FIGURE 3B.10). By pressing buttons on a laptop, the researchers can direct a rat—which carries a receiver, power source, and video camera on a backpack—to turn on cue, climb trees, scurry along branches, and turn around and come back down. Their work suggests future applications in search-and-rescue operations.

Do we humans also have limbic centers for pleasure? Indeed we do. To calm violent patients, one neurosurgeon implanted electrodes in such areas. Stimulated patients reported mild pleasure; however, unlike Olds' rats, they were not driven to a frenzy (Deutsch, 1972; Hooper & Teresi, 1986). Some researchers believe that addictive disorders, such as alcohol dependence, drug abuse, and binge eating, may stem from a *reward deficiency syndrome*—a genetically disposed deficiency in the natural brain systems for pleasure and well-being that leads people to crave whatever provides that missing pleasure or relieves negative feelings (Blum et al., 1996).

FIGURE 3B.11 locates the brain areas discussed in this unit, including the cerebral cortex, our next topic.

➤ **FIGURE 3B.10**

Ratbot on a pleasure cruise When stimulated by remote control, this rat could be guided to navigate across a field and even up a tree.

➤ **FIGURE 3B.11**
Brain structures and their functions

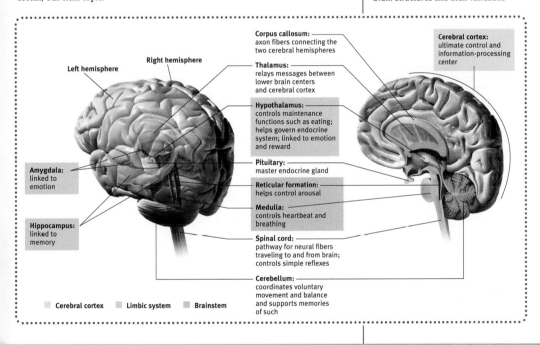

Left hemisphere

Right hemisphere

Corpus callosum: axon fibers connecting the two cerebral hemispheres

Cerebral cortex: ultimate control and information-processing center

Thalamus: relays messages between lower brain centers and cerebral cortex

Hypothalamus: controls maintenance functions such as eating; helps govern endocrine system; linked to emotion and reward

Amygdala: linked to emotion

Pituitary: master endocrine gland

Reticular formation: helps control arousal

Medulla: controls heartbeat and breathing

Hippocampus: linked to memory

Spinal cord: pathway for neural fibers traveling to and from brain; controls simple reflexes

Cerebellum: coordinates voluntary movement and balance and supports memories of such

Cerebral cortex   Limbic system   Brainstem

The neurotransmitters that work in reward centers are similar to drugs like cocaine and LSD. These drugs activate the reward centers, leading to the desire to take the drugs again. The pleasurable experience of taking drugs is due to this activation of the reward centers.

TROUBLESHOOTING

Students often confuse the names of the hypothalamus and the hippocampus. Help students use mnemonic devices for each part so that students can process the meaning of the word rather than relying on acoustic encoding.

TEACHING TIP

The connection between survival behavior and pleasurable sensations makes evolutionary sense. If behaviors such as eating, drinking, and sex are pleasurable, they are more likely to be repeated, thus leading to survival.

INTERCONNECTING

In Unit 6: Learning, students will learn about the Law of Effect, in which behaviors that are rewarded are more likely to be repeated and behaviors that are punished are not likely to be repeated. This law is supported physiologically by the discovery of reward centers in the brain.

TEACHING TIP

Neuroglia are another category of neural cells that provide the support network of cells surrounding the neurons and blood vessels of the brain and nervous system. They are thought to outnumber typical neurons 10 to 1. There are three types of neuroglia in the body:

- *Oligodendroglia* (o-lig-o-den-drog-glia) are cells found in the central nervous system (CNS) that produce myelin, the protective covering of axons that speed neural transmissions.

- *Schwann cells* perform the same function as oligodendroglia, but are found in the peripheral nervous system (PNS). Aside from location, the main difference between Schwann cells and oligodendroglia is that only Schwann cells can help axons regenerate.

- *Astrocytes* are star shaped and form most of the matrix in which neural cells are embedded and envelop blood vessels in the brain. They also absorb dead neural cells.

TEACHING TIP

The wrinkles on the brain are made by fissures and folds called gyri and sulci. Gyri (singular: gyrus) are the grooves in the brain. Sulci (singular: sulcus) are the humps in between the grooves.

● The people who first dissected and labeled the brain used the language of scholars—Latin and Greek. Their words are actually attempts at graphic description: For example, *cortex* means "bark," *cerebellum* is "little brain," and *thalamus* is "inner chamber." ●

::**cerebral** [seh-REE-bruhl] **cortex** the intricate fabric of interconnected neural cells covering the cerebral hemispheres; the body's ultimate control and information-processing center.

::**glial cells (glia)** cells in the nervous system that support, nourish, and protect neurons.

::**frontal lobes** portion of the cerebral cortex lying just behind the forehead; involved in speaking and muscle movements and in making plans and judgments.

::**parietal** [puh-RYE-uh-tuhl] **lobes** portion of the cerebral cortex lying at the top of the head and toward the rear; receives sensory input for touch and body position.

::**occipital** [ahk-SIP-uh-tuhl] **lobes** portion of the cerebral cortex lying at the back of the head; includes areas that receive information from the visual fields.

::**temporal lobes** portion of the cerebral cortex lying roughly above the ears; includes the auditory areas, each receiving information primarily from the opposite ear.

::**motor cortex** an area at the rear of the frontal lobes that controls voluntary movements.

The Cerebral Cortex

3: What functions are served by the various cerebral cortex regions?

OLDER BRAIN NETWORKS SUSTAIN BASIC LIFE functions and enable memory, emotions, and basic drives. Newer neural networks within the *cerebrum*—the two large hemispheres that contribute 85 percent of the brain's weight—form specialized work teams that enable our perceiving, thinking, and speaking. Covering those hemispheres, like bark on a tree, is the **cerebral cortex**, a thin surface layer of interconnected neural cells. It is your brain's thinking crown, your body's ultimate control and information-processing center.

As we move up the ladder of animal life, the cerebral cortex expands, tight genetic controls relax, and the organism's adaptability increases. Frogs and other amphibians with a small cortex operate extensively on preprogrammed genetic instructions. The larger cortex of mammals offers increased capacities for learning and thinking, enabling them to be more adaptable. What makes us distinctively human mostly arises from the complex functions of our cerebral cortex.

Structure of the Cortex

If you opened a human skull, exposing the brain, you would see a wrinkled organ, shaped somewhat like the meat of an oversized walnut. Without these wrinkles, a flattened cerebral cortex would require triple the area—roughly that of a very large pizza. The brain's ballooning left and right hemispheres are filled mainly with axons connecting the cortex to the brain's other regions. The cerebral cortex—that thin surface layer—contains some 20 to 23 billion nerve cells and 300 trillion synaptic connections (de Courten-Myers, 2005). Being human takes a lot of nerve.

Supporting these billions of nerve cells are nine times as many spidery **glial cells** ("glue cells"). Neurons are like queen bees; on their own they cannot feed or sheathe themselves. Glial cells are worker bees. They provide nutrients and insulating myelin, guide neural connections, and mop up ions and neurotransmitters. Glia may also play a role in learning and thinking. By "chatting" with neurons they may participate in information transmission and memory (Miller, 2005).

Moving up the ladder of animal life, the proportion of glia to neurons increases. A recent postmortem analysis of Einstein's brain did not find more or larger-than-usual neurons, but it did reveal a much greater concentration of glial cells than found in an average Albert's head (Fields, 2004).

Stepping back to consider the whole cortex, each hemisphere is divided into four *lobes*, geographic subdivisions separated by prominent *fissures*, or folds (**FIGURE 3B.12**). Starting at the front of your brain and moving over the top, there are the **frontal lobes** (behind your forehead), the **parietal lobes** (at the top and to the rear), and the **occipital lobes** (at the back of your head). Reversing direction and moving forward, just above your ears, you find the **temporal lobes**. Each of the four lobes carries out many functions, and many functions require the interplay of several lobes.

Functions of the Cortex

More than a century ago, autopsies of people who had been partially paralyzed or speechless revealed damaged cortical areas. But this rather crude evidence did not convince researchers that specific parts of the cortex perform specific complex functions. After all, if control of speech and movement were diffused across the cortex,

---

DEMO

Explain to students that the deeply convoluted surface of the brain is most strongly linked to intelligence. Because of its wrinkled appearance in humans, only about a third of it is visible on the surface. Illustrate the surface area of the cortex by taping together two 11" x 17" sheets of paper (large-size copy paper). Before crumpling the paper into a ball, say: "This sheet represents the approximate surface area of that thin sheet of neural tissue that we call the cerebral cortex. How can we fit it inside a skull small enough, along with the rest of the fetus, to be delivered through the mother's birth canal?" *(Nature's answer is to crumple it up.)*

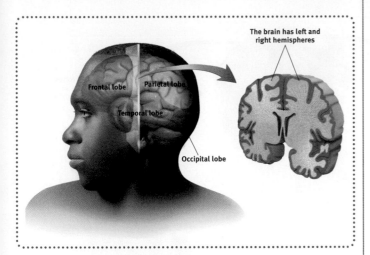

Frontal lobe

Parietal lobe

Temporal lobe

Occipital lobe

The brain has left and right hemispheres

➤ FIGURE 3B.12
The cortex and its basic subdivisions

damage to almost any area might produce the same effect. A television with its power cord cut would go dead, but we would be fooling ourselves if we thought we had "localized" the picture in the cord.

Motor Functions

Scientists had better luck in localizing simpler brain functions. For example, in 1870, when German physicians Gustav Fritsch and Eduard Hitzig applied mild electrical stimulation to parts of a dog's cortex, they made an important discovery: They could make parts of its body move. The effects were selective: Stimulation caused movement only when applied to an arch-shaped region at the back of the frontal lobe, running roughly ear-to-ear across the top of the brain. Moreover, stimulating parts of this region in the left or right hemisphere caused movements of specific body parts on the *opposite* side of the body. Fritsch and Hitzig had discovered what is now called the **motor cortex** (**FIGURE 3B.13** on the next page).

Mapping the Motor Cortex Lucky for brain surgeons and their patients, the brain has no sensory receptors. Knowing this, Otfrid Foerster and Wilder Penfield were able to map the motor cortex in hundreds of wide-awake patients by stimulating different cortical areas and observing the body's responses. They discovered that body areas requiring precise control, such as the fingers and mouth, occupied the greatest amount of cortical space.

Spanish neuroscientist José Delgado repeatedly demonstrated the mechanics of motor behavior. In one human patient, he stimulated a spot on the left motor cortex that triggered the right hand to make a fist. Asked to keep the fingers open during the next stimulation, the patient, whose fingers closed despite his best efforts, remarked, "I guess, Doctor, that your electricity is stronger than my will" (Delgado, 1969, p. 114).

More recently, scientists have been able to predict a monkey's arm motion a tenth of a second before it moves—by repeatedly measuring motor cortex activity preceding specific arm movements (Gibbs, 1996). Such findings, some researchers believe, have opened the door to a new generation of *prosthetics* (artificial body part replacements).

● *Demonstration:* Try moving your right hand in a circular motion, as if polishing a table. Now start your right foot doing the same motion synchronized with the hand. Now reverse the foot motion (but not the hand). Tough, huh? But easier if you try moving the *left* foot opposite to the right hand. The left and right limbs are controlled by opposite sides of the brain. So their opposed activities interfere less with each other. ●

TEACHING TIP

The lobes of the brain are demarcated by major gyri on the cortex:

- The frontal lobes are bordered in the rear by the central fissure, a long gyrus going vertically down the center of the cortex. This gyrus is more prominent on the left side.

- The temporal lobes are bordered on the top by the lateral fissure, a long gyrus running horizontally from front to back.

- The two hemispheres are separated by the longitudinal fissure, the largest of the gyri. This deep fissure separates the two hemispheres almost completely down to the corpus callosum.

TEACHING TIP

When Albert Einstein died in 1955, Dr. Thomas Harvey, with the family's consent, kept the brain for scientific study:

- While the overall size of Einstein's brain was average, the region called the inferior parietal lobe, where visual-spatial cognition, mathematical thought, and imagery of movement are controlled, was 15 percent wider than normal. Einstein's insights were often the result of visual images that he translated into mathematics. For example, his special theory of relativity was based on what he thought it would be like to ride through space on a beam of light.

- A feature known as the Sylvian fissure (a groove that normally runs through the brain tissue) was shorter than average. This meant that the brain cells were packed more closely together, permitting more interconnections and cross-referencing of information.

- Critics observe that while Einstein's brain may well be different, the cause-effect relationship is uncertain. The differences may be the result of strenuous mental exercise, not the cause of genius.

Lemonick, M. D. (1999, June 28). Was Einstein's brain built for brilliance? *Time*, p. 54.

Witelson, S. F., Kigar, D. L., & Harvey, T. (1999). The exceptional brain of Albert Einstein. *The Lancet, 353,* 2149–2153.

UNIT 3B

Help students realize that the lobes of the brain are plural—there are two of each lobe, one for each hemisphere. Often, students will talk about the "frontal lobe" and forget that there are actually two frontal, parietal, occipital, and temporal lobes each.

 TEACHING TIP

Figure 3B.13 features the sensory homunculus, a diagram showing how the cortex is parsed out to different parts of the body according to function. These diagrams show dramatically how much cortex is devoted to complex areas of the body like the face and hands and how little is devoted to rather simple areas such as the calf and back.

At this point, you may want to use **Classroom Exercise: *The Sensory Homunculus*** (p. 12) from Bolt's Teacher's Resource Binder.

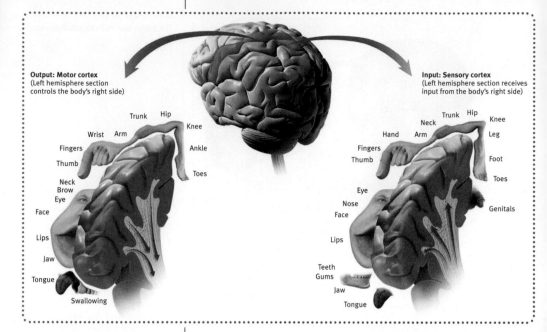

Output: Motor cortex
(Left hemisphere section controls the body's right side)

Input: Sensory cortex
(Left hemisphere section receives input from the body's right side)

➤ **FIGURE 3B.13**
Left hemisphere tissue devoted to each body part in the motor cortex and the sensory cortex As you can see from this classic though inexact representation, the amount of cortex devoted to a body part is not proportional to that part's size. Rather, the brain devotes more tissue to sensitive areas and to areas requiring precise control. Thus, the fingers have a greater representation in the cortex than does the upper arm.

Neural Prosthetics By similarly eavesdropping on the brain, could we enable someone—perhaps a paralyzed person—to move a robotic limb or command a cursor to write an e-mail or surf the Net? To find out, Brown University brain researchers implanted 100 tiny recording electrodes in the motor cortexes of three monkeys (Nicolelis & Chapin, 2002; Serruya et al., 2002). As the monkeys used a joystick to move a cursor to follow a moving red target (to gain rewards), the researchers matched the brain signals with the arm movements. Then they programmed a computer to monitor the signals and operate the joystick without the monkey's help. When a monkey merely thought about a move, the mind-reading computer moved the cursor with nearly the same proficiency as had the reward-seeking monkey. In a follow-up experiment, two monkeys were trained to control a robot arm that could reach for and grab food (Velliste et al., 2008).

Research has also recorded messages not from the motor neurons that directly control a monkey's arm, but from a brain area involved in planning and intention (Musallam et al., 2004). While the monkeys awaited a cue that told them to reach toward a spot (to get a juice reward) that had flashed on a screen in one of up to eight locations, a computer program recorded activity in this planning-intention brain area. By matching this neural brain activity to the monkey's subsequent pointing, the mind-reading researchers could now program a cursor to move in response to the monkey's thinking. Monkey think, computer do.

If this technique works with motor brain areas, why not use it to capture the words a person can think but cannot say (for example, after a stroke)? Neuroscientist Richard Andersen (2004, 2005) speculates that researchers could implant electrodes in speech areas, "ask a patient to think of different words and observe how the cells fire in different ways. So you build up your database, and then when the patient thinks of the word, you compare the signals with your database, and you can predict

 TROUBLESHOOTING TS

Help students remember that the motor cortex is in the frontal lobe and the sensory cortex is in the parietal lobe. The frontal lobe's decision-making function works with the motor cortex to create purposeful movement. The parietal lobe's association areas work with the sensory cortex to process sensory signals for accurate perception.

Mind over matter Guided by a tiny, 100-electrode brain implant, monkeys learned to control a mechanical arm that can grab snacks and put them in their mouth (Velliste et al., 2008). Implantable electrode grids are not yet permanently effective, but such research raises hopes that people with paralyzed limbs may someday be able to use their own brain signals to control computers and robotic prosthetic limbs.

the words they're thinking. Then you take this output and connect it to a speech synthesizer. This would be identical to what we're doing for motor control."

In 2004, the U.S. Food and Drug Administration approved the first clinical trial of neural prosthetics with paralyzed humans (Pollack, 2004, 2006). The first patient, a paralyzed 25-year-old man, was able to mentally control a television, draw shapes on a computer screen, and play video games—all thanks to an aspirin-sized chip with 100 microelectrodes recording activity in his motor cortex (Hochberg et al., 2006).

Sensory Functions

If the motor cortex sends messages out to the body, where does the cortex receive the incoming messages? Penfield also identified the cortical area that specializes in receiving information from the skin senses and from the movement of body parts. This area at the front of the parietal lobes, parallel to and just behind the motor cortex, we now call the **sensory cortex** (Figure 3B.13). Stimulate a point on the top of this band of tissue and a person may report being touched on the shoulder; stimulate some point on the side and the person may feel something on the face.

The more sensitive the body region, the larger the sensory cortex area devoted to it (Figure 3B.13). Your supersensitive lips project to a larger brain area than do your toes, which is one reason we kiss with our lips rather than touch toes. Rats have a large area of the brain devoted to their whisker sensations, and owls to their hearing sensations.

Scientists have identified additional areas where the cortex receives input from senses other than touch. At this moment, you are receiving visual information in the visual cortex in your occipital lobes, at the very back of your brain (**FIGURES 3B.14** and **3B.15** on the next page). A bad enough bash there would make you blind. Stimulated there, you might see flashes of light or dashes of color. (In a sense, we *do* have eyes in the back of our head!) From your occipital lobes, visual information goes to other areas that specialize in tasks such as identifying words, detecting emotions, and recognizing faces.

::**sensory cortex** area at the front of the parietal lobes that registers and processes body touch and movement sensations.

TEACHING TIP

Wilder Penfield is a famous name in neurosurgery. Penfield studied at Oxford on a Rhodes scholarship under Charles Sherrington, the discoverer of the synapse. Penfield, along with colleague Herbert Jasper, perfected a technique to treat epilepsy through surgery by selectively lesioning cells in the brain that triggered the seizures. By keeping patients conscious on the operating table, he was able to stimulate cells in the brain and map areas before destroying the offending cells.

TEACHING TIP

The sensory homunculus, largely created by Wilder Penfield through his mapping surgeries to treat epilepsy, has been essentially unaltered since their creation in the 1950s.

TEACHING TIP

At this point, you may want to use **Classroom Exercise: *Neuroscience and Moral Judgments*** (p. 10) from Bolt's Teacher's Resource Binder.

> ➤ **FIGURE 3B.14**
New technology shows the brain in action This fMRI (functional MRI) scan shows the visual cortex in the occipital lobes activated (color representation of increased bloodflow) as a research participant looks at a photo. When the person stops looking, the region instantly calms down.

> ➤ **FIGURE 3B.15**
The visual cortex and auditory cortex The visual cortex of the occipital lobes at the rear of your brain receives input from your eyes. The auditory cortex, in your temporal lobes—above your ears—receives information from your ears.

::**association areas** areas of the cerebral cortex that are not involved in primary motor or sensory functions; rather, they are involved in higher mental functions such as learning, remembering, thinking, and speaking.

INTERCONNECTING

Help students realize that the auditory hallucinations people with schizophrenia experience are triggered in the brain without external stimulation. People with schizophrenia are actually hearing voices, but those voices have no external basis. The MRI scans of these patients show that there is a biological basis for these types of hallucinations.

TEACHING TIP

- The *frontal lobe* controls thinking and judgment, so have students tap their foreheads like they are thinking through a difficult decision.

- The *temporal lobe* controls hearing, and it is located just beside the ears.

- The *occipital lobe* controls vision, so have students recall a time when they've gotten hit in the back of the head. Typically when this happens, people "see stars," since their visual system is momentarily impaired.

- The *parietal lobe* controls touch and sensory processing, so have students scratch the tops of their heads like they are washing their hair. This will help them remember that touch is controlled by that part of the "head."

Any sound you now hear is processed by your auditory cortex in your temporal lobes (Figure 3B.15). (If you think of your clenched fist as your brain, and hold it in front of you, your thumb would roughly correspond to one of your temporal lobes.) Most of this auditory information travels a circuitous route from one ear to the auditory receiving area above your opposite ear. If stimulated there, you might hear a sound. MRI scans of people with schizophrenia reveal active auditory areas in the temporal lobes during auditory hallucinations (Lennox et al., 1999). Even the phantom ringing sound experienced by people with hearing loss is—if heard in one ear—associated with activity in the temporal lobe on the brain's opposite side (Muhlnickel, 1998).

Association Areas

So far, we have pointed out small areas of the cortex that either receive sensory input or direct muscular output. In humans, that leaves a full three-fourths of the thin, wrinkled layer, the cerebral cortex, uncommitted to sensory or muscular activity. What, then, goes on in this vast region of the brain? Neurons in these **association areas** (the peach-colored areas in **FIGURE 3B.16**) integrate information. They link sensory inputs with stored memories—a very important part of thinking.

> ➤ **FIGURE 3B.16**
Areas of the cortex in four mammals More intelligent animals have increased "uncommitted" or association areas of the cortex. These vast areas of the brain are responsible for integrating and acting on information received and processed by sensory areas.

Rat
Cat
Chimpanzee
Human
■ Motor areas
■ Sensory areas
■ Association areas

TEACHING TIP

The idea that we only use ten percent of our brains is a myth that was developed in the last century. As brain research techniques have evolved, scientists have found that most of the brain is active at any given moment. Those areas that were thought to be unused were probably the association areas described in the text.

Electrically probing the association areas doesn't trigger any observable response. So, unlike the sensory and motor areas, association area functions cannot be neatly mapped. Their silence has led to what Donald McBurney (1996, p. 44) calls "one of the hardiest weeds in the garden of psychology": the claim that we ordinarily use only 10 percent of our brains. (If true, wouldn't this imply a 90 percent chance that a bullet to your brain would land in an unused area?) Surgically lesioned animals and brain-damaged humans bear witness that association areas are not dormant. Rather, these areas interpret, integrate, and act on information processed by the sensory areas.

Association areas are found in all four lobes. In the frontal lobes, they enable judgment, planning, and processing of new memories. People with damaged frontal lobes may have intact memories, high scores on intelligence tests, and great cake-baking skills. Yet they would not be able to plan ahead to *begin* baking a cake for a birthday party (Huey et al., 2006).

Frontal lobe damage also can alter personality, removing a person's inhibitions. Consider the classic case of railroad worker Phineas Gage. One afternoon in 1848, Gage, then 25 years old, was packing gunpowder into a rock with a tamping iron. A spark ignited the gunpowder, shooting the rod up through his left cheek and out the top of his skull, leaving his frontal lobes massively damaged (FIGURE 3B.17). To everyone's amazement, he was immediately able to sit up and speak, and after the wound healed he returned to work. But the affable, soft-spoken Phineas Gage was now irritable, profane, and dishonest. Although his mental abilities and memories were intact, his personality was not. This person, said his friends, was "no longer Gage." He eventually lost his job and ended up earning his living as a fairground exhibit.

With his frontal lobes ruptured, Gage's moral compass had disconnected from his behavior. Similar impairments to moral judgment have appeared in more recent studies of people with damaged frontal lobes. Not only may they become less inhibited (without the frontal lobe brakes on their impulses), but their moral judgments seem unrestrained by normal emotions. Would you advocate pushing someone in front of a runaway boxcar to save five others? Most people do not, but those with damage to a brain area behind the eyes often do (Koenigs et al., 2007).

Association areas also perform other mental functions. In the parietal lobes, parts of which were large and unusually shaped in Einstein's normal-weight brain, they enable mathematical and spatial reasoning (Witelson et al., 1999). An area on the underside of the right temporal lobe enables us to recognize faces. If a stroke or head injury destroyed this area of your brain, you would still be able to describe facial features and to recognize someone's gender and approximate age, yet be strangely unable to identify the person as, say, your grandmother.

Nevertheless, we should be wary of using pictures of brain "hot spots" to create a new phrenology that locates complex functions in precise brain areas (Uttal, 2001). Complex mental functions don't reside in any one place. There is no one spot in a rat's small association cortex that, when damaged, will obliterate its ability to learn or remember a maze. Memory, language, and attention result from the synchronized activity among distinct brain areas (Knight, 2007).

➤ FIGURE 3B.17
Phineas Gage reconsidered Using measurements of his skull (which was kept as a medical record) and modern neuroimaging techniques, researcher Hanna Damasio and her colleagues (1994) have reconstructed the probable path of the rod through Gage's brain.

TEACHING TIP

The story of Phineas Gage has become one of the most famous in all of psychology. The world in which he lived was shocked by his injury, but mainly because he survived and was able to perform most daily functions. His complete personality change was an early case study showing how the frontal lobes work with other parts of the brain to create a working whole.

INTERCONNECTING

Brain research relies heavily on case studies to learn more about functioning and anatomy in humans. Most brain research would be unethical to perform on both humans and nonhuman animals, so researchers have to wait for naturally occurring injuries to happen in order to learn more about how the brain works. Ask your students, "How many of you would volunteer to have part of your brain lesioned to learn more about the cause of Alzheimer's disease or the effects of brain cancer?" It's likely that none would seriously volunteer for such research.

TROUBLESHOOTING

Myers points out that we should be wary of thinking that the brain has "hot spots" of functioning, avoiding the idea that certain functions reside in one area of the brain or another. This is an important point to make with students just learning about biological bases of behavior. What we learn at this point in psychology is the most basic understanding of neuroscience. The whole picture of the field is much more complex since brain function is interconnected.

UNIT 3B

::**aphasia** impairment of language, usually caused by left hemisphere damage either to Broca's area (impairing speaking) or to Wernicke's area (impairing understanding).

::**Broca's area** controls language expression—an area, usually in the left frontal lobe, that directs the muscle movements involved in speech.

::**Wernicke's area** controls language reception—a brain area involved in language comprehension and expression; usually in the left temporal lobe.

INTERCONNECTING

The study of language is one of the most complex fields of study. Just studying the complexity of how language is processed in the brain provides a clue to how difficult it is to master an in-depth knowledge of how language works. Learn more about language in Unit 7B.

TEACHING TIP

Is language only located in the left hemisphere? Michael Gazzaniga reports the case of V. J., a left-handed and divided-brain woman whose case challenges notions of where the capacity for language resides. When a word is presented to her left visual field and thus processed by the right half of her brain, she can write it but not say it. When a word is presented to her right visual field and thus processed by the left hemisphere, she can say it but not write it. This is the first clear scientific evidence that in some people the capacities for spoken and written language may be located in different hemispheres. Linguist Steven Pinker thinks that V. J.'s case provides evidence that reading and writing rose separately from spoken language and may be wired into the brain wherever there are "spare areas."

Language

4: What brain areas are involved in language processing?

We think of speaking and reading, or writing and reading, or singing and speaking as merely different examples of the same general ability—language. But consider this curious finding: **Aphasia**, an impaired use of language, can result from damage to any one of several cortical areas. Even more curious, some people with aphasia can speak fluently but cannot read (despite good vision), while others can comprehend what they read but cannot speak. Still others can write but not read, read but not write, read numbers but not letters, or sing but not speak. What does this tell us about the mystery of how we use language, and how did researchers solve this mystery?

Clue 1 In 1865, French physician Paul Broca reported that after damage to a specific area of the left frontal lobe (later called Broca's area) a person would struggle to speak words while still being able to sing familiar songs and comprehend speech. Damage to Broca's area disrupts speaking.

Clue 2 In 1874, German investigator Carl Wernicke discovered that after damage to a specific area of the left temporal lobe (Wernicke's area) people could speak only meaningless words. Asked to describe a picture that showed two boys stealing cookies behind a woman's back, one patient responded: "Mother is away her working her work to get her better, but when she's looking the two boys looking the other part. She's working another time" (Geschwind, 1979). Damage to Wernicke's area also disrupts understanding.

Clue 3 A third brain area, the angular gyrus, is involved in reading aloud. It receives visual information from the visual area and recodes it into an auditory form, which Wernicke's area uses to derive its meaning. Damage to the angular gyrus leaves a person able to speak and understand, but unable to read aloud.

Clue 4 Nerve fibers interconnect these brain areas.

A century after Broca's and Wernicke's findings, Norman Geschwind assembled these and other clues into an explanation of how we use language (FIGURES 3B.18 and 3B.19). When you read aloud, the words (1) register in the visual area, (2) are relayed to a second brain area, the angular gyrus, which transforms the words into an auditory code that (3) is received and understood in the nearby Wernicke's area, and (4) is sent to Broca's area, which (5) controls the motor cortex as it creates the pronounced word. Depending on which link in this chain is damaged, a different form of aphasia occurs.

Today's neuroscience continues to enrich our understanding of language processing. We now know that more sites are involved than those portrayed in Figure 3B.19, and that the "map" can vary from person to person. Moreover, fMRI scans reveal that different neural networks are activated by nouns and verbs, and by one's native language and a second language learned later in life (Perani & Abutalebi, 2005; Shapiro et al., 2006). For example, adults who learned a second language early in life use the *same* patch of frontal lobe tissue when recounting an event in either the native or the second language. Those who learned their second tongue after childhood display activity in an adjacent brain area while using their second language (Kim et al., 1997).

Still, the big point to remember is this: *In processing language, as in other forms of information processing, the brain operates by dividing its mental functions—speaking, perceiving, thinking, remembering—into subfunctions.* Your conscious experience of reading this page *seems* indivisible, but your brain is computing each word's form, sound, and meaning using different neural networks (Posner & Carr, 1992). We will see this also in Unit 4, in the discussion of vision. Right now, assuming you have sight, you are experiencing a whole visual scene as if your eyes were video cameras projecting the scene into your brain. Actually, your brain is breaking that scene into specialized

TEACHING TIP

Help students remember what Broca's area is responsible for by relating the story of the area's discovery. Paul Broca was a French doctor in the late nineteenth century. In working with a patient named "Tan" (since that syllable was the only thing the patient could utter), Broca theorized that the damaged region in the frontal left hemisphere was responsible for spoken language, which was confirmed about a century later when CT scans of Tan's brain revealed the damaged area.

➤ FIGURE 3B.18
A simplified model of brain areas involved in language processing

Within the figure:
- **5. Motor cortex** (word is pronounced)
- **2. Angular gyrus** (transforms visual representations into an auditory code)
- **4. Broca's area** (controls speech muscles via the motor cortex)
- **1. Visual cortex** (receives written words as visual stimulation)
- **3. Wernicke's area** (interprets auditory code)

subtasks, such as discerning color, depth, movement, and form. And in vision as in language, a localized trauma that destroys one of these neural work teams may cause people to lose just one aspect of processing, as when a stroke destroys the ability to perceive movement. In both systems, each specialized neural network, having simultaneously done its own thing, then feeds its information to higher-level networks that combine the atoms of experience and relay them to progressively higher-level association areas, enabling us to recognize a face as "Grandmother."

This helps explain another funny finding. Functional MRI scans show that jokes playing on meaning ("Why don't sharks bite lawyers? . . . Professional courtesy") are processed in a different brain area than jokes playing on words ("What kind of lights did Noah use on the ark? . . . Flood lights") (Goel & Dolan, 2001). Scientists have even been able to predict, from the brain's response to various concrete nouns (things we experience with our senses), the brain's response to other concrete nouns (Mitchell et al., 2008). Think about it: *What you experience as a continuous, indivisible stream of experience is actually but the visible*

➤ FIGURE 3B.19
Brain activity when hearing, seeing, and speaking words PET scans such as these detect the activity of different areas of the brain.

(a) Hearing words (auditory cortex and Wernicke's area)
(b) Seeing words (visual cortex and angular gyrus)
(c) Speaking words (Broca's area and the motor cortex)

TEACHING TIP

The majority of left-handed people process language in the left hemisphere. The other lefties fall into two groups. Some have all language abilities in the right hemisphere. The second group shows a puzzling mixed pattern. But nobody has tracked these exceptions carefully enough to know exactly where their language abilities lie.

INTERCONNECTING

Help students identify the different lobes of the brain in Figure 3B.19. This will provide extra practice in learning the locations of the lobes on the cortex.

TEACHING TIP

At this point, you may want to use **Lecture/Discussion Topic: *The Smart-Talk Syndrome*** (p. 13) from Bolt's Teacher's Resource Binder.

tip of a subdivided information-processing iceberg, most of which lies beneath the surface of your awareness.

To sum up, the mind's subsystems are localized in particular brain regions, yet the brain acts as a unified whole. Moving your hand; recognizing faces; perceiving scenes; comprehending language—all depend on specific neural networks. Yet complex functions such as listening, learning, and loving involve the coordination of many brain areas. Together, these two principles—specialization and integration—describe the brain's functioning.

The Brain's Plasticity

5: To what extent can a damaged brain reorganize itself?

Our brains are sculpted not only by our genes but also by our experiences. MRI scans show that well-practiced pianists have a larger-than-usual auditory cortex area that encodes piano sounds (Bavelier et al., 2000; Pantev et al., 1998). In Unit 9, we'll focus more on how experience molds the brain, but for now, let's turn to evidence from studies of the brain's **plasticity,** its ability to modify itself after some types of damage.

Unlike cut skin, severed neurons usually do not regenerate (if your spinal cord were severed, you would probably be permanently paralyzed). And some very specific brain functions seem preassigned to particular areas. One newborn who suffered damage to the facial recognition areas on both temporal lobes never regained a normal ability to recognize faces (Farah et al., 2000). But there is good news: Some of the brain's neural tissue can *reorganize* in response to damage. It happens within all of us, as the brain repairs itself after little mishaps.

Our brains are most plastic when we are young children (Kolb, 1989; see also FIGURE 3B.20). *Constraint-induced therapy* aims to rewire brains by restraining a fully functioning limb and forcing use of the "bad hand" or the uncooperative leg. Gradually, the therapy reprograms the brain, improving the dexterity of a brain-damaged child or even an adult stroke victim (Taub, 2004). One stroke victim, a surgeon in his fifties, was put to work cleaning tables, with his good arm and hand restrained. Slowly, the bad arm recovered its skills. As the damaged brain functions migrated to other brain regions, he gradually learned to write again and even to play tennis (Doidge, 2007).

The brain's plasticity is good news for those who are blind or deaf. Blindness or deafness makes unused brain areas available for other uses (Amedi et al., 2005). If a blind person uses one finger to read Braille, the brain area dedicated to that finger expands as the sense of touch invades the visual cortex that normally helps people see (Barinaga, 1992a; Sadato et al., 1996). In Deaf people whose native language is sign, the temporal lobe area normally dedicated to hearing waits in vain for stimulation. Finally, it looks for

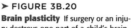

➤ **FIGURE 3B.20**

Brain plasticity If surgery or an injury destroys one part of a child's brain or, as in the case of this 6-year-old, even an entire *hemisphere* (removed to eliminate seizures), the brain will compensate by putting other areas to work. One Johns Hopkins medical team reflected on the child hemispherectomies they had performed. Although use of the opposite hand is compromised, they reported being "awed" by how well children retain their memory, personality, and humor after removal of either brain hemisphere (Vining et al., 1997). The younger the child, the greater the chance that the remaining hemisphere can take over the functions of the one that was surgically removed (Choi, 2008).

other signals to process, such as those from the visual system. That helps explain why some studies find that Deaf people have enhanced peripheral vision (Bosworth & Dobkins, 1999).

Plasticity is especially evident after serious damage. If a slow-growing left hemisphere tumor disrupts language, the right hemisphere may compensate (Thiel et al., 2006). Lose a finger and the sensory cortex that received its input will begin to receive input from the adjacent fingers, which then become more sensitive (Fox, 1984). Lost fingers also feature in another mysterious phenomenon. As Figure 3B.13 shows, the hand is between the sensory cortex's face and arm regions. When stroking the arm of someone whose hand had been amputated, V. S. Ramachandran found the person felt the sensations not only on the area stroked but also on the nonexistent ("phantom") fingers. Sensory fibers that terminate on adjacent areas had invaded the brain area vacated by the hand.

Although brain modification often takes the form of reorganization, evidence suggests that, contrary to long-held belief, adult mice and humans can also generate new brain cells (Jessberger et al., 2008). Monkey brains illustrate **neurogenesis** by forming thousands of new neurons each day. These baby neurons originate deep in the brain and may then migrate elsewhere and form connections with neighboring neurons (Gould, 2007). Master stem cells that can develop into any type of brain cell have also been discovered in the human embryo. If mass-produced in a lab and injected into a damaged brain, might neural stem cells turn themselves into replacements for lost brain cells? Might we someday be able to rebuild damaged brains, much as we reseed damaged lawns? Might new drugs spur the production of new nerve cells? Stay tuned. Today's biotech companies are hard at work on such possibilities (Gage, 2003). In the meantime, we can all benefit from other natural promoters of neurogenesis, such as exercise, sleep, and nonstressful but stimulating environments (Iso et al., 2007; Pereira et al., 2007; Stranahan et al., 2006).

Our Divided Brain

6: What do split brains reveal about the functions of our two brain hemispheres?

FOR MORE THAN A CENTURY, CLINICAL evidence has shown that the brain's two sides serve differing functions. This hemispheric specialization (or *lateralization*) is apparent after brain damage. Accidents, strokes, and tumors in the left hemisphere can impair reading, writing, speaking, arithmetic reasoning, and understanding. Similar lesions in the right hemisphere have effects that are less visibly dramatic.

By 1960, many interpreted these differences as evidence that the left hemisphere is the "dominant" or "major" hemisphere, and its silent companion to the right is the "subordinate" or "minor" hemisphere. Then researchers found that the "minor" right hemisphere was not so limited after all. The story of this discovery is a fascinating chapter in psychology's history.

Splitting the Brain

In 1961, two Los Angeles neurosurgeons, Philip Vogel and Joseph Bogen, speculated that major epileptic seizures were caused by an amplification of abnormal brain activity bouncing back and forth between the two cerebral hemispheres. If so, they

::**plasticity** the brain's ability to change, especially during childhood, by reorganizing after damage or by building new pathways based on experience.

::**neurogenesis** the formation of new neurons.

INTERCONNECTING

Phantom limb sensations can also be discussed in Unit 4: Sensation and Perception. V. S. Ramachandran's work with phantom limb sensations shows the interaction of sensation and perception as the brain tries to deal with the loss of a limb.

TEACHING TIP

Christopher Reeve devoted his later life to spinal cord research in an effort to find effective treatments for spinal cord injuries. Through intensive physical therapy, Reeve was able to regain some functioning in his lungs and his fingers, famously moving his finger during a televised event. His work showed that there is some hope for those with spinal cord damage to regain functioning, either through plasticity or neurogenesis.

 TEACHING TIP

Roger Sperry won the Nobel Prize for Medicine and Physiology in 1981 for his work on split-brain research. Starting out his academic career with a degree in English from Oberlin College, he quickly moved to Ph.D. work in zoology and postdoctoral work at the Yerkes Primate Laboratory under Karl Lashley. Dr. Sperry died in 1994.

UNIT 3B

➤ **FIGURE 3B.21**
The corpus callosum This large band of neural fibers connects the two brain hemispheres. To photograph the half brain shown at left, a surgeon separated the hemispheres by cutting through the corpus callosum and lower brain regions. In the view on the right, brain tissue has been cut back to expose the corpus callosum and bundles of fibers coming out from it.

wondered, could they put an end to this biological tennis game by severing the **corpus callosum** (FIGURE 3B.21), the wide band of axon fibers connecting the two hemispheres and carrying messages between them?

Vogel and Bogen knew that psychologists Roger Sperry, Ronald Myers, and Michael Gazzaniga had divided the brains of cats and monkeys in this manner, with no serious ill effects. So the surgeons operated. The result? The seizures were all but eliminated. Moreover, the patients with these **split brains** were surprisingly normal, their personality and intellect hardly affected. Waking from surgery, one even joked that he had a "splitting headache" (Gazzaniga, 1967).

Sperry and Gazzaniga's studies of people with split brains provide a key to understanding the two hemispheres' complementary functions. As FIGURE 3B.22 explains, the peculiar nature of our visual wiring enabled the researchers to send information to a patient's left or right hemisphere. As the person stared at a spot, they flashed a stimulus to its right or left. They could do this with you, too, but in your intact brain, the hemisphere receiving the information would instantly pass the news to its partner across the valley. Not so in patients who had undergone split-brain surgery. The phone cables responsible for transmitting messages from one hemisphere to the other—the corpus callosum—had been severed. This enabled the researchers to quiz each hemisphere separately.

In an early experiment, Gazzaniga (1967) asked these patients to stare at a dot as he flashed HE·ART on a screen (FIGURE 3B.23). Thus, HE appeared in their left visual field (which transmits to the right hemisphere) and ART in the right field (which transmits to the left hemisphere). When he then asked what they had seen, the patients said they had seen ART. But when asked to point to the word with their left hand (controlled by the right hemisphere), they were startled when they pointed to HE. Given an opportunity to express itself, each

➤ **FIGURE 3B.22**
The information highway from eye to brain Information from the left half of your field of vision goes to your right hemisphere, and information from the right half of your visual field goes to your left hemisphere, which usually controls speech. (Note, however, that each eye receives sensory information from both the right and left visual fields.) Data received by either hemisphere are quickly transmitted to the other across the corpus callosum. In a person with a severed corpus callosum, this information sharing does not take place.

(a) "Look at the dot."

(b) Two words separated by a dot are momentarily projected.

(c) "What word did you see?" or "Point with your left hand to the word you saw."

➤ **FIGURE 3B.23**
Testing the divided brain When an experimenter flashes the word HEART across the visual field, a woman with a split brain reports seeing the portion of the word transmitted to her left hemisphere. However, if asked to indicate with her left hand what she saw, she points to the portion of the word transmitted to her right hemisphere. (From Gazzaniga, 1983.)

hemisphere reported what it had seen. The right hemisphere (controlling the left hand) intuitively knew what it could not verbally report.

When a picture of a spoon was flashed to their right hemisphere, the patients could not *say* what they had viewed. But when asked to *identify* what they had viewed by feeling an assortment of hidden objects with their left hand, they readily selected the spoon. If the experimenter said, "Right!" the patient might reply, "What? Right? How could I possibly pick out the right object when I don't know what I saw?" It is, of course, the left hemisphere doing the talking here, bewildered by what the nonverbal right hemisphere knows.

A few people who have had split-brain surgery have been for a time bothered by the unruly independence of their left hand, which might unbutton a shirt while the right hand buttoned it, or put grocery store items back on the shelf after the right hand put them in the cart. It was as if each hemisphere was thinking "I've half a mind to wear my green (blue) shirt today." Indeed, said Sperry (1964), split-brain surgery leaves people "with two separate minds." With a split brain, both hemispheres can comprehend and follow an instruction to copy—*simultaneously*—different figures with the left and right hands (Franz et al., 2000; see also **FIGURE 3B.24** on the next page). (Reading these reports, I fantasize a person enjoying a solitary game of "rock, paper, scissors"—left versus right hand.)

When the "two minds" are at odds, the left hemisphere does mental gymnastics to rationalize reactions it does not understand. If a patient follows an order sent to the right hemisphere ("Walk"), a strange thing happens. Unaware of the order,

::**corpus callosum** [KOR-pus kah-LOW-sum] the large band of neural fibers connecting the two brain hemispheres and carrying messages between them.

::**split brain** a condition resulting from surgery that isolates the brain's two hemispheres by cutting the fibers (mainly those of the corpus callosum) connecting them.

TROUBLESHOOTING

Students often leave this section with the impression that life is difficult for split-brain patients. In fact, the patients only experience difficulty in the first months after surgery. As time passes, the "two separate minds" begin to figure out how to work together. Help students understand that split-brain patients do not experience problems in daily life because the optic chiasm is not severed in the surgery. The optic chiasm is the place where the nerves connecting the eyes and the brain cross, leading to cross-hemispheric processing. Split-brain patients do receive visual information from both visual fields, so the abnormalities are only noticeable in specialized laboratory conditions.

TEACHING TIP

Point out to students that the results of split-brain research may be due in part to the condition of the patients' brains after experiencing years of debilitating epilepsy. Could the brain's organization in these patients be due to epilepsy? Or is the specialization of the brain the same in all people? This question is difficult to answer without doing empirical research, which would generally be considered unethical.

TEACHING TIP

At this point, you may want to use **Classroom Exercise:** *Behavioral Effects of the Split-Brain Operation* (p. 15) from Bolt's Teacher's Resource Binder.

UNIT 3B

CRITICAL THINKING

Ask students whether they ever had a teacher try to gear his or her class toward educating the "whole brain." Have them debate whether such practices were helpful. The debate should focus on whether the positive effects of "right-brain techniques" are the result of a placebo or Hawthorne effect. Have students choose to defend the affirmative or the negative.

RESEARCH

Have students research programs that claim to educate people on "both sides of the brain."

- What techniques do they use to accomplish their goals?

- How have these programs used scientific research well? How have they misinterpreted the research?

- What concerns about education today do these programs try to address?

➤ **FIGURE 3B.24**

Try this! Joe, who has had split-brain surgery, can simultaneously draw two different shapes.

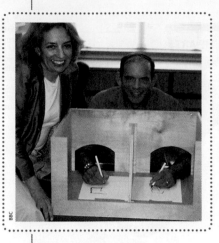

● *Question:* If we flashed a red light to the right hemisphere of a person with a split brain and flashed a green light to the left hemisphere, would each observe its own color? Would the person be aware that the colors differ? What would the person verbally report seeing? (Answers below.)●

Answers: Yes, No. Green.

the left hemisphere doesn't know why the patient begins walking. Yet, when asked why, the patient doesn't say "I don't know." Instead, the interpretive left hemisphere improvises—"I'm going into the house to get a Coke." Thus, Michael Gazzaniga (1988), who considers these patients "The most fascinating people on earth," concludes that the conscious left hemisphere is an "interpreter" or press agent that instantly constructs theories to explain our behavior.

These studies reveal that the left hemisphere is more active when a person deliberates over decisions (Rogers, 2003). When the rational left brain is active, people more often discount disagreeable information (Drake, 1993). The right hemisphere understands simple requests, easily perceives objects, and is more engaged when quick, intuitive responses are needed. The right side of the brain also surpasses the left at copying drawings and at recognizing faces. The right hemisphere is skilled at perceiving emotion and at portraying emotions through the more expressive left side of the face (**FIGURE 3B.25**). Right-hemisphere damage therefore more greatly disrupts emotion processing and social conduct (Tranel et al., 2002).

Most of the body's paired organs—kidneys, lungs, breasts—perform identical functions, providing a backup system should one side fail. Not so the brain's two halves, which can simultaneously carry out different functions with minimal duplication of effort. The result is a biologically odd but smart couple, each seemingly with a mind of its own.

➤ **FIGURE 3B.25**

Which one is happier? Look at the center of one face, then the other. Does one appear happier? Most people say the right face does. Some researchers think this is because the right hemisphere, which is skilled in emotion processing, receives information from the left half of each face (when looking at its center).

Right-Left Differences in the Intact Brain

SO, WHAT ABOUT THE 99.99+ PERCENT OF US with undivided brains? Does each of *our* hemispheres also perform distinct functions? Several different types of studies indicate they do.

TEACHING TIP

Tap into your students' creativity by having them write short stories using different parts of the brain as characters. Each story character should be a brain part whose function relates to the character's actions, feelings, or motives. Use the stories to make sure that the characters accurately reflect the brain part they represent. Request that volunteers read their work aloud or make the stories available for other students to read.

When a person performs a *perceptual* task, for example, brain waves, bloodflow, and glucose consumption reveal increased activity in the *right* hemisphere. When the person speaks or calculates, activity increases in the *left* hemisphere.

A dramatic demonstration of hemispheric specialization happens before some types of brain surgery. To check the location of language centers, the surgeon injects a sedative into the neck artery feeding blood to the left hemisphere. Before the injection, the patient is lying down, arms in the air, chatting with the doctor. You can probably predict what happens when the drug flows into the artery going to the left hemisphere: Within seconds, the person's right arm falls limp. The patient also usually becomes speechless until the drug wears off. When the drug enters the artery to the right hemisphere, the *left* arm falls limp, but the person can still speak.

Which hemisphere would you suppose enables sign language among deaf people? The right, because of its visual-spatial superiority? Or the left, because it typically processes language? Studies reveal that, just as hearing people usually use the left hemisphere to process speech, deaf people use the left hemisphere to process sign language (Corina et al., 1992; Hickok et al., 2001). A stroke in the left hemisphere will disrupt a deaf person's signing, much as it would disrupt a hearing person's speaking. The same brain area is similarly involved in both spoken and signed speech production (Corina, 1998). To the brain, language is language, whether spoken or signed.

Although the left hemisphere is adept at making quick, literal interpretations of language, the right hemisphere excels in making inferences (Beeman & Chiarello, 1998; Bowden & Beeman, 1998; Mason & Just, 2004). Primed with the flashed word *foot*, the left hemisphere will be especially quick to recognize the closely associated word *heel*. But if primed with *foot, cry,* and *glass,* the right hemisphere will more quickly recognize another word distantly related to all three *(cut)*. And if given an insightlike problem—"What word goes with *boot, summer,* and *ground?*"—the right hemisphere more quickly than the left recognizes the solution—*camp*. As one patient explained after a right-hemisphere stroke, "I understand words, but I'm missing the subtleties."

The right hemisphere also helps us modulate our speech to make meaning clear—as when we ask "What's that in the road ahead?" instead of "What's that in the road, a head?" (Heller, 1990).

The right hemisphere also seems to help orchestrate our sense of self. People who suffer partial paralysis will sometimes obstinately deny their impairment—strangely claiming they can move a paralyzed limb—if the damage is to the right hemisphere (Berti et al., 2005). With right-brain damage, some patients have difficulty perceiving who other people are in relation to themselves, as in the case of a man who saw medical caretakers as family (Feinberg & Keenan, 2005). Others fail to recognize themselves in a mirror, or assign ownership of a limb to someone else ("that's my husband's arm"). The power of the right brain appeared in an experiment in which people with normal brains viewed a series of images that progressively morphed from the face of a co-worker into their own face. As people recognized themselves, parts of their right brain displayed sudden activity. But when magnetic stimulation disrupted their normal right-brain activity, they had difficulty recognizing themselves in the morphed photos (Uddin et al., 2005, 2006).

Simply looking at the two hemispheres, so alike to the naked eye, who would suppose they contribute uniquely to the harmony of the whole? Yet a variety of observations—of people with split brains and people with normal brains—converge beautifully, leaving little doubt that we have unified brains with specialized parts.

● Are you a "righty" or a "lefty"? See Close-Up: Brain Organization and Handedness, next page, for more information about how our brain's wiring differs. ●

TROUBLESHOOTING

Help students see that basic language processing is a left hemisphere activity, as Myers points out by citing the research that Deaf people process sign language in the left hemisphere. However, notice in the other citations how the right hemisphere is responsible for more complex understandings and interpretations of language. Working together, the hemispheres help us have a rich, complex understanding of language.

UNIT 3B

Survey students to see how many "lefties" and "righties" you have in the class. You may want to get students to create a survey asking questions derived from the text about the benefits or deficits related to handedness. This data collection exercise would help reinforce the scientific method and reveal interesting information about the attitudes toward handedness among your students.

TEACHING TIP

Have students experiment with handedness on their own by seeing if they can train their non-dominant hand to catch and throw a ball or write their name legibly. They should hold back their dominant hand and try to accomplish the new skill over time. Have them report their success (or lack thereof) to the class.

CLOSE-UP

Brain Organization and Handedness

7: How does handedness relate to brain organization?

Nearly 90 percent of us are primarily right-handed (Leask & Beaton, 2007; Medland et al., 2004; Peters et al., 2006). Some 10 percent of us (somewhat more among males, somewhat less among females) are left-handed. (A few people write with their right hand and throw a ball with their left, or vice versa.) Almost all right-handers (96 percent) process speech primarily in the left hemisphere, which tends to be the slightly larger hemisphere (Hopkins, 2006). Left-handers are more diverse. Seven in ten process speech in the left hemisphere, as right-handers do. The rest either process language in the right hemisphere or use both hemispheres.

> • Most people also kick with their right foot, look through a microscope with their right eye, and (had you noticed?) kiss the right way—with their head tilted right (Güntürkün, 2003). •

Is Handedness Inherited?
Judging from prehistoric human cave drawings, tools, and hand and arm bones, this veer to the right occurred long ago (Corballis, 1989; Steele, 2000). Right-handedness prevails in all human cultures. Moreover, it appears prior to culture's impact: Ultrasound observations of fetal thumb-sucking reveal that more than 9 in 10 fetuses suck the right hand's thumb (Hepper et al., 1990, 2004). Such findings, along with the universal prevalence of right-handers, indicate that either genes or some prenatal factors influence handedness.

> • Evidence that challenges a genetic explanation of handedness: Handedness is one of but a few traits that genetically identical twins are not especially likely to share (Halpern & Coren, 1990). •

So, Is It All Right to Be Left-Handed?
Judging by our everyday conversation, left-handedness is not all right. To be "coming out of left field" is hardly better than to be "gauche" (derived from the French word for "left"). On the other hand, right-handedness is "right on," which any "righteous" "right-hand man" "in his right mind" usually is.

Left-handers are more numerous than usual among those with reading disabilities, allergies, and migraine headaches (Geschwind & Behan, 1984). But in Iran, where students report which hand they write with when taking the university entrance exam, lefties outperform righties in all subjects (Noroozian et al., 2003). Left-handedness is also more common among musicians, mathematicians, professional baseball and cricket players,[2] architects, and artists, including such luminaries as Michelangelo, Leonardo da Vinci, and Picasso. Although left-handers must tolerate elbow jostling at the dinner table, right-handed desks, and awkward scissors, the pros and cons of being a lefty seem roughly equal.

[2]Strategic factors explain the higher-than-normal percentage of lefties in sports. For example, it helps a soccer team to have left-footed players on the left side of the field (Wood & Aggleton, 1989). In golf, however, no left-hander won the Masters tournament until Canadian Mike Weir did so in 2003.

AP Photo/Nati Harnik, File

The rarest of baseball players: an ambidextrous pitcher Using a glove with two thumbs, Creighton University pitcher Pat Venditte, shown here in a 2008 game, pitched to right-handed batters with his right hand, then switched to face left-handed batters with his left hand. After one switch-hitter switched sides of the plate, Venditte switched pitching arms, which triggered the batter to switch again, and so on. The umpires ultimately ended the comedy routine by applying a little-known rule: A pitcher must declare which arm he will use before throwing his first pitch to a batter (Schwarz, 2007).

TEACHING TIP

At this point, you may want to use **Classroom Exercise/Student Project:** *The Wagner Preference Inventory* (p. 16) and **Lecture/Discussion Topics:** *Left-Handedness* (p. 18) and *The Right Brain Movement* (p. 20) from Bolt's Teacher's Resource Binder.

The Brain and Consciousness

8: What is the "dual processing" being revealed by today's cognitive neuroscience?

IN TODAY'S SCIENCE, ONE of the most hotly pursued research quests is to understand the biology of **consciousness**. Evolutionary psychologists speculate that consciousness must offer a reproductive advantage (Barash, 2006). Perhaps consciousness helps us act in our long-term interests (by considering consequences) rather than merely seeking short-term pleasure and avoiding pain. Or perhaps consciousness promotes our survival by anticipating how we seem to others and helping us read their minds. ("He looks really angry! I'd better run!") Even so, that leaves us with the so-called "hard-problem": How do brain cells jabbering to one another create our awareness of the taste of a taco, the pain of a toothache, the feeling of fright?

Cognitive Neuroscience

Scientists assume, in the words of neuroscientist Marvin Minsky (1986, p. 287), that "the mind is what the brain does." We just don't know *how* it does it. Given all the world's chemicals, computer chips, and energy, we still don't have a clue *how* to make a conscious robot. Yet today's **cognitive neuroscience**—the interdisciplinary study of the brain activity linked with our mental processes—is taking the first small step by relating specific brain states to conscious experiences. We know, for example, that the upper brainstem contributes to consciousness because some children born without a cerebral cortex exhibit signs of consciousness (Merker, 2007).

Another stunning demonstration of some level of consciousness appeared in brain scans of a noncommunicative patient—a 23-year-old woman who had been in a car accident and showed no outward signs of conscious awareness (Owen et al., 2006). When researchers asked her to *imagine* playing tennis or moving around her home, fMRI scans revealed brain activity like that of healthy volunteers. As she imagined playing tennis, for example, an area of her brain controlling arm and leg movements became active (**FIGURE 3B.26**). Even in a motionless body, the researchers concluded, the brain—and the mind—may still be active.

However, most cognitive neuroscientists are exploring and mapping the *conscious* functions of the cortex. Based on your cortical activation patterns, they can now, in some limited ways, read your mind. They can, for example, tell which of 10 similar objects (hammer, drill, and so forth) you are viewing (Shinkareva et al., 2008). Despite such

::**consciousness** our awareness of ourselves and our environment.

::**cognitive neuroscience** the interdisciplinary study of the brain activity linked with cognition (including perception, thinking, memory, and language).

➤ **FIGURE 3B.26**

Evidence of awareness? When asked to imagine playing tennis or navigating her home, a vegetative patient's brain (top) exhibited activity similar to a healthy person's brain (bottom). Although the case may be an exception, researchers wonder if such fMRI scans might enable a "conversation" with unresponsive patients, by instructing them, for example, to answer yes to a question by imagining playing tennis, and *no* by imagining walking around their home.

Courtesy: Adrian M. Owen, MRC Cognition and Brain Sciences Unit, University of Cambridge

Patient

Healthy Volunteers

Tennis Imagery   Spatial Navigation Imagery

UNIT 3B

Help students see that the idea of dual processing is reinforced in our study of memory in Unit 7A. We process new information both explicitly and implicitly. These two ways of remembering information are stored in different parts of the brain. The complexity of the brain is what makes it truly remarkable to study.

TROUBLESHOOTING

Students often find so-called "blindsight" confusing. Not only can people have blindness like that described by Myers in the text, but if people have damage to the occipital lobe, they can also be blind to understanding what they see with their working eyes. They won't be able to identify objects or even be able to say that they see anything recognizable. If the eyes work, some aspect of vision will be processed in the brain. Whether we can understand what we see, however, is dependent on the brain working as it should.

INTERCONNECTING

Have students create their own visual illusions to see whether they can fool their visual system. They can create the "hollow face illusion" to see if they experience this phenomenon of dual processing—seeing one thing, but processing another.

::**dual processing** the principle that information is often simultaneously processed on separate conscious and unconscious tracks.

> ▶ **FIGURE 3B.27**
The hollow face illusion What you see (an illusory protruding face from a reverse mask, as in the box at upper right) may differ from what you do (reach for a speck on the face inside the mask).

Adapted from: Milner, A. D. & Goodale, M. A. (2006). *The visual brain in action* (2nd ed.). Oxford University Press.

advances, much disagreement remains. One research group theorizes that conscious experiences arise from specific neuron circuits firing in a specific manner. Another sees conscious experiences as produced by the synchronized activity of the whole brain (Koch & Greenfield, 2007). How the brain produces the mind remains a mystery.

Dual Processing

Many cognitive neuroscience discoveries tell us of a particular brain region that becomes active with a particular conscious experience. Such findings strike many people as interesting but not mind-blowing. (If everything psychological is simultaneously biological, then our ideas, emotions, and spirituality must all, somehow, be embodied.) What *is* mind-blowing to many of us is the growing evidence that we have, so to speak, two minds, each supported by its own neural equipment.

At any moment, you and I are aware of little more than what's on the screen of our consciousness. But one of the grand ideas of recent cognitive neuroscience is that much of our brain work occurs off stage, out of sight. We saw this in the discussion of the conscious "left-brain" and more intuitive "right-brain" and in the older brain functions that effortlessly sustain our living and perceiving. Later units will explore our hidden mind at work in research on unconscious *priming*, on conscious (*explicit*) and unconscious (*implicit*) memories, on conscious versus automatic prejudices, and on the out-of-sight processing that enables sudden insights and creative moments. Perception, memory, thinking, language, and attitudes all operate on two levels—a conscious, deliberate "high road" and an unconscious, automatic "low road." Today's researchers call this **dual processing**. We know more than we know we know.

The Two-Track Mind

A scientific story illustrates the mind's two levels. Sometimes science-aided critical thinking confirms widely held beliefs. But sometimes, as this story illustrates, science is stranger than science fiction.

During my sojourns at Scotland's University of St. Andrews, I came to know cognitive neuroscientists Melvyn Goodale and David Milner (2004, 2006). A local woman, whom they call D. F., was overcome by carbon monoxide one day while showering. The resulting brain damage left her unable to recognize and discriminate objects visually. Yet she was only partly blind, for she would act as if she could see. Asked to slip a postcard into a vertical or horizontal mail slot, she could do so without error. Although unable to report the width of a block in front of her, she could grasp it with just the right finger-thumb distance.

How could this be? Don't we have one visual system? Goodale and Milner knew from animal research that the eye sends information simultaneously to different brain areas, which have different tasks. Sure enough, a scan of D. F.'s brain activity revealed normal activity in the area concerned with reaching for and grasping objects, but damage in the area concerned with consciously recognizing objects.

So, would the reverse damage lead to the opposite symptoms? Indeed, there are a few such patients—who can see and recognize objects but have difficulty pointing toward or grasping them.

How strangely intricate is this thing we call vision, conclude Goodale and Milner in their aptly titled book, *Sight Unseen*. We may think of our vision as one system that controls our visually guided actions, but it is actually a dual-processing system. A *visual perception track* enables us "to create the mental furniture that allows us to think about the world"—to recognize things and to plan future actions. A *visual action track* guides our moment-to-moment actions.

On rare occasions, the two conflict. Shown the *hollow face illusion*, people will mistakenly perceive the inside of a mask as a protruding face (**FIGURE 3B.27**). Yet

TECHNOLOGY RESOURCES

These resources will be helpful for teaching the concepts in this portion of the unit:

- *Videos: Digital Media Archive: Psychology,* 1st ed., *Video Clip 2: Brain Structures; Video Clip 3: Brain Imaging; Video Clip 22: Gleason's Wug Test; Video Clip 26: Self-Stimulation in Rats*
- *PsychSim 5: Brain and Behavior; Hemispheric Specialization*
- *Videos: Scientific American Frontiers,* 2nd ed., *Segment 5: Mind Reading and Segment 6: Image-Guided Surgery; Brain Plasticity: Rewiring the Visual Cortex; Segment 8: Old Brain, New Tricks; Segment 7: Severed Corpus Callosum*

they will unhesitatingly and accurately reach into the inverted mask to flick off a buglike target stuck on the face. What their conscious mind doesn't know, their hand does.

This big idea—that much of our everyday thinking, feeling, and acting operates outside our conscious awareness—"is a difficult one for people to accept," report New York University psychologists John Bargh and Tanya Chartrand (1999). We are understandably biased to believe that our own intentions and deliberate choices rule our lives. But in the mind's downstairs, there is much, much more to being human.

So, consciousness, though enabling us to exert voluntary control and to communicate our mental states to others, is but the tip of the information-processing iceberg. Beneath the surface, unconscious information processing occurs simultaneously on many parallel tracks. When we look at a bird flying, we are consciously aware of the result of our cognitive processing ("It's a hummingbird!") but not of our subprocessing of the bird's color, form, movement, distance, and identity.

Today's neuroscientists are identifying neural activity that precedes consciousness. In some provocative experiments, Benjamin Libet (1985, 2004) observed that when you move your wrist at will, you consciously experience the decision to move it about 0.2 seconds before the actual movement. No surprise there. But your brain waves jump about 0.35 seconds ahead of your conscious perception of your decision (FIGURE 3B.28)! Thus, before you know it, your brain seems headed toward your decision to move your wrist. Likewise, if asked to press a button when you feel a tap, you can respond in 1/10th of a second—less time than it takes to become conscious that you have responded (Wegner, 2002). In a follow-up experiment, fMRI brain scans enabled researchers to predict—with 60 percent accuracy and up to 7 seconds ahead—participants' decisions to press a button with their left or right finger (Soon et al., 2008). The startling conclusion: Consciousness sometimes arrives late to the decision-making party.

All of this unconscious information processing occurs simultaneously on multiple parallel tracks. Traveling by car on a familiar route, your hands and feet do the driving while your mind rehearses your upcoming day. Running on automatic pilot allows your consciousness—your mind's CEO—to monitor the whole system and deal with new challenges, while many assistants automatically take care of routine business.

Serial conscious processing, though slower than parallel processing, is skilled at solving new problems, which require our focused attention. Try this: If you are right-handed, you can move your right foot in a smooth counterclockwise circle, and you can write the number 3 repeatedly with your right hand—but probably not at the same time. (If you are musically inclined, try something equally difficult: Tap a steady three times with your left hand while tapping four times with your right hand.) Both tasks require conscious attention, which can be in only one place at a time. If time is nature's way of keeping everything from happening at once, then consciousness is nature's way of keeping us from thinking and doing everything at once.

➤ **FIGURE 3B.28**

Is the brain ahead of the mind? In this study, volunteers watched a computer clock sweep through a full revolution every 2.56 seconds. They noted the time at which they decided to move their wrist. About one-third of a second before that decision, their brain wave activity jumped, indicating a *readiness potential* to move. Watching a slow-motion replay, the researchers were able to predict when a person was about to decide to move (following which, the wrist did move) (Libet, 1985, 2004).

BEFORE YOU MOVE ON . . .

➤ **ASK YOURSELF**

Can you recall a time when, your attention focused on one thing, you were oblivious to something else (perhaps to pain, to someone's approach, or to background music)?

➤ **TEST YOURSELF 2**

What are the mind's two tracks, as revealed by studies of "dual processing"?

Answers to the Test Yourself questions can be found in Appendix E at the end of the book.

INTERCONNECTING

Much of this research on dual processing and the two-track mind suggests that some of Freud's ideas about the influence of the unconscious on behavior and mental processes are valid. The research does not validate Freud's claims about what the unconscious contains or the meaning of unconscious thoughts and feelings, but it does indicate that the unconscious is more influential than we realize.

At this point, you may want to use **Lecture/Discussion Topic:** *The Mind-Body Problem* (p. 21) and **Classroom Exercise:** *The Dualism Scale* (p. 22) from Bolt's Teacher's Resource Binder.

DEMO

Have students try the activities Myers describes on this page. Have them report their experiences to the class, discussing whether they processed the information serially or dually. You may also want to have them conduct some simple demonstrations with students in different areas of expertise, such as drummers versus math scholars on the tapping exercise, to see if there are differences between groups.

At this point, you may want to use **Lecture/Discussion Topics:** *Automatic Processing* (p. 22) and *Psychological Distance and Evaluative Judgments* (p. 23) from Bolt's Teacher's Resource Binder.

- *Psychology Video Tool Kit: Mapping the Brain Through Electrical Stimulation; Planning, Life Goals, and the Frontal Lobe; Compulsive Gambling and the Brain's Pleasure Center; Language and Brain Plasticity; Rewiring the Brain; The Split Brain: Lessons on Language, Vision, and Free Will; The Split Brain: Lessons on Cognition and the Cerebral Hemispheres*

- *ActivePsych: Scientific American Frontiers Teaching Modules, 3rd ed.: Neuroimaging: Assessing What's Cool; Digital Media Archive, 2nd ed.: The Brain's Reward Center; Scientific American Frontiers Teaching Modules, 3rd ed.: Brain and Behavior: Phineas Gage*

Technology Resources continued

ANSWERS to Multiple-Choice Questions

1. **e.** medulla.
2. **b.** dual processing.
3. **e.** the functions of various brain regions.
4. **b.** memory problems.
5. **d.** that someone is tickling you.
6. **a.** consciousness.
7. **a.** hypothalamus.
8. **c.** MRI.
9. **c.** glial cells.
10. **d.** Recognizing a friend's face.
11. **c.** be able to draw a spoon with her left hand but would not be able to say she had seen a spoon.
12. **e.** ability of brain tissue to take on new functions.
13. **c.** became less aggressive.
14. **c.** limbic system.
15. **b.** Reticular formation

UNIT REVIEW: The Brain

The Tools of Discovery: Having Our Head Examined

1: How do neuroscientists study the brain's connections to behavior and mind?

Clinical observations and *lesioning* reveal the general effects of brain damage. *CT* and *MRI* scans reveal brain structures, and *EEG, PET,* and *fMRI* recordings reveal brain activity.

Older Brain Structures

2: What are the functions of important lower-level brain structures?

The *brainstem,* the oldest part of the brain, is responsible for automatic survival functions. Its components are the *medulla* (controls heartbeat and breathing), the pons (helps coordinate movements), and the *reticular formation* (affects arousal). The *thalamus,* the brain's sensory switchboard, sits above the brainstem. The *cerebellum,* at the rear of the brainstem, coordinates muscle movement and helps process sensory information.

The *limbic system* is linked to emotions, memory, and drives. Its neural centers include the *amygdala* (involved in responses of aggression and fear) and the *hypothalamus* (involved in various bodily maintenance functions, pleasurable rewards, and the control of the hormonal system). The hypothalamus controls the pituitary (the "master gland") by stimulating it to trigger the release of hormones. The hippocampus processes memory.

The Cerebral Cortex

3: What functions are served by the various cerebral cortex regions?

In each hemisphere the *cerebral cortex* has four lobes, the *frontal, parietal, occipital,* and *temporal.* Each lobe performs many functions and interacts with other areas of the cortex. The *motor cortex* controls voluntary movements. The *sensory cortex* registers and processes body sensations. Body parts requiring precise control (in the motor cortex) or those that are especially sensitive (in the sensory cortex) occupy the greatest amount of space. Most of the brain's cortex—the major portion of each of the four lobes—is devoted to *association areas,* which integrate information involved in learning, remembering, thinking, and other higher-level functions.

4: What brain areas are involved in language processing?

When you read aloud, your brain's visual cortex registers words as visual stimuli, the angular gyrus transforms those visual representations into auditory codes, *Wernicke's area* interprets those codes and sends the message to *Broca's area,* which controls the motor cortex as it creates the pronounced words. But we now know that language results from the integration of many specific neural networks performing specialized subtasks in many parts of the brain.

5: To what extent can a damaged brain reorganize itself?

If one hemisphere is damaged early in life, the other will pick up many of its functions. This *plasticity* diminishes later in life. Some brain areas are capable of *neurogenesis* (forming new neurons).

Our Divided Brain

6: What do split brains reveal about the functions of our two brain hemispheres?

Split-brain research (experiments on people with a severed *corpus callosum*) has confirmed that in most people, the left hemisphere is the more verbal, and that the right hemisphere excels in visual perception and the recognition of emotion. Studies of healthy people with intact brains confirm that each hemisphere makes unique contributions to the integrated functioning of the brain.

7: How does handedness relate to brain organization?

About 10 percent of us are left-handed. Almost all right-handers process speech in the left hemisphere, as do more than half of all left-handers.

The Brain and Consciousness

8: What is the "dual processing" being revealed by today's cognitive neuroscience?

Cognitive neuroscientists and others studying the brain mechanisms underlying *consciousness* and cognition have discovered a two-track human mind, each with its own neural processing. This *dual processing* affects our perception, memory, and attitudes at an explicit, conscious level and at an implicit, unconscious level.

Terms and Concepts to Remember

TECHNOLOGY RESOURCES

 Technology Resources continued from p. 91

Revisited; Scientific American Frontiers Teaching Modules, 3rd ed.: *Brain Plasticity: Rewiring the Visual Cortex; Scientific American Frontiers Teaching Modules,* 3rd ed.: *Achieving Hemispheric Balance: Improving Sports Performance; Scientific American Frontiers Teaching Modules,* 3rd ed.: *Hidden Prejudice: The Implicit Association Test*

- *Videos: The Brain,* 2nd ed., *Module 1: Organization and Evaluation of Brain Function; Module 6: Language and Speech: Broca's and Wernicke's Areas; Module 5: The Divided Brain; Module 7: Brain Anomaly and Plasticity: Hydrocephalus; Module 8: Language Processing in the Brain; Module 25: The Frontal Lobes and Behavior: The Story of Phineas Gage; Module 32: Neurorehabilitation*

AP* Practice Test Questions ◄ ·······························

Multiple-Choice Questions

1. Breathing and heartbeat are controlled by the
a. pons.
b. corpus callosum.
c. parietal lobe.
d. hippocampus.
e. medulla.

2. Perception, thinking, and language can operate at conscious, deliberate levels and also at unconscious, automatic levels. This best describes
a. cognitive neuroscience.
b. dual processing.
c. selective attention.
d. selective inattention.
e. change blindness.

3. A PET scan best allows researchers to determine
a. the presence of tumors in the brain.
b. electrical activity on the surface of the brain.
c. the size of the internal structures of the brain.
d. the location of strokes.
e. the functions of various brain regions.

4. Damage to the hippocampus would result in
a. difficulties with balance and coordination.
b. memory problems.
c. the false sensation of burning in parts of the body.
d. emotional outbursts.
e. death.

5. Surgical stimulation of the sensory cortex might result in the false sensation
a. of music.
b. of flashes of colored light.
c. that someone is whispering your name.
d. that someone is tickling you.
e. of a bad odor.

6. Awareness of ourselves and our environment best describes
a. consciousness.
b. dual processing.
c. inattentional blindness.
d. change blindness.
e. cognitive neuroscience.

7. The link between the nervous system and the endocrine system is maintained by the
a. hypothalamus.
b. temporal lobe.
c. cerebellum.
d. thalamus.
e. motor cortex.

8. A researcher interested in determining the size of a particular area of the brain would be most likely to use a(n)
a. lesion.
b. EEG.
c. MRI.
d. fMRI.
e. PET scan.

9. The support cells that provide nourishment and help the brain in numerous other ways are called
a. neurons.
b. interneurons.
c. glial cells.
d. endocrine cells.
e. myelin cells.

10. Which of the following is a task more likely to be accomplished by the right hemisphere of the brain?
a. Solving a mathematical equation.
b. Reading.
c. Making a brief oral presentation to a class.
d. Recognizing a friend's face.
e. Solving a logic problem.

11. If you flashed a picture of a spoon to the left visual field of a person whose corpus callosum had been severed (so it was transmitted to her right hemisphere), she would
a. be able to draw a spoon with her right hand but would not be able to say she had seen a spoon.
b. be confused about whether she had seen a spoon.
c. be able to draw a spoon with her left hand but would not be able to say she had seen a spoon.
d. be able to tell you she had seen a spoon.
e. be able to tell you she had seen something that rhymes with spoon (for example, "the Moon").

12. Brain plasticity refers to the
a. feel of healthy human brain tissue.
b. ability of the brain to transfer information from one hemisphere to the other.
c. way a brain gets larger as a child grows.
d. wide variety of functions performed by the human brain.
e. ability of brain tissue to take on new functions.

13. When Heinrich Klüver and neurosurgeon Paul Bucy surgically lesioned the amygdala of a rhesus monkey's brain, the monkey
a. lost its ability to coordinate movement.
b. died because its heartbeat became irregular.
c. became less aggressive.
d. lost its memory of where food was stored.
e. sank into an irreversible coma.

14. The reward deficiency syndrome argues that addictive disorders may be partially explained by genetic flaws in the
a. brainstem.
b. cerebral cortex.
c. limbic system.
d. endocrine system.
e. cerebrum.

15. An individual experiences brain damage that produces a coma. Which part of the brain was probably damaged?
a. Corpus callosum
b. Reticular formation
c. Frontal lobe
d. Cerebellum
e. Limbic system

Free-Response Question

You have been hired to write and direct short, educational films covering a variety of different brain injuries. In five short paragraphs, explain five ideas you have for scripts. In each case, create a character who has suffered a brain injury. Include the name of the brain part injured and a description of the loss of function that occurs as a result of that injury.

*AP is a trademark registered and/or owned by the College Board, which was not involved in the production of, and does not endorse, this product.

 WEB

Multiple-choice self-test and more may be found at www.worthpublishers.com/myers

Rubric for Grading the Free-Response Question

This is a 10-point question. Scoring depends on the scenarios created by the student. Each of the five paragraphs is worth two points—one point for mentioning a brain part and one point for connecting damage to that part to the appropriate loss of function. For example, it would be worth two points if a student described a condition that damaged a person's hippocampus and indicated that there would be a loss of memory as a result.

- *Videos: The Mind, 2nd ed., Module 6: Brain Mechanisms of Pleasure and Addiction; Module 7: The Frontal Lobes: Cognition and Awareness; Module 18: Effects of Mental and Physical Activity on Brain/Mind*
- *Videos: Psychology: The Human Experience, Module 16: Language Centers in the Brain; Module 4: A Case Study of Brain Damage; Module 5: Brain Plasticity*

Pacing Guide

Use the following guide to determine how many instructional days to devote to this portion of the unit depending on the type of course you teach:

Year-long course: 3–4 days
Block schedule/Semester-long
course: 2–3 days

This entire unit (Parts A, B, & C) encompasses 8–10 percent of the AP Exam. Spending an appropriate amount of time on this unit will help students do well on the AP Exam.

 TEACHING TIP

Teach this unit early in the course so students can get the foundational knowledge offered by this material. Understanding the concepts in this unit is important to mastering the entire course content. However, due to the amount of information covered in this unit, it has been broken down into three parts. Helping students chunk the information will help them learn a large amount of very important material more easily.

 INTERCONNECTING

Keep in mind that the following units will also rely heavily on a thorough understanding of the biological bases of behavior:

Unit 4: Sensation and Perception
Unit 5: States of Consciousness
Unit 7: Part A: Memory
Unit 8: Part B: Emotions, Stress, and Health
Unit 12: Abnormal Psychology
Unit 13: Treatment of Psychological Disorders

Biological Bases of Behavior:
3C—Genetics, Evolutionary Psychology, and Behavior

Behind the story of our human brain—surely the most awesome thing on Earth—is the essence of our universal human attributes and our individual traits. What makes you *you?* In important ways, we are each unique. We look different. We sound different. We have varying personalities, interests, and cultural and family backgrounds.

We are also the leaves of one tree. Our human family shares not only a common biological heritage—cut us and we bleed—but also common behavioral tendencies. Our shared brain architecture predisposes us to sense the world, develop language, and feel hunger through identical mechanisms. Whether we live in the Arctic or the tropics, we prefer sweet tastes to sour. We divide the color spectrum into similar colors. And we feel drawn to behaviors that produce and protect offspring.

Our kinship appears in our social behaviors as well. Whether named Wong, Nkomo, Smith, or Gonzales, we start fearing strangers at about eight months, and as teenagers and adults we prefer the company of those with attitudes and attributes similar to our own. Coming from different parts of the globe, we know how to read one another's smiles and frowns. As members of one species, we affiliate, conform, return favors, punish offenses, organize hierarchies of status, and grieve a child's death. A visitor from outer space could drop in anywhere and find humans dancing and feasting, singing and worshiping, playing sports and games, laughing and crying, living in families and forming groups. Taken together, such universal behaviors define our human nature.

What causes our striking diversity, and also our shared human nature? How much are human differences shaped by our differing genes? And how much by our *environment*—by every external influence, from maternal nutrition while in the womb to social support while nearing the tomb? This unit begins to tell the complex story of how our genes (*nature*) and environments (*nurture*) define us.

The nurture of nature Parents everywhere wonder: Will my baby grow up to be peaceful or aggressive? Homely or attractive? Successful or struggling at every step? What comes built in, and what is nurtured—and how? Research reveals that nature and nurture together shape our development—every step of the way.

94

Suggested Readings

Harris, J. R. (1998). *The nurture assumption.* New York: Free Press.

Horstman, J. (2009). *The* Scientific American *day in the life of your brain.* New York: Jossey-Bass.

Pinker, S. (2002). *The blank slate: The modern denial of human nature.* New York: Viking.

Ramachandran, V. S., & Blakeslee, S. (1998). *Phantoms in the brain: Probing the mysteries of the human mind.* New York: William Morrow.

Sacks, O. (1973). *Awakenings.* New York: HarperCollins.

Sacks, O. (1985). *The man who mistook his wife for a hat.* New York: Summit Books.

Behavior Genetics: Predicting Individual Differences

1: What are genes, and how do behavior geneticists explain our individual differences?

IF JADEN AGASSI, SON OF TENNIS STARS Andre Agassi and Stephanie Graf, grows up to be a tennis star, should we attribute his superior talent to his Grand Slam genes? To his growing up in a tennis-rich environment? To high expectations? Such questions intrigue **behavior geneticists**, who study our differences and weigh the effects and interplay of heredity and **environment**.

"Thanks for almost everything, Dad"

Genes: Our Codes for Life

Barely more than a century ago, few would have guessed that every cell nucleus in your body contains the genetic master code for your entire body. It's as if every room in the Pentagon had a book containing the architect's plans for the entire structure. The plans for your own book of life run to 46 chapters—23 donated by your mother (from her egg) and 23 by your father (from his sperm). Each of these 46 chapters, called a **chromosome**, is composed of a coiled chain of the molecule **DNA** *(deoxyribonucleic acid)*. **Genes**, small segments of the giant DNA molecules, form the words of those chapters (**FIGURE 3C.1**). All told, you have 30,000 or so gene words. Genes can be either active *(expressed)* or inactive. Environmental events "turn on" genes, rather like hot water enabling a tea bag

➤ **FIGURE 3C.1**
The human building blocks The nucleus of every human cell contains chromosomes, each of which is made up of two strands of DNA connected in a double helix.

Cell

Chromosome

Gene

Nucleus

DNA

::behavior genetics the study of the relative power and limits of genetic and environmental influences on behavior.

::environment every non-genetic influence, from prenatal nutrition to the people and things around us.

::chromosomes threadlike structures made of DNA molecules that contain the genes.

::DNA *(deoxyribonucleic acid)* a complex molecule containing the genetic information that makes up the chromosomes.

::genes the biochemical units of heredity that make up the chromosomes; segments of DNA capable of synthesizing a protein.

Key Terms

Behavior Genetics: Predicting Individual Differences

behavior genetics
environment
chromosomes
DNA (deoxyribonucleic acid)
genes
genome
identical twins
fraternal twins
heritability
interaction
molecular genetics

Evolutionary Psychology: Understanding Human Nature

evolutionary psychology
natural selection
mutation

Key People

Thomas Bouchard
David Buss
Francis Collins
Charles Darwin
Alice Eagly
David Lykken
Robert Plomin
Wendy Wood

UNIT 3C

"Your DNA and mine are 99.9 percent the same . . . At the DNA level, we are clearly all part of one big worldwide family."

Francis Collins,
Human Genome Project director, 2007

"We share half our genes with the banana."

Evolutionary biologist Robert May,
president of Britain's Royal Society, 2001

➤ **FIGURE 3C.2**
Same fertilized egg, same genes; different eggs, different genes Identical twins develop from a single fertilized egg, fraternal twins from two.

::**genome** the complete instructions for making an organism, consisting of all the genetic material in that organism's chromosomes.

::**identical twins** twins who develop from a single fertilized egg that splits in two, creating two genetically identical organisms.

::**fraternal twins** twins who develop from separate fertilized eggs. They are genetically no closer than brothers and sisters, but they share a fetal environment.

to express its flavor. When turned on, genes provide the code for creating *protein molecules,* the building blocks of physical development.

Genetically speaking, every other human is close to being your identical twin. Human **genome** researchers have discovered the common sequence within human DNA. It is this shared genetic profile that makes us humans, rather than chimpanzees or tulips.

Actually, we aren't all that different from our chimpanzee cousins; with them we share about 96 percent of our DNA sequence (Mikkelsen et al., 2005). At "functionally important" DNA sites, reports one molecular genetics team, the human-chimpanzee DNA similarity is 99.4 percent (Wildman et al., 2003). Yet that wee difference matters. Despite some remarkable abilities, chimpanzees grunt. Shakespeare intricately wove some 24,000 words to form his literary masterpieces. And small differences matter among chimpanzees, too. Two species, common chimpanzees and bonobos, differ by much less than 1 percent of their genomes, yet they display markedly differing behaviors. Chimpanzees are aggressive and male-dominated. Bonobos are peaceable and female led.

Geneticists and psychologists are interested in the occasional variations found at particular gene sites in human DNA. Slight person-to-person variations from the common pattern give clues to our uniqueness—why one person has a disease that another does not, why one person is short and another tall, why one is outgoing and another shy.

Most of our traits are influenced by many genes. How tall you are, for example, reflects the size of your face, vertebrae, leg bones, and so forth—each of which may be influenced by different genes interacting with your environment. Complex traits such as intelligence, happiness, and aggressiveness are similarly influenced by groups of genes. Thus our genetic predispositions—our genetically influenced traits—help explain both our shared human nature and our human diversity.

Twin and Adoption Studies

To scientifically tease apart the influences of environment and heredity, behavior geneticists would need to design two types of experiments. The first would control the home environment while varying heredity. The second would control heredity while varying the home environment. Such experiments with human infants would be unethical, but happily for our purposes, nature has done this work for us.

Identical Versus Fraternal Twins

Identical twins, who develop from a single fertilized egg that splits in two, are *genetically* identical (**FIGURE 3C.2**). They are nature's own human clones—indeed, clones who share not only the same genes but the same conception, uterus, birth date, and usually the same cultural history. Two slight qualifications:

- Although identical twins have the same genes, they don't always have the same *number of copies* of those genes. That may help explain why one twin may be more at risk for certain illnesses (Bruder et al., 2008).

- Most identical twins share a placenta during prenatal development, but one of every three sets has two separate placentas. One twin's placenta may provide slightly better nourishment, which may contribute to identical twin differences (Davis et al., 1995; Phelps et al., 1997; Sokoll et al., 1995).

> "It will inevitably be revealed that there are strong genetic components associated with more aspects of what we attribute to human existence including personality subtypes, language capabilities, mechanical abilities, intelligence, sexual activities and preferences, intuitive thinking, quality of memory, willpower, temperament, athletic abilities, etc."
>
> Genomics researcher, J. Craig Venter, 2006

Identical twins Curiously, twinning rates vary by race. The rate among Caucasians is roughly twice that of Asians and half that of Africans. In Africa and Asia, most twins are identical. In Western countries, most twins are fraternal, and fraternal twins are increasing with the use of fertility drugs (Hall, 2003; Steinhauer, 1999).

Fraternal twins develop from separate fertilized eggs. They share a fetal environment, but they are genetically no more similar than ordinary brothers and sisters.

Shared genes can translate into shared experiences. A person whose identical twin has Alzheimer's disease, for example, has a 60 percent risk of getting the disease; if the affected twin is fraternal, the risk is only 30 percent (Plomin et al., 1997).

Are identical twins, being genetic clones of one another, also behaviorally more similar than fraternal twins? Studies of thousands of twin pairs in Sweden, Finland, and Australia provide a consistent answer: On both extraversion (outgoingness) and neuroticism (emotional instability), identical twins are much more similar than fraternal twins.

If genes influence traits such as emotional instability, might they also influence the social effects of such traits? To find out, Matt McGue and David Lykken (1992) studied divorce rates among 1500 same-sex, middle-aged twin pairs. Their result: If you have a fraternal twin who has divorced, the odds of your divorcing go up 1.6 times (compared with having a not-divorced twin). If you have an identical twin who has divorced, the odds of your divorcing go up 5.5 times. From such data, McGue and Lykken estimate that people's differing divorce risks are about 50 percent attributable to genetic factors.

When John Loehlin and Robert Nichols (1976) gave a battery of questionnaires to 850 U.S. twin pairs, identical twins, more than fraternal twins, also reported being treated alike. So, did their experience rather than their genes account for their similarity? No, said Loehlin and Nichols; identical twins whose parents treated them alike were not psychologically more alike than identical twins who were treated less similarly. In explaining individual differences, genes matter.

Separated Twins

Imagine the following science fiction experiment: A mad scientist decides to separate identical twins at birth, then rear them in differing environments. Better yet, consider a *true* story:

On a chilly February morning in 1979, some time after divorcing his first wife, Linda, Jim Lewis awoke in his modest home next to his second wife, Betty. Determined that this marriage would work, Jim made a habit of leaving love notes to Betty

- Sweden has the world's largest national twin registry—140,000 living and dead twin pairs—which form part of a massive registry of 600,000 twins currently being sampled in the world's largest twin study (Wheelwright, 2004; www.genomeutwin.org). •

At this point, you may want to use **Lecture/Discussion Topic:** *The Genetic Revolution* (p. 4) from Bolt's Teacher's Resource Binder.

🛟 **TEACHING TIP**

- Identical twins are also referred to as **monozygotic** twins. They come from one zygote that split during early pregnancy.

- Fraternal twins are also referred to as **dizygotic** twins. They come from two different eggs produced during the same menstrual cycle that were fertilized at the same time.

At this point, you may want to use **Lecture/Discussion Topic:** *"Mom Always Liked You Best"* (p. 7) from Bolt's Teacher's Resource Binder.

🛟 **TEACHING TIP**

Identical twins are unique in that they share 100 percent of the same genes, but, while sharing the same genotype, they can have different phenotypes.

- Some identical twins are mirror images of each other (one being left-handed, the other right-handed; one having a mole on the left side of the face while the other has one on the right, etc.).

- Others may have different personalities and interests, showing that heritability of a trait doesn't mean it will occur even in two people who share the same genes.

- Fraternal twins, even though they may look alike and act alike, are only as similar to one another as any sibling combination.

UNIT 3C

RESEARCH

Have students research other stories of identical twins separated at birth.

- What similarities did the twins share? How were they different?
- How did each twin feel growing up—did they sense they had a twin or did they not feel a connection to their sibling?
- How did they feel when they reunited with their twin?

● Twins Lorraine and Levinia Christmas, driving to deliver Christmas presents to each other near Flitcham, England, collided (Shepherd, 1997). ●

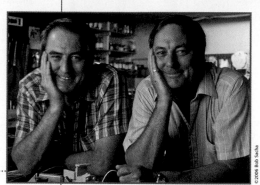

▼ **Identical twins are people two** Identical twins Jim Lewis and Jim Springer were separated shortly after birth and raised in different homes without awareness of each other. Research has shown remarkable similarities in the life choices of separated identical twins, lending support to the idea that genes influence personality.

"In some domains it looks as though our identical twins reared apart are . . . just as similar as identical twins reared together. Now that's an amazing finding and I can assure you none of us would have expected that degree of similarity."

Thomas Bouchard (1981)

● Bouchard's famous twin research was, appropriately enough, conducted in Minneapolis, the "Twin City" (with St. Paul), and home to the Minnesota Twins baseball team. ●

around the house. As he lay in bed he thought about others he had loved, including his son, James Alan, and his faithful dog, Toy.

Jim was looking forward to spending part of the day in his basement woodworking shop, where he had put in many happy hours building furniture, picture frames, and other items, including a white bench now circling a tree in his front yard. Jim also liked to spend free time driving his Chevy, watching stock-car racing, and drinking Miller Lite beer.

Jim was basically healthy, except for occasional half-day migraine headaches and blood pressure that was a little high, perhaps related to his chain-smoking habit. He had become overweight a while back but had shed some of the pounds. Having undergone a vasectomy, he was done having children.

What was extraordinary about Jim Lewis, however, was that at that same moment (I am not making this up) there existed another man—also named Jim—for whom all these things (right down to the dog's name) were also true.[1] This other Jim—Jim Springer—just happened, 38 years earlier, to have been his womb-mate. Thirty-seven days after their birth, these genetically identical twins were separated, adopted by blue-collar families, and reared with no contact or knowledge of each other's whereabouts until the day Jim Lewis received a call from his genetic clone (who, having been told he had a twin, set out to find him).

One month later, the brothers became the first twin pair tested by University of Minnesota psychologist Thomas Bouchard and his colleagues, beginning a study of separated twins that extends to the present (Holden, 1980a,b; Wright, 1998). Given tests measuring their personality, intelligence, heart rate, and brain waves, the Jim twins—despite 38 years of separation—were virtually as alike as the same person tested twice. Their voice intonations and inflections were so similar that, hearing a playback of an earlier interview, Jim Springer guessed "That's me." Wrong—it was his brother.

Identical twins Oskar Stohr and Jack Yufe presented equally striking similarities. One was raised by his grandmother in Germany as a Catholic and a Nazi, while the other was raised by his father in the Caribbean as a Jew. Nevertheless, they shared traits and habits galore. They liked spicy foods and sweet liqueurs, fell asleep in front of the television, flushed the toilet before using it, stored rubber bands on their wrists, and dipped buttered toast in their coffee. Stohr was domineering toward women and yelled at his wife, as did Yufe before he and his wife separated. Both married women named Dorothy Jane Scheckelburger. Okay, the last item is a joke. But as Judith Rich Harris (2006) notes, it is hardly weirder than some other reported similarities.

Aided by publicity in magazine and newspaper stories, Bouchard and his colleagues (1990; DiLalla et al., 1996; Segal, 1999) located and studied 80 pairs of identical twins reared apart. They continued to find similarities not only of tastes and physical attributes but also of personality, abilities, attitudes, interests, and even fears.

In Sweden, Nancy Pedersen and her co-workers (1988) identified 99 separated identical twin pairs and more than 200 separated fraternal twin pairs. Compared with equivalent samples of identical twins reared together, the separated identical twins had somewhat

[1]Actually, this description of the two Jims errs in one respect: Jim Lewis named his son James Alan. Jim Springer named his James Allan.

DEMO

While the stories of the two Jims and Oskar and Jack are extraordinary, it is very common for relative strangers to share many things in common. Create a biographical scavenger hunt for your students by having them find other people in the class who share the same birthday, clothing size, shoe size, height, weight, favorite color, favorite movie, etc. Have students conduct data analysis to determine how common similarities are among their peers in class. Students will likely find they have more in common with their peers than they have differences. This points to the influence of similar environments on development.

At this point, you may want to use **Classroom Exercise: Striking Similarities** (p. 5) from Bolt's Teacher's Resource Binder.

less identical personalities (characteristic patterns of thinking, feeling, and acting). Still, separated twins were more alike if genetically identical than if fraternal. And separation shortly after birth (rather than, say, at age 8) did not amplify their personality differences.

Stories of startling twin similarities do not impress Bouchard's critics, who remind us that "the plural of *anecdote* is not *data*." They contend that if any two strangers were to spend hours comparing their behaviors and life histories, they would probably discover many coincidental similarities. If researchers created a control group of biologically unrelated pairs of the same age, sex, and ethnicity, who had not grown up together but who were as similar to one another in economic and cultural background as are many of the separated twin pairs, wouldn't these pairs also exhibit striking similarities (Joseph, 2001)? Bouchard replies that separated fraternal twins do not exhibit similarities comparable to those of separated identical twins. Twin researcher Nancy Segal (2000) notes that *virtual twins*—same-age, biologically unrelated siblings—are also much more dissimilar.

Even the more impressive data from personality assessments are clouded by the reunion of many of the separated twins some years before they were tested. Moreover, identical twins share an appearance, and the responses it evokes, and adoption agencies tend to place separated twins in similar homes. Despite these criticisms, the striking twin-study results helped shift scientific thinking toward a greater appreciation of genetic influences.

Biological Versus Adoptive Relatives

For behavior geneticists, nature's second type of real-life experiment—adoption—creates two groups: *genetic relatives* (biological parents and siblings) and *environmental relatives* (adoptive parents and siblings). For any given trait, we can therefore ask whether adopted children are more like their biological parents, who contributed their genes, or their adoptive parents, who contribute a home environment. While sharing that home environment, do adopted siblings also come to share traits?

The stunning finding from studies of hundreds of adoptive families is that people who grow up together, whether biologically related or not, do not much resemble one another in personality (McGue & Bouchard, 1998; Plomin et al., 1998; Rowe, 1990). In traits such as extraversion and agreeableness, adoptees are more similar to their biological parents than to their caregiving adoptive parents.

The finding is important enough to bear repeating: The environment shared by a family's children has virtually no discernible impact on their personalities. Two adopted children reared in the same home are no more likely to share personality traits with each other than with the child down the block. Heredity shapes other primates' personalities, too. Macaque monkeys raised by foster mothers exhibit social behaviors that resemble their biological, rather than foster, mothers (Maestripieri, 2003). Add all this to the similarity of identical twins, whether they grow up together or apart, and the effect of a shared rearing environment seems shockingly modest.

 Nature or nurture or both? When talent runs in families, as with the Williams sisters, how do heredity and environment together do their work?

What we have here is perhaps "the most important puzzle in the history of psychology," contends Steven Pinker (2002): Why are children in the same family so different? Why does shared family environment have so little effect on children's personalities? Is it because each sibling experiences unique peer influences and life events? Because sibling relationships ricochet off each other, amplifying their differences? Because siblings—despite sharing half their genes—have very different combinations of genes and may evoke very different kinds of parenting? Such questions fuel behavior geneticists' curiosity.

● Coincidences are not unique to twins. Patricia Kern of Colorado was born March 13, 1941, and named Patricia Ann Campbell. Patricia DiBiasi of Oregon also was born March 13, 1941, and named Patricia Ann Campbell. Both had fathers named Robert, worked as bookkeepers, and at the time of this comparison had children ages 21 and 19. Both studied cosmetology, enjoyed oil painting as a hobby, and married military men, within 11 days of each other. They are not genetically related (from an AP report, May 2, 1983). ●

"We carry to our graves the essence of the zygote that was first us."
Mary Pipher, *Seeking Peace: Chronicles of the Worst Buddhist in the World*, 2009

"Mom may be holding a full house while Dad has a straight flush, yet when Junior gets a random half of each of their cards his poker hand may be a loser."
David Lykken (2001)

TROUBLESHOOTING

Myers quotes Thomas Bouchard's critics who say, "The plural of anecdote is not data." This quote highlights a major theme of psychological science: We must balance our personal experience with data from scientific research. While we may know of someone's experience that counters research findings, data from research shows how these experiences occur among the population. Individual differences do occur, but we should not be so bold as to generalize from those individual experiences to the population as a whole.

At this point, you may want to use **Lecture/Discussion Topic: *Genetic Influences on Psychological Traits*** (p. 7) from Bolt's Teacher's Resource Binder

TEACHING TIP

You may have students who have been adopted. Be sensitive to their possible feelings and visible reactions as you discuss research concerning the impact of nature and nurture on the development of adopted children. Some students in your class may know, for example, that their biological parents had substance abuse problems or other psychological issues, and this knowledge may cause them concern over whether they will face similar challenges. Help them see that while a trait may be heritable, that doesn't necessarily mean that the trait will manifest itself.

TEACHING TIP

Author Judith Rich Harris in the book *The Nurture Assumption* proposed that parents do not have as much influence on the development of their children as people generally believe. In his book *The Blank Slate: The Modern Denial of Human Nature*, Steven Pinker also argues that infants are not born blank, but with a structure that influences how they behave and think. Have students consider the following:

● How much of your behavior would you attribute to biology? How much to environment? Why? ● How would you feel if you knew that your genes had the greatest influence on your behavior? Why?

At this point, you may want to use **Lecture/Discussion Topic: *Nature and Nurture*** (p. 8) from Bolt's Teacher's Resource Binder.

UNIT 3C

INTERCONNECTING

Note that Myers references Unit 7B for further explanation of heritability. Use this opportunity to show a practical application of heritability with students.

INTERCONNECTING

John B. Watson, the father of behaviorism, believed that environment was the single biggest determinant of behavior and mental processes. He famously wrote in his 1930 book *Behaviorism*:

Give me a dozen healthy infants, well-formed, and my own specified world to bring them up in and I'll guarantee to take any one at random and train him to become any type of specialist I might select—doctor, lawyer, artist, merchant-chief and, yes, even beggar-man and thief, regardless of his talents, penchants, tendencies, abilities, vocations, and race of his ancestors. I am going beyond my facts and I admit it, but so have the advocates of the contrary and they have been doing it for many thousands of years. (p. 82)

• The greater uniformity of adoptive homes—mostly healthy, nurturing homes—helps explain the lack of striking differences when comparing child outcomes of different adoptive homes (Stoolmiller, 1999). •

"The title of my science project is 'My Little Brother: Nature or Nurture.'"

The minimal shared-environment effect does not, however, mean that adoptive parenting is a fruitless venture. The genetic leash may limit the family environment's influence on personality, but parents do influence their children's attitudes, values, manners, faith, and politics (Reifman & Cleveland, 2007). A pair of adopted children or identical twins *will*, especially during adolescence, have more similar religious beliefs if reared together (Kelley & De Graaf, 1997; Koenig et al., 2005; Rohan & Zanna, 1996). Parenting matters!

Moreover, in adoptive homes, child neglect and abuse and even parental divorce are rare. (Adoptive parents are carefully screened; natural parents are not.) So it is not surprising that, despite a somewhat greater risk of psychological disorder, most adopted children thrive, especially when adopted as infants (Loehlin et al., 2007; van IJzendoorn & Juffer, 2006; Wierzbicki, 1993). Seven in eight report feeling strongly attached to one or both adoptive parents. As children of self-giving parents, they grow up to be more self-giving and altruistic than average (Sharma et al., 1998). Many score higher than their biological parents on intelligence tests, and most grow into happier and more stable adults. In one Swedish study, infant adoptees grew up with fewer problems than were experienced by children whose biological mothers had initially registered them for adoption but then decided to raise the children themselves (Bohman & Sigvardsson, 1990). Regardless of personality differences between parents and their adoptees, children benefit from adoption.

Heritability

2: What is heritability, and how does it relate to individuals and groups?

Using twin and adoption studies, behavior geneticists can mathematically estimate the **heritability** of a trait—the extent to which variation among individuals can be attributed to their differing genes. As Unit 7B will emphasize, if the heritability of intelligence is, say, 50 percent, this does *not* mean that *your* intelligence is 50 percent genetic. (If the heritability of height is 90 percent, this does not mean that a 60-inch-tall woman can credit her genes for 54 inches and her environment for the other 6 inches.) Rather, it means that genetic influence explains 50 percent of the observed variation *among people*. This point is so often misunderstood that I repeat: We can never say what percentage of an *individual's* personality or intelligence is inherited. It makes no sense to say that your personality is due *x* percent to your heredity and *y* percent to your environment. Heritability refers instead to the extent to which *differences among people* are attributable to genes.

Even this conclusion must be qualified, because heritability can vary from study to study. Consider humorist Mark Twain's (1835–1910) proposal to raise boys in barrels to age 12, feeding them through a hole. If we were to follow his suggestion, the boys would all emerge with lower-than-normal intelligence scores at age 12; yet, given their equal environments, their test score differences could be explained only by their heredity. In this case, heritability—differences due to genes—would be near 100 percent. As environments become more similar, heredity as a source of differences necessarily becomes more important. If all schools were of uniform quality, all families equally loving, and all neighborhoods equally healthy, then heritability would increase (because differences due to environment would decrease). At the other extreme, if all people had similar heredities but were raised in drastically different environments (some in barrels, some in luxury homes), heritability would be much lower.

Group Differences

If genetic influences help explain individual diversity in traits such as aggressiveness, can the same be said of group differences between men and women, or between people of different races? Not necessarily. Individual differences in height and weight, for example,

TROUBLESHOOTING

Students may have some difficulty understanding the concept of heritability. Help them break down the word into its component parts:

- *Herit-* is part of the more familiar word "inherit." To inherit means to possess something that someone else has given you. We inherit our traits and qualities from our parents.

- *-ability* as a suffix means "capable." If a trait is genetically passed on from one generation to the next, then it

is capable of showing up in the children of people who possess that quality.

- Help students see that a heritable trait is one that is capable of being passed down from parent to child.

are highly heritable; yet nutritional rather than genetic influences explain why, as a group, today's adults are taller and heavier than those of a century ago. The two groups differ, but not because human genes have changed in a mere century's eyeblink of time.

As with height and weight, so with personality and intelligence scores: Heritable individual differences need not imply heritable group differences. If some individuals are genetically disposed to be more aggressive than others, that needn't explain why some groups are more aggressive than others. Putting people in a new social context can change their aggressiveness. Today's peaceful Scandinavians carry many genes inherited from their Viking warrior ancestors.

Nature and Nurture

Among our similarities, the most important—the behavioral hallmark of our species—is our enormous adaptive capacity. Some human traits, such as having two eyes, develop the same in virtually every environment. But other traits are expressed only in particular environments. Go barefoot for a summer and you will develop toughened, callused feet—a biological adaptation to friction. Meanwhile, your shod neighbor will remain a tenderfoot. The difference between the two of you is, of course, an effect of environment. But it is also the product of a biological mechanism—adaptation. Our shared biology enables our developed diversity (Buss, 1991).

An analogy may help: Genes and environment—nature and nurture—work together like two hands clapping. Genes not only code for particular proteins, they also respond to environments. An African butterfly that is green in summer turns brown in fall, thanks to a temperature-controlled genetic switch. The genes that produce brown in one situation produce green in another. Thus, genes are *self-regulating*. Rather than acting as blueprints that lead to the same result no matter the context, genes react. People with identical genes but differing experiences therefore have similar though not identical minds. One twin may fall in love with someone quite different from the co-twin's love.

As we will see in Unit 12, at least one known gene will, in response to major life stresses, code for a protein that controls a neurotransmitter involved in depression. By itself, the gene doesn't cause depression, but it is part of the recipe. Likewise, the breast-feeding boost to later intelligence that we noted in Unit 2 turns out to be true only for the 90 percent of infants with a gene that assists in breaking down fatty acids present in human milk (Caspi et al., 2007). Studies of 1037 New Zealand adults and 2232 English 12- and 13-year olds found no breast-feeding boost among those not carrying the gene. As so often happens, nature and nurture work together.

Thus, asking whether your personality is more a product of your genes or your environment is like asking whether the area of a field is more the result of its length or its width. We could, however, ask whether the differing areas of various fields are more the result of *differences* in their length or their width, and also whether person-to-person personality differences are influenced more by nature or nurture. Human differences result from both genetic and environmental influences. Thus (to give a preview of a future unit), eating disorders are genetically influenced: Some individuals are more at risk than others. But culture also bends the twig, for eating disorders are primarily a contemporary Western cultural phenomenon.

Gene-Environment Interaction

To say that genes and experience are *both* important is true. But more precisely, they **interact**. Imagine two babies, one genetically predisposed to be attractive, sociable, and easygoing, the other less so. Assume further that the first baby attracts more affectionate and stimulating care than the second and so develops into a warmer and more outgoing person. As the two children grow older, the more naturally outgoing child more often seeks activities and friends that encourage further social confidence.

::**heritability** the proportion of variation among individuals that we can attribute to genes. The heritability of a trait may vary, depending on the range of populations and environments studied.

::**interaction** the interplay that occurs when the effect of one factor (such as environment) depends on another factor (such as heredity).

> "Men's natures are alike; it is their habits that carry them far apart."
> Confucius, *Analects*, 500 B.C.E.

Emphasize that just because a trait is heritable does not mean it will affect an individual or that it will be a defining trait of a group. Heritability only demonstrates the extent to which a trait is explainable by genetics, but not the extent to which the trait will affect behavior in an individual or group outside of environmental influences.

INTERCONNECTING

Myers notes that Unit 12 will discuss a genetic tendency toward depression or other psychological disorders. Scientists have found numerous genes in recent years that predispose people to a wide range of physical and psychological conditions. Help students see that genetics alone does not guarantee that a person will develop a condition, only that it will be more likely to occur if the right environmental influences interact with those genes.

CRITICAL THINKING

Students often have preconceptions about the nature/nurture dynamic. Inspire critical thinking in your students by playing devil's advocate for both sides of the debate of nature/nurture. When you do this, students who strongly believe that either nature or nurture is wholly definitive will see that both interact in determining human behavior.

TROUBLESHOOTING

Students often discount the interaction of genes and the environment. They especially don't believe that a person's genetics can influence his or her environment. Use the pictures on page 102 of Will Ferrell and Zac Efron as examples of this interaction effect. Have students also do research on whether the way one looks affects prospects for getting a job or a promotion. Some research already done suggests that people who are judged as attractive physically are more likely to get a job or a promotion over those judged less attractive, demonstrating the influence of genes on environment.

INTERCONNECTING

The phrase, "bottom-up," is also used in Unit 5: Sensation and Perception to describe situations in which sensory information is processed before perceptual expectations. When we use bottom-up processing, we are taking in all pieces of sensory information, beginning at the microscopic level, before processing the meaning, or macroscopic level. In the case of molecular genetics, bottom-up refers to beginning at a micro level of understanding.

> "Heredity deals the cards; environment plays the hand."
> Psychologist Charles L. Brewer (1990)

Gene-environment interaction People respond differently to Will Ferrell, left, than to fellow actor Zac Efron, right.

What has caused their resulting personality differences? Neither heredity nor experience dances alone. Environments trigger gene activity. (Scientists are now exploring environmental influences on when particular genes generate proteins.) The other partner in the dance—our genetically influenced traits—also *evoke* significant responses in others. Thus, a student's impulsivity and aggression may evoke an angry response from a teacher who otherwise reacts warmly to the student's model classmates. Parents, too, may treat their own children differently; one child elicits punishment, another does not. In such cases, the child's nature and the parents' nurture interact. Neither operates apart from the other. Gene and scene dance together.

Evocative interactions may help explain why identical twins reared in different families recall their parents' warmth as remarkably similar—almost as similar as if they had had the same parents (Plomin et al., 1988, 1991, 1994). Fraternal twins have more differing recollections of their early family life—even if reared in the same family! "Children experience us as different parents, depending on their own qualities," noted Sandra Scarr (1990). Moreover, as we grow older we also *select* environments well suited to our natures.

So, from conception onward, we are the product of a cascade of interactions between our genetic predispositions and our surrounding environments. Our genes affect how people react to and influence us. Biological appearances have social consequences. So, forget nature *versus* nurture; think nature *via* nurture.

The New Frontier: Molecular Genetics

3: What is the promise of molecular genetics research?

Behavior geneticists have progressed beyond asking, "Do genes influence behavior?" The new frontier of behavior-genetics research draws on "bottom-up" **molecular genetics** as it seeks to identify *specific genes* influencing behavior.

As we have already seen, most human traits are influenced by teams of genes. For example, twin and adoption studies tell us that heredity influences body weight, but there is no single "obesity gene." More likely, some genes influence how quickly the stomach tells the brain, "I'm full." Others might dictate how much fuel the muscles need, how many calories are burned off by fidgeting, and how efficiently the body converts extra calories into fat (Vogel, 1999). The goal of *molecular behavior genetics* is to find some of the many genes that influence normal human traits, such as body weight, sexual orientation, and extraversion, and also to explore the mechanisms that control gene expression (Tsankova et al., 2007).

Genetic tests can now reveal at-risk populations for many diseases. The search continues in labs worldwide, where molecular geneticists are teaming with psychologists to pinpoint genes that put people at risk for such genetically influenced disorders as learning disabilities, depression, schizophrenia, and alcohol dependence. (In Unit 12, for example, we will take note of a worldwide research effort to sleuth the genes that make people vulnerable to the emotional swings of bipolar disorder, formerly known as manic-depressive disorder.) To tease out the implicated genes, molecular behavior geneticists seek links between certain genes or chromosome segments and specific disorders. First, they find families that have had the disorder across several generations. Then they draw blood or take cheek swabs from both affected and unaffected family members and examine their DNA, looking for differences. "The most powerful potential for DNA," note Robert Plomin and John Crabbe (2000), "is to predict risk so that steps can be taken to prevent problems before they happen."

Aided by inexpensive DNA-scanning techniques, medical personnel are becoming able to give would-be parents a readout on how their fetus' genes differ from the normal pattern

TROUBLESHOOTING

Students may not appreciate the importance of the concept of predisposition. While a person's genetic code will determine many physical and personal qualities such as eye color, hair color, height, weight, and extraversion/introversion, these qualities interact with the environment to influence things like popularity, interests, and dating choices. Even identical twins, who share 100 percent of the same genes, can differ in many ways depending on even slightly different environmental influences that occur.

and what this might mean. With this benefit come risks. Might labeling a fetus, for example, "at risk for a learning disorder" lead to discrimination? Prenatal screening poses ethical dilemmas. In China and India, where boys are highly valued, testing for an offspring's sex has enabled selective abortions resulting in millions—yes, millions—of "missing women."

Assuming it were possible, should prospective parents take their eggs and sperm to a genetics lab for screening before combining them to produce an embryo? Should we enable parents to screen their fertilized eggs for health—and for brains or beauty? Progress is a double-edged sword, raising both hopeful possibilities and difficult problems. By selecting out certain traits, we may deprive ourselves of future Handels and van Goghs, Churchills and Lincolns, Tolstoys and Dickinsons—troubled people all.

"I thought that sperm-bank donors remained anonymous."

BEFORE YOU MOVE ON . . .

➤ **ASK YOURSELF**

Would you want genetic tests on your unborn offspring? What would you do if you knew your child would be destined for hemophilia? A learning disability? A high risk of depression? Do you think society would benefit or lose if such embryos were aborted?

➤ **TEST YOURSELF 1**

What is *heritability*?

Answers to the Test Yourself questions can be found in Appendix E at the end of the book.

Evolutionary Psychology: Understanding Human Nature

4: How do evolutionary psychologists use natural selection to explain behavior tendencies?

BEHAVIOR GENETICISTS EXPLORE THE genetic and environmental roots of human differences. **Evolutionary psychologists** instead focus mostly on what makes us so much alike as humans. They use Charles Darwin's principle of **natural selection** to understand the roots of behavior and mental processes. Richard Dawkins (2007) calls natural selection "arguably the most momentous idea ever to occur to a human mind." The idea, simplified, is this:

- Organisms' varied offspring compete for survival.
- Certain biological and behavioral variations increase organisms' reproductive and survival chances in their particular environment.
- Offspring that survive are more likely to pass their genes to ensuing generations.
- Thus, over time, population characteristics may change.

To see these principles at work, let's consider a straightforward example in foxes.

Natural Selection and Adaptation

A fox is a wild and wary animal. If you capture a fox and try to befriend it, be careful. Stick your hand in the cage and, if the timid fox cannot flee, it may make a snack of your fingers. Dmitry Belyaev, of the Russian Academy of Science's Institute of Cytology and Genetics, wondered how our human ancestors had domesticated dogs from their equally wild wolf forebears. Might he, within a comparatively short stretch of time, accomplish a similar feat by transforming the fearful fox into a friendly fox?

::**molecular genetics** the subfield of biology that studies the molecular structure and function of genes.

::**evolutionary psychology** the study of the evolution of behavior and the mind, using principles of natural selection.

::**natural selection** the principle that, among the range of inherited trait variations, those that lead to increased reproduction and survival will most likely be passed on to succeeding generations.

CRITICAL THINKING

Have students debate the merits of molecular genetics. Do the benefits of this research for finding cures to disease outweigh the potential misuse of selective breeding? Be sure to infuse discussion of heritability into these discussions to help students apply their knowledge.

TROUBLESHOOTING

Evolution is a controversial subject in many parts of the country. In some communities the majority of people view the theory of evolution as a direct contradiction of religious teaching. Be aware of your local community's views regarding evolution so that you can address students' questions in a thoughtful, sensitive way.

CRITICAL THINKING

Now that Darwin's ideas about evolution are more than 150 years old, have students debate whether they agree with Dawkins' quote that natural selection is "arguably the most momentous idea ever to occur to a human mind." Help them use the information from this unit to discuss the merits and unanswered questions about evolution.

UNIT 3C

TROUBLESHOOTING

Remind students that this discussion of evolutionary psychology is not about how one species evolves into another species over time. Rather, this discussion is about how genetics and environment interact, leading to changes in genetics to fit the environment. It is also about how traits that lead to survival are more likely to be passed down. If students can focus on these aspects of evolution instead of the controversial ones, the discussion can be productive for the AP Exam.

L. N. Trut, American Scientist (1999) 87: 160–169

From wary to winsome More than 40 years into the fox-breeding experiment, most of the offspring are devoted, affectionate, and capable of forming strong bonds with people.

::**mutation** a random error in gene replication that leads to a change.

To find out, Belyaev set to work with 30 male and 100 female foxes. From their offspring he selected and mated the tamest 5 percent of males and 20 percent of females. (He measured tameness by the foxes' responses to attempts to feed, handle, and stroke them.) Over more than 30 generations of foxes, Belyaev and his successor, Lyudmila Trut, repeated that simple procedure. Forty years and 45,000 foxes later, they had a new breed of foxes that, in Trut's (1999) words, are "docile, eager to please, and unmistakably domesticated. . . . Before our eyes, 'the Beast' has turned into 'beauty,' as the aggressive behavior of our herd's wild [ancestors] entirely disappeared." So friendly and eager for human contact are the foxes, so inclined to whimper to attract attention and to lick people like affectionate dogs, that the cash-strapped institute seized on a way to raise funds—marketing its foxes to people as house pets.

When certain traits are *selected*—by conferring a reproductive advantage to an individual or a species—those traits, over time, will prevail. Dog breeders, as Robert Plomin and his colleagues (1997) remind us, have given us sheepdogs that herd, retrievers that retrieve, trackers that track, and pointers that point. Psychologists, too, have bred dogs, mice, and rats whose genes predispose them to be serene or reactive, quick learners or slow.

Does natural selection also explain our human tendencies? Nature has indeed selected advantageous variations from among the **mutations** (random errors in gene replication) and from the new gene combinations produced at each human conception. But the tight genetic leash that predisposes a dog's retrieving, a cat's pouncing, or an ant's nest building is looser on humans. The genes selected during our ancestral history provide more than a long leash; they endow us with a great capacity to learn and therefore to *adapt* to life in varied environments, from the tundra to the jungle. Genes and experience together wire the brain. Our adaptive flexibility in responding to different environments contributes to our *fitness*—our ability to survive and reproduce.

Evolutionary Success Helps Explain Similarities

Although human differences grab our attention, our deep similarities also demand explanation. And in the big picture, our lives are remarkably alike. Visit the international arrivals area at Amsterdam's Schiphol Airport, a world hub where arriving passengers meet their excited loved ones. There you will see the same delighted joy in the faces of Indonesian grandmothers, Chinese children, and homecoming Dutch. Evolutionary psychologist Steven Pinker (2002, p. 73) believes it is no wonder that our emotions, drives, and reasoning "have a common logic across cultures." Our shared human traits "were shaped by natural selection acting over the course of human evolution."

Our behavioral and biological similarities arise from our shared human genome. No more than 5 percent of the genetic differences among humans arise from population group differences. Some 95 percent of genetic variation exists within populations (Rosenberg et al., 2002). The typical genetic difference between two Icelandic villagers or between two Kenyans is much greater than the *average* difference between the two groups. Thus, noted geneticist Richard Lewontin (1982), if after a worldwide catastrophe only Icelanders or Kenyans survived, the human species would suffer only "a trivial reduction" in its genetic diversity.

And how did we develop this shared human genome? At the dawn of human history, our ancestors faced certain questions: Who is my ally, who my foe? What food should I eat? With whom should I mate? Some individuals answered those questions more successfully than others. For example, some women's experience of nausea in the critical first three months of pregnancy predisposes their avoiding certain bitter, strongly flavored, and novel foods. Avoiding such foods has survival value, since they are the very foods most often toxic to embryonic development (Schmitt & Pilcher, 2004). Early humans disposed to eat nourishing rather than poisonous food survived to contribute their genes to later generations. Those who deemed leopards "nice to pet" often did not.

 TEACHING TIP

At this point, you may want to use **Lecture/Discussion Topic:** *Gene-Environment Correlation* (p. 9) from Bolt's Teacher's Resource Binder.

Similarly successful were those whose mating helped them produce and nurture offspring. Over generations, the genes of individuals not so disposed tended to be lost from the human gene pool. As genes contributing to success continued to be selected, behavioral tendencies and thinking and learning capacities emerged that prepared our Stone Age ancestors to survive, reproduce, and send their genes into the future.

Outdated Tendencies

As inheritors of this prehistoric genetic legacy, we are predisposed to behave in ways that promoted our ancestors' surviving and reproducing. We love the taste of sweets and fats, which once were hard to come by but which prepared our ancestors to survive famines. With famine now rare in Western cultures, and sweets and fats beckoning us from school cafeterias, store shelves, fast-food outlets, and vending machines, obesity has become a growing problem. Our natural dispositions, rooted deep in history, are mismatched with today's junk-food environment (Colarelli & Dettman, 2003). We are, in some ways, biologically prepared for a world that no longer exists.

Evolutionary Psychology Today

Darwin's theory of evolution has been an organizing principle for biology for a long time. Jared Diamond (2001) notes that "virtually no contemporary scientists believe that Darwin was basically wrong." Today, Darwin's theory lives on in "the second Darwinian revolution": the application of evolutionary principles to psychology. In concluding *On the Origin of Species*, Darwin (1859, p. 346) anticipated this, foreseeing "open fields for far more important researches. Psychology will be based on a new foundation."

Evolutionary psychologists have addressed questions such as these:

- Why do infants start to fear strangers about the time they become mobile?
- Why are biological fathers so much less likely than unrelated boyfriends to abuse and murder the children with whom they share a home?
- Why do so many more people have phobias about spiders, snakes, and heights than about more dangerous threats, such as guns and electricity?
- Why do humans share some universal moral ideas?
- How are men and women alike? How and why do men's and women's sexuality differ?

We will address such questions in later units. To see how evolutionary psychologists think and reason, let's pause now to explore that last question.

An Evolutionary Explanation of Human Sexuality

5: How might an evolutionary psychologist explain gender differences in sexuality and mating preferences?

Having faced many similar challenges throughout history, men and women have adapted in similar ways. Whether male or female, we eat the same foods, avoid the same predators, and perceive, learn, and remember similarly. It is only in those domains where we have faced differing adaptive challenges—most obviously in behaviors related to reproduction—that we differ, say evolutionary psychologists.

Gender Differences in Sexuality

Differ we do, report psychologists Roy Baumeister, Kathleen Catanese, and Kathleen Vohs (2001). They invite us to consider whether women or men have the stronger sex drive. Who desires more frequent sex, thinks more about sex, initiates more sex, and sacrifices more to gain sex? The answers, they report, are *men, men, men,* and *men.* For example, in one BBC survey of more than 200,000 people in 53 nations, men everywhere more

---

• Despite high infant mortality and rampant disease in past millennia, not one of your countless ancestors died childless. •

• Those who are troubled by an apparent conflict between scientific and religious accounts of human origins may find it helpful to recall (Unit 1) that different perspectives of life can be complementary. For example, the scientific account attempts to tell us *when* and *how*; religious creation stories usually aim to tell about an ultimate *who* and *why*. As Galileo explained to the Grand Duchess Christina, "The Bible teaches how to go to heaven, not how the heavens go." •

INTERCONNECTING

Myers lists several questions that evolutionary psychologists have addressed. Point students toward a more thorough understanding of these questions addressed in future units:

- Question 1: Unit 9
- Question 2: Unit 9 and Unit 12
- Question 3: Unit 12
- Question 4: Unit 14

Guide students towards these units if they have questions about how evolutionary psychologists have tried to answer these questions.

CRITICAL THINKING

Have students discuss why they eat and what they eat. Have them discuss whether the evolutionary perspective can explain their own eating habits.

TEACHING TIP

At this point, you may want to use **Lecture/Discussion Topic: *Designer Babies?*** (p. 10) from Bolt's Teacher's Resource Binder.

UNIT 3C

RESEARCH

Have students examine what today's teens believe to be attractive. They can do this in several ways:

- Take a sample of magazines directed more toward men (*Sports Illustrated, Men's Health*, etc.) and women's magazines (*Vogue, Glamour, Redbook*, etc.) as well as magazines that are considered neutral (news magazines, etc.) to see how the people in advertisements are portrayed. Have students count the qualities of the people shown in the ads—hair color, whether they are smiling or not, etc. Do these data support an evolutionary perspective on attraction?

- Compile pictures of people from different demographics (tall, short, blond, brunette, red hair, ethnic identity, etc.). Have volunteers rate how attractive each person in the picture is, analyzing the data to determine whether a pattern emerges. Do these data support an evolutionary perspective?

strongly agreed that "I have a strong sex drive" and "It doesn't take much to get me sexually excited" (Lippa, 2008). Indeed, "with few exceptions anywhere in the world," report cross-cultural psychologist Marshall Segall and his colleagues (1990, p. 244), "males are more likely than females to initiate sexual activity."

Men also have a lower threshold for perceiving warm responses as a sexual come-on. In study after study, men more often than women attribute a woman's friendliness to sexual interest (Abbey, 1987; Johnson et al., 1991). Misattributing women's cordiality as a come-on helps explain—but does not excuse—men's greater sexual assertiveness (Kolivas & Gross, 2007). The unfortunate results can range from sexual harassment to date rape.

Natural Selection and Mating Preferences

As biologists use natural selection to explain the mating behaviors of many species, so evolutionary psychologists use natural selection to explain a worldwide human sexuality difference: Women's approach to sex is usually more relational, and men's more recreational (Schmitt, 2005, 2007). The explanation goes like this: While a woman usually incubates and nurses one infant at a time, a male can spread his genes through other females. Our natural yearnings are our genes' way of reproducing themselves. In our ancestral history, women most often sent their genes into the future by pairing wisely, men by pairing widely. "Humans are living fossils—collections of mechanisms produced by prior selection pressures," says evolutionary psychologist David Buss (1995).

And what do heterosexual men and women find attractive in the other sex? Some aspects of attractiveness cross place and time. Men in a wide range of cultures, from Australia to Zambia (**FIGURE 3C.3**), judge women as more attractive if they have a youthful

> **► FIGURE 3C.3**
> **Worldwide mating preferences** In a wide range of cultures studied (indicated by the red dots), men more than women preferred physical features suggesting youth and health—and reproductive potential. Women more than men preferred mates with resources and social status. Researchers credit (or blame) natural selection (Buss, 1994).

appearance (Buss, 1994). Evolutionary psychologists say that men who were drawn to healthy, fertile-appearing women—women with smooth skin and a youthful shape suggesting many childbearing years to come—stood a better chance of sending their genes into the future. And sure enough, men feel most attracted to women whose waists are (or are surgically altered to be) roughly a third narrower than their hips—a sign of future fertility. Moreover, just as evolutionary psychology predicts, men are most attracted to women who, in the ancestral past (when ovulation began later than today), were at ages associated with peak fertility. Thus teen boys are most excited by a woman several years older than themselves, report Douglas Kenrick and his colleagues (in press). Midtwenties men prefer women around their own age.

And older men prefer younger women. This pattern, they report, consistently appears across European singles ads, Indian marital ads, and marriage records from North and South America, Africa, and the Philippines (Singh, 1993; Singh & Randall, 2007).

Women, in turn, prefer stick-around dads over likely cads. They are attracted to men who seem mature, dominant, bold, and affluent (Singh, 1995). They prefer mates with the potential for long-term mating and investment in their joint offspring (Gangestad & Simpson, 2000). Such attributes, say the evolutionary psychologists, connote a capacity to support and protect (Buss, 1996, 2000; Geary, 1998). In one experiment, women skillfully discerned which men most liked looking at baby pictures, and they rated those men higher as potential long-term mates (Roney et al., 2006).

There is a principle at work here, say evolutionary psychologists: Nature selects behaviors that increase the likelihood of sending one's genes into the future. As mobile gene machines, we are designed to prefer whatever worked for our ancestors in their environments. They were predisposed to act in ways that would leave grandchildren—had they not been, we wouldn't be here. And as carriers of their genetic legacy, we are similarly predisposed.

"What about you, Walter—how do you feel about same-age marriage?"

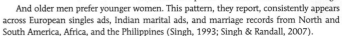

TEACHING TIP

At this point, you may want to use **Lecture/Discussion Topic: *Evolutionary Psychology*** (p. 10) from Bolt's Teacher's Resource Binder.

Critiquing the Evolutionary Perspective

6: What are the key criticisms of evolutionary psychology?

Without disputing nature's selection of traits that enhance gene survival, critics see problems with evolutionary psychology. It often, they say, starts with an effect (such as the gender sexuality difference) and works backward to propose an explanation. So let's imagine a different observation and reason backward. If men were uniformly loyal to their mates, might we not reason that the children of these committed, supportive fathers would more often survive to perpetuate their genes? Might not men also be better off bonded to one woman—both to increase their odds of impregnation and to keep her from the advances of competing men? Might not a ritualized bond—a marriage—also spare women from chronic male harassment? Such suggestions are, in fact, evolutionary explanations for why humans tend to pair off monogamously. One can hardly lose at hindsight explanation, which is, said paleontologist Stephen Jay Gould (1997), mere "speculation [and] guesswork in the cocktail party mode."

Some also worry about the social consequences of evolutionary psychology. Does it suggest a genetic determinism that strikes at the heart of progressive efforts to remake society (Rose, 1999)? Does it undercut moral responsibility? Could it be used to rationalize "high-status men marrying a series of young, fertile women" (Looy, 2001)?

Much of who we are is *not* hard-wired, agree evolutionary psychologists. What's considered attractive does vary somewhat with time and place. The voluptuous Marilyn Monroe ideal of the 1950s has been replaced by the twenty-first-century, leaner, yet still curvy athletic image. Moreover, cultural expectations can bend the genders. If socialized to value lifelong commitment, men may sexually bond with one partner; if socialized to accept casual sex, women may willingly have sex with many partners.

Social expectations also shape gender differences in mate preferences. Show Alice Eagly and Wendy Wood (1999; Wood & Eagly, 2002, 2007) a culture with gender inequality—where men are providers and women are homemakers—and they will show you a culture where men strongly desire youth and domestic skill in their potential mates, and where women seek status and earning potential in their mates. Show Eagly and Wood a culture with gender equality, and they will show you a culture with smaller gender differences in mate preferences.

Evolutionary psychologists reassure us that the sexes, having faced similar adaptive problems, are far more alike than different. They stress that humans have a great capacity for learning and social progress. (We come equipped to adapt and survive, whether living in igloos or tree houses.) They point to the coherence and explanatory power of evolutionary principles, especially those offering testable predictions (for example, that we will favor others to the extent that they share our genes or can later reciprocate our favors). And they remind us that the study of how we came to be need not dictate how we *ought* to be. Understanding our propensities sometimes helps us overcome them.

"I had a nice time, Steve. Would you like to come in, settle down, and raise a family?"

BEFORE YOU MOVE ON . . .

➤ **ASK YOURSELF**

Whose reasoning do you find most persuasive—that of evolutionary psychologists or their critics? Why?

➤ **TEST YOURSELF 2**

What are the three main criticisms of evolutionary psychology's explanations?

Answers to the Test Yourself questions can be found in Appendix E at the end of the book.

TROUBLESHOOTING

Address several misunderstandings about evolutionary theory:

- Evolution does not imply genetic determinism.
- Behavior can be changed.
- Evolutionary theory does not assume that organisms can compute complex mathematical formulas.
- Current adaptive mechanisms in human are not "optimally designed."
- Organisms do not have a conscious or unconscious goal of maximizing gene reproduction.

Buss, D. M. (1999). *Evolutionary psychology: The new science of the mind.* Needham Heights, MA: Allyn & Bacon.

 TEACHING TIP

Social Darwinism, the application of Darwin's theories to social behaviors and institutions, is a philosophy that was often cited in the early days of evolutionary theory to justify the then-current state of society which strictly separated rich from poor and one race from another. Some people used to justify keeping classes and races separate to avoid contaminating the "superior" gene pool. In actuality, genetic diversity is more beneficial from an evolutionary perspective than genetic similarity. This misapplication of Darwin's ideas led to many policies that hurt people rather than helped.

At this point, you may want to use **Classroom Exercise: Mate Preferences** (p. 13) from Bolt's Teacher's Resource Binder.

 TEACHING TIP

At this point, you may want to use **Lecture/Discussion Topic: Misunderstanding Evolutionary Theory and Psychology** (p. 12) from Bolt's Teacher's Resource Binder.

It may seem that this extended discussion of nature/nurture and evolutionary psychology is a digression rather than a necessity for AP Psychology. However, students often misunderstand this issue in general and evolution in particular. Making sure students leave this topic with a thorough understanding of the nature/nurture issue is crucial to their understanding of future content in the course.

CRITICAL THINKING

While the text is very clear about the interaction of nature and nurture, this belief has only emerged in the last few decades. For many years, people battled from one extreme to the other, in both science and philosophy:

- Plato and Aristotle argued about whether people already knew the great truths of life (Idealism) or whether great truths are learned through experience (Empiricism).

- John Locke and Jean-Jacques Rousseau argued over whether an individual is born as a *tabula rasa* ("blank slate") or with unfulfilled potential.

- Freud and Watson argued over whether people were born with innate, unchecked tendencies (the id) or as "balls of putty" ready to be shaped by experience.

Culture matters As this exhibit at San Diego's Museum of Man illustrates, children learn their culture. A baby's foot can step into any culture. ▲

Reflections on Nature and Nurture

"THERE ARE TRIVIAL TRUTHS AND GREAT truths," reflected the physicist Niels Bohr on some of the paradoxes of modern science. "The opposite of a trivial truth is plainly false. The opposite of a great truth is also true." It appears true that our ancestral history helped form us as a species. Where there is variation, natural selection, and heredity, there will be evolution. The unique gene combination created when our mother's egg engulfed our father's sperm predisposed both our shared humanity and our individual differences. This is a great truth about human nature. Genes form us.

But it also is true that our experiences form us. In our families and in our peer relationships, we learn ways of thinking and acting. Differences initiated by our nature may be amplified by our nurture. If their genes and hormones predispose males to be more physically aggressive than females, culture may magnify this gender difference through norms that encourage males to be macho and females to be the kinder, gentler sex. If men are encouraged toward roles that demand physical power, and women toward more nurturing roles, each may then exhibit the actions expected of those who fill such roles and find themselves shaped accordingly. Roles remake their players. Presidents in time become more presidential, servants more servile. Gender roles similarly shape us.

But gender roles are converging. Brute strength has become increasingly irrelevant to power and status (think Bill Gates and Oprah Winfrey). Thus both women and men are now seen as "fully capable of effectively carrying out organizational roles at all levels," note Wendy Wood and Alice Eagly (2002). And as women's employment in formerly male occupations has increased, gender differences in traditional masculinity or femininity and in what one seeks in a mate have diminished (Twenge, 1997). As the roles we play change over time, we change with them.

* * *

If nature and nurture jointly form us, are we "nothing but" the product of nature and nurture? Are we rigidly determined?

We *are* the product of nature and nurture (**FIGURE 3C.4**), but we are also an open system. Genes are all-pervasive but not all-powerful; people may defy their genetic bent to reproduce, by electing celibacy. Culture, too, is all-pervasive but not all-powerful; people may defy peer pressures and do the opposite of the expected. To excuse our failings by blaming our nature and nurture is what philosopher-novelist Jean-Paul Sartre called "bad faith"—attributing responsibility for one's fate to bad genes or bad influences.

In reality, we are both the creatures and the creators of our worlds. We are—it is a great truth—the products of our genes and environments. Nevertheless (another great truth) the stream of causation that shapes the future runs through our present choices. Our decisions today design our environments tomorrow. Mind matters. The human environment is not like the weather—something that just happens. We are its architects. Our hopes, goals, and expectations influence our future. And that is what enables cultures to vary and to change so quickly.

* * *

I know from my mail and from public opinion surveys that some readers feel troubled by the naturalism and evolutionism of contemporary science. Particularly in the United States there is a wide gulf between scientific and lay thinking about evolution. "The idea that human minds are the product of evolution is . . . unassailable fact," declared a 2007 editorial in *Nature*, a leading science magazine. That sentiment concurs with a 2006 statement of "evidence-based facts" about evolution jointly issued by the national science academies of 66 nations (IAP, 2006). In *The Language of God*,

At this point, you may want to use **Classroom Exercise:** *Evolutionary Psychology* (p. 11) from Bolt's Teacher's Resource Binder.

Human Genome Project director Francis Collins (2006, pp. 141, 146), a self-described evangelical Christian, compiles the "utterly compelling" evidence that leads him to conclude that Darwin's big idea is "unquestionably correct." Yet a 2007 Gallup survey reports that half of U.S. adults do not believe in evolution's role in "how human beings came to exist on Earth" (Newport, 2007). Many of those who dispute the scientific story worry that a science of behavior (and evolutionary science in particular) will destroy our sense of the beauty, mystery, and spiritual significance of the human creature. For those concerned, I offer some reassuring thoughts.

When Isaac Newton explained the rainbow in terms of light of differing wavelengths, the poet Keats feared that Newton had destroyed the rainbow's mysterious beauty. Yet, notes Richard Dawkins (1998) in *Unweaving the Rainbow*, Newton's analysis led to an even deeper mystery—Einstein's theory of special relativity. Moreover, nothing about Newton's optics need diminish our appreciation for the dramatic elegance of a rainbow arching across a brightening sky.

When Galileo assembled evidence that the Earth revolved around the Sun, not vice versa, he did not offer irrefutable proof for his theory. Rather, he offered a coherent explanation for a variety of observations, such as the changing shadows cast by the Moon's mountains. His explanation eventually won the day because it described and explained things in a way that made sense, that hung together. Darwin's theory of evolution likewise is a coherent view of natural history. It offers an organizing principle that unifies various observations.

Francis Collins is not the only person of faith to find the scientific idea of human origins congenial with his spirituality. In the fifth century, St. Augustine (quoted by Wilford, 1999) wrote, "The universe was brought into being in a less than fully formed state, but was gifted with the capacity to transform itself from unformed matter into a truly marvelous array of structures and life forms." Some 1600 years later, Pope John Paul II in 1996 welcomed a science-religion dialogue, finding it noteworthy that evolutionary theory "has been progressively accepted by researchers, following a series of discoveries in various fields of knowledge."

Meanwhile, many people of science are awestruck at the emerging understanding of the universe and the human creature. It boggles the mind—the entire universe popping out of a point some 14 billion years ago, and instantly inflating to cosmological size. Had the energy of this Big Bang been the tiniest bit less, the universe would have collapsed back on itself. Had it been the tiniest bit more, the result would have been a soup too thin to support life. Astronomer Sir Martin Rees has described *Just Six Numbers* (1999), any one of which, if changed ever so slightly, would produce a cosmos in which life could not exist. Had gravity been a tad bit stronger or weaker, or had the weight of a carbon proton been a wee bit different, our universe just wouldn't have worked.

What caused this almost-too-good-to-be-true, finely tuned universe? Why is there something rather than nothing? How did it come to be, in the words of Harvard-Smithsonian astrophysicist Owen Gingerich (1999), "so extraordinarily right, that it seemed the universe had been expressly designed to produce intelligent, sentient beings"? Is there a benevolent superintelligence behind it all? Have there instead been an infinite number of universes born and we just happen to be the lucky inhabitants

Biological influences:
• Shared human genome
• Individual genetic variations
• Prenatal environment
• Sex-related genes, hormones, and physiology

Psychological influences:
• Gene-environment interaction
• Neurological effect of early experiences
• Responses evoked by our own personality, gender, etc.
• Beliefs, feelings, and expectations

Individual development

Social-cultural influences:
• Parental influences
• Peer influences
• Cultural attitudes and norms

➤ **FIGURE 3C.4**
The biopsychosocial approach to development

"Let's hope that it's not true; but if it is true, let's hope that it doesn't become widely known."

Lady Ashley,
commenting on Darwin's theory

"Is it not stirring to understand how the world actually works—that white light is made of colors, that color measures light waves, that transparent air reflects light . . . ? It does no harm to the romance of the sunset to know a little about it."

Carl Sagan, *Skies of Other Worlds*, 1988

 TEACHING TIP

The biopsychosocial model is fundamental to an understanding of modern psychology. It may be useful to have students make a poster of Figure 3C.4 for your wall so they can be reminded of this model throughout the course.

 RESEARCH

Encourage students to do historical studies of the events described here regarding the controversies science and religion have endured through the centuries. Have students consider whether the handling of these scientific discoveries by religious authorities has helped or hurt both science and religion through the years.

TEACHING TIP

At this point, you may want to use **Classroom Exercises:** *Darwinian Grandparenting* (p. 11) or *Self-Efficacy* (p. 14) from Bolt's Teacher's Resource Binder.

UNIT 3C

of one that, by chance, was exquisitely fine-tuned to give birth to us? Or does that idea violate *Occam's razor*, the principle that we should prefer the simplest of competing explanations? On such matters, a humble, awed, scientific silence is appropriate, suggested philosopher Ludwig Wittgenstein: "Whereof one cannot speak, thereof one must be silent."

Rather than fearing science, we can welcome its enlarging our understanding and awakening our sense of awe. In *The Fragile Species*, Lewis Thomas (1992) described his utter amazement that the Earth in time gave rise to bacteria and eventually to Bach's Mass in B Minor. In a short 4 billion years, life on Earth has come from nothing to structures as complex as a 6-billion-unit strand of DNA and the incomprehensible intricacy of the human brain. Atoms no different from those in a rock somehow formed dynamic entities that became conscious. Nature, says cosmologist Paul Davies (2007), seems cunningly and ingeniously devised to produce extraordinary, self-replicating, information-processing systems—us. Although we appear to have been created from dust, over eons of time, the end result is a priceless creature, one rich with potential beyond our imagining.

BEFORE YOU MOVE ON . . .

➤ ASK YOURSELF

How have your heredity and your environment influenced who you are today? Can you recall an important time when you determined your own fate in a way that was at odds with pressure you felt from either your heredity or your environment?

➤ TEST YOURSELF 3

How does the biopsychosocial approach explain our individual development?

Answers to the Test Yourself questions can be found in Appendix E at the end of the book.

* * *

We have glimpsed the truth of this unit's overriding principle: Everything psychological is simultaneously biological. This unit has focused on how our thoughts, feelings, and actions arise from our specialized yet integrated brain. In units to come, we will further explore the significance of the biological revolution in psychology.

From nineteenth-century phrenology to today's neuroscience, we have come a long way. Yet what is unknown still dwarfs what is known. We can describe the brain. We can learn the functions of its parts. We can study how the parts communicate. But how do we get mind out of meat? How does the electrochemical whir in a hunk of tissue the size of a head of lettuce give rise to elation, a creative idea, or that memory of Grandmother?

➤ FIGURE 3C.5

Mind and brain as holistic system In Roger Sperry's view, the brain creates and controls the emergent mind, which in turn influences the brain. (Think vividly about biting into a lemon and you may salivate.)

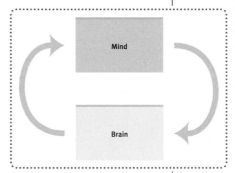

Much as gas and air can give rise to something different—fire—so also, believed Roger Sperry, does the complex human brain give rise to something different: consciousness. The mind, he argued, emerges from the brain's dance of ions, yet is not reducible to it. Cells cannot be fully explained by the actions of atoms, nor minds by the activity of cells. Psychology is rooted in biology, which is rooted in chemistry, which is rooted in physics. Yet psychology is more than applied physics. As Jerome Kagan (1998) reminds us, the meaning of the Gettysburg Address is not reducible to neural activity. Morality and responsibility become possible when we understand the mind as a "holistic system," said Sperry (1992) (**FIGURE 3C.5**). We are not mere jabbering robots.

The mind seeking to understand the brain—that is indeed among the ultimate scientific challenges. And so it will always be. To paraphrase cosmologist John Barrow, a brain simple enough to be understood is too simple to produce a mind able to understand it.

INTERCONNECTING

Remind students that events that seem random are not all that rare. Just because an event is random does not mean it is unlikely. The idea that random mutations in genetics over time have resulted in today's current technological, social, and artistic achievements is not unlikely, only random.

TEACHING TIP

Help students see how amazing the last century was for advancements in psychology and biology. Consider that the following ideas were unfathomable to people in 1909:

- Neurons fire using an ion-exchange system.

- Machines can see the brain at work in real time.

- Language is processed mainly in the left hemisphere.

- Humans share 99.9% of the genetic code with chimpanzees.

TEACHING TIP

At this point, you may want to use **Lecture/Discussion Topic: *Evolutionary Theory and Gender Differences in Motivation*** (p. 14) from Bolt's Teacher's Resource Binder.

UNIT REVIEW: Genetics, Evolutionary Psychology, and Behavior

Behavior Genetics: Predicting Individual Differences

1: What are genes, and how do behavior geneticists explain our individual differences?

Chromosomes are coils of *DNA* containing *gene* segments that, when "turned on" (expressed), code for the proteins that form our body's building blocks. Most human traits are influenced by many genes acting together. *Behavior geneticists* seek to quantify genetic and *environmental* influences on our traits. Studies of *identical twins*, *fraternal twins*, and adoptive families help specify the influence of genetic nature and of environmental nurture, and the *interaction* between them (meaning that the effect of each depends on the other).

2: What is heritability, and how does it relate to individuals and groups?

Heritability describes the extent to which variation among members of a group can be attributed to genes. Heritable individual differences in traits such as height or intelligence need not explain group differences. Genes mostly explain why some are taller than others, but not why people today are taller than a century ago.

3: What is the promise of molecular genetics research?

Molecular geneticists study the molecular structure and function of genes. Psychologists and molecular geneticists are cooperating to identify specific genes—or more often, teams of genes—that put people at risk for disorders.

Evolutionary Psychology: Understanding Human Nature

4: How do evolutionary psychologists use natural selection to explain behavior tendencies?

Evolutionary psychologists seek to understand how *natural selection* has shaped our traits and behavior tendencies. The principle of natural selection states that variations increasing the odds of reproducing and surviving are most likely to be passed on to future generations. Some variations arise from *mutations* (random errors in gene replication), others from new gene combinations at conception. Charles Darwin, whose theory of evolution has for a long time been an organizing principle in biology, anticipated the contemporary application of evolutionary principles in psychology.

5: How might an evolutionary psychologist explain gender differences in sexuality and mating preferences?

Men more than women think about sex and misinterpret friendliness as sexual interest. Women more than men do not approve of casual sex and have a relational view of sexual activity. Applying principles of natural selection, evolutionary psychologists reason that men's attraction to multiple healthy, fertile-appearing partners increases their chances of spreading their genes widely. Because women incubate and nurse babies, they increase their own and their children's chances of survival by searching for mates with the resources and the potential for long-term investment in their joint offspring.

6: What are the key criticisms of evolutionary psychology?

Critics argue that evolutionary psychologists start with an effect and work backward to an explanation, that the evolutionary perspective gives too little emphasis to social influences, and that the evolutionary viewpoint absolves people from taking responsibility for their sexual behavior. Evolutionary psychologists respond that understanding our predispositions can help us overcome them. They also cite the value of testable predictions based on evolutionary principles, as well as the coherence and explanatory power of those principles.

Terms and Concepts to Remember

behavior genetics, p. 95
environment, p. 95
chromosomes, p. 95
DNA (*deoxyribonucleic acid*), p. 95
genes, p. 95

genome, p. 96
identical twins, p. 96
fraternal twins, p. 97
heritability, p. 100
interaction, p. 101

molecular genetics, p. 102
evolutionary psychology, p. 103
natural selection, p. 103
mutation, p. 104

UNIT 3C

ANSWERS to Multiple-Choice Questions

1. **a.** it analyzes after the fact using hindsight.
2. **a.** natural selection.
3. **b.** This perspective discounts important genetics influences.
4. **c.** he discovered almost unbelievable similarities between adult identical twins who had been separated near birth.
5. **e.** heritability.
6. **d.** exists in its entirety in every cell of your body.
7. **b.** Men are attracted to women who appear fertile and capable of bearing children.
8. **b.** Women tend to seek men who can provide protection for their children because this has increased the survival rate of children in the past.
9. **a.** 23 chromosomes.
10. **c.** they are the same age and are usually raised in similar environments, but they do not have the same genetic code.
11. **e.** group variation in a trait that can be explained by genetics.
12. **d.** chromosomes.
13. **a.** molecular genetics.
14. **c.** interaction.
15. **d.** evaluate whether adopted children more closely resemble their adoptive parents or their biological parents.

> **AP* Practice Test Questions** ◄ ·

Multiple-Choice Questions

1. One major criticism of the evolutionary perspective in psychology is that
   a. it analyzes after the fact using hindsight.
   b. it attempts to extend a biological theory into a psychological realm.
   c. there is very little evidence to support it.
   d. it has not been around long enough to "stand the test of time."
   e. it seems to apply in certain cultures but not in others.

2. Evolutionary psychologists seek to understand how traits and behavioral tendencies have been shaped by
   a. natural selection.
   b. genes.
   c. prenatal nutrition.
   d. DNA.
   e. chromosomes.

3. Which of the following is *not* one of the main criticisms of the evolutionary psychology explanation of human sexuality?
   a. This perspective starts with an effect and works backward to propose an explanation.
   b. This perspective discounts important genetics influences.
   c. Unethical and immoral men could use such explanations to rationalize their behavior toward women.
   d. This explanation overlooks the effects of cultural expectations and socialization.
   e. This explanation does not consider the importance of individual choices in any given situation.

4. Thomas Bouchard's study of twins is notable, because
   a. it demonstrated that peer influence is more important than parental influence in the development of personality traits.
   b. it proved that the influence of parental environment becomes more and more important as children grow into adults.
   c. he discovered almost unbelievable similarities between adult identical twins who had been separated near birth.
   d. fraternal twins showed almost as much similarity as identical twins when they reached adulthood.
   e. it provided evidence that heritability is less important than researchers previously suspected.

5. The extent to which variation among members of a group can be attributed to genes is called
   a. fraternal genetics.
   b. maternal genetics.
   c. behavior genetics.
   d. interaction.
   e. heritability.

6. Your genetic code
   a. exists only in the cells of the nervous system.
   b. disappears gradually as the developmental processes it governs are completed.
   c. is influenced by early environmental experiences.
   d. exists in its entirety in every cell of your body.
   e. exists only in the cells of the reproductive system.

7. Which of the following statements has been supported by the research of evolutionary psychologists?
   a. Women are attracted to men who appear virile.
   b. Men are attracted to women who appear fertile and capable of bearing children.
   c. The connection between sex and pleasure is mostly determined by culture.
   d. The same factors determine sexual attraction in both males and females.
   e. Most adults are attracted to partners that in some way remind them of their parents.

8. Which of the following is an example of a phenomenon that could be explained by natural selection?
   a. A squirrel discovers that if it hides food in a particular tree it will not be discovered by other animals.
   b. Women tend to seek men who can provide protection for their children because this has increased the survival rate of children in the past.
   c. World records are set at every Olympic competition, suggesting that human athletic performance continues to improve.
   d. Children in some countries are much less likely to die from childhood diseases than are children in other countries.
   e. After several months, children are likely to select a well-balanced diet if they are allowed to plan their own menus without adult supervision.

TECHNOLOGY RESOURCES

These resources will be helpful for teaching the concepts in this portion of the unit:

- *Psychology Video Tool Kit: Ethics in Human Research: Violating One's Privacy; Nature Versus Nurture: Growing Up Apart; 100-Years-Old and Counting: Psychological and Biological Factors; Genes and Personality; Designer Babies; The Nature-Nurture Issue; Evolutionary Psychology and Sex Differences*
- *Video: The Brain,* 2nd ed., *Module 12: Huntington's Disease*
- *Video: The Mind,* 2nd ed., *Module 16: The Effect of Aging on Cognitive Function: Nature/Nurture*

9. When the mother's egg and the father's sperm unite, each contributes
a. 23 chromosomes.
b. 1 chromosome pair.
c. 23 chromosome pairs.
d. 30,000 chromosome pairs.
e. 30,000 chromosomes.

10. Researchers find the study of fraternal twins important, because
a. they share similar environments and the same genetic code.
b. data collected concerning their similarities is necessary for calculating heritability.
c. they are the same age and are usually raised in similar environments, but they do not have the same genetic code.
d. results allow us to determine exactly how disorders ranging from heart disease to schizophrenia are inherited.
e. they are typically raised in less similar environments than non-twin siblings.

11. Heritability refers to the percentage of
a. group variation in a trait that can be explained by environment.
b. traits shared by identical twins.
c. traits shared by fraternal twins.
d. traits shared by adopted children and their birth parents.
e. group variation in a trait that can be explained by genetics.

12. Threadlike structures made of DNA molecules that contain the genes are called
a. cell nuclei.
b. deoxyribonucleic acids.
c. genomes.
d. chromosomes.
e. mutations.

13. The study of specific genes and teams of genes that influence behavior is called
a. molecular genetics.
b. evolutionary psychology.
c. behavior genetics.
d. heritability.
e. natural selection.

14. The interplay of environment and heredity is called
a. heritability.
b. mutation.
c. interaction.
d. molecular genetics.
e. behavior genetics.

15. In an effort to reveal genetic influences on personality, researchers use adoption studies mainly to
a. compare adopted children with nonadopted children.
b. study the effect of prior neglect on adopted children.
c. study the effect of a child's age at adoption.
d. evaluate whether adopted children more closely resemble their adoptive parents or their biological parents.
e. consider the effects of adoption on a child's manners and values.

Free-Response Question

Explain the difference between fraternal and identical twins. How do twin studies help us understand the effects of nature and nurture?

WEB

Multiple-choice self-tests and more may be found at www.worthpublishers.com/myers

- *Video: Scientific American Frontiers Teaching Modules, 3rd ed.: Genes and Personality: Understanding Williams Syndrome*
- *Video: Scientific American Frontiers, 2nd ed., Segment 22, Bypass Genes*
- *PsychSim 5: Mind-Reading Monkeys; Dating and Mating*

Rubric for Grading the Free-Response Question

This is a 5-point question. Allow one point (up to two) for each adequate discussion of the differences between fraternal and identical twins. Allow one point (up to three) for reasons given explaining the importance of twin studies for understanding the effects of nature and nurture. Modify the rubric by adding or subtracting concepts depending on what was emphasized in class.

Differences between fraternal and identical twins:

- Fraternal twins develop from separate fertilized eggs. Identical twins develop from a single fertilized egg that splits into two separate zygotes.

- Fraternal twins are genetically no more similar than ordinary brothers and sisters. Identical twins are genetically identical.

How twin studies help us understand the effects of nature and nurture:

- Studies of identical twins raised apart provide instances where genes are the same, but environment is different, giving us a better picture of the role of genetic factors on behaviors. Where traits in the separated twins are similar, despite the differing environments in which they were raised, we can determine that genetics played a larger role than environment.

- We can compare fraternal twins raised together with identical twins raised together to get a better understanding of the role of environmental factors on development. In this case the environments are the same, but the genetics differ (genetically identical for the identical twins, and not identical for the fraternal twins). When raised together, identical twins are much more similar than fraternal twins, which suggests the power of genetic influences.

- We can compare identical twins raised apart with identical twins raised together. Identical twins raised together are even more similar than identical twins raised apart, which suggests that environmental factors do play some role in development as well.

UNIT 4

Pacing Guide

Use the following guide to determine how many instructional days to devote to this unit depending on the type of course you teach:

Year-long course   5–7 days
Block schedule/Semester-long course: 3–4 days

This unit encompasses 6–8 percent of the AP Exam. Spending an appropriate amount of time on this unit will help students do well on the AP Exam.

 TEACHING TIP

This unit provides numerous opportunities for active learning. Don't be afraid to use your time teaching this unit to do the activities suggested in the text and in Bolt's Teacher's Resource Binder, which accompanies this text. Students will understand the information better if they are able to experience the material firsthand.

114

Suggested Readings

Cialdini, R. B. (1993). *Influence: Science and practice* (3rd ed.). New York: HarperCollins.

Goleman, D. (1985). *Vital lies, simple truths*. New York: Simon and Schuster.

Levine, M., & Shefner, J. (1991). *Sensation and perception* (2nd ed.). Belmont, CA: Wadsworth.

Matlin, M., & Foley, H. (1997). *Sensation and perception* (4th ed.). Boston: Allyn & Bacon.

Melzack, R., & Wall, P. D. (1983). *The challenge of pain*. New York: Basic Books.

Sacks, O. (1987). *The man who mistook his wife for a hat*. New York: Summit.

Schiffman, H. R. (1996). *Sensation and perception* (4th ed.). New York: Wiley.

Shepard, R. N. (1990). *Mind sights*. New York: Freeman.

Sensation and Perception

"I have perfect vision," explains my colleague, Heather Sellers, an acclaimed writer and writing teacher. Her vision may be fine, but there is a problem with her perception. She cannot recognize faces.

In her memoir, *Face First,* Sellers (2010) tells of awkward moments resulting from her lifelong *prosopagnosia*—face blindness.

In college, on a date at the Spaghetti Station, I returned from the bathroom and plunked myself down in the wrong booth, facing the wrong man. I remained unaware he was not my date even as my date (a stranger to me) accosted Wrong Booth Guy, and then stormed out of the Station. I can't distinguish actors in movies and on television. I do not recognize myself in photos or video. I can't recognize my stepsons in the soccer pick-up line; I failed to determine which husband was mine at a party, in the mall, at the market.

Her inability to recognize acquaintances means that people sometimes perceive her as snobby or aloof. "Why did you walk past me?" someone might later ask. Similar to those of us with hearing loss who fake hearing during trite social conversation, Sellers sometimes fakes recognition. She often smiles at people she passes, in case she knows them. Or she pretends to know the person with whom she is talking. (To avoid the stress associated with such perception failures, people with serious hearing loss or with prosopagnosia often shy away from busy social situations.) But there is an upside: When encountering someone who previously irritated her, she typically won't feel ill will, because she doesn't recognize the person.

This curious mix of "perfect vision" and face blindness illustrates the distinction between *sensation* and *perception.* When Sellers looks at a friend, her sensation is normal: Her sensory receptors detect the same information yours would, and they transmit that information to her brain. And her perception—the organization and interpretation of sensory information that enables her to consciously recognize objects—is almost normal. Thus, she may recognize people from their hair, their gait, their voice, or their particular physique, just not their face. She can see the elements of their face—the nose, the eyes, and the chin—and yet, at a party, "[I introduce myself] to my colleague Gloria THREE TIMES." Her experience is much like the struggle you or I would have trying to recognize a specific penguin in a group of waddling penguins.

Thanks to an area on the underside of your brain's right hemisphere, you can recognize a human face (but not a penguin's) in one-seventh of a second. As soon as you detect a face, you recognize it (Jacques & Rossion, 2006). How do you do it?

Twenty-four hours a day, all kinds of stimuli from the outside world bombard your body. Meanwhile, in a silent, cushioned, inner world, your brain floats in utter darkness. By itself, it sees nothing. It hears nothing. It feels nothing. *So, how does the world out there get in?*

To phrase the question scientifically: How do we construct our representations of the external world? How do a campfire's flicker, crackle, and smoky scent activate neural connections? And how, from this living neurochemistry, do we create our conscious

115

Key People

Richard Axel	Ronald Melzack
Georg von Bekésy	James Randi
Linda Buck	Herman von Helmholtz
Gustav Fechner	Richard Walk
Eleanor Gibson	Patrick Wall
Ewald Hering	Ernst Weber
David Hubel	Torsten Wiesel
Harry McGurk	Thomas Young

Key Terms

Sensing the World: Some Basic Principles
sensation
perception
bottom-up processing
top-down processing
selective attention
inattentional blindness
change blindness
psychophysics
absolute threshold
signal detection theory
subliminal
priming
difference threshold
Weber's Law
sensory adaptation

Vision

transduction	retina
wavelength	accommodation
hue	rods
intensity	cones
pupil	optic nerve
iris	blind spot
lens	fovea

feature detectors
parallel processing
Young-Helmholtz trichromatic (three color) theory
opponent process theory

Hearing

audition	cochlea
frequency	inner ear
pitch	place theory
middle ear	frequency theory

conduction hearing loss
sensorineural hearing loss
cochlear implant

Other Senses
kinesthesis
vestibular sense
gate-control theory
sensory interaction

 Key Terms continued

UNIT 4

experience of the fire's motion and temperature, its aroma and beauty? In search of answers to such questions, let's look more closely at what psychologists have learned about how we sense and perceive the world around us.

Sensing the World: Some Basic Principles

1: What are sensation and perception? What do we mean by bottom-up processing and top-down processing?

IN OUR EVERYDAY EXPERIENCES, **sensation** and **perception** blend into one continuous process. In this unit, we slow down that process to study its parts.

We start with the sensory receptors and work up to higher levels of processing. Psychologists refer to sensory analysis that starts at the entry level as **bottom-up processing.** But our minds also *interpret* what our senses *detect*. We construct perceptions drawing both on sensations coming bottom-up to the brain and on our experience and expectations, which psychologists call **top-down processing.** For example, as our brain deciphers the information in FIGURE 4.1, bottom-up processing enables our sensory systems to detect the lines, angles, and colors that form the horses, rider, and surroundings. Using top-down processing we consider the painting's title, notice the apprehensive expressions, and then direct our attention to aspects of the painting that will give those observations meaning.

Nature's sensory gifts suit each recipient's needs. They enable each organism to obtain essential information. Consider:

- A frog, which feeds on flying insects, has eyes with receptor cells that fire only in response to small, dark, moving objects. A frog could starve to death knee-deep in motionless flies. But let one zoom by and the frog's "bug detector" cells snap awake.

➤ **FIGURE 4.1**
What's going on here? Our sensory and perceptual processes work together to help us sort out the complex images, including the hidden faces in this Bev Doolittle painting, *The Forest Has Eyes.*

Detail, The Forest Has Eyes by Bev Doolittle © The Greenwich Workshop, Inc., Trumbull, CT.

WEB CONNECT

Use any or all of the following Internet sites to help prepare for this unit:

- Hugh Foley's page at www.skidmore.edu/~hfoley/ perception.htm
- Psychology Tutorials at http://psych.hanover.edu/ Krantz/tutor.html
- The Internet Psychology Lab (IPL) at www.ipsych.com/
- Interactive Eye at www.nei.nih. gov/health/eyediagram/

 TEACHING TIP

The Online Psychology Laboratory (OPL) is an excellent Web site that has online experiments in all areas of psychology, especially sensation and perception, that students can participate in and download results to analyze. Using a computer lab, students can participate in several different experiments or participate in experiments you choose by accessing http://opl.apa.org/Main.aspx

INTERCONNECTING

Students may more readily identify top-down processing with stereotyping since both use previous expectations to make judgments about the world around us. Help students understand that while stereotyping can be negative, it can also be very efficient for people as they interact with certain stimuli. Without top-down processing, we would have to interpret the world as if it were constantly new. It would be like having to relearn how to add in math class every single day!

TROUBLESHOOTING

Students may get bottom-up and top-down processing confused. Help students remember the difference between the two concepts with these tips:

- Bottom-up processing—we process this way when we have no prior knowledge. We start at the bottom and work our way up.
- Top-down processing—we process this way when we have prior knowledge. We start at the top and have to work to process details.

- A male silkworm moth has receptors so sensitive to the female sex-attractant odor that a single female need release only a billionth of an ounce per second to attract every male silkworm moth within a mile. That is why there continue to be silkworms.

- We are similarly equipped to detect the important features of our environment. Our ears are most sensitive to sound frequencies that include human voice consonants and a baby's cry.

We begin the exploration of our sensory gifts with some basic questions that cut across all of our sensory systems: Where is the border between our conscious and unconscious awareness, and what stimuli cross that threshold?

Selective Attention

2: How are we affected by selective attention?

Through **selective attention,** your conscious awareness focuses, like a flashlight beam, on only a very limited aspect of all that you experience. By one estimate, your five senses take in 11,000,000 bits of information per second, of which you consciously process about 40 (Wilson, 2002). Yet your mind's unconscious track intuitively makes great use of the other 10,999,960 bits. Until reading this sentence, for example, you have been unaware that your shoes are pressing against your feet or that your nose is in your line of vision. Now, suddenly, your attentional spotlight shifts. Your feet feel encased, your nose stubbornly intrudes on the page before you. While attending to these words, you've also been blocking from awareness information coming from your peripheral vision. But you can change that. As you stare at the X below, notice what surrounds the book (the edges of the page, your desktop, and so forth).

X

Another example of selective attention, the *cocktail party effect,* is your ability to attend to only one voice among many. (Let another voice speak your name at a party and your cognitive radar, operating on the mind's other track, will instantly bring that voice into consciousness. You may tune in just long enough to decide whether to join in or to ignore the conversation.)

Focused listening comes at a cost. Imagine hearing two conversations over a headset, one in each ear, and being asked to repeat the message in your left ear while it is spoken. When paying attention to what is being said in your left ear, you won't perceive what is said in your right. Asked later what language your right ear heard, you may draw a blank (though you could report the speaker's gender and loudness).

Selective Attention and Accidents

Talk on the phone while driving and your selective attention will shift back and forth from the road to the phone. But when a demanding situation requires your full attention, you'll probably stop talking. This process of switching attentional gears, especially when shifting to complex tasks, can entail a slight and sometimes fatal delay in coping (Rubenstein et al., 2001). The U.S. National Highway Traffic Safety Administration (2006) estimates that almost 80 percent of vehicle crashes involve driver distraction. In University of Utah driving-simulation experiments, students conversing on cell phones were slower to detect and respond to traffic signals, billboards, and other cars (Strayer & Johnston, 2001; Strayer et al., 2003).

::**sensation** the process by which our sensory receptors and nervous system receive and represent stimulus energies from our environment.

::**perception** the process of organizing and interpreting sensory information, enabling us to recognize meaningful objects and events.

::**bottom-up processing** analysis that begins with the sensory receptors and works up to the brain's integration of sensory information.

::**top-down processing** information processing guided by higher-level mental processes, as when we construct perceptions drawing on our experience and expectations.

::**selective attention** the focusing of conscious awareness on a particular stimulus.

 Key Terms continued from p. 115

Perceptual Organization

gestalt
figure-ground
grouping
depth perception
visual cliff
binocular cues
retinal disparity
monocular cues
phi phenomenon
perceptual constancy
color constancy

Perceptual Interpretation

perceptual adaptation
perceptual set

Is There Extrasensory Perception?

extrasensory perception (ESP)
parapsychology

 TEACHING TIP

People with ADHD (attention deficit hyperactivity disorder) seem to lack the ability to be selectively attentive. Instead of filtering out unimportant stimuli in order to focus on important ones, they attend to all stimuli in the environment, making it difficult, if not impossible, to process information correctly.

 TEACHING TIP

When people get so caught up in an experience that they miss out on obvious stimuli in the environment, they are said to be having a *flow* experience. Flow, a term coined by Mihalyi Csikszentmihalyi (cheek-sent-me-high), involves being skilled at a challenging task that takes away our sense of self-consciousness and awareness of time and the presence of others around us.

 TEACHING TIP

Apply selective attention to students' lives by having them share experiences where they were either so caught up in an activity that they missed something obvious in the environment, or when the environment was so distracting that they couldn't concentrate. Students with attention difficulties may be reassured to know that others are frequently unable to concentrate or that they, too, have times where their own intense concentration makes them miss things.

RESEARCH

Have students conduct research about laws governing cell phone use while driving. Have students see whether research into attention was used to craft or justify the laws.

TEACHING TIP

Have students speculate how selective attention is related to the evolutionary perspective.

- If we had to attend to every stimulus in the environment, we might be hindered from action.
- However, if we miss important stimuli in the environment due to attention that is too selective, we may fall victim to all sorts of trouble—falls, car accidents, etc.

::**inattentional blindness** failing to see visible objects when our attention is directed elsewhere.

::**change blindness** failing to notice changes in the environment.

Because attention is selective, attending to a phone call (or a GPS navigation system or a DVD player) causes inattention to other things. Thus, when Suzanne McEvoy and her University of Sydney colleagues (2005, 2007) analyzed phone records for the moments before a car crash, they found that cell-phone users (even with hands-free sets) were four times more at risk. Having a passenger increased risk only 1.6 times. Texting drains even more attention, putting long-haul truckers at a 23 times greater risk of a collision than when not texting (VTTI, 2009).

The effects of distraction on driving also appeared in an experiment that asked drivers to pull off at a freeway rest stop 8 miles ahead. Of drivers conversing with a passenger, 88 percent did so. Of those talking on a cell phone, 50 percent drove on by (Strayer & Drews, 2007). Even hands-free cell-phone talking is more distracting than a conversation with passengers, who can see the driving demands and pause the conversation.

▼ **Driven to distraction** In driving-simulation experiments, people whose attention is diverted by cell phone conversation make more driving errors.

SALLY FORTH

Walking while talking can also pose dangers, as one naturalistic observation of Ohio State University pedestrians found (Nasar et al., 2008). Half the people on cell phones and only a quarter without this distraction exhibited unsafe road crossing, such as by crossing when a car was approaching. It's like trying to listen to someone while checking an incoming text message: attention, at any precise moment, is in one place.

Selective Inattention

At the level of conscious awareness, we are "blind" to all but a tiny sliver of the immense array of visual stimuli constantly before us. Ulric Neisser (1979) and Robert Becklen and Daniel Cervone (1983) demonstrated this dramatically by showing people a one-minute video in which images of three black-shirted men tossing a basketball were superimposed over the images of three white-shirted players. The viewers' supposed task was to press a key every time a black-shirted player passed the ball. Most focused their attention so completely on the game that they failed to notice a young woman carrying an umbrella saunter across the screen midway through the video. When researchers replayed the video, viewers were astonished to see her. With their attention directed elsewhere, they exhibited **inattentional blindness** (Mack & Rock, 2000). In a recent repeat of the experiment, smart-aleck researchers Daniel Simons and Christopher Chabris (1999) sent a gorilla-suited assistant through the swirl of players (**FIGURE 4.2**). During its 5- to 9-second cameo appearance, the gorilla paused to thump its chest. Still, half the conscientious pass-counting participants failed to see it.

In other experiments, people have also exhibited a blindness to change. After a brief visual interruption, a big Coke bottle may disappear, a railing may rise, clothing

Daniel Simons, University of Illinois

➤ **FIGURE 4.2**

Gorillas in our midst When attending to one task (counting basketball passes by one of the three-person teams) about half the viewers displayed inattentional blindness by failing to notice a clearly visible gorilla passing through.

TEACHING TIP

- You may want to use **Lecture/Discussion Topics:** *Sensation Versus Perception* (p. 4) or *Top-Down Processing* (p. 5) from Bolt's Teacher's Resource Binder.
- You may want to use **Classroom Exercises:** *A Scale to Assess Sensory-Processing Sensitivity* (p. 5) or *Human Senses Demonstration Kits* (p. 6) from Bolt's Teacher's Resource Binder.

color may change, but, more often than not, viewers won't notice (Resnick et al., 1997; Simons, 1996; Simons & Ambinder, 2005). This form of inattentional blindness is called **change blindness.** It has occurred among people giving directions to a construction worker who, unnoticed by two-thirds of them, is replaced by another construction worker (**FIGURE 4.3**). Out of sight, out of mind. *Change deafness* can also occur. In one experiment, 40 percent of people focused on repeating a list of sometimes challenging words failed to notice a change in the person speaking (Vitevitch, 2003).

➤ **FIGURE 4.3**

Change blindness While a man (white hair) provides directions to a construction worker, two experimenters rudely pass between them carrying a door. During this interruption, the original worker switches places with another person wearing different colored clothing. Most people, focused on their direction giving, do not notice the switch.

An equally astonishing form of inattention is the *choice blindness* discovered by a Swedish research team. Petter Johansson and his colleagues (2005) showed 120 volunteers two female faces for 2 to 5 or more seconds and asked them which face was more attractive. The researchers then put the photos face down and handed viewers the one they had chosen, inviting them to explain their choice. But on 3 of 15 occasions, the tricky researchers used sleight-of-hand to switch the photos—showing viewers the face they had *not* chosen. Not only did people seldom notice the deception (on only 13 percent of the switches), they readily explained why they preferred the face they had actually rejected. "I chose her because she smiled," said one person (after picking the solemn-faced one). Asked later whether they would notice such a switch in a "hypothetical experiment," 84 percent insisted they would. They exhibited a blindness the researchers call (can you see the twinkle in their eyes?) *choice-blindness blindness.*

Some stimuli, however, are so powerful, so strikingly distinct, that we experience *pop-out*, as with the only smiling face in **FIGURE 4.4**. We don't choose to attend to these stimuli; they draw our eye and demand our attention.

Our selective attention extends even into our sleep, as we will see in Unit 5, when we are oblivious to most but not all of what is happening around us. We may feel "dead to the world," but we are not.

➤ **FIGURE 4.4**
The pop-out phenomenon

● Magicians exploit our change blindness by selectively riveting our attention on one hand's dramatic act with inattention to the change accomplished by the other hand. ●

WEB CONNECT

Students may be interested in learning more about change blindness by visiting the Web site created by Daniel J. Simons from the University of Illinois. He and his team research attention issues, and they have created several videos students can watch that demonstrates our blindness to change. http://viscog.beckman.illinois.edu/djs_lab/

TEACHING TIP

Relate choice blindness to implicit associations. Harvard researchers have been examining how our unconscious associations affect prejudice and discrimination. Have students take the Implicit Associations Test online: https://implicit.harvard.edu/implicit/

BEFORE YOU MOVE ON . . .

➤ **ASK YOURSELF**

Can you recall a recent time when, your attention focused on one thing, you were oblivious to something else (perhaps to pain, to someone's approach, or to background music)?

➤ **TEST YOURSELF 1**

What is the rough distinction between sensation and perception?

Answers to the Test Yourself questions can be found in Appendix E at the end of the book.

 TEACHING TIP

● You may want to use **Lecture/Discussion Topics:** *Inattentional Blindness* (p. 8) or *Change Blindness* (p. 9) or *Mindsight—A Sixth Sense?* (p. 10) from Bolt's Teacher's Resource Binder.

● You may want to use **Classroom Exercises:** *Mindful Attention Awareness Scale* (p. 6) or *Field Dependence–Independence* (p. 6) or *Human Earphones* (p. 7) from Bolt's Teacher's Resource Binder.

UNIT 4

As long ago as 1888, Joseph Jastrow speculated that lapses of attention, slight fatigue, and other psychological changes could cause fluctuations in the absolute threshold.

TEACHING TIP

Gustav Fechner (1801–1887) developed three methods of experimental measurement used to study sensory phenomenon:

- **Method of limits.** Begin with a minimal stimulus and increase it until the subject can perceive it. This method helps determine the "just noticeable difference."

- **Method of right and wrong cases**. Present identical stimuli repeatedly—either single stimuli at the threshold or pairs of stimuli that are very similar. The subject responds "Yes" if perceived or if a difference exists or "No" if not perceived or different.

- **Method of adjustment**. Adjust a comparison stimulus until it appears identical to the standard stimulus. Every error is recorded and after many trials, the average error is computed. It, too, provides a measure of just noticeable difference.

TROUBLESHOOTING

Students may wonder why anyone cares about signal detection theory. The research in this area is especially important to fields where attention to detail amid environmental distractions is paramount—air traffic controllers, security screeners, law enforcement, and even common car drivers.

::**psychophysics** the study of relationships between the physical characteristics of stimuli, such as their intensity, and our psychological experience of them.

::**absolute threshold** the minimum stimulation needed to detect a particular stimulus 50 percent of the time.

Thresholds

3: What are the absolute and difference thresholds, and do stimuli below the absolute threshold have any influence?

We exist in a sea of energy. At this moment, you and I are being struck by X-rays and radio waves, ultraviolet and infrared light, and sound waves of very high and very low frequencies. To all of these we are blind and deaf. Other animals detect a world that lies beyond human experience (Hughes, 1999). Migrating birds stay on course aided by an internal magnetic compass. Bats and dolphins locate prey with sonar (bouncing echoing sound off objects). On a cloudy day, bees navigate by detecting polarized light from an invisible (to us) sun.

The shades on our own senses are open just a crack, allowing us only a restricted awareness of this vast sea of energy. Let's see what **psychophysics** has discovered about the physical energy we can detect and its effect on our psychological experience.

Absolute Thresholds

To some kinds of stimuli we are exquisitely sensitive. Standing atop a mountain on an utterly dark, clear night, most of us could see a candle flame atop another mountain 30 miles away. We could feel the wing of a bee falling on our cheek. We could smell a single drop of perfume in a three-room apartment (Galanter, 1962).

German scientist and philosopher Gustav Fechner (1801–1887) studied our awareness of these faint stimuli and called them our **absolute thresholds**—the minimum stimulation necessary to detect a particular light, sound, pressure, taste, or odor 50 percent of the time (**FIGURE 4.5**). To test your absolute threshold for sounds, a hearing specialist would expose each of your ears to varying sound levels. For each tone, the test would define where half

➤ **FIGURE 4.5**
Absolute threshold Can I detect this sound? An *absolute threshold* is the intensity at which we can detect a stimulus half the time. Hearing tests locate these thresholds for sounds at various frequency levels. Stimuli we detect less than 50 percent of the time are *subliminal*.

• Try out this old riddle on a couple of friends. "You're driving a bus with 12 passengers. At your first stop, 6 passengers get off. At the second stop, 3 get off. At the third stop, 2 more get off but 3 new people get on. What color are the bus driver's eyes?" Do your friends detect the signal—who is the bus driver?—amid the accompanying noise? •

the time you correctly detect the sound and half the time you do not. For each of your senses, that 50-50 recognition point defines your absolute threshold.

Absolute thresholds may vary with age. Sensitivity to high-pitched sounds declines with normal aging, leaving older ears in need of louder sound to hear a high-pitched cell-phone ring. That fact of life, as we will see in Unit 9, has been exploited by some students using a "mosquito" ringtone their teachers are unlikely to hear, and by some Welsh shopkeepers broadcasting annoying sounds that help disperse loitering teens without repelling older adults.

DEMO

Have students place an alarm clock (or wristwatch) on a table in a quiet room. They should move away so that they can no longer hear the ticking, then gradually move toward the clock until they begin to hear the sound. This is the "momentary" threshold. If they remain in place, occasionally they won't be able to hear the sound and will need to step forward to reach threshold. At other times the sound will get louder and they will be able to step back. This changing sensitivity indicates that the "absolute threshold" is anything but absolute.

Coren, S., Ward, L. M., & Enns, J. T. (1999). *Sensation and perception* (5th ed.). Fort Worth, TX: Harcourt Brace.

Signal Detection

Detecting a weak stimulus, or signal, depends not only on the signal's strength (such as a hearing-test tone) but also on our psychological state—our experience, expectations, motivation, and alertness. **Signal detection theory** predicts when we will detect weak signals (measured as our ratio of "hits" to "false alarms"). Signal detection theorists seek to understand why people respond differently to the same stimuli (have you ever noticed that some teachers are much more likely than others to detect student cheating on a test?), and why the same person's reactions vary as circumstances change. Exhausted parents will notice the faintest whimper from a newborn's cradle while failing to notice louder, unimportant sounds.

In a horror-filled wartime situation, failure to detect an intruder could be fatal. Mindful of many comrades' deaths, soldiers and police in Iraq probably became more likely to notice—and fire at—an almost imperceptible noise. With such heightened responsiveness come more false alarms, as when the U.S. military fired on an approaching car that was rushing an Italian journalist to freedom, killing the Italian intelligence officer who had rescued her. In peacetime, when survival is not threatened, the same soldiers would require a stronger signal before sensing danger.

Signal detection can also have life-or-death consequences when people are responsible for watching an airport scanner for weapons, monitoring patients from an intensive-care nursing station, or detecting radar blips. Studies have shown, for example, that people's ability to catch a faint signal diminishes after about 30 minutes. But this diminishing response depends on the task, on the time of day, and even on whether the participants periodically exercise (Warm & Dember, 1986). To help motivate airport baggage screeners, the U.S. Transportation Security Administration periodically adds images of guns, knives, and other threatening objects into bag X-rays. When the signal is detected, the system congratulates the screener and the image disappears (Winerman, 2006). Experience matters, too. In one experiment, 10 hours of action video game playing—scanning for and instantly responding to any intrusion—increased novice players' signal detection skills (Green & Bavelier, 2003). (See Unit 14 for research on less positive social effects of violent video games.)

Subliminal Stimulation

Hoping to penetrate our unconscious, entrepreneurs offer recordings that supposedly speak directly to our brains to help us lose weight, stop smoking, or improve our memories. Masked by soothing ocean sounds, unheard messages ("I am thin," "Smoke tastes bad," or "I do well on tests. I have total recall of information") will, they say, influence our behavior. Such claims make two assumptions: (1) We can unconsciously sense **subliminal** (literally, "below threshold") stimuli, and (2) without our awareness, these stimuli have extraordinary suggestive powers. Can we? Do they?

Can we sense stimuli below our absolute thresholds? In one sense, the answer is clearly *yes*. Remember that an "absolute" threshold is merely the point at which we detect a stimulus *half the time*. At or slightly below this threshold, we will still detect the stimulus some of the time.

Can we be affected by stimuli so weak as to be unnoticed? Under certain conditions, the answer is *yes*. An invisible image or word can briefly **prime** your response to a later question. In a typical experiment, the image or word is quickly flashed, then replaced by a *masking stimulus* that interrupts the brain's processing before conscious perception. For example, one experiment subliminally flashed either emotionally positive scenes (kittens, a romantic couple) or negative scenes (a werewolf, a dead body) an instant before participants viewed slides of people (Krosnick et al., 1992). The participants consciously perceived either scene as only a flash of light. Yet the people somehow looked nicer if their

::signal detection theory a theory predicting how and when we detect the presence of a faint stimulus (*signal*) amid background stimulation (*noise*). Assumes there is no single absolute threshold and that detection depends partly on a person's experience, expectations, motivation, and alertness.

::subliminal below one's absolute threshold for conscious awareness.

::priming the activation, often unconsciously, of certain associations, thus predisposing one's perception, memory, or response.

Signal detection How soon would you notice an incoming text message? Fairly quickly if (1) you are expecting a particular message, (2) it is important that you detect it, and (3) you are alert.

2009 Jutta Klee/AbleImages/ PhotoLibrary

TEACHING TIP

Anthony Pratkanis identified factors that contribute to the public's beliefs regarding subliminal influence.

- *Popular accounts of subliminal influence appeal to the "pop" psychology of the day.*

- *Popular accounts link subliminal influence to the issue of the day.* Subliminal influence first emerged as a national concern after the Korean War when brainwashing and hypnotic suggestion captured the nation's imagination in films such as *The Manchurian Candidate.*

- *Many of the popular articles fail to report scientific evidence that is critical of claims for subliminal persuasion.*

- *Belief in subliminal persuasion may serve a need for many individuals.* Subliminal persuasion takes on a supernatural "the devil made me do it" quality capable of explaining why Americans engage in irrational consumer behavior.

Pratkanis, A. (1990, August). *Subliminal sorcery then and now: Who is seducing whom?* Paper presented at the 98th Annual Convention of the American Psychological Association, Boston, MA.

RESEARCH

With federal takeover of airport screening as a result of the September 11th attacks, accurate signal detection by Transportation Safety Administration (TSA) employees remains an important concern. Contact a nearby TSA office or air traffic control office to ask if representatives from your class might interview a supervisor about the following issues in signal detection:

- What policies do you have in place that increase accurate signal detection?

- What training programs do you use to equip screeners to make accurate calls about stimuli?

- Do you offer incentives based on accurate performance? Why or why not?

- Does your office engage in periodic checks of accurate signal detection? What methods do you use to study this area?

UNIT 4

Some students may have heard that movie theatres in the 1950s used subliminal advertising to increase sales of popcorn and soda. They placed frames that said, "buy popcorn" and "buy Coke" within movies, which was supposed to encourage people to subliminally want to purchase concessions. This advertising ploy actually never happened. The source of the myth, James Vicary, actually lied about experiments he conducted at a New Jersey movie theatre. His lie, however, led the Federal Communications Commission to ban so-called "subliminal advertising" in 1974.

Source: www.snopes.com

 INTERCONNECTING

While subliminal advertising may not work, priming does. If we are exposed to stimuli about a specific subject, we are more likely to recognize information about that subject in the environment. This phenomenon is related to context effects, which is discussed in more detail in Unit 7A.

> "The heart has its reasons which reason does not know."
> Pascal, *Pensées*, 1670

Subliminal persuasion? Although subliminally presented stimuli *can* subtly influence people, experiments discount attempts at subliminal advertising and self-improvement. (The playful message here is not actually subliminal—because you can easily perceive it.) ▲

The LORD is my shepherd;
I shall not want.
He maketh me to lie down
in green pastures:
he leadeth me
beside the still waters.
He restoreth my soul:
he leadeth me
in the paths of righteousness
for his name's sake.
Yea, though I walk through the valley
of the shadow of death,
I will fear no evil:
for thou art with me;
thy rod and thy staff
they comfort me.
Thou preparest a table before me
in the presence of mine enemies:
thou anointest my head with oil,
my cup runneth over.
Surely goodness and mercy
shall follow me
all the days of my life:
and I will dwell
in the house of the LORD
for ever.

The difference threshold In this computer-generated copy of the Twenty-third Psalm, each line of the typeface changes imperceptibly. How many lines are required for you to experience a just noticeable difference? ▲

image immediately followed unperceived kittens rather than an unperceived werewolf. Another experiment exposed people to subliminal pleasant, neutral, or unpleasant odors (Li et al., 2007). Despite having no awareness of the odors, the participants rated a neutral-expression face as more likable after exposure to pleasant rather than unpleasant smells.

This experiment illustrates an intriguing phenomenon: Sometimes we *feel* what we do not know and cannot describe. An imperceptibly brief stimulus often triggers a weak response that *can* be detected by brain scanning (Blankenburg et al., 2003; Haynes & Rees, 2005, 2006). The conclusion (turn up the volume here): *Much of our information processing occurs automatically, out of sight, off the radar screen of our conscious mind.*

But does the fact of subliminal *sensation* verify entrepreneurial claims of subliminal *persuasion?* Can advertisers really manipulate us with "hidden persuasion"? The near-consensus among researchers is *no.* Their verdict is similar to that of astronomers who say of astrologers, *yes,* they are right that stars and planets are out there; but *no,* the celestial bodies don't directly affect us. The laboratory research reveals a *subtle, fleeting* effect. Priming thirsty people with the subliminal word *thirst* might therefore, for a brief interval, make a thirst-quenching beverage ad more persuasive (Strahan et al., 2002). Likewise, priming thirsty people with Lipton Ice Tea may increase their choosing the primed brand (Karremans et al., 2006). But the subliminal-message hucksters claim something different: a *powerful, enduring* effect on behavior.

To test whether commercial subliminal recordings have an effect beyond that of a placebo (the effect of one's belief in them), Anthony Greenwald and his colleagues (1991, 1992) randomly assigned university students to listen daily for five weeks to commercial subliminal messages claiming to improve either self-esteem or memory. But the researchers played a very practical joke and switched half of the labels. Some students *thought* they were receiving affirmations of self-esteem when they actually were hearing the memory enhancement message. Others got the self-esteem message but thought their memory was being recharged.

Were the recordings effective? Students' scores on tests for both self-esteem and memory, taken before and after the five weeks, revealed no effects. And yet, those who *thought* they had heard a memory recording *believed* their memory had improved. A similar result occurred for those who thought they had heard a self-esteem recording. The recordings had no effects, yet the students *perceived* themselves receiving the benefits they *expected.* When reading this research, one hears echoes of the testimonies that ooze from the mail-order catalogs. Some customers, having bought what is not supposed to be heard (and having indeed not heard it!) offer testimonials like, "I really know that your tapes were invaluable in reprogramming my mind." Over a decade, Greenwald conducted 16 double-blind experiments evaluating subliminal self-help tapes. His results were uniform: Not one had any therapeutic effect (Greenwald, 1992). His conclusion: "Subliminal procedures offer little or nothing of value to the marketing practitioner" (Pratkanis & Greenwald, 1988).

Difference Thresholds

To function effectively, we need absolute thresholds low enough to allow us to detect important sights, sounds, textures, tastes, and smells. We also need to detect small differences among stimuli. A musician must detect minute discrepancies in an instrument's tuning. Students in the hallway must detect the sound of their friends' voices amid all the other voices. Even after living two years in Scotland, sheep *baa's* all sound alike to my ears. But not to those of ewes, which I have observed streaking, after shearing, directly to the *baa* of their lamb amid the chorus of other distressed lambs.

The **difference threshold,** also called the *just noticeable difference (jnd)*, is the minimum difference a person (or sheep) can detect between any two stimuli half the time. That detectable difference increases with the size of the stimulus. Thus, if you

---

- You may want to use **Lecture/Discussion Topics:** *Gustav Fechner and Psychophysics* (p. 10) or *Subliminal Smells* (p. 11) or *Subliminal Persuasion* (p. 12) or *Applying Weber's Law* (p. 13) from Bolt's Teacher's Resource Binder.

- You may want to use **Student Projects:** *The Variability of the Absolute Threshold* (p. 11) or *Understanding Weber's Law* (p. 12) from Bolt's Teacher's Resource Binder.

add 1 ounce to a 10-ounce weight, you will detect the difference; add 1 ounce to a 100-ounce weight and you probably will not. More than a century ago, Ernst Weber noted something so simple and so widely applicable that we still refer to it as **Weber's law:** For their difference to be perceptible, two stimuli must differ by a constant *proportion*—not a constant amount. The exact proportion varies, depending on the stimulus. For the average person to perceive their differences, two lights must differ in intensity by 8 percent. Two objects must differ in weight by 2 percent. And two tones must differ in frequency by only 0.3 percent (Teghtsoonian, 1971). For example, to be perceptibly different, a 50-ounce weight must differ from another by about an ounce, a 100-ounce weight by about two ounces.

Sensory Adaptation

4: What is the function of sensory adaptation?

Entering your neighbors' living room, you smell a musty odor. You wonder how they can stand it, but within minutes you no longer notice it. **Sensory adaptation**—our diminishing sensitivity to an unchanging stimulus—has come to your rescue. (To experience this phenomenon, move your watch up your wrist an inch: You will feel it—but only for a few moments.) After constant exposure to a stimulus, our nerve cells fire less frequently.

Why, then, if we stare at an object without flinching, does it not vanish from sight? Because, unnoticed by us, our eyes are always moving, flitting from one spot to another enough to guarantee that stimulation on the eyes' receptors continually changes (**FIGURE 4.6**).

What if we actually could stop our eyes from moving? Would sights seem to vanish, as odors do? To find out, psychologists have devised ingenious instruments for maintaining a constant image on the eye's inner surface. Imagine that we have fitted a volunteer, Mary, with one of these instruments—a miniature projector mounted on a contact lens (**FIGURE 4.7a**, next page). When Mary's eye moves, the image from the projector moves as well. So everywhere that Mary looks, the scene is sure to go.

::difference threshold the minimum difference between two stimuli required for detection 50 percent of the time. We experience the difference threshold as a *just noticeable difference (jnd)*.

::Weber's law the principle that, to be perceived as different, two stimuli must differ by a constant percentage (rather than a constant amount).

::sensory adaptation diminished sensitivity as a consequence of constant stimulation.

> "We need above all to know about changes; no one wants or needs to be reminded 16 hours a day that his shoes are on."
> Neuroscientist David Hubel [1979]

• For 9 in 10 people—but for only 1 in 3 of those with schizophrenia—this eye flutter turns off when the eye is following a moving target (Holzman & Matthyss, 1990). •

➤ **FIGURE 4.6**
The jumpy eye University of Edinburgh psychologist John Henderson (2007) illustrates how a person's gaze jumps from one spot to another every third of a second or so. Eye-tracking equipment shows how a typical person views a photograph of Edinburgh's Princes Street Gardens. Circles represent fixations, and the numbers indicate the time of fixation in milliseconds (300 milliseconds = three-tenths of a second).

DEMO

Weber's law can be applied to many situations. Robert Cialdini suggests students imagine a man who wants to buy a three-piece suit and a sweater. If you were the salesperson, which should you show him first in order to get him to spend the most money? You might think it best to sell the sweater first. Having spent a lot on a suit, the customer might be reluctant to spend more on a sweater. However, sales motivation analysts suggest the opposite. Sell the suit first because the additional cost of the sweater will not be so readily noticed. If the man has just paid $300 for a suit, an additional $75 for a sweater will not seem excessive. The same applies to other accessories, such as a shirt or shoes. As a rule, people will almost always pay more for accessories if they buy them after rather than before a more expensive purchase.

Cialdini, R. B. (1993). *Influence: Science and practice* (3rd ed.). New York: HarperCollins.

TEACHING TIP

A fun way to demonstrate the importance of sensory adaptation is to ask students what a day would be like if they felt different items they wore on a daily basis like a wristwatch, glasses, socks, etc. Be descriptive as you ask students about these items they are wearing, questions like: "Do you feel your socks gripping your ankles? your watch squeezing your wrist?" Students become squirmy as they "feel" these items rather intensely!

DEMO

To apply Weber's Law, students need three quarters, two envelopes, and a pair of shoes. Have them place one quarter in one envelope and the remaining two quarters in the other. Lifting each envelope, they can easily determine which is heavier. Now have them put each envelope in a shoe. When they lift the shoes, one at a time, the weight difference will be imperceptible.

Coren, S., Ward, L. M., & Enns, J. T. (2003). *Sensation and perception* (6th ed.). New York: Wiley.

UNIT 4

Divide students into small groups and have one person in the group complete a simple task, such as completing a crossword puzzle or word find. Have the other members of the group test different types of noise interference on the person's ability to complete the task. They should record their results. Have them consider the following questions:

- Does noise with words (reading a story) interfere more than noise without words (static or yelling "blah, blah")?

- Does music with words interfere more than music without words?

- How loud does the noise have to be for it to become distracting?

WEB CONNECT

Use the following Web site to enhance students' understanding of our visual system:

- Vision Science at www.visionscience.com/ VisionScience.html

➤ **FIGURE 4.7**

Sensory adaptation: now you see it, now you don't! (a) A projector mounted on a contact lens makes the projected image move with the eye. (b) Initially, the person sees the stabilized image, but soon she sees fragments fading and reappearing. (From "Stabilized images on the retina," by R. M. Pritchard.)

(a)   (b)

> "My suspicion is that the universe is not only queerer than we suppose, but queerer than we can suppose."
>
> J. B. S. Haldane, *Possible Worlds*, 1927

::**transduction** conversion of one form of energy into another. In sensation, the transforming of stimulus energies, such as sights, sounds, and smells, into neural impulses our brains can interpret.

::**wavelength** the distance from the peak of one light or sound wave to the peak of the next. Electromagnetic wavelengths vary from the short blips of cosmic rays to the long pulses of radio transmission.

::**hue** the dimension of color that is determined by the wavelength of light; what we know as the color names *blue, green,* and so forth.

::**intensity** the amount of energy in a light or sound wave, which we perceive as brightness or loudness, as determined by the wave's amplitude.

If we project the profile of a face through such an instrument, what will Mary see? At first, she will see the complete profile. But within a few seconds, as her sensory system begins to fatigue, things will get weird. Bit by bit, the image will vanish, only later to reappear and then disappear—in recognizable fragments or as a whole (Figure 4.7b).

Although sensory adaptation reduces our sensitivity, it offers an important benefit: freedom to focus on *informative* changes in our environment without being distracted by the constant chatter of uninformative background stimulation. Our sensory receptors are alert to novelty; bore them with repetition and they free our attention for more important things. Stinky or heavily perfumed classmates don't notice their odor because, like you and me, they adapt to what's constant and detect only change. This reinforces a fundamental lesson: *We perceive the world not exactly as it is, but as it is useful for us to perceive it.*

Our sensitivity to changing stimulation helps explain television's attention-grabbing power. Cuts, edits, zooms, pans, sudden noises—all demand attention, even from TV researchers: During interesting conversations, notes Percy Tannenbaum (2002), "I cannot for the life of me stop from periodically glancing over to the screen."

Sensory thresholds and adaptation are only two of the commonalities shared by the senses. All our senses receive sensory stimulation, transform it into neural information, and deliver that information to the brain. How do the senses work? How do we see? Hear? Smell? Taste? Feel pain? Keep our balance?

Vision

5: What is the energy that we see as visible light?

ONE OF NATURE'S GREAT WONDERS IS neither bizarre nor remote, but commonplace: How does our material body construct our conscious visual experience? How do we transform particles of light energy into colorful sights?

Part of this genius is our ability to convert one sort of energy to another. Our eyes, for example, receive light energy and **transduce** (transform) it into neural messages that our brain then processes into what we consciously see. How does such a taken-for-granted yet remarkable thing happen?

The Stimulus Input: Light Energy

Scientifically speaking, what strikes our eyes is not color but pulses of electromagnetic energy that our visual system perceives as color. What we see as visible light is but a thin slice of the whole spectrum of electromagnetic energy. As **FIGURE 4.8** illustrates, this *electromagnetic spectrum* ranges from imperceptibly short waves of gamma rays, to

 TEACHING TIP

Team with your school's physics instructor to give a lesson on the physics of light. Light is an interesting phenomenon that behaves both like waves and like particles. Our ability to see color depends on the wave properties of light. Objects reflect the wavelength of their colors back to the eye and absorb all other wavelengths of light. A possible guest speaker for this lesson could be an astrophysicist, who might address such issues as how astrophysicists use the properties of light to determine the age of the universe.

> **FIGURE 4.8**
The spectrum of electromagnetic energy This spectrum ranges from gamma rays as short as the diameter of an atom to radio waves over a mile long. The narrow band of wavelengths visible to the human eye (shown enlarged) extends from the shorter waves of blue-violet light to the longer waves of red light.

the narrow band we see as visible light, to the long waves of radio transmission. Other organisms are sensitive to differing portions of the spectrum. Bees, for instance, cannot see red but can see ultraviolet light.

Two physical characteristics of light help determine our sensory experience of them. Light's **wavelength**—the distance from one wave peak to the next (**FIGURE 4.9a**)—determines its **hue** (the color we experience, such as blue or green). **Intensity,** the amount of energy in light waves (determined by a wave's *amplitude,* or height), influences brightness (Figure 4.9b). To understand *how* we transform physical energy into color and meaning, we first need to understand vision's window, the eye.

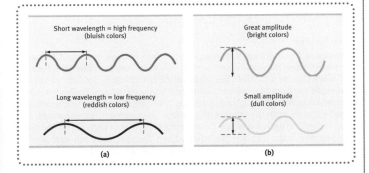

> **FIGURE 4.9**
The physical properties of waves
(a) Waves vary in wavelength (the distance between successive peaks). Frequency, the number of complete wavelengths that can pass a point in a given time, depends on the wavelength. The shorter the wavelength, the higher the frequency. (b) Waves also vary in amplitude (the height from peak to trough). Wave amplitude determines the intensity of colors.

TEACHING TIP

Have students draw with the appropriate colored crayon what the different wavelengths of light would look like. For instance, a bright red color would have a long wavelength with a great (tall) amplitude while a dull blue color would have a short wavelength with a small (short) amplitude. Have them consult a physics textbook or search online for help with different colors in between. Students with learning difficulties might appreciate this more tactile approach to understanding the relationship between colors and wavelength.

TROUBLESHOOTING

Vision and audition use similar terms to discuss the different stimuli that are processed by our visual and auditory systems. This is because both visual and auditory stimuli work in waves, so the characteristics of waves are similar for both light and sound.

- Wavelength—determines the quality of the waves (for vision, color; for sound, pitch)
- Amplitude—determines the intensity of the waves (for vision, brightness; for sound, loudness)

TEACHING TIP

You may want to use **Classroom Exercise:** *The Hermann Grid* (p. 14) or **Student Project:** *Locating the Retinal Blood Vessels* (p. 14) or **Student Projects/Classroom Exercises:** *Rods, Cones, and Color Vision* (p. 14) or *Locating the Blind Spot* (p. 15) from Bolt's Teacher's Resource Binder.

UNIT 4

TEACHING TIP

Invite your school's art/photography teacher to teach the students about how a camera is similar to the eye. Cameras use the eye as a model for how much light to let in to create a correct photograph of a given image or situation. Have the teacher discuss any of the following:

- Why certain film is important to use for different situations and images

- Why a flash is important and when it should be used

- Creative ways photographers use the camera's features to take interesting pictures

DEMO

Nearsightedness occurs when the lens focuses objects in front of the retina. *Farsightedness* occurs when the lens focuses objects behind the retina. Using an overhead projector, have students imagine the screen is the retina. When the projector is blurred in either direction, you have to move the projector or the screen in order to focus it.

TROUBLESHOOTING

The word *accommodation* means different things in different contexts. For this unit, accommodation means the ways in which the muscles of the eye change the shape of the lens to focus light onto the retina. In Unit 9, accommodation means the ways in which we change our schemas to incorporate new information we learn.

➤ **FIGURE 4.10**

The eye Light rays reflected from the candle pass through the cornea, pupil, and lens. The curvature and thickness of the lens change to bring either nearby or distant objects into focus on the retina. Rays from the top of the candle strike the bottom of the retina and those from the left side of the candle strike the right side of the retina. The candle's retinal image is thus upside-down and reversed.

::pupil the adjustable opening in the center of the eye through which light enters.

::iris a ring of muscle tissue that forms the colored portion of the eye around the pupil and controls the size of the pupil opening.

::lens the transparent structure behind the pupil that changes shape to help focus images on the retina.

::retina the light-sensitive inner surface of the eye, containing the receptor rods and cones plus layers of neurons that begin the processing of visual information.

::accommodation the process by which the eye's lens changes shape to focus near or far objects on the retina.

::rods retinal receptors that detect black, white, and gray; necessary for peripheral and twilight vision, when cones don't respond.

::cones retinal receptor cells that are concentrated near the center of the retina and that function in daylight or in well-lit conditions. The cones detect fine detail and give rise to color sensations.

::optic nerve the nerve that carries neural impulses from the eye to the brain.

::blind spot the point at which the optic nerve leaves the eye, creating a "blind" spot because no receptor cells are located there.

::fovea the central focal point in the retina, around which the eye's cones cluster.

The Eye

6: How does the eye transform light energy into neural messages?

Light enters the eye through the *cornea,* which protects the eye and bends light to provide focus (**FIGURE 4.10**). The light then passes through the **pupil,** a small adjustable opening surrounded by the **iris,** a colored muscle that adjusts light intake. The iris dilates or constricts in response to light intensity and even to inner emotions. (When we're feeling amorous, our telltale dilated pupils and dark eyes subtly signal our interest.) Each iris is so distinctive that an iris-scanning machine could confirm your identity.

Behind the pupil is a **lens** that focuses incoming light rays into an image on the **retina,** a multilayered tissue on the eyeball's sensitive inner surface. The lens focuses the rays by changing its curvature in a process called **accommodation.**

For centuries, scientists knew that when an image of a candle passes through a small opening, it casts an inverted mirror image on a dark wall behind. If the retina receives this sort of upside-down image, as in Figure 4.10, how can we see the world right side up? The ever-curious Leonardo da Vinci had an idea: Perhaps the eye's watery fluids bend the light rays, reinverting the image to the upright position as it reaches the retina. But then in 1604, the astronomer and optics expert Johannes Kepler showed that the retina does receive upside-down images of the world (Crombie, 1964). And how could we understand such a world? "I leave it," said the befuddled Kepler, "to natural philosophers."

Eventually, the answer became clear: The retina doesn't "see" a whole image. Rather, its millions of receptor cells convert particles of light energy into neural impulses and forward those to the brain. *There,* the impulses are reassembled into a perceived, upright-seeming image.

The Retina

If you could follow a single light-energy particle into your eye, you would first make your way through the retina's outer layer of cells to its buried receptor cells, the **rods** and **cones** (**FIGURE 4.11**). There, you would see the light energy trigger chemical changes that would spark neural signals, activating neighboring *bipolar cells.* The bipolar cells in turn would activate the neighboring *ganglion cells.* Following the particle's path, you would see axons from this network of ganglion cells converging, like the strands of a rope, to form the **optic nerve** that carries information to your brain (where the thalamus will receive and distribute the information). The optic nerve can send nearly 1 million messages at once through its nearly 1 million ganglion fibers. (The auditory nerve, which enables hearing, carries much less information through its mere 30,000

TEACHING TIP

What is *red eye,* that annoying red dot that appears in people's eyes in pictures, and why does it occur? Usually, red eye occurs in pictures where the surrounding illumination is dim, so the camera's flash must be used to take an accurate picture. The flash is so quick that the iris doesn't have time to contract, making the pupil big enough to see right through to the red retina! Cameras with so-called "red eye reduction" features provide a series of quick flashes that warn the eye that a picture is about to be taken. The iris reacts to the light pulses and shrinks the pupil down so the retina is protected from the bright flash.

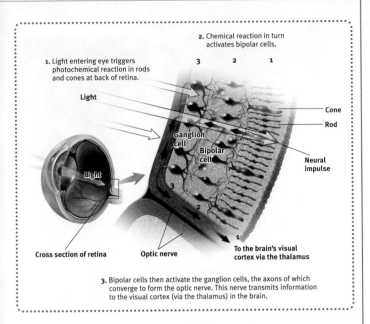

1. Light entering eye triggers photochemical reaction in rods and cones at back of retina.

2. Chemical reaction in turn activates bipolar cells.

Light

Ganglion cell

Bipolar cell

Cone

Rod

Neural impulse

Light

Cross section of retina

Optic nerve

To the brain's visual cortex via the thalamus

3. Bipolar cells then activate the ganglion cells, the axons of which converge to form the optic nerve. This nerve transmits information to the visual cortex (via the thalamus) in the brain.

➤ FIGURE 4.11
The retina's reaction to light

fibers.) Where the optic nerve leaves the eye there are no receptor cells—creating a **blind spot** (FIGURE 4.12). Close one eye and you won't see a black hole on your TV screen, however. Without seeking your approval, your brain fills in the hole.

Rods and cones differ in their geography and in the tasks they handle (TABLE 4.1, next page). Cones cluster in and around the **fovea,** the retina's area of central focus (see Figure 4.10). Many cones have their own hotline to the brain—bipolar cells that help relay the cone's individual message to the visual cortex, which devotes a large area to input from the fovea. These direct connections preserve the cones' precise information, making them better able to detect fine detail. Rods have no such hotline; they share bipolar cells with other rods, sending combined messages. To experience this difference in sensitivity to details, pick a word in this sentence and stare directly at it, focusing its image on the cones in your fovea. Notice that words a few inches off to the

➤ FIGURE 4.12
The blind spot There are no receptor cells where the optic nerve leaves the eye (see Figure 4.10). This creates a blind spot in your vision. To demonstrate, close your left eye, look at the spot, and move the page to a distance from your face (about a foot) at which the car disappears. The blind spot does not normally impair your vision, because your eyes are moving and because one eye catches what the other misses.

Cameras with so-called "red-eye reduction" features provide a series of quick flashes that warn the eye that a picture is about to be taken. The iris reacts to the light and shrinks the pupil down so the retina is protected from the bright flash. Have students conduct an experiment to see which type of red-eye reduction flash leads to the lowest amount of red eye in a picture. Be sure they include students who have both light colored eyes and darker colored eyes to control for eye color.

TEACHING TIP

By deliberately aiming the blind spot, one can block out any appropriately sized object. Legend has it that King Charles II of England did this with his courtiers. V. S. Ramachandran reports, "He used to make their heads disappear. One story is that he used to do it to people he had sentenced to die, to see what they would look like without their heads."

DEMO

Extend the text's blind-spot activity by having students notice what exactly fills the space where the blind spot is. The space is actually white, not gray or black as one would expect. Students can even draw a line around the car. This time they will notice the line continues as the brain creates what fills the blind spot based on the surrounding stimuli.

DEMO

Have students test their foveal vision in the dark as a homework project. Have them go in their backyards or in a dark room and try to focus their central vision on an image. They should reflect on how detailed the image appears. Then, have them look at the image in their peripheral vision, focusing their foveal vision just to the side of the image they want to see. They should note that the image becomes clearer and more detailed when they don't look at it dead-on, because in dim light the cones in the fovea are not activated but the rods in the periphery are.

UNIT 4

DEMO

Our eyes take a significant amount of time to adjust to darkness and back to light because two different types of cells process the different levels of light. Have students measure how long it takes to make the light-dark adaptation. Divide students into small groups and expose one group member to different levels of light. Have them record the time it took for the student to first see in the dark and first open both eyes without irritation in bright light (after being in the dark). Be sure students record results over several trials to get an average time of adaptation. Take the groups' data and combine them into an average class result.

TROUBLESHOOTING

The cells that make up the retina seem backward. The rods and cones are located at the very back of the retina. The bipolar and ganglion cells are stacked on top of the rods and cones in layers. The light is interpreted by the rods and cones first, even though the light passes through the bipolar and ganglion cells before it hits those light-sensitive cells.

::**feature detectors** nerve cells in the brain that respond to specific features of the stimulus, such as shape, angle, or movement.

TABLE 4.1

RECEPTORS IN THE HUMAN EYE: ROD-SHAPED RODS AND CONE-SHAPED CONES		
	Cones	Rods
Number	6 million	120 million
Location in retina	Center	Periphery
Sensitivity in dim light	Low	High
Color sensitivity	High	Low
Detail sensitivity	High	Low

Omikron/Photo Researchers, Inc.

side appear blurred? Their image strikes the more peripheral region of your retina, where rods predominate. The next time you are driving or biking, note, too, that you can detect a car in your peripheral vision well before perceiving its details.

Cones also enable you to perceive color. In dim light they become ineffectual, so you see no colors. Rods, which enable black-and-white vision, remain sensitive in dim light, and several rods will funnel their faint energy output onto a single bipolar cell. Thus, cones and rods each provide a special sensitivity—cones to detail and color, and rods to faint light.

When you enter a darkened theater or turn off the light at night, your pupils dilate to allow more light to reach your retina. It typically takes 20 minutes or more before your eyes fully adapt. You can demonstrate dark adaptation by closing or covering one eye for up to 20 minutes. Then make the light in the room not quite bright enough to read this book with your open eye. Now open the dark-adapted eye and read (easily). This period of dark adaptation parallels the average natural twilight transition between the sun's setting and darkness.

Some nocturnal animals, such as toads, mice, rats, and bats, have retinas made up almost entirely of rods, allowing them to function well in dim light. These creatures probably have very poor color vision. Knowing just this much about the eye, can you imagine why a cat sees so much better at night than you do?[1]

Visual Information Processing

7: How does the brain process visual information?

Visual information percolates through progressively more abstract levels. At the entry level, the retina processes information before routing it via the thalamus to the brain's cortex. The retina's neural layers—which are actually brain tissue that migrates to the eye during early fetal development—don't just pass along electrical impulses; they also help to encode and analyze the sensory information. The third neural layer in a frog's eye, for example, contains the "bug detector" cells that fire only in response to moving flylike stimuli.

After processing by your retina's nearly 130 million receptor rods and cones, information travels to your bipolar cells, then to your million or so ganglion cells, through their axons making up the optic nerve, to your brain. Any given retinal area relays its information to a corresponding location in the visual cortex, in the occipital lobe at the back of your brain (FIGURE 4.13).

[1]There are at least two reasons: (1) A cat's pupils can open much wider than yours, letting in more light; (2) a cat has a higher proportion of light-sensitive rods (Moser, 1987). But there is a trade-off: With fewer cones, a cat sees neither details nor color as well as you do.

DEMO

Since cones detect color and rods do not, students might not realize that their peripheral vision is very poor at judging color. Have a student sit in a chair and fixate on a point straight ahead. Stand to the side of the student, at a 180-degree angle, with a colored marker or piece of colored paper against a neutral background. Move in a semicircle toward the student's center of vision, asking periodically if the student can tell what color the marker is. Repeated guessing will prove incorrect until the marker is close to the center of the field of vision where the cones reside.

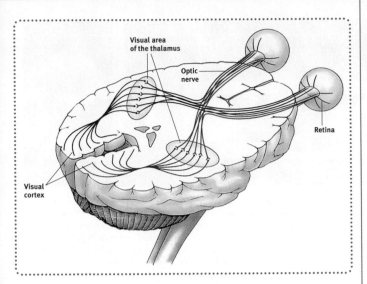

➤ FIGURE 4.13
Pathway from the eyes to the visual cortex Ganglion axons forming the optic nerve run to the thalamus, where they synapse with neurons that run to the visual cortex.

INTERCONNECTING

Connect to neuroscience in Unit 3B by reminding students that visual processing occurs in the occipital lobe of the brain rather than in the eye. The occipital lobe is located in the back of the brain, just above the cerebellum.

The same sensitivity that enables retinal cells to fire messages can lead them to misfire as well. Turn your eyes to the left, close them, and then gently rub the right side of your right eyelid with your fingertip. Note the patch of light to the left, moving as your finger moves. Why do you see light? Why at the left?

Your retinal cells are so responsive that even pressure triggers them. But your brain interprets their firing as light. Moreover, it interprets the light as coming from the left—the normal direction of light that activates the right side of the retina.

Feature Detection

Nobel Prize winners David Hubel and Torsten Wiesel (1979) demonstrated that neurons in the occipital lobe's visual cortex receive information from individual ganglion cells in the retina. These **feature detector** cells derive their name from their ability to respond to a scene's specific features—to particular edges, lines, angles, and movements.

Feature detectors in the visual cortex pass such information to other cortical areas where teams of cells *(supercell clusters)* respond to more complex patterns. One temporal lobe area just behind your right ear, for example, enables you to perceive faces. If this region were damaged, you might recognize other forms and objects, but, like Heather Sellers, not familiar faces. Functional MRI (fMRI) scans show other brain areas lighting up when people view other object categories (Downing et al., 2001). Damage in these areas blocks other perceptions while sparing face recognition. Amazingly specific combinations of activity may appear (**FIGURE 4.14**). "We can tell if a person is looking at a shoe, a chair, or a face, based on the pattern of their brain activity," notes researcher James Haxby (2001).

Psychologist David Perrett and his colleagues (1988, 1992, 1994) reported that for biologically important objects and events, monkey brains (and surely ours as well)

| ■ Faces | ■ Chairs |
| ■ Houses | ■ Houses and Chairs |

➤ FIGURE 4.14
The telltale brain Looking at faces, houses, and chairs activates different brain areas in this right-facing brain.

TEACHING TIP

You may want to use **Classroom Exercises:** *The Color Vision Screening Inventory and Color Blindness* (p. 17) or *Subjective Colors* (p. 18) from Bolt's Teacher's Resource Binder.

UNIT 4

Remind students that the human brain is uniquely capable of parallel processing, as discussed in Unit 3B. Computers process serially, only able to do one process at a time. Humans can process multiple types of stimuli from the environment, making us more efficient in understanding the world than computers. In fact, our visual system is so adept at parallel processing and, thus, so complicated, that no computer has been invented that can re-create it.

TEACHING TIP

Those with blindsight, argues Anthony Marcel of Cambridge University, have superb vision but they don't know they can see. Employing a high-speed camera, Marcel tracked the subjects' arms, hands, and fingers as they reached for objects they could not consciously see. The films indicate that their reach was quite precise. This suggests that their vision remains intact; only the neural areas that bring vision into awareness are impaired.

▼ **Well-developed supercells** In this 2007 World Cup match, Brazil's Marta instantly processed visual information about the positions and movements of Australia's defenders and goalkeeper (Melissa Barbieri) and somehow managed to get the ball around them all and into the net.

have a "vast visual encyclopedia" distributed as cells that specialize in responding to one type of stimulus—such as a specific gaze, head angle, posture, or body movement. Other supercell clusters integrate this information and fire only when the cues collectively indicate the direction of someone's attention and approach. This instant analysis, which aided our ancestors' survival, also helps a soccer goalkeeper anticipate the direction of an impending kick, and a driver anticipate a pedestrian's next movement.

Parallel Processing

Unlike most computers, which do step-by-step *serial processing*, our brain engages in **parallel processing:** doing many things at once. The brain divides a visual scene into subdimensions, such as color, movement, form, and depth (**FIGURE 4.15**), and works on each aspect simultaneously (Livingstone & Hubel, 1988). We then construct our perceptions by integrating the separate but parallel work of these different visual teams.

To recognize a face, for example, the brain integrates information that the retina projects to several visual cortex areas, compares it to stored information, and enables you to recognize the image as, say, your grandmother. The whole process of facial recognition requires tremendous brain power—30 percent of the cortex (10 times the brain area devoted to hearing). If researchers temporarily disrupt the brain's face-processing areas with magnetic pulses, people are unable to recognize faces. They will, however, be able to recognize houses; the brain's face-perception process differs from its object-perception process (McKone et al., 2007; Pitcher et al., 2007).

Destroying or disabling the neural workstation for other visual subtasks produces different peculiar results, as happened to "Mrs. M." (Hoffman, 1998). Since a stroke damaged areas near the rear of both sides of her brain, she can no longer perceive movement. People in a room seem "suddenly here or there but I have not seen them

➤ **FIGURE 4.15**

Parallel processing Studies of patients with brain damage suggest that the brain delegates the work of processing color, motion, form, and depth to different areas. After taking a scene apart, how does the brain integrate these subdimensions into the perceived image? The answer to this question is the Holy Grail of vision research.

| Color | Motion | Form | Depth |

TEACHING TIP

You may want to use **Lecture/Discussion Topic:** *Blindsight* (p. 16) or **Classroom Exercise/Student Project:** *Movement Aftereffects* (p. 15) from Bolt's Teacher's Resource Binder.

moving." Pouring tea into a cup is a challenge because the fluid appears frozen—she cannot perceive it rising in the cup.

Others with stroke or surgery damage to their brain's visual cortex have experienced *blindsight*, a localized area of blindness in part of their field of vision (Weiskrantz, 1986). Shown a series of sticks in the blind field, they report seeing nothing. Yet when asked to guess whether the sticks are vertical or horizontal, their visual intuition typically offers the correct response. When told, "You got them all right," they are astounded. There is, it seems, a second "mind"—a parallel processing system—operating unseen. (Recall Unit 3B's discussion of how the separate visual systems for perception and action illustrate dual processing—the two-track mind.)

It's not just brain-injured people who have two visual information systems, as Jennifer Boyer and her colleagues (2005) showed in studies of people without such injuries. Using magnetic pulses to shut down the brain's primary visual cortex area, the researchers showed these temporarily disabled people a horizontal or vertical line, or a red or green dot. Although they reported seeing nothing, the participants were right 75 percent of the time in guessing the line orientation and 81 percent right in guessing the dot color.

A scientific understanding of visual information processing leaves many neuropsychologists awestruck. As Roger Sperry (1985) observed, the "insights of science give added, not lessened, reasons for awe, respect, and reverence." Think about it: As you look at someone, visual information is transduced and sent to your brain as millions of neural impulses, then constructed into its component features, and finally, in some as-yet mysterious way, composed into a meaningful image, which you compare with previously stored images and recognize: "That's Sara!" Likewise, as you read this page, the printed squiggles are transmitted by reflected light rays onto your retina, which triggers a process that sends formless nerve impulses to several areas of your brain, which integrates the information and decodes meaning, thus completing the transfer of information across time and space from my mind to your mind. The whole process (**FIGURE 4.16**) is more complex than taking apart a

::**parallel processing** the processing of many aspects of a problem simultaneously; the brain's natural mode of information processing for many functions, including vision. Contrasts with the step-by-step (serial) processing of most computers and of conscious problem solving.

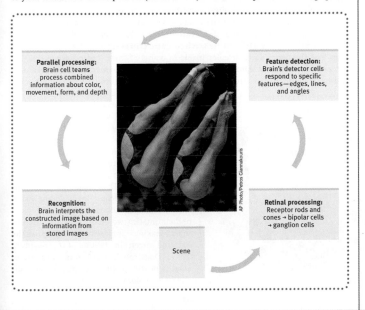

➤ **FIGURE 4.16**
A simplified summary of visual information processing

WEB CONNECT

Blindsight occurs when people experience damage to the visual cortex of the brain. Their eyes are fully functioning, but they report they cannot see even when they demonstrate that they can. For an interesting demonstration of blindsight as well as additional description of the phenomenon, have students visit http://serendip.brynmawr.edu/bb/blindsight.html

TEACHING TIP

Use Figure 4.16 to show how much work goes into processing a simple visual image. The complexity of this process is still fascinating to researchers.

TEACHING TIP

People who are colorblind see the color they are deficient in as a shade of muted gray or brown. They've been trained, however, to identify that muted "color" as red, blue, or green (depending on their deficiency), so unless tested, they usually do not know they are colorblind!

TROUBLESHOOTING

Student often ask, "How do I know I am seeing the same color as someone else?" The answer is simple—the wavelength of light determines the color, so in a properly functioning eye and brain, the color will be processed the same. However, what we call color shades can vary significantly, especially in advertising. Acquire several catalogues of clothing companies or go to their Web sites and compare what they call similar hues of color for clothes they sell. Are forest and hunter the same shade of green? Students can also make a list of the different names for hues in the same color family (reds, blues, greens, browns, etc.).

"I am . . . wonderfully made."
King David, Psalm 139:14

"Only mind has sight and hearing; all things else are deaf and blind."
Epicharmus, *Fragments*, 550 B.C.E.

car, piece by piece, transporting it to a different location, then having specialized workers reconstruct it. That all of this happens instantly, effortlessly, and continuously is indeed awesome.

Color Vision

8: What theories help us understand color vision?

We talk as though objects possess color: "A tomato is red." Perhaps you have pondered the old question, "If a tree falls in the forest and no one hears it, does it make a sound?" We can ask the same of color: If no one sees the tomato, is it red?

The answer is *no*. First, the tomato is everything *but* red, because it *rejects* (reflects) the long wavelengths of red. Second, the tomato's color is our mental construction. As Isaac Newton (1704) noted, "The [light] rays are not colored." Color, like all aspects of vision, resides not in the object but in the theater of our brains, as evidenced by our dreaming in color.

In the study of vision, one of the most basic and intriguing mysteries is how we see the world in color. How, from the light energy striking the retina, does the brain manufacture our experience of color—and of such a multitude of colors? Our difference threshold for colors is so low that we can discriminate some 7 million different color variations (Geldard, 1972).

At least most of us can. For about 1 person in 50, vision is color deficient—and that person is usually male, because the defect is genetically sex-linked. To understand why some people's vision is color deficient, it will help to first understand how normal color vision works.

Modern detective work on the mystery of color vision began in the nineteenth century when Hermann von Helmholtz built on the insights of an English physicist, Thomas Young. Knowing that any color can be created by combining the light waves of three primary colors—red, green, and blue—Young and von Helmholtz inferred that the eye must have three corresponding types of color receptors. Years later, researchers measured the response of various cones to different color stimuli and confirmed the **Young-Helmholtz trichromatic (three-color) theory,** which implies that the cones do their color magic in teams of three. Indeed, the retina has three types of color receptors, each especially sensitive to one of three colors. And those colors are, in fact, red, green, and blue. When we stimulate combinations of these cones, we see other colors. For example, there are no receptors especially sensitive to yellow. Yet when both red-sensitive and green-sensitive cones are stimulated, we see yellow.

Most people with color-deficient vision are not actually "colorblind." They simply lack functioning red- or green-sensitive cones, or sometimes both. Their vision—perhaps unknown to them, because their lifelong vision *seems* normal—is monochromatic (one-color) or dichromatic (two-color) instead of trichromatic, making it impossible to distinguish the red and green in **FIGURE 4.17** (Boynton, 1979). Dogs, too, lack receptors for the wavelengths of red, giving them only limited, dichromatic color vision (Neitz et al., 1989).

➤ **FIGURE 4.17**
Color-deficient vision People who suffer red-green deficiency have trouble perceiving the number within the design.

TROUBLESHOOTING

Students have a hard time accepting that both theories of color vision are likely correct. Since visual processing occurs in both the eye and the brain, both theories of color vision may work in each context. However, testing these theories in humans is currently not possible, because we do not possess the technology to study the retina in action.

UNIT 4

➤ FIGURE 4.18
Afterimage effect Stare at the center of the flag for a minute and then shift your eyes to the dot in the white space beside it. What do you see? (After tiring your neural response to black, green, and yellow, you should see their opponent colors.) Stare at a white wall and note how the size of the flag grows with the projection distance!

But trichromatic theory cannot solve all parts of the color vision mystery, as Ewald Hering soon noted. For example, we see yellow when mixing red and green light. But how is it that those blind to red and green can often still see yellow? And why does yellow appear to be a pure color and not a mixture of red and green, the way purple is of red and blue?

Hering, a physiologist, found a clue in the well-known occurrence of *afterimages*. When you stare at a green square for a while and then look at a white sheet of paper, you see red, green's *opponent color*. Stare at a yellow square and you will later see its opponent color, blue, on the white paper (as in the flag demonstration in **FIGURE 4.18**). Hering surmised that there must be two additional color processes, one responsible for red-versus-green perception, and one for blue-versus-yellow.

A century later, researchers confirmed Hering's **opponent-process theory**. As visual information leaves the receptor cells, we analyze it in terms of three sets of opponent colors: *red-green, yellow-blue,* and *white-black*. In the retina and in the thalamus (where impulses from the retina are relayed en route to the visual cortex), some neurons are turned "on" by red but turned "off" by green. Others are turned on by green but off by red (DeValois & DeValois, 1975).

Opponent processes explain afterimages, such as in the flag demonstration, in which we tire our green response by staring at green. When we then stare at white (which contains all colors, including red), only the red part of the green-red pairing will fire normally.

The present solution to the mystery of color vision is therefore roughly this: Color processing occurs in two stages. The retina's red, green, and blue cones respond in varying degrees to different color stimuli, as the Young-Helmholtz trichromatic theory suggested. Their signals are then processed by the nervous system's opponent-process cells, en route to the visual cortex.

BEFORE YOU MOVE ON . . .

➤ ASK YOURSELF
If you were forced to give up one sense, which would it be? Why?

➤ TEST YOURSELF 2
What is the rapid sequence of events that occurs when you see and recognize someone you know?

Answers to the Test Yourself questions can be found in Appendix E at the end of the book.

Hearing

FOR HUMANS, VISION IS THE MAJOR SENSE. More of our brain cortex is devoted to vision than to any other sense. Yet without our senses of hearing, touch, body position

::Young-Helmholtz trichromatic (three-color) theory the theory that the retina contains three different color receptors—one most sensitive to red, one to green, one to blue—which, when stimulated in combination, can produce the perception of any color.

::opponent-process theory the theory that opposing retinal processes (red-green, yellow-blue, white-black) enable color vision. For example, some cells are stimulated by green and inhibited by red; others are stimulated by red and inhibited by green.

WEB CONNECT

Afterimages are not limited to color vision. Students can see afterimages of movement as well. For a vivid example of movement after effects, invite students to visit http://dogfeathers.com/java/spirals.html. They will view the Counter-Rotating Spirals illusion and learn more of the history of motion aftereffects.

INTERCONNECTING

Opponent processes occur in many different contexts. Here, in Unit 4, the perception of color operates as an opponent process as one color works only when the other color does not. In Unit 3A, the sympathetic and parasympathetic nervous systems work as an opponent process. When one system is active, the other is not.

TEACHING TIP

Team teach a lesson in subtractive and additive color mixing with your school's art teacher. Encourage students to combine colors in different levels to create some of the 7 million different hues the human eye can see.

UNIT 4

DEMO

Have band students bring in instruments that they play to demonstrate how vibrations work with the different instruments.

- What produces the vibrations in each instrument?

- How does the instrument produce louder and softer sounds?

RESEARCH

Have students measure the decibels of different sounds common to school like the bells that signal class changes, hall noise, and different teachers' voices. Do these sounds fall within the safe range of decibels?

::**audition** the sense or act of hearing.

::**frequency** the number of complete wavelengths that pass a point in a given time (for example, per second).

::**pitch** a tone's experienced highness or lowness; depends on frequency.

::**middle ear** the chamber between the eardrum and cochlea containing three tiny bones (hammer, anvil, and stirrup) that concentrate the vibrations of the eardrum on the cochlea's oval window.

::**cochlea** [KOHK-lee-uh] a coiled, bony, fluid-filled tube in the inner ear through which sound waves trigger nerve impulses.

::**inner ear** the innermost part of the ear, containing the cochlea, semicircular canals, and vestibular sacs.

and movement, taste, and smell, our capacities for experiencing the world would be vastly diminished.

Like our other senses, our **audition,** or hearing, is highly adaptive. We hear a wide range of sounds, but we hear best those sounds with frequencies in a range corresponding to that of the human voice. We also are acutely sensitive to faint sounds, an obvious boon for our ancestors' survival when hunting or being hunted, or for detecting a child's whimper. (If our ears were much more sensitive, we would hear a constant hiss from the movement of air molecules.)

We are also remarkably attuned to variations in sounds. We easily detect differences among thousands of human voices: Walking between classes, we immediately recognize the voice of a friend behind us. A fraction of a second after a spoken word stimulates receptors in the inner ear, millions of neurons have simultaneously coordinated in extracting the essential features, comparing them with past experience, and identifying the stimulus (Freeman, 1991). For hearing as for seeing, we will consider the fundamental question: How do we do it?

The Stimulus Input: Sound Waves

9: What are the characteristics of air pressure waves that we hear as sound?

Draw a bow across a violin, and the resulting stimulus energy is sound waves—jostling molecules of air, each bumping into the next, like a shove transmitted through a concert hall's crowded exit tunnel. The resulting waves of compressed and expanded air are like the ripples on a pond circling out from where a stone has been tossed. As we swim in our ocean of moving air molecules, our ears detect these brief air pressure changes. Exposed to a loud, low bass sound—perhaps from a bass guitar or a cello—we can also *feel* the vibration, and we hear by both air and bone conduction.

The ears then transform the vibrating air into nerve impulses, which our brain decodes as sounds. The strength, or *amplitude,* of sound waves (recall Figure 4.9, which illustrated amplitude in relation to vision) determines their *loudness*. Waves also vary in length, and therefore in **frequency.** Their frequency determines the **pitch** we experience: Long waves have low frequency—and low pitch. Short waves have high frequency—and high pitch. A violin produces much shorter, faster sound waves than does a cello.

We measure sounds in decibels. The absolute threshold for hearing is arbitrarily defined as zero decibels. Every 10 decibels correspond to a tenfold increase in sound intensity. Thus, normal conversation (60 decibels) is 10,000 times more intense than a 20-decibel whisper. And a temporarily tolerable 100-decibel passing subway train is 10 billion times more intense than the faintest detectable sound.

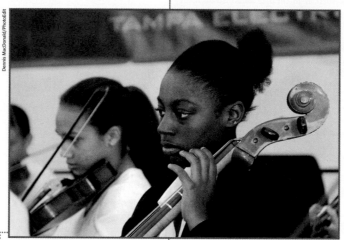

Dennis MacDonald/PhotoEdit

The sounds of music A violin's short, fast waves create a high pitch, a cello's longer, slower waves a lower pitch. Differences in the waves' height, or amplitude, also create differing degrees of loudness. ▲

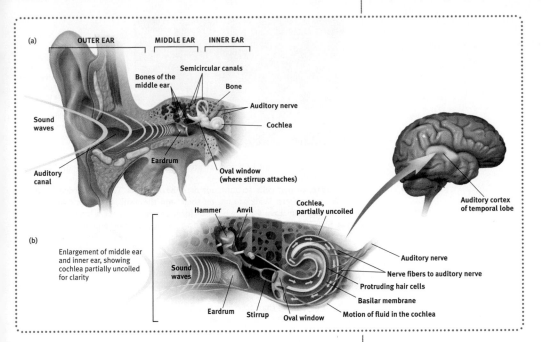

(a)

OUTER EAR   MIDDLE EAR   INNER EAR

Semicircular canals

Bones of the middle ear

Bone

Auditory nerve

Cochlea

Sound waves

Eardrum

Oval window (where stirrup attaches)

Auditory canal

Auditory cortex of temporal lobe

Cochlea, partially uncoiled

Hammer   Anvil

(b)

Enlargement of middle ear and inner ear, showing cochlea partially uncoiled for clarity

Sound waves

Auditory nerve

Nerve fibers to auditory nerve

Protruding hair cells

Basilar membrane

Eardrum   Stirrup   Oval window   Motion of fluid in the cochlea

The Ear

10: How does the ear transform sound energy into neural messages?

To hear, we must somehow convert sound waves into neural activity. The human ear accomplishes this feat through an intricate mechanical chain reaction (**FIGURE 4.19**). First, the visible *outer ear* channels the sound waves through the auditory canal to the *eardrum,* a tight membrane that vibrates with the waves. The **middle ear** then transmits the eardrum's vibrations through a piston made of three tiny bones (the *hammer, anvil,* and *stirrup*) to the **cochlea,** a snail-shaped tube in the **inner ear.** The incoming vibrations cause the cochlea's membrane (the *oval window*) to vibrate, jostling the fluid that fills the tube. This motion causes ripples in the *basilar membrane,* bending the *hair cells* lining its surface, not unlike the wind bending a wheat field. Hair cell movement triggers impulses in the adjacent nerve cells, whose axons converge to form the *auditory nerve,* which sends neural messages (via the thalamus) to the *temporal lobe's auditory cortex.* From vibrating air to moving piston to fluid waves to electrical impulses to the brain: Voila! We hear.

My vote for the most intriguing part of the hearing process is the hair cells. A Howard Hughes Medical Institute (2008) report on these "quivering bundles that let us hear" marvels at their "extreme sensitivity and extreme speed." A cochlea has 16,000 of them, which sounds like a lot until we compare that with an eye's 130 million or so photoreceptors. But consider their responsiveness. Deflect the tiny bundles of cilia on the tip of a hair cell by the width of an atom—the equivalent of displacing the top of the Eiffel Tower by half an inch—and the

➤ FIGURE 4.19

Hear here: How we transform sound waves into nerve impulses that our brain interprets (a) The outer ear funnels sound waves to the eardrum. The bones of the middle ear amplify and relay the eardrum's vibrations through the oval window into the fluid-filled cochlea. (b) As shown in this detail of the middle and inner ear, the resulting pressure changes in the cochlear fluid cause the basilar membrane to ripple, bending the hair cells on the surface. Hair cell movements trigger impulses at the base of the nerve cells, whose fibers converge to form the auditory nerve, which sends neural messages to the thalamus and on to the auditory cortex.

 TEACHING TIP

The technical name for the collection of bones in the middle ear is *ossicles*. Each bone also has a more technical name:

- Hammer—malleus
- Anvil—incus
- Stirrups—stapes

 DEMO

Why does our own voice sound unfamiliar when we hear it on tape? When we listen to ourselves speak, we hear both the sound conducted by air waves to the outer ear and that carried directly to the auditory nerve by bone conduction. The latter is easily demonstrated by clicking the teeth or munching popcorn, or by striking the prongs of a fork on a table and quickly applying its handle to the bone behind the ear. An even more resounding effect will be produced if the handle is clenched between the teeth. The strictly air-conducted sound that others normally hear (like a sound we hear when our voice is on tape) is thinner. Students can hear the sound waves conducted by bone if they plug their ears and talk in a normal voice.

Fisher, J. (1979). *Body magic.* New York: Stein and Day.

 DEMO

Students can also demonstrate bone-conducted sound with a metal coat hanger tied to the center of a thin string about four feet long. They should first press one end of the string into each ear with the tips of the index fingers while plugging their ears. Then they should ask someone to tap the coat hanger with a knife or fork. John Fisher reports that the effect will sound like the city of London's famous clock Big Ben.

UNIT 4

People who are deaf due to a defect in either the inner or middle ear may still be able to hear by bone conduction. When Beethoven became deaf, he could still hear a piano being played by placing one end of his walking stick against it and gripping the other end between his teeth. To determine the nature and degree of their hearing loss, deaf violinists reportedly applied their teeth to some part of their vibrating instruments. If they could not hear sound, they concluded that the auditory nerves were the problem and the deafness was past cure.

Be kind to your inner ear's hair cells When vibrating in response to sound, the hair cells shown here lining the cochlea produce an electrical signal.

alert hair cell, thanks to a special protein at its tip, triggers a neural response (Corey et al., 2004).

Damage to hair cells accounts for most hearing loss. They have been likened to thick carpet fibers. Walk around on them and they will spring back with a quick vacuuming. But leave a heavy piece of furniture on them for a long time and they may never rebound. As a general rule, if we cannot talk over a noise, it is potentially harmful, especially if prolonged and repeated (Roesser, 1998). Such experiences are common when sound exceeds 100 decibels, as happens in venues from frenzied sports arenas to bagpipe bands to iPods playing near maximum volume (FIGURE 4.20). Ringing of the ears after exposure to loud machinery or music indicates that we have been bad to our unhappy hair cells. As pain alerts us to possible bodily harm, ringing of the ears alerts us to possible hearing damage. It is hearing's equivalent of bleeding.

Teen boys more than teen girls or adults blast themselves with loud volumes for long periods (Zogby, 2006). Males' greater noise exposure may help explain why men's hearing tends to be less acute than women's. But male or female, those who spend many hours in a loud nightclub, behind a power mower, or above a jackhammer should wear earplugs. "Earplugs or walk away," say hearing educators.

➤ **FIGURE 4.20**
The intensity of some common sounds At close range, the thunder that follows lightning has 120-decibel intensity.

You may want to use **Lecture/Discussion Topics:** *Hearing Loss* (p. 19) or *A Quiet World—Living with Hearing Loss* (p. 20) from Bolt's Teacher's Resource Binder.

Perceiving Loudness

So, how do we detect loudness? It is not, as I would have guessed, from the intensity of a hair cell's response. Rather, a soft, pure tone activates only the few hair cells attuned to its frequency. Given louder sounds, its neighbor hair cells also respond. Thus, the brain can interpret loudness from the *number* of activated hair cells.

If a hair cell loses sensitivity to soft sounds, it may still respond to loud sounds. This helps explain another surprise: Really loud sounds may seem loud both to people with hearing loss and to those with normal hearing. As a person with hearing loss, I used to wonder when exposed to really loud music what it must sound like to people with normal hearing. Now I realize it can sound much the same; where we differ is in our sensation of soft sounds. This is why we hard-of-hearing people do not want *all* sounds (loud and soft) amplified. We like sound *compressed*—which means harder-to-hear sounds are amplified more than loud sounds (a feature of today's digital hearing aids).

Perceiving Pitch

> **11:** What theories help us understand pitch perception?

How do we know whether a sound is the high-frequency, high-pitched chirp of a bird or the low-frequency, low-pitched roar of a truck? Current thinking on how we discriminate pitch, like current thinking on how we discriminate color, combines two theories.

Hermann von Helmholtz's **place theory** presumes that we hear different pitches because different sound waves trigger activity at different places along the cochlea's basilar membrane. Thus, the brain determines a sound's pitch by recognizing the specific place (on the membrane) that is generating the neural signal. When Nobel laureate-to-be Georg von Békésy (1957) cut holes in the cochleas of guinea pigs and human cadavers and looked inside with a microscope, he discovered that the cochlea vibrated, rather like a shaken bedsheet, in response to sound. High frequencies produced large vibrations near the beginning of the cochlea's membrane, low frequencies near the end.

But there is a problem with place theory. It can explain how we hear high-pitched sounds, but not how we hear low-pitched sounds, because the neural signals generated by low-pitched sounds are not so neatly localized on the basilar membrane. **Frequency theory** suggests an alternative explanation: The brain reads pitch by monitoring the frequency of neural impulses traveling up the auditory nerve. The whole basilar membrane vibrates with the incoming sound wave, triggering neural impulses to the brain at the same rate as the sound wave. If the sound wave has a frequency of 100 waves per second, then 100 pulses per second travel up the auditory nerve.

Frequency theory can explain how we perceive low-pitched sounds. But it, too, is problematic: An individual neuron cannot fire faster than 1000 times per second. How, then, can we sense sounds with frequencies above 1000 waves per second (roughly the upper third of a piano keyboard)? Enter the *volley principle:* Like soldiers who alternate firing so that some can shoot while others reload, neural cells can alternate firing. By firing in rapid succession, they can achieve a *combined frequency* above 1000 waves per second.

Thus, place theory best explains how we sense high pitches, frequency theory best explains how we sense low pitches, and some combination of place and frequency seems to handle the pitches in the intermediate range.

::**place theory** in hearing, the theory that links the pitch we hear with the place where the cochlea's membrane is stimulated.

::**frequency theory** in hearing, the theory that the rate of nerve impulses traveling up the auditory nerve matches the frequency of a tone, thus enabling us to sense its pitch.

UNIT 4

Invite a volunteer to sit with eyes closed in a chair facing the class. Clap at varying locations around the volunteer's head. The person will confidently and accurately locate sounds coming from either side (which strike the two ears differently) but will have more difficulty locating sound in the 360-degree plane equidistant between the two ears (overhead, in back, or in front).

 TEACHING TIP

Ask students why dogs cock their heads to one side or another when they listen to sounds. Explain that dogs and other animals do that to identify the direction of the sound and hear it better.

::**conduction hearing loss** hearing loss caused by damage to the mechanical system that conducts sound waves to the cochlea.

::**sensorineural hearing loss** hearing loss caused by damage to the cochlea's receptor cells or to the auditory nerves; also called *nerve deafness*.

::**cochlear implant** a device for converting sounds into electrical signals and stimulating the auditory nerve through electrodes threaded into the cochlea.

➤ **FIGURE 4.21**
How we locate sounds Sound waves strike one ear sooner and more intensely than the other. From this information, our nimble brain computes the sound's location. As you might therefore expect, people who lose all hearing in one ear often have difficulty locating sounds.

• Experiments are also under way to restore vision—with a bionic retina (a 2-millimeter-diameter microchip with photoreceptors that stimulate damaged retinal cells), and with a video camera and computer that stimulate the visual cortex. In test trials, both devices have enabled blind people to gain partial sight (Boahen, 2005; Steenhuysen, 2002). •

Locating Sounds

12: How do we locate sounds?

Why don't we have one big ear—perhaps above our one nose? The better to hear you, as the wolf said to Red Riding Hood. As the placement of our eyes allows us to sense visual depth, so the placement of our two ears allows us to enjoy stereophonic ("three-dimensional") hearing.

Two ears are better than one for at least two reasons: If a car to the right honks, your right ear receives a more *intense* sound, and it receives sound slightly *sooner* than your left ear (**FIGURE 4.21**). Because sound travels 750 miles per hour and our ears are but 6 inches apart, the intensity difference and the time lag are extremely small. However, our supersensitive auditory system can detect such minute differences (Brown & Deffenbacher, 1979; Middlebrooks & Green, 1991). A just noticeable difference in the direction of two sound sources corresponds to a time difference of just 0.000027 second! To simulate what the ears experience with sound from varying locations, audio software can emit sound from two stereo speakers with varying time delays and intensity. The result: We may perceive a bee buzzing loudly in one ear, then flying around the room and returning to buzz near the other ear (Harvey, 2002).

So how well do you suppose we do at locating a sound that is equidistant from our two ears, such as those that come from directly ahead, behind, overhead, or beneath us? Not very well. Why? Because such sounds strike the two ears simultaneously. Sit with closed eyes while a friend snaps fingers around your head. You will easily point to the sound when it comes from either side, but you will likely make some mistakes when it comes from directly ahead, behind, above, or below. That is why, when trying to pinpoint a sound, you cock your head, so that your two ears will receive slightly different messages.

Hearing Loss and Deaf Culture

13: What are the common causes of hearing loss, and why does controversy surround cochlear implants?

The ear's intricate and delicate structure makes it vulnerable to damage. Problems with the mechanical system that conducts sound waves to the cochlea cause **conduction hearing loss.** If the eardrum is punctured or if the tiny bones of the middle ear lose their ability to vibrate, the ear's ability to conduct vibrations diminishes.

Damage to the cochlea's hair cell receptors or their associated nerves can cause the more common **sensorineural hearing loss** (or *nerve deafness*). Occasionally, disease causes sensorineural hearing loss, but more often the culprits are biological changes linked with heredity, aging, and prolonged exposure to ear-splitting noise or music. (See Close-Up: Living in a Silent World.)

For now, the only way to restore hearing for people with nerve deafness is a sort of bionic ear—a **cochlear implant.** This electronic device translates sounds into electrical signals that, wired into the cochlea's nerves, convey some information about sound to the brain. The implant helps children become proficient in oral communication (especially if they receive it as preschoolers or even before age 1) (Dettman et al., 2007; Schorr et al., 2005). The latest cochlear implants also can help restore hearing for most adults (though not for those whose adult brain never learned to process sound during childhood). By 2003, some 60,000 people worldwide had cochlear implants, and millions more were potential candidates (Gates & Miyamoto, 2003).

 TEACHING TIP

You may want to use **Classroom Exercise:** *Locating Sounds* (p. 19) from Bolt's Teacher's Resource Binder.

Living in a Silent World

The world's 500 million people who live with hearing loss are a diverse group (Phonak, 2007). Some are profoundly deaf; others have limited hearing. Some were deaf prelingually (before developing language); others have known the hearing world. Some sign and identify with the language-based Deaf culture; more, especially those who lost their hearing postlingually, are "oral" and converse with the hearing world by reading lips or reading written notes. Still others move between the two cultures.

Despite its many variations, living without hearing poses challenges. When older people with hearing loss must expend effort to hear words, they have less remaining cognitive capacity available to remember and comprehend them (Wingfield et al., 2005). In several studies, people with hearing loss, especially if not wearing hearing aids, have also reported feeling sadder, being less socially engaged, and more often experiencing others' irritation (Chisolm et al., 2007; Fellinger et al., 2007; National Council on Aging, 1999).

Deaf children who grow up around other Deaf people more often identify with Deaf culture and feel positive self-esteem. If raised in a signing household, whether by Deaf or hearing parents, they also express higher self-esteem and feel more accepted (Bat-Chava, 1993, 1994).

Separated from a supportive community, Deaf people face many challenges (Braden, 1994). Unable to communicate in customary ways, speaking and signing playmates may struggle to coordinate their play. And because academic subjects are rooted in *spoken* languages, signing students' school achievement may suffer. Adolescents may feel socially excluded, with a resulting low self-confidence.

Even adults whose hearing becomes impaired later in life may experience a sort of shyness. "It's almost universal among the deaf to want to cause hearing people as little fuss as possible," observed Henry Kisor (1990, p. 244), a Chicago newspaper editor and columnist who lost his hearing at age 3. "We can be self-effacing and diffident to the point of invisibility. Sometimes this tendency can be crippling. I must fight it all the time." Helen Keller, both blind and deaf, noted, "Blindness cuts people off from things. Deafness cuts people off from people."

I understand. My mother, with whom we communicated by writing notes on an erasable "magic pad," spent her last dozen years in a silent world, largely withdrawn from the

Signs of success Deaf participants in a spelling bee offer applause to a contestant.

AP Photo/Seth Perlman

stress and strain of trying to interact with people outside a small circle of family and old friends. With my own hearing declining on a trajectory toward hers, I find myself sitting front and center at plays and meetings, seeking quiet corners in restaurants, and asking my wife to make necessary calls to friends whose accents differ from ours. I do benefit from cool technology that, at the press of a button, can transform my hearing aids into in-the-ear loudspeakers for the broadcast of phone, TV, and public address system sound (see www.hearingloop.org). Yet I still experience frustration when, with or without hearing aids, I can't hear the joke everyone else is guffawing over; when, after repeated tries, I just can't catch that exasperated person's question and can't fake my way around it; when family members give up and say, "Oh, never mind" after trying three times to tell me something unimportant.

As she aged, my mother came to feel that seeking social interaction was simply not worth the effort. However, I share newspaper columnist Kisor's belief that communication is worth the effort (p. 246): "So, . . . I will grit my teeth and plunge ahead." To reach out, to connect, to communicate with others, even across a chasm of silence, is to affirm our humanity as social creatures.

The use of cochlear implants is hotly debated. On the one side are the hearing parents of more than 90 percent of all deaf children. Most of these parents want their children to experience their world of sound and talk. If an implant is to be effective, they cannot delay the decision until their child reaches the age of consent. On the other side are Deaf culture advocates, who object to using the implants on children who were deaf prelingually. The National Association of the Deaf, for example, argues that deafness is *not* a disability because native

RESEARCH

Have students research how many colleges and universities offer sign language as a "foreign language" option for students.

- Should American Sign Language (Ameslan) be an option for fulfilling a "foreign language" requirement?

- How is Ameslan different from English speech?

TEACHING TIP

Have students discuss how people in the hearing world view those who are deaf. According to the text, people who are deaf do not necessarily view themselves as disabled. In fact, they feel that they have certain advantages over their hearing peers. Discuss ways that the hearing world can be more inclusive of those in the Deaf community.

Hardware for hearing An X-ray image shows a cochlear implant's array of wires leading to 12 stimulation sites on the auditory nerve.

Wolfgang Gstottner. (2004) American Scientist, Vol. 92, Number 5. (p. 437)

• Deaf culture advocates prefer capitalizing "Deaf" when referring to people with deafness, and to the Deaf community in general. In referring to children without hearing, "deaf" is usually lowercased because young children have not yet had the opportunity to make an informed decision about whether they are a part of the Deaf community. I have followed this style throughout my text. •

"By placing my hand on a person's lips and throat, I gain an idea of many specific vibrations, and interpret them: a boy's chuckle, a man's 'Whew!' of surprise, the 'Hem!' of annoyance or perplexity, the moan of pain, a scream, a whisper, a rasp, a sob, a choke, and a gasp."

Helen Keller, 1908

signers are not linguistically disabled. In his 1960 book *Sign Language Structure,* Gallaudet University linguist William Stokoe showed what even native signers had not fully understood: Sign is a complete language with its own grammar, syntax, and meanings.

Deaf culture advocates sometimes further contend that deafness could as well be considered "vision enhancement" as "hearing impairment." People who lose one channel of sensation do seem to compensate with a slight enhancement of their other sensory abilities (Backman & Dixon, 1992; Levy & Langer, 1992). Some examples:

- Blind musicians (think Stevie Wonder) are more likely than sighted ones to develop perfect pitch (Hamilton, 2000).
- With one ear plugged, blind people are also more accurate than sighted people at locating a sound source (Gougoux et al., 2005; Lessard et al., 1998).
- Close your eyes and with your hands indicate the width of a one-dozen egg carton. Blind individuals, report University of Otago researchers, can do this more accurately than sighted people (Smith et al., 2005).
- People who have been deaf from birth exhibit enhanced attention to their peripheral vision (Bavelier et al., 2006). Their auditory cortex, starved for sensory input, remains largely intact but becomes responsive to touch and to visual input (Emmorey et al., 2003; Finney et al., 2001; Penhune et al., 2003).

Close your eyes and immediately you, too, will notice your attention being drawn to your other senses. In one experiment, people who had spent 90 minutes sitting quietly blindfolded became more accurate in their location of sounds (Lewald, 2007). When kissing, lovers minimize distraction and increase their touch sensitivity by closing their eyes.

BEFORE YOU MOVE ON . . .

➤ ASK YOURSELF
If you are a hearing person, imagine that you had been born deaf. Do you think you would want to receive a cochlear implant? Does it surprise you that most lifelong Deaf adults do not desire implants for themselves or their children?

➤ TEST YOURSELF 3
What are the basic steps in transforming sound waves into perceived sound?

Answers to the Test Yourself questions can be found in Appendix E at the end of the book.

Other Senses

ALTHOUGH OUR BRAINS GIVE SEEING and hearing priority in the allocation of cortical tissue, extraordinary happenings occur within our four other senses—our senses of touch, body position and movement, taste, and smell. Sharks and dogs rely on their extraordinary sense of smell, aided by large brain areas devoted to this system. Without our own senses of touch, body position and movement, taste, and smell, we humans would also be seriously handicapped, and our capacities for enjoying the world would be devastatingly diminished.

Touch

14: How do we sense touch and sense our body's position and movement? How do we experience pain?

Although it may not be the first sense to come to mind, touch is vital. Right from the start, touch is essential to our development. Infant rats deprived of their mother's grooming produce less growth hormone and have a lower metabolic rate—a good way to keep alive until the mother returns, but a reaction that stunts growth if prolonged. Infant monkeys allowed to see, hear, and smell—but not touch—their mother become desperately unhappy; those separated by a screen with holes that allow touching are much less miserable. As you will see in Unit 9, premature human babies gain weight faster and go home sooner if they are stimulated by hand massage. As lovers, we yearn to touch—to kiss, to stroke, to snuggle. And even strangers, touching only their forearms and separated by a curtain, can communicate anger, fear, disgust, love, gratitude, and sympathy at well above chance levels (Hertenstein et al., 2006).

Humorist Dave Barry may be right to jest that your skin "keeps people from seeing the inside of your body, which is repulsive, and it prevents your organs from falling onto the ground." But skin does much more. Our "sense of touch" is actually a mix of distinct senses, with different types of specialized nerve endings within the skin. Touching various spots on the skin with a soft hair, a warm or cool wire, and the point of a pin reveals that some spots are especially sensitive to pressure, others to warmth, others to cold, still others to pain.

Surprisingly, there is no simple relationship between what we feel at a given spot and the type of specialized nerve ending found there. Only pressure has identifiable receptors. Other skin sensations are variations of the basic four (pressure, warmth, cold, and pain):

- Stroking adjacent pressure spots creates a tickle.
- Repeated gentle stroking of a pain spot creates an itching sensation.
- Touching adjacent cold and pressure spots triggers a sense of wetness, which you can experience by touching dry, cold metal.
- Stimulating nearby cold and warm spots produces the sensation of hot (**FIGURE 4.22**).

Touch sensations involve more than tactile stimulation, however. A self-produced tickle produces less somatosensory cortex activation than the same tickle would from something or someone else (Blakemore et al., 1998). (The brain is wise enough to be most sensitive to unexpected stimulation.) This

The precious sense of touch As William James wrote in his *Principles of Psychology* (1890), "Touch is both the alpha and omega of affection."

➤ **FIGURE 4.22**

Warm + cold = hot When ice-cold water passes through one coil and comfortably warm water through another, we perceive the combined sensation as burning hot.

TEACHING TIP

There are two types of skin, the largest organ in the human body:

- *Hairy skin* contains hair cells, which detect movement and pressure.
- *Glabrous skin* contains no hair cells, so the receptors in this type of skin are more sensitive. Glabrous skin is found mainly on the palms of the hands, bottoms of the feet, and on the lips.

You may want to use **Classroom Exercises:** *Two-Point Thresholds* (p. 21) or *Touch Localization* (p. 23) or *Nystagmus* (p. 24) or *Vision and Balance* (p. 24) from Bolt's Teacher's Resource Binder.

DEMO

The skin senses variations of cold and warm which, when combined, make something feel hot. Donald Mershon suggests a convenient demonstration that utilizes an ice-cube tray (one that makes the very small cubes). First fill every other row in either direction with water and freeze. Then, being careful not to slop water to produce melting, fill the empty row with warm water. Have a student place his or her hand over the surface of the tray to feel the heat.

UNIT 4

People who lose their kinesthetic sense, also called *proprioception,* lose the ability to move unless they can see themselves move. When they see their bodies, their brains are able to process what needs to be done to move. In the dark, these people become limp and collapse.

RESEARCH

Invite a local dance instructor or figure skating instructor to come to class to discuss how dancers and figure skaters maintain their balance when completing those amazing spins and turns.

You may want to use **Lecture/ Discussion Topics:** *The Amazing Capabilities of Touch* (p. 21) or *The Remarkable Case of Ian Waterman* (p. 23) from Bolt's Teacher's Resource Binder.

INTERCONNECTING

Pain is mainly governed by nerves known as "free nerve endings," which are not directly connected to any specific nervous system. Pain seems to be regulated within its own system, working where needed to signal the body to a painful stimulus. Nervous systems are discussed in more detail in Unit 3A.

> ➤ FIGURE 4.23
> **The rubber-hand illusion** When a researcher simultaneously touches a volunteer's real and fake hands, the volunteer feels as though the seen fake hand is her own (MacLachlan et al., 2003).

Michal Cizek/AFP/Getty Images

The intricate vestibular sense These Cirque du Soleil performers can thank their inner ears for the information that enables their brains to monitor their bodies' position so expertly. ▲

top-down influence on touch sensation also appears in the *rubber-hand illusion.* Imagine yourself looking at a realistic rubber hand while your own hand is hidden (**FIGURE 4.23**). If an experimenter simultaneously touches your fake and real hands, you likely will perceive the rubber hand as your own and sense it being touched. Even just "stroking" the fake hand with a laser light produces, for most people, an illusory sensation of warmth or touch in their unseen real hand (Durgin et al., 2007). Touch is not only a bottom-up property of your senses but also a top-down product of your brain and your expectations.

Important sensors in your joints, tendons, bones, and ears, as well as your skin sensors enable your **kinesthesis**—your sense of the position and movement of your body parts. By closing your eyes or plugging your ears you can momentarily imagine being without sight or sound. But what would it be like to live without touch or kinesthesis—without, therefore, being able to sense the positions of your limbs when you wake during the night? Ian Waterman of Hampshire, England, knows. In 1972, at age 19, Waterman contracted a rare viral infection that destroyed the nerves that enabled his sense of light touch and of body position and movement. People with this condition report feeling disembodied, as though their body is dead, not real, not theirs (Sacks, 1985). With prolonged practice, Waterman has learned to walk and eat—by visually focusing on his limbs and directing them accordingly. But if the lights go out, he crumples to the floor (Azar, 1998). Even for the rest of us, vision interacts with kinesthesis. Stand with your right heel in front of your left toes. Easy. Now close your eyes and you will probably wobble.

A companion **vestibular sense** monitors your head's (and thus your body's) position and movement. The biological gyroscopes for this sense of equilibrium are in your inner ear. The *semicircular canals,* which look like a three-dimensional pretzel (Figure 4.19a), and the *vestibular sacs,* which connect the canals with the cochlea, contain fluid that moves when your head rotates or tilts. This movement stimulates hairlike receptors, which send messages to the cerebellum at the back of the brain, thus enabling you to sense your body position and to maintain your balance.

If you twirl around and then come to an abrupt halt, neither the fluid in your semicircular canals nor your kinesthetic receptors will immediately return to their neutral state. The dizzy aftereffect fools your brain with the sensation that you're still spinning. This illustrates a principle that underlies perceptual illusions: Mechanisms that normally give us an accurate experience of the world can, under special conditions, fool us. Understanding how we get fooled provides clues to how our perceptual system works.

Pain

Be thankful for occasional pain. Pain is your body's way of telling you something has gone wrong. Drawing your attention to a burn, a break, or a sprain, pain orders you

DEMO

Our ability to maintain balance depends to some extent on visual cues. Students can experience this for themselves by standing on one foot for 30 seconds first with their eyes open, then with their eyes closed. The latter is more difficult, because the vestibular and visual systems working together enable us to maintain balance. If students spin around a few times, thus disrupting their vestibular sense, and then close their eyes, they will find it impossible to balance on one foot.

to change your behavior—"Stay off that turned ankle!" The rare people born without the ability to feel pain may experience severe injury or even die before early adulthood. Without the discomfort that makes us occasionally shift position, their joints fall from excess strain, and without the warnings of pain, the effects of unchecked infections and injuries accumulate (Neese, 1991).

More numerous are those who live with chronic pain, which is rather like an alarm that won't shut off. The suffering of such people, and of those with persistent or recurring backaches, arthritis, headaches, and cancer-related pain, prompts two questions: What is pain? How might we control it?

Understanding Pain

Our pain experiences vary widely, depending on our physiology, our experiences and attention, and our surrounding culture (Gatchel et al., 2007). Thus, our feelings of pain combine both bottom-up sensations and top-down processes.

Biological Influences The pain system, unlike vision, is not located in a simple neural cord running from a sensing device to a definable area in the brain. Moreover, there is no one type of stimulus that triggers pain (as light triggers vision). Instead, there are different *nociceptors*—sensory receptors that detect hurtful temperatures, pressure, or chemicals (**FIGURE 4.24**).

Although no theory of pain explains all available findings, psychologist Ronald Melzack and biologist Patrick Wall's (1965, 1983) classic **gate-control theory**

A pain-free, problematic life Ashlyn Blocker (right), shown here with her mother and sister, has a rare genetic disorder. She feels neither pain nor extreme hot and cold. She must frequently be checked for accidentally self-inflicted injuries that she herself cannot feel. "Some people would say [that feeling no pain is] a good thing," says her mother. "But no, it's not. Pain's there for a reason. It lets your body know something's wrong and it needs to be fixed. I'd give anything for her to feel pain" (quoted by Bynum, 2004).

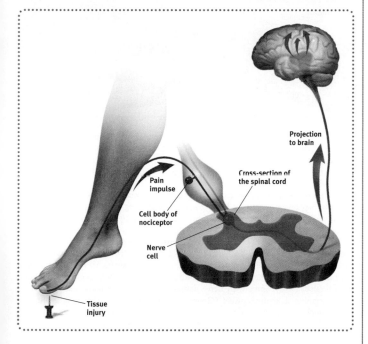

::**kinesthesis** [kin-ehs-THEE-sehs] the system for sensing the position and movement of individual body parts.

::**vestibular sense** the sense of body movement and position, including the sense of balance.

::**gate-control theory** the theory that the spinal cord contains a neurological "gate" that blocks pain signals or allows them to pass on to the brain. The "gate" is opened by the activity of pain signals traveling up small nerve fibers and is closed by activity in larger fibers or by information coming from the brain.

➤ FIGURE 4.24

The pain circuit Sensory receptors (nociceptors) respond to potentially damaging stimuli by sending an impulse to the spinal cord, which passes the message to the brain, which interprets the signal as pain.

TEACHING TIP

Point out that Dennis Turk and his colleagues have defined three subtypes of people who are evaluated at pain centers.

- **Dysfunctional** patients report high levels of pain and psychological distress and believe they have little control over their lives and are extremely inactive.

- **Interpersonally distressed** patients feel they have little social support and report that significant others don't take their pain seriously.

- **Adaptive copers** report far less pain and social distress than people in the other two groups and continue to function at a relatively high level.

Treatments for pain include **hypnosis, acupuncture, physiotherapy, ultrasound, biofeedback, relaxation**, and **electrical stimulation**. Many clinics also use some form of behavioral treatment, which is based on the assumption that pain has become a learned behavior pattern that can be changed.

 TEACHING TIP

The gate-control theory of pain helps explain why people aren't always aware of pain. Pain signals can be controlled by the brain. The brain can sometimes choose which pain to consider and which to ignore, blocking off pain signals in the spinal cord that it chooses to ignore. This theory explains why pain is related to the severity of the injury incurred and why athletes can ignore major injuries. Research indicates that when surgical patients were told what to expect following surgery and to relax to reduce their pain, they needed fewer painkillers and were sent home 2.7 days earlier than a control group. Research also indicates that up to 35 percent of patients with pathological pain obtain relief from a placebo that contains no active ingredients. These examples show that there is more to pain than what stimulates the sense receptors.

TEACHING TIP

The gate-control theory of pain may explain why acupuncture works. Acupuncture is the ancient Chinese practice of inserting needles into the skin at certain points to alleviate pain. This practice may work because the needles create a competing sensation that blocks the pain signals. The brain could also be releasing endorphins to counteract the numerous pain sensations that acupuncture creates, thus alleviating pain.

INTERCONNECTING

Refer students to the Unit 3A discussion of endorphins, the body's natural painkillers. These endogenous morphines work to alleviate pain and inhibit substance P, the body's pain neurotransmitter.

TEACHING TIP

Phantom limb sensations occur when a person feels the presence of a limb after it has been lost. At times, people can experience intense pain in the limbs that are no longer there. Contact a surgeon who specializes in amputations to ask about how doctors treat patients with phantom limb pain and sensations.

> "When belly with bad pains doth swell,
> It matters naught what else goes
> well."
> Sadi, *The Gulistan*, 1258

> "Pain is increased by attending to it."
> Charles Darwin, *Expression of Emotions in
> Man and Animals*, 1872

provides a useful model. The spinal cord contains small nerve fibers that conduct most pain signals, and larger fibers that conduct most other sensory signals. Melzack and Wall theorized that the spinal cord contains a neurological "gate." When tissue is injured, the small fibers activate and open the gate, and you feel pain. Large-fiber activity closes the gate, blocking pain signals and preventing them from reaching the brain. Thus, one way to treat chronic pain is to stimulate (by massage, by electric stimulation, or by acupuncture) "gate-closing" activity in the large neural fibers (Wall, 2000). Rubbing the area around your stubbed toe will create competing stimulation that will block some pain messages.

But pain is not merely a physical phenomenon of injured nerves sending impulses to the brain—like pulling on a rope to ring a bell. Melzack and Wall noted that brain-to-spinal-cord messages can also close the gate, helping to explain some striking influences on pain. When we are distracted from pain (a psychological influence) and soothed by the release of *endorphins,* our natural painkillers (a biological influence), our experience of pain may be greatly diminished. Sports injuries may go unnoticed until the after-game shower. People who carry a gene that boosts the availability of endorphins are less bothered by pain, and their brain is less responsive to pain (Zubieta et al., 2003). Others, who carry a mutated gene that disrupts pain circuit neurotransmission, may be unable to experience pain (Cox et al., 2006). Such discoveries may point the way toward new pain medications that mimic these genetic effects.

Playing with pain In a 2008 NBA championship series game, Boston Celtics star Paul Pierce screamed in pain after an opposing player stepped on his right foot, causing his knee to twist and pop. After being carried off the court, he came back and played through the pain, which reclaimed his attention after the game's end.
▲

The brain can also create pain, as it does in people's experiences of *phantom limb sensations,* when it misinterprets the spontaneous central nervous system activity that occurs in the absence of normal sensory input. As the dreamer may see with eyes closed, so some 7 in 10 amputees may feel pain or movement in nonexistent limbs, notes Melzack (1992, 2005). (An amputee may also try to step off a bed onto a phantom limb or to lift a cup with a phantom hand.) Even those born without a limb sometimes perceive sensations from the absent arm or leg. The brain, Melzack (1998) surmises, comes prepared to anticipate "that it will be getting information from a body that has limbs."

A similar phenomenon occurs with other senses. People with hearing loss often experience the sound of silence: phantom sounds—a ringing-in-the-ears sensation known as *tinnitus.* Those who lose vision to glaucoma, cataracts, diabetes, or macular degeneration may experience phantom sights—nonthreatening hallucinations (Ramachandran & Blakeslee, 1998). Some with nerve damage have had taste phantoms, such as ice water seeming sickeningly sweet (Goode, 1999). Others have experienced phantom smells, such as nonexistent rotten food. The point to remember: *We feel, see, hear, taste, and smell with our brain,* which can sense even without functioning senses.

RESEARCH

Some people are born without the ability to feel pain. While this may seem like a great condition to have, it is actually horribly tragic. To understand the situation, explore the following questions in a class discussion:

- Why would it be bad not to feel pain? *(Pain allows us to determine injury, sickness, and danger.)*

- What might be the expected lifespan of someone who can't feel pain? *(People born with this condition do not live long past the teen years. They often die of normally painful illnesses that they don't feel.)*

Psychological Influences The psychological effects of distraction are clear in the stories of athletes who, focused on winning, play through the pain. Carrie Armel and Vilayanur Ramachandran (2003) cleverly illustrated psychological influences on pain with another version of the rubber-hand illusion. They bent a finger slightly backward on the unseen hands of 16 volunteers, while simultaneously "hurting" (severely bending) a finger on a visible fake rubber hand. The volunteers felt as if their real finger were being bent, and they responded with increased skin perspiration.

We also seem to edit our *memories* of pain, which often differ from the pain we actually experienced. In experiments, and after medical procedures, people overlook a pain's duration. Their memory snapshots instead record two factors: First, people tend to record pain's *peak* moment, which can lead them to recall variable pain, with peaks, as worse (Stone et al., 2005). Second, they register how much pain they felt at the *end,* as Daniel Kahneman and his co-researchers (1993) discovered when they asked people to immerse one hand in painfully cold water for 60 seconds, and then the other hand in the same painfully cold water for 60 seconds followed by a slightly less painful 30 seconds more. Which of these experiences would you expect to recall as most painful?

Curiously, when asked which trial they would prefer to repeat, most preferred the longer trial, with more net pain—but less pain at the end. A physician used this principle with patients undergoing colon exams—lengthening the discomfort by a minute, but lessening its intensity (Kahneman, 1999). Although the extended milder discomfort added to their net pain experience, patients experiencing this taper-down treatment later recalled the exam as less painful than did those whose pain ended abruptly.

Social-Cultural Influences Our perception of pain also varies with our social situation and our cultural traditions. We tend to perceive more pain when others also seem to be experiencing pain (Symbaluk et al., 1997). This may help explain other apparent social aspects of pain, as when pockets of Australian keyboard operators during the mid-1980s suffered outbreaks of severe pain during typing or other repetitive work—without any discernible physical abnormalities (Gawande, 1998). Sometimes the pain in sprain is mainly in the brain—literally. When feeling empathy for another's pain, a person's own brain activity may partly mirror that of the other's brain in pain (Singer et al., 2004).

Thus, our perception of pain is a biopsychosocial phenomenon (**FIGURE 4.25**). Viewing pain this way can help us better understand how to cope with pain and treat it.

Controlling Pain

If pain is where body meets mind—if it is both a physical and a psychological phenomenon—then it should be treatable both physically and psychologically. Depending on the type of symptoms, pain control clinics select one or more therapies from a list that includes drugs, surgery, acupuncture, electrical stimulation, massage, exercise, hypnosis, relaxation training, and thought distraction.

➤ FIGURE 4.25

Biopsychosocial approach to pain Our experience of pain is much more than neural messages sent to the brain.

Biological influences:
- activity in spinal cord's large and small fibers
- genetic differences in endorphin production
- the brain's interpretation of CNS activity

Psychological influences:
- attention to pain
- learning based on experience
- expectations

Social-cultural influences:
- presence of others
- empathy for others' pain
- cultural expectations

Personal experience of pain

INTERCONNECTING

Link our perception of pain to the following concepts from other units:

- From Unit 7A: Pain can be remembered differently depending on our moods, according to mood-congruent memory. If we are in a good mood when we experience pain, our memories of it may not be negative.

- From Unit 14: Cultural differences affect how we perceive pain, or what type of pain we may perceive as being negative. If we know pain is coming, and if we expect it to be part of a growth experience, we may not be bothered by it.

TEACHING TIP

Reinforce the biopsychosocial approach with students by using Figure 4.25. Students should leave AP Psychology knowing that psychological phenomena are complex, influenced by multiple variables.

TEACHING TIP

You may want to use **Lecture/Discussion Topics:** *Amputating a Phantom Limb* (p. 25) or *Cultural Differences in Pain* (p. 25) or *Pain Control* (p. 26) or **Classroom Exercise:** *The Revised Reducer–Augmenter Scale* (p. 24) from Bolt's Teacher's Resource Binder.

UNIT 4

INTERCONNECTING

Remind students about the importance of placebos in research, as discussed in Unit 2. Having a "fake" treatment for your control condition (or at least a treatment that mimics the status quo), helps ensure that just getting treatment is not causing a difference in groups.

INTERCONNECTING

Some researchers believe that hypnosis, discussed in Unit 5, can be effective in relieving pain. Others believe that hypnosis is just an elaborate way to distract people from obvious stimuli. Regardless of the method, diverting one's attention from pain can be helpful in alleviating its effects.

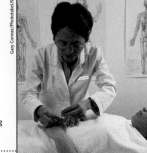

Seeking relief This acupuncturist is attempting to help this woman gain relief from back pain by using needles on points of the patient's hand.

Even an inert placebo can help, by dampening the brain's attention and responses to painful experiences—mimicking analgesic drugs (Wager, 2005). After being injected in the jaw with a stinging saltwater solution, men in one experiment were given a placebo that was said to relieve pain. They immediately felt better, a result associated with activity in a brain area that releases natural pain-killing opiates (Scott et al., 2007; Zubieta et al., 2005). Being given fake pain-killing chemicals caused the brain to dispense real ones. "Believing becomes reality," noted one commentator (Thernstrom, 2006), as "the mind unites with the body."

Another experiment pitted two placebos—fake pills and pretend acupuncture—against each other (Kaptchuk et al., 2006). People with persistent arm pain (270 of them) received either sham acupuncture (with trick needles that retracted without puncturing the skin) or blue cornstarch pills that looked like pills often prescribed for strain injury. A fourth of those receiving the nonexistent needle pricks and 31 percent of those receiving the pills complained of side effects, such as painful skin or dry mouth and fatigue. After two months, both groups were reporting less pain, with the fake acupuncture group reporting the greater pain drop.

Distracting people with pleasant images ("Think of a warm, comfortable environment") or drawing their attention away from the painful stimulation ("Count backward by 3's") is an especially effective way to increase pain tolerance (Fernandez & Turk, 1989; McCaul & Malott, 1984). A well-trained nurse may distract needle-shy patients by chatting with them and asking them to look away when inserting the needle. For burn victims receiving excruciating wound care, an even more effective distraction comes from immersion in a computer-generated 3-D world, like the snow scene in FIGURE 4.26. Functional MRI (fMRI) scans reveal that playing in the virtual reality reduces the brain's pain-related activity (Hoffman, 2004). Because pain is in the brain, diverting the brain's attention may bring relief.

➤ **FIGURE 4.26**
Virtual-reality pain control For burn victims undergoing painful skin repair, an escape into virtual reality can powerfully distract attention, thus reducing pain and the brain's response to painful stimulation. The MRI scans (far right) illustrate a lowered pain response when the patient is distracted.

No Distraction   Distraction

Taste

15: How do we experience taste?

Like touch, our sense of taste involves several basic sensations. Taste's sensations were once thought to be sweet, sour, salty, and bitter, with all others stemming from mixtures of these four (McBurney & Gent, 1979). Then, as investigators searched for specialized nerve fibers for the four taste sensations, they encountered a receptor for what we now know is a fifth—the savory meaty taste of *umami*, best experienced as the flavor enhancer monosodium glutamate.

Tastes exist for more than our pleasure (see **TABLE 4.2**). Pleasing tastes attracted our ancestors to energy- or protein-rich foods that enabled their survival. Aversive tastes deterred them from new foods that might be toxic. We see the inheritance of this biological wisdom in today's 2- to 6-year-olds, who are typically fussy eaters, especially when offered new meats or bitter-tasting vegetables, such as spinach and Brussels sprouts (Cooke et al., 2003). Meat and plant toxins were both potentially dangerous sources of food poisoning for our ancestors, especially for children. Given repeated small tastes of disliked new foods, children will, however, typically begin to accept them (Wardle et al., 2003).

Taste is a chemical sense. Inside each little bump on the top and sides of your tongue are 200 or more taste buds, each containing a pore that catches food chemicals. Into each taste bud pore, 50 to 100 taste receptor cells project antennalike hairs that sense food molecules. Some receptors respond mostly to sweet-tasting molecules, others to salty-, sour-, umami-, or bitter-tasting ones. It doesn't take much to trigger a response that alerts your brain's temporal lobe. If a stream of water is pumped across your tongue, the addition of a concentrated salty or sweet taste for but one-tenth of a second will get your attention (Kelling & Halpern, 1983). When a friend asks for "just a taste" of your soft drink, you can squeeze off the straw after a mere fraction of a second.

Taste receptors reproduce themselves every week or two, so when you burn your tongue with hot pizza it hardly matters. However, as you grow older, the number of taste buds decreases, as does taste sensitivity (Cowart, 1981). (No wonder adults enjoy strong-tasting foods that children resist.) Smoking and alcohol use accelerate these declines. Those who lose their sense of taste report that food tastes like "straw" and is hard to swallow (Cowart, 2005).

Essential as taste buds are, there's more to taste than meets the tongue. As with other senses, your expectations influence your brain's response. When people are forewarned that an unpleasant taste is coming, their brain responds more actively to negative tastes, which they rate as very unpleasant. When led to believe that the *same taste* will be merely mildly unpleasant, the brain region that responds to aversive tastes is less active, and the participants rate the taste as less unpleasant (Nitschke et al., 2006). Likewise, when adults are told that a wine costs $90 rather than its real $10 price, the inexpensive wine tastes better and triggers more activity in a brain area that responds to pleasant experiences (Plassmann et al., 2008). As happens with the pain placebo effect, the brain's thinking frontal lobes offer information that other brain regions act upon.

Sensory Interaction

Taste also illustrates another curious phenomenon. Hold your nose, close your eyes, and have someone feed you various foods. A slice of apple may be indistinguishable from a chunk of raw potato; a piece of steak may taste like cardboard; without their smells, a cup of cold coffee may be hard to distinguish from a glass of Gatorade. To savor a taste, we normally breathe the aroma through our nose—which is why eating is not much fun when you have a bad cold. Smell can also change our perception of taste: A drink's strawberry odor enhances our perception of its sweetness. This is **sensory interaction** at work—the principle that one sense may influence another. Smell plus texture plus taste equals flavor.

Sensory interaction similarly influences what we hear. If I (as a person with hearing loss) watch a video with simultaneous captioning, I have no trouble hearing the words I am seeing (and may therefore think I don't need the captioning). If I then turn off the captioning, I suddenly realize I need it (**FIGURE 4.27**, next page). But what

::**sensory interaction** the principle that one sense may influence another, as when the smell of food influences its taste.

TABLE 4.2

THE SURVIVAL FUNCTIONS OF BASIC TASTES

Taste	Indicates
Sweet	Energy source
Salty	Sodium essential to physiological processes
Sour	Potentially toxic acid
Bitter	Potential poisons
Umami	Proteins to grow and repair tissue

(Adapted from Cowart, 2005.)

UNIT 4

 TEACHING TIP

Psychologists Marcia Pelchat and Patricia Pliner devised an experiment to find out whether it is the novelty of a food or something else that prompts people to spurn it. They gave two groups of people identical foods. When the foods were accurately named—"chopped tomatoes," "oatmeal," and "beefsteak"—the subjects were quite willing to taste them. When the foods were referred to as "pendula fruit," "lat," and "langua steaks," subjects were far less cooperative.

 TEACHING TIP

People seem to have a built-in preference for sweet foods. They find bitter and sour foods unpleasant; they like salty foods at low concentrations but dislike them at high concentrations. In one study of infants, sweet substances elicited sucking and, in some cases, smiling. Sour tastes produced "lip pursing and wrinkling of the nose," and bitter tastes prompted "opening of the mouth with the upper lip elevated and protrusion of the tongue." These reactions make good evolutionary sense, because bitter or sour plants are often toxic, while the sweeter ones tend to be nutritious.

➤ **FIGURE 4.27**
Sensory interaction When a hard-of-hearing listener sees an animated face forming the words being spoken at the other end of a phone line, the words become easier to understand (Knight, 2004).

Courtesy of RNID www.rnid.org.uk

• Impress your friends with your new word for the day: People unable to see are said to experience blindness. People unable to hear experience deafness. People unable to smell experience *anosmia*. •

"There could be a stack of truck tires burning in the living room, and I wouldn't necessarily smell it. Whereas my wife can detect a lone spoiled grape two houses away."
Dave Barry, 2005

do you suppose happens if we *see* a speaker saying one syllable while we *hear* another? Surprise: We may perceive a third syllable that blends both inputs. Seeing the mouth movements for *ga* while hearing *ba* we may perceive *da*—a phenomenon known as the *McGurk effect*, after its discoverers, psychologist Harry McGurk and his assistant John MacDonald (1976).

Much the same is true with vision and touch. A weak flicker of light that we have trouble perceiving becomes more visible when accompanied by a short burst of sound (Kayser, 2007). In detecting events, the brain can combine simultaneous visual and touch signals, thanks to neurons projecting from the somatosensory cortex back to the visual cortex (Macaluso et al., 2000).

So, the senses interact: Seeing, hearing, touching, tasting, and smelling are not totally separate channels. In interpreting the world, the brain blends their inputs. In a few select individuals, the senses become joined in a phenomenon called *synaesthesia*, where one sort of sensation (such as hearing sound) produces another (such as seeing color). Thus, hearing music or seeing a specific number may activate color-sensitive cortex regions and trigger a sensation of color (Brang et al., 2008; Hubbard et al., 2005). Seeing the number 3 may evoke a taste sensation (Ward, 2003). For many people, an odor, perhaps of mint or chocolate, may evoke a sensation of taste (Stevenson & Tomiczek, 2007).

Smell

16: How do we experience smell?

Inhale, exhale. Inhale, exhale. Breaths come in pairs—except at two moments: birth and death. Between those two moments, you will daily inhale and exhale nearly 20,000 breaths of life-sustaining air, bathing your nostrils in a stream of scent-laden molecules. The resulting experiences of smell (*olfaction*) are strikingly intimate: You inhale something of whatever or whoever it is you smell.

Like taste, smell is a chemical sense. We smell something when molecules of a substance carried in the air reach a tiny cluster of 5 million or more receptor cells at the top of each nasal cavity (**FIGURE 4.28**). These olfactory receptor cells, waving like sea anemones on a reef, respond selectively—to the aroma of a cake baking, to a wisp of smoke, to a friend's fragrance. Instantly, they alert the brain through their axon fibers. Being an old, primitive sense, olfactory neurons bypass the brain's sensory switchboard, the thalamus.

Even nursing infants and their mothers have a literal chemistry to their relationship. They quickly learn to recognize each other's scents (McCarthy, 1986). Aided by smell, a mother fur seal returning to a beach crowded with pups will find her own. Our own sense of smell is less impressive than the acuteness of our seeing and hearing. Looking out across a garden, we see its forms and colors in exquisite detail and hear a variety of birds singing, yet we smell little of it without sticking our nose into the blossoms.

Odor molecules come in many shapes and sizes—so many, in fact, that it takes many different receptors to detect them. A large family of genes designs the 350 or so receptor proteins that recognize particular odor molecules (Miller, 2004). Richard

TEACHING TIP

You may want to use **Lecture/Discussion Topics:** *Taste Preferences* (p. 29) or *Synaesthesia* (p. 30) or **Classroom Exercises:** *Taste: The Basic Taste Sensations* (p. 28) or *Genetic Effects in Taste* (p. 28) or **Classroom Exercise/Student Project:** *Taste* (p. 30) or **Student Project:** *Mapping Your Tongue* (p. 29) from Bolt's Teacher's Resource Binder.

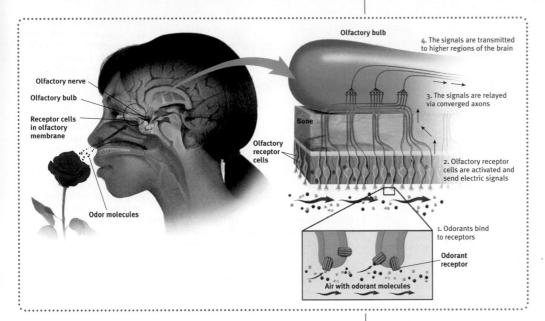

➤ FIGURE 4.28
The sense of smell If you are to smell a flower, airborne molecules of its fragrance must reach receptors at the top of your nose. Sniffing swirls air up to the receptors, enhancing the aroma. The receptor cells send messages to the brain's olfactory bulb, and then onward to the temporal lobe's primary smell cortex and to the parts of the limbic system involved in memory and emotion.

• Humans have 10 to 20 million olfactory receptors. A bloodhound has some 200 million (Herz, 2001). •

> "The smell and taste of things bears unfaltering, in the tiny and almost impalpable drop of their essence, the vast structure of recollection."
> French novelist Marcel Proust, in *Remembrance of Things Past* [1913], describing how the aroma and flavor of a bit of cake soaked in tea resurrected long-forgotten memories of the old family house.

Axel and Linda Buck (1991) discovered (in work for which they received a 2004 Nobel Prize) that these receptor proteins are embedded on the surface of nasal cavity neurons. As a key slips into a lock, so odor molecules slip into these receptors. Yet we don't seem to have a distinct receptor for each detectable odor. This suggests that some odors trigger a combination of receptors, in patterns that are interpreted by the olfactory cortex. As the English alphabet's 26 letters can combine to form many words, so odor molecules bind to different receptor arrays, producing the 10,000 odors we can detect (Malnic et al., 1999). It is the combinations of olfactory receptors, which activate different neuron patterns, that allow us to distinguish between the aromas of fresh-brewed and hours-old coffee (Zou et al., 2005).

The ability to identify scents peaks in early adulthood and gradually declines thereafter, with women's smelling ability tending to surpass men's (**FIGURE 4.29**, on the next page). Despite our skill at discriminating scents, we aren't very good at describing them. Words more readily portray the sound of coffee brewing than its aroma. Compared with how we experience and remember sights and sounds, smells are almost primitive and certainly harder to describe and recall (Richardson & Zucco, 1989; Zucco, 2003).

As any dog or cat with a good nose could tell us, we each have our own identifiable chemical signature. (One noteworthy exception: A dog will follow the tracks of one identical twin as though they had been made by the other [Thomas, 1974].) Animals that have many times more olfactory receptors than we do also use their sense of smell to communicate and to navigate. Long before the shark can see its prey, or the moth its mate, odors direct their way. Migrating salmon follow faint olfactory cues back to their home stream. If exposed in a hatchery to one of two odorant chemicals, they will, when returning two years later, seek whichever stream near their release site is spiked with the familiar smell (Barinaga, 1999).

For humans, too, the attractiveness of smells depends on learned associations (Herz, 2001). Babies are not born with a built-in preference for the smell of their

INTERCONNECTING

As a link to neuroscience, inform students that smell is the only sense where the signals do not go directly to the thalamus before being processed. In fact, smell is processed near the prefrontal cortex before it is sent along, which may help explain why smell can trigger powerful memories since that part of the brain works with the limbic system to process emotional memories.

TEACHING TIP

Can we tell if a person is male or female on the basis of odor alone? Research indicates that we can:

- Patricia Wallace had blindfolded subjects sniff a thoroughly washed hand held one-half inch from their nose. Her subjects could discriminate male from female hands with over 80 percent accuracy. Female sniffers were more accurate than male sniffers.

- Richard Doty and his colleagues had college students assess breath odor of subjects who sat on the other side of a partition and exhaled through a plastic tube. Most judges scored better than chance, and again females outperformed males.

- Mark Russel had college freshmen wear T-shirts for 24 hours after which the shirts were individually placed in sealed containers. Each subject was then presented with three containers—one holding his or her own shirt, a second holding the shirt of an unknown female, and a third holding the shirt of an unknown male. The vast majority were able to identify their own shirt and which belonged to a male and female.

TEACHING TIP

You may want to use **Lecture/Discussion Topics:** *Anosmia* (p. 31) or *Gender-Related Odors* (p. 33) or *Pheromones* (p. 33) or *Fragrance Effects* (p. 34) from Bolt's Teacher's Resource Binder.

UNIT 4

TEACHING TIP

Are there human pheromones? The most promising evidence comes from researchers investigating the menstrual "synchrony" in women who live or work together. Martha McClintock and Kathleen Stern recruited a group of 29 women and asked nine of them to wear pads under their arms for several hours, either before or just after ovulation. When the pads were then wiped under the noses of the other women, the results were startling: Smelling pre-ovulation pads shortened their menstrual cycles by as many 14 days, while ovulation phase pads increased cycles by as many as 12 days. McClintock is continuing her research with an eye on possible applications. Pheromone treatments designed to regulate ovulation could serve as fertility enhancers for couples who want to conceive and as contraceptives for those who don't.

➤ **FIGURE 4.29**
Age, sex, and sense of smell Among the 1.2 million people who responded to a *National Geographic* scratch-and-sniff survey, women and younger adults most successfully identified six sample odors (from Wysocki & Gilbert, 1989). Smokers and people with Alzheimer's, Parkinson's, or alcohol dependence typically experience a diminished sense of smell (Doty, 2001).

➤ **FIGURE 4.30**
The olfactory brain Information from the taste buds (yellow arrow) travels to an area of the temporal lobe not far from where the brain receives olfactory information, which interacts with taste. The brain's circuitry for smell (red arrow) also connects with areas involved in memory storage, which helps explain why a smell can trigger a memory explosion.

mother's breast; as they nurse, their preference builds. After a good experience becomes associated with a particular scent, people come to like that scent, which helps explain why people in the United States tend to like the smell of wintergreen (which they associate with candy and gum) more than do those in Great Britain (where it often is associated with medicine). In another example of odors evoking unpleasant emotions, Rachel Herz and her colleagues (2004) frustrated Brown University students with a rigged computer game in a scented room. Later, if exposed to the same odor while working on a verbal task, the students' frustration was rekindled and they gave up sooner than others exposed to a different odor or no odor.

Though it's difficult to recall odors by name, we have a remarkable capacity to recognize long-forgotten odors and their associated memories (Engen, 1987; Schab, 1991). The smell of the sea, the scent of a perfume, or an aroma of a favorite relative's kitchen can bring to mind a happy time. It's a phenomenon understood by the British travel agent chain Lunn Poly. To evoke memories of lounging on sunny, warm beaches, the company once piped the aroma of coconut suntan oil into its shops (Fracassini, 2000).

Our brain's circuitry helps explain this power to evoke feelings and memories (**FIGURE 4.30**). A hotline runs between the brain area receiving information from the nose and the brain's ancient limbic centers associated with memory and emotion. Smell is primitive. Eons before the elaborate analytical areas of our cerebral cortex had fully evolved, our mammalian ancestors sniffed for food—and for predators.

BEFORE YOU MOVE ON . . .

➤ **ASK YOURSELF**

Can you recall a time when, with your attention focused on some activity, you felt no pain from a wound or injury?

➤ **TEST YOURSELF 4**

How does our system for sensing smell differ from our sensory systems for vision, touch, and taste?

Answers to the Test Yourself questions can be found in Appendix E at the end of the book.

TEACHING TIP

You may want to use **Classroom Exercise:** *Identifying Odors* (p. 32) from Bolt's Teacher's Resource Binder.

Perceptual Organization

17: How did the Gestalt psychologists understand perceptual organization?

WE HAVE EXAMINED THE PROCESSES by which we sense sights and sounds, touch and movement, tastes and smells. Now our central question is: how do we see not just shapes and colors, but a rose in bloom, a loved one's face, a beautiful sunset? How do we hear not just a mix of pitches and rhythms, but a friend's cry of pain, the hum of distant traffic, a symphony? In short, how do we organize and interpret our sensations so that they become meaningful perceptions?

Early in the twentieth century, a group of German psychologists noticed that when given a cluster of sensations, people tend to organize them into a **gestalt,** a German word meaning a "form" or a "whole." For example, look at the Necker cube in FIGURE 4.31. Note that the individual elements of the figure are really nothing but eight blue circles, each containing three converging white lines. When we view them all together, however, we see a *whole,* a cube. The Gestalt psychologists, who had wide-ranging interests, were fond of saying that in perception the whole may exceed the sum of its parts. Combine sodium, a corrosive metal, with chlorine, a poisonous gas, and something very different emerges: salt. Likewise, a unique perceived form emerges from a stimulus' components (Rock & Palmer, 1990).

Over the years, the Gestalt psychologists provided compelling demonstrations and described principles by which we organize our sensations into perceptions. As you read further about these principles, keep in mind the fundamental truth they illustrate: *Our brain does more than register information about the world.* Perception is not just opening a shutter and letting a picture print itself on the brain. We constantly filter sensory information and infer perceptions in ways that make sense to us. Mind matters.

Form Perception

18: How do figure-ground and grouping principles contribute to our perceptions?

Imagine designing a video/computer system that, like your eye/brain system, can recognize faces at a glance. What abilities would it need?

Figure and Ground

To start with, the system would need to recognize faces as distinct from their backgrounds. Likewise, our first perceptual task is to perceive any object (the figure) as distinct from its surroundings (the ground). Among the voices you hear at a party, the one you attend to becomes the figure; all others, part of the ground. As you read, the words are the figure; the white paper, the ground. In FIGURE 4.32, the **figure-ground** relationship continually reverses—but always we organize the stimulus into a figure seen against a ground. Such reversible figure-and-ground illustrations demonstrate again that the same stimulus can trigger more than one perception.

::**gestalt** an organized whole. Gestalt psychologists emphasized our tendency to integrate pieces of information into meaningful wholes.

::**figure-ground** the organization of the visual field into objects (the *figures*) that stand out from their surroundings (the *ground*).

➤ **FIGURE 4.31**
A Necker cube What do you see: circles with white lines, or a cube? If you stare at the cube, you may notice that it reverses location, moving the tiny X in the center from the front edge to the back. At times, the cube may seem to float in front of the page, with circles behind it; other times the circles may become holes in the page through which the cube appears, as though it were floating behind the page. There is far more to perception than meets the eye. (From Bradley et al., 1976.)

➤ **FIGURE 4.32**
Reversible figure and ground

Time-Saving Suggestion, © 2003 Roger N. Shepard.

TROUBLESHOOTING

Students may not understand the Gestalt psychologists' view that the whole is greater than the sum of its parts. Have them imagine how much the different elements that make up the human body are worth. Even though those elements may be valuable, their combined value making up the human body is more valuable than they ever could be on their own.

TEACHING TIP

Have students create their own tessellations like the one in Figure 4.32. This picture is similar to tessellations created by M. C. Escher, whose drawings capitalized on figure-ground illusions to create fanciful, yet impossible, pictures. A tessellation is a repeating geometric pattern, and the ones in the figure and those that Escher created would combine tessellations with figure-ground illusions where two geometric patterns would repeat at the same time—one as a figure and one as a ground.

DEMO

Students can discover auditory figure-ground illusions by simply repeating aloud a word such as *say*. It will shift abruptly to *ace* and back again to *say*.

UNIT 4

TROUBLESHOOTING

Students typically find Gestalt grouping principles to be very mundane and obvious. Remind students that the Gestalt psychologists were the first to study systematically how people perceive whole objects. Before their work, people took these grouping principles for granted.

TEACHING TIP

Use the following examples of two of the Gestalt grouping principles to help students remember them:

- Proximity: We perceive items that are close to each other as being together. Have students imagine their reactions when someone they do not know well walks in step with them down the hall. Typically, people feel discomfort when this happens because of their proximity to the other person. We do not like to be grouped together with people we do not know well.

- Similarity: Items that look the same are usually grouped together. Have students imagine their reactions when someone they do not know well wears the same outfit or shirt as they do. Typically, they are uncomfortable with this since we do not like being grouped with people we do not know well.

Proximity   Similarity

Continuity   Connectedness

➤ **FIGURE 4.33**
Organizing stimuli into groups We could perceive the stimuli shown here in many ways, yet people everywhere see them similarly. The Gestalt psychologists believed this shows that the brain follows rules to order sensory information into wholes.

Grouping

Having discriminated figure from ground, we (and our video/computer system) now have to organize the figure into a meaningful form. Some basic features of a scene—such as color, movement, and light/dark contrast—we process instantly and automatically (Treisman, 1987). To bring order and form to these basic sensations, our minds follow certain rules for **grouping** stimuli together. These rules, identified by the Gestalt psychologists and applied even by infants, illustrate the idea that the perceived whole differs from the sum of its parts (Quinn et al., 2002; Rock & Palmer, 1990):

Proximity We group nearby figures together, as in FIGURE 4.33. We see three sets of two lines, not six separate lines.

Similarity We group similar figures together. We see the triangles and circles as vertical columns of similar shapes, not as horizontal rows of dissimilar shapes.

Continuity We perceive smooth, continuous patterns rather than discontinuous ones. The pattern in the lower-left corner of Figure 4.33 could be a series of alternating semicircles, but we perceive it as two continuous lines—one wavy, one straight.

Connectedness Because they are uniform and linked, we perceive each set of two dots and the line between them as a single unit.

Closure We fill in gaps to create a complete, whole object. Thus we assume that the circles (below left) are complete but partially blocked by the (illusory) triangle. Add nothing more than little line segments that close off the circles (below right) and now your brain stops constructing a triangle.

Such principles usually help us construct reality. Sometimes, however, they lead us astray, as when we look at the doghouse in FIGURE 4.34.

➤ **FIGURE 4.34**
Grouping principles What's the secret to this impossible doghouse? You probably perceive this doghouse as a gestalt—a whole (though impossible) structure. Actually, your brain imposes this sense of wholeness on the picture. As Figure 4.39 shows, Gestalt grouping principles such as closure and continuity are at work here.

Photo by Walter Wick. Reprinted from GAMES Magazine. © 1983 PCS Games Limited Partnership

TEACHING TIP

You may want to use **Lecture/Discussion Topics:** *Object Recognition* (p. 37) or *Visual Agnosia* (p. 38) or **Classroom Exercise:** *Perceptual Illusions and Principles* (p. 36) or **Classroom Exercise/Student Project:** *The Wundt-Jastrow Illusion* (p. 35) or **Student Projects:** *Playing Cards and Illusions* (p. 37) or *Instant Object Recognition* (p. 37) from Bolt's Teacher's Resource Binder.

Depth Perception

19: How do we see the world in three dimensions?

From the two-dimensional images falling on our retinas, we somehow organize three-dimensional perceptions. **Depth perception,** seeing objects in three dimensions, enables us to estimate their distance from us. At a glance, we estimate the distance of an oncoming car or the height of a house. This ability is partly innate. Eleanor Gibson and Richard Walk (1960) discovered this using a miniature cliff with a drop-off covered by sturdy glass. Gibson's inspiration for these experiments occurred while she was picnicking on the rim of the Grand Canyon. She wondered: Would a toddler peering over the rim perceive the dangerous drop-off and draw back?

Back in their Cornell University laboratory, Gibson and Walk placed 6- to 14-month-old infants on the edge of a safe canyon—a **visual cliff** (FIGURE 4.35). When the infants' mothers then coaxed them to crawl out onto the glass, most refused to do so, indicating that they could perceive depth. Crawling infants come to the lab after lots of learning. Yet newborn animals with virtually no visual experience—young kittens, a day-old goat, and newly hatched chicks—respond similarly. To Gibson and Walk, this suggested that mobile newborn animals come prepared to perceive depth.

Each species, by the time it is mobile, has the perceptual abilities it needs. But if biological maturation predisposes our wariness of heights, experience amplifies it. Infants' wariness increases with their experiences of crawling, no matter when they begin to crawl (Campos et al., 1992). And judging from what they will reach for, 7-month-olds use the cast shadow of a toy to perceive its distance, while 5-month-olds don't (Yonas & Granrud, 2006). This suggests that in human infants, depth perception grows with age.

How do we do it? How do we transform two differing two-dimensional retinal images into a single three-dimensional perception? The process begins with depth cues, some that depend on the use of two eyes, and others that are available to each eye separately.

Binocular Cues

Try this: With both eyes open, hold two pens or pencils in front of you and touch their tips together. Now do so with one eye closed. With one eye, the task becomes noticeably more difficult, demonstrating the importance of **binocular cues** in judging the distance of nearby objects. Two eyes are better than one.

Because our eyes are about 2½ inches apart, our retinas receive slightly different images of the world. When the brain compares these two images, the difference between them—their **retinal disparity**—provides one important binocular cue to the relative distance of different objects. When you hold your fingers directly in front of your nose, your retinas receive quite different views. (You can see this if you close one eye and then the other, or create a finger sausage as in FIGURE 4.36, next page.) At a greater distance—say, when you hold your fingers at arm's length—the disparity is smaller.

➤ FIGURE 4.35

Visual cliff Eleanor Gibson and Richard Walk devised this miniature cliff with a glass-covered drop-off to determine whether crawling infants and newborn animals can perceive depth. Even when coaxed, infants are reluctant to venture onto the glass over the cliff.

::**grouping** the perceptual tendency to organize stimuli into coherent groups.

::**depth perception** the ability to see objects in three dimensions although the images that strike the retina are two-dimensional; allows us to judge distance.

::**visual cliff** a laboratory device for testing depth perception in infants and young animals.

::**binocular cues** depth cues, such as retinal disparity, that depend on the use of two eyes.

::**retinal disparity** a binocular cue for perceiving depth: By comparing images from the retinas in the two eyes, the brain computes distance—the greater the disparity (difference) between the two images, the closer the object.

INTERCONNECTING

Refer students to Unit 9, for a thorough discussion of infant development. The visual cliff study, a classic in the field, helped demonstrate how infants perceive depth and ways to measure infant perceptions without relying on language.

TEACHING TIP

Seeing depth is achieved because we have two eyes in the front of our heads. Animals with eyes on the sides of their heads need that type of vision to scan for danger around them. Peripheral vision is much better at detecting motion, so having better peripheral vision with eyes on the sides of the head gives an evolutionary advantage to animals that are typically hunted. Predators do not need to be on the look out for danger—they are the danger! They need to determine distances between them and their prey, which requires the depth perception that binocular vision provides.

DEMO

Relate retinal disparity to real life by having students recall a time when they were lying down watching television. Ask them if they ever had their vision in one eye obscured by a pillow or blanket they were lying with. If so, then they probably had to shift their position to correct the obstruction or close one eye—watching TV and a pillow at the same time is not very enjoyable!

WEB CONNECT

Some people cannot see depth well because of different conditions that hinder the eyes' ability to see in stereo. Check out www.vision3d.com to find the answers to the following questions:

- What is amblyopia? (*lazy eye*) What are some treatments for this condition?

- What is strabismus? (*deflected eye; crossed eyes or wall eyes*). What are some treatments for this condition?

- How are vision problems related to learning disabilities and dyslexia?

UNIT 4

DEMO

Try to round up some Viewmasters to demonstrate retinal disparity in class. Students can view the images with one eye closed and both eyes open to see how the same image is projected in two slightly different places to capitalize on our perception of depth.

DEMO

Have students roll a sheet of paper into a tube and raise it to their right eye like a telescope. Tell them to look through it, focusing on a blank wall in front of them. Next, have them hold their open left hand beside the tube and continue to focus ahead. The images received by the two eyes will fuse, and the hole in the tube will appear to be in the student's hand. They may need to slide the hand alongside the tube until they find the precise spot where the hole appears to go through the very center of the palm.

Fisher, J. (1979). *Body magic*. New York: Stein and Day.

WEB CONNECT

In a computer lab or as a home-work assignment, have students try out some of the 3D vision games found at www.vision3d.com.

- Eye Hop Game: www.vision3d. com/ehop.html
- Framing Game: www.vision3d. com/frame.html
- Reversible figures: www.vision3d.com/optical/ puzzles.html

➤ **FIGURE 4.36**
The floating finger sausage Hold your two index fingers about 5 inches in front of your eyes, with their tips a half-inch apart. Now look beyond them and note the weird result. Move your fingers out farther and the retinal disparity—and the finger sausage—will shrink.

::**monocular cues** depth cues, such as interposition and linear perspective, available to either eye alone.

The creators of 3-D (three-dimensional) movies simulate or exaggerate retinal disparity by photographing a scene with two cameras placed a few inches apart (a feature we might want to build into our seeing computer). When we view the movie through special glasses that allow the left eye to see the image from the left camera and the right eye the image from the right camera, the 3-D effect mimics or exaggerates normal retinal disparity. Similarly, twin cameras in airplanes can take photos of terrain for integration into 3-D maps.

Monocular Cues

How do we judge whether a person is 10 or 100 meters away? In both cases, retinal disparity while looking straight ahead is slight. At such distances, we depend on **monocular cues** (available to each eye separately). Monocular cues also influence our everyday perceptions. Is the St. Louis Gateway Arch (**FIGURE 4.37**)—the world's largest human-made illusion—taller than it is wide? Or wider than it is tall? To most of us, it appears taller. Actually, its height and width are equal. Relative height is a possible contributor to this unexplained *horizontal-vertical illusion*—our perceiving vertical dimensions as longer than identical horizontal dimensions. No wonder people (even experienced bartenders) pour less juice when given a tall, thin glass rather than a short, wide glass (Wansink & van Ittersum, 2003, 2005).

➤ **FIGURE 4.37**
The St. Louis Gateway Arch Which is greater: its height or width?

Rick Friedman/Black Star

Another monocular depth cue, the light-and-shadow effect, may have contributed to several accidents when the steps of our new campus field house were unfortunately painted black on the step's edge (making it seem farther away) and bright silver on the flat surface of the step below (making it seem closer). The seeming result was the misperception of no step-down, and (for some) sprained ankles and backs. **FIGURE 4.38** illustrates relative height, light and shadow, and other monocular cues.

DEMO

Have students close one eye, point their two forefingers toward each other, and then bring them together quickly. They are likely to miss. An even more difficult test is to have them hold a pencil in each hand and bring the points together. It is important, of course, that their hands not be at arm's length. If they repeat either test, they ought to drop their arms out of view before they try again. This will eliminate the perception of any depth cues from the position of the hands and arms.

Relative height We perceive objects higher in our field of vision as farther away. Because we perceive the lower part of a figure-ground illustration as closer, we perceive it as figure (Vecera et al., 2002). Invert the illustration above and the black becomes ground, like a night sky.

Relative size If we assume two objects are similar in size, *most* people perceive the one that casts the smaller retinal image as farther away.

Interposition If one object partially blocks our view of another, we perceive it as closer. The depth cues provided by interposition make this an impossible scene.

THE FREIGHT ELEVATOR FOR THE MAN WHO HAS EVERYTHING

Linear perspective Parallel lines, such as railroad tracks, appear to converge with distance. The more they converge, the greater their perceived distance.

Light and shadow Nearby objects reflect more light to our eyes. Thus, given two identical objects, the dimmer one seems farther away. Shading, too, produces a sense of depth consistent with our assumption that light comes from above. Invert the illustration below and the hollow in the bottom row will become a hill.

Fixation point

Relative motion As we move, objects that are actually stable may appear to move. If while riding on a bus you fix your gaze on some object—say, a house—the objects beyond the fixation point appear to move with you; objects in front of the fixation point appear to move backward. The farther those objects are from the fixation point, the faster they seem to move.

Direction of passenger's motion →

➤ **FIGURE 4.38**
Monocular depth cues

Motion Perception

20: How do we perceive motion?

Imagine that you could perceive the world as having color, form, and depth but that you could not see motion. Not only would you be unable to bike or drive, you would have trouble writing, eating, and walking.

Students may feel that the monocular depth cues are more common sense than psychology. Emphasize that without these cues, many forms of entertainment—from art to television to movies—would lack the visual richness and beauty they possess. Monocular depth cues help make the world a more visually interesting place!

TEACHING TIP

Many of these depth cues rely on previous knowledge in order to work. If we don't know already how large an object is, then the relative size cue becomes meaningless. Here is where top-down processing is most useful in helping us accurately understand the world.

You may want to use **Lecture/ Discussion Topic:** *Autostereograms* (p. 40) or **Classroom Exercise:** *Binocular Vision* (p. 40) or **Classroom Exercise/Student Project:** *Binocular Vision Versus Monocular Vision* (p. 40) from Bolt's Teacher's Resource Binder.

DEMO

Divide students into small groups and have them compile a portfolio of examples of monocular depth cues. Have them bring in their own magazines (or collect back issues from your library) to look for examples of each type of monocular cue, collecting them in a scrapbook or poster and identifying the one that each picture exemplifies.

Max Wertheimer, the founder of Gestalt psychology, used an everyday phenomenon to explain his theory. Wertheimer observed the *phi phenomenon*, where individual flashing lights could be made to look like they were chasing each other by putting them in a timed sequence. He noticed that by looking at each light individually, you lost the whole effect of the lights chasing each other. He felt that studying individual behaviors took away from appreciating the whole person.

DEMO

Boston's Museum of Science offers a wonderful online lesson in which students can create a realistic and natural picture using linear perspective. Called Leonardo's Window, this lesson asks students to tape some acetate onto a window and trace the lines found in the natural world outside to create a painting. For more instructions, see www.mos.org/sln/Leonardo/UsingLeosWindow.html.

TEACHING TIP

While we can see depth with only one eye, it is much more difficult to perceive depth with one eye closed than with both eyes open. Animals with eyes on the sides of their heads (birds, rabbits, etc.) tend to compensate for their lack of depth perception by moving their heads around a lot to as they try to look around objects. This type of movement that creates depth is called *monocular parallax*.

➤ **FIGURE 4.39**

The solution Another view of the impossible doghouse in Figure 4.34 reveals the secrets of this illusion. From the photo angle in Figure 4.34, the grouping principle of closure leads us to perceive the boards as continuous.

➤ **FIGURE 4.40**

Perceiving shape Do the tops of these tables have different dimensions? They appear to. But—believe it or not—they are identical. (Measure and see.) With both tables, we adjust our perceptions relative to our viewing angle.

Normally your brain computes motion based partly on its assumption that shrinking objects are retreating (not getting smaller) and enlarging objects are approaching. But you are imperfect at motion perception. Large objects, such as trains, appear to move more slowly than smaller objects, such as cars moving at the same speed. (Perhaps at an airport you've noticed that jumbo jets seem to land more slowly than little jets.)

To catch a fly ball, softball or cricket players (unlike drivers) want to achieve a collision—with the ball that's flying their way. To accomplish that, they follow an unconscious rule—one they can't explain but know intuitively: Run to keep the ball at a constantly increasing angle of gaze (McBeath et al., 1995). A dog catching a Frisbee does the same (Shaffer et al., 2004).

The brain will also perceive continuous movement in a rapid series of slightly varying images (a phenomenon called *stroboscopic movement*). As film animation artists know well, you can create this illusion by flashing 24 still pictures a second. The motion we then see in popular action adventures is not in the film, which merely presents a superfast slide show. The motion is constructed in our heads. Marquees and holiday lights create another illusion of movement using the **phi phenomenon.** When two adjacent stationary lights blink on and off in quick succession, we perceive a single light moving back and forth between them. Lighted signs exploit the phi phenomenon with a succession of lights that creates the impression of, say, a moving arrow.

All of these illusions reinforce a fundamental lesson: Perception is not merely a projection of the world onto our brain. Rather, sensations are disassembled into information bits that the brain, using both bottom-up and top-down processing, then reassembles into its own functional model of the external world. *Our brain constructs our perceptions.*

Perceptual Constancy

21: How do perceptual constancies help us organize our sensations into meaningful perceptions?

So far, we have noted that our video/computer system must first perceive objects as we do—as having a distinct form, location, and perhaps motion. Its next task is to recognize objects without being deceived by changes in their shape, size, brightness, or color—an ability we call **perceptual constancy.** Regardless of our viewing angle, distance, and illumination, this top-down process lets us identify people and things in less time than it takes to draw a breath. This human perceptual feat, which has intrigued researchers for decades, provides a monumental challenge for our perceiving computer.

Shape and Size Constancies

Sometimes an object whose actual shape cannot change *seems* to change shape with the angle of our view (**FIGURE 4.40**). More often, thanks to *shape constancy*, we perceive the form of familiar objects, such as the door in **FIGURE 4.41**, as constant even while our retinal image of it changes.

Thanks to *size constancy*, we perceive objects as having a constant size, even while our distance from them varies. We assume a car is large enough to carry people, even when we see its tiny image from two blocks away. This illustrates the close connection between perceived *distance* and perceived *size*. Perceiving an object's distance gives us cues to its size. Likewise, knowing its general size—that the object is a car—provides us with cues to its distance.

TEACHING TIP

Cite an interesting example of depth cues working to create an illusion of reality by discussing the proportions of Michelangelo's sculpture, *The Pieta*. *The Pieta* depicts the Virgin Mary holding her dead son Jesus. While the figure of Christ is life-like and proportional to reality, if the figure of Mary were to rise to her feet and stand erect, she would be over 7 feet tall! But to look at the sculpture, one would never notice Mary was so much larger than her son in reality.

➤ FIGURE 4.41

Shape constancy A door casts an increasingly trapezoidal image on our retinas as it opens, yet we still perceive it as rectangular.

::**phi phenomenon** an illusion of movement created when two or more adjacent lights blink on and off in quick succession.

::**perceptual constancy** perceiving objects as unchanging (having consistent shapes, size, lightness, and color) even as illumination and retinal images change.

It is a marvel how effortlessly size perception occurs. Given an object's perceived distance and the size of its image on our retinas, we instantly and unconsciously infer the object's size. Although the monsters in **FIGURE 4.42a** cast the same retinal images, the linear perspective tells our brain that the monster in pursuit is farther away. We therefore perceive it as larger.

This interplay between perceived size and perceived distance helps explain several well-known illusions. For example, can you imagine why the Moon looks up to 50 percent larger when near the horizon than when high in the sky? For at least 22 centuries, scholars have debated this question (Hershenson, 1989). One reason for the *Moon illusion* is that cues to objects' distances make the horizon Moon—like the distant monster in Figure 4.42a and the distant bar in the *Ponzo illusion* in Figure 4.42b—appear farther away and therefore larger than the Moon high in the night sky (Kaufman & Kaufman, 2000). Take away these distance cues—by looking at the horizon Moon (or each monster or each bar) through a paper tube—and the object immediately shrinks.

Size-distance relationships also explain why in **FIGURE 4.43** the two same-age girls seem so different in size. As the diagram reveals, the girls are actually about the same size, but the room is distorted. Viewed with one eye through a peephole, its trapezoidal walls produce the same images as those of a normal rectangular room viewed with both eyes. Presented with the camera's one-eyed view, the brain makes the reasonable assumption that the room *is* normal and each girl is therefore the same distance from us. And given the different sizes of their images on the retina, our brain ends up calculating that the girls are very different in size.

Our occasional misperceptions reveal the workings of our normally effective perceptual processes. The perceived relationship between distance and size is usually

(a)   (b)

➤ FIGURE 4.42

The interplay between perceived size and distance (a) The monocular cues for distance (such as linear perspective and relative height) make the pursuing monster look larger than the pursued. It isn't. (b) This visual trick, called the Ponzo illusion, is based on the same principle as the fleeing monsters. The two red bars cast identical-size images on our retinas. But experience tells us that a more distant object can create the same-size image as a nearer one only if it is actually larger. As a result, we perceive the bar that seems farther away as larger.

➤ FIGURE 4.43

The illusion of the shrinking and growing girls This distorted room, designed by Adelbert Ames, appears to have a normal rectangular shape when viewed through a peephole with one eye. The girl in the right corner appears disproportionately large because we judge her size based on the false assumption that she is the same distance away as the girl in the far corner.

TEACHING TIP

When Spanish conquistadors explored the Southwestern United States, their perception was tricked as they looked down on the Colorado River from the rim of the Grand Canyon. What they perceived to be a small running creek about 6 feet wide was actually a raging river over a mile wide! The perceptual cues from the top of the canyon fooled them into thinking the river was much smaller than it really was.

DEMO

Have students hold a hand in front of them at arm's length and move it toward their head, then away; they will perceive no change in size. The size of the retinal image is, of course, changing. Now, have students hold the forefinger of their left hand about 8 inches in front of their face and focus on it. They should then position their right hand at arm's length, past their left forefinger. While maintaining fixation on their left fingertip, they should move their right hand toward and away from their face. Although their focus should be on the finger, they should also notice the image of the hand as it moves. It will change dramatically in size.

TEACHING TIP

Have students imagine how disturbing the world would be if we suddenly lost our ability to perceive constancy. What if objects seemed to grow larger as they approached? What if objects appeared to change shape when they moved? What if color became different in different levels of light? "My monster little brother" would take on a whole new meaning if he grew and changed shapes and colors right before your eyes!

UNIT 4

Bring in two sets of men's dress socks—one dark blue and one black. In dim light, have students identify what color the socks are. Do the same in brighter light. While the task may be easier, it is still not definitive until both colors of socks are compared to each other. Sometimes blue and black are difficult to distinguish in dim light, which is why getting dressed in the dark can often bring about mismatches when choosing dark socks or shoes to wear!

Courtesy Edward Adelson

➤ **FIGURE 4.44**

Relative luminance Squares A and B are identical in color, believe it or not. (If you don't believe me, photocopy the illustration, cut out the squares, and compare.) But we perceive B as lighter, thanks to its surrounding context.

"From there to here, from here to there, funny things are everywhere."
Dr. Seuss, *One Fish, Two Fish, Red Fish, Blue Fish*, 1960

➤ **FIGURE 4.45**

Color depends on context Believe it or not, these three blue disks are identical in color.

R. Beau Lotto at University College, London

valid. But under special circumstances it can lead us astray—as when helping to create the Moon illusion and the Ames illusion.

Lightness Constancy

White paper reflects 90 percent of the light falling on it; black paper, only 10 percent. In sunlight, a black paper may reflect 100 times more light than does a white paper viewed indoors, but it still looks black (McBurney & Collings, 1984). This illustrates *lightness constancy* (also called *brightness constancy*); we perceive an object as having a constant lightness even while its illumination varies.

Perceived lightness depends on *relative luminance*—the amount of light an object reflects relative to its surroundings (**FIGURE 4.44**). If you view sunlit black paper through a narrow tube so nothing else is visible, it may look gray, because in bright sunshine it reflects a fair amount of light. View it without the tube and it is again black, because it reflects much less light than the objects around it.

Color Constancy

As light changes, a red apple in a fruit bowl retains its redness. This happens because our experience of color depends on something more than the wavelength information received by the cones in our retina. That something more is the surrounding *context*. If you view only part of a red apple, its color will seem to change as the light changes. But if you see the whole apple as one item in a bowl of fresh fruits, its color will remain roughly constant as the lighting and wavelengths shift—a phenomenon known as **color constancy.** Dorothea Jameson (1985) noted that a chip colored blue under indoor lighting matches the wavelengths reflected by a gold chip in sunlight. Yet bring a bluebird indoors and it won't look like a goldfinch. Likewise, a green leaf hanging from a brown branch may, when the illumination changes, reflect the same light energy that formerly came from the brown branch. Yet to us the leaf stays greenish and the branch stays brownish. Put on yellow-tinted ski goggles and the snow, after a second, looks as white as before.

Though we take color constancy for granted, the phenomenon is truly remarkable. It demonstrates that our experience of color comes not just from the object—the color is not in the isolated leaf—but from everything around it as well. You and I see color thanks to our brains' computations of the light reflected by any object *relative to its surrounding objects*. But only if we grew up with normal light, it seems. Monkeys raised under a restricted range of wavelengths later have great difficulty recognizing the same color when illumination varies (Sugita, 2004).

In a context that does not vary, we maintain color constancy. But what if we change the context? Because the brain computes the color of an object relative to its context, the perceived color changes (as is dramatically apparent in **FIGURE 4.45**). This principle—that we perceive objects not in isolation but in their environmental context—matters to artists, interior decorators, and clothing designers. Our perception of the color of a wall or of a streak of paint on a canvas is determined not just by the paint in the can but by the surrounding colors. The take-home lesson: Comparisons govern perceptions.

TEACHING TIP

You may want to use **Lecture/Discussion Topic:** *Auditory Organization* (p. 43) or **Classroom Exercises:** *Variation in the Size of the Retinal Image* (p. 41) or *Perceived Distance and Perceived Size* (p. 41) or *Binocular Disparity and Size Constancy* (p. 42) or *Brightness Contrast* (p. 42) or **Classroom Exercise/Student Project:** *Perceived Lunar Size* (p. 42) from Bolt's Teacher's Resource Binder.

* * *

Form perception, depth perception, motion perception, and perceptual constancy illuminate how we organize our visual experiences. Perceptual organization applies to other senses, too. It explains why we perceive a clock's steady tick not as a *tick-tick-tick-tick* but as grouped sounds, say, *TICK-tick, TICK-tick*. Listening to an unfamiliar language, we have trouble hearing where one word stops and the next one begins. Listening to our own language, we automatically hear distinct words. This, too, reflects perceptual organization. But it is more, for we even organize a string of letters—THEDOGATEMEAT—into words that make an intelligible phrase, more likely "The dog ate meat" than "The do gate me at" (McBurney & Collings, 1984). This process involves not only the organization we've been discussing, but also interpretation—discerning meaning in what we perceive—the topic we turn to next.

BEFORE YOU MOVE ON . . .

➤ **ASK YOURSELF**

Try drawing a realistic depiction of the scene from your window. Which monocular cues will you use in your drawing?

➤ **TEST YOURSELF 5**

What do we mean when we say that, in perception, "the whole is greater than the sum of its parts"?

Answers to the Test Yourself questions can be found in Appendix E at the end of the book.

Perceptual Interpretation

PHILOSOPHERS HAVE DEBATED WHETHER our perceptual abilities should be credited to our nature or our nurture. To what extent do we *learn* to perceive? German philosopher Immanuel Kant (1724–1804) maintained that knowledge comes from our *inborn* ways of organizing sensory experiences. Indeed, we come equipped to process sensory information. But British philosopher John Locke (1632–1704) argued that through our experiences we also *learn* to perceive the world. Indeed, we learn to link an object's distance with its size. So, just how important is experience? How radically does it shape our perceptual interpretations?

Sensory Deprivation and Restored Vision

22: What does research on sensory deprivation and restored vision reveal about the effects of experience on perception?

Writing to John Locke, a friend asked a question that would test the idea that experience shapes perceptions. If "a man born blind, and now adult, [was] taught by his touch to distinguish between a cube and a sphere" could he, if made to see, visually distinguish the two? Locke's answer was *no*, because the man would never have learned to see the difference.

This clever question has since been put to the test with a few dozen adults who, though blind from birth, have gained sight (Gregory, 1978; von Senden, 1932). Most were born with cataracts—clouded lenses that allowed them to see only light and

::**color constancy** perceiving familiar objects as having consistent color, even if changing illumination alters the wavelengths reflected by the object.

> "Let us then suppose the mind to be, as we say, white paper void of all characters, without any ideas: How comes it to be furnished? . . . To this I answer, in one word, from EXPERIENCE."
>
> John Locke, *An Essay Concerning Human Understanding*, 1690

DEMO

The importance of perceptual constancy is demonstrated in the following passage:

I cdnuolt blveiee taht I cluod aulaclty uesdnatnrd waht I was rdanieg. Takhns to the phaonmneal pweor of the hmuan mnid, aoccdrnig to rscheearch at Cmabrigde Uinervtisy, it deosn't mttaer in waht oredr the ltteers in a wrod are, the olny iprmoatnt tihng is taht the frist and lsat ltteer be in the rghit pclae. The rset can be a taotl mses and you can sitll raed it wouthit a porbelm. Tihs is bcuseae the huamn mnid deos not raed ervey lteter by istlef, but the wrod as a wlohe. Amzanig, huh? Yaeh and I awlyas tghuhot slpeling was ipmorantt! if you can raed tihs, psas it on!!"

While this popular Internet message was not really based on a study by Cambridge University, and its scientific validity is in serious doubt, the fact that people can still decipher this paragraph is testimony to the power of the brain to make sense out of nonsense. Have students discuss ways to test the claims of this passage scientifically.

INTERCONNECTING

Critical periods are discussed both here and in Unit 9. Be sure to help students connect this discussion with the later one.

You may want to use **Lecture/Discussion Topic:** *Cases of Restored Vision* (p. 43) from Bolt's Teacher's Resource Binder.

TEACHING TIP

Myers describes experiments in which infant animals were outfitted with goggles through which they could only see diffuse, unpatterned light. Use of this type of apparatus is called a ganzfeld procedure. This procedure is often used to create an experience of sensory deprivation.

You may want to use **Classroom Exercises:** *Perceptual Organization* (p. 38) or *An Auditory Analogue of the Visual Reversible Figure* (p. 39) or *The Ganzfeld* (p. 39) from Bolt's Teacher's Resource Binder.

Learning to see At age 3, Mike May lost his vision in an explosion. On March 7, 2000, after a new cornea restored vision to his right eye, he got his first look at his wife and children. Alas, although signals were reaching his long dormant visual cortex, it lacked the experience to interpret them. Faces, apart from features such as hair, were not recognizable. Expressions eluded him. Yet he can see an object in motion and is gradually learning to navigate his world and to marvel at such things as dust floating in sunlight (Abrams, 2002). ▲

Perceptual adaptation "Oops, missed," thinks researcher Hubert Dolezal as he views the world through inverting goggles. Yet, believe it or not, kittens, monkeys, and humans can adapt to an inverted world. ▲

shadows, rather as someone might see a foggy image through a Ping-Pong ball sliced in half. After surgery, the patients could tell the difference between figure and ground and could sense colors. This suggests that we are born with these aspects of perception. But much as Locke supposed, they often could not by sight recognize objects that were familiar by touch.

In experiments with infant kittens and monkeys, researchers have outfitted the young animals with goggles through which they could see only diffuse, unpatterned light (Wiesel, 1982). After infancy, when the goggles were removed, these animals' reactions were much like those of humans born with cataracts. Their eyes were healthy. Their retinas still sent signals to their visual cortex. But the brain's cortical cells had not developed normal connections. Thus, the animals remained functionally blind to shape. Experience guides and sustains the brain's development as it forms pathways that affect our perceptions.

In both humans and animals, similar sensory restrictions later in life do no permanent damage. When researchers cover an adult animal's eye for several months, its vision will be unaffected after the eye patch is removed. When surgeons remove cataracts that develop during late adulthood, most people are thrilled at the return to normal vision. The effect of sensory restriction on infant cats, monkeys, and humans suggests there is a *critical period* (Unit 9) for normal sensory and perceptual development. Nurture sculpts what nature has endowed.

Perceptual Adaptation

23: How adaptable is our ability to perceive?

Given a new pair of glasses, we may feel a little strange, even dizzy. Within a day or two, we adjust. Our **perceptual adaptation** to changed visual input makes the world seem normal again. But imagine a far more dramatic new pair of glasses—one that shifts the apparent location of objects 40 degrees to the left. When you first put them on and toss a ball to a friend, it sails off to the left. Walking forward to shake hands with the person, you veer to the left.

Could you adapt to this distorted world? Chicks cannot. When fitted with such lenses, they continue to peck where food grains seem to be (Hess, 1956; Rossi, 1968). But we humans adapt to distorting lenses quickly. Within a few minutes, your throws would again be accurate, your stride on target. Remove the lenses and you would experience an aftereffect. At first your throws would err in the opposite direction, sailing off to the right. But again, within minutes you would adjust.

Indeed, given an even more radical pair of glasses—one that literally turns the world upside down—you could still adapt. Psychologist George Stratton (1896) experienced this when he invented, and for eight days wore, a device that flipped left to right and up to down, making him the first person to experience a right-side-up retinal image while standing upright. The ground was up, the sky was down.

At first, when Stratton wanted to walk, he found himself searching for his feet, which were now "up." Eating was nearly impossible. He became nauseated and depressed. But Stratton persisted, and by the eighth day he could comfortably reach for an object in the right direction and walk without bumping into things. When Stratton finally removed the headgear, he readapted quickly.

In later experiments, people wearing the optical gear have even been able to ride a motorcycle, ski the Alps, and fly an airplane (Dolezal, 1982; Kohler, 1962). The world around them still seemed above their heads or on the wrong side. But by actively moving about in these topsy-turvy worlds, they adapted to the context and learned to coordinate their movements.

DEMO

Create or purchase visual distortion goggles for students to use in class (You can purchase goggles from www.psychkits.com). Have students toss soft balls to each other as they wear the goggles. After a few tries, they will find they can throw accurately. Then have them take off the goggles. They will need a few more tries to throw accurately again, since their vision will be distorted in the opposite way from what it was while they were wearing the goggles.

Sara Nadar, © 1990 Roger N. Shepard

➤ FIGURE 4.46

Perceptual set Show a friend either the left or right image. Then show the center image and ask, "What do you see?" Whether your friend reports seeing a saxophonist or a woman's face will likely depend on which of the other two drawings was viewed first. In each of those images, the meaning is clear, and it will establish perceptual expectations.

Perceptual Set

24: How do our expectations, contexts, and emotions influence our perceptions?

As everyone knows, to see is to believe. As we less fully appreciate, to believe is to see. Our experiences, assumptions, and expectations may give us a **perceptual set,** or mental predisposition, that greatly influences (top-down) what we perceive. People perceive an adult-child pair as looking more alike when told they are parent and child (Bressan & Dal Martello, 2002). And consider: Is the image in the center picture of FIGURE 4.46 a man playing a saxophone or a woman's face? What we see in such a drawing can be influenced by first looking at either of the two unambiguous versions (Boring, 1930).

Once we have formed a wrong idea about reality, we have more difficulty seeing the truth. Everyday examples of perceptual set abound. In 1972, a British newspaper published genuine, unretouched photographs of a "monster" in Scotland's Loch Ness—"the most amazing pictures ever taken," stated the paper. If this information creates in you the same perceptual set it did in most of the paper's readers, you, too, will see the monster in the photo reproduced in FIGURE 4.47a. But when Steuart Campbell (1986) approached the photos with a different perceptual set, he saw a curved tree trunk—as had others the day the photo was shot. With this different perceptual set, you may now notice that the object is floating motionless, without any rippling water or wake around it—hardly what we would expect of a lively monster.

Perceptual set can similarly influence what we hear. Consider the kindly airline pilot who, on a takeoff run, looked over at his depressed co-pilot and said, "Cheer up."

::**perceptual adaptation** in vision, the ability to adjust to an artificially displaced or even inverted visual field.

::**perceptual set** a mental predisposition to perceive one thing and not another.

"The temptation to form premature theories upon insufficient data is the bane of our profession."
Sherlock Holmes, in Arthur Conan Doyle's *The Valley of Fear,* 1914

• When shown the phrase
Mary had a
a little lamb
many people perceive what they expect, and miss the repeated word. Did you? •

(a)

(b)

Frank Searle, photo Adams/Corbis-Sygma

Dick Ruhl

➤ FIGURE 4.47

Believing is seeing What do you perceive in these photos? (a) Is this Nessie, the Loch Ness monster, or a log? (b) Are these flying saucers or clouds? We often perceive what we expect to see.

DEMO

Ask your class to shout out the answers to the following questions. "What do these letters spell?" (Write *folk* on the board.) "How about these?" (Write *croak.*) "And what do these letters spell?" (Write *soak.*) "What do we call the white of an egg?" Students will respond, "yolk" even though the answer is "egg white."

INTERCONNECTING

Perceptual set is similar to priming. What we expect to see is often influenced by what is around us.

DEMO

Use figure-ground illusions like the one in Figure 4.46 to demonstrate perceptual set. Tell half the class to imagine an orchestra while the other half imagines a runway fashion show. See how many in each group see the musician or the woman.

> IT'S AMAZING HOW PEOPLE SLOW DOWN WHEN YOU POINT A HAIR DRYER AT THEM.

The co-pilot heard the usual "Gear up" and promptly raised the wheels—before they left the ground (Reason & Mycielska, 1982). Perceptual set also influenced some bar patrons invited to sample free beer (Lee et al., 2006). When researchers added a few drops of vinegar to a brand-name beer, the tasters preferred it—unless they had been told they were drinking vinegar-laced beer and thus expected, and usually experienced, a worse taste. Perceptual set also influences preschool children's taste preferences. By a 6 to 1 margin in one experiment, they judged french fries as tasting better when served in a McDonald's bag rather than a plain white bag (Robinson et al., 2007). Clearly, much of what we perceive comes not just from the world "out there" but also from what's behind our eyes and between our ears.

What determines our perceptual set? Through experience we form concepts, or *schemas,* that organize and interpret unfamiliar information (see Unit 9). Our preexisting schemas for male saxophonists and women's faces, for monsters and tree trunks, for clouds and UFOs, all influence how we interpret ambiguous sensations with top-down processing.

Our schemas for faces prime us to see facial patterns even in random configurations, such as the Moon's landscape, clouds, rocks, or cinnamon buns. Kieran Lee, Graham Byatt, and Gillian Rhodes (2000) demonstrated how we recognize people by facial features that cartoonists can caricature. For but a fraction of a second they showed University of Western Australia students three versions of familiar faces—the actual face, a computer-created caricature that accentuated the differences between this face and the average face, and an "anticaricature" that muted the distinctive features. As **FIGURE 4.48** shows, the students more accurately recognized the caricatured faces than the actual ones. A caricatured Arnold Schwarzenegger is more recognizably Schwarzenegger than Schwarzenegger himself!

> ➤ **FIGURE 4.48**
> **Recognizing faces** When briefly flashed, a caricature of Arnold Schwarzenegger was more accurately recognized than Schwarzenegger himself. Ditto for other familiar male faces.

Percentage of students correctly recognizing face

Anticaricature   Actual   Caricature

Anticaricature   Actual   Caricature

Kieran Lee/FaceLab, Department of Psychology, University of Western Australia

Context Effects

A given stimulus may trigger radically different perceptions, partly because of our differing set, but also because of the immediate context. Some examples:

- Imagine hearing a noise interrupted by the words "eel is on the wagon." Likely, you would actually perceive the first word as *wheel*. Given "eel is on the orange," you would hear *peel*. This curious phenomenon, discovered by Richard Warren, suggests that the brain can work backward in time to allow a later stimulus to determine how we perceive an earlier one. The context creates an expectation that, top-down, influences our perception as we match our bottom-up signal against it (Grossberg, 1995).

> FIGURE 4.49
Context effects: the magician's cabinet Is the box in the far left frame lying on the floor or hanging from the ceiling? What about the one on the far right? In each case, the context defined by the inquisitive rabbits guides our perceptions. (From Shepard, 1990.)

- Did the pursuing monster in Figure 4.42a look aggressive? Did the identical pursued one seem frightened? If so, you experienced a context effect.
- Is the "magician's cabinet" in **FIGURE 4.49** sitting on the floor or hanging from the ceiling? How we perceive it depends on the context defined by the rabbits.
- How tall is the shorter player in **FIGURE 4.50**?

Even hearing sad rather than happy music can predispose people to perceive a sad meaning in spoken homophonic words—*mourning* rather than *morning, die* rather than *dye, pain* rather than *pane* (Halberstadt et al., 1995).

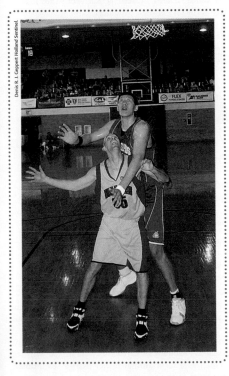

Denis R. J. Geppert Holland Sentinel.

> FIGURE 4.50
Big and "little" The "little guy" shown here is actually a 6'9" former Hope College basketball center who towers over me. But he seemed like a short player when matched in a semi-pro game against the world's tallest basketball player, 7'9" Sun Ming Ming from China.

The effects of perceptual set and context show how experience helps us construct perception. In everyday life, for example, stereotypes about gender (another instance of perceptual set) can color perception. Without the obvious cues of pink or blue,

"We hear and apprehend only what we already half know."
Henry David Thoreau, *Journal,* 1860

Use the figures on these pages to demonstrate to students these perceptual concepts. Have students find their own examples of these as well to create a library of visual illusions to use with students.

Research on context shows that situations can have a powerful effect on behavior:

- Studying should not occur while lying in bed. Students who do this often associate studying with sleeping since they study where they sleep. For effective studying, a designated place should be created where all the necessary supplies are available.

- Sleep researchers assisting those suffering from insomnia also suggest designating the bed for sleeping only and not for watching TV or reading. People may come to associate the bed with those other activities rather than with sleeping, which can hinder their ability to fall asleep easily.

TROUBLESHOOTING

The picture at the top of page 164 is an excellent example of how culture influences perception. Most Westerners have no trouble interpreting the scene of people sitting inside a dwelling. They do not confuse the window with a box on the woman's head. However, those from other cultures that do not share the same perceptual sets perceive the scene differently. Help students see the perspective of others with this picture.

RESEARCH

Have your teaching colleagues provide baby pictures of themselves or their children that do not give away the baby's gender. Have students guess what gender the baby is, having them identify what cues they are using to determine the gender. You can discuss with students how we use our schemas and perceptual sets to make sense of ambiguous stimuli.

> "When you're hitting the ball, it comes at you looking like a grapefruit. When you're not, it looks like a blackeyed pea."
>
> Former major league baseball player George Scott

Culture and context effects What is above the woman's head? In one study, nearly all the East Africans who were questioned said the woman was balancing a metal box or can on her head and that the family was sitting under a tree. Westerners, for whom corners and boxlike architecture are more common, were more likely to perceive the family as being indoors, with the woman sitting under a window. (Adapted from Gregory & Gombrich, 1973.)

people will struggle over whether to call the new baby "he" or "she." But told an infant is "David," people (especially children) may perceive "him" as bigger and stronger than if the same infant is called "Diana" (Stern & Karraker, 1989). Some differences, it seems, exist merely in the eyes of their beholders.

Given a perceptual set—"this is a girl"—people see a more feminine baby.

Emotion and Motivation

Perceptions are influenced, top-down, not only by our expectations and by the context, but also by our emotions. Dennis Proffitt (2006a,b) and others have demonstrated this with clever experiments showing that

- walking destinations look farther away to those who have been fatigued by prior exercise.
- a hill looks steeper to those wearing a heavy backpack or just exposed to sad, heavy classical music rather than light, bouncy music.
- a target seems farther away to those throwing a heavy rather than a light object at it.

Even a softball appears bigger when you are hitting well, observed Jessica Witt and Proffitt (2005), after asking players to choose a circle the size of the ball they had just hit well or poorly.

Motives also matter. In Cornell University experiments, students viewed ambiguous figures, such as the horse/seal in **FIGURE 4.51**. If rewards were linked with seeing one category of stimulus (such as a farm animal rather than a sea animal), then, after just a one-second exposure to the drawing, viewers tended instantly to perceive an example of their hoped-for category (Balcetis & Dunning, 2006). (To confirm the participants' honesty in reporting their perceptions, the researchers in one experiment redefined the to-be-rewarded perception after the viewing. Still,

INTERCONNECTING

Link this discussion of Emotion and Motivation to the discussion of the same topics in Units 8A and 8B. How we perceive the world is influenced by our current emotional state and whether we are motivated to notice details.

people reported perceiving a stimulus from their originally hoped-for category.)

Emotions color our social perceptions, too. Spouses who feel loved and appreciated perceive less threat in stressful marital events—"He's just having a bad day" (Murray et al., 2003). Professional referees, if told a soccer team has a history of aggressive behavior, will assign more penalty cards after watching videotaped fouls (Jones et al., 2002). Lee Ross invites us to recall our own perceptions in different contexts: "Ever notice that when you're driving you hate pedestrians, the way they saunter through the crosswalk, almost daring you to hit them, but when you're walking you hate drivers?" (Jaffe, 2004).

To return to the question "Is perception innate or learned?" we can answer: It's both. The river of perception is fed by sensation, cognition, and emotion. And that is why we need multiple levels of analysis (**FIGURE 4.52**). "Simple" perceptions are the brain's creative products.

> ➤ FIGURE 4.51
> **Ambiguous horse/seal figure** If motivated to perceive farm animals, about 7 in 10 people immediately perceived a horse. If motivated to perceive a sea animal, about 7 in 10 perceived a seal.

"Ambiguity of form: Old and new" by G. H. Fisher, 1968, Perception and Psychophysics, 4, 189–192. Copyright 1968 by Psychonomic Society, Inc.

> ➤ FIGURE 4.52
> **Perception is a biopsychosocial phenomenon** Psychologists study how we perceive with different levels of analysis, from the biological to the social-cultural.

Biological influences:
• sensory analysis
• unlearned visual phenomena
• critical period for sensory development

Psychological influences:
• selective attention
• learned schemas
• Gestalt principles
• context effects
• perceptual set

Perception: Our version of reality

Social-cultural influences:
• cultural assumptions and expectations

"Have you ever noticed that anyone driving slower than you is an idiot, and anyone going faster is a maniac?"
George Carlin, *George Carlin on Campus*, 1984

BEFORE YOU MOVE ON . . .

➤ **ASK YOURSELF**
Can you recall a time when your expectations have predisposed how you perceived a person (or group of people)?

➤ **TEST YOURSELF 6**
What type of evidence shows that, indeed, "there is more to perception than meets the senses"?

Answers to the Test Yourself questions can be found in Appendix E at the end of the book.

INTERCONNECTING

Link this discussion to the actor-observer bias, discussed in Unit 14. When we are participants in an activity, we view it differently than if we are an observer.

TEACHING TIP

Which type of animal do your students see in Figure 4.51? Extend this activity by asking students how long it took them to see the "other" animal. Have students speculate why it takes so long to adjust our perceptual set.

INTERCONNECTING

Use Figure 4.52 to reinforce the biopsychosocial model. Perception occurs as a result of biological, psychological, and social influences, as discussed in this unit. Make sure students appreciate this interplay of variables.

Is There Extrasensory Perception?

25: What are the claims of ESP, and what have most research psychologists concluded after putting these claims to the test?

CAN WE PERCEIVE ONLY WHAT WE sense? Or, as nearly half of Americans believe, are we capable of **extrasensory perception (ESP)** without sensory input (AP, 2007; Moore, 2005)?

Are there indeed people—any people—who can read minds, see through walls, or foretell the future? Five British universities have **parapsychology** units staffed by Ph.D. graduates of Edinburgh University's parapsychology program (Turpin, 2005). Sweden's Lund University, the Netherlands' Utrecht University, and Australia's University of Adelaide also have added faculty chairs or research units for parapsychology. Parapsychologists in such places do experiments that search for possible ESP and other paranormal phenomena. But other research psychologists and scientists—including 96 percent of the scientists in the U.S. National Academy of Sciences—are skeptical that such phenomena exist (McConnell, 1991). If ESP is real, we would need to overturn the scientific understanding that we are creatures whose minds are tied to our physical brains and whose perceptual experiences of the world are built of sensations. Sometimes new evidence does overturn our scientific preconceptions. Science, as we will see throughout this book, offers us various surprises—about the extent of the unconscious mind, about the effects of emotions on health, about what heals and what doesn't, and much more. Before we evaluate claims of ESP, let's review them.

Claims of ESP

Claims of paranormal phenomena ("psi") include astrological predictions, psychic healing, communication with the dead, and out-of-body experiences. But the most testable and (for a perception discussion) most relevant claims are for three varieties of ESP:

- *Telepathy*, or mind-to-mind communication—one person sending thoughts to another or perceiving another's thoughts.
- *Clairvoyance*, or perceiving remote events, such as sensing that a friend's house is on fire.
- *Precognition*, or perceiving future events, such as a political leader's death or a sporting event's outcome.

Closely linked with these are claims of *psychokinesis (PK)*, or "mind over matter," such as levitating a table or influencing the roll of a die (**FIGURE 4.53**). (The claim is illustrated by the wry request, "Will all those who believe in psychokinesis please raise my hand?")

Premonitions or Pretensions?

Can psychics see into the future? Although one might wish for a psychic stock forecaster, the tallied forecasts of "leading psychics" reveal meager accuracy. No greedy—or charitable—psychic has been able to predict the outcome of a lottery jackpot, or to make billions on the stock market. During the 1990s, tabloid psychics were all wrong in predicting surprising events. (Madonna did not become a gospel singer, the Statue of Liberty did not lose both its arms in a terrorist blast, Queen Elizabeth did not

● There would also be some people, notes Michael Shermer (1999), who would have no need for caller ID, who would never lose at "rock, paper, scissors," and for whom we could never have a surprise party. ●

SNAPSHOTS

➤ **FIGURE 4.53**
Parapsychological concepts

abdicate her throne to enter a convent.) And the new-century psychics missed the big-news events, such as the horror of 9/11. (Where were the psychics on 9/10 when we needed them? Why, despite a $50 million reward offered, could none of them help locate Osama bin Laden after 9/11?) Gene Emery (2004), who has tracked annual psychic forecasts for 26 years, reports that almost never have unusual predictions come true, and virtually never have psychics anticipated any of the year's headline events.

Analyses of psychic visions offered to police departments reveal that these, too, are no more accurate than guesses made by others (Reiser, 1982). Psychics working with the police do, however, generate hundreds of predictions. This increases the odds of an occasional correct guess, which psychics can then report to the media. Moreover, vague predictions can later be interpreted ("retrofitted") to match events that provide a perceptual set for "understanding" them. Nostradamus, a sixteenth-century French psychic, explained in an unguarded moment that his ambiguous prophecies "could not possibly be understood till they were interpreted after the event and by it."

Police departments are wise to all this. When Jane Ayers Sweat and Mark Durm (1993) asked the police departments of America's 50 largest cities whether they ever used psychics, 65 percent said they never had. Of those that had, not one had found it helpful.

Are the spontaneous "visions" of everyday people any more accurate? Consider our dreams. Do they foretell the future, as people often believe? Or do they only seem to do so because we are more likely to recall or reconstruct dreams that appear to have come true? Two Harvard psychologists (Murray & Wheeler, 1937) tested the prophetic power of dreams after aviator Charles Lindbergh's baby son was kidnapped and murdered in 1932, but before the body was discovered. When the researchers invited the public to report their dreams about the child, 1300 visionaries submitted dream reports. How many accurately envisioned the child dead? Five percent. And how many also correctly anticipated the body's location—buried among trees? Only 4 of the 1300. Although this number was surely no better than chance, to those 4 dreamers the accuracy of their apparent precognitions must have seemed uncanny.

Throughout the day, each of us imagines many events. Given the billions of events in the world each day, and given enough days, some stunning coincidences are sure to occur. By one careful estimate, chance alone would predict that more than a thousand times a day someone on Earth will think of someone and then within the ensuing five minutes will learn of the person's death (Charpak & Broch, 2004). With enough time and people, the improbable becomes inevitable.

That was the experience of comics writer John Byrne (2003). Six months after his Spider-Man story about a New York blackout appeared, New York suffered a massive blackout. A subsequent Spider-Man story line involved a major earthquake in Japan. "And again," he recalled, "the real thing happened in the month the issue hit the stands." Later, when working on a Superman comic book, he "had the Man of Steel fly to the rescue when disaster beset the NASA space shuttle. The [1986] *Challenger* tragedy happened almost immediately thereafter" (with time for the issue to be redrawn). "Most recently, and chilling, came when I was writing and drawing Wonder Woman and did a story in which the title character was killed as a prelude to her becoming a goddess." The issue's cover "was done as a newspaper front page, with the headline 'Princess Diana Dies.' (Diana is Wonder Woman's real name.) That issue went on sale on a Thursday. The following Saturday . . . I don't have to tell you, do I?"

Putting ESP to Experimental Test

In the past, there have been all kinds of strange ideas—that bumps on the head reveal character traits, that bloodletting is a cure-all, that each sperm cell contains a miniature

> "A person who talks a lot is sometimes right."
> Spanish proverb

::**extrasensory perception (ESP)** the controversial claim that perception can occur apart from sensory input; includes telepathy, clairvoyance, and precognition.

::**parapsychology** the study of paranormal phenomena, including ESP and psychokinesis.

WEB CONNECT

The following Web sites offer information about scientific testing of psychic phenomena:

- The James Randi Educational Foundation homepage at www.randi.org

- The Rhine Research Center Web site at www.rhine.org

After searching these sites, have students address the following questions:

- Why are psychics generally unwilling to be scientifically tested?

- Do you think paranormal phenomena is a worthy scientific subject to study? Why or why not?

INTERCONNECTING

Remind students of the following concepts from scientific thinking in Unit 2:

- Correlation does not mean causation. Just because events occur together does not mean that they cause each other.

- Confirmation bias occurs when we only look for evidence that supports our beliefs and ignore evidence that refutes them. Many people believe in parapsychology because they rely only on the evidence that supports their belief.

TEACHING TIP

You may want to use **Classroom Exercises:** *Belief in ESP Scale* (p. 49) or *ESP Tricks* (p. 50) from Bolt's Teacher's Resource Binder.

INTERCONNECTING

Have students create their own experimental conditions under which they would like to test ESP. Use this activity as a check of their knowledge of research methodology learned from Unit 2.

Testing psychic powers in the British population Hertfordshire University psychologist Richard Wiseman created a "mind machine" to see if people can influence or predict a coin toss. Using a touch-sensitive screen, visitors to festivals around the country were given four attempts to call heads or tails. Using a random-number generator, a computer then decided the outcome. When the experiment concluded in January 2000, nearly 28,000 people had predicted 110,972 tosses—with 49.8 percent correct.

> "At the heart of science is an essential tension between two seemingly contradictory attitudes—an openness to new ideas, no matter how bizarre or counterintuitive they may be, and the most ruthless skeptical scrutiny of all ideas, old and new."
>
> Carl Sagan (1987)

> "A psychic is an actor playing the role of a psychic."
>
> Psychologist-magician Daryl Bem (1984)

BIZARRO   By DAN PIRARO

Which supposed psychic ability does Psychic Pizza claim?

person. Faced with such claims—or with claims of mind-reading or out-of-body travel or communication with the dead—how can we separate bizarre ideas from those that sound bizarre but are true? At the heart of science is a simple answer: *Test them to see if they work.* If they do, so much the better for the ideas. If they don't, so much the better for our skepticism.

This scientific attitude has led both believers and skeptics to agree that what parapsychology needs is a reproducible phenomenon and a theory to explain it. Parapsychologist Rhea White (1998) spoke for many in saying that "the image of parapsychology that comes to my mind, based on nearly 44 years in the field, is that of a small airplane [that] has been perpetually taxiing down the runway of the Empirical Science Airport since 1882 . . . its movement punctuated occasionally by lifting a few feet off the ground only to bump back down on the tarmac once again. It has never taken off for any sustained flight."

Seeking a reproducible phenomenon, how might we test ESP claims in a controlled experiment? An experiment differs from a staged demonstration. In the laboratory, the experimenter controls what the "psychic" sees and hears. On stage, the psychic controls what the audience sees and hears. Time and again, skeptics note, so-called psychics have exploited unquestioning audiences with mind-blowing performances in which they *appeared* to communicate with the spirits of the dead, read minds, or levitate objects—only to have it revealed that their acts were nothing more than the illusions of stage magicians.

The search for a valid and reliable test of ESP has resulted in thousands of experiments. Some 380 of them have assessed people's efforts to influence computer-generated random sequences of ones and zeros. In some small experiments, the tally of the desired number has exceeded chance by 1 or 2 percent, an effect that disappears when larger experiments are added to the mix (Bösch et al. 2006a,b; Radin et al., 2006; Wilson & Shadish, 2006).

Another set of experiments has invited "senders" to telepathically transmit one of four visual images to "receivers" deprived of sensation in a nearby chamber (Bem & Honorton, 1994). The result? A reported 32 percent accurate response rate, surpassing the chance rate of 25 percent. But follow-up studies have (depending on who was summarizing the results) failed to replicate the phenomenon or produced mixed results (Bem et al., 2001; Milton & Wiseman, 2002; Storm, 2000, 2003).

TEACHING TIP

You may want to use **Student Project: *The Psychic Challenge*** (p. 50) from Bolt's Teacher's Resource Binder.

If ESP nevertheless exists, might it subtly register in the brain? To find out, Harvard researchers Samuel Moulton and Stephen Kosslyn (2008) had a sender try to send one of two pictures telepathically to a receiver lying in an fMRI machine. In these pairs (mostly couples, friends, or twins), the receivers guessed the picture's content correctly at the level of chance (50.0 percent). Moreover, their brains responded no differently when later viewing the actual pictures "sent" by ESP. "These findings," concluded the researchers, "are the strongest evidence yet obtained against the existence of paranormal mental phenomena."

From 1998 to 2010, one skeptic, magician James Randi, offered $1 million "to anyone who proves a genuine psychic power under proper observing conditions" (Randi, 1999, 2008). French, Australian, and Indian groups have parallel offers of up to 200,000 euros to anyone with demonstrable paranormal abilities (CFI, 2003). Large as these sums are, the scientific seal of approval would be worth far more to anyone whose claims could be authenticated. To refute those who say there is no ESP, one need only produce a single person who can demonstrate a single, reproducible ESP phenomenon. (To refute those who say pigs can't talk would take but one talking pig.) So far, no such person has emerged. Randi's offer has been publicized for years and dozens of people have been tested, sometimes under the scrutiny of an independent panel of judges. Still, nothing.

The Quigmans by Buddy Hickerson; © 1990, Los Angeles Times Syndicate. Reprinted with permission.

BEFORE YOU MOVE ON . . .

➤ ASK YOURSELF

Have you ever had what felt like an ESP experience? Can you think of an explanation other than ESP for that experience?

➤ TEST YOURSELF 7

What psychic ability is being claimed by the sports channel in the cartoon above?

Answers to the Test Yourself questions can be found in Appendix E at the end of the book.

* * *

To feel awe and to gain a deep reverence for life, we need look no further than our own perceptual system and its capacity for organizing formless nerve impulses into colorful sights, vivid sounds, and evocative smells. As Shakespeare's Hamlet recognized, "There are more things in Heaven and Earth, Horatio, than are dreamt of in your philosophy." Within our ordinary sensory and perceptual experiences lies much that is truly extraordinary—surely much more than has so far been dreamt of in our psychology.

> "People's desire to believe in the paranormal is stronger than all the evidence that it does not exist."
> Susan Blackmore,
> "Blackmore's first law," 2004

> "So, how does the mind work? I don't know. You don't know. Pinker doesn't know. And, I rather suspect, such is the current state of the art, that if God were to tell us, we wouldn't understand."
> Jerry Fodor,
> "Reply to Steven Pinker," 2005

TEACHING TIP

You may want to use **Student Project/Classroom Exercise:** *Testing for ESP* (p. 53) from Bolt's Teacher's Resource Binder.

UNIT REVIEW: Sensation and Perception

Sensing the World: Some Basic Principles

1: What are sensation and perception? What do we mean by bottom-up processing and top-down processing?

Sensation is the process by which our sensory receptors and nervous system receive and represent stimulus energies from our environment. *Perception* is the process of organizing and interpreting this information. Although we view sensation and perception separately to analyze and discuss them, they are actually parts of one continuous process. *Bottom-up processing* is sensory analysis that begins at the entry level, with information flowing from the sensory receptors to the brain. *Top-down processing* is analysis that begins with the brain and flows down, filtering information through our experience and expectations to produce perceptions.

2: How are we affected by selective attention?

We *selectively attend* to, and process, a very limited aspect of incoming information, blocking out most, often shifting the spotlight of our attention from one thing to another. We even display *inattentional blindness* to events and changes in our visual world.

3: What are the absolute and difference thresholds, and do stimuli below the absolute threshold have any influence?

Our *absolute threshold* for any stimulus is the minimum stimulation necessary for us to be consciously aware of it 50 percent of the time. *Signal detection theory* demonstrates that individual absolute thresholds vary, depending on the strength of the signal and also on our experience, expectations, motivation, and alertness. Our *difference threshold* (also called just noticeable difference, or JND) is the barely noticeable difference we discern between two stimuli 50 percent of the time. *Priming* shows that we can process some information from stimuli below our absolute threshold for conscious awareness. But the effect is too fleeting to enable people to exploit us with *subliminal* messages. *Weber's law* states that two stimuli must differ by a constant proportion to be perceived as different.

4: What is the function of sensory adaptation?

Sensory adaptation (our diminished sensitivity to constant or routine odors, sounds, and touches) focuses our attention on informative changes in our environment.

Vision

5: What is the energy that we see as visible light?

Each sense receives stimulation, transforms (*transduces*) it into neural signals, and sends these neural messages to the brain. In vision, the signals consist of light-energy particles from a thin slice of the broad spectrum of electromagnetic energy. The *hue* we perceive in a light depends on its *wavelength*, and its brightness depends on its *intensity*.

6: How does the eye transform light energy into neural messages?

After entering the eye and being focused by a *lens*, light-energy particles strike the eye's inner surface, the *retina*. The retina's light-sensitive *rods* and color-sensitive *cones* convert the light energy into neural impulses which, after processing by bipolar and ganglion cells, travel through the *optic nerve* to the brain.

7: How does the brain process visual information?

Impulses travel along the optic nerve, to the thalamus, and on to the visual cortex. In the visual cortex, *feature detectors* respond to specific features of the visual stimulus. Higher-level supercells integrate this pool of data for processing in other cortical areas. *Parallel processing* in the brain handles many aspects of a problem simultaneously, and separate neural teams work on visual subtasks (color, movement, depth, and form). Other neural teams integrate the results, comparing them with stored information, and enabling perceptions.

8: What theories help us understand color vision?

The *Young-Helmholtz trichromatic (three-color) theory* proposed that the retina contains three types of color receptors. Contemporary research has found three types of cones, each most sensitive to the wavelengths of one of the three primary colors of light (red, green, or blue). Hering's *opponent-process theory* proposed three additional color processes (red-versus-green, blue-versus-yellow, black-versus-white). Contemporary research has confirmed that, en route to the brain, neurons in the retina and the thalamus code the color-related information from the cones into pairs of opponent colors. Thus we know that color processing occurs in these two stages.

Hearing

9: What are the characteristics of air pressure waves that we hear as sound?

Sound waves are bands of compressed and expanded air. Our ears detect these changes in air pressure and transform them into neural impulses, which the brain decodes as sound. Sound waves vary in *frequency*, which we experience as differing *pitch*, and amplitude, which we perceive as differing loudness.

10: How does the ear transform sound energy into neural messages?

The outer ear is the visible portion of the ear. The *middle ear* is the chamber between the eardrum and *cochlea*. The *inner ear* consists of the cochlea, semicircular canals, and vestibular sacs. Through a mechanical chain of events, sound waves traveling through the auditory canal cause tiny vibrations in the eardrum. The bones of the middle ear amplify the vibrations and relay them to the fluid-filled cochlea. Rippling of the basilar membrane, caused by pressure changes in the cochlear fluid, causes movement of the tiny hair cells, triggering neural messages to be sent (via the thalamus) to the auditory cortex in the brain.

11: What theories help us understand pitch perception?

Place theory proposes that our brain interprets a particular pitch by decoding the place where a sound wave stimulates the cochlea's basilar membrane. *Frequency theory* proposes that the brain deciphers the frequency of the pulses traveling to the brain. Place theory explains how we hear high-pitched sounds; frequency theory explains how we hear low-pitched sounds; and some combination of the two helps explain how we hear sounds in the middle range.

12: How do we locate sounds?

Sound waves strike one ear sooner and more intensely than the other. The brain analyzes the minute differences in the sounds received by the two ears and computes the sound's source.

13: What are the common causes of hearing loss, and why does controversy surround cochlear implants?

Conduction hearing loss results from damage to the mechanical system that transmits sound waves to the cochlea. *Sensorineural hearing loss* (or nerve deafness) results from damage to the cochlea's hair cells or their associated nerves. Diseases and accidents can cause hearing loss, but age-related disorders and prolonged exposure to loud noises are more common causes. *Cochlear implants* restore hearing for some people, but many in the Deaf community believe cochlear implants are unnecessary for people who have been Deaf from birth and who can speak their own language, sign.

Other Senses

14: How do we sense touch and sense our body's position and movement? How do we experience pain?

Our sense of touch is actually several senses—pressure, warmth, cold, and pain—that combine to produce other sensations, such as "hot." Through *kinesthesis,* we sense the position and movement of body parts. We monitor the body's position and maintain our balance with our *vestibular sense.* Pain is an alarm system that draws our attention to some physical problem. One theory of pain is that a *"gate"* in the spinal cord either opens to permit pain signals traveling up small nerve fibers to reach the brain, or closes to prevent their passage. The biopsychosocial approach views pain as the sum of three sets of forces: biological influences, such as nerve fibers sending messages to the brain; psychological influences, such as our expectations; and social-cultural influences, such as the presence of others.

15: How do we experience taste?

Taste, a chemical sense, is a composite of five basic sensations—sweet, sour, salty, bitter, and umami—and of the aromas that interact with information from the taste receptor cells of the taste buds. The influence of smell on our sense of taste is an example of *sensory interaction,* the ability of one sense to influence another.

16: How do we experience smell?

Smell is a chemical sense. Some 5 million olfactory receptor cells, with their approximately 350 different receptor proteins, recognize individual odor molecules. The receptor cells send messages to the brain's olfactory bulb, then to the temporal lobe and to parts of the limbic system. Odors can spontaneously evoke memories and feelings, due in part to the close connections between brain areas that process smell and memory.

Perceptual Organization

17: How did the Gestalt psychologists understand perceptual organization?

Gestalt psychologists searched for rules by which the brain organizes fragments of sensory data into *gestalts* (from the German word for "whole"), or meaningful forms. In pointing out that the whole is more than the sum of its parts, they noted that we filter sensory information and infer perceptions in ways that make sense to us.

18: How do figure-ground and grouping principles contribute to our perceptions?

To recognize an object, we must first perceive it (see it as a *figure*) as distinct from its surroundings (the *ground*). We bring order and form to stimuli by organizing them into meaningful *groups,* following the rules of proximity, similarity, continuity, connectedness, and closure.

19: How do we see the world in three dimensions?

Depth perception is our ability to see objects in three dimensions and judge distance. The *visual cliff,* and other research, demonstrates that many species perceive the world in three dimensions at, or very soon after, birth. *Binocular cues,* such as *retinal disparity,* are depth cues that rely on information from both eyes. *Monocular cues* (such as relative size, interposition, relative height, relative motion, linear perspective, and light and shadow) let us judge depth using information transmitted by only one eye.

20: How do we perceive motion?

As objects move, we assume that shrinking objects are retreating and enlarging objects are approaching. But sometimes we miscalculate. A quick succession of images on the retina can create an illusion of movement, as in stroboscopic movement or the *phi phenomenon.*

21: How do perceptual constancies help us organize our sensations into meaningful perceptions?

Perceptual constancy enables us to perceive objects as stable despite the changing image they cast on our retinas. Shape constancy is our ability to perceive familiar objects (such as an opening door) as unchanging in shape. Size constancy is the perception of objects as unchanging in size despite their changing retinal images. Sometimes we misread distance cues and reach the wrong conclusions, as in the Moon illusion. With lightness constancy, we perceive an object as having a constant lightness even when illumination changes. With *color constancy,* we perceive consistent color in objects, even though the lighting and wavelengths shift.

TECHNOLOGY RESOURCES

These resources will be helpful for teaching the concepts in this unit:

- *Video: Psychology: The Human Experience, Module 8: Sensation and Perception*

- *Videos: Digital Media Archive: Psychology,* 1st ed., *Video Clip 23: Neisser's Selective Attention Test; Video Clip 5: Depth Cues; Video Clip 4: Müller-Lyer Illusion*

- *ActivePsych: Digital Media Archive,* 2nd ed.: *A Variety of Visual Illusions; The Visual Cliff*

- *Psychology Video Tool Kit: "Blindsight": Seeing Without Awareness; Automatic Skills: Disrupting a Pilot's Performance; Visual Attention: There's a Gorilla on the Court; Visual Attention: Piecing Things Together; Losing One's Touch: Living Without Proprioception; Phantom Limb Sensations; Pickpockets, Placebos, and Pain: The Role of Expectations; Coping With Pain; "Supertasters"; The "Red Hot" Chili-Eating Contest:*

Technology Resources continued

ANSWERS to Multiple-Choice Questions

1. **c.** allow light into the eye.
2. **d.** feature detectors.
3. **c.** absolute thresholds.
4. **c.** We know that the brightness of a printed page has not changed as it moves from sunlight into shadow.
5. **c.** perceptual set.
6. **d.** transduce
7. **b.** The intensity of pain at the end of the event.
8. **a.** rate at which the basilar membrane vibrates.
9. **d.** A cook can just barely taste the salt she has added to her soup.
10. **c.** how an organized whole is formed out of its component pieces.
11. **d.** transmit sound waves to the cochlea.
12. **c.** Dizziness and a loss of balance.
13. **e.** Figure-ground
14. **a.** relative motion.
15. **b.** The effect that our experiences and expectations have on perception.

Perceptual Interpretation

22: What does research on sensory restriction and restored vision reveal about the effects of experience?
People born blind who later regain sight lack the experience to recognize shapes, forms, and complete faces. Animals who have had restricted visual input suffer enduring visual handicaps. There is a critical period for some aspects of sensory and perceptual development. Without early stimulation, the brain's neural organization does not develop normally.

23: How adaptable is our ability to perceive?
Perceptual adaptation is evident when people are given glasses that shift the world to the left, right, or upside-down. People are initially disoriented, but they manage to adapt to the new context.

24: How do our expectations, contexts, and emotions influence our perceptions?
Perceptual set is a mental predisposition that functions as a lens through which we perceive the world. Our learned concepts (schemas) prime us to organize and interpret ambiguous stimuli in certain ways. The surrounding context helps create expectations that guide our perceptions. Emotional context colors our interpretations as well.

Is There Extrasensory Perception?

25: What are the claims of ESP, and what have most research psychologists concluded after putting these claims to the test?
The three most testable forms of *extrasensory perception (ESP)* are telepathy (mind-to-mind communication), clairvoyance (perceiving remote events), and precognition (perceiving future events). Most research psychologists believe that people are not capable of perception without sensory input. *Parapsychologists* have been unable to replicate ESP phenomena under controlled conditions.

Terms and Concepts to Remember

sensation, p. 116
perception, p. 116
bottom-up processing, p. 116
top-down processing, p. 116
selective attention, p. 117
inattentional blindness, p. 118
change blindness, p. 119
psychophysics, p. 120
absolute threshold, p. 120
signal detection theory, p. 121
subliminal, p. 121
priming, p. 121
difference threshold, p. 122
Weber's law, p. 123
sensory adaptation, p. 123
transduction, p. 124
wavelength, p. 125
hue, p. 125
intensity, p. 125
pupil, p. 126
iris, p. 126
lens, p. 126

retina, p. 126
accommodation, p. 126
rods, p. 126
cones, p. 126
optic nerve, p. 126
blind spot, p. 127
fovea, p. 127
feature detectors, p. 129
parallel processing, p. 130
Young-Helmholtz trichromatic (three-color) theory, p. 132
opponent-process theory, p. 133
audition, p. 134
frequency, p. 134
pitch, p. 134
middle ear, p. 135
cochlea [KOHK-lee-uh], p. 135
inner ear, p. 135
place theory, p. 137
frequency theory, p. 137
conduction hearing loss, p. 138
sensorineural hearing loss, p. 138

cochlear implant, p. 138
kinesthesis [kin-ehs-THEE-sehs], p. 142
vestibular sense, p. 142
gate-control theory, p. 143
sensory interaction, p. 147
gestalt, p. 151
figure-ground, p. 151
grouping, p. 152
depth perception, p. 153
visual cliff, p. 153
binocular cues, p. 153
retinal disparity, p. 153
monocular cues, p. 154
phi phenomenon, p. 156
perceptual constancy, p. 156
color constancy, p. 158
perceptual adaptation, p. 160
perceptual set, p. 161
extrasensory perception (ESP), p. 166
parapsychology, p. 166

 ## AP* Practice Test Questions

Multiple-Choice Questions

1. The purpose of the pupil is to
   a. focus light on the retina.
   b. process color.
   c. allow light into the eye.
   d. enable night vision.
   e. detect specific shapes.

2. Cells that can respond to specific edges, lines, angles, and movements are called
   a. rods.
   b. cones.
   c. ganglion cells.
   d. feature detectors.
   e. bipolar cells.

3. Signal detection theory is most closely associated with
   a. vision.
   b. sensory adaptation.
   c. absolute thresholds.
   d. hearing.
   e. context effects.

 TECHNOLOGY RESOURCES

>> **Technology Resources** continued from p. 171

Sensitivity to Taste; Synaesthesia: The Man Who Tastes Words; Seeing the World Upside Down

- *Videos: The Mind*, 2nd ed., *Module 9: Studying the Effects of Subliminal Stimulation on the Mind; Module 20: Phantom Limb Pain; Module 21: Treating Chronic Pain*
- *Videos: Scientific American Frontiers*, 2nd ed., *Segment 9: Smart Glasses; Segment 12: Tasters and Supertasters; Segment 10: Lights, Camera, Magic!; Segment 11: Cockpit Confusion; Segment 2: Water, Water Everywhere*

4. Which of the following represents perceptual constancy?
   a. We recognize the taste of McDonald's food each time we eat it.
   b. In photos with people, the people almost always are perceived as figure and everything else as ground.
   c. We know that the brightness of a printed page has not changed as it moves from sunlight into shadow.
   d. From the time they are very young, most people can recognize the smell of a dentist's office.
   e. The cold water in a lake doesn't seem so cold after you have been swimming in it for a few minutes.

5. Our tendency to see faces in clouds and other ambiguous stimuli is partly based on
   a. selective attention.
   b. ESP.
   c. perceptual set.
   d. shape constancy.
   e. bottom-up processing.

6. Our rods and cones _____ electromagnetic energy into neural messages.
   a. adapt
   b. accommodate
   c. parallel process
   d. transduce
   e. perceptually set

7. Which of the following is most likely to influence our memory of a painful event?
   a. The overall length of the event.
   b. The intensity of pain at the end of the event.
   c. The reason for the pain.
   d. The amount of rest you've had in the 24 hours preceding the event.
   e. The specific part of the body that experiences the pain.

8. Frequency theory relates to the
   a. rate at which the basilar membrane vibrates.
   b. number of fibers in the auditory nerve.
   c. point at which the basilar membrane exhibits the most vibration.
   d. decibel level of a sound.
   e. number of hair cells in each cochlea.

9. All except one of the following demonstrate a *difference* threshold. The exception represents an *absolute* threshold. Which of the following represents an absolute threshold?
   a. A guitar player knows that his D string has just gone out of tune.
   b. A photographer can tell that the natural light available for a photograph has just faded slightly.
   c. Your friend amazes you by correctly identifying unlabeled glasses of Coke and Pepsi.
   d. A cook can just barely taste the salt she has added to her soup.
   e. Your mom throws out the milk because she says the taste is "off."

10. The Gestalt psychologists were interested in
    a. depth perception and how it allows us to survive in the world.
    b. why we see an object near us as closer rather than larger.
    c. how an organized whole is formed out of its component pieces.
    d. what the smallest units of perception are.
    e. the similarities between shape constancy and size constancy.

11. The hammer, anvil, and stirrup
    a. process only high frequency sounds.
    b. process only low frequency sounds.
    c. make up a frame that supports the eardrum.
    d. transmit sound waves to the cochlea.
    e. hold the hair cells that enable hearing.

12. Which of the following might result from a disruption of your vestibular sense?
    a. Inability to detect the position of your arm without looking at it.
    b. Loss of the ability to detect bitter tastes.
    c. Dizziness and a loss of balance.
    d. An inability to detect pain.
    e. Loss of color vision.

13. Which of the following is *not* a Gestalt grouping principle?
    a. Proximity
    b. Similarity
    c. Closure
    d. Continuity
    e. Figure-ground

14. The two monocular depth cues that are most responsible for our ability to know that a jet flying high overhead is at an elevation of several miles are relative size and
    a. relative motion.
    b. retinal disparity.
    c. interposition.
    d. light and shadow.
    e. linear perspective.

15. Which of the following phrases describes top-down processing?
    a. The entry level data captured by our various sensory systems.
    b. The effect that our experiences and expectations have on perception.
    c. Our tendency to scan a visual field from top to bottom.
    d. Our inclination to follow a predetermined set of steps, beginning with step 1, to process sound.
    e. The fact that information is processed by the higher regions of the brain before it reaches the lower brain.

Free-Response Question

A musician is walking home alone late one night and is startled when a dog in a yard to his left barks unexpectedly. Respond to each of the following regarding the musician's ability to hear the bark.

- Trace the path that the sound waves travel as they enter the ear and proceed to the receptor cells for hearing.
- Trace the path that the neural impulses created by the bark travel from the receptor cells into the brain.
- Using two theories of pitch perception, explain how the brain might process the pitch of the dog's bark.
- Explain how the musician would know that the bark originated to his left even without seeing the dog.

 WEB

Multiple-choice self-tests and more may be found at www.worthpublishers.com/myers

Rubric for Grading the Free-Response Question

This is a 9-point question. The teacher should require enough description for each point to be assured of the students' understanding.

Trace the path that sound waves follow:

- 1 point for the auditory canal and eardrum
- 1 point for the bones of the middle ear
- 1 point for the cochlea

Trace the path of the neural impulses:

- 1 point for the hair cells
- 1 point for the thalamus and temporal lobes

Pitch perception:

- 1 point for place theory and its role in perceiving a high-pitched bark
- 1 point for frequency theory and its role in perceiving a low-pitched bark

Sound localization:

- 1 point for a more intense sound from the left
- 1 point for a louder sound from the left

- *Videos: The Brain, 2nd ed., Module 8: Visual Information Processing: Elementary Concepts; Module 9: Visual Information Processing: Perception; Module 11: Sensory–Motor Integration; Module 10: Perception: Inverted Vision*
- *PsychSim 5: Colorful World; The Auditory System; Visual Illusions*

UNIT 5

Pacing Guide

Use the following guide to determine how many instructional days to devote to this unit depending on the type of course you teach:

Year-long course: 2–3 days
Block schedule/Semester-long course: 1–2 days

This unit encompasses 2–4 percent of the AP Exam. Spending an appropriate amount of time on this unit will help students do well on the AP Exam.

 TEACHING TIP

Even though this unit does not encompass a large portion of the AP Exam, the concepts are certainly important and interesting to students. While you may not spend a lot of time on this unit, you should emphasize to students that any content can show up on the AP Exam, making this content "fair game" for multiple-choice or free-response questions.

 INTERCONNECTING

Keep in mind how the concepts in this unit are reinforced in other units:

Unit 3: Biological Bases of
          Behavior
Unit 4: Sensation and Perception
Unit 7: Part A: Memory
Unit 8: Part B: Emotions, Stress,
          and Health
Unit 12: Abnormal Psychology
Unit 13: Treatment of
          Psychological Disorders

174

Suggested Readings

Bachman, J. (1997). *Smoking, drinking, and drug use in young adulthood: The impact of new freedoms and new responsibilities.* Mahwah, NJ: Lawrence Erlbaum.

Carroll, C. (1996). *Drugs in modern society,* 4th ed. Madison, WI: Brown and Benchmark.

Coren, S. (1996). *Sleep thieves.* New York: Free Press.

Dement, W. C. (1978). *Some must watch while some must sleep.* New York: Norton.

Dement, W. C., & Vaughan, C. (1999). *The promise of sleep.* New York: Delacorte Press.

Fromm, E., & Nash, M. R. (Eds.). (1992). *Contemporary hypnosis research.* New York: Guilford Press.

States of Consciousness

onsciousness can be a funny thing. It offers us weird experiences, as when entering sleep or leaving a dream, and sometimes it leaves us wondering who is really in control. After putting me under the influence of nitrous oxide, my dentist tells me to turn my head to the left. My conscious mind resists: "No way," I silently say. "You can't boss me around!" Whereupon my robotic head, ignoring my conscious mind, turns obligingly under the dentist's control.

During my noontime pickup basketball games, I am sometimes mildly irritated as my body passes the ball while my conscious mind is saying, "No, stop, you fool! Peter is going to intercept!" Alas, my body completes the pass on its own. Other times, notes psychologist Daniel Wegner (2002) in *Illusion of Conscious Will,* people believe their consciousness is controlling their actions when it isn't. In one experiment, people co-controlled a computer mouse with a partner (who was actually the experimenter's accomplice). Even when the partner caused the mouse to stop on a predetermined square, the participants perceived that *they* had caused it to stop there.

And then there are those times when consciousness seems to split. Reading *Green Eggs and Ham* to one of my preschoolers for the umpteenth time, my obliging mouth could say the words while my mind wandered elsewhere. And if someone asks what you're doing for lunch while you're texting, it's not a problem. Your fingers complete the message as you suggest getting tacos.

Was my drug-induced dental experience akin to people's experiences with other *psychoactive drugs* (mood- and perception-altering substances)? Was my automatic obedience to my dentist like people's responses to a hypnotist? Or does a split in consciousness, like those that we have when our mind goes elsewhere while reading or texting, explain people's behavior while under hypnosis? And during sleep, when and why do those weird dream experiences occur?

But first questions first: What is *consciousness?* Every science has concepts so fundamental they are nearly impossible to define. Biologists agree on what is alive but not on precisely what life is. In physics, *matter* and *energy* elude simple definition. To psychologists, consciousness is similarly a fundamental yet slippery concept.

At its beginning, *psychology* was "the description and explanation of states of consciousness" (Ladd, 1887). But during the first half of the twentieth century, the difficulty of scientifically studying consciousness led many psychologists—including those in the emerging school of *behaviorism* (Unit 6)—to turn to direct observations of behavior. By the 1960s, psychology had nearly lost consciousness and was defining itself as "the science of behavior." Consciousness was likened to a car's speedometer: "It doesn't make the car go, it just reflects what's happening" (Seligman, 1991, p. 24).

"Neither [psychologist] Steve Pinker nor I can explain human subjective consciousness. . . . We don't understand it."
Evolutionary biologist Richard Dawkins (1999)

"Psychology must discard all reference to consciousness."
Behaviorist John B. Watson (1913)

175

Key Terms

Sleep and Dreams

consciousness
circadian rhythm
REM sleep
alpha waves
sleep
hallucinations
delta waves
NREM sleep
insomnia
narcolepsy
sleep apnea
night terrors
dream
manifest content
latent content
REM rebound

Hypnosis

hypnosis
posthypnotic suggestion
dissociation

Drugs and Consciousness

psychoactive drugs
tolerance
withdrawal
physical dependence
psychological dependence
addiction
depressants
barbiturates
opiates
stimulants
amphetamines
methamphetamine
Ecstasy (MDMA)
hallucinogens
LSD
near-death experience
THC

Gauld, A. (1992). *A history of hypnotism.* New York: Cambridge University Press.

Maas, J. B. (1998). *Power sleep.* New York: Villard.

Key People

Eugene Aserinsky
Stanley Coren
William Dement
Sigmund Freud
Ernest Hilgard
Albert Hofmann
Nathaniel Kleitman
Nicholas Spanos

UNIT 5

INTERCONNECTING

Be sure students understand the content presented in Unit 3C and Unit 4 about the two-track mind and selective attention. The study of the brain and consciousness demonstrate that we are able to process many things at the same time, with much of that information being processed unconsciously.

At this point, you may want to use **Student Project:** *A Penny for Your Thoughts* (p. 2) from Bolt's Teacher's Resource Binder, which accompanies this text.

TROUBLESHOOTING

Help students see that what we know about unconscious processing is different from Freud's ideas about the unconscious mind. Freud's view of the unconscious described it as a repository of childhood experiences that influenced behavior without our conscious knowledge. The modern understanding of the unconscious views it as a parallel processing system that enables us to deal with all sorts of information and stimuli outside of the conscious. This system helps us to be more cognitively efficient.

➤ FIGURE 5.1

States of consciousness In addition to normal, waking awareness, consciousness comes to us in altered states, including daydreaming, sleeping, meditating, and drug-induced hallucinating.

Some states occur spontaneously	Daydreaming	Drowsiness	Dreaming
Some are physiologically induced	Hallucinations	Orgasm	Food or oxygen starvation
Some are psychologically induced	Sensory deprivation	Hypnosis	Meditation

After 1960, mental concepts began to reemerge. Advances in neuroscience made it possible to relate brain activity to sleeping, dreaming, and other mental states. Researchers began studying consciousness altered by hypnosis and drugs. Psychologists of all persuasions were affirming the importance of *cognition,* or mental processes. Psychology was regaining consciousness.

For most psychologists today, **consciousness** is *our awareness of ourselves and our environment.* As we saw in Unit 3B, our conscious awareness is one part of the *dual processing* that goes on in our two-track minds. Although much of our information processing is conscious, much is unconscious and automatic—outside our awareness. Unit 4 highlighted our *selective attention,* which directs the spotlight of our awareness, allowing us to assemble information from many sources as we reflect on our past and plan for our future. We are also attentive when we learn a complex concept or behavior—say, riding a bike—making us aware of obstacles that we have to steer around and how to use the brakes. With practice, riding a bike no longer requires our undivided attention, freeing us to focus our attention on other things. As we do so, we experience what the early psychologist William James called a continuous "stream of consciousness," with each moment flowing into the next. Over the course of a day, we also flit between a variety of *states of consciousness,* including sleeping, waking, and other altered states (**FIGURE 5.1**).

Sleep and Dreams

SLEEP—THE IRRESISTIBLE TEMPTER TO whom we inevitably succumb. Sleep—the equalizer of seniors and second graders. Sleep—sweet, renewing, mysterious sleep.

Even when you are deeply asleep, your perceptual window is actually not completely shut. You move around on your bed, but you manage not to fall out. The occasional roar of passing vehicles may leave your deep sleep undisturbed, but a cry from a baby's nursery quickly interrupts it. So does the sound of your name. EEG recordings confirm that the brain's auditory cortex responds to sound stimuli even during sleep (Kutas, 1990). And when we are asleep, as when we are awake, we process most information outside our conscious awareness.

> "I love to sleep. Do you? Isn't it great? It really is the best of both worlds. You get to be alive and unconscious."
> Comedian Rita Rudner, 1993

Many of sleep's mysteries are now being solved as some people sleep, attached to recording devices, while others observe. By recording brain waves and muscle movements, and by observing and occasionally waking sleepers, researchers are glimpsing things that a thousand years of common sense never told us. Perhaps you can anticipate some of their discoveries. Are the following statements true or false?

1. When people dream of performing some activity, their limbs often move in concert with the dream.

2. Older adults sleep more than young adults.

3. Sleepwalkers are acting out their dreams.

4. Sleep experts recommend treating insomnia with an occasional sleeping pill.

5. Some people dream every night; others seldom dream.

All these statements (adapted from Palladino & Carducci, 1983) are false. To see why, read on.

Biological Rhythms and Sleep

1: How do our biological rhythms influence our daily functioning?

Like the ocean, life has its rhythmic tides. Over varying time periods, our bodies fluctuate, and with them, our minds. Let's look more closely at two of those biological rhythms—our 24-hour biological clock and our 90-minute sleep cycle.

Circadian Rhythm

The rhythm of the day parallels the rhythm of life—from our waking at a new day's birth to our nightly return to what Shakespeare called "death's counterfeit." Our bodies roughly synchronize with the 24-hour cycle of day and night through a biological clock called the **circadian rhythm** (from the Latin *circa,* "about," and *diem,* "day"). Body temperature rises as morning approaches, peaks during the day, dips for a time in early afternoon (when many people take siestas), and then begins to drop again before we go to sleep. Thinking is sharpest and memory most accurate when we are at our daily peak in circadian arousal. Pulling an all-nighter, we may feel groggiest about 4:00 A.M., and then we get a second wind after our normal wake-up time arrives.

Bright light in the morning tweaks the circadian clock by activating light-sensitive retinal proteins. These proteins control the circadian clock by triggering signals to the brain's *suprachiasmatic nucleus (SCN)*—a pair of grain-of-rice-sized, 20,000-cell clusters in the hypothalamus (Foster, 2004). The SCN does its job in part by causing the brain's pineal gland to decrease its production of the sleep-inducing hormone *melatonin* in the morning or increase it in the evening (**FIGURE 5.2**).

Bright light at night helps delay sleep, thus resetting our biological clock when we stay up late and sleep in on weekends (Oren & Terman, 1998). Sleep often eludes those who sleep till noon on Sunday and then

::**consciousness** our awareness of ourselves and our environment.

::**circadian** [ser-KAY-dee-an] **rhythm** the biological clock; regular bodily rhythms (for example, of temperature and wakefulness) that occur on a 24-hour cycle.

• Dolphins, porpoises, and whales sleep with one side of their brain at a time (Miller et al., 2008). •

• At about age 20 (slightly earlier for women), we begin to shift from being evening-energized "owls" to being morning-loving "larks" (Roenneberg et al., 2004). Most 20-year-olds are owls, with performance improving across the day (May & Hasher, 1998). Most older adults are larks, with performance declining as the day wears on. Retirement homes are typically quiet by mid-evening; in university dorms, the day is far from over. •

➤ **FIGURE 5.2**
The biological clock Light striking the retina signals the suprachiasmatic nucleus (SCN) to suppress the pineal gland's production of the sleep hormone melatonin. At night, the SCN quiets down, allowing the pineal gland to release melatonin into the bloodstream.

Suprachiasmatic nucleus — Pineal gland — Melatonin production suppressed — Light

Melatonin produced — Blood flow

TEACHING TIP

In contrast to the sleep induced by most drugs, melatonin-induced sleep seems remarkably normal.

- The stages of both non-REM and REM occur at the usual hours and last the usual amount of time.

- Most users do not seem to feel drowsy or experience side effects.

- Melatonin seems to promote sleep at any time of day.

- Repeated doses at certain times of day or night can alter circadian body rhythms.

The data suggest that melatonin may be helpful for people

- who need to sleep during the day (i.e. night shift workers or those who fly across time zones).

- who are taking drugs which inhibit normal melatonin synthesis.

- who are patients with diseases that cause insomnia.

Haimov, I., & Lavie, P. (1996). Melatonin—A soporific hormone. *Current Directions in Psychological Science, 5,* 106–111.

TEACHING TIP

The waves people exhibit when they are awake and active are called beta waves. These are high frequency, low amplitude waves. Theta waves characterize the transition from stage 1 to stage 2. Theta waves are slower, so they have higher amplitude and lower frequency than alpha waves, the type of waves that are present as we move from relaxation to deeper sleep.

• If our natural circadian rhythm were attuned to a 23-hour cycle, would we instead need to discipline ourselves to stay up later at night and sleep in longer in the morning? •

::**REM sleep** rapid eye movement sleep; a recurring sleep stage during which vivid dreams commonly occur. Also known as *paradoxical sleep,* because the muscles are relaxed (except for minor twitches) but other body systems are active.

::**alpha waves** the relatively slow brain waves of a relaxed, awake state.

::**sleep** periodic, natural loss of consciousness—as distinct from unconsciousness resulting from a coma, general anesthesia, or hibernation. (Adapted from Dement, 1999.)

::**hallucinations** false sensory experiences, such as seeing something in the absence of an external visual stimulus.

---

go to bed just 11 hours later in preparation for the new school week. They are like New Yorkers whose biology is on California time. But what about North Americans who fly to Europe, and who need to be up when their circadian rhythm cries "Sleep!"? Studies in the laboratory and with shift workers find that bright light—spending the next day outdoors—helps reset the biological clock (Czeisler et al., 1986, 1989; Eastman et al., 1995).

Curiously—given that our ancestors' body clocks were attuned to the rising and setting sun of the 24-hour day—many of today's young adults adopt something closer to a 25-hour day, by staying up too late to get 8 hours of sleep. For this, we can thank (or blame) Thomas Edison, inventor of the light bulb. Being bathed in light disrupts our 24-hour biological clock (Czeisler et al., 1999; Dement, 1999). This helps explain why, until our later years, we must discipline ourselves to go to bed and force ourselves to get up. Most animals, too, when placed under unnatural constant illumination, will exceed a 24-hour day. Artificial light delays sleep.

Sleep Stages

2: What is the biological rhythm of our sleep?

As sleep overtakes us and different parts of our brain's cortex stop communicating, consciousness fades (Massimini et al., 2005). But our still-active sleeping brain does not emit a constant dial tone, because sleep has its own biological rhythm. About every 90 minutes, we pass through a cycle of five distinct sleep stages. This elementary fact apparently was unknown until 8-year-old Armond Aserinsky went to bed one night in 1952. His father, Eugene, a University of Chicago graduate student, needed to test an electroencephalograph (EEG) he had been repairing that day (Aserinsky, 1988; Seligman & Yellen, 1987). Placing electrodes near Armond's eyes to record the rolling eye movements then believed to occur during sleep, Aserinsky watched the machine go wild, tracing deep zigzags on the graph paper. Could the machine still be broken? As the night proceeded and the activity periodically recurred, Aserinsky finally realized that the fast, jerky eye movements were accompanied by energetic brain activity. Awakened during one such episode, Armond reported having a dream. Aserinsky had discovered what we now know as **REM sleep** (rapid *eye m*ovement sleep).

To find out if similar cycles occur during adult sleep, Nathaniel Kleitman (1960) and Aserinsky pioneered procedures that have now been used with thousands of volunteers. To appreciate their methods and findings, imagine yourself in their lab. As the hour grows late, you feel sleepy and you yawn in response to reduced brain metabolism. (Yawning, which can be socially contagious, stretches your neck muscles and increases your heart rate, which increases your alertness [Moorcroft, 2003]). When you are ready for bed, the researcher tapes electrodes to your scalp (to detect your brain waves), just outside the corners of your eyes (to detect eye movements), and on your chin (to detect muscle tension) (**FIGURE 5.3**). Other devices allow the researcher to record your heart rate, your respiration rate, and your genital arousal.

When you are in bed with your eyes closed, the researcher in the next room sees on the EEG the relatively slow **alpha waves** of your awake but relaxed state (**FIGURE 5.4**). As you adapt to all this equipment, you grow tired and, in an unremembered moment, slip into **sleep.** The transition is marked by the slowed breathing and the irregular brain waves of Stage 1 (**FIGURE 5.5**).

In one of his 15,000 research participants, William Dement (1999) observed the moment the brain's perceptual window to the outside world slammed shut. Dement

---

RESEARCH

Have students conduct a sleep survey with a representative sample of students at your school. They should ask how much sleep students get each night, whether they nap in class or feel extremely tired during the day, and why they may or may not get enough sleep each night.

- Be sure to get approval from an Institutional Review Board and obtain informed consent from subjects before embarking on any research project.

➤ FIGURE 5.3
Measuring sleep activity Sleep researchers measure brain-wave activity, eye movements, and muscle tension by electrodes that pick up weak electrical signals from the brain, eye, and facial muscles. (From Dement, 1978.)

asked this sleep-deprived young man, lying on his back with eyelids taped open, to press a button every time a strobe light flashed in his eyes (about every 6 seconds). After a few minutes the young man missed one. Asked why, he said, "Because there was no flash." But there was a flash. He missed it because (as his brain activity revealed) he had fallen asleep for 2 seconds. Unaware that he had done so, he had missed not only the flash 6 inches from his nose but also the abrupt moment of his entry into sleep.

During this brief Stage 1 sleep you may experience fantastic images, resembling **hallucinations**—sensory experiences that occur without a sensory stimulus. You may have a sensation of falling (at which moment your body may suddenly jerk) or of floating weightlessly. Such *hypnagogic* sensations may later be incorporated into memories. People who claim to have been abducted by aliens—often shortly after getting into bed—commonly recall being floated off or pinned down on their beds (Clancy, 2005).

You then relax more deeply and begin about 20 minutes of Stage 2 sleep, characterized by the periodic appearance of *sleep spindles*—bursts of rapid, rhythmic brainwave activity (see Figure 5.4). Although you could still be awakened without too much

➤ FIGURE 5.5
The moment of sleep We seem unaware of the moment we fall into sleep, but someone eavesdropping on our brain waves could tell. (From Dement, 1999.)

➤ FIGURE 5.4
Brain waves and sleep stages The regular alpha waves of an awake, relaxed state are quite different from the slower, larger delta waves of deep Stage 4 sleep. Although the rapid REM sleep waves resemble the near-waking Stage 1 sleep waves, the body is more aroused during REM sleep than during Stage 1 sleep. (From Dement, 1978.)

TEACHING TIP

Another type of wave found in sleep stage 2 is the K-complex. As you can see in Figure 5.4, in stage 2 there is a sharp upturn followed by a rapid downturn of the wave, looking similar to a heartbeat pattern on an EKG. This wave is the precursor to the large delta waves that characterize stages 3 and 4 sleep.

TEACHING TIP

Be sure to point out the name for the hallucinations people experience when they are in the early stages of sleep—hypnagogic sensations. This term may show up on the AP Exam.

At this point, you may want to use **Student Project: *Catching the Hypnagogic State*** (p. 7) from Bolt's Teacher's Resource Binder.

INTERCONNECTING

The device used to measure sleep waves is the EEG—electroencephalogram—which was discussed in Unit 3. This device captures the electrical activity given off by the neurons as they fire action potentials. The speed with which the action potentials occur creates the brain wave patterns seen during wakefulness and sleep. Sleep researchers use other devices during sleep studies to measure eye movements and muscle activity to gain a better understanding of the physiology of sleep.

TROUBLESHOOTING

Use Figure 5.4 to help students identify the different types of brain waves characterizing the different stages of sleep. A diagram like this may show up on the AP Exam. Students could need to identify which waves go with each stage.

UNIT 5

● To catch your own hypnagogic experiences after going to bed, you might have a "snooze" alarm awaken you every five minutes. ●

● Horses, which spend 92 percent of each day standing and can sleep standing, must lie down for REM sleep (Morrison, 2003). ●

difficulty, you are now clearly asleep. Sleeptalking—usually garbled or nonsensical—can occur during Stage 2 or any other sleep stage (Mahowald & Ettinger, 1990).

Then for the next few minutes you go through the transitional Stage 3 to the deep sleep of Stage 4. First in Stage 3, and increasingly in Stage 4, your brain emits large, slow **delta waves.** These two slow-wave stages last for about 30 minutes, during which you would be hard to awaken. Ever say to classmates, "That thunder was so loud last night," only to have them respond, "What thunder?" Those who missed the storm may have been in delta sleep. Curiously, it is at the end of the deep sleep of Stage 4 that children may wet the bed or begin sleepwalking. About 20 percent of 3- to 12-year-olds have at least one episode of sleepwalking, usually lasting 2 to 10 minutes; some 5 percent have repeated episodes (Giles et al., 1994).

REM Sleep

About an hour after you first fall asleep, a strange thing happens. You leave behind the stages known as **NREM sleep.** Rather than continuing in deep slumber, you ascend from your initial sleep dive. Returning through Stage 3 and Stage 2 (where you spend about half your night), you enter the most intriguing sleep phase—REM sleep (**FIGURE 5.6**). For about 10 minutes, your brain waves become rapid and saw-toothed, more like those of the nearly awake Stage 1 sleep. But unlike Stage 1 sleep, during REM sleep your heart rate rises, your breathing becomes rapid and irregular, and every half-minute or so your eyes dart around in a momentary burst of activity behind closed lids. Because anyone watching a sleeper's eyes can notice these REM bursts, it is amazing that science was ignorant of REM sleep until 1952.

Except during very scary dreams, your genitals become aroused during REM sleep, and you have an erection or increased vaginal lubrication, regardless of whether the dream's content is sexual (Karacan et al., 1966). Men's common "morning erection" stems from the night's last REM period, often just before waking.

Although your brain's motor cortex is active during REM sleep, your brainstem blocks its messages, leaving muscles relaxed—so relaxed that, except for an occasional finger, toe, or facial twitch, you are essentially paralyzed. Moreover, you cannot easily

➤ **FIGURE 5.6**
The stages in a typical night's sleep Most people pass through the five-stage sleep cycle (graph a) several times, with the periods of Stage 4 sleep and then Stage 3 sleep diminishing and REM sleep periods increasing in duration. Graph b plots this increasing REM sleep and decreasing deep sleep based on data from 30 young adults. (From Cartwright, 1978; Webb, 1992.)

be awakened. Thus, REM sleep is sometimes called *paradoxical sleep*, with the body internally aroused and externally calm.

More intriguing than the paradoxical nature of REM sleep is what the rapid eye movements announce: the beginning of a dream. Even those who claim they never dream will, more than 80 percent of the time, recall a dream after being awakened during REM sleep. Unlike the fleeting images of Stage 1 sleep ("I was thinking about my test today," or "I was trying to borrow something from someone"), REM sleep dreams are often emotional, usually storylike, and more richly hallucinatory, including visual, auditory, and other sensory details:

> My girlfriend and I were at some friends' house, but our friends weren't there. Their TV had been left on, but otherwise it was very quiet. After we wandered around for a while, their dogs finally noticed us and barked and growled loudly, with bared teeth.

The sleep cycle repeats itself about every 90 minutes. As the night wears on, deep Stage 4 sleep gets progressively briefer and then disappears. The REM and Stage 2 sleep periods get longer (see Figure 5.6b). By morning, 20 to 25 percent of our average night's sleep—some 100 minutes—has been REM sleep. Thirty-seven percent of people report rarely or never having dreams "that you can remember the next morning" (Moore, 2004). Unknown to those people, they spend about 600 hours a year experiencing some 1500 dreams, or more than 100,000 dreams over a typical lifetime—dreams swallowed by the night but never acted out, thanks to REM's protective paralysis.

Some sleep deeply, some not The fluctuating sleep cycle enables safe sleep for these soldiers on the battlefield. One benefit of communal sleeping is that someone will probably be awake or easily roused in the event of a threat. ▲

Why Do We Sleep?

The idea that "everyone needs 8 hours of sleep" is untrue. Newborns spend nearly two-thirds of their day asleep, most adults no more than one-third. Age-related differences in average sleeping time are rivaled by the differences among individuals at any age. Some people thrive with fewer than 6 hours per night; others regularly rack up 9 hours or more. Such sleep patterns may be genetically influenced. When Wilse Webb and Scott Campbell (1983) checked the pattern and duration of sleep among fraternal and identical twins, only the identical twins were strikingly similar.

Sleep patterns are also culturally influenced. In the United States and Canada, for example, adults average just over 8 hours per night (Hurst, 2008; Robinson & Martin, 2007).

"Boy are my eyes tired! I had REM sleep all night long."

• People rarely snore during dreams. When REM starts, snoring stops. •

::**delta waves** the large, slow brain waves associated with deep sleep.

::**NREM sleep** non–rapid eye movement sleep; encompasses all sleep stages except for REM sleep.

UNIT 5

TEACHING TIP

The importance of sleep cannot be ignored, especially in today's fast-paced society. Use the following activity to help students evaluate how sleep may positively affect their lives:

On the left half of a piece of paper, have students list three ways in which they would like to improve in school subjects or extracurricular and social activities. After you discuss the importance of getting enough sleep, have students speculate how the three items they listed might improve if they changed or modified some of their sleep habits. Encourage them to write the possible improvements on the right side of the piece of paper. These comparisons may help students determine ways in which they can correct unhealthy sleep habits.

CRITICAL THINKING

Have students brainstorm about possible reasons why teenagers resist getting 8 to 10 hours of sleep a night. Have them consider work, academic, familial, physiological, and social reasons for the prevalence of sleep deprivation among teens. Discuss ways they can counter these negative influences on getting a good night's sleep.

At this point, you may want to use **Classroom Exercise: *Am I Sleep Deprived?*** (p. 8) from Bolt's Teacher's Resource Binder.

• In 1989, Michael Doucette was named America's Safest Driving Teen. In 1990, while driving home from college, he fell asleep at the wheel and collided with an oncoming car, killing both himself and the other driver. Michael's driving instructor later acknowledged never having mentioned sleep deprivation and drowsy driving (Dement, 1999). •

• In a 2001 Gallup poll, 61 percent of men, but only 47 percent of women, said they got enough sleep. •

Sleepless and suffering These fatigued, sleep-deprived earthquake rescue workers in China may experience a depressed immune system, impaired concentration, and greater vulnerability to accidents.

Reuters/China Daily (China)

(The weeknight sleep of many students and workers falls short of this average [NSF, 2008].) North Americans are nevertheless sleeping less than their counterparts a century ago. Thanks to modern light bulbs, shift work, the Internet, and social diversions, those who would have gone to bed at 9:00 P.M. are now up until 11:00 P.M. or later. Thomas Edison (1948) was pleased to accept credit for this, believing that less sleep meant more productive time and greater opportunities.

Allowed to sleep unhindered, most adults will sleep at least 9 hours a night, reports Stanley Coren (1996). With that much sleep, we awake refreshed, sustain better moods, and perform more efficient and accurate work. Compare that with a succession of 5-hour nights, when we accumulate a sleep debt that cannot be paid off by one long marathon sleep. "The brain keeps an accurate count of sleep debt for at least two weeks," says William Dement (1999, p. 64). With our body yearning for sleep, we will begin to feel terrible. Trying to stay awake, we will eventually lose. In the tiredness battle, sleep always wins. It's easy to spot students who have stayed up late to study for a test or finish a term paper: they are often fighting the "nods" (their heads bobbing downward) as they try to stay awake.

Obviously, then, we need sleep. Sleep commands roughly one-third of our lives—some 25 years, on average. But why? It seems an easy question to answer: Just keep people awake for several days and note how they deteriorate. If you were a volunteer in such an experiment, how do you think it would affect your body and mind? You would, of course, become terribly drowsy—especially during the hours when your biological clock programs you to sleep. But could the lack of sleep physically damage you? Would it noticeably alter your biochemistry or body organs? Would you become emotionally disturbed? Mentally disoriented?

The Effects of Sleep Loss

3: How does sleep loss affect us?

Good news! Psychologists have discovered a treatment that strengthens memory, increases concentration, boosts mood, moderates hunger and obesity, fortifies the disease-fighting immune system, and lessens the risk of fatal accidents. Even better news: The treatment feels good, it can be self-administered, the supplies are limitless, and it's available free! If you are a typical high school senior, often going to bed near midnight and dragged out of bed six or seven hours later by the dreaded alarm, the treatment is simple: Each night add an hour to your sleep.

The U.S. Navy and the National Institutes of Health have demonstrated the benefits of unrestricted sleep in experiments in which volunteers spent 14 hours daily in bed for at least a week. For the first few days, the volunteers averaged 12 hours of sleep a day or more, apparently paying off a sleep debt that averaged 25 to 30 hours. That accomplished, they then settled back to 7.5 to 9 hours nightly and, with no sleep debt, felt energized and happier (Dement, 1999). In one Gallup survey (Mason, 2005), 63 percent of adults who reported getting the sleep they need also reported being "very satisfied" with their personal life (as did only 36 percent of those needing more sleep). When Daniel Kahneman and his colleagues (2004) invited 909 working women to report on their daily moods, they were struck by what mattered little, such as money (so long as they were not battling poverty). And they were struck by what mattered a lot—less time pressure at work and a good night's sleep.

Unfortunately, many of us are suffering from patterns that not only leave us sleepy but also thwart our having an energized feeling of well-

RESEARCH

Have students record their sleep habits for a week, including a weekend. Then have them calculate the average number of hours of sleep they get each night, comparing weekend sleep with weeknight sleep. Discuss with students how their sleep patterns may be affecting their daily performance. Ask them what prevents them from getting more sleep and how getting one hour more a night would affect their quality of life.

At this point, you may want to use **Student Project: *Keeping a Sleep Diary*** (p. 6) from Bolt's Teacher's Resource Binder.

being (Mikulincer et al., 1989). Teens who typically need 8 or 9 hours of sleep now average less than 7 hours—nearly 2 hours less each night than did their counterparts of 80 years ago (Holden, 1993; Maas, 1999). In one survey, 28 percent of high school students acknowledged falling asleep in class at least once a week (Sleep Foundation, 2006). When the going gets boring, the students start snoring.

Even when awake, students often function below their peak. And they know it: Four in five American teens and three in five 18- to 29-year-olds wish they could get more sleep on weekdays (Mason, 2003, 2005). Yet that teen who staggers glumly out of bed in response to an unwelcome alarm, yawns through morning classes, and feels half-depressed much of the day may be energized at 11 P.M. and mindless of the next day's looming sleepiness (Carskadon, 2002).

Sleep researcher William Dement (1997) reports that at Stanford University, 80 percent of students are "dangerously sleep deprived . . . Sleep deprivation [entails] difficulty studying, diminished productivity, tendency to make mistakes, irritability, fatigue." A large sleep debt "makes you stupid," says Dement (1999, p. 231).

It can also make you fatter. Sleep deprivation increases the hunger-arousing hormone ghrelin and decreases its hunger-suppressing partner, leptin. It also increases the stress hormone cortisol, which stimulates the body to make fat. Sure enough, children and adults who sleep less than normal are fatter than those who sleep more (Chen et al., 2008; Knutson et al., 2007; Schoenborn & Adams, 2008).

• To test whether you are one of the many sleep-deprived students, see TABLE 5.1. •

TABLE 5.1

Cornell University psychologist James Maas reports that most students suffer the consequences of sleeping less than they should. To see if you are in that group, answer the following true-false questions:

True	False	
____	____	1. I need an alarm clock in order to wake up at the appropriate time.
____	____	2. It's a struggle for me to get out of bed in the morning.
____	____	3. Weekday mornings I hit the snooze bar several times to get more sleep.
____	____	4. I feel tired, irritable, and stressed out during the week.
____	____	5. I have trouble concentrating and remembering.
____	____	6. I feel slow with critical thinking, problem solving, and being creative.
____	____	7. I often fall asleep watching TV.
____	____	8. I often fall asleep in boring meetings or lectures or in warm rooms.
____	____	9. I often fall asleep after heavy meals.
____	____	10. I often fall asleep while relaxing after dinner.
____	____	11. I often fall asleep within five minutes of getting into bed.
____	____	12. I often feel drowsy while driving.
____	____	13. I often sleep extra hours on weekend mornings.
____	____	14. I often need a nap to get through the day.
____	____	15. I have dark circles around my eyes.

If you answered "true" to three or more items, you probably are not getting enough sleep. To determine your sleep needs, Maas recommends that you "go to bed 15 minutes earlier than usual every night for the next week—and continue this practice by adding 15 more minutes each week—until you wake without an alarm clock and feel alert all day." (Quiz reprinted with permission from James B. Maas, *Power sleep: The revolutionary program that prepares your mind and body for peak performance* [New York: HarperCollins, 1999].)

TEACHING TIP

Relate to students the story of Randy Gardner, a high school student who in 1969 attempted to stay awake for as long as possible. Gardner eventually stayed awake for 11 days, but he experienced frightening symptoms as a result of his sleep loss. He developed a heart murmur, slurred his speech, and couldn't attend to a conversation for more than a few moments. He hallucinated that street signs were people, and he believed himself to be an African American football star—even though he was not African American and did not play football. When people confronted him with the truth, he called them racist. Once Gardner began sleeping again, his symptoms disappeared. He was back to his regular sleep pattern within 3–4 days of ending his marathon of wakefulness.

At this point, you may want to use **Lecture/Discussion Topic:** *How Long Can Humans Stay Awake?* (p. 8) from Bolt's Teacher's Resource Binder.

DEMO

Have students take the sleep deprivation quiz in Table 5.1. Have them evaluate whether the quiz indicates sleep deprivation. Then have them reflect on why they may be sleep deprived. Challenge them to consider ways in which lack of sleep has adversely affected their lives and what they can realistically do to add more sleep to their daily schedules.

At this point, you may want to use **Classroom Exercise:** *The Sleep IQ Test* (p. 4) from Bolt's Teacher's Resource Binder.

CRITICAL THINKING

If the benefits of sleep are so clear, why does Western culture seem to disdain it? Have students consider the factors that keep people in the U.S. and other industrialized cultures from sleeping. How do economic factors play into the lack of sleep? What about social influences? How can policymakers encourage people to get more sleep?

At this point, you may want to use **Classroom Exercise/Student Project:** *Epworth Sleepiness Scale* (p. 9) from Bolt's Teacher's Resource Binder.

TEACHING TIP

Ask students if they have ever fallen asleep while they were bored. Most students will raise their hands. Tell them that boredom actually does not cause drowsiness. In fact, boredom causes restless behavior, like fidgeting or impatience. When people fall asleep while bored, it is an indication of sleep deprivation. If students are falling asleep in class, this is a sure sign they are not getting enough sleep during the night.

And experimental sleep deprivation of adults increases appetite and eating (Nixon et al., 2008; Patel et al., 2006; Spiegel et al., 2004; Van Cauter et al., 2007). This may help explain the common weight gain among sleep-deprived students (although a review of 11 studies reveals that the mythical college student's "freshman 15" is, on average, closer to a "first-year 4" [Hull et al., 2007]).

In addition to making us more vulnerable to obesity, sleep deprivation can suppress immune cells that fight off viral infections and cancer (Motivala & Irwin, 2007). This may help explain why people who sleep 7 to 8 hours a night tend to outlive those who are chronically sleep deprived, and why older adults who have no difficulty falling or staying asleep tend to live longer than their sleep-deprived age-mates (Dement, 1999; Dew et al., 2003). When infections do set in, we typically sleep more, boosting our immune cells.

Chronic sleep debt also alters metabolic and hormonal functioning in ways that mimic aging and are conducive to hypertension and memory impairment (Spiegel et al., 1999; Taheri, 2004). Other effects include irritability, slowed performance, and impaired creativity, concentration, and communication (Harrison & Horne, 2000). Reaction times slow and errors increase on visual tasks similar to those involved in airport baggage screening, performing surgery, and reading X-rays (Horowitz et al., 2003).

Sleep deprivation can be devastating for driving, piloting, and equipment operating. Driver fatigue contributes to an estimated 20 percent of American traffic accidents (Brody, 2002) and to some 30 percent of Australian highway deaths (Maas, 1999). Consider the timing of four industrial disasters—the 1989 *Exxon Valdez* tanker hitting rocks and spilling millions of gallons of oil on the shores of Alaska; Union Carbide's 1984 release of toxic gas killing thousands in Bhopal, India; and the 1979 (Three Mile Island) and 1986 (Chernobyl) nuclear accidents—all occurred after midnight, when operators in charge were likely to be drowsiest and unresponsive to signals that require an alert response. When sleepy frontal lobes confront an unexpected situation, misfortune often results.

Stanley Coren capitalized on what is, for many North Americans, a semi-annual sleep-manipulation experiment—the "spring forward" to "daylight savings" time and "fall backward" to "standard" time. Searching millions of records, Coren found that in both Canada and the United States, accidents increase immediately after the time change that shortens sleep (**FIGURE 5.7**).

But let's put all this positively: To manage your life with enough sleep to awaken naturally and well rested is to be more alert, productive, happy, healthy, and safe.

> "Drowsiness is red alert!"
> William Dement, *The Promise of Sleep*, 1999

➤ **FIGURE 5.7**

Canadian traffic accidents On the Monday after the spring time change, when people lose one hour of sleep, accidents increased as compared with the Monday before. In the fall, traffic accidents normally increase because of greater snow, ice, and darkness, but they diminished after the time change. (Adapted from Coren, 1996.)

Sleep Theories

4: What is sleep's function?

So, nature charges us for our sleep debt. But why do we have this need for sleep?

We have very few answers, but sleep may have evolved for five reasons: First, *sleep protects*. When darkness precluded our distant ancestors' hunting and food gathering and made travel treacherous, they were better off asleep in a cave, out of harm's way. Those who didn't try to navigate around rocks and cliffs at night were more likely to leave descendants. This fits a broader principle: A species' sleep pattern tends to suit its ecological niche. Animals with the greatest need to graze and the least ability to hide tend to sleep less. Elephants and horses sleep 3 to 4 hours a day, gorillas 12 hours, and cats 14 hours. For bats and eastern chipmunks, both of which sleep 20 hours, to live is hardly more than to eat and to sleep (Moorcroft, 2003). (Would you rather be like a giraffe and sleep 2 hours a day or a bat and sleep 20?)

Second, *sleep helps us recuperate*. It helps restore and repair brain tissue. Bats and other animals with high waking metabolism burn a lot of calories, producing a lot of *free radicals*, molecules that are toxic to neurons. Sleeping a lot gives resting neurons time to repair themselves, while allowing unused connections to weaken (Siegel, 2003; Vyazovski et al., 2008). Think of it this way: When consciousness leaves your house, brain construction workers come in for a makeover.

But sleep is not just for keeping us safe and for repairing our brain. New research reveals that *sleep is for making memories*—for restoring and rebuilding our fading memories of the day's experiences. People trained to perform tasks recall them better after a night's sleep, or even after a short nap, than after several hours awake (Walker & Stickgold, 2006). And in both humans and rats, neural activity during slow-wave sleep reenacts and promotes recall of prior novel experiences (Peigneux et al., 2004; Ribeiro et al., 2004). In one experiment, people were exposed to the scent of roses while learning the locations of various picture cards. When reexposed to the scent during slow-wave sleep, their memory scratch pad—the hippocampus—was reactivated, and they remembered the picture placements with almost perfect accuracy the next day (Rasch et al., 2007).

Sleep also feeds creative thinking. On occasion, dreams have inspired noteworthy literary, artistic, and scientific achievements, such as the dream that clued chemist August Kekulé to the structure of benzene (Ross, 2006). More commonplace is the boost that a complete night's sleep gives to our thinking and learning. After working on a task, then sleeping on it, people solve problems more insightfully than do those who stay awake (Wagner et al., 2004). They can also, after sleep, better discern connections among different novel pieces of information (Ellenbogen et al., 2007). Even 15-month-olds, if retested after a nap, better recall relationships among novel words (Gómez et al., 2006). To think smart and see connections, it often pays to sleep on it.

Finally, *sleep may play a role in the growth process*. During deep sleep, the pituitary gland releases a growth hormone. As we age, we release less of this hormone and spend less time in deep sleep (Pekkanen, 1982). Such discoveries are beginning to solve the ongoing riddle of sleep.

So when it's time to sleep, pay attention to your body. Ignore that last text message, resist the urge to update your Facebook profile, and succumb to sleep, the gentle tyrant.

Sleep Disorders

5: What are the major sleep disorders?

No matter what their normal need for sleep, 1 in 10 adults, and 1 in 4 older adults, complain of **insomnia**—not an occasional inability to

::**insomnia** recurring problems in falling or staying asleep.

> "Sleep faster, we need the pillows."
> *Yiddish proverb*

> "Corduroy pillows make headlines."
> *Anonymous*

Economic-recession stress can rob sleep A National Sleep Foundation (2009) survey found 27 percent of people reporting sleeplessness related to the economy and their personal finances and employment. Higher stress levels, and more restless sleep, may plague those who are unemployed, or underemployed, and seeking new jobs, such as these people.

UNIT 5

TEACHING TIP

Gregg Jacobs and his colleagues report much better success in treating insomnia when a combination of behavioral techniques is used. Subjects who had serious difficulty falling asleep were told to try the following strategies.

- Sleep restriction: Do not spend more than seven hours in bed. Avoid naps, and arise at the same time every morning, including weekends.

- Stimulus control: Go to bed only when sleepy, and use the bed only for sleep or relaxing activities. If you cannot fall asleep within 20 minutes, stop trying and do something relaxing.

- Relaxation response training: Use soothing visual imagery, rhythmic breathing, and muscle relaxation to calm yourself.

Jacobs, G., Benson, H., & Friedman, R. (1993). Home-based central nervous system assessment of a multifactor behavioral intervention for chronic sleep-onset insomnia. *Behavior Therapy*, *24*, 159–174.

At this point, you may want to use **Lecture/Discussion Topic: *Treating Insomnia*** (p. 11) from Bolt's Teacher's Resource Binder.

INTERCONNECTING

Narcolepsy is often treated using powerful stimulants, called amphetamines, to keep the patient's brain from going into the REM patterns that are most restful. Amphetamines are discussed in greater detail later in the unit.

> "The lion and the lamb shall lie down together, but the lamb will not be very sleepy."
>
> Woody Allen, in the movie *Love and Death*, 1975

> "Sleep is like love or happiness. If you pursue it too ardently it will elude you."
>
> Wilse Webb, 1992

> "In 1757 Benjamin Franklin gave us the axiom, 'Early to bed, early to rise, makes a man healthy, wealthy, and wise.' It would be more accurate to say 'consistently to bed and consistently to rise . . . ' "
>
> James B. Maas, *Power Sleep*, 1999

off the mark.com   by Mark Parisi

LET ME GET THIS STRAIGHT, IT'S BEEN TWO CONSECUTIVE HOURS SINCE YOU'VE SLEPT?

WHEN CATS EXPERIENCE INSOMNIA

---

sleep when anxious or excited, but persistent problems in falling or staying asleep (Irwin et al., 2006).

From middle age on, sleep is seldom uninterrupted. Being occasionally awakened becomes the norm, not something to fret over or treat with medication. And some people do fret unnecessarily about their sleep (Coren, 1996). In laboratory studies, insomnia complainers do sleep less than others, but they typically overestimate—by about double—how long it takes them to fall asleep. They also underestimate by nearly half how long they actually have slept. Even if we have been awake only an hour or two, we may *think* we have had very little sleep because it's the waking part we remember.

The most common quick fixes for true insomnia—sleeping pills and alcohol—can aggravate the problem, reducing REM sleep and leaving the person with next-day blahs. Relying on sleeping pills—sales of which soared 60 percent from 2000 to 2006 (Saul, 2007)—the person may need increasing doses to get an effect. Then, when the drug is discontinued, the insomnia can worsen.

Scientists are searching for natural chemicals that are abundant during sleep, hoping they might be synthesized as a sleep aid without side effects. In the meantime, sleep experts offer other natural alternatives:

- Exercise regularly but not in the late evening. (Late afternoon is best.)

- Avoid all caffeine after early afternoon, and avoid rich foods before bedtime. Instead, try a glass of milk, which provides raw materials for the manufacture of serotonin, a neurotransmitter that facilitates sleep.

- Relax before bedtime, using dimmer light.

- Sleep on a regular schedule (rise at the same time even after a restless night) and avoid naps. Sticking to a schedule boosts daytime alertness, too, as shown in an experiment in which University of Arizona students averaged 7.5 hours of sleep a night on either a varying or consistent schedule (Manber et al., 1996).

- Hide the clock face so you aren't tempted to check it repeatedly.

- Reassure yourself that a temporary loss of sleep causes no great harm.

- Realize that for any stressed organism, being vigilant is natural and adaptive. A personal conflict during the day often means a fitful sleep that night (Åkerstedt et al., 2007; Brissette & Cohen, 2002). Managing your stress levels will enable more restful sleeping. (See Unit 8B and Appendix C for more on stress.)

- If all else fails, settle for less sleep, either going to bed later or getting up earlier.

Rarer but also more troublesome than insomnia are the sleep disorders *narcolepsy*, *sleep apnea*, *night terrors*, and *sleepwalking*.

Narcolepsy (from *narco*, "numbness," and *lepsy*, "seizure") sufferers experience periodic, overwhelming sleepiness. Attacks usually last less than 5 minutes but sometimes occur at the most inopportune times, perhaps just after taking a terrific swing at a softball or when laughing loudly, shouting angrily, or having sex (Dement, 1978, 1999). In severe cases, the person may collapse directly into a brief period of REM sleep, with its accompanying loss of muscular tension. People with narcolepsy—1 in 2000 of us, estimates the Stanford University Center for Narcolepsy (2002)—must therefore live with extra caution. As a traffic menace, "snoozing is second only to boozing," says the American Sleep Disorders Association, and those with narcolepsy are especially at risk (Aldrich, 1989).

At the twentieth century's end, researchers discovered a gene causing narcolepsy in dogs (Lin et al., 1999; Taheri, 2004). Genes help sculpt the brain, and neuroscientists are searching the brain for abnormalities linked with narcolepsy. One team of researchers discovered a relative absence of a hypothalamic neural center that produces *orexin* (also called hypocretin), a neurotransmitter linked to alertness (Taheri et al., 2002; Thannickal et al., 2000). (That discovery has led to the clinical testing of a new sleeping pill that works by blocking orexin's arousing activity.)

TEACHING TIP

Point out to students that insomnia is not just an inability to fall asleep quickly, but it is also an inability to stay asleep. Patients with insomnia often cannot sleep throughout the night, waking up in the middle of the night and then having trouble falling back asleep.

Narcolepsy, it is now clear, is a brain disease; it is not just "in your mind." And this gives hope that narcolepsy might be effectively relieved by a drug that mimics the missing orexin and can sneak through the blood-brain barrier (Fujiki et al., 2003; Siegel, 2000). In the meantime, physicians are prescribing other drugs to relieve narcolepsy's sleepiness in humans.

Sleep apnea also puts millions of people at increased risk of traffic accidents (Teran-Santos et al., 1999). Although 1 in 20 of us has this disorder, it was unknown before modern sleep research. *Apnea* means "with no breath," and people with this condition intermittently stop breathing during sleep. After an airless minute or so, decreased blood oxygen arouses them and they wake up enough to snort in air for a few seconds, in a process that repeats hundreds of times each night, depriving them of slow-wave sleep. Apart from complaints of sleepiness and irritability during the day—and their mate's complaints about their loud "snoring"—apnea sufferers are often unaware of their disorder. The next morning they have no recall of these episodes, and may just report feeling fatigued and depressed (Peppard et al., 2006).

Sleep apnea is associated with obesity, and as the number of obese people in the United States has increased, so has this disorder, particularly among overweight men, including some football players (Keller, 2007). Anyone who snores at night, feels tired during the day, and possibly has high blood pressure as well (increasing the risk of a stroke or heart attack) should be checked for apnea (Dement, 1999). A physician may prescribe a masklike device with an air pump that keeps the sleeper's airway open and breathing regular. If one doesn't mind looking a little goofy in the dark (imagine a snorkeler at a slumber party), the treatment can effectively treat both the apnea and associated depressed energy and mood.

Unlike sleep apnea, **night terrors** target mostly children, who may sit up or walk around, talk incoherently, experience a doubling of heart and breathing rates, and appear terrified (Hartmann, 1981). They seldom wake up fully during an episode and recall little or nothing the next morning—at most, a fleeting, frightening image. Night terrors are not nightmares (which, like other dreams, typically occur during early morning REM sleep); night terrors usually occur during the first few hours of Stage 4.

Children also are most prone to *sleepwalking*—another Stage 4 sleep disorder—and to *sleeptalking*, conditions that run in families. Finnish twin studies reveal that occasional childhood sleepwalking occurs for about one-third of those with a sleepwalking fraternal twin and half of those with a sleepwalking identical twin. The same is true for sleeptalking (Hublin et al., 1997, 1998). Sleepwalking is usually harmless and unrecalled the next morning. Sleepwalkers typically return to bed on their own or are guided there by a family member. Young children, who have the deepest and lengthiest Stage 4 sleep, are the most likely to experience both night terrors and sleepwalking. As we grow older and deep Stage 4 sleep diminishes, so do night terrors and sleepwalking. After being sleep deprived, people sleep more deeply, which increases any tendency to sleepwalk (Zadra et al., 2008).

Dreams

6: What do we dream?

Now playing at an inner theater near you: the premiere showing of a sleeping person's vivid dream. This never-before-seen mental movie features captivating characters wrapped in a plot so original and unlikely, yet so intricate and so seemingly real, that the viewer later marvels at its creation.

• Imagine observing a person with narcolepsy in medieval times. Might such symptoms (especially the instant dreams from dropping into REM sleep) have seemed like demon possession? •

Archivo Iconografico, S.A./Corbis

Did Brahms need his own lullabies? Cranky, overweight, and nap-prone, Johannes Brahms exhibited common symptoms of sleep apnea (Margolis, 2000). ▲

::**narcolepsy** a sleep disorder characterized by uncontrollable sleep attacks. The sufferer may lapse directly into REM sleep, often at inopportune times.

::**sleep apnea** a sleep disorder characterized by temporary cessations of breathing during sleep and repeated momentary awakenings.

::**night terrors** a sleep disorder characterized by high arousal and an appearance of being terrified; unlike nightmares, night terrors occur during Stage 4 sleep, within two or three hours of falling asleep, and are seldom remembered.

UNIT 5

 TEACHING TIP

Stanley Krippner and his colleagues compared the dreams of more than 400 Argentinean, Brazilian, and American adults:

- Americans tended to dream about animals and food, whereas Brazilians had more sexual and emotional dreams.

- Americans and Argentineans reported more dreams about architecture than Brazilians.

- Argentineans reported more dreams about aggression and good fortune than Brazilians or Americans.

Americans from different parts of the country differed in dream content:

- Northeasterners have dreams with images of time, activity, streets, and architecture.

- Southerners dream of nature, good fortune, emotion, and family members.

- Westerners dream about architecture, objects, negative emotions, and indoor settings.

Krippner found some differences between the genders:

- In the U.S., men were more likely to dream about aggression and tools; women were more likely to dream about children, clothes, food, and friendly interactions.

- There were relatively few gender differences in dreams within the Latin-American sample. Other researchers have found that Mexican women's dreams are significantly more emotional than men's.

At this point, you may want to use **Student Project: Remembering Night Dreams** (p. 12) from Bolt's Teacher's Resource Binder.

Waking from a troubling dream, wrenched by its emotions, who among us has not wondered about this weird state of consciousness? How can our brain so creatively, colorfully, and completely construct this alternative, conscious world? In the shadowland between our dreaming and waking consciousness, we may even wonder for a moment which is real.

Discovering the link between REM sleep and dreaming opened a new era in dream research. Instead of relying on someone's hazy recall hours or days after having a dream, researchers could catch dreams as they happened. They could awaken people during or within 3 minutes after a REM sleep period and hear a vivid account.

What We Dream

REM **dreams**—"hallucinations of the sleeping mind" (Loftus & Ketcham, 1994, p. 67)—are vivid, emotional, and bizarre. They are unlike daydreams, which tend to involve the familiar details of our life—perhaps picturing ourselves explaining to a teacher why a paper will be late, or replaying in our mind personal encounters we relish or regret. The dreams of REM sleep are so vivid we may confuse them with reality. Awakening from a nightmare, a 4-year-old may be sure there is a bear in the house.

We spend six years of our life in dreams, many of which are anything but sweet. For both women and men, 8 in 10 dreams are marked by at least one negative event or emotion (Domhoff, 2007). People commonly dream of repeatedly failing in an attempt to do something; of being attacked, pursued, or rejected; or of experiencing misfortune (Hall et al., 1982). Dreams with sexual imagery occur less often than you might think. In one study, only 1 dream in 10 among young men and 1 in 30 among young women had sexual overtones (Domhoff, 1996). More commonly, the story line of our dreams—what Sigmund Freud called their **manifest content**—incorporates traces of previous days' nonsexual experiences and preoccupations (De Koninck, 2000):

- After suffering a trauma, people commonly report nightmares (Levin & Nielsen, 2007). One sample of Americans who were recording their dreams during September 2001 reported an increase in threatening dreams following the 9/11 attack (Propper et al., 2007).

- After playing a computer game for seven hours and then being awakened repeatedly during their first hour of sleep, 3 in 4 people reported experiencing images of the game (Stickgold et al., 2000).

- People in hunter-gatherer societies often dream of animals; urban Japanese rarely do (Mestel, 1997).

- Compared with nonmusicians, musicians report twice as many dreams of music (Uga et al., 2006).

Sensory stimuli in our sleeping environment may also intrude. A particular odor or the telephone's ringing may be instantly and ingeniously woven into the dream story. In a classic experiment, William Dement and Edward Wolpert (1958) lightly sprayed cold water on dreamers' faces. Compared with sleepers who did not get the cold-water treatment, these people were more likely to dream about a waterfall, a leaky roof, or even about being sprayed by someone. Even while in REM sleep, focused on internal stimuli, we maintain some awareness of changes in our external environment.

So, could we learn a foreign language by hearing it played while we sleep? If only it were so easy. While sleeping we can learn to associate a sound with a mild electric shock (and to react to the sound accordingly). But we do not remember recorded information played while we are soundly asleep (Eich, 1990; Wyatt & Bootzin, 1994). In fact, anything that happens during the 5 minutes just before we fall asleep

> "I do not believe that I am now dreaming, but I cannot prove that I am not."
> Philosopher Bertrand Russell (1872–1970)

> • Would you suppose that people dream if blind from birth? Studies of blind people in France, Hungary, Egypt, and the United States all found them dreaming of using their nonvisual senses—hearing, touching, smelling, tasting (Buquet, 1988; Taha, 1972; Vekassy, 1977). •

> "For what one has dwelt on by day, these things are seen in visions of the night."
> Menander of Athens
> (342–292 B.C.E.), *Fragments*

> "Follow your dreams, except for that one where you're naked at work."
> Attributed to Henny Youngman

 TEACHING TIP

Point out to students that Freud's theory of dreams had two parts, which are discussed separately in this unit. Freud called the plot of the dream the manifest content, and he also had a name for the symbolic meaning of dreams—latent content. This hidden content of dreams was supposed to reflect our unconscious thoughts and desires, which Freud theorized were often too difficult to deal with while we were awake. Freud believed that dreams were the "royal road" to the unconscious, shedding light on these forbidden thoughts and feelings we kept hidden from ourselves and the world.

is typically lost from memory (Roth et al., 1988). This explains why sleep apnea patients, who repeatedly awaken with a gasp and then immediately fall back to sleep, do not recall the episodes. It also explains why dreams that momentarily awaken us are mostly forgotten by morning. To remember a dream, get up and stay awake for a few minutes.

MAXINE

www.maxine.net —© 2001 Marian Henley— mkhenley@prodigy.net

Why We Dream

7: What is the function of dreams?

Dream theorists have proposed several explanations of why we dream, including these:

To satisfy our own wishes. In 1900, in his landmark book *The Interpretation of Dreams,* Freud offered what he thought was "the most valuable of all the discoveries it has been my good fortune to make": Dreams provide a psychic safety valve that discharges otherwise unacceptable feelings. According to Freud, a dream's *manifest* (apparent) *content* is a censored, symbolic version of its **latent content,** which consists of unconscious drives and wishes that would be threatening if expressed directly. Although most dreams have no overt sexual imagery, Freud nevertheless believed that most adult dreams can be "traced back by analysis to erotic wishes." Thus, a gun might be a disguised representation of a penis.

Freud considered dreams the key to understanding our inner conflicts. However, his critics say it is time to wake up from Freud's dream theory, which is a scientific nightmare. Based on the accumulated science, "there is no reason to believe any of Freud's specific claims about dreams and their purposes," notes dream researcher William Domhoff (2003). Some contend that even if dreams are symbolic, they could be interpreted any way one wished. Others maintain that dreams hide nothing. A dream about a gun is a dream about a gun. Legend has it that even Freud, who loved to smoke cigars, acknowledged that "sometimes, a cigar is just a cigar." Freud's wish-fulfillment theory of dreams has in large part given way to other theories.

To file away memories. Researchers who see dreams as *information processing* believe that dreams may help sift, sort, and fix the day's experiences in our memory. As we noted earlier, people tested the next day generally improve on a learned task after a night of memory consolidation. Even after two nights of recovery sleep, those who have been deprived of both slow-wave and REM sleep don't do as well as those who sleep undisturbed on their new learning (Stickgold et al., 2000, 2001). People who hear unusual phrases or learn to find hidden visual images before bedtime remember

 A popular sleep myth: If you dream you are falling and hit the ground (or if you dream of dying), you die. (Unfortunately, those who could confirm these ideas are not around to do so. Some people, however, have had such dreams and are alive to report them.) •

> "When people interpret [a dream] as if it were meaningful and then sell those interpretations, it's quackery."
> Sleep researcher J. Allan Hobson (1995)

::**dream** a sequence of images, emotions, and thoughts passing through a sleeping person's mind. Dreams are notable for their hallucinatory imagery, discontinuities, and incongruities, and for the dreamer's delusional acceptance of the content and later difficulties remembering it.

::**manifest content** according to Freud, the remembered story line of a dream (as distinct from its latent, or hidden, content).

::**latent content** according to Freud, the underlying meaning of a dream (as distinct from its manifest content).

TEACHING TIP

The activation-synthesis theory of dreams, discussed in this section of the unit, helps explain why dreams tend to be random and bizarre. Without external stimulation and information to help organize the signals fired from neurons, the brain does its best to make sense of the signals. The brain puts the signals together into a story. Often, the stories it puts together don't make much sense to the waking mind.

CRITICAL THINKING

Students are fascinated by dream analysis. Popularized by Sigmund Freud as being the key to understanding our unconscious thoughts, dream analysis is still used by some psychoanalysts to help clients understand the causes of their current life problems. Typically, however, these professionals leave most of the interpretation up to the client, forgoing the practice of imposing symbolic interpretation on the patient. Most dream interpretation books on the market today are not based on scientific testing and shouldn't be used as evaluation tools.

 TEACHING TIP

At this point, you may want to use **Student Project:** *Dreaming and Problem Solving* (p. 13) from Bolt's Teacher's Resource Binder.

UNIT 5

RESEARCH

Have students correlate GPA with hours of sleep to try to replicate the findings of the Wolfson and Carskadon study. Have students hypothesize reasons why those with higher GPAs may get more sleep than those with lower GPAs. Have students share their experiences with sleep and academic achievement.

CRITICAL THINKING

Does the sleep bulimia as described by Robert Stickgold occur with your students? Have students discuss whether they use the weekend to play catch up on their sleep or whether they become night owls during the weekend, staying up extremely late participating in social activities. Have them discuss the effect of this erratic sleep behavior on their daily performance.

INTERCONNECTING

Point out to students how sleep differences occur in a developmental pattern, with infants spending up to 16 hours a day sleeping. Older adults actually sleep about 1 hour less a night than their younger counterparts. Unit 9 describes this in more detail, but students should be aware of the developmental differences in sleep patterns.

° Rapid eye movements also stir the liquid behind the cornea; this delivers fresh oxygen to corneal cells, preventing their suffocation °

➤ **FIGURE 5.8**

Sleep across the life span As we age, our sleep patterns change. During our first few months, we spend progressively less time in REM sleep. During our first 20 years, we spend progressively less time asleep. (Adapted from Snyder & Scott, 1972.)

less the next morning if awakened every time they begin REM sleep than they do if awakened during other sleep stages (Empson & Clarke, 1970; Karni & Sagi, 1994).

Brain scans confirm the link between REM sleep and memory. The brain regions that buzz as rats learn to navigate a maze, or as people learn to perform a visual-discrimination task, buzz again during later REM sleep (Louie & Wilson, 2001; Maquet, 2001). So precise are these activity patterns that scientists can tell where in the maze the rat would be if awake.

Some researchers are unpersuaded by these studies (Siegel, 2001; Vertes & Siegel, 2005). They note that memory consolidation may occur independent of dreaming, including during NREM sleep. But this much seems true: A night of solid sleep (and dreaming) has an important place in our lives. To sleep, perchance to remember. This is important news for students, many of whom, researcher Robert Stickgold (2000) believes, suffer from a kind of sleep bulimia—binge-sleeping on the weekend. "If you don't get good sleep and enough sleep after you learn new stuff, you won't integrate it effectively into your memories," he warns. That helps explain why high school students with high grades average 25 minutes more sleep a night and go to bed 40 minutes earlier than their lower-achieving classmates (Wolfson & Carskadon, 1998).

To develop and preserve neural pathways. Some researchers speculate that dreams may also serve a *physiological* function. Perhaps the brain activity associated with REM sleep provides the sleeping brain with periodic stimulation. This theory makes developmental sense. As you will see in Unit 9, stimulating experiences develop and preserve the brain's neural pathways. Infants, whose neural networks are fast developing, spend much of their abundant sleep time in REM sleep (**FIGURE 5.8**).

To make sense of neural static. Other theories propose that dreams erupt from neural activity spreading upward from the brainstem (Antrobus, 1991; Hobson, 2003, 2004). According to one version—the *activation-synthesis* theory—this neural activity is random, and dreams are the brain's attempt to make sense of it. Much as a neurosurgeon can produce hallucinations by stimulating different parts of a patient's cortex, so can stimulation originating within the brain. These internal stimuli activate brain areas that process visual images, but not the visual cortex area, which receives raw input from the eyes. As Freud might have expected, PET scans of sleeping people also reveal increased activity in the emotion-related limbic system (in the amygdala) during REM sleep. In contrast, frontal lobe regions responsible for inhibition and logical thinking seem to idle, which may explain why our dreams are less inhibited than we are (Maquet et al., 1996). Add the limbic system's emotional tone to the brain's visual bursts and—Voila!—we dream. Damage either the limbic system or the visual centers active during dreaming, and dreaming itself may be impaired (Domhoff, 2003).

To reflect cognitive development. Some dream researchers dispute both the Freudian and activation-synthesis theories, preferring instead to see dreams as part of brain maturation and cognitive development (Domhoff, 2003; Foulkes, 1999). For example, prior to age 9, children's dreams seem more like a slide show and less like an active story in which the dreamer is an actor. Dreams overlap with waking cognition and feature coherent speech. They draw on our concepts and knowledge. TABLE 5.2 compares major dream theories.

 Question: Does eating spicy foods cause one to dream more? *Answer:* Any food that causes you to awaken more increases your chance of recalling a dream (Moorcroft, 2003).

TABLE 5.2

DREAM THEORIES

Theory	Explanation	Critical Considerations
Freud's wish-fulfillment	Dreams provide a "psychic safety valve"—expressing otherwise unacceptable feelings; contain manifest (remembered) content and a deeper layer of latent content—a hidden meaning.	Lacks any scientific support; dreams may be interpreted in many different ways.
Information-processing	Dreams help us sort out the day's events and consolidate our memories.	But why do we sometimes dream about things we have not experienced?
Physiological function	Regular brain stimulation from REM sleep may help develop and preserve neural pathways.	This may be true, but it does not explain why we experience *meaningful* dreams.
Activation-synthesis	REM sleep triggers neural activity that evokes random visual memories, which our sleeping brain weaves into stories.	The individual's brain is weaving the stories, which still tells us something about the dreamer.
Cognitive development	Dream content reflects dreamers' cognitive development—their knowledge and understanding.	Does not address the neuroscience of dreams.

Although sleep researchers debate dreams' function—and some are skeptical that dreams serve any function—there is one thing they agree on: We need REM sleep. Deprived of it by repeatedly being awakened, people return more and more quickly to the REM stage after falling back to sleep. When finally allowed to sleep undisturbed, they literally sleep like babies—with increased REM sleep, a phenomenon called **REM rebound.** Withdrawing REM-suppressing sleeping medications also increases REM sleep, but with accompanying nightmares.

Most other mammals also experience REM rebound, suggesting that the causes and functions of REM sleep are deeply biological. That REM sleep occurs in mammals—and not in animals such as fish, whose behavior is less influenced by learning—also fits the information-processing theory of dreams.

So does this mean that because dreams serve physiological functions and extend normal cognition, they are psychologically meaningless? Not necessarily. Every psychologically meaningful experience involves an active brain. We are once again reminded of a basic principle: *Biological and psychological explanations of behavior are partners, not competitors.* Dreams may be akin to abstract art—open to more than one meaningful interpretation.

Dreams are a fascinating altered state of consciousness. But they are not the only altered states. Hypnosis and drugs can also alter conscious awareness.

::**REM rebound** the tendency for REM sleep to increase following REM sleep deprivation (created by repeated awakenings during REM sleep).

TEACHING TIP

What do contemporary research-ers believe about hypnosis? Students can browse the Society for Psychological Hypnosis's Web site www.apa.org/divisions/div30/

CRITICAL THINKING

Stage hypnotists make ready use of our openness to sugges-tion when they announce to their audience that they will begin to experience itching sensations on various parts of their body . . . on their head . . . arms . . . back . . . legs. To underscore the sugges-tion, the performer may casually but not obtrusively scratch himself. Before long, many in the audience follow suit.

BEFORE YOU MOVE ON . . .

> ➤ **ASK YOURSELF**

In some countries, such as Britain, the school day for teenagers runs from about 9:00 A.M. to 4:00 P.M. In other countries, such as the United States, the teen school day often runs from 8:00 A.M. to 3:00 P.M., or even 7:00 A.M. to 2:00 P.M. Early to rise isn't making kids wise, say critics—it's making them sleepy. For optimal alertness and well-being, teens need 8 to 9 hours of sleep a night. So, should early-start schools move to a later start time, even if it requires buying more buses or switching start times with elementary schools? Or is this impractical, and would it do little to remedy the tired-teen problem?

> ➤ **TEST YOURSELF 1**

Are you getting enough sleep? What might you ask yourself to answer this question?

Answers to the Test Yourself questions can be found in Appendix E at the end of the book.

Hypnosis

8: What is hypnosis, and what powers does a hypnotist have over a hypnotized subject?

IMAGINE YOU ARE ABOUT TO BE hypnotized. The hypnotist invites you to sit back, fix your gaze on a spot high on the wall, and relax. In a quiet voice the hypnotist sug-gests, "Your eyes are growing tired . . . Your eyelids are becoming heavy . . . now heavier and heavier . . . They are beginning to close . . . You are becoming more deeply relaxed . . . Your breathing is now deep and regular . . . Your muscles are becoming more and more relaxed. Your whole body is beginning to feel like lead."

After a few minutes of this *hypnotic induction,* you may experience **hypnosis.** When the hypnotist suggests, "Your eyelids are shutting so tight that you cannot open them even if you try," it may indeed seem beyond your control to open your eyelids. Told to forget the number 6, you may be puzzled when you count 11 fingers on your hands. Invited to smell a sensuous perfume that is actually ammonia, you may linger delight-edly over its pungent odor. Told that you cannot see a certain object, such as a chair, you may indeed report that it is not there, although you manage to avoid the chair when walking around (illustrating once again that two-track mind of yours).

But is hypnosis really an *altered* state of consciousness? Let's start with some agreed-upon facts.

Facts and Falsehoods

Those who study hypnosis have agreed that its power resides not in the hypnotist but in the subject's openness to suggestion (Bowers, 1984). Hypnotists have no magical mind-control power; they merely engage people's ability to focus on certain images or behaviors. But how open to suggestions are we?

Can Anyone Experience Hypnosis?

To some extent, we are all open to suggestion. When people stand upright with their eyes closed and are told that they are swaying back and forth, most will indeed sway a little. In fact, *postural sway* is one of the items assessed on the Stanford Hypnotic Sus-ceptibility Scale. People who respond to such suggestions without hypnosis are the same people who respond with hypnosis (Kirsch & Braffman, 2001).

::**hypnosis** a social interaction in which one person (the hypnotist) suggests to another (the subject) that certain per-ceptions, feelings, thoughts, or behav-iors will spontaneously occur.

TEACHING TIP

At this point, you may want to use any of the following exercises: **Classroom Exercises:** *Attitudes Toward Hypnosis Scale* (p. 14*); Hypnosis as Heightened Suggestibility* (p. 14*); The Creative Imagination Scale* (p. 15*); Hypnosis—A Stage Demonstration* (p. 16) from Bolt's Teacher's Resource Binder.

After giving a brief hypnotic induction, a hypnotist suggests a series of experiences ranging from easy (your outstretched arms will move together) to difficult (with eyes open, you will see a nonexistent person). Highly hypnotizable people—say, the 20 percent who can carry out a suggestion not to smell or react to a bottle of ammonia held under their nose—are those who easily become deeply absorbed in imaginative activities (Barnier & McConkey, 2004; Silva & Kirsch, 1992). Typically, they have rich fantasy lives and become absorbed in the imaginary events of a novel or movie. (Perhaps you can recall being riveted by a movie into a trancelike state, oblivious to the people or noise surrounding you.) Many researchers refer to hypnotic "susceptibility" as hypnotic *ability*—the ability to focus attention totally on a task, to become imaginatively absorbed in it, to entertain fanciful possibilities.

Indeed, anyone who can turn attention inward and imagine is able to experience some degree of hypnosis—because that's what hypnosis is. And virtually anyone will experience hypnotic responsiveness if led to *expect* it. Imagine being asked to stare at a high spot and then hearing that "your eyes are growing tired . . . your eyelids are becoming heavy." With such strain, anyone's eyes would get tired. (Try looking up for 30 seconds.) But you likely would attribute your heavy eyelids to the hypnotist's abilities and then become more open to other suggestions.

Can Hypnosis Enhance Recall of Forgotten Events?

Can hypnotic procedures enable people to recall kindergarten classmates? To retrieve forgotten or suppressed details of a crime? Should testimony obtained under hypnosis be admissible in court?

Most people believe (wrongly, as Unit 7A will explain) that our experiences are all "in there," recorded in our brain and available for recall if only we can break through our own defenses (Loftus, 1980). In one community survey, 3 in 4 people agreed with the inaccurate statement that hypnosis enables people to "recover accurate memories as far back as birth" (Johnson & Hauck, 1999). But 60 years of research disputes such claims of age regression—the supposed ability to relive childhood experiences. Age-regressed people act as they believe children would, but they typically miss the mark by outperforming real children of the specified age (Silverman & Retzlaff, 1986). They may, for example, feel childlike and print much as they know a 6-year-old would. But they sometimes do so with perfect spelling and typically without any change in their adult brain waves, reflexes, and perceptions.

"Hypnotically refreshed" memories combine fact with fiction. Without either person being aware of what is going on, a hypnotist's hints—"Did you hear loud noises?"—can plant ideas that become the subject's pseudomemory. Thus, American, Australian, and British courts generally ban testimony from witnesses who have been hypnotized (Druckman & Bjork, 1994; Gibson, 1995; McConkey, 1995).

Other striking examples of memories created under hypnosis come from the thousands of people who since 1980 have reported being abducted by UFOs. Most such reports have come from people who are predisposed to believe in aliens, are highly hypnotizable, and have undergone hypnosis (Newman & Baumeister, 1996; Nickell, 1996).

Can Hypnosis Force People to Act Against Their Will?

Researchers have induced hypnotized people to perform an apparently dangerous act: plunging one hand briefly into fuming "acid," then throwing the "acid" in a researcher's face (Orne & Evans, 1965). Interviewed a day later, these people exhibited no memory of their acts and emphatically denied they would ever follow such orders.

Had hypnosis given the hypnotist a special power to control others against their will? To find out, researchers Martin Orne and Frederich Evans unleashed

> "Hypnosis is not a psychological truth serum and to regard it as such has been a source of considerable mischief."
>
> Researcher Kenneth Bowers (1987)

• See Unit 7A for a more detailed discussion of how people may construct false memories. •

TEACHING TIP

Irving Kirsch and Steven Jay Lynn provide an excellent review of the literature on hypnosis, including the question of whether hypnosis produces an out-of-the-ordinary, trancelike, "altered" state of consciousness. Research indicates the following:

- The ability to be hypnotized does not indicate gullibility or weakness.

- Participants retain the ability to control their behavior during hypnosis.

- Spontaneous posthypnotic amnesia is relatively rare.

- Hypnosis is not a dangerous procedure when practiced by qualified researchers and clinicians.

- Hypnosis does not increase the accuracy of memory.

- Hypnosis does not foster a literal re-experiencing of childhood events.

Kirsch, I., & Lynn, S. J. (1995). The altered state of hypnosis: Changes in the theoretical landscape. *American Psychologist, 50,* 846–858.

> "It wasn't what I expected. But facts are facts, and if one is proved to be wrong, one must just be humble about it and start again."
> Agatha Christie's Miss Marple

::**posthypnotic suggestion** a suggestion, made during a hypnosis session, to be carried out after the subject is no longer hypnotized; used by some clinicians to help control undesired symptoms and behaviors.

::**dissociation** a split in consciousness, which allows some thoughts and behaviors to occur simultaneously with others.

that enemy of so many illusory beliefs—the control group. Orne asked other individuals to *pretend* they were hypnotized. Laboratory assistants, unaware that those in the experiment's control group had not been hypnotized, treated both groups the same. The result? All the *un*hypnotized participants (perhaps believing that the laboratory context assured safety) performed the same acts as those who were hypnotized.

Such studies illustrate a principle that Unit 14 emphasizes: An authoritative person in a legitimate context can induce people—hypnotized or not—to perform some unlikely acts. Hypnosis researcher Nicholas Spanos (1982) put it directly: "The overt behaviors of hypnotic subjects are well within normal limits."

Can Hypnosis Be Therapeutic?

Hypnotherapists try to help patients harness their own healing powers (Baker, 1987). **Posthypnotic suggestions** have helped alleviate headaches, asthma, and stress-related skin disorders. One woman, who for more than 20 years suffered from open sores all over her body, was asked to imagine herself swimming in shimmering, sunlit liquids that would cleanse her skin, and to experience her skin as smooth and unblemished. Within three months her sores had disappeared (Bowers, 1984).

In one statistical digest of 18 studies, the average client whose therapy was supplemented with hypnosis showed greater improvement than 70 percent of other therapy patients (Kirsch et al., 1995, 1996). Hypnosis seemed especially helpful for the treatment of obesity. However, drug, alcohol, and smoking addictions have not responded well to hypnosis (Nash, 2001). In controlled studies, hypnosis speeds the disappearance of warts, but so do the same positive suggestions given without hypnosis (Spanos, 1991, 1996).

Can Hypnosis Alleviate Pain?

Yes, hypnosis *can* relieve pain (Druckman & Bjork, 1994; Patterson, 2004). When unhypnotized people put their arm in an ice bath, they feel intense pain within 25 seconds. When hypnotized people do the same after being given suggestions to feel no pain, they indeed report feeling little pain. As some dentists know, even light hypnosis can reduce fear, thus reducing hypersensitivity to pain.

Nearly 10 percent of us can become so deeply hypnotized that we can even undergo major surgery without anesthesia. Half of us can gain at least some pain relief from hypnosis. In surgical experiments, hypnotized patients have required less medication, recovered sooner, and left the hospital earlier than unhypnotized controls, thanks to the inhibition of pain-related brain activity (Askay & Patterson, 2007; Spiegel, 2007). The surgical use of hypnosis has flourished in Europe, where one Belgian medical team has performed more than 5000 surgeries with a combination of hypnosis, local anesthesia, and a mild sedative (Song, 2006).

Explaining the Hypnotized State

9: Is hypnosis an extension of normal consciousness or an altered state?

We have seen that hypnosis involves heightened suggestibility. We have also seen that hypnotic procedures do not endow a person with special powers. But they can sometimes help people overcome stress-related ailments and cope with pain. So, just what *is* hypnosis? And is hypnosis an *altered* state of consciousness?

INTERCONNECTING

Link the concept of lost or hidden memories with Freudian theory. Sigmund Freud developed the idea that people repress difficult experiences from childhood in the subconscious or unconscious, which must be brought to the consciousness so they do not interfere with adult life. Hypnosis and dream interpretation were two ways Freud believed these experiences and memories could be revealed.

Hypnosis as a Social Phenomenon

Some researchers believe that hypnotic phenomena reflect the workings of normal consciousness and the power of social influence (Lynn et al., 1990; Spanos & Coe, 1992). They point out how powerfully our interpretations and attentional spotlight influence our ordinary perceptions.

Does this mean that people are consciously faking hypnosis? No—like actors caught up in their roles, subjects begin to feel and behave in ways appropriate for "good hypnotic subjects." The more they like and trust the hypnotist, the more they allow that person to direct their attention and fantasies (Gfeller et al., 1987). "The hypnotist's ideas become the subject's thoughts," explained Theodore Barber (2000), "and the subject's thoughts produce the hypnotic experiences and behaviors." If told to scratch their ear later when they hear the word *psychology*, subjects will likely do so only if they think the experiment is still under way (and scratching is therefore expected). If an experimenter eliminates their motivation for acting hypnotized—by stating that hypnosis reveals their "gullibility"—subjects become unresponsive.

Based on such findings, advocates of the *social influence theory* contend that hypnotic phenomena—like the behaviors associated with other supposed altered states, such as dissociative identity disorder (Unit 12) and spirit or demon possession—are an extension of everyday social behavior, not something unique to hypnosis (Spanos, 1994, 1996).

Hypnosis as Divided Consciousness

Most hypnosis researchers grant that normal social and cognitive processes play a part in hypnosis, but they nevertheless believe hypnosis is more than inducing someone to play the role of "good subject." For one thing, hypnotized subjects will sometimes carry out suggested behaviors on cue, even when they believe no one is watching (Perugini et al., 1998). Moreover, distinctive brain activity accompanies hypnosis. When deeply hypnotized people in one experiment were asked to imagine a color, areas of their brain lit up as if they were really seeing the color. Mere imagination had become—to the hypnotized person's brain—a compelling hallucination (Kosslyn et al., 2000). Another experiment invited hypnotizable or nonhypnotizable people to say the color of letters—an easy task that slows if, say, green letters form the conflicting word RED (Raz et al., 2005). When given a suggestion to focus on the color and to perceive the letters as irrelevant gibberish, easily hypnotized people became much less slowed by the word-color conflict. (Brain areas that decode words and detect conflict remained inactive.)

These results would not have surprised famed researcher Ernest Hilgard (1986, 1992), who believed hypnosis involves not only social influence but also a special state of **dissociation**—a split between different levels of consciousness. Hilgard viewed hypnotic dissociation as a vivid form of everyday mind splits—similar to doodling while listening to a teacher or keying in the end of a sentence while starting a conversation. Hilgard felt that when, for example, hypnotized people lower their arm into an ice bath, as in **FIGURE 5.9**, hypnosis dissociates the sensation of the pain stimulus (of which the

Attention is diverted from a painful ice bath. How?

Divided-consciousness theory:
Hypnosis has caused a split in awareness.

Social influence theory:
The subject is so caught up in the hypnotized role that she ignores the cold.

Courtesy of News and Publications Service, Stanford University

➤ **FIGURE 5.9**

Dissociation or role-playing? This hypnotized woman tested by Ernest Hilgard exhibited no pain when her arm was placed in an ice bath. But asked to press a key if some part of her felt the pain, she did so. To Hilgard, this was evidence of dissociation, or divided consciousness. Proponents of social influence theory, however, maintain that people responding this way are caught up in playing the role of "good subject."

RESEARCH

Divide students into groups and have them research how hypnosis is portrayed in different types of movies and television shows. If possible, have them bring in clips to demonstrate their conclusions.

- How do legal shows and movies portray hypnosis?

- How do comedic and cartoon shows and movies portray hypnosis?

- Do either type of media cite the drawbacks or limitations of hypnosis? What claims are made about what hypnosis is capable of providing?

INTERCONNECTING

What other explanations can students come up with to explain hypnotic behavior? Have students research the following social psychology concepts related to the social influence theory. They should apply their research by explaining orally or in writing how these concepts reinforce the social influence theory:

- Conformity

- Peer pressure

- Groupthink

- Social desirability

At this point, you may want to use **Lecture/Discussion Topic: *Is Hypnosis an Altered State of Consciousness?*** (p. 17) from Bolt's Teacher's Resource Binder.

DEMO

Tell your students to close their eyes and imagine they are cutting a lemon . . . a large . . . sour . . . bitter lemon . . . so full of juice that it drips over their fingers onto the floor. Imagine now sucking the juice from the same fruit.

- What's happening? Are they salivating? Why or why not?

- How does this demonstration mimic hypnotic suggestion?

- What about this demonstration was particularly vivid?

UNIT 5

➤ **FIGURE 5.10**
Levels of analysis for hypnosis Using a biopsychosocial approach, researchers explore hypnosis from complementary perspectives.

Biological influences:
• distinctive brain activity
• unconscious information processing

Psychological influences:
• focused attention
• expectations
• heightened suggestibility
• dissociation between normal sensations and conscious awareness

Hypnosis

Social-cultural influences:
• presence of an authoritative person in legitimate context
• role-playing "good subject"

subjects are still aware) from the emotional suffering that defines their experience of pain. The ice water therefore feels cold—very cold—but not painful.

Hypnotic pain relief may also result from another form of dual processing we've discussed—*selective attention*—as when an injured athlete, caught up in the competition, feels little or no pain until the game ends. Support for this view comes from PET scans showing that hypnosis reduces brain activity in a region that processes painful stimuli, but not in the sensory cortex, which receives the raw sensory input (Rainville et al., 1997). Hypnosis does not block sensory input, but it may block our *attention* to those stimuli.

Although the divided-consciousness theory of hypnosis is controversial, this much seems clear: There is, without doubt, much more to thinking and acting than we are conscious of. Our information processing, which starts with selective attention, is divided into simultaneous conscious and nonconscious realms. In hypnosis as in life, *much of our behavior occurs on autopilot.* We have two-track minds.

Yet, there is also little doubt that social influences do play an important role in hypnosis. So, might the two views—social influence and divided consciousness—be bridged? Researchers John Kihlstrom and Kevin McConkey (1990) believe there is no contradiction between the two approaches, which are converging toward a *unified account of hypnosis.* Hypnosis, they suggest, is an extension *both* of normal principles of social influence *and* of everyday dissociations between our conscious awareness and our automatic behaviors. Hypnosis researchers are moving beyond the "hypnosis is social influence" *versus* "hypnosis is divided consciousness" debate (Killeen & Nash, 2003; Woody & McConkey, 2003). They are instead exploring how brain activity, attention, and social influences interact to affect hypnotic phenomena (**FIGURE 5.10**).

RESEARCH

Some obstetricians have begun teaching their pregnant patients to self-hypnotize so they can use hypnosis to alleviate the pain of labor. Some doctors and patients report that there are no feelings of pain, even without the use of drugs. Research the extent of the use of self-hypnosis for women going through labor.

- What techniques are important for being successful with self-hypnosis?

- Are the results just as likely to occur with relaxation techniques? Why or why not?

- How popular is the technique? Have there been any studies on its effectiveness?

- Are there concerns about the use of drugs during labor that would prompt people to choose hypnosis over drugs?

- Are there dangers with self-hypnosis? How does one come out of it? Are there liability issues or ethical obligations for doctors who advocate this practice?

TEACHING TIP

Ernest Hilgard is considered to be one of the most influential psychologists of the 20th century. After joining the faculty at Stanford in 1933, he pursued many interests, one of which was hypnosis. Hypnosis was viewed as largely the tool of magicians and quacks, but Hilgard's scientific studies of the phenomenon helped shed light on why it worked for some people and what applications were beneficial. He developed the Stanford Hypnotic Suggestibility Scale, which helped to standardize the study of hypnosis.

"The total possible consciousness may be split into parts which co-exist but mutually ignore each other."
William James, *Principles of Psychology*, 1890

::**psychoactive drug** a chemical substance that alters perceptions and moods.

::**tolerance** the diminishing effect with regular use of the same dose of a drug, requiring the user to take larger and larger doses before experiencing the drug's effect.

::**withdrawal** the discomfort and distress that follow discontinuing the use of an addictive drug.

::**physical dependence** a physiological need for a drug, marked by unpleasant withdrawal symptoms when the drug is discontinued.

::**psychological dependence** a psychological need to use a drug, such as to relieve negative emotions.

::**addiction** compulsive drug craving and use, despite adverse consequences.

BEFORE YOU MOVE ON . . .

➤ **ASK YOURSELF**

You've read about two examples of dissociated consciousness: talking while texting, and thinking about something else while reading a child a bedtime story. Can you think of another example that you have experienced?

➤ **TEST YOURSELF 2**

When is the use of hypnosis potentially harmful, and when can hypnosis be used to help?

Answers to the Test Yourself questions can be found in Appendix E at the end of the book.

INTERCONNECTING

The problems of hypnotic suggestion have called into question the diagnosis of dissociative identity disorder, formerly known as multiple personality disorder. Have students research the criticism against DID as a legitimate psychological disorder:

- Why has DID come into question in recent years?

- What are some arguments for and against its legitimacy?

- What role does hypnosis play in this debate?

- What position has the American Psychiatric Association taken on this disorder? Is it still included in the current version of DSM? Are there plans to remove it from the manual?

Drugs and Consciousness

THERE IS CONTROVERSY ABOUT WHETHER hypnosis uniquely alters consciousness, but there is little dispute that some drugs do. **Psychoactive drugs** are chemicals that change perceptions and moods through their actions at the neural synapses (see Unit 3A). Let's imagine a day in the life of a legal-drug user. It begins with a wake-up latte. By midday, several cigarettes have calmed frazzled nerves before an appointment at the plastic surgeon's office for wrinkle-smoothing Botox injections. A diet pill before dinner helps stem the appetite, and its stimulating effects can later be partially offset with a glass of wine and two Tylenol PMs. And if performance needs enhancing, there are beta blockers for onstage performers, Viagra for middle-aged men, hormone-delivering "libido patches" for middle-aged women, and Adderall for students hoping to focus their concentration. Before drifting off into REM-depressed sleep, our hypothetical drug user is dismayed by news reports of pill-sharing, pill-popping college students and of celebrity deaths attributed to accidental overdoses of lethal drug combinations.

Dependence and Addiction

10: What are tolerance, dependence, and addiction, and what are some common misconceptions about addiction?

Why might a person who rarely drinks alcohol get tipsy on one can of beer, but a heavy drinker show few effects until the second six-pack? Continued use of alcohol and other psychoactive drugs produces **tolerance.** As the user's brain adapts its chemistry to offset the drug effect (a process called *neuroadaptation*), the user requires larger and larger doses to experience the same effect (**FIGURE 5.11**). Despite the connotations of alcohol "tolerance," the brain, heart, and liver of a person addicted to alcohol suffer damage from the excessive alcohol being "tolerated."

Users who stop taking psychoactive drugs may experience the undesirable side effects of **withdrawal.** As the body responds to the drug's absence, the user may feel physical pain and intense cravings, indicating **physical dependence.** People can also develop **psychological dependence,** particularly for stress-relieving drugs. Such drugs, although not physically addictive, can become an important part of the user's life, often as a way of relieving negative emotions. With either physical or psychological dependence, the user's primary focus may be obtaining and using the drug.

Misconceptions About Addiction

An **addiction** is a compulsive craving for a substance despite adverse consequences and often with physical symptoms such as aches, nausea, and distress following sudden withdrawal. Worldwide, reports the World Health Organization (2008), 90 million people suffer from such problems related to alcohol and other drugs.

In recent pop psychology, the supposedly irresistible seduction of addiction has been extended to cover many behaviors formerly considered bad habits or even sins. Has the concept been stretched too far? Are addictions as irresistible as commonly believed? Many drug researchers argue that the following three common beliefs about addiction are *myths:*

"Just tell me where you kids got the idea to take so many drugs."

➤ **FIGURE 5.11**

Drug tolerance With repeated exposure to a psychoactive drug, the drug's effect lessens. Thus, it takes bigger doses to get the desired effect.

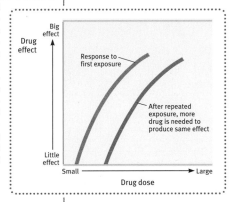

The odds of getting hooked after trying various drugs:

Marijuana	9%
Alcohol	15%
Heroin	23%
Tobacco	32%

Source: National Academy of Science, Institute of Medicine (Brody, 2003).

INTERCONNECTING

Drugs can have such an effect on the body because they are chemically similar to the brain's natural neurotransmitters. Some commonly known drugs and the neurotransmitters they are similar to are as follows:

- Cocaine is chemically similar to dopamine.
- LSD is chemically similar to serotonin.
- Opiates are chemically similar to endorphins. Even the name *endorphins* is a combination of the NT's technical name *endogenous morphines. Endogenous* means "naturally occurring."

UNIT 5

Battling student misconceptions can be difficult because beliefs tend to persist even in the face of disconfirming evidence. Student beliefs about drug use and addiction can be powerfully persistent since their popular culture often seems to validate these myths. Use this opportunity to dispel some of these persistent myths.

TEACHING TIP

Contact a local psychologist who specializes in substance dependence to get his or her thoughts on the various addictions found in the U.S. population.

- Do they feel addictions to the Internet, shopping, or sex have the same fundamental basis as substance dependence? Why or why not?

- Do they treat all addictions to substances the same? Why or why not?

"About 70 percent of Americans have tried illicit drugs, but . . . only a *few* percent have done so in the last month. . . . Past age 35, the casual use of illegal drugs virtually ceases." Having sampled the pleasures and their aftereffects, "most people eventually walk away."

Neuropsychologist Michael Gazzaniga (1997)

"That is not one of the seven habits of highly effective people."

Myth 1. Addictive drugs quickly corrupt; for example, morphine taken to control pain is powerfully addictive and often leads to heroin abuse. People given morphine to control pain rarely develop the cravings of the addict who uses morphine as a mood-altering drug (Melzack, 1990). But some people—perhaps 10 percent—do indeed have a hard time using a psychoactive drug in moderation or stopping altogether. Even so, controlled, occasional users of drugs such as alcohol and marijuana far outnumber those addicted to these substances (Gazzaniga, 1988; Siegel, 1990). "Even for a very addictive drug like cocaine, only 15 to 16 percent of people become addicted within 10 years of first use," report Terry Robinson and Kent Berridge (2003). Much the same is true for rats, only some of which become compulsively addicted to cocaine (Deroche-Garmonet et al., 2004).

Myth 2. Addictions cannot be overcome voluntarily; therapy is required. Addictions can be powerful, and some addicts do benefit from treatment programs. Alcoholics Anonymous, for example, has supported many people in overcoming their alcohol dependence. But the recovery rates of treated and untreated groups differ less than one might suppose. Helpful as therapy or group support may be, people often recover on their own.

Moreover, viewing addiction as a disease, as diabetes is a disease, can undermine self-confidence and the will to change cravings that, without treatment, "one cannot fight." And that, critics say, would be unfortunate, for many people do voluntarily stop using addictive drugs, without treatment. Most of America's 41 million ex-smokers kicked the habit on their own, usually after prior failed efforts or treatments.

Myth 3. We can extend the concept of addiction to cover not just drug dependencies, but a whole spectrum of repetitive, pleasure-seeking behaviors. We can, and we have, but should we? The addiction-as-disease-needing-treatment idea has been suggested for a host of driven behaviors, including too much eating, shopping, exercise, sex, gambling, and work. Initially, we may use the term metaphorically ("I'm a science fiction addict"), but if we begin taking the metaphor as reality, addiction can become an all-purpose excuse. Those who embezzle to feed their "gambling addiction," surf the Web half the night to satisfy their "Internet addiction," or abuse or betray to indulge their "sex addiction" can then explain away their behavior as an illness.

Sometimes, though, behaviors such as gambling, playing video games, or surfing the Internet do become compulsive and dysfunctional, much like abusive drug taking (Griffiths, 2001; Hoeft et al., 2008). Some Internet users, for example, do display an apparent inability to resist logging on, and staying on, even when this excessive use impairs their work and relationships (Ko et al., 2005). So, there may be justification for stretching the addiction concept to cover certain social behaviors. Debates over the addiction-as-disease model continue.

Psychoactive Drugs

11: What are depressants, and what are their effects?

The three major categories of psychoactive drugs—*depressants, stimulants,* and *hallucinogens*—all do their work at the brain's synapses. They stimulate, inhibit, or mimic the activity of the brain's own chemical messengers, the neurotransmitters. Our culturally influenced expectations also play a role in the way these drugs affect us (Ward, 1994). If one culture assumes that a particular drug produces euphoria (or aggression or sexual arousal) and another does not, each culture may find its expectations fulfilled.

 TEACHING TIP

At this point, you may want to use **Student Project:** *Understanding Addiction* (p. 18) from Bolt's Teacher's Resource Binder.

Depressants

Depressants are drugs such as alcohol, barbiturates (tranquilizers), and opiates that calm neural activity and slow body functions.

Alcohol True or false? In large amounts, alcohol is a depressant; in small amounts, it is a stimulant. *False.* Low doses of alcohol may, indeed, enliven a drinker, but they do so by slowing brain activity that controls judgment and inhibitions. Alcohol lowers our inhibitions, slows neural processing, disrupts memory formation, and reduces self-awareness.

Disinhibition Alcohol is an equal-opportunity drug: It increases harmful tendencies—as when angered people become aggressive after drinking. And it increases helpful tendencies—as when tipsy restaurant patrons leave extravagant tips (M. Lynn, 1988). The urges you would feel if sober are the ones you will more likely act upon when intoxicated.

Slowed Neural Processing Low doses of alcohol relax the drinker by slowing sympathetic nervous system activity. In larger doses, alcohol can become a staggering problem: Reactions slow, speech slurs, skilled performance deteriorates. Paired with sleep deprivation, alcohol is a potent sedative. (Although either sleep deprivation or drinking can put a driver at risk, their combination is deadlier yet.) These physical effects, combined with lowered inhibitions, contribute to alcohol's worst consequences—the several hundred thousand lives claimed worldwide each year in alcohol-related accidents and violent crime. Car accidents occur despite most drinkers' belief (when sober) that driving under the influence of alcohol is wrong and despite their insisting that they would not do so. Yet, as blood-alcohol levels rise and moral judgments falter, people's qualms about drinking and driving lessen. Virtually all will drive home from a bar, even if given a breathalyzer test and told they are intoxicated (Denton & Krebs, 1990; MacDonald et al., 1995).

Memory Disruption Alcohol also disrupts the processing of recent experiences into long-term memories. Thus, heavy drinkers may not recall people they met the night before or what they said or did while intoxicated. These blackouts result partly from the way alcohol suppresses REM sleep, which helps fix the day's experiences into permanent memories.

The effects of heavy drinking on the brain and cognition can be long-term. In rats, at a development period corresponding to human adolescence, binge-drinking diminishes the genesis of nerve cells, impairs the growth of synaptic connections, and contributes to nerve cell death (Crews et al., 2006, 2007). MRI scans show another way prolonged and excessive drinking can affect cognition (**FIGURE 5.12**). It can shrink the brain, especially in women, who have less of a stomach enzyme that digests alcohol

Dangerous disinhibition Alcohol consumption leads to feelings of invincibility, which become especially dangerous behind the wheel of a car, such as this one totaled by a teenage drunk driver. This Colorado University Alcohol Awareness Week exhibit prompted many students to post their own anti-drinking pledges (white flags).

➤ **FIGURE 5.12**
Alcohol dependence shrinks the brain MRI scans show brain shrinkage in women with alcohol dependence (left) compared with women in a control group (right).

Scan of woman with alcohol dependence

Scan of woman without alcohol dependence

::**depressants** drugs (such as alcohol, barbiturates, and opiates) that reduce neural activity and slow body functions.

Many antidepressants are known as SSRIs or selective serotonin reuptake inhibitors. These drugs block the reabsorption of serotonin so it is left in the synapse longer. Some disorders that these drugs are effective in treating include depression, bulimia nervosa, obsessive-compulsive disorder, anorexia nervosa, and panic disorder.

CRITICAL THINKING

Alcohol is a controversial drug. Its misuse has led to countless tragedies. Moderate, thoughtful use is linked to significant health benefits. Have students explore the following questions related to alcohol consumption:

- Why have efforts to prohibit alcohol sale and consumption failed in the past?

- Are current laws that regulate alcohol sale and consumption effective? Why or why not? What laws or enforcement techniques should be enacted to have an effect?

- What are some of the health benefits of alcohol consumption? What recommendations do doctors give for healthful alcohol consumption?

- Should there be different blood alcohol limits for men and women considering how the drug affects each gender differently? Why or why not?

RESEARCH

Have students explore the advertising techniques alcohol distributors use:

- Is there a common theme about the type of scenes depicted in the ads? Describe it.

- At what type of audience is the ad aiming?

- Are there laws that limit what alcohol advertising can depict? Are there limits to where they can advertise?

At this point, you may want to use **Classroom Exercise:** *Alcohol Expectancies* (p. 21) from Bolt's Teacher's Resource Binder.

UNIT 5

INTERCONNECTING

Explain to students that expectancy effects are similar to the placebo effect. Both involve the mind convincing the body that an effect will occur. The effects that the body expects may or may not be the actual effects of the drug or treatment, or the effects may be an exaggerated effect of the drug or treatment.

RESEARCH

Have students explore the rates of violent crime that occur while under the influence of alcohol:

- What percentage of murders occurs while either the victim or assailant is under the influence?

- What percentage of sexual assaults occurs while either the victim or assailant is under the influence? Does this percentage change depending on the age of either?

- How does the influence of alcohol affect other violent crimes such as theft, battery or domestic abuse?

INTERCONNECTING

Alcohol has been shown to affect the hippocampus, the area of the brain that is responsible for forming new memories. This effect helps explain why people who drink heavily lose their memories of the time they were intoxicated.

::**barbiturates** drugs that depress the activity of the central nervous system, reducing anxiety but impairing memory and judgment.

::**opiates** opium and its derivatives, such as morphine and heroin; they depress neural activity, temporarily lessening pain and anxiety.

::**stimulants** drugs (such as caffeine, nicotine, and the more powerful amphetamines, cocaine, and Ecstasy) that excite neural activity and speed up body functions.

::**amphetamines** drugs that stimulate neural activity, causing speeded-up body functions and associated energy and mood changes.

::**methamphetamine** a powerfully addictive drug that stimulates the central nervous system, with speeded-up body functions and associated energy and mood changes; over time, appears to reduce baseline dopamine levels.

• A University of Illinois campus survey showed that before sexual assaults, 80 percent of the male assailants and 70 percent of the female victims had been drinking (Camper, 1990). Another survey of 89,874 American collegians found alcohol or drugs involved in 79 percent of unwanted sexual intercourse experiences (Presley et al., 1997). •

(Wuethrich, 2001). Girls and young women can also become addicted to alcohol more quickly than boys and young men do, and they are at risk for lung, brain, and liver damage at lower consumption levels (CASA, 2003).

Reduced Self-Awareness and Self-Control Alcohol not only impairs judgment and memory, it also reduces self-awareness (Hull et al., 1986). This may help explain why people who want to suppress their awareness of failures or shortcomings are more likely to drink than are those who feel good about themselves. Losing a business deal, a game, or a romantic partner sometimes elicits a drinking binge. Excess drinking is especially common when people with low self-esteem experience pain in a romantic relationship (DeHart et al., 2008). By focusing attention on the immediate situation and away from any future consequences, alcohol also lessens impulse control (Steele & Josephs, 1990). In surveys of rapists, more than half acknowledge drinking before committing their offense (Seto & Barbaree, 1995).

Expectancy Effects As with other psychoactive drugs, alcohol's behavioral effects stem not only from its alteration of brain chemistry but also from the user's expectations. When people believe that alcohol affects social behavior in certain ways, and believe, rightly or wrongly, that they have been drinking alcohol, they will behave accordingly (Leigh, 1989). David Abrams and Terence Wilson (1983) demonstrated this in a now-classic experiment. They gave Rutgers University men who volunteered for a study on "alcohol and sexual stimulation" either an alcoholic or a nonalcoholic drink. (Both had strong tastes that masked any alcohol.) In each group, half the participants thought they were drinking alcohol and half thought they were not. After watching an erotic movie clip, the men who thought they had consumed alcohol were more likely to report having strong sexual fantasies and feeling guilt-free. Being able to attribute their sexual responses to alcohol released their inhibitions—whether they actually had drunk alcohol or not. If, as commonly believed, liquor is the quicker pick-her-upper, the effect lies partly in that powerful sex organ, the mind.

Alcohol + Sex = The Perfect Storm Alcohol's effects on self-control and social expectations often converge in sexual situations. More than 600 studies have explored the link between drinking and risky sex, with "the overwhelming majority" finding the two correlated (Cooper, 2006). But of course correlations do not come with causal arrows attached. In this case, three factors appear to influence the correlation.

1. Underlying "third variables," such as sensation-seeking and peer influences, simultaneously push people toward both drinking and risky sex.

2. The desire for sex leads people to drink and to get their partners to drink. Sexually coercive college men, for example, may lower their dates' sexual inhibitions by getting them to drink (Abbey, 1991; Mosher & Anderson, 1986).

3. Drinking disinhibits, and when sexually aroused, men become more disposed to sexual aggression, and men and women more disposed to casual sex (Davis et al., 2006; Grello et al., 2006). University women under alcohol's influence find an attractive but sexually promiscuous man a more appealing potential date than they do when sober. It seems, surmise Sheila Murphy and her colleagues (1998), "that when people have been drinking, the restraining forces of reason may weaken and yield under the pressure of their desires."

Barbiturates The **barbiturate** drugs, or *tranquilizers*, mimic the effects of alcohol. Because they depress nervous system activity, barbiturates such as Nembutal, Seconal, and Amytal are sometimes prescribed to induce sleep or reduce anxiety. In larger doses, they can lead to impaired memory and judgment or even death. If combined with alcohol—as sometimes happens when people take a sleeping pill after an evening of heavy drinking—the total depressive effect on body functions can be lethal.

TEACHING TIP

Laudanum was a common medicine used in the Victorian era to treat a variety of different ailments. Most successfully, it was used as a painkiller and a cough suppressant. It was also found to help with loose stool. Mothers used it often to soothe their fussy babies. What made laudanum so effective? It was a special mixture of alcohol and opium. Doctors in the Victorian period were so impressed with the medicinal properties of opium and laudanum that they neglected to tell their patients about its addictive properties. Officials in the U.S. banned the practice of prescribing opium in 1914.

Opiates The **opiates**—opium and its derivatives—also depress neural functioning. When abusing the opiates, which include *heroin*, a user's pupils constrict, breathing slows, and lethargy sets in, as blissful pleasure replaces pain and anxiety. But for this short-term pleasure the user may pay a long-term price: a gnawing craving for another fix, a need for progressively larger doses, and the extreme discomfort of withdrawal. When repeatedly flooded with an artificial opiate, the brain eventually stops producing its own opiates, the *endorphins*. If the artificial opiate is then withdrawn, the brain lacks the normal level of these painkilling neurotransmitters. Those who cannot or choose not to tolerate this state may pay an ultimate price—death by overdose. Opiates include the *narcotics*, such as codeine and morphine, which physicians prescribe for pain relief.

Stimulants

12: What are stimulants, and what are their effects?

Stimulants such as caffeine and nicotine temporarily excite neural activity and arouse body functions. People use these substances to stay awake, lose weight, or boost mood or athletic performance. This category of drugs also includes **amphetamines,** the even more powerful cocaine, *Ecstasy* (a stimulant as well as a mild hallucinogen), and **methamphetamine** ("speed"), which is chemically related to its parent drug, *amphetamine* (NIDA, 2002, 2005). All strong stimulants increase heart and breathing rates and cause pupils to dilate, appetite to diminish (because blood sugar increases), and energy and self-confidence to rise. And, as with other drugs, the benefits of stimulants come with a price. These substances can be addictive and may induce an aftermath crash into fatigue, headaches, irritability, and depression (Silverman et al., 1992).

Methamphetamine Methamphetamine has even greater effects, which can include eight hours or so of heightened energy and euphoria. The drug triggers the release of the neurotransmitter dopamine, which stimulates brain cells that enhance energy and mood. In response to a typical amphetamine dose, men show a higher rate of dopamine release than do women, which helps explain their higher addiction rate (Munro et al., 2006).

Over time, methamphetamine may reduce baseline dopamine levels, leaving the user with permanently depressed functioning. This drug is highly addictive, and its possible aftereffects include irritability, insomnia, hypertension, seizures, social isolation, depression, and occasional violent outbursts (Homer et al., 2008). The British government now classifies *crystal meth,* the highly addictive crystalized form of methamphetamine, alongside cocaine and heroin as one of the most dangerous drugs (BBC, 2006).

Dramatic drug-induced decline This woman's methamphetamine addiction led to obvious physical changes. Her decline is evident in these two photos, taken at age 36 (left) and, after four years of addiction, at age 40 (right).

Meth bust As use of the dangerously addictive stimulant methamphetamine has increased, enforcement agencies have increased their efforts to snuff out the labs that produce it.

INTERCONNECTING

Link information about amphetamines to neuroscience by pointing out that recent research has shown that detoxified former methamphetamine users had lost some key dopamine transporters, which are crucial to movement, verbal performance, and memory. Patients with Parkinson's disease have similar decreases in these dopamine transporters.

RESEARCH

Methamphetamine (aka crystal meth) use has been on the increase in the U.S. in recent years. Have students conduct research on the prevalence of crystal meth use in their local community. Also have them consider the economic impact crystal meth use has had on the community. Discuss with them how information about addiction explains the virulent use of meth in some communities.

TEACHING TIP

At this point, you may want to use **Lecture/Discussion Topic:** *Caffeine—Is It Harmful?* (p. 21) from Bolt's Teacher's Resource Binder.

UNIT 5

RESEARCH

Have students research the effects of caffeine. They should investigate both the negative effects and the health benefits that caffeinated products have. While caffeine may not be dangerous in and of itself, the products that contain caffeine (coffee, sodas, and so on), are not considered healthful products.

TEACHING TIP

Brainstorm with students about the availability of caffeinated products in your school:

- Are there vending machines that dispense caffeinated products?
- How available is coffee to students and teachers?
- Are students allowed to carry caffeinated drinks to class? Why or why not?
- Does the lunchroom serve caffeinated products?

RESEARCH

Tobacco companies have come under intense scrutiny over the last decade as states have sued them to get reimbursement for the medical expenses of tobacco users. The companies agreed to a record-setting agreement to settle the claims brought by the states as the legal costs began to mount.

- What were the details of this settlement?
- What did the companies have to do differently as a result?
- What benefits did the states get from settling? What rights did they relinquish regarding future litigation?

> "There is an overwhelming medical and scientific consensus that cigarette smoking causes lung cancer, heart disease, emphysema, and other serious diseases in smokers. Smokers are far more likely to develop serious diseases, like lung cancer, than nonsmokers."
> Philip Morris Companies Inc., 1999

> • Smoke a cigarette and nature will charge you 12 minutes—ironically, just about the length of time you spend smoking it (*Discover*, 1996). •

> "A cigarette in the hands of a Hollywood star on screen is a gun aimed at a 12- or 14-year-old."
> Screenwriter Joe Eszterhas, 2002

Caffeine Caffeine, the world's most widely consumed psychoactive substance, can now be found not only in coffee, tea, and soda but also in fruit juices, mints, energy drinks, bars, and gels—and even in soap. Coffees and teas vary in their caffeine content, with a cup of drip coffee surprisingly having more caffeine than a shot of espresso, and teas having less. A mild dose of caffeine typically lasts three or four hours, which—if taken in the evening—may be long enough to impair sleep. Like other drugs, caffeine used regularly and in heavy doses produces tolerance: Its stimulating effects lessen. And discontinuing heavy caffeine intake often produces withdrawal symptoms, including fatigue and headache.

Nicotine Imagine that cigarettes were harmless—except, once in every 25,000 packs, an occasional innocent-looking one is filled with dynamite instead of tobacco. Not such a bad risk of having your head blown off. But with 250 million packs a day consumed worldwide, we could expect more than 10,000 gruesome daily deaths (more than three times the 9/11 fatalities each and every day)—surely enough to have cigarettes banned everywhere.[1]

The lost lives from these dynamite-loaded cigarettes approximate those from today's actual cigarettes. Each year throughout the world, tobacco kills nearly 5.4 million of its 1.3 billion customers, reports the World Health Organization (WHO). (Imagine the outrage if terrorists took down an equivalent of 25 loaded jumbo jets today, let alone tomorrow and every day thereafter.) And by 2030, annual deaths will increase to 8 million, according to WHO predictions. That means that *1 billion* (say that number slowly) twenty-first-century people may be killed by tobacco (WHO, 2008).

A teen-to-the-grave smoker has a 50 percent chance of dying from the habit, and the death is often agonizing and premature, as the Philip Morris company acknowledged in 2001. Responding to Czech Republic complaints about the health-care costs of tobacco, Philip Morris reassured the Czechs that there was actually a net "health-care cost savings due to early mortality" and the resulting savings on pensions and elderly housing (Herbert, 2001).

Eliminating smoking would increase life expectancy more than any other preventive measure. Why, then, do so many people smoke?

Nic-a-teen Aware that virtually all smokers start as teenagers—and that sales would plummet if no teens were enticed to smoke—cigarette companies target teens. They have portrayed tough, appealing, socially adept smokers in hopes that teens will imitate. Teen smoking went up in the 1990s (Brody, 2001), coinciding with an increased number of appealing smokers in popular films, including a younger Johnny Depp in this 1999 film, *The Source*. ▲

Russel Einhorn/The Gamma Liaison Network

Smoking usually begins during early adolescence. (If you make it to college without the cigarette manufacturers attracting your business, they almost surely never will.) Adolescents, self-conscious and often thinking the world is watching their every move, are vulnerable to smoking's allure. They may first light up to imitate glamorous celebrities, or to project a mature image, or to get the social reward of being accepted

---

[1]This analogy, adapted here with world-based numbers, was suggested by mathematician Sam Saunders, as reported by K. C. Cole (1998).

RESEARCH

Have students create and distribute a survey of their peers about caffeine consumption:

- How many students at your school would consider themselves addicted to caffeine?
- How do students generally get their caffeine "fix"? Does the school provide this drug to students? In what ways?
- Is there a stigma associated with caffeine consumption? Why or why not?
- Why do students consume caffeinated products?
- Are students concerned about their caffeine consumption? Why or why not?

➤ **FIGURE 5.13**
Peer influence Kids don't smoke if their friends don't (Philip Morris, 2003). A correlation-causation question: Does the close link between teen smoking and friends' smoking reflect peer influence? Teens seeking similar friends? Or both?

by other smokers (Cin et al., 2007; Tickle et al., 2006). Mindful of these tendencies, cigarette companies have effectively modeled smoking with themes that appeal to youths: sophistication, independence, adventure-seeking, social approval. Typically, teens who start smoking also have friends who smoke, who suggest its pleasures, and who offer them cigarettes (Eiser, 1985; Evans et al., 1988; Rose et al., 1999). Among teens whose parents and best friends are nonsmokers, the smoking rate is close to zero (Moss et al., 1992; also see **FIGURE 5.13**).

Those addicted to nicotine find it very hard to quit because tobacco products are as powerfully and quickly addictive as heroin and cocaine. As with other addictions, a smoker becomes dependent; each year fewer than one of every seven smokers who want to quit will do so. Smokers also develop tolerance, eventually needing larger and larger doses to get the same effect. Quitting causes nicotine-withdrawal symptoms, including craving, insomnia, anxiety, and irritability. Even attempts to quit within the first weeks of smoking often fail as nicotine cravings set in (DiFranza, 2008). And all it takes to relieve this aversive state is a cigarette—a portable nicotine dispenser.

Nicotine, like other addictive drugs, is not only compulsive and mood-altering, it is also reinforcing. Smoking delivers its hit of nicotine within 7 seconds, triggering the release of epinephrine and norepinephrine, which in turn diminish appetite and boost alertness and mental efficiency (**FIGURE 5.14**). At the same time, nicotine stimulates the central nervous system to release neurotransmitters that calm anxiety and

> Humorist Dave Barry (1995) recalling why he smoked his first cigarette the summer he turned 15: "Arguments against smoking: 'It's a repulsive addiction that slowly but surely turns you into a gasping, gray-skinned, tumor-ridden invalid, hacking up brownish gobs of toxic waste from your one remaining lung.' Arguments for smoking: 'Other teenagers are doing it.' Case closed! Let's light up!"

• Asked "If you had to do it all over again, would you start smoking?" more than 85 percent of adult smokers answer *No* (Slovic et al., 2002). •

1. Arouses the brain to a state of increased alertness

2. Increases heart rate and blood pressure

3. At high levels, relaxes muscles and triggers the release of neurotransmitters that may reduce stress

4. Reduces circulation to extremities

5. Suppresses appetite for carbohydrates

➤ **FIGURE 5.14**
Where there's smoke . . . : The physiological effects of nicotine Nicotine reaches the brain within 7 seconds, twice as fast as intravenous heroin. Within minutes, the amount in the blood soars.

UNIT 5

INTERCONNECTING

Reinforce your study of neurotransmitters and action potentials with Figure 5.15, which shows how drugs affect the action at the synapse. You will know here whether students learned the material in Unit 3A. If students can understand this material after having learned about action potentials, they will have successfully transferred their learning from one unit to another.

CRITICAL THINKING

The United States has a strained relationship with some countries due to cocaine trafficking. In Peru, for example, cultivation of the coca bush is legal, as long as farmers sell their crop to the state. But studies show that farmers can make much more money selling to illegal markets, making cocaine a problem in the developing world. Some leaders in foreign countries and groups within the U.S. argue that if the U.S. government would crack down on the demand of people who use drugs, then drug traffickers would not find dealing to be as profitable, thus ending the drug problem altogether.

- What should the U.S. government do to curb the drug trade? Have efforts been successful in the past?

- Should the U.S. government cut off diplomatic and economic ties with drug trafficking countries? Why or why not?

> "To cease smoking is the easiest thing I ever did; I ought to know because I've done it a thousand times."
>
> Mark Twain, 1835–1910

• The recipe for Coca-Cola originally included an extract of the coca plant, creating a cocaine tonic for tired older people. Between 1896 and 1905, Coke was indeed "the real thing." •

reduce sensitivity to pain. For example, nicotine stimulates the release of dopamine and (like heroin and morphine) opioids (Nowak, 1994; Scott et al., 2004). These rewards keep people smoking even when they wish they could stop—indeed, even when they know they are committing slow-motion suicide (Saad, 2002). An informative exception: Brain-injured patients who have lost a prune-size frontal lobe region called the *insula*—an area that lights up when people crave drugs—are able to give up cigarettes instantly (Naqvi et al., 2007).

Nevertheless, half of all Americans who have ever smoked have quit, and 81 percent of those who haven't yet quit wish to (Jones, 2007). For those who endure, the acute craving and withdrawal symptoms gradually dissipate over the ensuing six months (Ward et al., 1997). These nonsmokers may live not only healthier but also happier. Smoking correlates with higher rates of depression, chronic disabilities, and divorce (Doherty & Doherty, 1998; Vita et al., 1998). Healthy living seems to add both years to life and life to years.

Cocaine Cocaine use offers a fast track from euphoria to crash. When sniffed ("snorted"), and especially when injected or smoked ("free-based"), cocaine enters the bloodstream quickly. The result: a "rush" of euphoria that depletes the brain's supply of the neurotransmitters dopamine, serotonin, and norepinephrine (FIGURE 5.15). Within 15 to 30 minutes, a crash of agitated depression follows as the drug's effect wears off.

In national surveys, 5 percent of U.S. high school seniors and 4 percent of British 18- to 24-year-olds reported having tried cocaine during the past year (Home Office, 2003; Johnston et al., 2009). Nearly half of the drug-using seniors had smoked *crack*, a crystallized form of cocaine. This faster-working, potent form of the drug produces a briefer but more intense high, a more intense crash, and a craving for more, which wanes after several hours only to return several days later (Gawin, 1991).

Cocaine-addicted monkeys have pressed levers more than 12,000 times to gain one cocaine injection (Siegel, 1990). Many regular cocaine users—animal and human—do become addicted. In situations that trigger aggression, ingesting cocaine

➤ FIGURE 5.15
Cocaine euphoria and crash

(a) Neurotransmitters carry a message from a sending neuron across a synapse to receptor sites on a receiving neuron.

(b) The sending neuron normally reabsorbs excess neurotransmitter molecules, a process called reuptake.

(c) By binding to the sites that normally reabsorb neurotransmitter molecules, cocaine blocks reuptake of dopamine, norepinephrine, and serotonin (Ray & Ksir, 1990). The extra neurotransmitter molecules therefore remain in the synapse, intensifying their normal mood-altering effects and producing a euphoric rush. When the cocaine level drops, the absence of these neurotransmitters produces a crash.

TEACHING TIP

Sigmund Freud was indeed a strong advocate of the use of cocaine in his early years. He took the drug himself on a daily basis and advised its use as a treatment for mental and physical disorders (such as asthma), as an aphrodisiac, and as a local anesthetic. Freud was even hired by two pharmaceutical firms, Merck and Parke-Davis, to promote the use of their cocaine-based products.

may heighten reactions. Caged rats fight when given foot shocks, and they fight even more when given cocaine and foot shocks. Likewise, humans who voluntarily ingest high cocaine doses in laboratory experiments impose higher shock levels on a presumed opponent than do those receiving a placebo (Licata et al., 1993). Cocaine use may also lead to emotional disturbances, suspiciousness, convulsions, cardiac arrest, or respiratory failure.

As with all psychoactive drugs, cocaine's psychological effects depend not only on the dosage and form consumed but also on the situation and the user's expectations and personality. Given a placebo, cocaine users who *think* they are taking cocaine often have a cocainelike experience (Van Dyke & Byck, 1982).

Ecstasy **Ecstasy**, a street name for **MDMA** (methylenedioxymethamphetamine), is both a stimulant and a mild hallucinogen. As an amphetamine derivative, it triggers dopamine release. But its major effect is releasing stored serotonin and blocking its reabsorption, thus prolonging serotonin's feel-good flood (Braun, 2001). About a half-hour after taking an Ecstasy pill, users enter a three- to four-hour period of feelings of emotional elevation and, given a social context, connectedness with those around them ("I love everyone").

During the late 1990s, Ecstasy's popularity soared as a "club drug" taken at nightclubs and all-night raves (Landry, 2002). There are, however, reasons not to be ecstatic about Ecstasy. One is its dehydrating effect, which—when combined with prolonged dancing—can lead to severe overheating, increased blood pressure, and death. Another is that long-term, repeated leaching of brain serotonin can damage serotonin-producing neurons, leading to decreased output and increased risk of permanently depressed mood (Croft et al., 2001; McCann et al., 2001; Roiser et al., 2005). Ecstasy also suppresses the disease-fighting immune system, impairs memory and other cognitive functions, and disrupts sleep by interfering with serotonin's control of the circadian clock (Laws & Kokkalis, 2007; Pacifici et al., 2001; Schilt et al., 2007). Ecstasy delights for the night but dispirits the morrow.

Hallucinogens

13: What are hallucinogens, and what are their effects?

Hallucinogens distort perceptions and evoke sensory images in the absence of sensory input (which is why these drugs are also called *psychedelics,* meaning "mind-manifesting"). Some, such as LSD and MDMA (Ecstasy), are synthetic. Others, including the mild hallucinogen marijuana, are natural substances.

LSD In 1943, Albert Hofmann reported perceiving "an uninterrupted stream of fantastic pictures, extraordinary shapes with intense, kaleidoscopic play of colors" (Siegel, 1984). Hofmann, a chemist, created—and on one Friday afternoon in April 1943 accidentally ingested—**LSD** (lysergic acid diethylamide). The result reminded him of a childhood mystical experience that had left him longing for another glimpse of "a miraculous, powerful, unfathomable reality" (Smith, 2006).

LSD and other powerful hallucinogens are chemically similar to (and therefore block the actions of) a subtype of the neurotransmitter serotonin (Jacobs, 1987). The emotions of an LSD trip vary from euphoria to detachment to panic. The user's current mood and expectations color the emotional experience, but the perceptual distortions and hallucinations have some commonalities. Psychologist Ronald Siegel (1982) reports that whether you provoke your brain to hallucinate by drugs, loss of oxygen, or extreme sensory deprivation, "it will hallucinate in basically the same way." The experience typically begins with simple geometric forms, such as a lattice, a cobweb, or a spiral. The next phase consists of more meaningful images; some may be superimposed on

> "Cocaine makes you a new man. And the first thing that new man wants is more cocaine."
>
> Comedian George Carlin (1937–2008)

::**Ecstasy (MDMA)** a synthetic stimulant and mild hallucinogen. Produces euphoria and social intimacy, but with short-term health risks and longer-term harm to serotonin-producing neurons and to mood and cognition.

::**hallucinogens** psychedelic ("mind-manifesting") drugs, such as LSD, that distort perceptions and evoke sensory images in the absence of sensory input.

::**LSD** a powerful hallucinogenic drug; also known as acid *(lysergic acid diethylamide).*

 TEACHING TIP

Ecstasy, or MDMA, is a highly addictive and dangerous drug. As Myers points out, studies show that taking Ecstasy only once can lead to significant degeneration of serotonin neurons in the brain. This finding seems to be the basis of the popular notion that taking Ecstasy causes "holes in the brain." While it does not produce visible holes, it does cause significant damage, which is about as close to making holes in the brain as you can get.

 TEACHING TIP

Flashbacks are associated with LSD use. These experiences can occur days, months, or years after an initial trip. Flashbacks can be as intense as the original trip, but because of their unpredictable nature, they are often terrifying for the user.

 TEACHING TIP

At this point, you may want to use **Lecture/Discussion Topics:** *The LSD Experience* (p. 22) or *Near-Death Experiences* (p. 23) from Bolt's Teacher's Resource Binder.

TEACHING TIP

TEACHING TIP

Students may have heard before that marijuana is considered to be a "gateway" drug, which means that it leads users to desire harder drugs like heroin. A study of 311 sets of identical and fraternal twins in Australia found that those teens who used marijuana early (before age 17) were two to five times more likely to use harder drugs later in life. In each of these sets of twins, one twin was a user while the other was not, helping to control for confounding factors like genetics and environment.

TEACHING TIP

- Marijuana smokers typically take longer drags on the marijuana cigarette than on traditional cigarettes.

- Marijuana cigarettes are not usually filtered as tobacco cigarettes are.

At this point, you may want to use **Lecture/Discussion Topic:** *Is Marijuana Good Medicine?* (p. 24) from Bolt's Teacher's Resource Binder.

➤ **FIGURE 5.16**
Near-death vision or hallucination? Psychologist Ronald Siegel (1977) reported that people under the influence of hallucinogenic drugs often see "a bright light in the center of the field of vision. . . . The location of this point of light create[s] a tunnel-like perspective."

a tunnel or funnel, others may be replays of past emotional experiences. As the hallucination peaks, people frequently feel separated from their body and experience dreamlike scenes so real that they may become panic-stricken or harm themselves.

These sensations are strikingly similar to the **near-death experience,** an altered state of consciousness reported by about one-third of those who survive a brush with death, as when revived from cardiac arrest (Moody, 1976; Ring, 1980; Schnaper, 1980). Many experience visions of tunnels (**FIGURE 5.16**), bright lights or beings of light, a replay of old memories, and out-of-body sensations (Siegel, 1980). Given that oxygen deprivation and other insults to the brain are known to produce hallucinations, it is difficult to resist wondering whether a brain under stress manufactures the near-death experiences. Patients who have experienced temporal lobe seizures have reported similarly profound mystical experiences, as have solitary sailors and polar explorers while enduring monotony, isolation, and cold (Suedfeld & Mocellin, 1987).

Marijuana Marijuana consists of the leaves and flowers of the hemp plant, which for 5000 years has been cultivated for its fiber. Whether smoked or eaten, marijuana's major active ingredient, **THC** (delta-9-tetrahydrocannabinol), produces a mix of effects. (Smoking gets the drug into the brain in about 7 seconds, producing a greater effect than does eating the drug, which causes its peak concentration to be reached at a slower, unpredictable rate.) Like alcohol, marijuana relaxes, disinhibits, and may produce a euphoric high. But marijuana is also a mild hallucinogen, amplifying sensitivity to colors, sounds, tastes, and smells. And unlike alcohol, which the body eliminates within hours, THC and its by-products linger in the body for a month or more. Thus, contrary to the usual tolerance phenomenon, regular users may achieve a high with smaller amounts of the drug than occasional users would need to get the same effect.

A user's experience can vary with the situation. If the person feels anxious or depressed, using marijuana may intensify these feelings. And studies controlling for other drug use and personal traits have found that the more one uses marijuana, the greater one's risk of anxiety, depression, or possibly schizophrenia (Hall, 2006; Murray et al., 2007; Patton et al., 2002). Daily use bodes a worse outcome than infrequent use.

The National Academy of Sciences (1982, 1999) and National Institute on Drug Abuse (2004) have identified other marijuana consequences. Like alcohol, marijuana

::**near-death experience** an altered state of consciousness reported after a close brush with death (such as through cardiac arrest); often similar to drug-induced hallucinations.

::**THC** the major active ingredient in marijuana; triggers a variety of effects, including mild hallucinations.

RESEARCH

Cancer and AIDS advocacy groups have been pushing for the legalization of marijuana for medicinal purposes. Marijuana has been shown to help curb the nausea associated with chemotherapy for cancer and AIDS, helping patients to keep their strength up as they endure uncomfortable treatments. Explore laws across the country that address the medical use of marijuana.

- How many states authorize the medical use of marijuana?

- How does the federal government handle cases of people authorized to use marijuana medicinally?

- Does the federal government supply the drug to people authorized to use marijuana medically? Why or why not?

impairs the motor coordination, perceptual skills, and reaction time necessary for safely operating an automobile or other machine. "THC causes animals to misjudge events," reported Ronald Siegel (1990, p. 163). "Pigeons wait too long to respond to buzzers or lights that tell them food is available for brief periods; and rats turn the wrong way in mazes." Marijuana also disrupts memory formation and interferes with immediate recall of information learned only a few minutes before. Such cognitive effects outlast the period of smoking (Messinis et al., 2006). Prenatal exposure through maternal marijuana use also impairs brain development (Berghuis et al., 2007; Huizink & Mulder, 2006). Heavy adult use for over 20 years is associated with a shrinkage of brain areas that process memories and emotions (Yücel et al., 2008).

Scientists have shed light on marijuana's cognitive, mood, and motor effects with the discovery of concentrations of THC-sensitive receptors in the brain's frontal lobes, limbic system, and motor cortex (Iversen, 2000). As the 1970s discovery of receptors for morphine put researchers on the trail of morphinelike neurotransmitters (the endorphins), so the recent discovery of *cannabinoid receptors* has led to a successful hunt for naturally occurring THC-like molecules that bind with cannabinoid receptors. These molecules may naturally control pain. If so, this may help explain why marijuana can be therapeutic for those who suffer the pain, nausea, and severe weight loss associated with AIDS (Watson et al., 2000). Such uses have motivated legislation in some states to make the drug legally available for medical purposes. To avoid the toxicity of marijuana smoke—which, like cigarette smoke, can cause cancer, lung damage, and pregnancy complications—the Institute of Medicine recommends medical inhalers to deliver the THC.

* * *

Despite their differences, the psychoactive drugs summarized in **TABLE 5.3** share a common feature: They trigger negative aftereffects that offset their immediate positive effects and grow stronger with repetition. And that helps explain both tolerance and withdrawal. As the opposing, negative aftereffects grow stronger, it takes larger and larger doses to produce the desired high (tolerance), causing the aftereffects to worsen in the drug's absence (withdrawal). This in turn creates a need to switch off the withdrawal symptoms by taking yet more of the drug.

> "How strange would appear to be this thing that men call pleasure! And how curiously it is related to what is thought to be its opposite, pain! . . . Wherever the one is found, the other follows up behind."
>
> Plato, *Phaedo*, fourth century B.C.E.

 TEACHING TIP

A study released by the Substance Abuse and Mental Health Services Administration (SAMHSA) showed that teen marijuana use increased by about 20 percent during the last half of the 1990s. In 1994, 43 percent of teens treated for substance abuse used marijuana, but in 1999, the number of teens treated for marijuana was 60 percent.

TABLE 5.3

A GUIDE TO SELECTED PSYCHOACTIVE DRUGS

Drug	Type	Pleasurable Effects	Adverse Effects
Alcohol	Depressant	Initial high followed by relaxation and disinhibition	Depression, memory loss, organ damage, impaired reactions
Heroin	Depressant	Rush of euphoria, relief from pain	Depressed physiology, agonizing withdrawal
Caffeine	Stimulant	Increased alertness and wakefulness	Anxiety, restlessness, and insomnia in high doses; uncomfortable withdrawal
Methamphetamine	Stimulant	Euphoria, alertness, energy	Irritability, insomnia, hypertension, seizures
Cocaine	Stimulant	Rush of euphoria, confidence, energy	Cardiovascular stress, suspiciousness, depressive crash
Nicotine	Stimulant	Arousal and relaxation, sense of well-being	Heart disease, cancer
Ecstasy (MDMA)	Stimulant; mild hallucinogen	Emotional elevation, disinhibition	Dehydration, overheating, depressed mood, impaired cognitive and immune functioning
Marijuana	Mild hallucinogen	Enhanced sensation, relief of pain, distortion of time, relaxation	Impaired learning and memory, increased risk of psychological disorders, lung damage from smoke

UNIT 5

INTERCONNECTING

Teens often feel as though their own behavior does not qualify as addictive or destructive behavior. They attribute their own behavior to situational factors and the behavior of others to dispositional factors—a type of attribution known as the fundamental attribution error. Students will say they drink or take drugs due to factors such as stress or social pressure. They will say that others drink or take drugs due to weakness or bad decision making. Help students evaluate their own behavior critically, asking themselves whether their own behavior would qualify as destructive.

CRITICAL THINKING

Have students evaluate whether the educational and public service campaigns they've been exposed to over the years have influenced their choices to take drugs or drink alcohol. Brainstorm with students the most effective elements of these campaigns that would help children and teenagers stay off drugs.

Warning signs of alcohol dependence

- Drinking binges
- Regretting things done or said when drunk
- Feeling low or guilty after drinking
- Failing to honor a resolve to drink less
- Drinking to alleviate depression or anxiety
- Avoiding family or friends when drinking

➤ **FIGURE 5.17**

Trends in drug use The percentage of U.S. high school seniors who report having used alcohol, marijuana, or cocaine during the past 30 days declined from the late 1970s to 1992, when it partially rebounded for a few years. (From Johnston et al., 2009.)

Influences on Drug Use

14: Why do some people become regular users of consciousness-altering drugs?

Drug use by North American youths increased during the 1970s. Then, with increased drug education and a more realistic and deglamorized media depiction of taking drugs, drug use declined sharply. After the early 1990s, the cultural antidrug voice softened, and drugs for a time were again glamorized in some music and films. Consider these marijuana-related trends:

- In the University of Michigan's annual survey of 15,000 U.S. high school seniors, the proportion who believe there is "great risk" in regular marijuana use rose from 35 percent in 1978 to 79 percent in 1991, then retreated to 52 percent in 2008 (Johnston et al., 2009).
- After peaking in 1978, marijuana use by U.S. high school seniors declined through 1992, then rose, but has recently been tapering off (**FIGURE 5.17**). Among Canadian 15- to 24-year-olds, 23 percent report using marijuana monthly, weekly, or daily (Health Canada, 2007).

For some adolescents, occasional drug use represents thrill seeking. Why, though, do other adolescents become regular drug users? In search of answers, researchers have engaged biological, psychological, and social-cultural levels of analysis.

Biological Influences

Some people may be biologically vulnerable to particular drugs. For example, evidence accumulates that heredity influences some aspects of alcohol abuse problems, especially those appearing by early adulthood (Crabbe, 2002):

- Adopted individuals are more susceptible to alcohol dependence if one or both biological parents have a history of it.
- Having an identical rather than fraternal twin with alcohol dependence puts one at increased risk for alcohol problems (Kendler et al., 2002). (In marijuana use also, identical twins more closely resemble one another than do fraternal twins.)

[Figure 5.17: Line graph titled "High school seniors reporting drug use" showing percentages from 0% to 80% on the y-axis and Years from 1975 to '07 on the x-axis, with three lines labeled Alcohol, Marijuana/hashish, and Cocaine.]

TEACHING TIP

At this point, you may want to use **Lecture/Discussion Topic:** *Factors in Drug Use* (p. 25) from Bolt's Teacher's Resource Binder.

- Boys who at age 6 are excitable, impulsive, and fearless (genetically influenced traits) are more likely as teens to smoke, drink, and use other drugs (Masse & Tremblay, 1997).
- Researchers have bred rats and mice that prefer alcoholic drinks to water. One such strain has reduced levels of the brain chemical NPY. Mice engineered to *overproduce* NPY are very sensitive to alcohol's sedating effect and drink little (Thiele et al., 1998).
- Researchers have identified genes that are more common among people and animals predisposed to alcohol dependence, and they are seeking genes that contribute to tobacco addiction (NIH, 2006; Nurnberger & Bierut, 2007). These culprit genes seemingly produce deficiencies in the brain's natural dopamine reward system, which is impacted by addictive drugs. When repeated, the drugs trigger dopamine-produced pleasure but also disrupt normal dopamine balance. Studies of how drugs reprogram the brain's reward systems raise hopes for anti-addiction drugs that might block or blunt the effects of alcohol and other drugs (Miller, 2008; Wilson & Kuhn, 2005).

Psychological and Social-Cultural Influences

Psychological and social-cultural influences also contribute to drug use (**FIGURE 5.18**). In their studies of youths and young adults, Michael Newcomb and L. L. Harlow (1986) found that one psychological factor is the feeling that one's life is meaningless and directionless, a common feeling among school dropouts who subsist without job skills, without privilege, and with little hope. When young unmarried adults leave home, alcohol and other drug use increases; when they marry and have children, it decreases (Bachman et al., 1997).

Heavy users of alcohol, marijuana, and cocaine often display other psychological influences. Many have experienced significant stress or failure and are depressed. Females with a history of depression, eating disorders, or sexual or physical abuse are at risk for substance addiction, as are those undergoing school or neighborhood transitions (CASA, 2003; Logan et al., 2002). Monkeys, too, develop a taste for alcohol when stressed by permanent separation from their mother at birth (Small, 2002). By temporarily dulling the pain of self-awareness, alcohol may offer a way to avoid coping with depression, anger, anxiety, or insomnia. As Unit 6 explains, behavior is often controlled more by its immediate consequences than by its later ones.

Especially for teenagers, drug use also has social roots. Most teen drinking is done for social reasons, not as a way to cope with problems (Kuntsche et al., 2005). Social influence also appears in the differing rates of drug use across cultural and ethnic groups. For example, a 2003 survey of 100,000 teens in 35 European countries found that marijuana use in the prior 30 days ranged from zero to 1 percent in Romania and Sweden to 20 to 22 percent in Britain, Switzerland, and France (ESPAD, 2003). Independent U.S. government studies of drug use in households nationwide and among high schoolers in all regions reveal that African-American teens have sharply lower rates of drinking, smoking, and cocaine use (Johnston et al., 2007). Alcohol and other drug addiction rates have also been extremely low in the United States among Orthodox Jews, Mormons, the Amish, and Mennonites (Trimble, 1994). Relatively drug-free small towns and rural areas tend to constrain any genetic predisposition to drug use, report Lisa Legrand and her colleagues (2005). For those whose genetic predispositions nudge them toward substance use, "cities offer more opportunities" and less supervision.

➤ **FIGURE 5.18**
Levels of analysis for drug use
The biopsychosocial approach enables researchers to investigate drug use from complementary perspectives.

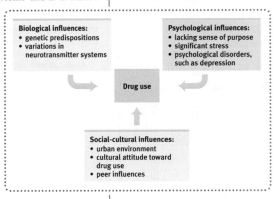

Biological influences:
- genetic predispositions
- variations in neurotransmitter systems

Psychological influences:
- lacking sense of purpose
- significant stress
- psychological disorders, such as depression

Drug use

Social-cultural influences:
- urban environment
- cultural attitude toward drug use
- peer influences

● In the real world, alcohol accounts for one-sixth or less of beverage use. In TV land, drinking alcohol occurs more often than the combined drinking of coffee, tea, soft drinks, and water (Gerbner, 1990). ●

Culture and alcohol
Percentage of adults drinking weekly or more:

United States	30%
Canada	40%
Britain	58%

(Gallup Poll, from Moore, 2006)

INTERCONNECTING

Remind students that in Unit 3, we learned that having a genetic trait does not guarantee the display of that trait. Simply because children display traits that are correlated to future drug use does not mean they will become drug users. Remember, correlation does not mean causation!

TEACHING TIP

Drug use is commonly seen among the poor and the wealthy. Those in poverty often live in environments that provide little outlet for entertainment or opportunity. People in poverty often turn to drug use as recreation or to mask the emotional and psychological pain poverty often brings. Those who are wealthy often have too many options for entertainment and opportunity is often too easy. People who are wealthy turn to drug use because they can afford the recreation or they may mask the pressure or pain being wealthy may cause.

INTERCONNECTING

Help students see that peer pressure does not usually present itself in obvious ways. Normative social influence occurs when people are rewarded or punished by social engagement or isolation for behaviors they exhibit. Rarely do peers say, "Hey, I won't like you if you don't use drugs." Typically, peers will engage with those who do drugs and isolate those who do not, implicitly applying the peer pressure that leads to drug use.

TABLE 5.4

FACTS ABOUT "HIGHER" EDUCATION

College and university students drink more alcohol than their nonstudent peers and exhibit 2.5 times the general population's rate of substance abuse.

Fraternity and sorority members report nearly twice the binge drinking rate of nonmembers.

Since 1993, campus smoking rates have declined, alcohol use has been steady, and abuse of prescription opioids, stimulants, tranquilizers, and sedatives has increased, as has marijuana use.

Source: NCASA, 2007.

SNAPSHOTS

Whether in cities or rural areas, peers influence attitudes about drugs. They also throw the parties and provide the drugs. If an adolescent's friends use drugs, the odds are that he or she will, too. If the friends do not, the opportunity may not even arise. Teens who come from happy families, who do not begin drinking before age 14, and who do well in school tend not to use drugs, largely because they rarely associate with those who do (Bachman et al., 2007; Hingson et al., 2006; Oetting & Beauvais, 1987, 1990).

Peer influence, however, is not just a matter of what friends do and say but also of what adolescents *believe* friends are doing and favoring. In one survey of sixth graders in 22 U.S. states, 14 percent believed their friends had smoked marijuana, though only 4 percent acknowledged doing so (Wren, 1999). University students are not immune to such misperceptions: Drinking dominates social occasions partly because students overestimate their fellow students' enthusiasm for alcohol and underestimate their views of its risks (Prentice & Miller, 1993; Self, 1994) **(TABLE 5.4)**.

People whose beginning use was influenced by their peers are more likely to stop using drugs when friends stop or the social network changes (Kandel & Raveis, 1989). One study that followed 12,000 adults over 32 years found that smokers tend to quit in clusters (Christakis & Fowler, 2008). Within a social network, the odds of a person's quitting increased when a spouse, friend, or co-worker stopped smoking. Similarly, most soldiers who became drug-addicted while in Vietnam ceased their drug use after returning home (Robins et al., 1974).

As always with correlations, the traffic between friends' drug use and our own may be two-way: Our friends influence us. Social networks matter. But we also select as friends those who share our likes and dislikes.

What do the findings on drug use suggest for drug prevention and treatment programs? Three channels of influence seem possible:

- Educate young people about the long-term costs of a drug's temporary pleasures.
- Help young people find other ways to boost their self-esteem and purpose in life.
- Attempt to modify peer associations or to "inoculate" youths against peer pressures by training them in refusal skills.

People rarely abuse drugs if they understand the physical and psychological costs, feel good about themselves and the direction their lives are taking, and are in a peer group that disapproves of using drugs. These educational, psychological, and social factors may help explain why 42 percent of U.S. high school dropouts, but only 15 percent of college graduates, smoke (Ladd, 1998).

BEFORE YOU MOVE ON . . .

➤ ASK YOURSELF

Drinking dominates parties when students overestimate other students' enthusiasm for alcohol. Do you think such misperceptions exist at your high school? How might you find out?

➤ TEST YOURSELF 3

A U.S. government survey of 27,616 current or former alcohol drinkers found that 40 percent of those who began drinking before age 15 grew dependent on alcohol. The same was true of only 10 percent of those who first imbibed at age 21 or 22 (Grant & Dawson, 1998). What possible explanations might there be for this correlation between early use and later abuse?

Answers to the Test Yourself questions can be found in Appendix E at the end of the book.

TROUBLESHOOTING

Students will tend to protest the findings of the studies Myers cites regarding the predictors of drug and alcohol use among teens. They will cite their own experience or the experiences of their friends as evidence that the studies are wrong. Remind them that the plural of anecdote is not data. Also point out that these are correlated predictors, not guarantees. Many factors contribute to whether someone will become a drug or alcohol user, and those presented here are only some of those factors. Awareness of what might lead to such behavior is a good first step in avoiding the bad outcomes.

TEACHING TIP

At this point, you may want to use **Student Project: *Debates on Drugs and Society*** (p. 25) from Bolt's Teacher's Resource Binder.

UNIT REVIEW: States of Consciousness

Sleep and Dreams

1: How do our biological rhythms influence our daily functioning?

Our internal biological rhythms create periodic physiological fluctuations. The *circadian rhythm's* 24-hour cycle regulates our daily schedule of sleeping and waking, in part in response to light on the retina, triggering alterations in the level of sleep-inducing melatonin. Shifts in schedules can reset our biological clock.

2: What is the biological rhythm of our sleep?

Another biological rhythm is the *sleep* stages. We cycle through five sleep stages in about 90 minutes. Leaving the *alpha waves* of the awake, relaxed stage, we descend into transitional Stage 1 sleep, often with the sensation of falling or floating. Stage 2 sleep (in which we spend the most time) follows about 20 minutes later, with its characteristic sleep spindles. Then follow Stages 3 and 4, together lasting about 30 minutes, with large, slow *delta waves*. All these stages are referred to as *NREM sleep*. Reversing course, we retrace our path, but with one difference: About an hour after falling asleep, we begin periods of *REM* (rapid eye movement) *sleep*. Most dreaming occurs in this fifth stage (also known as paradoxical sleep) of internal arousal but outward paralysis. During a normal night's sleep, periods of Stages 3 and 4 sleep shorten and REM sleep lengthens.

3: How does sleep loss affect us?

Sleep deprivation causes fatigue and impairs concentration, creativity, and communication. It also can lead to obesity, hypertension, a suppressed immune system, irritability, and slowed performance (with greater vulnerability to accidents).

4: What is sleep's function?

Sleep may have played a protective role in human evolution by keeping people safe during potentially dangerous periods. Sleep also gives the brain time to heal, as it restores and repairs damaged neurons. During sleep, we restore and rebuild memories of the day's experiences. A good night's sleep promotes creative problem solving the next day. Finally, sleep encourages growth; the pituitary gland secretes a growth hormone in Stage 4 sleep.

5: What are the major sleep disorders?

The disorders of sleep include *insomnia* (recurring wakefulness), *narcolepsy* (sudden uncontrollable sleepiness or lapsing into REM sleep), *sleep apnea* (the stopping of breathing while asleep), *night terrors* (high arousal and the appearance of being terrified), sleepwalking, and sleeptalking. Sleep apnea mainly targets overweight men. Children are most prone to night terrors, sleepwalking, and sleeptalking.

6: What do we dream?

We usually *dream* of ordinary events and everyday experiences, most involving some anxiety or misfortune. Fewer than 10 percent (and less among women) of dreams have any sexual content. Most dreams occur during REM sleep; those that happen during NREM sleep tend to be vague fleeting images.

7: What is the function of dreams?

There are five major views of the function of dreams. (1) Freudian: to provide a safety valve, with *manifest content* (or story line) acting as a censored version of *latent content* (some underlying meaning that gratifies our unconscious wishes). (2) The information-processing perspective: to sort out the day's experiences and fix them in memory. (3) Brain stimulation: to preserve neural pathways in the brain. (4) The activation-synthesis explanation: to make sense of neural static our brain tries to weave into a story line. (5) The brain-maturation/cognitive-development perspective: dreams represent the dreamer's level of development, knowledge, and understanding. Most sleep theorists agree that REM sleep and its associated dreams serve an important function, as shown by the *REM rebound* that occurs following REM deprivation.

Hypnosis

8: What is hypnosis, and what powers does a hypnotist have over a hypnotized subject?

Hypnosis is a social interaction in which one person suggests to another that certain perceptions, feelings, thoughts, or behaviors will spontaneously occur. Hypnotized people are no more vulnerable to acting against their will than unhypnotized people are, and hypnosis does not enhance recall of forgotten events (it may even evoke false memories). Hypnotized people, like unhypnotized people, may perform unlikely acts when told to do so by an authoritative person. *Posthypnotic suggestions* have helped people harness their own healing powers but have not been very effective in treating addiction. Hypnosis can help relieve pain.

9: Is hypnosis an extension of normal consciousness or an altered state?

Many psychologists believe that hypnosis is a form of normal social influence and that hypnotized people act out the role of "good subject." Other psychologists view hypnosis as a *dissociation*—a split between normal sensations and conscious awareness. A unified account of hypnosis melds these two views and studies how brain activity, attention, and social influences interact in hypnosis.

Drugs and Consciousness

10: What are tolerance, dependence, and addiction, and what are some common misconceptions about addiction?

Psychoactive drugs alter perceptions and moods. Their continued use produces *tolerance* (requiring larger doses to achieve the same effect) and may lead to *physical* or *psychological dependence*. *Addiction* is compulsive drug craving and use. Three

ANSWERS to Multiple-Choice Questions

1. **e.** narcolepsy.
2. **e.** Delta
3. **c.** caffeine.
4. **b.** the production of melatonin.
5. **d.** sleep spindles.
6. **a.** Decreased concentration
7. **d.** Crystal meth
8. **a.** hypnosis.
9. **a.** hallucinogens.
10. **c.** paradoxical.
11. **b.** endorphins.
12. **d.** alcohol.
13. **e.** Dissociation
14. **a.** consciousness.
15. **b.** tolerance.

Rubric for Grading the Free-Response Question

This is a 13-point question. Allow one point for an adequate discussion of each of the following concepts or terms, with one point for each of the two confounding factors. Modify the rubric by adding or subtracting terms depending on what was emphasized in class.

Depressants (1 point)—drugs such as alcohol, barbiturates (tranquilizers), and opiates that calm neural activity and slow body functions.

Stimulants (1 point)—drugs such as nicotine, caffeine, and methamphetamine that temporarily excite neural activity and arouse body functions.

Hallucinogens (1 point)—drugs such as LSD and marijuana that distort perceptions and evoke sensory images in the absence of sensory input.

Hypothesis (1 point)—a testable prediction involving a drug and its impact on improving sleep.

common misconceptions about addiction are that (1) addictive drugs quickly corrupt; (2) therapy is always required to overcome addiction; and (3) the concept of addiction can meaningfully be extended beyond chemical dependence to a wide range of other behaviors.

11: What are depressants, and what are their effects?
Depressants, such as alcohol, *barbiturates*, and the *opiates* (which include narcotics), dampen neural activity and slow body functions. Alcohol tends to disinhibit—it increases the likelihood that we will act on our impulses, whether harmful or helpful. Alcohol also slows nervous system activity and impairs judgment, disrupts memory processes by suppressing REM sleep, and reduces self-awareness. User expectations strongly influence alcohol's behavioral effects.

12: What are stimulants, and what are their effects?
Stimulants—caffeine, nicotine, the *amphetamines,* cocaine, and *Ecstasy*—excite neural activity and speed up body functions. All are highly addictive. Nicotine's effects make smoking a difficult habit to kick, but the percentage of Americans who smoke is nevertheless decreasing. Continued use of *methamphetamine* may permanently reduce dopamine production. Cocaine gives users a 15- to 30-minute high, followed by a crash. Its risks include cardiovascular stress and suspiciousness. Ecstasy is a combined stimulant and mild hallucinogen that produces a euphoric high and feelings of intimacy. Its users risk immune system suppression, permanent damage to mood and memory, and (if taken during physical activity) dehydration and escalating body temperatures.

13: What are hallucinogens, and what are their effects?
Hallucinogens—such as *LSD* and marijuana—distort perceptions and evoke *hallucinations*—sensory images in the absence of sensory input. The user's mood and expectations influence the effects of LSD, but common experiences are hallucinations and emotions varying from euphoria to panic. People who have experienced a *near-death experience* during a life-threatening illness or accident have reported sensations that closely parallel drug-induced hallucinations, possibly reflecting a brain under stress. Marijuana's main ingredient, *THC*, may trigger feelings of disinhibition, euphoria, relaxation, relief from pain, and intense sensitivity to sensory stimuli. It may also increase feelings of depression or anxiety, impair motor coordination and reaction time, disrupt memory formation, and damage lung tissue (because of the inhaled smoke).

14: Why do some people become regular users of consciousness-altering drugs?
Psychological factors (such as stress, depression, and hopelessness) and social factors (such as peer pressure) combine to lead many people to experiment with—and sometimes become dependent on—drugs. Cultural and ethnic groups have differing rates of drug use. Some people may be biologically more likely to become dependent on drugs such as alcohol. Each type of influence—biological, psychological, and social-cultural—offers a possible path for drug prevention and treatment programs.

Terms and Concepts to Remember

TECHNOLOGY RESOURCES

These resources will be helpful for teaching the concepts in this portion of the unit:

- *Videos: The Brain,* 2nd ed., *Module 13: Sleep and Circadian Rhythms; Module 14: Sleep: Brain Functions; Module 15: REM Sleep and Dreaming**
- *Video: Psychology: The Human Experience, Module 9: Circadian Rhythms*
- *Psychology Video Tool Kit: Sleep and Sleeplessness; Sleep Terror Disorder; Hypnosis: Medical and Psychological Applications; Hypnosis: An Altered Mental State?; The Nature and Abuse of Ecstasy (MDMA); The Medical Use of Marijuana; The Effects of Sleep Deprivation: Three Brave Souls*

AP* Practice Test Questions ◀ •

Multiple-Choice Questions

1. Sudden sleep attacks at inopportune times best describes
a. sleep apnea.
b. insomnia.
c. night terrors.
d. sleepwalking.
e. narcolepsy.

2. Deep sleep occurs in which stage?
a. Hypnagogic
b. REM
c. Alpha
d. Stage 1
e. Delta

3. Fruit juices, energy drinks, mints, soap, and soda have all been known to contain
a. marijuana.
b. cocaine.
c. caffeine.
d. nicotine.
e. crystal meth.

4. The pineal gland's role in sleep involves
a. activating the suprachiasmatic nucleus.
b. the production of melatonin.
c. the location of hypnagogic images.
d. remembering dreams upon waking.
e. emitting alpha waves.

5. Bursts of rapid, rhythmic brain-wave activity while sleeping are called
a. hallucinations.
b. circadian rhythms.
c. alpha waves.
d. sleep spindles.
e. delta waves.

6. Which of the following is *least likely* to occur as a result of good sleep habits?
a. Decreased concentration
b. Better immune system
c. Strengthened memory
d. Lower serious accident rate
e. Decreased obesity

7. In addition to cocaine and heroin, what drug does the British government consider one of the most dangerous?
a. Alcohol
b. Marijuana
c. Endorphins
d. Crystal meth
e. Nicotine

8. Stress-related disorders, asthma, and headaches have been successfully alleviated using
a. hypnosis.
b. serotonin.
c. leptin.
d. melatonin.
e. tolerance.

9. The three major categories of drugs include depressants, stimulants, and
a. hallucinogens.
b. barbiturates.
c. amphetamines.
d. caffeine.
e. alcohol.

10. Jarod's muscles are relaxed, his body is basically paralyzed, and he is hard to awaken. His sleep state would most likely be called
a. sleep apnea.
b. hypnagogic.
c. paradoxical.
d. delta.
e. sleep deprivation.

11. The brain's own opiates are called
a. barbiturates.
b. endorphins.
c. tranquilizers.
d. Nembutal.
e. Seconal.

12. Slowed reactions, slurred speech, and decreased skill performance are associated with abuse of
a. nicotine.
b. methamphetamine.
c. caffeine.
d. alcohol.
e. Ecstasy.

13. What did Ernest Hilgard call a split between different levels of consciousness?
a. Hypnagogic imagery
b. REM sleep
c. Delta waves
d. Spindles
e. Dissociation

14. Awareness of ourselves and our environment best describes
a. consciousness.
b. circadian rhythm.
c. hallucinations.
d. the biological clock.
e. hypnotism.

15. The brain's adaptation to a drug's chemistry, requiring larger and larger doses to experience the same effect, is called
a. withdrawal.
b. tolerance.
c. physical dependence.
d. psychological dependence.
e. disinhibiting.

Free-Response Question

Describe the three major categories of drugs. Design an experiment that would determine whether a drug in one of the categories helps improve sleep. Be sure to correctly use the following concepts in the natural context of your response.

- Hypothesis
- Operational definitions of sleep and improved sleep
- Independent and dependent variables
- Control and experimental groups
- Population and sample
- Two possible confounding factors

 WEB

Multiple-choice self-tests and more may be found at www.worthpublishers.com/myers

 Rubric continued

Operational definitions (1 point)—a statement of procedures used to define "sleep" and "improved sleep." For example, "sleep" might be defined as the amount of time spent asleep per night, as measured by EEG recordings in a sleep lab. And "improved sleep" might be defined as the amount of increased sleep per night as measured by EEG recordings in a sleep lab.

Independent variable (1 point)—the drug being tested

Dependent variable (1 point)—results of the drug, in this case, the impact on improved sleep

Control group (1 point)—is not given the drug, but otherwise experiences the same conditions that the experimental group experiences

Experimental group (1 point)—receives the drug

Population (1 point)—the large group being studied, and to which results may be applied

Sample (1 point)—the subset of the population involved in the experiment

Confounding factors (2 points)—list two; options include but are not limited to the following:

Amount of sleep received the night before the experiment starts

Hunger of the participant

Ability to adapt to having electrodes on one's head

Noise occurring during sleep time

Stress (i.e., relationship, academic, financial)

- *Videos: Scientific American Frontiers,* 2nd ed., *Segment 13: Catching Catnaps; Segment 15: Can You Beat Jet Lag?; Segment 14: What's in a Dream?*
- *PsychSim 5: EEG and Sleep Stages; Your Mind on Drugs*
- *ActivePsych: Digital Media Archive,* 2nd ed.: *Narcoleptic Dogs; The Brain's Reward Center*
- *Videos: The Mind,* 2nd ed., *Module 2: Hypnotic Dissociation and Pain Relief; Module 30: Treating Drug Addiction: A Behavioral Approach; Module 22: Depressants and Their Addictive Effect on the Brain; Module 29: Alcohol Addiction: Hereditary Factors*

UNIT 6

Pacing Guide

Use the following guide to determine how many instructional days to devote to this unit depending on the type of course you teach:

Year-long course: 7–9 days
Block schedule/Semester-long course: 3–5 days

This unit encompasses 7–9 percent of the AP Exam. Spending an appropriate amount of time on this unit will help students do well on the AP Exam.

INTERCONNECTING

Point out to students that the learning described in this unit is a largely behaviorist view of learning. The concepts in this unit are basic to our understanding of human and nonhuman animal learning, but the unit only scratches the surface when addressing the cognitive aspects of learning.

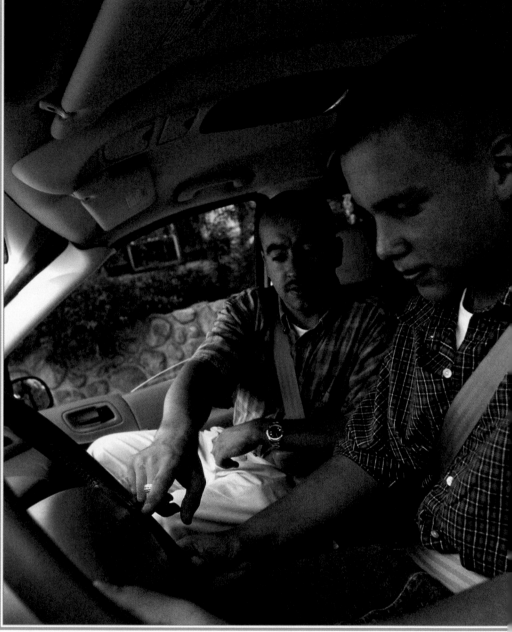

214

Suggested Readings

Black, A. H., & Perokasy, W. F. (Eds.) (1972). *Classical conditioning II: Current theory.* New York: Appleton-Century-Crofts.

Cialdini, R. B. (1993). *Influence: Science and practice* (3rd ed.). New York: HarperCollins.

Logue, A. W. (1995). *Self-control: Waiting until tomorrow for what you want today.* Englewood Cliffs, NJ: Prentice Hall.

Skinner, B. F. (1971). *Beyond freedom and dignity.* New York: Knopf.

Skinner, B. F. (1948). *Walden two.* New York: Macmillan.

Learning

When a chinook salmon first emerges from its egg in a stream's gravel bed, its genes provide most of the behavioral instructions it needs for life. It knows instinctively how and where to swim, what to eat, and how to protect itself. Following a built-in plan, the young salmon soon begins its trek to the sea. After some four years in the ocean, the mature salmon returns to its birthplace. It navigates hundreds of miles to the mouth of its home river and then, guided by the scent of its home stream, begins an upstream odyssey to its ancestral spawning ground. Once there, the salmon seeks out the best temperature, gravel, and water flow for breeding. It then mates and, its life mission accomplished, dies.

Unlike salmon, we are not born with a genetic plan for life. Much of what we do we learn from experience. Although we struggle to find the life direction a salmon is born with, our learning gives us more flexibility. We can learn how to build grass huts or snow shelters, submarines or space stations, and thereby adjust to almost any environment.

© 1986 by Sidney Harris, American Scientist Magazine.

"Actually, sex just isn't that important to me."

Indeed, nature's most important gift to us may be our *adaptability*—our capacity to learn new behaviors that help us cope with changing circumstances.

Learning breeds hope. What is learnable we can potentially teach—a fact that encourages parents, teachers, coaches, and animal trainers. What has been learned we can potentially change by new learning—an assumption that underlies counseling, psychotherapy, and rehabilitation programs. No matter how unhappy, unsuccessful, or unloving we are, that need not be the end of our story.

No topic is closer to the heart of psychology than **learning,** *a relatively permanent behavior change due to experience.* In earlier units we considered the learning of faulty thinking patterns, of visual perceptions, of a drug's expected effect. In later units we will see how learning shapes our thought and language, our motivations and emotions, our personalities and attitudes. This unit examines three types of learning: *classical conditioning, operant conditioning,* and *observational learning.*

How Do We Learn?

1: What are some basic forms of learning?

MORE THAN 200 YEARS AGO, philosophers such as John Locke and David Hume echoed Aristotle's conclusion from 2000 years earlier: We learn by *association.* Our minds naturally connect events that occur in sequence. Suppose you see and smell freshly baked bread, eat some, and find it satisfying. The next time you see and smell fresh bread, that experience will lead you to expect that eating it will once again be satisfying. So, too, with sounds. If

"Learning is the eye of the mind."
> Thomas Drake,
> *Bibliotheca Scholastica Instructissima,* 1633

::**learning** a relatively permanent change in an organism's behavior due to experience.

215

Key People

Little Albert
Albert Bandura
Edward Deci
John Garcia
Ivan Pavlov
Rosalie Rayner
Robert Rescorla
Giacomo Rizzolatti

Richard Ryan
Martin Seligman
B. F. Skinner
Edward L. Thorndike
Edward Chase Tolman
Allan Wagner
John Watson

Key Terms

learning
habituation
associative learning

Classical Conditioning

classical conditioning
behaviorism
unconditioned response (UR)
unconditioned stimulus (US)
conditioned response (CR)
conditioned stimulus (CS)
acquisition
higher-order conditioning
extinction
spontaneous recovery
generalization
discrimination
learned helplessness

Operant Conditioning

respondent behavior
operant conditioning
operant behavior
law of effect
operant chamber
shaping
discriminative stimulus
reinforcer
positive reinforcement
negative reinforcement
primary reinforcer
conditioned reinforcer
continuous reinforcement
partial (intermittent) reinforcement
fixed-ratio schedule
variable-ratio schedule
fixed-interval schedule
variable-interval schedule
punishment
cognitive map
latent learning
insight
intrinsic motivation
extrinsic motivation
biofeedback

Key Terms continued »

Use the definition of learning to help students understand the perspective this unit is taking about learning:

- **Relatively permanent:** Note to students that learning should have staying power. Real learning is not fleeting or temporary, like when they "learn something just for the test."

- **Change in an organism's behavior:** Point out that we know learning has occurred when the behavior has changed. Before learning, behavior happens in one way. After learning, behavior occurs differently.

- **Due to experience:** Learning does not occur in a vacuum. Learning results from experience, either directly or indirectly.

At this time, you may want to use **Classroom Exercise: *Defining Learning*** (p. 3) from Bolt's Teacher's Resource Binder, which accompanies this text.

TROUBLESHOOTING

Students may confuse habituation with adaptation, a concept discussed in Unit 4. These concepts, while similar, are quite different from each other.

- With habituation, we eventually lose our sensitivity to an oft-repeated stimulus. Once habituation occurs, we will have reduced sensitivity to that stimulus, even if the stimulus changes.

- Adaptation occurs when we get used to a continuous, unchanging stimulus. As long as the stimulus is unchanging, we will eventually not notice it at all. When the stimulus changes, however, our sensitivity to the stimulus will go back to original levels.

In short, adaptation is recoverable. Habituation is not.

Nature without appropriate nurture
Keiko—the killer whale of Free Willy fame—had all the right genes for being dropped right back into his Icelandic home waters. But lacking life experience, he required caregivers to his life's end in a Norwegian fjord. ▲

• Most of us would be unable to name the order of the songs on our favorite CD or playlist. Yet, hearing the end of one piece cues (by association) an anticipation of the next. Likewise, when singing your national anthem, you associate the end of each line with the beginning of the next. (Pick a line out of the middle and notice how much harder it is to recall the *previous* line.) •

you associate a sound with a frightening consequence, hearing the sound alone may trigger your fear. As one 4-year-old exclaimed after watching a TV character get mugged, "If I had heard that music, I wouldn't have gone around the corner!" (Wells, 1981).

Learned associations also feed our habitual behaviors (Wood & Neal, 2007). As we repeat behaviors in a given context—the sleeping posture we associate with bed, our walking routes from class to class, our eating popcorn in a movie theater—the behaviors become associated with the contexts. Our next experience of the context then automatically triggers the habitual response. Such associations can make it hard to kick a smoking habit; when back in the smoking context, the urge to light up can be powerful (Siegel, 2005).

Other animals also learn by association. Disturbed by a squirt of water, the sea slug *Aplysia* protectively withdraws its gill. If the squirts continue, as happens naturally in choppy water, the withdrawal response diminishes. We say the slug **habituates**. But if the sea slug repeatedly receives an electric shock just after being squirted, its withdrawal response to the squirt instead grows stronger. The animal relates the squirt to the impending shock. Complex animals can learn to relate their own behavior to its outcomes. Seals in an aquarium will repeat behaviors, such as slapping and barking, that prompt people to toss them a herring.

By linking two events that occur close together, both the sea slug and the seals exhibit **associative learning.** The sea slug associates the squirt with an impending shock; the seal associates slapping and barking with a herring treat. Each animal has learned something important to its survival: predicting the immediate future.

The significance of an animal's learning is illustrated by the challenges captive-bred animals face when introduced to the wild. After being bred and raised in captivity, 11 Mexican gray wolves—extinct in the United States since 1977—were released in Arizona's Apache National Forest in 1998. Eight months later, a lone survivor was recaptured. The pen-reared wolves had learned how to hunt—and to move 100 feet away from people—but had not learned to run from a human with a gun. Their story is not unusual. Twentieth-century records document 145 reintroductions of 115 species. Of those, only 11 percent produced self-sustaining populations in the wild. Successful adaptation requires both nature (the needed genetic predispositions) and nurture (a history of appropriate learning).

Conditioning is the process of learning associations. In *classical conditioning*, we learn to associate two stimuli and thus to anticipate events. We learn that a flash of lightning signals an impending crack of thunder, so when lightning flashes nearby, we start to brace ourselves (FIGURE 6.1).

➤ **FIGURE 6.1**
Classical conditioning

At this time, you may want to use **Lecture/Discussion Topic: *Cultural Beliefs About Learning: Mind or Virtue?*** (p. 3) from Bolt's Teacher's Resource Binder.

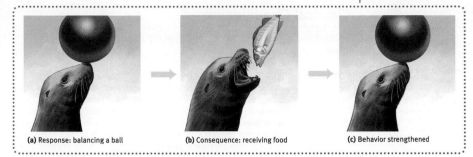

(a) Response: balancing a ball   (b) Consequence: receiving food   (c) Behavior strengthened

In *operant conditioning,* we learn to associate a response (our behavior) and its consequence and thus to repeat acts followed by good results (FIGURE 6.2) and avoid acts followed by bad results.

To simplify, we will explore these two types of associative learning separately. Often, though, they occur together, as on one Japanese cattle ranch, where the clever rancher outfitted his herd with electronic pagers, which he calls from his cell phone. After a week of training, the animals learn to associate two stimuli—the beep on their pager and the arrival of food (classical conditioning). But they also learn to associate their hustling to the food trough with the pleasure of eating (operant conditioning).

The concept of association by conditioning provokes questions: What principles influence the learning and the loss of associations? How can these principles be applied? And what really are the associations: Does the beep on a steer's pager evoke a mental representation of food, to which the steer responds by coming to the trough? Or does it make little sense to explain conditioned associations in terms of cognition? (In Unit 7B, we will see how the brain stores and retrieves learning.)

Conditioning is not the only form of learning. Through *observational learning,* we learn from others' experiences. Chimpanzees, too, may learn behaviors merely by watching others perform them. If one sees another solve a puzzle and gain a food reward, the observer may perform the trick more quickly.

By conditioning and by observation we humans learn and adapt to our environments. We learn to expect and prepare for significant events such as food or pain *(classical conditioning).* We also learn to repeat acts that bring good results and to avoid acts that bring bad results *(operant conditioning).* By watching others we learn new behaviors *(observational learning).* And through language, we also learn things we have neither experienced nor observed.

BEFORE YOU MOVE ON . . .

➤ ASK YOURSELF

Can you remember some example from your childhood of learning through classical conditioning—perhaps salivating at the sound or smell of some delicious food cooking in your family kitchen? Can you remember an example of operant conditioning, when you repeated (or decided not to repeat) a behavior because you liked (or hated) its consequences? Can you recall watching someone else perform some act and later repeating or avoiding that act?

➤ TEST YOURSELF 1

As we develop, we learn cues that lead us to expect and prepare for good and bad events. We learn to repeat behaviors that bring rewards. And we watch others and learn. What do psychologists call these three types of learning?

Answers to the Test Yourself questions can be found in Appendix E at the end of the book.

➤ FIGURE 6.2
Operant conditioning

::**habituation** an organism's decreasing response to a stimulus with repeated exposure to it.

::**associative learning** learning that certain events occur together. The events may be two stimuli (as in classical conditioning) or a response and its consequences (as in operant conditioning).

 Key Terms continued from p. 215

Learning by Observation
observational learning
modeling
mirror neurons
prosocial behavior

TEACHING TIP

Associative learning is the blanket term for all the types of conditioning discussed in this unit. This unit deals with types of conditioning in which organisms associate one stimulus or experience with another.

At this time, you may want to use **Lecture/Discussion Topic:** *The Association Principle* (p. 9) from Bolt's Teacher's Resource Binder.

INTERCONNECTING

Point out that Unit 7A discusses the connection between memory and learning. For decades during the twentieth century, behaviorists resisted this connection, because memory and cognition were not as measurable as associative learning.

::**classical conditioning** a type of learning in which one learns to link two or more stimuli and anticipate events.

::**behaviorism** the view that psychology (1) should be an objective science that (2) studies behavior without reference to mental processes. Most research psychologists today agree with (1) but not with (2).

::**unconditioned response (UR)** in classical conditioning, the unlearned, naturally occurring response to the unconditioned stimulus (US), such as salivation when food is in the mouth.

::**unconditioned stimulus (US)** in classical conditioning, a stimulus that unconditionally—naturally and automatically—triggers a response.

::**conditioned response (CR)** in classical conditioning, the learned response to a previously neutral (but now conditioned) stimulus (CS).

::**conditioned stimulus (CS)** in classical conditioning, an originally irrelevant stimulus that, after association with an unconditioned stimulus (US), comes to trigger a conditioned response.

Ivan Pavlov "Experimental investigation . . . should lay a solid foundation for a future true science of psychology" (1927).

Classical Conditioning

2: What is classical conditioning, and how did Pavlov's work influence behaviorism?

FOR MANY PEOPLE, THE NAME IVAN Pavlov (1849–1936) rings a bell. His early twentieth-century experiments—now psychology's most famous research—are classics, and the phenomenon he explored we justly call **classical conditioning.**

Pavlov's work also laid the foundation for many of psychologist John B. Watson's ideas. In searching for laws underlying learning, Watson (1913) urged his colleagues to discard reference to inner thoughts, feelings, and motives. The science of psychology should instead study how organisms respond to stimuli in their environments, said Watson: "Its theoretical goal is the prediction and control of behavior. Introspection forms no essential part of its methods." Simply said, psychology should be an objective science based on observable behavior. This view, which influenced North American psychology during the first half of the twentieth century, Watson called **behaviorism.** Watson and Pavlov shared both a disdain for "mentalistic" concepts (such as consciousness) and a belief that the basic laws of learning were the same for all animals—whether dogs or humans. Few researchers today propose that psychology should ignore mental processes, but most now agree that classical conditioning is a basic form of learning by which all organisms adapt to their environment.

Pavlov's Experiments

3: How does a neutral stimulus become a conditioned stimulus?

Pavlov was driven by a lifelong passion for research. After setting aside his initial plan to follow his father into the Russian Orthodox priesthood, Pavlov received a medical degree at age 33 and spent the next two decades studying the digestive system. This work earned him Russia's first Nobel Prize in 1904. But it was his novel experiments on learning, to which he devoted the last three decades of his life, that earned this feisty scientist his place in history.

Pavlov's new direction came when his creative mind seized on an incidental observation. Without fail, putting food in a dog's mouth caused the animal to salivate. Moreover, the dog began salivating not only to the taste of the food, but also to the mere sight of the food, or the food dish, or the person delivering the food, or even the sound of that person's approaching footsteps. At first, Pavlov considered these "psychic secretions" an annoyance—until he realized they pointed to a simple but important form of learning.

Pavlov and his assistants tried to imagine what the dog was thinking and feeling as it drooled in anticipation of the food. This only led them into fruitless debates. So, to explore the phenomenon more objectively, they experimented. To eliminate other possible influences, they isolated the dog in a small room, secured it in a harness, and attached a device to divert its saliva to a measuring instrument. From the next room, they presented food—first by sliding in a food bowl, later by blowing meat powder into the dog's mouth at a precise moment. They then paired various *neutral events*—something the dog could see or hear but didn't associate with food—with food in the dog's mouth. If a sight or sound regularly signaled the arrival of food, would the dog learn the link? If so, would it begin salivating in anticipation of the food?

The answers proved to be *yes* and *yes*. Just before placing food in the dog's mouth to produce salivation, Pavlov sounded a tone. After several pairings of tone and food, the dog, anticipating the meat powder, began salivating to the tone alone. In later experiments,

---

UNIT 6

BEFORE CONDITIONING

US (food in mouth) → UR (salivation)

An unconditioned stimulus (US) produces an unconditioned response (UR).

Neutral stimulus (tone) → No salivation

A neutral stimulus produces no salivation response.

DURING CONDITIONING

Neutral stimulus (tone) + US (food in mouth) → UR (salivation)

The unconditioned stimulus is repeatedly presented just after the neutral stimulus. The unconditioned stimulus continues to produce an unconditioned response.

AFTER CONDITIONING

CS (tone) → CR (salivation)

The neutral stimulus alone now produces a conditioned response (CR), thereby becoming a conditioned stimulus (CS).

a buzzer, a light, a touch on the leg, even the sight of a circle set off the drooling.[1] (This procedure works with people, too. When hungry young Londoners viewed abstract figures before smelling peanut butter or vanilla, their brains soon were responding in anticipation to the abstract images alone [Gottfried et al., 2003]).

Because salivation in response to food in the mouth was unlearned, Pavlov called it an **unconditioned response (UR).** Food in the mouth automatically, *unconditionally,* triggers a dog's salivary reflex (FIGURE 6.3). Thus, Pavlov called the food stimulus an **unconditioned stimulus (US).**

Salivation in response to the tone was *conditional* upon the dog's learning the association between the tone and the food. Today we call this learned response the **conditioned response (CR).** The previously neutral (in this context) tone stimulus that now triggered the conditional salivation we call the **conditioned stimulus (CS).** Distinguishing these two kinds of stimuli and responses is easy: Conditioned = learned; *unconditioned = unlearned.*

Let's check your understanding with a second example. An experimenter sounds a tone just before delivering an air puff, which causes your eye to blink. After several repetitions, you blink to the tone alone. What is the US? The UR? The CS? The CR?[2]

PEANUTS

THE EARS HEAR THE CAN OPENER..

RIGHT AWAY THE STOMACH KNOWS THAT SUPPER IS COMING..

HOW DO THE EARS TELL THE STOMACH?

I'VE NEVER BEEN ABLE TO FIGURE THAT OUT..

PEANUTS reprinted by permission of United Feature Syndicate, Inc.

_____

[1]The "buzzer" (English translation) was perhaps Pavlov's supposed bell—a small electric bell (Tully, 2003).

[2]US = air puff; UR = blink to air puff; CS = tone after procedure; CR = blink to tone

> **FIGURE 6.3**
> **Pavlov's classic experiment** Pavlov presented a neutral stimulus (a tone) just before an unconditioned stimulus (food in mouth). The neutral stimulus then became a conditioned stimulus, producing a conditioned response.

UNIT 6

TEACHING TIP

Using a question format like the one in the margin is excellent practice for AP Exam questions. You can create classical conditioning scenarios yourself or challenge students to come up with scenarios to test their peers.

TEACHING TIP

Timing is very important to successful classical conditioning. Studies have shown that the CS must precede the US by about ½ to 1 second in order to bring about the CR. Other types of timing that can occur with classical conditioning include the following:

- Delayed conditioning: The CS precedes the US, but they overlap just a little. This is the best situation for conditioning, especially if the time delay between CS and US is short.

- Trace conditioning: The CS precedes the US and they do not overlap. The longer the time delay between the CS and US, the more difficult conditioning is.

- Simultaneous conditioning: The CS occurs at the same time as the US. This is not a good idea because it results in poor conditioning. The CS doesn't predict the US at all in this situation.

- Backward conditioning: The CS follows the US. Little or no conditioning takes place, unless the response is biologically predisposed.

● Check yourself: If the aroma of cake baking sets your mouth to watering, what is the US? The CS? The CR? (Answers below.)

Remember:
US = Unconditioned Stimulus
UR = Unconditioned Response
CS = Conditioned Stimulus
CR = Conditioned Response ●

The cake (and its taste) are the US. The associated aroma is the CS. Salivation to the aroma is the CR.

::**acquisition** in classical conditioning, the initial stage, when one links a neutral stimulus and an unconditioned stimulus so that the neutral stimulus begins triggering the conditioned response. In operant conditioning, the strengthening of a reinforced response.

::**higher-order conditioning** a procedure in which the conditioned stimulus in one conditioning experience is paired with a new neutral stimulus, creating a second (often weaker) conditioned stimulus. For example, an animal that has learned that a tone predicts food might then learn that a light predicts the tone and begin responding to the light alone. (Also called *second-order conditioning*.)

::**extinction** the diminishing of a conditioned response; occurs in classical conditioning when an unconditioned stimulus (US) does not follow a conditioned stimulus (CS); occurs in operant conditioning when a response is no longer reinforced.

::**spontaneous recovery** the reappearance, after a pause, of an extinguished conditioned response.

If Pavlov's demonstration of associative learning was so simple, what did he do for the next three decades? What discoveries did his research factory publish in his 532 papers on salivary conditioning (Windholz, 1997)? He and his associates explored five major conditioning processes: *acquisition, extinction, spontaneous recovery, generalization,* and *discrimination.*

Acquisition

4: In classical conditioning, what are the processes of acquisition, extinction, spontaneous recovery, generalization, and discrimination?

To understand the **acquisition,** or initial learning, of the stimulus-response relationship, Pavlov and his associates had to confront the question of timing: How much time should elapse between presenting the neutral stimulus (the tone, the light, the touch) and the unconditioned stimulus? In most cases, not much—half a second usually works well.

What do you suppose would happen if the food (US) appeared before the tone (CS) rather than after? Would conditioning occur?

Not likely. With but a few exceptions, conditioning doesn't happen when the CS follows the US. Remember, classical conditioning is biologically adaptive because it helps humans and other animals *prepare* for good or bad events. To Pavlov's dogs, the tone (CS) signaled an important biological event—the arrival of food (US). To deer in the forest, the snapping of a twig (CS) may signal a predator's approach (US). If the good or bad event had already occurred, the CS would not likely signal anything significant.

Michael Domjan (1992, 1994, 2005) showed how a CS can signal another important biological event, by conditioning the sexual arousal of male Japanese quail. Just before presenting an approachable female, the researchers turned on a red light. Over time, as the red light continued to herald the female's arrival, the light caused the male quail to become excited. They developed a preference for their cage's red-light district, and when a female appeared, they mated with her more quickly and released more semen and sperm (Matthews et al., 2007). All in all, the quail's capacity for classical conditioning gives it a reproductive edge. Again we see the larger lesson: *Conditioning helps an animal survive and reproduce—by responding to cues that help it gain food, avoid dangers, locate mates, and produce offspring* (Hollis, 1997).

In humans, too, objects, smells, and sights associated with sexual pleasure—even a geometric figure in one experiment—can become conditioned stimuli for sexual arousal (Byrne, 1982). Psychologist Michael Tirrell (1990) recalls: "My first girlfriend loved onions, so I came to associate onion breath with kissing. Before long, onion breath sent tingles up and down my spine. Oh what a feeling!" (FIGURE 6.4)

Through **higher-order conditioning,** a new neutral stimulus can become a new conditioned stimulus. All that's required is for it to become associated with a previously conditioned stimulus. If a tone regularly signals food and produces salivation, then a light that becomes associated with the tone may also begin to trigger salivation. Although this higher-order conditioning (also called *second-order conditioning*) tends to be weaker than first-stage conditioning, it influences our everyday lives. Imagine that something makes us very afraid (perhaps a big dog associated with a previous dog bite). If something else, such as the sound of a barking dog, brings to mind that big dog, the bark alone may make us feel a little afraid.

Associations can influence attitudes (De Houwer et al., 2001; Park et al., 2007). As Andy Field (2006) showed British children novel cartoon characters alongside either ice cream (*Yum!*) or Brussels sprouts (*Yuk!*), the children came to like best the ice-cream-

DEMO

Pete Cherniss of Riverside Poly High School in California suggests using a yardstick with brass reinforcements on both ends to demonstrate classical conditioning. Ask for a volunteer to name a color that is neutral to him or her, one he or she neither likes nor dislikes. Then ask the volunteer to close his/her eyes. Tell the class to observe the person as you go behind the volunteer and say the color (very nonchalantly) followed by immediately snapping the ruler loudly. Students can easily identify the US, UR, CS and CR. Also introduce discrimination and generalization with the same example.

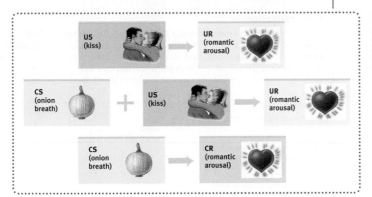

➤ **FIGURE 6.4**
An unexpected CS Onion breath does not usually arouse romantic feelings. But when repeatedly paired with a kiss, it can become a CS and do just that.

associated characters. Michael Olson and Russell Fazio (2001) classically conditioned adults' attitudes, using little-known Pokémon characters. The participants, playing the role of a security guard monitoring a video screen, viewed a stream of words, images, and Pokémon characters. Their task, they were told, was to respond to one target Pokémon character by pressing a button. Unnoticed by the participants, when two other Pokémon characters appeared on the screen, one was consistently associated with various positive words and images (such as *awesome* or a hot fudge sundae); the other appeared with negative words and images (such as *awful* or a cockroach). Without any conscious memory for the pairings, the participants formed more gut-level positive attitudes for the characters associated with the positive stimuli.

Follow-up studies indicate that conditioned likes and dislikes are even stronger when people notice and are aware of the associations they have learned (De Houwer et al., 2005a,b; Pleyers et al., 2007). Cognition matters.

Extinction and Spontaneous Recovery

After conditioning, what happens if the CS occurs repeatedly without the US? Will the CS continue to elicit the CR? Pavlov discovered that when he sounded the tone again and again without presenting food, the dogs salivated less and less. Their declining salivation illustrates **extinction,** the diminished responding that occurs when the CS (tone) no longer signals an impending US (food).

Pavlov found, however, that if he allowed several hours to elapse before sounding the tone again, the salivation to the tone would reappear spontaneously (**FIGURE 6.5**). This **spontaneous recovery**—the reappearance of a (weakened) CR after a pause—suggested to Pavlov that extinction was suppressing the CR rather than eliminating it.

After breaking up with his fire-breathing heartthrob, Tirrell also experienced extinction and spontaneous recovery. He recalls that "the smell of onion breath (CS), no longer paired with the kissing (US), lost its ability to shiver my timbers. Occasionally, though, after not sensing the aroma for a long while, smelling onion breath awakens a small version of the emotional response I once felt."

➤ **FIGURE 6.5**
Idealized curve of acquisition, extinction, and spontaneous recovery The rising curve shows that the CR rapidly grows stronger as the CS and US are repeatedly paired *(acquisition),* then weakens as the CS is presented alone *(extinction).* After a pause, the CR reappears *(spontaneous recovery).*

TROUBLESHOOTING

The term "extinction" is used throughout this unit for both classical and operant conditioning. In both cases, the term refers to the loss of the learned response or behavior. The only difference for each type of conditioning is how the extinction occurs.

- For classical conditioning, extinction occurs when the US is no longer paired with the CS.
- For operant conditioning, extinction occurs when the reinforcement is no longer paired with the behavior.

TROUBLESHOOTING

Spontaneous recovery occurs only after extinction has occurred. In order to see spontaneous recovery, you do not need to reintroduce the unconditioned stimulus. Even though the recovered response is weaker, it is recovered after extinction, as though it never went away in the first place.

DEMO

There are several active ways to demonstrate classical conditioning with students. You may want to use any or all of these activities found in Bolt's Teacher's Resource Binder:

- **Classroom Exercise:** *Classical Conditioning Using Potato Chips and Lemonade Powder* (p. 4)
- **Classroom Exercise:** *Classical Conditioning: Preparing for an Important Event* (p. 5)
- **Classroom Exercise:** *Classical Conditioning With a Watergun* (p. 6)
- **Student Project:** *Conditioning the Eyeblink* (p. 7)

Stimulus generalization

"I don't care if she's a tape dispenser. I love her."

Generalization

Pavlov and his students noticed that a dog conditioned to the sound of one tone also responded somewhat to the sound of a different tone that had never been paired with food. Likewise, a dog conditioned to salivate when rubbed would also drool a bit when scratched (Windholz, 1989) or when touched on a different body part (**FIGURE 6.6**). This tendency to respond to stimuli similar to the CS is called **generalization.**

CRITICAL THINKING

Remind students that they respond to stimuli at school everyday—for instance, the sound of the bell that signals a class change. Have students hypothesize how students would react if that sound were changed in any way. For example:

- How long do they think it would take for students to realize what the new sound meant?

- Do they think students could be trained to respond to only one type of bell?

- How do they think school administrators use the concepts of generalization and discrimination in daily school situations?

TEACHING TIP

Generalization is quite automatic, as Myers describes. Discrimination, on the other hand, occurs as the result of overtraining, exposing the organism to the desired stimulus so many times that a response to anything similar doesn't occur. This process is similar to the training it takes to become an expert at a task.

➤ **FIGURE 6.6**
Generalization Pavlov demonstrated generalization by attaching miniature vibrators to various parts of a dog's body. After conditioning salivation to stimulation of the thigh, he stimulated other areas. The closer a stimulated spot was to the dog's thigh, the stronger the conditioned response. (From Pavlov, 1927.)

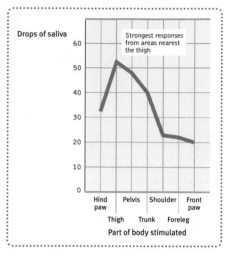

Drops of saliva

Strongest responses from areas nearest the thigh

60
50
40
30
20
10
0

Hind paw | Pelvis | Shoulder | Front paw
Thigh | Trunk | Foreleg

Part of body stimulated

Generalization can be adaptive, as when toddlers taught to fear moving cars also become afraid of moving trucks and motorcycles. So automatic is generalization that one Argentine writer who underwent torture still recoils with fear when he sees black shoes—his first glimpse of his torturers as they approached his cell. Generalization of anxiety reactions has been demonstrated in laboratory studies comparing abused with nonabused children (**FIGURE 6.7**). Shown an angry face on a computer screen, abused children's brain-wave responses are dramatically stronger and longer lasting (Pollak et al., 1998).

Because of generalization, stimuli similar to naturally disgusting or appealing objects will, by association, evoke some disgust or liking. Normally desirable foods, such as fudge, are unappealing when shaped to resemble dog feces (Rozin et al., 1986). Adults with childlike facial features (round face, large forehead, small chin, large eyes) are perceived as having childlike warmth, submissiveness, and naïveté (Berry & McArthur, 1986). In both cases, people's emotional reactions to one stimulus generalize to similar stimuli.

➤ **FIGURE 6.7**
Child abuse leaves tracks in the brain Seth Pollak (University of Wisconsin–Madison) reports that abused children's sensitized brains react more strongly to angry faces. This generalized anxiety response may help explain why child abuse puts children at greater risk for psychological disorders.

Discrimination

Pavlov's dogs also learned to respond to the sound of a particular tone and *not* to other tones. **Discrimination** is the learned ability to *distinguish* between a conditioned stimulus (which predicts the US) and other irrelevant stimuli. Being able to recognize differences is adaptive. Slightly different stimuli can be followed by vastly different consequences. Confronted by a guard dog, your heart may race; confronted by a guide dog, it probably will not.

Extending Pavlov's Understanding

5: Do cognitive processes and biological constraints affect classical conditioning?

In their dismissal of "mentalistic" concepts such as consciousness, Pavlov and Watson underestimated the importance of *cognitive processes* (thoughts, perceptions, expectations) and *biological constraints* on an organism's learning capacity.

Cognitive Processes

The early behaviorists believed that rats' and dogs' learned behaviors could be reduced to mindless mechanisms, so there was no need to consider cognition. But Robert Rescorla and Allan Wagner (1972) showed that an animal can learn the *predictability* of an event. If a shock always is preceded by a tone, and then may also be preceded by a light that accompanies the tone, a rat will react with fear to the tone but not to the light. Although the light is always followed by the shock, it adds no new information; the tone is a better predictor. The more predictable the association, the stronger the conditioned response. It's as if the animal learns an *expectancy,* an awareness of how likely it is that the US will occur.

Researcher Martin Seligman (1975, 1991) and others found that dogs strapped in a harness and given repeated shocks, with no opportunity to avoid them, learned a sense of helplessness. Later placed in another situation where they *could* escape the punishment by simply leaping a hurdle, the dogs cowered as if without hope. In contrast, animals able to escape the first shocks learned personal control and easily escaped the shocks in the new situation. People, too, when repeatedly faced with traumatic events over which they have no control, come to feel helpless, hopeless, and depressed. Psychologists call this passive resignation **learned helplessness**. (More on this concept and its relation to our sense of control in Unit 10.)

Such experiments help explain why classical conditioning treatments that ignore cognition often have limited success. For example, people receiving therapy for alcohol dependency may be given alcohol spiked with a nauseating drug. Will they then associate alcohol with sickness? If classical conditioning were merely a matter of "stamping in" stimulus associations, we might hope so, and to some extent this does occur (as we will see in Unit 13). However, the awareness that the nausea is induced by the drug, not the alcohol, often weakens the association between drinking alcohol and feeling sick. So, even in classical conditioning, it is (especially with humans) not simply the CS–US association but also the thought that counts.

Biological Predispositions

Ever since Charles Darwin, scientists have assumed that all animals share a common evolutionary history and thus commonalities in their makeup and functioning. Pavlov and Watson, for example, believed that the basic laws of learning were essentially similar in all animals. So it should make little difference whether one studied pigeons or people. Moreover, it seemed that any natural response could be conditioned to any neutral stimulus. As learning researcher Gregory Kimble proclaimed in 1956, "Just about any activity of which the organism is capable can be conditioned and . . . these responses can be conditioned to any stimulus that the organism can perceive" (p. 195).

Twenty-five years later, Kimble (1981) humbly acknowledged that "half a thousand" scientific reports had proven him wrong. More than the early behaviorists realized, an animal's capacity for conditioning is constrained by its biology. Each species' predispositions prepare it to learn the associations that enhance its survival. Environments are not the whole story.

::**generalization** the tendency, once a response has been conditioned, for stimuli similar to the conditioned stimulus to elicit similar responses.

::**discrimination** in classical conditioning, the learned ability to distinguish between a conditioned stimulus and stimuli that do not signal an unconditioned stimulus.

::**learned helplessness** the hopelessness and passive resignation an animal or human learns when unable to avoid repeated aversive events.

"All brains are, in essence, anticipation machines."
Daniel C. Dennett, *Consciousness Explained,* 1991

 TEACHING TIP

Rescorla and Wagner's idea that the predictability of the CS determined whether conditioning occurred was revolutionary to behaviorism. Predictability is a cognitive process, requiring thought to occur.

INTERCONNECTING

Learned helplessness has been found to be one of the roots of depression, which is discussed in Unit 12. Seligman and his colleagues have developed therapeutic techniques that help people unlearn this helplessness.

 TEACHING TIP

Seligman and Meier's studies in learned helplessness didn't just reveal the helpless pattern of behavior. Some of the dogs in their studies never gave up, trying different ways to escape the shock. Seligman became curious about these dogs and their different reactions to the uncontrollable situation. Through this research, he and his colleagues developed the idea of learned optimism, and they have formulated ways to help people develop ways to be more optimistic and less helpless.

 TEACHING TIP

At this time, you may want to use **Lecture/Discussion Topics:** *Cognitive Processes in Learning* (p. 8) or *Biological Predispositions* (p. 9) from Bolt's Teacher's Resource Binder.

UNIT 6

Taste aversions are particularly good for illustrating classical conditioning. Share one of your own and explain it in terms of conditioning principles. If asked, students are sure to volunteer aversions of their own. Martin Bolt of Calvin College told his students of the origin of his aversion to commercially produced frozen chicken dinners. He once stored such a dinner in the freezer compartment of his department's refrigerator. When he went to retrieve it, he found it in the company of a frozen laboratory rat. A student assistant, not knowing how to dispose of the deceased animal, had carefully packaged it in plastic and temporarily placed it in the freezer. He now finds all such dinners repulsive.

At this time, you may want to use **Lecture/Discussion Topic:** *Human Taste Aversions* (p. 5) from Bolt's Teacher's Resource Binder.

John Garcia As the laboring son of California farmworkers, Garcia attended school only in the off-season during his early childhood years. After entering junior college in his late twenties, and earning his Ph.D. in his late forties, he received the American Psychological Association's Distinguished Scientific Contribution Award "for his highly original, pioneering research in conditioning and learning." He was also elected to the National Academy of Sciences. ▲

Taste aversion If you became violently ill after eating seafood, you probably would have a hard time eating it again. The smell and taste would have become a CS for nausea. This learning occurs readily because our biology prepares us to learn taste aversions to toxic foods. ▲

John Garcia was among those who challenged the prevailing idea that all associations can be learned equally well. While researching the effects of radiation on laboratory animals, Garcia and Robert Koelling (1966) noticed that rats began to avoid drinking water from the plastic bottles in radiation chambers. Could classical conditioning be the culprit? Might the rats have linked the plastic-tasting water (a CS) to the sickness (UR) triggered by the radiation (US)?

To test their hunch, Garcia and Koelling gave the rats a particular taste, sight, or sound (CS) and later also gave them radiation or drugs (US) that led to nausea and vomiting (UR). Two startling findings emerged: First, even if sickened as late as several hours after tasting a particular novel flavor, the rats thereafter avoided that flavor. This appeared to violate the notion that for conditioning to occur, the US must immediately follow the CS.

Second, the sickened rats developed aversions to tastes but not to sights or sounds. This contradicted the behaviorists' idea that any perceivable stimulus could serve as a CS. But it made adaptive sense, because for rats the easiest way to identify tainted food is to taste it. (If sickened after sampling a new food, they thereafter avoid the food—which makes it difficult to eradicate a population of "bait-shy" rats by poisoning.)

Humans, too, seem biologically prepared to learn some associations rather than others. If you become violently ill four hours after eating contaminated seafood, you will probably develop an aversion to the taste of the seafood but not to the sight of the associated restaurant, its plates, the people you were with, or the music you heard there. In contrast, birds, which hunt by sight, appear biologically primed to develop aversions to the *sight* of tainted food (Nicolaus et al., 1983). Organisms are predisposed to learn associations that help them adapt.

Remember those Japanese quail that were conditioned to get excited by a red light that signaled a receptive female's arrival? Michael Domjan and his colleagues (2004) report that such conditioning is even speedier, stronger, and more durable when the CS is *ecologically relevant*—something similar to stimuli associated with sexual activity in the natural environment, such as the stuffed head of a female quail. In the real world, observes Domjan (2005), conditioned stimuli have a natural association with the unconditioned stimuli they predict.

This may help explain why we humans seem to be naturally disposed to learn associations between the color red and women's sexuality, note Andrew Elliot and Daniela Niesta (2008). Female primates display red when nearing ovulation. In human females, enhanced bloodflow produces the red blush of flirtation and sexual excitation. Does the frequent pairing of red and sex—with Valentine's hearts, red-light districts, and red lipstick—naturally enhance men's attraction to women? Elliot and Niesta's experiments consistently suggest that, without men's awareness, it does (**FIGURE 6.8**).

Garcia's early findings on taste aversion were met with an onslaught of criticism. As the German philosopher Arthur Schopenhauer (1788–1860) once said, important ideas are first ridiculed, then attacked, and finally taken for granted. In Garcia's case, the leading journals refused to publish his work. The findings were impossible, said some critics. But, as often happens in science, Garcia and Koelling's taste-aversion research is now basic textbook material. It is also a good example of experiments that began with the discomfort of some laboratory animals and ended by enhancing the welfare of many others. In another conditioned taste-aversion study, coyotes and wolves that were tempted into eating sheep carcasses laced with a sickening poison developed an aversion to sheep meat (Gustavson et al., 1974, 1976). Two wolves later penned with a live sheep seemed actually to fear it. The study not only saved the sheep from their predators, but also saved the sheep-shunning coyotes and wolves from angry ranchers and farmers who had wanted to destroy them. Later applications of Garcia and Koelling's findings have prevented baboons from raiding African gardens,

Some drug treatment programs use taste aversion techniques to get patients to quit using drugs. Have students investigate these programs:

- How do these treatment programs use taste aversions to get people to quit?
- Are they successful? Why or why not?
- Is it ethical to make someone sick on purpose, even if you are trying to help him or her overcome a devastating illness? Why or why not?

Courtesy of Kathryn Brownson, Hope College

 FIGURE 6.8
Romantic red In a series of experiments that controlled for other factors (such as the brightness of the image), men found women more attractive and sexually desirable when framed in red (Elliot & Niesta, 2008).

raccoons from attacking chickens, and ravens and crows from feeding on crane eggs—all while preserving predators who occupy an important ecological niche (Garcia & Gustavson, 1997).

All these cases support Darwin's principle that natural selection favors traits that aid survival. Our ancestors who readily learned taste aversions were unlikely to eat the same toxic food again and were more likely to survive and leave descendants. Nausea, like anxiety, pain, and other bad feelings, serves a good purpose. Like a low-oil warning on a car dashboard, each alerts the body to a threat (Neese, 1991).

The discovery of biological constraints—our readiness to learn adaptive associations such as taste aversions—affirms the value of different levels of analysis, including the biological and cognitive (**FIGURE 6.9**), when we seek to understand phenomena such as learning. And once again, we see an important principle at work: *Learning enables animals to adapt to their environments.* Responding to stimuli that announce significant events, such as food or pain, is adaptive. So is a genetic predisposition to associate a CS with a US that follows predictably and immediately: Causes often immediately precede effects.

Often, but not always, as we saw in the taste-aversion findings. Adaptation also sheds light on this exception. The ability to discern that effect need not follow cause immediately—that poisoned food can cause sickness quite a while after it has been

> "All animals are on a voyage through time, navigating toward futures that promote their survival and away from futures that threaten it. Pleasure and pain are the stars by which they steer."
>
> Psychologists Daniel T. Gilbert and Timothy D. Wilson, "Prospection: Experiencing the Future," 2007

> "Once bitten, twice shy."
>
> G. F. Northall, *Folk-Phrases*, 1894

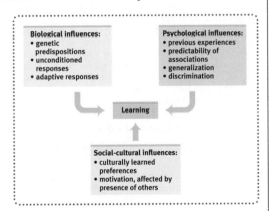

Biological influences:
• genetic predispositions
• unconditioned responses
• adaptive responses

Psychological influences:
• previous experiences
• predictability of associations
• generalization
• discrimination

Learning

Social-cultural influences:
• culturally learned preferences
• motivation, affected by presence of others

 FIGURE 6.9
Biopsychosocial influences on learning Today's learning theorists recognize that our learning results not only from environmental experiences, but also from cognitive and biological influences.

UNIT 6

TEACHING TIP

Students may not appreciate the contributions Pavlov made to psychology, which were great even though he was not a psychologist. His work set the stage for behaviorism to emerge, leading to numerous discoveries about learning and behavior that still are respected today. Emphasize to students the importance of Pavlov's work.

TEACHING TIP

Fortunately, what can be learned can be unlearned or reconditioned to a different stimulus. When cancer patients develop aversions after chemotherapy, doctors can use conditioning techniques to help them extinguish those aversions.

INTERCONNECTING

Many common phobias are learned through classical conditioning. They can also be deconditioned, using the same classical conditioning processes. The most common form of therapy for phobias is called systematic desensitization (Unit 13). Patients are gradually taught to associate feelings of relaxation with what they fear instead of associating feelings of anxiety with the feared object or activity.

> ➤ **FIGURE 6.10**
> **Nausea conditioning in cancer patients**

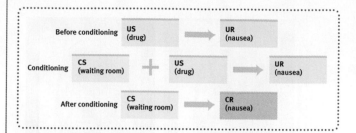

eaten—gives animals an adaptive advantage. Occasionally, however, our predispositions trick us. When chemotherapy triggers nausea and vomiting more than an hour following treatment, cancer patients may over time develop classically conditioned nausea (and sometimes anxiety) to the sights, sounds, and smells associated with the clinic (**FIGURE 6.10**) (Hall, 1997). Merely returning to the clinic's waiting room or seeing the nurses can provoke these conditioned feelings (Burish & Carey, 1986; Davey, 1992). Under normal circumstances, such revulsion to sickening stimuli would be adaptive.

Pavlov's Legacy

6: Why is Pavlov's work important?

What, then, remains of Pavlov's ideas? A great deal. Most psychologists agree that classical conditioning is a basic form of learning. Judged by today's knowledge of cognitive processes and biological predispositions, Pavlov's ideas were incomplete. But if we see further than Pavlov did, it is because we stand on his shoulders.

Why does Pavlov's work remain so important? If he had merely taught us that old dogs can learn new tricks, his experiments would long ago have been forgotten. Why should we care that dogs can be conditioned to salivate at the sound of a tone? The importance lies first in this finding: *Many other responses to many other stimuli can be classically conditioned in many other organisms*—in fact, in every species tested, from earthworms to fish to dogs to monkeys to people (Schwartz, 1984). Thus, classical conditioning is one way that virtually all organisms learn to adapt to their environment.

Second, *Pavlov showed us how a process such as learning can be studied objectively.* He was proud that his methods involved virtually no subjective judgments or guesses about what went on in a dog's mind. The salivary response is a behavior measurable in cubic centimeters of saliva. Pavlov's success therefore suggested a scientific model for how the young discipline of psychology might proceed—by isolating the basic building blocks of complex behaviors and studying them with objective laboratory procedures.

Applications of Classical Conditioning

7: What have been some applications of classical conditioning?

Other units in this text—on consciousness, motivation, emotion, health, psychological disorders, and therapy—show how Pavlov's principles of classical conditioning apply to human health and well-being. Two examples:

> "[Psychology's] factual and theoretical developments in this century—which have changed the study of mind and behavior as radically as genetics changed the study of heredity—have all been the product of objective analysis—that is to say, behavioristic analysis."
>
> Psychologist Donald Hebb (1980)

- Former drug users often feel a craving when they are again in the drug-using context—with people or in places they associate with previous highs. Thus, drug counselors advise addicts to steer clear of people and settings that may trigger these cravings (Siegel, 2005).

- Classical conditioning even works on the body's disease-fighting immune system. When a particular taste accompanies a drug that influences immune responses, the taste by itself may come to produce an immune response (Ader & Cohen, 1985).

Pavlov's work also provided a basis for John Watson's (1913) idea that human emotions and behaviors, though biologically influenced, are mainly a bundle of conditioned responses. Working with an 11-month-old named Albert, Watson and Rosalie Rayner (1920; Harris, 1979) showed how specific fears might be conditioned. Like most infants, "Little Albert" feared loud noises but not white rats. Watson and Rayner presented a white rat and, as Little Albert reached to touch it, struck a hammer against a steel bar just behind his head. After seven repeats of seeing the rat and hearing the frightening noise, Albert burst into tears at the mere sight of the rat (an ethically troublesome study by today's standards). What is more, five days later Albert showed generalization of his conditioned response by reacting with fear to a rabbit, a dog, and a sealskin coat, but not to dissimilar objects such as toys.

Although Little Albert's fate is unknown, Watson's is not. After losing his professorship at Johns Hopkins University over an affair with Rayner (whom he later married), he became the J. Walter Thompson advertising agency's resident psychologist. There he used his knowledge of associative learning to conceive many successful campaigns, including the classic one for Maxwell House coffee that helped make the "coffee break" an American custom (Hunt, 1993).

Some psychologists, noting that Albert's fear wasn't learned quickly, had difficulty repeating Watson and Rayner's findings with other children. Nevertheless, Little Albert's case has had legendary significance for many psychologists. Some have wondered if each of us might not be a walking repository of conditioned emotions (see Close-Up: Trauma as Classical Conditioning on the next page). Might extinction procedures or even new conditioning help us change our unwanted responses to emotion-arousing stimuli? One patient, who for 30 years had feared going into an elevator alone, did just that. Following his therapist's advice, he forced himself to enter 20 elevators a day. Within 10 days, his fear had nearly extinguished (Ellis & Becker, 1982). In Units 12 and 13, we will see more examples of how psychologists use behavioral techniques to treat emotional disorders and promote personal growth.

• In Watson and Rayner's experiment, what was the US? The UR? The CS? The CR? (Answers below.) •

The US was the loud noise; the UR was the startled fear response; the CS was the rat; the CR was fear.

Brown Brothers

John B. Watson Watson (1924) admitted to "going beyond my facts" when offering his famous boast: "Give me a dozen healthy infants, well-formed, and my own specified world to bring them up in and I'll guarantee to take any one at random and train him to become any type of specialist I might select— doctor, lawyer, artist, merchant-chief, and, yes, even beggar-man and thief, regardless of his talents, penchants, tendencies, abilities, vocations, and race of his ancestors."

BEFORE YOU MOVE ON . . .

➤ **ASK YOURSELF**

How have your emotions or behaviors been classically conditioned?

➤ **TEST YOURSELF 2**

In slasher movies, sexually arousing images of women are sometimes paired with violence against women. Based on classical conditioning principles, what might be an effect of this pairing?

Answers to the Test Yourself questions can be found in Appendix E at the end of the book.

TROUBLESHOOTING

Help students see the difference between classical and operant conditioning—classical conditioning focuses on whether one stimulus predicts another to cause a response. Operant conditioning focuses on whether our behavior is rewarded or punished.

CLOSE-UP

Trauma as Classical Conditioning

"A burnt child dreads the fire," says a medieval proverb. Experiments with dogs reveal that, indeed, if a painful stimulus is sufficiently powerful, a single event is sometimes enough to traumatize the animal when it again faces the situation. The human counterparts to these experiments can be tragic, as illustrated by one woman's experience of being attacked and raped, and conditioned to a period of fear. Her fear (CR) was most powerfully associated with particular locations and people (CS), but it generalized to other places and people. Note, too, how her traumatic experience robbed her of the normally relaxing associations with such stimuli as home and bed.

> Four months ago I was raped. In the middle of the night I awoke to the sound of someone outside my bedroom. Thinking my housemate was coming home, I called out her name. Someone began walking slowly toward me, and then I realized. I screamed and fought, but there were two of them. One held my legs, while the other put a hand over my mouth and a knife to my throat and said, "Shut up . . . or we'll kill you." Never have I been so terrified and helpless. They both raped me, one brutally. As they then searched my room for money and valuables, my housemate came home. They brought her into my room, raped her, and left us both tied up on my bed.

We never slept another night in that apartment. We were too terrified. Still, when I go to bed at night—always with the bedroom light left on—the memory of them entering my room repeats itself endlessly. I was an independent person who had lived alone or with other women for four years; now I can't even think about spending a night alone. When I drive by our old apartment, or when I have to go into an empty house, my heart pounds and I sweat. I am afraid of strangers, especially men, and the more they resemble my attackers the more I fear them. My housemate shares many of my fears and is frightened when entering our new apartment. I'm afraid to stay in the same town, I'm afraid it will happen again, I'm afraid to go to bed. I dread falling asleep.

Eleven years later this woman could report—as do many trauma victims (Gluhoski & Wortman, 1996)—that her conditioned fears had mostly extinguished:

> The frequency and intensity of my fears have subsided. Still, I remain cautious about personal safety and occasionally have nightmares about my experience. But more important is my renewed ability to laugh, love, and trust—both old friends and new. Life is once again joyful. I have survived.

(From personal correspondence, with permission.)

::**respondent behavior** behavior that occurs as an automatic response to some stimulus.

::**operant conditioning** a type of learning in which behavior is strengthened if followed by a reinforcer or diminished if followed by a punisher.

::**operant behavior** behavior that operates on the environment, producing consequences.

::**law of effect** Thorndike's principle that behaviors followed by favorable consequences become more likely, and that behaviors followed by unfavorable consequences become less likely.

::**operant chamber** in operant conditioning research, a chamber (also known as a *Skinner box*) containing a bar or key that an animal can manipulate to obtain a food or water reinforcer; attached devices record the animal's rate of bar pressing or key pecking.

::**shaping** an operant conditioning procedure in which reinforcers guide behavior toward closer and closer approximations of the desired behavior.

Operant Conditioning

8: What is operant conditioning, and how does it differ from classical conditioning?

IT'S ONE THING TO CLASSICALLY CONDITION a dog to salivate at the sound of a tone, or a child to fear moving cars. To teach an elephant to walk on its hind legs or a child to say *please*, we must turn to another type of learning—*operant conditioning.*

Classical conditioning and operant conditioning are both forms of associative learning, yet their difference is straightforward:

- *Classical conditioning* forms associations between stimuli (a CS and the US it signals). It also involves **respondent behavior**—actions that are automatic responses to a stimulus (such as salivating in response to meat powder and later in response to a tone).

- In **operant conditioning**, organisms associate their own actions with consequences. Actions followed by reinforcers increase; those followed by punishers decrease. Behavior that *operates* on the environment to *produce* rewarding or punishing stimuli is called **operant behavior.**

We can therefore distinguish classical from operant conditioning by asking: *Is the organism learning associations between events it does not control* (classical conditioning)? *Or is it learning associations between its behavior and resulting events* (operant conditioning)?

TEACHING TIP

At this time, you may want to use **Classroom Exercise/Student Project:** *A Build-It-Yourself Skinner Box* (p. 11) from Bolt's Teacher's Resource Binder.

Yale University Library

Skinner's Experiments

B. F. Skinner (1904–1990) was a college English major and an aspiring writer who, seeking a new direction, entered graduate school in psychology. He went on to become modern behaviorism's most influential and controversial figure. Skinner's work elaborated what psychologist Edward L. Thorndike (1874–1949) called the **law of effect:** Rewarded behavior is likely to recur (**FIGURE 6.11**). Using Thorndike's law of effect as a starting point, Skinner developed a *behavioral technology* that revealed principles of *behavior control.* These principles also enabled him to teach pigeons such unpigeonlike behaviors as walking in a figure 8, playing Ping-Pong, and keeping a missile on course by pecking at a screen target.

For his pioneering studies, Skinner designed an **operant chamber,** popularly known as a *Skinner box* (**FIGURE 6.12**). The box has a bar or key that an animal presses or pecks to release a reward of food or water, and a device that records these responses. Operant conditioning experiments have done far more than teach us how to pull habits out of a rat. They have explored the precise conditions that foster efficient and enduring learning.

 FIGURE 6.11
Cat in a puzzle box Thorndike (1898) used a fish reward to entice cats to find their way out of a puzzle box (above right) through a series of maneuvers. The cats' performance tended to improve with successive trials (above left), illustrating Thorndike's *law of effect.* (Adapted from Thorndike, 1898.)

 FIGURE 6.12
A Skinner box Inside the box, the rat presses a bar for a food reward. Outside, a measuring device (not shown here) records the animal's accumulated responses.

Shaping Behavior

In his experiments, Skinner used **shaping,** a procedure in which *reinforcers,* such as food, gradually guide an animal's actions toward a desired behavior. Imagine that you wanted to condition a hungry rat to press a bar. First, you would watch how the animal naturally behaves, so that you could build on its existing behaviors. You might give the rat a food reward each time it approaches the bar. Once the rat is approaching regularly, you would require it to move closer before rewarding it, then closer still. Finally, you would require it to touch the bar before you gave it the food. With this method of *successive approximations,* you reward responses that are ever-closer to the final desired behavior, and you ignore all other responses. By making rewards contingent on desired behaviors, researchers and animal trainers gradually shape complex behaviors.

Khamis Ramadhan/Panapress/Getty Images

Shaping rats to save lives A Gambian giant pouched rat, having been shaped to sniff out land mines, receives a bite of banana after successfully locating a mine during training in Mozambique.

CRITICAL THINKING

Skinner not only trained animals in operant chambers (Skinner boxes), he also developed a device called an air crib, which was designed to house infants to train them. Have students discuss the ethical concerns that people might have about Skinner's practices of training animals and children in boxes or air cribs.

- How do animal rights activists feel about the use of animals in psychological experiments?

- Why might people have a hard time accepting the air crib as a child-rearing technique? Would parents who used such a device be considered abusive? Why or why not?

TEACHING TIP

Help students see the importance of Thorndike's law of effect. A law in science refers to an idea that is true at all times—like Newton's law of gravity or the law of thermodynamics. There are very few laws in psychology because psychology is such a young science and behavior is quite complex and difficult to discuss in unequivocal terms such as laws. Thorndike's law of effect is an example of a way in which behavior works all the time—when a behavior is rewarded, it continues, and when a behavior is punished, it discontinues.

TEACHING TIP

B. F. Skinner's work with animals spurred research and work in training all kinds of animals to serve useful purposes. In World War II, Skinner trained pigeons to guide missiles to their targets. While the military at that time didn't buy into Skinner's pigeons (nobody wanted to admit they used ordinary pigeons to win the war), these animals were more effective than humans at identifying their targets. Jim Simmons, Ph.D., a Navy scientist, trained pigeons for the Coast Guard to conduct search and rescue missions. While humans were 38 percent accurate at identifying targets, pigeons were 93 percent accurate—and they didn't get bored after being on duty for hours.

Azar, B. (Oct. 2002). Pigeons as baggage screeners, rats as rescuers. *Monitor on Psychology, 33* (9), 42.

TEACHING TIP

Make sure students understand that shaping is crucial to operant conditioning. Shaping is important because humans and nonhuman animals rarely perform desired behaviors (especially complicated ones) the first time around. They need some type of hint as to whether they are on the right track in order to perform.

INTERCONNECTING

Notice how the concept of discrimination is used differently with operant conditioning than it was used with classical conditioning. With operant conditioning, discrimination is used to show which type of stimulus gets the reaction that is reinforced.

TROUBLESHOOTING

The example about Billy needing his shoes tied shows the difficulties with identifying elements of operant conditioning. For Billy, whining is reinforced, which will cause him to continue whining to get his father's attention. For Billy's father, his response to the whining is reinforcing, making Billy's whining stop. Identifying reinforcement depends on the perspective of the person or animal being reinforced.

At this time, you may want to use **Lecture/Discussion Topic:** *Examples of Negative Reinforcement* (p. 12) from Bolt's Teacher's Resource Binder.

A **discriminating creature** University of Windsor psychologist Dale Woodyard uses a food reward to train this manatee to discriminate between objects of different shapes, colors, and sizes. Manatees remember such responses for a year or more.

::discriminative stimulus in operant conditioning, a stimulus that elicits a response after association with reinforcement (in contrast to related stimuli not associated with reinforcement).

::reinforcer in operant conditioning, any event that *strengthens* the behavior it follows.

::positive reinforcement increasing behaviors by presenting positive stimuli, such as food. A positive reinforcer is any stimulus that, when *presented* after a response, strengthens the response.

::negative reinforcement increasing behaviors by stopping or reducing negative stimuli, such as shock. A negative reinforcer is any stimulus that, when *removed* after a response, strengthens the response. (*Note:* negative reinforcement is not punishment.)

::primary reinforcer an innately reinforcing stimulus, such as one that satisfies a biological need.

::conditioned reinforcer a stimulus that gains its reinforcing power through its association with a primary reinforcer; also known as a *secondary reinforcer*.

Shaping can also help us understand what nonverbal organisms perceive. Can a dog distinguish red and green? Can a baby hear the difference between lower- and higher-pitched tones? If we can shape them to respond to one stimulus and not to another, then we know they can perceive the difference. Such experiments have even shown that some animals can form concepts. If an experimenter reinforces a pigeon for pecking after seeing a human face, but not after seeing other images, the pigeon learns to recognize human faces (Herrnstein & Loveland, 1964). In this experiment, a face is a **discriminative stimulus;** like a green traffic light, it signals that a response will be reinforced. After being trained to discriminate among flowers, people, cars, and chairs, pigeons can usually identify the category in which a new pictured object belongs (Bhatt et al., 1988; Wasserman, 1993). They have even been trained to discriminate between Bach's music and Stravinsky's (Porter & Neuringer, 1984).

In everyday life, we continually reward and shape others' behavior, said Skinner, but we often do so unintentionally. Billy's whining, for example, annoys his mystified parents, but look how they typically deal with Billy:

Billy: Could you tie my shoes?
Father: (Continues reading paper.)
Billy: Dad, I need my shoes tied.
Father: Uh, yeah, just a minute.
Billy: DAAAAD! TIE MY SHOES!
Father: How many times have I told you not to whine? Now, which shoe do we do first?

Billy's whining is reinforced, because he gets something desirable—his dad's attention. Dad's response is reinforced because it gets rid of something aversive—Billy's whining.

Or consider a teacher who pastes gold stars on a wall chart after the names of children scoring 100 percent on spelling tests. As everyone can then see, some children consistently do perfect work. The others, who take the same test and may have worked harder than the academic all-stars, get no rewards. The teacher would be better advised to apply the principles of operant conditioning—to reinforce all spellers for gradual improvements (successive approximations toward perfect spelling of words they find challenging).

HI AND LOIS

Types of Reinforcers

9: What are the basic types of reinforcers?

People often refer rather loosely to the power of "rewards." This idea gains a more precise meaning in Skinner's concept of a **reinforcer:** any event that strengthens (increases the frequency of) a preceding response. A reinforcer may be a tangible reward, such as food or money. It may be praise or attention—even being yelled at, for a child hungry for attention. Or it may be an activity—borrowing the family car after doing the dishes, or taking a break after an hour of study.

DEMO

While discussing operant conditioning, interrupt your lecture and say, "Oh, by the way, before I forget again . . ." and complete the sentence by asking a question that will get either an almost totally positive or negative response. All students will usually raise a hand. Immediately, tell students to freeze in their positions. Ask, "Did anyone ask you to raise your hands or even mention anything about raising hands?" Explain that students are conditioned to discriminate when to raise their hands—that is, in response to a teacher's request but not to others' requests.

Stork, E. (1992). Operant conditioning: Role in human behavior. In R. Brown, R. D. Franz, B. Ibarra, & M. Sullivan, (Eds.), *Learning.* Washington, D.C.: APA.

Although anything that serves to increase behavior is a reinforcer, reinforcers vary with circumstances. What's reinforcing to one person (rock concert tickets) may not be to another. What's reinforcing in one situation (food when hungry) may not be in another.

Up to now, we've really been discussing **positive reinforcement,** which strengthens a response by *presenting* a typically pleasurable stimulus after a response. But there are *two* basic kinds of reinforcement (TABLE 6.1). **Negative reinforcement** *strengthens* a response by *reducing* or *removing* something undesirable or unpleasant, as when an organism escapes an aversive situation. Taking aspirin may relieve your headache, and pushing the snooze button will silence your annoying alarm. These welcome results (end of pain, end of alarm) provide negative reinforcement and increase the odds that you will repeat these behaviors. For drug addicts, the negative reinforcement of ending withdrawal pangs can be a compelling reason to resume using (Baker et al., 2004). Note that contrary to popular usage, *negative reinforcement is not punishment.* (*Advice:* Repeat the last five words in your mind, because this is one of psychology's most often misunderstood concepts.) Rather, negative reinforcement *removes* a punishing (aversive) event.

Sometimes negative and positive reinforcement coincide. Imagine a worried student who, after goofing off and getting a bad test grade, studies harder for the next test. This increased effort may be negatively reinforced by reduced anxiety, and positively reinforced by a better grade. Whether it works by reducing something aversive, or by giving something desirable, *reinforcement is any consequence that strengthens behavior.*

Positive reinforcement A heat lamp positively reinforces this Taronga Zoo meerkat's behavior during a cold snap in Sydney, Australia. ▲

• Remember whining Billy? In that example, whose behavior was positively reinforced and whose was negatively reinforced? (Answer below.) •

Billy's whining was positively reinforced, because Billy got something desirable—his father's attention. His dad's response to the whining (doing what Billy wanted) was negatively reinforced, because it got rid of Billy's annoying whining.

TABLE 6.1

WAYS TO INCREASE BEHAVIOR

Operant Conditioning Term	Description	Examples
Positive reinforcement	Add a desirable stimulus	Getting a hug; receiving a paycheck
Negative reinforcement	Remove an aversive stimulus	Fastening seatbelt to turn off beeping

Primary and Conditioned Reinforcers Primary reinforcers—getting food when hungry or having a painful headache go away—are unlearned. They are innately satisfying. **Conditioned reinforcers,** also called *secondary reinforcers,* get their power through learned association with primary reinforcers. If a rat in a Skinner box learns that a light reliably signals that food is coming, the rat will work to turn on the light. The light has become a conditioned reinforcer associated with food. Our lives are filled with conditioned reinforcers—money, good grades, a pleasant tone of voice—each of which has been linked with more basic rewards. If money is a conditioned reinforcer—if people's desire for money is derived from their desire for food—then hunger should also make people more money-hungry, reasoned one European research team (Briers et al., 2006). Indeed, in their experiments, people were less likely to donate to charity when food deprived, and less likely to share money with fellow participants when in a room with hunger-arousing aromas.

Immediate and Delayed Reinforcers Let's return to the imaginary shaping experiment in which you were conditioning a rat to press a bar. Before performing this "wanted" behavior, the hungry rat will engage in a sequence of "unwanted" behaviors—scratching, sniffing, and moving around. If you present food immediately after any one of these behaviors, the rat will likely repeat that rewarded behavior. But what if the rat presses the bar while you are distracted, and you delay giving the reinforcer? If the delay lasts longer than 30 seconds, the rat will not learn to press the bar. You

UNIT 6

"Oh, not bad. The light comes on, I press the bar, they write me a check. How about you?"

Delayed gratification is a skill many parents want their children to have. People who can delay gratification are able to achieve more in life. Have students consider the following questions:

- What types of "real world" rewards occur on a delayed schedule?

- Did you learn to wait for rewards? Why or why not?

- Does the media encourage people to delay gratification? Why or why not?

At this time, you may want to use **Classroom Exercise: Consideration of Future Consequences Scale** (p. 12) from Bolt's Teacher's Resource Binder.

TEACHING TIP

Help students understand that there are only two main types of reinforcement schedules—continuous and partial (intermittent) schedules. The different ratio and interval schedules described in the text are all partial schedules.

TROUBLESHOOTING

Continuous schedules are excellent for training behavior quickly. If you want quick results, reinforce after every desired behavior occurs. The problem with continuous reinforcement, however, is that it also extinguishes quickly. Once the reinforcement ends, so does the desired behavior. If you want the behavior to stick, you'll need to transition to a partial schedule, which is more resistant to extinction.

At this time, you may want to use **Classroom Exercise: Partial Reinforcement Schedules** (p. 13) from Bolt's Teacher's Resource Binder.

> "The charm of fishing is that it is the pursuit of what is elusive but attainable, a perpetual series of occasions for hope."
>
> Scottish author John Buchan (1875–1940)

::**continuous reinforcement** reinforcing the desired response every time it occurs.

::**partial (intermittent) reinforcement** reinforcing a response only part of the time; results in slower acquisition of a response but much greater resistance to extinction than does continuous reinforcement.

::**fixed-ratio schedule** in operant conditioning, a reinforcement schedule that reinforces a response only after a specified number of responses.

will have reinforced other incidental behaviors—more sniffing and moving—that intervened after the bar press.

Unlike rats, humans do respond to delayed reinforcers: the paycheck at the end of the week, the good grade at the end of the term, the trophy at the end of the season. Indeed, to function effectively we must learn to delay gratification. In laboratory testing, some 4-year-olds show this ability. In choosing a candy, they prefer having a big one tomorrow to munching on a small one right now. Learning to control our impulses in order to achieve more valued rewards is a big step toward maturity (Logue, 1998a,b). No wonder children who make such choices tend to become socially competent and high-achieving adults (Mischel et al., 1989).

But to our detriment, small but immediate consequences (the enjoyment of watching late-night TV, for example) are sometimes more alluring than big but delayed consequences (not feeling sluggish tomorrow). For many teens, the immediate gratification of risky, unprotected sex in passionate moments prevails over the delayed gratifications of safe sex or saved sex (Loewenstein & Furstenberg, 1991). And for too many of us, the immediate rewards of today's gas-guzzling vehicles, air travel, and air conditioning have prevailed over the bigger future consequences of global climate change, rising seas, and extreme weather.

Reinforcement Schedules

10: How do different reinforcement schedules affect behavior?

So far, most of our examples have assumed **continuous reinforcement:** Reinforcing the desired response every time it occurs. Under such conditions, learning occurs rapidly, which makes continuous reinforcement preferable until a behavior is mastered. But extinction also occurs rapidly. When reinforcement stops—when we stop delivering food after the rat presses the bar—the behavior soon stops. If a normally dependable candy machine fails to deliver a chocolate bar twice in a row, we stop putting money into it (although a week later we may exhibit spontaneous recovery by trying again).

Real life rarely provides continuous reinforcement. Salespeople do not make a sale with every pitch, nor do anglers get a bite with every cast. But they persist because their efforts have occasionally been rewarded. This persistence is typical with **partial (intermittent) reinforcement** schedules, in which responses are sometimes reinforced, sometimes not. Although initial learning is slower, intermittent reinforcement produces greater *resistance to extinction* than is found with continuous reinforcement. Imagine a pigeon that has learned to peck a key to obtain food. When the experimenter gradually phases out the delivery of food until it occurs only rarely and unpredictably, pigeons may peck 150,000 times without a reward (Skinner, 1953). Slot machines reward gamblers in much the same way—occasionally and unpredictably. And like pigeons, slot players keep trying, time and time again. With intermittent reinforcement, hope springs eternal. Lesson for parents: Partial reinforcement also works with children. *Occasionally* giving in to children's tantrums for the sake of peace and quiet intermittently reinforces the tantrums. This is the very best procedure for making a behavior persist.

Skinner (1961) and his collaborators compared four schedules of partial reinforcement. Some are rigidly fixed, some unpredictably variable.

Fixed-ratio schedules reinforce behavior after a set number of responses. Just as coffee shops reward us with a free drink after every 10 purchased, laboratory animals may be reinforced on a fixed ratio of, say, one reinforcer for every 30 responses. Once conditioned, the animal will pause only briefly after a reinforcer and will then return to a high rate of responding (FIGURE 6.13).

RESEARCH

Have students survey a representative sample of students to see if they would prefer to delay gratification rather than get immediate gratification. The survey should present different situations that offer a choice of delaying or getting immediate gratification.

- Be sure to obtain permission from an Institutional Review Board as well as securing informed consent before conducting any research on human subjects.

➤ FIGURE 6.13
Intermittent reinforcement schedules Skinner's laboratory pigeons produced these response patterns to each of four reinforcement schedules. (Reinforcers are indicated by diagonal marks.) For people, as for pigeons, reinforcement linked to number of responses (a *ratio* schedule) produces a higher response rate than reinforcement linked to amount of time elapsed (an *interval* schedule). But the predictability of the reward also matters. An unpredictable (*variable*) schedule produces more consistent responding than does a predictable (*fixed*) schedule.

Variable-ratio schedules provide reinforcers after an unpredictable number of responses. This is what slot-machine players and fly-casting anglers experience—unpredictable reinforcement—and what makes gambling and fly fishing so hard to extinguish even when both are getting nothing for something. Like the fixed-ratio schedule, the variable-ratio schedule produces high rates of responding, because reinforcers increase as the number of responses increases.

Fixed-interval schedules reinforce the first response after a fixed time period. Like people checking more frequently for the mail as the delivery time approaches, or checking to see if the Jell-O has set, pigeons on a fixed-interval schedule peck a key more frequently as the anticipated time for reward draws near, producing a choppy stop-start pattern (see Figure 6.13) rather than a steady rate of response.

Variable-interval schedules reinforce the first response after *varying* time intervals. Like the "You've got mail" that finally rewards persistence in rechecking for e-mail, variable-interval schedules tend to produce slow, steady responding. This makes sense, because there is no knowing when the waiting will be over (**TABLE 6.2**).

Animal behaviors differ, yet Skinner (1956) contended that the reinforcement principles of operant conditioning are universal. It matters little, he said, what response, what reinforcer, or what species you use. The effect of a given reinforcement schedule is pretty much the same: "Pigeon, rat, monkey, which is which? It doesn't matter. . . . Behavior shows astonishingly similar properties."

TABLE 6.2		
SCHEDULES OF REINFORCEMENT		
	Fixed	**Variable**
Ratio	*Every so many:* reinforcement after every n[th] behavior, such as buy 10 coffees, get 1 free, or pay per product unit produced	*After an unpredictable number:* reinforcement after a random number of behaviors, as when playing slot machines or fly-casting
Interval	*Every so often:* reinforcement for behavior after a fixed time, such as Tuesday discount prices	*Unpredictably often:* reinforcement for behavior after a random amount of time, as in checking for e-mail

● Door-to-door salespeople are reinforced by which schedule? People checking the oven to see if the cookies are done are on which schedule? Airline frequent-flyer programs that offer a free flight after every 25,000 miles of travel use which reinforcement schedule? (Answers below.) ●

Door-to-door salespeople are reinforced on a variable-ratio schedule (after varying numbers of rings). Cookie checkers are reinforced on a fixed-interval schedule. Frequent-flyer programs use a fixed-ratio schedule.

::**variable-ratio schedule** in operant conditioning, a reinforcement schedule that reinforces a response after an unpredictable number of responses.

::**fixed-interval schedule** in operant conditioning, a reinforcement schedule that reinforces a response only after a specified time has elapsed.

::**variable-interval schedule** in operant conditioning, a reinforcement schedule that reinforces a response at unpredictable time intervals.

 TEACHING TIP

The pattern of reinforcement shown during a fixed-interval reinforcement schedule is called scooping. Animals and people trained on this schedule tend to wait until the time interval is drawing near before performing the behavior, which results in the scooped look of the graph charting the behavior.

CRITICAL THINKING

Many teachers give grades on a continuous reinforcement schedule, awarding points for every assignment students turn in. Have students consider the impact of this type of reinforcement on learning:

- Do you get grades for every assignment you turn in? Why or why not?

- How do you feel if a teacher doesn't give grades for every assignment?

- What unintended consequences might occur when teachers use continuous reinforcement?

TEACHING TIP

Be sure students can discriminate the difference between interval and ratio schedules.

- **Interval schedules** involve a time element—time must pass before reinforcement will occur. The subject must be behaving at the right time to get reinforcement.

- **Ratio schedules** are dependent on the behavior itself—a certain number of behaviors are needed before reinforcement will occur.

 TROUBLESHOOTING

Variable-interval schedules are difficult to remember because they are simply about waiting until a behavior occurs before reinforcement is given. Students have to be continuously studying and waiting for a quiz to occur on this schedule. Help students remember this by reminding them that an interval schedule requires the subject to be performing the behavior when the reinforcement comes.

UNIT 6

TROUBLESHOOTING

The distinction between negative reinforcement and punishment is one of the most often confused concepts in psychology. Help students figure out the difference:

- **Negative reinforcement** encourages behavior. When something unpleasant ceases, the behavior that caused it to stop is reinforced.

- **Punishment** discourages behavior. Behavior that is unwanted is punished, making it less likely for that behavior to continue.

At this time, you may want to use **Classroom Exercise:** *Negative Reinforcement Versus Punishment* (p. 13) from Bolt's Teacher's Resource Binder.

TROUBLESHOOTING

Table 6.3 describes a concept called "positive punishment." Help students understand that this is not a desirable type of punishment. Rather, the words "positive" and "negative" when referring to reinforcement and punishment mean "adding" and "subtracting" respectively. When we add a punishing stimulus for a behavior, then it is considered positive punishment.

TABLE 6.3

WAYS TO DECREASE BEHAVIOR

Type of Punisher	Description	Possible Examples
Positive punishment	Administer an aversive stimulus	Spanking; a parking ticket
Negative punishment	Withdraw a desirable stimulus	Time-out from privileges (such as time with friends); revoked driver's license

Punishment

11: How does punishment affect behavior?

Reinforcement increases a behavior; **punishment** does the opposite. A *punisher* is any consequence that *decreases* the frequency of a preceding behavior (**TABLE 6.3**).

Swift and sure punishers can powerfully restrain unwanted behavior. The rat that is shocked after touching a forbidden object and the child who loses a treat after running into the street will learn not to repeat the behavior. A dog that has learned to come running at the sound of an electric can opener will stop coming if its owner starts running the machine to attract the dog and banish it to the basement.

Sureness and swiftness are also marks of effective criminal punishment, note John Darley and Adam Alter (in press). Studies show that criminal behavior, much of it impulsive, is not deterred by the threat of severe sentences. Thus, when Arizona introduced an exceptionally harsh sentence for first-time drunk drivers, it did not affect the drunk-driving rate. But when Kansas City started patrolling a high crime area to increase the sureness and swiftness of punishment, crime dropped dramatically.

So, how should we interpret the punishment studies in relation to parenting practices? Many psychologists and supporters of nonviolent parenting note four drawbacks of physically punishing children (Gershoff, 2002; Marshall, 2002).

1. ***Punished behavior is suppressed, not forgotten.*** This suppression, though temporary, may (negatively) reinforce parents' punishing behavior. The child swears, the parent swats, the parent hears no more swearing and feels the punishment successfully stopped the behavior. No wonder spanking is a hit with so many U.S. parents of 3- and 4-year-olds—more than 9 in 10 of whom acknowledge spanking their children (Kazdin & Benjet, 2003).

2. ***Punishment teaches discrimination.*** Was the punishment effective in putting an end to the swearing? Or did the child simply learn that it's not okay to swear around the house, but it is okay to swear elsewhere?

3. ***Punishment can teach fear.*** The child may associate fear not only with the undesirable behavior but also with the person who delivered the punishment or the place it occurred. Thus, children may learn to fear a punishing teacher and try to avoid school. For such reasons, most European countries and most U.S. states now ban hitting children in schools (StopHitting.com, 2009). Eleven countries, including those in Scandinavia, further outlaw hitting by parents, giving children the same legal protection given to spouses (EPOCH, 2000).

4. ***Physical punishment may increase aggressiveness by modeling aggression as a way to cope with problems.*** We know that many aggressive delinquents and abusive parents come from abusive families (Straus & Gelles, 1980; Straus et al., 1997). But some researchers note a problem with studies that find that spanked children are at increased risk for aggression (and depression and low self-esteem). Well, yes, they say, just as people who have undergone psychotherapy are more

::**punishment** an event that *decreases* the behavior that it follows.

INTERCONNECTING

Connect punishment to classical conditioning by showing how spanking can lead to an association between the parent and pain:

- US: spanking
- CS: Parent's upraised hand that does the spanking
- UR: fear and crying from pain

If the parent's upraised hand is paired often enough with the pain of a spanking, children can begin to associate the gesture with the pain and fear their own parents. This unintended consequence can lead to children not trusting their parents at an early age.

likely to suffer depression—because they had preexisting problems that triggered the treatments (Larzelere, 2000, 2004). Which is the chicken and which is the egg? The correlations don't hand us an answer.

If one adjusts for preexisting antisocial behavior, then an occasional single swat or two to misbehaving 2- to 6-year-olds looks more effective (Baumrind et al., 2002; Larzelere & Kuhn, 2005). That is especially so if the swat is used only as a backup when milder disciplinary tactics (such as a *time-out,* removing them from reinforcing surroundings) fail, and when the swat is combined with a generous dose of reasoning and reinforcing. Remember: *Punishment tells you what not to do; reinforcement tells you what to do.* This dual approach can be effective. When children with self-destructive behaviors bite themselves or bang their heads, they may be mildly punished (say, with a squirt of water in the face), but they may also be rewarded (with positive attention and food) when they behave well. In class, teachers can give feedback on papers by saying, "No, but try this . . ." and "Yes, that's it!" Such responses reduce unwanted behavior while reinforcing more desirable alternatives.

Parents of delinquent youth are often unaware of how to achieve desirable behaviors without screaming or hitting their children (Patterson et al., 1982). Training programs can help reframe contingencies from dire threats to positive incentives—turning "You clean up your room this minute or no dinner!" to "You're welcome at the dinner table after you get your room cleaned up." When you stop to think about it, many threats of punishment are just as forceful, and perhaps more effective, if rephrased positively. Thus, "If you don't get your homework done, there'll be no car" would better be phrased as . . .

What punishment often teaches, said Skinner, is how to avoid it. Most psychologists now favor an emphasis on reinforcement: Notice people behaving well and commend them for it.

Extending Skinner's Understanding

12: Do cognitive processes and biological constraints affect operant conditioning?

Skinner granted the existence of private thought processes and the biological underpinnings of behavior. Nevertheless, many psychologists criticized him for discounting the importance of these influences.

Cognition and Operant Conditioning

A mere eight days before dying of leukemia, Skinner (1990) stood before the American Psychological Association convention for one final critique of "cognitive science," which he viewed as a throwback to early twentieth-century introspectionism. Skinner died resisting the growing belief that cognitive processes—thoughts, perceptions, expectations—have a necessary place in the science of psychology and even in our understanding of conditioning. (He regarded thoughts and emotions as behaviors that follow the same laws as other behaviors.) Yet we have seen several hints that cognitive processes might be at work in operant learning. For example, animals on a fixed-interval reinforcement schedule respond more and more frequently as the time approaches when a response will produce a reinforcer. Although a strict behaviorist would object to talk of "expectations," the animals behave as if they expected that repeating the response would soon produce the reward.

Latent Learning Evidence of cognitive processes has also come from studying rats in mazes, including classic studies by Edward Chase Tolman (1886–1959) and C.H.

● For more information on animal behavior, see books by (I am not making this up) Robin Fox and Lionel Tiger. ●

CRITICAL THINKING

Spanking is a controversial punishment technique employed by many parents and school systems across the country. Have students consider the following questions:

- Were you spanked as a child? Why or why not?
- What reasons might parents have for spanking their children?
- What reasons might parents have for not spanking their children?
- Where is the line between spanking and child abuse?
- Is spanking successful? Why or why not?

 ### TEACHING TIP

Have students recall their early childhood memories of learning how to do something, like riding a bike. How did they learn? What operant conditioning techniques did their "teacher" use with them?

 ### TEACHING TIP

At this time, you may want to use **Classroom Exercise: *The Sensitivity to Punishment and Sensitivity to Reward Questionnaire*** (p. 15) from Bolt's Teacher's Resource Binder.

Even though the original studies on cognitive maps were done with rats, people form cognitive maps in many circumstances. For instance, ninth graders first coming to the high school often take time in the summer to walk through the building, forming a cognitive map of the school. When they arrive at school for the first day, they will navigate the school better than those students who don't take time to learn the layout during the summer.

At this time, you may want to use **Lecture/Discussion Topic:** *Mindful Learning* (p. 17) from Bolt's Teacher's Resource Binder.

"Bathroom? Sure, it's just down the hall to the left, jog right, left, another left, straight past two more lefts, then right, and it's at the end of the third corridor on your right."

Honzik that were done in Skinner's youth. After exploring a maze for 10 days, rats received a food reward at the end of the maze. They quickly demonstrated their prior learning of the maze—by immediately completing it as quickly as (and even faster than) rats that had been reinforced for running the maze all along (Tolman & Honzik, 1930). It seems that rats exploring a maze, with no obvious reward, are like people sightseeing in a new town. They seem to develop a **cognitive map**, a mental representation of the maze. This map, and their learning, is not demonstrated until the experimenter places food in the maze's goal box, which motivates the sightseeing rats to run the maze as quickly as possible—and typically as fast or faster than the rats that had been reinforced with food for running the maze.

During their explorations, the rats have seemingly experienced **latent learning**—learning that becomes apparent only when there is some incentive to demonstrate it. Children, too, may learn from watching a parent but demonstrate the learning only much later, as needed. The point to remember: *There is more to learning than associating a response with a consequence; there is also cognition.* In Unit 7B, we will encounter more striking evidence of cognitive abilities in solving problems and in using language.

Insight Learning Some learning occurs after little or no systematic interaction with our environment. For example, we may puzzle over a problem, and suddenly, the pieces fall together as we perceive the solution in a sudden flash of **insight.** Ten-year-old Johnny Appleton displayed insight in solving a problem that had stumped construction workers: how to rescue a young robin that had fallen into a narrow 30-inch-deep hole in a cement-block wall. Johnny's solution: Slowly pour in sand, giving the bird enough time to keep its feet on top of the constantly rising sand (Ruchlis, 1990).

Intrinsic Motivation The cognitive perspective has also led to an important qualification concerning the power of rewards: Promising people a reward for a task they already enjoy can backfire. Many think that offering tangible rewards will boost anyone's interest in an activity. Actually, in experiments, children promised a payoff for playing with an interesting puzzle or toy later play with the toy less than do their unpaid counterparts (Deci et al., 1999; Tang & Hall, 1995). It is as if the children think, "If I have to be bribed into doing this, it must not be worth doing for its own sake."

Pure love If this girl were suddenly told that she must look after her baby cousin from now on, she might lose some of the joy that her intrinsic motivation to care for him has provided.

RESEARCH

Have students replicate the Tolman and Honzik latent learning experiment. Construct two mazes and have one group of laboratory rats run through one maze while the other group doesn't get that opportunity. Then, train the rats using operant conditioning to run the maze. Time each group to see which one learns the maze the fastest.

- Be sure to get approval from an Institutional Review Board and follow the guidelines for caring for animals as defined by the APA Ethics Code.

Excessive rewards can undermine **intrinsic motivation**—the desire to perform a behavior effectively and for its own sake. **Extrinsic motivation** is the desire to behave in certain ways to receive external rewards or avoid threatened punishment.

To sense the difference, think about your experience in this course. Are you feeling pressured to finish this reading before a deadline? Worried about your grade? Eager for rewards that depend on your doing well? If yes, then you are extrinsically motivated (as, to some extent, almost all students must be). Are you also finding the course material interesting? Does learning it make you feel more competent? If there were no grade at stake, might you be curious enough to want to learn the material for its own sake? If yes, intrinsic motivation also fuels your efforts. Intrinsically motivated people work and play in search of enjoyment, interest, self-expression, or challenge.

Youth sports coaches who aim to promote enduring interest in an activity, not just to pressure players into winning, should focus on the intrinsic joy of playing and of reaching one's potential, note motivation researchers Edward Deci and Richard Ryan (1985, 1992, 2002). Giving people choices also enhances their intrinsic motivation (Patall et al., 2008). Nevertheless, rewards can be effective if used neither to bribe nor to control but to signal a job well done (Boggiano et al., 1985). "Most improved player" awards, for example, can boost feelings of competence and increase enjoyment of a sport. Rightly administered, rewards can raise performance and spark creativity (Eisenberger & Rhoades, 2001; Henderlong & Lepper, 2002). And extrinsic rewards (such as the college scholarships and jobs that often follow good grades) are here to stay.

Biological Predispositions

As with classical conditioning, an animal's natural predispositions constrain its capacity for operant conditioning. Using food as a reinforcer, you can easily condition a hamster to dig or to rear up because these actions are among the animal's natural food-searching behaviors. But you won't be so successful if you use food as a reinforcer to shape other hamster behaviors, such as face washing, that aren't normally associated with food or hunger (Shettleworth, 1973). Similarly, you could easily teach pigeons to flap their wings to avoid being shocked, and to peck to obtain food, because fleeing with their wings and eating with their beaks are natural pigeon behaviors. However, they would have a hard time learning to peck to avoid a shock, or to flap their wings to obtain food (Foree & LoLordo, 1973). The principle: *Biological constraints predispose organisms to learn associations that are naturally adaptive.*

After witnessing the power of operant technology, Skinner's students Keller Breland and Marian Breland (1961; Bailey & Gillaspy, 2005) began training dogs, cats, chickens, parakeets, turkeys, pigs, ducks, and hamsters, and they eventually left their graduate studies to form an animal training company. Over the ensuing 47 years they trained more than 15,000 animals from 140 species for movies, traveling shows, corporations, amusement parks, and the government. They also trained animal trainers, including Sea World's first director of training.

At first, the Brelands presumed that operant principles would work on almost any response an animal could make. But along the way, they confronted the constraints of biological predispositions. In one act, pigs trained to pick up large wooden "dollars" and deposit them in a piggy bank began to drift back to their natural ways. They would drop the coin, push it with their snouts as pigs are prone to do, pick it up again, and then repeat the sequence—delaying their food reinforcer. This *instinctive drift* occurred as the animals reverted to their biologically predisposed patterns.

::**cognitive map** a mental representation of the layout of one's environment. For example, after exploring a maze, rats act as if they have learned a cognitive map of it.

::**latent learning** learning that occurs but is not apparent until there is an incentive to demonstrate it.

::**insight** a sudden and often novel realization of the solution to a problem.

::**intrinsic motivation** a desire to perform a behavior effectively for its own sake.

::**extrinsic motivation** a desire to perform a behavior to receive promised rewards or avoid threatened punishment.

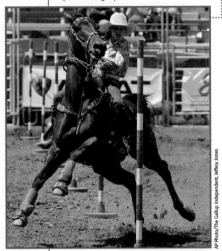

▼ **Natural athlete** Animals can most easily learn and retain behaviors that draw on their biological predispositions, such as horses' inborn ability to move around obstacles with speed and agility.

> "Never try to teach a pig to sing. It wastes your time and annoys the pig."
>
> Mark Twain (1835–1910)

 TEACHING TIP

At this time, you may want to use **Lecture/Discussion Topic:** *The Overjustification Effect* (p. 16) from Bolt's Teacher's Resource Binder.

 TEACHING TIP

The overjustification effect occurs when extrinsic motivation overrides intrinsic motivation. This concept is related to cognitive dissonance. In **cognitive dissonance,** subjects try to reconcile a conflict between attitudes and actions. In doing so, they often change their attitudes to support the actions others see.

In one experiment, subjects pretended to like a boring task, and then were paid either $1 or $20. Those who were paid $1 said afterward they liked the task more, because they had no other incentive to like it—their payment didn't justify liking the activity for the money.

This effect helps to explain why teachers, police officers, and firefighters devote long, hard hours to their jobs for relatively little pay—and why professional athletes and celebrities often complain about being rich and famous!

 INTERCONNECTING

Biological predispositions work similarly with operant and classical conditioning. Only certain behaviors are likely to elicit responses. You can teach people and animals a wide variety of behaviors, but you can't teach them any behavior you desire.

 TEACHING TIP

Emphasize the concept of instinctive drift, mentioned on the bottom on page 237. Since this is not a bold word, students may miss this important concept. Even trained animals act naturally, regardless of whether a trained behavior is being reinforced.

TEACHING TIP

Skinner believed the following: Human freedom and dignity are illusions. Denial that we are controlled by our environment leaves us vulnerable to outside control. When we demand freedom, what we really mean is freedom from aversive consequences and not freedom to make choices. We can have "freedom" but only by arranging our own consequences and not by leaving it to "fate" or the "government."

At this time, you may want to use **Lecture/Discussion Topics:** *Skinner's Last Days* (p. 18) or *Beyond Freedom and Dignity* (p. 19) from Bolt's Teacher's Resource Binder.

TEACHING TIP

Communal societies began to emerge using Skinner's operant conditioning principles. Have students explore the Web sites of the two societies, mentioned below, that are still in existence today:

- Los Horcones in the mountains of Mexico maintains a Web site at www.loshorcones.org/index_eng.html. Of special interest at the site is the section "Misunderstandings About Behavior Analysis and Radical Behaviorism," which tries to refute common objections to the use of Skinnerian concepts in daily life.

- Twin Oaks, a community in rural Virginia, maintains a large Web site at www.twinoaks.org that describes its policies and activities, including Saturday tours and a 3-week visitor program.

B. F. Skinner "I am sometimes asked, 'Do you think of yourself as you think of the organisms you study?' The answer is yes. So far as I know, my behavior at any given moment has been nothing more than the product of my genetic endowment, my personal history, and the current setting" (1983). ▲

 Computer-assisted learning
Computers have helped realize Skinner's goal of individually paced instruction with immediate feedback. ▼

Skinner's Legacy

B. F. Skinner was one of the most controversial intellectual figures of the late twentieth century. He stirred a hornet's nest with his outspoken beliefs. He repeatedly insisted that external influences (not internal thoughts and feelings) shape behavior. And he urged people to use operant principles to influence others' behavior at school, work, and home. Knowing that behavior is shaped by its results, he said we should use rewards to evoke more desirable behavior.

Skinner's critics objected, saying that he dehumanized people by neglecting their personal freedom and by seeking to control their actions. Skinner's reply: External consequences already haphazardly control people's behavior. Why not administer those consequences toward human betterment? Wouldn't reinforcers be more humane than the punishments used in homes, schools, and prisons? And if it is humbling to think that our history has shaped us, doesn't this very idea also give us hope that we can shape our future?

Applications of Operant Conditioning

13: How might operant conditioning principles be applied at school, in sports, at work, at home, and for self-improvement?

In later units we will see how psychologists apply operant conditioning principles to help people moderate high blood pressure or gain social skills. Reinforcement technologies are also at work in schools, sports, workplaces, and homes (Flora, 2004), and these principles can support our self-improvement as well.

At School A generation ago, Skinner and others worked toward a day when teaching machines and textbooks would shape learning in small steps, immediately reinforcing correct responses. Such machines and texts, they said, would revolutionize education and free teachers to focus on each student's special needs.

Stand in Skinner's shoes for a moment and imagine two math teachers, each with a class of students ranging from whiz kids to slow learners. Teacher A gives the whole class the same lesson, knowing that the bright kids will breeze through the math concepts, and the slower ones will be frustrated and fail. With so many different children, how could one teacher guide them individually? Teacher B, faced with a similar class, paces the material according to each student's rate of learning and provides prompt feedback, with positive reinforcement, to both the slow and the fast learners. Thinking as Skinner did, how might you achieve the individualized instruction of Teacher B?

Computers were Skinner's final hope. "Good instruction demands two things," he said. "Students must be told immediately whether what they do is right or wrong and, when right, they must be directed to the step to be taken next." Thus, the computer could be Teacher B—pacing math drills to the student's rate of learning, quizzing the student to find gaps in understanding, giving immediate feedback, and keeping flawless records. To the end of his life, Skinner (1986, 1988, 1989) believed his ideal was achievable. Although the predicted education revolution has not occurred, today's interactive student software, Web-based learning, and online testing bring us closer than ever before to achieving his ideal.

In Sports Reinforcement principles can enhance athletic performance as well. Again, the key is to shape behavior, by first reinforcing small successes and then gradually increasing the challenge. Thomas Simek and Richard O'Brien (1981, 1988) applied these principles to teaching golf and baseball by starting with easily

TEACHING TIP

At this time, you may want to use **Lecture/Discussion Topic:** *Walden Two and the Twin Oaks Community* (p. 21) from Bolt's Teacher's Resource Binder.

reinforced responses. Golf students learn putting by starting with very short putts. As they build mastery, they eventually step back farther and farther. Likewise, novice batters begin with half swings at an oversized ball pitched from 10 feet away, giving them the immediate pleasure of smacking the ball. As the hitters' confidence builds with their success and they achieve mastery at each level, the pitcher gradually moves back—to 15, then 22, 30, and 40.5 feet—and eventually introduces a standard baseball. Compared with children taught by conventional methods, those trained by this behavioral method show, in both testing and game situations, faster skill improvement.

In sports as in the laboratory, the accidental timing of rewards can produce superstitious behaviors. If a Skinner box food dispenser gives a pellet of food every 15 minutes, whatever the animal happened to be doing just before the food arrives (perhaps scratching itself) is more likely to be repeated and reinforced, which occasionally can produce a persistent superstitious behavior. Likewise, if a baseball or softball player gets a hit after tapping the plate with the bat he or she may be more likely to do so again. Over time the player may experience partial reinforcement for what becomes a superstitious behavior.

At Work Skinner's ideas have also shown up in the workplace. Knowing that reinforcers influence productivity, many organizations have invited employees to share the risks and rewards of company ownership. Others focus on reinforcing a job well done. Rewards are most likely to increase productivity if the desired performance has been well-defined and is achievable. The message for managers? *Reward specific, achievable behaviors, not vaguely defined "merit."* Even criticism triggers the least resentment and the greatest performance boost when specific and considerate (Baron, 1988).

Operant conditioning also reminds us that reinforcement should be *immediate.* IBM legend Thomas Watson understood. When he observed an achievement, he wrote the employee a check on the spot (Peters & Waterman, 1982). But rewards need not be material, or lavish. An effective manager may simply walk the floor and sincerely affirm people for good work, or write notes of appreciation for a completed project. As Skinner said, "How much richer would the whole world be if the reinforcers in daily life were more effectively contingent on productive work?"

At Home As we have seen, parents can apply operant conditioning practices. Parent-training researchers remind us that parents who say "Get ready for bed" but cave in to protests or defiance reinforce whining and arguing (Wierson & Forehand, 1994). Exasperated, they may then yell or gesture menacingly. When the child, now frightened, obeys, that in turn reinforces the parents' angry behavior. Over time, a destructive parent-child relationship develops.

To disrupt this cycle, parents should remember the basic rule of shaping: *Notice people doing something right and affirm them for it.* Give children attention and other reinforcers when they are behaving *well* (Wierson & Forehand, 1994). Target a specific behavior, reward it, and watch it increase. When children misbehave or are defiant, don't yell at them or hit them. Simply explain the misbehavior and give them a time-out.

For Self-Improvement Finally, we can use operant conditioning principles to improve our own lives (see Close-Up: Training Our Partners on the next page). To build up your *self-control,* you need to reinforce your own desired behaviors and extinguish the undesired ones. Psychologists suggest taking these steps:

1. *State your goal—to cease smoking, eat less, exercise more, or stop procrastinating—in measurable terms, and announce it.* You might, for example,

CRITICAL THINKING

Have students imagine what it would be like if they only received reinforcement for perfect performance. Would they be a student who learns how to behave perfectly? Or would they be frustrated and fail? This thought exercise might help them see the value of operant conditioning research on their own lives.

TEACHING TIP

Skinner's research on "superstitious" behavior in pigeons can be presented in class to illustrate both the power of reinforcement and its application to everyday life. According to Skinner, a superstitious behavior is a response that is accidentally reinforced—that is, there is no prearranged contingency between the response and reinforcement. Because the behavior and reinforcement occur together, the behavior is repeated and, by chance, is again followed by reinforcement. This process may explain why we carry a half dollar as a good luck piece, wear the same slacks when taking tests, and step over cracks in the sidewalk.

DEMO

Use any of these active learning experiences with students to demonstrate elements of operant conditioning. All are found in Bolt's Teacher's Resource Binder.

- **Student Project:** *Modifying an Existing Behavior* (p. 23)
- **Student Project/Classroom Exercise:** *Conditioning the Teacher's Behavior* (p. 21)
- **Student Project/Classroom Exercise:** *Biodots and Biofeedback in the Classroom* (p. 23)

UNIT 6

Fables about students conditioning their teachers' behaviors are legion. You have perhaps heard and even told your class how students have shaped their teachers to stand only in one corner of the room or face in one direction. W. Lambert Gardiner tells, tongue in cheek, how one class laughed more uproariously at their teacher's jokes as he moved toward the right side of the room until they were able to condition him right out the door.

RESEARCH

Psychologist David Allison of Columbia University reported an application of operant conditioning principles to both weight control and leisure management in children. The researchers created TVs that turned on and stayed on when the children pedaled a stationary bike. Children who had to pedal to watch TV biked an average of an hour a week while the others biked an average of only eight minutes. The pedal group watched one hour of TV per week and decreased overall body fat, while the non-pedal group watched 20 hours and saw no difference in weight.

Have your students design a research study that uses operant conditioning to control a negative behavior. Consider the following behaviors:

- Smoking
- Nail biting
- Procrastination with school work

CLOSE-UP

Training Our Partners

By Amy Sutherland

For a book I was writing about a school for exotic animal trainers, I started commuting from Maine to California, where I spent my days watching students do the seemingly impossible: teaching hyenas to pirouette on command, cougars to offer their paws for a nail clipping, and baboons to skateboard.

I listened, rapt, as professional trainers explained how they taught dolphins to flip and elephants to paint. Eventually it hit me that the same techniques might work on that stubborn but lovable species, the American husband.

The central lesson I learned from exotic animal trainers is that I should reward behavior I like and ignore behavior I don't. After all, you don't get a sea lion to balance a ball on the end of its nose by nagging. The same goes for the American husband.

Back in Maine, I began thanking Scott if he threw one dirty shirt into the hamper. If he threw in two, I'd kiss him. Meanwhile, I would step over any soiled clothes on the floor without one sharp word, though I did sometimes kick them under the bed. But as he basked in my appreciation, the piles became smaller.

I was using what trainers call "approximations," rewarding the small steps toward learning a whole new behavior.... Once I started thinking this way, I couldn't stop. At the school in California, I'd be scribbling notes on how to walk an emu or have a wolf accept you as a pack member, but I'd be thinking, "I can't wait to try this on Scott...."

After two years of exotic animal training, my marriage is far smoother, my husband much easier to love. I used to take his faults personally; his dirty clothes on the floor were an affront, a symbol of how he didn't care enough about me. But thinking of my husband as an exotic species gave me the distance I needed to consider our differences more objectively.

"I wrote another five hundred words. Can I have another cookie?"

> "O! This learning, what a thing it is."
> William Shakespeare, *The Taming of the Shrew,* 1597

aim to boost your study time by an hour a day and share that goal with some close friends.

2. ***Monitor how often you engage in your desired behavior.*** You might log your current study time, noting under what conditions you do and don't study. (When I began writing textbooks, I logged how I spent my time each day and was amazed to discover how much time I was wasting.)

3. ***Reinforce the desired behavior.*** To increase your study time, give yourself a reward (a snack or some activity you enjoy) only after you finish your extra hour of study. Agree with your friends that you will join them for weekend activities only if you have met your realistic weekly studying goal.

4. ***Reduce the rewards gradually.*** As your new behaviors become more habitual, give yourself a mental pat on the back instead of a cookie.

In addition, we can literally learn from ourselves. There is some evidence that when we have feedback about our bodily responses, we can sometimes change those responses. (See Close-Up: Biofeedback.)

Contrasting Classical and Operant Conditioning

Both classical and operant conditioning are forms of associative learning, and both involve acquisition, extinction, spontaneous recovery, generalization, and discrimination. The similarities are sufficient to make some researchers wonder if a single stimulus-response learning process might explain them both (Donahoe & Vegas, 2004). Their procedural difference is this: Through classical (Pavlovian) conditioning, an organism associates different stimuli that it does not control and responds automatically (respondent behaviors) (**TABLE 6.4**). Through operant conditioning, an organism associates its operant behaviors—those that act on its environment to produce rewarding or punishing stimuli—with their consequences. Cognitive processes and biological predispositions influence both classical and operant conditioning.

At this time, you may want to use **Classroom Exercises: *A Token Economy*** (p. 20) or ***Assessing Self-Reinforcement*** (p. 23) from Bolt's Teacher's Resource Binder.

Biofeedback

Knowing the damaging effects of stress, could we train people to counteract stress, bringing their heart rate and blood pressure under conscious control? When a few psychologists started experimenting with this idea, many of their colleagues thought them foolish. After all, these functions are controlled by the autonomic ("involuntary") nervous system. Then, in the late 1960s, experiments by respected psychologists made the skeptics wonder. Neal Miller, for one, found that rats could modify their heartbeat if given pleasurable brain stimulation when their heartbeat increased or decreased. Later research revealed that some paralyzed humans could also learn to control their blood pressure (Miller & Brucker, 1979).

Miller was experimenting with **biofeedback**, a system of recording, amplifying, and feeding back information about subtle physiological responses. Biofeedback instruments mirror the results of a person's own efforts, thereby allowing the person to learn techniques for controlling a particular physiological response (**FIGURE 6.14**). After a decade of study, however, researchers decided the initial claims for biofeedback were overblown and oversold (Miller, 1985). A 1995 National Institutes of Health panel declared that biofeedback works best on tension headaches.

System receives signal

Amplifies signal

Processes signal

Feedback

Displays signal

➤ **FIGURE 6.14**

Biofeedback systems
Biofeedback systems—such as this one, which records tension in the forehead muscle of a headache sufferer—allow people to monitor their subtle physiological responses. As this man relaxes his forehead muscle, the pointer on the display screen (or a tone) may go lower.

::biofeedback a system for electronically recording, amplifying, and feeding back information regarding a subtle physiological state, such as blood pressure or muscle tension.

TABLE 6.4

COMPARISON OF CLASSICAL AND OPERANT CONDITIONING

	Classical Conditioning	Operant Conditioning
Basic idea	Organisms learn associations between events they don't control.	Organisms learn associations between their behavior and resulting events.
Response	Involuntary, automatic.	Voluntary, operates on environment.
Acquisition	Associating events; CS announces US.	Associating response with a consequence (reinforcer or punisher).
Extinction	CR decreases when CS is repeatedly presented alone.	Responding decreases when reinforcement stops.
Spontaneous recovery	The reappearance, after a rest period, of an extinguished CR.	The reappearance, after a rest period, of an extinguished response.
Generalization	The tendency to respond to stimuli similar to the CS.	Organisms' responses to similar stimuli are also reinforced.
Discrimination	The learned ability to distinguish between a CS and other stimuli that do not signal a US.	Organisms learn that certain responses, but not others, will be reinforced.
Cognitive processes	Organisms develop expectation that CS signals the arrival of US.	Organisms develop expectation that a response will be reinforced or punished; they also exhibit latent learning, without reinforcement.
Biological predispositions	Natural predispositions constrain what stimuli and responses can easily be associated.	Organisms best learn behaviors similar to their natural behaviors; unnatural behaviors instinctively drift back toward natural ones.

 TEACHING TIP

Use Table 6.4 to emphasize the differences between classical and operant conditioning. Students often get these two paradigms confused, so giving them the tools to understand the differences will be helpful.

INTERCONNECTING

Biofeedback is one way in which learning and biopsychology intersect. By using cognitive strategies to help control our physical reactions, we can learn how to relax. This type of therapy can be helpful for people with stress-related illnesses.

 TEACHING TIP

At this time, you may want to use **Classroom Exercise: *Conditioning Honeybees, Wasps, and Fish*** (p. 24) from Bolt's Teacher's Resource Binder.

TEACHING TIP

Ask students why observational learning is beneficial from an evolutionary perspective. Without the ability to learn by watching others, people would have to learn things the "hard way," which doesn't always lead to optimal chances of survival.

TEACHING TIP

In one study, preschool children, chosen because they were terrified of dogs, merely watched a little boy playing happily with a dog for 20 minutes. As a result of this experience, 67 percent were willing to climb into a playpen with a dog and remain confined there, petting and scratching the dog, while everyone else left the room. Their observations seemed to have a lasting positive effect. One month later the children were more willing than ever to approach dogs.

Cialdini, R. (1993). *Influence: Science and practice* (3rd ed.). New York: HarperCollins.

➤ **FIGURE 6.15**
Cognitive imitation When Monkey A (below left) sees Monkey B touch four pictures on a display screen in a certain order to gain a banana, Monkey A learns to imitate that order, even when shown a different configuration (Subiaul et al., 2004).

➤ **ASK YOURSELF**

Can you recall a time when a teacher, coach, family member, or employer helped you learn something by shaping your behavior in little steps until you achieved your goal?

➤ **TEST YOURSELF 3**

Positive reinforcement, negative reinforcement, positive punishment, and *negative punishment* are tricky concepts for many students. Can you fit the right term in the four spaces in this table? I'll do the first one (positive reinforcement) for you.

Type of Stimulus	Give It	Take It Away
Desired (for example, a compliment):	*Positive reinforcement*	
Undesired/aversive (for example, an insult):		

Answers to the Test Yourself questions can be found in Appendix E at the end of the book.

Learning by Observation

14: What is observational learning, and how is it enabled by mirror neurons?

FROM DROOLING DOGS, RUNNING RATS, and pecking pigeons we have learned much about the basic processes of learning. But conditioning principles don't tell us the whole story. Higher animals, especially humans, can learn without direct experience, through **observational learning,** also called *social learning,* because we learn by observing and imitating others. A child who sees his sister burn her fingers on a hot stove learns not to touch it. And a monkey watching another selecting certain pictures to gain treats learns to imitate that behavior (**FIGURE 6.15**). We learn all kinds of specific behaviors by observing and imitating models, a process called **modeling.** Lord Chesterfield (1694–1773) had the idea: "We are, in truth, more than half what we are by imitation."

We can glimpse the roots of observational learning in other species. Rats, pigeons, crows, and gorillas all observe others and learn (Byrne & Russon, 1998; Dugatkin,

Monkey A's screen   Monkey B's screen

TEACHING TIP

At this time, you may want to use **Lecture/Discussion Topic:** *Germans Who Helped Jews Escape* (p. 25) from Bolt's Teacher's Resource Binder.

2002). So do monkeys. Rhesus macaque monkeys rarely make up quickly after a fight—unless they grow up with forgiving older macaques. Then, more often than not, their fights, too, are quickly followed by reconciliation (de Waal & Johanowicz, 1993). Monkey see, monkey do. Chimpanzees learn all sorts of foraging and tool use behaviors by observation, which then are transmitted across generations within their local culture (Hopper et al., 2008; Whiten et al., 2007).

Imitation is all the more striking in humans. Our catch-phrases, hem lengths, ceremonies, foods, traditions, vices, and fads all spread by one person copying another. Even as 2½-year-olds, when many of our mental abilities were near those of chimpanzees, we considerably surpassed chimps at social tasks such as imitating another's solution to a problem (Herrmann et al., 2007).

Mirrors in the Brain

On a 1991 hot summer day in Parma, Italy, a lab monkey awaited its researchers' return from lunch. The researchers had implanted wires next to its motor cortex, in a frontal lobe brain region that enabled the monkey to plan and enact movements. When the monkey moved a peanut into its mouth, for example, the monitoring device would buzz. That day, as one of the researchers reentered the lab, ice cream cone in hand, the monkey stared at him. As the student raised the cone to lick it, the monkey's monitor again buzzed—as if the motionless monkey had itself moved (Blakeslee, 2006; Iacoboni, 2008).

Having earlier observed the same weird result when the monkey watched humans or other monkeys move peanuts to their mouths, the flabbergasted researchers, led by Giacomo Rizzolatti (2002, 2006), eventually surmised that they had stumbled onto a previously unknown type of neuron: **mirror neurons,** whose activity provides a neural basis for imitation and observational learning. When a monkey grasps, holds, or tears something, these neurons fire. And they likewise fire when the monkey observes another doing so. When one monkey sees, these neurons mirror what another monkey does.

It's not just monkey business. Imitation shapes even very young humans' behavior. Shortly after birth, a baby may imitate an adult who sticks out his tongue. By 8 to 16 months, infants imitate various novel gestures (Jones, 2007). By age 12 months, they begin looking where an adult is looking (Brooks & Meltzoff, 2005). And by age 14 months (**FIGURE 6.16** on the next page), children imitate acts modeled on TV (Meltzoff, 1988; Meltzoff & Moore, 1989, 1997). Children see, children do.

PET scans of different brain areas reveal that humans, like monkeys, have a mirror neuron system that supports empathy and imitation (Iacoboni, 2008). As we observe another's action, our brain generates an inner simulation, enabling us to experience the other's experience within ourselves. Mirror neurons help give rise to children's empathy and to their ability to infer another's mental state, an ability known as *theory of mind*. As noted in Unit 9, people with autism display reduced imitative yawning and mirror neuron activity—"broken mirrors," some have said (Ramachandran & Oberman, 2006; Senju et al., 2007; Williams et al., 2006).

For most of us, however, our mirror neurons make emotions contagious. We grasp others' states of mind—often feeling what they feel—by mental simulation. We find it harder to frown when viewing a smile than when viewing a frown (Dimberg et al., 2000, 2002). We find ourselves yawning after observing another's yawn, laughing when others laugh. When watching movies, a scorpion crawling up someone's leg makes us tighten up; observing a passionate kiss, we may notice our own

Children see, children do? Children who often experience physical punishment tend to display more aggression.
▲

::**observational learning** learning by observing others. Also called *social learning*.

::**modeling** the process of observing and imitating a specific behavior.

::**mirror neurons** frontal lobe neurons that fire when performing certain actions or when observing another doing so. The brain's mirroring of another's action may enable imitation and empathy.

TEACHING TIP

Have students ask younger children who their role models are. Students can also ask older people who their role models were when they were growing up. They can compare the children's and older people's choices to their own role models.

INTERCONNECTING

The pictures in Figure 6.17 show PET scans, which were discussed in Unit 3B. PET scans use radio-active sugars to track which neurons are active during certain activities. This scan shows mirror neurons in action.

➤ **FIGURE 6.16**
Learning from observation
This 14-month-old boy in Andrew Meltzoff's laboratory is imitating behavior he has seen on TV. In the top photo the infant leans forward and carefully watches the adult pull apart a toy. In the middle photo he has been given the toy. In the bottom photo he pulls the toy apart, imitating what he has seen the adult do.

Meltzoff, A. N. (1988). Imitation of televised models by infants. *Child Development*, 59, 1221–1229. Photos courtesy of A. N. Meltzoff and M. Hanuk.

lips puckering. Seeing a loved one's pain, our faces mirror their emotion. But as **FIGURE 6.17** shows, so do our brains. In this fMRI scan, the pain imagined by an empathic romantic partner has triggered some of the same brain activity experienced by the loved one actually having the pain (Singer et al., 2004). Even fiction reading may trigger such activity, as we mentally simulate the experiences described (Mar & Oatley, 2008). The bottom line: *Our brain's mirror neurons underlie our intensely social nature.*

➤ **FIGURE 6.17**
Experienced and imagined pain in the brain Brain activity related to actual pain (left) is mirrored in the brain of an observing loved one (right). Empathy in the brain shows up in emotional brain areas, but not in the somatosensory cortex, which receives the physical pain input.

Pain   Empathy

Reprinted with permission from The American Association for the Advancement of Science, Sobaul et al., *Science* 305:407-410 (2004) ©2004 AAAS.

Bandura's Experiments

Picture this scene from a famous experiment by Albert Bandura, the pioneering researcher of observational learning (Bandura et al., 1961). A preschool child

TEACHING TIP

At this time, you may want to use **Lecture/Discussion Topic:** *Media Violence and Aggression* (p. 26) from Bolt's Teacher's Resource Binder.

works on a drawing. An adult in another part of the room is building with Tinkertoys. As the child watches, the adult gets up and for nearly 10 minutes pounds, kicks, and throws around the room a large inflated Bobo doll, yelling, "Sock him in the nose. . . . Hit him down. . . . Kick him."

The child is then taken to another room filled with appealing toys. Soon the experimenter returns and tells the child she has decided to save these good toys "for the other children." She takes the now-frustrated child to a third adjacent room containing a few toys, including a Bobo doll. Left alone, what does the child do?

Compared with children not exposed to the adult model, those who viewed the model's actions were much more likely to lash out at the doll. Apparently, observing the aggressive outburst lowered their inhibitions. But something more was also at work, for the children imitated the very acts they had observed and used the very words they had heard (**FIGURE 6.18**).

What determines whether we will imitate a model? Bandura believes part of the answer is reinforcements and punishments—those received by the model as well as by the imitator. By watching, we learn to anticipate a behavior's consequences in situations like those we are observing. We are especially likely to imitate people we perceive as similar to ourselves, as successful, or as admirable.

Albert Bandura "The Bobo doll follows me wherever I go. The photographs are published in every introductory psychology text and virtually every undergraduate takes introductory psychology. I recently checked into a Washington hotel. The clerk at the desk asked, 'Aren't you the psychologist who did the Bobo doll experiment?' I answered, 'I am afraid that will be my legacy.' He replied, 'That deserves an upgrade. I will put you in a suite in the quiet part of the hotel'" (2005).

> **FIGURE 6.18**
The famous Bobo doll experiment
Notice how the children's actions directly imitate the adult's.

Applications of Observational Learning

The big news from Bandura's studies is that we look and we learn. Models—in one's family or neighborhood, or on TV—may have effects—good or bad. Many business organizations effectively use *behavior modeling* to train communications, sales, and customer service skills (Taylor et al., 2005). Trainees gain skills faster when they not only are told the needed skills but also are able to observe the skills being modeled effectively by experienced workers (or actors simulating them).

"Children need models more than they need critics."
Joseph Joubert, *Pensées*, 1842

INTERCONNECTING

Albert Bandura is one of the more prolific and respected scientists of his generation. Not only is he famous for the Bobo doll studies described in this unit, he also developed the theories of reciprocal determinism discussed in Unit 10 and self-efficacy (related to an internal locus of control, which is also discussed in Unit 10).

TEACHING TIP

Vicarious learning is a type of observational learning. Vicarious learning depends on the learner understanding consequences. Observational learning can occur without consequences.

TEACHING TIP

At this time, you may want to use **Lecture/Discussion Topic:** *Parents and Television Watching* (p. 27) from Bolt's Teacher's Resource Binder.

UNIT 6

RESEARCH

Students can improve a skill by choosing a role model and observing his or her behavior over a period of time. Students can engage in a project in which they identify someone who possesses a skill they want to improve in their lives. Through interviews with and observation of the role model, the students can learn techniques to change their behavior. Students can demonstrate their new-found skills in a class "talent show."

TEACHING TIP

The study of Germans who helped Jews during the Holocaust can provide a good introduction to the significance of observational learning on prosocial behavior. Perry London found that rescuers shared personality characteristics: 1) a spirit of adventurousness, 2) intense identification with a parental model of moral conduct, and 3) a sense of being socially marginal, typified by a rescuer who reported that he had stuttered as a child, and had been friendless. Samuel and Pearl Oliner also showed that those who rescued Jews were motivated by three factors: 1) a commitment to justice, 2) conformity to social norms such as helping others, and 3) empathy for the suffering of others.

London, P. (1970). The rescuers: Motivational hypotheses about Christians who saved Jews from the Nazis. In J. Macaulay & L. Berkowitz (Eds.), *Altruism and helping behavior*. Orlando, FL: Academic Press.

Oliner, S., & Oliner, P. (1988). *The altruistic personality: Rescuers of Jews in Nazi Europe.* New York: Macmillan.

::**prosocial behavior** positive, constructive, helpful behavior. The opposite of antisocial behavior.

Prosocial Effects

15: What is the impact of prosocial modeling and of antisocial modeling?

The good news is that **prosocial** (positive, helpful) models can have prosocial effects. To encourage children to read, read to them and surround them with books and people who read. To increase the odds that your children will practice your religion, worship and attend religious activities with them. People who exemplify nonviolent, helpful behavior can prompt similar behavior in others. India's Mahatma Gandhi and America's

▼ **A model player** Los Angeles Galaxy soccer star David Beckham provided a powerful role model for aspiring players at this youth soccer clinic in Harlem. As the sixteenth-century proverb states, "Example is better than precept."

Martin Luther King, Jr., both drew on the power of modeling, making nonviolent action a powerful force for social change in both countries. Parents are also powerful models. European Christians who risked their lives to rescue Jews from the Nazis usually had a close relationship with at least one parent who modeled a strong moral or humanitarian concern; this was also true for U.S. civil rights activists in the 1960s (London, 1970; Oliner & Oliner, 1988). The observational learning of morality begins early. Socially responsive toddlers who readily imitate their parents tend to become preschoolers with a strong internalized conscience (Forman et al., 2004).

Models are most effective when their actions and words are consistent. Sometimes, however, models say one thing and do another. Many parents seem to operate according to the principle "Do as I *say*, not as I do." Experiments suggest that children learn to do both (Rice & Grusec, 1975; Rushton, 1975). Exposed to a hypocrite, they tend to imitate the hypocrisy by doing what the model did and saying what the model said.

RESEARCH

Celebrity endorsements are a multi-billion dollar business. Have students research the impact of celebrity endorsements on people's beliefs about the quality of products.

- Have students count the number of ads in popular magazines that have a celebrity endorsing the product. Compare their findings to the number of ads without celebrity endorsement.
- Students can create a survey that asks people to rank their preferences for several products, some with celebrity endorsers and others without.

Antisocial Effects

The bad news is that observational learning may have *antisocial effects*. This helps us understand why abusive parents might have aggressive children, and why many men who beat their wives had wife-battering fathers (Stith et al., 2000). Critics note that being aggressive could be passed along by parents' genes. But with monkeys we know it can be environmental. In study after study, young monkeys separated from their mothers and subjected to high levels of aggression grew up to be aggressive themselves (Chamove, 1980). The lessons we learn as children are not easily unlearned as adults, and they are sometimes visited on future generations.

TV is a powerful source of observational learning. While watching TV, children may "learn" that bullying is an effective way to control others, that free and easy sex brings pleasure without later misery or disease, or that men should be tough and women gentle. And they have ample time to learn such lessons. During their first 18 years, most children in developed countries spend more time watching TV than they spend in school. In the United States, where 9 in 10 teens watch TV daily, someone who lives to age 75 will have spent 9 years staring at the tube (Gallup, 2002; Kubey & Csikszentmihalyi, 2002). With more than 1 billion TV sets playing in homes worldwide, CNN reaching 150 countries, and MTV broadcasting in 17 languages, television has created a global pop culture (Gundersen, 2001; Lippman, 1992).

Television viewers are learning about life from a rather peculiar storyteller, one that reflects the culture's mythology but not its reality. During the late twentieth century, the average child viewed some 8000 TV murders and 100,000 other acts of violence before finishing elementary school (Huston et al., 1992). If we include cable programming and video rentals, the violence numbers escalate. An analysis of more than 3000 network and cable programs aired in the 1996–1997 season revealed that nearly 6 in 10 featured violence, that 74 percent of the violence went unpunished, that 58 percent did not show the victims' pain, that nearly half the incidents involved "justified" violence, and that nearly half involved an attractive perpetrator. These conditions define the recipe for the *violence-viewing effect* described in many studies (Donnerstein, 1998).

How much are we affected by repeated exposure to violent programs? Was the judge who in 1993 tried two British 10-year-olds for murdering a 2-year-old right to suspect that the pair had been influenced by "violent video films"? Were the American media right to think that the teen assassins who killed 13 of their Columbine High School classmates had been influenced by repeated exposure to *Natural Born Killers* and splatter games such as *Doom?* To understand whether violence viewing leads to violent behavior, researchers have done some 600 correlational and experimental studies (Anderson & Gentile, 2008; Comstock, 2008; Murray, 2008).

Correlational studies do support this link:

- In the United States and Canada, homicide rates doubled between 1957 and 1974, just when TV was introduced and spreading. Moreover, census regions with later dates for TV service also had homicide rates that jumped later.
- White South Africans were first introduced to TV in 1975. A similar near-doubling of the homicide rate began after 1975 (Centerwall, 1989).
- Elementary schoolchildren with heavy exposure to media violence (via TV, videos, and video games) also tend to get into more fights (**FIGURE 6.19** next page).

But as we know from Unit 2, correlation does not imply causation. So these studies do not prove that viewing violence causes aggression (Freedman, 1988; McGuire, 1986). Maybe aggressive children prefer violent programs. Maybe abused or neglected children are both more aggressive and more often left in front of the TV. Maybe violent programs simply reflect, rather than affect, violent trends.

"The problem with television is that the people must sit and keep their eyes glued to a screen: The average American family hasn't time for it. Therefore the showmen are convinced that . . . television will never be a serious competitor of [radio] broadcasting."
New York Times, 1939

• TV's greatest effect may stem from what it displaces. Children and adults who spend 4 hours a day watching TV spend 4 fewer hours in active pursuits—talking, studying, playing, reading, or socializing with friends. What would you have done with your extra time if you had never watched TV, and how might you therefore be different? •

"Thirty seconds worth of glorification of a soap bar sells soap. Twenty-five minutes worth of glorification of violence sells violence."
U.S. Senator Paul Simon, Remarks to the Communitarian Network, 1993

UNIT 6

TEACHING TIP

Observational learning subtly influences behavior in many different ways:

- Television executives seem to know what they are doing when they use canned laughter. Experiments indicate that the technique causes an audience to laugh louder and more often when humorous material is presented.

- Advertisers love to tell us that their product is the "fastest growing" or "largest selling." The fact that many others are using it prompts us to buy it.

- Bartenders and baristas seed their tip jars with a few dollar bills to demonstrate appropriate customer behavior.

- The producers of charity telethons devote a great deal of time to listing the viewers who have already pledged contributions on the premise that others will follow suit.

Cialdini, R. (1993). *Influence: Science and practice* (3rd ed.). New York: HarperCollins.

INTERCONNECTING

Students may have already protested that many people watch violence in the media and play violent video games and do not ultimately turn to violence to solve problems. Remind them that just because research suggests that exposure to media violence tends to lead to more expressions of aggression does not mean that *every* person exposed to media violence will become more aggressive. As Unit 14 explains, many other factors also contribute to aggressive behavior. Still, it would be unwise not to consider the effects of the media to which we expose ourselves.

➤ **FIGURE 6.19**
Media violence viewing predicts future aggressive behavior Douglas Gentile and his colleagues (2004) studied more than 400 third to fifth graders. After controlling for existing differences in hostility and aggression, the researchers reported increased aggression in those heavily exposed to violent television, videos, and video games.

● Gallup surveys asked American teens (Mazzuca, 2002): "Do you feel there is too much violence in the movies, or not?"
1977: 42 percent said yes.
1999: 23 percent said yes. ●

Violence viewing leads to violent play Research has shown that viewing media violence does lead to increased expression of aggression in the viewers, as with these boys imitating pro wrestlers.

To pin down causation, psychologists use experiments. In this case, researchers randomly assigned some viewers to observe violence and others to watch entertaining nonviolence. Does viewing cruelty prepare people, when irritated, to react more cruelly? To some extent, it does. "The consensus among most of the research community," reported the National Institute of Mental Health (1982), "is that violence on television does lead to aggressive behavior by children and teenagers who watch the programs." This is especially so when an attractive person commits seemingly justified, realistic violence that goes unpunished and causes no visible pain or harm (Donnerstein, 1998).

The violence-viewing effect seems to stem from at least two factors. One is *imitation* (Geen & Thomas, 1986). As we noted earlier, children as young as 14 months will imitate acts they observe on TV. As they watch, their mirror neurons simulate the behavior, and after this inner rehearsal they become more likely to act it out. One research team observed a sevenfold increase in violent play immediately after children viewed *Power Rangers* (Boyatzis et al., 1995). These children, like those we saw earlier in the Bobo doll experiment, often precisely imitated the models' violent acts, including flying karate kicks. Imitation may also have played a role in the first eight days after the 1999 Columbine High School massacre, when every U.S. state except Vermont had to deal with copycat threats or incidents. Pennsylvania alone had 60 threats of school violence (Cooper, 1999).

Prolonged exposure to violence also *desensitizes* viewers; they become more indifferent to it when later viewing a brawl, whether on TV or in real life (Rule & Ferguson, 1986). Adult males who spent three evenings watching sexually violent movies became progressively less bothered by the rapes and slashings. Compared with those in a control group, the film watchers later expressed less sympathy for domestic violence victims, and they rated the victims' injuries as less severe (Mullin & Linz, 1995).

Indeed, suggested Edward Donnerstein and his co-researchers (1987), an evil psychologist could hardly imagine a better way to make people indifferent to brutality than to expose them to a graded series of scenes, from fights to killings to the mutilations in slasher movies. Watching cruelty fosters indifference.

"Don't you understand? This is life, this is what is happening. We can't switch to another channel."

BEFORE YOU MOVE ON . . .

➤ ASK YOURSELF

Who has been a significant role model for you? For whom are you a model?

➤ TEST YOURSELF 4

Jason's parents and older friends all smoke, but they advise him not to. Juan's parents and friends don't smoke, but they say nothing to deter him from doing so. Will Jason or Juan be more likely to start smoking?

Answers to the Test Yourself questions can be found in Appendix E at the end of the book.

* * *

Our knowledge of learning principles comes from the work of thousands of investigators. This unit has focused on the ideas of a few pioneers—Ivan Pavlov, John Watson, B. F. Skinner, and Albert Bandura. They illustrate the impact that can result from single-minded devotion to a few well-defined problems and ideas. These researchers defined the issues and impressed on us the importance of learning. As their legacy demonstrates, intellectual history is often made by people who risk going to extremes in pushing ideas to their limits (Simonton, 2000).

RESEARCH

Have students call local day care centers to ask about their policies for letting children watch violent cartoons and movies. Ask the teachers of these students if they've ever noticed children imitating the behaviors of cartoon or movie characters. Analyze this survey data to see if there is a trend of children imitating behavior.

CRITICAL THINKING

European cultures tend to view media violence as a taboo and restrict how much can be shown on television and in movies. Research how other cultures view violence in the media. Are juvenile crime rates higher or lower than those in the United States in cultures that restrict media violence?

UNIT 6

UNIT REVIEW: Learning

How Do We Learn?

1: What are some basic forms of learning?

Learning is a relatively permanent change in an organism's behavior due to experience. In *associative learning*, we learn to associate two stimuli (as in classical conditioning) or a response and its consequences (as in operant conditioning). In observational learning, we learn by watching others' experiences and examples.

Classical Conditioning

2: What is classical conditioning, and how did Pavlov's work influence behaviorism?

Classical conditioning is a type of learning in which an organism comes to associate stimuli. Pavlov's work on classical conditioning laid the foundation for *behaviorism*, the view that psychology should be an objective science that studies behavior without reference to mental processes.

3: How does a neutral stimulus become a conditioned stimulus?

In classical conditioning, a *UR* is an event that occurs naturally (such as salivation), in response to some stimulus. A *US* is something that naturally and automatically (without learning) triggers the unlearned response (as food in the mouth triggers salivation). A *CS* is a previously irrelevant stimulus (such as a bell) that, through learning, comes to be associated with some unlearned response (salivating). A *CR* is the learned response (salivating) to the originally irrelevant but now conditioned stimulus.

4: In classical conditioning, what are the processes of acquisition, extinction, spontaneous recovery, generalization, and discrimination?

In classical conditioning, *acquisition* is associating a CS with the US. Acquisition occurs most readily when a CS is presented just before (ideally, about a half-second before) a US, preparing the organism for the upcoming event. This finding supports the view that classical conditioning is biologically adaptive. *Extinction* is diminished responding when the CS no longer signals an impending US. *Spontaneous recovery* is the appearance of a formerly extinguished response, following a rest period. *Generalization* is the tendency to respond to stimuli that are similar to a CS. *Discrimination* is the learned ability to distinguish between a CS and other irrelevant stimuli.

5: Do cognitive processes and biological constraints affect classical conditioning?

The behaviorists' optimism that in any species, any response can be conditioned to any stimulus has been tempered. Conditioning principles, we now know, are cognitively and bio-

logically constrained. In classical conditioning, animals learn when to expect a US, and they may be aware of the link between stimuli and responses. Moreover, because of biological predispositions, learning some associations is easier than learning others. Learning is adaptive: Each species learns behaviors that aid its survival.

6: Why is Pavlov's work important?

Pavlov taught us that significant psychological phenomena can be studied objectively, and that classical conditioning is a basic form of learning that applies to all species. Later research modified this finding somewhat by showing that in many species cognition and biological predispositions place some limits on conditioning.

7: What have been some applications of classical conditioning?

Classical conditioning techniques are used in treatment programs for those recovering from drug abuse and to condition more appropriate responses in therapy for emotional disorders. The body's immune system also appears to respond to classical conditioning.

Operant Conditioning

8: What is operant conditioning, and how does it differ from classical conditioning?

In *operant conditioning*, an organism learns associations between its own behavior and resulting events; this form of conditioning involves *operant behavior* (behavior that operates on the environment, producing consequences). In classical conditioning, the organism forms associations between stimuli—behaviors it does not control; this form of conditioning involves *respondent behavior* (automatic responses to some stimulus).

Expanding on Edward Thorndike's *law of effect*, B. F. Skinner and others found that the behavior of rats or pigeons placed in an *operant chamber* (Skinner box) can be *shaped* by using *reinforcers* to guide closer and closer approximations of the desired behavior.

9: What are the basic types of reinforcers?

Positive reinforcement adds something desirable to increase the frequency of a behavior. *Negative reinforcement* removes something undesirable to increase the frequency of a behavior. *Primary reinforcers* (such as receiving food when hungry or having nausea end during an illness) are innately satisfying—no learning is required. *Conditioned* (or secondary) *reinforcers* (such as cash) are satisfying because we have learned to associate them with more basic rewards (such as the food or medicine we buy with them). Immediate reinforcers (such as unprotected sex) offer immediate payback; delayed rein-

TECHNOLOGY RESOURCES

These resources will be helpful for teaching the concepts in this unit:

- *PsychSim 5: Classical Conditioning; Operant Conditioning; Maze Learning; Monkey See, Monkey Do*

- *Feature Film: Jaws* (p. 4 in Bolt's Teacher's Resource Binder)

- *Videos: Digital Media Archive*, 1st ed.: *Video Clip 6: Pavlov's Discovery of Classical Conditioning* (also in the *Psychology Video Tool Kit*); *Video Clip 7: Watson's Little Albert; Video Clip 8: Thorndike's Puzzle Box* (also in the *Psychology Video Tool Kit*); *Video Clip 9: B. F. Skinner Interview; Video Clip 10: Cognitive Maps* forcers (such as a weekly paycheck) require the ability to delay gratification.

10: How do different reinforcement schedules affect behavior?

In *continuous reinforcement* (reinforcing desired responses every time they occur), learning is rapid, but so is extinction if rewards cease. In *partial (intermittent) reinforcement,* initial learning is slower, but the behavior is much more resistant to extinction. *Fixed-ratio schedules* offer rewards after a set number of responses; *variable-ratio schedules,* after an unpredictable number. *Fixed-interval schedules* offer rewards after set time periods; *variable-interval schedules,* after unpredictable time periods.

11: How does punishment affect behavior?

Punishment attempts to decrease the frequency of a behavior (a child's disobedience) by administering an undesirable consequence (such as spanking) or withdrawing something desirable (such as taking away a favorite toy). Undesirable side effects can include suppressing rather than changing unwanted behaviors, teaching aggression, creating fear, encouraging discrimination (so that the undesirable behavior appears when the punisher is not present), and fostering depression and low self-esteem.

12: Do cognitive processes and biological constraints affect operant conditioning?

Skinner underestimated the limits that cognitive and biological constraints place on conditioning. Research on *cognitive mapping, latent learning,* and *insight* demonstrate the importance of cognitive processes in learning. Excessive rewards can undermine *intrinsic motivation.* Training that attempts to override biological constraints will probably not endure because the animals will revert to their predisposed patterns.

13: How might operant conditioning principles be applied at school, in sports, at work, at home, and for self-improvement?

At school, teachers can use shaping techniques to guide students' behaviors, and they can use interactive software and Web sites to provide immediate feedback. In sports, coaches can build players' skills and self-confidence by rewarding small improvements. At work, managers can boost productivity and morale by rewarding well-defined and achievable behaviors. At home, parents can reward behaviors they consider desirable, but not those that are undesirable. We can shape our own behaviors by stating our goals, monitoring the frequency of desired behaviors, reinforcing desired behaviors, and cutting back on incentives as behaviors become habitual.

Learning by Observation

14: What is observational learning, and how is it enabled by mirror neurons?

Albert Bandura's experiments on *observational learning* (also called social learning), demonstrate how we observe and imitate others. *Mirror neurons,* located in the brain's frontal lobes, demonstrate a neural basis for observational learning. They fire when we perform certain actions (such as responding to pain or moving our mouth to form words), or when we observe someone else performing those actions.

15: What is the impact of prosocial modeling and of antisocial modeling?

Children tend to imitate what a model does and says, whether the behavior being *modeled* is *prosocial* (positive, constructive, and helpful) or antisocial. If a model's actions and words are inconsistent, children may imitate the hypocrisy they observe.

Terms and Concepts to Remember

learning, p. 215	acquisition, p. 220	operant behavior, p. 228
habituation, p. 216	higher-order conditioning, p. 220	law of effect, p. 229
associative learning, p. 216	extinction, p. 221	operant chamber, p. 229
classical conditioning, p. 218	spontaneous recovery, p. 221	shaping, p. 229
behaviorism, p. 218	generalization, p. 222	discriminative stimulus, p. 230
unconditioned response (UR), p. 219	discrimination, p. 222	reinforcer, p. 230
unconditioned stimulus (US), p. 219	learned helplessness, p. 223	positive reinforcement, p 231
conditioned response (CR), p. 219	respondent behavior, p. 228	negative reinforcement, p. 231
conditioned stimulus (CS), p. 219	operant conditioning, p. 228	primary reinforcer, p. 231

- *Videos: Psychology: The Human Experience, Module 10: Classical Conditioning; Module 11: Operant Conditioning; Module 12: Cognitive Processes in Learning*
- *Psychology Video Tool Kit: Classical Conditioning and the Immune System: Combating Lupus; Overcoming Fear; Do Video Games Teach People to Be Violent?; Program 3: Brain and Behavior: A Contemporary Phineas Gage*
- *Videos: Digital Media Archive, 2nd ed.: The Research of Carolyn Rovee-Collier: Learning and Memory in Preverbal Infants; Bandura on Social Learning With Clips From Original Experiment*
- *TV Episode: The Office: Jim Conditions Dwight* (p. 25 in Bolt's Teacher's Resource Binder)

UNIT 6

ANSWERS to Multiple-Choice Questions

1. **d.** may happen frequently because if the punished person stops misbehaving for a while this reinforces the punisher.

2. **a.** A mother playing catch with her daughter gradually backs up to increase the distance between the two of them.

3. **c.** be the mechanism by which the brain accomplishes observational learning.

4. **a.** A rabbit that has been conditioned to blink to a tone also blinks when a similar tone is sounded.

5. **a.** children are likely to imitate the behavior of adults.

6. **e.** the importance of cognitive factors in classical conditioning.

7. **d.** states that rewarded behavior is more likely to happen again.

8. **d.** pair a neutral stimulus with an unconditioned stimulus several times.

9. **e.** a discriminative stimulus.

10. **b.** negative reinforcement.

11. **b.** there are biological predispositions involved in learning.

12. **b.** variable interval

13. **a.** spontaneous recovery.

14. **c.** cognition plays an important role in operant conditioning.

15. **c.** behaviorism.

TECHNOLOGY RESOURCES

Technology Resources for Unit 6 can be found on pp. 250–251.

> AP* Practice Test Questions

Multiple-Choice Questions

1. Punishment
   a. is a good way to increase a behavior as long as it is not used too frequently.
   b. may create problems in the short term but rarely produces long-term negative side effects.
   c. is effective because it is a quick, direct way of informing the learner of what behavior is expected.
   d. may happen frequently because if the punished person stops misbehaving for a while this reinforces the punisher.
   e. should never be used in the opinion of most psychologists.

2. Which of the following is an application of shaping?
   a. A mother playing catch with her daughter gradually backs up to increase the distance between the two of them.
   b. A pigeon pecks a disk 25 times for an opportunity to receive a food reinforcement.
   c. A rat presses a bar when a green light is on but not when a red light is on.
   d. A rat gradually stops pressing a bar when it no longer receives a food reinforcement.
   e. A gambler continues to play a slot machine even though he has won nothing on his last 20 plays.

3. Mirror neurons may
   a. allow an organism to replace an unconditioned response with a conditioned response.
   b. help produce intrinsic motivation in some children.
   c. be the mechanism by which the brain accomplishes observational learning.
   d. produce the neural associations that are the basis of both classical and operant conditioning.
   e. explain why modeling prosocial behavior is more effective than modeling negative behavior.

4. Which of the following illustrates generalization?
   a. A rabbit that has been conditioned to blink to a tone also blinks when a similar tone is sounded.
   b. A dog salivates to a tone but not to a buzzer.
   c. A light is turned on repeatedly until a rat stops flexing its paw when it's turned on.
   d. A pigeon whose disk pecking response has been extinguished is placed in a Skinner box three hours later and begins pecking the disk again.
   e. A child is startled when the doorbell rings.

5. Albert Bandura's Bobo doll experiments demonstrated that
   a. children are likely to imitate the behavior of adults.
   b. there may be a correlation between televised violence and aggressive behavior, but it is probably not a cause-effect relationship.
   c. children are more likely to copy what adults say than what adults do.
   d. allowing children to watch too much television is detrimental to their development.
   e. observational learning can explain the development of fears in children.

6. Robert Rescorla and Allan Wagner conducted experiments that established
   a. that the acquisition of a CR depends on pairing the CS and the US.
   b. that different species respond differently to classical conditioning situations.
   c. the current belief that classical conditioning is really a form of operant conditioning.
   d. that mirror neurons form the biological basis of classical conditioning.
   e. the importance of cognitive factors in classical conditioning.

Rubric for Grading the Free-Response Question

This is a 15-point question. You should require enough description for each point to be assured of the students' understanding.

Ivan Pavlov

- 1 point for identifying classical conditioning as the type of learning.
- 1 point for citing Pavlov's research on the conditioned salivary response in dogs as the nature of the research.
- 1 point for an implication of the research. Responses will vary, but one possibility is to describe how a person might begin salivating when she hears her mother call her to dinner.

7. Edward Thorndike's law of effect
a. establishes the difference between positive and negative reinforcement.
b. shows that behavior maintained by partial reinforcement is more resistant to extinction than behavior maintained by continuous reinforcement.
c. demonstrates how shaping can be used to establish operant conditioning.
d. states that rewarded behavior is more likely to happen again.
e. relates to the limited effectiveness of punishment.

8. To produce the acquisition of a conditioned response, one should
a. repeatedly present an unconditioned response.
b. administer the conditioned stimulus without the unconditioned stimulus.
c. make sure that the conditioned stimulus comes at least one minute before the unconditioned stimulus.
d. pair a neutral stimulus with an unconditioned stimulus several times.
e. present the conditioned stimulus until it starts to produce an unconditioned response.

9. To determine just what an organism can learn to distinguish, you would use
a. generalization.
b. a variable ratio schedule of reinforcement.
c. a fixed ratio schedule of reinforcement.
d. extinction.
e. a discriminative stimulus.

10. A student studies long and hard to avoid the bad feelings associated with a low grade on a test. In this case, the studying behavior is being strengthened because of
a. positive reinforcement.
b. negative reinforcement.
c. delayed reinforcement.
d. primary reinforcement.
e. conditioned reinforcement.

11. Taste aversion research has demonstrated that
a. taste is the most fundamental of the senses.
b. there are biological predispositions involved in learning.
c. animals must evaluate a situation cognitively before taste aversion develops.
d. taste aversion is a universal survival mechanism.
e. a US must occur within seconds of a CS for conditioning to occur.

12. Mary checks her phone a couple times an hour for incoming text messages. Her behavior is being maintained on a _____ reinforcement schedule.
a. fixed interval
b. variable interval
c. variable ratio
d. fixed ratio
e. continuous

13. A dog is trained to salivate when it hears a tone. Then the tone is sounded repeatedly without a US until the dog stops salivating. Later, when the tone sounds again, the dog salivates again. This is a description of
a. spontaneous recovery.
b. extinction.
c. generalization.
d. discrimination.
e. acquisition.

14. Latent learning demonstrates that
a. punishment is an ineffective means of controlling behavior.
b. negative reinforcement should be avoided when possible.
c. cognition plays an important role in operant conditioning.
d. conditioned reinforcers are more effective than primary reinforcers.
e. shaping is usually not necessary for operant conditioning.

15. Classical and operant conditioning were both initially based on the principles of
a. cognitive psychology.
b. biological psychology.
c. behaviorism.
d. evolution.
e. animal thought processes.

Free-Response Question

Many pioneering researchers have devoted their careers to understanding how we learn. For each of the following individuals, identify the type of learning researched, briefly explain the nature of the research conducted, and provide an implication of the research for human behavior in the real world.
• Ivan Pavlov
• John Watson
• John Garcia
• B. F. Skinner
• Albert Bandura

 WEB
Multiple-choice self-tests and more may be found at www.worthpublishers.com/myers

John Watson
- 1 point for identifying classical conditioning as the type of learning.
- 1 point for citing Watson's research on the conditioned fear response in Little Albert as the nature of the research.
- 1 point for an implication of the research. Responses will vary, but one possibility is to describe how a child might learn to fear storms because of the association between the storm and a loud boom of thunder.

John Garcia
- 1 point for identifying classical conditioning as the type of learning.

 Rubric continued

- 1 point for citing Garcia's research on taste aversion in rats as the nature of the research.
- 1 point for an implication of the research. Responses will vary, but one possibility is to describe how a person might develop an aversion to cheese soup if that person ate cheese soup when already sick with the stomach flu.

B. F. Skinner
- 1 point for identifying operant conditioning as the type of learning.
- 1 point for citing Skinner's research on the effects of reinforcement or punishment as the nature of the research.
- 1 point for an implication of the research. Responses abound. Any application of the effect of reinforcement or punishment on real-life behavior will score this point.

Albert Bandura
- 1 point for identifying observational learning as the type of learning.
- 1 point for citing Bandura's Bobo doll research on children's imitation of aggressive behavior as the nature of the research.
- 1 point for an implication of the research. Any application of someone imitating behavior modeled by another person will score this point.

Pacing Guide

Use the following guide to determine how many instructional days to devote to this portion of the unit depending on the type of course you teach:

Year-long course: 8–10 days
Block schedule/Semester-long course: 4–5 days

This entire unit (Parts A & B) encompasses 8–10 percent of the AP Exam. Spending an appropriate amount of time on this unit will help students do well on the AP Exam.

INTERCONNECTING

This unit, like biological bases of behavior, is one that is often referenced in other units. Consider teaching this unit early in the course so students can use the concepts in this unit for their personal studying. This unit is broken down into two smaller units. Help students process the wealth of information found in this unit by using the concepts and techniques discussed within.

254

Suggested Readings

Baddeley, A. (1998). *Human memory: Theory and practice* (rev. ed.). Boston: Allyn & Bacon.

Hilts, P. J. (1995). *Memory's ghost: The strange tale of Mr. M. and the nature of memory.* New York: Simon & Schuster.

Pinker, S. (1997). *How the mind works.* New York: W. W. Norton.

Schacter, D. L. (2001). *The seven sins of memory: How the mind forgets and remembers.* New York: Houghton-Mifflin.

Cognition:
7A—Memory

Be thankful for memory. We take it for granted, except when it malfunctions. But it is our memory that accounts for time and defines our life. It is our memory that enables us to recognize family, speak our language, find our way home, and locate food and water. It is our memory that enables us to enjoy an experience and then mentally replay and enjoy it again. Our shared memories help bind us together as Irish or Aussies, as Serbs or Albanians. And it is our memories that occasionally pit us against those whose offenses we cannot forget.

In large part, you are what you remember. Without memory, your storehouse of accumulated learning, there would be no savoring of past joys, no guilt or anger over painful recollections. You would instead live in an enduring present, each moment fresh. But each person would be a stranger, every language foreign, every task—dressing, eating, biking—a new challenge. You would even be a stranger to yourself, lacking that continuous sense of self that extends from your distant past to your momentary present. "If you lose the ability to recall your old memories then you have no life," suggested memory researcher James McGaugh (2003). "You might as well be a rutabaga or a cabbage."

The Phenomenon of Memory

TO A PSYCHOLOGIST, **memory** is learning that has persisted over time, information that has been stored and can be retrieved.

Research on memory's extremes has helped us understand how memory works. At age 92, my father suffered a small stroke that had but one peculiar effect. His genial personality was intact. He was as mobile as before. He knew us and while poring over family photo albums could reminisce in detail about his past. But he had lost most of his ability to lay down new memories of conversations and everyday episodes. He could not tell me what day of the week it was. Told repeatedly of his brother-in-law's death, he expressed surprise each time he heard the news.

"Waiter, I'd like to order, unless I've eaten, in which case bring me the check."

::**memory** the persistence of learning over time through the storage and retrieval of information.

Key Terms

The Phenomenon of Memory
memory

Information Processing
encoding
storage
retrieval
sensory memory
short-term memory
long-term memory
working memory
parallel processing
automatic processing
effortful processing
rehearsal
spacing effect
serial position effect
visual encoding
acoustic encoding
semantic encoding
imagery
mnemonics
chunking
iconic memory
echoic memory
long-term potentiation (LTP)
flashbulb memory
amnesia
implicit memory
explicit memory
hippocampus
recall
recognition
relearning
priming
déjà vu
mood congruent memory

Forgetting
proactive interference
retroactive interference
repression

Memory Construction
misinformation effect
source amnesia

Key People

Richard Atkinson
Alan Baddeley
Fergus Craik
Hermann Ebbinghaus
Eric Kandel
Jeffrey Karpicke
Karl Lashley
Elizabeth Loftus

H. M. (Henry Molaison)
Rajan Mahadevan
George Miller
Henry Roediger
Oliver Sacks
Daniel Schacter
James Schwartz
Richard Shiffrin

George Sperling
Endel Tulving

TEACHING TIP

Have students consider what life would be like with no memory. As Myers points out, our memory makes life easier because we retain the details of each day and the tasks we need to know to get through each day.

- With no memory, how would you answer the question: How are you today?

- With no memory, who would you be? How would your identity be affected?

At this time, you may want to use **Student Project/Classroom Exercise:** *Self-Defining Memories* (p. 3) from Bolt's Teacher's Resource Binder, which accompanies this text.

INTERCONNECTING

The cognitive revolution in psychology that occurred in the 1960s and 1970s helped dethrone behaviorism as the dominant perspective in psychology. One of the driving forces in this cognitive revolution was the application of computer models to behavior and mental processes.

TEACHING TIP

Help students understand that the information-processing model of memory is merely a simple explanation of a very complex topic. Memory is more complicated than this model makes it seem, but the basic structure of the model helps drive research into how memory works. As students progress through studies in psychology, they will learn more about Baddeley's model and other models that describe neural networks.

::**encoding** the processing of information into the memory system—for example, by extracting meaning.

::**storage** the retention of encoded information over time.

::**retrieval** the process of getting information out of memory storage.

::**sensory memory** the immediate, very brief recording of sensory information in the memory system.

::**short-term memory** activated memory that holds a few items briefly, such as the seven digits of a phone number while dialing, before the information is stored or forgotten.

::**long-term memory** the relatively permanent and limitless storehouse of the memory system. Includes knowledge, skills, and experiences.

At the other extreme are people who would be medal winners in a memory Olympics, such as Russian journalist Shereshevskii, or S, who had merely to listen while other reporters scribbled notes (Luria, 1968). Where you and I could parrot back a string of about 7—maybe even 9—digits, S could repeat up to 70, provided they were read about 3 seconds apart in an otherwise silent room. Moreover, he could recall digits or words backward as easily as forward. His accuracy was unerring, even when recalling a list as much as 15 years later, after having memorized hundreds of others. "Yes, yes," he might recall. "This was a series you gave me once when we were in your apartment. . . . You were sitting at the table and I in the rocking chair. . . . You were wearing a gray suit and you looked at me like this. . . ."

Amazing? Yes, but consider your own pretty staggering capacity for remembering countless voices, sounds, and songs; tastes, smells, and textures; faces, places, and happenings. Imagine viewing more than 2500 slides of faces and places, for only 10 seconds each. Later you see 280 of these slides, paired with others not previously seen. If you are like the participants in this experiment by Ralph Haber (1970), you would recognize 90 percent of those you had seen before.

➤ **FIGURE 7A.1**
What is this?

Or imagine yourself looking at a picture fragment, such as the one in **FIGURE 7A.1**. Also imagine that you had seen the complete picture (**FIGURE 7A.3**) for a couple of seconds 17 years earlier. Given this experience in a real experiment (Mitchell, 2006), people were more likely to identify previously seen objects than were members of a control group who had not seen complete drawings. Moreover, like the cicada insect that reemerges every 17 years, the picture memory reappeared even for those who had no conscious recollection of participating in the long-ago experiment!

How do we accomplish such memory feats? How can we remember things we have not thought about for years, yet forget the name of someone we met a minute ago? How are memories stored in our brains? Why do some painful memories persist, like unwelcome houseguests, while other memories leave too quickly? How can two people's memories of the same event be so different? Why will you be likely later in this unit to misrecall this sentence: *"The angry rioter threw the rock at the window"*? How can we improve our memories? These will be among the questions we consider as we review more than a century of research on memory.

TEACHING TIP

The San Francisco Exploratorium Web site includes a number of fascinating memory demonstrations and activities at www.exploratorium.edu/memory/index.html. Have students explore this site, complete several of the activities and respond to the following questions:

- How well did you do on the memory tasks?

- Are the types of memory games highlighted in the site related to the type of memory you use in school? Why or why not?

Information Processing

1: How do psychologists describe the human memory system?

A MODEL OF HOW MEMORY WORKS can help us think about how we form and retrieve memories. One model that has often been used is a computer's information-processing system, which is in some ways similar to human memory. To remember any event, we must *get information into our brain* (**encoding**), *retain that information* (**storage**), and later *get it back out* (**retrieval**). A computer also *encodes, stores,* and *retrieves* information. First, it translates input (keystrokes) into an electronic language, much as the brain encodes sensory information into a neural language. The computer permanently stores vast amounts of information on a drive, from which it can later be retrieved.

Like all analogies, the computer model has its limits. Our memories are less literal and more fragile than a computer's. Moreover, most computers process information speedily but sequentially, even while alternating between tasks. The brain is slower but does many things at once.

Psychologists have proposed several information-processing models of memory. One modern model, *connectionism,* views memories as emerging from interconnected neural networks. Specific memories arise from particular activation patterns within these networks. In an older but easier-to-picture model, Richard Atkinson and Richard Shiffrin (1968) proposed that we form memories in three stages:

1. We first record to-be-remembered information as a fleeting **sensory memory.**

2. From there, we process information into a **short-term memory** bin, where we encode it through *rehearsal.*

3. Finally, information moves into **long-term memory** for later retrieval.

Although historically important and helpfully simple, this three-step process is limited and fallible. In this unit, we use a *modified version of the three-stage processing model of memory* (**FIGURE 7A.2**). This updated model accommodates two important new concepts:

▶ **FIGURE 7A.2**

A modified three-stage processing model of memory Atkinson and Shiffrin's classic three-step model helps us to think about how memories are processed, but today's researchers recognize other ways long-term memories form. For example, some information slips into long-term memory via a "back door," without our consciously attending to it. And so much active processing occurs in the short-term memory stage that many now prefer the term *working memory.*

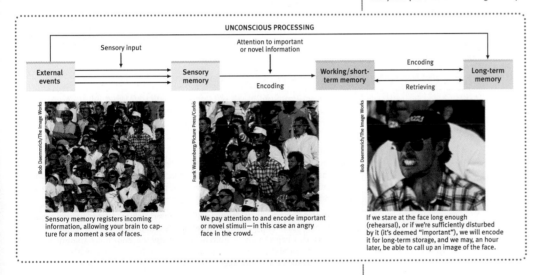

Sensory memory registers incoming information, allowing your brain to capture for a moment a sea of faces.

We pay attention to and encode important or novel stimuli—in this case an angry face in the crowd.

If we stare at the face long enough (rehearsal), or if we're sufficiently disturbed by it (it's deemed "important"), we will encode it for long-term storage, and we may, an hour later, be able to call up an image of the face.

TROUBLESHOOTING

Students often confuse short-term memory in casual conversation, believing that things that they remember for days or weeks and then forget are only stored in short-term memory. Their casual understanding of this term is mistaken. True short-term memory only lasts about a minute or so. Memories that stay with us for longer, but not permanently, are stored in working memory.

INTERCONNECTING

The complexity of the neural network allows for parallel processing. As discussed in Unit 3A, the more dendrites neurons have, the more complex the connections can be. This complexity gives us the ability to process many items at once, which is much more efficient.

DEMO

To demonstrate working memory and the limits of short-term memory, use the following demonstration. Ask your students if they can recite the second sentence of the Pledge of Allegiance. Everyone will think this is easy and will think through the entire pledge before realizing it consists of a single sentence.

At this time, you may want to use **Classroom Exercise:** *Remembering the Seven Dwarfs* (p. 4) from Bolt's Teacher's Resource Binder.

UNIT 7A

TEACHING TIP

Hermann Ebbinghaus spent hours each day testing his memory theories on himself. Ebbinghaus was a methodical researcher. To control for meaning as a variable, he memorized CVCs—consonant-vowel-consonant letter combinations. Examples of CVCs include ZUG, BIH, and NOK.

TEACHING TIP

Students often feel as though effortful processing is undesirable because they are afraid it will take too much time and energy. They feel overwhelmed with balancing all their classes and other interests. Emphasize to students what Myers points out: Effortful processing can become automatic. With enough practice, students can study more efficiently if they put in the effortful work in the beginning.

At this time, you may want to use **Classroom Exercise: Automatic Processing** (p. 6) from Bolt's Teacher's Resource Binder.

::**working memory** a newer understanding of short-term memory that focuses on conscious, active processing of incoming auditory and visual-spatial information, and of information retrieved from long-term memory.

::**parallel processing** the processing of many aspects of a problem simultaneously; the brain's natural mode of information processing for many functions. Contrasts with the step-by-step (serial) processing of most computers and of conscious problem solving.

::**automatic processing** unconscious encoding of incidental information, such as space, time, and frequency, and of well-learned information, such as word meanings.

::**effortful processing** encoding that requires attention and conscious effort.

::**rehearsal** the conscious repetition of information, either to maintain it in consciousness or to encode it for storage.

➤ **FIGURE 7A.3**

Now you know People who had seen this complete image were, 17 years later, more likely to recognize the fragment in Figure 7A.1.

- Some information, as you will see later in this unit, skips Atkinson and Shiffrin's first two stages and is processed directly and automatically into long-term memory, without our conscious awareness.
- **Working memory,** a newer understanding of Atkinson and Shiffrin's second stage, concentrates on the active processing of information in this intermediate stage. Because we cannot possibly focus on all the information bombarding our senses at once, we shine the flashlight beam of our attention on certain incoming stimuli—often those that are novel or important. We process these incoming stimuli, along with information we retrieve from long-term memory, in temporary working memory. Working memory associates new and old information and solves problems (Baddeley, 2001, 2002; Engle, 2002).

People's working memory capacity differs. Imagine being shown a letter of the alphabet, then asked a simple question, then being shown another letter, followed by another question, and so on. Those who can juggle the most mental balls—who can remember the most letters despite the interruptions—tend in everyday life to exhibit high intelligence and to better maintain their focus on tasks (Kane et al., 2007; Unsworth & Engle, 2007). When beeped to report in at various times, they are less likely than others to report that their mind was wandering from their current activity.

Let's use our updated model now to look more closely at how we encode, store, and retrieve information.

BEFORE YOU MOVE ON . . .

➤ **ASK YOURSELF**

How have you used the three parts of your memory system (encoding, storage, and retrieval) in learning something new today?

➤ **TEST YOURSELF 1**

Memory includes (in alphabetical order) long-term memory, sensory memory, and working/short-term memory. What's the correct order of these three memory stages?

Answers to the Test Yourself questions can be found in Appendix E at the end of the book.

Encoding: Getting Information In

2: What information do we encode automatically? What information do we encode effortfully, and how does the distribution of practice influence retention?

How We Encode

Some information, such as the route you walked to your last class, you process with great ease, freeing your memory system to focus on less familiar events. But to retain novel information, such as a friend's new cell phone number, you need to pay attention and try hard.

Automatic Processing Unlike most computers, which do step-by-step *serial processing,* our brain engages in **parallel processing:** doing many things at once. Thanks to this capacity for simultaneous activity, an enormous amount of multitasking goes on without your conscious attention. For example, without conscious effort you **automatically process** information about

DEMO

Reading is an activity most students in high school take for granted. Students who read on grade level process the words without much thought or effort. Because of this automaticity, students can misread the most simple sentence. Show students the following poem:

Spring is the
The most beautiful
Time of the year.

Ask students what is wrong with the sentence. Many will not immediately notice the repeated word "the" in the poem. This demonstrates the limits of automatic processing.

- *space.* While studying, you often encode the place on a page or in your notebook where certain material appears; later, when struggling to recall that information, you may visualize its location.
- *time.* While going about your day, you unintentionally note the sequence of the day's events. Later, when you realize you've left your backpack somewhere, you can re-create that sequence and retrace your steps.
- *frequency.* You effortlessly keep track of how many times things happen, thus enabling you to realize "this is the third time I've run into her today."
- *well-learned information.* For example, when you see words in your native language, perhaps on the side of a delivery truck, you cannot help but register their meanings. At such times, automatic processing is so effortless that it is difficult to shut off.

Deciphering words was not always so easy. When you first learned to read, you sounded out individual letters to figure out what words they made. With effort, you plodded slowly through a mere 20 to 50 words on a page. Reading, like some other forms of processing, initially requires attention and effort, but with experience and practice becomes automatic. Imagine now learning to read reversed sentences like this:

.citamotua emoceb nac gnissecorp luftroffE

At first, this requires effort, but after enough practice, you would also perform this task much more automatically. We develop many skills in this way. We learn to drive, to text message, to speak a new language first with great effort, then more automatically.

Effortful Processing We encode and retain vast amounts of information automatically, but we remember other types of information, such as this unit's concepts, only with effort and attention (**FIGURE 7A.4**). **Effortful processing** often produces durable and accessible memories.

When learning novel information such as vocabulary terms, we can boost our memory through **rehearsal,** or conscious repetition. The pioneering researcher of verbal memory, German philosopher Hermann Ebbinghaus (1850–1909), showed this after becoming impatient with philosophical speculations about memory. Ebbinghaus decided he would scientifically study his own learning and forgetting of novel verbal materials.

To create novel verbal material for his learning experiments, Ebbinghaus formed a list of all possible nonsense syllables by sandwiching one vowel between two consonants. He then randomly selected a sample of the syllables, practiced them, and tested himself. To get a feel for his experiments, rapidly read aloud, eight times over, the following list (from Baddeley, 1982). Then try to recall the items:

JIH, BAZ, FUB, YOX, SUJ, XIR, DAX, LEQ, VUM, PID, KEL, WAV, TUV, ZOF, GEK, HIW.

The day after learning such a list, Ebbinghaus could recall few of the syllables. But were they entirely forgotten? As **FIGURE 7A.5** (next page) portrays, the more frequently he repeated the list aloud on day 1, the fewer repetitions he required to relearn the list on day 2. Here, then, was a simple beginning principle: *The amount remembered depends on the time spent learning.* Even after we learn material, additional rehearsal *(overlearning)* increases retention. For students,

➤ **FIGURE 7A.4**
Automatic versus effortful processing
Some information, such as where you ate dinner yesterday, you process automatically. Other information, such as this unit's concepts, requires effort to encode and remember.

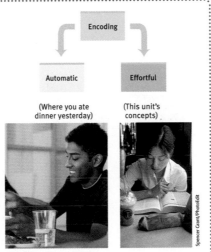

Encoding

Automatic | Effortful

(Where you ate dinner yesterday) | (This unit's concepts)

Spencer Grant/PhotoEdit

"He should test his memory by reciting the verses."
Abdur-Rahman Abdul Khaliq, "Memorizing the Quran"

UNIT 7A

RESEARCH

Divide students into groups and have one group memorize a list of 30 nonsense words based on whether the word sounds like another word. The other group should memorize the same list but try to associate a meaning with the nonsense word. See which group memorizes more words.

At this time, you may want to use **Classroom Exercise: *Rehearsal and the Twelve Days of Christmas*** (p. 7) from Bolt's Teacher's Resource Binder.

TEACHING TIP

Create a PowerPoint presentation in which you call out a word at the same time you show a picture related to the word. After you present the final picture, have students get out a sheet of paper. Ask them to write down the word you called out when you show the pictures again. This time, however, show the pictures in a different order than the original trial. Students should find they have no trouble remembering the words.

At this time, you may want to use **Classroom Exercise: *Serial Position Effect in Recalling U.S. Presidents*** (p. 7) from Bolt's Teacher's Resource Binder.

Time in minutes taken to relearn list on day 2

As rehearsal increases, relearning time decreases

Number of repetitions of list on day 1

➤ **FIGURE 7A.5**

Ebbinghaus' retention curve Ebbinghaus found that the more times he practiced a list of nonsense syllables on day 1, the fewer repetitions he required to relearn it on day 2. Said simply, the more time we spend learning novel information, the more we retain. (From Baddeley, 1982.)

"The mind is slow in unlearning what it has been long in learning."
Roman philosopher Seneca [4 B.C.E.–65 C.E.]

this means that it is important to continue to rehearse course material even after you know it. *The point to remember:* For novel verbal information, practice—effortful processing—does indeed make perfect.

Later research revealed more about how to lay down enduring memories. To paraphrase Ebbinghaus (1885), those who learn quickly also forget quickly. We retain information better when our rehearsal is distributed over time (as when learning classmates' names), a phenomenon called the **spacing effect.** More than 300 experiments over the last century consistently reveal the benefits of spacing learning times (Cepeda et al., 2006). *Massed practice* (cramming) can produce speedy short-term learning and feelings of confidence. But *distributed study time* produces better long-term recall. After studying long enough to master the material, further study at that time becomes inefficient, note Doug Rohrer and Harold Pashler (2007). Better to spend that extra reviewing time later—a day later if you need to remember something 10 days hence, or a month later if you need to remember something 6 months hence.

In a 9-year experiment, Harry Bahrick and three of his family members (1993) practiced foreign language word translations for a given number of times, at intervals ranging from 14 to 56 days. Their consistent finding: The longer the space between practice sessions, the better their retention up to 5 years later. The practical implication? Spreading out learning—over a semester or a year, rather than over a shorter term—should help you not only on comprehensive final exams, but also in retaining the information for a lifetime. Repeated quizzing of previously studied material also helps, a phenomenon that Henry Roediger and Jeffrey Karpicke (2006) call the *testing effect*, adding, "Testing is a powerful means of improving learning, not just assessing it." In one of their studies, students recalled the meaning of 40 previously learned Swahili words much better if tested repeatedly than if they spent the same time restudying the words (Karpicke & Roediger, 2008). *So here is another point to remember:* Spaced study and self-assessment beat cramming.

Another phenomenon, the **serial position effect,** further illustrates the benefits of rehearsal. As an everyday parallel, imagine it's your first day in a new job, and your manager is introducing co-workers. As you meet each one, you repeat (rehearse) all their names, starting from the beginning. By the time you meet the last person, you will have spent more time rehearsing the earlier names than the later ones; thus, the next day you will probably more easily recall the earlier names. Also, learning the first few names may interfere with your learning the later ones.

Experimenters have demonstrated the serial position effect by showing people a list of items (words, names, dates, even odors) and then immediately asking them to recall the items in any order (Reed, 2000). As people struggle to recall the list, they often remember the last and first items better than they do those in the middle (**FIGURE 7A.6**). Perhaps because the last items are still in working memory, people briefly recall them especially quickly and well (*a recency effect*). But after a delay—after they shift their attention from the last items—their recall is best for the first items (*a primacy effect*).

Sometimes, however, rehearsal is not enough to store new information for later recall (Craik & Watkins, 1973; Greene, 1987). To understand why this happens, we need to know more about how we encode information for processing into long-term memory.

DEMO

Students can see for themselves whether cramming or distributed rehearsal is more effective. Divide students into two groups—the "cramming" group and the distributed rehearsal group. Give students some material to study, whether it is from this unit, another unit, or even unrelated material. Tell the students that they will have a quiz on the material in one week's time. The cramming group should only study the night before the quiz. The distributed rehearsal group should study 15–30 minutes per night for the entire week. Compare the scores of each group to see which one earned the higher scores.

Immediate recall: last items best (recency effect)

Later recall: only first items recalled well (primacy effect)

Percentage of words recalled

Position of word in list

AP Photo/Musadeq Sadeq, Pool

➤ **FIGURE 7A.6**

The serial position effect Immediately after Australian Prime Minister Kevin Rudd introduces this long line of officials to Afghan President Hamid Karzai, President Karzai will probably recall the names of the last few people best. But later Karzai may recall the first few people best. (From Craik & Watkins, 1973.)

What We Encode

3: What effortful processing methods aid in forming memories?

Processing our sensory input is like sorting through e-mail. Some items we instantly discard. Others we open, read, and retain. We process information by encoding its meaning, encoding its image, or mentally organizing it.

Levels of Processing When processing verbal information for storage, we usually encode its meaning, associating it with what we already know or imagine. Whether we hear *eye-screem* as "ice cream" or "I scream" depends on how the context and our experience guide us to interpret and encode the sounds. (Remember, our working memories interact with our long-term memories.)

Can you repeat the sentence about the rioter that I gave you at this unit's beginning? ("The angry rioter threw . . .") Perhaps, like those in an experiment by William Brewer (1977), you recalled the rioter sentence by the meaning you encoded when you read it (for example, "The angry rioter threw the rock *through* the window") and not as it was written ("The angry rioter threw the rock *at* the window"). Referring to such recall, Gordon Bower and Daniel Morrow (1990) liken our minds to theater directors who, given a raw script, imagine a finished stage production. Asked later what we heard or read, we recall not the literal text but *what we encoded.* Thus, studying for a test, you may remember your class notes rather than the class itself.

What kind of encoding do you think yields the best memory of verbal information? **Visual encoding** of images? **Acoustic encoding** of sounds? **Semantic encoding** of meaning? Each of these levels of processing has its own brain system (Poldrack & Wagner, 2004). And each can help. For example, acoustic encoding enhances the memorability and seeming truth of rhyming aphorisms. "What sobriety conceals, alcohol reveals" seems more accurate than "what sobriety conceals, alcohol unmasks" (McGlone & Tofighbakhsh, 2000). Attorney Johnnie Cochran's celebrated plea to O. J. Simpson's murder trial jury—"If the glove doesn't fit, you must acquit"—was also more easily remembered than had Cochran said, "If the glove doesn't fit, you must find him not guilty!"

To compare visual, acoustic, and semantic encoding, Fergus Craik and Endel Tulving (1975) flashed a word at people. Then they asked a question that required the viewers

• Here is another sentence I will ask you about later: The fish attacked the swimmer. •

::**spacing effect** the tendency for distributed study or practice to yield better long-term retention than is achieved through massed study or practice.

::**serial position effect** our tendency to recall best the last and first items in a list.

::**visual encoding** the encoding of picture images.

::**acoustic encoding** the encoding of sound, especially the sound of words.

::**semantic encoding** the encoding of meaning, including the meaning of words.

RESEARCH

Have students develop their own paragraphs that describe a common activity in general terms like the paragraph that describes doing laundry on page 262. Then, have them share their paragraphs with other students, giving some the context and leaving others in the dark. Have them record whether knowing the context influenced how much of the paragraph their volunteers remembered. Remember to get approval for all research with human participants.

At this time, you may want to use **Classroom Exercise:** *Meaning and Memory* (p. 8) from Bolt's Teacher's Resource Binder.

CRITICAL THINKING

Visual and acoustic processing are effective in helping people remember information from the environment, but the level of recall is not as good as with semantic encoding. Have students consider the following experiences:

- When studying, you claim you can "see" the page on which you wrote the information, and you even remember what color highlighter you used to mark the information. However, you just can't remember what the word or concept is.

- In literature class, you have a hard time remembering Hamlet's "To be or not to be" soliloquy. Yet, you remember every word of Jay-Z's new album.

Have students discuss why these experiences occur in terms of the power and limitations of visual and acoustic encoding.

UNIT 7A

INTERCONNECTING

The self-reference effect is important to all learning. As you teach this unit (and every unit, really), try to get students to relate their own stories about the concepts. In this vein, you may ask students to use journal writing to help them better remember information when they relate it to their own life.

TEACHING TIP

Add the mnemonic devices below to the text's discussion to help students understand how their own memory techniques relate to this material:

- The **first-letter technique** is most useful when the order of items is important. This involves taking the first letter of each word and forming a new word or a sentence from these letters. Either ROY G. BIV or "Richard Of York Gains Battles in Vain" is used to remember the colors of the spectrum. (See page 264.)

- In the **substitution technique**, letters are used to replace numbers. For example, a T may be substituted for 1, N for 2, M for 3, etc. The letters may then be used to make up words or sentences. Businesses will sometimes help potential customers remember their phone number by using the letters associated with the numbers on the keypad to compose a familiar word.

At this time, you may want to use **Lecture/Discussion Topic: Mnemonic Devices** (p. 9) from Bolt's Teacher's Resource Binder.

● How many *F*s are in the following sentence?
FINISHED FILES ARE THE RESULTS OF YEARS OF SCIENTIFIC STUDY COMBINED WITH THE EXPERIENCE OF YEARS. (Answer below.) ●

Partly because your initial processing of the letters was primarily acoustic rather than visual, you probably missed some of the six *F*s, especially those that sound like a *V* rather than an *F*.

➤ FIGURE 7A.7
Levels of processing Processing a word deeply—by its meaning (semantic encoding)—produces better recognition of it at a later time than does shallow processing by attending to its appearance or sound. (From Craik & Tulving, 1975.)

to process the word at one of three levels (1) visually (the appearance of the letters), (2) acoustically (the sound of the word), or (3) semantically (the meaning of the word). To experience the task yourself, rapidly answer the following questions:

Sample Questions to Elicit Processing	Word Flashed	Yes	No
1. Is the word in capital letters?	CHAIR	___	___
2. Does the word rhyme with train?	brain	___	___
3. Would the word fit in this sentence?			
The girl put the _____ on the table.	gun	___	___

Which type of processing would best prepare you to recognize the word at a later time? In Craik and Tulving's experiment, the deeper, semantic processing—question 3—yielded much better memory than the "shallow processing" elicited by question 2 and especially by question 1 (**FIGURE 7A.7**).

But given too raw a script, we have trouble creating a mental model. Put yourself in the place of the students who John Bransford and Marcia Johnson (1972) asked to remember the following recorded passage:

> The procedure is actually quite simple. First you arrange things into different groups. Of course, one pile may be sufficient depending on how much there is to do. . . . After the procedure is completed one arranges the materials into different groups again. Then they can be put into their appropriate places. Eventually they will be used once more and the whole cycle will then have to be repeated. However, that is part of life.

When the students heard the paragraph you have just read, without a meaningful context, they remembered little of it. When told the paragraph described washing clothes (something meaningful to them), they remembered much more of it—as you probably could now after rereading it. Processing a word deeply—by its meaning (*semantic encoding*)—produces better recognition later than does shallow processing, such as attending to its appearance (*visual encoding*) or sound (*acoustic encoding*) (Craik & Tulving, 1975).

Such research suggests the benefits of rephrasing what we read and hear into meaningful terms. People often ask actors how they learn "all those lines." They do it by first coming to understand the flow of meaning, report psychologist-actor team Helga Noice and Tony Noice (2006). "One actor divided a half-page of dialogue into three [intentions]: 'to flatter,' 'to draw him out,' and 'to allay his

TEACHING TIP

The first mnemonic based on visual imagery was devised by the Greek poet Simonides in about 500 B.C.E. Simonides was invited to give a recitation in honor of an athletic champion at a banquet. After the poem, Simonides was called out of the banquet hall, and then the floor of the hall collapsed, killing and mutilating all the guests. The bodies were unrecognizable. However, by remembering where most of the guests had been sitting at the time he left, Simonides could identify the victims. The experience led Simonides to devise the method of loci.

fears.'" With this meaningful sequence in mind, the actor more easily remembers the lines.

From his experiments on himself, Ebbinghaus estimated that, compared with learning nonsense material, learning meaningful material required one-tenth the effort. As memory researcher Wayne Wickelgren (1977, p. 346) noted, "The time you spend thinking about material you are reading and relating it to previously stored material is about the most useful thing you can do in learning any new subject matter." *The point to remember:* The amount remembered depends both on the time spent learning and on your making it meaningful.

We have especially good recall for information we can meaningfully relate to ourselves. Asked how well certain adjectives describe someone else, we often forget them; asked how well the adjectives describe us, we—especially those from individualistic Western cultures—remember the words well. This phenomenon is called the *self-reference effect* (Symons & Johnson, 1997; Wagar & Cohen, 2003). So, you will profit from taking time to find personal meaning in what you are studying. Information deemed "relevant to me" is processed more deeply and remains more accessible.

Visual Encoding Why is it that we struggle to remember formulas, definitions, and dates, yet we can easily remember where we were yesterday, who was with us, where we sat, and what we wore? One difference is the greater ease of remembering mental pictures. Our earliest memories—probably of something that happened at age 3 or 4—involve visual **imagery**. We more easily remember concrete words, which lend themselves to visual mental images, than we do abstract, low-imagery words. (When I quiz you later, which three of these words—*typewriter, void, cigarette, inherent, fire, process*—will you most likely recall?) If you still recall the rock-throwing rioter sentence, it is probably not only because of the meaning you encoded but also because the sentence lent itself to a visual image. Memory for concrete nouns, such as "cigarette," is aided by encoding them *both* semantically and visually (Marschark et al., 1987; Paivio, 1986). Two codes are better than one.

Thanks to this durability of vivid images, our memory of an experience is often colored by its best or worst moment—the best moment of pleasure or joy, and the worst moment of pain or frustration (Fredrickson & Kahneman, 1993). Recalling the high points while forgetting the mundane may explain the phenomenon of *rosy retrospection* (Mitchell et al., 1997): People tend to recall events such as a camping trip more positively than they judged them at the time. The muggy heat and long lines of that visit to Disney World fade in the glow of vivid surroundings, food, and rides.

Imagery is at the heart of many **mnemonic** (nih-MON-ik) devices (so named after the Greek word for "memory"). Ancient Greek scholars and orators developed mnemonics to help them retrieve lengthy memorized passages and speeches. Some modern mnemonic devices rely on both acoustic and visual codes. For example, the *peg-word system* requires you to memorize a jingle: *"One is a bun; two is a shoe; three is a tree; four is a door; five is a hive; six is sticks; seven is heaven; eight is a gate; nine is swine; ten is a hen."* Without much effort, you will soon be able to count by peg-words instead of numbers: *bun, shoe, tree* . . . and then to visually associate the peg-words with to-be-remembered items. Now you are ready to challenge anyone to give you a grocery list to remember. Carrots? Stick them into the imaginary bun. Milk? Fill the shoe with it. Paper towels? Drape them over the tree branch. Think *bun, shoe, tree* and you see their associated

::**imagery** mental pictures; a powerful aid to effortful processing, especially when combined with semantic encoding.

::**mnemonics** [nih-MON-iks] memory aids, especially those techniques that use vivid imagery and organizational devices.

SALLY FORTH

Rosy retrospection A happy fact of life: For most people, the negative emotion recalled from bad events fades more rapidly than the positive emotion recalled from good events (Walker et al., 2003).

DEMO

Have students apply the method of loci with the following activity:

To remember 10 items on a grocery list—honey, dog food, sugar, oranges, ice cream, peanut butter, bread, pork chops, milk, and potato chips—take your students on a hypothetical tour of a house. Begin in the kitchen and see honey dripping down into the toaster on the counter and a giant St. Bernard eating his dog food on top of the kitchen table. Proceed to the living room, where sugar is embedded in the shag carpet, oranges are under the davenport pillows, peanut butter is stuck between the piano keys, and ice cream is in the roaring fireplace. Go up the stairs, with a slice of bread on each step. Pork chops are floating in the bathtub, milk is tipped over on the dresser in the bedroom, and potato chips are stuck between the bedsheets. When you get to the supermarket, re-tour your house. Ask students, "What's in the toaster . . . on the kitchen table . . . in the living room carpet . . .?"

 TEACHING TIP

Why are phone numbers divided into groups of three and four numbers? Why are social security numbers divided into three numbers, then two numbers, and then four numbers? Because with chunking, people can remember more pieces of information. By dividing the numbers into smaller groups, people are more likely to remember the entire list of numbers.

 DEMO

Without telling your class why, ask volunteers to give you single words to remember. (To simplify this task, specify that the words must name concrete objects.) Have the students recite the words for you at three- to five-second intervals and as they do, mentally use the "peg-word" system (cited in the text) to remember them (one-bun, two-shoe, three-tree, four-door, five-hive, six-sticks, seven-heaven, eight-gate, nine-swine, ten-hen). Behind your back, have a student quickly record them on the chalkboard in the order they are given. After all ten have been given, immediately give them back both backward and forward. In addition, tell them what the third, sixth, and ninth words were.

TEACHING TIP

Often students complain about studying for long hours only to do poorly on the test. Use this unit to reinforce the idea that *time spent studying* does not necessarily equal *quality of time spent studying*. Students who use mnemonic devices, chunking, and hierarchies understand the material better and can recall the material more readily than those who attempt to memorize or simply repeat the material over and over again. Encourage students to use the techniques described in this unit on the upcoming tests. With practice, they should spend less time studying but see more reward.

At this time, you may want to use **Classroom Exercise:** *Chunking* (p. 11) from Bolt's Teacher's Resource Binder.

TEACHING TIP

Students often resist outlining the chapter for class assignments. Point out to them that understanding the chapter organization is key to remembering the material. If they spend quality time with this type of assignment, they will ultimately spend less time studying later since they established a good foundation for learning the material throughout the unit.

images: carrots, milk, paper towels. With few errors (Bugelski et al., 1968), you will be able to recall the items in any order and to name any given item. Memory whizzes understand the power of such systems. A study of star performers in the World Memory Championships showed them not to have exceptional intelligence, but rather to be superior at using spatial mnemonic strategies (Maguire et al., 2003).

Organizing Information for Encoding Mnemonic devices can also help organize material for our later retrieval. When Bransford and Johnson's laundry paragraph became meaningful, we could mentally organize its sentences into a sequence. We process information more easily when we can organize it into meaningful units or structures.

➤ **FIGURE 7A.8**
Effects of chunking on memory When we organize information into meaningful units, such as letters, words, and phrases, we recall it more easily. (From Hintzman, 1978.)

1. ◁ ⊃ ฿ ⍹ ∩ ⊥ ℸ
2. K L C I S N E

3. KLCISNE NVESE YNA NI CSTTIH TNDO
4. NICKELS SEVEN ANY IN STITCH DONT

5. NICKELS SEVEN ANY IN STITCH DONT SAVES AGO A SCORE TIME AND NINE WOODEN FOUR YEARS TAKE

6. DONT TAKE ANY WOODEN NICKELS FOUR SCORE AND SEVEN YEARS AGO A STITCH IN TIME SAVES NINE

Chunking Glance for a few seconds at row 1 of **FIGURE 7A.8**, then look away and try to reproduce what you saw. Impossible, yes? But you can easily reproduce the second row, which is no less complex. Similarly, you will probably find row 4 much easier to remember than row 3, although both contain the same letters. And you could remember the sixth cluster more easily than the fifth, although both contain the same words.

As these units demonstrate, we more easily recall information when we can organize it into familiar, manageable chunks. **Chunking** occurs so naturally that we take it for granted. If you are a native English speaker, you can reproduce perfectly the 150 or so line segments that make up the words in the three phrases of item 6 in Figure 7A.8. It would astonish someone unfamiliar with the language.

➤ **FIGURE 7A.9**
An example of chunking—for those who read Chinese After looking at these characters, can you reproduce them exactly? If so, you are literate in Chinese.

春
夏
秋
冬

I am similarly awed at the ability of someone literate in Chinese to glance at **FIGURE 7A.9** and then to reproduce all of the strokes; or of a chess master who, after a 5-second look at the board during a game, can recall the exact positions of most of the pieces (Chase & Simon, 1973); or of a varsity basketball player who, given a 4-second glance at a basketball play, can recall the positions of the players (Allard & Burnett, 1985). We all remember information best when we can organize it into personally meaningful arrangements.

Chunking can also be used as a mnemonic technique to recall unfamiliar material. Want to remember the colors of the rainbow in order of wavelength? Think of the mnemonic ROY G. BIV (red, *orange, yellow, green, blue, indigo, violet*). Need to recall the names of North America's five Great Lakes? Just remember HOMES (*Huron, Ontario, Michigan, Erie, Superior*). In each case, we chunk information into a more familiar form by creating a word (called an *acronym*) from the first letters of the to-be-remembered items.

DEMO

Read aloud the following string of numbers: 1 7 7 6 1 8 1 2 1 8 6 1 1 9 1 7 1 9 4 1 1 9 6 3 1 9 8 6 2 0 0 2. Have students write down as many numbers as they can recall.

Then read aloud the same numbers, chunking them in the following way: 1776, 1812, 1861, 1917, 1941, 1963, 1986, 2002. Now have students write down as many of the numbers as they remember. They will demonstrate the power of chunking to remember large amounts of information.

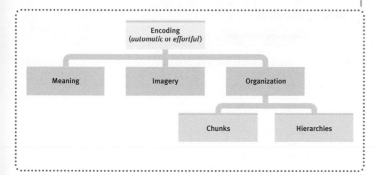

Organization benefits memory When we organize words or concepts into hierarchical groups, as illustrated here with concepts in this unit, we remember them better than when we see them presented randomly.

Hierarchies When people develop expertise in an area, they process information not only in chunks but also in *hierarchies* composed of a few broad concepts divided and subdivided into narrower concepts and facts. This unit, for example, aims not only to teach you the elementary facts of memory but also to help you organize these facts around broad principles, such as *encoding;* subprinciples, such as *automatic* and *effortful processing;* and still more specific concepts, such as *meaning, imagery,* and *organization* (**FIGURE 7A.10**).

Organizing knowledge into hierarchies helps us retrieve information efficiently. Gordon Bower and his colleagues (1969) demonstrated this by presenting words either randomly or grouped into categories. When the words were organized into groups, recall was two to three times better. Such results show the benefits of organizing what you study—of paying special attention to unit outlines, headings, preview questions, summaries, and self-test questions. If you can master a unit's concepts within their overall organization, your recall should be effective at test time. Taking class and text notes in outline format—a type of hierarchical organization—may also prove helpful.

BEFORE YOU MOVE ON . . .

➤ **ASK YOURSELF**

Can you think of three ways to employ the principles in this section to improve your own learning and retention of important ideas?

➤ **TEST YOURSELF 2**

What would be the most effective strategy to learn and retain a list of names of key historical figures for a week? For a year?

Answers to the Test Yourself questions can be found in Appendix E at the end of the book.

Storage: Retaining Information

At the heart of memory is storage. If you later recall something you experienced, you must, somehow, have stored and retrieved it. Anything stored in long-term memory lies dormant, waiting to be reconstructed by a cue. What is our memory storage capacity? Let's start with the first memory store noted in the modified three-stage processing model (Figure 7A.2)—our fleeting sensory memory.

• In the discussion of encoding imagery, I gave you six words and told you I would quiz you about them later. How many of these words can you now recall? Of these, how many are high-imagery words? How many are low-imagery? (You can check your list against the six inverted words below.) •

Typewriter, void, cigarette, inherent, fire, process.

::chunking organizing items into familiar, manageable units; often occurs automatically.

UNIT 7A

TROUBLESHOOTING

Even though our capacity for storing long-term memories is essentially limitless, memory is not a recording of events. You cannot rewind memory to retrieve memories accurately. Memory has an amazing capacity, but the actual memories that are stored are interfered with by attention issues, prior knowledge, and memory decay. Help students understand this important principle of memory.

K	Z	R
Q	B	T
S	G	N

➤ **FIGURE 7A.11**
Momentary photographic memory
When George Sperling flashed a group of letters similar to this for one-twentieth of a second, people could recall only about half of the letters. But when signaled to recall a particular row immediately after the letters had disappeared, they could do so with near-perfect accuracy.

• The Magical Number Seven has become psychology's contribution to an intriguing list of magic sevens—the seven wonders of the world, the seven seas, the seven deadly sins, the seven primary colors, the seven musical scale notes, the seven days of the week—seven magical sevens. •

Sensory Memory

4: What is sensory memory?

How much of this page could you sense and recall with less exposure than a lightning flash? Researcher George Sperling (1960) asked people to do something similar when he showed them, for only one-twentieth of a second, three rows of three letters each (**FIGURE 7A.11**). After the nine letters disappeared, people could recall only about half of them.

Was it because they had insufficient time to glimpse them? No, Sperling cleverly demonstrated that people actually *could* see and recall all the letters, but only momentarily. Rather than ask them to recall all nine letters at once, Sperling sounded a high, medium, or low tone immediately *after* flashing the nine letters. This cue directed participants to report only the letters of the top, middle, or bottom row, respectively. Now they rarely missed a letter, showing that all nine letters were momentarily available for recall.

Sperling's experiment revealed that we have a fleeting photographic memory called **iconic memory.** For a few tenths of a second, our eyes register an exact representation of a scene and we can recall any part of it in amazing detail. But if Sperling delayed the tone signal by more than half a second, the image faded and participants again recalled only about half the letters. Our visual screen clears quickly, as new images are superimposed over old ones.

We also have an impeccable, though fleeting, memory for auditory stimuli, called **echoic memory** (Cowan, 1988; Lu et al., 1992). Picture yourself in class, as your attention veers to thoughts of the weekend. If your mildly irked teacher tests your attention by asking, "What did I just say?" you can recover the teacher's last few words from your mind's echo chamber. Auditory echoes tend to linger for 3 or 4 seconds. Experiments on echoic and iconic memory have helped us understand the initial recording of sensory information in the memory system.

Working/Short-Term Memory

5: What are the duration and capacity of short-term and of long-term memory?

Among the vast amounts of information registered by our sensory memory, we illuminate some with our attentional flashlight. We also retrieve information from long-term storage for "on-screen" display. But unless our working memory meaningfully encodes or rehearses that information, it quickly disappears from our short-term store. During your finger's trip from phone book to phone, a telephone number may evaporate.

To find out how quickly a short-term memory will disappear, Lloyd Peterson and Margaret Peterson (1959) asked people to remember three-consonant groups, such as *CHJ*. To prevent rehearsal, the researchers asked them, for example, to start at 100 and count aloud backward by threes. After 3 seconds, people recalled the letters only about half the time; after 12 seconds, they seldom recalled them at all (**FIGURE 7A.12**). Without active processing, short-term memories have a limited life.

Short-term memory is limited not only in duration but also in capacity, typically storing about seven bits of information (give or take two). George Miller (1956) enshrined this recall capacity as the *Magical Number Seven, plus or minus two*. Not surprisingly, when some phone companies began requiring all callers to dial a three-digit area code in addition to a seven-digit number, many people reported trouble retaining the just-looked-up number.

TEACHING TIP

- The current world record for memorizing digits of pi is held by Chao Lu of China, who memorized 67,890 digits.
- Dominic O'Brien of Great Britain memorized 54 decks of cards, totaling 2808 cards—a world record.
- Ben Pridmore, also of Great Britain, memorized 96 historical dates in 5 minutes. He also set the world record of memorizing a single shuffled deck of cards in under 30 seconds.

➤ **FIGURE 7A.12**
Short-term memory decay Unless rehearsed, verbal information may be quickly forgotten. (From Peterson & Peterson, 1959; see also Brown, 1958.)

::**iconic memory** a momentary sensory memory of visual stimuli; a photographic or picture-image memory lasting no more than a few tenths of a second.

::**echoic memory** a momentary sensory memory of auditory stimuli; if attention is elsewhere, sounds and words can still be recalled within 3 or 4 seconds.

Our short-term recall is slightly better for random digits (as in a phone number) than for random letters, which may have similar sounds. It is slightly better for what we hear than for what we see. Both children and adults have short-term recall for roughly as many words as they can speak in 2 seconds (Cowan, 1994; Hulme & Tordoff, 1989). Compared with spoken English words, signs in American Sign Language take longer to articulate. And sure enough, short-term memory can hold fewer signs than spoken words (Wilson & Emmorey, 2006).

Without rehearsal, most of us actually retain in short-term memory only about four information chunks (for example, letters meaningfully grouped as BBC, FBI, KGB, CIA) (Cowan, 2001; Jonides et al., 2008). Suppressing rehearsal by saying *the, the, the* while hearing random digits also reduces memory to about four items. The basic principle: *At any given moment, we can consciously process only a very limited amount of information.*

Long-Term Memory

In Sir Arthur Conan Doyle's *A Study in Scarlet,* Sherlock Holmes offers a popular theory of memory capacity:

> I consider that a man's brain originally is like a little empty attic, and you have to stock it with such furniture as you choose. . . . It is a mistake to think that that little room has elastic walls and can distend to any extent. Depend upon it, there comes a time when for every addition of knowledge you forget something that you knew before.

Contrary to Holmes' belief, our capacity for storing long-term memories is essentially limitless. Our brains are *not* like attics, which once filled can store more items only if we discard old ones.

The point is vividly illustrated by those who have performed phenomenal memory feats (**TABLE 7A.1**, next page). Consider the 1990s tests of psychologist Rajan Mahadevan's memory. Given a block of 10 digits from the first 30,000 or so digits of pi, Rajan, after a few moments of mental searching for the string, would pick up the series from there, firing numbers like a machine gun (Delaney et al., 1999; Thompson et al., 1993). He could also repeat 50 random digits—backward. It is not a genetic gift, he said; anyone could learn to do it. But given the genetic influence on so many human traits, and knowing that Rajan's father memorized Shakespeare's complete works, one wonders. We are reminded that many psychological phenomena, including memory capacity, can be studied by means of different levels of analysis, including the biological.

R.J. Erwin/Photo Researchers

Clark's Nutcracker Among animals, one contender for champion memorist would be a mere birdbrain—the Clark's Nutcracker—which during winter and early spring can locate up to 6000 caches of pine seeds it had previously buried (Shettleworth, 1993).

● Pi in the sky: In 2006, Japan's Akira Haraguchi reportedly recited the first 100,000 digits of pi, topping the world record by more than 30,000 digits (Associated Press, 2006). ●

UNIT 7A

TABLE 7A.1

WORLD MEMORY CHAMPIONSHIP RECORDS

From world memory competitions, here are some current records, as of 2008:

Contest/Description	Record
Speed cards Shortest time to memorize a shuffled pack of 52 playing cards	26 seconds
One-hour cards Most cards memorized in one hour (52 points for every pack correct; 26 points if 1 mistake)	1404 points
Speed numbers Most random digits memorized in 5 minutes	396 digits
Names and faces Most first and last names memorized in 15 minutes after being shown cards with faces (1 point for every correctly spelled first or last name; ½ point for every phonetically correct but incorrectly spelled name)	181 points
Binary digits Most binary digits (101101, etc.) memorized in 30 minutes when presented in rows of 30 digits	4140 digits

Sources: www.usamemoriad.com and www.worldmemorychampionship.com

Storing Memories in the Brain

6: How does the brain store our memories?

I marveled at my aging mother-in-law, a retired pianist and organist. At age 88 her blind eyes could no longer read music. But let her sit at a keyboard and she would flawlessly play any of hundreds of hymns, including ones she had not thought of for 20 years. Where did her brain store those thousands of sequenced notes?

For a time, some surgeons and memory researchers believed that flashbacks triggered by brain stimulation during surgery indicated that our whole past, not just well-practiced music, is "in there," in complete detail, just waiting to be relived. But when Elizabeth Loftus and Geoffrey Loftus (1980) analyzed the vivid "memories" triggered by brain stimulation, they found that the seeming flashbacks appeared to have been invented, not relived. Psychologist Karl Lashley (1950) further demonstrated that memories do not reside in single, specific spots. He trained rats to find their way out of a maze, then cut out pieces of their cortexes and retested their memory. Amazingly, no matter which small brain section he removed, the rats retained at least a partial memory of how to navigate the maze. So, despite the brain's vast storage capacity, we do not store information as libraries store their books, in discrete, precise locations.

Synaptic Changes Looking for clues to the brain's storage system, contemporary memory researchers have searched for a *memory trace*. Although the brain represents a memory in distributed groups of neurons, those nerve cells must communicate through their synapses (Tsien, 2007). Thus, the quest to understand the physical basis of memory—for how information becomes incarnated in matter—has sparked study of the synaptic meeting places where neurons communicate with one another via their neurotransmitter messengers.

We know that experience does modify the brain's neural networks; given increased activity in a particular pathway, neural interconnections form or strengthen. Eric Kandel and James Schwartz (1982) observed such changes in the sending neurons of

> "Our memories are flexible and superimposable, a panoramic blackboard with an endless supply of chalk and erasers."
> Elizabeth Loftus and Katherine Ketcham, *The Myth of Repressed Memory*, 1994

> "The biology of the mind will be as scientifically important to this [new] century as the biology of the gene [was] to the twentieth century."
> Eric Kandel, acceptance remarks for the 2000 Nobel Prize

a simple animal, the California sea slug, *Aplysia.* Its mere 20,000 or so nerve cells are unusually large and accessible, enabling the researchers to observe synaptic changes during learning. Unit 6 noted how the sea slug can be classically conditioned (with electric shock) to reflexively withdraw its gills when squirted with water, much as a shell-shocked soldier jumps at the sound of a snapping twig. By observing the slug's neural connections before and after conditioning, Kandel and Schwartz pinpointed changes. When learning occurs, the slug releases more of the neurotransmitter *serotonin* at certain synapses. These synapses then become more efficient at transmitting signals.

Increased synaptic efficiency makes for more efficient neural circuits. In experiments, rapidly stimulating certain memory-circuit connections has increased their sensitivity for hours or even weeks to come. The sending neuron now needs less prompting to release its neurotransmitter, and the receiving neuron's receptor sites may increase (**FIGURE 7A.13**). This prolonged strengthening of potential neural firing, called **long-term potentiation (LTP),** provides a neural basis for learning and remembering associations (Lynch, 2002; Whitlock et al., 2006). Several lines of evidence confirm that LTP is a physical basis for memory:

- Drugs that block LTP interfere with learning (Lynch & Staubli, 1991).
- Mutant mice engineered to lack an enzyme needed for LTP can't learn their way out of a maze (Silva et al., 1992).
- Rats given a drug that enhances LTP will learn a maze with half the usual number of mistakes (Service, 1994).
- Injecting rats with a chemical that blocks the preservation of LTP erases recent learning (Pastalkova et al., 2006).

Aplysia The California sea slug, which neuroscientist Eric Kandel studied for 45 years, has increased our understanding of the neural basis of learning.

Jeff Rotman

Both photos: From N. Toni et al., *Nature*, 402, Nov. 25, 1999. Courtesy of Dominique Muller.

➤ **FIGURE 7A.13**
Doubled receptor sites
Electron microscope images show just one receptor site (gray) reaching toward a sending neuron before long-term potentiation (left) and two sites after LTP (right). A doubling of the receptor sites means that the receiving neuron has increased sensitivity for detecting the presence of the neurotransmitter molecules that may be released by the sending neuron. (From Toni et al., 1999.)

Some memory-biology explorers have helped found pharmaceutical companies that are competing to develop and test memory-boosting drugs. Their target market includes millions of people with Alzheimer's disease, millions more with *mild cognitive impairment* that often becomes Alzheimer's, and countless millions who would love to turn back the clock on age-related memory decline. From expanding memories perhaps will come bulging profits.

One approach is developing drugs that boost production of the protein CREB, which can switch genes off or on. You may recall that genes code the production of protein molecules. With repeated neural firing, a nerve cell's genes produce synapse-strengthening proteins, enabling LTP (Fields, 2005). Boosting CREB production might lead to increased production of proteins that help reshape synapses and consolidate a short-term memory into a long-term memory. Sea slugs, mice, and fruit flies with enhanced CREB production have displayed enhanced memories.

::**long-term potentiation (LTP)** an increase in a synapse's firing potential after brief, rapid stimulation. Believed to be a neural basis for learning and memory.

::**flashbulb memory** a clear memory of an emotionally significant moment or event.

::**amnesia** the loss of memory.

• Although ECT for depression disrupts memory for recent experiences, it leaves most memories intact (see Unit 13). •

▼
Severe stress sears in memories Significantly stressful events, such as the disastrous 2007 California wildfires, may be an indelible part of the memories of those who experienced them.

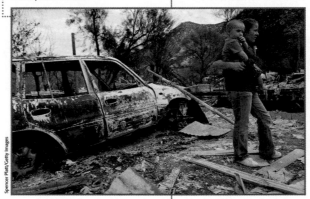

Spencer Platt/Getty Images

• If you suffered a traumatic experience, would you want to take a drug to blunt that memory? •

• Which is more important—your experiences or your memories of them? •

Another approach is developing drugs that boost *glutamate*, a neurotransmitter that enhances synaptic communication (LTP). It remains to be seen whether such drugs can boost memory without nasty side effects and without cluttering our minds with trivia best forgotten. In the meantime, one effective, safe, and free memory enhancer is already available for high schoolers everywhere: study followed by adequate sleep! (See Unit 5.)

After long-term potentiation has occurred, passing an electric current through the brain won't disrupt old memories. But the current will wipe out very recent memories. Such is the experience both of laboratory animals and of depressed people given electroconvulsive therapy (ECT). A blow to the head can do the same. Football players and boxers momentarily knocked unconscious typically have no memory of events just before the knock-out (Yarnell & Lynch, 1970). Their working memory had no time to consolidate the information into long-term memory before the lights went out.

Stress Hormones and Memory Researchers interested in the biology of the mind have also looked closely at the influence of emotions and stress hormones on memory. When we are excited or stressed, emotion-triggered stress hormones make more glucose energy available to fuel brain activity, signaling the brain that something important has happened. Moreover, the amygdala, two emotion-processing clusters in the limbic system, boosts activity and available proteins in the brain's memory-forming areas (Buchanan, 2007; Kensinger, 2007). The result? Arousal can sear certain events into the brain, while disrupting memory for neutral events around the same time (Birnbaum et al., 2004; Brewin et al., 2007).

"Stronger emotional experiences make for stronger, more reliable memories," says James McGaugh (1994, 2003). After traumatic experiences—an episode of school violence, a house fire, a rape—vivid recollections of the horrific event may intrude again and again. It is as if they were burned in. This makes adaptive sense. Memory serves to predict the future and to alert us to potential dangers.

Conversely, weaker emotion means weaker memories. People given a drug that blocks the effects of stress hormones will later have more trouble remembering the details of an upsetting story (Cahill, 1994). That connection is appreciated by those working to develop drugs that, when taken after a traumatic experience, might blunt intrusive memories. In one experiment, victims of car accidents, rapes, and other traumas received either one such drug, propranolol, or a placebo for 10 days following their horrific event. When tested three months later, half the placebo group but none of the drug-treated group showed signs of stress disorder (Pitman et al., 2002, 2005).

Emotion-triggered hormonal changes help explain why we long remember exciting or shocking events, such as our first kiss or our whereabouts when learning of a friend's death. In a 2006 Pew survey, 95 percent of American adults said they could recall exactly where they were or what they were doing when they first heard the news of the 9/11 attack. This perceived clarity of memories of surprising, significant events leads some psychologists to call them **flashbulb memories.** It's as if the brain commands, "Capture this!" The people who experienced a 1989 San Francisco earthquake did just that. A year and a half later, they had perfect recall of where they had been and what they were doing (verified by their recorded thoughts

INTERCONNECTING

Glutamate is the body's most commonly occurring excitatory neurotransmitter. Most action potentials involve glutamate at some point in the process.

TEACHING TIP

Point out to students that one more hour of sleep a night can dramatically improve performance. Most of what we think is typical forgetfulness or a careless error is likely the result of inadequate sleep. Encourage your students to try getting one more hour of sleep each night for two weeks. Have them notice whether their performance at school, work, or home improves during this time.

RESEARCH

Discuss with students the flashbulb memories people from each generation seem to share. Have students interview parents, grandparents, and older siblings or friends about these flashbulb memories of the past:

  The bombing of Pearl Harbor
  Kennedy's assassination
  The bicentennial
  Ronald Reagan's attempted assassination
  The *Challenger* explosion

Princess Diana's death
September 11th
Michael Jackson's death
President Obama's election and/or inauguration

• How vividly do they remember their whereabouts?
• What emotional reactions did they have about the event?

within a day or two of the quake). Others' memories for the circumstances under which they merely *heard* about the quake were more prone to errors (Neisser et al., 1991; Palmer et al., 1991). Flashbulb memories that people relive, rehearse, and discuss may also come to err (Talarico et al., 2003). Although our flashbulb memories are noteworthy for their vividness and the confidence with which we recall them, misinformation can seep into them (Talarico & Rubin, 2007).

There are other limits to stress-enhanced remembering. When *prolonged*—as in sustained abuse or combat—stress can act like acid, corroding neural connections and shrinking the brain area (the hippocampus) that is vital for laying down memories (more on this in Unit 8B). Moreover, when sudden stress hormones are flowing, older memories may be blocked. It is true for stressed rats trying to find their way to a hidden target (de Quervain et al., 1998). And it is true for those of us whose mind has gone blank while making a class presentation.

Storing Implicit and Explicit Memories A memory-to-be enters the cortex through the senses, then wends its way into the brain's depths. Precisely where it goes depends on the type of information, as dramatically illustrated by those who, as in the case of my father mentioned earlier, suffer from a type of **amnesia** in which they are unable to form new memories.

The most famous case, a patient known to every neuroscientist as H. M., experienced in 1953 the necessary surgical removal of a brain area involved in laying new conscious memories of facts and experiences. The brain tissue loss left his older memories intact. But converting new experiences to long-term storage was another matter. For example, over practice sessions H. M. became skilled at what is for anyone an initially difficult task: tracing the mirrored outline of a star. Yet, having no memory for doing the task he remarked to researcher Brenda Milner, after many practice trials, that "this was easier than I thought it would be" (Carey, 2008). "I've known H. M. since 1962, and he still doesn't know who I am," noted his longtime researcher Suzanne Corkin (Adelson, 2005).

Neurologist Oliver Sacks (1985, pp. 26–27) described another such patient, Jimmie, who had brain damage. Jimmie had no memories—thus, no sense of elapsed time—beyond his injury in 1945. Asked in 1975 to name the U.S. President, he replied, "FDR's dead. Truman's at the helm."

When Jimmie gave his age as 19, Sacks set a mirror before him: "Look in the mirror and tell me what you see. Is that a 19-year-old looking out from the mirror?"

Jimmie turned ashen, gripped the chair, cursed, then became frantic: "What's going on? What's happened to me? Is this a nightmare? Am I crazy? Is this a joke?" When his attention was diverted to some children playing baseball, his panic ended, the dreadful mirror forgotten.

Sacks showed Jimmie a photo from *National Geographic*. "What is this?" he asked. "It's the Moon," Jimmie replied.

"No, it's not," Sacks answered. "It's a picture of the Earth taken from the Moon."

"Doc, you're kidding? Someone would've had to get a camera up there!"

"Naturally."

"Hell! You're joking—how the hell would you do that?" Jimmie's wonder was that of a bright young man from 60 years ago reacting with amazement to his travel back to the future.

Careful testing of these unique people reveals something even stranger: Although incapable of recalling new facts or anything they have done recently, Jimmie and others with similar conditions can learn. Shown hard-to-find figures in pictures (in the *Where's Waldo?* series), they can quickly spot them again later. They can find their way to the bathroom, though without being able to tell you where it is. They can learn to read mirror-image writing or do a jigsaw puzzle, and they have even been taught complicated job skills (Schacter, 1992, 1996; Xu & Corkin, 2001). And they can be

"The most important patient in the history of brain science." So said the *New York Times* of H. M., revealed at his death in 2008 to be Henry Molaison. H. M. died at age 82 in a Connecticut nursing home.
▲

TEACHING TIP

Several documented cases exist of people who have lost the ability to form new memories. One such case involves a musician named Clive Wearing. Having lost his memory due to an illness, Wearing lived his life in the momentary present, experiencing fleeting realizations of his condition.

At this time, you may want to use **Lecture/Discussion Topic: *Explicit-Implicit Memory and Clive Wearing*** (p. 14) from Bolt's Teacher's Resource Binder.

TEACHING TIP

In 2009, researchers at the Brain Observatory sectioned the brain of Henry Molaison, psychology's most famous amnesiac. They collected 2401 sections during a live video feed shown throughout the world via the Internet. The team is working to post the slides of each section online for public access. During this process, students can read the H. M. Tech Blog and see what projects the observatory is working on: http://thebrainobservatory.ucsd.edu/hm_live.php

UNIT 7A

TROUBLESHOOTING

Students may confuse implicit and explicit memories. Help them understand the difference by using this mnemonic device:

- Explicit memories are typically easy to <u>ex</u>plain. These are memories that usually involve episodes we experience or facts we learn.

- Implicit memories are typically <u>im</u>possible to explain. These are memories that usually involve skills we learn.

TEACHING TIP

Studies have shown that patients with Korsakoff's syndrome have smaller hippocampi than normal. Korsakoff's is a dementia-like disease linked to chronic alcohol dependence. Patients' memories slowly erode, leaving them lost in the past.

classically conditioned. However, *they do all these things with no awareness of having learned them.*

These amnesia victims are in some ways like people with brain damage who cannot consciously recognize faces but whose physiological responses to familiar faces reveal an implicit (unconscious) recognition. Their behaviors challenge the idea that memory is a single, unified, conscious system. Instead, we seem to have two memory systems operating in tandem (**FIGURE 7A.14**). Whatever has destroyed *conscious* recall in these individuals with amnesia has not destroyed their *unconscious* capacity for learning. They can learn *how* to do something—called **implicit memory** (*nondeclarative memory*). Some implicit memories are of motor skills, such as bike riding or playing an instrument (*procedural memory*). Although implicitly knowing how to do something, these people may not know and be able to declare that they know—called **explicit memory** (*declarative memory*).

> **FIGURE 7A.14**

Memory subsystems We process and store our explicit and implicit memories separately. Thus, people with brain damage may lose explicit memory (becoming amnesic), yet display implicit memory for material they cannot consciously recall.

"[Brain-scanning] technologies are revolutionizing the study of the brain and mind in the same way that the telescope revolutionized the study of the heavens."

Endel Tulving (1996)

Having read a story once, they will read it faster a second time, showing implicit memory. But there will be no explicit memory, for they cannot recall having seen the story before. If repeatedly shown the word *perfume,* they will not recall having seen it. But if asked the first word that comes to mind in response to the letters *per,* they say *perfume,* readily displaying their learning. Using such tasks, even Alzheimer's patients, whose explicit memories for people and events are lost, display an ability to form new implicit memories (Lustig & Buckner, 2004).

The Hippocampus These remarkable stories provoke us to wonder: Do our explicit and implicit memory systems involve separate brain regions? Brain scans, such as PET scans of people recalling words (Squire, 1992), and autopsies of people who had amnesia, reveal that new explicit memories of names, images, and events are laid down via the **hippocampus,** a temporal lobe neural center that also forms part of the brain's limbic system (**FIGURE 7A.15**; Anderson et al., 2007).

Damage to the hippocampus therefore disrupts some types of memory. Chickadees and other birds can store food in hundreds of places and return to these unmarked caches months later, but not if their hippocampus has been removed (Kamil & Cheng, 2001; Sherry & Vaccarino, 1989). Like the cortex, the hippocampus is lateralized. (You have two of them, one just above each ear and about an inch and a half straight in.) Damage to one or the other seems to produce different results. With left-hippocampus damage, people have trouble remembering verbal information, but they have no trouble recalling visual designs and locations. With right-hippocampus damage, the problem is reversed (Schacter, 1996).

New research also pinpoints the functions of subregions of the hippocampus. One part is active as people learn to associate names with faces (Zeineh et al., 2003). Another part is active as memory whizzes engage in spatial mnemonics (Maguire et al.,

➤ FIGURE 7A.15
The hippocampus Explicit memories for facts and episodes are processed in the hippocampus and fed to other brain regions for storage.

::**implicit memory** retention independent of conscious recollection. (Also called *nondeclarative* or *procedural memory*.)

::**explicit memory** memory of facts and experiences that one can consciously know and "declare." (Also called *declarative memory*.)

::**hippocampus** a neural center that is located in the limbic system; helps process explicit memories for storage.

2003b). The rear area, which processes spatial memory, also grows bigger the longer a London cabbie has been navigating the maze of city streets (Maguire et al., 2003a).

The hippocampus is active during slow-wave sleep, as memories are processed and filed for later retrieval. The greater the hippocampus activity during sleep after a training experience, the better the next day's memory (Peigneux et al., 2004). But those memories are not permanently stored in the hippocampus. Instead, it seems to act as a loading dock where the brain registers and temporarily holds the elements of a remembered episode—its smell, feel, sound, and location. Then, like older files shifted to a basement storeroom, memories migrate for storage elsewhere. Removing the hippocampus 3 hours after rats learn the location of some tasty new food disrupts this process and prevents long-term memory formation; removal 48 hours later does not (Tse et al., 2007). Sleep supports this memory consolidation. During sleep, our hippocampus and brain cortex display simultaneous activity rhythms, as if they were having a dialogue (Euston et al., 2007; Mehta, 2007). Researchers suspect that the brain is replaying the day's experiences as it transfers them to the cortex for long-term storage.

Once stored, our mental encores of these past experiences activate various parts of the frontal and temporal lobes (Fink et al., 1996; Gabrieli et al., 1996; Markowitsch, 1995). Recalling a telephone number and holding it in working memory, for example, would activate a region of the left frontal cortex; recalling a party scene would more likely activate a region of the right hemisphere.

The Cerebellum Although your hippocampus is a temporary processing site for your *explicit* memories, you could lose it and still lay down memories for skills and conditioned associations. Joseph LeDoux (1996) recounts the story of a brain-damaged patient whose amnesia left her unable to recognize her physician as, each day, he shook her hand and introduced himself. One day, after reaching for his hand, she yanked hers back, for the physician had pricked her with a tack in his palm. The next time he returned to introduce himself she refused to shake his hand but couldn't explain why. Having been classically conditioned, she just wouldn't do it.

The *cerebellum*, the brain region extending out from the rear of the brainstem, plays a key role in forming and storing the implicit memories created by classical conditioning. With a damaged cerebellum, people cannot develop certain conditioned reflexes, such as associating a

Cerebellum

Cerebellum The cerebellum plays an important part in our forming and storing of implicit memories.

INTERCONNECTING

This section highlighting the brain areas responsible for memory can serve as a refresher for biopsychology content covered in Unit 3B. Use this content as a mini-review in biopsychology for the AP Exam.

TEACHING TIP

Once a memory reaches long-term memory, it is there for an unlimited amount of time—unless the person has a disorder that affects where new memories are stored. Dementia refers to a list of over 100 disorders.

- **Alzheimer's Disease** was first identified by the German neurologist Alois Alzheimer in 1906. He first described senile plaque, which is a buildup of protein in the brain that causes neurons to die. The causes of these plaques are unknown. Alzheimer's patients also seem to lack neurotransmitters such as acetylcholine. As people age, their risk of Alzheimer's increases. Diagnosing Alzheimer's is becoming more efficient, but a definitive diagnosis occurs only after death when an autopsy is performed.

- **Korsakoff's Syndrome** seems to be related to alcohol consumption over a number of years. The alcohol does not cause Korsakoff's directly—a lack of thiamine (vitamin B1) leads to the disorder. Those with alcohol dependence tend to have poor eating habits, which leads to the vitamin deficiency. An interesting component of Korsakoff's syndrome is confabulation, where patients will make up information that fills in the memory gaps. Patients will have detailed stories about people they've met and places they've been when these stories could not possibly be true.

Remind students what a conditioned response involves. Conditioned responses are those that are associated with a conditioned stimulus. These are the learned responses. If the disruption of the cerebellum causes a failure to learn this type of response, the cerebellum is likely involved in learning new skills.

RESEARCH

Have students research which school subjects are more likely to involve recall versus recognition tests.

- Survey teachers in other courses about the types of test formats they use most often.

- Conduct a chi-square analysis to see which subjects give recall tests versus recognition tests.

- Have students draw conclusions about why certain subjects might give certain types of tests. Also have them speculate about the impact of standardized tests on test formats.

::**recall** a measure of memory in which the person must retrieve information learned earlier, as on a fill-in-the-blank test.

::**recognition** a measure of memory in which the person need only identify items previously learned, as on a multiple-choice test.

::**relearning** a measure of memory that assesses the amount of time saved when learning material for a second time.

::**priming** the activation, often unconsciously, of particular associations in memory.

tone with an impending puff of air—and thus do not blink in anticipation of the puff (Daum & Schugens, 1996; Green & Woodruff-Pak, 2000). By methodically disrupting the function of different pathways in the cortex and cerebellum of rabbits, researchers have shown that rabbits also fail to learn a conditioned eyeblink response when the cerebellum is temporarily deactivated (Krupa et al., 1993; Steinmetz, 1999). Implicit memory formation needs the cerebellum.

Our dual explicit-implicit memory system helps explain *infantile amnesia*: The implicit reactions and skills we learned during infancy reach far into our future, yet as adults we recall nothing (explicitly) of our first three years. Children's explicit memories have a seeming half-life. In one study, events experienced and discussed with one's mother at age 3 were 60 percent remembered at age 7 but only 34 percent remembered at age 9 (Bauer et al., 2007). As adults, our conscious memory of our first three years is blank because we index so much of our explicit memory by words that nonspeaking children have not learned, but also because the hippocampus is one of the last brain structures to mature.

Our two-track memory system reinforces an important principle introduced in the earlier description of *parallel processing*: Mental feats such as vision, thinking, and memory may seem to be single abilities, but they are not. Rather, we split information into different components for separate and simultaneous processing.

BEFORE YOU MOVE ON . . .

➤ **ASK YOURSELF**

Can you name an instance in which stress has helped you remember something, and another instance in which stress has interfered with remembering something?

➤ **TEST YOURSELF 3**

Your friend tells you that her father experienced brain damage in an accident. She wonders if psychology can explain why he can still play checkers very well but has a hard time holding a sensible conversation. What can you tell her?

Answers to the Test Yourself questions can be found in Appendix E at the end of the book.

Retrieval: Getting Information Out

7: How do we get information out of memory?

To remember an event requires more than getting it in (encoding) and retaining it (storage). To most people, memory is **recall,** the ability to retrieve information not in conscious awareness. To a psychologist, memory is any sign that something learned has been retained. So **recognizing** or more quickly **relearning** information also indicates memory.

Long after you cannot recall most of the people in your high school graduating class, you may still be able to recognize their yearbook pictures from a photographic lineup and pick their names from a list of names. Harry Bahrick and his colleagues (1975) reported that people who had graduated 25 years earlier could not *recall* many of their old classmates, but they could *recognize* 90 percent of their pictures and names. If you are like most students, you, too, could likely recognize more names of the Seven Dwarfs than you could recall (Miserandino, 1991).

Our recognition memory is impressively quick and vast. "Is your friend wearing a new or old outfit?" "Old." "Is this five-second movie clip from a film you've ever seen?" "Yes." "Have you ever seen this person before—this minor variation on the same old human features (two eyes, one nose, and so on)?" "No." Before the mouth can form our answer to any of millions of such questions, the mind knows, and knows that it knows.

Our speed at relearning also reveals memory. If you once learned something and then forgot it, you probably will relearn it more quickly your second time around. When you study for a final exam or resurrect a language used in early childhood, the relearning is easier. Tests of recognition and of time spent relearning confirm the point: We remember more than we can recall.

Retrieval Cues

Imagine a spider suspended in the middle of her web, held up by the many strands extending outward from her in all directions to different points (perhaps a window sill, a tree branch, a leaf on a shrub). If you were to trace a pathway to the spider, you would first need to create a path from one of these anchor points and then follow the strand down into the web.

The process of retrieving a memory follows a similar principle, because memories are held in storage by a web of associations, each piece of information interconnected with others. When you encode into memory a target piece of information, such as the name of the person sitting next to you in class, you associate with it other bits of information about your surroundings, mood, seating position, and so on. These bits can serve as *retrieval cues*, anchor points you can use to access the target information when you want to retrieve it later. The more retrieval cues you have, the better your chances of finding a route to the suspended memory.

Do you recall the gist of the second sentence I asked you to remember, in the discussion of what we encode? If not, does the word *shark* serve as a retrieval cue? Experiments show that *shark* (likely what you visualized) more readily retrieves the image you stored than does the sentence's actual word, *fish* (Anderson et al., 1976). (The sentence was "The fish attacked the swimmer.")

Mnemonic devices—ROY G. BIV; HOMES; bun, shoe, tree—provide us with handy retrieval cues. But the best retrieval cues come from associations we form at the time we encode a memory. Tastes, smells, and sights often evoke our recall of associated episodes. To call up visual cues when trying to recall something, we may mentally place ourselves in the original context. After losing his sight, John Hull (1990, p. 174) described his difficulty recalling such details: "I knew I had been somewhere, and had done particular things with certain people, but where? I could not put the conversations . . . into a context. There was no background, no features against which to identify the place. Normally, the memories of people you have spoken to during the day are stored in frames which include the background."

The features Hull was mourning are the strands we activate to retrieve a specific memory from its web of associations. Philosopher-psychologist William James referred to this process, which we call **priming,** as the "wakening of associations." Often our associations are activated, or primed, without our awareness. As **FIGURE 7A.16** (next page) indicates, seeing or hearing the word *rabbit* primes associations with *hare,* even though we may not recall having seen or heard *rabbit.*

Priming is often "memoryless memory"—invisible memory without explicit remembering. If, walking down a hallway, you see a poster of a missing child,

Remembering things past Even if Oprah Winfrey and Brad Pitt had not become famous, their high school classmates would most likely still recognize their yearbook photos.
▲

• Multiple-choice questions test our
a. recall.
b. recognition.
c. relearning.

Fill-in-the-blank questions test our _____.

(Answers below.) •

Multiple-choice questions test recognition. Fill-in-the-blank questions test recall.

"Memory is not like a container that gradually fills up; it is more like a tree growing hooks onto which memories are hung."
Peter Russell, *The Brain Book,* 1979

"Let me refresh your memory. It was the night before Christmas and all through the house not a creature was stirring until you landed a sled, drawn by reindeer, on the plaintiff's home, causing extensive damage to the roof and chimney."

INTERCONNECTING

Priming works not only with memory: Our behaviors can be primed in social situations as well. Our biases and prejudices can be primed in certain social situations as well, as we will see in Unit 14.

TEACHING TIP

How powerful is context to memory? Have students spend some time trying to remember events from their childhood. Challenge students who can to then visit a place where they spent a lot of time during childhood (an elementary school, a childhood home, a playground, etc.). Have them spend some time trying to remember the events but now in the environmental context of those memories.

- How much easier was it to remember the events in the environmental context?
- Did other memories come flooding back while you were in the context?

TEACHING TIP

Encourage students to spend time studying for tests in your classroom, even in the desks they sit in during class. This will capitalize on the context effect when they take the test on the material at a later time.

• Ask a friend two rapid-fire questions: (a) How do you pronounce the word spelled by the letters s-h-o-p? (b) What do you do when you come to a green light? If your friend answers "stop" to the second question, you have demonstrated priming. •

::**déjà vu** that eerie sense that "I've experienced this before." Cues from the current situation may subconsciously trigger retrieval of an earlier experience.

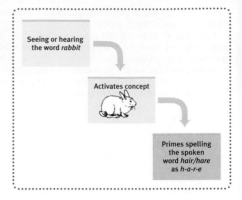

➤ **FIGURE 7A.16**
Priming—awakening associations After seeing or hearing rabbit, we are later more likely to spell the spoken word as h-a-r-e. The spreading of associations unconsciously activates related associations. This phenomenon is called priming. (Adapted from Bower, 1986.)

you will then unconsciously be primed to interpret an ambiguous adult-child interaction as a possible kidnapping (James, 1986). Although you don't consciously remember the poster, it predisposes your interpretation. Meeting someone who reminds us of someone we've previously met can awaken our associated feelings about that earlier person, which may transfer into the new context (Andersen & Saribay, 2005; Lewicki, 1985). (And as we saw in Unit 4, even subliminal stimuli can briefly prime responses to later stimuli.)

Context Effects

8: How do external contexts and internal emotions influence memory retrieval?

Putting yourself back in the context where you experienced something can prime your memory retrieval. Duncan Godden and Alan Baddeley (1975) discovered this when they had scuba divers listen to a list of words in two different settings, either 10 feet underwater or sitting on the beach. As **FIGURE 7A.17** illustrates, the divers recalled more words when they were retested in the same place.

You may have experienced similar context effects. Consider this scenario: While taking notes from this book, you realize you need to sharpen your pencil. You get up and walk downstairs, but then you cannot remember why. After returning to your desk it hits you: "I wanted to sharpen this pencil!" What happens to create this frustrating experience? In one context (desk, reading psychology), you realize your pencil needs sharpening. When you go downstairs into a different context, you have few cues to lead you back to that thought. When you are once again at your desk, you are back in the context in which you encoded the thought "This pencil is dull."

In several experiments, Carolyn Rovee-Collier (1993) found that a familiar context can activate memories even in 3-month-olds. After infants learned that kicking a crib mobile would make it move (via a connecting ribbon from the ankle), the infants kicked more when tested again in the same crib with the same bumper than when in a different context.

Sometimes, being in a context similar to one we've been in before may trigger the experience of **déjà vu** (French for "already seen"). Two-thirds of us have experienced this fleeting, eerie sense that "I've been in this exact situation before," but it happens most commonly to well-educated, imaginative young adults, especially when tired or stressed (Brown, 2003, 2004; McAneny, 1996). Some wonder, "How could I recognize

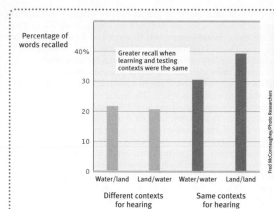

Percentage of words recalled

Greater recall when learning and testing contexts were the same

Fred McConnaughey/Photo Researchers

Water/land   Land/water   Water/water   Land/land

Different contexts for hearing and recall   Same contexts for hearing and recall

a situation I'm experiencing for the first time?" Others may think of reincarnation ("I must have experienced this in a previous life") or precognition ("I viewed this scene in my mind before experiencing it").

Posing the question differently ("Why do I feel as though I recognize this situation?"), we can see how our memory system might produce déjà vu (Alcock, 1981). The current situation may be loaded with cues that unconsciously retrieve an earlier, similar experience. (We take in and retain vast amounts of information while hardly noticing and often forgetting where it came from.) Thus, if in a similar context you see a stranger who looks and walks like one of your friends, the similarity may give rise to an eerie feeling of recognition. Having awakened a shadow of that earlier experience, you may think, "I've seen that person in this situation before."

Or perhaps, suggests James Lampinen (2002), a situation seems familiar when moderately similar to several events. Imagine you briefly encounter my dad, my brothers, my sister, my children, and a few weeks later meet me. You might think, "I've been with this guy before." Although no one in my family looks or acts just like me (lucky them), their looks and gestures are somewhat like mine and I might form a "global match" to what you had experienced.

Yet another theory, among more than 50 proposed, attributes déjà vu to our dual processing. Recall that we assemble our perceptions from information processing that occurs simultaneously on multiple tracks. If there's a slight neural hiccup and one track's signal is delayed, perhaps it feels like a repeat of the earlier one, creating an illusion that we are now reexperiencing something (Brown, 2004b).

Moods and Memories

Associated words, events, and contexts are not the only retrieval cues. Events in the past may have aroused a specific *emotion* that later primes us to recall its associated events. Cognitive psychologist Gordon Bower (1983) explained it this way: "An emotion is like a library room into which we place memory records. We best retrieve those records by returning to that emotional room." What we learn in one state—be it drunk or sober—may be more easily recalled when we are again in that state, a subtle phenomenon called *state-dependent memory*. What people learn when drunk they don't recall well in *any* state (alcohol disrupts storage). But they recall it slightly better when again drunk. Someone who hides money when drunk may forget the location until drunk again.

➤ **FIGURE 7A.17**

The effects of context on memory
Words heard underwater are best recalled underwater; words heard on land are best recalled on land. (Adapted from Godden & Baddeley, 1975.)

> "Do you ever get that strange feeling of vujà dé? Not déjà vu; vujà dé. It's the distinct sense that, somehow, something just happened that has never happened before. Nothing seems familiar. And then suddenly the feeling is gone. Vujà dé."
>
> George Carlin (1937–2008), in *Funny Times*, December 2001

©The New Yorker Collection, 2005 David Sipress from cartoonbank.com. All rights reserved

"I can't remember what we're arguing about, either. Let's keep yelling, and maybe it will come back to us."

INTERCONNECTING

Connect this discussion of déjà vu with discussions later in the unit on reconstructed memories. Both phenomena result when we do not pay close enough attention to the details around us. Our dual-processing minds still process the information, but without conscious processing, that information can become skewed.

At this time, you may want to use **Lecture/Discussion Topic: *The Déjà Vu Illusion*** (p. 16) from Bolt's Teacher's Resource Binder.

RESEARCH

Does the state-dependent effect work with caffeine and sugar, both of which students likely consume while studying? Have students research the literature on state-dependent memories to see if any studies exist on these variables. Students can also do anecdotal research, recording how much caffeine and sugar they consume while studying and whether they consume the same amount before taking the test to see if their recall is affected.

UNIT 7A

DEMO

The Pollyanna Principle states that pleasant items and events are usually processed more efficiently and accurately than less pleasant items. Margaret Matlin suggests a classroom demonstration of the principle. Students need two sheets of paper. Have them make three columns of numbers from 1 to 10 on the first sheet. In the first column, they should list 10 vegetables in any order they wish; in the second, 10 fruits; in the last column, 10 teachers. On the second sheet, they should arrange each of the lists in alphabetical order. After doing so, they should put the original lists aside and then rank each item on the second sheet with respect to the other items on the list. For example, they should give their favorite vegetable a rank of 1 and their least favorite vegetable a rank of 10. Finally, ask them to transfer each of the ranks back to the original list. Thus, each of the 10 items on each of the three lists should have a rank. Students will likely have recalled the more favored items before less favored items.

Matlin, M. (1998). *Cognition* (4th ed.). Fort Worth, TX: Harcourt.

For more information, see **Classroom Exercise: *The Pollyanna Principle*** (p. 17) from Bolt's Teacher's Resource Binder.

> "When a feeling was there, they felt as if it would never go; when it was gone, they felt as if it had never been; when it returned, they felt as if it had never gone."
> George MacDonald, *What's Mine's Mine*, 1886

• Moods influence not only our memories but also how we *interpret* other people's behavior. In a bad mood we read someone's look as a glare and feel even worse; in a good mood we encode the same look as interest and feel even better. Passions exaggerate. •

> "Amnesia seeps into the crevices of our brains, and amnesia heals."
> Joyce Carol Oates, "Words Fail, Memory Blurs, Life Wins," 2001

Our mood states provide an example of memory's state dependence. Emotions that accompany good or bad events become retrieval cues (Fiedler et al., 2001). Thus, our memories are somewhat **mood-congruent.** If you've had a bad evening—your date never showed, your Toledo Mud Hens hat disappeared, your TV went out 10 minutes before the end of a mystery—your gloomy mood may facilitate recalling other bad times. Being depressed sours memories by priming negative associations, which we then use to explain our current mood. If put in a buoyant mood—whether under hypnosis or just by the day's events (a World Cup soccer victory for the German participants in one study)—people recall the world through rose-colored glasses (DeSteno et al., 2000; Forgas et al., 1984; Schwarz et al., 1987). They judge themselves competent and effective, other people benevolent, happy events more likely.

Knowing this mood-memory connection, we should not be surprised that in some studies *currently* depressed people recall their parents as rejecting, punitive, and guilt-promoting, whereas *formerly* depressed people describe their parents much as do those who have never suffered depression (Lewinsohn & Rosenbaum, 1987; Lewis, 1992). Similarly, adolescents' ratings of parental warmth in one week give little clue to how they will rate their parents six weeks later (Bornstein et al., 1991). When teens are down, their parents seem inhuman; as their mood brightens, their parents morph from devils into angels. In a good or bad mood, we persist in attributing to reality our own changing judgments and memories.

Our mood's effect on retrieval helps explain why our moods persist. When happy, we recall happy events and therefore see the world as a happy place, which helps prolong our good mood. When depressed, we recall sad events, which darkens our interpretations of current events. For those of us with a predisposition to depression, this process can help maintain a vicious, dark cycle.

BEFORE YOU MOVE ON . . .

➤ **ASK YOURSELF**
What sort of mood have you been in lately? How has your mood colored your memories, perceptions, and expectations?

➤ **TEST YOURSELF 4**
You have just watched a movie that includes a chocolate factory. After the chocolate factory is out of mind, you nevertheless feel a strange urge for a chocolate bar. How do you explain this in terms of priming?

Answers to the Test Yourself questions can be found in Appendix E at the end of the book.

Forgetting

9: Why do we forget?

AMID ALL THE APPLAUSE FOR MEMORY—all the efforts to understand it, all the books on how to improve it—have any voices been heard in praise of forgetting? William James (1890, p. 680) was such a voice: "If we remembered everything, we should on most occasions be as ill off as if we remembered nothing." To discard the clutter of useless or out-of-date information—where we parked the car yesterday, an old locker combination, restaurant orders already cooked and served—is surely a blessing. The Russian memory whiz S, whom we met at the beginning of this unit, was haunted by his junk heap of memories. They dominated his consciousness. He had difficulty thinking abstractly—generalizing, organizing, evaluating. After reading a story, he could recite it but would struggle to summarize its gist.

INTERCONNECTING

Daniel Simons and Daniel Levin's findings on **change blindness** provide remarkable examples of how forgetting may reflect encoding failure. This occurs when people fail to detect changes in objects or scenes that occur over time, as we saw in Unit 4.

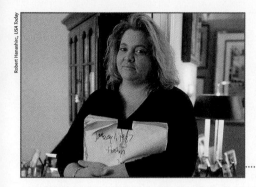

The woman who can't forget "A. J." in real life is Jill Price, who, with writer Bart Davis, told her story in a 2008 published memoir. Price remembers every day of her life since age 14 with detailed clarity, including both the joys and the unforgotten hurts.

A more recent case of a life overtaken by memory is "A. J.," whose experience has been studied and verified by a University of California at Irvine research team (Parker et al., 2006). A. J., who has identified herself as Jill Price, describes her memory as "like a running movie that never stops. It's like a split screen. I'll be talking to someone and seeing something else. . . . Whenever I see a date flash on the television (or anywhere for that matter) I automatically go back to that day and remember where I was, what I was doing, what day it fell on, and on and on and on and on. It is nonstop, uncontrollable, and totally exhausting." A good memory is helpful, but so is the ability to forget. If a memory-enhancing pill becomes available, it had better not be *too* effective.

More often, however, our memory dismays and frustrates us. Memories are quirky. My own memory can easily call up such episodes as that wonderful first kiss with the woman I love or trivial facts like the air mileage from London to Detroit. Then it abandons me when I discover I have failed to encode, store, or retrieve my new colleague's name or where I left my sunglasses. Memory researcher Daniel Schacter (1999) enumerates seven ways our memories fail us—the seven sins of memory, he calls them:

Three sins of forgetting:

- *Absent-mindedness*—inattention to details leads to encoding failure (our mind is elsewhere as we lay down the car keys).
- *Transience*—storage decay over time (after we part ways with former classmates, unused information fades).
- *Blocking*—inaccessibility of stored information (seeing an actor in an old movie, we feel the name on the tip of our tongue but experience retrieval failure—we cannot get it out).

Three sins of distortion:

- *Misattribution*—confusing the source of information (putting words in someone else's mouth or remembering a dream as an actual happening).
- *Suggestibility*—the lingering effects of misinformation (a leading question "Did Mr. Jones touch your private parts?"—later becomes a young child's false memory).
- *Bias*—belief-colored recollections (current feelings toward a friend may color our recalled initial feelings).

One sin of intrusion:

- *Persistence*—unwanted memories (being haunted by images of a sexual assault).

Let's first consider the sins of forgetting, then those of distortion and intrusion.

 Cellist Yo-Yo Ma forgot his 266-year-old, $2.5 million cello in a New York taxi. (He later recovered it.)

"Oh, is that today?"

::**mood-congruent memory** the tendency to recall experiences that are consistent with one's current good or bad mood.

DEMO

To demonstrate retrieval, obtain a copy of each student's transcript from the guidance counselor. Have students list the classes they took and the grades they received each year beginning in 9th grade. Once they feel they've exhausted their memories, give them a copy of their transcript. Comparing their remembered list with the actual one, they should count the number of errors. Which type of information was more memorable—classes or grades?

At this time, you may want to use **Student Project/Classroom Exercise:** *Retrieval Cues* (p. 15) from Bolt's Teacher's Resource Binder.

TEACHING TIP

Daniel Simons maintains a Web site with streaming video of change blindness and other visual and cognitive phenomena: http://viscog.beckman.uiuc.edu/djs_lab/demos.html.

At this time, you may want to use **Lecture/Discussion Topic:** *Change Blindness* (p. 18) from Bolt's Teacher's Resource Binder.

UNIT 7A

TEACHING TIP

How can students decrease the forgetting curve described by Ebbinghaus? If students would take several minutes to review information they learned right after a particular class, they might retain more information for a longer period of time, increasing the likelihood of long-term storage occurring.

DEMO

Demonstrate encoding failure by posing the following questions:

- What is the color of the top stripe of the American flag? The bottom stripe? How many red and how many white stripes does it have? (Red; Red; 7 red and 6 white)

- Most wooden pencils are not round. How many sides do they typically have? (Six)

- In what hand does the Statue of Liberty hold her torch? (Right)

- The White House is pictured on the back of a $20 bill. What is on the back of a $10 bill? (Treasury Building) A $5 bill? (Lincoln Memorial) A $1 bill? (The word "One")

- What four words besides "In God We Trust" appear on most U.S. coins? (United States of America)

Albrecht, K. (1980). *Brain power.* Englewood Cliffs, NJ: Prentice Hall.

> ➤ **FIGURE 7A.18**
> **Forgetting as encoding failure**
> We cannot remember what we have not encoded.

"Each of us finds that in [our] own life every moment of time is completely filled. [We are] bombarded every second by sensations, emotions, thoughts . . . nine-tenths of which [we] must simply ignore. The past [is] a roaring cataract of billions upon billions of such moments: Any one of them too complex to grasp in its entirety, and the aggregate beyond all imagination. . . . At every tick of the clock, in every inhabited part of the world, an unimaginable richness and variety of 'history' falls off the world into total oblivion."

English novelist-critic C. S. Lewis (1967)

Encoding Failure

Much of what we sense we never notice, and what we fail to encode, we will never remember (**FIGURE 7A.18**). Age can affect encoding efficiency. The brain areas that jump into action when young adults encode new information are less responsive in older adults. This slower encoding helps explain age-related memory decline (Grady et al., 1995).

But no matter how young we are, we selectively attend to few of the myriad sights and sounds continually bombarding us. Consider this example: You have probably looked at thousands of pennies in your lifetime. You can surely recall their color and size, but can you recall what the side with the head looks like? If not, let's make the memory test easier: Can you recognize the real U.S. penny in **FIGURE 7A.19**? Most people cannot (Nickerson & Adams, 1979). Of the eight critical features (Lincoln's head, date, "In God we trust," and so on), the average person spontaneously remembers only three. Likewise, few British people can draw from memory the one-pence coin (Richardson, 1993). The details of these coins are not very meaningful—nor are they essential for distinguishing them from other coins—and few of us have made the effort to encode them. As we noted earlier, we encode some information—where we had dinner yesterday—automatically; other types of information—like the concepts in this unit—require effortful processing. Without effort, many memories never form.

> ➤ **FIGURE 7A.19**
> **Test your memory** Which one of these pennies is the real thing? (From Nickerson & Adams, 1979.) Answer below.

The first penny (a) is the real penny.

Storage Decay

Even after encoding something well, we sometimes later forget it. To study the durability of stored memories, Ebbinghaus (1885) learned more lists of nonsense syllables and measured how much he retained when relearning each list, from 20 minutes to

Percentage of
list retained
when relearning

Retention
drops,

then levels off.

Time in days since learning list

Hermann Ebbinghaus (1850–1909)

30 days later. The result, confirmed by later experiments, was his famous forgetting curve: The course of forgetting is initially rapid, then levels off with time (**FIGURE 7A.20**; Wixted & Ebbesen, 1991). One such experiment was Harry Bahrick's (1984) study of the forgetting curve for Spanish vocabulary learned in school. Compared with those just completing a high school or college Spanish course, people 3 years out of school had forgotten much of what they had learned (**FIGURE 7A.21**). However, what people remembered then, they still remembered 25 and more years later. Their forgetting had leveled off.

One explanation for these forgetting curves is a gradual fading of the physical memory trace. Cognitive neuroscientists are getting closer to solving the mystery of the physical storage of memory and are increasing our understanding of how memory storage could decay. But memories fade for other reasons, including the accumulation of learning that disrupts our retrieval.

➤ FIGURE 7A.20

Ebbinghaus' forgetting curve After learning lists of nonsense syllables, Ebbinghaus studied how much he retained up to 30 days later. He found that memory for novel information fades quickly, then levels out. (Adapted from Ebbinghaus, 1885.)

➤ FIGURE 7A.21

The forgetting curve for Spanish learned in school Compared with people just completing a Spanish course, those 3 years out of the course remembered much less. Compared with the 3-year group, however, those who studied Spanish even longer ago did not forget much more. (Adapted from Bahrick, 1984.)

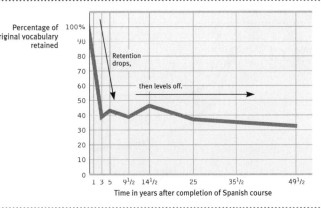

Percentage of
original vocabulary
retained

Retention
drops,

then levels off.

Time in years after completion of Spanish course

TEACHING TIP

Introduce students to the **tip-of-the-tongue phenomenon.** Have students ever had the feeling that they knew a name but were unable to retrieve it? Explain that this experience is called the tip-of-the-tongue (TOT) phenomenon, which occurs when the retrieval process does not produce a complete response but produces parts that must be constructed into a whole. Most fundamentally, it shows how forgetting may result from retrieval failure, rather than encoding or storage failure.

At this time, you may want to use **Classroom Exercise: *The Tip-of-the-Tongue Phenomenon and Capital Cities*** (p. 20) from Bolt's Teacher's Resource Binder.

DEMO

Ask volunteers to maintain a forgetting journal for at least a couple of weeks. They are to record specific instances of having forgotten something, such as forgetting names, appointments, intentions, or routes; repetitive checking (e.g., Did I turn the stove off?); and the tip-of-the-tongue phenomenon. They should write down the situation, any factors relevant to the forgetting (for example, their emotional state or focus of attention), and some judgment as to why the forgetting occurred. They should note whether the forgotten material was recalled. Students should also record unusual instances of remembering—for example, the sudden remembrance of something forgotten. Students should describe the conditions surrounding the unexpected retrieval. Reading only a few journals will reveal examples of nearly every concept presented in a memory unit. You might also ask students to suggest possible remedies for their specific forgetting problems.

Terry, W. S. (1984). A "forgetting journal" for memory courses. *Teaching of Psychology, 11*(2), 111–112.

UNIT 7A

TS

TROUBLESHOOTING

Help students remember the difference between proactive and retroactive interference by using the following mnemonics:

- The prefix *pro-* means "before," and proactive interference is defined by previous memories—those coming *before* now—blocking newer memories.

- The prefix *retro-* means "backward," and retroactive interference is defined by previous memories being blocked by newer memories—newer memories *go back* and seemingly erase older ones.

TEACHING TIP

Figure 7A.22 is an excellent way to help students remember the organization of the information in this unit. Use this figure to review the material so students can understand how memory is organized.

➤ **FIGURE 7A.22**
Retrieval failure
We store in long-term memory what's important to us or what we've rehearsed. But sometimes even stored information cannot be accessed, which leads to forgetting.

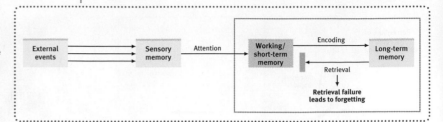

• Deaf persons fluent in sign language experience a parallel "tip of the fingers" phenomenon (Thompson et al., 2005). •

➤ **FIGURE 7A.23**
Retroactive interference More forgetting occurred when a person stayed awake and experienced other new material. (From Jenkins & Dallenbach, 1924.)

Percentage of syllables recalled

Without interfering events, recall is better.

After sleep

After remaining awake

Hours elapsed after learning syllables

Retrieval Failure

We have seen that forgotten events are like books you can't find in your high school library—some because they were never acquired (not encoded), others because they were discarded (stored memories decay).

But there is a third possibility: The book may be there but inaccessible because we don't have enough information to look it up and retrieve it. How frustrating when we know information is "in there," but we cannot get it out (**FIGURE 7A.22**), as when a name lies poised on the tip of our tongue, waiting to be retrieved. Given retrieval cues ("It begins with an *M*"), we may easily retrieve the elusive memory. Retrieval problems contribute to the occasional memory failures of older adults, who more frequently are frustrated by tip-of-the-tongue forgetting (Abrams, 2008). Often, forgetting is not memories discarded but memories unretrieved.

Interference

Learning some items may interfere with retrieving others, especially when the items are similar. If someone gives you a phone number, you may be able to recall it later. But if two more people give you their numbers, each successive number will be more difficult to recall. Likewise, if you buy a new combination lock, your memory of the old one may interfere. Such **proactive** *(forward-acting)* **interference** occurs when something you learned earlier disrupts your recall of something you experience later. As you collect more and more information, your mental attic never fills, but it certainly gets cluttered. Tuning out the clutter helps us focus. Sometimes forgetting is adaptive.

Retroactive *(backward-acting)* **interference** occurs when new information makes it harder to recall something you learned earlier. It is rather like a second stone tossed in a pond, disrupting the waves rippling out from the first. (See Close-Up: Retrieving Passwords.)

Information presented in the hour before sleep is protected from retroactive interference because the opportunity for interfering events is minimized. Researchers John Jenkins and Karl Dallenbach (1924) discovered this in a now-classic experiment. Day after day, two people each learned some nonsense syllables, then tried to recall them after up to eight hours of being awake or asleep at night. As **FIGURE 7A.23** shows,

Retrieving Passwords

There's something that you need lots of, and that your grandparents at your age didn't: passwords. To log into your e-mail, retrieve your voice mail, draw cash from a machine, access your phone card, use the copy machine, or persuade the keypad to open the building door, you need to remember your password. A typical student faces eight demands for passwords, report Alan Brown and his colleagues (2004).

With so many passwords needed, what's a person to do? As **FIGURE 7A.24** illustrates, we are plagued by proactive interference from irrelevant old information and retroactive interference from other newly learned information.

Memory researcher Henry Roediger takes a simple approach to storing all the important phone, PIN, and code numbers in his life: "I have a sheet in my shirt pocket with all the numbers I need," says Roediger (2001), adding that he can't mentally store them all, so why bother? Other strategies may help those who do not want to lose their PINs in the wash. First, *duplicate.* The average student uses four different passwords to meet those eight needs. Second, *harness retrieval cues.* Surveys in Britain and the United States reveal that about half of our passwords harness a familiar name or date. Others often involve familiar phone or identification numbers.

Third, in online banking or other situations where security is essential, *use a mix of letters and numbers,* advise Brown and his colleagues. After composing such a password, rehearse it,

> ➤ **FIGURE 7A.24**
> **Proactive and retroactive interference**

then rehearse it a day later, and continue rehearsing at increasing intervals. In such ways, long-term memories will form and be retrievable at the cash and copy machines.

---

forgetting occurred more rapidly after being awake and involved with other activities. The investigators surmised that "forgetting is not so much a matter of the decay of old impressions and associations as it is a matter of interference, inhibition, or obliteration of the old by the new" (1924, p. 612). Later experiments have confirmed the benefits of sleep and found that the hour before a night's sleep is indeed a good time to commit information to memory (Benson & Feinberg, 1977; Fowler et al., 1973; Nesca & Koulack, 1994). But not the seconds just before sleep; information presented then is seldom remembered (Wyatt & Bootzin, 1994). Nor is recorded information played during sleep, although the ears do register it (Wood et al., 1992).

Interference is an important cause of forgetting, and it may explain why ads viewed during attention-grabbing violent or sexual TV programs are so forgettable (Bushman & Bonacci, 2002). But we should not overstate the point. Sometimes old information can facilitate our learning of new information. Knowing Latin may help us to learn French—a phenomenon called *positive transfer.* It is when old and new information compete with each other that interference occurs.

Motivated Forgetting

To remember our past is often to revise it. Years ago, the huge cookie jar in our kitchen was jammed with freshly baked chocolate chip cookies. Still more were cooling across racks on the counter. Twenty-four hours later, not a crumb was left. Who had taken them? During that time, my wife, three children, and I were the only people in the house. So while memories were still fresh, I conducted a little memory test. Andy

::**proactive interference** the disruptive effect of prior learning on the recall of new information.

::**retroactive interference** the disruptive effect of new learning on the recall of old information.

Figure 7A.24 can be helpful to teach about interference. These concepts are some of the most often confused, so the more reinforcement you can give students, the better. Have students also consider how interference affects their lives, from calling people by the wrong name to forgetting their current or former phone numbers or locker combinations.

INTERCONNECTING

This discussion of repression continues in Unit 10. The concept of repression is so engrained in popular culture, but its validity as an actual phenomenon is controversial at best. Later in Unit 7A, Elizabeth Loftus's work counters the Freudian notion of repression. Have students debate whether they feel repression actually occurs or not.

At this time, you may want to use **Classroom Exercise:** *Repression or Inadequate Retrieval Cues?* (p. 21) from Bolt's Teacher's Resource Binder.

TEACHING TIP

Students are likely very confident that their memories are accurate. Help students appreciate that their memories for any experience are accurate only right after the occurrence. If students rehearse what they have experienced immediately after the event, they will have more accurate memories in the future.

acknowledged wolfing down as many as 20. Peter admitted eating 15. Laura guessed she had stuffed her then-6-year-old body with 15 cookies. My wife, Carol, recalled eating 6, and I remembered consuming 15 and taking 18 more to the office. We sheepishly accepted responsibility for 89 cookies. Still, we had not come close; there had been 160.

This would not have surprised Michael Ross and his colleagues (1981), who time and again showed that people unknowingly revise their own histories. One group of people, told the benefits of frequent tooth brushing, then recalled (more than others did) having frequently brushed their teeth in the preceding two weeks.

Even Ralph Haber, a memory researcher whose demonstration of people's remarkable recall of 2500 faces and places we encountered earlier, has found his own memory sometimes unreliable. In one instance, his recollection was distorted by his motivation to see himself as boldly leaving home despite being loved by a mother who wanted him nearby. Thus, he recalled choosing to leave the University of Michigan to go to graduate school at Stanford. In his memory, he "leapt for joy" when the Stanford admission came, and he enthusiastically prepared to head west. Twenty-five years later he visited Michigan for his mother's eightieth birthday. Reading the letters he had sent her over the years, he was startled to discover himself explaining his decision to stay at Michigan, until yielding to his mother's passionate plea that he accept the Stanford offer. Sometimes, note Carol Tavris and Elliot Aronson (2007) in recording this story, memory is an "unreliable, self-serving historian" (p. 6, 79).

Why do our memories fail us? Why did my family and I not remember the number of cookies each of us had eaten? As **FIGURE 7A.25** reminds us, we automatically encode sensory information in amazing detail. So was it an encoding problem? Or a storage problem—might our memories of cookies, like Ebbinghaus' memory of nonsense syllables, have vanished almost as fast as the cookies themselves? Or was the information still intact but irretrievable because it would be embarrassing to remember?[1]

Sigmund Freud might have argued that our memory systems self-censored this information. He proposed that we **repress** painful memories to protect our self-concept and to minimize anxiety. But the submerged memory will linger, he believed, to be retrieved by some later cue or during therapy. Here is a sample case. A woman had an intense, unexplained fear of running water. One day her aunt whispered, "I have never told." Like relighting a blown-out candle, these words cued the woman's memory of an incident when, as a disobedient young child, she had wandered away from a family picnic and become trapped under a waterfall—until being rescued by her aunt, who promised not to tell her parents (Kihlstrom, 1990).

Repression was central to Freud's psychology (see Unit 10) and became part of psychology's lore. Most everyone—including 9 in 10 university students—believes that "memories for painful experiences are sometimes pushed into unconsciousness" (Brown et al., 1996). Therapists often assume it. Yet increasing numbers of memory researchers think repression rarely, if ever, occurs. People's efforts to intentionally forget neutral material often succeed, but not when the to-be-forgotten material is emotional (Payne & Corrigan, 2007). Thus, we may have intrusive memories of the very traumatic experiences we would most like to forget.

> ➤ **FIGURE 7A.25**
> **When do we forget?** Forgetting can occur at any memory stage. As we process information, we filter, alter, or lose much of it.

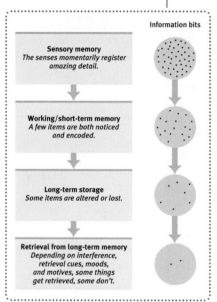

[1] One of my cookie-scarfing sons, on reading this in his father's textbook years later, confessed he had fibbed "a little."

➤ ASK YOURSELF

Most people, especially as they grow older, wish for a better memory. Is that true of you? Or do you more often wish you could better discard old memories?

➤ TEST YOURSELF 5

Can you offer an example of proactive interference?

Answers to the Test Yourself questions can be found in Appendix E at the end of the book.

Memory Construction

10: How do misinformation, imagination, and source amnesia influence our memory construction? How real-seeming are false memories?

PICTURE YOURSELF having this experience:

You go to a fancy restaurant for dinner. You are seated at a table with a white tablecloth. You study the menu. You tell the server you want prime rib, medium rare, a baked potato with sour cream, and a salad with blue cheese dressing. You also order some iced tea from the beverage list. A few minutes later the server returns with your salad. Later the rest of the meal arrives. You enjoy it all, except the prime rib is a bit overdone.

Were I immediately to quiz you on this paragraph (adapted from Hyde, 1983), you could surely retrieve considerable detail. For example, without looking back, answer the following questions:

1. What kind of salad dressing did you order?
2. Was the tablecloth red checked?
3. What did you order to drink?
4. Did the server give you a menu?

You were probably able to recall exactly what you ordered, and maybe even the tablecloth color. But did the server give you a menu? Not in the paragraph given. Nevertheless, many answer *yes*. We often construct our memories as we encode them, and we may also alter our memories as we withdraw them from our memory bank. Like scientists who infer a dinosaur's appearance from its remains, we infer our past from stored information plus what we later imagined, expected, saw, and heard. We don't just retrieve memories, we reweave them, notes Daniel Gilbert (2006, p. 79): "Information acquired after an event alters memory of the event."

Misinformation and Imagination Effects

In more than 200 experiments, involving more than 20,000 people, Elizabeth Loftus has shown how eyewitnesses similarly reconstruct their memories when later questioned. In one classic experiment, Loftus and John Palmer showed a film of a traffic accident and then quizzed people about what they had seen (Loftus & Palmer, 1974). Those asked, "How fast were the cars going when they *smashed* into each other?" gave higher speed estimates than those asked, "How fast were the cars going when they *hit* each other?" A week later, the researchers asked both groups if they recalled seeing any broken glass. Those who had heard *smashed* were more than twice as likely to report seeing glass fragments (**FIGURE 7A.26**, next page). In fact, the film showed no broken glass.

::**repression** in psychoanalytic theory, the basic defense mechanism that banishes from consciousness anxiety-arousing thoughts, feelings, and memories.

> "Memory isn't like reading a book; it's more like writing a book from fragmentary notes."
> Psychologist John F. Kihlstrom (1994)

Gary Wells' Web site at www.psychology.iastate.edu/faculty/gwells/homepage.htm provides numerous resources for extending the text discussion of eyewitness recall. Included are video clips for students to test their own eyewitness accuracy, current research reports, and the recently published U.S. Department of Justice national guidelines on eyewitness evidence.

Tell students about Frederick Bartlett's constructive memory processes:

- **Leveling:** Material in the story gets simplified, because the teller makes judgments about which details are important.

- **Sharpening:** The teller also makes judgments about what information is important, and highlights or overemphasizes details.

- **Assimilation:** The teller also changes details for a better fit with his or her own background or knowledge.

How much influence does the media have on our beliefs about eyewitness testimony? Have students watch an episode or two of any of the crime dramas on network television. Students can evaluate whether these television shows accurately portray what the research suggests about eyewitness testimony and memory construction.

- Did the police in the show ask leading questions of witnesses?

- Did the attorneys rely too heavily on the word of witnesses?

- Was a line-up used? If so, did it follow what research suggests is proper procedure? (See Gary Wells' Web site cited above for details of this research.)

UNIT 7A

RESEARCH

Have students do a literature review about the misinformation effect by focusing on the following questions, which Elizabeth Loftus points out are the main issues that have occupied researchers:

- When are people susceptible to misinformation? People are prone to misinformation when time allows the original memory to fade. Forewarning people that a narrative may be misleading enables them to resist its influence.

- Who is susceptible to misinformation? Young children are particularly susceptible to the misinformation effect.

- What happens to the original memory? Some have argued that the original memory traces are changed by post-event information.

- Do people genuinely believe the misinformation? Misleading information can turn a lie into memory's truth. It can cause people to believe that they saw things that never really existed or that they saw things differently from the way things actually were.

> ▶ **FIGURE 7A.26**
> **Memory construction** When people who had seen the film of a car accident were later asked a leading question, they recalled a more serious accident than they had witnessed. (From Loftus, 1979.)

Leading question: *"About how fast were the cars going when they smashed into each other?"*

Depiction of actual accident

Memory construction

> "Memory is insubstantial. Things keep replacing it. Your batch of snapshots will both fix and ruin your memory. . . . You can't remember anything from your trip except the wretched collection of snapshots."
>
> Annie Dillard, "To Fashion a Text," 1988

In many follow-up experiments around the world, people have witnessed an event, received or not received misleading information about it, and then taken a memory test. The repeated result is a **misinformation effect:** After exposure to subtle misinformation, many people misremember. They have misrecalled a yield sign as a stop sign, hammers as screwdrivers, Coke cans as peanut cans, *Vogue* magazine as *Mademoiselle*, "Dr. Henderson" as "Dr. Davidson," breakfast cereal as eggs, and a clean-shaven man as a man with a mustache (Loftus et al., 1992). One experiment showed people digitally altered photos depicting themselves (a pasted image from a childhood family album) taking a hot air balloon ride. After seeing this three times over two weeks, half the participants "remembered" the nonexistent experience, often in rich detail (Wade et al., 2002). The human mind comes with built-in Photoshopping software.

So unwitting is the misinformation effect that we may later find it nearly impossible to discriminate between our memories of real and suggested events (Schooler et al., 1986). Perhaps you can recall recounting an experience and filling in memory gaps with plausible guesses and assumptions. We all do it, and after more retellings, we may recall the guessed details—now absorbed into our memories—as if we had actually observed them (Roediger et al., 1993). Others' vivid retelling of an event may also implant false memories.

Even repeatedly *imagining* nonexistent actions and events can create false memories. Students who repeatedly imagined simple acts such as breaking a toothpick or picking up a stapler later experienced this *imagination inflation;* they were more likely than others to think they had actually done such things during the experiment's first phase (Goff & Roediger, 1998; Seamon et al., 2006). Similarly, one in four American and British university students asked to imagine certain childhood events, such as breaking a window with their hand or having a skin sample removed from a finger, later recalled the imagined event as something that had really happened (Garry et al., 1996; Mazzoni & Memon, 2003). Imagination inflation occurs partly because visualizing something and actually perceiving it activate similar brain areas (Gonsalves et al., 2004).

Imagined events later seem more familiar, and familiar things seem more real. Thus, the more vividly we can imagine things, the more likely we are to inflate them into memories (Loftus, 2001; Porter et al., 2000). People who believe aliens transported them to spaceships for medical exams tend to have powerful imaginations and, in memory tests, to be more susceptible to false memories (Clancy, 2005). Those who believe they have recovered memories of childhood sexual abuse likewise tend to have vivid imaginations and to score high on false memory tests (Clancy et al., 2000; McNally, 2003).

To see how far the mind's search for a fact will go in creating a fiction, Richard Wiseman and his University of Hertfordshire colleagues (1999) staged eight séances, each attended by 25 curious people. During each session, the medium—actually a professional actor and magician—urged everyone to concentrate on the moving table. Although it never moved, he suggested it had: "That's good. Lift the table up. That's

---

⊙ **TEACHING TIP**

At this time, you may want to use **Lecture/Discussion Topics:** *Misremembering the Causes of Behavior* (p. 24) or *The Misinformation Effect* (p. 24) from Bolt's Teacher's Resource Binder.

good. Keep concentrating. Keep the table in the air." When questioned two weeks later, 1 in 3 participants recalled actually having seen the table levitate.

Psychologists are not immune to memory construction. Famed child psychologist Jean Piaget was startled as an adult to learn that a vivid, detailed memory from his childhood—a nursemaid's thwarting his kidnapping—was utterly false. Piaget apparently constructed the memory from the many retellings of the story he had heard (which his nursemaid, after undergoing a religious conversion, later confessed had never happened).

> "It isn't so astonishing, the number of things I can remember, as the number of things I can remember that aren't so."
>
> Mark Twain (1835–1910)

DOONESBURY

By Garry Trudeau DOONESBURY © 1994 G. B. Trudeau. Reprinted with permission of UNIVERSAL PRESS SYNDICATE.

Source Amnesia

Piaget remembered, but attributed his memory to the wrong sources (to his own experience rather than to his nursemaid's stories). Among the frailest parts of a memory is its source. Thus, we may recognize someone but have no idea where we have seen the person. We may dream an event and later be unsure whether it really happened. We may hear something and later recall seeing it (Henkel et al., 2000). In all these cases of **source amnesia** (also called *source misattribution*), we retain the memory of the event, but not of the context in which we acquired it.

Debra Poole and Stephen Lindsay (1995, 2001, 2002) demonstrated source amnesia among preschoolers. They had the children interact with "Mr. Science," who engaged them in activities such as blowing up a balloon with baking soda and vinegar. Three months later, on three successive days, their parents read them a story describing some things the children had experienced with Mr. Science and some they had not. When a new interviewer asked what Mr. Science had done with them—"Did Mr. Science have a machine with ropes to pull?"—4 in 10 children spontaneously recalled him doing things that had happened only in the story.

Discerning True and False Memories

Because memory is reconstruction as well as reproduction, we can't be sure whether a memory is real by how real it feels. Much as perceptual illusions may seem like real perceptions, unreal memories *feel* like real memories.

* Authors and songwriters sometimes suffer source amnesia. They think an idea came from their own creative imagination, when in fact they are unintentionally plagiarizing something they earlier read or heard. *

::**misinformation effect** incorporating misleading information into one's memory of an event.

::**source amnesia** attributing to the wrong source an event we have experienced, heard about, read about, or imagined. (Also called *source misattribution*.) Source amnesia, along with the misinformation effect, is at the heart of many false memories.

TEACHING TIP

Jean Piaget is a famous victim of a false memory. He tells the story of being kidnapped as a small child, a story he believed to be true until he was 15 years old:

> I was sitting in my pram, which my nurse was pushing in the Champs Élysées, when a man tried to kidnap me. I was held in by the strap fastened round me while my nurse bravely tried to stand between me and the thief. She received various scratches, and I can still see vaguely those on her face. Then a crowd gathered, a policeman with a short cloak and a white baton came up, and the man took to his heels. I can still see the whole scene, and can even place it near the tube station. When I was about fifteen, my parents received a letter from my former nurse saying she had been converted to the Salvation Army. She wanted to confess her past faults, and in particular to return the watch she had been given as a reward on this occasion. She had made up the whole story, faking the scratches. I, therefore, must have heard, as a child, the account of this story, which my parents believed, and projected into the past in the form of a visual memory.

Piaget, J. (1962). *Play, dreams, and imitation in childhood.* New York: W. W. Norton.

TEACHING TIP

Help students see how source amnesia contributes to "the rumor mill." Often, students will hear a story about another student, and in the retelling of the story, misattribute the source. Have students discuss how the misattribution of sources can have negative effects on the sharing of stories among people.

DEMO

Give students a list of words related to a certain topic, such as sleep or movies or school. However, do NOT include the word *sleep* or *movies* or *school* in the list of words you give. When asked to recall the list of words, many students will swear that you called out the topic word when you actually did not. This demonstrates how even confident memories can be wrong.

TROUBLESHOOTING

One main reason why memories are so fallible is that our imaginations and expectations are very powerful. When we experience an event, we are also processing what the event means to us and how well the event fits into our schemas and expectations. This dual processing causes us to insert imagined circumstances and expectations into the situation. While this helps us understand our experiences better, it does not help us remember situations accurately.

➤ FIGURE 7A.27

Our assumptions alter our perceptual memories Researchers showed people faces with computer-blended expressions, such as the angry/happy face in (a), then asked them to explain why the person was either angry or happy. Those asked to explain an "angry" expression later (when sliding a bar on a morphing movie to identify the earlier-seen face) remembered an angrier face, such as the one shown in (b).

(a)   (b)

Indeed, note today's researchers, memories are akin to perceptions—perceptions of the past (Koriat et al., 2000). And as Jamin Halberstadt and Paul Niedenthal (2001) showed, people's initial interpretations influence their perceptual memories. They invited New Zealand university students to view morphed faces that expressed a mix of emotions, such as anger and happiness (**FIGURE 7A.27a**), and to imagine and explain "why this person is feeling angry [or happy]." A half-hour later, the researchers asked the students to view a computer video showing a morphed transition from the angry to happy face, and to slide a bar to change the face's expression until it matched the expression they had seen earlier. Students who had explained anger ("This woman is angry because her best friend has cheated on her with her boyfriend") recalled the face as angrier (Figure 7A.27b) than did those who had explained happiness ("This woman is very happy that everyone remembered her birthday").

So could we judge a memory's reality by its persistence? Again, the answer is *no*. Memory researchers Charles Brainerd and Valerie Reyna (Brainerd et al., 1995, 1998, 2002) note that memories we derive from experience have more detail than memories we derive from imagination. Memories of imagined experiences are more restricted to the *gist* of the supposed event—the associated meanings and feelings. Because gist memories are durable, children's false memories sometimes outlast their true memories, especially as children mature and become better able to process the gist (Brainerd & Poole, 1997). Thus, therapists or investigators who ask for the gist rather than the details run a greater risk of eliciting false memories.

False memories created by suggested misinformation and misattributed sources may *feel* as real as true memories and may be very persistent. Imagine that I were to read aloud a list of words such as *candy, sugar, honey,* and *taste.* Later, I ask you to recognize the presented words from a larger list. If you are at all like the people tested by Henry Roediger and Kathleen McDermott (1995), you would err three out of four times—by falsely remembering a nonpresented similar word, such as *sweet.* We more easily remember the gist than the words themselves.

In experiments on eyewitness testimony, researchers have repeatedly found that the most confident and consistent eyewitnesses are the most persuasive; however, they often are not the most accurate. Eyewitnesses, whether right or wrong, express roughly similar self-assurance (Bothwell et al., 1987; Cutler & Penrod, 1989; Wells & Murray, 1984).

Memory construction helps explain why 79 percent of 200 convicts exonerated by later DNA testing had been misjudged based on faulty eyewitness identification (Garrett, 2008). It explains why "hypnotically refreshed" memories of crimes so easily incorporate errors, some of which originate with the hypnotist's leading questions ("Did you hear loud noises?"). It explains why dating partners who fall in love *over*estimate their first impressions of one another ("It was love at first sight"), while those who break up *under*estimate their earlier liking ("We never really clicked")

TEACHING TIP

At this time, you may want to use **Classroom Exercises:** *Eyewitness Testimony— What Have We Learned?* (p. 26) or *Eyewitness Recall* (p. 27) from Bolt's Teacher's Resource Binder.

(McFarland & Ross, 1987). And it explains why people asked how they felt 10 years ago about marijuana or gender issues recall attitudes closer to their current views than to the views they had actually reported a decade earlier (Markus, 1986). How people feel today seems to be how they have always felt. What people know today seems to be what they have always known (Mazzoni & Vannucci, 2007; and recall from Unit 2 our tendency to *hindsight bias*).

One research team interviewed 73 ninth-grade boys and then reinterviewed them 35 years later. When asked to recall how they had reported their attitudes, activities, and experiences, most men recalled statements that matched their actual prior responses at a rate no better than chance. Only 1 in 3 now remembered receiving physical punishment, though as ninth-graders 82 percent had said they had (Offer et al., 2000). As George Vaillant (1977, p. 197) noted after following adult lives through time, "It is all too common for caterpillars to become butterflies and then to maintain that in their youth they had been little butterflies. Maturation makes liars of us all."

Australian psychologist Donald Thompson found his own work on memory distortion ironically haunting him when authorities brought him in for questioning about a rape. Although he was a near-perfect match to the victim's memory of the rapist, he had an airtight alibi. Just before the rape occurred, Thompson was being interviewed on live television. He could not possibly have made it to the crime scene. Then it came to light that the victim had been watching the interview—ironically about face recognition—and had experienced source amnesia, confusing her memories of Thompson with those of the rapist (Schacter, 1996).

Recognizing that the misinformation effect can occur as police and attorneys ask questions framed by their own understandings of an event, Ronald Fisher, Edward Geiselman, and their colleagues (1987, 1992) have trained police interviewers to ask less suggestive, more effective questions. To activate retrieval cues, the detective first asks witnesses to visualize the scene—the weather, time of day, lighting, sounds, smells, positions of objects, and their mood. Then the witness tells in detail, and without interruption, every point recalled, no matter how trivial. Only then does the detective ask evocative follow-up questions: "Was there anything unusual about the person's appearance or clothing?" When this *cognitive interview technique* is used, accurate recall increases (Wells et al., 2006).

Children's Eyewitness Recall

If memories can be sincere, yet sincerely wrong, might children's recollections of sexual abuse be prone to error? Stephen Ceci (1993) thinks "it would be truly awful to ever lose sight of the enormity of child abuse." Yet, as we have seen, interviewers who ask leading questions can plant false memories. Ceci and Maggie Bruck's (1993, 1995) studies of children's memories have sensitized them to children's suggestibility. For example, they asked 3-year-olds to show on anatomically correct dolls where a pediatrician had touched them. Fifty-five percent of the children who had not received genital examinations pointed to either genital or anal areas. And when the researchers used suggestive interviewing techniques, they found that most preschoolers and many older children could be induced to report false events, such as seeing a thief steal food in their day-care center (Bruck & Ceci, 1999, 2004). In another experiment, preschoolers merely *overheard* an erroneous remark that a magician's missing rabbit had gotten loose in their classroom. Later, when the children were suggestively questioned, 78 percent of them recalled actually seeing the rabbit (Principe et al., 2006).

In one study, Ceci and Bruck had a child choose a card from a deck of possible happenings and an adult then read from the card. For example, "Think real hard, and tell me if this ever happened to you. Can you remember going to the hospital with a

 • In experiments with adults, suggestive questions ("In fresh water, do snakes swim upside down for about half the time?") are often misremembered as statements (Pandelaere & Dewitte, 2006). •

 RESEARCH

Movies and television sensationalize recovered memories. The most famous example of a movie depicting recovered memories is *Sybil*, in which a young woman remembers childhood abuse by her mother and manifests multiple personalities (dissociative identity disorder) to cope with the memories. Have students examine the depiction of recovered memories in movies and television shows to see if the depictions are in line with current psychological scholarship.

 TEACHING TIP

Elizabeth Loftus's students conducted a study in which two female students left a bag on a bench. While they were a short distance away, a male student walked over to the bag, pretended to pull out an object and stuff it under his coat. He then quickly scurried away. The women immediately returned and one, noting the bag had been tampered with, cried out, "Oh, no, my tape recorder is missing." She described how her boss had loaned it to her for a special reason, that it was very expensive, etc. The two women then talked to the people in the area. The student whose "tape recorder" had been stolen asked eyewitnesses for their telephone numbers "in case we need it for insurance purposes." Most gladly provided them. A week later an "insurance agent" called the eyewitnesses. All were asked, "Did you see the tape recorder?" Although there had been no tape recorder, over half the eyewitnesses remembered seeing it and nearly all could describe it in reasonably good detail. The descriptions were very diverse: some saw it as gray, others as black, some claimed it was in a case, others said it was not, some even said it had an antenna. In short, their descriptions indicated a vivid "memory" for a nonexistent tape recorder.

Loftus, E. (1979). *Eyewitness testimony.* Cambridge, MA: Harvard University Press.

UNIT 7A

Many states enacted legislation that enabled people previously barred from suing by statutes of limitations to sue for injury suffered as a result of childhood abuse at any time within three years of the time they remembered the abuse. Have students research the laws in your state regarding the use of recovered memory testimony in criminal cases.

- Are these types of memories admissible in court?
- Have there been any cases in your state where a person was put on trial based on a recovered memory? If so, what was the outcome of the case?
- Are recovered memories treated differently in court than eyewitness testimony?

TEACHING TIP

Loftus and her colleagues have also done work on "impossible memories" to show that reconstructed memories are not just amalgamations of actual experiences. Loftus and her colleagues had people imagine going to Disney World and seeing Warner Brothers cartoon characters (Bugs Bunny, Daffy Duck, etc.) —an event that would be impossible. When later asked to recall a childhood visit to Disney World, people recalled seeing Warner Brothers cartoon characters, even though this was not possible, further demonstrating her ideas about reconstructed memories.

> "[The] research leads me to worry about the possibility of false allegations. It is not a tribute to one's scientific integrity to walk down the middle of the road if the data are more to one side."
>
> Stephen Ceci (1993)

• Like children (whose frontal lobes have not fully matured), older adults—especially those whose frontal lobe functioning has declined—are more susceptible than younger adults to false memories. This makes older adults more vulnerable to scams, as when a repairperson overcharges by falsely claiming, "I told you it would cost x, and you agreed to pay" (Jacoby et al., 2005; Jacoby & Rhodes, 2006; Roediger & Geraci, 2007; Roediger & McDaniel, 2007). •

mousetrap on your finger?" After 10 weekly interviews, with the same adult repeatedly asking children to think about several real and fictitious events, a new adult asked the same question. The stunning result: 58 percent of preschoolers produced false (often vivid) stories regarding one or more events they had never experienced, as this little boy did (Ceci et al., 1994):

> My brother Colin was trying to get Blowtorch [an action figure] from me, and I wouldn't let him take it from me, so he pushed me into the wood pile where the mousetrap was. And then my finger got caught in it. And then we went to the hospital, and my mommy, daddy, and Colin drove me there, to the hospital in our van, because it was far away. And the doctor put a bandage on this finger.

Given such detailed stories, professional psychologists who specialize in interviewing children were often fooled. They could not reliably separate real memories from false ones. Nor could the children themselves. The above child, reminded that his parents had told him several times that the mousetrap incident never happened—that he had imagined it—protested, "But it really did happen. I remember it!"

Does this mean that children can never be accurate eyewitnesses? No. If questioned about their experiences in neutral words they understand, children often accurately recall what happened and who did it (Goodman, 2006; Howe, 1997; Pipe, 1996). When interviewers use less suggestive, more effective techniques, even 4- to 5-year-old children produce more accurate recall (Holliday & Albon, 2004; Pipe et al., 2004). Children are especially accurate when they have not talked with involved adults prior to the interview and when their disclosure is made in a first interview with a neutral person who asks nonleading questions.

Repressed or Constructed Memories of Abuse?

11: What is the controversy related to claims of repressed and recovered memories?

There are two tragedies related to adult recollections of child abuse. One is trauma survivors being disbelieved when telling their secret. The other is innocent people being falsely accused. What, then, shall we say about clinicians who have guided people in "recovering" memories of childhood abuse? Are they triggering false memories that damage innocent adults? Or are they uncovering the truth?

In one American survey, the average therapist estimated that 11 percent of the population—some 34 million people—have repressed memories of childhood sexual abuse (Kamena, 1998). In another survey, of British and American doctoral-level therapists, 7 in 10 said they had used techniques such as hypnosis or drugs to help clients recover suspected repressed memories of childhood sexual abuse (Poole et al., 1995).

Some have reasoned with patients that "people who've been abused often have your symptoms, so you probably were abused. Let's see if, aided by hypnosis or drugs, or helped to dig back and visualize your trauma, you can recover it." As we might expect from the research on source amnesia and the misinformation effect, patients exposed to such techniques may form an image of a threatening person. With further visualization, the image grows more vivid, leaving the patient stunned, angry, and ready to confront or sue the equally stunned and devastated parent, relative, or clergy member, who then vigorously denies the accusation. After 32 therapy sessions, one woman recalled her father abusing her when she was 15 months old.

Without questioning the professionalism of most therapists, critics have charged that clinicians who use "memory work" techniques such as "guided imagery," hypnosis, and dream analysis to recover memories "are nothing more than merchants of mental chaos, and, in fact, constitute a blight on the entire field of psychotherapy"

TEACHING TIP

At this time, you may want to use **Student Project:** *Constructive Memory* (p. 23) from Bolt's Teacher's Resource Binder.

(Loftus et al., 1995). "Thousands of families were cruelly ripped apart," with "previously loving adult daughters" suddenly accusing fathers, noted Martin Gardner (2006) in his commentary on North America's "greatest mental health scandal." Irate clinicians countered that those who dispute recovered memories of abuse add to abused people's trauma and play into the hands of child molesters.

In an effort to find a sensible common ground that might resolve this ideological battle—psychology's "memory war"—study panels have been convened and public statements made by the American Medical, American Psychological, and American Psychiatric Associations; the Australian Psychological Society; the British Psychological Society; and the Canadian Psychiatric Association. Those committed to protecting abused children and those committed to protecting wrongly accused adults agree on the following:

- *Sexual abuse happens.* And it happens more often than we once supposed. There is no characteristic "survivor syndrome" (Kendall-Tackett et al., 1993). However, sexual abuse is a traumatic betrayal that can leave its victims predisposed to problems ranging from sexual dysfunction to depression (Freyd et al., 2007).

- *Injustice happens.* Some innocent people have been falsely convicted. And some guilty people have evaded responsibility by casting doubt on their truth-telling accusers.

- *Forgetting happens.* Many of those actually abused were either very young when abused or may not have understood the meaning of their experience—circumstances under which forgetting is common. Forgetting isolated past events, both negative and positive, is an ordinary part of everyday life.

- *Recovered memories are commonplace.* Cued by a remark or an experience, we recover memories of long-forgotten events, both pleasant and unpleasant. What is debated is whether the unconscious mind sometimes *forcibly represses* painful experiences and, if so, whether these can be retrieved by certain therapist-aided techniques. (Memories that surface naturally are more likely to be corroborated than are therapist-assisted recollections Geraerts et al., 2007.)

- *Memories of things happening before age 3 are unreliable.* As our earlier discussion of infantile amnesia pointed out, people do not reliably recall happenings of any sort from their first three years. Most psychologists—including most clinical and counseling psychologists—therefore doubt "recovered" memories of abuse during infancy (Gore-Felton et al., 2000; Knapp & VandeCreek, 2000). The older a child's age when suffering sexual abuse, and the more severe it was, the more likely it is to be remembered (Goodman et al., 2003).

- *Memories "recovered" under hypnosis or the influence of drugs are especially unreliable.* "Age-regressed" hypnotized subjects incorporate suggestions into their memories, even memories of "past lives."

- *Memories, whether real or false, can be emotionally upsetting.* Both the accuser and the accused may suffer when what was born of mere suggestion becomes, like an actual trauma, a stinging memory that drives bodily stress (McNally, 2003, 2007). People knocked unconscious in unremembered accidents have later developed stress disorders after being haunted by memories they constructed from photos, news reports, and friends' accounts (Bryant, 2001).

To more closely approximate therapist-aided recall, Elizabeth Loftus and her colleagues (1996) have experimentally implanted false memories of childhood traumas. In one study, she had a trusted family member recall for a teenager three real childhood experiences and a false one—a vivid account of the child being lost

> "When memories are 'recovered' after long periods of amnesia, particularly when extraordinary means were used to secure the recovery of memory, there is a high probability that the memories are false."
>
> Royal College of Psychiatrists Working Group on Reported Recovered Memories of Child Sexual Abuse [Brandon et al., 1998]

TODAY'S SPECIAL GUEST

BRUNDAGE MORNALD, OF BATTLE CREEK, MONTANA

UNDER HYPNOSIS, MR. MORNALD RECOVERED LONG-BURIED MEMORIES OF A PERFECTLY NORMAL, HAPPY CHILDHOOD.

Have students research recent efforts to exonerate individuals accused of crimes through eyewitness testimony. The most famous of these efforts is The Innocence Project, which, as of January 2010, had exonerated 249 prisoners. Check out their work at www.innocenceproject.org/.

▼
Elizabeth Loftus "The research findings for which I am being honored now generated a level of hostility and opposition I could never have foreseen. People wrote threatening letters, warning me that my reputation and even my safety were in jeopardy if I continued along these lines. At some universities, armed guards were provided to accompany me during speeches."
Elizabeth Loftus, on receiving the Association for Psychological Science's William James Fellow Award, 2001

for an extended time in a shopping mall at age 5 until being rescued by an older person. Two days later, one participant, Chris, said, "That day I was so scared that I would never see my family again." Two days after that, he began to visualize the flannel shirt, bald head, and glasses of the old man who supposedly had found him. Told the story was made up, Chris was incredulous: "I thought I remembered being lost . . . and looking around for the guys. I do remember that, and then crying, and Mom coming up and saying, 'Where were you? Don't you . . . ever do that again.'" In other experiments, a third of participants have become wrongly convinced that they almost drowned as a child, and about half were led to falsely recall an awful experience, such as a vicious animal attack (Heaps & Nash, 2001; Porter et al., 1999).

Such is the memory construction process by which people can recall being abducted by aliens, victimized by a satanic cult, molested in a crib, or living a past life. Thousands of reasonable, normally functioning human beings, notes Loftus, "speak in terror-stricken voices about their experience aboard flying saucers. They *remember*, clearly and vividly, being abducted by aliens" (Loftus & Ketcham, 1994, p. 66).

Loftus knows firsthand the phenomenon she studies. At a family reunion, an uncle told her that at age 14 she found her mother's drowned body. Shocked, she denied it. But the uncle was adamant, and over the next three days she began to wonder if *she* had a repressed memory. "Maybe that's why I'm so obsessed with this topic." As the now-upset Loftus pondered her uncle's suggestion, she "recovered" an image of her mother lying in the pool, face down, and of herself finding the body. "I started putting everything into place. Maybe that's why I'm such a workaholic. Maybe that's why I'm so emotional when I think about her even though she died in 1959."

Then her brother called. Their uncle now remembered what other relatives also confirmed. Aunt Pearl, not Loftus, had found the body (Loftus & Ketcham, 1994; Monaghan, 1992).

Loftus also knows firsthand the reality of sexual abuse. A male baby-sitter molested her when she was 6 years old. She has not forgotten. And that makes her wary of those whom she sees as trivializing real abuse by suggesting uncorroborated traumatic experiences, then accepting them uncritically as fact. The enemies of the truly victimized are not only those who prey and those who deny, she says, but those whose writings and allegations "are bound to lead to an increased likelihood that society in

● **Although scorned by some trauma therapists, Loftus has been elected president of the science-oriented Association for Psychological Science, awarded psychology's biggest prize ($200,000), and elected to the U.S. National Academy of Sciences and the Royal Society of Edinburgh.** ●

🛟 **TEACHING TIP**

At this time, you may want to use **Lecture/Discussion Topics:** *True Photos and False Memories* (p. 25) or *False Memories Surrounding the Iraq War* (p. 26) from Bolt's Teacher's Resource Binder.

general will disbelieve the genuine cases of childhood sexual abuse that truly deserve our sustained attention" (Loftus, 1993).

So, does repression ever occur? Or is this concept—the cornerstone of Freud's theory and of so much popular psychology—misleading? In Unit 10, we will return to this hotly debated issue. As we will see, this much now appears certain: The most common response to a traumatic experience (witnessing a parent's murder, experiencing the horrors of a Nazi death camp, being terrorized by a hijacker or a rapist, escaping the collapsing World Trade Center towers, surviving an Asian tsunami) is not banishment of the experience into the unconscious. Rather, such experiences are typically etched on the mind as vivid, persistent, haunting memories (Porter & Peace, 2007). Playwright Eugene O'Neill understood. As one of the characters in his *Strange Interlude* (1928) exclaimed, "The devil! . . . What beastly incidents our memories insist on cherishing!"

> "Horror sears memory, leaving . . . the consuming memories of atrocity."
> Robert Kraft, *Memory Perceived: Recalling the Holocaust,* 2002

BEFORE YOU MOVE ON . . .

➤ **ASK YOURSELF**

Could you be an impartial jury member in a trial of a parent accused of sexual abuse based on a recovered memory, or of a therapist being sued for creating a false memory of abuse?

➤ **TEST YOURSELF 6**

Source amnesia occurs when we attribute to the wrong source an event we have experienced, heard about, read about, or imagined. What might life be like if we remembered all our waking experiences as well as all our dreams?

Answers to the Test Yourself questions can be found in Appendix E at the end of the book.

Improving Memory

12: How can an understanding of memory contribute to more effective study techniques?

NOW AND THEN WE ARE DISMAYED AT our forgetfulness—at our embarrassing inability to recall someone's name, at forgetting to bring up a point in conversation, at not bringing along something important, at finding ourselves standing in a room unable to recall why we are there (Herrmann, 1982). Is there anything we can do to minimize such memory misdeeds? Much as biology benefits medicine and botany benefits agriculture, so can the psychology of memory benefit education. Sprinkled throughout this unit and summarized here for easy reference are concrete suggestions for improving memory. The SQ3R—*Survey, Question, Read, Rehearse, Review*—study technique introduced in this book's Unit 1 incorporates several of these strategies.

Study repeatedly. To master material, use distributed (spaced) practice. To learn a concept, provide yourself with many separate study sessions: Take advantage of life's little intervals—riding on the bus, walking to lunch, waiting for class to start. To memorize specific facts or figures, suggests Thomas Landauer (2001), "rehearse the name or number you are trying to memorize, wait a few seconds, rehearse again, wait a little longer, rehearse again, then wait longer still and rehearse yet again. The waits should be as long as possible without losing the information." New memories are weak; exercise them and they will strengthen. Speed-reading (skimming) complex material—with minimal rehearsal—yields little retention. Rehearsal and critical reflection help more. It pays to study actively.

> "I have discovered that it is of some use when you lie in bed at night and gaze into the darkness to repeat in your mind the things you have been studying. Not only does it help the understanding, but also the memory."
> Leonardo da Vinci (1452–1519)

INTERCONNECTING

While Freud believed that awful memories were repressed, research shows that memories of terrible, tragic events are often encoded as flashbulb memories, vividly recalled at a later time. Often, people report remembering not only the chronology of these events, but also details related to all their senses—sights, sounds, smells, tastes, and tactile sensations.

TEACHING TIP

Encourage students to break their study sessions up into separate sessions, as the text suggests. Studying in depth for 15–20 minutes can yield more benefit than studying for hours on end simply repeating the material.

TEACHING TIP

At this time, you may want to use **Lecture/Discussion Topics:** *Repressed Memories of Abuse* (p. 29) or *The Misinformation Effect and False Confessions* (p. 30) from Bolt's Teacher's Resource Binder.

UNIT 7A

"Knit each new thing on to some
acquisition already there."
William James, *Principles of Psychology*, 1890

Make the material meaningful. To build a network of retrieval cues, take text
and class notes in your own words. (Mindlessly repeating someone else's words
is relatively ineffective.) To apply the concepts to your own life, form images, understand and organize information, relate the material to what you already know
or have experienced, and put it in your own words. Increase retrieval cues by
forming associations. Without such cues, you may find yourself stuck when a
question uses phrasing different from the rote forms you memorized.

Activate retrieval cues. Mentally re-create the situation and the mood in which
your original learning occurred. Return to the same location. Jog your memory by
allowing one thought to cue the next.

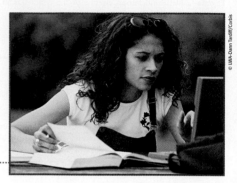

▼
Thinking and memory
Most of what we know is
not the result of efforts to
memorize. We learn because
we're curious and because
we spend time thinking about
our experiences. Actively
thinking as we read, by
rehearsing and relating ideas,
yields the best retention.

Use mnemonic devices. Associate items with peg-words. Make up a story that incorporates vivid images of the items. Chunk information into acronyms. Create
rhythmic rhymes ("*i* before *e*, except after *c*").

Minimize interference. Study before sleeping. Do not schedule back-to-back
study times for topics that are likely to interfere with each other, such as Spanish
and French.

Sleep more. During sleep, the brain organizes and consolidates information for
long-term memory. Sleep deprivation disrupts this process.

**Test your own knowledge, both to rehearse it and to help determine what you do
not yet know.** Don't be lulled into overconfidence by your ability to recognize information. Test your recall using the learning objective questions that appear at
the beginning of this text's main sections. Outline sections on a blank page. Define the terms and concepts listed at each unit's end before turning back to their
definitions. Take the practice tests found at the end of each unit.

BEFORE YOU MOVE ON . . .

➤ **ASK YOURSELF**

Which of the study and memory strategies suggested in this section will work best
for you?

➤ **TEST YOURSELF 7**

What are the recommended memory strategies you just read about? (One advised
rehearsing to-be-remembered material. What were the others?)

Answers to the Test Yourself questions can be found in Appendix E at the end of the book.

UNIT REVIEW: Memory

Information Processing

1: How do psychologists describe the human memory system?

Memory is the persistence of learning over time. The Atkinson-Shiffrin classic three-stage memory model (*encoding, storage,* and *retrieval*) suggests that we (1) register fleeting *sensory memories,* some of which are (2) processed into conscious *short-term memories,* a tiny fraction of which are (3) encoded for *long-term memory* and, possibly, later retrieval. Contemporary memory researchers note that we also register some information automatically, bypassing the first two stages. And they prefer the term *working memory* (rather than short-term memory) to emphasize the active processing in the second stage.

2: What information do we encode automatically? What information do we encode effortfully, and how does the distribution of practice influence retention?

With *parallel processing,* the brain handles many aspects of a problem simultaneously. *Automatic processing* happens unconsciously, as we absorb information (space, time, frequency, well-learned material) in our environment. *Effortful processing* (of meaning, *imagery,* organization) requires conscious attention and deliberate effort. The *spacing effect* is our tendency to retain information more easily if we practice it repeatedly (spaced study) than if we practice it in one long session (massed practice, or cramming). The *serial position effect* is our tendency to recall the first item (the primacy effect) and the last item (the recency effect) in a long list more easily than we recall the intervening items.

3: What effortful processing methods aid in forming memories?

Visual encoding (of images) and *acoustic encoding* (of sounds) engage shallower processing than *semantic encoding* (of meaning). We process verbal information best when we make it relevant to ourselves (the self-reference effect). Encoding imagery, as when using some *mnemonic* devices, also supports memory, because vivid images are memorable. *Chunking* and hierarchies help organize information for easier retrieval.

4: What is sensory memory?

As information enters the memory system through our senses, we briefly register and store visual images via *iconic memory,* in which picture images last no more than a few tenths of a second. We register and store sounds via *echoic memory,* where echoes of auditory stimuli may linger as long as 3 or 4 seconds.

5: What are the duration and capacity of short-term and of long-term memory?

At any given time, we can focus on and process only about seven items of information (either new or retrieved from our memory store). Without *rehearsal,* information disappears from short-term memory within seconds. Our capacity for storing information permanently in long-term memory is essentially unlimited.

6: How does the brain store our memories?

Researchers are exploring memory-related changes within and between single neurons. *Long-term potentiation (LTP)* appears to be the neural basis of learning and memory. Stress triggers hormonal changes that arouse brain areas and can produce indelible memories. We are particularly likely to remember vivid events that form *flashbulb memories.* We have two memory systems. *Explicit* (declarative) *memories* of general knowledge, facts, and experiences are processed by the *hippocampus. Implicit* (nondeclarative or procedural) *memories* of skills and conditioned responses are processed by other parts of the brain, including the cerebellum.

7: How do we get information out of memory?

Recall is the ability to retrieve information not in conscious awareness; a fill-in-the-blank question tests recall. *Recognition* is the ability to identify items previously learned; a multiple-choice question tests recognition. *Relearning* is the ability to master previously stored information more quickly than you originally learned it. Retrieval cues catch our attention and tweak our web of associations, helping to move target information into conscious awareness. *Priming* is the process of activating associations (often unconsciously).

8: How do external contexts and internal emotions influence memory retrieval?

The context in which we originally experienced an event or encoded a thought can flood our memories with retrieval cues, leading us to the target memory. In a different but similar context, such cues may trick us into retrieving a memory, a feeling known as *déjà vu.* Specific emotions can prime us to retrieve memories consistent with that state. *Mood-congruent memory,* for example, primes us to interpret others' behavior in ways consistent with our current emotions.

Forgetting

9: Why do we forget?

We may fail to encode information for entry into our memory system. Memories may fade after storage—rapidly at first, and then leveling off, a trend known as the forgetting curve. We may experience retrieval failure, when old and new material compete, when we don't have adequate retrieval cues, or possibly, in rare instances, because of motivated forgetting, or *repression.* In *proactive interference,* something learned in the past interferes with our ability to recall something recently learned. In *retroactive interference,* something recently learned interferes with something learned in the past.

Memory Construction

10: How do misinformation, imagination, and source amnesia influence our memory construction? How real-seeming are false memories?

If children or adults are subtly exposed to *misinformation* after an event, or if they repeatedly imagine and rehearse an event that never occurred, they may incorporate misleading details

ANSWERS to Multiple-Choice Questions

1. **c** capacity of short-term memory.

2. **c** Memories are formed in the brain when a synapse changes to allow for more efficient transfer of information.

3. **a** The ability to find a hidden *Where's Waldo?* figure with practice.

4. **e** Memories are often a blend of correct and incorrect information.

5. **a** semantically.

6. **a** chunking.

7. **d** The amygdala help make sure we remember events that trigger strong emotional responses.

8. **e** Alp is unable to remember the middle of a list of vocabulary words as well as he remembers the first or last words on the list.

9. **e** massed rehearsal.

10. **b** context effects.

11. **d** new information.

12. **c** rehearsal.

13. **d** Stephen misremembers a dream as something that really happened.

14. **b** hierarchy.

15. **a** most forgetting occurs early on and then levels off.

---

into their memory of what actually happened. When we reassemble a memory during retrieval, we may successfully retrieve something we have heard, read or imagined, but attribute it to the wrong source (*source amnesia*). False memories feel like true memories and are equally durable. Constructed memories are usually limited to the gist of the event.

11: What is the controversy related to claims of repressed and recovered memories?
This controversy between memory researchers and some well-meaning therapists is related to whether most memories of early childhood abuse are repressed and can be recovered by means of leading questions and/or hypnosis during therapy. Psychologists now tend to agree that: (1) Abuse happens, and can leave lasting scars. (2) Some innocent people have been falsely convicted of abuse that never happened, and some true abusers have used the controversy over recovered memories to avoid punishment.

(3) Forgetting isolated past events, good or bad, is an ordinary part of life. (4) Recovering good and bad memories, triggered by some memory cue, is commonplace. (5) Infantile amnesia—the inability to recall memories from the first three years of life—makes recovery of very early childhood memories unlikely. (6) Memories obtained under the influence of hypnosis or drugs or therapy are unreliable. (7) Both real and false memories cause stress and suffering.

Improving Memory
12: How can an understanding of memory contribute to more effective study techniques?
Research on memory suggests concrete strategies for improving memory. These include studying repeatedly, making material personally meaningful, activating retrieval cues, using mnemonic devices, minimizing interference, getting adequate sleep, and self-testing.

Terms and Concepts to Remember

memory, p. 255
encoding, p. 257
storage, p. 257
retrieval, p. 257
sensory memory, p. 257
short-term memory, p. 257
long-term memory, p. 257
working memory, p. 258
parallel processing, p. 258
automatic processing, p. 258
effortful processing, p. 259
rehearsal, p. 259
spacing effect, p. 260

serial position effect, p. 260
visual encoding, p. 261
acoustic encoding, p. 261
semantic encoding, p. 261
imagery, p. 263
mnemonics [nih-MON-iks], p. 263
chunking, p. 264
iconic memory, p. 266
echoic memory, p. 266
long-term potentiation (LTP), p. 269
flashbulb memory, p. 270
amnesia, p. 271
implicit memory, p. 272

explicit memory, p. 272
hippocampus, p. 272
recall, p. 274
recognition, p. 274
relearning, p. 274
priming, p. 275
déjà vu, p. 276
mood-congruent memory, p. 278
proactive interference, p. 282
retroactive interference, p. 282
repression, p. 284
misinformation effect, p. 286
source amnesia, p. 287

 AP* Practice Test Questions ◄ ·······································

Multiple-Choice Questions

1. The "magical number seven, plus or minus two" refers to the
   a. ideal number of times to rehearse information in the first encoding session.
   b. number of seconds information stays in short-term memory without rehearsal.
   c. capacity of short-term memory.
   d. number of seconds information stays in echoic storage.
   e. number of years most long-term memories last.

2. Which of the following describes long-term potentiation?
   a. When attempting to retrieve information, it is easier to recognize than to recall.
   b. Constructed memories have the potential to be either accurate or inaccurate.
   c. Memories are formed in the brain when a synapse changes to allow for more efficient transfer of information.
   d. Implicit memories are processed by the cerebellum instead of by the hippocampus.
   e. Information is transferred from working memory to long-term memory.

3. Which of the following is an example of implicit memory?
   a. The ability to find a hidden *Where's Waldo?* figure with practice.
   b. The ability to retrieve from memory the details of an assignment that is due tomorrow.
   c. The ability to vividly recall significant events like the 9/11 attacks in New York City and Washington, D.C.
   d. The ability to remember the details of your last birthday party.
   e. The ability of people to recognize names and pictures of their classmates many years after they have graduated.

TECHNOLOGY RESOURCES

These resources will be helpful for teaching the concepts in this portion of the unit:

- *Videos: Psychology: The Human Experience, Module 13: What Is Memory?; Module 14: Flashbulb Memories*

- *Videos: The Mind, 2nd ed., Module 10: Life Without Memory: The Case of Clive Wearing, Part 1; Module 11: Clive Wearing, Part 2: Living Without Memory*

- *Videos: Digital Media Archive: Psychology, 1st ed.: Video Clip 24: Aging and Memory; Video Clip 25: Clive Wearing: Living Without Memory; 2nd ed: Journey Into Memory*

- *Psychology Video Tool Kit: An Amazing Memory; Living Without Memory; Brain Fingerprinting: Memory, Recognition, and Lie Detection; Creating False Memories:*

4. Which of the following statements concerning memory is true?

a. Hypnosis, when used as a component of therapy, usually improves the accuracy of memory.

b. One aspect of memory that is usually accurate is the source of the remembered information.

c. Children's memories of abuse are always accurate.

d. Memories we are more certain of are more likely to be accurate.

e. Memories are often a blend of correct and incorrect information.

5. The basketball players could remember the main points of their coach's halftime talk, but not her exact words. This is because they encoded the information

a. semantically.

b. acoustically.

c. visually.

d. shallowly.

e. automatically.

6. When someone provides his phone number to another person, he usually pauses after the area code and again after the next three numbers. This pattern underscores the importance of

a. chunking.

b. the serial position effect.

c. semantic encoding.

d. auditory encoding.

e. automatic processing.

7. Which of the following is true regarding the role of the amygdala in memory?

a. The amygdala help process implicit memories.

b. The amygdala support Freud's ideas about memory because they allow us to repress memories of trauma.

c. The amygdala produce long-term potentiation in the brain.

d. The amygdala help make sure we remember events that trigger strong emotional responses.

e. The amygdala are active when the retrieval of a long-term memory is primed.

8. Which of the following illustrates the serial position effect?

a. The only name Kensie remembers from the people she met at the party is Spencer, because she thought he was particularly good looking.

b. Kimia has trouble remembering information from the book's first unit when she reviews for semester finals.

c. It's easy for Brittney to remember that carbon's atomic number is 6 because her birthday is on December 6.

d. Kyle was not able to remember the names of all of his new co-workers after one week on the job, but he could after two weeks.

e. Alp is unable to remember the middle of a list of vocabulary words as well as he remembers the first or last words on the list.

9. Mnemonic devices are *least* likely to be dependent upon

a. imagery.

b. acronyms.

c. rhymes.

d. stories.

e. massed rehearsal.

10. You are likely to remember more psychology in your psychology classroom than in other environments because of

a. mood congruence.

b. context effects.

c. state-dependency.

d. proactive interference.

e. retroactive interference.

11. All of the following kinds of information tend to be automatically processed *except*

a. space information.

b. time information.

c. frequency information.

d. new information.

e. well-learned information.

12. Hermann Ebbinghaus is considered a pioneer in memory research because he established the importance of

a. semantic encoding.

b. mnemonic devices.

c. rehearsal.

d. iconic storage.

e. long-term potentiation.

13. Which of the following is an example of source amnesia?

a. Iva can't remember the details of a horrifying event because she has repressed them.

b. Mary has entirely forgotten about an incident in grade school until her friend reminds her of the event.

c. Michael can't remember this year's locker combination because he confuses it with last year's combination.

d. Stephen misremembers a dream as something that really happened.

e. Anna, who is trying to lose weight, is unable to remember several of the between-meal snacks she had yesterday.

14. Chemistry teachers almost always present elements within the context of the periodic table. The periodic table is useful because it is a(n)

a. example of chunking.

b. hierarchy.

c. mnemonic device.

d. example of iconic storage.

e. massed rehearsal strategy.

15. Hermann Ebbinghaus' forgetting curve indicates that

a. most forgetting occurs early on and then levels off.

b. we forget more rapidly as additional time passes.

c. forgetting is relatively constant over time.

d. forgetting is related to many factors, but time is not one of them.

e. we are more likely to forget items in the middle of a list than at the beginning or the end.

Free-Response Question

A good friend, unhappy over his low grades in Japanese class, has asked you for advice about how to improve his memory. Explain how human memories are processed. Include specific recommendations for improving memory.

 WEB

Multiple-choice self-tests and more may be found at www.worthpublishers.com/myers

Rubric for Grading the Free-Response Question

This is a 10-point question. You should require enough description for each point to be assured of the students' understanding.

Explanation of human memory processing:

- 1 point for a description of encoding as the stage where information gets into the brain.

- 3 points for identifying the three stages of memory storage: sensory storage, short-term/working memory, and long-term memory.

- 1 point for discussing retrieval as the process of getting information back out of memory.

Specific recommendations:

- Up to 4 points for explanations of encoding strategies discussed in the text. These would include effective use of rehearsal, chunking, the spacing effect, the serial position effect, levels of encoding (visual, acoustic, semantic), or mnemonics.

- 1 point for explanations of retrieval strategies discussed in the text. These would include effective use of priming, retrieval cues, or mood congruence.

A Laboratory Study; Repression: Reality or Myth?; A Pill for Forgetting; Retrieval: A Journey Into Memory

- *PsychSim 5: Iconic Memory, Short-Term Memory, When Memory Fails; Forgetting; Trusting Your Memory*

- *Videos: The Brain, 2nd ed., Module 20: A Super-Memorist Advises on Study Strategies; Module 16: The Locus of Learning and Memory; Module 18: Living With Amnesia: The Hippocampus and Memory; Module 17: Learning as Synaptic Change*

- *Videos: Scientific American Frontiers, 2nd ed., Segment 16: Remembering What Matters; Segment 17: True or False?*

- *ActivePsych: Scientific American Frontiers Teaching Modules, 3rd ed.: Aging and Memory: Studying Alzheimer's Disease, Enhancing Memory: The Role of Emotion; Memory Loss: A Case Study*

Pacing Guide

Use the following guide to determine how many instructional days to devote to this portion of the unit depending on the type of course you teach:

Year-long course: 8–10 days
Block schedule/Semester-long course: 4–5 days

This entire unit (Parts A & B) encompasses 8–10 percent of the AP Exam. Spending an appropriate amount of time on this unit will help students do well on the AP Exam.

INTERCONNECTING

This content links well with concepts in other units:

- Thinking: Connect this content with Unit 2, Research Methods, where Myers discusses scientific thinking.

- Problem solving: Connect this content with Unit 14, Social Psychology, where Myers discusses stereotyping.

- Creativity: Connect this content with Unit 11, Testing and Individual Differences, where Myers discusses definitions of intelligence.

- Language: Connect this content with Unit 9, Developmental Psychology, where Myers discusses cognitive development.

Cognition:
7B—Thinking, Problem Solving, Creativity, and Language

Throughout history, we humans have both bemoaned our foolishness and celebrated our wisdom. The poet T. S. Eliot was struck by "the hollow men . . . Headpiece filled with straw." But Shakespeare's Hamlet extolled the human species as "noble in reason! . . . infinite in faculties! . . . in apprehension how like a god!" In the preceding units, we have likewise marveled at both our abilities and our errors.

We have studied the human brain—3 pounds of wet tissue the size of a small cabbage, yet containing circuitry more complex than the planet's data networks. We have relished our sensory system, which disassembles visual stimuli into millions of nerve impulses, distributes them for parallel processing, and then reassembles them into colorful perceptions. We have pondered the ease with which our two-track mind processes information, consciously and unconsciously. Little wonder that our species has had the collective genius to invent the camera, the car, and the computer; to unlock the atom and crack the genetic code; to travel out to space and into the oceans' depths.

Yet we have also seen that our species is kin to the other animals. We are influenced by the same principles that produce learning in rats and pigeons. As one pundit said, echoing Pavlov, "How like a dog!" We have noted that we assimilate reality into our preconceptions and succumb to perceptual illusions. We have seen how easily we deceive ourselves about pseudopsychic claims and hypnotic feats.

In this unit, we encounter further instances of these two images of the human condition—the rational and the irrational. We started in Unit 7A with *memory*, studying how we receive, perceive, store, and retrieve information. Here in Unit 7B we will consider how our cognitive system uses all that information. We will look at our flair for language and consider how and why it develops. And we will reflect on how deserving we are of our name, *Homo sapiens*—wise human.

> "The average newspaper boy in Pittsburgh knows more about the universe than did Galileo, Aristotle, Leonardo, or any of those other guys who were so smart they only needed one name."
> *Daniel Gilbert, Stumbling on Happiness, 2006*

::**cognition** the mental activities associated with thinking, knowing, remembering, and communicating.

::**concept** a mental grouping of similar objects, events, ideas, or people.

::**prototype** a mental image or best example of a category. Matching new items to a prototype provides a quick and easy method for sorting items into categories (as when comparing feathered creatures to a prototypical bird, such as a robin).

Thinking

THINKING, or **cognition**, refers to all the mental activities associated with thinking, knowing, remembering, and communicating. *Cognitive psychologists* study these activities, including the logical and sometimes illogical ways in which we create concepts, solve problems, make decisions, and form judgments.

Concepts

1: What are the functions of concepts?

To think about the countless events, objects, and people in our world, we simplify things. We form **concepts**—mental groupings of similar objects, events, ideas, and people. The concept *chair* includes many items—a baby's high chair, a reclining chair, a dentist's chair—all of which are for sitting. Chairs vary, but it is their common features that define the concept of *chair*.

Suggested Readings

Budiansky, S. (1998). *If a lion could talk: Animal intelligence and the evolution of consciousness.* New York: Free Press.

Lutz, W. (1989). *Doublespeak.* New York: HarperCollins.

Pinker, S. (1997). *How the mind works.* New York: W. W. Norton.

Restak, R. M. (1988). *The mind.* New York: Bantam Books.

Stanovich, K. (1998). *How to think straight about psychology* (5th ed.). New York: HarperCollins.

Imagine life without concepts. We would need a different name for every object and idea. We could not ask a child to "throw the ball" because there would be no concept of *ball* (or *throw*). Instead of saying, "They were angry," we would have to describe expressions, intensities, and words. Such concepts as *ball* and *anger* give us much information with little cognitive effort.

To further simplify things, we organize concepts into category *hierarchies*. Cab drivers organize their cities into geographical sectors, which subdivide into neighborhoods, and again into blocks. Once our categories exist, we use them efficiently. Shown a bird, car, or food, people need no more time to identify an item's category than to perceive that something is there. "As soon as you know it is there, you know what it is," report Kalanit Grill-Spector and Nancy Kanwisher (2005).

We form some concepts by *definition*. Told that a triangle has three sides, we thereafter classify all three-sided geometric forms as triangles. More often, however, we form our concepts by developing **prototypes**— a mental image or best example that incorporates all the features we associate with a category (Rosch, 1978). The more closely something matches our prototype of a concept, the more readily we recognize it as an example of the concept. A robin and a penguin both satisfy our definition of *bird*: a two-footed animal that has wings and feathers and hatches from an egg. Yet people agree more quickly that "a robin is a bird" than that "a penguin is a bird." For most of us, the robin is the birdier bird; it more closely resembles our bird prototype.

A bird and a . . . ?
It takes a bit longer to conceptualize a penguin as a bird because it doesn't match our prototype of a small, feathered, flying creature.

Once we place an item in a category, our memory of it later shifts toward the category prototype. Olivier Corneille and his colleagues (2004) found memory shifts after showing Belgian students ethnically mixed faces. For example, when shown a face that was a blend of 70 percent of the features of a Caucasian person and 30 percent of an Asian person, people categorized the face as Caucasian and later recalled having seen a more prototypically Caucasian person (Corneille et al., 2004). (They were more likely to recall an 80 percent Caucasian face than the 70 percent Caucasian they actually saw.) If shown a 70 percent Asian face, they later recalled a more prototypically Asian face (**FIGURE 7B.1**). A follow-up study found the phenomenon with gender as well. Those shown 70 percent male faces categorized them as male (no surprise there), and then later misrecalled them as even more prototypically male (Huart et al., 2005).

➤ **FIGURE 7B.1**
Face categorization influences recollection
For example, shown a face that was 70 percent Caucasian, people tended to classify the person as Caucasian and to recollect the face as more Caucasian than it was. (From Corneille et al., 2004.)

| 90% CA | 80% CA | 70% CA | 60% CA | 50%/50% | 60% AS | 70% AS | 80% AS | 90% AS |

"*Attention, everyone! I'd like to introduce the newest member of our family.*"

Key Terms

Thinking
cognition
concept
prototype
algorithm
heuristic
insight
creativity
confirmation bias
fixation
mental set
functional fixedness
representativeness heuristic
availability heuristic
overconfidence
belief perseverance
intuition
framing

Language
language
phoneme
morpheme
grammar
semantics
syntax
babbling stage
one-word stage
two-word stage
telegraphic speech

Thinking and Language
linguistic determinism

Tversky, A., & Kahneman, D. (1980). Causal schemas in judgments under uncertainty. In M. Fishbeinn (Ed.), *Progress in social psychology, Vol. 1.* Hillsdale, NJ: Erlbaum.

Wade, C., & Tavris, C. (1993). *Critical & creative thinking: The case of love and war.* New York: HarperCollins.

Key People

Noam Chomsky
Daniel Kahneman
Wolfgang Köhler
Wallace Lambert
Steven Pinker
Dean Keith Simonton
B. F. Skinner
Robert Sternberg

Shelley Taylor
Amos Tversky
Peter Wason
Benjamin Lee Whorf

UNIT 7B

INTERCONNECTING

Link the discussion of concepts with Jean Piaget's idea of schemas (Unit 9). Piaget called the basic unit of cognition a schema, and upon these schemas people would base their conceptions of the world. As people process information, they will either assimilate it or accommodate it. Assimilation involves putting the new information into an existing category. Accommodation requires one to change or adapt a category to suit the new information that conflicted with or added to the old category.

TEACHING TIP

Have students create a list of the different concepts that are represented in your classroom. Try to narrow down all the objects into the simplest concept possible—furniture, floor covering, shelving, books, etc. Then, have students look around your classroom and create a list of their own. Once they've done all they can, form different groups to come up with one class list. Compare the class list to yours to see how well they compare. Debate will surely ensue over what the simplest concepts are and how to categorize certain items.

At this point, you may want to use **Classroom Exercise/Student Project:** *The Need for Cognition Scale* (p. 3) from Bolt's Teacher's Resource Binder, which accompanies this text.

Heuristic searching To search for hot cocoa mix, you could search every supermarket aisle (an algorithm), or you could check the breakfast, beverage, and baking supplies sections (heuristics). The heuristics approach is often speedier, but an algorithmic search guarantees you will find it eventually.

➤ **FIGURE 7B.2**
The Aha! moment A burst of right temporal lobe activity accompanies insight solutions to word problems (Jung-Beeman et al., 2004).

Move away from our prototypes, and category boundaries may blur. Is a tomato a fruit? Is a 17-year-old female a girl or a woman? Is a whale a fish or a mammal? Because this marine animal fails to match our prototype, we are slower to recognize it as a mammal. Similarly, we are slow to perceive an illness when our symptoms don't fit one of our disease prototypes (Bishop, 1991). People whose heart attack symptoms (shortness of breath, exhaustion, a dull weight in the chest) don't match their prototype of a heart attack (sharp chest pain) may not seek help. And when discrimination doesn't fit our prejudice prototypes—of White against Black, male against female, young against old—we often fail to notice it. People more easily detect male prejudice against females than female against males or female against females (Inman & Baron, 1996; Marti et al., 2000). So, concepts, like other mental shortcuts we will encounter, speed and guide our thinking. But they don't always make us wise.

Solving Problems

One tribute to our rationality is our problem-solving skill in coping with novel situations. What's the best route around this traffic jam? How shall we handle a friend's criticism? How can we get in the house without our keys?

Strategies

2: What strategies assist our problem solving?

Some problems we solve through *trial and error*. Thomas Edison tried thousands of light bulb filaments before stumbling upon one that worked. For other problems, we use **algorithms**, step-by-step procedures that guarantee a solution. But step-by-step algorithms can be laborious and exasperating. For example, to find another word using all the letters in *SPLOYOCHYG*, we could try each letter in each position, but we would need to generate and examine the 907,200 resulting permutations. In such cases, we often resort to simpler strategies called **heuristics**. Thus, we might reduce the number of options in our *SPLOYOCHYG* example by excluding rare letter combinations, such as two Y's together. By using heuristics and then applying trial and error, we may hit upon the answer (which you can see by turning the page).

Sometimes, no problem-solving strategy seems to be at work at all, and we arrive at a solution to a problem with **insight**. Teams of researchers have identified brain activity associated with sudden flashes of insight (Jung-Beeman et al., 2004; Sandkühler & Bhattacharya, 2008). They gave people a problem: Think of a word that will form a compound word or phrase with each of three words in a set (such as *pine, crab,* and *sauce*), and press a button to sound a bell when you know the answer. (If you need a hint: The word is a fruit.[1]) All the while, the researchers mapped the problem solver's brain activity, using fMRIs (functional MRIs) or EEGs. In the first experiment, about half the solutions were by a sudden Aha! insight, which typically was preceded by frontal lobe activity involved in focusing attention and was accompanied by a burst of activity in the right temporal lobe, just above the ear (**FIGURE 7B.2**).

We also are not the only creatures to display insight, as psychologist Wolfgang Köhler (1925) demonstrated in an experiment with Sultan, a chimpanzee. Köhler placed a piece of fruit and a long stick well beyond Sultan's reach, and a short stick inside his cage. Spying the short stick, Sultan grabbed it and tried to reach the fruit. After several unsuccessful attempts, Sultan dropped the stick and seemed to survey the situation. Then suddenly, as if thinking "Aha!" he jumped up, seized the short stick

[1]The word is *apple*: pineapple, crabapple, applesauce.

RESEARCH

On their next visit to a store of any kind, have the students notice the number of different categories into which the store's managers have divided the items they sell. Challenge them to write down the different categories they notice and bring those lists to class. Then have students compare how different stores categorize merchandise. If there are several branches of a particular store in your area, have students visit each one to see if their organizational structures are similar.

again, and used it to pull in the longer stick—which he then used to reach the fruit. This evidence of animal cognition, said Köhler, showed that there is more to learning than conditioning. What is more, apes will even exhibit foresight, by storing a tool that they can use to retrieve food the next day (Mulcahy & Call, 2006).

As you perhaps experienced in solving the *pine-crab-sauce* problem, insight often pops into the mind with striking suddenness, with no prior sense that one is "getting warmer" or feeling close to the answer (Knoblich & Oellinger, 2006; Metcalfe, 1986). When the "Eureka moment" hits us, we feel a sense of satisfaction, a feeling of happiness. The joy of a joke may similarly lie in our sudden comprehension of an unexpected ending or a double meaning, as in this one (a highly rated joke among 40,000 submitted in an Internet humor study [Wiseman, 2002]):

Sherlock Holmes and Dr. Watson are going camping. They pitch their tent under the stars and go to sleep. Sometime in the middle of the night Holmes wakes Watson up.

Holmes: "Watson, look up at the stars, and tell me what you deduce."
Watson: "I see millions of stars and even if a few of those have planets, it's quite likely there are some planets like Earth, and if there are a few planets like Earth out there, there might also be life. What does it tell you, Holmes?"
Holmes: "Watson, you idiot, somebody has stolen our tent!"

Creativity

3: What is creativity, and what fosters it?

Pierre de Fermat, a seventeenth-century mischievous genius, challenged mathematicians of his day to match his solutions to various number theory problems. His most famous challenge—*Fermat's last theorem*—baffled the greatest mathematical minds, even after a $2 million prize (in today's dollars) was offered in 1908 to whoever first created a proof.

Princeton mathematician Andrew Wiles had pondered the problem for more than 30 years and had come to the brink of a solution. Then, one morning, out of the blue, the final "incredible revelation" struck him. "It was so indescribably beautiful; it was so simple and so elegant. I couldn't understand how I'd missed it and I just stared at it in disbelief for 20 minutes. Then during the day I walked around the department, and I'd keep coming back to my desk looking to see if it was still there. It was still there. I couldn't contain myself, I was so excited. It was the most important moment of my working life" (Singh, 1997, p. 25).

Wiles' incredible moment illustrates **creativity**—the ability to produce ideas that are both novel and valuable. Studies suggest that a certain level of aptitude is necessary but not sufficient for creativity. Exceptionally creative architects, mathematicians, scientists, and engineers usually score no higher on intelligence tests than do their less creative peers (MacKinnon & Hall, 1972; Simonton, 2000). So, clearly there is more to creativity than what intelligence tests reveal. Indeed, the two kinds of thinking engage different brain areas. Intelligence tests, which demand a single correct answer, require *convergent thinking*. Creativity tests (*How many uses can you think of for a brick?*) require *divergent thinking*. Injury to the left parietal lobe damages the convergent thinking required by intelligence test scores and for school success. Injury to certain areas of the frontal lobes can leave reading, writing, and arithmetic skills intact but destroy imagination (Kolb & Whishaw, 2006).

Robert Sternberg and his colleagues have identified five components of creativity (Sternberg, 1988, 2003; Sternberg & Lubart, 1991, 1992):

1. *Expertise,* a well-developed base of knowledge, furnishes the ideas, images, and phrases we use as mental building blocks. "Chance favors only the prepared mind," observed Louis Pasteur. The more blocks we have, the more chances we have to combine them in novel ways. Wiles' well-developed base of knowledge put the needed theorems and methods at his disposal.

::**algorithm** a methodical, logical rule or procedure that guarantees solving a particular problem. Contrasts with the usually speedier—but also more error-prone—use of *heuristics*.

::**heuristic** a simple thinking strategy that often allows us to make judgments and solve problems efficiently; usually speedier but also more error-prone than *algorithms*.

::**insight** a sudden and often novel realization of the solution to a problem; it contrasts with strategy-based solutions.

::**creativity** the ability to produce novel and valuable ideas.

● After picking up a Nobel Prize in Stockholm, physicist Richard Feynman stopped in Queens, New York, to look at his high school record. "My grades were not as good as I remembered," he reported, "and my IQ was [a good, though unexceptional] 124" (Faber, 1987). ●

"If you would allow me any talent, it's simply this: I can, for whatever reason, reach down into my own brain, feel around in all the mush, find and extract something from my persona, and then graft it onto an idea."

Cartoonist Gary Larson,
The Complete Far Side, 2003

INTERCONNECTING

Robert Sternberg, a former president of the APA, does extensive work on his theory of intelligence, which he calls the theory of successful intelligence. His theory proposes three parts to intelligence—practical, analytical, and creative.

TROUBLESHOOTING

Students often get *convergent* and *divergent* thinking confused. Help them see the difference by focusing on the root words: *converge* (meaning, to come together to one point) and *diverge* (meaning, to separate into multiple points). Convergent thinking requires focusing on one answer, while divergent thinking asks people to consider multiple answers.

INTERCONNECTING

Intrinsic motivation is discussed more thoroughly in Unit 8A. Intrinsic motivation is different from extrinsic motivation, which is based on external rewards rather than internal ones. People who are creative don't necessarily need external rewards in order to pursue their interests.

"For the love of God, is there a doctor in the house?"

Everyone held up their crackers as David threw the cheese log into the ceiling fan.

Imaginative thinking Cartoonists often display creativity as they see things in new ways or make unusual connections.

• Answer to SPLOYOCHYG anagram on previous page: PSYCHOLOGY. •

> "The human understanding, when any proposition has been once laid down . . . forces everything else to add fresh support and confirmation."
> Francis Bacon, *Novum Organum*, 1620

2. **Imaginative thinking skills** provide the ability to see things in novel ways, to recognize patterns, and to make connections. Having mastered a problem's basic elements, we redefine or explore it in a new way. Copernicus first developed expertise regarding the solar system and its planets, and then creatively defined the system as revolving around the Sun, not the Earth. Wiles' imaginative solution combined two partial solutions.

3. **A venturesome personality** seeks new experiences, tolerates ambiguity and risk, and perseveres in overcoming obstacles. Inventor Thomas Edison tried countless substances before finding the right one for his light bulb filament. Wiles said he labored in near-isolation from the mathematics community partly to stay focused and avoid distraction. Venturing encounters with different cultures also fosters creativity (Leung et al., 2008).

4. **Intrinsic motivation** is being driven more by interest, satisfaction, and challenge than by external pressures (Amabile & Hennessey, 1992). Creative people focus less on extrinsic motivators—meeting deadlines, impressing people, or making money—than on the pleasure and stimulation of the work itself. Asked how he solved such difficult scientific problems, Isaac Newton reportedly answered, "By thinking about them all the time." Wiles concurred: "I was so obsessed by this problem that for eight years I was thinking about it all the time—when I woke up in the morning to when I went to sleep at night" (Singh & Riber, 1997).

5. **A creative environment** sparks, supports, and refines creative ideas. After studying the careers of 2026 prominent scientists and inventors, Dean Keith Simonton (1992) noted that the most eminent among them were mentored, challenged, and supported by their relationships with colleagues. Even Wiles stood on the shoulders of others and wrestled his problem with the collaboration of a former student. Creativity-fostering environments often support contemplation. After Jonas Salk solved a problem that led to the polio vaccine while in a monastery, he designed the Salk Institute to provide contemplative spaces where scientists could work without interruption (Sternberg, 2006).

Obstacles to Problem Solving

4: What obstacles hinder our problem solving?

Inventive as we can be in solving problems, the correct answer may elude us. Two cognitive tendencies—*confirmation bias* and *fixation*—often lead us astray.

Confirmation Bias We seek evidence verifying our ideas more eagerly than we seek evidence that might refute them (Klayman & Ha, 1987; Skov & Sherman, 1986). This

TEACHING TIP

At this point, you may want to use **Classroom Exercises:** *Differences in Thinking Styles* (p. 4) or *Cognitive Complexity* (p. 5) or *Introducing Prototypes* (p. 5) from Bolt's Teacher's Resource Binder.

tendency, known as **confirmation bias**, is a major obstacle to problem solving. Peter Wason (1960) demonstrated the confirmation bias by giving British university students the three-number sequence 2-4-6 and asking them to guess the rule he had used to devise the series. (The rule was simple: any three ascending numbers.) Before submitting answers, students generated their own sets of three numbers, and Wason told them whether their sets conformed to his rule. Once they felt *certain* they had the rule, they were to announce it. The result? Seldom right but never in doubt. Most of Wason's students formed a wrong idea ("Maybe it's counting by twos") and then searched only for evidence confirming the wrong rule (by testing 6-8-10, 100-102-104, and so forth).

"Ordinary people," said Wason (1981), "evade facts, become inconsistent, or systematically defend themselves against the threat of new information relevant to the issue." The results are sometimes momentous. The United States launched its war against Iraq on the assumption that Saddam Hussein possessed weapons of mass destruction (WMD) that posed an immediate threat. When that assumption turned out to be false, confirmation bias was one of the flaws in the judgment process identified by the bipartisan U.S. Senate Select Committee on Intelligence (2004). Administration analysts "had a tendency to accept information which supported [their presumptions] . . . more readily than information which contradicted" them. Sources denying such weapons were deemed "either lying or not knowledgeable about Iraq's problems, while those sources who reported ongoing WMD activities were seen as having provided valuable information."

Fixation Once we incorrectly represent a problem, it's hard to restructure how we approach it. If the solution to the matchstick problem in FIGURE 7B.3 eludes you, you may be experiencing **fixation**—the inability to see a problem from a fresh perspective. (See the solution in FIGURE 7B.5 on the next page.)

Two examples of fixation are *mental set* and *functional fixedness*. As a perceptual set predisposes what we perceive, a **mental set** predisposes how we think. Mental set refers to our tendency to approach a problem with the mind-set of what has worked for us previously. Indeed, solutions that worked in the past often do work on new problems. Consider:

Given the sequence O-T-T-F-?-?-?, what are the final three letters?

Most people have difficulty recognizing that the three final letters are *F*(ive), *S*(ix), and *S*(even). But solving this problem may make the next one easier:

Given the sequence J-F-M-A-?-?-?, what are the final three letters? (If you don't get this one, ask yourself what month it is.)

Sometimes, however, a mental set based on what worked in the past precludes our finding a new solution to a new problem. Our mental set from our past experiences with matchsticks predisposes our arranging them in two dimensions.

Another type of fixation—our tendency to think of only the familiar functions for objects, without imagining alternative uses goes by the awkward but appropriate label **functional fixedness**. A person may ransack the house for a screwdriver when a coin would have turned the screw. As an example, try the candle-mounting problem in FIGURE 7B.4. Did you experience functional fixedness? If so, see FIGURE 7B.6 (on the next page). Perceiving and relating familiar things in new ways is part of creativity.

Making Decisions and Forming Judgments

5: How do heuristics, overconfidence, and belief perseverance influence our decisions and judgments?

When making each day's hundreds of judgments and decisions (*Is it worth the bother to take a jacket? Can I trust this person? Should I shoot the basketball or pass to the player who's hot?*), we seldom take the time and effort to reason systematically. We just follow

➤ **FIGURE 7B.3**
The matchstick problem How would you arrange six matches to form four equilateral triangles?

➤ **FIGURE 7B.4**
The candle-mounting problem Using these materials, how would you mount the candle on a bulletin board? (From Duncker, 1945.)

::**confirmation bias** a tendency to search for information that supports our preconceptions and to ignore or distort contradictory evidence.

::**fixation** the inability to see a problem from a new perspective, by employing a different mental set.

::**mental set** a tendency to approach a problem in one particular way, often a way that has been successful in the past.

::**functional fixedness** the tendency to think of things only in terms of their usual functions; an impediment to problem solving.

UNIT 7B

You can also demonstrate how heuristics leads to error by asking students to imagine they are offered a bet. A die with four green sides and two red ones will be rolled several times. They can be paid $25 if RGRRR or GRGRRR occurs. (Write each one on the chalkboard.) Which sequence do they think is more likely to pay off? Most will choose GRGRRR.

In fact, when Tversky and Kahneman posed this choice, either hypothetically or by offering hard cash, at least two-thirds chose that sequence. While the sequence is more representative of a die with four green faces (because green sides outnumber red sides), in actuality it is only two-thirds as likely because it is the same as the first alternative with the addition of a "G" (which has the probability of two-thirds on any given roll).

INTERCONNECTING

The representativeness heuristic is a form of stereotyping. We judge people according to the likelihood that they fit our representation of groups to which we feel they should belong.

➤ **FIGURE 7B.5**
Solution to the matchstick problem To solve this problem, you must view it from a new perspective, breaking the fixation of limiting solutions to two dimensions.

➤ **FIGURE 7B.6**
Solution to the candle-mounting problem Solving this problem requires recognizing that a matchbox can have other functions besides holding matches. (From Duncker, 1945.)

our intuition. After interviewing policymakers in government, business, and education, social psychologist Irving Janis (1986) concluded that they "often do not use a reflective problem-solving approach. How do they usually arrive at their decisions? If you ask, they are likely to tell you . . . they do it mostly by *the seat of their pants*."

Using and Misusing Heuristics

When we need to act quickly, those mental shortcuts we call heuristics often do help us overcome analysis paralysis. Thanks to our mind's automatic information processing, intuitive judgments are instantaneous. But the price we sometimes pay for this efficiency—quick but bad judgments—can be costly. Research by cognitive psychologists Amos Tversky and Daniel Kahneman (1974) on the *representativeness* and *availability heuristics* showed how these generally helpful shortcuts can lead even the smartest people into dumb decisions. (Their joint work on decision making received a 2002 Nobel Prize, although sadly, only Kahneman was alive to receive the honor.)

The Representativeness Heuristic To judge the likelihood of things in terms of how well they represent particular prototypes is to use the **representativeness heuristic**. To illustrate, consider:

> A stranger tells you about a person who is short, slim, and likes to read poetry, and then asks you to guess whether this person is more likely to be a professor of classics at an Ivy League university or a truck driver (adapted from Nisbett & Ross, 1980). Which would be the better guess?

Did you answer "professor"? Many people do, because the description seems more *representative* of Ivy League scholars than of truck drivers. The representativeness heuristic enabled you to make a snap judgment. But it also led you to ignore other relevant information. When I help people think through this question, the conversation goes something like this:

Question: First, let's figure out how many professors fit the description. How many Ivy League universities do you suppose there are?
Answer: Oh, about 10, I suppose.
Question: How many classics professors would you guess there are at each?
Answer: Maybe 4.
Question: Okay, that's 40 Ivy League classics professors. What fraction of these are short and slim?

::**representativeness heuristic** judging the likelihood of things in terms of how well they seem to represent, or match, particular prototypes; may lead us to ignore other relevant information.

::**availability heuristic** estimating the likelihood of events based on their availability in memory; if instances come readily to mind (perhaps because of their vividness), we presume such events are common.

At this point, you may want to use **Lecture/Discussion Topics: *The Projective Way of Knowing*** (p. 15) or ***The Sunk Cost Fallacy*** (p. 17) or ***Risks in Everyday Life*** (p. 17) or ***Perceiving Risk and the Fear of Global Warming*** (p. 16) or ***The Disjunction Fallacy or Irrational Prudence*** (p. 21) or ***Thinking Errors and International Conflict*** (p. 21) from Bolt's Teacher's Resource Binder.

"In creating these problems, we didn't set out to fool people. All our problems fooled us, too."
Amos Tversky (1985)

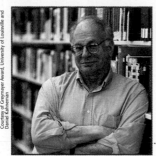

"Intuitive thinking [is] fine most of the time. . . . But sometimes that habit of mind gets us in trouble."
Daniel Kahneman (2005)

Answer: Let's say half.
Question: And, of these 20, how many like to read poetry?
Answer: I'd say half—10 professors.
Question: Okay, now let's figure how many truck drivers fit the description. How many truck drivers do you suppose there are?
Answer: Maybe 400,000.
Question: What fraction are short and slim?
Answer: Not many—perhaps 1 in 8.
Question: Of these 50,000, what percentage like to read poetry?
Answer: Truck drivers who like poetry? Maybe 1 in 100—oh, oh, I get it—that leaves 500 short, slim, poetry-reading truck drivers.
Comment: Yup. So, even if we accept your stereotype that the description is more representative of classics professors than of truck drivers, the odds are 50 to 1 that this person is a truck driver.

The representativeness heuristic influences many of our daily decisions. To judge the likelihood of something, we intuitively compare it with our mental representation of that category—of, say, what truck drivers are like. If the two match, that fact usually overrides other considerations of statistics or logic.

The Availability Heuristic The **availability heuristic** operates when we base our judgments on how mentally available information is. Anything that enables information to "pop into mind" quickly and with little effort—its recency, vividness, or distinctiveness—can increase its perceived availability, making it seem commonplace. Casinos entice us to gamble by signaling even small wins with bells and lights—making them vividly memorable—while keeping big losses soundlessly invisible. And if someone from a particular ethnic group commits a terrorist act, our readily available memory of the dramatic event may shape our impression of the whole group. When statistical reality is pitted against a single vivid case, the memorable case often wins. The mass killing of civilians may seem on the increase of late, thanks to memorably available terrorism and genocide. Actually, such horrors have declined sharply since the late 1980s (Pinker, 2007; U.S. Department of State, 2004).

Even during 9/11's horrific year, terrorist acts claimed comparatively few lives, note risk researchers (see **FIGURE 7B.7**, next page). Yet in 2007, a poll showed "terrorism" was Americans' top priority for Congress and the President, and that responding to global climate change—which some scientists regard as a future "Armageddon in slow motion"—was one of the lowest priorities (Pew, 2007). Emotion-laden images

"The problem is I can't tell the difference between a deeply wise, intuitive nudge from the Universe and one of my own bone-headed ideas!"

"Don't believe everything you think."
Bumper sticker

One area that relies on people using the availability heuristic is gambling. Have students research the probability of winning the lottery or casino games like blackjack or slot machines.

- How many lottery tickets are sold in a year and how much revenue do different casino games bring in?

- Do the odds of winning seem good or bad?

- How do the revenues that gambling bring in compare to the odds of winning?

- Would you participate in any of these games considering the odds of winning? Why or why not?

- Does buying more tickets increase one's chances of winning? Why or why not?

At this point, you may want to use **Classroom Exercises: *Dice Games to Demonstrate Problem Solving*** (p. 7) or ***The "Aha!" Experience*** (p. 8) or ***Assessing Creativity*** (p. 10) or ***Confirmation Bias*** (p. 12) or ***Functional Fixedness*** (p. 13) or **Student Projects: *The Tower of Hanoi Problem*** (p. 6) or ***Problem-Solving Strategies*** (p. 7) from Bolt's Teacher's Resource Binder.

TEACHING TIP

At this point, you may want to use **Classroom Exercises: *The Representativeness Heuristic*** (p. 13) or ***The Base-Rate Fallacy*** (p. 14) or ***The Availability Heuristic*** (p. 14) or ***The Anchoring Heuristic or Bias*** (p. 16) from Bolt's Teacher's Resource Binder.

UNIT 7B

DEMO

Demonstrate overconfidence by having students guess about the following figures about crime. The FBI classifies crime in the United States into two categories—violent crimes, such as murder, rape, robbery, and assault; and property crimes, such as burglary, larceny, or car theft. Pose the following questions to your students:

- What percentage of crimes would you estimate are violent rather than property crimes? (*12 percent. In 1996, there were 1,682,280 violent crimes reported and 11,791,300 property crimes.*)

- What percentage of accused felons plead insanity? What percentage are acquitted? (*Less than 1 percent of all accused felons plead insanity and only a quarter of those are ultimately acquitted.*)

- What percentage of convictions for felony crimes are obtained through trial instead of plea bargaining? (*Less than 10 percent of convictions for felony crimes are obtained through a trial; more than 90 percent result from plea bargaining.*)

> ➤ **FIGURE 7B.7**
> **Risk of death from various causes in the United States, 2001** (Data assembled from various government sources by Randall Marshall et al., 2007.)

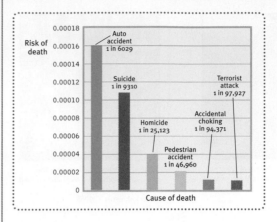

> "The human understanding is most excited by that which strikes and enters the mind at once and suddenly, and by which the imagination is immediately filled and inflated. It then begins almost imperceptibly to conceive and suppose that everything is similar to the few objects which have taken possession of the mind."
>
> Francis Bacon,
> *Novum Organum*, 1620

of terror exacerbate our fears of terrorism by harnessing the availability heuristic, notes political scientist Cass Sunstein (2007). We fear flying because we play in our heads a tape of 9/11 or some other air disaster. We fear letting our children walk to school because we play in our heads tapes of abducted and brutalized children. We fear swimming in ocean waters because we replay *Jaws* in our heads. And so, thanks to these readily available images, we come to fear extremely rare events. Meanwhile, the lack of comparably available images of global climate change leaves most people little concerned. (For more on the power of vivid cases, turn the page to see Thinking Critically About: The Fear Factor.)

We reason emotionally and neglect probabilities, points out psychologist Paul Slovic (2007). We overfeel and underthink. In one experiment, Deborah Small, George Lowenstein, and Slovic (2007) found that donations to a starving 7-year-old child were greater when her image was *not* accompanied by statistical information about the millions of needy African children like her. "If I look at the mass I will never act," Mother Teresa reportedly said. "If I look at the one, I will."

> ▼ **Predict your own behavior** When will you finish reading this unit?

Overconfidence

Our use of intuitive heuristics when forming judgments, our eagerness to confirm the beliefs we already hold, and our knack for explaining away failures combine to create **overconfidence**, a tendency to overestimate the accuracy of our knowledge and judgments. Across various tasks, people overestimate what their performance was, is, or will be (Metcalfe, 1998).

People are also more confident than correct when answering such questions as, "Is absinthe a liqueur or a precious stone?" (It's a licorice-flavored liqueur.) On questions where only 60 percent of people answer correctly, respondents typically

DEMO

Perhaps the simplest demonstration of overconfidence is to have students predict their score on a multiple-choice or another type of short-answer test immediately after they have completed it (have them note their estimate at the top of the test). The majority will overestimate the number of questions they got right. While the strength of this tendency will depend on the amount of feedback they have received on previous tests, some students continue to overestimate throughout the semester.

feel 75 percent confident. Even those who feel 100 percent certain err about 15 percent of the time (Fischhoff et al., 1977).

Overconfidence plagues decisions outside the laboratory, too. It was an overconfident Lyndon Johnson who waged war with North Vietnam and an overconfident George W. Bush who marched into Iraq to eliminate supposed weapons of mass destruction. On a smaller scale, overconfidence drives stockbrokers and investment managers to market their ability to outperform stock market averages, despite overwhelming evidence to the contrary (Malkiel, 2004). A purchase of stock X, recommended by a broker who judges this to be the time to buy, is usually balanced by a sale made by someone who judges this to be the time to sell. Despite their confidence, buyer and seller cannot both be right.

Students are routinely overconfident about how quickly they can do assignments and write papers, typically expecting to finish ahead of schedule (Buehler et al., 1994). In fact, the projects generally take about twice the number of days predicted. Despite our painful underestimates, we remain overly confident of our next prediction. More-over, anticipating how much we will accomplish, we then overestimate our future free time (Zauberman & Lynch, 2005). Believing we will have more free time next month than we do today, we happily accept invitations, only to discover we're just as busy when the day rolls around.

Failing to appreciate our potential for error can have serious consequences, but overconfidence does have adaptive value. People who err on the side of overconfidence live more happily, find it easier to make tough decisions, and seem more credible than those who lack self-confidence (Baumeister, 1989; Taylor, 1989). Moreover, given prompt and clear feedback—as weather forecasters receive after each day's predictions—we can learn to be more realistic about the accuracy of our judgments (Fischhoff, 1982). The wisdom to know when we know a thing and when we do not is born of experience.

The Belief Perseverance Phenomenon

Our readiness to fear the wrong things and to be overconfident in our judgments is startling. Equally startling is our tendency to cling to our beliefs in the face of contrary evidence. **Belief perseverance** often fuels social conflict, as it did in one study of people with opposing views of capital punishment (Lord et al., 1979). Those on both sides studied two supposedly new research findings, one supporting and the other refuting the claim that the death penalty deters crime. Each side was more impressed by the study supporting its own beliefs, and each readily disputed the other study. Thus, showing the pro- and anti-capital-punishment groups the *same* mixed evidence actually *increased* their disagreement.

If you want to rein in the belief perseverance phenomenon, a simple remedy exists. *Consider the opposite.* When Charles Lord and his colleagues (1984) repeated the capital-punishment study, they asked some participants to be "as *objective* and *unbiased* as possible." The plea did nothing to reduce biased evaluations of evidence. They asked another group to consider "whether you would have made the same high or low evaluations had exactly the same study produced results on the *other* side of the issue." Having imagined and pondered *opposite* findings, these people became much less biased in their evaluations of the evidence.

The more we come to appreciate why our beliefs might be true, the more tightly we cling to them. Once people have explained to themselves why they believe a child is "gifted" or "learning disabled," or why candidate X or Y will be a better commander-in-chief, or why company Z makes a product worth owning, they tend to ignore evidence undermining that belief. Prejudice persists. As we will see in Unit 14, once beliefs form and get justified, it takes more compelling evidence to change them than it did to create them.

"I'm happy to say that my final judgment of a case is almost always consistent with my prejudgment of the case."

::**overconfidence** the tendency to be more confident than correct—to over-estimate the accuracy of our beliefs and judgments.

::**belief perseverance** clinging to one's initial conceptions after the basis on which they were formed has been discredited.

INTERCONNECTING

Link this discussion of overconfidence with Unit 14's discussion of groupthink. With groupthink, a charismatic leader can cause others in a group to suppress any objections they may have about an idea in order to preserve group harmony. The leader, then, believes that everyone agrees with him/her since no one is objecting. This feeds the feeling of overconfidence in the doomed idea.

TEACHING TIP

Myers points out that overconfidence has its benefits. It is important to point out to students that many of the concepts in this unit—heuristics, framing, overconfidence, belief perseverance—do have their drawbacks, but if they did not have any value, people would not rely on them so much. If we use these concepts in this unit appropriately, they can add value to our lives by making decision making easier.

INTERCONNECTING

Belief perseverance may be an underlying reason for the results found in the "Pygmalion in the Classroom" study by Robert Rosenthal and colleagues in 1972. This famous study demonstrated that teachers' expectations can influence whether students perform well in school. Teachers who believe their students are not capable may not change their minds if they see evidence to the contrary.

TEACHING TIP

People perceive certain situations to be dangerous when a memorable tragedy occurs, even when that activity isn't as dangerous as more common activities. For example, people will be afraid of flying because they've seen coverage of a plane crash, but have no fear of driving, which is a much more dangerous activity than flying. Have students discuss their feelings about the following activities in light of recent, vivid tragedies:

- Flying on airplanes following September 11th
- Working in tall buildings following September 11th
- Traveling on a space shuttle following the *Columbia* accident
- Being kidnapped from their homes by a stranger following reports of missing children disappearing under similar circumstances

THINKING CRITICALLY ABOUT

The Fear Factor—Do We Fear the Right Things?

"Most people reason dramatically, not quantitatively," said Oliver Wendell Holmes. After 9/11, many people feared flying more than driving. (In a 2006 Gallup survey, only 40 percent reported being "not afraid at all" to fly.) Yet Americans were—mile for mile—230 times more likely to die in an automobile crash than on a commercial flight in the months between 2003 and 2005 (National Safety Council, 2008). In a late-2001 essay, I calculated that if—because of 9/11—we flew 20 percent less and instead drove half those unflown miles, about 800 more people would die in traffic accidents in the year after 9/11 (Myers, 2001). In checking this estimate against actual accident data (why didn't I think of that?), German psychologist Gerd Gigerenzer (2004) found that the last three months of 2001 did indeed produce significantly more U.S. traffic fatalities than the three-month average in the previous five years (**FIGURE 7B.8**). Long after 9/11, the dead terrorists were still killing Americans. As air travel gradually recovered during 2002 through 2005, U.S. commercial flights carried nearly 2.5 billion passengers, with no deaths on a major airline big jet (McMurray, 2006; Miller, 2005). Meanwhile, 172,000 Americans died in traffic accidents. For most people, the most dangerous aspect of airline flying is the drive to the airport.

Why do we fear the wrong things? Why do we judge terrorism to be a greater risk than accidents—which kill nearly as many per *week* in just the United States as did terrorism (2527 deaths worldwide) in all of the 1990s (Johnson, 2001)? Even with the horror of 9/11, more Americans in 2001 died of food poisoning (which scares few) than of terrorism (which scares many). Psychological science has identified four influences on our intuitions about risk. Together they explain why we sometimes fret over remote possibilities while ignoring much higher probabilities.

First, *we fear what our ancestral history has prepared us to fear*. Human emotions were road tested in the Stone Age. Our old brain prepares us to fear yesterday's risks: snakes,

FIGURE 7B.8
Still killing Americans Images of 9/11 etched a sharper image in our minds than did the millions of fatality-free flights on U.S. airlines during 2002 and after. Such dramatic events, being readily available to memory, shape our perceptions of risk. In the three months after 2001, those faulty perceptions led more people to travel, and some to die, by car. (Adapted from Gigerenzer, 2004.)

AP/Wide World Photos

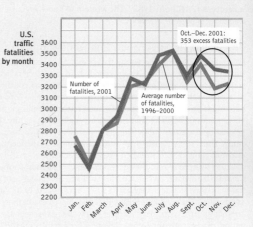

The Perils and Powers of Intuition

6: How do smart thinkers use intuition?

::**intuition** an effortless, immediate, automatic feeling or thought, as contrasted with explicit, conscious reasoning.

We have seen how our irrational thinking can plague our efforts to solve problems, make wise decisions, form valid judgments, and reason logically. Intuition also feeds our gut fears and prejudices. Moreover, these perils of **intuition** appear even

TEACHING TIP

At this point, you may want to use **Classroom Exercise: *The Overconfidence Phenomenon*** (p. 18) from Bolt's Teacher's Resource Binder.

Ian Berry/Magnum Photos

Dramatic deaths in bunches breed concern and fear The memorable 2004 South Asian tsunami that killed some 230,000 people stirred an outpouring of concern and new tsunami-warning technology. Meanwhile, a "silent tsunami" of poverty-related malaria was killing about that many of the world's children every three months, according to the World Health Organization.

lizards, and spiders (which combined now kill relatively few in developed countries). And it prepares us to fear confinement and heights, and therefore flying.

Second, *we fear what we cannot control*. Driving we control, flying we do not.

Third, *we fear what is immediate*. Threats related to flying are mostly telescoped into the moments of takeoff and landing, while the dangers of driving are diffused across many moments to come, each trivially dangerous. Similarly, many smokers (whose habit shortens their lives, on average, by about five years) fret openly before flying (which, averaged across people, shortens life by one day). Smoking's toxicity kills in the distant future.

Fourth, *we fear what is most readily available in memory*. Powerful, available memories—like the image of United Flight 175 slicing into the World Trade Center—serve as our measuring rods as we intuitively judge risks. Thousands of safe car trips have extinguished our anxieties about driving.

Vivid events also distort our comprehension of risks and probable outcomes. We comprehend disasters that have killed people dramatically, in bunches. But we fear too little those threats that will claim lives undramatically, one by one, and in the distant future. As Bill Gates has noted, each year a half-million children worldwide—the equivalent of four 747s full of children every day—die quietly, one by one, from rotavirus, and we hear nothing of it (Glass, 2004). Dramatic outcomes make us gasp; probabilities we hardly grasp.

Nevertheless, we must "learn to protect ourselves and our families against future terrorist attacks," warns a U.S. Department of Homeland Security ad that appeared periodically in my local newspaper, advising us to buy and store the food supplies, duct tape, and battery-powered radios we'll need if "there's a terrorist attack on your city." With 4 in 10 Americans being at least somewhat worried "that you or someone in your family will become a victim of terrorism," the "Be afraid!" message—be afraid not just of a terrorist attack on somebody somewhere, but of one on you and your place—has been heard (Carroll, 2005).

The point to remember: It is perfectly normal to fear purposeful violence from those who hate us. When terrorists strike again, we will all recoil in horror. But smart thinkers will remember this: *Check your fears against the facts and resist those who serve their own purposes by cultivating a culture of fear.* By so doing, we can take away the terrorists' most omnipresent weapon: exaggerated fear.

> "Fearful people are more dependent, more easily manipulated and controlled, more susceptible to deceptively simple, strong, tough measures and hard-line postures."
> Media researcher George Gerbner to U.S. Congressional Subcommittee on Communications, 1981

when people are offered extra pay for thinking smart, even when they are asked to justify their answers, and even when they are expert physicians or clinicians (Shafir & LeBoeuf, 2002). From this you might conclude that our heads are indeed filled with straw.

But we must not abandon hope for human rationality. Today's cognitive scientists are also revealing intuition's powers, as you can see throughout this book (**TABLE 7B.1**, next page). For the most part, our cognition's instant, intuitive reactions enable

TEACHING TIP

Have students list the top five things of which they are afraid. Have them evaluate whether their fears are based on the reasons for fear stated in the text:

- Is the fear related to evolutionary history?
- Is the fear something you cannot control?
- Is the fear immediate?
- Is the fear the result of the availability heuristic?

INTERCONNECTING

Connect this discussion of fear to the discussion of theories of emotion in Unit 8B. Fear is a well-researched emotion, so our knowledge of how it develops—and how it can be conquered—is vast.

UNIT 7B

TEACHING TIP

Table 7B.1 is an excellent way to review the unit's concepts and connect these concepts to other parts of the course. Helping students see how these concepts are interconnected is an excellent way to build critical thinking skills and promote higher order thinking.

INTERCONNECTING

The two-track mind is a recurring idea in psychology. Parallel processing, discussed in Unit 7A, is one way our two-track mind works. We can work consciously on one task while thinking unconsciously about other tasks. This often results in creative thinking and insight, as discussed elsewhere in this unit.

TABLE 7B.1

INTUITION'S PERILS AND POWERS (TEXT UNIT NUMBERS FOLLOW)

Intuition's Dozen Deadly Sins	Evidence of Intuition's Powers
• *Hindsight bias*—looking back on events, we falsely surmise that we knew it all along. (2)	• *Blindsight*—brain-damaged persons' "sight unseen" as their bodies react to things and faces not consciously recognized. (3B)
• *Illusory correlation*—intuitively perceiving a relationship where none exists. (2)	• *Right-brain thinking*—split-brain persons displaying knowledge they cannot verbalize. (3B)
• *Memory construction*—influenced by our present moods and by misinformation, we may form false memories. (7A)	• *Infants' intuitive learning*—of language and physics. (7B, 9)
• *Representativeness and availability heuristics*—fast and frugal heuristics become quick and dirty when leading us into illogical and incorrect judgments. (7B)	• *Moral intuition*—quick gut feelings that precede moral reasoning. (9)
• *Overconfidence*—our intuitive assessments of our own knowledge are often more confident than correct. (2, 7B)	• *Divided attention and priming*—unattended information processed by the mind's downstairs radar watchers. (5, 7A)
• *Belief perseverance and confirmation bias*—thanks partly to our preference for confirming information, beliefs are often resilient, even after their foundation is discredited. (2, 7B)	• *Everyday perception*—the instant parallel processing and integration of complex information streams. (4, 7A)
• *Framing*—judgments flip-flop, depending on how the same issue or information is posed. (7B)	• *Automatic processing*—the cognitive autopilot that guides us through most of life. (various)
• *Interviewer illusion*—inflated confidence in one's discernment based on interview alone. (Appendix B)	• *Implicit memory*—remembering *how* to do something without knowing *that* one knows. (7A)
• *Mispredicting our own feelings*—we often mispredict the intensity and duration of our emotions. (8B)	• *Heuristics*—those fast and frugal mental shortcuts that normally serve us well enough. (7B)
• *Self-serving bias*—in various ways, we exhibit inflated self-assessments. (10)	• *Intuitive expertise*—phenomena of unconscious learning, expert learning, and physical genius. (7B, 10, 11)
• *Fundamental attribution error*—overly attributing others' behavior to their dispositions by discounting unnoticed situational forces. (14)	• *Creativity*—the sometimes-spontaneous appearance of novel and valuable ideas. (7B)
• *Mispredicting our own behavior*—our intuitive self-predictions often go astray. (14)	• *Social and emotional intelligence*—the intuitive know-how to comprehend and manage ourselves in social situations and to perceive and express emotions. (11)
	• *The wisdom of the body*—when instant responses are needed, the brain's emotional pathways bypass the cortex; hunches sometimes precede rational understanding. (8B)
	• *Thin slices*—detecting traits from mere seconds of behavior. (10)
	• *Dual attitude system*—as we have two ways of knowing (unconscious and conscious) and two ways of remembering (implicit and explicit), we also have gut-level and rational attitude responses. (14)

us to react quickly and *usually* adaptively. They do so thanks, first, to our fast and frugal heuristics that enable us, for example, to intuitively assume that fuzzy-looking objects are far away, which they usually are (except on foggy mornings). Our learned associations also spawn the intuitions of our two-track mind. If a stranger looks like someone who previously harmed or threatened us, we may—without consciously recalling the earlier experience—react warily. (The learned association surfaces as a gut feeling.)

In showing how everyday heuristics usually make us smart (and only sometimes make us dumb), Gigerenzer (2004, 2007) asked both American and German university students, "Which city has more inhabitants: San Diego or San Antonio?" After thinking a moment, 62 percent of the Americans guessed right: San Diego. But German students, many of whom had not heard of San Antonio (apologies to our Texas friends), used a fast and frugal intuitive heuristic: Pick the one you recognize. With less knowledge but an adaptive heuristic, 100 percent of the German respondents answered correctly.

University of Amsterdam psychologist Ap Dijksterhuis and his colleagues (2006a,b) discovered the surprising power of unconscious intuition in experiments that showed people complex information about potential apartments (or roommates or art posters). They invited some participants to state their immediate preference after reading a dozen pieces of information about each of four apartments. A second group, given several minutes to analyze the information, tended to make slightly smarter decisions. But wisest of all, in study after study, was a third group, whose attention was distracted for a time. This enabled their minds to process the complex information unconsciously and to arrive at a more satisfying result. Faced with complex decisions involving many factors, the best advice may indeed be to take our time—to "sleep on it"—and to await the intuitive result of our unconscious processing.

Intuition is huge. More than we realize, thinking occurs off-screen, with the results occasionally displayed on-screen. Intuition is adaptive. It feeds our expertise, our creativity, our love, and our spirituality. And intuition, smart intuition, is born of experience. Chess masters can look at a board and intuitively know the right move. Playing "blitz chess," where every move is made after barely more than a glance, they display a hardly diminished skill (Burns, 2004). Experienced chicken sexers can tell you a chick's sex at a glance, yet cannot tell you how they do it. In each case, the immediate insight describes acquired, speedy expertise that feels like instant intuition. Experienced nurses, firefighters, art critics, car mechanics, hockey players, and you, for anything in which you develop a deep and special knowledge, learn to size up many a situation in an eyeblink. Intuition is recognition, observed Nobel laureate psychologist-economist Herbert Simon (2001). It is analysis "frozen into habit."

So, intuition—fast, automatic, unreasoned feeling and thought—harvests our experience and guides our lives. Intuition is powerful, often wise, but sometimes perilous, and especially so when we overfeel and underthink, as we do when judging risks. Today's psychological science enhances our appreciation for intuition. But it also reminds us to check our intuitions against reality. Our two-track mind makes sweet harmony as smart, critical thinking listens to the creative whispers of our vast unseen mind, and builds upon it by evaluating evidence, testing conclusions, and planning for the future.

The Effects of Framing

7: What is framing?

A further test of rationality is whether the same issue, presented in two different but logically equivalent ways, will elicit the same answer. For example, one surgeon tells someone that 10 percent of people die while undergoing a particular surgery. Another tells someone that 90 percent survive. The information is the same. The effect is not. To both patients and physicians, the risk seems greater to those who hear that 10 percent will *die* (Marteau, 1989; McNeil et al., 1988; Rothman & Salovey, 1997).

The effects of **framing**, the way we present an issue, are sometimes striking. Nine in 10 college students rate a condom as effective if it has a supposed "95 percent success rate" in stopping the HIV virus that causes AIDS; only 4 in 10 think it successful given a "5 percent failure rate" (Linville et al., 1992). And people express more surprise when a 1-in-20 event happens than when an equivalent 10-in-200 event happens (Denes-Raj et al., 1995). To scare people, frame risks as numbers, not percentages. People told that a chemical exposure is projected to kill 10 of every 10 million people (imagine 10 dead people!) feel more frightened than if told the fatality risk is an infinitesimal .000001 (Kraus et al., 1992).

▼ **Chick sexing** When acquired expertise becomes an automatic habit, as it is for experienced chick sexers, it feels like intuition. At a glance, they just know.

Jean-Philippe Ksiazek/AFP

::**framing** the way an issue is posed; how an issue is framed can significantly affect decisions and judgments.

INTERCONNECTING

Myers suggests that sleeping on a problem may produce the best results for decision making. Refer students to Unit 5 for a discussion of the work of William Dement, who showed that people can solve brain teasers better after having slept on the problem. Remind students that a good night's sleep is one of the most important factors in good performance.

INTERCONNECTING

Chicken sexers rely on procedural memory to perform their jobs, a concept discussed in Unit 7A. Procedural memory is often implicit, meaning people have a difficult time explaining how they perform a skill.

 TEACHING TIP

People can be seduced by the way products are framed. For example, people may buy more during a "25 percent off" sale even though they may end up spending more money than they would if there hadn't been a sale. Also, people tend to overeat foods that are labeled "low-fat," believing that more of that food is the same as smaller servings of higher-fat foods, instead of realizing that the amount of fat they consume in either case is about the same.

RESEARCH

Have students create two different surveys on the same topic. Each survey should differ in how the questions are framed.

- Students should distribute the surveys randomly to matched sets of participants—meaning participants with similar qualities are divided into each group to ensure that similar types of people answer each type of survey.

- Conduct some statistical analysis on each set of data, seeing how each group differed in its answers. Did students see a framing effect? Why or why not?

Consider how the framing effect influences political and business decisions. Politicians know to frame their position on public assistance as "aid to the needy" if they are for it and "welfare" if not. Merchants mark up their "regular prices" to appear to offer huge savings on "sale prices." A $100 coat marked down from $150 by Store X can seem like a better deal than the same coat priced regularly at $100 by Store Y (Urbany et al., 1988). And ground beef described as "75 percent lean" seems much more appealing than beef that is "25 percent fat" (Levin & Gaeth, 1988; Sanford et al., 2002). Likewise, a price difference between gas purchased by credit card versus cash feels better if framed as a "cash discount" rather than a "credit card fee."

Framing research also finds a powerful application in the definition of options, which can be posed in ways that nudge people toward better decisions (Thaler & Sunstein, 2008).

- *Preferred portion size depends on framing.* If a restaurant offers a regular and an alternative "small-sized" menu option, most people will elect the larger option. If the restaurant makes the small portion the default option and relabels the larger option as "supersized," more people will choose the smaller portion (Schwartz, 2007).

- *Why choosing to be an organ donor depends on where you live.* In many European countries as well as North America, people can decide whether they want to be organ donors when renewing their driver's license. In countries where the default option is *yes*, but people can opt out, nearly 100 percent agree to be donors. In the United States, Canada, Britain, and Germany, where the default option is *no* but people can "opt in," only about 1 in 4 agree to be donors (Johnson & Goldstein, 2003).

- *How to help employees decide to save for their retirement.* A 2006 U.S. pension law recognized the huge effect of framing options. Previously, employees who wanted to defer part of their compensation to a 401(k) retirement plan typically had to elect to lower their take-home pay, which most people are averse to doing. Now companies are being encouraged to enroll their employees automatically but to allow them to opt out (thereby raising their take-home pay). In both plans, the choice was the employee's. But under the "opt-out" rather than "opt-in" option, enrollments soared from 49 to 86 percent (Madrian & Shea, 2001).

The point to remember: Those who understand the power of framing can use it to influence our decisions.

BEFORE YOU MOVE ON . . .

➤ ASK YOURSELF

People's perceptions of risk, often biased by vivid images from movies or the news, are surprisingly unrelated to actual risks. (People may hide in the basement during thunderstorms but fail to buckle their seat belts in the car.) What are the things you fear? Are some of those fears out of proportion to statistical risk? Are you failing, in other areas of your life, to take reasonable precautions?

➤ TEST YOURSELF 1

The availability heuristic is a quick-and-easy but sometimes misleading guide to judging reality. What is the availability heuristic?

Answers to the Test Yourself questions can be found in Appendix E at the end of the book.

TEACHING TIP

At this point, you may want to use **Classroom Exercises: *Framing Decisions*** (p. 19) or ***Framing Alternatives and Human Irrationality*** (p. 20) from Bolt's Teacher's Resource Binder.

Language

THE STRIKING EFFECTS OF ISSUE framing illustrate the power of **language**—our spoken, written, or signed words and the ways we combine them as we think and communicate. Humans have long and proudly proclaimed that language sets us above all other animals. "When we study human language," asserted linguist Noam Chomsky (1972), "we are approaching what some might call the 'human essence,' the qualities of mind that are, so far as we know, unique [to humans]." To cognitive scientist Steven Pinker (1990), language is "the jewel in the crown of cognition."

Imagine an alien species that could pass thoughts from one head to another merely by pulsating air molecules in the space between them. Perhaps these weird creatures could inhabit a future Spielberg movie? Actually, we are those creatures! When we speak, our brain and voice box conjure up air pressure waves that we send banging against another's eardrum—enabling us to transfer thoughts from our brain into theirs. As Pinker (1998) notes, we sometimes sit for hours "listening to other people make noise as they exhale, because those hisses and squeaks contain *information*." And thanks to all those funny sounds created in our heads from the air pressure waves we send out, adds Bernard Guerin (2003), we get people's attention, we get them to do things, and we maintain relationships. Depending on how you vibrate the air after opening your mouth, you may get slapped or kissed.

But language is more than vibrating air. As I create this paragraph, my fingers on a keyboard generate electronic binary numbers that get translated into squiggles of dried carbon pressed onto stretched wood pulp on the page in front of you. When transmitted by reflected light rays into your retina, the printed squiggles trigger formless nerve impulses that project to several areas of your brain, which integrates the information, compares it to stored information, and decodes meaning. Thanks to language, we have transferred meaning from one mind to another. Whether spoken, written, or signed, language enables us not only to communicate but to transmit civilization's accumulated knowledge across generations. Monkeys mostly know what they see. Thanks to language, we know much that we've never seen.

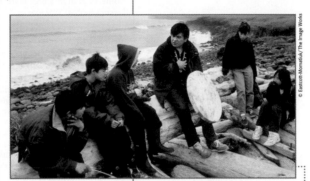

Language transmits culture Words and grammar differ from culture to culture. But in every society, language allows people to transmit their accumulated knowledge from one generation to the next. Here, a group of Aleut Alaska Native youth on St. Paul Island learn from a traditional storyteller the history of their homeland in light of modern-day environmental concerns.
▲

Language Structure

8: What are the structural components of a language?

Consider how we might go about inventing a language. For a spoken language, we would need three building blocks.

Phonemes

First, we would need a set of basic sounds, which linguists call **phonemes**. To say *bat* we utter the phonemes *b, a,* and *t. Chat* also has three phonemes—*ch, a,* and *t.* Linguists surveying nearly 500 languages have identified 869 different phonemes in human speech (Holt, 2002; Maddieson, 1984). No one language uses all of them. English uses about 40; other languages, anywhere from half to more than twice that many.

::**language** our spoken, written, or signed words and the ways we combine them to communicate meaning.

::**phoneme** in language, the smallest distinctive sound unit.

TEACHING TIP

Some scholars have called language the most complex body of knowledge known to humanity. Consider this: Languages are composed of a limited number of symbols that can be combined according to particular rules. These symbols and rules can then be put together to create an unlimited number of messages. As long as someone is using the basic symbols and follows the basic rules of the language, he or she can be understood! What an amazing ability we have!

RESEARCH

Show students that even language that doesn't make meaningful sense can still be grammatically correct—and be understood:

- What is so unusual about the sentence below? (Aside from the fact it does not make a lot of sense.) "Jackdaws love my big sphinx of quartz."

Answer: It's the shortest sentence in the English language that includes every letter of the alphabet.

RESEARCH

Have students research how many phonemes the world languages taught in your school contain as compared to English. In addition, ask students from other cultures that are represented in your student body to discuss the sound structure of their languages.

- Which language has more than English? Which has less?
- What are some of the phonemes in the world languages taught at your school that are not found in English?
- What other languages are represented at your school? What are some unique phonemes found in those languages?

UNIT 7B

CULTURAL CONNECTIONS

The number of phonemes varies from as few as 11 in Rotokas (Papua New Guinea) and 12 in Hawaiian to as many as 141 in !Xu~ (southern Africa, in the Kalahari desert).

- In some languages, there are only 2 or 3 vowel sounds, as in some dialects of the Abkhaz language (republic of Georgia), in the Arabic language, in some Australian Aboriginal languages, and in many Native American languages. By contrast, in the Punjabi language (India), there are over 25 vowel sounds. The most common vowel sounds are those found in English: a, e, i, o, and, u.

- Consonant sounds also vary. Rotokas contains 6 consonants while !Xu~ contains over 100, including several Click consonants. The most common consonants are p, t, and k, but not all languages have these. For example, Hawai'ian lacks the t sound, and the Mohawk language lacks the p sound, but all known languages have at least two of the three.

- One of the rarest sounds is found in the Czech language: "r hacek" (found in the name Dvořăk); that sound is unique to that language.

Source: Wikipedia: The Free Encyclopedia. www.wikipedia.org/wiki/Phoneme

At this point, you may want to use **Lecture/Discussion Topic: Vanishing Languages** (p. 22) from Bolt's Teacher's Resource Binder.

• How many morphemes are in the word cats? How many phonemes? (Answers below.) •

Two morphemes—cat and s, and four phonemes—c, a, t, and s.

From The Wall Street Journal—permission Cartoon Features Syndicate.

"Let me get this straight now. Is what you want to build a jean factory or a gene factory?"

• Slightly more than half the world's 6000 languages are spoken by fewer than 10,000 people. And slightly more than half the world's population speaks one of the top 20 languages (Gibbs, 2002). •

Within a language, changes in phonemes produce changes in meaning. In English, varying the vowel sound between b and t creates 12 different meanings: *bait, bat, beat/beet, bet, bit, bite, boat, boot, bought, bout,* and *but* (Fromkin & Rodman, 1983). Generally, though, consonant phonemes carry more information than do vowel phonemes. The treth ef thes stetement shed be evedent frem thes bref demenstretien.

People who grow up learning one set of phonemes usually have difficulty pronouncing those of another language. The native English speaker may smile at the native German speaker's difficulties with the *th* sound, which can make *this* sound like *dis*. But the German speaker smiles back at the problems English speakers have rolling the German *r* or pronouncing the breathy *ch* in *ich*, the German word for *I*.

Sign language also has phonemelike building blocks defined by hand shapes and movements. Like speakers, native signers of one of the 200+ sign languages may have difficulty with the phonemes of another. Chinese native signers who come to America and learn sign usually sign with an accent, notes researcher Ursula Bellugi (1994).

Morphemes

But sounds alone do not make a language. The second building block is the **morpheme**, the smallest unit of language that carries meaning. In English, a few morphemes are also phonemes—the personal pronoun *I*, for instance, or the *s* that indicates plural. But most morphemes are combinations of two or more phonemes. Some, like b*at*, are words, but others are only parts of words. Morphemes include prefixes and suffixes, such as the *pre-* in *preview* or the *-ed* that shows past tense.

Grammar

Finally, our new language must have a **grammar**, a system of rules (*semantics* and *syntax*) in a given language that enables us to communicate with and understand others. **Semantics** is the set of rules we use to derive meaning from morphemes, words, and even sentences. In English, a semantic rule tells us that adding *-ed* to *laugh* means that it happened in the past. **Syntax** refers to the rules we use to order words into sentences. One rule of English syntax says that adjectives usually come before nouns, so we say *white house*. Spanish adjectives usually reverse this order, as in *casa blanca*. The English rules of syntax allow the sentence *They are hunting dogs*. Given the context, semantics will tell us whether it refers to dogs that seek animals or people who seek dogs.

In all 6000 human languages, the grammar is intricately complex. "There are 'Stone Age' societies, but they do not have 'Stone Age' languages" (Pinker, 1995). Contrary to the illusion that less-educated people speak ungrammatically, they simply speak a different dialect. To a linguist, "ain't got none" is grammatically equal to "doesn't have any." (It has the same syntax.)

Note, however, that language becomes increasingly more complex as you move from one level to the next. In English, for example, the relatively small number of 40 or so phonemes can be combined to form more than 100,000 morphemes, which alone or in combination produce the 616,500 word forms in the *Oxford English Dictionary* (including 290,500 main entries such as *meat* and 326,000 subentries such as *meat eater*). We can then use these words to create an infinite number of sentences, most of which (like this one) are original. Like life itself constructed from the genetic code's simple alphabet, language is complexity built of simplicity. I know that you can know why I worry that you think this sentence is starting to get too complex, but that complexity—and our capacity to communicate and comprehend it—is what distinguishes human language capacity (Hauser et al., 2002).

🛟 TEACHING TIP

Have students discuss ways they do not use grammar correctly in everyday speech.

- Point out that "Me and him are going to the store" is incorrect grammar—wrong pronoun case usage to be exact. Another rule ignored in everyday speech involves pronoun-antecedent agreement [everybody has their notebook in class—incorrect].

- Point out that many nouns and adjectives have become verbs or taken on new meanings. For example, bad has several connotations, meaning both "good" and "bad." The brand name Google has become a verb—"I've been googled."

Language Development

Make a quick guess: How many words did you learn during the years between your first birthday and your high school graduation? The answer is about 60,000 (Bloom, 2000; McMurray, 2007). That averages (after age 1) to nearly 3500 words each year, or nearly 10 each day! How you did it—how the 3500 words a year you learned could so far outnumber the roughly 200 words a year that your schoolteachers consciously taught you—is one of the great human wonders.

Before you were able to add 2 + 2, you were creating your own original and grammatically appropriate sentences. Most of us would have trouble stating our language's rules for ordering words to form sentences. Yet as preschoolers, you comprehended and spoke with a facility that puts to shame your fellow students now struggling to learn a foreign language.

We humans have an astonishing facility for language. With remarkable efficiency, we selectively sample tens of thousands of words in memory, effortlessly assemble them with near-perfect syntax, and spew them out at a rate of three words (with a dozen or so phonemes) a second (Vigliocco & Hartsuiker, 2002). Seldom do we form sentences in our minds before speaking them. Rather they organize themselves on the fly as we speak. And while doing all this, we also adapt our utterances to our social and cultural context, following rules for speaking (*How far apart should we stand?*) and listening (*Is it OK to interrupt?*). Given how many ways there are to mess up, it's amazing that we can master this social dance. So, when and how does it happen?

When Do We Learn Language?

9: What are the milestones in language development?

Receptive Language Children's language development moves from simplicity to complexity. Infants start without language (*in fantis* means "not speaking"). Yet by 4 months of age, babies can discriminate speech sounds (Stager & Werker, 1997). They can also read lips: They prefer to look at a face that matches a sound, so we know they can recognize that *ah* comes from wide open lips and *ee* from a mouth with corners pulled back (Kuhl & Meltzoff, 1982). This period marks the beginning of the development of babies' *receptive language*, their ability to comprehend speech. At seven months and beyond, babies grow in their power to do what you and I find difficult when listening to an unfamiliar language: segmenting spoken sounds into individual words. Moreover, their adeptness at this task, as judged by their listening patterns, predicts their language abilities at ages 2 and 5 (Newman et al., 2006).

Productive Language Babies' *productive language*, their ability to produce words, matures after their receptive language. Around 4 months of age, babies enter the **babbling stage**, in which they spontaneously utter a variety of sounds, such as *ah-goo*. Babbling is not an imitation of adult speech, for it includes sounds from various languages, even those not spoken in the household. From this early babbling, a listener could not identify an infant as being, say, French, Korean, or Ethiopian. Deaf infants who observe their Deaf parents signing begin to babble more with their hands (Petitto & Marentette, 1991). Before nurture molds our speech, nature enables a wide range of possible sounds. Many of these natural babbling sounds are consonant-vowel pairs formed by simply bunching the tongue in the front of the mouth (*da-da, na-na, ta-ta*) or by opening and closing the lips (*ma-ma*), both of which babies do naturally for feeding (MacNeilage & Davis, 2000).

By the time infants are about 10 months old, their babbling has changed so that a trained ear can identify the language of the household (de Boysson-Bardies et al., 1989). Sounds and intonations outside that language begin to disappear. Without

 Although you probably know between 60,000 and 80,000 words, you use only 150 words for about half of what you say. •

::**morpheme** in a language, the smallest unit that carries meaning; may be a word or a part of a word (such as a prefix).

::**grammar** in a language, a system of rules that enables us to communicate with and understand others.

::**semantics** the set of rules by which we derive meaning from morphemes, words, and sentences in a given language; also, the study of meaning.

::**syntax** the rules for combining words into grammatically sensible sentences in a given language.

::**babbling stage** beginning at about 4 months, the stage of speech development in which the infant spontaneously utters various sounds at first unrelated to the household language.

Grammar is more than just a set of rules students learn in English class.

- *Mechanics* are rules that govern how language is written. These are the concepts around which most English grammar lessons are structured. Use of commas, capitalization, and end mark rules are considered part of English mechanics.

- *Pragmatics* are the usually unwritten rules about what language is appropriate to use at particular times. People use language differently in a job interview than when they are hanging out with friends.

RESEARCH

Have students create their own ambiguous sentences by playing with *dangling modifiers*. A dangling modifier is a grammatical error where a word or phrase is not located in front of or near the word it modifies. For example, consider the sentence "Happy to be home, the bed looked like a comfortable place to take a nap." Now, just who is happy to be home? The bed? It is according to this sentence.

TEACHING TIP

Holographic speech appears around one year of age and involves using single words to stand for a whole sentence of meaning. For example, the word "ball" could mean "I want the ball" or "Where is the ball?" depending on the inflection.

At this point, you may want to use **Lecture/Discussion Topics: *Language Development*** (p. 24) or ***Bilingualism*** (p. 24) from Bolt's Teacher's Resource Binder.

TEACHING TIP

Babies even younger than 4 months old use language. *Cooing* occurs at around 3 to 5 weeks of age. Infants at this age will repeat basic vowel sounds without using consonants.

TROUBLESHOOTING

Students often read charts like Table 7B.2 and believe the timeline given is set in stone. Remind students that the developmental milestones provided here are averages. In development, the sequence of language development is set, but the timeline is not. Babies vary in when they reach these milestones.

RESEARCH

Ask a local daycare center to record the different types of language usage children at their center use. Have them focus on recordings of babbling, one-word, and two-word language usage and ways children over-generalize grammar rules.

- What are the consonants most used by infants in the babbling stage?

- What are the common words young children use in the one-word stage?

- What types of verbs and modifiers are added most by children in the two-word stage?

- What are some examples of over-generalized words children in the center are using? Are the caregivers correcting them? Why or why not?

exposure to other languages, babies become functionally deaf to speech sounds outside their native language (Pallier et al., 2001). This explains why adults who speak only English cannot discriminate certain Japanese sounds within speech, and why Japanese adults with no training in English cannot distinguish between the English *r* and *l*. Thus, *la-la-ra-ra* may, to a Japanese-speaking adult, sound like the same syllable repeated. A Japanese-speaking person told that the train station is "just after the next light" may wonder, "The next what? After the street veering right, or farther down, after the traffic light?"

Around their first birthday (the exact age varies from child to child), most children enter the **one-word stage.** They have already learned that sounds carry meanings, and if repeatedly trained to associate, say, *fish* with a picture of a fish, 1-year-olds will look at a fish when a researcher says "Fish, fish! Look at the fish!" (Schafer, 2005). Not surprisingly, they now begin to use sounds—usually only one barely recognizable syllable, such as *ma* or *da*—to communicate meaning. But family members quickly learn to understand, and gradually the infant's language conforms more to the family's language. At this one-word stage, an inflected word may equal a sentence. "Doggy!" may mean "Look at the dog out there!"

At about 18 months, children's word learning explodes from about a word per week to a word per day. By their second birthday, most have entered the **two-word stage.** They start uttering two-word sentences (TABLE 7B.2) in **telegraphic speech**: Like the old-fashioned telegrams (TERMS ACCEPTED. SEND MONEY), this early form of speech contains mostly nouns and verbs (*Want juice*). Also like telegrams, it follows rules of syntax; the words are in a sensible order. English-speaking children typically place adjectives before nouns—*big doggy* rather than *doggy big*.

Once children move out of the two-word stage, they quickly begin uttering longer phrases (Fromkin & Rodman, 1983). If they get a late start on learning a particular language, for example after receiving a cochlear implant or being an international adoptee, their language development still proceeds through the same sequence, although usually at a faster pace (Ertmer et al., 2007; Snedeker et al., 2007). By early elementary school, children understand complex sentences and begin to enjoy the humor conveyed by double meanings: "You never starve in the desert because of all the sand-which-is there."

"Got idea. Talk better. Combine words. Make sentences."

© 1994 by Sidney Harris.

TABLE 7B.2

SUMMARY OF LANGUAGE DEVELOPMENT

Month (approximate)	Stage
4	Babbles many speech sounds.
10	Babbling resembles household language.
12	One-word stage.
24	Two-word, telegraphic speech.
24+	Language develops rapidly into complete sentences.

::one-word stage the stage in speech development, from about age 1 to 2, during which a child speaks mostly in single words.

::two-word stage beginning about age 2, the stage in speech development during which a child speaks mostly two-word statements.

::telegraphic speech early speech stage in which a child speaks like a telegram—"go car"—using mostly nouns and verbs.

Explaining Language Development

10: How do we learn language?

Attempts to explain how we acquire language have sparked a spirited intellectual controversy. The nature-nurture debate surfaces again and, here as elsewhere, appreciation for innate predisposition and the nature-nurture interaction has grown.

Skinner: Operant Learning Behaviorist B. F. Skinner (1957) believed we can explain language development with familiar learning principles, such as *association* (of the sights of things with the sounds of words); *imitation* (of the words and syntax modeled by others); and *reinforcement* (with smiles and hugs when the child says something right). Thus, Skinner (1985) argued, babies learn to talk in many of the same ways that animals learn to peck keys and press bars: "Verbal behavior evidently came into existence when, through a critical step in the evolution of the human species, the vocal musculature became susceptible to operant conditioning." And it's not just humans. Song-learning birds also acquire their "language" aided by imitation (Haesler, 2007).

TEACHING TIP

Have students attempt to communicate to each other only using telegraphic speech. Have them combine verbs, adjectives, and nouns together to relate an episode from the previous day. Have them discuss the difficulty of the task.

At this point, you may want to use **Lecture/Discussion Topic: *Universals of Language*** (p. 23) from Bolt's Teacher's Resource Binder.

Chomsky: Inborn Universal Grammar Linguist Noam Chomsky (1959, 1987) has likened Skinner's ideas to filling a bottle with water. But developing language is not just being "filled up" with the right kinds of experiences, Chomsky insisted. Children acquire untaught words and grammar at a rate too extraordinary to be explained solely by learning principles. They generate all sorts of sentences they have never heard, sometimes with novel errors. (No parent teaches the sentence, "I hate you, Daddy.") Moreover, many of the errors young children make result from overgeneralizing logical grammatical rules, such as adding *-ed* to form the past tense (de Cuevas, 1990):

> Child: My teacher holded the baby rabbits and we petted them.
> Mother: Did you say your teacher held the baby rabbits?
> Child: Yes.
> Mother: Did you say she held them tightly?
> Child: No, she holded them loosely.

Chomsky instead views language development much like "helping a flower to grow in its own way." Given adequate nurture, language will naturally occur. It just "happens to the child." And the reason it happens is that we come prewired with a sort of switch box—a *language acquisition device*. It is as if the switches need to be turned either "on" or "off" for us to understand and produce language. As we hear language, the switches get set for the language we are to learn.

Underlying human language, Chomsky says, is a *universal grammar*: All human languages therefore have the same grammatical building blocks, such as nouns and verbs, subjects and objects, negations and questions. Thus, we readily learn the specific grammar of whatever language we experience, whether spoken or signed (Bavelier et al., 2003). And no matter what that language is, we start speaking mostly in nouns *(kitty, da-da)* rather than verbs and adjectives (Bornstein et al., 2004). It happens so naturally—as naturally as birds learning to fly—that training hardly helps.

Many psychologists believe we benefit from both Skinner's and Chomsky's views. Children's genes design complex brain wiring that prepares them to learn language as they interact with their caregivers. Skinner's emphasis on learning helps explain how infants acquire their language as they interact with others. Chomsky's emphasis on our built-in readiness to learn grammar rules helps explain why preschoolers acquire language so readily and use grammar so well. Once again, we see biology and experience working together.

Statistical Learning and Critical Periods Human infants display a remarkable ability to learn statistical aspects of human speech. When you or I listen to an unfamiliar language, the syllables all run together. Someone unfamiliar with English might, for example, hear *United Nations* as "Uneye Tednay Shuns." Well before our first birthday, our brains were not only discerning word breaks, they were statistically analyzing which syllables, as in "hap-py-ba-by," most often go together. Jenny Saffran and her colleagues (1996; 1999) showed this by exposing 8-month-old infants to a computer voice speaking an unbroken, monotone string of nonsense syllables *(bidakupadotigolabubidaku . . .)*. After just two minutes of exposure, the infants were able to recognize (as indicated by their attention) three-syllable sequences that appeared repeatedly.

Other research offers further testimony to infants' surprising knack for soaking up language. For example, 7-month-old infants can learn simple sentence structures. After repeatedly hearing syllable sequences that follow one rule, such as *ga-ti-ga* and *li-na-li* (an ABA pattern), they listen longer to syllables in a different sequence, such as *wo-fe-fe* (an ABB pattern) rather than *wo-fe-wo*. Their detecting the difference between the two patterns supports the idea that babies come with a built-in readiness to learn grammatical rules (Marcus et al., 1999).

• Under Chomsky's influence, some researchers also infer a "universal moral grammar"—an innate sense of right and wrong—that comes prewired by evolution and gets refined by culture (Hauser, 2006; Mikhail, 2007). •

Susan Meiselas/Magnum Photos

Creating a language Brought together as if on a desert island (actually a school), Nicaragua's young deaf children over time drew upon sign gestures from home to create their own Nicaraguan Sign Language, complete with words and intricate grammar. Our biological predisposition for language does not create language in a vacuum. But activated by a social context, nature and nurture work creatively together (Osborne, 1999; Sandler et al., 2005; Senghas & Coppola, 2001).
▲ . . . .

UNIT 7B

TROUBLESHOOTING

Most researchers recognize a distinction between "critical" and "sensitive" periods. Typically, critical periods are more rigid than sensitive periods. Critical periods suggest a finite amount of time during which a skill must be learned. Sensitive periods suggest an ideal amount of time during which a skill ought to be learned, but if the skill is not learned in time, it can be learned eventually, but perhaps not as easily.

 TEACHING TIP

Linguistic competence refers to the ability to produce and understand utterances we have never heard before. Ronald Macaulay illustrates this with the following sentence: "Karl Marx was playing bridge with Abraham Lincoln, Winston Churchill, and Mary Queen of Scots when Tarzan walked in." No listener has ever encountered this sentence before but anyone who speaks English would immediately understand it.

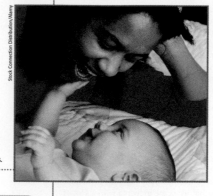

▼ **A natural talent** Human infants come with a remarkable capacity to soak up language. But the particular language they learn will reflect their unique interactions with others.

> "Childhood is the time for language, no doubt about it. Young children, the younger the better, are good at it; it is child's play. It is a onetime gift to the species."
>
> Lewis Thomas,
> *The Fragile Species*, 1992

▼ **No means no—no matter how you say it!** Deaf children of Deaf-signing parents and hearing children of hearing parents have much in common. They develop language skills at about the same rate, and they are equally effective at opposing parental wishes and demanding their way.

> "Children can learn multiple languages without an accent and with good grammar, if they are exposed to the language before puberty. But after puberty, it's very difficult to learn a second language so well. Similarly, when I first went to Japan, I was told not even to bother trying to bow, that there were something like a dozen different bows and I was always going to 'bow with an accent.'"
>
> Psychologist Stephen M. Kosslyn,
> "The World in the Brain," 2008

But are we capable of performing this same feat of statistical analysis throughout our life span? Many researchers believe not. Childhood seems to represent a *critical* (or "sensitive") *period* for mastering certain aspects of language (Hernandez & Li, 2007). Deaf children who gain hearing with cochlear implants by age 2 develop better oral speech than do those who receive implants after age 4 (Greers, 2004). And whether children are deaf or hearing, later-than-usual exposure to language (at age 2 or 3) unleashes their brain's idle language capacity, producing a rush of language. But children who have not been exposed to either a spoken or a signed language during their early years (by about age 7) gradually lose their ability to master *any* language. Natively deaf children who learn sign language after age 9 never learn it as well as those who become deaf at age 9 after learning English. They also never learn English as well as other natively deaf children who learned sign in infancy (Mayberry et al., 2002). The striking conclusion: When a young brain does not learn *any* language, its language-learning capacity never fully develops.

After the window for learning language closes, learning a second language seems more difficult. People who learn a second language as adults usually speak it with the accent of their first. Grammar learning is similarly more difficult. Jacqueline Johnson and Elissa Newport (1991) asked Korean and Chinese immigrants to identify whether each of 276 English sentences (*"Yesterday the hunter shoots a deer"*) was grammatically correct or incorrect. Some test-takers had arrived in the United States in early childhood, others as adults, but all had been in the country for approximately 10 years. Nevertheless, as **FIGURE 7B.9** reveals, those who learned their second language early learned it best. The older the age at which one emigrates to a new country, the harder it is to learn its language (Hakuta et al., 2003).

The impact of early experiences is also evident in language learning in the 90+ percent of deaf children born to hearing-nonsigning parents. These children typically do not experience language during their early years. Compared with children exposed to sign language from birth, those who learn to sign as teens or adults are like immigrants who learn English after childhood. They can master the basic words and learn to order them, but they never become as fluent as native signers in producing and comprehending subtle grammatical differences (Newman et al., 2002). Moreover, the late-learners show less brain activity in right hemisphere regions that are active as native signers read sign language (Newman et al., 2002). As a flower's growth will be stunted without nourishment, so, too, children will typically become linguistically stunted if isolated from language during the critical period for its acquisition. The altered brain activity in those deprived of early language raises a question: How does the maturing brain normally process language?

* * *

Returning to our debate about how deserving we are of our name *Homo sapiens*, let's pause to issue an interim report card. On decision making and judgment, our error-

---

? **CRITICAL THINKING**

Since children can learn languages easier than adults, many educators and linguists believe that second (and even third) languages should be taught in elementary school rather than high school. Explore this issue with your students:

- Are world languages taught in elementary schools in your district? Why or why not?

- Is world language instruction the same in elementary schools as it is in high schools, with an emphasis on grammar, vocabulary, and conversational speaking? Why or why not?

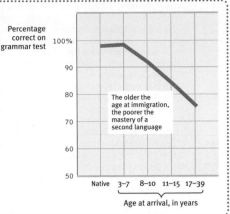

Percentage correct on grammar test

The older the age at immigration, the poorer the mastery of a second language

Age at arrival, in years

➤ FIGURE 7B.9

New language learning gets harder with age Young children have a readiness to learn language. Ten years after coming to the United States, Asian immigrants took a grammar test. Although there is no sharply defined critical period for second language learning, those who arrived before age 8 understood American English grammar as well as native speakers did. Those who arrived later did not. (From Johnson & Newport, 1991.)

CULTURAL CONNECTIONS

With their permission, have students who speak different languages at home discuss their experiences with learning a new language. Have students compare and contrast their own experiences learning a second language without an immersion experience.

CRITICAL THINKING

Have students give grades like Myers does for problem solving, thinking, creativity, and other cognitive abilities. Have them write a short paragraph justifying each grade.

prone species might rate a C+. On problem solving, where humans are inventive yet vulnerable to fixation, we would probably receive a better grade, perhaps a B. On cognitive efficiency, our fallible but quick heuristics earn us an A. And when it comes to our creativity and our learning and using language, the awestruck experts would surely award the human species an A+.

BEFORE YOU MOVE ON . . .

➤ **ASK YOURSELF**

There has been controversy at some universities about allowing fluency in sign language to fulfill a second-language requirement for an undergraduate degree. What is your opinion?

➤ **TEST YOURSELF 2**

If children are not yet speaking, is there any reason to think they would benefit from parents and other caregivers reading to them?

Answers to the Test Yourself questions can be found in Appendix E at the end of the book.

Thinking and Language

11: What is the relationship between language and thinking?

THINKING AND LANGUAGE INTRICATELY intertwine. Asking which comes first is one of psychology's chicken-and-egg questions. Do our ideas come first and we wait for words to name them? Or are our thoughts conceived in words and therefore unthinkable without them?

Language Influences Thinking

Linguist Benjamin Lee Whorf contended that language determines the way we think. According to Whorf's (1956) **linguistic determinism** hypothesis, different languages impose different conceptions of reality: "Language itself shapes a man's basic

"It is the way systems interact and have a dynamic interdependence that is—unless one has lost all sense of wonder—quite awe-inspiring."
Simon Conway Morris, "The Boyle Lecture," 2005

::**linguistic determinism** Whorf's hypothesis that language determines the way we think.

 TEACHING TIP

At this point, you may want to use **Classroom Exercise: *Doublespeak*** (p. 27) from Bolt's Teacher's Resource Binder.

UNIT 7B

CRITICAL THINKING

Give students some simple words—big, good, person, go—and have them come up with as many different synonyms for those words as they can generate. Have them discuss how the meanings of the synonyms are different. You can use this discussion as an opportunity to teach students about *denotation* and *connotation*.

- **Denotation** is the explicit definition of the word. It is commonly thought of as the dictionary definition.

- **Connotation** is the underlying, secondary meaning of the word. It is commonly thought of as the emotional or contextual meaning.

> "Language is not a straight jacket."
> Psychologist Lila Gleitman,
> American Association for the
> Advancement of Science Convention, 2002

● Before reading on, use a pen or pencil to sketch this idea: "The girl pushes the boy." Now see the inverted margin note below. ●

How did you illustrate "the girl pushes the boy."? Anne Maass and Aurore Russo (2003) report that people whose language reads from left to right mostly position the pushing girl on the left. Those who read and write Arabic, a right-to-left language, mostly place her on the right. This spatial bias appears only in those old enough to have learned their culture's writing system (Dobel et al., 2007).

● Perceived distances between cities also grow when two cities are in different countries rather than in the same country (Burris & Branscombe, 2005). ●

➤ FIGURE 7B.10

Language and perception Emre Özgen (2004) reports that when people view blocks of equally different colors, they perceive those with different names as more different. Thus the "green" and "blue" in contrast A may appear to differ more than the two similarly different blues in contrast B.

ideas." The Hopi, Whorf noted, have no past tense for their verbs. Therefore, he contended, a Hopi could not so readily *think* about the past.

To say that language *determines* the way we think is much too strong. But to those who speak two dissimilar languages, such as English and Japanese, it seems obvious that a person may think differently in different languages (Brown, 1986). Unlike English, which has a rich vocabulary for self-focused emotions such as anger, Japanese has more words for interpersonal emotions such as sympathy (Markus & Kitayama, 1991). Many bilinguals report that they have different senses of self, depending on which language they are using (Matsumoto, 1994). They may even reveal different personality profiles when taking the same test in their two languages (Dinges & Hull, 1992). "Learn a new language and get a new soul," says a Czech proverb.

Michael Ross, Elaine Xun, and Anne Wilson (2002) demonstrated this by inviting China-born, bilingual University of Waterloo students to describe themselves in English or Chinese. English-language versions of self-descriptions fit typical Canadian profiles: Students expressed mostly positive self-statements and moods. Responding in Chinese, students gave typically Chinese self-descriptions: They reported more agreement with Chinese values and roughly equal positive and negative self-statements and moods. Their language use seemed to shape how they thought of themselves.

A similar personality change occurs as people shift between the cultural frames associated with English and Spanish. English speakers score higher than Spanish speakers on measures of extraversion, agreeableness, and conscientiousness. But is this a language effect? Nairán Ramírez-Esparza and her co-workers (2006) wondered. So they had samples of bicultural, bilingual Americans and Mexicans take the tests in each language. Sure enough, when using English they expressed their somewhat more extraverted, agreeable, and conscientious selves (and the differences were not due to how the questionnaires were translated).

So our words may not *determine* what we think, but they do *influence* our thinking (Hardin & Banaji, 1993; Özgen, 2004). We use our language in forming categories. In Brazil, the isolated Piraha tribespeople have words for the numbers *1* and *2*, but numbers above that are simply "many." Thus if shown 7 nuts in a row, they find it very difficult to lay out the same number from their own pile (Gordon, 2004).

Words also influence our thinking about colors. Whether we live in New Mexico, New South Wales, or New Guinea, we *see* colors much the same, but we use our native language to *classify* and *remember* colors (Davidoff, 2004; Roberson et al., 2004, 2005). If that language is English, you might view three colors and call two of them "yellow" and one of them "blue." Later you would likely see and recall the yellows as being more similar. But if you were a member of Papua New Guinea's Berinmo tribe, which has words for two different shades of yellow, you would better recall the distinctions between the two yellows.

Perceived differences grow when we assign different names to colors. On the color spectrum, blue blends into green—until we draw a dividing line between the portions we call "blue" and "green." Although equally different on the color spectrum (FIGURE 7B.10), two different "blues" (or two different "greens") that share the same name are harder to distinguish than two items with the different names "blue" and "green" (Özgen, 2004).

Given words' subtle influence on thinking, we do well to choose our words carefully. Does it make any difference whether I write, "A child learns language as *he* interacts with *his* caregivers" or "Children learn language as *they* interact with *their* caregivers"? Many studies have found that it does. When hearing the generic *he* (as in "the artist and his work") people are more likely to picture a male (Henley, 1989; Ng, 1990). If *he* and *his* were truly gender-free, we shouldn't skip a beat when hearing that "man, like other mammals, nurses his young."

To expand language is to expand the ability to think. As Unit 9 points out, young children's thinking develops hand in hand with their language (Gopnik & Meltzoff, 1986). Indeed, it is very difficult to think about or conceptualize certain abstract ideas (commitment, freedom, or

TEACHING TIP

At this point, you may want to use **Lecture/Discussion Topic:** *The Vocabulary of Taste* (p. 25) from Bolt's Teacher's Resource Binder.

rhyming) without language! And what is true for preschoolers is true for everyone: *It pays to increase your word power.* That's why most textbooks, including this one, introduce new words—to teach new ideas and new ways of thinking. And that is why psychologist Steven Pinker (2007) titled his book on language *The Stuff of Thought*.

Increased word power helps explain what McGill University researcher Wallace Lambert (1992; Lambert et al., 1993) calls the *bilingual advantage*. Bilingual children, who learn to inhibit one language while using the other, are also better able to inhibit their attention to irrelevant information. If asked to say whether a sentence (*"Why is the cat barking so loudly?"*) is grammatically correct, they can more efficiently focus on the grammar alone (Bialystok, 2001; Carlson & Meltzoff, 2008).

> "All words are pegs to hang ideas on."
> Henry Ward Beecher,
> *Proverbs from Plymouth Pulpit, 1887*

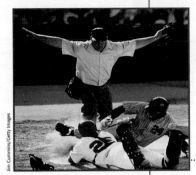

Lambert helped devise a Canadian program that immerses English-speaking children in French. (From 1981 to 2001, the number of non-Quebec Canadian children immersed in French rose from 65,000 to 297,000 [Statistics Canada, 2007].) For most of their first three years in school, the English-speaking children are taught entirely in French, and thereafter gradually shift by the end of their schooling to classes mostly in English. Not surprisingly, the children attain a natural French fluency unrivaled by other methods of language teaching. Moreover, compared with similarly capable children in control groups, they do so without detriment to their English fluency, and with increased aptitude scores, creativity, and appreciation for French-Canadian culture (Genesee & Gándara, 1999; Lazaruk, 2007).

A safe sign We have outfielder William Hoy to thank for baseball sign language. The first deaf player to join the major leagues (1892), he invented hand signals for "Strike!," "Safe!" (shown here) and "Yerr Out!" (Pollard, 1992). Such gestures worked so well that referees in all sports now use invented signs, and fans are fluent in sports sign language.

Whether we are deaf or hearing, minority or majority, language links us to one another. Language also connects us to the past and the future. "To destroy a people, destroy their language," observed poet Joy Harjo.

Thinking in Images

When you are alone, do you talk to yourself? Is "thinking" simply conversing with yourself? Without a doubt, words convey ideas. But aren't there times when ideas precede words? To turn on the cold water in your bathroom, in which direction do you turn the handle? To answer this question, you probably thought not in words but with *implicit* (nondeclarative, procedural) memory—a mental picture of how you do it (see Unit 7A).

Indeed, we often think in images. Artists think in images. So do composers, poets, mathematicians, athletes, and scientists. Albert Einstein reported that he achieved some of his greatest insights through visual images and later put them into words. Pianist Liu Chi Kung showed the value of thinking in images. One year after placing second in the 1958 Tschaikovsky piano competition, Liu was imprisoned during China's cultural revolution. Soon after his release, after seven years without touching a piano, he was back on tour, the critics judging his musicianship better than ever. How did he continue to develop without practice? "I did practice," said Liu, "every day. I rehearsed every piece I had ever played, note by note, in my mind" (Garfield, 1986).

For someone who has learned a skill, such as ballet dancing, even *watching* the activity will activate the brain's internal simulation of it, reported one British research team after collecting fMRIs as people watched videos (Calvo-Merino et al., 2004). So, too, will imagining an activity. **FIGURE 7B.11** shows an fMRI

• Many native English speakers, including most Americans, are monolingual. Most humans are bilingual or multilingual. Does monolingualism limit people's ability to comprehend the thinking of other cultures? •

➤ **FIGURE 7B.11**

The power of imagination Imagining a physical activity triggers action in the same brain areas that are triggered when actually performing that activity. These fMRIs show a person imagining the experience of pain, which activates some of the same areas in the brain as the actual experience of pain.

TEACHING TIP

Hope theory, formulated by the late C. R. Snyder, reinforces Myers' discussion of the importance of process simulation. According to hope theory, goals are important for having hope, but a goal alone is not enough. One must have pathways for reaching those goals and agency (beliefs about capability) for achieving those goals. Shelley Taylor's and C. R. Snyder's research seems complementary here.

A thoughtful art Playing the piano engages thinking without language. In the absence of a piano, mental practice can sustain one's skill. ▲

➤ **FIGURE 7B.12**

The interplay of thought and language The traffic runs both ways between thinking and language. Thinking affects our language, which affects our thought.

 What time is it now? When I asked you (in the section on overconfidence) to estimate how quickly you would finish this unit, did you underestimate or overestimate? ●

of a person imagining the experience of pain, activating neural networks that are active during actual pain (Grèzes & Decety, 2001).

Small wonder, then, that "mental practice has become a standard part of training" for Olympic athletes (Suinn, 1997). One experiment on mental practice and basketball foul shooting tracked the University of Tennessee women's team over 35 games (Savoy & Beitel, 1996). During that time, the team's free-throw shooting increased from approximately 52 percent in games following standard physical practice to some 65 percent after mental practice. Players had repeatedly imagined making foul shots under various conditions, including being "trash-talked" by their opposition. In a dramatic conclusion, Tennessee won the national championship game in overtime, thanks in part to their foul shooting.

Mental rehearsal can also help you achieve an academic goal, as Shelley Taylor and her UCLA colleagues (1998) demonstrated with two groups of introductory psychology students facing a midterm exam one week later. (Scores of other students formed a control group, not engaging in any mental simulation.) The first group was told to spend five minutes each day visualizing themselves scanning the posted grade list, seeing their A, beaming with joy, and feeling proud. This daily *outcome simulation* had little effect, adding only 2 points to their exam-scores average. Another group spent five minutes each day visualizing themselves effectively studying—reading the chapters, going over notes, eliminating distractions, declining an offer to go out. This daily *process simulation* paid off—this second group began studying sooner, spent more time at it, and beat the others' average by 8 points. *The point to remember:* It's better to spend your fantasy time planning how to get somewhere than to dwell on the imagined destination.

Experiments on thinking without language bring us back to a principle we've seen in earlier units: Much of our information processing occurs outside of consciousness and beyond language. Inside our ever-active brain, many streams of activity flow in parallel, function automatically, are remembered implicitly, and only occasionally surface as conscious words.

* * *

What, then, should we say about the relationship between thinking and language? As we have seen, language does influence our thinking. But if thinking did not also affect language, there would never be any new words. And new words and new combinations of old words express new ideas. The basketball term *slam dunk* was coined after the act itself had become fairly common. So, let us say that *thinking affects our language, which then affects our thought* (**FIGURE 7B.12**).

Psychological research on thinking and language mirrors the mixed views of our species by those in fields such as literature and religion. The human mind is simultaneously capable of striking intellectual failures and of striking intellectual power. Misjudgments are common and can have disastrous consequences. So we do well to appreciate our capacity for error. Yet our efficient heuristics often serve us well. Moreover, our ingenuity at problem solving and our extraordinary power of language mark humankind as almost "infinite in faculties."

BEFORE YOU MOVE ON . . .

➤ **ASK YOURSELF**

Do you use certain words or gestures that only your family or closest circle of friends would understand? Can you envision using these words or gestures to construct a language, as the Nicaraguan children did in building their version of sign?

➤ **TEST YOURSELF 3**

To say that "words are the mother of ideas" assumes the truth of what concept?

Answers to the Test Yourself questions can be found in Appendix E at the end of the book.

TEACHING TIP

At this point, you may want to use **Classroom Exercises:** *Introducing Imagery Research* (p. 28) or *Mental Imagery* (p. 28) or *Creating a Mental Model* (p. 30) from Bolt's Teacher's Resource Binder.

UNIT REVIEW: Thinking, Problem Solving, Creativity, and Language

Thinking

1: What are the functions of concepts?

Cognition is a term covering all the mental activities associated with thinking, knowing, remembering, and communicating. We use *concepts*, mental groupings of similar objects, events, ideas, or people, to simplify and order the world around us. In creating hierarchies, we subdivide these categories into smaller and more detailed units. We form some concepts, such as triangles, by definition (three-sided objects), but we form most around *prototypes*, or best examples of a category.

2: What strategies assist our problem solving?

An *algorithm* is a time-consuming but thorough set of rules or procedures (such as a step-by-step description for evacuating a building during a fire) that guarantees a solution to a problem. A *heuristic* is a simpler thinking strategy (such as running for an exit if you smell smoke) that may allow us to solve problems quickly, but sometimes leads us to incorrect solutions. *Insight* is not a strategy-based solution, but rather a sudden flash of inspiration that solves a problem.

3: What is creativity, and what fosters it?

Creativity is the ability to produce novel and valuable ideas. It correlates somewhat with intelligence, but beyond a score of 120, that correlation dwindles. It also correlates with expertise, imaginative thinking skills, a venturesome personality, intrinsic motivation, and the support offered by a creative environment.

4: What obstacles hinder our problem solving?

Obstacles to successful problem solving are the *confirmation bias*, which predisposes us to verify rather than challenge our hypotheses, and *fixation*, such as *mental set* and *functional fixedness*, which may prevent us from taking the fresh perspective that would let us solve the problem.

5: How do heuristics, overconfidence, and belief perseverance influence our decisions and judgments?

The *representativeness heuristic* leads us to judge the likelihood of things in terms of how they represent our prototype for a group of items. The *availability heuristic* leads us to judge the likelihood of things based on how readily they come to mind, which often leads us to fear the wrong things. We are often more confident than correct. Once we have formed a belief and explained it, the explanation may linger in our minds even if the belief gets discredited—the result is *belief perseverance*. A remedy for belief perseverance is to consider how we might have explained an opposite result.

6: How do smart thinkers use intuition?

Although it sometimes leads us astray, human *intuition*—effortless, immediate, automatic feeling or thought—can give us instant help when we need it. Experts in a field grow adept at making quick, shrewd judgments. Smart thinkers will welcome their intuitions but check them against available evidence.

7: What is framing?

Framing is the way a question or statement is worded. Subtle wording differences can dramatically alter our responses.

Language

8: What are the structural components of a language?

Phonemes are a language's basic units of sound. *Morphemes* are the elementary units of meaning. *Grammar*—the system of rules that enables us to communicate—includes *semantics* (rules for deriving meaning) and *syntax* (rules for ordering words into sentences).

9: What are the milestones in language development?

The timing varies from one child to another, but all children follow the same sequence. At about 4 months of age, infants *babble*, making sounds found in languages located all over the world. By about 10 months, their babbling contains only the sounds found in their household language. Around 12 months of age, children begin to speak in single words. This *one-word stage* evolves into *two-word (telegraphic)* utterances before their second birthday, after which they begin speaking in full sentences.

10: How do we learn language?

Behaviorist B. F. Skinner proposed that we learn language by the familiar principles of association (of sights of things with sounds of words), imitation (of words and syntax modeled by others), and reinforcement (with smiles and hugs after saying something right). Linguist Noam Chomsky argues that we are born with a language acquisition device that biologically prepares us to learn language and that equips us with a universal grammar, which we use to learn a specific language. Cognitive researchers believe childhood is a critical period for learning spoken and signed language.

Thinking and Language

11: What is the relationship between language and thinking?

Although Whorf's *linguistic determinism* hypothesis suggested that language determines thought, it is more accurate to say that language influences thought. Different languages embody different ways of thinking, and immersion in bilingual education can enhance thinking. We often think in images when we use implicit (nondeclarative, procedural) memory—our unconscious memory system for motor and cognitive skills and classically and operantly conditioned associations. Thinking in images can increase our skills when we mentally practice upcoming events.

UNIT 7B

ANSWERS to Multiple-Choice Questions

1. **c.** concepts.
2. **d.** framing.
3. **b.** Recalling published reports of corporate fraud to estimate how much fraud occurs in American business.
4. **e.** A golden retriever (dog)
5. **a.** B. F. Skinner
6. **d.** fixation.
7. **b.** syntax.
8. **a.** images.
9. **d.** units of sound in a language.
10. **e.** overconfidence.
11. **d.** A position of ignorance
12. **c.** intuition.
13. **a.** Deciding that a new kid in school is a nerd because he looks like a nerd.
14. **b.** influence language has on thinking.
15. **a.** exposure to language in early childhood.

Terms and Concepts to Remember

cognition, p. 298
concept, p. 298
prototype, p. 299
algorithm, p. 300
heuristic, p. 300
insight, p. 300
creativity, p. 301
confirmation bias, p. 303
fixation, p. 303
mental set, p. 303

functional fixedness, p. 303
representativeness heuristic, p. 304
availability heuristic, p. 305
overconfidence, p. 306
belief perseverance, p. 307
intuition, p. 308
framing, p. 311
language, p. 313
phoneme, p. 313
morpheme, p. 314

grammar, p. 314
semantics, p. 314
syntax, p. 314
babbling stage, p. 315
one-word stage, p. 316
two-word stage, p. 316
telegraphic speech, p. 316
linguistic determinism, p. 319

AP* Practice Test Questions

Multiple-Choice Questions

1. "Chair," "freedom," and "ball" are all
   a. phonemes.
   b. heuristics.
   c. concepts.
   d. telegraphic utterances.
   e. prototypes.

2. People are more concerned about a medical procedure when told it has a 10 percent death rate than they are when told it has a 90 percent survival rate. This is because of
   a. belief perseverance.
   b. insight.
   c. intuition.
   d. framing.
   e. confirmation bias.

3. Which of the following illustrates a heuristic?
   a. Calculating the area of a rectangle by multiplying the length times the width.
   b. Recalling published reports of corporate fraud to estimate how much fraud occurs in American business.
   c. Looking in each room of your home to find your sleeping cat.
   d. Following a new recipe to bake a cake for your friend.
   e. Trying every key on your mom's key ring until you find the one that unlocks the seldom-used storeroom in the basement.

4. Which of the following represents a prototype for the concept indicated in parentheses?
   a. A whale (mammal)
   b. An ostrich (bird)
   c. A beanbag chair (chair)
   d. An igloo (house)
   e. A golden retriever (dog)

5. Who proposed the idea that language development could be explained with the principles of learning?
   a. B. F. Skinner
   b. Noam Chomsky
   c. Steven Pinker
   d. Benjamin Lee Whorf
   e. Paul Broca

6. The inability to see a problem from a fresh perspective is called
   a. confirmation bias.
   b. insight.
   c. representativeness.
   d. fixation.
   e. availability.

7. In English, we know to put adjectives before nouns because of
   a. semantics.
   b. syntax.
   c. statistical learning.
   d. algorithms.
   e. practice during the babbling stage.

8. Mental rehearsal can improve athletic performance because of the effectiveness of thinking in
   a. images.
   b. morphemes.
   c. telegraphic speech.
   d. semantics.
   e. phonemes.

9. Phonemes are
   a. units of meaning in a language.
   b. a form of syntax.
   c. the basis of grammar.
   d. units of sound in a language.
   e. a form of telegraphic speech.

10. People often underestimate the amount of time it will take to complete a project because of
    a. belief perseverance.
    b. framing.
    c. intuition.
    d. the availability heuristic.
    e. overconfidence.

11. According to Robert Sternberg, which of the following is *not* a component of creativity?
    a. A venturesome personality
    b. Imaginative thinking skills
    c. A creative environment
    d. A position of ignorance
    e. Intrinsic motivation

*AP is a trademark registered and/or owned by the College Board, which was not involved in the production of, and does not endorse, this product.

TECHNOLOGY RESOURCES

These resources will be helpful for teaching the concepts in this portion of the unit:

- *PsychSim 5: My Head Is Spinning; Dueling Brains*
- *Videos: Scientific American Frontiers,* 2nd ed., *Segment 28: Teaching Computers to Think; Segment 18: Talking Babies; Segment 21: Born to Talk*
- *Videos: The Mind,* 2nd ed., *Module 28: Language and Culture; Module 25: Human Language: Signed and Spoken; Module 23: Infant Speech Sound Discrimination; Module 24: Language Predisposition*
- *Video: Digital Media Archive: Psychology,* 1st ed., *Video Clip 21: Chomsky's View of Language Development*

12. German students unfamiliar with American geography guessed that San Diego was larger than San Antonio more frequently than American students made this correct identification. The German students were effectively using
   a. framing.
   b. the representativeness heuristic.
   c. intuition.
   d. belief perseverance.
   e. mental set.

13. Which of the following demonstrates the representativeness heuristic?
   a. Deciding that a new kid in school is a nerd because he looks like a nerd.
   b. Fearing air travel because of memories of plane crashes.
   c. Checking in every drawer to find some matches because matches are usually in drawers.
   d. Having the solution to a word problem pop into your head because you have just successfully solved a similar problem.
   e. Applying for jobs in several local grocery stores because your best friend just got a job in a grocery store.

14. Benjamin Lee Whorf's linguistic determinism hypothesis relates to the
   a. influence thinking has on language.
   b. influence language has on thinking.
   c. role of the language acquisition device.
   d. importance of critical periods in language development.
   e. development of language in nonhuman animals.

15. Noam Chomsky believes that all we need to acquire language is
   a. exposure to language in early childhood.
   b. instruction in grammar.
   c. reinforcement for babbling and other early verbal behaviors.
   d. imitation and drill.
   e. linguistic determinism.

Free-Response Question

Describe the positions of B. F. Skinner and Noam Chomsky in their debate concerning the development of language. Include an explanation of how learning principles and universal grammar relate to language development. Provide evidence or an example that supports each of these scientists' perspectives.

WEB
Multiple-choice self-tests and more may be found at www.worthpublishers.com/myers

Rubric for Grading the Free-Response Question

This is a 6-point question. You should require enough description for each point to be assured of the students' understanding.

B. F. Skinner

- Up to 2 points for Skinner's position: learning principles such as association, imitation, and reinforcement account for the development of language.

- 1 point for evidence or an example supporting Skinner's position. Answers will vary, but should focus on the effect of learning. For example, a child might learn the word "cow" because her mother praises her when she identifies a cow with the proper word when looking at a picture book.

Noam Chomsky

- Up to 2 points for Chomsky's position: an inborn language acquisition device and universal grammar account for the development of language.

- 1 point for evidence or an example supporting Chomsky's position. Answers will vary, but should focus on the effect of inborn abilities. For example, a child might say, "I goed to the store," because he has overgeneralized the grammatical rule for past tense, even though he has never had "goed" modeled for him.

- *ActivePsych: Digital Media Archive*, 2nd ed.: *Learning Language: Language Development in Infants and Toddlers*

- *Video: Scientific American Frontiers Teaching Modules*, 3rd ed.: *Genes and Personality: Understanding Williams Syndrome*

- *Psychology Video Tool Kit: Learning Through Visualization: A Gymnast Acquires New Skills*

Pacing Guide

Use the following guide to determine how many instructional days to devote to this portion of the unit depending on the type of course you teach:

Year-long course: 5–7 days
Block schedule/Semester-long course: 3–4 days

This entire unit (Parts A & B) encompasses 6–8 percent of the AP Exam. Spending an appropriate amount of time on this unit will help students do well on the AP Exam.

TROUBLESHOOTING

This unit addresses content that may be controversial in some communities. Help your students see the science of these topics. Guide students to use this information to make informed choices about their own behavior.

INTERCONNECTING

Motivation is closely tied to both neuroscience and cognition. Help students see the interplay between these two areas in motivation. This will help students see the connections across previously learned material.

326

Suggested Readings

Burger, J. M. (1992). *Desire for control.* New York: Plenum Press.

Frankl, V. (1959). *Man's search for meaning.* New York: Washington Square Press.

Harris, M. (1987). *The sacred cow and the abominable pig.* New York: Simon & Schuster, Inc.

Snyder, C. R. (1994). *The psychology of hope.* New York: Free Press.

Motivation and Emotion:
8A—Motivation

After an ill-fated Saturday morning in the spring of 2003, experienced mountaineer Aron Ralston understands the extent to which motivation can energize and direct behavior. Having bagged nearly all of Colorado's tallest peaks, many of them solo and in winter, Ralston ventured some solo canyon hiking that seemed so risk-free he didn't bother to tell anyone where he was going. In Utah's narrow Bluejohn Canyon, just 150 yards above his final rappel, he was climbing over an 800-pound rock when disaster struck: It shifted and pinned his right wrist and arm. He was, as the title of his book says, caught *Between a Rock and a Hard Place*.

Realizing no one would be rescuing him, Ralston tried with all his might to dislodge the rock. Then, with his dull pocket knife, he tried chipping away at the rock. When that, too, failed, he rigged up ropes to lift the rock. Alas, nothing worked. Hour after hour, then cold night after cold night, he was stuck.

By Tuesday, he had run out of food and water. On Wednesday, as thirst and hunger gnawed, he began saving and sipping his own urine. Using his video recorder, he said his good-byes to family and friends, for whom he now felt intense love: "So again love to everyone. Bring love and peace and happiness and beautiful lives into the world in my honor. Thank you. Love you."

On Thursday, surprised to find himself still alive, Ralston had a seemingly divine insight into his reproductive future, a vision of a preschool boy being scooped up by a one-armed man. With this inspiration, he summoned his remaining strength and his enormous will to live and, over the next hour, willfully broke his bones and then proceeded to use that dull knife to cut off his arm. The moment after putting on a tourniquet, chopping the last piece of skin, and breaking free—and before rappelling with his bleeding half-arm down a 65-foot cliff and hiking 5 miles until finding someone—he was, in his own words, "just reeling with this euphoria . . . having been dead and standing in my grave, leaving my last will and testament, etching 'Rest in peace' on

Motivation personified Aron Ralston's motivation to live and belong energized and directed his sacrificing half of his arm.
▲

Key Terms

motivation

Motivational Concepts
instinct
drive-reduction theory
homeostasis
incentive
hierarchy of needs

Hunger
glucose
set point
basal metabolic rate
anorexia nervosa
bulimia nervosa
binge-eating disorder

Sexual Motivation
sexual response cycle
refractory period
estrogens
testosterone
sexual orientation

Key People

Roy Baumeister
Daryl Bem
Walter Cannon
Charles Darwin
Virginia Johnson
Simon LeVay
Abraham Maslow

William Masters
A. L. Washburn

TEACHING TIP

An effective way to introduce the nature and diversity of human motivation is to ask students, "Why do you think people go to college?" Answers will cover the full range of human motives, from "Eventually they have to earn a living" to "They simply want to know, to increase their competence." The discussion provides an excellent opportunity to illustrate that motivation has both energizing and directional aspects. The diversity of answers also provides a good lead-in to Maslow's hierarchy of motives.

At this point, you may want to use **Lecture/Discussion Topic: Maslow's Hierarchy** (p. 4) or **Student Project/Classroom Exercise: *An Assessment of Your Present Needs*** (p. 4) or **Classroom Exercise: *A Short Measure of Self-Actualization*** (p. 5) from Bolt's Teacher's Resource Binder, which accompanies this text.

 TEACHING TIP

Human instincts have been hard to pinpoint since humans behave so individualistically. Have students compare and contrast behavior of animals and humans, trying to isolate what might be considered instincts for humans.

- What types of behavior are "inherited, preprogrammed, complex behaviors that occur throughout" the human and animal species?

- Where can we draw the line between individual behavior and instinctive behavior?

- Does drive-reduction theory help differentiate between what is considered an instinct and what is an individual behavior? Why or why not?

the wall, all of that, gone and then replaced with having my life again. It was undoubtedly the sweetest moment that I will ever experience" (Ralston, 2004).

Ralston's thirst and hunger, his sense of belonging to others, and his brute will to live and become a father highlight the force of **motivation**: a need or desire that *energizes* behavior and *directs* it toward a goal. His intense emotional experiences of love and joy demonstrate the close ties between our feelings, or *emotions*, and our motivated behaviors. In this unit, we explore our motivations and emotions, and the health effects of intense or prolonged emotions such as anger or stress.

Motivational Concepts

1: From what perspectives do psychologists view motivated behavior?

LET'S STEP BACK NOW AND CONSIDER four perspectives psychologists have used in their attempt to understand motivated behaviors. *Instinct theory* (now replaced by the *evolutionary perspective*) focuses on genetically predisposed behaviors. *Drive-reduction theory* focuses on how our inner pushes and external pulls interact. *Arousal theory* focuses on finding the right level of stimulation. And Abraham Maslow's *hierarchy of needs* describes how some of our needs take priority over others.

Instincts and Evolutionary Psychology

Early in the twentieth century, as the influence of Charles Darwin's evolutionary theory grew, it became fashionable to classify all sorts of behaviors as instincts. If people criticized themselves, it was because of their "self-abasement instinct." If they boasted, it reflected their "self-assertion instinct." After scanning 500 books, one sociologist compiled a list of 5759 supposed human instincts! Before long, this fad for naming instincts collapsed under its own weight. Rather than *explaining* human behaviors, the early instinct theorists were simply *naming* them. It was like "explaining" a bright child's low grades by labeling the child an "underachiever." To name a behavior is *not* to explain it.

To qualify as an **instinct**, a complex behavior must have a fixed pattern throughout a species and be unlearned (Tinbergen, 1951). Such behaviors are common in other species (recall the return of salmon to their birthplace in Unit 6; we will see this in imprinting birds in Unit 9). Human behavior, too, exhibits certain unlearned fixed

"What do you think . . . should we get started on that motivation research or not?"

▼ **Same motive, different wiring** The more complex the nervous system, the more adaptable the organism. Both the people and the weaver bird satisfy their need for shelter in ways that reflect their inherited capacities. The people's behavior is flexible; they can learn whatever skills they need to build a house. The bird's behavior pattern is fixed; it can build only this kind of nest.

 INTERCONNECTING

Darwin's theory of evolution plays a large role in psychology. Many psychologists use this theory as a basis for investigating certain behaviors, from social interactions to emotions, such as fear. Help students see the importance of this theory.

At this point, you may want to use **Lecture/Discussion Topic: *Evolutionary Psychology*** (p. 3) from Bolt's Teacher's Resource Binder.

patterns, including infants' innate reflexes for rooting and sucking. Most psychologists, though, view human behavior as directed both by physiological needs and by psychological wants.

Although instinct theory failed to explain human motives, the underlying assumption that genes predispose species-typical behavior remains as strong as ever. We saw this in Unit 3C's evolutionary explanation of our human similarities. We saw this again in Unit 6's discussion of animals' biological predispositions to learn certain behaviors. And we will see this in later discussions of how evolution might influence our phobias, our helping behaviors, and our romantic attractions.

Drives and Incentives

When the original instinct theory of motivation collapsed, it was replaced by **drive-reduction theory**—the idea that a physiological need creates an aroused state that drives the organism to reduce the need by, say, eating or drinking. With few exceptions, when a physiological need increases, so does a psychological *drive*—an aroused, motivated state.

The physiological aim of drive reduction is **homeostasis**—the maintenance of a steady internal state. An example of homeostasis (literally "staying the same") is the body's temperature-regulation system, which works like a room thermostat. Both systems operate through feedback loops: Sensors feed room temperature to a control device. If the room temperature cools, the control device switches on the furnace. Likewise, if our body temperature cools, blood vessels constrict to conserve warmth, and we feel driven to put on more clothes or seek a warmer environment (**FIGURE 8A.1**).

Not only are we *pushed* by our "need" to reduce drives, we also are *pulled* by **incentives**—positive or negative stimuli that lure or repel us. This is one way our individual learning histories influence our motives. Depending on our learning, the aroma of good food, whether freshly baked pizza or freshly toasted ants, can motivate our behavior. So can the sight of those we find attractive or threatening.

When there is both a need and an incentive, we feel strongly driven. The food-deprived person who smells baking bread feels a strong hunger drive. In the presence of that drive, the baking bread becomes a compelling incentive. For each motive, we can therefore ask, "How is it pushed by our inborn physiological needs and pulled by incentives in the environment?"

Optimum Arousal

We are much more than homeostatic systems, however. Some motivated behaviors actually *increase* arousal. Well-fed animals will leave their shelter to explore and gain information, seemingly in the absence of any need-based drive. Curiosity drives monkeys to monkey around trying to figure out how to unlock a latch that opens nothing or how to open a window that allows them to see outside their room (Butler, 1954). It drives the 9-month-old infant who investigates every accessible corner of the house. It drives you to read this text, and it drives the scientists whose work this text discusses. And it drives explorers and adventurers, such

---

::**motivation** a need or desire that energizes and directs behavior.

::**instinct** a complex behavior that is rigidly patterned throughout a species and is unlearned.

::**drive-reduction theory** the idea that a physiological need creates an aroused tension state (a drive) that motivates an organism to satisfy the need.

::**homeostasis** a tendency to maintain a balanced or constant internal state; the regulation of any aspect of body chemistry, such as blood glucose, around a particular level.

::**incentive** a positive or negative environmental stimulus that motivates behavior.

➤ **FIGURE 8A.1**

Drive-reduction theory Drive-reduction motivation arises from *homeostasis*—an organism's natural tendency to maintain a steady internal state. Thus, if we are water deprived, our thirst drives us to drink and to restore the body's normal state.

The text here does not discuss directly the Yerkes-Dodson curve, an inverted U-shaped graph that shows the relationship between performance and stress. As stress increases from minimal, performance also increases. However, once stress reaches a moderately high level, performance peaks. More stress leads to decreased performance beyond the high point. Therefore, an optimum level of performance occurs when stress is moderate.

DEMO

Using jigsaw puzzles of varying degrees of difficulty, set up three different centers, each having a timer. Have students try to put together the puzzle under varying degrees of stress in each center.

- Students should time themselves putting together each puzzle in 5-, 15-, and 30-second intervals.

- Have them record how many pieces they put in correctly in each timed trial.

- Students should then chart their levels of arousal on a graph. Did their performance get better under higher stress? Why or why not?

TROUBLESHOOTING

Arousal and *stimulation* are two words which will likely elicit giggles and chuckles from students of varying degrees of maturity. Help students see that these words can mean more than the popular connotations they possess.

At this point, you may want to use **Classroom Exercises:** *Exploration Index* (p. 4) or *Sensation-Seeking Scale* (p. 4) from Bolt's Teacher's Resource Binder.

Driven by curiosity Baby monkeys and young children are fascinated by things they've never handled before. Their drive to explore the relatively unfamiliar is one of several motives that do not fill any immediate physiological need.

as Aron Ralston and George Mallory. Asked why he wanted to climb Mount Everest, the *New York Times* reported that Mallory answered, "Because it is there." Those who, like Mallory and Ralston, enjoy high arousal are most likely to enjoy intense music, novel foods, and risky behaviors (Zuckerman, 1979).

So, human motivation aims not to eliminate arousal but to seek optimum levels of arousal. Having all our biological needs satisfied, we feel driven to experience stimulation and we hunger for information. We are "infovores," say neuroscientists Irving Biederman and Edward Vessel (2006), after identifying brain mechanisms that reward us for acquiring information. Lacking stimulation, we feel bored and look for a way to increase arousal to some optimum level. However, with too much stimulation comes stress, and we then look for a way to decrease arousal.

A Hierarchy of Motives

Some needs take priority over others. At this moment, with your needs for air and water hopefully satisfied, other motives—such as your desire to achieve (discussed in Appendix B)—are energizing and directing your behavior. Let your need for water go unsatisfied and your thirst will preoccupy you. Just ask Aron Ralston. Deprived of air, your thirst would disappear.

Abraham Maslow (1970) described these priorities as a **hierarchy of needs** (**FIGURE 8A.2**). At the base of this pyramid are our physiological needs, such as those for food and water. Only if these needs are met are we prompted to meet our need for safety, and then to satisfy the uniquely human needs to give and receive love and to enjoy self-esteem. Beyond this, said Maslow (1971), lies the need to actualize one's full potential. (More on self-esteem and self-actualization in Unit 10.)

Near the end of his life, Maslow proposed that some people also reach a level of self-transcendence. At the self-actualization level, people seek to realize their own potential. At the self-transcendence level, people strive for meaning, purpose, and communion that is beyond the self, that is *transpersonal* (Koltko-Rivera, 2006).

Maslow's hierarchy is somewhat arbitrary; the order of such needs is not universally fixed. People have starved themselves to make a political statement. Nevertheless, the simple idea that some motives are more compelling than others provides a framework for thinking about motivation. Life-satisfaction surveys in 39 nations support this basic idea (Oishi et al., 1999). In poorer nations that lack easy access to money and the food and shelter it buys, financial satisfaction more strongly predicts feelings of well-being. In wealthy nations, where most are able to meet basic needs, home-life satisfaction is a better predictor. Self-esteem matters most in individualist nations, whose citizens tend to focus more on personal achievements than on family and community identity.

"Hunger is the most urgent form of poverty."

Alliance to End Hunger, 2002

::**hierarchy of needs** Maslow's pyramid of human needs, beginning at the base with physiological needs that must first be satisfied before higher-level safety needs and then psychological needs become active.

Myron Zuckerman argues that people differ in the amount of stimulation they need or want. He and others have identified four forms of sensation-seeking:

Thrill- and Adventure-Seeking Some people may seek excitement in risky but socially acceptable activities such as parachute jumping, skydiving, and race-car driving.

Experience-Seeking This represents the desire to seek sensation through the mind, the senses, and a nonconforming lifestyle.

Disinhibition Those who have chosen the middle-class lifestyle but find it boring may seek escape in social drinking and partying.

Boredom Susceptibility This occurs when people have a low tolerance for experiences that are repetitious or constant.

FIGURE 8A.2

Maslow's hierarchy of needs Once our lower-level needs are met, we are prompted to satisfy our higher-level needs. (From Maslow, 1970.) For survivors of the disastrous 2007 Bangladeshi flood, such as this man carefully carrying his precious load of clean water, satisfying very basic needs for water, food, and safety become top priority. Higher-level needs on Maslow's hierarchy, such as respect, self-actualization, and meaning, tend to become far less important during such times.

Let's now consider three representative motives, beginning at the physiological level with hunger and working up through sexual motivation and the need to belong. At each level, we shall see how experience interacts with biology.

BEFORE YOU MOVE ON . . .

➤ **ASK YOURSELF**

Consider your own experiences in relation to Maslow's hierarchy of needs. Have you ever experienced true hunger or thirst that displaced your concern for other, higher-level needs? Do you usually feel safe? Loved? Confident? How often do you feel you are able to address what Maslow called your "self-actualization" needs?

➤ **TEST YOURSELF 1**

While on a long road trip, you suddenly feel very hungry. You see a diner that looks pretty deserted and creepy, but you are *really* hungry, so you stop anyway. What motivational perspective would most easily explain this behavior, and why?

Answers to the Test Yourself questions can be found in Appendix E at the end of the book.

Hunger

A VIVID DEMONSTRATION OF THE supremacy of physiological needs came from starvation experiences in World War II prison camps. David Mandel (1983), a Nazi concentration camp survivor, recalled how a starving "father and son would fight over a piece of bread. Like dogs." One father, whose 20-year-old son stole his bread from under his pillow while he slept, went into a deep depression, asking over and over how his son could do such a thing. The next day the father died. "Hunger does something to you that's hard to describe," Mandel explained.

CULTURAL CONNECTIONS

Do people in other cultures regard the fulfillment of basic needs as an important road to self-actualization? Have students study different cultural and religious teachings about how to achieve the ultimate in life. Is it the same road that Maslow described in his hierarchy?

TEACHING TIP

Viktor Frankl's *Man's Search for Meaning* is an excellent resource for lectures on the hierarchy of needs. Frankl describes his 3 years as an inmate in the Nazi concentration camps at Auschwitz and Dachau. Along with his fellow prisoners, he suffered malnourishment, disease, separation from family, physical torture, and the constant threat of death. He later calculated his odds of surviving at less than one in twenty-eight. He concluded that a critical factor in survival was whether an inmate still found purpose in living. From these experiences Frankl developed his theory of personality and his approach to psychotherapy, called logotherapy.

TEACHING TIP

At this point, you may want to use **Classroom Exercises: *Self-Transcendence Inventory*** (p. 5) or ***The Meaning in Life Questionnaire*** (p. 5) from Bolt's Teacher's Resource Binder.

Hunger is a good motivated behavior to focus on, because it involves physiology and psychology at the same time. If people only ate to satisfy a physiological need, hunger would be a simple process. However, people eat not only to relieve hunger, but they also eat to feel comforted, to socialize, or to relieve boredom. People also refuse to eat for a variety of reasons—to exert control, to lose weight, or to make a political statement. Studying hunger can help you teach your students about the facets of motivated behavior efficiently.

::**glucose** the form of sugar that circulates in the blood and provides the major source of energy for body tissues. When its level is low, we feel hunger.

> "Nobody wants to kiss when they are hungry."
> Dorothea Dix, 1801–1887

To learn more about the results of semistarvation, a research team led by physiologist Ancel Keys (1950), the creator of World War II Army K rations, fed 36 male volunteers—all conscientious objectors to the war—just enough to maintain their initial weight. Then, for six months, they cut this food level in half. The effects soon became visible. Without thinking about it, the men began conserving energy; they appeared listless and apathetic. After dropping rapidly, their body weights eventually stabilized at about 25 percent below their starting weights. Especially dramatic were the psychological effects. Consistent with Maslow's idea of a needs hierarchy, the men became food-obsessed. They talked food. They daydreamed food. They collected recipes, read cookbooks, and feasted their eyes on delectable forbidden foods. Preoccupied with their unfulfilled basic need, they lost interest in sex and social activities. As one participant reported, "If we see a show, the most interesting part of it is contained in scenes where people are eating. I couldn't laugh at the funniest picture in the world, and love scenes are completely dull."

The semistarved men's preoccupations illustrate the power of activated motives to hijack our consciousness. When we are hungry, thirsty, fatigued, or sexually aroused, little else may seem to matter. When you're not, food, water, sleep, or sex just don't seem like such big things in your life, now or ever. (You may recall from Unit 7A a parallel effect of our current good or bad mood on our memories.) In University of Amsterdam studies, Loran Nordgren and his colleagues (2006, 2007) found that people in a motivational "hot" state (from fatigue, hunger, or sexual arousal) become more aware of having had such feelings in the past and more sympathetic to how fatigue, hunger, or sexual arousal might drive others' behavior. Similarly, if preschool children are made to feel thirsty (by eating salty pretzels), they understandably want water; but unlike children who are not thirsty, they also choose water over pretzels for "tomorrow" (Atance & Meltzoff, 2006). Motives matter mightily. Grocery shop with an empty stomach and you are more likely to think that those jelly-filled doughnuts are just what you've always loved and will be wanting tomorrow.

The Physiology of Hunger

2: What physiological factors produce hunger?

Keys' semistarved volunteers felt their hunger in response to a homeostatic system designed to maintain normal body weight and an adequate nutrient supply. But what precisely triggers hunger? Is it the pangs of an empty stomach? That is how it feels. And so it seemed after A. L. Washburn, working with Walter Cannon (Cannon & Washburn, 1912), intentionally swallowed a balloon. When inflated to fill his stomach, the balloon transmitted his stomach contractions to a recording device (**FIGURE 8A.3**). While his stomach was being monitored, Washburn pressed a key each time he felt hungry. The discovery: Washburn was indeed having stomach contractions whenever he felt hungry.

> "The full person does not understand the needs of the hungry."
> Irish proverb

GARFIELD

At this point, you may want to use **Classroom Exercise:** *Motivations-to-Eat Scale* (p. 7) from Bolt's Teacher's Resource Binder.

Washburn swallows balloon, which measures stomach contractions.

Washburn presses key each time he feels hungry.

Stomach contractions

Hunger pangs

Time in minutes

➤ FIGURE 8A.3
Monitoring stomach contractions Using this procedure, Washburn showed that stomach contractions (transmitted by the stomach balloon) accompany our feelings of hunger (indicated by a key press). (From Cannon, 1929.)

Would hunger persist without stomach pangs? To answer that question, researchers removed some rats' stomachs and attached their esophagi to their small intestines (Tsang, 1938). Did the rats continue to eat? Indeed they did. Some hunger persists similarly in humans whose ulcerated or cancerous stomachs have been removed.

If the pangs of an empty stomach are not the only source of hunger, what else matters?

Body Chemistry and the Brain

People and other animals automatically regulate their caloric intake to prevent energy deficits and maintain a stable body weight. This suggests that somehow, somewhere, the body is keeping tabs on its available resources. One such resource is the blood sugar **glucose**. Increases in the hormone *insulin* (secreted by the pancreas) diminish blood glucose, partly by converting it to stored fat. If your blood glucose level drops, you won't consciously feel this change. But your brain, which is automatically monitoring your blood chemistry and your body's internal state, will trigger hunger. Signals from your stomach, intestines, and liver (indicating whether glucose is being deposited or withdrawn) all signal your brain to motivate eating or not.

But how does the brain integrate and respond to these messages? More than a half-century ago, researchers began unraveling this puzzle when they located hunger controls within the *hypothalamus*, that small but complex neural traffic intersection deep in the brain (**FIGURE 8A.4**).

Two distinct hypothalamic centers influence eating. Activity along the sides of the hypothalamus (the *lateral hypothalamus*) brings on hunger. If electrically stimulated there, well-fed animals begin to eat. (If the area is destroyed, even starving animals have no interest in food.) Recent research helps explain this behavior. When a rat is food-deprived, its blood sugar levels wane and the lateral hypothalamus churns out the hunger-triggering hormone *orexin*. When given orexin, rats become ravenously hungry (Sakurai et al., 1998).

Activity in the second center—the lower mid-hypothalamus (the *ventromedial hypothalamus*)—depresses hunger. Stimulate this area and an animal will stop eating; destroy it and the animal's stomach and intestines will process food more rapidly, causing it to become extremely fat (Duggan & Booth, 1986; Hoebel & Teitelbaum, 1966). This discovery helped explain why some patients with tumors near the base of the brain (in what we now realize is the hypothalamus) eat excessively and become very overweight (Miller, 1995). Rats with mid-hypothalamus lesions eat more often,

Pix° Elation from Fran Heyl Associates

➤ FIGURE 8A.4
The hypothalamus As we saw in Unit 3B, the hypothalamus (colored red) performs various body maintenance functions, including control of hunger. Blood vessels supply the hypothalamus, enabling it to respond to our current blood chemistry as well as to incoming neural information about the body's state.

Richard Howard

Evidence for the brain's control of eating A lesion near the ventromedial area of the hypothalamus caused this rat's weight to triple.
▲

 TEACHING TIP

Extremes in blood sugar levels can be harmful to one's health.

- **Hypoglycemia** occurs when blood sugar levels run too low through a lack of food. This condition is accompanied by feelings of dizziness and weakness.

- **Hyperglycemia** occurs when blood sugar levels run too high. This condition, also known as diabetes, is caused by cells in the pancreas that do not metabolize carbohydrates.

 TROUBLESHOOTING

The lateral hypothalamus (LH) is the part of the brain that controls the desire to eat. When this structure is stimulated, a rat will eat without becoming satiated. The ventromedial hypothalamus (VMH) is the part of the brain that controls satiety. When this is stimulated, a rat will starve to death, acting as though it has eaten and does not need food. These parts are often confused. Use this mnemonic to help students remember the difference:

- Lateral hypothalamus (LH) gives one a **L**arge **H**unger, or the desire to eat.

- Ventromedial hypothalamus (VMH) gives one **V**ery **M**inute **H**unger, or the feeling of satiety.

TEACHING TIP

Even though the names of these hormones are not in bold, they are important for students to know. Be sure students pay attention to the descriptions of each so they can know which hormones are important for feeling hunger and which are important for feeling satiety.

RESEARCH

Research into the role of the hypothalamus in weight control has raised hope of a weight-control pill that triggers the appropriate part of this region of the brain either to feel hungry or to feel satiated. In a class discussion, elicit students' responses to the following questions:

- Why would such a pill be popular?

- How would this pill affect eating habits of people over time?

- What might be some long-term effects on health from the use of this pill?

➤ **FIGURE 8A.5**
The appetite hormones
Insulin: Secreted by pancreas; controls blood glucose.
Leptin: Secreted by fat cells; when abundant, causes brain to increase metabolism and decrease hunger.
Orexin: Hunger-triggering hormone secreted by hypothalamus.
Ghrelin: Secreted by empty stomach; sends "I'm hungry" signals to the brain.
Obestatin: Secreted by stomach; sends out "I'm full" signals to the brain.
PYY: Digestive tract hormone; sends "I'm *not* hungry" signals to the brain.

produce more fat, and use less fat for energy, rather like a miser who runs every bit of extra money to the bank and resists taking any out (Pinel, 1993).

In addition to producing orexin, the hypothalamus monitors levels of the body's other appetite hormones (**FIGURE 8A.5**). One of these is *ghrelin*, a hunger-arousing hormone secreted by an empty stomach. When people with severe obesity undergo bypass surgery that seals off part of the stomach, the remaining stomach then produces much less ghrelin, and their appetite lessens (Lemonick, 2002). *Obestatin*, a sister hormone to ghrelin, is produced by the same gene, but obestatin sends out a fullness signal that suppresses hunger (Zhang et al., 2005). Other appetite-suppressants include *PYY*, a hormone secreted by the digestive tract, and *leptin*, a protein that is secreted by fat cells and acts to diminish the rewarding pleasure of food (Farooqi et al., 2007).

Experimental manipulation of appetite hormones has raised hopes for an appetite-reducing medication. Such a nose spray or skin patch might counteract the body's hunger-producing chemicals, or mimic or increase the levels of hunger-dampening chemicals. The recent ups and downs of excitement over PYY illustrate the intense search for a substance that might someday be a treatment, if not a magic bullet, for obesity. The initial report that PYY suppresses appetite in mice was followed by a skeptical statement from 12 laboratories reporting a big fat disappointment: The PYY finding did not replicate. But a few months later, this was followed by newer studies using different methods that *did* find at least a temporary appetite-suppressing effect (Gura, 2004).

The complex interaction of appetite hormones and brain activity may help explain the body's apparent predisposition to maintain itself at a particular weight level. When semistarved rats fall below their normal weight, this "weight thermostat" signals the body to restore the lost weight: Hunger increases and energy expenditure decreases. If body weight rises—as happens when rats are force-fed—hunger decreases and energy expenditure increases. This stable weight toward which semistarved and overstuffed rats return is their **set point** (Keesey & Corbett, 1983). In rats and humans, heredity influences body type and set point.

Our bodies regulate weight through the control of food intake, energy output, and **basal metabolic rate**—the rate of energy expenditure for maintaining basic body functions when the body is at rest. By the end of their 24 weeks of semistarvation, the men who participated in Keys' experiment had stabilized at three-quarters of their normal weight, while taking in half of their previous calories. How did they manage this? By reducing their energy expenditure, partly through inactivity but partly because of a 29 percent drop in their basal metabolic rate.

Some researchers, however, doubt that our bodies have a preset tendency to maintain optimum weight (Assanand et al., 1998). They point out that slow, sustained changes in body weight can alter one's set point, and that psychological factors also sometimes drive our feelings of hunger. Given unlimited access to a wide variety of tasty foods, people and other animals tend to overeat and gain weight (Raynor & Epstein, 2001). For all these reasons, some researchers have abandoned the idea of a biologically fixed *set point*. They prefer the term *settling point* to indicate the level at which a person's weight settles in response to caloric intake and expenditure (which are influenced by environment as well as biology).

The Psychology of Hunger

3: What psychological and cultural factors influence hunger?

Our eagerness to eat is indeed pushed by our physiological state—our body chemistry and hypothalamic activity. Yet there is more to hunger than meets the stomach. This was strikingly apparent when Paul Rozin and his trickster colleagues (1998) tested two patients with amnesia who had no memory for events occurring more than a minute ago. If, 20 minutes after eating a normal lunch, the patients were offered another, both readily consumed it . . . and usually a third meal offered 20 minutes after the second was finished. This suggests that part of knowing when to eat is our memory of our last meal. As time passes since we last ate, we anticipate eating again and start feeling hungry.

Psychological influences on eating behavior are most striking when the desire to be thin overwhelms normal homeostatic pressures.

Taste Preferences: Biology and Culture

Body chemistry and environmental factors together influence not only when we feel hungry, but also what we hunger for—our taste preferences. When feeling tense or depressed, do you crave starchy, carbohydrate-laden foods? Carbohydrates help boost levels of the neurotransmitter serotonin, which has calming effects. When stressed, even rats find it extra rewarding to scarf Oreos (Artiga et al., 2007; Boggiano et al., 2005).

Our preferences for sweet and salty tastes are genetic and universal. Other taste preferences are conditioned, as when people given highly salted foods develop a liking for excess salt (Beauchamp, 1987), or when people who have been sickened by a food develop an aversion to it. (The frequency of children's illnesses provides many chances for them to learn food aversions.)

Culture affects taste, too. Bedouins enjoy eating the eye of a camel, which most North Americans would find repulsive. But then North Americans and Europeans shun horse, dog, and rat meat, all of which are prized elsewhere.

• Over the next 40 years you will eat about 20 tons of food. If, during those years, you increase your daily intake by just .01 ounce more than required for your energy needs, you will gain 24 pounds (Martin et al., 1991). •

"Never get a tattoo when you're drunk and hungry."

::**set point** the point at which an individual's "weight thermostat" is supposedly set. When the body falls below this weight, an increase in hunger and a lowered metabolic rate may act to restore the lost weight.

::**basal metabolic rate** the body's resting rate of energy expenditure.

 TEACHING TIP

Taste preferences often seem arbitrary and irrational. Muslims and Jews don't eat pigs, Hindus don't eat cows, and Westerners are unlikely to eat bugs. Muslims and Jews consider the pig unclean, Hindus believe the cow is sacred, and Westerners are usually disgusted by the thought of eating an ant. An anthropologist at the University of Florida argues that all taste preferences ultimately result from a careful calculation of rewards and costs. Our disgust with ants and termites, for example, originated because gathering them was a waste of energy. Many other foods were more readily available and hence more easily acquired. Not so for certain Amazonian tribes, who regard a stick full of crawling ants or termites to be a real delicacy.

 TEACHING TIP

At this point, you may want to use **Lecture/Discussion Topic:** *Taste Preferences—Learned and Genetic* (p. 6) from Bolt's Teacher's Resource Binder.

 TEACHING TIP

Mention some of the following findings about the importance of taste preferences and hunger:

- Some researchers argue that at some point in human evolution, being a supertaster may have improved chances of survival in parts of the world where there were many poisonous plants, since these tend to taste bitter. On the other hand, being a nontaster could have been an advantage in safer environments.
- Supertasters seem to be more sensitive to tastes because they have more taste buds on their tongues.
- Supertasters tend to find bitter foods nastily bitter and sweet foods excessively sweet. Dairy fat tastes creamier, chili peppers are hotter, and carbonated beverages may seem unpleasantly bubbly.
- Supertasters find that saccharin has an unpleasant aftertaste; nontasters are likely to say it tastes fine.
- Female supertasters are less likely to be overweight and appear to have better cholesterol levels.

An acquired taste For Alaska Natives (left), but not for most other North Americans, whale blubber is a tasty treat. For these Campa Indians in Peru (right), roasted ants are similarly delicious. People everywhere learn to enjoy the foods prescribed by their culture.

TEACHING TIP

The text suggests that culture has a large impact on our eating habits and taste preferences. With permission, interview students from other cultures to find out what foods they eat in their culture that are different from foods eaten in American culture. Also, have students research how other cultures view body images—whether thin is "in" elsewhere in the world.

TEACHING TIP

The studies in unit bias discussed here relate to whether people are "internal eaters," those who eat based on internal cues, such as hunger, or "external eaters," those who eat when food is available. Discuss with students whether they believe they are "internals" or "externals." What foods can they resist? What can they not resist? What environmental or cultural factors influence their eating habits? This discussion will help students apply this knowledge to their own lives.

Rats themselves tend to avoid unfamiliar foods (Sclafani, 1995). So do we, especially those that are animal-based. In experiments, people have tried novel fruit drinks or ethnic foods. With repeated exposure, their appreciation for the new taste typically increases; moreover, exposure to one set of novel foods increases our willingness to try another (Pliner, 1982; Pliner et al., 1993). *Neophobia* (dislike of things unfamiliar) surely was adaptive for our ancestors, protecting them from potentially toxic substances.

Other taste preferences are also adaptive. For example, the spices most commonly used in hot-climate recipes—where food, especially meat, spoils more quickly—inhibit the growth of bacteria (**FIGURE 8A.6**). Pregnancy-related nausea is another example of adaptive taste preferences. Its associated food aversions peak about the tenth week, when the developing embryo is most vulnerable to toxins.

The Ecology of Eating

To a surprising extent, situations also control our eating. You perhaps have noticed one situational phenomenon, though you likely have underestimated its power: People eat more when eating with others (Herman et al., 2003; Hetherington et al., 2006). As we will see in Unit 14, the presence of others tends to amplify our natural behavior tendencies (a phenomenon called *social facilitation*, which helps explain why, after a party or a feast, we may realize that we have overeaten).

Another aspect of the ecology of eating, which Andrew Geier and his colleagues (2006) call *unit bias*, occurs with similar mindlessness. In collaboration with researchers at France's National Center for Scientific Research, they explored a possible explanation of why French waistlines are smaller than American waistlines. From soda drinks to yogurt sizes, the French offer foods in smaller portion sizes. Does it matter? (One could as well order two small sandwiches as one large one.)

To find out, the investigators offered people varieties of free snacks. For example, in the lobby of an apartment house, they laid out either full or half pretzels, big or little Tootsie Rolls, or a big bowl of M&M's with either a small or large serving scoop. Their consistent result: Offered a supersized standard portion, people put away more calories. Another research team led by Brian Wansink (2006) invited some Americans to help themselves to ice cream. They, too, found a unit bias: Even nutrition experts took 31 percent more when given a big rather than small bowl, and 15 percent more when scooping it with a big scoop rather than a small one. For cultures struggling with rising obesity rates, the principle—that ecology influences eating—implies a practical message: Reduce standard portion sizes, and serve food with smaller bowls, plates, and utensils.

> **FIGURE 8A.6**

Hot cultures like hot spices Countries with hot climates, in which food historically spoiled more quickly, feature recipes with more bacteria-inhibiting spices (Sherman & Flaxman, 2001). India averages nearly 10 spices per meat recipe; Finland, 2 spices.

TEACHING TIP

At this point, you may want to use **Lecture/Discussion Topic:** *Environmental Factors in Eating* (p. 8) from Bolt's Teacher's Resource Binder.

Eating Disorders

4: How do anorexia nervosa, bulimia nervosa, and binge-eating disorder demonstrate the influence of psychological forces on physiologically motivated behaviors?

Our bodies are naturally disposed to maintain a normal weight, including stored energy reserves for times when food becomes unavailable. Yet sometimes psychological influences overwhelm biological wisdom. This becomes painfully clear in three eating disorders.

- **Anorexia nervosa** typically begins as a weight-loss diet. People with anorexia—usually adolescents and 3 out of 4 times females—drop significantly (15 percent or more) below normal weight. Yet they feel fat, fear gaining weight, and remain obsessed with losing weight. About half of those with anorexia display a binge-purge-depression cycle.

- **Bulimia nervosa** may also be triggered by a weight-loss diet, broken by gorging on forbidden foods. Binge-purge eaters—mostly women in their late teens or early twenties—eat the way some people with alcohol dependency drink—in spurts, sometimes influenced by friends who are bingeing (Crandall, 1988). In a cycle of repeating episodes, overeating is followed by compensatory purging (through vomiting or laxative use) or fasting or excessive exercise (Wonderlich et al., 2007). Preoccupied with food (craving sweet and high-fat foods), and fearful of becoming overweight, binge-purge eaters experience bouts of depression and anxiety, most severe during and following binges (Hinz & Williamson, 1987; Johnson et al., 2002). Unlike anorexia, bulimia is marked by weight fluctuations within or above normal ranges, making the condition easy to hide.

- Those who do significant binge eating, followed by remorse—but do not purge, fast, or exercise excessively—are said to have **binge-eating disorder**.

A national study funded by the U.S. National Institute of Mental Health reports that, at some point during their lifetime, 0.6 percent of people meet the criteria for anorexia, 1 percent for bulimia, and 2.8 percent for binge-eating disorder (Hudson et al., 2007). So, how can we explain these disorders?

Eating disorders do *not* provide (as some have speculated) a telltale sign of childhood sexual abuse (Smolak & Murnen, 2002; Stice, 2002). The family environment may provide a fertile ground for the growth of eating disorders in other ways, however.

- Mothers of girls with eating disorders tend to focus on their own weight and on their daughters' weight and appearance (Pike & Rodin, 1991).

- Families of bulimia patients have a higher-than-usual incidence of childhood obesity and negative self-evaluation (Jacobi et al., 2004).

- Families of anorexia patients tend to be competitive, high-achieving, and protective (Pate et al., 1992; Yates, 1989, 1990).

::**anorexia nervosa** an eating disorder in which a person (usually an adolescent female) diets and becomes significantly (15 percent or more) underweight, yet, still feeling fat, continues to starve.

::**bulimia nervosa** an eating disorder characterized by episodes of overeating, usually of high-calorie foods, followed by vomiting, laxative use, fasting, or excessive exercise.

::**binge-eating disorder** significant binge-eating episodes, followed by distress, disgust, or guilt, but without the compensatory purging, fasting, or excessive exercise that marks bulimia nervosa.

▼ **Dying to be thin** Anorexia was identified and named in the 1870s, when it appeared among affluent adolescent girls (Brumberg, 2000). This 1930s photo illustrates the physical condition (left). Many modern-day celebrities have struggled publicly with eating disorders, as when actress Mary-Kate Olsen (right) was admitted to a rehabilitation clinic in Utah for six weeks in 2004 for treatment of anorexia.

Reprinted by permission of *The New England Journal of Medicine*, 207, (Oct. 5, 1932), 611–617.

Reuters/Lucas Jackson (USA)

UNIT 8A

RESEARCH

Have students, both male and female, take their measurements (chest, waist, hip, and leg plus arm circumference) and calculate the averages of these measurements and share that information with the class.

- Into what size clothes would someone with these measurements fit?

- Do magazines portray people who look like they have these measurements?

- Do you feel as though you are the same, smaller, or larger than people featured in magazine ads? Why or why not? How does this make you feel about your body image?

> "Diana remained throughout a very insecure person at heart, almost childlike in her desire to do good for others, so she could release herself from deep feelings of unworthiness, of which her eating disorders were merely a symptom."
>
> Charles, Ninth Earl of Spencer, eulogizing his sister Princess Diana, 1997

"Thanks, but we don't eat."

> "Why do women have such low self-esteem? There are many complex psychological and societal reasons, by which I mean Barbie."
>
> Dave Barry, 1999

"Gee, I had no idea you were married to a supermodel."

Anorexia sufferers often have low self-evaluations, set perfectionist standards, fret about falling short of expectations, and are intensely concerned with how others perceive them (Pieters et al., 2007; Polivy & Herman, 2002; Striegel-Moore et al., 1993, 2007). Some of these factors also predict teen boys' pursuit of unrealistic muscularity (Ricciardelli & McCabe, 2004).

Genetics may influence susceptibility to eating disorders. Twins are somewhat more likely to share the disorder if they are identical rather than fraternal (Fairburn et al., 1999; Kaplan, 2004). In follow-up molecular studies, scientists are searching for culprit genes, which may influence the body's available serotonin and estrogen (Klump & Culbert, 2007).

But these disorders also have cultural and gender components. Body ideals vary across culture and time. In India, women students rate their ideal shape as close to their actual shape. In much of Africa—where plumpness means prosperous and thinness can signal poverty, AIDS, and hunger—bigger seems better (Knickmeyer, 2001).

Bigger does not seem better in Western cultures, where, according to 222 studies of 141,000 people, the rise in eating disorders over the last 50 years has coincided with a dramatic increase in women having a poor body image (Feingold & Mazzella, 1998). In one national survey, nearly one-half of all U.S. women reported feeling negative about their appearance and preoccupied with being or becoming overweight (Cash & Henry, 1995).

Gender differences in body image have surfaced in several studies. In one study of New Zealand university students and 3500 British bank and university staff, men were more likely to *be* overweight and women were more likely to *perceive* themselves as overweight (Emslie et al., 2001; Miller & Halberstadt, 2005). In another study at the University of Michigan, men and women donned either a sweater or a swimsuit and completed a math test while alone in a changing room (Fredrickson et al., 1998). For the women but not the men, wearing the swimsuit triggered self-consciousness and shame that disrupted their math performance. That surely explains why a survey of 52,677 adults found that 16 percent of men and 31 percent of women avoid wearing a swimsuit in public (Frederick et al., 2006). In another informal survey of 60,000 people, 9 in 10 women said they would rather have a perfect body than have a mate with a perfect body; 6 of 10 men preferred the reverse (Lever, 2003).

Those most vulnerable to eating disorders are also those (usually women) who most idealize thinness and have the greatest body dissatisfaction (Striegel-Moore & Bulik, 2007). Should it surprise us, then, that when women view real and doctored images of unnaturally thin models and celebrities, they often feel ashamed, depressed, and dissatisfied with their own bodies—the very attitudes that predispose eating disorders (Grabe et al., 2008)? Eric Stice and his colleagues (2001) tested this idea by giving some adolescent girls (but not others) a 15-month subscription to an American teen-fashion magazine. Compared with their counterparts who had not received the magazine, vulnerable girls—defined as those who were already dissatisfied, idealizing thinness, and lacking social support—exhibited increased body dissatisfaction and eating disorder tendencies. But even ultra-thin models do not reflect the impossible

---

TEACHING TIP

At this point, you may want to use **Classroom Exercises:** *A Survey of Eating Habits* (p. 8) or *Assessing Body Image* (p. 10) from Bolt's Teacher's Resource Binder.

"Skeletons on parade" A recent article used this headline in criticizing superthin models. Do such models make self-starvation fashionable?

standard of the classic Barbie doll, who had, when adjusted to a height of 5 feet 7 inches, a 32–16–29 figure (Norton et al., 1996).

It seems clear that the sickness of today's eating disorders lies in part within our weight-obsessed culture—a culture that says, in countless ways, "Fat is bad," that motivates millions of women to be "always dieting," and that encourages eating binges by pressuring women to live in a constant state of semistarvation. If cultural learning contributes to eating behavior (**FIGURE 8A.7**), then might prevention programs increase acceptance of one's body? From their review of 66 prevention studies, Stice and his colleagues (2007) answer *yes*, and especially if the programs are interactive and focused on girls over age 15.

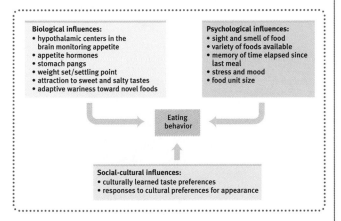

Biological influences:
• hypothalamic centers in the brain monitoring appetite
• appetite hormones
• stomach pangs
• weight set/settling point
• attraction to sweet and salty tastes
• adaptive wariness toward novel foods

Psychological influences:
• sight and smell of food
• variety of foods available
• memory of time elapsed since last meal
• stress and mood
• food unit size

Eating behavior

Social-cultural influences:
• culturally learned taste preferences
• responses to cultural preferences for appearance

➤ **FIGURE 8A.7**
Levels of analysis for our hunger motivation Clearly, we are biologically driven to eat, yet psychological and social-cultural factors strongly influence what, when, and how much we eat.

INTERCONNECTING

In Figure 8A.7, Myers shows the biopsychosocial model in action with eating behavior. Help students see how the model works in this context which is similar to ways the model works in other contexts studied before. Use this model throughout the course to help students see how modern psychology approaches behaviors and mental processes.

TEACHING TIP

Psychology Today conducted readership surveys of body image in 1996. The results are not considered representative because they are based on the first 4000 people to respond to the five-page questionnaire, but the findings are interesting nonetheless:

• A total of 89 percent of women respondents said they want to lose weight; 22 percent of the males said they want to gain weight.

• 15 percent of the women and 11 percent of the men said they would sacrifice more than five years of their lives to be the weight they want.

• Body dissatisfaction affected those women who described themselves as feminists (32 percent) as well as those who said they were more traditional (49 percent). Feminists did indicate that they were less willing to use such drastic measures as vomiting to control their weight.

• Pregnancy was increasingly being viewed as an encumbrance to body image. Some women said they were choosing not to have children for this reason.

• Teasing during childhood or adolescence had a lasting effect on women's feelings about their bodies.

• More than three out of ten women said that models in the media made them feel angry and resentful. Media models made more than four out of ten women feel insecure.

TEACHING TIP

Have students calculate their own BMI using the formula on this page. Have them identify on the chart where their BMI would fit. Have them discuss reasons why BMI might be a good measure of obesity and why it might not be a good measure of obesity. Supporters claim BMI is good because it doesn't just consider weight. BMI also considers one's height as well. Critics claim that other factors, such as metabolism, blood pressure, cholesterol levels, and muscle mass are all important factors in determining obesity, yet BMI does not consider these factors.

TEACHING TIP

Body fat is important for many body functions, including brain processing and reproductive health. Babies need fat to help stimulate neuronal growth. Pre-teens and teens need fat to experience puberty and to continue to be reproductively healthy. Girls with little to no body fat can experience a disruption in their menstrual cycle, and evidence indicates that boys with little to no body fat have decreased sperm counts.

Obesity and Weight Control

5: What factors predispose some people to become and remain obese?

Why do some people gain weight while others eat the same amount and seldom add a pound? And why do so few overweight people win the battle of the bulge? Is there weight-loss hope for the 66 percent of Americans who, according to the Centers for Disease Control, are overweight?

Our bodies store fat for good reasons. Fat is an ideal form of stored energy—a high-calorie fuel reserve to carry the body through periods when food is scarce—a common occurrence in the feast-or-famine existence of our prehistoric ancestors. (Think of that spare tire around the middle as an energy storehouse—biology's counterpart to a hiker's waist-borne snack pack.) No wonder that in most developing societies today, as in Europe in earlier centuries—in fact, wherever people face famine—obesity signals affluence and social status (Furnham & Baguma, 1994).

In those parts of the world where food and sweets are now abundantly available, the rule that once served our hungry distant ancestors (*When you find energy-rich fat or sugar, eat it!*) has become dysfunctional.

Worldwide, estimates the World Health Organization (WHO) (2007), more than 1 billion people are overweight, and 300 million of them are clinically *obese* (defined by WHO as a body mass index of 30 or more—see **FIGURE 8A.8**). In the United States, the adult obesity rate has more than doubled in the last 40 years, reaching 34 percent, and child-teen obesity has quadrupled (CDC, 2007; NCHS, 2007). Australia classifies 54 percent of its population as overweight or obese, with Canada close behind at 49 percent, and France at 42 percent (Australian Bureau of Statistics, 2007; Statistics Canada, 2007). In all these and many other countries, rising obesity rates trail the American rates by just a few years and are projected to increase further, resulting in a "global epidemic" of diabetes (Yach et al., 2006).

> "If we do nothing, in a few years the French will be as fat as Americans."
> Olivier Andrault, food expert with the French Union of Consumers, 2007

➤ **FIGURE 8A.8**

Obesity measured as body mass index (BMI) U.S. government guidelines encourage a BMI under 25. The World Health Organization and many countries define *obesity* as a BMI of 30 or more (although muscular bodies may also have a high BMI). The shading in this graph is based on BMI measurements for these heights and weights. BMI is calculated by using the following formula:

$$\frac{\text{Weight in kg (pounds} \times .45)}{\text{Squared height in meters (inches} \div 39.4)^2} = \text{BMI}$$

RESEARCH

Have students keep a food diary for at least a week. They should record all the food they eat and beverages they drink. At the end of the week, have them reflect on the following questions:

- Compare your eating choices with the FDA's food pyramid. Do your eating habits reflect the recommendations for a healthy diet? Why or why not?

- Why did you eat what you ate and drink what you drank? What were the motives that drove your choices?

- After reflecting upon your eating choices, what would you change? Why? What would you keep the same? Why?

➤ **FIGURE 8A.9**
Obesity and mortality Relative risk of death among healthy nonsmokers rises with extremely high or low body mass index. (Data from 14-year study of 1.05 million Americans, Calle et al., 1999.)

Being slightly overweight poses only modest health risks (Dolan et al., 2007; Gibbs, 2005). Fitness matters more than being a little overweight. But significant obesity increases the risk of diabetes, high blood pressure, heart disease, gallstones, arthritis, and certain types of cancer, thus shortening life expectancy (Olshansky et al., 2005). The risks are greater for apple-shaped people who carry their weight in pot bellies than for pear-shaped people with ample hips and thighs (Greenwood, 1989; Price et al., 2006). New research also has linked women's obesity to their risk of late-life Alzheimer's disease and brain tissue loss (Gustafson et al., 2003, 2004).

Not surprisingly, then, one study (Calle et al., 1999) that followed more than 1 million Americans over 14 years revealed that being significantly overweight can cut life short (**FIGURE 8A.9**). Those overweight at age 40 die three years earlier than their slim counterparts, reports another long-term study (Peeters et al., 2003). The death rate is especially high among very overweight men. Understandably, in 2004 the U.S. Medicare system began recognizing obesity as an illness. And in 2008 in Japan, a new national law mandated waistline measurements as part of annual checkups for those ages 40 to 74, with dieting guidance and re-education for those persistently over 33.5 inches for men and 35.4 inches for women (Onishi, 2008).

The Social Effects of Obesity

Obesity can also be socially toxic, by affecting both how you are treated and how you feel about yourself. Obese people know the stereotype: slow, lazy, and sloppy (Crandall, 1994, 1995; Ryckman et al., 1989). Widen people's images on a video monitor (making them look fatter) and observers suddenly rate them as less sincere, less friendly, meaner, and more obnoxious (Gardner & Tockerman, 1994). The social effects of obesity were clear in a study that followed 370 obese 16- to 24-year-old women (Gortmaker et al., 1993). When restudied seven years later, two-thirds of the women were still obese. They also were making less money—$7000 a year less—than an equally intelligent comparison group of some 5000 nonobese women. And they were less likely to be married. In personal ads, men often state their preference for, and women often advertise, slimness (Miller et al., 2000; Smith et al., 1990).

Regina Pingitore and her colleagues (1994) demonstrated weight discrimination in a clever experiment. They filmed mock job interviews in which professional actors appeared

> Obesity stereotype: "The [obesity lawsuit] bill says, 'Don't run off and file a lawsuit if you are fat.' It says, 'Look in the mirror because you're the one to blame.'"
> U.S. Senator F. James Sensenbrenner, 2004

TROUBLESHOOTING

Help students understand the difference between type 1 and type 2 diabetes.

- Type 1 diabetes, also known as juvenile diabetes, is typically diagnosed in early childhood or adolescence. People with this disorder are more often than not insulin dependent and require consistent monitoring of their blood glucose levels.

- Type 2 diabetes is often known as adult-onset diabetes and can result from lifestyle choices such as inactivity and poor diet. Typically, adults with a BMI of 25 or above and a genetic history of diabetes are more at risk for developing type 2 diabetes.

INTERCONNECTING

Students typically think of prejudice in terms of race or ethnicity. They do not think about how appearance can be the subject of prejudice. Help them see that the same principles studied in Unit 14 apply to the way people look, not only with skin color, but also with weight, height, or even hair color.

TEACHING TIP

At this point, you may want to use **Lecture/Discussion Topics:** *Paul Rozin's History of Eating* (p. 10) or *Genes, Exercise, and Weight Control* (p. 11) or *Losing Weight* (p. 11) or *Maintaining Weight Loss* (p. 12) or *The National Weight Control Registry* (p. 12) or *A Twinkie Tax—Is Fighting Fat a Social Responsibility?* (p. 13) from Bolt's Teacher's Resource Binder.

UNIT 8A

CRITICAL THINKING

The airline industry has been grappling with weight discrimination for many years. Weight limitations are a critical concern for the industry, because overweight planes can experience difficulty in flight. Have students debate the following issues regarding weight discrimination on airplanes:

- For many years, flight attendants were required to maintain certain weights. Many women who served as flight attendants felt the policy was more about customer service than plane weight distributions. Should flight attendants be required to maintain a certain weight? In what ways might this be perceived as discriminatory?

- In recent years, airlines have shrunk the sizes of seats in most sections of most airplanes to accommodate more paying customers. Passengers who are overweight often take up more room than the seat allows. Should airlines require these customers to pay for more than one seat? Why or why not?

> "For fat students, the school experience is one of almost constant harassment."
>
> Report on Size Discrimination, National Education Association, 1994

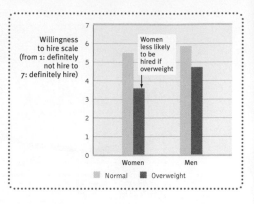

> **FIGURE 8A.10**
> **Gender and weight discrimination** When women applicants were made to look overweight, university students were less willing to think they would hire them. Among men applicants, weight mattered less. (Data from Pingitore et al., 1994.)

either as normal-weight or as overweight applicants (wearing makeup and prostheses to make them look 30 pounds heavier). When appearing overweight, the same person—using the same lines, intonations, and gestures—was rated less worthy of hiring (**FIGURE 8A.10**). The weight bias was especially strong against women. Other studies reveal that weight discrimination, though hardly discussed, is greater than race and gender discrimination. It occurs at every stage of the employment cycle—hiring, placement, promotion, compensation, discipline, and discharge—and is, indeed, much more likely to affect women (Roehling et al., 1999, 2007). Anti-fat prejudice even extends to applicants who are *seen* with an obese person (Hebl & Mannix, 2003)! This prejudice appears early. Children scorn fat children and express less liking of normal-weight children who are seen with an obese child (Penny & Haddock, 2007; Puhl & Latner, 2007).

In national studies of U.S. adults, obesity has been associated with lower psychological well-being, especially among women, and with a 25 percent increase in depression and anxiety (Bookwala & Boyar, 2008; Petry et al., 2008; Simon et al., 2006). Likewise, German and British people who feel overweight report lower than average psychological well-being (Oswald & Powdthavee, 2007). In studies of patients especially unhappy with their weight—those who had lost an average of 100 pounds after short-cutting digestion with intestinal bypass surgery—4 in 5 said their children had asked them not to attend school functions. And 9 in 10 said they would rather have a leg amputated than be obese again (Rand & Macgregor, 1990, 1991).

Why don't obese people drop their excess baggage and free themselves of all this pain? An answer lies in the physiology of fat.

The Physiology of Obesity

Research on the physiology of obesity challenges the stereotype of severely overweight people being weak-willed gluttons. First, consider the arithmetic of weight gain: People get fat by consuming more calories than they expend. The energy equivalent of a pound of fat is 3500 calories; therefore, dieters have been told they will lose a pound for every 3500-calorie reduction in their diet. Surprise: This conclusion is false. (Read on.)

Fat Cells The immediate determinants of body fat are the size and number of fat cells. A typical adult has 30 to 40 billion of these miniature fuel tanks, half of which lie near the skin's surface. A fat cell can vary from relatively empty, like a deflated balloon, to overly full. In an obese person, fat cells may swell to two or three times their normal size and then divide or trigger nearby immature fat cells to divide—resulting in up to 75 billion fat cells (Hirsch, 2003). Once the number of fat cells increases—

TEACHING TIP

Help students in your class be sensitive to students who are overweight, especially in light of Myers' conclusions that obesity is not necessarily the result of a weak willpower. Help them see that obesity is just as complicated a behavioral and psychological issue as any other issue studied in this book.

due to genetic predisposition, early childhood eating patterns, or adult overeating—it never decreases (**FIGURE 8A.11**). On a diet, fat cells may shrink, but their number does not (Sjöstrum, 1980; Spalding et al., 2008).

Set Point and Metabolism Once we become fat, we require less food to maintain our weight than we did to attain it. Why? Because compared with other tissue, fat has a lower metabolic rate—it takes less food energy to maintain. When an overweight person's body drops below its previous set point (or settling point), the person's hunger increases and metabolism decreases. Thus, the body adapts to starvation by burning off fewer calories.

In a classic month-long experiment (Bray, 1969), obese patients whose daily food intake was reduced from 3500 to 450 calories lost only 6 percent of their weight—partly because their bodies reacted as though they were being starved, and their metabolic rates dropped about 15 percent (**FIGURE 8A.12**). That is why reducing your food intake by 3500 calories may not reduce your weight by 1 pound. That is also why further weight loss comes slowly following the rapid losses during the initial three weeks or so of a rigorous diet. And that is why amounts of food that worked to maintain weight before a diet began may increase it when a diet ends—the body is still conserving energy. Given two people who weigh and look the same, the formerly

► **FIGURE 8A.11**
Fat cells We store energy in fat cells, which become larger and more numerous if we are obese, and smaller (but still more numerous) if we then lose weight. (Adapted from Jules Hirsch, 2003.)

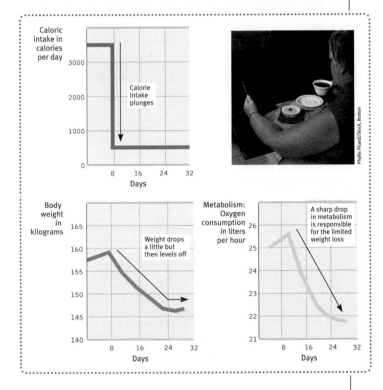

► **FIGURE 8A.12**
The effects of a severe diet on obese patients' body weight and metabolism After seven days on a 3500-calorie diet, six obese patients were given only 450 calories a day for the next 24 days. Body weight declined only 6 percent and then leveled off, because metabolism dropped about 15 percent. (From Bray, 1969.)

UNIT 8A

TEACHING TIP

Teens tend to have faster metabolisms than adults, mainly because their bodies expend so much energy growing. However, when the growth process stops (typically around ages 18 to 20), people tend to gain weight. This corresponds with the early years of college, when many college students gain the "Freshman 15." Help students see that they need to maintain their current levels of exercise and have healthy eating habits when they enter college to avoid this fate.

TEACHING TIP

Students can get a glimpse of what they will look like as adults if they look at their parents. They may not like this, but it is largely true. As Myers points out, our weight is correlated with the weights of other members of our family. In addition, we learn eating and exercise habits from our families. Encourage students to set some long-term goals about eating and exercise by thinking about what they want to look like in 20 years. Have them sketch out a plan for how they will accomplish a fit and healthy lifestyle during the next 20 years.

overweight one will likely need to eat fewer calories to maintain that weight than will the never-overweight one. (Who said life is fair?)

Thirty years after the Bray study, researchers performed a reverse experiment (Levine et al., 1999). They overfed volunteers an extra 1000 calories a day for eight weeks. Those who gained the least weight tended to spend the extra caloric energy by fidgeting more. Lean people are naturally disposed to fidget and move about more (and to burn more calories) than are energy-conserving overweight people who tend to sit still longer, report James Levine and his colleagues (2005). (How did the researchers know this? They outfitted people with undergarments that for 10 days monitored their movements every half-second.) These individual differences in resting metabolism help explain why two people of the same height, age, and activity level can maintain the same weight, even if one of them eats much less than the other does.

The Genetic Factor Do our genes predispose us to fidget or sit still? Possibly. Studies do reveal a genetic influence on body weight. Consider:

- Despite shared family meals, adoptive siblings' body weights are uncorrelated with one another or with those of their adoptive parents. Rather, people's weights resemble those of their biological parents (Grilo & Pogue-Geile, 1991).
- Identical twins have closely similar weights, even when reared apart (Plomin et al., 1997; Stunkard et al., 1990). Across studies, their weight correlates +.74. The much lower +.32 correlation among fraternal twins suggests that genes explain two-thirds of our varying body mass (Maes et al., 1997).
- Given an obese parent, a boy is three times, and a girl six times, more likely to be obese than their counterparts with normal-weight parents (Carrière, 2003).
- Scientists have discovered many different genes that influence body weight. One gene scan of 40,000 people worldwide identified a variant of a gene called *FTO*, which nearly doubles the risk of becoming obese (Flier & Maratos-Flier, 2007; Frayling et al., 2007). Researchers hope that identifying such culprit genes will lead them to the trail of the hunger-signaling proteins encoded by those genes.

So, the specifics of our genes predispose the size of our jeans. But the genetic influence is surely complex, with different genes, like differing band members, making music by playing together. Some genes might influence when our intestines signal "full," with others dictating how efficiently we burn calories or convert extra calories to fat, and, yes, still others prompting us to fidget or sit still.

The Food and Activity Factors Genes tell an important part of the obesity story. But research reveals that environmental factors are mighty important, too. *Sleep loss* is one such factor. Studies in France, Japan, Spain, the United States, and Switzerland all show that children and adults who skimp on sleep are more vulnerable to obesity (Keith et al., 2006; Taheri, 2004a,b). With sleep deprivation, the levels of leptin (which reports body fat to the brain) fall and ghrelin (the stomach hormone that stimulates appetite) rise.

Social influence is another factor. One research team followed the social networks of 12,067 people whom they had closely studied for 32 years (Christakis & Fowler, 2007). Their discovery: People were most likely to become obese when a friend became obese. If the friend who became obese is a close friend, the odds of one's likewise becoming obese almost tripled. (Their analysis showed that the correlation among friends' weights was not simply a matter of seeking out similar people as friends.) Friends matter.

The strongest evidence that environment as well as genes influences weight comes from our fattening world. Although the developed nations lead the trend, people *across the globe* are getting heavier. In Mexico, reports obesity researcher Barry Popkin (2007), the percentage of overweight people has expanded from 1 in 10 in 1989, to nearly 7 in 10 today. Changing *food consumption* and *activity levels* are at work. Sugar-

INTERCONNECTING

Remind students about the critical importance of sleep. Myers reminds us here that sleep loss can lead to obesity. Remind students of the aspects of sleep described in Unit 5—the ability of sleep to help with memory, performance, and, in this case, weight management. Also remind them of how little sleep teenagers feel they need or want. Ask whether the research would suggest that weight difficulties may be due to inadequate sleep.

laden soft drinks and activity-inhibiting TV watching are spreading across the world. So are energy-rich cooking oils and energy-saving tools, trucks, and cars.

Western cultures especially have become like animal feedlots (where farmers fatten inactive animals). In a massive long-term study of 50,000 nurses, researchers found—even after controlling for exercise, smoking, age, and diet—that each two-hour increase in daily TV watching predicted a 23 percent obesity increase and a 7 percent diabetes increase (Hu et al., 2003). Other studies show that people living in walking-dependent communities such as Manhattan tend to weigh less than more sedentary folks in car-dependent suburbs (Ewing et al., 2003). Among Ontario's Old Order Amish, where farming and gardening is labor intensive and pedometers reveal that men walk nine miles a day and women seven miles, the obesity rate is one-seventh the U.S. rate (Bassett et al., 2004).

Inactivity is compounded by ever-larger food unit portions of high-calorie foods. Compared with our counterparts in the early 1900s, we are eating a higher-fat, higher-sugar diet, expending fewer calories, and suffering higher rates of diabetes at younger ages (Popkin, 2007). Just since 1971, women are eating 300 more calories a day and men nearly 200 calories more (O'Connor, 2004). And they are eating three times as many meals in fast-food restaurants (Farley & Cohen, 2001). Today's teens consume twice as much soda as milk—the reverse of a quarter-century ago (Brownell & Nestle, 2004).

On most North American college campuses, yesterday's cafeteria line with limited choices has been replaced by today's food buffet, with multiple serving stations offering all-you-can-eat entrees and make-your-own waffles washed down with limitless soft drinks (Brody, 2003). For many, the understandable result is the "freshman 15"—or, more typically, the "freshman 5" (Holm-Denoma et al., 2008). Small wonder that your parents and grandparents at age 30 likely weighed less than you will. Since 1960, the average adult American has grown one inch and gained 23 pounds (Ogden et al., 2004). Taken together, Big Macs, Double Whoppers, sugar-laden drinks, and inactivity form a weapon of mass destruction.

The "bottom" line: New stadiums, theaters, and subway cars are widening their own seats to accommodate this population growth (Hampson, 2000). Washington State Ferries abandoned a 50-year-old standard of 18 inches per person: "Eighteen-inch butts are a thing of the past," explained a spokesperson (Shepherd, 1999). New York City, facing a large problem with Big Apple bottoms, has mostly replaced 17.5-inch bucket-style subway seats with bucketless seats (Hampson, 2000). In the end, today's people need more room.

If the changing environment explains the expanding obesity problem, then environmental reform is part of the remedy, reasoned the 53 European health ministers who signed a new World Health Organization anti-obesity charter (Cheng, 2006). The charter beckons the private sector to "substantially reduce" its advertising of fatty, sugary foods to children and commits governments to increasing the availability of healthy foods and roadways that promote cycling and walking. In the United States, several states, including Arizona, California, and Kentucky, are now setting nutritional standards for school-provided food and drink (Tumulty, 2006).

Psychologist Kelly Brownell (2002) has been campaigning for these and other environmental reforms:

- Establish a fast-food–free zone around schools.
- Slap an extra tax on calorie-laden junk food and soft drinks. We're reducing smoking with increased cigarette taxes. Why not, for the same reason, institute a "Twinkie Tax"?
- Use the revenues to subsidize healthy foods and to finance health-supportive nutritional advertising.

Too much food, and too little It is ironic that in a world where 800 million still live with hunger, obesity rates continue to rise in Western countries, endangering the lives of the severely overweight (Pinstrup-Andersen & Cheng, 2007; Popkin, 2007).

"We put fast food on every corner, we put junk food in schools, we got rid of P.E., we put candy and soda at the checkout stand of every retail outlet you can think of. The results are in. It worked."

Harold Goldstein, Executive Director of the California Center for Public Health Advocacy, 2009, when imagining a vast U.S. national experiment to encourage weight gain

RESEARCH

Have students collect children's magazines and watch children's TV shows, counting the number of advertisements for candy, soda, and other junk foods (including fast foods). Have them use this data to speculate about the influence of this type of media on children's eating habits.

INTERCONNECTING

Remind students that media is influential in changing behavior. Remind students of Bandura's research with the Bobo doll from Unit 6. In that study, children copied the actions of role models seen in videos. If children see advertisements for fast food, candy, and soda throughout the day, they will be more likely to want to eat and drink those types of foods, contributing to childhood obesity.

We will revisit this lesson in Unit 11's study of individual differences: There can be high levels of *heritability* (genetic influence on individual differences) without heredity explaining group differences. Genes mostly determine why one person today is heavier than another. Environment mostly determines why people today are heavier than their counterparts 50 years ago. Our eating behavior also demonstrates the now familiar interaction among biological, psychological, and social-cultural factors.

Losing Weight

Perhaps you are shaking your head: "Slim chance I have of becoming and staying thin. If I lose weight on a diet, my metabolism slows and my hungry fat cells cry out, 'Feed me!' I'm fated for fat!" Indeed, the condition of an obese person's body reduced to average weight is much like that of a semistarved body. Held under normal set point, the body "thinks" it is starving. Having lost weight, formerly obese people look normal, but their fat cells may be abnormally small, their metabolism slowed, and their minds obsessed with food.

The battle of the bulge rages on as intensely as ever, and it is most intense among those with two X chromosomes. Nearly two-thirds of women and half of men say they want to lose weight; about half of those women and men say they are "seriously trying"(Moore, 2006). Asked if they would rather "be five years younger or weigh 15 pounds less," 29 percent of men and 48 percent of women said they would prefer losing the weight (Responsive Community, 1996).

With fat cells, settling points, metabolism, and genetic and environmental factors all tirelessly conspiring against shedding excess pounds, what advice can psychology offer these people? Perhaps the most important point is that permanent weight loss is not easy. Millions can attest that it is possible to lose weight; they have done it lots of times. But short of drastic surgery to tie off part of the stomach and small intestine, most who succeed on a weight-loss program eventually regain the lost weight or more (Mann et al., 2007).

Those who do manage to keep pounds off set realistic and moderate goals, undertaking programs that modify their life-style and ongoing eating behavior. They realize that being moderately heavy is less risky than being extremely thin (Ernsberger & Koletsky, 1999). They lose weight gradually: "A reasonable time line for a 10 percent reduction in body weight is six months," advised the National Institutes of Health (1998). And they exercise regularly. For other helpful hints, see Close-Up: Waist Management.

A losing battle Ryan Benson lost 122 pounds to win the first season of the TV reality show *The Biggest Loser*. But then, like so many, he found maintaining the loss an even bigger challenge.

INTERCONNECTING

Heritability is a difficult concept for students to understand. Remind them that heritability refers to the tendency of traits to be attributable to genes in a group, not in individuals. An individual's likelihood of having a certain genetic trait is not explained by heritability. Yet, as a member of a group, the trait can be explained by heritability.

TEACHING TIP

Shows like *The Biggest Loser* (NBC) and *Celebrity Fit Club* (VH1) feature contestants losing large amounts of weight under controlled circumstances. Contestants live away from their homes and have the benefit of personal chefs and trainers. They tend to lose significant, amazing amounts of weight over the course of a few months. Their real test, however, comes when they return home from their experience. Many of these contestants, like Ryan Benson, go on to gain back much, if not all, of their original weight. Only those who maintain their levels of healthy eating and exercise manage to keep the weight off.

TEACHING TIP

Setting realistic goals is key to losing weight effectively. While those with much weight to lose will lose weight more quickly initially, their goal should not be to lose too much weight too quickly. Steady, moderate weight loss can be longer lasting than quick, intense weight loss.

Waist Management

People struggling with obesity are well advised to seek medical evaluation and guidance. For others who wish to take off a few pounds, researchers have offered these tips.

Begin only if you feel motivated and self-disciplined. For most people, permanent weight loss requires making a career of staying thin—a lifelong change in eating habits combined with gradually increased exercise.

Minimize exposure to tempting food cues. Keep tempting foods out of the house or out of sight. Go to the supermarket only on a full stomach, and avoid the sweets and chips aisles. Eat simple meals, with only a few different foods; given more variety, people consume more.

Take steps to boost your metabolism. Inactive people are often overweight (**FIGURE 8A.13**). In a 1980s study of 6671 young people 12 to 17 years old, and in a 1990s follow-up study of 4063 individuals 8 to 16 years old, obesity was more common among those who watched the most TV (Andersen et al., 1998; Dietz & Gortmaker, 1985). Of course, overweight people may avoid activity, preferring to sit and watch TV. But the association between TV watching and obesity remained when many other factors were controlled, suggesting that inactivity and snacking while watching TV do contribute to obesity. The good news is that one of the few predictors of successful long-term weight loss is exercise, both during and after changing your eating patterns (Jeffery et al., 2000; McGuire et al., 1999; Wadden et al., 1998). Exercise, supported by 7 to 8 hours sleep a night, empties fat cells, builds muscle, speeds up metabolism, and helps lower your settling point (Bennett, 1995; Kolata, 1987; Thompson et al., 1982).

Eat healthy foods. Whole grains, fruits, vegetables, and healthy fats such as those found in olive oil and fish help regulate appetite and artery-clogging cholesterol (Taubes, 2001, 2002). Better crispy greens than Krispy Kremes.

Don't starve all day and eat one big meal at night. This eating pattern, common among overweight people, slows metabolism. Moreover, those who eat a balanced breakfast are, by late morning, more alert and less fatigued (Spring et al., 1992).

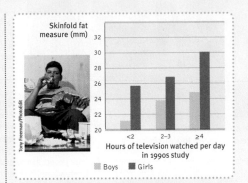

Skinfold fat measure (mm)

Hours of television watched per day in 1990s study

☐ Boys ■ Girls

FIGURE 8A.13

American idle: Couch potatoes beware—TV watching correlates with obesity As life-styles have become more sedentary and TV watching has increased, so has the percentage of overweight people in Britain, North America, and elsewhere. When California children were placed in a TV-reduction educational program, they watched less—and lost weight (Robinson, 1999).

Beware of the binge. Especially for men, eating more slowly leads to eating less (Martin et al., 2007). Among people who do consciously restrain their eating, drinking alcohol or feeling anxious or depressed can unleash the urge to eat (Herman & Polivy, 1980). So can being distracted from monitoring your eating (Ward & Mann, 2000). (Ever notice that you eat more when out with friends?) Once the diet is broken, the person often thinks "What the heck" and then binges (Polivy & Herman, 1985, 1987). A lapse need not become a full collapse: Remember, most people occasionally lapse.

Although mindful that preserving weight loss is a constant challenge, Stanley Schachter (1982) was less pessimistic than most of today's obesity researchers about the dieter's chances of success. He recognized the overwhelming rate of failure among those in structured weight-loss programs, but he also noted that these people are a special group who probably have been unable to help themselves. Moreover, the failure rates recorded for these programs are based on single attempts at weight loss. Perhaps when people try repeatedly to lose weight, more of them do eventually succeed. When Schachter interviewed people, he found that one-fourth had at one time been significantly overweight and had tried to slim down. Of these, 6 of 10 had *succeeded:* They weighed at least 10 percent less than their maximum prediet weight (an average loss of 35 pounds) and were no longer obese. A 1993 survey of 90,000 *Consumer Reports* readers found 25 percent of dieters claiming an enduring weight loss. Aided by media publicity, the National Weight Control Registry has identified more than 4000 people who have maintained significant weight loss

UNIT 8A

TEACHING TIP

Encourage students to strive for healthy eating habits rather than strive for thinness or an "ideal" weight. Myers points out that striving to be thin has significant health and psychological consequences. Reframing the issue may help students be more successful in the long run.

Successful weight loss After losing 110 pounds, former Arkansas governor and U.S. presidential candidate Mike Huckabee poses with a girl who weighs what he lost. "Look at Huckabee," said his longtime adversary, former U.S. President Bill Clinton. "You've got to consume less and burn more. There is no other alternative. And to do that, you've got to change the culture."

for at least one year and are being studied over time. On average, these people have lost 60 pounds and kept it off for five years, virtually always with continued diet and exercise.

These findings hint that prospects for losing weight may be somewhat brighter than the dismal conclusions drawn from following patients who undergo a single weight-loss program. This pattern would be similar to the one found in stop-smoking programs, which tend to be (1) effective in the short run and (2) ineffective in the long run, even though (3) many people are former smokers.

There is another option for overweight people, and one chosen by 13 percent of the people Schachter interviewed: to accept one's weight. We all do well to note that researchers have *not* identified guilt, hostility, oral fixation, or any similar personality maladjustment as causes of obesity. Nor is obesity simply a matter of lack of willpower. Dieters are more likely to binge when under stress or after breaking their diets, which may be largely a consequence of their constant dieting. Indeed, the relentless pursuit of thinness puts people at risk not only for binge eating and food obsession, but also for weight fluctuations, malnutrition, smoking, depression, and harmful side effects of weight-loss drugs (Cogan & Ernsberger, 1999).

"Fat is not a four-letter world," proclaims the National Association to Advance Fat Acceptance, so "a waist is a terrible thing to mind." Such statements discount the health risks linked with significant obesity, but they do convey a valid point: It is surely better to accept oneself as a bit heavy than to diet and binge and feel continually out of control and guilty. Fans loved Oprah Winfrey before she lost 67 pounds. They loved her after she put them back on. They loved her when she shed them again. And they will love her still, chubby or not.

BEFORE YOU MOVE ON . . .

➤ **ASK YOURSELF**

Do you feel in touch with your body's hunger signals? Do you eat when your body needs food? Or do you tend to be more externally influenced by enticing foods even when you're full?

➤ **TEST YOURSELF 2**

You are traveling and have not eaten anything in eight hours. As your long-awaited favorite dish is placed in front of you, your mouth waters. Even imagining this may set your mouth to watering. What triggers this anticipatory drooling?

Answers to the Test Yourself questions can be found in Appendix E at the end of the book.

Sexual Motivation

"It is a near-universal experience, the invisible clause on one's birth certificate stipulating that one will, upon reaching maturity, feel the urge to engage in activities often associated with the issuance of more birth certificates."
Science writer Natalie Angier, 2007

SEX IS PART OF LIFE. HAD THIS NOT been so for all your ancestors, you would not be reading this book. Sexual motivation is nature's clever way of making people procreate, thus enabling our species' survival. When two people feel attracted, they hardly stop to think of themselves as guided by their genes. As the pleasure we take in eating is nature's inventive method of getting our body nourishment, so the desires and pleasures of sex are our genes' way of preserving and spreading themselves. Life is sexually transmitted.

TROUBLESHOOTING

You may teach in a community that may regard classroom lessons about sex to be controversial. Be sensitive to the concerns of your community so you can be discerning about how to teach this material. If certain topics would be too inflammatory, help students see how the scientific method tries to examine these issues rather than engaging in debates about what findings are "right" or "wrong." While material from this section of the book could be addressed on the AP Exam, it will most likely be one or two multiple-choice questions or one part of one free-response question at the most. Do not feel you have to dwell on this material if doing so would lead to tension and strife.

The Physiology of Sex

Like hunger, sexual arousal depends on the interplay of internal and external stimuli. To understand sexual motivation, we must consider both.

The Sexual Response Cycle

6: What stages mark the human sexual response cycle?

In the 1960s, gynecologist-obstetrician William Masters and his collaborator Virginia Johnson (1966) made headlines by recording the physiological responses of volunteers who masturbated or had intercourse. With the help of 382 female and 312 male volunteers—a somewhat atypical sample, consisting only of people able and willing to display arousal and orgasm while being observed in a laboratory—Masters and Johnson monitored or filmed more than 10,000 sexual "cycles." Their description of the **sexual response cycle** identified four stages, similar in men and women. During the initial *excitement phase*, the genital areas become engorged with blood, a woman's vagina expands and secretes lubricant, and her breasts and nipples may enlarge.

"I love the idea of there being two sexes, don't you?"

In the *plateau phase*, excitement peaks as breathing, pulse, and blood pressure rates continue to increase. The penis becomes fully engorged and some fluid—frequently containing enough live sperm to enable conception—may appear at its tip. Vaginal secretion continues to increase.

Masters and Johnson observed muscle contractions all over the body during *orgasm*; these were accompanied by further increases in breathing, pulse, and blood pressure rates. A woman's arousal and orgasm facilitate conception by positioning the uterus to receive sperm, and drawing the sperm further inward. A woman's orgasm therefore not only reinforces intercourse, which is essential to natural reproduction, it also increases retention of deposited sperm (Furlow & Thornhill, 1996). In the excitement of the moment, men and women are hardly aware of all this as their rhythmic genital contractions create a pleasurable feeling of sexual release.

The feeling apparently is much the same for both sexes. In one study, a panel of experts could not reliably distinguish between descriptions of orgasm written by men and those written by women (Vance & Wagner, 1976). University of Groningen neuroscientist Gerg Holstege and his colleagues (2003a,b) understand why. They discovered that when men and women undergo PET scans while having orgasms, the same subcortical brain regions glow. And when people who are passionately in love undergo fMRI (functional MRI) scans while viewing photos of their beloved or of a stranger, men's and women's brain responses to their partner are pretty similar (Fisher et al., 2002).

The body gradually returns to its unaroused state as the engorged genital blood vessels release their accumulated blood—relatively quickly if orgasm has occurred, relatively slowly otherwise. (It's like the nasal tickle that goes away rapidly if you have sneezed, slowly otherwise.) During this *resolution phase*, the male enters a **refractory period**, lasting from a few minutes to a day or more, during which he is incapable of another orgasm. The female's much shorter refractory period may enable her to have more orgasms if restimulated during or soon after resolution.

::**sexual response cycle** the four stages of sexual responding described by Masters and Johnson—excitement, plateau, orgasm, and resolution.

::**refractory period** a resting period after orgasm, during which a man cannot achieve another orgasm.

INTERCONNECTING

The sexual response stages are similar to Hans Selye's General Adaptation Syndrome (GAS), which describes the body's physiological response to stress (Unit 8B). First, the GAS describes the alarm reaction phase, in which the body recognizes and prepares to tackle the stress, similar to the excitement phase of sex. Then, the GAS describes the resistance phase, in which the body fights the stress for an indefinite amount of time, much like the plateau phase. Finally, the body either conquers the stress or exhausts resources to handle the stress further, resulting in the exhaustion phase of GAS. This is similar to the orgasm and resolution phases of the sexual response cycle. Thus, the body's reaction to stress is not much different than the body's reaction to sex!

INTERCONNECTING

Remind students of the neuronal refractory period from Unit 3A. Once they have fired an action potential, neurons must become repolarized so they can be ready to fire another action potential. There is a slight rest period between all action potentials fired by neurons in the entire nervous system.

© The New Yorker Collection, 1993, Robert Mankoff from cartoonbank.com. All rights reserved.

TEACHING TIP

Students may be surprised to read that women secrete testosterone. In fact, men and women secrete both sex hormones, but men secrete more testosterone than women, and women secrete more estrogens than men. However, as Myers points out, testosterone plays a role for both men and women in their levels of sexual desire.

INTERCONNECTING

Connect this topic with developmental psychology and Unit 9 by discussing how the onset of puberty has changed for both boys and girls in the last 100 years. About 100 years ago, girls used to mature sexually around 15 years of age. However, girls sexually mature today at around 12 years old. Along with this backwards trend, the average age of marriage has increased from 22 (100 years ago) to about 25 years of age (today). If today's teens are going to abstain from sex until marriage, they must wait over 12 years between the onset of puberty until marriage.

• In a National Center for Health Statistics survey of adult Americans, using computer-assisted self-interviews that guaranteed privacy, nearly 98 percent of 30- to 59-year-olds reported having had sex (Fryar et al., 2007). •

"Fill'er up with testosterone."

::**estrogens** sex hormones, such as estradiol, secreted in greater amounts by females than by males and contributing to female sex characteristics. In nonhuman female mammals, estrogen levels peak during ovulation, promoting sexual receptivity.

::**testosterone** the most important of the male sex hormones. Both males and females have it, but the additional testosterone in males stimulates the growth of the male sex organs in the fetus and the development of the male sex characteristics during puberty.

Hormones and Sexual Behavior

7: Do hormones influence human sexual motivation?

Sex hormones have two effects: They direct the physical development of male and female sex characteristics, and (especially in nonhuman animals) they activate sexual behavior. In most mammals, nature neatly synchronizes sex with fertility. The female becomes sexually receptive (in animals, being "in heat") when secretion of the female hormones, the **estrogens** (such as estradiol), peak during ovulation. In experiments, researchers can stimulate receptivity by injecting female animals with estrogen. Male hormone levels are more constant, and researchers cannot so easily manipulate the sexual behavior of male animals with hormones (Feder, 1984). Nevertheless, castrated male rats—having lost their testes, which manufacture the male sex hormone **testosterone**—gradually lose much of their interest in receptive females. They gradually regain it if injected with testosterone.

In humans, hormones more loosely influence sexual behavior, although sexual desire rises slightly at ovulation among women with mates (Pillsworth et al., 2004). One study invited partnered women not at risk for pregnancy to keep a diary of their sexual activity. (These women were either using intrauterine devices or had undergone surgery to prevent pregnancy.) On the days around ovulation, intercourse was 24 percent more frequent (Wilcox et al., 2004). Other studies find that women fantasize more about sex with desirable partners and wear more sexually attractive clothing around ovulation (Haselton et al., 2006; Pillsworth & Haselton, 2006; Sheldon et al., 2006).

Women's sexuality differs from that of other mammalian females in being more responsive to testosterone levels than to estrogen levels (Meston & Frohlich, 2000; Reichman, 1998). If a woman's natural testosterone level drops, as happens with removal of the ovaries or adrenal glands, her sexual interest may wane. But testosterone-replacement therapy sometimes restores diminished sexual appetite. That is the finding of experiments with hundreds of surgically or naturally menopausal women, for whom a testosterone-replacement patch restored sexual activity, arousal, and desire more than did a placebo (Braunstein et al., 2005; Buster et al., 2005; Davis et al., 2003; Kroll et al., 2004).

In men, normal fluctuations in testosterone levels, from man to man and hour to hour, have little effect on sexual drive (Byrne, 1982). Indeed, fluctuations in male hormones are partly a *response* to sexual stimulation. When James Dabbs and his colleagues (1987, 2000) had heterosexual male collegians converse separately with another male student and with a female student, the men's testosterone levels rose with the social arousal, but especially after talking with the female. Thus, sexual arousal can be a cause as well as a consequence of increased testosterone levels.

Although normal short-term hormonal changes have little effect on men's and women's desire, large hormonal shifts over the life span have a greater effect. A person's interest in dating and sexual stimulation usually increases with the pubertal surge in sex hormones, as happens with male testosterone levels during puberty. When adult men are castrated, sex drive typically falls as testosterone levels decline (Hucker & Bain, 1990). Male sex offenders taking Depo-Provera, a drug that reduces testosterone level to that of a prepubertal boy, similarly lose much of their sexual urge (Money et al., 1983).

In later life, as sex hormone levels decline, the frequency of sexual fantasies and intercourse declines as well (Leitenberg & Henning, 1995). For men with abnormally low testosterone levels, testosterone-replacement therapy often increases sexual desire and also energy and vitality (Yates, 2000).

To summarize: We might compare human sex hormones, especially testosterone, to the fuel in a car. Without fuel, a car will not run. But if the fuel level is minimally adequate, adding more fuel to the gas tank won't change how the car runs. The analogy is imperfect, because hormones and sexual motivation interact. However, the analogy correctly suggests that biology is a necessary but not sufficient explanation of human sexual behavior. The hormonal fuel is essential, but so are the psychological stimuli that turn on the engine, keep it running, and shift it into high gear.

The Psychology of Sex

8: How do internal and external stimuli influence sexual motivation?

Hunger and sex are different sorts of motivations. Hunger responds to a *need*. If we do not eat, we die. Sex is not in this sense a need. If we do not have sex, we may feel like dying, but we do not. Nevertheless, there are similarities between hunger and sexual motivation. Both depend on internal physiological factors. And both are influenced by external and imagined stimuli, as well as cultural expectations (**FIGURE 8A.14**).

External Stimuli

Many studies confirm that men become aroused when they see, hear, or read erotic material. Surprising to many (because sexually explicit materials are sold mostly to men) is that most women—at least the less-inhibited women who volunteer to participate in such studies—report or exhibit nearly as much arousal to the same stimuli (Heiman, 1975; Stockton & Murnen, 1992). (Their brains do, however, respond differently, with fMRI scans revealing a more active amygdala in men viewing erotica [Hamann et al., 2004].)

Can sexually explicit material have adverse effects? Research indicates that it can. Depictions of women being sexually coerced—and enjoying it—tend to increase viewers' acceptance of the false idea that women enjoy rape, and they tend to increase male viewers' willingness to hurt women (Malamuth & Check, 1981; Zillmann, 1989). Viewing images of sexually attractive women and men may also lead people to devalue their own partners and relationships. After male collegians view TV or magazine depictions of sexually attractive women, they often find an average woman, or

> "Ours is a society which stimulates interest in sex by constant titillation.... Cinema, television, and all the formidable array of our marketing technology project our very effective forms of titillation and our prejudices about man as a sexy animal into every corner of every hovel in the world."
>
> Germaine Greer, 1984

Biological influences:
- sexual maturity
- sex hormones, especially testosterone
- sexual orientation

Psychological influences:
- exposure to stimulating conditions
- sexual fantasies

Sexual motivation

Social-cultural influences:
- family and society values
- religious and personal values
- cultural expectations
- media

➤ **FIGURE 8A.14**
Levels of analysis for sexual motivation
Compared with our motivation for eating, our sexual motivation is less influenced by biological factors. Psychological and social-cultural factors play a bigger role.

 TEACHING TIP

Point out to students how sex is not a need, but rather a desire, unlike hunger. Discuss with students how the physical drive for sex is different from a motivational standpoint from the drive to eat. The sex drive can be suppressed until the urge subsides, which would be unwise to do with hunger.

INTERCONNECTING

Remind students that the amygdala is the brain's "emotion center," responsible for processing the body's signals to determine the emotional response necessary for the situation.

TEACHING TIP

Figure 8A.14 shows the biopsychosocial model for sexual motivation. Use this to reinforce the integrated use of psychological explanations for complex behaviors like sex.

UNIT 8A

RESEARCH

Have students get into small groups to research laws and policies concerning sex education in your state. With the class, discuss these programs and how they differ in various communities.

- Do the policies differ from school system to school system?

- Why were policies adopted in certain communities?

- What does psychological research say about the effectiveness of different types of sex education programs?

- Now that a vaccine is available for the human papilloma virus (HPV), which causes pelvic inflammatory disease (PID) and can lead to cervical cancer, several states are debating whether to make the vaccine mandatory for all teenage girls. Should states mandate this vaccine like they mandate the measles vaccine for children? Why or why not?

• Sexually explicit TV programs also divert attention from TV ads, making the ads more forgettable. Ads embedded in nonsexual and nonviolent programs more often produce memory for the products (Bushman & Bonacci, 2002). •

"Will your child learn to multiply before she learns to subtract?"
Anti–teen-pregnancy poster,
Children's Defense Fund

---

their own girlfriend or wife, less attractive (Kenrick & Gutierres, 1980; Kenrick et al., 1989; Weaver et al., 1984). Viewing X-rated sex films similarly tends to diminish people's satisfaction with their own sexual partner (Zillmann, 1989). Some sex researchers suspect that reading or watching erotica may create expectations that few men and women can fulfill.

Imagined Stimuli

The brain, it has been said, is our most significant sex organ. The stimuli inside our heads—our imagination—can influence sexual arousal and desire. People who, because of a spinal cord injury, have no genital sensation can still feel sexual desire (Willmuth, 1987). Consider, too, the erotic potential of dreams. Sleep researchers have discovered that genital arousal accompanies all types of dreams, even though most dreams have no sexual content. But in nearly all men and some 40 percent of women, dreams sometimes contain sexual imagery that leads to orgasm (Wells, 1986). In men, nighttime orgasm and nocturnal emissions ("wet dreams") are more likely when orgasm has not occurred recently.

About 95 percent of both men and women say they have had sexual fantasies. Men (whether gay or straight) fantasize about sex more often, more physically, and less romantically. They also prefer less personal and faster-paced sexual content in books and videos (Leitenberg & Henning, 1995). Fantasizing about sex does *not* indicate a sexual problem or dissatisfaction. If anything, sexually active people have more sexual fantasies.

Adolescent Sexuality

9: What factors influence teen sexuality, teen pregnancy, and risk of sexually transmitted infections?

Adolescents' physical maturation fosters a sexual dimension to their emerging identity. Yet sexual expression varies dramatically with time and culture. Among American women born before 1900, a mere 3 percent had experienced premarital sex by age 18 (Smith, 1998). In 2005, 47 percent of high school students acknowledged having had sexual intercourse (CDC, 2006). Teen intercourse rates are roughly similar in Western Europe and in Latin America, but much lower in Arab and Asian countries and among North Americans of Asian descent (McLaughlin et al., 1997; Wellings et al., 2006). Given the wide variation across time and place, it's no surprise that a recent twin study found that environmental factors accounted for almost three-fourths of the individual variation in age of sexual initiation (Bricker et al., 2006). Family and cultural values matter.

Sex during the teen years is often unprotected, leading to risks of pregnancy and *sexually transmitted infections* (STIs, also called *STDs* for *sexually transmitted diseases*).

Teen Pregnancy

Compared with European teens, American teens have a lower rate of contraceptive use and thus a higher rate of teen pregnancy and abortion (Call et al., 2002). Why?

Ignorance One survey of Canadian teens revealed some real gaps in knowledge about sex and sexual health (Ipsos, 2006). Although 9 in 10 claimed to be knowledgeable, many were unaware that STIs can be transmitted through oral sex (which two-thirds had engaged in); only 19 percent had heard of HPV (human papillomavirus, a leading cause of genital warts and cervical cancer); and only 37 percent mentioned infertility as a possible result of chlamydia. Most teens also overestimate their peers' sexual activity, a misperception that may influence their own behavior (Child Trends, 2001). Countering ignorance with contraceptive sex education "does not increase adolescent sexual activity" (Surgeon General, 2001), but a World Health Organization report found that it does increase "intention to practice safer sex," and may even *delay* "rather than hasten the onset of sexual activity" (Wellings et al., 2006).

Minimal communication about birth control Many teenagers are uncomfortable discussing contraception with their parents, partners, and peers. Teens who talk freely with parents and are in an exclusive relationship with a partner with whom they communicate openly are more likely to use contraceptives (Aspy et al., 2007; Milan & Kilmann, 1987).

Guilt related to sexual activity In one survey, 72 percent of sexually active 12- to 17-year-old American girls said they regretted having had sex (Reuters, 2000). Sexual inhibitions or ambivalence can reduce sexual activity, but they may also reduce attempts at birth control if passion overwhelms intentions (Gerrard & Luus, 1995; MacDonald & Hynie, 2008).

Alcohol use Sexually active teens are typically alcohol-using teens (Albert et al., 2003; ASA, 2004), and those who use alcohol prior to sex are less likely to use condoms (Kotchick et al., 2001). By depressing the brain centers that control judgment, inhibition, and self-awareness, alcohol tends to break down normal restraints, a phenomenon well known to sexually coercive males.

Mass media norms of unprotected promiscuity Media help write the "social scripts" that affect our perceptions and actions. So what sexual scripts do today's media write on our minds? An average hour of prime-time television on the three major U.S. networks contains approximately 15 sexual acts, words, and innuendos. The partners are usually unmarried, with no prior romantic relationship, and few communicate any concern for birth control or sexually transmitted infections (Brown et al., 2002; Kunkel, 2001; Sapolsky & Tabarlet, 1991). The more sexual content adolescents view (even when controlling for other predictors of early sexual activity), the more likely they are to perceive their peers as sexually active, to develop sexually permissive attitudes, and to experience early intercourse (Escobar-Chaves et al., 2005; Martino et al., 2005; Ward & Friedman, 2006).

Sexually Transmitted Infections

Unprotected sex has led to increased rates of sexually transmitted infections. Two-thirds of new infections occur in people under 25 (CASA, 2004). Teenage girls, because of their not yet fully mature biological development and lower levels of protective antibodies, seem especially vulnerable (Dehne & Riedner, 2005; Guttmacher, 1994). A recent Centers for Disease Control study of sexually experienced 14- to 19-year-old U.S. females found 39.5 percent had STIs (Forhan et al., 2008).

Consider this: If someone uses a method that is 98 percent effective in preventing pregnancy or infection, there is a 2 percent chance of failure in the first such use. Surprisingly to many people, given 30 such uses, the risk would accumulate to nearly a 50 percent chance of failure at some point. Moreover, when people feel drawn to a partner, they become motivated to underestimate risks (Knäuper el al., 2005).

Given these odds, the rapid spread of STIs is not surprising. Condoms offer little protection against certain skin-to-skin STIs (Medical Institute, 1994; NIH, 2001). Across the available studies, condoms have, however, been 80 percent effective in preventing transmission of HIV (human immunodeficiency virus—the virus that causes AIDS) from an infected partner (Weller & Davis-Beaty, 2002; WHO, 2003). The effects were clear when Thailand promoted 100 percent condom use by commercial sex workers. Over a four-year period, as condom use soared from 14 to 94 percent, the annual number of bacterial STIs plummeted from 410,406 to 27,362 (WHO, 2000).

In the United States, STI facts of life have led to another response: a greater emphasis on teen abstinence within some comprehensive sex-education programs. A National Longitudinal Study of Adolescent Health among 12,000 teens found several predictors of sexual restraint:

> "All of us who make motion pictures are teachers, teachers with very loud voices."
>
> Film producer George Lucas, Academy Award ceremonies, 1992

INTERCONNECTING

Help students see how alcohol use can lead to decreased inhibition by referring them to Unit 5. In that unit, Myers discusses the effects of several different types of drugs, including alcohol. Alcohol is a nervous system depressant, which means it lowers inhibitions for the behaviors people would normally avoid.

INTERCONNECTING

Connect the studies presented here with Bandura's Bobo doll studies from Unit 6. Bandura showed that children will copy role models' behaviors. Teens may also be copying adult behaviors they see on television and in movies that depict sexual behavior.

TEACHING TIP

At this point, you may want to use **Lecture/Discussion Topic:** *Virginity Pledges* (p. 14) from Bolt's Teacher's Resource Binder.

RESEARCH

Sexually transmitted infections are a problem in the U.S. Many students are unaware of the pervasiveness of STIs and the dangers associated with them. Have students do research on any of the following STIs:

- chlamydia
- syphilis
- HIV/AIDS
- gonorrhea
- pelvic inflammatory disease (PID) and cervical cancer
- herpes

Students should address the following questions about the disease:

- What are the symptoms of the disease?
- How many people are infected each year?
- What is the prognosis for this disease? Are there any treatments/cures available?

 TEACHING TIP

Overall, the research showing what qualities lead to sexual restraint all related to one overarching idea—engagement. Students who are engaged in school (learning), their religion, their families, and in prosocial projects seem to buffer themselves against early sexual experiences.

::**sexual orientation** an enduring sexual attraction toward members of either one's own sex (homosexual orientation) or the other sex (heterosexual orientation).

High intelligence Teens with high rather than average intelligence test scores more often delay sex, evidently because they appreciate possible negative consequences and are more focused on future achievement than on here-and-now pleasures (Halpern et al., 2000).

Religious engagement Actively religious teens and adults more often reserve sex for marital commitment (Rostosky et al., 2004; Smith, 1998).

Father presence In studies following hundreds of New Zealand and U.S. girls from age 5 to 18, a father's absence was linked to sexual activity before age 16 and teen pregnancy (Ellis et al., 2003). These associations held even after adjusting for other adverse influences, such as poverty.

Participation in service learning programs Several experiments have found lower pregnancy rates among teens volunteering as tutors or teachers' aides or participating in community projects, than found among comparable teens randomly assigned to control conditions (Kirby, 2002; O'Donnell et al., 2002). Researchers are unsure why. Does service learning promote a sense of personal competence, control, and responsibility? Does it encourage more future-oriented thinking? Or does it simply reduce opportunities for unprotected sex?

* * *

In recent history, the pendulum of sexual values has swung from the European eroticism of the early 1800s to the conservative Victorian era of the late 1800s, from the libertine flapper era of the 1920s to the family values period of the 1950s. The pendulum may have begun a new swing toward commitment in the twenty-first century, with declining teen birth rates since 1991. This decline reflects both increasing condom use among sexually active high school students (from 46 to 63 percent between 1991 and 2005) and decreasing sexual intercourse (from 54 to 47 percent) (CDC, 2006).

Sexual Orientation

10: What has research taught us about sexual orientation?

To motivate is to energize and direct behavior. So far, we have considered the energizing of sexual motivation but not its direction. We express the direction of our sexual interest in our **sexual orientation**—our enduring sexual attraction toward members of our own sex (*homosexual orientation*) or the other sex (*heterosexual orientation*). Cultures vary in their attitudes toward homosexuality. In Chile, 32 percent of people say they think homosexuality "is never justified," as do 50 percent of people in the United States and 98 percent in Kenya and Nigeria (Pew, 2006). As far as we know, all cultures in all times have been predominantly heterosexual (Bullough, 1990). Whether a culture condemns or accepts homosexuality, heterosexuality prevails and homosexuality survives.

Gay men and lesbians often recall childhood play preferences like those of the other sex (Bailey & Zucker, 1995). But most homosexual people report not becoming aware of same-sex attraction until during or shortly after puberty, and not thinking of themselves as gay or lesbian (their socially influenced identity) until later in their teens or twenties (Garnets & Kimmel, 1990; Hammack, 2005). As adolescents, their friendship quality is similar to that of "straight" teenagers, and as adults, their partnerships are "remarkably similar" to heterosexual couples in love and satisfaction (Busseri et al., 2006; Peplau & Fingerhut, 2007).

Sexual Orientation Statistics

How many people are exclusively homosexual? About 10 percent, as the popular press has often assumed? A little more than 20 percent, as average Americans estimated in a 2002 Gallup survey (Robinson, 2002)? Not according to more than a dozen national surveys in the early 1990s, which explored sexual orientation in Europe and the United States, using methods that protected the respondents' anonymity. The most accurate figure seems to be about 3 or 4 percent of men and 1 or 2 percent of women (Laumann et al., 1994; Mosher et al., 2005; Smith, 1998). Estimates derived from the sexual activity of unmarried partners

 In one British survey, of the 18,876 people contacted, 1 percent were seemingly asexual, having "never felt sexually attracted to anyone at all" (Bogaert, 2004, 2006). ·

TEACHING TIP

Some of your students may be dealing with issues concerning sexuality, both heterosexual and homosexual. Discussions of homosexuality may be sensitive. Be aware of your community's understanding of the research concerning this issue. Determine how you can promote informed tolerance for individual people who may be dealing with questions in this area.

reported in the 2000 U.S. Census suggest that 2.5 percent of the population is gay or lesbian (Tarmann, 2002). Fewer than 1 percent of survey respondents—for example, 12 people out of 7076 Dutch adults in one survey (Sandfort et al., 2001)—reported being actively bisexual. A larger number of adults in that study reported having had an isolated homosexual experience. And most people report having had an occasional homosexual fantasy. Health experts find it helpful to know sexual statistics, but numbers do not decide issues of human rights.

What does it feel like to be homosexual in a heterosexual culture? If you are heterosexual, one way to understand is to imagine how you would feel if you were ostracized or fired for openly admitting or displaying your feelings toward someone of the other sex; if you overheard people making crude jokes about heterosexual people; if most movies, TV shows, and advertisements portrayed (or implied) homosexuality; and if your family members were pleading with you to change your heterosexual lifestyle and to enter into a homosexual marriage.

Sexual orientation is not an indicator of mental health. "Homosexuality, in and of itself, is not associated with mental disorders or emotional or social problems," declares the American Psychological Association (2007). But some homosexual individuals, especially during adolescence, struggle with their sexual attractions and are at increased risk for thinking about and attempting suicide (Balsam et al., 2005; Kitts, 2005; Plöderl & Fartacek, 2005). They may at first try to ignore or deny their desires, hoping they will go away. But they don't. The feelings typically persist, as do those of heterosexual people—who are similarly incapable of becoming homosexual (Haldeman, 1994, 2002; Myers & Scanzoni, 2005). Most of today's psychologists therefore view sexual orientation as neither willfully chosen nor willfully changed. Sexual orientation in some ways is like handedness: Most people are one way, some the other. A very few are truly ambidextrous. Regardless, the way one is endures.

This conclusion is most strongly established for men. Compared with men's sexual orientation, women's tends to be less strongly felt and potentially more fluid and changing (Chivers, 2005; Diamond, 2007; Peplau & Garnets, 2000). Men's lesser sexual variability is apparent in many ways, notes Roy Baumeister (2000). Across time, across cultures, across situations, and across differing levels of education, religious observance, and peer influence, adult women's sexual drive and interests are more flexible and varying than are adult men's. Women, more than men, for example, prefer to alternate periods of high sexual activity with periods of almost none, and are somewhat more likely than men to feel and act on bisexual attractions (Mosher et al., 2005).

In men, a high sex drive is associated with increased attraction to women (if heterosexual) or men (if homosexual). In women, a high sex drive is associated with increased attraction to both men and women (Lippa, 2006, 2007). When shown pictures of heterosexual couples, in either erotic or nonerotic contexts, heterosexual men look mostly at the woman while heterosexual women look more equally at both the man and the woman (Lykins et al., 2008). And when shown sexually explicit film clips, men's genital and subjective sexual arousal is mostly to preferred sexual stimuli (for heterosexual viewers, depictions of women). Women respond more nonspecifically to depictions of sexual activity involving males or females (Chivers et al., 2007). Baumeister calls this phenomenon the gender difference in *erotic plasticity*.

Origins of Sexual Orientation

Where do these enduring preferences—heterosexual or homosexual—come from? See if you can anticipate the consensus that has emerged from hundreds of research studies by responding *yes* or *no* to the following questions:

1. Is homosexuality linked with problems in a child's relationships with parents, such as with a domineering mother and an ineffectual father, or a possessive mother and a hostile father?

2. Does homosexuality involve a fear or hatred of people of the other gender, leading individuals to direct their sexual desires toward members of their own sex?

In one study of self-described heterosexual, bisexual, and homosexual men, those who described themselves as bisexual responded as did homosexual men—with genital arousal primarily to same-sex erotic stimuli (Rieger et al., 2005). They also exhibit interests and traits more like gay than heterosexual men (Lippa, 2005).

Personal values affect sexual orientation less than they affect other forms of sexual behavior. Compared with people who rarely attend religious services, for example, those who attend regularly are one-third as likely to have cohabited before marriage, and they report having had many fewer sex partners. But (if male) they are just as likely to be homosexual (Smith, 1998).

Note that the scientific question is not "What causes homosexuality?" (or "What causes heterosexuality?") but "What causes differing sexual orientations?" In pursuit of answers, psychological science compares the backgrounds and physiology of people whose sexual orientations *differ*.

TEACHING TIP

As recently as the 1970s, the American Psychiatric Association classified homosexuality as a mental illness in its *Diagnostic and Statistical Manual of Mental Disorders* (or DSM). Today, psychiatrists and psychologists alike do not view homosexuality as a mental disorder.

TROUBLESHOOTING

You may want to use the following terms that more accurately define the different types of orientations:

- **Lesbian** refers to homosexual women.

- **Gay** refers to homosexual men.

- **Bisexual** refers to men and women who prefer sex with both men and women.

- **Transgendered** refers to people who have undergone (or who are undergoing) sexual transformation or who believe themselves to be a different gender than the one they inhabit currently.

- **Questioning** refers to those who are questioning their sexual orientation, but have not yet decided whether they are homosexual, heterosexual, or bisexual.

TROUBLESHOOTING

Regardless of your community's religious beliefs, the findings presented in this section of the unit are based on scientific methodology. Help your students be critical thinkers about this issue.

INTERCONNECTING

Many studies about homosexual orientation are correlational. Remind students that correlation does not mean causation. The causes of homosexuality are not known, but these findings do point to potential variables that may influence homosexuality.

> "Efforts to change sexual orientation are unlikely to be successful and involve some risk of harm."
> American Psychological Association, 2009

3. Is sexual orientation linked with levels of sex hormones currently in the blood?

4. As children, were many homosexuals molested, seduced, or otherwise sexually victimized by an adult homosexual?

The answer to all these questions appears to be *no* (Storms, 1983). In interviews with nearly 1000 homosexuals and 500 heterosexuals, Kinsey Institute investigators assessed nearly every imaginable psychological cause of homosexuality—parental relationships, childhood sexual experiences, peer relationships, dating experiences (Bell et al., 1981; Hammersmith, 1982). Their findings: Homosexuals are no more likely than heterosexuals to have been smothered by maternal love, neglected by their father, or sexually abused. And consider this: If "distant fathers" were more likely to produce homosexual sons, then shouldn't boys growing up in father-absent homes more often be gay? (They are not.) And shouldn't the rising number of such homes have led to a noticeable increase in the gay population? (It has not.)

Homosexual people do, however, appear more often in certain populations. One study (Ludwig, 1995) of the biographies of 1004 eminent people found homosexual and bisexual people overrepresented, especially among poets (24 percent), fiction writers (21 percent), and artists and musicians (15 percent). Gay more than straight men also express interest in occupations that attract many women, such as decorator, florist, and flight attendant (Lippa, 2002). (Given that some 96 percent of men are not gay, most men in such occupations may nevertheless be straight.)

Men who have older brothers are also somewhat more likely to be gay, report Ray Blanchard (1997, 2008) and Anthony Bogaert (2003)—about one-third more likely for each additional older brother. If the odds of homosexuality are roughly 2 percent among first sons, they would rise to nearly 3 percent among second sons, 4 percent for third sons, and so on for each additional older brother (see **FIGURE 8A.15**). The reason for this curious phenomenon—the *fraternal birth-order effect*—is unclear. Blanchard suspects a defensive maternal immune response to foreign substances produced by male fetuses. With each pregnancy with a male fetus, the maternal antibodies may become stronger and may prevent the fetus' brain from developing in a male-typical pattern. Consistent with this biological explanation, the fraternal birth-order effect occurs only in men with older brothers from the same mother (whether reared together or not). Sexual orientation is unaffected by adoptive brothers (Bogaert, 2006). The birth-order effect on sexual orientation is not found among women with older sisters, women who were wombmates of twin brothers, and men who are not right-handed (Rose et al., 2002).

The bottom line from a half-century's theory and research: If there are environmental factors that influence sexual orientation, we do not yet know what they are. This reality has motivated researchers to consider more carefully the possible biological influences on orientation, including evidence of homosexuality in the animal world, and the influences of differing brain centers, genetics, and prenatal hormone exposure.

Same-Sex Attraction in Animals At Coney Island's New York Aquarium, penguins Wendell and Cass spent several years as devoted same-sex partners. Central Park Zoo penguins Silo and Roy show similar devotion. Biologist Bruce Bagemihl (1999) has identified several hundred species in which at least occasional same-sex relations have been observed. Grizzlies, gorillas, monkeys, flamingos, and owls are all on the long list. Among rams, for example, some 6 to 10 percent—to sheep-breeding ranchers, the "duds"—display same-sex attraction by shunning ewes and seeking to mount other males (Perkins & Fitzgerald, 1997). Some degree of homosexuality seems to be a natural part of the animal world.

➤ **FIGURE 8A.15**

The fraternal birth-order effect
Researcher Ray Blanchard (2008) offers these approximate curves depicting a man's likelihood of homosexuality as a function of his number of older brothers. This correlation has been found in several studies, but only among right-handed men.

The Brain and Sexual Orientation Researcher Simon LeVay (1991) studied sections of the hypothalamus taken from deceased heterosexual and homosexual people. As a gay scientist, LeVay wanted to do "something connected with my gay identity." To avoid biasing the results, he did a *blind study*, not knowing which donors were gay. For nine months he peered through his microscope at a cell cluster he thought might be important. Then, one morning, he broke the codes: One cell cluster was reliably larger in heterosexual men than in women and homosexual men. "I was almost in a state of shock," LeVay said (1994). "I took a walk by myself on the cliffs over the ocean. I sat for half an hour just thinking what this might mean."

It should not surprise us that brains differ with sexual orientation, a finding confirmed by a recent discovery that gay men and straight women have brain hemispheres of similar size, whereas in lesbian women and straight men, the right hemisphere is larger (Savic & Lindström, 2008). Remember our maxim: *Everything psychological is simultaneously biological.* But when do such brain differences begin? At conception? In the womb? During childhood or adolescence? Does experience produce these differences? Or is it genes or prenatal hormones (or genes via prenatal hormones)?

LeVay does not view the hypothalamic center as a sexual orientation center; rather, he sees it as an important part of the neural pathway engaged in sexual behavior. He acknowledges that sexual behavior patterns may influence the brain's anatomy. In fish, birds, rats, and humans, brain structures vary with experience—including sexual experience, reports sex researcher Marc Breedlove (1997). But LeVay believes it more likely that brain anatomy influences sexual orientation. His hunch seems confirmed by the discovery of a similar hypothalamic difference between the 7 to 10 percent of male sheep that display same-sex attraction and the 90+ percent attracted to females (Larkin et al., 2002; Roselli et al., 2002, 2004). Moreover, report University of London psychologists Qazi Rahman and Glenn Wilson (2003), "the neuroanatomical correlates of male homosexuality differentiate very early postnatally, if not prenatally."

Responses to hormone-derived sexual scents also point to a brain difference (Savic et al., 2005). When straight women are given a whiff of a scent derived from men's sweat, their hypothalamus lights up in an area governing sexual arousal. Gay men's brains respond similarly to the men's scent. But straight men's brains show the arousal response only to a female hormone derivative. Gays and lesbians similarly differ from their straight counterparts in other studies of brain responses to sex-related sweat odors and to pictures of male and female faces (Kranz & Ishai, 2006; Martins et al., 2005).

Genes and Sexual Orientation Are these sexuality-related brain differences genetically influenced? Evidence does indicate a genetic influence on sexual orientation. "First, homosexuality does appear to run in families," note Brian Mustanski and Michael Bailey (2003). "Second, twin studies have established that genes play a substantial role in explaining individual differences in sexual orientation." Identical twins are somewhat more likely than fraternal twins to share a homosexual orientation (Lángström et al., 2008). (Because sexual orientations differ in many identical twin pairs, especially female twins, we know that other factors besides genes are at work.)

Experimenters have also, by genetic manipulations, created female fruit flies that during courtship act like males (pursuing other females) and males that act like females (Demir & Dickson, 2005). "We have shown that a single gene in the fruit fly is sufficient to determine all aspects of the flies' sexual orientation and behavior," explained Barry Dickson (2005). With humans, it's likely that multiple genes, possibly in interaction with other influences, shape sexual orientation. One study financed by the U.S. National Institutes of Health is analyzing the genes of more than 1000 gay brothers in search of such genetic markers.

Juliet and Juliet Boston's beloved swan couple, "Romeo and Juliet," were discovered actually to be, as are many other animal partners, a same-sex pair.

TEACHING TIP

The studies of brain differences in men and women, gay or straight, are not experimental, so their conclusions are limited. These results may be due to a variety of factors, one of which is the sexual orientation of the donor. The brain science of sexual orientation is very young. Students should consider the types of studies needed to come to solid conclusions about the biology of sexual orientation.

UNIT 8A

TEACHING TIP

Use Table 8A.1 to summarize the book's presentation of sexual orientation. Myers cites numerous studies, and this table gives students a concise picture of the important findings.

TROUBLESHOOTING

Regardless of how students may view sexual orientation, there is no excuse for negative prejudice or discrimination against people they might feel are different sexually. All students deserve to be treated tolerantly. Help students to be intolerant of intolerance.

> "Modern scientific research indicates that sexual orientation is . . . partly determined by genetics, but more specifically by hormonal activity in the womb."
>
> Glenn Wilson and Qazi Rahman, *Born Gay: The Psychobiology of Sex Orientation*, 2005

Prenatal Hormones and Sexual Orientation Elevated rates of homosexual orientation in identical *and* fraternal twins suggest that not just shared genetics but also a shared prenatal environment may be a factor. In animals and some exceptional human cases, abnormal prenatal hormone conditions have altered a fetus' sexual orientation. German researcher Gunter Dorner (1976, 1988) pioneered research on the influence of prenatal hormones by manipulating a fetal rat's exposure to male hormones, thereby "inverting" its sexual orientation. In other studies, when pregnant sheep were injected with testosterone during a critical period of fetal development, their female offspring later showed homosexual behavior (Money, 1987).

A critical period for the human brain's neural-hormonal control system may exist between the middle of the second and fifth months after conception (Ellis & Ames, 1987; Gladue, 1990; Meyer-Bahlburg, 1995). Exposure to the hormone levels typically experienced by female fetuses during this time appears to predispose the person (whether female or male) to be attracted to males in later life.

On several traits, gays and lesbians appear to fall midway between straight females and males (**TABLE 8A.1**). For example, lesbians' cochlea and hearing systems develop in a way that is intermediate between those of heterosexual females and heterosexual males, which seems attributable to prenatal hormonal influence (McFadden, 2002). Fingerprint ridge counts may also differ. Although most people have more fingerprint ridges on their right hand than on their left, some studies find a greater right-left difference in heterosexual males than in females and gay males (Hall & Kimura, 1994; Mustanski et al., 2002; Sanders et al., 2002). Given that fingerprint ridges are complete by the sixteenth fetal week, this difference may be due to prenatal hormones. Prenatal hormones also are a possible explanation

TABLE 8A.1

BIOLOGICAL CORRELATES OF SEXUAL ORIENTATION

On average (the evidence is strongest for males), various biological and behavioral traits of gays and lesbians fall between those of straight men and straight women. Tentative findings—some in need of replication—include these:

Brain differences

- Brain asymmetry is greater in straight men and lesbian women.
- One hypothalamic cell cluster is larger in straight men than in women and gay men; same difference is found in male sheep displaying other-sex versus same-sex attraction.
- Gay men's hypothalamus reacts as does a straight woman's to the smell of sex-related hormones.

Genetic influences

- Shared sexual orientation is higher among identical twins than among fraternal twins.
- Sexual attraction in fruit flies can be genetically manipulated.

Prenatal hormonal influences

- Altered prenatal hormone exposure may lead to homosexuality in humans and other animals.
- Right-handed men with several older biological brothers are more likely to be gay.

These brain differences and genetic and prenatal influences may contribute to observed gay-straight differences in

• spatial abilities.	• gender nonconformity.
• fingerprint ridge counts.	• age of onset of puberty in males.
• auditory system development.	• male body size.
• handedness.	• sleep length.
• occupational preferences.	• physical aggression.
• relative finger lengths.	• male eating disorders.

for why data from 20 studies revealed that "homosexual participants had 39 percent greater odds of being non–right-handed" (Lalumière et al., 2000).

Another you-never-would-have-guessed-it gay-straight difference appears in studies showing that gay men's spatial abilities resemble those typical of straight women (Cohen, 2002; Gladue, 1994; McCormick & Witelson, 1991; Sanders & Wright, 1997). On mental rotation tasks such as the one illustrated in **FIGURE 8A.16**, straight men tend to outscore women. Studies by Qazi Rahman and colleagues (2003, 2008) find that, as on a number of other measures, the scores of gays and lesbians fall between those of heterosexual males and females. But straight women and gays both outperform straight men at remembering objects' spatial locations in tasks like those found in memory games (Hassan & Rahman, 2007).

Because the physiological evidence is preliminary and controversial, some scientists remain skeptical. Rather than specifying sexual orientation, they suggest, biological factors may predispose a *temperament* that influences sexuality "in the context of individual learning and experience" (Byne & Parsons, 1993). Daryl Bem (1996, 1998, 2000) has theorized that genes code for prenatal hormones and brain anatomy, which predispose temperaments that lead children to prefer gender-typical or gender-atypical activities and friends. These preferences may later lead children to feel attracted to whichever sex feels different from their own. The dissimilar-seeming sex (whether or not it conforms to one's own anatomy) becomes associated with anxiety and other forms of arousal, which are eventually transformed into romantic arousal. The exotic becomes erotic.

Regardless of the process, the consistency of the brain, genetic, and prenatal findings has swung the pendulum toward a biological explanation of sexual orientation (Rahman & Wilson, 2003). This helps explain why sexual orientation is so difficult to change, and why a BBC Internet study of more than 200,000 people found the same gay-straight differences in personality and interests worldwide (Lippa, 2007a,b, 2008).

Still, some people wonder: Should the cause of sexual orientation matter? Perhaps it shouldn't, but people's assumptions matter. Those who believe—as do 41 percent of Americans and most gays and lesbians—that sexual orientation is biologically disposed also tend to express more accepting attitudes toward homosexual people (Allen et al., 1996; Gallup polls; Haslam & Levy, 2006; Kaiser, 2001; Whitley, 1990).

➤ **FIGURE 8A.16**

Spatial abilities and sexual orientation
Which of the four figures can be rotated to match the target figure at the top? Straight males tend to find this an easier task than do straight females, with gays and lesbians intermediate. (From Rahman et al., 2003, with 60 people tested in each group.)

BEFORE YOU MOVE ON . . .

➤ **ASK YOURSELF**
What do you think would be an effective strategy for reducing teen pregnancy?

➤ **TEST YOURSELF 3**
How might the evolutionary perspective, drive-reduction theory, and arousal theory explain our sexual motivation?

Answers to the Test Yourself questions can be found in Appendix E at the end of the book.

The Need to Belong

11: What evidence points to our human need to belong?

SEPARATED FROM FRIENDS OR FAMILY—isolated in prison, alone at a new school, living in a foreign land—most people feel keenly their lost connections with important others. We are what Aristotle called *the social animal*. "Without friends," wrote Aristotle in his *Nichomachean Ethics*, "no one would choose to live, though he had all other

 TEACHING TIP

Have students discuss the social influences on sex role behaviors. Have them consider how we regard children who engage in atypical activities for their gender—boys who play with dolls or girls who play with trucks.

● How accepting are we of those types of behaviors?

● Does engaging in atypical sex role behaviors make one homosexual? Why not?

 TEACHING TIP

Do your students use words like "gay" or "retarded" as synonyms for "stupid"? This is a common practice with today's teens. Encourage students to refrain from this use of these words. Those who are homosexual or questioning or who have special needs (or have siblings with special needs) may find the use of these terms to be offensive and demeaning. It is a small way to encourage tolerance among your students.

UNIT 8A

INTERCONNECTING

Erik Erikson's theory of psycho-social development (discussed in Unit 9) addressed the need to belong in the stage of young adulthood. In the *intimacy vs. isolation* stage, adults must find meaningful relationships or feel isolated from their peers and society. Typically, this intimacy is found in marriage, but adults who do not marry can find these types of relationships with close friends, nuclear family members, or colleagues.

> "The only thing that really matters in life are your relationships to other people."
>
> George Vaillant, 2009, when asked what he had learned from his study following 238 Harvard University men from the 1930s to the end of their lives.

Separation amplifies the felt need to belong In the film *Cast Away*, Chuck Noland (played by Tom Hanks) is stranded alone on a desert island for four years after a plane crash. He combats social starvation by talking with his girlfriend's snapshot and a volleyball he names Wilson.

20th Century Fox/DreamWorks/The Kobal Collection

goods." Although healthy people vary in their wish for privacy and solitude, most of us seek to affiliate with others, even to become strongly attached to certain others in enduring, close relationships. Human beings, contended the personality theorist Alfred Adler, have an "urge to community" (Ferguson, 1989, 2001). Roy Baumeister and Mark Leary (1995) have assembled evidence for this deep *need to belong*.

Aiding Survival

Social bonds boosted our ancestors' survival rate. By keeping children close to their caregivers, attachments served as a powerful survival impulse. As adults, those who formed attachments were more likely to reproduce and to co-nurture their offspring to maturity. To be "wretched" literally means, in its Middle English origin (*wrecche*), to be without kin nearby.

Survival also was enhanced by cooperation. In solo combat, our ancestors were not the toughest predators. But as hunters, they learned that six hands were better than two. As foragers, they gained protection from predators and enemies by traveling in groups. Those who felt a need to belong survived and reproduced most successfully, and their genes now predominate. We are innately social creatures. People in every society on Earth belong to groups (and, as Unit 14 explains, prefer and favor "us" over "them").

Do you have close friends—people with whom you freely disclose your ups and downs? As we shall see later in this unit, people who feel supported by close relationships are not only happier, they also live with better health and at lower risk for psychological disorder and premature death than do those who lack social support. Married people, for example, are less at risk for depression, suicide, and early death than are unattached people.

Wanting to Belong

The need to belong colors our thoughts and emotions. We spend a great deal of time thinking about actual and hoped-for relationships. When relationships form, we often feel joy. Falling in mutual love, people have been known to feel their cheeks ache from their irrepressible grins. Asked, "What is necessary for your happiness?" or "What is it that makes your life meaningful?" most people mention—before anything else—close, satisfying relationships with family, friends, or romantic partners (Berscheid, 1985). Happiness hits close to home.

Pause a moment to consider: What was your most satisfying moment in the past week? Kennon Sheldon and his colleagues (2001) asked that question of American and South Korean collegians, then asked them to rate how much this peak experience had satisfied various needs. In both countries, the satisfaction of self-esteem and relatedness-belonging needs were the top two contributors to the peak moment. Another study found that *very* happy students are not distinguished by their money but by their "rich and satisfying close relationships" (Diener & Seligman, 2002). The need to belong runs deeper, it seems, than any need to be rich. When our need for relatedness is satisfied in balance with two other basic psychological needs—*autonomy* and *competence*—the result is a deep sense of well-being (Deci & Ryan, 2002; Patrick et al., 2007; Sheldon & Niemiec, 2006). To feel connected, free, and capable is to enjoy a good life.

South Africans have a word for the human bonds that define us all. *Ubuntu* (oo-BOON-too), explained Desmond Tutu (1999), expresses the fact that "my humanity is caught up, is inextricably bound up, in yours." A Zulu maxim captures the idea: *Umuntu ngumuntu ngabantu*—"a person is a person through other persons."

When we feel included, accepted, and loved by those important to us, our self-esteem rides high. Indeed, say Mark Leary and his colleagues (1998), self-esteem is a gauge of how valued and accepted we feel. Much of our social behavior therefore aims to increase our belonging—our social acceptance and inclusion. To avoid rejection, we generally conform to group standards and seek to make favorable impressions (more on this in

Unit 14). To win friendship and esteem, we monitor our behavior, hoping to create the right impressions. Seeking love and belonging, we spend billions on clothes, cosmetics, and diet and fitness aids—all motivated by our quest for acceptance. In one recent survey of entering American collegians, 86 percent reported spending some time on social networking sites such as Facebook (Pryor et al., 2007).

Like sexual motivation, which feeds both love and exploitation, the need to belong feeds both deep attachments and menacing threats. Out of our need to define a "we" come loving families, faithful friendships, and team spirit, but also gangs, ethnic rivalries, and fanatic nationalism.

Sustaining Relationships

For most of us, familiarity breeds liking, not contempt. Thrown together in groups at school, at band camp, on a ski trip, we later resist breaking those social bonds—we promise to call, to write, to come back for reunions. Parting, we feel distress. You don't need to look far to see people spending hours speaking into a BlackBerry, video-chatting on computers, sustaining their relationships with absent people by talking, texting, and e-mailing.

When the fear of being alone seems worse than the pain of emotional or physical abuse, attachments can keep people in abusive relationships. Even when bad relationships break, people suffer. After separations, feelings of loneliness and anger—and sometimes even a strange desire to be near the former partner—linger. In one 16-nation survey, and repeated in U.S. surveys, separated and divorced people have been half as likely as married people to say they were "very happy" (Inglehart, 1990; NORC, 2007).

The need to connect Six days a week, women from the Philippines work as "domestic helpers" in 154,000 Hong Kong households. On Sundays, they throng to the central business district to picnic, dance, sing, talk, and laugh. "Humanity could stage no greater display of happiness," reported one observer (*Economist,* 2001).

Our fear of being alone has some basis in reality. Children who move through a series of foster homes, with repeated disruption of budding attachments, may come to have difficulty forming deep attachments. And children reared in institutions without a sense of belonging to anyone, or locked away at home under extreme neglect, become pathetic creatures—withdrawn, frightened, speechless.

When something threatens or dissolves our social ties, negative emotions—anxiety, loneliness, jealousy, guilt—overwhelm us. The bereaved often feel life is empty, pointless. Even the first days away from home at camp or first weeks at college can be distressing. For immigrants and refugees moving alone to new places, the stress and loneliness can be depressing. But if feelings of acceptance and connection build, so do self-esteem, positive feelings, and desires to help rather than hurt others (Buckley & Leary, 2001). After years of placing individual refugee and immigrant families in isolated communities, U.S. policies today encourage *chain migration* (Pipher, 2002). The second refugee Sudanese family settling in a town generally has an easier adjustment than the first.

The Pain of Ostracism

Sometimes, though, the need to belong is denied. Perhaps you can recall such a time, when you felt excluded or ignored or shunned. Perhaps you received the silent treatment. Perhaps others avoided you, or averted their eyes in your presence, or even mocked you behind your back.

Social psychologist Kipling Williams (2007) and his colleagues have studied such experiences of *ostracism*—of social exclusion—in both natural and laboratory settings. Worldwide, humans control social behavior via the punishing effects of severe ostracism—of exile, imprisonment, and solitary confinement. For children, even a brief time-out in isolation can be punishing. Asked to describe personal episodes that made them feel especially good about themselves, people often think of some achievement.

INTERCONNECTING

Social psychologists call the phenomenon where familiarity breeds liking the *mere exposure effect*. With this effect, simply being exposed to a stimulus repeatedly and consistently causes one to like that stimulus more. It explains why an annoying song (or little brother or sister) can be remembered fondly or enjoyed.

TEACHING TIP

At this point, you may want to use **Classroom Exercises:** *The Need to Affiliate* (p. 15) or *Measures and Issues Related to the Need to Belong* (p. 15) or *Fear of Negative Evaluation Scale* (p. 17) or *Demonstrating Ostracism: The Train Ride* (p. 18) from Bolt's Teacher's Resource Binder.

UNIT 8A

A violent response to social exclusion
Most socially excluded teens do not commit violence, but some do. Charles "Andy" Williams, described by a classmate as someone his peers derided as "freak, dork, nerd, stuff like that," went on a shooting spree at his suburban California high school, killing 2 and wounding 13 (Bowles & Kasindorf, 2001).

 Note: The researchers later debriefed and reassured the participants. •

TEACHING TIP

Use this presentation of social ostracism to discuss the effects of bullying on students. While students typically think of bullying as a physical act (fighting or overtly threatening behavior), bullying can also be social. Socially isolating other students, either by spreading rumors or making them sit alone in class or the cafeteria, can be bullying just as much as fighting is. In fact, some psychologists believe that bullying like this is more detrimental than fighting. Many school shooters, like the one depicted on this page, were often the victim of some type of social-isolation bullying.

But asked what made them feel especially *bad* about themselves, they will—about four times in five—describe a relationship difficulty (Pillemer et al., 2007).

To be shunned—given the cold shoulder or the silent treatment, with others' eyes avoiding yours—is to have one's need to belong threatened (Williams & Zadro, 2001). "It's the meanest thing you can do to someone, especially if you know they can't fight back. I never should have been born," said Lea, a lifelong victim of the silent treatment by her mother and grandmother. Like Lea, people often respond to social ostracism with depressed moods, initial efforts to restore their acceptance, and then withdrawal. After two years of silent treatment by his employer, Richard reported, "I came home every night and cried. I lost 25 pounds, had no self-esteem and felt that I wasn't worthy."

To experience ostracism is to experience real pain, as Kipling Williams and his colleagues were surprised to discover in their studies of *cyber-ostracism* (Gonsalkorale & Williams, 2006). (Perhaps you can recall the feeling of being ignored by someone you tried to friend on Facebook, or having an e-mail go unanswered.) Such ostracism, they discovered, even by strangers or by a despised outgroup, such as the Australian branch of the KKK, takes a toll: It elicits increased activity in a brain area, the *anterior cingulate cortex*, that also activates in response to physical pain (Eisenberger et al., 2003). Psychologically, we seem to experience social pain with the same emotional unpleasantness that marks physical pain (MacDonald & Leary, 2005). And pain, whatever its source, focuses our attention and motivates corrective action.

Rejected and unable to remedy the situation, people may seek new friends—or they may turn nasty. In a series of experiments, Jean Twenge and her collaborators (2001, 2002, 2007; Baumeister et al., 2002; Maner et al., 2007) told some students (who had taken a personality test) that they were "the type likely to end up alone later in life," or that people they had met didn't want them in a group that was forming. They told other students that they would have "rewarding relationships throughout life," or that "everyone chose you as someone they'd like to work with." Those excluded became much more likely to engage in self-defeating behaviors and to underperform on aptitude tests. The rejection also interfered with their empathy for others and made them more likely to act in disparaging or aggressive ways against those who had excluded them (blasting them with noise, for example). "If intelligent, well-adjusted, successful university students can turn aggressive in response to a small laboratory experience of social exclusion," noted the research team, "it is disturbing to imagine the aggressive tendencies that might arise from a series of important rejections or chronic exclusion from desired groups in actual social life." Indeed, reports Williams (2007), ostracism "weaves through case after case of school violence."

BEFORE YOU MOVE ON . . .

➤ **ASK YOURSELF**

Have there been times when you felt "out of the loop" with family and friends, or even ostracized by them? How did you respond?

➤ **TEST YOURSELF 4**

How might the evolutionary perspective, drive-reduction theory, and arousal theory explain our affiliation needs?

Answers to the Test Yourself questions can be found in Appendix E at the end of the book.

* * *

We have seen that identifiable physiological mechanisms drive some motives, such as hunger (though learned tastes and cultural expectations matter, too). Other motives, such as our need for affiliation, are more obviously driven by psychological factors, such as the social rewards that come from belonging. What unifies all motives is their common effect: the energizing and directing of behavior.

TEACHING TIP

At this point, you may want to use **Lecture/Discussion Topics: *Fear of Intimacy Scale*** (p. 15) or ***Social Ostracism*** (p. 17) or ***Does Social Rejection Literally Feel Cold?*** (p. 19) from Bolt's Teacher's Resource Binder.

UNIT REVIEW: Motivation

Motivational Concepts

1: From what perspectives do psychologists view motivated behavior?

The *instinct*/evolutionary perspective explores genetic influences on complex behaviors. *Drive-reduction theory* explores how physiological needs create aroused tension states (drives) that direct us to satisfy those needs. Arousal theory proposes a *motivation* for behaviors, such as curiosity-driven behaviors, that do not reduce physiological needs. Maslow's *hierarchy of needs* proposes a pyramid of human needs, from basic needs, such as hunger and thirst, up to higher-level needs, such as self-actualization and self-transcendence.

Hunger

2: What physiological factors produce hunger?

Hunger's pangs correspond to the stomach's contractions, but hunger also has other causes. Appetite hormones include insulin (controls blood *glucose*), leptin (secreted by fat cells), orexin (secreted by the hypothalamus), ghrelin (secreted by an empty stomach), obestatin (secreted by the stomach), and PYY (secreted by digestive tract). Two areas of the hypothalamus regulate the body's weight by affecting feelings of hunger and satiety. The body may have a *set point* (a biologically fixed tendency to maintain an optimum weight) or a looser settling point (also influenced by the environment).

3: What psychological and cultural factors influence hunger?

Hunger also reflects learning, our memory of when we last ate, and our expectation of when we should eat again. Humans as a species prefer certain tastes (such as sweet and salty) but we satisfy those preferences with specific foods prescribed by our situation and our culture. Some taste preferences, such as the avoidance of new foods or of foods that have made us ill, have survival value.

4: How do anorexia nervosa, bulimia nervosa, and binge-eating disorder demonstrate the influence of psychological forces on physiologically motivated behaviors?

In these eating disorders, psychological factors may overwhelm the homeostatic drive to maintain a balanced internal state. People with *anorexia nervosa* (usually adolescent females) starve themselves but continue to diet because they view themselves as fat. Those with *bulimia nervosa* binge and purge in secret (primarily females in their late teens and twenties). Those with *binge-eating disorder* binge but do not purge. Cultural pressures, low self-esteem, and negative emotions interact with stressful life experiences to produce eating disorders. Twin research also indicates, however, that these disorders may have a genetic component.

5: What factors predispose some people to become and remain obese?

The lack of exercise combined with the abundance of high-calorie food has led to increased rates of obesity, showing the influence of environment. Twin and adoption studies indicate that body weight is also genetically influenced (in the number of fat cells and *basal metabolic rate*). Thus, genes and environment interact to produce obesity. Those wishing to lose weight are advised to make a lifelong change in habits, minimize exposure to tempting food cues, boost energy expenditure through exercise, eat healthy foods, space meals throughout the day, beware of the binge, and forgive the occasional lapse.

Sexual Motivation

6: What stages mark the human sexual response cycle?

Masters and Johnson described four stages in the human *sexual response cycle*: excitement, plateau, orgasm (which seems to involve similar feelings and brain activity in males and females), and resolution. In the resolution phase, males experience a *refractory period*, during which renewed arousal and orgasm are impossible.

7: Do hormones influence human sexual motivation?

The female *estrogen* and male *testosterone* hormones influence human sexual behavior less directly than they influence nonhuman animals. Unlike other mammalian females, women's sexuality is more responsive to testosterone level than to estrogen level. Short-term shifts in testosterone level are normal in men, partly in response to stimulation.

8: How do internal and external stimuli influence sexual motivation?

Erotic material and other external stimuli can trigger sexual arousal in both men and women, although the activated brain areas differ somewhat. Men respond more specifically to sexual depictions involving their preferred sex. Sexually explicit material may lead people to perceive their partners as comparatively less appealing and to devalue their relationships. Sexually coercive material tends to increase viewers' acceptance of rape and violence toward women. Fantasies (imagined stimuli) also influence sexual arousal.

9: What factors influence teen sexuality, teen pregnancy, and risk of sexually transmitted infections?

Rates of teen intercourse vary from culture to culture and era to era. Factors contributing to teen pregnancy include ignorance; minimal communication about contraception with parents, partners, and peers; guilt related to sexual activity; alcohol use; and mass media norms of unprotected and impulsive sexuality. STIs—sexually

UNIT 8A

ANSWERS to Multiple-Choice Questions

1. **b** Drive-reduction theory
2. **b** ostracism.
3. **d** Arousal theory
4. **d** The body reacts as if it's being starved and metabolic rates drop.
5. **e** lost interest in social activities.
6. **a** Increased body dissatisfaction.
7. **b** Fat is a fuel reserve during periods when food is scarce.
8. **d** Motivation
9. **c** an overweight person was rated less worthy of hiring for a job.
10. **c** helps to describe human motivation.
11. **e** Ignorance
12. **a** biology.
13. **c** Homeostasis
14. **a** Tumor in the hypothalamus.
15. **a** Plateau

transmitted infections—have spread rapidly. Attempts to protect teens through comprehensive sex-education programs include contraceptive and abstinence education. High intelligence, religiosity, father presence, and participation in service learning programs are predictors of teen sexual restraint.

10: What has research taught us about sexual orientation? There is no research evidence that environmental influences determine *sexual orientation*. Support for biological influences on orientation includes the presence of same-sex behaviors in many animal species, straight-gay differences in body and brain characteristics, higher rates of a homosexual

orientation in certain families, and the discovery of a critical period of prenatal development during which exposure to certain hormones affects orientation.

The Need to Belong
11: What evidence points to our human need to belong? Our need to affiliate or belong—to feel connected and identified with others—had survival value for our ancestors, which may explain why humans in every society live in groups. Societies everywhere control behavior with the threat of ostracism or shunning others. When socially excluded, people may engage in self-defeating behaviors (performing below their ability) or in antisocial behaviors.

Terms and Concepts to Remember

motivation, p. 328
instinct, p. 328
drive-reduction theory, p. 329
homeostasis, p. 329
incentive, p. 329
hierarchy of needs, p. 330

glucose, p. 333
set point, p. 335
basal metabolic rate, p. 335
anorexia nervosa, p. 337
bulimia nervosa, p. 337
binge-eating disorder, p. 337

sexual response cycle, p. 349
refractory period, p. 349
estrogens, p. 350
testosterone, p. 350
sexual orientation, p. 354

 AP* Practice Test Questions

Multiple-Choice Questions

1. _____ is the idea that physiological needs create an aroused state that motivates an organism to reduce the need.
   a. Instinct theory
   b. Drive-reduction theory
   c. Self-assertion instinct
   d. Arousal theory
   e. Hierarchy of needs

2. Attempts to control social behavior by using the punishing effects of isolation is an example of
   a. attachment disorder.
   b. ostracism.
   c. exploitation.
   d. wanting to belong.
   e. conforming.

   *AP is a trademark registered and/or owned by the College Board, which was not involved in the production of, and does not endorse, this product.

3. _____ explains why, when our biological needs are satisfied, we may still feel driven to experience stimulation.
   a. Incentive
   b. Homeostasis
   c. Instinct
   d. Arousal theory
   e. Physiology

4. Why does weight loss come slowly following a rapid loss during the initial three weeks of a rigorous diet?
   a. The number of fat cells makes further weight loss impossible.
   b. When a person's hunger increases, metabolism increases.
   c. When an obese person's set point has been reached, weight loss increases dramatically.
   d. The body reacts as if it's being starved and metabolic rates drop.
   e. An obese person cannot maintain a rigorous weight loss diet.

5. Research conducted by Ancel Keys on semistarvation found that men who were given just enough food to stabilize their weight at 25 percent below their starting weight
   a. became obsessed with physical exercise.
   b. were more interpersonally outgoing.
   c. showed increases in mental cognition.
   d. were in a state of homeostasis.
   e. lost interest in social activities.

6. In Eric Stice's study of adolescent girls, vulnerable girls were more likely to exhibit which of the following tendencies?
   a. Increased body dissatisfaction.
   b. Less self-consciousness.
   c. Increased acceptance of their own body image.
   d. Reduction in eating disorders.
   e. Decrease in academic performance.

 TECHNOLOGY RESOURCES

These resources will be helpful for teaching the concepts in this portion of the unit:

- *Video: Psychology: The Human Experience, Module 18: What Is Motivation?*
- *Psychology Video Tool Kit: Purging Food; Overcoming Anorexia Nervosa; Self-Image: Body Dissatisfaction Among Teenage Girls; Eating and Weight Gain: A Role for Fidgeting; Eating and Weight Gain: Genetic Engineering*
- *PsychSim 5: Hunger and the Fat Rat*

7. Which of the following is the best biological explanation for why the human body stores fat?

a. Fat signals affluence and social status.
b. Fat is a fuel reserve during periods when food is scarce.
c. Fat is a display of abundant food sources.
d. Fat keeps the body warm in winter climates.
e. Fat combats the global epidemic of diabetes.

8. What do we call a need or desire that energizes and directs behavior?

a. Incentive
b. Refractory period
c. Emotion
d. Motivation
e. Instinct

9. In a weight discrimination study, Regina Pingitore and her colleagues demonstrated that

a. overweight men are rated less worthy than overweight women.
b. there is a correlation between a person's weight and intelligence.
c. an overweight person was rated less worthy of hiring for a job.
d. overweight people make as much money as non-overweight people.
e. overweight people, on average, are as satisfied as their non-overweight peers.

10. Abraham Maslow's hierarchy of needs is a framework that

a. aims to eliminate arousal.
b. explains our homeostatic system.
c. helps to describe human motivation.
d. helps people reach self-transcendence.
e. is universally fixed.

11. Which of the following will likely increase an adolescent's odds of pregnancy or contracting a sexually transmitted disease?

a. High intelligence
b. Father presence
c. Religious engagement
d. Sexual orientation
e. Ignorance

12. Current research suggests that sexual orientation is most likely a result of

a. biology.
b. intelligence.
c. social problems.
d. mental health.
e. culture.

13. What is the tendency to maintain a balanced or constant internal state?

a. Hierarchy of needs
b. Basal metabolic rate
c. Homeostasis
d. Instinct
e. Motivation

14. A person who eats excessively and never seems to feel full may have which of the following conditions?

a. Tumor in the hypothalamus.
b. Too much insulin.
c. Stomach ulcer.
d. Stomach bypass surgery.
e. Too much obestatin.

15. Which of the following is one of the stages of the sexual response cycle described by Masters and Johnson?

a. Plateau
b. Refractory
c. Attraction
d. Compensation
e. Bingeing

Free-Response Question

Explain four challenges faced by those attempting to lose weight. What are four steps one can take to avoid obesity?

WEB

Multiple-choice self-tests and more may be found at www.worthpublishers.com/myers

Rubric for Grading the Free-Response Question

This is an 8-point question. Allow one point (up to four) for adequately describing challenges faced, and one point (up to four) for each correct obesity-avoiding step. Modify the rubric by adding or subtracting terms depending on what was emphasized in class.

Challenges include but are not limited to:

- Once the number of fat cells increases, it never decreases.
- Once we become fat, we require less food to maintain our weight than we did to attain it.
- The body adapts to starvation by lowering its metabolism and burning off fewer calories.
- Genetics: Given an obese parent, a boy is three times, and a girl six times, more likely to be obese than their counterparts with normal-weight parents.

Steps to avoid obesity include but are not limited to:

- Stay physically active.
- Watch portion sizes to be sure they don't become unhealthfully large.
- Get your sleep: Children and adults who skimp on sleep are more vulnerable to obesity.
- Social influence: People are more likely to become obese if their friends are obese. Those who stay slim encourage their friends to do likewise.
- People who need to lose weight should set realistic and moderate goals, undertaking programs that modify lifestyle and ongoing eating behavior.

UNIT 8B

Pacing Guide

Use the following guide to determine how many instructional days to devote to this portion of the unit depending on the type of course you teach:

Year-long course: 5–7 days
Block schedule/Semester-long course: 3–4 days

This entire unit (Parts A & B) encompasses 6–8 percent of the AP Exam. Spending an appropriate amount of time on this unit will help students do well on the AP Exam.

Motivation and Emotion:
8B—Emotions, Stress, and Health

Motivated behavior often is driven by powerful emotions that color and sometimes disrupt our lives. I will never forget the day I went to a huge store to drop off film and brought along Peter, my toddler first-born child. As I set Peter down on his feet and prepared to complete the paperwork, a passerby warned, "You'd better be careful or you'll lose that boy!" Not more than a few breaths later, after dropping the film in the slot, I turned and found no Peter beside me.

With mild anxiety, I peered around one end of the counter. No Peter in sight. With slightly more anxiety, I peered around the other end. No Peter there, either. Now, with my heart accelerating, I circled the neighboring counters. Still no Peter anywhere. As anxiety turned to panic, I began racing up and down the store aisles. He was nowhere to be found. Apprised of my alarm, the store manager used the public-address system to ask customers to assist in looking for a missing child. Soon after, I passed the customer who had warned me. "I told you that you were going to lose him!" he scorned. With visions of kidnapping (strangers routinely adored that beautiful child), I braced for the possibility that my negligence had caused me to lose what I loved above all else, and that I might have to return home and face my wife without our only child.

But then, as I passed the customer service counter yet again, there he was, having been found and returned by some obliging customer! In an instant, the arousal of terror spilled into ecstasy. Clutching my son, with tears suddenly flowing, I found myself unable to speak my thanks and stumbled out of the store awash in grateful joy.

Where do such emotions come from? Why do we have them? What are they made of? Emotions are our body's adaptive response. They exist not to give us interesting experiences but to enhance our survival. When we face challenges, emotions focus our attention and energize our action. Our heart races. Our pace quickens. All our senses go on high alert. Receiving unexpected good news, we may find our eyes tearing. We raise our hands triumphantly. We feel exuberance and a newfound confidence. Yet when prolonged and experienced as stress, emotions can also have a damaging effect on our health, as we will see.

Theories of Emotion

1: What are the components of an emotion?

AS MY ANGUISHED SEARCH for Peter illustrates, **emotions** are a mix of (1) physiological arousal (heart pounding), (2) expressive behaviors (quickened pace), and (3) consciously experienced thoughts (is this a kidnapping?) and feelings (a sense of fear, and later joy). The puzzle for psychologists has been figuring out how these three pieces fit together.

Suggested Readings

Axtell, R. E. (1998). *Gestures: The do's and taboos of body language around the world.* Hoboken, NJ: John Wiley & Sons.

Carlson, J., & Hatfield, E. (1992). *Psychology of emotion.* Fort Worth, TX: Harcourt Brace Jovanovich.

Deaux, K., Dane, F., & Wrightsman, L. (1993). *Social psychology in the 90s* (6th ed.). Pacific Grove, CA: Brooks/Cole.

LeDoux, J. (1998). *The emotional brain: The mysterious underpinnings of emotional life.* New York: Simon & Schuster.

Parkinson, B., Totterdell, P., Briner, R. B., & Reynolds, S. (1996). *Changing moods: The psychology of mood and mood regulation.* New York: Longman.

Pinker, S. (1997). *How the mind works.* New York: Norton.

There are two controversies over the interplay of our physiology, expressions, and experience in emotions. The first, a chicken-and-egg debate, is old: Does your physiological arousal precede or follow your emotional experience? (Did I first notice my heart racing and my faster step, and then feel anxious dread about losing Peter? Or did my sense of fear come first, stirring my heart and legs to respond?) The second controversy concerns the interaction between thinking and feeling: Does cognition always precede emotion? (Did I *think* about the kidnapping threat before reacting emotionally?)

Common sense tells most of us that we cry because we are sad, lash out because we are angry, tremble because we are afraid. First comes conscious awareness, then the physiological trimmings. But to pioneering psychologist William James, this commonsense view of emotion was backward. According to James, "We feel sorry because we cry, angry because we strike, afraid because we tremble" (1890, p. 1066). Perhaps you can recall a time when your car skidded on slick pavement. As it careened crazily, you countersteered and regained control. Just after the fishtail ended, you noticed your racing heart and then, shaking with fright, you felt the whoosh of emotion. Your feeling of fear *followed* your body's response. James' idea, also proposed by Danish physiologist Carl Lange, is called the **James-Lange theory**. First comes a distinct physiological response, then (as we observe that response) comes our experienced emotion.

This James-Lange theory struck U.S. physiologist Walter Cannon as implausible. Cannon thought the body's responses were not distinct enough to evoke the different emotions. Does a racing heart signal fear, anger, or love? Also, changes in heart rate, perspiration, and body temperature seemed too slow to trigger sudden emotion. Cannon, and later another physiologist, Philip Bard, concluded that our physiological arousal and our emotional experience occur *simultaneously*: The emotion-triggering stimulus is routed simultaneously to the brain's cortex, causing the subjective awareness of emotion, and to the sympathetic nervous system, causing the body's arousal. This **Cannon-Bard theory** implies that your heart begins pounding *as* you experience fear; one does not cause the other. Our physiological response and experienced emotion are separate.

Let's check your understanding of the James-Lange and Cannon-Bard theories. Imagine that your brain could not sense your heart pounding or your stomach churning. According to each theory, how would this affect your experienced emotions?

Cannon and Bard would have expected you to experience emotions normally because they believed emotions occur separately from (though simultaneously with) the body's arousal. James and Lange would have expected greatly diminished emotions because they believed that to experience emotion you must first perceive your body's arousal.

Stanley Schachter and Jerome Singer (1962) proposed a third theory: that our physiology and our cognitions—perceptions, memories, and interpretations—together create emotion. In their **two-factor theory**, emotions therefore have two ingredients: physical arousal and a cognitive label (**FIGURE 8B.1** on the next page). Like James and Lange, Schachter and Singer presumed that our experience of emotion grows from our awareness of our body's arousal. Yet like Cannon and Bard, Schachter and Singer also believed that emotions are physiologically similar. Thus, in their view, an emotional experience requires a conscious interpretation of the arousal.

AP Photo/Steve Pope

Joy Expressed According to the James-Lange theory, we don't just smile because we share our teammates' joy. We also share the joy because we are smiling with them.

> ● Not only emotion, but most psychological phenomena (vision, sleep, memory, sex, and so forth) can be approached these three ways—physiologically, behaviorally, and cognitively. ●

::**emotion** a response of the whole organism, involving (1) physiological arousal, (2) expressive behaviors, and (3) conscious experience.

::**James-Lange theory** the theory that our experience of emotion is our awareness of our physiological responses to emotion-arousing stimuli.

::**Cannon-Bard theory** the theory that an emotion-arousing stimulus simultaneously triggers (1) physiological responses and (2) the subjective experience of emotion.

::**two-factor theory** the Schachter-Singer theory that to experience emotion one must (1) be physically aroused and (2) cognitively label the arousal.

367

Key Terms

Theories of Emotion

emotion
James-Lange theory
Cannon-Bard theory
two-factor theory

Embodied Emotion

polygraph

Expressed Emotion

facial feedback

Experienced Emotion

catharsis
feel-good, do-good phenomenon
well-being
adaptation-level phenomenon
relative deprivation

Stress and Health

behavioral medicine
health psychology
stress
general adaptation syndrome (GAS)
coronary heart disease
Type A
Type B
psychophysiological illness
psychoneuroimmunology (PNI)
lymphocytes

Key People

Philip Bard
Walter Cannon
Ed Diener
Paul Ekman
Meyer Friedman
William James
Carl Lange
Richard Lazarus

Joseph LeDoux
Ray Rosenman
Robert Rosenthal
Stanley Schachter
Hans Selye
Jerome Singer
Shelley Taylor
Robert Zajonc

TEACHING TIP

William James has long been considered one of the greatest minds in psychology, even though he never took a course in his field. He wrote the first textbook of psychology, *Principles of Psychology*; taught the first course in psychology offered in America (at Harvard); and conducted experiments in psychology about the same time as Wilhelm Wundt (the widely regarded "father of psychology"). Yet, James hated doing experiments because he felt they were tedious and dismissed being called a "psychologist." And not only was he related to Walter Cannon, his brother was the famous author Henry James.

At this point, you may want to use **Classroom Exercise:** *Need for Affect Scale* (p. 3) from Bolt's Teacher's Resource Binder, which accompanies this text.

TROUBLESHOOTING

The theories of emotion can be difficult to keep straight. Each theory uses the same terminology to discuss emotions—namely, physiological arousal and cognitive labeling. These concepts, however, are presented in different orders, depending on the theory. Help students organize these theories by presenting them on a visual flowchart, like the one in Figure 8B.1.

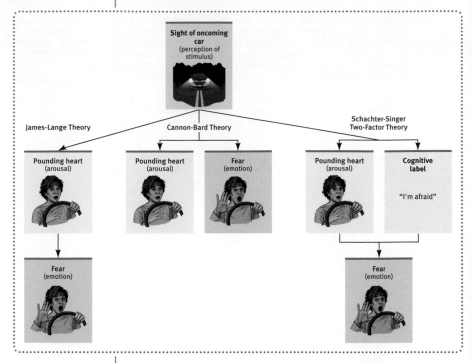

➤ **FIGURE 8B.1**
Theories of emotion

To assess the James-Lange, Cannon-Bard, and two-factor theories, we'll consider in the next section the answers researchers have gleaned to three questions:

- Does physiological arousal always precede emotional experience?
- Are different emotions marked by distinct physiological responses?
- What is the connection between what we *think* and how we *feel*?

BEFORE YOU MOVE ON . . .

➤ **ASK YOURSELF**

Can you remember a time when you began to feel upset or uneasy and only later labeled those feelings?

➤ **TEST YOURSELF 1**

Christine is holding her 8-month-old baby when a fierce dog appears out of nowhere and, with teeth bared, leaps for the baby's face. Christine immediately ducks for cover to protect the baby, screams at the dog, then notices that her heart is banging in her chest and she's broken out in a cold sweat. How would the James-Lange, Cannon-Bard, and two-factor theories explain Christine's emotional reaction?

Answers to the Test Yourself questions can be found in Appendix E at the end of the book.

TEACHING TIP

Have students relate a time when they felt the same type of physical feeling for different emotions.

- What emotions have similar physical bases?
- Have you ever tried to convince yourself that you were feeling a different emotion? How did you do it? Were you effective?

Embodied Emotion

WHETHER YOU ARE EAGERLY ANTICIPATING a long-awaited vacation, falling in love, or grieving a death, you need little convincing that emotions involve the body. Feeling without a body is like breathing without lungs. Some physical responses are easy to notice, others—many taking place at the level of brain neurons—happen without your awareness.

Emotions and the Autonomic Nervous System

2: What is the link between emotional arousal and the autonomic nervous system?

As we learned in Unit 3A, in a crisis it is your *autonomic nervous system (ANS)* that mobilizes your body for action and calms it when the crisis passes (**FIGURE 8B.2**). Without any conscious effort, your body's response to danger is wonderfully coordinated and adaptive—preparing you to *fight or flee*.

The *sympathetic division* of your ANS directs your adrenal glands to release the stress hormones epinephrine (adrenaline) and norepinephrine (noradrenaline). Influenced by this energy-enhancing hormonal surge, your liver pours extra sugar into your bloodstream. To help burn the sugar, your respiration increases to supply needed oxygen. Your heart rate and blood pressure increase. Your digestion slows, diverting blood from your internal organs to your muscles. With blood sugar driven into the large muscles, running becomes easier. Your pupils dilate, letting in more light. To cool your stirred-up body, you perspire. If wounded, your blood would clot more quickly.

When the crisis passes, the *parasympathetic division* of your ANS takes over, calming your body. Its neural centers inhibit further release of stress hormones, but those already in your bloodstream will linger awhile, so arousal diminishes gradually.

In many situations, arousal is adaptive. When you're taking a test, for example, it pays to be moderately aroused—alert but not trembling with nervousness (**FIGURE 8B.3** on the next page). But too little arousal (think sleepiness) can be disruptive, and prolonged high arousal can tax the body (more on this later in this unit).

> "Fear lends wings to his feet."
> Virgil, *Aeneid*, 19 B.C.E.

➤ **FIGURE 8B.2**
Emotional arousal Like a crisis control center, the autonomic nervous system arouses the body in a crisis and calms it when danger passes.

Autonomic Nervous System Controls Physiological Arousal

Sympathetic division (arousing)		Parasympathetic division (calming)
Pupils dilate	EYES	Pupils contract
Decreases	SALIVATION	Increases
Perspires	SKIN	Dries
Increases	RESPIRATION	Decreases
Accelerates	HEART	Slows
Inhibits	DIGESTION	Activates
Secrete stress hormones	ADRENAL GLANDS	Decrease secretion of stress hormones

UNIT 8B

Ralph Adolphs and his colleagues at the University of Iowa report the case of a 30-year-old woman known as S.M., who seems to know no fear and has trouble seeing it in others. A rare genetic disorder has destroyed the amygdala in this otherwise healthy woman. When Adolphs showed the woman dozens of photographs of common facial expressions, she could readily identify pure happiness, disgust, and surprise. However, she had difficulty identifying mixed emotions. Fearful expressions mystified her completely. Judging from the woman's responses in conversation, Adolphs suspects that the damage to her amygdala means that she not only fails to recognize fear but also does not feel it at a gut level. S.M. seems adroit at recognizing rationally when she should be afraid based on cues such as loud voices, dark alleys, or cars speeding at her and thus manages to stay out of harm's way. Because everyday life is rich with such signals, the woman functions fairly normally and claims she does not feel at all impaired.

Adolphs, R., et al. (1994). Impaired recognition of emotion in facial expressions following bilateral damage to the human amygdala. *Nature, 372,* 669–672.

> ➤ **FIGURE 8B.3**
> **Arousal and performance** Performance peaks at lower levels of arousal for difficult tasks, and at higher levels for easy or well-learned tasks. Thus, runners excel when aroused by competition. But facing a difficult test, high anxiety may disrupt performance. Teaching anxious students how to relax before a test can therefore enable them to perform better (Hembree, 1988).

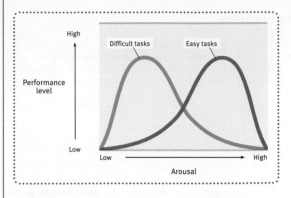

Emotional arousal Elated excitement and panicky fear involve similar physiological arousal. That allows us to flip rapidly between the two emotions.

> "No one ever told me that grief felt so much like fear. I am not afraid, but the sensation is like being afraid. The same fluttering in the stomach, the same restlessness, the yawning. I keep on swallowing."
>
> C. S. Lewis,
> *A Grief Observed,* 1961

• In 1966, a young man named Charles Whitman killed his wife and mother and then climbed to the top of a tower at the University of Texas and shot 38 people. An autopsy later revealed a tumor pressing against his amygdala, which may have contributed to his violence. •

Physiological Similarities Among Specific Emotions

3: Do different emotions activate different physiological and brain-pattern responses?

Imagine conducting an experiment measuring the physiological responses of emotion. In each of four rooms, you have someone watching a movie: In the first, the person is viewing a horror show; in the second, an anger-provoking film; in the third, a sexually arousing film; in the fourth, an utterly boring movie. From the control center you monitor each person's physiological responses, measuring perspiration, breathing, and heart rates. Do you think you could tell who is frightened? Who is angry? Who is sexually aroused? Who is bored?

With training, you could probably pick out the bored viewer. But discerning physiological differences among fear, anger, and sexual arousal would be much more difficult (Barrett, 2006). Different emotions do not have sharply distinct biological signatures.

To you and me, sexual arousal, fear, and anger nevertheless *feel* different. And, despite similar arousal, emotions often *look* different. People may appear "paralyzed with fear" or "ready to explode." So, does research pinpoint any distinct physiological or brain-pattern indicators of each emotion? Sometimes. Read on.

Physiological Differences Among Specific Emotions

Researchers have found some real, though subtle, physiological distinctions among the emotions. The finger temperatures and hormone secretions that accompany fear and rage do sometimes differ (Ax, 1953; Levenson, 1992). And, though fear and joy can prompt similar increased heart rate, they stimulate different facial muscles. During fear, brow muscles tense. During joy, muscles in the cheeks and under the eyes pull into a smile (Witvliet & Vrana, 1995).

Emotions differ much more in the brain circuits they use (Panksepp, 2007). Compared with observers watching angry faces, those watching (and subtly mimicking) fearful faces show more activity in their amygdala, the emotional control center in the brain's limbic system (Whalen et al., 2001). (The amygdala also offers a shortcut for some of our emotional responses, as you'll see later in this unit.)

Have students simulate different emotional reactions to the point where they physically experience the emotion. For example, students can increase their breathing and try to cry to simulate fear or sadness, or they can begin to laugh hysterically to simulate happiness or joy.

• Did this exercise create an emotional feeling in you? Why or why not?

• What theory does this exercise support? Why?

At this point, you may want to use **Classroom Exercises:** *Facial Feedback and the James-Lange Theory of Emotion* (p. 4) or *A Process Model of Emotion Regulation* (p. 4) from Bolt's Teacher's Resource Binder.

Brain scans and EEG recordings show that emotions also activate different areas of the brain's cortex, with some tendency for negative emotions to be linked to the right hemisphere and positive emotions to the left. Disgust, for example, triggers more activity in the right prefrontal cortex than in the left. Depression-prone people, and those with generally negative personalities, also show more right frontal lobe activity (Harmon-Jones et al., 2002).

Positive moods tend to trigger more left frontal lobe activity. People with positive personalities—exuberant infants and alert, enthusiastic, energized, and persistently goal-directed adults—also show more activity in the left frontal lobe than in the right (Davidson, 2000, 2003; Urry et al., 2004). Indeed, the more a person's baseline frontal lobe activity tilts left—or is made to tilt left by perceptual activity—the more upbeat the person typically is (Drake & Myers, 2006). Brain injury can also tilt activity to the left. One man, having lost part of his right frontal lobe in brain surgery, became (his not-unhappy wife reported) less irritable and more affectionate (Goleman, 1995). After a right-hemisphere stroke at age 92, my father lived the last two years of his life with happy gratitude and hardly a complaint or negative emotion.

The left frontal lobe's rich supply of dopamine receptors may help explain why a peppy left hemisphere predicts a perky personality. A neural pathway that increases dopamine levels runs from the frontal lobes to a nearby cluster of neurons, the *nucleus accumbens*. This small region lights up when people experience natural or drug-induced pleasures. In case studies, electrical stimulation of the nucleus accumbens of depressed patients has triggered smiles, laughter, and giddy euphoria (Okun et al., 2004).

* * *

We have seen that emotions as varied as fear, joy, and anger involve a similar general autonomic arousal (as in similar heart rate). We have also seen that there are real, if subtle, physiological and brain differences among the emotions. How does this new evidence affect the assessment of the James-Lange, Cannon-Bard, and two-factor theories of emotion? The evidence of real distinctions among the emotions makes the James-Lange theory plausible. Further support comes from observations of people with severed spinal cords. Psychologist George Hohmann (1966) asked 25 soldiers who suffered such injuries in World War II to recall emotion-arousing incidents that occurred before and after their spinal injuries. Those with lower-spine injuries, who had lost sensation only in their legs, reported little change in their emotions. But as James and Lange would have expected, those who could feel nothing below the neck reported a considerable decrease in emotional intensity. The anger, as one man confessed, "just doesn't have the heat to it that it used to. It's a mental kind of anger." Those with high spinal-cord injury experienced their emotions more above the neck. They reported increases in weeping, lumps in the throat, and getting choked up when worshipping, saying good-bye, or watching a touching movie. Such evidence, some researchers believe, confirms the view that our feelings are "mostly shadows" of our bodily responses and behaviors (Damasio, 2003).

Does this mean that Cannon and Bard were wrong? No. Most researchers now agree that our experienced emotions also involve cognition, the topic we turn to next (Averill, 1993; Barrett, 2006). Whether we fear the man behind us on a dark street depends entirely on whether we interpret his actions as threatening or friendly. So, with James and Lange we can say that our body's reactions are an important ingredient of emotion. And with Cannon and Bard we can say that there is more to the experience of emotion than reading our body's responses. If that were not the case, lie detectors would be foolproof, which they are not (see Thinking Critically About: Lie Detection on the next page). As the two-factor theory indicates, emotions involve the labels we put on our bodily states.

 TEACHING TIP

The amygdala is part of the limbic system of the brain. Along with the amygdala, the hippocampus and the basal ganglia make up this structure. A scientist named James Papez (rhymes with "apes") theorized that this part of the brain was responsible for expression of emotion, so the region was originally called *Papez' Circuit*.

At this point, you may want to use **Classroom Exercise: *Estimating the Effects of Test Error*** (p. 9) or **Student Project: *Assessing Brain Asymmetry*** (p. 8) or **Lecture/Discussion Topics: *Cognitive Appraisals and Emotion*** (p. 11) or **Public and Private Self-Consciousness** (p. 11) from Bolt's Teacher's Resource Binder.

 TEACHING TIP

At this point, you may want to use **Classroom Exercise: *Sensation-Seeking Scale*** (p. 5) or **Lecture/Discussion Topics: *Oxytocin and Trust*** (p. 7) or ***The Brain and Emotion*** (p. 7) *or **Government Confidence in the Polygraph*** (p. 8) or ***Interviewing for Integrity*** (p. 9) from Bolt's Teacher's Resource Binder.

Donna Desforges and Thomas Lee conducted a study that demonstrated the difficulty of detecting deception. The cues people use when they are actually trying to deceive are speech hesitation, increased vocal pitch, blinking, and pupil dilation. Studies at Michigan State University suggest that deceivers tend to use shorter sentences and talk for shorter durations. They tend to make more speech errors, such as stuttering and mispronunciation. They often pause longer between words and take longer to respond to a question or comment. In addition, they often use a lot of hand gestures, fidget with their collars, run their fingers through their hair, or twiddle their thumbs.

At this point, you may want to use **Classroom Exercises: *The Mood Awareness Scale*** (p. 12) or ***Emotional Expressivity Scale*** (p. 12) from Bolt's Teacher's Resource Binder.

Have students research local, state, and federal laws concerning the use of polygraphs in criminal investigations. Have them address the following questions:

- Have laws regarding the use of polygraphs changed due to research on their ineffectiveness?

- Why are law enforcement officials so confident in the use of polygraphs in investigations?

THINKING CRITICALLY ABOUT

Lie Detection

Can polygraph tests like this identify liars?
To learn more, read on.

The creators and users of the *lie detector*, or **polygraph**, have believed that our physical indicators of emotion can provide a telltale equivalent of Pinocchio's nose. Actually, polygraphs do not literally detect lies, and their accuracy has been questioned as our understanding of physiological measures of emotion has grown.

Polygraphs measure the changes in breathing, cardiovascular activity, and perspiration that accompany emotion. An examiner monitors these responses as you answer questions. Some items, called *control questions*, aim to make anyone a little nervous. If asked, "In the last 20 years, have you ever taken something that didn't belong to you?" many people will tell a white lie and say *no*, and the polygraph will detect arousal. If your physiological reactions to *critical questions* ("Did you ever steal anything from your previous employer?") are weaker than to control questions, the examiner infers you are telling the truth.

But there are two problems: First, our physiological arousal is much the same from one emotion to another—anxiety, irritation, and guilt all prompt similar physiological reactivity. Second, these tests err about one-third of the time, especially when innocent people respond with heightened tension to the accusations implied by the critical questions (**FIGURE 8B.4**). Many rape victims, for example, "fail" lie detector tests when reacting emotionally while telling the truth about their assailant (Lykken, 1991).

A 2002 U.S. National Academy of Sciences report noted that "no spy has ever been caught [by] using the polygraph." It is not for lack of trying. The FBI, CIA, and Departments of Defense and Energy in the United States have spent millions of dollars testing tens of thousands of employees. Meanwhile Aldrich Ames, who enjoyed an unexplained lavish life-style as a Russian spy within the CIA, went undetected. Ames "took scores of polygraph tests and passed them all," noted Robert Park (1999). "Nobody thought to investigate the source of his sudden wealth—after all, he was passing the lie detector tests." The truth is, lie detectors can lie.

A more effective approach to lie detection uses the *guilty knowledge test*, which assesses a suspect's physiological responses to crime-scene details known only to the police and the guilty person (Ben-Shakhar & Elaad, 2003). If a camera and computer had been stolen, for example, presumably only a guilty person would react strongly to the specific brand names of these items. Given enough such specific probes, an innocent person will seldom be wrongly accused.

Several twenty-first-century research teams are exploring new ways to nab liars. Some are developing computer software that compares the language of truth tellers and of liars

::**polygraph** a machine, commonly used in attempts to detect lies, that measures several of the physiological responses accompanying emotion (such as perspiration and cardiovascular and breathing changes).

Cognition and Emotion

4: To experience emotions, must we consciously interpret and label them?

What is the connection between what we *think* and how we *feel?* Which is the chicken and which the egg? Can we experience emotion apart from thinking? Or do we become what we think?

Cognition Can Define Emotion

Sometimes our arousal response to one event spills over into our response to the next event. Imagine arriving home after an invigorating run and finding a

---

At this point, you may want to use **Classroom Exercises: *Nonverbal Communication*** (p. 13) or ***"Reading the Mind in the Eyes" Test: Sample Items*** (p. 13) or ***Difficulty in Detecting Deception*** (p. 14) from Bolt's Teacher's Resource Binder.

> **FIGURE 8B.4**
How often do lie detectors lie? Benjamin Kleinmuntz and Julian Szucko (1984) had polygraph experts study the polygraph data of 50 theft suspects who later confessed to being guilty and 50 suspects whose innocence was later established by someone's confession. Had the polygraph experts been the judges, more than one-third of the innocent would have been declared guilty, and almost one-fourth of the guilty would have been declared innocent.

> **FIGURE 8B.5**
Liar, liar, brain's on fire An fMRI scan identified two brain areas that became especially active when a participant lied about holding a five of clubs.

teach law enforcement officers to detect the presumed fleeting signals of deceit in facial expressions.

Other researchers are going straight to the seat of deceit—the brain. EEG recordings have revealed brain waves indicating familiarity with crime scenes, and fMRI scans have shown liars' brains lighting up in places that honest people's brains do not (Langleben et al., 2002, 2005, 2006). Pinocchio's giveaway signal of lying may be not the length of his nose, but rather the telltale activity in places such as his left frontal lobe and anterior cingulate cortex, which become active when the brain inhibits truth telling (**FIGURE 8B.5**). A new $10 million Law and Neuroscience Project, led by psychologist Michael Gazzaniga, aims to assess the new technology's appropriate uses by those seeking to identify terrorists, convict criminals, and protect the innocent (Dingfelder, 2007).

(who use fewer first-person pronouns and more negative-emotion words). Other software analyzes facial microexpressions linked with lying (Adelson, 2004; Newman et al., 2003). Psychologist Paul Ekman (2003) has run training seminars to

message that you got a longed-for job. With arousal lingering from the run, would you feel more elated than if you received this news after awakening from a nap?

To find out whether this *spillover effect* exists, Stanley Schachter and Jerome Singer (1962) aroused college men with injections of the hormone epinephrine (adrenaline). Picture yourself as one of their participants: After receiving the injection, you go to a waiting room, where you find yourself with another person (actually an accomplice of the experimenters) who is acting either euphoric or irritated. As you observe this person, you begin to feel your heart race, your body flush, and your breathing become more rapid. If told to expect these effects from the injection, what would you feel? Schachter and Singer's volunteers felt little emotion—because they attributed their arousal to the drug. But if told the

UNIT 8B

INTERCONNECTING

Link Robert Zajonc's arguments to a discussion of reflexes. Because reflexes work by passing on messages that control movement before processing in the brain occurs, we can avoid dangerous situations without having to take time to think about them.

Reuters/Corbis

▼ **The spillover effect** Arousal from a soccer match can fuel anger, which can descend into rioting or other violent confrontations.

> "Feelings that one interprets as fear in the presence of a sheer drop may be interpreted as lust in the presence of a sheer blouse."
>
> Daniel Gilbert, *Stumbling on Happiness*, 2006

● Can you recall liking something or someone immediately, without knowing why? ●

injection would produce no effects, what would you feel? Perhaps you would react, as another group of participants did, by "catching" the apparent emotion of the person you are with—becoming happy if the accomplice is acting euphoric, and testy if the accomplice is acting irritated.

This discovery—that a stirred-up state can be experienced as one emotion or another very different one, depending on how we interpret and label it—has been replicated in dozens of experiments. Insult people who have just been aroused by pedaling an exercise bike or watching rock videos and they will find it easy to misattribute their arousal to the provocation. Their anger will exceed that of people similarly provoked but not previously aroused. Likewise, sexually aroused people react with more hostility in anger-provoking situations. And, vice versa—the arousal that lingers after an intense argument or a frightening experience may intensify sexual passion (Palace, 1995). Just as the Schachter-Singer two-factor theory predicts, arousal + label = emotion. Emotional arousal may not be as undifferentiated as Schachter and Singer believed, but arousal from emotions as diverse as anger, fear, and sexual excitement can indeed spill from one emotion to another (Reisenzein, 1983; Sinclair et al., 1994; Zillmann, 1986). *The point to remember: Arousal fuels emotion; cognition channels it.*

Cognition Does Not Always Precede Emotion

Is the heart always subject to the mind? Robert Zajonc (pronounced ZI-yence; 1980, 1984a) has contended that we actually have many emotional reactions apart from, or even before, our interpretations of a situation. Imagine receiving some unsettling news. You discover that you've forgotten an important deadline, or that you've hurt someone's feelings. As the ongoing conversation distracts your attention, you lose awareness of the bad news. Yet the feeling still churns. You feel a little bad. You know there's a reason, but for the moment you can't put your finger on it. The arousal lingers, but without a label.

In earlier units, we noted that when people repeatedly view stimuli flashed too briefly for them to interpret, much less label, they nevertheless come to prefer those stimuli. Without being consciously aware of having seen the stimuli, they rather like them. As a University of Amsterdam study confirms, we seem to have an acutely sensitive automatic radar for emotionally significant information (Zeelenberg et al., 2006). When researchers flashed a four-letter positive or negative word (such as *kiss* or *dead*), people more readily identified it than a similarly common neutral word (*fact*).

A subliminally flashed stimulus, such as a smiling or angry face or a disgusting scene, can also prime a mood or specific emotion and lead us to feel better or worse about a follow-up stimulus (Murphy et al., 1995; Ruys & Stapel, 2008). In one set of experiments, thirsty people were given a fruit-flavored drink after viewing a subliminally flashed (thus unperceived) face. Those exposed to a happy face drank about 50 percent more than those exposed to a neutral face (Berridge & Winkielman, 2003). Those flashed an angry face drank substantially less.

(a) The speedy low road

(b) The thinking high road

➤ FIGURE 8B.6

The brain's shortcut for emotions In the two-track brain, sensory input may be routed (a) directly to the amygdala (via the thalamus) for an instant emotional reaction or (b) to the cortex for analysis.

Lazarus studied the importance of preparing a person for emotion. He and his associates documented that a person's emotional reactions to witnessing a film on a painful event could be lessened by describing the procedure in a matter-of-fact way, or the emotional reactions could be heightened by emphasizing the pain the subject was experiencing.

- How could this research be used by doctors to help their patients before surgery?
- How can parents use this research to help rear their children?
- How could activists use this information to motivate people to join the cause?

Neuroscience research helps us understand these surprising findings. Like speedy reflexes that operate apart from the brain's thinking cortex, some emotions take what Joseph LeDoux (2002) calls the "low road," via neural pathways that bypass the cortex (which offers the alternative "high road" pathway). One low-road pathway runs from the eye or ear via the thalamus to the amygdala, bypassing the cortex (**FIGURE 8B.6**). This shortcut enables our greased-lightning emotional response before our intellect intervenes. So speedy is the amygdala reaction that we may be unaware of what's transpired (Dimberg et al., 2000). In one fascinating experiment, Paul Whalen and his colleagues (2004) used fMRI scans to observe the amygdala's response to subliminally presented fearful eyes (**FIGURE 8B.7**). Compared with a control condition that presented the whites of happy eyes, the fearful eyes triggered increased amygdala activity (despite no one's being aware of seeing them).

> "Oh! ye'll tak' the high road and I'll tak' the low road, An' I'll be in Scotland afore ye."
>
> Traditional Scottish song
> "Bonnie Banks o' Loch Lomond"

Fearful   Happy

➤ FIGURE 8B.7

The brain's sensitivity to threats Even when fearful eyes (left) were flashed too briefly for people to consciously perceive them, fMRI scans revealed that their hypervigilant amygdala was alerted (Whalen et al., 2004). The happy eyes on the right did not have this effect.

UNIT 8B

Richard Lazarus conducted experiments using mild electrical shock on his patients. He noticed that they would react to the shock without realizing it. He called this ability to react emotionally without conscious awareness "subception."

The amygdala sends more neural projections up to the cortex than it receives back. This makes it easier for our feelings to hijack our thinking than for our thinking to rule our feelings, noted LeDoux and Jorge Armony (1999). In the forest, we jump at the sound of rustling bushes nearby, leaving the cortex to decide later whether the sound was made by a predator or just the wind. Such an experience supports Zajonc's belief that *some* of our emotional reactions involve no deliberate thinking.

Emotion researcher Richard Lazarus (1991, 1998) conceded that our brains process and react to vast amounts of information without our conscious awareness, and he willingly granted that some emotional responses do not require *conscious* thinking. Much of our emotional life operates via the automatic, effortless, speedy low road. But, he noted, even instantaneously felt emotions require some sort of cognitive appraisal of the situation; otherwise, how would we *know* what we are reacting to? The appraisal may be effortless and we may not be conscious of it, but it is still a mental function. To know whether something is good or bad, the brain must have some idea of what it is (Storbeck et al., 2006). Thus, emotions arise when we *appraise* an event as beneficial or harmful to our well-being, whether we truly know it is or not. We appraise the sound of the rustling bushes as the presence of a threat. Later, we realize that it was "just the wind."

To sum up, as Zajonc and LeDoux have demonstrated, some emotional responses—especially simple likes, dislikes, and fears—involve no conscious thinking (**FIGURE 8B.8**). We may fear a spider, even if we "know" it is harmless. Such responses are difficult to alter by changing our thinking.

> ➤ **FIGURE 8B.8**
> **Another example of dual processing: two routes to emotion** Zajonc and LeDoux have emphasized that some emotional responses are immediate, before any conscious appraisal. Lazarus, Schachter, and Singer emphasized that our appraisal and labeling of events also determine our emotional responses.

The emotional brain even influences people's political decisions, leading many to vote for candidates they automatically *like* over a candidate expressing positions more like their own. When voters undergo brain imaging while watching candidates, their emotion circuits are more engaged than their rational frontal lobes (Westen, 2007).

But like other emotions—including moods such as depression and complex feelings such as hatred, guilt, happiness, and love—our feelings about politics are, as Lazarus, Schachter, and Singer predicted, greatly influenced by our memories, expectations, and interpretations. Highly emotional people are intense partly because of their interpretations. They may *personalize* events as being somehow directed at them, and they may *generalize* their experiences by blowing single incidents out of proportion (Larsen & Diener, 1987). In dealing with complex emotions, as you will see in Unit 12, learning to *think* more positively can help people *feel* better. Even though the emotional low road functions automatically, the thinking high road allows us to retake some control over our emotional life.

A dramatic testimony to the interplay of emotion and cognition comes from the brain-damaged, seemingly emotionless patients studied by Antonio Damasio (1994, 2003). He devised a simple card-game task on which, over trials, people could make or lose money. Without brain damage, most people make money as the emotions generated by their unconscious brain figure things out ahead of their conscious reasoning. Without these feelings to inform their thinking, the emotionless patients typically *lose* money. This demonstrates once again that our two-track minds include a smart unconsciousness. Automatic emotion and conscious thinking together weave the fabric of our minds (Forgas, 2008).

Blow up several balloons and secure a stick pin so you can pop the balloons at a given time. Replicate the procedure Lazarus used to prepare people for emotional reactions. Establish a baseline reaction by popping one balloon at a random point, catching the class off guard. Then run one trial in which you explain matter-of-factly that you will be popping the balloon, preparing them for the uncomfortable experience of hearing it pop. Then, run another trial in which you emphasize how painful it is to hear a balloon pop. Dramatize the "pain" as much as possible. Ask the students after the second trial how your preparation in each instance changed their "subception" of the event.

➤ **ASK YOURSELF**

Can you think of a recent time when you noticed your body's reactions to an emotionally charged situation, such as a difficult social setting or perhaps even a test or game you were worrying about in advance? Did you perceive the situation as a challenge or a threat? How well did you do?

➤ **TEST YOURSELF 2**

How do the two divisions of the autonomic nervous system help us respond to and recover from a crisis, and why is this relevant to the study of emotions?

Answers to the Test Yourself questions can be found in Appendix E at the end of the book.

Expressed Emotion

5: How do we communicate nonverbally?

THERE IS A SIMPLER METHOD OF deciphering people's emotions: We read their bodies, listen to their tone of voice, and study their faces. People's expressive behavior reveals their emotion. Does this nonverbal language vary with culture, or is it universal? And do our expressions influence our experienced emotions?

> "Your face, my thane, is a book where men may read strange matters."
>
> Lady Macbeth to her husband, in William Shakespeare's *Macbeth*

Detecting Emotion

All of us communicate nonverbally as well as verbally. To Westerners, a firm handshake immediately conveys an outgoing, expressive personality (Chaplin et al., 2000). With a gaze, an averted glance, or a stare we can communicate intimacy, submission, or dominance (Kleinke, 1986). Among those passionately in love, gazing into each other's eyes is typically prolonged and mutual (Rubin, 1970). Joan Kellerman, James Lewis, and James Laird (1989) wondered if intimate gazes would stir such feelings between strangers. To find out, they asked unacquainted male-female pairs to gaze intently for two minutes either at each other's hands or into each other's eyes. After separating, the eye gazers reported feeling a tingle of attraction and affection.

Most of us are good enough at reading nonverbal cues to decipher the emotions in an old silent film. We are especially good at detecting threats. Even when hearing emotions conveyed in another language, people most readily detect anger (Scherer et al., 2001). When viewing subliminally flashed words, we more often sense the presence of a negative word, such as *snake* or *bomb* (Dijksterhuis & Aarts, 2003). And in a crowd of faces, a single angry face will "pop out" faster than a single happy one (Fox et al., 2000; Hansen & Hansen, 1988; Öhman et al., 2001).

Experience can sensitize us to particular emotions, as shown by experiments using a series of faces (like those in **FIGURE 8B.9** on the next page) that morphed from fear (or sadness) to anger. Viewing such faces, physically abused children are much quicker than other children to spot the signals of anger. Shown a face that is 60 percent fear and 40 percent anger, they are as likely to perceive anger as fear. Their perceptions become sensitively attuned to glimmers of danger that nonabused children miss.

Hard-to-control facial muscles reveal signs of emotions you may be trying to conceal. Lifting just the inner part of your eyebrows, which few people do consciously,

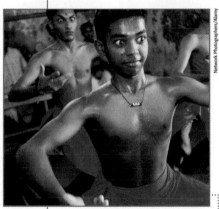

Network Photographers/Alamy

A silent language of emotion Hindu classic dance uses the face and body to effectively convey 10 different emotions (Hejmadi et al., 2000).

Ask students, "Are fears common the world over?" Have students identify cultures other than their own to research about what people in different cultures fear and how those fears are most commonly expressed.

According to Roger G. Axtell, there is one "ultimate gesture" that carries a certain welcome characteristic, unlike any other single gesture. This "ultimate gesture" is known everywhere in the world. It is absolutely universal. It is rarely, if ever, misunderstood. Primitive tribes and world leaders alike know and use it. Scientists believe this particular gesture actually releases chemicals called endorphins into the system to create a feeling of mild euphoria.

What is this singular signal, this ultimate giant of all gestures? (The smile!)

Axtell, R. E. (1998) *Gestures: The do's and taboos of body language around the world.* Hoboken, NJ: John Wiley & Sons.

At this point, you may want to use **Lecture/Discussion Topic:** *Cultural Differences in Emotional Expression* (p. 14) from Bolt's Teacher's Resource Binder.

Used by permission of S. D. Pollak, D. J. Kistler, and the National Academy of Science

DEMO

People who are self-conscious in public are sensitive to social rejection and may be less inclined to express their true emotions. Have students pretend to draw a capital E on their forehead using their dominant hand. What direction does the "E" face? If it is oriented so that someone looking at the student would have seen it in the correct position, it is likely that the student is high in public self-consciousness. According to a study by R. Glen Hass, people who are low in public self-consciousness are more likely to draw an E from an internal perspective.

TEACHING TIP

Barbara Frederickson of UNC-Chapel Hill has proposed the broaden-and-build theory of emotions. While negative emotions narrow one's perspective, positive emotions broaden perspective and build toward more positive emotions. Frederickson proposes that positive emotions lead to more positive thoughts and actions in the future.

At this point, you may want to use **Lecture/Discussion Topic: *Elevation—A New Positive Emotion*** (p. 20) from Bolt's Teacher's Resource Binder.

➤ **FIGURE 8B.9**
Experience influences how we perceive emotions Viewing the morphed middle face above, evenly mixing fear with anger, physically abused children were more likely than nonabused children to perceive the face as angry (Pollak & Kistler, 2002; Pollak & Tolley-Schell, 2003).

Dr. Paul Ekman, University of California at San Francisco

Which of Paul Ekman's smiles is feigned, which natural? The smile on the right engages the facial muscles of a natural smile.

• Injected as part of the war on wrinkles, Botox paralyzes facial muscles that create wrinkles, allowing the overlying skin to relax and smooth. By erasing the subtle expressions of frown lines or smiling eyes, might this cosmetic procedure hide subtle emotions? •

reveals distress or worry. Eyebrows raised and pulled together signal fear. Activated muscles under the eyes and raised cheeks suggest a natural smile, called a *Duchenne smile*, in honor of the French physician who described it. A feigned smile, such as one we make for a photographer, often continues for more than 4 or 5 seconds. Most authentic expressions have faded by that time. Feigned smiles are also switched on and off more abruptly than is a genuine happy smile (Bugental, 1986).

Our brains are rather amazing detectors of subtle expressions. Elisha Babad, Frank Bernieri, and Robert Rosenthal (1991) discovered just *how* amazing after filming teachers talking to unseen schoolchildren. A mere 10-second clip of either the teacher's voice or face provided enough clues for both young and old viewers to determine whether the teacher liked and admired the child he or she was addressing. In another experiment, a glimpse of a face for even one-tenth of a second was enough for people to judge someone's trustworthiness (Willis & Todorov, 2006). When researchers blur faces or hide them in distracting information, people still display remarkable skill at recognizing distinct emotions (Smith et al., 2005). Exposing different facial parts shows the eyes and mouth to be most revealing, with fear and anger read mostly from the eyes, and happiness from the mouth (Adolphs, 2006).

Despite our brain's emotion-detecting skill, we find it difficult to detect deceiving expressions (Porter & ten Brinke, 2008). People worldwide believe that one telltale sign of lying is averting one's gaze (Bond et al., 2006). Perhaps this is what former President George W. Bush had in mind when telling U.S. troops in Baghdad that he had come "to look at Prime Minister Maliki in the eyes and determine whether or not he is as dedicated to a free Iraq as you are" (Burns & Filkins, 2006). Yet in one digest of 206 studies of discerning truth from lies, people were just 54 percent accurate—barely better than a coin toss (Bond & DePaulo, 2006). Moreover, contrary to claims that some experts can spot lies, the available research indicates that virtually no one beats chance by much (Bond & DePaulo, 2008).

Some of us are, however, more sensitive than others to physical cues. Robert Rosenthal, Judith Hall, and their colleagues (1979) discovered this by showing hundreds of people brief film clips of portions of a person's emotionally expressive face or body, sometimes accompanied by a garbled voice. For example, after a 2-second scene revealing only the face of an upset woman, the researchers would ask whether the woman was criticizing someone for being late or was talking about her divorce. Rosenthal and Hall reported that, given such "thin slices," some people are much better than others at detecting emotion. Introverts tend to excel at reading others' emotions, although extraverts are generally easier to read (Ambady et al., 1995).

Gestures, facial expressions, and tones of voice are all absent in electronic communication. E-mail sometimes includes sideways *emoticons*, such as ;-) for a knowing wink and :-(for a frown. But text messages, e-mail, tweets, and non-video Internet chats and posts otherwise lack nonverbal cues to status, personality, and age. Nobody knows what you look or sound like, or anything about your background; you are judged solely on your words. When first meeting face-to-face with someone met electronically, people are often surprised at the person they encounter.

It's also easy to misread texts or e-mails, where the absence of expressive e-motion can make for ambiguous emotion. So can the absence of those vocal nuances by which we signal that a statement is serious, kidding, or sarcastic. Research by Justin Kruger and his colleagues (2005) shows that communicators often think their "just kidding" intent is equally clear, whether e-mailed or spoken. But they commonly exhibit egocentrism by not foreseeing misinterpretations in the absence of nonverbal cues.

Gender, Emotion, and Nonverbal Behavior

Is women's intuition, as so many believe, superior to men's? Consider: As Jackie Larsen left her Grand Marais, Minnesota, church prayer group one April 2001 morning, she encountered Christopher Bono, a clean-cut, well-mannered youth. Bono's car had broken down, and he said he was looking for a ride to meet friends in Thunder Bay. When Bono later appeared in Larsen's shop, where she had promised to help him phone his friends, she felt a pain in her stomach. Intuitively sensing that something was very wrong with this young man, she insisted that they talk outside on the sidewalk. "I said, 'I am a mother and I have to talk to you like a mother. . . . I can tell by your manners that you have a nice mother.'" At the mention of his mother, Bono's eyes fixed on her. "I don't know where my mother is," he said.

As the conversation ended, Larsen directed Bono back to the church to meet the pastor. She also called the police and suggested that they trace his license plates. The car was registered to his mother in southern Illinois. When police went to her apartment, they found blood all over and Lucia Bono dead in the bathtub. Christopher Bono, 16, was charged with first-degree murder (Biggs, 2001).

Was it a coincidence that Larsen, who saw through Bono's calm exterior, was a woman? Some psychologists would say *no*. In her analysis of 125 studies of sensitivity to nonverbal cues, Judith Hall (1984, 1987) discerned that, when given "thin slices," women generally surpass men at reading people's emotional cues. Women's nonverbal sensitivity also gives them an edge in spotting lies (DePaulo, 1994). And women have surpassed men in discerning whether a male-female couple is a genuine romantic couple or a posed phony couple, and in discerning which of two people in a photo is the other's supervisor (Barnes & Sternberg, 1989).

Women's nonverbal sensitivity helps explain their greater emotional literacy. Invited by Lisa Feldman Barrett and her colleagues (2000) to describe how they would feel in certain situations, men described simpler emotional reactions. You might like to try this yourself: Ask some people how they might feel when saying good-bye to friends they will no longer see very often after graduation. Barrett's work suggests you are more likely to hear males say, simply, "I'll feel bad," and to hear females express more complex emotions: "It will be bittersweet; I'll feel both happy and sad."

Women's skill at decoding others' emotions may also contribute to their greater emotional responsiveness in both positive and negative situations (Grossman & Wood, 1993; Sprecher & Sedikides, 1993; Stoppard & Gruchy, 1993). In studies of 23,000 people from 26 cultures around the world, women more than men reported themselves open to feelings (Costa et al., 2001). That helps explain the extremely strong perception that emotionality is "more true of women"—a perception expressed by nearly 100 percent of 18- to 29-year-old Americans (Newport, 2001).

One exception: Anger strikes most people as a more masculine emotion. Ask someone to imagine an angry face, then ask them: Is it male, as it seemed to be for three in four Arizona State University students (Becker et al., 2007)? The researchers also found that people are quicker to see anger on men's faces. And if a gender-neutral face is made to look angry, most people perceive it as male. If smiling, it's more likely to be perceived as female (**FIGURE 8B.10**, next page).

➤ **FIGURE 8B.10**
Angry = Male When Vaughn Becker and his colleagues (2007) manipulated a gender-neutral face, people were more likely to see it as a male when they gave it an angry expression.

INTERCONNECTING

Link the expression of empathy with Unit 6's discussion of mirror neurons. Mirror neurons comprise neural systems that activate when we are imagining what other people are feeling or doing. Some researchers think that mirror neurons are the physiological mechanism of empathy.

CRITICAL THINKING

Have students debate whether the differences between the genders in emotional expression are due to biology or environment. Are men and women physically different from an emotional standpoint? Or does society teach women and men to express emotions differently? Have them cite evidence from the unit in their responses.

When surveyed, women are also far more likely than men to describe themselves as empathic. If you have *empathy*, you identify with others and imagine what it must be like to walk in their shoes. You rejoice with those who rejoice and weep with those who weep. Physiological measures of empathy, such as one's heart rate while seeing another's distress, reveal a much smaller gender gap than is reported in surveys (Eisenberg & Lennon, 1983). Nevertheless, females are more likely to *express* empathy—to cry and to report distress when observing someone in distress. Ann Kring and Albert Gordon (1998) observed this gender difference in videotapes of men and women students watching film clips that were sad (children with a dying parent), happy (slapstick comedy), or frightening (a man nearly falling off the ledge of a tall building). As **FIGURE 8B.11** shows, the women reacted more visibly to each film type. Women also tend to experience emotional events (such as viewing pictures of mutilation) more deeply—with more brain activation in areas sensitive to emotion—and then to remember the scenes better three weeks later (Canli et al., 2002).

In another exploration of gender and facial expression, Harold Hill and Alan Johnston (2001) animated an image of an average head with expressions (smirks, head tosses, raised eyebrows) that had been digitally captured from the faces of London University students as they read a joke. Despite having no anatomical clues to gender, observers could usually detect gender in the telltale expressions.

➤ **FIGURE 8B.11**
Gender and expressiveness Although male and female students did not differ dramatically in self-reported emotions or physiological responses while viewing emotional films, the women's faces *showed* much more emotion. (From Kring & Gordon, 1998.)

Culture and Emotional Expression

6: Are nonverbal expressions of emotion universally understood?

The meaning of gestures varies with the culture. Some years ago, psychologist Otto Klineberg (1938) observed that in Chinese literature people clapped their hands to express worry or disappointment, laughed a great "Ho-Ho" to express anger, and stuck out their tongues to show surprise. Similarly, the North American "thumbs up" and "A-OK" signs are considered insults in certain other cultures. (When former U.S. President Richard Nixon made the latter sign in Brazil, he didn't realize he was offering a crude insult.) Just how important cultural definitions of gestures can be was demonstrated in 1968, when North Korea

CULTURAL CONNECTIONS

Have students explore how people in different cultures express the following emotions: love and affection, fear, discomfort or displeasure, and anger.

Students can also interview peers from other cultures about how they express these emotions and how they might be learning to adapt their emotional expression habits to American cultural standards.

publicized photos of supposedly happy officers from a captured U.S. Navy spy ship. In the photo, three of the men raised their middle fingers; they had told captors it was a "Hawaiian good luck sign" (Fleming & Scott, 1991).

Do facial expressions also have different meanings in different cultures? To find out, two investigative teams—one led by Paul Ekman, Wallace Friesen, and others (1975, 1987, 1994), the other by Carroll Izard (1977, 1994)—showed photographs of various facial expressions to people in different parts of the world and asked them to guess the emotion. You can try this matching task yourself by pairing the six emotions with the six faces of FIGURE 8B.12.

Ekman & Matsumoto, Japanese and Caucasian Facial Expression of Emotion

Regardless of your cultural background, you probably did pretty well. A smile's a smile the world around. Ditto for anger, and to a lesser extent the other basic expressions (Elfenbein & Ambady, 1999). (There is no culture where people frown when they are happy.) Thus, a glimpse at competitors' spontaneous expressions following an Olympic judo competition gives a very good clue about who won, no matter their country (Matsumoto & Willingham, 2006).

Do people from different cultures share these similarities because they share experiences, such as American movies or the BBC and CNN broadcasts? Apparently not. Ekman and his team asked isolated people in New Guinea to display various emotions in response to such statements as, "Pretend your child has died." When the researchers showed tapes of the New Guineans' facial reactions to North American collegians, the students read them easily.

Facial expressions do contain some nonverbal accents that provide clues to one's culture (Marsh et al., 2003). So it is not surprising that data from 182 studies show slightly enhanced accuracy when people judge emotions from their own culture (Elfenbein & Ambady, 2002, 2003a,b). Still, the telltale signs of emotion generally cross cultures. Even our emotional *display rules* (such as expressing more emotion to fellow group members than to outsiders) cross world cultures (Matsumoto et al., 2008).

Children's facial expressions—even those of blind children who have never seen a face—are also universal (Eibl-Eibesfeldt, 1971). People blind from birth spontaneously exhibit the common facial expressions associated with such emotions as joy, sadness, fear, and anger (Galati et al., 1997). The world over, children cry when distressed, shake their heads when defiant, and smile when they are happy.

➤ FIGURE 8B.12

Culture-specific or culturally universal expressions? As people of differing cultures and races, do our faces speak differing languages? Which face expresses disgust? Anger? Fear? Happiness? Sadness? Surprise? (From Matsumoto & Ekman, 1989.) (Answers below.)

From left to right, top to bottom: happiness, surprise, fear, sadness, anger, disgust.

"For news of the heart, ask the face."
Guinean proverb

RESEARCH

Have students replicate the study by Matsumoto and Ekman by showing the pictures of the different emotional expressions to different students (as in Figure 8B.12). Have them choose from a scale what emotion goes with each facial expression. Students can see how good people are at identifying different emotional reactions.

TEACHING TIP

Continue to reinforce the bio-psychosocial perspective with Figure 8B.13. Emotions rely heavily on the interplay of biological, psychological, and social-cultural determinants. Have students choose one particular emotion and create lists of biological, psychological, and social-cultural factors that determine the expression of that emotion.

INTERCONNECTING

Have students discuss how differences in emotional expression may occur in collectivist versus individualist cultures (Unit 10). What specific types of emotions are likely to be different in these different types of cultures? What fundamental philosophies of life might contribute to this difference in emotional expression?

TEACHING TIP

At this point, you may want to use **Classroom Exercise/Student Project:** *The Affect Intensity Measure* (p. 16) or **Student Project:** *The Relationship Between Affect and Personality Traits* (p. 18) from Bolt's Teacher's Resource Binder.

• While weightless, astronauts' internal bodily fluids move toward their upper body and their faces become puffy. This makes nonverbal communication more difficult, increasing the risks of misunderstanding, especially among multinational crews (Gelman, 1989). •

The discovery that facial muscles speak a fairly universal language would not have surprised pioneering emotion researcher Charles Darwin (1809–1882). He speculated that in prehistoric times, before our ancestors communicated in words, their ability to convey threats, greetings, and submission with facial expressions helped them survive. That shared heritage, he believed, is why all humans express the basic emotions with similar facial expressions. A sneer, for example, retains elements of an animal baring its teeth in a snarl. Emotional expressions may enhance our survival in other ways, too. Surprise raises the eyebrows and widens the eyes, enabling us to take in more information. Disgust wrinkles the nose, closing it from foul odors.

Smiles, too, are social phenomena as well as emotional reflexes. Bowlers seldom smile when they score a strike—they smile when they turn to face their companions (Jones et al., 1991; Kraut & Johnston, 1979). Even euphoric winners of Olympic gold medals typically don't smile when they are awaiting their ceremony but do when interacting with officials and facing the crowd and cameras (Fernández-Dols & Ruiz-Belda, 1995).

It has been adaptive for us to interpret faces in particular contexts. (Recall the aggressive or frightened monsters from Unit 4.) People judge an angry face set in a frightening situation as afraid. They judge a fearful face set in a painful situation as pained (Carroll & Russell, 1996). Movie directors harness this phenomenon by creating contexts and soundtracks that amplify our perceptions of particular emotions.

Although cultures share a universal facial language for basic emotions, they differ in how much emotion they express. Cultures that encourage individuality, as in Western Europe, Australia, New Zealand, and North America, display mostly visible emotions (van Hemert et al., 2007). In Chinese culture, which encourages people to adjust to others, personal emotions are less visibly displayed (Tsai et al., 2007). Ditto Japan, where people infer emotion more from the surrounding context, and where the difficult-to-control eyes convey more emotion than the mouth, which is so expressive in North America (Masuda et al., 2008; Yuki et al., 2007). Eyes convey emotion in many ways. When someone asks you a question that requires some thinking, are you more likely to look up or down? In Japan, people typically look down, which displays respect for others. Canadians typically look up (McCarthy et al., 2006).

Cultural differences also exist within nations. The Irish and their Irish-American descendants tend to be more expressive than Scandinavians and their Scandinavian-American descendants (Tsai & Chentsova-Dutton, 2003). And that reminds us of a familiar lesson: Like most psychological events, emotion is best understood not only as a biological and cognitive phenomenon, but also as a social-cultural phenomenon (**FIGURE 8B.13**).

➤ **FIGURE 8B.13**
Levels of analysis for the study of emotion As with other psychological phenomena, researchers explore emotion at biological, psychological, and social-cultural levels.

CRITICAL THINKING

Regardless of culture or gender, students should be able to identify correctly what emotion is being expressed. Pose the following questions to students after having them complete the research exercise suggested at the bottom of page 381:

• Why is it important to study how and why emotions are expressed?

• Does the knowledge that emotional expression is universal change your attitude about people from other cultures and the opposite gender? Why or why not?

Encourage your students to recognize that emotions unify us as a human race. Since we all share these basic responses to the environment, we are really less different than we may appear.

The Effects of Facial Expressions

7: Do our facial expressions influence our feelings?

As William James struggled with feelings of depression and grief, he came to believe that we can control emotions by going "through the outward movements" of any emotion we want to experience. "To feel cheerful," he advised, "sit up cheerfully, look around cheerfully, and act as if cheerfulness were already there."

Studies of emotional effects of facial expressions reveal precisely what James might have predicted. Expressions not only communicate emotion, they also amplify and regulate it. In his 1872 book, *The Expression of the Emotions in Man and Animals*, Darwin contended that "the free expression by outward signs of an emotion intensifies it. . . . He who gives way to violent gestures will increase his rage."

Was Darwin right? Let's test Darwin's hypothesis: Fake a big grin. Now scowl. Can you feel the "smile therapy" difference? Participants in dozens of experiments have felt a difference. For example, James Laird and his colleagues (1974, 1984, 1989) subtly induced students to make a frowning expression by asking them to "contract these muscles" and "pull your brows together" (supposedly to help the researchers attach facial electrodes). The results? The students reported feeling a little angry. People instructed to mold their faces in ways that express other basic emotions also experienced those emotions (FIGURE 8B.14). For example, they reported feeling more fear than anger, disgust, or sadness when made to construct a fearful expression: "Raise your eyebrows. And open your eyes wide. Move your whole head back, so that your chin is tucked in a little bit, and let your mouth relax and hang open a little" (Duclos et al., 1989). The face is more than a billboard that displays our feelings; *it also feeds our feelings*.

In the absence of competing emotions, this **facial feedback** effect is subtle yet detectable. Students induced to smile have felt happier and recalled happier memories than did frowners. Just activating one of the smiling muscles by holding a pen in the teeth (rather than with the lips, which activates a frowning muscle) is enough to make cartoons seem more amusing (Strack et al., 1988). A heartier smile—made not just with the mouth but with raised cheeks that crinkle the eyes—enhances positive feelings even more when you are reacting to something pleasant or funny (Soussignan, 2001). Smile warmly on the outside and you feel better on the inside. When smiling you will even more quickly understand sentences that describe pleasant events (Havas et al., 2007). Scowl and the whole world seems to scowl back.

Two new studies demonstrate the power of facial feedback. In one, Tiffany Ito and her colleagues (2006) used the pen-in-the-teeth procedure to induce happiness while people viewed pictures of faces. If they had viewed Black rather than White faces, they later, on an Implicit Attitude Test, exhibited lessened racial bias against Blacks. The good feeling had spread by association. Another study used Botox injections to paralyze the frowning muscles of 10 depressed patients (Finzi & Wasserman, 2006). Two months after the treatment, 9 of the 10 nonfrowning patients were no longer depressed. (This intriguing study awaits replication with an untreated control group.)

Sara Snodgrass and her associates (1986) observed the *behavior feedback* phenomenon with walking. You can duplicate the participants' experience: Walk for a few minutes with short, shuffling steps, keeping your eyes downcast. Now walk around taking long strides, with your arms swinging and your eyes looking straight ahead. Can you feel your mood shift? Going through the motions awakens the emotions.

> "Whenever I feel afraid
> I hold my head erect
> And whistle a happy tune."
> Richard Rodgers and Oscar Hammerstein,
> *The King and I*, 1958

> ➤ FIGURE 8B.14
> **How to make people frown without telling them to frown** Randy Larsen, Margaret Kasimatis, and Kurt Frey's (1992) solution: Attach two golf tees above the eyebrows and ask the participants to make the tee tips touch. Participants felt sad while viewing scenes of war, sickness, and starvation, and even sadder with their "sad face" muscles activated.

● A request from your author: Smile often as you read this book. ●

::**facial feedback** the effect of facial expressions on experienced emotions, as when a facial expression of anger or happiness intensifies feelings of anger or happiness.

DEMO

Have students practice facial feedback on each other. Each pair of students should write two sentences, one delivering good news and one delivering bad news. For example, the good news may be "You have just won the lottery!" and the bad news may be "You have just failed your math class." Have the students then attach golf tees to their eyebrows as shown in Figure 8B.14. Have students deliver both types of news with both happy expressions and sad expressions. They should report their feelings as they expressed the news and as they received the news. Did the type of facial expression affect either the expression or reception of the news?

DEMO

Have students try the behavior feedback activity described on page 383. Does the way they carry themselves affect how they feel? Have students discuss whether the phrase "dress for success" may be a way people have embodied this phenomenon.

Have students create their own list of "basic" emotions. Have them list as many different emotions as they can come up with, narrowing them down into categories. Have students compare their list of basic emotions with each other and the book. Most likely, students will see general agreement among their lists.

One small way to become more empathic is to let your own face mimic another person's expression (Vaughn & Lanzetta, 1981). Acting as another acts helps us feel what another feels. Indeed, natural mimicry of others' emotions helps explain why emotions are contagious (Dimberg et al., 2000; Neumann & Strack, 2000). Blocking people's natural mimicry, for example, by having them bite a pencil with their teeth, impairs their ability to recognize others' emotions (Oberman et al., 2007).

BEFORE YOU MOVE ON . . .

➤ **ASK YOURSELF**

Can you think of one situation in which you would like to change the way you feel, and create a simple plan for doing so? For instance, if you would like to feel more cheerful on your way to class tomorrow morning rather than dragging yourself there, you might try walking briskly—with head held high and a pleasant expression on your face.

➤ **TEST YOURSELF 3**

Who tends to express more emotion—men or women? How do we know the answer to that question?

Answers to the Test Yourself questions can be found in Appendix E at the end of the book.

Experienced Emotion

HOW MANY DISTINCT EMOTIONS ARE there? Carroll Izard (1977) isolated 10 basic emotions (joy, interest-excitement, surprise, sadness, anger, disgust, contempt, fear, shame, and guilt), most of which are present in infancy (**FIGURE 8B.15**). Jessica

(a) Joy (mouth forming smile, cheeks lifted, twinkle in eye)

(b) Anger (brows drawn together and downward, eyes fixed, mouth squarish)

(c) Interest (brows raised or knitted, mouth softly rounded, lips may be pursed)

➤ **FIGURE 8B.15**
Infants' naturally occurring emotions To identify the emotions present from birth, Carroll Izard analyzed the facial expressions of infants.

(d) Disgust (nose wrinkled, upper lip raised, tongue pushed outward)

(e) Surprise (brows raised, eyes widened, mouth rounded in oval shape)

(f) Sadness (brow's inner corners raised, mouth corners drawn down)

(g) Fear (brows level, drawn in and up, eyelids lifted, mouth corners retracted)

At this point, you may want to use **Classroom Exercises: *The Affect Grid*** (p. 16) or ***Brief Measures of Positive and Negative Affect—The PANAS Scales*** (p. 17) or ***Individual Differences in Emotional Complexity*** (p. 17) or ***The Disgust Scale*** (p. 18) or ***Envy and Jealousy*** (p. 20) from Bolt's Teacher's Resource Binder.

Tracey and Richard Robins (2004) believe that pride is also a distinct emotion, signaled by a small smile, head slightly tilted back, and an open posture. And Phillip Shaver and his colleagues (1996) believe that love, too, may be a basic emotion. But Izard has argued that other emotions are combinations of these 10, with love, for example, being a mixture of joy and interest-excitement.

The ingredients of emotion include not only physiology and expressive behavior but also our conscious experience. Varied people, including Estonians, Poles, Greeks, Chinese, and Canadians, place emotional experience along the two dimensions illustrated in FIGURE 8B.16—pleasant/positive-versus-unpleasant/negative *valence*, and low-versus-high *arousal* (Russell et al., 1989, 1999a,b; Watson et al., 1999). On the valence and arousal dimensions, *terrified* is more frightened (more unpleasant and aroused) than *afraid*, *enraged* is angrier than *angry*, *delighted* is happier than *happy*.

Let's take a closer look at three of these emotions: fear, anger, and happiness. What functions do they serve? What influences our experience of each?

Fear

8: What is the function of fear, and how do we learn fears?

Fear can be poisonous. It can torment us, rob us of sleep, and preoccupy our thinking. People can be literally scared to death. Fear can also be contagious. In 1903, someone yelled "Fire!" as a fire broke out in Chicago's Iroquois Theater. Eddie Foy, the comedian on stage at the time, tried to reassure the crowd by calling out, "Don't get excited. There's no danger. Take it easy!" Alas, the crowd panicked. During the 10 minutes it took the fire department to arrive and quickly extinguish the flames, more than 500 people perished, most of them trampled or smothered in a stampede. Bodies were piled 7 or 8 feet deep in the stairways, and many of the faces bore heel marks (Brown, 1965).

More often, fear is adaptive. It's an alarm system that prepares our bodies to flee from danger. Fear of real or imagined enemies binds people together as families, tribes, and nations. Fear of injury protects us from harm. Fear of punishment or retaliation restrains our harming one another. Fear helps us focus on a problem and rehearse coping strategies. Fearful expressions improve peripheral vision and speed eye movements, thus boosting sensory input (Susskind et al., 2008).

Learning Fear

People can be afraid of almost anything—"afraid of truth, afraid of fortune, afraid of death, and afraid of each other," observed Ralph Waldo Emerson. The "politics of fear" builds upon people's fear—fear of terrorists, fear of immigrants, fear of criminals. Why so many fears? Recall from Unit 6 that infants come to fear furry objects associated with frightening noises. When infants begin to crawl, they learn from their falls and near-falls—and become increasingly afraid of heights (Campos et al., 1992). Through such conditioning, the short list of naturally painful and frightening events can multiply into a long list of human fears—fear of driving or flying, fear of mice or cockroaches, fear of closed or open spaces, fear of failure or success, fear of another race or nation.

Learning by observation extends the list. Susan Mineka (1985, 2002) sought to explain why nearly all monkeys reared in the wild fear snakes, yet lab-reared monkeys

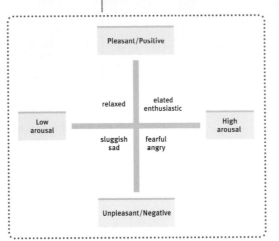

> **FIGURE 8B.16**
> **Two dimensions of emotion** James Russell, David Watson, Auke Tellegen, and others describe emotions as variations on two dimensions—arousal (low versus high) and valence (pleasant versus unpleasant feeling).

• One explanation of sudden death caused by a voodoo "curse" is that the terrified person's parasympathetic nervous system, which calms the body, overreacts to the extreme arousal by slowing the heart to a stop (Seligman, 1974). •

Compared to other mental disorders, phobias are relatively easy to treat. Usually, phobias are learned responses to a stimulus, so they can be extinguished using traditional conditioning techniques, such as systematic desensitization. Typically, however, most people do not seek treatment for their phobias because they do not necessarily interfere with daily life.

INTERCONNECTING

Connect learned fears with Bandura's observational learning, from Unit 6. Bandura showed that simply watching others behave can cause the observer to learn the behavior without actually experiencing the stimuli for themselves. This same phenomenon is shown with the lab-reared monkeys learning to fear snakes like their wild counterparts.

do not. Surely, most wild monkeys do not actually suffer snake bites. Do they learn their fear through observation? To find out, Mineka experimented with six monkeys reared in the wild (all strongly fearful of snakes) and their lab-reared offspring (virtually none of which feared snakes). After repeatedly observing their parents or peers refusing to reach for food in the presence of a snake, the younger monkeys developed a similar strong fear of snakes. When retested three months later, their learned fear persisted. Humans likewise learn fears by observing others (Olsson et al., 2007). This suggests that our fears include the fears we learn from our parents and friends.

The Biology of Fear

We may be biologically prepared to learn some fears more quickly than others. Monkeys learn to fear snakes even by watching tapes of monkeys reacting fearfully to a snake; but they *don't* learn to fear flowers when clever editing transposes the seemingly feared stimulus into a flower (Cook & Mineka, 1991). We humans quickly learn to fear snakes, spiders, and cliffs—fears that probably helped our ancestors survive (Öhman & Mineka, 2003). But our Stone Age fears leave us unprepared for high-tech dangers—cars, electricity, bombs, and global climate change—all of which are now far more dangerous.

➤ **FIGURE 8B.17**

The amygdala—a neural key to fear learning Nerves running out from these knots of neural tissue, one on either side of the brain's center, carry messages that control heart rate, sweating, stress hormones, attention, and other engines that rev up in threatening situations.

 Units 12 and 13 discuss how such phobias develop and are treated. ◦

One key to fear learning lies in the amygdala, that limbic system neural center deep in the brain (**FIGURE 8B.17**). The amygdala plays a key role in associating various emotions, including fear, with certain situations (Barinaga, 1992b; Reijmers et al., 2007). Rabbits learn to react with fear to a tone that predicts an impending small shock—unless their amygdala is damaged. If rats have their amygdala deactivated by a drug that blocks the strengthening of neural connections, they, too, show no fear learning.

The amygdala is similarly involved in human fears. If an experimenter repeatedly blasts people with a blaring horn after showing a blue slide, they will begin to react emotionally to the slide (as measured by the electricity conducted by their perspiring skin). If they have suffered damage to the nearby hippocampus, they still show the emotional reaction—an implicit memory—but they won't be able to remember why. If they have instead suffered amygdala damage, they will consciously remember the conditioning but will show no emotional effect of it (Schacter, 1996). Patients who have lost use of their amygdala are unusually trusting of scary-looking people (Adolphs et al., 1998).

Of course, there are people whose fears seem to fall outside the average range. Some, with *phobias*, have intense fears of specific objects (such as bugs) or situations (such as public speaking) that disrupt their ability to cope. Others—courageous heroes and remorseless criminals—are less fearful than most of us. Astronauts and adventurers who have "the right stuff"—who can keep their wits and function coolly and effectively in times of severe stress—seem to thrive on risk. So, too, do con artists and killers who calmly charm their intended victims. In laboratory tests, they exhibit little fear of a tone that predictably precedes a painful electric shock.

Experience helps shape such fearfulness or fearlessness, but so do our genes. (As we will see in Unit 9, genes influence our temperament—our emotional reactivity.) Among

At this point, you may want to use **Lecture/Discussion Topics:** *The Amygdala and Fear* (p. 22) or *Scared to Death* (p. 22) from Bolt's Teacher's Resource Binder.

ootie boe/Alamy

Hard-wired fears
Entertainment businesses exploit our survival circuits. Although we can know that amusement park deaths are extremely rare, our fear alarm system nevertheless gives us an adrenaline rush and sweaty palms during a free-flying fair ride.

identical twins, one twin's level of fearfulness is similar to the other's—even when they have been reared separately (Lykken, 1982). Scientists have isolated a gene that influences the amygdala's response to frightening situations (Hariri et al., 2002). People with a short version of this gene have less of a protein that speeds the reuptake of the neurotransmitter serotonin. With more serotonin available to activate their amygdala neurons, people with this short gene exhibit a revved-up amygdala response to frightening pictures.

Anger

9: What are the causes and consequences of anger?

Anger, the sages have said, is "a short madness" (Horace, 65–8 B.C.E.) that "carries the mind away" (Virgil, 70–19 B.C.E.) and can be "many times more hurtful than the injury that caused it" (Thomas Fuller, 1654–1734). But they have also said that "noble anger" (William Shakespeare, 1564–1616) "makes any coward brave" (Cato, 234–149 B.C.E.) and "brings back . . . strength" (Virgil).

What makes us angry? Sometimes anger is a response to a friend or loved one's perceived misdeeds, especially when the person's act seems willful, unjustified, and avoidable (Averill, 1983). But small hassles and blameless annoyances—foul odors, high temperatures, dead cell phones, traffic jams, aches and pains—also have the power to make us angry (Berkowitz, 1990).

Anger can harm us. As you'll see later in this unit, chronic hostility is linked to heart disease. How, then, can we rid ourselves of our anger? In a Gallup survey of teens, boys more than girls reported walking away from the situation or working it off with exercise; girls more often reported talking with a friend, listening to music, or writing (Ray, 2005). Popular books and articles on aggression at times advise that even releasing angry feelings as hostile outbursts can be better than internalizing them. When irritated, should we lash out at the offender? Are advice columnists right in urging us to teach children to vent their anger? Are "recovery" therapists right in encouraging us to rage at our divorced parents, imaginatively curse the boss, or confront our childhood abuser?

Encouraging people to vent their rage is typical in individualized cultures, but it would seldom be heard in cultures where people's identity is centered more on the group. People who keenly sense their *inter*dependence see anger as a threat to group harmony (Markus & Kitayama, 1991). In Tahiti, for instance, people learn to be considerate and gentle. In Japan, from infancy on, angry expressions are less common than in Western cultures.

RESEARCH

Situational rage has become a national problem, often with devastating consequences. Several different types of rage have emerged in recent years: road rage, workplace rage, even "surf rage." Consider the following questions in a full class discussion:

- Why does expressing instant anger over minor annoyances lead to health problems in the future?

- Why do you think the incidence of rage-related situations has increased in recent years?

- What are some techniques people can use to deal with their feelings of instant rage?

- What are some reasons why "blowing off steam" or expressing rage only intensifies hostile feelings?

TEACHING TIP

At this point, you may want to use **Lecture/Discussion Topics:** *Angry Driving* (p. 24) or *Do We Need to Vent Our Rage?* (p. 26) or **Classroom Exercise:** *The Anger Discomfort Scale* (p. 25) from Bolt's Teacher's Resource Binder.

TROUBLESHOOTING

Students often believe that letting off a little steam is a good way to deal with anger. Point out that the research demonstrates the impotency of catharsis. Some research even suggests that catharsis is harmful! Help students see that a cooling-off period, along with engaging in behaviors that promote positive emotions, will help them feel less angry in the long run.

INTERCONNECTING

You may want to connect to the Unit 14 concept known as the frustration-aggression principle. Researchers believe that much of the aggression people feel results from a frustrating experience—an experience in which a goal is blocked. People who are late for an appointment, who don't get the answer they hope for, who get cut off in traffic or conversation feel frustrated, which can lead to their acting aggressively toward the person or situation that caused the frustration.

A cool culture Domestic violence is rare in Micronesia. This photo of community life on Pulap Island suggests one possible reason: Family life takes place in the open. Relatives and neighbors who witness angry outbursts can step in before the emotion escalates into child, spouse, or elder abuse.

SIX CHIX

The catharsis myth: Is it true?

The Western "vent your anger" advice presumes that through aggressive action or fantasy we can achieve emotional release, or **catharsis**. Experimenters report that *sometimes* when people retaliate against a provoker, they may indeed calm down. But this tends to be true only *if* their counterattack is directed against the provoker, *if* their retaliation seems justifiable, and *if* their target is not intimidating (Geen & Quanty, 1977; Hokanson & Edelman, 1966). In short, expressing anger can be *temporarily* calming *if* it does not leave us feeling guilty or anxious.

However, despite the temporary afterglow, catharsis usually fails to cleanse one's rage. More often, expressing anger breeds more anger. For one thing, it may provoke further retaliation, thus escalating a minor conflict into a major confrontation. For another, expressing anger can magnify anger. (Recall the behavior feedback research: Acting angry can make us feel angrier.) Ebbe Ebbesen and his colleagues (1975) saw this when they interviewed 100 frustrated engineers and technicians just laid off by an aerospace company. They asked some of the workers questions that released hostility, such as, "What instances can you think of where the company has not been fair with you?" When these people later filled out a questionnaire that assessed their attitudes toward the company, did this opportunity to "drain off" their hostility reduce it? Quite the contrary. Compared with those who had not vented their anger, those who had let it all out exhibited *more* hostility. Even when provoked people hit a punching bag *believing* it will be cathartic, the effect is the opposite—leading them to exhibit *more* cruelty (Bushman et al., 1999). And when they wallop a punching bag while ruminating about the person who angered them, they become even more aggressive when given a chance for revenge. "Venting to reduce anger is like using gasoline to put out a fire," concluded researcher Brad Bushman (2002).

When anger fuels physically or verbally aggressive acts we later regret, it becomes maladaptive. Anger primes prejudice. After 9/11, Americans who responded with anger more than fear displayed intolerance for immigrants and Muslims (DeSteno et al., 2004; Skitka et al., 2004). Angry outbursts that temporarily calm us are dangerous in another way: They may be reinforcing and therefore habit forming. If stressed managers find they can drain off some of their tension by berating an employee, then the next time they feel irritated and tense they may be more likely to explode again. Think about it: The next time you are angry you are likely to do whatever has relieved your anger in the past.

What, then, is the best way to handle our anger? Experts offer two suggestions. First, wait. You can bring down the level of physiological arousal of anger by waiting.

TEACHING TIP

At this point, you may want to use **Classroom Exercise/Student Project:** *The Multidimensional Anger Inventory* (p. 24) or **Student Project:** *Monitoring Anger* (p. 24) from Bolt's Teacher's Resource Binder.

"It is true of the body as of arrows," noted Carol Tavris (1982), "what goes up must come down. Any emotional arousal will simmer down if you just wait long enough." Second, deal with anger in a way that involves neither being chronically angry over every little annoyance, nor sulking and rehearsing your grievances. Ruminating inwardly about the causes of your anger serves only to increase it (Rusting & Nolen-Hoeksema, 1998). Calm yourself by exercising, playing an instrument, or talking it through with a friend.

Anger does communicate strength and competence (Tiedens, 2001). It can benefit a relationship when it expresses a grievance in ways that promote reconciliation rather than retaliation. Controlled expressions of anger are more adaptive than either hostile outbursts or pent-up angry feelings. When James Averill (1983) asked people to recall or keep careful records of their experiences with anger, they often recalled reacting assertively rather than hurtfully. Their anger frequently led them to discuss the conflicts with the offender, thereby lessening the aggravation. Civility means not only keeping silent about trivial irritations but also communicating important ones clearly and assertively. A nonaccusing statement of feeling—perhaps letting a sibling know that "I get irritated when you mess up my room while I'm away"—can help resolve the conflicts that cause anger.

What if someone else's behavior really hurts you? Research commends the age-old response of forgiveness. Without letting the offender off the hook or inviting further harm, forgiveness releases anger and calms the body. To explore the bodily effects of forgiveness, Charlotte Witvliet and her co-researchers (2001) invited college students to recall an incident when someone had hurt them. As the students mentally rehearsed forgiveness, their negative feelings—and their perspiration, blood pressure, heart rate, and facial tension—all were lower than when they rehearsed their grudges.

Happiness

10: What are the causes and consequences of happiness?

"How to gain, how to keep, how to recover happiness is in fact for most men at all times the secret motive for all they do," observed William James (1902, p. 76). Understandably so, for one's state of happiness or unhappiness colors everything. People who are happy perceive the world as safer, feel more confident, make decisions more easily, rate job applicants more favorably, are more cooperative and tolerant, and live healthier and more energized and satisfied lives (Briñol et al., 2007; Lyubomirsky et al., 2005; Pressman & Cohen, 2005). When your mood is gloomy and your thinking preoccupied, life as a whole seems depressing and meaningless. Let your mood brighten, and your thinking broadens and becomes more playful and creative (Amabile et al., 2005; Fredrickson, 2006; King et al., 2006). Your relationships, your self-image, and your hopes for the future also seem more promising. Positive emotions fuel upward spirals.

This helps explain why college students' happiness helps predict their life course. In one study, women who smiled happily (rather than smiling artificially or not at all) in 1950s college yearbook photos were more likely to be married, and happily so, in middle age (Harker & Keltner, 2001). In another study, which surveyed thousands of U.S. college students in 1976 and restudied them at age 37, happy students had gone on to earn significantly more money than their less-happy-than-average peers (Diener et al., 2002). Nonetheless, it's also true that social reforms are often launched, as well as great literature written, by those not extremely happy with how things are (Oishi et al., 2007).

"Anger will never disappear so long as thoughts of resentment are cherished in the mind."

The Buddha, 500 B.C.E.

::**catharsis** emotional release. The catharsis hypothesis maintains that "releasing" aggressive energy (through action or fantasy) relieves aggressive urges.

TEACHING TIP

Have students make a "Top Ten" list of things that will make them happy. Have them categorize the list into things that are "material" and "non-material." Create a master list from their individual ones to see which category is larger.

CRITICAL THINKING

Before World War II, two of psychology's goals focused on studying the positive aspects of life. Since World War II, the field has focused on curing illness rather than identifying positive qualities. Set aside time for small groups of students to discuss the following questions about positive subjective experiences:

- Why are mental illnesses easier to study than positive traits?

- What prejudices might lead some to disregard the study of positive qualities?

- How might knowing the qualities of positive experiences lead to greater knowledge of our health?

RESEARCH

Have students work with partners or in small groups to check in your school's biology and health textbooks for references to the relationship between positive experiences and health. Have them use their findings to respond to the following questions:

- How many references to the relationship between positive experiences and health are there in each text? How many pages are devoted to this relationship?

- Which type of textbook has more references to the positivity/health link? Why might this be?

- How do these books describe this link? Do they seem biased? If so, how?

INTERCONNECTING

The feel-good, do-good phenomenon is much like the behavior feedback hypothesis presented earlier in the unit. If we do good things, we will feel good, making it more likely that we will do more good things in the future.

TEACHING TIP

One way to study happiness is to examine the lives of "paragons" of happiness. Have students think of the happiest person they know and interview him or her about why he or she is so happy.

- Do these people view themselves as happy? Why or why not?

- What is their attitude about taking compliments?

- What is their attitude about handling difficulties in life?

- Do they consciously do anything to maintain happiness in their lives? Why or why not?

- How can you learn to be happier by following their examples?

At this point, you may want to use **Lecture/Discussion Topics:** *Two Dimensions of Positive Affect* (p. 27) or *Money and Happiness* (p. 29) or *Rising Happiness and Freedom of Choice* (p. 29) or *Laughter* (p. 31) from Bolt's Teacher's Resource Binder.

::**feel-good, do-good phenomenon** people's tendency to be helpful when already in a good mood.

::**well-being** self-perceived happiness or satisfaction with life. Used along with measures of objective well-being (for example, physical and economic indicators) to evaluate people's quality of life.

Moreover—and this is one of psychology's most consistent findings—when we feel happy we more often help others. In study after study, a mood-boosting experience (finding money, succeeding on a challenging task, recalling a happy event) has made people more likely to give money, pick up someone's dropped papers, volunteer time, and do other good deeds. Psychologists call it the **feel-good, do-good phenomenon** (Salovey, 1990). Happiness doesn't just feel good, it does good. (Doing good also promotes good feeling, a phenomenon harnessed by some happiness coaches and instructors as they assign people to perform a daily "random act of kindness" and to record the results.)

Despite the significance of happiness, psychology throughout its history has more often focused on negative emotions. Since 1887, *Psychological Abstracts* (a guide to psychology's literature) has included, as of this writing, 14,889 articles mentioning anger, 93,371 mentioning anxiety, and 120,897 mentioning depression. For every 17 articles on these topics, only 1 dealt with the positive emotions of joy (1789), life satisfaction (6255), or happiness (5764). There is, of course, good reason to focus on negative emotions; they can make our lives miserable and drive us to seek help. But researchers are becoming increasingly interested in **well-being**, assessed either as feelings of happiness (sometimes defined as a high ratio of positive to negative feelings) or as a sense of satisfaction with life. A new *positive psychology* is on the rise (see Unit 10).

The Short Life of Emotional Ups and Downs

In their happiness research, psychologists have studied influences on both our temporary moods and our long-term life satisfaction. When studying people's hour-by-hour moods, David Watson (2000) and Daniel Kahneman and his colleagues (2004) discovered that positive emotion rises over the early to middle part of most days (FIGURE 8B.18). Stressful events—an argument, a sick child, a car problem—trigger bad moods. No surprise there. But by the next day, the gloom nearly always lifts (Affleck et al., 1994; Bolger et al., 1989; Stone & Neale, 1984). If anything, people tend to rebound from bad days to a *better*-than-usual good mood the following day. When in a bad mood, can you usually depend on rebounding within a day or two? Are your times of elation similarly hard to sustain? Over the long run, our emotional ups and downs tend to balance.

Apart from prolonged grief over the loss of a loved one or lingering anxiety after a trauma (such as child abuse, rape, or the terrors of war), even tragedy is not permanently depressing:

➤ **FIGURE 8B.18**

Moods across the day When psychologist David Watson (2000) sampled nearly 4500 mood reports from 150 people, he found this pattern of variation from the average levels of positive and negative emotions.

- Learning that one is HIV-positive is devastating. But after five weeks of adapting to the grim news, those who have tested positive report feeling less emotionally distraught than they had expected (Sieff et al., 1999).

- Kidney dialysis patients recognize that their health is relatively poor, yet in their moment-to-moment experiences they report being just as happy as healthy nonpatients (Riis et al., 2005).

- European 8- to 12-year-olds with cerebral palsy experience normal psychological well-being (Dickinson et al., 2007).

"If you are a paraplegic," explains Daniel Kahneman (2005), "you will gradually start thinking of other things, and the more time you spend thinking of other things the less miserable you are going to be." A major disability often leaves people less happy than

DEMO

Have students brainstorm about flow activities they regularly engage in. Challenge them to participate in a flow activity within the next few days, reflecting afterward about how that experience made them feel:

- Why did you engage in the flow activity? Did you choose to do it but sacrificed other activities? Why or why not?

- Did engaging in this activity affect your mood for the rest of the day? Why or why not? Did a good mood extend into the next day? Why or why not?

- How can you experience more flow in your life?

average, yet happier than able-bodied people with depression (Kübler et al., 2005; Lucas, 2007a,b; Oswald & Powdthavee, 2006; Schwartz & Estrin, 2004). Even patients "locked-in" a motionless body "rarely want to die," report Eimar Smith and Mark Delargy (2005), which "counters a popular misconception that such patients would have been better off dead."

In less life-threatening contexts, the pattern continues. Those involved in romantic relationships often expect their lives would be utterly deflated by a breakup. Actually, after a recovery period, those who do suffer breakups are not noticeably less happy than those who don't (Gilbert et al., 1998). The surprising reality: *We overestimate the duration of our emotions and underestimate our capacity to adapt.*

Positive emotions are similarly hard to sustain. In *Rethinking Happiness: The Science of Psychological Wealth*, Ed Diener and Robert Biswas-Diener (2009) illustrate the short life of most emotions with daily happiness reports of a 21-year-old student undergoing treatment for Hodgkins disease, a cancer of the immune system. Midway through his 80 daily reports, the young man learned the treatment had effectively wiped out his cancer. As **FIGURE 8B.19** shows, on the day he received this wonderful news, he was elated. But although the ensuing month was relatively free of down-in-the-dumps days, his emotions soon returned to near their previous level, with fluctuations in response to daily events.

Wealth and Well-Being

"*Do you think you would be happier if you made more money?*" *Yes*, replied 73 percent of Americans in a 2006 Gallup poll. How important is "Being very well off financially?" In recent years, this has, for entering U.S. collegians, been ranked first or second among 21 possible objectives. Some 3 in 4 students rate their top two objectives—being "very well off" and "raising a family"—as "extremely important" or "essential" (**FIGURE 8B.20** on the next page).

Human resilience Seven weeks after her 1994 wedding, Anna Putt of South Midlands, England, shown here with her husband, Des, suffered a brainstem stroke that left her "locked-in." For months after, she recalls, "I was paralyzed from the neck down and was unable to communicate. These were VERY frightening times. But with encouragement from family, friends, faith, and medical staff, I tried to keep positive." In the ensuing three years, she became able to "talk" (by nodding at letters), to steer an electric wheelchair with her head, and to use a computer (by nodding while wearing spectacles that guide a cursor). Despite her paralysis, she reports that "I enjoy going out in the fresh air. My motto is 'Don't look back, move forward.' God would not want me to stop trying and I have no intention of doing so. Life is what you make of it!"

> "Weeping may tarry for the night, but joy comes with the morning."
> Psalm 30:5

➤ **FIGURE 8B.19 The short life of strong emotions** A university student's daily reports of negative and positive moods revealed day-to-day fluctuations, punctuated by temporary elation on the day he learned that he was now cancer free. (From Diener & Biswas-Diener, 2009.)

TEACHING TIP

Several factors influence the extent of positive subjective experiences:

- *Temperament:* Inborn qualities help determine how well people interact with the environment.

- *Learned positive outlook on life:* People learn optimism and hope through experience.

- *Strongly held important values and goals related to these values:* People who have clear goals and make progress working toward them report higher levels of subjective well-being.

- *Cultural differences:* Psychological measures, such as self-esteem, more accurately predict positive subjective experience in individualistic cultures (United States or Western European cultures) than in collectivist ones (Japanese or communal-based cultures).

- *Age:* People's age brings a wealth of perspective and experience that colors how they view life situations.

Source: Williamson, G. (2000). Extending the activity restriction model of depressed affect: Evidence from a sample of breast cancer patients. *Health Psychology, 19,* 339–347.

At this point, you may want to use *Classroom Exercises: What Is Satisfying About Satisfying Events?* (p. 27) or *Happiness Measures* (p. 28) or *Orientations to Happiness and Life Satisfaction* (p. 28) from Bolt's Teacher's Resource Binder.

TROUBLESHOOTING

People who live without disabilities or illness often feel pity for those who do. They believe that no one would want to live with a life-altering condition or have to depend on others for basic needs (such as feeding or bathing). Yet, research overwhelmingly suggests that people who live with disabilities or illness report high levels of well-being and satisfaction with life. Perhaps these people tend to value each day more than those who do not live with life-altering issues, perhaps not taking for granted simple pleasures and annoyances of life.

UNIT 8B

CRITICAL THINKING

Have students examine why those in Denmark report such high levels of happiness. Denmark has among the highest taxes of any European nation. Denmark is not known for its exports or cuisine. In fact, many students won't even know where Denmark is on a map! Here are some reasons Danes cite for their happiness:

- Denmark has efficiently run government institutions, such as public transportation and child care. Trains tend to run on time in Denmark, and parents are only responsible for 25 percent of child care costs.

- Working overtime is not an expectation for Danes. Danes have a 37-hour work week. The work day ends around 4:30 p.m. each day. Danes expect to spend significant amounts of time with family.

- Low expectations for what will happen are a key part of Danish consciousness. Some researchers feel Danes are happy simply because they do not have high expectations for how life will turn out. If you set the bar low, you will almost surely clear it!

Source: *BBC News Magazine,* April, 2007.

➤ **FIGURE 8B.20**

The changing materialism of entering collegians Surveys of more than 200,000 entering U.S. collegians per year have revealed an increasing desire for wealth after 1970. (From *The American Freshman* surveys, UCLA, 1966 to 2007.)

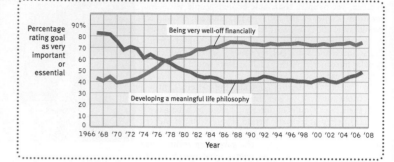

- In World Values Surveys in 97 countries (Inglehart, 2008) and in Gallup (2008) surveys in 130 countries, the highest self-reported happiness was found in Denmark. •

"Money won't make you happy, Waldron. So instead of a raise, I'm giving a Prozac."

> "Americans say that money doesn't bring happiness. But it helps you to live with misery in comfort."
> Farah Pahlavi, exiled widow of the wealthy Shah of Iran, 2004

There is evidence that wealth, to a point, correlates with well-being. Consider:

- Within most countries, though especially in poor countries, individuals with lots of money are typically happier than those who struggle to afford life's basic needs (Diener & Biswas-Diener, 2009; Howell & Howell, 2008). They also often enjoy better health than those stressed by poverty and lack of control over their lives.

- People in rich countries are also somewhat happier than those in poor countries (Inglehart, 2009).

- Those who have experienced a recent windfall from a lottery, an inheritance, or a surging economy typically feel some elation (Diener & Oishi, 2000; Gardner & Oswald, 2007).

So, it seems that money enough to buy your way out of hunger and hopelessness also buys some happiness. But once one has enough money for comfort and security, piling up more and more matters less and less. This *diminishing returns* phenomenon is familiar to economists as *diminishing marginal utility* and to you as the second piece of dessert satisfying you less than the first. As Robert Cummins (2006) confirms with Australian data, the power of more money to increase happiness is significant at low incomes and diminishes as income rises. A $1000 annual wage increase does a lot more for the average person in Malawi than for the average person in Switzerland. This implies, he adds, that raising low incomes will do more to increase human well-being than raising high incomes.

The income-happiness correlation seemingly occurs because more income produces greater happiness. But perhaps, note John Cacioppo and his collaborators (2008), more happiness produces greater income. So it was among the middle-aged adults whom they studied over time: Today's happiness predicted tomorrow's income better than today's income predicted tomorrow's happiness. (Recall that after graduation, happy collegians likewise outearn their less happy fellow students.)

And consider this: During the last four decades, the average U.S. citizen's buying power almost tripled. Did this greater wealth—enabling twice as many cars per person, not to mention iPods, laptops, and camera cell phones—also buy more happiness? As **FIGURE 8B.21** shows, the average American, though certainly richer, is not a bit happier. In 1957, some 35 percent said they were "very happy," as did slightly fewer—32 percent—in 2008. Much the same has been true of Europe, Australia, and Japan, where people enjoy better nutrition, health care, education, and science, and they are somewhat happier than those in very poor countries (Diener & Biswas-Diener, 2002, 2009; Speth, 2008). Yet their increasing real incomes have *not* produced increasing happiness. This finding lobs a bombshell at modern

TEACHING TIP

Do your students believe that money can buy happiness? Have students discuss why people may have this belief and what evidence they can think of that would help them keep the wealth-to-happiness ratio in perspective.

FIGURE 8B.21
Does money buy happiness? It surely helps us to avoid certain types of pain. Yet, though buying power has almost tripled since the 1950s, the average American's reported happiness has remained almost unchanged. (Happiness data from National Opinion Research Center surveys; income data from *Historical Statistics of the United States and Economic Indicators.*)

materialism: *Economic growth in affluent countries has provided no apparent boost to morale or social well-being.*

Ironically, those who strive hardest for wealth tend to live with lower well-being, a finding that "comes through very strongly in every culture I've looked at," reported Richard Ryan (1999). This is especially so for those seeking money to prove themselves, gain power, or show off rather than support their families (Srivastava et al., 2001). Ryan's collaborator, Tim Kasser (2000, 2002), concluded from their studies that those who instead strive for "intimacy, personal growth, and contribution to the community" experience a higher quality of life.

If we are richer and healthier than were our grandparents at our age, but no happier, should our national priorities focus more on advancing psychological well-being? In Bhutan, King Jigme Singye Wangchuk said that "gross national happiness is more important than gross national product." Bhutan's prime minister framed his annual report in terms of Bhutan's four pillars of progress toward national happiness: "The promotion of equitable and sustainable socio-economic development, preservation and promotion of cultural values, conservation of the natural environment, and establishment of good governance" (Esty, 2004). Diener (2006), supported by 52 colleagues, has proposed ways in which nations might measure national well-being. "Policymakers should be interested in well-being not only because of its inherent value to citizens, but also because individuals' well-being can have positive spillover benefits for the society as a whole."

Two Psychological Phenomena: Adaptation and Comparison

Two psychological principles explain why, for those who are not poor, more money buys little more than a temporary surge of happiness and why our emotions seem

"Australians are three times richer than their parents and grandparents were in the 1950s, but they are not happier."
The Australia Institute,
"A Well-Being Manifesto," 2005

"But on the positive side, money can't buy happiness—so who cares?"

"No happiness lasts for long."
Seneca, *Agamemnon*, 60 C.E.

TEACHING TIP

Have students ponder how research might support these two maxims:

- *"You can't go home again."* Research into adaptation-level phenomena suggests that once we experience a new place or a new item, it is difficult to accept the earlier status quo. We compare today's experience with yesterday's, often thinking today's is better.

- *"They're keeping up with the Joneses."* Research into relative deprivation suggests that we compare our happiness to the happiness of others. We believe that people who have more stuff or who seem happier must be happier than we are.

TROUBLESHOOTING

Notice how relative deprivation works in two ways:

- We compare upwardly—we compare ourselves to people who seem to have more than we do. We tend to think those people are happier than we are. Typically, we overestimate the happiness of wealthy people.

- We compare downwardly—we compare ourselves with those less fortunate, feeling thankful that we are not as unhappy as those in poverty must be. Typically, we underestimate the happiness of poor people.

::adaptation-level phenomenon our tendency to form judgments (of sounds, of lights, of income) relative to a neutral level defined by our prior experience.

::relative deprivation the perception that we are worse off relative to those with whom we compare ourselves.

> "Continued pleasures wear off.... Pleasure is always contingent upon change and disappears with continuous satisfaction."
>
> Dutch psychologist Nico Frijda (1988)

> "I have a 'fortune cookie maxim' that I'm very proud of: Nothing in life is quite as important as you think it is while you are thinking about it. So, nothing will ever make you as happy as you think it will."
>
> Nobel laureate psychologist Daniel Kahneman, Gallup interview, "What Were They Thinking?" 2005

"Shortly after I realized I had plenty, I realized there was plenty more."

attached to elastic bands that pull us back from highs or lows. In its own way, each principle suggests that happiness is relative.

Happiness and Prior Experience The **adaptation-level phenomenon** describes our tendency to judge various stimuli relative to those we have previously experienced. As psychologist Harry Helson (1898–1977) explained, we adjust our *neutral* levels—the points at which sounds seem neither loud nor soft, temperatures neither hot nor cold, events neither pleasant nor unpleasant—based on our experience. We then notice and react to variations up or down from these levels.

Thus, if our current condition—our income, academic average, or social prestige—increases, we feel an initial surge of pleasure. We then adapt to this new level of achievement, come to consider it normal, and require something even better to give us another surge of happiness. From my childhood, I can recall the thrill of watching my family's first 12-inch, black-and-white TV. Now, after viewing a movie on a family member's 60-inch high-definition screen, I am unimpressed by my once wonderful 27-inch TV. Having adapted upward, I perceive as neutral what I once experienced as positive. Satisfaction and dissatisfaction, success and failure—all are relative to our recent experience. Satisfaction, as Ryan (1999) said, "has a short half-life."

HI & LOIS

The point is not that, so far as long-term happiness goes, nothing really matters. Despite our remarkable adaptiveness and resilience, after being struck by a severe disability, we may not rebound all the way back to our former emotions (Diener et al., 2006). Moreover, there are some things we can do to enhance our happiness (see Close-Up: How to Be Happier).

Happiness and Others' Attainments Happiness is relative not only to our past experience but also to our comparisons with others (Lyubomirsky, 2001). We are always comparing ourselves with others. And whether we feel good or bad depends on who those others are. We are slow-witted or clumsy only when others are smarter or more agile.

Two examples: To explain the frustration expressed by U.S. Air Corps soldiers during World War II, researchers formulated the concept of **relative deprivation**—the sense that we are worse off than others with whom we compare ourselves. Despite a relatively rapid promotion rate for the group, many soldiers were frustrated about their own promotion rates (Merton & Kitt, 1950). Apparently, seeing so many others being promoted inflated the soldiers' expectations. And when expectations soar above attainments, the result is disappointment. Alex Rodriguez's 10-year, $275 million baseball contract surely made him temporarily happy, but it likely also diminished other star players' satisfaction with their lesser, multimillion-dollar contracts. Likewise, the economic surge that has made some urban Chinese newly affluent appears to have fueled among others a sense of relative deprivation (Burkholder, 2005a,b).

Such comparisons help us understand why the middle-and upper-income people in a given country, who can compare themselves with the relatively poor, tend to be slightly more satisfied with life than their less fortunate compatriots. Nevertheless,

TEACHING TIP

At this point, you may want to use **Classroom Exercises:** *Adaptation Level* (p. 30) or *Relative Deprivation* (p. 30) from Bolt's Teacher's Resource Binder.

CLOSE-UP

How to Be Happier

Happiness, like cholesterol level, is a genetically influenced trait. Yet as cholesterol is also influenced by diet and exercise, so our happiness is to some extent under our personal control. Here are some research-based suggestions for improving your mood and increasing your satisfaction with life.

1. **Realize that enduring happiness may not come from financial success.** People adapt to changing circumstances. Thus wealth is like health: Its utter absence breeds misery, but having it (or any circumstance we long for) doesn't guarantee happiness.

2. **Take control of your time.** Happy people feel in control of their lives. To master your use of time, set goals and break them into daily aims. Although we often overestimate how much we will accomplish in any given day (leaving us frustrated), we generally underestimate how much we can accomplish in a year, given just a little progress every day.

3. **Act happy.** We can sometimes act ourselves into a happier frame of mind. Manipulated into a smiling expression, people feel better; when they scowl, the whole world seems to scowl back. So put on a happy face. Talk as *if* you feel positive self-esteem, are optimistic, and are outgoing. Going through the motions can trigger the emotions.

4. **Seek work and leisure that engage your skills.** Happy people often are in a zone called *flow*—totally absorbed in enjoyable tasks that challenge but don't overwhelm them. Passive forms of leisure (watching TV) often provide less flow experience than gardening, socializing, or craft work. Take time to savor such pleasant experiences.

5. **Join the "movement" movement.** Aerobic exercise can relieve mild depression and anxiety and promote health and energy. Sound minds reside in sound bodies. Off your duffs, couch potatoes.

6. **Give your body the sleep it wants.** Happy people live active vigorous lives yet reserve time for renewing sleep and solitude. Many people suffer from sleep debt, with resulting fatigue, diminished alertness, and gloomy moods.

7. **Give priority to close relationships.** Intimate friendships with those who care deeply about you can help you weather difficult times. Confiding is good for soul and body. Resolve to nurture your closest relationships by *not* taking your loved ones for granted, by displaying to them the sort of kindness you display to others, by affirming them, by playing together and sharing together.

8. **Focus beyond self.** Reach out to those in need. Happiness increases helpfulness (those who feel good do good). But doing good also makes one feel good.

9. **Count your blessings and record your gratitude.** Keeping a gratitude journal heightens well-being (Emmons, 2007; Seligman et al., 2005). Try pausing each day to record positive events and why they occurred. Express your gratitude to others.

10. **Nurture your spiritual self.** For many people, faith provides a support community, a reason to focus beyond self, and a sense of purpose and hope. That helps explain why people active in faith communities report greater-than-average happiness and often cope well with crisis.

Digested from David G. Myers, *The Pursuit of Happiness* (Harper, 1993).

INTERCONNECTING

Several pieces of advice Myers gives in the "How to Be Happier" box are related to content covered in other parts of the text:

- *Act happy.* In this unit, Myers discusses the "behavior feedback" hypothesis, in which people who act in certain ways will feel that way.

- *Join the "movement" movement.* In Appendix C, students may read how engaging in aerobic exercise helps boost serotonin levels, which contributes to alleviating depression.

- *Give your body the sleep it needs.* In Unit 5, Myers discusses the research showing that getting one more hour of sleep a night can boost productivity, which in turn, can boost feelings of competency.

once people reach a moderate income level, further increases buy little more happiness. Why? Because as people climb the ladder of success they mostly compare themselves with peers who are at or above their current level (Gruder, 1977; Suls & Tesch, 1978). "Beggars do not envy millionaires, though of course they will envy other beggars who are more successful," noted Bertrand Russell (1930, p. 90). Thus, "Napoleon envied Caesar, Caesar envied Alexander, and Alexander, I daresay, envied Hercules, who never existed. You cannot, therefore, get away from envy by means of success alone, for there will always be in history or legend some person even more successful than you are" (pp. 68–69).

Just as comparing ourselves with those who are better off creates envy, so counting our blessings as we compare ourselves with those worse off boosts our contentment. Marshall Dermer and his colleagues (1979) demonstrated this by asking University of Wisconsin-Milwaukee women to study others' deprivation and suffering. After viewing vivid depictions of how grim life was in Milwaukee in 1900, or after imagining and then writing about various personal tragedies, such as being burned and disfigured, the women expressed greater satisfaction with their own lives. Similarly, when mildly depressed people read about someone who is even more depressed, they feel somewhat better (Gibbons, 1986). "I cried because I had no shoes," states a Persian saying, "until I met a man who had no feet."

• The effect of comparison with others helps explain why students of a given level of academic ability tend to have a higher academic self-concept if they attend a school where most other students are not exceptionally able (Marsh & Parker, 1984). If you were near the top of your graduating class, you might feel inferior upon entering a college or university where all students were near the top of their class. •

DEMO

Research suggests that writing down things for which we are grateful can boost mood. Have students take a short measure of life satisfaction or happiness each day for a week. Then, have students write down three things for which they are thankful each night before they go to bed. Also have them continue their measurement of life satisfaction or happiness each morning. Compare their pre-gratitude/post-gratitude measure of happiness to see if writing down the things for which they were grateful helped boost their mood.

UNIT 8B

TEACHING TIP

Notice that happiness is not a cure-all. Researchers suggest that being happy is good, but being happy while ignoring responsibilities or major negative life events is not psychologically healthy. And, as Table 8B.1 suggests, happiness does not cure wrinkles!

CRITICAL THINKING

The research in this unit suggests that women are more emotionally variable than men. In fact, Table 8B.1 shows that women are both more happy and more sad than men. Have students discuss the benefits and drawbacks that women have with their emotional variability. Does this variability help women experience fewer ill health effects (such as heart disease or other stress-related illnesses)? Does this variability hurt women in business or social experiences?

Predictors of Happiness

If, as the adaptation-level phenomenon implies, our emotions tend to rebound toward our normal, why are some people normally so joyful and others so gloomy? The answers vary somewhat by culture. Self-esteem matters more to individualistic Westerners, social acceptance matters more to those in communal cultures (Diener et al., 2003). But across many countries, research does reveal several predictors of happiness (**TABLE 8B.1**).

TABLE 8B.1

HAPPINESS IS . . .

Researchers Have Found That Happy People Tend to	However, Happiness Seems Not Much Related to Other Factors, Such as
Have high self-esteem (in individualistic countries).	Age.
Be optimistic, outgoing, and agreeable.	Gender (women are more often depressed, but also more often joyful).
Have close friendships or a satisfying marriage.	Parenthood (having children or not).
Have work and leisure that engage their skills.	Physical attractiveness.
Have a meaningful religious faith.	
Sleep well and exercise.	

Sources: Summarized from DeNeve & Cooper (1998), Diener et al. (2003), Lucas et al. (2004), Myers (1993, 2000), Myers & Diener (1995, 1996), and Steel et al. (2008).

"I could cry when I think of the years I wasted accumulating money, only to learn that my cheerful disposition is genetic."

● Studies of chimpanzees in zoos reveal that happiness in chimpanzees, as rated by 200 employees, is also genetically influenced (Weiss et al., 2000, 2002). ●

Although tasks and relationships affect our happiness, genes matter, too. From their study of 254 identical and fraternal twins, David Lykken and Auke Tellegen (1996) estimated that 50 percent of the difference among people's happiness ratings is heritable. Other twin studies report similar or slightly less heritability (Lucas, 2008). Genes influence the personality traits that mark happy lives (Weiss et al., 2008). Thus even identical twins raised apart are often similarly happy.

But when researchers have followed thousands of lives over two decades, they observe that people's "happiness set point" is not fixed (Lucas & Donnellan, 2007). Satisfaction may rise or fall, and happiness can be influenced by factors that are under our control. A striking example: In a long-term study of people in Germany, married partners were as similarly satisfied with their lives as were identical twins (Schimmack & Lucas, 2007). Genes matter. But as this study hints, relationship quality matters, too.

Our studies of happiness remind us that emotions combine physiological activation (left hemisphere especially), expressive behaviors (smiles), and conscious thoughts ("I was so ready for that test!") and feelings (pride, satisfaction). Fear, anger, happiness, and so much else have this in common: They are biopsychosocial phenomena. Our genetic predispositions, brain activity, outlooks, experiences, relationships, and cultures jointly form us.

BEFORE YOU MOVE ON . . .

➤ ASK YOURSELF

If we learn our emotional responses, we may be able to learn new responses to replace old ones. Would you like to change any of your emotional responses? Do you feel you are too easily provoked to anger or fear, for instance? How might you go about changing your behavior or your thinking in order to change your emotional reactions?

➤ TEST YOURSELF 4

What things do (and do not) predict self-reported happiness?

Answers to the Test Yourself questions can be found in Appendix E at the end of the book.

TEACHING TIP

At this point, you may want to use **Student Project: *Constructing a Family Health History*** (p. 32) from Bolt's Teacher's Resource Binder.

Stress and Health

HOW OFTEN DO YOU EXPERIENCE stress in your daily life? Never? Rarely? Sometimes? Or frequently? When Gallup put that question to a national sample in late 2007, three in four said "sometimes" or "frequently." Slightly over half of those under age 55 also said they generally did not have enough time to do what they wanted to do (Carroll, 2008). And you?

For many students, the high school years, with their new relationships and more demanding challenges, prove stressful. Deadlines become relentless and intense at the end of each semester. The time demands of volunteering, sports, college prep courses, and college applications combine with occasional family tensions and success pressures. Sometimes it's enough to give you a headache or disrupt sleep.

If such stress endures, it can also bring on (in those of us who are physiologically predisposed) skin rashes, asthma attacks, or high blood pressure *(hypertension)*. It can also increase our risk for serious illness and death. To study how stress and healthy and unhealthy behaviors influence health and illness, psychologists and physicians created the interdisciplinary field of **behavioral medicine**, integrating behavioral and medical knowledge. **Health psychology** provides psychology's contribution to behavioral medicine. For psychologists, health is more than "merely the slowest possible rate at which one can die" (Prairie Home Companion, 1999). Health psychologists ask: How do our emotions and personality influence our risk of disease? What attitudes and behaviors help prevent illness and promote health and well-being? How do our perceptions of a situation determine the stress we feel? How can we reduce or control stress?

Stress and Illness

11: What is stress?

You think roller coasters are scary? Imagine the stress of being 21-year-old Ben Carpenter on the world's wildest and fastest wheelchair ride. As he crossed an intersection on a sunny summer afternoon in 2007, the light changed. A large truck, whose driver didn't see him, started moving into the intersection. As they bumped, the wheelchair turned to face forward, its handles becoming stuck in the grille. And off they went, the driver unable to hear Ben's cries for help. As they sped down the highway about an hour from my home, passing motorists caught the bizarre sight of a truck pushing a wheelchair at 50 mph and started calling 911. (The first caller: "You are not going to believe this. There is a semi truck pushing a guy in a wheelchair on Red Arrow Highway!") One passerby was an undercover police officer, who did a quick U-turn, followed the truck to its destination a couple of miles from where the incident started, and informed the disbelieving driver that he had a passenger hooked in his grille. "It was very scary," said Ben, who has muscular dystrophy.

Stress is a slippery concept. We sometimes use the word informally to describe threats or challenges ("Ben was under a lot of stress"), and at other times our responses ("Ben experienced acute stress"). To a psychologist, the dangerous truck ride was a *stressor*. Ben's physical and emotional responses were a *stress reaction*. And the process by which he related to the threat was *stress*.

Thus, **stress** is not just a stimulus or a response. It is the process by which we appraise and cope with environmental threats and challenges (**FIGURE 8B.22** on the next page). Stress arises less from events themselves than from how we appraise them (Lazarus, 1998). One person, alone in a house, dismisses

::**behavioral medicine** an interdisciplinary field that integrates behavioral and medical knowledge and applies that knowledge to health and disease.

::**health psychology** a subfield of psychology that provides psychology's contribution to behavioral medicine.

::**stress** the process by which we perceive and respond to certain events, called *stressors*, that we appraise as threatening or challenging.

Extreme stress Ben Carpenter experienced the wildest of rides after his wheelchair got stuck in a truck's grille.

 TEACHING TIP

Stress comes in two types.

- **Distress** is stress perceived as being negative—those events we typically think of when we think of "stress."

- **Eustress** is stress perceived as being positive, but which still carries with it heightened arousal.

Both types of stress, endured over a prolonged period of time, can lead to harmful physical effects, even though eustress is more pleasant to endure.

 TEACHING TIP

Studies of stressors have shown that people's number one fear is speaking in public. Second to this fear is the fear of dying. Citing this finding, comedian Jerry Seinfeld has joked that people are more afraid of giving the eulogy at a funeral than being in the casket!

 DEMO

Have students brainstorm about different stressors they encounter in a regular school day. Assign each of several small groups a different stressor, challenging them to come up with at least three positive ways to deal with the stress. Have them try to think of ways that are realistic for people their age. Then have them share their ideas with the group at large, discussing why teens don't always handle stress very well.

UNIT 8B

➤ **FIGURE 8B.22**
Stress appraisal The events of our lives flow through a psychological filter. How we appraise an event influences how much stress we experience and how effectively we respond.

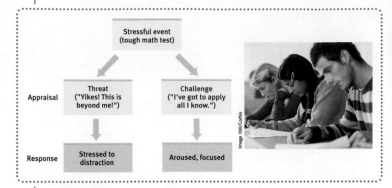

its creaking sounds and experiences no stress; someone else suspects an intruder and becomes alarmed. One person regards a new job as a welcome challenge; someone else appraises it as risking failure.

When short-lived, or when perceived as challenges, stressors can have positive effects. A momentary stress can mobilize the immune system for fending off infections and healing wounds (Segerstrom, 2007). Stress also arouses and motivates us to conquer problems. Championship athletes, successful entertainers, and great teachers and leaders all thrive and excel when aroused by a challenge (Blascovich et al., 2004). Having conquered cancer or rebounded from a lost job, some people emerge with stronger self-esteem and a deepened spirituality and sense of purpose. Indeed, some stress early in life is conducive to later emotional resilience (Landauer & Whiting, 1979). Adversity can beget growth.

But stressors can also threaten us. And experiencing severe or prolonged stress may harm us. Children's physiological responses to severe child abuse put them at later risk of chronic disease (Repetti et al., 2002). Those who had post-traumatic stress reactions to heavy combat in the Vietnam war went on to suffer greatly elevated rates of circulatory, digestive, respiratory, and infectious diseases (Boscarino, 1997).

The Stress Response System

Medical interest in stress dates back to Hippocrates (460–377 B.C.E.). But it was not until the 1920s that Walter Cannon (1929) confirmed that the stress response is part of a unified mind-body system. He observed that extreme cold, lack of oxygen, and emotion-arousing incidents all trigger an outpouring of the stress hormones epinephrine and norepinephrine from the central core of the adrenal glands. This is but one part of the sympathetic nervous system's response. When alerted by any of a number of brain pathways, the sympathetic nervous system, as we have seen, increases heart rate and respiration, diverts blood from digestion to the skeletal muscles, dulls pain, and releases sugar and fat from the body's stores—all to prepare the body for the wonderfully adaptive response that Cannon called *fight or flight* (see Figure 8B.2).

Since Cannon's time, physiologists have identified an additional stress response system. On orders from the cerebral cortex (via the hypothalamus and pituitary gland), the outer part of the adrenal glands secrete *glucocorticoid* stress hormones such as *cortisol*. The two stress hormone systems work at different speeds, explains biologist Robert Sapolsky (2003): "In a fight-or-flight scenario, epinephrine is the one handing out guns; glucocorticoids are the ones drawing up blueprints for new aircraft carriers needed for the war effort." The epinephrine guns were firing at high speed during an experiment inadvertently conducted by British Airways on an April 23, 1999, flight from San Francisco to London. Three hours after takeoff, a mistakenly played message told passengers the plane was about to crash into the sea. Although the flight crew immediately recognized the error and tried to calm the terrified passengers, several required medical assistance (Associated Press, 1999). These passengers can empathize with those on a 2005 JetBlue flight as it circled Southern California for hours with faulty landing gear. Many of the plane's passengers became severely distressed, some crying, by the "surreal" experience of watching onboard satellite TV news broadcasts speculating on their fate (Nguyen, 2005).

There are alternatives to fight or flight. One is a common response to the stress of a loved one's death: Withdraw. Pull back. Conserve energy. Faced with an extreme disaster, such as a ship sinking, some people become paralyzed by fear. Another stress response, especially common among women, report Shelley Taylor and her colleagues (2000), is to seek and give support: *Tend and befriend*.

Facing stress, men more often than women tend to socially withdraw, turn to alcohol, or become aggressive. Women more often respond to stress by nurturing and banding together, which Taylor (2006) attributes partly to *oxytocin*, a stress-moderating hormone associated with pair-bonding in animals and released by cuddling, massage, and breast-feeding in humans.

Canadian scientist Hans Selye's (1936, 1976) 40 years of research on stress extended Cannon's findings and helped make stress a major concept in both psychology and medicine. Selye studied animals' reactions to various stressors, such as electric shock, surgical trauma, and immobilizing restraint. He discovered that the body's adaptive response to stress was so general—like a single burglar alarm that sounds no matter what intrudes—that he called it the **general adaptation syndrome (GAS).**

Selye saw the GAS as having three phases (**FIGURE 8B.23**). Let's say you suffer a physical or emotional trauma. In Phase 1, you experience an *alarm reaction* due to the sudden activation of your sympathetic nervous system. Your heart rate zooms. Blood is diverted to your skeletal muscles. You feel the faintness of shock. With your resources mobilized, you are now ready to fight the challenge during Phase 2, *resistance*. Your temperature, blood pressure, and respiration remain high, and there is a sudden outpouring of hormones. If persistent, the stress may eventually deplete your body's reserves during Phase 3, *exhaustion*. With exhaustion, you are more vulnerable to illness or even, in extreme cases, collapse and death.

::**general adaptation syndrome (GAS)** Selye's concept of the body's adaptive response to stress in three phases—alarm, resistance, exhaustion.

➤ **FIGURE 8B.23**
Selye's general adaptation syndrome
This girl being carried to freedom and medical attention managed to escape her terrorist captors in a three-day school holdup in North Ossetia in 2004. After such a trauma, the body enters an alarm phase of temporary shock. From this it rebounds, as stress resistance rises. If the stress is prolonged, as it was for the 400 school hostages and their waiting loved ones, wear and tear may lead to exhaustion.

High

The body's resistance to stress can only last so long before exhaustion sets in

Stress resistance

Stressor occurs

Low

| Phase 1 Alarm reaction (mobilize resources) | Phase 2 Resistance (cope with stressor) | Phase 3 Exhaustion (reserves depleted) |

EPA/Yuri Kochetkov/Landov

TEACHING TIP

Using Figure 8B.23, have students identify the different phases of Hans Selye's general adaptation syndrome. Cover up the different phases, having students identify orally or on paper what the different phases are called and what they entail. This will help you assess whether students understand the syndrome and whether any of this needs to be re-addressed.

"You may be suffering from what's known as full-nest syndrome."

Have students research some significant catastrophes (wars, natural disasters, etc.) that have occurred throughout history. Have them analyze how well the people and nations affected by these catastrophes dealt with stress before, during, and after the event:

- Were general conditions particularly stable before the catastrophe? Why or why not?

- Why did the catastrophe take place? Was someone or something to blame or was the event completely unpredictable and controllable? Why? How did this affect the collective psyche?

- What was the immediate impact of the catastrophe on the people or nation?

- How long did the effects of the catastrophe last?

- Did the people or nation emerge stronger from the catastrophe? Why or why not?

Few medical experts today quarrel with Selye's basic point: Although the human body comes designed to cope with temporary stress, prolonged stress can produce physical deterioration. The brain's production of new neurons slows (Mirescu & Gould, 2006). In one study, women who suffered enduring stress as caregivers for children with serious disorders displayed a symptom that is a normal part of the aging process—shorter bits of DNA at the ends of their chromosomes (Epel et al., 2004). When these DNA pieces, called *telomeres*, get too short, the cell can no longer divide, and it ultimately dies. The most stressed women had cells that looked a decade older than their chronological age, which may help explain why severe stress seems to age people. Even fearful, easily stressed rats have been found to die sooner (after about 600 days) than their more confident siblings, which average 700-day life spans (Cavigelli & McClintock, 2003). Such findings serve as further incentives to today's health psychologists, as they ask: What causes stress? And how does stress affect us?

Stressful Life Events

12: What events provoke stress responses?

Research has focused on our responses to three types of stressors: catastrophes, significant life changes, and daily hassles.

Catastrophes Catastrophes are unpredictable large-scale events, such as war and natural disasters, that nearly everyone appraises as threatening. Although people often provide one another with aid as well as comfort after such events, the health consequences can be significant. In the three weeks after the 9/11 terrorist attacks, two-thirds of Americans surveyed by University of Michigan researchers said they were having some trouble concentrating and sleeping (Wahlberg, 2001). In another national survey, New Yorkers were especially likely to report such symptoms (NSF, 2001). Sleeping pill prescriptions rose by a reported 28 percent in the New York area (HMHL, 2002).

Toxic stress On the day of its 1994 earthquake, Los Angeles experienced a fivefold increase in sudden-death heart attacks—especially in the first two hours after the quake and near its epicenter. Physical exertion (running, lifting debris) was a factor in only 13 percent of the deaths, leaving stress as the likely trigger for the others (Muller & Verrier, 1996).

Do other community disasters usually produce effects this great? After digesting data from 52 studies of catastrophic floods, hurricanes, and fires, Anthony Rubonis and Leonard Bickman (1991) found the typical effect more modest but nonetheless genuine. In disaster's wake, rates of psychological disorders such as depression and anxiety rose an average 17 percent. In the four months after Hurricane Katrina, New Orleans reportedly experienced a tripled suicide rate (Saulny, 2006). Refugees fleeing their homeland also suffer increased rates of psychological disorders. Their stress is twofold: the trauma of uprooting and family separation, and the challenges of adjusting to a foreign culture's new language, ethnicity, climate, and social norms (Pipher, 2002; Williams & Berry, 1991). In years to come, relocations necessitated by climate change may also produce such effects.

Significant Life Changes The second type of life-event stressor is a significant personal life change—the death of a loved one, the loss of a job, leaving home, a marriage, a divorce. Life transitions and insecurities are often keenly felt during young adulthood. That helps explain why, when 15,000 Canadian adults were asked whether "You are trying to take on too many things at once," responses indicated highest stress levels among the youngest adults. The same

---

is true of Americans: Half of adults under age 50 report "frequent" stress, as do fewer than 30 percent of those over 50 (Saad, 2001).

Some psychologists study the health effects of life changes by following people over time to see if such events precede illnesses. Others compare the life changes recalled by those who have or have not suffered a specific health problem, such as a heart attack. A review of these studies commissioned by the U.S. National Academy of Sciences revealed that people recently widowed, fired, or divorced are more vulnerable to disease (Dohrenwend et al., 1982). A Finnish study of 96,000 widowed people confirmed the phenomenon: Their risk of death doubled in the week following their partner's death (Kaprio et al., 1987). Experiencing a cluster of crises puts one even more at risk.

Daily Hassles As we noted earlier, our happiness stems less from enduring good fortune than from our response to daily events—a hoped-for medical result, a perfect test score, a gratifying Facebook comment, your team's winning the big game.

This principle works for negative events, too. Everyday annoyances—rush-hour traffic, aggravating housemates, long lines at the store, too many things to do, e-mail spam, and obnoxious cell-phone talkers—may be the most significant sources of stress (Kohn & Macdonald, 1992; Lazarus, 1990; Ruffin, 1993). Although some people can simply shrug off such hassles, others are "driven up the wall" by them. People's difficulties in letting go of unattainable goals is another everyday stressor with health consequences (Miller & Wrosch, 2007).

Over time, these little stressors can add up and take a toll on our health and well-being. Hypertension rates are high among residents of impoverished areas where the stresses that accompany inadequate income, unemployment, solo parenting, and overcrowding are part of daily life for many people. In Europe, hypertension rates are likewise highest in countries where people express the least satisfaction with their lives (**FIGURE 8B.24**).

For minority populations, daily pressures may be compounded by racism, which—like other stressors—can have both psychological and physical consequences. Thinking that some of the people you encounter each day will distrust you, dislike you, or doubt your abilities makes daily life stressful. Such stress takes a toll on the health of many African-Americans, driving up blood pressure levels (Clark et al., 1999; Mays et al., 2007).

A 2009 Pew survey of 2969 American adults asked, "Is the recession causing stress in your family?"

Age	Yes responses
18–49	52%
50–64	58%
65+	38%

➤ **FIGURE 8B.24**
Where life satisfaction is high, hypertension rates are low (From data gleaned from European nations by David Blanchflower and Andrew Oswald, 2008.)

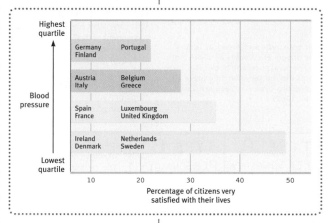

Stress and the Heart

13: Why are some of us more prone than others to coronary heart disease?

Elevated blood pressure is just one of the factors that increase the risk of **coronary heart disease**, the closing of the vessels that nourish the heart muscle. Although infrequent before 1900, this condition became by the 1950s North America's leading cause of death, and it remains so today. In addition to hypertension and a family history of the disease, many behavioral and physiological factors—smoking, obesity, a

::**coronary heart disease** the clogging of the vessels that nourish the heart muscle; the leading cause of death in North America.

 TEACHING TIP

Richard Lazarus and his colleagues suggest that daily hassles, such as petty annoyances, frustrations, and unpleasant surprises, may cause us more grief than life's major stressful events. The impact of hassles on health depends on their frequency, duration, and intensity. A person's response to daily hassles depends on **personality**, **coping style**, and **how the rest of the day has gone**.

CULTURAL CONNECTIONS

Using available resources, including the Internet, have students work independently or with partners to research stress in other countries by considering the following questions:

• What types of daily stressors are common in that country?

• What type of cultural expectation exists about handling stress?

• How has that particular country dealt with a major catastrophic event in its history?

• What are the instances of depression and suicide among people of that country/culture? What do these statistics say about how the country/culture deals with stress?

If permission is granted, international students could be interviewed for personal opinions and information about how other cultures deal with stress.

 TEACHING TIP

The counterparts to daily hassles are **daily uplifts**—pleasant and satisfying experiences, such as hearing good news, getting a good night's sleep, or solving a difficult problem. Just as hassles may cause changes that result in illness, uplifts may serve as emotional buffers.

::**Type A** Friedman and Rosenman's term for competitive, hard-driving, impatient, verbally aggressive, and anger-prone people.

::**Type B** Friedman and Rosenman's term for easygoing, relaxed people.

::**psychophysiological illness** literally, "mind-body" illness; any stress-related physical illness, such as hypertension and some headaches.

::**psychoneuroimmunology (PNI)** the study of how psychological, neural, and endocrine processes together affect the immune system and resulting health.

::**lymphocytes** the two types of white blood cells that are part of the body's immune system: *B lymphocytes* form in the *bone* marrow and release antibodies that fight bacterial infections; *T lymphocytes* form in the *thymus* and other lymphatic tissue and attack cancer cells, viruses, and foreign substances.

• In both India and America, Type A bus drivers are literally hard-driving: They brake, pass, and honk their horns more often than their more easygoing Type B colleagues (Evans et al., 1987). •

 "The fire you kindle for your enemy often burns you more than him." Chinese proverb

high-fat diet, physical inactivity, and an elevated cholesterol level—increase the risk of heart disease. The psychological factors of stress and personality also play a big role.

In a now-classic study, Meyer Friedman, Ray Rosenman, and their colleagues tested the idea that stress increases vulnerability to heart disease (Friedman & Ulmer, 1984). They measured the blood cholesterol level and clotting speed of 40 U.S. tax accountants. They found that from January through March, both of these coronary warning indicators were completely normal. Then, as the accountants began scrambling to finish their clients' tax returns before the April 15 filing deadline, their cholesterol and clotting measures rose to dangerous levels. In May and June, with the deadline past, the measures returned to normal. The researchers' hunch had paid off: Stress predicted heart attack risk.

The stage was set for Friedman and Rosenman's classic nine-year study of more than 3000 healthy men aged 35 to 59. At the start of the study, they interviewed each man for 15 minutes about his work and eating habits. During the interview, they noted the man's manner of talking and other behavioral patterns. Those who seemed the most reactive, competitive, hard-driving, impatient, time-conscious, supermotivated, verbally aggressive, and easily angered they called **Type A**. The roughly equal number who were more easygoing they called **Type B**. Which group do you suppose turned out to be the most coronary prone?

By the time the study was complete, 257 men had suffered heart attacks; 69 percent of them were Type A. Moreover, not one of the "pure" Type Bs—the most mellow and laid-back of their group—had suffered a heart attack.

As often happens in science, this exciting discovery provoked enormous public interest. But after the honeymoon period, in which the finding seemed definitive and revolutionary, other researchers began asking: Is the finding reliable? If so, what is the toxic component of the Type A profile: Time-consciousness? Competitiveness? Anger?

More recent research has revealed that Type A's toxic core is negative emotions—especially the anger associated with an aggressively reactive temperament (Smith, 2006; Williams, 1993). Type A individuals are more often "combat ready." You may recall from this unit's discussion of anger that when we are harassed or challenged, our active sympathetic nervous system redistributes bloodflow to our muscles and away from internal organs such as the liver, which normally removes cholesterol and fat from the blood. Thus, a Type A person's blood may contain excess cholesterol and fat that later get deposited around the heart. Further stress—sometimes conflicts brought on by the person's own abrasiveness—may trigger the altered heart rhythms that, in those with weakened hearts, can cause sudden death (Kamarck & Jennings, 1991). Hostility also correlates with other risk factors, such as smoking, drinking, and obesity (Bunde & Suls, 2006). In important ways, people's minds and hearts interact.

The effect of an anger-prone personality appears most noticeably in studies in which interviewers assess verbal assertiveness and emotional intensity. (If you pause in the middle of a sentence, an intense, anger-prone person may jump in and finish it for you.) One study of young and middle-aged adults found that those who react with anger over little things are the most coronary-prone, and suppressing negative emotions only heightens the risk (Kupper & Denollet, 2007). Another study followed 13,000 middle-aged people for 5 years (Williams et al., 2000). Among those with normal blood pressure, people who had scored high on anger were three times more likely to have had heart attacks, even after researchers controlled for smoking and weight. The link between anger and heart attacks also appeared in a study that followed 1055 male medical students over an average of 36 years. Those who had reported being hot-tempered were five times more likely to have had a heart attack by age 55 (Chang et al., 2002). As Charles Spielberger and Perry London (1982) put it, rage "seems to lash back and strike us in the heart muscle."

Pessimism seems to be similarly toxic. Laura Kubzansky and her colleagues (2001) studied 1306 initially healthy men who a decade earlier had scored as optimists, pessimists, or neither. Even after other risk factors such as smoking had been ruled out,

---

 TEACHING TIP

Redford Williams' *The Trusting Heart: Great News About Type A Behavior* discusses overcoming the hostile and cynical elements of Type A behavior. After showing how hostility and cynical mistrust seem to be the lethal aspects of the Type A syndrome, Williams suggests that the route to a more trusting heart requires three things.

- First, Type A's must reduce cynical mistrust of others.

- Second, they must reduce the frequency and intensity with which they experience anger, frustration, irritation, and rage.

- Third, they must learn to treat others with kindness and consideration and to develop their assertiveness skills for unavoidable situations.

TROUBLESHOOTING

Point out to students that a high-energy and stressful life is not the main contributor to coronary heart disease. If Type A personalities deal with stress by reacting negatively—with hostility and combativeness—they will be more likely to experience coronary heart disease.

TEACHING TIP

At this point, you may want to use **Lecture/Discussion Topics: *Broken Heart Syndrome*** (p. 36) or ***Type D Personality*** (p. 37) or **Classroom Exercise: *Hostility and Its Alleviation*** (p. 36) from Bolt's Teacher's Resource Binder.

pessimists were more than twice as likely as optimists to develop heart disease (FIGURE 8B.25).

Depression, too, can be lethal. The accumulated evidence from 57 studies suggests that "depression substantially increases the risk of death, especially death by unnatural causes and cardiovascular disease" (Wulsin et al., 1999). One study of 7406 women age 67 or older found that among those with no depressive symptoms, 7 percent died within six years, as did 24 percent of those with six or more depressive symptoms (Whooley & Browner, 1998). In the years following a heart attack, people with high scores for depression are four times more likely than their low-scoring counterparts to develop further heart problems (Frasure-Smith & Lesperance, 2005). Depression is disheartening.

Recent research suggests that heart disease and depression may both result when chronic stress triggers persistent inflammation (Matthews, 2005; Miller & Blackwell, 2006). Stress, as we will see, disrupts the body's disease-fighting immune system, thus enabling the body to focus its energies on fleeing or fighting the threat. Yet stress hormones enhance one immune response, the production of proteins that contribute to the inflammation. Although inflammation helps fight infections, persistent inflammation can produce problems such as asthma or clogged arteries, and even, it now seems, depression (see FIGURE 8B.26).

Stress and Susceptibility to Disease

14: How does stress make us more vulnerable to disease?

Not so long ago, the term *psychosomatic* described psychologically caused physical symptoms. To laypeople, the term implied that the symptoms were unreal—"merely" psychosomatic. To avoid such connotations and to better describe the genuine physiological effects of psychological states, most experts today refer instead to stress-related **psychophysiological illnesses**, such as hypertension and some headaches. Stress also affects our resistance to disease, and this understanding has led to the burgeoning development of the field of **psychoneuroimmunology (PNI).** PNI studies how *psychological, neural,* and endocrine processes affect our *immune* system (psychoneuro-immunology), and how all these factors influence our health and wellness.

Psychoneuroimmunology

Hundreds of new experiments reveal the nervous and endocrine systems' influence on the immune system (Sternberg, 2001). Your immune system is a complex surveillance system that defends your body by isolating and destroying bacteria, viruses, and other foreign substances. This system includes two types of white blood cells, called **lymphocytes**. *B lymphocytes* form in the *b*one marrow and release antibodies that fight bacterial infections. *T lymphocytes* form in the *t*hymus and other lymphatic tissue and attack cancer cells, viruses, and foreign substances—even "good" ones, such as transplanted organs. Two other important agents of the immune system are the *macrophage* ("big eater"), which identifies, pursues, and ingests harmful invaders and worn-out cells (FIGURE 8B.27, on the next page), and the *natural killer cells* (NK cells), which pursue diseased cells (such as those infected by viruses or cancer). Age, nutrition, genetics, body temperature, and stress all influence the immune system's activity.

Your immune system can err in two directions. Responding too strongly, it may attack the body's own tissues, causing arthritis or an allergic reaction. Underreacting, it may allow a dormant herpes virus to erupt or cancer cells to multiply. Women are immunologically stronger than men,

 FIGURE 8B.25
Pessimism and heart disease A Harvard School of Public Health team found that compared with optimistic men, pessimistic men have a more than doubled risk of developing heart disease over a 10-year period. (From Kubzansky et al., 2001.)

> "A cheerful heart is a good medicine, but a downcast spirit dries up the bones."
>
> Proverbs 17:22

 FIGURE 8B.26
Stress→inflammation↔heart disease and depression Gregory Miller and Ekin Blackwell (2006) report that chronic stress leads to persistent inflammation, which heightens the risk of both depression and clogged arteries.

UNIT 8B

Illness tends to occur around times of stress. For students, stressful times usually occur around exam time. Have students consider the following questions:

- Do you feel most stressed around exam time at your school? Why or why not?

- How could you personally reduce your stress level at exam time?

- How do your teachers and administrators try to reduce the stress of exam time?

- What other things could be done to make exam time less stressful?

➤ **FIGURE 8B.27**

The immune system in action A large macrophage (at top) is about to trap and ingest a tiny bacterium (lower right). Macrophages constantly patrol our bodies in search of invaders—such as this *Escherichia coli* bacterium—and debris, such as worn-out red blood cells.

"When the heart is at ease, the body is healthy."

Chinese proverb

making them less susceptible to infections (Morell, 1995). But this very strength also makes them more susceptible to self-attacking diseases, such as lupus and multiple sclerosis.

Your immune system is not a headless horseman. The brain regulates the secretion of stress hormones, which suppress the disease-fighting lymphocytes. Thus, when animals are physically restrained, given unavoidable electric shocks, or subjected to noise, crowding, cold water, social defeat, or maternal separation, their immune systems become less active (Maier et al., 1994). One study monitored immune responses in 43 monkeys over six months (Cohen et al., 1992). Twenty-one were stressed by being housed with new roommates—three or four new monkeys—each month. (To empathize with the monkeys, recall the stress of leaving home to attend school or summer camp, and imagine having to repeat this experience monthly.) Compared with monkeys left in stable groups, the socially disrupted monkeys experienced weakened immune systems. Stress similarly depresses the immune system of humans. Consider some striking and consistent results:

- Surgical wounds heal more slowly in stressed animals and humans. In one experiment, dental students received punch wounds (precise small holes punched in the skin). Compared with wounds placed during summer vacation, those placed three days before a major exam healed 40 percent more slowly. In fact, reported Janice Kiecolt-Glaser and her co-researchers (1998), "no student healed as rapidly during this stressful period as during vacation."

- Compared with the healing of punch wounds in unstressed married couples, either the stress of a 30-minute marital spat or ongoing marital conflict caused punch wounds to take a day or two longer to heal (Kiecolt-Glaser et al., 2005).

- In another experiment, 47 percent of participants living stress-filled lives developed colds after a virus was dropped in their noses, as did only 27 percent of those living relatively free of stress (**FIGURE 8B.28**). In follow-up research, the happiest and most relaxed people were likewise markedly less vulnerable to an experimentally delivered cold virus (Cohen et al., 2003, 2006).

- Managing stress may be life-sustaining. The one personality trait shared by 169 centenarians (people over 100) is their ability to manage stress well (Perls et al., 1999).

The stress effect on immunity makes physiological sense (Maier et al., 1994). It takes energy to fight infections and maintain fevers. Thus, when diseased, our bodies reduce muscular energy output by inactivity and increased sleep. But stress creates a competing energy need. Stress triggers an aroused fight-or-flight response, diverting energy from the disease-fighting immune system to the muscles and brain, rendering

➤ **FIGURE 8B.28**

Stress and colds In an experiment by Sheldon Cohen and colleagues (1991), people with the highest life stress scores were also most vulnerable when exposed to an experimentally delivered cold virus.

Divide students into groups and have them list the three most stressful things teens deal with on a daily basis. Then have them list some explanations why these things happen and why they are stressful. As students present their reasons to the class, have them analyze whether the attributions are optimistic or pessimistic. Help students see that optimistic thinking empowers people to seek ways to change stressful situations while pessimistic thinking does not provide a way out of a stressful circumstance.

us more vulnerable to illness (see Figure 8B.2). *The bottom line:* Stress does not make us sick, but it does alter our immune functioning, making us less able to resist infection and more prone to heart disease.

Stress and AIDS

AIDS has become the world's fourth leading cause of death and the number one killer in Africa. As its name tells us, AIDS is an immune disorder—an *acquired immune deficiency syndrome* caused by the *human immunodeficiency virus (HIV)*, which is spread by the exchange of bodily fluids, primarily semen and blood. If a disease spread by human contact kills slowly, as does AIDS, it ironically can be lethal to more people: Those who carry the virus have time to spread it, often without realizing they are infected. When the HIV infection manifests itself as AIDS, some years after the initial infection, the person has difficulty fighting off other diseases, such as pneumonia. Worldwide, reports the United Nations, more than 20 million people have died of AIDS (UNAIDS, 2008). (In the United States, where "only" a half-million of these fatalities have occurred, AIDS has killed more people than did combat in all the twentieth-century wars.) In 2007, worldwide some 2.7 million—half of them women—were infected with HIV, often without their awareness (UNAIDS, 2008).

So if stress restrains the immune system's response to infections, could it also exacerbate the *course* of AIDS? Researchers have found that stress and negative emotions do correlate with (a) a progression from HIV infection to AIDS, and (b) the speed of decline in those infected (Bower et al., 1998; Kiecolt-Glaser & Glaser, 1995; Leserman et al., 1999). HIV-infected men faced with stressful life circumstances, such as the loss of a partner, exhibit somewhat greater immune suppression and a faster disease progression.

Would efforts to reduce stress help control the disease? Although the benefits are small compared with available drug treatments, the answer appears again to be *yes*. Educational initiatives, bereavement support groups, cognitive therapy, relaxation training, and exercise programs that reduce distress have all had positive consequences for HIV-positive individuals (Baum & Posluszny, 1999; McCain et al., 2008; Schneiderman, 1999). Better yet is preventing HIV infection, which is the focus of many educational programs, such as the ABC (*abstinence, being faithful, condom use*) program used in many countries, with seeming success in Uganda (Altman, 2004; USAID, 2004).

Stress and Cancer

Stress and negative emotions have also been linked to cancer's rate of progression. To explore a possible connection between stress and cancer, experimenters have implanted tumor cells into rodents or given them *carcinogens* (cancer-producing substances). Those rodents also exposed to uncontrollable stress, such as inescapable shocks, were more prone to cancer (Sklar & Anisman, 1981). With immune systems weakened by stress, tumors developed sooner and grew larger.

Some investigators have reported that people are at increased risk for cancer within a year after experiencing depression, helplessness, or bereavement. One large Swedish study revealed that people with a history of workplace stress had 5.5 times greater risk of colon cancer than those who reported no such problems, a difference not attributable to differing age, smoking, drinking, or physical characteristics (Courtney et al., 1993). Other researchers have found no link between stress and human cancer (Edelman & Kidman, 1997; Fox, 1998; Petticrew et al., 1999, 2002). Concentration camp survivors and former prisoners of war, for example, have not exhibited elevated cancer rates.

● In North America and Western Europe, 75 percent of people with AIDS are men. In Sub-Saharan Africa, 60 percent of people with AIDS are women (and among 15- to 24-year-olds, 75 percent are women). Girls' thin layer of cervical cells makes them especially vulnerable (Altman, 2004; UNAIDS, 2005). ●

Africa is ground zero for AIDS In Lesotho, Uganda, and elsewhere, the "ABC" Campaign—Abstinence, Be faithful, and use Condoms—forms part of prevention efforts.
▲

TROUBLESHOOTING

Help students appreciate the difference between being HIV-positive and having AIDS. Being HIV-positive means that one is infected with the virus that causes AIDS. Having AIDS means that one has symptoms of diseases that result from a deficient immune system.

RESEARCH

Contact local oncologists to see what they think about a stress-cancer link.

● Do they see a link between cancer and stress in their own practice? Why or why not?

● How do they suggest their patients deal with stress?

● What support groups are available in your area for cancer patients?

UNIT 8B

RESEARCH

Have students research times during the school year when students are absent the most. Students may need to research attendance records for the past few years to see if any patterns of attendance seem to materialize.

- Do dips in attendance occur before or after stressful times, such as around exam time?

- Are later days of the week (Thursdays and Fridays) more often missed than earlier days (Mondays and Tuesdays)? If so, could this be due to stress?

"I didn't give myself cancer."
Mayor Barbara Boggs Sigmund,
1939–1990, Princeton, New Jersey

• When organic causes of illness are unknown, it is tempting to invent psychological explanations. Before the germ that causes tuberculosis was discovered, personality explanations of TB were popular (Sontag, 1978). •

One danger in hyping reports on attitudes and cancer is that some patients may then blame themselves for their illness—"If only I had been more expressive, relaxed, and hopeful." A corollary danger is a "wellness macho" among the healthy, who take credit for their "healthy character" and lay a guilt trip on the ill: "She has cancer? That's what you get for holding your feelings in and being so nice." Dying thus becomes the ultimate failure.

The emerging view seems to be that stress does *not* create cancer cells. At worst, it may affect their growth by weakening the body's natural defenses against proliferating malignant cells (Antoni & Lutgendorf, 2007). Although a relaxed, hopeful state may enhance these defenses, we should be aware of the thin line that divides science from wishful thinking. The powerful biological processes at work in advanced cancer or AIDS are not likely to be completely derailed by avoiding stress or maintaining a relaxed but determined spirit (Anderson, 2002; Kessler et al., 1991).

* * *

We can view the stress effect on our disease resistance as a price we pay for the benefits of stress (FIGURE 8B.29). Stress invigorates our lives by arousing and motivating us. An unstressed life would hardly be challenging or productive. Moreover, it pays to spend our resources in fighting or fleeing an external threat. But we do so at the cost of diminished resources for fighting internal threats to health. When the stress is momentary, the cost is negligible. When uncontrollable aggravations persist, the cost may become considerable.

➤ FIGURE 8B.29
Stress can have a variety of health-related consequences This is especially so when experienced by "disease-prone" angry, depressed, or anxious persons.

Behavioral medicine research provides yet another reminder of one of contemporary psychology's overriding themes: *Mind and body interact; everything psychological is simultaneously physiological.* Psychological states are physiological events that influence other parts of our physiological system. Just pausing to *think* about biting into an orange section—the sweet, tangy juice from the pulpy fruit flooding across your tongue—can trigger salivation. As the Indian sage Santi Parva recognized more than 4000 years ago, "Mental disorders arise from physical causes, and likewise physical disorders arise from mental causes." There is an interplay between our heads and our health. We are biopsychosocial systems.

BEFORE YOU MOVE ON . . .

➤ **ASK YOURSELF**

What are the stresses in your own life? How intensely do you respond to them? Are there changes you could make to avoid the persistent stressors in your life?

➤ **TEST YOURSELF 5**

What are the basic links in our stress response system?

Answers to the Test Yourself questions can be found in Appendix E at the end of the book.

 TEACHING TIP

Each generation deals with unique stressors. Students today confront pressures from parents, peers, and teachers as they move from junior high to high school and beyond. The goal of this unit is to help students understand what stress is and recognize it in their lives. You may wish to have students read Appendix C, Promoting Health, at some point (perhaps after the AP Exam is administered and you have the luxury of more time) so that they can learn more about coping with and managing stress.

UNIT REVIEW: Emotions, Stress, and Health

Theories of Emotion

1: What are the components of an emotion?

*Emotion*s are psychological responses of the whole organism involving an interplay among (1) physiological arousal, (2) expressive behaviors, and (3) conscious experience (**FIGURE 8B.30**).

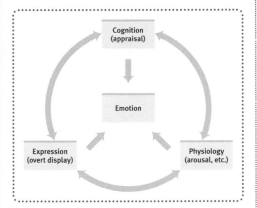

➤ **FIGURE 8B.30**

The ingredients of emotion From the interplay of physiology, expression, and cognition comes emotion.

Three theories support different combinations of these responses. The *James-Lange theory* maintains that our emotional feelings follow our body's response to the emotion-inducing stimuli. The *Cannon-Bard theory* proposes that our body responds to emotion at the same time that we experience the emotion (one does not cause the other). The *two-factor theory* holds that our emotions have two ingredients: physical arousal and a cognitive label.

Embodied Emotion

2: What is the link between emotional arousal and the autonomic nervous system?

Emotions are both psychological and physiological. Much of the physiological activity is controlled by the autonomic nervous system's sympathetic (arousing) and parasympathetic (calming) divisions. Our performance on a task is usually best when arousal is moderate, though this varies with the difficulty of the task.

3: Do different emotions activate different physiological and brain-pattern responses?

Emotions may be similarly arousing, but there are some subtle physiological responses that distinguish them. More meaningful differences have been found in activity in the brain's cortical areas, in use of brain pathways, and in secretion of hormones associated with different emotions. *Polygraphs* measure several physiological indicators of emotion, but they are not accurate enough to justify their widespread use in business and law enforcement. The use of guilty knowledge questions and new forms of technology may produce better indications of lying.

4: To experience emotions, must we consciously interpret and label them?

Schachter and Singer's two-factor theory of emotion contends that the cognitive labels we put on our states of arousal are an essential ingredient of emotion. Lazarus agreed that cognition is essential: Many important emotions arise from our interpretations or inferences. Zajonc and LeDoux, however, believe that some simple emotional responses occur instantly, not only outside our conscious awareness but before any cognitive processing occurs. The interplay between emotion and cognition again illustrates our two-track mind.

Expressed Emotion

5: How do we communicate nonverbally?

Much of our communication is through the silent language of the body. Even very thin (seconds-long) filmed slices of behavior can reveal feelings. Women tend to be better at reading people's emotional cues.

6: Are nonverbal expressions of emotion universally understood?

Some gestures are culturally determined. Facial expressions, such as those of happiness and fear, are common the world over. Cultures differ in the amount of emotion they express.

7: Do our facial expressions influence our feelings?

Expressions do more than communicate emotion to others. They also amplify the felt emotion and signal the body to respond accordingly.

Experienced Emotion

8: What is the function of fear, and how do we learn fears?

Fear has adaptive value because it helps us avoid threats and, when necessary, cope with them. We are predisposed to some fears, and we learn others through conditioning and observation.

9: What are the causes and consequences of anger?

Anger is most often evoked by events that not only are frustrating or insulting but also are interpreted as willful, unjustified, and avoidable. Blowing off steam (*catharsis*) may be temporarily calming, but in the long run it does not reduce anger. Expressing anger can actually make us angrier.

TECHNOLOGY RESOURCES

These resources will be helpful for teaching the concepts in this portion of the unit:

- *Video: The Brain,* 2nd ed., *Module 21: Emotions, Stress, and Health*

- *Psychology Video Tool Kit: Emotion = Arousal Plus Interpretation; Brain Fingerprinting: Memory, Recognition, and Lie Detection; Emotions and Facial Expression; The Development of Disgust; Do Body Smells Reveal Fear and Happiness?; Rage: One Man's Story and Treatment;*

Rage: One Woman's Story and Treatment; A Happiness Trait?; The Search for Happiness; Measuring Stress While Running With the Bulls; The Stress Response; Stress and the Immune System: Caretakers and Risk; Fighting Cancer: Mobilizing the Immune System

- *Videos: Psychology: The Human Experience, Module 20: The Physiology of Emotions; Module 35: What Is Stress?*

Technology Resources continued

UNIT 8B

ANSWERS to Multiple-Choice Questions

1. **e.** Schachter-Singer two-factor theory
2. **b.** largely dependent upon our bodily responses and behaviors.
3. **d.** adrenal glands.
4. **d.** diminishing returns.
5. **c.** anger.
6. **c.** Left frontal lobe
7. **e.** Exercise, play an instrument, or talk with a friend.
8. **a.** Surgical wounds heal more slowly in stressed humans.
9. **c.** Adaptation-level phenomenon
10. **a.** the spillover effect.
11. **c.** Facial signs of emotion are generally understood across world cultures.
12. **a.** Keep a gratitude journal, and "count your blessings."
13. **b.** no deliberate thinking.
14. **d.** facial feedback.
15. **b.** Resistance

10: What are the causes and consequences of happiness?
A good mood boosts people's perceptions of the world and their willingness to help others (the *feel-good, do-good phenomenon*). The moods triggered by the day's good or bad events seldom last beyond that day. Even significant good events, such as a substantial rise in income, seldom increase happiness for long. We can explain the relativity of happiness with the *adaptation-level phenomenon* and the *relative deprivation* principle. Nevertheless, some people are usually happier than others, and researchers have identified factors that predict *well-being*.

Stress and Health
11: What is stress?
Walter Cannon viewed *stress*, the process by which we appraise and respond to events that challenge or threaten us, as a "fight-or-flight" system. Hans Selye saw it as a three-phase (alarm-resistance-exhaustion) *general adaptation syndrome (GAS)*.

12: What events provoke stress responses?
Modern research on stress assesses the health consequences of catastrophic events, significant life changes, and daily hassles. The events that tend to provoke stress responses are those that we perceive as both negative and uncontrollable.

13: Why are some of us more prone than others to coronary heart disease?
Coronary heart disease, North America's number one cause of death, has been linked with the competitive, hard-driving, impatient, and (especially) anger-prone *Type A* personality. Under stress, the body of a reactive, hostile person secretes more of the hormones that accelerate the buildup of plaque on the heart's artery walls. *Type B* personalities are more relaxed and easygoing. Chronic stress also contributes to persistent inflammation, which heightens the risk of clogged arteries and depression.

14: How does stress make us more vulnerable to disease?
Stress diverts energy from the immune system, inhibiting the activities of its B and T *lymphocytes*, macrophages, and NK cells. Although stress does not cause diseases such as AIDS and cancer, it may influence their progression.

Terms and Concepts to Remember

emotion, p. 366
James-Lange theory, p. 367
Cannon-Bard theory, p. 367
two-factor theory, p. 367
polygraph, p. 372
facial feedback, p. 383
catharsis, p. 388
feel-good, do-good phenomenon, p. 390

well-being, p. 390
adaptation-level phenomenon, p. 394
relative deprivation, p. 394
behavioral medicine, p. 397
health psychology, p. 397
stress, p. 397
general adaptation syndrome (GAS), p. 399

coronary heart disease, p. 401
Type A, p. 402
Type B, p. 402
psychophysiological illness, p. 403
psychoneuroimmunology (PNI), p. 403
lymphocytes, p. 403

 AP* Practice Test Questions

Multiple-Choice Questions

1. Emotions are a mix of consciously experienced thoughts, expressive behaviors, and physiological arousal. Which theory emphasized the importance of the consciously experienced thoughts?
   a. Facial feedback theory
   b. James-Lange theory
   c. Arousal and performance theory
   d. Fight-or-flight theory
   e. Schachter-Singer two-factor theory

*AP is a trademark registered and/or owned by the College Board, which was not involved in the production of, and does not endorse, this product.

2. Interviews conducted with people who have spinal cord injuries suggest to researchers that emotions are
   a. entirely cognitive—requiring no physical response to be intense.
   b. largely dependent upon our bodily responses and behaviors.
   c. mostly a social response to surrounding factors.
   d. mostly a cultural reaction to context.
   e. mostly psychological.

3. The stress hormones epinephrine and norepinephrine are released from the
   a. parasympathetic nervous system.
   b. hippocampus.
   c. tend-and-befriend response.
   d. adrenal glands.
   e. hypothalamus.

4. Research shows that once we have enough money for comfort and security, piling up more money does not make us happier. This is an example of
   a. relative deprivation.
   b. well-being.
   c. the feel-good, do-good phenomenon.
   d. diminishing returns.
   e. catharsis.

5. When hearing emotions conveyed in another language, people most readily detect
   a. sadness.
   b. happiness.
   c. anger.
   d. fear.
   e. surprise.

TECHNOLOGY RESOURCES

 Technology Resources continued from p. 407

- *Videos: Digital Media Archive: Psychology,* 1st ed., *Video Clip 27: Reading Nonverbal Communication; Video Clip 28: Ekman's Studies on Facial Expressions of Emotion; Video Clip 38: Stress on the Job; Video Clip 39: Selye's Stress Response Studies;* 2nd ed.: *Ekman's Facial Expression Research: Detecting "Microexpressions"*

- *PsychSim 5: Catching Liars; Expressing Emotion; All Stressed Out*

- *Video: The Mind,* 2nd ed., *Module 4: Cognition and the Immune System: Mind/Body Interaction*

6. Brain scans and EEG recordings show positive emotions most often activate which brain section?
   a. Right temporal lobe
   b. Cerebellum
   c. Left frontal lobe
   d. Left temporal lobe
   e. Right parietal lobe

7. Which of the following is the best way to handle your anger?
   a. Ruminate inwardly about the causes of your anger.
   b. List all of the reasons why you are angry.
   c. Vent your anger at the person who provoked you.
   d. Take your frustrations out on a punching bag.
   e. Exercise, play an instrument, or talk with a friend.

8. Which of the following statements about stress is *true*?
   a. Surgical wounds heal more slowly in stressed humans.
   b. Stress has no effect on those exposed to cold viruses.
   c. There is no correlation between stress and longevity.
   d. Stress makes us more resistant to infection and heart disease.
   e. Anxiety, irritation, and guilt all prompt very different stress responses.

9. What describes our tendency to judge various stimuli relative to those we have previously experienced?
   a. Relative deprivation
   b. Tend-and-befriend response
   c. Adaptation-level phenomenon
   d. Fight-or-flight response
   e. General adaptation syndrome

10. An irritated person interacts with someone who is happy, causing him or her to become happy as well. This exemplifies
    a. the spillover effect.
    b. the James-Lange theory.
    c. the two-factory theory.
    d. the Cannon-Bard theory.
    e. arousal and performance.

11. Which of the following statements about nonverbal expression is *true*?
    a. People blind from birth cannot exhibit common facial expressions.
    b. The meaning of gestures is the same across cultures.
    c. Facial signs of emotion are generally understood across world cultures.
    d. People from different cultures have difficulty understanding nonverbal expressions.
    e. Nonverbal expression is not reliably interpreted within a culture.

12. Which of the following is a research-based suggestion for improving your mood and increasing your satisfaction with life?
    a. Keep a gratitude journal, and "count your blessings."
    b. Let others make most of your decisions for you.
    c. Give priority to multiple, less-intimate relationships.
    d. Avoid activities involving faith communities.
    e. Stay away from flow experiences.

13. Through their research, Robert Zajonc and Joseph LeDoux have demonstrated that some emotional responses, especially simple likes, dislikes, and fears, involve
    a. intentional cognitive appraisal.
    b. no deliberate thinking.
    c. harmful physiological reactions.
    d. complex feelings.
    e. processing in the cortex.

14. Smiling warmly on the outside so you feel better on the inside is an example of
    a. relative deprivation.
    b. mimicry.
    c. empathy.
    d. facial feedback.
    e. catharsis.

15. After an alarming event, your temperature, blood pressure, and respiration are high, and you have an outpouring of hormones. Hans Selye would most likely guess that you are in which general adaptation syndrome phase?
    a. Exhaustion
    b. Resistance
    c. Immobilization
    d. Collapse
    e. Shock

Free-Response Question

A friend approaches you, clearly "down in the dumps," and expresses a desire to be happier. Given your understanding of well-being, what advice can you give your friend?

> **WEB**
> Multiple-choice self-tests and more may be found at www.worthpublishers.com/myers

Rubric for Grading the Free-Response Question

This is an 8-point question. Allow one point for an adequate discussion of any eight of the following concepts or terms dealing with increasing mood and well-being. Modify the rubric by adding or subtracting terms depending on what was emphasized in class.

- Realize that happiness may not be contingent on financial success. Having wealth does not guarantee happiness.
- Take control of your time. Set goals, have daily aims, and realize that happy people often feel in control of their lives.
- Act happy. Talk as if you are optimistic and outgoing. Going through the motions can trigger the emotions.

» Rubric continued

- Seek work and leisure that engage your skills. Happy people often are in a zone called "flow"—absorbed in tasks that challenge but don't overwhelm them. Take time to savor such pleasant experiences.

- Exercise. Aerobic exercise can relieve mild depression and anxiety and promote health and energy.

- Sleep. Many people suffer from sleep debt, with resulting fatigue, diminished alertness, and gloomy moods.

- Give priority to close relationships. Intimate friendships with those who care deeply about you can help you weather difficult times. Resolve to nurture your closest relationships by not taking your loved ones for granted, and by displaying to them the sort of kindness you display to others.

- Focus beyond self. Reach out to those in need. Helpfulness increases happiness.

- Keep track of what is going well. Pause daily to record positive events and why they occurred.

- Express and record your gratitude. Express your gratitude to others. Keeping a gratitude journal heightens well-being.

- Nurture your spiritual self. People who are active in faith communities report greater-than-average happiness and often cope well with crisis.

UNIT 9

Pacing Guide

Use the following guide to determine how many instructional days to devote to this unit depending on the type of course you teach:

Year-long course: 6–9 days
Block schedule/Semester-long course: 4–5 days

This unit encompasses 7–9 percent of the AP Exam. Spending an appropriate amount of time on this unit will help students do well on the AP Exam.

TEACHING TIP

Consider assigning students to conduct developmental research using case studies by having students conduct in-depth interviews and interactions with people experiencing developmental milestones—young children (ages 3 to 6 years old), adolescents (both older and younger than your students) or older adults (age 65 and older). Students can present their cases using a variety of methods, including video, scrapbooks, or PowerPoint presentations.

410

Suggested Readings

Albom, M. (1997). *Tuesdays with Morrie.* New York: Doubleday.

Blum, D. (2004). *Love at goon park: Harry Harlow and the science of affection.* New York: Berkley Trade.

Brown, L. M. (1998). *Raising their voices: The politics of girls' anger.* Cambridge, MA: Harvard University Press.

Cohen, D. B. (1999). *Stranger in the nest: Do parents really shape their child's personality, intelligence, or character?* New York: John Wiley.

Csikszentmihalyi, M., Rathunde, K., & Whalen, S. (1993). *Talented teenagers: The roots of success and failure.* Cambridge: Cambridge University Press.

Gottman, J. (1999). *The seven principles for making marriage work.* New York: Crown.

Inhelder, B., & Piaget, J. (1959). *The growth of logical thinking from childhood to adolescence.* New York: Basic Books.

Kagan, J. (1994). *Galen's prophecy: Temperament in human nature.* New York: Basic Books.

Myers, D. G. (1995). *The pursuit of happiness.* New York: Avon.

Developmental Psychology

As we journey through life—from womb to tomb—when and how do we develop? Virtually all of us began walking around age 1 and talking by age 2. As children, we engaged in social play in preparation for life's work. As teenagers, you and your classmates all smile and cry, love and loathe, and occasionally ponder the fact that someday, life will end. **Developmental psychology** examines how people are continually developing—physically, cognitively, and socially—from infancy through old age. Much of its research centers on three major issues:

1. ***Nature and nurture:*** How do genetic inheritance (*our nature*) and experience (*the nurture we receive*) influence our development?

2. ***Continuity and stages:*** Is development a gradual, continuous process like riding an escalator, or does it proceed through a sequence of separate stages, like climbing rungs on a ladder?

3. ***Stability and change:*** Do our early personality traits persist through life, or do we become different persons as we age?

In Units 1 and 3C, we engaged the nature and nurture issue. At this unit's end, we will also reflect on the continuity and stability issues.

::**developmental psychology** a branch of psychology that studies physical, cognitive, and social change throughout the life span.

Prenatal Development and the Newborn

1: How does life develop before birth?

Conception

Nothing is more natural than a species reproducing itself. Yet nothing is more wondrous. With humans, the process starts when a woman's ovary releases a mature egg—a cell roughly the size of the period at the end of this sentence. The woman was born with all the immature eggs she would ever have, although only 1 in 5000 will ever mature and be released. A man, in contrast, begins producing sperm cells at puberty. For the rest of his life, 24 hours a day, he will be a nonstop sperm factory, although the rate of production—in the beginning more than 1000 sperm during the second it takes to read this phrase—will slow with age.

Like space voyagers approaching a huge planet, the 200 million or more deposited sperm begin their race upstream, approaching a cell 85,000 times their own size. The relatively few reaching the egg release digestive enzymes that eat away its protective coating (**FIGURE 9.1**, next page). As soon as one sperm begins to penetrate and is welcomed in, the egg's surface blocks out the others. Before half a day elapses, the egg nucleus and the sperm nucleus fuse. The two have become one. Consider it your most fortunate of moments. Among 200

"Nature is all that a man brings with him into the world; nurture is every influence that affects him after his birth."
Francis Galton,
English Men of Science, 1874

Key People

Mary Ainsworth
Paul Baltes
Albert Bandura
John Bowlby
Mihaly Csikszentmihalyi
Erik Erikson
Carol Gilligan

Jonathan Haidt
G. Stanley Hall
Harry Harlow
Judith Harris
Lawrence Kohlberg
Konrad Lorenz
Jean Piaget

Mark Rosenzweig
Sandra Scarr
Lev Vygotsky

Key Terms

developmental psychology

Prenatal Development and the Newborn

zygote
embryo
fetus
teratogens
fetal alcohol syndrome (FAS)
habituation

Infancy and Childhood

maturation
cognition
schema
assimilation
accommodation
sensorimotor stage
object permanence
preoperational stage
conservation
egocentrism
theory of mind
concrete operational stage
formal operational stage

autism
stranger anxiety
attachment
critical period
imprinting
temperament
basic trust
self-concept
gender typing
social learning theory

gender
aggression
X chromosome
Y chromosome
testosterone
role
gender role
gender identity

Adolescence

adolescence
puberty
primary sex characteristics
secondary sex characteristics
menarche
identity
social identity
intimacy
emerging adulthood

Key Terms continued »

UNIT 9

(a)   (b)

➤ **FIGURE 9.1**

Life is sexually transmitted (a) Sperm cells surround an ovum. (b) As one sperm penetrates the egg's jellylike outer coating, a series of chemical events begins that will cause sperm and egg to fuse into a single cell. If all goes well, that cell will subdivide again and again to emerge 9 months later as a 100-trillion-cell human being.

First known photo of Olympic swimming champ Michael Phelps
(If the playful cartoonist were to convey literal truth, a second arrow would also point to the egg that contributed the other half of Michael Phelps' genes.)

● **Prenatal development**
zygote: conception to 2 weeks
embryo: 2 weeks through 8 weeks
fetus: 9 weeks to birth ●

CRITICAL THINKING

Fertility has become an important social issue in recent years, with more women postponing child-bearing and new technologies emerging that address infertility. Explore the following ethical questions about fertility issues:

- Some women harvest their eggs to conceive later in life, building a career before having children. What are the pros and cons of having children later in life? What societal implications will this practice produce?

- What should become of unused frozen embryos? Explain the reasons behind your answer.

- Should human cloning be allowed? Why or why not?

TEACHING TIP

According to the National Center for Health Statistics (2001), about 50 more males than females are born per 1000 babies each year. More babies are born in August than any other month, and more babies are born on Tuesdays, regardless of race.

Ventura, S. J., et. al. (April 17, 2001). *National vital statistics report: Births: Final data for 1999*. Volume 49, 1. Atlanta, GA: Centers for Disease Control.

---

million sperm, the one needed to make you, in combination with that one particular egg, won the race.

Prenatal Development

Fewer than half of all fertilized eggs, called **zygotes,** survive beyond the first 2 weeks (Grobstein, 1979; Hall, 2004). But for you and me, good fortune prevailed. One cell became 2, then 4—each just like the first—until this cell division produced a zygote of some 100 cells within the first week. Then the cells began to differentiate—to specialize in structure and function. How identical cells do this—as if one decides "I'll become a brain, you become intestines!"—is a puzzle that scientists are just beginning to solve.

About 10 days after conception, the zygote attaches to the mother's uterine wall, beginning approximately 37 weeks of the closest human relationship. The zygote's inner cells become the **embryo** (FIGURE 9.2a). Over the next 6 weeks, organs begin to form and function. The heart begins to beat.

By 9 weeks after conception, the embryo looks unmistakably human (Figure 9.2c). It is now a **fetus** (Latin for "offspring" or "young one"). During the sixth month, organs such as the stomach have developed enough to allow a prematurely born fetus a chance of survival. At this point, the fetus is also responsive to sound (Hepper, 2005). Microphone readings taken inside the uterus have revealed that the fetus is exposed to the sound of its mother's muffled voice (Ecklund-Flores, 1992). Immediately after birth, when newborns emerge from living 38 or so weeks underwater, they prefer this voice to another woman's or to their father's voice (Busnel et al., 1992; DeCasper et al., 1984, 1986, 1994).

At each prenatal stage, genetic *and* environmental factors affect our development. The *placenta*, which formed as the zygote's outer cells attached to the uterine wall, transfers nutrients and oxygen from mother to fetus. A healthy and well-nourished

---

CRITICAL THINKING

Thirteen states can terminate parental rights if evidence of substance abuse exists during pregnancy. Eight states require doctors to report if evidence of prenatal substance abuse exists. Guide a class discussion with the following questions:

- How do you think the criminal justice system should deal with mothers who abuse drugs during pregnancy?

- If states pursue offenders of this crime, how do you think society, in general, would be affected?

Source: *State policies in brief*. (2002, July). New York: The Alan Guttmacher Institute. Retrieved from the World Wide Web: www.guttmacher.org/statecenter/spibs/spib_SADP.pdf.

Images courtesy of Lennart Nilsson/Albert Bonniers Publishing Company

(a)   (b)   (c)

mother helps form a healthy baby-to-be. The placenta also screens out many potentially harmful substances. But some substances slip by, including **teratogens,** which are harmful agents such as viruses and drugs. If the mother carries the HIV virus, her baby may also. If she is a heroin addict, her baby will be born a heroin addict. A pregnant woman never smokes alone; she and her fetus both experience reduced blood oxygen and a shot of nicotine. If she is a heavy smoker, her fetus may receive fewer nutrients and be born underweight and at risk for various problems (Pringle et al., 2005).

There is no known safe amount of alcohol during pregnancy. Alcohol enters the woman's bloodstream—and her fetus'—and depresses activity in both their central nervous systems. A pregnant mother's alcohol use may prime her offspring to like alcohol. Teens whose mothers drank when pregnant are at risk for heavy drinking and alcohol dependence. In experiments, when pregnant rats drink alcohol, their young offspring later display a liking for alcohol's odor (Youngentob et al., 2007). Even light drinking can affect the fetal brain (Braun, 1996; Ikonomidou et al., 2000), and persistent heavy drinking will put the fetus at risk for birth defects and intellectual disability. For 1 in about 800 infants, the effects are visible as **fetal alcohol syndrome (FAS),** marked by a small, misproportioned head and lifelong brain abnormalities (May & Gossage, 2001).

The Competent Newborn

2: What are some newborn abilities, and how do researchers explore infants' mental abilities?

Having survived prenatal hazards, we as newborns came equipped with automatic responses ideally suited for our survival. We withdrew our limbs to escape pain. If a cloth over our face interfered with our breathing, we turned our head from side to side and swiped at it.

New parents are often in awe of the coordinated sequence of reflexes by which their baby gets food. When something touches their cheek, babies turn toward that touch, open their mouth, and vigorously *root* for a nipple. Finding one, they

➤ **FIGURE 9.2**

Prenatal development (a) The embryo grows and develops rapidly. At 40 days, the spine is visible and the arms and legs are beginning to grow. (b) By the end of the second month, when the fetal period begins, facial features, hands, and feet have formed. (c) As the fetus enters the fourth month, its 3 ounces could fit in the palm of your hand.

"You shall conceive and bear a son. So then drink no wine or strong drink."
Judges 13:7

::zygote the fertilized egg; it enters a 2-week period of rapid cell division and develops into an embryo.

::embryo the developing human organism from about 2 weeks after fertilization through the second month.

::fetus the developing human organism from 9 weeks after conception to birth.

::teratogens agents, such as chemicals and viruses, that can reach the embryo or fetus during prenatal development and cause harm.

::fetal alcohol syndrome (FAS) physical and cognitive abnormalities in children caused by a pregnant woman's heavy drinking. In severe cases, symptoms include noticeable facial misproportions.

 Key Terms continued from p. 411

Adulthood

menopause
cross-sectional study
longitudinal study
crystallized intelligence
fluid intelligence
social clock

RESEARCH

Fertility technologies increase the likelihood of multiple fetuses developing in one pregnancy, resulting in famous births of multiples including the McCaughey sextuplets of Iowa, the Harris sextuplets of Alabama, and the Suleman octuplets most recently in 2009. Research and discuss the following with students about multiple births:

- What advances in technology make it more likely that multiples can survive?

- What developmental problems can parents of multiples expect?

- What kind of community responses do parents of multiples receive?

- What ethical dilemmas do doctors and parents face with multiple fetuses developing in one pregnancy?

 TEACHING TIP

You may have students who are parents already. Encourage them to discuss their childrearing practices and what it is like to be a teen parent so they can learn to be the best parents they can be, using psychological research as their guide.

TEACHING TIP

If you are up for a lively discussion, you might organize a structured debate on any of the following issues related to prenatal development:

- When "life" begins

- Genetic testing of fetuses for abnormalities

- Human cloning

- Stem cell research

UNIT 9

Habituation is an often-confused concept. Help students understand how habituation works. Once the stimulus becomes familiar and expected, our sensitivity to it decreases. We do not respond as strongly to it as we did in the beginning. An example of this is when people watch scary movies. When they first watch a scary movie, they react very strongly to the frightening scenes. However, the more they watch scary movies, the less they may respond to startling or gory scenes; they become habituated.

TEACHING TIP

The research techniques Myers describes here have revolutionized the study of psychology. Now that scientists can interpret infant behaviors, we can know more about how infants think and come close to answering questions about when different psychological phenomena begin to emerge.

At this time, you may want to use **Classroom Exercise: *Introducing Central Issues in Developmental Psychology*** (p. 4) from Bolt's Teacher's Resource Binder, which accompanies this text.

Prepared to feed and eat Animals are predisposed to respond to their offsprings' cries for nourishment.

"I felt like a man trapped in a woman's body. Then I was born."
Comedian Chris Bliss

::**habituation** decreasing responsiveness with repeated stimulation. As infants gain familiarity with repeated exposure to a visual stimulus, their interest wanes and they look away sooner.

➤ **FIGURE 9.3**
Quick—which is the cat? Researchers used cat-dog hybrid images such as these to test how infants categorize animals.

automatically close on it and begin *sucking*—which itself requires a coordinated sequence of reflexive *tonguing, swallowing,* and *breathing.* Failing to find satisfaction, the hungry baby may *cry*—a behavior parents find highly unpleasant and very rewarding to relieve.

The pioneering American psychologist William James presumed that the newborn experiences a "blooming, buzzing confusion." Until the 1960s, few people disagreed. It was said that, apart from a blur of meaningless light and dark shades, newborns could not see. But then scientists discovered that babies can tell you a lot—if you know how to ask. To ask, you must capitalize on what babies can do—gaze, suck, turn their heads. So, equipped with eye-tracking machines and pacifiers wired to electronic gear, researchers set out to answer parents' age-old questions: What can my baby see, hear, smell, and think?

One technique developmental researchers use to answer such questions is a simple form of learning called **habituation**—a decrease in responding with repeated stimulation. A novel stimulus gets attention when first presented. But the more often the stimulus is presented, the weaker the response becomes. This seeming boredom with familiar stimuli gives us a way to ask infants what they see and remember.

Janine Spencer, Paul Quinn, and their colleagues (1997; Quinn, 2002) used a *novelty-preference procedure* to ask 4-month-olds how they recognize cats or dogs. The researchers first showed the infants a series of images of cats and dogs. Which of the two animals in **FIGURE 9.3** do you think the infants would find more novel (measured in looking time) after seeing a series of cats? It was the hybrid animal with the dog's head (or with a cat's head, if they had previously viewed a series of dogs). This suggests that infants, like adults, focus first on the face, not the body.

Indeed, we are born preferring sights and sounds that facilitate social responsiveness. As newborns, we turn our heads in the direction of human voices. We gaze longer at a drawing of a facelike image (**FIGURE 9.4**) than at a bull's-eye pattern; yet we gaze more at a bull's-eye pattern—which has contrasts much like those of the human

Children with birth defects are treated differently depending on what culture they are born into. Have students identify a culture they are interested in and explore the following questions:

- Do superstitions exist in the culture regarding how birth defects are explained? Describe them.

- What types of support services are available for children with birth defects and their families?

- How much prenatal education is available to expectant mothers regarding teratogens and nutrition?

eye—than at a solid disk (Fantz, 1961). We prefer to look at objects 8 to 12 inches away. Wonder of wonders, that just happens to be the approximate distance between a nursing infant's eyes and its mother's (Maurer & Maurer, 1988).

Within days after birth, our brain's neural networks were stamped with the smell of our mother's body. Thus, a week-old nursing baby, placed between a gauze pad from its mother's bra and one from another nursing mother, will usually turn toward the smell of its own mother's pad (MacFarlane, 1978). At 3 weeks, if given a pacifier that sometimes turns on recordings of its mother's voice and sometimes that of a female stranger's, an infant will suck more vigorously when it hears its now-familiar mother's voice (Mills & Melhuish, 1974). So not only could we as young infants see what we needed to see, and smell and hear well, we were already using our sensory equipment to learn.

> FIGURE 9.4

Newborns' preference for faces When shown these two stimuli with the same elements, Italian newborns spent nearly twice as many seconds looking at the facelike image (Johnson & Morton, 1991). Canadian newborns—average age 53 minutes in one study—display the same apparently inborn preference to look toward faces (Mondloch et al., 1999).

BEFORE YOU MOVE ON . . .

> **ASK YOURSELF**

Are you surprised by the news of infants' competencies? Remember *hindsight bias* from Unit 2? Is this one of those cases where it feels like you "knew it all along"?

> **TEST YOURSELF 1**

Your friend's older sister—a regular drinker—hopes to become pregnant soon and has stopped drinking. Why is this a good idea? What negative effects might alcohol consumed during pregnancy have on a developing fetus?

Answers to the Test Yourself questions can be found in Appendix E at the end of the book.

Infancy and Childhood

DURING INFANCY, A BABY GROWS from newborn to toddler, and during childhood from toddler to teenager. We all traveled this path, developing physically, cognitively, and socially. From infancy on, brain and mind—neural hardware and cognitive software—develop together.

Physical Development

3: During infancy and childhood, how do the brain and motor skills develop?

Brain Development

In your mother's womb, your developing brain formed nerve cells at the explosive rate of nearly one-quarter million per minute. The developing brain cortex actually overproduces neurons, with the number peaking at 28 weeks and then subsiding to a stable 23 billion or so at birth (Rabinowicz et al., 1996, 1999; de Courten-Myers, 2002). On the day you were born, you had most of the brain cells you would ever have. However, your nervous system was immature: After birth, the branching neural networks that eventually enabled you to walk, talk, and remember had a wild growth spurt (FIGURE 9.5). From ages 3 to 6,

"It is a rare privilege to watch the birth, growth, and first feeble struggles of a living human mind."
Annie Sullivan, in Helen Keller's *The Story of My Life*, 1903

> FIGURE 9.5

Drawings of human cerebral cortex sections In humans, the brain is immature at birth. As the child matures, the neural networks grow increasingly more complex.

At birth   3 months   15 months

TEACHING TIP

The APGAR test is a quick physical test given to every newborn at birth. Scores are given at 1 and 5 minutes after birth. If problems exist, then another test is given at 10 minutes after birth. A score of 7 to 10 is considered normal. Infants scoring 4–6 might need resuscitation, while scores under 3 require immediate resuscitation. APGAR is an acronym for the following tests:

A = Activity or muscle tone. Muscle movements are measured.

P = Pulse. Ideally, babies have a heart rate of over 100 beats per minute.

G = Grimace or reflex irritability. Active babies sneeze and cough during suctioning of the mucus in their noses and mouths.

A = Appearance. Doctors look for normal skin color. Blue-gray or pale skin color is not a good sign.

R = Respiration. Babies should be crying and breathing regularly.

TEACHING TIP

At this time, you may want to use **Lecture/Discussion Topic:** *Prenatal Sensory Development* (p. 8) from Bolt's Teacher's Resource Binder.

"This is the path to adulthood. You're here."

The presence of certain reflexes at birth signal normal neurological development. Other reflexes infants possess at birth include the following:

- *Babinski reflex* The toes flare out and then curl back in when the bottom of the foot is stroked.

- *Moro reflex* Arms are thrust out and the back is arched in response to surprise or a sudden noise or movement.

- *Plantar reflex* The toes will curl in when the ball of the foot is pressed.

- *Swimming reflex* If submerged in water for a short period of time, babies hold their breath and pump their arms and legs.

- *Stepping reflex* Infants move feet up and down as if they are walking when held up over a flat surface.

the most rapid growth was in your frontal lobes, which enable rational planning. This helps explain why preschoolers display a rapidly developing ability to control their attention and behavior (Garon et al., 2008).

The association areas—those linked with thinking, memory, and language—are the last cortical areas to develop. As they do, mental abilities surge (Chugani & Phelps, 1986; Thatcher et al., 1987). Fiber pathways supporting language and agility proliferate into puberty, after which a *pruning process* shuts down excess connections and strengthens others (Paus et al., 1999; Thompson et al., 2000).

As a flower unfolds in accord with its genetic instructions, so do we, in the orderly sequence of biological growth processes called **maturation**. Maturation decrees many of our commonalities—from standing before walking, to using nouns before adjectives. Severe deprivation or abuse can retard development, and ample experiences talking and reading with parents will help sculpt neural connections. Yet the genetic growth tendencies are inborn. Maturation sets the basic course of development; experience adjusts it.

Motor Development

The developing brain enables physical coordination. As an infant's muscles and nervous system mature, more complicated skills emerge. With occasional exceptions, the motor development sequence is universal. Babies roll over before they sit unsupported, and they usually creep on all fours before they walk (**FIGURE 9.6**). These behaviors reflect not imitation but a maturing nervous system; blind children, too, crawl before they walk.

There are, however, individual differences in timing. In the United States, for example, 25 percent of all babies walk by age 11 months, 50 percent within a week after their first birthday, and 90 percent by age 15 months (Frankenburg et al., 1992). The recommended infant *back-to-sleep position* (putting babies to sleep on their backs to reduce the risk of a smothering crib death) has been associated with somewhat later crawling but not with later walking (Davis et al., 1998; Lipsitt, 2003).

Genes play a major role in motor development. Identical twins typically begin sitting up and walking on nearly the same day (Wilson, 1979). Maturation—including the rapid development of the cerebellum at the back of the brain—creates our readiness to learn walking at about age 1. Experience before that time has a limited effect. This is true for other physical skills, including bowel and bladder control. Before

• In the eight years following the 1994 launch of a U.S. "Back to Sleep" educational campaign, the number of infants sleeping on their stomachs dropped from 70 to 11 percent—and SIDS (Sudden Infant Death Syndrome) deaths fell by half (Braiker, 2005). •

➤ **FIGURE 9.6**
Triumphant toddlers Sit, crawl, walk, run—the sequence of these motor development milestones is the same the world around, though babies reach them at varying ages.

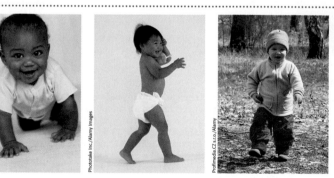

Recent research suggests that infants with a low level of serotonin may be more at risk for Sudden Infant Death Syndrome (SIDS). This research suggests that serotonin plays a role in the brainstem to help with breathing, sleeping, and waking. When babies exhale, they expel carbon dioxide, and that carbon dioxide may linger nearby if there is not enough space around the baby's mouth and nose. Normally, this would trigger a release of serotonin, which would cause the baby to wake up and move his or her head. Babies with low serotonin levels do not respond this way to carbon dioxide inhalation, thus resulting in higher risk of death. This finding helps explain why having infants sleep on their backs has helped reduce the number of SIDS-related deaths.

necessary muscular and neural maturation, parents shouldn't expect pleading or punishment to produce successful toilet training.

Maturation and Infant Memory

Our earliest memories seldom predate our third birthday. We see this *infantile amnesia* in the memories of some preschoolers who experienced an emergency fire evacuation caused by a burning popcorn maker. Seven years later, they were able to recall the alarm and what caused it—*if* they were 4 to 5 years old at the time. Those experiencing the event as 3-year-olds could not remember the cause and usually misrecalled being already outside when the alarm sounded (Pillemer, 1995). Other studies confirm that the average age of earliest conscious memory is 3.5 years (Bauer, 2002). By 4 to 5 years, childhood amnesia is giving way to remembered experiences (Bruce et al., 2000). But even into adolescence, the brain areas underlying memory, such as the hippocampus and frontal lobes, continue to mature (Bauer, 2007).

Although we *consciously* recall little from before age 4, our memory was processing information during those early years. In 1965, while finishing her doctoral work, Carolyn Rovee-Collier observed an infant memory. She was also a new mom, whose colicky 2-month-old, Benjamin, could be calmed by moving a crib mobile. Weary of bonking the mobile, she strung a cloth ribbon connecting the mobile to Benjamin's foot. Soon, he was kicking his foot to move the mobile. Thinking about her unintended home experiment, Rovee-Collier realized that, contrary to popular opinion at that time, babies are capable of learning. To know for sure that little Benjamin wasn't just a whiz kid, Rovee-Collier had to repeat the experiment with other infants (Rovee-Collier, 1989, 1999). Sure enough, they, too, soon kicked more when linked to a mobile, both on the day of the experiment and the day after. They had learned the link between moving legs and moving mobile. If, however, she hitched them to a different mobile the next day, the infants showed no learning. Their actions indicated that they remembered the original mobile and recognized the difference. Moreover, when tethered to a familiar mobile a month later, they remembered the association and again began kicking (FIGURE 9.7).

Evidence of early processing also appeared in a study in which 10-year-olds were shown photos of preschoolers and asked to spot their former classmates. Although they consciously recognized only 1 in 5 of their onetime compatriots, their physiological responses (measured as skin perspiration) were greater to their former classmates whether or not they consciously recognized them (Newcombe et al., 2000). What the conscious mind does not know and cannot express in words, the nervous system somehow remembers.

Cognitive Development

4: From the perspective of Piaget and of today's researchers, how does a child's mind develop?

Cognition refers to all the mental activities associated with thinking, knowing, remembering, and communicating. Somewhere on your precarious journey "from

---

::**maturation** biological growth processes that enable orderly changes in behavior, relatively uninfluenced by experience.

::**cognition** all the mental activities associated with thinking, knowing, remembering, and communicating

• Can you recall your first day of preschool (or your third birthday party)? •

Michael Newman/Photo Edit

➤ FIGURE 9.7

Infant at work Babies only 3 months old can learn that kicking moves a mobile, and they can retain that learning for a month. (From Rovee-Collier, 1989, 1997.)

"Who knows the thoughts of a child?"
Poet Nora Perry

 TEACHING TIP

At this time, you may want to use **Classroom Exercise:** *Identifying Developmental Landmarks* (p. 8) from Bolt's Teacher's Resource Binder.

 CULTURAL CONNECTIONS

Certain cultural groups in Africa have shown that maturational milestones can occur in the same order but on different schedules. Have students explore the developmental timelines for a variety of groups in African countries to determine whether maturational milestones occur at different times. Students will likely note that while the timing of events may differ from culture to culture, the order of development does not differ.

TEACHING TIP

Sensory development in fetuses follows a specific pattern:

- 7 ½ weeks: The fetus will flex its head away from stimulation around the mouth. By month's end the ears begin to take shape.

- 12–15 weeks: Touch receptors around the mouth have developed. The fetus can grasp, frown, squint, and grimace. It may suck its thumb and swallow.

- 20–24 weeks: The senses of taste and smell have now formed. The fetus can feel movement and may respond to sound.

- 25–27 weeks: Some babies born prematurely can survive. Nerve supply to the ears is complete. Brain scans show response to touch and to light.

- 32 weeks: The eyes open in the womb and the fetus may see its environment. Neural circuits are as advanced as a newborn's. Brain scans show periods of deep sleep.

Ohnuma, K. (1987, July/August). Making senses. *Hippocrates,* p. 73.

UNIT 9

::**schema** a concept or framework that organizes and interprets information.

::**assimilation** interpreting our new experiences in terms of our existing schemas.

::**accommodation** adapting our current understandings (schemas) to incorporate new information.

> "Childhood has its own way of seeing, thinking, and feeling, and there is nothing more foolish than the attempt to put ours in its place."
> Philosopher Jean-Jacques Rousseau, 1798

▼ **Jean Piaget (1896–1980)** "If we examine the intellectual development of the individual or of the whole of humanity, we shall find that the human spirit goes through a certain number of stages, each different than the other" (1930).

egghood to personhood" (Broks, 2007), you became conscious. When was that, and how did your mind unfold from there? Developmental psychologist Jean Piaget (pronounced Pee-ah-ZHAY) spent his life searching for the answers to such questions. His interest began in 1920, when he was in Paris developing questions for children's intelligence tests. While administering the tests, Piaget became intrigued by children's *wrong* answers, which, he noted, were often strikingly similar among children of a given age. Where others saw childish mistakes, Piaget saw intelligence at work.

A half-century spent with children convinced Piaget that a child's mind is not a miniature model of an adult's. Thanks partly to his work, we now understand that children reason *differently*, in "wildly illogical ways about problems whose solutions are self-evident to adults" (Brainerd, 1996).

Piaget's studies led him to believe that a child's mind develops through a series of stages, in an upward march from the newborn's simple reflexes to the adult's abstract reasoning power. Thus, an 8-year-old can comprehend things a toddler cannot, such as the analogy that "getting an idea is like having a light turn on in your head," or that a miniature slide is too small for sliding, and a miniature car is much too small to get into (**FIGURE 9.8**). But our adult minds likewise engage in reasoning uncomprehended by 8-year-olds.

Piaget's core idea is that the driving force behind our intellectual progression is an unceasing struggle to make sense of our experiences: "Children are active thinkers, constantly trying to construct more advanced understandings of the world" (Siegler & Ellis, 1996). To this end, the maturing brain builds **schemas,** concepts or mental molds into which we pour our experiences (**FIGURE 9.9**). By adulthood we have built countless schemas, ranging from *cats* and *dogs* to our concept of *love.*

To explain how we use and adjust our schemas, Piaget proposed two more concepts. First, we **assimilate** new experiences—we interpret them in terms of our current understandings (schemas). Having a simple schema for *cow,* for example, a toddler may call all four-legged animals *cows.* But as we interact with the world, we also adjust, or **accommodate,** our schemas to incorporate information

➤ **FIGURE 9.8**
Scale errors Psychologists Judy DeLoache, David Uttal, and Karl Rosengren (2004) report that 18- to 30-month-old children may fail to take the size of an object into account when trying to perform impossible actions with it. At left, a 21-month-old attempts to slide down a miniature slide. At right, a 24-month-old opens the door to a miniature car and tries to step inside.

provided by new experiences. Thus, the child soon learns that the original *cow* schema is too broad and accommodates by refining the category (**FIGURE 9.10**).

Piaget believed that as children construct their understandings while interacting with the world, they experience spurts of change, followed by greater stability as they move from one cognitive plateau to the next. He viewed these plateaus as forming stages. Let's consider Piaget's stages now, in the light of current thinking.

➤ FIGURE 9.9
An impossible object Look carefully at the "devil's tuning fork." Now look away—no, better first study it some more—and then look away and draw it. . . . Not so easy, is it? This is an impossible object; you have no schema for such an image.

Two-year-old Gabriella has learned the schema for *cow* from her picture books.

Gabriella sees a moose and calls it a "cow." She is trying to assimilate this new animal into an existing schema. Her mother tells her, "No, it's a moose."

Gabriella accommodates her schema for large, shaggy animals and continues to modify that schema to include "mommy moose," "baby moose," and so forth.

Piaget's Theory and Current Thinking

Piaget proposed that children progress through four stages of cognitive development, each with distinctive characteristics that permit specific kinds of thinking (**TABLE 9.1**, next page).

Sensorimotor Stage In the **sensorimotor stage,** from birth to nearly age 2, babies take in the world through their senses and actions—through looking, hearing, touching, mouthing, and grasping.

Very young babies seem to live in the present: Out of sight is out of mind. In one test, Piaget showed an infant an appealing toy and then flopped his beret over it. Before the age of 6 months, the infant acted as if it ceased to exist. Young infants lack **object permanence**—the awareness that objects continue to exist when not perceived (**FIGURE 9.11**). By 8 months, infants begin exhibiting memory for things

➤ FIGURE 9.10
Pouring experience into mental molds

::**sensorimotor stage** in Piaget's theory, the stage (from birth to about 2 years of age) during which infants know the world mostly in terms of their sensory impressions and motor activities.

::**object permanence** the awareness that things continue to exist even when not perceived.

➤ FIGURE 9.11
Object permanence Infants younger than 6 months seldom understand that things continue to exist when they are out of sight. But for this infant, out of sight is definitely not out of mind.

Doug Goodman

Another example of simple schemas comes from the Disney movie *Bambi*. When the young Bambi is sniffing the flowers with his rabbit friend Thumper, a little skunk pokes his head up through the flowers to say hello. Bambi, having just learned the word "flower," immediately calls the skunk "Flower," mistaking him for what he was smelling. Bambi didn't accommodate his schema for flowers after meeting the skunk.

After infants have mastered object permanence, they engage in something called *directed groping*. With this, babies will move in different ways to achieve a goal. They may use sticks or other objects to help them get other objects.

At this time, you may want to use **Lecture/Discussion Topics:** *Preoperational Thought and Moral Development* (p. 12) or *Vygotsky's Sociocultural Theory of Cognitive Development* (p. 13) from Bolt's Teacher's Resource Binder.

Help students remember the sensorimotor stage by breaking down the word itself into *sensory* and *motor*. Remind students that babies are sensory beings—they look intently on stimuli that interest them and listen to soothing sounds. Babies are also constantly moving. They move their bodies, often by accident, to discover what they are capable of and what objects within their reach can do.

UNIT 9

TABLE 9.1

PIAGET'S STAGES OF COGNITIVE DEVELOPMENT

Typical Age Range	Description of Stage	Developmental Phenomena
Birth to nearly 2 years	*Sensorimotor* Experiencing the world through senses and actions (looking, hearing, touching, mouthing, and grasping)	• Object permanence • Stranger anxiety
2 to about 6 or 7 years	*Preoperational* Representing things with words and images; using intuitive rather than logical reasoning	• Pretend play • Egocentrism
About 7 to 11 years	*Concrete operational* Thinking logically about concrete events; grasping concrete analogies and performing arithmetical operations	• Conservation • Mathematical transformations
About 12 through adulthood	*Formal operational* Abstract reasoning	• Abstract logic • Potential for mature moral reasoning

---

TEACHING TIP

The sensorimotor stage can be broken down into three different substages:

- *Primary Circular Reactions* involve babies experimenting with their own bodies. They enjoy moving their arms and legs and making noises with their mouths.

- *Secondary Circular Reactions* occur when babies respond to other people or objects. They will repeat actions over and over to get the desired response (such as a smile from Mommy).

- *Tertiary Circular Reactions* take babies even further as they explore the outside world. Usually, they will accidentally cause an event to occur, for example, by kicking a ball. Then, they will devise new activities with that object to make it do other things, like bouncing the ball or putting it in a box and taking it out over and over again.

::**preoperational stage** in Piaget's theory, the stage (from 2 to about 6 or 7 years of age) during which a child learns to use language but does not yet comprehend the mental operations of concrete logic.

::**conservation** the principle (which Piaget believed to be a part of concrete operational reasoning) that properties such as mass, volume, and number remain the same despite changes in the forms of objects.

::**egocentrism** in Piaget's theory, the preoperational child's difficulty taking another's point of view.

> ➤ **FIGURE 9.12**
> **Infants can discriminate between possible and impossible objects** After habituating to the stimulus on the left, 4-month-olds stared longer if shown the impossible version of the cube—where one of the back vertical bars crosses over a front horizontal bar (Shuwairi et al., 2007).

---

no longer seen. If you hide a toy, the infant will momentarily look for it. Within another month or two, the infant will look for it even after being restrained for several seconds.

But does object permanence in fact blossom at 8 months, much as tulips blossom in spring? Today's researchers see development as more continuous than Piaget did, and they believe object permanence unfolds gradually. Even young infants will at least momentarily look for a toy where they saw it hidden a second before (Wang et al., 2004).

Researchers believe Piaget and his followers underestimated young children's competence. Consider some simple experiments that demonstrate baby logic:

- Like adults staring in disbelief at a magic trick (the "Whoa!" look), infants look longer at an unexpected and unfamiliar scene of a car seeming to pass through a solid object, a ball stopping in midair, or an object violating object permanence by magically disappearing (Baillargeon, 1995, 2008; Wellman & Gelman, 1992). In another clever experiment, Sarah Shuwairi and her colleagues (2007) exposed 4-month-olds to a picture of a cube (**FIGURE 9.12**) with one small area covered. After the infants had habituated to this image, they stared longer when shown an impossible rather than possible version of the cube. Babies, it seems, have a more intuitive grasp of simple laws of physics than Piaget realized.

- Babies also have a head for numbers. Karen Wynn (1992, 2000) showed 5-month-olds one or two objects. Then she hid the objects behind a screen, and visibly removed or added one (**FIGURE 9.13**). When she lifted the screen, the infants sometimes did a double take, staring longer when shown a wrong number of objects. But were they just responding to a greater or smaller mass of objects, rather than a change in number (Feigenson et al., 2002)? Later experiments showed that babies' number sense extends to larger numbers and such things as drumbeats and motions (McCrink & Wynn, 2004; Spelke & Kinzler, 2007; Wynn et al., 2002). If accustomed to a Daffy Duck puppet jumping three times on stage, they show surprise if it jumps only twice. Clearly, infants are smarter than Piaget appreciated. Even as babies, we had a lot on our minds.

Then either: possible outcome
5. Screen drops... revealing 1 object

1. Objects placed in case 2. Screen comes up 3. Empty hand enters 4. One object removed

or: impossible outcome
5. Screen drops... revealing 2 objects

Preoperational Stage Piaget believed that until about age 6 or 7, children are in a **preoperational stage**—too young to perform mental operations. For a 5-year-old, the milk that seems "too much" in a tall, narrow glass may become an acceptable amount if poured into a short, wide glass. Focusing only on the height dimension, this child cannot perform the operation of mentally pouring the milk back, because she lacks the concept of **conservation**—the principle that quantity remains the same despite changes in shape (**FIGURE 9.14**).

Piaget did not view the stage transitions as abrupt. Even so, symbolic thinking appears at an earlier age than he supposed. Judy DeLoache (1987) discovered this when she showed children a model of a room and hid a model toy in it (a miniature stuffed dog behind a miniature couch). The 2½-year-olds easily remembered where to find the miniature toy, but they could not use the model to locate an actual stuffed dog behind a couch in a real room. Three-year-olds—only 6 months older—usually went right to the actual stuffed animal in the real room, showing they *could* think of the model as a symbol for the room. Piaget probably would have been surprised.

➤ **FIGURE 9.13**

Baby math Shown a numerically impossible outcome, 5-month-old infants stare longer. (From Wynn, 1992.)

• Question: If most 2½-year-olds do not understand how miniature toys can symbolize real objects, should anatomically correct dolls be used when questioning such children about alleged physical or sexual abuse? Judy DeLoache (1995) reports that "very young children do not find it natural or easy to use a doll as a representation of themselves. •

Bianca Moscatelli/Worth Publishers

Egocentrism Piaget contended that preschool children are **egocentric**: They have difficulty perceiving things from another's point of view. Asked to "show Mommy your picture," 2-year-old Gabriella holds the picture up facing her own eyes. Three-year-old Gray makes himself "invisible" by putting his hands over his eyes, assuming that if he can't see his grandparents, they can't see him. Children's conversations also reveal their egocentrism, as one young boy demonstrated (Phillips, 1969, p. 61):

➤ **FIGURE 9.14**

Piaget's test of conservation This preoperational child does not yet understand the principle of conservation of substance. When the milk is poured into a tall, narrow glass, it suddenly seems like "more" than when it was in the shorter, wider glass. In another year or so, she will understand that the volume stays the same.

UNIT 9

"It's too late, Roger—they've seen us."

Roger has not outgrown his early childhood egocentrism.

TEACHING TIP

Egocentrism manifests in children in several different ways:

- *Collective monologues*: Children will appear to be talking to each other in a dialogue, but they are really talking about two completely different subjects.

- *Animism*: Children believe that nature is alive and controllable by them or their parents. They often believe natural things, such as trees or the sun, have feelings.

- *Artificialism:* Children believe natural phenomena are created by people, for instance, that mountains were created by someone piling up a bunch of dirt.

At this time, you may want to use **Student Projects:** *Egocentrism* (p. 10) or *Conservation, Seriation, and Class Inclusion* (p. 11) from Bolt's Teacher's Resource Binder.

• Use your finger to trace a capital E on your forehead. When Adam Galinsky and his colleagues (2006) invited people to do that, they were more egocentric—less likely to draw it from the perspective of someone looking at them—if they were first made to feel powerful. Other studies confirm that feeling powerful reduces people's sensitivity to how others see, think, and feel. •

Family Circus ® Bil Keane

TELL ME, JEFFY, WHAT WAS THIS FUN DREAM ABOUT LAST NIGHT?

8-21

"Don't you remember, Grandma? You were in it with me."

::**theory of mind** people's ideas about their own and others' mental states—about their feelings, perceptions, and thoughts, and the behaviors these might predict.

::**concrete operational stage** in Piaget's theory, the stage of cognitive development (from about 6 or 7 to 11 years of age) during which children gain the mental operations that enable them to think logically about concrete events.

"Do you have a brother?"
"Yes."
"What's his name?"
"Jim."
"Does Jim have a brother?"
"No."

Like Gabriella, TV-watching preschoolers who block your view of the TV assume that you see what they see. They simply have not yet developed the ability to take another's viewpoint. Even teens and adults often overestimate the extent to which others share their opinion and perspectives. We assume that something will be clear to others if it is clear to us, or that text message recipients will "hear" our "just kidding" intent (Epley et al., 2004; Kruger et al., 2005). Children, however, are even more susceptible to this *curse of knowledge.*

Theory of Mind When Little Red Riding Hood realizes her "grandmother" is really a wolf, she swiftly revises her ideas about the creature's intentions and races away. Preschoolers, although still egocentric, develop this ability to infer others' mental states when they begin forming a **theory of mind** (a term first coined by psychologists David Premack and Guy Woodruff, to describe chimpanzees' seeming ability to read intentions).

As children's ability to take another's perspective develops, they seek to understand what made a playmate angry, when a sibling will share, and what might make a parent buy a toy. And they begin to tease, empathize, and persuade. Between about 3½ and 4½, children worldwide come to realize that others may hold false beliefs (Callaghan et al., 2005; Sabbagh et al., 2006). Jennifer Jenkins and Janet Astington (1996) showed Toronto children a Band-Aids box and asked them what was inside. Expecting Band-Aids, the children were surprised to discover that the box actually contained pencils. Asked what a child who had never seen the box would think was inside, 3-year-olds typically answered "pencils." By age 4 to 5, the children's theory of mind had leapt forward, and they anticipated their friends' false belief that the box would hold Band-Aids.

In a follow-up experiment, children see a doll named Sally leaving her ball in a red cupboard (FIGURE 9.15). Another doll, Anne, then moves the ball to a blue cupboard. Researchers then pose a question: When Sally returns, where will she look for the ball? Children with *autism* (see Close-Up: Autism, on the next page) have difficulty understanding that Sally's state of mind differs from their own—that Sally, not knowing the ball has been moved, will return to the red cupboard. They also have difficulty reflecting on their own mental states. They are, for example, less likely to use the personal pronouns *I* and *me*. Deaf children who have hearing parents and minimal communication opportunities have similar difficulty inferring others' states of mind (Peterson & Siegal, 1999).

Our abilities to perform mental operations, to think symbolically, and to take another's perspective are not absent in the preoperational stage and then miraculously present in later stages. Rather, these abilities begin to show up early and continue to develop gradually (Wellman et al., 2001). For example, we are able to appreciate others' perceptions and feelings before we can appreciate others' *beliefs* (Saxe & Powell, 2006).

By age 7, children become increasingly capable of thinking in words and of using words to work out solutions to problems. They do this, noted the Russian psychologist Lev Vygotsky (1896–1934), by internalizing

Lev Vygotsky (1896–1934) Vygotsky, a Russian developmental psychologist, pictured here with his daughter, studied how a child's mind feeds on the language of social interaction.

James V. Wertsch/Washington University

DEMO

Invite a group of preoperational children to class (or visit their school) and conduct Piagetian tasks with them. Warn students that the younger children who are solidly preoperational will be pleased at their great performance on the tasks but older children, who are moving toward concrete operations, may wonder if they are being tricked or if your students are a little dim themselves! Overall, your students should encourage the children regardless of their responses. If they get the "wrong" answers, that does not reflect on their intelligence.

their culture's language and relying on inner speech. Parents who say "No, no!" when pulling a child's hand away from a cake are giving the child a self-control tool. When later needing to resist temptation, the child may likewise say "No, no!" Second-graders who mutter to themselves while doing math problems grasp third-grade math better the following year (Berk, 1994). Whether out loud or inaudibly, talking to themselves helps children control their behavior and emotions and master new skills.

Concrete Operational Stage By about 6 or 7 years of age, said Piaget, children enter the **concrete operational stage.** Given concrete materials, they begin to grasp conservation. Understanding that change in form does not mean change in quantity, they can mentally pour milk back and forth between glasses of different shapes. They also enjoy jokes that allow them to use this new understanding:

> Mr. Jones went into a restaurant and ordered a whole pizza for his dinner. When the waiter asked if he wanted it cut into 6 or 8 pieces, Mr. Jones said, "Oh, you'd better make it 6, I could never eat 8 pieces!" (McGhee, 1976)

Piaget believed that during the concrete operational stage, children fully gain the mental ability to comprehend mathematical transformations and conservation. When my daughter, Laura, was 6, I was astonished at her inability to reverse simple arithmetic. Asked, "What is 8 plus 4?" she required 5 seconds to compute "12," and another 5 seconds to then compute 12 minus 4. By age 8, she could answer a reversed question instantly.

Formal Operational Stage By age 12, our reasoning expands from the purely concrete (involving actual experience) to encompass abstract thinking (involving imagined realities and symbols). As children approach adolescence, said Piaget, many become capable of solving hypothetical propositions and deducing consequences: If this, then that. Systematic reasoning, what Piaget called **formal operational** thinking, is now within their grasp.

Although full-blown logic and reasoning await adolescence, the rudiments of formal operational thinking begin earlier than Piaget realized. Consider this simple problem:

> If John is in school, then Mary is in school. John is in school. What can you say about Mary?

Formal operational thinkers have no trouble answering correctly. But neither do most 7-year-olds (Suppes, 1982).

Reflecting on Piaget's Theory

What remains of Piaget's ideas about the child's mind? Plenty—enough to merit his being singled out by *Time* magazine as one of the twentieth century's 20 most influential scientists and thinkers and rated in a survey of British psychologists as the greatest psychologist of that century (*Psychologist*, 2003). Piaget identified significant cognitive milestones and stimulated worldwide interest in how the mind develops. His emphasis was less on the ages at which children typically reach specific milestones than on their sequence. Studies around the globe, from aboriginal Australia to Algeria to North America, have confirmed that human cognition unfolds basically in the sequence Piaget described (Lourenco & Machado, 1996; Segall et al., 1990).

This is Sally. This is Anne.

Sally puts her ball in the red cupboard.

Sally goes away.

Anne moves the ball to the blue cupboard.

Where will Sally look for her ball?

➤ **FIGURE 9.15**

Testing children's theory of mind This simple problem illustrates how researchers explore children's presumptions about others' mental states. (Inspired by Baron-Cohen et al., 1985.)

> "Assessing the impact of Piaget on developmental psychology is like assessing the impact of Shakespeare on English literature."
> Developmental psychologist Harry Beilin [1992]

::**formal operational stage** in Piaget's theory, the stage of cognitive development (normally beginning about age 12) during which people begin to think logically about abstract concepts.

DEMO

Set up a lab practicum in which students must identify different Piagetian tasks and what concept each task measures.

TROUBLESHOOTING

Students should understand that developmental milestones aren't etched in stone—in some children they occur earlier, and in some they occur later. Parents who don't understand these time ranges may endure unnecessary worry and heartache as they wait for their child to develop "on time."

At this time, you may want to use **Classroom Exercises:** *The Autism-Spectrum Quotient* (p. 10) or *"Reading the Mind in the Eyes" Test: Sample Items* (p. 10) or *Assessing Empathizing and Systemizing* (p. 11) from Bolt's Teacher's Resource Binder.

CLOSE-UP

Autism and "Mind-Blindness"

Autism This speech-language pathologist is helping a boy with autism learn to form sounds and words. Autism, which afflicts four boys for every girl, is marked by deficient social communication and difficulty in grasping others' states of mind.

Diagnoses of **autism**, a disorder marked by communication deficiencies and repetitive behaviors, have been increasing, according to recent estimates. Once believed to affect 1 in 2500 children, autism or a related disorder will now strike 1 in 150 American children and, in Britain's London area, 1 in 86 children (Baird et al., 2006; CDC, 2007; Lilienfeld & Arkowitz, 2007). Some people have attributed the modern "autism epidemic" to small amounts of mercury in childhood vaccines, leading nearly 5000 parents of children with autism to file a 2007 lawsuit against the U.S. government. But the mercury-laden ingredient was removed from vaccines in 2001, and autism rates have reportedly not dropped since then (Normand & Dallery, 2007; Schechter & Grether, 2008). Moreover, the increase in autism diagnoses has been offset by a decrease in the number of children considered "cognitively disabled" or "learning disabled," which suggests a relabeling of children's disorders (Gernsbacher et al., 2005; Grinker, 2007; Shattuck, 2006).

We do know that the underlying source of autism's symptoms seems to be poor communication among brain regions that normally work together to let us take another's viewpoint. This effect appears to result from an unknown number of autism-related genes interacting with the environment in as yet poorly understood ways (Blakeslee, 2005; Wickelgren, 2005).

People with autism are therefore said to have an impaired theory of mind (Rajendran & Mitchell, 2007). They have difficulty inferring others' thoughts and feelings. They do not appreciate that playmates and parents might view things differently. Mindreading that most find intuitive *(Is that face conveying a happy smile, a self-satisfied smirk, or a contemptuous sneer?)* is difficult for those with autism. Most children learn that another child's pouting mouth signals sadness, and that twinkling eyes mean happiness or mischief. A child with autism fails to understand these signals (Frith & Frith, 2001).

To encompass the variations in autism, today's researchers refer to *Autism spectrum disorder*. One variation in this spectrum is *Asperger syndrome*, a "high-functioning" form of autism. Asperger syndrome is marked by normal intelligence, often accompanied by exceptional skill or talent in a specific area, but deficient social and communication skills (and thus an inability to form normal peer relationships).

Psychologist Simon Baron-Cohen (2008) proposes that autism, which afflicts four boys for every girl, represents an "extreme male brain." Girls are naturally predisposed to be "empathizers," he contends. They are better at reading facial expressions and gestures—a challenging task for those with autism. And, although the sexes overlap, boys are, he believes, better "systemizers"—understanding things according to rules or laws, as in mathematical and mechanical systems.

"If two 'systemizers' have a child, this will increase the risk of the child having autism," Baron-Cohen theorizes. And because of *assortative mating*—people's tendency to seek spouses who share their interests—two systemizers will indeed often mate. "I do not discount environmental factors," he notes. "I'm just saying, don't forget about biology."

Biology's influence appears in studies of identical twins. If one twin is diagnosed with autism, the chances are 70 percent that the identical co-twin will be as well (Sebat et al., 2007). The younger sibling of a child with autism also is at a heightened risk of 15 percent or so (Sutcliffe, 2008). Random genetic mutations in sperm-producing cells may also play a role. As men age, these mutations become more frequent, which may help explain why an over-40 man has a much higher risk of father-

---

::autism a disorder that appears in childhood and is marked by deficient communication, social interaction, and understanding of others' states of mind.

However, today's researchers see development as more continuous than did Piaget. By detecting the beginnings of each type of thinking at earlier ages, they have revealed conceptual abilities Piaget missed. Moreover, they see formal logic as a smaller part of cognition than he did. Piaget would not be surprised that today, as part of our own cognitive development, we are adapting his ideas to accommodate new findings.

Piaget's emphasis on how the child's mind grows through interaction with the physical environment is complemented by Vygotsky's emphasis on how the child's mind grows through interaction with the *social* environment. If Piaget's child was a

---

TEACHING TIP

The American Psychiatric Association's new *Diagnostic and Statistical Manual of Mental Disorders, Volume 5*, which is now scheduled to be published in 2013, may change the criteria for diagnosing autism disorders. Instead of differentiating among many types of autism, the *DSM-V* may collapse all autistic disorders into a category called Autism Spectrum Disorders. Asperger's syndrome, a form of high-functioning autism, may no longer be included in the new manual.

ing a child with autism than does a man under 30 (Reichenberg et al., 2007). Genetic influences appear to do their damage by altering brain synapses (Crawley, 2007; Garber, 2007).

Biology's role in autism also appears in studies comparing the brain's functioning in those with and without autism. People without autism often yawn after seeing others yawn. And as they view and imitate another's smiling or frowning, they feel something of what the other is feeling, thanks to their brain's *mirror neurons* (Unit 6). Not so among those with autism, who are less imitative and whose brain areas involved in mirroring others' actions are much less active (Dapretto et al., 2006; Perra et al., 2008; Senju et al., 2007). For example, when people with autism watch another person's hand movements, their brain displays less than normal mirroring activity (Oberman & Ramachandran, 2007; Théoret et al., 2005).

Such discoveries have launched explorations of treatments that might alleviate some of autism's symptoms by triggering mirror neuron activity (Ramachandran & Oberman, 2006). For example, seeking to "systemize empathy," Baron-Cohen and his Cambridge University colleagues (2007; Golan et al., 2007)

collaborated with Britain's National Autistic Society and a film production company. Knowing that television shows with vehicles have been most popular for kids with autism, they created a series of animations that graft emotion-conveying faces onto toy tram, train, and tractor characters in a pretend boy's bedroom (**FIGURE 9.16**). After the boy leaves for school, the characters come to life and have experiences that lead them to display various emotions (which I predict you would enjoy viewing at www.thetransporters.com). The children expressed a surprising ability to generalize what they had learned to a new, real context. By the end of the intervention, their previously deficient ability to recognize emotions on real faces now equaled that of children without autism.

(a) Emotion-conveying faces grafted onto toy trains

➤ **FIGURE 9.16**

Transported into a world of emotion (a) A research team at Cambridge University's Autism Research Centre introduced children with autism to emotions experienced and displayed by toy vehicles. (b) After four weeks of viewing animations, the children displayed a markedly increased ability to recognize emotions in human as well as the toy faces.

(b) Matching new scenes and faces (and data for two trials)

"The neighbor's dog has bitten people before. He is barking at Louise."

Point to the face that shows how Louise is feeling.

Accuracy scores

After intervention, children with autism become better able to identify which facial emotion matches the context.

Time 1   Time 2
■ Typical control   ■ Faces intervention

© Crown copyright MMVI, www.thetransporters.com, courtesy Changing Media Development

young scientist, Vygotsky's was a young apprentice. By mentoring children and giving them new words, parents and others provide a temporary *scaffold* from which children can step to higher levels of thinking (Renninger & Granott, 2005). Language, an important ingredient of social mentoring, provides the building blocks for thinking, noted Vygotsky (who was born the same year as Piaget, but died prematurely of tuberculosis). Effective mentoring occurs when children are developmentally ready to learn a new skill. For Vygotsky, a child's *zone of proximal development* was the zone between what they could learn with and without help.

TEACHING TIP

Lev Vygotsky was a pioneer of developmental psychology, but he has been less known in the West than Piaget. One of Vygotsky's contributions to development psychology is his description of the *zone of proximal development*. Vygotsky believed that children learn best by interacting with others. In fact, children will not likely move to the next level of understanding without help from peers or role models. The peer/role model influence helps the child move through the development zone to the next level of understanding.

Explain to students that if they are trying to approach a child with stranger anxiety, they should keep the following in mind:

- *Get permission from his or her parent before approaching.* If the parent greets you in a positive way, the child will be more likely to view you as friendly.

- *Approach the child on his or her level.* Crouch down to the child's eye level so he or she doesn't feel intimidated by your height.

- *Ask him or her to interact with you in a casual way.* For example, ask the child to give you "five" or to tell you what kittens say.

- *If the child is very shy or nervous around you, back off and play with his or her toys.* The child will soon get over his or her inhibitions and play with you.

::**stranger anxiety** the fear of strangers that infants commonly display, beginning by about 8 months of age.

::**attachment** an emotional tie with another person; shown in young children by their seeking closeness to the caregiver and showing distress on separation.

::**critical period** an optimal period shortly after birth when an organism's exposure to certain stimuli or experiences produces proper development.

::**imprinting** the process by which certain animals form attachments during a critical period very early in life.

Stranger anxiety A newly emerging ability to evaluate people as unfamiliar and possibly threatening helps protect babies 8 months and older. ▲

Implications for Parents and Teachers Future parents and teachers remember: Young children are incapable of adult logic. Preschoolers find it easier to follow positive instructions ("Hold the puppy gently") than negative ones ("Don't squeeze the puppy"). Preschoolers who stand in the way when others are trying to watch TV simply have not learned to take another's viewpoint. What seems simple and obvious to us—getting off a teeter-totter will cause a friend on the other end to crash—may be incomprehensible to a 3-year-old. Also remember that children are not passive receptacles waiting to be filled with knowledge. Better to build on what they already know, engaging them in concrete demonstrations and stimulating them to think for themselves. And, finally, accept children's cognitive immaturity as adaptive. It is nature's strategy for keeping children close to protective adults and providing time for learning and socialization (Bjorklund & Green, 1992).

Social Development

5: How do parent-infant attachment bonds form?

From birth, babies in all cultures are social creatures, developing an intense bond with their caregivers. Infants come to prefer familiar faces and voices, then to coo and gurgle when given their mother's or father's attention. Soon after object permanence emerges and children become mobile, a curious thing happens. At about 8 months, they develop **stranger anxiety.** They may greet strangers by crying and reaching for familiar caregivers. "No! Don't leave me!" their distress seems to say. At about this age, children have schemas for familiar faces; when they cannot assimilate the new face into these remembered schemas, they become distressed (Kagan, 1984). Once again, we see an important principle: *The brain, mind, and social-emotional behavior develop together.*

Origins of Attachment

By 12 months, infants typically cling tightly to a parent when they are frightened or expect separation. Reunited after being separated, they shower the parent with smiles and hugs. No social behavior is more striking than this intense and mutual infant-parent bond. This **attachment** bond is a powerful survival impulse that keeps infants close to their caregivers. Infants become attached to those—typically their parents—who are comfortable and familiar. For many years, developmental psychologists reasoned that infants became attached to those who satisfied their need for nourishment. It made sense. But an accidental finding overturned this explanation.

Body Contact During the 1950s, University of Wisconsin psychologists Harry Harlow and Margaret Harlow bred monkeys for their learning studies. To equalize the infant monkeys' experiences and to isolate any disease, they separated them from their mothers shortly after birth and raised them in sanitary individual cages, which included a cheesecloth baby blanket (Harlow et al., 1971). Then came a surprise: When their blankets were taken to be laundered, the monkeys became distressed.

The Harlows recognized that this intense attachment to the blanket contradicted the idea that attachment derives from an association with nourishment. But how could they show this more convincingly? To pit the drawing power of a food source against the contact comfort of the blanket, they created two artificial mothers. One was a bare wire cylinder with a wooden head and an attached feeding bottle, the other a cylinder wrapped with terry cloth.

When raised with both, the monkeys overwhelmingly preferred the comfy cloth mother (**FIGURE 9.17**). Like human infants clinging to their mothers, the monkeys would cling to their cloth mothers when anxious. When venturing into the environment,

The Harlows' work on parental love came about during a time when psychologists and physicians believed that isolating children would protect them from disease. The Harlows went against the establishment in psychology, which at that time was centered on a behaviorist view—if it can't be seen, it shouldn't be studied.

they used her as a secure base, as if attached to her by an invisible elastic band that stretched only so far before pulling them back. Researchers soon learned that other qualities—rocking, warmth, and feeding—made the cloth mother even more appealing.

Human infants, too, become attached to parents who are soft and warm and who rock, feed, and pat. Much parent-infant emotional communication occurs via touch (Hertenstein et al., 2006), which can be either soothing (snuggles) or arousing (tickles). Human attachment also consists of one person providing another with a safe haven when distressed and a secure base from which to explore. As we mature, our secure base and safe haven shift—from parents to peers and partners (Cassidy & Shaver, 1999). But at all ages we are social creatures. We gain strength when someone offers, by words and actions, a safe haven: "I will be here. I am interested in you. Come what may, I will actively support you" (Crowell & Waters, 1994).

Familiarity Contact is one key to attachment. Another is familiarity. In many animals, attachments based on familiarity likewise form during a **critical period**—an optimal period when certain events must take place to facilitate proper development (Bornstein, 1989). For goslings, ducklings, or chicks, that period falls in the hours shortly after hatching, when the first moving object they see is normally their mother. From then on, the young fowl follow her, and her alone.

Konrad Lorenz (1937) explored this rigid attachment process, called **imprinting.** He wondered: What would ducklings do if he was the first moving creature they observed? What they did was follow him around: Everywhere that Konrad went, the ducks were sure to go. Further tests revealed that although baby birds imprint best to their own species, they also will imprint to a variety of moving objects—an animal of another species, a box on wheels, a bouncing ball (Colombo, 1982; Johnson, 1992). And, once formed, this attachment is difficult to reverse.

Children—unlike ducklings—do not imprint. However, they do become attached during a less precisely defined *sensitive period* to what they've known. *Mere exposure* to people and things fosters fondness (see Unit 14). Children like to reread the same books, rewatch the same movies, reenact family traditions. They prefer to eat familiar foods, live in the same familiar neighborhood, attend school with the same old friends. Familiarity is a safety signal. Familiarity breeds content.

Attachment Differences: Temperament and Parenting

6: How have psychologists studied attachment differences, and what have they learned about the effects of temperament and parenting?

What accounts for children's attachment differences? Placed in a *strange situation* (usually a laboratory playroom), about 60 percent of infants display *secure attachment.* In

➤ FIGURE 9.17
The Harlows' mothers
Psychologists Harry Harlow and Margaret Harlow raised monkeys with two artificial mothers—one a bare wire cylinder with a wooden head and an attached feeding bottle, the other a cylinder with no bottle but covered with foam rubber and wrapped with terry cloth. The Harlows' discovery surprised many psychologists: The infants much preferred contact with the comfortable cloth mother, even while feeding from the nourishing mother.

Harlow Primate Laboratory, University of Wisconsin

● Lee Kirkpatrick (1999) reports that for some people a perceived relationship with God functions as do other attachments, by providing a secure base for exploration and a safe haven when threatened. ●

Alastair Miller

Attachment When French pilot Christian Moullec took off in his microlight plane, his imprinted geese, which he had raised since their hatching, followed closely.

RESEARCH

The Harlows went further in their research and studied the effects of abuse and neglect on infants. They would subject their monkeys to isolation, neglect, and even abuse to see if they adapted and what their responses would be. Have students explore these issues that the Harlows' research uncovered:

● Should the same ethical constraints be imposed on animal research that exist for human subjects? Why or why not?

● Did the Harlows' studies imply that women should be the primary caregivers for infants? Why or why not?

INTERCONNECTING

Link *familiarity* to social psychology by reminding students that the concept relates to the principle of the mere exposure effect. This effect demonstrates that being around an object long enough will cause one to develop an affection for the object. We tend to find objects, people, and places appealing and comfortable because we are around these things for extended periods of time.

RESEARCH

Have students explore the relationship between premature birth and parental contact. Have them interview a local obstetrician, pediatrician, or neonatal physician about the health care procedures for infants born prematurely, both in the past and today.

● What illnesses are premature infants prone to?

● How can human contact affect a newborn's health? What biological processes does human contact seem to impact?

TEACHING TIP

Mary Ainsworth worked for much of her career with John Bowlby, another leading figure in developmental psychology. It was Bowlby who developed the idea of separation anxiety. He believed this feeling was different from fear, which resulted from environmental cues, and different from anger or hostility, which resulted from being rejected by parents and family.

At this time, you may want to use **Lecture/Discussion Topic: Attachment Style, Compassion, and Self-Esteem** (p. 14) or **Classroom Exercise/Student Project: Measures of Attachment Type** (p. 13) from Bolt's Teacher's Resource Binder.

➤ **FIGURE 9.18**
Social deprivation and fear Monkeys raised with artificial mothers were terror-stricken when placed in strange situations without their surrogate mothers. (Today's climate of greater respect for animal welfare prevents such primate studies.)

"Oh, he's cute, all right, but he's got the temperament of a car alarm."

their mother's presence they play comfortably, happily exploring their new environment. When she leaves, they are distressed; when she returns, they seek contact with her. Other infants avoid attachment or show *insecure attachment.* They are less likely to explore their surroundings; they may even cling to their mother. When she leaves, they either cry loudly and remain upset or seem indifferent to her departure and return (Ainsworth, 1973, 1989; Kagan, 1995; van IJzendoorn & Kroonenberg, 1988).

Mary Ainsworth (1979), who designed the strange situation experiments, studied attachment differences by observing mother-infant pairs at home during their first six months. Later she observed the 1-year-old infants in a strange situation without their mothers. Sensitive, responsive mothers—those who noticed what their babies were doing and responded appropriately—had infants who exhibited secure attachment. Insensitive, unresponsive mothers—mothers who attended to their babies when they felt like doing so but ignored them at other times—had infants who often became insecurely attached. The Harlows' monkey studies, with unresponsive artificial mothers, produced even more striking effects. When put in strange situations without their artificial mothers, the deprived infants were terrified (**FIGURE 9.18**).

Follow-up studies have confirmed that sensitive mothers—and fathers—tend to have securely attached infants (De Wolff & van IJzendoorn, 1997). But what explains the correlation? Is attachment style the *result* of parenting? Or is attachment style the result of genetically influenced **temperament**—a person's characteristic emotional reactivity and intensity?

As most parents will tell you after having their second child, babies differ even before gulping their first breath. One quickly apparent aspect of personality is an infant's temperament—whether reactive, intense, and fidgety, or easygoing, quiet, and placid. From the first weeks of life, *difficult* babies are more irritable, intense, and unpredictable. *Easy* babies are cheerful, relaxed, and predictable in feeding and sleeping. *Slow-to-warm-up* infants tend to resist or withdraw from new people and situations (Chess & Thomas, 1987; Thomas & Chess, 1977).

Temperament differences tend to persist. Consider:

- The most emotionally reactive newborns tend also to be the most reactive 9-month-olds (Wilson & Matheny, 1986; Worobey & Blajda, 1989).
- Exceptionally inhibited and fearful 2-year-olds often are still relatively shy as 8-year-olds; about half will become introverted adolescents (Kagan et al., 1992, 1994).
- The most emotionally intense preschoolers tend to be relatively intense young adults (Larsen & Diener, 1987). In one study of more than 900 New Zealanders, emotionally reactive and impulsive 3-year-olds developed into somewhat more impulsive, aggressive, and conflict-prone 21-year-olds (Caspi, 2000).

Heredity predisposes temperament differences (Rothbart, 2007). As we have seen, identical twins have more similar personalities, including temperament, than do fraternal twins. Physiological tests reveal that anxious, inhibited infants have high and variable heart rates and a reactive nervous system, and that they become more physiologically aroused when facing new or strange situations (Kagan & Snidman, 2004). One form of a gene that regulates the neurotransmitter serotonin predisposes a fearful temperament and, in combination with unsupportive caregiving, an inhibited child (Fox et al., 2007). Such evidence adds to the emerging conclusion that our biologically rooted temperament helps form our enduring personality (McCrae et al., 2000, 2007; Rothbart et al., 2000).

By neglecting such inborn differences, chides Judith Harris (1998), the parenting studies are like "comparing foxhounds reared in kennels with poodles reared in apartments." So, to separate nature and nurture, Dutch researcher Dymphna van den Boom (1990, 1995) varied parenting while controlling temperament. (Pause and think: If you were the researcher, how might you have done this?)

 TROUBLESHOOTING

It is important to remind students that children are usually distressed when their parents leave them, so being distressed at a parent's absence is not a sign of weak attachment. How infants behave when their parents are absent and how they react when their parents return from being absent indicates the level of attachment.

Van den Boom's solution was to randomly assign one hundred 6-to 9-month-old temperamentally difficult infants to either an experimental condition, in which mothers received personal training in sensitive responding, or to a control condition in which they did not. At 12 months of age, 68 percent of the experimental-condition infants were rated securely attached, as were only 28 percent of the control-condition infants. Other studies have also found that intervention programs can increase parental sensitivity and, to a lesser extent, infant attachment security (Bakermans-Kranenburg et al., 2003; Van Zeijl et al., 2006).

As these examples indicate, researchers have more often studied mother care than father care. Infants who lack a caring mother are said to suffer "maternal deprivation"; those lacking a father's care merely experience "father absence." This reflects a wider attitude in which "fathering a child" has meant impregnating, and "mothering" has meant nurturing. But fathers are more than just mobile sperm banks. Across nearly 100 studies worldwide, a father's love and acceptance have been comparable to a mother's love in predicting their offspring's health and well-being (Rohner & Veneziano, 2001). In one mammoth British study following 7259 children from birth to adulthood, those whose fathers were most involved in parenting (through outings, reading to them, and taking an interest in their education) tended to achieve more in school, even after controlling for many other factors, such as parental education and family wealth (Flouri & Buchanan, 2004).

Whether children live with one parent or two, are cared for at home or in a day-care center, live in North America, Guatemala, or the Kalahari Desert, their anxiety over separation from parents peaks at around 13 months, then gradually declines (**FIGURE 9.19**). Does this mean our need for and love of others also fades away? Hardly. Our capacity for love grows, and our pleasure in touching and holding those we love never ceases. The power of early attachment does nonetheless gradually relax, allowing us to move out into a wider range of situations, communicate with strangers more freely, and stay emotionally attached to loved ones despite distance.

Developmental theorist Erik Erikson (1902–1994), working in collaboration with his wife, Joan Erikson, said that securely attached children approach life with a sense of **basic trust**—a sense that the world is predictable and reliable. He attributed basic trust not to environment or inborn temperament, but to early parenting. He theorized that infants blessed with sensitive, loving caregivers form a lifelong attitude of trust rather than fear. (Later we'll consider Erikson's other stages of development.)

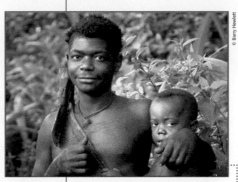
Fantastic father Among the Aka people of Central Africa, fathers form an especially close bond with their infants, even suckling the babies with their own nipples when hunger makes the child impatient for Mother's return. According to anthropologist Barry Hewlett (1991), fathers in this culture are holding or within reach of their babies 47 percent of the time.

> "We need fathers to realize that responsibility does not end at conception. We need them to realize that what makes you a man is not the ability to have a child—it's the courage to raise one."
> Barack Obama, Father's Day sermon, 2008

> "Out of the conflict between trust and mistrust, the infant develops hope, which is the earliest form of what gradually becomes faith in adults."
> Erik Erikson (1983)

➤ **FIGURE 9.19 Infants' distress over separation from parents** In an experiment, groups of infants were left by their mothers in an unfamiliar room. In both groups, the percentage who cried when the mother left peaked at about 13 months. Whether the infant had experienced day care made little difference. (From Kagan, 1976.)

::**temperament** a person's characteristic emotional reactivity and intensity.

::**basic trust** according to Erik Erikson, a sense that the world is predictable and trustworthy; said to be formed during infancy by appropriate experiences with responsive caregivers.

TEACHING TIP

Mary Ainsworth instituted an experimental procedure called the "Strange Situation" to study attachment. Parent and infant are introduced alone to the room. Parent watches while infant explores. Then, Stranger enters, talks with Parent, then approaches infant. Parent leaves inconspicuously.

- *First separation episode:* Stranger's behavior is geared to that of infant.
- *First reunion episode:* Parent greets and comforts infant, then leaves again.
- *Second separation episode:* Infant is alone.
- *Continuation of second separation episode:* Stranger enters and gears behavior to that of infant.
- *Second reunion episode:* Parent enters, greets infant, and picks up infant; stranger leaves inconspicuously.

Ainsworth, M. D. S., Blehar, M. C., Waters, E., & Wall, S. (1978). *Patterns of attachment: A psychological study of the strange situation.* Hillsdale, N.J.: Erlbaum.

TEACHING TIP

Ainsworth suggested two main types of attachment—secure and insecure. Parents who are slow or inconsistent in their responses to their children can foster insecure attachments. Have students explore advice available to new parents about attachment:

- How can parents balance response to needs and a concern with spoiling their babies?
- Do babies cry in different ways to express different needs? How can parents know when their child is crying for a need or crying for attention?
- How can parents foster an easy transition to childcare?

UNIT 9

International adoptions are on the rise in recent years, and concerns about the quality of care in orphanages in foreign countries has increased as adoptive parents must overcome neglect and ill treatment suffered by their new children. Have students explore the policies for international adoptions and the quality of childcare in orphanages in different countries around the world.

Spanking has become a controversial issue in parenting today. Have students research and discuss the following questions related to spanking:

- Should parents spank their children? When, why, and under what conditions? Why not?

- Do states have laws making a distinction between spanking and abuse? What are the distinctions?

Although debate continues, many researchers now believe that our early attachments form the foundation for our adult relationships and our comfort with affection and intimacy (Birnbaum et al., 2006; Fraley, 2002). Adult styles of romantic love do tend to exhibit secure, trusting attachment; insecure, anxious attachment; or the avoidance of attachment (Feeney & Noller, 1990; Shaver & Mikulincer, 2007; Rholes & Simpson, 2004). Moreover, these adult attachment styles in turn affect relationships with our children, as avoidant people find parenting more stressful and unsatisfying (Rholes et al., 2006). Attachment style is also associated with motivation, note Andrew Elliot and Harry Reis (2003). Securely attached people exhibit less fear of failure and a greater drive to achieve.

Deprivation of Attachment

7: Do parental neglect, family disruption, or day care affect children's attachments?

If secure attachment nurtures social competence, what happens when circumstances prevent a child from forming attachments? In all of psychology, there is no sadder research literature. Babies reared in institutions without the stimulation and attention of a regular caregiver, or locked away at home under conditions of abuse or extreme neglect, are often withdrawn, frightened, even speechless. Those abandoned in Romanian orphanages during the 1980s looked "frighteningly like [the Harlows'] monkeys" (Carlson, 1995). If institutionalized more than 8 months, they often bore lasting emotional scars (Chisholm, 1998; Malinosky-Rummell & Hansen, 1993; Rutter et al., 1998).

The Harlows' monkeys bore similar scars if reared in total isolation, without even an artificial mother. As adults, when placed with other monkeys their age, they either cowered in fright or lashed out in aggression. When they reached sexual maturity, most were incapable of mating. If artificially impregnated, females often were neglectful, abusive, even murderous toward their first-born. An experiment with primates confirms the abuse-breeds-abuse phenomenon. Whether reared by biological or adoptive mothers, 9 of 16 females who were abused by their mothers became abusive parents, as did no female reared by a nonabusive mother (Maestripieri, 2005).

In humans, too, the unloved sometimes become the unloving. Most abusive parents—and many condemned murderers—report having been neglected or battered as children (Kempe & Kempe, 1978; Lewis et al., 1988). But does this mean that today's victim is predictably tomorrow's victimizer? No. Though most abusers were indeed abused, most abused children do *not* later become violent criminals or abusive parents. Most children growing up under adversity (as did the surviving children of the Holocaust) are *resilient*; they become normal adults (Helmreich, 1992; Masten, 2001).

But others, especially those who experience no sharp break from their abusive past, don't bounce back so readily. Some 30 percent of people who have been abused do abuse their children—a rate lower than that found in the primate study, but four times the U.S. national rate of child abuse (Dumont et al., 2007; Kaufman & Zigler, 1987; Widom, 1989a,b).

Extreme early trauma seems to leave footprints on the brain. If repeatedly threatened and attacked while young, normally placid golden hamsters grow up to be cowards when caged with same-sized hamsters, or bullies when caged with weaker ones (Ferris, 1996). Such animals show changes in the brain chemical serotonin, which calms aggressive impulses. A similarly sluggish serotonin response has been found in abused children who become aggressive teens and adults. "Stress can set off a ripple of hormonal changes that permanently wire a child's brain to cope with a malevolent world," concludes abuse researcher Martin Teicher (2002).

> "What is learned in the cradle, lasts to the grave."
>
> French proverb

At this time, you may want to use **Feature Film and Lecture/Discussion Topic:** *Places in the Heart* and *Spanking* (p. 17) from Bolt's Teacher's Resource Binder.

Such findings help explain why young children terrorized through physical abuse or wartime atrocities (being beaten, witnessing torture, and living in constant fear) may suffer other lasting wounds—often nightmares, depression, and an adolescence troubled by substance abuse, binge eating, or aggression (Kendall-Tackett et al., 1993, 2004; Polusny & Follette, 1995; Trickett & McBride-Chang, 1995). Child sexual abuse, especially if severe and prolonged, places children at increased risk for health problems, psychological disorders, substance abuse, and criminality (Freyd et al., 2005; Tyler, 2002). Abuse victims are at considerable risk for depression *if* they carry a gene variation that spurs stress-hormone production (Bradley et al., 2008). As we will see again and again, behavior and emotion arise from a particular environment interacting with particular genes.

Disruption of Attachment What happens to an infant when attachment is disrupted? Separated from their families, infants—both monkeys and humans—become upset and, before long, withdrawn and even despairing (Bowlby, 1973; Mineka & Suomi, 1978). Fearing that the stress of separation might cause lasting damage (and when in doubt, acting to protect parents' rights), courts are usually reluctant to remove children from their homes.

If placed in a more positive and stable environment, most infants recover from the separation distress. In studies of adopted children, Leon Yarrow and his co-workers (1973) found that when children between 6 and 16 months of age were removed from their foster mothers, they initially had difficulties eating, sleeping, and relating to their new mothers. But when these children were studied at age 10, little visible effect remained. Thus, they fared no worse than children placed before the age of 6 months (with little accompanying distress). Likewise, socially deprived but adequately nourished Romanian orphans who were adopted into a loving home during infancy or early childhood usually progressed rapidly, especially in their cognitive development. If removed and adopted after age 2, however, they were at risk for attachment problems. Foster care that prevents attachment by moving a child through a series of foster families can be very disruptive. So can repeated and prolonged removals from a mother.

Adults also suffer when attachment bonds are severed. Whether through death or separation, a break produces a predictable sequence. Agitated preoccupation with the lost partner is followed by deep sadness and, eventually, the beginnings of emotional detachment and a return to normal living (Hazan & Shaver, 1994). Newly separated couples who have long ago ceased feeling affection are sometimes surprised at their desire to be near the former partner. Deep and longstanding attachments seldom break quickly. Detaching is a process, not an event.

Does Day Care Affect Attachment? In the mid-twentieth century, when Mom-at-home was the social norm, researchers asked, "Is day care bad for children? Does it disrupt children's attachments to their parents?" For the high-quality day-care programs usually studied, the answer was *no*. In *Mother Care/Other Care*, developmental psychologist Sandra Scarr (1986) explained that children are "biologically sturdy individuals . . . who can thrive in a wide variety of life situations." Scarr spoke for many developmental psychologists, whose research has uncovered no major impact of maternal employment on children's development (Erel et al., 2000; Goldberg et al., 2008).

Research then shifted to the effects of differing quality of day care on different types and ages of children. Scarr (1997) explained: Around the world, "high-quality child care consists of warm, supportive interactions with adults in a safe, healthy, and stimulating environment. . . . Poor care is boring and unresponsive to children's needs." Newer research not only confirms that day-care quality matters, but also finds that family poverty often consigns children to lower-quality day care, as well as more family instability and turmoil, more authoritarian parenting (imposing strict rules and demanding obedience), more time in front of the television, and less access to books (Love et al., 2003; Evans, 2004).

An example of high-quality day care Research has shown that young children thrive socially and intellectually in safe, stimulating environments with a ratio of one caregiver for every three or four children.

INTERCONNECTING

Myers mentions that avoidant people find parenting more stressful. One type of personality disorder is avoidant personality, in which people shun relationships with others and avoid social situations. They find socializing with others so uncomfortable that they would rather be alone than around people.

TROUBLESHOOTING

Some of your students may have been—or currently are—victims of abuse from their parents or caregivers. Be sensitive to this reality and help students see that the cycle of abuse does not have to continue.

TEACHING TIP

At this time, you may want to use **Classroom Exercises:** *EAS Temperament Survey* (p. 15) or *Dimensions of Parenting* (p. 16) or *Parental Authority Questionnaire* (p. 16) or *Parenting and Children's Traits* (p. 18) from Bolt's Teacher's Resource Binder.

UNIT 9

CRITICAL THINKING

CRITICAL THINKING

Structure a formal or informal debate about the impact of nature and/or nurture in childrearing. Since evidence exists for both, the debate should be lively. Some resolutions students may debate include:

- People born with learning disabilities can only expect a certain level of achievement in school.

- Children in daycare are more likely to be behavior problems at home and at school.

- Children born in poverty are more likely to be poor learners.

 TEACHING TIP

Children who are adopted from orphanages may be behind in their physical development. They may be underweight and lack muscle control. However, once adopted, these children typically catch up in development, due to better nutrition and more attentive care.

::**self-concept** our understanding and evaluation of who we are.

One ongoing study in 10 American cities has followed 1100 children since the age of 1 month. The researchers found that at ages 4½ to 6, those children who had spent the most time in day care had slightly advanced thinking and language skills. They also had an increased rate of aggressiveness and defiance (NICHD, 2002, 2003, 2006). To developmental psychologist Eleanor Maccoby (2003), the positive correlation between increased rate of problem behaviors and time spent in child care suggests "some risk for some children spending extended time in some day-care settings as they're now organized." But the child's temperament, the parents' sensitivity, and the family's economic and educational level mattered more than time spent in day care.

To be a day-care researcher and "to follow the data" can be controversial, notes researcher Jay Belsky (2003). Both opponents and advocates of day care have strong feelings. "As a result," says Belsky, "the scientist who is willing to report unpopular results is all too frequently blamed for generating them." Just as weather forecasters can report rain but love sunshine, so scientists aim to reveal and report the way things are, even when they wish it were otherwise.

Children's ability to thrive under varied types of responsive caregiving should not surprise us, given cultural variations in attachment patterns. Westernized attachment features one or two caregivers and their offspring. In other cultures, such as the Efe of Zaire, multiple caregivers are the norm (Field, 1996; Whaley et al., 2002). Even before the mother holds her newborn, the baby is passed among several women. In the weeks to come, the infant will be constantly held (and fed) by other women. The result is strong multiple attachments. As an African proverb says, "It takes a village to raise a child."

There is little disagreement that the many preschool children left *alone* for part of their parents' working hours deserve better. So do the children who merely exist for 9 hours a day in minimally equipped, understaffed centers. What all children need is a consistent, warm relationship with people whom they can learn to trust. The importance of such relationships extends beyond the preschool years, as Finnish psychologist Lea Pulkkinen (2006) observed in her career-long study of 285 individuals tracked from age 8 to 42. Her observation that adult monitoring of children was associated with favorable outcomes led her to undertake, with support from Finland's parliament, a nationwide program of adult-supervised activities for all first and second graders (Pulkkinen, 2004; Rose, 2004).

Self-Concept

8: How do children's self-concepts develop, and how are children's traits related to parenting styles?

Self-awareness Mirror images fascinate infants from the age of about 6 months. Only at about 18 months, however, does the child recognize that the image in the mirror is "me."

Infancy's major social achievement is attachment. *Childhood's* major social achievement is a positive sense of self. By the end of childhood, at about age 12, most children have developed a **self-concept**—an understanding and assessment of who they are. (Their *self-esteem* is how they feel about who they are.) Parents often wonder when and how this sense of self develops. "Is my baby girl aware of herself—does she know she is a person distinct from everyone else?"

Of course we cannot ask the baby directly, but we can again capitalize on what she can do—letting her *behavior* provide clues to the beginnings of her self-awareness. In 1877, biologist Charles Darwin offered one idea: Self-awareness begins when we recognize ourselves in a mirror. By this indicator, self-recognition emerges gradually over about a year, starting in roughly the sixth month as the child reaches toward the mirror to touch her image as if it were another child (Courage & Howe, 2002; Damon & Hart, 1982, 1988, 1992).

But how can we know when the child recognizes that the girl in the mirror is indeed herself, not just an agreeable playmate? In a simple variation of the mirror procedure, researchers sneakily dabbed rouge on children's noses before placing them in front of the mirror. At about 15 to 18 months, children will begin to touch their own noses when they see the red spot in the mirror (Butterworth, 1992; Gallup & Suarez, 1986). Apparently, 18-month-olds have a schema of how their face should look, and they wonder, "What is that spot doing on *my* face?"

Beginning with this simple self-recognition, the child's self-concept gradually strengthens. By school age, children start to describe themselves in terms of their gender, group memberships, and psychological traits, and they compare themselves with other children (Newman & Ruble, 1988; Stipek, 1992). They come to see themselves as good and skillful in some ways but not others. They form a concept of which traits, ideally, they would like to have. By age 8 or 10, their self-image is quite stable.

As adolescents and adults, will our self-esteem be lower if we have experienced adoption? That's what Dutch researchers Femmie Juffer and Marinus van IJzendoorn (2007) predicted, given that some adopted children will have suffered early neglect or abuse, will know that their biological parents gave them up, and will often look different from their adoptive parents. To check their presumption, they mined data from 88 studies comparing the self-esteem scores of 10,977 adoptees and 33,862 nonadoptees. To their surprise, they found "no difference in self-esteem." This was true even for transracial and international adoptees. Many adoptees face challenges, the researchers acknowledge, but "supported by the large investment of adoptive families" they display resilience.

Children's views of themselves affect their actions. Children who form a positive self-concept are more confident, independent, optimistic, assertive, and sociable (Maccoby, 1980). This then raises important questions: How can parents encourage a positive yet realistic self-concept?

Parenting Styles

Some parents spank, some reason. Some are strict, some are lax. Some show little affection, some liberally hug and kiss. Do such differences in parenting styles affect children?

The most heavily researched aspect of parenting has been how, and to what extent, parents seek to control their children. Investigators have identified three parenting styles:

1. **Authoritarian** parents impose rules and expect obedience: "Don't interrupt." "Keep your room clean." "Don't stay out late or you'll be grounded." "Why? Because I said so."
2. **Permissive** parents submit to their children's desires. They make few demands and use little punishment.
3. **Authoritative** parents are both demanding and responsive. They exert control by setting rules and enforcing them, but they also explain the reasons for rules. And, especially with older children, they encourage open discussion when making the rules and allow exceptions.

Too hard, too soft, and just right, these styles have been called. Studies by Stanley Coopersmith (1967), Diana Baumrind (1996), and John Buri and others (1988) reveal that children with the highest self-esteem, self-reliance, and social competence usually have warm, concerned, *authoritative* parents. (Those with authoritarian parents tend to have less social skill and self-esteem, and those with permissive parents tend to be more aggressive and immature.) The participants in most studies have been middle-class White families, and some critics suggest that effective parenting may vary by culture. Yet

Self-aware animals After prolonged exposure to mirrors, several species—chimpanzees, orangutans, gorillas, dolphins, elephants, and magpies—have similarly demonstrated self-recognition of their mirror image (Gallup, 1970: Reiss & Marino, 2001; Prior et al., 2008). In an experiment by Joshua Plotnik and colleagues (2006), an Asian elephant, when facing a mirror, repeatedly used her trunk to touch an "X" painted above her eye (but not a similar mark above the other eye that was visible only under black light).

AP Photo/National Academy of Sciences, Courtesy of Joshua Plotnik, Frans de Waal, and Diana Reiss

INTERCONNECTING

Emphasize that correlational studies linking parenting style with certain childhood outcomes are not necessarily revealing cause and effect. For example, children's traits might influence parenting more than vice versa.

TEACHING TIP

Help students remember the different types of parenting styles by associating each with a famous historical figure:

- *Authoritarian* can be associated with any oppressive dictator, from Hitler to Hussein.
- *Permissive* can be associated with the "laissez-faire" type of government that Thomas Jefferson advocated.
- *Authoritative* can be associated with the U.S. President, who is a symbol of democracy, where individuals are expected to be rational and law-abiding.

UNIT 9

::**gender** in psychology, the biologically and socially influenced characteristics by which people define *male* and *female*.

CRITICAL THINKING

Have students discuss whether our temperament influences our caregivers, or whether our caregivers influence our temperament. According to the research cited here, a child's temperament may affect how their parents interact with them.

CULTURAL CONNECTIONS

Have students interview people from different cultures about the way they were reared. Have them compare and contrast childrearing practices in the United States with those of different cultures.

- Are the childrearing practices in the other culture, in general, better or worse than those in the United States?

- Which practices would you adopt for your own future children? Which would you reject? Why?

studies with families of other races and in more than 200 cultures worldwide confirm the social and academic correlates of loving and authoritative parenting (Rohner & Veneziano, 2001; Sorkhabi, 2005; Steinberg & Morris, 2001). And the effects are stronger when children are embedded in *authoritative communities* with connected adults who model a good life (Commission on Children at Risk, 2003).

A word of caution: The association between certain parenting styles (being firm but open) and certain childhood outcomes (social competence) is correlational. *Correlation is not causation.* Here are two possible alternative explanations for this parenting-competence link. (Can you imagine others?)

- Children's traits may influence parenting more than vice versa. Parental warmth and control vary somewhat from child to child, even in the same family (Holden & Miller, 1999). So perhaps socially mature, agreeable, easygoing children *evoke* greater trust and warmth from their parents, and less competent and less cooperative children elicit less. Twin studies support this possibility (Kendler, 1996).

- Some underlying third factor may be at work. Perhaps, for example, competent parents and their competent children share genes that predispose social competence. Twin studies also support this possibility (South et al., 2008).

Parents struggling with conflicting advice and with the stresses of child-rearing should remember that *all advice reflects the advice-giver's values.* For those who prize unquestioning obedience from a child, an authoritarian style may have the desired effect. For those who value children's sociability and self-reliance, authoritative firm-but-open parenting is advisable.

Culture and Child-Rearing

Child-rearing practices reflect cultural values that vary across time and place. Do you prefer children who are independent or children who comply? If you live in a Westernized culture, the odds are you prefer independence. "You are responsible for yourself," Western families and schools tell their children. "Follow your conscience. Be true to yourself. Discover your gifts. Set your own goals." A half-century and more ago, Western cultural values placed greater priority on obedience, respect, and sensitivity to others (Alwin, 1990; Remley, 1988). "Be true to your traditions," parents then taught their children. "Be loyal to your heritage and country. Show respect toward your parents and other superiors." Cultures can change.

Many Asians and Africans live in cultures that value emotional closeness. Rather than being given their own bedrooms and entrusted to day care, infants and toddlers may sleep with their mothers and spend their days close to a family member (Morelli et al., 1992; Whiting & Edwards, 1988). These cultures encourage a strong sense of *family self*—a feeling that what shames the child shames the family, and what brings honor to the family brings honor to the self.

Cultures vary In Scotland's Orkney Islands' town of Stromness, social trust has enabled parents to park their toddlers outside of shops.

Copyright Steve Reeh

Children across place and time have thrived under various child-rearing systems. Upper-class British parents traditionally handed off routine caregiving to nannies, then sent their children off to boarding school at about age 10. These children generally grew up to be pillars of British society, just like their parents and their boarding-school peers. In the African Gusii society, babies nurse freely but spend most of the day on their mother's back—with lots of body contact but little face-to-face and language interaction. When the mother becomes pregnant, the toddler is weaned and handed over to someone else, often an older sibling. Westerners may wonder about the negative effects of this lack of verbal interaction, but then the African Gusii would in turn wonder about Western mothers pushing their babies around in strollers and leaving them in playpens and car seats

INTERCONNECTING

Connect this discussion of culture and child-rearing to Unit 14's discussion of individualist versus collectivist cultures. Collectivist cultures, such as those in Asia or Africa, often value communal connections and family over individual goals. Individualist cultures, such as the predominant culture in the United States and many European cultures, value individual goals and pride. The values people in these two orientations may pass on to their children would likely differ significantly.

(Small, 1997). Such diversity in child-rearing cautions us against presuming that our culture's way is the only way to rear children successfully.

Gender Development

As we saw in Unit 7B, we humans share an irresistible urge to organize our worlds into simple categories. Among the ways we classify people—as tall or short, fat or slim, smart or dull—one stands out: At your birth, everyone wanted to know, "Boy or girl?" Our biological sex in turn helps define our **gender**, the biological and social characteristics by which people define *male* or *female*. Under the influence of our culture, our gender influences our social development.

Gender Similarities and Differences

9: What are some ways in which males and females tend to be alike and to differ?

Having faced similar adaptive challenges, we are in most ways alike. Men and women are not from different planets—Mars and Venus—but from the same planet Earth. Tell me whether you are male or female and you give me virtually no clues to your vocabulary, intelligence, and happiness, or to the mechanisms by which you see, hear, learn, and remember. Your "opposite" sex is, in reality, your very similar sex. And should we be surprised? Among your 46 chromosomes, 45 are unisex.

But males and females also differ, and differences command attention. Some much-talked-about differences are actually quite modest, as Janet Hyde (2005) illustrated by graphically representing the gender difference in self-esteem scores, across many studies (**FIGURE 9.20**). Some differences are more striking. Compared with the average man, the average woman enters puberty two years sooner, lives five years longer, carries 70 percent more fat, has 40 percent less muscle, and is 5 inches shorter. Other gender differences appear throughout this book. Women smell fainter odors, express emotions more freely, and are offered help more often. They are doubly vulnerable to depression and anxiety, and their risk of developing eating disorders is 10 times greater. But then men are some 4 times more likely to commit suicide or suffer alcohol dependence. They are far more often diagnosed with autism, color-blindness, attention-deficit hyperactivity disorder (as children), and antisocial personality disorder (as adults). Choose your gender and pick your vulnerability.

Parental involvement promotes development Parents in every culture facilitate their children's discovery of their world, but cultures differ in what they deem important. Asian cultures place more emphasis on school and hard work than do North American cultures. This may help explain why Japanese and Taiwanese children get higher scores on mathematics achievement tests.

➤ **FIGURE 9.20**

Much ado about a small difference Janet Hyde (2005) shows us two normal distributions that differ by the approximate magnitude (0.21 standard deviations) of the gender difference in self-esteem, averaged over all available samples. Moreover, though we can identify gender differences, the variation among individual women and among individual men greatly exceeds the difference between the average woman and man.

Have students discuss what evolutionary advantages there might be for gender differences such as aggression and social connectedness. How might men who are aggressive be more likely to survive? How might women who are more socially connected be more likely to survive?

Have students use their knowledge of the development of stereotypes and prejudice to discuss why women may not hold many positions of power in governments around the world. Discuss how generalizations about women (they are moody due to hormones; they are too emotional) may contribute to this imbalance of power.

::**aggression** physical or verbal behavior intended to hurt someone.

• Women's 2009 representations in national parliaments ranged from 10% in the Arab States to 17% in the United States and 22% in Canada to 41% in Scandinavia (IPU, 2009). •

Every man for himself, or tend and befriend? Gender differences in the way we interact with others begin to appear at a very young age. ▲

How much does biology bend the genders? What portion of our differences is socially constructed—by the gender roles our culture assigns us, and by how we are socialized as children? To answer those questions, let's look more closely at some average gender differences in aggression, social power, and social connectedness.

Gender and Aggression In surveys, men admit to more **aggression** than do women, and experiments confirm that men tend to behave more aggressively, such as by administering what they believe are more painful electric shocks (Bettencourt & Kernahan, 1997). The aggression gender gap pertains to *physical* aggression (such as hitting) rather than verbal, *relational* aggression (such as excluding someone). The gender gap in physical aggression appears in everyday life at various ages and in various cultures, especially those with gender inequality (Archer, 2004, 2006). In dating relationships, violent acts (such as slaps and thrown objects) are often mutual (Straus, 2008). Violent crime rates more strikingly illustrate the gender difference. The male-to-female arrest ratio for murder, for example, is 10 to 1 in the United States and almost 7 to 1 in Canada (FBI, 2007; Statistics Canada, 2007).

Throughout the world, hunting, fighting, and warring are primarily men's activities (Wood & Eagly, 2002, 2007). Men also express more support for war. The Iraq war, for example, has consistently been supported more by American men than by American women (Newport et al., 2007).

Gender and Social Power Around the world, from Nigeria to New Zealand, people have perceived men as more dominant, forceful, and independent, women as more deferential, nurturant, and affiliative (Williams & Best, 1990). Indeed, in most societies men *are* socially dominant. When groups form, whether as juries or companies, leadership tends to go to males (Colarelli et al., 2006). Men worldwide place more importance on power and achievement (Schwartz & Rubel, 2005). As leaders, men tend to be more directive, even autocratic; women tend to be more democratic, more welcoming of subordinates' participation in decision making (Eagly & Carli, 2007; van Engen & Willemsen, 2004). When people interact, men are more likely to utter opinions, women to express support (Aries, 1987; Wood, 1987). These differences carry into everyday behavior, where men are more likely to act as powerful people often do—talking assertively, interrupting, initiating touches, staring more, and smiling less (Hall, 1987; Leaper & Ayres, 2007; Major et al., 1990).

Such behaviors help sustain social power inequities. When political leaders are elected, they usually are men, who held 82 percent of the seats in the world's governing parliaments in 2008 (IPU, 2009). When salaries are paid, those in traditionally male occupations receive more.

Gender and Social Connectedness To Carol Gilligan and her colleagues (1982, 1990), the "normal" struggle to create a separate identity describes Western individualist males more than relationship-oriented females. Gilligan believes females tend to differ from males both in being less concerned with viewing themselves as separate individuals and in being more concerned with "making connections."

These gender differences in connectedness surface early in children's play, and they continue with age. Boys typically play in large groups with an activity focus and little intimate discussion (Rose & Rudolph, 2006). Girls usually play in smaller groups, often with one friend. Their play is less competitive than boys' and more imitative of social relationships. Both in play and other settings, females are more open and responsive to feedback than are males (Maccoby, 1990; Roberts, 1991). Asked difficult questions—"Do you have any idea why the sky is blue?" "Do you have any idea why shorter people live longer?"—men are more likely than women to hazard answers rather than admit they don't know, a phenomenon Traci Giuliano and her colleagues (1998a,b) call the *male answer syndrome*.

Females are more *interdependent* than males. As teens, girls spend more time with friends and less time alone (Wong & Csikszentmihalyi, 1991). As late adolescents, they spend more time on social-networking Internet sites (Pryor et al., 2007). As adults, women take more pleasure in talking face-to-face, and they tend to use conversation more to explore relationships. Men enjoy doing activities side-by-side, and they tend to use conversation to communicate solutions (Tannen, 1990; Wright, 1989). The communication difference is apparent even in student e-mails, from which people in one New Zealand study could correctly guess the author's gender two-thirds of the time (Thomson & Murachver, 2001).

These gender differences are sometimes reflected in patterns of phone communication. In France, women make 63 percent of phone calls and, when talking to a woman, stay connected longer (7.2 minutes) than men do when talking to other men (4.6 minutes) (Smoreda & Licoppe, 2000). So, does this confirm the idea that women are just more talkative? To check that presumption, Matthias Mehl and his colleagues (2007) counted the number of words 396 college students spoke in the course of an average day. (How many words would you guess you speak a day?) They found that talkativeness varied enormously—by 45,000 words between their most and least talkative participants. But contrary to stereotypes of jabbering women, both men and women averaged about 16,000 words daily.

Women worldwide orient their interests and vocation more to people and less to things (Lippa, 2005, 2006, 2008). In the workplace, they often are less driven by money and status and are more likely to choose reduced work hours (Pinker, 2008). In the home, they provide most of the care to the very young and the very old. Women also purchase 85 percent of greeting cards (*Time*, 1997). Women's emphasis on caring helps explain another interesting finding: Although 69 percent of people say they have a close relationship with their father, 90 percent feel close to their mother (Hugick, 1989). When wanting understanding and someone with whom to share worries and hurts, both men and women usually turn to women, and both report their friendships with women to be more intimate, enjoyable, and nurturing (Rubin, 1985; Sapadin, 1988).

Bonds and feelings of support are even stronger among women than among men (Rossi & Rossi, 1993). Women's ties—as mothers, daughters, sisters, aunts, and grandmothers—bind families together. As friends, women talk more often and more openly (Berndt, 1992; Dindia & Allen, 1992). And when they themselves must cope with stress, women more than men turn to others for support—they *tend and befriend* (Tamres et al., 2002; Taylor, 2002).

As empowered people generally do, men value freedom and self-reliance, which helps explain why men of all ages, worldwide, are less religious (less God-focused) and pray less (Benson, 1992; Stark, 2002). Men also dominate the ranks of professional skeptics. All 10 winners and 14 runners-up on the *Skeptical Inquirer* list of outstanding twentieth-century rationalist skeptics were men. In the Science and the Paranormal section of the 2007 Prometheus Books catalog (from the leading publisher of skepticism), one can find 94 male and 4 female authors. In one Skeptics Society survey, nearly 4 in 5 respondents were men (Shermer, 1999). Women, it appears, are more open to spirituality (and are far more likely to author books on spirituality than on skepticism).

Gender differences in power, connectedness, and other traits peak in late adolescence and early adulthood—the very years most commonly studied (also the years of dating and mating). As teenagers, girls become progressively less assertive and more

• *Question:* Why does it take 200 million sperm to fertilize one egg? *Answer:* Because they won't stop for directions. •

RESEARCH

Have students take a sample of one day's postings on a social network site (Facebook, Twitter, Google Buzz, etc.) and count the number of posts by their male and female friends. Collect the data as a class to see if significant gender differences emerge.

RESEARCH

Have your students watch a video clip from a television show or movie. Then have them write a summary of what the clip was about. Students should only put their gender as identification on the paper. Collect these summaries and distribute them back to students randomly. Have students count the number of words used in the summary. They should add their data to a spreadsheet or whiteboard so you can calculate the differences in word usage between guys and girls.

TEACHING TIP

At this time, you may want to use **Classroom Exercises:** *Gender Roles in the Home* (p. 24) or *Learning Gender Roles* (p. 24) or *Sex-Role Egalitarianism Scale (SRES)* (p. 25) from Bolt's Teacher's Resource Binder.

TEACHING TIP

Sex-linked traits are those that are passed down to the child by the mother through the X chromosome. Typically, these traits are recessive, so when the father passes along another X chromosome (thus resulting in a female), his chromosome dominates the recessive gene. Therefore, most sex-linked traits are exhibited in males, since they only have one X chromosome. Color blindness is an example of this type of trait.

INTERCONNECTING

Use this content as a review of the concepts discussed in Unit 3B. Help students remember the parts of the brain that are responsible for various behaviors.

> "In the long years liker must they grow; The man be more of woman, she of man."
> Alfred Lord Tennyson, *The Princess*, 1847

Courtesy of Nick Downes.

::**X chromosome** the sex chromosome found in both men and women. Females have two X chromosomes; males have one. An X chromosome from each parent produces a female child.

::**Y chromosome** the sex chromosome found only in males. When paired with an X chromosome from the mother, it produces a male child.

::**testosterone** the most important of the male sex hormones. Both males and females have it, but the additional testosterone in males stimulates the growth of the male sex organs in the fetus and the development of the male sex characteristics during puberty.

---

flirtatious; boys become more domineering and unexpressive. But by age 50, these differences have diminished. Men become more empathic and less domineering and women, especially if working, become more assertive and self-confident (Kasen et al., 2006; Maccoby, 1998).

The Nature of Gender

10: How do nature and nurture together form our gender?

What explains our gender diversity? Is biology destiny? Are we shaped by our cultures? A biopsychosocial view suggests it is both, thanks to the interplay among our biological dispositions, our developmental experiences, and our current situations (Wood & Eagly, 2002, 2007).

In domains where men and women have faced similar challenges—regulating heat with sweat, developing tastes that nourish, growing calluses where the skin meets friction—the sexes are similar. Even when describing the ideal mate, both men and women put traits such as "kind," "honest," and "intelligent" at the top of their lists. But in domains pertinent to mating, evolutionary psychologists contend, guys act like guys whether they are elephants or elephant seals, rural peasants or corporate presidents. Such gender differences may be influenced genetically, by our differing *sex chromosomes* and, physiologically, from our differing concentrations of *sex hormones.*

Males and females are variations on a single form. Seven weeks after conception, you were anatomically indistinguishable from someone of the other sex. Then your genes activated your biological sex, which was determined by your twenty-third pair of chromosomes, the two sex chromosomes. From your mother, you received an **X chromosome.** From your father, you received the one chromosome out of 46 that is not unisex—either another X chromosome, making you a girl, or a **Y chromosome,** making you a boy. The Y chromosome includes a single gene that throws a master switch triggering the testes to develop and produce the principal male hormone, **testosterone.** Females also have testosterone, but less of it. The male's greater output of testosterone starts the development of external male sex organs at about the seventh week.

Another key period for sexual differentiation falls during the fourth and fifth prenatal months, when sex hormones bathe the fetal brain and influence its wiring. Different patterns for males and females develop under the influence of the male's greater testosterone and the female's ovarian hormones (Hines, 2004; Udry, 2000). Recent research confirms male-female differences during development in brain areas with abundant sex hormone receptors (Cahill, 2005). In adulthood, parts of the frontal lobes, an area involved in verbal fluency, are reportedly thicker in women. Part of the parietal cortex, a key area for space perception, is thicker in men. Other studies report gender differences in the hippocampus, the amygdala, and the volume of brain *gray matter* (the neural bodies) versus *white matter* (the axons and dendrites).

Given sex hormones' influence on development, what do you suppose happens when glandular malfunction or hormone injections expose a female embryo to excess testosterone? These genetically female infants are born with masculine-appearing genitals, which can either be accepted or altered surgically. Until puberty, such females tend to act in more aggressive "tomboyish" ways than do most girls, and they dress and play in ways more typical of boys than of girls (Berenbaum & Hines, 1992; Ehrhardt, 1987). Given a choice of toys, they (like boys) are more likely to play with cars and guns than with dolls and crayons. Most—like nearly all girls with traditionally feminine interests—become heterosexual. Moreover, the hormones do not reverse their gender identity; they view themselves as girls, not boys (Berenbaum & Bailey, 2003).

 TEACHING TIP

At this time, you may want to use **Lecture/Discussion Topics:** *Gender Differences in Personality?* (p. 19) or *Are Women More Social?* (p. 21) or *Innate Sex Differences* (p. 22) from Bolt's Teacher's Resource Binder.

Is the tomboyish behavior of these girls due to the prenatal hormones? If so, may we conclude that biological sex differences produce behavioral gender differences? Vervet monkeys seem to suggest one answer. Male vervets, like most little boys, will spend more time playing with "masculine" toys such as trucks, and female vervets, like most little girls, will choose "feminine" toys such as dolls (Hines, 2004). Moreover, experiments with many species, from rats to monkeys, confirm that female embryos given male hormones will later exhibit a typically masculine appearance and more aggressive behavior (Hines & Green, 1991). But a more complex picture emerges when we consider social influences. Girls who were prenatally exposed to excess testosterone frequently look masculine and are known to be "different," so perhaps people also treat them more like boys. Thus, the effect of early exposure to sex hormones is both direct, in the girl's biological appearance, and indirect, in the influence of social experiences that shape her. Like a sculptor's two hands shaping a lump of clay, nature and nurture work together.

"Sex matters," concludes the National Academy of Sciences (2001). In combination with the environment, sex-related genes and physiology "result in behavioral and cognitive differences between males and females."

The Nurture of Gender

Although biologically influenced, gender is also socially constructed. What biology initiates, culture accentuates.

Gender Roles Sex indeed matters. But from a biopsychosocial perspective, culture and the immediate situation matter, too. *Culture* is everything shared by a group and transmitted across generations. We can see culture's shaping power in the social expectations that guide men's and women's behavior. In psychology, as in the theater, a **role** refers to a cluster of prescribed actions—the behaviors we expect of those who occupy a particular social position. One set of norms defines our culture's **gender roles**—our expectations about the way men and women should behave. In the United States it has, especially in previous decades, traditionally been men who initiate dates, drive the car, and pick up the check, and women who decorate the home, buy and care for the children's clothes, and select the wedding gifts.

Gender roles exist outside the home, too. Compared with employed women, employed men in the United States spend about an hour and a half more on the job each day and about one hour less on household activities and caregiving (Amato et al., 2007; Bureau of Labor Statistics, 2004; Fisher et al., 2006). I do not have to tell you which parent, about 90 percent of the time in two-parent U.S. families, has stayed home with a sick child, arranged for the baby-sitter, or called the doctor (Maccoby, 1995). In Australia, women devote 54 percent more time to unpaid household work and 71 percent more time to child care than do men (Trewin, 2001).

Gender roles can smooth social relations, saving awkward decisions about who does the laundry this week and who mows the lawn. But they often do so at a cost: If we deviate from such conventions, we may feel anxious.

Do gender roles reflect what is biologically natural for men and women? Or do cultures construct them? Gender-role diversity over time and space indicates that culture has a big influence. Nomadic societies of food-gathering people have only a minimal division of labor by sex. Boys and girls receive much the same upbringing. In agricultural societies, where women work in the fields close to home, and men roam more freely herding livestock, children typically socialize into more distinct gender roles (Segall et al., 1990; Van Leeuwen, 1978).

::role a set of expectations (norms) about a social position, defining how those in the position ought to behave.

::gender role a set of expected behaviors for males or for females.

"Genes, by themselves, are like seeds dropped onto pavement: powerless to produce anything."
Primatologist Frans B. M. de Waal (1999)

"Sex brought us together, but gender drove us apart."

The gendered tsunami In Sri Lanka, Indonesia, and India, the gendered division of labor helps explain the excess of female deaths from the 2004 tsunami. In some villages, 80 percent of those killed were women, who were mostly at home while the men were more likely to be at sea fishing or doing out-of-the-home chores (Oxfam, 2005).

TEACHING TIP

Have students brainstorm about different gender expectations and roles they subscribe to in their generation. How many of these expectations and roles come from their parents? How many come from the prevailing culture? How many buck the trends of previous generations?

INTERCONNECTING

The anxiety we might feel when we do not follow social roles results from normative social influence (Unit 14). With normative social influence, people behave in ways that gain acceptance from others. When they do not behave in socially expected ways, others will shun them or disapprove, provoking feelings of anxiety.

TEACHING TIP

At this time, you may want to use **Lecture/Discussion Topics:** *Abnormal Sex Chromosome Patterns* (p. 22) or *Who Does the Housework?* (p. 23) from Bolt's Teacher's Resource Binder.

UNIT 9

Albert Bandura is a primary name to connect with social learning theory. He is one of the 20th century's most prolific and influential psychologists, providing psychology with not only social learning theory, but reciprocal determinism, self-efficacy, and social-cognitive theory.

Remind students that earlier in the unit they learned about Jean Piaget and his conceptualization of schemas. Students need to remember how schemas are developed—through the processes of assimilation and accommodation.

➤ **FIGURE 9.21**

Women and the professions Law, medicine, and psychology have been attracting more and more women. (Data from professional associations reported by A. Cynkar, 2007.)

"How is it gendered?"

Among industrialized countries, gender roles and attitudes vary widely (UNICEF, 2006). Australia and the Scandinavian countries offer the greatest gender equity, Middle Eastern and North African countries the least (Social Watch, 2006). And consider: Would you say life is more satisfying when both spouses work for pay and share child care? If so, you would agree with most people in 41 of 44 countries, according to a Pew Global Attitudes survey (2003). Even so, the culture-to-culture differences were huge, ranging from Egypt, where people disagreed 2 to 1, to Vietnam, where people agreed 11 to 1.

Attitudes about gender roles also vary over time. At the opening of the twentieth century, only one country—New Zealand—granted women the right to vote (Briscoe, 1997). By the late 1960s and early 1970s, with the flick of an apron, the number of U.S. college women hoping to be full-time homemakers had plunged. And in the three decades after 1976, the percentage of women in medical, law, and psychology programs roughly doubled (**FIGURE 9.21**).

Gender ideas vary not only across cultures and over time, but also across generations. When families emigrate from Asia to Canada and the United States, their children tend to grow up with peers from a new culture. Many immigrant children, especially girls, feel torn between the competing sets of gender-role norms presented by peers and parents (Dion & Dion, 2001).

Gender and Child-Rearing As society assigns each of us to a gender, the social category of male or female, the inevitable result is our strong **gender identity,** our sense of *being* male or female. To varying extents, we also become **gender typed.** That is, some boys more than others exhibit traditionally masculine traits and interests, and some girls more than others become distinctly feminine.

Social learning theory assumes that children learn gender-linked behaviors by observing and imitating and by being rewarded or punished. "Nicole, you're such a good mommy to your dolls"; "Big boys don't cry, Alex." But parental modeling and rewarding of male-female differences aren't enough to explain gender typing (Lytton & Romney, 1991). In fact, even when their families discourage traditional gender typing, children usually organize themselves into "boy worlds" and "girl worlds," each guided by rules for what boys and girls do.

Cognition (thinking) also matters. In your own childhood, as you struggled to comprehend the world, you—like other children—formed schemas that helped you make sense of your world. One of these was a schema for your own gender (Bem, 1987, 1993). Your *gender schema* then became a lens through which you viewed your experiences. Social learning shapes gender schemas. Before age 1, children begin to discriminate male and female voices and faces (Martin et al., 2002). After age 2, language forces children to begin organizing their worlds on the basis of gender. English, for example, uses the pronouns *he* and *she;* other languages classify objects as masculine ("*le* train") or feminine ("*la* table").

Young children are "gender detectives," explain Carol Lynn Martin and Diane Ruble (2004). Once they grasp that two sorts of people exist—and that they are of one sort—they search for clues about gender, and they find them in language, dress, toys, and songs. Girls, they may decide, are the ones with long hair. Having divided the human world in half, 3-year-olds will then like their own sex better and seek out their own kind for play. And having compared themselves with their concept of gender, they will adjust their behavior accordingly ("I am male—thus, masculine, strong, aggressive," or "I am female—therefore, feminine, sweet, and helpful"). The rigidity of boy-girl stereotypes peaks at about age 5 or 6. If the new neighbor is a boy, a 6-year-old girl may just assume he cannot share her interests. For young children, gender looms large.

➤ **ASK YOURSELF**

Do you consider yourself strongly gender typed or *not* strongly gender typed? What factors do you think have contributed to your feelings of masculinity or femininity?

➤ **TEST YOURSELF 3**

What are gender roles, and what do their variations tell us about our human capacity for learning and adaptation?

Answers to the Test Yourself questions can be found in Appendix E at the end of the book.

* * *

The investment in raising a child buys many years not only of joy and love but of worry and irritation. Yet for most people who become parents, a child is one's biological and social legacy—one's personal investment in the human future. Remind young adults of their mortality and they will express increased desire for children (Wisman & Goldenberg, 2005). To paraphrase psychiatrist Carl Jung, we reach backward into our parents and forward into our children, and through their children into a future we will never see, but about which we must therefore care.

> "You are the bows from which your children as living arrows are sent forth."
>
> Kahlil Gibran, *The Prophet*, 1923

Parents and Peers

11: To what extent is our development shaped by early stimulation, by parents, and by peers?

WE ARE NOT "BLANK SLATES," note Douglas Kenrick and his colleagues (2009). We are more like coloring books, with certain lines predisposed and experience filling in our picture. We are formed by nature *and* nurture. But what are the most influential components of our nurture? How do our early experiences, our family and peer relationships, and all our other experiences guide our development and contribute to our diversity?

Parents and Early Experiences

The formative nurture that conspires with nature begins at conception, as we have seen, with the prenatal environment in the womb. Embryos receive differing nutrition and varying levels of exposure to toxic agents. Nurture then continues outside the womb, where our early experiences foster brain development.

Experience and Brain Development

Our genes dictate our overall brain architecture, but experience fills in the details, developing neural connections and preparing our brain for thought and language and other later experiences. So how do early experiences leave their "marks" in the brain? Mark Rosenzweig and David Krech opened a window on that process when they raised some young rats in solitary confinement and others in a communal playground. When they later analyzed the rats' brains, those who died with the most toys had won. The rats living in the enriched environment, which simulated a natural environment, usually developed a heavier and thicker brain cortex (**FIGURE 9.22**, next page).

::**gender identity** our sense of being male or female.

::**gender typing** the acquisition of a traditional masculine or feminine role.

::**social learning theory** the theory that we learn social behavior by observing and imitating and by being rewarded or punished.

INTERCONNECTING

Remind students that it's not the size of the brain that matters—it's the complexity of it. Brains that are more complex have more dendritic interconnections than brains that don't. Enriched brains are not larger than non-enriched brains, they are just more complex. Rosenzweig's research helped shed light on this fact.

UNIT 9

TEACHING TIP

For several years, many parents believed that exposing their babies to classical music would increase intelligence later in life. This was known as the Mozart Effect, and the practice seemed to be the key to making smart babies. Unfortunately, the Mozart Effect was based on one study, and subsequent studies have shown that the effect does not have the impact on intellectual development that proponents claimed it had.

➤ **FIGURE 9.22**

Experience affects brain development Mark Rosenzweig and David Krech raised rats either alone in an environment without playthings, or with other rats in an environment enriched with playthings changed daily. In 14 of 16 repetitions of this basic experiment, rats in the enriched environment developed significantly more cerebral cortex (relative to the rest of the brain's tissue) than did those in the impoverished environment.

Impoverished environment · Impoverished rat brain cell · Enriched environment · Enriched rat brain cell

Rosenzweig was so surprised by this discovery that he repeated the experiment several times before publishing his findings (Renner & Rosenzweig, 1987; Rosenzweig, 1984). So great are the effects that, shown brief video clips of rats, you could tell from their activity and curiosity whether their environment had been impoverished or enriched (Renner & Renner, 1993). Bryan Kolb and Ian Whishaw (1998) noted extraordinary changes after 60 days in the enriched environment; the rats' brain weights increased 7 to 10 percent and the number of synapses mushroomed by about 20 percent.

Such results have motivated improvements in environments for laboratory, farm, and zoo animals—and for children in institutions. Stimulation by touch or massage also benefits infant rats and premature babies (Field et al., 2007). "Handled" infants of both species develop faster neurologically and gain weight more rapidly. By giving preemies massage therapy, neonatal intensive care units now help them to go home sooner (Field et al., 2006).

Both nature and nurture sculpt our synapses. After brain maturation provides us with an abundance of neural connections, our experiences trigger a pruning process. Sights and smells, touches and tugs activate connections and strengthen them. Unused neural pathways weaken and degenerate. Similar to pathways through a forest, popular paths are broadened and less-traveled paths gradually disappear. The result by puberty is a massive loss of unemployed connections.

Here at the juncture of nurture and nature is the biological reality of early childhood learning. During early childhood—while excess connections are still on call—youngsters can most easily master such skills as the grammar and accent of another language. Lacking any exposure to language before adolescence, a person will never master any language (see Unit 7B).

Likewise, lacking visual experience during the early years, people whose vision is restored by cataract removal never achieve normal perceptions (see Unit 4). The brain cells normally assigned to vision have died or been diverted to other uses. For us to have optimum brain development, normal stimulation during the early years is critical. The maturing brain's rule: Use it or lose it.

The brain's development does not, however, end with childhood. As we saw in Unit 3B's discussion of brain plasticity, our neural tissue is ever changing. If a monkey is trained to push a lever with a finger several thousand times a day, the brain tissue controlling that finger will change to reflect the experience. Human brains work similarly (**FIGURE 9.23**). Whether learning to keyboard or skateboard, we perform with increasing skill as our brain incorporates the learning.

▼ **Stringing the circuits young** String musicians who started playing before age 12 have larger and more complex neural circuits controlling the note-making left-hand fingers than do string musicians whose training started later (Elbert et al., 1995).

Courtesy of C. Brune

"Genes and experiences are just two ways of doing the same thing—wiring synapses."

Joseph LeDoux, *The Synaptic Self*, 2002

➤ FIGURE 9.23

A trained brain A well-learned finger-tapping task activates more motor cortex neurons (orange area, right) than were active in the same brain before training (left). (From Karni et al., 1998.)

How Much Credit (or Blame) Do Parents Deserve?

In procreation, a woman and a man shuffle their gene decks and deal a life-forming hand to their child-to-be, who is then subjected to countless influences beyond their control. Parents, nonetheless, feel enormous satisfaction in their children's successes, and feel guilt or shame over their failures. They beam over the child who wins an award. They wonder where they went wrong with the child who is repeatedly called into the principal's office. Freudian psychiatry and psychology have been among the sources of such ideas, by blaming problems from asthma to schizophrenia on "bad mothering." Society reinforces such parent-blaming: Believing that parents shape their offspring as a potter molds clay, people readily praise parents for their children's virtues and blame them for their children's vices. Popular culture endlessly proclaims the psychological harm toxic parents inflict on their fragile children. No wonder that it can seem risky to have and raise children.

But do parents really produce future adults with an inner wounded child by being (take your pick from the toxic-parent lists) overbearing—or uninvolved? Pushy—or ineffectual? Overprotective—or distant? Are children really so easily wounded? If so, should we then blame our parents for our failings, and ourselves for our children's failings? Or does all the talk of wounding fragile children through normal parental mistakes trivialize the brutality of real abuse?

Peter Neubauer and Alexander Neubauer (1990, pp. 20–21) illustrate how, with hindsight, we may inappropriately credit or blame our parents:

> Identical twin men, now age 30, were separated at birth and raised in different countries by their respective adoptive parents. Both kept their lives neat—neat to the point of pathology. Their clothes were preened, appointments met precisely on time, hands scrubbed regularly to a raw, red color. When the first was asked why he felt the need to be so clean, his answer was plain.
>
> "My mother. When I was growing up she always kept the house perfectly ordered. She insisted on every little thing returned to its proper place, the clocks—we had dozens of clocks—each set to the same noonday chime. She insisted on this, you see. I learned from her. What else could I do?"
>
> The man's identical twin, just as much a perfectionist with soap and water, explained his own behavior this way: "The reason is quite simple. I'm reacting to my mother, who was an absolute slob."

Parents do matter. The power of parenting to shape our differences is clearest at the extremes—the abused who become abusive, the neglected who become neglectful, the

• Even among chimpanzees, when one infant is hurt by another, the victim's mother will often attack the offender's mother (Goodall, 1968). •

"So I blame you for everything—whose fault is that?"

TEACHING TIP

Freudian psychologists (most notably, Freud himself) often blamed all manner of mental illness on "bad mothering." Freud believed that schizophrenia was a result of mothers being too overbearing. Today, we realize that many mental illnesses, including schizophrenia, are biologically based. The mothers and fathers of persons with mental illness no longer need to struggle with guilt regarding their parenting techniques.

loved but firmly handled children who become self-confident and socially competent. The power of the family environment also frequently shows up in children's political attitudes, religious beliefs, and personal manners. And it appears in the remarkable academic and vocational successes of children of the refugee "boat people" fleeing Vietnam and Cambodia—successes attributed to close-knit, supportive, even demanding families (Caplan et al., 1992).

Yet in personality measures, shared environmental influences—including, as we have seen, the home influences siblings share—typically account for less than 10 percent of children's differences. In the words of behavior geneticists Robert Plomin and Denise Daniels (1987), "Two children in the same family [are on average] as different from one another as are pairs of children selected randomly from the population." To developmental psychologist Sandra Scarr (1993), this implies that "parents should be given less credit for kids who turn out great and blamed less for kids who don't." Knowing children are not easily sculpted by parental nurture, perhaps parents can relax a bit more and love their children for who they are.

Peer Influence

As children mature, what other experiences do the work of nurturing? At all ages, but especially during childhood and adolescence, we seek to fit in with groups and are subject to group influences.

Consider the power of peers (Harris, 1998, 2000):

- Preschoolers who disdain a certain food often will eat that food if put at a table with a group of children who like it.
- Children who hear English spoken with one accent at home and another in the neighborhood and at school will invariably adopt the accent of their peers, not their parents. Accents (and slang) reflect culture, "and children get their culture from their peers," notes Harris (2007).
- Teens who start smoking typically have friends who model smoking, suggest its pleasures, and offer cigarettes (J. S. Rose et al., 1999; R. J. Rose et al., 2003). Part of this peer similarity may result from a *selection effect,* as kids seek out peers with similar attitudes and interests. Those who smoke (or don't) may select as friends those who also smoke (or don't).

Howard Gardner (1998) concludes that parents and peers are complementary:

> Parents are more important when it comes to education, discipline, responsibility, orderliness, charitableness, and ways of interacting with authority figures. Peers are more important for learning cooperation, for finding the road to popularity, for inventing styles of interaction among people of the same age. Youngsters may find their peers more interesting, but they will look to their parents when contemplating their own futures. Moreover, parents [often] choose the neighborhoods and schools that supply the peers.

As Gardner points out, parents can influence the culture that shapes the peer group, by helping to select their children's neighborhood and schools. And because neighborhood influences matter, parents may want to become involved in intervention programs for youth that aim at a whole school or neighborhood. If the vapors of a toxic climate are seeping into a child's life, that climate—not just the child—needs reforming.

"To be frank, officer, my parents never set boundaries."

"If you want to blame your parents for your own adult problems, you are entitled to blame the genes they gave you, but you are not entitled—by any facts I know—to blame the way they treated you. . . . We are not prisoners of our past."

Martin Seligman, *What You Can Change and What You Can't,* 1994

"Men resemble the times more than they resemble their fathers."

Ancient Arab proverb

Ole Graf/zefa/Corbis

Peer power As we develop, we play, date, and partner with peers. No wonder children and youths are so sensitive and responsive to peer influences.

TEACHING TIP

While peers may influence slang, food, and fashion preferences, parents are more influential when it comes to values, political beliefs, and manners. Thus, parents may not be able to keep their children from getting tattoos or the latest trendy jacket, but children would rather get their parents' advice when picking political candidates.

TEACHING TIP

At this time, you may want to use **Classroom Exercise:** *Introducing Adolescent Development* (p. 26) from Bolt's Teacher's Resource Binder.

BEFORE YOU MOVE ON . . .

➤ **ASK YOURSELF**

To what extent, and in what ways, have your peers and your parents helped shape who you are?

➤ **TEST YOURSELF 4**

To predict whether a teenager smokes, ask how many of the teen's friends smoke. One explanation for this correlation is peer influence. What's another?

Answers to the Test Yourself questions can be found in Appendix E at the end of the book.

Adolescence

MANY PSYCHOLOGISTS ONCE BELIEVED that childhood sets our traits. Today's developmental psychologists see development as lifelong. At a five-year high school reunion, former best friends may be surprised at their divergence; a decade later, they may have trouble sustaining a conversation.

As the life-span perspective emerged, psychologists began to look at how maturation and experience shape us not only in infancy and childhood, but also in adolescence and beyond. **Adolescence**—the years spent morphing from child to adult—starts with the physical beginnings of sexual maturity and ends with the social achievement of independent adult status (which means that in some cultures, where teens are self-supporting, adolescence hardly exists).

In industrialized countries, what are the teen years like? In Leo Tolstoy's *Anna Karenina,* the teen years were "that blissful time when childhood is just coming to an end, and out of that vast circle, happy and gay, a path takes shape." But another teenager, Anne Frank, writing in her diary while hiding from the Nazis, described tumultuous teen emotions:

> My treatment varies so much. One day Anne is so sensible and is allowed to know every-thing; and the next day I hear that Anne is just a silly little goat who doesn't know any-thing at all and imagines that she's learned a wonderful lot from books. . . . Oh, so many things bubble up inside me as I lie in bed, having to put up with people I'm fed up with, who always misinterpret my intentions.

G. Stanley Hall (1904), one of the first psychologists to describe adolescence, be-lieved that this tension between biological maturity and social dependence creates a period of "storm and stress." Indeed, after age 30, many who grow up in independence-fostering Western cultures look back on their teenage years as a time they would not want to relive, a time when their peers' social approval was imperative, their sense of direction in life was in flux, and their feeling of alienation from their parents was deepest (Arnett, 1999; Macfarlane, 1964).

But for many, adolescence is a time of vitality without the cares of adulthood, a time of rewarding friendships, of heightened idealism and a growing sense of life's exciting possibilities.

Physical Development

12: What physical changes mark adolescence?

Adolescence begins with **puberty,** the time when we mature sexually. Puberty follows a surge of hormones, which may intensify moods and which trigger a two-year period of rapid physical development, usually beginning at about age 11 in girls and at about

> "It takes a village to raise a child."
> African proverb

 ● How will you look back on your life 10 years from now? Are you making choices that someday you will recollect with satisfaction? ●

::**adolescence** the transition period from childhood to adulthood, extending from puberty to independence.

::**puberty** the period of sexual matura-tion, during which a person becomes capable of reproducing.

 INTERCONNECTING

G. Stanley Hall is considered the father of American psychology. He studied under Wilhelm Wundt in Leipzig, Germany, learning the new science of psychology in the first experimental lab to be established. Hall later went on to be president of Clark University in Worcester, Massachusetts, where he fostered a thriving psychology department that trained most of the United States' early psychologists, including Lewis Terman, Francis Cecil Sumner, and Margaret Floy Washburn. He also estab-lished the American Psychological Association (APA) in his living room near the Clark campus.

::**primary sex characteristics** the body structures (ovaries, testes, and external genitalia) that make sexual reproduction possible.

::**secondary sex characteristics** nonreproductive sexual characteristics, such as female breasts and hips, male voice quality, and body hair.

age 13 in boys. About the time of puberty, boys' growth propels them to greater height than their female counterparts (**FIGURE 9.24**). During this growth spurt, the **primary sex characteristics**—the reproductive organs and external genitalia—develop dramatically. So do **secondary sex characteristics,** the nonreproductive traits such as breasts and hips in girls, facial hair and deepened voice in boys, pubic and underarm hair in both sexes (**FIGURE 9.25**). A year or two before puberty, however, boys and girls often feel the first stirrings of physical attraction toward someone (McClintock & Herdt, 1996).

➤ **FIGURE 9.24**
Height differences Throughout childhood, boys and girls are similar in height. At puberty, girls surge ahead briefly, but then boys overtake them at about age 14. (Data from Tanner, 1978.) Studies suggest that sexual development and growth spurts are beginning somewhat earlier than was the case a half-century ago (Herman-Giddens et al., 2001).

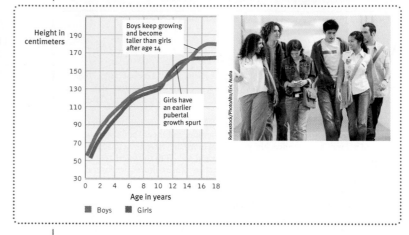

➤ **FIGURE 9.25**
Body changes at puberty At about age 11 in girls and age 13 in boys, a surge of hormones triggers a variety of physical changes.

In girls, puberty starts with breast development, which now often begins by age 10 (Brody, 1999). But puberty's landmarks are the first ejaculation in boys, usually by about age 14, and the first menstrual period in girls, usually within a year of age 12½

CRITICAL THINKING

Teen pregnancy is a controversial issue in many parts of the country. Have students explore the following questions related to this issue:

- What are the health risks of having a baby in the teen years?

- What policies does your school have about pregnant teens? How do other students in school view pregnant students?

- Should teen couples who are pregnant get married? Why or why not?

(Anderson et al., 2003). The first menstrual period, called **menarche** (meh-NAR-key), is a memorable event. Nearly all adult women recall it and remember experiencing a mixture of feelings—pride, excitement, embarrassment, and apprehension (Greif & Ulman, 1982; Woods et al., 1983). Girls who have been prepared for menarche usually experience it as a positive life transition. Most men similarly recall their first ejaculation (*spermarche*), which usually occurs as a nocturnal emission (Fuller & Downs, 1990).

Just as in the earlier life stages, the *sequence* of physical changes in puberty (for example, breast buds and visible pubic hair before menarche) is far more predictable than their *timing*. Some girls start their growth spurt at 9, some boys as late as age 16. Though such variations have little effect on height at maturity, they may have psychological consequences. For boys, early maturation pays dividends: Being stronger and more athletic during their early teen years, they tend to be more popular, self-assured, and independent, though also more at risk for alcohol use, delinquency, and premature sexual activity (Lynne et al., 2007; Steinberg & Morris, 2001). For girls, early maturation can be stressful (Mendle et al., 2007). If a young girl's body is out of sync with her own emotional maturity and her friends' physical development and experiences, she may begin associating with older adolescents or may suffer teasing or sexual harassment. It is not only when we mature that counts, but how people react to our genetically influenced physical development. Remember: *Heredity and environment interact.*

An adolescent's brain is also a work in progress. Until puberty, brain cells increase their connections, like trees growing more roots and branches. Then, during adolescence, comes a selective pruning of unused neurons and connections (Blakemore, 2008). What we don't use, we lose. It's rather like traffic engineers reducing congestion by eliminating certain streets and constructing new beltways that move traffic more efficiently.

As teens mature, their frontal lobes also continue to develop. The growth of *myelin*, the fatty tissue that forms around axons and speeds neurotransmission, enables better communication with other brain regions (Kuhn, 2006; Silveri et al., 2006). These developments bring improved judgment, impulse control, and the ability to plan for the long term.

Frontal lobe maturation lags the emotional limbic system. Puberty's hormonal surge and limbic system development help explain teens' occasional impulsiveness, risky behaviors, emotional storms—slamming doors and turning up the music (Casey et al., 2008). No wonder younger teens (whose unfinished frontal lobes aren't yet fully equipped for making long-term plans and curbing impulses) so often succumb to the lure of smoking, which most adult smokers could tell them they will later regret. Teens actually don't underestimate the risks of smoking—or driving fast or unprotected sex—they just, when reasoning from their gut, weigh the benefits more heavily (Reyna & Farley, 2006; Steinberg, 2007).

So, when Junior drives recklessly and academically self-destructs, should his parents reassure themselves that "he can't help it; his frontal cortex isn't yet fully grown"? They can at least take hope: The brain with which Junior begins his teens differs from the brain with which he will end his teens. Unless he slows his brain development with heavy drinking—leaving him prone to impulsivity and addiction—his frontal lobes will continue maturing until about age 25 (Beckman, 2004; Crews et al., 2007).

In 2004, the American Psychological Association joined seven other medical and mental health associations in filing U.S. Supreme Court briefs, arguing against the death penalty for 16- and 17-years-olds. The briefs documented the teen brain's immaturity "in areas that bear upon adolescent decision-making." Teens are "less

::**menarche** [meh-NAR-key] the first menstrual period.

● Menarche appears to occur a few months earlier, on average, for girls who have experienced stresses related to father absence or sexual abuse (Vigil et al., 2005; Zabin et al., 2005). ●

"Young man, go to your room and stay there until your cerebral cortex matures."

"If a gun is put in the control of the prefrontal cortex of a hurt and vengeful 15-year-old, and it is pointed at a human target, it will very likely go off."

National Institutes of Health brain scientist Daniel R. Weinberger, "A Brain Too Young for Good Judgment," 2001

CULTURAL CONNECTIONS

Have students research coming-of-age rituals (rites of passage) and how adolescence is viewed in cultures that are Native American, tribal African, African-American, Muslim, Hispanic, Indian, Eastern European, Western European, or Asian. Encourage students to present their findings to the class as a written paper, oral presentation, or poster.

TEACHING TIP

The timing of puberty can be socially and psychologically important. In Western cultures, early puberty in males is viewed as desirable. Boys who go through puberty early are viewed as being more competent and receive more attention from girls and athletic coaches. Early puberty in girls, however, is not always advantageous. Girls often feel awkward if they mature too early, and many early-blooming girls will become sexually active earlier than their later-maturing peers.

 TEACHING TIP

At this time, you may want to use **Student Project:** *Interviewing Adolescents* (p. 26) or *Lecture/Discussion Topic: Is 16 Too Young to Drive a Car?* (p. 27) or **Student Project:** *Writing About Puberty* (p. 27) from Bolt's Teacher's Resource Binder.

UNIT 9

Adolescents experience egocentrism, but in a different way from children. With adolescent egocentrism, teens experience the *imaginary audience phenomenon* in which they believe others are always paying attention to them, especially their flaws. Also, they feel that no one else has experienced life exactly as they have, referred to as the *"nobody understands me"* phenomenon.

CRITICAL THINKING

Because teens often grapple with what is moral, pose the following questions to help them focus on their definitions of morality:

- What does it mean to be a moral person?
- What stage of morality (based on Kohlberg) would you say you and your friends are in most of the time?
- Does the definition of morality change with a situation or does it remain the same all the time?

---

guilty by reason of adolescence," suggested psychologist Laurence Steinberg and law professor Elizabeth Scott (2003). In 2005, by a 5-to-4 margin, the Court concurred, declaring juvenile death penalties unconstitutional.

Cognitive Development

13: How did Piaget, Kohlberg, and later researchers describe adolescent cognitive and moral development?

As young teenagers become capable of thinking about their thinking, and of thinking about other people's thinking, they begin imagining what other people are thinking about *them*. (Adolescents might worry less if they understood their peers' similar preoccupation.) As their cognitive abilities mature, many begin to think about what is ideally possible and compare that with the imperfect reality of their society, their parents, and even themselves.

Developing Reasoning Power

During the early teen years, reasoning is often self-focused. Adolescents may think their private experiences are unique, something parents just could not understand: "But, Mom, *you* don't really know how it feels to be in love" (Elkind, 1978).

Gradually, though, most achieve the intellectual summit Piaget called *formal operations,* and they become more capable of abstract reasoning. Adolescents ponder and debate human nature, good and evil, truth and justice. Having left behind the concrete images of early childhood, they may now seek a deeper conception of God and existence (Elkind, 1970; Worthington, 1989). The ability to reason hypothetically and deduce consequences also enables them to detect inconsistencies in others' reasoning and to spot hypocrisy. This can lead to heated debates with parents and silent vows never to lose sight of their own ideals (Peterson et al., 1986).

Developing Morality

Two crucial tasks of childhood and adolescence are discerning right from wrong and developing character—the psychological muscles for controlling impulses. Much of

"When the pilot told us to brace and grab our ankles, the first thing that went through my mind was that we must all look pretty stupid."
Jeremiah Rawlings, age 12, after a 1989 DC-10 crash in Sioux City, Iowa

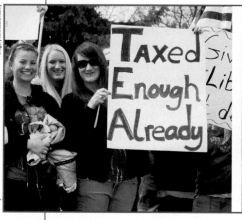

"Ben is in his first year of high school, and he's questioning all the right things."

Demonstrating their reasoning ability These teens are demonstrating their ability to think logically about abstract topics. According to Piaget, they are in the final cognitive stage, formal operations.

CRITICAL THINKING

Have students break into groups and study youth-led activism, including such movements as the protests against the Vietnam War and the French Revolution.

- How have youth influenced these movements?
- What impact have youth had on other revolutionary movements, such as the American Revolution and the Civil War?
- How do current activist groups effectively use the energy and enthusiasm of youth to forward their agendas?
- How does government seek to involve youth in its workings?

our morality is rooted in gut-level reactions, for which the mind seeks rationalization (Haidt, 2006). Often, reason justifies passions such as disgust or liking. Yet to be a moral person is to *think* morally and *act* accordingly.

Piaget (1932) believed that children's moral judgments build on their cognitive development. Agreeing with Piaget, Lawrence Kohlberg (1981, 1984) sought to describe the development of *moral reasoning,* the thinking that occurs as we consider right and wrong. Kohlberg posed moral dilemmas (for example, whether a person should steal medicine to save a loved one's life) and asked children, adolescents, and adults if the action was right or wrong. He then analyzed their answers for evidence of stages of moral thinking.

His findings led him to believe that as we develop intellectually, we pass through three basic levels of moral thinking:

- *Preconventional morality* Before age 9, most children's morality focuses on self-interest: They obey rules either to avoid punishment or to gain concrete rewards.
- *Conventional morality* By early adolescence, morality focuses on caring for others and on upholding laws and social rules, simply because they are the laws and rules.
- *Postconventional morality* With the abstract reasoning of formal operational thought, people may reach a third moral level. Actions are judged "right" because they flow from people's rights or from self-defined, basic ethical principles.

Kohlberg claimed these levels form a moral ladder. As with all stage theories, the sequence is unvarying. We begin on the bottom rung and ascend to varying heights.

Research confirms that children in various cultures progress from Kohlberg's preconventional level into his conventional level (Gibbs et al., 2007). The postconventional level is more controversial. It appears mostly in the European and North American educated middle class, which prizes *individualism*—giving priority to one's own goals rather than to group goals (Eckensberger, 1994; Miller & Bersoff, 1995). Critics therefore contend that Kohlberg's theory is biased against the moral reasoning of members of collectivist societies such as China and India. Moreover, people's thinking about real-world moral choices also engages their emotions, and moral feelings don't easily fit into Kohlberg's neat stages (Krebs & Denton, 2005).

Moral Feeling The mind makes moral judgments as it makes aesthetic judgments— quickly and automatically. We feel disgust when seeing people engaged in degrading or subhuman acts, and we feel *elevation*—a tingly, warm, glowing feeling in the chest— when seeing people display exceptional generosity, compassion, or courage.

One woman recalled driving through her snowy neighborhood with three young men as they passed "an elderly woman with a shovel in her driveway. I did not think much of it, when one of the guys in the back asked the driver to let him off there. . . . When I saw him jump out of the back seat and approach the lady, my mouth dropped in shock as I realized that he was offering to shovel her walk for her." Witnessing this unexpected goodness triggered elevation: "I felt like jumping out of the car and hugging this guy. I felt like singing and running, or skipping and laughing. I felt like saying nice things about people" (Haidt, 2000).

In Jonathan Haidt's (2002, 2007, 2008) *social intuitionist* account of morality, moral feelings precede moral reasoning. "Could human morality really be run by the moral emotions," he wonders, "while moral reasoning struts about pretending to be in control?" Indeed, he surmises, "moral judgment involves quick gut feelings, or affectively laden intuitions, which then trigger moral reasoning." Moral reasoning—our mind's press secretary—aims to convince ourselves and others of what we intuitively feel.

"It is a delightful harmony when doing and saying go together."
Michel Eyquem de Montaigne (1533–1592)

Moral reasoning New Orleans Hurricane Katrina victims were faced with a moral dilemma: Should they help themselves to household necessities? Their reasoning likely reflected different levels of moral thinking, even if they behaved similarly.

"I am a bit suspicious of any theory that says that the highest moral stage is one in which people talk like college professors."
James Q. Wilson, *The Moral Sense,* 1993

TROUBLESHOOTING

Kohlberg used the term "conventional" in his theory to describe what type of morality was commonly found in society. Conventional morality was the stage he found most prevalent among people in general society. Pre-conventional morality was found in people before they joined society as "adults." Kohlberg believed that a type of postconventional morality existed, but he was unable to find enough people to study over a long period of time to validate it.

TEACHING TIP

Kohlberg didn't believe that people could skip stages of moral development. He, like Piaget, believed that each stage built on the one before it, so skipping stages was not likely. His theory would fit into a "continuity versus stages" argument in favor of a stage theory of development.

TEACHING TIP

Kohlberg believed that social interaction encouraged moral growth. He felt that formal education offered the best opportunities for moral development. He also believed that subjects presented with moral dilemmas similar to the ones described in the text would see how reasonable the higher stages of morality were, encouraging them to aspire for deeper moral development.

At this time, you may want to use **Classroom Exercises:** *Formal Operational Thought* (p. 28) or *Kohlberg's Theory of Moral Development* (p. 28) from Bolt's Teacher's Resource Binder.

RESEARCH

Conduct some active research with your students by having them present moral dilemmas to their classmates. Participants should write out a paragraph explaining how they would respond to the dilemmas. Analyze the results to determine the level of moral development into which each participant seems to fit. Be sure to keep the following in mind:

- Have students obtain informed consent.

- Code the paragraphs to ensure anonymity of the participants.

- Create a rubric for analyzing the paragraphs. What words or phrases will indicate each level of moral development?

- Have several students analyze each paragraph and compare their evaluations to ensure reliability.

- Designate students to write up the research like a scholarly paper. Consider submitting your findings to a student journal.

The social intuitionist explanation of morality finds support from a study of moral paradoxes. Imagine seeing a runaway trolley headed for five people. All will certainly be killed unless you throw a switch that diverts the trolley onto another track, where it will kill one person. Should you throw the switch?

Most say *yes*. Kill one, save five. Now imagine the same dilemma, except that your opportunity to save the five requires you to push a large stranger onto the tracks, where he will die as his body stops the trolley. Kill one, save five?

The logic is the same, but most say *no*. Seeking to understand why, a Princeton research team led by Joshua Greene (2001) used brain imaging to spy on people's neural responses as they contemplated such dilemmas. Only when given the body-pushing type of moral dilemma did their brain's emotion areas light up. Despite the identical logic, the personal dilemma engaged emotions that altered moral judgment. Moral judgment is more than thinking; it is also gut-level feeling.

The gut feelings that drive our moral judgments turn out to be widely shared. To neuroscientist Marc Hauser (2006) this suggests that humans are hard-wired for moral feelings. Faced with moral choices, people across the world, with similar evolved brains, display similar moral intuitions. For example, is it acceptable to kill a healthy man who walks into a hospital that has five dying patients who could be saved by harvesting his organs? Most people say *no*. We all seem to unconsciously assume that harm caused by an action is worse than harm caused by failing to act (Cushman et al., 2006). With damage to a brain area that underlies emotions, however, people apply more coldly calculating reasoning to moral dilemmas (Koenigs et al., 2007).

Moral Action Our moral thinking and feeling surely affect our moral talk. But sometimes talk is cheap and emotions are fleeting. Morality involves *doing* the right thing, and what we do also depends on social influences. As political theorist Hannah Arendt (1963) observed, many Nazi concentration camp guards during World War II were ordinary "moral" people who were corrupted by a powerfully evil situation.

Nevertheless, as our *thinking* matures, our *behavior* also becomes less selfish and more caring (Krebs & Van Hesteren, 1994; Miller et al., 1996). Today's character education programs therefore tend to focus both on moral issues and on *doing* the right thing. They teach children *empathy* for others' feelings, and also the self-discipline needed to restrain one's own impulses—to delay small gratifications now to enable bigger rewards later. Those who do learn to *delay gratification* become more socially responsible, academically successful, and productive (Funder & Block, 1989; Mischel et al., 1988, 1989). In service-learning programs, teens tutor, clean up their neighborhoods, and assist older people, and their sense of competence and desire to serve increase at the same time that their school absenteeism and drop-out rates diminish (Andersen, 1998; Piliavin, 2003). Moral action feeds moral attitudes.

Social Development

14: What are the social tasks and challenges of adolescence?

Theorist Erik Erikson (1963) contended that each stage of life has its own *psychosocial* task, a crisis that needs resolution. Young children wrestle with issues of *trust*, then *autonomy* (independence), then *initiative* (**TABLE 9.2**). School-age children strive for *competence*, feeling able and productive. But for people your age, the task, said Erikson, is to synthesize past, present, and future possibilities into a clearer sense of self. Adolescents wonder, "Who am I as an individual? What do I want to do with my life? What values should I live by? What do I believe in?" Erikson called this quest the adolescent's *search for identity*.

As sometimes happens in psychology, Erikson's interests were bred by his own life experience. As the son of a Jewish mother and a Danish Gentile father, Erikson was

"This might not be ethical. Is that a problem for anybody?"

Drawing by Vietor; © 1987 The New Yorker Magazine, Inc.

> On humanity's need to delay gratification in response to global climate change: "The benefits of strong early action considerably outweigh the costs."
> *The Economics of Climate Change*, UK Government Economic Service, 2007

::identity our sense of self; according to Erikson, the adolescent's task is to solidify a sense of self by testing and integrating various roles.

::social identity the "we" aspect of our self-concept; the part of our answer to "Who am I?" that comes from our group memberships.

TEACHING TIP

Erik Erikson was a student of Sigmund Freud, which explains why his theory looks similar to his mentor's *psychosexual* stages of development. Erikson believed that social influences were more important to development than sexual impulses, so he crafted his theory to highlight different influences than those supported by his teacher.

TABLE 9.2

ERIKSON'S STAGES OF PSYCHOSOCIAL DEVELOPMENT

Stage (approximate age)	Issue	Description of Task
Infancy (to 1 year)	Trust vs. mistrust	If needs are dependably met, infants develop a sense of basic trust.
Toddlerhood (1 to 3 years)	Autonomy vs. shame and doubt	Toddlers learn to exercise their will and do things for themselves, or they doubt their abilities.
Preschool (3 to 6 years)	Initiative vs. guilt	Preschoolers learn to initiate tasks and carry out plans, or they feel guilty about their efforts to be independent.
Elementary school (6 years to puberty)	Industry vs. inferiority	Children learn the pleasure of applying themselves to tasks, or they feel inferior.
Adolescence (teen years into 20s)	Identity vs. role confusion	Teenagers work at refining a sense of self by testing roles and then integrating them to form a single identity, or they become confused about who they are.
Young adulthood (20s to early 40s)	Intimacy vs. isolation	Young adults struggle to form close relationships and to gain the capacity for intimate love, or they feel socially isolated.
Middle adulthood (40s to 60s)	Generativity vs. stagnation	In middle age, people discover a sense of contributing to the world, usually through family and work, or they may feel a lack of purpose.
Late adulthood (late 60s and up)	Integrity vs. despair	Reflecting on his or her life, an older adult may feel a sense of satisfaction or failure.

Competence vs. inferiority

Intimacy vs. isolation

"doubly an outsider," reports Morton Hunt (1993, p. 391). He was "scorned as a Jew in school but mocked as a Gentile in the synagogue because of his blond hair and blue eyes." Such episodes fueled his interest in the adolescent struggle for identity.

Forming an Identity

To refine their sense of identity, adolescents in individualistic cultures usually try out different "selves" in different situations. They may act out one self at home, another with friends or on Facebook, and still another at school or on World of Warcraft. If two situations overlap—as when a teenager brings home friends—the discomfort can be considerable. The teen asks, "Which self should I be? Which is the real me?" The resolution is a self-definition that unifies the various selves into a consistent and comfortable sense of who one is—an **identity.**

For both adolescents and adults, group identities often form around how we differ from those around us. When living in Britain, I became conscious of my Americanness. When spending time with my daughter in Africa, I become conscious of my minority (White) race. When surrounded by women, I am mindful of my gender identity. For international students, for those of a minority ethnic group, for people with a disability, for those on a team, a **social identity** often forms around their distinctiveness.

But not always. Erikson noticed that some adolescents forge their identity early, simply by adopting their parents' values and expectations. (Traditional, less individualistic cultures inform adolescents about who they are, rather than encouraging them to decide on their own.) Other adolescents may adopt an identity defined in opposition to parents but in conformity with a particular peer group—jocks, preps, geeks, band kids, debaters.

"Self-consciousness, the recognition of a creature by itself as a 'self,' [cannot] exist except in contrast with an 'other,' a something which is not the self."

C. S. Lewis, *The Problem of Pain*, 1940

CRITICAL THINKING

Have your students write down ten different answers to the question, "Who am I?" listing only those things that, if lost, would make a real difference in their sense of identity—for instance, their roles or responsibilities, groups they belong to, beliefs, personality traits, needs, feelings, or behavior patterns.

When they have finished, ask them to imagine what life would be like if the items they listed were no longer true—for instance, what would the loss of a parent mean to those who wrote down "son" or "daughter"? After the students have reviewed items in this way, ask them to order their lists in terms of importance.

Bugen, L. A. (1979). *Death and dying: Theory, research, practice.* Dubuque, IA: Wm. C. Brown.

 TEACHING TIP

In outlining Erikson's theory in class, you might ask students to include in their notes for each stage the name of a person they know who exemplifies the stage. The theory is likely to become less abstract and more meaningful as they check the stages against the reality of living examples.

 TEACHING TIP

At this time, you may want to use **Classroom Exercises:** *Erikson's Stages* (p. 29) or *Objective Measure of Ego-Identity Status* (p. 30) or *Who Am I?* (p. 30) or *The Life Cycle* (p. 31) from Bolt's Teacher's Resource Binder.

Girls describe their friendships as more intimate than do boys. Although some researchers have suggested that this is merely a matter of style, others suggest that male friendships are less intimate because boys trust their friends less than girls do. The sex difference does not simply reflect a developmental delay for boys; adult women also tend to have more intimate friends than do men.

CRITICAL THINKING

Erikson saw the importance of adolescent identity seeking when he worked with the Oglala Lakota Indians. In their culture, young males would go off on their own to have an identity-determining dream that would guide the courses of their lives. When the U.S. government tried to assimilate the Lakota into American society, the tribe lost this rite of passage, and consequently the young males of the culture were denied this method of finding an identity.

Explore rites of passage with your students:

● What rites of passage do American youth go through to achieve adulthood?

● Do these rites help form a sense of identity? Why or why not?

Who shall I be today? By varying the way they look, adolescents try out different "selves." Although we eventually form a consistent and stable sense of identity, the self we present may change with the situation. ▲

● See Unit 8A for a complete discussion of adolescent sexuality. ●

"She says she's someone from your past who gave birth to you, and raised you, and sacrificed everything so you could have whatever you wanted."

"I love u guys."
Emily Keyes' final text message to her parents before dying in a Colorado school shooting, 2006

Most young people do develop a sense of contentment with their lives. When American teens were asked whether a series of statements described them, 81 percent said *yes* to "I would choose my life the way it is right now." But others never quite seem to find themselves: The other 19 percent agreed with "I wish I were somebody else." In response to another question, 28 percent agreed that "I often wonder why I exist" (Lyons, 2004). Reflecting on their existence, 75 percent of American collegians say they "discuss religion/spirituality" with friends, "pray," and agree that "we are all spiritual beings" and "search for meaning/purpose in life" (Astin et al., 2004; Bryant & Astin, 2008). This would not surprise Stanford psychologist William Damon and his colleagues (2003), who contend that a key task of adolescent development is to achieve a purpose—a desire to accomplish something personally meaningful that makes a difference to the world beyond oneself.

The late teen years, when many people like you in industrialized countries begin attending college or working full time, provide new opportunities for trying out possible roles. Here is something for you to remember: Many college seniors have achieved a clearer identity and a more positive self-concept than they had as first-year students (Waterman, 1988). This could be one of the reasons why that first year of college is such a challenge. In several nationwide studies, researchers have given young Americans tests of self-esteem. (Sample item: "I am able to do things as well as most other people.") During the early to mid-teen years, self-esteem falls and, for girls, depression scores often increase, but then self-image rebounds during the late teens and twenties (Robins et al., 2002; Twenge & Campbell, 2001; Twenge & Nolen-Hoeksema, 2002).

Identity also becomes more personalized. Daniel Hart (1988) asked American youths of various ages to imagine a machine that would clone (a) what you think and feel, (b) your appearance, or (c) your relationships with friends and family. When he then asked which clone would be "closest to being you?" three-fourths of the seventh-graders chose (c), the clone with the same social network. In contrast, three-fourths of the ninth-graders chose (a), the one with their individual thoughts and feelings.

Erikson contended that the adolescent identity stage is followed in young adulthood by a developing capacity for **intimacy.** With a clear and comfortable sense of who you are, said Erikson, you are ready to form emotionally close relationships. Such relationships are, for most of us, a source of great pleasure. When Mihaly Csikszentmihalyi (pronounced chick-SENT-me-hi) and Jeremy Hunter (2003) used a beeper to sample the daily experiences of American teens, they found them unhappiest when alone and happiest when with friends. As Aristotle long ago recognized, we humans are "the social animal." Relationships matter.

Parent and Peer Relationships

This next research finding will not surprise you: As adolescents in Western cultures seek to form their own identities, they begin to pull away from their parents (Shanahan et al., 2007). The preschooler who can't be close enough to her mother, who loves to touch and cling to her, becomes the 14-year-old who wouldn't be caught dead holding hands with Mom. The transition occurs gradually (FIGURE 9.26). By adolescence, arguments occur more often, usually over mundane things—household chores, bedtime, homework (Tesser et al., 1989). Parent-child conflict during the transition to adolescence tends to be greater with first-born than with second-born children (Shanahan et al., 2007).

For a minority of parents and their adolescents, differences lead to real splits and great stress (Steinberg & Morris, 2001). But most disagreements are at the level of harmless bickering. And most adolescents—6000 of them in 10 countries, from Australia to Bangladesh to Turkey—have said that they like their parents (Offer et al., 1988). "We usually get along but . . . ," adolescents often report (Galambos, 1992; Steinberg, 1987).

Create a "forming identity" chart with four columns, labeling them with the following four subheadings that depict characteristics of adolescence: experimentation, rebellion, "self"-ishness, and optimism. Under each heading, have students brainstorm about situations in which adolescents demonstrate *healthy* experimentation, rebellion, "self"-ishness, and optimism. While students may snicker about the unhealthy ways to demonstrate these identity-seeking arenas, encourage them to think critically about ways adolescents can achieve an identity without causing harm to themselves or others.

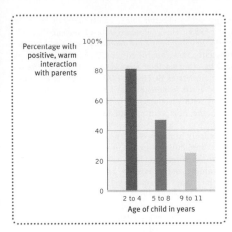

➤ FIGURE 9.26
The changing parent-child relationship Interviews from a large, national study of Canadian families reveal that the typically close, warm relationships between parents and preschoolers loosen as children become older. (Data from Statistics Canada, 1999.)

::**intimacy** in Erikson's theory, the ability to form close, loving relationships; a primary developmental task in late adolescence and early adulthood.

Positive parent-teen relations and positive peer relations often go hand-in-hand. High school girls who have the most affectionate relationships with their mothers tend also to enjoy the most intimate friendships with girlfriends (Gold & Yanof, 1985). And teens who feel close to their parents tend to be healthy and happy and to do well in school (Resnick et al., 1997). Of course, we can state this correlation the other way: Misbehaving teens are more likely to have tense relationships with parents and other adults.

Adolescence is typically a time of diminishing parental influence and growing peer influence. Asked in a survey if they had "ever had a serious talk" with their child about illegal drugs, 85 percent of American parents answered yes. But if the parents had indeed given this earnest advice, many teens apparently had tuned it out: Only 45 percent could recall such a talk (Morin & Brossard, 1997).

Heredity does much of the heavy lifting in forming individual differences in temperament and personality, and parent and peer influences do much of the rest. Most teens are herd animals. They talk, dress, and act more like their peers than their parents. What their friends are, they often become, and what "everybody's doing," they often do. In teen calls to hotline counseling services, peer relationships are the most discussed topic (Boehm et al., 1999). For those who feel excluded, the pain is acute. "The social atmosphere in most high schools is poisonously clique-driven and exclusionary," observed social psychologist Elliot Aronson (2001). Most excluded "students suffer in silence. . . . A small number act out in violent ways against their classmates." Those who withdraw are vulnerable to loneliness, low self-esteem, and depression (Steinberg & Morris, 2001). Peer approval matters.

Teens see their parents as having more influence in other areas—for example, in shaping their religious faith and in thinking about college and career choices (*Emerging Trends*, 1997). A Gallup Youth Survey reveals that most share their parent's political views (Lyons, 2005).

Emerging Adulthood

15: What is emerging adulthood?

In young adulthood, emotional ties with parents loosen further. During their early twenties, many people still lean heavily on their parents. But by the late twenties,

"How was my day? How was my day? Must you micromanage my life?"

Nine times out of ten, it's all about peer pressure.

TEACHING TIP

James Marcia expanded on Erikson's theory of identity formation. He established four distinct ways adolescents can express identity formation:

- *Identity achievement*, in which adolescents arrive at a sense of identity on their own after considering their options.
- *Identity diffusion*, in which adolescents lack commitment to any goal.
- *Moratorium*, in which adolescents are still in a crisis period searching for an identity but not yet coming to a conclusion.
- *Foreclosure*, in which adolescents make a commitment to an identity without experiencing a crisis. Usually, the adolescent will make an identity decision based on the expectations of others rather than their own choices.

DEMO

Studies show that adolescent students usually choose values and moral beliefs their parents taught them rather than those their friends may employ. Pose the following dilemma:

- You and your friends find a sheet of paper that your teacher probably had lost. On the paper are the questions and answers for a test that you are going to have tomorrow. Your friends all plan to study from this sheet, and they want you to go along with them. You don't think you should, but they tell you to do it anyway. What would you really do: Study from the sheet or not study from it?

CRITICAL THINKING

Divide students into groups to think about their plans for after high school graduation. Present the following questions as discussion starting points:

- Where do you see yourself one year from now? Five years? Ten years? Twenty years?

- What is your attitude about going to college? Why do you feel you have this attitude?

- What are your career/work plans?

- Do you feel your plans for the next few years are solid or do you hope your purpose in life will reveal itself soon?

CRITICAL THINKING

Students may be curious about why physical maturity is occurring earlier in modern youth. Consider the following questions:

- What factors have contributed to earlier physical development in teens? *(increased body fat and stress hormones)*

- What impact has early sexual development had on society?

- Are there cultures where sexual maturity happens later than in the U.S.? Earlier? Why are those cultures different?

::**emerging adulthood** for some people in modern cultures, a period from the late teens to mid-twenties, bridging the gap between adolescent dependence and full independence and responsible adulthood.

"When I was your age, I was an adult."

➤ **FIGURE 9.27**

The transition to adulthood is being stretched from both ends In the 1890s, the average interval between a woman's first menstrual period and marriage, which typically marked a transition to adulthood, was about 7 years; in industrialized countries today it is about 12 years (Guttmacher, 1994, 2000). Although many adults are unmarried, later marriage combines with prolonged education and earlier menarche to help stretch out the transition to adulthood.

most feel more comfortably independent and better able to empathize with parents as fellow adults (Frank, 1988; White, 1983). This graduation from adolescence to adulthood is now taking longer.

In the Western world, adolescence now roughly corresponds to the teen years. At earlier times, and still today in other parts of the world, this slice of the life span has been much smaller (Baumeister & Tice, 1986). Shortly after sexual maturity, such societies bestowed adult responsibilities and status on the young person, often marking the event with an elaborate initiation—a public *rite of passage*. With society's blessing, the new adult would then work, marry, and have children.

When schooling became compulsory in many Western countries, independence began occurring later. In industrialized cultures from Europe to Australia, adolescents are now taking more time to finish college, leave the nest, and establish careers. In the United States, for example, the average age at first marriage varies by ethnic group but has increased more than 4 years since 1960 (to 27 for men, 25 for women).

While cultural traditions were changing, Western adolescents were also beginning to develop earlier. Today's earlier sexual maturity is related both to increased body fat (which can support pregnancy and nursing) and to weakened parent-child bonds, including absent fathers (Ellis, 2004). Together, delayed independence and earlier sexual maturity have widened the once-brief interlude between biological maturity and social independence (**FIGURE 9.27**).

Especially for those still in school, the time from 18 to the mid-twenties is an increasingly not-yet-settled phase of life, which some now call **emerging adulthood** (Arnett, 2006, 2007; Reitzle, 2006). Unlike some other cultures with an abrupt transition to adulthood, Westerners typically ease their way into their new status. Those who leave home for college, for example, are separated from parents and, more than ever before, managing their time and priorities. Yet they may remain dependent on their parents' financial and emotional support and may return home for holidays. For many others, their parents' home may be the only affordable place to live. No longer adolescents, these emerging adults have not yet assumed full adult responsibilities and independence, and they feel "in between." But adulthood emerges gradually, and often with diminishing bouts of depression or anger and increased self-esteem (Galambos et al., 2006).

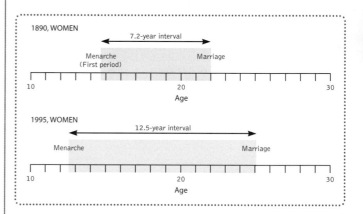

➤ **ASK YOURSELF**

What have been your best and worst experiences during adolescence? How have your experiences been influenced by environmental factors, such as your cultural context, and how have they been influenced by your inborn traits?

➤ **TEST YOURSELF 5**

How has the transition from childhood to adulthood changed in Western cultures in the last century or so?

Answers to the Test Yourself questions can be found in Appendix E at the end of the book.

Adulthood

AT ONE TIME, PSYCHOLOGISTS VIEWED the center-of-life years between adolescence and old age as one long plateau. No longer. Those who follow the unfolding of people's adult lives now believe our development continues.

It is more difficult to generalize about adulthood stages than about life's early years. If you know that James is a 1-year-old and Jamal is a 10-year-old, you could say a great deal about each child. Not so with adults who differ by a similar number of years. The boss may be 30 or 60; the marathon runner may be 20 or 50; the 19-year-old may be a parent who supports a child or a child who receives an allowance. Yet our life courses are in some ways similar. Physically, cognitively, and especially socially, we are at age 50 different from our 25-year-old selves.

Adult abilities vary widely Eighty-seven-year-olds: Don't try this. In 2002, George Blair became the world's oldest barefoot water skier, 18 days after his eighty-seventh birthday.

Physical Development

16: What physical changes occur during middle and late adulthood?

Our physical abilities—muscular strength, reaction time, sensory keenness, and cardiac output—all crest by the mid-twenties. Like the declining daylight after the summer solstice, the decline of physical prowess begins imperceptibly. Athletes are

> "I am still learning."
> Michelangelo, 1560, at age 85

● How old does a person have to be before you think of him or her as old? The average 18- to 29-year-old says 67. The average person 60 and over says 76 (Yankelovich, 1995). ●

Survey your students regarding whether they have made concrete plans for life after high school. Depending on the time in the school year, most have probably not chosen a college or decided what type of work they will do after high school. Maybe seeing that others around them are just as undecided about the immediate future will help them relax about the stressful life choices they will be making in the next few months and years.

Has the modern conception of the stages of adulthood changed in the last century? Brainstorm with students what factors may have led people in U.S. society to reevaluate their conception of adulthood.

● What effect does better health care have on the definitions of adulthood?

● Why did the federal government choose the age 65 to grant people Social Security? Why not younger or older?

At this time, you may want to use **Lecture/Discussion Topic:** *Emerging Adulthood* (p. 32) from Bolt's Teacher's Resource Binder.

RESEARCH

More and more, there are older professional athletes who still perform well into their forties. Research who these athletes are and how their statistics have changed over the years.

- What differences have they experienced in their playing time or position over the years due to physical changes?

- What medical advances have they been able to take advantage of to prolong their athletic careers?

- Contact any or all of the athletes your students have researched to ask them how their physical abilities have changed their athletic careers as they age. How do they feel about their aging? How have they adapted?

TEACHING TIP

Studies show that the two major symptoms that are attributable to menopause are hot flashes and vaginal atrophy—when the lining of the vagina becomes dry, making intercourse uncomfortable. What about the other symptoms that seem also to be involved in menopause, such as irritability? These other symptoms seem more affected by individual differences and are not necessarily the norm.

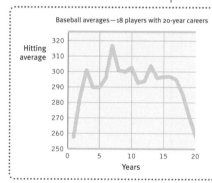

"Happy fortieth. I'll take the muscle tone in your upper arms, the girlish timbre of your voice, your amazing tolerance for caffeine, and your ability to digest french fries. The rest of you can stay."

"If the truth were known, we'd have to diagnose [older women] as having P.M.F.—Post-Menstrual Freedom."
Social psychologist Jacqueline Goodchilds (1987)

"The things that stop you having sex with age are exactly the same as those that stop you riding a bicycle (bad health, thinking it looks silly, no bicycle)."
Alex Comfort, *The Joy of Sex,* 2002

➤ **FIGURE 9.28**

Gradually accelerating decline An analysis of aging and batting averages of all twentieth-century major league baseball players revealed a gradual but accelerating decline in players' later years (Schall & Smith, 2000). The career performance record of the great Willie Mays is illustrative.

often the first to notice. World-class sprinters and swimmers peak by their early twenties. Women—who mature earlier than men—also peak earlier. But most of us—especially those of us whose daily lives do not require top physical performance—hardly perceive the early signs of decline.

Physical Changes in Middle Adulthood

Middle-aged (post-40) athletes know all too well that physical decline gradually accelerates (**FIGURE 9.28**). As a 67-year-old who plays basketball, I now find myself occasionally wondering whether my team really needs me to run for that loose ball. But even diminished vigor is sufficient for normal activities. Moreover, during early and middle adulthood, physical vigor has less to do with age than with a person's health and exercise habits. Many of today's physically fit 50-year-olds run 4 miles with ease, while sedentary 25-year-olds find themselves huffing and puffing up two flights of stairs.

Aging also brings a gradual decline in fertility. For a 35- to 39-year-old woman, the chances of getting pregnant after a single act of intercourse are only half those of a woman 19 to 26 (Dunson et al., 2002). A woman's foremost biological sign of aging, the onset of **menopause,** ends her menstrual cycles, usually within a few years of age 50. Her expectations and attitudes will influence the emotional impact of this event. Does she see it as a sign that she is losing her femininity and growing old? Or does she view it as liberation from menstrual periods and fears of pregnancy? As is often the case, our expectations influence our perceptions.

Data from Africa support an evolutionary theory of menopause: Infants with a living maternal grandmother—typically a caring and invested family member without young children of her own—have had a greater chance of survival (Shanley et al., 2007).

Men experience no equivalent to menopause—no cessation of fertility, no sharp drop in sex hormones. They do experience a gradual decline in sperm count, testosterone level, and speed of erection and ejaculation. Some may also experience distress related to their perception of declining virility and physical capacities. But most age without such problems.

In a national survey of Canadians age 40 to 64, only 3 in 10 rated their sex life as less enjoyable than during their twenties (Wright, 2006). After middle age, most men and women remain capable of satisfying sexual activity. In another survey by the National Council on Aging, 39 percent of people over 60 expressed satisfaction with the amount of sex they were having and 39 percent said they wished for sex more frequently (Leary, 1998). And in an American Association of Retired Persons sexuality survey, it was not until age 75 or older that most women and nearly half of men reported little sexual desire (DeLamater & Sill, 2005).

Baseball averages—18 players with 20-year careers

Baseball averages over 20 years for Willie Mays

RESEARCH

Have students research the effects of older fathers on childhood development. Several celebrities have fathered children in old age, including Tony Randall and Clint Eastwood. Do children of older fathers deal with different developmental issues than children of younger parents? Why or why not?

Physical Changes in Later Life

Is old age "more to be feared than death" (Juvenal, *Satires*)? Or is life "most delightful when it is on the downward slope" (Seneca, *Epistulae ad Lucilium*)? What is it like to grow old? To gauge your own understanding, take the following true/false quiz:

1. Older people become more susceptible to short-term illnesses.

2. During old age many of the brain's neurons die.

3. If they live to be 90 or older, most people eventually become senile.

4. Recognition memory—the ability to identify things previously experienced—declines with age.

5. Life satisfaction peaks in the fifties and then gradually declines after age 65.

Life Expectancy The above statements—all false—are among the misconceptions about aging exploded by recent research. Worldwide, life expectancy at birth increased from 49 years in 1950 to 67 in 2004—and to 80 and beyond in some developed countries (PRB, 2004; Sivard, 1996). This increasing life expectancy (humanity's greatest achievement, say some) combines with decreasing birthrates to make older adults a bigger and bigger population segment, which provides an increasing demand for cruise ships, hearing aids, retirement villages, and nursing homes.

By 2050, about 35 percent of Europe's population likely will be over age 60 (Fernández-Ballesteros & Caprara, 2003). Clearly, countries that have depended on children to care for the aged are destined for a "demographic tsunami." Russia and Western Europe are also headed for depopulation—from 146 million to 104 million people in Russia by 2050, projects the United Nations (Brooks, 2005). "When an entire continent, healthier, wealthier, and more secure than ever before, fails to create the human future in the most elemental sense—by creating the next generation—something very serious is afoot," states George Weigel (2005).

Life expectancy differs for males and females; males are more prone to dying. Although 126 male embryos begin life for every 100 females who do so, the sex ratio is down to 105 males for every 100 females at birth (Strickland, 1992). During the first year, male infants' death rates exceed females' by one-fourth. Women outlive men by 4 years worldwide and by 5 to 6 years in Canada, the United States, and Australia. (Rather than marrying a man older than themselves, 20-year-old women who want a husband who shares their life expectancy should wait for the 15-year-old boys to mature.) By age 100, females outnumber males 5 to 1.

But few of us live to 100. Even if no one died before age 50, and cancer, heart disease, and infectious illness were eliminated, average life expectancy would still increase only to about 85 or a few years beyond (Barinaga, 1991). The body ages. Its cells stop reproducing. It becomes frail. It becomes vulnerable to tiny insults—hot weather, a fall, a mild infection—that *your* body easily handles.

With age (especially when accentuated by smoking, obesity, or stress), people's chromosome tips, called *telomeres*, wear down, much as the tip of a shoelace frays. As these protective tips shorten, aging cells may die without being replaced with perfect genetic replicas (Blackburn et al., 2007; Valdes et al., 2005; Zhang et al., 2007).

Why do we eventually wear out? Why don't we, like the bristlecone pine trees, rockfish, and some social insect queens, grow older without withering? One theory, proposed by evolutionary biologists, speculates that the answer relates to our survival as a species: We pass on our genes most successfully when we raise our young and then stop consuming resources. Once we've fulfilled our gene-reproducing and nurturing task, there are no natural selection pressures against genes that cause degeneration in later life (Olshansky et al., 1993; Sapolsky & Finch, 1991).

The human spirit also affects life expectancy. As we saw in Unit 8B, chronic anger and depression increase our risk of ill health and premature death. Researchers have

::menopause the time of natural cessation of menstruation; also refers to the biological changes a woman experiences as her ability to reproduce declines.

World record for longevity? French woman Jeanne Calment, the oldest human in history with authenticated age, died in 1998 at age 122. At age 100, she was still riding a bike. At age 114, she became the oldest film actor ever, by portraying herself in *Vincent and Me.*

Aging researchers

CULTURAL CONNECTIONS

Have students research how growing old is viewed in cultures that are Native American, tribal African, African-American, Muslim, Hispanic, Indian, Eastern European, Western European, or Asian. Encourage students to present their findings to the class as an oral report.

TEACHING TIP

Some students may have grandparents or parents who are dealing with the effects of growing older. Help them discuss their frustrations with these effects and guide them toward more sensitive ways of interacting with older people in their lives.

At this time, you may want to use **Lecture/Discussion Topic: *2002—American Perceptions of Aging in the Twenty-First Century*** (p. 33) from Bolt's Teacher's Resource Binder.

DEMO

What is it like to age physically? Students may get frustrated with older people as they move around in the world more slowly than teens. Have them experience what it is like to have arthritis, lowered visual acuity, and lower auditory thresholds by simulating these ailments using tape, gloves, modified glasses, and earplugs. As they are physically impaired, they can try to do simple tasks, such as write checks, see road signs, read menus, and hear instructions.

In Figure 9.30, Myers shows how sensory abilities decrease dramatically as people age into their 70s. However, students should notice that, for the most part, sensory acuity is relatively stable for most of adulthood. In fact, some sensory abilities get *better* in early to mid-adulthood before tapering off in later adulthood.

You can find an example of the "mosquito" tone on the Internet. Some students may find that they cannot hear the sound. Sensitivity to the sound is largely dependent on the level of exposure to extremely loud noises. If students are attending loud concerts or listening to their iPods loudly, they may be damaging their hearing more than they realize.

➤ **FIGURE 9.29**
Postponing a date with the grim reaper? The total number of daily U.S. deaths from 1987 to 2002 increased on the days following Christmas. To researchers Mitsuru Shimizu and Brett Pelham (2008), this adds to the growing evidence of a death-deferral phenomenon.

> "For some reason, possibly to save ink, the restaurants had started printing their menus in letters the height of bacteria."
> Dave Barry, *Dave Barry Turns Fifty*, 1998

• Most stairway falls taken by older people occur on the top step, precisely where the person typically descends from a window-lit hallway into the darker stairwell (Fozard & Popkin, 1978). Our knowledge of aging could be used to design environments that would reduce such accidents (National Research Council, 1990). •

➤ **FIGURE 9.30**
The aging senses Sight, smell, and hearing all are less acute among those over age 70. (From Doty et al., 1984.)

even observed an intriguing *death-deferral* phenomenon. For example, Mitsuru Shimizu and Brett Pelham (2008) report that, in one recent 15-year-period, 2000 to 3000 more Americans died on the two days after Christmas than on Christmas and the two days before (**FIGURE 9.29**). And the death rate *increases* when people reach their birthdays, as it did for those who survived to the milestone first day of the new millennium.

Sensory Abilities Although physical decline begins in early adulthood, we are not usually acutely aware of it until later life. Visual sharpness diminishes, and distance perception and adaptation to changes in light level are less acute. Muscle strength, reaction time, and stamina also diminish noticeably, as do vision, the sense of smell, and hearing (**FIGURE 9.30**). In later life, the stairs get steeper, the print gets smaller, and other people seem to mumble more. In Wales, teens' loitering around a convenience store has been discouraged by a device that emits an aversive high-pitched sound that almost no one over 30 can hear (Lyall, 2005). Some students use that pitch to their advantage with ringtones that their instructors cannot hear (Vitello, 2006).

With age, the eye's pupil shrinks and its lens becomes less transparent, reducing the amount of light reaching the retina. In fact, a 65-year-old retina receives only about one-third as much light as its 20-year-old counterpart (Kline & Schieber, 1985). Thus, to see as well as a 20-year-old when reading or driving, a 65-year-old needs three times as much light—a reason for buying cars with untinted windshields. This also explains why older people sometimes ask younger people, "Don't you need better light for reading?"

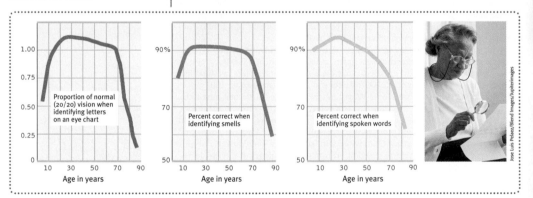

In the UK, many shopkeepers used the mosquito tone to keep groups of teenagers from loitering around their stores. However, these tones were also disturbing to children and infants, causing them to cry and become upset when exposed to the noise.

At this time, you may want to use **Classroom Exercise/Student Project: *Is There a Prime of Life?*** (p. 33) from Bolt's Teacher's Resource Binder.

Health For those growing older, there is both bad and good news about health. The bad news: The body's disease-fighting immune system weakens, making older people more susceptible to life-threatening ailments such as cancer and pneumonia. The good news: Thanks partly to a lifetime's accumulation of antibodies, those over 65 suffer fewer short-term ailments, such as common flu and cold viruses. They are, for example, half as likely as 20-year-olds and one-fifth as likely as preschoolers to suffer upper respiratory flu each year (National Center for Health Statistics, 1990). This helps explain why older workers have lower absenteeism rates (Rhodes, 1983).

Aging levies a tax on the brain by slowing our neural processing. Up to the teen years, we process information with greater and greater speed (Fry & Hale, 1996; Kail, 1991). But compared to you, older people take a bit more time to react, to solve perceptual puzzles, even to remember names (Bashore et al., 1997; Verhaeghen & Salthouse, 1997). The lag is greatest on complex tasks (Cerrella, 1985; Poon, 1987). At video games, most 70-year-olds are no match for a 20-year-old. And, as FIGURE 9.31 indicates, fatal accident rates per mile driven increase sharply after age 75. By age 85, they exceed the 16-year-old level. Nevertheless, because older people drive less, they account for fewer than 10 percent of crashes (Coughlin et al., 2004).

Brain regions important to memory begin to atrophy during aging (Schacter, 1996). In young adulthood, a small, gradual net loss of brain cells begins, contributing by age 80 to a brain-weight reduction of 5 percent or so. Earlier, we noted that late-maturing frontal lobes help account for teen impulsivity. Late in life, atrophy of the inhibition-controlling frontal lobes seemingly explains older people's occasional blunt questions ("Have you put on weight?") and frank comments (von Hippel, 2007).

In addition to enhancing muscles, bones, and energy and helping to prevent obesity and heart disease, exercising the body feeds the brain and helps compensate for cell loss (Coleman & Flood, 1986). Physical exercise stimulates brain cell development and neural connections, thanks perhaps to increased oxygen and nutrient flow (Kempermann et al., 1998; Pereira et al., 2007). That may explain why active older adults tend to be mentally quick older adults, and why, across 20 studies, sedentary older adults randomly assigned to aerobic exercise programs have exhibited enhanced memory and sharpened judgment (Colcombe & Kramer, 2003; Colcombe et al., 2004; Weuve et al., 2004). Exercise also promotes neurogenesis (the birth of new nerve cells) in the hippocampus, a brain region important for memory (Pereira et al., 2007). And exercise helps maintain the telomeres protecting the ends of chromosomes (Cherkas et al., 2008). We are more likely to rust from disuse than to wear out from overuse.

➤ FIGURE 9.31

Age and driver fatalities Slowing reactions contribute to increased accident risks among those 75 and older, and their greater fragility increases their risk of death when accidents happen (NHTSA, 2000). Would you favor driver exams based on performance, not age, to screen out those whose slow reactions or sensory impairments indicate accident risk?

UNIT 9

RESEARCH

Ask students to conduct more in-depth research about Alzheimer's disease and senile dementia.

- What are the causes, symptoms, and treatments for each?

- How can doctors make a definitive diagnosis for either? Are they often misdiagnosed?

- What are some early warning signs?

- What percentage of older people gets these disorders?

At this time, you may want to use **Classroom Exercise: Alzheimer's Quiz** (p. 36) from Bolt's Teacher's Resource Binder.

> "We're keeping people alive so they can live long enough to get Alzheimer's disease."
>
> Steve McConnell, Alzheimer's Association Vice President, 2007

Dementia and Alzheimer's Disease Some adults do, unfortunately, suffer a substantial loss of brain cells. Up to age 95, the incidence of mental disintegration doubles roughly every 5 years (**FIGURE 9.32**). A series of small strokes, a brain tumor, or alcohol dependence can progressively damage the brain, causing that mental erosion we call *dementia*. So, too, can the feared brain ailment, *Alzheimer's disease*, which strikes 3 percent of the world's population by age 75. Alzheimer's symptoms are *not* normal aging. (Occasionally forgetting where you laid the car keys is no cause for alarm; forgetting how to get home may suggest Alzheimer's.)

➤ **FIGURE 9.32**
Incidence of dementia (mental disintegration) by age Risk of dementia due to Alzheimer's disease or a series of strokes doubles about every 5 years in later life. (From Jorm et al., 1987, based on 22 studies in industrial nations.)

Alzheimer's destroys even the brightest of minds. First memory deteriorates, then reasoning. Robert Sayre (1979) recalls his father shouting at his afflicted mother to "think harder," while his mother, confused, embarrassed, on the verge of tears, randomly searched the house for lost objects. A diminishing sense of smell is associated with the pathology that foretells Alzheimer's (Wilson et al., 2007). As the disease runs its course, after 5 to 20 years, the person becomes emotionally flat, then disoriented and disinhibited, then incontinent, and finally mentally vacant—a sort of living death, a mere body stripped of much of its humanity.

Underlying the symptoms of Alzheimer's is a loss of brain cells and deterioration of neurons that produce the neurotransmitter acetylcholine. Deprived of this vital chemical messenger, memory and thinking suffer. An autopsy reveals two telltale abnormalities in these acetylcholine-producing neurons: shriveled protein filaments in the cell body, and plaques (globs of degenerating tissue) at the tips of neuron branches. In one line of research, scientists are working to develop drugs that will block proteins from aggregating into plaques or that will lower the levels of the culprit protein, much as cholesterol-lowering drugs help prevent heart disease (Grady, 2007; Wolfe, 2006).

Researchers are gaining insights into the chemical, neural, and genetic roots of Alzheimer's (Gatz, 2007; Rogaeva et al., 2007). In people at risk for this disease, brain scans (**FIGURE 9.33**) reveal—before symptoms appear—the telltale degeneration of critical brain cells and diminished activity in brain areas affected by Alzheimer's (Apostolova et al., 2006; Johnson et al., 2006; Wu & Small, 2006). When the person is memorizing words, they also show diffuse brain activity, as if more exertion was required to achieve the same performance (Bookheimer et al., 2000). Physically active, nonobese people are less at risk for Alzheimer's (Abbott et al., 2004; Gustafson

RESEARCH

Have students research laws regarding health care of older people in the United States.

- When are older people eligible for Medicare? What benefits does it offer compared to private insurance?

- What benefits are available to care for people with Alzheimer's disease or senile dementia? Are nursing homes the only alternative?

- When people are diagnosed with a degenerative neurological disorder, do they lose any privileges as citizens, such as driving or voting? Why or why not?

> FIGURE 9.33
Predicting Alzheimer's disease During a memory test, MRI scans of the brains of people at risk for Alzheimer's (left) revealed more intense activity (yellow, followed by orange and red) when compared with normal brains (right). As brain scans and genetic tests make it possible to identify those likely to suffer Alzheimer's, would you want to be tested? At what age?

et al., 2003; Marx, 2005). So, too, are those with an active, challenged mind—often the mind of an educated, active reader (Wilson & Bennett, 2003). As with muscles, so with the brain: Those who use it, less often lose it.

Cognitive Development

17: How do memory and intelligence change with age?

Among the most intriguing developmental psychology questions is whether adult cognitive abilities, such as memory, intelligence, and creativity, parallel the gradually accelerating decline of physical abilities.

Aging and Memory

As we age, we remember some things well. Looking back in later life, people asked to recall the one or two most important events over the last half-century tend to name events from their teens or twenties (Conway et al., 2005; Rubin et al., 1998). Whatever people experience around this time of life—Barack Obama's election, the Iraq war, the events of 9/11, the civil rights movement—becomes pivotal (Pillemer, 1998; Schuman & Scott, 1989). Our teens and twenties are a time of so many memorable "firsts"—first kiss, first job, first going to college or university, first meeting your parents-in-law.

Early adulthood is indeed a peak time for some types of learning and remembering. In one experiment, Thomas Crook and Robin West (1990) invited 1205 people to learn some names. Fourteen videotaped people said their names, using a common format: "Hi, I'm Larry." Then the same individuals reappeared and said, for example, "I'm from Philadelphia"—thus providing visual *and* voice cues for remembering their name. As **FIGURE 9.34** shows, everyone remembered more names after a second and third replay of the introductions, but younger adults consistently surpassed older adults. Perhaps it is not surprising, then, that nearly two-thirds of people over age 40 say their memory is worse than it was 10 years ago (KRC, 2001).

But consider another experiment (Schonfield & Robertson, 1966), in which adults of various ages learned a list of 24 words. Without giving any clues, the researchers then asked some to *recall* as many words as they could from the list, and others simply to *recognize* words, using multiple-choice questions. Although younger adults had better recall, no age-related memory decline appeared on

● What experiences from your high school years do you think you may never forget? (These years, and the next few, will be among the times of your life you may remember most easily when you are 50.) ●

> FIGURE 9.34
Tests of recall Recalling new names introduced once, twice, or three times is easier for younger adults than for older ones. (Data from Crook & West, 1990.)

 TEACHING TIP

Point out that even teenagers have a more difficult time than younger children when it comes to learning a foreign language. Ask students if they had an easier time learning a new video game when they were in middle school compared to now. While learning new tricks seems to be easiest for the young, being even younger than a teenager seems to be advantageous for learning some types of tricks.

At this time, you may want to use **Student Projects:** *Attitudes Toward the Elderly* (p. 35) or *Growing Old* (p. 36) from Bolt's Teacher's Resource Binder.

TEACHING TIP

Divide students into two groups. Assign one group the adage "Can't teach an old dog new tricks" and the other group the adage "Never too late to learn." Have them come up with evidence and examples supporting each statement and then share those lists with the class as a whole. Revisit those lists after reading this section to see what the evidence seems to support.

UNIT 9

TEACHING TIP

Have students share instances in which they forgot to do something simple. Also have them relate stories of older people who seem to have good memories. Compare the types of memory lapses that seem to occur in teens with those that seem to occur in older adults.

TEACHING TIP

Market Facts Inc. asked, "What is the ideal age?" of more than 1000 adults. Most respondents, regardless of their actual age, said they feel and act as if they are in their mid-thirties. Both men and women wanted to be about 32 years old. The sexes differed, however, on the age they considered to be "old." Men thought old age occurred in the late sixties, and women said being old began in one's seventies. "Psychological age," suggested the pollsters, "may be just as important as real age when trying to understand people's behavior and such things as their buying decisions."

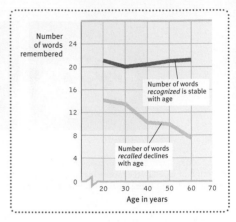

➤ **FIGURE 9.35**
Recall and recognition in adulthood In this experiment, the ability to *recall* new information declined during early and middle adulthood, but the ability to *recognize* new information did not. (From Schonfield & Robertson, 1966.)

the recognition tests (**FIGURE 9.35**). So, how well older people remember depends: Are they being asked simply to *recognize* what they have tried to memorize (minimal decline) or to *recall* it without clues (greater decline)?

Prospective memory ("Remember to . . .") remains strong when events help trigger memories, as when walking by a convenience store triggers a "Pick up milk!" memory. Time-based tasks ("Remember the 3:00 P.M. meeting") prove somewhat more challenging for older people. Habitual tasks, such as remembering to take medications three times daily, can be especially challenging (Einstein et al., 1990, 1995, 1998). Teens and young adults surpass both young children and 70-year-olds at remembering to do something (Zimmerman & Meier, 2006). To minimize problems associated with declining prospective memory, older adults rely more on time management and on using reminder cues, such as notes to themselves (Henry et al., 2004).

Those who study our capacity to learn and remember are aware of one other important complication: Right through our later years, we continue to diverge. Younger adults differ in their abilities to learn and remember, but 70-year-olds differ much more. "Differences between the most and least able 70-year-olds become much greater than between the most and least able 50-year-olds," reports Oxford researcher Patrick Rabbitt (2006). Some 70-year-olds perform below nearly all 20-year-olds; other 70-year-olds match or outdo the average 20-year-old.

But no matter how quick or slow we are, remembering seems also to depend on the type of information we are trying to retrieve. If the information is meaningless—nonsense syllables or unimportant events—then the older we are, the more errors we are likely to make. If the information is *meaningful,* older people's rich web of existing knowledge will help them to catch it, though they may take longer than younger adults to *produce* the words and things they know (Burke & Shafto, 2004). (Quick-thinking game show winners are usually younger to middle-aged adults.) Older people's capacity to learn and remember *skills* also declines less than their verbal recall (Graf, 1990; Labouvie-Vief & Schell, 1982; Perlmutter, 1983).

Aging and Intelligence

What happens to our broader intellectual powers as we age? Do they gradually decline, as does our ability to recall new material? Or do they remain constant, as does our ability to recognize meaningful material? The quest for answers to these questions makes an interesting research story, one that illustrates psychology's self-correcting process (Woodruff-Pak, 1989). This research developed in phases.

TEACHING TIP

At this time, you may want to use **Lecture/Discussion Topics:** *Achievement in Later Life* (p. 37) or *Living to 100* (p. 38) from Bolt's Teacher's Resource Binder.

Phase I: Cross-Sectional Evidence for Intellectual Decline In **cross-sectional studies,** researchers at one point in time test and compare people of various ages. When giving intelligence tests to representative samples of people, researchers consistently find that older adults give fewer correct answers than do younger adults. David Wechsler (1972), creator of the most widely used adult intelligence test, therefore concluded that "the decline of mental ability with age is part of the general [aging] process of the organism as a whole."

For a long time, this rather dismal view of mental decline went unchallenged. Many corporations established mandatory retirement policies, assuming the companies would benefit by replacing aging workers with younger, presumably more capable, employees. As everyone "knows," you can't teach an old dog new tricks.

Phase II: Longitudinal Evidence for Intellectual Stability After colleges began giving intelligence tests to entering students about 1920, several psychologists saw their chance to study intelligence **longitudinally**—retesting the same people over a period of years. What they expected to find was a decrease in intelligence after about age 30 (Schaie & Geiwitz, 1982). What they actually found was a surprise: Until late in life, intelligence remained stable (**FIGURE 9.36**). On some tests, it even increased.

How then are we to account for the cross-sectional findings? In retrospect, researchers saw the problem. When cross-sectional studies compared 70-year-olds and 30-year-olds, it compared people not only of two different ages but of two different eras. It compared generally less-educated people (born, say, in the early 1900s) with better-educated people (born after 1950), people raised in large families with people raised in smaller families, people growing up in less affluent families with people raised in more affluent families.

According to this more optimistic view, the myth that intelligence sharply declines with age was laid to rest. At age 70, John Rock developed the birth control pill. At age 78, Grandma Moses took up painting, and she was still painting after age 100. At age 81—and 17 years from the end of his college football coaching career—Amos Alonzo Stagg was named coach of the year. At age 89, architect Frank Lloyd Wright designed New York City's Guggenheim Museum. As everyone "knows," given good health you're never too old to learn.

Phase III: It All Depends With "everyone knowing" two different and opposing facts about age and intelligence, something was clearly wrong. As it turns out, longitudinal studies have their own potential pitfalls. Those who survive to the end of longitudinal studies may be bright, healthy people whose intelligence is least likely to decline. (Perhaps people who died younger and were removed from the study had declining intelligence.) Adjusting for the loss of participants, as did a study following more than 2000 people over age 75 in Cambridge, England, reveals a steeper intelligence decline. This is especially so as people age after 85 (Brayne et al., 1999).

Research is further complicated by the finding that intelligence is not a single trait, but rather several distinct abilities (Unit 11). Intelligence tests that assess speed of thinking may place older adults at a disadvantage because of their slower neural mechanisms for processing information. Meeting old friends on the street, names rise to the mind's surface more slowly—"like air bubbles in molasses," said David Lykken (1999). But slower processing need not mean less intelligent. When given tests that assess general vocabulary, knowledge, and ability to integrate information, older adults generally fare well (Craik, 1986). Older Canadians surpass younger Canadians at answering questions such as, "Which province

::**cross-sectional study** a study in which people of different ages are compared with one another.

::**longitudinal study** research in which the same people are restudied and retested over a long period.

➤ **FIGURE 9.36**
Cross-sectional versus longitudinal testing of intelligence at various ages In this test of one type of verbal intelligence (inductive reasoning), the cross-sectional method produced declining scores with age. The longitudinal method (in which the same people were retested over a period of years) produced a slight rise in scores well into adulthood. (Adapted from Schaie, 1994.)

● Like older people, older gorillas process information more slowly (Anderson et al., 2005). ●

INTERCONNECTING

Remind students that cross-sectional and longitudinal research can be experimental or correlational in nature. Researchers can use these types of designs to conduct experiments or surveys at different times or with different cohorts of participants.

TROUBLESHOOTING

Help students see how cross-sectional and longitudinal research can have its benefits and drawbacks:

● Cross-sectional research is more efficient, in that participants are studied at one time. However, cross-sectional research is more susceptible to individual differences.

● Longitudinal research is less efficient, often taking years to complete. In addition, participant attrition is a problem. However, longitudinal research is less susceptible to individual differences, because participants are compared to themselves.

UNIT 9

RESEARCH

Have one group of students research lists of awards for writing (e.g., Pulitzer Prize, National Book Award, etc.). Explore which novels were written by people older and younger than 50 and how old the writer was when he or she won the award.

- Are more "great" novels written by older people?

- Do more book prizes go to younger writers or older writers?

Have another group of students research winners of top math and science prizes (e.g., Nobel Prizes, Fields Medals, etc.).

- In the citations for these awards, how old was the researcher when he or she was engaging in the work that earned him or her the prize?

Compare the ages of people successful in literature with those successful in math and science. Does age seem to be a factor, as the text suggests? Why or why not?

---

was once called New Caledonia?" And in four studies in which players were given 15 minutes to fill in words in *New York Times* crossword puzzles, the highest average performance was achieved by adults in their fifties, sixties, and seventies (**FIGURE 9.37**).

> "In youth we learn, in age we understand."
>
> Marie Von Ebner-Eschenbach, *Aphorisms*, 1883

German researcher Paul Baltes and his colleagues (1993, 1994, 1999) developed "wisdom" tests that assess "expert knowledge about life in general and good judgment and advice about how to conduct oneself in the face of complex, uncertain circumstances." Their results suggest that older adults more than hold their own on these tests, too. Thus, despite 30-year-olds' quick-thinking smarts, we usually select older-than-thirties people to be president of the company, the college, or the country. Age is sage. To paraphrase one 60-year-old, "Forty years ago I had a great memory, but I was a fool."

So the answers to our age-and-intelligence questions depend on what we assess and how we assess it. **Crystallized intelligence**—our accumulated knowledge as reflected in vocabulary and analogies tests—*increases* up to old age. **Fluid intelligence**—our ability to reason speedily and abstractly, as when solving novel logic problems—*decreases* slowly up to age 75 or so, then more rapidly, especially after age 85 (Cattell, 1963; Horn, 1982). We can see this pattern in the intelligence scores of a national sample of adults (Kaufman et al., 1989). After adjustments for education, verbal scores (reflecting crystallized intelligence) held relatively steady from ages 20 to 74. Nonverbal, puzzle-solving intelligence declined. With age we lose and we win. We lose recall memory and processing speed, but we gain vocabulary and knowledge (Park et al., 2002). Our decisions also become less distorted by negative emotions such as anxiety, depression, and anger (Blanchard-Fields, 2007; Carstensen & Mikels, 2005).

These cognitive differences help explain why mathematicians and scientists produce much of their most creative work during their late twenties or early thirties, whereas those in literature, history, and philosophy tend to produce their best work in their forties, fifties, and beyond, after accumulating more knowledge (Simonton, 1988, 1990). For example, poets (who depend on fluid intelligence) reach their peak output earlier than prose authors (who need a deeper knowledge reservoir), a finding observed in every major literary tradition, for both living and dead languages.

Despite age-related cognitive changes, studies in several countries indicate that age is only a modest predictor of abilities such as memory and intelligence. Mental ability

➤ **FIGURE 9.37**

Word power grows with age In four studies summarized by Timothy Salthouse (2004), older crossword puzzle players excelled when given 15 minutes with a *New York Times* puzzle.

TEACHING TIP

Crystallized intelligence is the type of intelligence involved in learning skills, such as riding a bike or ice skating. Once you learn, you can still perform the skill after many years of no practice. While the skill may not be very polished after a long period of inactivity, the task can still be performed.

more strongly correlates with proximity to death. Tell me whether someone is 70, 80, or 90, and you haven't told me much about the person's mental sharpness. But if you tell me whether someone is 8 months or 8 years from death, regardless of age, you'll give me a better clue to the person's mental ability. Especially in the last three or four years of life, cognitive decline typically accelerates (Wilson et al., 2007). Researchers call this near-death drop *terminal decline* (Backman & MacDonald, 2006).

Social Development

18: What themes and influences mark our social journey from early adulthood to death?

Many differences between younger and older adults are created by significant life events. A new job means new relationships, new expectations, and new demands. Marriage brings the joy of intimacy and the stress of merging your life with another's. The birth of a child introduces responsibilities and alters your life focus. The death of a loved one creates an irreplaceable loss. Do these adult life events shape a sequence of life changes?

Adulthood's Ages and Stages

As people enter their forties, they undergo a transition to middle adulthood, a time when they realize that life will soon be mostly behind instead of ahead of them. Some psychologists have argued that for many the *midlife transition* is a crisis, a time of great struggle, regret, or even feeling struck down by life. The popular image of the midlife crisis is an early-forties man who forsakes his family for a younger girlfriend and a hot sports car. But the fact—reported by large samples of people—is that unhappiness, job dissatisfaction, marital dissatisfaction, divorce, anxiety, and suicide do *not* surge during the early forties (Hunter & Sundel, 1989; Mroczek & Kolarz, 1998). Divorce, for example, is most common among those in their twenties, suicide among those in their seventies and eighties. One study of emotional instability in nearly 10,000 men and women found "not the slightest evidence" that distress peaks anywhere in the midlife age range (**FIGURE 9.38**). For the 1 in 4 adults who do report experiencing a life crisis, the trigger is not age, but a major event, such as illness, divorce, or job loss (Lachman, 2004).

Life events trigger transitions to new life stages at varying ages. The **social clock**—the definition of "the right time" to leave home, get a job, marry, have children, and retire—varies from era to era and culture to culture. In Western Europe, fewer than

::**crystallized intelligence** our accumulated knowledge and verbal skills; tends to increase with age.

::**fluid intelligence** our ability to reason speedily and abstractly; tends to decrease during late adulthood.

::**social clock** the culturally preferred timing of social events such as marriage, parenthood, and retirement.

> "Midway in the journey of our life I found myself in a dark wood, for the straight way was lost."
>
> Dante, *The Divine Comedy*, 1314

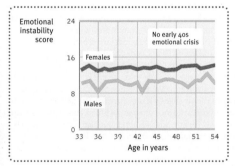

> **FIGURE 9.38**
> **Early forties midlife crises?** Among 10,000 people responding to a national health survey, there was no early forties increase in emotional instability ("neuroticism") scores. (From McCrae & Costa, 1990.)

CULTURAL CONNECTIONS

Explore other cultural differences in the social clock.

- How do other cultures (including Hispanic/Latin, European, African, Arabic, etc.) view the timing of marriage and childrearing?

- Do the immigrants from these cultures adopt the U.S. social clock or do they keep their own cultural traditions? How many generations tend to pass before U.S. customs are chosen over traditional ones?

CRITICAL THINKING

Ask students what significant life events their families have experienced since they were born. Have they moved? Changed jobs, either voluntarily or involuntarily? Added family members, either through birth, adoption, or caregiving? What effect have these life events had on the lives of their parents and their relationship with their parents?

 TEACHING TIP

Many of your students may be children of divorced parents. While the research shows that is common today, many students may feel alone and confused when their parents split. Encourage healthy discussion of how to handle being a child of divorce so students know they are part of a growing segment of society that knows what divorce is like firsthand.

10 percent of men over 65 remain in the work force, as do 16 percent in the United States, 36 percent in Japan, and 69 percent in Mexico (Davies et al., 1991). And the once-rigid sequence for many Western women—of student to worker to wife to at-home mom to worker again—has loosened. Contemporary women occupy these roles in any order or all at once. The social clock still ticks, but people feel freer about being out of sync with it.

Even *chance events* can have lasting significance because they often deflect us down one road rather than another (Bandura, 1982). Romantic attraction, for example, is often influenced by chance encounters. Albert Bandura (2005) recalls the ironic true story of a book editor who came to one of Bandura's lectures on the "Psychology of Chance Encounters and Life Paths"—and ended up marrying the woman who happened to sit next to him. The sequence that led to my authoring this book (which was not my idea) began with my being seated near, and getting to know, a distinguished colleague at an international conference.

Thus, chance events, including romantic encounters, can change our lives. Consider one study of identical twins, who tend to make similar choices of friends, clothes, vacations, jobs, and so on. So, if your identical twin became engaged to someone, wouldn't you (being in so many ways the same as your twin) expect to also feel attracted to this person? Surprisingly, only half the identical twins recalled really liking their co-twin's selection, and only 5 percent said, "I could have fallen for my twin's partner." Researchers David Lykken and Auke Tellegen (1993) surmise that romantic love is rather like ducklings' imprinting: Given repeated exposure to someone after childhood, you may form a bond (infatuation) with almost any available person who has a roughly similar background and level of attractiveness and who reciprocates your affections.

> "The important events of a person's life are the products of chains of highly improbable occurrences."
> Joseph Traub, "Traub's Law," 2003

Adulthood's Commitments

Two basic aspects of our lives dominate adulthood. Erik Erikson called them *intimacy* (forming close relationships) and *generativity* (being productive and supporting future generations). Researchers have chosen various terms—*affiliation* and *achievement, attachment* and *productivity, commitment* and *competence.* Sigmund Freud (1935) put it most simply: The healthy adult, he said, is one who can *love* and *work.*

Love We typically flirt, fall in love, and commit—one person at a time. "Pair-bonding is a trademark of the human animal," observed anthropologist Helen Fisher (1993). From an evolutionary perspective, relatively monogamous pairing makes sense: Parents who cooperated to nurture their children to maturity were more likely to have their genes passed along to posterity than were parents who didn't.

> "One can live magnificently in this world if one knows how to work and how to love."
> Leo Tolstoy, 1856

Adult bonds of love are most satisfying and enduring when marked by a similarity of interests and values, a sharing of emotional and material support, and intimate self-disclosure (see Unit 14). Couples who seal their love with commitment—via (in one study) marriage for heterosexual couples and civil unions for homosexual couples—more often endure (Balsam et al., 2008). Marriage bonds are especially likely to last when couples marry after age 20 and are well educated. Compared with their counterparts of 40 years ago, people in Western countries *are* better educated and marrying later. Yet, ironically, they are nearly twice as likely to divorce. (Both Canada and the United States now have about one divorce for every two marriages [Bureau of the Census, 2007], and in Europe, divorce is only slightly less common.) The divorce rate partly reflects women's lessened economic dependence on men and men and women's rising expectations. We now hope not only for an enduring bond, but also for a mate who is a wage earner, caregiver, intimate friend, and warm and responsive lover.

Might test-driving life together in a "trial marriage" minimize divorce risk? In a 2001 Gallup survey of American twenty-somethings, 62 percent thought it would

 TEACHING TIP

Have students develop a pamphlet or presentation for younger children about how to handle being a child of divorce. Encourage them to contact local psychologists who specialize in counseling children and families dealing with divorce for research-based tips they can offer others. This type of activity can help students deal with feelings they may have about their experiences with divorce.

(Whitehead & Popenoe, 2001). In reality, in Europe, Canada, and the United States, those who cohabit before marriage have had *higher* rates of divorce and marital dysfunction than those who did not cohabit (Dush et al., 2003; Popenoe & Whitehead, 2002). The risk appears greatest for cohabiting prior to engagement (Kline et al., 2004).

Two factors help explain why American children born to cohabiting parents are about five times more likely to experience their parents' separation than are children born to married parents (Osborne et al., 2007). First, cohabiters tend to be initially less committed to the ideal of enduring marriage. Second, they become even less marriage-supporting while cohabiting.

Nonetheless, the institution of marriage endures. Worldwide, reports the United Nations, 9 in 10 heterosexual adults marry. And marriage is a predictor of happiness, health, sexual satisfaction, and income. National Opinion Research Center surveys of more than 40,000 Americans since 1972 reveal that 40 percent of married adults, though only 23 percent of unmarried adults, have reported being "very happy." Lesbian couples, too, report greater well-being than those who are alone (Peplau & Fingerhut, 2007; Wayment & Peplau, 1995). Moreover, neighborhoods with high marriage rates typically have low rates of social pathologies such as crime, delinquency, and emotional disorders among children (Myers & Scanzoni, 2005).

Marriages that last are not always devoid of conflict. Some couples fight but also shower one another with affection. Other couples never raise their voices yet also seldom praise one another or nuzzle. Both styles can last. After observing the interactions of 2000 couples, John Gottman (1994) reported one indicator of marital success: at least a five-to-one ratio of positive to negative interactions. Stable marriages provide five times more instances of smiling, touching, complimenting, and laughing than of sarcasm, criticism, and insults. So, if you want to predict which newlyweds will stay together, don't pay attention to how passionately they are in love. The couples who make it are more often those who refrain from putting down their partners. To prevent a cancerous negativity, successful couples learn to fight fair (to state feelings without insulting) and to steer conflict away from chaos with comments like "I know it's not your fault" or "I'll just be quiet for a moment and listen."

Often, love bears children. For most people, this most enduring of life changes is a happy event. "I feel an overwhelming love for my children unlike anything I feel for anyone else," said 93 percent of American mothers in a national survey (Erickson & Aird, 2005). Many fathers feel the same. A few weeks after the birth of my first child I was suddenly struck by a realization: "So *this* is how my parents felt about me!"

When children begin to absorb time, money, and emotional energy, satisfaction with the marriage itself may decline. This is especially likely among employed women who, more than they expected, carry the traditional burden of doing the chores at home. Putting effort into creating an equitable relationship can thus pay double dividends: a more satisfying marriage, which breeds better parent-child relations (Erel & Burman, 1995).

Lisa B./Corbis

Love Intimacy, attachment, commitment—love by whatever name—is central to healthy and happy adulthood.

 What do you think? Does marriage correlate with happiness because marital support and intimacy breed happiness, because happy people more often marry and stay married, or both?

TEACHING TIP

Amy Wrzesniewski of NYU studies whether people view their occupations as jobs, careers, or callings. In one study of hospital janitors, she found that these people fell into one of these categories. Janitors who viewed their work as a job wouldn't work overtime unless paid extra. Janitors who viewed work as a career would work for advancement and recognition from superiors. Those who viewed being a janitor as a calling would participate in patient care, talking with patients and helping them get things they needed. One's attitude about an occupation can determine how positively one views that work.

Although love bears children, children eventually leave home. This departure is a significant and sometimes difficult event. For most people, however, an empty nest is a happy place (Adelmann et al., 1989; Glenn, 1975). Compared with middle-aged women with children still at home, those living in an empty nest report greater happiness and greater enjoyment of their marriage. Many parents experience a "post-launch honeymoon," especially if they maintain close relationships with their children (White & Edwards, 1990). As Daniel Gilbert (2006) has said, "The only known symptom of 'empty nest syndrome' is increased smiling."

Work For many adults, the answer to "Who are you?" depends a great deal on the answer to "What do you do?" For women and men, choosing a career path is difficult, especially in today's changing work environment. During the first two years of college or university, few students can predict their later careers. Most shift from their initially intended majors, many find their postcollege employment in fields not directly related to their majors, and most will change careers (Rothstein, 1980). In the end, happiness is about having work that fits your interests and provides you with a sense of competence and accomplishment. It is having a close, supportive companion who cheers your accomplishments (Gable et al., 2006). And for some, it includes having children who love you and whom you love and feel proud of.

▼ **Job satisfaction and life satisfaction** Work can provide us with a sense of identity and competence and opportunities for accomplishment. Perhaps this is why challenging and interesting occupations enhance people's happiness.

Well-Being Across the Life Span

To live is to grow older. This moment marks the oldest you have ever been and the youngest you will henceforth be. That means we all can look back with satisfaction or regret, and forward with hope or dread. When asked what they would have done differently if they could relive their lives, people's most common answer is "Taken my education more seriously and worked harder at it" (Kinnier & Metha, 1989; Roese & Summerville, 2005). Other regrets—"I should have told my father I loved him," "I regret that I never went to Europe"—also focus less on mistakes made than on the things one *failed* to do (Gilovich & Medvec, 1995).

From the teens to midlife, people typically experience a strengthening sense of identity, confidence, and self-esteem (Miner-Rubino et al., 2004; Robins & Trzesniewski, 2005). In later life, challenges arise: Income shrinks, work is often taken away, the body deteriorates, recall fades, energy wanes, family members and friends die or move away, and the great enemy, death, looms ever closer. Small wonder that most presume that happiness declines in later life (Lacey et al., 2006). But

"I hope I die before I get old," wrote The Who's Pete Townshend—when he was 20.

TEACHING TIP

At this time, you may want to use **Classroom Exercise: *Selective Optimization With Compensation*** (p. 37) from Bolt's Teacher's Resource Binder.

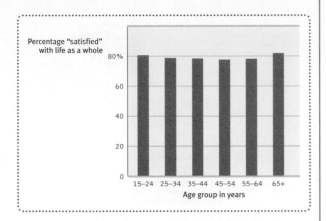

Percentage "satisfied" with life as a whole

> **FIGURE 9.39**

Age and life satisfaction With the tasks of early adulthood behind them, many older adults have more time to pursue personal interests. No wonder their satisfaction with life remains high, and may even rise if they are healthy and active. As this graph, based on surveys of 170,000 people in 16 countries shows, age differences in life satisfaction are small. (Data from Inglehart, 1990.)

RESEARCH

Research findings have suggested that a higher perceived purpose in life is associated with less fear of death. Help students explore the issue of death with these questions:

- What are the different socially acceptable ways people should feel about death?

- Did American poet Jesse Stuart speak the truth when, in recovering from a near-fatal heart attack, he said, "No man really begins to live until he has come close to dying"?

- Do you think acceptance of the inevitability of death is what gives meaning to life? Explain your answer.

the over-65 years are not notably unhappy, as Ronald Inglehart (1990) discovered when he amassed interviews conducted during the 1980s with representative samples of nearly 170,000 people in 16 nations (**FIGURE 9.39**). Newer surveys of some 2 million people worldwide confirm that happiness is slightly higher among both young and older adults than among those middle-aged. Moreover, national studies in both Britain and Australia reveal that the risk of depression tapers off in later life (Blanchflower & Oswald, 2008; Troller et al., 2007).

If anything, positive feelings grow after midlife and negative feelings subside (Charles et al., 2001; Mroczek, 2001). Consider:

- Older adults increasingly use words that convey positive emotions (Pennebaker & Stone, 2003).

- Older adults attend less and less to negative information. For example, they are slower than younger adults to perceive negative faces (Carstensen & Mikels, 2005).

- The amygdala, a neural processing center for emotions, shows diminishing activity in older adults in response to negative events, but it maintains its responsiveness to positive events (Mather et al., 2004; Williams et al., 2006).

- Brain-wave reactions to negative images diminish with age (Kisley et al., 2007).

Moreover, at all ages, the bad feelings we associate with negative events fade faster than do the good feelings we associate with positive events (Walker et al., 2003). This contributes to most older people's sense that life, on balance, has been mostly good. Given that growing older is an outcome of living (an outcome nearly all of us prefer to early dying), the positivity of later life is comforting. More and more people flourish into later life, thanks to biological, psychological, and social-cultural influences (**FIGURE 9.40**, next page).

The resilience of well-being across the life span obscures some interesting age-related emotional differences. Although life satisfaction does not decline with age, it often wanes in the terminal decline phase, as death approaches (Gerstorf et al., 2008). Also, as the years go by, feelings mellow (Costa et al., 1987; Diener et al., 1986). Highs become less high, lows less low. Thus, although we are less often depressed, and our *average* feeling level tends to remain stable, with age we also find ourselves less often feeling excited, intensely proud, and on top of the world. Compliments provoke less elation and criticisms less despair, as both become merely additional feedback atop a mountain of accumulated praise and blame.

> "At twenty we worry about what others think of us. At forty we don't care what others think of us. At sixty we discover they haven't been thinking about us at all."
> Anonymous

> "The best thing about being 100 is *no peer pressure.*"
> Lewis W. Kuester, 2005, on turning 100

UNIT 9

Be sensitive to students who may have experienced a death in their lives. Some students may want to talk about their loss while others may not. You may want to let students know in advance that you will be teaching about death and dying so they can let you know whether they are comfortable with the topic.

Have students write their own obituaries. Model the obituaries after those found in the newspaper. They should write what they want people to remember about them, reflecting on what they anticipate their lifespan will be.

At this time, you may want to use **Student Project:** *Preparing an Obituary* (p. 40) from Bolt's Teacher's Resource Binder.

➤ **FIGURE 9.40**
Biopsychosocial influences on successful aging Numerous biological, psychological, and social-cultural factors affect the way we age. With the right genes, we have a good chance of aging successfully if we maintain a positive outlook and stay mentally and physically active, as well as connected to family and friends in the community.

Psychologists Mihaly Csikszentmihalyi and Reed Larson (1984) mapped people's emotional terrain by periodically signaling them with electronic beepers to report their current activities and feelings. They found that teenagers typically come down from elation or up from gloom in less than an hour. Adult moods are less extreme but more enduring. For most people, old age offers less intense joy but greater contentment and increased spirituality, especially for those who remain socially engaged (Harlow & Cantor, 1996; Wink & Dillon, 2002). As we age, life becomes less an emotional roller coaster.

Death and Dying

Most of us will suffer and cope with the deaths of relatives and friends. Usually, the most difficult separation is from a spouse—a loss suffered by five times more women than men. When, as usually happens, death comes at an expected late-life time, the grieving may be relatively short-lived. (**FIGURE 9.41** shows the typical emotions before and after a spouse's death.) But even 20 years after losing a spouse, people still talk about the long-lost partner once a month on average (Carnelley et al., 2006).

Grief is especially severe when the death of a loved one comes suddenly and before its expected time on the social clock. The sudden illness that claims a 45-year-old life partner or the accidental death of a child may trigger a year or more of memory-laden mourning that eventually subsides to a mild depression (Lehman et al., 1987).

For some, however, the loss is unbearable. One study, following more than 1 million Danes over the last half of the twentieth century, found that more than 17,000 people had suffered the death of a child under 18. In the five years following that death, 3 percent of them had a first psychiatric hospitalization. This rate was 67 percent higher than the rate recorded for parents who had not lost a child (Li et al., 2005).

"Donald is such a fatalist—he's convinced he's going to grow old and die."

"Love—why, I'll tell you what love is: It's you at 75 and her at 71, each of you listening for the other's step in the next room, each afraid that a sudden silence, a sudden cry, could mean a lifetime's talk is over."
Brian Moore, *The Luck of Ginger Coffey*, 1960

RESEARCH

Have students explore what laws exist that prohibit ageism.

- Has ageism been given the same protections as racism? Why or why not?
- Is ageism more or less prohibited than gender discrimination? Why or why not?
- Do analysts predict that ageism will be given greater emphasis with the aging of the Baby Boomer generation? Why or why not?
- Do laws concerning ageism protect both the old and young alike? Why or why not?

Even so, the normal range of reactions to a loved one's death is wider than most suppose. Some cultures encourage public weeping and wailing; others hide grief. Within any culture, individuals differ. Given similar losses, some people grieve hard and long, others are more resilient (Ott et al., 2007). Contrary to popular misconceptions, however,

- terminally ill and bereaved people do not go through identical predictable stages, such as denial before anger (Nolen-Hoeksema & Larson, 1999). A Yale study following 233 bereaved individuals through time did, however, find that yearning for the loved one reached a high point four months after the loss, with anger peaking, on average, about a month later (Maciejewski et al., 2007).

- those who express the strongest grief immediately do not purge their grief more quickly (Bonanno & Kaltman, 1999; Wortman & Silver, 1989).

- bereavement therapy and self-help groups offer support, but there is similar healing power in the passing of time and the support of friends—and also in giving support and help to others (Brown et al., 2008). Grieving spouses who talk often with others or who receive grief counseling adjust about as well as those who grieve more privately (Bonanno, 2001, 2004; Genevro, 2003; Stroebe et al., 2001, 2002, 2005).

We can be grateful for the waning of death-denying attitudes. Facing death with dignity and openness helps people complete the life cycle with a sense of life's meaningfulness and unity—the sense that their existence has been good and that life and death are parts of an ongoing cycle. Although death may be unwelcome, life itself can be affirmed even at death. This is especially so for people who review their lives not with despair but with what Erik Erikson called a sense of *integrity*—a feeling that one's life has been meaningful and worthwhile.

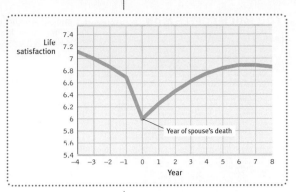

> ➤ **FIGURE 9.41**
> **Life satisfaction before, during the year of, and after a spouse's death** Richard Lucas and his collaborators (2003) examined longitudinal annual surveys of more than 30,000 Germans. The researchers identified 513 married people who experienced the death of a spouse and did not remarry. They found that life satisfaction began to dip during the prewidowhood year, dropped significantly during the year of the spouse's death, and then eventually rebounded to nearly the earlier level. (*Source:* Richard Lucas.)

> "Consider, friend, as you pass by, as you are now, so once was I. As I am now, you too shall be. Prepare, therefore, to follow me."
> Scottish tombstone epitaph

BEFORE YOU MOVE ON . . .

➤ ASK YOURSELF

In what ways are you looking forward to adulthood? What concerns do you have about your own transition into adulthood, and how do you think you might address them?

➤ TEST YOURSELF 6

Research has shown that living together before marriage predicts an increased likelihood of future divorce. Can you imagine two possible explanations for this correlation?

Answers to the Test Yourself questions can be found in Appendix E at the end of the book.

Reflections on Three Major Developmental Issues

WE BEGAN OUR SURVEY OF DEVELOPMENTAL psychology by identifying three pervasive issues: (1) how development is steered by genes and by experience, (2) whether development is a gradual, continuous process or a series of discrete stages,

TEACHING TIP

Have students construct a "life line" on a line they draw across a piece of notebook paper. They should label their birthday on the far left, project their death date on the far right, and show the day's date at the appropriate place along this continuum. Students should note important events from their childhood and adolescence to the left and some future life events to the right of the day's date.

Encourage students to compare and contrast events on their lifelines with a classmate. Finally, allow volunteers to tell the class what they learned from the exercise and how it relates to concepts about adulthood and aging that they read about in this module.

Brick, Peggy. (1981). The life cycle. In L. T. Benjamin & K. D. Lowman (Eds.), *Activities handbook for the teaching of psychology* (pp. 128–130). Washington, D.C.: American Psychological Association.

TROUBLESHOOTING

Many students will have heard of Elizabeth Kübler-Ross's theory about the stages of dying. While research does not support predictable stages, you may want to review Kübler-Ross's stages so students have a point of reference for this discussion:

- Denial
- Anger
- Bargaining
- Depression
- Acceptance

UNIT 9

TOO MUCH COFFEE MAN BY SHANNON WHEELER

LIFE:

PLAY, PLAY, PLAY, PLAY, PLAY, PLAY, PLAY, PLAY, PLAY,
PLAY, PLAY, PLAY, PLAY, PLAY, PLAY, PLAY, PLAY, PLAY,
PLAY, PLAY, PLAY, PLAY, PLAY, PLAY, PLAY, PLAY, PLAY,
PLAY, SCHOOL, PLAY, SCHOOL, PLAY, SCHOOL, PLAY, SCHOOL,
SCHOOL, SCHOOL, SCHOOL, SCHOOL, SCHOOL, SCHOOL, SCHOOL,
SCHOOL, SCHOOL, SCHOOL, SCHOOL, SCHOOL, SCHOOL, SCHOOL,
FIRST LOVE, BRIEF HAPPINESS, BREAK UP, REGRET, SCHOOL,
SCHOOL, SCHOOL, SCHOOL, SCHOOL, SCHOOL, SCHOOL, SCHOOL,
SCHOOL, SCHOOL, SCHOOL, SCHOOL, SCHOOL, SCHOOL, SCHOOL,
PLAY, WORK, PLAY, WORK, PLAY, WORK, PLAY, WORK,
IDEALISM, EFFORT, REJECTION, FAILURE, WORK, EFFORT, FAILURE,
COMPROMISE, WORK, WORK, WORK, WORK, WORK, WORK, PLAY,
COMMITMENT, WORK, WORK, WORK, WORK, WORK, WORK, PLAY,
WORK, WORK, WORK, WORK, WORK, WORK, WORK, WORK, PLAY,
WORK, WORK, WORK, WORK, WORK, WORK, WORK, WORK, PLAY,
WORK, WORK, WORK, WORK, WORK, WORK, WORK, WORK, PLAY,
WORK, WORK, WORK, WORK, WORK, WORK, WORK, WORK, PLAY,
WORK, WORK, WORK, WORK, WORK, WORK, WORK, WORK, PLAY,
WORK, WORK, WORK, WORK, WORK, WORK, WORK, WORK, PLAY,
WORK, WORK, WORK, WORK, WORK, WORK, WORK, WORK, PLAY,
WORK, WORK, WORK, WORK, WORK, WORK, WORK, WORK, PLAY,
WORK, WORK, WORK, WORK, WORK, WORK, WORK, WORK, PLAY,
WORK, WORK, WORK, WORK, WORK, WORK, WORK, WORK, PLAY,
WORK, WORK, WORK, WORK, WORK, WORK, WORK, WORK, PLAY,
WORK, WORK, WORK, WORK, WORK, WORK, WORK, WORK, PLAY,
RETIRE, PLAY, DIE.

©Shannon Wheeler

Stages of the life cycle

and (3) whether development is characterized more by stability over time or by change. We have considered the first issue in Units 1 and 3C. It is time to reflect on all three now.

Nature and Nurture

Studies of the inheritance of temperament, and of twins and adopted children (in Unit 3C), confirm that nature *and* nurture influence development. Genes *and* environment, biological *and* social factors direct our life courses, and their effects intertwine.

Continuity and Stages

Do adults differ from infants as a giant redwood differs from its seedling—a difference created by gradual, cumulative growth? Or do they differ as a butterfly differs from a caterpillar—a difference of distinct stages?

Generally speaking, researchers who emphasize experience and learning see development as a slow, continuous shaping process. Those who emphasize biological maturation tend to see development as a sequence of genetically predisposed stages or steps: Although progress through the various stages may be quick or slow, everyone passes through the stages in the same order.

Are there clear-cut stages of psychological development, as there are physical stages such as walking before running? We have considered the stage theories of Jean Piaget on cognitive development, Lawrence Kohlberg on moral development, and Erik Erikson on psychosocial development (FIGURE 9.42). And we have seen their stage theories criticized: Young children have some abilities Piaget attributed to later stages. Kohlberg's work reflected a worldview characteristic of educated people in individualistic cultures and emphasized thinking over acting. Adult life does not progress through the fixed, predictable series of steps Erikson envisioned.

Although research casts doubt on the idea that life proceeds through neatly defined, age-linked stages, the stage concept remains useful. The human brain does experience growth spurts during childhood and puberty that correspond roughly to Piaget's stages (Thatcher et al., 1987). And stage theories contribute a developmental perspective on the whole life span, by suggesting how people of one age think and act differently when they arrive at a later age.

➤ **FIGURE 9.42**
Comparing the stage theories (With thanks to Dr. Sandra Gibbs, Muskegon Community College, for inspiring this illustration.)

Lawrence Kohlberg			
Preconventional morality		Conventional morality	(Postconventional morality?)

Erik Erikson							
Basic Trust	Autonomy	Initiative	Competence	Identity	Intimacy	Generativity	Integrity

Jean Piaget			
Sensorimotor	Preoperational	Concrete operational	Formal operational

Birth | 1 yr. | 2 yrs. | 3 yrs. | 4 yrs. | 5 yrs. | 6 yrs. | 7 yrs. | 8 yrs. | 9 yrs. | 10 yrs. | 11 yrs. | 12 yrs. | 13 yrs. | 14 yrs. | Death

Stability and Change

This leads us to the final question: Over time, are people's personalities consistent, or do they change? If reunited with a long-lost grade school friend, would you instantly recognize that "it's the same old Andy"? Or does a person befriended during one period of life seem like a different person at a later period? (That was the experience of one male friend of mine who failed to recognize a former classmate at his 40-year college reunion. The aghast classmate to whom he spoke was his long-ago ex-wife.)

Researchers who have followed lives through time have found evidence for both stability and change. There is continuity to personality and yet, happily for troubled children and adolescents, life is a process of becoming: The struggles of the present may be laying a foundation for a happier tomorrow. More specifically, researchers generally agree on the following points:

1. The first two years of life provide a poor basis for predicting a person's eventual traits (Kagan et al., 1978, 1998). Older children and adolescents also change. Although delinquent children have elevated rates of later work problems, substance abuse, and crime, many confused and troubled children have blossomed into mature, successful adults (Moffitt et al., 2002; Roberts et al., 2001; Thomas & Chess, 1986).

2. As people grow older, personality gradually stabilizes (Hampson & Goldberg, 2006; Johnson et al., 2005; Terracciano et al., 2006). Some characteristics, such as temperament, are more stable than others, such as social attitudes (Moss & Susman, 1980). When a research team led by Avshalom Caspi (2003) studied 1000 New Zealanders from age 3 to 26, they were struck by the consistency of temperament and emotionality across time.

3. In some ways, we all change with age. Most shy, fearful toddlers begin opening up by age 4, and most people become more self-disciplined, stable, agreeable, and self-confident in the years after adolescence (McCrae & Costa, 1994; Roberts et al., 2003, 2006, 2008). Many irresponsible 18-year-olds have matured into 40-year-old business or cultural leaders. Such changes can occur without changing a person's position *relative to others* of the same age. The hard-driving young adult may mellow by later life, yet still be a relatively hard-driving senior citizen.

Finally, we should remember that life requires *both* stability and change. Stability enables us to depend on others, provides our identity, and motivates our concern for the healthy development of children. Change motivates our concerns about present influences, sustains our hope for a brighter future, and lets us adapt and grow with experience.

As adults grow older, there is continuity of self.

"As at 7, so at 70."
    Jewish proverb

"At 70, I would say the advantage is that you take life more calmly. You know that 'this, too, shall pass'!"
    Eleanor Roosevelt, 1954

BEFORE YOU MOVE ON . . .

➤ ASK YOURSELF

Are you the same person you were as a preschooler? An 8-year-old? A 12-year-old? How are you different? How are you the same?

➤ TEST YOURSELF 7

What findings in psychology support the concept of stages in development and the idea of stability in personality across the life span? What findings challenge these ideas?

Answers to the Test Yourself questions can be found in Appendix E at the end of the book.

TEACHING TIP

TEACHING TIP

Help students distinguish what is enduring and what is transient. Personality traits, such as the Big Five personality traits, tend to endure with only variation in intensity as we age. Preferences, such as our political or music preferences, tend to vary significantly as we age.

UNIT 9

TECHNOLOGY RESOURCES

These resources will be helpful for teaching the concepts in this portion of the unit:

- *Video series: Transitions Throughout the Life Span*

- *Videos: The Mind, 2nd ed., Module 12: Teratogens and Their Effects on the Developing Brain and Mind; Module 13: Capabilities of the Newborn; Module 14: Infant Cognitive Development; Module 15: Social Development in Infancy; Module 17: Aging and Memory; Module 18: Effects of Mental and Physical Activity on Brain/Mind; Module 19: Understanding Alzheimer's Disease*

- *PsychSim 5: Conception to Birth; Cognitive Development; Who Am I?; Signs of Aging*

- *ActivePsych: Digital Media Archive, 2nd ed.: Prenatal Animation: Fetal Development; The Scale Errors; Moral Development: The Heinz Dilemma A–H*

- *Videos: Digital Media Archive, 1st ed., Video Clip 13: Testing Competency in the Newborn; Video Clip 14: Reflexes in the Newborn; Video Clip 15: Object Permanence; Video Clip 16: Stranger Anxiety; Video Clip 18: Piaget's Conservation Task; Video Clip 19: Body Part Counting System; Video Clip 12: Harlow's Studies on Dependency in Monkeys; Video Clip 17: Morelli's Strange Situation Test; Video Clip 20: Erikson's Stages of Psychosocial Development—Trust Versus Mistrust;*

- *Videos: Digital Media Archive, 2nd ed.: Prenatal Brain Development: From Conception to Birth; Piaget's Conservation-of-Liquid Task A and B (also in the Psychology Video Tool Kit); Piaget's Conservation-of-Numbers Task; The Development*

UNIT REVIEW: Developmental Psychology

Prenatal Development and the Newborn

1: How does life develop before birth?

Developmental psychologists study physical, mental, and social changes throughout the life span. The life cycle begins at conception, when one sperm cell unites with an egg to form a *zygote*. Attached to the uterine wall, the developing *embryo's* body organs begin to form and function. By 9 weeks, the *fetus* is recognizably human. *Teratogens* are potentially harmful agents that can pass through the placental screen and harm the developing embryo or fetus, as happens with *fetal alcohol syndrome*.

2: What are some newborn abilities, and how do researchers explore infants' mental abilities?

Newborns are born with sensory equipment and reflexes that facilitate their survival and their social interactions with adults. For example, they quickly learn to discriminate their mother's smell and sound. Researchers use techniques that test *habituation*, such as the novelty-preference procedure, to explore infants' abilities.

Infancy and Childhood

3: During infancy and childhood, how do the brain and motor skills develop?

The brain's nerve cells are sculpted by heredity and experience; their interconnections multiply rapidly after birth. Pruning of unused connections begins to occur around puberty. Our complex motor skills—sitting, standing, walking—develop in a predictable sequence whose timing is a function of individual *maturation* and culture. We lose conscious memories of experiences from before about age 2½, in part because major areas of the brain have not yet matured.

4: From the perspective of Piaget and of today's researchers, how does a child's mind develop?

Piaget proposed that through *assimilation* and *accommodation*, children actively construct and modify their understanding of the world. They form *schemas* that help them organize their experiences. Progressing from the simplicity of the *sensorimotor stage* of the first two years, in which they develop *object permanence*, children move to more complex ways of thinking. In the *preoperational stage* they develop a *theory of mind* (absent in children with *autism*), but they are *egocentric* and unable to perform simple logical operations. At about age 6 or 7, they enter the *concrete operational stage* and can perform concrete operations, such as those required to comprehend the principle of *conservation*. By about age 12, children enter the *formal operational stage* and can reason systematically. Research supports the sequence Piaget proposed for the unfolding of human *cognition*, but it also shows that young children are more capable, and their development more continuous, than he believed.

5: How do parent–infant attachment bonds form?

At about 8 months, infants separated from their caregivers display *stranger anxiety*. Infants form *attachments* not simply because parents gratify biological needs but, more important, because they are comfortable, familiar, and responsive. Ducks and other animals have a more rigid attachment process, called *imprinting*, that occurs during a *critical period*. Neglect or abuse can disrupt the attachment process. Infants' differing attachment styles reflect both their individual temperament and the responsiveness of their parents and child-care providers.

6: How have psychologists studied attachment differences, and what have they learned about the effects of temperament and parenting?

Attachment has been studied in strange situation experiments, which show that some children are securely attached and others are insecurely attached. Sensitive, responsive parents tend to have securely attached children. Adult relationships seem to reflect the attachment styles of early childhood, lending support to Erikson's idea that *basic trust* is formed in infancy by our experiences with responsive caregivers. Yet it's become clear that *temperament*—our characteristic emotional reactivity and intensity—also plays a huge role in how our attachment patterns form.

7: Do parental neglect, family disruption, or day care affect children's attachments?

Children are very resilient. But those who are moved repeatedly, severely neglected by their parents, or otherwise prevented from forming attachments by age 2 may be at risk for attachment problems. Quality day care, with responsive adults interacting with children in a safe and stimulating environment, does not appear to harm children's thinking and language skills. Some studies have linked extensive time in day care with increased aggressiveness and defiance, but other factors—the child's temperament, the parents' sensitivity, and the family's economic and educational levels and culture—also matter.

8: How do children's self-concepts develop, and how are children's traits related to parenting styles?

Self-concept, a sense of one's identity and personal worth, emerges gradually. At 15 to 18 months, children recognize themselves in a mirror. By school age, they can describe many of their own traits, and by age 8 to 10 their self-image is stable. Parenting styles—authoritarian, permissive, and authoritative—reflect varying degrees of control. Children with high self-esteem tend to have authoritative parents and to be self-reliant and socially competent, but the direction of cause and effect in this relationship is not clear.

>> Technology Resources continued

of Tangles and Plaques in Alzheimer's Disease; Can the Immune System Be Used to Combat Alzheimer's Disease?

- *Videos: Scientific American Frontiers, 2nd ed., Segments 25: The Magic Years, and 27: A Change of Mind; Segment 23: Bringing up Monkey*

- *Videos: Scientific American Frontiers Teaching Modules, 3rd ed.: Cognitive Development: Overcoming Attentional Inertia; Childhood Disorder: Understanding Autism; Moral Thinking and Emotion: A Challenging Dilemma; Aging and Memory: Studying Alzheimer's Disease*

- *Psychology Video Tool Kit: Theory of Mind: Taking the Perspective of Others; The Two Faces of Autism; Today's Overscheduled Children; Sexual Identity Goes Awry; The Art of Listening: Males Versus Females; Love: The Mind-Body Connection; Are Today's*

9: What are some ways in which males and females tend to be alike and to differ?
Human males and females are more alike than different, thanks to their similar genetic makeup. Regardless of our gender, we see, hear, learn, and remember similarly. Males and females do differ in body fat, muscle, height, age of onset of puberty, and life expectancy; in vulnerability to certain disorders; and in *aggression,* social power, and social connectedness.

10: How do nature and nurture together form our gender?
Biological sex is determined by the twenty-third pair of chromosomes, to which the mother contributes an *X chromosome* and the father either an X (producing a female) or a *Y chromosome* (producing a male). A Y chromosome triggers additional *testosterone* release and male sex organs. *Gender* refers to the characteristics, whether biologically or socially influenced, by which people define male and female. Sex-related genes and hormones influence gender differences in behavior, possibly by influencing brain development. We also learn *gender roles,* which vary with culture, across place and time. *Social learning theory* proposes that we learn *gender identity* as we learn other things—through reinforcement, punishment, and observation.

Parents and Peers

11: To what extent is our development shaped by early stimulation, by parents, and by peers?
During maturation, a child's brain changes as neural connections increase in areas associated with stimulating activity, and unused synapses degenerate. Parents influence their children in areas such as manners and political and religious beliefs, but not in other areas, such as personality. Language and other behaviors are shaped by peer groups, as children adjust to fit in. By choosing their children's neighborhoods and schools, parents can exert some influence over peer group culture.

Adolescence

12: What physical changes mark adolescence?
Adolescence is the transition period between *puberty* and social independence. During these years, both *primary* and *secondary sex characteristics* develop dramatically. Boys seem to benefit from "early" maturation, girls from "late" maturation. The brain's frontal lobes mature during adolescence and the early twenties, enabling improved judgment, impulse control, and long-term planning.

13: How did Piaget, Kohlberg, and later researchers describe adolescent cognitive and moral development?
Piaget theorized that adolescents develop a capacity for formal operations and that this development is the foundation for moral judgment. Kohlberg proposed a stage theory of moral reasoning, from a preconventional morality of self-interest, to a conventional morality concerned with upholding laws and social rules, to (in some people) a postconventional morality of universal ethical principles. Kohlberg's critics note that morality lies in actions and emotions as well as thinking, and that his postconventional level represents morality from the perspective of individualist, middle-class people.

14: What are the social tasks and challenges of adolescence?
Erikson theorized that a chief task of adolescence is solidifying one's sense of self—one's *identity.* This often means "trying on" a number of different roles. During adolescence, parental influence diminishes and peer influence increases.

15: What is emerging adulthood?
The transition from adolescence to adulthood is now taking longer. *Emerging adulthood* is the period from age 18 to the mid-twenties, when many young people are not yet fully independent. But observers note that this stage is found mostly in today's Western cultures.

Adulthood

16: What physical changes occur during middle and late adulthood?
Muscular strength, reaction time, sensory abilities, and cardiac output begin to decline in the late twenties and continue throughout middle and late adulthood. Around age 50, *menopause* ends women's period of fertility but usually does not trigger psychological problems or interfere with a satisfying sex life. Men do not undergo a similar sharp drop in hormone levels or fertility.

17: How do memory and intelligence change with age?
As the years pass, recall begins to decline, especially for meaningless information, but recognition memory remains strong. *Cross-sectional* and *longitudinal studies* have shown that *fluid intelligence* declines in later life but *crystallized intelligence* does not.

18: What themes and influences mark our social journey from early adulthood to death?
Adults do not progress through an orderly sequence of age-related social stages. More important are life events, and the loosening of strict dictates of the *social clock*—the culturally preferred timing of social events. The dominant themes of adulthood are love and work, which Erikson called *intimacy* and *generativity.* Life satisfaction tends to remain high across the life span.

Girls Academically Superior to Boys?; Teen Boys: Emerging Sexuality; Teen Girls: Emerging Sexuality; Do Adolescents Lack Empathy?; Echo Boomers: Understanding Today's College Students; Alzheimer's Disease; Old Age: Thinking and Moving at the Same Time; Healthy Aging: The Power of Positive Thinking

- *Videos: Psychology: The Human Experience, Module 21: Attachment; Module 1: Gender Roles; Module 24: Gender Role Stereotypes; Module 22: Adolescence: Independence From Parents and Identity Formation; Module 23: Stages of Adult Development*

- *Videos: The Brain, 2nd ed., Module 3: Gender Development: Social Influences; Module 19: Alzheimer's Disease; Module 31: Brain Transplants in Parkinson's Patients*

UNIT 9

ANSWERS to Multiple-Choice Questions

1. **c.** cognitively.
2. **b.** Alzheimer's disease.
3. **d.** critical
4. **c.** Older people become less susceptible to short-term illnesses.
5. **a.** Postconventional
6. **a.** Sensitive, responsive caregivers
7. **b.** emotional reactivity.
8. **a.** decreases slowly with age.
9. **e.** a zygote.
10. **d.** a positive sense of self.
11. **d.** Formal operational
12. **a.** social clock.
13. **e.** habituation.
14. **c.** Time spent in day care
15. **b.** identity.

Rubric for Grading the Free-Response Question

This is a 12-point question. Each developmental theory receives a maximum of 4 points for accurate **identification** (1 point), **explanation** (2 points), and **criticism** (1 point). Modify the rubric by adding or subtracting terms depending on what was emphasized in class.

Identification: 1 point for each correctly identified theory
I. Piaget—Cognitive development
II. Erikson—Psychosocial development
III. Kohlberg—Moral development

Explanation: 1 point for each correctly mentioned theoretical aspect (2 points maximum for each developmental theory)

I. PIAGET
A. Mentioning all stages (sensorimotor, preoperational, concrete operational, formal operational) earns 1 point
B. Describe each stage (1 point):
   1. Sensorimotor—experiencing the world through senses
   2. Preoperational—representing

things with words and images; using intuitive reasoning
   3. Concrete operational—thinking logically about concrete events
   4. Formal operational—using abstract reasoning
C. Correctly identifying two of the phenomena in any stage (1 point per stage, up to 2 points) For example:
Sensorimotor
   1. Experiencing the world through senses
   2. Object permanence
   3. Stranger anxiety
Preoperational

   1. Representing things with words and images
   2. Pretend play
   3. Egocentrism
Concrete operational
   1. performing arithmetical operations
   2. Conservation
   3. Grasping concrete analogies
Formal operational
   1. Abstract reasoning
   2. Abstract logic
   3. Potential for mature moral reasoning

II. ERIKSON
A. Mentioning 4 of the 8 issues (trust vs.

Terms and Concepts to Remember

developmental psychology, p. 411
zygote, p. 412
embryo, p. 412
fetus, p. 412
teratogens, p. 413
fetal alcohol syndrome (FAS), p. 413
habituation, p. 414
maturation, p. 416
cognition, p. 417
schema, p. 418
assimilation, p. 418
accommodation, p. 418
sensorimotor stage, p. 419
object permanence, p. 419
preoperational stage, p. 421
conservation, p. 421
egocentrism, p. 421
theory of mind, p. 422

concrete operational stage, p. 423
formal operational stage, p. 423
autism, p. 424
stranger anxiety, p. 426
attachment, p. 426
critical period, p. 427
imprinting, p. 427
temperament, p. 428
basic trust, p. 429
self-concept, p. 432
gender, p. 435
aggression, p. 436
X chromosome, p. 438
Y chromosome, p. 438
testosterone, p. 438
role, p. 439
gender role, p. 439
gender identity, p. 440

gender typing, p. 440
social learning theory, p. 440
adolescence, p. 445
puberty, p. 445
primary sex characteristics, p. 446
secondary sex characteristics, p. 446
menarche [meh-NAR-key], p. 447
identity, p. 451
social identity, p. 451
intimacy, p. 452
emerging adulthood, p. 454
menopause, p. 456
cross-sectional study, p. 463
longitudinal study, p. 463
crystallized intelligence, p. 464
fluid intelligence, p. 464
social clock, p. 465

 AP* Practice Test Questions

Multiple-Choice Questions

1. Jean Piaget's development theory focused on how humans grow
   a. socially.
   b. morally.
   c. cognitively.
   d. physically.
   e. egocentrically.

2. The loss of brain cells, the deterioration of neurons that produce acetylcholine, and the formation of plaques at the ends of neuron branches is indicative of
   a. the death-deferral phenomenon.
   b. Alzheimer's disease.
   c. crystallized intelligence.
   d. multiple sclerosis.
   e. normal aging.

*AP is a trademark registered and/or owned by the College Board, which was not involved in the production of, and does not endorse, this product.

3. A time when certain events must take place to facilitate proper development is called the _____ period.
   a. conservation
   b. preoperational
   c. attachment
   d. critical
   e. assimilation

4. Which of the following is *true*?
   a. During old age, many of the brain's neurons die.
   b. If we live to be 90 or older, most of us will eventually become senile.
   c. Older people become less susceptible to short-term illnesses.
   d. Recognition memory—the ability to identify things previously experienced—declines with age.
   e. Life satisfaction peaks in the 50s and then gradually declines after age 65.

5. According to Kohlberg, what kind of morality is exhibited when actions are judged "right" because they flow from basic ethical principles?
   a. Postconventional
   b. Preconventional
   c. Conventional
   d. Preoperational
   e. Formal operational

6. According to Mary Ainsworth's research on attachment, what would a child need most to become "securely attached"?
   a. Sensitive, responsive caregivers
   b. The right temperament
   c. A terry-cloth wrapped "surrogate" mother
   d. An imprinting experience shortly after birth
   e. The right diet

7. Temperament refers to an infant's
   a. susceptibility to infection and disease.
   b. emotional reactivity.
   c. general intelligence.
   d. level of anger.
   e. ability to learn from situations.

8. Fluid intelligence—our ability to reason speedily and abstractly—
   a. decreases slowly with age.
   b. has not been measured over time.
   c. increases slowly with age.
   d. does not change until about age 75.
   e. remains unchanged if we exercise.

9. Once a sperm penetrates the cell wall of an egg and fertilizes it, this structure is known as
   a. an embryo.
   b. a fetus.
   c. placenta.
   d. a teratogen.
   e. a zygote.

10. Researchers suggest that infancy's major social achievement is attachment. *Childhood's* major social achievement is developing
    a. basic trust.
    b. into a sexually mature person.
    c. intimacy.
    d. a positive sense of self.
    e. object permanence.

11. Most adolescents can ponder and debate human nature, good and evil, truth and justice. According to Piaget, this is due to the emergence of which stage?
    a. Concrete operational
    b. Sensorimotor
    c. Preoperational
    d. Formal operational
    e. Accommodation

12. The sense of when to leave home, get a job, or marry is also referred to as the
    a. social clock.
    b. midlife crisis.
    c. critical period.
    d. life span.
    e. theory of mind.

13. The more often the stimulus is presented, the weaker the response becomes. Developmental researchers call this decrease in responding with repeated stimulation
    a. stagnation.
    b. attachment.
    c. autonomy.
    d. imprinting.
    e. habituation.

14. Eleanor Maccoby's research found which of the following factors to be the *least* positively correlated with problem behavior in preschool children?
    a. Parent income
    b. Parent education level
    c. Time spent in day care
    d. Child's temperament
    e. Parent sensitivity

15. According to Erikson's psychosocial theory of development, the crisis that needs resolution for adolescents involves the search for
    a. trust.
    b. identity.
    c. autonomy.
    d. initiative.
    e. worth.

Free-Response Question

Explain the stage theories of Jean Piaget, Erik Erikson, and Lawrence Kohlberg. Include a valid criticism of each.

WEB

Multiple-choice self-tests and more may be found at www.worthpublishers.com/myers

 Rubric continued

on their lives and feel a sense of satisfaction, or they feel failure.

III. KOHLBERG
A. Mentioning all levels (preconventional, conventional, postconventional) earns 1 point.
B. Correctly describing a level (1 point per level, up to 2 points). For example:
   1. Preconventional: Morality focuses on self-interest and obeying rules to avoid punishment or gain concrete rewards.
   2. Conventional: Morality focuses on caring for others and upholding laws because they are the laws.
   3. Postconventional: Actions are judged "right" because they flow from people's rights or basic ethical principles.

Criticism: 1 point for an accurate criticism of a theory (1 point per theory). Criticisms may include but are not limited to the following.

I. PIAGET
A. Researchers today see development as more continuous than Piaget did.
B. Piaget missed identifying some of children's conceptual abilities.
C. Formal logic is seen as a smaller part of cognition than Piaget thought.

II. ERIKSON
A. Researchers today see development as more continuous than Erikson did.
B. Erikson's theory may have been overly influenced by his upbringing.

III. KOHLBERG
A. Researchers contend that Kohlberg's theory is biased against women and members of collectivist societies.
B. Real-world moral choices don't always fit into Kohlberg's levels.
C. Morality lies in actions and emotions as well as in thinking.

mistrust, autonomy vs. shame, initiative vs. guilt, industry vs. inferiority, identity vs. role confusion, intimacy vs. isolation, generativity vs. stagnation, integrity vs. despair) earns 1 point
B. Correctly describing a task in any stage (1 point per stage, up to 2 points) For example:
   1. Trust vs. mistrust: If needs are met, infants develop trust.
   2. Autonomy vs. shame: Toddlers learn to exercise their will and do things for themselves, or they doubt abilities.
   3. Initiative vs. guilt: Preschoolers learn to initiate tasks, or they feel guilty about their efforts to be independent.
   4. Industry vs. inferiority: Children learn the pleasure of applying themselves to tasks, or they feel inferior.
   5. Identity vs. role confusion: Teenagers test roles and integrate them into a single identity, or becoming confused.
   6. Intimacy vs. isolation: Young adults form close relationships, or feel socially isolated.
   7. Generativity vs. stagnation: Middle-aged people feel they are contributing to the world, or they feel a lack of purpose.
   8. Integrity vs. despair: Older people reflect

UNIT 10

Pacing Guide

Use the following guide to determine how many instructional days to devote to this unit depending on the type of course you teach:

Year-long course: 4–6 days
Block schedule/Semester-long
course: 3–4 days

This unit encompasses 5–7 percent of the AP Exam. Spending an appropriate amount of time on this unit will help students do well on the AP Exam.

🛟 TEACHING TIP

At this point, you may want to use **Lecture/Discussion Topic:** *Issues in Personality Theory* (p. 4) or **Classroom Exercises:** *Introducing Personality* (p. 3) or *Your Theory of Personality* (p. 4) from Bolt's Teacher's Resource Binder, which accompanies this text.

478

Suggested Readings

Dolnick, E. (1998). *Madness on the couch: Blaming the victim in the heyday of psychoanalysis*. New York: Simon & Schuster.

Gay, P. (1997). *Freud: A life for our time*. New York: W. W. Norton.

Loftus, E., & Ketcham, K. (1994). *The myth of repressed memory: False memories and allegations of sexual abuse*. New York: St. Martin's Press.

Nye, R. D. (1992). *Three psychologies: Perspectives from Freud, Skinner, and Rogers* (4th ed.). Pacific Grove, CA: Brooks/Cole.

Seligman, M. E. P. (1998). *Learned optimism: How to change your mind and your life* (2nd. ed.). New York: Pocket Books.

Zimbardo, P. G. (1977). *Shyness*. Reading, MA: Addison-Wesley.

Personality

Lord of the Rings hobbit-hero Frodo Baggins knew that throughout his difficult journey there was one who would never fail him—his loyal and ever-cheerful companion, Sam Gamgee. Even before they left their beloved hometown, Frodo warned Sam that the journey would not be easy.

"It is going to be very dangerous, Sam. It is already dangerous. Most likely neither of us will come back."

"If you don't come back, sir, then I shan't, that's certain," said Sam. "[The Elves told me] 'Don't you leave him!' Leave him! I said. I never mean to. I am going with him, if he climbs to the Moon; and if any of those Black Riders try to stop him, they have Sam Gamgee to reckon with." (J. R. R. Tolkien, *The Fellowship of the Ring*, p. 96)

And so they did! Later in the story, when it becomes clear that Frodo's path will lead him into the land of Mordor, it is Sam who insists he will be at Frodo's side, come what may. It is Sam who lifts Frodo's spirits with songs and stories from their boyhood. And it is Sam whom Frodo leans upon when he can barely take another step. When Frodo is overcome by the evil of the ring he carries, it is Sam who saves him. In the end, it is Sam who helps Frodo successfully reach the end of his journey. Sam Gamgee—cheerful, optimistic, emotionally stable—never falters in his faithfulness or his belief that they will overcome the threatening darkness.

As he appears and reappears throughout the series, Tolkien's Sam Gamgee exhibits the distinctive and enduring behaviors that define **personality**—a person's characteristic pattern of thinking, feeling, and acting. It

is, suggest Dan McAdams and Jennifer Pals (2006), "an individual's unique variation on the general evolutionary design for human nature," which gets expressed in one's traits and cultural situation. Earlier units have focused on our shared paths—our similar ways of developing, perceiving, learning, remembering, thinking, and feeling. This unit focuses on what makes us unique.

Much of this book deals with personality. In earlier units, we considered biological influences on personality, personality development across the life span, and personality-related aspects of learning, motivation, emotion, and health. In later units we will study disorders of personality and social influences on personality.

In this unit we begin with two grand theories that have become part of our cultural legacy. These historically significant perspectives helped establish the field of personality psychology and raised key issues still being addressed in today's research and clinical work.

- Sigmund Freud's *psychoanalytic* theory proposed that childhood sexuality and unconscious motivations influence personality.
- The *humanistic* approach focused on our inner capacities for growth and self-fulfillment.

These classic theories, which offer sweeping perspectives on human nature, are complemented by what this unit goes on to explore: today's more focused and down-to-earth scientific research of specific aspects of personality.

::**personality** an individual's characteristic pattern of thinking, feeling, and acting.

479

Key Terms

personality

The Psychoanalytic Perspective

free association   id

psychoanalysis   ego

unconscious   superego

psychosexual stages

Oedipus complex

identification

fixation

defense mechanisms

repression   rationalization

regression   displacement

reaction formation   sublimation

projection   denial

collective unconscious

projective test

Thematic Apperception Test (TAT)

Rorschach inkblot test

terror-management theory

The Humanistic Perspective

self-actualization

unconditional positive regard

self-concept

The Trait Perspective

trait

personality inventory

Minnesota Multiphasic Personality Inventory (MMPI)

empirically derived test

The Social-Cognitive Perspective

social-cognitive perspective

reciprocal determinism

personal control

external locus of control

internal locus of control

positive psychology

Exploring the Self

self   self-serving bias

spotlight effect   individualism

self-esteem   collectivism

Key People

Alfred Adler

Gordon Allport

Albert Bandura

Roy Baumiester

Katharine Briggs

Isabel Briggs Myers

Hans Eysenck

Sybil Eysenck

Sigmund Freud

Karen Horney

Carl Jung

Ellen Langer

Hazel Markus

Abraham Maslow

Henry Murray

Judith Rodin

Carl Rogers

Hermann Rorschach

Julian Rotter

Barry Schwartz

Martin Seligman

UNIT 10

William Revelle of Northwestern University directs the Personality Project at www.personality-project.org. It has separate sections devoted to recommended readings, academic and nonacademic Web pages, psychological organizations, and "special advice for students."

TEACHING TIP

List the following terms on the board or overhead, asking students to describe what these terms mean to them. All of these terms are part of our common vocabulary thanks to Freud!

- Fixated—To be stuck on a particular object or way of behaving

- Repressed—To have suppressed thoughts, feelings, or memories that are too painful to bear

- Regressed—To act in a more immature way

- Anal-retentive—To be obsessively neat and organized

- Oedipus complex—A condition in which a boy loves his mother and hates his father

- Rationalize—To explain away a problem or justify one's own behavior

INTERCONNECTING

Link this discussion of hypnosis with Unit 5's treatment of the workings of this controversial psychotherapeutic technique. Unit 5 explains that some people are more easily hypnotized than others, because they are more susceptible to suggestion by authority figures.

::**free association** in psychoanalysis, a method of exploring the unconscious in which the person relaxes and says whatever comes to mind, no matter how trivial or embarrassing.

::**psychoanalysis** Freud's theory of personality that attributes thoughts and actions to unconscious motives and conflicts; the techniques used in treating psychological disorders by seeking to expose and interpret unconscious tensions.

::**unconscious** according to Freud, a reservoir of mostly unacceptable thoughts, wishes, feelings, and memories. According to contemporary psychologists, information processing of which we are unaware.

::**id** a reservoir of unconscious psychic energy that, according to Freud, strives to satisfy basic sexual and aggressive drives. The id operates on the *pleasure principle,* demanding immediate gratification.

::**ego** the largely conscious, "executive" part of personality that, according to Freud, mediates among the demands of the id, superego, and reality. The ego operates on the *reality principle,* satisfying the id's desires in ways that will realistically bring pleasure rather than pain.

Sigmund Freud, 1856–1939 "I was the only worker in a new field." ▲

Today's personality researchers study the basic dimensions of personality, the biological roots of these basic dimensions, and the interaction of persons and environments. They also study self-esteem, self-serving bias, and cultural influences on one's sense of self. And they study the unconscious mind—with findings that probably would have surprised Freud himself.

The Psychoanalytic Perspective

1: What was Freud's view of personality and its development?

LOVE HIM OR HATE HIM, SIGMUND Freud has profoundly influenced Western culture. Ask 100 people on the street to name a notable deceased psychologist, suggests Keith Stanovich (1996, p. 1), and "Freud would be the winner hands down." In the popular mind, he is to psychology's history what Elvis Presley is to rock music's history. Freud's influence lingers in literary and film interpretation, psychiatry, and clinical psychology. So, who was Freud, and what did he teach?

Long before entering the University of Vienna in 1873, a youthful Sigmund Freud showed signs of independence and brilliance. He had a prodigious memory and so loved reading plays, poetry, and philosophy that he once ran up a bookstore debt beyond his means. As a teen he often took his evening meal in his tiny bedroom in order to lose no time from his studies. After medical school he set up a private practice, specializing in nervous disorders. Before long, however, he faced patients whose disorders made no neurological sense. For example, a patient might have lost all feeling in a hand—yet there is no sensory nerve that, if damaged, would numb the entire hand and nothing else. Freud's search for a cause for such disorders set his mind running in a direction destined to change human self-understanding.

Exploring the Unconscious

Might some neurological disorders have psychological causes? Observing patients led Freud to his "discovery" of the unconscious. He speculated that lost feeling in one's hand might be caused by a fear of touching one's genitals; that unexplained blindness or deafness might be caused by not wanting to see or hear something that aroused intense anxiety. Freud at first thought hypnosis might unlock the door to the unconscious, but his patients displayed an uneven capacity for hypnosis. He then turned to **free association,** in which he told the patient to relax and say whatever came to mind, no matter how embarrassing or trivial. Freud assumed that a line of mental dominoes had fallen from his patients' distant past to their troubled present. Free association, he believed, would allow him to retrace that line, following a chain of thought leading into the patient's unconscious, where painful unconscious memories, often from childhood, could be retrieved and released. Freud called his theory of personality and the associated treatment techniques **psychoanalysis.**

Basic to Freud's theory was his belief that the mind is mostly hidden (**FIGURE 10.1**). Our conscious awareness is like the part of an iceberg that floats above the surface. Beneath our awareness is the larger **unconscious** mind with its thoughts, wishes, feelings, and memories. Some of these thoughts we store temporarily in a *preconscious* area, from which we can retrieve them into conscious awareness. Of greater interest to Freud was the mass of unacceptable passions and thoughts that he believed we *repress,* or forcibly block from our consciousness because they would be too unsettling to acknowledge. Freud believed that, although we are not consciously aware of them, these troublesome feelings and ideas powerfully influence us, sometimes gaining

TEACHING TIP

Sigmund Freud was not a psychologist; during the time he received his education, there were only one or two "psychology" programs in the world. Freud was trained as a neurologist and treated mostly women with what were commonly called "neuroses." These neuroses typically had a sexual component due, at least in part, to the Victorian social norm of sexual prudence that was prevalent during his lifetime.

► **FIGURE 10.1**

Freud's idea of the mind's structure
Psychologists have used an iceberg image to illustrate Freud's idea that the mind is mostly hidden beneath the conscious surface. Note that the id is totally unconscious, but ego and superego operate both consciously and unconsciously. Unlike the parts of a frozen iceberg, however, the id, ego, and superego interact.

"Good morning, beheaded—uh, I mean beloved."

expression in disguised forms—the work we choose, the beliefs we hold, our daily habits, our troubling symptoms.

For Freud the determinist, nothing was ever accidental. He believed he could glimpse the unconscious seeping not only into people's free associations, beliefs, habits, and symptoms but also into slips of the tongue and pen. He illustrated with a financially stressed patient who, not wanting any large pills, said, "Please do not give me any bills, because I cannot swallow them." Similarly, Freud viewed jokes as expressions of repressed sexual and aggressive tendencies, and dreams as the "royal road to the unconscious." The remembered content of dreams (their *manifest content*) he believed to be a censored expression of the dreamer's unconscious wishes (the dream's *latent content*). In his dream analyses, Freud searched for patients' inner conflicts.

Personality Structure

In Freud's view, human personality—including its emotions and strivings—arises from a conflict between impulse and restraint—between our aggressive, pleasure-seeking biological urges and our internalized social controls over these urges. Freud believed personality is the result of our efforts to resolve this basic conflict—to express these impulses in ways that bring satisfaction without also bringing guilt or punishment. To understand the mind's dynamics during this conflict, Freud proposed three interacting systems: the *id*, *ego*, and *superego* (Figure 10.1).

The **id's** unconscious psychic energy constantly strives to satisfy basic drives to survive, reproduce, and aggress. The id operates on the *pleasure principle:* It seeks immediate gratification. To envision an id-dominated person, think of a newborn infant crying out for satisfaction, caring nothing for the outside world's conditions and demands. Or think of people with a present rather than future time perspective—those who often use tobacco, alcohol, and other drugs, and would sooner party now than sacrifice today's pleasure for future success and happiness (Keough et al., 1999).

As the **ego** develops, the young child responds to the real world. The ego, operating on the *reality principle*, seeks to gratify the id's impulses in realistic ways that will bring long-term pleasure. (Imagine what would happen if, lacking an ego, we expressed all our unrestrained sexual or aggressive impulses.) The ego contains our partly conscious perceptions, thoughts, judgments, and memories.

INSTANT CASH

"Fifty is plenty."   *"Hundred and fifty."*
The ego struggles to reconcile the demands of superego and id, said Freud.

UNIT 10

::**superego** the part of personality that, according to Freud, represents internalized ideals and provides standards for judgment (the conscience) and for future aspirations.

::**psychosexual stages** the childhood stages of development (oral, anal, phallic, latency, genital) during which, according to Freud, the id's pleasure-seeking energies focus on distinct erogenous zones.

::**Oedipus** [ED-uh-puss] **complex** according to Freud, a boy's sexual desires toward his mother and feelings of jealousy and hatred for the rival father.

::**identification** the process by which, according to Freud, children incorporate their parents' values into their developing superegos.

::**fixation** according to Freud, a lingering focus of pleasure-seeking energies at an earlier psychosexual stage, in which conflicts were unresolved.

::**defense mechanisms** in psychoanalytic theory, the ego's protective methods of reducing anxiety by unconsciously distorting reality.

::**repression** in psychoanalytic theory, the basic defense mechanism that banishes anxiety-arousing thoughts, feelings, and memories from consciousness.

::**regression** psychoanalytic defense mechanism in which an individual faced with anxiety retreats to a more infantile psychosexual stage, where some psychic energy remains fixated.

::**reaction formation** psychoanalytic defense mechanism by which the ego unconsciously switches unacceptable impulses into their opposites. Thus, people may express feelings that are the opposite of their anxiety-arousing unconscious feelings.

▼

Identification Freud believed that children cope with threatening feelings of competition with their same-sex parent by identifying with that parent.

From the K. Vandevelde private collection

Around age 4 or 5, Freud theorized, a child's ego recognizes the demands of the newly emerging **superego,** the voice of our moral compass (conscience) that forces the ego to consider not only the real but the *ideal*. The superego focuses on how we *ought* to behave. It strives for perfection, judging actions and producing positive feelings of pride or negative feelings of guilt. Someone with an exceptionally strong superego may be virtuous yet guilt-ridden; another with a weak superego may be wantonly self-indulgent and remorseless.

Because the superego's demands often oppose the id's, the ego struggles to reconcile the two. It is the personality "executive," mediating the impulsive demands of the id, the restraining demands of the superego, and the real-life demands of the external world. If chaste Jane feels sexually attracted to John, she may satisfy both id and superego by joining a volunteer organization that John attends regularly.

Personality Development

Analysis of his patients' histories convinced Freud that personality forms during life's first few years. He concluded that children pass through a series of **psychosexual stages,** during which the id's pleasure-seeking energies focus on distinct pleasure-sensitive areas of the body called *erogenous zones* (**TABLE 10.1**).

Freud believed that during the *phallic stage* boys seek genital stimulation, and they develop both unconscious sexual desires for their mother and jealousy and hatred for their father, whom they consider a rival. Given these feelings, boys supposedly also experience guilt and a lurking fear of punishment, perhaps by castration, from their father. Freud called this collection of feelings the **Oedipus complex** after the Greek legend of Oedipus, who unknowingly killed his father and married his mother. Some psychoanalysts in Freud's era believed that girls experienced a parallel *Electra complex*.

TABLE 10.1

FREUD'S PSYCHOSEXUAL STAGES	
Stage	**Focus**
Oral (0–18 months)	Pleasure centers on the mouth—sucking, biting, chewing
Anal (18–36 months)	Pleasure focuses on bowel and bladder elimination; coping with demands for control
Phallic (3–6 years)	Pleasure zone is the genitals; coping with incestuous sexual feelings
Latency (6 to puberty)	Dormant sexual feelings
Genital (puberty on)	Maturation of sexual interests

Children eventually cope with the threatening feelings, said Freud, by repressing them and by identifying with (trying to become like) the rival parent. It's as though something inside the child decides, "If you can't beat 'em [the parent of the same sex], join 'em." Through this **identification** process, children's superegos gain strength as they incorporate many of their parents' values. Freud believed that identification with the same-sex parent provides what psychologists now call our *gender identity*—our sense of being male or female. Freud presumed that our early childhood relations—especially with parents and caregivers—influence our developing identity, personality, and frailties.

In Freud's view, conflicts unresolved during earlier psychosexual stages could surface as maladaptive behavior in the adult years. At any point in the oral, anal, or phallic stages, strong conflict could lock, or **fixate,** the person's pleasure-seeking energies in that stage. A person who had been either orally overindulged or deprived (perhaps by abrupt, early weaning) might fixate at the oral stage. This orally fixated adult could exhibit either passive dependence (like that of a nursing infant) or an exaggerated denial of this dependence (by acting tough or uttering biting sarcasm). Or the person might continue to seek oral gratification by smoking or excessive eating. In such ways, Freud suggested, the twig of personality is bent at an early age.

Defense Mechanisms

2: How did Freud think people defended themselves against anxiety?

Anxiety, said Freud, is the price we pay for civilization. As members of social groups, we must control our sexual and aggressive impulses, not act them out. But sometimes the ego fears losing control of this inner war between the id and superego. The presumed result is a dark cloud of unfocused anxiety that leaves us feeling unsettled but unsure why.

Freud proposed that the ego protects itself with **defense mechanisms**—tactics that reduce or redirect anxiety by distorting reality. Here are eight examples.

- **Repression** banishes anxiety-arousing wishes from consciousness. According to Freud, *repression underlies all the other defense mechanisms*, each of which disguises threatening impulses and keeps them from reaching consciousness. Freud believed that repression explains why we do not remember our childhood lust for our parent of the other sex. However, he also believed that repression is often incomplete, with repressed urges seeping out in dream symbols and slips of the tongue.

- **Regression** allows us to retreat to an earlier, more infantile stage of development. Facing the anxious first days of school, a child may regress to the oral comfort of thumb-sucking. Juvenile monkeys, when anxious, retreat to infantile clinging to their mothers or to one another (Suomi, 1987). Even homesick new college students may long for the security and comfort of home.

- In **reaction formation,** the ego unconsciously makes unacceptable impulses look like their opposites. En route to consciousness, the unacceptable proposition "I hate Dad" becomes "I love him." Timidity becomes daring. Feelings of inadequacy become bravado.

- **Projection** disguises threatening impulses by attributing them to others. Thus, "He doesn't trust me" may be a projection of the actual feeling "I don't trust him" or "I don't trust myself." An El Salvadoran saying captures the idea: "The thief thinks everyone else is a thief."

- **Rationalization** occurs when we unconsciously generate self-justifying explanations to hide from ourselves the real reasons for our actions. Thus, habitual drinkers may say they drink with their friends "just to be sociable." Students who fail to study may rationalize, "All work and no play makes Jack [or Jill] a dull person."

- **Displacement** diverts sexual or aggressive impulses toward an object or person that is psychologically more acceptable than the one that aroused the feelings.

"Oh, for goodness' sake! Smoke!"

::projection psychoanalytic defense mechanism by which people disguise their own threatening impulses by attributing them to others.

::rationalization psychoanalytic defense mechanism that offers self-justifying explanations in place of the real, more threatening, unconscious reasons for one's actions.

::displacement psychoanalytic defense mechanism that shifts sexual or aggressive impulses toward a more acceptable or less threatening object or person, as when redirecting anger toward a safer outlet.

VStock/Alamy

Barbara Von Hoffmann/Animals Animals

Regression Faced with a mild stressor, children and young orangutans will regress, retreating to the comfort of earlier behaviors. ▲

"The lady doth protest too much, methinks."
William Shakespeare, *Hamlet,* 1600

 TEACHING TIP

Have students create some type of sentence in which each word starts with the first letter of a defense mechanism. Challenge them to create a very useful sentence that describes the function of defense mechanisms that can help them remember even better. In fact, you may want to have a contest to see who can come up with the best sentence.

 TEACHING TIP

Some of the most famous fixations occurred during the oral and anal stages:

- If someone were weaned too early, then he or she would show signs of oral fixation later in life—always putting objects in the mouth, chain smoking, or overeating.

- In the anal stage, fixation occurs in one of two ways. If potty training occurs too early, a person can become *anal-retentive* (overly neat and fussy about organization and details). If potty training is not encouraged or allowed to happen haphazardly, the person can become *anal-expulsive* (overly slovenly and messy).

At this point, you may want to use **Classroom Exercise:** *Fifteen Freudian Principle Statements* (p. 6) or **Lecture/Discussion Topics:** *Freudian Slips* (p. 7) or *Freud's View of Humor* (p. 8) or *The Case of Little Hans* (p. 9) from Bolt's Teacher's Resource Binder.

 TEACHING TIP

Students may be familiar with the defense mechanisms as they are described, but the terminology may be confusing or difficult to remember. Have them create a narrative using the defense mechanisms as characters. Each mechanism should behave according to the description given in the text. As students create their stories, you can assess whether they understood these concepts and help those who didn't understand get a better picture of what each of the defense mechanisms is.

At this point, you may want to use **Classroom Exercises:** *Demonstrating Personality Structure* (p. 6) or *Defense Mechanisms* (p. 9) or *Defense Mechanism Miniskits* (p. 10) from Bolt's Teacher's Resource Binder.

UNIT 10

::**sublimation** psychoanalytic defense mechanism by which people re-channel their unacceptable impulses into socially approved activities.

::**denial** psychoanalytic defense mechanism by which people refuse to believe or even to perceive painful realities.

::**collective unconscious** Carl Jung's concept of a shared, inherited reservoir of memory traces from our species' history.

Children who fear expressing anger against their parents may displace it by kicking the family pet. Students upset over a test may snap at a friend.

- **Sublimation** is the transformation of unacceptable impulses into socially valued motivations. Sublimation is therefore socially adaptive and may even be a wellspring for great cultural and artistic achievements. Freud suggested that Leonardo da Vinci's paintings of Madonnas were a sublimation of his longing for intimacy with his mother, who was separated from him at an early age.

- **Denial** protects the person from real events that are painful to accept, either by rejecting a fact or its seriousness. Dying patients may deny the gravity of their illness. Parents may deny their child's misconduct. Spouses may deny evidence of their partner's affairs.

Note that these defense mechanisms are not conscious self-presentation tactics. Rather, they function indirectly and unconsciously, reducing anxiety by disguising some threatening impulse. Just as the body unconsciously defends itself against disease, so also, believed Freud, does the ego unconsciously defend itself against anxiety. Defense mechanisms protect our self-understanding.

BEFORE YOU MOVE ON . . .

> **ASK YOURSELF**

How would you describe *your* personality? What characteristics make up your typical patterns of thinking, feeling, and acting?

> **TEST YOURSELF 1**

What, according to Freud, were some of the important defense mechanisms, and what do they defend against?

Answers to the Test Yourself questions can be found in Appendix E at the end of the book.

The Neo-Freudian and Psychodynamic Theorists

3: Which of Freud's ideas did his followers accept or reject?

Freud's writings were controversial, but they soon attracted followers, mostly young, ambitious physicians who formed an inner circle around their strong-minded leader. These pioneering psychoanalysts and others, whom we now call *neo-Freudians*, accepted Freud's basic ideas: the personality structures of id, ego, and superego; the importance of the unconscious; the shaping of personality in childhood; and the dynamics of anxiety and the defense mechanisms. But they veered away from Freud in two important ways. First, they placed more emphasis on the conscious mind's role in interpreting experience and in coping with the environment. And second, they doubted that sex and aggression were all-consuming motivations. Instead, they tended to emphasize loftier motives and social interactions. The following examples illustrate.

Alfred Adler and Karen Horney (pronounced HORN-eye) agreed with Freud that childhood is important. But they believed that childhood *social,* not sexual, tensions are crucial for personality formation (Ferguson, 2003). Adler (who had proposed the still-popular idea of the *inferiority complex*) himself struggled to overcome childhood illnesses and accidents, and he believed that much of our behavior is driven by efforts to conquer childhood feelings of inferiority, feelings that trigger our strivings for superiority and power. Horney said childhood anxiety, caused by the dependent child's sense of helplessness, triggers our desire for love and security. Horney countered Freud's assumptions that women have weak

TEACHING TIP

Remind students of the way Freudian conceptualizations of "envy" have permeated our culture. Freud believed that girls developed penis envy, never forgiving their mothers for castrating them at birth. In the Disney/Pixar movie *Toy Story*, when Buzz Lightyear arrives in Andy's room, all the other toys but Woody are impressed with Buzz's laser light. As Woody protests that Buzz's laser is "just a lightbulb," Hamm the piggy bank asks Mr. Potato Head, "What's with Woody?" Mr. Potato Head leans over and whispers, "Laser envy."

TEACHING TIP

Karen Horney fully developed the idea of neurosis, or a driving need for something or someone. She believed neuroses helped to make life bearable, giving us a sense of something to strive for. Only when people didn't fulfill a need or became obsessed with a particular neurotic need did these neuroses become problematic and interfere with life. The 10 neurotic needs she identified can be divided into three main categories:

- *Compliance,* including needs for affection, a partner, and to simplify one's life.

- *Aggression,* including needs for power, exploitation of others, prestige, personal admiration, and personal achievement.

- *Withdrawal,* including needs for independence and perfection.

WEB CONNECT

Sigmund Freud and his ideas were perhaps some of the most influential and controversial of the 20th century. Have students prepare a report or series of reports on Freud and his influence on popular culture. Students can use Freud Net: The Abraham A. Brill Library at www.psychoanalysis.org/resources-library.html as a rich resource for finding information about Freud on the Internet. Maintained by the New York Psychoanalytic Institute, it contains a huge collection of books and articles on the life and work of Freud as well as links to "Sigmund Freud on the Internet."

Alfred Adler "The individual feels at home in life and feels his existence to be worthwhile just so far as he is useful to others and is overcoming feelings of inferiority" (*Problems of Neurosis*, 1964).

Karen Horney "The view that women are infantile and emotional creatures, and as such, incapable of responsibility and independence is the work of the masculine tendency to lower women's self-respect" (*Feminine Psychology*, 1932).

Carl Jung "From the living fountain of instinct flows everything that is creative; hence the unconscious is the very source of the creative impulse" (*The Structure and Dynamics of the Psyche*, 1960).

superegos and suffer "penis envy," and she attempted to balance the bias she detected in this masculine view of psychology.

Unlike other neo-Freudians, Carl Jung (pronounced YOO-ng)—Freud's disciple-turned-dissenter—placed less emphasis on social factors and agreed with Freud that the unconscious exerts a powerful influence. But to Jung, the unconscious contains more than our repressed thoughts and feelings. He believed we also have a **collective unconscious,** a common reservoir of images derived from our species' universal experiences. Jung said that the collective unconscious explains why, for many people, spiritual concerns are deeply rooted and why people in different cultures share certain myths and images, such as mother as a symbol of nurturance. (Today's psychologists discount the idea of inherited experiences. But many do believe that our shared evolutionary history shaped some universal dispositions.)

Freud died in 1939. Since then, some of his ideas have been incorporated into *psychodynamic theory.* "Most contemporary dynamic theorists and therapists are not wedded to the idea that sex is the basis of personality," noted Drew Westen (1996). They "do not talk about ids and egos, and do not go around classifying their patients as oral, anal, or phallic characters." What they do assume, with Freud, is that much of our mental life is unconscious; that we often struggle with inner conflicts among our wishes, fears, and values; and that childhood shapes our personality and ways of becoming attached to others.

Assessing Unconscious Processes

4: What are projective tests, and how are they used?

Personality assessment tools are useful to those who study personality or provide therapy. Such tools differ because they are tailored to specific theories. How might clinicians working in the Freudian tradition attempt to assess personality characteristics?

The first requirement would be some sort of a road into the unconscious, to track down residue from early childhood experiences—something to move beyond surface pretensions and reveal hidden conflicts and impulses. (Recall that Freud believed free association and dream interpretation could reveal the unconscious.) Objective assessment tools, such as agree-disagree or true-false questionnaires, would be inadequate because they would merely tap the conscious surface.

"The female . . . acknowledges the fact of her castration, and with it, too, the superiority of the male and her own inferiority; but she rebels against this unwelcome state of affairs."
Sigmund Freud, *Female Sexuality*, 1931

"The forward thrust of the antlers shows a determined personality, yet the small sun indicates a lack of self-confidence. . . ."

"We don't see things as they are; we see things as we are."
The Talmud

INTERCONNECTING

INTERCONNECTING

Link Adler's view of the importance of social tensions to Erik Erikson's theory of psychosocial development. Erikson, also a student of Freud's, supported many of Freud's primary ideas but rejected the emphasis on sexuality in childhood. His eight-stage theory outlines different social crises people must overcome in order to proceed to the next stage of development.

TEACHING TIP

Part of Jung's theory of the collective unconscious is his description of archetypes. Archetypes can be found in many classic and modern works of literature. Have students bring in their favorite piece of literature and identify archetypes found in those works. Some common archetypes include the following:

- Hero (Savior or Deliverer)
- The Quest (undertaking of a long journey in which battles, trials, and challenges take place to accomplish some lofty purpose)
- The Scapegoat (when the Hero must die or sacrifice something to save others)
- The Great or Good Mother (represents warmth, fertility, abundance)
- The Terrible Mother or Witch (represents danger, fear, or death)
- The Soul-Mate or Princess (represents inspiration or fulfillment)

TEACHING TIP

Jung developed his theories of the collective unconscious by studying people who experienced hallucinations as a result of a mental disorder. These hallucinations could not be explained by a past experience, which would fit in with traditional Freudian analysis, so Jung hypothesized that we must share a collective unconscious buried deep in our brains that contained experiences that occurred as a part of our shared evolutionary history.

At this point, you may want to use **Lecture/Discussion Topic:** *Freud's Legacy and the Neo-Analytic Movement* (p. 11) from Bolt's Teacher's Resource Binder.

Help students remember the term "projective" tests by linking that term to Freud's defense mechanism of projection. With projection, clients would attribute their negative feelings to someone or something else, making it safer for them to have those types of feelings. Projective tests enable people to apply their feelings to a picture, which the analyst interprets to explain hidden feelings and experiences.

 TEACHING TIP

Hermann Rorschach was a Swiss psychoanalyst who developed the famous inkblot test. Even though the test enjoyed popularity in the 1940s, '50s, and '60s, he did not experience success with the test in his lifetime. He had difficulty finding a publisher, and when his book *Psychodiagnostik* came out in 1921, it was poorly received. He died of complications from appendicitis in 1922 at the age of 37.

➤ **FIGURE 10.2**

The TAT This clinician presumes that the hopes, fears, and interests expressed in this boy's descriptions of a series of ambiguous pictures in the Thematic Apperception Test (TAT) are projections of his inner feelings.

➤ **FIGURE 10.3**

The Rorschach test In this projective test, people tell what they see in a series of symmetrical inkblots. Some who use this test are confident that the interpretation of ambiguous stimuli will reveal unconscious aspects of the test-taker's personality. Others use it as an ice-breaker or to supplement other information.

"The Rorschach Inkblot Test has been resoundingly discredited.... I call it the Dracula of psychological tests, because no one has been able to drive a stake through the cursed thing's heart."

Carol Tavris, "Mind Games: Psychological Warfare Between Therapists and Scientists," 2003

Projective tests aim to provide this "psychological X-ray," by asking test-takers to describe an ambiguous stimulus or tell a story about it. Henry Murray introduced one such test, the **Thematic Apperception Test (TAT),** in which people view ambiguous pictures and then make up stories about them (**FIGURE 10.2**). One use of storytelling has been to assess achievement motivation. Shown a daydreaming boy, those who imagine he is fantasizing about an achievement are presumed to be projecting their own goals.

The most widely used projective test is the famous **Rorschach inkblot test,** in which people describe what they see in a series of inkblots (**FIGURE 10.3**). Swiss psychiatrist Hermann Rorschach (pronounced ROAR-shock) based it on a childhood game in which he and his friends dripped ink on a paper, folded it, and then said what they saw in the resulting blot (Sdorow, 2005). Do you see predatory animals or weapons? Perhaps you have aggressive tendencies. But is this a reasonable assumption?

Clinicians' and critics' answers differ. Some clinicians cherish the Rorschach, even offering Rorschach-based assessments of criminals' violence potential to judges. Others view it as a helpful diagnostic tool, a source of suggestive leads, or an ice-breaker and a revealing interview technique. The Society for Personality Assessment (2005) commends "its responsible use" (which would *not* include inferring past child sexual abuse). And—in response to past criticisms of test scoring and interpretation (Sechrest et al., 1998)—a research-based, computer-aided tool has been designed to improve agreement among raters and enhance the test's validity (Erdberg, 1990; Exner, 2003).

But the evidence is insufficient to its revilers, who insist the Rorschach is no emotional MRI. They argue that only a few of the many Rorschach-derived scores, such as ones for hostility and anxiety, have demonstrated validity (Wood, 2006). Moreover, they say, these tests are not reliable. Inkblot assessments diagnose many normal adults as pathological (Wood et al., 2003, 2006). Alternative projective assessment techniques fare little better. "Even seasoned professionals can be fooled by their intuitions and their faith in tools that lack strong evidence of effectiveness," warned Scott Lilienfeld, James Wood, and Howard Garb (2001). "When a substantial body of research demonstrates that old intuitions are wrong, it is time to adopt new ways of thinking." Freud himself might have agreed. He probably would have been more interested in the therapist–patient interactions that take place during the testing process.

 TEACHING TIP

At this point, you may want to use **Lecture/Discussion Topics:** *Unconscious Insights* (p. 11) or *Terror-Management Theory and the Scrooge Effect* (p. 12) or **Classroom Exercise:** *The False Consensus Effect* (p. 13) from Bolt's Teacher's Resource Binder.

Evaluating the Psychoanalytic Perspective

5: How do contemporary psychologists view Freud and the unconscious?

Contradictory Evidence from Modern Research

We critique Freud from an early twenty-first-century perspective, a perspective that itself will be subject to revision. Freud did not have access to neurotransmitter or DNA studies, or to all that we have since learned about human development, thinking, and emotion. To criticize his theory by comparing it with current concepts, some say, is like criticizing Henry Ford's Model T by comparing it with today's hybrid cars. (How tempting it always is to judge people in the past from our perspective in the present.)

But both Freud's admirers and his critics agree that research contradicts many of his specific ideas. Today's developmental psychologists see our development as lifelong, not fixed in childhood. They doubt that infants' neural networks are mature enough to sustain as much emotional trauma as Freud assumed. Some think Freud overestimated parental influence and underestimated child abuse and peer influence. They also doubt that conscience and gender identity form as the child resolves the Oedipus complex at age 5 or 6. We gain our gender identity earlier and become strongly masculine or feminine even without a same-sex parent present. And they note that Freud's ideas about childhood sexuality arose from his skepticism of stories of childhood sexual abuse told by his female patients—stories that some scholars believe he attributed to their own childhood sexual wishes and conflicts (Esterson, 2001; Powell & Boer, 1994). Today, we understand how Freud's questioning might have created false memories of abuse, but we also know that childhood sexual abuse does happen.

As we saw in Unit 5, new ideas about why we dream dispute Freud's belief that dreams disguise and fulfill wishes. And slips of the tongue can be explained as competition between similar verbal choices in our memory network. Someone who says "I don't want to do that—it's a lot of brothel" may simply be blending *bother* and *trouble* (Foss & Hakes, 1978). Researchers find little support for Freud's idea that defense mechanisms disguise sexual and aggressive impulses (though our cognitive gymnastics do indeed work to protect our self-esteem). History also has failed to support another of Freud's ideas—that suppressed sexuality causes psychological disorders. From Freud's time to ours, sexual inhibition has diminished; psychological disorders have not.

Is Repression a Myth?

Freud's entire psychoanalytic theory rests on his assumption that the human mind often *represses* offending wishes, banishing them into the unconscious until they resurface, like long lost books in a dusty attic. Recover and resolve childhood's conflicted wishes, and emotional healing should follow. Under Freud's influence, repression became a widely accepted concept, used to explain hypnotic phenomena and psychological disorders. Freud's followers extended repression to explain apparently lost and recovered memories of childhood traumas (Boag, 2006; Cheit, 1998; Erdelyi, 2006). In one survey, 88 percent of university students believed that painful experiences commonly get pushed out of awareness and into the unconscious (Garry et al., 1994).

Today's researchers acknowledge that we sometimes spare our egos by neglecting information that is threatening (Green et al., 2008). Yet, many contend that repression, if it ever occurs, is a rare mental response to terrible trauma. "Repression folklore is . . . partly refuted, partly untested, and partly untestable," said Elizabeth Loftus (1995). Even those who have witnessed a parent's murder or survived Nazi death camps retain their unrepressed memories of the horror (Helmreich, 1992, 1994;

> "Many aspects of Freudian theory are indeed out of date, and they should be: Freud died in 1939, and he has been slow to undertake further revisions."
> — Psychologist Drew Westen (1998)

> "For seven and a half years I've worked alongside President Reagan. We've had triumphs. Made some mistakes. We've had some sex . . . uh . . . setbacks."
> — George H. W. Bush, 1988

> "I remember your name perfectly but I just can't think of your face."
> — Oxford professor W. A. Spooner, 1844–1930, famous for his linguistic flip-flops (*spoonerisms*). Spooner rebuked one student for "fighting a liar in the quadrangle" and another who "hissed my mystery lecture," adding "You have tasted two worms."

::projective test a personality test, such as the Rorschach or TAT, that provides ambiguous stimuli designed to trigger projection of one's inner dynamics.

::Thematic Apperception Test (TAT) a projective test in which people express their inner feelings and interests through the stories they make up about ambiguous scenes.

::Rorschach inkblot test the most widely used projective test, a set of 10 inkblots, designed by Hermann Rorschach; seeks to identify people's inner feelings by analyzing their interpretations of the blots.

INTERCONNECTING

Freud and his students based most of their theories on case studies rather than experimentation. Have students explore the importance of scientific investigation:

- Why are case studies not as reliable as experimentation?

- What type of people did Freud and his students analyze? How might this population skew the development of the theory?

- How might modern scientists test Freud's theory more scientifically?

DEMO

Have students visit one of the many Web sites that provide interactive personality tests. Ask your students to take a test to see if it provides an accurate assessment of some aspect of their personality. Is there any evidence of the inventory's validity or reliability? Are norms provided and, if so, on whom are they based? Was the test empirically derived?

- Personality Online at www.personalityonline.com distinguishes between serious tests such as the Keirsey Temperament Sorter and entertaining-fun tests such as the Love-Type Test and the Color Test.

- Personality Tests on the Web at www.2h.com/Tests/personality.phtml provides dozens of links to interactive tests measuring such constructs as self-esteem, lifestyle, and assertiveness.

- QueenDom.Com at http://queendom.com provides links to advice columns and articles on personality and mental health.

UNIT 10

INTERCONNECTING

Link the discussion of the Modern Unconscious Mind to the discussions in Unit 3B and Unit 5 of the two-track mind and states of consciousness. Modern psychologists are finding robust evidence for a vibrant unconscious mind that helps us process stimuli from the environment with great efficiency. While this modern conceptualization is not quite what Freud had in mind, it does support Freud's idea that our conscious awareness is not all that is going on with us at any given moment.

INTERCONNECTING

Myers provides several connections to other parts of the text in this section. You may want to have students make a web diagram that connects consciousness to these other concepts, displaying it on your wall or bulletin board as a reminder of how psychology is interconnected.

> "The overall findings . . . seriously challenge the classical psychoanalytic notion of repression."
> Psychologist Yacov Rofé, "Does Repression Exist?" 2008

> "During the Holocaust, many children . . . were forced to endure the unendurable. For those who continue to suffer [the] pain is still present, many years later, as real as it was on the day it occurred."
> Eric Zillmer, Molly Harrower, Barry Ritzler, and Robert Archer, *The Quest for the Nazi Personality*, 1995

::**terror-management theory** a theory of death-related anxiety; explores people's emotional and behavioral responses to reminders of their impending death.

Malmquist, 1986; Pennebaker, 1990). "Dozens of formal studies have yielded not a single convincing case of repression in the entire literature on trauma," concludes personality researcher John Kihlstrom (2006). Ditto for the world's literature, reports a Harvard team that offered $1000 to anyone who could provide a pre-1800 medical or even fictional example of a healthy person who had blocked out a specific traumatic event and retrieved it a year or more later (Pope et al., 2007). Surely, if such often occurred, someone would have noticed. But despite wide publicity, no such case was unearthed. (After their paper was published, one person did come up with a 1786 opera in which a woman apparently forgets discovering her dead lover after a duel [Pettus, 2008].)

Some researchers believe that extreme, prolonged stress, such as the stress some severely abused children experience, might disrupt memory by damaging the hippocampus (Schacter, 1996). But the far more common reality is that high stress and associated stress hormones enhance memory (see Unit 7A). Indeed, rape, torture, and other traumatic events haunt survivors, who experience unwanted flashbacks. They are seared onto the soul. "You see the babies," said Holocaust survivor Sally H. (1979). "You see the screaming mothers. You see hanging people. You sit and you see that face there. It's something you don't forget."

The Modern Unconscious Mind

Freud was right about at least one thing: We indeed have limited access to all that goes on in our minds (Erdelyi, 1985, 1988, 2006; Kihlstrom, 1990). In experiments, people have learned to anticipate the computer screen quadrant in which a character will appear next, even before being able to articulate the underlying rule (Lewicki et al., 1992, 1997). Research confirms the reality of unconscious *implicit learning* (Fletcher et al., 2005; Frensch & Rünger, 2003). Our two-track mind has a vast out-of-sight realm.

Nevertheless, the "iceberg" notion held by today's research psychologists differs from Freud's—so much so, argues Anthony Greenwald (1992), that it is time to abandon Freud's view of the unconscious. As we saw in earlier units, many now think of the unconscious not as seething passions and repressive censoring but as cooler information processing that occurs without our awareness. To these researchers, the unconscious also involves

- the schemas that automatically control our perceptions and interpretations (Unit 4).
- the priming by stimuli to which we have not consciously attended (Units 4 and 7A).
- the right-hemisphere activity that enables the split-brain patient's left hand to carry out an instruction the patient cannot verbalize (Unit 3B).
- the parallel processing of different aspects of vision and thinking (Units 4 and 7B).
- the implicit memories that operate without conscious recall, even among those with amnesia (Unit 7B).
- the emotions that activate instantly, before conscious analysis (Unit 8B).
- the self-concept and stereotypes that automatically and unconsciously influence how we process information about ourselves and others (Unit 14).

More than we realize, we fly on autopilot. Our lives are guided by off-screen, out-of-sight, unconscious information processing. The unconscious mind is huge. This understanding of unconscious information processing is more like the pre-Freudian view of an underground, unattended stream of thought from which spontaneous behavior and creative ideas surface (Bargh & Morsella, 2008).

Recent research has also provided some support for Freud's idea of defense mechanisms (even if they don't work exactly as Freud supposed). For example, Roy Baumeister and his colleagues (1998) found that people tend to see their foibles and attitudes in others, a phenomenon that Freud called projection and that today's researchers call the *false consensus effect*, the tendency to overestimate the extent to which others share our beliefs and behaviors. People who cheat on their taxes or break speed limits tend to think many others do likewise. Supportive evidence is meager for other defenses, such as displacement, that are tied to instinctual energy. More evidence exists for defenses, such as reaction formation, that defend self-esteem. Defense mechanisms, Baumeister concluded, are motivated less by the seething impulses that Freud presumed than by our need to protect our self-image.

Finally, recent history has supported Freud's idea that we defend ourselves against anxiety. Again, however, the contemporary idea differs from Freud's. Jeff Greenberg, Sheldon Solomon, and Tom Pyszczynski (1997) have proposed that one source of anxiety is "the terror resulting from our awareness of vulnerability and death." More than 200 studies testing their **terror-management theory** show that thinking about one's mortality—for example, by writing a short essay on dying and its associated emotions—provokes various terror-management defenses. For example, death anxiety increases prejudice—contempt for others and esteem for oneself (Koole et al., 2006).

Faced with a threatening world, people act not only to enhance their self-esteem but also to adhere more strongly to worldviews that answer questions about life's meaning. The prospect of death promotes religious sentiments, and deep religious convictions enable people to be less defensive—less likely to rise in defense of their worldview—when reminded of death (Jonas & Fischer, 2006; Norenzayan & Hansen, 2006). Moreover, they cleave to close relationships (Mikulincer et al., 2003). The events of 9/11—a striking experience of the terror of death—led trapped World Trade Center occupants to spend their last moments calling loved ones, and led most Americans to reach out to family and friends.

Freud's Ideas as Scientific Theory

Psychologists also criticize Freud's theory for its scientific shortcomings. Recall from Unit 2 that good scientific theories explain observations and offer testable hypotheses. Freud's theory rests on few objective observations, and parts of it offer few testable hypotheses. (For Freud, his own recollections and interpretations of patients' free associations, dreams, and slips were evidence enough.)

What is the most serious problem with Freud's theory? It offers after-the-fact explanations of any characteristic (of one person's smoking, another's fear of horses, another's sexual orientation) yet fails to *predict* such behaviors and traits. If you feel angry at your mother's death, you illustrate his theory because "your unresolved childhood dependency needs are threatened." If you do not feel angry, you again illustrate his theory because "you are repressing your anger." That, said Calvin Hall and Gardner Lindzey (1978, p. 68), "is like betting on a horse after the race has been run." A good theory makes testable predictions.

For such reasons, some of Freud's critics offer harsh words. They see a decaying Freudian edifice built on the swamplands of childhood sexuality, repression, dream analysis, and after-the-fact speculation. "When we stand on [Freud's] shoulders, we

"I don't want to attain immortality through my work; I want to attain immortality by not dying."

Woody Allen

"It says, 'Someday you will die.'"

"I sought the Lord, and he answered me and delivered me out of all my terror."

Psalm 34:4

"We are arguing like a man who should say, 'If there were an invisible cat in that chair, the chair would look empty; but the chair does look empty; therefore there is an invisible cat in it.'"

C. S. Lewis, *Four Loves*, 1958

TROUBLESHOOTING

Students may read about Baumeister's false consensus effect and Greenberg, Solomon, and Pyszczynski's terror-management theory and think they are just repackaging Freud for modern sensibilities. Help students see that their research is helping to refine the theory, discarding parts of Freud's theory that are not empirically validated and retaining those aspects that stand the test of scientific scrutiny.

INTERCONNECTING

Much of Freud's theory fails the test of falsifiability—his theory does not allow for it to be false. When people would challenge Freud's interpretations of their experiences, he would say they were being "resistant." The theory proved itself, making it difficult to test hypotheses in scientifically valid ways.

PEANUTS

I'VE JUST COME UP WITH THE PERFECT THEORY

IT'S MY THEORY THAT BEETHOVEN WOULD HAVE WRITTEN EVEN BETTER MUSIC IF HE HAD BEEN MARRIED!

WHAT'S SO PERFECT ABOUT THAT THEORY?

IT CAN'T BE PROVED ONE WAY OR THE OTHER!

UNIT 10

::**self-actualization** according to Maslow, one of the ultimate psychological needs that arises after basic physical and psychological needs are met and self-esteem is achieved; the motivation to fulfill one's potential.

::**unconditional positive regard** according to Rogers, an attitude of total acceptance toward another person.

TROUBLESHOOTING

Help students see that Freudian theory is not part of most psychology curricula in the nation's colleges and universities. Although covered in courses such as introductory psychology and history of psychology, Freud's theories are not part of the mainstream discipline. When it is used as a therapeutic technique, it is included as part of an eclectic approach.

TEACHING TIP

Humanistic psychology is often called the "third force" in psychology. Prior to the 1960s, psychologists were divided into two main camps—behaviorists and psychoanalysts. When the humanistic psychologists came to the forefront, their perspective on human behavior felt like a breath of fresh air.

only discover that we're looking further in the wrong direction," said John Kihlstrom (1997). To Freud's most searing critic, Frederick Crews (1998), what is original about Freud's ideas is not good, and what is good is not original (the unconscious mind is an idea that dates back to Plato).

So, should psychology post a "Do Not Resuscitate" order on this old theory? Freud's supporters object. To criticize Freudian theory for not making testable predictions is, they say, like criticizing baseball for not being an aerobic exercise, something it was never intended to be. Freud never claimed that psychoanalysis was predictive science. He merely claimed that, looking back, psychoanalysts could find meaning in our state of mind (Rieff, 1979).

Supporters also note that some of Freud's ideas *are* enduring. It was Freud who drew our attention to the unconscious and the irrational, to our self-protective defenses, to the importance of human sexuality, and to the tension between our biological impulses and our social well-being. It was Freud who challenged our self-righteousness, punctured our pretensions, and reminded us of our potential for evil.

In science, Darwin's legacy lives while Freud's is waning (Bornstein, 2001). Almost 9 in 10 American college courses that reference psychoanalysis are, according to one national survey, outside of psychology departments (Cohen, 2007). In the popular culture, Freud's legacy lives on. Some ideas that many people assume to be true—that childhood experiences mold personality, that dreams have meaning, that many behaviors have disguised motives—are part of that legacy. His early twentieth-century concepts penetrate our twenty-first-century language. Without realizing their source, we may speak of *ego, repression, projection, complex* (as in "inferiority complex"), *sibling rivalry, Freudian slips,* and *fixation.* "Freud's premises may have undergone a steady decline in currency within academia for many years," noted Martin Seligman (1994), "but Hollywood, the talk shows, many therapists, and the general public still love them."

BEFORE YOU MOVE ON . . .

> **ASK YOURSELF**

What understanding and impressions of Freud did you bring to this unit? Have they changed in any way after reading this section?

> **TEST YOURSELF 2**

How does today's psychological science assess Freud's theory?

Answers to the Test Yourself questions can be found in Appendix E at the end of the book.

The Humanistic Perspective

6: How did humanistic psychologists view personality, and what was their goal in studying personality?

BY THE 1960S, SOME PERSONALITY psychologists had become discontented with the negativity of Freudian theory and the mechanistic psychology of B. F. Skinner's behaviorism. In contrast to Freud's study of the base motives of "sick" people, these *humanistic psychologists* focused on the ways "healthy" people strive for self-determination and self-realization. In contrast to behaviorism's scientific objectivity, they studied people through their own self-reported experiences and feelings.

Two pioneering theorists—Abraham Maslow (1908–1970) and Carl Rogers (1902–1987)—offered a *third-force perspective* that emphasized human potential.

TEACHING TIP

At this point, you may want to use **Lecture/Discussion Topic: *Obstacles to Self-Actualization*** (p. 13) from Bolt's Teacher's Resource Binder.

Abraham Maslow's Self-Actualizing Person

Maslow proposed that we are motivated by a hierarchy of needs (Unit 8A). If our physiological needs are met, we become concerned with personal safety; if we achieve a sense of security, we then seek to love, to be loved, and to love ourselves; with our love needs satisfied, we seek self-esteem. Having achieved self-esteem, we ultimately seek **self-actualization** (the process of fulfilling our potential) and *self-transcendence* (meaning, purpose, and communion beyond the self).

Maslow (1970) developed his ideas by studying healthy, creative people rather than troubled clinical cases. He based his description of self-actualization on a study of those who seemed notable for their rich and productive lives—among them, Abraham Lincoln, Thomas Jefferson, and Eleanor Roosevelt. Maslow reported that these people shared certain characteristics: They were self-aware and self-accepting, open and spontaneous, loving and caring, and not paralyzed by others' opinions. Secure in their sense of who they were, their interests were problem-centered rather than self-centered. They focused their energies on a particular task, one they often regarded as their mission in life. Most enjoyed a few deep relationships rather than many superficial ones. Many had been moved by spiritual or personal *peak experiences* that surpassed ordinary consciousness.

These, said Maslow, are mature adult qualities, ones found in those who have learned enough about life to be compassionate, to have outgrown their mixed feelings toward their parents, to have found their calling, to have "acquired enough courage to be unpopular, to be unashamed about being openly virtuous, etc." Maslow's work with college students led him to speculate that those likely to become self-actualizing adults were likable, caring, "privately affectionate to those of their elders who deserve it," and "secretly uneasy about the cruelty, meanness, and mob spirit so often found in young people."

Abraham Maslow "Any theory of motivation that is worthy of attention must deal with the highest capacities of the healthy and strong person as well as with the defensive maneuvers of crippled spirits" (*Motivation and Personality*, 1970).

Carl Rogers' Person-Centered Perspective

Fellow humanistic psychologist Carl Rogers agreed with much of Maslow's thinking. Rogers believed that people are basically good and are endowed with self-actualizing tendencies. Unless thwarted by an environment that inhibits growth, each of us is like an acorn, primed for growth and fulfillment. Rogers (1980) believed that a growth-promoting climate required three conditions—genuineness, acceptance, and empathy.

According to Rogers, people nurture our growth by being *genuine*—by being open with their own feelings, dropping their facades, and being transparent and self-disclosing.

People also nurture our growth by being *accepting*—by offering us what Rogers called **unconditional positive regard.** This is an attitude of grace, an attitude that values us even knowing our failings. It is a profound relief to drop our pretenses, confess our worst feelings, and discover that we are still accepted. In a good marriage, a close family, or an intimate friendship, we are free to be spontaneous without fearing the loss of others' esteem.

Finally, people nurture our growth by being *empathic*—by sharing and mirroring our feelings and reflecting our meanings. "Rarely do we listen with real understanding, true empathy," said Rogers. "Yet listening, of this very special kind, is one of the most potent forces for change that I know."

Genuineness, acceptance, and empathy are the water, sun, and nutrients that enable people to grow like vigorous oak trees, according to Rogers. For "as persons are accepted and prized, they tend to develop a more caring attitude toward themselves"

A father *not* offering unconditional positive regard:

P. BYRNES.

"Just remember, son, it doesn't matter whether you win or lose—unless you want Daddy's love."

DEMO

Have students do a quick demonstration on the limitations of case study research. Have students pick a few qualities that can be measured in all people—height, weight, shoe size, favorite foods (or colors, music, movies, etc.). Have them choose three or four people and do in-depth interviews about these issues. Then have them take a formal, randomized survey of these issues from a representative population of students in the school. They should then compare the results from the case studies with the results from the survey to see how well the case study information generalized to the public at large. Students should see that information from a few people does not accurately reflect information from the population at large.

CULTURAL CONNECTIONS

Have students find and talk with a variety of self-actualized people who have lived in different cultural groups inside and outside the United States.

- What roles in society did these people hold?
- What types of things were they able to accomplish?
- Did they inspire others to follow their examples?
- Did people outside their culture recognize them for their efforts? Why or why not?

DEMO

Have students divide into groups and come up with experiences that contradict Maslow's hierarchy of needs, which is the basis for his theory of self-actualization. Some examples you can use to get them started might include the following:

- Can students learn when they are hungry?
- Why do people go on hunger strikes to protest a cause they believe in?
- Why are there such things as "starving artists"?

Traditional humanistic therapy was individualized, personal, lengthy, and extensive. Because of this personal attention, it was also expensive. With managed-care costs skyrocketing, this type of therapy would not be viewed as practical or efficient today. Have students explore what insurance companies typically cover regarding psychotherapy.

- What type of therapy is generally covered by insurance plans?
- How long can a patient participate in therapy?
- Does the therapist have discretion to increase the length of time a person can stay in therapy? Why or why not?

TEACHING TIP

At this point, you may want to use **Classroom Exercise/Student Project:** *Perceived Self Versus Ideal Self* (p. 14) from Bolt's Teacher's Resource Binder.

The picture of empathy Being open and sharing confidences is easier when the listener shows real understanding. Within such relationships people can relax and fully express their true selves.

Image Source/Jupiterimages

::**self-concept** all our thoughts and feelings about ourselves, in answer to the question, "Who am I?"

(Rogers, 1980, p. 116). As persons are empathically heard, "it becomes possible for them to listen more accurately to the flow of inner experiencings."

Writer Calvin Trillin (2006) recalls an example of parental genuineness and acceptance at a camp for children with severe disorders, where his wife, Alice, worked. L., a "magical child," had genetic diseases that meant she had to be tube-fed and could walk only with difficulty. Alice recalled,

> One day, when we were playing duck-duck-goose, I was sitting behind her and she asked me to hold her mail for her while she took her turn to be chased around the circle. It took her a while to make the circuit, and I had time to see that on top of the pile [of mail] was a note from her mom. Then I did something truly awful. . . . I simply had to know what this child's parents could have done to make her so spectacular, to make her the most optimistic, most enthusiastic, most hopeful human being I had ever encountered. I snuck a quick look at the note, and my eyes fell on this sentence: "If God had given us all of the children in the world to choose from, L., we would only have chosen you." Before L. got back to her place in the circle, I showed the note to Bud, who was sitting next to me. "Quick. Read this," I whispered. "It's the secret of life."

Maslow and Rogers would have smiled knowingly. For them a central feature of personality is one's **self-concept**—all the thoughts and feelings we have in response to the question, "Who am I?" If our self-concept is positive, we tend to act and perceive the world positively. If it is negative—if in our own eyes we fall far short of our *ideal self*—said Rogers, we feel dissatisfied and unhappy. A worthwhile goal for therapists, parents, teachers, and friends is therefore, he said, to help others know, accept, and be true to themselves.

Assessing the Self

7: How did humanistic psychologists assess a person's sense of self?

Humanistic psychologists sometimes assessed personality by asking people to fill out questionnaires that would evaluate their self-concept. One questionnaire, inspired by Carl Rogers, asked people to describe themselves both as they would *ideally* like to be and as they *actually* are. When the ideal and the actual self are nearly alike, said Rogers, the self-concept is positive. Assessing his clients' personal growth during therapy, he looked for successively closer ratings of actual and ideal selves.

Some humanistic psychologists believed that any standardized assessment of personality, even a questionnaire, is depersonalizing. Rather than forcing the person to respond to narrow categories, these humanistic psychologists presumed that interviews and intimate conversation would provide a better understanding of each person's unique experiences.

Evaluating the Humanistic Perspective

8: How has the humanistic perspective influenced psychology? What criticisms has it faced?

One thing said of Freud can also be said of the humanistic psychologists: Their impact has been pervasive. Maslow's and Rogers' ideas have influenced counseling, education, child-rearing, and management.

They have also influenced—sometimes in ways they did not intend—much of today's popular psychology. Is a positive self-concept the key to happiness and success? Do acceptance and empathy nurture positive feelings about oneself? Are people basically good and capable of self-improvement? Many people answer *yes, yes,* and *yes.* Responding

TEACHING TIP

Not much analysis occurred in person-centered therapy. To facilitate unconditional positive regard, genuineness, and empathy, Rogers would answer questions with questions. "How does that make you feel?" was a common question Rogers would ask. Rogers felt that if people received the attention and acceptance that they needed, they could cure themselves. The therapist was merely there to provide that support.

to a 1992 *Newsweek* Gallup poll, 9 in 10 people rated self-esteem as very important for "motivating a person to work hard and succeed." Humanistic psychology's message has been heard.

The prominence of the humanistic perspective set off a backlash of criticism. First, said the critics, its concepts are vague and *subjective*. Consider Maslow's description of self-actualizing people as open, spontaneous, loving, self-accepting, and productive. Is this a scientific description? Isn't it merely a description of the theorist's own values and ideals? Maslow, noted M. Brewster Smith (1978), offered impressions of his own personal heroes. Imagine another theorist who began with a different set of heroes—perhaps Napoleon, John D. Rockefeller, Sr., and former U.S. Vice President Dick Cheney. This theorist would likely describe self-actualizing people as "undeterred by others' needs and opinions," "motivated to achieve," and "comfortable with power."

Critics also objected to the idea that, as Rogers put it, "The only question which matters is, 'Am I living in a way which is deeply satisfying to me, and which truly expresses me?'" (quoted by Wallach & Wallach, 1985). As we will see, the *individualism* encouraged by humanistic psychology—trusting and acting on one's feelings, being true to oneself, fulfilling oneself—can, the critics have said, lead to self-indulgence, selfishness, and an erosion of moral restraints (Campbell & Specht, 1985; Wallach & Wallach, 1983). Indeed, it is those who focus beyond themselves who are most likely to experience social support, to enjoy life, and to cope effectively with stress (Crandall, 1984).

Humanistic psychologists reply that a secure, nondefensive self-acceptance is actually the first step toward loving others. Indeed, people who feel intrinsically liked and accepted—for who they are, not just for their achievements—exhibit less-defensive attitudes (Schimel et al., 2001).

A final accusation leveled against humanistic psychology is that it is *naive,* that it fails to appreciate the reality of our human capacity for evil. Faced with global climate change, overpopulation, terrorism, and the spread of nuclear weapons, we may become apathetic from either of two rationalizations. One is a naive optimism that denies the threat ("People are basically good; everything will work out"). The other is a dark despair ("It's hopeless; why try?"). Action requires enough realism to fuel concern and enough optimism to provide hope. Humanistic psychology, say the critics, encourages the needed hope but not the equally necessary realism about evil.

"We do pretty well when you stop to think that people are basically good."

CULTURAL CONNECTIONS

Rogers' ideas about humanistic psychology do seem to favor an individualistic perspective on the self. This is one of the theories that cross-cultural psychologists use as evidence of the fact that many ideas in psychology need to be tested in samples outside of those in Western nations. This way, we can know whether these phenomena are universal or influenced by culture.

BEFORE YOU MOVE ON . . .

➤ **ASK YOURSELF**

Have you had someone in your life who accepted you unconditionally? Do you think this person helped you to know yourself better and to develop a better image of yourself?

➤ **TEST YOURSELF 3**

What does it mean to be "empathic"? To be "self-actualized"?

Answers to the Test Yourself questions can be found in Appendix E at the end of the book.

The Trait Perspective

9: How do psychologists use traits to describe personality?

RATHER THAN FOCUSING ON UNCONSCIOUS FORCES and thwarted growth opportunities, some researchers attempt to define personality in terms of stable and enduring behavior patterns, such as Sam Gamgee's loyalty and optimism. This perspective

 TEACHING TIP

When Gordon Allport went to visit Freud, the esteemed psychoanalyst sat quietly waiting for the conversation to start. After a long period of time, Allport impulsively told the story of a young boy becoming upset on the bus because he had to sit in the same seat a dirty old man had occupied earlier. Allport proposed that maybe the boy learned to be preoccupied with neatness from his domineering mother. Freud commented, "And that little boy was you?" Allport from then on felt that psychoanalysis tried to delve too deeply into behavior, just as behaviorism didn't delve deeply enough.

UNIT 10

CRITICAL THINKING

Ask students to list individually the traits they believe to be positive and negative. Divide students into groups and have them compare their lists to see how many traits they have in common in each list. Then compile a class list of desirable and undesirable traits.

- Were more positive than negative qualities present? Why or why not?

- Do students strive to cultivate any of these qualities? Why or why not?

- Are these traits inborn or learned? Why do you think so?

 TEACHING TIP

The Greeks identified four bodily fluids as the humors that governed behavior, which are the precursors of today's personality types. They believed that a person had a particular personality type if an excess of a particular fluid was present.

- *Blood* was responsible for making people sanguine in personality.

- *Black bile* was responsible for the melancholic personality.

- *Yellow bile* was blamed for the phlegmatic personality.

- *Green bile* was determined to be the cause of the choleric personality.

::**trait** a characteristic pattern of behavior or a disposition to feel and act, as assessed by self-report inventories and peer reports.

Jon Stewart: The extravert Trait labels such as *extraversion* can describe our temperament and typical behaviors.

can be traced in part to a remarkable meeting in 1919, when Gordon Allport, a curious 22-year-old psychology student, interviewed Sigmund Freud in Vienna. Allport soon discovered just how preoccupied the founder of psychoanalysis was with finding hidden motives, even in Allport's own behavior during the interview. That experience ultimately led Allport to do what Freud did not do—to describe personality in terms of fundamental **traits**—people's characteristic behaviors and conscious motives (such as the curiosity that actually motivated Allport to see Freud). Meeting Freud, said Allport, "taught me that [psychoanalysis], for all its merits, may plunge too deep, and that psychologists would do well to give full recognition to manifest motives before probing the unconscious." Allport came to define personality in terms of identifiable behavior patterns. He was concerned less with *explaining* individual traits than with *describing* them.

Like Allport, Isabel Briggs Myers (1987) and her mother, Katharine Briggs, wanted to describe important personality differences. They attempted to sort people according to Carl Jung's personality types, based on their responses to 126 questions. The *Myers-Briggs Type Indicator (MBTI)*, available in 21 languages, is taken by more than 2 million people a year, mostly for counseling, leadership training, and work-team development (CPP, 2008). It offers choices, such as "Do you usually value sentiment more than logic, or value logic more than sentiment?" Then it counts the test-taker's preferences, labels them as indicating, say, a "feeling type," or "thinking type," and feeds them back to the person in complimentary terms. Feeling types, for example, are told they are sensitive to values and are "sympathetic, appreciative, and tactful"; thinking types are told they "prefer an objective standard of truth" and are "good at analyzing." (Every type has its strengths, so everyone is affirmed.)

Most people agree with their announced type profile, which mirrors their declared preferences. They may also accept their label as a basis for being matched with work partners and tasks that supposedly suit their temperaments. A National Research Council report noted, however, that despite the test's popularity in business and career counseling, its initial use outran research on its value as a predictor of job performance, and "the popularity of this instrument in the absence of proven scientific worth is troublesome" (Druckman & Bjork, 1991, p. 101; see also Pittenger, 1993). Although research on the MBTI has been accumulating since those cautionary words were expressed, the test remains mostly a counseling and coaching tool, not a research instrument.

Exploring Traits

Classifying people as one or another distinct personality type fails to capture their full individuality. We are each a unique complex of multiple traits. So how else could we describe our personalities? We might describe an apple by placing it along several trait dimensions—relatively large or small, red or yellow, sweet or sour. By placing people on several trait dimensions simultaneously, psychologists can describe countless individual personality variations. (Remember from Unit 4 that variations on just three color dimensions—hue, saturation, and brightness—create many thousands of colors.)

What trait dimensions describe personality? If you had an upcoming blind date, what personality traits might give you an accurate sense of the person? Allport and his associate H. S. Odbert (1936) counted all the words in an unabridged dictionary with which one could describe people. How many were there? Almost 18,000! How, then, could psychologists condense the list to a manageable number of basic traits?

 TEACHING TIP

At this point, you may want to use **Lecture/Discussion Topic: *Personality Traits of U.S. Presidents*** (p. 15) or **Classroom Exercises: *Extraversion and Emotional Stability*** (p. 14) or ***Shyness*** (p. 15) from Bolt's Teacher's Resource Binder.

Factor Analysis

One way has been to propose traits, such as anxiety, that some theory regards as basic. A newer technique is *factor analysis,* a statistical procedure (described in Unit 11) that identifies clusters of correlated test items that tap basic components of intelligence (such as spatial ability or verbal skill). Imagine that people who describe themselves as outgoing also tend to say that they like excitement and practical jokes and dislike quiet reading. Such a statistically correlated cluster of behaviors reflects a basic factor, or trait—in this case, *extraversion*.

British psychologists Hans Eysenck and Sybil Eysenck (pronounced EYE-zink) believed that we can reduce many of our normal individual variations to two or three dimensions, including *extraversion–introversion* and *emotional stability–instability* (**FIGURE 10.4**). People in 35 countries around the world, from China to Uganda to Russia, have taken the *Eysenck Personality Questionnaire.* When their answers were analyzed, the extraversion and emotionality factors inevitably emerged as basic personality dimensions (Eysenck, 1990, 1992). The Eysencks believed that these factors are genetically influenced, and research supports this belief.

UNSTABLE

Moody   Touchy
Anxious   Restless
Rigid   Aggressive
Sober   Excitable
Pessimistic   Changeable
Reserved   Impulsive
Unsociable   Optimistic
Quiet   Active

INTROVERTED — **EXTRAVERTED**

Passive   Sociable
Careful   Outgoing
Thoughtful   Talkative
Peaceful   Responsive
Controlled   Easygoing
Reliable   Lively
Even-tempered   Carefree
Calm   Leadership

STABLE

Biology and Personality

Brain-activity scans of extraverts add to the growing list of traits and mental states that have been explored with brain-imaging procedures. (That list includes intelligence, impulsivity, addictive cravings, lying, sexual attraction, aggressiveness, empathy, spiritual experience, and even racial and political attitudes [Olson, 2005].) Such studies indicate that extraverts seek stimulation because their normal *brain arousal* is relatively low. For example, PET scans show that a frontal lobe area involved in behavior inhibition is less active in extraverts than in introverts (Johnson et al., 1999). Dopamine and dopamine-related neural activity tend to be higher in extraverts (Wacker et al., 2006).

Our biology influences our personality in other ways as well. As you may recall from Unit 3C, our *genes* have much to say about the temperament and behavioral style that help define our personality. Jerome Kagan, for example, has attributed differences in children's shyness and inhibition to their *autonomic nervous system reactivity.* Given a reactive autonomic nervous system, we respond to stress with

➤ **FIGURE 10.4**

Two personality dimensions Mapmakers can tell us a lot by using two axes (north-south and east-west). Hans Eysenck and Sybil Eysenck used two primary personality factors—extraversion–introversion and stability–instability—as axes for describing personality variation. Varying combinations define other, more specific traits. (From Eysenck & Eysenck, 1963.)

TEACHING TIP

Raymond Cattell, an early pioneer of factor analysis, took three different measurements from people to arrive at a factor analysis of their personality. These different data sets would be correlated to determine a person's personality:

- L-data was comprised of events from a person's daily life. He would collect statistical information on daily behavior (number of accidents, visits to the doctor, etc.).

- Q-data was quantitative, resulting from answers to self-report questionnaires. Subjects would take several different personality tests as part of his research.

- T-data came from more "objective" measures of personality that didn't rely on self-report (which could be unreliable or incorrect). He would use the thematic apperception test, Rorschach inkblot test, and word association tests for this component.

WEB CONNECT

Have students learn more about Gordon Allport's contributions to psychology by having them visit http://webspace.ship.edu/cgboer/allport.html. Allport was the first person to use the word "trait" to describe personality, and his theory is considered to be fundamental to modern study of personality. At this site, students can also take a quiz modeled after Allport's original personality tests.

TEACHING TIP

William Sheldon developed a controversial body type-personality theory. From the late 1800s to the mid-1900s, many prestigious U.S. universities would take nude "posture photos" of every freshman entering each year. These photos were taken supposedly to determine who needed remedial posture classes. In reality, eugenic theorists used the pictures to develop a database of the elite to reinforce notions of racial superiority of white people. Sheldon, who took some of these photographs, developed his theory of body type determining personality from analyzing these photographs. Over 20,000 of these photographs are stored in Smithsonian archives.

CRITICAL THINKING

Personality theories do not seek to place value judgments on people's behavior. They merely describe how people behave and try to categorize those behaviors so we can all understand each other better. But do some personality traits seem more desirable than others? Have students explore how personality theory can be used to stereotype others:

- Which personality dimensions seem more desirable than others? Would you want to be classified as "unstable" and "introverted"—which would mean you were "depressed"?

- Do you see some personality traits as being linked to the behavior of women or men? How could this be limiting to either gender?

TEACHING TIP

Complement the text discussion of the MMPI with coverage of the NEO-PI-R. The NEO-PI-R (Neuroticism-Extraversion-Openness Personality Inventory, Revised) and its successor, the NEO Five Factor Inventory (NEO-FFI), were developed by Paul Costa and Robert McCrae in an effort to assess the major domains in the five-factor model of personality described in the text. In contrast to the MMPI, which measures psychological disorders, the NEOs are designed to measure "normal" personality.

Liebert, R., & Liebert, L. (1998). *Personality: Strategies and issues* (8th ed.). Pacific Grove, CA: Brooks/Cole.

greater anxiety and inhibition. The fearless, curious child may become the rock-climbing or fast-driving adult.

Samuel Gosling and his colleagues (2003; Jones & Gosling, 2005) report that personality differences among dogs (in energy, affection, reactivity, and curious intelligence) are as evident, and as consistently judged, as personality differences among humans. Monkeys, chimpanzees, orangutans, and even birds have stable personalities (Weiss et al., 2006). Among the Great Tit (a European relative of the American chickadee), bold birds more quickly inspect new objects and explore trees (Groothuis & Carere, 2005; Verbeek et al., 1994). By selective breeding, researchers can produce bold or shy birds. Both have their place in natural history. In lean years, bold birds are more likely to find food; in abundant years, shy birds feed with less risk.

Assessing Traits

10: What are personality inventories, and what are their strengths and weaknesses as trait-assessment tools?

If stable and enduring traits guide our actions, can we devise valid and reliable tests of them? Several trait assessment techniques exist—some more valid than others (turn the page to see Thinking Critically About: How to Be a "Successful" Astrologer or Palm Reader). Some profile a person's behavior patterns—often providing quick assessments of a single trait, such as extraversion, anxiety, or self-esteem. **Personality inventories**—longer questionnaires covering a wide range of feelings and behaviors— are designed to assess several traits at once.

The classic personality inventory is the **Minnesota Multiphasic Personality Inventory (MMPI).** Although it assesses "abnormal" personality tendencies rather than normal personality traits, the MMPI illustrates a good way of developing a personality inventory. One of its creators, Starke Hathaway (1960), compared his effort to that of Alfred Binet. Binet, as you will see in Unit 11, developed the first intelligence test by selecting items that identified children who would probably have trouble progressing normally in French schools. The MMPI items, too, were **empirically derived.** That is, from a large pool of items, Hathaway and his colleagues selected those on which particular diagnostic groups differed. They then grouped the questions into 10 clinical scales, including scales that assess depressive tendencies, masculinity–femininity, and introversion–extraversion.

Hathaway and others initially gave hundreds of true-false statements ("No one seems to understand me"; "I get all the sympathy I should"; "I like poetry") to groups of psychologically disordered patients and to "normal" people. They retained any statement—no matter how silly it sounded—on which the patient group's answer differed from that of the normal group. "Nothing in the newspaper interests me except the comics" may seem senseless, but it just so happened that depressed people were more likely to answer *true*. (Nevertheless, people have had fun spoofing the MMPI with their own mock items: "Weeping brings tears to my eyes," "Frantic screams make me nervous," and "I stay in the bathtub until I look like a raisin" [Frankel et al., 1983].) Today's MMPI-2 also has scales assessing, for instance, work attitudes, family problems, and anger.

In contrast to the subjectivity of most projective tests, personality inventories are scored objectively—so objectively that a computer can administer and score them. (The computer can also provide descriptions of people who previously responded similarly.) Objectivity does not, however, guarantee validity. For example, individuals taking the MMPI for employment purposes can give socially desirable answers to create a good impression. But in so doing they may also score high on a *lie scale* that

::personality inventory a questionnaire (often with *true-false* or *agree-disagree* items) on which people respond to items designed to gauge a wide range of feelings and behaviors; used to assess selected personality traits.

::Minnesota Multiphasic Personality Inventory (MMPI) the most widely researched and clinically used of all personality tests. Originally developed to identify emotional disorders (still considered its most appropriate use), this test is now used for many other screening purposes.

::empirically derived test a test (such as the MMPI) developed by testing a pool of items and then selecting those that discriminate between groups.

TEACHING TIP

At this point, you may want to use **Lecture/Discussion Topic:** *The NEO Personality Inventory* (p. 18) or **Classroom Exercises:** *Empirically Derived Tests and the Importance of Cross-Validation* (p. 16) or *Assessing Social Desirability* (p. 16) or *The Self-Monitoring Scale* (p. 17) from Bolt's Teacher's Resource Binder.

assesses faking (as when people respond *false* to a universally true statement such as "I get angry sometimes"). The objectivity of the MMPI has contributed to its popularity and to its translation into more than 100 languages.

The Big Five Factors

11: Which traits seem to provide the most useful information about personality variation?

Today's trait researchers believe that simple trait factors, such as the Eysencks' introverted–extraverted and unstable–stable dimensions, are important, but they do not tell the whole story. A slightly expanded set of factors—dubbed the *Big Five*— does a better job (Costa & McCrae, 2006; John & Srivastava, 1999). If a test specifies where you are on the five dimensions (conscientiousness, agreeableness, neuroticism, openness, and extraversion; see **TABLE 10.2**), it has said much of what there is to say about your personality. Around the world—across 56 nations and 29 languages in one study (Schmitt et al., 2007)—people describe others in terms roughly consistent with this list. The Big Five may not be the last word, but for now, at least, it is the winning number in the personality lottery. The Big Five—today's "common currency for personality psychology" (Funder, 2001)—has been the most active personality research topic since the early 1990s and is currently our best approximation of the basic trait dimensions.

TABLE 10.2

THE "BIG FIVE" PERSONALITY FACTORS

(*Memory tip:* Picturing a **CANOE** will help you recall these.)

Trait Dimension	Endpoints of the Dimension	
Conscientiousness	Organized	⟷	Disorganized
	Careful	⟷	Careless
	Disciplined	⟷	Impulsive
Agreeableness	Soft-hearted	⟷	Ruthless
	Trusting	⟷	Suspicious
	Helpful	⟷	Uncooperative
Neuroticism (emotional stability vs. instability)	Calm	⟷	Anxious
	Secure	⟷	Insecure
	Self-satisfied	⟷	Self-pitying
Openness	Imaginative	⟷	Practical
	Preference for variety	⟷	Preference for routine
	Independent	⟷	Conforming
Extraversion	Sociable	⟷	Retiring
	Fun-loving	⟷	Sober
	Affectionate	⟷	Reserved

Source: Adapted from McCrae & Costa (1986, p. 1002).

TROUBLESHOOTING

Have students use the mnemonic for the Big Five personality factors that Myers suggests—CANOE. They can also use OCEAN, if they prefer. Remind them that mnemonics are best when they are relevant to the person.

TEACHING TIP

Pearson Assessments, publishers of the MMPI-2, recommends the following applications for their test:

- Assess major symptoms of social and personal maladjustment.
- Identify suitable candidates for high-risk public safety positions.
- Support classification, treatment, and management decisions in criminal justice and correctional settings.

- Give a strong empirical foundation for a clinician's expert testimony.
- Assess medical patients and design effective treatment strategies, including chronic pain management.
- Evaluate participants in substance abuse programs and select appropriate treatment approaches.
- Support college and career counseling recommendations.
- Provide valuable insight for marriage and family counseling.

Source: www.pearsonassessments.com/tests/mmpi_2.htm

INTERCONNECTING

Lie detectors have been shown to be unreliable (Unit 8B), and people regularly give false answers to psychological surveys, both intentionally and unintentionally. What do psychologists do about this problem?

- How do psychologists evaluate the reliability and validity of tests they give?

- How do standardization and norming help provide better results?

- What are the problems with lie detectors? Why aren't they reliable?

- How do psychologists avoid problems such as social desirability and lying?

RESEARCH

Cut daily horoscope predictions out of the newspaper for several different zodiac signs. Code each prediction so only you know which prediction belongs to which sign. Place them all on one page, and have students rate which one they think is their horoscope. Then calculate whether students were right.

How to Be a "Successful" Astrologer or Palm Reader

Can we discern people's traits from the alignment of the stars and planets at the time of their birth? From their handwriting? From lines on their palms?

Astronomers scoff at the naiveté of astrology—the constellations have shifted in the millennia since astrologers formulated their predictions (Kelly, 1997, 1998). Humorists mock it: "No offense," wrote Dave Barry, "but if you take the horoscope seriously your frontal lobes are the size of Raisinets." Psychologists instead ask questions: Does it work? Can astrologers surpass chance when given someone's birth date and asked to identify the person from a short lineup of different personality descriptions? Can people pick out their own horoscopes from a lineup of horoscopes?

The consistent answers have been *no, no,* and *no* (British Psychological Society, 1993; Carlson, 1985; Kelly, 1997). For example, one researcher examined census data from 20 million married people in England and Wales and found that "astrological sign has no impact on the probability of marrying—and staying married to—someone of any other sign" (Voas, 2008).

Graphologists, who make predictions from handwriting samples, have similarly been found to do no better than chance when trying to discern people's occupations from examining several pages of their handwriting (Beyerstein & Beyerstein, 1992; Dean et al., 1992). Nevertheless, graphologists—and introductory psychology students—will often *perceive* correlations between personality and handwriting even where there are none (King & Koehler, 2000).

If all these perceived correlations evaporate under close scrutiny, how do astrologers, palm readers, and crystal-ball gazers persuade millions of people worldwide to buy their services? Ray Hyman (1981), palm reader turned research psychologist, has revealed some of their suckering methods.

The first technique, the "stock spiel," builds on the observation that each of us is in some ways like no one else and in other ways just like everyone. That some things are true of us all enables the "seer" to offer statements that seem impressively accurate: "I sense that you worry about things more than you let on, even to your best friends." A number of such generally true statements can be combined into a personality description. Imagine that you take a personality test and then receive the following character sketch:

> You have a strong need for other people to like and to admire you. You have a tendency to be critical of yourself. . . . You pride yourself on being an independent thinker and do not accept other opinions without satisfactory proof. You have found it unwise to be too frank in revealing yourself to others. At times you are extraverted, affable, sociable; at other times you are introverted, wary, and reserved. Some of your aspirations tend to be pretty unrealistic (Davies, 1997; Forer, 1949).

In experiments, college students have received stock assessments like this one, drawn from statements in a newsstand astrology book. When they think the bogus, generic feedback was prepared just for them and when it is favorable, they nearly always rate the description as either "good" or "excellent" (Davies, 1997). Even skeptics, given a

The recent wave of Big Five research explores various questions:

- **How stable are these traits?** In adulthood, the Big Five traits are quite stable. Some tendencies—neuroticism (emotional instability), extraversion, and openness—wane a bit during early and middle adulthood, and others (agreeableness and conscientiousness) rise (McCrae et al., 1999; Vaidya et al., 2002). Conscientiousness increases the most during people's twenties, as people mature and learn to manage their jobs and relationships. Agreeableness increases the most during people's thirties and continues to increase through their sixties (Srivastava et al., 2003).

- **How heritable are they?** Heritability (the extent to which individual differences are attributable to genes) varies with the diversity of people studied. But it generally runs

DEMO

Students can see trait theory and the controversies surrounding it by visiting the Keirsey Temperament Web Site at http://keirsey.com/. Students can take the Keirsey Temperament Sorter II, a personality test that includes four scales assessing the dimensions of extraversion versus introversion, intuiting versus sensing, feeling versus thinking, and judging versus perceiving.

- Ask students if they agree with their scored profile. The Keirsey Temperament Sorter tends to be positive and

may largely explain why people find themselves in agreement.

- Is there reason to believe that the Keirsey Temperament Sorter has greater validity?

- Does the site offer empirical support for its claims?

flattering description attributed to an astrologer, begin to think that "maybe there's something to this astrology stuff after all" (Glick et al., 1989). An astrologer, it has been said, is someone "prepared to tell you what you think of yourself" (Jones, 2000).

French psychologist Michael Gauguelin offered a free personal horoscope in an ad he placed in a Paris newspaper. Ninety-four percent of those receiving the horoscope praised the description as accurate. Whose horoscope had they all received? That of France's Dr. Petiot, a notorious mass murderer (Kurtz, 1983). This acceptance of stock, positive descriptions is called the *Barnum effect*, named in honor of master showman P. T. Barnum's dictum, "There's a sucker born every minute."

A second technique used by seers is to "read" our clothing, physical features, nonverbal gestures, and reactions to what they are saying. Imagine yourself as the character reader visited by a young woman in her late twenties or early thirties. Hyman described the woman as "wearing expensive jewelry, a wedding band, and a black dress of cheap material. The observant reader noted that she was wearing shoes which were advertised for people with foot trouble." Do these clues suggest anything?

Drawing on these observations, the character reader proceeded to amaze his client with his insights. He assumed the woman had come to see him, as did most of his female customers, because of a love or financial problem. The black dress and the wedding band led him to reason that her husband had died recently. The expensive jewelry suggested she had been financially comfortable during the marriage, but the cheap dress suggested her husband's death had left her impoverished. The therapeutic shoes signified she was now on her feet more than she had been used to, implying that she had been working to support herself since her husband's death. Based on these insights, the reader correctly guessed that the woman was wondering if she should remarry in hope of ending her economic hardship. No wonder, say the skeptics, that when mediums cannot see the person who has come to them, their clients cannot recognize the reading that was meant for them from among other readings (O'Keeffe & Wiseman, 2005).

"Madame Zelinski can provide an even more accurate reading with your date of birth and Social Security number."

If you are not as shrewd as this character reader, Hyman says it hardly matters. If people seek you out for a reading, start with some safe sympathy: "I sense you're having some problems lately. You seem unsure what to do. I get the feeling another person is involved." Then tell them what they want to hear. Memorize some Barnum statements from astrology and fortune-telling manuals and use them liberally. Tell people it is their responsibility to cooperate by relating your message to their specific experiences. Later they will recall that you predicted those specific details. Phrase statements as questions, and when you detect a positive response assert the statement strongly. Finally, be a good listener, and later, in different words, reveal to people what they earlier revealed to you. If you dupe them, they will come.

Better yet, beware of those who, by exploiting people with these techniques, are fortune takers rather than fortune tellers.

---

50 percent or a tad more for each dimension, and genetic influences are similar in different nations (Loehlin et al., 1998; Yamagata et al., 2006).

- **Do the Big Five traits predict other personal attributes?** Yes, and here are some examples: Highly conscientious people earn better high school and university grades (Conard, 2006; Noftle & Robins, 2007). They also are more likely to be morning types (sometimes called "larks"); evening types ("owls") are marginally more extraverted (Jackson & Gerard, 1996). If one partner scores lower than the other on agreeableness, stability, and openness, marital and sexual satisfaction may suffer (Botwin et al., 1997; Donnellan et al., 2004).

By exploring such questions, Big Five research has sustained trait psychology and renewed appreciation for the importance of personality.

Conscientiousness has been shown to be the best predictor of successful job performance. Have students contact those working in human resources, personnel management, and job placement to explore how many use personality testing to hire and promote people in their organization.

- What types of organizations use personality testing? If they don't use personality tests, why don't they?

- What types of personality tests do employers use?

- What personality traits are they looking for specifically? What traits have they found to be most indicative of successful employees?

TEACHING TIP

Former President Reagan and his wife consulted astrologers to gain insight into certain political situations they were dealing with. Was he the only influential world leader—or leader of the U.S.—who relied on astrology for insight into the future? Have students research world leaders throughout history to see how many have consulted psychics when making policy decisions.

One famous case you might have students research in depth regards the last czar of Russia, Nicholas III, and his wife Alexandra. Alexandra fell under the influence of the infamous Rasputin, a mystic who led her to make decisions that some blame for the downfall of czarist Russia and the rise of communism.

DEMO

Teen magazines hardly let an issue go by without offering some type of quiz—love quizzes, personality quizzes, and friendship quizzes. Have students collect several teen magazines and assess what these tests measure.

- What do these tests claim to measure? Do the questions seem to lead toward that logical conclusion? Why or why not?

- Are these tests reliable—can you take them at different times and get the same results? Why or why not?

TEACHING TIP

Trait psychologists and social-cognitive psychologists debate how we attribute (or explain) people's behavior. Trait psychologists focus on dispositions—inborn qualities that are relatively consistent over a lifetime. Social-cognitive psychologists emphasize the power of situations on human behavior, which change from moment to moment.

INTERCONNECTING

Connect the person-situation controversy with the actor-observer bias. In the actor-observer bias, those who are participants in an event (actors) tend to explain the event in terms of situational factors. Those who are observing the event (observers) explain the event in terms of dispositional, or personality, factors. Learn more about this bias in Unit 14.

> "There is as much difference between us and ourselves, as between us and others."
>
> Michel de Montaigne, *Essays*, 1588

● Roughly speaking, the temporary, external influences on behavior are the focus of social psychology, and the enduring, inner influences are the focus of personality psychology. In actuality, behavior always depends on the interaction of persons with situations. ●

● Change and consistency can co-exist. If all people were to become somewhat less shy with age, there would be personality change, but also relative stability and predictability. ●

"Mr. Coughlin over there was the founder of one of the first motorcycle gangs."

➤ **FIGURE 10.5**

Personality stability With age, personality traits become more stable, as reflected in the correlation of trait scores with follow-up scores seven years later. (Data from Roberts & DelVecchio, 2000.)

Evaluating the Trait Perspective

12: Does research support the consistency of personality traits over time and across situations?

Are our personality traits stable and enduring? Or does our behavior depend on where and with whom we find ourselves? J. R. R. Tolkien created characters, like the loyal Sam Gamgee, whose personality traits were consistent across various times and places. The Italian playwright Luigi Pirandello had a different view. For him, personality was ever-changing, tailored to the particular role or situation. In one of Pirandello's plays, Lamberto Laudisi describes himself: "I am really what you take me to be; though, my dear madam, that does not prevent me from also being really what your husband, my sister, my niece, and Signora Cini take me to be—because they also are absolutely right!" To which Signora Sirelli responds, "In other words you are a different person for each of us."

The Person-Situation Controversy

Who, then, typifies human personality, Tolkien's consistent Sam Gamgee or Pirandello's inconsistent Laudisi? Both. Our behavior is influenced by the interaction of our inner disposition with our environment. Still, the question lingers: Which is *more* important? Are we *more* as Tolkien or as Pirandello imagined us to be?

When we explore this *person-situation controversy,* we look for genuine personality traits that persist over time *and* across situations. Are some people dependably conscientious and others unreliable, some cheerful and others dour, some friendly and outgoing and others shy? If we are to consider friendliness a trait, friendly people must act friendly at different times and places. Do they?

In Unit 9, we considered research that has followed lives through time. We noted that some scholars (especially those who study infants) are impressed with personality change; others are struck by personality stability during adulthood. As **FIGURE 10.5** illustrates, data from 152 long-term studies reveal that personality trait scores are positively correlated with scores obtained seven years later, and that as people grow older their personality stabilizes. Interests may change—the avid collector of tropical fish may become an avid gardener. Careers may change—the determined salesperson may become a determined social worker. Relationships may change—the hostile spouse may start over with a new partner. But most people recognize their traits as their own, note Robert McCrae and Paul Costa (1994), "and it is well that they do. A person's recognition of the inevitability

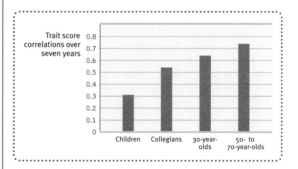

Trait score correlations over seven years

Children Collegians 30-year-olds 50- to 70-year-olds

TEACHING TIP

At this point, you may want to use **Lecture/Discussion Topics**: *Evolution and the Big Five Personality Traits* (p. 18) or *Personality Traits in the Workplace* (p. 21) or *The Hogan Personality Inventory* (p. 21) or **Classroom Exercise**: *"Big Five" Inventories* (p. 19) from Bolt's Teacher's Resource Binder.

of his or her one and only personality is . . . the culminating wisdom of a lifetime." So most people—including most psychologists—would probably side with Tolkien's assumption of stability of personality traits. Moreover, our traits are socially significant. They influence our health, our thinking, and our job performance (Deary & Matthews, 1993; Hogan, 1998). Studies that follow lives through time show that personality traits rival socioeconomic status and cognitive ability as predictors of mortality, divorce, and occupational attainment (Roberts et al., 2007).

Although our personality *traits* may be both stable and potent, the consistency of our specific *behaviors* from one situation to the next is another matter. As Walter Mischel (1968, 1984, 2004) has pointed out, people do not act with predictable consistency. Mischel's studies of college students' conscientiousness revealed but a modest relationship between a student's being conscientious on one occasion (say, showing up for class on time) and being similarly conscientious on another occasion (say, turning in assignments on time). Pirandello would not have been surprised. If you've noticed how outgoing you are in some situations and how reserved you are in others, perhaps you're not surprised either (though for certain traits, Mischel reports, you may accurately assess yourself as more consistent).

This inconsistency in behaviors also makes personality test scores weak predictors of behaviors. People's scores on an extraversion test, for example, do not neatly predict how sociable they actually will be on any given occasion. If we remember such results, says Mischel, we will be more cautious about labeling and pigeonholing individuals. Years in advance, science can tell us the phase of the Moon for any given date. A day in advance, meteorologists can often predict the weather. But we are much further from being able to predict how *you* will feel and act tomorrow.

However, people's *average* outgoingness, happiness, or carelessness over many situations is predictable (Epstein, 1983a,b). When rating someone's shyness or agreeableness, this consistency enables people who know someone well to agree on their ratings (Kenrick & Funder, 1988). By collecting snippets of people's daily experience via body-worn recording devices, Matthias Mehl and his colleagues (2006) confirmed that extraverts really do talk more. (I have repeatedly vowed to cut back on my jabbering and joking during my noontime pickup basketball games with friends. Alas, moments later, the irrepressible chatterbox inevitably reoccupies my body.) As our best friends can verify, we do have genetically influenced personality traits. And those traits even lurk, report Samuel Gosling and his colleagues in a series of studies, in our

- *music preferences*. Classical, jazz, blues, and folk music lovers tend to be open to experience and verbally intelligent; country, pop, and religious music lovers tend to be cheerful, outgoing, and conscientious (Rentfrow & Gosling, 2003, 2006). On first meeting, students often disclose their music preferences to each other; in doing so, they are swapping information about their personalities.

- *bedrooms and offices*. Our personal spaces display our identity and leave a behavioral residue (in our scattered laundry or neat desktop). And that helps explain why just a few minutes' inspection of our living and working spaces can enable someone to assess with reasonable accuracy our conscientiousness, our openness to new experiences, and even our emotional stability (Gosling et al., 2002).

- *personal Web sites*. Is a personal Web site or a Facebook profile also a canvas for self-expression? Or is it an opportunity for people to present themselves in

"I'm going to France—I'm a different person in France."

Have students discuss what type of experiments they would set up to test the predictive validity of personality assessments, such as the Myers-Briggs Type Indicator or any of the trait measures. Have them decide what variables they want the MBTI to predict and how they would test it.

Remind students that whole group behavior is more predictable than individual behavior. You may want to show them the normal curve again, reminding them that while the majority of scores fall near the average, there are scores that are outliers, which vary significantly from the norm.

TEACHING TIP

At this point, you may want to use **Lecture/Discussion Topic:** *The HEXACO Model of Personality Structure* (p. 21) or **Classroom Exercise:** *Astrology and the Barnum Effect* (p. 22) from Bolt's Teacher's Resource Binder.

Our spaces express our personalities
Even at "zero acquaintance," people can discern something of others' personality from glimpsing their Web site, bedroom, or office. So, what is your read on University of Texas researcher Samuel Gosling? ▲

John Langford Photography

TEACHING TIP

With the popularity of online social networking forums, such as Facebook, Google Buzz, and Twitter, relationships have become more complicated. From "friending" to online dating, starting, maintaining, and ending relationships involves a very complex web. Have students discuss the following regarding online relationships:

- Do you start or maintain relationships (friendly or otherwise) with people you do not know in "real" life? Why or why not?

- How can you tell if someone is being genuine online? What are some of your own criteria for determining someone's personality?

- What are some etiquette rules for communicating your desire to joke around with others? Expressing your anger or displeasure? Using sarcasm?

::**social-cognitive perspective** views behavior as influenced by the interaction between people's traits (including their thinking) and their social context.

::**reciprocal determinism** the interacting influences of behavior, internal cognition, and environment.

false or misleading ways? It's more the former (Gosling et al., 2007; Marcus et al., 2006; Vazire & Gosling, 2004). Visitors to personal Web sites quickly gain important clues to the owner's extraversion, conscientiousness, and openness to experience.

- *e-mail.* If you have ever felt you could detect someone's personality from the writing voice in their e-mail, you are right!! What a cool, exciting finding!!! (if you catch my drift). People's ratings of others' personalities based solely on their e-mails correlate with actual personality scores on measures such as extraversion and neuroticism (Gill et al., 2006; Oberlander & Gill, 2006). Extraverts, for example, use more adjectives.

In unfamiliar, formal situations—perhaps as a guest in the home of a person from another culture—our traits remain hidden as we carefully attend to social cues. In familiar, informal situations—just hanging out with friends—we feel less constrained, allowing our traits to emerge (Buss, 1989). In these informal situations, our expressive styles—our animation, manner of speaking, and gestures—are impressively consistent. That's why those very thin slices of someone's behavior—even just three 2-second clips of a teacher—can be revealing (Ambady & Rosenthal, 1992, 1993).

Some people are naturally expressive (and therefore talented at pantomime and charades); others are less expressive (and therefore better poker players). To evaluate people's voluntary control over their expressiveness, Bella DePaulo and her colleagues (1992) asked people to *act* as expressive or inhibited as possible while stating opinions. Their remarkable findings: Inexpressive people, even when feigning expressiveness, were less expressive than expressive people acting naturally. Similarly, expressive people, even when trying to seem inhibited, were less inhibited than inexpressive people acting naturally. It's hard to be someone you're not, or not to be what you are.

Even our conversational word use expresses our personality. For example, in hour-long interviews, expressive, assertive people used more words expressing certainty, as in "I have *always* enjoyed computers and the Internet and that is *certainly* where I want to focus my attention" (Fast & Funder, 2008). The irrepressibility of expressiveness explains why we can size up how outgoing someone is within seconds. Picture this experiment by Maurice Levesque and David Kenny (1993). They seated groups of four university women around a table and asked each woman merely to state her name, year in school, hometown, and college residence. Judging from just these few seconds of verbal and nonverbal behavior, the women were then to guess one another's talkativeness. (How do you think you would do in guessing someone's talkativeness, based on such a small glimpse of their behavior?) When later correlated with how talkative each woman actually was during a series of one-on-one taped conversations, the snap judgments proved reasonably accurate. Despite situational variations in behavior, personality came shining through. Someone who seemed smart or outgoing in one situation tended to seem (to someone else) smart or outgoing in another. When we judge an expressive trait such as outgoingness, thin slices of behavior can be revealing.

To sum up, we can say that at any moment the immediate situation powerfully influences a person's behavior, especially when the situation makes clear demands. We can better predict drivers' behavior at traffic lights from knowing the color of the lights than from knowing the drivers' personalities. Thus, teachers may perceive certain students as subdued (based on their classroom behavior), but friends may perceive them as pretty wild (based on their party behavior). Averaging our behavior across many occasions does, however, reveal distinct personality traits. Traits exist. We differ. And our differences matter.

BEFORE YOU MOVE ON . . .

➤ **ASK YOURSELF**

Where would you place yourself on the five personality dimensions—conscientiousness, agreeableness, neuroticism (emotional stability versus instability), openness, and extraversion? Where might your family and friends place you?

➤ **TEST YOURSELF 4**

What is the person-situation controversy?

Answers to the Test Yourself questions can be found in Appendix E at the end of the book.

The Social-Cognitive Perspective

13: In the view of social-cognitive psychologists, what mutual influences shape an individual's personality?

TODAY'S PSYCHOLOGICAL SCIENCE views individuals as biopsychosocial organisms. The **social-cognitive perspective** on personality proposed by Albert Bandura (1986, 2006, 2008) emphasizes the interaction of our traits with our situations. Much as nature and nurture always work together, so do individuals and their situations.

Social-cognitive theorists believe we learn many of our behaviors either through conditioning or by observing others and modeling our behavior after theirs. (That is the "social" part.) They also emphasize the importance of mental processes: What we *think* about our situations affects our behavior. (That is the "cognitive" part.) This perspective is sometimes considered a *cognitive-behavioral approach* to personality, but it goes considerably beyond behaviorism. Instead of focusing solely on how our environment *controls* us, as behaviorists do, social-cognitive theorists focus on how we and our environment *interact:* How do we interpret and respond to external events? How do our schemas, our memories, and our expectations influence our behavior patterns?

Reciprocal Influences

Bandura (1986, 2006) views the person-environment interaction as **reciprocal determinism.** "Behavior, internal personal factors, and environmental influences," he said, "all operate as interlocking determinants of each other" (**FIGURE 10.6** on the next page). For example, children's TV-viewing habits (past behavior) influence their viewing preferences (internal factor), which influence how television (environmental factor) affects their current behavior. The influences are mutual.

Consider three specific ways in which individuals and environments interact:

1. **Different people choose different environments.** The school you attend, the reading you do, the TV programs you watch, the music you listen to, the friends you associate with—all are part of an environment you have chosen, based partly on your dispositions (Ickes et al., 1997). You choose your environment and it then shapes you.

INTERCONNECTING

Albert Bandura is most well known for studying how television violence relates to aggression. His famous experiment exposed children to a video of an adult who either played aggressively or nonaggressively with a Bobo clown doll, a tall, inflated doll with sand in the bottom to keep it upright. Children who watched the aggressive play were more likely to play aggressively with the Bobo doll than children who watched the nonaggressive play.

TEACHING TIP

Extend the text discussion of the social-cognitive perspective on personality by introducing George Kelly's personal construct theory. Kelly argued that we use bipolar personal constructs to interpret and predict events. For example, we might use the personal constructs warm–cold, flexible–dogmatic, intelligent–unintelligent, tall–short to create an image of a new acquaintance. Using these bipolars, a person might conclude that the stranger is warm, flexible, intelligent, and tall. One may use further bipolar constructs to judge the nature of his intelligence, for example, academically intelligent–common sense intelligent.

 TEACHING TIP

At this point, you may want to use **Lecture/Discussion Topics:** *Perceived Efficacy and Acquirable Skills* (p. 23) or *George Kelly's Personal Construct Theory* (p. 23) from Bolt's Teacher's Resource Binder.

UNIT 10

TEACHING TIP

The term *reciprocal determinism* may be difficult for some students to understand. Help them understand this term by breaking down each word, then bringing them together again as they learn the definition. Be sure they understand what the words "reciprocal" and "determinism" mean.

- *Reciprocal* refers to two or more parties exchanging something—in this case, information. So in this theory, thoughts, environment, and behaviors are interacting, exchanging information about how and why we behave.

- *Determinism* refers to the inevitable consequences of actions. Consequences are determined by actions that precede them, so with this theory, our actions are determined by the interaction of the environment and our thoughts.

➤ **FIGURE 10.6**
Reciprocal determinism The social-cognitive perspective proposes that our personalities are shaped by the interaction of our personal traits (including our thoughts and feelings), our environment, and our behaviors.

2. ***Our personalities shape how we interpret and react to events.*** Anxious people, for example, are attuned to potentially threatening events (Eysenck et al., 1987). Thus, they perceive the world as threatening, and they react accordingly.

3. ***Our personalities help create situations to which we react.*** Many experiments reveal that how we view and treat people influences how they in turn treat us. If we expect someone to be angry with us, we may give the person a cold shoulder, touching off the very anger we expect. If we have an easygoing, positive disposition, we will likely enjoy close, supportive friendships (Donnellan et al., 2005; Kendler, 1997).

In such ways, we are both the products and the architects of our environments.

If all this has a familiar ring, it may be because it parallels and reinforces a pervasive theme in psychology and in this book: *Behavior emerges from the interplay of external and internal influences.* Boiling water turns an egg hard and a potato soft. A threatening environment turns one person into a hero, another into a scoundrel. *At every moment,* our behavior is influenced by our biology, our social and cultural experiences, and our cognition and dispositions (**FIGURE 10.7**).

➤ **FIGURE 10.7**
The biopsychosocial approach to the study of personality As with other psychological phenomena, personality is fruitfully studied at multiple levels.

TEACHING TIP

Students can remember the reciprocal determinism theory with the following acronym:

A = Affect or thoughts and emotions

B = Behaviors

C = Consequences

Personal Control

14: What are the causes and consequences of personal control?

In studying how we interact with our environment, social-cognitive psychologists emphasize our sense of **personal control**—whether we learn to see ourselves as controlling, or as controlled by, our environment. Psychologists have two basic ways to study the effect of personal control (or any personality factor). One: *correlate* people's feelings of control with their behaviors and achievements. Two: *experiment*, by raising or lowering people's sense of control and noting the effects.

Internal Versus External Locus of Control

Consider your own feelings of control. Do you believe that your life is beyond your control? That the world is run by a few powerful people? That getting a good job depends mainly on being in the right place at the right time? Or do you more strongly believe that what happens to you is your own doing? That the average person can influence government decisions? That being a success is a matter of hard work?

Hundreds of studies have compared people who differ in their perceptions of control. On the one side are those who have what psychologist Julian Rotter called an **external locus of control**—the perception that chance or outside forces determine their fate. On the other are those who perceive an **internal locus of control,** who believe that they control their own destiny. In study after study, "internals" achieve more in school and work, act more independently, enjoy better health, and feel less depressed than do "externals" (Lefcourt, 1982; Ng et al., 2006). Moreover, they are better at delaying gratification and coping with various stressors, including marital problems (Miller et al., 1986).

Depleting and Strengthening Self-Control

Self-control—the ability to control impulses and delay gratification—in turn predicts good adjustment, better grades, and social success, report June Tangney and her colleagues (2004). Students who plan their day's activities and then live out their day as planned are also at low risk for depression (Nezlek, 2001).

None of us experiences unvarying self-control. Like a muscle, self-control temporarily weakens after an exertion, replenishes with rest, and becomes stronger with exercise, report Roy Baumeister and Julia Exline (2000). Exercising willpower can deplete your mental energy and even deplete the blood sugar and neural activity associated with mental focus (Inzlicht & Gutsell, 2007). In one experiment, hungry people who had resisted the temptation to eat chocolate chip cookies gave up sooner on a tedious task than those who had not resisted the cookies. People also become less restrained in their aggressive responses to provocation and in their sexuality after expending willpower on laboratory tasks, such as stifling prejudice or saying the color of words (for example, "red" even if the red-colored word was *green*) (DeWall et al., 2007; Gaillot & Baumeister, 2007). But giving people energy-boosting sugar (in a naturally sweetened rather than an artificially sweetened lemonade)—as experimenters did in another experiment—strengthened the research participants' effortful thinking (Masicampo & Baumeister, 2008).

In the long run, self-control requires attention and energy. People who practice self-regulation through physical exercise and time-managed study programs can develop their self-regulation capacity. Strengthened self-control is seen both in their performance on laboratory tasks and in their improved self-management of eating, drinking, smoking, and household chores (Oaten & Cheng, 2006a,b). Develop your self-discipline in one area of your life and your strengthened self-control may spill over into other areas as well.

::**personal control** the extent to which people perceive control over their environment rather than feeling helpless.

::**external locus of control** the perception that chance or outside forces beyond your personal control determine your fate.

::**internal locus of control** the perception that you control your own fate.

Exercising self-control Exercising helps us practice self-regulation, which then bubbles over to increased self-control in other areas of our lives.

(c) Simon Winnall/ Getty Images

 TEACHING TIP

You may want to show students a clip from the movie *Schindler's List* showing Oskar Schindler talking to the commandant's maid about loss of personal control in her life. (Note, however, that this is an R-rated movie, so you may need permission to show it to your class, and you will definitely want to preview this clip.) After showing this powerful clip, form small groups to discuss the following questions:

- Briefly describe a time in your life when your efforts seemed to make little difference. What effects did those feelings have on you?

- Concentration camp and prison inmates experience little control over their lives. What other groups are likely to feel the same? What do you think are the long-term effects on them?

- How do you think gender, age, and race might influence one's feelings of control? How might religious faith influence one's feelings of control?

- What are the most important factors influencing one's sense of control?

 TEACHING TIP

At this point, you may want to use **Lecture/Discussion Topic:** *Locus of Control* (p. 24) or **Classroom Exercises:** *Satisficers Versus Maximizers* (p. 25) from Bolt's Teacher's Resource Binder.

 INTERCONNECTING

Link discussion of locus of control with motivation. Intrinsic motivation is similar to internal locus of control. When we are motivated by internal factors such as the desire to learn or personal feelings of goodness, then we are likely to feel in control of our feelings toward a situation. When we are motivated by extrinsic factors such as getting good grades or other rewards, then we are at the mercy of others to determine our feelings of self worth. This becomes an integral factor in creating an external locus of control.

UNIT 10

TEACHING TIP

Ellen Langer and Judith Rodin conducted an important study about perceived control in nursing homes. For one group of nursing home patients, Langer and Rodin allowed for them to determine certain aspects of their environments—whether to have plants in their rooms or whether they wanted to paint their rooms a different color. The other group of patients were not given control, as most nursing home patients are normally treated. Those patients who were given choice were more likely to live longer and be healthier than those who had no control over their choices.

TEACHING TIP

Martin Seligman's research with the depressed dogs led to his revolutionary identification of learned helplessness. But his move to research in optimism had its beginnings in the study of these depressed dogs. Most dogs developed learned helplessness when they were placed in a situation over which they had no control. But some of the dogs in the uncontrollable situation would not lie down and give up. They would continually try to escape the situation even though they received no feedback that their efforts were successful. That observation led Seligman to wonder what made certain dogs behave this way, and whether such inextinguishable optimism could be learned.

Benefits of Personal Control

As we saw in Unit 6, people who feel helpless and oppressed often perceive control as external and may develop *learned helplessness*. This perception may then deepen their feelings of resignation (**FIGURE 10.8**).

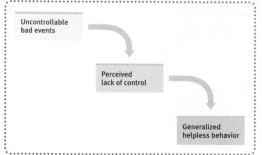

➤ **FIGURE 10.8**
Learned helplessness When animals and people experience no control over repeated bad events, they often learn helplessness.

Part of the shock we feel in an unfamiliar culture comes from a diminished sense of control when we are unsure how people in the new environment will respond (Triandis, 1994). Similarly, people given little control over their world in prisons, factories, schools, and nursing homes experience lower morale and increased stress. Measures that increase control—allowing prisoners to move chairs and control room lights and the TV, having workers participate in decision making, offering nursing home patients choices about their environment—noticeably improve health and morale (Humphrey et al., 2007; Ruback et al., 1986; Wener et al., 1987). When Gallup pollsters asked workers whether they could personalize their workspace, those who answered *yes* were 55 percent more likely also to report high engagement with their work (Krueger & Killham, 2006). Telecommuters likewise tend to be both satisfied with their jobs and productive, especially when given control over their time (Gajendran & Harrison, 2007). (Those working from home three or more days a week do, however, feel more isolation from co-workers.)

In one famous study of nursing home patients, 93 percent of those encouraged to exert more control became more alert, active, and happy (Rodin, 1986). As researcher Ellen Langer (1983, p. 291) concluded, "perceived control is basic to human functioning." She recommended that "for the young and old alike," it is important that we create environments that enhance our sense of control and personal efficacy. No wonder so many people like their iPods and DVRs, which give them control of the content and timing of their entertainment.

The verdict of these studies is reassuring: Under conditions of personal freedom and empowerment, people thrive. Small wonder that the citizens of stable democracies report higher levels of happiness (Inglehart, 1990, 2009). Shortly before the democratic revolution in the former East Germany, psychologists Gabriele Oettingen and Martin Seligman (1990) studied the telltale body language of working-class men in East and West Berlin bars. Compared with their counterparts on the other side of the Wall, the empowered West Berliners much more often laughed, sat upright rather than slumped, and had upward- rather than downward-turned mouths.

Happy are those who choose their own path These happy East Berliners, crossing over to West Berlin after the wall came down in 1989, seem to personify this sentiment from the Roman philosopher Seneca.

Some freedom and control is better than none, notes Barry Schwartz (2000, 2004). But does ever-increasing choice breed ever-happier lives? Actually, no. Schwartz notes that the "excess of freedom" in today's Western cultures contributes to decreasing life satisfaction, increased depression, and sometimes paralysis. Increased consumer choices, as when buying a car or phone, are not an unmixed blessing. After choosing among 30 brands of jam or chocolate, people express less satisfaction than those choosing among a half-dozen options (Iyengar & Lepper, 2000). This *tyranny of choice* brings information overload and a greater likelihood that we will feel regret over some of the unchosen options.

TEACHING TIP

At this point, you may want to use **Classroom Exercises:** *The Life Orientation Test and Optimism* (p. 26) or *Defensive Pessimism* (p. 27) from Bolt's Teacher's Resource Binder.

Optimism Versus Pessimism

One measure of how helpless or effective you feel is where you stand on optimism-pessimism. How do you characteristically explain negative and positive events? Perhaps you have known students whose *attributional style* is pessimistic—who attribute poor performance to their lack of ability ("I can't do this") or to situations enduringly beyond their control ("There is nothing I can do about it"). Such students are more likely to persist in getting low grades than are students who adopt the more hopeful attitude that effort, good study habits, and self-discipline can make a difference (Noel et al., 1987; Peterson & Barrett, 1987). Mere fantasies do not fuel motivation and success, but realistic positive expectations do (Oettingen & Mayer, 2002).

Optimism and Health Health, too, benefits from a basic optimism. As we saw in Unit 8B, a depressed hopelessness dampens the body's disease-fighting immune system. In repeated studies, optimists have outlived pessimists or lived with fewer illnesses. When dating couples wrestle with conflicts, optimists and their partners see each other as engaging constructively. They tend then to feel more supported and satisfied with the resolution and with their relationship (Srivastava et al., 2006). Expect good things from others, and often you will get what you expect. Such studies helped point Seligman toward proposing a more positive psychology (see Close-Up: Toward a More Positive Psychology on the next page).

Excessive Optimism If positive thinking in the face of adversity pays dividends, so, too, can a dash of realism (Schneider, 2001). Self-disparaging explanations of past failures can depress ambition, but realistic anxiety over possible *future* failures can fuel energetic efforts to avoid the dreaded fate (Goodhart, 1986; Norem, 2001; Showers, 1992). Students concerned about failing an upcoming test may study thoroughly and outperform their equally able but more confident peers. Edward Chang (2001) reports that, compared with European-American students, Asian-American students express somewhat greater pessimism—which he suspects helps explain their impressive academic achievements. Success requires enough optimism to provide hope and enough pessimism to prevent complacency. We want our airline pilots to be mindful of worst-possible outcomes.

Excessive optimism can blind us to real risks. Neil Weinstein (1980, 1982, 1996) has shown how our natural positive-thinking bias can promote "an unrealistic optimism about future life events." Most late adolescents see themselves as much less vulnerable than their peers to the HIV virus that causes AIDS (Abrams, 1991). Most college students perceive themselves as less likely than their average classmate to develop drinking problems, drop out of school, or have a heart attack by age 40. Many credit-card users, unrealistically optimistic about how they will use their charge cards, elect cards with low fees and high interest (Yang et al., 2006). These and others—who optimistically deny the effects of smoking, venture into ill-fated relationships, and outwit themselves in dozens of other ways—remind us that, like pride, blind optimism may go before a fall.

Our natural positive-thinking bias does seem to vanish, however, when we are bracing ourselves for feedback, such as test results (Carroll et al., 2006). (Have you ever noticed that, as a game nears its end, the outcome seems more in doubt when your team is ahead than when it is behind?) Positive illusions also vanish after a traumatic personal experience—as they did for victims of a catastrophic California earthquake, who had to give up their illusions of being less vulnerable than others to earthquakes (Helweg-Larsen, 1999).

Blindness to One's Own Incompetence Ironically, people often are most overconfident when most incompetent. That's because it often takes competence to recognize competence, as Justin Kruger and David Dunning noted (1999). They found that

Positive expectations often motivate eventual success.

"We just haven't been flapping them hard enough."

"O God, give us grace to accept with serenity the things that cannot be changed, courage to change the things which should be changed, and the wisdom to distinguish the one from the other."

Reinhold Niebuhr,
"The Serenity Prayer," 1943

"Pessimism is like optimism, only less dangerous."

Mignon McLaughlin,
The Neurotic's Notebook, 1963

"I didn't think it could happen to me."

Earvin "Magic" Johnson, *My Life*,
1993 [after contracting HIV]

INTERCONNECTING

You might link this discussion of explanatory style with the Appendix C discussion of promoting wellness. The positive health effects of optimistic thinking are discussed in detail in Appendix C.

TEACHING TIP

Positive psychology is a hot topic in psychology in the 21st century, but some critics feel that overemphasizing the good at the expense of the bad gives an imbalanced view of psychology. As Myers points out here, being too optimistic about future events may lead to poor decisions and risks. Having a balanced explanatory style seems to be most beneficial.

DEMO

Have students imagine that they have just failed a psychology test. Have them write down two or three reasons why they would have failed. Then have them look over their reasons to assess what type of locus of control they feel those reasons indicate.

UNIT 10

Before World War II, psychology had three main areas of focus: to cure mental illness, to cultivate genius and talent, and to find what makes life fulfilling. After the horrors of World War II, psychology focused full throttle on diagnosing and treating mental illness—with much success. Why was study of the good life left behind? Have students discuss the following questions related to studying the good in life:

- Is the study of positive qualities just as important as understanding illness? Why or why not?

- Why would researchers feel hesitant about studying positive qualities rather than negative ones?

- Is the study of positive qualities more difficult than studying negative ones? Why or why not?

CLOSE-UP

Toward a More Positive Psychology

Courtesy of Martin E. P. Seligman, Ph.D, Director, Positive Psychology Center/University of Pennsylvania

Martin E. P. Seligman "The main purpose of a positive psychology is to measure, understand, and then build the human strengths and the civic virtues."

During its first century, psychology understandably focused much of its attention on understanding and alleviating negative states. Psychologists have studied abuse and anxiety, depression and disease, prejudice and poverty. As Unit 8B noted, articles on selected negative emotions since 1887 have outnumbered those on positive emotions by 17 to 1.

In ages past, notes American Psychological Association past-president Martin Seligman (2002), times of relative peace and prosperity have enabled cultures to turn their attention from repairing weakness and damage to promoting "the highest qualities of life." Prosperous fifth-century Athens nurtured philosophy and democracy. Flourishing fifteenth-century Florence nurtured great art. Victorian England, flush with the bounty of the British Empire, nurtured honor, discipline, and duty. In this millennium, Seligman believes, thriving Western cultures have a parallel opportunity to create, as a "humane, scientific monument," a more **positive psychology**—a psychology concerned not only with weakness and damage but also with strength and virtue. Thanks to his own leadership and to some $30 million in funding, the new positive psychology movement has gained strength (Seligman, 2004).

Positive psychology shares with humanistic psychology an interest in advancing human fulfillment, but its methodology is scientific. From these roots have grown not only the new studies of happiness and health (Unit 8B), but also the shift in emphasis from learned helplessness and depression to optimism and thriving. "Positive psychology," say Seligman and colleagues (2005), "is an umbrella term for the study of positive emotions, positive character traits, and enabling institutions."

Taken together, satisfaction with the past, happiness with the present, and optimism about the future define the movement's first pillar: *positive emotions.* Happiness, Seligman argues, is a by-product of a pleasant, engaged, and meaningful life.

Positive psychology is about building not just a pleasant life, says Seligman, but also a *good life* that engages one's skills, and a *meaningful life* that points beyond oneself. Thus, the second pillar, *positive character,* focuses on exploring and enhancing creativity, courage, compassion, integrity, self-control, leadership, wisdom, and spirituality. Current research examines the roots and fruits of such characteristics, sometimes by studying individuals who exemplify them in extraordinary ways.

The third pillar, *positive groups, communities, and cultures,* seeks to foster a positive social ecology, including healthy families, communal neighborhoods, effective schools, socially responsible media, and civil dialogue.

Will psychology have a more positive mission in this century? Without slighting the need to repair damage and cure disease, positive psychology's proponents hope so. With *American Psychologist* and British *Psychologist* special issues devoted to positive psychology; with lots of books; with networked scientists working in worldwide research groups; and with prizes, research awards, summer institutes, and a graduate program promoting positive psychology scholarship, these psychologists have reason to be positive.

> "The living-room [Scrabble] player is lucky. . . . He has no idea how miserably he fails with almost every turn, how many possible words or optimal plays slip by unnoticed."
>
> Stefan Fatsis, *Word Freak,* 2001

::**positive psychology** the scientific study of optimal human functioning; aims to discover and promote strengths and virtues that enable individuals and communities to thrive.

most students scoring at the low end of grammar and logic tests believed they had scored in the top half. If you do not know what good grammar is, you may be unaware that your grammar is poor. This "ignorance of one's own incompetence" phenomenon has a parallel, as I can confirm, in hard-of-hearing people's difficulty recognizing their own hearing loss. We're not so much "in denial" as we are simply unaware of what we don't hear. If I fail to hear my friend calling my name, the friend notices my inattention. But for me it's a nonevent. I hear what I hear—which, to me, seems pretty normal.

The difficulty in recognizing one's own incompetence helps explain why so many low-scoring students are dumbfounded after doing badly on a test. If you don't know all the Scrabble word possibilities you've overlooked, you may feel pretty smart—until someone points them out. As Deanna Caputo and Dunning (2005) demonstrate in experiments that re-create this phenomenon, our ignorance of what we don't know helps sustain our confidence in our own abilities.

DOONESBURY

To judge one's competence and predict one's future performance, it often pays to invite others' assessments, notes Dunning (2006). Based on studies in which both individuals and their acquaintances predict their future, we can hazard some advice: If you are a junior doctor and want to predict how well you will do on a surgical skills exam, don't rate yourself—ask your peers for their candid prediction. If you're a Naval officer and need to assess your leadership ability don't rate yourself—ask your fellow officers. And if you're in love and want to predict whether it will last, don't listen to your heart—ask your friends.

Assessing Behavior in Situations

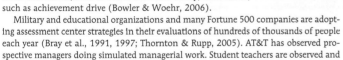

15: What underlying principle guides social-cognitive psychologists in their assessment of people's behavior and beliefs?

Social-cognitive psychologists explore how people interact with situations. To predict behavior, they often observe behavior in realistic situations.

The idea, though effective, is not new. One ambitious example was the U.S. Army's World War II strategy for assessing candidates for spy missions. Rather than using paper-and-pencil tests, Army psychologists subjected the candidates to simulated undercover conditions. They tested their ability to handle stress, solve problems, maintain leadership, and withstand intense interrogation without blowing their cover. Although time-consuming and expensive, this assessment of behavior in a realistic situation helped predict later success on actual spy missions (OSS Assessment Staff, 1948). Modern studies indicate that assessment center exercises are more revealing of some dimensions, such as communication ability, than others, such as achievement drive (Bowler & Woehr, 2006).

Military and educational organizations and many Fortune 500 companies are adopting assessment center strategies in their evaluations of hundreds of thousands of people each year (Bray et al., 1991, 1997; Thornton & Rupp, 2005). AT&T has observed prospective managers doing simulated managerial work. Student teachers are observed and

Assessing behavior in situations Reality TV shows, such as Donald Trump's *The Apprentice,* may take "show me" job interviews to the extreme, but they do illustrate a valid point. Seeing how a potential employee behaves in a job-relevant situation helps predict job performance.
▲ ....

 TEACHING TIP

Explanatory style, or the way we explain events in our lives, falls into three categories:

- *Permanence*—the belief that life events will have a permanent effect on us. Optimists believe that bad events are temporary and good events are permanent. Pessimists believe the opposite—the effects of bad events are permanent and the effects of good events are transient.

- *Pervasiveness*—the belief that life events have ripple-effect impacts on other areas of life. Optimists believe that good experiences will spill over into other areas while bad events are isolated to a particular circumstance. Pessimists believe that bad events impact other areas, expecting failure in one area to cause problems in others.

- *Personal*—the belief that life events are due to some personality trait that is unchangeable. Optimists believe that good events are personal while bad events are due to circumstances. Pessimists believe that good events are circumstantial and bad events are due to personal faults.

CRITICAL THINKING ?

Have students come up with some pessimistic explanations for failing a test. Then have them apply the following methods of disputing these thoughts:

- Alternative seeking: Students should come up with alternative explanations that are more optimistic.

- Evidence seeking: Students should cite evidence that disputes negative thoughts like "I am stupid."

- De-catastrophizing: Students should come up with reasons why this particular test grade is not the end of the world.

UNIT 10

The trait and social-cognitive theories presented in this unit try to be more scientific than intuitive. Have students evaluate the scientific practices of the trait theory and the social-cultural theory.

- Is the use of objective tests or real-life simulations better scientific practice? Why?

- What are the limitations of each type of scientific practice in explaining human behavior?

- How can a union of the two perspectives lead to a greater understanding of human behavior?

::**self** in contemporary psychology, assumed to be the center of personality, the organizer of our thoughts, feelings, and actions.

• A *New York Times* analysis of 100 rampage murders over the last half-century revealed that 55 of the killers had regularly exploded in anger and 63 had threatened violence (Goodstein & Glaberson, 2000). Most didn't, out of the blue, "just snap." •

evaluated several times. Many colleges assess potential faculty members' teaching abilities by observing them teach and assess graduate students' potential via internships and student teaching. Armies assess their soldiers by observing them during military exercises. Most American cities with populations of 50,000 or more have used assessment centers in evaluating police and fire officers (Lowry, 1997).

These procedures exploit the principle that the best means of predicting future behavior is neither a personality test nor an interviewer's intuition. Rather, it is the person's past behavior patterns in similar situations (Mischel, 1981; Ouellette & Wood, 1998; Schmidt & Hunter, 1998). As long as the situation and the person remain much the same, the best predictor of future job performance is past job performance; the best predictor of future grades is past grades; the best predictor of future aggressiveness is past aggressiveness; the best predictor of drug use in young adulthood is drug use in high school. If you can't check the person's past behavior, the next-best thing is to create an assessment situation that simulates the task so you can see how the person handles it.

Evaluating the Social-Cognitive Perspective

16: What has the social-cognitive perspective contributed to the study of personality, and what criticisms has it faced?

The social-cognitive perspective on personality sensitizes researchers to how situations affect, and are affected by, individuals. More than other perspectives, it builds from psychological research on learning and cognition.

Critics charge that the social-cognitive perspective focuses so much on the situation that it fails to appreciate the person's inner traits. Where is the person in this view of personality, ask the dissenters, and where are human emotions? True, the situation does guide our behavior. But, say the critics, in many instances our unconscious motives, our emotions, and our pervasive traits shine through. Personality traits have been shown to predict behavior at work, love, and play. Our biologically influenced traits really do matter. Consider Percy Ray Pridgen and Charles Gill. Each faced the same situation: They had jointly won a $90 million lottery jackpot (Harriston, 1993). When Pridgen learned of the winning numbers, he began trembling uncontrollably, huddled with a friend behind a bathroom door while confirming the win, then sobbed. When Gill heard the news, he told his wife and then went to sleep.

BEFORE YOU MOVE ON . . .

➤ ASK YOURSELF
Are you a pessimist? Do you tend to have low expectations and to attribute bad events to your inability or to circumstances beyond your control? Or are you an optimist, perhaps even being excessively optimistic at times? How has either tendency influenced your choices thus far?

➤ TEST YOURSELF 5
How do personal control and optimism influence behavior?

Answers to the Test Yourself questions can be found in Appendix E at the end of the book.

* * *

As we have seen, researchers investigate personality using various methods that serve differing purposes. For a synopsis and comparison of these methods, see **TABLE 10.3**.

TABLE 10.3

COMPARING RESEARCH METHODS USED TO INVESTIGATE PERSONALITY

Research Method	Description	Perspectives incorporating this method	Benefits	Weaknesses
Case study	In-depth study of one.	Psychoanalytic, humanistic	Less expensive than other methods.	May not generalize to the larger population.
Survey	Systematic questioning of a random sample of the population.	Trait, social-cognitive, positive psychology	Results tend to be reliable and can be generalized to the larger population.	May be expensive; correlational findings.
Projective tests (e.g., TAT and Rorschach)	Ambiguous stimuli designed to trigger projection of inner dynamics.	Psychodynamic	Designed to get beneath the conscious surface of a person's self-understanding; may be a good ice-breaker.	Results have weak validity and reliability.
Personality Inventories, such as Myers-Briggs, the MMPI, and (thanks to factor analysis) the Big Five	Objectively scored groups of questions designed to identify personality dispositions.	Trait	Generally reliable and empirically validated.	Explore limited number of traits.
Observation	Studying how individuals react in different situations.	Social-cognitive	Allows researchers to study the effects of environmental factors on the way an individual's personality is expressed.	Results may not apply to the larger population.
Experimentation	Manipulate variables, with random assignment to conditions.	Social-cognitive	Discerns cause and effect.	Some variables cannot feasibly or ethically be manipulated.

Exploring the Self

17: Are we helped or hindered by high self-esteem?

PSYCHOLOGY'S CONCERN WITH PEOPLE'S sense of self dates back at least to William James, who devoted more than 100 pages of his 1890 *Principles of Psychology* to the topic. By 1943, Gordon Allport lamented that the self had become "lost to view." Although humanistic psychology's emphasis on the self did not instigate much scientific research, it did help renew the concept of self and keep it alive. Now, more than a century after James, the self is one of Western psychology's most vigorously researched topics. Every year, new studies galore appear on self-esteem, self-disclosure, self-awareness, self-schemas, self-monitoring, and so forth. Underlying this research is an assumption that the **self**, as organizer of our thoughts, feelings, and actions, is the center of personality.

One example of thinking about self is the concept of *possible selves* put forth by Hazel Markus and her colleagues (Cross & Markus, 1991; Markus & Nurius, 1986). Your possible selves include your visions of the self you dream of becoming—the rich self, the successful self, the loved and admired self. They also include the self you fear becoming—the unemployed self, the lonely self, the academically failed self. Such possible selves motivate us by laying out specific goals and calling forth the energy to work toward them. University of Michigan students in a combined undergraduate/medical school program earn higher grades if they undergo the program with a clear vision of themselves as successful doctors. Dreams do often give birth to achievements.

Our self-focused perspective may motivate us, but it can also lead us to presume too readily that others are noticing and evaluating us. Thomas Gilovich (1996)

▼

Possible selves By giving them a chance to try out many possible selves, pretend games offer children important opportunities to develop emotionally, socially, and cognitively. This young boy may or may not grow up to be a physician, but playing adult roles will certainly bear fruit in terms of an expanded vision of what he might become.

Sybil Shackman

"The first step to better times is to imagine them."

Chinese fortune cookie

INTERCONNECTING

Using Table 10.3, review with students the different types of research methodologies first presented in Unit 2. Students will likely be asked about research methods throughout the AP Exam, so a thorough understanding of what these methodologies are and how to distinguish them in real-world situations is important for success on the AP Exam.

DEMO

Have students write down their possible selves:

- The self they hope to become
- The self they fear they will become
- The self they think they are to their friends
- The self they think they are with their family
- The self they are at school

UNIT 10

INTERCONNECTING

Connect the *spotlight effect* with adolescent egocentrism. Teens often feel as though everyone is thinking about them. They believe everyone is preoccupied with the things they are preoccupied about—their looks, their behavior, etc. However, most teens are pre-occupied with themselves, making it difficult to be preoccupied with anyone else.

TROUBLESHOOTING

Self-esteem is a feeling of self worth, while self-efficacy is our beliefs about how capable we feel we are. Typically, self-esteem and self-efficacy go together.

LOW SELF-ESTEEM

"There's a lot of talk about self-esteem these days. It seems pretty basic to me. If you want to feel proud of yourself, you've got to do things you can be proud of."

Oseola McCarty, Mississippi laundry worker, after donating $150,000 to the University of Southern Mississippi

demonstrated this **spotlight effect** by having individual Cornell University students don Barry Manilow T-shirts before entering a room with other students. Feeling self-conscious, the T-shirt wearers guessed that nearly half their peers would take note of the shirt as they walked in. In reality, only 23 percent did. This absence of attention applies not only to our dorky clothes and bad hair but also to our nervousness, irritation, or attraction: Fewer people notice than we presume (Gilovich & Savitsky, 1999). Others are also less aware than we suppose of the variability—the ups and downs—of our appearance and performance (Gilovich et al., 2002). Even after a blunder (setting off a library alarm, showing up in the wrong clothes), we stick out like a sore thumb less than we imagine (Savitsky et al., 2001). Knowing about the spotlight effect can be empowering. Help public speakers to understand that their natural nervousness is not so apparent to their audience and their speaking performance improves (Savitsky & Gilovich, 2003).

The Benefits of Self-Esteem

How we feel about ourselves is also important. High **self-esteem**—a feeling of self-worth—pays dividends. People who feel good about themselves (who strongly agree with self-affirming questionnaire statements such as, "I am fun to be with") have fewer sleepless nights; succumb less easily to pressures to conform; are more persistent at difficult tasks; are less shy, anxious, and lonely; and are just plain happier (Greenberg, 2008; Leary, 1999; Murray et al., 2002; Watson et al., 2002). Moreover, today's self-esteem sometimes predicts tomorrow's achievements. In one study of 297 Finnish university students, self-esteem scores predicted employment, salary, and job satisfaction a decade later (Salmela-Aro & Nurmi, 2007).

Is high self-esteem really "the armor that protects kids" from life's problems? Some psychologists have their doubts (Baumeister, 2006; Dawes, 1994; Leary, 1999; Seligman, 1994, 2002). Although children's academic self-concept—their confidence that they can do well in a subject—predicts school achievement, general self-image does not (Marsh & Craven, 2006; Swann et al., 2007; Trautwein et al., 2006). Maybe self-esteem simply reflects reality. Maybe feeling good *follows* doing well. Maybe it's a side effect of meeting challenges and surmounting difficulties. Maybe self-esteem is a gauge that reads out the state of our relationships with others. If so, isn't pushing the gauge artificially higher akin to forcing a car's low fuel gauge to display "full"? And if problems and failures cause low self-esteem, won't the best boost therefore come not so much from our repeatedly telling children how wonderful they are as from their own effective coping and hard-won achievements?

However, experiments do reveal an *effect* of low self-esteem. Temporarily deflate people's self-image (say, by telling them they did poorly on an aptitude test or by disparaging their personality) and they will be more likely to disparage others or to express heightened racial prejudice (Ybarra, 1999). Those who are negative about themselves also tend to be thin-skinned and judgmental (Baumgardner et al., 1989; Pelham, 1993). In experiments, people made to feel insecure often become excessively critical, as if to impress others with their own brilliance (Amabile, 1983). Such findings are consistent with Maslow's and Rogers' presumptions that a healthy self-image pays dividends. Accept yourself and you'll find it easier to accept others. Disparage yourself and you will be prone to the floccinaucinihilipilification[1] of others. Said more simply, some "love their neighbors as themselves"; others loathe their neighbors as themselves. People who are down on themselves tend to be down on other things and people.

[1] I couldn't resist throwing that in. But don't worry, you won't be tested on floccinaucinihilipilification, which is the act of estimating something as worthless (and was the longest nontechnical word in the first edition of the *Oxford English Dictionary*).

TEACHING TIP

At this point, you may want to use **Classroom Exercise: *Self-Efficacy Scale*** (p. 23) from Bolt's Teacher's Resource Binder.

Self-Serving Bias

Carl Rogers (1958) once objected to the religious doctrine that humanity's problems arise from excessive self-love, or pride. He noted that most people he had known "despise themselves, regard themselves as worthless and unlovable." Mark Twain had a similar idea: "No man, deep down in the privacy of his heart, has any considerable respect for himself."

Actually, most of us have a good reputation with ourselves. In studies of self-esteem, even those who score low respond in the midrange of possible scores. (A low-self-esteem person responds to statements such as "I have good ideas" with qualifying adjectives such as *somewhat* or *sometimes*.) Moreover, one of psychology's most provocative and firmly established recent conclusions concerns our potent **self-serving bias**—our readiness to perceive ourselves favorably (Mezulis et al., 2004; Myers, 2008). Consider these findings:

People accept more responsibility for good deeds than for bad, and for successes than for failures. Athletes often privately credit their victories to their own prowess, and their losses to bad breaks, lousy officiating, or the other team's exceptional performance. After receiving poor grades on a test, most students in a half-dozen studies criticized the test, not themselves. On insurance forms, drivers have explained accidents in such words as: "An invisible car came out of nowhere, struck my car, and vanished." "As I reached an intersection, a hedge sprang up, obscuring my vision, and I did not see the other car." "A pedestrian hit me and went under my car." The question "What have I done to deserve this?" is one we usually ask of our troubles, not our successes—those, we assume we deserve.

PEANUTS

Most people see themselves as better than average. This is true for nearly any commonplace behavior that is subjectively assessed and socially desirable. In national surveys, most business executives say they are more ethical than their average counterpart. In several studies, 90 percent of business managers and more than 90 percent of college professors rated their performance as superior to that of their average peer. In Australia, 86 percent of people rate their job performance as above average, and only 1 percent as below average. The phenomenon, which reflects the overestimation of self rather than the underestimation of others (Epley & Dunning, 2000), is less striking in Asia, where people value modesty (Heine & Hamamura, 2007). Yet self-serving biases have been observed worldwide: among Dutch, Australian, and Chinese students; Japanese drivers; Indian Hindus; and French people of most walks of life. In every one of 53 countries surveyed, people expressed self-esteem above the midpoint of the most widely used scale (Schmitt & Allik, 2005).

Ironically, people even see themselves as more immune than others to self-serving bias (Pronin, 2007). The world, it seems, is Garrison Keillor's Lake Wobegon writ large—a place where "all the women are strong, all the men are good-looking, and all the children are above average." And so are the pets. Three in four owners believe their pet is smarter than average (Nier, 2004).

::**spotlight effect** overestimating others' noticing and evaluating our appearance, performance, and blunders (as if we presume a spotlight shines on us).

::**self-esteem** one's feelings of high or low self-worth.

::**self-serving bias** a readiness to perceive oneself favorably.

"To love oneself is the beginning of a life-long romance."
Oscar Wilde, *An Ideal Husband*, 1895

TEACHING TIP

Just as athletes take credit for victories and not for their defeats, fans of athletic teams do the same. When their favorite team wins, everyone shouts, "We won!" When their team loses, everyone shouts, "They lost!" It seems that the self-serving bias is not limited to our own deeds.

INTERCONNECTING

Connect the idea that we see ourselves as better than average with the phenomenon of *overconfidence*, presented in Unit 2. When asked to predict future performance or whether we think we have an answer correct on a test, we are very likely to think the best. We tend to be more confident than correct in most instances.

TEACHING TIP

At this point, you may want to use **Classroom Exercises/Student Projects:** *Possible Selves* (p. 28) or *Exploring Possible Selves as Roadmaps to the Future* (p. 29) from Bolt's Teacher's Resource Binder.

UNIT 10

INTERCONNECTING

Remind students about Alfred Adler, who coined the term *inferiority complex.* An inferiority complex occurs when we underestimate our own capabilities. By contrast, some people also experience a *superiority complex,* in which they overestimate their capabilities.

TEACHING TIP

At this point, you may want to use **Lecture/Discussion Topics:** *The Dark Side of Self-Esteem* (p. 31) or *The Sociometer Theory of Self-Esteem* (p. 32) from Bolt's Teacher's Resource Binder.

> "The [self-]portraits that we actually believe, when we are given freedom to voice them, are dramatically more positive than reality can sustain."
> Shelley Taylor, *Positive Illusions,* 1989

Self-serving bias flies in the face of pop psychology. "All of us have inferiority complexes," wrote John Powell (1989, p. 15). "Those who seem not to have such a complex are only pretending." But additional findings remove any doubts (Myers, 2008):

- We remember and justify our past actions in self-enhancing ways.
- We exhibit an inflated confidence in our beliefs and judgments.
- We overestimate how desirably *we* would act in situations where most people behave less than admirably.
- We often seek out favorable, self-enhancing information.
- We are quicker to believe flattering descriptions of ourselves than unflattering ones, and we are impressed with psychological tests that make us look good.
- We shore up our self-image by *over*estimating the commonality of our foibles and by *under*estimating the commonality of our strengths.
- We see ourselves making better-than-average contributions to our groups (but so do our teammates, which explains why group members' self-contribution estimates usually total more than 100 percent).
- We exhibit group pride—a tendency to see our group (our school, our country, our race, our children, even our pets) as superior.

Moreover, pride, as religion and literature together remind us, does often go before a fall. Self-serving perceptions underlie conflicts ranging from blaming one's spouse for marital discord to arrogantly promoting one's own ethnic superiority. Finding their self-esteem threatened, people with large egos may do more than put others down; they may react violently. "Aryan pride" fueled Nazi atrocities. "These biases have the effect of making wars more likely to begin and more difficult to end," note Daniel Kahneman and Jonathan Renshon (2007).

We can see these tendencies even in children, where the recipe for frequent fighting mixes high self-esteem with social rejection. The most aggressive children tend to have high self-regard that gets punctured by other kids' dislike (van Boxtel et al.,

TEACHING TIP

At this point, you may want to use **Classroom Exercises:** *Rosenberg Self-Esteem Scale* (p. 29) or *A Single-Item Measure of Self-Esteem (SISE)* (p. 29) or *Contingencies of Self-Worth Scale* (p. 30) or *Self-Concept Clarity* (p. 32) from Bolt's Teacher's Resource Binder.

2004). Similarly, an adolescent or adult with a swelled head that gets deflated by insult is potentially dangerous. Brad Bushman and Roy Baumeister (1998) experimented with this "dark side of high self-esteem." They had 540 undergraduate volunteers write a paragraph, in response to which another supposed student gave them either praise ("Great essay!") or stinging criticism ("One of the worst essays I have read!"). Then the essay writers played a reaction-time game against the other student. After wins, they could assault their opponent with noise of any intensity for any duration.

Can you anticipate the result? After criticism, those with unrealistically high self-esteem were "exceptionally aggressive." They delivered three times the auditory torture of those with normal self-esteem. Threatened egotism, more than low self-esteem, it seems, predisposes aggression. "Encouraging people to feel good about themselves when they haven't earned it" poses problems, Baumeister (2001) concluded. "Conceited, self-important individuals turn nasty toward those who puncture their bubbles of self-love."

After tracking self-importance across the last several decades, psychologist Jean Twenge (2006; Twenge et al., 2008) reports that today's new generation—Generation Me, she calls it—expresses more narcissism (by agreeing more often with statements such as, "If I ruled the world, it would be a better place," or "I think I am a special person"). Agreement with such statements correlates with materialism, the desire to be famous, inflated expectations, more hookups with fewer committed relationships, more gambling, and more cheating, all of which have been on the rise as narcissism has increased.

Despite the demonstrated perils of pride, many people reject the idea of self-serving bias, insisting it overlooks those who feel worthless and unlovable and seem to despise themselves. If self-serving bias prevails, why do so many people disparage themselves? For three reasons: Sometimes self-directed put-downs are subtly strategic: They elicit reassuring strokes. Saying "No one likes me" may at least elicit "But not everyone has met you!" Other times, such as before a game or a test, self-disparaging comments prepare us for possible failure. The coach who extols the superior strength of the upcoming opponent makes a loss understandable, a victory noteworthy. And finally, self-disparagement also frequently pertains to one's old self. People are much more critical of their distant past selves than of their current selves—even when they have not changed (Wilson & Ross, 2001). "At 18, I was a jerk; today I'm more sensitive." In their own eyes, chumps yesterday, champs today.

Even so, it's true: All of us some of the time, and some of us much of the time, do feel inferior—especially when we compare ourselves with those who are a step or two higher on the ladder of status, looks, income, or ability. The deeper and more frequently we have such feelings, the more unhappy, even depressed, we are. But for most people, thinking has a naturally positive bias.

While recognizing the dark side of self-serving bias and self-esteem, some researchers prefer isolating the effects of two types of self-esteem—defensive and secure (Kernis, 2003; Lambird & Mann, 2006; Ryan & Deci, 2004). *Defensive self-esteem* is fragile. It focuses on sustaining itself, which makes failures and criticism feel threatening. Such egotism exposes one to perceived threats, which feed anger and disorder, note Jennifer Crocker and Lora Park (2004). Thus, like low

> "The enthusiastic claims of the self-esteem movement mostly range from fantasy to hogwash. The effects of self-esteem are small, limited, and not all good."
>
> Roy Baumeister (1996)

> "If you compare yourself with others, you may become vain and bitter; for always there will be greater and lesser persons than yourself."
>
> Max Ehrmann, "Desiderata," 1927

Developing real esteem Researchers suggest that the best way to develop our self-esteem is to earn it by way of hard-won accomplishments, as these dancers have done. By contrast, false praise seems to build up a defensive self-esteem that can lead to aggression in the face of more realistic assessments.

Reflexstock/First Light/Steve La

TEACHING TIP

Much of the criticism of the self-esteem movement centers on the giving of false praise. As Myers points out, false praise can lead to defensive self-esteem, which can lead to aggression. Many schools and recreational sports leagues give trophies and prizes to all students, regardless of performance. These well-meaning adults want to help children feel better about themselves, but children are aware when their performance is not as good as someone else's. This false praise can actually have a detrimental effect.

TEACHING TIP

At this point, you may want to use **Classroom Exercises: *The Name-Letter Effect*** (p. 32) or ***Biased Self-Ratings*** (p. 33) or ***Self-Handicapping*** (p. 34) or ***Taking Credit for Success, Denying Responsibility for Failure*** (p. 34) from Bolt's Teacher's Resource Binder.

UNIT 10

self-esteem, defensive self-esteem correlates with aggressive and antisocial behavior (Donnellan et al., 2005).

Secure self-esteem is less fragile, because it is less contingent on external evaluations. To feel accepted for who we are, and not for our looks, wealth, or acclaim, relieves pressures to succeed and enables us to focus beyond ourselves. By losing ourselves in relationships and purposes larger than self, Crocker and Park add, we may achieve a more secure self-esteem and greater quality of life.

BEFORE YOU MOVE ON . . .

> ### ▶ ASK YOURSELF

What possible selves do you dream of—or fear—becoming? To what extent do these imagined selves motivate you now?

> ### ▶ TEST YOURSELF 6

In a 1997 Gallup poll, White Americans estimated 44 percent of their fellow White Americans to be high in prejudice (scoring them 5 or higher on a 10-point scale). How many rated themselves similarly high in prejudice? Just 14 percent. What phenomenon does this illustrate?

Answers to the Test Yourself questions can be found in Appendix E at the end of the book.

CRITICAL THINKING

Individualism and collectivism form some of the psychological basis for the economic systems of capitalism and communism, respectively. Invite your school's government teacher to discuss capitalism and communism.

- What are the fundamental principles that underlie these systems?

- How are these systems similar to individualism and collectivism?

- How might living under these systems lead to people valuing individualistic or collectivistic ideals?

Culture and the Self

18: How do individualist and collectivist cultural influences affect people?

Cultures vary in the extent to which they give priority to the nurturing and expression of personal identity or group identity. To grasp the difference, imagine that someone were to rip away your social connections, making you a solitary refugee in a foreign land. How much of your identity would remain intact? The answer would depend in large part on whether you give greater priority to the independent self that marks **individualism** or to the interdependent self that marks **collectivism.**

If as our solitary traveler you pride yourself on your individualism, a great deal of your identity would remain intact—the very core of your being, the

▼
Uniform requirements
People in individualist Western cultures sometimes see traditional Japanese culture as confining. But from the Japanese perspective, the same tradition may express a "serenity that comes to people who know exactly what to expect from each other" (Weisz et al., 1984).

🛟 TEACHING TIP

Set up a communication (via e-mail or pen pals) with a school in a collectivist culture.

- How is their school day different from yours?

- What kinds of classes do they take? Are they required or selected? Why or why not?

- What does their school prepare its students for? College? Technical school? Employment?

- What are the likes and dislikes of the students?

- What type of social activities do the students participate in?

sense of "me," the awareness of your personal convictions and values. Individualists (often people from North America, Western Europe, Australia, or New Zealand) give relatively greater priority to personal goals and define their identity mostly in terms of personal attributes (Schimmack et al., 2005). They strive for personal control and individual achievement. In American culture, with its relatively big "I" and small "we," 85 percent of people say it is possible "to pretty much be who you want to be" (Sampson, 2000).

Individualists share the human need to belong. They join groups. But they are less focused on group harmony and doing their duty to the group (Brewer & Chen, 2007). Being more self-contained, individualists also move in and out of social groups more easily. They feel relatively free to switch places of worship, leave one job for another, or even leave their extended families and migrate to a new place. Marriage is often for as long as they both shall love.

If set adrift in a foreign land as a collectivist, you might experience a greater loss of identity. Cut off from family, groups, and loyal friends, you would lose the connections that have defined who you are. In a collectivist culture, group identifications provide a sense of belonging, a set of values, a network of caring individuals, an assurance of security. In return, collectivists have deeper, more stable attachments to their groups, often their family, clan, or company. In South Korea, for example, people place less value on expressing a consistent, unique self-concept, and more on tradition and shared practices (Choi & Choi, 2002).

Valuing communal solidarity, people in collectivist cultures place a premium on preserving group spirit and making sure others never lose face. What people say reflects not only what they feel (their inner attitudes) but what they presume others feel (Kashima et al., 1992). Avoiding direct confrontation, blunt honesty, and uncomfortable topics, people often defer to others' wishes and display a polite, self-effacing humility (Markus & Kitayama, 1991). In new groups, they may be shy and more easily embarrassed than their individualist counterparts (Singelis et al., 1995, 1999). Compared with Westerners, people in Japanese and Chinese cultures, for example, exhibit greater shyness toward strangers and greater concern for social harmony and loyalty (Bond, 1988; Cheek & Melchior, 1990; Triandis, 1994). Elders and superiors receive respect, and duty to family may trump personal career preferences. When the priority is "we," not "me," that individualized latte—"decaf, single shot, skinny, extra hot"—that feels so good to a North American in a coffee shop might sound more like a selfish demand in Seoul (Kim & Markus, 1999).

To be sure, there is diversity within cultures. Even in the most individualistic countries, some people manifest collectivist values. And there are regional differences within cultures, such as the spirit of individualism in Japan's "northern frontier" island of Hokkaido (Kitayama et al., 2006). But in general, people (especially men) in competitive, individualist cultures have more personal freedom, are less geographically bound to their families, enjoy more privacy, and take more pride in personal achievements (**TABLE 10.4** on the next page). During the 2000 and 2002 Olympic games, U.S. gold medal winners and the U.S. media

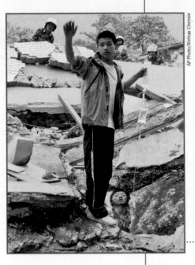

Interdependence This young man is helping a fellow student who became trapped in the rubble that was their school after a devastating earthquake shook China in 2008. By identifying strongly with family and other groups, Chinese people tend to have a collectivist sense of "we" and an accompanying support network of care, which may have helped them struggle through the aftermath of this disaster.

::**individualism** giving priority to one's own goals over group goals and defining one's identity in terms of personal attributes rather than group identifications.

::**collectivism** giving priority to the goals of one's group (often one's extended family or work group) and defining one's identity accordingly.

CULTURAL CONNECTIONS

First-generation immigrants often keep up with their cultural traditions while second-generation immigrants, their children who were likely born in the U.S., struggle to find a balance between cultural heritage and Americanization. Have students explore this phenomenon:

● How do first-generation immigrants hold on to cultural traditions?

● What pressures do second-generation immigrants have to be both traditional and "American"?

● How do second-generation immigrants from collectivist cultures deal with the contrasting cultural influence in their new home?

TEACHING TIP

Have students explore culturally specific behaviors and customs. They can interview people from a different culture, look up information about that culture on the Internet, or research different books that contain cultural information. These differences in culture that are uncovered should help students understand diverse cultural traditions.

TEACHING TIP

At this point, you may want to use **Lecture/Discussion Topic:** *Individualism Versus Collectivism* (p. 36) or **Classroom Exercises:** *Assessing Individualism/Collectivism* (p. 35) or *Independent and Interdependent Selves* (p. 35) from Bolt's Teacher's Resource Binder.

UNIT 10

TEACHING TIP

Have students write a reflective paper about their cultural experiences. Recall your first (or a recent) experience of cultural difference. How did it happen? How did you feel? Given the importance of cultural context, explain how the following may be considered ethnic and cultural stumbling blocks:

- Language and nonverbal communications
- Ethnocentricity
- Culture- and class-related values
- Racism and stereotypes

Adapted from Ernst, R. M. (Jan. 1997) *A Matter of Context.* Presentation to the National Institute for the Teaching of Psychology. St. Petersburg, Florida.

CRITICAL THINKING

Personality tests are not the only psychological assessments that have been accused of cultural, gender, and racial bias. Intelligence tests have also been criticized for being biased. Have students explore the issue of bias in intelligence testing:

- How are culturally biased questions worded?
- What is the racial and cultural makeup of people who do well on intelligence tests? Do these figures hint at a bias? Why or why not?
- How could tests be biased against a particular gender?
- What would be the implications of culturally biased tests?
- How can intelligence tests overcome these biases?

TABLE 10.4

VALUE CONTRASTS BETWEEN INDIVIDUALISM AND COLLECTIVISM

Concept	Individualism	Collectivism
Self	Independent (identity from individual traits)	Interdependent (identity from belonging)
Life task	Discover and express one's uniqueness	Maintain connections, fit in, perform role
What matters	Me—personal achievement and fulfillment; rights and liberties; self-esteem	Us—group goals and solidarity; social responsibilities and relationships; family duty
Coping method	Change reality	Accommodate to reality
Morality	Defined by individuals (self-based)	Defined by social networks (duty-based)
Relationships	Many, often temporary or casual; confrontation acceptable	Few, close and enduring; harmony valued
Attributing behavior	Behavior reflects one's personality and attitudes	Behavior reflects social norms and roles

Sources: Adapted from Thomas Schoeneman (1994) and Harry Triandis (1994).

> "One needs to cultivate the spirit of sacrificing the *little me* to achieve the benefits of the *big me.*"
>
> Chinese saying

covering them attributed the achievements mostly to the athletes themselves (Markus et al., 2006). "I think I just stayed focused," explained swimming gold medalist Misty Hyman. "It was time to show the world what I could do. I am just glad I was able to do it." Japan's gold medalist in the women's marathon, Naoko Takahashi, had a different explanation: "Here is the best coach in the world, the best manager in the world, and all of the people who support me—all of these things were getting together and became a gold medal." Even when describing friends, Westerners tend to use trait-describing adjectives ("she is helpful"), whereas East Asians more often use verbs that describe behaviors in context ("she helps her friends") (Maass et al., 2006).

Individualism's benefits can come at the cost of more loneliness, more divorce, more homicide, and more stress-related disease (Popenoe, 1993; Triandis et al., 1988). People in individualist cultures demand more romance and personal fulfillment in marriage, subjecting the relationship to more pressure (Dion & Dion, 1993). In one survey, "keeping romance alive" was rated as important to a good marriage by 78 percent of U.S. women but only 29 percent of Japanese women (*American Enterprise*, 1992). In China, love songs often express enduring commitment and friendship (Rothbaum & Tsang, 1998). As one song put it, "We will be together from now on. . . . I will never change from now to forever."

BEFORE YOU MOVE ON . . .

➤ ASK YOURSELF

Which concept best describes you—collectivist or individualist? Do you fit completely in either category, or are you sometimes a collectivist and sometimes an individualist?

➤ TEST YOURSELF 7

How do individualist and collectivist cultures differ?

Answers to the Test Yourself questions can be found in Appendix E at the end of the book.

UNIT REVIEW: Personality

The Psychoanalytic Perspective

1: What was Freud's view of personality and its development?

Sigmund Freud's treatment of emotional disorders led him to believe that they spring from *unconscious* dynamics, which he sought to analyze through *free association* and dreams. He referred to his theory and techniques as *psychoanalysis*. He saw *personality* as composed of pleasure-seeking psychic impulses (the *id*), a reality-oriented executive (the *ego*), and an internalized set of ideals (the *superego*). He believed that children develop through *psychosexual stages*, and that failure to resolve conflicts associated with a particular stage may result in *fixation* at that stage.

2: How did Freud think people defended themselves against anxiety?

Tensions between the demands of id and superego cause anxiety. The ego copes by using *defense mechanisms*, especially *repression*.

3: Which of Freud's ideas did his followers accept or reject?

Neo-Freudians Alfred Adler, Karen Horney, and Carl Jung accepted many of Freud's ideas. But Adler and Horney argued that we have motives other than sex and aggression and that the ego's conscious control is greater than Freud supposed, and Jung proposed a *collective unconscious*. Psychodynamic theorists share Freud's view that unconscious mental processes, inner conflicts, and childhood experiences are important influences on personality.

4: What are projective tests, and how are they used?

Projective tests attempt to assess personality by presenting ambiguous stimuli designed to reveal the unconscious. Although projective tests, such as the *Rorschach inkblots*, have questionable reliability and validity, many clinicians continue to use them.

5: How do contemporary psychologists view Freud and the unconscious?

Today's research psychologists note that Freud's theory offers only after-the-fact explanations, and that repression rarely occurs. Current information-processing research confirms that our access to all that goes on in our mind is very limited, but it does not support Freud's view of the unconscious. Rather, the unconscious consists of schemas that control our perceptions; priming; parallel processing that occurs without our conscious knowledge; implicit memories of learned skills; instantly activated emotions; and self-concepts and stereotypes that filter information about ourselves and others. There is also little support for the idea of defense mechanisms. Psychology's false consensus effect (the tendency to overestimate the extent to which others share our beliefs and behaviors) does, however, bear a resemblance to Freud's *projection*, and *reaction formation* also seems to happen.

Nevertheless, Freud drew psychology's attention to the unconscious, to the struggle to cope with anxiety and sexuality, and to the conflict between biological impulses and social restraints. His cultural impact has been enormous.

The Humanistic Perspective

6: How did humanistic psychologists view personality, and what was their goal in studying personality?

Humanistic psychologists sought to turn psychology's attention toward the growth potential of healthy people. Abraham Maslow believed that if basic human needs are fulfilled, people will strive toward *self-actualization*. To nurture growth in others, Carl Rogers advised being genuine, accepting, and empathic. In this climate of *unconditional positive regard*, he believed, people can develop a deeper self-awareness and a more realistic and positive *self-concept*.

7: How did humanistic psychologists assess a person's sense of self?

Humanistic psychologists assessed personality through questionnaires on which people reported their self-concept, and in therapy by seeking to understand their clients' subjective personal experiences.

8: How has the humanistic perspective influenced psychology? What criticisms has it faced?

Humanistic psychology helped to renew psychology's interest in the concept of self. Nevertheless, humanistic psychology's critics complained that its concepts were vague and subjective, its values Western and self-centered, and its assumptions naively optimistic.

The Trait Perspective

9: How do psychologists use traits to describe personality?

Rather than explain the hidden aspects of personality, *trait* theorists attempt to describe our stable and enduring characteristics. Through factor analysis, researchers have isolated important dimensions of personality. Genetic predispositions influence many traits.

10: What are personality inventories, and what are their strengths and weaknesses as trait-assessment tools?

Personality inventories (like the *MMPI*) are questionnaires on which people respond to items designed to gauge a wide range of feelings and behaviors. Items on the test are *empirically derived*, and the tests are objectively scored. But people can fake their answers to create a good impression, and the ease of computerized testing may lead to misuse of these tests.

11: Which traits seem to provide the most useful information about personality variation?

The Big Five personality dimensions—conscientiousness, agreeableness, neuroticism (emotional stability versus instability), openness, and extraversion—offer a reasonably comprehensive picture of personality.

ANSWERS to Multiple-Choice Questions

1. **d.** Self-control
2. **e.** emphasizes the interaction of our traits with our situations.
3. **c.** learned helplessness.
4. **c.** Repression
5. **b.** the self-serving bias.
6. **c.** Self-actualization
7. **a.** self-concept
8. **a.** psychoanalysis
9. **e.** personality inventories.
10. **b.** giving priority to group goals.
11. **d.** evil.
12. **d.** the spotlight effect.
13. **a.** became exceptionally aggressive.
14. **b.** unconditional positive regard.
15. **c.** reciprocal determinism.

12: Does research support the consistency of personality traits over time and across situations?
Although people's traits persist over time, their behaviors vary widely from situation to situation. Despite these variations, a person's average behavior across different situations tends to be fairly consistent.

The Social-Cognitive Perspective

13: In the view of social-cognitive psychologists, what mutual influences shape an individual's personality?
The *social-cognitive perspective* applies principles of learning, cognition, and social behavior to personality, with particular emphasis on the ways in which our personality influences and is influenced by our interaction with the environment. It assumes *reciprocal determinism*—that personal-cognitive factors interact with the environment to influence people's behavior.

14: What are the causes and consequences of personal control?
By studying how people vary in their perceived *locus of control* (*external* or *internal*), researchers have found that a sense of *personal control* helps people to cope with life. Research on personal control evolved into research on the effects of optimism and pessimism, which led to a broader *positive psychology* movement.

15: What underlying principle guides social-cognitive psychologists in their assessment of people's behavior and beliefs?
Social-cognitive researchers study how people interact with their situations. They tend to believe that the best way to predict someone's behavior in a given situation is to observe that person's behavior in similar situations.

16: What has the social-cognitive perspective contributed to the study of personality, and what criticisms has it faced?
Though faulted for underemphasizing the importance of unconscious dynamics, emotions, and inner traits, the social-cognitive perspective builds on psychology's well-established concepts of learning and cognition and reminds us of the power of social situations.

Exploring the Self

17: Are we helped or hindered by high self-esteem?
In contemporary psychology, the *self* is assumed to be the center of personality, the organizer of our thoughts, feelings, and actions. Research confirms the benefits of high *self-esteem*, but it also warns of the dangers of unrealistically high self-esteem. The *self-serving bias* leads us to perceive ourselves favorably, often causing us to overestimate our abilities and underestimate our faults.

18: How do individualist and collectivist cultural influences affect people?
Cultures based on self-reliant *individualism,* like those of most of the United States, Canada, Australia, and Western Europe, value personal independence and individual achievement. Identity is defined in terms of self-esteem, personal goals and attributes, and personal rights and liberties. Cultures based on socially connected *collectivism,* like those of many parts of Asia and Africa, value interdependence, tradition, and harmony, and they define identity in terms of group goals and commitments and belonging to one's group. Within any culture, the degree of individualism or collectivism varies from person to person.

Terms and Concepts to Remember

TECHNOLOGY RESOURCES

These resources will be helpful for teaching the concepts in this unit:

- *Videos: Psychology: The Human Experience, Module 26: Origins of Personality; Module 29: Personality Traits; Module 28: Personality Testing for Career Choice; Module 27: The Social/Cognitive Model*

- *Psychology Video Tool Kit: Personality Structure: Id, Ego, and Superego; Repression: Reality or Myth?; Self-Image: Body Dissatisfaction Among Teenage Girls*

- *ActivePsych: Scientific American Frontiers Teaching Modules,* 3rd ed.: *Genes and Personality: Understanding Williams Syndrome; Psychology Video Tool Kit: Genes and Personality; A Happiness Trait?; Personality and the Brain*

- *PsychSim 5: Helplessly Hoping*

AP* Practice Test Questions

Multiple-Choice Questions

1. What do we call the ability to control impulses and delay gratification?
a. Self-actualization
b. External locus of control
c. Independence
d. Self-control
e. Self-esteem

2. Albert Bandura proposed the social-cognitive perspective, which
a. explains the nature-nurture debate.
b. predicts human behavior.
c. focuses on how our environment controls us.
d. explains human motivation.
e. emphasizes the interaction of our traits with our situations.

3. People given little control over their world in prisons, factories, schools, and nursing homes experience
a. personal control.
b. reciprocal determinism.
c. learned helplessness.
d. self-actualization.
e. projection.

4. According to Sigmund Freud, which of the following defense mechanisms buries threatening or upsetting events outside of consciousness?
a. Regression
b. Displacement
c. Repression
d. Projection
e. Rationalization

5. Athletes who often privately credit their victories to their own prowess, and their losses to bad breaks, lousy officiating, or the other team's exceptional performance are exhibiting
a. a low self-esteem.
b. the self-serving bias.
c. pessimism.
d. the spotlight effect.
e. incompetence.

6. What did Abraham Maslow call the process of fulfilling our potential?
a. Love needs
b. Self-esteem
c. Self-actualization
d. Self-transcendence
e. Hierarchy of needs

7. Our _____ consists of all the thoughts and feelings we have in response to the question, "Who am I?"
a. self-concept
b. ideal self
c. self-esteem
d. empathy
e. self-acceptance

8. Sigmund Freud called his theory of personality and the associated treatment techniques
a. psychoanalysis.
b. the humanistic approach.
c. the self-concept.
d. the psychosexual stages.
e. free association.

9. Questionnaires covering a wide range of feelings and behaviors designed to assess several traits at once are called
a. factor analysis studies.
b. peer reports.
c. achievement tests.
d. cognition tests.
e. personality inventories.

10. Collectivist cultures are characterized by members
a. developing a strong sense of self.
b. giving priority to group goals.
c. forming casual, often temporary relationships.
d. achieving personal goals.
e. discovering how they are different from the group.

11. Critics of humanistic psychology have suggested that this theory fails to appreciate the reality of our human capacity for
a. empathy.
b. love.
c. negativity.
d. evil.
e. laziness.

12. Our self-focused perspective may motivate us, but it can also lead us to presume too readily that others are noticing and evaluating us. This is called
a. self-monitoring.
b. self-schemas.
c. possible selves.
d. the spotlight effect.
e. the social-cognitive perspective.

13. Brad Bushman and Roy Baumeister found that when criticized, people with unrealistically high self-esteem
a. became exceptionally aggressive.
b. were more receptive to the criticism.
c. became easily depressed.
d. worked harder to do better the next time.
e. quit the task without completing it.

14. According to Carl Rogers, when we are in a good marriage, a close family, or an intimate friendship, we are free to be spontaneous without fearing the loss of others' esteem. He called the accepting attitude that enables this freedom
a. a peak experience.
b. unconditional positive regard.
c. self-transcendence.
d. humanistic psychology.
e. our self-concept.

15. Children's TV-viewing habits (past behavior) influence their viewing preferences (internal personal factor), which influence how television (environmental factor) affects their current behavior. This is an example of
a. personal control.
b. learned helplessness.
c. reciprocal determinism.
d. the Big Five traits.
e. implicit learning.

Free-Response Question

Explain the relationship of the following as they relate to well-being: self-serving bias, self-esteem, locus of control, self-actualization, and reciprocal determinism.

 WEB

Multiple-choice self-tests and more may be found at www.worthpublishers.com/myers

---

Rubric for Grading the Free-Response Question

This is a 10-point question. One point is awarded for accurate connections of the concepts to well-being. Students can earn two points per concept (10 points total). Modify the rubric by adding or subtracting terms depending on what was emphasized in class.

Self-serving bias (Name at least two of the following in order to earn the 2 points.)

Relationship to well-being—Our readiness to perceive ourselves favorably:

1. increases the likelihood of remembering favorable events.
2. decreases the likelihood of remembering unfavorable events.
3. increases self-esteem, which can lead to a multitude of benefits.
4. increases positive interpretations of any given event.

Self-esteem (Name at least two of the following in order to earn the 2 points.)
Relationship to well-being—Those with a feeling of self-worth:

Rubric continued

1. sleep better.
2. are less shy.
3. are happier.
4. are less lonely.

Locus of control (Name at least two of the following in order to earn the 2 points.)

Relationship to well-being—The sense of environmental control (internal locus of control) leads to:
1. achieving more in school.
2. enjoying better health.
3. feeling less depressed.
4. coping better with stress.

Self-actualization (Name at least two of the following in order to earn the 2 points.)
Relationship to well-being—Fulfilling our potential leads to:
1. an increased sense of meaning.
2. an increased sense of purpose.
3. greater self-esteem, which can have a multitude of benefits.
4. greater helpfulness, which leads to more happiness.

Reciprocal determinism (Name at least two of the following in order to earn the 2 points.)

Relationship to well-being—The person-environment interaction affects:
1. the environment one chooses, which in turn shapes an individual. Selection of a positive environment would increase well-being.
2. interpretation of events. Those with an optimistic outlook would be attuned to a favorable interpretation of events, and less attuned to a threatening interpretation of events.
3. how we create situations to which we react. Those with positive dispositions likely enjoy close, supportive friendships, which increases well-being.

Pacing Guide

Use the following guide to determine how many instructional days to devote to this unit depending on the type of course you teach:

Year-long course: 4–6 days
Block schedule/Semester-long course: 3–4 days

This unit encompasses 5–7 percent of the AP Exam. Spending an appropriate amount of time on this unit will help students do well on the AP Exam.

 TEACHING TIP

At this point, you may want to use **Lecture/Discussion Topic:** *Twelve Interesting Facts About Intelligence* (p. 3) or **Classroom Exercises/Student Projects:** *What Is Intelligence?* (p. 3) or *Designing and Administering an Intelligence Test* (p. 3) from Bolt's Teacher's Resource Binder, which accompanies this text.

522

Suggested Readings

Budiansky, S. (1998). *If a lion could talk: Animal intelligence and the evolution of consciousness.* New York: Free Press.

Csikszentmihalyi, M. (1996). *Creativity: The work and lives of 91 eminent people.* New York: HarperCollins.

Deary, I. J. (2001). *Intelligence: A very short introduction.* Oxford: Oxford University Press.

Gardner, H. (1999). *Multiple intelligences for the 21st century.* New York: Basic Books.

Gould, S. J. (1981). *The mismeasure of man.* New York: W. W. Norton.

Sternberg, R. (1988). *The triarchic mind.* New York: Viking Penguin.

Sternberg, R. J., Forsythe, G. B., Hedlund, J., Horvath, J., Snook, S., Williams, W. M., Wagner, R. K., & Grigorenko, E. L. (2000). *Practical intelligence.* New York: Cambridge University Press.

Testing and Individual Differences

Three huge controversies have sparked recent debate in and beyond psychology. First is the "memory war," over whether traumatic experiences are repressed and can later be recovered, with therapeutic benefit. The second great controversy is the "gender war," over the extent to which nature and nurture shape our behaviors as men and women. In this unit, we meet the "intelligence war": Does each of us have an inborn general mental capacity (intelligence), and can we quantify this capacity as a meaningful number?

School boards, courts, and scientists debate the use and fairness of tests that attempt to assess people's mental abilities and assign them a score. Is intelligence testing a constructive way to guide people toward suitable opportunities? Or is it a potent, discriminatory weapon camouflaged as science? First, some basic questions:

- What is intelligence?
- How can we best assess it?
- To what extent does it result from heredity rather than environment?
- What do test score differences among individuals and groups really mean? Should we use such differences to track abilities of public school students, to admit them to colleges or universities, to hire them?

This unit offers answers. It will also remind you that there are a variety of mental gifts and that the recipe for high achievement in any field blends talent and grit.

Hands-on healing Intelligence can be defined in a variety of ways, and as a socially constructed concept, its meaning varies from culture to culture. This folk healer in Peru displays his intelligence in his knowledge about his medicinal plants and understanding of the needs of the people he is helping.

Key Terms

What Is Intelligence?
intelligence test
intelligence
general intelligence (g)
factor analysis
savant syndrome
emotional intelligence

Assessing Intelligence
mental age
Stanford-Binet
intelligence quotient (IQ)
achievement tests
aptitude tests
Wechsler Adult Intelligence Scale (WAIS)
standardization
normal curve
reliability
validity
content validity
predictive validity

The Dynamics of Intelligence
intellectual disability
Down syndrome

Genetic and Environmental Influences on Intelligence
stereotype threat

Key People

Wade, C., & Tavris, C. (1993). *Critical & creative thinking: The case of love and war.* New York: HarperCollins.

Wallace, D. B., & Gruber, H. E. (Eds.) (1989). *Creative people at work: Twelve cognitive case studies.* New York: Oxford University Press.

Joshua Aronson
Alfred Binet
David Caruso
James Flynn
Francis Galton
Howard Gardner
John Mayer

Peter Salovey
Sandra Scarr
Théodore Simon
Charles Spearman
Claude Steele
William Stern
Robert Sternberg

Lewis Terman
L. L. Thurstone
David Wechsler

TEACHING TIP

Introduce this module by asking your students to list behaviors they believe to be distinctively characteristic of either particularly intelligent or of particularly unintelligent people. In research studies, the behaviors normally listed generally fall into three classes: practical problem-solving skills, verbal skills, and social competence.

TROUBLESHOOTING

The central debate in intelligence-testing circles is how intelligence is defined. The two main camps—the generalists and the multiples (my own names for them!)—argue their respective viewpoints, outlined in this unit. Students probably have their own naturally developed views of the definition of intelligence, so help them identify on which side of the debate their own definitions fall. This will help them engage the self-reference effect, so that they can feel more personally connected to particular philosophical ideas about intelligence.

What Is Intelligence?

PSYCHOLOGISTS DEBATE: SHOULD WE consider intelligence as one aptitude or many? As linked to cognitive speed? As neurologically measurable? Yet, intelligence experts do agree on this: Although people have differing abilities, intelligence is a concept and not a "thing." When we refer to someone's "IQ" (short for *intelligence quotient*) as if it were a fixed and objectively real trait like height, we commit a reasoning error called *reification*—viewing an abstract, immaterial concept as if it were a concrete thing. To reify is to invent a concept, give it a name, and then convince ourselves that such a thing objectively exists in the world. When someone says, "She has an IQ of 120," they are reifying IQ; they are imagining IQ to be a thing this person *has*, rather than a score she once obtained on a particular **intelligence test**. Better to say, "She scored 120 on the intelligence test."

Intelligence is a socially constructed concept: Cultures deem "intelligent" whatever attributes enable success in those cultures (Sternberg & Kaufman, 1998). In the Amazon rain forest, intelligence may be understanding the medicinal qualities of local plants; in an Ontario high school, it may be superior performance on cognitive tasks. In each context, **intelligence** is the ability to learn from experience, solve problems, and use knowledge to adapt to new situations. In research studies, *intelligence* is what intelligence tests measure. Historically, as we will see, that has been the sort of problem solving displayed as "school smarts."

Is Intelligence One General Ability or Several Specific Abilities?

1: What arguments support intelligence as one general mental ability, and what arguments support the idea of multiple distinct identities?

You probably know some people with talents in science, others who excel at the humanities, and still others gifted in athletics, art, music, or dance. You may also know a talented artist who is dumbfounded by the simplest mathematical problems, or a brilliant math student with little aptitude for literary discussion. Are all of these people intelligent? Could you rate their intelligence on a single scale? Or would you need several different scales?

Charles Spearman (1863–1945) believed we have one **general intelligence** (often shortened to **g**). He granted that people often have special abilities that stand out. Spearman had helped develop **factor analysis,** a statistical procedure that identifies clusters of related items. He had noted that those who score high in one area, such as verbal intelligence, typically score higher than average in other areas, such as spatial or reasoning ability. Spearman believed a common skill set, the g factor, underlies all of our intelligent behavior, from navigating the sea to excelling in school.

This idea of a general mental capacity expressed by a single intelligence score was controversial in Spearman's day, and it remains so in our own. One of Spearman's early opponents was L. L. Thurstone (1887–1955). Thurstone gave 56 different tests to people and mathematically identified seven clusters of primary mental abilities (word fluency, verbal comprehension, spatial ability, perceptual speed, numerical ability, inductive reasoning, and memory). Thurstone did not rank people on a single scale of general aptitude. But when other investigators studied the profiles of the people Thurstone had tested, they detected a persistent tendency: Those who excelled in one of the seven clusters generally scored well on the others. So, the investigators concluded, there was still some evidence of a g factor.

> • *New York Times* interviewer Deborah Solomon, 2004: "What is your IQ?"
> Physicist Stephen Hawking: "I have no idea. People who boast about their IQ are losers." •

> "*g* is one of the most reliable and valid measures in the behavioral domain . . . and it predicts important social outcomes such as educational and occupational levels far better than any other trait."
> Behavior geneticist Robert Plomin (1999)

TEACHING TIP

At this point, you may want to use **Lecture/Discussion Topic:** *Intelligence as the Capacity to Adapt* (p. 5) from Bolt's Teacher's Resource Binder.

We might, then, liken mental abilities to physical abilities. Athleticism is not one thing but many. The ability to run fast is distinct from the strength needed for power lifting, which is distinct from the eye-hand coordination required to throw a ball on target. A champion weightlifter rarely has the potential to be a skilled ice skater. Yet there remains some tendency for good things to come packaged together—for running speed and throwing accuracy to correlate, thanks to general athletic ability. So, too, with intelligence. Several distinct abilities tend to cluster together and to correlate enough to define a small general intelligence factor.

Satoshi Kanazawa (2004) argues that general intelligence evolved as a form of intelligence that helps people solve *novel* problems—how to stop a fire from spreading, how to find food during a drought, how to reunite with one's band on the other side of a flooded river. More common problems—such as how to mate or how to read a stranger's face or how to find your way back to camp—require a different sort of intelligence. Kanazawa asserts that general intelligence scores *do* correlate with the ability to solve various novel problems (like those found in academic and many vocational situations) but do not much correlate with individuals' skills in *evolutionarily familiar* situations—such as marrying and parenting, forming close friendships, displaying social competence, and navigating without maps.

Theories of Multiple Intelligences

2: How do Gardner's and Sternberg's theories of multiple intelligences differ?

Since the mid-1980s some psychologists have sought to extend the definition of *intelligence* beyond Spearman's and Thurstone's academic smarts. They acknowledge that people who score well on one sort of cognitive test have some tendency to score well on another. But maybe this occurs not because they express an underlying general intelligence but rather because, over time, different abilities interact and feed one another, rather as a speedy runner's throwing ability improves after being engaged in sports that develop both running and throwing abilities (van der Maas et al., 2006).

Gardner's Eight Intelligences Howard Gardner (1983, 2006) views intelligence as multiple abilities that come in packages. Gardner finds evidence for this view in studies of people with diminished or exceptional abilities. Brain damage, for example, may destroy one ability but leave others intact. And consider people with **savant syndrome,** who often score low on intelligence tests but have an island of brilliance (Treffert & Wallace, 2002). Some have virtually no language ability, yet are able to compute numbers as quickly and accurately as an electronic calculator, or identify almost instantly the day of the week that corresponds to any given date in history, or render incredible works of art or musical performances (Miller, 1999). About 4 in 5 people with savant syndrome are males, and many also have autism, a developmental disorder (see Unit 9).

The late memory whiz Kim Peek, a savant who did not have autism, was the inspiration for the movie *Rain Man*. In 8 to 10 seconds, he could read and remember a page, and he learned 9000 books, including Shakespeare and the Bible, by heart. He learned maps from the front of phone books, and he could provide MapQuest-like travel directions within any major U.S. city. Yet he could not button his clothes. And he had little capacity for abstract concepts. Asked by his father at a restaurant to "lower your voice," he slid lower in his chair to lower his voice box. Asked for Lincoln's Gettysburg Address, he responded, "227 North West Front Street. But he only stayed there one night—he gave the speech the next day" (Treffert & Christensen, 2005).

::**intelligence test** a method for assessing an individual's mental aptitudes and comparing them with those of others, using numerical scores.

::**intelligence** mental quality consisting of the ability to learn from experience, solve problems, and use knowledge to adapt to new situations.

::**general intelligence (g)** a general intelligence factor that, according to Spearman and others, underlies specific mental abilities and is therefore measured by every task on an intelligence test.

::**factor analysis** a statistical procedure that identifies clusters of related items (called *factors*) on a test; used to identify different dimensions of performance that underlie a person's total score.

::**savant syndrome** a condition in which a person otherwise limited in mental ability has an exceptional specific skill, such as in computation or drawing.

TEACHING TIP

Robert J. Gregory provides an illustration of intelligent behavior as the ability to learn from experience, to solve problems, and to use knowledge to adapt to new situations:

A 61-year-old newspaper vendor with moderate intellectual disabilities was well-known to community mental health professionals. However, he managed his own affairs with minimal supervision. Both eccentric and fiercely independent, he stored canned goods in his freezer and swore at caseworkers who stopped by to inquire about his well-being. He maintained his independence by selling papers from a street side newsstand. The papers cost a quarter, and he refused payment other than a quarter or a dollar— an arrangement his customers had learned to live with. However, one day the price of a newspaper increased to 35 cents. He now had to learn to deal with nickels and dimes as well as quarters and dollars. The amount of learning required to adapt to this new environmental demand exceeded his intellectual abilities and, sadly, he was soon out of business.

Gregory, R. (1992). *Psychological testing: History, principles, and applications.* Boston: Allyn & Bacon.

CRITICAL THINKING

Howard Gardner supports his theory of multiple intelligences with the following statements:

- Brain damage has isolated specific types of intelligence in some individuals.

- Savants, prodigies, and other exceptional individuals exist.

- There is an identifiable core set of operations, which are basic kinds of information-processing operations or mechanisms that deal with one specific kind of input.

- We each have a distinctive developmental history, along with a definite set of "end-state" achievements.

- Multiple intelligences are supported by our evolutionary history; they make sense from an adaptive perspective.

- Experimental and psychological tasks support the idea of multiple intelligences.

- Psychometric findings also support the idea of multiple intelligences.

UNIT 11

TEACHING TIP

Gardner's most intriguing argument for his theory is that separate neural centers underlie various intelligences. He provides numerous case studies of patients who have lost all language abilities because of damage to the speech centers in the left hemisphere of the brain, but who still retain the capacity to be musicians, visual artists, and engineers. He describes patients who have difficulty with spatial representation and other visual tasks because of right-hemisphere damage, but who retain their linguistic abilities. Gardner provides neurological data for personal intelligences. For example, although a lobotomy may cause little impairment of linguistic or logical-mathematical intelligence, it can be disastrous for self-understanding and interpersonal relationships.

INTERCONNECTING

Gardner's theory of multiple intelligences is largely based on case study research. While the use of case studies is a valid and informative research method, the results from this type of research are not generalizable to the population at large. The effect of individual differences influences case studies significantly, making it difficult to say that the variable of interest— in this case, intelligence—is the reason for those differences.

TEACHING TIP

At this point, you may want to use **Lecture/Discussion Topics**: *Kim Peek's Brain* (p. 7) or *Gardner's Theory of Multiple Intelligences* (p. 7) from Bolt's Teacher's Resource Binder.

Islands of genius: Savant syndrome After a 30-minute helicopter ride and a visit to the top of a skyscraper, British savant artist Stephen Wiltshire began seven days of drawing that reproduced the Tokyo skyline.

TABLE 11.1

GARDNER'S EIGHT INTELLIGENCES

Aptitude	Exemplar
1. Linguistic	T. S. Eliot, poet
2. Logical-mathematical	Albert Einstein, scientist
3. Musical	Igor Stravinsky, composer
4. Spatial	Pablo Picasso, artist
5. Bodily-kinesthetic	Martha Graham, dancer
6. Intrapersonal (self)	Sigmund Freud, psychiatrist
7. Interpersonal (other people)	Mahatma Gandhi, leader
8. Naturalist	Charles Darwin, naturalist

• Gardner (1998) has also speculated about a ninth possible intelligence—*existential intelligence*—the ability "to ponder large questions about life, death, existence." •

Spatial intelligence genius In 1998, World Checkers Champion Ron "Suki" King of Barbados set a new record by simultaneously playing 385 players in 3 hours and 44 minutes. Thus, while his opponents often had hours to plot their game moves, King could only devote about 35 seconds to each game. Yet he still managed to win all 385 games!

Using such evidence, Gardner argues that we do not have *an* intelligence, but rather *multiple intelligences*. He identifies a total of eight (**TABLE 11.1**), including the verbal and mathematical aptitudes assessed by standard tests. Thus, the computer programmer, the poet, the street-smart adolescent who becomes a crafty executive, and the basketball team's point guard exhibit different kinds of intelligence (Gardner, 1998). He notes,

> If a person is strong (or weak) in telling stories, solving mathematical proofs, navigating around unfamiliar terrain, learning an unfamiliar song, mastering a new game that entails dexterity, understanding others, or understanding himself, one simply does not know whether comparable strengths (or weaknesses) will be found in other areas.

A general intelligence score is therefore like the overall rating of a city—which tells you something but doesn't give you much specific information about its schools, streets, or nightlife.

Wouldn't it be wonderful if the world were so just, responds intelligence researcher Sandra Scarr (1989). Wouldn't it be nice if being weak in one area would be compensated by genius in some other area? Alas, the world is not just. General intelligence scores predict performance on various complex tasks, in various jobs, and in varied countries; *g* matters (Bertua et al., 2005; Gottfredson, 2002a,b, 2003a,b; Rindermann, 2007). In two digests of more than 100 data sets, academic intelligence scores that predicted graduate school success also predicted later job success (Kuncel et al., 2004; Strenze, 2007; see also **FIGURE 11.1**).

Even so, "success" is not a one-ingredient recipe. High intelligence may help you get into a good college and ultimately a desired profession, but it won't make you successful once there. The recipe for success combines talent with *grit*: Those who become highly successful are also

TEACHING TIP

Unlike the theories for general intelligence, Gardner's multiple intelligence theory has not yet produced a valid and reliable test to assess whether people have multiple intelligences or which type of intelligence people might have. Some have criticized Gardner's theory for this lack of a test, saying that the theory borders more on philosophy than science.

➤ FIGURE 11.1

Smart and rich? Jay Zagorsky (2007) tracked 7403 participants in the U.S. National Longitudinal Survey of Youth across 25 years. As shown in this scatterplot, their intelligence scores correlated +.30 with their later income.

conscientious, well-connected, and doggedly energetic. Anders Ericsson (2002, 2007; Ericsson et al., 2007) reports a *10-year rule:* A common ingredient of expert performance in chess, dancing, sports, computer programming, music, and medicine is "about 10 years of intense, daily practice."

Sternberg's Three Intelligences Robert Sternberg (1985, 1999, 2003) agrees that there is more to success than traditional intelligence. And he agrees with Gardner's idea of multiple intelligences. But he proposes a *triarchic theory* of three, not eight, intelligences:

- *Analytical (academic problem-solving) intelligence* is assessed by intelligence tests, which present well-defined problems having a single right answer. Such tests predict school grades reasonably well and vocational success more modestly.

- *Creative intelligence* is demonstrated in reacting adaptively to novel situations and generating novel ideas.

- *Practical intelligence* is required for everyday tasks, which may be ill-defined, with multiple solutions. Managerial success, for example, depends less on academic problem-solving skills than on a shrewd ability to manage oneself, one's tasks, and other people. Sternberg and Richard Wagner's (1993, 1995) test of practical managerial intelligence measures skill at writing effective memos, motivating people, delegating tasks and responsibilities, reading people, and promoting one's own career. Business executives who score relatively high on this test tend to earn high salaries and receive high performance ratings.

With support from the U.S. College Board (which administers the Advanced Placement program as well as the widely used SAT Reasoning Test to U.S. college and university applicants), Sternberg (2006, 2007) and a team of collaborators have developed new measures of creativity (such as thinking up a caption for an untitled cartoon) and practical thinking (such as figuring out how to move a large bed up a winding staircase). Their initial data indicate that these more comprehensive assessments improve prediction of American students' first-year college grades, and they do so with reduced ethnic-group differences.

● For more on how self-disciplined grit feeds achievement, see Appendix B. ●

"You have to be careful, if you're good at something, to make sure you don't think you're good at other things that you aren't necessarily so good at. . . . Because I've been very successful at [software development] people come in and expect that I have wisdom about topics that I don't."

Bill Gates (1998)

Street smarts This child selling candy on the streets of Manaus, Brazil, is developing practical intelligence at a very young age.

David R. Frazier Photolibrary, Inc./Alamy

TEACHING TIP

Thomas Armstrong's *7 Kinds of Smart* is a very useful resource for classroom lectures, discussions, and exercises relating to Gardner's theory. Written as a self-help book, it describes the intelligences, provides checklists for assessing one's strengths and weaknesses, includes suggestions for developing each intelligence, and concludes with an extensive list of additional resources.

Armstrong, T. (1999). *7 kinds of smart: Identifying and developing your many intelligences, Revised and updated with information on 2 new kinds of smart.* New York: Penguin.

WEB CONNECT

Have students explore the practical implications of multiple intelligences via Howard Gardner's Project Zero Web site: www.pz.harvard.edu

TEACHING TIP

At this point, you may want to use **Lecture/Discussion Topics:** *Successful Intelligence* (p. 10) or *The Psychology of Wisdom* (p. 12) or **Classroom Exercise:** *Sternberg's Balance Theory of Wisdom* (p. 13) from Bolt's Teacher's Resource Binder.

CRITICAL THINKING

Robert Sternberg uses the following activity to get people thinking about intelligence. You can use it to help students evaluate their definitions of intelligence. Divide students into small groups and have them brainstorm about the following. Discuss their thoughts as a whole class.

- Think of a time when you learned something significant. Think about the way that you learned it.

- What did you do to learn this significant thing?

- Were you changed afterwards?

TROUBLESHOOTING

Students may get the different theories and theorists confused. Use Table 11.2 to review these theories and help students identify the strengths and weaknesses of each theory.

TEACHING TIP

Psychologist Walter Mischel tested children's impulse control (an aspect of emotional intelligence) with the marshmallow challenge. He offered 4-year-olds a marshmallow and told them if they were willing to wait while he ran an errand, they could have two marshmallows on his return. Some grabbed the treat the minute he left. Some lasted a few minutes before giving in. In the seemingly endless 15- to 20-minute interval, others resisted in a variety of ways. They covered their eyes, sang to themselves, played games with their hands and feet, and tried to sleep. Twelve to 14 years later, those who resisted at 4 were more socially competent, personally effective, and self-assertive. They were less likely to freeze under stress and pursued challenges even in the face of difficulties. They were more self-reliant, confident, trustworthy, and dependable. When again evaluated as high school graduates, the resisters were better students than those who acted on whim. They also had dramatically higher scores on their SAT tests (over 200 points higher than the other group).

Although Sternberg and Gardner differ on specific points, they agree that multiple abilities can contribute to life success. (Neither candidate in the 2000 U.S. presidential election had scored exceptionally high on college entrance aptitude tests, Sternberg [2000] noted, yet both became influential.) The two theorists also agree that the differing varieties of giftedness add spice to life and challenges for education. Under their influence, many teachers have been trained to appreciate the varieties of ability and to apply multiple intelligence theory in their classrooms. TABLE 11.2 compares these different ways of defining *intelligence*.

TABLE 11.2

COMPARING THEORIES OF INTELLIGENCE

Theory	Summary	Strengths	Other Considerations
Spearman's general intelligence (g)	A basic intelligence predicts our abilities in varied academic areas.	Different abilities, such as verbal and spatial, do have some tendency to correlate.	Human abilities are too diverse to be encapsulated by a single general intelligence factor.
Thurstone's primary mental abilities	Our intelligence may be broken down into seven factors: word fluency, verbal comprehension, spatial ability, perceptual speed, numerical ability, inductive reasoning, and memory.	A single g score is not as informative as scores for seven primary mental abilities.	Even Thurstone's seven mental abilities show a tendency to cluster, suggesting an underlying g factor.
Gardner's multiple intelligences	Our abilities are best classified into eight independent intelligences, which include a broad range of skills beyond traditional school smarts.	Intelligence is more than just verbal and mathematical skills. Other abilities are equally important to our human adaptability.	Should all of our abilities be considered *intelligences*? Shouldn't some be called less vital *talents*?
Sternberg's triarchic	Our intelligence is best classified into three areas that predict real-world success: analytical, creative, and practical.	These three facets can be reliably measured.	1. These three facets may be less independent than Sternberg thought and may actually share an underlying g factor. 2. Additional testing is needed to determine whether these facets can reliably predict success.

Emotional Intelligence

3: What makes up emotional intelligence?

"You're wise, but you lack tree smarts."

Also distinct from academic intelligence is *social intelligence*—the know-how involved in comprehending social situations and managing oneself successfully. The concept was first proposed in 1920 by psychologist Edward Thorndike, who noted, "The best mechanic in a factory may fail as a foreman for lack of social intelligence" (Goleman, 2006, p. 83). Like Thorndike, later psychologists have marveled that high-aptitude people are "not, by a wide margin, more effective . . . in achieving better marriages, in successfully raising their children, and in achieving better mental and physical well-being" (Epstein & Meier, 1989). Others have explored the difficulty that some rationally smart people have in processing and managing social information (Cantor & Kihlstrom, 1987; Weis & Süß, 2007). This idea is especially significant for an aspect of social intelligence that John Mayer, Peter Salovey, and David Caruso (2002, 2008) have called **emotional intelligence.** They have developed a test that assesses four emotional intelligence components, which are the abilities to

- *perceive* emotions (to recognize them in faces, music, and stories).
- *understand* emotions (to predict them and how they change and blend).

WEB CONNECT

John Mayer, one of the leaders in emotional intelligence, maintains a Web site that discusses the major issues in emotional intelligence. Have students explore this site to learn more about emotional intelligence and how it is measured: www.unh.edu/emotional_intelligence.

- *manage* emotions (to know how to express them in varied situations).
- *use* emotions to enable adaptive or creative thinking.

Mindful of popular misuses of their concept, Mayer, Salovey, and Caruso caution against stretching "emotional intelligence" to include varied traits such as self-esteem and optimism, although emotionally intelligent people are self-aware. In both the United States and Germany, those scoring high on managing emotions enjoy higher-quality interactions with friends (Lopes et al., 2004). They avoid being hijacked by overwhelming depression, anxiety, or anger. They can read others' emotions and know what to say to soothe a grieving friend, encourage a colleague, and manage a conflict. Such findings may help explain why, across 69 studies in many countries, those scoring high in emotional intelligence also exhibit modestly better job performance (Van Rooy & Viswesvaran, 2004; Zeidner et al., 2008). They can delay gratification in pursuit of long-range rewards, rather than being overtaken by immediate impulses. Simply said, they are emotionally in tune with others, and thus they often succeed in career, marriage, and parenting situations where academically smarter (but emotionally less intelligent) people fail (Ciarrochi et al., 2006).

Brain damage reports have provided extreme examples of the results of diminished emotional intelligence in people with high general intelligence. Neuroscientist Antonio Damasio (1994) told of Elliot, who had a brain tumor removed: "I never saw a tinge of emotion in my many hours of conversation with him, no sadness, no impatience, no frustration." Shown disturbing pictures of injured people, destroyed communities, and natural disasters, Elliot showed—and realized he felt—no emotion. He knew but he could not feel. Unable to intuitively adjust his behavior in response to others' feelings, Elliot lost his job. He went bankrupt. His marriage collapsed. He remarried and divorced again. At last report, he was dependent on a disability check and custodial care from a sibling.

Some scholars, however, are concerned that emotional intelligence stretches the concept of intelligence too far. Multiple-intelligence man Howard Gardner (1999) welcomes our stretching the concept into the realms of space, music, and information about ourselves and others. But let us also, he says, respect emotional sensitivity, creativity, and motivation as important but different. Stretch "intelligence" to include everything we prize and it will lose its meaning.

Is Intelligence Neurologically Measurable?

4: To what extent is intelligence related to brain anatomy and neural processing speed?

Using today's neuroscience tools, might we link differences in people's intelligence test performance to dissimilarities in the heart of smarts—the brain? Might we anticipate a future brain test of intelligence?

Brain Size and Complexity

After the brilliant English poet Lord Byron died in 1824, doctors discovered that his brain was a massive 5 pounds, not the normal 3 pounds. Three years later, Beethoven died and his brain was found to have exceptionally numerous and deep convolutions. Such observations set brain scientists off studying the brains of other geniuses at their wits' end (Burrell, 2005). Do people with big brains have big smarts?

Alas, some geniuses had small brains, and some dim-witted criminals had brains like Byron's. More recent studies that directly measure brain volume using MRI scans do reveal correlations of about +.33 between brain size (adjusted for body size) and

::**emotional intelligence** the ability to perceive, understand, manage, and use emotions.

CRITICAL THINKING

Is emotional intelligence a product of heredity or environment? Have students consider this question based on their knowledge from previous units, such as Unit 3C and Unit 9. Are children born with the ability to succeed socially and be self-aware? Or do socially reinforcing experiences breed socially intelligent people?

"I worry about [intelligence] definitions that collapse assessments of our cognitive powers with statements about the kind of human beings we favor."

Howard Gardner, "Rethinking the Concept of Intelligence," 2000

• Recall from Unit 2 that the lowest correlation, −1.0, represents perfect disagreement between two sets of scores—as one score goes up, the other goes down. A correlation of zero represents no association. The highest correlation, +1.0, represents perfect agreement—as the first score goes up, so does the second. •

TEACHING TIP

At this point, you may want to use **Lecture/Discussion Topics:** *Myths About Emotional Intelligence* (p. 16) or *Emotional Intelligence: An Ability or Collection of Eclectic Traits?* (p. 16) or *Fostering Children's Emotional Intelligence* (p. 17) or *Intelligence, Self-Discipline, and Academic Performance* (p. 18) or **Classroom Exercises:** *Ten Facets of Emotional Intelligence* (p. 14) or *Emotional Intelligence Scale* (p. 15) or *"Reading the Mind in the Eyes" Test: Sample Items* (p. 15) from Bolt's Teacher's Resource Binder.

UNIT 11

INTERCONNECTING

Myers reminds students about how to interpret correlation coefficients, so extend this by reminding students about the third-variable problem with correlations. If two variables correlate, they may cause each other, but the cause may also be another variable altogether. In the case of intelligence and brain size, note how Myers points out that genes, nutrition, environmental stimulation, or some other combination may be the reason why brain size and intelligence seem to go together. The conclusions we can make about this relationship are very limited.

INTERCONNECTING

The prefrontal cortex seems to house the executive functions of humans. We use our prefrontal cortex to make decisions about how to express emotions, which choice to make when faced with an ethical dilemma, and how far to throw a Frisbee. Individuals with damage to the prefrontal cortex typically display more immature decisions and social difficulties.

● A sperm whale's brain is about 6 times heavier than your brain. ●

"I am, somehow, less interested in the weight and convolutions of Einstein's brain than in the near certainty that people of equal talent have lived and died in cotton fields and sweatshops."
Stephen Jay Gould, *The Panda's Thumb*, 1992

➤ FIGURE 11.2
Gray matter matters A frontal view of the brain shows some of the areas where gray matter is concentrated in people with high intelligence scores, and where *g* may therefore be concentrated. (From Haier et al., 2004.)

intelligence score (Carey, 2007; McDaniel, 2005). Moreover, as adults age, brain size and nonverbal intelligence test scores fall in concert (Bigler et al., 1995).

One review of 37 brain-imaging studies revealed associations between intelligence and brain size and activity in specific areas, especially within the frontal and parietal lobes (Jung & Haier, 2007). Sandra Witelson would not have been surprised. With the brains of 91 Canadians as a comparison base, Witelson and her colleagues (1999) seized an opportunity to study Einstein's brain. Although not notably heavier or larger in total size than the typical Canadian's brain, Einstein's brain was 15 percent larger in the parietal lobe's lower region—which just happens to be a center for processing mathematical and spatial information. Certain other areas were a tad smaller than average. With different mental functions competing for the brain's real estate, these observations may offer a clue to why Einstein, like some other great physicists such as Richard Feynman and Edward Teller, was slow in learning to talk (Pinker, 1999).

If intelligence does modestly correlate with brain size, the cause could be differing genes, nutrition, environmental stimulation, some combination of these, or perhaps something else. Recall from earlier units that experience alters the brain. Rats raised in a stimulating rather than deprived environment develop thicker, heavier cortexes. And learning leaves detectable traces in the brain's neural connections. "Intelligence is due to the development of neural connections in response to the environment," notes University of Sydney psychologist Dennis Garlick (2003).

Postmortem brain analyses reveal that highly educated people die with more synapses—17 percent more in one study—than their less-educated counterparts (Orlovskaya et al., 1999). This does not tell us whether people grow synapses with education, or people with more synapses seek more education, or both. But other evidence suggests that highly intelligent people differ in their *neural plasticity*—their ability during childhood and adolescence to adapt and grow neural connections in response to their environment (Garlick, 2002, 2003).

One study repeatedly scanned the brains of 307 children and teens ages 5 to 19. The surprising result: Kids with average intelligence scores showed modest cortex thickening and thinning—with a peak thickness at age 8, suggesting a short developmental window (Shaw et al., 2006). The most intelligent 7-year-olds had a *thinner* brain cortex, which progressively thickened up to age 11 to 13, before thinning with the natural pruning of unused connections. Agile minds came with agile brains.

Efforts to link brain structure with cognition continue. One research team, led by psychologist Richard Haier (2004; Colom et al., 2006), correlated intelligence scores from 47 adult volunteers with scans that measured their volume of *gray matter* (neural cell bodies) and *white matter* (axons and dendrites) in various brain regions.

Higher intelligence scores were linked with more gray matter in areas known to be involved in memory, attention, and language (**FIGURE 11.2**).

Brain Function

Even if the modest correlations between brain anatomy and intelligence prove reliable, they only begin to explain intelligence differences. Searching for other explanations, neuroscientists are studying the brain's functioning.

As people contemplate a variety of questions like those found on intelligence tests, a frontal lobe area just above the outer edge of the eyebrows becomes especially active—in the left brain for verbal questions, and on both sides for spatial questions (Duncan et al., 2000). Information from various brain areas seems to converge in this spot, suggesting to researcher John Duncan (2000) that it may be a "global workspace for organizing and coordinating information" and that some people may be "blessed with a workspace that functions very, very well."

 TEACHING TIP

At this point, you may want to use **Classroom Exercises: *The Factor Analysis Approach*** (p. 5) or ***Questionnaire for Business Management*** (p. 11) from Bolt's Teacher's Resource Binder.

Are more intelligent people literally more quick-witted, much as today's speedier computer chips enable more powerful computing than did their predecessors? On some tasks they seem to be. Earl Hunt (1983) found that verbal intelligence scores are predictable from the speed with which people retrieve information from memory. Those who recognize quickly that *sink* and *wink* are different words, or that *A* and *a* share the same name, tend to score high in verbal ability. Extremely precocious 12- to 14-year-old college students are especially quick in responding to such tasks (Jensen, 1989). To try to define *quick-wittedness*, researchers are taking a close look at speed of perception and speed of neural processing of information.

Perceptual Speed Across many studies, the correlation between intelligence score and the speed of taking in perceptual information tends to be about +.3 to +.5 (Deary & Der, 2005; Sheppard & Vernon, 2008). A typical experiment flashes an incomplete stimulus, as in **FIGURE 11.3**, then a *masking image*—another image that overrides the lingering afterimage of the incomplete stimulus. The researcher then asks participants whether the long side appeared on the right or left. How much stimulus inspection time do you think you would need to answer correctly 80 percent of the time? Perhaps .01 second? Or .02 second? Those who perceive very quickly tend to score somewhat higher on intelligence tests, particularly on tests based on perceptual rather than verbal problem solving.

Stimulus → Mask

Question: Long side on left or right?

➤ **FIGURE 11.3**
An inspection time task A stimulus is flashed before being overridden by a masking image. How long would you need to glimpse the stimulus at the left to answer the question? People who can perceive the stimulus very quickly tend to score somewhat higher on intelligence tests. (Adapted from Deary & Stough, 1996.)

Neurological Speed Do the quicker processing and perceptions of highly intelligent people reflect greater neural processing speed? Repeated studies have found that their brain waves do register a simple stimulus (such as a flash of light or a beeped tone) more quickly and with greater complexity (Caryl, 1994; Deary & Caryl, 1993; Reed & Jensen, 1992). The evoked brain response also tends to be slightly faster when people with high rather than low intelligence scores perform a simple task, such as pushing a button when an *X* appears on a screen (McGarry-Roberts et al., 1992).

Neural processing speed on a simple task seems far removed from the untimed responses to complex intelligence test items, such as, "In what way are *wool* and *cotton* alike?" As yet, notes intelligence expert Nathan Brody (1992, 2001), we have no firm understanding of *why* fast reactions on simple tasks should predict intelligence test performance, though he suspects they reflect one's "core information processing ability." Philip Vernon (1983) has speculated that "faster cognitive processing may allow more information to be acquired." Perhaps people who more quickly process information accumulate more information—about wool, cotton, and millions of other things. Or perhaps, as one Australian-Dutch research team has found, processing speed and intelligence may correlate not because one causes the other but because they share an underlying genetic influence (Luciano et al., 2005).

The neurological approach to understanding intelligence (and so many other things in psychology) is currently in its heyday. Will this new research reduce what we now call the *g* factor to simple measures of underlying brain activity? Or are these efforts totally wrongheaded because what we call intelligence is not a single general trait but several culturally adaptive skills? The controversies surrounding the nature of intelligence are a long way from resolution.

CRITICAL THINKING

Many schools subscribe to the idea that perceptual and neurological speed are indicative of intelligence. These schools assess students with timed tests, and students who are identified as requiring special education are given extended time for taking tests. This type of practice implicitly communicates that schools equate processing speed with intelligence. Have students debate whether these practices are helpful or harmful to student learning.

INTERCONNECTING

Remind students that just because two variables are correlated does not mean they are causally linked. Faster processing on simple tasks is related to intelligence, but whether faster processing is a cause of intelligence is still unknown.

TEACHING TIP

At this point, you may want to use **Classroom Exercise:** *The Autism-Spectrum Quotient* (p. 11) or **Lecture/Discussion Topic:** *Reaction Time, Intelligence, and Longevity* (p. 18) from Bolt's Teacher's Resource Binder.

UNIT 11

CRITICAL THINKING

Intelligence tests were created to help students, which they still do when they are used to identify students who need more help and enrichment. But they have also hurt some students since identification for special services can lead to prejudice and discrimination. Have students discuss the benefits and drawbacks of intelligence testing in today's schools:

- Is it better to separate students into ability groups or to have mainstreamed classes? Why?

- Are intelligence tests the main way students are identified for special services in school? What other assessments are used to identify students who need extra help?

- How can intelligence tests keep students back? How can they help students succeed?

::**mental age** a measure of intelligence test performance devised by Binet; the chronological age that most typically corresponds to a given level of performance. Thus, a child who does as well as the average 8-year-old is said to have a mental age of 8.

BEFORE YOU MOVE ON . . .

➤ **ASK YOURSELF**

The modern concept of multiple intelligences (as proposed by Gardner and Sternberg) assumes that the analytical school smarts measured by traditional intelligence tests are important abilities but that other abilities are also important. Different people have different gifts. What are yours?

➤ **TEST YOURSELF 1**

Joseph, a Harvard Law School student, has a straight-A average, writes for the *Harvard Law Review*, and will clerk for a Supreme Court justice next year. His grandmother, Judith, is very proud of him, saying he is way more intelligent than she ever was. But Joseph is also very proud of Judith: As a young woman, she was imprisoned by the Nazis. When the war ended, she walked out of Germany, contacted an agency helping refugees, and began a new life in the United States as an assistant chef in her cousin's restaurant. According to the definition of *intelligence* in this unit, is Joseph the only intelligent person in this story? Why or why not?

Answers to the Test Yourself questions can be found in Appendix E at the end of the book.

Assessing Intelligence

HOW DO WE ASSESS INTELLIGENCE? And what makes a test credible? Answering those questions begins with a look at why psychologists created tests of mental abilities and how they have used those tests.

The Origins of Intelligence Testing

5: When and why were intelligence tests created?

Some societies concern themselves with promoting the collective welfare of the family, community, and society. Other societies emphasize individual opportunity. Plato, a pioneer of the individualist tradition, wrote more than 2000 years ago in *The Republic* that "no two persons are born exactly alike; but each differs from the other in natural endowments, one being suited for one occupation and the other for another." As heirs to Plato's individualism, people in Western societies have pondered how and why individuals differ in mental ability.

Western attempts to assess such differences began in earnest more than a century ago. The English scientist Francis Galton (1822–1911) had a fascination with measuring human traits. When his cousin Charles Darwin proposed that nature selects successful traits through the survival of the fittest, Galton wondered if it might be possible to measure "natural ability" and to encourage those of high ability to mate with one another. At the 1884 London Exposition, more than 10,000 visitors received his assessment of their "intellectual strengths" based on such things as reaction time, sensory acuity, muscular power, and body proportions. But alas, on these measures, eminent adults and high-achieving students did not outscore those supposedly not so bright. Nor did the measures correlate with each other.

Although Galton's quest for a simple intelligence measure failed, he gave us some statistical techniques that we still use (as well as the phrase "nature and nurture"). And his persistent belief in the inheritance of eminence and genius—reflected in the title of his book, *Hereditary Genius*—illustrates an important lesson from both the

---

 TEACHING TIP

At this point, you may want to use **Classroom Exercise: *A World War I IQ Test*** (p. 19) from Bolt's Teacher's Resource Binder.

history of intelligence research and the history of science: Although science itself strives for objectivity, individual scientists are affected by their own assumptions and attitudes.

Alfred Binet: Predicting School Achievement

The modern intelligence-testing movement began at the turn of the twentieth century, when France passed a law requiring that all children attend school. Some children, including many newcomers to Paris, seemed incapable of benefiting from the regular school curriculum and in need of special classes. But how could the schools objectively identify children with special needs?

The French government hesitated to trust teachers' subjective judgments of children's learning potential. Academic slowness might merely reflect inadequate prior education. Also, teachers might prejudge children on the basis of their social backgrounds. To minimize bias, France's minister of public education in 1904 commissioned Alfred Binet (1857–1911) and others to study the problem.

Binet and his collaborator, Théodore Simon, began by assuming that all children follow the same course of intellectual development but that some develop more rapidly. On tests, therefore, a "dull" child should perform as does a typical younger child, and a "bright" child as does a typical older child. Thus, their goal became measuring each child's **mental age,** the level of performance typically associated with a certain chronological age. The average 9-year-old, for example, has a mental age of 9. Children with below-average mental ages, such as 9-year-olds who perform at the level of a typical 7-year-old, would struggle with schoolwork considered normal for their age.

To measure mental age, Binet and Simon theorized that mental aptitude, like athletic aptitude, is a general capacity that shows up in various ways. After testing a variety of reasoning and problem-solving questions on Binet's two daughters, and then on "bright" and "backward" Parisian schoolchildren, Binet and Simon identified items that would predict how well French children would handle their schoolwork.

Note that Binet and Simon made no assumptions concerning *why* a particular child was slow, average, or precocious. Binet personally leaned toward an environmental explanation. To raise the capacities of low-scoring children, he recommended "mental orthopedics" that would train them to develop their attention span and self-discipline. He believed his intelligence test did not measure inborn intelligence as a meter stick measures height. Rather, it had a single practical purpose: to identify French schoolchildren needing special attention. Binet hoped his test would be used to improve children's education, but he also feared it would be used to label children and limit their opportunities (Gould, 1981).

Lewis Terman: The Innate IQ

Binet's fears were realized soon after his death in 1911, when others adapted his tests for use as a numerical measure of inherited intelligence. This began when Stanford University professor Lewis Terman (1877–1956) found that the Paris-developed questions and age norms worked poorly with California schoolchildren. Adapting some of Binet's original items, adding others, and establishing new age norms, Terman extended the upper end of the test's range from teenag-

National Library of Medicine

Alfred Binet "Some recent philosophers have given their moral approval to the deplorable verdict that an individual's intelligence is a fixed quantity, one which cannot be augmented. We must protest and act against this brutal pessimism" (Binet, 1909, p. 141).

"The IQ test was invented to predict academic performance, nothing else. If we wanted something that would predict life success, we'd have to invent another test completely." Social psychologist Robert Zajonc (1984b)

 TEACHING TIP

Alfred Binet believed that intelligence equaled good judgment. He was quoted in a publication he wrote with Théodore Simon to say, "A person may be a moron or an imbecile if he is lacking in judgment; but with good judgment he can never be either."

Source: The University of Indiana's *History of Influences in Development of Intelligence Theory and Testing* online database: www.indiana.edu/~intell

TEACHING TIP

At this point, you may want to use **Student Project:** *Joining Mensa* (p. 19) from Bolt's Teacher's Resource Binder.

 INTERCONNECTING

Binet and Simon's work with intelligence tests influenced another famous developmental psychologist—Jean Piaget. Théodore Simon put a young Jean Piaget in charge of standardizing another colleague's reasoning test for Parisian schoolchildren, a move which many believe led Piaget to become fascinated with how children develop intellectually.

UNIT 11

ers to "superior adults." He also gave his revision the name it retains today—the **Stanford-Binet.**

From such tests, German psychologist William Stern derived the famous **intelligence quotient,** or **IQ.** The IQ was simply a person's mental age divided by chronological age and multiplied by 100 to get rid of the decimal point:

$$IQ = \frac{mental\ age}{chronological\ age} \times 100$$

Thus, an average child, whose mental and chronological ages are the same, has an IQ of 100. But an 8-year-old who answers questions as would a typical 10-year-old has an IQ of 125.

Mrs. Randolph takes mother's pride too far.

The original IQ formula worked fairly well for children but not for adults. (Should a 40-year-old who does as well on the test as an average 20-year-old be assigned an IQ of only 50?) Most current intelligence tests, including the Stanford-Binet, no longer compute an IQ (though the term *IQ* still lingers in everyday vocabulary as a shorthand expression for "intelligence test score"). Instead, they represent the test-taker's performance *relative* to the *average performance of others the same age.* This average performance is arbitrarily assigned a score of 100, and about two-thirds of all test-takers fall between 85 and 115.

Terman promoted the widespread use of intelligence testing. His motive was to "take account of the inequalities of children in original endowment" by assessing their "vocational fitness." In sympathy with *eugenics*—a much-criticized nineteenth-century movement that proposed measuring human traits and using the results to encourage only smart and fit people to reproduce—Terman (1916, pp. 91–92) envisioned that the use of intelligence tests would "ultimately result in curtailing the reproduction of feeble-mindedness and in the elimination of an enormous amount of crime, pauperism, and industrial inefficiency" (p. 7).

With Terman's help, the U.S. government developed new tests to evaluate both newly arriving immigrants and World War I army recruits—the world's first mass administration of an intelligence test. To some psychologists, the results indicated the inferiority of people not sharing their Anglo-Saxon heritage. Such findings were part of the cultural climate that led to a 1924 immigration law that reduced Southern and Eastern European immigration quotas to less than a fifth of those for Northern and Western Europe.

Binet probably would have been horrified that his test had been adapted and used to draw such conclusions. Indeed, such sweeping judgments did become an embarrassment to most of those who championed testing. Even Terman came to appreciate that test scores reflected not only people's innate mental abilities but also their education and their familiarity with the culture assumed by the test. Nevertheless, abuses of the early intelligence tests serve to remind us that science can be value-laden. Behind a screen of scientific objectivity, ideology sometimes lurks.

::**Stanford-Binet** the widely used American revision (by Terman at Stanford University) of Binet's original intelligence test.

::**intelligence quotient (IQ)** defined originally as the ratio of mental age *(ma)* to chronological age *(ca)* multiplied by 100 (thus, IQ = *ma/ca* × 100). On contemporary intelligence tests, the average performance for a given age is assigned a score of 100.

::**achievement tests** tests designed to assess what a person has learned.

::**aptitude tests** tests designed to predict a person's future performance; *aptitude* is the capacity to learn.

::**Wechsler Adult Intelligence Scale (WAIS)** the WAIS is the most widely used intelligence test; contains verbal and performance (nonverbal) subtests.

 TROUBLESHOOTING

Many students confuse the individuals who came up with the formula for the intelligence quotient (IQ). Alfred Binet and Théodore Simon came up with the concept of mental age, which is the score achieved on the test. Help students remember, though, that William Stern came up with the formula, and Lewis Terman used the formula with his Stanford-Binet Test.

 TEACHING TIP

People in Terman's time believed that bright children became maladjusted adults. Terman's Termites were a group of gifted children chosen to show that such children became talented, adjusted adults. Terman found that the gifted were taller, healthier, physically better developed, and superior in leadership and social adaptability. Terman believed that gifted children should be treated differently:

- They should be identified as early as possible in childhood.
- They should be accelerated through school.
- They should have a differentiated curriculum and instruction.
- They should have specially trained teachers.
- They should be viewed as a national resource for the betterment of society.
- They should be allowed to develop in whatever directions their talents and interests dictate.

Source: The University of Indiana's *History of Influences in Development of Intelligence Theory and Testing* online database: www.indiana.edu/~intell

 TEACHING TIP

Emphasize to students that 100 is considered a "normal" score on an intelligence test. Intelligence tests are routinely re-standardized so that the 100 score is the accurate normal score. That way, generational effects in nutrition, education, and knowledge can be taken into account.

Modern Tests of Mental Abilities

6: What's the difference between aptitude and achievement tests, and how can we develop and evaluate them?

By this point in your life, you've faced dozens of ability tests: school tests of basic reading and math skills, course exams, intelligence tests, and driver's license exams, to name just a few. Psychologists classify such tests as either **achievement tests,** intended to *reflect* what you have learned, or **aptitude tests,** intended to *predict* your ability to learn a new skill. Exams covering what you have learned in this course (like the Advanced Placement Psychology Examination) are achievement tests. A college entrance exam, which seeks to predict your ability to do college work, is an aptitude test—a "thinly disguised intelligence test," says Howard Gardner (1999). Indeed, report Meredith Frey and Douglas Detterman (2004), total scores on the U.S. SAT (formerly called the U.S. Scholastic Aptitude Test) correlated +.82 with general intelligence scores in a national sample of 14- to 21-year-olds (FIGURE 11.4).

Actually, the differences between achievement and aptitude tests are not so clear-cut. Your *achieved* vocabulary influences your score on most aptitude tests. Similarly, your *aptitudes* for learning and test-taking influence your grades on achievement tests. Most tests, whether labeled achievement or aptitude, assess both ability and its development. Practically speaking, however, achievement tests assess current performance and aptitude tests predict future performance.

Psychologist David Wechsler created what is now the most widely used intelligence test, the **Wechsler Adult Intelligence Scale (WAIS),** with a version for school-age children (the *Wechsler Intelligence Scale for Children* [*WISC*]), and another for preschool children. As illustrated in FIGURE 11.5 (on the next page), the WAIS consists of 11 subtests broken into verbal and performance areas. It yields not only an overall intelligence score, as does the Stanford-Binet, but also separate scores for verbal comprehension, perceptual organization, working memory, and processing speed. Striking differences among these scores can provide clues to cognitive strengths or weaknesses that teachers or therapists can build upon. For example, a low verbal comprehension score combined with high scores on other subtests could indicate a reading or language disability. Other comparisons can help a psychologist or psychiatrist establish a rehabilitation plan for a stroke patient. Such uses are possible, of course, only when we can trust the test results.

Matching patterns Block design puzzles test the ability to analyze patterns. Wechsler's individually administered intelligence test comes in forms suited for adults and children.

▲

➤ **FIGURE 11.4**

Close cousins: Aptitude and intelligence scores A scatterplot shows the close correlation between intelligence scores and verbal and quantitative SAT scores. (From Frey and Detterman, 2004.)

RESEARCH

Have students determine which standardized tests are given in your school district that qualify as achievement tests and which qualify as aptitude tests.

● How well have they done on each respective type of test?

● Did they take either type seriously? Why or why not?

TEACHING TIP

Studies have shown that standardized aptitude tests like the SAT and ACT are not as good at predicting future college success as GPA and class rank. Robert Sternberg and his colleagues have recently been testing a new version of the SAT that takes into account Sternberg's theory of successful intelligence. Initial findings show that the new version seems to do better at predicting college success.

TEACHING TIP

David Wechsler developed his intelligence test in reaction to criticism that the Stanford-Binet and similar tests were biased toward English language speakers. His performance-oriented items test nonverbal abilities, giving those who do not speak English as their first language a chance to demonstrate elements of intelligence.

INTERCONNECTING

Help students know the difference between "standardizing" and "norming":

- *Standardizing* involves testing in conditions that are as similar as possible. Students experience this process whenever they take standardized tests in school. Tests that require all test givers to read the same set of directions, and to allow the same amounts of time for all test takers, are being offered under standardized conditions.

- *Norming* involves taking the scores from the test and graphing them. With a large sample of data, the normal curve usually results. The properties of the normal curve, shown in Figure 11.6, then apply to the set of data.

TEACHING TIP

Have students brainstorm the qualities of a bad test.

- What do they particularly hate about bad tests?

- What are qualities of bad multiple choice, matching, fill-in-the-blank, and essay tests?

- How can bad tests be made better?

Thorndike et al., Measurement and evaluation in psychology and education, 5e, © 1990. Published by Prentice Hall.

Getty Images/Stockdisc

➤ **FIGURE 11.5**
Sample items from the Wechsler Adult Intelligence Scale (WAIS) subtests (Adapted from Thorndike & Hagen, 1977.)

::**standardization** defining meaningful scores by comparison with the performance of a pretested group.

::**normal curve** the symmetrical, bell-shaped curve that describes the distribution of many physical and psychological attributes. Most scores fall near the average, and fewer and fewer scores lie near the extremes.

Principles of Test Construction

To be widely accepted, psychological tests must meet three criteria: They must be *standardized, reliable, and valid.* The Stanford-Binet and Wechsler tests meet these requirements.

Standardization

The number of questions you answer correctly on an intelligence test would tell us almost nothing. To evaluate your performance, we need a basis for comparing it with others' performance. To enable meaningful comparisons, test-makers first give the test to a representative sample of people. When you later take the test following the same procedures, your score can be compared with the sample's scores to determine your position relative to others. This process of defining meaningful scores relative to a pretested group is called **standardization.**

Group members' scores typically are distributed in a bell-shaped pattern that forms the **normal curve** shown in FIGURE 11.6. No matter what we measure—heights, weights, or mental aptitudes—people's scores tend to form this roughly symmetrical shape. On an intelligence test, we call the midpoint, the average score, 100. Moving out from the average, toward either extreme, we find fewer and fewer people. For both the Stanford-Binet and the Wechsler tests, a person's score indicates whether that person's performance fell above or below the average. As Figure 11.6 shows, a performance higher than all but 2 percent of all scores earns an intelligence score of 130. A performance lower than 98 percent of all scores earns an intelligence score of 70.

DEMO

Have students construct their own version of the Wechsler tests by coming up with different items for each of the subtests highlighted in Figure 11.5. Have them try to administer their tests, comparing people's scores with their GPA:

- Verbal: General Information, Similarities, Arithmetic Reasoning, Vocabulary, Comprehension, Digit Span

- Performance: Picture Completion, Picture Arrangement, Block Design, Object Assembly, and Digit-Symbol Substitution

➤ FIGURE 11.6
The normal curve Scores on aptitude tests tend to form a normal, or bell-shaped, curve around an average score. For the Wechsler scale, for example, the average score is 100.

To keep the average score near 100, the Stanford-Binet and the Wechsler scales are periodically restandardized. If you took the WAIS Third Edition recently, your performance was compared with a standardization sample who took the test during 1996, not to David Wechsler's initial 1930s sample. If you compared the performance of the most recent standardization sample with that of the 1930s sample, do you suppose you would find rising or declining test performance? Amazingly—given that college entrance aptitude scores were dropping during the 1960s and 1970s—intelligence test performance has been improving. This worldwide phenomenon is called the *Flynn effect*, in honor of New Zealand researcher James Flynn (1987, 2007), who first calculated its magnitude. As **FIGURE 11.7** indicates, the average person's intelligence test score 80 years ago was—by today's standard—only a 76! Such rising performance has been observed in 20 countries, from Canada to rural Australia (Daley et al., 2003). Although the gains have recently reversed in Scandinavia, the historic increase is now widely accepted as an important phenomenon (Sundet et al., 2004; Teasdale & Owen, 2005, 2008).

The Flynn effect's cause is a mystery (Neisser, 1997a, 1998). Did it result from greater test sophistication? (But the gains began before testing was widespread.) Better nutrition? As the nutrition explanation would predict, people have gotten not only smarter but taller. Moreover, the increases have been greatest at the lowest economic levels, which have gained the most from improved nutrition (Colom et al., 2005). Or did the Flynn effect stem from more education? More stimulating environments? Less childhood disease? Smaller families and more parental investment?

➤ FIGURE 11.7
Getting smarter? In every country studied, intelligence test performance rose during the twentieth century, as shown here with American Wechsler and Stanford-Binet test performance between 1918 and 1989. In Britain, test scores have risen 27 points since 1942. (From Hogan, 1995.) Very recent data indicate this trend may have leveled off or may even be reversing.

INTERCONNECTING

The properties of the graph in Figure 11.6 are important to know for the AP Exam. Remind students about their knowledge of this graph from their study of Unit 2. You may also want to point out that the AP Exam scores are determined by the normal curve. Sixty-eight percent of students will make a 3, 13.5 percent will make a 4, and 2 percent will make a 5.

TEACHING TIP

James R. Flynn, a professor and social activist in New Zealand, has campaigned for over 25 years to question the notion that non-White ethnic groups are intellectually inferior because of their lower average scores on intelligence tests. Flynn proceeded to document the intelligence test scores from over 20 countries and found that overall intelligence test scores have risen anywhere from 5 to 25 points from the beginning of the 20th century—regardless of race, ethnicity, or cultural background. This rise in test scores has perplexed researchers and caused many to question whether intelligence tests actually measure intelligence. Flynn believes that intelligence tests actually measure problem-solving skills, which weakly correlate to intelligence.

TEACHING TIP

At this point, you may want to use **Classroom Exercises:** *Issues in Testing* (p. 20) or *Reliability and Validity* (p. 22) or *Remote Associates Test* (p. 22) from Bolt's Teacher's Resource Binder.

TEACHING TIP

Students can take standardized college admissions tests as many times as they'd like in order to try for higher scores, but they do not take the same test each time. Companies such as Educational Testing Service have several versions of the tests they administer that have undergone tests of reliability against each other so that students don't compromise their results by remembering items from previous test-taking opportunities.

TROUBLESHOOTING

Help students remember the difference between predictive and content validity:

- *Predictive* validity is pretty self-explanatory. Remind students that a test should predict what it is supposed to predict in order to have predictive validity. Driver's tests should predict good driving habits; the ACT and SAT should predict college performance.

- *Content* validity occurs when tests measure what they are supposed to measure. We want our tests to measure what we have learned. The AP Exam in Psychology should contain items about psychology. The driver's test should not contain items about psychology.

::**reliability** the extent to which a test yields consistent results, as assessed by the consistency of scores on two halves of the test, or on retesting.

::**validity** the extent to which a test measures or predicts what it is supposed to. (See also *content validity* and *predictive validity*.)

::**content validity** the extent to which a test samples the behavior that is of interest.

::**predictive validity** the success with which a test predicts the behavior it is designed to predict; it is assessed by computing the correlation between test scores and the criterion behavior. (Also called *criterion-related validity*.)

Regardless of what combination of factors explains the rise in intelligence test scores, the phenomenon counters one concern of some hereditarians—that the higher twentieth-century birthrates among those with lower scores would shove human intelligence scores downward (Lynn & Harvey, 2008). Seeking to explain the rising scores, and mindful of global mixing, one scholar has even speculated about the influence of a genetic phenomenon comparable to "hybrid vigor," which occurs in agriculture when cross-breeding produces corn or livestock superior to the parent plants or animals (Mingroni, 2004, 2007).

Reliability

Knowing where you stand in comparison to a standardization group still won't tell us much about your intelligence unless the test has **reliability**—unless it yields dependably consistent scores. To check a test's reliability, researchers retest people. They may use the same test or they may split the test in half and see whether odd-question scores and even-question scores agree. If the two scores generally agree, or *correlate*, the test is reliable. The higher the correlation between the *test-retest* or the *split-half* scores, the higher the test's reliability. The tests we have considered so far—the Stanford-Binet, the WAIS, and the WISC—all have reliabilities of about +.9, which is very high. When retested, people's scores generally match their first score closely.

Validity

High reliability does not ensure a test's **validity**—the extent to which the test actually measures or predicts what it promises. If you use an inaccurate tape measure to measure people's heights, your height report would have high reliability (consistency) but low validity. It is enough for some tests that they have **content validity**, meaning the test taps the pertinent behavior, or *criterion*. The road test for a driver's license has content validity because it samples the tasks a driver routinely faces. Course exams have content validity if they assess one's mastery of a representative sample of course material. But we expect intelligence tests to have **predictive validity:** They should predict the criterion of future performance, and to some extent they do.

Are general aptitude tests as predictive as they are reliable? As critics are fond of noting, the answer is plainly *no*. The predictive power of aptitude tests is fairly strong in the early school years, but later it weakens. Academic aptitude test scores are reasonably good predictors of achievement for children ages 6 to 12, where the correlation between intelligence score and school performance is about +.6 (Jensen, 1980). Intelligence scores correlate even more closely with scores on *achievement tests:* +.81 in one comparison of 70,000 English children's intelligence scores at age 11 to their academic achievement in national exams at age 16 (Deary et al., 2007). The SAT, used in the United States as a college entrance exam, is less successful in predicting first-year college grades; here, the correlation is less than +.5 (Willingham et al., 1990). By the time we get to the Graduate Record Examination (GRE; an aptitude test similar to the SAT but for those applying to graduate school), the correlation with graduate school performance is an even more modest but still significant +.4 (Kuncel & Hezlett, 2007).

Why does the predictive power of aptitude scores diminish as students move up the educational ladder? Consider a parallel situation: Among all American or Canadian football linemen, body weight correlates with success. A 300-pound player tends to overwhelm a 200-pound opponent. But within the narrow 280- to 320-pound range typically found at the professional level, the correlation between weight and success becomes negligible (**FIGURE 11.8**). The narrower the *range* of weights,

TEACHING TIP

Another very valid test students take is the driver's test. To get a driver's license, one must demonstrate knowledge of the rules of the road and the ability to drive well. A test can't be more valid than that! Have students brainstorm about other performance-based tests that measure with validity what they are designed to measure.

At this point, you may want to use **Classroom Exercise/Student Project:** *Understanding Predictive Validity* (p. 21) from Bolt's Teacher's Resource Binder.

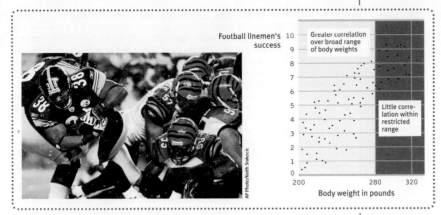

Football linemen's success

Greater correlation over broad range of body weights

Little correlation within restricted range

Body weight in pounds

AP Photo/Keith Srakocic

the lower the predictive power of body weight becomes. If an elite university takes only those students who have very high aptitude scores, those scores cannot possibly predict much. This will be true even if the test has excellent predictive validity with a more diverse sample of students. So, when we validate a test using a wide range of people but then use it with a restricted range of people, it loses much of its predictive validity.

➤ FIGURE 11.8

Diminishing predictive power Let's imagine a correlation between football linemen's body weight and their success on the field. Note how insignificant the relationship becomes when we narrow the range of weight to 280 to 320 pounds. As the range of data under consideration narrows, its predictive power diminishes.

BEFORE YOU MOVE ON . . .

➤ ASK YOURSELF

Are you working to the potential reflected in your standardized test scores? What, other than your aptitude, is affecting your school performance?

➤ TEST YOURSELF 2

What was the purpose of Binet's pioneering intelligence test?

Answers to the Test Yourself questions can be found in Appendix E at the end of the book.

The Dynamics of Intelligence

WE NOW CAN ADDRESS SOME AGE-OLD questions about the dynamics of human intelligence—about its stability over the life span, and about the extremes of intelligence.

Stability or Change?

7: How stable are intelligence scores over the life span?

If we retested people periodically throughout their lives, would their intelligence scores be stable? Unit 9 explored the stability of mental abilities in later life. What about the stability of intelligence scores early in life?

Developmental researchers have left few stones unturned in their search for indicators of infants' later intelligence. Unable to talk with infants, they have assessed

UNIT 11

INTERCONNECTING

Remind students of the types of experimental techniques created by developmental psychologists, as noted in Unit 9. Some of the techniques involve studying how infants attend to stimuli. The more attention they give particular stimuli, the more they are processing the information about those stimuli.

 TEACHING TIP

The APGAR test is perhaps the first standardized test people take in their lives. The APGAR is a part of standard procedure for assessing newborn development. APGAR is an acronym referring to the following abilities all newborns should possess in the first moments of life:

A = Activity (muscle tone). Babies should move actively from the very beginning.

P = Pulse. A pulse rate above 100 beats per minute is considered ideal.

G = Grimace. When a puff of air is blown in the babies' faces, they should sneeze, cough, and pull away.

A = Appearance. Skin color should be normal over the entire body.

R = Respiration. Babies should be breathing well and crying.

> "My dear Adele, I am 4 years old and I can read any English book. I can say all the Latin substantives and adjectives and active verbs besides 52 lines of Latin poetry."
>
> Francis Galton, letter to his sister, 1827

• Ironically, SAT and GRE scores correlate better with each other than either does with its intended criterion, school achievement. Thus, their reliability far exceeds their predictive validity. If either test was much affected by coaching, luck, or how one feels on the test day (as so many people believe), such reliability would be impossible. •

what they can observe—everything from birth weight, to the relative lengths of different toes, to age of sitting up alone. None of these measures provides any useful prediction of intelligence scores at much later ages (Bell & Waldrop, 1989; Broman, 1989). Perhaps, as developmental psychologist Nancy Bayley reflected in 1949, "we have not yet found the right tests." Someday, she speculated, we might find "infant behaviors which are characteristic of underlying intellectual functions" and which will predict later intelligence. Some studies have found that infants who quickly grow bored with a picture—who, given a choice, prefer to look at a new one—score higher on tests of brain speed and intelligence up to 21 years later, but the prediction is crude (Fagan et al., 2007; Kavsek, 2004; Tasbihsazan et al., 2003).

So, new parents who are wondering about their baby's intelligence and anxiously comparing their baby to others can relax. Except for extremely impaired or very precocious children, casual observation and intelligence tests before age 3 only modestly predict children's future aptitudes (Humphreys & Davey, 1988; Tasbihsazan et al., 2003). For example, children who are early talkers—speaking in sentences typical of 3-year-olds by age 20 months—are not especially likely to be reading by age 4½ (Crain-Thoreson & Dale, 1992). (A better predictor of early reading is having parents who have read lots of stories to their child.) Remember that even Albert Einstein was slow in learning to talk (Quasha, 1980).

By age 4, however, children's performance on intelligence tests begins to predict their adolescent and adult scores. Moreover, high-scoring adolescents tend to have been early readers. One study surveyed the parents of 187 American seventh- and eighth-graders who had taken a college aptitude test as part of a seven-state talent search and had scored considerably higher than most high school seniors. If their parents' memories can be trusted, more than half of this precocious group of adolescents began reading by age 4 and more than 80 percent were reading by age 5 (Van Tassel-Baska, 1983). Not surprisingly, then, intelligence tests given to 5-year-olds do predict school achievement (Tramontana et al., 1988).

After about age 7, intelligence test scores, though certainly not fixed, stabilize (Bloom, 1964). Thus, the consistency of scores over time increases with the age of the child. The remarkable stability of aptitude scores by late adolescence is seen in a U.S. Educational Testing Service study of 23,000 students who took the SAT and then later took the GRE (Angoff, 1988). On either test, verbal scores correlated only modestly with math scores—revealing that these two aptitudes are distinct. Yet scores on the SAT verbal test correlated +.86 with the scores on the GRE verbal tests taken four to five years later. An equally astonishing +.86 correlation occurred between the two math tests. Given the time lapse and differing educational experiences of these 23,000 students, the stability of their aptitude scores is remarkable.

Ian Deary and his colleagues (2004) recently set a record for long-term follow-up. Their amazing study was enabled by their country, Scotland, doing something that no nation has done before or since. On Monday morning, June 1, 1932, essentially every child in the country who had been born in 1921—87,498 children at ages 10½ to 11½—was given an intelligence test. The aim was to identify working-class children who would benefit from further education. Sixty-five years later to the day, Patricia Whalley, the wife of Deary's co-worker, Lawrence Whalley, discovered the test results on dusty storeroom shelves at the Scottish Council for Research in Education, not far from Deary's Edinburgh University office. "This will change our lives," Deary replied when Whalley told him the news.

And so it has, with dozens of studies of the stability and the predictive capacity of these early test results. For example, when the intelligence test administered to 11-year-old Scots in 1932 was readministered to 542 survivors as turn-of-the-millennium 80-year-olds, the correlation between the two sets of scores—after some 70 years of varied life experiences—was striking (**FIGURE 11.9**). High-scoring 11-year-olds

INTERCONNECTING

The work conducted by Ian Deary and his colleagues is an example of longitudinal research, discussed in detail in Unit 9.

Intelligence endures When Ian Deary and his colleagues (2004) retested 80 year-old Scots, using an intelligence test they had taken as 11-year-olds, their scores across seven decades correlated +.66.

also were more likely to be living independently as 77-year-olds and were less likely to have suffered late-onset Alzheimer's disease (Starr et al., 2000; Whalley et al., 2000). Among girls scoring in the highest 25 percent, 70 percent were still alive at age 76—as were only 45 percent of those scoring in the lowest 25 percent (**FIGURE 11.10**). (World War II prematurely ended the lives of many of the male test-takers.) Another study that followed 93 nuns confirmed that those exhibiting less verbal ability in essays written when entering their convent in their teens were more at risk for Alzheimer's disease after age 75 (Snowdon et al., 1996).

> "Whether you live to collect your old-age pension depends in part on your IQ at age 11."
> Ian Deary, "Intelligence, Health, and Death," 2005

➤ FIGURE 11.10
Living smart Women scoring in the highest 25 percent on the Scottish national intelligence test at age 11 tended to live longer than those who scored in the lowest 25 percent. (From Whalley & Deary, 2001.)

Extremes of Intelligence

8: What are the traits of those at the low and high intelligence extremes?

One way to glimpse the validity and significance of any test is to compare people who score at the two extremes of the normal curve. The two groups should differ noticeably, and they do.

INTERCONNECTING

Remind students that Figure 11.9 represents a scatterplot, first discussed in Unit 2. In addition, this figure shows a positive correlation, since the slope of the graph is positive.

INTERCONNECTING

Those who remain mentally active by engaging in mentally challenging activities in old age are more likely to live longer and have a smaller incidence of Alzheimer's disease. However, causation is uncertain because all these things could be caused by a third factor—having a higher IQ from the start.

UNIT 11

::**intellectual disability** (formerly referred to as *mental retardation*) a condition of limited mental ability, indicated by an intelligence score of 70 or below and difficulty in adapting to the demands of life; varies from mild to profound.

::**Down syndrome** a condition of intellectual disability and associated physical disorders caused by an extra copy of chromosome 21.

The Low Extreme

At one extreme of the normal curve are those whose intelligence test scores fall at 70 or below. To be labeled as having an **intellectual disability** (formerly referred to as *mental retardation*), a child must have both a low test score and difficulty adapting to the normal demands of independent living. Only about 1 percent of the population meets both criteria, with males outnumbering females by 50 percent (American Psychiatric Association, 1994). As **TABLE 11.3** indicates, most individuals with intellectual disabilities can, with support, live in mainstream society.

Intellectual disabilities sometimes have a known physical cause. **Down syndrome,** for example, is a disorder of varying severity caused by an extra chromosome 21 in the person's genetic makeup.

During the last two centuries, the pendulum of opinion about how best to care for Americans with intellectual disabilities has made a complete swing. Until the mid-nineteenth century, they were cared for at home. Many of those with the most severe disabilities died, but people with less significant challenges often found a place in a farm-based society. Then, residential schools for slow learners were established. By the twentieth century, many of these institutions had become warehouses, providing residents little attention, no privacy, and no hope. Parents often were told to separate themselves permanently from their impaired child before they became attached.

In the last half of the twentieth century, the pendulum swung back to normalization—encouraging people to live in their own communities as normally as their functioning permits. Children with mild intellectual disabilities are educated in less restrictive environments, and many are integrated, or *mainstreamed,* into regular classrooms. Most grow up with their own families, then move into a protected living arrangement, such as a group home. The hope, and often the reality, is a happier and more dignified life.

But think about another reason people diagnosed with mild intellectual disabilities—those just below the 70 score on an intelligence test used to draw the line on who has a disability—might be better able to live independently today than many decades ago. Recall that, thanks to the Flynn effect, the tests have been periodically restandardized. When that happens, individuals who scored near 70 suddenly lose about 6 IQ points, and two people with the same ability level could thus be classified differently depending on when they were tested (Kanaya et al., 2003). As the number of people diagnosed with intellectual disabilities suddenly jumps, more people become eligible for special education and for Social Security payments for those with a mental disability. And in the United States (one of only a few countries with the death penalty), fewer people are eligible for execution—the U.S. Supreme Court ruled in 2002 that the execution of people with intellectual disabilities is

TABLE 11.3

DEGREES OF INTELLECTUAL DISABILITY

Level	Approximate Intelligence Scores	Adaptation to Demands of Life
Mild	50–70	May learn academic skills up to sixth-grade level. Adults may, with assistance, achieve self-supporting social and vocational skills.
Moderate	35–50	May progress to second-grade level academically. Adults may contribute to their own support by laboring in sheltered workshops.
Severe	20–35	May learn to talk and to perform simple work tasks under close supervision but are generally unable to profit from vocational training.
Profound	Below 20	Require constant aid and supervision.

Source: Reprinted with permission from the *Diagnostic and Statistical Manual of Mental Disorders,* Fourth Edition, text revision. Copyright 2000 American Psychiatric Association.

TEACHING TIP

The American Association on Intellectual and Developmental Disabilities (AAIDD) is an organization of professionals dedicated to the study of intellectual disability. The group's mission statement reads, "AAIDD promotes progressive policies, sound research, effective practices, and universal human rights for people with intellectual and developmental disabilities." The group was founded in 1876, but has been responsible for defining intellectual disability since 1921.

WEB CONNECT

Have students go to the AAIDD's Web site, listed below, to see their current definition for intellectual disability. www.aamr.org

- Does this definition fit into their schema for mental retardation? Why or why not?

- How does this definition change their perspective of people considered mentally retarded?

- How are the intellectual and adaptive components of the definition different?

CRITICAL THINKING

More whites are identified as gifted and more African-American boys are identified as needing special education services than any other racial, ethnic or gender group. Have students explore why:

- Do intelligence tests seem to favor white males? Why?

- Are intelligence tests the only thing to blame in this disparity? Why or why not?

- What legal problems have schools faced for these disparities? What have been the courts' solutions?

- What impact has President George W. Bush's "No Child Left Behind" act had on bridging the achievement gap?

- How can schools shrink the achievement gap?

"cruel and unusual punishment." For people near that score of 70, intelligence testing can be a high-stakes competition.

The High Extreme

In one famous project begun in 1921, Lewis Terman studied more than 1500 California schoolchildren with IQ scores over 135. Contrary to the popular notion that intellectually gifted children are frequently maladjusted because they are "in a different world" from their nongifted peers, Terman's high-scoring children, like those in later studies, were healthy, well-adjusted, and unusually successful academically (Lubinski & Benbow, 2006; Stanley, 1997). When restudied over the next seven decades, most people in Terman's group had attained high levels of education (Austin et al., 2002; Holahan & Sears, 1995). They included many doctors, lawyers, professors, scientists, and writers, but no Nobel Prize winners.

A more recent study of precocious youths who aced the math SAT at age 13—by scoring in the top quarter of 1 percent of their age group—were at age 33 twice as likely to have patents as were those in the bottom quarter of the top 1 percent (Wai et al., 2005). And they were more likely to have earned a Ph.D.—1 in 3, compared with 1 in 5 from the lower part of the top 1 percent. Compared with the math aces, 13-year-olds scoring high on verbal aptitude were more likely to have become humanities professors or written a novel (Park et al., 2007).

These whiz kids remind me of Jean Piaget, who by age 7 was devoting his free time to studying birds, fossils, and machines; who by age 15 was publishing scientific articles on mollusks; and who later went on to become the twentieth century's most famous developmental psychologist (Hunt, 1993). Children with extraordinary academic gifts are sometimes more isolated, introverted, and in their own worlds (Winner, 2000). But most thrive.

Is there a gifted education program in your school? There are critics who question many of the assumptions of currently popular "gifted child" programs, such as the belief that only 3 to 5 percent of children are gifted and that it pays to identify and "track" these special few—segregating them in special classes and giving them academic enrichment not available to the other 95 percent. Critics note that tracking by aptitude sometimes creates a *self-fulfilling prophecy:* Those implicitly labeled "ungifted" may be influenced to become so (Lipsey & Wilson, 1993; Slavin & Braddock, 1993). Denying lower-ability students opportunities for enriched education can widen the achievement gap between ability groups and increase their social isolation from one another (Carnegie, 1989; Stevenson & Lee, 1990). Because minority and low-income youth are more often placed in lower academic groups, tracking can also promote segregation and prejudice—hardly, note critics, a healthy preparation for working and living in a multicultural society.

Critics and proponents of gifted education do, however, agree on this: Children have differing gifts. Some are especially good at math, others at verbal reasoning, others at art, still others at social leadership. Educating children as if all were alike is as naive as assuming that giftedness is something, like blue eyes, that you either have or do not have. One need not hang labels on children to affirm their special talents and to challenge them all at the frontiers of their own ability and understanding. By providing *appropriate developmental placement* suited to each child's talents, we can promote both equity and excellence for all (Colangelo et al., 2004; Lubinski & Benbow, 2000; Sternberg & Grigorenko, 2000).

• Terman did test two future Nobel laureates in physics but they failed to score above his gifted sample cut-off (Hulbert, 2005). •

"Joining Mensa means that you are a genius. . . . I worried about the arbitrary 132 cut-off point, until I met someone with an IQ of 131 and, honestly, he was a bit slow on the uptake."

Steve Martin, 1997

AP Photo/Anne Ryan

▼
The extremes of intelligence Sho Yano was playing Mozart by age 4, aced the SAT at age 8, and graduated summa cum laude from Loyola University at age 12, at which age he began combined Ph.D.–M.D. studies at the University of Chicago.

INTERCONNECTING

Refer students to Unit 3C for more discussion of the dynamics of the nature and nurture debate.

 TEACHING TIP

Identical twins are unique in that they share 100 percent of the same genes, but while sharing the same genotype, they can have different phenotypes.

- Some identical twins are mirror-images of each other (one being left-handed, the other right, one having a mole on the left side of the face while the other has one on the right, etc.).

- Others may have different personalities and interests, showing that heritability of a trait doesn't mean it will occur even in two people who share the same genes.

- Fraternal twins, even though they may look alike and act alike, are only as similar to one another as any two siblings.

"I told my parents that if grades were so important they should have paid for a smarter egg donor."

> "There are more studies addressing the genetics of *g* [general intelligence] than any other human characteristic."
>
> Robert Plomin (1999)

Genetic and Environmental Influences on Intelligence

9: What does evidence reveal about hereditary and environmental influences on intelligence?

INTELLIGENCE RUNS IN FAMILIES. But why? Are our intellectual abilities mostly inherited? Or are they molded by our environment?

Few issues arouse such passion or have such serious political implications. Consider: If we mainly inherit our differing mental abilities, and if success reflects those abilities, then people's socioeconomic standing will correspond to their inborn differences. This could lead to those on top believing that their intellectual birthright justifies their social positions.

But if mental abilities are primarily nurtured by the environments that raise and inform us, then children from disadvantaged environments can expect to lead disadvantaged lives. In this case, people's standing will result from their unequal opportunities.

For now, as best we can, let's set aside such political implications and examine the evidence.

Twin and Adoption Studies

Do people who share the same genes also share comparable mental abilities? As you can see from **FIGURE 11.11**, which summarizes many studies, the answer is clearly *yes*. In support of the genetic contribution to intelligence, researchers cite three sets of findings:

- The intelligence test scores of identical twins reared together are virtually as similar as those of the same person taking the same test twice (Lykken, 1999; Plomin, 2001). (The scores of fraternal twins, who typically share only half their genes, are much less similar.) Likewise, the test scores of identical twins reared separately are similar enough to have led twin researcher Thomas Bouchard (1996a) to estimate that "about 70 percent" of intelligence test score variation "can be attributed to genetic variation." Other estimates range from 50 to 75 percent (Devlin et al., 1997; Neisser et al., 1996; Plomin, 2003). For simple reaction time tasks that measure processing speed, estimates range from 30 to 50 percent (Beaujean, 2005).

 TEACHING TIP

At this point, you may want to use **Lecture/Discussion Topic:** *Genes and Intelligence* (p. 25) from Bolt's Teacher's Resource Binder.

> **FIGURE 11.11**
Intelligence: Nature and nurture The most genetically similar people have the most similar intelligence scores. Remember: 1.0 indicates a perfect correlation; zero indicates no correlation at all. (Data from McGue et al., 1993.)

- Brain scans reveal that identical twins have very similar gray matter volume, and that their brains (unlike those of fraternal twins) are virtually the same in areas associated with verbal and spatial intelligence (Thompson et al., 2001).
- Are there genes for genius? Today's researchers have identified chromosomal regions important to intelligence, and they have pinpointed specific genes that seemingly influence variations in intelligence and learning disabilities (Dick et al., 2007; Plomin & Kovas, 2005; Posthuma & de Geus, 2006). Intelligence appears to be *polygenetic*, meaning many genes seem to be involved, with each gene accounting for much less than 1 percent of intelligence variations (Butcher et al., 2008).

But other evidence points to the effects of environment. Studies show that adoption enhances the intelligence scores of mistreated or neglected children (van IJzendoorn & Juffer, 2005, 2006). And fraternal twins, who are genetically no more alike than any other siblings—but who are treated more alike because they are the same age—tend to score more alike than other siblings. So if shared environment matters, do children in adoptive families share similar aptitudes?

Seeking to disentangle genes and environment, researchers have compared the intelligence test scores of adopted children with those of their adoptive siblings and with those of (a) their biological parents, the providers of their genes, and (b) their adoptive parents, the providers of their home environment. During childhood, the intelligence test scores of adoptive siblings correlate modestly. Over time, adopted children accumulate experience in their differing adoptive families. So would you expect the family environment effect to grow with age and the genetic legacy effect to shrink?

If you would, behavior geneticists have a surprise for you. Mental similarities between adopted children and their adoptive families wane with age, until the correlation approaches zero by adulthood (McGue et al., 1993). This is even true of "virtual twins"—same age, biologically unrelated siblings reared together from infancy (Segal et al., 2007). Genetic influences—not environmental ones—become more apparent as we accumulate life experience (Bouchard, 1995, 1996b). Identical twins' similarities, for example, continue or increase into their eighties (McClearn et al., 1997; Plomin et al., 1997). Similarly, adopted children's intelligence scores over time become more like those of their biological parents (**FIGURE 11.12** on the next page).

 TEACHING TIP

You may have students who are adoptees. Be sensitive to them as you discuss research concerning the impact of nature and nurture on their development. Some adoptees may know that their biological parents had substance abuse problems or other psychological issues, and this knowledge may cause them concern over whether they will turn out like their biological parents. Help them see that while a trait may be heritable, it doesn't necessarily mean that the trait will manifest itself.

TEACHING TIP

Point out in Figure 11.11 that the correlation of IQ for identical twins is not +1.00. Therefore, genes are not the sole predictor of high IQ scores. If they were, then identical twins, who share 100 percent of the same genes, would have a +1.00 correlation of their respective intelligence scores.

 TEACHING TIP

Author Judith Rich Harris in the book *The Nurture Assumption* proposed that parents do not have as much influence on the development of their children as is generally believed. In his book *The Blank Slate: The Modern Denial of Human Nature,* Steven Pinker also argues that as infants we are not born blank, but with a structure that influences how we behave and think. Have students consider the following:

- How much of your behavior would you attribute to biology? How much to environment? Why?

- How would you feel knowing that your genes mostly influence your behavior? Why?

- Why might people in Western societies feel more comfortable with the idea that environment is the major influence on behavior?

UNIT 11

➤ **FIGURE 11.12**
Who do adopted children resemble? As the years went by in their adoptive families, children's verbal ability scores became modestly more like their *biological* parents' scores. (Adapted from Plomin & DeFries, 1998.)

Child-parent correlation in verbal ability scores

Legend:
Children and their birth parents
Adopted children and their birth parents
Adopted children and their adoptive parents

(3 years, 16 years)

Heritability

Recall from Unit 3C the meaning of *heritability*. As noted earlier, estimates of the heritability of intelligence—the variation in intelligence test scores attributable to genetic factors—put it at about 50 percent. Does this mean your genes are responsible for 50 percent of your intelligence and your environment for the rest? No. It means we credit heredity with 50 percent of the variation in intelligence among people being studied. This point is so often misunderstood that I repeat: Heritability never pertains to an individual, only to why people differ from one another.

Heritability differences among people due to genes can vary from study to study. Where environments vary widely, as they do among children of less-educated parents, environmental differences are more predictive of intelligence scores (Rowe et al., 1999; Turkheimer et al., 2003). Recall from Unit 3C Mark Twain's fantasy of raising boys in barrels to age 12, feeding them through a hole. Given the boys' equal environments, differences in their individual intelligence test scores at age 12 could be explained only by their heredity. Thus, heritability for their differences would be nearly 100 percent. But if we raise people with similar heredities in drastically different environments (barrels versus advantaged homes), the environment effect will be huge, and heritability will therefore be lower. In a world of clones, heritability would be zero.

Remember, too, that genes and environment work together. If you try out for a basketball team and are just slightly taller and quicker than others, notes James Flynn (2003, 2007), you will more likely be picked, play more, and get more coaching. The same would be true for your separated identical twin—who might, *not just for genetic reasons,* also come to excel at basketball. Likewise, if you have a natural aptitude for academics, you will more likely stay in school, read books, and ask questions—all of which will amplify your cognitive brain power. Thanks to such gene-environment interaction, modest genetic advantages can be socially multiplied into big performance advantages. Our genes shape the experiences that shape us.

Environmental Influences

Genes make a difference. Even if we were all raised in the same intellectually stimulating environment, we would have differing aptitudes. But life experiences also matter. Human environments are rarely as impoverished as the dark and barren cages

---

TEACHING TIP

Stephen Jay Gould argued that even though intelligence is largely heritable (70 percent by his estimates), racial and cultural differences in intelligence are not necessarily genetic. For example, height, as a trait, is about 95 percent heritable. Imagine a group of malnourished Africans whose average height is several inches less than that of North Americans. The Africans would not remain shorter if they were properly fed. Similarly, the average height in Japan has gone up several inches since World War II, but no one argues that the Japanese gene pool has changed.

Gould, S. J. (1981). *The mismeasure of man.* New York: Norton.

TROUBLESHOOTING **TS**

Students may have some difficulty understanding the concept of heritability. Help them break down the word into its component parts:

- *Herit-* comes from the word "inherit." To inherit means to possess something that someone else has given you. We inherit our traits and qualities from our parents.

- *-ability* as a suffix means "capable." If a trait is genetically passed on from one generation to the next, then it is capable of showing up in the children of people who possess that quality.

- Help students see that a heritable trait is one that is capable of being passed down from parent to child.

At this point, you may want to use **Lecture/Discussion Topic: Misunderstanding Heritability** (p. 26) from Bolt's Teacher's Resource Binder.

● A check on your understanding of heritability: If environments become more equal, the heritability of intelligence would
a. increase.
b. decrease.
c. be unchanged.
(Answer below.) ●

Heritability—variation explained by genetic influences—will *increase* as environmental variation decreases.

"Selective breeding has given me an aptitude for the law, but I still love fetching a dead duck out of freezing water."

TROUBLESHOOTING

Emphasize that just because a trait is heritable does not mean it will affect an individual or that it will be a defining trait of a group. Heritability only demonstrates the extent to which a trait is explainable by genetics, not the extent to which the trait will affect behavior in an individual or group outside of environmental influences.

inhabited by deprived rats that develop thinner-than-normal brain cortexes (see Unit 9). Yet severe deprivation does leave footprints on the brain.

Early Environmental Influences

We have seen that biology and experience intertwine. Nowhere is this more apparent than in impoverished human environments such as J. McVicker Hunt (1982) observed in a destitute Iranian orphanage. The typical child Hunt observed there could not sit up unassisted at age 2 or walk at age 4. The little care the infants received was not in response to their crying, cooing, or other behaviors, so the children developed little sense of personal control over their environment. They were instead becoming passive "glum lumps." Extreme deprivation was bludgeoning native intelligence.

Aware of both the dramatic effects of early experiences and the impact of early intervention, Hunt began a program of *tutored human enrichment*. He trained caregivers to play language-fostering games with 11 infants, imitating the babies' babbling, then engaging them in vocal follow-the-leader, and finally teaching them sounds from the Persian language. The results were dramatic. By 22 months of age, the infants could name more than 50 objects and body parts and so charmed visitors that most were adopted—an unprecedented success for the orphanage. (Institutionalized Romanian orphans also have benefited cognitively if transferred early to more enriched home care [Nelson et al., 2007].)

Hunt's findings are an extreme case of a more general finding: Among the poor, environmental conditions can override genetic differences, depressing cognitive development. Unlike children of affluence, siblings within impoverished families have more similar intelligence scores (Turkheimer et al., 2003). Schools with lots of poverty-level children often have less-qualified teachers, as one study of 1450 Virginia schools found. And even after controlling for poverty, having less-qualified teachers predicted lower achievement scores (Tuerk, 2005). Malnutrition also plays a role. Relieve infant malnutrition with nutritional supplements, and poverty's effect on physical and cognitive development lessens (Brown & Pollitt, 1996).

Do studies of such early interventions indicate that providing an "enriched" environment can "give your child a superior intellect," as some popular books claim? Most experts are doubtful (Bruer, 1999). Although malnutrition, sensory deprivation, and social isolation can retard normal brain development, there is no environmental recipe for fast-forwarding a normal infant into a genius. All babies should have normal exposure to sights, sounds, and speech. Beyond that, Sandra Scarr's (1984) verdict still is widely shared: "Parents who are very concerned about providing special educational lessons for their babies are wasting their time."

Still, explorations of intelligence promotion continue. One widely publicized but now-discounted finding, dubbed the "Mozart effect," suggested that listening to classical music boosted cognitive ability. Other research has, however, revealed small but enduring cognitive benefits to either keyboard or vocal music training (Schellenberg, 2005, 2006). The music-training effect appears unexplained by the greater parental income and education of music-trained children; it may result from improved attention focus or abstract thinking ability. Other researchers hold out hope that *targeted training* of specific abilities (rather like a body builder doing curls to strengthen biceps and sit-ups to strengthen abdominal muscles) might build mental muscles (Kosslyn, 2007).

Schooling and Intelligence

Later in childhood, schooling is one intervention that pays dividends reflected in intelligence scores. Schooling and intelligence interact, and both enhance later income (Ceci & Williams, 1997). Hunt was a strong believer in the ability of education to boost children's chances for success by developing their cognitive and social skills. Indeed, his

Devastating neglect Romanian orphans who had minimal interaction with caregivers, such as this child in the Lagunul Pentro Copii orphanage in 1990, suffered delayed development.

"There is a large body of evidence indicating that there is little if anything to be gained by exposing middle-class children to early education."
Developmental psychologist
Edward F. Zigler (1987)

INTERCONNECTING

John B. Watson, the father of behaviorism, believed that environment was the single biggest determinant of behavior and mental processes. He famously wrote in his 1930 book *Behaviorism:*

"Give me a dozen healthy infants, well-formed, and my own specified world to bring them up in and I'll guarantee to take any one at random and train him to become any type of specialist I might select—doctor, lawyer, artist, merchant-chief and, yes, even beggar-man and thief, regardless of his talents, penchants, tendencies, abilities, vocations, and race of his ancestors. I am going beyond my facts and I admit it, but so have the advocates of the contrary and they have been doing it for many thousands of years." (p. 82)

TEACHING TIP

For several years, many parents believed that exposing their babies to classical music would increase intelligence later in life. This was known as the Mozart Effect, and the practice seemed to be the key to making smart babies. Unfortunately, the Mozart Effect was based on one study, and subsequent studies have shown that the effect does not have the impact on intellectual development that proponents claimed it had.

Getting a Head Start Project Head Start offers educational activities designed to increase readiness for schoolwork and expand children's notions of where school might lead them. Here children in a classroom learn about colors, and children on a field trip prepare for the annual Head Start parade in Boston. ▲

INTERCONNECTING

Remind students that earlier in the unit they learned that Alfred Binet and Théodore Simon developed the first intelligence tests to identify children who were ready for schooling. Programs like Head Start try to help students who are not ready for schooling become ready.

TEACHING TIP

Many critics and supporters of Head Start believe that the program went forward to large-scale application in U.S. public schools before it was ready. Smaller scale tests of the program showed promise, and overeager policymakers began implementing the program on a large scale quickly. Some of these later adopters didn't follow program protocols, resulting in poor outcomes. Head Start's mixed results demonstrates the importance of rigorous testing of such programs to discover what can be generalized and what cannot.

"It is our choices . . . that show what we truly are, far more than our abilities."
Professor Dumbledore to Harry Potter in J. K. Rowling's *Harry Potter and the Chamber of Secrets*, 1999

1961 book, *Intelligence and Experience*, helped launch Project Head Start in 1965. Head Start, a U.S. government-funded preschool program, serves more than 900,000 children, most of whom come from families below the poverty level (Head Start, 2005).

Does it succeed? Researchers study Head Start and other preschool programs such as Sure Start in Britain by comparing children who experience the program with their counterparts who don't. Quality programs, offering individual attention, increase children's school readiness, which decreases their likelihood of repeating a grade or being placed in special education. Generally, the aptitude benefits dissipate over time (reminding us that life experience *after* Head Start matters, too). Psychologist Edward Zigler, the program's first director, nevertheless believes there are long-term benefits (Ripple & Zigler, 2003; Zigler & Styfco, 2001). High-quality preschool programs can provide at least a small boost to emotional intelligence—creating better attitudes toward learning and reducing school dropouts and criminality (Reynolds et al., 2001).

Genes and experience together weave the intelligence fabric. But what we accomplish with our intelligence depends also on our own beliefs and motivation, reports Carol Dweck (2006, 2007). Those who believe that intelligence is biologically fixed and unchanging tend to focus on proving and defending their identity. Those who instead believe that intelligence is changeable will focus more on learning and growing. Seeing that it pays to have a "growth mindset" rather than a "fixed mindset," Dweck has developed interventions that effectively teach early teens that the brain is like a muscle that grows stronger with use as neuron connections grow. Indeed, as we noted earlier, superior achievements in fields from sports to science to music arise from disciplined effort and sustained practice (Ericsson et al., 2007).

Group Differences in Intelligence Test Scores

10: How and why do gender and racial groups differ in mental ability scores?

If there were no group differences in aptitude scores, psychologists could politely debate hereditary and environmental influences in their ivory towers. But there are group differences. What are they? And what shall we make of them?

Gender Similarities and Differences

In science, as in everyday life, differences, not similarities, excite interest. Compared with the anatomical and physiological similarities between men and women, our differences are relatively minor. Yet it is the differences we find exciting. Similarly, in the

TEACHING TIP

Beliefs about intelligence are related to how well students do on tests. Carol Dweck's research has shown that students who have a "performance orientation" believe that intelligence is fixed and immutable. These students tend to give up when they do poorly on tests. Students who have a "mastery orientation" believe that intelligence is environmental and changeable. These students will believe learning is the result of hard work and effort.

At this point, you may want to use **Classroom Exercise: *Incremental Versus Entity Theories of Intelligence*** (p. 27) from Bolt's Teacher's Resource Binder.

psychological domain, gender similarities vastly outnumber gender differences. We are all so much alike. In that 1932 testing of all Scottish 11-year-olds, for example, girls' average intelligence score was 100.6 and boys' was 100.5 (Deary et al., 2003). On a 2001 to 2003 Cognitive Ability Test administered to 324,000 British 11- and 12-year-olds, boys averaged 99.1 and girls a similar 99.9 (Strand et al., 2006). So far as *g* is concerned, boys and girls, men and women, are the same species. Yet, most people find differences more newsworthy. And here they are:

Spelling Females are better spellers: At the end of high school, only 30 percent of U.S. males spell better than the average female (Lubinski & Benbow, 1992).

Verbal ability Females excel at verbal fluency and remembering words (Halpern et al., 2007). And, year after year, among nearly 200,000 students taking Germany's Test for Medical Studies, young women have surpassed men in remembering facts from short medical cases (Stumpf & Jackson, 1994). (My wife, who remembers many of my experiences for me, tells me that if she died I'd be a man without a past.)

Nonverbal memory Females have an edge in remembering and locating objects (Voyer et al., 2007). In studies of more than 100,000 American adolescents, girls also modestly surpassed boys in memory for picture associations (Hedges & Nowell, 1995).

Sensation Females are more sensitive to touch, taste, and odor.

Emotion-detecting ability Females are better emotion detectors. Robert Rosenthal, Judith Hall, and their colleagues (1979; McClure, 2000) discovered this while studying sensitivity to emotional cues (an aspect of emotional intelligence). They showed hundreds of people brief film clips of portions of a person's emotionally expressive face or body, sometimes with a garbled voice added. For example, after showing a 2-second scene revealing only the face of an upset woman, the researchers asked people to guess whether the woman was criticizing someone for being late or was talking about her divorce. Rosenthal and Hall found that some people, many of them women, are much better emotion detectors than others. Such skills may explain women's somewhat greater responsiveness in both positive and negative emotional situations (see Unit 8B).

Could this ability also have helped our ancestral mothers read emotions in their infants and would-be lovers, in turn fueling cultural tendencies to encourage women's empathic skills? Some evolutionary psychologists believe so.

Math and spatial aptitudes On math tests given to more than 3 million representatively sampled people in 100 independent studies (Hyde et al., 1990, 2008). But again—despite greater diversity within the genders than between them—group differences make the news. In 20 of 21 countries, females displayed an edge in math computation, but males scored higher in math problem solving (Bronner, 1998; Hedges & Nowell, 1995). In Western countries, virtually all math prodigies participating in the International Mathematics Olympiad

○ Despite the gender equivalence in intelligence test scores, males are more likely than females to overestimate their own test scores. Both males and females tend to rate their father's scores higher than their mother's, their brothers' scores higher than their sisters', and their sons' scores higher than their daughters' (Furnham, 2001; Furnham et al., 2002a,b, 2004a,b,c). ○

○ In the first 56 years of the college Putnam Mathematical Competition, all of the nearly 300 awardees were men (Arenson, 1997). In 1997, a woman broke the male grip by joining 5 men in the winner's circle. In 1998, Melanie Wood became the first female member of a U.S. Math Olympics Team (Shulman, 2000). Her training began at an early age: When mall-shopping with her then-4-year-old daughter, Melanie's mother would alleviate her child's boredom by giving her linear equations to solve. ○

World Math Olympics champs After outscoring thousands of their U.S. peers, these young people became the U.S. Math Team in 2002 and placed third in the worldwide competition.

RESEARCH

Have students research who has won the Nobel Prizes and other major awards, such as the Field medal (in mathematics).

- How many of the winners have been men?
- How many women have been nominated?
- What factors might explain this disparity?

INTERCONNECTING

Much of the research cited in this section is referenced in other units:

- Spelling and verbal ability— Unit 7B
- Nonverbal memory—Unit 7A
- Sensation—Unit 4
- Emotion-detecting ability— Unit 8B
- Math and spatial aptitudes— Unit 7B

DEMO

Conduct a "Mental Ability Olympics" between boys and girls in your class. Create contests that test the abilities discussed in this section and pit girls against boys in each class. Once the contests are over and prizes awarded (at your discretion, of course!), debrief students by asking them the following:

- Which gender did better in each contest?
- Did they see average differences in results as well as individual differences?
- What other variables, besides gender, might explain the results of these contests? (You may suggest prior schooling differences, such as exposure to honors or AP courses, or parents' levels of education.)

➤ **FIGURE 11.13**

The mental rotation test This is a test of spatial abilities. (From Vandenberg & Kuse, 1978.) (Answer below.)

The first and fourth alternatives.

Which two circles contain a configuration of blocks identical to the one in the circle at the left?
Standard   Alternatives

TEACHING TIP

Emphasize to students that behavior is complex, so finding simple ways in which gender differences occur in cognition is not likely. Students should remember that the ability tested is only as good as the question being asked. We cannot generalize differences based on a few different types of questions posed to a few different people.

INTERCONNECTING

Point out how influential social expectations and situational forces are on behavior. Unit 14 presents a thorough discussion of the variety of social circumstances that can affect how individuals behave.

---

have been males. (More female math prodigies have, however, reached the top levels in non-Western countries, such as China [Halpern, 1991]).

The score differences are sharpest at the extremes. Among 12- to 14-year-olds scoring extremely high on SAT math, boys have outnumbered girls 13 to 1, and within that precocious group, the boys more often went on to earn a degree in the inorganic sciences and engineering (Benbow et al., 2000). In the United States, males also have an edge in the annual physics and computer science Advanced Placement exams (Stumpf & Stanley, 1998).

Men are 99 percent of the world's chess grandmasters, a difference attributable to the much greater number of boys beginning to play competitive chess. Understanding *why* boys more than girls enter competitive chess is a challenge for future research (Chabris & Glickman, 2006).

The average male edge seems most reliable in spatial ability tests like the one shown in **FIGURE 11.13**, which involves speedily rotating three-dimensional objects in one's mind (Collins & Kimura, 1997; Halpern, 2000). Exposure to high levels of male sex hormones during the prenatal period does enhance spatial abilities (Berenbaum et al., 1995). So, one recent experiment indicates, does action video game playing (Feng et al., 2007). Spatial abilities skills help when fitting suitcases into a car trunk, playing chess, or doing certain types of geometry problems.

From an evolutionary perspective (Geary, 1995, 1996; Halpern et al., 2007), those same skills helped our ancestral fathers track prey and make their way home. The survival of our ancestral mothers may have benefited more from a keen memory for the location of edible plants—a legacy that lives today in women's superior memory for objects and their location.

Evolutionary psychologist Steven Pinker (2005) argues that biological as well as social influences appear to affect gender differences in life priorities (women's greater interest in people versus men's in money and things), in risk-taking (with men more reckless), and in math reasoning and spatial abilities. Such differences are, he notes, observed across cultures, stable over time, influenced by prenatal hormones, and observed in genetic boys raised as girls. Other researchers are exploring a brain basis for male-female cognitive differences (Halpern et al., 2007).

Elizabeth Spelke (2005), however, urges caution in charting male-female intellectual worlds. It oversimplifies to say that women have more "verbal ability" and men more "math ability." Women excel at verbal fluency, men at verbal analogies. Women excel at rapid math calculations, men at rapid math reasoning. Women excel at remembering objects' spatial positions, men at remembering geometric layouts.

Other critics urge us to remember that social expectations and divergent opportunities shape boys' and girls' interests and abilities (Crawford et al., 1995; Eccles et al., 1990). Gender-equal cultures, such as Sweden and Iceland, exhibit little of the gender math gap found in gender-unequal cultures, such as Turkey and Korea (Guiso et al., 2008). In the United States, the male edge in math problem solving is detectable only after elementary school. Traditionally, math and science have been

---

TEACHING TIP

At this point, you may want to use **Lecture/Discussion Topic: *Teaching Intelligence*** (p. 26) from Bolt's Teacher's Resource Binder.

Nature or nurture? At this 2005 Google Inc.-sponsored computer coding competition, programmers competed for cash prizes and possible jobs. What do you think accounted for the fact that only one of the 100 finalists was female?

CRITICAL THINKING

Have students discuss the academic disciplines that have traditionally been encouraged for men and for women. Discuss why they think men were encouraged to take more math and science courses and why women were encouraged to take more humanities and arts courses. Have students share whether they feel times have changed for women and men. Do members of each gender feel welcome in one anothers' academic worlds? Why or why not?

considered masculine subjects, but as more parents encourage their daughters to develop their abilities in math and science, the gender gap is narrowing (Nowell & Hedges, 1998). In some fields, including psychology, women now earn most of the Ph.D.s. Yet, notes Diane Halpern (2005) with a twinkle in her eye, "no one has asked if men have the innate ability to succeed in those academic disciplines where *they* are underrepresented."

Greater male variability Finally, intelligence research consistently reports a peculiar tendency for males' mental ability scores to vary more than females' (Halpern et al., 2007). Thus, boys outnumber girls at both the low extreme and the high extreme (Kleinfeld, 1998; Strand et al., 2006; also see **FIGURE 11.14**). Boys are, therefore, more often found in special education classes. They talk later. They stutter more.

➤ **FIGURE 11.14**

Gender and variability In the 1932 intelligence testing of nearly 90,000 Scottish 11-year-olds, the average IQ score for girls and boys was essentially identical. But as other studies have found, boys were overrepresented at the low and high extremes. (Adapted from Deary et al., 2003.)

Percentage of boys vs. girls at each score level

[Graph showing percentage (0–100%) vs. IQ score (60–140) with curves for Boys and Girls]

Ethnic Similarities and Differences

Fueling the group-differences debate are two other disturbing but agreed-upon facts:

- Racial groups differ in their average intelligence test scores.
- High-scoring people (and groups) are more likely to attain high levels of education and income.

TEACHING TIP

At this point, you may want to use **Lecture/Discussion Topic: *Environmental Explanation of Group Differences*** (p. 29) from Bolt's Teacher's Resource Binder.

CULTURAL CONNECTIONS

In Africa, intelligence includes skills that help to establish and maintain harmonious and stable intergroup relations. Chewa adults in Zambia emphasize social responsibility, cooperation, and obedience as important to intelligence. Similarly, Kenyan parents emphasize responsible participation in family and social life as important aspects of intelligence. In Zimbabwe, the word for intelligence, *ngware*, means to be prudent and cautious, particularly in social relationships.

Sternberg, R. J., & Kaufman, J. C. (1998). Human abilities. In J. T. Spence, J. M. Darley, & D. J. Foss (Eds.), *Annual Review of Psychology*, Volume 49, (pp. 479-502). Palo Alto, CA: Annual Reviews.

CULTURAL CONNECTIONS

Joseph Glick's study of Liberia's Kpelle tribesmen provides a classic example of adaptive intelligence. Glick asked the tribesmen to sort a group of objects sensibly. To his puzzlement, they insisted on grouping the objects by function (for example, placing a potato with a hoe) rather than by taxonomy (placing the potato with other foods). After Glick demonstrated the "correct" answer, one of the tribesmen remarked that only a stupid person would sort things that way. When Glick thereafter asked tribesmen to sort items the way a stupid person would, they sorted them taxonomically without hesitation or difficulty.

A statement by 52 intelligence researchers explained: "The bell curve for Whites is centered roughly around IQ 100; the bell curve for American Blacks roughly around 85; and those for different subgroups of Hispanics roughly midway between those for Whites and Blacks" (Avery et al., 1994). Comparable results come from other academic aptitude tests. In recent years, the Black-White difference has diminished somewhat, and among children has dropped to 10 points in some studies (Dickens & Flynn, 2006). Yet the test score gap stubbornly persists, and other studies suggest the gap stopped narrowing among those born after 1970 (Murray, 2006, 2007).

There are differences among other groups as well. New Zealanders of European descent outscore native Maori New Zealanders. Israeli Jews outscore Israeli Arabs. Most Japanese outscore the stigmatized Japanese minority, the Burakumin. And those who can hear outscore those born deaf (Braden, 1994; Steele, 1990; Zeidner, 1990).

Everyone further agrees that such *group* differences provide little basis for judging individuals. Women outlive men by six years, but knowing someone's sex doesn't tell us with any precision how long that person will live. Even Charles Murray and Richard Herrnstein (1994), whose writings drew attention to Black-White differences, reminded us that "millions of Blacks have higher IQs than the average White."

Swedes and Bantus differ in complexion and language. That first factor is genetic, the second environmental. So what about intelligence scores?

As we have seen, heredity contributes to individual differences in intelligence. Does that mean it also contributes to group differences? Some psychologists believe it does, perhaps because of the world's differing climates and survival challenges (Herrnstein & Murray, 1994; Lynn, 1991, 2001; Rushton & Jensen, 2005, 2006).

But we have also seen that group differences in a heritable trait may be entirely environmental, as in our earlier barrel-versus-home–reared boys example. Consider one of nature's experiments: Allow some children to grow up hearing their culture's dominant language, while others, born deaf, do not. Then give both groups an intelligence test rooted in the dominant language, and (no surprise) those with expertise in that language will score highest. Although individual performance differences may be substantially genetic, the group difference is not (FIGURE 11.15).

Also consider: If each identical twin were exactly as tall as his or her co-twin, heritability would be 100 percent. Imagine that we then separated some young twins and gave only half of them a nutritious diet, and that the well-nourished twins all grew to be exactly 3 inches taller than their counterparts—an environmental effect

● In prosperous country X everyone eats all they want. In country Y the rich are well fed, but the semistarved poor are often thin. In which country will the heritability of body weight be greater? (Answer below.) ●

Heritability—differences due to genes—will be greater in country X, where environmental differences in nutrition are minimal.

● Since 1830, the average Dutch man has grown from 5 feet 5 inches to nearly 6 feet. ●

➤ **FIGURE 11.15**

Group differences and environmental impact Even if the variation between members within a group reflects genetic differences, the average difference between groups may be wholly due to the environment. Imagine that seeds from the same mixture are sown in different soils. Although height differences *within* each window box will be genetic, the height difference *between* the two groups will be environmental. (From Lewontin, 1976.)

Variation within group

Variation within group

Seeds

Poor soil

Fertile soil

Difference between groups

TEACHING TIP

At this point, you may want to use **Lecture/Discussion Topic: *Intelligence as Culturally Defined*** (p. 30) or **Classroom Exercise: *Blacks as a "Castelike" Minority*** (p. 28) from Bolt's Teacher's Resource Binder.

comparable to that actually observed in both Britain and America, where adolescents are several inches taller than their counterparts were a half-century ago. What would the heritability of height now be for our well-nourished twins? Still 100 percent, because the variation in height within the group would remain entirely predictable from the heights of their mal-nourished identical siblings. So even perfect heritability within groups would not eliminate the possibility of a strong environmental impact on the group differences.

Might the racial gap be similarly environmental? Consider:

Genetics research reveals that under the skin, the races are remarkably alike (Cavalli-Sforza et al., 1994; Lewontin, 1982). Individual differences within a race are much greater than differences between races. The average genetic difference between two Icelandic villagers or between two Kenyans greatly exceeds the group difference between Icelanders and Kenyans. Moreover, looks can deceive. Light-skinned Europeans and dark-skinned Africans are genetically closer than are dark-skinned Africans and dark-skinned Aboriginal Australians.

Race is not a neatly defined biological category. Some scholars argue that there is a reality to race, noting that there are genetic markers for race (the continent of one's ancestry) and that medical risks (such as skin cancer or high blood pressure) vary by race. Behavioral traits may also vary by race. "No runner of Asian or European descent—a majority of the world's population—has broken 10 seconds in the 100-meter dash, but dozens of runners of West African descent have done so," observes psychologist David Rowe (2005). Many social scientists, though, see race primarily as a social construction without well-defined physical boundaries (Helms et al., 2005; Smedley & Smedley, 2005; Sternberg et al., 2005). People with varying ancestry may categorize themselves in the same race. Moreover, with increasingly mixed ancestries, more and more people defy neat racial categorization.

Asian students outperform North American students on math achievement and aptitude tests. But this difference appears to be a recent phenomenon and may reflect conscientiousness more than competence. Asian students also attend school 30 percent more days per year and spend much more time in and out of school studying math (Geary et al., 1996; Larson & Verma, 1999; Stevenson, 1992).

The intelligence test performance of today's better-fed, better-educated, and more test-prepared population exceeds that of the 1930s population—by the same margin that the intelligence test score of the average White today exceeds that of the average Black. No one attributes the generational group difference to genetics.

White and Black infants have scored equally well on an infant intelligence measure (preference for looking at novel stimuli—a crude predictor of future intelligence scores [Fagan, 1992]).

When Blacks and Whites have or receive the same pertinent knowledge, they exhibit similar information-processing skill. "The data support the view that cultural

Nature's own morphing Nature draws no sharp boundaries between races, which blend gradually one into the next around the Earth. Thanks to the human urge to classify, however, people socially define themselves in racial categories, which become catch-all labels for physical features, social identity, and nationality.

© Paul Almasy/Corbis; © Rob Howard/Corbis;
© Barbara Bannister; Gallo Images/Corbis;
© David Turnley/Corbis; © Dave Bartruff/Corbis;
© Haruyoshi Yamaguchi/Corbis;
© Richard T. Nowitz/Corbis; © Owen Franken/Corbis;
© Paul Almasy/Corbis; © John-Francis Bourke/zefa/Corbis

The culture of scholarship The children of Indochinese refugee families studied by Nathan Caplan, Marcella Choy, and James Whitmore (1992) typically excel in school. On weekday nights after dinner, the family clears the table and begins homework. Family cooperation is valued, and older siblings help younger ones.

TEACHING TIP

Lewis Terman was part of the eugenics movement, which started in the nineteenth century. The eugenics movement believed that only the "fit" should be allowed to reproduce. In this view, societal problems like poverty were a result of the "feebleminded" reproducing at a faster rate than the mentally strong. Terman believed that people from certain ethnic groups and cultures were more feebleminded than others, as evidenced by immigrants from those groups being more likely to be poor. He pushed to have his intelligence tests used as a requirement for entry into the U.S. He was part of a committee that used intelligence testing on military recruits for World War I to identify which recruits would be trained for specialized jobs and which ones would be sent to the front lines as regular infantry.

TROUBLESHOOTING

The idea that race is not a biological category may come as a surprise to some students. Many researchers today regard our racial categories as socially constructed. We categorize people according to easily discernible differences, like skin color, in order to make sense of the world. There is no real basis beyond the surface qualities to justify racial categories.

CRITICAL THINKING

Eugenics came to fruition during Hitler's Nazi regime. By selectively eliminating certain ethnic groups and people with "undesirable" traits (such as handicaps, diseases, and lower intelligence levels), the Nazis hoped to create a "master" race that rivaled no other in the world. Today's growing research in genetic therapy to eliminate disease has come under scrutiny as a rebirth of the eugenics movement. Some critics believe that gene therapy could just as easily be used for genetic enhancements as it could be used to treat genetic disorders. Explore these questions with students regarding gene therapy:

- Would you support gene therapy to combat diseases such as Alzheimer's and Parkinson's? Why or why not?
- Would you support gene therapy to enhance traits like intelligence and height? Why or why not?
- Should ethical limits be placed on genetic research? Why or why not?

Have students find at least one major accomplishment discovered or developed by each of the following cultural groups throughout history:

- Greeks
- Romans
- Chinese
- People of the Indus Valley in Asia
- Russians
- Aztecs
- Mayans
- Incas
- Japanese
- Arabs

TEACHING TIP

At this point, you may want to use **Lecture/Discussion Topics: *Intelligence as Culturally Defined*** (p. 30) or ***The SAT: A Case Study in Testing*** (p. 30) or ***Unanswered Questions About Intelligence*** (p. 32) or **Classroom Exercise: *Culture-Biased and Culture-Fair Tests*** (p. 29) from Bolt's Teacher's Resource Binder.

> "Do not obtain your slaves from Britain, because they are so stupid and so utterly incapable of being taught."
>
> Cicero, 106–43 B.C.E.

::**stereotype threat** a self-confirming concern that one will be evaluated based on a negative stereotype.

differences in the provision of information may account for racial differences in IQ," report researchers Joseph Fagan and Cynthia Holland (2007).

In different eras, different ethnic groups have experienced golden ages—periods of remarkable achievement. Twenty-five-hundred years ago, it was the Greeks and the Egyptians, then the Romans; in the eighth and ninth centuries, genius seemed to reside in the Arab world; 500 years ago it was the Aztec Indians and the peoples of Northern Europe. Today, people marvel at Asians' technological genius. Cultures rise and fall over centuries; genes do not. That fact makes it difficult to attribute a natural superiority to any race.

Moreover, consider the striking results of a national study that looked back over the mental test performances of White and Black young adults after graduation from college. From eighth grade through the early high school years, the average aptitude scores of the White students increased, while those of the Black students decreased—creating a gap that reached its widest point at about the time that high school students like you take college admissions tests. But during college, the Black students' scores increased "more than four times as much" as those of their White counterparts, thus greatly decreasing the aptitude gap. "It is not surprising," concluded researcher Joel Myerson and his colleagues (1998), "that as Black and White students complete more grades in high school environments that differ in quality, the gap in cognitive test scores widens. At the college level, however, where Black and White students are exposed to educational environments of comparable quality . . . many Blacks are able to make remarkable gains, closing the gap in test scores."

The Question of Bias

11: Are intelligence tests inappropriately biased?

If one assumes that race is a meaningful concept, the debate over race differences in intelligence divides into three camps, note Earl Hunt and Jerry Carlson (2007):

- There are genetically disposed race differences in intelligence.
- There are socially influenced race differences in intelligence.
- There are race differences in test scores, but the tests are inappropriate or biased.

Are intelligence tests biased? The answer depends on which of two very different definitions of *bias* are used, and on an understanding of stereotypes.

Two Meanings of Bias

A test may be considered biased if it detects not only innate differences in intelligence but also performance differences caused by cultural experiences. This in fact happened to Eastern European immigrants in the early 1900s. Lacking the experience to answer questions about their new culture, many were classified as feeble-minded. David Wechsler, who entered the United States as a 6-year-old Romanian just before this group, designed the WAIS.

In this popular sense, intelligence tests are biased. They measure your developed abilities, which reflect, in part, your education and experiences. You may have read examples of intelligence test items that make middle-class assumptions (for example, that a cup goes with a saucer, or, as in one of the sample test items from the WAIS [Figure 11.5], that people buy insurance to protect the value of their homes and possessions). Do such items bias the test against those who do not use saucers or do not have enough possessions to make the cost of insurance relevant? Could such questions explain racial differences in test performance? If

---

DEMO

One way to demonstrate bias to your students is to take one of your typical unit tests and replace certain words with more complex synonyms to see if students still understand the questions. You can find these types of synonyms using a regular thesaurus or by using more technical jargon.

so, are tests a vehicle for discrimination, consigning potentially capable children to dead-end classes and jobs?

Defenders of aptitude testing note that racial group differences are at least as great on nonverbal items, such as counting digits backward (Jensen, 1983, 1998). Moreover, they add, blaming the test for a group's lower scores is like blaming a messenger for bad news. Why blame the tests for exposing unequal experiences and opportunities? If, because of malnutrition, people were to suffer stunted growth, would you blame the measuring stick that reveals it? If unequal past experiences predict unequal future achievements, a valid aptitude test will detect such inequalities.

The second meaning of *bias*—its *scientific* meaning—is different. It hinges on a test's validity—on whether it predicts future behavior only for some groups of test-takers. For example, if the U.S. SAT accurately predicted the college achievement of women but not that of men, then the test would be biased. In this statistical meaning of the term, the near-consensus among psychologists (as summarized by the U.S. National Research Council's Committee on Ability Testing and the American Psychological Association's Task Force on Intelligence) is that the major U.S. aptitude tests are *not* biased (Hunt & Carlson, 2007; Neisser et al., 1996; Wigdor & Garner, 1982). The tests' predictive validity is roughly the same for women and men, for Blacks and Whites, and for rich and poor. If an intelligence test score of 95 predicts slightly below-average grades, that rough prediction usually applies equally to both genders and all ethnic and economic groups.

Test-Takers' Expectations

Throughout this text, we have seen that our expectations and attitudes can influence our perceptions and behaviors. Once again, we find this effect in intelligence testing. When Steven Spencer and his colleagues (1997) gave a difficult math test to equally capable men and women, women did not perform as well as men—except when they had been led to expect that women usually do as well as men on the test. Otherwise, the women apparently felt apprehensive, and it affected their performance. With Claude Steele and Joshua Aronson, Spencer (2002) also observed this self-fulfilling **stereotype threat** when Black students, taking verbal aptitude tests under conditions designed to make them feel threatened, performed at a lower level. Critics note that stereotype threat does not fully account for the Black-White aptitude score difference (Sackett et al., 2004, 2008). But it does help explain why Blacks have scored higher when tested by Blacks than when tested by Whites (Danso & Esses, 2001; Inzlicht & Ben-Zeev, 2000). And it gives us insight into why women have scored higher on math tests when no male test-takers were in the group, and why women's chess play drops sharply when they *think* they are playing a male rather than female opponent (Maass et al., 2008).

Steele (1995, 1997) concluded that telling students they probably won't succeed (as is sometimes implied by remedial "minority support" programs) functions as a stereotype that can erode test and school performance. Over time, such students may detach their self-esteem from academics and look for recognition elsewhere. Indeed, as African-American boys progress from eighth to twelfth grade, they tend to underachieve as the disconnect between their grades and their self-esteem becomes pronounced (Osborne, 1997). One experiment randomly assigned some African-American seventh-graders to write for 15 minutes about their most important values (Cohen et al., 2006). That simple exercise in self-affirmation had the apparent effect of boosting their semester grade point average by 0.26 in a first experiment and 0.34 in a replication. Minority students in university programs that challenge them to believe in their potential, or to focus on the idea that intelligence

> "Political equality is a commitment to universal human rights, and to policies that treat people as individuals rather than representatives of groups; it is not an empirical claim that all groups are indistinguishable."
>
> Steven Pinker (2006)

> "Math class is tough!"
>
> "Teen talk" talking Barbie doll (introduced February 1992, recalled October 1992)

TROUBLESHOOTING

Stereotype threat occurs only when the stereotype is activated. If Black and White students were to take any particular test together, the threat would only be activated if the teacher or another student pointed out that White children do better or that Black children do worse on the particular test. Then, students in the stereotyped group may embody the negative expectation even if their own personal past performance would suggest they would excel.

TEACHING TIP

Point out to students that the threat works also with White students who are compared negatively to other groups, such as Asians on math tests. If White students are told that Asians typically score better than Whites on a particular test, the White students will underperform on the test.

CRITICAL THINKING

Herrnstein and Murray published a very controversial book entitled *The Bell Curve* in which they argue that intelligence differences have led to social and economic problems. Have students debate some of their conclusions:

- Not only is IQ shaped more by genes than by environment, but no means have been found to raise it significantly;

- current social interventions such as job quotas merely serve to undercut productivity if they require lowered standards;

- as a nation, the United States is becoming genetically stratified, deepening tension between the haves and the have-nots; and

- because of present welfare policies, low-IQ people are propagating profusely, dragging down the nation's intelligence level at the same time that low-level jobs are disappearing and social ills are swelling.

Untestable compassion Intelligence test scores are only one part of the picture of a whole person. They don't measure the abilities, talent, and commitment of, for example, people who devote their lives to helping others.

"Almost all the joyful things of life are outside the measure of IQ tests."
Madeleine L'Engle, *A Circle of Quiet*, 1972

is malleable and not fixed, have likewise produced markedly higher grades and had lower dropout rates (Wilson, 2006).

What, then, can we realistically conclude about aptitude tests and bias? The tests do seem biased (appropriately so, some would say) in one sense—sensitivity to performance differences caused by cultural experience. But they are not biased in the scientific sense of making valid statistical predictions for different groups.

Bottom line: Are the tests discriminatory? Again, the answer can be *yes* or *no*. In one sense, *yes*, their purpose is to discriminate—to distinguish among individuals. In another sense, *no*, their purpose is to reduce discrimination by reducing reliance on subjective criteria for school and job placement—who you know, what school you're from, or whether you are the "right kind of person." Civil service aptitude tests, for example, were devised to discriminate more fairly and objectively by reducing the political, racial, and ethnic discrimination that preceded their use. Banning aptitude tests would lead those who decide on jobs and admissions to rely more on other considerations, such as their personal opinions.

Perhaps, then, our goals for tests of mental abilities should be threefold. First, we should realize the benefits Alfred Binet foresaw—to enable schools to recognize who might profit most from early intervention. Second, we must remain alert to Binet's fear that intelligence test scores may be misinterpreted as literal measures of a person's worth and potential. And finally, we must remember that the competence that general intelligence tests sample is important; it helps enable success in some life paths. But it reflects only one aspect of personal competence. Our practical intelligence and emotional intelligence matter, too, as do other forms of creativity, talent, and character. The carpenter's spatial ability differs from the programmer's logical ability, which differs from the poet's verbal ability. Because there are many ways of being successful, our differences are variations of human adaptability.

BEFORE YOU MOVE ON . . .

➤ **ASK YOURSELF**

How have genetic and environmental influences shaped your intelligence?

➤ **TEST YOURSELF 4**

As society succeeds in creating equality of opportunity, it will also increase the heritability of ability. The heritability of intelligence scores will be greater in a society marked by equal opportunity than in a society of peasants and aristocrats. Why?

Answers to the Test Yourself questions can be found in Appendix E at the end of the book.

TEACHING TIP

Create a chart with two columns—one labeled benefits and one labeled drawbacks. Have students list reasons supporting and rejecting the use of intelligence tests in schools, for admissions, and for job placement. Ask students the following:

- Has your view of intelligence tests changed after reading this unit? Why or why not?

- Would you recommend that people submit to intelligence tests for any purpose? Why or why not?

- How can schools make good, responsible use of intelligence test information?

UNIT REVIEW: Testing and Individual Differences

What Is Intelligence?

1: What arguments support intelligence as one general mental ability, and what arguments support the idea of multiple distinct abilities?

Factor analysis is a statistical procedure that has revealed some underlying commonalities in different mental abilities. Spearman named this common factor the *g* factor. Thurstone argued against defining *intelligence* so narrowly as just one score. He identified seven different clusters of mental abilities. Yet there remained a tendency for high scorers in one of his clusters to score high in other clusters as well. Our *g* scores seem most predictive in novel situations and do not much correlate with skills in evolutionarily familiar situations.

2: How do Gardner's and Sternberg's theories of multiple intelligences differ?

Gardner proposes eight independent intelligences: linguistic, logical-mathematical, musical, spatial, bodily-kinesthetic, intrapersonal, interpersonal, and naturalist. Sternberg's theory has proposed three intelligence domains: analytical (academic problem-solving), creative, and practical. (For more on the single-intelligence/multiple-intelligences debate, see Table 11.2.)

3: What makes up emotional intelligence?

Emotional intelligence is the ability to perceive, understand, manage, and use emotions. Those with higher emotional intelligence tend to achieve greater personal and professional success. However, critics question whether we stretch the idea of intelligence too far when we apply it to emotions.

4: To what extent is intelligence related to brain anatomy and neural processing speed?

Recent studies indicate some correlation (about +.33) between brain size (adjusted for body size) and intelligence score. Highly educated or intelligent people exhibit an above-average volume of synapses and gray matter. People who score high on *intelligence tests* tend also to have speedy brains that retrieve information and perceive stimuli quickly.

Assessing Intelligence

5: When and why were intelligence tests created?

In France in 1904, Alfred Binet started the modern intelligence-testing movement by developing questions that helped predict children's future progress in the Paris school system. Lewis Terman of Stanford University revised Binet's work for use in the United States. Terman believed his *Stanford-Binet* could help guide people toward appropriate opportunities, but more than Binet, he believed intelligence is inherited. During the early part of the twentieth century, intelligence tests were sometimes used to "document" scientists' assumptions about the innate inferiority of certain ethnic and immigrant groups.

6: What's the difference between aptitude and achievement tests, and how can we develop and evaluate them?

Aptitude tests are designed to predict what you *can learn*. *Achievement tests* are designed to assess what you *have learned*. The *WAIS (Wechsler Adult Intelligence Scale)*, an aptitude test, is the most widely used intelligence test for adults. Such tests must be *standardized*, by giving the test to a representative sample of future test-takers to establish a basis for meaningful score comparisons. The distribution of test scores often forms a *normal*, bell-shaped *curve*. Tests must also be *reliable*, by yielding consistent scores (on two halves of the test, or when people are retested). And they must be *valid*. A valid test measures or predicts what it is supposed to. *Content validity* is the extent to which a test samples the pertinent behavior (as a driving test measures driving ability). *Predictive validity* is the extent to which the test predicts a behavior it is designed to predict (aptitude tests have predictive ability if they can predict future achievements).

The Dynamics of Intelligence

7: How stable are intelligence scores over the life span?

The stability of intelligence test scores increases with age. By age 4, scores fluctuate somewhat but begin to predict adolescent and adult scores. At about age 7, scores become fairly stable and consistent.

8: What are the traits of those at the low and high intelligence extremes?

Those with intelligence test scores below 70, the cut-off mark for the diagnosis of an *intellectual disability* (formerly referred to as mental retardation), vary from near-normal to those requiring constant aid and supervision. *Down syndrome* is a form of intellectual disability with a physical cause—an extra copy of chromosome 21. High-scoring people, contrary to popular myths, tend to be healthy and well-adjusted, as well as unusually successful academically. Schools sometimes "track" such children, separating them from those with lower scores. Such programs can become self-fulfilling prophecies as children live up to—or down to—others' perceptions of their ability.

Genetic and Environmental Influences on Intelligence

9: What does evidence reveal about hereditary and environmental influences on intelligence?

Studies of twins, family members, and adoptees together point to a significant hereditary contribution to intelligence scores. The search is under way for genes that together contribute to intelligence. Yet research also provides evidence of environmental influence. The intelligence test scores of fraternal twins raised together are more similar than those of other siblings, and the scores of identical twins raised apart are slightly less

UNIT 11

ANSWERS to Multiple-Choice Questions

1. **b.** 70.
2. **a.** general intelligence.
3. **e.** It is reliable but not valid.
4. **d.** spatial ability.
5. **c.** measurement is to prediction.
6. **b.** savant syndrome.
7. **c.** Practical intelligence
8. **e.** gradual improvement in intelligence test scores over the last several decades.
9. **d.** emotional intelligence.
10. **c.** the amount of group variation in intelligence that can be attributed to genetics.
11. **e.** number of synapses between neurons.
12. **d.** David Wechsler.
13. **a.** predictive validity.
14. **a.** predict how children would do in school.
15. **b.** mental age to his or her chronological age.

similar (though still very highly correlated) than the scores of identical twins raised together. Other studies, of children reared in extremely impoverished, enriched, or culturally different environments, indicate that life experiences can significantly influence intelligence test performance.

10: How and why do gender and racial groups differ in mental ability scores?
Males and females average the same in overall intelligence. There are, however, some small but intriguing gender differences in specific abilities. Girls are better spellers, more verbally fluent, better at locating objects, better at detecting emotions, and more sensitive to touch, taste, and color. Boys outperform girls at spatial ability and related mathematics, though girls outperform boys in math computation. Boys also outnumber girls at the low and high extremes of mental abilities. Psychologists debate evolutionary, brain-based, and cultural explana-

tions of such gender differences. As a group, Whites score higher than their Hispanic and Black counterparts, though the gap is not as great as it was half a century and more ago. The evidence suggests that environmental differences are largely, perhaps entirely, responsible for these group differences.

11: Are intelligence tests inappropriately biased?
Aptitude tests aim to predict how well a test-taker will perform in a given situation. So they are necessarily "biased" in the sense that they are sensitive to performance differences caused by cultural experience. But bias can also mean what psychologists commonly mean by the term—that a test predicts less accurately for one group than for another. In this sense of the term, most experts consider the major aptitude tests unbiased. *Stereotype threat*, a self-confirming concern that one will be evaluated based on a negative stereotype, affects performance on all kinds of tests.

Terms and Concepts to Remember

intelligence test, p. 524
intelligence, p. 524
general intelligence (*g*), p. 524
factor analysis, p. 524
savant syndrome, p. 525
emotional intelligence, p. 528
mental age, p. 533
Stanford-Binet, p. 534

intelligence quotient (IQ), p. 534
achievement tests, p. 535
aptitude tests, p. 535
Wechsler Adult Intelligence Scale (WAIS), p. 535
standardization, p. 536
normal curve, p. 536
reliability, p. 538

validity, p. 538
content validity, p. 538
predictive validity, p. 538
intellectual disability, p. 542
Down syndrome, p. 542
stereotype threat, p. 555

 AP* Practice Test Questions

Multiple-Choice Questions

1. Children are said to have an intellectual disability if they have difficulty adapting to the demands of independent living and have IQ scores below
   a. 60.
   b. 70.
   c. 80.
   d. 90.
   e. 100.

2. Charles Spearman's *g* refers to
   a. general intelligence.
   b. grouped intelligence factors.
   c. genetic intelligence.
   d. generated creativity.
   e. generalized reliability.

   *AP is a trademark registered and/or owned by the College Board, which was not involved in the production of, and does not endorse, this product.

3. What would be true of a thermometer that always reads three degrees off?
   a. It is valid but not reliable.
   b. It is both reliable and valid.
   c. It is neither reliable nor valid.
   d. It is not valid but you cannot determine if it is reliable from the information given.
   e. It is reliable but not valid.

4. In general, males score higher than females on tests of
   a. spelling.
   b. verbal fluency.
   c. emotion detection.
   d. spatial ability.
   e. sensitivity to touch, taste, and odor.

5. Achievement tests are to aptitude tests as
   a. verbal performance is to spatial performance.
   b. elementary school skills are to secondary school skills.
   c. measurement is to prediction.
   d. reliability is to validity.
   e. general intelligence is to multiple intelligences.

6. Howard Gardner found evidence of multiple intelligences in individuals who scored low on intelligence but had an area of exceptional ability—for example, to make complex calculations. These people have
   a. the Flynn effect.
   b. savant syndrome.
   c. advanced mental age.
   d. Wechsler syndrome.
   e. intelligence heritability.

 TECHNOLOGY RESOURCES

These resources will be helpful for teaching the concepts in this unit:

- *PsychSim 5: Get Smart*
- *Psychology Video Tool Kit: Savant Music Skills; Savant Art Skills: In Autism and Dementia; Locking Away the "Feebleminded": A Shameful History*
- *Video: Psychology: The Human Experience, Module 17: Pros and Cons of Intelligence Tests*

- *ActivePsych: Digital Media Archive, 2nd ed.: Psychologist Ellen Winner Discusses "Gifted Children"; Hothouse Babies: Mother Tries to Teach Her Two-Year-Old Multiplication*
- *Video: The Brain, 2nd ed., Module 4: Intelligence and Culture*

7. Which of the following does Robert Sternberg include as a type of intelligence?
a. Naturalistic intelligence
b. General intelligence
c. Practical intelligence
d. Savant intelligence
e. Kinesthetic intelligence

8. The Flynn effect refers to the
a. superiority of certain racial and ethnic groups on intelligence tests.
b. fact that male performance on math tests is more extreme (that is, more very high and very low scores) than is female performance.
c. stereotype threat that might cause some Black students to underperform on standardized tests.
d. predictive ability of intelligence tests.
e. gradual improvement in intelligence test scores over the last several decades.

9. The ability to perceive, understand, manage, and use emotions is called
a. interpersonal intelligence.
b. general intelligence.
c. practical intelligence.
d. emotional intelligence.
e. adaptive intelligence.

10. Heritability of intelligence refers to
a. the extent to which a person's intelligence is caused by genetics.
b. the effect of adoption on the intelligence of adopted children.
c. the amount of group variation in intelligence that can be attributed to genetics.
d. the extent to which the quality of schools and other environmental factors determine intelligence.
e. the correlation between intelligence test scores of identical twins.

11. The neurological basis of intelligence is most dependent on the
a. overall number of neurons.
b. quantity of specific neurotransmitters.
c. development of the left hemisphere.
d. development of the right hemisphere.
e. number of synapses between neurons.

12. The most widely used modern intelligence test was developed by
a. Alfred Binet.
b. Louis Terman.
c. Robert Sternberg.
d. David Wechsler.
e. Howard Gardner.

13. Students who do well on college entrance exams generally do well in college. This helps establish that these exams have
a. predictive validity.
b. split-half reliability.
c. content validity.
d. test-retest reliability.
e. standard validity.

14. The purpose of Alfred Binet's early intelligence test was to
a. predict how children would do in school.
b. identify differences among ethnic and racial groups.
c. help French graduates find the occupation in which they were most likely to succeed.
d. establish the scientific definition of intelligence.
e. facilitate "genetic breeding" experiments.

15. The intelligence quotient compares a child's
a. aptitude to his or her school performance.
b. mental age to his or her chronological age.
c. intelligence to his or her siblings' intelligence.
d. intelligence to his or her parents' intelligence.
e. math intelligence to his or her verbal intelligence.

Free-Response Question

Assume you are going to develop a new test to predict job success for aspiring novelists. Consider how each of the following concepts relates to your task, and describe how you would attempt to accomplish each for your new test.
• Content validity
• Predictive validity
• Standardization
• Reliability

> **WEB**
> Multiple-choice self-tests and more may be found at www.worthpublishers.com/myers

Rubric for Grading the Free-Response Question

This is an 8-point question. You should require enough description for each point to be assured of the students' understanding.

Content validity

• 1 point for establishing what content validity is: the extent to which a test taps pertinent behavior.

• 1 point for applying the concept to the question: the test has to clearly be about novel writing, and not some other, unrelated behavior like mathematical skill.

Predictive validity

• 1 point for establishing what predictive validity is: the extent to which a test predicts future performance.

 Rubric continued

• 1 point for applying the concept to the question: aspiring novelists who do well on the test would have to be more likely to be successful novelists than those who don't do well on the test.

Standardization

• 1 point for establishing what standardization is: the process of defining meaningful scores in relation to a pretested group.

• 1 point for applying the concept to the question: the test should be pretested with a representative group of writers in order to determine what a meaningful score would be (for example, determining what the mean is).

Reliability

• 1 point for establishing what reliability is: the extent to which a test yields dependably consistent scores.

• 1 point for applying the concept to the question: the test should be given to some individuals twice to make sure there is a reasonably high positive correlation between the two groups of scores (test-retest reliability).

UNIT 12

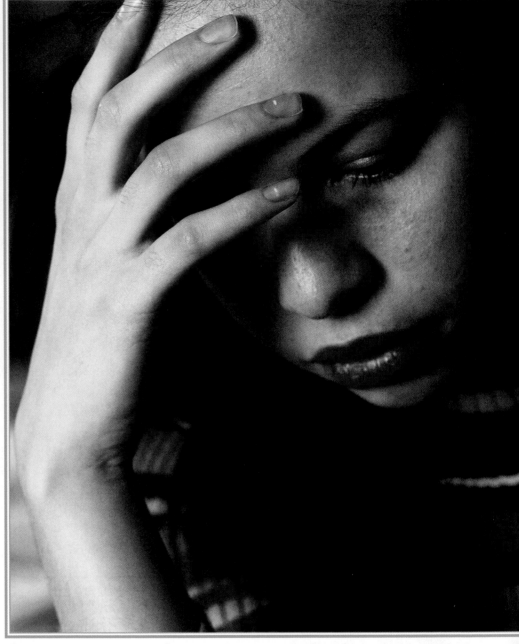

Pacing Guide

Use the following guide to determine how many instructional days to devote to this unit depending on the type of course you teach:

Year-long course: 6–9 days
Block schedule/Semester-long course: 4–6 days

This unit encompasses 7–9 percent of the AP Exam. Spending an appropriate amount of time on this unit will help students do well on the AP Exam.

 TEACHING TIP

Before reading the unit, have students form groups of four or five and develop a definition for "psychological disorder." Instruct them to be specific, identifying criteria they would apply to draw the line between normality and abnormality. Have each group report its definition to the class.

Spend the rest of the session considering the difficulty of defining the term. End the session by sharing the following four criteria: *atypical, disturbing, maladaptive,* and *unjustifiable.*

At this time you may want to use **Lecture/Discussion Topic:** *Using Case Studies to Teach Psychological Disorders* (p. 4) or **Student Project:** *Diagnosing a "Star"* (p. 4) from Bolt's Teacher's Resource Binder, which accompanies this text.

560

Suggested Readings

Chesler, P. (1972, 1989). *Women and madness.* San Diego: Harcourt Brace Jovanovich.

Jamison, K. R. (1995). *An unquiet mind.* New York: Knopf.

Johnson, A. B. (1990). *Out of Bedlam: The truth about deinstitutionalization.* New York: Basic Books.

Seligman, M. (1990). *Learned optimism.* New York: Knopf.

Spanos, N. P. (2001). *Multiple identities and false memories: A socio-cognitive perspective.* Washington, D.C.: APA Books.

Summers, M., & Hollander, E. (2000). *Everything in its place: My trials and triumphs over obsessive compulsive disorder.* New York: J. P. Tarcher.

Szasz, T. S. (1994). *Cruel compassion: Psychiatric control of society's unwanted.* New York: Wiley.

Wedding, D., & Boyd, M. A. (1999). *Movies and mental illness.* New York: McGraw-Hill.

Abnormal Psychology

I felt the need to clean my room at home in Indianapolis every Sunday and would spend four to five hours at it. I would take every book out of the bookcase, dust and put it back. At the time I loved doing it. Then I didn't want to do it anymore, but I couldn't stop. The clothes in my closet hung exactly two fingers apart. . . . I made a ritual of touching the wall in my bedroom before I went out because something bad would happen if I didn't do it the right way. I had a constant anxiety about it as a kid, and it made me think for the first time that I might be nuts.

Marc, diagnosed with obsessive-compulsive disorder
(from Summers, 1996)

Whenever I get depressed it's because I've lost a sense of self. I can't find reasons to like myself. I think I'm ugly. I think no one likes me. . . . I become grumpy and short-tempered. Nobody wants to be around me. I'm left alone. Being alone confirms that I am ugly and not worth being with. I think I'm responsible for everything that goes wrong.

Greta, diagnosed with depression
(from Thorne, 1993, p. 21)

Voices, like the roar of a crowd, came. I felt like Jesus; I was being crucified. It was dark. . . . I just continued to huddle under the blanket, feeling weak, laid bare and defenseless in a cruel world I could no longer understand.

Stuart, diagnosed with schizophrenia
(from Emmons et al., 1997)

People are fascinated by the exceptional, the unusual, the abnormal. "The sun shines and warms and lights us and we have no curiosity to know why this is so," observed Ralph Waldo Emerson, "but we ask the reason of all evil, of pain, and hunger, and [unusual] people." But why such fascination with disturbed people? Do we see in them something of ourselves? At various moments, all of us feel, think, or act the way disturbed people do much of the time. We, too, get anxious, depressed, withdrawn, suspicious, or deluded, just less intensely and more briefly. It's no wonder that studying psychological disorders may at times evoke an eerie sense of self-recognition, one that illuminates the dynamics of our own personality. "To study the abnormal is the best way of understanding the normal," proposed William James (1842–1910).

Another reason for our curiosity is that so many of us have felt, either personally or through friends or family, the bewilderment and pain of a psychological disorder that may bring unexplained physical symptoms, irrational fears, or a feeling that life is not worth living. Indeed, as members of the human family, most of us will at some point encounter a psychologically disturbed person.

The World Health Organization (WHO, 2008) reports that, worldwide, some 450 million people suffer from mental or behavioral disorders. These disorders account for 15.4 percent of the years of life lost due to death or disability—scoring slightly below

561

Key People

Christopher Peterson
Philippe Pinel
David Rosenhan
Martin Seligman

Key Terms

Perspectives on Psychological Disorders

psychological disorder
attention-deficit hyperactivity disorder (ADHD)
medical model
DSM-IV-TR

Anxiety Disorders

anxiety disorders
generalized anxiety disorder
panic disorder
phobia
obsessive-compulsive disorder (OCD)
post-traumatic stress disorder (PTSD)
post-traumatic growth

Somatoform Disorders

somatoform disorders
conversion disorder
hypochondriasis

Dissociative Disorders

dissociative disorders
dissociative identity disorder (DID)

Mood Disorders

mood disorders
major depressive disorder
mania
bipolar disorder

Schizophrenia

schizophrenia
delusions

Personality Disorders

personality disorders
antisocial personality disorder

UNIT 12

CULTURAL CONNECTIONS

Some cultures have very different social practices that may be considered abnormal to people in U.S. culture:

- Hissing is a polite way to show respect for superiors in Japan.

- Among the Karaki of New Guinea, a man is considered abnormal if he has not engaged in homosexual behavior before marriage.

- Public displays of affection between men and women in Thailand are unacceptable. Interestingly, however, men holding hands is considered a sign of friendship. Additionally, the use of straws is considered vulgar.

RESEARCH

Have students investigate the behavior of people throughout history that might be considered abnormal according to today's standards of behavior:

- What health practices were popular among people in earlier times? (*Consider the use of leeches to rid patients of "bad blood," as well as a practice by ancient cultures of cutting a hole in the skull to release evil spirits that "caused" migraines or epilepsy.*)

- What social practices were popular in earlier times? (*Consider that bundling was a common practice in Colonial America when a young man came to visit his girlfriend's home and had to stay overnight. The mother would sew the suitor into the bed, making it difficult for him to take advantage of her daughter.*)

cardiovascular conditions and slightly above cancer (Murray & Lopez, 1996). Rates and symptoms of psychological disorders vary by culture, but no known society is free of two terrible maladies: depression and schizophrenia (Baumeister & Härter, 2007; Draguns, 1990a,b, 1997). Before we examine disorders in depth, however, let's consider some more basic questions.

Perspectives on Psychological Disorders

MOST PEOPLE WOULD AGREE THAT someone who is too depressed to get out of bed for weeks at a time has a psychological disorder. But what about those who, having experienced a loss, are unable to resume their usual social activities? Where should we draw the line between sadness and depression? Between zany creativity and bizarre irrationality? Between normality and abnormality? Let's start with these questions:

- How should we *define* psychological disorders?
- How should we *understand* disorders—as sicknesses that need to be diagnosed and cured, or as natural responses to a troubling environment?
- How should we *classify* psychological disorders? And can we do so in a way that allows us to help people without stigmatizing them with *labels?*

> "Who in the rainbow can draw the line where the violet tint ends and the orange tint begins? Distinctly we see the difference of the colors, but where exactly does the one first blendingly enter into the other? So with sanity and insanity."
>
> Herman Melville, *Billy Budd, Sailor,* 1924

Defining Psychological Disorders

1: How should we draw the line between normality and disorder?

Mental health workers view **psychological disorders** as patterns of thoughts, feelings, or behaviors that are deviant, distressful, and dysfunctional (Comer, 2004).

Being different (*deviant*) from most other people in one's culture is *part* of what it takes to define a psychological disorder. As the reclusive poet Emily Dickinson observed in 1862,

Assent—and you are sane—
Demur—you're straightaway dangerous—
and handled with a Chain.

Standards for deviant behavior vary by context and by culture. In one context—wartime—mass killing may be viewed as normal and even heroic. In some contexts, people are presumed deranged when they hear voices. But in cultures practicing ancestor worship, people may claim to talk with the dead and not be seen as disordered because other people find them rational (Friedrich, 1987).

Standards for deviance also vary with time. From 1952 through December 9, 1973, homosexuality was classified as an illness. By day's end on December 10, it was not. The American Psychiatric Association had dropped homosexuality as a disorder because more and more of its members no longer viewed it as a psychological problem. (Later research has revealed that the stigma and stresses associated with being homosexual do, however, increase the risk of mental health problems [Meyer, 2003].) In this new century, controversy swirls over the frequent diagnosing of children with *attention-deficit hyperactivity disorder* (see Thinking Critically About: ADHD—Normal High Energy or Genuine Disorder?).

Culture and normality Men of the West African Wodaabe tribe put on elaborate makeup and costumes to attract women. In Western society, the same behavior would break behavioral norms and might be judged abnormal.

Carol Beckwith

CRITICAL THINKING ?

Have students consider that statistically speaking, any behavior is atypical if it is not exhibited by 68 percent of the people in a particular group or culture. What common behaviors would be considered abnormal if we followed this definition of abnormality? Who would suffer discrimination if this standard were enforced?

- What religious practices would be considered abnormal for your community?
- What ways of life would be abnormal? Single-parent households? Two-parent households?
- What ethnic groups would be considered abnormal?
- What styles of dress? What music preferences? What post–high school choices?

ADHD—Normal High Energy or Genuine Disorder?

Eight-year-old Todd has always been energetic. At home, he chatters away and darts from one activity to the next, rarely settling down to read a book or focus on a game. At play, he is reckless and overreacts when playmates bump into him or take one of his toys. At school, his exasperated teacher complains that fidgety Todd doesn't listen, follow instructions, or stay in his seat and do his lessons.

If taken for a psychological evaluation, Todd may be diagnosed with **attention-deficit hyperactivity disorder (ADHD),** as are some 4 percent of children who display at least one of its key symptoms (extreme inattention, hyperactivity, and impulsivity) (NIMH, 2003).

To skeptics, being distractible, fidgety, and impulsive sounds like a "disorder" caused by a single genetic variation: a Y chromosome. And sure enough, ADHD is diagnosed two to three times more often in boys than in girls. Does energetic child + boring school = ADHD overdiagnosis? Is the label being applied to healthy schoolchildren who, in more natural outdoor environments, would seem perfectly normal?

Skeptics think so. In the decade after 1987, they note, the proportion of American children being treated for ADHD nearly quadrupled (Olfson et al., 2003). By 2005, a Gallup survey showed that 10 percent of American 13- to 17-year-olds were being medicated for ADHD (Mason, 2005). How commonplace the diagnosis is depends in part on teacher referrals. Some teachers refer lots of kids for ADHD assessment, others none. ADHD rates have varied by a factor of 10 in different counties of New York State (Carlson, 2000).

On the other side of the debate are those who argue that the more frequent diagnoses of ADHD today reflect increased awareness of the disorder, especially in those areas where rates are highest. They acknowledge that diagnoses can be subjective and sometimes inconsistent—ADHD is not as objectively defined as is a broken arm. Nevertheless, declared the World Federation for Mental Health (2005), "there is strong agreement among the international scientific community that ADHD is a real neurobiological disorder whose existence should no longer be debated." In neuroimaging studies, ADHD has associations with certain brain activity patterns, notes a consensus statement by 75 researchers (Barkley et al., 2002).

What, then, is known about ADHD's causes? It is not caused by too much sugar or poor schools. (Researchers have found, however, that toddlers who watch lots of TV are, at age 7, more likely than average to display ADHD symptoms [Christakis et al., 2004].) It often coexists with a learning disorder or with defiant and temper-prone behavior. The U.S. National Institute of Mental Health (1999, 2003) reports that ADHD is heritable, and research teams are sleuthing the culprit genes (Brookes et al., 2006). It is treatable with nonaddictive medications such as Ritalin and Adderall, which are stimulants but help calm hyperactivity and increase one's ability to sit and focus on a task. Psychological therapies, such as those focused on shaping behaviors in the classroom and at home, have also helped address the distress of ADHD.

New research is seeking not only more information on causes but also a more objective assessment of ADHD. Possibilities include a physical measure of fidgeting, an eye-tracking device that gauges ability to focus on and follow spots of light, and more detailed brain imaging (Ashtari et al., 2004; Pavlidis, 2005; Teicher, 2002).

Other research is targeting effects of long-term use of stimulant drugs. About 80 percent of children medicated for ADHD still require medication as teens, as do 50 percent or more as adults. People appear to tolerate long-term use with no increased risk of substance abuse (Biederman et al., 1999). However, one major long-term study found that medication benefits had disappeared after three years (Jensen et al., 2007). A possible explanation comes from another recent study that used brain imaging to observe the development of children diagnosed with ADHD (Shaw et al., 2007). Compared with their peers, these children's brain maturation was normal but lagged by about three years, with delayed thinning, or pruning, of the frontal cerebral cortex. Thus, many fidgety, hyperactive 5-year-olds mature into normal teens.

The bottom line: Extreme inattention, hyperactivity, and impulsivity can derail social, academic, and vocational achievements, and these symptoms can be treated with medication and other treatment. But the debate continues over whether normal rambunctiousness is too often diagnosed as a psychiatric disorder, and whether there is a cost to the long-term use of stimulant drugs in treating ADHD.

But there is more to a disorder than being deviant. Olympic gold medalists deviate from the norm in their physical abilities, and society honors them. To be considered disordered, deviant behavior usually causes the person *distress*. Marc, Greta, and Stuart were all clearly distressed by their behaviors.

Deviant and distressful behaviors are more likely to be considered disordered when also judged to be a *harmful dysfunction* (Wakefield, 1992, 2006). Marc's distracting obsessive behaviors, for example, interfered with his work and leisure. By this measuring stick, even typical behaviors, such as the occasional despondency many students feel, may signal a psychological disorder *if* they become disabling. Dysfunction is key to defining a disorder: An intense fear of spiders may be deviant, but if it doesn't impair your life it is not a disorder.

::**psychological disorder** deviant, distressful, and dysfunctional patterns of thoughts, feelings, or behaviors.

::**attention-deficit hyperactivity disorder (ADHD)** a psychological disorder marked by the appearance by age 7 of one or more of three key symptoms: extreme inattention, hyperactivity, and impulsivity.

CRITICAL THINKING

Respect for diversity sounds like a wonderful ideal, but how should we react when it clashes with some deeply held value, such as gender equality? Consider the following issues:

- Should the U.S. government be accepting of brutality such as genital mutilation of women that is common in certain African countries?

- Female U.S. military personnel in Saudi Arabia have fought against regulations that require them to wear a veil outside their bases. Should these personnel be forced to follow Saudi law or U.S. customs?

- Should we object to the law in Saudi Arabia that forbids women to drive?

- In Sudan, a woman may not leave the country without the permission of her husband, father, or brother. Should we object to such a practice?

- What are the limits of tolerance? What types of cultural practices should we accept from other cultures and to what should we object?

TEACHING TIP

Some of your students may be identified as having Attention-Deficit Hyperactivity Disorder (ADHD). Point out to students that the *DSM* criteria do not include a diagnosis of Attention-Deficit Disorder (ADD), only ADHD. If students are willing, encourage them to share how they process information and external stimuli.

TEACHING TIP

Have students brainstorm about behaviors that, when taken out of context, could be considered abnormal. Some ideas to get them started might include the following:

- Having a heated argument with someone
- Praying aloud or chanting outside of a religious service
- Dancing in excitement over getting a good grade or hearing good news

At this time you may want to use **Classroom Exercises**: *Introducing Psychological Disorders* (p. 5) or *Defining Psychological Disorder* (p. 5) or **Student Project**: *Encounters with a "Mentally Ill" Person* (p. 6) from Bolt's Teacher's Resource Binder.

Philippe Pinel, once the personal physician to Napoleon, devoted his life to helping the mentally ill when he directed the Paris men's asylum. Some patients there had been chained to the walls for decades. During his tenure, death rates for patients went from 60 percent to 10 percent.

Have students research the treatment of the mentally ill throughout history. Use these ideas as a research starting point:

- When and where was the first hospital for the mentally ill opened? (*The Society of Friends [Quakers] opened the first private institution in 1813. The oldest government-run mental institution is St. Elizabeth's in Washington, D.C.*)

- What qualified a person to be committed in earlier times? (*People could be committed for any reason. Men could have their wives committed if they wanted a divorce, and girls who became pregnant out of wedlock were sometimes also institutionalized.*)

Dorothea Dix began her crusade for humane treatment of mentally ill patients when she began tutoring inmates at a women's prison. Men and women who were mentally ill or disabled were being housed with hardened female criminals. Dix took her reforms to all existing states and to Europe.

Yesterday's "therapy" In other times and places, psychologically disordered people sometimes received brutal treatments, including the trephination evident in this Stone Age skull. Drilling skull holes like these may have been an attempt to release evil spirits and cure those with mental disorders. Did this patient survive the "cure"?

"Moral treatment" Under Philippe Pinel's influence, hospitals sometimes sponsored patient dances, such as the "Lunatic Ball" depicted in this painting by George Bellows (*Dance in a Madhouse*).

> "It's no measure of health to be well adjusted to a profoundly sick society."
> Krishnamurti, 1895–1986

• In Malaysia, *amok* describes a sudden outburst of violent behavior (thus the phrase "run amok"). •

Understanding Psychological Disorders

2: What perspectives can help us understand psychological disorders?

To explain puzzling behavior, people in earlier times often presumed that strange forces—the movements of the stars, godlike powers, or evil spirits—were at work. Had you lived during the Middle Ages, you might have said "The devil made him do it," and you might have approved of a cure to rid the evil force by exorcising the demon. Until the last two centuries, "mad" people were sometimes caged in zoolike conditions or given "therapies" appropriate to a demon: beatings, burning, or castration. In other times, therapy included trephination (drilling holes in the skull), pulling teeth, removing lengths of intestines, cauterizing the clitoris, or giving transfusions of animal blood (Farina, 1982).

The Medical Model

In opposition to brutal treatments, reformers, including Philippe Pinel (1745–1826) in France, insisted that madness is not demon possession but a sickness of the mind caused by severe stresses and inhumane conditions. For Pinel and others, "moral treatment" included boosting patients' morale by unchaining them and talking with them, and by replacing brutality with gentleness, isolation with activity, and filth with clean air and sunshine.

By the 1800s, the discovery that syphilis infects the brain and distorts the mind provided the impetus for further reform. Hospitals replaced asylums, and the medical world began searching for physical causes of mental disorders, and for treatments that would cure them. Today, this **medical model** is recognizable in the terminology of the mental *health* movement: A mental *illness* (also called a psychopathology) needs to be *diagnosed* on the basis of its *symptoms* and *cured* through *therapy*, which may include *treatment* in a psychiatric *hospital*.

George Wesley Bellows, *Dance in a Madhouse*, 1907. © 1997 The Art Institute of Chicago

The medical perspective has gained credibility from recent discoveries that genetically influenced abnormalities in brain structure and biochemistry contribute to many disorders. But as we will see, psychological factors, such as enduring or traumatic stress, also play an important role.

The Biopsychosocial Approach

Today's psychologists contend that *all* behavior, whether called normal or disordered, arises from the interaction of nature (genetic and physiological factors) and nurture (past and present experiences). To presume that a person is "mentally ill," they say, attributes the condition to a "sickness" that must be found and cured. But instead or additionally, there may be a difficulty in the person's environment, in the person's current interpretations of events, or in the person's bad habits and poor social skills.

Evidence of such effects comes from links between specific disorders and cultures (Beardsley, 1994; Castillo, 1997). Cultures differ in their sources of stress, and they produce different ways of coping. The eating disorders anorexia nervosa and bulimia nervosa, for example, occur mostly in Western cultures. Latin America lays claim to *susto*, a condition marked by severe anxiety, restlessness, and a fear of black magic.

At this point, you may want to use **Student Projects/Classroom Exercises: *Adult ADHD Screening Test*** (p. 6) or ***Normality and the Sexes*** (p. 7) from Bolt's Teacher's Resource Binder.

Taijin-kyofusho, social anxiety about one's appearance combined with a readiness to blush and a fear of eye contact, appears in Japan. Such disorders may share an underlying dynamic (such as anxiety) while differing in the symptoms (an eating problem or a type of fear) manifested in a particular culture. But not all disorders are culture-bound. As noted earlier, depression and schizophrenia occur worldwide. From Asia to Africa and across the Americas, schizophrenia's symptoms often include irrationality and incoherent speech.

To assess the whole set of influences—genetic predispositions and physiological states; inner psychological dynamics; and social and cultural circumstances—the biopsychosocial model helps (**FIGURE 12.1**). This approach recognizes that mind and body are inseparable. Negative emotions contribute to physical illness, and physical abnormalities contribute to negative emotions. We are mind embodied.

Classifying Psychological Disorders

3: How and why do clinicians classify psychological disorders?

In biology and the other sciences, classification creates order. To classify an animal as a "mammal" says a great deal—that it is warm-blooded, has hair or fur, and nourishes its young with milk. In psychiatry and psychology, too, classification orders and describes symptoms. To classify a person's disorder as "schizophrenia" suggests that the person talks incoherently; hallucinates or has delusions (bizarre beliefs); shows either little emotion or inappropriate emotion; or is socially withdrawn. "Schizophrenia" provides a handy shorthand for describing a complex disorder.

In psychiatry and psychology, diagnostic classification aims not only to describe a disorder but also to predict its future course, imply appropriate treatment, and stimulate research into its causes. Indeed, to study a disorder we must first name and describe it. A current authoritative scheme for classifying psychological disorders is the **DSM-IV-TR**. This volume is the American Psychiatric Association's *Diagnostic and Statistical Manual of Mental Disorders,* Fourth Edition, updated as a 2000 "text revision"; a more substantially revised DSM-V will appear in 2012. (A set of case illustrations accompanying the DSM-IV-TR provides several of this book's examples.) The DSM-IV-TR was developed in coordination with the tenth edition of the World Health Organization's *International Classification of Diseases* (ICD-10), which covers both medical and psychological disorders.

Despite its medical terminology (*diagnosing, symptoms, illness*), most practitioners find the DSM-IV-TR a helpful and practical tool. It is also financially necessary: North American health insurance companies usually require an ICD diagnosis before they pay for therapy.

The DSM-IV-TR defines a diagnostic process and 16 clinical syndromes (**TABLE 12.1** on the next page). Without presuming to explain their causes, it describes various disorders including *psychotic disorders,* in which a person loses contact with reality and experiences irrational ideas and distorted perceptions. To be helpful and useful, these categories and diagnostic guidelines must be reliable, and to a reasonable extent they are. If one psychiatrist or psychologist diagnoses someone as having, say, catatonic schizophrenia, the chances are good that another mental health worker will independently give the same diagnosis. Following these guidelines, clinicians answer a series of objective questions about observable behaviors, such as, "Is the person afraid to leave home?" In one study, 16 psychologists used this structured-interview procedure to

> **FIGURE 12.1**
The biopsychosocial approach to psychological disorders Today's psychology studies how biological, psychological, and social-cultural factors interact to produce specific psychological disorders.

"I'm always like this, and my family was wondering if you could prescribe a mild depressant."

::**medical model** the concept that diseases, in this case psychological disorders, have physical causes that can be *diagnosed, treated,* and, in most cases, *cured,* often through treatment in a *hospital.*

::**DSM-IV-TR** the American Psychiatric Association's *Diagnostic and Statistical Manual of Mental Disorders,* Fourth Edition, updated as a 2000 "text revision"; a widely used system for classifying psychological disorders.

TEACHING TIP

It is important for students to know the five "Axis" diagnostic criteria used in the *DSM*. These criteria help doctors determine not only the type of mental illness a person has, but also some contributing factors that probably need to be dealt with in order to get the primary mental illness symptoms under control.

TEACHING TIP

The *DSM* diagnostic criteria are important not only for doctors deciding what type of mental illness a person might have, but also for health care for the mentally ill in general. Insurance companies require that mental illness diagnoses reference the *DSM* system in order to pay for services to treat the disorder. The use of the *DSM* by insurance providers makes any changes to the *DSM* very important.

TABLE 12.1

HOW ARE PSYCHOLOGICAL DISORDERS DIAGNOSED?

Based on assessments, interviews, and observations, many clinicians diagnose by answering the following questions from the five levels, or *axes*, of the DSM-IV-TR. (Unit numbers in parentheses locate the topics in this text.)

Axis I Is a *Clinical Syndrome* present?

Using specifically defined criteria, clinicians may select none, one, or more syndromes from the following list:

- Disorders usually first diagnosed in infancy, childhood, and adolescence
- Delirium, dementia, amnesia, and other cognitive disorders (Unit 9)
- Mental disorders due to a general medical condition (formerly referred to as *organic disorders*)
- Substance-related disorders (Unit 5)
- Schizophrenia and other psychotic disorders (this unit)
- Mood disorders (this unit)
- Anxiety disorders (this unit)
- Somatoform disorders (this unit)
- Factitious disorders (intentionally faked)
- Dissociative disorders (this unit)
- Eating disorders (Unit 8A)
- Sexual disorders and gender identity disorder
- Sleep disorders (Unit 5)
- Impulse-control disorders not classified elsewhere
- Adjustment disorders
- Other conditions that may be a focus of clinical attention

Axis II Is a *Personality Disorder* or *Mental Retardation* present?
Clinicians may or may not also select one of these two conditions.

Axis III Is a *General Medical Condition,* such as diabetes, hypertension, or arthritis, also present?

Axis IV Are *Psychosocial* or *Environmental Problems,* such as school or housing issues, also present?

Axis V What is the *Global Assessment* of this person's functioning?
Clinicians assign a code from 0–100.

---

diagnose 75 psychiatric patients as suffering from (1) depression, (2) generalized anxiety, or (3) some other disorder (Riskind et al., 1987). Without knowing the first psychologist's diagnosis, another psychologist viewed a videotape of each interview and offered a second opinion. For 83 percent of the patients, the two opinions agreed.

Some critics have faulted the manual for casting too wide a net and bringing "almost any kind of behavior within the compass of psychiatry" (Eysenck et al., 1983). Others note that as the number of disorder categories has swelled (from 60 in the 1950s' DSM to 400 in today's), so has the number of adults who meet the criteria for at least one of them—26 percent in any year, according to the U.S. National Institute of Mental Health (2008), and 46 percent at some time in their lives (Kessler et al., 2005). The number of children diagnosed with psychological disorders has also mushroomed, tripling to 6 million children since the early 1990s, according to some reports (Carey, 2006). Today's adolescent mood swings are more often taken to be "bipolar disorder." Temper tantrums, arguing, touchiness, and spitefulness are more often taken to be "oppositional defiant disorder." Inattentive, impulsive, fidgety children are more often taken to have ADHD. As a complement to the DSM, some psychologists are offering a manual of human strengths and virtues (see Close-Up: The "un-DSM"—A Diagnostic Manual of Human Strengths).

CRITICAL THINKING

Have students consider the following as they learn about the strengths and virtues classified by the "un-DSM":

- What would be some ways researchers could validate that these strengths are universally held?

- Are people born with these strengths and virtues, or can these be developed?

- Some of these strengths are not demonstrated unless a crisis situation occurs (e.g., courage). How can a person know if he/she has this strength if the situation has not occurred that would lead to demonstrating it?

- Are some of the strengths and virtues more desirable then others? Why or why not?

The "un-DSM"—A Diagnostic Manual of Human Strengths

Psychologists Christopher Peterson and Martin Seligman (2004) have noted the usefulness of the DSM-IV-TR in ordering and defining dysfunctions. Would it not also be useful, these researchers ask, to have a companion catalog of human strengths—the thinking-feeling-action tendencies that contribute to the *good* life, for self and others?

The result, *The Values in Action Classification of Strengths*, resembles the DSM-IV-TR in proposing a research-based common vocabulary. A questionnaire, which has been taken by some 1 million people worldwide (at www.viastrengths.org), assesses six clusters of 24 strengths:

- *Wisdom and knowledge*—curiosity; love of learning; critical judgment and open-mindedness; creativity; and perspective (wisdom)

- *Courage (overcoming opposition)*—bravery/valor; industry and perseverance; integrity and honesty; and vitality (zest and enthusiasm)

- *Humanity*—love; kindness; and social intelligence

- *Justice*—citizenship and teamwork; fairness and equity; and leadership

- *Temperance*—humility; self-control; prudence and caution; and forgiveness and mercy

- *Transcendence*—appreciation of beauty, awe/wonder; gratitude; hope and optimism; playfulness and humor; and spirituality and purpose

Building strengths by rebuilding bikes This volunteer-run bicycle shop was established in New Orleans to repair the bikes that survived Hurricane Katrina. The teens working here are modeling strengths related to humanity and justice.

This classification of human strengths is another expression of the *positive psychology movement* (Unit 10). Psychological science seeks to understand and help alleviate human ills and evils, agree positive psychology advocates, but also to understand and promote human strengths and virtues.

Labeling Psychological Disorders

4: Why do some psychologists criticize the use of diagnostic labels?

The DSM has other critics who register a more fundamental complaint—that these labels are at best arbitrary and at worst value judgments masquerading as science. Once we label a person, we view that person differently (Farina, 1982). Labels create preconceptions that guide our perceptions and our interpretations.

In a now-classic study of the biasing power of labels, David Rosenhan (1973) and seven others went to hospital admissions offices, complaining of "hearing voices" saying *empty, hollow,* and *thud*. Apart from this complaint and giving false names and occupations, they answered questions truthfully. All eight normal people were misdiagnosed with disorders.

Should we be surprised? As one psychiatrist noted, if someone swallows blood, goes to an emergency room, and spits it up, should we fault the doctor for diagnosing a bleeding ulcer? Surely not. But what followed the diagnosis in the Rosenhan study was startling. Until being released an average of 19 days later, the "patients" exhibited no further symptoms. Yet after analyzing their (quite normal) life histories, clinicians were able to "discover" the causes of their disorders, such as reacting with mixed emotions about a parent. Even the routine behavior of taking notes was misinterpreted as a symptom.

> "One of the unpardonable sins, in the eyes of most people, is for a man to go about unlabeled. The world regards such a person as the police do an unmuzzled dog, not under proper control."
>
> T. H. Huxley, *Evolution and Ethics*, 1893

CRITICAL THINKING

Ask students whether psychological well-being simply refers to the absence of disorder. Are people mentally sound if they do not suffer from anxiety, depression, or other forms of psychological symptomology? What characteristics mark psychological well-being? Carol D. Ryff is one of many psychologists who argues that we must define mental health in terms of the positive. She identifies the following six core dimensions of well-being:

- *Self-acceptance.* A person not only has a positive attitude toward the self but accepts multiple aspects of the self—good and bad, past, present, and future.

- *Positive relations with other people.* Healthy people have warm, satisfying, and trusting interpersonal relationships.

- *Autonomy.* The person is independent, self-determining, and self-controlled.

- *Environmental mastery.* The healthy are able to choose or create contexts that are supportive of personal needs or values.

- *Purpose in life.* The person has both goals and a sense of directedness.

- *Personal growth.* Healthy people see themselves as growing and expanding.

Ryff, C. D. (1995). Psychological well-being in adult life. *Current Directions in Psychological Science, 4,* 99–103.

TEACHING TIP

At this point, you may want to use **Lecture/Discussion Topics:** *Tourette Syndrome* (p. 7) or *Culture-Bound Disorders* (p. 8) or **Classroom Exercise:** *Multiple Causation* (p. 8) from Bolt's Teacher's Resource Binder.

UNIT 12

CRITICAL THINKING

Ask students which of the following they feel is less stigmatizing:

- Calling someone a "schizophrenic"?
- Calling someone a "person with schizophrenia"?

Help students see that the first label doesn't recognize the person at all and implies that the person is the condition. The second label acknowledges the person and places the mental illness in the same categories as other, less stigmatizing labels.

CRITICAL THINKING

How might the issue of labeling affect teachers? Studies show that labeling of students can bias a teacher's treatment of a particular student. However, knowing a student's diagnosis can help a teacher get that student the help he or she needs to succeed. How can a balance be reached? Have students brainstorm about ways teachers can be aware of labels but sensitive to the limitations labels can place on students:

- What type of training should teachers go through to help them be more sensitive to the power of labels?
- Should teachers and students be informed of their labels? Why or why not?
- How can teachers and students be proactive about learning disabilities?

> "What's the use of their having names," the Gnat said, "if they won't answer to them?"
> "No use to *them*," said Alice; "but it's useful to the people that name them, I suppose."
>
> Lewis Carroll,
> *Through the Looking-Glass*, 1871

::**anxiety disorders** psychological disorders characterized by distressing, persistent anxiety or maladaptive behaviors that reduce anxiety.

Labels matter. When people watched videotaped interviews, those told the interviewees were job applicants perceived them as normal (Langer et al., 1974, 1980). Those who thought they were watching psychiatric or cancer patients perceived them as "different from most people." Therapists who thought an interviewee was a psychiatric patient perceived him as "frightened of his own aggressive impulses," a "passive, dependent type," and so forth. A label can, as Rosenhan discovered, have "a life and an influence of its own."

Surveys in Europe and North America have demonstrated the stigmatizing power of labels (Page, 1977). Getting a job or finding a place to rent can be a challenge for those known to be just released from prison—or a mental hospital. But as we are coming to understand that many psychological disorders are diseases of the brain, not failures of character, the stigma seems to be lifting (Solomon, 1996). Public figures are feeling freer to "come out" and speak with candor about their struggles with disorders such as depression. And the more contact people have with individuals with disorders, the more accepting their attitudes are (Kolodziej & Johnson, 1996).

Nevertheless, stereotypes linger in media portrayals of psychological disorders. Some are reasonably accurate and sympathetic. But too often people with disorders are portrayed as objects of humor or ridicule (*As Good as It Gets*), as homicidal maniacs (Hannibal Lecter in *Silence of the Lambs*), or as freaks (Nairn, 2007). Apart from the few who experience threatening delusions and hallucinated voices that command a violent act, mental disorders seldom lead to violence (Harris & Lurigio, 2007). In real life, people with disorders are more likely to be victims than perpetrators of violence (Marley & Bulia, 2001). Indeed, reports the U.S. Surgeon General's Office (1999, p. 7), "There is very little risk of violence or harm to a stranger from casual contact with an individual who has a mental disorder." (Although most people with psychological disorders are not violent, those who are create a moral dilemma for society. For more on this topic, see Thinking Critically About: Insanity and Responsibility.)

Not only can labels bias perceptions, they can also change reality. When teachers are told certain students are "gifted," when students expect someone to be "hostile," or when interviewers check to see whether someone is "extraverted," they may act in ways that elicit the very behavior expected (Snyder, 1984). Someone who was led to think you are nasty may treat you coldly, leading you to respond as a mean-spirited person would. Labels can serve as *self-fulfilling prophecies*.

But let us remember the *benefits* of diagnostic labels. Mental health professionals use labels to communicate about their cases, to comprehend the underlying causes, and to discern effective treatment programs.

BEFORE YOU MOVE ON . . .

> **ASK YOURSELF**

How would you draw the line between sending disturbed criminals to prisons or to mental hospitals? Would the person's history (for example, having suffered child abuse) influence your decisions?

> **TEST YOURSELF 1**

What is the biopsychosocial perspective, and why is it important in our understanding of psychological disorders?

Answers to the Test Yourself questions can be found in Appendix E at the end of the book.

DEMO

Have students watch episodes of popular television shows that depict people with mental illness.

- Have them compare the portrayal with the *DSM-IV-TR* diagnostic criteria to see if they match.
- Students can also evaluate whether they think the portrayal promotes sensitivity or further stigma toward the particular mental illness.

Insanity and Responsibility

"My brain . . . my genes . . . my bad upbringing made me do it." Such defenses were anticipated by Shakespeare's *Hamlet*. If I wrong someone when not myself, he explained, "then Hamlet does it not, Hamlet denies it. Who does it then? His madness." Such is the essence of a legal insanity defense, created in 1843 after a deluded Scotsman tried to shoot the prime minister (who he thought was persecuting him) but killed an assistant by mistake. Like U.S. President Ronald Reagan's near-assassin, John Hinckley, Scotsman Daniel M'Naughten was sent to a mental hospital rather than to prison.

In both cases, the public was outraged. "Hinckley Insane, Public Mad," declared one headline. And they were mad again when a deranged Jeffrey Dahmer in 1991 admitted murdering 15 young men and eating parts of their bodies. They were mad in 1998 when 15-year-old Kip Kinkel, driven by "those voices in my head," killed his parents and 2 fellow Springfield, Oregon, students and wounded 25 others. And they were mad in 2002 when Andrea Yates, after being taken off her antipsychotic medication, was tried in Texas for drowning her five children. All of these people were sent to jails, not hospitals, following their arrests (though later, after another trial, Yates was instead hospitalized).

Most people with psychological disorders are not violent. But what should society do with those who are? A 1999 U.S. Justice Department study found that about 16 percent of U.S. jail and prison inmates had severe mental disorders. This is roughly 100,000 more than the 183,000 psychiatric inpatients in all types of U.S. hospitals (Bureau of the Census, 2004; Butterfield, 1999). Many people who have been executed or are now on death row have been limited by intellectual disability or motivated by delusional voices. The State of Arkansas forcibly medicated one murderer with schizophrenia, Charles Singleton, with antipsychotic drugs—in order to make him mentally competent, so that he could then be put to death.

Jail or hospital? Two weeks after being taken off antipsychotic medication by her psychiatrist, Andrea Yates drowned her five children, ages 7, 5, 3, 2, and 6 months, in her bathtub, apparently believing she was sparing them "the fires of hell." Although she was psychotic, one jury rejected the insanity defense, believing Yates still could have discerned right from wrong. On retrial, a second jury found her not guilty by reason of insanity.

Which of Yates' two juries made the right decision? The first, which decided that people who commit such rare but terrible crimes should be held responsible? Or the second, which decided to blame the "madness" that clouds their vision? As we come to better understand the biological and environmental basis for all human behavior, from generosity to vandalism, when should we—and should we not—hold people accountable for their actions?

Anxiety Disorders

5: What are anxiety disorders, and how do they differ from ordinary worries and fears?

ANXIETY IS PART OF LIFE. Speaking in front of a class, looking out from a mountaintop, or waiting to play in a big game, any one of us might feel anxious. At times we may feel enough anxiety to avoid making eye contact or talking with someone—"shyness," we call it. Fortunately for most of us, our uneasiness is not intense and persistent. If it becomes so, we may have one of the **anxiety disorders,** marked by distressing, persistent anxiety or dysfunctional anxiety-reducing behaviors. Let's consider these five:

▼

Coping with anxiety "The only way I knew how to deal with it was to write a song about it," musician Billie Joe Armstrong of Green Day explained, referring to his song "Basket Case," which chronicles a personal struggle with anxiety disorders.

A landmark study conducted in 1962 by J. B. Calhoun demonstrated that high population density causes abnormal behavior in rat populations. Calhoun allowed rats to live in an overcrowded environment for 16 months. Some of the pathological behaviors he observed included the following:

- Aggression: There was increased fighting among male rats for dominance, and periodic senseless fighting with females, juveniles, and less active males.

- Submissiveness: Non-dominant male rats became unusually submissive and acted as though they were in a hypnotic trance.

- Sexual deviance: Non-dominant males would not follow normal rat "rules" for mating. This included following females into burrows and often eating the young found inside.

- Nesting abnormalities: The female rats would eventually fail to build nests, having their babies directly on the floor.

- High infant mortality: Rates ranged from 80–96 percent.

At this point, you may want to use **Classroom Exercise:** *The Effects of Labeling* (p. 9) or **Lecture/Discussion Topic:** *Mental Health as Flourishing* (p. 9) from Bolt's Teacher's Resource Binder.

UNIT 12

SNAPSHOTS

Obsessing about obsessive-compulsive disorder.

TEACHING TIP

Patients who have generalized anxiety disorder (GAD) often also have major depression, an illness discussed later in this unit. Effexor, a drug manufactured by Wyeth-Ayerst, has been shown to be effective in treating both GAD and major depression. Paxil, an antidepressant drug in the same class as Prozac and Zoloft, is a serotonin reuptake inhibitor and is also approved for use to treat GAD as well as social phobia and panic disorder.

TEACHING TIP

Agoraphobia, or the fear of being in open spaces or in public, often accompanies panic disorder. Since people experience panic attacks at uncontrollable times and in uncontrollable situations, they will often develop a fear of being out in public and having a panic attack. This fear leaves them suffering in their homes, afraid even to leave at all.

• Gender and anxiety: Eight months after 9/11, more U.S. women (34 percent) than men (19 percent) told Gallup (2002) they were still less willing than before 9/11 to go into skyscrapers or fly on planes. In early 2003, more women (57 percent) than men (36 percent) were "somewhat worried" about becoming a terrorist victim (Jones, 2003). •

::**generalized anxiety disorder** an anxiety disorder in which a person is continually tense, apprehensive, and in a state of autonomic nervous system arousal.

::**panic disorder** an anxiety disorder marked by unpredictable minutes-long episodes of intense dread in which a person experiences terror and accompanying chest pain, choking, or other frightening sensations.

::**phobia** an anxiety disorder marked by a persistent, irrational fear and avoidance of a specific object, activity, or situation.

::**obsessive-compulsive disorder (OCD)** an anxiety disorder characterized by unwanted repetitive thoughts (obsessions) and/or actions (compulsions).

- *Generalized anxiety disorder*, in which a person is unexplainably and continually tense and uneasy
- *Panic disorder*, in which a person experiences sudden episodes of intense dread
- *Phobias*, in which a person feels irrationally and intensely afraid of a specific object or situation
- *Obsessive-compulsive disorder*, in which a person is troubled by repetitive thoughts or actions
- *Post-traumatic stress disorder*, in which a person has lingering memories, nightmares, and other symptoms for weeks after a severely threatening, uncontrollable event

In its own way, each anxiety disorder harms quality of life (Olatunji et al., 2007). Our most anxious days are typically our unhappiest days (Kashdan & Steger, 2006). For people with generalized anxiety disorder, that adds up to a lot of unhappiness.

Generalized Anxiety Disorder

For the past two years, Tom, a 27-year-old electrician, has been bothered by dizziness, sweating palms, heart palpitations, and ringing in his ears. He feels edgy and sometimes finds himself shaking. With reasonable success, he hides his symptoms from his family and co-workers. But he allows himself few other social contacts, and occasionally he has to leave work. His family doctor and a neurologist can find no physical problem.

Tom's unfocused, out-of-control, negative feelings suggest **generalized anxiety disorder.** The symptoms of this disorder are commonplace; their persistence is not. People with this condition (two-thirds are women) worry continually, and they are often jittery, agitated, and sleep-deprived. Concentration is difficult, as attention switches from worry to worry, and their tension and apprehension may leak out through furrowed brows, twitching eyelids, trembling, perspiration, or fidgeting.

One of the worst characteristics of this disorder is that the person cannot identify, and therefore cannot deal with or avoid, its cause. To use Sigmund Freud's term, the anxiety is *free-floating*. Generalized anxiety disorder is often accompanied by depressed mood, but even without depression it tends to be disabling (Hunt et al., 2004; Moffitt et al., 2007b). Moreover, it may lead to physical problems, such as high blood pressure.

Many people with generalized anxiety disorder were maltreated and inhibited as children (Moffitt et al., 2007a). As time passes, however, emotions tend to mellow, and by age 50, generalized anxiety disorder becomes rare (Rubio & López-Ibor, 2007).

Panic Disorder

Panic disorder is an anxiety tornado. It strikes suddenly, wreaks havoc, and disappears. For the 1 person in 75 with this disorder, anxiety suddenly escalates into a terrifying *panic attack*—a minutes-long episode of intense fear that something horrible is about to happen. Heart palpitations, shortness of breath, choking sensations, trembling, or dizziness typically accompany the panic, which may be misperceived as a heart attack or other serious physical ailment. Smokers have at least a doubled risk of panic disorder (Zvolensky & Bernstein, 2005). Because nicotine is a stimulant, lighting up doesn't lighten up.

One woman recalled suddenly feeling "hot and as though I couldn't breathe. My heart was racing and I started to sweat and tremble and I was sure I was going to faint. Then my fingers started to feel numb and tingly and things seemed unreal. It was so bad I wondered if I was dying and asked my husband to take me to the emergency room. By the time we got there (about 10 minutes) the worst of the attack was over and I just felt washed out" (Greist et al., 1986).

TEACHING TIP

At this point, you may want to use **Classroom Exercises:** *Penn State Worry Questionnaire* (p. 10) or *Taylor Manifest Anxiety Scale* (p. 10) or *The Posttraumatic Cognitions Inventory (PTCI)* (p. 11) or **Lecture/Discussion Topic:** *Discovery Health Channel Phobia Study* (p. 11) or **Classroom Exercises:** *Fear Survey* (p. 12) or *Social Phobia* (p. 12) from Bolt's Teacher's Resource Binder.

Phobias

Phobias are anxiety disorders in which an irrational fear causes the person to avoid some object, activity, or situation. Many people accept their phobias and live with them, but others are incapacitated by their efforts to avoid the feared situation. Marilyn, an otherwise healthy and happy 28-year-old, so fears thunderstorms that she feels anxious as soon as a weather forecaster mentions possible storms later in the week. If her husband is away and a storm is forecast, she may stay with a close relative. During a storm, she hides from windows and buries her head to avoid seeing the lightning.

Other *specific phobias* may focus on animals, insects, heights, blood, or close spaces (**FIGURE 12.2**). People avoid the stimulus that arouses the fear, hiding during thunderstorms or avoiding high places.

Not all phobias have such specific triggers. *Social phobia* is shyness taken to an extreme. Those with a social phobia, an intense fear of being scrutinized by others, avoid potentially embarrassing social situations, such as speaking up, eating out, or going to parties—or will sweat, tremble, or have diarrhea when doing so.

People who have experienced several panic attacks may come to fear the fear itself and avoid situations where the panic has struck before. If the fear is intense enough, it may become *agoraphobia,* fear or avoidance of situations in which escape might be difficult or help unavailable when panic strikes. Given such fear, people may avoid being outside the home, in a crowd, on a bus, or on an elevator.

After spending five years sailing the world, Charles Darwin began suffering panic disorder at age 28. Because of the attacks, he moved to the country, avoided social gatherings, and traveled only in his wife's company. But the relative seclusion did free him to focus on developing his evolutionary theory. "Even ill health," he reflected, "has saved me from the distraction of society and its amusements" (quoted in Ma, 1997).

➤ FIGURE 12.2
Some common and uncommon specific fears This national interview study identified the commonality of various specific fears. A strong fear becomes a phobia if it provokes a compelling but irrational desire to avoid the dreaded object or situation. (From Curtis et al., 1998.)

Obsessive-Compulsive Disorder

As with generalized anxiety and phobias, we can see aspects of our own behavior in **obsessive-compulsive disorder (OCD).** We may at times be obsessed with senseless or offensive thoughts that will not go away. Or we may engage in compulsive behaviors, rigidly checking, ordering, and cleaning before guests arrive, or lining up books and pencils "just so" before studying.

Obsessive thoughts and compulsive behaviors cross the fine line between normality and disorder when they persistently interfere with everyday living and cause the person distress. Checking to see that you locked the door is normal; checking 10 times is not. Washing your hands is normal; washing so often that your skin becomes raw is not. (**TABLE 12.2** on the next page offers more examples.) At some time during their lives, often during their late teens or twenties, 2 to 3 percent of people cross that line from normal preoccupations and fussiness to debilitating disorder (Karno et al., 1988). The obsessive thoughts become so haunting, the compulsive rituals so senselessly time-consuming, that effective functioning becomes impossible.

OCD advocate Comedian and TV host Howie Mandel knows the reality of obsessive-compulsive disorder. He has used humor to deal with his own challenges and to help others understand the disorder. Mandel also suffers a germ phobia that prompted him to shave his head to "feel cleaner."

🛟 **TEACHING TIP**

Former Nickelodeon game show host Marc Summers suffers from obsessive-compulsive disorder. Students may remember him as the host of *Double Dare* and *Family Double Dare*, game shows that daily subjected him and contestants on the show to getting splattered with slime and goo. He often felt consumed by anxiety as he struggled to put on a cheerful face as the show's host. Currently, he hosts a nationally syndicated talk show and is the national spokesman for the Obsessive-Compulsive Foundation.

CRITICAL THINKING

Phobias are one of the most successfully treated disorders around, yet few people with phobias seek treatment for them. Have students contemplate why this might be:

- Why would people be reluctant to get treatment for their everyday fears? (*Everyday fears might not be crippling or disruptive. Also, people may successfully avoid their fear object, not seeing the need to rid themselves of the fear.*)

- What types of fears are more crippling than others? Why?

CULTURAL CONNECTIONS

Have students explore whether the things feared most by people in the U.S. are similar to those things that are feared in other countries.

- Do people in other cultures fear speaking in public as much as U.S. people seem to?

- Do fears differ among people of different socio-economic groups? Why or why not?

- Do people in countries who have experienced war have higher incidences of certain anxiety disorders? Which kinds?

WEB CONNECT

Have students explore the Internet to see how many different types of phobias they can find.

- What is the most obscure phobia they found?

- What was the most common phobia listed?

UNIT 12

TEACHING TIP

Compulsions manifest themselves in several different ways:

- Hoarders collect things and have a hard time throwing anything away because they are plagued by fears of losing something or needing something that they've thrown away. So, they keep everything, including leftover food, papers, and broken items.

- Checkers will recheck actions they have performed over again. For example, they fear they did not turn off the oven, so they will recheck a certain number of times before they feel better. The number of checks needed to relieve anxiety increases with each experience.

- Counters will count everything, from steps they take to words people say to them. They can become preoccupied with counting something seemingly unimportant to the point of stopping their daily progress.

- Cleaners will clean excessively. Often, this cleaning will need to be done a certain number of times in order to relieve the anxiety.

At this point, you may want to use **Lecture/Discussion Topic: *Obsessive Thoughts*** (p. 14) or **Classroom Exercise: *Obsessive-Compulsive Disorder*** (p. 13) from Bolt's Teacher's Resource Binder.

TABLE 12.2

COMMON OBSESSIONS AND COMPULSIONS AMONG CHILDREN AND ADOLESCENTS WITH OBSESSIVE-COMPULSIVE DISORDER

Thought or Behavior	Percentage Reporting Symptom
Obsessions *(repetitive thoughts)*	
Concern with dirt, germs, or toxins	40
Something terrible happening (fire, death, illness)	24
Symmetry, order, or exactness	17
Compulsions *(repetitive behaviors)*	
Excessive hand washing, bathing, tooth brushing, or grooming	85
Repeating rituals (in/out of a door, up/down from a chair)	51
Checking doors, locks, appliances, car brakes, homework	46

Source: Adapted from Rapoport, 1989.

OCD is more common among teens and young adults than among older people (Samuels & Nestadt, 1997). A 40-year follow-up study of 144 Swedish people diagnosed with the disorder found that, for most, the obsessions and compulsions had gradually lessened, though only 1 in 5 had completely recovered (Skoog & Skoog, 1999).

Post-Traumatic Stress Disorder

As an Army infantry scout during the Iraq war, Jesse "saw the murder of children, women. It was just horrible for anyone to experience." After calling in a helicopter strike on one house where he had seen ammunition crates carried in, he heard the screams of children from within. "I didn't know there were kids there," he recalls. Back home in Texas, he suffered "real bad flashbacks" (Welch, 2005).

Our memories exist in part to protect us in the future. So there is biological wisdom in not being able to forget our most emotional or traumatic experiences—our greatest embarrassments, our worst accidents, our most horrid experiences. But sometimes, for some of us, the unforgettable takes over our lives. The complaints of battle-scarred veterans such as Jesse—recurring haunting memories and nightmares, a numbed social withdrawal, jumpy anxiety, insomnia—are typical of what once was called "shellshock" or "battle fatigue" and now is called **post-traumatic stress disorder (PTSD)** (Hoge et al., 2004; Kessler, 2000).

PTSD symptoms have also been reported by survivors of accidents, disasters, and violent and sexual assaults (including an estimated two-thirds of prostitutes) (Brewin et al., 1999; Farley et al., 1998; Taylor et al., 1998). A month after the 9/11 terrorist attacks, a survey of Manhattan residents indicated that 8.5 percent were suffering PTSD, most as a result of the attack (Galea et al., 2002). Among those living near the World Trade Center, 20 percent reported such telltale signs as nightmares, severe anxiety, and fear of public places (Susser et al., 2002).

To pin down the frequency of this disorder, the U.S. Centers for Disease Control (1988) compared 7000 Vietnam combat veterans with 7000 noncombat veterans who served during the same years. On average, according to a recent reanalysis, 19 percent of all Vietnam veterans reported PTSD symptoms. The rate varied from 10 percent among those who had never seen combat to 32 percent among those who had experienced heavy combat (Dohrenwend et al., 2006). Similar variations in rates have been found among people who have experienced a natural disaster or have been kidnapped, held captive, tortured, or raped (Brewin et al., 2000; Brody, 2000; Kessler, 2000; Stone, 2005).

AP Photo/Lawrence Journal-World, Thad Allender

Bringing the war home Many war veterans, such as this sergeant at a Veterans Administration hospital, have recently been treated for post-traumatic stress disorder.

TROUBLESHOOTING

Help students differentiate between obsessive-compulsive disorder and obsessive-compulsive personality disorder:

- OCD is an *anxiety disorder* characterized by obsessive thoughts with corresponding compulsions. People with OCD are likely to lead lives where strict routines become essential, repeating tasks over and over again to find relief from their anxieties.

- OCPD is a *personality disorder* characterized by an obsessive need for neatness, order, and symmetry. People with OCPD are more likely to be called "neat freaks" or "anal-retentive."

The toll seems at least as high for veterans of the Iraq war, where 1 in 6 U.S. combat infantry personnel has reported symptoms of PTSD, depression, or severe anxiety in the months after returning home (Hoge et al., 2006, 2007). In one study of 103,788 veterans returning from Iraq and Afghanistan, 1 in 4 was diagnosed with a psychological disorder, most frequently PTSD (Seal et al., 2007). The extent of the PTSD problem was clear in the disability payments made to U.S. veterans in the decade following the mid-1990s: All forms of mental illness decreased, except PTSD, which nearly tripled, producing a $4.3 billion bill to taxpayers (Satel, 2006).

So what determines whether a person develops PTSD after a traumatic event? Research indicates that the greater one's emotional distress during a trauma, the higher the risk for post-traumatic symptoms (Ozer et al., 2003). Among New Yorkers who witnessed the 9/11 attacks, PTSD was doubled for survivors who were inside rather than outside the World Trade Center (Bonanno et al., 2006). And the more frequent an assault experience, the more adverse the long-term outcomes tend to be (Golding, 1999).

A sensitive limbic system seems to increase vulnerability, by flooding the body with stress hormones again and again as images of the traumatic experience erupt into consciousness (Kosslyn, 2005; Ozer & Weiss, 2004). Genes may also play a role. Some combat-exposed men have identical twins who did not experience combat. But these nonexposed co-twins tend to share their brother's risk for cognitive difficulties, such as unfocused attention. Such findings suggest that some PTSD symptoms may actually be genetically predisposed (Gilbertson et al., 2006).

Some psychologists believe that PTSD has been overdiagnosed, due partly to a broadening definition of *trauma* (which originally meant direct exposure to threatened death or serious injury, as during combat or rape [McNally, 2003]). PTSD is actually infrequent, say those critics, and well-intentioned attempts to have people relive the trauma may exacerbate their emotions and pathologize normal stress reactions (Wakefield & Spitzer, 2002). "Debriefing" survivors right after a trauma by getting them to revisit the experience and vent emotions has actually proven generally ineffective and sometimes harmful (Devilly et al., 2006; McNally et al., 2003; Rose et al., 2003).

Other researchers are interested in the impressive *survivor resiliency* of those who do *not* develop PTSD (Bonanno, 2004, 2005). About half of adults experience at least one traumatic event in their lifetime, but only about 1 in 10 women and 1 in 20 men develop PTSD (Olff et al., 2007; Ozer & Weiss, 2004; Tolin & Foa, 2006). More than 9 in 10 New Yorkers, although stunned and grief-stricken by 9/11, did *not* respond pathologically. By the following January, the stress symptoms of the rest had mostly subsided (Galea et al., 2002). Similarly, most combat-stressed veterans and most political dissidents who survive dozens of episodes of torture do not later exhibit PTSD (Mineka & Zinbarg, 1996).

Psychologist Peter Suedfeld (1998, 2000; Cassel & Suedfeld, 2006), who as a boy survived the Holocaust under deprived conditions while his mother died in Auschwitz, has documented the resilience of Holocaust survivors, most of whom lived productive lives. "It is not always true that 'What doesn't kill you makes you stronger,' but it is often true," he reports. And "what doesn't kill you may reveal to you just how strong you really are." Fellow Holocaust survivor Ervin Staub (Staub & Vollhardt, 2008) has described "altruism born of suffering." Although nothing justifies terror and victimization, those who have suffered, he reports, often develop a greater-than-usual sensitivity to suffering and empathy for others who suffer, an increased sense of responsibility, and an enlarged capacity for caring. Staub is a living example of his own work. After being spared from being sent to Auschwitz thanks to a heroic intervention, his lifelong mission has been to understand why some people perpetrate evil, some stand by, and some work to prevent it.

Indeed, suffering can lead to "benefit finding" (Helgeson et al., 2006), what Richard Tedeschi and Lawrence Calhoun (2004) call **post-traumatic growth.** Tedeschi and

::**post-traumatic stress disorder (PTSD)** an anxiety disorder characterized by haunting memories, nightmares, social withdrawal, jumpy anxiety, and/or insomnia that lingers for four weeks or more after a traumatic experience.

::**post-traumatic growth** positive psychological changes as a result of struggling with extremely challenging circumstances and life crises.

"'Tis an ill wind that blows no good."
English proverb

Today, 24-hour news channels show up-to-the-minute coverage of war and disaster. People can watch violence as it happens. While this represents an advance in TV journalism, it exposes everyday people to experiences that could lead to post-traumatic stress disorder (PTSD).

- How does viewing trauma on TV affect people who haven't experienced the tragedy or conflict firsthand?

- Can people develop PTSD vicariously? How different are experiences with PTSD from those who developed it vicariously compared to those who developed it through firsthand experience with trauma?

- How did coverage of the events of the September 11, 2001 attacks and Hurricane Katrina affect the viewing public?

- Were lessons learned from coverage of the first Gulf War applied to coverage of the Iraq War? Why or why not?

INTERCONNECTING

Link PTSD to flashbulb memories. Have students recall a powerful memory of a traumatic event that they've experienced.

- Do they remember vividly where they were when they heard about someone famous dying?

- Do their parents remember vividly the 9/11 attacks, the *Challenger* accident, Ronald Reagan's assassination attempt, or when John Lennon was killed?

RESEARCH

Have students interview people who have experienced trauma to see how they coped with the stress involved with a particularly tragic event. Some people you may consider interviewing might include the following:

- Survivors of the Holocaust or soldiers in World War II

- Soldiers from the Korean, Vietnam, or Iraq War

- People who remember the assassinations of the 1960s

- Survivors or witnesses of the September 11, 2001, tragedy

- Evacuees of Hurricane Katrina

INTERCONNECTING

Review with students the components of classical conditioning that lead to Little Albert developing a fear of white, furry objects (Unit 6):

- Unconditioned stimulus (US)— loud "bang" that occurred when the lead pipes were struck

- Unconditioned response (UR)— fear of the loud "bang"

- Conditioned stimulus (CS)— white, furry objects

- Conditioned response (CR)— fear, but this time in response to the white, furry object

Have students recall that the fear response John Watson cultivated so easily was reversed in other patients by his student Mary Cover Jones. She used classical conditioning to remove a fear response from individuals who had developed a fear of a certain object. She used a pleasant US, like candy or food, so patients could associate the pleasant feeling with the object they had come to fear.

Calhoun have found that the struggle with challenging crises, such as facing cancer, often leads people later to report an increased appreciation for life, more meaningful relationships, increased personal strength, changed priorities, and a richer spiritual life. This idea—that suffering has transformative power—is also found in Judaism, Christianity, Hinduism, Buddhism, and Islam. Out of even our worst experiences some good can come. Like the body, the mind has great recuperative powers.

Understanding Anxiety Disorders

6: What produces the thoughts and feelings that mark anxiety disorders?

Anxiety is both a feeling and a cognition, a doubt-laden appraisal of one's safety or social skill. How do these anxious feelings and cognitions arise? Freud's psychoanalytic theory proposed that, beginning in childhood, people *repress* intolerable impulses, ideas, and feelings and that this submerged mental energy sometimes produces mystifying symptoms, such as anxiety. Today's psychologists have turned to two contemporary perspectives—learning and biological.

The Learning Perspective

Fear Conditioning When bad events happen unpredictably and uncontrollably, anxiety often develops (Field, 2006; Mineka & Zinbarg, 2006). Recall from Unit 6 that dogs learn to fear neutral stimuli associated with shock and that infants come to fear furry objects associated with frightening noises. Using classical conditioning, researchers have also created chronically anxious, ulcer-prone rats by giving them unpredictable electric shocks (Schwartz, 1984). Like assault victims who report feeling anxious when returning to the scene of the crime, the rats become apprehensive in their lab environment. This link between conditioned fear and general anxiety helps explain why anxious people are hyperattentive to possible threats, and how panic-prone people come to associate anxiety with certain cues (Bar-Haim et al., 2007; Bouton et al., 2001). In one survey, 58 percent of those with social phobia experienced their disorder after a traumatic event (Ost & Hugdahl, 1981).

Through conditioning, the short list of naturally painful and frightening events can multiply into a long list of human fears. My car was once struck by another whose driver missed a stop sign. For months afterward, I felt a twinge of unease when any car approached from a side street. Marilyn's phobia may have been similarly conditioned during a terrifying or painful experience associated with a thunderstorm.

Two specific learning processes can contribute to such anxiety. The first, *stimulus generalization,* occurs, for example, when a person attacked by a fierce dog later develops a fear of *all* dogs. The second learning process, *reinforcement,* helps maintain our phobias and compulsions after they arise. Avoiding or escaping the feared situation reduces anxiety, thus reinforcing the phobic behavior. Feeling anxious or fearing a panic attack, a person may go inside and be reinforced by feeling calmer (Antony et al., 1992). Compulsive behaviors operate similarly. If washing your hands relieves your feelings of anxiety, you may wash your hands again when those feelings return.

Observational Learning We may also learn fear through observational learning— by observing others' fears. As Susan Mineka (1985) demonstrated, wild monkeys transmit their fear of snakes to their watchful offspring. Human parents similarly transmit fears to their children. Moreover, just observing someone receiving a mild electric shock after a conditioned stimulus produces fear learning similar to that produced by direct experience (Olsson & Phelps, 2004).

TEACHING TIP

At this point, you may want to use **Lecture/Discussion Topic:** *Concentration Camp Survival* (p. 15) from Bolt's Teacher's Resource Binder.

The Biological Perspective

There is, however, more to anxiety than conditioning and observational learning. The biological perspective can help us understand why few people develop lasting phobias after suffering traumas, why we learn some fears more readily, and why some individuals are more vulnerable.

Natural Selection We humans seem biologically prepared to fear threats faced by our ancestors. Our phobias focus on such specific fears: spiders, snakes, and other animals; close spaces and heights; storms and darkness. (Those fearless about these occasional threats were less likely to survive and leave descendants.) Thus, even in Britain, with only one poisonous snake species, people often fear snakes. And preschool children more speedily detect snakes in a scene than flowers, caterpillars, or frogs (LoBue & DeLoache, 2008). It is easy to condition and hard to extinguish fears of such stimuli (Davey, 1995; Öhman, 1986).

Our modern fears can also have an evolutionary explanation. For example, a fear of flying may come from our biological predisposition to fear confinement and heights. Moreover, consider what people tend *not* to learn to fear. World War II air raids produced remarkably few lasting phobias. As the air blitzes continued, the British, Japanese, and German populations became not more panicked, but rather more indifferent to planes outside their immediate neighborhoods (Mineka & Zinbarg, 1996). Evolution has not prepared us to fear bombs dropping from the sky.

Just as our phobias focus on dangers faced by our ancestors, our compulsive acts typically exaggerate behaviors that contributed to our species' survival. Grooming gone wild becomes hair pulling. Washing up becomes ritual hand washing. Checking territorial boundaries becomes rechecking an already locked door (Rapoport, 1989).

Genes Some people more than others seem predisposed to anxiety. Genes matter. Pair a traumatic event with a sensitive, high-strung temperament and the result may be a new phobia.

Among monkeys, fearfulness runs in families. Individual monkeys react more strongly to stress if their close biological relatives are anxiously reactive (Suomi, 1986). In humans, vulnerability to anxiety disorders rises when an afflicted relative is an identical twin (Hettema et al., 2001; Kendler et al., 1992, 1999, 2002a,b). Identical twins also may develop similar phobias, even when raised separately (Carey, 1990; Eckert et al., 1981). One pair of 35-year-old female identical twins independently became so afraid of water that each would wade in the ocean backward and only up to the knees.

With the genetic contribution to anxiety disorders established, researchers are now sleuthing specific genes that put people at risk. One research team has identified 17 genes that appear to be expressed with typical anxiety disorder symptoms (Hovatta et al., 2005). Another team found genes associated specifically with OCD (Hu et al., 2006).

Genes influence disorders by regulating neurotransmitters. Some studies point to an *anxiety gene* that affects brain levels of serotonin, a neurotransmitter that influences sleep and mood (Canli, 2008). Other studies implicate genes that regulate the neurotransmitter *glutamate* (Lafleur et al., 2006; Welch et al., 2007). With too much glutamate, the brain's alarm centers become overactive.

The Brain Generalized anxiety, panic attacks, PTSD, and even obsessions and compulsions are manifested biologically as an overarousal of brain areas involved in impulse control and habitual behaviors. When the disordered brain detects that something is amiss, it seems to generate a mental hiccup of repeating thoughts or actions (Gehring et al., 2000). Brain scans of people with OCD reveal elevated activity in specific brain areas during behaviors such as compulsive hand washing, checking, ordering, or hoarding (Mataix-Cols et al., 2004, 2005). As **FIGURE 12.3** shows, the *anterior cingulate cortex,* a

Fearless Fearing heights is certainly an adaptive response. The biological perspective helps us understand why most people would be terrified in this situation, and why some individuals—like this rider performing a "backflip tabletop" trick in a BMX event—seem free of that fear.

▶ **FIGURE 12.3**

An obsessive-compulsive brain
Neuroscientist Stefan Ursu and his colleagues (2003) used functional magnetic resonance imaging (fMRI) scans to compare the brains of those with and without OCD as they engaged in a challenging cognitive task. The fMRI scans of those with OCD showed elevated activity in the anterior cingulate cortex in the brain's frontal area.

UNIT 12

TEACHING TIP

Somatoform disorders are not as commonly diagnosed as they used to be. In fact, the proposed revisions to the *DSM-V* (likely to be published in 2013) suggest combining somatization disorder, hypochondriasis, undifferentiated somatoform disorder, and pain disorder into a new category entitled "Complex Somatic Symptom Disorder" (CSSD). This new diagnosis addresses several issues cited by clinicians and researchers:

- Significant overlap exists among these disorders, making them difficult to diagnose consistently.

- Treatments for these disorders are essentially similar.

- The new combined diagnosis—CSSD—promises to be more reliable and valid than diagnosing the other disorders separately.

The authors of the new *DSM* recommendations hope this new disorder will make diagnosis more consistent and less confusing than the separate disorders have been in the past.

INTERCONNECTING

One contributor to somatoform illnesses may be stress. Remind students of the physical effects of stress as discussed in Unit 8B. Some of the symptoms of stress-related illness may seem familiar as they study somatoform disorders.

---

brain region that monitors our actions and checks for errors, seems especially likely to be hyperactive in those with OCD (Ursu et al., 2003). Fear-learning experiences that traumatize the brain can also create fear circuits within the amygdala (Etkin & Wager, 2007; Kolassa & Elbert, 2007; Maren, 2007). Some antidepressant drugs dampen this fear-circuit activity and its associated obsessive-compulsive behavior.

The biological perspective cannot by itself explain all aspects of anxiety disorders, such as the sharp increase in the anxiety levels of both children and college students over the last half-century, which appears to be related to fraying social support accompanying family breakup (Twenge, 2006). It is nevertheless clear that biology underlies anxiety.

BEFORE YOU MOVE ON . . .

> **ASK YOURSELF**

Can you recall a fear that you have learned? What role, if any, was played by fear conditioning and by observational learning?

> **TEST YOURSELF 2**

How do generalized anxiety disorder, panic disorder, phobias, obsessive-compulsive disorder, and post-traumatic stress disorder differ?

Answers to the Test Yourself questions can be found in Appendix E at the end of the book.

Somatoform Disorders

7: What are somatoform disorders?

AMONG THE MOST COMMON PROBLEMS bringing people into doctors' offices are "medically unexplained illnesses" (Johnson, 2008). Ellen becomes dizzy and nauseated in the late afternoon—shortly before she expects her husband home. Neither her primary care physician nor the neurologist he sent her to could identify a physical cause. They suspect her symptoms have an unconscious psychological origin, possibly triggered by her mixed feelings about her husband. In **somatoform disorders,** such as Ellen's, the distressing symptoms take a somatic (bodily) form without apparent physical causes. One person may have a variety of complaints—vomiting, dizziness, blurred vision, difficulty in swallowing. Another may experience severe and prolonged pain.

Culture has a big effect on people's physical complaints and how they explain them (Kirmayer & Sartorius, 2007). In China, psychological explanations of anxiety and depression are socially less acceptable than in many Western countries, and people less often express the emotional aspects of distress. The Chinese appear more sensitive to—and more willing to report—the physical symptoms of their distress (Ryder et al., 2008). Mr. Wu, a 36-year-old technician in Hunan, illustrates one of China's most common psychological disorders (Spitzer & Skodol, 2000). He finds work difficult because of his insomnia, fatigue, weakness, and headaches. Chinese herbs and Western medicines provide no relief. To his Chinese clinician, who treats the bodily symptoms, he seems not so much depressed as exhausted. Similar, generalized bodily complaints have often been observed in African cultures (Binitie, 1975).

Even to people in the West, somatic symptoms are familiar. To a lesser extent, we have all experienced inexplicable physical symptoms under stress. It is little comfort to be told that the problem is "all in your head." Although the symptoms may be psychological in origin, they are nevertheless genuinely felt.

::**somatoform disorder** psychological disorder in which the symptoms take a somatic (bodily) form without apparent physical cause. (See *conversion disorder* and *hypochondriasis*.)

::**conversion disorder** a rare somatoform disorder in which a person experiences very specific genuine physical symptoms for which no physiological basis can be found.

::**hypochondriasis** a somatoform disorder in which a person interprets normal physical sensations as symptoms of a disease.

::**dissociative disorders** disorders in which conscious awareness becomes separated (dissociated) from previous memories, thoughts, and feelings.

TEACHING TIP

At this point, you may want to use **Lecture/Discussion Topic:** *Factitious Disorder* (p. 15) from Bolt's Teacher's Resource Binder.

One type of somatoform disorder, more common in Freud's day than in ours, is **conversion disorder,** so called because anxiety presumably is converted into a physical symptom. (As we noted in Unit 10, Freud's effort to treat and understand psychological disorders stemmed from his puzzlement over ailments that had no physiological basis.) A patient with a conversion disorder might, for example, lose sensation in a way that makes no neurological sense. Yet the physical symptoms would be real; sticking pins in the affected area would produce no response. Other conversion disorder symptoms might be unexplained paralysis, blindness, or an inability to swallow. In each case, the person would be strangely indifferent to the problem.

As you can imagine, somatoform disorders send people not to a psychologist or psychiatrist but to a physician. This is especially true of those who experience **hypochondriasis.** In this relatively common somatoform disorder, people interpret normal sensations (a stomach cramp today, a headache tomorrow) as symptoms of a dreaded disease. Sympathy or temporary relief from everyday demands may reinforce such complaints. No amount of reassurance by any physician convinces the patient that the trivial symptoms do not reflect a serious illness. So the patient moves on to another physician, seeking and receiving more medical attention—but failing to confront the disorder's psychological root.

BEFORE YOU MOVE ON . . .

➤ ASK YOURSELF

Can you recall (as most people can) times when you have fretted needlessly over a normal bodily sensation?

➤ TEST YOURSELF 3

What does somatoform mean?

Answers to the Test Yourself questions can be found in Appendix E at the end of the book.

Dissociative Disorders

8: What are dissociative disorders, and why are they controversial?

AMONG THE MOST BEWILDERING DISORDERS are the rare **dissociative disorders.** These are disorders of consciousness, in which a person appears to experience a sudden loss of memory or change in identity, often in response to an overwhelmingly stressful situation. One Vietnam veteran who was haunted by his comrades' deaths, and who had left his World Trade Center office shortly before the 9/11 attack, lost memory for his personal identity (a rare disorder called *fugue state*). He disappeared en route to work one day and was discovered six months later in a Chicago homeless shelter, reportedly with no memory of his identity or family (Stone, 2006). In such cases, the person's conscious awareness is said to *dissociate* (become separated) from painful memories, thoughts, and feelings. (Note that this explanation presumes the existence of repressed memories, which, as we noted in Units 7A and 10, have been questioned by memory researchers.)

Dissociation itself is not so rare. Now and then, many people may have a sense of being unreal, of being separated from their body, of watching themselves as if in a movie. Sometimes we may say, "I was not myself at the time." Perhaps you can recall getting in your car and driving to some unintended location while your mind was preoccupied elsewhere. Facing trauma, such detachment may actually protect a person from being overwhelmed by emotion.

Multiple personalities Chris Sizemore's story, *The Three Faces of Eve,* gave early visibility to what is now called *dissociative identity disorder.*

Lois Bernstein/Gamma Liaison

Dissociative identity disorder (DID) is so controversial partly because the claims of patients are so difficult to confirm. Typically, DID is not diagnosed until later in life when alleged perpetrators might have died or evidence of past abuse or trauma has been lost.

- Does such difficulty in confirming trauma necessarily deny the claims of patients?

- How do investigators prove claims of abuse that happened long ago?

TROUBLESHOOTING

If you show any of the popular films that depict dissociative identity disorder, help students watch with a critical eye. The goal of movies is not to depict reality, but to entertain and tell a compelling story. The movie may or may not be an accurate depiction of what actually happened.

::**dissociative identity disorder (DID)** a rare dissociative disorder in which a person exhibits two or more distinct and alternating personalities. Formerly called *multiple personality disorder*.

The "Hillside Strangler" Kenneth Bianchi is shown here at his trial. ▲

"Pretense may become reality."
Chinese proverb

"Would it be possible to speak with the personality that pays the bills?"

Dissociative Identity Disorder

A massive dissociation of self from ordinary consciousness characterizes those with **dissociative identity disorder (DID),** in which two or more distinct identities are said to alternately control the person's behavior. Each personality has its own voice and mannerisms. Thus the person may be prim and proper one moment, loud and flirtatious the next. Typically, the original personality denies any awareness of the other(s).

People diagnosed with DID (formerly called *multiple personality disorder*) are usually not violent, but cases have been reported of dissociations into a "good" and a "bad" (or aggressive) personality—a modest version of the Dr. Jekyll/Mr. Hyde split immortalized in Robert Louis Stevenson's story. One unusual case involved Kenneth Bianchi, accused in the "Hillside Strangler" rapes and murders of 10 California women. During a hypnosis session with Bianchi, psychologist John Watkins (1984) "called forth" a hidden personality: "I've talked a bit to Ken, but I think that perhaps there might be another part of Ken that . . . maybe feels somewhat differently from the part that I've talked to. . . . Would you talk with me, Part, by saying, 'I'm here'?" Bianchi answered "Yes" and then claimed to be "Steve."

Speaking as Steve, Bianchi stated that he hated Ken because Ken was nice and that he (Steve), aided by a cousin, had murdered women. He also claimed Ken knew nothing about Steve's existence and was innocent of the murders. Was Bianchi's second personality a ruse, simply a way of disavowing responsibility for his actions? Indeed, Bianchi—a practiced liar who had read about multiple personality in psychology books—was later convicted.

Understanding Dissociative Identity Disorder

Skeptics question whether DID is a genuine disorder or an extension of our normal capacity for personality shifts. Nicholas Spanos (1986, 1994, 1996) asked college students to pretend they were accused murderers being examined by a psychiatrist. Given the same hypnotic treatment Bianchi received, most spontaneously expressed a second personality. This discovery made Spanos wonder: Are dissociative identities simply a more extreme version of our capacity to vary the "selves" we present—as when we display a goofy, loud self while hanging out with friends, and a subdued, respectful self around grandparents? Are clinicians who discover multiple personalities merely triggering role-playing by fantasy-prone people? Do these patients, like actors who commonly report "losing themselves" in their roles, then convince themselves of the authenticity of their own role enactments? Spanos was no stranger to this line of thinking. In a related research area, he had also raised these questions about the hypnotic state. Given that most DID patients are highly hypnotizable, whatever explains one condition—dissociation or role-playing—may help explain the other.

Skeptics also find it suspicious that the disorder is so localized in time and space. Between 1930 and 1960, the number of DID diagnoses in North America was 2 per decade. In the 1980s, when the DSM contained the first formal code for this disorder, the number of reported cases had exploded to more than 20,000 (McHugh, 1995a). The average number of displayed personalities also mushroomed—from 3 to 12 per patient (Goff & Simms, 1993). Outside North America, the disorder is much less prevalent, although in other cultures some people are said to be "possessed" by an alien spirit (Aldridge-Morris, 1989; Kluft, 1991). In Britain, DID—which some consider "a wacky American fad" (Cohen, 1995)—is rare. In India and Japan, it is essentially nonexistent.

Such findings, skeptics say, point to a cultural phenomenon—a disorder created by therapists in a particular social context (Merskey, 1992). Patients do not enter therapy saying "Allow me to introduce myselves." Rather, note skeptics, some therapists—often practitioners of hypnosis (Goff, 1993; Piper, 1998)—go fishing for multiple

Two other dissociative disorders should also be learned:

- Dissociative amnesia: Patients suffer from a complete loss of identity. They forget who they are due to a trauma.

- Dissociative fugue: Patients suffer the identity loss as in dissociative amnesia, but these patients also travel away from home, often showing up as a "John/Jane Doe" in another community far away.

personalities: "Have you ever felt like another part of you does things you can't control? Does this part of you have a name? Can I talk to the angry part of you?" Once patients permit a therapist to talk, by name, "to the part of you that says those angry things" they have begun acting out the fantasy. The result may be a real phenomenon, which vulnerable patients may experience as another self.

Other psychologists disagree, finding support for DID as a genuine disorder in the distinct brain and body states associated with differing personalities (Putnam, 1991). Handedness, for example, sometimes switches with personality (Henninger, 1992). Ophthalmologists have detected shifting visual acuity and eye-muscle balance as patients switched personalities, changes that did not occur among control group members trying to simulate DID (Miller et al., 1991). Dissociative disorder patients also have exhibited heightened activity in brain areas associated with the control and inhibition of traumatic memories (Elzinga et al., 2007).

Researchers and clinicians have interpreted DID symptoms from psychoanalytic and learning perspectives. Both views agree that the symptoms are ways of dealing with anxiety. Psychoanalysts see them as defenses against the anxiety caused by the eruption of unacceptable impulses; a wanton second personality enables the discharge of forbidden impulses. Learning theorists see dissociative disorders as behaviors reinforced by anxiety reduction.

Other clinicians include dissociative disorders under the umbrella of post-traumatic disorders—a natural, protective response to "histories of childhood trauma" (Putnam, 1995; Spiegel, 2008). Many DID patients recall suffering physical, sexual, or emotional abuse as children (Gleaves, 1996; Lilienfeld et al., 1999). In one study of 12 murderers diagnosed with DID, 11 had suffered severe, torturous child abuse (Lewis et al., 1997). One was set afire by his parents. Another was used in child pornography and was scarred from being made to sit on a stove burner. Some critics wonder, however, whether vivid imagination or therapist suggestion contributes to such recollections (Kihlstrom, 2005).

So the debate continues. On one side are those who believe multiple personalities are the desperate efforts of the traumatized to detach from a horrific existence. On the other are the skeptics who think DID is a condition contrived by fantasy-prone, emotionally vulnerable people, and constructed out of the therapist-patient interaction. If the skeptics' view wins, predicted psychiatrist Paul McHugh (1995b), "this epidemic will end in the way that the witch craze ended in Salem. The [multiple personality phenomenon] will be seen as manufactured."

> "Though this be madness, yet there is method in 't."
> William Shakespeare, *Hamlet*, 1600

BEFORE YOU MOVE ON . . .

➤ **ASK YOURSELF**

In a more normal way, do you ever flip between displays of different aspects of your personality?

➤ **TEST YOURSELF 4**

The psychoanalytic and learning perspectives agree that dissociative identity disorder symptoms are ways of dealing with anxiety. How do their explanations differ?

Answers to the Test Yourself questions can be found in Appendix E at the end of the book.

Mood Disorders

9: What are mood disorders, and what forms do they take?

THE EMOTIONAL EXTREMES of **mood disorders** come in two principal forms: (1) *major depressive disorder*, with its prolonged hopelessness and lethargy, and

::**mood disorders** psychological disorders characterized by emotional extremes. See *major depressive disorder, mania,* and *bipolar disorder.*

CRITICAL THINKING

Women's health issues have only recently begun to be distinguished from men's health issues. Contemporaries of Freud believed that women who attended college suffered from shrunken ovaries since they did not bear as many children as their less-educated sisters. Mental illnesses such as dissociative and somatoform disorders were often only reported in women in the past. Have students explore old stereotypes and new advances in women's health:

- What were some other common beliefs about women's health issues?

- What kind of influence did Freud and others have on the study of women's health?

- When did women's health issues start to get serious attention as being distinct from men's health issues?

- What advances have been made in recent years that have allowed women's health issues to be better understood?

INTERCONNECTING

Remind students of Elizabeth Loftus's work questioning the validity of repressed memories. Many DID patients experience memory loss with at least one alternate personality. Have students consider whether this type of memory loss can be related to research done by Loftus and others.

TEACHING TIP

At this point, you may want to use **Classroom Exercise:** *The Curious Experiences Inventory* (p. 16) or **Lecture/Discussion Topics:** *Psychogenic Versus Organic Amnesia* (p. 16) or *The Dissociative Disorders Interview Schedule and Dissociative Identity Disorder* (p. 17) from Bolt's Teacher's Resource Binder.

TEACHING TIP

There are several different types of mood disorders that are not classified in the *DSM*. Have students research the following two examples, concentrating on why they are not included in the *DSM*:

- Seasonal affective disorder
- Postpartum depression

TEACHING TIP

National Depression Screening Day, created by Harvard psychiatrist Douglas G. Jacobs in 1991, has since been repeated every year in early October. Each year, the number of sites staffed by mental health professionals has grown. The free screening includes completion of a self-rating depression scale; a 20-minute talk on the causes, symptoms, and treatment of the disorder, during which participants may ask questions; and 5 minutes alone with a mental health professional. No diagnosis or treatment is provided, but based on the scale scores and the clinician's probing, participants learn if they need more evaluation.

● For some people, recurring depression during winter's dark months constitutes a *seasonal affective disorder*. For others, winter darkness means more blue moods. When asked "Have you cried today?" Americans answered "Yes" more often in the winter.

Percentage answering *yes*

	Men	Women
August	4%	7%
December	8%	21%

Source: Time/CNN survey, 1994 ●

> "My life had come to a sudden stop. I was able to breathe, to eat, to drink, to sleep. I could not, indeed, help doing so; but there was no real life in me."
>
> Leo Tolstoy, *My Confession*, 1887

> "Depression . . . is well adapted to make a creature guard itself against any great or sudden evil."
>
> Charles Darwin, *The Life and Letters of Charles Darwin*, 1887

> "If someone offered you a pill that would make you permanently happy, you would be well advised to run fast and run far. Emotion is a compass that tells us what to do, and a compass that is perpetually stuck on NORTH is worthless."
>
> Daniel Gilbert, "The Science of Happiness," 2006

(2) *bipolar disorder* (formerly called *manic-depressive disorder*), in which a person alternates between depression and mania, an overexcited, hyperactive state.

Major Depressive Disorder

If you are like most high school students, at some time during this year—more likely the dark months of winter than the bright days of summer—you will probably experience a few of depression's symptoms. You may feel deeply discouraged about the future, dissatisfied with your life, or socially isolated. You may lack the energy to get things done or even to force yourself out of bed; be unable to concentrate, eat, or sleep normally; or even wonder if you would be better off dead. Perhaps academic success came easily to you in middle school, and now you find that disappointing grades jeopardize your goals. Maybe social stresses, such as feeling you don't belong or experiencing the end of a romance, have plunged you into despair. And maybe brooding has at times only worsened your self-torment. You are not alone. In one survey of American high school students, 29 percent "felt so sad or hopeless almost every day for 2 or more weeks in a row that they stopped doing some usual activities" (CDC, 2008). In another survey of 90,000 American college and university students, 44 percent reported that on one or more occasions within the last school year, they had felt "so depressed it was difficult to function" (ACHA, 2006).

Depression has been called the "common cold" of psychological disorders—an expression that effectively describes its pervasiveness but not its seriousness. Although phobias are more common, depression is the number-one reason people seek mental health services. At some point during their lifetime, depressive disorders have plagued 12 percent of Canadian adults and 13 percent of U.S. adults (Hasin et al., 2005; Patten et al., 2006). Moreover, it is the leading cause of disability worldwide (WHO, 2002). In any given year, a depressive episode plagues 5.8 percent of men and 9.5 percent of women, reports the World Health Organization.

As anxiety is a response to the threat of future loss, depressed mood is often a response to past and current loss. About one in four people diagnosed with depression is simply struggling with the normal emotional impact of a significant loss, such as a loved one's death, a ruptured marriage, a lost job (Wakefield et al., 2007). To feel bad in reaction to profoundly sad events is to be in touch with reality. In such times, depression is like a car's refueling light—a signal that warns us to stop and take appropriate measures. Recall that, biologically speaking, life's purpose is not happiness but survival and reproduction. Coughing, vomiting, and various forms of pain protect the body from dangerous toxins. Similarly, depression is a sort of psychic hibernation: It slows us down, defuses aggression, and restrains risk taking (Allen & Badcock, 2003). To grind temporarily to a halt and ruminate, as depressed people do, is to reassess one's life when feeling threatened, and to redirect energy in more promising ways (Watkins, 2008). There is sense to suffering.

But when does this response become seriously maladaptive? Joy, contentment, sadness, and despair are different points on a continuum, points at which any of us may be found at any given moment. The difference between a blue mood after bad news and a mood disorder is like the difference between gasping for breath after a hard run and being chronically short of breath.

Major depressive disorder occurs when at least five signs of depression (including lethargy, feelings of worthlessness, or loss of interest in family, friends, and activities) last two or more weeks and are not caused by drugs or a medical condition. To sense what major depression feels like, suggest some clinicians, imagine combining the anguish of grief with the sluggishness of jet lag.

TEACHING TIP

Students may be interested in dysthymic disorder, a depressive state lasting more than two years. In children and adolescents, the depressive state need only last one year. Patients must also present two or more of the following symptoms:

- poor appetite or overeating
- insomnia (lack of sleeping) or hypersomnia (too much sleep)
- low energy or fatigue
- low self-esteem
- poor concentration or difficulty making decisions
- feelings of hopelessness

Bipolar Disorder

With or without therapy, episodes of major depression usually end, and people temporarily or permanently return to their previous behavior patterns. However, some people rebound to, or sometimes start with, the opposite emotional extreme—the euphoric, hyperactive, wildly optimistic state of **mania.** If depression is living in slow motion, mania is fast forward. Alternating between depression and mania signals **bipolar disorder.**

Adolescent mood swings, from rage to bubbly, can, when prolonged, produce a bipolar diagnosis. Between 1994 and 2003, U.S. National Center for Health Statistics annual physician surveys revealed an astonishing 40-fold increase in diagnoses of bipolar disorder in those 19 and under—from an estimated 20,000 to 800,000 (Carey, 2007; Moreno et al., 2007). The new popularity of the diagnosis, given in two-thirds of the cases to boys, has been a boon to companies whose drugs are prescribed to lessen mood swings.

During the manic phase, people with bipolar disorder are typically overtalkative, overactive, and elated (though easily irritated if crossed); have little need for sleep; and show fewer sexual inhibitions. Speech is loud, flighty, and hard to interrupt. They find advice irritating, yet they need protection from their own poor judgment, which may lead to reckless spending or unsafe sex.

To simulate mania's racing thoughts, such as you may have experienced when excited about a new idea, Emily Pronin and Daniel Wegner (2006) invited students to read a series of statements at either double or half the normal reading speed. Those who had just raced through the material reported feeling happier, more powerful, more energetic, and more creative. A racing mind arouses an upbeat mood.

Creativity and bipolar disorder History has given us many creative artists, composers, and writers with bipolar disorder, including (left to right) Walt Whitman, Virginia Woolf, Samuel Clemens (Mark Twain), and Ernest Hemingway.

In milder forms, mania's energy and free-flowing thinking does fuel creativity. George Frideric Handel (1685–1759), who may have suffered from a mild form of bipolar disorder, composed his nearly four-hour-long *Messiah* during three weeks of intense, creative energy (Keynes, 1980). Robert Schumann composed 51 musical works during two years of mania (1840 and 1849) and none during 1844, when he was severely depressed (Slater & Meyer, 1959). Those who rely on precision and logic, such as architects, designers, and journalists, suffer bipolar disorder less often than do those who rely on emotional expression and vivid imagery, reports Arnold Ludwig (1995). Composers, artists, poets, novelists, and entertainers seem especially prone (Jamison, 1993, 1995; Kaufman & Baer, 2002; Ludwig, 1995).

It is as true of emotions as of everything else: What goes up comes down. Before long, the elated mood either returns to normal or plunges into a depression. Though bipolar disorder is much less common than major depressive disorder, it is often more dysfunctional, claiming twice as many lost workdays yearly (Kessler et al., 2006). Among adults, it afflicts men and women about equally.

> "All the people in history, literature, art, whom I most admire: Mozart, Shakespeare, Homer, El Greco, St. John, Chekhov, Gregory of Nyssa, Dostoevsky, Emily Brontë: not one of them would qualify for a mental-health certificate."
>
> Madeleine L'Engle, *A Circle of Quiet*, 1972

::major depressive disorder a mood disorder in which a person experiences, in the absence of drugs or a medical condition, two or more weeks of significantly depressed moods, feelings of worthlessness, and diminished interest or pleasure in most activities.

::mania a mood disorder marked by a hyperactive, wildly optimistic state.

::bipolar disorder a mood disorder in which the person alternates between the hopelessness and lethargy of depression and the overexcited state of mania. (Formerly called *manic-depressive disorder.*)

TEACHING TIP

Bipolar disorder comes in two types:

- Bipolar Disorder I is the classic diagnosis of this disorder. Patients experience periods of inflated mood followed by depressive episodes occurring in cycles.

- Bipolar Disorder II is a milder form of bipolar disorder in which patients experience at least one episode of hypomania (a period of elevated mood, but without psychosis) and at least one major depressive episode.

TEACHING TIP

Give students an idea of mania by reading the following account:

> When I start going into a high, I no longer feel like an ordinary housewife. Instead, I feel organized and accomplished, and I begin to feel I am my most creative self. I can write poetry easily. I can compose melodies without effort. I can paint. . . . I see myself as being able to accomplish a great deal for the good of people. . . . I feel able to accomplish a great deal for the good of my family and others. I feel pleasure, a sense of euphoria or elation. I want it to last forever. I don't seem to need much sleep. I've lost weight and feel healthy, and I like myself. I've just bought six new dresses, in fact, and they look quite good on me . . . I feel capable of speaking and doing good in politics. I would like to help people with problems similar to mine so they won't feel hopeless.

Fieve, R. R. (1975). *Mood swing.* New York: Morrow. (p. 17.)

TEACHING TIP

At this point, you may want to use **Classroom Exercises:** *Depression Scales* (p. 17) or *The Automatic Thoughts Questionnaire* (p. 18) or *Depression and Memory* (p. 18) or *Loneliness* (p. 18) or **Lecture/Discussion Topic:** *Bipolar Disorder* (p. 19) from Bolt's Teacher's Resource Binder.

Understanding Mood Disorders

10: What causes mood disorders, and what might explain the Western world's rising incidence of depression among youth and young adults?

In thousands of studies, psychologists have been accumulating evidence to help explain mood disorders and suggest more effective ways to treat and prevent them. Researcher Peter Lewinsohn and his colleagues (1985, 1998, 2003) have summarized the facts that any theory of depression must explain, including the following:

- *Many behavioral and cognitive changes accompany depression.* People trapped in a depressed mood are inactive and feel unmotivated. They are sensitive to negative happenings, more often recall negative information, and expect negative outcomes (my team will lose, my grades will fall, my love will fail). When the mood lifts, these behavioral and cognitive accompaniments disappear. Nearly half the time, people also exhibit symptoms of another disorder, such as anxiety or substance abuse.

- *Depression is widespread.* Its commonality suggests that its causes, too, must be common.

- *Compared with men, women are nearly twice as vulnerable to major depression* (FIGURE 12.4). This gender gap begins in adolescence; preadolescent girls are not more depression-prone than boys (Hyde et al., 2008). The factors that put women at risk for depression (genetic predispositions, child abuse, low self-esteem, marital problems, and so forth) similarly put men at risk (Kendler et al., 2006). Yet women are more vulnerable to disorders involving internalized states, such as depression, anxiety, and inhibited sexual desire. Men's disorders tend to be more external—alcohol abuse, antisocial conduct, lack of impulse control. When women get sad, they often get sadder than men do. When men get mad, they often get madder than women do.

- *Most major depressive episodes self-terminate.* Therapy tends to speed recovery, yet most people suffering major depression eventually return to normal even without professional help. The plague of depression comes and, a few weeks or months later, it goes, though it sometimes recurs (Burcusa & Iacono, 2007). About 50 percent of those who recover from depression will suffer another episode within two years. Recovery is more likely to be permanent the later the first episode strikes, the longer the person stays well, the fewer the previous episodes, the less stress experienced, and the more social support received (Belsher & Costello, 1988; Fergusson & Woodward, 2002; Kendler et al., 2001).

The emotional lives of men and women?

➤ FIGURE 12.4
Gender and major depression
Interviews with 38,000 adults in 10 countries confirm what many smaller studies have found: Women's risk of major depression is nearly double that of men's. Lifetime risk of depression also varies by culture—from 1.5 percent in Taiwan to 19 percent in Beirut. (Data from Weissman et al., 1996.)

Percentage of 18- to 84-year-olds experiencing major depression at some point in life

Around the world, women are more susceptible to depression

USA · Edmonton · Puerto Rico · Paris · Germany · Florence · Beirut · Taiwan · Korea · New Zealand

Males   Females

- *Stressful events related to work, marriage, and close relationships often precede depression.* A family member's death, a job loss, a marital crisis, or a physical assault increase one's risk of depression. If stress-related anxiety is a "crackling, menacing brushfire," notes biologist Robert Sapolsky (2003), "depression is a suffocating heavy blanket thrown on top of it." One long-term study (Kendler, 1998) tracked rates of depression in 2000 people. The risk of depression ranged from less than 1 percent among those who had experienced no stressful life event in the preceding month to 24 percent among those who had experienced three such events in that month. Major events such as Hurricane Katrina and 9/11 have increased anxiety and mood disorders (Galea et al., 2007; Person et al., 2006). But generally, depression results more often from a pileup of stresses than from a single loss or failure (Keller et al., 2007; van der Werf et al., 2006).

- *With each new generation, depression is striking earlier (now often in the late teens) and affecting more people.* This is true in Canada, the United States, England, France, Germany, Italy, Lebanon, New Zealand, Puerto Rico, and Taiwan (Collishaw et al., 2007; Cross-National Collaborative Group, 1992; Twenge et al., 2008). In one study, 12 percent of Australian adolescents reported symptoms of depression (Sawyer et al., 2000). Most hid it from their parents; almost 90 percent of those parents perceived their depressed teen as *not* suffering depression. In North America, today's young adults are three times more likely than their grandparents to report having recently—or ever—suffered depression (despite the grandparents' many more years of being at risk). The increase appears partly authentic, but it may also reflect today's young adults' greater willingness to disclose depression.

Researchers may accept these facts without agreeing how best to explain them. For example, proponents of Sigmund Freud's psychoanalytic theory (or the more modern psychodynamic approach) have an idea: Depression often occurs when significant losses, such as the breakup of a current romantic relationship, evoke feelings associated with losses experienced in childhood (the intimate relationship with one's mother, for example). Alternatively, these theorists may view depression as unresolved anger toward one's parents, turned inward against oneself.

Most contemporary researchers propose biological and cognitive explanations of depression, often combined in a biopsychosocial perspective.

The Biological Perspective

Most recent mental health research dollars have funded explorations of biological influences on mood disorders. Areas of interest have been genetic predispositions, brain activity, and biochemical imbalances.

Genetic Influences We have long known that mood disorders run in families. As one researcher noted, emotions are "postcards from our genes" (Plotkin, 1994). The risk of major depression and bipolar disorder increases if you have a parent or sibling with the disorder (Sullivan et al., 2000). If one identical twin is diagnosed with major depressive disorder, the chances are about 1 in 2 that at some time the other twin will be, too. If one identical twin has bipolar disorder, the chances are 7 in 10 that the other twin will at some point be diagnosed similarly. Among fraternal twins, the corresponding odds are just under 2 in 10 (Tsuang & Faraone, 1990). The greater similarity among identical twins holds even among twins reared apart (DiLalla et al., 1996). Summarizing the major twin studies, Kenneth Kendler and his co-researchers (2006) estimate that the *heritability* of major depression is 35 to 40 percent.

Adopted people who suffer a mood disorder often have close biological relatives who suffer mood disorders, become dependent on alcohol, or commit suicide (Wender et al., 1986). (Close-Up: Suicide, next page, reports more research findings.)

> "I see depression as the plague of the modern era."
>
> Lewis Judd, former chief,
> National Institute of Mental Health, 2000

Down Came the Rain Actress Brooke Shields chronicled her disabling postpartum depression in this 2005 book.

INTERCONNECTING

Remind students that being genetically predisposed to a condition such as depression does not mean one is guaranteed to get the disease. Mitigating environmental circumstances can help a person who is genetically predisposed to depression to avoid the symptoms or incidence of disease.

TEACHING TIP

Invite a psychologist to class who specializes in treating mood disorders.

- What method or methods of treatment does he or she prefer?
- What current research is being done on mood disorders?
- What are the rates of mood disorders among high school students?

 TEACHING TIP

At this point, you may want to use **Lecture/Discussion Topics:** *The Sadder-but-Wiser Effect* (p. 20) or *Cognitive Errors in Depression* (p. 21) or *Commitment to the Common Good* (p. 25) or **Classroom Exercises:** *Attributions for an Overdrawn Checking Account* (p. 21) or *The Body Investment Scale and Self-Mutilation* (p. 22) or *Understanding Suicide* (p. 23) or *The Expanded Revised Facts on Suicide Quiz* (p. 24) from Bolt's Teacher's Resource Binder.

Suicide may be a sensitive subject, especially if students have known someone who has attempted or committed suicide. Students may also have attempted suicide and not shared that with others. Students generally struggle with questions of life's purpose, and these feelings are normal. Remind students that any indication of someone contemplating suicide should be taken seriously.

TEACHING TIP

What reasons do people give for being lonely? One survey sorted them into five major categories.

1. Being unattached. Having no spouse or partner, particularly breaking up with a spouse or significant other.

2. Alienation. Being misunderstood and feeling different; not being needed and having no close friends.

3. Being alone. Coming home to an empty house.

4. Forced isolation. Being hospitalized or housebound; having no transportation.

5. Dislocation. Being away from home; starting a new job or school; traveling often.

CLOSE-UP

Suicide

> "But life, being weary of these worldly bars, Never lacks power to dismiss itself."
> William Shakespeare, *Julius Caesar*, 1599

Each year nearly 1 million despairing people worldwide will elect a permanent solution to what might have been a temporary problem (WHO, 2008). Comparing the suicide rates of different groups, researchers have found

- **national differences:** Britain's, Italy's, and Spain's suicide rates are little more than half those of Canada, Australia, and the United States. Austria's and Finland's are about double (WHO, 2008). Within Europe, the most suicide-prone people (Lithuanians) have been 14 times more likely to kill themselves than the least (Greeks).

- **racial differences:** Within the United States, Whites are nearly twice as likely as Blacks to kill themselves (NIMH, 2002).

- **gender differences:** Women are much more likely than men to attempt suicide (WHO, 2008). But men are two to four times more likely (depending on the country) to succeed (**FIGURE 12.5**). Men use more lethal methods, such as firing a bullet into the head, the method of choice in 6 of 10 U.S. suicides.

- **age differences and trends:** In late adulthood, rates increase, dramatically so among men (Figure 12.5). In the last half of the twentieth century, the global rate of annual suicide deaths rose from 10 to 18 per 100,000 (WHO, 2008).

- **other group differences:** Suicide rates are much higher among the rich, the nonreligious, and those who are single, widowed, or divorced (Hoyer & Lund, 1993; Stack,

1992; Stengel, 1981). Gay and lesbian youth much more often suffer distress and attempt suicide than do their heterosexual peers (Goldfried, 2001). Among 1.3 million Swedish military conscripts at age 18, thinner men were more likely than their rounder age-mates to later commit suicide (Magnusson et al., 2006). In England and Wales, there is a 17 percent increased risk of suicide among those born in the spring and early summer rather than autumn (Salib & Cortina-Borja, 2006).

The risk of suicide is at least five times greater for those who have been depressed than for the general population (Bostwick & Pankratz, 2000). People seldom commit suicide while in the depths of depression, when energy and initiative are lacking. It is when they begin to rebound and become capable of following through that the risk increases. Compared with people who suffer no disorder, those with alcohol dependency are roughly 100 times more likely to commit suicide; some 3 percent of them do (Murphy & Wetzel, 1990). Even among people who have attempted suicide, those who abuse alcohol are five times more likely than others to kill themselves eventually (Beck & Steer, 1989). Teenage suicides are often linked with drug and alcohol abuse; the final act may follow a traumatic event, such as a romantic breakup or a guilt-provoking antisocial act (Fowler et al., 1986; Kolata, 1986). Because suicide is so often an impulsive act, environmental barriers (such as jump barriers on high bridges and the unavailability of loaded guns) can reduce suicides (Anderson, 2008). Although common sense might suggest that a determined person would simply find another way to complete the act, such restrictions give time for self-destructive impulses to subside.

▼ Gene-hunters' pursuit of bipolar-DNA links Linkage studies seek to identify aberrant genes in family members suffering a disorder. These Pennsylvania Amish family members—an isolated population sharing a common lifestyle and some vulnerability to bipolar disorder—have volunteered for such studies.

To tease out the genes that put people at risk for depression, some researchers have turned to *linkage analysis*. After finding families in which the disorder appears across several generations, geneticists examine DNA from affected and unaffected family members, looking for differences. Linkage analysis points us to a chromosome neighborhood, note behavior genetics researchers Robert Plomin and Peter McGuffin (2003); "a house-to-house search is then needed to find the culprit gene." Such studies are reinforcing the view that depression is a complex condition. Many genes probably work together, producing a mosaic of small effects that interact with other factors to put some people at greater risk. If the culprit gene variations can be identified, they may open the door to more effective drug therapy (Hu et al., 2007; McMahon et al., 2006; Paddock et al., 2007).

> ➤ FIGURE 12.5
>
> **Suicide rates by gender and age** Worldwide suicide rates are higher among males than among females. The highest rates of all are found among older men. (From *Statistical Abstract,* 2008.)

Social suggestion may trigger suicide. Following highly publicized suicides and TV programs featuring suicide, known suicides increase. So do fatal auto and private airplane "accidents." One six-year study tracked suicide cases among all 1.2 million people who lived in metropolitan Stockholm at any time during the 1990s (Hedström et al., 2008). Men exposed to a family suicide were 8 times more likely to commit suicide than were nonexposed men. Although that phenomenon may be partly attributable to family genes, shared genetic predispositions do not explain why men exposed to a co-worker's suicide were 3.5 times more likely to commit suicide, compared with non-exposed men.

Suicide is not necessarily an act of hostility or revenge. The elderly sometimes choose death as an alternative to current or future suffering. In people of all ages, suicide may be a way of switching off unendurable pain and relieving a perceived burden on family members. "People desire death when two fundamental needs are frustrated to the point of extinction," notes Thomas Joiner (2006, p. 47): "The need to belong with or connect to others, and the need to feel effective with or to influence others."

In retrospect, families and friends may recall signs that they believe should have forewarned them—verbal hints, giving possessions away, or withdrawal and preoccupation with death. But few who talk of suicide or think suicidal thoughts (a number that includes one-third of all adolescents and college students) actually attempt suicide, and few of those who attempt it complete the act (Yip, 1998). U.S. hospital emergency rooms, for example, log a half-million visits as a result of attempted suicides each year (Surgeon General, 1999). But about 30,000 do succeed, one-third of whom have tried to kill themselves previously. Most discussed it beforehand. So, if a friend talks suicide to you, it's important to listen and to direct the person to professional help. Anyone who threatens suicide is at least sending a signal of feeling desperate or despondent.

The Depressed Brain Using modern technology, researchers are also gaining insight into brain activity during depressed and manic states, and into the effects of certain neurotransmitters during these states. One study gave 13 elite Canadian swimmers the wrenching experience of watching a video of the swim in which they failed to make the Olympic team or failed at the Olympic games (Davis et al., 2008). Functional MRI (fMRI) scans showed the bummed-out swimmers experiencing brain activity patterns akin to those of patients with depressed moods.

Many studies have found less activity in the brain during slowed-down depressive states, and more activity during periods of mania (**FIGURE 12.6** on the next page). The left frontal lobe, which is active during positive emotions, is likely to be inactive during depressed states (Davidson et al., 2002). In one study of people with severe depression, MRI scans found their frontal lobes 7 percent smaller than normal (Coffey et al., 1993). Other studies show that the *hippocampus,* the memory-processing center linked with the brain's emotional circuitry, is vulnerable to stress-related damage.

TEACHING TIP

Have students divide into groups and come up with several serious, helpful responses they might give to a friend, family member, or acquaintance who might communicate they are contemplating suicide.

- What would their response be to someone who seems preoccupied with death?

- What would their response be to someone who tried to give them a prized possession?

- What would they say to someone who told them they were contemplating suicide?

TEACHING TIP

How do people cope with loneliness? Rubenstein and Shaver have found four major strategies.

- "Sad passivity" includes sleeping, drinking, overeating, and watching TV.

- "Social contact" may involve calling a friend or visiting someone.

- "Active solitude" takes the form of studying, reading, exercising, or going to a movie.

- "Distractions" include spending money and going shopping.

Rubenstein, C. M., & Shaver, P. (1982). *In search of intimacy.* New York: Delacorte Press.

Have students research the neurotransmitters most related to mood disorders. Extend the research to include the types of drugs used to treat these conditions. Have students discover how the drugs act on the neural sites to affect behavior.

 TEACHING TIP

Research shows that patients with mood disorders respond best to treatments that use both medical therapies (i.e., drugs) and cognitive/behavioral therapy. Each alone does not seem to be as effective as both combined.

➤ **FIGURE 12.6**

The ups and downs of bipolar disorder
These top-facing PET scans show that brain energy consumption rises and falls with the patient's emotional switches. Red areas are where the brain rapidly consumes glucose.

| Depressed state (May 17) | Manic state (May 18) | Depressed state (May 27) |

Courtesy of Lewis Baxter and Michael E. Phelps, UCLA School of Medicine

Biochemical Influences At least two neurotransmitter systems play a role in mood disorders. The first, *norepinephrine,* which increases arousal and boosts mood, is scarce during depression and overabundant during mania. (Drugs that alleviate mania reduce norepinephrine.) Most people with a history of depression also have a history of habitual smoking. This may indicate an attempt to self-medicate with inhaled nicotine, which can temporarily increase norepinephrine and boost mood (HMHL, 2002).

The second neurotransmitter, *serotonin,* is also scarce during depression. Some genes now under scrutiny provide codes for a protein that controls serotonin activity (Plomin & McGuffin, 2003). A widely publicized study of New Zealand young adults seemed to identify a serotonin-controlling gene that, in combination with significant stress, formed a recipe for depression (Caspi et al., 2003; Moffitt et al., 2006). Alas, other recent studies failed to replicate the finding (Risch et al., 2009). But stay tuned: Science grows by fits and starts.

Drugs that relieve depression tend to increase norepinephrine or serotonin supplies by blocking either their reuptake (as Prozac, Zoloft, and Paxil do with serotonin) or their chemical breakdown. Repetitive physical exercise, such as jogging, reduces depression as it increases serotonin (Ilardi et al., 2007; Jacobs, 1994). Boosting serotonin may promote recovery from depression by stimulating hippocampus neuron growth (Airan et al., 2007; Jacobs et al., 2000).

The Social-Cognitive Perspective

Depression is a whole-body disorder. Biological influences contribute to depression but don't fully explain it. The social-cognitive perspective explores the roles of thinking and acting.

Depressed people view life through dark glasses. Their intensely negative assumptions about themselves, their situation, and their future lead them to magnify bad experiences and minimize good ones. Listen to Norman, a Canadian college professor, recalling his depression:

> I [despaired] of ever being human again. I honestly felt subhuman, lower than the lowest vermin. Furthermore, I was self-deprecatory and could not understand why anyone would want to associate with me, let alone love me. . . . I was positive that I was a fraud and a phony and that I didn't deserve my Ph.D. I didn't deserve to have tenure; I didn't deserve to be a Full Professor. . . . I didn't deserve the research grants I had been awarded; I couldn't understand how I had written books and journal articles. . . . I must have conned a lot of people. (Endler, 1982, pp. 45–49)

Self-defeating beliefs and a *negative explanatory style* feed depression's vicious cycle.

Negative Thoughts and Negative Moods Interact Self-defeating beliefs may arise from *learned helplessness.* As we saw in Units 6 and 10, both dogs and humans act depressed, passive, and withdrawn after experiencing uncontrollable painful events. Learned helplessness is more common in women than in men, and women may respond more strongly to stress (Hankin & Abramson, 2001; Mazure et al., 2002; Nolen-Hoeksema, 2001, 2003). For example, 38 percent of women and 17 percent of men entering American colleges and universities report feeling "frequently overwhelmed by all I have to do" (Pryor et al., 2006). (Men report spending more of their time in "light anxiety" activities such as sports, TV watching, and partying, possibly avoiding activities that might make them feel overwhelmed.) This may help explain why, beginning in their early teens, women are nearly twice as vulnerable to depression (Kessler, 2001). Susan Nolen-Hoeksema (2003) believes women's higher risk of depression may also be related to what she describes as their tendency to *overthink*—to ruminate, to endlessly rehash something in one's mind. Women often have vivid recall for both wonderful and horrid experiences; men more vaguely recall such experiences (Seidlitz & Diener, 1998). The gender difference in emotional memory may feed women's greater rumination over negative events and explain why fewer men than women report being frequently overwhelmed on entering college.

But why do life's unavoidable failures lead some people—women or men—and not others to become depressed? The answer lies partly in their *explanatory style*—who or what they blame for their failures. Think how you might feel if you failed a test. If you can externalize the blame ("What an unfair test!"), you are more likely to feel angry. But if you blame yourself, you probably will feel stupid and depressed.

So it is with depressed people, who tend to explain bad events in terms that are *stable* ("It's going to last forever"), *global* ("It's going to affect everything I do"), and *internal* ("It's all my fault") (**FIGURE 12.7**). Depression-prone people respond to bad events in an especially self-focused, self-blaming way (Mor & Winquist, 2002; Pyszczynski et al., 1991; Wood et al., 1990a,b). Their self-esteem fluctuates more rapidly up with boosts and down with threats (Butler et al., 1994).

The result of these pessimistic, overgeneralized, self-blaming attributions may be a depressing sense of hopelessness (Abramson et al., 1989; Panzarella et al., 2006). As

Susan Nolen-Hoeksema "This epidemic of morbid meditation is a disease that women suffer much more than men. Women can ruminate about anything and everything—our appearance, our families, our career, our health." (*Women Who Think Too Much: How to Break Free of Overthinking and Reclaim Your Life*, 2003) ▲

> "I have learned to accept my mistakes by referring them to a personal history which was not of my making."
> B. F. Skinner, 1983

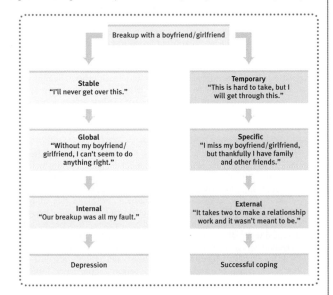

Breakup with a boyfriend/girlfriend

| Stable "I'll never get over this." | Temporary "This is hard to take, but I will get through this." |

| Global "Without my boyfriend/girlfriend, I can't seem to do anything right." | Specific "I miss my boyfriend/girlfriend, but thankfully I have family and other friends." |

| Internal "Our breakup was all my fault." | External "It takes two to make a relationship work and it wasn't meant to be." |

| Depression | Successful coping |

► **FIGURE 12.7**
Explanatory style and depression

TEACHING TIP

Explanatory style and learned helplessness help explain depression, but what about explanations for mania? Have students brainstorm about different psychological explanations for mania:

- How might learning theorists explain mania?

- What attributions might a person in a manic state make about his or her behavior? Would the person be optimistic or pessimistic?

DEMO

Ask students to imagine that they have just been notified by their bank that their account is overdrawn. Have them write down in a sentence or two what they believe to be the single most important cause. Then, in thinking about what they have written, have them answer the following questions:

- Does the cause you describe reflect more about you (internal) or something more about other people or circumstances (external)?

- Is the cause something that is permanent/stable (likely to be present in the future), or is the cause temporary?

- Is the cause something that influences other areas of your life (global) or only your account balance (specific)?

Ask for volunteers to share some of their answers and reiterate that attributions for events that are internal, stable, and global are most likely to be associated with depression.

INTERCONNECTING

Remind students that learned helplessness, an early experimental basis for explanatory style, has its roots in classical conditioning. Using classical conditioning techniques, Seligman and Maier found that dogs learned to be helpless in the face of uncontrollable stimuli. This lead them to wonder whether depression has its roots in learning theory.

INTERCONNECTING

Peter Barnett and Ian Gotlib point out that certain types of thinking may be related to depression, but they might not be the causes of depression. Further experimental evidence is needed to determine the exact causes of the illness.

Might Charlie Brown be helped by an optimism-training program?

PEANUTS

Reprinted by permission of United Feature Syndicate, Inc.

• From 1985 to 2004, Americans indeed reported fewer close relationships with co-workers, extended family, and neighbors, and thus had fewer people with whom they could discuss meaningful matters. The number of people with no confidantes increased from 10 to 25 percent (McPherson et al., 2006). •

"Man never reasons so much and becomes so introspective as when he suffers, since he is anxious to get at the cause of his sufferings."

Luigi Pirandello, *Six Characters in Search of an Author*, 1922

Martin Seligman has noted, "A recipe for severe depression is preexisting pessimism encountering failure" (1991, p. 78). What then might we expect of new college students who are not depressed but do exhibit a pessimistic explanatory style? Lauren Alloy and her collaborators (1999) monitored Temple University and University of Wisconsin students every 6 weeks for 2.5 years. Among those identified as having a pessimistic thinking style, 17 percent had a first episode of major depression, as did only 1 percent of those who began college with an optimistic thinking style. Follow-up research found that new students exhibiting optimism developed more social support, which contributes to a lowered risk of depression (Brissette et al., 2002).

Seligman (1991, 1995) contends that depression is common among young Westerners because the rise of individualism and the decline of commitment to religion and family have forced young people to take personal responsibility for failure or rejection. In non-Western cultures, where close-knit relationships and cooperation are the norm, major depression is less common and less tied to self-blame over personal failure (WHO, 2004). In Japan, for example, depressed people instead tend to report feeling shame over letting others down (Draguns, 1990a).

There is, however, a chicken-and-egg problem with the social-cognitive explanation of depression. Self-defeating beliefs, negative attributions, and self-blame surely do support depression. Peter Barnett and Ian Gotlib (1988) note that such cognitions *coincide* with a depressed mood and are *indicators* of depression. But do they *cause* depression, any more than a speedometer's reading of 70 mph causes a car's speed? Before or after being depressed, people's thoughts are less negative. Perhaps this is because, as we noted in our discussion of state-dependent memory (Unit 7A), a depressed mood triggers negative thoughts. If you temporarily put people in a bad or sad mood, their memories, judgments, and expectations suddenly become more pessimistic.

Joseph Forgas and his associates (1984) provided a striking demonstration of the mood effect. First, they filmed people talking to each other. The next day, they put those participants in a good or bad mood via hypnosis and had them watch the tape of themselves. The happy participants detected in their screen selves more positive than negative behaviors; the unhappy participants more often saw themselves behaving negatively.

Depression's Vicious Cycle Depression, as we have seen, is often brought on by stressful experiences—losing a job, getting divorced or rejected, suffering physical trauma—by anything that disrupts our sense of who we are and why we are worthy human beings. This disruption in turn leads to brooding, which amplifies negative feelings. But being withdrawn, self-focused, and complaining can by itself elicit rejection (Furr & Funder, 1998; Gotlib & Hammen, 1992). In one study, researchers Stephen Strack and James Coyne (1983) noted that "depressed persons induced hostility, depression, and anxiety in others and got rejected. Their guesses that they were not accepted were not a matter of cognitive distortion." Indeed, people in the throes of depression are at high risk for divorce, job loss, and other stressful life events. Weary of the person's fatigue, hopeless attitude, and lethargy, a spouse may threaten to leave or a boss may begin to question the person's competence. (This provides another example of genetic–environmental interaction: People genetically predisposed to depression more often experience depressing events.) The losses and stress only serve to compound the original depression. Rejection and depression feed each other. Misery may love another's company, but company does not love another's misery.

We can now assemble some of the pieces of the depression puzzle (**FIGURE 12.8**): (1) Negative, stressful events interpreted through (2) a ruminating, pessimistic explanatory style create (3) a hopeless, depressed state that (4) hampers the way the person thinks and acts. This, in turn, fuels (1) negative, stressful experiences such as rejection.

None of us is immune to the dejection, diminished self-esteem, and negative thinking brought on by rejection or defeat. As Edward Hirt and his colleagues (1992) demonstrated, even small losses can temporarily sour our thinking. They studied some avid Indiana University basketball fans who seemed to regard the team as an extension of themselves. After the fans watched their team lose or win, the researchers asked them to predict the team's future performance and their own. After a loss, the morose fans offered bleaker assessments not only of the team's future but also of their own likely performance at throwing darts, solving anagrams, and getting a date. When things aren't going our way, it may seem as though they never will.

It is a cycle we can all recognize. Bad moods feed on themselves: When we *feel* down, we *think* negatively and remember bad experiences. On the brighter side, we can break the cycle of depression at any of these points—by moving to a different environment, by reversing our self-blame and negative attributions, by turning our attention outward, or by engaging in more pleasant activities and more competent behavior.

Winston Churchill called depression a "black dog" that periodically hounded him. Poet Emily Dickinson was so afraid of bursting into tears in public that she spent much of her adult life in seclusion (Patterson, 1951). As each of these lives reminds us, people can and do struggle through depression. Most regain their capacity to love, to work, and even to succeed at the highest levels.

➤ **FIGURE 12.8**

The vicious cycle of depressed thinking
Cognitive therapists attempt to break this cycle, as we will see in Unit 13, by changing the way depressed people process events. Psychiatrists attempt to alter with medication the biological roots of persistently depressed moods.

BEFORE YOU MOVE ON . . .

➤ **ASK YOURSELF**

Has your high school experience been a challenging time for you? What advice would you have for other students about to enter high school?

➤ **TEST YOURSELF 5**

What does it mean to say that "depression is the common cold of psychological disorders"?

Answers to the Test Yourself questions can be found in Appendix E at the end of the book.

Schizophrenia

11: What patterns of thinking, perceiving, feeling, and behaving characterize schizophrenia?

IF DEPRESSION IS THE COMMON COLD of psychological disorders, chronic schizophrenia is the cancer. Nearly 1 in 100 people will develop schizophrenia, joining the estimated 24 million across the world who suffer one of humanity's most dreaded disorders (WHO, 2008).

 TEACHING TIP

Barbara Frederickson of the University of North Carolina, Chapel Hill, has proposed a theory of positive emotions. While negative emotions make us selfish and closed to the world around us, positive emotions broaden and build our lives. When experiencing positive emotions, people tend to be helpful and spread their good feelings around. Frederickson calls this theory the "broaden and build" theory.

 TEACHING TIP

Arrange a field trip to a local mental health care facility to learn more about the most common disorders found in mental institutions. Students can tour the facility and meet with staff psychologists or psychiatrists to learn more about how schizophrenia is treated. You may also want to bring donations of clothing, personal hygiene products, and games for patients to use while they stay in the facility.

 TEACHING TIP

Children as young as 12 have developed symptoms of schizophrenia. The onset of the disorder typically occurs during the late teen and early adult years. Full-blown psychotic episodes (where patients lose touch with reality) may not occur until the patient is out on his or her own, away from family and friends who have supported that person in the past.

UNIT 12

::**schizophrenia** a group of severe disorders characterized by disorganized and delusional thinking, disturbed perceptions, and inappropriate emotions and actions.

::**delusions** false beliefs, often of persecution or grandeur, that may accompany psychotic disorders.

Symptoms of Schizophrenia

Literally translated, **schizophrenia** means "split mind." It refers not to a multiple-personality split but rather to a split from reality that shows itself in disorganized thinking, disturbed perceptions, and inappropriate emotions and actions.

Disorganized Thinking

Imagine trying to communicate with Maxine, a young woman whose thoughts spill out in no logical order. Her biographer, Susan Sheehan (1982, p. 25), observed her saying aloud to no one in particular, "This morning, when I was at Hillside [Hospital], I was making a movie. I was surrounded by movie stars. . . . I'm Mary Poppins. Is this room painted blue to get me upset? My grandmother died four weeks after my eighteenth birthday."

As this strange monologue illustrates, the thinking of a person with schizophrenia is fragmented, bizarre, and often distorted by false beliefs called **delusions** ("I'm Mary Poppins"). Those with *paranoid* tendencies are particularly prone to delusions of persecution. Even within sentences, jumbled ideas may create what is called *word salad*. One young man begged for "a little more allegro in the treatment," and suggested that "liberationary movement with a view to the widening of the horizon" will "ergo extort some wit in lectures."

Disorganized thoughts may result from a breakdown in *selective attention*. Recall from Unit 4 that we normally have a remarkable capacity for giving our undivided attention to one set of sensory stimuli while filtering out others. Those with schizophrenia cannot do this. Thus, irrelevant, minute stimuli, such as the grooves on a brick or the inflections of a voice, may distract their attention from a bigger event or a speaker's meaning. As one former patient recalled, "What had happened to me . . . was a breakdown in the filter, and a hodge-podge of unrelated stimuli were distracting me from things which should have had my undivided attention" (MacDonald, 1960, p. 218). This selective-attention difficulty is but one of dozens of cognitive differences associated with schizophrenia (Reichenberg & Harvey, 2007).

Disturbed Perceptions

A person with schizophrenia may have *hallucinations* (sensory experiences without sensory stimulation), seeing, feeling, tasting, or smelling things that are not there. Most often, however, the hallucinations are auditory, frequently voices making insulting remarks or giving orders. The voices may tell the patient that she is bad or that

RESEARCH

Some famous criminals have claimed that voices told them to commit their crimes. They also held ideas that seemed delusional. Have students research the following cases:

- David Berkowitz (the "Son of Sam"). This case involved a young man who claimed his neighbor's dog was possessed by Satan and told him to kill. Berkowitz confessed to killing six people in New York City over the course of a year.

- John Hinkley. Hinkley attempted to assassinate President Ronald Reagan to attract the attention of Jodie Foster, the Hollywood actress and director.

- John David Chapman. Chapman killed John Lennon because he felt the "devil" side of him told him to.

TROUBLESHOOTING

Help students remember the difference between delusions and hallucinations:

- Delusions are false beliefs. These are a dysfunction of our cognitive systems.

- Hallucinations are false perceptions. These are a dysfunction of our perceptual systems.

▼
Art by people diagnosed with schizophrenia
Commenting on the kind of artwork shown here, poet and art critic John Ashbery wrote: "The lure of the work is strong, but so is the terror of the unanswerable riddles it proposes."

August Natterer, *Witch's Head, The Prinzhorn Collection, University of Heidelberg*

Photos of paintings by Krannert Museum, University of Illinois at Urbana-Champaign

WEB CONNECT

Access a free online computer simulation available through UC-Davis that simulates hallucinations that people with schizophrenia might experience. Students will need to set up a free account with Second Life, the online virtual world: www.ucdmc.ucdavis.edu/ais/virtualhallucinations/.

she must burn herself with a cigarette lighter. Imagine your own reaction if a dream broke into your waking consciousness. When the unreal seems real, the resulting perceptions are at best bizarre, at worst terrifying.

Inappropriate Emotions and Actions

The emotions of schizophrenia are often utterly inappropriate, split off from reality. Maxine laughed after recalling her grandmother's death. On other occasions, she cried when others laughed, or became angry for no apparent reason. Others with schizophrenia lapse into an emotionless state of *flat affect*.

Motor behavior may also be inappropriate. Some perform senseless, compulsive acts, such as continually rocking or rubbing an arm. Others, who exhibit *catatonia*, may remain motionless for hours and then become agitated.

As you can imagine, such disorganized thinking, disturbed perceptions, and inappropriate emotions and actions profoundly disrupt social relationships and make it difficult to hold a job. Even those with dissociative identity disorder may continue to function in everyday life, but less so those with schizophrenia. During their most severe periods, those with schizophrenia live in a private inner world, preoccupied with illogical ideas and unreal images. Given a supportive environment, some eventually recover to enjoy a normal life or experience bouts of schizophrenia only intermittently. Others remain socially withdrawn and isolated throughout much of their lives.

Onset and Development of Schizophrenia

Schizophrenia typically strikes as young people are maturing into adulthood. Although it only afflicts 1 in 100 people, it knows no national boundaries, and it affects both males and females—though men tend to be struck earlier, more severely, and slightly more often (Aleman et al., 2003; Picchioni & Murray, 2007). Studies of Swedish and Danish male populations reveal that thin young men, and those who were not breast fed, are more vulnerable (Sørensen et al., 2005, 2006; Zammit et al., 2007).

For some, schizophrenia will appear suddenly, seemingly as a reaction to stress. For others, as was the case with Maxine, schizophrenia develops gradually, emerging from a long history of social inadequacy (which helps explain why those predisposed to schizophrenia often end up in the lower socioeconomic levels, or even homeless). We have thus far described schizophrenia as if it were a single disorder. Actually, it is a cluster of disorders. The subtypes share some common features, but they also have some distinguishing symptoms (**TABLE 12.3**). Schizophrenia patients with *positive symptoms* may experience hallucinations, talk in disorganized and deluded ways, and exhibit inappropriate laughter, tears, or rage. Those with *negative symptoms* have toneless voices, expressionless faces, or mute and rigid bodies. Thus, positive symptoms

TABLE 12.3

SUBTYPES OF SCHIZOPHRENIA	
Paranoid	Preoccupation with delusions or hallucinations, often with themes of persecution or grandiosity
Disorganized	Disorganized speech or behavior, or flat or inappropriate emotion
Catatonic	Immobility (or excessive, purposeless movement), extreme negativism, and/or parrotlike repeating of another's speech or movements
Undifferentiated	Many and varied symptoms
Residual	Withdrawal, after hallucinations and delusions have disappeared

> "When someone asks me to explain schizophrenia I tell them, you know how sometimes in your dreams you are in them yourself and some of them feel like real nightmares? My schizophrenia was like I was walking through a dream. But everything around me was real. At times, today's world seems so boring and I wonder if I would like to step back into the schizophrenic dream, but then I remember all the scary and horrifying experiences."
>
> Stuart Emmons, with Craig Geisler, Kalman J. Kaplan, and Martin Harrow, *Living With Schizophrenia*, 1997

TEACHING TIP

Extend the discussion of schizophrenia to include autism. Social withdrawal is prominent in both autism and schizophrenia. Autism is diagnosed at an early age (always by age 3). The diagnosis of schizophrenia occurs between 15 and 30 years. The incidence of schizophrenia in males and females is about equal, while autism occurs mostly in males. James Kalat identifies nine behaviors of the autistic child.

1. Social isolation
2. Stereotyped behaviors, such as rocking back and forth, biting hands, and staring
3. Resistance to any change in routine
4. Abnormal, often extreme, responses to sensory stimuli
5. Insensitivity to pain
6. Inappropriate emotional expression
7. Disturbances of movement
8. Poor development of speech
9. Specific, limited, intellectual problems

Kalat, J. (1998). *Biological psychology* (9th ed.). Pacific Grove, CA: Brooks/Cole.

TEACHING TIP

Paranoid schizophrenia is the most widely recognizable form of the disorder. Movies depicting people with paranoid schizophrenia as either bumbling oddballs or psychopathic killers reinforce stereotypes of these patients.

TEACHING TIP

People with schizophrenia will exhibit other striking symptoms of their disorder:

- Loose associations occur in patients with disorganized schizophrenia as they link events and memories that don't seem to fit together logically.
- Neologisms are words that patients create, usually as part of the "word salad" symptom. They will make up words that make no logical sense.

are the *presence* of inappropriate behaviors, and negative symptoms are the *absence* of appropriate behaviors. Because schizophrenia is a cluster of disorders, these varied symptoms could have more than one cause.

One rule holds true around the world: When schizophrenia is a slow-developing process (called *chronic,* or *process, schizophrenia*), recovery is doubtful (WHO, 1979). Those with chronic schizophrenia often exhibit the persistent and incapacitating negative symptom of withdrawal (Kirkpatrick et al., 2006). Men, whose schizophrenia develops on average four years earlier than women's, more often exhibit negative symptoms and chronic schizophrenia (Räsänen et al., 2000). When previously well-adjusted people develop schizophrenia rapidly (called *acute,* or *reactive, schizophrenia*) following particular life stresses, recovery is much more likely. They more often have the positive symptoms that are more likely to respond to drug therapy (Fenton & McGlashan, 1991, 1994; Fowles, 1992).

Understanding Schizophrenia

12: What causes schizophrenia?

Schizophrenia is not only the most dreaded psychological disorder but also one of the most heavily researched. Most of the new research studies link it with brain abnormalities and genetic predispositions. Schizophrenia is a disease of the brain exhibited in symptoms of the mind.

Brain Abnormalities

Might imbalances in brain chemistry underlie schizophrenia? Scientists have long known that strange behavior can have strange chemical causes. The saying "mad as a hatter" refers to the psychological deterioration of British hatmakers whose brains, it was later discovered, were slowly poisoned as they moistened the brims of mercury-laden felt hats with their lips (Smith, 1983). As we saw in Unit 5, scientists are clarifying the mechanism by which chemicals such as LSD produce hallucinations. These discoveries hint that schizophrenia symptoms might have a biochemical key.

Dopamine Overactivity Researchers discovered one such key when they examined schizophrenia patients' brains after death and found an excess of receptors for *dopamine*—a sixfold excess for the so-called D4 dopamine receptor (Seeman et al., 1993; Wong et al., 1986). They speculate that such a high level may intensify brain signals in schizophrenia, creating positive symptoms such as hallucinations and paranoia. As we might therefore expect, drugs that block dopamine receptors often lessen these symptoms; drugs that increase dopamine levels, such as amphetamines and cocaine, sometimes intensify them (Swerdlow & Koob, 1987). Dopamine overactivity may underlie patients' overreactions to irrelevant external and internal stimuli.

Dopamine-blocking drugs have little effect on persistent negative symptoms of withdrawal. Researchers are exploring the excitatory neurotransmitter glutamate. Impaired glutamate activity appears to be another source of schizophrenia symptoms (Javitt & Coyle, 2004). Drugs that interfere with glutamate receptors can produce schizophrenialike negative symptoms.

Abnormal Brain Activity and Anatomy Modern brain-scanning techniques reveal that many people with chronic schizophrenia have abnormal activity in multiple brain areas. Some have abnormally low brain activity in the frontal lobes, which are critical for reasoning, planning, and problem solving (Morey et al., 2005; Pettegrew et al., 1993; Resnick, 1992). People diagnosed with schizophrenia also display a noticeable decline in the brain waves that reflect synchronized neural firing in the frontal

● **About 60 percent of schizophrenia patients smoke, often heavily. Nicotine apparently stimulates certain brain receptors, which helps focus attention (Javitt & Coyle, 2004).** ●

lobes (Spencer et al., 2004; Symond et al., 2005). Out-of-sync neurons may disrupt the integrated functioning of neural networks, possibly contributing to schizophrenia symptoms.

One study took PET scans of brain activity while people were hallucinating (Silbersweig et al., 1995). When participants heard a voice or saw something, their brain became vigorously active in several core regions, including the thalamus, a structure deep in the brain that filters incoming sensory signals and transmits them to the cortex. Another PET scan study of people with paranoia found increased activity in the amygdala, a fear-processing center (Epstein et al., 1998).

Many studies have found enlarged, fluid-filled areas and a corresponding shrinkage of cerebral tissue in people with schizophrenia (Wright et al., 2000). Some studies have even found such abnormalities in the brains of people who would *later* develop this disorder, and in their close relatives (Boos et al., 2007; Job et al., 2006). The greater the shrinkage, the more severe the thought disorder (Collinson et al., 2003; Nelson et al., 1998; Shenton, 1992). One smaller-than-normal area is the cortex. Another is the thalamus, which may explain why people with schizophrenia have difficulty filtering sensory input and focusing attention (Andreasen et al., 1994). The bottom line of various studies is that schizophrenia involves not one isolated brain abnormality but problems with several brain regions and their interconnections (Andreasen, 1997, 2001).

Naturally, scientists wonder what causes these abnormalities. Some suspect a mishap during prenatal development or delivery. Two known risk factors for schizophrenia are low birth weight and oxygen deprivation during delivery (Buka et al., 1999; Zornberg et al., 2000). Famine may also increase risks. People conceived during the peak of the Dutch wartime famine later displayed a doubled rate of schizophrenia, as did those conceived during the famine of 1959 to 1961 in eastern China (St. Clair et al., 2005; Susser et al., 1996).

Maternal Virus During Pregnancy Consider another possible culprit: a maternal viral infection that impairs fetal brain development (Patterson, 2007). Can you imagine some ways to test this fetal-virus idea? Scientists have asked the following:

- *Are people at increased risk of schizophrenia if, during the middle of their fetal development, their country experienced a flu epidemic?* The repeated answer is *yes* (Mednick et al., 1994; Murray et al., 1992; Wright et al., 1995).
- *Are people born in densely populated areas, where viral diseases spread more readily, at greater risk for schizophrenia?* The answer, confirmed in a study of 1.75 million Danes, is *yes* (Jablensky, 1999; Mortensen, 1999).
- *Are those born during the winter and spring months—after the fall-winter flu season—also at increased risk?* The answer is again *yes*, at 5 to 8 percent increased risk (Torrey et al., 1997, 2002).
- *In the Southern Hemisphere, where the seasons are the reverse of the Northern Hemisphere, are the months of above-average schizophrenia births similarly reversed?* Again, the answer is *yes*, though somewhat less so. In Australia, for example, people born between August and October are at greater risk—*unless* they migrated from the Northern Hemisphere, in which case their risk is greater if they were born between January and March (McGrath et al., 1995, 1999).
- *Are mothers who report being sick with influenza during pregnancy more likely to bear children who develop schizophrenia?* In one study of nearly 8000 women, the answer was *yes*. The schizophrenia risk increased from the customary 1 percent to about 2 percent—but only when infections occurred during the second trimester (Brown et al., 2000).

Studying the neurophysiology of schizophrenia Psychiatrist E. Fuller Torrey is collecting the brains of hundreds of those who died as young adults and suffered disorders such as schizophrenia and bipolar disorder. Torrey is making tissue samples available to researchers worldwide. ▲

TEACHING TIP

Recent research using brain imaging techniques has shed some light on the biological basis of schizophrenia.

- People who develop schizophrenia have abnormal brain activity before the onset of symptoms, showing that schizophrenia may be a developmental disorder.

- MRI studies show that gray matter in the brains of people with schizophrenia is markedly less dense than in people with no schizophrenia.

- Studies have also shown that people who have auditory hallucinations experience temporal lobe activation, indicating that they really are hearing voices, even though the voices are not present.

TEACHING TIP

Michael Gorman suggests that students read Mark Vonnegut's *The Eden Express,* which is an autobiographical account of the author's schizophrenic breakdown and recovery. Vonnegut (son of author Kurt Vonnegut) describes his hallucinating, his suicide attempts, and his struggle to recover. He attributes his cure to thorazine, but other factors contributed as well. Students can complete any of the following projects:

- An analysis of the depiction of schizophrenia in light of modern knowledge

- A reflective paper focusing on the student's reaction to Vonnegut's story

- A creative story based on Vonnegut's account

Gorman, M. (1984). Using *The Eden Express* to teach introductory psychology. *Teaching of Psychology, 11(1),* 39–40.

TEACHING TIP

At this point, you may want to use **Classroom Exercise:** *Magical Ideation Scale* (p. 26) or **Lecture/Discussion Topic:** *Infantile Autism* (p. 26) or **Student Project: The Eden Express** *and Schizophrenia* (p. 26) from Bolt's Teacher's Resource Binder.

UNIT 12

TEACHING TIP

Remind students that a genetic predisposition does not guarantee that one will get a disorder such as schizophrenia. Environmental and behavioral influences help determine whether someone with a predisposition will develop the disorder.

TROUBLESHOOTING

Students may be confused to learn that identical twins may not share a placenta. Identical twins are defined by their shared DNA, not by a shared placenta.

- *Does blood drawn from pregnant women whose offspring develop schizophrenia show higher-than-normal levels of antibodies that suggest a viral infection?* In one study of 27 women whose children later developed schizophrenia, the answer was *yes* (Buka et al., 2001). And the answer was again *yes* in a huge California study, which collected blood samples from some 20,000 pregnant women during the 1950s and 1960s. Some children born of those pregnancies were later diagnosed with schizophrenia. When antibodies in the mother's blood indicated she had been exposed to influenza during the first half of the pregnancy, the child's risk of developing schizophrenia tripled. Flu during the second half of the pregnancy produced no such increase (Brown et al., 2004).

These converging lines of evidence suggest that fetal-virus infections play a contributing role in the development of schizophrenia. They also strengthen the recommendation that "women who will be more than three months pregnant during the flu season" have a flu shot (CDC, 2003).

Why might a second-trimester maternal flu bout put fetuses at risk? Is it the virus itself? The mother's immune response to it? Medications taken? (Wyatt et al., 2001). Does the infection weaken the brain's supportive glial cells, leading to reduced synaptic connections (Moises et al., 2002)? In time, answers may become available.

Genetic Factors

Fetal-virus infections do appear to increase the odds that a child will develop schizophrenia. But this theory cannot tell us why some 98 percent of women who catch the flu during their second trimester of pregnancy bear children who do *not* develop schizophrenia. Might people also inherit a predisposition to this disorder? The evidence strongly suggests that, *yes*, some do. The nearly 1-in-100 odds of any person's being diagnosed with schizophrenia become about 1 in 10 among those whose sibling or parent has the disorder, and close to 1 in 2 if the affected sibling is an identical twin (**FIGURE 12.9**). And, although only a dozen or so such cases are on record, the co-twin of an identical twin with schizophrenia retains that 1-in-2 chance when the twins are reared apart (Plomin et al., 1997).

Remember, though, that identical twins also share a prenatal environment. About two-thirds also share a placenta and the blood it supplies; the other one-third have two single placentas. If an identical twin has schizophrenia, the co-twin's chances of being similarly afflicted are 6 in 10 if they shared a placenta. If they had separate placentas, as do fraternal twins, the chances are only 1 in 10 (Davis et al., 1995a,b; Phelps et al., 1997). Twins who share a placenta are more likely to experience the same prenatal viruses. So it is possible that shared germs as well as shared genes produce identical twin similarities.

➤ **FIGURE 12.9**
Risk of developing schizophrenia The lifetime risk of developing schizophrenia varies with one's genetic relatedness to someone having this disorder. Across countries, barely more than 1 in 10 fraternal twins, but some 5 in 10 identical twins, share a schizophrenia diagnosis. (Adapted from Gottesman, 2001.)

RESEARCH

Have students examine how heritable other mental illnesses are. They can find statistics related to how likely a child is to develop a disorder the parent has. Consider the following conditions:

- Depression and bipolar disorder
- Anxiety disorders
- Somatoform disorders
- Substance-related disorders
- Personality disorders

Adoption studies, however, confirm that the genetic link is real (Gottesman, 1991). Children adopted by someone who develops schizophrenia seldom "catch" the disorder. Rather, adopted children have an elevated risk if a biological parent is diagnosed with schizophrenia.

With the genetic factor established, researchers are now sleuthing specific genes that, in some combination, might predispose schizophrenia-inducing brain abnormalities (Marx, 2007; Millar et al., 2005; Williams et al., 2007). (It is not our genes but our brains that directly control our behavior.) Some of these genes influence the effects of dopamine and other neurotransmitters in the brain. Others affect the production of *myelin*, a fatty substance that coats the axons of nerve cells and lets impulses travel at high speed through neural networks.

Although the genetic contribution to schizophrenia is beyond question, the genetic formula is not as straightforward as the inheritance of eye color. A complex disorder such as schizophrenia is surely influenced by multiple genes with small effects, but identifying these genes has proven difficult (McClellan et al., 2007; Sanders et al., 2008; Walsh et al., 2008). And even within this context, other factors—such as the prenatal viral infections, nutritional deprivation, and oxygen deprivation at birth mentioned earlier—may somehow help to "turn on" the genes that predispose some of us to this disease. As we have so often seen, nature and nurture interact. Neither hand claps alone.

Our knowledge of human genetics and of genetic influences on maladies such as schizophrenia is exploding, thanks partly to millions of new U.S. National Institute of Mental Health dollars focused on solving the schizophrenia riddle. In 2007, one privately funded new research center announced its ambitious aim: "To unambiguously diagnose patients with psychiatric disorders based on their DNA sequence in 10 years' time" (Holden, 2007). So, can scientists develop genetic tests that reveal who is at risk? If so, will people in the future subject their embryos to genetic testing (and gene repair or abortion) if they are at risk for this or some other psychological or physical malady? Might they take their egg and sperm to a genetics lab for screening before combining them to produce an embryo? Or will children be tested for genetic risks and given appropriate preventive treatments? In this brave new twenty-first-century world, such questions await answers.

Schizophrenia in identical twins When twins differ, only the one afflicted with schizophrenia typically has enlarged, fluid-filled cranial cavities (right) (Suddath et al., 1990). The difference between the twins implies some nongenetic factor, such as a virus, is also at work.

No schizophrenia   Schizophrenia

The Genain quadruplets The odds of any four people picked at random all being diagnosed with schizophrenia are 1 in 100 million. But genetically identical sisters Nora, Iris, Myra, and Hester Genain all have the disease. Two of the sisters have more severe forms of the disorder than the others, suggesting the influence of environmental as well as biological factors.

Psychological Factors

If prenatal viruses and genetic predispositions do not, by themselves, cause schizophrenia, neither do family or social factors alone. Psychologists who once attributed schizophrenia to cold and capricious "refrigerator mothers" have long since abandoned this idea. It remains true, as Susan Nicol and Irving Gottesman (1983) noted almost three decades ago, that "no environmental causes have been discovered that will invariably, or even with moderate probability, produce schizophrenia in persons who are not related to" a person with schizophrenia.

Hoping to identify environmental triggers of schizophrenia, several investigators are following the development of "high-risk" children, such as those born to a parent with schizophrenia or exposed to prenatal risks (Freedman et al., 1998; Olin & Mednick, 1996; Susser, 1999). One study followed 163 teens and early-twenties adults who had

Both photos: Courtesy of Daniel R. Weinberger, M.D., NIH-NIMH/NSC

Courtesy of Genain family

TEACHING TIP

The first and last names of the quadruplets featured here were changed to protect their privacy as they became recurrent research subjects. They share the unique distinction of being the only set of multiples who share this mental illness. All became schizophrenic by age 25, but in addition to sharing the same gene code, they also shared a nightmarish family life, suffering abuse from their father and ambivalence from their mother. The least ill of the four, Myra, seemed to be her mother's favorite and managed to avoid some of her father's abuse, reinforcing the idea of the interplay between heredity and environment.

UNIT 12

CRITICAL THINKING

Personality disorders are difficult to diagnose and treat, because the behaviors are enduring and rigid. Have students discuss why people may be unable to recognize that someone has a personality disorder:

- Where is the line between being eccentric, anxious, or odd and having a personality disorder?

- How might treatment be difficult?

TEACHING TIP

Students may be curious about the other personality disorders identified in the *DSM-IV-TR:*

- Cluster A includes paranoid, schizoid, and schizotypal. People with illnesses from this group of disorders exhibit odd or eccentric behavior.

- Cluster B includes antisocial, borderline, histrionic, and narcissistic. This group focuses on disorders that demonstrate dramatic or impulsive behavior.

- Cluster C includes avoidant, dependent, and obsessive-compulsive personalities. These are the anxiety-related disorders.

The *DSM-V* might eliminate these categories in favor of a more generalized way to diagnose personality disorders.

::**personality disorders** psychological disorders characterized by inflexible and enduring behavior patterns that impair social functioning.

::**antisocial personality disorder** a personality disorder in which the person (usually a man) exhibits a lack of conscience for wrongdoing, even toward friends and family members. May be aggressive and ruthless or a clever con artist.

Antisocial personality? Dennis Rader, known as the "BTK killer" in Kansas, was convicted in 2005 of killing 10 people over a 30-year span. Rader exhibited the extreme lack of conscience that marks antisocial personality disorder.

two relatives with schizophrenia. During the 2.5-year study, the 20 percent who developed schizophrenia displayed some tendency to withdraw socially and behave oddly before the onset of the disorder (Johnstone et al., 2005). By comparing the experiences of high-risk and low-risk children who do and do not develop schizophrenia, researchers have so far pinpointed the following possible early warning signs:

- A mother whose schizophrenia was severe and long-lasting
- Birth complications, often involving oxygen deprivation and low birth weight
- Separation from parents
- Short attention span and poor muscle coordination
- Disruptive or withdrawn behavior
- Emotional unpredictability
- Poor peer relations and solo play

* * *

Most of us can relate more easily to the ups and downs of mood disorders than to the strange thoughts, perceptions, and behaviors of schizophrenia. Sometimes our thoughts do jump around, but we do not talk nonsensically. Occasionally we feel unjustly suspicious of someone, but we do not fear that the world is plotting against us. Often our perceptions err, but rarely do we see or hear things that are not there. We have felt regret after laughing at someone's misfortune, but we rarely giggle in response to bad news. At times we just want to be alone, but we do not live in social isolation. However, millions of people around the world do talk strangely, suffer delusions, hear nonexistent voices, see things that are not there, laugh or cry at inappropriate times, or withdraw into private imaginary worlds. The quest to solve the cruel puzzle of schizophrenia therefore continues, and more vigorously than ever.

BEFORE YOU MOVE ON . . .

➤ **ASK YOURSELF**

Do you think the media accurately portrays the behavior of people suffering from schizophrenia? Why or why not?

➤ **TEST YOURSELF 6**

How do researchers believe that biological and environmental factors interact in the onset of schizophrenia?

Answers to the Test Yourself questions can be found in Appendix E at the end of the book.

Personality Disorders

13: What characteristics are typical of personality disorders?

SOME DYSFUNCTIONAL BEHAVIOR patterns impair people's social functioning without depression or delusions. Among them are **personality disorders,** disruptive, inflexible, and enduring behavior patterns that impair one's social functioning. One cluster of these disorders expresses anxiety, such as a fearful sensitivity to rejection that predisposes the withdrawn *avoidant personality disorder.* A second cluster expresses eccentric behaviors, such as the emotionless disengagement of *schizoid personality disorder.* A third cluster exhibits dramatic or impulsive behaviors, such as the attention-getting *histrionic personality disorder* and the self-focused and self-inflating *narcissistic personality disorder.* The personality disorders categories are not sharply distinguished, however, and likely will be revised in the next DSM revision (Clark, 2007; Widiger & Trull, 2007).

TROUBLESHOOTING

Paranoid personality disorder and schizoid personality disorder are different from schizophrenia only by a matter of degree. While people with schizophrenia experience psychotic episodes when they lose touch with reality, people with these personality disorders do not have these extreme experiences. Their behavior is odd, eccentric, and disturbing, but it does not impair daily life in the way that schizophrenia does.

Antisocial Personality Disorder

The most troubling and heavily researched personality disorder is the **antisocial personality disorder.** The person (formerly called a *sociopath* or a *psychopath*) is typically a male whose lack of conscience becomes plain before age 15, as he begins to lie, steal, fight, or display unrestrained sexual behavior (Cale & Lilienfeld, 2002). About half of such children become antisocial adults—unable to keep a job, irresponsible as a spouse and parent, and assaultive or otherwise criminal (Farrington, 1991). When the antisocial personality combines a keen intelligence with amorality, the result may be a charming and clever con artist—or worse.

Despite their antisocial behavior, many criminals do not fit the description of antisocial personality disorder. Why? Because they actually show responsible concern for their friends and family members. Antisocial personalities feel and fear little, and in extreme cases, the results can be horrifyingly tragic. Henry Lee Lucas confessed that during his 32 years of crime, he had bludgeoned, suffocated, stabbed, shot, or mutilated some 360 women, men, and children—the first (a woman) at age 13. During the last 6 years of his reign of terror, Lucas teamed with Elwood Toole, who reportedly slaughtered about 50 people he "didn't think was worth living anyhow." It ended when Lucas confessed to stabbing and dismembering his 15-year-old common-law wife, who was Toole's niece.

The antisocial personality expresses little regret over violating others' rights. "Once I've done a crime, I just forget it," said Lucas. Toole was equally matter-of-fact: "I think of killing like smoking a cigarette, like another habit" (Darrach & Norris, 1984).

Understanding Antisocial Personality Disorder

Antisocial personality disorder is woven of both biological and psychological strands. No single gene codes for a complex behavior such as crime, but twin and adoption studies reveal that biological relatives of those with antisocial and unemotional tendencies are at increased risk for antisocial behavior (Larsson et al., 2007; Livesley & Jang, 2008). The genetic vulnerability of people with antisocial and unemotional tendencies appears as a fearless approach to life. Awaiting aversive events, such as electric shocks or loud noises, they show little autonomic nervous system arousal (Hare, 1975; van Goozen et al., 2007). Even as youngsters, before committing any crime, they react with lower levels of stress hormones than do others their age (**FIGURE 12.10**).

Some studies have detected the early signs of antisocial behavior in children as young as ages 3 to 6 (Caspi et al., 1996; Tremblay et al., 1994). Boys who later became aggressive or antisocial adolescents tended, as young children, to have been impulsive, uninhibited, unconcerned with social rewards, and low in anxiety. If channeled in more productive directions, such fearlessness may lead to courageous heroism, adventurism, or star-level athleticism (Poulton & Milne, 2002). Lacking a sense of social responsibility, the same disposition may produce a cool con artist or killer (Lykken, 1995). The genes that put people at risk for antisocial behavior also put people at risk for dependence on alcohol and other drugs, which helps explain why these disorders often appear in combination (Dick, 2007).

Many criminals, like this one, exhibit a sense of conscience and responsibility in other areas of their life, and thus do **not** exhibit antisocial personality disorder.

"Thursday is out. I have jury duty."

➤ **FIGURE 12.10**

Cold-blooded arousability and risk of crime Levels of the stress hormone adrenaline were measured in two groups of 13-year-old Swedish boys. In both stressful and nonstressful situations, those who would later be convicted of a crime (as 18- to 26-year-olds) showed relatively low arousal. (From Magnusson, 1990.)

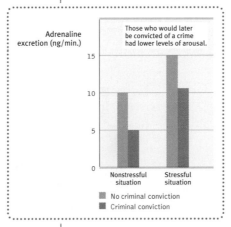

Adrenaline excretion (ng/min.)

Those who would later be convicted of a crime had lower levels of arousal.

- No criminal conviction
- Criminal conviction

The terms psychopath and sociopath are synonymous. These words are actually legal terms and not used as psychological diagnoses.

 TEACHING TIP

Harvey Cleckley identifies the following characteristics of antisocial personality disorder.

- Superficial charm and high intelligence.
- Poise, rationality, absence of neurotic anxiety.
- Lack of a sense of personal responsibility.
- Untruthfulness, insincerity, callousness, manipulativeness.
- Antisocial behavior without regret or shame.
- Poor judgment and failure to learn from experience.
- Inability to establish lasting, close relationships with others.
- Lack of insight into personal motivations.

Cleckley, H. (1976). *The mask of sanity* (5th ed.). St. Louis: Mosby.

RESEARCH

While all serial killers are antisocial, not all those with antisocial disorder are serial killers. Have students explore the lives and crimes of these serial killers, all of whom are believed to have had antisocial personality disorder:

- Ted Bundy
- Kenneth Bianchi (the Hillside Strangler)
- Jeffrey Dahmer
- Aileen Wuornos, America's only known female serial killer

UNIT 12

INTERCONNECTING

Remind students how PET scans, as shown in Figure 12.11, are conducted. Patients are injected with a slightly radioactive glucose (sugar) that is used as fuel for active brain cells. The scanning machine measures how much glucose is being used by the cells as the patient engages in different activities.

TEACHING TIP

At this point, you may want to use **Lecture/Discussion Topic:** *Narcissistic Personality Disorder* (p. 27) or **Classroom Exercises:** *Schizotypal Personality Questionnaire* (p. 28) or *Antisocial Personality Disorder* (p. 28) from Bolt's Teacher's Resource Binder.

Normal   Murderer

Courtesy of Adrian Raine, University of Southern California

➤ **FIGURE 12.11**

Murderous minds These top-facing PET scans illustrate reduced activation (less red and yellow) in a murderer's frontal cortex—a brain area that helps brake impulsive, aggressive behavior. (From Raine, 1999.)

➤ **FIGURE 12.12**

Biopsychosocial roots of crime Danish male babies whose backgrounds were marked both by obstetrical complications and social stresses associated with poverty were twice as likely to be criminal offenders by ages 20 to 22 as those in either the biological or social risk groups. (From Raine et al., 1996.)

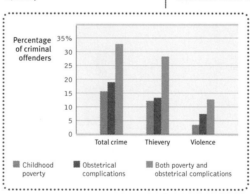

Genetic influences help wire the brain. Adrian Raine (1999, 2005) compared PET scans of 41 murderers' brains with those from people of similar age and sex. Raine found reduced activity in the murderers' frontal lobes, an area of the cortex that helps control impulses (**FIGURE 12.11**). This reduction was especially apparent in those who murdered impulsively. In a follow-up study, Raine and his team (2000) found that violent repeat offenders had 11 percent less frontal lobe tissue than normal. This helps explain why people with antisocial personality disorder exhibit marked deficits in frontal lobe cognitive functions, such as planning, organization, and inhibition (Morgan & Lilienfeld, 2000). Compared with people who feel and display empathy, their brains also respond less to facial displays of others' distress (Deeley et al., 2006).

Perhaps a biologically based fearlessness, as well as early environment, helps explain the reunion of long-separated sisters Joyce Lott, 27, and Mary Jones, 29—in a South Carolina prison where both were sent on drug charges. After a newspaper story about their reunion, their long-lost half-brother Frank Strickland called. He explained it would be a while before he could come see them—because he, too, was in jail, on drug, burglary, and larceny charges (Shepherd et al., 1990). According to a 2004 U.S. Justice Department report, 48 percent of 2 million state prison inmates say they have had incarcerated relatives (Johnson, 2008).

Genetics alone is hardly the whole story of antisocial crime, however. Relative to 1960, the average American in 1995 (before the late 1990s crime decline) was twice as likely to be murdered, four times as likely to report being raped, four times as likely to report being robbed, and five times as likely to report being assaulted (FBI, *Uniform Crime Reports*). Violent crime was also surging in other Western nations. Yet the human gene pool had hardly changed. Or consider the British social experiment begun in 1787, exiling 160,000 criminals to Australia. The descendants of these exiles, carrying their ancestors' supposed "criminal genes," helped create a civilized democracy whose crime rate is similar to Britain's. Genetic predispositions do put some individuals more at risk for antisocial conduct than others; biological as well as environmental influences explain why 5 to 6 percent of offenders commit 50 to 60 percent of crimes (Lyman, 1996). But we must look to social-cultural factors to explain the modern epidemic of violence.

A study of criminal tendencies among young Danish men illustrates the usefulness of a complete biopsychosocial perspective. A research team led by Adrian Raine (1996) checked criminal records on nearly 400 men at ages 20 to 22, knowing that these men either had experienced biological risk factors at birth (such as premature birth) or came from family backgrounds marked by poverty and family instability. The researchers then compared each of these two groups with a third *biosocial* group whose lives were marked by *both* the biological and social risk factors. The biosocial group had double the risk of committing crime (**FIGURE 12.12**). Similar findings emerged from a famous study that followed 1037 children for a quarter-century: Two combined factors—childhood maltreatment and a gene that altered neurotransmitter balance—predicted antisocial problems (Caspi et al., 2002). Neither "bad" genes alone nor a "bad" environment alone predisposed later antisocial behavior. Rather, genes predisposed some children to be more sensitive to maltreatment. Within "genetically vulnerable segments of the population," environmental influences matter—for better or for worse (Belsky et al., 2007; Moffitt, 2005). With antisocial behavior, as with so much else, nature and nurture interact.

Percentage of criminal offenders

35%
30
25
20
15
10
5
0

      Total crime   Thievery   Violence

■ Childhood poverty   ■ Obstetrical complications   ■ Both poverty and obstetrical complications

TEACHING TIP

Divide students into small groups and provide them with case studies of people with different personality disorders. After they read each case study, have them decide which disorder is described. Then have students come together to see if they all agreed on the diagnosis. They may also come up with their own case studies to see if other students can correctly diagnose the disorders.

Rates of Psychological Disorders

14: How many people suffer, or have suffered, from a psychological disorder?

WHO IS MOST VULNERABLE TO psychological disorders? At what times of life? To answer such questions, various countries have conducted lengthy, structured interviews with representative samples of thousands of their citizens. After asking hundreds of questions that probed for symptoms—"Has there ever been a period of two weeks or more when you felt like you wanted to die?"—the researchers have estimated the current, prior-year, and lifetime prevalence of various disorders.

How many people have, or have had, a psychological disorder? More than most of us suppose:

- The U.S. National Institute of Mental Health (2008, based on Kessler et al., 2005) estimates that 26 percent of adult Americans "suffer from a diagnosable mental disorder in a given year" (**TABLE 12.4**).

- National population surveys reveal differing annual rates in Australia (16 percent), Germany (31 percent), and the Netherlands (23 percent) (Baumeister & Härter, 2007).

- A twenty-first-century World Health Organization (2004) study—based on 90-minute interviews of 60,463 people—estimated the number of prior-year mental disorders in 20 countries. As **FIGURE 12.13** displays, the lowest rate of reported mental disorders was in Shanghai, the highest rate in the United States. Moreover, immigrants to the United States from Mexico, Africa, and Asia average better mental health than their native U.S. counterparts (Breslau et al., 2007). For example, compared with people who have recently immigrated from Mexico, Mexican-Americans born in the United States are at greater risk of mental disorder.

Who is most vulnerable to mental disorders? As we have seen, the answer varies with the disorder. One predictor of mental

TABLE 12.4

PERCENTAGE OF AMERICANS REPORTING SELECTED PSYCHOLOGICAL DISORDERS IN THE PAST YEAR

Psychological Disorder	Percentage
Generalized anxiety	3.1
Social phobia	6.8
Phobia of specific object or situation	8.7
Mood disorder	9.5
Obsessive-compulsive disorder	1.0
Schizophrenia	1.1
Post-traumatic stress disorder (PTSD)	3.5
Attention-deficit hyperactivity disorder (ADHD)	4.1
Any mental disorder	26.2

Source: National Institute of Mental Health, 2008.

 Does a full Moon trigger "madness" in some people? James Rotton and I. W. Kelly (1985) examined data from 37 studies that related lunar phase to crime, homicides, crisis calls, and mental hospital admissions. Their conclusion: There is virtually no evidence of "Moon madness." Nor does lunar phase correlate with suicides, assaults, emergency room visits, or traffic disasters (Martin et al., 1992; Raison et al., 1999). ●

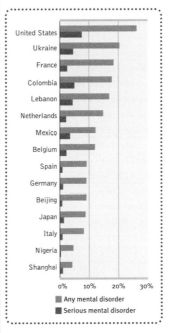

> **FIGURE 12.13**

Prior-year prevalence of disorders in selected areas From World Health Organization (2004) interviews in 20 countries.

UNIT 12

Positive psychology seeks to provide a balance to what is becoming popularly known as "negative psychology," the study of mental illness. As research continues in what leads to optimal functioning, we may discover ways in which biological, psychological, and social-cultural factors not only lead to less risk for mental illness, but greater potential for thriving. Have students consider the following:

- An imbalance of neurotransmitters seems to lead to mental illness. Could some imbalances lead to positive behavioral outcomes?

- What parenting techniques lead to children doing well in life?

- Which ways of coping with stress lead to better mental health? Which ways are only moderately effective?

At this point, you may want to use **Lecture/Discussion Topic: The Commonality of Psychological Disorders** (p. 29) from Bolt's Teacher's Resource Binder.

TABLE 12.5

RISK AND PROTECTIVE FACTORS FOR MENTAL DISORDERS

Risk Factors	Protective Factors
Academic failure	Aerobic exercise
Birth complications	Community offering empowerment, opportunity, and security
Caring for chronically ill or patients with dementia	Economic independence
Child abuse and neglect	Feelings of security
Chronic insomnia	Feelings of mastery and control
Chronic pain	Effective parenting
Family disorganization or conflict	Literacy
Low birth weight	Positive attachment and early bonding
Low socioeconomic status	Positive parent-child relationships
Medical illness	Problem-solving skills
Neurochemical imbalance	Resilient coping with stress and adversity
Parental mental illness	Self-esteem
Parental substance abuse	Social and work skills
Personal loss and bereavement	Social support from family and friends
Poor work skills and habits	
Reading disabilities	
Sensory disabilities	
Social incompetence	
Stressful life events	
Substance abuse	
Trauma experiences	

Source: World Health Organization (2004a,b).

disorder, poverty, crosses ethnic and gender lines. The incidence of serious psychological disorders is doubly high among those below the poverty line (Centers for Disease Control, 1992). Like so many other correlations, the poverty-disorder association raises a chicken-and-egg question: Does poverty cause disorders? Or do disorders cause poverty? It is both, though the answer varies with the disorder. Schizophrenia understandably leads to poverty. Yet the stresses and demoralization of poverty can also precipitate disorders, especially depression in women and substance abuse in men (Dohrenwend et al., 1992). In one natural experiment on the poverty-pathology link, researchers tracked rates of behavior problems in North Carolina Native American children as economic development enabled a dramatic reduction in their community's poverty rate. As the study began, children of poverty exhibited more deviant and aggressive behaviors. After four years, children whose families had moved above the poverty line exhibited a 40 percent decrease in the behavior problems, while those who continued in their previous positions below or above the poverty line exhibited no change (Costello et al., 2003).

As **TABLE 12.5** indicates, there is a wide range of risk and protective factors for mental disorders. At what times of life do disorders strike? Usually by early adulthood. "Over 75 percent of our sample with any disorder had experienced its first symptoms by age 24," reported Lee Robins and Darrel Regier (1991, p. 331). The symptoms of antisocial personality disorder and of phobias are among the earliest to appear, at a median age of 8 and 10, respectively. Symptoms of alcohol dependency, obsessive-compulsive disorder, bipolar disorder, and schizophrenia appear at a median age near 20. Major depression often hits somewhat later, at a median age of 25. Such findings make clear the need for research and treatment to help the growing number of people, especially teenagers and young adults, who suffer the bewilderment and pain of a psychological disorder.

Although mindful of the pain, we can also be encouraged by the many successful people—including Leonardo da Vinci, Isaac Newton, and Leo Tolstoy—who pursued brilliant careers while enduring psychological difficulties. So have 18 U.S. presidents, including the periodically depressed Abraham Lincoln, according to one psychiatric analysis of their biographies (Davidson et al., 2006). The bewilderment, fear, and sorrow caused by psychological disorders are real. But, as Unit 13 shows, hope, too, is real.

BEFORE YOU MOVE ON . . .

> **ASK YOURSELF**

Do you have a family member or friend who has experienced a psychological disorder? If so, has anything you have read in this unit increased your understanding of the challenges that person has been facing?

> **TEST YOURSELF 8**

What is the relationship between poverty and psychological disorders?

Answers to the Test Yourself questions can be found in Appendix E at the end of the book.

These resources will be helpful for teaching the concepts in this unit:

- *Psychology Video Tool Kit: ADHD and the Family; Post-partum Psychosis: The Case of Andrea Yates; Obsessive-Compulsive Disorder: A Young Mother's Struggle; Those Who Hoard; Post-Traumatic Stress Disorder: A Vietnam Combat Veteran; PTSD: Returning from Iraq; Fear, PTSD, and the Brain; Beyond Perfection: Female Body Dysmorphic Disorder; Depression; Suicide: Case of the "3-Star"*

- *Chef; John Nash: "A Beautiful Mind"; Trichotillomania: Pulling Out One's Hair*

- *Videos: Scientific American Frontiers, 2nd ed., Segment 33: Cop Psychiatrists; Segment 32: Arachnophobia*

- *Videos: Digital Media Archive: Psychology, 1st ed., Video Clip 32: Gender Identity Disorder; Video Clip 31: Multiple Personality Disorder; Video Clip 33: Mood Disorders; Video Clip 29: The Schizophrenic Brain; Video Clip 30: The Mind of the Psychopath*

UNIT REVIEW: Abnormal Psychology

Perspectives on Psychological Disorders

1: How should we draw the line between normality and disorder?

Psychologists and psychiatrists consider behavior disordered when it is deviant, distressful, and dysfunctional. The definition of deviant varies with context and culture. It also varies with time; for example, some children who might have been judged rambunctious a few decades ago now are being diagnosed with *attention-deficit hyperactivity disorder*.

2: What perspectives can help us understand psychological disorders?

The *medical model* assumes that *psychological disorders* are mental illnesses that can be diagnosed on the basis of their symptoms and cured through therapy, sometimes in a hospital. The biopsychosocial perspective assumes that disordered behavior, like other behavior, arises from genetic predispositions and physiological states; inner psychological dynamics; and social-cultural circumstances.

3: How and why do clinicians classify psychological disorders?

The fourth edition (text revised) of the American Psychiatric Association's *Diagnostic and Statistical Manual of Mental Disorders (DSM-IV-TR)* provides diagnostic labels and descriptions that aid mental health professionals by providing a common language and shared concepts for communication and research. Most U.S. health insurance organizations require DSM-IV-TR diagnoses before they will pay for therapy.

4: Why do some psychologists criticize the use of diagnostic labels?

Labels can create preconceptions that unfairly stigmatize people and can bias our perceptions of their past and present behavior. The label "insanity"—used in some legal defenses—raises moral and ethical questions about how a society should treat people who have disorders and have committed crimes.

Anxiety Disorders

5: What are anxiety disorders, and how do they differ from ordinary worries and fears?

Anxiety is classified as a psychological disorder only when it becomes distressing or persistent, or is characterized by maladaptive behaviors intended to reduce it.

People with *generalized anxiety disorder* feel persistently and uncontrollably tense and apprehensive, for no apparent reason. In the more extreme *panic disorder*, anxiety escalates into periodic episodes of intense dread. Those with a *phobia* may be irrationally afraid of a specific object or situation. Persistent and repetitive thoughts (obsessions) and actions (compulsions) characterize *obsessive-compulsive disorder*. Symptoms of *post-traumatic stress disorder* include four or more weeks of haunting memories, nightmares, social withdrawal, jumpy anxiety, and sleep problems following some traumatic and uncontrollable event.

6: What produces the thoughts and feelings that mark anxiety disorders?

Freud viewed *anxiety disorders* as the manifestation of mental energy associated with the discharge of repressed impulses. Psychologists working from the learning perspective view anxiety disorders as a product of fear conditioning, stimulus generalization, reinforcement of fearful behaviors, and observational learning of others' fear. Those working from the biological perspective consider the role that fears of life-threatening animals, objects, or situations played in natural selection and evolution; the genetic inheritance of a high level of emotional reactivity; and abnormal responses in the brain's fear circuits.

Somatoform Disorders

7: What are somatoform disorders?

Somatoform disorders present a somatic (bodily) symptom—some physiologically unexplained but genuinely felt ailment. With *conversion disorder*, anxiety appears converted to a physical symptom that has no reasonable neurological basis. *Hypochondriasis* is the more common interpretation of normal sensations as a dreaded disorder.

Dissociative Disorders

8: What are dissociative disorders, and why are they controversial?

Dissociative disorders are conditions in which conscious awareness seems to become separated from previous memories, thoughts, and feelings. Skeptics note that *dissociative identity disorder*, formerly known as multiple personality disorder, increased dramatically in the late twentieth century, that it is rarely found outside North America, and that it may reflect role-playing by people who are vulnerable to therapists' suggestions. Others view this disorder as a manifestation of feelings of anxiety, or as a response learned when behaviors are reinforced by reductions in feelings of anxiety.

Mood Disorders

9: What are mood disorders, and what forms do they take?

Mood disorders are characterized by emotional extremes. A person with *major depressive disorder* experiences two or more weeks of seriously depressed moods and feelings of worthlessness, takes little interest in most activities, and derives little pleasure from them. These feelings are not caused by drugs or a medical condition. People with the less common condition of *bipolar disorder* experience not only depression but also *mania*, episodes of hyperactive and wildly optimistic impulsive behavior.

10: What causes mood disorders, and what might explain the Western world's rising incidence of depression among youth and young adults?

The biological perspective on depression focuses on genetic predispositions and on abnormalities in brain structures and functions (including those found in neurotransmitter systems). The social-cognitive perspective examines the influence of cyclic

TEACHING TIP

Students may notice that the risk factors for mental illness outnumber the protective factors. Some reasons for this imbalance may include the following:

- The protective factors may inoculate against several types of illness, whereas the risk factors may be particular to certain disorders.

- The emphasis on pathology since World War II has given us more evidence for what leads to mental illness and less evidence about what inoculates against it.

- *ActivePsych: Digital Media Archive*, 2nd ed.: *Experiencing Anxiety; Schizophrenia: New Definitions, New Therapies; Overcoming Schizophrenia: John Nash's Beautiful Mind*

- *PsychSim 5: Mystery Client; Losing Touch With Reality*

- *Videos: Psychology: The Human Experience, Module 37: Three Anxiety Disorders; Module 36: Obsessive-Compulsive Disorder; Module 38: Mood Disorders: Major Depression and Bipolar Disorder; Module 39: Schizophrenia*

- *Videos: The Brain*, 2nd ed., *Module 23: Multiple Personality; Module 26: Schizophrenia: Symptoms; Module 29: Autism; Module 27: Schizophrenia: Etiology*

- *Videos: The Mind*, 2nd ed., *Module 31: Mood Disorders: Mania and Depression; Module 32: Mood Disorders: Hereditary Factors; Module 35: The Mind of the Psychopath*

ANSWERS to Multiple-Choice Questions

1. **b.** Someone suffering from depression will get better only with therapy or medication.
2. **c.** have a parent or sibling with the disorder.
3. **e.** Psychological disorders
4. **d.** bipolar disorder.
5. **a.** schizophrenia.
6. **b.** whose sibling or parent has the disorder.
7. **c.** Bipolar disorder
8. **e.** hallucinations.
9. **a.** depression.
10. **c.** abnormal activity in multiple brain areas.
11. **a.** antisocial personality disorder
12. **d.** explanatory style.
13. **d.** schizophrenia.
14. **e.** nature and nurture.
15. **a.** is unexplainably and continually tense and uneasy.

self-defeating beliefs, learned helplessness, negative attributions, and stressful experiences. The biopsychosocial approach considers influences interacting on many levels (**FIGURE 12.14**). Increased rates of depression among young Westerners may be due to the rise of individualism and the decline of commitment to religion and family, but this is a correlational finding, so the cause-effect relationship is not yet clear.

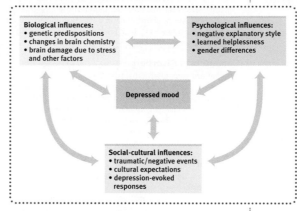

➤ **FIGURE 12.14**

Biopsychosocial approach to depression Seriously depressed moods result from a combination of interacting factors. Altering any one component can alter the others.

Schizophrenia

11: What patterns of thinking, perceiving, feeling, and behaving characterize schizophrenia?

Schizophrenia is a group of disorders that typically strike during late adolescence, affect men very slightly more than women, and seem to occur in all cultures. Symptoms of schizophrenia are disorganized and delusional thinking, disturbed perceptions, and inappropriate emotions and actions. *Delusions* are false beliefs; hallucinations are sensory experiences without sensory stimulation. Schizophrenia may

emerge gradually from a chronic history of social inadequacy (in which case the outlook is dim) or suddenly in reaction to stress (in which case the prospects for recovery are brighter).

12: What causes schizophrenia?

People with schizophrenia have increased receptors for the neurotransmitter dopamine, which may intensify the positive symptoms of schizophrenia. Brain abnormalities associated with schizophrenia include enlarged, fluid-filled cerebral cavities and corresponding decreases in the cortex. Brain scans reveal abnormal activity in the frontal lobes, thalamus, and amygdala. Malfunctions in multiple brain regions and their connections apparently interact to produce the symptoms of schizophrenia. Research support is mounting for the causal effects of a virus suffered during pregnancy. Twin and adoption studies also point to a genetic predisposition that interacts with environmental factors to produce schizophrenia.

Personality Disorders

13: What characteristics are typical of personality disorders?

Personality disorders are enduring, maladaptive patterns of behavior that impair social functioning. *Antisocial personality disorder* is characterized by a lack of conscience and, sometimes, by aggressive and fearless behavior. Genetic predispositions may interact with environment to produce the altered brain activity associated with this disorder.

Rates of Psychological Disorders

14: How many people suffer, or have suffered, from a psychological disorder?

Mental health surveys in many countries provide varying estimates of the rates of psychological disorders. Poverty is a predictor of mental illness. Conditions and experiences associated with poverty contribute to the development of mental disorders, but some mental disorders, such as schizophrenia, can drive people into poverty. Among Americans who have ever experienced a psychological disorder, the three most common are phobias, alcohol dependency, and mood disorder.

Terms and Concepts to Remember

TECHNOLOGY RESOURCES

Technology Resources for Unit 12 can be found on pp. 600–601.

Rubric for Grading the Free-Response Question

This is a 5-point question. One point is awarded for an accurate example explaining how each concept either alleviates or contributes to the development of depression (5 points total). Students need not provide both an alleviation and development example. Modify the rubric by adding or subtracting terms depending on what was emphasized in class.

Genetics

Development: A person can be genetically predisposed to depression, increasing (or decreasing) the likelihood of experiencing depression over a lifetime.

Alleviation: A person can be genetically predisposed to
1. overcoming depression.

AP* Practice Test Questions ◄ ·····································

Multiple-Choice Questions

1. Which of the following statements is *false*?
a. Many behavioral and cognitive changes accompany depression.
b. Someone suffering from depression will get better only with therapy or medication.
c. Compared with men, women are nearly twice as vulnerable to major depression.
d. Stressful events related to work, marriage, and close relationships often precede depression.
e. With each new generation, depression is striking earlier and affecting more people.

2. The risk of major depression and bipolar disorder dramatically increases if you
a. have suffered a debilitating injury.
b. have an adoptive parent that has the disorder.
c. have a parent or sibling with the disorder.
d. have a life-threatening illness.
e. have above-average intelligence.

3. What do mental health workers call patterns of thoughts, feelings, or behaviors that are deviant, distressful, and dysfunctional?
a. Interactions of nature and nurture
b. Physiological states
c. Genetic predispositions
d. Psychological factors
e. Psychological disorders

4. Adolescent mood swings are often misdiagnosed as
a. schizophrenia.
b. temper tantrums.
c. oppositional defiant disorder.
d. bipolar disorder.
e. ADHD.

5. A split from reality that shows itself in disorganized thinking, disturbed perceptions, and inappropriate emotions and actions is called
a. schizophrenia.
b. a phobia.
c. depression.
d. bipolar disorder.
e. anxiety.

6. The nearly 1-in-100 odds of any person being diagnosed with schizophrenia become about 1 in 10 among those
a. who also suffer anxiety disorder.
b. whose sibling or parent has the disorder.
c. who have been diagnosed with depression.
d. who live with someone diagnosed with schizophrenia.
e. whose identical twin has schizophrenia.

7. Which of the following is *not* an anxiety disorder?
a. Generalized anxiety disorder
b. Phobias
c. Bipolar disorder
d. Obsessive-compulsive disorder
e. Post-traumatic stress disorder

8. Sensory experiences without sensory stimulation are called
a. word salads.
b. delusions.
c. paranoid thoughts.
d. ruminations.
e. hallucinations.

9. The number one reason people seek mental health services is
a. depression.
b. bipolar disorder.
c. post-traumatic stress disorder.
d. dissociative identity disorder.
e. hypochondriasis.

10. Brain-scanning techniques reveal that people with chronic schizophrenia tend to have
a. abnormally high brain activity in the frontal lobes.
b. a noticeable increase in the brain waves that reflect synchronized neural firing.
c. abnormal activity in multiple brain areas.
d. decreased activity in the amygdala.
e. normal amounts of cerebral tissue.

11. People with _____ show little regret over violating others' rights.
a. antisocial personality disorder
b. avoidant personality disorder
c. schizoid personality disorder
d. histrionic personality disorder
e. narcissistic personality disorder

12. Our way of thinking—who or what we blame for our successes and failures—is called
a. stability.
b. emotional memory.
c. the social-cognitive perspective.
d. explanatory style.
e. dissociative reasoning.

13. Although some psychological disorders are culture-bound, others are universal. For example, in every known culture some people suffer from
a. bulimia nervosa.
b. anorexia nervosa.
c. susto.
d. schizophrenia.
e. taijin-kyofusho.

14. Today's psychologists contend that all behavior, whether it is called normal or disordered, arises from the interaction of
a. genetics and physiology.
b. children and parents.
c. symptoms and therapy.
d. diagnosis and cure.
e. nature and nurture.

15. Generalized anxiety disorder is diagnosed when a person
a. is unexplainably and continually tense and uneasy.
b. experiences sudden episodes of intense dread.
c. feels irrationally and intensely afraid of a specific object or situation.
d. is troubled by repetitive thoughts or actions.
e. has nightmares for weeks after a severe, uncontrollable event.

Free-Response Question

Using specific examples, explain the role of the following in either the alleviation or the development of depression:
- Genetics
- Explanatory style
- Alcohol
- Psychotherapy
- Drug therapy

 WEB

Multiple-choice self-tests and more may be found at www.worthpublishers.com/myers

---

2. responding favorably to antidepressant medication.

Explanatory style
Development: Those with negative, self-defeating thoughts are more likely to experience depression.
Alleviation: Those who develop positive, healthy self-talk and reduce self-blame are more likely to rebound from depression.

Alcohol
Development: Alcohol abuse can lead to bad decisions that negatively affect relationships, employment, achievement, etc., all of which could contribute to depression.

 Rubric continued

Alleviation: drinking temporarily elevates mood, decreasing the feeling of depression.

Psychotherapy
Development: Psychotherapy does not contribute to the development of depression.
Alleviation: Therapies used to help alleviate depression include the following.

A. Psychodynamic therapy focuses on patients' current conflicts and unconscious defenses by searching for themes common to many past and present relationships.

B. Interpersonal therapy (brief version of psychodynamic therapy) deals with current symptoms rather than the origins of unconscious conflicts.

C. Client-centered (humanistic) therapy utilizes active listening and unconditional positive regard to provide a growth-fostering environment.

D. Behavior therapy modifies the problem itself (as opposed to promoting self-awareness), using techniques such as counterconditioning, systematic desensitization, virtual reality exposure therapy, aversive conditioning, or token economies.

E. Cognitive therapy changes self-defeating thinking by training people to look at themselves in new, more positive ways.

Drug (Biomedical) Therapy
Development: Biomedical therapy does not contribute to the development of depression.
Alleviation: Antidepressant drugs increase the availability of serotonin and norepinephrine, which can help lift depression.

UNIT 13

Pacing Guide

Use the following guide to determine how many instructional days to devote to this unit depending on the type of course you teach:

Year-long course: 3–5 days
Block schedule/Semester-long course: 2–3 days

This unit encompasses 5–7 percent of the AP Exam. Spending an appropriate amount of time on this unit will help students do well on the AP Exam.

 TEACHING TIP

At this point, you may want to use **Introductory Exercise:** *Fact or Falsehood?* (p. 3) or **Lecture/ Discussion Topic**: *The Availability and Adequacy of Treatment* (p. 4) or **Classroom Exercises:** *Therapist Role-Playing* (p. 3) or *Attitudes Toward Seeking Professional Psychological Help* (p. 3) from Bolt's Teacher's Resource Binder, which accompanies this text.

604

Suggested Readings

Axline, V. (1964). *Dibs: In search of self.* Boston, MA: Houghton Mifflin.

Balter, M., & Katz, R. (1987). *Nobody's child.* Reading, MA: Addison-Wesley.

Dolnick, E. (1998). *Madness on the couch: Blaming the victim in the heyday of psychoanalysis.* New York: Simon & Schuster.

Johnson, A. B. (1990). *Out of Bedlam: The truth about deinstitutionalization.* New York: Basic Books.

Seligman, M. E. P. (1994). *What you can change & what you can't.* New York: Knopf.

Szasz, T. S. (1994). *Cruel compassion: Psychiatric control of society's unwanted.* New York: Wiley.

Winerip, M. (1994). *9 Highland Road: Sane living for the mentally ill.* New York: Vintage Books.

Treatment of Psychological Disorders

Today we comprehend deep outer space and can state with certainty the chemical composition of Jupiter's atmosphere. But in understanding and treating the disturbances of deep inner space—the psychological disorders described in Unit 12—we are only beginning to make real progress. In the 2200 years since Eratosthenes correctly estimated the Earth's circumference, we have charted the heavens, cracked the genetic code, and eliminated or found cures for all sorts of diseases. Meanwhile, we have treated psychological disorders with a bewildering array of harsh and gentle methods: by cutting holes in the head and by giving warm baths and massages; by restraining, bleeding, or "beating the devil" out of people and by placing them in sunny, serene environments; by administering drugs and electric shocks and by talking—talking about childhood experiences, about current feelings, about maladaptive thoughts and behaviors.

The transition from brutal to gentler treatments occurred thanks to the efforts of reformers such as Philippe Pinel in France and Dorothea Dix in the United States, Canada, and Scotland. Both advocated constructing mental hospitals to offer more humane methods of treatment. But times have once again changed, and the introduction of therapeutic drugs and community-based treatment programs has largely emptied mental health hospitals since the mid-1950s.

Culver Pictures

Dorothea Dix (1802–1887) "I . . . call your attention to the state of the Insane Persons confined within this Commonwealth, in cages."

Today's mental health therapies can be classified into two main categories, and the favored treatment depends on both the disorder and the therapist's viewpoint. Learning-related disorders, such as phobias, are likely candidates for *psychotherapy,* in which a trained therapist uses psychological techniques to assist someone seeking to overcome difficulties or achieve personal growth. Biologically influenced disorders, such as schizophrenia, will often be treated with *biomedical therapy*—a prescribed medication or medical procedure that acts directly on the patient's nervous system.

Depending on the client and the problem, some therapists—particularly the many

605

Key People

Aaron Beck

Dorothea Dix

Albert Ellis

Sigmund Freud

Mary Cover Jones

Carl Rogers

Benjamin Rush

Joseph Wolpe

Key Terms

eclectic approach

The Psychological Therapies

psychotherapy

psychoanalysis

resistance

interpretation

transference

psychodynamic therapy

insight therapies

client-centered therapy

active listening

unconditional positive regard

behavior therapy

counterconditioning

exposure therapies

systematic desensitization

virtual reality exposure therapy

aversive conditioning

token economy

cognitive therapy

cognitive-behavioral therapy

family therapy

Evaluating Psychotherapies

regression toward the mean

meta-analysis

evidence-based practice

The Biomedical Therapies

biomedical therapy

psychopharmacology

antipsychotic drugs

tardive dyskinesia

antianxiety drugs

antidepressant drugs

electroconvulsive therapy (ECT)

repetitive transcranial magnetic stimulation (rTMS)

psychosurgery

lobotomy

Preventing Psychological Disorders

resilience

UNIT 13

INTERCONNECTING

Before Freud, psychology was a new science concerned more with describing the human experience than developing effective therapeutic techniques.

- Structuralism, the school founded by Wilhelm Wundt in 1879, sought to describe what consciousness was, positing that people shared common experiences and perceptions about the world.

- Functionalism, a school favored by G. Stanley Hall in the U.S., stated that describing sensations was not as important as knowing how the mind worked.

INTERCONNECTING

Review the stages of development in Freud's theory (from Unit 10):

- *Oral stage* spans from birth to about 18 months. Infants are gratified by activities like sucking and biting. Early weaning may lead to bad habits like overeating or smoking.

- *Anal stage* spans the potty-training years. Children have to balance societal demands with their own desires. If a person is trained too early, an anal-retentive personality may develop.

- *Phallic stage* lasts until school starts. Young children face such Freudian issues as the Oedipus complex, penis envy, and castration anxiety.

- *Latency stage*, occurring during the elementary school years, occurs when children learn gender roles by associating with same-sex friends.

- *Genital stage* starts at puberty. Freud believed if people do not engage in sexual experiences, they will have problems later in life.

The history of treatment As William Hogarth's (1697–1764) painting of London's St. Mary of Bethlehem hospital (commonly called Bedlam) depicts, visitors to eighteenth-century mental hospitals paid to gawk at patients, as though they were viewing zoo animals. Benjamin Rush (1746–1813), a founder of the movement for more humane treatment of the mentally ill, designed the chair on the far right "for the benefit of maniacal patients." He believed the restraints would help them regain their sensibilities.

::**eclectic approach** an approach to psychotherapy that, depending on the client's problems, uses techniques from various forms of therapy.

::**psychotherapy** treatment involving psychological techniques; consists of interactions between a trained therapist and someone seeking to overcome psychological difficulties or achieve personal growth.

::**psychoanalysis** Sigmund Freud's therapeutic technique. Freud believed the patient's free associations, resistances, dreams, and transferences—and the therapist's interpretations of them—released previously repressed feelings, allowing the patient to gain self-insight.

::**resistance** in psychoanalysis, the blocking from consciousness of anxiety-laden material.

::**interpretation** in psychoanalysis, the analyst's noting supposed dream meanings, resistances, and other significant behaviors and events in order to promote insight.

::**transference** in psychoanalysis, the patient's transfer to the analyst of emotions linked with other relationships (such as love or hatred for a parent).

using a biopsychosocial approach—draw from a variety of techniques. Many patients receive drug therapy in combination with psychotherapy. Half of all psychotherapists describe themselves as taking an **eclectic approach,** using a blend of therapies (Beitman et al., 1989; Castonguay & Goldfried, 1994). *Psychotherapy integration* attempts to combine a selection of assorted techniques into a single, coherent system.

The Psychological Therapies

AMONG THE DOZENS OF TYPES of **psychotherapy,** we will look at only the most influential. Each is built on one or more of psychology's major theories: psychoanalytic, humanistic, behavioral, and cognitive. Most of these techniques can be used one-on-one or in groups.

Psychoanalysis

1: What are the aims and methods of psychoanalysis, and how have they been adapted in psychodynamic therapy?

Sigmund Freud's **psychoanalysis** was the first of the psychological therapies, and its terminology has crept into our modern vocabulary. Few clinicians today practice therapy as Freud did, but some of his techniques and assumptions survive, especially in the *psychodynamic therapies*.

Aims

Because Freud assumed that many psychological problems are fueled by childhood's residue of repressed impulses and conflicts (see Unit 10), he and his students sought to bring these repressed feelings into patients' conscious awareness. By gaining insight into the origins of the disorder—by excavating their childhood past and fulfilling the ancient imperative to "know thyself" in a deep way—patients then work through the buried feelings and take responsibility for their own growth. Psychoanalytic theory presumes that healthier, less anxious living becomes possible when people release the energy they had previously devoted to id-ego-superego conflicts.

TEACHING TIP

Dorothea Dix began her crusade for humane treatment of mentally ill patients when she began tutoring inmates at a women's prison. Men and women who were mentally ill or disabled were being housed with hardened female criminals. Dix took her reforms to all existing states and to Europe.

Freud's consulting room
Freud's office was rich with antiquities from around the world, including artwork related to his ideas about unconscious motives. His famous couch, piled high with pillows, placed patients in a comfortable reclining position facing away from him to help them focus inward.

Methods

Psychoanalysis is historical reconstruction. Psychoanalytic theory emphasizes the formative power of childhood experiences, and thus aims to unearth the past in hope of unmasking the present. But how?

After trying hypnosis and discarding it as unreliable, Freud turned to *free association*. Imagine yourself as a patient using free association. First, you relax, perhaps by lying on a couch. To help you focus on your own thoughts and feelings, the psychoanalyst may sit out of your line of vision. You say aloud whatever comes to your mind, at one moment an early childhood memory, at another a dream or recent experience. It sounds easy, but soon you notice how often you edit your thoughts as you speak, omitting what seems trivial, irrelevant, or shameful. Even in the safe presence of the analyst, you may pause momentarily before uttering an embarrassing thought. You may joke or change the subject to something less threatening. Sometimes your mind goes blank or you find yourself unable to remember important details.

To the psychoanalyst, these blocks in the flow of your free associations indicate **resistance**. They hint that anxiety lurks and you are defending against sensitive material. The analyst will note your resistances and then **interpret** their meaning, providing *insight* into your underlying wishes, feelings, and conflicts. If offered at the right moment, this interpretation—of, say, your not wanting to talk about your mother—may illuminate what you are avoiding and demonstrate how this resistance fits with other pieces of your psychological puzzle.

Freud believed that another clue to unconscious conflicts is your dreams' *latent content*—their underlying but censored meaning. Thus, after inviting you to report a dream, the analyst may offer a *dream analysis*, suggesting its meaning.

During many such sessions you will probably disclose to your analyst more of yourself than you have ever revealed to anyone else, much of it pertaining to your earliest memories. You may find yourself experiencing strong positive or negative feelings for your analyst, who may suggest you are **transferring** to your analyst feelings you experienced in earlier relationships with family members or other important people. By exposing feelings you have previously defended against, such as dependency or mingled love and anger, transference will give you a belated chance to work through them, with your analyst's help. Examining your feelings may also give you insight into your current relationships, not just those of early childhood.

Psychoanalysts acknowledge the criticism that their interpretations cannot be proven or disproven. But they insist that interpretations often are a great help to patients. Psychoanalysis, they say, is therapy, not science.

Traditional psychoanalysis takes time, up to several years of several sessions a week, and it is expensive. (Three times a week for just two years at more than $100 per hour comes to at

"You say, 'Off with her head' but what I'm hearing is, 'I feel neglected.'"

> "I haven't seen my analyst in 200 years. He was a strict Freudian. If I'd been going all this time, I'd probably almost be cured by now."
>
> Woody Allen, after awakening from suspended animation in the movie *Sleeper*

UNIT 13

"Your problems make my fee seem insignificant."

"Look, making you happy is out of the question, but I can give you a compelling narrative for your misery."

RESEARCH

Insurance coverage for mental health limits the amount of time a person can spend in therapy. Have students find out what mental health coverage they have through their parents or legal guardians or what coverage is provided to people in jobs they'd like to have after graduation or college.

- How much time in outpatient therapy can a person spend in a calendar year?

- How much time in inpatient therapy can a person spend in a calendar year?

- Do insurance companies specify what type of mental health therapy they will provide?

- What type of coverage does the state pay for through Medicaid?

TEACHING TIP

Interpersonal Psychotherapy (IPT) is a short-term therapy that has been shown to be effective for treating depression. Depression isn't caused by interpersonal events alone, but it usually has an interpersonal component, affecting relationships. Types of interpersonal events that are concentrated on in IPT include the following:

- Interpersonal disputes and conflicts

- Role transitions (such as becoming a parent or losing a parent)

- Grief that goes beyond the normal bereavement period

- Deficits patients have in starting and maintaining relationships

---

least $30,000.) Outside of France, Germany, Quebec, and New York City, relatively few therapists offer it (Goode, 2003). In the United States, at least, this is not surprising, given that U.S. managed health care limits the types and length of insured mental health services.

Psychodynamic Therapy

Influenced by Freud, **psychodynamic therapists** try to understand a patient's current symptoms by focusing on themes across important relationships, including childhood experiences and the therapist relationship. They also help the person explore and gain perspective on defended-against thoughts and feelings. But these therapists may talk to the patient face to face (rather than out of the patient's line of vision), once a week (rather than several times weekly), and for only a few weeks or months (rather than several years).

No brief excerpt can exemplify the way psychodynamic therapy interprets a patient's conflict. But the following interaction between therapist David Malan (1978, pp. 133–134) and a depressed patient illustrates the goal of enabling insight by looking for common, recurring themes, especially in relationships.

Malan: I get the feeling that you're the sort of person who needs to keep active. If you don't keep active, then something goes wrong. Is that true?

Patient: Yes.

Malan: I get a second feeling about you and that is that you must, underneath all this, have an awful lot of very strong and upsetting feelings. Somehow they're there but you aren't really quite in touch with them. Isn't this right? I feel you've been like that as long as you can remember.

Patient: For quite a few years, whenever I really sat down and thought about it I got depressed, so I tried not to think about it.

Malan: You see, you've established a pattern, haven't you? You're even like that here with me, because in spite of the fact that you're in some trouble and you feel that the bottom is falling out of your world, the way you're telling me this is just as if there wasn't anything wrong.

Notice how Malan interpreted the woman's earlier remarks (when she did most of the talking) and suggested that her relationship with him reveals a characteristic pattern of behavior? He was suggesting insights into her problems.

Interpersonal psychotherapy, a brief (12- to 16-session) variation of psychodynamic therapy, has been effective in treating depression (Weissman, 1999). Interpersonal psychotherapy aims to help people gain insight into the roots of their difficulties, but its goal is symptom relief in the here and now, not overall personality change. Rather than focusing mostly on undoing past hurts and offering interpretations, the therapist focuses primarily on current relationships and on helping people improve their relationship skills.

The case of Anna (not her real name), a 34-year-old married professional, illustrates these goals. Five months after receiving a promotion, with accompanying increased responsibilities and longer hours, Anna experienced increased tensions with her husband over his wish for a second child. She began feeling depressed, had trouble sleeping, became irritable, and was gaining weight. A typical psychodynamic therapist might have helped Anna gain insight into her angry impulses and her defenses against anger. An interpersonal therapist similarly wanted Anna to gain these insights, but also engaged her thinking on more immediate issues—how she could balance work and home, resolve the dispute with her husband, and express her emotions more effectively (Markowitz et al., 1998).

▼ **Face-to-face therapy** In this type of therapy session, the couch has disappeared. But the influence of psychoanalytic theory may not have, especially if the therapist probes for the origin of the patient's symptoms by seeking information from the patient's childhood.

DEMO

Present case studies from various abnormal psychology textbooks and have students explain the person's behavior from a particular perspective. You may assign students a particular perspective and have them come up with a case study that reflects common disorders that therapists from that perspective would likely treat. Then have them describe what type of treatment that type of therapist would recommend to this new "patient."

At this point, you may want to use **Lecture/Discussion Topic: Good Candidates for Psychoanalysis** (p. 5) from Bolt's Teacher's Resource Binder.

Humanistic Therapies

2: What are the basic themes of humanistic therapy, such as Rogers' client-centered approach?

The humanistic perspective (Unit 10) has emphasized people's inherent potential for self-fulfillment. Not surprisingly, humanistic therapists aim to boost self-fulfillment by helping people grow in self-awareness and self-acceptance. Like psychoanalytic therapies, humanistic therapies have attempted to reduce the inner conflicts that are impeding natural developmental growth by providing clients with new insights. Indeed, the psychoanalytic and humanistic therapies are often referred to as **insight therapies.** But humanistic therapists differ from psychoanalysts in focusing on

- the *present* and *future* more than the past. They explore feelings as they occur, rather than achieving insights into the childhood origins of the feelings.
- *conscious* rather than unconscious thoughts.
- taking immediate *responsibility* for one's feelings and actions, rather than uncovering hidden determinants.
- promoting growth instead of curing illness. Thus, those in therapy became "clients" rather than "patients" (a change many therapists have since adopted).

Carl Rogers (1902–1987) developed the widely used humanistic technique he called **client-centered therapy,** which focuses on the person's conscious self-perceptions. In this *nondirective therapy,* the therapist listens, without judging or interpreting, and seeks to refrain from directing the client toward certain insights.

Believing that most people already possess the resources for growth, Rogers (1961, 1980) encouraged therapists to exhibit *genuineness, acceptance,* and *empathy.* When therapists drop their facades and genuinely express their true feelings, when they enable their clients to feel unconditionally accepted, and when they empathically sense and reflect their clients' feelings, the clients may deepen their self-understanding and self-acceptance (Hill & Nakayama, 2000). As Rogers (1980, p. 10) explained,

Hearing has consequences. When I truly hear a person and the meanings that are important to him at that moment, hearing not simply his words, but him, and when I let him know that I have heard his own private personal meanings, many things happen. There is first of all a grateful look. He feels released. He wants to tell me more about his world. He surges forth in a new sense of freedom. He becomes more open to the process of change.

I have often noticed that the more deeply I hear the meanings of the person, the more there is that happens. Almost always, when a person realizes he has been deeply heard, his eyes moisten. I think in some real sense he is weeping for joy. It is as though he were saying, "Thank God, somebody heard me. Someone knows what it's like to be me."

"Hearing" refers to Rogers' technique of **active listening**—echoing, restating, and seeking clarification of what the person expresses (verbally or nonverbally) and acknowledging the expressed feelings. Active listening is now an accepted part of therapeutic counseling practices in many high schools, colleges, and clinics. The counselor listens attentively and interrupts only to restate and confirm feelings, to accept what is being expressed, or to seek clarification. The following brief excerpt between Rogers and a male client illustrates how he sought to provide a psychological mirror that would help clients see themselves more clearly.

Rogers: Feeling that now, hm? That you're just no good to yourself, no good to anybody. Never will be any good to anybody. Just that you're completely worthless, huh?—Those really are lousy feelings. Just feel that you're no good at all, hm?

::**psychodynamic therapy** therapy deriving from the psychoanalytic tradition that views individuals as responding to unconscious forces and childhood experiences, and that seeks to enhance self-insight.

::**insight therapies** a variety of therapies that aim to improve psychological functioning by increasing the client's awareness of underlying motives and defenses.

::**client-centered therapy** a humanistic therapy, developed by Carl Rogers, in which the therapist uses techniques such as active listening within a genuine, accepting, empathic environment to facilitate clients' growth. (Also called *person-centered therapy.*)

::**active listening** empathic listening in which the listener echoes, restates, and clarifies. A feature of Rogers' client-centered therapy.

> "We have two ears and one mouth that we may listen the more and talk the less."
>
> Zeno, 335–263 B.C.E., *Diogenes Laertius*

TROUBLESHOOTING

Not much analysis occurred in person-centered therapy. To facilitate unconditional positive regard, genuineness, and empathy, Rogers would answer questions with questions. "How does that make you feel?" was a common question Rogers would ask when clients would discuss their feelings. Rogers felt that if people received the attention and acceptance that they needed, they could cure themselves. The therapist was merely there to provide that support.

INTERCONNECTING

Link humanistic therapy to Abraham Maslow's hierarchy of needs (Unit 8A). Instead of explaining behavior in terms of buried unconscious feelings and desires, Maslow believed that full human potential could be achieved if certain basic needs were met. Maslow theorized that people could not appreciate beauty if they were worried about where their next meal was coming from or if they did not have a loving relationship with others.

CRITICAL THINKING

Have students consider the effect of calling people patients instead of clients.

- How does the use of each term affect the whole therapeutic relationship?
- In what other situations have semantics (the meaning of different words) affected how different jobs, issues, and roles in society are viewed? (*To get the conversation started, suggest that garbage collectors are called sanitation engineers, overthrowing a political leader is called regime change, and one comedienne called herself a "domestic goddess" rather than housewife.*)

TEACHING TIP

Virginia Axline, a student of Carl Rogers, has extended the client-centered approach to the treatment of children in play therapy. She has written *Dibs: In Search of Self*, a book that is extremely popular with students. This book can be assigned in preparation for class discussion of the humanistic therapies, and particularly of Rogers' nondirective approach. The more general humanistic themes of becoming aware of one's feelings as they occur, of emphasizing conscious rather than unconscious material, of encouraging responsibility for one's actions, and of promoting growth and fulfillment are also clearly evident in the book.

You can have students write a paper identifying the important elements of client-centered therapy (for example, active listening, genuineness, acceptance, empathy) used with Dibs.

CRITICAL THINKING

Would too much unconditional positive regard be a bad thing? Have students consider the following questions:

- How could unconditional positive regard lead to unwarranted self-esteem?

- Why would people in therapy benefit most from unconditional positive regard?

Client: Yeah. *(Muttering in low, discouraged voice)* That's what this guy I went to town with just the other day told me.

Rogers: This guy that you went to town with really told you that you were no good? Is that what you're saying? Did I get that right?

Client: M-hm.

Rogers: I guess the meaning of that if I get it right is that here's somebody that—meant something to you and what does he think of you? Why, he's told you that he thinks you're no good at all. And that just really knocks the props out from under you. *(Client weeps quietly.)* It just brings the tears. *(Silence of 20 seconds)*

Client: *(Rather defiantly)* I don't care though.

Rogers: You tell yourself you don't care at all, but somehow I guess some part of you cares because some part of you weeps over it.

(Meador & Rogers, 1984, p. 167)

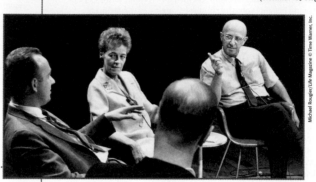

▼ Active listening Carl Rogers (right) empathized with a client during this group therapy session.

::**unconditional positive regard** a caring, accepting, nonjudgmental attitude, which Carl Rogers believed would help clients to develop self-awareness and self-acceptance.

::**behavior therapy** therapy that applies learning principles to the elimination of unwanted behaviors.

::**counterconditioning** a behavior therapy procedure that uses classical conditioning to evoke new responses to stimuli that are triggering unwanted behaviors; includes *exposure therapies* and *aversive conditioning*.

::**exposure therapies** behavioral techniques, such as systematic desensitization, that treat anxieties by exposing people (in imagination or actuality) to the things they fear and avoid.

::**systematic desensitization** a type of exposure therapy that associates a pleasant relaxed state with gradually increasing anxiety-triggering stimuli. Commonly used to treat phobias.

Can a therapist be a perfect mirror, without selecting and interpreting what is reflected? Rogers conceded that one cannot be *totally* nondirective. Nevertheless, he believed that the therapist's most important contribution is to accept and understand the client. Given a nonjudgmental, grace-filled environment that provides **unconditional positive regard,** people may accept even their worst traits and feel valued and whole.

If you want to listen more actively in your own relationships, three hints may help:

1. *Paraphrase.* Rather than saying "I know how you feel," check your understandings by summarizing the speaker's words in your own words.

2. *Invite clarification.* "What might be an example of that?" may encourage the speaker to say more.

3. *Reflect feelings.* "It sounds frustrating" might mirror what you're sensing from the speaker's body language and intensity.

Behavior Therapies

3: What are the assumptions and techniques of the behavior therapies?

The insight therapies assume that many psychological problems diminish as self-awareness grows. Traditional psychoanalysts expect problems to subside as people gain insight into their unresolved and unconscious tensions. Humanistic therapists expect problems to diminish as people get in touch with their feelings. Proponents of

TEACHING TIP

Have students create their own scripts that utilize the principles of active listening. They can present their "conversations" to the class, discussing whether their interpretations of Rogerian technique would be helpful.

At this point, you may want to use **Lecture/Discussion Topic:** *Computer-Assisted Psychotherapy* (p. 5) or **Classroom Exercises:** *Understanding Empathy* (p. 7) or *Role-Playing to Demonstrate Client-Centered Therapy* (p. 7) or *The Self-Concealment Scale* (p. 8) or *The Imposter Phenomenon* (p. 8) or **Student Project:** *Dibs and Play Therapy* (p. 8) from Bolt's Teacher's Resource Binder.

behavior therapy, however, doubt the healing power of self-awareness. (You can become aware of why you are highly anxious during tests and still be anxious.) They assume that problem behaviors *are* the problems, and the application of learning principles can eliminate them. Rather than delving deeply below the surface looking for inner causes, behavior therapists view maladaptive symptoms—such as phobias or other anxiety disorders—as learned behaviors that can be replaced by constructive behaviors.

Classical Conditioning Techniques

One cluster of behavior therapies derives from principles developed in Ivan Pavlov's early twentieth-century conditioning experiments (Unit 6). As Pavlov and others showed, we learn various behaviors and emotions through classical conditioning. Could maladaptive symptoms be examples of conditioned responses? If so, might reconditioning be a solution? Learning theorist O. H. Mowrer thought so and developed a successful conditioning therapy for chronic bed-wetters. The child sleeps on a liquid-sensitive pad connected to an alarm. Moisture on the pad triggers the alarm, waking the child. With sufficient repetition, this association of urinary relaxation with waking up stops the bedwetting. In three out of four cases the treatment is effective, and the success provides a boost to the child's self-image (Christophersen & Edwards, 1992; Houts et al., 1994).

Another example: If a claustrophobic fear of elevators is a learned aversion to the stimulus of being in a confined space, then might one unlearn that association by undergoing another round of conditioning to replace the fear response? **Counterconditioning** pairs the trigger stimulus (in this case, the enclosed space of the elevator) with a new response (relaxation) that is incompatible with fear. And indeed, behavior therapists have successfully counterconditioned people with this fear. Two specific counterconditioning techniques—*exposure therapy* and *aversive conditioning*—replace unwanted responses.

Exposure Therapies Picture this scene reported in 1924 by behaviorist psychologist Mary Cover Jones: Three-year-old Peter is petrified of rabbits and other furry objects. Jones plans to replace Peter's fear of rabbits with a conditioned response incompatible with fear. Her strategy is to associate the fear-evoking rabbit with the pleasurable, relaxed response associated with eating.

As Peter begins his midafternoon snack, Jones introduces a caged rabbit on the other side of the huge room. Peter, eagerly munching away on his crackers and drinking his milk, hardly notices. On succeeding days, she gradually moves the rabbit closer and closer. Within two months, Peter is tolerating the rabbit in his lap, even stroking it while he eats. Moreover, his fear of other furry objects subsides as well, having been *countered*, or replaced, by a relaxed state that cannot coexist with fear (Fisher, 1984; Jones, 1924).

Unfortunately for those who might have been helped by her counterconditioning procedures, Jones' story of Peter and the rabbit did not immediately become part of psychology's lore. It was more than 30 years later that psychiatrist Joseph Wolpe (1958; Wolpe & Plaud, 1997) refined Jones' technique into what are now the most widely used types of behavior therapies: **exposure therapies,** which expose people to what they normally avoid. As people can habituate to the sound of planes passing over their new home, so, with repeated exposure, can they become less anxiously responsive to things that once petrified them (Deacon & Abramowitz, 2004).

One widely used exposure therapy is **systematic desensitization.** Wolpe assumed, as did Jones, that you cannot be simultaneously anxious

 What might a psychoanalyst say about Mowrer's therapy for bed-wetting? How might a behavior therapist reply? •

THE FAR SIDE® BY GARY LARSON

Professor Gallagher and his controversial technique of simultaneously confronting the fear of heights, snakes, and the dark.

The Far Side® by Gary Larson © 1986 FarWorks, Inc. All Rights Reserved. The "Far Side" and the Larson signature are registered trademarks of FarWorks, Inc. Used with permission.

INTERCONNECTING

Remind students that Mary Cover Jones was a student of John Watson. Watson had demonstrated in 1929 that fear could be learned through classical conditioning with his infamous Little Albert study. Mary Cover Jones later showed that people could unlearn fear by associating that object with positive stimuli, work that undergirds the premise of systematic desensitization.

TEACHING TIP

An extreme and controversial form of systematic desensitization is called flooding. In flooding, patients are immersed in the object or situation that they fear. Imagine being thrown into a swimming pool if you fear the water or having roaches crawl all over you if you fear them. The idea of this type of therapy is to show the person that they have no reason to fear the item, and experiencing it in this way will lead to less fear later.

TEACHING TIP

At this point, you may want to use **Classroom Exercise:** *Using Systematic Desensitization to Treat Eraser Phobia* (p. 9) from Bolt's Teacher's Resource Binder.

RESEARCH

Classical and operant conditioning techniques can be used for many different disorders and issues, from addictions to laziness. Have students research how classical conditioning is used in popular treatment programs for various life problems including the following:

- Self-injurious behavior in autistic children
- Addictions
- Children who are couch potatoes

UNIT 13

::**virtual reality exposure therapy**
An anxiety treatment that progressively exposes people to simulations of their greatest fears, such as airplane flying, spiders, or public speaking.

::**aversive conditioning** a type of counterconditioning that associates an unpleasant state (such as nausea) with an unwanted behavior (such as drinking alcohol).

and relaxed. Therefore, if you can repeatedly relax when facing anxiety-provoking stimuli, you can gradually eliminate your anxiety. The trick is to proceed gradually. Let's see how this might work with a common phobia. Imagine yourself afraid of public speaking. A behavior therapist might first ask for your help in constructing a hierarchy of anxiety-triggering speaking situations. Yours might range from mildly anxiety-provoking situations, perhaps speaking up in a small group of friends, to panic-provoking situations, such as having to address a large audience.

Next, using *progressive relaxation,* the therapist would train you to relax one muscle group after another, until you achieve a drowsy state of complete relaxation and comfort. Then the therapist would ask you to imagine, with your eyes closed, a mildly anxiety-arousing situation: You are at lunch with a group of friends and are trying to decide whether to speak up. If imagining the scene causes you to feel any anxiety, you would signal your tension by raising your finger, and the therapist would instruct you to switch off the mental image and go back to deep relaxation. This imagined scene is repeatedly paired with relaxation until you feel no trace of anxiety.

The therapist would progress up the constructed anxiety hierarchy, using the relaxed state to desensitize you to each imagined situation. After several sessions, you move to actual situations and practice what you had only imagined before, beginning with relatively easy tasks and gradually moving to more anxiety-filled ones. Conquering your anxiety in an actual situation, not just in your imagination, raises your self-confidence (Foa & Kozak, 1986; Williams, 1987). Eventually, you may even become a confident public speaker.

When an anxiety-arousing situation is too expensive, difficult, or embarrassing to re-create, **virtual reality exposure therapy** offers an efficient middle ground. Wearing a head-mounted display unit that projects a three-dimensional virtual world, you would view a lifelike series of scenes. As your head turns, motion sensors would adjust the scene. Experiments led by several research teams have treated many different people with many different fears—flying, heights, particular animals, and public speaking (Gregg & Tarrier, 2007; Powers & Emmelkamp, 2008; Rothbaum, 2006). People who fear flying, for example, can peer out a virtual window of a simulated plane, feel vibrations, and hear the engine roar as the plane taxis down the runway and takes off. In initial experiments, those experiencing virtual reality exposure therapy have had greater relief from their fears—in real life—than have those in control groups.

Developments in virtual reality therapy suggest the possibility of designing simulated worlds in which patients create an avatar (a computer representation of oneself), through which they can try out new behaviors in virtual environments (Gorini, 2007). For example, someone with a social phobia might visit a virtual party or group discussion, which others join over time.

▼
Virtual reality exposure therapy Within the confines of a room, virtual reality technology exposes people to vivid simulations of feared stimuli, such as a plane's takeoff.

Aversive Conditioning In systematic desensitization, the goal is substituting a positive (relaxed) response for a negative (fearful) response to a *harmless* stimulus. In **aversive conditioning,** the goal is substituting a negative (aversive) response for a positive response to a *harmful* stimulus (such as alcohol). Thus, aversive conditioning is the reverse of systematic desensitization—it seeks to condition an aversion to something the person *should* avoid.

The procedure is simple: It associates the unwanted behavior with unpleasant feelings. To treat nail biting, one can paint the fingernails with a nasty-tasting nail polish (Baskind, 1997). To treat alcohol dependency, an aversion therapist offers the client appealing drinks laced with a drug that produces severe nausea. By linking alcohol with violent nausea (recall the taste-aversion experiments with rats and coyotes in Unit 6), the therapist seeks to transform the person's reaction to alcohol from positive to negative (FIGURE 13.1).

Does aversive conditioning work? In the short run it may. Arthur Wiens and Carol Menustik (1983) studied 685 patients with alcohol dependency who completed an aversion therapy program at a Portland, Oregon, hospital. One year later, after returning for several booster treatments of alcohol-sickness pairings, 63 percent were still successfully abstaining. But after three years, only 33 percent had remained abstinent.

The problem, as we saw in Unit 6, is that cognition influences conditioning. People know that outside the therapist's office they can drink without fear of nausea. Their ability to discriminate between the aversive conditioning situation and all other situations can limit the treatment's effectiveness. Thus, therapists often use aversive conditioning in combination with other treatments.

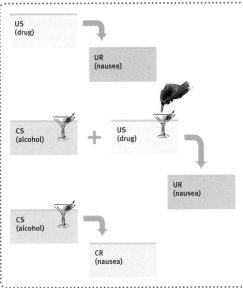

► FIGURE 13.1
Aversion therapy for alcohol dependency After repeatedly imbibing an alcoholic drink mixed with a drug that produces severe nausea, some people with a history of alcohol abuse develop at least a temporary conditioned aversion to alcohol. (Remember: US is unconditioned stimulus, UR is unconditioned response, CS is conditioned stimulus, and CR is conditioned response.)

Operant Conditioning

A basic concept in operant conditioning (Unit 6) is that voluntary behaviors are strongly influenced by their consequences. Knowing this, behavior therapists can practice *behavior modification*—reinforcing desired behaviors, and withholding reinforcement or enacting punishment for undesired behaviors. Using operant conditioning to solve specific behavior problems has raised hopes for some otherwise hopeless cases. Children with an intellectual disability have been taught to care for themselves. Socially withdrawn children with autism have learned to interact. People with schizophrenia have been helped to behave more rationally in their hospital ward. In such cases, therapists use positive reinforcers to shape behavior in a step-by-step manner, rewarding closer and closer approximations of the desired behavior.

In extreme cases, treatment must be intensive. In one study, researchers worked with 19 withdrawn, uncommunicative 3-year-olds with autism. Each participated in a 2-year program in which their parents spent 40 hours a week attempting to shape their behavior (Lovaas, 1987). The combination of positively reinforcing desired

🛟 **TEACHING TIP**

Students may find it amusing that even *The Simpsons*™ have delved into aversive conditioning. In the first season, in 1990, in an episode entitled "There's No Disgrace Like Home," Homer Simpson, the family patriarch, decides that his family needs therapy after a disastrous experience at his company's picnic. At the end of the show, each family member is hooked up to an electroshock therapy machine and gets to administer a shock to another whenever an unwelcome comment or action occurs.

🛟 **TEACHING TIP**

Alzheimer's patients have difficulty being conditioned to blink in response to a tone that previously signaled an impending air puff. The opposite is true in people with obsessive-compulsive disorder (OCD). Under certain conditions, people with OCD condition three times faster than people without OCD. The finding is consistent with the idea that victims of anxiety disorders suffer a susceptibility to aversive conditioning. People with autism condition faster than those without autism. Those with autism seem to over-attend to neutral stimuli, which facilitates the conditioning process and causes mistimed learned responses.

Azar, B. (1999, March). Classical conditioning could link disorders and brain dysfunction, researchers suggest. *APA Monitor,* p. 17.

INTERCONNECTING

Remind students about the Unit 6 discussion of taste aversion. Martin Bolt told his students about his aversion to commercially produced frozen chicken dinners. Once, he had stored a dinner in the freezer compartment of his department's refrigerator. When he went to retrieve it, he found it in the company of a frozen laboratory rat. A student assistant, not knowing how to dispose of the deceased animal, had carefully packaged it in plastic and temporarily placed it in the freezer. Bolt always found such dinners repulsive after this experience.

::**token economy** an operant conditioning procedure in which people earn a token of some sort for exhibiting a desired behavior and can later exchange the tokens for various privileges or treats.

::**cognitive therapy** therapy that teaches people new, more adaptive ways of thinking and acting; based on the assumption that thoughts intervene between events and our emotional reactions.

behaviors, and ignoring or punishing aggressive and self-abusive behaviors, worked wonders for some. By first grade, 9 of the 19 children were functioning successfully in school and exhibiting normal intelligence. In a group of 40 comparable children not undergoing this treatment (which involves sustained effort), only one showed similar improvement.

Rewards used to modify behavior vary. For some people, the reinforcing power of attention or praise is sufficient. Others require concrete rewards, such as food. In institutional settings, therapists may create a **token economy.** When people display appropriate behavior, such as getting out of bed, washing, dressing, eating, talking coherently, cleaning up their rooms, or playing cooperatively, they receive a token or plastic coin as a positive reinforcer. Later, they can exchange their accumulated tokens for various rewards, such as candy, TV time, trips to town, or better living quarters. Token economies have been successfully applied in various settings (homes, classrooms, hospitals, institutions for the delinquent) and among members of various populations (including disturbed children and people with schizophrenia and other mental disabilities).

Critics of behavior modification express two concerns. The first is practical: *How durable are the behaviors?* Will people become so dependent on extrinsic rewards that the appropriate behaviors will stop when the reinforcers stop, as may happen when they leave the institution? Proponents of behavior modification believe the behaviors will endure if therapists wean patients from the tokens by shifting them toward other rewards, such as social approval, more typical of life outside the institution. They also point out that the appropriate behaviors themselves can be intrinsically rewarding. For example, as a withdrawn person becomes more socially competent, the intrinsic satisfactions of social interaction may help the person maintain the behavior.

The second concern is ethical: *Is it right for one human to control another's behavior?* Those who set up token economies deprive people of something they desire and decide which behaviors to reinforce. To critics, this whole process has an authoritarian taint. Advocates reply that some patients request the therapy. Moreover, control already exists; rewards and punishers are already maintaining destructive behavior patterns. So why not reinforce adaptive behavior instead? Treatment with positive rewards is more humane than being institutionalized or punished, they argue, and the right to effective treatment and an improved life justifies temporary deprivation.

Cognitive Therapies

4: What are the goals and techniques of the cognitive therapies?

▼ **Cognitive therapy for eating disorders aided by journaling** Cognitive therapists guide people toward new ways of explaining their good and bad experiences. By recording each day's positive events and how she has enabled those events, this young woman may become more mindful of her self-control and more optimistic in her outlook.

We have seen how behavior therapists treat specific fears and problem behaviors. But how do they deal with major depression? Or with generalized anxiety, in which anxiety has no focus and developing a hierarchy of anxiety-triggering situations is difficult? Behavior therapists treating these less clearly defined psychological problems have had help from the same *cognitive revolution* that has profoundly changed other areas of psychology during the last five decades.

The **cognitive therapies** assume that our thinking colors our feelings (**FIGURE 13.2**).

TEACHING TIP

Ask students whether they have ever participated in a token economy. If they say yes, have them list different situations that use a token economy. If they say no, ask them if they have ever received a report card or a "conduct grade." Students are not paid to go to school and behave themselves while there, but teachers do give grades that are designed to evaluate the performance of students both academically and behaviorally. Additionally, many elementary school classrooms use token economies. Children who behave get to pick a prize out of a "treasure box" or cash in "good behavior dollars" for goodies or privileges.

TEACHING TIP

At this point, you may want to use **Classroom Exercises:** *Modeling* (p. 11) or *Assessing Assertiveness* (p. 12) or **Student Projects:** *Practicing Systematic Desensitization* (p. 10) or *Modifying an Existing Behavior* (p. 12) from Bolt's Teacher's Resource Binder.

TEACHING TIP

B. F. Skinner believed that living a life based on operant conditioning principles would actually make people more free; they would be in control of their environments. Communist and totalitarian governments, however, use classical and operant conditioning principles to keep people's behavior in check. Have students explore how totalitarian governments use conditioning to limit people's freedom:

● How do these governments use variable reinforcement schedules to produce fear and superstitions?

● How is brainwashing accomplished with conditioning procedures?

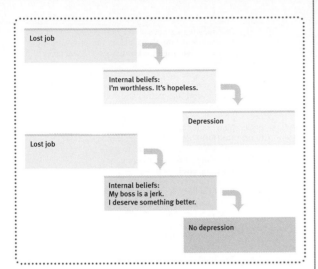

> FIGURE 13.2
A cognitive perspective on psychological disorders The person's emotional reactions are produced not directly by the event but by the person's thoughts in response to the event.

Between the event and our response lies the mind. Self-blaming and overgeneralized explanations of bad events are often an integral part of the vicious cycle of depression (see Unit 12). The depressed person interprets a suggestion as criticism, disagreement as dislike, praise as flattery, friendliness as pity. Ruminating on such thoughts sustains the negative thinking. If such thinking patterns can be learned, then surely they can be replaced. Cognitive therapists therefore try in various ways to teach people new, more constructive ways of thinking. If people are miserable, they can be helped to change their minds.

Beck's Therapy for Depression

Cognitive therapist Aaron Beck was originally trained in Freudian techniques. As Beck analyzed the dreams of depressed people, he found recurring negative themes of loss, rejection, and abandonment that extended into their waking thoughts. Such negativity even extends into therapy, as clients recall and rehearse their failings and worst impulses (Kelly, 2000). With cognitive therapy, Beck and his colleagues (1979) have sought to reverse clients' *catastrophizing* beliefs about themselves, their situations, and their futures. Gentle questioning seeks to reveal irrational thinking, and then to persuade people to remove the dark glasses through which they view life (Beck et al., 1979, pp. 145–146):

> Client: I agree with the descriptions of me but I guess I don't agree that the way I think makes me depressed.
> Beck: How do you understand it?
> Client: I get depressed when things go wrong. Like when I fail a test.
> Beck: How can failing a test make you depressed?
> Client: Well, if I fail I'll never get into law school.
> Beck: So failing the test means a lot to you. But if failing a test could drive people into clinical depression, wouldn't you expect everyone who failed the test to have a depression? . . . Did everyone who failed get depressed enough to require treatment?
> Client: No, but it depends on how important the test was to the person.
> Beck: Right, and who decides the importance?

> "Life does not consist mainly, or even largely, of facts and happenings. It consists mainly of the storm of thoughts that are forever blowing through one's mind."
> Mark Twain, 1835–1910

INTERCONNECTING

Link cognitive therapy to optimistic thinking. Optimistic thinking has three important qualities:

- **Temporary, not permanent.** Pessimists believe that bad events will become a permanent fixture in their lives, whereas optimists believe that bad events are temporary.

- **Circumstantial, not personal.** Pessimists believe that bad events are a result of some personal flaw that cannot be changed, while optimists believe that bad events are the result of circumstances that can be controlled.

- **Localized, not pervasive.** Pessimists believe that a bad experience in one area of life will influence other areas, causing havoc throughout one's life. Optimists believe that bad events will remain isolated in time, not affecting later decisions or opportunities as much.

 TEACHING TIP

At this point, you may want to use **Lecture/Discussion Topics**: *Strategies to Correct One's Thinking* (p. 13) or *Overcoming the Fear of Public Speaking* (p. 14) or **Classroom Exercise**: *Frequency of Self-Reinforcement Questionnaire* (p. 14) or **Student Project**: *Mood-Memory Repair* (p. 15) from Bolt's Teacher's Resource Binder.

UNIT 13

INTERCONNECTING

Remind students about the different types of compulsions people with obsessive-compulsive disorder (OCD) demonstrate. Compulsions manifest themselves in several different ways:

- Hoarders collect things and have a hard time throwing anything away. People who hoard are usually plagued by fears of losing something or needing something that they've thrown away. So, they keep everything, including leftover food, papers, and broken items.

- Checkers will recheck actions they have performed over and over again. They may fear they did not turn off the oven or lock the door, and they may need to recheck a certain number of times before they will feel better. Unfortunately, the number of rechecks needed to relieve anxiety may increase with each experience.

- Counters will count everything, from steps they take to words people say to them. They will become preoccupied with counting something seemingly unimportant to the point of stopping their daily progress in life.

- Cleaners will clean either their hands or surfaces excessively. Often, this cleaning will need to be done a certain number of times in order to relieve the anxiety.

PEANUTS

Drawing by Charles Schulz; © 1956 Reprinted by permission of United Feature Syndicate, Inc.

"The trouble with most therapy is that it helps you to feel better. But you don't get better. You have to back it up with action, action, action."

Psychologist Albert Ellis (1913–2007)

Client: I do.
Beck: And so, what we have to examine is your way of viewing the test (or the way that you think about the test) and how it affects your chances of getting into law school. Do you agree?
Client: Right.
Beck: Do you agree that the way you interpret the results of the test will affect you? You might feel depressed, you might have trouble sleeping, not feel like eating, and you might even wonder if you should drop out of the course.
Client: I have been thinking that I wasn't going to make it. Yes, I agree.
Beck: Now what did failing mean?
Client: *(tearful)* That I couldn't get into law school.
Beck: And what does that mean to you?
Client: That I'm just not smart enough.
Beck: Anything else?
Client: That I can never be happy.
Beck: And how do these thoughts make you feel?
Client: Very unhappy.
Beck: So it is the meaning of failing a test that makes you very unhappy. In fact, believing that you can never be happy is a powerful factor in producing unhappiness. So, you get yourself into a trap—by definition, failure to get into law school equals "I can never be happy."

We often think in words. Therefore, getting people to change what they say to themselves is an effective way to change their thinking. Perhaps you can identify with the anxious students who, before a test, make matters worse with self-defeating thoughts: "This test's probably going to be impossible. All these other students seem so relaxed and confident. I wish I were better prepared. Anyhow, I'm so nervous I'll forget everything." To change such negative self-talk, Donald Meichenbaum (1977, 1985) has offered *stress inoculation training*: teaching people to restructure their thinking in stressful situations. Sometimes it may be enough simply to say more positive things to oneself: "Relax. The test may be hard, but it will be hard for everyone else, too. I studied harder than most people. Besides, I don't need a perfect score to get a good grade." After being trained to dispute their negative thoughts, depression-prone children, teens, and college students exhibit a greatly reduced rate of future depression (Seligman, 2002; Seligman et al., 2009). To a large extent, it *is* the thought that counts.

Cognitive-Behavioral Therapy

Cognitive-behavioral therapy, a widely practiced integrative therapy, aims not only to alter the way people think (cognitive therapy), but also to alter the way they act (behavior therapy). It seeks to make people aware of their irrational negative thinking, to replace it with new ways of thinking, *and to practice* the more positive approach in everyday settings. Anxiety and mood disorders share a common problem: emotion regulation. An effective treatment program for these emotional disorders trains people both to replace their catastrophizing thinking with more realistic appraisals, and to practice behaviors that are incompatible with their problem (Moses & Barlow, 2006). A person with a fear of social situations, for example, might learn new ways of thinking, but also practice approaching people.

In one study, people learned to prevent compulsive behaviors by relabeling their obsessive thoughts (Schwartz et al., 1996). Feeling the urge to wash their hands again, they would tell themselves, "I'm having a compulsive urge," and attribute it to their brain's abnormal activity, as previously viewed in their PET scans. Instead of giving in to the urge, they would then spend 15 minutes in an

CRITICAL THINKING

Combination therapies tend to be more effective than single therapeutic approaches. Have students ponder why this might be so:

- How do combination therapies address the different explanations for human behavior?

- For what other disorders are combination therapies effective?

enjoyable, alternative behavior, such as practicing an instrument, taking a walk, or gardening. This helped "unstick" the brain by shifting attention and engaging other brain areas. For two or three months, the weekly therapy sessions continued, with relabeling and refocusing practice at home. By the study's end, most participants' symptoms had diminished and their PET scans revealed normalized brain activity. Many other studies confirm cognitive-behavioral therapy's effectiveness for those suffering anxiety or depression (Covin et al., 2008; Mitte, 2005; Norton & Price, 2007).

Group and Family Therapies

5: What are the aims and benefits of group and family therapy?

Except for traditional psychoanalysis, most therapies may also occur in small groups. Group therapy does not provide the same degree of therapist involvement with each client. However, it saves therapists' time and clients' money—and it often is no less effective than individual therapy (Fuhriman & Burlingame, 1994). Therapists frequently suggest group therapy for people experiencing family conflicts or for those whose behavior is distressing to others. For up to 90 minutes a week, the therapist guides the interactions of a group of people as they engage issues and react to one another.

Group sessions also offer a unique benefit: The social context allows people both to discover that others have problems similar to their own and to receive feedback as they try out new ways of behaving. It can be a relief to find that you are not alone—to learn that others, despite their apparent composure, share your problems and your troublesome feelings. It can also be reassuring to hear that you yourself look poised even though you feel anxious and self-conscious.

One special type of group interaction, **family therapy,** assumes that no person is an island, that we live and grow in relation to others, especially our families. We struggle to differentiate ourselves from our families, but we also need to connect with them emotionally. Some of our problem behaviors arise from the tension between these two tendencies, which can create family stress.

Unlike most psychotherapy, which focuses on what happens inside the person's own skin, family therapists work with family members to heal relationships and to mobilize family resources. They tend to view the family as a system in which each person's actions trigger reactions from others, and they help family members discover their role within their family's social system. A child's rebellion, for example, affects and is affected by other family tensions. Therapists also attempt—usually with some success, research suggests—to open up communication within the family or to help family members discover new ways of preventing or resolving conflicts (Hazelrigg et al., 1987; Shadish et al., 1993).

A wide range of people participate in self-help and support groups (Yalom, 1985). One analysis (Davison et al., 2000) of online support groups and more than 14,000 self-help groups reports that most support groups focus on stigmatized or hard-to-discuss illnesses. AIDS patients are 250 times more likely than hypertension patients to be in support

::**cognitive-behavioral therapy** a popular integrative therapy that combines cognitive therapy (changing self-defeating thinking) with behavior therapy (changing behavior).

::**family therapy** therapy that treats the family as a system. Views an individual's unwanted behaviors as influenced by, or directed at, other family members.

Family therapy This type of therapy often acts as a preventive mental health strategy. The therapist helps family members understand how their ways of relating to one another create problems. The treatment's emphasis is not on changing the individuals but on changing their relationships and interactions.

RESEARCH

Many support groups utilize therapeutic techniques as they provide a network of people who depend on each other for support and aid. Contact local support group organizations to ask what type of therapeutic techniques they use in their sessions:

● Are sessions lead by a qualified or certified therapist? Why or why not?

● What rules for discussion are followed by the group?

● How much contact do group members have outside of the support group meetings?

● What types of planned activities does the group provide?

 CRITICAL THINKING

Have students discuss the advantages and disadvantages of family therapy. Some questions they may consider in their discussion include the following:

● If a patient has a dysfunctional family life, how might individual therapy be only partially effective?

● Might a person be less willing to open up about personal issues if the rest of the family knew about these feelings? Why or why not?

RESEARCH

Have students research how many non-psychiatric therapy services are available in your city or area. They can use the phone book to find listings of clinical psychologists in private practice, community mental health centers, halfway houses, crisis hotlines, and similar services that do not rely on psychiatrists to perform psychotherapy.

 TEACHING TIP

Have students contact a support group and ask if it would be appropriate for them to sit in on a therapy session. If the group is comfortable with visitors, have students attend a meeting, keeping the following in mind:

- How many people attended that particular meeting? Was this attendance average? If not, why?

- Who seemed to be in charge of the session? Was it a therapist or a group member?

- What were the qualifications of the group's leader?

- Did there seem to be a lesson or objective to the meeting or was the session open to free discussion? Why was this particular method used?

• With more than 2 million members worldwide, AA is said to be "the largest organization on Earth that nobody wanted to join" (Finlay, 2000). •

groups. Those struggling with anorexia and alcohol dependency often join groups; those with migraines and ulcers do not. People with hearing loss have national organizations with local chapters; people with vision loss more often cope without such groups.

The grandparent of support groups, Alcoholics Anonymous (AA), reports having more than 2 million members in 114,000 groups worldwide. Its famous 12-step program, emulated by many other self-help groups, asks members to admit their powerlessness, to seek help from a higher power and from one another, and (the twelfth step) to take the message to others in need of it. In one eight-year, $27 million investigation, AA participants reduced their drinking sharply, although so did those assigned to cognitive-behavioral therapy or to "motivational therapy" (Project Match, 1997). Other studies have similarly found that 12-step programs such as AA have helped reduce alcohol dependence comparably to other treatment interventions (Ferri et al., 2006; Moos & Moos, 2005). The more meetings patients attend, the greater their alcohol abstinence (Moos & Moos, 2006). In one study of 2300 veterans who sought treatment for alcohol dependency, a high level of AA involvement was followed by diminished alcohol problems (McKellar et al., 2003).

In an individualistic age, with more and more people living alone or feeling isolated, the popularity of support groups—for the addicted, the bereaved, the divorced, or simply those seeking fellowship and growth—seems to reflect a longing for community and connectedness. More than 100 million Americans belong to small religious, interest, or self-help groups that meet regularly—and 9 in 10 report that group members "support each other emotionally" (Gallup, 1994).

* * *

For a synopsis of the main forms of psychotherapy we've been discussing, see **TABLE 13.1**.

TABLE 13.1

COMPARISON OF A SAMPLE OF MAJOR PSYCHOTHERAPIES

Therapy	Assumed Problem	Therapy Aims	Method
Psychodynamic	Unconscious forces and childhood experiences	Reduced anxiety through self-insight	Analysis and interpretation
Client-centered	Barriers to self-understanding and self-acceptance	Personal growth through self-insight	Active listening and unconditional positive regard
Behavior	Maladaptive behaviors	Extinction of maladaptive behaviors, and relearning of more adaptive behaviors	Counterconditioning, exposure, desensitization, aversive conditioning, and operant conditioning
Cognitive	Negative, self-defeating thinking	Healthier thinking and self-talk	Reveal and reverse self-blaming
Family	Stressful relationships	Relationship healing	Understanding family social system; exploring roles; improving communication

BEFORE YOU MOVE ON . . .

> **ASK YOURSELF**

Critics say that behavior modification techniques, such as those used in token economies, are inhumane. Do you agree or disagree? Why?

> **TEST YOURSELF 1**

What is the major distinction between the underlying assumptions in insight therapies and in behavior therapies?

Answers to the Test Yourself questions can be found in Appendix E at the end of the book.

 TEACHING TIP

For a fun informal assessment, have students identify fictional characters who seem to have some type of mental disorder. What type of treatment would they recommend for that disorder? This activity can help you know whether students know the symptoms of major mental illnesses and the appropriate treatments for those disorders.

Evaluating Psychotherapies

ADVICE COLUMNISTS FREQUENTLY URGE their troubled letter writers to get professional help: "Don't give up. Find a therapist who can help you. Make an appointment."

Therapists can verify that many Americans share this confidence in psychotherapy's effectiveness. Before 1950, psychiatrists were the primary providers of mental health care. Today, surging demands for psychotherapy mean that people are also seeking help from clinical and counseling psychologists; clinical social workers; pastoral, marital, abuse, and school counselors; and psychiatric nurses. In 2004, for example, 7.4 percent of Americans reported "undergoing counseling for mental or emotional problems," a 25 percent increase since 1991 (Smith, 2005). With such an enormous outlay of time as well as money, effort, and hope, it is important to ask: Are the millions of people worldwide justified in placing such hope in psychotherapy?

Is Psychotherapy Effective?

6: Does psychotherapy work? Who decides?

The question, though simply put, is not simply answered. Measuring therapy's effectiveness is not like taking your body's temperature to see if your fever has gone away. If you and I were to undergo psychotherapy, how would we assess its effectiveness? By how we feel about our progress? How our therapist feels about it? How our friends and family feel about it? How our behavior has changed?

Clients' Perceptions

If clients' testimonials were the only measuring stick, we could strongly affirm the effectiveness of psychotherapy. When 2900 *Consumer Reports* readers (1995; Kotkin et al., 1996; Seligman, 1995) related their experiences with mental health professionals, 89 percent said they were at least "fairly well satisfied." Among those who recalled feeling *fair* or *very poor* when beginning therapy, 9 in 10 now were feeling *very good, good,* or at least *so-so*. We have their word for it—and who should know better?

We should not dismiss these testimonials lightly. But for several reasons, client testimonials do not persuade psychotherapy's skeptics:

- **People often enter therapy in crisis**. When, with the normal ebb and flow of events, the crisis passes, people may attribute their improvement to the therapy.
- **Clients may need to believe the therapy was worth the effort.** To admit investing time and money in something ineffective is like admitting to having one's car serviced repeatedly by a mechanic who never fixes it. Self-justification is a powerful human motive.
- **Clients generally speak kindly of their therapists.** Even if the problems remain, say the critics, clients "work hard to find something positive to say. The therapist had been very understanding, the client had gained a new perspective, he learned to communicate better, his mind was eased, anything at all so as not to have to say treatment was a failure" (Zilbergeld, 1983, p. 117).

As earlier units document, we are prone to selective and biased recall and to making judgments that confirm our beliefs. Consider the testimonials gathered in a massive experiment with over 500 Massachusetts boys, aged 5 to 13 years, many of whom seemed bound for delinquency. By the toss of a coin, half the boys were assigned to a 5-year treatment program. The treated boys were visited by counselors twice a month. They participated in community programs, and they received academic tutoring, medical attention, and family assistance as needed. Some 30 years later, Joan McCord

UNIT 13

::**regression toward the mean** the tendency for extreme or unusual scores to fall back (regress) toward their average.

::**meta-analysis** a procedure for statistically combining the results of many different research studies.

INTERCONNECTING

Remind students that in Unit 2 Myers discussed the benefits and drawbacks of case study research. The benefits include a detailed understanding of a case and the ability to conduct research that would be unethical in experimental situations. The drawbacks include the lack of generalizability and the lack of control over confounding variables.

CRITICAL THINKING

Unfortunately, many people who have psychological disorders do not have a clear-cut diagnosis, making it difficult to conduct clean outcome research that is free of confounding variables. Have students brainstorm about why clear-cut diagnoses are difficult to make:

- How does a patient's level of candor or openness contribute to the ability of the therapist to diagnose the problem?

- How can substance abuse interfere with an accurate diagnosis?

> "Fortunately, [psycho]analysis is not the only way to resolve inner conflicts. Life itself still remains a very effective therapist."
> Karen Horney, *Our Inner Conflicts*, 1945

(1978, 1979) located 485 participants, sent them questionnaires, and checked public records from courts, mental hospitals, and other sources. Was the treatment successful?

Client testimonials yielded encouraging results, even glowing reports. Some men noted that, had it not been for their counselors, "I would probably be in jail," "My life would have gone the other way," or "I think I would have ended up in a life of crime." Court records offered apparent support: Even among the "difficult" boys in the treatment group, 66 percent had no official juvenile crime record.

But recall psychology's most powerful tool for sorting reality from wishful thinking: the *control group*. For every boy in the treatment group, there was a similar boy in a control group receiving no counseling. Of these untreated men, *70 percent* had no juvenile record. On several other measures, such as a record of having committed a second crime, alcohol dependence, death rate, and job satisfaction, the untreated men exhibited slightly *fewer* problems. The glowing testimonials of those treated had been unintentionally deceiving.

Clinicians' Perceptions

Do clinicians' perceptions give us any more reason to celebrate? Case studies of successful treatment abound. The problem is that clients justify entering psychotherapy by emphasizing their unhappiness, justify leaving by emphasizing their well-being, and stay in touch only if satisfied. Therapists treasure compliments from clients as they say good-bye or later express their gratitude, but they hear little from clients who experience only temporary relief and seek out new therapists for their recurring problems. Thus, the same person—with the same recurring anxieties, depression, or marital difficulty—may be a "success" story in several therapists' files.

Because most people enter therapy when they are extremely unhappy, and usually leave when they are less extremely unhappy, most therapists, like most clients, testify to therapy's success—regardless of the treatment (see Thinking Critically About: "Regressing" From Unusual to Usual).

Outcome Research

How, then, can we objectively measure the effectiveness of psychotherapy if neither clients nor clinicians can tell us? How can we determine what types of people and problems are best helped, and by what type of psychotherapy?

In search of answers, psychologists have turned to controlled research studies. Similar research in the 1800s transformed the field of medicine. Physicians, skeptical of many of the fashionable treatments (bleeding, purging, infusions of plant and metal substances), began to realize that many patients got better on their own, without these treatments, and that others died in spite of them. Sorting fact from superstition required following patients with and without a particular treatment. Typhoid fever patients, for example, often improved after being bled, convincing most physicians that the treatment worked. Not until a control group was given mere bed rest—and 70 percent were observed to improve after five weeks of fever—did physicians learn, to their shock, that the bleeding was worthless (Thomas, 1992).

In psychology, the opening challenge to the effectiveness of psychotherapy was issued by British psychologist Hans Eysenck (1952). Launching a spirited debate, he summarized studies showing that two-thirds of those receiving psychotherapy for nonpsychotic disorders improved markedly. To this day, no one disputes that optimistic estimate.

Why, then, are we still debating psychotherapy's effectiveness? Because Eysenck also reported similar improvement among *untreated* persons, such as those who were on waiting lists. With or without psychotherapy, he said, roughly two-thirds improved noticeably. Time was a great healer.

INTERCONNECTING

Remind students of the placebo effect. This effect, in which people's belief in a therapy can lead to their actually feeling better, helps explain why 29 percent of people did get better while on a placebo. But this does not compare to the 50 percent success rate of real treatment programs.

THINKING CRITICALLY ABOUT

"Regressing" From Unusual to Usual

Clients' and therapists' perceptions of therapy's effectiveness are vulnerable to inflation from two phenomena. One is the *placebo effect*—the power of belief in a treatment. If you think a treatment is going to be effective, it just may be (thanks to the healing power of your positive expectation).

The second phenomenon is **regression toward the mean**—the tendency for unusual events (or emotions) to "regress" (return) to their average state. Thus, extraordinary happenings (feeling low) tend to be followed by more ordinary ones (a return to our more usual state). Indeed, when things hit bottom, whatever we try—going to a psychotherapist, starting yoga, doing aerobic exercise—is more likely to be followed by improvement than by further descent.

> "Once you become sensitized to it, you see regression everywhere."
>
> Psychologist Daniel Kahneman (1985)

The point may seem obvious, yet we regularly miss it: We sometimes attribute what may be a normal regression (the expected return to normal) to something we have done. Consider:

- Students who score much lower or higher on a test than they usually do are likely, when retested, to return toward their average.
- Unusual ESP subjects who defy chance when first tested nearly always lose their "psychic powers" when retested (a phenomenon parapsychologists have called the *decline effect*).
- Coaches often yell at their players after an unusually bad first half. They may then feel rewarded for having done so when the team's performance improves (returns to normal) during the second half.

In each case, the cause-effect link may be genuine. It is more likely, however, that each is an instance of the natural tendency for behavior to regress from the unusual to the more usual. And this defines the task for therapy-efficacy research: Does the client's improvement following a particular therapy exceed what could be expected from the placebo and regression effects alone, shown by comparison with control groups?

> "The real purpose of [the] scientific method is to make sure Nature hasn't misled you into thinking you know something that you actually don't."
>
> Robert Pirsig,
> *Zen and the Art of Motorcycle Maintenance*, 1974

Later research revealed shortcomings in Eysenck's analyses; his sample was small (only 24 studies of psychotherapy outcomes in 1952). Today, hundreds of studies are available. The best are *randomized clinical trials,* in which researchers randomly assign people on a waiting list to therapy or to no therapy, and later evaluate everyone, using tests and the reports of people who don't know whether therapy was given. The results of many such studies are then digested by a means of **meta-analysis,** a statistical procedure that combines the conclusions of a large number of different studies. Simply said, meta-analyses give us the bottom-line results of lots of studies.

Psychotherapists welcomed the first meta-analysis of some 475 psychotherapy outcome studies (Smith et al., 1980). It showed that the average therapy client ends up better off than 80 percent of the untreated individuals on waiting lists (**FIGURE 13.3** on the next page). The claim is modest—by definition, about 50 percent of untreated people also are better off than the average untreated person. Nevertheless, Mary Lee Smith and her colleagues exulted that "psychotherapy benefits people of all ages as reliably as schooling educates them, medicine cures them, or business turns a profit" (p. 183).

More than five dozen subsequent summaries have now examined this question (Kopta et al., 1999; Shadish et al., 2000). Their verdict echoes the results of the earlier outcome studies: *Those not undergoing therapy often improve, but those undergoing therapy are more likely to improve.*

Is psychotherapy also cost-effective? Again, the answer is *yes.* Studies show that when people seek psychological treatment, their search for other medical treatment drops—by 16 percent in one digest of 91 studies (Chiles et al., 1999). Given the staggering annual cost of psychological disorders and substance abuse—crime, accidents,

TROUBLESHOOTING

Regression toward the mean is a statistical term students may not be familiar with. Have students recall their study of the normal curve (Units 2 and 11). In a normal curve, the mean identifies where the center of the data lies. If students were to chart their test scores in your class, they would come up with an average. While individual tests may show significant deviation from the mean, only multiple, consistently different test scores over time would shift the mean in either direction on the graph. So, one unusual performance (or behavior, or thought, or experience) is just that—unusual—and our behavior is bound to return to our "normal."

At this point, you may want to use **Classroom Exercise: *Regression Toward the Mean and Aspiration Level*** (p. 18) from Bolt's Teacher's Resource Binder.

 TEACHING TIP

While the phrase *randomized clinical trials* is not a bold vocabulary word, it is an important phrase for students to know. This type of experimental procedure is considered the "gold standard" for outcome research. As students become consumers of psychological and medical therapy, they should talk to their providers about whether they use treatments that have undergone this type of procedure.

TEACHING TIP

A classic meta-analysis was conducted by Mary Lee Smith and her colleagues to determine whether psychotherapy was effective. These researchers found that overall, most psychotherapies were effective, and all demonstrated about the same levels of effectiveness. Interestingly, the researchers found that around 35–40 percent of people got better simply by deciding they needed to seek psychological treatment. It seems that admitting you have a problem is a significant first step toward healing.

The graph in Figure 13.3 is an important one for students to understand. Not only does this graph demonstrate the importance of seeking psychological therapy when people experience mental illness, but it also demonstrates concepts in statistics, such as significant differences and normal distributions. Review these concepts with students using this graph.

Have students come up with an experiment that tests the efficacy of a therapeutic intervention. The intervention does not have to be specific, but the experimental methodology should include a control group and an experimental group, blind or double-blind procedures, and randomization techniques. Have students also discuss the ethical considerations involved in conducting an efficacy experiment.

➤ **FIGURE 13.3**
Treatment versus no treatment These two normal distribution curves based on data from 475 studies show the improvement of untreated people and psychotherapy clients. The outcome for the average therapy client surpassed that for 80 percent of the untreated people. (Adapted from Smith et al., 1980.)

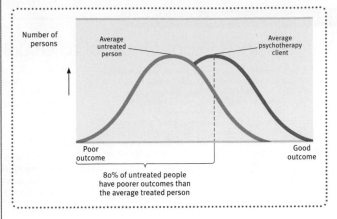

lost work, and treatment—psychotherapy seems to be a good investment, much like money spent on prenatal and well-baby care. Both *reduce* long-term costs. Boosting employees' psychological well-being, for example, can lower medical costs, improve work efficiency, and diminish absenteeism.

But note that the claim—that psychotherapy, *on average*, is somewhat effective—refers to no one therapy in particular. It is like reassuring lung-cancer patients that "on average," medical treatment of health problems is effective. What people want to know is the effectiveness of a *particular* treatment for their specific problems.

The Relative Effectiveness of Different Therapies

7: Are some therapies more effective than others?

So what can we tell people considering therapy, and those paying for it, about *which* psychotherapy will be most effective for their problem? The statistical summaries and surveys fail to pinpoint any one type of therapy as generally superior (Smith et al., 1977, 1980). Clients seemed equally satisfied, *Consumer Reports* concluded, whether treated by a psychiatrist, psychologist, or social worker; whether seen in a group or individual context; whether the therapist had extensive or relatively limited training and experience (Seligman, 1995). Other studies concur. There is little if any connection between clinicians' experience, training, supervision, and licensing and their clients' outcomes (Luborsky et al., 2002; Wampold, 2007).

So, was the dodo bird in *Alice in Wonderland* right: "Everyone has won and all must have prizes"? Not quite. Some forms of therapy get prizes for particular problems. Behavioral conditioning therapies, for example, have achieved especially favorable results with specific behavior problems, such as bed-wetting, phobias, compulsions, and marital problems (Bowers & Clum, 1988; Hunsley & DiGiulio, 2002; Shadish & Baldwin, 2005). And new studies confirm cognitive therapy's effectiveness in coping with depression and reducing suicide risk (Brown et al., 2005; DeRubeis et al., 2005; Hollon et al., 2005).

Moreover, we can say that therapy is most effective when the problem is clear-cut (Singer, 1981; Westen & Morrison, 2001). Those who experience phobias or panic, who are unassertive, or who seek more family harmony can hope for improvement. Those with less-focused problems, such as depression and anxiety, usually benefit in the short term but often relapse later. And those with the negative symptoms of

> "Whatever differences in treatment efficacy exist, they appear to be extremely small, at best."
> Bruce Wampold et al. [1997]

> "Different sores have different salves."
> English proverb

At this point, you may want to use **Lecture/Discussion Topics:** *Writing About Emotional Experiences as Therapy* (p. 20) or *Psychological Treatments Versus Psychotherapy* (p. 21) from Bolt's Teacher's Resource Binder.

chronic schizophrenia or a desire to change their entire personality are unlikely to benefit from psychotherapy alone (Pfammatter et al., 2006; Zilbergeld, 1983). The more specific the problem, the greater the hope.

But no prizes—and little or no scientific support—go to other therapies (Arkowitz & Lilienfeld, 2006). We would all therefore be wise to avoid the following unsupported approaches.

- **Energy therapies** propose to manipulate people's invisible energy fields.
- **Recovered-memory therapies** aim to unearth "repressed memories" of early child abuse (Unit 7A).
- **Rebirthing therapies** engage people in reenacting the supposed trauma of their birth.
- **Facilitated communication** has an assistant touch the typing hand of a child with autism.
- **Crisis debriefing** forces people to verbalize, rehearse, and "process" their traumatic experiences.

But this question—which therapies get prizes and which do not?—lies at the heart of a serious controversy some call psychology's civil war. To what extent should science guide both clinical practice and the willingness of health care providers and insurers to pay for psychotherapy? On the one side are research psychologists using scientific methods to extend the list of well-defined and validated therapies for various disorders. On the other side are nonscientist therapists who view their practice as more art than science, saying that people are too complex and therapy too intuitive to describe in a manual or test in an experiment. Between these two factions stand the science-oriented clinicians, who believe that by basing practice on evidence and making mental health professionals accountable for effectiveness, therapy will only gain in credibility. Moreover, the public will be protected from pseudotherapies, and therapists will be protected from accusations of sounding like snake-oil salespeople—"Trust me, I know it works, I've seen it work."

To encourage **evidence-based practice** in psychology, the American Psychological Association (2006; Spring, 2007) has followed the Institute of Medicine's lead, advocating that clinicians integrate the best available research with clinical expertise and patient preferences and characteristics. Available therapies "should be rigorously evaluated" and then applied by clinicians who are mindful of their skills and of each patient's unique situation (**FIGURE 13.4**). Increasingly, insurer and government support for mental health services requires evidence-based practice. In late 2007, for example, Britain's National Health Service announced that it would pour the equivalent of $600 million into training new mental health workers in evidence-based practices (such as cognitive-behavioral therapy) and to disseminating information about such treatments (DeAngelis, 2008).

Evaluating Alternative Therapies

8: How do alternative therapies fare under scientific scrutiny?

The tendency of many abnormal states of mind to return to normal, combined with the placebo effect, creates fertile soil for pseudotherapies. Bolstered by anecdotes, heralded by the media, and praised on the Internet, alternative therapies can spread like wildfire. In one national survey, 57 percent of those with a history of anxiety attacks and 54 percent of those with a history of depression had used alternative treatments, such as herbal medicine, massage, and spiritual healing (Kessler et al., 2001).

Testimonials aside, what does the evidence say about alternative therapies? This is a tough question, because there is no evidence for or against most of them, though

::**evidence-based practice** clinical decision-making that integrates the best available research with clinical expertise and patient characteristics and preferences.

➤ FIGURE 13.4
Evidence-based clinical decision-making The ideal clinical decision-making is a three-legged stool, upheld by research evidence, clinical expertise, and knowledge of the patient.

TEACHING TIP

Have students research the unsubstantiated therapeutic practices Myers lists here. Have students generate a list of maladies these practices aim to treat and how scientific research has debunked their use. Be mindful that some students or their families may have participated in these practices in the past. Help them see that while they may have thought they were effective in the past, research does not support their general effectiveness.

TEACHING TIP

Myers refers to "psychology's civil war." Some students may wonder what he means by this phrase. Since the beginning of psychology, clinicians (those who treat people with mental illness or other psychological issues) and academics (those who research psychological phenomena) have battled over which emphasis is more important to psychology.

- The academics believe that understanding psychological phenomena and testing the effectiveness of therapy is the necessary first step to being a discipline that is taken seriously by other scientists and the public at large.

- The clinicians believe that much research lacks a practical component, making it less useful for helping individuals in crisis. They argue that clients who are helped demonstrate the effectiveness of therapy.

WEB CONNECT

Another therapy that has been debunked is therapeutic touch therapy, in which a practitioner will attempt to manipulate the "auras" and "energy fields" around a person's body to promote healing. Therapeutic touch therapy (which does not, ironically, involve any actual touching) should not be confused with touch therapy. Touch therapy involves actual massage therapy to treat different illnesses. Touch therapy can increase weight in premature babies, alleviate depression, reduce stress hormone levels, and improve immune response. For more information about Touch Therapy, refer to the Touch Research Institute Web page at www.miami.edu/touch-research/.

UNIT 13

TEACHING TIP

At this point, you may want to use **Lecture/Discussion Topics:** *Pets in Therapy* (p. 21) or *Trepanation* (p. 22) or *Autobiographies* (p. 22) from Bolt's Teacher's Resource Binder.

their proponents often feel personal experience is evidence enough. Some, however, have been the subject of controlled research. Let's consider two of them. As we do, remember that sifting sense from nonsense requires the scientific attitude: being skeptical but not cynical, open to surprises but not gullible.

Eye Movement Desensitization and Reprocessing (EMDR)

EMDR (eye movement desensitization and reprocessing) is a therapy adored by thou-sands and dismissed by thousands more as a sham—"an excellent vehicle for illustrat-ing the differences between scientific and pseudoscientific therapy techniques," suggested James Herbert and seven others (2000). Francine Shapiro (1989, 2007) developed EMDR one day while walking in a park and observing that anxious thoughts vanished as her eyes spontaneously darted about. Offering her novel anxiety treat-ment to others, she had people imagine traumatic scenes while she triggered eye movements by waving her finger in front of their eyes, supposedly enabling them to unlock and reprocess previously frozen memories. After she tried this on 22 people haunted by old traumatic memories, and all reported marked reductions in their dis-tress after just one therapeutic session, the extraordinary result evoked an enormous response from mental health professionals. To date, nearly 70,000 of them, from more than 75 countries, have undergone training (EMDR, 2008). Not since the sim-ilarly charismatic Franz Anton Mesmer introduced *animal magnetism* (hypnosis) more than two centuries ago (also after feeling inspired by an outdoor experience) has a new therapy attracted so many devotees so quickly.

Does it work? For 84 to 100 percent of single-trauma victims participating in four studies, the answer was *yes,* reported Shapiro (1999, 2002). (When EMDR did not fare well in other trials, Shapiro argued that the therapists were not properly trained.) More-over, the treatment need take no more than three 90-minute sessions. The Society of Clinical Psychology task force on empirically validated treatments acknowledges that the treatment is "probably efficacious" for the treatment of nonmilitary post-traumatic stress disorder (PTSD)(Chambless et al., 1997; see also Bisson & Andrew, 2007; Seidler & Wagner, 2006). Encouraged by their seeming successes, EMDR therapists are now applying the technique to other anxiety disorders, such as panic disorder, and, with Shapiro's (1995, 2002) encouragement, to a wide range of complaints, including pain, grief, paranoid schizophrenia, rage, and guilt.

Why, wonder the skeptics, would rapidly moving one's eyes while recalling trau-mas be therapeutic? Indeed, it seems eye movements are *not* the therapeutic ingredi-ent. In trials in which people imagined traumatic scenes and tapped a finger, or just stared straight ahead while the therapist's finger wagged, the therapeutic results were the same (Devilly, 2003). EMDR does work better than doing nothing, acknowledge the skeptics (Lilienfeld & Arkowitz, 2007), but many suspect that what is therapeutic is the combination of exposure therapy—repeatedly associating with traumatic mem-ories a safe and reassuring context that provides some emotional distance from the experience—and a robust placebo effect. Had Mesmer's pseudotherapy been compared with no treatment at all, it, too (thanks to the healing power of positive belief), might have been found "probably efficacious," observed Richard McNally (1999).

> "Studies indicate that EMDR is just as effective with fixed eyes. If that conclusion is right, what's useful in the therapy [chiefly behavioral desensitization] is not new, and what's new is superfluous."
> *Harvard Mental Health Letter,* 2002

Light Exposure Therapy

Have you ever found yourself oversleeping, gaining weight, and feeling lethargic dur-ing the dark mornings and overcast days of winter? There likely was a survival advan-tage to your distant ancestors' slowing down and conserving energy during the dark days of winter. For some people, however, especially women and those living far from the equator, the wintertime blahs constitute a form of depression known as *seasonal affective disorder,* for which the appropriate acronym is SAD. To counteract these dark spirits, National Institute of Mental Health researchers in the early 1980s had an

RESEARCH

Have students comb through magazines and newspapers to see what types of alternative therapy are advertised.

- What claims of effectiveness do these ads make?
- What type of credentials do the practitioners possess?
- What type of disorders do these therapies claim to treat?

idea: Give SAD people a timed daily dose of intense light. Sure enough, people reported they felt better.

Was this a bright idea, or another dim-witted example of the placebo effect, attributable to people's expectations? Recent studies shed some light. One exposed some people with SAD to 90 minutes of bright light and others to a sham placebo treatment—a hissing "negative ion generator" about which the staff expressed similar enthusiasm (but which, unknown to the participants, was not turned on). After four weeks of treatment, 61 percent of those exposed to morning light had greatly improved, as had 50 percent of those exposed to evening light and 32 percent of those exposed to the placebo (Eastman et al., 1998). Other studies have found that 30 minutes of exposure to 10,000-lux white fluorescent light produced relief for more than half the people receiving morning light therapy and for one-third receiving evening light therapy (Terman et al., 1998, 2001). From 20 carefully controlled trials we have a verdict (Golden et al., 2005): Morning bright light does indeed dim SAD symptoms for many people. Moreover, it does so as effectively as taking antidepressant drugs or undergoing cognitive-behavioral therapy (Lam et al., 2006; Rohan et al., 2007). The effects are clear in brain scans; this therapy sparks activity in a brain region that influences the body's arousal and hormones (Ishida et al., 2005).

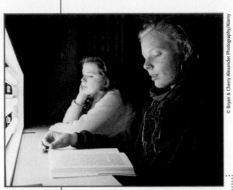

Light therapy To counteract winter depression, some people spend time each morning exposed to intense light that mimics natural outdoor light. These Norwegian high school students receive regular light therapy at school during the winter months. In the United States, light boxes to counteract SAD are available from health supply and lighting stores.

Commonalities Among Psychotherapies

9: What three elements are shared by all forms of psychotherapy?

The scientific attitude helps us sift sense from nonsense as we consider new forms of therapy. Might it also help explain why studies have found little correlation between therapists' training and experience and clients' outcomes? In search of some answers, Jerome Frank (1982), Marvin Goldfried (Goldfried & Padawer, 1982), Hans Strupp (1986), and Bruce Wampold (2001, 2007) have studied the common ingredients of various therapies. They suggest they all offer at least three benefits: *hope for demoralized people; a new perspective* on oneself and the world; and *an empathic, trusting, caring relationship.*

Hope for Demoralized People

People seeking therapy typically feel anxious, depressed, devoid of self-esteem, and incapable of turning things around. What any therapy offers is the expectation that, with commitment from the therapy seeker, things can and will get better. This belief, apart from any therapeutic technique, may function as a placebo, improving morale, creating feelings of self-efficacy, and diminishing symptoms (Prioleau et al., 1983). Statistical analyses showing that improvement is greater for placebo-treated people than for untreated people suggest that one way therapies help is by harnessing the client's own healing powers. And that, says psychiatrist Jerome Frank, helps us understand why all sorts of treatments—including some folk healing rites that are powerless apart from the participants' belief—may in their own time and place produce cures.

A New Perspective

Every therapy also offers people a plausible explanation of their symptoms and an alternative way of looking at themselves or responding to their world. Armed with a believable fresh perspective, they may approach life with a new attitude, open to making changes in their behaviors and their views of themselves.

"I utilize the best from Freud, the best from Jung, and the best from my Uncle Marty, a very smart fellow."

 TEACHING TIP

Seasonal affective disorder (SAD) is not included in the *DSM-IV-TR* and is not recommended for inclusion in the proposed *DSM-V.* Have students ponder why it isn't and what qualifies a disorder to be included in this diagnostic tool.

- How many people suffer from SAD?

- How do psychiatrists decide which disorders are included in the *DSM?*

 TEACHING TIP

C. R. Snyder developed a theory of hope that helps show why hope may be important for demoralized people. Snyder proposed three components to hope:

- Goals: People with clear, concrete, and challenging yet attainable goals were more likely to make plans for the future and believe in themselves.

- Agency: People with high agency—beliefs about their abilities and capabilities for action—tend to be more willing to pursue goals and accomplish them.

- Pathways: People who develop multiple pathways for achieving goals have higher hope and are more likely to thrive, even after failure.

 TEACHING TIP

At this point, you may want to use **Lecture/Discussion Topic:** *Evaluating Self-Help Resources* (p. 23) from Bolt's Teacher's Resource Binder.

UNIT 13

INTERCONNECTING

Remind students that Carl Rogers was the leading advocate of the importance of the client-therapist relationship. He developed his client-centered therapy as a response to the very therapist-heavy approach of Freud and his students. In Freudian therapy, the therapist is in control and tells clients what they are thinking, feeling, and remembering. In client-centered therapy, the client is the one in control, receiving active listening and unconditional positive regard from the therapist.

An Empathic, Trusting, Caring Relationship

To say that therapy outcome is unrelated to training and experience is not to say all *therapists* are equally effective. No matter what therapeutic technique they use, effective therapists are empathic people who seek to understand another's experience; who communicate their care and concern to the client; and who earn the client's trust and respect through respectful listening, reassurance, and advice. Marvin Goldfried and his associates (1998) found these qualities in taped therapy sessions from 36 recognized master therapists. Some were cognitive-behavioral therapists, others were psychodynamic-interpersonal therapists. Regardless, the striking finding was how *similar* they were during the parts of their sessions they considered most significant. At key moments, the empathic therapists of both persuasions would help clients evaluate themselves, link one aspect of their life with another, and gain insight into their interactions with others.

A caring relationship Effective therapists form a bond of trust with their patients.

The emotional bond between therapist and client—the *therapeutic alliance*—is a key aspect of effective therapy (Klein et al., 2003; Wampold, 2001). One U.S. National Institute of Mental Health depression-treatment study confirmed that the most effective therapists were those who were perceived as most empathic and caring and who established the closest therapeutic bonds with their clients (Blatt et al., 1996). That all therapies offer hope through a fresh perspective offered by a caring person is what also enables paraprofessionals (briefly trained caregivers) to assist so many troubled people so effectively (Christensen & Jacobson, 1994).

These three common elements are also part of what the growing numbers of self-help and support groups offer their members. And they are part of what traditional healers have offered (Jackson, 1992). Healers everywhere—special people to whom others disclose their suffering, whether psychiatrists, witch doctors, or shamans—have listened in order to understand and to empathize, reassure, advise, console, interpret, or explain (Torrey, 1986). Such qualities may explain why people who feel supported by close relationships—who enjoy the fellowship and friendship of caring people—are less likely to need or seek therapy (Frank, 1982; O'Connor & Brown, 1984).

* * *

To recap, people who seek help usually improve. So do many of those who do not undergo psychotherapy, and that is a tribute to our human resourcefulness and our capacity to care for one another. Nevertheless, though the therapist's orientation and experience appear not to matter much, people who receive some psychotherapy usually improve more than those who do not. People with clear-cut, specific problems tend to improve the most.

Culture and Values in Psychotherapy

10: How do culture and values influence the therapist-client relationship?

All therapies offer hope, and nearly all therapists attempt to enhance their clients' sensitivity, openness, personal responsibility, and sense of purpose (Jensen & Bergin, 1988). But in matters of cultural and moral diversity, therapists differ from one another and may differ from their clients (Delaney et al., 2007; Kelly, 1990).

These differences can become significant when a therapist from one culture meets a client from another. In North America, Europe, and Australia, for example, most

---

⦿ TEACHING TIP

At this point, you may want to use **Lecture/Discussion Topic:** *Mental Health Values of Professional Therapists* (p. 24) or **Student Project:** *Applying the Major Therapies* (p. 25) from Bolt's Teacher's Resource Binder.

therapists reflect their culture's individualism, which often gives priority to personal desires and identity. Clients who are immigrants from Asian countries, where people are mindful of others' expectations, may have trouble relating to therapies that require them to think only of their own well-being. Such differences help explain some minority populations' reluctance to use mental health services and to prematurely terminate therapy (Sue, 2006). In one experiment, Asian-American clients matched with counselors who shared their cultural values (rather than mismatched with those who did not) perceived more counselor empathy and felt a stronger alliance with the counselor (Kim et al., 2005). Recognizing that therapists and clients may differ in their values, communication styles, and language, many therapy training programs now provide training in cultural sensitivity and recruit members of underrepresented cultural groups.

Another area of potential value conflict is religion. Highly religious people may prefer and benefit from religiously similar therapists (Smith et al., 2007; Wade et al., 2006; Worthington et al., 1996). They may have trouble establishing an emotional bond with a therapist who does not share their values. (For those thinking about seeking therapy, Close-Up: A Consumer's Guide to Psychotherapists offers some tips on when to seek help and how to start searching for a therapist who shares your perspective and goals.)

CLOSE-UP

A Consumer's Guide to Psychotherapists

Life for everyone is marked by a mix of serenity and stress, blessing and bereavement, good moods and bad. So, when should we seek a mental health professional's help? The American Psychological Association offers these common trouble signals:

- Feelings of hopelessness
- Deep and lasting depression
- Self-destructive behavior, such as alcohol and drug abuse
- Disruptive fears

- Sudden mood shifts
- Thoughts of suicide
- Compulsive rituals, such as hand washing

In looking for a therapist, you may want to have a preliminary consultation with two or three. You can describe your problem and learn each therapist's treatment approach. You can ask questions about the therapist's values, credentials (**TABLE 13.2**), and fees. And, knowing the importance of the emotional bond between therapist and client, you can assess your own feelings about each of them.

TABLE 13.2

THERAPISTS AND THEIR TRAINING

Type	Description
Counselors	Marriage and family counselors specialize in problems arising from family relations. Pastoral counselors provide counseling to countless people. Abuse counselors work with substance abusers and with spouse and child abusers and their victims.
Clinical or psychiatric social workers	A two-year master of social work graduate program plus postgraduate supervision prepares some social workers to offer psychotherapy, mostly to people with everyday personal and family problems. About half have earned the National Association of Social Workers' designation of clinical social worker.
Clinical psychologists	Most are psychologists with a Ph.D. or Psy.D. and expertise in research, assessment, and therapy, supplemented by a supervised internship and, often, post-doctoral training. About half work in agencies and institutions, half in private practice.
Psychiatrists	Psychiatrists are physicians who specialize in the treatment of psychological disorders. Not all psychiatrists have had extensive training in psychotherapy, but as M.D.s they can prescribe medications. Thus, they tend to see those with the most serious problems. Many have their own private practice.

Have students contact your state's licensure board to find out what types of training one must receive in order to practice psychotherapy legally.

- What is the minimum amount of training one must receive in order to gain licensure?

- How many licensed practitioners are in your state? Your area?

- Do people have to pass an exam to get licensed? Which one(s)? Do they get an opportunity to take it again if they fail the first time? How many times can they take it?

- What should potential clients look for to ensure their therapist is state-licensed?

TROUBLESHOOTING

Remind students about the difference between psychologists and psychiatrists:

- Psychologists are trained in Ph.D. programs that emphasize psychological bases for mental illness and provide clinical training. Except in two states and the military, clinical psychologists cannot prescribe medication.

- Psychiatrists are trained in medical schools as doctors first, followed by a residency or fellowship specializing in psychiatry. The emphasis of most psychiatrists is more medical than psychological. All psychiatrists who are properly licensed can prescribe medication.

UNIT 13

::**biomedical therapy** prescribed medications or medical procedures that act directly on the patient's nervous system.

::**psychopharmacology** the study of the effects of drugs on mind and behavior.

::**antipsychotic drugs** drugs used to treat schizophrenia and other forms of severe thought disorder.

::**tardive dyskinesia** involuntary movements of the facial muscles, tongue, and limbs; a possible neurotoxic side effect of long-term use of antipsychotic drugs that target certain dopamine receptors.

TEACHING TIP

Even though *rational-emotive therapy* is not listed as a bold vocabulary word, students need to know about this therapy for the AP Exam. Rational-emotive therapy is quite aggressive in its approach to dealing with cognitive issues. Albert Ellis would often employ a technique called "thought stopping," in which he would yell "STOP" at patients when they expressed a thought that was self-defeating or detrimental.

TEACHING TIP

Before 1972, over 5200 patients were housed at Bryce State Mental Hospital in Alabama, but the facility was only designed to hold around 800. Doors in the older portions of the building, built in 1851, are short on the bottom by about a foot, which allowed caretakers at the hospital to slide food trays under them so that the couple hundred or so patients could scramble for their nourishment. A Supreme Court case, called the Wyatt case, stopped such inhumane practices at the facility. Today, Bryce houses roughly 400 patients in modern buildings. Patients are afforded private and semi-private living quarters and are rarely housed for more than 6 months.

Albert Ellis, who advocated an aggressive *rational-emotive therapy,* and Allen Bergin, co-editor of the *Handbook of Psychotherapy and Behavior Change,* illustrated how sharply therapists can differ, and how those differences can affect their view of a healthy person. Ellis (1980) assumed that "no one and nothing is supreme," that "self-gratification" should be encouraged, and that "unequivocal love, commitment, service, and . . . fidelity to any interpersonal commitment, especially marriage, leads to harmful consequences." Bergin (1980) assumed the opposite—that "because God is supreme, humility and the acceptance of divine authority are virtues," that "self-control and committed love and self-sacrifice are to be encouraged," and that "infidelity to any interpersonal commitment, especially marriage, leads to harmful consequences."

Bergin and Ellis disagreed more radically than most therapists on what values are healthiest. In so doing, however, they agreed on a more general point: Psychotherapists' personal beliefs influence their practice. Because clients tend to adopt their therapists' values (Worthington et al., 1996), some psychologists believe therapists should divulge those values more openly.

BEFORE YOU MOVE ON . . .

> ### ASK YOURSELF
> Without trying to play therapist, how might you use the helping principles discussed in this unit with a friend who is anxious?

> ### TEST YOURSELF 2
> How does the placebo effect bias clients' appraisals of the effectiveness of psychotherapies?

Answers to the Test Yourself questions can be found in Appendix E at the end of the book.

The Biomedical Therapies

PSYCHOTHERAPY IS ONE WAY TO TREAT psychological disorders. The other, often used with serious disorders, is **biomedical therapy**—physically changing the brain's functioning by altering its chemistry with drugs, or affecting its circuitry with electroconvulsive shock, magnetic impulses, or psychosurgery. Psychologists can provide psychological therapies. But with a few exceptions, only psychiatrists (as medical doctors) offer biomedical therapies.

Drug Therapies

11: What are the drug therapies? What criticisms have been leveled against drug therapies?

"The mentally ill were out of the hospital, but in many cases they were simply out on the streets, less agitated but lost, still disabled but now uncared for."
Lewis Thomas, *Late Night Thoughts on Listening to Mahler's Ninth Symphony,* 1983

By far the most widely used biomedical treatments today are the drug therapies. Since the 1950s, discoveries in **psychopharmacology** (the study of drug effects on mind and behavior) have revolutionized the treatment of people with severe disorders, liberating hundreds of thousands from hospital confinement. Thanks to drug therapy—and to efforts to minimize involuntary hospitalization and to support people with community mental health programs—the resident population of U.S. state and county mental hospitals is a small fraction of what it was a half-century ago (**FIGURE 13.5**). For some unable to care for themselves, however, release from hospitals has meant homelessness, not liberation.

Almost any new treatment, including drug therapy, is greeted by an initial wave of enthusiasm as many people apparently improve. But that enthusiasm often diminishes after researchers subtract the rates of (1) normal recovery among untreated

TEACHING TIP

People who weren't mentally ill were routinely committed involuntarily to mental hospitals up until the early 1970s. In many states, family members could commit a relative for any reason. Young women who became pregnant out of wedlock could be committed, as could wives of men who wanted a divorce. People with mild mental retardation and unwed mothers were often placed in the same large, impersonal rooms that violent criminals and those with schizophrenia occupied. If you weren't mentally ill before entering a mental hospital before 1972, you certainly would question your sanity by the time you left.

U.S. state and county mental hospital residents, in thousands

700
600
500
400
300
200
100
0

Introduction of antipsychotic drugs

Rapid decline in the state and county mental hospital population

1900 1910 1920 1930 1940 1950 1960 1970 1980 1990 2000
Year

➤ **FIGURE 13.5**

The emptying of U.S. mental hospitals
After the widespread introduction of antipsychotic drugs, starting in about 1955, the number of residents in state and county mental hospitals declined sharply. But in the rush to deinstitutionalize the mentally ill, many people who were ill-equipped to care for themselves were left homeless on city streets. (Data from the U.S. National Institute of Mental Health and Bureau of the Census, 2004.)

persons and (2) recovery due to the placebo effect, which arises from the positive expectations of patients and mental health workers alike. So, to evaluate the effectiveness of any new drug, researchers give half the patients the drug, and the other half a similar-appearing placebo. Because neither the staff nor the patients know who gets which, this is called a *double-blind procedure*. The good news: In double-blind studies, several types of drugs have proven useful in treating psychological disorders.

Antipsychotic Drugs

The revolution in drug therapy for psychological disorders began with the accidental discovery that certain drugs, used for other medical purposes, calmed patients with *psychoses* (disorders in which hallucinations or delusions indicate some loss of contact with reality). These **antipsychotic drugs,** such as chlorpromazine (sold as Thorazine), dampened responsiveness to irrelevant stimuli. Thus, they provided the most help to patients experiencing positive symptoms of schizophrenia, such as auditory hallucinations and paranoia (Lehman et al., 1998; Lenzenweger et al., 1989).

The molecules of most conventional antipsychotic drugs are similar enough to molecules of the neurotransmitter dopamine to occupy its receptor sites and block its activity. This finding reinforces the idea that an overactive dopamine system contributes to schizophrenia. Antipsychotics are powerful drugs. Some can produce sluggishness, tremors, and twitches similar to those of Parkinson's disease, which is marked by too little dopamine (Kaplan & Saddock, 1989). Long-term use of these medications can also produce **tardive dyskinesia** with involuntary movements of the facial muscles (such as grimacing), tongue, and limbs.

Patients exhibiting the negative symptoms of schizophrenia, such as apathy and withdrawal, often do not respond well to conventional antipsychotic drugs. Newer *atypical antipsychotics,* such as clozapine (marketed since 1989 as Clozaril), target both dopamine and serotonin receptors. This helps alleviate negative symptoms, sometimes enabling "awakenings" in these individuals. Atypical antipsychotics may also help those who have positive symptoms but have not responded to other drugs.

Although not more effective in controlling schizophrenia symptoms, many of the newer antipsychotics have fewer conventional side effects. But they may increase the risk of obesity and diabetes (Lieberman et al., 2005, 2006). One new drug now undergoing testing stimulates receptors for the amino acid called glutamate. An initial trial has raised hopes that it may reduce schizophrenia symptoms with fewer side effects (Berenson, 2007).

"Our psychopharmacologist is a genius."

Drug or placebo effect? For many people, depression lifts while taking an antidepressant drug. But people given a placebo may experience the same effect. Double-blind clinical trials suggest that, especially for those with severe depression, antidepressant drugs do have at least a modest clinical effect.

• **Perhaps you can guess an occasional side effect of L-dopa, a drug that raises dopamine levels for Parkinson's patients: hallucinations.** •

 TROUBLESHOOTING

Distinguish between a drug's main effects and side effects for students:

- Main effects are the effects the drugs are supposed to create in patients. Antianxiety drugs and antidepressant drugs are supposed to create decreased anxiety and depression in patients who take them.

- Side effects are unintended consequences of taking drugs. Patients may experience nausea, headaches, sexual side effects, and exacerbation of other medical conditions if they take certain drugs. Side effects can vary from person to person.

TEACHING TIP

Remind students that a psychosis involves a break with reality. Breaks with reality can include delusions (false beliefs) and hallucinations (false perceptions). Researchers believe that these breaks with reality are the result of biochemical imbalances in the brain, which helps explain why antipsychotic drugs help patients who experience these problems.

 RESEARCH

Have students research the different types of drugs for treatment of psychosis.

- How are Clozaril and Risperdal different from Thorazine?

- Do all these drugs bind exclusively to dopamine receptors? If not, what receptors do they bind to?

- Does insurance offer benefits for long-term use of these drugs? Why or why not?

At this point, you may want to use **Lecture/Discussion Topics:** *SSRI Antidepressants* (p. 25) or *Cosmetic Psychopharmacology* (p. 25) or *A Pill for Stage Fright (Anxiety)* (p. 26) from Bolt's Teacher's Resource Binder.

UNIT 13

INTERCONNECTING

GABA, or gamma-aminobutyric acid, is an amino acid that acts like a neurotransmitter throughout the body. GABA and its alter ego glutamate are more plentiful than any other neurotransmitter in the body. While glutamate is excitatory, GABA is inhibitory, acting on the presynaptic cell to cause it to stop releasing its particular neurotransmitter into the synapse. By boosting GABA, antianxiety drugs stop the overabundance of neurotransmitters that cause tension.

CRITICAL THINKING

In 2002, a reality-TV show followed the late model and actress Anna Nicole Smith as she tried to deal with the daily hassles of life. In one episode, she confessed that her dog had to take Prozac. The cameras showed a dog who seemed highly sedated and "spaced out." This sparked discussion about whether pets should be given medication to control their unruly, odd, or eccentric behavior. Have students discuss whether pets should be treated for psychological disorders:

- Do the drug companies that manufacture these drugs recommend their use with pets? Why or why not?

- What type of credentials does one need to have to be called a "pet psychiatrist"?

- What do veterinary medical associations say about the use of human drugs on animals?

::**antianxiety drugs** drugs used to control anxiety and agitation.

::**antidepressant drugs** drugs used to treat depression; also increasingly prescribed for anxiety. Different types work by altering the availability of various neurotransmitters.

• On U.S. college campuses, the 9 percent of counseling center visitors taking psychiatric medication in 1994 nearly tripled, to 24.5 percent in 2004 (Duenwald, 2004). •

Despite the drawbacks, antipsychotic drugs, combined with life-skills programs and family support, have enabled hundreds of thousands of people with schizophrenia who had been consigned to the back wards of mental hospitals to return to work and to near-normal lives (Leucht et al., 2003).

Antianxiety Drugs

Like alcohol, **antianxiety drugs**, such as Xanax or Ativan, depress central nervous system activity (and so should not be used in combination with alcohol). Antianxiety drugs are often used in combination with psychological therapy. A new antianxiety drug, the antibiotic D-cycloserine, acts upon a receptor that facilitates the extinction of learned fears. Experiments indicate that the drug enhances the benefits of exposure therapy and helps relieve the symptoms of PTSD and obsessive-compulsive disorder (Davis, 2005; Kushner et al., 2007).

A criticism sometimes made of the behavior therapies—that they reduce symptoms without resolving underlying problems—is also made of antianxiety drugs. Unlike the behavior therapies, however, these substances may be used as an ongoing treatment. "Popping a Xanax" at the first sign of tension can produce psychological dependence; the immediate relief reinforces a person's tendency to take drugs when anxious. Antianxiety drugs can also cause physiological dependence. After heavy use, people who stop taking them may experience increased anxiety, insomnia, and other withdrawal symptoms.

Over the dozen years at the end of the twentieth century, the rate of outpatient treatment for anxiety disorders nearly doubled. The proportion of psychiatric patients receiving medication during that time increased from 52 to 70 percent (Olfson et al., 2004). And the new standard drug treatment for anxiety disorders? Antidepressants.

Antidepressant Drugs

The **antidepressants** were named for their ability to lift people up from a state of depression, and this was their main use until recently. The label is a bit of a misnomer now that these drugs are increasingly being used to successfully treat anxiety disorders such as obsessive-compulsive disorder. They work by increasing the availability of norepinephrine or serotonin, neurotransmitters that elevate arousal and mood and appear scarce during depression. Fluoxetine, which tens of millions of users worldwide have known as Prozac, partially blocks the reabsorption and removal of serotonin from synapses (FIGURE 13.6). Because they slow the synaptic vacuuming up of serotonin, Prozac and its cousins Zoloft and Paxil are called *selective-serotonin-reuptake-inhibitors (SSRIs)*. Other antidepressants work by blocking the reabsorption or breakdown of both norepinephrine and serotonin. Though effective, these dual-action drugs have more potential side effects, such as dry mouth, weight gain, hypertension, or dizzy spells (Anderson, 2000; Mulrow, 1999). Administering them by means of a patch, bypassing the intestines and liver, helps reduce such side effects (Bodkin & Amsterdam, 2002).

After the introduction of SSRI drugs, the percentage of patients receiving medication for depression jumped dramatically, from 70 percent in 1987, the year before SSRIs were introduced, to 89 percent in 2001 (Olfson et al., 2003; Stafford et al., 2001). In the United States, 11 percent of women and 5 percent of men take antidepressants (Barber, 2008).

Be advised: Patients with depression who begin taking antidepressants do not wake up the next day singing "It's a beautiful day!" Although the drugs begin to influence neurotransmission within hours, their full psychological effect often requires four weeks (and may involve a side effect of diminished sexual desire). One possible reason for the delay is that increased serotonin promotes *neurogenesis*—the

INTERCONNECTING

Link discussion of the relief of tension to negative reinforcement (Unit 6). Reinforcement is designed to encourage a behavior by either giving a reward or taking away something unpleasant. Negative reinforcement does the latter, taking away something that the person wants to avoid. In cases of anxiety, people are going to be more likely to take their drugs to relieve feelings of anxiety and tension because the drugs do take those feelings away. While this is effective in the short term, the strong power of negative reinforcement may encourage people to take drugs any time they feel anxious—even in situations they could handle without using drugs.

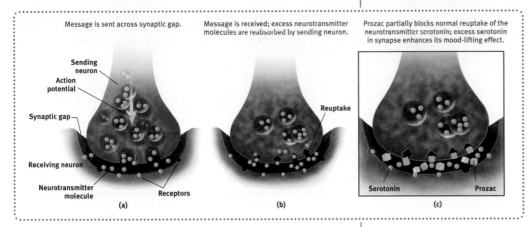

Message is sent across synaptic gap.

Message is received; excess neurotransmitter molecules are reabsorbed by sending neuron.

Prozac partially blocks normal reuptake of the neurotransmitter serotonin; excess serotonin in synapse enhances its mood-lifting effect.

(a)   (b)   (c)

➤ **FIGURE 13.6**
Biology of antidepressants Shown here is the action of Prozac, which partially blocks the reuptake of serotonin.

birth of new brain cells, perhaps reversing stress-induced loss of neurons (Becker & Wojtowicz, 2007; Jacobs, 2004).

Antidepressant drugs are not the only way to give the body a lift. Aerobic exercise, which helps calm people who feel anxious and energize those who feel depressed, does about as much good for some people with mild to moderate depression, and has additional positive side effects (more on this topic later in this unit). Cognitive therapy, by helping people reverse their habitual negative thinking style, can boost the drug-aided relief from depression and reduce the post-treatment risk of relapse (Hollon et al., 2002; Keller et al., 2000; Vittengl et al., 2007). Better yet, some studies suggest, is to attack depression from both above and below (Goldapple et al., 2004; TADS, 2004). Use antidepressant drugs (which work, bottom-up, on the emotion-forming limbic system) in conjunction with cognitive-behavioral therapy (which works, top-down, starting with changed frontal lobe activity).

Researchers generally agree that people with depression often improve after a month on antidepressants. But after allowing for natural recovery (the return to normal called *spontaneous recovery*) and the placebo effect, how big is the drug effect? Not big, report Irving Kirsch and his colleagues (1998, 2002). Their analyses of double-blind clinical trials indicate that placebos accounted for about 75 percent of the active drug's effect. In a follow-up review that included unpublished clinical trials, the antidepressant drug effect was again modest (Kirsch et al., 2008). The placebo effect was less for those with severe depression, which made the added benefit of the drug somewhat greater for them. "Given these results, there seems little reason to prescribe antidepressant medication to any but the most severely depressed patients, unless alternative treatments have failed," Kirsch concluded (BBC, 2008). For about 1 in 4 people who do not respond to a particular antidepressant, switching to another does bring relief (Rush et al., 2006). Scientists dream of a not-too-far-off day when patients may be screened for genetic variations that will indicate drugs to use or avoid.

Although the effects of drug therapy are less exciting than many TV ads suggest, they also are less frightening than other stories have warned. Some people taking Prozac, for example, have committed suicide, but their numbers seem fewer than we would expect from the millions of depressed people now taking that medication. Moreover, a large British study revealed that the ups and downs of adolescent SSRI

"If this doesn't help you don't worry, it's a placebo."

"No twisted thought without a twisted molecule."
Attributed to psychologist Ralph Gerard

 TEACHING TIP

Depression is a cyclic disorder, so many patients suffer relapses, which longer drug therapy may prevent. A February 2003 study published in the medical journal *The Lancet* shows that long-term use of antidepressants reduces the number of relapses patients experience. Researchers in England, along with other researchers in Britain, Japan, and the United States reviewed data from 33 trials involving over 4000 depressed patients. In these trials, patients had finished the standard course of treatment (four to six months) and were offered an opportunity to continue treatment. One group of patients received a placebo while the other group took antidepressants.

 TEACHING TIP

Remind students that even biomedical therapies need to be subjected to randomized controlled clinical trials. The effectiveness of medical therapies is just as important to understand as the effectiveness of psychological therapies.

 RESEARCH

Have students research the different drugs mentioned above:

- What type of receptors do drugs like Valium, Librium, and Xanax bind with?
- What are the side effects of taking these drugs?
- Are they addicting? If so, how are patients monitored to prevent addiction?

- How are selective serotonin reuptake inhibitors (SSRIs) different from monamine oxidase inhibitors (MAOIs)? (*MAOIs are older types of drugs that are more dangerous when taken in overdose than SSRIs*)
- What type of side effects do SSRIs have?
- How effective are these different types of drugs?

TEACHING TIP

Insulin coma therapy was common in the early part of the 20th century. John Forbes Nash, the Nobel-prize-winning economist whose story was told in the Academy Award™-winning motion picture *A Beautiful Mind*, endured this therapy as a treatment for his paranoid schizophrenia. This type of therapy was shown to be highly effective—over 70 percent of patients showed improvements of psychotic symptoms—but the therapy was difficult to control and not long lasting. Other famous people subjected to insulin coma therapy were the first Secretary of Defense James Forrestal (who eventually committed suicide) and Zelda Fitzgerald, wife of the author F. Scott Fitzgerald.

> "Lithium prevents my seductive but disastrous highs, diminishes my depressions, clears out the wool and webbing from my disordered thinking, slows me down, gentles me out, keeps me from ruining my career and relationships, keeps me out of a hospital, alive, and makes psychotherapy possible."
>
> Kay Redfield Jamison, *An Unquiet Mind*, 1995

"First of all I think you should know that last quarter's sales figures are interfering with my mood-stabilizing drugs."

▼
ECT proponent In her book, *Shock: The Healing Power of Electroconvulsive Therapy* (2006), Kitty Dukakis writes, "I used to . . . be unable to shake the dread even when I was feeling good, because I knew the bad feelings would return. ECT has wiped away that foreboding. It has given me a sense of control, of hope."

prescriptions over time were unrelated to the adolescent suicide rate (Wheeler et al., 2008). Prozac users who commit suicide are like cell-phone users who get brain cancer. Given the millions of people taking Prozac and using cell phones, alarming anecdotes tell us nothing.

The question critical thinkers want answered is this: Do these groups suffer an elevated *rate* of suicide and brain cancer? The answer in each case appears to be *no* (Grunebaum et al., 2004; Paulos, 1995; Tollefson et al., 1993, 1994). Some researchers have speculated that the start of drug therapy may give formerly inert people enough energy to act on their depression, which could make for a temporary heightened suicide risk. But three recent studies of between 70,000 and 439,000 patients concur that, in the long run, patients attempt fewer suicides if treated with antidepressants (Gibbons et al., 2007; Simon & Savarino, 2007; Sønergård et al., 2006).

Mood-Stabilizing Medications

In addition to antipsychotic, antianxiety, and antidepressant drugs, psychiatrists have *mood-stabilizing drugs* in their arsenal. The simple salt *lithium* can be an effective mood stabilizer for those suffering the emotional highs and lows of bipolar disorder. Australian physician John Cade discovered this in the 1940s when he administered lithium to a patient with severe mania. Although Cade's reasoning was misguided—he thought lithium had calmed excitable guinea pigs when actually it had made them sick—his patient became perfectly well in less than a week (Snyder, 1986). After suffering mood swings for years, about 7 in 10 people with bipolar disorder benefit from a long-term daily dose of this cheap salt (Solomon et al., 1995). Their risk of suicide is but one-sixth that of bipolar patients not taking lithium (Tondo et al., 1997). Although we do not fully understand why, lithium works. And so does Depakote, a drug originally used to treat epilepsy and more recently found effective in the control of manic episodes associated with bipolar disorder.

Brain Stimulation

12: How effective is electroconvulsive therapy, and what other brain-stimulation options may offer relief from severe depression?

Electroconvulsive Therapy

A more controversial brain manipulation occurs through shock treatment, or **electroconvulsive therapy (ECT).** When ECT was first introduced in 1938, the wide-awake patient was strapped to a table and jolted with roughly 100 volts of electricity to the brain, producing racking convulsions and brief unconsciousness. ECT therefore gained a barbaric image, one that lingers. Today, however, the patient receives a general anesthetic and a muscle relaxant (to prevent injury from convulsions) before a psychiatrist delivers 30 to 60 seconds of electrical current to the patient's brain (**FIGURE 13.7**). Within 30 minutes, the patient awakens and remembers nothing of the treatment or of the preceding hours. After three such sessions each week for two to four weeks, 80

CRITICAL THINKING

Have students divide into groups to discuss how they would feel about using any of the therapies discussed in this unit to treat a mental illness in themselves or a loved one.

- Would you consider antianxiety, antidepressant, or antipsychotic drugs as a treatment for a mental illness? Why or why not?

- Would you encourage a loved one to receive ECT to treat depression? Why or why not?

- What advice would you give a loved one if they were faced with these treatment options?

> **FIGURE 13.7**
Electroconvulsive therapy Although controversial, ECT is often an effective treatment for depression that does not respond to drug therapy.

percent or more of people receiving ECT improve markedly, showing some memory loss for the treatment period but no discernible brain damage. Study after study confirms that ECT is an effective treatment for severe depression in patients who have not responded to drug therapy (Pagnin et al., 2004; UK ECT Review Group, 2003). A leading medical journal concluded that "the results of ECT in treating severe depression are among the most positive treatment effects in all of medicine" (Glass, 2001).

How does ECT alleviate severe depression? After more than 50 years, no one knows for sure. One recipient likened ECT to the smallpox vaccine, which was saving lives before we knew how it worked. It's also like restarting your computer, which solves many a problem even if you don't know why. Perhaps the shock-induced seizures calm neural centers where overactivity produces depression. ECT, like antidepressant drugs and exercise, also appears to boost the production of new brain cells (Bolwig & Madsen, 2007).

ECT reduces suicidal thoughts and is credited with saving many from suicide (Kellner et al., 2005). It is now administered with briefer pulses, sometimes only to the brain's right side and with less memory disruption (HMHL, 2007). Yet no matter how impressive the results, the idea of electrically shocking people into convulsions still strikes many as barbaric, especially given our ignorance about why ECT works. Moreover, about 4 in 10 ECT-treated patients relapse into depression within six months (Kellner et al., 2006). Nevertheless, in the minds of many psychiatrists and patients, ECT is a lesser evil than severe depression's misery, anguish, and risk of suicide. As research psychologist Norman Endler (1982) reported after ECT alleviated his deep depression, "A miracle had happened in two weeks."

• The medical use of electricity is an ancient practice. Physicians treated the Roman Emperor Claudius (10 B.C.E–54 C.E.) for headaches by pressing electric eels to his temples. •

::**electroconvulsive therapy (ECT)**
a biomedical therapy for severely depressed patients in which a brief electric current is sent through the brain of an anesthetized patient.

The aim of ECT is to produce a seizure in the brain, similar to that which occurs spontaneously in some types of epilepsy. In fact, research suggests that without a seizure, ECT is ineffective. A small electric current passes through two electrodes placed on the patient's head. Only a portion of this current reaches the brain because most of it is deflected by the skull. Since muscle relaxants may interfere with breathing, an anesthesiologist administers oxygen. The muscle relaxants often block all outward signs of a seizure, and so the patient's brain waves must be monitored. The entire procedure takes about five minutes, and complications are rare.

TROUBLESHOOTING

ECT has gotten a bad rap in such movies as *One Flew Over the Cuckoo's Nest*, a film from the late 1970s starring a young Jack Nicholson and Louise Fletcher (both of whom won Oscars for their portrayals). In that movie, Nicholson's character is subjected to ECT as a way to control him rather than treat him. Today, ECT is only used for patients whose depression is so deep they do not respond positively to other treatments. The electrical stimulation seems to jump start neural communication, leading to improved mood.

RESEARCH

Since patients sleep through electroconvulsive therapy, it should come as no surprise that in one study 82 percent rated ECT as equally or no less upsetting than going to the dentist. Have students explore how ECT has changed over the years to become an effective, humane treatment for major depression:

• What techniques were used in the past to administer ECT?

• What procedures are used today that make the treatment less unpleasant?

TEACHING TIP

It may seem to students that rTMS may be one of those "debunked" therapies mentioned earlier in the text. Little research shows that magnets improve health in other areas. However, rTMS seems to work similarly to ECT, stimulating electrical activity in the brain. Since all neural communication is electrical, it should be logical that forces that affect electrical currents, like magnets, should work on the brain.

Alternative Neurostimulation Therapies

Some patients with chronic depression have found relief through a chest implant that intermittently stimulates the vagus nerve, which sends signals to the brain's mood-related limbic system (Fitzgerald & Daskalakis, 2008; George & Belmaker, 2007; Marangell et al., 2007). Two other techniques—magnetic stimulation and deep-brain stimulation—are also raising hopes for gentler alternatives that jump-start neural circuits in the depressed brain.

Magnetic Stimulation Depressed moods seem to improve when repeated pulses surge through a magnetic coil held close to a person's skull (FIGURE 13.8). Unlike deep-brain stimulation, the magnetic energy penetrates only to the brain's surface (though tests are under way with a higher energy field that penetrates more deeply). The painless procedure—called **repetitive transcranial magnetic stimulation (rTMS)**—is performed on wide-awake patients over several weeks. Unlike ECT, the rTMS procedure produces no seizures, memory loss, or other side effects.

In one double-blind experiment, 67 Israelis with major depression were randomly assigned to two groups (Klein et al., 1999). One group received rTMS daily for two weeks, while the other received sham treatments (without magnetic stimulation). At the end of the two weeks, half the stimulated patients showed at least a 50 percent improvement in their scores on a depression scale, as did only a quarter of the placebo group. One possible explanation is that the stimulation energizes depressed patients' relatively inactive left frontal lobe (Helmuth, 2001). When repeatedly stimulated, nerve cells can form functioning circuits through long-term potentiation (LTP), a process described in Unit 7A.

Other clinical experiments have had mixed results. Some have found little effects from rTMS treatment. However, several recent studies using the latest techniques

➤ **FIGURE 13.8**
Magnets for the mind Repetitive transcranial magnetic stimulation (rTMS) sends a painless magnetic field through the skull to the surface of the cortex. Pulses can be used to stimulate or dampen activity in various cortical areas. (From George, 2003.)

TEACHING TIP

At this point, you may want to use **Lecture/Discussion Topic:** *Electroconvulsive Therapy* (p. 27) from Bolt's Teacher's Resource Binder.

A depression switch?
By comparing the brains of patients with and without depression, researcher Helen Mayberg identified a brain area that appears active in people who are depressed or sad, and whose activity may be calmed by deep-brain stimulation.

have produced significant relief from depression, as compared with sham treatments (George & Belmaker, 2007; Gross et al., 2007; O'Reardon et al., 2007).

Deep-Brain Stimulation Other patients whose depression has resisted both drugs that flood the body and ECT that jolts at least half the brain have benefited from an experimental treatment pinpointed at a brain depression center. Neuroscientist Helen Mayberg and her colleagues (2005, 2006, 2007; Dobbs, 2006) have been focusing on a cortex area that bridges the thinking frontal lobes to the limbic system. They have discovered that this area, which is overactive in the brain of a depressed or temporarily sad person, becomes calm when treated by ECT or antidepressants. To experimentally excite neurons that inhibit this negative emotion-feeding activity, Mayberg drew upon the deep-brain stimulation technology sometimes used to treat Parkinson's tremors. Among an initial 12 patients receiving implanted electrodes and a pacemaker stimulator, 8 experienced relief. Some felt suddenly more aware and became more talkative and engaged; others improved only slightly if at all. Future research will explore whether Mayberg has discovered a switch that can lift depression. Other researchers are following up on reports that deep-brain stimulation can offer relief to people with obsessive-compulsive disorder.

Psychosurgery

13: What is psychosurgery?

Because its effects are irreversible, **psychosurgery**—surgery that removes or destroys brain tissue—is the most drastic and the least-used biomedical intervention for changing behavior. In the 1930s, Portuguese physician Egas Moniz developed what became the best-known psychosurgical operation: the **lobotomy.** Moniz found that cutting the nerves connecting the frontal lobes with the emotion-controlling centers of the inner brain calmed uncontrollably emotional and violent patients. In a crude but easy and inexpensive procedure that took only about 10 minutes, a neurosurgeon would shock the patient into a coma, hammer an icepicklike instrument through each eye socket into the brain, and then wiggle it to sever connections running up to the frontal lobes. Tens of thousands of severely disturbed people—including President John F. Kennedy's sister, Rosemary—were "lobotomized" between 1936 and 1954, and Moniz was honored with a Nobel Prize (Valenstein, 1986).

Although the intention was simply to disconnect emotion from thought, a lobotomy's effect was often more drastic: It usually decreased the person's misery or tension, but also produced a permanently lethargic, immature, uncreative person.

::**repetitive transcranial magnetic stimulation (rTMS)** the application of repeated pulses of magnetic energy to the brain; used to stimulate or suppress brain activity.

::**psychosurgery** surgery that removes or destroys brain tissue in an effort to change behavior.

::**lobotomy** a now-rare psychosurgical procedure once used to calm uncontrollably emotional or violent patients. The procedure cut the nerves connecting the frontal lobes to the emotion-controlling centers of the inner brain.

TEACHING TIP

At this point, you may want to use **Lecture/Discussion Topic: *Cingulotomy*** (p. 27) from Bolt's Teacher's Resource Binder.

TEACHING TIP

Lobotomies would have died out much more quickly as a therapeutic treatment had it not been for Walter Freeman, an American physician. Freeman and James Watts developed the "Freeman-Watts Standard Procedure," which set guidelines for the surgery. Freeman grew weary of the length and messiness of the Moniz-style operation, so he developed the "ice pick lobotomy." In this gruesome procedure, Freeman would insert a traditional ice pick into the eye sockets of anesthetized patients and, with a small mallet, tap the pick through the bone into the prefrontal cortex. He would then swipe the pick back and forth to sever the connections to the prefrontal cortex. Freeman would have his interns time him as he performed operations. Other neurosurgeons watching the procedure would faint at the sight. Even James Watts broke his ties with Freeman.

TEACHING TIP

Today, psychosurgery is much more precise and targeted than the lobotomies of old. Our greater understanding of brain anatomy and function allows surgeons to pinpoint areas of trouble rather than taking out or damaging whole sections of the brain. Patients are typically awake during brain surgery so doctors can stimulate the areas in and around the trouble site to determine what needs to be fixed and what needs to be left alone.

UNIT 13

INTERCONNECTING

Remind students about how the life-style changes suggested here are discussed in other units:

- Aerobic exercise is discussed as producing health benefits in Unit 8B.

- Adequate sleep is mentioned several times as important to good health, cognition, and behavior, but it is discussed in detail in Unit 5.

- Light exposure is discussed earlier in this unit.

- Social connection is discussed extensively in Unit 8A (need to belong) and Unit 14.

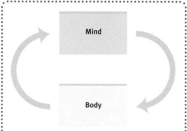

> **FIGURE 13.9**

Mind-body interaction The biomedical therapies assume that mind and body are a unit: Affect one and you will affect the other.

During the 1950s, after some 35,000 people had been lobotomized in the United States alone, calming drugs became available and psychosurgery was largely abandoned. Today, lobotomies are history, and other psychosurgery is used only in extreme cases. For example, if a patient suffers uncontrollable seizures, surgeons can deactivate the specific nerve clusters that cause or transmit the convulsions. MRI-guided precision surgery is also occasionally done to cut the circuits involved in severe obsessive-compulsive disorder (Sachdev & Sachdev, 1997). Because these procedures are irreversible, however, neurosurgeons perform them only as a last resort.

Therapeutic Life-Style Change

14: How, by caring for their bodies with a healthy life-style, might people find some relief from depression?

The effectiveness of the biomedical therapies reminds us of a fundamental lesson: We find it convenient to talk of separate psychological and biological influences, but everything psychological is also biological (**FIGURE 13.9**). Every thought and feeling depends on the functioning brain. Every creative idea, every moment of joy or anger, every period of depression emerges from the electrochemical activity of the living brain. The influence is two-way: When psychotherapy relieves obsessive-compulsive behavior, PET scans reveal a calmer brain (Schwartz et al., 1996).

Anxiety disorders, major depression, bipolar disorder, and schizophrenia are all biological events. As we have seen over and again, *a human being is an integrated biopsychosocial system.* For years, we have trusted our bodies to physicians and our minds to psychiatrists and psychologists. That neat separation no longer seems valid. Stress affects body chemistry and health. And chemical imbalances, whatever their cause, can produce schizophrenia and depression.

That lesson is being applied by Stephen Ilardi and his colleagues (2008) in their training seminars promoting *therapeutic life-style change.* Human brains and bodies were designed for physical activity and social engagement, they note. Our ancestors hunted, gathered, and built in groups, with little evidence of disabling depression. Indeed, those whose way of life entails strenuous physical activity, strong community ties, sunlight exposure, and plenty of sleep (think of foraging bands in Papua New Guinea, or Amish farming communities in North America) rarely experience depression. "Simply put: Humans were never designed for the sedentary, disengaged, socially isolated, poorly nourished, sleep-deprived pace of twenty-first-century American life."

The Ilardi team was impressed by this research showing that regular aerobic exercise and a complete night's sleep boost mood and energy. So they invited small groups of people with depression to undergo a 12-week training program with the following goals:

- *Aerobic exercise,* 30 minutes a day, at least 3 times weekly (increases fitness and vitality, stimulates endorphins)
- *Adequate sleep,* with a goal of 7 to 8 hours a night (increases energy and alertness, boosts immunity)
- *Light exposure,* at least 30 minutes each morning with a light box (amplifies arousal, influences hormones)
- *Social connection,* with less alone time and at least two meaningful social engagements weekly (satisfying the human need to belong)

 TEACHING TIP

At this point, you may want to use **Lecture/Discussion Topic: *Therapeutic Life-Style Change*** (p. 28) from Bolt's Teacher's Resource Binder.

Healthier life-styles Researchers suggest that *therapeutic life-style change* can be an effective antidote for people with depression. The changes include managing sleep time, spending more time outdoors (or with a light box), getting more exercise, and developing more social connections.

INTERCONNECTING

A focus on mental health rather than mental illness is a hallmark of positive psychology, a movement to study optimal functioning and bring a balanced perspective to psychology.

- *Anti-rumination*, by identifying and redirecting negative thoughts (enhancing positive thinking)
- *Nutritional supplements*, including a daily fish oil supplement with omega-3 fatty acids (for healthy brain functioning)

In one study of 74 people, 77 percent of those who completed the program experienced relief from depressive symptoms, compared with a 19 percent rate in those assigned to a treatment-as-usual control condition. Future research will seek to replicate this striking result of life-style change, and also to identify which of the treatment components (additively or in some combination) produce the therapeutic effect. But there seems little reason to doubt the truth of the Latin adage, *Mens sana in corpore sano:* "A healthy mind in a healthy body."

BEFORE YOU MOVE ON . . .

➤ **ASK YOURSELF**

If a troubled friend asked, how would you summarize the available biomedical therapies?

➤ **TEST YOURSELF 3**

How do researchers evaluate the effectiveness of particular drug therapies?

Answers to the Test Yourself questions can be found in Appendix E at the end of the book.

Preventing Psychological Disorders

15: What is the rationale for preventive mental health programs?

IF LIFE-STYLE CHANGE CAN HELP *reverse* some of the symptoms of psychological disorders, might such change also *prevent* some disorders by building individuals' **resilience**—an ability to cope with stress and recover from adversity?

resilience the personal strength that helps most people cope with stress and recover from adversity and even trauma.

Faced with unforeseen trauma, most adults exhibit resilience. This was true of New Yorkers in the aftermath of 9/11, especially those who enjoyed supportive close relationships and who had not recently experienced other stressful events (Bonanno et al., 2007).

Many psychological disorders are understandable responses to a disturbing and stressful society. We have seen that psychotherapies and biomedical therapies tend to locate the cause of psychological disorders within the person with the disorder. These therapies try to treat people by giving them insight into their problems, by changing their thinking, or by helping them gain control with drugs. Yet according to the preventive view, it is not just the person who needs treatment, but also the person's social context. Better to prevent a problem by reforming a sick situation and by developing people's coping competencies than to wait for a problem to arise and then treat it.

A story about the rescue of a drowning person from a rushing river illustrates this viewpoint: Having successfully administered first aid to the first victim, the rescuer spots another struggling person and pulls her out, too. After a half-dozen repetitions, the rescuer suddenly turns and starts running away while the river sweeps yet another floundering person into view. "Aren't you going to rescue that fellow?" asks a bystander. "Heck no," the rescuer replies. "I'm going upstream to find out what's pushing all these people in."

> "It is better to prevent than to cure."
> Peruvian folk wisdom

Preventive mental health is upstream work. It seeks to prevent psychological casualties by identifying and alleviating the conditions that cause them. As George Albee (1986) pointed out, there is abundant evidence that poverty, meaningless work, constant criticism, unemployment, racism, and sexism undermine people's sense of competence, personal control, and self-esteem. Such stresses increase their risk of depression, alcohol dependency, and suicide.

We who care about preventing psychological casualties should, Albee contended, support programs that alleviate these demoralizing situations. We eliminated smallpox not by treating the afflicted but by inoculating the unafflicted. We conquered yellow fever in many parts of the world by controlling mosquitoes. Preventing psychological problems means empowering those who have learned an attitude of helplessness, changing environments that breed loneliness, renewing the disintegrating family, and bolstering parents' and teachers' skills at nurturing children's achievements and resulting self-esteem. Indeed, "Everything aimed at improving the human condition, at making life more fulfilling and meaningful, may be considered part of primary prevention of mental or emotional disturbance" (Kessler & Albee, 1975, p. 557). That includes the cognitive training that promotes positive thinking in children at risk for depression (Gillham et al., 2006).

> "Mental disorders arise from physical ones, and likewise physical disorders arise from mental ones."
> *The Mahabharata,* c. 200 C.E.

BEFORE YOU MOVE ON . . .

➤ ASK YOURSELF

Can you think of a specific way that improving the environment in your own community might prevent some psychological disorders among its residents?

➤ TEST YOURSELF 4

What is the difference between preventive mental health and psychological or biomedical therapy?

Answers to the Test Yourself questions can be found in Appendix E at the end of the book.

UNIT REVIEW: Treatment of Psychological Disorders

The Psychological Therapies

Psychotherapy consists of interactions between a trained therapist and someone seeking to overcome psychological difficulties or achieve personal growth. The major psychotherapies derive from the psychoanalytic, humanistic, behavioral, and cognitive perspectives on psychology. Today, many therapists combine aspects of these perspectives in an *eclectic approach* or psychotherapy integration, sometimes in a group setting.

1: What are the aims and methods of psychoanalysis, and how have they been adapted in psychodynamic therapy?

Through *psychoanalysis*, Sigmund Freud and his students aimed to help people gain insight into the unconscious origins of their disorders, to work through the accompanying feelings, and to take responsibility for their own growth. Techniques included free association, dream analysis, and *interpretation* of *resistances* and *transference* to the therapist of long-repressed feelings. Contemporary *psychodynamic therapy* has been influenced by traditional psychoanalysis but is briefer and less expensive. It focuses on a patient's current conflicts and defenses by searching for themes common to many past and present important relationships. Interpersonal therapy (a brief 12- to 16-session form of psychodynamic therapy) deals primarily with current symptoms (such as depression) rather than the origins of unconscious conflicts.

2: What are the basic themes of humanistic therapy, such as Rogers' client-centered approach?

Humanistic therapists have focused on clients' current conscious feelings and on their taking responsibility for their own growth. Carl Rogers' *client-centered therapy* proposed that therapists' most important contributions are to function as a psychological mirror through *active listening* and to provide a growth-fostering environment of *unconditional positive regard,* characterized by genuineness, acceptance, and empathy. The humanistic and psychoanalytic therapies are known as *insight therapies.*

3: What are the assumptions and techniques of the behavior therapies?

Behavior therapists do not attempt to explain the origin of problems or to promote self-awareness. Instead, they attempt to modify the problem behaviors. Thus, they may *countercondition* behaviors through *exposure therapies*, such as *systematic desensitization, virtual reality exposure therapy*, or *aversive conditioning*. Or they may apply operant conditioning principles with behavior modification techniques, such as in *token economies*.

4: What are the goals and techniques of the cognitive therapies?

The *cognitive therapies*, such as Aaron Beck's cognitive therapy for depression, aim to change self-defeating thinking by training people to look at themselves in new, more positive ways. The widely researched and practiced *cognitive-behavioral therapy* also helps clients to regularly practice new ways of thinking and talking.

5: What are the aims and benefits of group and family therapy?

Group therapy sessions can help more people and cost less per person than individual therapy would. Clients may benefit from knowing others have similar problems and from getting feedback and reassurance. *Family therapy* views a family as an interactive system and attempts to help members discover the roles they play and to learn to communicate more openly and directly.

Evaluating Psychotherapies

6: Does psychotherapy work? Who decides?

Because the positive testimonials of clients and therapists cannot prove that therapy is actually effective, psychologists have conducted hundreds of outcome studies of psychotherapy using *meta-analyses*. Studies of randomized clinical trials indicate that people who remain untreated often improve, but those who receive psychotherapy are more likely to improve, regardless of the kind or duration of therapy. Placebo treatments or the sympathy and friendly counsel of paraprofessionals also tend to produce more improvement than no treatment at all.

7: Are some therapies more effective than others?

No one type of psychotherapy is generally superior to all others. Therapy is most effective for those with clear-cut, specific problems. Some therapies are more effective for specific disorders, such as behavioral conditioning for treating phobias and compulsions. *Evidence-based practice* integrates the best available research with clinicians' expertise and patients' characteristics and preferences.

8: How do alternative therapies fare under scientific scrutiny?

Controlled research has not supported the claims of eye movement and desensitization (EMDR) therapy. Light exposure therapy does seem to relieve the symptoms of seasonal affective disorder (SAD).

9: What three elements are shared by all forms of psychotherapy?

All psychotherapies offer new hope for demoralized people; a fresh perspective; and (if the therapist is effective) an empathic, trusting, and caring relationship.

10: How do culture and values influence the therapist-client relationship?

Therapists differ in the values that influence their aims. These differences may create problems when therapists work with clients with different cultural or religious perspectives. A person

---

TECHNOLOGY RESOURCES

These resources will be helpful for teaching the concepts in this portion of the unit:

- *Videos: Psychology: The Human Experience, Module 40: Problems in Living; Module 41: Empirically Validated Therapies*

- *Videos: Digital Media Archive: Psychology, 2nd ed., Video Clip 35: Treatment of Drug Addiction; Video Clip 36: Early Treatment of Mental Disorders; Video Clip 34: Schizophrenia; Video Clip 37: Electroconvulsive Therapy*

- *Psychology Video Tool Kit: Early Treatment of Mental Disorders; Outpatient Commitment: Forcing Persons into Mental Health Treatment; Treating OCD: Exposure and Response Prevention; City of Gheel: Community Mental Health at Its Best; Dealing With Panic; Mentally Ill Chemical Abusers: A Community Problem; When Treatment Leads to Execution: Mental Health and the Law*

- *PsychSim 5: Computer Therapist; Mystery Therapist*

Technology Resources continued

UNIT 13

ANSWERS to Multiple-Choice Questions

1. **b.** behavior
2. **e.** Both approaches are generally considered insight therapies.
3. **a.** Eclectic
4. **d.** deep-brain stimulation.
5. **a.** Antidepressant
6. **c.** ECT
7. **a.** active listening.
8. **c.** transference.
9. **b.** Psychodynamic
10. **e.** Cognitive-behavioral
11. **c.** Group
12. **c.** Cognitive therapy
13. **d.** dopamine
14. **a.** Sleeping fewer than 7 hours per night
15. **d.** Cognitive

seeking therapy may want to ask about the therapist's treatment approach, values, credentials, and fees.

The Biomedical Therapies

The *biomedical therapies* treat psychological disorders with medications or medical procedures that act directly on a patient's nervous system.

11: What are the drug therapies? What criticisms have been leveled against drug therapies?

Drug therapy is the most widely used biomedical therapy. The *antipsychotic drugs*, used in treating schizophrenia, block dopamine activity. Some can have serious side effects, including *tardive dyskinesia* (with involuntary movements of facial muscles, tongue, and limbs) or increased risk of obesity and diabetes. *Antianxiety drugs*, which depress central nervous system activity, are used to treat anxiety disorders. These drugs can be physically and psychologically addictive. *Antidepressant drugs*, which increase the availability of serotonin and norepinephrine, are used for depression, with modest effectiveness beyond that of placebo drugs. Lithium and Depakote are mood stabilizers prescribed for those with bipolar disorder.

12: How effective is electroconvulsive therapy, and what other brain-stimulation options may offer relief from severe depression?

Electroconvulsive therapy (ECT), in which a brief electric current is sent through the brain of an anesthetized patient, is an effective, last-resort treatment for severely depressed people who have not responded to other therapy. Newer alternative treatments for depression include *repetitive transcranial magnetic stimulation (rTMS)* and, in preliminary clinical experiments, deep-brain stimulation that calms an overactive brain region linked with negative emotions.

13: What is psychosurgery?

Psychosurgery removes or destroys brain tissue in hopes of modifying behavior. Radical psychosurgical procedures such as *lobotomy* were once popular, but neurosurgeons now rarely perform brain surgery to change behavior or moods. Brain surgery is a treatment of last resort because its effects are irreversible.

14: How, by caring for their bodies with a healthy lifestyle, might people find some relief from depression?

A healthy mind usually lives in a healthy body. Depressed people who undergo a program of aerobic exercise, adequate sleep, light exposure, social engagement, negative-thought reduction, and better nutrition often gain some relief.

Preventing Psychological Disorders

15: What is the rationale for preventive mental health programs?

Faced with stress or trauma, people generally exhibit *resilience*, which helps them cope successfully. Preventive mental health programs are based on the idea that many psychological disorders could be prevented by changing oppressive, esteem-destroying environments into more benevolent, nurturing environments that foster individual growth and self-confidence and build resilience.

Terms and Concepts to Remember

eclectic approach, p. 606
psychotherapy, p. 606
psychoanalysis, p. 606
resistance, p. 607
interpretation, p. 607
transference, p. 607
psychodynamic therapy, p. 608
insight therapies, p. 609
client-centered therapy, p. 609
active listening, p. 609
unconditional positive regard, p. 610
behavior therapy, p. 611

counterconditioning, p. 611
exposure therapies, p. 611
systematic desensitization, p. 611
virtual reality exposure therapy, p. 612
aversive conditioning, p. 613
token economy, p. 614
cognitive therapy, p. 614
cognitive-behavioral therapy, p. 616
family therapy, p. 617
regression toward the mean, p. 621
meta-analysis, p. 621
evidence-based practice, p. 623

biomedical therapy, p. 628
psychopharmacology, p. 628
antipsychotic drugs, p. 629
tardive dyskinesia, p. 629
antianxiety drugs, p. 630
antidepressant drugs, p. 630
electroconvulsive therapy (ECT), p. 632
repetitive transcranial magnetic stimulation (rTMS), p. 634
psychosurgery, p. 635
lobotomy, p. 635
resilience, p. 637

TECHNOLOGY RESOURCES

>> Technology Resources continued from p. 639

- *ActivePsych: Digital Media Archive*, 2nd ed.: *Therapy in the Real World: The Use of Real-Life Exposure to Treat Phobias; The Therapeutic Effect of Antipsychotic Drugs; Schizophrenia: New Definitions, New Therapies; Undesired Effects of Conventional Antipsychotic Drugs*

- *Videos: The Mind*, 2nd ed., *Module 30: Treating Drug Addiction: A Behavioral Approach; Module 3: The Placebo Effect: Mind-Body Relationship; Module 33: Mood Disorders:* *Medication and Talk Therapy; Module 34: Treating Depression: Electroconvulsive Therapy (ECT)*

- *Video: Scientific American Frontiers*, 2nd ed., *Segment 31: Virtual Fear*

- *Video: The Brain*, 2nd ed., *Module 28: Schizophrenia: Pharmacological Treatment*

AP* Practice Test Questions

Multiple-Choice Questions

1. In an effort to help a child overcome a fear of dogs, a _____ therapist might pair a trigger stimulus (something associated with dogs) with a new stimulus that causes a response that is incompatible with fear (for example, an appealing snack or toy).
   a. psychodynamic
   b. behavior
   c. biomedical
   d. client-centered
   e. humanistic

2. Which of the following is a similarity between humanistic and psychoanalytic therapies?
   a. Both approaches focus on the present more than the past.
   b. Both approaches are more concerned with conscious than unconscious feelings.
   c. Both approaches focus on taking immediate responsibility for one's feelings.
   d. Both approaches focus on growth instead of curing illness.
   e. Both approaches are generally considered insight therapies.

3. A psychotherapist professing to use a blend of therapies is practicing what kind of approach?
   a. Eclectic
   b. Psychodynamic
   c. Cognitive
   d. Cognitive-behavioral
   e. Humanistic

4. Some patients whose depression has resisted drugs have benefited from an experimental treatment called
   a. transference.
   b. meta-analysis.
   c. antipsychotic drugs.
   d. deep-brain stimulation.
   e. resistance.

5. Which kind of drug is most closely associated with increasing the availability of norepinephrine or serotonin?
   a. Antidepressant
   b. Antipsychotic
   c. Antianxiety
   d. Mood-stabilizing
   e. Muscle relaxant

6. Which of the following is seen as an effective treatment for severe depression?
   a. Lobotomy
   b. Token economy
   c. ECT
   d. Crisis debriefing
   e. EMDR therapy

7. Echoing, restating, and seeking clarification of what a person expresses (verbally or nonverbally) in a therapy session is called
   a. active listening.
   b. virtual reality exposure therapy.
   c. systematic desensitization.
   d. family therapy.
   e. classical conditioning.

8. Most psychodynamic therapists would contend that experiencing strong positive or negative feelings for your analyst is a sign of
   a. counterconditioning.
   b. meta-analysis.
   c. transference.
   d. tardive dyskinesia.
   e. aversive conditioning.

9. Which kind of therapist would be most likely to note the following during a session: "Blocks in the flow of free associations indicate resistance"?
   a. Cognitive
   b. Psychodynamic
   c. Rogerian
   d. Behavioral
   e. Client-centered

10. Which kind of therapy is most closely associated with the goal of altering actions and thoughts?
    a. Rational-emotive
    b. Psychodynamic
    c. Client-centered
    d. Family
    e. Cognitive-behavioral

11. Allowing people to discover, in a social context, that others have problems similar to their own is a unique benefit of what kind of therapy?
    a. Psychodynamic
    b. Psychopharmacological
    c. Group
    d. Cognitive
    e. Humanistic

12. Which of the following therapeutic approaches is scientifically supported?
    a. Recovered-memory therapies
    b. Rebirthing therapies
    c. Cognitive therapy
    d. Energy therapies
    e. Crisis debriefing

13. Most conventional antipsychotic drugs are similar enough to molecules of the neurotransmitter _____ to occupy its receptor sites and block its activity.
    a. adrenaline
    b. epinephrine
    c. serotonin
    d. dopamine
    e. acetylcholine

14. Which of the following is *not* recommended by therapists as a way to help prevent or get over depression?
    a. Sleeping fewer than 7 hours per night
    b. Aerobic exercise
    c. Light exposure
    d. Social connecting
    e. Anti-rumination strategies

15. A psychotherapist states, "Getting people to change what they say to themselves is an effective way to change their thinking." This statement best exemplifies which kind of therapeutic approach?
    a. Behavioral
    b. Psychodynamic
    c. Biomedical
    d. Cognitive
    e. Active listening

Free-Response Question

Describe and discuss two advantages for each of the following psychotherapies.
- Psychodynamic
- Client-centered
- Counterconditioning
- Cognitive-behavioral

Do not use an advantage more than once.

*AP is a trademark registered and/or owned by the College Board, which was not involved in the production of, and does not endorse, this product.

 WEB

Multiple-choice self-tests and more may be found at www.worthpublishers.com/myers

Rubric for Grading the Free-Response Question

This is an 8-point question. Allow one point for an adequate discussion or description of a psychotherapy's advantage (maximum 2 points per psychotherapy). Modify the rubric by adding or subtracting terms depending on what was emphasized in class.

Note: All psychotherapies share the following advantages.
1. new hope for demoralized people
2. a fresh perspective
3. an empathic, trusting, and caring relationship

Psychodynamic Advantages

- Provides insight into unconscious origins.
- Works through the feelings associated with unconscious origins.
- Patients learn to take responsibility for their own growth.
- Reduces the inner conflicts impeding growth by providing new insights.

 Rubric continued

Client-Centered Advantages

- Utilizes active listening to provide a growth-fostering environment.
- Utilizes unconditional positive regard to provide a growth-fostering environment.
- Boosts self-fulfillment by helping people grow in self-awareness and self-acceptance.
- Reduces the inner conflicts impeding growth by providing new insights.

Counterconditioning Advantages

- Pairs the trigger stimulus with a new response that is incompatible with the problematic behavior.
- Repeated exposure decreases problematic responses to the target stimuli.
- Systematic desensitization is a type of counterconditioning that eliminates anxiety through repeated association of a relaxed state with increasingly anxiety-provoking stimuli.

Cognitive-Behavioral Advantages

- Seeks to make people aware of their irrational negative thinking, to replace it with new ways of thinking, and to practice the more rational approach in everyday settings.
- Trains people in emotional regulation—replacing catastrophizing thinking with more realistic appraisals.
- Trains people to practice behaviors that are incompatible with a problem.

Pacing Guide

Use the following guide to determine how many instructional days to devote to this unit depending on the type of course you teach:

Year-long course: 8–10 days
Block schedule/Semester-long course: 5–7 days

This unit encompasses 8–10 percent of the AP Exam. Spending an appropriate amount of time on this unit will help students do well on the AP Exam.

 TEACHING TIP

Students often underestimate the influence of others on their behavior. As teens search for their own individual identity, they may deny that peer pressure, conformity, and obedience dictate many of their choices and behaviors. Have students ponder the following questions:

- Why do you obey some rules and disobey others at your school?

- Have you ever been convinced by friends to do something you knew was wrong? To do something you knew was right?

- Do you consider yourself a conformist? Nonconformist? Why?

At this time, you may want to use **Introductory Exercise: Fact or Falsehood?** (p. 3) or **Lecture/Discussion Topic: Social Psychology's Most Important Lessons** (p. 3) from Bolt's Teacher's Resource Binder, which accompanies this text.

642

Suggested Readings

Aronson, E. (2008). *The social animal* (10th ed.). New York: Worth Publishers.

Cialdini, R. B. (1998). *Influence: The psychology of persuasion.* New York: William Morrow.

Janis, I. L. (1982). *Groupthink.* Boston, MA: Houghton Mifflin.

Lerner, M. (1980). *The belief in a just world.* New York: Plenum.

Marsh, P. (Ed.). (1988). *Eye to eye: How people interact.* Topsfield, MA: Salem House Publishers.

Milgram, S. (1974). *Obedience to authority.* New York: HarperCollins.

Social Psychology

Although still young, this twenty-first century has dramatically reminded us that we are social animals whose lives and cultures revolve around how we think about, influence, and relate to one another.

On September 11, 2001, nineteen men with box cutters achieved an act of catastrophic violence that triggered fright, outrage, and a lust for revenge. But it also triggered an outpouring of compassion and care, including gifts of more money, food, clothing, and teddy bears than New Yorkers could possibly use. What drives people to feel such hatred that they would destroy thousands of innocent lives? And what motivates the heroic altruism of those who died trying to save others and of the many more who reached out to those coping with loss?

Echoes of these questions resurfaced after genocide plagued the Darfur region of Sudan beginning in 2003, and during the war in Iraq, where survey-based estimates of deaths ranged from 151,000 to more than 1 million from 2002 through 2006 (Iraq Family Study, 2008; ORB, 2008). What factors affect the decision making of our world leaders? And how can we transform the closed fists of international conflict into the open arms of peace and cooperation?

This century has also challenged Americans' preconceived notions about race, gender, and age. The unprecedented 2008 U.S. presidential contest involved a 60-year-old White woman (Hillary Clinton), a 46-year-old African-American man (Barack Obama), and a 71-year-old White man (John McCain). Knowing that a difference of but a few votes could change the course of history, donors contributed hundreds of millions of dollars in the hope of influencing people's opinions. How do we form our attitudes, and how do those attitudes affect our actions?

As each day's news has brought updates on acts of hate or heroism, defeats or victories, many of us have lived out our own experiences with love and loss. Why are we attracted to some people but not others, and what spurs friendship and romance?

Human connections are powerful and can be perilous. Yet "we cannot live for ourselves alone," remarked the novelist Herman Melville. "Our lives are connected by a thousand invisible threads." **Social psychologists** explore these connections by scientifically studying how we *think about, influence,* and *relate to* one another.

Social Thinking

OUR SOCIAL BEHAVIOR arises from our social cognition. Especially when the unexpected occurs, we analyze why people act as they do. Does her warmth reflect romantic interest, or is that how she relates to everyone? Does his absenteeism signify illness? Laziness? A stressful work atmosphere?

SOCIAL THINKING
Attributing Behavior to Persons or to Situations
Attitudes and Actions
Close-Up: Abu Ghraib Prison—An "Atrocity-Producing Situation"?
SOCIAL INFLUENCE
Conformity and Obedience
Group Influence
Cultural Influence
The Power of Individuals
SOCIAL RELATIONS
Prejudice
Close-Up: Automatic Prejudice
Aggression
Close-Up: Parallels Between Smoking Effects and Media Violence Effects
Attraction
Close-Up: Online Matchmaking and Speed Dating
Altruism
Conflict and Peacemaking

• Recall from Unit 10 that personality psychologists study the enduring, inner determinants of behavior that help to explain why *different people* act differently in a given situation. Social psychologists study the social influences that help explain why the *same person* will act differently in *different situations.* •

::social psychology the scientific study of how we think about, influence, and relate to one another.

643

Key Terms

social psychology

Social Thinking

attribution theory
fundamental attribution error
attitude
central route persuasion
peripheral route persuasion
foot-in-the-door phenomenon
role
cognitive dissonance theory

Social Influence

conformity
normative social influence
informational social influence
social facilitation
social loafing
deindividuation
group polarization
groupthink
culture
norm
personal space

Social Relations

prejudice
stereotype
discrimination
ingroup
outgroup
ingroup bias
scapegoat theory
other-race effect
just-world phenomenon
aggression
frustration-aggression principle
mere-exposure effect
passionate love
companionate love
equity
self-disclosure
altruism
bystander effect
social exchange theory
reciprocity norm
social-responsibility norm

Oliner, S., & Oliner, P. (1988). *The altruistic personality: Rescuers of Jews in Nazi Europe.* New York: Macmillan.

Patterson, J., & Kim, P. (1991). *The day America told the truth.* New York: Prentice Hall.

Key People

Solomon Asch
Robert Cialdini
John Darley
Leon Festinger
Irving Janis
Bibb Latané
Stanley Milgram
Muzafer Sherif
Philip Zimbardo

Key Terms continued

UNIT 14

INTERCONNECTING

Link discussion of attribution to explanatory style in positive psychology (Unit 12). We make certain attributions (or explanations) about our own behavior that are either situational or dispositional.

- Optimists are more likely to attribute good events to dispositions and bad events to situations.

- Pessimists, who are more likely to suffer depression, will make dispositional attributions for bad events and situational attributions for good events.

CRITICAL THINKING

Have students consider the following questions to get them thinking about situational versus dispositional attribution:

- If a very good friend gets angry with you, how would you explain his or her behavior? If that same friend does something nice for you, how would you explain the behavior?

- If someone you have recently gotten to know walks by you in the hall but doesn't say hello (even as you try to say hello to them), what would you think about them? Why?

- Are your thoughts about your good friend's behavior different than your thoughts about someone you're only acquainted with? Why or why not?

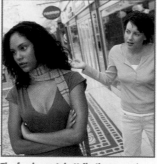

The fundamental attribution error If our new friend acts grouchy, we may decide she's a grouchy person. She may be more likely to explain her behavior as a result of losing sleep over a family worry, missing the bus to school, or having a fight with her boyfriend.

Actor and observer perspectives make for differing attributions During their contentious U.S. presidential primaries in 2008, Barack Obama was criticized for seeming—in this camera perspective that faces him—to turn a cold shoulder to his opponent, Hillary Clinton. Obama later explained that he had greeted her earlier, and here was turning to speak to (as a picture shot from behind him might have shown) the unseen person to his left. In laboratory experiments, when a camera shows the actor's perspective, observers better appreciate the situation's influence.

Was the horror of 9/11 the work of crazed people, or of ordinary people corrupted by life events?

Attributing Behavior to Persons or to Situations

1: How do we tend to explain others' behavior and our own?

After studying how people explain others' behavior, Fritz Heider (1958) proposed an **attribution theory.** Heider noted that people usually attribute others' behavior either to their internal dispositions or to their external situations. A teacher, for example, may wonder whether a student's hostility reflects an aggressive personality (a *dispositional attribution*) or a reaction to stress or abuse (a *situational attribution*).

In class, we notice that Juliette seldom talks; over coffee, Jack talks nonstop. Attributing their behaviors to their personal dispositions, we decide Juliette is shy and Jack is outgoing. Because people do have enduring personality traits, such attributions are sometimes valid. However, we often fall prey to the **fundamental attribution error,** by overestimating the influence of personality and underestimating the influence of situations. In class, Jack may be as quiet as Juliette. Catch Juliette as the lead in the high school musical and you may hardly recognize your quiet classmate.

An experiment by David Napolitan and George Goethals (1979) illustrated the phenomenon. They had Williams College students talk, one at a time, with a young woman who acted either aloof and critical or warm and friendly. Beforehand, they told half the students that the woman's behavior would be spontaneous. They told the other half the truth—that she had been instructed to *act* friendly (or unfriendly). What do you suppose was the effect of being told the truth?

There was no effect. The students disregarded the information. If the woman acted friendly, they inferred she really was a warm person. If she acted unfriendly, they inferred she really was a cold person. In other words, they attributed her behavior to her personal disposition *even when told that her behavior was situational*—that she was merely acting that way for the purposes of the experiment. Although the fundamental attribution error occurs in all cultures studied, this tendency to attribute behavior to people's dispositions runs especially strong in individualistic Western countries. In East Asian cultures, for example, people are more sensitive to the power of the situation (Masuda & Kitayama, 2004).

You have surely committed the fundamental attribution error. In judging whether your AP psychology teacher is shy or outgoing, you have perhaps by now inferred that he or she has an outgoing personality. But you know your teacher only from the classroom, a situation that demands outgoing behavior. Catch the teacher in a different situation and you might be surprised. Outside their assigned roles, teachers seem less teacherly, presidents less presidential, servants less servile.

Your teacher, on the other hand, observes his or her own behavior in many different situations—in the classroom, in meetings, at home—and so might say, "Me, outgoing? It all depends on the situation. In class or with good friends, yes, I'm outgoing. But at professional meetings I'm really rather shy." When explaining the behavior of those we know well and see in varied situations, we are sensitive to how behavior changes with the situation

TROUBLESHOOTING

Social psychology is different from sociology. Social psychology considers how *individuals* interact with each other and society at large. Sociologists explore the behavior of *groups and cultures* as they interact internally and externally.

At this time, you may want to use **Lecture/Discussion Topic:** *Attribution and Models of Helping* (p. 6) or **Classroom Exercises:** *The Fundamental Attribution Error* (p. 4) or *Students' Perceptions of You* (p. 5) from Bolt's Teacher's Resource Binder.

(Idson & Mischel, 2001). After behaving badly, we also recognize how the situation affected our own behavior (recall the *self-serving bias* discussed in Unit 10). What about our own intentional and admirable actions? Those we more often attribute to our own good reasons than to situational causes (Malle, 2006; Malle et al., 2007).

When explaining *others'* behavior, particularly the behavior of strangers we have observed in only one type of situation, we often commit the fundamental attribution error: We disregard the situation and leap to unwarranted conclusions about their personality traits. Many people initially assumed the 9/11 terrorists were obviously crazy, when actually they went unnoticed in their neighborhoods, health clubs, and favorite restaurants.

Researchers who have reversed the perspectives of actor and observer—by having each view a replay of the situation filmed from the other's perspective—have also reversed the attributions (Lassiter & Irvine, 1986; Storms, 1973). Seeing the world from the actor's perspective, the observers better appreciate the situation. (As you act, your eyes look outward; you see others' faces, not your own.) Taking the observer's point of view, the actors better appreciate their own personal style. Reflecting on our past selves of 5 or 10 years ago also switches our perspective. We now adopt an observer's perspective and attribute our behavior mostly to our traits (Pronin & Ross, 2006). Likewise, in another 5 or 10 years, our today's self may seem like another person.

The Effects of Attribution

In everyday life we often struggle to explain others' actions. A jury must decide whether a shooting was malicious or in self-defense. An interviewer must judge whether the applicant's geniality is genuine. A person must decide whether to interpret another's friendliness as genuine, or motivated by self-interest (she just needs a ride). When we make such judgments, our attributions—either to the person or to the situation—have important consequences (Fincham & Bradbury, 1993; Fletcher et al., 1990). Happily married couples attribute a spouse's tart-tongued remark to a temporary situation ("She must have had a bad day at work"). Unhappily married couples attribute the same remark to a mean disposition ("Why did I marry such a hostile person?").

Or consider the political effects of attribution. How do you explain poverty or unemployment? Researchers in Britain, India, Australia, and the United States (Furnham, 1982; Pandey et al., 1982; Wagstaff, 1982; Zucker & Weiner, 1993) report that political conservatives tend to attribute such social problems to the personal dispositions of the poor and unemployed themselves: "People generally get what they deserve. Those who don't work are often freeloaders. Anybody who takes the initiative can still get ahead." "Society is not to blame for crime, criminals are," said one conservative U.S. presidential candidate (Dole, 1996). Political liberals (and social scientists) are more likely to blame past and present situations: "If you or I had to live with the same poor education, lack of opportunity, and discrimination, would we be any better off?" To understand and prevent terrorism, they say, consider the situations that breed terrorists. Better to drain the swamps than swat the mosquitoes.

Managers' attributions also have effects. In evaluating employees, they are likely to attribute poor performance to personal factors, such as low ability or lack of motivation. But remember the actor's viewpoint: Workers doing poorly on a job recognize situational influences, such as inadequate supplies, poor working conditions, difficult co-workers, or impossible demands (Rice, 1985).

The point to remember: Our attributions—to individuals' dispositions or to their situations—should be made carefully. They have real consequences.

"Otis, shout at that man to pull himself together."

• Some 7 in 10 college women report having experienced a man misattributing her friendliness as a sexual come-on (Jacques-Tiura et al., 2007). •

An attribution question Some people blamed the New Orleans residents for not evacuating before the predicted 2005 Hurricane Katrina. Others attributed their inaction to the situation—to their not having cars or not being offered bus transportation.

 Key Terms continued from p. 643

conflict
social trap
mirror-image perceptions
self-fulfilling prophecy
superordinate goals
GRIT

TEACHING TIP

People will make attributions depending on their level of involvement in a situation. Have students determine what types of attributions the actors and observers made in the following situation:

In 1979, rock fans were waiting to get into a concert by The Who. When the Coliseum doors were opened, several fans were trampled to death. *Time* magazine later received a letter from an outside observer and one from an actor participant. How do their attributions differ?

• The observer:

"The violently destructive message that The Who and other rock groups deliver leaves me little surprised that they attract a mob that will trample human beings to death to gain better seats. Of greater concern is a respected news magazine's adulation of this sick phenomenon."

• The actor:

"While standing in the crowd at Riverfront Coliseum, I distinctly remember feeling that I was being punished for being a rock fan. My sister and I joked about this, unaware of the horror happening around us. Later, those jokes came back to us grimly as we watched the news. How many lives will be lost before the punitive and inhuman policy of festival seating at rock concerts is outlawed?"

 INTERCONNECTING

Link the discussion of attributions to stereotypes and prejudice. If people hold strong stereotypes or prejudices toward a particular group of people, they are likely to make a dispositional attribution for their behaviors. These people would explain similar behavior by people in their own groups using situational attributions instead.

TEACHING TIP

When we are aware of our attitudes, they are more likely to guide our actions. Researchers have made participants more aware by installing mirrors in the laboratory. This is called the "looking glass effect."

- Edward Diener and Mark Wallbom noted that nearly all college students say that cheating is morally wrong. They had students work on an anagram-solving task that was presumably an IQ test. They told them to stop when a bell sounded. Left alone, 71 percent cheated by working past the bell. For students working in front of a mirror, only 7 percent cheated.

- Brad Bushman found that people who can see their reflections eat less unhealthy food than those who can't see themselves. Bushman and his colleagues asked college students to try full-fat, low-fat, and fat-free cream cheese. Participants in a room with a mirror ate less of the full-fat spread than did those with no mirror.

Diener, E., & Wallbom, M. (1976). Effects of self-awareness on antinormative behavior. *Journal of Research in Personality, 10*, 107–111.

Haugen, P. (1999, May/June). The looking glass effect. *Psychology Today,* p. 24.

::**attitude** feelings, often influenced by our beliefs, that predispose us to respond in a particular way to objects, people, and events.

::**central route persuasion** attitude change path in which interested people focus on the arguments and respond with favorable thoughts.

::**peripheral route persuasion** attitude change path in which people are influenced by incidental cues, such as a speaker's attractiveness.

::**foot-in-the-door phenomenon** the tendency for people who have first agreed to a small request to comply later with a larger request.

::**role** a set of expectations (norms) about a social position, defining how those in the position ought to behave.

➤ **FIGURE 14.1**
Attitudes follow behavior Cooperative actions, such as those performed by people on sports teams, feed mutual liking. Such attitudes, in turn, promote positive behavior.

Attitudes and Actions

2: Does what we think affect what we do, or does what we do affect what we think?

Attitudes are feelings, often influenced by our beliefs, that predispose our reactions to objects, people, and events. If we *believe* someone is mean, we may *feel* dislike for the person and *act* unfriendly.

Attitudes Affect Actions

Our attitudes often predict our behavior. Al Gore's movie *An Inconvenient Truth* and the Alliance for Climate Protection it has spawned have a simple premise: Public opinion about the reality and dangers of global climate change can change, with effects on both personal behaviors and public policies. Indeed, by the end of 2007, an analysis of international opinion surveys by WorldPublicOpinion.org showed "widespread and growing concern about climate change. Large majorities believe that human activity causes climate change and favor policies designed to reduce emissions." Thanks to the mass persuasion campaign, many corporations, as well as campuses, are now going green.

This tidal wave of change has occurred as people have engaged scientific evidence and arguments and responded with favorable thoughts. Such **central route persuasion** occurs mostly when people are naturally analytical or involved in the issue. When issues don't engage systematic thinking, persuasion may occur through a faster **peripheral route,** as people respond to incidental cues, such as endorsements by respected people, and make snap judgments. Because central route persuasion is more thoughtful and less superficial, it is more durable and more likely to influence behavior.

Other factors, including the external situation, also influence behavior. Strong social pressures can weaken the attitude-behavior connection (Wallace et al., 2005). For example, the American public's overwhelming support for former President George W. Bush's preparation to attack Iraq motivated Democratic leaders to vote to support Bush's war plan, despite their private reservations (Nagourney, 2002). Nevertheless, attitudes do affect behavior when external influences are minimal, especially when the attitude is stable, specific to the behavior, and easily recalled (Glasman & Albarracín, 2006). One experiment used vivid, easily recalled information to persuade people that sustained tanning put them at risk for future skin cancer. One month later, 72 percent of the participants, and only 16 percent of those in a waiting list control group, had lighter skin (McClendon & Prentice-Dunn, 2001).

Actions Affect Attitudes

Now consider a more surprising principle: Not only will people sometimes stand up for what they believe, they will also come to believe in the idea they have supported. Many streams of evidence confirm that *attitudes follow behavior* (**FIGURE 14.1**).

The Foot-in-the-Door Phenomenon Inducing people to act against their beliefs can affect their attitude. During the Korean war, many captured U.S. soldiers were imprisoned in war camps run by Chinese communists. Without using brutality, the captors secured the prisoners' collaboration in various activities. Some merely ran errands or accepted favors. Others made radio appeals and false confessions. Still others informed on fellow prisoners and divulged military information. When the war ended, 21 prisoners chose to stay with the communists. More returned home "brainwashed"—convinced that communism was a good thing for Asia.

TROUBLESHOOTING

Help students remember the different routes to persuasion:

- Central route is more direct, focusing on the heart of the issue being discussed. The issues are the heart (or center) of the matter.

- Peripheral route is more indirect, focusing on things that really may not have any direct connection to the issue at hand. Students can remember what peripheral vision is from Unit 4—our vision of things on the outer edge of the visual field. Celebrity endorsements, a peripheral route to persuasion, are not central to supporting an issue.

A key ingredient of the Chinese "thought-control" program was its effective use of the **foot-in-the-door phenomenon**—a tendency for people who agree to a small action to comply later with a larger one. The Chinese began with harmless requests but gradually escalated their demands (Schein, 1956). Having "trained" the prisoners to speak or write trivial statements, the communists then asked them to copy or create something more important—noting, perhaps, the flaws of capitalism. Then, perhaps to gain privileges, the prisoners participated in group discussions, wrote self-criticisms, or uttered public confessions. After doing so, they often adjusted their beliefs toward consistency with their public acts.

The point is simple: To get people to agree to something big, "start small and build," said Robert Cialdini (1993). Knowing this, you can be wary of those who would exploit you with the tactic. This chicken-and-egg spiral, of actions-feeding-attitudes-feeding-actions, enables behavior to escalate. A trivial act makes the next act easier. Succumb to a temptation and you will find the next temptation harder to resist.

Dozens of experiments have simulated part of the war prisoners' experience by coaxing people into acting against their attitudes or violating their moral standards. The nearly inevitable result: Doing becomes believing. When people are induced to harm an innocent victim—by making nasty comments or delivering electric shocks—they then begin to disparage their victim. If induced to speak or write on behalf of a position they have qualms about, they begin to believe their own words.

Fortunately, the attitudes-follow-behavior principle works as well for good deeds as for bad. The foot-in-the-door tactic has helped boost charitable contributions, blood donations, and product sales. In one experiment, researchers posing as safe-driving volunteers asked Californians to permit the installation of a large, poorly lettered "Drive Carefully" sign in their front yards. Only 17 percent consented. They approached other home owners with a small request first: Would they display a 3-inch-high "Be a Safe Driver" sign? Nearly all readily agreed. When reapproached two weeks later to allow the large, ugly sign in their front yards, 76 percent consented (Freedman & Fraser, 1966). To secure a big commitment, it often pays to put your foot in the door: Start small and build.

Racial attitudes likewise follow behavior. In the years immediately following the introduction of school desegregation in the United States and the passage of the Civil Rights Act of 1964, White Americans expressed diminishing racial prejudice. And as Americans in different regions came to act more alike—thanks to more uniform national standards against discrimination—they began to think more alike. Experiments confirm the observation: Moral action strengthens moral convictions.

Role-Playing Affects Attitudes When you adopt a new **role**—when you leave middle school and start high school, become a college student, or begin a new job—you strive to follow the social prescriptions. At first, your behaviors may feel phony, because you are *acting* a role. The first weeks in the military feel artificial—as if one is pretending to be a soldier. The first weeks of a marriage may feel like "playing house." Before long, however, what began as play-acting in the theater of life becomes *you*.

Researchers have confirmed this effect by assessing people's attitudes before and after they adopt a new role, sometimes in laboratory situations, sometimes in everyday situations, such as before and after taking a job. In one famous laboratory study, male college students volunteered to spend time in a simulated prison devised by Stanford psychologist Philip Zimbardo (1972). Some he randomly designated as guards; he gave them uniforms, billy clubs, and whistles and instructed them to enforce certain rules. The remainder became prisoners; they were locked in barren cells and forced to wear humiliating outfits. After a day or two in which the volunteers self-consciously "played"

"If the King destroys a man, that's proof to the King it must have been a bad man."

Thomas Cromwell, in Robert Bolt's *A Man for All Seasons*, 1960

"Fake it until you make it."

Alcoholics Anonymous saying

UNIT 14

The power of the situation In Philip Zimbardo's Stanford prison simulation, a toxic situation triggered degrading behaviors among those assigned to the guard role. ▲

TEACHING TIP

Other techniques influence actions and attitudes:

- Low-ball technique. Students were asked to participate in a laboratory experiment at 7:00 A.M. Only 24 percent came. When students agreed to participate without knowing the time and then were told the early time, 53 percent showed up!

- Brainwashing. Used on American POWs during the Korean War, the captors had the prisoners write a series of essays, each representing a more serious attack on the U.S. government. Slowly each writer's attitude tended to change to become consistent with his words.

- Write-it-down technique. Once a customer fills out a sales agreement, they commit to the purchase.

- "Fifty-words-or-less" testimonials. Why are manufacturers of toothpaste, breakfast cereal, and chewing gum so eager to get people to compose a short personal statement that begins, "Why I like. . ."? To get as many people as possible to go on record as favoring the product. Saying is believing!

TEACHING TIP

At this time, you may want to use **Lecture/Discussion Topics:** *The Looking Glass Effect* (p. 6) or *The Theory of Reasoned Action* (p. 7) or *Actions Influence Attitudes* (p. 7) or *The Justification of Effort* (p. 8) or *Revisiting the Stanford Prison Experiment* (p. 9) or *Abu Ghraib Prison and Social Psychology* (p. 10) from Bolt's Teacher's Resource Binder.

their roles, the simulation became real—too real. Most of the guards developed disparaging attitudes, and some devised cruel and degrading routines. One by one, the prisoners broke down, rebelled, or became passively resigned, causing Zimbardo to call off the study after only six days. More recently, similar situations have played themselves out in the real world—as in Iraq at the Abu Ghraib prison (see Close-Up: Abu Ghraib Prison—An "Atrocity-Producing Situation"?).

Greece's military junta during the early 1970s took advantage of the effects of role-playing to train men to become torturers (Staub, 1989). The men's indoctrination into their roles occurred in small steps. First, the trainee stood guard outside the interrogation cells—the "foot in the door." Next, he stood guard inside. Only then was he ready to become actively involved in the questioning and torture. As the nineteenth-century writer Nathaniel Hawthorne noted, "No man, for any considerable period, can wear one face to himself and another to the multitude without finally getting bewildered as to which may be true." What we do, we gradually become.

Psychologists add a cautionary note: In Zimbardo's prison simulation, at Abu Ghraib prison, and in other atrocity-producing situations, some people succumb to the situation and others do not (Carnahan & McFarland, 2007; Haslam & Reicher, 2007; Mastroianni & Reed, 2006; Zimbardo, 2007). Person and situation interact. Water has the power to dissolve some substances, notes John Johnson (2007), but not all. In a watery situation, salt dissolves, sand does not. So also, when put in with rotten apples, some people, but not others, become bad apples.

Cognitive Dissonance: Relief From Tension So far we have seen that actions can affect attitudes, sometimes turning prisoners into collaborators, doubters into believers, mere acquaintances into friends, and compliant guards into abusers. But why? One explanation is that when we become aware that our attitudes and actions don't coincide, we experience tension, or *cognitive dissonance*. To relieve this tension, according to the **cognitive dissonance theory** proposed by Leon Festinger, we often bring our attitudes into line with our actions. It is as if we rationalize, "If I chose to do it (or say it), I must believe in it." The less coerced and more responsible we feel for a troubling act, the more dissonance we feel. The more dissonance we feel, the more motivated we are to find consistency, such as changing our attitudes to help justify the act.

The U.S. invasion of Iraq was mainly premised on the presumed threat of Saddam Hussein's weapons of mass destruction (WMD). As the war began, only 38 percent of Americans surveyed said the war was justified even if Iraq did not have WMD (Gallup, 2003). Nearly 80 percent believed such weapons would be found (Duffy, 2003; Newport et al., 2003). When no WMD were found, many Americans felt dissonance, which was heightened by their awareness of the war's financial and human costs, by scenes of chaos in Iraq, and by inflamed anti-American and pro-terrorist sentiments in some parts of the world.

To reduce dissonance, some people revised their memories of the main rationale for going to war, which then became liberating an oppressed people and promoting democracy in the Middle East. Before long, the once-minority opinion became the majority view: 58 percent of Americans said they supported the war even if there were no WMD (Gallup, 2003). "Whether or not they find weapons of mass destruction doesn't matter," explained Republican pollster Frank Luntz (2003), "because the rationale for the war changed." It was not until late 2004, when hopes for a flourishing peace waned, that Americans' support for the war dropped below 50 percent.

> Regarding President Lyndon Johnson's commitment to the Vietnam war: "A president who justifies his actions only to the public might be induced to change them. A president who has justified his actions to himself, believing that he has *the truth*, becomes impervious to self-correction."
>
> Carol Tavris and Elliot Aronson, *Mistakes Were Made (But Not by Me)*, 2007

"Look, I have my misgivings, too, but what choice do we have except stay the course?"

MANKOFF

WEB CONNECT

Philip Zimbardo created a simulated prison and randomly assigned college students to play either the role of guard or prisoner. A Web-based slide show at www.prisonexp.org provides a detailed account of this fascinating study that demonstrates how role playing can powerfully shape attitudes and even self-identity. Narrated slides show how the guards developed degrading routines and, in only six days, the prisoners broke down, rebelled, or became passively resigned. Students can provide an oral or written report on their visit to this Web site. Helpful discussion questions accompany the slide program and can be printed for classroom use.

TEACHING TIP

CLOSE-UP

Abu Ghraib Prison—An "Atrocity-Producing Situation"?

Bad apples or bad barrels? Like the Stanford Prison Experiment in 1971, the real-life Abu Ghraib prison fiasco in 2004 was a powerfully toxic situation, contends social psychologist Philip Zimbardo.

Originally published in the New Yorker

As the first photos emerged in 2004 from Iraq's Abu Ghraib prison, the civilized world was shocked. The photos showed U.S. military guards stripping prisoners naked, placing hoods on them, stacking them in piles, prodding them with electricity, taunting them with attack dogs, and subjecting them to sleep deprivation, humiliation, and extreme stress. Was the problem, as so many people initially supposed, a few bad apples—a few irresponsible or sadistic guards? That was the U.S. Army's seeming verdict when it court-martialed and imprisoned some of the guards, and then cleared four of the five top commanding officers responsible for Abu Ghraib's policies and operations. The lower-level military guards were "sick bastards," explained the defense attorney for one of the commanding officers (Tarbert, 2004).

Many social psychologists, however, reminded us that a toxic situation can make even good apples go bad (Fiske et al., 2004). "When ordinary people are put in a novel, evil place, such as most prisons, Situations Win, People Lose," offered Philip Zimbardo (2004), adding, "That is true for the majority of people in all the relevant social psychological research done over the past 40 years."

Consider the situation, explained Zimbardo. The guards, some of them model soldier-reservists with no prior criminal or sadistic history, were exhausted from working 12-hour shifts, seven days a week. They were dealing with an enemy, and their prejudices were heightened by fears of lethal attacks and by the violent deaths of many fellow soldiers. They were put in an understaffed guard role, with minimal training and supervision. They were then encouraged to "soften up" for interrogation detainees who had been denied access to the Red Cross. "When you put that set of horrendous work conditions and external factors together, it creates an evil barrel. You could put virtually anybody in it and you're going to get this kind of evil behavior" (Zimbardo, 2005). Atrocious behaviors often emerge in atrocious situations.

Dozens of experiments have explored cognitive dissonance by making people feel responsible for behavior that is inconsistent with their attitudes and that has foreseeable consequences. As a participant in one of these experiments, you might agree for a measly $2 to help a researcher by writing an essay that supports something you don't believe in (perhaps a tuition increase). Feeling responsible for the statements (which are not consistent with your attitudes), you would probably feel dissonance, especially if you thought an administrator would be reading your essay. How could you reduce the uncomfortable dissonance? One way would be to start believing your phony words. Your pretense would become your reality.

The attitudes-follow-behavior principle has a heartening implication: Although we cannot directly control all our feelings, we can influence them by altering our behavior. (Recall from Unit 8B the emotional effects of facial expressions and of body postures.) If we are down in the dumps, we can do as cognitive therapists advise and talk in more positive, self-accepting ways with fewer self-put-downs. If we are unloving, we can become more loving by behaving as if we were so—by doing thoughtful things, expressing affection, giving affirmation. "Assume a virtue, if you have it not," says Hamlet to his mother. "For use can almost change the stamp of nature."

::cognitive dissonance theory the theory that we act to reduce the discomfort (dissonance) we feel when two of our thoughts (cognitions) are inconsistent. For example, when our awareness of our attitudes and of our actions clash, we can reduce the resulting dissonance by changing our attitudes.

 TEACHING TIP

Engage students in a discussion of college hazing techniques, which are often perpetuated by cognitive dissonance. During fraternity pledging, first year students are run through activities designed to test their limits. One pledge was told to dig his "own grave." After he complied with orders to lie flat in the finished hole, the sides collapsed and suffocated him before his fraternity brothers could dig him out. Another pledge choked to death after repeatedly trying to swallow a large slab of raw liver soaked in oil. Why do hazing activities persist? As a result of their efforts, new fraternity members may find the group more attractive and worthwhile.

 TEACHING TIP

At this time, you may want to use **Classroom Exercise: *Introducing Cognitive Dissonance Theory*** (p. 8) from Bolt's Teacher's Resource Binder.

 DEMO

To demonstrate the "low-ball" technique, you will need the help of a confederate.

- Offer a "free day" in exchange for an after-school study hall. You will negotiate with the principal, but they must make an offer first. Suggest 30 minutes. Send a confederate to the office with the offer. The student will come back with the principal's "counteroffer": they must spend 2 hours after school. Send back another offer of an hour and a half. This time, the principal "agrees."

- Will students take the new offer? Probably. Discuss how this "low-ball" technique works off of foot-in-the-door and cognitive dissonance.

UNIT 14

650 UNIT 14 :: SOCIAL PSYCHOLOGY

CRITICAL THINKING

Conformity is a controversial issue among teens who want to fit in, but who also each want to be a distinct person at the same time. Have students discuss conformity in your school:

- Are the majority of students conformists or nonconformists? Why?

- Is there pressure among students at your school to dress a certain way or like certain types of music? Why or why not?

- Was there more pressure to conform in middle school as compared to high school? Why or why not?

- Where is the line between conformity and nonconformity? Is a group of nonconformists conforming to each other or nonconforming against society?

🛟 TEACHING TIP

At this time, you may want to use **Lecture/Discussion Topics:** *Mimicry and Prosocial Behavior* (p. 10) or *Social Exclusion and Mimicry* (p. 11) or *The Seattle Windshield Pitting Epidemic* (p. 11) or *Obedience in Everyday Life* (p. 14) from Bolt's Teacher's Resource Binder.

"Sit all day in a moping posture, sigh, and reply to everything with a dismal voice, and your melancholy lingers. . . . If we wish to conquer undesirable emotional tendencies in ourselves, we must . . . go through the outward movements of those contrary dispositions which we prefer to cultivate."

William James, *Principles of Psychology*, 1890

The point to remember: Cruel acts shape the self. But so do acts of good will. Act as though you like someone, and you soon will. Changing our behavior can change how we think about others and how we feel about ourselves.

BEFORE YOU MOVE ON . . .

> ### ➤ ASK YOURSELF

Do you have an attitude or tendency you would like to change? Using the attitudes-follow-behavior principle, how might you go about changing that attitude?

> ### ➤ TEST YOURSELF 1

Driving to school one snowy day, Marco narrowly misses a car that slides through a red light. "Slow down! What a terrible driver," he thinks to himself. Moments later, Marco himself slips through an intersection and yelps, "Wow! These roads are awful. The city plows need to get out here." What social psychology principle has Marco just demonstrated? Explain.

Answers to the Test Yourself questions can be found in Appendix E at the end of the book.

Social Influence

SOCIAL PSYCHOLOGY'S GREAT LESSON is the enormous power of social influence. This influence can be seen in our conformity, our compliance, and our group behavior. Suicides, bomb threats, airplane hijackings, and UFO sightings all have a curious tendency to come in clusters. On most high school campuses, jeans are the dress code; on New York's Wall Street or London's Bond Street, dress suits are the norm. When we know how to act, how to groom, how to talk, life functions smoothly. Armed with social influence principles, advertisers, fund raisers, and campaign workers aim to sway our decisions to buy, to donate, to vote. Isolated with others who share their grievances, dissenters may gradually become rebels, and rebels may become terrorists. Let's examine the pull of these social strings. How strong are they? How do they operate?

Conformity and Obedience

3: What do experiments on conformity and compliance reveal about the power of social influence?

Niche conformity Are these students asserting their individuality or identifying themselves with others of the same microculture?

Behavior is contagious. Consider:

- A cluster of people stand gazing upward, and passersby pause to do likewise.

- Baristas and street musicians know to "seed" their tip containers with money to suggest that others have given.

- One person laughs, coughs, or yawns, and others in the group soon do the same. Chimpanzees, too, are more likely to yawn after observing another chimpanzee yawn (Anderson et al., 2004).

- "Sickness" can also be psychologically contagious. In the anxious 9/11 aftermath, more than two dozen elementary and middle schools had outbreaks of children reporting red rashes, sometimes causing parents to wonder whether biological terrorism was at work (Talbot, 2002). Some cases may have been

---

DEMO

If students feel conformity is not really an issue with them, ask them a question in which you will get a totally positive or negative response. How many students raise their hands? Who told them to raise their hands? While this activity demonstrates the power of conditioning, it also shows how students conform to the behavior the school demands from them—like raising hands in response to teacher requests.

Adapted from Stork, E. (1992). Operant conditioning: Role in human behavior. In Sullivan, M., Blair-Broeker, C., Lindenberg, T., & Carlisle, A., (Eds.) (1992) *Learning.* Washington, DC: American Psychological Association.

stress-related, but mostly, health experts concluded, people were just noticing normal early acne, insect bites, eczema, and dry skin from overheated classrooms.

We are natural mimics—an effect Tanya Chartrand and John Bargh (1999) have called the *chameleon effect*. Unconsciously mimicking others' expressions, postures, and voice tones helps us feel what they are feeling. This helps explain why we feel happier around happy people than around depressed ones, and why studies of groups of British nurses and accountants reveal *mood linkage*—sharing up and down moods (Totterdell et al., 1998). Just hearing someone reading a neutral text in either a happy- or sad-sounding voice creates "mood contagion" in listeners (Neumann & Strack, 2000).

Chartrand and Bargh demonstrated the chameleon effect when they had students work in a room alongside a confederate working for the experimenter. Sometimes the confederates rubbed their face; on other occasions, they shook their foot. Sure enough, participants tended to rub their own face when with the face-rubbing person and shake their own foot when with the foot-shaking person. Such automatic mimicry is part of empathy. Empathic people yawn more after seeing others yawn (Morrison, 2007). And empathic, mimicking people are liked more. Those most eager to fit in with a group seem intuitively to know this, for they are especially prone to unconscious mimicry (Lakin & Chartrand, 2003).

NON SEQUITUR   by WILEY

NON SEQUITUR © 2000 Wiley. Dist. by Universal Press Syndicate. Reprinted with permission.

Sometimes the effects of suggestibility are more serious. In the eight days following the 1999 shooting rampage at Colorado's Columbine High School, every U.S. state except Vermont experienced threats of copycat violence. Pennsylvania alone recorded 60 such threats (Cooper, 1999). Sociologist David Phillips and his colleagues (1985, 1989) found that suicides, too, sometimes increase following a highly publicized suicide. In the wake of screen idol Marilyn Monroe's suicide on August 6, 1962, for example, the number of suicides in the United States exceeded the usual August count by 200. Within a one-year period, one London psychiatric unit experienced 14 patient suicides (Joiner, 1999). In the days after Saddam Hussein's widely publicized execution in Iraq, there were cases of boys in Turkey, Pakistan, Yemen, Saudi Arabia, and the United States who hung themselves, apparently accidently, after slipping nooses around their own heads (AP, 2007).

What causes suicide clusters? Do people act similarly because of their influence on one another? Or because they are simultaneously exposed to the same events and conditions? Seeking answers, social psychologists have conducted experiments on group pressure and conformity.

Group Pressure and Conformity

Suggestibility is a subtle type of **conformity**—adjusting our behavior or thinking toward some group standard. To study conformity, Solomon Asch (1955) devised a

::conformity adjusting one's behavior or thinking to coincide with a group standard.

UNIT 14

Standard line   1 2 3
Comparison lines

➤ **FIGURE 14.2**

Asch's conformity experiments Which of the three comparison lines is equal to the standard line? What do you suppose most people would say after hearing five others say, "Line 3"? In this photo from one of Asch's experiments, the student in the center shows the severe discomfort that comes from disagreeing with the responses of other group members (in this case, confederates of the experimenter).

TEACHING TIP

Have students notice that the correct answer among the comparison lines is quite obvious. There should have been no question as to which line to choose, but the power of conformity to the group lead normally confident people to choose the wrong answer instead of the right one.

TEACHING TIP

Suggest to students an ethical issue, such as participating in cheating or bullying another student, where they would need to stand against a crowd in order to do the right thing. Would they vote their conscience or go with the crowd? Discuss with students what personal qualities and situations would lead a person to be more likely to vote his or her conscience.

> "Have you ever noticed how one example—good or bad—can prompt others to follow? How one illegally parked car can give permission for others to do likewise? How one racial joke can fuel another?"
>
> Marian Wright Edelman, *The Measure of Our Success*, 1992

::**normative social influence** influence resulting from a person's desire to gain approval or avoid disapproval.

::**informational social influence** influence resulting from one's willingness to accept others' opinions about reality.

simple test. As a participant in what you believe is a study of visual perception, you arrive at the experiment location in time to take a seat at a table where five people are already seated. The experimenter asks which of three comparison lines is identical to a standard line (**FIGURE 14.2**). You see clearly that the answer is Line 2 and await your turn to say so after the others. Your boredom with this experiment begins to show when the next set of lines proves equally easy.

Now comes the third trial, and the correct answer seems just as clear-cut, but the first person gives what strikes you as a wrong answer: "Line 3." When the second person and then the third and fourth give the same wrong answer, you sit up straight and squint. When the fifth person agrees with the first four, you feel your heart begin to pound. The experimenter then looks to you for your answer. Torn between the unanimity of your five fellow respondents and the evidence of your own eyes, you feel tense and much less sure of yourself than you were moments ago. You hesitate before answering, wondering whether you should suffer the discomfort of being the oddball. What answer do you give?

In the experiments conducted by Asch and others after him, thousands of college students have experienced this conflict. Answering such questions alone, they erred less than 1 percent of the time. But the odds were quite different when several others—confederates working for the experimenter—answered incorrectly. Although most people told the truth even when others did not, Asch nevertheless was disturbed by his result: More than one-third of the time, these "intelligent and well-meaning" college-student participants were then "willing to call white black" by going along with the group.

Conditions That Strengthen Conformity Asch's procedure became the model for later investigations. Although experiments have not always found so much conformity, they do reveal that conformity increases when

- one is made to feel incompetent or insecure.
- the group has at least three people.
- the group is unanimous. (The dissent of just one other person greatly increases social courage.)
- one admires the group's status and attractiveness.
- one has made no prior commitment to any response.
- others in the group observe one's behavior.
- one's culture strongly encourages respect for social standards.

Thus, we might predict the behavior of Austin, an enthusiastic but insecure new student government member: Noting that the 10 other members appear unanimous in their plans for a fund raiser, Austin is unlikely to voice his dissent.

CULTURAL CONNECTIONS

Have students examine which cultures are more likely to encourage conformity.

- What are the qualities of cultures that encourage conformity?
- What types of government do these cultures have? Are they all communistic, democratic, or a mixture of both?
- On whom do these cultures encourage conformity—government officials, families, adults, or all of the above?
- How do these cultures handle people who don't conform? Do they suffer formalized punishment (jail, fines, etc.) or more informal social punishment (shunning, lack of job advancement, etc.)?

Reasons for Conforming Fish swim in schools. Birds fly in flocks. And humans, too, tend to go with their group, to think what it thinks and do what it does. Researchers have seen this in college residence halls, where over time students' attitudes become more similar to those living near them (Cullum & Harton, 2007). But why? Why do we clap when others clap, eat as others eat, believe what others believe, even see what others see? Frequently, it is to avoid rejection or to gain social approval. In such cases, we are responding to what social psychologists call **normative social influence.** We are sensitive to social norms—understood rules for accepted and expected behavior—because the price we pay for being different may be severe.

"I love the little ways you're identical to everyone else."

Respecting norms is not the only reason we conform: Groups may provide valuable information, and only an uncommonly stubborn person will never listen to others. When we accept others' opinions about reality, we are responding to **informational social influence.** "Those who never retract their opinions love themselves more than they love truth," observed the eighteenth-century French essayist Joseph Joubert. As Rebecca Denton demonstrated in 2004, sometimes it pays to assume others are right and to follow their lead. Denton set a record for the furthest distance driven on the wrong side of a British divided highway—30 miles, with only one minor sideswipe, before the motorway ran out and police were able to puncture her tires. Denton later explained that she thought the hundreds of other drivers coming at her were all on the wrong side of the road (Woolcock, 2004).

Robert Baron and his colleagues (1996) cleverly demonstrated our openness to informational influence on tough, important judgments. They modernized the Asch experiment by showing University of Iowa students a slide of a stimulus person, followed by a slide of a four-person lineup (**FIGURE 14.3**). Their experiment made the task either easy (viewing the lineup for five seconds) or difficult (viewing the lineup for but half a second). It also led them to think their judgments were either unimportant (just a preliminary test of some eyewitness identification procedures) or important (establishing norms for an actual police procedure, with a $20 award to the most accurate participants). When the accuracy of their judgments seemed important, people rarely conformed when the task was easy, but they conformed half the time when the task was difficult. If we are unsure of what is right, and if being right matters, we are receptive to others' opinions.

Our view of social influence as bad or good depends on our values. When influence supports what we approve, we applaud those who are "open-minded" and "sensitive" enough to be "responsive." When influence supports what we disapprove, we scorn the

➤ **FIGURE 14.3**
Informational influence Sample task: After seeing Slides 1 and 2, participants judged which person in Slide 2 was the same as the person in Slide 1. (From Baron et al., 1996.)

DEMO

Stanley Milgram asked his students to violate a social norm, such as asking another passenger for his or her seat on a city bus or subway. One graduate student reported: "I just couldn't go on. It was one of the most difficult things I ever did in my life." Unconvinced, Milgram tried it himself. He approached a seated passenger but the words "seemed lodged in my trachea and would simply not emerge. I stood there frozen, then retreated, the mission unfulfilled." He finally choked out the request: "Excuse me, sir, may I have your seat?" To Milgram's surprise, the man gave up his seat! In taking the man's seat, Milgram observed, "I was overwhelmed by the need to behave in a way that would justify my request. My head sank between my knees . . . I actually felt as if I were going to perish." Not until he left the train did his tension dissipate. This experiment demonstrated several social principles:

- Enormous inhibitory anxiety ordinarily prevents us from breaking social norms.

- We have a powerful need to justify our actions after violating a norm.

- The power of immediate circumstances on our feelings and behavior is immense.

 TEACHING TIP

Most people will yield to the majority opinion even when it conflicts with their own. When asked how we would respond in the Asch situation, we predict we would resist group pressure. We underestimate the power of social forces. Students can imagine themselves violating some less-than-earthshaking norms: standing in the middle of a class, greeting some distinguished city officials by their first names, munching popcorn at a piano recital, wearing shorts to a place of worship.

- How would they feel in these situations?

- What consequences would they endure for violating these norms? Is that why they conform?

Stanley Milgram did his research during a time when people were dealing with the consequences of the Holocaust and watching the Nuremberg trials. People believed the German people were evil for being complicit in the Holocaust, and Milgram, himself a Jew, wanted to demonstrate the power of social situations on people's behavior. Have students research this particularly painful time in history:

- What techniques did Hitler and his propaganda officers use to convince the German people to comply with the Holocaust?

- Highlight some examples of German citizens who tried to save Jews from the genocide. Why were these people able to disobey?

Stanley Milgram (1933–1984) This social psychologist's obedience experiments "belong to the self-understanding of literate people in our age" (Sabini, 1986). ▲

Courtesy of CUNY Graduate School and University Center

"submissive conformity" of those who comply with others' wishes. As we saw in Unit 10, cultures vary in the extent to which they value individualism or collectivism. Western Europeans and people in most English-speaking countries tend to prize individualism more than conformity and obedience. These values are reflected in social influence experiments that have been conducted in 17 countries: In individualist cultures, conformity rates are lower (Bond & Smith, 1996). In the individualistic United States, university students tend to see themselves, in domains ranging from consumer purchases to political views, as less conforming than others (Pronin et al., 2007). We are, in our own eyes, individuals amid a crowd of sheep. Thus, tattoos, once a symbol of nonconformity, may lose their appeal if they become too popular.

Obedience

Social psychologist Stanley Milgram (1963, 1974), a student of Solomon Asch, knew that people often comply with social pressures. But how would they respond to outright commands? To find out, he undertook what have become social psychology's most famous and controversial experiments. Imagine yourself as one of the nearly 1000 participants in Milgram's 20 experiments.

Responding to an advertisement, you come to Yale University's psychology department to participate in an experiment. Professor Milgram's assistant explains that the study concerns the effect of punishment on learning. You and another person draw slips from a hat to see who will be the "teacher" (which your slip says) and who will be the "learner." The learner is then led to an adjoining room and strapped into a chair that is wired through the wall to an electric shock machine. You sit in front of the machine, which has switches labeled with voltages. Your task: to teach and then test the learner on a list of word pairs. You are to punish the learner for wrong answers by delivering brief electric shocks, beginning with a switch labeled "15 Volts—Slight Shock." After each of the learner's errors, you are to move up to the next higher voltage. With each flick of a switch, lights flash, relay switches click on, and an electric buzzing fills the air.

Complying with the experimenter's instructions, you hear the learner grunt when you flick the third, fourth, and fifth switches. After you activate the eighth switch (labeled "120 Volts—Moderate Shock"), the learner shouts that the shocks are painful. After the tenth switch ("150 Volts—Strong Shock"), he cries, "Get me out of here! I won't be in the experiment anymore! I refuse to go on!" Hearing these pleas, you draw back. But the experimenter prods you: "Please continue—the experiment requires that you continue." If you still resist, he insists, "It is absolutely essential that you continue," or "You have no other choice, you *must* go on."

Obeying, you hear the learner's protests escalate to shrieks of agony as you continue to raise the shock level with each succeeding error. After the 330-volt level, the learner refuses to answer and falls silent. Still, the experimenter pushes you toward the final, 450-volt switch, ordering you to ask the questions and, if no correct answer is given, to administer the next shock level.

How far do you think you would follow the experimenter's commands? In a survey Milgram conducted before the experiment, most people declared they would stop playing such a sadistic-seeming role soon after the learner first indicated pain and certainly before he shrieked in agony. This also was the prediction made by each of 40 psychiatrists Milgram asked to guess the outcome. When Milgram actually conducted the experiment with men aged 20 to 50, he was astonished to find that 63 percent complied fully—right up to the last switch. Ten later studies that included women found women's compliance rates were similar to men's (Blass, 1999).

Did the teachers figure out the hoax—that no shock was being delivered? Did they correctly guess the learner was a confederate who only pretended to feel the shocks? Did they realize the experiment was really testing their willingness to comply with commands to inflict punishment? No. The teachers typically displayed genuine distress:

At this time, you may want to use **Student Project:** *Violating a Social Norm* (p. 13) from Bolt's Teacher's Resource Binder.

They perspired, trembled, laughed nervously, and bit their lips. In a recent virtual reality re-creation of these experiments, participants responded much as did Milgram's participants, including perspiration and racing heart, when shocking a virtual woman on a screen in front of them (Slater et al., 2006).

Milgram's use of deception and stress triggered a debate over his research ethics. In his own defense, Milgram pointed out that, after the participants learned of the deception and actual research purposes, virtually none regretted taking part (though perhaps by then the participants had reduced their dissonance). When 40 of the teachers who had agonized most were later interviewed by a psychiatrist, none appeared to be suffering emotional aftereffects. All in all, said Milgram, the experiments provoked less enduring stress than university students experience when facing and failing big exams (Blass, 1996).

Wondering whether the participants obeyed because the learners' protests were not convincing, Milgram repeated the experiment with 40 new teachers. This time his confederate mentioned a "slight heart condition" while being strapped into the chair, and then he complained and screamed more intensely as the shocks became more punishing. Still, 65 percent of the new teachers complied fully (**FIGURE 14.4**).

➤ **FIGURE 14.4**
Milgram's follow-up obedience experiment In a repeat of the earlier experiment, 65 percent of the adult male "teachers" fully obeyed the experimenter's commands to continue. They did so despite the "learner's" earlier mention of a heart condition and despite hearing cries of protest after 150 volts and agonized protests after 330 volts. (Data from Milgram, 1974.)

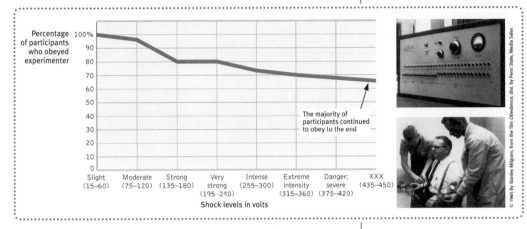

Percentage of participants who obeyed experimenter

The majority of participants continued to obey to the end

Shock levels in volts:
Slight (15–60), Moderate (75–120), Strong (135–180), Very strong (195–240), Intense (255–300), Extreme intensity (315–360), Danger: severe (375–420), XXX (435–450)

In later experiments, Milgram discovered that subtle details of a situation powerfully influence people. When he varied the social conditions, the proportion of fully compliant participants varied from 0 to 93 percent. Obedience was highest when

- the person giving the orders was close at hand and was perceived to be a legitimate authority figure. (Such was the case in 2005 when Temple University's basketball coach sent a 250-pound bench player, Nehemiah Ingram, into a game with instructions to commit "hard fouls." Following orders, Ingram fouled out in four minutes after breaking an opposing player's right arm.)
- the authority figure was supported by a prestigious institution. Compliance was somewhat lower when Milgram dissociated his experiments from Yale University.
- the victim was depersonalized or at a distance, even in another room. (Similarly, in combat with an enemy they can see, many soldiers either do not fire their rifles or do not aim them properly. Such refusals to kill are rare among those who operate more distant artillery or aircraft weapons [Padgett, 1989].)
- there were no role models for defiance; that is, no other participants were seen disobeying the experimenter.

"Drive off the cliff, James, I want to commit suicide."

TEACHING TIP

Subjects in Milgram's studies were actually sheep, not wolves. Milgram designed an alternative experiment in which the "teacher" could select any shock levels on the generator without any coercion. Describe this procedure, asking students to make the following predictions:

- On the average, what shock level do you think the teacher chose for the learner?
- What percentage of teachers do you think set the shock at the highest setting of 450 volts?

Milgram reports that only one subject pressed the maximum shock, and in general the shock level remained in the 45-to-60-volt range. Students typically overestimate the level of shock subjects would choose, thinking they are wolves, not sheep.

Safer, M. (1980). Attributing evil to the subject, not the situation. *Personality and Social Psychology Bulletin, 6,* 205–209.

INTERCONNECTING

Discuss with students the ethical issues that arise out of experiments like Stanley Milgram's obedience study:

- Does the APA Ethics Code allow for deception? Why or why not?
- Would this study be approved by an Institutional Review Board today? Why or why not?
- What responsibilities do researchers have for the well-being of participants?

For more information on the APA Ethics Code, see the document online at www.apa.org/ethics.

TEACHING TIP

At this time, you may want to use **Lecture/Discussion Topics**: *Deviance in the Dark* (p. 16) or *Understanding Terrorism* (p. 17) from Bolt's Teacher's Resource Binder.

Standing up for democracy Some individuals—roughly one in three in Milgram's experiments—resist social coercion, as did this unarmed man in Beijing, by single-handedly challenging an advancing line of tanks the day after the 1989 Tiananmen Square student uprising was suppressed.

TEACHING TIP

We can learn from the minority of Milgram's participants who confronted authority. Gretchen Brandt, a young medical technician, provides one fascinating example to present in class. She emigrated from Germany 5 years before the studies. Speaking with a thick German accent, she coolly turned to the experimenter at different points and inquired, "Shall I continue?" At the delivery of 210 volts she announced firmly, "Well, I'm sorry, I don't think we should continue." In spite of the experimenter's prompts, she refused to go further and the study ended. Gretchen never appeared tense or nervous. She simply stated that she "did not want to be responsible for any harm to the learner." Milgram notes that her straightforward, courteous demeanor seemed to make disobedience a simple and rational deed. What made her different? Gretchen grew to adolescence in Nazi Germany and, for the greater part of her youth, was exposed to Hitler's propaganda. When asked about the influence of her background, she simply remarked, "Perhaps we have seen too much pain."

Milgram, S. (1974). *Obedience to authority.* New York: Harper & Row.

The power of legitimate, close-at-hand authorities is dramatically apparent in stories of those who complied with orders to carry out the Holocaust atrocities, and those who didn't. Obedience alone does not explain the Holocaust; anti-Semitic ideology produced eager killers as well (Mastroianni, 2002). But obedience was a factor. In the summer of 1942, nearly 500 middle-aged German reserve police officers were dispatched to German-occupied Jozefow, Poland. On July 13, the group's visibly upset commander informed his recruits, mostly family men, that they had been ordered to round up the village's Jews, who were said to be aiding the enemy. Able-bodied men were to be sent to work camps, and all the rest were to be shot on the spot. Given a chance to refuse participation in the executions, only about a dozen immediately did so. Within 17 hours, the remaining 485 officers killed 1500 helpless women, children, and elderly by shooting them in the back of the head as they lay face down. Hearing the pleas of the victims, and seeing the gruesome results, some 20 percent of the officers did eventually dissent, managing either to miss their victims or to wander away and hide until the slaughter was over (Browning, 1992). But in real life, as in Milgram's experiments, the disobedient were the minority.

Another story was being played out in the French village of Le Chambon, where French Jews destined for deportation to Germany were being sheltered by villagers who openly defied orders to cooperate with the "New Order." The villagers' ancestors had themselves been persecuted and their pastors had been teaching them to "resist whenever our adversaries will demand of us obedience contrary to the orders of the Gospel" (Rochat, 1993). Ordered by police to give a list of sheltered Jews, the head pastor modeled defiance: "I don't know of Jews, I only know of human beings." Without realizing how long and terrible the war would be, or how much punishment and poverty they would suffer, the resisters made an initial commitment to resist. Supported by their beliefs, their role models, their interactions with one another, and their own initial acts, they remained defiant to the war's end.

Lessons From the Conformity and Obedience Studies

What do the Asch and Milgram experiments teach us about ourselves? How does judging the length of a line or flicking a shock switch relate to everyday social behavior? Recall from Unit 2 that psychological experiments aim not to re-create the literal behaviors of everyday life but to capture and explore the underlying processes that shape those behaviors. Asch and Milgram devised experiments in which the participants had to choose between adhering to their own standards and being responsive to others, a dilemma we all face frequently.

In Milgram's experiments, participants were also torn between what they should respond to—the pleas of the victim or the orders of the experimenter. Their moral sense warned them not to harm another, yet it also prompted them to obey the experimenter and to be a good research participant. With kindness and obedience on a collision course, obedience usually won.

Such experiments demonstrate that strong social influences can make people conform to falsehoods or capitulate to cruelty. "The most fundamental lesson of our study," Milgram noted, is that "ordinary people, simply doing their jobs, and without any particular hostility on their part, can become agents in a terrible destructive process" (1974, p. 6). Milgram did not entrap his teachers by asking them first to zap learners with enough electricity to make their hair stand on end. Rather, he exploited the foot-in-the-door effect, beginning with a little tickle of electricity and escalating step by step. In the minds of those throwing the switches, the small action became

> "I was only following orders."
> Adolf Eichmann, Director of Nazi deportation of Jews to concentration camps

RESEARCH

Most colleges and universities have banned hazing for fraternities, sororities, and clubs on campus. Why does it still persist? Have students contact university student relations departments, fraternity and sorority members, and alumni of these organizations to discuss hazing practices past and present:

- What are current university policies regarding hazing? What sanctions will be enacted for organizations that haze?

- How did the university view hazing in the past?

- How do the fraternities' and sororities' national organizations view hazing?

- Did alumni endure hazing? How did they view it then? Would they condone their children enduring hazing?

justified, making the next act tolerable. In Jozefow, in Le Chambon, and in Milgram's experiments, those who resisted usually did so early. After the first acts of compliance or resistance, attitudes began to follow and justify behavior.

So it happens when people succumb, gradually, to evil. In any society, great evils sometimes grow out of people's compliance with lesser evils. The Nazi leaders suspected that most German civil servants would resist shooting or gassing Jews directly, but they found them surprisingly willing to handle the paperwork of the Holocaust (Silver & Geller, 1978). Likewise, when Milgram asked 40 men to administer the learning test while someone else did the shocking, 93 percent complied. Contrary to images of devilish villains, cruelty does not require monstrous characters; all it takes is ordinary people corrupted by an evil situation—ordinary soldiers who follow orders to torture prisoners, ordinary students who follow orders to haze initiates into their group, ordinary employees who follow orders to produce and market harmful products. Before leading the 9/11 attacks, Mohammed Atta reportedly was a sane, rational person who had been a "good boy" and an excellent student from a close-knit family—not someone who fits our image of a barbaric monster.

> "The normal reaction to an abnormal situation is abnormal behavior."
> James Waller, *Becoming Evil: How Ordinary People Commit Genocide and Mass Killing*, 2007

Group Influence

How do groups affect our behavior? To find out, social psychologists study the various influences that operate in the simplest of groups—one person in the presence of another—and those that operate in more complex groups, such as families, teams, and committees.

Individual Behavior in the Presence of Others

4: How is our behavior affected by the presence of others or by being part of a group?

Appropriately, social psychology's first experiments focused on the simplest of all questions about social behavior: How are we influenced by people watching us or joining us in various activities?

Social Facilitation Having noticed that cyclists' racing times were faster when they competed against each other than when they competed with a clock, Norman Triplett (1898) hypothesized that the presence of others boosts performance. To test his hypothesis, Triplett had adolescents wind a fishing reel as rapidly as possible. He discovered that they wound the reel faster in the presence of someone doing the same thing. This phenomenon of stronger performance in others' presence is called **social facilitation.** For example, after a light turns green, drivers take about 15 percent less time to travel the first 100 yards when another car is beside them at the intersection than when they are alone (Towler, 1986).

But on tougher tasks (learning nonsense syllables or solving complex multiplication problems), people perform *less* well when observers or others working on the same task are present. Further studies revealed why the presence of others sometimes helps and sometimes hinders performance (Guerin, 1986; Zajonc, 1965). When

::**social facilitation** stronger responses on simple or well-learned tasks in the presence of others.

Courtesy Hope College Public Relations

Social facilitation Skilled athletes often find they are "on" before an audience. What they do well, they do even better when people are watching.

INTERCONNECTING

Relate social facilitation with test anxiety. While some people feel distinct anxiety any time they take a test, most people only feel anxiety if they are not prepared for an assessment. Edward Thorndike proposed the "Law of Readiness," which states in part that if a person is not ready for a performance, he or she will feel frustrated and will actively seek to avoid the performance. If the person is ready, then he or she will be willing and ready to perform.

CRITICAL THINKING

If performance on tasks diminishes when we are not good at that task, consider the following scenarios:

- Should students schedule when they take tests so that they can take them when they are ready? Why or why not?

- Should students be allowed to give oral presentations in front of the teacher if they believe their project isn't very good or if they are uncomfortable with their public speaking ability? Why or why not?

 TEACHING TIP

At this time, you may want to use **Lecture/Discussion Topic: *Groupthink*** (p. 17) or **Classroom Exercises: *Deindividuation*** (p. 16) or ***Group Polarization*** (p. 16) or ***The Wisdom of Crowds*** (p. 18) from Bolt's Teacher's Resource Binder.

INTERCONNECTING

The Yerkes-Dodson Law also addresses how arousal impacts performance (Figure 8B.3, page 370). This law states that there needs to be an optimal level of arousal present if we want to perform our best. Too little arousal means performance is half-hearted. Too much arousal leads performance to be sloppy.

UNIT 14

CRITICAL THINKING

If social loafing in group work is such a problem, why do teachers still use it? Have students brainstorm about ways to minimize social loafing in group projects:

- Should teachers stop using group projects altogether? Why or why not?

- Does having group members evaluate each other minimize social loafing? Why or why not?

- Does assigning roles help minimize social loafing? Why or why not?

- How can group members motivate each other to work their hardest during group work?

RESEARCH

Have students research your school's sports teams' statistics. Do they notice signs of social facilitation in the following stats?

- Home wins versus away wins for team sports such as football, soccer, basketball, and baseball

- Home wins versus away wins for individual sports such as track, wrestling, and cross-country

- Individual records/best games accomplished at home or away for all sports (For example, do basketball players hit more free throws at home or away? Do track athletes run faster at home or away? Do football players individually have higher stats for home games or away games?)

---

others observe us, we become aroused. This arousal strengthens the most *likely* response—the correct one on an easy task, an incorrect one on a difficult task. Thus, when we are being observed, we perform well-learned tasks more quickly and accurately, and unmastered tasks less quickly and accurately.

James Michaels and his associates (1982) found that expert pool players who made 71 percent of their shots when alone made 80 percent when four people came to watch them. Poor shooters, who made 36 percent of their shots when alone, made only 25 percent when watched. The energizing effect of an enthusiastic audience probably contributes to the home advantage enjoyed by various sports teams. Studies of more than 80,000 college and professional athletic events in Canada, the United States, and England reveal that home teams win about 6 in 10 games (somewhat fewer for baseball and football, somewhat more for basketball and soccer—see **TABLE 14.1**).

TABLE 14.1

HOME ADVANTAGE IN MAJOR TEAM SPORTS

Sport	Games Studied	Home Team Winning Percentage
Baseball	23,034	53.5%
Football	2,592	57.3
Ice hockey	4,322	61.1
Basketball	13,596	64.4
Soccer	37,202	69.0

From Courneya & Carron (1992).

The point to remember: What you do well, you are likely to do even better in front of an audience, especially a friendly audience; what you normally find difficult may seem all but impossible when you are being watched.

Social facilitation also helps explain a funny effect of crowding: Comedy routines that are mildly amusing to people in an uncrowded room seem funnier in a densely packed room (Aiello et al., 1983; Freedman & Perlick, 1979). As comedians and actors know, a "good house" is a full one. The arousal triggered by crowding amplifies other reactions, too. If sitting close to one another, participants in experiments like a friendly person even more, an unfriendly person even less (Schiffenbauer & Schiavo, 1976; Storms & Thomas, 1977). The practical lesson: If choosing a room for a class or setting up chairs for a gathering, have barely enough seating.

Social Loafing Social facilitation experiments test the effect of others' presence on performance on an individual task, such as shooting pool. But what happens to performance when people perform the task as a group? In a team tug-of-war, for example, do you suppose your effort would be more than, less than, or the same as the effort you would exert in a one-on-one tug-of-war? To find out, Alan Ingham and his fellow researchers (1974) asked blindfolded University of Massachusetts students to "pull as hard as you can" on a rope. When Ingham fooled the students into believing three others were also pulling behind them, they exerted only 82 percent as much effort as when they knew they were pulling alone.

Bibb Latané and others (1981; Jackson & Williams, 1988) describe this diminished effort as **social loafing.** In 78 experiments conducted in the United States, India, Thailand, Japan, China, and Taiwan, social loafing occurred on various tasks, though it was especially common among men in individualistic cultures (Karau & Williams, 1993). In one of Latané's experiments, blindfolded people seated in a group clapped or shouted as loud as they could while listening through headphones to the sound of loud clapping or shouting. When told they were doing it with the others, the participants produced about one-third less noise than when they thought their individual efforts were identifiable.

Why this social loafing? First, people acting as part of a group feel less accountable and therefore worry less about what others think. Second, they may view their contribution as dispensable (Harkins & Szymanski, 1989; Kerr & Bruun, 1983). As many leaders of organizations know—and as you have perhaps observed on student group assignments—if group members share equally in the benefits regardless of how much they contribute, some may slack off. Unless highly motivated and identified with their group, they may free ride on the other group members' efforts.

Deindividuation So, the presence of others can arouse people (as in the social facilitation experiments) or can diminish their feelings of responsibility (as in the social

---

DEMO

Take students to your school's gym and have some volunteers try to shoot baskets with the class acting as either a supportive home crowd or a hostile away crowd (not too hostile—just booing and being distracting). Have someone record the number of shots each volunteer made under each condition.

- Did the volunteers perform better under friendly or hostile conditions?

- How much experience did each volunteer have at shooting baskets? Did a basketball team member do better in the "away crowd" condition than someone who has never played before? Why or why not?

loafing experiments). But sometimes the presence of others both arouses people *and* diminishes their sense of responsibility. The result can be uninhibited behavior ranging from a food fight in the school cafeteria or screaming at a basketball referee to vandalism or rioting. Abandoning normal restraints to the power of the group is termed **deindividuation.** To be deindividuated is to be less self-conscious and less restrained when in a group situation.

Deindividuation often occurs when group participation makes people feel aroused and anonymous. In one experiment, New York University women dressed in depersonalizing Ku Klux Klan–style hoods delivered twice as much electric shock to a victim as did identifiable women (Zimbardo, 1970). (As in all such experiments, the "victim" did not actually receive the shocks.) Similarly, tribal warriors who depersonalize themselves with face paints or masks are more likely than those with exposed faces to kill, torture, or mutilate captured enemies (Watson, 1973). Whether in a mob, at a rock concert, at a ballgame, or at worship, to lose self-consciousness (to become deindividuated) is to become more responsive to the group experience.

Effects of Group Interaction

5: What are group polarization and groupthink?

We have examined the conditions under which being in the *presence* of others can

- motivate people to exert themselves or tempt them to free ride on the efforts of others.
- make easy tasks easier and difficult tasks harder.
- enhance humor or fuel mob violence.

Research shows that *interacting* with others can similarly have both bad and good effects.

Group Polarization Educational researchers have noted that, over time, initial differences between groups of college students tend to grow. If the first-year students at College X tend to be more intellectually oriented than those at College Y, that difference will probably be amplified by the time they are seniors. And if the political conservatism of students who join fraternities and sororities is greater than that of students who do not, the gap in the political attitudes of the two groups will probably widen as they progress through college (Wilson et al., 1975). Similarly, notes Eleanor Maccoby (2002) from her decades of observing gender development, girls talk more intimately than boys do and play and fantasize less aggressively—and these gender differences widen over time as they interact mostly with their own gender.

This enhancement of a group's prevailing tendencies—called **group polarization**—occurs when people within a group discuss an idea that most of them either favor or oppose. Group polarization can have beneficial results, as when it amplifies a sought-after spiritual awareness or reinforces the resolve of those in a self-help group, or strengthens feelings of tolerance in a low-prejudice group. But it can also have dire consequences. George Bishop and I discovered that when high-prejudice students discussed racial issues, they became *more* prejudiced (**FIGURE 14.5**). (Low-prejudice students became even more accepting.) The experiment's ideological separation and polarization finds a seeming parallel in the growing polarization of American politics. The percentage of landslide counties—voting 60 percent or more for one presidential candidate—increased from 26 percent in 1976 to 48 percent in 2004 (Bishop, 2004). More and more, people are living near and learning from others

::**social loafing** the tendency for people in a group to exert less effort when pooling their efforts toward attaining a common goal than when individually accountable.

::**deindividuation** the loss of self-awareness and self-restraint occurring in group situations that foster arousal and anonymity.

::**group polarization** the enhancement of a group's prevailing inclinations through discussion within the group.

➤ **FIGURE 14.5**

Group polarization If a group is like-minded, discussion strengthens its prevailing opinions. Talking over racial issues increased prejudice in a high-prejudice group of high school students and decreased it in a low-prejudice group (Myers & Bishop, 1970).

UNIT 14

RESEARCH

Groupthink has impacted several famous historical events. Have students research the following events, citing how groupthink was either avoided or led to dreadful consequences:

- The space shuttle *Columbia* disaster
- The Bay of Pigs
- The Cuban Missile Crisis
- The Vietnam conflict
- The buildup to the Iraq war

TROUBLESHOOTING

Students may get conformity and groupthink confused. Help them distinguish these concepts using these explanations:

- Groupthink occurs when people suppress their opinions (also known as "self-censoring") in order to maintain perceived group harmony. People in groupthink situations do not want to be the "odd one out."

- Groupthink also reflects the presence of a charismatic leader. Everyone in the group seems to be going along with the leader, making it difficult to speak out.

- Conformity occurs simply when people don't want to be different. They are not necessarily self-censoring. Rather, they are going along due to normative or informational social influence.

---

who think as they do. One experiment brought together small groups of citizens in liberal Boulder, Colorado, and other groups down in conservative Colorado Springs, to discuss global climate change, affirmative action, and same-sex unions. Although the discussions increased agreement within groups, those in Boulder generally moved further left and those in Colorado Springs moved further right (Schkade et al., 2006). Thus ideological separation + deliberation = polarization between groups.

The polarizing effect of interaction among the like-minded applies also to suicide terrorists. After analyzing terrorist organizations around the world, psychologists Clark McCauley and Mary Segal (1987; McCauley, 2002) noted that the terrorist mentality does not erupt suddenly. Rather, it usually arises among people who get together because of a grievance and then become more and more extreme as they interact in isolation from any moderating influences. Increasingly, group members (who may be isolated with other "brothers" and "sisters" in camps) categorize the world as "us" against "them" (Moghaddam, 2005; Qirko, 2004). Suicide terrorism is virtually never done on a personal whim, reports researcher Ariel Merari (2002). The like-minded echo chamber will continue to polarize people, speculates the 2006 U.S. National Intelligence Estimate: "We assess that the operational threat from self-radicalized cells will grow."

The Internet provides a medium for group polarization. Its tens of thousands of virtual groups enable bereaved parents, peacemakers, and teachers to find solace and support from kindred spirits. But the Internet also enables people who share interests in government conspiracy, extraterrestrial visitors, White supremacy, or citizen militias to find one another and to find support for their shared suspicions (McKenna & Bargh, 1998).

Groupthink Does group interaction ever distort important decisions? Social psychologist Irving Janis began to think so as he read historian Arthur M. Schlesinger Jr.'s account of how President John F. Kennedy and his advisers blundered into an ill-fated plan to invade Cuba with 1400 CIA-trained Cuban exiles. When the invaders were easily captured and soon linked to the U.S. government, Kennedy wondered in hindsight, "How could we have been so stupid?"

To find out, Janis (1982) studied the decision-making procedures that led to the fiasco. He discovered that the soaring morale of the recently elected president and his advisers fostered undue confidence in the plan. To preserve the good group feeling, any dissenting views were suppressed or self-censored, especially after President Kennedy voiced his enthusiasm for the scheme. Since no one spoke strongly against the idea, everyone assumed consensus support. To describe this harmonious but unrealistic group thinking, Janis coined the term **groupthink.**

Janis and others then examined other historical fiascos—the failure to anticipate the 1941 Japanese attack on Pearl Harbor, the escalation of the Vietnam war, the U.S. Watergate cover-up, the Chernobyl nuclear reactor accident (Reason, 1987), and the U.S. space shuttle *Challenger* explosion (Esser & Lindoerfer, 1989). They discovered that in these cases, too, groupthink was fed by overconfidence, conformity, self-justification, and group polarization.

Groupthink surfaced again, reported the bipartisan U.S. Senate Intelligence Committee (2004), when "personnel involved in the Iraq WMD issue demonstrated several aspects of groupthink: examining few alternatives, selective gathering of information, pressure to conform within the group or withhold criticism, and collective rationalization." This groupthink led analysts to "interpret ambiguous evidence as conclusively indicative of a WMD program as well as ignore or minimize evidence that Iraq did not have [WMD] programs."

Despite such fiascos and tragedies, two heads are better than one in solving some types of problems. Knowing this, Janis also studied instances in which U.S. presidents and their advisers collectively made good decisions, such as when the Truman

---

> "One's impulse to blow the whistle on this nonsense was simply undone by the circumstances of the discussion."
>
> Arthur M. Schlesinger, Jr.,
> *A Thousand Days*, 1965

> "One of the dangers in a White House, based on my reading of history, is that you get wrapped up in groupthink, and everybody agrees with everything, and there's no discussion and there are not dissenting views."
>
> Barack Obama, *New York Daily News*,
> December 1, 2008

> "Truth springs from argument among friends."
>
> Philosopher David Hume, 1711–1776

TEACHING TIP

As preparation for the AP Exam, have students explain how a group can be positively and negatively influenced in a short paper. Students should be able to accurately describe social facilitation and, at times, group polarization on the positive side and social loafing, deindividuation, and groupthink on the negative side.

administration formulated the Marshall Plan, which offered assistance to Europe after World War II, and when the Kennedy administration worked to keep the Soviets from installing missiles in Cuba. In such instances—and in the business world, too, Janis believed—groupthink is prevented when a leader welcomes various opinions, invites experts' critiques of developing plans, and assigns people to identify possible problems. Just as the suppression of dissent bends a group toward bad decisions, so open debate often shapes good ones. This is especially so with diverse groups, whose varied perspectives enable creative or superior outcomes (Nemeth & Ormiston, 2007; Page, 2007). None of us is as smart as all of us.

Cultural Influence

6: How do cultural norms affect our behavior?

As social creatures, our human readiness to learn from and adapt to those around us includes the influences of our surrounding culture. We come equipped with a huge cerebral hard drive ready to receive many gigabytes of cultural software.

Culture is the behaviors, ideas, attitudes, values, and traditions shared by a group of people and transmitted from one generation to the next (Brislin, 1988). Human nature, notes Roy Baumeister (2005), seems designed for culture. We are social animals, but more. Wolves are social animals; they live and hunt in packs. Ants are incessantly social, never alone. But "culture is a better way of being social," notes Baumeister. Wolves function pretty much as they did 10,000 years ago. You and I enjoy things unknown to most of our century-ago ancestors, including electricity, indoor plumbing, antibiotics, and the Internet. Culture works.

Primates exhibit the rudiments of culture, with local customs of tool use, grooming, and courtship. Younger chimpanzees and macaque monkeys sometimes invent customs—potato washing, in one famous example—and pass them on to their peers and offspring. But human culture does more. It supports our species' survival and reproduction by enabling social and economic systems that give us an edge.

Thanks to our mastery of language, we humans enjoy the *preservation of innovation*. Within the span of this day, I have, thanks to my culture, made good use of Post-it Notes, Google, and a single-shot skinny latte. On a grander scale, we have culture's accumulated knowledge to thank for the last century's 30-year extension of the average life expectancy in most countries where this book is being read. Moreover, culture enables an efficient *division of labor*. Although one lucky person gets his name on this book's cover, the product actually results from the coordination and commitment of a team of women and men, no one of whom could produce it alone.

Across cultures, we differ in our language, our monetary systems, our sports, which fork—if any—we eat with, even which side of the road we drive on. But beneath these differences is our great similarity—our capacity for culture. Culture provides the shared and transmitted customs and beliefs that enable us to communicate, to exchange money for things, to play, to eat, and to drive with agreed-upon rules and without crashing into one another. This shared capacity for culture enables our striking group differences. Human nature manifests human diversity.

If we all lived in homogeneous ethnic groups in separate regions of the world, as some people still do, cultural diversity would be less relevant. In Japan, almost 99 percent of the country's 127 million people are of Japanese descent. Internal cultural differences are therefore minimal compared with those found in Los Angeles, where the public schools recently taught 82 different languages, or in Toronto or Vancouver, where minorities are one-third of the population and many are immigrants (as are 13.4 percent of all Canadians and 23 percent of Australians) (Axiss, 2007; Statistics Canada, 2002). I am ever mindful that the readers of this book are

> "If you have an apple and I have an apple and we exchange apples then you and I will still each have one apple. But if you have an idea and I have an idea and we exchange these ideas, then each of us will have two ideas."
>
> Attributed to dramatist George Bernard Shaw, 1856–1950

::**groupthink** the mode of thinking that occurs when the desire for harmony in a decision-making group overrides a realistic appraisal of alternatives.

::**culture** the enduring behaviors, ideas, attitudes, values, and traditions shared by a group of people and transmitted from one generation to the next.

RESEARCH

Have students do a character study of famous individuals who stood up against the majority to enact positive change, exploring the qualities and beliefs they possessed that enabled them to stand firm. Encourage students to find examples not found on this list that represent diverse cultural backgrounds:

- Martin Luther King, Jr.
- Che Guevara
- William Wallace (whose story was featured in the movie *Braveheart*)
- Martin Luther
- Galileo Galilei
- Joan of Arc

 TEACHING TIP

David Matsumoto defines culture not as nationalities or ethnic groups, but in regards to shared experiences. He says that the influential factors for determining a culture are as follows:

- Relative affluence. The relative wealth of people in a culture helps distinguish them from others.
- Population density. The conditions under which people live (crowded apartment buildings or wide, open prairies) help distinguish cultural groups.
- Technology access. How accessible technology (computers versus hand tools) is helps determine culture.
- Climate. Cultural practices can be largely determined by climate conditions—arid or wet, hot or cold.

 TEACHING TIP

At this time, you may want to use **Lecture/Discussion Topics:** *Understanding Cultural Differences in Relation to Individual Differences* (p. 18) or *The Geography of Time* (p. 19) or *Differences in Cultural Norms* (p. 20) or **Classroom Exercise:** *Intercultural Learning Activities* (p. 20) or **Classroom Exercise/Student Project:** *Cross-Cultural Dialogues* (p. 20) from Bolt's Teacher's Resource Binder.

UNIT 14

Cultures differ Behavior seen as appropriate in one culture may violate the norms of another group. In Arab societies, but not in Western cultures, men often greet one another with a kiss.

culturally diverse. Your ancestors reach from Australia to Africa and from Singapore to Sweden.

Variation Across Cultures

We see our adaptability in cultural variations among our beliefs and our values, in how we raise our children and bury our dead, and in what we wear (or whether we wear anything at all). Riding along with a unified culture is like biking with the wind: As it carries us along, we hardly notice it is there. When we try riding *against* the wind we feel its force. Face to face with a different culture, we become aware of the cultural winds. Visiting Europe, most North Americans notice the smaller cars, the left-handed use of the fork, the uninhibited attire on the beaches. Stationed in Iraq, Afghanistan, and Kuwait, American and European soldiers alike realized how liberal their home cultures were. Arriving in North America, visitors from Japan and India struggle to understand why so many people wear their dirty *street* shoes in the house.

Each cultural group evolves its own **norms**—rules for accepted and expected behavior. Many South Asians, for example, use only the right hand's fingers for eating. The British have a norm for orderly waiting in line. Sometimes social expectations seem oppressive: "Why should it matter how I dress?" Yet, norms grease the social machinery and free us from self-preoccupation. Knowing when to clap or bow, how to behave on the first day of school, and what sorts of gestures and compliments are appropriate—whether to greet people by shaking hands or kissing each cheek, for example—we can relax and enjoy one another without fear of embarrassment or insult.

When cultures collide, their differing norms often befuddle. For example, if someone invades our **personal space**—the portable buffer zone we like to maintain around our bodies—we feel uncomfortable. Scandinavians, North Americans, and the British have traditionally preferred more personal space than do Latin Americans, Arabs, and the French (Sommer, 1969). At a social gathering, a Mexican seeking a comfortable conversation distance may end up walking around a room with a backpedaling Canadian. (You can experience this at a party by playing Space Invader as you talk with someone.) To the Canadian, the Mexican may seem intrusive; to the Mexican, the Canadian may seem standoffish.

Cultures also vary in their expressiveness. Those with roots in northern European culture have perceived people from Mediterranean cultures as warm and charming but inefficient. The Mediterraneans, in turn, have seen northern Europeans as efficient but cold and preoccupied with punctuality (Triandis, 1981).

Cultures vary in their pace of life, too. People from time-conscious Japan—where bank clocks keep exact time, pedestrians walk briskly, and postal clerks fill requests speedily—may find themselves growing impatient when visiting Indonesia, where clocks keep less accurate time and the pace of life is more leisurely (Levine & Norenzayan, 1999). In adjusting to their host countries, the first wave of U.S. Peace Corps volunteers reported that two of their greatest culture shocks, after the language differences, were the differing pace of life and the people's differing sense of punctuality (Spradley & Phillips, 1972).

Variation Over Time

Consider, too, how rapidly cultures may change over time. English poet Geoffrey Chaucer (1342–1400) is separated from a modern Briton by only 20 generations, but the two would converse with great difficulty. In the thin slice of history since 1960, most Western cultures have changed with remarkable speed. Middle-class people fly to places they once only read about, text those they once postal-mailed, and work in air-conditioned comfort where they once sweltered. They enjoy the convenience of online shopping, anywhere-anytime electronic communication, and—enriched by

TEACHING TIP

Have students explore culturally specific behaviors and customs. They can interview people from that culture, look up information about that culture on the Internet, or research different books that contain cultural information. These differences in culture that are uncovered should help students understand diverse cultural traditions.

RESEARCH

Have students conduct an informal survey of their friends, family, and neighbors to see what they consider to be rude within their culture:

- What do you consider rude? Why do you consider it rude?
- What kind of politeness to you expect from others? Why?
- Do you confront people who are rude or impolite? Why or why not?

CULTURAL CONNECTIONS

Have students write a reflective paper about their cultural experiences. Recall your first (or a recent) experience of cultural difference. How did it happen? How did you feel? Given the importance of cultural context, explain how the following may be considered ethnic and cultural stumbling blocks:

- Language and nonverbal communications
- Ethnocentricity
- Culture- and class-related values
- Racism and stereotypes

Adapted from Ernst, R. M. (1997, January). *A Matter of Context.* Presentation to the National Institute for the Teaching of Psychology, St. Petersburg, FL.

doubled per-person real income—eating out more than twice as often as did their elders back in the culture of 1960. With greater economic independence, today's women are more likely to marry for love and less likely to endure abusive relationships out of economic need. Many minority groups enjoy expanded human rights.

But some changes seem not so wonderfully positive. Had you fallen asleep in the United States in 1960 and awakened today, you would open your eyes to a culture with more divorce, delinquency, and depression. You would also find North Americans—like their counterparts in Britain, Australia, and New Zealand—spending more hours at work, fewer hours sleeping, and fewer hours with friends and family (Frank, 1999; Putnam, 2000).

Whether we love or loathe these changes, we cannot fail to be impressed by their breathtaking speed. And we cannot explain them by changes in the human gene pool, which evolves far too slowly to account for high-speed cultural transformations. Cultures vary. Cultures change. And cultures shape our lives.

The Power of Individuals

7: How much power do we have as individuals? Can a minority sway a majority?

In affirming the power of social influence, we must not overlook our power as individuals. *Social control* (the power of the situation) and *personal control* (the power of the individual) interact. People aren't sheep. When feeling pressured, we may react by doing the opposite of what is expected, thereby reasserting our sense of freedom (Brehm & Brehm, 1981).

Three individual soldiers asserted their personal control in response to the abuse of Iraqi prisoners at Abu Ghraib prison (O'Connor, 2004). Lt. David Sutton put an end to one incident, which he reported to his commanders. Navy dog-handler William Kimbro refused pressure to participate in improper interrogations using his attack dogs. Specialist Joseph Darby brought visual images of the horrors into the light of day, providing incontestable evidence of the atrocities. Each risked ridicule or even court-martial for not following orders.

As these three soldiers discovered, committed individuals can sway the majority and make social history. Were this not so, communism would have remained an obscure theory, Christianity would be a small Middle Eastern sect, and Rosa Parks' refusal to sit at the back of the bus would not have ignited the U.S. civil rights movement. Technological history, too, is often made by innovative minorities who overcome the majority's resistance to change. To many, the railroad was a nonsensical idea; some farmers even feared that train noise would prevent hens from laying eggs. People derided Robert Fulton's steamboat as "Fulton's Folly." As Fulton later said, "Never did a single encouraging remark, a bright hope, a warm wish, cross my path." Much the same reaction greeted the printing press, the telegraph, the incandescent lamp, and the typewriter (Cantril & Bumstead, 1960).

European social psychologists have sought to better understand *minority influence*—the power of one or two individuals to sway majorities (Moscovici, 1985). They investigated groups in which one or two individuals consistently expressed a controversial attitude or an unusual perceptual judgment. They repeatedly found that a minority that unswervingly holds to its position is far more successful in swaying the majority than is a minority that waffles. Holding consistently to a minority opinion will not make you popular, but it may make you influential. This is especially so if your self-confidence stimulates others to consider why you react as you do.

::**norm** an understood rule for accepted and expected behavior. Norms prescribe "proper" behavior.

::**personal space** the buffer zone we like to maintain around our bodies.

Margaret Bourke-White/*Life* Magazine. © 1946 Time Warner, Inc.

Gandhi As the life of Hindu nationalist and spiritual leader Mahatma Gandhi powerfully testifies, a consistent and persistent minority voice can sometimes sway the majority. Gandhi's nonviolent appeals and fasts were instrumental in winning India's independence from Britain in 1947.
▲

TEACHING TIP

This unit primarily focuses on ways in which groups influence behavior negatively. Students may miss the ways in which group influence can be positive. Have students create a chart in which they list the ways in which groups influence individuals both positively and negatively. This may help them understand the nuances of these concepts.

TEACHING TIP

Remind students that it only takes one voice to break conformity. This may explain why these individuals were able to stand against such significant foes.

TEACHING TIP

At this time, you may want to use **Student Project:** *A Personal Cultural History* (p. 21) from Bolt's Teacher's Resource Binder.

UNIT 14

TROUBLESHOOTING

Adults who lived through the civil rights movement know that prejudice and discrimination involved clashes among people of different racial or ethnic groups. Today, students are confronted with prejudice and discrimination based on religion, race, ethnicity, sexual orientation, and body type. Help students see the varied ways people hold prejudices and discriminate against each other. This will help them apply studies regarding one type of prejudice with another.

::**prejudice** an unjustifiable (and usually negative) attitude toward a group and its members. Prejudice generally involves stereotyped beliefs, negative feelings, and a predisposition to discriminatory action.

::**stereotype** a generalized (sometimes accurate but often overgeneralized) belief about a group of people.

::**discrimination** unjustifiable negative *behavior* toward a group and its members.

Although people often follow the majority view publicly, they may privately develop sympathy for the minority view. Even when a minority's influence is not yet visible, it may be persuading some members of the majority to rethink their views (Wood et al., 1994). The powers of social influence are enormous, but so are the powers of the committed individual.

BEFORE YOU MOVE ON . . .

➤ **ASK YOURSELF**

What two examples of social influence have you experienced this week? (Remember, influence may be informational.)

➤ **TEST YOURSELF 2**

You are organizing a Town Hall–style meeting of fiercely competitive political candidates. To add to the fun, friends have suggested handing out masks of the candidates' faces for supporters to wear. What phenomenon might these masks engage?

Answers to the Test Yourself questions can be found in Appendix E at the end of the book.

Social Relations

WE HAVE SAMPLED HOW WE *THINK* about and *influence* one another. Now we come to social psychology's third focus—how we *relate* to one another. What causes us to harm or to help or to fall in love? How can we move a destructive conflict toward a just peace? We will ponder the bad and the good: from prejudice and aggression to attraction, altruism, and peacemaking.

Prejudice

8: What is prejudice?

Prejudice means "prejudgment." It is an unjustifiable and usually negative attitude toward a group—often a different cultural, ethnic, or gender group. Like all attitudes, **prejudice** is a mixture of *beliefs* (in this case called **stereotypes**), *emotions* (hostility, envy, or fear), and predispositions to *action* (to **discriminate**). To *believe* that obese people are gluttonous, to *feel* dislike for an obese person, and to be hesitant to hire or date an obese person is to be prejudiced. Prejudice is a negative *attitude;* discrimination is a negative *behavior*.

How Prejudiced Are People?

To learn about levels of prejudice, we can assess what people say and what they do. Judging by what Americans say, gender and racial attitudes have changed dramatically in the last half-century. The one-third of Americans who in 1937 told Gallup they would vote for a qualified woman whom their party nominated for president soared to 89 percent in 2007. Support for all forms of racial contact, including interracial marriage (**FIGURE 14.6**), has also dramatically increased. Nearly everyone agrees that children of all races should attend the same schools and that women and men should receive the same pay for the same job.

Yet as *overt* prejudice wanes, *subtle* prejudice lingers. Despite increased verbal support for interracial marriage, many people admit that in socially intimate settings (dating, dancing, marrying) they would feel uncomfortable with someone of another

TEACHING TIP

In 1942, fewer than one-third of whites supported school integration. Today, nearly everyone agrees that children of all races should attend the same schools. Still, prejudice persists. Opinions about interracial contacts reveal prejudice. In one survey, only 3 percent of whites wouldn't want their child to attend an integrated school, but 57 percent would be unhappy if their child married a black person.

Patterson, J., & Kim, P. (1991). *The day America told the truth*. New York: Prentice Hall.

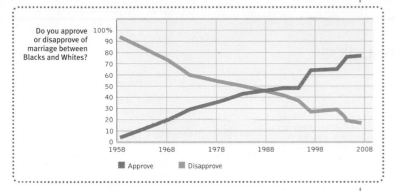

➤ FIGURE 14.6
Prejudice over time Americans' approval of interracial marriage has soared over the past half-century. (Gallup surveys reported by Carroll, 2007.)

INTERCONNECTING

Link this discussion of prejudice with framing, as discussed in Unit 7B. People will respond in a prejudiced fashion or not, depending on how the situation is framed. If we are aware of the effects of framing, we are less likely to succumb to it.

race. And in Western Europe, where many "guest workers" and refugees settled at the end of the twentieth century, "modern prejudice"—rejecting immigrant minorities as job applicants for supposedly nonracial reasons—has been replacing blatant prejudice (Jackson et al., 2001; Lester, 2004; Pettigrew, 1998, 2006). A slew of recent experiments illustrates that prejudice can be not only subtle but also automatic and unconscious (see Close-Up: Automatic Prejudice, next page).

Nevertheless, overt prejudice still surfaces in public settings. In several U.S. states where Black motorists are a minority of the drivers and speeders on interstate highways, they have been the majority of those stopped and searched by state police (Lamberth, 1998; Staples, 1999a,b). In the Los Angeles area, 1115 landlords received identically worded e-mails from a would-be tenant (actually a researcher) expressing interest in vacant apartments advertised online. Encouraging replies came back to 56 percent of notes signed "Tyrell Jackson," to 66 percent signed "Said Al-Rahman," and to 89 percent of those signed "Patrick McDougall" (Carpusor & Loges, 2006).

In the aftermath of 9/11 and the Iraq war, 4 in 10 Americans acknowledged "some feelings of prejudice against Muslims," and about half of non-Muslims in Western Europe and the United States perceived Muslims as "violent" (Saad, 2006; Wike & Grim, 2007). Muslims reciprocated the negativity, with most in Jordan, Egypt, Turkey, and Britain seeing Westerners as "greedy" and "immoral."

In most places in the world, gays and lesbians cannot comfortably acknowledge who they are and whom they love. Gender prejudice and discrimination persist, too. Despite gender equality in intelligence scores, people tend to perceive their fathers as more intelligent than their mothers (Furnham & Rawles, 1995). In Saudi Arabia, women are not allowed to drive. In Western countries, we pay more to those (usually men) who drive machines that take care of our streets than to those (usually women) who take care of our children. Worldwide, women are more likely to live in poverty (Lipps, 1999), and their 69 percent literacy rate is well below men's 83 percent (PRB, 2002).

Female infants are no longer left out on a hillside to die of exposure, as was the practice in ancient Greece. Yet even today boys are often valued more than their sisters. With testing that enables sex-selective abortions, several south Asian countries, including certain regions of China and India, have experienced a shortfall in female births. Natural female mortality and the normal male-to-female newborn ratio (105-to-100) hardly explain the world's estimated 101 million (say that number slowly) "missing women" (Sen, 2003). In 2005, China's newborn sex ratio reportedly reached 118 boys for every 100 girls (AP, 2007). With demographic predictions of 40 million Chinese bachelors unable to find mates, China has declared that sex-selective abortions—gender genocide—are now a criminal offense.

"Unhappily the world has yet to learn how to live with diversity."

Pope John Paul II,
Address to the United Nations, 1995

• In the aftermath of China's one-child social policy and sex-selective abortions, the looming excess of young Chinese men may impact Chinese society. Imbalanced population sex ratios have historically influenced gender roles. Places with a shortage of unmarried women have stressed sexual morality and traditional women's roles (Guttentag & Secord, 1983). Such places—with lots of unmarried men, as in some frontier towns, immigrant ghettos, and mining camps—have also tended to have high violence rates (Hvistendahl, 2008). •

WEB CONNECT

Have students prepare a one- to two-page profile of one of the hate groups described on the www.tolerance.org Web site, which is a project of the Southern Poverty Law Center.

- How are the beliefs of this particular group prejudiced? What stereotypes do they hold and against whom?

- What type of discrimination do they recommend people take against those they hate?

- Does the First Amendment protect this type of behavior? Why or why not?

UNIT 14

Automatic Prejudice

As we have seen throughout this book, we process information on two levels: conscious and unconscious. To some extent, our thinking, our memories, and our attitudes are *explicit*—on the radar screen of our awareness. And to an even greater extent, to-day's researchers believe, they are *implicit*—below the radar, out of sight. Modern studies of implicit, automatic attitudes indicate that prejudice is often more of an unthinking knee-jerk response than a decision. Consider these findings on U.S. racial prejudice:

Implicit racial associations Asked to tap keys to associate words and images, people more quickly associate positive words such as *happy* or *peace* with positive objects such as flowers, and negative words such as *rotten* or *ugly* with insects. Extend-ing these Implicit Association Tests, Anthony Greenwald and his colleagues (1998) showed that even people who deny harboring racial prejudice may carry negative associations. For example, 9 in 10 White respondents took longer to identify pleasant words (such as *peace* and *paradise*) as "good" when presented with Black-sounding names (such as *Latisha* and *Darnell*) rather than White-sounding names (such as *Katie* and *Ian*). Moreover, peo-ple who more quickly associate good things with White names or faces also are the quickest to perceive anger and apparent threat in Black faces (Hugenberg & Bodenhausen, 2003). (By 2008, more than 6 million people had taken the Implicit Asso-ciation Test, as you can at www.implicit.harvard.edu.)

Unconscious patronization Kent Harber (1998) asked White university women to evaluate a flawed essay said to be written by a Black or a White fellow student. When they believed the writer was Black, the women gave markedly higher ratings and never ex-pressed the harsh criticisms they assigned to White-authored es-says, such as "When I read college work this bad I just want to lay my head down on the table and cry." Did the evaluators calibrate their evaluations to their racial stereotypes, Harber wondered, leading them to patronize the Black writers with less exacting standards? If used in real-world evaluations, such low expecta-tions and the resulting "inflated praise and insufficient criticism" could hinder minority student achievement. (To preclude such bias, many teachers read essays while "blind" to their authors.)

Race-influenced perceptions Two research teams were in-terested in the shooting of an unarmed man in the doorway of his Bronx apartment building by officers who mistook his wal-let for a gun. Each research team reenacted the situation with a video, asking viewers to press buttons quickly to "shoot" or not shoot men who suddenly appeared on screen holding either a gun or a harmless object such as a flashlight or bottle (Correll et al., 2002, 2007; Greenwald et al., 2003). People (both Blacks and Whites, in one of the studies) more often mistakenly shot targets who were Black. Priming people with a flashed Black rather than White face also makes them more likely then to misperceive a flashed tool as a gun (**FIGURE 14.7**).

Seeing Black Several studies show that the more a person's features are perceived as typical of their racial category, the more likely they are to elicit race-based responding (Maddox, 2004). In one study of 182 police officers, Jennifer Eberhardt and her collab-

"There are still barriers and biases out there, often unconscious."

> Senator Hillary Rodham Clinton, 2008 U.S. presidential primary concession speech

orators (2004; 2006) found that "Black faces looked more criminal to police officers; the more Black, the more criminal." In a follow-up study, they found people more willing to give the death sentence to Black defendants having the most stereotypically Black features.

Reflexive bodily responses Today's biopsychosocial ap-proach has stimulated neuroscience studies that measure peo-ple's instant responses to viewing White and Black faces. These studies have detected implicit prejudice in people's facial-mus-cle responses and in the activation of their amygdala, the emo-tion-processing center (Cunningham et al., 2004; Eberhardt, 2005; Vanman et al., 2004). Even people who consciously ex-press little prejudice may give off telltale signals as their body responds selectively to another's race.

If your own gut check sometimes reveals feelings you would rather not have about other people, be assured that you are not alone. It is what we do with our feelings that matters. By monitoring our feelings and actions, and by replacing old hab-its with new ones based on new friendships, we can work to free ourselves from prejudice.

> **FIGURE 14.7**

Race primes perceptions In experiments by Keith Payne (2006), people viewed a White or Black face, immediately fol-lowed by a gun or hand tool, which was then quickly obscured by a "visual mask" on the screen. Participants were more likely to misperceive a tool as a gun when it was preceded by a Black rather than White face.

Visual mask

INTERCONNECTING

Link stereotyping to Jean Piaget's concept of schema (Unit 9). As children, we categorize the world around us into schemas. We form schemas for everything, from people to animals to plants. When we learn something new, we assimilate that information into our existing schemas. When what we learn conflicts with a schema, we will need to adjust our schemas through a process called accom-modation. Hopefully, prejudiced schemas are accommodated quickly when we learn positive qualities about a person or group of people!

WEB CONNECT

Students can test their own implicit prejudices with the Harvard Implicit Association Test (IAT) found online at http://implicit.harvard.edu. The researchers have posted several versions of the IAT, including items that test for age, gender-career, Arab-Muslim, disability, Native American/Alaska Native, race, reli-gion, and weight prejudices.

TEACHING TIP

At this time, you may want to use **Lecture/Discussion Topic:** *Racial Prejudice* (p. 22) or **Classroom Exercises:** *Subtle Prejudice and the Ambivalent Sexism Inventory* (p. 23) from Bolt's Teacher's Resource Binder.

DEMO

Divide students into homogeneous groups according to race, gender, or school group affiliation (band members, athletes, drama members, etc.). Have them write down the positive and negative stereotypes others have for their group.

- Which parts of the stereotype do you like? Which do you not like?
- Do all members of your group fit the stereotypes? Why or why not?
- How can your group communicate to others that its members don't necessarily all fit the stereotype?

Suppose that you could only have one child. Would you prefer that it be a boy or a girl? When Gallup asked that question of Americans, two-thirds expressed a gender preference, and for two-thirds of those—in 2003 as in 1941—it was for a boy (Lyons, 2003).

But the news isn't all bad for girls and women. Most people also *feel* more positively about women in general than they do about men (Eagly, 1994; Haddock & Zanna, 1994). People worldwide see women as having some traits (such as nurturance, sensitivity, and less aggressiveness) that most people prefer (Glick et al., 2004; Swim, 1994). That may explain why women tend to like women more than men like men (Rudman & Goodwin, 2004). And perhaps that is also why people prefer slightly feminized computer-generated faces—men's and women's—to slightly masculinized faces. Researcher David Perrett and his colleagues (1998) speculate that a slightly feminized male face connotes kindness, cooperativeness, and other traits of a good father. When the British Broadcasting Corporation invited 18,000 women to guess which of the men in **FIGURE 14.8** was most likely to place a personal ad seeking "a special lady to love and cherish forever," which one do you think they picked?

Social Roots of Prejudice

9: What are the social and emotional roots of prejudice?

Why does prejudice arise? Inequalities, social divisions, and emotional scapegoating are partly responsible.

Social Inequalities When some people have money, power, and prestige and others do not, the "haves" usually develop attitudes that justify things as they are. In the extreme case, slave "owners" perceived slaves as innately lazy, ignorant, and irresponsible—as having the very traits that "justified" enslaving them. More commonly, women have been perceived as unassertive but sensitive and therefore suited for the caretaking tasks they have traditionally performed (Hoffman & Hurst, 1990). In short, stereotypes rationalize inequalities.

Discrimination also increases stereotyping and prejudice through the reactions it provokes in its victims. In his classic 1954 book, *The Nature of Prejudice*, Gordon Allport noted that being a victim of discrimination can produce either self-blame or anger. Both reactions may create new grounds for prejudice through the classic *blame-the-victim* dynamic. If the circumstances of poverty breed a higher crime rate, someone can then use the higher crime rate to justify continuing the discrimination against those who live in poverty.

Us and Them: Ingroup and Outgroup Thanks to our ancestral need to belong, we are a group bound species. Our ancestors, living in a world where neighboring tribes occasionally raided and pillaged one another's camps, knew that there was safety in solidarity (those who didn't band together left fewer descendants). Whether hunting, defending, or attacking, 10 hands were better than 2. Dividing the world into "us" and "them" entails racism and war, but it also provides the benefits of communal solidarity. Thus we cheer for our groups, kill for them, die for them. Indeed, we

(a)   (b)

Professor Dave Perrett, St. Andrews University

➤ **FIGURE 14.8**
Who do you like best? Which one placed an ad seeking "a special lady to love and cherish forever"? (Answer below.)

Research suggests that subtly feminized features convey a likable image, which people tend to associate more with committed dads than with promiscuous cads. Thus, 66 percent of the women picked computer-generated face (b) in response to both of these questions.

▼ **French fury** Members of France's marginalized ethnic groups reached the tipping point for tolerance in 2005, when they began destructive rioting

Eric Travers/EPA/Landov

UNIT 14

TROUBLESHOOTING

Remind students that sometimes having a group identity is desirable. Sports teams and performing groups like the choir or band would be less effective if everyone didn't dress the same or bond on a personal level.

DEMO

Illustrate how easy it is to fall victim to ingroup bias. Divide the class on the basis of some arbitrary characteristic (wearing sneakers or having blue eyes), making sure that at least one-third of the students are in a given group. When you have defined the groups, have them sit together. Ask each group to compile a list of reasons why those in the other group are not like them.

Each group usually begins by listing neutral reasons, which quickly become more derogatory. If the groups overhear each other's less complimentary reasons, the hostility heightens. At the end of the exercise, the groups should share their lists. Students quickly learn how easily we categorize and develop ingroup bias.

Teaching in the psychological sciences (TIPS-Online Discussion Group), Mueller, J. (1995, February 11). *Teaching about prejudice and discrimination.*

▼ **The ingroup** Basketball fans, shown here from my own college during a game against their archrival, share a social identity that defines "us" (the ingroup) and "them" (the outgroup).

"All good people agree,
And all good people say
All nice people, like Us, are We
And every one else is They.
But if you cross over the sea
Instead of over the way
You may end by (think of it)
Looking on We
As only a sort of They."

Rudyard Kipling, "We and They," 1926

define who we are—our identities—partly in terms of our groups. Australian psychologists John Turner (1987, 2007) and Michael Hogg (1996, 2006) note that through our *social identities* we associate ourselves with certain groups and contrast ourselves with others. When Ian identifies himself as a man, an Aussie, a Labourite, a University of Sydney student, a Catholic, and a MacGregor, he knows who he is, and so do we.

Ironically, we often reserve our most intense dislike for outgroup rivals most like us. Freud (1922, p. 42) long ago recognized that animosities formed around small differences: "Of two neighboring towns, each is the other's most jealous rival; every little canton looks down upon the others with contempt. Closely related races keep one another at arm's length; the South German cannot endure the North German, the Englishman casts every kind of aspersion upon the Scot, the Spaniard despises the Portuguese." In surveys, 7 in 10 Japanese express an unfavorable view of China, and 7 in 10 Chinese similarly dislike Japan (Pew, 2006). Hostilities between the Iraqi Sunni and Shia, the Rwandan Hutu and Tutsi, and the Northern Ireland Protestant and Catholic have pitted ingroups against outgroups who, on a world diversity scale, are much more alike than different.

As an occasional resident of Scotland, I've witnessed many examples of *The Xenophobe's Guide to the Scots* observation—that Scots divide non-Scots "into two main groups: (1) The English; (2) The Rest." As rabid Chicago Cubs fans are happy if either the Cubs win or the Chicago White Sox lose, so rabid fans of Scottish soccer rejoice in either a Scotland victory or an England defeat. "Phew! They lost," rejoiced one Scottish tabloid's front-page headline after England's 1996 Euro Cup defeat—by Germany, no less. Perhaps you, too, can recall being most conscious of your school identity when competing with an archrival school.

Numerical minorities, such as the Scots in Britain, are especially conscious of their social identities. The 5 million Scots are more conscious of their national identity vis-à-vis the neighboring 51 million English than vice versa. Likewise, the 4 million New Zealanders are more conscious of their identity vis-à-vis the 21 million Australians, and they are more likely to root for Australia's sports opponents (Halberstadt et al., 2006).

The social definition of who we are also implies who we are not. Mentally drawing a circle that defines "us" (the **ingroup**) excludes "them" (the **outgroup**). Such group identifications typically promote an **ingroup bias**—a favoring of one's own group. Even arbitrarily creating an us-them distinction—by grouping people with the toss of a coin—leads people to show favoritism to their own group when dividing any rewards (Tajfel, 1982; Wilder, 1981).

The urge to distinguish enemies from friends and to have one's group be dominant predisposes prejudice against strangers (Whitley, 1999). To Greeks of the classical era, all non-Greeks were "barbarians." In our own era, most children believe their school is better than all other schools in town. Many high school students form cliques—jocks, emos, skaters, gangsters, freaks, geeks—and disparage those outside their own group. Even chimpanzees have been seen to wipe clean the spot where they were touched by a chimpanzee from another group (Goodall, 1986).

Emotional Roots of Prejudice

Prejudice springs not only from the divisions of society but also from the passions of the heart. Facing the terror of death tends to heighten patriotism and produce loathing

CRITICAL THINKING ?

Most schools have loosely defined cliques that separate people. Have students brainstorm about the different cliques that exist in your school, noting particular behaviors that set each group apart:

- How many different cliques are there in your school? What defines these groups?
- How do these groups differentiate themselves from the others?
- Where do these groups hang out during down times at school? Where do they eat lunch? If someone from another group or a new kid enters their areas, how do they react?

and aggression toward "them"—those who threaten one's world (Pyszczynski et al., 2002). Recalling such terror may alter attitudes, as happened to participants when Mark Landau and eight others (2004) reminded them of their own mortality or of the terror of 9/11. This terror reminder led to their expressing increased support for then-President George W. Bush.

Prejudice may also express anger. According to the **scapegoat theory** of prejudice, finding someone to blame when things go wrong can provide a target for one's anger. Following 9/11, some outraged people lashed out at innocent Arab-Americans, about whom negative stereotypes blossomed. Calls to eliminate Saddam Hussein, whom Americans had been grudgingly tolerating, also increased. "Fear and anger create aggression, and aggression against citizens of different ethnicity or race creates racism and, in turn, new forms of terrorism," noted Philip Zimbardo (2001).

Evidence for the scapegoat theory comes from high prejudice levels among economically frustrated people and from experiments in which a temporary frustration intensifies prejudice. In experiments, students who experience failure or are made to feel insecure will often restore their self-esteem by disparaging a rival school or another person (Cialdini & Richardson, 1980; Crocker et al., 1987). To boost our own sense of status, it helps to have others to denigrate. That is why a rival's misfortune sometimes provides a twinge of pleasure. By contrast, those made to feel loved and supported become more open to and accepting of others who differ (Mikulincer & Shaver, 2001).

Cognitive Roots of Prejudice

10: What are the cognitive roots of prejudice?

Prejudice springs not only from a culture's divisions and the heart's passions, but also from the mind's natural workings. Stereotyped beliefs are a by-product of how we cognitively simplify the world.

Categorization One way we simplify our world is to categorize. A chemist categorizes molecules as organic and inorganic. A football coach categorizes offensive players as running backs, linemen, or receivers. A mental health professional categorizes psychological disorders by types. In categorizing people into groups, however, we often stereotype them, biasing our perceptions of their diversity. We recognize how greatly *we* differ from other individuals in *our* groups. But we overestimate the similarity of those within other groups (we perceive *outgroup homogeneity*). "They"—the members of some other group—seem to look and act alike, but "we" are diverse (Bothwell et al., 1989). To those in one ethnic group, members of another often seem more alike than they really are in appearance, personality, and attitudes. This greater recognition for own-race faces—called the **other-race effect,** or *own-race bias*—emerges during infancy, between 3 and 9 months of age (Kelly et al., 2007).

With experience, however, people get better at recognizing individual faces from another group. People of European descent, for example, more accurately identify individual African faces if they have watched a great deal of basketball on television, exposing them to many African-heritage faces (Li et al., 1996). And the longer Chinese people have resided in a Western country, the less they exhibit the other-race effect (Hancock & Rhodes, 2008).

Vivid Cases As we saw in Unit 7B, we often judge the frequency of events by instances that readily come to mind. In a classic experiment, Myron Rothbart and his colleagues (1978) demonstrated this ability to overgeneralize from vivid, memorable cases. They divided University of Oregon student volunteers into two groups, then showed them information about 50 men. The first group's list included 10 men arrested for nonviolent

> "If the Tiber reaches the walls, if the Nile does not rise to the fields, if the sky doesn't move or the Earth does, if there is famine, if there is plague, the cry is at once: 'The Christians to the lion!'"
>
> Tertullian, *Apologeticus*, 197 C.E.

• One seeming antidote to prejudice is intelligence. In a large national study, British children with high intelligence scores at age 10 typically expressed low prejudice at age 30 (Deary et al., 2008). •

::**ingroup** "Us"—people with whom we share a common identity.

::**outgroup** "Them"—those perceived as different or apart from our ingroup.

::**ingroup bias** the tendency to favor our own group.

::**scapegoat theory** the theory that prejudice offers an outlet for anger by providing someone to blame.

::**other-race effect** the tendency to recall faces of one's own race more accurately than faces of other races. Also called the *cross-race effect* and the *own-race bias*.

CULTURAL CONNECTIONS

The term "scapegoat" comes from the Hebrew tradition of Yom Kippur. According to the Torah, on Yom Kippur, the Day of Atonement for the people of Israel, the high priest would designate a goat which would symbolically bear the sins of the entire nation. This goat would then be sent out into the wilderness to fend for itself, carrying away the sins of the people for another year.

INTERCONNECTING

Remind students that the term for making judgments based on vivid cases is called the "availability heuristic" (Unit 7B).

TEACHING TIP

At this time, you may want to use **Classroom Exercises: Ingroup Bias** (p. 24) or ***Belief in a Just World*** (p. 25) or **Classroom Exercise/Student Project: *Measuring Stereotypes*** (p. 21) from Bolt's Teacher's Resource Binder.

TEACHING TIP

The other-race effect (or outgroup homogeneity) comes into play when people are giving descriptions of people from other races. People tend to focus on the traits that typically differentiate people within their own race. For instance, White people tend to focus on traits like hair and eye color when describing others, which can be meaningless when describing Blacks or Asians, most of whom share similar hair and eye color.

CRITICAL THINKING

Recently, Lakshmi Raman and Gerald Winer reported that some adults believe physical illness can be a payback for bad behavior. Even victims themselves may attribute their serious illness to bad choices. Just weeks before his death from pancreatic cancer, actor Michael Landon stated,

> "I think I have it because for most of my life, though I was never a drunk, I drank too much. I also smoked too many cigarettes and ate a lot of wrong things. And if you do that, even if you think you are too strong to get anything, somehow you're going to pay."

- Do you believe that illness is payback for mistakes in life? For example, do you think that AIDS is a punishment for people who have lived a risky life? Would this apply to all people with AIDS? Why or why not?

- If you were diagnosed with a terminal illness, would you wonder what you did to deserve such an illness? Why or why not?

➤ **FIGURE 14.9**

Vivid cases feed stereotypes The 9/11 Muslim terrorists created, in many minds, an exaggerated stereotype of Muslims as terror-prone. Actually, reported a U.S. National Research Council panel on terrorism, when offering the inexact illustration at right, most terrorists are not Muslim and "the vast majority of Islamic people have no connection with and do not sympathize with terrorism" (Smelser & Mitchell, 2002).

::just-world phenomenon the tendency for people to believe the world is just and that people therefore get what they deserve and deserve what they get.

::aggression any physical or verbal behavior intended to hurt or destroy.

crimes, such as forgery. The second group's list included 10 men arrested for violent crimes, such as assault. Later, when both groups recalled how many men on their list had committed any sort of crime, the second group overestimated the number. Vivid (violent) cases are readily available to our memory and therefore influence our judgments of a group (**FIGURE 14.9**).

The Just-World Phenomenon As we noted earlier, people often justify their prejudice by blaming its victims. Bystanders, too, may blame victims by assuming the world is just and therefore "people get what they deserve." In experiments, merely observing someone receive painful shocks has led many people to think less of the victim (Lerner, 1980). This **just-world phenomenon** reflects an idea we commonly teach our children—that good is rewarded and evil is punished. From this it is but a short leap to assume that those who succeed must be good and those who suffer must be bad. Such reasoning enables the rich to see both their own wealth and the poor's misfortune as justly deserved. As one German civilian is said to have remarked when visiting the Bergen-Belsen concentration camp shortly after World War II, "What terrible criminals these prisoners must have been to receive such treatment."

Hindsight bias is also at work here (Carli & Leonard, 1989). Have you ever heard people say that rape victims, abused spouses, or people with AIDS got what they deserved? In some countries, women who have been raped have been sentenced to severe punishment for having violated a law against adultery (Mydans, 2002). An experiment by Ronnie Janoff-Bulman and her collaborators (1985) illustrates this phenomenon of blaming the victim. When given a detailed account of a date that ended with the woman being raped, people perceived the woman's behavior as at least partly to blame. In hindsight, they thought, "She should have known better." (Blaming the victim also serves to reassure people that it couldn't happen to them.) Others, given the same account with the rape ending deleted, did not perceive the woman's behavior as inviting rape.

Aggression

The most destructive force in our social relations is aggression. In psychology, *aggression* has a more precise meaning than it does in everyday usage. The assertive, persistent salesperson is not aggressive. Nor is the dentist who makes you wince with pain. But the person who passes along a vicious rumor about you, the person who verbally assaults you, and the attacker who mugs you are aggressive. Thus, to a psychologist, **aggression** is any physical or verbal behavior intended to hurt or destroy, whether done reactively out of hostility or proactively as a calculated means to an end. Thus, murders and assaults that occurred as hostile outbursts are aggression. So were the 110 million war-related deaths that took place during the last century, many of which were cool and calculated.

TEACHING TIP

In a test of the just-world phenomenon, you could have students participate in a study presumably on the perception of emotional cues. One of the participants (actually a confederate) would be selected to perform a memory task. She would receive what appears to be a painful shock for each error; the other students would be asked to observe and note her emotional responses. Do you think the students would respond with compassion and sympathy? No. Results from similar experiments indicate that when the observers are powerless to alter her fate, they tend to reject and devalue her. Subsequent research has suggested that this is particularly true of those who have a strong belief in a just world.

Aggression research shows that behavior emerges from the interaction of biology and experience. For a gun to fire, the trigger must be pulled; with some people, as with hair-trigger guns, it doesn't take much to trip an explosion. Let us look first at biological factors that influence our thresholds for aggressive behavior, then at the psychological factors that pull the trigger.

The Biology of Aggression

11: What biological factors make us more prone to hurt one another?

Aggression varies too widely from culture to culture, era to era, and person to person to be considered an unlearned instinct. But biology does *influence* aggression. Stimuli that trigger aggressive behavior operate through our biological system. We can look for biological influences at three levels—genetic, neural, and biochemical. Our genes engineer our individual nervous systems, which operate electrochemically.

Genetic Influences Animals have been bred for aggressiveness—sometimes for sport, sometimes for research. Pit bulls and cocker spaniels are formed by differing genes. Twin studies suggest that genes influence human aggression as well (Miles & Carey, 1997; Rowe et al., 1999). If one identical twin admits to "having a violent temper," the other twin will often independently admit the same. Fraternal twins are much less likely to respond similarly. Researchers are now searching for genetic markers found in those who commit the most violence. (One is already well known and is carried by half the human race: the Y chromosome.)

Neural Influences Animal and human brains have neural systems that, when stimulated, either inhibit or produce aggressive behavior (Moyer, 1983). Consider:

- The domineering leader of a caged monkey colony had a radio-controlled electrode implanted in a brain area that, when stimulated, inhibits aggression. When researchers placed the button that activated the electrode in the colony's cage, one small monkey learned to push it every time the boss became threatening.

- A mild-mannered woman had an electrode implanted in her brain's limbic system (in the amygdala) by neurosurgeons seeking to diagnose a disorder. Because the brain has no sensory receptors, she was unable to feel the stimulation. But at the flick of a switch she snarled, "Take my blood pressure. Take it now," then stood up and began to strike the doctor.

- One intensive evaluation of 15 death-row inmates revealed that all 15 had suffered a severe head injury. Although most neurologically impaired people are not violent, researcher Dorothy Lewis and her colleagues (1986) inferred that unrecognized neurological disorders may be one ingredient in the violence recipe. Other studies of violent criminals have revealed diminished activity in the frontal lobes, which play an important role in controlling impulses (Amen et al., 1996; Davidson et al., 2000; Raine, 1999, 2005).

So, does the brain have a "violence center" that produces aggression when stimulated? Actually, no one spot in the brain controls aggression, because aggression is a complex behavior that occurs in particular contexts. Rather, the brain has neural systems that, given provocation, will *facilitate* aggression. And it has a frontal lobe system for inhibiting aggression, making aggression more likely if this system is damaged, inactive, disconnected, or not yet fully mature.

Biochemical Influences Hormones, alcohol, and other substances in the blood influence the neural systems that control aggression. A raging bull will become a

In the last 40 years in the United States, well over 1 million people—more than all deaths in all wars in American history—have been killed by firearms in nonwar settings. Compared with people of the same sex, race, age, and neighborhood, those who keep a gun in the home (ironically, often for protection) are nearly three times more likely to be murdered in the home—nearly always by a family member or close acquaintance. For every self-defense use of a gun in the home, there are 4 unintentional shootings, 7 criminal assaults or homicides, and 11 attempted or completed suicides (Kellermann et al., 1993, 1997, 1998).

"It's a guy thing."

CRITICAL THINKING

Ask your students, "Do you think people are more likely to express anger today than they used to be?" When Scripps Howard News Service and Ohio University posed this question to 815 adults across the United States in mid-1999, 88 percent answered yes. A total of 26 percent said that they themselves felt more anger than they used to feel. Yet, contrary to popular perception, the rate of school violence (often the result of expressions of anger) is actually going down.

 TEACHING TIP

Have students make a chart with two columns—one labeled "Appropriate Aggression" and one labeled "Inappropriate Aggression." Have them brainstorm together about what aggression society deems as appropriate and what behavior is inappropriate. Then create a class list to see if everyone agrees on what is an appropriate expression of aggression:

- Which list is longer—appropriate or inappropriate?

- Does there seem to be a gender difference in the perception of appropriate aggression?

- Do students from different cultural backgrounds have different ideas about what is appropriate?

 TEACHING TIP

At this time, you may want to use **Lecture/Discussion Topics:** *Workplace Violence and the Conditional Reasoning Test of Aggression* (p. 26) or *Genocide* (p. 27) or *Relational Aggression in the Media* (p. 28) or *Do We Need to Vent Our Rage?* (p. 29) from Bolt's Teacher's Resource Binder.

Karl Ammann/Getty Images

INTERCONNECTING

Link discussion of testosterone and biochemistry to the endocrine system (Unit 3A). Some major endocrine glands include the following:

- Adrenal glands (located atop the kidneys)—adrenaline and noradrenaline
- Pancreas—insulin, which regulates body sugar levels
- Thyroid—calcitonin, which regulates calcium and phosphorus levels in the body
- Ovaries—estrogen and progesterone
- Testes—testosterone

A lean, mean, fighting machine—the testosterone-laden female hyena The hyena's unusual embryology pumps testosterone into female fetuses. The result is revved-up young female hyenas who seem born to fight. ▲

"We could avoid two-thirds of all crime simply by putting all able-bodied young men in cryogenic sleep from the age of 12 through 28."

David T. Lykken, *The Antisocial Personalities*, 1995

gentle Ferdinand when castration reduces its testosterone level. The same is true of castrated mice. When injected with testosterone, however, the castrated mice once again become aggressive.

Although humans are less sensitive to hormonal changes, violent criminals tend to be muscular young males with lower-than-average intelligence scores, low levels of the neurotransmitter serotonin, and higher-than-average testosterone levels (Dabbs et al., 2001a; Pendick, 1994). Drugs that sharply reduce their testosterone levels also subdue their aggressive tendencies. High testosterone correlates with irritability, assertiveness, impulsiveness, and low tolerance for frustration—qualities that predispose somewhat more aggressive responses to provocation (Dabbs et al., 2001b; Harris, 1999). Among both teenage boys and adult men, high testosterone levels correlate with delinquency, hard drug use, and aggressive-bullying responses to frustration (Berman et al., 1993; Dabbs & Morris, 1990; Olweus et al., 1988). With age, testosterone levels—and aggressiveness—diminish. Hormonally charged, aggressive 17-year-olds mature into hormonally quieter and gentler 70-year-olds.

The traffic between hormones and behavior is two-way. Testosterone heightens dominance and aggressiveness. But dominating behavior also boosts testosterone levels (Mazur & Booth, 1998). One study measured testosterone levels in the saliva of male college basketball fans before and after a big game. Testosterone levels swelled among the victorious fans and sank among the dejected ones (Bernhardt et al., 1998). Handling and describing a gun also has been found to increase testosterone in research participants' saliva and to increase the amount of hot sauce they put in water they believe another person will drink (Klinesmith et al., 2006).

For both biological and psychological reasons, alcohol unleashes aggressive responses to frustration (Bushman, 1993; Ito et al., 1996; Taylor & Chermack, 1993). Just *thinking* you've imbibed alcohol has some effect; but so, too, does unknowingly ingesting alcohol slipped into a drink. Unless people are distracted, alcohol tends to focus their attention on a provocation rather than on inhibitory cues (Giancola & Corman, 2007). Police data and prison surveys reinforce conclusions drawn from experiments on alcohol and aggression: Aggression-prone people are more likely to drink and to become violent when intoxicated (White et al., 1993). People who have been drinking commit 4 in 10 violent crimes and 3 in 4 acts of spousal abuse (Greenfeld, 1998).

Psychological and Social-Cultural Factors in Aggression

12: What psychological factors may trigger aggressive behavior?

Biological factors influence the ease with which aggression is triggered. But what psychological factors pull the trigger?

Aversive Events Although suffering sometimes builds character, it may also bring out the worst in us. Studies in which animals or humans experience unpleasant events reveal that those made miserable often make others miserable (Berkowitz, 1983, 1989).

Being blocked short of a goal also increases people's readiness to aggress. This phenomenon is called the **frustration-aggression principle:** Frustration creates anger, which may in some people generate aggression, especially in the presence of an aggressive cue, such as a gun. One analysis of 27,667 hit-by-pitch major league baseball incidents between 1960 and 2004 found pitchers were most likely to hit batters when

---

⊛ **TEACHING TIP**

At this time, you may want to use **Classroom Exercise:** *Defining Aggression* (p. 26) from Bolt's Teacher's Resource Binder.

frustrated by the previous batter's hitting a home run, by the current batter's hitting a home run the last time at bat, or by a teammate's having been hit by a pitch in the previous half inning (Timmerman, 2007).

Recall that organisms often respond to stress with a *fight-or-flight reaction*. After the frustration and stress of 9/11, Americans responded with a readiness to fight. Terrorism similarly may spring from a desire for revenge, sometimes after a friend or family member has been killed or injured. Contrary to the popular idea that poverty breeds terrorists, suicide bombers and those who support them actually tend to be neither uneducated nor desperately poor (Krueger, 2007). The 9/11 suicide bombers, for example, were mostly educated men from wealthy Saudi Arabia (McDermott, 2005). Frustration (and aggression) arise less from deprivation than from the gap between reality and expectations, which may rise with education and attainments.

Like frustration, other aversive stimuli—physical pain, personal insults, foul odors, hot temperatures, cigarette smoke, and a host of others—can also evoke hostility. For example, violent crime and spousal abuse rates are higher during hotter years, seasons, months, and days (**FIGURE 14.10**). When people get overheated, they think, feel, and act more aggressively. From the available data, Craig Anderson and his colleagues (2000) have projected that, other things being equal, global warming of 4 degrees Fahrenheit (about 2 degrees centigrade) would induce more than 50,000 additional assaults and murders in the United States alone.

Social and Cultural Influences Aggression may be a natural response to aversive events, but learning can alter natural reactions. Animals naturally eat when they are hungry. But if appropriately rewarded or punished, they can be taught either to overeat or to starve.

Our reactions are more likely to be aggressive in situations where experience has taught us that aggression pays. Children whose aggression successfully intimidates other children may become more aggressive. Animals that have successfully fought to get food or mates become increasingly ferocious.

Ostracism, as we noted in Unit 8A, can also be a real pain. In a series of studies, Jean Twenge and her collaborators (2001, 2002, 2003) told some people that others whom they had met didn't want them in their group, or that a personality test indicated they "were likely to end up alone later in life." People led to feel socially excluded were later more likely to disparage or even deliver a blast of noise to someone who insulted them. This rejection-induced aggression brings to mind various North American and European school shootings, committed by youths who had been shunned, mocked, and sometimes bullied by peers, as reportedly was also the case in 2007 with Virginia Tech mass murderer Seung-Hui Cho. Other studies confirm that rejection often intensifies aggression (Catanese & Tice, 2005; Gaertner & Iuzzini, 2005).

Different cultures model, reinforce, and evoke different tendencies toward violence. For example, crime rates are higher (and average happiness is lower) in countries marked by a great disparity between rich and poor (Triandis, 1994). Richard Nisbett and Dov Cohen (1996) have shown how violence can vary by culture within a country. They analyzed violence among White Americans in southern towns settled by Scots-Irish herders whose tradition emphasized

::**frustration-aggression principle** the principle that frustration—the blocking of an attempt to achieve some goal—creates anger, which can generate aggression.

➤ **FIGURE 14.10**

Uncomfortably hot weather and aggressive reactions Between 1980 and 1982 in Houston, murders and rapes were more common on days over 91 degrees Fahrenheit (33 degrees centigrade), as shown in the graph. This finding is consistent with those from laboratory experiments in which people working in a hot room react to provocations with greater hostility. (From Anderson & Anderson, 1984.)

INTERCONNECTING

Frustration is typically defined as the failure to achieve a desired goal. Have students discuss why being blocked from achieving a goal might lead to frustration and then aggression. Also discuss ways to keep frustration from building into aggression, citing research from Unit 8B.

TEACHING TIP

Psychologists in the late 1930s proposed that frustration was the cause of aggression. Research seems to point to several ways that frustration is linked to aggression:

- If the aggression helps to alleviate the frustration, aggression is more likely to occur.

- If a goal is almost accomplished, and frustration is experienced, aggression is more likely.

- If an aggressive stimulus is seen while frustration is experienced, aggression is more likely.

Does frustration always lead to aggression? No, but environmental factors can determine when a frustrating situation will lead to someone acting aggressively.

CULTURAL CONNECTIONS

Compare crime rates in the U.S. and other countries to see if people in the U.S. are the perpetrators and victims of more aggressive forms of crime.

- Consider all aggressive forms of crime—from murder to assault. Does the U.S. have higher rates of these crimes than other countries?

- How does the U.S. compare to other Westernized countries? How do we compare to developing or third world countries?

- Do these statistics mean that people living in the U.S. are more aggressive than people living in other countries?

INTERCONNECTING

Quiz students on how aggression can be reinforced. Remind students that reinforcement occurs when we are rewarded, or when something unpleasant is taken away because we behave a certain way. If a child is looking for attention and learns that a parent will offer attention for aggressive behavior, then the child will learn to be aggressive to get attention.

"manly honor," the use of arms to protect one's flock, and a history of coercive slavery. Their cultural descendants, Nisbett and Cohen found, have triple the homicide rates and are more supportive of physically punishing children, of warfare initiatives, and of uncontrolled gun ownership than are their White counterparts in New England towns settled by the more traditionally peaceful Puritan, Quaker, and Dutch farmer-artisans.

Social influence also appears in high violence rates among cultures and families that experience minimal father care (Triandis, 1994). Even after controlling for parental education, race, income, and teen motherhood, American male youths from father-absent homes have double their peers' incarceration rate (Harper & McLanahan, 2004).

It is important, however, to note how many people are leading gentle, even heroic lives amid social stresses, reminding us again that individuals differ. The person matters. That people differ over time and place reminds us that environments also differ, and situations matter. Yesterday's plundering Vikings have become today's peace-promoting Scandinavians. Like all behavior, aggression arises from the interaction of persons and situations.

Once established, however, aggressive behavior patterns are difficult to change. To foster a kinder, gentler world we had best model and reward sensitivity and cooperation from an early age, perhaps by training parents to discipline without modeling violence. Modeling violence—screaming and hitting—is precisely what exasperated parents often do. Parents of delinquent youngsters typically discipline with beatings, thus modeling aggression as a method of dealing with problems (Patterson et al., 1982, 1992). They also frequently cave into (reward) their children's tears and temper tantrums.

Parent-training programs advise a more positive approach. They encourage parents to reinforce desirable behaviors and to frame statements positively ("When you finish loading the dishwasher you can go play," rather than "If you don't load the dishwasher, there'll be no playing"). One *aggression-replacement program* has brought down re-arrest rates of juvenile offenders and gang members by teaching the youths and their parents communication skills, training them to control anger, and encouraging more thoughtful moral reasoning (Goldstein et al., 1998).

Observing Models of Aggression Parents are hardly the only aggression models. As we noted in Unit 6, observing TV violence tends to desensitize people to cruelty and prime them to respond aggressively when provoked. Does this media effect extend to sexual violence? We do know that sexually coercive men typically are sexually promiscuous and hostile in their relationships with women (**FIGURE 14.11**). We also know from surveys of American and Australian teens and university students that viewing X-rated films and Internet pornography is several times higher among males than among females (Carroll et al., 2008; Flood, 2007; Wolak et al., 2007). Might sexually explicit media models contribute to sexually aggressive tendencies?

Content analyses reveal that most X-rated films have depicted quick, casual sex between strangers, but that scenes of rape and sexual exploitation of women by men are also common (Cowan et al., 1988; NCTV, 1987; Yang & Linz, 1990). Rape scenes often portray the victim at first fleeing and resisting her attacker, but then becoming aroused and finally driven to ecstasy. In less graphic form, the same unrealistic script—she resists, he persists, she melts—is commonplace on TV and in romance novels. In *Gone With the Wind*, Scarlett O'Hara is carried to bed screaming and wakes up singing. Most rapists accept this *rape myth*—the idea that some women invite or enjoy rape and get "swept away" while being "taken" (Brinson, 1992). (In actuality, rape is traumatic, and it frequently harms women's reproductive and psychological health [Golding, 1996].) Compared with those who watch little television, men and women who watch a great deal are more likely to accept the rape myth (Kahlor & Morrison, 2007).

> "Why do we kill people who kill people to show that killing people is wrong?"
> National Coalition to Abolish the Death Penalty, 1992

➤ FIGURE 14.11

Men who sexually coerce women The recipe for coercion against women combines an impersonal approach to sex with a hostile masculinity. (Adapted from Malamuth, 1996.)

INTERCONNECTING

Link viewing television violence to Albert Bandura's famous Bobo doll studies (Unit 6). Bandura and his colleagues showed young children videos of adults playing with a Bobo doll (an inflated doll with sand in the bottom that rights itself whenever it is knocked over). For one group of children, adults were seen acting aggressively toward the doll. The other group saw the adults playing nicely. How did the children react when put in a room with a Bobo doll? Those who saw the aggressive behavior played aggressively in response. Those who saw the nice behavior played nicely.

When interviewed, Canadian and U.S. sex offenders (rapists, child molesters, and serial killers) report a greater-than-usual appetite for sexually explicit and sexually violent materials—materials typically labeled as *pornography* (Marshall, 1989; Oddone-Paolucci et al., 2000; Ressler et al., 1988). For example, the Los Angeles Police Department has reported that pornography was "conspicuously present" in 62 percent of its extrafamilial childhood sexual abuse cases during the 1980s (Bennett, 1991). High pornography consumption also has predicted greater sexual aggressiveness among university men, even after controlling for other predictors of antisocial behavior (Vega & Malamuth, 2007). But are the sexual aggressors merely, as sex researcher John Money (1988) suspected, using pornography "as an alibi to explain to themselves and their captors what otherwise is inexplicable"?

Laboratory experiments reveal that repeatedly watching X-rated films (even if nonviolent) later makes one's own partner seem less attractive, makes a woman's friendliness seem more sexual, and makes sexual aggression seem less serious (Harris, 1994). In one such experiment, Dolf Zillmann and Jennings Bryant (1984) showed undergraduates six brief, sexually explicit films each week for six weeks. A control group viewed nonerotic films during the same six-week period. Three weeks later, both groups read a newspaper report about a man convicted but not yet sentenced for raping a hitchhiker. When asked to suggest an appropriate prison term, those who had viewed sexually explicit films recommended sentences half as long as those recommended by the control group.

Experiments cannot elicit actual sexual violence, but they can assess a man's willingness to hurt a woman. Often the research gauges the effect of violent versus nonviolent erotic films on men's willingness to deliver supposed electric shocks to women who had earlier provoked the men. These experiments suggest that it's not the eroticism but rather the depictions of sexual *violence* (whether in R-rated slasher films or X-rated films) that most directly affect men's acceptance and performance of aggression against women. A conference of 21 social scientists, including many of the researchers who conducted these experiments, produced a consensus (Surgeon General, 1986): "Pornography that portrays sexual aggression as pleasurable for the victim increases the acceptance of the use of coercion in sexual relations." Contrary to much popular opinion, viewing such depictions does not provide an outlet for bottled-up impulses. Rather, "In laboratory studies measuring short-term effects, exposure to violent pornography increases punitive behavior toward women."

Acquiring Social Scripts Significant behaviors, such as violence, usually have many determinants, making any single explanation an oversimplification. Asking what causes violence is therefore like asking what causes cancer. Those who study the effects of asbestos exposure on cancer rates may remind us that asbestos is indeed a cancer cause, albeit only one among many. Likewise, report Neil Malamuth and his colleagues (1991, 1995), several factors can create a predisposition to sexual violence. They include the media but also dominance motives, disinhibition by alcohol, and a history of child abuse. Still, if media depictions of violence can disinhibit and desensitize; if viewing sexual violence fosters hostile, domineering attitudes and behaviors; and if viewing pornography leads viewers to trivialize rape, devalue their partners, and engage in uncommitted sex, then media influence is not a minor issue.

Social psychologists attribute the media's influence partly to the *social scripts* (mental tapes for how to act, provided by our culture) they portray. When we find ourselves in new situations, uncertain how to act, we rely on social scripts. After so many action films, youngsters may acquire a script that gets played when they face real-life conflicts. Challenged, they may "act like a man" by intimidating or eliminating the threat. Likewise, after viewing the multiple sexual innuendoes and acts found in most prime-time TV hours—often involving impulsive or short-term relationships—youths may acquire sexual scripts they later enact in real-life relationships (Kunkel et

• In follow-up studies, Zillmann (1989) found that after massive exposure to X-rated sexual films, men and women became more accepting of extramarital sex, of women's sexual submission to men, and of a man's seducing a 12-year-old girl. As people heavily exposed to televised crime perceive the world as more dangerous, so people heavily exposed to pornography see the world as more sexual. •

RESEARCH

Have students watch several different types of television shows to see how many acts of violence are shown. Suggest that they watch a news broadcast (both local and national), a sitcom, a police drama, a medical drama, and a nonspecific drama (family or relational shows). Be sure to define operationally what an "act of violence" is before viewing.

- How many acts of violence occurred overall? How many occurred in each show?

- Does one type of program depict more violence than others?

- What was different about the violence depicted on the different types of shows?

- How did watching this violence affect you? Would you feel comfortable letting young children watch the acts you saw?

UNIT 14

RESEARCH

Have students research the popularity of violent video games and survey their own video game collections.

- What are the most popular video games today? How many of them are considered violent?
- What impact does the rating system have on the popularity of a particular video game?
- Do students own many violent video games?
- Do students feel violent video games affect their behavior?

INTERCONNECTING

Students may have already protested that many people watch violence in the media and play violent video games and do not ultimately turn to violence to solve problems. Remind them that just because research suggests that exposure to media violence tends to lead to more expressions of aggression does not mean that *every* person exposed to media violence will become more aggressive. As the text explains, many other factors also contribute to aggressive behavior. Still, it would be unwise not to consider the effects of the media to which we expose ourselves.

al., 2001; Sapolsky & Tabarlet, 1991). Music lyrics also write social scripts. In one set of experiments, German university men who listened to woman-hating song lyrics administered the most hot chili sauce to a woman and recalled more negative feelings and beliefs about women. Man-hating song lyrics had a similar effect on the aggressive behavior of women listeners (Fischer & Greitemeyer, 2006).

Might public consciousness be raised by making people aware of the information you have just been reading? (See also Close-Up: Parallels Between Smoking Effects and Media Violence Effects.) In the 1940s, movies often depicted African-Americans as childlike superstitious buffoons. Today, we would not tolerate such images. In the 1960s and 1970s, some rock music and movies glamorized drug use. Responding to a tidal change in cultural attitudes, the entertainment industry now more often portrays the dark side of drug use. In response to growing public concern about violence in the media, television violence levels declined in the early 1990s (Gerbner et al., 1993). The growing sensitivity to violence has raised hopes that entertainers, producers, and audiences might someday look back with embarrassment on the days when movies "entertained" people with scenes of torture, mutilation, and sexual coercion.

Do Video Games Teach, or Release, Violence? Violent video games became an issue for public debate after teen assassins in more than a dozen places seemed to mimic the carnage in the splatter games they had so often played (Anderson, 2004a). In 2002, two Grand Rapids, Michigan, teens and a man in his early twenties spent part of a night drinking beer and playing *Grand Theft Auto III,* using cars to run down simulated pedestrians, before beating them with fists and leaving a bloody body behind (Kolker, 2002). Then they went out on a real drive, spotted a 38-year-old man on a bicycle, ran him down with their car, got out, stomped and punched him, and returned home to play the game some more. (The man, a father of three, died six days later.)

Interactive games transport the player into their own vivid reality. When youths play *Grand Theft Auto: San Andreas,* they can carjack vehicles; run down pedestrians; do drive-by shootings; pick up a prostitute, have sex with her, and then kill her. When youths play such games, do they learn social scripts?

Most abused children don't become abusive adults. Most social drinkers don't become alcohol dependent. And most youths who spend hundreds of hours in these

▼ **Desensitizing people to violence**

Mark C. Burnett/Stock, Boston

CLOSE-UP

Parallels Between Smoking Effects and Media Violence Effects

Researchers Brad Bushman and Craig Anderson (2001) note that the correlation between viewing violence and behaving aggressively nearly equals the correlation between smoking and lung cancer. They also note other parallels:

1. Not everyone who smokes gets lung cancer.
2. Smoking is only one cause of lung cancer, although an important one.
3. The first cigarette can nauseate, but the sickening effect lessens with repetition.
4. The short-term effect of one cigarette is minor and dissipates within an hour or so.
5. The long-term, cumulative effect of smoking can be severe.
6. Corporate interests have denied the smoking–lung cancer link.

1. Not everyone who watches violence becomes aggressive.
2. Viewing violence is only one cause of aggression, although an important one.
3. The first violence exposure can upset, but the upset lessens with repetition.
4. One violent TV program can prime aggressive thoughts and behaviors, but the effect dissipates within an hour or so.
5. The long-term, cumulative effect of viewing violence is increased likelihood of habitual aggression.
6. Corporate interests have denied the viewing violence–aggression link.

mass murder simulators don't become teen assassins. Still, we wonder: If, as research has shown, passively viewing violence elevates aggressive responses to provocation and lowers sensitivity to cruelty, what will be the effect of actively role-playing aggression? Although very few will commit slaughter, how many will become desensitized to violence and more open to violent acts?

Thirty-eight studies of more than 7000 people offer some answers (Anderson et al., 2004). One study (Ballard & Wiest, 1998) observed a rising level of arousal and feelings of hostility in college men as they played *Mortal Kombat*. Other studies have found that video games can prime aggressive thoughts and increase aggression. Consider this report from Craig Anderson and Karen Dill (2000): University men who have spent the most hours playing violent video games tend to be the most physically aggressive (for example, to acknowledge having hit or attacked someone else). In one experiment, people randomly assigned to play a game involving bloody murders with groaning victims (rather than to play nonviolent *Myst*) became more hostile. On a follow-up task, they also were more likely to blast intense noise at a fellow student. Those with extensive experience in violent video gaming also display desensitization to violent images, as shown by blunted brain responses (Bartholow et al., 2006).

Studies of young adolescents by Douglas Gentile and his co-researchers (2004; 2007) further reveal that kids who play a lot of violent video games see the world as more hostile, get into more arguments and fights, and get worse grades (those hours aren't spent reading or studying). Ah, but is this merely because naturally hostile kids are drawn to such games? *No,* says Gentile. Even among violent-game players scoring low in hostility, 38 percent had been in fights. That figure is nearly 10 times the rate (4 percent) found among their nongaming counterparts. Moreover, over time, the nongamers became more likely to have fights only if they started playing the violent games. Anderson and his colleagues (2007) believe that, due partly to the more active participation and rewarded violence of game play, violent video games have even greater effects on aggressive behavior and cognition than do violent television and movies.

Although much remains to be learned, these studies again disconfirm the *catharsis hypothesis*—the idea that we feel better if we "blow off steam" by venting our emotions (Unit 8B). Playing violent video games *increases* aggressive thoughts, emotions, and behaviors. One video game company's CEO rationalizes that we are "violent by nature [and] need release valves." "It's a way to process violent feelings and anxieties through a fantasy medium," adds a prominent civil liberties lawyer in explaining her hunch that playing violent games calms violent tendencies (Heins, 2004). Actually, expressing anger breeds more anger, and practicing violence breeds more violence. Tomorrow's games may have even greater effects. Social psychologists Susan Persky and Jim Blascovich (2005) created a violent video game for students to play on either a desktop computer or by putting on a headset and stepping into a virtual reality. As they predicted, the virtual reality more dramatically heightened aggressive feelings and behavior during and after the play.

To sum up, research reveals biological, psychological, and social-cultural influences on aggressive behavior. Like so much else, aggression is a biopsychosocial phenomenon (**FIGURE 14.12**).

"We are what we repeatedly do."
Aristotle

> **FIGURE 14.12**

Biopsychosocial understanding of aggression Because many factors contribute to aggressive behavior, there are many ways to change such behavior, including learning anger management and communication skills, and avoiding violent media and video games.

TEACHING TIP

Psychological research offers limited support for the catharsis hypothesis, which states that people experience a release (catharsis) when they vent their anger. Laboratory tests of catharsis have produced mixed results at best. One study found that when students were allowed to counterattack someone who had provoked them, their blood pressure more quickly returned to normal. The calming effect seems to occur, however, only when the target is one's actual tormenter, the retaliation is justified, and the target is non-intimidating.

Does the viewing of aggression prove cathartic? Alfred Hitchcock once said, "One of television's great contributions is that it brought murder back into the home where it belongs. Seeing a murder on television can be good therapy. It can help work off one's antagonisms. If you have no antagonisms, the commercials will give you some." Once again, research is not supportive. Spectators of football, wrestling, and hockey exhibit more hostility after watching the event than before. Similarly, after a war a nation's murder rate tends to increase, not decrease. The near consensus in the research community is that viewing television violence increases aggression in the viewer.

TEACHING TIP

Use Figure 14.12 to highlight the biopsychosocial model of aggression. This model should help students review the main issues related to aggression and remember that explanations of behavior are complex and encompass many variables.

UNIT 14

TEACHING TIP

Relate two anecdotes to illustrate how familiarity breeds fondness rather than contempt.

- Several years ago the Associated Press carried the following story from Corvallis, Oregon: A mysterious student has been attending a class at Oregon State University for the past 2 months enveloped in a big, black bag. Only his bare feet show. Each Monday, Wednesday, and Friday at 11 o'clock in the morning, the black bag sits on a small table near the back of the classroom. Professor Charles Goetzinger knows the identity of the person inside, but none of the students do. Goetzinger said the students' attitudes changed from hostility toward the black bag to curiosity and finally to friendship.

- In 1972, a small town in Ecuador was confronted with how to deal with their new mayor, Pulvapies. Pulvapies was fairly elected, beating his nearest opponent by a comfortable margin. There was one problem: Pulvapies was a foot deodorant! During the election, the manufacturer thought it would be clever to post billboards and distribute flyers saying: "For mayor: Honorable Pulvapies." Little did he realize that his deodorant would be elected.

Familiarity breeds acceptance When this rare white penguin was born in the Sydney, Australia, zoo, his tuxedoed peers ostracized him. Zookeepers thought they would need to dye him black to gain acceptance. But after three weeks of contact, the other penguins came to accept him.

Attraction

Pause a moment and think about your relationships with two people—a close friend, and someone who stirs in you feelings of romantic love. What is the psychological chemistry that binds us together in these special sorts of attachments that help us cope with all other relationships? Social psychology suggests some answers.

The Psychology of Attraction

13: Why do we befriend or fall in love with some people but not with others?

We endlessly wonder how we can win others' affection and what makes our own affections flourish or fade. Does familiarity breed contempt, or does it intensify our affection? Do birds of a feather flock together, or do opposites attract? Is beauty only skin deep, or does attractiveness matter greatly? Consider three ingredients of our liking for one another: proximity, physical attractiveness, and similarity.

Proximity Before friendships become close, they must begin. *Proximity*—geographic nearness—is friendship's most powerful predictor. Proximity provides opportunities for aggression, but much more often it breeds liking. Study after study reveals that people are most inclined to like, and even to marry, those who live in the same neighborhood, who sit nearby in class, who work in the same office, who share the same parking lot, who eat in the same cafeteria. Look around. (For more on modern ways to connect people, see Close-Up: Online Matchmaking and Speed Dating.)

Why is proximity so conducive to liking? Obviously, part of the answer is the greater availability of those we often meet. But there is more to it than that. For one thing, repeated exposure to novel stimuli—be they nonsense syllables, musical selections, geometric figures, Chinese characters, human faces, or the letters of our own name—increases our liking for them (Moreland & Zajonc, 1982; Nuttin, 1987; Zajonc, 2001). People are even somewhat more likely to marry someone whose familiar-sounding first or last name resembles their own (Jones et al., 2004).

This phenomenon is the **mere exposure effect.** Within certain limits (Bornstein, 1989, 1999), familiarity breeds fondness. Richard Moreland and Scott Beach (1992) demonstrated this by having four equally attractive women silently attend a 200-student class for zero, 5, 10, or 15 class sessions. At the end of the course, students were shown slides of each woman and asked to rate each one's attractiveness. The most attractive? The ones they'd seen most often. The phenomenon will come as no surprise to the young Taiwanese man who wrote more than 700 letters to his girlfriend, urging her to marry him. She did marry—the mail carrier (Steinberg, 1993).

No face is more familiar than one's own. And that helps explain an interesting finding from Lisa DeBruine's research (2004): Men liked other men, and women liked other women, when their faces incorporated some morphed features of their own. When DeBruine (2002) had McMaster University students play a game with a supposed other player, they also were more trusting and cooperative when the other person's image had some features of their own face morphed into it. In me I trust. (See also **FIGURE 14.13.**)

The mere exposure effect The mere exposure effect applies even to ourselves. Because the human face is not perfectly symmetrical, the face we see in the mirror is not the same as the one our friends see. Most of us prefer the familiar mirror image, while our friends like the reverse (Mita et al., 1977). The Chris Martin (Coldplay lead singer) known to his fans is at left. The person he sees in the mirror each morning is shown at right, and that's the photo he would probably prefer.

TEACHING TIP

Have students consider the following aphorisms:

- Birds of a feather flock together.
- Opposites attract.

Which is true? Are they both? How can that be?

Online Matchmaking and Speed Dating

If you have not found a romantic partner in your immediate proximity, why not cast a wider net? In the United States, 16 million people have tried online dating and matchmaking services, as have an estimated 14 million more in China, 10 million in India, and tens of millions in other countries (Cullen & Masters, 2008).

Although published research on the effectiveness of Internet matchmaking services is sparse, this much seems well established: Some people dishonestly represent their age, attractiveness, occupation, or other details, and thus are not who they seem to be. Nevertheless, Katelyn McKenna and John Bargh and their colleagues have found that, on average, Internet-formed friendships and romantic relationships are more likely than relationships formed in person to last beyond two years (Bargh et al. 2002, 2004; McKenna & Bargh, 1998, 2000; McKenna et al., 2002). In one of their studies, people disclosed more, with less posturing, to those whom they met online. When conversing online with someone for 20 minutes, they felt more liking for that person than they did for someone they had met and talked with face to face. This was true even when (unknown to them) it was the same person! Small wonder that Internet friendships often feel as real and important to people as in-person relationships.

Speed dating is in-person matchmaking. People rotate through 3- to 8-minute conversations with a succession of prospective partners, deciding after each if they'd like to see the person again. Researchers report that 4 minutes is often enough for participants to form a feeling about the conversational partner and to register whether the partner likes them (Eastwick & Finkel, 2008a,b). It also is enough for researchers to have begun using speed dating as a vehicle for studying influences on people's first impressions of potential romantic partners.

"I can't wait to see what you're like online."

Voter | George Bush | 60:40 blend

➤ **FIGURE 14.13**
I like the candidate who looks a bit like dear old me Jeremy Bailenson and his colleagues (2005) incorporated morphed features of voters' faces into the faces of 2004 U.S. presidential candidates George Bush and John Kerry. Without conscious awareness of their own incorporated features, the participants became more likely to favor the candidate whose face incorporated some of their own features.

For our ancestors, the mere exposure effect was adaptive. What was familiar was generally safe and approachable. What was unfamiliar was more often dangerous and threatening. Evolution seems to have hard-wired into us the tendency to bond with those who are familiar and to be wary of those who are unfamiliar (Zajonc, 1998). Gut-level prejudice against those culturally different may thus be a primitive, automatic emotional response (Devine, 1995). It's what we do with our knee-jerk prejudice that matters, suggest researchers. Do we let those feelings control our behavior? Or do we monitor our feelings and act in ways that reflect our conscious valuing of human equality?

Physical Attractiveness Once proximity affords you contact, what most affects your first impressions: The person's sincerity? Intelligence? Personality? Hundreds of

::**mere exposure effect** the phenomenon that repeated exposure to novel stimuli increases liking of them.

UNIT 14

RESEARCH

Have students conduct research on attractiveness. Have them collect pictures of "attractive" and "unattractive" people and show them to various participants. Participants should be asked to respond to questions that ask them to guess what kind of job, personality, and education the person in the picture has. Compare the types of answers for the "attractive" and "unattractive" people to determine whether there seem to be more positive predictions for the "attractive" people.

Be sure to obtain Institutional Review Board approval and informed consent for all research endeavors.

RESEARCH

Have students consider their favorite movies and TV shows, and have them describe the physical appearance of the villains and the heroes.

- Are people who are villainous or less than heroic portrayed as physically attractive? Why or why not?
- How are the heroes physically different from the villains?

When Neanderthals fall in love.

"Personal beauty is a greater recommendation than any letter of introduction."

Aristotle, *Apothegems*, 330 B.C.E

• Percentage of Men and Women Who "Constantly Think About Their Looks"

	Men	Women
Canada	18%	20%
United States	17	27
Mexico	40	45
Venezuela	47	65

From Roper Starch survey, reported by McCool (1999). •

• *New York Times* columnist Maureen Dowd on liposuction (January 19, 2000): "Women in the 50's vacuumed. Women in the 00's are vacuumed. Our Hoovers have turned on us!" •

experiments reveal that it is something far more superficial: Appearance. For people taught that "beauty is only skin deep" and that "appearances can be deceiving," the power of physical attractiveness is unnerving.

In one early study, Elaine Hatfield and her co-workers (Walster et al., 1966) randomly matched new University of Minnesota students for a Welcome Week dance. Before the dance, each student took a battery of personality and aptitude tests. On the night of the blind date, the couples danced and talked for more than two hours and then took a brief intermission to rate their dates. What determined whether they liked each other? As far as the researchers could determine, only one thing mattered: Physical attractiveness (which had been rated by the researchers beforehand). Both the men and the women liked good-looking dates best. Although women are more likely than men to say that another's looks don't affect them (Lippa, 2007), a man's looks do affect women's behavior (Feingold, 1990; Sprecher, 1989; Woll, 1986). Recent speed-dating experiments confirm that attractiveness influences first impressions for both sexes (Belot & Francesconi, 2006; Finkel & Eastwick, 2008).

People's physical attractiveness also predicts their frequency of dating, their feelings of popularity, and others' initial impressions of their personalities. We perceive attractive people to be healthier, happier, more sensitive, more successful, and more socially skilled, though not more honest or compassionate (Eagly et al., 1991; Feingold, 1992; Hatfield & Sprecher, 1986). Attractive, well-dressed people are more likely to make a favorable impression on potential employers and to enjoy occupational success (Cash & Janda, 1984; Langlois et al., 2000; Solomon, 1987). Income analyses show a penalty for plainness or obesity and a premium for beauty (Engemann & Owyang, 2005).

An analysis of 100 top-grossing films since 1940 found that attractive characters were portrayed as morally superior to unattractive characters (Smith et al., 1999). But Hollywood modeling doesn't explain why, to judge from their gazing times, even babies prefer attractive over unattractive faces (Langlois et al., 1987). So do some blind people, as University of Birmingham professor John Hull (1990, p. 23) discovered after going blind. A colleague's remarks on a woman's beauty would strangely affect his feelings. He found this "deplorable. . . . What can it matter to me what sighted men think of women . . . yet I do care what sighted men think, and I do not seem able to throw off this prejudice."

The importance of looks seems unfair and unenlightened. Why should it matter? Two thousand years ago the Roman statesman Cicero felt the same way: "The final good and the supreme duty of the wise person is to resist appearance." Cicero might be reassured by two other findings.

First, people's attractiveness is surprisingly unrelated to their self-esteem and happiness (Diener et al., 1995; Major et al., 1984). One reason may be that, except after comparing themselves with superattractive people, few people (thanks, perhaps, to the mere exposure effect) view themselves as unattractive (Thornton & Moore, 1993). Another reason is that strikingly attractive people are sometimes suspicious that praise for their work may simply be a reaction to their looks. When less attractive people are praised, they are more likely to accept it as sincere (Berscheid, 1981).

Cicero might also find comfort in knowing that attractiveness judgments are relative. The standards by which judges crown Miss Universe hardly apply to the whole planet. Rather, beauty is in the eye of the culture—our standards for beauty reflect our time and place. Hoping to look attractive, people in different cultures have pierced their noses, lengthened their necks, bound their feet, and dyed or painted their skin and hair. They have gorged themselves to achieve a full figure or liposuctioned fat to achieve a slim one, applied chemicals hoping to rid themselves of unwanted hair or to

TEACHING TIP

At this time, you may want to use **Classroom Exercises: *Using Personal Ads to Teach Interpersonal Attraction*** (p. 29) or ***Assessing Friendship*** (p. 31) or ***The Pairing Game*** (p. 32) or ***Matching, the Contrast Effect, and Relationship Satisfaction*** (p. 33) or ***Love Styles*** (p. 33) or ***The Trust Scale*** (p. 34) or ***The Minding Scale*** (p. 34) or ***Solitude: Bane or Blessing?*** (p. 35) from Bolt's Teacher's Resource Binder.

In the eye of the beholder Conceptions of attractiveness vary by culture. Moreover, the current concept of attractiveness in the KwaZulu-Natal province of South Africa; the city of Sana'a, Yemen; and in southern California may well change in the future.

regrow wanted hair, strapped on leather garments to make their breasts seem smaller or surgically filled their breasts with silicone and put on Wonderbras to make them look bigger.

For women in North America, the ultra-thin ideal of the Roaring Twenties gave way to the soft, voluptuous Marilyn Monroe ideal of the 1950s, only to be replaced by today's lean yet busty ideal. Americans now spend more on beauty supplies than on education and social services combined and, when still not satisfied, undergo 12 million cosmetic medical treatments each year, including plastic surgery, Botox skin smoothing, and laser hair removal—not even counting procedures for teeth capping or whitening (ASAPS, 2008). But the result of the beauty race since 1970 has been that more and more women feel *un*happy with their appearance (Feingold & Mazella, 1998).

Some aspects of attractiveness, however, do cross place and time (Cunningham et al., 2005; Langlois et al., 2000). As we noted in Unit 3C, men in a wide range of cultures, from Australia to Zambia, judge women as more attractive if they have a youthful appearance. Women feel attracted to healthy-looking men, but especially to those who seem mature, dominant, and affluent.

People everywhere also seem to prefer physical features—noses, legs, physiques—that are neither unusually large nor small. An averaged face is attractive (**FIGURE 14.14**). In one clever demonstration of this, Judith Langlois and Lori Roggman (1990) digitized the faces of up to 32 college students and used a computer to average them. Students judged the averaged, composite faces as more attractive than 96 percent of the individual faces. One reason is that averaged faces are symmetrical, and people with symmetrical faces and bodies are more sexually attractive (Rhodes et al., 1999; Singh, 1995; Thornhill & Gangestad, 1994). Merge either half of your face with its mirror image and your symmetrical new face would boost your attractiveness a notch.

 Women have 91 percent of cosmetic procedures (ASAPS, 2008). Women also recall others' appearance better than do men (Mast & Hall, 2006).

▶ **FIGURE 14.14**

Average is attractive Which of these faces offered by University of St. Andrews psychologist David Perrett (2002) is most attractive? Most people say it's the face on the right—of a nonexistent person that is the average composite of these three plus 57 other actual faces.

RESEARCH

Collect fashion magazine cover photos of women from today and compare them with cover photos of women from 30, 40, and 50 years ago.

- How were the women physically different in the past?

- How was makeup applied differently? How were hairstyles different? Are women more "natural" today than in years past?

 TEACHING TIP

At this time, you may want to use **Classroom Exercise/Student Project**: *The Mere Exposure Effect* (p. 30) from Bolt's Teacher's Resource Binder.

CULTURAL CONNECTIONS

Have students obtain fashion magazines from different cultures to see how their standards of beauty are different from and similar to those in the United States.

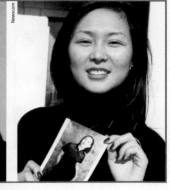

▼
Extreme makeover Greater wealth and concerns about appearance in China have led to increasing numbers of women seeking to alter their appearance. This woman underwent six months of grueling plastic surgery to transform her eyes, nose, chin, breasts, abdomen, bottom, legs, and skin in hopes of obtaining a career in film.

TEACHING TIP

Students may insist that opposites do attract. They will cite examples of people who are part of their intimate circle who are vastly different from them. Have them discuss these differences to see whether these people they mention really are different:

- How are you different from the person who you consider an "opposite"? Is it in areas that include strongly held values and beliefs? For example, are you friends with someone who is a racist when you are strongly against racism?

- Does the friend you consider an "opposite" represent the opposite values of your parents? If so, that could represent the attraction of this friendship.

▼
Beauty grows with mere exposure Herman Miller, Inc.'s famed Aeron chair initially received high comfort ratings but abysmal beauty ratings. To some it looked like "lawn furniture" or "a giant prehistoric insect" (Gladwell, 2005). But then, with design awards, media visibility, and imitators, the ugly duckling came to be the company's best-selling chair ever and to be seen as beautiful. With people, too, beauty lies partly in the beholder's eye and can grow with exposure.

"Love has ever in view the absolute loveliness of that which it beholds."
George MacDonald, *Unspoken Sermons*, 1867

● In Italy and the United States, people also like political candidates who share their own self-perceived personality traits. In 2004, John Kerry was seen as open-minded and George Bush as loyal and sincere, and each was favored by voters who saw those traits in themselves (Caprara et al., 2007). ●

Cultural standards aside, attractiveness also depends on our feelings about the person. If led to believe that someone has appealing traits (such as being honest, humorous, and polite rather than rude, unfair, and abusive) people perceive the person as more physically attractive (Lewandowski et al., 2007). In a Rodgers and Hammerstein musical, Prince Charming asks Cinderella, "Do I love you because you're beautiful, or are you beautiful because I love you?" Chances are it's both. As we see our loved ones again and again, their physical imperfections grow less noticeable and their attractiveness grows more apparent (Beaman & Klentz, 1983; Gross & Crofton, 1977). Shakespeare said it in *A Midsummer Night's Dream:* "Love looks not with the eyes, but with the mind." Come to love someone and watch beauty grow.

Similarity Let's say that proximity has brought you into contact with someone and that your appearance has made an acceptable first impression. What now influences whether acquaintances develop into friends? For example, as you get to know someone better, is the chemistry better if you are opposites or if you are alike?

It makes a good story—extremely different types living in harmonious union: Rat, Mole, and Badger in *The Wind in the Willows,* Frog and Toad in Arnold Lobel's books. The stories delight us by expressing what we seldom experience, for we tend *not* to like dissimilar people (Rosenbaum, 1986). In real life, opposites retract. Birds that flock together usually *are* of a feather. Friends and couples are far more likely to share common attitudes, beliefs, and interests (and, for that matter, age, religion, race, education, intelligence, smoking behavior, and economic status) than are randomly paired people. Moreover, the more alike people are, the more their liking endures (Byrne, 1971). Journalist Walter Lippmann was right to suppose that love is best sustained "when the lovers love many things together, and not merely each other." Similarity breeds content. Dissimilarity often fosters disfavor, which helps explain many straight men's disapproval of gay men who are doubly dissimilar from themselves in sexual orientation and gender roles (Lehavot & Lambert, 2007).

Proximity, attractiveness, and similarity are not the only determinants of attraction. We also like those who like us. This is especially so when our self-image is low. When we believe someone likes us, we feel good and respond to them warmly, which leads them to like us even more (Curtis & Miller, 1986). To be liked is powerfully rewarding.

Indeed, a simple *reward theory of attraction*—that we will like those whose behavior is rewarding to us and that we will continue relationships that offer more rewards than costs—can explain all the findings we have considered so far. When a person lives or works in close proximity with someone else, it costs less time and effort to develop the friendship and enjoy its benefits. Attractive people are aesthetically pleasing, and associating with them can be socially rewarding. Those with similar views reward us by validating our own.

Romantic Love

14: How does romantic love typically change as time passes?

Occasionally, people move quickly from initial impressions, to friendship, to the more intense, complex, and mysterious state of romantic love. Elaine Hatfield (1988) distinguishes two types of love: temporary passionate love and a more enduring companionate love.

Passionate Love Noting that arousal is a key ingredient of **passionate love,** Hatfield suggests that the two-factor theory of emotion (Unit 8B) can help us understand this intense positive absorption in another. The theory assumes that (1) emotions have two ingredients—physical arousal plus cognitive appraisal—and that (2) arousal from any source can enhance one emotion or another, depending on how we interpret and label the arousal.

In tests of this theory, college men have been aroused by fright, by running in place, by viewing erotic materials, or by listening to humorous or repulsive monologues. They were then introduced to an attractive woman and asked to rate her (or their girlfriend). Unlike unaroused men, those who were stirred up attributed some of their arousal to the woman or girlfriend and felt more attracted to her (Carducci et al., 1978; Dermer & Pyszczynski, 1978; White & Kight, 1984).

Outside the laboratory, Donald Dutton and Arthur Aron (1974, 1989) went to two bridges across British Columbia's rocky Capilano River. One, a swaying footbridge, was 230 feet above the rocks; the other was low and solid. An attractive young female accomplice intercepted men coming off each bridge, sought their help in filling out a short questionnaire, and then offered her phone number in case they wanted to hear more about her project. Far more of those who had just crossed the high bridge—which left their hearts pounding—accepted the number and later called the woman. To be revved up and to associate some of that arousal with a desirable person is to feel the pull of passion. Adrenaline makes the heart grow fonder.

Companionate Love Although the spark of romantic love often endures, the intense absorption in the other, the thrill of the romance, the giddy "floating on a cloud" feeling typically fades. Does this mean the French are correct in saying that "love makes the time pass and time makes love pass"? Or can friendship and commitment keep a relationship going after the passion cools?

HI & LOIS

Reprinted with special permission of King Features Syndicate.

Bill looked at Susan, Susan at Bill. Suddenly death didn't seem like an option. This was love at first sight.

::**passionate love** an aroused state of intense positive absorption in another, usually present at the beginning of a love relationship.

CULTURAL CONNECTIONS

Investigate the success of arranged marriages. If students in your school are from cultures where marriages are arranged, have them come and discuss this custom with your class. You may even invite their parents to class if they feel comfortable doing so.

- How long do arranged marriages typically last?

- Do couples in arranged marriages grow to love each other? Why or why not?

- Do young people who will have marriages arranged agree with the practice? Why or why not?

- Would your students trust their parents to find a suitable mate? Why or why not?

INTERCONNECTING

Remind students which two factors are included in the two-factor theory of emotion (Unit 8B):

- Physiological response
- Cognitive label

According to this theory, both factors must be present in order to experience an emotion. Stanley Schachter and Jerome Singer developed this theory.

RESEARCH

The divorce rate is much higher today than it was when your students' grandparents were getting married. Have students investigate why people get divorced:

- Are the values of society different today than they were a generation ago regarding divorce?

- What are some common reasons people cite for getting a divorce? Do these reasons point to a lack of companionship between the spouses?

MATRIMONY

COURTSHIP

Sometimes passionate love becomes enduring companionate love, sometimes not (invert the picture) What, in addition to similar attitudes and interests, predicts long-term loving attachment? ▲

"When two people are under the influence of the most violent, most insane, most delusive, and most transient of passions, they are required to swear that they will remain in that excited, abnormal, and exhausting condition continuously until death do them part."

George Bernard Shaw, "Getting Married," 1908

▼ **Love is an ancient thing** In 2007, a 5000- to 6000-year-old "Romeo and Juliet" young couple was unearthed locked in embrace, near Rome.

Hatfield reports that as love matures it becomes a steadier **companionate love**—a deep, affectionate attachment. There may be adaptive wisdom to this change from passion to attachment (Reis & Aron, 2008). Passionate love often produces children, whose survival is aided by the parents' waning obsession with one another. Social psychologist Ellen Berscheid and her colleagues (1984) noted that the failure to appreciate passionate love's limited half-life can doom a relationship: "If the inevitable odds against eternal passionate love in a relationship were better understood, more people might choose to be satisfied with the quieter feelings of satisfaction and contentment." Indeed, recognizing the short duration of passionate love, some societies have deemed such feelings an irrational reason for marrying. Better, such cultures say, to choose (or have someone choose for you) a partner with a compatible background and interests. Non-Western cultures, where people rate love less important for marriage, do have lower divorce rates (Levine et al., 1995).

One key to a gratifying and enduring relationship is **equity:** Both partners receive in proportion to what they give. When equity exists—when both partners freely give and receive, when they share decision making—their chances for sustained and satisfying companionate love are good (Gray-Little & Burks, 1983; Van Yperen & Buunk, 1990). In one national survey, "sharing household chores" ranked third, after "faithfulness" and a "happy sexual relationship," on a list of nine things people associated with successful marriages. "I like hugs. I like kisses. But what I really love is help with the dishes," summarized the Pew Research Center (2007).

Equity's importance extends beyond marriage. Mutually sharing self and possessions, giving and getting emotional support, promoting and caring about each other's welfare are at the core of every type of loving relationship (Sternberg & Grajek, 1984). It is true for lovers, for parent and child, and for intimate friends.

Another vital ingredient of loving relationships is **self-disclosure,** the revealing of intimate details about ourselves—our likes and dislikes, our dreams and worries, our proud and shameful moments. "When I am with my friend," noted the Roman statesman Seneca, "me thinks I am alone, and as much at liberty to speak anything as to think it." Self-disclosure breeds liking, and liking breeds self-disclosure (Collins & Miller, 1994). As one person reveals a little, the other reciprocates, the first then reveals more, and on and on, as friends or lovers move to deeper intimacy. Each increase in intimacy rekindles passion (Baumeister & Bratslavsky, 1999).

One experiment marched pairs of volunteer college students through 45 minutes of increasingly self-disclosing conversation—from "When did you last sing to yourself?" to "When did you last cry in front of another person? By yourself?" By the experiment's end, those experiencing the escalating intimacy felt remarkably close to their conversation partner, much closer than others who had spent the time with small-talk questions, such as "What was your high school like?" (Aron et al., 1997). Given self-disclosing intimacy plus mutually supportive equality, the odds favor enduring companionate love.

Intimacy can also grow from pausing to ponder and write our feelings. Richard Slatcher and James Pennebaker (2006) discovered this when they invited one person from each of 86 dating couples to spend 20 minutes a day over three days either writing their deepest thoughts

DEMO

Have students come up with a list of self-disclosing questions. Then have them partner with someone they don't know well and answer the questions for each other.

- How did they feel about each other before this exercise?

- What new things did they learn about each other?

- What was the most interesting thing they learned? What things would they like to know more about?

and feelings about the relationship or writing merely about their daily activities. Those who wrote their feelings expressed more emotion in their instant messages with their partners in the days following, and 77 percent were still dating three months later (compared with 52 percent of those who had written about their activities).

Altruism

15: When are we most—and least—likely to help?

Carl Wilkens, a Seventh Day Adventist missionary, was living with his family in Kigali, Rwanda, when Hutu militia began to slaughter the Tutsi in 1994. The U.S. government, church leaders, and friends all implored Wilkens to leave. He refused. After evacuating his family, and even after every other American had left Kigali, he alone stayed and contested the 800,000-person genocide. When the militia came to kill him and his Tutsi servants, Wilkens' Hutu neighbors deterred them. Despite repeated death threats, he spent his days running roadblocks to take food and water to orphanages and to negotiate, plead, and bully his way through the bloodshed, saving lives time and again. "It just seemed the right thing to do," he later explained (Kristof, 2004).

Elsewhere in Kigali, Paul Rusesabagina, a Hutu married to a Tutsi and the acting manager of a luxury hotel, was sheltering more than 1200 terrified Tutsis and moderate Hutus. When international peacemakers abandoned the city and hostile militia threatened his guests in the "Hotel Rwanda" (as it came to be called in a 2004 movie), the courageous Rusesabagina began cashing in past favors, bribing the militia, and telephoning influential persons abroad to bring pressure on local authorities, thereby sparing the lives of the hotel's occupants from the surrounding chaos.

Such selfless goodness exemplifies **altruism**—the unselfish regard for the welfare of others. Altruism became a major concern of social psychologists after an especially vile act of sexual violence. On March 13, 1964, a stalker repeatedly stabbed Kitty Genovese, then raped her as she lay dying outside her Queens, New York, apartment at 3:30 A.M. "Oh, my God, he stabbed me!" Genovese screamed into the early morning stillness. "Please help me!" Windows opened and lights went on as neighbors—38 of them, according to an initial *New York Times* report, though the number was later contested—heard her screams. Her attacker fled and then returned to stab and rape her again. Not until he had fled for good did anyone so much as call the police, at 3:50 A.M.

> "Probably no single incident has caused social psychologists to pay as much attention to an aspect of social behavior as Kitty Genovese's murder."
> R. Lance Shotland (1984)

Bystander Intervention

Reflecting on initial reports of the Genovese murder and other such tragedies, most commentators were outraged by the bystanders' "apathy" and "indifference." Rather than blaming the onlookers, social psychologists John Darley and Bibb Latané (1968b) attributed their inaction to an important situational factor—the presence of others. Given certain circumstances, they suspected, most of us might behave similarly.

After staging emergencies under various conditions, Darley and Latané assembled their findings into a decision scheme: We will help only if the situation enables us first to *notice* the incident, then to *interpret* it as an emergency, and finally to *assume responsibility* for helping (**FIGURE 14.15**, next page). At each step, the presence of other bystanders turns people away from the path that leads to helping. In the laboratory and on the street, people in a group of strangers are more likely than solitary individuals to keep their eyes focused on what they themselves are doing or where they are going. If they notice an unusual situation, they may infer from the blasé reactions of the other passersby that the situation is not an emergency. "The person lying on the sidewalk must be drunk," they think, and move on.

::companionate love the deep affectionate attachment we feel for those with whom our lives are intertwined.

::equity a condition in which people receive from a relationship in proportion to what they give to it.

::self-disclosure revealing intimate aspects of oneself to others.

::altruism unselfish regard for the welfare of others.

RESEARCH

Have students research back issues of the local paper for stories of people who acted heroically. Contact these people if possible and interview them over the phone, asking them about their particular act of courage.

- What caused them to help in the first place?

- How did they feel before, during, and after the event? Why weren't they paralyzed by fear or more concerned for their own safety?

- Have they received recognition for their heroic acts? How did that recognition make them feel?

WEB CONNECT

Andrew Carnegie was inspired to establish the Hero Fund Commission in 1904 after two attempted rescues from a coal-mining disaster in which both rescuers died. Carnegie set aside $5 million to compensate rescuers or their families. The commission has recognized more than 8300 acts of heroism. In addition to the medal, awardees or their survivors receive $3500 and, occasionally, a pension or scholarship. For more information, go to the commission's Web site at www.carnegiehero.org.

DEMO

It is usually fairly easy to have students both enjoy and learn from performing a random act of kindness. After performing an act of kindness, students should write a brief paper describing the act, the recipient's reaction, and their own reaction. Recipients' reactions, particularly when the recipient is not grateful, provide the basis for a lively classroom discussion. Extend the text discussion of altruism by asking students to reflect on why some recipients might have a negative reaction to receiving help.

Teaching in the psychological sciences (TIPS-Online Discussion Group), Radmacher, S. (1997, January 19). *Social psychology projects.*

> ➤ **FIGURE 14.15**
> **The decision-making process for by-stander intervention** Before helping, one must first notice an emergency, then correct-ly interpret it, and then feel responsible. (From Darley & Latané, 1968b.)

RESEARCH

While the story of Kitty Genovese is tragic and horrific, there are other stories of people who *did* help in such situations. Have students investigate some of these stories, noting how they are different from cases like Kitty Genovese's.

- Many people both in and out of Nazi Germany helped Jews escape the Holocaust. Why did these people risk their own lives to help these people their society had deemed unworthy?

- White Southerners in the Confederate South helped establish and maintain the Underground Railroad, the vehicle that helped thousands of slaves escape to freedom. What caused these people to rebel against their society's norms and laws?

INTERCONNECTING

Link the bystander effect with deindividuation and social loafing.

- When individuals are in a crowd, they are less likely to behave rationally. Their sense of responsibility will diffuse, causing them to do things like riot, loot, or vandalize.

- When people are in a group, they are less likely to exert their best effort, especially if they believe others are available to help.

But sometimes the emergency is unambiguous and people still fail to help. The witnesses looking out through their windows initially were reported to have noticed the incident, correctly interpreted the emergency, and yet failed to assume responsi-bility. Why? To find out, Darley and Latané (1968a) simulated a physical emergency in their laboratory. University students participated in a discussion over an intercom. Each student was in a separate cubicle, and only the person whose microphone was switched on could be heard. One of the students was an accomplice of the experi-menters. When his turn came, he made sounds as though he were having an epileptic seizure and called for help.

How did the other students react? As **FIGURE 14.16** shows, those who believed only they could hear the victim—and therefore thought they bore total responsibility for helping him—usually went to his aid. Those who thought others also could hear were more likely to ignore the victim. When more people shared responsibility for help-ing—when there was a *diffusion of responsibility*—any single listener was less likely to help.

In hundreds of additional experiments, psychologists have studied the factors that influence bystanders' willingness to relay an emer-gency phone call, aid a stranded motorist, donate blood, pick up dropped books, contribute money, and give time. For example, Latané, James Dabbs (1975), and 145 collaborators took 1497 eleva-tor rides in three cities and "accidentally" dropped coins or pencils in front of 4813 fellow passengers. The women coin droppers were more likely to receive help than were the men—a gender difference often reported by other researchers (Eagly & Crowley, 1986). But the major finding was the **bystander effect**—any particular bystander was less likely to give aid with other bystanders present. When alone with the person in need, 40 percent helped; in the presence of five other by-standers, only 20 percent helped.

From their observations of behavior in tens of thousands of such situations, altruism researchers have discerned some additional patterns. The *best* odds of our helping someone occur when

- the person appears to need and deserve help.
- the person is in some way similar to us.
- we have just observed someone else being helpful.
- we are not in a hurry.
- we are in a small town or rural area.
- we are feeling guilty.
- we are focused on others and not preoccupied.
- we are in a good mood.

[Figure 14.16 graph]
Percentage attempting to help (y-axis: 0 to 90%)
Number of others presumed available to help (x-axis: 1 to 4)
"Fewer people help if others seem available"

> ➤ **FIGURE 14.16**
> **Responses to a simulated physical emergency** When people thought they alone heard the calls for help from a person they believed to be having an epileptic sei-zure, they usually helped. But when they thought four others were also hearing the calls, fewer than a third responded. (From Darley & Latané, 1968a.)

🛟 **TEACHING TIP**

The results of the original Darley and Latané studies were robust. When bystanders were alone, 85 percent would go for help. When they were in a crowd, only 31 per-cent went for help. So if you need help, hope that there isn't a big crowd around!

At this time, you may want to use **Lecture/Discussion Topic:** *Case Studies in Helping* (p. 36) from Bolt's Teacher's Resource Binder.

This last result, that happy people are helpful people, is one of the most consistent findings in all of psychology. No matter how people are cheered—whether by being made to feel successful and intelligent, by thinking happy thoughts, by finding money, or even by receiving a posthypnotic suggestion—they become more generous and more eager to help (Carlson et al., 1988).

The Norms for Helping

Why do we help? One widely held view is that self-interest underlies all human interactions, that our constant goal is to maximize rewards and minimize costs. Accountants call it *cost-benefit analysis*. Philosophers call it *utilitarianism*. Social psychologists call it **social exchange theory.** If you are pondering whether to donate blood, you may weigh the costs of doing so (time, discomfort, and anxiety) against the benefits (reduced guilt, social approval, and good feelings). If the rewards you anticipate from helping exceed the costs, you will help.

For most people, helping is intrinsically rewarding. Making charitable donations activates brain areas associated with reward (Harbaugh et al., 2007). That helps explain some findings by Elizabeth Dunn and her colleagues (2008). People who give more money away are happier than those who spend their money almost entirely on themselves. Employees who receive a windfall bonus, for example, are later happier if they have done something for other people with it. In one experiment, researchers gave people an envelope with cash and told them either to spend it on themselves or on others. Which group do you suppose was happiest at the day's end? It was, indeed, those assigned to the spend-it-on-others condition.

But why does helpfulness breed happiness (as well as the reverse)? And why do we leave tips for people we will never see again and give directions to strangers? In part because we have been socialized to do so, through norms that prescribe how we *ought* to behave, often to our mutual benefit. Through socialization, we learn the **reciprocity norm,** the expectation that we should return help, not harm, to those who have helped us. In our relations with others of similar status, the reciprocity norm compels us to give (in favors, gifts, or social invitations) about as much as we receive. We also learn a **social-responsibility norm:** that we should help those who need our help—young children and others who cannot give as much as they receive—even if the costs outweigh the benefits. In repeated Gallup surveys, people who each week attend religious services often exhibit the social-responsibility norm: They report volunteering more than twice as many hours in helping the poor and infirm than do those who rarely or never attend religious services (Hodgkinson & Weitzman, 1992; Independent Sector, 2002). They also give away three times as much money.

A social-responsibility norm was active on January 2, 2007, as construction worker Wesley Autrey and his 6- and 4-year-old daughters were awaiting a New York City subway train. Before them a man collapsed in a seizure, got up, then stumbled to the platform's edge and fell onto the tracks. With train headlights approaching, "I had to make a split decision," Autrey later recalled (Buckley, 2007). His decision, as his girls looked on in horror, was to leap from the platform, push the man off the tracks and into a foot-deep space between them, and lay atop him. As the train screeched to a halt, five cars traveled just above his head, leaving grease on his knit cap. When Autrey cried out, "I've got two daughters up there. Let them know their father is okay," the onlookers erupted into applause.

> "Oh, make us happy and you make us good!"
> Robert Browning, *The Ring and the Book,* 1868

::**bystander effect** the tendency for any given bystander to be less likely to give aid if other bystanders are present.

::**social exchange theory** the theory that our social behavior is an exchange process, the aim of which is to maximize benefits and minimize costs.

::**reciprocity norm** an expectation that people will help, not hurt, those who have helped them.

::**social-responsibility norm** an expectation that people will help those dependent upon them.

Subway hero Wesley Autrey: "I don't feel like I did something spectacular; I just saw someone who needed help."

DEMO

Have student pairs go to a public area in school. The "displayer" should walk or stand about 5 feet in front of the "coder" and make eye contact with a single oncoming subject. The displayer should then signal the coder discreetly to observe the respondent's facial expression.

In the original study, over half the subjects responded to a smile with a smile, but few subjects responded to a frown with a frown. The reciprocity norm may explain that we should respond in kind to rewarding actions. A frown generally represents unfriendly or negative affect. Passersby seemed to respond to a frown with a look of bewilderment. Females were more likely to smile than males. People were more likely to smile at a female. Did your students find similar results? Why or why not?

Hinsz, V., & Tomhave, J. (1991). Smile and (half) the world smiles with you, frown and you frown alone. *Personality and Social Psychology Bulletin, 17,* 586–592.

TEACHING TIP

At this time, you may want to use **Lecture/Discussion Topics:** *Europeans Who Helped Jews Escape* (p. 38) or **Classroom Exercise:** *Why Do People Volunteer?* (p. 37) or **Student Project: A Random Act of Kindness** (p. 38) from Bolt's Teacher's Resource Binder.

TEACHING TIP

Reciprocity is a powerful social norm.

- A professor sent holiday cards to strangers. Cards poured back from people who had never met him.
- Many people who receive free samples in the supermarket find it difficult to return only trash. They buy the product even if they do not need it.

Cialdini, R. (1998). *Influence: The psychology of persuasion.* New York: William Morrow.

Researchers identify five specific strategies for dealing with social conflict. Consider the hypothetical case of Peter, who is looking forward to a vacation at a mountain lodge. His wife wants to go to a seaside resort.

- He can respond by **contending** or arguing for the mountain vacation, even threatening to go alone. Concern only about his own needs would lead to this.

- He can **yield** to his wife's preference. Concern only for others' needs might lead to this.

- He can take a **problem-solving approach** and find a vacation that satisfies both. Concerns for self and others can lead to problem solving.

- He can be **inactive** and hope the disagreement will evaporate. When both concerns for self and others are weak, inaction is the likely approach.

- Peter can **withdraw** from the controversy by deciding not to take any vacation. The model makes no prediction about the antecedents of withdrawing.

Pruitt, D., Rubin, J., & Kim, S. (1994). *Social conflict: Escalation, stalemate, and settlement* (2nd ed.). New York: McGraw-Hill.

Conflict and Peacemaking

16: How do social traps and mirror-image perceptions fuel social conflict?

We live in surprising times. With astonishing speed, late-twentieth-century democratic movements swept away totalitarian rule in Eastern European countries, and hopes for a new world order displaced the Cold War chill. And yet, the twenty-first century began with terrorist acts and war, and the world continued to spend $2 billion every day for arms and armies—money that could have been used for housing, nutrition, education, and health care. Knowing that wars begin in human minds, psychologists have wondered: What in the human mind causes destructive conflict? How might the perceived threats of social diversity be replaced by a spirit of cooperation?

To a social psychologist, a **conflict** is a perceived incompatibility of actions, goals, or ideas. The elements of conflict are much the same at all levels, from nations at war, to cultural disputes within a society, to individuals in a marital dispute. In each situation, people become enmeshed in a potentially destructive social process that can produce results no one wants. Among the destructive processes are social traps and distorted perceptions.

Social Traps

In some situations, we support our collective well-being by pursuing our personal interests. As capitalist Adam Smith wrote in *The Wealth of Nations* (1776), "It is not from the benevolence of the butcher, the brewer, or the baker that we expect our dinner, but from their regard to their own interest." In other situations, we harm our collective well-being by pursuing our personal interests. Such situations are **social traps.**

Consider the simple game matrix in FIGURE 14.17, which is similar to those used in experiments with countless thousands of people. Both sides can win or both can lose, depending on the players' individual choices. Pretend you are Person 1, and that you and Person 2 will each receive the amount shown after you separately choose either A or B. (You might invite someone to look at the matrix with you and take the role of Person 2.) Which do you choose—A or B?

You and Person 2 are caught in a dilemma. If you both choose A, you both benefit, making $5 each. Neither of you benefits if you both choose B, for neither of you makes anything. Nevertheless, on any single trial you serve your own interests if you choose B: You can't lose, and you might make $10. But the same is true for the other person. Hence, the social trap: As long as you both pursue your own immediate best interest and choose B, you will both end up with nothing—the typical result—when you could have made $5.

Many real-life situations similarly pit our individual interests against our communal well-being. Individual whalers reasoned that the few whales they took would not threaten the species and that if they didn't take them others would anyway. The result: Some species of whales became endangered. Ditto for the bison hunters of yesterday and the elephant-tusk poachers of today. Individual car owners and home owners reason, "It would cost me comfort or money to buy a more fuel-efficient car and furnace. Besides, the fossil fuels I burn don't noticeably add to the greenhouse gases." When enough others reason similarly, the collective result threatens disaster—global climate change, rising seas, and more extreme weather.

Social traps challenge us to find ways of reconciling our right to pursue our personal well-being with our responsibility for the well-being of all. Psychologists are therefore exploring ways to convince people to cooperate for

➤ **FIGURE 14.17**

Social-trap game matrix By pursuing our self-interest and not trusting others, we can end up losers. To illustrate this, imagine playing the game below. The peach triangles show the outcomes for Person 1, which depend on the choices made by both players. If you were Person 1, would you choose A or B? (This game is called a *non–zero-sum* game because the outcomes need not add up to zero; both sides can win or both can lose.)

Have students sit around a shallow bowl that initially contains ten metal nuts. State that the goal is to accumulate as many nuts as possible. Each student may take as many as he or she wants, and every ten seconds the number of nuts remaining in the bowl will be doubled. What happens? Unless students are allowed some time to devise a strategy for conservation, 65 percent of the groups will never reach the first ten-second replenishment. Often they knocked the bowl off the table grabbing for their share!

their mutual betterment—through agreed-upon *regulations,* through better *communication,* and through promoting *awareness of our responsibilities* toward community, nation, and the whole of humanity (Dawes, 1980; Linder, 1982; Sato, 1987). Given effective regulations, communication, and awareness, people more often cooperate, whether it be in playing a laboratory game or the real game of life.

Enemy Perceptions

Psychologists have noted that those in conflict have a curious tendency to form diabolical images of one another. These distorted images are ironically similar, so similar in fact that we call them **mirror-image perceptions:** As we see "them"—as untrustworthy and evil intentioned—so "they" see us. Each demonizes the other.

Mirror-image perceptions often feed a vicious cycle of hostility. If Juan believes Maria is annoyed with him, he may snub her, causing her to act in ways that justify his perception. As with individuals, so with countries. Perceptions can become **self-fulfilling prophecies.** They may confirm themselves by influencing the other country to react in ways that seem to justify them.

People in conflict also tend to see their own actions as responses to provocation, not as the causes of what happens next. When responding to a perceived provocation they often hit back harder, though perceiving themselves as merely returning tit for tat. In one experiment, University College London volunteers used a mechanical device to press on another volunteer's finger, after feeling pressure on their own finger. Although their task was to reciprocate with the same amount of pressure, they typically responded with about 40 percent more force than they had just experienced. Despite seeking to respond only in kind, their touches soon escalated to hard presses, much as when each child after a fight claims that "I just poked him, but he hit me harder" (Shergill et al., 2003).

In the early twenty-first century, many Americans came to loathe Saddam Hussein. Like the "evil" Saddam Hussein, "some of today's tyrants are gripped by an implacable hatred of the United States of America," declared then-President George W. Bush (2001). "They hate our friends, they hate our values, they hate democracy and freedom and individual liberty. Many care little for the lives of their own people." Hussein (2002) reciprocated the perception, seeing the United States as "an evil tyrant" that, with Satan as its protector, lusted for oil and aggressively attacked those who "defend what is right."

The point is not that truth must lie midway between two such views (one may be more accurate). The point is that enemy perceptions often form mirror images. Moreover, as enemies change, so do perceptions. In American minds and media, the "bloodthirsty, cruel, treacherous" Japanese of World War II later became our "intelligent, hardworking, self-disciplined, resourceful allies" (Gallup, 1972).

How can we make peace? Can contact, cooperation, communication, and conciliation transform the antagonisms fed by prejudice and conflicts into attitudes that promote peace? Research indicates that, in some cases, they can.

Contact

17: How can we transform feelings of prejudice, aggression, and conflict into attitudes that promote peace?

Does it help to put two conflicting parties into close contact? It depends. When such contact is noncompetitive and between parties of equal status, such as retail clerks

Not in my ocean! Many people support alternative energy sources, including wind turbines. But proposals to construct wind farms in real-world neighborhoods elicit less support. One such proposal (shown in this visual simulation), for locating wind turbines off the coast of Massachusetts' Nantucket Island, produced heated debate over the future benefits of clean energy versus the costs of altering treasured ocean views and, possibly, migratory bird routes.

::**conflict** a perceived incompatibility of actions, goals, or ideas.

::**social trap** a situation in which the conflicting parties, by each rationally pursuing their self-interest, become caught in mutually destructive behavior.

::**mirror-image perceptions** mutual views often held by conflicting people, as when each side sees itself as ethical and peaceful and views the other side as evil and aggressive.

::**self-fulfilling prophecy** a belief that leads to its own fulfillment.

INTERCONNECTING

Link mirror-image perceptions with ingroup bias and other-race effect, discussed earlier in this unit. We tend to feel defensive and protective of our own group, and we tend to view those in the outgroup as being homogeneous and indistinguishable. These tendencies lead to quicker responses to others that may not be reasoned well, leading to rash behaviors and thoughts.

TROUBLESHOOTING

Students often get confused by self-fulfilling prophecies. Help them understand this concept better with this example:

- A student believes that she will not pass the next AP Psychology test.
- The student then does not study for the test, since she will fail anyway.
- The student fails the test, confirming her belief.
- The prophecy is fulfilled, even though her actions could have altered the prophecy.

Students need to know that their own subsequent action is what creates the self-fulfilling prophecy, not the belief itself.

::superordinate goals shared goals that override differences among people and require their cooperation.

WEB CONNECT

Do different racial, ethnic, cultural, or social groups re-segregate during lunch or other common activities at your school? If so, have your students participate in a version of a Mix-It-Up day (www.tolerance.org/mix-it-up), a project of the Southern Poverty Law Center. With Mix-It-Up, students sit with people from outside their ingroup during lunch, promoting contact and encouraging tolerance. Challenge students to continue this practice once a week.

working the same shift, it typically helps. Initially prejudiced co-workers of different races have, in such circumstances, usually come to accept one another.

This finding is confirmed by a statistical digest of more than 500 studies of face-to-face contact with outgroups (such as ethnic minorities, the elderly, and those with disabilities). Among the quarter-million people studied across 38 nations, contact has been correlated with, or in experimental studies has led to, more positive attitudes (Pettigrew & Tropp, 2006). Some examples:

- With interracial contact, South African Whites' and Blacks' "attitudes [have moved] into closer alignment" (Dixon et al., 2007).
- Heterosexuals' personal contact with gay people correlates with accepting attitudes. In one national survey, those who knowingly had a gay family member or close friend were twice as likely to support gay marriage as those who didn't—55 percent versus 25 percent (Neidorf & Morin, 2007).
- Even indirect contact with a member of an outgroup (via story reading or through a friend who has an outgroup friend) tends to reduce prejudice (Cameron & Rutland, 2006; Pettigrew et al., 2007).

However, mere contact is not always enough. In most desegregated schools, ethnic groups resegregate themselves in the lunchrooms and on the school grounds (Clack et al., 2005; Schofield, 1986). People in each group often think that they would welcome more contact with the other group, but they assume the other group does not reciprocate the wish (Richeson & Shelton, 2007). "I don't reach out to them, because I don't want to be rebuffed; they don't reach out to me, because they're just not interested." When such mirror-image misperceptions are corrected, friendships may then form and prejudices melt.

> "You cannot shake hands with a clenched fist."
>
> Indira Gandhi, 1971

Cooperation

To see if enemies could overcome their differences, researcher Muzafer Sherif (1966) first instigated conflict. He placed 22 Oklahoma City boys in two separate areas of a Boy Scout camp. He then put the two groups through a series of competitive activities, with prizes going to the victors. Before long, each group became intensely proud of itself and hostile to the other group's "sneaky," "smart-alecky stinkers." Food wars broke out during meals. Cabins were ransacked. Fistfights had to be broken up by members of the camp staff. When Sherif brought the two groups together, they avoided one another, except to taunt and threaten.

Nevertheless, within a few days Sherif transformed these young enemies into jovial comrades. He gave them **superordinate goals**—shared goals that overrode their differences and that could be achieved only through cooperation. A planned disruption of the camp water supply necessitated that all 22 boys work together to restore water. Renting a movie in those pre-DVD days required their pooled resources. A stalled

▼ **Superordinate goals override differences** Cooperative efforts to achieve shared goals are an effective way to break down social barriers.

truck needed the combined force of all the boys pulling and pushing together to get it moving. Having used isolation and competition to make strangers into enemies, Sherif used shared predicaments and goals to reconcile the enemies and make them friends. What reduced conflict was not mere contact, but *cooperative* contact.

A shared predicament—a fearsome external threat and a superordinate desire to overcome it—likewise had a powerfully unifying effect in the weeks after 9/11. Patriotism soared as Americans felt that "we" were under attack. Gallup-surveyed approval of "our President" shot up from 51 percent the week before the attack to a highest-ever level of 90 percent 10 days after, just surpassing the previous approval-rating record of 89 percent enjoyed by his father, George Bush, at the climax of the 1991 Persian Gulf war (Newport, 2002). In chat groups and everyday speech, even the word *we* (relative to *I*) surged in the immediate aftermath (Pennebaker, 2002).

 TEACHING TIP

At this time, you may want to use **Lecture/Discussion Topics:** *Five Dangerous Ideas* (p. 39) or *The Dual Concern Model of Social Conflict* (p. 40) or *The Jigsaw Technique* (p. 41) or **Classroom Exercise:** *The Missiles Game* (p. 39) from Bolt's Teacher's Resource Binder.

Cooperation has especially positive effects when it leads people to define a new, inclusive group that dissolves their former subgroups (Dovidio & Gaertner, 1999). Seat the members of two groups not on opposite sides, but alternately around the table. Give them a new, shared name. Have them work together. Such experiences change "us" and "them" into "we." Those once perceived as being in another group now are seen as part of one's own group. One 18-year-old New Jersey man would not be surprised. After 9/11, he explained a shift in his social identity: "I just thought of myself as Black. But now I feel like I'm an American, more than ever" (Sengupta, 2001). In one experiment, White Americans who read a newspaper article about a terrorist threat against all Americans subsequently expressed reduced prejudice against African-Americans (Dovidio et al., 2004).

During the 1970s, several teams of educational researchers simultaneously wondered: If cooperative contacts between members of rival groups encourage positive attitudes, could we apply this principle in multicultural schools? Could we promote interracial friendships by replacing competitive classroom situations with cooperative ones? And could cooperative learning maintain or even enhance student achievement? Many experiments with adolescents from 11 countries confirm that in all three cases, the answer is *yes* (Roseth, Johnson, & Johnson, 2008). Members of interracial groups who work together on projects and play together on athletic teams typically come to feel friendly toward those of another race. So do those who engage in cooperative classroom learning. So encouraging are these results that thousands of teachers have introduced interracial cooperative learning into their classrooms.

The power of cooperative activity to make friends of former enemies has led psychologists to urge increased international exchange and cooperation (Klineberg, 1984). As we engage in mutually beneficial trade, as we work to protect our common destiny on this fragile planet, and as we become more aware that our hopes and fears are shared, we can change misperceptions that feed conflict into a solidarity based on common interests.

Working toward shared goals enables diverse peoples to discover unity in their common values and superordinate identity. "Common values" are what we need, declared the chair of Britain's Commission for Racial Equality as ethnic tensions recently flared (Phillips, 2004). "There is no ethnicity here. We are all Rwandan," proclaimed Rwanda's government as it sought to resolve historic animosities between Tutsis and Hutus (Lacey, 2004). Western democracies have largely been spared ethnic tribal warfare because their different racial groups have shared so many of the very same goals, noted sociologist Amitai Etzioni (1999). In the United States, these shared goals include fair treatment for all, higher moral standards, and a wish that all high school graduates "understand the common history and ideas that tie all Americans together." Although diversity commands attention, we are—as working toward shared goals reminds us—more alike than different.

"We often forget how much unites all the members of humanity," declared President Ronald Reagan in 1987. "Perhaps we need some outside, universal threat to recognize this common bond." Echoing those words, climate protection advocate Al Gore (2007) noted, "We—all of us—now face a universal threat [which] requires us, in Reagan's phrase, to unite in recognition of our common bond."

Communication

When real-life conflicts become intense, a third-party mediator—a marriage counselor, labor mediator, diplomat, community volunteer—may facilitate much-needed communication (Rubin et al., 1994). Mediators help each party to voice its viewpoint and to understand the other's. By leading each side to think about the other's underlying needs and goals, the mediator aims to replace a competitive *win-lose* orientation with a cooperative *win-win* orientation that offers a mutually beneficial resolution. A classic example: Two friends, after quarreling over an orange, agreed to split it. One squeezed his half for juice. The other used the peel from her half to make a cake. If

> "Most of us have overlapping identities which unite us with very different groups. We *can* love what we are, without hating what—and who—we are *not*. We can thrive in our own tradition, even as we learn from others."
>
> Former U.N. Secretary-General Kofi Annan, Nobel Prize Lecture, 2001

> "I am prepared this day to declare myself a citizen of the world, and to invite everyone everywhere to embrace this broader vision of our interdependent world, our common quest for justice, and ultimately for Peace on Earth."
>
> Father Theodore Hesburgh, *The Human Imperative*, 1974

CRITICAL THINKING

Many teachers use cooperative learning groups, but are these groups truly cooperative? Discuss with students what a truly cooperative situation looks like, including the use of superordinate goals, common values, and mutual benefits.

- Do the groups they work in for projects at school reflect these qualities?

- Do the groups have any superordinate goals besides getting a good grade?

- Do the group members share common values such as hard work and attention to detail?

- How are groups typically graded? Do the grading practices reduce cooperation or improve it?

- How does social loafing fit into all this?

::**GRIT** *G*raduated and *R*eciprocated *I*nitiatives in *T*ension-Reduction—a strategy designed to decrease international tensions.

only the two had understood each other's motives, they could have hit on the win-win solution of one having all the juice, the other all the peel.

Such understanding and cooperative resolution is most needed, yet least likely, in times of anger or crisis (Bodenhausen et al., 1994; Tetlock, 1988).

Conciliation

When conflicts intensify, images become more stereotyped, judgments more rigid, and communication more difficult, or even impossible. Each party is likely to threaten, coerce, or retaliate. In the weeks before the Persian Gulf war, the first President George Bush threatened, in the full glare of publicity, to "kick Saddam's ass." Saddam Hussein communicated in kind, threatening to make Americans "swim in their own blood."

Under such conditions, is there an alternative to war or surrender? Social psychologist Charles Osgood (1962, 1980) advocated a strategy of *Graduated and Reciprocated Initiatives in Tension-Reduction,* nicknamed **GRIT.** In applying GRIT, one side first announces its recognition of mutual interests and its intent to reduce tensions. It then initiates one or more small, conciliatory acts. Without weakening one's retaliatory capability, this modest beginning opens the door for reciprocity by the other party. Should the enemy respond with hostility, one reciprocates in kind. But so, too, with any conciliatory response. Thus, U.S. President John Kennedy's gesture of stopping atmospheric nuclear tests began a series of reciprocated conciliatory acts that culminated in the 1993 atmospheric test-ban treaty.

In laboratory experiments, GRIT has been an effective strategy for increasing trust and cooperation (Lindskold et al., 1978, 1988). Even during intense personal conflict, when communication has been nonexistent, a small conciliatory gesture—a smile, a touch, a word of apology—may work wonders. Conciliations allow both parties to begin edging down the tension ladder to a safer rung where communication and mutual understanding can begin.

And how good that such can happen, for civilization advances not by cultural isolation—maintaining walls around ethnic enclaves—but by tapping the knowledge, the skills, and the arts that are each culture's legacy to the whole human race. Thomas Sowell (1991) observed that, thanks to cultural sharing, every modern society is enriched by a cultural mix. We have China to thank for paper and printing and for the magnetic compass that opened the great explorations. We have Egypt to thank for trigonometry. We have the Islamic world and India's Hindus to thank for our Arabic numerals. While celebrating and claiming these diverse cultural legacies, we can also welcome the enrichment of today's social diversity. We can view ourselves as instruments in a human orchestra. And we can therefore affirm our own culture's heritage while building bridges of communication, understanding, and cooperation across cultural traditions as we think about, influence, and relate to one another.

"To begin with, I would like to express my sincere thanks and deep appreciation for the opportunity to meet with you. While there are still profound differences between us, I think the very fact of my presence here today is a major breakthrough."

BEFORE YOU MOVE ON...

➤ **ASK YOURSELF**

Do you regret not getting along with some friend or family member? How might you go about reconciling that relationship?

➤ **TEST YOURSELF 3**

Why didn't anybody help Kitty Genovese? What social relations principle did this incident illustrate?

Answers to the Test Yourself questions can be found in Appendix E at the end of the book.

TECHNOLOGY RESOURCES

These resources will be helpful for teaching the concepts in this unit:

- *ActivePsych: Digital Media Archive,* 2nd ed.: *The Actor-Observer Difference in Attribution: Observe a Riot in Action; Zimbardo's Stanford Prison Experiment; Being Gay: Coming Out in the 21st Century*

- *Videos: Psychology: The Human Experience, Module 30: Social Cognition and Person Perception: The Blind Date; Module 33: Conformity; Module 34: Obedience: The Milgram Study; Module 2: Group Decision-Making; Module 31:*

Attitudes and Prejudicial Behavior; Module 32: Ethnocentrism and Prejudice

- *Psychology Video Tool Kit: The Stanford Prison Experiment: The Power of the Situation; Liking and Imitation: The Sincerest Form of Flattery; Obedience and Authority: A Laboratory Demonstration; The Wisdom of Groups; Competition and Aggression; Interpersonal Attraction: Clothes Make the Man; Love: The Mind-Body Connection; Bystander Apathy: Failing to Help Others in Distress; Whom Do We Help?*

UNIT REVIEW: Social Psychology

Social psychologists study how people think about, influence, and relate to one another.

Social Thinking

1: How do we tend to explain others' behavior and our own?
We generally explain people's behavior by *attributing* it to internal dispositions and/or to external situations. In committing the *fundamental attribution error*, we underestimate the influence of the situation on others' actions. When explaining our own behavior, we more often point to the situation. Our attributions influence our personal, legal, political, and workplace judgments.

2: Does what we think affect what we do, or does what we do affect what we think?
Attitudes influence behavior when other influences are minimal, and when the attitude is stable, specific to the behavior, and easily recalled.

Studies of the *foot-in-the-door phenomenon* and of *role*-playing reveal that our actions (especially those we feel responsible for) can also modify our attitudes. *Cognitive dissonance theory* proposes that behavior shapes attitudes because we feel discomfort when our actions and attitudes differ. We reduce the discomfort by bringing our attitudes more into line with what we have done.

Social Influence

3: What do experiments on conformity and compliance reveal about the power of social influence?
Asch's conformity studies demonstrated that under certain conditions people will *conform* to a group's judgment even when it is clearly incorrect. We may conform either to gain social approval (*normative social influence*) or because we welcome the information that others provide (*informational social influence*). In Milgram's famous experiments, people torn between obeying an experimenter and responding to another's pleas to stop the apparent shocks usually chose to obey orders. People most often obeyed when the person giving orders was nearby and was perceived as a legitimate authority figure; when the person giving orders was supported by a prestigious institution; when the victim was depersonalized or at a distance; and when no other person modeled defiance by disobeying.

4: How is our behavior affected by the presence of others or by being part of a group?
Social facilitation experiments reveal that the presence of either observers or co-actors can arouse individuals, boosting their performance on easy tasks but hindering it on difficult ones. When people pool their efforts toward a group goal, *social loafing* may occur as individuals free ride on others' efforts. *Deindividuation*—becoming less self-aware and self-restrained—may happen when people are both aroused and made to feel anonymous.

5: What are group polarization and groupthink?
Discussions among like-minded members often produce *group polarization*, as prevailing attitudes are intensified. This is one cause of *groupthink,* the tendency to suppress unwelcome information and make unrealistic decisions for the sake of group harmony. To prevent groupthink, leaders can welcome a variety of opinions, invite experts' critiques, and assign people to identify possible problems in developing plans.

6: How do cultural norms affect our behavior?
Cultural *norms* are rules for accepted and expected behaviors, ideas, attitudes, and values. Across places and over time *cultures* differ in their norms. Humans share a capacity for culture, and that shared capacity enables our striking human diversity by influencing our everyday attitudes and behaviors.

7: How much power do we have as individuals? Can a minority sway a majority?
The power of the group is great, but even a small minority may sway group opinion, especially when the minority expresses its views consistently.

Social Relations

8: What is prejudice?
Prejudice is a mixture of beliefs (often *stereotypes*), negative emotions, and predispositions to action. Prejudice may be overt (such as openly and consciously denying a particular ethnic group the right to vote) or subtle (such as feeling fearful when alone in an elevator with a stranger from a different racial or ethnic group).

9: What are the social and emotional roots of prejudice?
Social and economic inequalities may trigger prejudice as people in power attempt to justify the status quo or develop an *ingroup bias*. Fear and anger feed prejudice, and, when frustrated, we may focus our anger on a *scapegoat*.

10: What are the cognitive roots of prejudice?
In processing information, we tend to recognize diversity in our own groups but to overestimate similarities in other groups, as in the *other-race effect*. We also notice and remember vivid cases. These trends help create stereotypes. Favored social groups often rationalize their higher status with the *just-world phenomenon*.

11: What biological factors make us more prone to hurt one another?
Aggression is a complex behavior that results from an interaction between biology and experience. For example, genes influence our temperament, making us more or less likely to respond aggressively when frustrated in specific situations. Experiments stimulating portions of the brain (such as the amygdala and frontal lobes) have revealed neural systems in the brain that

- *Video: Scientific American Frontiers Series,* 2nd ed., *Segment 29: Superpower Ping-Pong*
- *Videos: Digital Media Archive: Psychology,* 1st ed., *Video Clip 41: Milgram's Obedience Studies; Video Clip 42: Schachter's Affiliation Experiment; Video Clip 40: Takooshian's Psychology of Bystanders*
- *ActivePsych: Scientific American Frontiers Teaching Modules,* 3rd ed.: *Hidden Prejudice: The Implicit Association Test*
- *Video: The Brain,* 2nd ed., *Module 24: Aggression, Violence, and the Brain*
- *PsychSim 5: Social Decision Making*

ANSWERS to Multiple-Choice Questions

1. **a.** group polarization.
2. **a.** People who agree to a small action are less likely to agree to a larger one later.
3. **a.** social identity.
4. **a.** ingroup bias.
5. **c.** attribution.
6. **b.** Playing violent video games decreases aggressive thoughts and behaviors.
7. **e.** minority influence.
8. **c.** aggression.
9. **e.** cognitive dissonance.
10. **d.** A physical behavior intended to hurt or destroy
11. **c.** social facilitation.
12. **b.** deindividuation.
13. **d.** a mirror-image perception.
14. **d.** adjusting our behavior or thinking toward some group standard.
15. **b.** the fundamental attribution error.

facilitate or inhibit aggression. Biochemical influences, such as testosterone and other hormones; alcohol (which disinhibits); and other substances also contribute to aggression.

12: What psychological factors may trigger aggressive behavior?

Frustration and other aversive events (such as heat, crowding, and provocation) can evoke hostility, especially in those rewarded for aggression, those who have learned aggression from role models, and those who have been influenced by media violence. Enacting violence in video games or viewing it in the media can desensitize people to cruelty and prime them to behave aggressively when provoked, or to view sexual aggression as more acceptable.

13: Why do we befriend or fall in love with some people but not with others?

Three factors are known to affect our liking for one another. Proximity—geographical nearness—is conducive to attraction, partly because *mere exposure* to novel stimuli enhances liking. Physical attractiveness increases social opportunities and influences the way we are perceived. As acquaintanceship moves toward friendship, similarity of attitudes and interests greatly increases liking.

14: How does romantic love typically change as time passes?

Passionate love is an aroused state that we cognitively label as love. The strong affection of *companionate love,* which often emerges as passionate love subsides, is enhanced by an *equitable* relationship and by intimate *self-disclosure.*

15: When are we most—and least—likely to help?

Altruism is unselfish regard for the well-being of others. We are less likely to help if others are present. This *bystander effect* is especially apparent in situations where the presence of others inhibits our noticing the event, interpreting it as an emergency, or assuming responsibility for offering help. Explanations of our willingness to help others focus on *social exchange theory* (the costs and benefits of helping); the intrinsic rewards of helping others; the *reciprocity norm* (we help those who help us); and the *social-responsibility norm* (we help those who need our help).

16: How do social traps and mirror-image perceptions fuel social conflict?

Social *conflicts* are situations in which people perceive their actions, goals, or ideas to be incompatible. In *social traps,* two or more individuals engage in mutually destructive behavior by rationally pursuing their own self-interests. People in conflict tend to expect the worst of each other, producing *mirror-image perceptions* that can become *self-fulfilling prophecies.*

17: How can we transform feelings of prejudice, aggression, and conflict into attitudes that promote peace?

Enemies sometimes become friends, especially when the circumstances favor equal-status contact, cooperation to achieve *superordinate goals,* understanding through communication, and reciprocated conciliatory gestures.

Terms and Concepts to Remember

TECHNOLOGY RESOURCES

Technology Resources for Unit 14 can be found on pp. 692–693.

Rubric for Grading the Free-Response Question

This is an 8-point question. Allow 1 point for an adequate explanation of how a phenomenon affects behavior (5 points total). Allow 1 point for an adequate explanation of how three of the five might perpetuate racial discrimination (3 points total). Modify the rubric by adding or subtracting terms depending on what was emphasized in class.

Examples of Language That Would Score the Behavior Points

Deindividuation affects behavior

1. by arousing people and diminishing the sense of responsibility in a group situation.
2. through the abandonment of normal restraints to the power of the group.

AP* Practice Test Questions ◄ ·······································

Multiple-Choice Questions

1. The enhancement of a group's prevailing tendencies occurs when people within a group discuss an idea that most of them either favor or oppose. This tendency is called
 a. group polarization.
 b. deindividuation.
 c. the just-world phenomenon.
 d. discrimination.
 e. categorization.

2. Which of the following statements about the foot-in-the-door phenomenon is *false*?
 a. People who agree to a small action are less likely to agree to a larger one later.
 b. The Chinese took advantage of this phenomenon in the thought control program they used on prisoners during the Korean war.
 c. To get people to agree to something big, start small and build.
 d. Succumb to a temptation and you will find the next temptation harder to resist.
 e. This phenomenon has been used to boost charitable contributions, blood donations, and product sales.

3. Associating ourselves with certain groups and contrasting ourselves with others is often referred to as establishing
 a. social identity.
 b. discrimination.
 c. a stereotype.
 d. prejudice.
 e. minority influence.

4. When we believe our school is better than all the other schools in town we exhibit
 a. ingroup bias.
 b. conformity.
 c. the scapegoat theory.
 d. discrimination.
 e. groupthink.

5. People frequently credit or blame either internal dispositions or external situations for others' behavior. This is called
 a. the foot-in-the-door phenomenon.
 b. the fundamental attribution error.
 c. attribution.
 d. social psychology.
 e. social thinking.

6. Which of the following statements is *false*?
 a. Violent video games have greater effects on aggressive behavior than violent movies.
 b. Playing violent video games decreases aggressive thoughts and behaviors.
 c. Observing television violence desensitizes people to cruelty and primes them to respond aggressively when provoked.
 d. Once established, aggressive behavior patterns are difficult to change.
 e. Children whose aggression successfully intimidates other children may become more aggressive.

7. Rosa Parks' refusal to sit at the back of the bus is an example of
 a. social thinking.
 b. group polarization.
 c. conformity.
 d. a stereotype.
 e. minority influence.

8. Any physical or verbal behavior intended to hurt or destroy is called
 a. the mere exposure effect.
 b. hindsight bias.
 c. aggression.
 d. the just-world phenomenon.
 e. the other-race effect.

9. When we become aware that our attitudes and actions don't coincide, we experience tension, or
 a. role playing.
 b. the fundamental attribution error.
 c. social pressure.
 d. social influence.
 e. cognitive dissonance.

10. Which of the following *least* describes prejudice?
 a. An unjustifiable attitude toward a group
 b. Schemas that influence how we notice and interpret events
 c. Preconceived ideas that bias our impressions of others' behavior
 d. A physical behavior intended to hurt or destroy
 e. Automatic and unconscious

11. Performing a task better in the presence of others is called
 a. compliance.
 b. group polarization.
 c. social facilitation.
 d. conformity.
 e. social loafing.

12. Becoming less self-conscious and less restrained when in a group situation is termed
 a. social loafing.
 b. deindividuation.
 c. social facilitation.
 d. obedience.
 e. cognitive dissonance.

13. If Juan believes Ngoc is annoyed with him, he may snub her, causing her to act in ways that justify his perception. This is an example of
 a. superordinate goals.
 b. tension-reduction.
 c. conciliation.
 d. a mirror-image perception.
 e. a social trap.

14. Conformity is best described as
 a. sharing our moods.
 b. unconsciously mimicking others.
 c. changing how we think about others.
 d. adjusting our behavior or thinking toward some group standard.
 e. bringing our attitudes in line with our actions.

15. When we overestimate the influence of personality, and underestimate the influence of situations, we are demonstrating
 a. the attitudes-follow-behavior principle.
 b. the fundamental attribution error.
 c. central route persuasion.
 d. the foot-in-the-door phenomenon.
 e. cognitive dissonance theory.

Free-Response Question

Explain how the following phenomena can affect behavior. Explain further how three of the five might play a role in perpetuating racial discrimination.
 • Deindividuation
 • Social loafing
 • Social facilitation
 • Obedience
 • Cognitive dissonance

 WEB

Multiple-choice self-tests and more may be found at www.worthpublishers.com/myers

Social loafing affects behavior
 1. because people acting as part of a group feel less accountable and worry less about what others think.
 2. because people in a group adopt the view that each individual's contributions are dispensable.
 3. because individuals slack off when they are in group situations where members share equally in the benefits of a task regardless of how much each contributes.

Social facilitation affects behavior by causing people to perform
 1. better in the presence of others while engaging in tasks at which they are skilled.

 Rubric continued

 2. worse in the presence of others while engaging in tasks at which they are not skilled.

Obedience affects behavior
 1. when people follow the orders of a legitimate authority figure to harm others even when a victim asks them to stop.
 2. more when the authority figure is supported by a prestigious institution.

Cognitive dissonance affects behavior
 1. by driving an individual to reduce discomfort when two thoughts are incompatible.
 2. when awareness of attitudes and actions clash, and one reduces the dissonance by changing attitudes.

Examples of Language That Would Score the Perpetuating Racism Points

Deindividuation: In a group, people with racist inclinations might lose their normal sense of restraint and shout racist comments or behave in racially discriminatory ways.

Social loafing does not appear to perpetuate racism.

Social facilitation: In a group, someone who is skilled at making racist statements will feel more confident in making racist statements.

Obedience: An authority figure who expresses racist views is more likely to be followed or believed by virtue of his or her position, spreading the racial prejudice.

Cognitive dissonance: If people's attitudes are non-racist, but they behave in racially discriminatory ways, they may work to reduce the dissonance by becoming more racially discriminatory in their attitudes.

Careers in Psychology

Jennifer Zwolinski
University of San Diego

What can you do with a degree in psychology? Lots!

If you major in psychology in college, you will graduate with a scientific mind-set and an awareness of basic principles of human behavior (biological mechanisms, development, cognition, psychological disorders, social interaction). This background will prepare you for success in many areas, including business, the helping professions, health services, marketing, law, sales, and teaching. You may even go on to graduate school for specialized training to become a psychology professional. This appendix describes the various levels of psychology education and some jobs available at those levels; psychology's specialized subfields; and ways you can improve your chances of admission to graduate school.

Preparing for a Career in Psychology

PSYCHOLOGY IS THE SECOND MOST POPULAR college major in the United States, second only to business (Princeton Review, 2005). Recent data show that more than 88,000 psychology majors graduate annually from U.S. colleges and universities (U.S. National Center for Education Statistics, 2007). An undergraduate degree in psychology can prepare you for a broad array of jobs in numerous fields after graduation. For a career that is more closely related to the field of psychology, you will need a graduate degree.

The Bachelor's Degree

If you major in psychology and earn a four-year bachelor's degree, you will have several possible career paths to follow (Cannon, 2005). First, you might consider employment after graduation in a variety of professional settings. Most students who graduate with psychology majors find work in for-profit organizations, especially in management, sales, and administration. **TABLE A.1** on the next page shows the top 10 occupations that employ people with a bachelor's degree in psychology.[1] If you choose to work more directly in the field of psychology, a bachelor's degree will qualify you to work as an assistant to psychologists, researchers, or other professionals in community mental health centers, vocational rehabilitation

[1]For a more comprehensive list of job titles, see Appleby (2006).

A-1

Appendix A

TEACHING TIP

Students should appreciate that they do not necessarily have to treat people with mental illness if they get a psychology degree. Psychology degrees provide skills that are applicable in a multitude of jobs, making psychology one of the most popular majors at colleges and universities in the U.S.

TEACHING TIP

Have students contact a local community college or four-year college/university or the post-high school institution they are interested in attending to see what the most popular majors are at that particular institution (as measured by the number of students who major in a particular field). Discuss the following questions with students:

- What factors might explain the diversity of popular college majors at a given institution?

- Does knowing what is the "popular" major at a particular institution you favor influence your own choice of major?

TABLE A.1

TOP 10 OCCUPATIONS THAT EMPLOY PEOPLE WITH A BACHELOR'S DEGREE IN PSYCHOLOGY

1. Top- and mid-level managers, executives, administrators
2. Sales occupations, including retail
3. Social workers
4. Other management-related occupations
5. Personnel, training, labor relations specialists
6. Other administrative occupations
7. Insurance, securities, real estate, business services
8. Other marketing and sales occupations
9. Registered nurses, pharmacists, therapists, physician assistants
10. Accountants, auditors, other financial specialists

Source: Fogg et al. (2004).

offices, and correctional programs (U.S. Bureau of Labor Statistics, 2008). A second option for psychology majors after graduation is to pursue a graduate degree in psychology. Approximately 42 percent of U.S. psychology majors go on to graduate school in psychology (Fogg et al., 2004). A third option is to pursue advanced training in other disciplines such as law, business, education, or medicine.

Clearly, psychology majors are marketable beyond the boundaries of psychology. Their sought-after skills include an ability to work and get along with others, a desire to understand oneself and others, adaptability to changing situations, and a capacity for problem solving (Landrum, 2001). Psychology majors also have a number of methodological skills that result from the focus on the scientific study of human and animal behavior. The study of statistics and research methodology contributes to a scientific mind-set that emphasizes exploring and managing uncertainty, critical and analytical skills, and logical thinking abilities. The ability to analyze data using statistics, conduct database searches, and integrate multiple sources of information would be helpful in a number of professional settings. Prospective employers will also appreciate the excellent written and oral communication skills among students who present their research projects at conferences and master the widely used American Psychological Association's (APA) writing style.

There are some things that all psychology majors can do to maximize success in college and, later, in the job market. Employers who hire people with only a bachelor's degree tend to favor individuals with strong interpersonal skills and practical experience as well as a good education (Cannon, 2005). It's not too early for you to begin planning how you can use your upcoming college education to improve your chances for success after college. Betsy Morgan and Ann Korschgen (1998) offer the following helpful tips for succeeding in college and increasing your chances of getting a job after graduation. Many of these tools will benefit students who plan to apply to graduate school as well.

1. *Get to know your instructors.* Talk with them about the field of psychology and get their advice on your career plan. Ask them to support you on an independent study internship or research project. By learning more about your skills and future aims,

faculty members can help you accomplish your goals. This may even result in an enthusiastic reference for future employment.

2. *Take courses that support your interests.* Although the psychology major offers a range of skills that will benefit you, don't assume the psychology curriculum will offer all the skills necessary in your area of interest. Add courses to increase your knowledge base and skills. This will show prospective employers, for example, that your specific interests are in line with the demands of the job.

3. *Familiarize yourself with available resources, such as campus career services and alumni.* If you are searching for a part-time job during your studies (or a full-time job after graduation), career services can help you identify and market your job skills and emphasize the knowledge and abilities you have in your resume. They can also help you to network with other alumni who are working in your area of interest and who can help you to prepare for the career that you want.

4. *Participate in at least one internship experience.* Students can gain relevant experience outside the classroom. Internships are offered during the school year as well as the summer break. Some are paid and others are not, but you may be able to earn course credit while completing your internship. In addition to trying out a possible career and gaining relevant work experience before you graduate, you will increase your support network of mentors who can provide supervision and support for your career goals as well as letters of support when you apply for jobs or to graduate school.

5. *Volunteer some of your time and talent to campus or community organizations, such as Psi Chi (the International Honor Society in Psychology) or your college's psychology club.* In addition to showing that you are an active citizen in your department, you will gain important skills, such as meeting and event planning, how to work with a group, and improved communication skills, all of which enhance your marketability.

Postgraduate Degrees

A graduate degree in psychology will give you proficiency in an area of psychological specialization. According to the U.S. Bureau of Labor Statistics (2008), psychologists with advanced degrees held approximately 166,000 jobs in 2006. Employment for psychologists is expected to grow 15 percent from 2006 to 2016, which is faster than the average for all occupations. The work settings for psychologists vary somewhat by type of graduate degree. As shown in **FIGURE A.1** on the next page, psychologists with a doctorate work primarily in universities and colleges; most people with a master's degree work in other educational institutions (such as public schools) and in for-profit companies. Among advanced degree recipients in 2005–2006, a total of 19,770 had master's degrees and 4921 earned doctoral degrees (U.S. National Center for Education Statistics, 2007).

The Master's Degree

A master's degree in psychology requires at least two years of full-time graduate study in a specific subfield of psychology. In addition to specialized course work in psychology, requirements usually include practical experience in an applied setting

On the job with a B.A. There are psychology-related jobs available even for those with only a B.A. degree. For example, this case manager working for a mental health organization in Florida is conducting a survey of the homeless people in her county to consider the best ways to address their needs.
▲

TEACHING TIP

While the psychology degree is widely useful regardless of your career choice, working in psychology typically requires a postgraduate degree. Help students see that the training for psychologists—both academic and clinical—is no more rigorous than training to be a doctor or lawyer.

TEACHING TIP

At this point, you may want to use **Student Project:** *Interviewing a Psychologist* (p. 3) from Bolt's Teacher's Resource Binder.

Appendix A

A-4 APPENDIX A: CAREERS IN PSYCHOLOGY

➤ **FIGURE A.1**
Work settings for psychology-degree recipients
Source: Fogg et al., 2004.

Chart categories: For-profit companies, State or local government, Not-for-profit organizations, Universities and 4-year colleges, Self-employed, Federal government, Other educational institutions. X-axis: 0% to 60%. Legend: Doctorate, MA/MS, BA/BS.

Because students often want to enter psychology as a career to "help people," assist these students in finding areas of psychology that capitalize on their interests. Also, help students realistically calculate how long it takes to earn a professional degree.

Prescription privileges Many psychologists would like the opportunity to prescribe medicines (normally reserved for *physicians* only) in order to expand the scope of clinical practice and to meet the need for psychiatric services in many parts of the United States. Psychologists in the U.S. military and in some U.S. states currently have prescription privileges.

Tom Stewart/Corbis

and/or a master's thesis reporting on an original research project. You might acquire a master's degree to do specialized work in psychology. As a graduate with a master's degree, you might handle research and data collection and analysis in a university, government, or private industry setting. You might work under the supervision of a psychologist with a doctorate, providing some clinical service such as therapy or testing. Or you might find a job in the health, government, industry, or education fields. You might also acquire a master's degree as a stepping stone for more advanced study in a doctoral program in psychology, which will considerably expand the number of employment opportunities available to you (Super & Super, 2001).

Doctoral Degrees

You will probably need five to seven years of graduate study in a specific subfield of psychology to get your doctoral degree. The degree you choose to pursue will depend on your career goals. You will probably choose to earn a doctor of philosophy (Ph.D.) in psychology if your career goals are geared toward conducting research, or a doctor of psychology (Psy.D.) if you are more interested in pursuing professional practice (clinical or therapeutic work). Training for the Ph.D. culminates in a dissertation (an extensive research paper you will be required to defend orally) based on original research. Courses in quantitative research methods, which include the use of computer-based analysis, are an important part of graduate study and are necessary to complete the dissertation. Psy.D. training may be based on clinical work and examinations rather than a dissertation. It is important to note, however, that psychologists with Psy.D. degrees are not the only ones who work in professional practice. Many psychologists who earn a Ph.D. in clinical or counseling

TEACHING TIP

At this point, you may want to use **Lecture/Discussion Topics: *What Do Employers Look for in Psychology Graduates?*** (p. 3) or ***Careers With a B.A. in Psychology*** (p. 4) from Bolt's Teacher's Resource Binder.

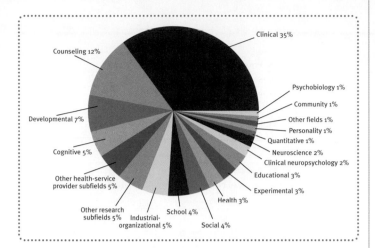

Counseling 12%
Clinical 35%
Developmental 7%
Psychobiology 1%
Community 1%
Cognitive 5%
Other fields 1%
Personality 1%
Quantitative 1%
Other health-service provider subfields 5%
Neuroscience 2%
Clinical neuropsychology 2%
Educational 3%
Experimental 3%
Health 3%
Other research subfields 5%
Industrial-organizational 5%
School 4%
Social 4%

➤ FIGURE A.2
U.S. psychology Ph.D.s by subfield
Source: National Science Foundation 2001
Survey of Doctorate Recipients. Compiled by
the American Psychological Association.

psychology conduct research and work in professional settings. If you pursue clinical and counseling psychology programs, you should expect at least a one-year internship in addition to the regular course work, clinical practice, and research.

FIGURE A.2 lists by subfield the 2001 psychology Ph.D.s earned in the United States. Clinical psychology is the most popular specialty area among those with doctorates in psychology. The largest employment growth areas for doctoral graduates have been in the for-profit and self-employment sectors, including health services providers, industrial-organizational psychology, and educational psychology. About one-third of doctoral-level psychologists are employed in academic settings (Fogg et al., 2004).

In 2001, a total of 73 percent of new doctoral respondents and 55 percent of new master's respondents indicated that their primary occupational position was their first choice. Most new graduates with a master's degree or a Ph.D. are fairly satisfied with their current positions overall in terms of salary, benefits, opportunities for personal development, supervisors, colleagues, and working conditions (Kohout & Wicherski, 2004; Singleton et al., 2003).

Subfields of Psychology

IF YOU ARE LIKE MOST PSYCHOLOGY STUDENTS, you may be unaware of the wide variety of specialties and work settings available in psychology (Terre & Stoddart, 2000). To date, the American Psychological Association (APA) has formed 56 divisions (TABLE A.2 on the next page). The following paragraphs (arranged alphabetically) describe some careers in the main specialty areas of psychology, most of which require a graduate degree in psychology.

Clinical psychologists promote psychological health in individuals, groups, and organizations. Some clinical psychologists specialize in specific psychological disorders. Others treat a range of disorders, from adjustment difficulties to severe psychopathology. Clinical psychologists might engage in research, teaching, assessment, and consultation. Some hold workshops and lectures on psychological issues for other professionals

TEACHING TIP

Two major professional psychology organizations fund research, publish journals, and establish ethical and practical guidelines for professionals to follow:

- The American Psychological Association (APA) was founded in 1892. It is the primary publisher of scholarly journals in the field and promotes research and practice through funding initiatives and conferences.

- The Association for Psychological Science (APS) was founded in 1988 to promote the development of scientific psychology. The APS strictly promotes research, application, and teaching of scientific psychology.

Appendix A

TEACHING TIP

Students may wonder why there is no Division 11. According to the APA Web site, Division 11 was "Abnormal Psychology and Psychotherapy. It had a short life—by 1946 it had joined Division 12 for the Division of Clinical and Abnormal Psychology; Division 11 remains vacant."

Source: www.apa.org.

TABLE A.2

APA Divisions by Number and Name

1. Society for General Psychology	29. Psychotherapy
2. Society for the Teaching of Psychology	30. Society of Psychological Hypnosis
3. Experimental Psychology	31. State, Provincial, and Territorial Psychological Association Affairs
4. There is currently no Division 4.	32. Society for Humanistic Psychology
5. Evaluation, Measurement, and Statistics	33. Intellectual and Developmental Disabilities
6. Behavioral Neuroscience and Comparative Psychology	34. Population and Environmental Psychology
7. Developmental Psychology	35. Society for the Psychology of Women
8. Society for Personality and Social Psychology	36. Psychology of Religion
9. Society for the Psychological Study of Social Issues (SPSSI)	37. Society for Child and Family Policy and Practice
10. Society for the Psychology of Aesthetics, Creativity, and the Arts	38. Health Psychology
11. There is currently no Division 11.	39. Psychoanalysis
12. Society of Clinical Psychology	40. Clinical Neuropsychology
13. Society of Consulting Psychology	41. American Psychology-Law Society
14. Society for Industrial and Organizational Psychology	42. Psychologists in Independent Practice
15. Educational Psychology	43. Society for Family Psychology
16. School Psychology	44. Society for the Psychological Study of Lesbian, Gay, and Bisexual Issues
17. Society of Counseling Psychology	45. Society for the Psychological Study of Ethnic Minority Issues
18. Psychologists in Public Service	46. Media Psychology
19. Society for Military Psychology	47. Exercise and Sport Psychology
20. Adult Development and Aging	48. Society for the Study of Peace, Conflict, and Violence: Peace Psychology Division
21. Applied Experimental and Engineering Psychology	49. Group Psychology and Group Psychotherapy
22. Rehabilitation Psychology	50. Addictions
23. Society for Consumer Psychology	51. Society for the Psychological Study of Men and Masculinity
24. Society for Theoretical and Philosophical Psychology	52. International Psychology
25. Behavior Analysis	53. Society of Clinical Child and Adolescent Psychology
26. Society for the History of Psychology	54. Society of Pediatric Psychology
27. Society for Community Research and Action: Division of Community Psychology	55. American Society for the Advancement of Pharmacotherapy
28. Psychopharmacology and Substance Abuse	56. Trauma Psychology

Source: American Psychological Association.

or for the public. Clinical psychologists work in a variety of settings, including private practice, mental health service organizations, schools, universities, industries, legal systems, medical systems, counseling centers, government agencies, and military services.

To become a clinical psychologist, you will need to earn a doctorate from a clinical psychology program. The APA sets the standards for clinical psychology graduate programs, offering accreditation (official recognition) to those who meet their standards. In all U.S. states, clinical psychologists working in independent practice must obtain a license to offer services such as therapy and testing.

Cognitive psychologists study thought processes and focus on such topics as perception, language, attention, problem solving, memory, judgment and decision making, forgetting, and intelligence. Recent areas of research interest include designing computer-based models of thought processes and identifying biological correlates of cognition. As a cognitive psychologist, you might work as a professor, industrial consultant, or human factors specialist in an educational or business setting.

Community psychologists move beyond focusing on specific individuals or families and deal with broad problems of mental health in community settings. These psychologists believe that human behavior is powerfully influenced by the interaction between people and their physical, social, political, and economic environments. They seek to improve individual functioning by enhancing environmental settings to promote psychological health. Community psychologists focus on prevention, promotion of positive mental health, and crisis intervention, with special attention to the problems of underserved groups and ethnic minorities. Given the shared emphasis on prevention, some community psychologists collaborate with professionals in other areas, such as public health. As a community psychologist, your work settings could include federal, state, and local departments of mental health, corrections, and welfare systems. You might conduct research or help evaluate research in health service settings, serve as an independent consultant for a private or government agency, or teach and consult as a college or university faculty member.

Counseling psychologists help people adjust to life transitions or make life-style changes. This field is very similar to clinical psychology, except that counseling psychologists typically help people with adjustment problems rather than severe psychopathology. Like clinical psychologists, counseling psychologists conduct therapy and provide assessments to individuals and groups. As a counseling psychologist, you would emphasize your clients' strengths, helping clients cope during a transitional time using their own skills, interests, and abilities. You might find yourself working in an academic setting as a faculty member or administrator or in a university counseling center, community mental health center, business, or private practice. As with clinical psychology, if you plan to work in independent practice you will need to obtain a state license to provide counseling services to the public.

Developmental psychologists conduct research in age-related behavioral changes and apply their scientific knowledge to educational, child care, policy, and related settings. As a developmental psychologist, you would investigate change across a broad range of topics, including the biological, social, psychological, and cognitive aspects of development. Developmental psychology informs a number of applied fields, including educational psychology, school psychology, child psychopathology, and gerontology. The field also informs public policy in areas such as education and child-care reform, maternal and child health, and attachment and adoption. You would probably specialize in behavior during infancy, childhood, adolescence, or middle or late adulthood. Your work setting could be an educational institution, day-care center, youth group program, or senior center.

Cognitive consulting Cognitive psychologists may advise businesses on how to operate more effectively by understanding the human factors involved.

Coping with disaster After Peru's deadly August 2007 earthquake, this community psychologist working with Médecins Sans Frontières (Doctors Without Borders) helped survivors cope with the loss of their homes, and the deaths of family members and friends for many.

INTERCONNECTING

Help students identify famous psychologists who work in each subfield:

Developmental psychologists: Sigmund Freud, Erik Erikson, Lawrence Kohlberg, and Jean Piaget all studied developmental stages of growth; Mary Ainsworth and John Bowlby studied attachment in infants and children; and Lev Vygotsky studied how other people spark cognitive development in children.

Cognitive psychologists: Albert Bandura studies observational learning and self-efficacy; and Robert Sternberg studies intelligence and wisdom.

Appendix A

INTERCONNECTING

Help students identify famous psychologists who work in each subfield:

Experimental/research psychologists: Most psychologists listed under other subfields would also be considered "experimental" or "research" psychologists, but some prominent names here might include Martin Seligman, the founder of positive psychology, and B. F. Skinner, a prominent behaviorist from the 20th century.

TEACHING TIP

Educational psychologists are different from school psychologists. Educational psychologists research issues related to teaching and learning. School psychologists work in school districts to assess students' learning needs and to give advice regarding mental health issues.

TEACHING TIP

At this point, you may want to use **Lecture/Discussion Topic: *Quantitative Psychology*** (p. 4) from Bolt's Teacher's Resource Binder.

Criminal profiling On the popular TV show *Law and Order: Special Victims Unit,* Dr. George Huang (played by B. D. Wong) is an FBI agent and psychiatrist who uses his background in forensic psychology to conduct criminal investigations.

Educational psychologists study the relationship between learning and our physical and social environments. They study the psychological processes involved in learning and develop strategies for enhancing the learning process. As an educational psychologist, you might work in a university—in a psychology department or a school of education. You might conduct basic research on topics related to learning or develop innovative methods of teaching to enhance the learning process. You might design effective tests including measures of aptitude and achievement. You might be employed by a school or government agency or charged with designing and implementing effective employee-training programs in a business setting.

Experimental psychologists are a diverse group of scientists who investigate a variety of basic behavioral processes in research involving humans and other animals. Prominent areas of study in experimental research include comparative methods of science, motivation, learning, thought, attention, memory, perception, and language. Most experimental psychologists identify with a particular subfield, such as cognitive psychology, depending on their area of study. It is also important to note that the experimental method for conducting research studies is not limited to the field of experimental psychology, as many other subfields rely on experimental methodology to conduct studies. As an experimental psychologist, you would most likely work in an academic setting, teaching courses and supervising students' research in addition to conducting your own research using experimental methodology. Or you might be employed by a research institution, zoo, business, industry affiliate, or government agency.

Forensic psychologists apply psychological principles to legal issues. They conduct research on the interface of law and psychology, help to create public policies related to mental health, help law-enforcement agencies in criminal investigations, or assist in forensic consultation involving jury selection and deliberation research. They also provide therapy and assessment to assist the legal community. Some forensic psychologists hold law degrees and provide clients with legal services as well. Although most forensic psychologists are clinical psychologists, they might have expertise in other areas of psychology, such as social or cognitive psychology. As a forensic psychologist, you might work in a university psychology department, law school, research organization, community mental health agency, law-enforcement agency, court, or correctional setting.

Health psychologists are researchers and practitioners concerned with psychology's contribution to promoting health and preventing disease. As applied psychologists or clinicians, they may help individuals lead healthier lives by designing, conducting, and evaluating programs to stop smoking, lose weight, improve sleep, manage pain, treat associated psychosocial problems with chronic and terminal illness, or prevent the spread of sexually transmitted infections. As researchers and clinicians, they identify conditions and practices associated with health and illness to help create effective interventions. In public service, health psychologists study and work to improve government policies and health care systems. As a health psychologist, you could be employed in a hospital, medical school, rehabilitation center, public health agency, college or university, or, if you are also a clinical psychologist, in private practice.

Industrial-organizational (I/O) psychologists study the relationship between people and their working environments. They may develop new ways to increase productivity, improve personnel selection, or promote job satisfaction in a business setting. Their interests include organizational structure and change, consumer behavior, and personnel selection and training. As an I/O psychologist, you might conduct workplace training or provide organizational analysis and development. You may find yourself working in business, industry, the government, or a college or university. Or you may be self-employed as a consultant or work for a management

RESEARCH

Forensic psychology has grown with the popularity of crime shows on TV.

- Have students research different jobs they could get with a forensic psychology degree.
- Contact the local police department to see if they employ a forensic psychologist. Inquire about the responsibilities such a person would have.

consulting firm. I/O psychology is especially welcoming of diverse academic backgrounds, and can be successfully paired with such fields as engineering, industrial design, business, and computer science.

Neuropsychologists investigate the relationship between neurological processes (structure and function of the brain) and behavior. As a neuropsychologist you might assess, diagnose, or treat disorders related to the central nervous system, such as Alzheimer's disease or stroke. You might also evaluate individuals for evidence of head injuries, learning and developmental disabilities (such as autism), and other psychiatric disorders (including ADHD). If you are a *clinical neuropsychologist,* you might work in the neurology, neurosurgery, or psychiatric unit of a hospital. Neuropsychologists also work in academic settings, where they conduct research and teach.

Psychometric and *quantitative psychologists* study the methods and techniques used to acquire psychological knowledge. A psychometrician may update existing neurocognitive or personality tests or devise new tests for use in clinical and school settings or in business and industry. These psychologists also administer, score, and interpret such tests. Quantitative psychologists collaborate with researchers to design, analyze, and interpret the results of research programs. As a psychometric or quantitative psychologist, you will need to be well trained in research methods, statistics, and computer technology. You will most likely be employed by a university or college, testing company, private research firm, or government agency.

Rehabilitation psychologists are researchers and practitioners who work with people who have lost optimal functioning after an accident, illness, or other event. As a rehabilitation psychologist, you would probably work in a medical rehabilitation institution or hospital. You might also work in a medical school, university, state or federal vocational rehabilitation agency, or in private practice serving people with physical disabilities.

School psychologists are involved in the assessment of and intervention for children and adolescents in educational settings. They diagnose and treat cognitive, social, and emotional problems that may negatively influence learning or overall functioning at school. As a school psychologist, you would collaborate with teachers, parents, and administrators, making recommendations to improve student learning. You would work in an academic setting, a federal or state government agency, a child guidance center, or a behavioral research laboratory.

Social psychologists are interested in our interactions with others. Social psychologists study how our beliefs, feelings, and behaviors are affected by and influence other people. They study topics such as attitudes, aggression, prejudice,

Class counselor School psychologists, who have their master's degree in psychology, may find themselves working with students individually or in groups, as well as in a consultative role for their school's administrators.

© Spencer Grant/ PhotoEdit

INTERCONNECTING

Help students identify famous psychologists who work in each subfield:

Neuropsychologists: Nobel Laureate Roger Sperry and his colleague Michael Gazzaniga work with split-brain research; Richard Davidson conducts functional MRI research to determine satisfaction with life and other positive traits.

Social psychologists: Stanley Milgram studied obedience; Solomon Asch studied conformity; and Philip Zimbardo studies the power of role playing on behavior.

RESEARCH

Have students research which universities offer graduate study in behavior genetics or related fields in neuropsychology.

● How many programs are there? Are any near where you live?

● What job opportunities are available to people who get a degree in behavior genetics?

interpersonal attraction, group behavior, and leadership. As a social psychologist, you would probably be a college or university faculty member. You might also work in organizational consultation, marketing research, or other applied psychology fields including social neuroscience. Some social psychologists work for hospitals, federal agencies, or businesses performing applied research.

As a **sport psychologist,** you would study the psychological factors that influence, and are influenced by, participation in sports and other physical activities. Professional activities of sports psychologists include coach education and athlete preparation, as well as research and teaching. Sports psychologists who also have a clinical or counseling degree can apply those skills to working with individuals with psychological problems such as anxiety or substance-abuse problems that might interfere with optimal performance. If you were not working in an academic or research setting, you would most likely work as part of a team or organization or in a private capacity.

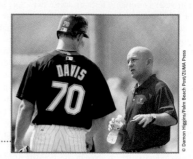

▼
Curing catchers Sports psychologists often work directly with athletes in an effort to help them improve their performance. Here the Florida Marlins team psychologist consults with catching prospect Brad Davis during spring training.

Preparing Early for Graduate Study in Psychology

COMPETITION FOR THE OPENINGS FOR advanced degrees in psychology is keen. If you plan to go to graduate school after college, there are a number of things you can do in advance to maximize your chances of gaining admission to the school of your choice.

The first step is to take full advantage of your opportunities in high school. By enrolling in challenging elective courses and working hard to develop an academic skill set, you will have paved the way for success in college. Successful students also take the time to learn effective study skills (seeking help from their teachers as needed) and to establish disciplined study habits. Involve yourself in extracurricular activities, gain some experience in the world of work with part-time jobs, and look for opportunities to volunteer in your school and community. In addition to helping you grow as a person, becoming a well-rounded student with high standards helps you to earn scholarships and increase your chances of being accepted by more colleges and universities.

During your first year on campus, continue to maximize opportunities and obtain the experience needed to gain admission to a competitive program. Kristy Arnold and Kelly Horrigan (2002) offer a number of suggestions to facilitate this process.

1. *Network.* Get to know faculty members and the psychology department by attending activities and meetings. This will be especially helpful when you apply to graduate school or for a professional position, because many applications require two to three letters of reference. Become involved in psychology clubs and in Psi

▼⋯

Membership benefits
Members of the Psi Chi
Honor Society, such as those
meeting here, enjoy edu-
cational and professional
benefits. They may attend
special Psi Chi sessions at
psychological conventions,
apply for research grants in
psychology or other academic awards, and read about
research advances in the
society's journal *Eye on Psi
Chi.* (For more information,
see www.psichi.org.)

Chi, the International Honor Society in Psychology. These meetings connect students with similar interests and expose them to a broader study of the field.

2. *Become actively involved in research as early as possible.* Start by doing simple
tasks such as data entry and data collection, and over time you will be prepared
to conduct your own research project under the supervision of a research mentor. Consider applying for summer research positions through your university
or from other organizations such as the American Psychological Association
Summer Science Institute (SSI) or the National Science Foundation Research
Experiences for Undergraduates (REU) program to test your interest in academic careers and to build your skills for future study in psychology.

3. *Volunteer or get a job in a psychology-related field.* Getting involved will show your
willingness to apply psychological concepts to real-world settings. Further, it will
showcase your ability to juggle a number of tasks successfully, such as work
and school—an important skill for graduate school success.

4. *Maintain good grades.* Demonstrate the ability to do well in graduate school
with successful completion of challenging courses, especially those related to
your interests. (See pages 14–15 and pages 293–294 for tips on how to do well
in this and other courses, and how to improve your retention of the information you are learning.)

In your junior year, you should begin studying for the Graduate Record Exam
(GRE), the standardized test that applicants to graduate school must complete. Many
graduate programs in psychology require both the General GRE and the Psychology
subject tests. If you start preparing early, you will be ready for success in your graduate school application and study.

* * *

So, the next time someone asks what you would do with a psychology degree, tell
them you will have a lot of options. You might use your acquired skills and understanding to get a job and succeed in any number of fields, or you might pursue graduate school and then career opportunities in associated professions. In any
case, what you learn about behavior and mental processes will surely enrich your
life (Hammer, 2003).

For More Information

www.apa.org (Web site for the American Psychological Association)

Actkinson, T. R. (2000). Master's and myth. *Eye on Psi Chi, 4,* 19–25.

American Psychological Association (2003). *Careers for the twenty-first century.* Washington, DC: Author.

American Psychological Association (2005). *Graduate study in psychology.* Washington, DC: Author.

Appleby, D. C. (2002). *The savvy psychology major.* Dubuque, IA: Kendall/Hunt.

Appleby, D. C. (2006). Occupations of interest to psychology majors from the Dictionary of Occupational Titles. *Eye on Psi Chi, 10,* 28–29.

Arnold, K., & Horrigan, K. (2002). Gaining admission into the graduate program of your choice. *Eye on Psi Chi, 7,* 1, 30–33.

Aubrecht, L. (2001). What can you do with a BA in psychology? *Eye on Psi Chi, 5,* 29–31.

Cannon, J. (2005). Career planning and opportunities: The bachelor's degree in psychology, *Eye on Psi Chi, 9,* 26–28.

Huss, M. (1996). Secrets to standing out from the pile: Getting into graduate school. *Psi Chi Newsletter,* 6–7.

Koch, G. (2001). Utilizing Psi Chi's programs to maximize learning and success. *Eye on Psi Chi, 10,* 22.

Kracen, A. C., & Wallace, I. J. (Eds.) (2008). *Applying to graduate school in psychology: Advice from successful students and prominent psychologists.* Washington, DC: American Psychological Association.

Lammers, B. (2000). Quick tips for applying to graduate school in psychology. *Eye on Psi Chi, 4,* 40–42.

Landrum, E. (2001). I'm getting my bachelor's degree in psychology. What can I do with it? *Eye on Psi Chi, 6,* 22–24.

LaRoche, K. (2004). Advantages of undergraduate research: A student's perspective. *Eye on Psi Chi, 8,* 20–21.

Morgan, B., & Korschgen, A. (2001). Psychology career exploration made easy. *Eye on Psi Chi, 5,* 35–36.

Schultheiss, D. E. P. (2008). *Psychology as a major: Is it right for me and what can I do with my degree?* Washington, DC: American Psychological Association.

Sternberg, R. (Ed.) (2002). *Career paths in psychology: Where your degree can take you.* Washington, DC: American Psychological Association.

AP* Practice Test Questions ◄ ···

Multiple-Choice Questions

1. Approximately what percentage of U.S. psychology majors attend graduate school in psychology?
a. 12 percent
b. 22 percent
c. 32 percent
d. 42 percent
e. 52 percent

2. Counseling psychologists are more likely to _____ than clinical psychologists.
a. treat serious psychopathology
b. prescribe medication
c. work in a school setting
d. have a Psy.D.
e. help people adjust to life transitions

3. The best time to begin preparations for a career in psychology is
a. when you begin applying to colleges.
b. no later than your first year of college.
c. when you have to declare a major.
d. in your first two years of college.
e. in your second two years of college.

4. The two most popular undergraduate majors in the United States are psychology and
a. education.
b. pre-med.
c. economics.
d. business.
e. humanities.

5. What degree do most psychologists in professional practice possess?
a. Ph.D.
b. Psy.D.
c. M.A.
d. M.S.
e. B.A.

6. Which of the following applies principles of psychology to legal issues?
a. Clinical psychology
b. Cognitive psychology
c. Forensic psychology
d. Community psychology
e. I/O psychology

7. The most popular specialty area in psychology is
a. educational psychology.
b. industrial-organizational psychology.
c. developmental psychology.
d. academic psychology.
e. clinical psychology.

8. Employment in psychology is expected to _____ between 2006 and 2016.
a. decline by about 15 percent
b. increase by about 15 percent
c. remain stable
d. decline by over 30 percent
e. increase by over 30 percent

9. Psychologists with a doctorate degree work primarily in
a. educational settings other than colleges and universities.
b. hospitals and clinics.
c. private practice.
d. colleges and universities.
e. business and industry.

10. Which of the following is not generally an area of research interest for a developmental psychologist?
a. Child care
b. Gerontology
c. Decision making
d. Infant attachment
e. Issues related to adoption

ANSWERS to Multiple-Choice Questions

1. a. 12 percent
2. e. help people adjust to life transitions
3. b. no later than your first year of college.
4. d. business.
5. b. Psy.D.
6. c. Forensic psychology
7. e. clinical psychology.
8. b. increase by about 15 percent
9. d. colleges and universities.
10. c. Decision making

Psychology at Work

The healthy life, said Sigmund Freud, is filled by love and by work. For most of us, work is life's biggest single waking activity. To live is to work.

The Nature of Work

WORK HELPS SATISFY SEVERAL LEVELS OF need identified in Maslow's pyramid of needs. Work supports us. Work connects us. Work defines us. Meeting someone for the first time, and wondering "Who are you?" we may ask, "So, what do you do?"

If we feel dissatisfied with our work-related pay, relationships, or identity, we may change where or for whom we work. Most people therefore have neither a single vocation nor a predictable career path. Two decades from now, most of you reading this book will be doing work you cannot now imagine. To prepare you and others for this unknown future, the colleges and universities you will attend will focus less on training your job skills and more on enlarging your capacities for understanding, thinking, and communicating in any work environment.

Amy Wrzesniewski and her colleagues (1997, 2001) have identified person-to-person variations in people's attitudes toward their work. Across various occupations, some people view their work as a *job*, an unfulfilling but necessary way to make money. Others view their work as a *career*, an opportunity to advance from one position to a better position. The rest—those who view their work as a *calling*, a fulfilling and socially useful activity—report the highest satisfaction with their work and with their lives.

This finding would not surprise Mihaly Csikszentmihalyi (1990, 1999), who has observed that people's quality of life increases when they are purposefully engaged. Between the anxiety of being overwhelmed and stressed, and the apathy of being underwhelmed and bored, lies a zone in which people experience **flow.** Csikszentmihalyi (chick-SENT-me-hi) formulated the flow concept after studying artists who spent hour after hour painting or sculpting with enormous concentration. Immersed in a project, they worked as if nothing else mattered, and then, when finished, they promptly forgot about it. The artists seemed driven less by the external rewards of producing art—money, praise, promotion—than by the intrinsic rewards of creating the work. Technology-related distractions can disrupt such flow. It takes time to refocus mental concentration after the distraction of a call, or a text or instant message. Thus, Microsoft is developing an *attentional user interface* that aims to "detect when users are available for communication, or when the user is in a state of flow" (Ullman, 2005).

Csikszentmihalyi's later observations—of dancers, chess players, surgeons, writers, parents, mountain climbers, sailors, and farmers; of Australians, North Americans,

• Sometimes, notes Gene Weingarten (2002), a humor writer knows "when to just get out of the way." Here are some sample job titles from the U.S. Department of Labor *Dictionary of Occupational Titles:* Animal impersonator, human projectile, banana ripening-room supervisor, impregnator, impregnator helper, dope sprayer, finger waver, rug scratcher, egg smeller, bottom buffer, cookie breaker, brain picker, hand pouncer, bosom presser, and mother repairer. •

::**flow** a completely involved, focused state of consciousness, with diminished awareness of self and time, resulting from optimal engagement of one's skills.

B-1

Key Terms

The Nature of Work
flow
industrial-organizational (I/O) psychology
personnel psychology
organizational psychology
human factors psychology

Personnel Psychology
structured interviews

Organizational Psychology
achievement motivation
task leadership
social leadership

DEMO

Have students brainstorm about flow activities they regularly engage in. Challenge them to participate in this activity within the next few days, reflecting afterward about how that flow experience made them feel:

- Why did you engage in the flow activity? Did you choose to do it but sacrificed other activities? Why or why not?

- How did being in flow make you feel?

- Did being in flow affect your mood for the rest of the day? Why or why not? Did a good mood extend into the next day? Why or why not?

- How can you experience more flow in your life?

Positive psychologists feel that studying the positive aspects of human behavior is important because being happy is not just the absence of being sad or ill. Have students discuss whether positive psychology is a legitimate way to study behavior:

- Is being happy more than just not being sad or ill?

- How is the study of positive traits similar to the study of negative qualities? How is it different?

- Should government sources fund positive psychology in the same way they fund "negative psychology"?

● Have you ever noticed that when you are immersed in an activity, time flies? And that when you are watching the clock, it seems to move more slowly? French researchers have confirmed that the more we attend to an event's duration, the longer it seems to last (Couli et al., 2004). ●

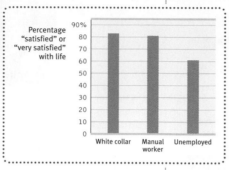

➤ **FIGURE B.1**

The bane of unemployment To want work but not have it is to feel less satisfied with life. These data are from 169,776 adults in 16 nations (Inglehart, 1990).

::**industrial-organizational (I/O) psychology** the application of psychological concepts and methods to optimizing human behavior in workplaces.

::**personnel psychology** a subfield of I/O psychology that focuses on employee recruitment, selection, placement, training, appraisal, and development.

::**organizational psychology** a subfield of I/O psychology that examines organizational influences on worker satisfaction and productivity and facilitates organizational change.

::**human factors psychology** a branch of psychology that explores how people and machines interact and how machines and physical environments can be made safe and easy to use.

Koreans, Japanese, and Italians; of people from their teens to their golden years—confirmed an overriding principle: It's exhilarating to flow with an activity that fully engages our skills. Flow experiences boost our sense of self-esteem, competence, and well-being. When the researchers beeped people at random intervals and asked them to report what they were doing and how much they were enjoying themselves, those who were vegetating usually reported little sense of flow and little satisfaction. People reported more positive feelings when interrupted while doing something active, something that engaged their skills, be it play or work. Other research indicates that in almost every industrialized nation, people have reported markedly lower well-being if unemployed (**FIGURE B.1**). Idleness may sound like bliss, but purposeful work enriches our lives.

In industrialized nations, work has been changing, from farming to manufacturing to *knowledge work*. More and more work is *outsourced* to temporary employees and consultants who communicate electronically from virtual workplaces in remote locations. (This book and its teaching package are developed and produced by a team of people in a dozen cities, from Alaska to Florida.) As work changes, will our attitudes toward our work also change? Will our satisfaction with work increase or decrease? Will the *psychological contract*—the subjective sense of mutual obligations between workers and employers—become more or less trusting and secure? These are among the questions that fascinate psychologists who study work-related behavior.

Industrial-organizational (I/O) psychology is a fast-growing profession that applies psychology's principles to the workplace (see Close-Up: I/O Psychology at Work). I/O psychology has three main subfields:

- **Personnel psychology** applies psychology's methods and principles to selecting and evaluating workers. Personnel psychologists match people with jobs, by identifying and placing well-suited candidates.

- **Organizational psychology** considers how work environments and management styles influence worker motivation, satisfaction, and productivity. Organizational psychologists modify jobs and supervision in ways that boost both morale and profits.

- **Human factors psychology** explores how machines and environments can be optimally designed to fit human abilities. Human factors psychologists study people's natural perceptions and inclinations to create user-friendly machines and work settings.

Personnel Psychology

1: How do personnel psychologists help organizations with employee selection, work placement, and performance appraisal?

PSYCHOLOGISTS CAN ASSIST ORGANIZATIONS at various stages of selecting and assessing employees. They may help identify needed job skills, decide upon selection methods, recruit and evaluate applicants, introduce and train new employees, and appraise their performance.

Harnessing Strengths

As a new AT&T human resource executive, psychologist Mary Tenopyr (1997) was assigned to solve a problem: Customer-service representatives were failing at a high

TEACHING TIP

At this point, you may want to use **Lecture/Discussion Topics:** *Flow* (p. 2) or *Flow in "Good Business"* (p. 4) from Bolt's Teacher's Resource Binder, which accompanies this text.

I/O Psychology at Work

As scientists, consultants, and management professionals, industrial-organizational psychologists are found working in varied areas:

Personnel Psychology

Selecting and placing employees

- Developing and validating assessment tools for selecting, placing, and promoting workers
- Analyzing job content
- Optimizing worker placement

Training and developing employees

- Identifying needs
- Designing training programs
- Evaluating training programs

Appraising performance

- Developing criteria
- Measuring individual performance
- Measuring organizational performance

Organizational Psychology

Developing organizations

- Analyzing organizational structures
- Maximizing worker satisfaction and productivity
- Facilitating organizational change

Enhancing quality of worklife

- Expanding individual productivity
- Identifying elements of satisfaction
- Redesigning jobs

Human Factors (Engineering) Psychology

- Designing optimum work environments
- Optimizing person-machine interactions
- Developing systems technologies

Source: Adapted from the Society of Industrial and Organizational Psychology (www.siop.org).

TEACHING TIP

At this point, you may want to use **Classroom Exercises:** *A Job, a Career, or a Vocation?* (p. 1) or *Assessing Flow* (p. 3) from Bolt's Teacher's Resource Binder.

---

rate. After concluding that many of the hires were ill-matched to the demands of their new job, Tenopyr developed a new selection instrument:

1. She asked new applicants to respond to various questions (without as yet making any use of their responses).

2. She followed up later to assess which of the applicants excelled on the job.

3. She identified the individual items on the earlier test that best predicted who would succeed.

The happy result of her data-driven work was a new test that enabled AT&T to identify likely-to-succeed customer representatives. Personnel selection techniques such as this one aim to match people's strengths with work that enables them and their organization to flourish. Marry the strengths of people with the tasks of organizations and the result is often prosperity and profit.

Your strengths are any enduring qualities that can be productively applied. Are you naturally curious? Persuasive? Charming? Persistent? Competitive? Analytical? Empathic? Organized? Articulate? Neat? Mechanical? Any such trait, if matched with suitable work, can function as a strength (Buckingham, 2007). (See Close-Up: Discovering Your Strengths on the next page.)

Gallup researchers Marcus Buckingham and Donald Clifton (2001) have argued that the first step to a stronger organization is instituting a strengths-based selection system. Thus, as a manager, you would first identify a group of the most effective people in any role—the ones you would want to hire more of—and compare their strengths with those of a group of the least effective people in that role. In defining these groups, you would try to measure performance as objectively as possible. In one Gallup study of more than 5000 telecommunications customer-service representatives, those evaluated most favorably by their managers were strong in

Artistic strengths At age 21, Henri Matisse was a sickly and often depressed lawyer's clerk. When his mother gave him a box of paints to cheer him up one day, he felt the darkness lift and his energy surge. He began to fill his days with painting and drawing and went on to art school and a life as one of the world's great painters. For Matisse, doing art felt like "a comfortable armchair." That is how exercising our strengths often feels.

Discovering Your Strengths

You can use some of the techniques personnel psychologists have developed to identify your own strengths and pinpoint types of work that will likely prove satisfying and successful. Buckingham and Clifton (2001) have suggested asking yourself:

- What activities give me pleasure? (Bringing order out of chaos? Playing host? Helping others? Challenging sloppy thinking?)
- What activities leave me wondering, "When can I do this again?" (Rather than "When will this be over?")
- What sorts of challenges do I relish? (And which do I dread?)
- What sorts of tasks do I learn easily? (And which do I struggle with?)

Some people find themselves in flow—their skills engaged and time flying—when teaching or selling or writing or cleaning or consoling or creating or repairing. If an activity feels good, if it comes easily, if you look forward to it, then look deeper and see your strengths at work.

Satisfied and successful people devote far less time to correcting their deficiencies than to accentuating their strengths. Top performers are "rarely well rounded," Buckingham and Clifton found (p. 26). Instead, they have sharpened their existing skills. Given the persistence of our traits and temperaments, we should focus not on our deficiencies, but rather on identifying and employing our talents. There may be limits to the benefits of assertiveness training if you are shy, for public speaking courses if you tend to be nervous and soft-spoken, or for drawing classes if you express your artistic side in stick figures.

But identifying your talents can help you recognize the activities you learn quickly and find absorbing. Knowing your strengths, you can develop them further.

As Robert Louis Stevenson said in *Familiar Studies of Men and Books* (1882), "To be what we are, and to become what we are capable of becoming, is the only end of life."

"harmony" and "responsibility," while those actually rated most effective by customers were strong in energy, assertiveness, and eagerness to learn.

An example: if you needed to hire new people in software development, and you had discovered that your best software developers are analytical, disciplined, and eager to learn, you would focus employment ads less on experience than on the identified strengths: "Do you take a logical and systematic approach to problem solving *[analytical]*? Are you a perfectionist who strives for timely completion of your projects *[disciplined]*? Do you want to learn to use Java, C++, and PHP *[eager to learn]*? If you can say *yes* to these questions, then please call . . ."

Identifying people's strengths and matching strengths to work is a first step toward workplace effectiveness. Personnel managers use various tools to assess applicants' strengths and decide who is best suited to the job (Sackett & Lievens, 2008). In Unit 11, we saw how psychologists assess candidates using ability tests. And in Unit 10, we explored personality tests and "assessment centers" that enable observations of behaviors on simulated job tasks. For now, let's consider the job interview.

Do Interviews Predict Performance?

Interviewers tend to feel confident in their ability to predict long-term job performance from an unstructured, get-acquainted interview. What's therefore shocking is how error-prone those predictions are. Whether predicting job or graduate school success, interviewers' judgments are weak predictors. From their review of 85 years of personnel-selection research, I/O psychologists Frank Schmidt and John Hunter (1998; Schmidt, 2002) determined that for all but less-skilled jobs, general mental ability best predicts on-the-job performance. Subjective overall evaluations from informal interviews are more useful than handwriting analysis (which is worthless). But informal interviews are less informative than aptitude tests, work samples, job knowledge tests, and past job performance. If there's a contest between what our gut tells us about someone and what test scores, work samples, and past performance tell us, we should distrust our gut.

> "Interviews are a terrible predictor of performance."
> Laszlo Bock, Google's Vice President, People Operations, 2007

The Interviewer Illusion

Interviewers often overrate their discernment, a phenomenon psychologist Richard Nisbett (1987) has labeled the *interviewer illusion.* "I have excellent interviewing skills, so I don't need reference checking as much as someone who doesn't have my ability to read people," is a comment sometimes heard by I/O consultants. Four factors explain this gap between interviewers' intuition and the resulting reality:

- *Interviews disclose the interviewee's good intentions, which are less revealing than habitual behaviors* (Ouellette & Wood, 1998). Intentions matter. People can change. But the best predictor of the person we will be is the person we have been. Wherever we go, we take ourselves along.

- *Interviewers more often follow the successful careers of those they have hired than the successful careers of those they have rejected and lost track of.* This missing feedback prevents interviewers from getting a reality check on their hiring ability.

- *Interviewers presume that people are what they seem to be in the interview situation.* As Unit 14 explained, when meeting others, we discount the enormous influence of varying situations and mistakenly presume that what we see is what we will get. But mountains of research on everything from chattiness to conscientiousness reveal that how we behave reflects not only our enduring traits, but also the details of the particular situation (such as wanting to impress in a job interview).

- *Interviewers' preconceptions and moods color how they perceive interviewees' responses* (Cable & Gilovich, 1998; Macan & Dipboye, 1994). If interviewers instantly like a person who perhaps is similar to themselves, they may interpret the person's assertiveness as indicating "confidence" rather than "arrogance." If told certain applicants have been prescreened, interviewers are disposed to judge them more favorably.

Traditional *unstructured interviews* do provide a sense of someone's personality—their expressiveness, warmth, and verbal ability, for example. But this information reveals less about the person's behavior toward others in different situations than most people suppose. Hoping to improve prediction and selection, personnel psychologists have put people in simulated work situations, scoured sources for information on past performance, aggregated evaluations from multiple interviews, administered tests, and developed job-specific interviews.

"Between the idea and reality . . . falls the shadow."
T. S. Eliot, *The Hollow Men*, 1925

Structured Interviews

Unlike casual conversation aimed at getting a feel for someone, **structured interviews** offer a disciplined method of collecting information. A personnel psychologist may analyze a job, script questions, and train interviewers. The interviewers then put the same questions, in the same order, to all applicants, and rate each applicant on established scales.

In an unstructured interview, someone might ask, "How organized are you?" "How well do you get along with people?" or "How do you handle stress?" Street-smart applicants know how to score high: "Although I sometimes drive myself too hard, I handle stress by prioritizing and delegating, and by making sure I leave time for sleep and exercise."

By contrast, structured interviews pinpoint strengths (attitudes, behaviors, knowledge, and skills) that distinguish high performers in a particular line of work. The process includes outlining job-specific situations and asking candidates to explain how they would handle them, and how they handled similar situations in their prior employment. "Tell me about a time when you were caught between conflicting demands, without time to accomplish both. How did you handle that?"

To reduce memory distortions and bias, the interviewer takes notes and makes ratings as the interview proceeds and avoids irrelevant and follow-up questions. The structured

::**structured interviews** interview process that asks the same job-relevant questions of all applicants, each of whom is rated on established scales.

interview therefore feels less warm, but that can be explained to the applicant: "This conversation won't typify how we relate to each other in this organization."

A review of 150 findings revealed that structured interviews had double the predictive accuracy of unstructured seat-of-the-pants interviews (Schmidt & Hunter, 1998; Wiesner & Cronshaw, 1988). Structured interviews also reduce bias, such as against overweight applicants (Kutcher & Bragger, 2004). Thanks partly to its greater reliability and partly to its job-analysis focus, the predictive power of one structured interview is roughly equal to that of the average judgment from three or four unstructured interviews (Huffcutt et al., 2001; Schmidt & Zimmerman, 2004).

If, instead, we let our intuitions bias the hiring process, notes Malcolm Gladwell (2000), then "all we will have done is replace the old-boy network, where you hired your nephew, with the new-boy network, where you hire whoever impressed you most when you shook his hand. Social progress, unless we're careful, can merely be the means by which we replace the obviously arbitrary with the not so obviously arbitrary."

To recap, personnel psychologists assist organizations in analyzing jobs, recruiting well-suited applicants, selecting and placing employees, and appraising their performance (**FIGURE B.2**)—the topic we turn to next.

➤ **FIGURE B.2**
Personnel psychologists' tasks
Personnel psychologists consult in human resources activities, from job definition to employee appraisal.

Appraising Performance

Performance appraisal serves organizational purposes: It helps decide who to retain, how to appropriately reward and pay people, and how to better harness employee strengths, sometimes with job shifts or promotions. Performance appraisal also serves individual purposes: Feedback affirms workers' strengths and helps motivate needed improvements.

Performance appraisal methods include

- *checklists* on which supervisors simply check specific behaviors that describe the worker ("always attends to customers' needs," "takes long breaks").
- *graphic rating scales* on which a supervisor checks, perhaps on a five-point scale, how often a worker is dependable, productive, and so forth.
- *behavior rating scales* on which a supervisor checks scaled behaviors that describe a worker's performance. If rating the extent to which a worker "follows procedures," the supervisor might mark the employee somewhere between "often takes short-cuts" and "always follows established procedures" (Levy, 2003).

In some organizations, performance feedback comes not only from supervisors but also from all organizational levels. If you join an organization that practices *360-degree feedback* (**FIGURE B.3**), you will rate yourself, your manager, and your other colleagues, and you will be rated by your manager, other colleagues, and customers (Green, 2002). The net result is often more open communication and more complete appraisal.

Performance appraisal, like other social judgments, is vulnerable to bias (Murphy & Cleveland, 1995). *Halo errors* occur when one's overall evaluation of an employee, or of a personal trait such as their friendliness, biases ratings of their specific work-related behaviors, such as their reliability. *Leniency* and *severity errors* reflect evaluators' tendencies to be either too easy or too harsh on everyone. *Recency errors* occur when raters focus only on easily remembered recent behavior. By using multiple raters and developing objective, job-relevant performance measures, personnel psychologists seek to support their organizations while also helping employees perceive the appraisal process as fair.

BEFORE YOU MOVE ON . . .

➤ Ask Yourself

What have you learned about your own strengths, and about the kind of career you might see yourself pursuing?

➤ Test Yourself 1

A human resources director explains to you that "I don't bother with tests or references. I can pick employees by my gut." Based on I/O psychology research, what concerns does this raise?

Answers to the Test Yourself questions can be found in Appendix E.

Organizational Psychology: Motivating Achievement

2: What is the role of organizational psychologists?

THE APPRAISAL OF WORK AND THE MATCHING of strengths to work matter, but so does overall motivation. Before considering how organizational psychologists assist with efforts to motivate employees and keep them engaged, let's take a closer look at why any employee might want to pursue high standards or difficult goals.

Think of someone you know who strives to succeed by excelling at any task where evaluation is possible. Now think of someone who is less driven. Psychologist Henry Murray (1938) defined the first person's **achievement motivation** as a desire for significant accomplishment, for mastering skills or ideas, for control, and for rapidly attaining a high standard.

As you might expect from their persistence and eagerness for realistic challenges, people with high achievement motivation do achieve more. One study followed the lives of 1528 California children whose intelligence test scores were in the top 1 percent. Forty years later, when researchers compared those who were most and least successful professionally, they found a motivational difference. Those most successful were more ambitious, energetic, and persistent. As children, they had more active hobbies. As adults, they participated in more groups and favored being sports participants to being spectators (Goleman, 1980). Gifted children are able learners. Accomplished adults are tenacious doers.

In other studies of both high school and university students, self-discipline has been a better predictor of school performance, attendance, and graduation honors than intelligence scores have been. "Discipline outdoes talent," concluded researchers

::**achievement motivation** a desire for significant accomplishment; for mastery of things, people, or ideas; for rapidly attaining a high standard.

➤ **FIGURE B.3**
360-degree feedback With multisource 360-degree feedback, one's knowledge, skills, and behaviors are rated by self and surrounding others. Teachers, for example, may be rated by their students, their principal, and their colleagues. After receiving all these ratings, teachers discuss the 360-degree feedback with their principal.

TEACHING TIP

Hope is a psychological concept related to achievement motivation. According to C. R. Snyder of the University of Kansas, hope is related to a person's goals and how they plan to achieve them. By setting realistic goals, people can start on the road to achievement. If people have goals that are 100 percent attainable (e.g., "I hope to watch an hour of TV today"), their hope is not high because the challenge is not great enough to require extra work. People who have completely unrealistic goals (e.g., "I hope I can train pigs to fly"), have low levels of hope, not because the challenges aren't great enough, but because they don't have the pathways or motivation to achieve them.

TEACHING TIP

Have students list their last three to five achievements and their last three to five failures on a sheet of paper. Next to each item, encourage them to write out a one- to two-sentence explanation for that achievement or failure.

What do they notice about these explanations? Are the achievement explanations celebrations or not? Do the failure explanations blame a personal fault or chalk it up to circumstances?

Remind students that optimists believe that good events are due to personal accomplishment, and that the effects will last for a long time and influence other areas of life. If students have pessimistic thinking about their accomplishments and failures, encourage them to come up with alternative explanations for these events that reflect more optimistic thinking.

Disciplined motivation feeds achievement Aware that he was far behind other students when beginning his graduate education in psychology, B. F. Skinner devised a daily discipline of rising at 6:00 A.M., studying until breakfast, then going to classes, labs, and the library. After dinner he studied some more, leaving no more than 15 unscheduled minutes each day, and later continued a disciplined daily routine as he became one of the twentieth century's most influential psychologists.

"The only place success comes before work is in the dictionary."

Former Green Bay Packers football coach Vince Lombardi

Engaged employees facilitate organizational success Best Buy's electronic goods stores have nearly identical product layout and operations manuals. Yet some stores have had much more engaged employees—and more profitable performance. The store with the highest worker-engagement scores has been in the top tenth of stores in having profits beyond budget. And the store with the least-engaged employees has been in the bottom tenth (Buckingham, 2001).

Angela Duckworth and Martin Seligman (2005, 2006), and it explains why girls get higher school grades than equally capable boys.

But discipline also refines talent. By their early twenties, top violinists have accumulated some 10,000 lifetime practice hours—double the practice time of other violin students aiming to be teachers (Ericsson et al., 2001, 2006, 2007). From his studies, Herbert Simon (1998), a psychologist who won the Nobel Prize in Economics, formed what Unit 11 called the *10-year rule:* That world-class experts in a field typically have invested "at least 10 years of hard work—say, 40 hours a week for 50 weeks a year." A study of outstanding scholars, athletes, and artists found that all were highly motivated and self-disciplined, willing to dedicate hours every day to the pursuit of their goals (Bloom, 1985). These superstar achievers were distinguished not so much by their extraordinary natural talent as by their extraordinary daily discipline. Great achievement, it seems, mixes a teaspoon of inspiration with a gallon of perspiration.

What distinguishes extremely successful individuals from their equally talented peers, note Duckworth and Seligman, is *grit*—passionate dedication to an ambitious, long-term goal. Although intelligence is distributed like a bell curve, achievements are not. That tells us that achievement involves much more than raw ability. And that is why organizational psychologists seek ways to engage and motivate ordinary people doing ordinary jobs.

Satisfaction and Engagement

Because work is such a big part of life, employee satisfaction is a priority concern for I/O psychologists. Satisfaction with work feeds satisfaction with life (see Close-Up: Doing Well While Doing Good). Moreover, as discussed in Appendix C, decreased job stress feeds improved health.

Does employee satisfaction also contribute to successful organizations? Positive moods at work do contribute to creativity, persistence, and helpfulness (Brief & Weiss, 2002). But are engaged, happy workers also less often absent? Less likely to quit? Less prone to theft? More punctual? More productive? Conclusive evidence of satisfaction's benefits is, some have said, the holy grail of I/O psychology. Statistical digests of prior research have found a modest positive correlation between individual job satisfaction and performance (Judge et al., 2001; Parker et al., 2003). In one analysis of 4500 employees at 42 British manufacturing companies, the most productive workers tended to be those in satisfying work environments (Patterson et al., 2004). But does satisfaction *produce* better job performance? The debate continues, with one analysis of past research indicating that satisfaction and performance correlate because both reflect job self-esteem ("I matter around here") and a sense that their efforts control their rewards (Bowling, 2007).

Nevertheless, some organizations do have a knack for cultivating more engaged and productive employees. In the United States, the *Fortune* "100 Best Companies to Work For" have also produced markedly higher-than-average returns for their investors (Fulmer et al., 2003). Other positive data come from the biggest-ever study, an analysis of Gallup data from more than 198,000 employees (turn the page for **TABLE B.1**) in nearly 8000 business units of 36 large companies (including some

Doing Well While Doing Good—"The Great Experiment"

At the end of the 1700s, the more than 1000 workers in the cotton mill at New Lanark, Scotland—many of them children drawn from Glasgow's poorhouses—worked 13-hour days and lived in grim conditions. Their education and sanitation were neglected, theft and drunkenness were commonplace, and most families occupied just one room.

On a visit to Glasgow, Welsh-born Robert Owen—an idealistic young cotton-mill manager—chanced to meet and fall in love with the mill owner's daughter. After their marriage, Owen, with several partners, purchased the mill and on the first day of the 1800s took control as its manager. Before long, he began what he said was "the most important experiment for the happiness of the human race that had yet been instituted at any time in any part of the world" (Owen, 1814). The exploitation of child and adult labor was, he observed, producing unhappy and inefficient workers. Believing that better working and living conditions could pay economic dividends, he undertook (with some resistance from his partners, whom he ultimately bought out) numerous innovations: a nursery for preschool children, education (with encouragement rather than corporal punishment), Sundays off, health care, paid sick days, unemployment pay for days when the mill could not operate, and a company store selling goods at reduced prices.

Owen also innovated a goals- and worker-assessment program that included detailed records of daily productivity and costs. By each employee's workstation, one of four colored boards indicated that person's performance for the previous day. Owen could walk through the mill and at a glance see how individuals were performing. There was, he said, "no beating, no abusive language. . . . I merely looked at the person and then at the color. . . . I could at once see by the expression [which color] was shown."

The commercial success that followed was essential to sustaining what became a movement toward humanitarian reforms. By 1816, with decades of profitability still ahead, Owen

Courtesy of New Lanark World Heritage Site

The great experiment New Lanark Mills, which today is preserved as a World Heritage Site (www.newlanark.org), provided an influential demonstration of how industries could do well while doing good. In its heyday, New Lanark was visited by many European royals and reformers who came to observe its vibrant workforce and prosperous business.

believed he had demonstrated "that society may be formed so as to exist without crime, without poverty, with health greatly improved, with little if any misery, and with intelligence and happiness increased a hundredfold." Although his Utopian vision has not been fulfilled, Owen's great experiment did lay the groundwork for employment practices that have today become accepted in much of the world.

1100 bank branches, 1200 stores, and 4200 teams or departments). James Harter, Frank Schmidt, and Theodore Hayes (2002) explored correlations between various measures of organizational success and *employee engagement*—the extent of workers' involvement, enthusiasm, and identification with their organizations. They found that engaged workers (compared with disengaged workers who are just putting in time) know what's expected of them, have what they need to do their work, feel fulfilled in their work, have regular opportunities to do what they do best, perceive that they are part of something significant, and have opportunities to learn and develop. They also found that business units with engaged employees have more loyal customers, less turnover, higher productivity, and greater profits. A follow-up analysis compared companies with top-quartile versus below-average employee engagement levels. Over a three-year period, earnings grew 2.6 times faster for the companies with highly engaged workers (Ott, 2007).

Appendix B

TEACHING TIP

At this point, you may want to use **Lecture/Discussion Topics:** *Organizational Citizenship* (p. 7) or *Managers' Implicit Assumptions About Personnel* (p. 8) or *Charisma* (p. 9) from Bolt's Teacher's Resource Binder.

TABLE B.1

THE GALLUP WORKPLACE AUDIT

Overall satisfaction—On a 5-point scale, where 5 is extremely satisfied and 1 is extremely dissatisfied, how satisfied are you with *(name of company)* as a place to work?_____

On a scale of 1 to 5, where 1 is strongly disagree and 5 is strongly agree, please indicate your agreement with the following items.

1. I know what is expected from me at work.
2. I have the materials and equipment I need to do my work right.
3. At work, I have the opportunity to do what I do best every day.
4. In the last seven days, I have received recognition or praise for doing good work.
5. My supervisor, or someone at work, seems to care about me as a person.
6. There is someone at work who encourages my development.
7. At work, my opinions seem to count.
8. The mission/purpose of my company makes me feel my job is important.
9. My associates (fellow employees) are committed to doing quality work.
10. I have a best friend at work.
11. In the last six months, someone at work has talked to me about my progress.
12. This last year, I have had opportunities at work to learn and grow.

Note: These statements are proprietary and copyrighted by The Gallup Organization. They may not be printed or reproduced in any manner without the written consent of The Gallup Organization. Reprinted here by permission.

Managing Well

Every leader dreams of managing in ways that enhance people's satisfaction, engagement, and productivity and their organization's success. Effective leaders harness job-relevant strengths, set goals, and choose an appropriate leadership style.

Harnessing Job-Relevant Strengths

"The major challenge for CEOs over the next 20 years will be the effective deployment of human assets," observed Marcus Buckingham (2001). That challenge is "about psychology. It's about getting [individuals] to be more productive, more focused, more fulfilled than [they were] yesterday." To do so, he and others have maintained, effective leaders want first to select the right people. Then, they aim to discern their employees' natural talents, adjust their work roles to suit their talents, and develop those talents into great strengths (**FIGURE B.4**). For example, should every teacher at

➤ **FIGURE B.4**
On the right path The Gallup Organization path to organizational success (adapted from Fleming, 2001).

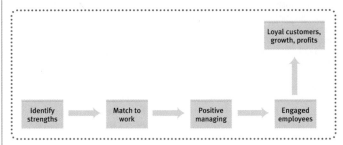

a high school be expected to teach the same level and number of students and engage in the same number of extracurricular activities? Or should each job description be tailored to harness a specific person's unique strengths?

As noted earlier in the discussion of personnel psychologists, our temperament and our traits tend to follow us throughout our lives. Managers who excel spend less time trying to instill talents that are not there and more time developing and drawing out what is there. Kenneth Tucker (2002) has noted that great managers

- start by helping people identify and measure their talents.
- match tasks to talents and then give people freedom to do what they do best.
- care how their people feel about their work.
- reinforce positive behaviors through recognition and reward.

Thus, rather than focusing on weaknesses and packing people off to training seminars to fix those problems, good managers focus training time on educating people about their strengths and building upon them (which means not promoting people into roles ill-suited to their strengths). In Gallup surveys, 77 percent of engaged workers, and only 23 percent of not-engaged workers, strongly agreed that "my supervisor focuses on my strengths or positive characteristics" (Krueger & Killham, 2005).

Celebrating engaged and productive employees in every organizational role builds upon a basic principle of operant conditioning (Unit 6): To teach a behavior, catch a person doing something right and reinforce it. It sounds simple, but many managers are like parents who, when their child returns home with near-perfect scores, focus on the one low score in a troublesome biology class and ignore the rest. "Sixty-five percent of Americans received NO praise or recognition in the workplace last year," reported the Gallup Organization (2004).

Positive coaching Larry Brown, an adviser to the youth sports organization the Positive Coaching Alliance, has been observed during practices to offer his players 4 to 5 positive comments for every negative comment (Insana, 2005). In 2004, his underdog Detroit Pistons won the National Basketball Association championship.

Setting Specific, Challenging Goals

In everyday life, our achievement goals sometimes involve approaching high levels of mastery or performance (perhaps mastering the material for this class and getting a high grade) and sometimes involve avoiding failure (Elliot & McGregor, 2001). In many situations, specific, challenging goals motivate achievement, especially when combined with progress reports (Johnson et al., 2006; Latham & Locke, 2007). Specific, measurable objectives, such as "finish gathering information for the history paper by Friday," serve to direct attention, promote effort, motivate persistence, and stimulate creative strategies.

When people state goals together with *subgoals* and *implementation intentions*—action plans that specify when, where, and how they will march toward achieving those goals—they become more focused in their work, and on-time completion becomes more likely (Burgess et al., 2004; Fishbach et al., 2006; Koestner et al., 2002). (Before beginning each new edition of this book, my editor, my associates, and I *manage by objectives*—we agree on target dates for the completion and editing of each unit draft.) So, to motivate high productivity, effective leaders work with people to define explicit goals, subgoals, and implementation plans, and then provide feedback on progress.

Choosing an Appropriate Leadership Style

Leadership varies from a boss-focused directive style to a democratic style that empowers workers in setting goals and strategies. Which works best may depend on the situation and the leader. The best leadership style for leading a discussion may not be the best style for leading troops on a charge (Fiedler, 1981). Moreover, different leaders are suited

Ezra Shaw/Getty Images

TEACHING TIP

At this point, you may want to use **Classroom Exercises:** *The Needs Assessment Questionnaire* (p. 6) or *Desire for Control* (p. 6) or *Achievement and Intrinsic Motivation* (p. 7) from Bolt's Teacher's Resource Binder.

Appendix B

Different types of leaders in business reflect different beliefs about achievement motivation.

- *Theory X* managers assume that workers are basically lazy, error-prone, and extrinsically motivated by money. Thus, workers need simple tasks, close monitoring, and incentives to produce more.

- In contrast, *Theory Y* managers assume that people are intrinsically motivated to work for reasons beyond money, for example, to promote self-esteem, enjoy satisfying interpersonal relations, and fulfill their potential.

> "Good leaders don't ask more than their constituents can give, but they often ask—and get—more than their constituents intended to give or thought it was possible to give."
> John W. Gardner, *Excellence*, 1984

::**task leadership** goal-oriented leadership that sets standards, organizes work, and focuses attention on goals.

::**social leadership** group-oriented leadership that builds teamwork, mediates conflict, and offers support.

to different styles. Some excel at **task leadership**—setting standards, organizing work, and focusing attention on goals. Being goal-oriented, task leaders are good at keeping a group centered on its mission. Typically, they have a directive style, which can work well if the leader is bright enough to give good orders (Fiedler, 1987).

Other managers excel at **social leadership**—explaining decisions, mediating conflicts, and building high-achieving teams (Evans & Dion, 1991). Social leaders often have a democratic style: They delegate authority and welcome the participation of team members. Many experiments show that social leadership is good for morale. Subordinates usually feel more satisfied and motivated and perform better when they participate in decision making (Cawley et al., 1998; Pereira & Osburn, 2007). Which style of leadership do you think is best in a student council?

Because effective leadership styles vary with the situation and the person, the once-popular *great person theory of leadership*—that all great leaders share certain traits—now seems overstated (Vroom & Jago, 2007; Wielkiewicz & Stelzner, 2005). The same coach may seem great or inferior depending on the strength of the team and its competition. But a leader's personality does matter (Zaccaro, 2007). Effective leaders tend to be neither extremely assertive (impairing social relationships) or unassertive (limiting task leadership) (Ames & Flynn, 2007). Effective leaders of laboratory groups, work teams, and large corporations also tend to exude *charisma* (House & Singh, 1987; Shamir et al., 1993). Their charisma blends a goal-based *vision*, clear *communication*, and optimism that *inspires* others to follow. In one study of 50 Dutch companies, the highest morale was at those firms with chief executives who most inspired their colleagues "to transcend their own self-interests for the sake of the collective" (de Hoogh et al., 2004). *Transformational leadership* of this kind motivates others to identify with and commit themselves to the group's mission. Transformational leaders, many of whom are natural extraverts, articulate high standards, inspire people to share their vision, and offer personal attention (Bono & Judge, 2004). The frequent result is more engaged, trusting, and effective workers (Turner et al., 2002). Women more than men tend to exhibit transformational leadership qualities. Alice Eagly (2007) believes this helps explain why companies with women in top management have recently tended to enjoy superior financial results, even after controlling for such variables as company size.

Peter Smith and Monir Tayeb (1989) compiled data from studies in India, Taiwan, and Iran indicating that effective managers—whether in coal mines, banks, or government offices—often exhibit a high degree of *both* task and social leadership. As achievement-minded people, effective managers certainly care about how well work is done, yet at the same time they are sensitive to their subordinates' needs. In one national survey of American workers, those in family-friendly organizations offering flexible-time hours reported feeling greater loyalty to their employers (Roehling et al., 2001).

Many successful businesses have also increased employee participation in making decisions, a management style common in Sweden and Japan and increasingly elsewhere (Naylor, 1990; Sundstrom et al., 1990). Although managers often think better of work they have directly supervised, studies reveal a *voice effect:* If given a chance to voice their opinion during a decision-making process, people will respond more positively to the decision (van den Bos & Spruijt, 2002). And, as noted earlier, positive, engaged employees are a mark of thriving organizations.

At this point, you may want to use **Classroom Exercises:** *Theory X and Y Orientation Scale* (p. 9) or *Assessing Leadership Style* (p. 10) from Bolt's Teacher's Resource Binder.

The rags-to-riches Harley-Davidson story illustrates the potential of inviting workers to participate in decision making (Teerlink & Ozley, 2000). In 1987, the struggling company began transforming its *command-and-control* management process to a *joint-vision process*. The aim: "To push decision-making, planning, and strategizing from a handful of people at the top, down throughout the organization. We wanted all the employees to think every day about how to improve the company," reported CEO Jeffrey Bleustein (2002). In the mid-1990s, Harley signed a cooperative agreement with its unions that included them "in decision-making in virtually every aspect of the business." Consensus decision-making can take longer, but "when the decision is made, it gets implemented quickly and the commitment is by the group," says Bleustein. The result has been more engaged workers and also more satisfied stockholders. Every $1 of Harley-Davidson stock purchased at the beginning of 1988 was worth $125 by mid-2005.

Sharing vision and decisions As CEO, Jeffrey Bleustein helped Harley-Davidson thrive, in part by replacing the organization's command-and-control management style with one based on company-wide consensus planning and decision making. ▲

Answers to the Test Yourself questions can be found in Appendix E.

BEFORE YOU MOVE ON . . .

➤ ASK YOURSELF

Are you highly motivated, or not highly motivated, to achieve in school? How has this affected your academic success? How might you improve upon your own achievement levels?

➤ TEST YOURSELF 2

What are the two basic types of leadership, and how do the most effective managers employ these leadership strategies?

Human Factors Psychology

3: How do human factors psychologists work to create user-friendly machines and work settings?

DESIGNS SOMETIMES NEGLECT THE HUMAN factor. Psychologist Donald Norman, an MIT alumnus with a Ph.D., bemoaned the complexity of assembling his new high-definition TV, receiver, speakers, digital recorder, DVD player, VCR, and seven remotes into a usable home theater system: "I was VP of Advanced Technology at Apple. I can program dozens of computers in dozens of languages. I understand television, really, I do. . . . It doesn't matter: I am overwhelmed."

How much easier life might be if engineers would routinely work with human factors psychologists to test their designs and instructions on real people. Human factors psychologists help to design appliances, machines, and work settings that fit our natural perceptions and inclinations. ATM machines are internally more complex than VCRs ever were, yet, thanks to human factors psychologists working with engineers, ATMs are easier to operate. TiVo has solved the TV recording problem with a simple select-and-click menu system ("record that one"). Apple has similarly engineered easy usability with the iPod and iPhone.

Norman (2001) hosts a Web site (www.jnd.org) that illustrates good designs that fit people (see **FIGURE B.5**, next page). Human factors psychologists also work at designing safe and efficient environments. An ideal kitchen layout, researchers have found, stores needed items close to their usage point and near eye level. It locates work areas to enable doing tasks in order, such as with a refrigerator, stove, and sink in a triangle. It creates counters that enable hands to work at or slightly below elbow height (Boehm-Davis, 2006).

Appendix B

Human-factors psychologists and industrial-organizational psychologists have similar job descriptions but work in different realms. Human-factors psychologists tend to work to improve human-machine interactions. I/O psychologists are more concerned with business and industrial environments that lead to productive workers and quality products.

➤ **FIGURE B.5**
Designing products that fit people Human factors psychologist Donald Norman offers these and other examples of effectively designed new products.

The Ride On Carry On foldable chair attachment "designed by a flight attendant mom," enables a small suitcase to double as a stroller.

The Oxo measuring cup allows the user to see the quantity from above.

The Chatsford Tea Pot comes with a built-in strainer.

Understanding human factors can do more than enable us to design for reduced frustration; it can help prevent accidents and avoid disaster (Boehm-Davis, 2005). Two-thirds of commercial air accidents, for example, have been caused by human error (Nickerson, 1998). After beginning commercial flights in the late 1960s, the Boeing 727 was involved in several landing accidents caused by pilot error. Psychologist Conrad Kraft (1978) noted a common setting for these accidents: All took place at night, and all involved landing short of the runway after crossing a dark stretch of water or unilluminated ground. Kraft reasoned that, beyond the runway, city lights would project a larger retinal image if on a rising terrain. This would make the ground seem farther away than it was. By re-creating these conditions in flight simulations, Kraft discovered that pilots were deceived into thinking they were flying higher than their actual altitudes (**FIGURE B.6**). Aided by Kraft's finding, the airlines began requiring the co-pilot to monitor the altimeter—calling out altitudes during the descent—and the accidents diminished.

➤ **FIGURE B.6**
The human factor in accidents Lacking distance cues when approaching a runway from over a dark surface, pilots simulating a night landing tended to fly too low. (From Kraft, 1978.)

Later Boeing psychologists worked on other human factors problems (Murray, 1998): How should airlines best train and manage mechanics to reduce the maintenance errors that underlie about 50 percent of flight delays and 15 percent of accidents? What illumination and typeface would make on-screen flight data easiest to read? How could warning messages be most effectively worded—as an action statement ("Pull Up") rather than a problem statement ("Ground Proximity")?

In studying human factors issues, psychologists' most powerful tool is theory-aided research. If an organization wonders what sort of Web design (Emphasizing content? Speed? Graphics?) would most effectively draw in visitors and entice them to return,

At this point, you may want to use the Technology Resource *Video: Scientific American Frontiers,* 2nd ed., *Segment 30: The Power of Persuasion.*

the psychologist will want to test responses to several alternatives. If NASA (National Aeronautics and Space Administration) wonders what sort of spacecraft design would best facilitate sleeping, work, and morale, their human factors psychologists will want to test the alternatives (**FIGURE B.7**).

Consider, finally, the available *assistive listening* technologies in various theaters, auditoriums, and places of worship. One technology, commonly available in the United States, requires a headset attached to a pocket-size receiver that detects infrared or FM signals from the room's sound system. The well-meaning people who design, purchase, and install these systems correctly understand that the technology puts sound directly into the user's ears. Alas, few people with hearing loss undergo the hassle and embarrassment of locating, requesting, wearing, and returning a conspicuous headset. Most such units therefore sit in closets. Britain, the Scandinavian countries, and Australia have instead installed *loop systems* (see www.hearingloop.org) that broadcast customized sound directly through a person's own hearing aid. When suitably equipped, a hearing aid can be transformed by a discrete touch of a switch into an in-the-ear loudspeaker. Offered convenient, inconspicuous, personalized sound, many more people elect to use assistive listening.

Designs that enable safe, easy, and effective interactions between people and technology often seem obvious after the fact. Why, then, aren't they more common? Technology developers sometimes mistakenly assume that others share their expertise—that what is clear to them will similarly be clear to others (Camerer et al., 1989; Nickerson, 1999). When people rap their knuckles on a table to convey a familiar tune (try this with a friend), they often expect their listener to recognize it. But for the listener, this is a near-impossible task (Newton, 1991). When you know a thing, it's hard to mentally simulate what it's like not to know, and that is called the *curse of knowledge*.

The point to remember: Designers and engineers should consider human abilities and behaviors by designing things to fit people, user-testing their inventions before production and distribution, and being mindful of the curse of knowledge.

The human factor in safe landings
Advanced cockpit design and rehearsed emergency procedures aided pilot Chesley "Sully" Sullenberger, a U.S. Air Force Academy graduate who studied psychology and human factors. In January 2009, Sullenberger's instantaneous decisions safely guided his disabled airliner onto New York City's Hudson River, where all 155 of the passengers and crew were safely evacuated.

➤ **FIGURE B.7**
How not to go mad while going to Mars Future astronauts headed to Mars will be confined in conditions of monotony, stress, and weightlessness for months on end. To help design and evaluate a workable human environment, such as for this Transit Habitation (Transhab) Module, NASA engages human factors psychologists (Weed, 2001; Wichman, 1992).

BEFORE YOU MOVE ON . . .

➤ **ASK YOURSELF**
What situations have you experienced (using new technology, visiting new or remodeled building spaces, taking various modes of transportation), where the design did not work well? What situations have you experienced where planners did a particularly good job matching machines and physical environments to our abilities and expectations?

➤ **TEST YOURSELF 3**
One of the ways human factors psychologists seek to reduce users' frustration and to improve safety is by watching out for the *curse of knowledge*. What exactly is this tendency?

Answers to the Test Yourself questions can be found in Appendix E.

 TEACHING TIP

October is National Ergonomics Month. Consider hosting a human-factors psychologist as a guest speaker or having students examine the ergonomics of products they interact with on a daily basis to present to the class during that month.

TEACHING TIP

Divide students into groups and have each team develop an advertisement for a product they use regularly (i.e., a certain type of toothpaste, iPods, Facebook, a particular brand of clothes, etc.). Conduct a consumer psychology study of each ad's effectiveness in "selling" the product.

Appendix B

TEACHING TIP

At this point, you may want to use **Lecture/Discussion Topics:** *Bad Human Designs* (p. 11) or *Banner Blindness and Web Design* (p. 11) from Bolt's Teacher's Resource Binder.

APPENDIX B REVIEW: Psychology at Work

Personnel Psychology

1: How do personnel psychologists help organizations with employee selection, work placement, and performance appraisal?

Personnel psychologists work with organizations to devise selection methods for new employees, recruit and evaluate applicants, design and evaluate training programs, identify people's strengths, analyze job content, and appraise individual and organizational performance. Subjective interviews foster the interviewer illusion; *structured interviews* pinpoint job-relevant strengths and are better predictors of performance. Checklists, graphic rating scales, and behavior rating scales are useful performance appraisal methods.

Organizational Psychology: Motivating Achievement

2: What is the role of organizational psychologists?

Organizational psychologists examine influences on worker satisfaction and productivity and facilitate organizational change. Employee engagement tends to correlate with organizational success. Leadership style may be goal-oriented *(task leadership)*, or group-oriented *(social leadership)*, or some combination of the two.

Human Factors Psychology

3: How do human factors psychologists work to create user-friendly machines and work settings?

Human factors psychologists contribute to human safety and improved design by encouraging developers and designers to consider human perceptual abilities, to avoid the curse of knowledge, and to test users to reveal perception-based problems.

Terms and Concepts to Remember

flow, p. B-1

industrial-organizational (I/O) psychology, p. B-2

personnel psychology, p. B-2

organizational psychology, p. B-2

human factors psychology, p. B-2

structured interviews, p. B-5

achievement motivation, p. B-7

task leadership, p. B-12

social leadership, p. B-12

AP* Practice Test Questions ◀ ···

Multiple-Choice Questions

1. Which of the following would fall within the realm of human factors psychology?
   a. Developing hiring procedures that enable businesses to hire the right person for a job.
   b. Applying successful motivational techniques in the workplace.
   c. Focusing on workers' rights to a safe work environment.
   d. Researching the fairest way for management and labor to negotiate contracts.
   e. Designing controls for a machine that allow people to operate it efficiently and safely.

2. A fast-growing profession that applies psychology's principles to the workplace is called
   a. industrial-organizational psychology.
   b. Gallup psychology.
   c. a psychological contract.
   d. attentional user interface.
   e. harnessing strengths.

3. Managers who excel at social leadership
   a. organize work tasks efficiently.
   b. keep work groups on task.
   c. set appropriate goals.
   d. produce high morale in their workers.
   e. are directive in their interactions with their workers.

4. Gallup researchers Marcus Buckingham and Donald Clifton have found that when employers institute a strengths-based selection system for hiring new employees, companies see
   a. an increase in employee intelligence.
   b. more employees working from home.
   c. an increase in workplace effectiveness.
   d. more employees going to school for advanced degrees.
   e. more demands from employees for organizational changes.

5. Mihaly Csikszentmihalyi has observed that between the anxiety of being overwhelmed and stressed, and the apathy of being underwhelmed and bored, lies a zone in which people experience
   a. a calling.
   b. external rewards.
   c. flow.
   d. dissatisfaction.
   e. distraction.

ANSWERS to Multiple-Choice Questions

1. e. Designing controls for a machine that allow people to operate it efficiently and safely.

2. a. industrial-organizational psychology.

3. d. produce high morale in their workers.

4. c. an increase in workplace effectiveness.

5. c. flow.

*AP is a trademark registered and/or owned by the College Board, which was not involved in the production of, and does not endorse, this product.

Promoting Health

Promoting health begins with implementing strategies that prevent illness and enhance wellness. Traditionally, people have thought about their health only when something goes wrong—visiting a physician for diagnosis and treatment. That, say health psychologists, is like ignoring a car's maintenance and going to a mechanic only when the car breaks down. Health maintenance includes alleviating stress, preventing illness, and promoting well-being.

Coping With Stress

1: What factors affect our ability to cope with stress?

STRESSORS ARE UNAVOIDABLE. THIS FACT, coupled with the fact that persistent stress correlates with heart disease, depression, and lowered immunity, gives us a clear message. We need to learn to **cope** with the stress in our lives. We address some stressors directly, with **problem-focused coping.** For example, if our impatience leads to a fight with a friend, we may go directly to that friend to work things out. If, despite our best efforts, we cannot get along with that friend, we may also incorporate an **emotion-focused coping,** such as reaching out to family members or other friends to help address our own emotional needs.

When challenged, some people tend to respond more with cool problem-focused coping, others with emotion-focused coping (Connor-Smith & Flachsbart, 2007). We tend to use problem-focused strategies when we feel a sense of control over a situation and think we can change the circumstances or change ourselves. We turn to emotion-focused strategies when we cannot—or *believe* we cannot—change a situation. We may, for example, seek emotional distance from a damaging relationship or keep busy with active hobbies to avoid falling back into a bad habit. Emotion-focused strategies can be nonadaptive, however, as when students worried about not keeping up with the reading in class go out to party to get it off their mind. Sometimes a problem-focused strategy (catching up with the reading) more effectively reduces stress and promotes long-term health and satisfaction.

Several factors affect our ability to cope successfully, including our feelings of personal control, our explanatory style, and our supportive connections.

Perceived Control

If two rats receive simultaneous shocks, but one can turn a wheel to stop the shocks (as illustrated in FIGURE C.1 on the next page), the helpless rat, but not the wheel turner,

COPING WITH STRESS
Perceived Control
Optimism and Health
Social Support
Close-Up: Pets Are Friends, Too
MANAGING STRESS
Aerobic Exercise
Biofeedback, Relaxation, and
Meditation
Thinking Critically About:
Complementary and Alternative
Medicine
Close-Up: The Relaxation
Response
Spirituality and Faith Communities

::**coping** alleviating stress using emotional, cognitive, or behavioral methods.

::**problem-focused coping** attempting to alleviate stress directly—by changing the stressor or the way we interact with that stressor.

::**emotion-focused coping** attempting to alleviate stress by avoiding or ignoring a stressor and attending to emotional needs related to one's stress reaction.

C-1

Key Terms

Coping With Stress
coping
problem-focused coping
emotion-focused coping

Managing Stress
aerobic exercise
biofeedback
complementary and alternative
 medicine (CAM)

TEACHING TIP

At this point, you may want to use **Lecture/Discussion Topics:** *The Health Belief Model* (p. 2) or *The Theory of Reasoned Action* (p. 2) from Bolt's Teacher's Resource Binder, which accompanies this text.

Appendix C

TEACHING TIP

At this point, you may want to use **Classroom Exercise:** *Unrealistic Optimism About Life Events* (p. 2) from Bolt's Teacher's Resource Binder.

➤ **FIGURE C.1**

Health consequences of a loss of control The "executive" rat at the left can switch off the tail shock by turning the wheel. Because it has control over the shock, it is no more likely to develop ulcers than is the unshocked control rat on the right. The "subordinate" rat in the center receives the same shocks as the executive rat, but with no control over the shocks. It is, therefore, more likely to develop ulcers. (Adapted from Weiss, 1977.)

becomes more susceptible to ulcers and lowered immunity to disease (Laudenslager & Reite, 1984). In humans, too, uncontrollable threats trigger the strongest stress responses (Dickerson & Kemeny, 2004). For example, a bacterial infection often combines with uncontrollable stress to produce the most severe ulcers (Overmier & Murison, 1997). To cure the ulcer, kill the bug with antibiotics and control the stomach's acid secretions with reduced stress.

Perceiving a loss of control, we become more vulnerable to ill health. Elderly nursing home residents who have little perceived control over their activities tend to decline faster and die sooner than do those given more control over their activities (Rodin, 1986). Workers given control over their work environment—by being able to adjust office furnishings and control interruptions and distractions—also experience less stress (O'Neill, 1993). This helps explain why British civil service workers at the executive grades outlive those at clerical or laboring grades, and why Finnish workers with low job stress are less than half as likely to die of cardiovascular disease (strokes or heart disease) as are those with a demanding job and little control. The more control workers have, the longer they live (Bosma et al., 1997, 1998; Kivimaki et al., 2002; Marmot et al., 1997).

Control may also help explain a well-established link between economic status and longevity. In one study of 843 grave markers in an old graveyard in Glasgow, Scotland, those with the costliest, highest pillars (indicating the most affluence) tended to have lived the longest (Carroll et al., 1994). Likewise, those living in Scottish regions with the least overcrowding and unemployment have the greatest longevity. There and elsewhere, high economic status predicts a lower risk of heart and respiratory diseases (Sapolsky, 2005). Wealthy predicts healthy among children, too (Chen, 2004). With higher economic status comes reduced risks of infant mortality, low birth weight, smoking, and violence. Even among other primates, those at the bottom of the social pecking order are more likely than their higher-status companions to become sick when exposed to a coldlike virus (Cohen et al., 1997). But for those high-status baboons and monkeys who frequently have to physically defend their dominant position, high status also entails stress (Sapolsky, 2005).

Researchers are debating the explanation for the income-health correlation, because poor health can lower income and because intelligence scores also correlate with both income and health (Kanazawa, 2006; Whalley & Deary, 2001). But this much seems clear: Poverty and diminished control can entail physiologically measurable stress, even among children (Evans & Kim, 2007).

Why does perceived loss of control predict health problems? Animal studies show—and human studies confirm—that losing control provokes an outpouring of stress hormones. When rats cannot control shock or when primates or humans feel unable to control their environment, stress hormone levels rise, blood pressure increases, and immune responses drop (Rodin, 1986; Sapolsky, 2005). Captive animals therefore experience more stress and are more vulnerable to disease than are wild animals (Roberts, 1988). The crowding that occurs in high-density neighborhoods, prisons, and college and university dorms is another source of diminished feelings of control—and of elevated levels of stress hormones and blood pressure (Fleming et al., 1987; Ostfeld et al., 1987).

Optimism and Health

Another influence on our ability to cope with stress is whether our basic outlook is optimistic or pessimistic. Psychologists Michael Scheier and Charles Carver (1992) have reported that *optimists*—people who agree with statements such as, "In uncertain times, I usually expect the best"—perceive more control, cope better with stressful events, and enjoy better health. During the last month of a semester, students previously identified as optimistic report less fatigue and fewer coughs, aches, and pains. And during the stressful first few weeks of law school, those who are optimistic ("It's unlikely that I will fail") enjoy better moods and stronger infection-thwarting immune systems (Segerstrom et al., 1998). Optimists also respond to stress with smaller increases in blood pressure, and they recover more quickly from heart bypass surgery.

Consider the consistency and startling magnitude of the optimism and positive emotions factor in several other studies:

- One research team followed 941 Dutch people, ages 65 to 85, for nearly a decade (Giltay et al., 2004, 2007). Among those in the lowest optimism quartile, 57 percent died, as did only 30 percent of the top optimism quartile.

- When Finnish researchers followed 2428 men for up to a decade, the number of deaths among those with a bleak, hopeless outlook was more than double that found among their optimistic counterparts (Everson et al., 1996).

- Another study asked 795 Americans, ages 64 to 79, if they were "hopeful about the future." When the researchers checked up on these folks about 5 years later, 29 percent of those answering *no* had died—more than double the 11 percent of deaths among those who said *yes* (Stern et al., 2001).

- A now-famous study followed up on 180 Catholic nuns who had written brief autobiographies at about 22 years of age. Despite living thereafter with similar life-styles and status, those who had expressed happiness, love, and other positive feelings lived an average 7 years longer than their more dour counterparts (Danner et al., 2001). By age 80, some 54 percent of those expressing few positive emotions had died, as had only 24 percent of the most positive-spirited.

Those who manage to find humor in life's daily events also seem to benefit. Among 54,000 adult Norwegians, those scoring in the top quarter on humor appreciation were 35 percent more likely to be alive 7 years later, and the difference was even greater within a cancer-patient subgroup (Svebak et al., 2007). There is not yet enough consistent evidence to suggest that "laughter is the best medicine" (Martin, 2001, 2002). But some studies suggest that mirthful humor (not hostile sarcasm) may defuse stress and strengthen immune activity (Berk et al., 2001; Kimata, 2001). People who laugh a lot (which arouses, massages muscles, and relaxes the body [Robinson, 1983]) also have exhibited a lower incidence of heart disease (Clark et al., 2001). In one experiment, laughter in response to a hilarious movie clip caused

Laughter among friends is good medicine Laughter arouses us, massages muscles, and then leaves us feeling relaxed (Robinson, 1983).

TEACHING TIP

At this point, you may want to use **Lecture/Discussion Topics:** *Stress, Positive Emotion, and Coping* (p. 4) or *Social Relationships and Health* (p. 7) or *Pets* (p. 7) from Bolt's Teacher's Resource Binder.

the blood vessels' inner lining to respond with improved tone and increased blood-flow, the opposite of what happened after people viewed a stressful movie clip (Miller, 2005). Perhaps future research will confirm that, indeed, those who laugh, last.

Social Support

Social support also matters. That's what James Coan and his colleagues (2006) discovered when they subjected happily married women to the threat of electric shock to an ankle while lying in an fMRI machine. During the experiment, some of the women held their husband's hand. Others held the hand of an anonymous person or no hand at all. While awaiting the occasional shocks, the women's brains were less active in threat-responsive areas if they held their husband's hand. This soothing benefit was greatest for those reporting the highest-quality marriages.

For most people, family relationships provide not only life's greatest heartaches (even when well-meaning, family intrusions can be stressful), but also its greatest comfort and joy. Peter Warr and Roy Payne (1982) asked a representative sample of British adults what, if anything, had emotionally strained them the day before. Their most frequent answer? "Family." But asked what prompted yesterday's times of pleasure, the same British sample, by an even larger margin, again answered "Family."

Seven massive investigations, each following thousands of people for several years, revealed that close relationships predict health. Compared with those having few social ties, people are less likely to die prematurely if supported by close relationships with friends, family, fellow workers, members of a faith community, or other support groups (Cohen, 1988; House et al., 1988; Nelson, 1988).

Carefully controlled studies indicate that married people live longer, healthier lives than the unmarried (Kaplan & Kronick, 2006; Wilson & Oswald, 2002). The National Center for Health Statistics (2004) reports that regardless of people's age, sex, race, and income, they tend to be healthier if married. In a seven-decades-long Harvard study, a good marriage at age 50 predicted healthy aging better than did a low cholesterol level at 50 (Vaillant, 2002). But, as Coan's study indicated, marital *functioning* also matters. Conflict-laden marriages are not conducive to health; positive, happy, supportive ones are (De Vogli et al., 2007; Kiecolt-Glaser & Newton, 2001). Moreover, middle-aged and older adults who live alone are more likely to smoke, be obese, and have high-cholesterol—and to have a doubled risk of heart attacks (Nielsen et al., 2006).

How can we explain this link between social support and health? Is it because healthy people are more supportive and marriage-prone? Possibly. But people with supportive friends and marriage partners eat better, exercise more, sleep better, and smoke less, and therefore cope with stress more effectively (Helgeson et al., 1998). Supportive friends can also help buffer immediate threats. Humans aren't the only source of stress-buffering comfort. After stressful events, Medicare patients who have a dog or other companionable pet are less likely to visit their doctor (Siegel, 1990). (See Close-Up: Pets Are Friends, Too.)

Environments that support our need to belong foster stronger immune functioning. Social ties and positive sociability even confer resistance to cold viruses. Sheldon Cohen and his colleagues (1997, 2004) demonstrated this by putting 276 healthy volunteers in quarantine for five days after administering nasal drops laden with a cold virus, and then repeating the experiment with 334 more volunteers. (In both experiments, the volunteers were paid $800 each to endure this experience.) The cold fact is that the effect of social ties is nothing to sneeze at. Age, race, sex, smoking, and other health habits being equal, those with the most social ties were least likely to catch a cold, and if they caught one, they produced less mucus. More sociability meant less susceptibility. More than 50 studies further reveal that social support calms the

> "Woe to one who is alone and falls and does not have another to help."
> Ecclesiastes 4:10

Pets Are Friends, Too

Have you ever wished for a friend who would love you just as you are, who is nonjudgmental, and who is always there for you, no matter your mood? For many tens of millions of people that friend exists, and it is a loyal dog or a friendly cat.

Many people describe their pet as a cherished family member who helps them feel calm, happy, and valued. Can pets also help people handle stress? If so, might pets have healing power? Karen Allen (2003) reports that, *yes*, pets have been found to increase the odds of survival after a heart attack, to relieve depression among AIDS patients, and to lower the level of blood lipids that contribute to cardiovascular risk. As nursing pioneer Florence Nightingale (1860) foresaw, "A small pet animal is often an excellent companion for the sick." Allen reports from her own research that women's blood pressure rises as they struggle with challenging math problems in the presence of a best friend or even a spouse, but much less so when accompanied by their dog.

So, would pets be good medicine for people who do not have pets? To find out, Allen studied a group of stockbrokers who lived alone, described their work as stressful, and had high blood pressure. She randomly selected half to adopt an animal shelter cat or dog. When later facing stress, these

Frank Siteman/Jupiterimages

new pet owners exhibited less than half the blood pressure increase of their counterparts without pets. The effect was greatest for those with few social contacts or friends. Her conclusion: For lowering blood pressure, pets are no substitute for effective drugs and exercise. But for those who enjoy animals, and especially for those who live alone, they are a healthy pleasure.

---

cardiovascular system, lowering blood pressure and stress hormones (Graham et al., 2006; Uchino et al., 1996, 1999).

Close relationships give us an opportunity to *confide* painful feelings, a social support component that has now been extensively studied (Frattaroli, 2006). In one study, health psychologists James Pennebaker and Robin O'Heeron (1984) contacted the surviving spouses of people who had committed suicide or died in car accidents. Those who bore their grief alone had more health problems than those who could express it openly. Talking about our troubles can be "open heart therapy."

Suppressing emotions can be detrimental to physical health. When Pennebaker surveyed more than 700 undergraduate women, he found that about 1 in 12 reported a traumatic sexual experience in childhood. Compared with women who had experienced nonsexual traumas, such as parental death or divorce, the sexually abused women—especially those who had kept their secret to themselves—reported more headaches and stomach ailments. Another study, of 437 Australian ambulance drivers, confirmed the ill effects of suppressing one's emotions after witnessing traumas (Wastell, 2002).

Even writing about personal traumas in a diary can help (Burton & King, 2008; Hemenover, 2003; Lyubomirsky et al., 2006). In one experiment, volunteers who did this had fewer health problems during the ensuing four to six months (Pennebaker, 1990). As one participant explained, "Although I have not talked with anyone about what I wrote, I was finally able to deal with it, work through the pain instead of trying to block it out. Now it doesn't hurt to think about it."

Talking about a stressful event can temporarily arouse people, but in the long run it calms them, by calming limbic system activity (Lieberman et al., 2007; Mendolia & Kleck, 1993). When Pennebaker and his colleagues (1989) invited 33 Holocaust survivors to spend two hours recalling their experiences, many did so in intimate detail never before disclosed. In the weeks following, most watched a tape of their recollections

⊕ **TEACHING TIP**

At this point, you may want to use **Classroom Exercises:** *Coping With Health Injuries and Problems Scale* (p. 3) or *Assessing Coping Strategies* (p. 3) or *Perceived Control* (p. 5) or *Savoring* (p. 5) or *The Life Orientation Scale and Optimism* (p. 6) or *Social Support Scale* (p. 6) or *Self-Concealment Scale* (p. 7) from Bolt's Teacher's Resource Binder.

TEACHING TIP

At this point, you may want to use the Technology Resources *Videos: The Brain,* 2nd ed., *Module 22: Coping With Stress: Control and Predictability* or *Scientific American Frontiers,* 2nd ed., *Segment 34: Sports Imports.*

and showed it to family and friends. Those who were most self-disclosing had the most improved health 14 months later. Confiding is good for the body and the soul.

BEFORE YOU MOVE ON . . .

➤ **ASK YOURSELF**

Can you remember a time when you felt better about some worrisome problem after discussing it with a friend or family member, or even after playing with your pet? How did that interaction help you to cope?

➤ **TEST YOURSELF 1**

How do problem-focused coping and emotion-focused coping differ?

Answers to the Test Yourself questions can be found in Appendix E.

Managing Stress

2: What tactics can we use to manage stress and reduce stress-related ailments?

HAVING A SENSE OF CONTROL, developing more optimistic thinking, and building social support can help us *experience* less stress and thus improve our health. Moreover, these factors interrelate: People who are upbeat about themselves and their future tend also to enjoy health-promoting social ties (Stinson et al., 2008). But sometimes we cannot alleviate stress and simply need to *manage* our stress. Aerobic exercise, biofeedback, relaxation, meditation, and spirituality may help us gather inner strength and lessen stress effects.

Aerobic Exercise

"Is there anyone here who specializes in stress management?"

Aerobic exercise is sustained exercise that increases heart and lung fitness. Jogging, swimming, and biking are common examples. Such exercise strengthens the body. Does it also boost the spirit?

Exercise and Mood

Many studies suggest that aerobic exercise can reduce stress, depression, and anxiety. For example, 3 in 10 American and Canadian people, and 2 in 10 British people, who do aerobic exercise at least three times a week also manage stressful events better, exhibit more self-confidence, feel more vigor, and feel depressed and fatigued less often than those who exercise less (McMurray, 2004). In a Gallup survey, nonexercisers were twice as likely as exercisers to report being "not too happy" (Brooks, 2002). But if we state this observation the other way around—that stressed and depressed people exercise less—cause and effect become unclear.

Experiments have resolved this ambiguity by randomly assigning stressed, depressed, or anxious people either to aerobic exercise or to other treatments. In one such experiment, Lisa McCann and David Holmes (1984) assigned one-third of a group of mildly depressed female college students to a program of aerobic exercise, one-third to a treatment of relaxation exercises, and the remaining third (a control group) to no treatment. As **FIGURE C.2** shows, 10 weeks later the women in the aerobic exercise program reported the greatest decrease in depression. Many of them had, quite literally,

::aerobic exercise sustained exercise that increases heart and lung fitness; may also alleviate depression and anxiety.

> ► FIGURE C.2
Aerobic exercise and depression Mildly depressed college women who participated in an aerobic exercise program showed markedly reduced depression, compared with those who did relaxation exercises or received no treatment. (From McCann & Holmes, 1984.)

run away from their troubles. Vigorous exercise provides a "substantial" immediate mood boost, reports David Watson (2000) from his monitoring of university students. Even a 10-minute walk stimulates two hours of increased well-being by raising energy levels and lowering tension (Thayer, 1987, 1993).

Other studies confirm that exercise reduces depression and anxiety and is therefore a useful adjunct to antidepressant drugs and psychotherapy (Dunn et al., 2005; Stathopoulou et al., 2006). Not only is exercise about as effective as drugs, some research suggests it better prevents symptom recurrence (Babyak et al., 2000; Salmon, 2001).

Researchers are now wondering *why* aerobic exercise alleviates negative emotions. Exercise orders up mood-boosting chemicals from our body's internal pharmacy—neurotransmitters such as norepinephrine, serotonin, and the endorphins (Jacobs, 1994; Salmon, 2001). Perhaps the emotional benefits of exercise are also a side effect of increased warmth and body arousal (counteracting depression's low arousal state), or of the muscle relaxation and sounder sleep that occur afterward. Or perhaps a sense of accomplishment and an improved physique enhance one's emotional state.

Exercise and Health

Other research reveals that exercise not only boosts our mood, but also strengthens the heart, increases bloodflow, keeps blood vessels open, and lowers both blood pressure and the blood pressure reaction to stress (Ford, 2002; Manson, 2002). Compared with inactive adults, people who exercise suffer half as many heart attacks (Powell et al., 1987). Exercise makes the muscles hungry for the "bad fats" that, if not used by the muscles, contribute to clogged arteries (Barinaga, 1997). One study following adult Finnish twins for nearly 20 years revealed that, other things being equal, occasional exercise (compared with no exercise) reduced the risk of death by 29 percent. Daily

The mood boost When one's energy or spirits are sagging, few things reboot the day better than exercising (as I can confirm from my daily noontime basketball). Aerobic exercise appears to counteract depression partly by increasing arousal (replacing depression's low-arousal state) and by doing naturally what Prozac does—increasing the brain's serotonin activity.

TEACHING TIP

At this point, you may want to use the Technology Resource *Psychology Video Tool Kit: Companionship and Support: Pets Fill the Void.*

Appendix C

At this point, you may want to use **Lecture/Discussion Topics:** *Fringe Medicine* (p. 10) or *Religion's Costs and Benefits* (p. 10) or *Spirituality and Health* (p. 11) from Bolt's Teacher's Resource Binder.

::**biofeedback** a system for electronically recording, amplifying, and feeding back information regarding a subtle physiological state, such as blood pressure or muscle tension.

::**complementary and alternative medicine (CAM)** as yet unproven health care treatments intended to supplement (complement) or serve as alternatives to conventional medicine, and which typically are not widely taught in medical schools, used in hospitals, or reimbursed by insurance companies. When research shows a therapy to be safe and effective, it usually then becomes part of accepted medical practice.

• Meditation is a modern phenomenon with a long history: "Sit down alone and in silence. Lower your head, shut your eyes, breathe out gently, and imagine yourself looking into your own heart. . . . As you breathe out, say 'Lord Jesus Christ, have mercy on me.' . . . Try to put all other thoughts aside. Be calm, be patient, and repeat the process very frequently" (Gregory of Sinai, died 1346). •

conditioning exercise reduced death risk by 43 percent (Kujala et al., 1998). In later life, regular exercise also predicts better cognitive functioning and reduced risk of dementia and Alzheimer's disease (Kramer & Erickson, 2007).

The genes passed down to us from our distant ancestors were those that enabled the physical activity essential to hunting, foraging, and farming. In muscle cells, those genes, when activated by exercise, respond by producing proteins. In the modern inactive person, these genes produce lower quantities of proteins and leave us susceptible to more than 20 chronic diseases, such as type-2 diabetes, cardiovascular disease, and cancer (Booth & Neufer, 2005). Inactivity is thus potentially toxic.

With less physical activity demanded of us to provide food, shelter, and mobility (machines do much of the work for us), our more sedentary life-style contributes to today's high rate of depression. Less exercise means less brain activity in areas essential for reward, motivation, and effective coping (Ilardi et al., 2007; Lambert, 2005, 2008). More exercise has beneficial effects similar to those of antidepressant drugs: In mice, exercise causes their brains to produce a molecule that acts as a natural antidepressant by stimulating the production of new neurons (Hunsberger et al., 2007).

By one estimate, moderate exercise adds not only quality of life (more energy and better mood) but also quantity of life—two additional years, on average. "Perhaps God does not subtract the time spent exercising from your allotted time on Earth," jested Martin Seligman (1994, p. 193).

Biofeedback, Relaxation, and Meditation

As we saw in Unit 6, **biofeedback** is a system of recording, amplifying, and feeding back information about subtle physiological responses. The years of rigorous testing and research on biofeedback exemplify the scientific attitude toward new but unproven health care treatment. (For more on this topic, see Thinking Critically About: Complementary and Alternative Medicine.)

Simple methods of relaxation, which require no expensive equipment, can produce many of the same results biofeedback once promised. For example, dozens of studies have found that relaxation procedures can help alleviate headaches, hypertension, anxiety, and insomnia (Nestoriuc et al., 2008; Stetter & Kupper, 2002). Such findings would not surprise Meyer Friedman and his colleagues. To find out whether teaching Type A heart attack victims to relax might reduce their risk of another attack, the researchers randomly assigned hundreds of middle-aged, male heart-attack survivors to one of two groups. The first group received standard advice from cardiologists concerning medications, diet, and exercise habits. The second group received similar advice plus continuing counseling on modifying their life-styles—how to slow down and relax by walking, talking, and eating more slowly; by smiling at others and laughing at themselves; by admitting mistakes; by taking time to enjoy life; and by renewing their religious faith. As **FIGURE C.3** (turn the page) indicates, during the ensuing three years, the second group experienced half as many repeat heart attacks as the first group. This, wrote the exuberant Friedman, was an unprecedented, spectacular reduction in heart-attack recurrence. A smaller-scale British study similarly divided heart-attack–prone people into control and life-style modification groups (Eysenck & Grossarth-Maticek, 1991). During the next 13 years, it also found a 50 percent reduction in death rate among those trained to alter their thinking and life-style. After suffering a heart attack at age 55, Friedman started taking his own behavioral medicine—and lived to age 90 (Wargo, 2007).

Cardiologist Herbert Benson (1996) became intrigued with meditative relaxation when he found that experienced meditators could decrease their blood pressure, heart rate, and oxygen consumption and raise their fingertip temperature. His study led him to what he calls the *relaxation response* (described in the Close-Up box, next page).

THINKING CRITICALLY ABOUT

Complementary and Alternative Medicine

One health care growth market is **complementary and alternative medicine (CAM),** which includes relaxation, acupuncture, massage therapy, homeopathy, spiritual healing, herbal remedies, chiropractic, and aromatherapy. In Germany, herbal remedies and homeopathy are enormously popular. In China, herbal therapies have long flourished, as have acupuncture and acupressure therapies that claim to correct "imbalances of energy flow" (called *Qi* or *Chi*) at identifiable points close to the skin. Andrew Weil's many books on alternative medicine have sold millions of copies, putting him on the cover of *Time* magazine.

Facing political pressure to explore these techniques, the U.S. National Institutes of Health (NIH) established the National Center for Complementary and Alternative Medicine, which the center defines as health care treatments not taught widely in medical schools, not usually reimbursed by insurance companies, and not used in hospitals (**TABLE C.1**).

So what shall we make of CAM? Some aspects, such as lifestyle changes and stress management, have acknowledged validity. And certain techniques have proved useful for specific ailments, such as acupuncture, massage therapy, and aromatherapy for pain relief in cancer patients (Fellowes et al., 2004). Do the other aspects offer, as some believe, a new medical paradigm?

Critics point out that people consult physicians for diagnosable, curable diseases and turn to CAM techniques for either incurable illnesses or when well but feeling subpar. Thus, an otherwise healthy person with a cold may try an herbal remedy and then credit the subsequent return to good health to CAM, rather than to the body's natural return to normal. CAM will seem especially effective with cyclical diseases, such as arthritis and allergies, as people seek therapy during the downturn and presume its effectiveness during the ensuing upturn. Add to this the healing power of belief—the *placebo effect*—plus the natural disappearance *(spontaneous remission)* of many diseases, and CAM practices are bound to seem effective, whether they are or not. One study of 302 migraine headache patients in Germany found that 51 percent of those receiving acupuncture treatment found relief, as did only 15 percent of those in a waiting list control group. But among a third group that received "sham acupuncture" (needles inserted at nonacupuncture points), 53 percent enjoyed relief. Such results, the investigators suspected, may indicate "a powerful placebo effect" (Linde et al., 2005).

As always, the way to discern what works and what does not is to experiment: Randomly assign patients to receive the therapy or a placebo control. Then ask the critical question: When neither the therapist nor the patient knows who is getting the real therapy, is the real therapy effective?

Much of today's mainstream medicine began as yesterday's alternative medicine. Natural botanical life has given us digitalis (from purple foxglove), morphine (from the opium poppy), and penicillin (from penicillium mold). In each case, the active ingredient was verified in controlled trials. We have medical and public health science to thank for the antibiotics, vaccines, surgical procedures, sanitation, and emergency medicine that helped lengthen our life expectancy by three decades during the last century.

"CAM changes continually," notes the National Center for Complementary and Alternative Medicine (2006), "as those therapies that are proven to be safe and effective become adopted into conventional health care." Indeed, said *New England Journal of Medicine* editors Marcia Angell and Jerome Kassirer (1998), "There cannot be two kinds of medicine—conventional and alternative. There is only medicine that has been adequately tested and medicine that has not, medicine that works and medicine that may or may not work. Once a treatment has been tested rigorously, it no longer matters whether it was considered alternative at the outset."

> "In God we trust. All others must have data."
> George Lundberg, Editor, *Journal of the American Medical Association,* 1998

TABLE C.1

FIVE DOMAINS OF COMPLEMENTARY AND ALTERNATIVE MEDICINE

Alternative medical systems	Therapies used in place of conventional medicine, including homeopathy in Western cultures and traditional Chinese medicine and Ayurveda in non-Western cultures.
Mind-body interventions	Techniques designed to enhance the mind's capacity to affect bodily function and symptoms, including meditation, prayer, mental healing, and therapies that use creative outlets such as art, music, or dance.
Biologically based therapies	Therapies using natural substances such as herbs, foods, and vitamins.
Manipulative and body-based methods	Based on manipulation and/or movement of one or more parts of the body, including chiropractic or osteopathic manipulation, and massage.
Energy therapies	Use presumed energy fields. Biofield therapies, such as qi gong, Reiki, and therapeutic touch, are intended to affect energy fields that purportedly surround and penetrate the human body. Bioelectromagnetic-based therapies involve the unconventional use of electromagnetic fields, such as pulsed or magnetic fields.

Source: Adapted from the National Center for Complementary and Alternative Medicine, NIH
http://nccam.nih.gov/health/whatiscam.

 TEACHING TIP

At this point, you may want to use **Classroom Exercise: *The Relaxation Response*** (p. 9) or **Classroom Exercise/Student Project: *Meditation*** (p. 10) from Bolt's Teacher's Resource Binder.

Appendix C

TEACHING TIP

At this point, you may want to use **Student Project/ Classroom Exercise:** *Biodots and Biofeedback in the Classroom* (p. 9) from Bolt's Teacher's Resource Binder.

➤ **FIGURE C.3**

Recurrent heart attacks and life-style modification The San Francisco Recurrent Coronary Prevention Project offered counseling from a cardiologist to survivors of heart attacks. Those who were also guided in modifying their Type A life-style suffered fewer repeat heart attacks. (From Friedman & Ulmer, 1984.)

● And then there are the mystics who seek to use the mind's power to enable novocaine-free cavity repair. Their aim: to transcend dental medication. ●

Tibetan Buddhists deep in meditation and Franciscan nuns deep in centering prayer report a diminished sense of self, space, and time. Brain scans reveal the neural footprints of such spiritual feelings during these mystical experiences: A part of the parietal lobe that tracks where we are in space is less active than usual, and a frontal lobe area involved in focused attention is more active (Cahn & Polich, 2006; Newberg & D'Aquili, 2001).

Psychologist Richard Davidson reports that Buddhist monks who are experienced in meditation display elevated levels of the left frontal lobe activity associated with positive emotions. To explore whether such activity is a *result* of meditation, Davidson and his colleagues (2003) ran baseline brain scans of volunteers who were *not* experienced meditators, and then randomly assigned them either to a control group or to an eight-week course in "mindfulness meditation." Compared with both the control group and their own baseline, the meditation participants exhibited noticeably more left-hemisphere activity, and also improved immune functioning after the training. Such effects may help explain the astonishing results of a study that randomly assigned 73 residents of homes for the elderly either to daily meditation or to none. After three years, one-fourth of the nonmeditators had died, but all the meditators were still alive (Alexander et al., 1989). A more recent study found that hypertension patients assigned to meditation training had (compared with other treatment groups) a 30 percent lower cardiovascular death rate over the ensuing 19-year study period (Schneider et al., 2005).

CLOSE-UP

The Relaxation Response

The relaxation response is a state of calm marked by relaxed muscles, slowed breathing and heart rate, and decreased blood pressure. Advocates such as cardiologist Herbert Benson claim lasting stress-reducing benefits when relaxation is practiced once or twice daily.

To experience the relaxation response, the Benson-Henry Institute for Mind Body Medicine recommends these steps: Sit quietly in a comfortable position. Close your eyes. Relax your muscles, starting with your feet, then your calves, and upward through your thighs, shoulders, neck, and head. Breathe slowly. As you exhale each breath, repeat a focus word, phrase, or prayer—something drawn from your own belief system. When other thoughts intrude, don't worry. Just return to your repetition and continue for 10 to 20 minutes. When finished, sit quietly for another minute or two, then open your eyes and sit for a few more moments.

Spirituality and Faith Communities

As humans suffered ills and sought healing throughout history, two healing traditions—religion and medicine—have joined hands in caring for them. Often those hands belonged to the same person—the spiritual leader was also the healer. Maimonides was a twelfth-century rabbi and a renowned physician. Hospitals, which were first established in monasteries and then spread by missionaries, often carry the names of saints or faith communities.

As medical science matured, healing and religion diverged. Rather than asking God to spare their children from smallpox, people were able to vaccinate them. Rather than seeking a spiritual healer when burning with bacterial fever, they were able to use antibiotics. Recently, however, religion and healing are converging once again. In 1992, 4 percent of American medical schools offered spirituality and health courses; in 2005, 75 percent did (Koenig, 2002; Puchalski, 2005). A National Library of Medicine MEDLINE search of *religion* or *spirituality* reveals 8294 articles between 2000 and 2007, more than three times the articles in the database's prior 35 years.

More than a thousand studies have sought to correlate the *faith factor* with health and healing. For example, Jeremy Kark and his colleagues (1996) compared the death rates for 3900 Israelis either in one of 11 religiously orthodox or in one of 11 matched, nonreligious collective settlements (kibbutz communities). The researchers reported that over a 16-year period, "belonging to a religious collective was associated with a strong protective effect" not explained by age or economic differences. In every age group, religious community members were about half as likely to have died as were their nonreligious counterparts. This is roughly comparable to the gender difference in mortality.

In response to such findings, Richard Sloan and his skeptical colleagues (1999, 2000, 2002, 2005) remind us that mere correlations can leave many factors uncontrolled. Consider one obvious possibility: Women are more religiously active than men, and women outlive men. So perhaps religious involvement is merely an expression of the gender effect on longevity.

However, several studies have found the correlation between religious involvement and life expectancy among men alone, and even more strongly among women (McCullough et al., 2000, 2005). One study that followed 5286 Californians over 28 years found that, after controlling for age, gender, ethnicity, and education, frequent religious attenders were 36 percent less likely to have died in any year (FIGURE C.4).

A U.S. National Health Interview Survey (Hummer et al., 1999) followed 21,204 people over 8 years. After controlling for age, sex, race, and region, researchers found that nonattenders were 1.87 times more likely to have died than were those attending more than weekly. This translated into a life expectancy at age 20 of 83 years for frequent attenders and 75 years for infrequent attenders (FIGURE C.5, next page).

These correlational findings do not indicate that nonattenders who start attending services and change nothing else will live 8 years longer. But they do indicate that as a *predictor* of health and longevity, religious involvement rivals nonsmoking and exercise effects. Such findings demand explanation. Can you imagine what intervening variables might account for the correlation?

First, religiously active people tend to have healthier life-styles; for example, they smoke and drink less (Lyons, 2002; Park, 2007; Strawbridge et al., 2001). Health-

➤ **FIGURE C.4**

Predictors of mortality: Not smoking, frequent exercise, and regular religious attendance Epidemiologist William Strawbridge and his co-workers (1997, 1999; Oman et al., 2002) followed 5286 Alameda, California, adults over 28 years. After adjusting for age and education, the researchers found that not smoking, regular exercise, and religious attendance all predicted a lowered risk of death in any given year. Women attending weekly religious services, for example, were only 54 percent as likely to die in a typical study year as were nonattenders.

Appendix C

At this point, you may want to use the Technology Resources *ActivePsych: Scientific American Frontiers Teaching Modules*, 3rd ed.: *Experience and Exercise: Generating New Brain Cells* or *Stress Management: The Relaxation Response.*

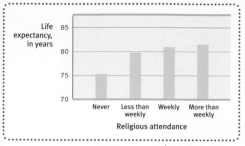

➤ **FIGURE C.5**

Religious attendance and life expectancy In a national health survey financed by the U.S. Centers for Disease Control and Prevention, religiously active people had longer life expectancies. (Data from Hummer et al., 1999.)

oriented, vegetarian Seventh Day Adventists have a longer-than-usual life expectancy (Berkel & de Waard, 1983). Religiously orthodox Israelis eat less fat than do their nonreligious compatriots. But such differences are not great enough to explain the dramatically reduced mortality that was found in the religious kibbutzim, argued the Israeli researchers. In American studies, too, about 75 percent of the longevity difference remains after controlling for unhealthy behaviors such as inactivity and smoking (Musick et al., 1999).

Social support is another variable that helps explain the faith factor (Ai et al., 2007; George et al., 2002). For Judaism, Christianity, and Islam, faith is not solo spirituality but a communal experience that helps satisfy the need to belong. The more than 350,000 faith communities in North America and the millions more elsewhere provide support networks for their active participants—people who are there for one another when misfortune strikes. Moreover, religion encourages another predictor of health and longevity—marriage. In the religious kibbutzim, for example, divorce has been almost nonexistent.

But even after controlling for gender, unhealthy behaviors, social ties, and preexisting health problems, the mortality studies find much of the mortality reduction remaining (George et al., 2000; Powell et al., 2003). Researchers therefore speculate that a third set of intervening variables is the stress protection and enhanced well-being associated with a coherent worldview, a sense of hope for the long-term future, feelings of ultimate acceptance, and the relaxed meditation of prayer or Sabbath observance (**FIGURE C.6**). These variables might also help to explain other findings among the religiously active, such as healthier immune functioning, fewer hospital admissions, and, for AIDS patients, fewer stress hormones and longer survival (Ironson et al., 2002; Koenig & Larson, 1998; Lutgendorf et al., 2004).

➤ **FIGURE C.6**

Possible explanations for the correlation between religious involvement and health/longevity

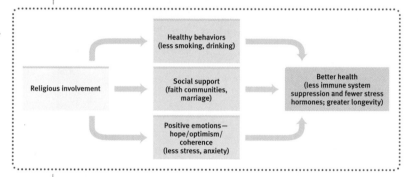

➤ **ASK YOURSELF**

What techniques do you currently use to manage stress? In what ways might you improve upon your stress management?

➤ **TEST YOURSELF 2**

Those who frequently attend religious services live longer, on average, than those who attend infrequently or not at all. What type of research finding is this, and what explanations might it have?

Answers to the Test Yourself questions can be found in Appendix E.

APPENDIX C REVIEW: Promoting Health

Coping With Stress

1: What factors affect our ability to cope with stress?

Having a sense of control, developing a more optimistic explanatory style, and building our base of social support can help us *cope* with stress emotionally, cognitively, or behaviorally. Direct, *problem-focused coping* strategies alleviate stress directly; *emotion-focused coping* tries to alleviate stress by attending to emotional needs. Optimists seem to cope more successfully with stress and enjoy better health.

Managing Stress

2: What tactics can we use to manage stress and reduce stress-related ailments?

Stress-management programs may include *aerobic exercise*, relaxation, and meditation. Learning to slow down and relax has helped lower rates of recurring heart attacks. Researchers are working toward understanding the active components of the religion-health correlation.

Terms and Concepts to Remember

coping, p. C-1
problem-focused coping, p. C-1
emotion-focused coping, p. C-1

aerobic exercise, p. C-6
biofeedback, p. C-8

complementary and alternative medicine (CAM), p. C-9

 AP* Practice Test Questions ◄ ···

Multiple-Choice Questions

1. What has helped to lower rates of recurring heart attacks?
   a. Confronting those who anger us.
   b. Ensuring one has a good income.
   c. Expressing our anger by "blowing off steam."
   d. Learning to slow down and relax.
   e. Avoiding social contacts.

2. You have a conflict with a friend and go directly to that person to work things out. This is an example of
   a. problem-focused coping.
   b. emotion-focused coping.
   c. biofeedback.
   d. catharsis.
   e. poor coping.

3. Perceived loss of control predicts health problems because it
   a. diminishes serotonin levels in the brain.
   b. diminishes norepinephrine levels in the brain.
   c. provokes the release of stress hormones.
   d. increases the quality of sleep.
   e. reduces the susceptibility to ulcers.

4. When Karen Allen studied the effects of pet ownership on highly stressed stockbrokers, she discovered that pet ownership
   a. actually increased stress because of the new responsibilities.
   b. helped decrease the stockbrokers' blood pressure.
   c. seemed to reduce blood pressure but increase cholesterol levels.
   d. led the stockbrokers to exercise more.
   e. had no measurable effect on stress levels but did elevate mood.

5. Which of the following statements about exercise is *not* true?
   a. Vigorous exercise provides a substantial and immediate mood boost.
   b. Exercise reduces depression and anxiety.
   c. In later life, regular exercise predicts better cognitive functioning.
   d. Regular exercise reduces the risk of dementia and Alzheimer's disease.
   e. Exercise causes less brain activity in areas essential for effective coping.

*AP is a trademark registered and/or owned by the College Board, which was not involved in the production of, and does not endorse, this product.

ANSWERS to Multiple-Choice Questions

1. d. Learning to slow down and relax.

2. a. problem-focused coping.

3. c. provokes the release of stress hormones.

4. b. helped decrease the stockbrokers' blood pressure.

5. e. Exercise causes less brain activity in areas essential for effective coping.

Animal Thinking and Language

If in our use of language we humans are, as the psalmist long ago rhapsodized, "little lower than God," where do other animals fit in the scheme of things? Are they "little lower than human"? Let's see what the research on animal thinking and language can tell us.

What Do Animals Think?

1: What do we know about animal thinking? Do other animals share our capacity for language?

WHAT DO ANIMALS THINK?

DO ANIMALS EXHIBIT LANGUAGE?

THE CASE OF THE APES

Close-Up: Talking Hands

TEACHING TIP

At this point, you may want to use **Lecture/Discussion Topic: *Do Animals Plan Ahead?*** (p. 1) from Bolt's Teacher's Resource Binder, which accompanies this text, or the Technology Resources *Psychology Video Tool Kit: How Intelligent Are Animals?* or *Can Chimpanzees Plan Ahead?*

ANIMALS ARE SMARTER THAN WE OFTEN realize. A baboon knows everyone's voices within its 80-member troop (Jolly, 2007). Sheep can recognize and remember individual faces (Morell, 2008). A marmoset can learn from and imitate others. Great apes and even monkeys can *form concepts*. When monkeys learn to classify cats and dogs, certain frontal lobe neurons in their brains fire in response to new "catlike" images, others to new "doglike" images (Freedman et al., 2001). Even pigeons—mere birdbrains—can sort objects (pictures of cars, cats, chairs, flowers). Shown a picture of a never-before-seen chair, pigeons will reliably peck a key that represents the category "chairs" (Wasserman, 1995).

Animals have also displayed some surprising abilities to solve problems. Chimpanzees, like humans, are shaped by reinforcement when they solve problems. Forest-dwelling chimpanzees have become *natural tool users* (Boesch-Achermann & Boesch, 1993). They break off a reed or a stick, strip the twigs and leaves, carry it to a termite mound, fish for termites by twisting it just so, and then carefully remove it without scraping off many termites. They even select different tools for different purposes—a heavy stick to puncture holes, a light, flexible stick for fishing (Sanz et al., 2004). One anthropologist, trying to mimic the chimpanzee's deft termite fishing, failed miserably.

Some animals also display a surprising *numerical ability*. Over two decades, Kyoto University researcher Tetsuro Matsuzawa (2007) has studied chimpanzees' ability to remember and relate numbers. In one experiment, a chimpanzee named Ai taps, in ascending order, numbers randomly displayed on a computer screen (**FIGURE D.1**, next page). If four or five of the numbers between 1 and 9 are flashed for no more than a second, and then replaced by white boxes, she does what a human cannot. Remembering the flashed numbers, she again taps the boxes in numerical order.

D-1

Appendix D

➤ **FIGURE D.1**

Chimpanzee bests humans It is adaptive for chimpanzees to be able to monitor lots of information in their natural environment. This might explain how chimpanzee Ai can remember and tap numbers in ascending order, even after they are covered by white boxes.

TEACHING TIP

At this point, you may want to use the Technology Resources *Video: Scientific American Frontiers,* 2nd ed., *Segment 20: Who Needs Words, Anyway?* or *ActivePsych: Digital Media Archive,* 2nd ed.: *Problem Solving in Genus Corvus (Crows, Ravens, and Magpies).*

Until his death in 2007, the grey parrot, Alex, also displayed a jaw-dropping numerical ability (Pepperberg, 2006). He not only could name and categorize objects, he displayed a comprehension of numbers up to 6. Thus, he could speak the number of objects, add two small clusters of objects and announce the sum, and indicate which of two numbers was greater. And he could answer when shown various groups of objects and asked, for example, "What color four?" (meaning "What's the color of the objects of which there are four?").

Researchers have found at least 39 local customs related to chimpanzee tool use, grooming, and courtship (Whiten & Boesch, 2001). One group may slurp ants directly from the stick, while another group plucks them off individually. One group may break nuts with a stone hammer, another with a wooden hammer. Or picture this actual laboratory experiment: Chimpanzee B observes Chimpanzee A as it obtains food, either by sliding or lifting a door. Then B follows the same lifting or sliding procedure. So does Chimpanzee C after observing B, and so forth. Chimp see, chimp do, unto the sixth generation (Bonnie et al., 2007; Horner et al., 2006).

To learn such customs, it helps to be a primate with a relatively large cortex (Whiten & van Schaik, 2007). But the chimpanzee group differences, along with differing dialects and hunting styles, seem not to be genetic. Rather, they are the chimpanzee equivalent of cultural diversity. Like humans, chimpanzees invent behaviors and *transmit cultural patterns* to their peers and offspring (**FIGURE D.2a**). So do orangutans and capuchin monkeys (Dindo et al., 2008; van Schaik et al., 2003). And so do some Australian dolphins (Figure D.2b), which have learned to break off sponges and wear them on their snouts while probing the sea floor for fish (Krützen et al., 2005).

Thus animals, and chimpanzees in particular, display remarkable talents. They form concepts, display insight, fashion tools, exhibit numerical abilities, and transmit local cultural behaviors. Chimpanzees and two species of monkeys can even read your intent. They would show more interest in a food container that you have intentionally grasped rather than one you flopped your hand on, as if by accident (Wood et al., 2007). Great apes, dolphins, and elephants have also demonstrated self-awareness (by recognizing themselves in a mirror). And as social creatures, chimpanzees have shown altruism, cooperation, and group aggression. But do they, like humans, exhibit language?

(a)   (b)

Do Animals Exhibit Language?

WITHOUT DOUBT, ANIMALS COMMUNICATE. Vervet monkeys have different alarm cries for different predators: a barking call for a leopard, a cough for an eagle, and a chuttering for a snake. Hearing the leopard alarm, other vervets climb the nearest tree. Hearing the eagle alarm, they rush into the bushes. Hearing the snake chutter, they stand up and scan the ground (Byrne, 1991). Whales also communicate, with clicks and wails. Honeybees do a dance that informs other bees of the direction and distance of the food source.

And what shall we say of dogs' ability to understand us? Border collie Rico knows and can fetch 200 items by name. Moreover, reports a team of psychologists at Leipzig's Max Planck Institute, if he is asked to retrieve a novel toy with a name he has never heard, Rico will pick out the novel item from among a group of familiar items (Kaminski et al., 2004). Hearing that novel word for the second time four weeks later, he as often as not retrieves the object. Such feats show animals' comprehension and communication. But is this language?

The Case of the Apes

THE GREATEST CHALLENGE TO OUR CLAIM to be the only language-using species has come from one of our closest genetic relatives, the chimpanzees. Psychologists Allen Gardner and Beatrix Gardner (1969) aroused enormous scientific and public interest when they taught sign language to the chimpanzee Washoe (c. 1965–2007). After four years, Washoe could use 132 signs; by age 32, 181 signs (Sanz et al., 1998). One *New York Times* reporter, having learned sign language from his deaf parents, visited Washoe and exclaimed, "Suddenly I realized I was conversing with a member of another species in my native tongue."

Further evidence of gestured "ape language" surfaced during the 1970s (see Close-Up: Talking Hands by turning the page). Usually apes sign just single words such as "that" or "gimme" (Bowman, 2003). But sometimes they string signs together to form intelligible sentences. Washoe signed, "You me go out, please." Apes even appear to combine words creatively. Washoe designated a swan as a "water bird." Koko, a gorilla trained by Francine Patterson (1978), reportedly described a long-nosed Pinocchio doll as an "elephant baby." Lana, a "talking" chimpanzee that

➤ **FIGURE D.2**
Cultural transmission (a) On the western bank of one Ivory Coast river, a youngster watches as its mother uses a stone hammer to open a nut. On the river's other side, a few miles away, chimpanzees do not follow this custom.
(b) This bottlenose dolphin in Shark Bay, Western Australia, is a member of a small group that uses marine sponges as protective gear when probing the sea floor for fish.

Comprehending canine Rico, a border collie with a 200-word vocabulary, can infer that an unfamiliar sound refers to a novel object.

• Seeing a doll floating in her water, Washoe signed, "Baby in my drink." •

▼
But is this language? Chimpanzees' ability to express themselves in American Sign Language (ASL) raises questions about the very nature of language. Here, the trainer is asking, "What is this?" The sign in response is "Baby." Does the response constitute language?

punched a crude computer keyboard that translated her entries into English, wanted her trainer's orange. She had no word for *orange,* but she did know her colors and the word for *apple,* so she improvised: "Tim give apple—which is orange" (Rumbaugh, 1977).

Granted, these vocabularies and sentences are simple, rather like those of a 2-year-old child (and nothing like your own 60,000 or so words, which you fluidly combine to create a limitless variety of sentences). Yet, as reports of ape language accumulated, it seemed that they might indeed be "little lower than human." Then, in the late 1970s, fascination with "talking apes" turned toward cynicism: Were the chimps language champs or were the researchers chumps? The ape language researchers were making monkeys of themselves, said the skeptics. Consider:

• Unlike speaking or signing children, who effortlessly soak up dozens of new words a week, apes gain their limited vocabularies only with great difficulty (Wynne, 2004, 2008). Saying that apes can learn language because they can sign words is like saying humans can fly because they can jump.

• Chimpanzees can make signs or push buttons in sequence to get a reward, but pigeons, too, can peck a sequence of keys to get grain (Straub et al., 1979). After training a chimpanzee he named Nim Chimsky, Herbert Terrace (1979) concluded that much of apes' signing is nothing more than aping their trainers' signs and learning that certain arm movements produce rewards.

• Presented with ambiguous information, people, thanks to their *perceptual set,* tend to see what they want or expect to see. Interpreting chimpanzee signs as language may be little more than the trainers' wishful thinking, claimed Terrace. (When Washoe signed *water bird,* she perhaps was separately naming *water* and *bird.*)

• "Give orange me give eat orange me eat orange . . ." is a far cry from the exquisite syntax of a 3-year-old (Anderson, 2004; Pinker, 1995). To the child, "you tickle" and "tickle you" communicate different ideas. A chimpanzee, lacking human syntax, might sign the phrases interchangeably.

In science as in politics, controversy can stimulate progress. Further evidence confirms chimpanzees' abilities to think and communicate. One surprising finding was of Washoe's training her adopted son in the signs she had learned. After her second infant died, Washoe became withdrawn when told, "Baby dead, baby gone, baby finished." Two weeks later, caretaker-researcher Roger Fouts (1992, 1997) signed better news: "I have baby for you." Washoe reacted with instant excitement, hair on end, swaggering and panting while signing over and again, "Baby, my baby." It took several hours for Washoe and the foster infant, Loulis, to warm to each other, whereupon she broke the ice by signing, "Come baby" and cuddling Loulis.

In the months that followed, Loulis picked up 68 signs simply by observing Washoe and three other language-trained chimpanzees. They now sign spontaneously, asking one another to *chase, tickle, hug, come,* or *groom.* People who sign are in near-perfect agreement about what the chimpanzees are saying, 90 percent of which pertains to social interaction, reassurance, or play (Fouts & Bodamer, 1987).

"He says he wants a lawyer."

Talking Hands

Chimpanzees' use of sign language builds upon their natural gestured words (such as a hand extended for "I want some"). Human language appears to have evolved from such gestured communications (Corballis, 2002, 2003; Pollick & de Waal, 2007). So, it's no wonder we talk and think with our hands:

- Gestures (pointing at a cup) pave the way for children's language (saying *cup,* while simultaneously pointing) (Iverson & Goldin-Meadow, 2005).
- Signed language readily develops among Deaf people.
- People gesture even when talking on the phone.

Gestured communication For hearing people, today's gestures may be less central to communication than for those who first used hand signals. Yet gestures remain naturally associated with spontaneous speech, especially speech that has spatial content.

- Congenitally blind people, like sighted people, gesture (Iverson & Goldin-Meadow, 1998). (And they do so even when they believe their listener is also blind.)
- Prohibiting gestures disrupts speech with spatial content, as when people try to describe an apartment's layout.
- Gesturing lightens a speaker's "cognitive load" (Goldin-Meadow, 2006). People told not to gesture put more effort into communicating with words alone, and are less able to remember recently learned words or numbers.

Gesture researcher Robert Krauss (1998) recalls his grandfather telling of two men walking on a bitter winter day. One chattered away while the second nodded, saying nothing. "Schmuel, why aren't you saying anything?" the first friend finally wondered. "Because," replied Schmuel, "I forgot my gloves."

 TEACHING TIP

At this point, you may want to use the Technology Resources *Video: The Mind,* 2nd ed., *Module 27: Animal Language.*

The chimpanzees are even modestly bilingual; they can translate spoken English words into signs (Shaw, 1989–1990).

Even more stunning was the report by Sue Savage-Rumbaugh and her colleagues (1993) of pygmy chimpanzees learning to *comprehend syntax* in English spoken to them. Kanzi, a pygmy chimpanzee with the seeming grammatical abilities of a human 2-year-old, happened onto language while observing his adoptive mother during language training. Kanzi has behaved intelligently whether asked, "Can you show me the light?" or "Can you bring me the [flash]light?" or "Can you turn the light on?" Kanzi also knows many spoken words, such as *snake, bite,* and *dog.* Given stuffed animals and asked—for the first time—to "make the dog bite the snake," he put the snake to the dog's mouth. For chimpanzees as for humans, early life is a critical time for learning language. Without early exposure to speech or word symbols, adults will not gain language competence (Rumbaugh & Savage-Rumbaugh, 1994).

The provocative claims that "apes share our capacity for language" and the skeptical counterclaims that "apes no use language" (as Washoe might have put it) have moved psychologists toward a greater appreciation of apes' remarkable abilities and

"[Our] view that [we are] unique from all other forms of animal life is being jarred to the core."
Duane Rumbaugh and
Sue Savage-Rumbaugh (1978)

At this point, you may want to use the Technology Resource *Psychology Video Tool Kit: Teaching Language to Chimpanzees*.

"Although humans make sounds with their mouths and occasionally look at each other, there is no solid evidence that they actually communicate with each other."

"Chimps do not develop language. But that is no shame on them; humans would surely do no better if trained to hoot and shriek like chimps, to perform the waggle-dance of the bee, or any of the other wonderful feats in nature's talent show."

Steve Pinker (1995)

of our own (Friend, 2004; Rumbaugh & Washburn, 2003). Most now agree that humans alone possess language, if by the term we mean verbal or signed expression of complex grammar. If we mean, more simply, an ability to communicate through a meaningful sequence of symbols, then apes are indeed capable of language.

Believing that animals could not think, Descartes and other philosophers argued that they were living robots without any moral rights. Animals, it has been said at one time or another, cannot plan, conceptualize, count, use tools, show compassion, or use language (Thorpe, 1974). Today, we know better. Animal researchers have shown us that primates exhibit insight, show family loyalty, communicate with one another, display altruism, transmit cultural patterns across generations, and comprehend the syntax of human speech. Accepting and working out the moral implications of all this is an unfinished task for our own thinking species.

BEFORE YOU MOVE ON . . .

➤ ASK YOURSELF
Can you think of a time when you felt an animal was communicating with you? How might you put such intuition to a test?

➤ TEST YOURSELF 1
If your dog barks at a stranger at the front door, does this qualify as language? What if the dog yips in a telltale way to let you know she needs to go out?

Answers to the Test Yourself questions can be found in Appendix E.

APPENDIX D REVIEW: Animal Thinking and Language

1: What do we know about animal thinking? Do other animals share our capacity for language?
Both humans and the great apes form concepts, display insight, use and create tools, exhibit numerical abilities, and transmit cultural innovations. A number of chimpanzees have learned to communicate with humans by signing or by pushing buttons wired to a computer, have developed vocabularies of nearly 200 words, have communicated by stringing these words together, and have taught their skills to younger animals. Only humans can master the verbal or signed expression of complex rules of syntax. Nevertheless, primates and other animals demonstrate impressive abilities to think and communicate.

 AP* Practice Test Questions ◄ ....

Multiple-Choice Questions

1. Skeptics like Herbert Terrace doubted the language abilities of apes partly because
   a. it was difficult for the ape's trainers to objectively interpret their data.
   b. they believed some researchers made up false data to support their case.
   c. apes were not able to use language among themselves.
   d. apes could only learn sign language, which is not considered a real language.
   e. apes could learn a maximum of about a dozen signs.

2. Which of the following is *not* true about animals?
   a. A baboon knows everyone's voices within its 80-member troop.
   b. Apes have shown the ability to learn close to 3000 sign words.
   c. Sheep can recognize and remember individual faces.
   d. A marmoset can learn from and imitate others.
   e. When monkeys learn to classify cats, frontal lobe neurons fire in response to new "catlike" images.

3. Researchers have found at least 39 local customs related to chimpanzee
   a. warlike and aggressive behaviors.
   b. signing and communicating of food preference.
   c. tool use, grooming, and courtship.
   d. food washing and preparing.
   e. dialects, hunting styles, and acculturation.

4. Which of the following examples comes from Tetsuro Matsuzawa's research demonstrating numerical ability in animals?
   a. A chimpanzee breaks off a stick, strips off the leaves, and fishes for dozens of termites.
   b. A dolphin uses sponges to protect its nose during multiple ocean bottom dives.
   c. A border collie fetches 200 items by name.
   d. A chimpanzee taps, in ascending order, numbers displayed on a computer screen.
   e. An ape describes a long-nosed doll as an "elephant baby."

5. Which of the following is *not* evidence pointing to the evolution of human language from gestured communication?
   a. Congenitally blind people, like sighted people, use gestures.
   b. Signed language readily develops among Deaf people.
   c. Speakers' "cognitive loads" lighten when they do not have to gesture.
   d. Prohibiting gestures disrupts speech with spatial content.
   e. Gestures (pointing to a cup) pave the way for children's language (saying *cup*, while simultaneously pointing).

ANSWERS to Multiple-Choice Questions

1. **a.** it was difficult for the ape's trainers to objectively interpret their data.
2. **b.** Apes have shown the ability to learn close to 3000 sign words.
3. **c.** tool use, grooming, and courtship.
4. **d.** A chimpanzee taps, in ascending order, numbers displayed on a computer screen.
5. **c.** Speakers' "cognitive loads" lighten when they do not have to gesture.

Answers to
Test Yourself Questions

Unit 1
Psychology's History and Approaches

1. **What event defined the founding of modern scientific psychology?**
   ANSWER: The founding of scientific psychology is often attributed to Wilhelm Wundt's opening of the University of Leipzig psychology laboratory in 1879. The new science of psychology was soon organized into different schools of thought, including *structuralism* (founded by Edward Bradford Titchener, using introspection to explore the elemental structure of the human mind) and *functionalism* (founded by William James, focusing on how mental and behavioral processes enable organisms to adapt, survive, and flourish). James also wrote an important psychology textbook, completed in 1890.

2. **What are psychology's major levels of analysis?**
   ANSWER: Psychology's three major levels of analysis are the biological, psychological, and social-cultural. The complementary insights of psychologists studying behavior and mental processes from the biological, evolutionary, psychodynamic, behavioral, cognitive, humanistic, and social-cultural perspectives offer a richer understanding than could usually be gained from any one viewpoint alone.

Unit 2
Research Strategies: Thinking Critically With Psychological Science

1. **What is the scientific attitude, and why is it important for critical thinking?**
   ANSWER: The scientific attitude combines *skeptical* testing of various claims and ideas with *humility* about one's own unexamined presumptions. Examining assumptions, searching for hidden values, evaluating evidence, and assessing conclusions are essential parts of critical thinking.

2. **Why, when testing a new drug to control blood pressure, would we learn more about its effectiveness from giving it to half of the participants in a group of 1000 than to all 1000 participants?**
   ANSWER: To determine whether this drug is medically effective—not just serving as a *placebo*—we must compare its effect on those randomly assigned to receive it (the experimental group) with those who receive a placebo (the control group). The only difference between the groups is whether they receive the actual drug. So, if blood pressure is lower in the experimental group, then we know that the drug itself has produced this effect, not just the participants' knowledge that they are being treated (placebo effect).

3. Consider a question posed by Christopher Jepson, David Krantz, and Richard Nisbett (1983) to University of Michigan introductory psychology students:

   The registrar's office at the University of Michigan has found that usually about 100 students in Arts and Sciences have perfect grades at the end of their first term at the University. However, only about 10 to 15 students graduate with perfect grades. What do you think is the most likely explanation for the fact that there are more perfect grades after one term than at graduation?

   ANSWER: Most students in the study came up with plausible causes for the drop in grades, such as, "Students tend to work harder at the beginning of their college careers than toward the end." Fewer than a third recognized the statistical phenomenon clearly at work: Averages based on fewer courses are more variable, which guarantees a greater number of extremely low and high grades at the end of the first term.

4. **How are human and animal research subjects protected?**
   ANSWER: Animal protection legislation, laboratory regulation and inspection, and local ethics committees serve to protect human and animal welfare. At universities, Institutional Review Boards screen research proposals. Ethical principles developed by international psychological organizations urge researchers using human participants to obtain *informed consent,* to protect them from harm and discomfort, to treat their personal information confidentially, and to fully *debrief* all participants.

Unit 3A
Neural Processing and the Endocrine System

1. **How do neurons communicate with one another?**
   ANSWER: A neuron fires when excitatory inputs exceed inhibitory inputs by a sufficient threshold. When the resulting impulse reaches the axon's end, it triggers the release of chemical messengers called *neurotransmitters.* After crossing a tiny gap, these molecules chemically activate receptor sites on neighboring neurons.

2. **How does information flow through your nervous system as you pick up a fork? Can you summarize this process?**
   ANSWER: Your central nervous system's hungry brain activates and guides the muscles of your arm and hand via your peripheral nervous system's motor neurons. As you pick up the fork, your brain processes the information from your sensory nervous system, enabling it to continue to guide the fork to your mouth. The functional circle starts with sensory input, continues with interneuron processing by the central nervous system, and finishes with motor output.

3. **Why is the pituitary gland called the "master gland"?**
   ANSWER: The pituitary gland, responding to signals from the hypothalamus, releases hormones that act as triggers. In response, other endocrine glands release their own hormones, which in turn influence brain and behavior.

Unit 3B
The Brain

1. **Within what brain region would damage be most likely to disrupt your ability to skip rope? Your ability to sense tastes or sounds? In what brain region would damage perhaps leave you in a coma? Without the very breath and heartbeat of life?**
   ANSWER: These regions are, respectively, the *cerebellum,* the *thalamus,* the *reticular formation,* and the *medulla.* These questions assess your understanding of the essential functions of the lower-level brain areas.

2. **What are the mind's two tracks, as revealed by studies of "dual processing"?**
ANSWER: The human brain has separate conscious and unconscious tracks that process information simultaneously. In vision, for example, the visual action track normally guides our conscious visual processing, while the visual perception track normally operates unconsciously, enabling our quick recognition of objects.

Unit 3C
Genetics, Evolutionary Psychology, and Behavior

1. **What is *heritability*?**
ANSWER: *Heritability* is the proportion of variation among individuals that we can attribute to genes. *Note:* Heritability is *not* the extent to which an *individual's* traits are genetically determined. Rather, it is the extent to which variation *among* individuals is due to their differing genes. For any trait, heritability can vary, depending on the population and range of environments studied.

2. **What are the three main criticisms of evolutionary psychology's explanations?**
ANSWER: Critics of evolutionary psychology's explanations point out that (1) they start with an effect and work backward to propose an explanation; (2) unethical and immoral men could use such explanations to rationalize their behavior toward women; and (3) this explanation overlooks the effects of cultural expectations and socialization.

3. **How does the biopsychosocial approach explain our individual development?**
ANSWER: The biopsychosocial approach considers all the factors that influence our individual development: biological factors (including evolution, genes, hormones, and brains), psychological factors (including our experiences, beliefs, feelings, and expectations), and social-cultural factors (including parental and peer influences and cultural attitudes and norms).

Unit 4
Sensation and Perception

1. **What is the rough distinction between sensation and perception?**
ANSWER: *Sensation* is the bottom-up process by which the physical sensory system receives and represents stimuli. *Perception* is the top-down mental process of organizing and interpreting sensory input. But in our everyday experiences, sensation and perception are different aspects of one continuous process.

2. **What is the rapid sequence of events that occurs when you see and recognize someone you know?**
ANSWER: Light waves reflect off the person and travel into your eye, where the *rods* and *cones* convert the light waves' energy into neural impulses sent to your brain. Your brain then processes the subdimensions of this visual input—including color, depth, movement, and form—separately but simultaneously, and integrates this information (along with previously stored information) into a conscious perception of the person you know.

3. **What are the basic steps in transforming sound waves into perceived sound?**
ANSWER: A simple figure offers a synopsis:

4. **How does our system for sensing smell differ from our sensory systems for vision, touch, and taste?**
ANSWER: We have three types of color receptors, four basic touch senses, and five taste sensations. But we have no basic smell receptors. Instead, 1000 odor receptors, individually and in combination, recognize some 10,000 discernible odors.

5. **What do we mean when we say that, in perception, "the whole is greater than the sum of its parts"?**
ANSWER: Gestalt psychologists used this saying to describe our perceptual tendency to organize clusters of sensations into meaningful forms or coherent groups.

6. **What type of evidence shows that, indeed, "there is more to perception than meets the senses"?**
ANSWER: We construct our perceptions based on both sensory input and—experiments show—on our assumptions, expectations, schemas, and perceptual sets, often influenced by the surrounding context.

7. **What psychic ability is being claimed by the sports channel cartoon at left?**
ANSWER: The psychic sports channel claims *precognition*—the ability to foresee future events.

Unit 5
States of Consciousness

1. **Are you getting enough sleep? What might you ask yourself to answer this question?**
ANSWER: You could start with the true/false questions in James Maas' sleep deprivation quiz in Table 5.1. Also, William Dement (1999, p. 73) has suggested considering these questions: "How often do you think about taking a quick snooze? How often do you rub your eyes and yawn during the day? How often do you feel like you really need some coffee?" Dement concluded that "each of these is a warning of a sleep debt that you ignore at your peril."

2. **When is the use of hypnosis potentially harmful, and when can hypnosis be used to help?**
ANSWER: Hypnosis is potentially harmful when therapists, seeking to "hypnotically refresh" memories, plant false memories. But posthypnotic suggestions have helped alleviate some ailments, and hypnosis can also help control pain.

3. A U.S. government survey of 27,616 current or former alcohol drinkers found that 40 percent of those who began drinking before age 15 grew dependent on alcohol. The same was true of only 10 percent of those who first imbibed at age 21 or 22 (Grant & Dawson, 1998). What possible explanations might there be for this correlation between early use and later abuse?

ANSWER: Possible explanations include (1) a biological predisposition to both early use and later abuse, (2) brain changes and taste preferences induced by early use, and (3) enduring habits, attitudes, activities, and/or peer relationships that are conducive to alcohol abuse.

Unit 6
Learning

1. As we develop, we learn cues that lead us to expect and prepare for good and bad events. We learn to repeat behaviors that bring rewards. And we watch others and learn. What do psychologists call these three types of learning?

ANSWER: Through *classical conditioning,* we learn cues that lead us to expect and prepare for good and bad events. Through *operant conditioning,* we learn to repeat behaviors that bring rewards. Through *observational learning,* we watch others and learn.

2. In slasher movies, sexually arousing images of women are sometimes paired with violence against women. Based on classical conditioning principles, what might be an effect of this pairing?

ANSWER: If viewing an attractive nude or semi-nude woman (a US) elicits sexual arousal (a UR), then pairing the US with a new stimulus (violence against women) could turn the violence into a conditioned stimulus (CS) that also becomes sexually arousing, a conditioned response (CR).

3. *Positive reinforcement, negative reinforcement, positive punishment,* and *negative punishment* are tricky concepts for many students. Can you fit the right term in the four spaces in this table? (I'll do the first one—positive reinforcement—for you.)

ANSWER:

Type of Stimulus	Give It	Take It Away
Desired (for example, a compliment):	*Positive reinforcement*	*Negative punishment*
Undesired/aversive (for example, an insult):	*Positive punishment*	*Negative reinforcement*

4. Jason's parents and older friends all smoke, but they advise him not to. Juan's parents and friends don't smoke, but they say nothing to deter him from doing so. Will Jason or Juan be more likely to start smoking?

ANSWER: Although both saying and doing can influence people, experiments suggest that children more often do as others do and say as they say. Generalizing this finding to smoking, we can expect that Jason will be more likely to start smoking.

Unit 7A
Memory

1. Memory includes (in alphabetical order) long-term memory, sensory memory, and working/short-term memory. What's the correct order of these three memory stages?

ANSWER: Sensory memory, working/short-term memory, long-term memory.

2. **What would be the most effective strategy to learn and retain a list of names of key historical figures for a week? For a year?**
Answer: For a week: Make the names personally meaningful. For a year: Overlearn the list and space out rehearsals over the course of several weeks.

3. **Your friend tells you that her father experienced brain damage in an accident. She wonders if psychology can explain why he can still play checkers very well but has a hard time holding a sensible conversation. What can you tell her?**
Answer: Our *explicit* (declarative) memories differ from our *implicit* memories of skills and procedures, such as playing checkers. Our implicit memories are processed by more ancient brain areas, which apparently escaped damage during the accident.

4. **You have just watched a movie that includes a chocolate factory. After the chocolate factory is out of mind, you nevertheless feel a strange urge for a chocolate bar. How do you explain this in terms of priming?**
Answer: *Priming* is the activation (often without our awareness) of associations. Seeing a chocolate factory in a movie, for example, might temporarily predispose you to crave a chocolate treat. Although you might not consciously remember the chocolate factory, it may prime how you interpret or recall events.

5. **Can you offer an example of proactive interference?**
Answer: *Proactive* (forward-acting) *interference* occurs when earlier learning disrupts your recall of a later experience. Proactive interference has occurred if learning names of new classmates in your first class makes it more difficult to learn the new names in your second class.

6. **Source amnesia occurs when we attribute to the wrong source an event we have experienced, heard about, read about, or imagined. What might life be like if we remembered all our waking experiences as well as all our dreams?**
Answer: Real experiences would be confused with those we dreamed. When meeting someone, we might therefore be unsure whether we were reacting to something they previously did or to something we dreamed they did. William Dement (1999, p. 298) thinks this "would put a great burden on your sanity. . . . I truly believe that the wall of memory is a blessed protection."

7. **What are the recommended memory strategies you just read about? (One advised rehearsing to-be-remembered material. What were the others?)**
Answer: Study repeatedly to boost long-term recall. Spend more time rehearsing or actively thinking about the material. Make the material personally meaningful. To remember a list of unfamiliar items, use mnemonic devices. Refresh your memory by activating retrieval cues. Recall events while they are fresh, before you encounter possible misinformation. Minimize interference. Test your own knowledge, both to rehearse it and to help determine what you do not yet know.

Unit 7B
Thinking, Problem Solving, Creativity, and Language

1. **The availability heuristic is a quick-and-easy but sometimes misleading guide to judging reality. What is the availability heuristic?**
Answer: The *availability heuristic* is our tendency to judge the likeliness of an event by how easily we can recall instances of it. Like all heuristics, this guide is efficient. But it can mislead, as it does when we attempt to judge various risks (for example, of plane travel).

2. **If children are not yet speaking, is there any reason to think they would benefit from parents and other caregivers reading to them?**
Answer: Indeed there is, because well before age one children are learning to detect words among the stream of spoken sounds and to discern grammatical rules. Before age one, they also are babbling with the phonemes of their own language. More than many parents realize, their infants are soaking up language. As researcher Peter Jusczyk reminds us, "Little ears are listening."

3. **To say that "words are the mother of ideas" assumes the truth of what concept?**
Answer: This phrase supports the *linguistic determinism hypothesis,* which asserts that language determines thought. Research indicates that this position is too extreme, but language does *influence* what we perceive and think.

Unit 8A
Motivation

1. **While on a long road trip, you suddenly feel very hungry. You see a diner that looks pretty deserted and creepy, but you are *really* hungry, so you stop anyway. What motivational theory would most easily explain this behavior, and why?**
Answer: *Drive-reduction theory*—the idea that physical needs create an aroused state that drives us to reduce the need—helps explain your behavior.

2. **You are traveling and have not eaten anything in eight hours. As your long-awaited favorite dish is placed in front of you, your mouth waters. Even imagining this may set your mouth to watering. What triggers this anticipatory drooling?**
Answer: You, like Pavlov's dogs, have learned through *classical conditioning* to respond to the cues—the sight and aroma—that signal the food about to enter your mouth. Both *physiological cues* (eight hours of deprivation have left you with low blood sugar) and *psychological cues* (the anticipation of the tasty meal) have heightened your experienced hunger.

3. **How might the evolutionary perspective, drive-reduction theory, and arousal theory explain our sexual motivation?**
Answer: *Drive-reduction theory* could imply that hormonal influences (from female estrogen and male testosterone) create a driven (physiologically aroused) state that compels us to reduce the drive. *Arousal theory* could add that people sometimes *seek* the pleasure and stimulation of arousal, with social-cultural influences on what leads people to feel aroused and how they seek optimum arousal levels. *Evolutionary psychologists* would remind us that those motivated to mate were more likely to leave descendants—us—than were others who lacked sexual motivation.

4. **How might the evolutionary perspective, drive-reduction theory, and arousal theory explain our affiliation needs?**
Answer: *Drive-reduction theory* might say that being threatened and afraid drives us to find safety in the company of others (thus reducing our aroused state). *Arousal theory* reminds us that we welcome optimal levels of arousal, and that the presence of others is arousing. *Evolutionary psychologists* have noted that our ancestors hunted and survived threats as group-dwelling creatures, finding food and safety in numbers. As their descendants, we therefore are disposed to live in groups, connected to supportive others.

Unit 8B
Emotions, Stress, and Health

1. **Christine is holding her 8-month-old baby when a fierce dog appears out of nowhere and, with teeth bared, leaps for the baby's face. Christine immediately ducks for cover to protect the baby, screams at the dog, then notices that her heart is banging in her chest and she's broken out in a cold sweat. How would the James-Lange, Cannon-Bard, and two-factor theories explain Christine's emotional reaction?**
Answer: The *James-Lange theory* would say that Christine's emotional reaction consists of her awareness of her physiological responses to the dog attack. The *Cannon-Bard theory* would say that her fear experience happened simultaneously with her physiological arousal. *Schachter and Singer's two-factor theory* would presume that her emotional reaction stemmed from her interpreting and labeling the arousal.

2. **How do the two divisions of the autonomic nervous system help us respond to and recover from a crisis, and why is this relevant to the study of emotions?**
Answer: The *sympathetic division* of the ANS arouses us, pumping out the stress hormones epinephrine and norepinephrine to prepare our body for fight or flight. The *parasympathetic division* of the ANS takes over when the crisis passes, restoring our body to a calm state. This is relevant to our study of emotions, because our physiological responses are a part of what creates our psychological experience of emotion. (The other part is our cognition—the expectations and experiences that affect our interpretation of a physiological state.)

3. **Who tends to express more emotion—men or women? How do we know the answer to that question?**
Answer: Women tend to surpass men not only as emotion detectors but also at expressing certain emotions (though men have slightly surpassed women in conveying anger). Researchers discovered this by showing people brief, silent clips of men's and women's faces expressing various emotions and by observing who is most skilled at reading and sending emotions.

4. **What things do (and do not) predict self-reported happiness?**
Answer: People's age, sex, and income give only modest clues to their happiness. Their personality traits, close relationships, "flow" in work and leisure, and religious faith do provide clues.

5. **What are the basic links in our stress response system?**
Answer: When alerted to a threat (to negative, uncontrollable events), our *sympathetic nervous system* arouses us. Heart rate and respiration increase. Blood is diverted from digestion to the skeletal muscles. The body releases sugar and fat to prepare for *fight or flight.* Simultaneously, the brain (via the *hypothalamus* and adjacent *pituitary gland*) orders the *adrenal glands* to secrete the stress hormone *cortisol.* The system is wonderfully adaptive. But if stress is continuous, health consequences and exhaustion may result.

Unit 9
Developmental Psychology

1. **Your friend's older sister—a regular drinker—hopes to become pregnant soon and has stopped drinking. Why is this a good idea? What negative effects might alcohol consumed during pregnancy have on a developing fetus?**
Answer: There is no known safe amount of alcohol during pregnancy, so your friend's older sister is wise to quit drinking before becoming pregnant. Harmful effects may occur even before a woman knows she is pregnant. If a woman drinks persistently and heavily during her pregnancy, the fetus will be at risk for severe physical and/or cognitive impairments (such as occurs with *fetal alcohol syndrome*).

2. **Use Piaget's first three stages of cognitive development to explain why children are not just miniature adults in the way they think.**
Answer: Infants in the *sensorimotor stage* tend to be focused only on their own perceptions of the world and may, for example, be unaware that objects continue to exist when unseen. A *preoperational* child is still egocentric and incapable of appreciating simple logic, such as the reversibility of operations. A preteen in the *concrete operational stage* is beginning to think logically about concrete events but not about abstract concepts.

3. **What are gender roles, and what do their variations tell us about our human capacity for learning and adaptation?**
Answer: *Gender roles* are social rules or norms for accepted and expected behavior for females and males. The norms associated with various roles, including gender roles, vary widely in different cultural contexts, which is proof that we are very capable of learning and adapting to the social demands of different environments.

4. **To predict whether a teenager smokes, ask how many of the teen's friends smoke. One explanation for this correlation is peer influence. What's another?**

   ANSWER: There may also be a *selection effect.* Adolescents tend to sort themselves into likeminded groups—the jocks, the geeks, the druggies, and so forth. Those who smoke may similarly seek out other teenagers who also smoke.

5. **How has the transition from childhood to adulthood changed in Western cultures in the last century or so?**

   ANSWER: In little more than a century, the gap between puberty and adult independence has widened from about 7 years to about 12 years. This longer adolescence gives us a chance to grow up a bit more before facing the "real world," but it also comes with its share of stressors, as sexually mature teens must wait many years before achieving true independence. In Western nations, this has led to a post-adolescent, not-yet-settled phase of life known as *emerging adulthood.*

6. **Research has shown that living together before marriage predicts an increased likelihood of future divorce. Can you imagine two possible explanations for this correlation?**

   ANSWER: William Axinn and Arland Thornton (1992) have reported data supporting two explanations. (1) The first explanation is an example of a *selection effect*—our tendency to seek out others who are similar to us. Cohabitation attracts people who are more open to terminating unsatisfying relationships. People who cohabit bring a more individualistic ethic to marriage, are more likely to see close relationships as temporary and fragile, are more accepting of divorce, and are about three times more likely after marriage to have an affair (Forste & Tanfer, 1996). (2) Axinn and Thornton's second explanation illustrates the *causal effect* of the experience of cohabitation. Over time, those who cohabit tend to become more approving of dissolving an unfulfilling union. This divorce-accepting attitude increases the odds of later divorce.

7. **What findings in psychology support the concept of stages in development and the idea of stability in personality across the life span? What findings challenge these ideas?**

   ANSWER: The idea of stages in development is supported by the work of Piaget (cognitive development), Kohlberg (moral development), and Erikson (psychosocial development), but it is challenged by findings that suggest change is more gradual and less culturally universal than these theorists supposed. Some personality traits, such as temperament, do exhibit remarkable stability across many years. But we do change in other ways, such as in our social attitudes, especially during life's early years.

Unit 10
Personality

1. **What, according to Freud, were some of the important defense mechanisms, and what do they defend against?**

   ANSWER: Freud believed repression to be the basic defense mechanism. Others include regression, reaction formation, projection, rationalization, and displacement. All supposedly serve to reduce anxiety.

2. **How does today's psychological science assess Freud's theory?**

   ANSWER: Modern research supports the phenomenon Freud called *projection* and current researchers call the *false consensus effect.* There is also some research support for self-esteem defenses, such as *reaction formation.* But there is little support for Freud's other defense mechanisms. Recent research does not support *repression,* which Freud viewed to be the basic defense mechanism. Recent research also does not support Freud's view of the unconscious but instead views the unconscious as part of our two-track mind—the many types and instances of information processing that take place out of our awareness, such as priming or parallel processing of various aspects of vision. It's also important to recognize, from a psychological science perspective, that Freudian theory does not enable predictions, and it tends to explain things after the fact.

3. **What does it mean to be "empathic"? To be "self-actualized"?**
ANSWER: To be *empathic* is to share and mirror another person's feelings. Carl Rogers believed that people nurture growth in others by being empathic. Abraham Maslow viewed *self-actualization*—the motivation to fulfill one's potential—as one of the ultimate psychological needs that arises after our physical needs are met. (The other ultimate psychological need is *self-transcendence*—meaning, purpose, and communion beyond the self.)

4. **What is the person-situation controversy?**
ANSWER: The *person-situation controversy* is the question of whether personality traits are consistent over time and across situations. Traits do tend to be consistent, though specific behaviors may vary with time and place.

5. **How do personal control and optimism influence behavior?**
ANSWER: If we lack a sense of *personal control* in our lives, we tend to feel helpless and depressed, and our health may suffer as a result. When facing adversity, realistic *optimism* leads to better moods, more persistence, and better health. Excessive optimism, however, can lead to complacency and can blind us to real risks and problems.

6. **In a 1997 Gallup poll, White Americans estimated 44 percent of their fellow White Americans to be high in prejudice (scoring them 5 or higher on a 10-point scale). How many rated themselves similarly high in prejudice? Just 14 percent. What phenomenon does this illustrate?**
ANSWER: This illustrates the general tendency to see ourselves as superior to the average other, which is one example of the *self-serving bias*.

7. **How do individualist and collectivist cultures differ?**
ANSWER: A culture that favors *individualism* gives priority to personal goals over group goals; people in that culture will tend to define their identity in terms of their own personal attributes. A culture that favors *collectivism* gives priority to group goals over individual goals; people in collectivist cultures tend to define their identity in terms of group identifications. Cultures vary in the extent to which they favor individualism or collectivism.

Unit 11
Testing and Individual Differences

1. **Joseph, a Harvard Law School student, has a straight-A average, writes for the *Harvard Law Review,* and will clerk for a Supreme Court justice next year. His grandmother, Judith, is very proud of him, saying that he is way more intelligent than she ever was. But Joseph is also very proud of Judith: As a young woman, she was imprisoned by the Nazis. When the war ended, she walked out of Germany, contacted an agency helping refugees, and began a new life in the United States as an assistant chef in her cousin's restaurant. According to the definition of *intelligence* in this module, is Joseph the only intelligent person in this story? Why or why not?**
ANSWER: Joseph is not the only intelligent person in this story. *Intelligence* is the ability to learn, solve problems, and adapt to new situations. Judith certainly demonstrates this quality as well, given all that she has accomplished.

2. **What was the purpose of Binet's pioneering intelligence test?**
ANSWER: Binet's original test and those built upon it were designed to predict school achievement.

3. **The Smiths have enrolled their 2-year-old son in a special program that promises to assess his IQ and, if he places in the top 5 percent of test-takers, to create a plan that will guarantee his admission to a top university at age 18. Why is this endeavor of questionable value?**
   Answer: This is a waste of money at best. First, IQ tests given before age 3 are only modestly reliable predictors of adult intelligence. Second, admission to a top university depends on more than simple IQ. Third, there are no known training programs that could guarantee this result. The Smiths would do better to read to their child, which predicts early reading and love of reading.

4. **As society succeeds in creating equality of opportunity, it will also increase the heritability of ability. The heritability of intelligence scores will be greater in a society marked by equal opportunity than in a society of peasants and aristocrats. Why?**
   Answer: Perfect environmental equality would create 100 percent heritability—because genes alone would account for any remaining human differences.

Unit 12
Abnormal Psychology

1. **What is the biopsychosocial perspective, and why is it important in our understanding of psychological disorders?**
   Answer: This contemporary perspective assumes that biological, psychological, and social-cultural influences combine to produce psychological disorders. Genes matter. The brain matters. Inner thoughts and feelings matter. Social and cultural influences matter. To get the whole integrated picture, a biopsychosocial perspective helps.

2. **How do generalized anxiety disorder, panic disorder, phobias, obsessive-compulsive disorder, and post-traumatic stress disorder differ?**
   Answer: *Generalized anxiety disorder* is unfocused tension, apprehension, and arousal. *Panic disorder* is marked by unpredictable episodes of intense dread accompanied by chest pain, choking, or other frightening sensations. Those with *phobias* focus anxiety on specific feared objects or situations. People suffering *obsessive-compulsive disorder* express anxiety through unwanted repetitive thoughts (obsessions) or actions (compulsions). In *post-traumatic stress disorder (PTSD),* anxiety may be accompanied by recurring memories and nightmares, social withdrawal, and insomnia for periods of four or more weeks after a traumatic event.

3. **What does somatoform mean?**
   Answer: Somatic symptoms are bodily symptoms. A *somatoform disorder* is one in which people express psychological distress through physical rather than psychological complaints and symptoms.

4. **The psychoanalytic and learning perspectives agree that dissociative identity disorder symptoms are ways of dealing with anxiety. How do their explanations differ?**
   Answer: The psychoanalytic explanation of DID *(dissociative identity disorder)* symptoms is that they are defenses against anxiety generated by unacceptable urges. The learning perspective attempts to explain these symptoms as behaviors that have been reinforced by relieving anxiety in the past. Others attempt to explain DID symptoms as detachment resulting from horrific experiences, such as childhood abuse.

5. **What does it mean to say that "depression is the common cold of psychological disorders"?**
   Answer: This expression describes the frequency of depression, but it is not meant to minimize the seriousness of this condition.

6. **How do researchers believe that biological and environmental factors interact in the onset of schizophrenia?**
   Answer: *Schizophrenia* has powerful biological roots, as evidenced by findings that those suffering schizophrenia have increased receptors for the neurotransmitter dopamine

(which may intensify the positive symptoms of schizophrenia); abnormal activity in the frontal lobes, thalamus, and amygdala; and such brain abnormalities as fluid-filled cerebral cavities. Malfunctions in multiple brain regions and their connections apparently interact to produce the symptoms of schizophrenia. Yet environment must play some role, because identical twins don't always share the expression of this disorder, and there is increasing evidence that a virus suffered by the mother during pregnancy can contribute to that baby's later developing schizophrenia.

7. **What contribution do genes make to the development of antisocial personality disorder?**
ANSWER: *Antisocial personality disorder*—in which a person exhibits a lack of conscience for wrongdoing—seems to have a strong genetic component. Twin and adoption studies show that biological relatives of people with this disorder are at increased risk for antisocial behavior. But the tendency to be fearless, when combined with a sense of social responsibility, can lead to heroism, adventurism, or athletic success.

8. **What is the relationship between poverty and psychological disorders?**
ANSWER: Poverty-related stressors can help trigger disorders, but disabling disorders can also contribute to poverty. Thus, poverty and disorder are often a chicken-and-egg situation, and it's hard to know which came first.

Unit 13
Treatment of Psychological Disorders

1. **What is the major distinction between the underlying assumptions in insight therapies and in behavior therapies?**
ANSWER: The *insight therapies*—psychoanalytic and humanistic therapies—seek to relieve problems by providing an understanding of their origins. *Behavior therapies* assume the problem behavior *is* the problem and treat it directly, paying less attention to its origins.

2. **How does the placebo effect bias clients' appraisals of the effectiveness of psychotherapies?**
ANSWER: The *placebo effect* is the healing power of *belief* in a treatment. Patients who expect a treatment to be effective may believe it was.

3. **How do researchers evaluate the effectiveness of particular drug therapies?**
ANSWER: Ideally, researchers assign people to treatment and no-treatment conditions to see if those who receive therapy improve more than those who don't. In many studies, the no-treatment comparison includes a placebo condition and follows a double-blind, controlled study format. If neither the therapist nor the client knows for sure whether the client has received the experimental treatment (for example, a drug), then any difference between the treated and untreated groups will reflect the treatment's actual effect.

4. **What is the difference between preventive mental health and psychological or biomedical therapy?**
ANSWER: Psychological and biomedical therapies attempt to relieve people's suffering from psychological disorders. Preventive mental health attempts to prevent suffering by identifying and eliminating the conditions that cause disorders, and by building individuals' *resilience.*

Unit 14
Social Psychology

1. **Driving to school one snowy day, Marco narrowly misses a car that slides through a red light. "Slow down! What a terrible driver," he thinks to himself. Moments later, Marco himself slides through an intersection and yelps, "Wow! These roads are awful. The city plows need to get out here." What social psychology principle has Marco just demonstrated? Explain.**
   ANSWER: By attributing the other person's behavior to the person ("What a terrible driver.") and his own, similar behavior to the situation ("These roads are awful."), Marco has exhibited the *fundamental attribution error*.

2. **You are organizing a Town Hall–style meeting of fiercely competitive political candidates. To add to the fun, friends have suggested handing out masks of the candidates' faces for supporters to wear. What phenomenon might these masks engage?**
   ANSWER: The anonymity provided by the masks, combined with the arousal of the contentious setting, might create *deindividuation* (lessened self-awareness and self-restraint).

3. **Why didn't anybody help Kitty Genovese? What social relations principle did this incident illustrate?**
   ANSWER: The incident illustrated the *bystander effect*. This occurs because, in the presence of others, an individual is less likely to notice a situation, correctly interpret it as an emergency, and then take responsibility for offering help.

Appendix A
Careers in Psychology

Appendix A contains no Test Yourself questions.

Appendix B
Psychology at Work

1. **A human resources director explains to you that "I don't bother with tests or references. I can pick employees by my gut." Based on I/O psychology research, what concerns does this raise?**
   ANSWER: Personnel interviewers tend to feel very confident in their ability to predict long-term job performance from informal interviews. Unfortunately, this is so often *not* the case that I/O psychologists have labeled the gap between interviewers' intuition and workplace reality the *interviewer illusion*. Four factors contribute: (1) interviews disclose prospective workers' good intentions, not their habitual behaviors; (2) interviewers tend to track the successful careers of those they hire, not the successful careers of those they reject; (3) interviewers presume people are what they seem to be in interviews; and (4) interviewers' preconceptions and moods color how they perceive interviewees' responses.

2. **What are the two basic types of leadership, and how do the most effective managers employ these leadership strategies?**
   ANSWER: *Task leadership* is goal-oriented. Managers using this style set standards, organize work, and focus attention on goals. *Social leadership* is group-oriented. Managers using this style build teamwork, mediate conflict, and offer support. Research indicates that effective managers exhibit both task and social leadership, depending on the situation and the person.

3. **One of the ways human factors psychologists seek to reduce users' frustration and to improve safety is by watching out for the *curse of knowledge*. What exactly is this tendency?**
ANSWER: The *curse of knowledge* is the tendency for engineers and other designers to assume falsely that others share their knowledge—that what's clear to them will be similarly clear to others.

Appendix C
Promoting Health

1. **How do problem-focused coping and emotion-focused coping differ?**
ANSWER: *Problem-focused coping* attempts to alleviate stress directly, by changing the stressor or the way we interact with it. *Emotion-focused coping* attempts to alleviate stress indirectly, by avoiding or ignoring the stressor and dealing with the emotions generated during our stress reaction.

2. **Those who frequently attend religious services live longer, on average, than those who attend infrequently or not at all. What type of research finding is this, and what explanations might it have?**
ANSWER: This is a correlational finding—frequent attendance at religious services is associated with (and predicts) health and longevity. But this is not a cause-effect statement. Longevity may be associated with religiosity because women (who tend to live longer than men) attend services more regularly, or because people in poor health are not able to attend services. But even controlling for these factors, the relationship remains, which indicates that the connection could reflect the healthy behaviors, stress-reducing social support, relaxed meditative state, optimistic outlook, and enhanced well-being often experienced by religiously active people.

Appendix D
Animal Thinking and Language

1. **If your dog barks at a stranger at the front door, does this qualify as language? What if the dog yips in a telltale way to let you know she needs to go out?**
ANSWER: These are definitely communications. But if language consists of words and the grammatical rules we use to combine them to communicate meaning, few scientists would label a dog's barking and yipping as language.

Glossary

absolute threshold the minimum stimulation needed to detect a particular stimulus 50 percent of the time. (p. 120)

accommodation (1) the process by which the eye's lens changes shape to focus near or far objects on the retina. (2) adapting our current understandings (schemas) to incorporate new information. (pp. 126, 418)

achievement motivation a desire for significant accomplishment; for mastery of things, people, or ideas; for rapidly attaining a high standard. (p. B-7)

achievement tests tests designed to assess what a person has learned. (p. 535)

acoustic encoding the encoding of sound, especially the sound of words. (p. 261)

acquisition in classical conditioning, the initial stage, when one links a neutral stimulus and an unconditioned stimulus so that the neutral stimulus begins triggering the conditioned response. In operant conditioning, the strengthening of a reinforced response. (p. 220)

action potential a neural impulse; a brief electrical charge that travels down an axon. (p. 53)

active listening empathic listening in which the listener echoes, restates, and clarifies. A feature of Rogers' client-centered therapy. (p. 609)

adaptation-level phenomenon our tendency to form judgments (of sounds, of lights, of income) relative to a neutral level defined by our prior experience. (p. 394)

addiction compulsive drug craving and use, despite adverse consequences. (p. 197)

adolescence the transition period from childhood to adulthood, extending from puberty to independence. (p. 445)

adrenal [ah-DREEN-el] **glands** a pair of endocrine glands that sit just above the kidneys and secrete hormones (epinephrine and norepinephrine) that help arouse the body in times of stress. (p. 63)

aerobic exercise sustained exercise that increases heart and lung fitness; may also alleviate depression and anxiety. (p. C-6)

aggression physical or verbal behavior intended to hurt someone. (pp. 436, 670)

algorithm a methodical, logical rule or procedure that guarantees solving a particular problem. Contrasts with the usually speedier— but also more error-prone—use of *heuristics*. (p. 300)

alpha waves the relatively slow brain waves of a relaxed, awake state. (p. 178)

altruism unselfish regard for the welfare of others. (p. 685)

amnesia the loss of memory. (p. 271)

amphetamines drugs that stimulate neural activity, causing speeded-up body functions and associated energy and mood changes. (p. 201)

amygdala [uh-MIG-duh-la] two lima bean–sized neural clusters in the limbic system; linked to emotion. (p. 71)

anorexia nervosa an eating disorder in which a person (usually an adolescent female) diets and becomes significantly (15 percent or more) underweight, yet, still feeling fat, continues to starve. (p. 337)

antianxiety drugs drugs used to control anxiety and agitation. (p. 630)

antidepressant drugs drugs used to treat depression; also increasingly prescribed for anxiety. Different types work by altering the availability of various neurotransmitters. (p. 630)

antipsychotic drugs drugs used to treat schizophrenia and other forms of severe thought disorder. (p. 629)

antisocial personality disorder a personality disorder in which the person (usually a man) exhibits a lack of conscience for wrongdoing, even toward friends and family members. May be aggressive and ruthless or a clever con artist. (p. 597)

anxiety disorders psychological disorders characterized by distressing, persistent anxiety or maladaptive behaviors that reduce anxiety. (p. 569)

aphasia impairment of language, usually caused by left hemisphere damage either to Broca's area (impairing speaking) or to Wernicke's area (impairing understanding). (p. 80)

applied research scientific study that aims to solve practical problems. (p. 13)

aptitude tests tests designed to predict a person's future performance; *aptitude* is the capacity to learn. (p. 535)

assimilation interpreting our new experience in terms of our existing schemas. (p. 418)

association areas areas of the cerebral cortex that are not involved in primary motor or sensory functions; rather, they are involved in higher mental functions such as learning, remembering, thinking, and speaking. (p. 78)

associative learning learning that certain events occur together. The events may be two stimuli (as in classical conditioning) or a response and its consequences (as in operant conditioning). (p. 216)

attachment an emotional tie with another person; shown in young children by their seeking closeness to the caregiver and showing distress on separation. (p. 426)

attention-deficit hyperactivity disorder (ADHD) a psychological disorder marked by the appearance by age 7 of one or more of three key symptoms extreme inattention, hyperactivity, and impulsivity. (p. 563)

attitude feelings, often influenced by our beliefs, that predispose us to respond in a particular way to objects, people, and events. (p. 646)

attribution theory the theory that we explain someone's behavior by crediting either the situation or the person's disposition. (p. 644)

audition the sense or act of hearing. (p. 134)

autism a disorder that appears in childhood and is marked by deficient communication, social interaction, and understanding of others' states of mind. (p. 424)

automatic processing unconscious encoding of incidental information, such as space, time, and frequency, and of well-learned information, such as word meanings. (p. 258)

autonomic [aw-tuh-NAHM-ik] **nervous system** the part of the peripheral nervous system that controls the glands and the muscles of the internal organs (such as the heart). Its sympathetic division arouses; its parasympathetic division calms. (p. 59)

availability heuristic estimating the likelihood of events based on their availability in memory; if instances come readily to mind (perhaps because of their vividness), we presume such events are common. (p. 305)

aversive conditioning a type of counterconditioning that associates an unpleasant state (such as nausea) with an unwanted behavior (such as drinking alcohol). (p. 613)

axon the extension of a neuron, ending in branching terminal fibers, through which messages pass to other neurons or to muscles or glands. (p. 53)

babbling stage beginning at about 4 months, the stage of speech development in which the infant spontaneously utters various sounds at first unrelated to the household language. (p. 315)

barbiturates drugs that depress the activity of the central nervous system, reducing anxiety but impairing memory and judgment. (p. 200)

basal metabolic rate the body's resting rate of energy expenditure. (p. 335)

basic research pure science that aims to increase the scientific knowledge base. (p. 13)

basic trust according to Erik Erikson, a sense that the world is predictable and trustworthy; said to be formed during infancy by appropriate experiences with responsive caregivers. (p. 429)

behavior genetics the study of the relative power and limits of genetic and environmental influences on behavior. (p. 95)

behavior therapy therapy that applies learning principles to the elimination of unwanted behaviors. (p. 611)

behavioral medicine an interdisciplinary field that integrates behavioral and medical knowledge and applies that knowledge to health and disease. (p. 397)

behavioral psychology the scientific study of observable behavior, and its explanation by principles of learning. (p. 10)

behaviorism the view that psychology (1) should be an objective science that (2) studies behavior without reference to mental processes. Most research psychologists today agree with (1) but not with (2). (pp. 6, 218)

belief perseverance clinging to one's initial conceptions after the basis on which they were formed has been discredited. (p. 307)

binge-eating disorder significant binge-eating episodes, followed by distress, disgust, or guilt, but without the compensatory purging, fasting, or excessive exercise that marks bulimia nervosa. (p. 337)

binocular cues depth cues, such as retinal disparity, that depend on the use of two eyes. (p. 153)

biofeedback a system for electronically recording, amplifying, and feeding back information regarding a subtle physiological state, such as blood pressure or muscle tension. (pp. 240, C-8)

biological psychology a branch of psychology concerned with the links between biology and behavior. (Some biological psychologists call themselves *behavioral neuroscientists, neuropsychologists, behavior geneticists, physiological psychologists,* or *biopsychologists.*) (pp. 10, 52)

biomedical therapy prescribed medications or medical procedures that act directly on the patient's nervous system. (p. 628)

biopsychosocial approach an integrated approach that incorporates biological, psychological, and social-cultural levels of analysis. (p. 10)

bipolar disorder a mood disorder in which the person alternates between the hopelessness and lethargy of depression and the overexcited state of mania. (Formerly called *manic-depressive disorder.*) (p. 581)

blind spot the point at which the optic nerve leaves the eye, creating a "blind" spot because no receptor cells are located there. (p. 127)

bottom-up processing analysis that begins with the sensory receptors and works up to the brain's integration of sensory information. (p. 116)

brainstem the oldest part and central core of the brain, beginning where the spinal cord swells as it enters the skull; the brainstem is responsible for automatic survival functions. (p. 69)

Broca's area controls language expression—an area, usually in the left frontal lobe, that directs the muscle movements involved in speech. (p. 80)

bulimia nervosa an eating disorder characterized by episodes of overeating, usually of high-calorie foods, followed by vomiting, laxative use, fasting, or excessive exercise. (p. 337)

bystander effect the tendency for any given bystander to be less likely to give aid if other bystanders are present. (p. 686)

Cannon-Bard theory the theory that an emotion-arousing stimulus simultaneously triggers (1) physiological responses and (2) the subjective experience of emotion. (p. 367)

case study an observation technique in which one person is studied in depth in the hope of revealing universal principles. (p. 26)

catharsis emotional release. The catharsis hypothesis maintains that "releasing" aggressive energy (through action or fantasy) relieves aggressive urges. (p. 388)

central nervous system (CNS) the brain and spinal cord. (p. 59)

central route persuasion attitude change path in which interested people focus on the arguments and respond with favorable thoughts. (p. 646)

cerebellum [sehr-uh-BELL-um] the "little brain" at the rear of the brainstem; functions include processing sensory input and coordinating movement output and balance. (p. 70)

cerebral [seh-REE-bruhl] **cortex** the intricate fabric of interconnected neural cells covering the cerebral hemispheres; the body's ultimate control and information-processing center. (p. 74)

change blindness failing to notice changes in the environment. (p. 119)

chromosomes threadlike structures made of DNA molecules that contain the genes. (p. 95)

chunking organizing items into familiar, manageable units; often occurs automatically. (p. 264)

circadian [ser-KAY-dee-an] **rhythm** the biological clock; regular bodily rhythms (for example, of temperature and wakefulness) that occur on a 24-hour cycle. (p. 177)

classical conditioning a type of learning in which one learns to link two or more stimuli and anticipate events. (p. 218)

client-centered therapy a humanistic therapy, developed by Carl Rogers, in which the therapist uses techniques such as active listening within a genuine, accepting, empathic environment to facilitate clients' growth. (Also called *person-centered therapy*.) (p. 609)

clinical psychology a branch of psychology that studies, assesses, and treats people with psychological disorders. (p. 13)

cochlea [KOHK-lee-uh] a coiled, bony, fluid-filled tube in the inner ear through which sound waves trigger nerve impulses. (p. 135)

cochlear implant a device for converting sounds into electrical signals and stimulating the auditory nerve through electrodes threaded into the cochlea. (p. 138)

cognition all the mental activities associated with thinking, knowing, remembering, and communicating. (pp. 298, 417)

cognitive-behavioral therapy a popular integrative therapy that combines cognitive therapy (changing self-defeating thinking) with behavior therapy (changing behavior). (p. 616)

cognitive dissonance theory the theory that we act to reduce the discomfort (dissonance) we feel when two of our thoughts (cognitions) are inconsistent. For example, when our awareness of our attitudes and of our actions clash, we can reduce the resulting dissonance by changing our attitudes. (p. 648)

cognitive map a mental representation of the layout of one's environment. For example, after exploring a maze, rats act as if they have learned a cognitive map of it. (p. 236)

cognitive neuroscience the interdisciplinary study of the brain activity linked with cognition (including perception, thinking, memory, and language). (pp. 7, 89)

cognitive psychology the scientific study of all the mental activities associated with thinking, knowing, remembering, and communicating. (p. 10)

cognitive therapy therapy that teaches people new, more adaptive ways of thinking and acting; based on the assumption that thoughts intervene between events and our emotional reactions. (p. 614)

collective unconscious Carl Jung's concept of a shared, inherited reservoir of memory traces from our species' history. (p. 485)

collectivism giving priority to goals of one's group (often one's extended family or work group) and defining one's identity accordingly. (p. 516)

color constancy perceiving familiar objects as having consistent color, even if changing illumination alters the wavelengths reflected by the object. (p. 158)

companionate love the deep affectionate attachment we feel for those with whom our lives are intertwined. (p. 684)

complementary and alternative medicine (CAM) as yet unproven health care treatments intended to supplement (complement) or serve as alternatives to conventional medicine, and which typically are not widely taught in medical schools, used in hospitals, or reimbursed by insurance companies. When research shows a therapy to be safe and effective, it usually then becomes part of accepted medical practice. (p. C-8)

concept a mental grouping of similar objects, events, ideas, or people. (p. 298)

concrete operational stage in Piaget's theory, the stage of cognitive development (from about 6 or 7 to 11 years of age) during which children gain the mental operations that enable them to think logically about concrete events. (p. 423)

conditioned reinforcer a stimulus that gains its reinforcing power through its association with a primary reinforcer; also known as a *secondary reinforcer*. (p. 231)

conditioned response (CR) in classical conditioning, the learned response to a previously neutral (but now conditioned) stimulus (CS). (p. 219)

conditioned stimulus (CS) in classical conditioning, an originally irrelevant stimulus that, after association with an unconditioned stimulus (US), comes to trigger a conditioned response. (p. 219)

conduction hearing loss hearing loss caused by damage to the mechanical system that conducts sound waves to the cochlea. (p. 138)

cones retinal receptor cells that are concentrated near the center of the retina and that function in daylight or in well-lit conditions. The cones detect fine detail and give rise to color sensations. (p. 126)

confirmation bias a tendency to search for information that supports our preconceptions and to ignore or distort contradictory evidence. (p. 303)

conflict a perceived incompatibility of actions, goals, or ideas. (p. 688)

conformity adjusting one's behavior or thinking to coincide with a group standard. (p. 651)

confounding variable a factor other than the independent variable that might produce an effect in an experiment. (p. 35)

consciousness our awareness of ourselves and our environment. (pp. 89, 176)

conservation the principle (which Piaget believed to be a part of concrete operational reasoning) that properties such as mass, volume, and number remain the same despite changes in the forms of objects. (p. 421)

content validity the extent to which a test samples the behavior that is of interest. (p. 538)

continuous reinforcement reinforcing the desired response every time it occurs. (p. 232)

control group in an experiment, the group that is *not* exposed to the treatment; contrasts with the experimental group and serves as a comparison for evaluating the effect of the treatment. (p. 35)

conversion disorder a rare somatoform disorder in which a person experiences very specific genuine physical symptoms for which no physiological basis can be found. (p. 577)

coping alleviating stress using emotional, cognitive, or behavioral methods. (p. C-1)

coronary heart disease the clogging of the vessels that nourish the heart muscle; the leading cause of death in many developed countries. (p. 401)

corpus callosum [KOR-pus kah-LOW-sum] the large band of neural fibers connecting the two brain hemispheres and carrying messages between them. (p. 84)

correlation a measure of the extent to which two factors vary together, and thus of how well either factor predicts the other. (p. 29)

correlation coefficient a statistical index of the relationship between two things (from −1 to +1). (p. 29)

counseling psychology a branch of psychology that assists people with problems in living (often related to school, work, or marriage) and in achieving greater well-being. (p. 13)

counterconditioning a behavior therapy procedure that uses classical conditioning to evoke new responses to stimuli that are triggering unwanted behaviors; includes *exposure therapies* and *aversive conditioning*. (p. 611)

creativity the ability to produce novel and valuable ideas. (p. 301)

critical period an optimal period shortly after birth when an organism's exposure to certain stimuli or experiences produces proper development. (p. 427)

critical thinking thinking that does not blindly accept arguments and conclusions. Rather, it examines assumptions, discerns hidden values, evaluates evidence, and assesses conclusions. (p. 24)

cross-sectional study a study in which people of different ages are compared with one another. (p. 463)

crystallized intelligence our accumulated knowledge and verbal skills; tends to increase with age. (p. 464)

CT (computed tomography) scan a series of X-ray photographs taken from different angles and combined by computer into a composite representation of a slice through the body. *Also called CAT scan.* (p. 68)

culture the enduring behaviors, ideas, attitudes, values and traditions shared by a group of people and transmitted from one generation to the next. (pp. 43, 661)

debriefing the postexperimental explanation of a study, including its purpose and any deceptions, to its participants. (p. 45)

defense mechanisms in psychoanalytic theory, the ego's protective methods of reducing anxiety by unconsciously distorting reality. (p. 483)

deindividuation the loss of self-awareness and self-restraint occurring in group situations that foster arousal and anonymity. (p. 659)

déjà vu that eerie sense that "I've experienced this before." Cues from the current situation may subconsciously trigger retrieval of an earlier experience. (p. 276)

delta waves the large, slow brain waves associated with deep sleep. (p. 180)

delusions false beliefs, often of persecution or grandeur, that may accompany psychotic disorders. (p. 590)

dendrite the bushy, branching extensions of a neuron that receive messages and conduct impulses toward the cell body. (p. 53)

denial psychoanalytic defense mechanism by which people refuse to believe or even to perceive painful realities. (p. 484)

dependent variable the outcome factor; the variable that may change in response to manipulations of the independent variable. (p. 35)

depressants drugs (such as alcohol, barbiturates, and opiates) that reduce neural activity and slow body functions. (p. 199)

depth perception the ability to see objects in three dimensions although the images that strike the retina are two-dimensional; allows us to judge distance. (p. 153)

developmental psychology a branch of psychology that studies physical, cognitive, and social change throughout the life span. (pp. 13, 411)

difference threshold the minimum difference between two stimuli required for detection 50 percent of the time. We experience the difference threshold as a *just noticeable difference (jnd)*. (p. 122)

discrimination (1) in classical conditioning, the learned ability to distinguish between a conditioned stimulus and stimuli that do not signal an unconditioned stimulus. (2) unjustifiable negative *behavior* toward a group and its members. (pp. 222, 664)

discriminative stimulus in operant conditioning, a stimulus that elicits a response after association with reinforcement (in contrast to related stimuli not associated with reinforcement). (p. 230)

displacement psychoanalytic defense mechanism that shifts sexual or aggressive impulses toward a more acceptable or less threatening object or person, as when redirecting anger toward a safer outlet. (p. 483)

dissociation a split in consciousness, which allows some thoughts and behaviors to occur simultaneously with others. (p. 195)

dissociative disorders disorders in which conscious awareness becomes separated (dissociated) from previous memories, thoughts, and feelings. (p. 577)

dissociative identity disorder (DID) a rare dissociative disorder in which a person exhibits two or more distinct and alternating personalities. Formerly called *multiple personality disorder.* (p. 578)

DNA (deoxyribonucleic acid) a complex molecule containing the genetic information that makes up the chromosomes. (p. 95)

double-blind procedure an experimental procedure in which both the research participants and the research staff are ignorant (blind) about whether the research participants have received the treatment or a placebo. Commonly used in drug-evaluation studies. (p. 35)

Down syndrome a condition of intellectual disability and associated physical disorders caused by an extra copy of chromosome 21. (p. 542)

dream a sequence of images, emotions, and thoughts passing through a sleeping person's mind. Dreams are notable for their hallucinatory imagery, discontinuities, and incongruities, and for the dreamer's delusional acceptance of the content and later difficulties remembering it. (p. 188)

drive-reduction theory the idea that a physiological need creates an aroused tension state (a drive) that motivates an organism to satisfy the need. (p. 329)

DSM-IV-TR the American Psychiatric Association's *Diagnostic and Statistical Manual of Mental Disorders*, Fourth Edition, updated as a 2000 "text revision"; a widely used system for classifying psychological disorders. (p. 565)

dual processing the principle that information is often simultaneously processed on separate conscious and unconscious tracks. (p. 90)

echoic memory a momentary sensory memory of auditory stimuli; if attention is elsewhere, sounds and words can still be recalled within 3 or 4 seconds. (p. 266)

eclectic approach an approach to psychotherapy that, depending on the client's problems, uses techniques from various forms of therapy. (p. 606)

Ecstasy (MDMA) a synthetic stimulant and mild hallucinogen. Produces euphoria and social intimacy, but with short-term health risks and longer-term harm to serotonin-producing neurons and to mood and cognition. (p. 205)

educational psychology the study of how psychological processes affect and can enhance teaching and learning. (p. 13)

effortful processing encoding that requires attention and conscious effort. (p. 259)

ego the largely conscious, "executive" part of personality that, according to Freud, mediates among the demands of the id, superego, and reality. The ego operates on the *reality principle,* satisfying the id's desires in ways that will realistically bring pleasure rather than pain. (p. 481)

egocentrism in Piaget's theory, the preoperational child's difficulty taking another's point of view. (p. 421)

electroconvulsive therapy (ECT) a biomedical therapy for severely depressed patients in which a brief electric current is sent through the brain of an anesthetized patient. (p. 632)

electroencephalogram (EEG) an amplified recording of the waves of electrical activity that sweep across the brain's surface. These waves are measured by electrodes placed on the scalp. (p. 67)

embryo the developing human organism from about 2 weeks after fertilization through the second month. (p. 412)

emerging adulthood for some people in modern cultures, a period from the late teens to mid-twenties, bridging the gap between adolescent dependence and full independence and responsible adulthood. (p. 454)

emotion a response of the whole organism, involving (1) physiological arousal, (2) expressive behaviors, and (3) conscious experience. (p. 366)

emotion-focused coping attempting to alleviate stress by avoiding or ignoring a stressor and attending to emotional needs related to one's stress reaction. (p. C-1)

emotional intelligence the ability to perceive, understand, manage, and use emotions. (p. 528)

empirically derived test a test (such as the MMPI) developed by testing a pool of items and then selecting those that discriminate between groups. (p. 496)

empiricism the view that knowledge originates in experience and that science should, therefore, rely on observation and experimentation. (p. 3)

encoding the processing of information into the memory system—for example, by extracting meaning. (p. 257)

endocrine [EN-duh-krin] **system** the body's "slow" chemical communication system; a set of glands that secrete hormones into the bloodstream. (p. 62)

endorphins [en-DOR-fins] "morphine within"—natural, opiatelike neurotransmitters linked to pain control and to pleasure. (p. 57)

environment every nongenetic influence, from prenatal nutrition to the people and things around us. (p. 95)

equity a condition in which people receive from a relationship in proportion to what they give to it. (p. 684)

estrogens sex hormones, such as estradiol, secreted in greater amounts by females than by males and contributing to female sex characteristics. In nonhuman female mammals, estrogen levels peak during ovulation, promoting sexual receptivity. (p. 350)

evidence-based practice clinical decision-making that integrates the best available research with clinical expertise and patient characteristics and preferences. (p. 623)

evolutionary psychology the study of the roots of behavior and mental processes using the principles of natural selection. (pp. 10, 103)

experiment a research method in which an investigator manipulates one or more factors (independent variables) to observe the effect on some behavior or mental process (the dependent variable). By *random assignment* of participants, the experimenter aims to control other relevant factors. (p. 34)

experimental group in an experiment, the group that is exposed to the treatment, that is, to one version of the independent variable. (p. 35)

experimental psychology the study of behavior and thinking using the experimental method. (p. 6)

explicit memory memory of facts and experiences that one can consciously know and "declare." (Also called *declarative memory*.) (p. 272)

exposure therapies behavioral techniques, such as systematic desensitization, that treat anxieties by exposing people (in imagination or actuality) to the things they fear and avoid. (p. 611)

external locus of control the perception that chance or outside forces beyond your personal control determine your fate. (p. 505)

extinction the diminishing of a conditioned response; occurs in classical conditioning when an unconditioned stimulus (US) does not follow a conditioned stimulus (CS); occurs in operant conditioning when a response is no longer reinforced. (p. 221)

extrasensory perception (ESP) the controversial claim that perception can occur apart from sensory input; includes telepathy, clairvoyance, and precognition. (p. 166)

extrinsic motivation a desire to perform a behavior to receive promised rewards or avoid threatened punishment. (p. 237)

facial feedback the effect of facial expressions on experienced emotions, as when a facial expression of anger or happiness intensifies feelings of anger or happiness. (p. 383)

factor analysis a statistical procedure that identifies clusters of related items (called *factors*) on a test; used to identify different dimensions of performance that underlie a person's total score. (p. 524)

family therapy therapy that treats the family as a system. Views an individual's unwanted behaviors as influenced by, or directed at, other family members. (p. 617)

feature detectors nerve cells in the brain that respond to specific features of the stimulus, such as shape, angle, or movement. (p. 129)

feel-good, do-good phenomenon people's tendency to be helpful when already in a good mood. (p. 390)

fetal alcohol syndrome (FAS) physical and cognitive abnormalities in children caused by a pregnant woman's heavy drinking. In severe cases, symptoms include noticeable facial misproportions. (p. 413)

fetus the developing human organism from 9 weeks after conception to birth. (p. 412)

figure-ground the organization of the visual field into objects (the *figures*) that stand out from their surroundings (the *ground*). (p. 151)

fixation (1) the inability to see a problem from a new perspective, by employing a different mental set. (2) according to Freud, a lingering focus of pleasure-seeking energies at an earlier psychosexual stage, in which conflicts were unresolved. (pp. 303, 483)

fixed-interval schedule in operant conditioning, a reinforcement schedule that reinforces a response only after a specified time has elapsed. (p. 233)

fixed-ratio schedule in operant conditioning, a reinforcement schedule that reinforces a response only after a specified number of responses. (p. 232)

flashbulb memory a clear memory of an emotionally significant moment or event. (p. 270)

flow a completely involved, focused state of consciousness, with diminished awareness of self and time, resulting from optimal engagement of one's skills. (p. B-1)

fluid intelligence our ability to reason speedily and abstractly; tends to decrease during late adulthood. (p. 464)

fMRI (functional MRI) a technique for revealing bloodflow and, therefore, brain activity by comparing successive MRI scans. fMRI scans show brain function. (p. 68)

foot-in-the-door phenomenon the tendency for people who have first agreed to a small request to comply later with a larger request. (p. 647)

formal operational stage in Piaget's theory, the stage of cognitive development (normally beginning about age 12) during which people begin to think logically about abstract concepts. (p. 423)

fovea the central focal point in the retina, around which the eye's cones cluster. (p. 127)

framing the way an issue is posed; how an issue is framed can significantly affect decisions and judgments. (p. 311)

fraternal twins twins who develop from separate fertilized eggs. They are genetically no closer than brothers and sisters, but they share a fetal environment. (p. 97)

free association in psychoanalysis, a method of exploring the unconscious in which the person relaxes and says whatever comes to mind, no matter how trivial or embarrassing. (p. 480)

frequency the number of complete wavelengths that pass a point in a given time (for example, per second). (p. 134)

frequency theory in hearing, the theory that the rate of nerve impulses traveling up the auditory nerve matches the frequency of a tone, thus enabling us to sense its pitch. (p. 137)

frontal lobes portion of the cerebral cortex lying just behind the forehead; involved in speaking and muscle movements and in making plans and judgments. (p. 74)

frustration-aggression principle the principle that frustration—the blocking of an attempt to achieve some goal—creates anger, which can generate aggression. (p. 672)

functional fixedness the tendency to think of things only in terms of their usual functions; an impediment to problem solving. (p. 303)

functionalism a school of psychology that focused on how our mental and behavioral processes function—how they enable us to adapt, survive, and flourish. (p. 5)

fundamental attribution error the tendency for observers, when analyzing another's behavior, to underestimate the impact of the situation and to overestimate the impact of personal disposition. (p. 644)

gate-control theory the theory that the spinal cord contains a neurological "gate" that blocks pain signals or allows them to pass on to the brain. The "gate" is opened by the activity of pain signals traveling up small nerve fibers and is closed by activity in larger fibers or by information coming from the brain. (p. 143)

gender in psychology, the biologically and socially influenced characteristics by which people define *male* and *female*. (p. 435)

gender identity our sense of being male or female. (p. 440)

gender role a set of expected behaviors for males or for females. (p. 439)

gender typing the acquisition of a traditional masculine or feminine role. (p. 440)

general adaptation syndrome (GAS) Selye's concept of the body's adaptive response to stress in three phases—alarm, resistance, exhaustion. (p. 399)

general intelligence (g) a general intelligence factor that, according to Spearman and others, underlies specific mental abilities and is therefore measured by every task on an intelligence test. (p. 524)

generalization the tendency, once a response has been conditioned, for stimuli similar to the conditioned stimulus to elicit similar responses. (p. 222)

generalized anxiety disorder an anxiety disorder in which a person is continually tense, apprehensive, and in a state of autonomic nervous system arousal. (p. 570)

genes the biochemical units of heredity that make up the chromosomes; segments of DNA capable of synthesizing a protein. (p. 95)

genome the complete instructions for making an organism, consisting of all the genetic material in that organism's chromosomes. (p. 96)

gestalt an organized whole. Gestalt psychologists emphasized our tendency to integrate pieces of information into meaningful wholes. (p. 151)

glial cells (glia) cells in the nervous system that support, nourish, and protect neurons. (p. 74)

glucose the form of sugar that circulates in the blood and provides the major source of energy for body tissues. When its level is low, we feel hunger. (p. 333)

grammar in a language, a system of rules that enables us to communicate with and understand others. (p. 314)

GRIT Graduated and Reciprocated Initiatives in Tension-Reduction—a strategy designed to decrease international tensions. (p. 692)

group polarization the enhancement of a group's prevailing inclinations through discussion within the group. (p. 659)

grouping the perceptual tendency to organize stimuli into coherent groups. (p. 152)

groupthink the mode of thinking that occurs when the desire for harmony in a decision-making group overrides a realistic appraisal of alternatives. (p. 660)

habituation decreasing responsiveness with repeated stimulation. As infants gain familiarity with repeated exposure to a visual stimulus, their interest wanes and they look away sooner. (pp. 216, 414)

hallucinations false sensory experiences, such as seeing something in the absence of an external visual stimulus. (p. 179)

hallucinogens psychedelic ("mind-manifesting") drugs, such as LSD, that distort perceptions and evoke sensory images in the absence of sensory input. (p. 205)

health psychology a subfield of psychology that provides psychology's contribution to behavioral medicine. (p. 397)

heritability the proportion of variation among individuals that we can attribute to genes. The heritability of a trait may vary, depending on the range of populations and environments studied. (p. 100)

heuristic a simple thinking strategy that often allows us to make judgments and solve problems efficiently; usually speedier but also more error-prone than *algorithms*. (p. 300)

hierarchy of needs Maslow's pyramid of human needs, beginning at the base with physiological needs that must first be satisfied before higher-level safety needs and then psychological needs become active. (p. 330)

higher-order conditioning a procedure in which the conditioned stimulus in one conditioning experience is paired with a new neutral stimulus, creating a second (often weaker) conditioned stimulus. For example, an animal that has learned that a tone predicts food might then learn that a light predicts the tone and begin responding to the light alone. (Also called *second-order conditioning*.) (p. 220)

hindsight bias the tendency to believe, after learning an outcome, that one would have foreseen it. (Also known as the *I-knew-it-all-along phenomenon*.) (p. 20)

hippocampus a neural center that is located in the limbic system; helps process explicit memories for storage. (p. 272)

homeostasis a tendency to maintain a balanced or constant internal state; the regulation of any aspect of body chemistry, such as blood glucose, around a particular level. (p. 329)

hormones chemical messengers that are manufactured by the endocrine glands, travel through the bloodstream, and affect other tissues. (p. 62)

hue the dimension of color that is determined by the wavelength of light; what we know as the color names *blue, green,* and so forth. (p. 125)

human factors psychology a branch of psychology that explores how people and machines interact and how machines and physical environments can be made safe and easy to use. (pp. 13, B-2)

humanistic psychology historically significant perspective that emphasized the growth potential of healthy people and the individual's potential for personal growth. (p. 6)

hypnosis a social interaction in which one person (the hypnotist) suggests to another (the subject) that certain perceptions, feelings, thoughts, or behaviors will spontaneously occur. (p. 192)

hypochondriasis a somatoform disorder in which a person interprets normal physical sensations as symptoms of a disease. (p. 577)

hypothalamus [hi-po-THAL-uh-muss] a neural structure lying below (*hypo*) the thalamus; it directs several maintenance activities (eating, drinking, body temperature), helps govern the endocrine system via the pituitary gland, and is linked to emotion and reward. (p. 72)

hypothesis a testable prediction, often implied by a theory. (p. 25)

iconic memory a momentary sensory memory of visual stimuli; a photographic or picture-image memory lasting no more than a few tenths of a second. (p. 266)

id a reservoir of unconscious psychic energy that, according to Freud, strives to satisfy basic sexual and aggressive drives. The id operates on the *pleasure principle,* demanding immediate gratification. (p. 481)

identical twins twins who develop from a single fertilized egg that splits in two, creating two genetically identical organisms. (p. 96)

identification the process by which, according to Freud, children incorporate their parents' values into their developing superegos. (p. 482)

identity our sense of self; according to Erikson, the adolescent's task is to solidify a sense of self by testing and integrating various roles. (p. 451)

illusory correlation the perception of a relationship where none exists. (p. 32)

imagery mental pictures; a powerful aid to effortful processing, especially when combined with semantic encoding. (p. 263)

implicit memory retention independent of conscious recollection. (Also called *nondeclarative* or *procedural memory*.) (p. 272)

imprinting the process by which certain animals form attachments during a critical period very early in life. (p. 427)

inattentional blindness failing to see visible objects when our attention is directed elsewhere. (p. 118)

incentive a positive or negative environmental stimulus that motivates behavior. (p. 329)

independent variable the experimental factor that is manipulated; the variable whose effect is being studied. (p. 35)

individualism giving priority to one's own goals over group goals and defining one's identity in terms of personal attributes rather than group identifications. (p. 516)

industrial-organizational (I/O) psychology the application of psychological concepts and methods to optimizing human behavior in workplaces. (pp. 13, B-2)

informational social influence influence resulting from one's willingness to accept others' opinions about reality. (p. 653)

informed consent an ethical principle that research participants be told enough to enable them to choose whether they wish to participate. (p. 45)

ingroup "Us"—people with whom we share a common identity. (p. 668)

ingroup bias the tendency to favor our own group. (p. 668)

inner ear the innermost part of the ear, containing the cochlea, semicircular canals, and vestibular sacs. (p. 135)

insight a sudden and often novel realization of the solution to a problem; it contrasts with strategy-based solutions. (pp. 236, 300)

insight therapies a variety of therapies that aim to improve psychological functioning by increasing the client's awareness of underlying motives and defenses. (p. 609)

insomnia recurring problems in falling or staying asleep. (p. 185)

instinct a complex behavior that is rigidly patterned throughout a species and is unlearned. (p. 328)

intellectual disability (formerly referred to as *mental retardation*) a condition of limited mental ability, indicated by an intelligence score of 70 or below and difficulty in adapting to the demands of life; varies from mild to profound. (p. 542)

intelligence mental quality consisting of the ability to learn from experience, solve problems, and use knowledge to adapt to new situations. (p. 524)

intelligence quotient (IQ) defined originally as the ratio of mental age (*ma*) to chronological age (*ca*) multiplied by 100 (thus, IQ = *ma/ca* × 100). On contemporary intelligence tests, the average performance for a given age is assigned a score of 100. (p. 534)

intelligence test a method for assessing an individual's mental aptitudes and comparing them with those of others, using numerical scores. (p. 524)

intensity the amount of energy in a light or sound wave, which we perceive as brightness or loudness, as determined by the wave's amplitude. (p. 125)

interaction the interplay that occurs when the effect of one factor (such as environment) depends on another factor (such as heredity). (p. 101)

internal locus of control the perception that you control your own fate. (p. 505)

interneurons neurons within the brain and spinal cord that communicate internally and intervene between the sensory inputs and motor outputs. (p. 53)

interpretation in psychoanalysis, the analyst's noting supposed dream meanings, resistances, and other significant behaviors and events in order to promote insight. (p. 607)

intimacy in Erikson's theory, the ability to form close, loving relationships; a primary developmental task in late adolescence and early adulthood. (p. 452)

intrinsic motivation a desire to perform a behavior effectively for its own sake. (p. 237)

intuition an effortless, immediate, automatic feeling or thought, as contrasted with explicit, conscious reasoning. (p. 308)

iris a ring of muscle tissue that forms the colored portion of the eye around the pupil and controls the size of the pupil opening. (p. 126)

James-Lange theory the theory that our experience of emotion is our awareness of our physiological responses to emotion-arousing stimuli. (p. 367)

just-world phenomenon the tendency for people to believe the world is just and that people therefore get what they deserve and deserve what they get. (p. 670)

kinesthesis [kin-ehs-THEE-sehs] the system for sensing the position and movement of individual body parts. (p. 142)

language our spoken, written, or signed words and the ways we combine them to communicate meaning. (p. 313)

latent content according to Freud, the underlying meaning of a dream (as distinct from its manifest content). (p. 189)

latent learning learning that occurs but is not apparent until there is an incentive to demonstrate it. (p. 236)

law of effect Thorndike's principle that behaviors followed by favorable consequences become more likely, and that behaviors followed by unfavorable consequences become less likely. (p. 229)

learned helplessness the hopelessness and passive resignation an animal or human learns when unable to avoid repeated aversive events. (p. 223)

learning a relatively permanent change in an organism's behavior due to experience. (p. 215)

lens the transparent structure behind the pupil that changes shape to help focus images on the retina. (p. 126)

lesion [LEE-zhuhn] tissue destruction. A brain lesion is a naturally or experimentally caused destruction of brain tissue. (p. 67)

levels of analysis the differing complementary views, from biological to psychological to social-cultural, for analyzing any given phenomenon. (p. 10)

limbic system doughnut-shaped neural system (including the *hippocampus, amygdala,* and *hypothalamus*) located below the cerebral hemispheres; associated with emotions and drives. (p. 71)

linguistic determinism Whorf's hypothesis that language determines the way we think. (p. 319)

lobotomy a now-rare psychosurgical procedure once used to calm uncontrollably emotional or violent patients. The procedure cut the nerves connecting the frontal lobes to the emotion-controlling centers of the inner brain. (p. 635)

long-term memory the relatively permanent and limitless storehouse of the memory system. Includes knowledge, skills, and experiences. (p. 257)

long-term potentiation (LTP) an increase in a synapse's firing potential after brief, rapid stimulation. Believed to be a neural basis for learning and memory. (p. 269)

longitudinal study research in which the same people are restudied and retested over a long period. (p. 463)

LSD a powerful hallucinogenic drug; also known as acid (*lysergic acid diethylamide*). (p. 205)

lymphocytes the two types of white blood cells that are part of the body's immune system *B* lymphocytes form in the *bone* marrow and release antibodies that fight bacterial infections; *T* lymphocytes form in the *thymus* and other lymphatic tissue and attack cancer cells, viruses, and foreign substances. (p. 403)

major depressive disorder a mood disorder in which a person experiences, in the absence of drugs or a medical condition, two or more weeks of significantly depressed moods, feelings of worthlessness, and diminished interest or pleasure in most activities. (p. 580)

mania a mood disorder marked by a hyperactive, wildly optimistic state. (p. 581)

manifest content according to Freud, the remembered story line of a dream (as distinct from its latent, or hidden, content). (p. 188)

maturation biological growth processes that enable orderly changes in behavior, relatively uninfluenced by experience. (p. 416)

mean the arithmetic average of a distribution, obtained by adding the scores and then dividing by the number of scores. (p. 38)

median the middle score in a distribution; half the scores are above it and half are below it. (p. 38)

medical model the concept that diseases, in this case psychological disorders, have physical causes that can be *diagnosed, treated,* and, in most cases, *cured,* often through treatment in a *hospital.* (p. 564)

medulla [muh-DUL-uh] the base of the brainstem; controls heartbeat and breathing. (p. 69)

memory the persistence of learning over time through the storage and retrieval of information. (p. 255)

menarche [meh-NAR-key] the first menstrual period. (p. 447)

menopause the time of natural cessation of menstruation; also refers to the biological changes a woman experiences as her ability to reproduce declines. (p. 456)

mental age a measure of intelligence test performance devised by Binet; the chronological age that most typically corresponds to a given level of performance. Thus, a child who does as well as the average 8-year-old is said to have a mental age of 8. (p. 533)

mental set a tendency to approach a problem in one particular way, often a way that has been successful in the past. (p. 303)

mere exposure effect the phenomenon that repeated exposure to novel stimuli increases liking of them. (p. 678)

meta-analysis a procedure for statistically combining the results of many different research studies. (p. 621)

methamphetamine a powerfully addictive drug that stimulates the central nervous system, with speeded-up body functions and associated energy and mood changes; over time, appears to reduce baseline dopamine levels. (p. 201)

middle ear the chamber between the eardrum and cochlea containing three tiny bones (hammer, anvil, and stirrup) that concentrate the vibrations of the eardrum on the cochlea's oval window. (p. 135)

Minnesota Multiphasic Personality Inventory (MMPI) the most widely researched and clinically used of all personality tests. Originally developed to identify emotional disorders (still considered its most appropriate use), this test is now used for many other screening purposes. (p. 496)

mirror-image perceptions mutual views often held by conflicting people, as when each side sees itself as ethical and peaceful and views the other side as evil and aggressive. (p. 689)

mirror neurons frontal lobe neurons that fire when performing certain actions or when observing another doing so. The brain's mirroring of another's action may enable imitation and empathy. (p. 243)

misinformation effect incorporating misleading information into one's memory of an event. (p. 286)

mnemonics [nih-MON-iks] memory aids, especially those techniques that use vivid imagery and organizational devices. (p. 263)

mode the most frequently occurring score(s) in a distribution. (p. 37)

modeling the process of observing and imitating a specific behavior. (p. 242)

molecular genetics the subfield of biology that studies the molecular structure and function of genes. (p. 102)

monocular cues depth cues, such as interposition and linear perspective, available to either eye alone. (p. 154)

mood-congruent memory the tendency to recall experiences that are consistent with one's current good or bad mood. (p. 278)

mood disorders psychological disorders characterized by emotional extremes. See *major depressive disorder, mania,* and *bipolar disorder*. (p. 579)

morpheme in a language, the smallest unit that carries meaning; may be a word or a part of a word (such as a prefix). (p. 314)

motivation a need or desire that energizes and directs behavior. (p. 328)

motor cortex an area at the rear of the frontal lobes that controls voluntary movements. (p. 75)

motor neurons neurons that carry outgoing information from the brain and spinal cord to the muscles and glands. (p. 53)

MRI (magnetic resonance imaging) a technique that uses magnetic fields and radio waves to produce computer-generated images of soft tissue. MRI scans show brain anatomy. (p. 68)

mutation a random error in gene replication that leads to a change. (p. 104)

myelin [MY-uh-lin] **sheath** a layer of fatty tissue segmentally encasing the fibers of many neurons; enables vastly greater transmission speed of neural impulses as the impulse hops from one node to the next. (p. 53)

narcolepsy a sleep disorder characterized by uncontrollable sleep attacks. The sufferer may lapse directly into REM sleep, often at inopportune times. (p. 186)

natural selection the principle that, among the range of inherited trait variations, those contributing to reproduction and survival will most likely be passed on to succeeding generations. (pp. 8, 103)

naturalistic observation observing and recording behavior in naturally occurring situations without trying to manipulate and control the situation. (p. 28)

nature-nurture issue the longstanding controversy over the relative contributions that genes and experience make to the development of psychological traits and behaviors. Today's science sees traits and behaviors arising from the interaction of nature and nurture. (p. 8)

near-death experience an altered state of consciousness reported after a close brush with death (such as through cardiac arrest); often similar to drug-induced hallucinations. (p. 206)

negative reinforcement increasing behaviors by stopping or reducing negative stimuli, such as shock. A negative reinforcer is any stimulus that, when *removed* after a response, strengthens the response. (*Note:* negative reinforcement is not punishment.) (p. 231)

nerves bundled axons that form neural "cables" connecting the central nervous system with muscles, glands, and sense organs. (p. 59)

nervous system the body's speedy, electrochemical communication network, consisting of all the nerve cells of the peripheral and central nervous systems. (p. 59)

neurogenesis the formation of new neurons. (p. 83)

neuron a nerve cell; the basic building block of the nervous system. (p. 53)

neurotransmitters chemical messengers that cross the synaptic gaps between neurons. When released by the sending neuron, neurotransmitters travel across the synapse and bind to receptor sites on the receiving neuron, thereby influencing whether that neuron will generate a neural impulse. (p. 55)

night terrors a sleep disorder characterized by high arousal and an appearance of being terrified; unlike nightmares, night terrors occur during Stage 4 sleep, within two or three hours of falling asleep, and are seldom remembered. (p. 187)

norm an understood rule for accepted and expected behavior. Norms prescribe "proper" behavior. (p. 662)

normal curve (*normal distribution*) a symmetrical, bell-shaped curve that describes the distribution of many types of data; most scores fall near the mean (68 percent fall within one standard deviation of it) and fewer and fewer near the extremes. (pp. 40, 536)

normative social influence influence resulting from a person's desire to gain approval or avoid disapproval. (p. 653)

NREM sleep non–rapid eye movement sleep; encompasses all sleep stages except for REM sleep. (p. 180)

object permanence the awareness that things continue to exist even when not perceived. (p. 419)

observational learning learning by observing others. Also called *social learning*. (p. 242)

obsessive-compulsive disorder (OCD) an anxiety disorder characterized by unwanted repetitive thoughts (obsessions) and/or actions (compulsions). (p. 571)

occipital [ahk-SIP-uh-tuhl] **lobes** portion of the cerebral cortex lying at the back of the head; includes areas that receive information from the visual fields. (p. 74)

Oedipus [ED-uh-puss] **complex** according to Freud, a boy's sexual desires toward his mother and feelings of jealousy and hatred for the rival father. (p. 482)

one-word stage the stage in speech development, from about age 1 to 2, during which a child speaks mostly in single words. (p. 316)

operant behavior behavior that operates on the environment, producing consequences. (p. 228)

operant chamber in operant conditioning research, a chamber (also known as a *Skinner box*) containing a bar or key that an animal can manipulate to obtain a food or water reinforcer; attached devices record the animal's rate of bar pressing or key pecking. (p. 229)

operant conditioning a type of learning in which behavior is strengthened if followed by a reinforcer or diminished if followed by a punisher. (p. 228)

operational definition a statement of the procedures (operations) used to define research variables. For example, *human intelligence* may be operationally defined as what an intelligence test measures. (p. 26)

opiates opium and its derivatives, such as morphine and heroin; they depress neural activity, temporarily lessening pain and anxiety. (p. 201)

opponent-process theory the theory that opposing retinal processes (red-green, yellow-blue, white-black) enable color vision. For example, some cells are stimulated by green and inhibited by red; others are stimulated by red and inhibited by green. (p. 133)

optic nerve the nerve that carries neural impulses from the eye to the brain. (p. 126)

organizational psychology a subfield of I/O psychology that examines organizational influences on worker satisfaction and productivity and facilitates organizational change. (p. B-2)

other-race effect the tendency to recall faces of one's own race more accurately than faces of other races. Also called the *cross-race effect* and the *own-race bias.* (p. 669)

outgroup "Them"—those perceived as different or apart from our ingroup. (p. 668)

overconfidence the tendency to be more confident than correct—to overestimate the accuracy of our beliefs and judgments. (p. 306)

panic disorder an anxiety disorder marked by unpredictable minutes-long episodes of intense dread in which a person experiences terror and accompanying chest pain, choking, or other frightening sensations. (p. 570)

parallel processing the processing of many aspects of a problem simultaneously; the brain's natural mode of information processing for many functions, including vision. Contrasts with the step-by-step (serial) processing of most computers and of conscious problem solving. (pp. 130, 258)

parapsychology the study of paranormal phenomena, including ESP and psychokinesis. (p. 166)

parasympathetic nervous system the division of the autonomic nervous system that calms the body, conserving its energy. (p. 60)

parietal [puh-RYE-uh-tuhl] **lobes** portion of the cerebral cortex lying at the top of the head and toward the rear; receives sensory input for touch and body position. (p. 74)

partial (intermittent) reinforcement reinforcing a response only part of the time; results in slower acquisition of a response but much greater resistance to extinction than does continuous reinforcement. (p. 232)

passionate love an aroused state of intense positive absorption in another, usually present at the beginning of a love relationship. (p. 683)

perception the process of organizing and interpreting sensory information, enabling us to recognize meaningful objects and events. (p. 116)

perceptual adaptation in vision, the ability to adjust to an artificially displaced or even inverted visual field. (p. 160)

perceptual constancy perceiving objects as unchanging (having consistent shapes, size, lightness, and color) even as illumination and retinal images change. (p. 156)

perceptual set a mental predisposition to perceive one thing and not another. (p. 161)

peripheral nervous system (PNS) the sensory and motor neurons that connect the central nervous system (CNS) to the rest of the body. (p. 59)

peripheral route persuasion attitude change path in which people are influenced by incidental cues, such as a speaker's attractiveness. (p. 646)

personal control the extent to which people perceive control over their environment rather than feeling helpless. (p. 505)

personal space the buffer zone we like to maintain around our bodies. (p. 662)

personality an individual's characteristic pattern of thinking, feeling, and acting. (p. 479)

personality disorders psychological disorders characterized by inflexible and enduring behavior patterns that impair social functioning. (p. 596)

personality inventory a questionnaire (often with *true-false* or *agree-disagree* items) on which people respond to items designed to gauge a wide range of feelings and behaviors; used to assess selected personality traits. (p. 496)

personality psychology the study of an individual's characteristic pattern of thinking, feeling, and acting. (p. 13)

personnel psychology a subfield of I/O psychology that focuses on employee recruitment, selection, placement, training, appraisal, and development. (p. B-2)

PET (positron emission tomography) scan a visual display of brain activity that detects where a radioactive form of glucose goes while the brain performs a given task. (p. 68)

phi phenomenon an illusion of movement created when two or more adjacent lights blink on and off in quick succession. (p. 156)

phobia an anxiety disorder marked by a persistent, irrational fear and avoidance of a specific object, activity, or situation. (p. 571)

phoneme in language, the smallest distinctive sound unit. (p. 313)

physical dependence a physiological need for a drug, marked by unpleasant withdrawal symptoms when the drug is discontinued. (p. 197)

pitch a tone's experienced highness or lowness; depends on frequency. (p. 134)

pituitary gland the endocrine system's most influential gland. Under the influence of the hypothalamus, the pituitary regulates growth and controls other endocrine glands. (p. 63)

place theory in hearing, the theory that links the pitch we hear with the place where the cochlea's membrane is stimulated. (p. 137)

placebo [pluh-SEE-bo; Latin for "I shall please"] **effect** experimental results caused by expectations alone; any effect on behavior caused by the administration of an inert substance or condition, which the recipient assumes is an active agent. (p. 35)

plasticity the brain's ability to change, especially during childhood, by reorganizing after damage or by building new pathways based on experience. (p. 82)

polygraph a machine, commonly used in attempts to detect lies, that measures several of the physiological responses accompanying emotion (such as perspiration and cardiovascular and breathing changes). (p. 372)

population all the cases in a group being studied, from which samples may be drawn. (*Note:* Except for national studies, this does *not* refer to a country's whole population.) (p. 28)

positive psychology the scientific study of optimal human functioning; aims to discover and promote strengths and virtues that enable individuals and communities to thrive. (p. 508)

positive reinforcement increasing behaviors by presenting positive stimuli, such as food. A positive reinforcer is any stimulus that, when *presented* after a response, strengthens the response. (p. 231)

posthypnotic suggestion a suggestion, made during a hypnosis session, to be carried out after the subject is no longer hypnotized; used by some clinicians to help control undesired symptoms and behaviors. (p. 194)

post-traumatic growth positive psychological changes as a result of struggling with extremely challenging circumstances and life crises. (p. 573)

post-traumatic stress disorder (PTSD) an anxiety disorder characterized by haunting memories, nightmares, social withdrawal, jumpy anxiety, and/or insomnia that lingers for four weeks or more after a traumatic experience. (p. 572)

predictive validity the success with which a test predicts the behavior it is designed to predict; it is assessed by computing the correlation between test scores and the criterion behavior. (Also called *criterion-related validity*.) (p. 538)

prejudice an unjustifiable (and usually negative) attitude toward a group and its members. Prejudice generally involves stereotyped beliefs, negative feelings, and a predisposition to discriminatory action. (p. 664)

preoperational stage in Piaget's theory, the stage (from 2 to about 6 or 7 years of age) during which a child learns to use language but does not yet comprehend the mental operations of concrete logic. (p. 421)

primary reinforcer an innately reinforcing stimulus, such as one that satisfies a biological need. (p. 231)

primary sex characteristics the body structures (ovaries, testes, and external genitalia) that make sexual reproduction possible. (p. 446)

priming the activation, often unconsciously, of certain associations, thus predisposing one's perception, memory, or response. (pp. 121, 275)

proactive interference the disruptive effect of prior learning on the recall of new information. (p. 282)

problem-focused coping attempting to alleviate stress directly—by changing the stressor or the way we interact with that stressor. (p. C-1)

projection psychoanalytic defense mechanism by which people disguise their own threatening impulses by attributing them to others. (p. 483)

projective test a personality test, such as the Rorschach or TAT, that provides ambiguous stimuli designed to trigger projection of one's inner dynamics. (p. 486)

prosocial behavior positive, constructive, helpful behavior. The opposite of antisocial behavior. (p. 246)

prototype a mental image or best example of a category. Matching new items to a prototype provides a quick and easy method for sorting items into categories (as when comparing feathered creatures to a prototypical bird, such as a robin). (p. 299)

psychiatry a branch of medicine dealing with psychological disorders; practiced by physicians who often provide medical (for example, drug) treatments as well as psychological therapy. (p. 13)

psychoactive drug a chemical substance that alters perceptions and moods. (p. 197)

psychoanalysis Freud's theory of personality and therapeutic technique that attributes thoughts and actions to unconscious motives and conflicts. Freud believed the patient's free associations, resistances, dreams, and transferences—and the therapist's interpretations of them—released previously repressed feelings, allowing the patient to gain self-insight. (pp. 480, 606)

psychodynamic psychology a branch of psychology that studies how unconscious drives and conflicts influence behavior, and uses that information to treat people with psychological disorders. (p. 10)

psychodynamic therapy therapy deriving from the psychoanalytic tradition that views individuals as responding to unconscious forces and childhood experiences, and that seeks to enhance self-insight. (p. 608)

psychological dependence a psychological need to use a drug, such as to relieve negative emotions. (p. 197)

psychological disorder deviant, distressful, and dysfunctional patterns of thoughts, feelings, or behaviors. (p. 562)

psychology the science of behavior and mental processes. (p. 7)

psychometrics the scientific study of the measurement of human abilities, attitudes, and traits. (p. 12)

psychoneuroimmunology (PNI) the study of how psychological, neural, and endocrine processes together affect the immune system and resulting health. (p. 403)

psychopharmacology the study of the effects of drugs on mind and behavior. (p. 628)

psychophysics the study of relationships between the physical characteristics of stimuli, such as their intensity, and our psychological experience of them. (p. 120)

psychophysiological illness literally, "mind-body" illness; any stress-related physical illness, such as hypertension and some headaches. (p. 403)

psychosexual stages the childhood stages of development (oral, anal, phallic, latency, genital) during which, according to Freud, the id's pleasure-seeking energies focus on distinct erogenous zones. (p. 482)

psychosurgery surgery that removes or destroys brain tissue in an effort to change behavior. (p. 635)

psychotherapy treatment involving psychological techniques; consists of interactions between a trained therapist and someone seeking to overcome psychological difficulties or achieve personal growth. (p. 606)

puberty the period of sexual maturation, during which a person becomes capable of reproducing. (p. 445)

punishment an event that *decreases* the behavior that it follows. (p. 234)

pupil the adjustable opening in the center of the eye through which light enters. (p. 126)

random assignment assigning participants to experimental and control groups by chance, thus minimizing preexisting differences between those assigned to the different groups. (p. 34)

random sample a sample that fairly represents a population because each member has an equal chance of inclusion. (p. 28)

range the difference between the highest and lowest scores in a distribution. (p. 39)

rationalization psychoanalytic defense mechanism that offers self-justifying explanations in place of the real, more threatening, unconscious reasons for one's actions. (p. 483)

reaction formation psychoanalytic defense mechanism by which the ego unconsciously switches unacceptable impulses into their opposites. Thus, people may express feelings that are the opposite of their anxiety-arousing unconscious feelings. (p. 483)

recall a measure of memory in which the person must retrieve information learned earlier, as on a fill-in-the-blank test. (p. 274)

reciprocal determinism the interacting influences of behavior, internal cognition, and environment. (p. 503)

reciprocity norm an expectation that people will help, not hurt, those who have helped them. (p. 687)

recognition a measure of memory in which the person need only identify items previously learned, as on a multiple-choice test. (p. 274)

reflex a simple, automatic response to a sensory stimulus, such as the knee-jerk response. (p. 61)

refractory period a resting period after orgasm, during which a man cannot achieve another orgasm. (p. 349)

regression psychoanalytic defense mechanism in which an individual faced with anxiety retreats to a more infantile psychosexual stage, where some psychic energy remains fixated. (p. 483)

regression toward the mean the tendency for extreme or unusual scores to fall back (regress) toward their average. (p. 621)

rehearsal the conscious repetition of information, either to maintain it in consciousness or to encode it for storage. (p. 259)

reinforcer in operant conditioning, any event that *strengthens* the behavior it follows. (p. 230)

relative deprivation the perception that we are worse off relative to those with whom we compare ourselves. (p. 394)

relearning a measure of memory that assesses the amount of time saved when learning material for a second time. (p. 274)

reliability the extent to which a test yields consistent results, as assessed by the consistency of scores on two halves of the test, or on retesting. (p. 538)

REM rebound the tendency for REM sleep to increase following REM sleep deprivation (created by repeated awakenings during REM sleep). (p. 191)

REM sleep rapid eye movement sleep; a recurring sleep stage during which vivid dreams commonly occur. Also known as *paradoxical sleep,* because the muscles are relaxed (except for minor twitches) but other body systems are active. (p. 178)

repetitive transcranial magnetic stimulation (rTMS) the application of repeated pulses of magnetic energy to the brain; used to stimulate or suppress brain activity. (p. 634)

replication repeating the essence of a research study, usually with different participants in different situations, to see whether the basic finding extends to other participants and circumstances. (p. 26)

representativeness heuristic judging the likelihood of things in terms of how well they seem to represent, or match, particular prototypes; may lead us to ignore other relevant information. (p. 304)

repression in psychoanalytic theory, the basic defense mechanism that banishes anxiety-arousing thoughts, feelings, and memories from consciousness. (pp. 284, 483)

resilience the personal strength that helps most people cope with stress and recover from adversity and even trauma. (p. 637)

resistance in psychoanalysis, the blocking from consciousness of anxiety-laden material. (p. 607)

respondent behavior behavior that occurs as an automatic response to some stimulus. (p. 228)

reticular formation a nerve network in the brainstem that plays an important role in controlling arousal. (p. 70)

retina the light-sensitive inner surface of the eye, containing the receptor rods and cones plus layers of neurons that begin the processing of visual information. (p. 126)

retinal disparity a binocular cue for perceiving depth By comparing images from the retinas in the two eyes, the brain computes distance—the greater the disparity (difference) between the two images, the closer the object. (p. 153)

retrieval the process of getting information out of memory storage. (p. 257)

retroactive interference the disruptive effect of new learning on the recall of old information. (p. 282)

reuptake a neurotransmitter's reabsorption by the sending neuron. (p. 55)

rods retinal receptors that detect black, white, and gray; necessary for peripheral and twilight vision, when cones don't respond. (p. 126)

role a set of expectations (norms) about a social position, defining how those in the position ought to behave. (pp. 439, 647)

Rorschach inkblot test the most widely used projective test, a set of 10 inkblots, designed by Hermann Rorschach; seeks to identify people's inner feelings by analyzing their interpretations of the blots. (p. 486)

savant syndrome a condition in which a person otherwise limited in mental ability has an exceptional specific skill, such as in computation or drawing. (p. 525)

scapegoat theory the theory that prejudice offers an outlet for anger by providing someone to blame. (p. 669)

scatterplot a graphed cluster of dots, each of which represents the values of two variables. The slope of the points suggests the direction of the relationship between the two variables. The amount of scatter suggests the strength of the correlation (little scatter indicates high correlation). (p. 29)

schema a concept or framework that organizes and interprets information. (p. 418)

schizophrenia a group of severe disorders characterized by disorganized and delusional thinking, disturbed perceptions, and inappropriate emotions and actions. (p. 590)

secondary sex characteristics nonreproductive sexual characteristics, such as female breasts and hips, male voice quality, and body hair. (p. 446)

selective attention the focusing of conscious awareness on a particular stimulus. (p. 117)

self in contemporary psychology, assumed to be the center of personality, the organizer of our thoughts, feelings, and actions. (p. 511)

self-actualization according to Maslow, one of the ultimate psychological needs that arises after basic physical and psychological needs are met and self-esteem is achieved; the motivation to fulfill one's potential. (p. 491)

self-concept all our thoughts and feelings about ourselves, in answer to the question, "Who am I?" (pp. 432, 492)

self-disclosure revealing intimate aspects of oneself to others. (p. 684)

self-esteem one's feelings of high or low self-worth. (p. 512)

self-fulfilling prophecy a belief that leads to its own fulfillment. (p. 689)

self-serving bias a readiness to perceive oneself favorably. (p. 513)

semantic encoding the encoding of meaning, including the meaning of words. (p. 261)

semantics the set of rules by which we derive meaning from morphemes, words, and sentences in a given language; also, the study of meaning. (p. 314)

sensation the process by which our sensory receptors and nervous system receive and represent stimulus energies from our environment. (p. 116)

sensorimotor stage in Piaget's theory, the stage (from birth to about 2 years of age) during which infants know the world mostly in terms of their sensory impressions and motor activities. (p. 419)

sensorineural hearing loss hearing loss caused by damage to the cochlea's receptor cells or to the auditory nerves; also called *nerve deafness.* (p. 138)

sensory adaptation diminished sensitivity as a consequence of constant stimulation. (p. 123)

sensory cortex area at the front of the parietal lobes that registers and processes body touch and movement sensations. (p. 77)

sensory interaction the principle that one sense may influence another, as when the smell of food influences its taste. (p. 147)

sensory memory the immediate, very brief recording of sensory information in the memory system. (p. 257)

sensory neurons neurons that carry incoming information from the sensory receptors to the brain and spinal cord. (p. 53)

serial position effect our tendency to recall best the last and first items in a list. (p. 260)

set point the point at which an individual's "weight thermostat" is supposedly set. When the body falls below this weight, an increase in hunger and a lowered metabolic rate may act to restore the lost weight. (p. 335)

sexual orientation an enduring sexual attraction toward members of either one's own sex (homosexual orientation) or the other sex (heterosexual orientation). (p. 354)

sexual response cycle the four stages of sexual responding described by Masters and Johnson—excitement, plateau, orgasm, and resolution. (p. 349)

shaping an operant conditioning procedure in which reinforcers guide behavior toward closer and closer approximations of the desired behavior. (p. 229)

short-term memory activated memory that holds a few items briefly, such as the seven digits of a phone number while dialing, before the information is stored or forgotten. (p. 257)

signal detection theory a theory predicting how and when we detect the presence of a faint stimulus (*signal*) amid background stimulation (*noise*). Assumes there is no single absolute threshold and that detection depends partly on a person's experience, expectations, motivation, and alertness. (p. 121)

sleep periodic, natural loss of consciousness—as distinct from un consciousness resulting from a coma, general anesthesia, or hibernation. (Adapted from Dement, 1999.) (p. 178)

sleep apnea a sleep disorder characterized by temporary cessations of breathing during sleep and repeated momentary awakenings. (p. 187)

social clock the culturally preferred timing of social events such as marriage, parenthood, and retirement. (p. 465)

social-cognitive perspective views behavior as influenced by the interaction between people's traits (including their thinking) and their social context. (p. 503)

social-cultural psychology the study of how situations and cultures affect our behavior and thinking. (p. 10)

social exchange theory the theory that our social behavior is an exchange process, the aim of which is to maximize benefits and minimize costs. (p. 687)

social facilitation stronger responses on simple or well-learned tasks in the presence of others. (p. 657)

social identity the "we" aspect of our self-concept; the part of our answer to "Who am I?" that comes from our group memberships. (p. 451)

social leadership group-oriented leadership that builds teamwork, mediates conflict, and offers support. (p. B-12)

social learning theory the theory that we learn social behavior by observing and imitating and by being rewarded or punished. (p. 440)

social loafing the tendency for people in a group to exert less effort when pooling their efforts toward attaining a common goal than when individually accountable. (p. 658)

social psychology the scientific study of how we think about, influence, and relate to one another. (pp. 13, 643)

social-responsibility norm an expectation that people will help those dependent upon them. (p. 687)

social trap a situation in which the conflicting parties, by each rationally pursuing their self-interest, become caught in mutually destructive behavior. (p. 688)

somatic nervous system the division of the peripheral nervous system that controls the body's skeletal muscles. Also called the *skeletal nervous system*. (p. 59)

somatoform disorder psychological disorder in which the symptoms take a somatic (bodily) form without apparent physical cause. (See *conversion disorder* and *hypochondriasis*.) (p. 576)

source amnesia attributing to the wrong source an event we have experienced, heard about, read about, or imagined. (Also called *source misattribution*.) Source amnesia, along with the misinformation effect, is at the heart of many false memories. (p. 287)

spacing effect the tendency for distributed study or practice to yield better long-term retention than is achieved through massed study or practice. (p. 260)

split brain a condition resulting from surgery that isolates the brain's two hemispheres by cutting the fibers (mainly those of the corpus callosum) connecting them. (p. 84)

spontaneous recovery the reappearance, after a pause, of an extinguished conditioned response. (p. 221)

spotlight effect overestimating others' noticing and evaluating our appearance, performance, and blunders (as if we presume a spotlight shines on us). (p. 512)

SQ3R a study method incorporating five steps *Survey, Question, Read, Rehearse, Review*. (p. 14)

standard deviation a computed measure of how much scores vary around the mean score. (p. 39)

standardization defining meaningful scores by comparison with the performance of a pretested group. (p. 536)

Stanford-Binet the widely used American revision (by Terman at Stanford University) of Binet's original intelligence test. (p. 534)

statistical significance a statistical statement of how likely it is that an obtained result occurred by chance. (p. 41)

stereotype a generalized (sometimes accurate but often overgeneralized) belief about a group of people. (p. 664)

stereotype threat a self-confirming concern that one will be evaluated based on a negative stereotype. (p. 555)

stimulants drugs (such as caffeine, nicotine, and the more powerful amphetamines, cocaine, and Ecstasy) that excite neural activity and speed up body functions. (p. 201)

storage the retention of encoded information over time. (p. 257)

stranger anxiety the fear of strangers that infants commonly display, beginning by about 8 months of age. (p. 426)

stress the process by which we perceive and respond to certain events, called *stressors*, that we appraise as threatening or challenging. (p. 397)

structuralism an early school of psychology that used introspection to explore the structural elements of the human mind. (p. 4)

structured interviews interview process that asks the same job-relevant questions of all applicants, each of whom is rated on established scales. (p. B-5)

sublimation psychoanalytic defense mechanism by which people re-channel their unacceptable impulses into socially approved activities. (p. 484)

subliminal below one's absolute threshold for conscious awareness. (p. 121)

superego the part of personality that, according to Freud, represents internalized ideals and provides standards for judgment (the conscience) and for future aspirations. (p. 482)

superordinate goals shared goals that override differences among people and require their cooperation. (p. 690)

survey a technique for ascertaining the self-reported attitudes or behaviors of a particular group, usually by questioning a representative, random sample of the group. (p. 27)

sympathetic nervous system the division of the autonomic nervous system that arouses the body, mobilizing its energy in stressful situations. (p. 59)

synapse [SIN-aps] the junction between the axon tip of the sending neuron and the dendrite or cell body of the receiving neuron. The tiny gap at this junction is called the *synaptic gap* or *synaptic cleft*. (p. 55)

syntax the rules for combining words into grammatically sensible sentences in a given language. (p. 314)

systematic desensitization a type of exposure therapy that associates a pleasant relaxed state with gradually increasing anxiety-triggering stimuli. Commonly used to treat phobias. (p. 611)

tardive dyskinesia involuntary movements of the facial muscles, tongue, and limbs; a possible neurotoxic side effect of long-term use of antipsychotic drugs that target certain dopamine receptors. (p. 629)

task leadership goal-oriented leadership that sets standards, organizes work, and focuses attention on goals. (p. B-12)

telegraphic speech early speech stage in which a child speaks like a telegram—"go car"—using mostly nouns and verbs. (p. 316)

temperament a person's characteristic emotional reactivity and intensity. (p. 428)

temporal lobes portion of the cerebral cortex lying roughly above the ears; includes the auditory areas, each receiving information primarily from the opposite ear. (p. 74)

teratogens agents, such as chemicals and viruses, that can reach the embryo or fetus during prenatal development and cause harm. (p. 413)

terror-management theory a theory of death-related anxiety; explores people's emotional and behavioral responses to reminders of their impending death. (p. 489)

testosterone the most important of the male sex hormones. Both males and females have it, but the additional testosterone in males stimulates the growth of the male sex organs in the fetus and the development of the male sex characteristics during puberty. (pp. 350, 438)

thalamus [THAL-uh-muss] the brain's sensory switchboard, located on top of the brainstem; it directs messages to the sensory receiving areas in the cortex and transmits replies to the cerebellum and medulla. (p. 70)

THC the major active ingredient in marijuana; triggers a variety of effects, including mild hallucinations. (p. 206)

Thematic Apperception Test (TAT) a projective test in which people express their inner feelings and interests through the stories they make up about ambiguous scenes. (p. 486)

theory an explanation using an integrated set of principles that organizes observations and predicts behaviors or events. (p. 25)

theory of mind people's ideas about their own and others' mental states—about their feelings, perceptions, and thoughts, and the behaviors these might predict. (p. 422)

threshold the level of stimulation required to trigger a neural impulse. (p. 54)

token economy an operant conditioning procedure in which people earn a token of some sort for exhibiting a desired behavior and can later exchange the tokens for various privileges or treats. (p. 614)

tolerance the diminishing effect with regular use of the same dose of a drug, requiring the user to take larger and larger doses before experiencing the drug's effect. (p. 197)

top-down processing information processing guided by higher-level mental processes, as when we construct perceptions drawing on our experience and expectations. (p. 116)

trait a characteristic pattern of behavior or a disposition to feel and act, as assessed by self-report inventories and peer reports. (p. 494)

transduction conversion of one form of energy into another. In sensation, the transforming of stimulus energies, such as sights, sounds, and smells, into neural impulses our brains can interpret. (p. 124)

transference in psychoanalysis, the patient's transfer to the analyst of emotions linked with other relationships (such as love or hatred for a parent). (p. 607)

two-factor theory the Schachter-Singer theory that to experience emotion one must (1) be physically aroused and (2) cognitively label the arousal. (p. 367)

two-word stage beginning about age 2, the stage in speech development during which a child speaks mostly two-word statements. (p. 316)

Type A Friedman and Rosenman's term for competitive, hard-driving, impatient, verbally aggressive, and anger-prone people. (p. 402)

Type B Friedman and Rosenman's term for easygoing, relaxed people. (p. 402)

unconditional positive regard a caring, accepting, nonjudgmental attitude, which Carl Rogers believed would help clients to develop self-awareness and self-acceptance. (pp. 491, 610)

unconditioned response (UR) in classical conditioning, the unlearned, naturally occurring response to the unconditioned stimulus (US), such as salivation when food is in the mouth. (p. 219)

unconditioned stimulus (US) in classical conditioning, a stimulus that unconditionally—naturally and automatically—triggers a response. (p. 219)

unconscious according to Freud, a reservoir of mostly unacceptable thoughts, wishes, feelings, and memories. According to contemporary psychologists, information processing of which we are unaware. (p. 480)

validity the extent to which a test measures or predicts what it is supposed to. (See also *content validity* and *predictive validity*.) (p. 538)

variable-interval schedule in operant conditioning, a reinforcement schedule that reinforces a response at unpredictable time intervals. (p. 233)

variable-ratio schedule in operant conditioning, a reinforcement schedule that reinforces a response after an unpredictable number of responses. (p. 233)

vestibular sense the sense of body movement and position, including the sense of balance. (p. 142)

virtual reality exposure therapy An anxiety treatment that progressively exposes people to simulations of their greatest fears, such as airplane flying, spiders, or public speaking. (p. 612)

visual cliff a laboratory device for testing depth perception in infants and young animals. (p. 153)

visual encoding the encoding of picture images. (p. 261)

wavelength the distance from the peak of one light or sound wave to the peak of the next. Electromagnetic wavelengths vary from the short blips of cosmic rays to the long pulses of radio transmission. (p. 125)

Weber's law the principle that, to be perceived as different, two stimuli must differ by a constant percentage (rather than a constant amount). (p. 123)

Wechsler Adult Intelligence Scale (WAIS) the WAIS is the most widely used intelligence test; contains verbal and performance (nonverbal) subtests. (p. 535)

well-being self-perceived happiness or satisfaction with life. Used along with measures of objective well-being (for example, physical and economic indicators) to evaluate people's quality of life. (p. 390)

Wernicke's area controls language reception—a brain area involved in language comprehension and expression; usually in the left temporal lobe. (p. 80)

withdrawal the discomfort and distress that follow discontinuing the use of an addictive drug. (p. 197)

working memory a newer understanding of short-term memory that focuses on conscious, active processing of incoming auditory and visual-spatial information, and of information retrieved from long-term memory. (p. 258)

X chromosome the sex chromosome found in both men and women. Females have two X chromosomes; males have one. An X chromosome from each parent produces a female child. (p. 438)

Y chromosome the sex chromosome found only in males. When paired with an X chromosome from the mother, it produces a male child. (p. 438)

Young-Helmholtz trichromatic (three-color) theory the theory that the retina contains three different color receptors—one most sensitive to red, one to green, one to blue—which, when stimulated in combination, can produce the perception of any color. (p. 132)

zygote the fertilized egg; it enters a 2-week period of rapid cell division and develops into an embryo. (p. 412)

Glosario en español

absolute threshold/umbral absoluto estímulo mínimo necesario para detectar un estímulo particular el cincuenta por ciento del tiempo. (pág. 120)

accommodation/adaptación (1) proceso por el que el lente del ojo cambia de forma para enfocar objetos lejanos o cercanos en la retina. (2) ajuste de nuestros conceptos actuales (esquemas) con el propósito de incorporar nueva información. (págs. 126, 418)

achievement motivation/motivación de logro deseo de alcanzar un logro significativo; de dominar cosas, personas o ideas; de alcanzar rápidamente un nivel muy alto. (pág. B-7)

achievement tests/prueba de rendimiento prueba diseñada para evaluar lo que una persona ha aprendido. (pág. 535)

acoustic encoding/codificación acústica codificación de sonido, sobre todo el sonido de palabras. (pág. 261)

acquisition/adquisición fase inicial del condicionamiento clásico en la que se asocia un estímulo neutro con un estímulo no condicionado de manera que el estímulo neutro comience a provocar la respuesta condicionada. En el condicionamiento operante, se refiere a la consolidación de una respuesta reforzada. (pág. 220)

action potential/potencial de acción impulso neural; carga eléctrica breve que se transmite por un axón. (pág. 53)

active listening/escucha activa escucha empática en la que el oyente hace eco, reitera y clarifica. Una característica de la terapia de Rogers centrada en el cliente. (pág. 609)

adaptation-level phenomenon/fenómeno del nivel de adaptación nuestra tendencia de formar juicios (de sonidos, de luces, de ingreso) relacionado a un nivel neutro definido por nuestra experiencia de antes. (pág. 394)

addiction/adicción deseo y uso compulsivo de una droga, a pesar de las consecuencias desfavorables. (pág. 197)

adolescence/adolescencia período de transición de la niñez a la madurez, extendiéndose de la pubertad a la independencia. (pág. 445)

adrenal [ah-DREEN-el] **glands/glándulas suprarrenales** par de glándulas endocrinas localizadas en la parte superior de los riñones. Estas glándulas secretan hormonas (epinefrina y norepinefrina) que estimulan el cuerpo permitiéndole responder al estrés. (pág. 63)

aerobic exercise/ejercicio aeróbico ejercicio continuo que fortalece el corazón y los pulmones; también puede aliviar la depresión y la ansiedad. (pág. C-6)

aggression/agresión comportamiento expresado de manera física o verbal con el propósito de herir a alguien. (págs. 436, 670)

algorithm/algoritmo regla metódica y lógica o un procedimiento que garantiza la solución de un problema particular. Se contrapone al uso de la *heurística* que es normalmente más rápido, pero también con más posibilidades de cometer errores. (pág. 300)

alpha waves/ritmo alfa ritmo con ondas cerebrales relativamente lentas que corresponden a un estado relajado y de vigilia. (pág. 178)

altruism/altruismo consideración desinteresada por el bienestar de otros. (pág. 685)

amnesia/amnesia pérdida de la memoria. (pág. 271)

amphetamines/anfetaminas drogas que estimulan la actividad neural, causando aceleración de las funciones corporales y de los niveles de energía asociadas con éstas así como cambios de humor. (pág. 201)

amygdala [uh-MIG-duh-la] **/amígdala** dos grupos neurales del tamaño de una almendra que forman parte del sistema límbico; están ligados a las emociones. (pág. 71)

anorexia nervosa/anorexia nervosa o nerviosa trastorno alimenticio en el que una persona (generalmente una muchacha adolescente) se pone a dieta y baja considerablemente de peso (el 15 por ciento o más) pero sigue sintiéndose gorda y continúa matándose de hambre. (pág. 337)

antianxiety drugs/medicamentos contra la ansiedad medicamentos que se emplean para aliviar la ansiedad y la agitación. (pág. 630)

antidepressant drugs/medicamentos antidepresivos medicación que se receta para tratar la depresión; también se receta cada vez más para tratar la ansiedad. Los distintos tipos de antidepresivos alteran la disponibilidad de diversos neurotransmisores. (pág. 630)

antipsychotic drugs/medicamentos antipsicóticos medicamentos que se emplean para tratar la esquizofrenia y otros tipos de trastornos graves del pensamiento. (pág. 629)

antisocial personality disorder/trastorno antisocial de la personalidad trastorno de la personalidad que se manifiesta cuando la persona (generalmente un hombre) no exhibe sentimiento de culpa por actuar con maldad, incluso hacia los amigos y miembros de la familia. Puede ser agresivo y cruel o un estafador listo. (pág. 597)

anxiety disorders/trastornos de ansiedad trastornos psicológicos que se caracterizan por la preocupación y tensión crónicas o comportamientos desadaptados que reducen la ansiedad. (pág. 569)

aphasia/afasia disfunción del centro del lenguaje generalmente causado por una lesión al hemisferio izquierdo ya sea en el área de Broca (problemas de articulación) o en el área de Wernicke (problemas de comprensión). (pág. 80)

applied research/investigación aplicada estudio científico cuyo objetivo es resolver los problemas prácticos. (pág. 13)

aptitude tests/prueba de aptitud prueba diseñada para predecir la actuación de una persona en el futuro; *la aptitud* es la capacidad de aprender. (pág. 535)

assimilation/asimilación interpretación de nuevas experiencias según los esquemas previamente existentes. (pág. 418)

association areas/áreas de asociación áreas de la corteza cerebral que no están involucradas en las funciones motoras o sensoriales primarias; más bien, están involucradas en las funciones mentales superiores como el aprender, recordar, pensar y hablar. (pág. 78)

associative learning/aprendizaje asociativo el aprender que ciertos eventos ocurren juntos. Los eventos pueden ser dos estímulos (como en el condicionamiento clásico) o una respuesta y sus consecuencias (como en el condicionamiento operante). (pág. 216)

attachment/apego vínculo emocional con otra persona; mostrado en niños pequeños quienes buscan cercanía física con la persona

GE-1

que los cuida y muestran angustia cuando se les separa de quien los cuida. (pág. 426)

attention-deficit hyperactivity disorder (ADHD) / trastorno de déficit de atención con hiperactividad trastorno psicológico marcado por la aparición antes de los 7 años de uno o más de estos tres síntomas claves: falta de atención extrema, hiperactividad e impulsividad. (pág. 563)

attitude/actitud sentimientos, a menudo basados en nuestras creencias, que nos predisponen para responder de una manera particular a objetos, personas y eventos. (pág. 646)

attribution theory/teoría de atribución teoría que propone que explicamos la conducta de una persona atribuyéndosela a la situación o a la disposición de esa persona. (pág. 644)

audition/audición sentido o acto de oír. (pág. 134)

autism/autismo trastorno que se manifiesta en la niñez y que está marcado por una comunicación deficiente, falta de interacción social, y una incapacidad para entender el estado de ánimo de los otros. (pág. 424)

automatic processing/procesamiento automático codificación inconsciente de información incidental, tal como el espacio, el tiempo y la frecuencia, y de información bien sabida, como el significado de las palabras. (pág. 258)

autonomic [aw-tuh-NAHM-ik] **nervous system/sistema nervioso autonómico** parte del sistema nervioso periférico que controla las glándulas y los músculos de los órganos internos (como el corazón). El sistema nervioso simpático alerta al cuerpo; el sistema nervioso parasimpático lo calma. (pág. 59)

availability heuristic/heurística de disponibilidad acto de estimar la probabilidad de un evento, basándose en la facilidad con la que es rememorado. Si los casos vienen prontamente a la mente (quizás debido a su intensidad), presumimos que tales eventos son comunes. (pág. 305)

aversive conditioning/condicionamiento aversivo paradigma de condicionamiento en el cual los efectos aversivos (naúsea) son asociados con estímulos externos no deseados (beber alcohol). (pág. 613)

axon/axón prolongación de una célula nerviosa a través de la cual viaja el impulso nervioso para transmitir mensajes a otra célula (de neuronas, músculos, o glándulas) mediante ramificaciones terminales. (pág. 53)

babbling stage/fase balbuciente fase del desarrollo del lenguaje que se da aproximadamente a los cuatro meses de edad, y en la cual el infante espontáneamente emite sonidos que al principio no están relacionados con el idioma de la casa. (pág. 315)

barbiturates/barbitúricos drogas que deprimen la actividad del sistema nervioso central, reduciendo la ansiedad; pero que afectan la memoria y el discernimiento. (pág. 200)

basal metabolic rate/tasa de metabolismo basal cantidad de energía requerida por el organismo en reposo absoluto. (pág. 335)

basic research/investigación básica ciencia pura que tiene como propósito aumentar la base del conocimiento científico. (pág. 13)

basic trust/confianza básica según Erik Erikson, la percepción de que el mundo es predecible y fidedigno; esta percepción se forma durante la infancia a través de experiencias apropiadas con cuidadores sensibles. (pág. 429)

behavior genetics/genética del comportamiento estudio del poder relativo y de los límites de las influencias genéticas y ambientales en el comportamiento. (pág. 95)

behavior therapy/terapia del comportamiento terapia que aplica los principios de aprendizaje para lograr la eliminación de comportamientos no deseados. (pág. 611)

behavioral medicine/medicina conductual campo interdisciplinario que integra el conocimiento conductual y el de la medicina y aplica ese conocimiento a la salud y a la enfermedad. (pág. 397)

behavioral psychology/psicología conductista el estudio científico del comportamiento observable, y su explicación por los principios de aprendizaje. (pág. 10)

behaviorism/conductismo posición de que la psicología (1) debe ser una ciencia objetiva que (2) estudia el comportamiento sin referencia a los procesos mentales. La mayoría de los psicólogos en investigación hoy están de acuerdo con (1) pero no con (2). (págs. 6, 218)

belief perseverance/perseverancia de las creencias tendencia de las personas de adherirse a sus concepciones iniciales aún después de que la base para estas creencias ha sido desacreditada. (pág. 307)

binge-eating disorder/trastorno de alimentación compulsiva episodios significativos de ingestión compulsiva de alimentos, seguidos de angustia, indignación o sentimientos de culpabilidad, que no están seguidos de las purgas, los ayunos o los ejercicios extremos con propósitos compensatorios que caracterizan a la bulimia nerviosa. (pág. 337)

binocular cues/indicadores binoculares indicadores de profundidad, tales como la disparidad de la retina, que dependen del uso de los dos ojos. (pág. 153)

biofeedback/bio-retroalimentación sistema para grabar electrónicamente, amplificando y retroalimentando información con respecto un estado fisiológico sutil, como presión arterial o tensión muscular. (págs. 240, C-8)

biological psychology/psicología biológica rama de la psicología cuya concentración es la conexión entre la biología y la conducta. (Algunos biopsicólogos se denominan *neurocientíficos conductuales, neuropsicólogos, geneticistas de la conducta, psicólogos fisiológicos* o *biopsicólogos*). (págs. 10, 52)

biomedical therapy/terapia biomédica medicamentos recetados o procedimientos médicos que actúan directamente en el sistema nervioso del paciente. (pág. 628)

biopsychosocial approach/enfoque biopsicosocial enfoque integrado que incorpora niveles de análisis biológicos, psicológicos y socioculturales. (pág. 10)

bipolar disorder/trastorno bipolar trastorno que afecta el estado de ánimo; la persona alterna entre la desesperanza y el letargo de la depresión y el estado eufórico de la manía. (Anteriormente llamado *trastorno maníaco-depresivo.*) (pág. 581)

blind spot/punto ciego punto en el que el nervio óptico abandona el ojo, creando un punto "ciego" porque no se encuentra ninguna célula receptora en este punto. (pág. 127)

bottom-up processing/procesamiento de abajo para arriba análisis que empieza con los receptores sensoriales y continúa para arriba hasta que llega al centro de integración sensorial del cerebro. (pág. 116)

brainstem/tronco encefálico parte más antigua y meollo del cerebro, empezando donde la médula espinal se inflama al entrar en el cráneo; el tronco encefálico es responsable por las funciones automáticas de supervivencia. (pág. 69)

Broca's area/área de Broca controla el procesamiento del lenguaje—una área del lóbulo frontal izquierdo, que dirige los movimientos musculares involucrados en el lenguaje y la producción del habla. (pág. 80)

bulimia nervosa/bulimia nerviosa trastorno de la alimentación caracterizado por episodios de ingestión masiva y descontrolada de alimentos, generalmente de alto contenido calórico, seguido por repetidos vómitos, uso de laxantes, ayuno o ejercicio excesivo. (pág. 337)

bystander effect/efecto espectador tendencia que tienen las personas a no brindar ayuda si hay otras personas presentes. (pág. 686)

Cannon-Bard theory/teoría de Cannon-Bard teoría de que un estímulo que despierta emociones simultáneamente puede provocar (1) respuestas fisiológicas y (2) la experiencia subjetiva de la emoción. (pág. 367)

case study/caso técnica de observación en la cual se estudia a una persona a profundidad con la esperanza de revelar principios universales. (pág. 26)

catharsis/catarsis descargo emocional. La hipótesis de catarsis mantiene que el "librar" la energía agresiva (a través de acción o fantasía) alivia los impulsos agresivos. (pág. 388)

central nervous system (CNS) / sistema nervioso central (SNC) el cerebro y la médula espinal. (pág. 59)

central route persuasion/la persuasión ruta central ruta de un cambio de actitud cuando las personas interesadas se centran en los argumentos y responden con pensamientos favorables. (pág. 646)

cerebellum [sehr-uh-BELL-um] **/cerebelo** "cerebro pequeño" situado en la parte posterior del tronco encefálico; sus funciones incluyen el proceso sensorial y la coordinación del movimiento y del equilibrio. (pág. 70)

cerebral [seh-REE-bruhl] **cortex/corteza cerebral** tejido intrincado de células neurales interconectadas que cubren los hemisferios cerebrales; el centro de control y procesamiento de información del cuerpo. (pág. 74)

change blindness/ceguera al cambio incapacidad de percibir cambios en el entorno. (pág. 119)

chromosomes/cromosomas estructuras semejantes a hilos conformados de moléculas de ADN que contienen los genes. (pág. 95)

chunking/división en pedazos el organizar los datos en unidades (pedazos) familiares y manejables; a menudo se da de manera automática. (pág. 264)

circadian [ser-KAY-dee-an] **rhythm/ritmo circadiano** reloj biológico; ritmos regulares del cuerpo (por ejemplo, temperatura y estado de vigilia) que ocurren en ciclos de 24 horas. (pág. 177)

classical conditioning/condicionamiento clásico tipo de aprendizaje en el cual un individuo aprende a asociar dos o más estímulos y a anticipar hechos. (pág. 218)

client-centered therapy/terapia centrado en el cliente terapia humanística, desarrollada por Carl Rogers, en la cual el terapeuta utiliz técnicas como el escuchar activamente dentro de un ambiente real de aceptación y empatía a fin de facilitar el crecimiento de los clientes. (También llamada *terapia centrada en la persona*) (pág. 609)

clinical psychology/psicología clínica rama de la psicología que estudia, evalúa y trata a las personas con trastornos psicológicos. (pág. 13)

cochlea [KOHK-lee-uh] **/cóclea** estructura ósea en forma de tubo enrollado en espiral, llena de fluídos, que se encuentra en el oído interno. A través de la cóclea las ondas sonoras activan los impulsos nerviosos. (pág. 135)

cochlear implant/implante coclear dispositivo que convierte sonidos en signos eléctricos y estimula el nervio auditorio a través de electrodos implantados en la cóclea. (pág. 138)

cognition/cognición todas las actividades mentales asociadas con el pensar, saber, recordar y comunicar. (págs. 298, 417)

cognitive-behavioral therapy/terapia cognitiva-conductual terapia popular que integra la terapia cognitiva (cambiar el pensamiento de autoderrota) y la terapia conductual (modificar la conducta) (pág. 616)

cognitive dissonance theory/teoría de la disonancia cognitiva teoría que dice que siempre que tenemos dos ideas, actitudes, u opiniones (cognición) que se contradicen (disonancia), hacemos algo para reducir esta disonancia. Por ejemplo, cuando la percepción de nuestras actitudes y la de nuestras acciones chocan, podemos reducir la disonancia resultante cambiando nuestras actitudes. (pág. 648)

cognitive map/mapa cognitivo representación mental del entorno familiar. Por ejemplo, después de explorar un laberinto, las ratas se comportan como si hubiesen aprendido un mapa cognitivo de éste. (pág. 236)

cognitive neuroscience/neurociencia cognitiva estudio interdisciplinario de la actividad cerebral relacionada con la cognición (incluye la percepción, el pensamiento, la memoria y el lenguaje). (págs. 7, 89)

cognitive psychology/psicología cognoscitiva el estudio científico de todas las actividades mentales se asoció con pensamiento, sabiendo, para recordar, y para comunicar. (pág. 10)

cognitive therapy/terapia cognitiva terapia que ayuda a los pacientes a pensar y actuar de un modo más realista y adaptativo. Está basada en el supuesto de que los pensamientos intervienen entre los eventos y nuestras reacciones emocionales. (pág. 614)

collective unconscious/inconsciente colectivo concepto de Carl Jung de un depósito de memorias de la historia de nuestra especie compartido por la humanidad. (pág. 485)

collectivism/colectivismo el dar prioridad al bien del grupo sobre el del individuo (generalmente la familia o grupo de trabajo), y definiendo de esta manera la identidad del individuo. (pág. 516)

color constancy/constancia de color el percibir que las superficies familiares parecen mantener la apariencia cromática incluso bajo condiciones luminosas muy diferentes. (pág. 158)

companionate love/amor compañero apego afectuoso profundo que sentimos por aquéllos con quienes nuestras vidas se entrelazan. (pág. 684)

complementary and alternative medicine (CAM) / medicina complementaria y alternativa tratamientos de salud que aún no se han puesto a prueba y tienen el propósito de complementar o de servir como alternativas a la medicina convencional; generalmente no se enseñan en las escuelas de medicina, no son utilizados en los hospitales, ni son reembolsados por las compañías de seguros. Cuando los estudios demuestran que una terapia es segura y eficaz, ésta pasa a formar parte de la práctica médica aceptada. (pág. C-8)

concept/concepto agrupación mental de objetos, eventos, ideas, o personas con características similares. (pág. 298)

concrete operational stage/etapa del pensamiento lógico-concreto en la teoría de Piaget, la fase del desarrollo cognitivo (desde aproximadamente los 6 o 7 años hasta los 11 años de edad) durante la cual los niños desarrollan las operaciones mentales que les permiten pensar lógicamente sobre eventos concretos. (pág. 423)

conditioned reinforcer/refuerzo condicionado también llamado *refuerzo secundario*. Un estímulo neutro es apareado con un reforzamiento primario hasta que asume las propiedades del primero. (pág. 231)

conditioned response (CR) / respuesta condicionada en el condicionamiento clásico, la respuesta aprendida a un estímulo previamente neutral (pero ahora condicionado) (pág. 219)

conditioned stimulus (CS) / estímulo condicionado en el condicionamiento clásico, un estímulo originalmente irrelevante que, después de ser asociado con un estímulo incondicionado (EI) produce una respuesta condicionada. (pág. 219)

conduction hearing loss/pérdida auditiva conductiva pérdida de audición causada por daño al sistema mecánico que conduce las ondas sonoras a la cóclea. (pág. 138)

cones/conos receptores de luz de la retina que se concentran cerca del centro de la retina y que funcionan a la luz del día o en condiciones con buena iluminación. Los conos ayudan a percibir el color y los detalles. (pág. 126)

confirmation bias/predisposición a buscar confirmación tendencia a buscar información que confirme nuestras ideas preconcebidas y a ignorar o distorsionar la evidencia contradictoria. (pág. 303)

conflict/conflicto incompatibilidad percibida de acciones, metas o ideas. (pág. 688)

conformity/conformidad el adaptar nuestro comportamiento o pensamiento para que coincida con una norma del grupo. (pág. 651)

confounding variable/variable de confusión Se dice de la variable, distinta de la variable independiente, que tendría influencia sobre la variable dependiente. Los investigadores deben controlar las variables de confusión para poder sacar conclusiones de causa y efecto durante un experimento. (pág. 35)

consciousness/conciencia percepción de nosotros mismos y de nuestro ambiente. (págs. 89, 176)

conservation/conservación principio de que las propiedades de masa, volumen y número no varían a pesar de los cambios en las formas de los objetos. (Piaget era de la opinión que éste formaba parte de la etapa operacional concreta). (pág. 421)

content validity/validez de contenido grado en el cual una prueba promueve el comportamiento que es de interés (como una prueba de conducir que promueve tareas relativas a la conducción. (pág. 538)

continuous reinforcement/refuerzo continuo el reforzar la respuesta deseada cada vez que ocurre. (pág. 232)

control group/grupo control en un experimento, grupo de participantes que no están expuestos al tratamiento en cuestión; contrasta con el grupo experimental y sirve como comparación para evaluar el efecto del tratamiento. (pág. 35)

conversion disorder/trastorno de conversión trastorno somatoforme poco común en el que una persona experimenta síntomas físicos genuinos y muy específicos que no se pueden relacionar con una base fisiológica. (pág. 577)

coping/afrontamiento el aliviar la tensión utilizando métodos emocionales, cognitivos o conductuales. (pág. C-1)

coronary heart disease/cardiopatía coronaria obstrucción de los vasos que nutren el músculo del corazón; la causa principal de muerte en muchos países desarrollados. (pág. 401)

corpus callosum [KOR-pus kah-LOW-sum] **/cuerpo calloso** banda grande de fibras neurales que conecta los dos hemisferios del cerebro y lleva mensajes entre ellos. (pág. 84)

correlation/correlación medida del grado en que dos factores varían juntos y por ende, si es que uno de ellos es capaz de predecir el otro. El coeficiente de correlación es la expresión matemática de relación yendo de −1 a +1. (pág. 29)

correlation coefficient/coeficiente de correlación índice estadístico de la relación entre dos cosas (de −1 a +1). (pág. 29)

counseling psychology/psicología de orientación división de la psicología que ayuda a las personas con problemas de la vida diaria (a menudo relacionados con la escuela, el trabajo o el matrimonio) y a lograr bienestar. (pág. 13)

counterconditioning/contracondicionamiento procedimiento de terapia conductual en el que se emplea el condicionamiento clásico para producir nuevas respuestas a estímulos que provocan conductas no deseadas; incluye *las terapias de exposición y el condicionamiento aversivo.* (pág. 611)

creativity/creatividad habilidad de producir ideas originales y valiosas. (pág. 301)

critical period/período crítico período óptimo poco después el nacimiento cuando la exposición de un organismo a ciertos estímulos o experiencias produce el desarrollo apropiado. (pág. 427)

critical thinking/pensamiento crítico pensamiento que no acepta argumentos y conclusiones a ciegas. Más bien examina las suposiciones, percibe los valores ocultos, analiza la evidencia y evalúa las conclusiones. (pág. 24)

cross-sectional study/estudio transversal estudio en el que se comparan personas de diferentes edades. (pág. 463)

crystallized intelligence/inteligencia cristalizada nuestro conocimiento acumulado y nuestras destrezas verbales; tiende a aumentar con la edad. (pág. 464)

CT (computed tomography) scan/tomografía computarizada (TC) una serie de fotografías de rayos X tomadas desde ángulos diferentes y combinadas mediante un ordenador en una representación compuesta de una sección del cuerpo. También se llama *CAT scan.* (pág. 68)

culture/cultura comportamientos duraderos, ideas, actitudes y tradiciones compartidos por un grupo de personas y transmitidos de una generación a la siguiente. (págs. 43, 661)

debriefing/aclaración postexperimental postexperimental la explicación de un estudio, incluyendo su finalidad y los engaños, a sus participantes. (pág. 45)

defense mechanisms/mecanismos de defensa en la teoría psicoanalítica, los métodos de protección del ego para reducir la ansiedad distorsionando la realidad inconcientemente. (pág. 483)

deindividuation/desindividualización pérdida de identidad personal y del sentido de responsabilidad en situaciones de grupo que fomentan la excitación y el anonimato. (pág. 659)

déjà vu/déjà vu sensación de haber vivido antes una experiencia específica. Señales de la presente situación pueden de manera subconsciente activar la recuperación de una experiencia previa. (pág. 276)

delta wave/sondas delta ondas cerebrales amplias y lentas asociadas con el sueño profundo. (pág. 180)

delusions/delirios creencias falsas, a menudo de persecución o grandeza, que pueden acompañar los trastornos psicóticos. (pág. 590)

dendrite/dendrita ramas de una neurona que reciben y orientan la información hacia el cuerpo celular. (pág. 53)

denial/negación mecanismo de defensa por el que las personas se niegan a creer o incluso a percibir realidades dolorosas. (pág. 484)

dependent variable/variable dependiente factor resultante; el factor que puede cambiar en respuesta a cambios en la variable independiente. (pág. 35)

depressants/depresivos drogas (como el alcohol, barbitúricos y opiatos) que hacen más lenta o reducen la actividad neuronal y física. (pág. 199)

depth perception/percepción de profundidad habilidad de ver objetos en tres dimensiones aunque las imágenes percibidas por la retina son bidimensionales. Esto nos permite juzgar la distancia. (pág. 153)

developmental psychology/psicología del desarrollo rama de la psicología que estudia el cambio físico, cognitivo y social a lo largo de la vida. (págs. 13, 411)

difference threshold/umbral diferencial diferencia mínima requerida para distinguir un estímulo de otro el cincuenta por ciento de las veces. Experimentamos el umbral diferencial como una diferencia apenas perceptible. (pág. 122)

discrimination/discriminación (1) en el condicionamiento clásico, la habilidad adquirida de distinguir entre un estímulo condicionado y aquellos estímulos que no señalan un estímulo sin condición. (2) comportamiento negativo injustificable hacia un grupo o sus miembros. (págs. 222, 664)

discriminative stimulus/estímulo discriminativo en el condicionamiento operante, un estímulo que provoca una respuesta después de la asociación con el refuerzo (en contraste a los estímulos relacionados no relacionados con el refuerzo). (pág. 230)

displacement/desplazamiento mecanismo de defensa psicoanalítico mediante el cual se cambian los impulsos sexuales o agresivos hacia un objeto o persona más aceptable o menos amenazante, como el redirigir la ira hacia un escape más seguro. (pág. 483)

dissociation/disociación separación de la conciencia que permite que algunos pensamientos y comportamientos ocurran simultáneamente con otros. (pág. 195)

dissociative disorders/trastornos disociativos trastornos en los que el conocimiento conciente se separa (se disocia) de los recuerdos, pensamientos y sentimientos anteriores. (pág. 577)

dissociative identity disorder (DID) / trastorno de identidad disociativo trastorno disociativo poco común en el que una persona exhibe dos o más personalidades distintas que se alternan. Anteriormente se denominaba *trastorno de personalidad múltiple.* (pág. 578)

DNA (deoxyribonucleic acid) / ADN (ácido desoxirribonucleico) molécula compleja que contiene la información genética de la que se constituyen los cromosomas. (pág. 95)

double-blind procedure/procedimiento doble ciego procedimiento experimental en el cual los participantes y el personal de la investigación ignoran (están ciegos) si los participantes de la investigación han recibido el tratamiento o un placebo. Normalmente se utiliza en los estudios de evaluación de drogas. (pág. 35)

Down syndrome/síndrome de Down retraso mental y trastornos físicos provocados por una copia adicional del vigésimo primer cromosoma. (pág. 542)

dream/sueño sucesión de imágenes, emociones y pensamientos que pasan a través de la mente de una persona durmiente. Los sueños se caracterizan por su fantasía alucinante, falta de ilación e incongruencias, y por la aceptación delirante del contenido de éstos de parte del soñador y las dificultades posteriores para recordarlo. (pág. 188)

drive-reduction theory/teoría de la reducción del impulso idea que una necesidad fisiológica crea un estado de excitación (un impulso) que motiva al organismo a satisfacer esta necesidad. (pág. 329)

DSM-IV-TR/DSM-IV-TR *Manual diagnóstico y estadístico de trastornos mentales,* Cuarta edición. Edición corregida y aumentada libro publicado y actualizado por la Asociación psiquiátrica estadounidense; sistema de amplia difusión para la clasificación de trastornos psicológicos. (pág. 565)

dual processing/procesamiento dual principio que afirma que la información a menudo se procesa por vías conscientes e inconscientes separadas. (pág. 90)

echoic memory/memoria ecoica memoria sensorial-auditiva de corto plazo; si la atención está en otra parte, se pueden recordar sonidos y palabras en los siguientes 3 ó 4 segundos. (pág. 266)

eclectic approach/aproximación ecléctica enfoque de la psicoterapia que, dependiendo de los problemas del cliente, utiliza técnicas de distintas formas de terapia. (pág. 606)

Ecstasy (MDMA) / éxtasis (MDMA) estimulante sintético y alucinógeno leve. Produce euforia e intimidad social, pero tiene riesgos de salud a corto plazo. Además, a largo plazo daña las neuronas que producen la serotonina, y afecta el ánimo y el proceso de cognición. (pág. 205)

educational psychology/psicología educativa el estudio de procesos cuán psicológicos afecta y puede aumentar la enseñanza y aprender. (pág. 13)

effortful processing/procesamiento con esfuerzo codificación que requiere atención y esfuerzo concientes. (pág. 259)

ego/ego parte conciente y ejecutiva de la personalidad que, de acuerdo a Freud, media entre las demandas del id, el superego, y la realidad. El ego opera bajo *el principio de realidad,* satisfaciendo los deseos del id en formas que de manera realista le brindarán placer y no dolor. (pág. 481)

egocentrism/egocentrismo en la teoría de Piaget, la dificultad de los niños en la etapa preoperacional de aceptar el punto de vista ajeno. (pág. 421)

electroconvulsive therapy (ECT) / terapia electroconvulsiva (TEC) terapia biomédica para pacientes severamente deprimidos en la que una corriente eléctrica de corta duración se envía a través del cerebro de un paciente anestesiado. (pág. 632)

electroencephalogram (EEG) / electroencefalograma (EEG) registro en el que se amplifican las ondas de actividad bioeléctrica del cerebro. Estas ondas son medidas a través de electrodos en el cuero cabelludo. (pág. 67)

embryo/embrión etapa de desarrollo en el organismo humano a partir de las dos semanas de fertilización hasta el segundo mes. (pág. 412)

emerging adulthood/adultez emergente entre algunos individuos de culturas modernas, etapa aproximadamente entre el final de la adolescencia y los veinticinco años de edad, en que se trata de salvar la brecha que se da entre la dependencia adolescente y la independencia completa del adulto responsable. (pág. 454)

emotion/emoción reacción que involucra a todo el organismo, e incluye (1) excitación fisiológica, (2) comportamientos expresivos y (3) experiencia conciente. (pág. 366)

emotion-focused coping/afrontamiento centrado en la emoción el intentar aliviar el estrés evitando o ignorando los factores estresantes, y atendiendo a las necesidades emocionales relacionadas con la reacción al estrés. (pág. C-1)

emotional intelligence/inteligencia emocional habilidad de percibir, entender, administrar y utilizar las emociones. (pág. 528)

empirically derived test/prueba empíricamente derivada prueba (tal como el MMPI) desarrollada a partir de un grupo de ítems y escogiendo aquéllos que discriminan entre grupos. (pág. 496)

empiricism/empirismo la vista que el conocimiento origina en la experiencia y en que ciencia debe, por lo tanto depende de observación y experimentación. (pág. 3)

encoding/codificación el procesar información al sistema de memoria—por ejemplo, extrayendo el significado. (pág. 257)

endocrine [EN-duh-krin] **system/sistema endocrino** sistema "lento" de comunicación química del cuerpo; un conjunto de glándulas que secretan hormonas al torrente sanguíneo. (pág. 62)

endorphins [en-DOR-fins] **/endorfinas** "morfina adentro"—neurotransmisores naturales similares a los opiatos que están asociados con el control del dolor y con el placer. (pág. 57)

environment/entorno toda influencia que no es de carácter genético, desde la nutrición prenatal hasta las personas y cosas que nos rodean. (pág. 95)

equity/equidad condición en la cual las personas reciben de manera proporcional lo que aportan a una relación. (pág. 684)

estrogens/estrógeno hormona sexual, por ejemplo, el estradiol, secretada en mayor cantidad en la mujer que en el hombre, que contribuye a formar las características sexuales de la mujer. En las mamíferas no humanas, los niveles de estrógeno alcanzan el nivel máximo durante la ovulación, promoviendo la receptividad sexual. (pág. 350)

evidence-based practice/práctica basada en la evidencia toma de decisiones que combina los mejores estudios disponibles con la experiencia clínica y las características y preferencias del paciente. (pág. 623)

evolutionary psychology/psicología evolutiva el estudio de las raíces de conducta y procesos mentales que utilizan los principios de selección natural. (págs. 10, 103)

experiment/experimento método de investigación en el que un científico manipula uno o más factores (variables independientes) para observar el efecto en algún comportamiento o proceso mental (variable dependiente). *La asignación aleatoria* de participantes tiene como finalidad el controlar otros factores pertinentes. (pág. 34)

experimental group/grupo experimental durante un experimento, grupo que está expuesto al tratamiento, o sea, la variable independiente. (pág. 35)

experimental psychology/psicología experimental el estudio de conducta y pensando utilizar el método experimental. (pág. 6)

explicit memory/memoria explícita recolección conciente de hechos y experiencias que uno puede "declarar." (También llamada *memoria declaratoria*). (pág. 272)

exposure therapies/terapias de exposición técnicas conductistas, como la insensibilización sistemática, que tratan los estados de ansiedad exponiendo a las personas (en su imaginación o en la realidad) a las cosas que temen y evitan. (pág. 611)

external locus of control/locus de control externo percepción de que nuestra suerte o las fuerzas externas que existen más allá de nuestro control, determinan nuestro destino. (pág. 505)

extinction/extinción debilitación de la respuesta condicionada (RC); en el condicionamiento clásico ocurre cuando el estímulo incondicionado (EI) no viene detrás del estímulo condicionado (EC). En el condicionamiento operante la extinción ocurre cuando ya no se refuerza una respuesta específica. (pág. 221)

extrasensory perception (ESP) / percepción extrasensorial (PES) afirmación controvertida de que es posible percibir por medios distintos de los cinco sentidos; incluye la telepatía, la clarividencia y la precognición. (pág. 166)

extrinsic motivation/motivación extrínseca deseo de desempeñar un comportamiento con el propósito de recibir recompensas prometidas o evitar amenazas de castigo. (pág. 237)

facial feedback/reacción facial el efecto de expresiones faciales en emociones experimentadas, como cuando una expresión facial de la ira o la felicidad intensifica sentimientos de la ira o la felicidad. (pág. 383)

factor analysis/análisis factorial procedimiento estadístico que identifica grupos de artículos relacionados (llamados *factores*) en una prueba. Se utiliza para identificar distintas dimensiones de desempeño que determinan el puntaje total que recibe una persona. (pág. 524)

family therapy/terapia de familia terapia en la que se considera que la familia es un sistema. Según esta terapia, los comportamientos no deseados de un individuo son influenciados por otros miembros de la familia o dirigidos a éstos. (pág. 617)

feature detectors/detectores de características neuronas en el cerebro que responden a características específicas de un estímulo tales como forma, ángulo o movimiento. (pág. 129)

feel-good, do-good phenomenon/fenómeno de sentirse bien, hacer el bien tendencia a ser serviciales cuando estamos de buen humor. (pág. 390)

fetal alcohol syndrome (FAS) / síndrome de alcoholismo fetal (SAF) anomalías físicas y cognitivas en los niños causadas por la ingestión de alcohol de las madres durante el embarazo. En casos agudos, los síntomas incluyen desproporciones faciales observables. (pág. 413)

fetus/feto organismo humano en vías de desarrollo a partir de las 9 semanas de concepción hasta el nacimiento. (pág. 412)

figure-ground/figura-fondo organización del campo visual en objetos (*figuras*) que se distinguen de sus ambientes (*fondos*). (pág. 151)

fixation/fijación (1) incapacidad de ver un problema desde una perspectiva nueva mediante el empleo de una postura mental distinta. (2) de acuerdo a Freud, un permanente foco de energía en busca de placer en una etapa psicosexual temprana cuando los conflictos todavía no estaban resueltos. (págs. 303, 483)

fixed-interval schedule/programa de intervalo fijo en el condicionamiento operante, un programa de refuerzo que sólo refuerza una respuesta después de un lapso de tiempo específico. (pág. 233)

fixed-ratio schedule/programa de frecuencia fija en el condicionamiento operante, un programa de refuerzo que sólo refuerza una respuesta después de un número específico de respuestas. (pág. 232)

flashbulb memory/memoria de flash memoria clara de un momento o evento emocionalmente significativo. (pág. 270)

flow/flujo el sentirse completamente involucrado en una actividad por sí mismo. El yo desaparece. El tiempo vuela. Todo el ser está involucrado y empleando las habilidades en todo su potencial. (pág. B-1)

fluid intelligence/inteligencia fluida capacidad que tenemos de razonar rápidamente y de manera abstracta; tiende a disminuir en los adultos muy mayores. (pág. 464)

fMRI (functional magnetic resonance imaging) / imágenes de resonancia magnética funcional técnica para observar la circulación sanguínea y, por lo tanto, la actividad cerebral comparando resultados sucesivos de exámenes de resonancia magnética. Los resultados del examen de resonancia magnética funcional muestran la función cerebral. (pág. 68)

foot-in-the-door phenomenon/fenómeno de pie en la puerta tendencia de la gente que ha accedido a algo pequeño en primer lugar, a después satisfacer una demanda más grande. (pág. 647)

formal operational stage/período operacional formal en la teoría de Piaget, el período en el desarrollo cognitivo (normalmente empieza a los 12 años) durante el que la persona empieza a pensar lógicamente sobre conceptos abstractos. (pág. 423)

fovea/fóvea punto central de enfoque de la retina alrededor del cual se agrupan los conos del ojo. (pág. 127)

framing/enmarcamiento manera como se presenta una situación; el cómo se enmarca una situación puede afectar de manera significativa las decisiones y juicios. (pág. 311)

fraternal twins/mellizos se desarrollan de dos óvulos fecundados distintos. Genéticamente no están más cercanos que los hermanos y hermanas; pero comparten un medio ambiente fetal. (pág. 97)

free association/asociación libre en psicoanálisis, un método de explorar el inconciente en el que la persona se relaja y dice lo primero que le viene a la mente, no importa cuán trivial o incómodo. (pág. 480)

frequency/frecuencia número de ondas completas que pasan un punto en un tiempo dado (por ejemplo, por segundo). (pág. 134)

frequency theory/teoría de frecuencia en la audición, la teoría que postula que la proporción de impulsos nerviosos que viaja por el nervio auditivo es igual a la frecuencia de un tono, permitiéndonos percibir el tono. (pág. 137)

frontal lobes/lóbulos frontales parte de la corteza cerebral que se halla inmediatamente detrás de la frente; tiene que ver con el habla y los movimientos musculares, así como la planificación y la formación de opiniones. (pág. 74)

frustration-aggression principle/principio de frustración-agresión principio de que la frustración—el bloqueo de un intento para lograr alguna meta—crea ira, la cual puede generar agresión. (pág. 672)

functional fixedness/fijación funcional tendencia de pensar en las cosas sólo en función de su uso más generalizado; un impedimento para resolver problemas. (pág. 303)

functionalism/funcionalismo escuela de la psicología que se concentraba en el funcionamiento de nuestros procesos mentales y conductuales y en cómo éstos nos permiten adaptarnos, sobrevivir y prosperar. (pág. 5)

fundamental attribution error/error fundamental de la atribución tendencia de los observadores, al analizar la conducta de otra persona, a subestimar el impacto de la situación y a sobrestimar el impacto de la disposición personal. (pág. 644)

gate-control theory/teoría de control de la puerta del dolor teoría de que la médula espinal contiene una "puerta" neurológica que bloquea las señales de dolor o les permite proseguir al cerebro. La "puerta" se abre por la actividad de las señales de dolor que viajan a través de pequeñas fibras nerviosas y se cierra por la actividad en las fibras más grandes o por información procedente del cerebro. (pág. 143)

gender/género en psicología, las características biológicas y sociales por las cuales la sociedad define *hombre y mujer.* (pág. 435)

gender identity/identidad de género sensación que tenemos de ser hombre o mujer. (pág. 440)

gender role/rol de género expectativas de cómo las mujeres y los hombres deben comportarse. (pág. 439)

gender typing/tipificación de género adquisición de un rol masculino o femenino tradicional. (pág. 440)

general adaptation syndrome (GAS) / síndrome de adaptación general (SAG) concepto de Selye que afirma que la respuesta de adaptación del cuerpo al estrés se presenta en los tres estados siguientes: alarma, resistencia y agotamiento. (pág. 399)

general intelligence (g) / factor g de inteligencia general factor de inteligencia general que de acuerdo a Spearman y otros subyace habilidades mentales específicas y es por lo tanto cuantificado por cada tarea de las pruebas de inteligencia. (pág. 524)

generalization/generalización tendencia, una vez que una respuesta ha sido condicionada, a que los estímulos similares al estímulo condicionado provoquen respuestas similares. (pág. 222)

generalized anxiety disorder/trastorno de ansiedad generalizado trastorno de ansiedad en el que la persona está constantemente tensa, aprensiva, y en estado de excitación del sistema nervioso autonómico. (pág. 570)

genes/gene unidades bioquímicas de la herencia que constituyen los cromosomas; un segmento de ADN capaz de sintetizar una proteína. (pág. 95)

genome/genoma instrucciones completas para crear un organismo; consiste de todo el material genético en los cromosomas de ese organismo. (pág. 96)

gestalt/Gestalt un todo organizado. Los psicólogos de la Gestalt ponen énfasis en nuestra tendencia a integrar segmentos de información en todos significativos. (pág. 151)

glial cells (glia)/células gliales células en el sistema nervioso que sostienen, nutren y protegen a las neuronas. (pág. 74)

glucose/glucosa forma de azúcar que circula en la sangre y provee de la mayor fuente de energía a los tejidos del cuerpo. Cuando su nivel es bajo, sentimos hambre. (pág. 333)

grammar/gramática en un idioma, un sistema de reglas que nos permite comunicarnos y entendernos con otros. (pág. 314)

GRIT/estrategia de de-escalamiento paso a paso GRIT (por sus siglas en inglés) estrategia diseñada para disminuir las tensiones internacionales. (pág. 692)

group polarization/efecto de polarización de grupo solidificación y fortalecimiento de las posiciones imperantes en un grupo a través de discusiones del grupo. (pág. 659)

grouping/agrupamiento tendencia perceptiva de organizar los estímulos en grupos coherentes. (pág. 152)

groupthink/pensamiento del grupo modo de pensar que ocurre cuando el deseo de armonía en un grupo de toma de decisiones anula la evaluación objetiva de las alternativas. (pág. 660)

habituation/habituación atenuación progresiva de una respuesta provocada por una estimulación repetitiva. Conforme los infantes se familiarizan con un estímulo visual debido su exposición repetida a éste, su interés desaparece y miran para otro lado más pronto. (págs. 216, 414)

hallucinations/alucinaciones percepciones sensoriales que no tienen relación con ningún evento externo. Por ejemplo, el ver algo sin ningún estímulo visual externo. (pág. 179)

hallucinogens/alucinógenos drogas psicodélicas ("que se manifiestan en la mente"), como el LSD que distorsionan las percepciones y evocan imágenes sensoriales sin ninguna inducción sensorial. (pág. 205)

health psychology/psicología de salud subdivisión de la psicología que contribuye a la medicina conductual. (pág. 397)

heritability/heredabilidad proporción de variación entre individuos que podemos atribuir a los genes. La heredabilidad de una característica puede variar dependiendo del rango de las poblaciones y de los ambientes estudiados. (pág. 100)

heuristic/heurística simple estrategia de pensamiento que nos permite formar juicios y resolver problemas de manera eficiente. Normalmente es más rápida que el utilizar *algoritmos;* pero también puede conducir a más errores. (pág. 300)

hierarchy of needs/jerarquía de necesidades pirámide de necesidades de Maslow, empezando en la base con las necesidades fisiológicas que se deben satisfacer antes de que se activen las necesidades de seguridad de nivel superior y luego las necesidades psicológicas. (pág. 330)

higher-order conditioning/condicionamiento de orden superior procedimiento en el que el estímulo condicionado de una experiencia condicionada se presenta a la vez que un nuevo estímulo neutral, creando un segundo (por lo general más débil) estímulo condicionado. Por ejemplo, un animal que ha aprendido que un tono precede un alimento, podría aprender que una luz precede el tono y responder sólo a la luz. (También se denomina *condicionamiento de segundo orden.)* (pág. 220)

hindsight bias/distorsión retrospectiva tendencia a creer después de saber un resultado, que uno lo habría previsto. (También conocido como el *fenómeno de "ya yo lo sabía".)* (pág. 20)

hippocampus/hipocampo centro neuronal que es parte del sistema límbico y contribuye al procesamiento de memorias explícitas para almacenarlas. (pág. 272)

homeostasis/homeóstasis tendencia a mantener un estado interior equilibrado; la regulación de cualquier aspecto químico del cuerpo, como la glucosa, a un nivel específico. (pág. 329)

hormones/hormonas mensajeros químicos producidos por las glándulas endocrinas que circulan en sangre y afectan a otros tejidos. (pág. 62)

hue/tono dimensión del color determinada por la longitud de onda de luz; lo que conocemos como los nombre de los colores: *azul, verde,* etc. (pág. 125)

human factors psychology/psicología de factores humanos división de psicología que explora cómo las personas y máquinas actúan recíprocamente y cómo las máquinas y los ambientes físicos pueden hacerse seguros y fáciles para usarse. (págs. 13, B-2)

humanistic psychology/psicología humanista perspectiva históricamente significativa que enfatizaba el potencial de crecimiento de las personas sanas y el potencial de crecimiento personal del individuo. (pág. 6)

hypnosis/hipnosis interacción social en la que una persona (el hipnotizador) le sugiere a otra (el sujeto) que ciertas percepciones, sentimientos, pensamientos o comportamientos ocurrirán espontáneamente. (pág. 192)

hypochondriasis/hipocondría trastorno somatoforme en el que una persona interpreta sensaciones físicas normales como síntomas de enfermedad. (pág. 577)

hypothalamus [hi-po-THAL-uh-muss] **/hipotálamo** estructura neural localizada debajo *(hipo)* del tálamo; regula varias actividades de mantenimiento (comer, beber y la temperatura corporal), contribuye a dirigir el sistema endocrino a través de la glándula pituitaria, y está conectado con las emociones y las recompensas. (pág. 72)

hypothesis/hipótesis predicción comprobable, a menudo implicada por una teoría. (pág. 25)

iconic memory/memoria icónica tipo de memoria sensorial momentánea que reacciona a los estímulos visuales; memoria fotográfica de imágenes que dura solo unas décimas de segundo. (pág. 266)

id/id contiene un depósito de energía psíquica inconciente que, según Freud, se esfuerza por satisfacer los impulsos sexuales y agresivos esenciales. El id opera bajo *el principio de placer,* exigiendo satisfacción inmediata. (pág. 481)

identical twins/gemelos monocigóticos se desarrollan a partir de un solo cigoto que se divide en dos, crando dos organismos con características genéticas idénticas. (pág. 96)

identification/identificación proceso en el que, según Freud, los niños incorporan los valores de sus padres en sus súper-egos en vías de desarrollo. (pág. 482)

identity/identidad idea que tenemos de nosotros mismos; según Erikson, el adolescente tiene la tarea de solidificar su sentido de identidad probando e integrando diversos modelos de conducta. (pág. 451)

illusory correlation/correlación ilusoria percepción de una relación dónde no hay ninguna. (pág. 32)

imagery/imágenes cuadros mentales; una ayuda poderosa para el procesamiento con esfuerzo, sobre todo cuando se combina con la codificación semántica. (pág. 263)

implicit memory/memoria implícita retención que es independiente de la memoria consciente. (También se denomina *memoria no declarativa* o *memoria procedimental.)* (pág. 272)

imprinting/impronta proceso en el que ciertos animales forman apegos durante un período crítico muy temprano en la vida. (pág. 427)

inattentional blindness/ceguera por falta de atención el no ver los objetos visibles cuando nuestra atención se dirige a otra parte. (pág. 118)

incentive/incentivo estímulo positivo o negativo medioambiental que motiva el comportamiento. (pág. 329)

independent variable/variable independiente factor experimental que se manipula; la variable cuyo efecto es el objeto de estudio. (pág. 35)

individualism/individualismo el dar prioridad a las propias metas sobre las metas del grupo y definir la propia identidad en términos de atributos personales en lugar de las identificaciones del grupo. (pág. 516)

industrial-organizational (I/O) psychology/psicología industrial y organizacional aplicación de conceptos y métodos psicológicos para optimizar el comportamiento humano en el centro de trabajo. (págs. 13, B-2)

informational social influence/influencia social informativa influencia resultante de la disposición de una persona para aceptar la opinión de los otros acerca de la realidad. (pág. 653)

informed consent/consentimiento informado un principio ético que participantes de investigación son dichos permitirlos bastante escoger si ellos desean participar. (pág. 45)

ingroup/endogrupo "nosotros": personas con las que tenemos una identidad en común. (pág. 668)

ingroup bias/favoritismo del endogrupo tendencia a favorecer al grupo al que pertenecemos. (pág. 668)

inner ear/oído interno parte más profunda de la oreja; contiene la cóclea, los canales semicirculares, y el vestíbulo. (pág. 135)

insight/sagacidad comprensión súbita y a menudo original de la solución a un problema en contraste con las soluciones basadas en estrategias. (págs. 236, 300)

insight therapies/terapias psicodinámicas variedad de terapias que tienen el propósito de mejorar el funcionamiento psicológico aumentando el nivel de conciencia que tiene el cliente de sus motivos y defensas subyacentes. (pág. 609)

insomnia/insomnio problemas recurrentes para dormir o quedarse dormido. (pág. 185)

instinct/instinto comportamiento complejo que está enraigado y es innato en cada especie. (pág. 328)

intellectual disability/discapacidad intelectual (anteriormente conocido como el retraso mental) cuadro de capacidad mental limitada marcada por un cociente intelectual de 70 o menos, y por la dificultad de adaptarse a las exigencias de la vida; varía de leve a profundo. (pág. 542)

intelligence/inteligencia calidad mental que consiste en la habilidad de aprender de la experiencia, resolver problemas y utilizar el conocimiento para adaptarse a nuevas situaciones. (pág. 524)

intelligence quotient (IQ) / cociente intelectual (CI) definido originalmente como la proporción entre la edad mental y edad cronológica multiplicada por 100. En las pruebas de inteligencia contemporáneas, se expresa de forma normalizada para que el CI medio en un grupo de edad sea 100. (pág. 534)

intelligence test/prueba de inteligencia método para evaluar las aptitudes mentales de un individuo y compararlas con las de otros utilizando puntajes numéricos. (pág. 524)

intensity/intensidad cantidad de energía en una onda de luz o en una onda sonora que percibimos como brillo o fuerza ,determinada por la amplitud de la onda. (pág. 125)

interaction/interacción acción que se ejerce recíprocamente cuando el efecto de un factor (como el ambiente) depende de otro factor (como la herencia). (pág. 101)

internal locus of control/locus de control interno impresión de que controlamos nuestro propio destino. (pág. 505)

interneurons/interneuronas neuronas del cerebro y la médula espinal que se comunican internamente e intervienen entre la estimulación sensorial y las respuestas motoras. (pág. 53)

interpretation/interpretación en psicoanálisis, las observaciones del analista con relación al significado de los sueños, las resistencias, y otros comportamientos y eventos significativos, a fin de promover la sagacidad. (pág. 607)

intimacy/intimidad en la teoría de Erikson, la habilidad de formar relaciones íntimas, amorosas. Una de las tareas principales del desarrollo de la adolescencia tardía y la adultez temprana. (pág. 452)

intrinsic motivation/motivación intrínseca deseo de expresar un comportamiento eficazmente por el comportamiento en sí. (pág. 237)

intuition/intuición sensación o pensamiento no esforzado, inmediato y automático, que contrasta con el razonamiento explícito y consciente. (pág. 308)

iris/iris anillo de tejido muscular que forma la porción coloreada del ojo alrededor de la pupila y controla el tamaño de la apertura de la pupila. (pág. 126)

James-Lange theory/teoría de James-Lange teoría que nuestra experiencia emocional es nuestra concicncia de nuestras respuestas fisiológicas a los estímulos que despiertan nuestras emociones. (pág. 367)

just-world phenomenon/hipótesis del "mundo justo" tendencia a creer que el mundo es justo y que las personas consiguen lo que se merecen y se merecen lo que consiguen. (pág. 670)

kinesthesis [kin-ehs-THEE-sehs] **/cinética** sistema que siente la posición y el movimiento de las partes individuales de cuerpo. (pág. 142)

language/lenguaje palabras habladas, escritas o en señas y las maneras que se combinan para comunicar significado. (pág. 313)

latent content/contenido latente según Freud, el significado subyacente de un sueño (distinto de su contenido manifiesto). (pág. 189)

latent learning/aprendizaje latente aprendizaje que ocurre; pero no es aparente hasta que aparece un incentivo para demostrarlo. (pág. 236)

law of effect/ley de efecto principio de Thorndike según el cual los comportamientos seguidos de consecuencias favorables son más probables y los comportamientos seguidos de consecuencias desfavorables son menos probables. (pág. 229)

learned helplessness/indefensión aprendida desesperación y resignación pasiva que un animal o un ser humano desarrollan cuando son incapaces de evitar repetidos eventos de aversión. (pág. 223)

learning/aprendizaje cambio relativamente permanente en el comportamiento de un organismo debido a la experiencia. (pág. 215)

lens/lente estructura transparente detrás de la pupila que cambia de forma para ayudar a enfocar las imágenes en la retina. (pág. 126)

lesion [LEE-zhuhn] **/lesión** destrucción del tejido. Una lesión cerebral es una destrucción del tejido cerebral ya sea por efectos naturales o experimentales. (pág. 67)

levels of analysis/niveles de análisis las distintas opiniones complementarias desde biológicas, pasando por las psicológicas, hasta socio-culturales, para analizar cualquier fenómeno. (pág. 10)

limbic system/sistema límbico sistema neuronal (que incluye *el hipocampo, la amígdala y el hipotálamo*) ubicado debajo de los hemisferios cerebrales; está asociado con las emociones y los instintos. (pág. 71)

linguistic determinism/determinismo lingüístico hipótesis de Whorf que el lenguaje determina la manera que pensamos. (pág. 319)

lobotomy/lobotomía procedimiento psicoquirúrgico actualmente inusual que se utilizó en una época para calmar a pacientes violentos o que padecían de emociones incontrolables. Mediante este procedimiento se separaba la conexión entre los lóbulos frontales y los centros de control de las emociones en las partes interiores del cerebro. (pág. 635)

long-term memory/memoria a largo plazo tipo de memoria relativamente permanente que mantiene grandes cantidades de información por un período largo de tiempo. Incluye el conocimiento, habilidades, y experiencias. (pág. 257)

long-term potentiation (LTP) / potenciación a largo plazo aumento en la eficiencia sináptica con breves y rápidas estimulaciones eléctricas repetitivas. Se cree que ésta es la base neuronal para el aprendizaje y la memoria. (pág. 269)

longitudinal study/estudio longitudinal investigación en la que las mismas personas son estudiadas y reexaminadas por un tiempo largo. (pág. 463)

LSD/LSD droga alucinógena poderosa; también conocido como *ácido (dietilamida del ácido lisérgico)*. (pág. 205)

lymphocytes/linfocitos dos tipos de glóbulos blancos que forman parte del sistema inmunológico: *los linfocitos del tipo B* se forman en la médula ósea y liberan anticuerpos que combaten las infecciones bacteriales; *los linfocitos del tipo T* se forman en el timo y en otro tejido linfático y atacan las células cancerosas, los virus y las sustancias extrañas. (pág. 403)

major depressive disorder/trastorno depresivo mayor trastorno del estado de ánimo en el cual una persona—sin una condición médica y sin el uso de drogas—se siente deprimida, inútil y muestra poco interés o placer en la mayoría de las actividades por un período de por lo menos dos semanas. (pág. 580)

mania/manía trastorno del estado de ánimo marcado por una condición hiperactiva y desenfrenadamente optimista. (pág. 581)

manifest content/contenido manifiesto según Freud, recuerdo de los eventos del sueño (distinto de su contenido latente u oculto). (pág. 188)

maturation/maduración procesos biológicos de crecimiento que permiten los cambios estructurados en el comportamiento y que no están relativamente influenciados por la experiencia. (pág. 416)

mean/media promedio aritmético de una distribución obtenidos sumando todos los puntajes y dividiendo el total por el número de puntajes. (pág. 38)

median/mediana punto medio en una distribución; la mitad de los puntajes están por encima y la mitad están por debajo de la mediana. (pág. 38)

medical model/modelo médico concepto que sostiene que las enfermedades tienen causas físicas que pueden *diagnosticarse, tratarse,* y, en la mayoría de los casos, *curarse.* Cuando es aplicado a los trastornos psíquicos, el modelo médico asume que estas enfermedades mentales pueden ser diagnosticadas basadas en sus síntomas y pueden curarse con terapia que puede incluir el tratamiento en un hospital psiquiátrico. (pág. 564)

medulla [muh-DUL-uh] **/médula** base del bulbo raquídeo; controla el latido del corazón y la respiración. (pág. 69)

memory/memoria el aprender de manera persistente a través del tiempo usando almacenaje y recuperación de la información. (pág. 255)

menarche [meh-NAR-key] **/menarquía** primer período menstrual. (pág. 447)

menopause/menopausia período en que la menstruación desaparece de manera natural; también se refiere a los cambios biológicos que una mujer experimenta al declinar su capacidad reproductora. (pág. 456)

mental age/edad mental medida de desempeño en pruebas de inteligencia diseñada por Bidet. La edad cronológica normalmente corresponde a un nivel dado de desempeño. Por ende, una criatura que se desempeña como una persona normal de ocho años, tiene una edad mental de ocho años. (pág. 533)

mental set/predisposición mental tipo de fijación en la cual el individuo trata de resolver un problema de una manera en particular que ha funcionado en el pasado. (pág. 303)

mere exposure effect/efecto de la mera exposición (EME) fenómeno que sostiene que la exposición repetida a estímulos novedosos aumenta su atracción. (pág. 678)

meta-analysis/metaanálisis procedimiento para combinar estadísticamente los resultados de distintos estudios de investigación. (pág. 621)

methamphetamine/metanfetamina droga poderosamente adictiva que estimula el sistema nervioso central con funciones corporales aceleradas y cambios de energía y estado de ánimo. Aparentemente, con el tiempo reduce los niveles mínimos de dopamina. (pág. 201)

middle ear/oído medio cámara entre el tímpano y cóclea que contiene tres huesos diminutos (martillo, yunque y estribo) que concentran las vibraciones del tímpano en la ventana ovalado de la cóclea. (pág. 135)

Minnesota Multiphasic Personality Inventory (MMPI) / Inventario multifásico de personalidad de Minesota (MMPI—por sus siglas en inglés) la prueba de personalidad más investigada y clínicamente utilizada. Originalmente se desarrolló para identificar trastornos emocionales (todavía se le considera éste su uso más apropiado), esta prueba hoy en día se utiliza con muchos otros propósitos. (pág. 496)

mirror-image perceptions/percepciones especulares opiniones mutuas que generalmente mantienen los individuos con sentimientos encontrados, por ejemplo, cuando uno de ellos se considera ético y pacífico y percibe al otro como malvado y agresivo. (pág. 689)

mirror neurons/neuronas espejo localizadas en la corteza cerebral, un grupo de neuronas que tienen la facultad de descargar impulsos tanto cuando el sujeto observa a otro realizar un movimiento como cuando es el sujeto quien lo hace. Este proceso de reflejar las acciones de otro puede posibilitar la imitación, el aprendizaje del lenguaje y la empatía. (pág. 243)

misinformation effect/efecto de desinformación el incorporar información engañosa en nuestra recolección de un evento. (pág. 286)

mnemonics [nih-MON-iks] **/mnemónica** ayudas de memoria, sobre todo esas técnicas que utilizan imágenes vívidas y dispositivos organizacionales. (pág. 263)

mode/moda el puntaje o puntajes que ocurren con mayor frecuencia en una distribución. (pág. 37)

modeling/modelado proceso de observar e imitar un comportamiento específico. (pág. 242)

molecular genetics/genética molecular división de la biología que estudia la estructura molecular y la función de los genes. (pág. 102)

monocular cues/indicaciones monoculares señales de profundidad como la interposición y la perspectiva lineal, que pueden ser extraídas de las imágenes de cada uno de los ojos. (pág. 154)

mood-congruent memory/memoria congruente con el humor tendencia a rememorar las experiencias que son consistentes con nuestro humor actual, bueno o malo. (pág. 278)

mood disorders/trastornos del estado de ánimo (también llamados trastornos afectivos) trastornos psicológicos caracterizados por estados extremos de ánimo. Véase *trastorno depresivo mayor, manía* y *trastorno bipolar.* (pág. 579)

morpheme/morfema en el lenguaje, la unidad más pequeña de significado; puede ser una palabra o parte de una palabra (como un prefijo). (pág. 314)

motivation/motivación necesidad o deseo que da energía y dirige el comportamiento. (pág. 328)

motor cortex/corteza motriz área en la parte posterior de los lóbulos frontales que controla los movimientos voluntarios. (pág. 75)

motor neurons/neuronas motrices neuronas que transmiten la información del cerebro y la médula espinal hacia los músculos y las glándulas. (pág. 53)

MRI (magnetic resonance imaging) / IRM (imágenes por resonancia magnética) técnica que utiliza campos magnéticos y ondas de radio para producir imágenes de tejidos blandos generadas por computadora. Las imágenes de resonancia magnética permiten observar la anatomía cerebral. (pág. 68)

mutation/mutación error aleatorio en la réplica de los genes que tiene como resultado un cambio. (pág. 104)

myelin [MY-uh-lin] **sheath/vaina de mielina** capa de tejido graso que encasilla las fibras de muchas neuronas, facilitando una mayor velocidad de impulsos neuronales ya que el impulso salta de un nódulo al siguiente. (pág. 53)

narcolepsy/narcolepsia trastorno del sueño caracterizado por ataques de somnolencia irresistibles con el sueño REM ocurriendo al inicio del sueño, a menudo en momentos inoportunos. (pág. 186)

natural selection/selección natural principio según el cual, entre la variedad de rasgos heredados, aquellos que contribuyen a la reproducción y la supervivencia tienen gran probabilidad de pasar a las generaciones futuras. (págs. 8, 103)

naturalistic observation/observación naturalista el observar y registrar la conducta en situaciones reales sin tratar de manipular y controlar la situación. (pág. 28)

nature-nurture issue/relación entre herencia y crianza larga controversia sobre las contribuciones relativas de los genes y la experiencia en el desarrollo de la conducta y los rasgos psicológicos. La ciencia actual considera que los rasgos y la conducta surgen de la interacción entre la herencia, o naturaleza, y la crianza. (pág. 8)

near-death experience/experiencia al borde de la muerte estado de alteración experimentado por personas que llegan al borde de la muerte, o que parecen morir pero luego retornan a la vida (por ejemplo, cuando uno sufre un paro cardíaco). Son similares a las alucinaciones inducidas por las drogas. (pág. 206)

negative reinforcement/refuerzo negativo aumento de conductas como consecuencia de la omisión o reducción de un estímulo negativo, como el electrochoque. Aquí se omite o retira un estímulo después de una respuesta o conducta, y como consecuencia se aumenta dicha conducta. (*Nota:* El refuerzo negativo no es castigo.) (pág. 231)

nerves/nervios conjunto de axones en forma de "cables" neurales que conectan el sistema nervioso central con los músculos, las glándulas y los órganos de los sentidos. (pág. 59)

nervous system/sistema nervioso veloz red electroquímica de comunicación del cuerpo que consiste de todas las células nerviosas del sistema periférico y del sistema nervioso central. (pág. 59)

neurogenesis/neurogénesis formación de nuevas neuronas. (pág. 83)

neuron/neurona célula nerviosa; el componente básico del sistema nervioso. (pág. 53)

neurotransmitters/neurotransmisores mensajeros químicos que atraviesan los espacios intersinápticos entre las neuronas. Cuando son liberados por una neurona emisora, los neurotransmisores pasan a través de la sinapsis y se acomodan en los receptores de la neurona receptora, influyendo en la generación de un impulso neural por parte de dicha neurona. (pág. 55)

night terrors/terrores nocturnos trastorno del sueño caracterizado por una gran excitación y la apariencia de estar aterrorizado; a diferencia de las pesadillas, los terrores nocturnos ocurren durante la etapa 4 del sueño, dos o tres horas después de dormirse, y raramente se recuerdan. (pág. 187)

norm/norma regla entendida de comportamiento aceptado y esperado. Las normas prescriben el comportamiento "apropiado". (pág. 662)

normal curve/curva normal (*distribución normal*) curva simétrica en forma de campana que describe la distribución de muchos tipos de datos. La mayoría de los puntajes están cerca de la media (68 por ciento están dentro de una desviación estándar de la misma) o promedio, y disminuyen en número conforme se acercan a los extremos. (págs. 40, 536)

normative social influence/influencia social normativa influencia que resulta del deseo de una persona de ganar aprobación o evitar desaprobación. (pág. 653)

NREM sleep/sueño de NREM (por sus siglas en inglés, llamado también sueño sin MOR—movimiento ocular rápido) el sueño no-rápido del movimiento del ojo; abarca todas etapas de sueño menos sueño de REM. (pág. 180)

object permanence/permanencia de objeto conocimiento que las cosas existen aunque no las veamos. (pág. 419)

observational learning/aprendizaje observacional el aprender observando a otros. (pág. 242)

obsessive-compulsive disorder (OCD) / trastorno obsesivo-compulsivo trastorno de ansiedad caracterizado por pensamientos repetitivos no deseados (obsesiones) y/o acciones (compulsiones). (pág. 571)

occipital [ahk-SIP-uh-tuhl] **lobes/lóbulos occipitales** porción de la corteza cerebral ubicada en la parte posterior de la cabeza; incluye las áreas que reciben información de los campos visuales. (pág. 74)

Oedipus [ED-uh-puss] **complex/complejo de Edipo** según Freud, los deseos sexuales de un muchacho hacia su madre y sentimientos de celos y odio para el padre rival. (pág. 482)

one-word stage/etapa holofrástica etapa en el desarrollo del habla, entre el año y los dos años, en la que el niño se expresa principalmente en palabras aisladas. (pág. 316)

operant behavior/comportamiento operante comportamiento que opera en el ambiente, produciendo consecuencias. (pág. 228)

operant chamber/cámara operante en los estudios del condicionamiento operante, cámara (también conocida como *caja de Skinner*) equipada con una barra o llave que un animal manipula para obtener un reforzador de comida o agua; unos dispositivos llevan un registro de las veces en que el animal aprieta la barra o picotea la llave. (pág. 229)

operant conditioning/condicionamiento operante aprendizaje donde el comportamiento se consolida si está seguido por un refuerzo o se atenúa si está seguido por un castigo. (pág. 228)

operational definition/definición operacional manifestación de los procedimientos (operaciones) utilizadas para definir las variables de investigación. Por ejemplo, *la inteligencia humana* puede ser operacionalmente definida como lo que mide una prueba de inteligencia. (pág. 26)

opiates/opiatas el opio y sus derivados tales como la morfina y la heroína; deprimen la actividad neuronal, disminuyendo el dolor y la ansiedad temporalmente. (pág. 201)

opponent-process theory/teoría de los procesos opuestos procesos opuestos en la retina (rojo-verde, amarillo-azul, blanco-negro) facilitan la visión de colores. Por ejemplo, algunas células son estimuladas por el verde e inhibidas por el rojo; otras están estimuladas por el rojo e inhibidas por el verde. (pág. 133)

optic nerve/nervio óptico nervio que transporta los impulsos neuronales del ojo al cerebro. (pág. 126)

organizational psychology/psicología organizacional subdivisión de la psicología industrial y organizacional que examina las influencias organizacionales en la satisfacción y productividad de los trabajadores, y facilita cambios organizacionales. (pág. B-2)

other-race effect/efecto de otras razas tendencia a recordar con mayor precisión los rostros de individuos de la raza a la cual uno pertenece que los rostros de individuos de otras razas. También se denomina *efecto interracial*. (pág. 669)

outgroup/exogrupo "ellos": personas que consideramos distintas o ajenas a nuestro endogrupo. (pág. 668)

overconfidence/confianza excesiva tendencia a estar más seguros de nosotros mismos que a estar en lo cierto, o sea, de sobreestimar la exactitud de nuestras creencias y opiniones. (pág. 306)

panic disorder/trastorno de pánico trastorno de ansiedad marcado por el inicio repentino y recurrente de episodios de aprehensión intensa o terror que pueden durar varios minutos. Incluyen dolor de pecho, sofocamiento, y otras sensaciones atemorizantes. (pág. 570)

parallel processing/procesamiento paralelo procesamiento simultáneo de varias partes de un problema; el modo natural del cerebro de procesar la información de muchas funciones, incluida la visión. Contrasta con el procesamiento paso a paso (en serie) de la mayoría de las computadoras y de la resolución consciente de problemas. (págs. 130, 258)

parapsychology/parapsicología estudio de fenómenos paranormales incluyendo la percepción extrasensorial y la psicoquinesis. (pág. 166)

parasympathetic nervous system/sistema nervioso autonómico parasimpático división del sistema nervioso autonómico que calma el cuerpo conservando su energía. (pág. 60)

parietal [puh-RYE-uh-tuhl] **lobes/lóbulos parietales** área de la corteza cerebral en la parte superior y hacia la parte posterior de la cabeza que recibe suministro sensorial para el tacto y la posición del cuerpo. (pág. 74)

partial (intermittent) reinforcement/refuerzo parcial (intermitente) refuerzo a una respuesta sólo parte del tiempo; tiene como resultado la adquisición más lenta de una respuesta pero mucho más resistente a la extinción que el refuerzo continuo. (pág. 232)

passionate love/amor apasionado estado excitado de intensa y positiva absorción en otro ser, normalmente presente al comienzo de una relación amorosa. (pág. 683)

perception/percepción proceso de organizar e interpretar la información sensorial, permitiéndonos reconocer los objetos y eventos significativos. (pág. 116)

perceptual adaptation/adaptación visual habilidad de acomodarnos a un campo visual artificialmente desplazado o hasta invertido. (pág. 160)

perceptual constancy/constancia perceptiva percepción de los objetos como constantes e inalterables (de forma, tamaño, luminosidad y color constantes) aunque cambien la iluminación y las imágenes en la retina. (pág. 156)

perceptual set/predisposición perceptiva predisposición mental para percibir una cosa y no otra. (pág. 161)

peripheral nervous system (PNS) / sistema nervioso periférico neuronas sensoriales y motrices que conectan el sistema nervioso central al resto del cuerpo. (pág. 59)

peripheral route persuasion/la persuasión ruta periférica ruta de un cambio de actitud en la que los individuos son influenciados por claves secundarias, por ejemplo, el atractivo físico de un orador. (pág. 646)

personal control/control personal sensación de que controlamos nuestro ambiente en lugar de sentirnos impotentes. (pág. 505)

personal space/espacio personal zona de seguridad que nos gusta mantener alrededor de nuestros cuerpos. (pág. 662)

personality/personalidad forma característica de pensar, sentir y actuar de un individuo. (pág. 479)

personality disorders/trastornos de la personalidad trastornos psicológicos caracterizados por modelos de comportamiento inflexibles y duraderos que impiden el funcionamiento social. (pág. 596)

personality inventory/inventario de personalidad cuestionario (a menudo con preguntas de *verdadero/falso,* estoy de *acuerdo/estoy* en desacuerdo) diseñado para medir un amplio rango de sentimientos y comportamientos, utilizados para evaluar ciertos rasgos de personalidad. (pág. 496)

personality psychology/psicología de personalidad el estudio de una pauta típica de individuo de pensamiento, de sentir, y de la actuación (pág. 13)

personnel psychology/psicología de personal subdivisión de la psicología industrial y organizacional que está enfocada en el reclutamiento, selección, colocación, entrenamiento, evaluación y desarrollo de los empleados. (pág. B-2)

PET (positron emission tomography) / TEP (tomografía por emission de positrons) presentación grafica de la actividad cerebral que detecta por dónde pasa una fórmula radiactiva de glucose mientras el cerebro realiza una tarea determinada. (pág. 68)

phi phenomenon/fenómeno fi ilusión de movimiento creado cuando dos o más luces adyacentes destellan en sucesión rápida. (pág. 156)

phobia/fobia trastorno de ansiedad marcado por un temor persistente e irracional y la evasión de un objeto, actividad, o situación específicos. (pág. 571)

phoneme/fonema en el lenguaje, la unidad de sonido más pequeña. (pág. 313)

physical dependence/dependencia física necesidad fisiológica de una droga, demostrada por un desagradable síndrome de abstinencia cuando se corta el suministro. (pág. 197)

pitch/tono propiedad de los *sonidos* que los caracteriza como agudos o graves, en función de su frecuencia (pág. 134)

pituitary gland/glándula pituitaria glándula más influyente del sistema endocrino. Bajo la influencia del hipotálamo, la pituitaria regula el crecimiento y controla otras glándulas endocrinas. (pág. 63)

place theory/teoría de ubicación en la audición, la teoría que relaciona al tono que oímos con el lugar dónde la membrana de la cóclea se estimula. (pág. 137)

placebo [pluh-SEE-bo] **effect/efecto de placebo** [del latín, "complaceré"] resultados experimentales causados exclusivamente por expectativas; cualquier efecto en el comportamiento causado por el suministro de una sustancia o condición inerte que el sujeto del experimento considera agente activo. (pág. 35)

plasticity/plasticidad capacidad del cerebro de cambiar, especialmente durante la niñez, reorganizándose después de sufrir una lesión o formando nuevas conexiones a partir de las experiencias del individuo. (pág. 82)

polygraph/polígrafo máquina utilizada para detectar mentiras que mide varias de las respuestas fisiológicas que acompañan la emoción (tales como la transpiración y los cambios cardiovasculares y de respiración). (pág. 372)

population/población todos los casos de un grupo de los que se pueden utilizar muestras para un estudio. (Nota: a excepción de los estudios nacionales, esto no se refiere a la población entera de un país.) (pág. 28)

positive psychology/psicología positiva estudio científico del funcionamiento humano óptimo cuya meta es descubrir y promover las fuerzas y las virtudes que permiten prosperar a individuos y comunidades. (pág. 508)

positive reinforcement/refuerzo positivo el aumentar la probabilidad de una conducta añadiendo estímulos positivos al entorno, como comida. Un refuerzo positivo es cualquier estímulo, presentado

después de la respuesta, que trae consigo que esa respuesta aumente o se repita en el futuro. (pág. 231)

posthypnotic suggestion/sugestión poshipnótica sugestión hecha durante una sesión de hipnosis, para que el sujeto la cumpla cuando ya no esté hipnotizado; técnica empleada por algunos médicos clínicos para tratar de controlar conductas y síntomas indeseados. (pág. 194)

post-traumatic growth/evolución post-traumática cambios psicológicos positivos que resultan de la lucha por superar circunstancias extremas y dificultades de la vida. (pág. 573)

post-traumatic stress disorder (PTSD) /trastorno de estrés post-traumático (TEPT) trastorno de ansiedad caracterizado por recuerdos obsesionantes, pesadillas, aislamiento social, ansiedad asustadiza, y/o insomnio que dura por cuatro semanas o más después de una experiencia traumática. (pág. 572)

predictive validity/validez predictiva éxito con cuál una prueba predice el comportamiento que está diseñada para predecir; se evalúa computando la correlación entre los puntajes de la prueba y el criterio de comportamiento. (También llamada *validez de criterio*). (pág. 538)

prejudice/prejuicio actitud injustificable (y normalmente negativa) hacia un grupo y sus miembros. El prejuicio generalmente implica creencias estereotipadas, sentimientos negativos y una predisposición a acción discriminatoria. (pág. 664)

preoperational stage/etapa preoperacional en la teoría de Piaget, la etapa (desde los 2 hasta los 6 o 7 años) durante la que el niño aprende a utilizar el lenguaje; pero todavía no comprende las operaciones mentales de lógica concreta. (pág. 421)

primary reinforcer/refuerzo primario estímulo natural de refuerzo, como cuando uno satisface una necesidad biológica. (pág. 231)

primary sex characteristics/características sexuales primarias estructuras del cuerpo (ovarios, testículos y los genitales externos) que hacen posible la reproducción sexual. (pág. 446)

priming/exposición previa activación normalmente inconsciente de ciertas asociaciones de la memoria, así predisponiendo una percepción, la memoria, o la respuesta. (págs. 121, 275)

proactive interference/interferencia proactiva efecto de interferencia cuando el material que ha sido aprendido anteriormente interrumpe el recordar material aprendido después. (pág. 282)

problem-focused coping/resolución enfocada en el problema el intentar aliviar la tensión directamente—cambiando la causa del estrés o la manera cómo interactuamos con ella. (pág. C-1)

projection/proyección mecanismo de defensa psicoanalítico por el que las personas enmascaran sus propios impulsos amenazantes atribuyéndolos a otros. (pág. 483)

projective test/prueba de proyección prueba de personalidad, como la de Rorschach o TAT, que proporciona estímulos ambiguos diseñados para activar las proyecciones de nuestra dinámica interna. (pág. 486)

prosocial behavior/comportamiento prosocial comportamiento positivo, constructivo, útil. Lo contrario del comportamiento antisocial. (pág. 246)

prototype/prototipo imagen mental o mejor ejemplo de una categoría. La comparación de elementos nuevos con un prototipo proporciona un método rápido y fácil de clasificar por categorías (como al comparar animales emplumados con un prototipo de ave, como el ruiseñor). (pág. 299)

psychiatry/psiquiatría división de la medicina que trata con trastornos psicológicos; practicado por médicos que a veces proporcionan tratamientos médicos (por ejemplo, drogas) así como terapia psicológica. (pág. 13)

psychoactive drug/droga psicoactiva sustancia química que altera las percepciones y el humor. (pág. 197)

psychoanalysis/psicoanálisis teoría de la personalidad de Freud y la técnica terapéutica que atribuye los pensamientos y acciones a los motivos y conflictos inconcientes. Freud creía que las asociaciones libres del paciente, las resistencias, los sueños y la transferencia—y las interpretaciones del terapeuta sobre ellos—liberaban los sentimientos previamente reprimidos, permitiendo al paciente ganar introspección. (págs. 480, 606)

psychodynamic psychology/psicología psicodinámica una rama de la psicología que estudia cuán inconsciente conduce y se opone conducta de influencia y utiliza la información para tratar a personas con desórdenes psicológicos. (pág. 10)

psychodynamic therapy/terapia psicodinámica terapia derivada de la tradición psicoanalítica, en la que se considera que las personas responden a fuerzas inconscientes y a experiencias de la niñez, y que tiene el propósito de aumentar el conocimiento de uno mismo. (pág. 608)

psychological dependence/dependencia psicológica necesidad psicológica de utilizar una droga, como para aliviar las emociones negativas. (pág. 197)

psychological disorder/trastorno psicológico modelos de comportamiento anticonvencional, angustioso, y disfuncional. (pág. 562)

psychology/psicología estudio científico del comportamiento y de los procesos mentales. (pág. 7)

psychometrics/psicometría el estudio científico de la medida de capacidades humanas, de las actitudes, y de los rasgos. (pág. 12)

psychoneuroimmunology (PNI) / psiconeuroinmunología estudio del efecto de los procesos psicológicos, neurales y endocrinos en el sistema de inmunidad y la salud resultante. (pág. 403)

psychopharmacology/psicofarmacología estudio de los efectos de las drogas en la mente y el comportamiento. (pág. 628)

psychophysics/psicofísica estudio de las relaciones entre las características físicas de los estímulos, como su intensidad, y nuestra experiencia psicológica de ellos. (pág. 120)

psychophysiological illness/enfermedad psicofisiológica término que significa literalmente "enfermedad de la mente y el cuerpo"; cualquier enfermedad física que tiene relación con el estrés, por ejemplo, la hipertensión y ciertos dolores de cabeza. (pág. 403)

psychosexual stages/etapas psicosexuales etapas del desarrollo infantil según Freud (oral, anal, fálica, latente, genital), durante las cuales la energía del id en busca de placer se enfoca en zonas erógenas específicas (pág. 482)

psychosurgery/psicocirugía cirugía que remueve o destruye tejido cerebral para cambiar el comportamiento. (pág. 635)

psychotherapy/psicoterapia tratamiento en el que se emplean técnicas psicológicas; consiste en interacciones entre un terapeuta especializado y una persona que desea superar dificultades psicológicas o lograr una evolución personal. (pág. 606)

puberty/pubertad período de maduración sexual durante el cual una persona adquiere la capacidad de reproducirse. (pág. 445)

punishment/castigo evento que *disminuye* el comportamiento que le precede. (pág. 234)

pupil/pupila apertura adaptable en el centro del ojo a través del cual la luz ingresa. (pág. 126)

random assignment/asignación aleatoria distribución al azar de participantes a grupos experimentales y de control para minimizar las diferencias preexistentes entre los participantes de cada grupo. (pág. 34)

random sample/muestra aleatoria muestra en la que cada elemento de la población tiene igual oportunidad de ser seleccionado. (pág. 28)

range/rango diferencia entre el puntaje más alto y el más bajo en una distribución. (pág. 39)

rationalization/racionalización mecanismo de defensa que ofrece explicaciones de autojustificación en vez de las razones reales, más amenazadoras e inconcientes para nuestras acciones. (pág. 483)

reaction formation/formación de reacción mecanismo de defensa psicoanalítico en el que el ego inconcientemente cambia los impulsos inaceptables por sus opuestos. Así, las personas pueden expresar sentimientos que son el opuesto de los sentimientos inconcientes que producen ansiedad. (pág. 483)

recall/recuerdo medida de la memoria en la que la persona debe recuperar información aprendida con anterioridad, como en las pruebas donde se debe llenar el espacio en blanco. (pág. 274)

reciprocal determinism/determinismo recíproco interacción de las influencias de conducta, cognición interna y entorno. (pág. 503)

reciprocity norm/norma de reciprocidad expectativa que las personas ayudarán y no herirán a aquellos que las han ayudado. (pág. 687)

recognition/reconocimiento medida de la memoria en la que la persona sólo debe identificar los artículos previamente aprendidos, como en una prueba de selección múltiple. (pág. 274)

reflex/reflejo reacción simple y automática a un estímulo sensorial, como el reflejo de la rodilla. (pág. 61)

refractory period/período refractario período de descanso después de un orgasmo durante el cual el hombre no puede tener otro orgasmo. (pág. 349)

regression/regresión mecanismo de defensa psicoanalítico en el cual un individuo enfrentado con la ansiedad retrocede a una etapa psicosexual más infantil dónde alguna energía psíquica quedó fijada. (pág. 483)

regression toward the mean/retroceso hacia el promedio tendencia de los puntajes extremos de regresar hacia el promedio. (pág. 621)

rehearsal/ensayo repetición conciente de información ya sea para mantenerla concientemente o para codificarla para almacenamiento. (pág. 259)

reinforcer/refuerzo en el condicionamiento operante, cualquier evento que fortalece la conducta que le precede. (pág. 230)

relative deprivation/privación relativa percepción de que uno está peor relativamente que aquellos a los que uno se compara. (pág. 394)

relearning/reaprendizaje medida de memoria que evalúa la cantidad de tiempo ahorrado cuando se aprende el material la segunda vez. (pág. 274)

reliability/fiabilidad medida en la que una prueba produce resultados parejos que son evaluados por la uniformidad de puntajes en dos partes de la misma o al administrarla nuevamente. (pág. 538)

REM rebound/rebote de REM aumento marcado del sueño REM como consecuencia de la privación del sueño REM (producida por despertares repetidos durante el sueño REM). (pág. 191)

REM sleep/sueño REM (por sus siglas en inglés, llamado también sueño MOR—movimiento ocular rápido) sueño con movimiento rápido de los ojos; etapa recurrente en el sueño durante la cual ocurren sueños vívidos. También se conoce como *sueño paradójico* porque los músculos están relajados (excepto por pequeños espasmos); pero el resto de los sistemas corporales se mantienen activos. (pág. 178)

repetitive transcranial magnetic stimulation (rTMS) / estimulación magnética transcraneal repetitiva (EMTr) aplicación repetitiva de pulsos de energía magnética al cerebro; utilizada para estimular o suprimir la actividad cerebral. (pág. 634)

replication/replicación el repetir la esencia de un estudio de investigación, usualmente con diferentes participantes y en diferentes situaciones para ver si las conclusiones básicas se extienden a otros participantes y circunstancias. (pág. 26)

representativeness heuristic/heurística de la representatividad estrategia para estimar la probabilidad de un suceso mediante la evaluación de su parecido o concordancia con ciertos prototipos; a veces conduce a ignorar datos relevantes. (pág. 304)

repression/represión en la teoría psicoanalítica, el mecanismo básico de defensa por medio del cual el sujeto elimina de su conciente aquellos pensamientos, emociones o recuerdos que le producen ansiedad. (págs. 284, 483)

resilience/capacidad de recuperación la fuerza personal que ayuda a la mayoría de las personas se enfrenta con énfasis y recupera de la adversidad e incluso trauma. (pág. 637)

resistance/resistencia en psicoanálisis, el bloquear del conciente aquello que está cargado de ansiedad. (pág. 607)

respondent behavior/conducta respondiente conducta que ocurre como respuesta automática a un estímulo. (pág. 228)

reticular formation/formación reticular red de nervios en el bulbo raquídeo que juega un papel importante en el control de la excitación. (pág. 70)

retina/retina superficie sensitiva a la luz en la parte interior del ojo que contiene los receptores de luz llamados bastoncillos y conos además de capas de neuronas que inician el procesamiento de la información visual. (pág. 126)

retinal disparity/disparidad retiniana clave binocular en la percepción de profundidad. El cerebro calcula distancias comparando las imágenes reflejadas en la retina de cada ojo. Cuanto más grande es la disparidad (diferencia) entre las dos imágenes, tanto más cerca está el objeto. (pág. 153)

retrieval/recuperación acto de sacar la información que está almacenada en la memoria. (pág. 257)

retroactive interference/interferencia retroactiva efecto de interferencia cuando el material que ha sido aprendido recientemente interrumpe el recordar material aprendido con anterioridad. (pág. 282)

reuptake/reabsorción reabsorción de un neurotransmisor por la neurona emisora. (pág. 55)

rods/bastoncillos receptores de la retina que detectan el negro, blanco y gris; necesarios para la visión periférica y en la penumbra cuando los conos no responden. (pág. 126)

role/rol conjunto de expectativas (normas) relacionadas a una posición social, definiendo como aquéllos en esa posición deben de comportarse. (págs. 439, 647)

Rorschach inkblot test/test de Rorschach prueba proyectiva de amplio uso, un conjunto de 10 manchas de tinta, diseñado por Hermann Rorschach; busca identificar los sentimientos internos de las personas analizando sus interpretaciones de las manchas. (pág. 486)

savant syndrome/síndrome de savant condición según la cual una persona de habilidad mental limitada, tiene una destreza excepcional en un campo como la computación o el dibujo. (pág. 525)

scapegoat theory/teoría del chivo expiatorio teoría que el prejuicio ofrece un escape para la cólera porque nos brinda a alguien que resulta útil como depositario de la agresión. (pág. 669)

scatterplot/diagramas de dispersión agrupaciones de puntos en una gráfica, cada una de las cuales representa el valor de dos variables.

La pendiente de los puntos representa la dirección de la relación entre las dos variables. La magnitud de la dispersión representa la fuerza de la correlación (a menor dispersión, mayor correlación). (pág. 29)

schema/esquema concepto o principio que organiza e interpreta la información. (pág. 418)

schizophrenia/esquizofrenia grupo de trastornos severos caracterizados por un pensamiento desorganizado y delirante, percepciones ofuscadas, así como emociones y acciones impropias. (pág. 590)

secondary sex characteristics/características sexuales secundarias características sexuales no reproductivas, como senos y caderas en las mujeres, timbre de voz y vello corporal en los hombres. (pág. 446)

selective attention/atención selectiva enfoque de la percepción consciente en un estímulo en particular. (pág. 117)

self/el yo en la psicología contemporánea, supuesto centro de la personalidad, organizador de nuestros pensamientos, sentimientos y acciones. (pág. 511)

self-actualization/autorrealización según Maslow, una de las necesidades psicológicas fundamentales que surge después de satisfacer las necesidades básicas, físicas y psicológicas, y de lograr la autoestima; motivación de satisfacer nuestro potencial. (pág. 491)

self-concept/autoconcepto todos nuestros pensamientos y sentimientos hacia nosotros mismos cuando respondemos a la pregunta: "¿quién soy yo?" (págs. 432, 492)

self-disclosure/autorevelación el revelar aspectos íntimos de uno mismo a otros. (pág. 684)

self-esteem/autoestima sentimiento valorativo positivo o negativo de nuestro ser. (pág. 512)

self-fulfilling prophecy/profecía uno mismo-satisfaciente una creencia que lleva a su propio cumplimiento. (pág. 689)

self-serving bias/tendencia al autoservicio tendencia a auto-percatarse de manera favorable. (pág. 513)

semantic encoding/codificación semántica codificación de significado, incluyendo el significado de las palabras. (pág. 261)

semantics/semántica conjunto de reglas de las que derivamos el significado de morfemas, palabras y frases en un idioma; también, el estudio del significado. (pág. 314)

sensation/sensación proceso por el cual los receptores sensoriales y el sistema nervioso reciben y procesan el estímulo del medio ambiente. (pág. 116)

sensorimotor stage/etapa sensorio-motriz en la teoría de Piaget, la etapa (0–2 años) durante la que los infantes conocen el mundo principalmente en términos de sus impresiones sensoriales y actividades motoras. (pág. 419)

sensorineural hearing loss/pérdida sensorio-neuronal del oído pérdida auditiva causada por daño a las células receptoras de la cóclea o a los nervios auditivos. También llamada sordera del nervio. (pág. 138)

sensory adaptation/adaptación sensorial sensibilidad disminuida como consecuencia del estímulo constante. (pág. 123)

sensory cortex/corteza sensorialauto área en el frente de los lóbulos parietales que registra y procesa las sensaciones de movimiento y tacto del cuerpo. (pág. 77)

sensory interaction/interacción sensorial principio que un sentido puede influir a otro, como cuando el olor de la comida influye en su sabor. (pág. 147)

sensory memory/memoria sensorial registro breve e inmediato de la información sensorial en el sistema de la memoria. (pág. 257)

sensory neurons/neuronas sensoriales neuronas que reciben la información relacionada con las sensaciones, de los receptores la transportan al sistema nervioso central. (pág. 53)

serial position effect/efecto de posición serial nuestra tendencia a recordar mejor los últimos y los primeros artículos en una lista. (pág. 260)

set point/punto fijo punto de equilibrio en el "termostato del peso" de un individuo. Cuando el cuerpo llega a un peso debajo de este punto, se produce un aumento en el hambre y una disminución en el índice metabólico, los cuales pueden actuar para restablecer el peso perdido. (pág. 335)

sexual orientation/orientación sexual atracción sexual perdurable hacia los miembros del mismo sexo (orientación homosexual) o del sexo opuesto (orientación heterosexual). (pág. 354)

sexual response cycle/ciclo de respuesta sexual las cuatro etapas de respuesta sexual descritas por Masters y Johnson—excitación, meseta, orgasmo y resolución. (pág. 349)

shaping/modelado por aproximaciones sucesivas procedimiento del condicionamiento operante donde el refuerzo guía la conducta para que ésta se aproxime más y más a la conducta deseada. (pág. 229)

short-term memory/memoria a corto plazo memoria activada que retiene algunos elementos por un corto tiempo,tales como los siete dígitos de un número telefónico mientras se marca, antes que la información se almacene o se olvide. (pág. 257)

signal detection theory/teoría de la detección de señales teoría que predice cómo y cuándo detectamos la presencia de un estímulo débil (*señal*) a pesar de la estimulación del ambiente (*ruido*). Asume que no hay ningún umbral absoluto y que la detección depende en parte de la experiencia de la persona, de sus expectativas, motivación, y vigilancia. (pág. 121)

sleep/sueño pérdida del conocimiento que es periódica y natural. Esto es distinto de la inconsciencia que puede resultar del estado de coma, anestesia general, o hibernación. (Adaptado de Dement, 1999.) (pág. 178)

sleep apnea/apnea del sueño trastorno de sueño caracterizado por cesaciones temporales de respiración durante el sueño y repetidos despertares momentáneos. (pág. 187)

social clock/reloj social manera que la sociedad tiene de marcar el tiempo adecuado de los eventos sociales, tales como matrimonio, paternidad y jubilación. (pág. 465)

social-cognitive perspective/perspectiva cognitivo-social enfoque según el cual la conducta es influenciada por la interacción entre los rasgos del individuo (incluida la forma de pensar) y su contexto social. (pág. 503)

social-cultural psychology/psicología social-cultural el estudio de cómo situaciones y culturas afectan nuestra conducta y el pensamiento. (pág. 10)

social exchange theory/teoría del intercambio social teoría que nuestra conducta social es un proceso de intercambio, cuyo objetivo es maximizar los beneficios y minimizar los costos. (pág. 687)

social facilitation/facilitación social respuestas más fuertes a las tareas simples o bien aprendidas en la presencia de otros. (pág. 657)

social identity/identidad social dentro de nuestro autoconcepto, parte a la que nos referimos como "nosotros"; la parte de nuestra respuesta a la pregunta "¿quién soy yo?" que tiene que ver con nuestras afiliaciones de grupo. (pág. 451)

social leadership/liderazgo social liderazgo orientado hacia el grupo que construye trabajo en grupo, media en el conflicto y ofrece apoyo. (pág. B-12)

social learning theory/teoría de aprendizaje social teoría que aprendemos la conducta social observando e imitando y al ser recompensados o castigados. (pág. 440)

social loafing/haraganería social tendencia de las personas en un grupo de realizar menos esfuerzo cuando juntan sus esfuerzos para lograr una meta común que cuando son responsables individualmente. (pág. 658)

social psychology/psicología social estudio científico del funcionamiento de la mente individual en un entorno social: pensamiento, influencia y relación entre las personas. (págs. 13, 643)

social-responsibility norm/norma de responsabilidad social posibilidad de que las personas ayudarán a aquellos que dependen de ellas. (pág. 687)

social trap/trampa social situación en la cual dos partes en conflicto, cada una persiguiendo racionalmente su propio interés, se ven atrapadas en conducta mutuamente destructiva. (pág. 688)

somatic nervous system/sistema nervioso somático división del sistema nervioso periférico que controla los músculos del esqueleto. También llamado *sistema nervioso del esqueleto*. (pág. 59)

somatoform disorder/trastorno somatoforme trastorno psicológico en el que los síntomas cobran carácter somático (del cuerpo) sin tener una causa física aparente. (Véase *trastorno de conversión* e *hipocondría*.) (pág. 576)

source amnesia/amnesia de la fuente el atribuir un origen erróneo a un evento que hemos experimentado, oído, leído o imaginado. (También se le conoce como *falsa atribución*). La amnesia de la fuente así como el efecto de desinformación, están en el corazón de muchas memorias falsas. (pág. 287)

spacing effect/efecto del aprendizaje espaciado tendencia a que el estudio o práctica distribuidos logren mejor retención a largo plazo que la que se logra a través de estudio o prácticas masivas. (pág. 260)

split brain/cerebro dividido estado a partir de una intervención quirúrgica en el que los dos hemisferios cerebrales quedan incomunicados mediante el corte de las fibras que los conectan (principalmente las del cuerpo calloso). (pág. 84)

spontaneous recovery/recuperación espontánea reaparición, después de una pausa, de una respuesta condicionada extinguida. (pág. 221)

spotlight effect/efecto reflector sobreestimación de lo que los demás advierten y evalúan de nuestra apariencia, desempeño y desatinos (como si estuviéramos apuntados por un reflector). (pág. 512)

SQ3R/método EPL2R técnica de estudio que combina los cinco pasos siguientes: *explorar, preguntar, leer, recitar y repasar*. (pág. 14)

standard deviation/desviación estándar medida calculada de cuánto varían los puntajes alrededor del promedio de la muestra. (pág. 39)

standardization/estandarización el definir puntajes significativos mediante la comparación del desempeño de un grupo examinado con anterioridad. (pág. 536)

Stanford-Binet/Stanford-Binet revisión (por Terman en la Universidad de Stanford) de la prueba original de inteligencia de Binet. Esta prueba revisada es usada extensamente. (pág. 534)

statistical significance/significado estadístico declaración estadística de cuán probable es que un resultado se haya obtenido por casualidad. (pág. 41)

stereotype/estereotipo creencia (a veces acertada; pero frecuentemente demasiado generalizada) sobre las características de un grupo. (pág. 664)

stereotype threat/amenaza del estereotipo preocupación personal que reconfirma el temor de ser evaluado sobre un base de un estereotipo negativo. (pág. 555)

stimulants/estimulantes drogas (como cafeína, nicotina y las anfetaminas más poderosas, cocaína y éxtasis) que excitan la actividad neuronal y aceleran las funciones corporales. (pág. 201)

storage/almacenamiento retención a través del tiempo de información codificada. (pág. 257)

stranger anxiety/miedo a los extraños miedo a los extraños que los infantes normalmente expresan a partir de los ocho meses. (pág. 426)

stress/estrés proceso a través del cual percibimos y respondemos a ciertos eventos llamados *estresores,* los cuales evaluamos como amenazantes o desafiantes. (pág. 397)

structuralism/estructuralismo escuela de los primeros años de la psicología, que empleaba la introspección para explorar los elementos estructurales de la mente humana. (pág. 4)

structured interviews/entrevistas estructuradas proceso mediante el cual en las entrevistas se hace las mismas preguntas a todos los postulantes, cada uno de los cuales será calificado de acuerdo a escalas establecidas. (pág. B-5)

sublimation/sublimación mecanismo de defensa del psicoanálisis por el que la gente reencauzar sus impulses inaceptable en actividades socialmente aprobado (pág. 484)

subliminal/subliminal debajo del umbral absoluto del nivel de conciencia. (pág. 121)

superego/superego parte de personalidad que, según Freud, representa los ideales interiorizados y provee de las normas para el juicio (la conciencia) y para las aspiraciones futuras. (pág. 482)

superordinate goals/metas comunes metas compartidas que hacen caso omiso de las diferencias entre las personas y que requieren su cooperación. (pág. 690)

survey/encuesta técnica para verificar las actitudes o conductas reportadas por las personas; usualmente se pregunta a una muestra aleatoria y representativa. (pág. 27)

sympathetic nervous system/sistema nervioso simpático división del sistema nervioso autonómico que en situaciones estresantes despierta al cuerpo y moviliza su energía. (pág. 59)

synapse [SIN-aps] **/sinapsis** intersección entre el extremo del axón de una neurona emisora y la dendrita o cuerpo celular de una neurona receptora. El pequeño espacio en esta intersección se denomina espacio intersináptico. (pág. 55)

syntax/sintaxis reglas para combinar las palabras y formar oraciones gramaticales en una lengua. (pág. 314)

systematic desensitization/desensibilización sistemática tipo de terapia de exposición en la que se asocia un estado tranquilo y placentero con estímulos graduales que producen ansiedad. Se emplea comúnmente para tratar fobias. (pág. 611)

tardive dyskinesia/disquinesia tardía movimientos involuntarios de los músculos del rostro, la lengua y las extremidades; probable efecto secundario por el uso a largo plazo de medicamentos antipsicóticos que actúan en ciertos receptores de dopamina. (pág. 629)

task leadership/liderazgo específico liderazgo orientado a metas específicas que establece las normas, organiza el trabajo y centra la atención en metas. (pág. B-12)

telegraphic speech/lenguaje telegráfico etapa en que un niño comienza a hablar expresándose en forma de telegrama ("dame" o "agua") y utilizando principalmente nombres y verbos. (pág. 316)

temperament/temperamento característica de reactividad emocional e intensidad de una persona. (pág. 428)

temporal lobes/lóbulos temporales porción de la corteza cerebral ubicada aproximadamente arriba de las orejas; incluye las áreas auditivas, cada una de las cuales recibe la información auditiva principalmente de la oreja opuesta. (pág. 74)

teratogens/teratógenos agentes químicos o virales que pueden afectar al embrión o al feto durante el desarrollo prenatal y causarle daño. (pág. 413)

terror-management theory/teoría de la gestión del terror explicación de la ansiedad relacionada con la muerte; explora las respuestas emocionales y conductuales de las personas a todo aquello que les haga recordar la muerte propia. (pág. 489)

testosterone/testosterona la más importante de las hormonas sexuales masculinas. Tanto los hombres como las mujeres la tienen, pero la testosterona adicional en los hombres estimula el crecimiento de los órganos sexuales masculinos en el feto y el desarrollo de las características sexuales masculinas durante la pubertad. (págs. 350, 438)

thalamus [THAL-uh-muss] **/tálamo** estructura cerebral ubicada sobre el bulbo raquídeo que funciona como una estación de relevo para dirigir información a las áreas sensoriales receptivas de la corteza cerebral y transmite respuestas al cerebelo y la médula. (pág. 70)

THC/THC principal sustancia activa encontrada en la marihuana, produce distintos efectos incluyendo alucinaciones leves. (pág. 206)

Thematic Apperception Test (TAT) / prueba de apercepción temática prueba psicológica proyectiva en la que las personas expresan sus sentimientos internos e intereses a través de historias que inventan a partir de escenas ambiguas. (pág. 486)

theory/teoría explicación que utiliza un conjunto integrado de principios que organiza y predice las observaciones. (pág. 25)

theory of mind/teoría de la mente ideas de la gente con relación a su estado de ánimo y al estado de ánimo de los demás—acerca de sus sentimientos, percepciones, y pensamientos y la conducta que éstos puedan predecir. (pág. 422)

threshold/umbral nivel de estímulo requerido para activar un impulso neuronal. (pág. 54)

token economy/economía de fichas procedimiento del condicionamiento operante en el cual las personas ganan fichas de algún tipo si exhiben una conducta aprobatoria y pueden cambiar las fichas por privilegios o regalos. (pág. 614)

tolerance/tolerancia efecto decreciente de la misma dosis de una droga después de un tiempo de uso, requiriendo que el usuario aumente la dosis para poder experimentar el efecto de la droga. (pág. 197)

top-down processing/procesamiento de arriba a abajo procesamiento de información dirigida por procesos mentales superiores, como cuando determinamos nuestras percepciones a partir de nuestra experiencia y nuestras expectativas. (pág. 116)

trait/rasgo patrón característico de conducta o una disposición para sentir y actuar tales como los reportaría una autoevaluación o evaluación por nuestros pares. (pág. 494)

transduction/transducción cualquier operación que transforma energía de determinado tipo en otro distinto. En el caso de los sistemas sensoriales, el transformar energía de estímulo, como visiones, sonidos y olores, en impulsos neuronales que nuestros cerebros son capaces de interpretar. (pág. 124)

transference/transferencia en el psicoanálisis, la transferencia de emociones ligadas a otras relaciones, del paciente al analista (como el amor u odio hacia uno de los padres). (pág. 607)

two-factor theory/teoría bifactorial teoría de Schachter y Singer que sostiene que para sentir una emoción, la persona debe (1) experimentar estimulación física y (2) clasificar la estimulación a nivel cognitivo. (pág. 367)

two-word stage/etapa de dos palabras a partir de los dos años, etapa del desarrollo del lenguaje durante la cual el niño emite mayormente frases de dos palabras. (pág. 316)

Type A/Tipo A término de Friedman y Rosenman para las personas competitivas, compulsivas, impacientes, verbalmente agresivas y con tendencia a enojarse. (pág. 402)

Type B/Tipo B término de Friedman y Rosenman para las personas tolerantes y relajadas. (pág. 402)

unconditional positive regard/consideración positiva incondicional según Rogers, actitud que no juzga, bondadosa y sin restricciones que conduce al desarrollo de la conciencia y la aceptación de uno mismo. (págs. 491, 610)

unconditioned response (UR) / respuesta incondicionada (RI) en el condicionamiento clásico, la respuesta no aprendida e innata que es producida por el estímulo incondicionado (EI) como la salivación cuando la comida está en la boca. (pág. 219)

unconditioned stimulus (US) / estímulo incondicionado (EI) en el condicionamiento clásico, un estímulo no condicionado—natural y automático—que produce una respuesta. (pág. 219)

unconscious/inconciente según Freud, un depósito de pensamientos, deseos, sentimiento y memorias en su mayoría inaceptables. Según los psicólogos contemporáneos, el procesamiento de información del cual no estamos alertas. (pág. 480)

validity/validez grado en que una prueba mide o predice lo que se supone debe medir o predecir (véase también *validez de contenido* y *validez predictiva*). (pág. 538)

variable-interval schedule/programa de intervalo variable en el condicionamiento operante, un horario de refuerzo que refuerza una respuesta después de intervalos de tiempo impredecibles. (pág. 233)

variable-ratio schedule/programa de razón variable en el condicionamiento operante, los reforzamientos ocurren después de una cantidad variable de respuestas, no después de un número fijo. Esta cantidad difiere de reforzamiento en reforzamiento (pág. 233)

vestibular sense/sentido vestibular sentido de movimiento del cuerpo y posición, incluyendo el sentido de equilibrio. (pág. 142)

virtual reality exposure therapy/terapia de exposición a una realidad virtual tratamiento de ansiedad que progresivamente expone a las personas a simulaciones de sus más grandes miedos, como volar en avión, arañas o hablar en público. (pág. 612)

visual cliff/precipicio visual dispositivo del laboratorio para examinar la percepción de profundidad en los infantes y animales jóvenes. (pág. 153)

visual encoding/codificación visual codificación de imágenes visuales. (pág. 261)

wavelength/longitud de onda distancia de la cresta de una onda de luz o sonido a la cresta de la próxima. Las longitudes de onda electromagnéticas varían desde los puntos de luz cortos de los rayos cósmicos hasta los pulsos largos de transmisión de radio. (pág. 125)

Weber's law/ley de Weber principio que, para que dos estímulos sean percibidos como diferentes, éstos deben variar en un porcentaje constante (en vez de en una cantidad constante). (pág. 123)

Wechsler Adult Intelligence Scale (WAIS) / escala de la Inteligencia de Wechsler para adultos prueba de inteligencia más ampliamente utilizada; contiene pruebas verbales y de desempeño (no verbales). (pág. 535)

well-being/bienestar la felicidad o la satisfacción auto percibidos con la vida. Utilizado junto con medidas del bienestar objetivo (por ejemplo, indicadores físicos y económicos) evaluar la calidad de personas de la vida. (pág. 390)

Wernicke's area/área de Wernicke controla la recepción del lenguaje. Un área del cerebro involucrada en la comprensión y la expresión del lenguaje; generalmente en el lóbulo temporal izquierdo. (pág. 80)

withdrawal/síndrome de abstinencia conjunto de síntomas que afectan a individuo cuando se ve privado bruscamente de alguna droga adictiva. (pág. 197)

working memory/memoria activa aproximación nueva a la memoria a corto plazo que involucra el procesamiento conciente y activo de la información auditiva y visual-espacial, además de la recuperación de información de la memoria a largo plazo. (pág. 258)

X chromosome/cromosoma X cromosoma del sexo encontrado en hombres y mujeres. Las mujeres tienen dos cromosomas X; los hombres tienen uno. Un cromosoma de X de cada progenitor produce una niña. (pág. 438)

Y chromosome/cromosoma Y cromosoma del sexo encontrado sólo en los hombres. Cuando se aparca con un cromosoma X de la madre, produce un niño. (pág. 438)

Young-Helmholtz trichromatic (three-color) theory/teoría tricromática (tricolor) de Young-Helmholtz teoría que la retina contiene tres tipos de receptores cromáticos—uno más sensible al rojo, otro al verde, otro al azul—que cuando se estimulan en combinación pueden producir la percepción de cualquier color. (pág. 132)

zygote/cigoto huevo fertilizado, que atraviesa por un período de dos semanas de división celular rápida y se convierte en un embrión. (pág. 412)

References

Abbey, A. (1987). Misperceptions of friendly behavior as sexual interest: A survey of naturally occurring incidents. *Psychology of Women Quarterly, 11,* 173-194. (p. 106)

Abbey, A. (1991). Acquaintance rape and alcohol consumption on college campuses: How are they linked? *Journal of American College Health, 39,* 165-169. (p. 200)

Abbott, R. D., White, L. R., Ross, G. W., Masaki, K. H., Curb, J. D., & Petrovitch, H. (2004). Walking and dementia in physically capable elderly men. *Journal of the American Medical Association, 292,* 1447-1453. (p. 460)

Abrams, D. B. (1991). AIDS: What young people believe and what they do. Paper presented at the British Association for the Advancement of Science conference. (p. 507)

Abrams, D. B., & Wilson, G. T. (1983). Alcohol, sexual arousal, and self-control. *Journal of Personality and Social Psychology, 45,* 188-198. (p. 200)

Abrams, L. (2008). Tip-of-the-tongue states yield language insights. *American Scientist, 96,* 234-239. (p. 282)

Abrams, M. (2002, June). Sight unseen—Restoring a blind man's vision is now a real possibility through stem-cell surgery. But even perfect eyes cannot see unless the brain has been taught to use them. *Discover, 23,* 54-60. (p. 160)

Abramson, L. Y., Metalsky, G. I., & Alloy, L. B. (1989). Hopelessness depression: A theory-based subtype. *Psychological Review, 96,* 358-372. (p. 587)

ACHA. (2006). *American College Health Association National College Health Assessment.* Baltimore, MD: American College Health Association (achancha.org). (p. 580)

Ackerman, D. (2004). *An alchemy of mind: The marvel and mystery of the brain.* New York: Scribner. (p. 55, 66)

Adelmann, P. K., Antonucci, T. C., Crohan, S. F., & Coleman, L. M. (1989). Empty nest, cohort, and employment in the well-being of midlife women. *Sex Roles, 20,* 173-189. (p. 468)

Adelson, R. (2004, August). Detecting deception. *APA Monitor,* pp. 70-73. (p. 373)

Adelson, R. (2005, September). Lessons from H. M. *Monitor on Psychology,* p. 59. (p. 271)

Ader, R., & Cohen, N. (1985). CNS-immune system interactions: Conditioning phenomena. *Behavioral and Brain Sciences, 8,* 379-394. (p. 227)

Adolphs, R. (2006). Perception and emotion: How we recognize facial expressions. *Current Directions in Psychological Science, 15,* 222-226. (p. 378)

Adolphs, R., Tranel, D., & Damasio, A. R. (1998). The human amygdala in social judgment. *Nature, 393,* 470-474. (p. 386)

Affleck, G., Tennen, H., Urrows, S., & Higgins, P. (1994). Person and contextual features of daily stress reactivity: Individual differences in relations of undesirable daily events with mood disturbance and chronic pain intensity. *Journal of Personality and Social Psychology, 66,* 329-340. (p. 390)

Ai, A. L., Park, C. L., Huang, B., Rodgers, W., & Tice, T. N. (2007). Psychosocial mediation of religious coping styles: A study of short-term psychological distress following cardiac surgery. *Personality and Social Psychology Bulletin, 33,* 867-882. (p. C-12)

Aiello, J. R., Thompson, D. D., & Brodzinsky, D. M. (1983). How funny is crowding anyway? Effects of room size, group size, and the introduction of humor. *Basic and Applied Social Psychology, 4,* 193-207. (p. 658)

Ainsworth, M. D. S. (1973). The development of infant-mother attachment. In B. Caldwell & H. Ricciuti (Eds.), *Review of child development research (Vol. 3).* Chicago: University of Chicago Press. (p. 428)

Ainsworth, M. D. S. (1979). Infant-mother attachment. *American Psychologist, 34,* 932-937. (p. 428)

Ainsworth, M. D. S. (1989). Attachments beyond infancy. *American Psychologist, 44,* 709-716. (p. 428)

Airan, R. D., Meltzer, L. A., Roy, M., Gong, Y., Chen, H., & Deisseroth, K. (2007). High-speed imaging reveals neurophysiological links to behavior in an animal model of depression. *Science, 317,* 819-823. (p. 586)

Åkerstedt, T., Kecklund, G., & Axelsson, J. (2007). Impaired sleep after bedtime stress and worries. *Biological Psychology, 76,* 170-173. (p. 186)

Albee, G. W. (1986). Toward a just society: Lessons from observations on the primary prevention of psychopathology. *American Psychologist, 41,* 891-898. (p. 638)

Albert, B., Brown, S., & Flanigan, C. M. (Eds.) (2003). *14 and younger: The sexual behavior of young adolescents.* Washington, DC: National Campaign to Prevent Teen Pregnancy. (p. 353)

Alcock, J. E. (1981). *Parapsychology: Science or magic?* Oxford: Pergamon. (p. 277)

Aldrich, M. S. (1989). Automobile accidents in patients with sleep disorders. *Sleep, 12,* 487-494. (p. 186)

Aldridge-Morris, R. (1989). *Multiple personality: An exercise in deception.* Hillsdale, NJ: Erlbaum. (p. 578)

Aleman, A., Kahn, R. S., & Selten, J-P. (2003). Sex differences in the risk of schizophrenia: Evidence from meta-analysis. *Archives of General Psychiatry, 60,* 565-571. (p. 591)

Alexander, C. N., Langer, E. J., Newman, R. I., Chandler, H. M., & Davies, J. L. (1989). Transcendental meditation, mindfulness, and longevity: An experimental study with the elderly. *Journal of Personality and Social Psychology, 57,* 950-964. (p. C-10)

Allard, F., & Burnett, N. (1985). Skill in sport. *Canadian Journal of Psychology, 39,* 294-312. (p. 264)

Allen, J. B., Repinski, D. J., Ballard, J. C., & Griffin, B. W. (1996). Beliefs about the etiology of homosexuality may influence attitudes toward homosexuals. Paper presented to the American Psychological Society convention. (p. 359)

Allen, K. (2003). Are pets a healthy pleasure? The influence of pets on blood pressure. *Current Directions in Psychological Science, 12,* 236-239. (p. C-5)

Allen, N. B., & Badcock, P. B. T. (2003). The social risk hypothesis of depressed mood: Evolutionary, psychosocial, and neurobiological perspectives. *Psychological Bulletin, 129,* 887-913. (p. 580)

Alloy, L. B., Abramson, L. Y., Whitehouse, W. G., Hogan, M. E., Tashman, N. A., Steinberg, D. L., Rose, D. T., & Donovan, P. (1999). Depressogenic cognitive styles: Predictive validity, information processing and personality characteristics, and developmental origins. *Behaviour Research and Therapy, 37,* 503-531. (p. 588)

Allport, G. W. (1954). *The nature of prejudice.* New York: Addison-Wesley. (pp. 27, 667)

Allport, G. W., & Odbert, H. S. (1936). Trait-names: A psycho-lexical study. *Psychological Monographs, 47*(1). (p. 494)

Altman, L. K. (2004, November 24). Female cases of HIV found rising worldwide. *New York Times* (www.nytimes.com). (p. 405)

Alwin, D. F. (1990). Historical changes in parental orientations to children. In N. Mandell (Ed.), *Sociological studies of child development (Vol. 3).* Greenwich, CT: JAI Press. (p. 434)

Amabile, T. M. (1983). *The social psychology of creativity.* New York: Springer-Verlag. (p. 512)

Amabile, T. M., Barsade, S. G., Mueller, J. S., & Staw, B. M. (2005). Affect and creativity at work. *Administrative Science Quarterly, 50,* 367-403. (p. 389)

Amabile, T. M., & Hennessey, B. A. (1992). The motivation for creativity in children. In A. K. Boggiano & T. S. Pittman (Eds.), *Achievement* *and motivation: A social-developmental perspective.* New York: Cambridge University Press. (p. 302)

Amato, P. R., Booth, A., Johnson, D. R., & Rogers, S. J. (2007). *Alone together: How marriage in America is changing.* Cambridge, MA: Harvard University Press. (p. 439)

Ambady, N., Hallahan, M., & Rosenthal, R. (1995). On judging and being judged accurately in zero-acquaintance situations. *Journal of Personality and Social Psychology, 69,* 518–529. (p. 378)

Ambady, N., & Rosenthal, R. (1992). Thin slices of expressive behavior as predictors of interpersonal consequences: A meta-analysis. *Psychological Bulletin, 111,* 256–274. (p. 502)

Ambady, N., & Rosenthal, R. (1993). Half a minute: Predicting teacher evaluations from thin slices of nonverbal behavior and physical attractiveness. *Journal of Personality and Social Psychology, 64,* 431–441. (p. 502)

Amedi, A., Merabet, L. B., Bermpohl, F., & Pascual-Leone, A. (2005). The occipital cortex in the blind: Lessons about plasticity and vision. *Current Directions in Psychological Science, 14,* 306–311. (p. 82)

Amen, D. G., Stubblefield, M., Carmichael, B., & Thisted, R. (1996). Brain SPECT findings and aggressiveness. *Annals of Clinical Psychiatry, 8,* 129–137. (p. 671)

American Enterprise. (1992, January/February). Women, men, marriages & ministers. p. 106. (p. 518)

American Psychiatric Association. (1994). *Diagnostic and statistical manual of mental disorders (Fourth Edition).* Washington, DC: American Psychiatric Press. (pp. 542, 565)

American Psychological Association. (1992). Ethical principles of psychologists and code of conduct. *American Psychologist, 47,* 1597–1611. (p. 45)

American Psychological Association. (2002). *Ethical principles of psychologists and code of conduct.* Washington, DC: American Psychological Association. (p. 45)

American Psychological Association. (2006). Evidence-based practice in psychology (from APA Presidential Task Force on Evidence-Based Practice). *American Psychologist, 61,* 271–285. (p. 623)

American Psychological Association. (2007). Answers to your questions about sexual orientation and homosexuality (www.apa.org. Accessed December 6, 2007). (p. 355)

Ames, D. R., & Flynn, F. J. (2007). What breaks a leader: The curvilinear relation between assertiveness and leadership. *Journal of Personality and Social Psychology, 92,* 307–324. (p. B-12)

Andersen, R. A. (2005, October). Dialogue: A locksmith for the mind. *Discover* (www.discovermagazine.com). (p. 76)

Andersen, R. A., Burdick, J. W., Musallam, S., Pesaran, B., & Cham, J. G. (2004). Cognitive neural prosthetics. *Trends in Cognitive Sciences, 8,* 486–493. (p. 76)

Andersen, R. E., Crespo, C. J., Bartlett, S. J., Cheskin, L. J., & Pratt, M. (1998). Relationship of physical activity and television watching with body weight and level of fatness among children. *Journal of the American Medical Association, 279,* 938–942. (p. 347)

Andersen, S. M. (1998). *Service Learning: A National Strategy for Youth Development.* A position paper issued by the Task Force on Education Policy. Washington, DC: Institute for Communitarian Policy Studies, George Washington University. (p. 450)

Andersen, S. M., & Saribay, S. A. (2005). The relational self and transference: Evoking motives, self-regulation, and emotions through activation of mental representations of significant others. In M. W. Baldwin (Ed.), *Interpersonal cognition.* New York: Guilford. (p. 276)

Anderson, A. K., & Phelps, E. A. (2000). Expression without recognition: Contributions of the human amygdala to emotional communication. *Psychological Science, 11,* 106–111. (p. 71)

Anderson, B. L. (2002). Biobehavioral outcomes following psychological interventions for cancer patients. *Journal of Consulting and Clinical Psychology, 70,* 590–610. (p. 406)

Anderson, C. A. (2004a). An update on the effects of playing violent video games. Journal of *Adolescence, 27,* 113–122. (p. 676)

Anderson, C. A., & Anderson, D. C. (1984). Ambient temperature and violent crime: Tests of the linear and curvilinear hypotheses. *Journal of Personality and Social Psychology, 46,* 91–97. (p. 673)

Anderson, C. A., Anderson, K. B., Dorr, N., DeNeve, K. M., & Flanagan, M. (2000). Temperature and aggression. In M. P. Zanna (Ed.), *Advances in Experimental Social Psychology.* San Diego: Academic Press. (p. 673)

Anderson, C. A., Carnagey, N. L., Flanagan, M., Benjamin, A. J., Jr., Eubanks, J., & Valentine, J. C. (2004). Violent video games: Specific effects of violent content on aggressive thoughts and behavior. *Advances in Experimental Social Psychology, 36,* 199–249. (p. 677)

Anderson, C. A., & Dill, K. E. (2000). Video games and aggressive thoughts, feelings, and behavior in the laboratory and in life. *Journal of Personality and Social Psychology, 78,* 772–790. (p. 677)

Anderson, C. A., & Gentile, D. A. (2008). Media violence, aggression, and public policy. In E. Borgida & S. Fiske (Eds.), *Beyond common sense: Psychological science in the courtroom.* Malden, MA: Blackwell. (p. 247)

Anderson, C. A., Gentile, D. A., & Buckley, K. E. (2007). *Violent video game effects on children and adolescents: Theory, research, and public policy.* New York: Oxford University Press. (pp. 272, 677)

Anderson, C. A., Lindsay, J. J., & Bushman, B. J. (1999). Research in the psychological laboratory: Truth or triviality? *Current Directions in Psychological Science, 8,* 3–9. (p. 43)

Anderson, I. M. (2000). Selective serotonin reuptake inhibitors versus tricyclic antidepressants: A meta-analysis of efficacy and tolerability. *Journal of Affective Disorders, 58,* 19–36. (p. 630)

Anderson, J. R., Myowa-Yamakoshi, M., & Matsuzawa, T. (2004). Contagious yawning in chimpanzees. *Biology Letters, 271,* S468–S470. (p. 650)

Anderson, R. C., Pichert, J. W., Goetz, E. T., Schallert, D. L., Stevens, K. V., & Trollip, S. R. (1976). Instantiation of general terms. *Journal of Verbal Learning and Verbal Behavior, 15,* 667–679. (p. 275)

Anderson, S. (2008, July 6). The urge to end it. *New York Times* (www.nytimes.com). (p. 584)

Anderson, S. E., Dallal, G. E., & Must, A. (2003). Relative weight and race influence average age at menarche: Results from two nationally representative surveys of U.S. girls studied 25 years apart. *Pediatrics, 111,* 844–850. (p. 447)

Anderson, S. R. (2004). *Doctor Dolittle's delusion: Animals and the uniqueness of human language.* New Haven: Yale University Press. (p. D-4)

Anderson, U. S., Stoinski, T. S., Bloomsmith, M. A., Marr, M. J., Anderson, D., & Maple, T. L. (2005). Relative numerous judgment and summation in young and old western lowland gorillas. *Journal of Comparative Psychology, 119,* 285–295. (p. 463)

Andreasen, N. C. (1997). Linking mind and brain in the study of mental illnesses: A project for a scientific psychopathology. *Science, 275,* 1586–1593. (p. 593)

Andreasen, N. C. (2001). *Brave new brain: Conquering mental illness in the era of the genome.* New York: Oxford University Press. (p. 593)

Andreasen, N. C., Arndt, S., Swayze, V., II, Cizadlo, T., & Flaum, M. (1994). Thalamic abnormalities in schizophrenia visualized through magnetic resonance image averaging. *Science, 266,* 294–298. (p. 593)

Angell, M., & Kassirer, J. P. (1998). Alternative medicine: The risks of untested and unregulated remedies. *New England Journal of Medicine, 17,* 839–841. (p. C-9)

Angelsen, N. K., Vik, T., Jacobsen, G., & Bakketeig, L. S. (2001). Breast feeding and cognitive development at age 1 and 5 years. *Archives of Disease in Childhood, 85,* 183–188. (p. 34)

Angoff, W. H. (1988, Winter). A philosophical discussion: The issues of test and item bias. *ETS Developments,* pp. 10–11. (p. 540)

Antoni, M. H., & Lutgendorf, S. (2007). Psychosocial factors and disease progression in cancer. *Current Directions in Psychological Science, 16,* 42–46. (p. 406)

Antony, M. M., Brown, T. A., & Barlow, D. H. (1992). Current perspectives on panic and panic disorder. *Current Directions in Psychological Science, 1,* 79–82. (p. 574)

Antrobus, J. (1991). Dreaming: Cognitive processes during cortical activation and high afferent thresholds. *Psychological Review, 98,* 96–121. (p. 190)

AP. (2007). AP-Ipsos poll of 1,013 U.S. adults taken October 16–18, 2007 and distributed via Associated Press. (p. 166)

AP. (2007). Kids copying execution accidentally hang selves. Associated Press, January 15, 2007 (*Grand Rapids Press,* p. A3). (p. 651)

AP. (2007, January 12). *China facing major gender imbalance.* Associated Press release. (p. 665)

APA. (2003, November). *Psychology careers for the twenty-first century.* Washington, DC: American Psychological Association. (p. 13)

Apostolova, L. G., Dutton, R. A., Dinov, I. D., Hayashi, K. M., Toga, A. W., Cummings, J. L., Thompson, P. M. (2006). Conversion of mild cognitive impairment to Alzheimer disease predicted by hippocampal atrophy maps. *Archives of Neurology, 63,* 693–699. (p. 460)

Appleby, D. (2006). Occupations of interest to psychology majors from the dictionary of occupational titles. *Eye on Psi Chi, 10,* 28–29. (p. A-1)

Archer, J. (2004). Sex differences in aggression in real-world settings: A meta-analytic review. Review of *General Psychology, 8,* 291–322. (p. 436)

Archer, J. (2006). Cross-cultural differences in physical aggression between partners: A social-role analysis. *Personality and Social Psychology Review, 10,* 133–153. (p. 436)

Arendt, H. (1963). *Eichmann in Jerusalem: A report on the banality of evil.* New York: Viking Press. (p. 450)

Arenson, K. W. (1997, May 4). Romanian woman breaks male grip on top math prize. *New York Times* News Service (in *Grand Rapids Press,* p. A7). (p. 549)

Aries, E. (1987). Gender and communication. In P. Shaver & C. Henrick (Eds.), *Review of Personality and Social Psychology, 7,* 149–176. (p. 436)

Arkowitz, H., & Lilienfeld, S. O. (2006, April/May). Psychotherapy on trial. *Scientific American: Mind,* pp. 42–49. (p. 623)

Armel, K. C., & Ramachandran, V. S. (2003). Projecting sensations to external objects: Evidence from skin conductance response. *Proceedings of the Royal Society of London. Series B. Biological Sciences, 270,* 1499–1506. (p. 145)

Arnett, J. J. (1999). Adolescent storm and stress, reconsidered. *American Psychologist, 54,* 317–326. (p. 445)

Arnett, J. J. (2006). Emerging adulthood: Understanding the new way of coming of age. In J. J. Arnett & J. L. Tanner (Eds.), *Emerging adults in America: Coming of age in the 21st century.* Washington, DC: American Psychological Association. (p. 454)

Arnett, J. J. (2007). Socialization in emerging adulthood: From the family to the wider world, from socialization to self-socialization. In J. E. Grusec & P. D. Hastings (Eds.), *Handbook of socialization: Theory and research.* New York: Guilford Press. (p. 454)

Arnold, K., & Horrigan, K. (2002). Gaining admission into the graduate program of your choice. *Eye on Psi Chi,* 30–33. (p. A-10)

Aron, A. P., Melinat, E., Aron, E. N., Vallone, R. D., & Bator, R. J. (1997). The experimental generation of interpersonal closeness: A procedure and some preliminary findings. *Personality and Social Psychology Bulletin, 23,* 363–377. (p. 684)

Aronson, E. (2001, April 13). Newsworthy violence. E-mail to SPSP discussion list, drawing from *Nobody Left to Hate.* New York: Freeman. (p. 453)

Artiga, A. I., Viana, J. B., Maldonado, C. R., Chandler-Laney, P. C., Oswald, K. D., & Boggiano, M. M. (2007). Body composition and endocrine status of long-term stress-induced binge-eating rats. *Physiology and Behavior, 91,* 424–431. (p. 335)

ASAPS. (2008). *Cosmetic procedures in 2007.* American Society for Aesthetic Plastic Surgery (www.surgery.org). (p. 681)

Asch, S. E. (1955). Opinions and social pressure. *Scientific American, 193,* 31–35. (p. 651)

Aserinsky, E. (1988, January 17). Personal communication. (p. 178)

Ashtari, M., Kumra, S., Clarke, T., Ardekani, B., Bhaskar, S., & Rhinewine, J. (2004, November 29). Diffusion tensor imaging of children with attention deficit/hyperactivity disorder. Paper presented at the Radiological Society of North America convention. (p. 563)

Askay, S. W., & Patterson, D. R. (2007). Hypnotic analgesia. *Expert Review of Neurotherapeutics, 7,* 1675–1683. (p. 194)

Aspy, C. B., Vesely, S. K., Oman, R. F., Rodine, S., Marshall, L., & McLeroy, K. (2007). Parental communication and youth sexual behaviour. *Journal of Adolescence, 30,* 449–466. (p. 353)

Assanand, S., Pinel, J. P. J., & Lehman, D. R. (1998). Personal theories of hunger and eating. *Journal of Applied Social Psychology, 28,* 998–1015. (p. 335)

Associated Press. (1999, April 26). Airline passengers mistakenly told plane would crash. *Grand Rapids Press,* p. A3. (p. 399)

Associated Press. (2006, October 4). *Man recites pi to 100,000 places.* (p. 267)

Astin, A. W., Astin, H. S., & Lindholm, J. A. (2004). *Spirituality in higher education: A national study of college students' search for meaning and purpose.* Los Angeles: Higher Education Research Institute, UCLA. (p. 452)

Atance, C. M., & Meltzoff, A. N. (2006). Preschoolers' current desires warp their choices for the future. *Psychological Science, 17,* 583–7. (p. 332)

Atkinson, R. C., & Shiffrin, R. M. (1968). Human memory: A control system and its control processes. In K. Spence (Ed.), *The psychology of learning and motivation* (Vol. 2). New York: Academic Press. (p. 257)

Austin, E. J., Deary, I. J., Whiteman, M. C., Fowkes, F. G. R., Pedersen, N. L., Rabbitt, P., Bent, N., & McInnes, L. (2002). Relationships between ability and personality: Does intelligence contribute positively to personal and social adjustment? *Personality and Individual Differences, 32,* 1391–1411. (p. 543)

Australian Bureau of Statistics. (2007, July 8). *Overweight and obesity.* (www.abs.gov.au). (p. 340)

Averill, J. R. (1983). Studies on anger and aggression: Implications for theories of emotion. *American Psychologist, 38,* 1145–1160. (pp. 387, 389)

Averill, J. R. (1993). William James's other theory of emotion. In M. E. Donnelly (Ed.), *Reinterpreting the legacy of William James.* Washington, DC: American Psychological Association. (p. 371)

Avery, R. D., & others. (1994, December 13). Mainstream science on intelligence. *Wall Street Journal,* p. A–18. (p. 552)

Ax, A. F. (1953). The physiological differentiation of fear and anger in humans. *Psychosomatic Medicine, 15,* 433–442. (p. 370)

Axinn, W. & Thornton, A. (1992). The relationship between cohabitation and divorce: Selectivity or causal influence? *Demography, 29,* 357–374. (p. E-9)

Axiss. (2007). Immigration and foreign population as percentage of total population: 1992 and 2003. *Axiss Australia, Australian Government* (www.axiss.gov.au). (p. 661)

Azar, B. (1998, June). Why can't this man feel whether or not he's standing up? *APA Monitor* (www.apa.org/monitor/jun98/touch.html). (p. 142)

Babad, E., Bernieri, F., & Rosenthal, R. (1991). Students as judges of teachers' verbal and nonverbal behavior. *American Educational Research Journal, 28,* 211–234. (p. 378)

Babyak, M., Blumenthal, J. A., Herman, S., Khatri, P., Doraiswamy, M., Moore, K., Craighead, W. W., Baldewics, T. T., & Krishnan, K. R. (2000). Exercise treatment for major depression: Maintenance of therapeutic benefit at ten months. *Psychosomatic Medicine, 62,* 633–638. (p. C-7)

Bachman, J., O'Malley, P. M., Schulenberg, J. E., Johnston, L. D., Freedman-Doan, P., & Messersmith, E. E. (2007). *The education-drug use connection: How successes and failures in school relate to adolescent smoking, drinking, drug use, and delinquency.* Mahwah, NJ: Erlbaum. (p. 210)

Bachman, J., Wadsworth, K., O'Malley, P., Johnston, L., & Schulenberg, J. (1997). *Smoking, drinking, and drug use in young adulthood: The impact of new freedoms and new responsibilities.* Mahwah, NJ: Erlbaum. (p. 209)

Backman, L., & Dixon, R. A. (1992). Psychological compensation: A theoretical framework. *Psychological Bulletin, 112,* 259–283. (p. 140)

Backman, L., & MacDonald, S. W. S. (2006). Death and cognition: Synthesis and outlook. *European Psychologist, 11,* 224–235. (p. 465)

Baddeley, A. D. (1982). *Your memory: A user's guide.* New York: Macmillan. (pp. 259, 260)

Baddeley, A. D. (2001). Is working memory still working? *American Psychologist, 56,* 849–864. (p. 258)

Baddeley, A. D. (2002, June). Is working memory still working? *European Psychologist, 7,* 85–97. (p. 258)

Bagemihl, B. (1999). *Biological exuberance: Animal homosexuality and natural diversity.* New York: St. Martins. (p. 356)

Bahrick, H. P. (1984). Semantic memory content in permastore: 50 years of memory for Spanish learned in school. *Journal of Experimental Psychology: General, 111,* 1–29. (p. 281)

Bahrick, H. P., Bahrick, L. E., Bahrick, A. S., & Bahrick, P. E. (1993). Maintenance of foreign language vocabulary and the spacing effect. *Psychological Science, 4,* 316–321. (p. 260)

Bahrick, H. P., Bahrick, P. O., & Wittlinger, R. P. (1975). Fifty years of memory for names and faces: A cross-sectional approach. *Journal of Experimental Psychology: General, 104,* 54–75. (p. 274)

Bailenson, J. N., Iyengar, S., & Yee, N. (2005). Facial identity capture and presidential candidate preference. Paper presented at the Annual Conference of the International Communication Association. (p. 679)

Bailey, J. M., & Zucker, K. J. (1995). Childhood sex-typed behavior and sexual orientation: A conceptual analysis and quantitative review. *Developmental Psychology, 31*, 43–55. (p. 354)

Bailey, R. E., & Gillaspy, Jr., J. A. (2005). Operant psychology goes to the fair: Marian and Keller Breland in the popular press, 1947–1966. *The Behavior Analyst, 28*, 143–159. (p. 237)

Baillargeon, R. (1995). A model of physical reasoning in infancy. In C. Rovee-Collier & L. P. Lipsitt (Eds.), *Advances in infancy research* (Vol. 9). Stamford, CT: Ablex. (p. 420)

Baillargeon, R. (2008). Innate ideas revisited: For a principle of persistence in infants' physical reasoning. *Perspectives in Psychological Science, 3*, 2–13. (p. 420)

Baird, G., Simonoff, E., Pickles, A., Chandler, S., Loucas, T., Meldrum, D., & Charman, T. (2006). Prevalence of disorders of the autism spectrum in a population cohort of children in South Thames: The special needs and autism project (SNAP). *The Lancet, 368*, 210–215. (p. 424)

Baker, E. L. (1987). The state of the art of clinical hypnosis. *International Journal of Clinical and Experimental Hypnosis, 35*, 203–214. (p. 194)

Baker, T. B., Piper, M. E., McCarthy, D. E., Majeskie, M. R., & Fiore, M. C. (2004). Addiction motivation reformulated: An affective processing model of negative reinforcement. *Psychological Review, 111*, 33–51. (p. 231)

Bakermans-Kranenburg, M. J., van IJzendoorn, M. H., & Juffer, F. (2003). Less is more: Meta-analyses of sensitivity and attachment interventions in early childhood. *Psychological Bulletin, 129*, 195–215. (p. 429)

Balcetis, E., & Dunning, D. (2006). See what you want to see: Motivational influences on visual perception. *Journal of Personality and Social Psychology, 91*, 612–625. (p. 164)

Ballard, M. E., & Wiest, J. R. (1998). Mortal Kombat: The effects of violent videogame play on males' hostility and cardiovascular responding. *Journal of Applied Social Psychology, 26*, 717–730. (p. 677)

Balsam, K. F., Beauchaine, T. P., Mickey, R. M., & Rothblum, E. D. (2005). Mental health of lesbian, gay, bisexual, and heterosexual siblings: Effects of gender, sexual orientation, and family. *Journal of Abnormal Psychology, 114*, 471–476. (p. 355)

Balsam, K. F., Beauchaine, T. P., Rothblum, E. S., & Solomon, S. E. (2008). Three-year follow-up of same-sex couples who had civil unions in Vermont, same-sex couples not in civil unions, and heterosexual married couples. *Developmental Psychology, 44*, 102–116. (p. 466)

Baltes, P. B. (1993). The aging mind: Potential and limits. *The Gerontologist, 33*, 580–594. (p. 464)

Baltes, P. B. (1994). Life-span developmental psychology: On the overall landscape of human development. Invited address, American Psychological Association convention. (p. 464)

Baltes, P. B., & Baltes, M. M. (1999, September-October). Harvesting the fruits of age: Growing older, growing wise. *Science and the Spirit*, pp. 11–14. (p. 464)

Bandura, A. (1982). The psychology of chance encounters and life paths. *American Psychologist, 37*, 747–755. (p. 466)

Bandura, A. (1986). *Social foundations of thought and action: A social-cognitive theory.* Englewood Cliffs, NJ: Prentice-Hall. (p. 503)

Bandura, A. (2005) The evolution of social cognitive theory. In K. G. Smith & M. A. Hitt (Eds.), *Great minds in management: The process of theory development.* Oxford: Oxford University Press. (pp. 245, 466)

Bandura, A. (2006). Toward a psychology of human agency. *Perspectives on Psychological Science, 1*, 164–180. (p. 503)

Bandura, A. (2008). An agentic perspective on positive psychology. In S. J. Lopez (Ed.), *The science of human flourishing.* Westport, CT: Praeger. (p. 503)

Bandura, A., Ross, D., & Ross, S. A. (1961). Transmission of aggression through imitation of aggressive models. *Journal of Abnormal and Social Psychology, 63*, 575–582. (p. 244)

Barash, D. P. (2006, July 14). I am, therefore I think. *Chronicle of Higher Education*, pp. B9, B10. (p. 89)

Barber, C. (2008, February/March). The medicated American. *Scientific American Mind*, pp. 45–51. (p. 630)

Barber, T. X. (2000). A deeper understanding of hypnosis: Its secrets, its nature, its essence. American *Journal of Clinical Hypnosis, 42*, 208–272. (p. 195)

Bargh, J. A., & Chartrand, T. L. (1999). The unbearable automaticity of being. *American Psychologist, 54*, 462–479. (p. 91)

Bargh, J. A., & McKenna, K. Y. A. (2004). The Internet and social life. *Annual Review of Psychology, 55*, 573–590. (p. 679)

Bargh, J. A., & Morsella, E. (2008). The unconscious mind. *Perspectives on Psychological Science, 3*, 73–79. (p. 488)

Bargh, J. A., McKenna, K. Y. A., & Fitzsimons, G. M. (2002). Bargh, J. A., McKenna, K. Y. A., & Fitzsimons, G. M. (2002). Can you see the real me? Activation and expression of the "true self" on the Internet. *Journal of Social Issues, 58*, 33–48. (p. 679)

Bar-Haim, Y., Lamy, D., Pergamin, L., Bakermans-Kranenburg, M. J., & van Ijzendoorn, M. H. (2007). Threat-related attentional bias in anxious and nonanxious individuals: A meta-analytic study. *Psychological Bulletin, 133*, 1–24. (p. 574)

Barinaga, M. B. (1991). How long is the human life-span? *Science, 254*, 936–938. (p. 457)

Barinaga, M. B. (1992a). The brain remaps its own contours. *Science, 258*, 216–218. (p. 82)

Barinaga, M. B. (1992b). How scary things get that way. *Science, 258*, 887–888. (p. 386)

Barinaga, M. B. (1997). How exercise works its magic. *Science, 276*, 1325. (p. C-7)

Barinaga, M. B. (1999). Salmon follow watery odors home. *Science, 286*, 705–706. (p. 149)

Barkley, R. A., & 74 others. (2002). International consensus statement (January 2002). *Clinical Child and Family Psychology Review, 5*, 2. (p. 563)

Barnes, M. L., & Sternberg, R. J. (1989). Social intelligence and decoding of nonverbal cues. *Intelligence, 13*, 263–287. (p. 379)

Barnett, P. A., & Gotlib, I. H. (1988). Psychosocial functioning and depression: Distinguishing among antecedents, concomitants, and consequences. *Psychological Bulletin, 104*, 97–126. (p. 588)

Barnier, A. J., & McConkey, K. M. (2004). Defining and identifying the highly hypnotizable person. In M. Heap, R. J. Brown, & D. A. Oakley (Eds.), *High hypnotisability: Theoretical, experimental and clinical issues.* London: Brunner-Routledge. (p. 193)

Baron, R. A. (1988). Negative effects of destructive criticism: Impact on conflict, self-efficacy, and task performance. *Journal of Applied Psychology, 73*, 199–207. (p. 239)

Baron, R. S., Vandello, J. A., & Brunsman, B. (1996). The forgotten variable in conformity research: Impact of task importance on social influence. *Journal of Personality and Social Psychology, 71*, 915–927. (p. 653)

Baron-Cohen, S. (2008). Autism, hypersystemizing, and truth. *Quarterly Journal of Experimental Psychology, 61*, 64–75. (p. 424)

Baron-Cohen, S., Golan, O., Chapman, E., & Granader, Y. (2007). Transported to a world of emotion. *The Psychologist, 20*, 76–77. (p. 425)

Baron-Cohen, S., Leslie, A. M., & Frith, U. (1985). Does the autistic child have a "theory of mind"? *Cognition, 21*, 37–46. (p. 423)

Barrett, L. F. (2006). Are emotions natural kinds? *Perspectives on Psychological Science, 1*, 28–58., 370. (p. 379)

Barrett, L. F., Lane, R. D., Sechrest, L., & Schwartz, G. E. (2000). Sex differences in emotional awareness. *Personality and Social Psychology Bulletin, 26*, 1027–1035. (p. 379)

Barry, D. (1995, September 17). Teen smokers, too, get cool, toxic, waste-blackened lungs. *Asbury Park Press*, p. D3. (p. 203)

Bartholow, B. C., Bushman, B. J., & Sestir, M. A. (2006). Chronic violent video game exposure and desensitization to violence: Behavioral and event-related brain potential data. *Journal of Experimental Social Psychology, 42*, 532–539. (p. 677)

Bashore, T. R., Ridderinkhof, K. R., & van der Molen, M. W. (1997). The decline of cognitive processing speed in old age. *Current Directions in Psychological Science, 6*, 163–169. (p. 459)

Baskind, D. E. (1997, December 14). Personal communication, from Delta College. (p. 613)

Bassett, D. R., Schneider, P. L., & Huntington, G. E. (2004). Physical activity in an Old Order Amish community. *Medicine and Science in Sports and Exercise, 36*, 79–85. (p. 345)

Bat-Chava, Y. (1993). Antecedents of self-esteem in deaf people: A meta-analytic review. *Rehabilitation Psychology, 38*(4), 221–234. (p. 139)

Bat-Chava, Y. (1994). Group identification and self-esteem of deaf adults. *Personality and Social Psychology Bulletin, 20,* 494–502. (p. 139)

Bauer, P. J. (2002). Long-term recall memory: Behavioral and neurodevelopmental changes in the first 2 years of life. *Current Directions in Psychology, 11,* 137–141. (p. 417)

Bauer, P. J. (2007). Recall in infancy: A neurodevelopmental account. *Current Directions in Psychological Science, 16,* 142–146. (pp. 274, 417)

Baum, A., & Posluszny, D. M. (1999). Health psychology: Mapping biobehavioral contributions to health and illness. *Annual Review of Psychology, 50,* 137–163. (p. 405)

Baumeister, H., & Härter, M. (2007). Prevalence of mental disorders based on general population surveys. *Social Psychiatry and Psychiatric Epidemiology, 42,* 537–546. (pp. 562, 599)

Baumeister, R. F. (1989). The optimal margin of illusion. *Journal of Social and Clinical Psychology, 8,* 176–189. (p. 307)

Baumeister, R. F. (1996). Should schools try to boost self-esteem? Beware the dark side. *American Educator, 20,* 14–19, 43. (p. 515)

Baumeister, R. F. (2000). Gender differences in erotic plasticity: The female sex drive as socially flexible and responsive. *Psychological Bulletin, 126,* 347–374. (p. 355)

Baumeister, R. F. (2001, April). Violent pride: Do people turn violent because of self-hate, or self-love? *Scientific American,* pp. 96–101. (p. 515)

Baumeister, R. F. (2005). *The cultural animal: Human nature, meaning, and social life.* New York: Oxford University Press. (p. 661)

Baumeister, R. F. (2006, August/September). Violent pride. *Scientific American Mind,* pp. 54–59. (p. 512)

Baumeister, R. F., & Bratslavsky, E. (1999). Passion, intimacy, and time: Passionate love as a function of change in intimacy. *Personality and Social Psychology Review, 3,* 49–67. (p. 684)

Baumeister, R. F., Catanese, K. R., & Vohs, K. D. (2001). Is there a gender difference in strength of sex drive? Theoretical views, conceptual distinctions, and a review of relevant evidence. *Personality and Social Psychology Review, 5,* 242–273. (p. 105)

Baumeister, R. F., Dale, K., & Sommer, K. L. (1998). Freudian defense mechanisms and empirical findings in modern personality and social psychology: Reaction formation, projection, displacement, undoing, isolation, sublimation, and denial. *Journal of Personality, 66,* 1081–1125. (p. 488)

Baumeister, R. F., & Exline, J. J. (2000). Self-control, morality, and human strength. *Journal of Social and Clinical Psychology, 19,* 29–42. (p. 505)

Baumeister, R. F., & Leary, M. R. (1995). The need to belong: Desire for interpersonal attachments as a fundamental human motivation. *Psychological Bulletin, 117,* 497–529. (p. 360)

Baumeister, R. F., & Tice, D. M. (1986). How adolescence became the struggle for self: A historical transformation of psychological development. In J. Suls & A. G. Greenwald (Eds.), *Psychological perspectives on the self* (Vol. 3). Hillsdale, NJ: Erlbaum. (p. 454)

Baumeister, R. F., Twenge, J. M., & Nuss, C. K. (2002). Effects of social exclusion on cognitive processes: Anticipated aloneness reduces intelligent thought. *Journal of Personality and Social Psychology, 83,* 817–827. (p. 362)

Baumgardner, A. H., Kaufman, C. M., & Levy, P. E. (1989). Regulating affect interpersonally: When low esteem leads to greater enhancement. *Journal of Personality and Social Psychology, 56,* 907–921. (p. 512)

Baumrind, D. (1996). The discipline controversy revisited. *Family Relations, 45,* 405–414. (p. 433)

Baumrind, D., Larzelere, R. E., & Cowan, P. A. (2002). Ordinary physical punishment: Is it harmful? Comment on Gershoff (2002). *Psychological Bulletin, 128,* 602–611. (p. 235)

Bavelier, D., Dye, M. W. G., & Hauser, P. C. (2006). Do deaf individuals see better? *Trends in Cognitive Sciences, 10,* 512–518. (p. 140)

Bavelier, D., Newport, E. L., & Supalla, T. (2003). Children need natural languages, signed or spoken. *Cerebrum, 5*(1), 19–32. (p. 317)

Bavelier, D., Tomann, A., Hutton, C., Mitchell, T., Corina, D., Liu, G., & Neville, H. (2000). Visual attention to the periphery is enhanced in congenitally deaf individuals. *Journal of Neuroscience, 20,* 1–6. (p. 82)

Bayley, N. (1949). Consistency and variability in the growth of intelligence from birth to eighteen years. *Journal of Genetic Psychology, 75,* 165–196. (p. 540)

BBC. (2006, June 14). Crystal meth to be Class A drug. *BBC News* (www.news.bbc.co.uk) . (p. 201)

BBC. (2008, February 26). Anti-depressants 'of little use.' *BBC News* (www.news.bbc.co.uk). (p. 631)

Beaman, A. L., & Klentz, B. (1983). The supposed physical attractiveness bias against supporters of the women's movement: A meta-analysis. *Personality and Social Psychology Bulletin, 9,* 544–550. (p. 682)

Beardsley, L. M. (1994). Medical diagnosis and treatment across cultures. In W. J. Lonner & R. Malpass (Eds.), *Psychology and culture.* Boston: Allyn & Bacon. (p. 564)

Beauchamp, G. K. (1987). The human preference for excess salt. *American Scientist, 75,* 27–33. (p. 335)

Beaujean, A. A. (2005). Heritability of cognitive abilities as measured by mental chronometric tasks: A meta-analysis. *Intelligence, 33,* 187–201. (p. 544)

Beck, A. T., & Steer, R. A. (1989). Clinical predictors of eventual suicide: A 5- to 10-year prospective study of suicide attempters. *Journal of Affective Disorders, 17,* 203–209. (p. 584)

Beck, A. T., Rush, A. J., Shaw, B. F., & Emery, G. (1979). *Cognitive therapy of depression.* New York: Guilford Press. (p. 615)

Becker, D. V., Kenrick, D. T., Neuberg, S. L., Blackwell, K. C., & Smith, D. M. (2007). The confounded nature of angry men and happy women. *Journal of Personality and Social Psychology, 92,* 179–190. (pp. 379, 380)

Becker, S., & Wojtowicz, J. M. (2007). A model of hippocampal neurogenesis in memory and mood disorders. *Trends in Cognitive Sciences, 11,* 70–76. (p. 631)

Becklen, R., & Cervone, D. (1983). Selective looking and the noticing of unexpected events. *Memory and Cognition, 11,* 601–608. (p. 118)

Beckman, M. (2004). Crime, culpability, and the adolescent brain. *Science, 305,* 596–599. (p. 447)

Beeman, M. J., & Chiarello, C. (1998). Complementary right- and left-hemisphere language comprehension. *Current Directions in Psychological Science, 7,* 2–8. (p. 87)

Beilin, H. (1992) Piaget's enduring contribution to developmental psychology. *Developmental Psychology, 28,* 191–204. (p. 423)

Beitman, B. D., Goldfried, M. R., & Norcross, J. C. (1989). The movement toward integrating the psychotherapies: An overview. *American Journal of Psychiatry, 146,* 138–147. (p. 606)

Bell, A. P., Weinberg, M. S., & Hammersmith, S. K. (1981). *Sexual preference: Its development in men and women.* Bloomington: Indiana University Press. (p. 356)

Bell, R. Q., & Waldrop, M. F. (1989). Achievement and cognitive correlates of minor physical anomalies in early development. In M. G. Bornstein & N. A. Krasnegor (Eds.), *Stability and continuity in mental development: Behavioral and biological perspectives.* Hillsdale, NJ: Erlbaum. (p. 540)

Bellugi, U. (1994, August). Quoted in P. Radetsky, Silence, signs, and wonder. *Discover,* pp. 60–68. (p. 314)

Belot, M., & Francesconi, M. (2006, November). *Can anyone be 'the one'? Evidence on mate selection from speed dating.* London: Centre for Economic Policy Research (www.cepr.org). (p. 680)

Belsher, G., & Costello, C. G. (1988). Relapse after recovery from unipolar depression: A critical review. *Psychological Bulletin, 104,* 84–96. (p. 582)

Belsky, J. (2003). The politicized science of day care: A personal and professional odyssey. *Family Policy Review 1*(2), 23–40. (p. 432)

Belsky, J., Bakermans-Kranenburg, M. J., & van Ijzendoorn, M. H. (2007). For better and for worse: Differential susceptibility to environmental influences. *Current Directions in Psychological Science, 16,* 300–304. (p. 598)

Bem, D. J. (1984). Quoted in *The Skeptical Inquirer, 8,* 194. (p. 168)

Bem, D. J. (1996). Exotic becomes erotic: A developmental theory of sexual orientation. *Psychological Review, 103,* 320–335. (p. 359)

Bem, D. J. (1998). Is EBE theory supported by the evidence? Is it androcentric? A reply to Peplau et al. (1998). *Psychological Review, 105,* 395–398. (p. 359)

Bem, D. J. (2000). Exotic becomes erotic: Interpreting the biological correlates of sexual orientation. *Archives of Sexual Behavior, 29,* 531–548. (p. 359)

Bem, D. J., & Honorton, C. (1994). Does psi exist? Replicable evidence for an anomalous process of information transfer. *Psychological Bulletin, 115,* 4–18. (p. 168)

Bem, D. J., Palmer, J., & Broughton, R. S. (2001). Updating the Ganzfeld database: A victim of its own success? *Journal of Parapsychology, 65,* 207–218. (p. 168)

Bem, S. L. (1987). Masculinity and femininity exist only in the mind of the perceiver. In J. M. Reinisch, L. A. Rosenblum, & S. A. Sanders (Eds.), *Masculinity/femininity: Basic perspectives.* New York: Oxford University Press. (p. 440)

Bem, S. L. (1993). *The lenses of gender.* New Haven: Yale University Press. (p. 440)

Benbow, C. P., Lubinski, D., Shea, D. L., & Eftekhari-Sanjani, H. (2000). Sex differences in mathematical reasoning ability at age 13: Their status 20 years later. *Psychological Science, 11,* 474–2000. (p. 550)

Bennett, R. (1991, February). Pornography and extrafamilial child sexual abuse: Examining the relationship. Unpublished manuscript, Los Angeles Police Department Sexually Exploited Child Unit. (p. 675)

Bennett, W. I. (1995). Beyond overeating. *New England Journal of Medicine, 332,* 673–674. (p. 347)

Ben-Shakhar, G., & Elaad, E. (2003). The validity of psychophysiological detection of information with the guilt knowledge test: A meta-analytic review. *Journal of Applied Psychology, 88,* 131–151. (p. 372)

Benson, H. (1996). *Timeless healing: The power and biology of belief.* New York: Scribner. (p. C-8)

Benson, K., & Feinberg, I. (1977). The beneficial effect of sleep in an extended Jenkins and Dallenbach paradigm. *Psychophysiology, 14,* 375–384. (p. 283)

Benson, P. L. (1992, Spring). Patterns of religious development in adolescence and adulthood. *PIRI Newsletter,* 2–9. (p. 437)

Berenbaum, S. A., & Bailey, J. M. (2003). Effects on gender identity of prenatal androgens and genital appearance: Evidence from girls with congenital adrenal hyperplasia. *Journal of Clinical Endocrinology and Metabolism, 88,* 1102–1106. (p. 438)

Berenbaum, S. A., & Hines, M. (1992). Early androgens are related to childhood sex-typed toy preferences. *Psychological Science, 3,* 203–206. (p. 438)

Berenbaum, S. A., Korman, K., & Leveroni, C. (1995). Early hormones and sex differences in cognitive abilities. *Learning and Individual Differences, 7,* 303–321. (p. 550)

Berenson, A. (2007, September 3). New schizophrenia drug shows promise in trials. *New York Times* (www.nytimes.com). (p. 629)

Berghuis, P., & 16 others. (2007). Hardwiring the brain: Endocannabinoids shape neuronal connectivity. *Science, 316,* 1212–1216. (p. 207)

Bergin, A. E. (1980). Psychotherapy and religious values. *Journal of Consulting and Clinical Psychology, 48,* 95–105. (p. 628)

Berk, L. E. (1994, November). Why children talk to themselves. *Scientific American,* pp. 78–83. (p. 423)

Berk, L. S., Felten, D. L., Tan, S. A., Bittman, B. B., & Westengard, J. (2001). Modulation of neuroimmune parameters during the eustress of humor-associated mirthful laughter. *Alternative Therapies, 7,* 62–76. (p. C-3)

Berkel, J., & de Waard, F. (1983). Mortality pattern and life expectancy of Seventh Day Adventists in the Netherlands. *International Journal of epidemiology, 12,* 455–459. (p. C-12)

Berkowitz, L. (1983). Aversively stimulated aggression: Some parallels and differences in research with animals and humans. *American Psychologist, 38,* 1135–1144. (p. 672)

Berkowitz, L. (1989). Frustration-aggression hypothesis: Examination and reformulation. *Psychological Bulletin, 106,* 59–73. (p. 672)

Berkowitz, L. (1990). On the formation and regulation of anger and aggression: A cognitive-neoassociationistic analysis. *American Psychologist, 45,* 494–503. (p. 387)

Berman, M., Gladue, B., & Taylor, S. (1993). The effects of hormones, Type A behavior pattern, and provocation on aggression in men. *Motivation and Emotion, 17,* 125–138. (p. 672)

Berndt, T. J. (1992). Friendship and friends' influence in adolescence. *Current Directions in Psychological Science, 1,* 156–159. (p. 437)

Bernhardt, P. C., Dabbs, J. M., Jr., Fielden, J. A., & Lutter, C. D. (1998). Testosterone changes during vicarious experiences of winning and losing among fans at sporting events. *Physiology and Behavior, 65,* 59–62. (p. 672)

Berridge, K. C., & Winkielman, P. (2003). What is an unconscious emotion? (The case of unconscious "liking"). *Cognition and Emotion, 17,* 181–211. (p. 374)

Berry, D. S., & McArthur, L. Z. (1986). Perceiving character in faces: The impact of age-related craniofacial changes on social perception. *Psychological Bulletin, 100,* 3–18. (p. 222)

Berscheid, E. (1981). An overview of the psychological effects of physical attractiveness and some comments upon the psychological effects of knowledge of the effects of physical attractiveness. In G. W. Lucker, K. Ribbens, & J. A. McNamara (Eds.), *Psychological aspects of facial form* (Craniofacial growth series). Ann Arbor: Center for Human Growth and Development, University of Michigan. (p. 680)

Berscheid, E. (1985). Interpersonal attraction. In G. Lindzey & E. Aronson (Eds.), *The handbook of social psychology.* New York: Random House. (p. 360)

Berscheid, E., Gangestad, S. W., & Kulakowski, D. (1984). Emotion in close relationships: Implications for relationship counseling. In S. D. Brown & R. W. Lent (Eds.), *Handbook of counseling psychology.* New York: Wiley. (p. 684)

Berti, A., Cottini, G., Gandola, M., Pia, L., Smania, N., Stracciari, A., Castiglioni, I., Vallar, G., & Paulesu, E. (2005). Shared cortical anatomy for motor awareness and motor control. *Science, 309,* 488–491. (p. 87)

Bertua, C., Anderson, N., & Salgado, J. F. (2005). The predictive validity of cognitive ability tests: A UK meta-analysis. *Journal of Occupational and Organizational Psychology, 78,* 387–409. (p. 526)

Bettencourt, B. A., & Kernahan, C. (1997). A meta-analysis of aggression in the presence of violent cues: Effects of gender differences and aversive provocation. *Aggressive Behavior, 23,* pp. 447–457. (p. 436)

Beyerstein, B., & Beyerstein, D. (Eds.) (1992). *The write stuff: Evaluations of graphology.* Buffalo, NY: Prometheus Books. (p. 498)

Bhatt, R. S., Wasserman, E. A., Reynolds, W. F., Jr., & Knauss, K. S. (1988). Conceptual behavior in pigeons: Categorization of both familiar and novel examples from four classes of natural and artificial stimuli. *Journal of Experimental Psychology: Animal Behavior Processes, 14,* 219–234. (p. 230)

Bialystok, E. (2001). *Bilingualism in development, language, literacy, and cognition.* New York: Cambridge University Press. (p. 321)

Biederman, I., & Vessel, E. A. (2006). Perceptual pleasure and the brain. *American Scientist, 94,* 247–253., 330)

Biederman, J., Wilens, T., Mick, E., Spencer, T., & Faraone, S. V. (1999). Pharmacotherapy of Attention-Deficit/Hyperactivity Disorder reduces risk for substance use disorder. *Pediatrics, 104,* 1–5. (p. 563)

Biggs, V. (2001, April 13). Murder suspect captured in Grand Marais. *Cook County News-Herald.* (p. 379)

Bigler, E. D., Johnson, S. C., Jackson, C., & Blatter, D. D. (1995). Aging, brain size, and IQ. *Intelligence, 21,* 109–119. (p. 530)

Binet, A. (1909). *Les idées mordermes sur les enfants.* Paris: Flammarion (quoted by A. Clarke & A. Clarke, Born to be bright. *The Psychologist, 19,* 409). (p. 533)

Binitie, A. (1975) A factor-analytical study of depression across cultures (African and European). *British Journal of Psychiatry, 127,* 559–563. (p. 576)

Birnbaum, G. E., Reis, H. T., Mikulincer, M., Gillath, O., & Orpaz, A. (2006). When sex is more than just sex: Attachment orientations, sexual experience, and relationship quality. *Journal of Personality and Social Psychology, 91,* 929–943. (p. 430)

Birnbaum, S. G., Yuan, P. X., Wang, M., Vijayraghavan, S., Bloom, A. K., Davis, D. J., Gobeski, K. T., Sweatt, J. D., Manhi, H. K., & Arnsten, A. F. T. (2004). Protein kinase C overactivity impairs prefrontal cortical regulation of working memory. *Science, 306,* 882–884. (p. 270)

Bishop, G. D. (1991). Understanding the understanding of illness: Lay disease representations. In J. A. Skelton & R. T. Croyle (Eds.), *Mental representation in health and illness.* New York: Springer-Verlag. (p. 300)

Bishop, G. D. (2004, November 22). Personal correspondence, and earlier articles on "The great divide" in the *Austin Statesman.* (p. 659)

Bisson, J., & Andrew, M. (2007). Psychological treatment of post-traumatic stress disorder (PTSD). *Cochrane Database of Systematic Reviews 2007,* Issue 3. Art. No: CD003388. (p. 624)

Bjork, R. A. (2000, July/August). Toward one world of psychological science. *APS Observer,* p. 3. (p. 8)

Bjorklund, D. F., & Green, B. L. (1992). The adaptive nature of cognitive immaturity. *American Psychologist, 47,* 46–54. (p. 426)

Blackburn, E. H., Greider, C. W., & Szostak, J. W. (2007). Telomeres and telomerase: The path from maize, *Tetrahymena* and yeast to human cancer and aging. *Nature Medicine, 12*(10), vii–xii. (p. 457)

Blakemore, S-J. (2008). Development of the social brain during adolescence. *Quarterly Journal of Experimental Psychology, 61,* 40–49. (p. 447)

Blakemore, S-J., Wolpert, D. M., & Frith, C. D. (1998). Central cancellation of self-produced tickle sensation. *Nature Neuroscience, 1,* 635–640. (p. 141)

Blakeslee, S. (2005, February 8). Focus narrows in search for autism's cause. *New York Times* (www.nytimes.com). (p. 424)

Blakeslee, S. (2006, January 10). Cells that read minds. *New York Times* (www.nytimes.com). (p. 243)

Blanchard, R. (1997). Birth order and sibling sex ratio in homosexual versus heterosexual males and females. *Annual Review of Sex Research, 8,* 27–67. (p. 356)

Blanchard, R. (2008). Review and theory of handedness, birth order, and homosexuality in men. *Laterality, 13,* 51–70. (p. 356)

Blanchard-Fields, F. (2007). Everyday problem solving and emotion: An adult developmental perspective. *Current Directions in Psychological Science, 16,* 26–31. (p. 464)

Blanchflower, D. G., & Oswald, A. J. (2008). Hypertension and happiness across nations. *Journal of Health Economics, 27,* 218–233. (pp. 401, 469)

Blank, H., Musch, J., & Pohl, R. F. (2007). Hindsight bias: On being wise after the event. *Social Cognition, 25,* 1–9. (p. 20)

Blankenburg, F., Taskin, B., Ruben, J., Moosmann, M., Ritter, P., Curio, G., & Villringer, A. (2003). Imperceptive stimuli and sensory processing impediment. *Science, 299,* 1864. (p. 122)

Blascovich, J., Seery, M. D., Mugridge, C. A., Norris, R. K., & Weisbuch, M. (2004). Predicting athletic performance from cardiovascular indexes of challenge and threat. *Journal of Experimental Social Psychology, 40,* 683–688. (p. 398)

Blass, T. (1996). Stanley Milgram: A life of inventiveness and controversy. In G. A. Kimble, C. A. Boneau, & M. Wertheimer (Eds.), *Portraits of pioneers in psychology (Vol. II)*. Washington, DC and Mahwah, NJ: American Psychological Association and Lawrence Erlbaum Publishers. (p. 655)

Blass, T. (1999). The Milgram paradigm after 35 years: Some things we now know about obedience to authority. *Journal of Applied Social Psychology, 29,* 955–978. (p. 654)

Blatt, S. J., Sanislow, C. A., III, Zuroff, D. C., & Pilkonis, P. (1996). Characteristics of effective therapists: Further analyses of data from the National Institute of Mental Health Treatment of Depression Collaborative Research Program. *Journal of Consulting and Clinical Psychology, 64,* 1276–1284. (p. 626)

Bleustein, J. (2002, June 15). Quoted in "Harley retooled," by S. S. Smith, *American Way Magazine.* (p. B-13)

Bloom, B. C. (Ed.). (1985). *Developing talent in young people.* New York: Ballantine. (p. B-8)

Bloom, B. J. (1964). *Stability and change in human characteristics.* New York: Wiley. (p. 540)

Bloom, F. E. (1993, January/February). What's new in neurotransmitters. *BrainWork,* pp. 7–9. (p. 55)

Bloom, P. (2000). *How children learn the meanings of words.* Cambridge, MA: MIT Press. (p. 315)

Blum, K., Cull, J. G., Braverman, E. R., & Comings, D. E. (1996). Reward deficiency syndrome. *American Scientist, 84,* 132–14. (p. 73)

Boag, S. (2006). Freudian repression, the common view, and pathological science. *Review of General Psychology, 10,* 74–86. (p. 487)

Boahen, K. (2005, May). Neuromorphic microchips. *Scientific American,* pp. 56–63. (p. 138)

Bodenhausen, G. V., Sheppard, L. A., & Kramer, G. P. (1994). Negative affect and social judgment: The differential impact of anger and sadness. *European Journal of Social Psychology, 24,* 45–62. (p. 692)

Bodkin, J. A., & Amsterdam, J. D. (2002). Transdermal selegiline in major depression: A double-blind, placebo-controlled, parallel-group study in outpatients. *American Journal of Psychiatry, 159,* 1869–1875. (p. 630)

Boehm, K. E., Schondel, C. K., Marlowe, A. L., & Manke-Mitchell, L. (1999). Teens' concerns: A national evaluation. *Adolescence, 34,* 523–528. (p. 453)

Boehm-Davis, D. A. (2005). Improving product safety and effectiveness in the home. *Reviews of Human Factors and Ergonomics, 1,* 219–253. (p. B-14)

Boehm-Davis, D. A. (2006). Improving product safety and effectiveness in the home. In R. S. Nickerson (Ed.), *Reviews of human factors and ergonomics.* Volume 1 (pp. 219–253). Santa Monica, CA: Human Factors and Ergonomics Society. (p. B-13)

Boesch-Achermann, H., & Boesch, C. (1993). Tool use in wild chimpanzees: New light from dark forests. *Current Directions in Psychological Science, 2,* 18–21. (p. D-1)

Bogaert, A. F. (2003). Number of older brothers and sexual orientation: New texts and the attraction/behavior distinction in two national probability samples. *Journal of Personality and Social Psychology, 84,* 644–652. (p. 356)

Bogaert, A. F. (2004). Asexuality: Prevalence and associated factors in a national probability sample. *Journal of Sex Research, 41,* 279–287. (p. 354)

Bogaert, A. F. (2006). Biological versus nonbiological older brothers and men's sexual orientation. *Proceedings of the National Academy of Sciences, 103,* 10771–10774. (p. 354)

Bogaert, A. F. (2006). Toward a conceptual understanding of asexuality. *Review of General Psychology, 10,* 241–250. (p. 356)

Boggiano, A. K., Harackiewicz, J. M., Bessette, M. M., & Main, D. S. (1985). Increasing children's interest through performance-contingent reward. *Social Cognition, 3,* 400–411. (p. 237)

Boggiano, M. M., Chandler, P. C., Viana, J. B., Oswald, K. D., Maldonado, C. R., & Wauford, P. K. (2005). Combined dieting and stress evoke exaggerated responses to opioids in binge-eating rats. *Behavioral Neuroscience, 119,* 1207–1214. (p. 335)

Bohman, M., & Sigvardsson, S. (1990). Outcome in adoption: Lessons from longitudinal studies. In D. Brodzinsky & M. Schechter (Eds.), *The psychology of adoption.* New York: Oxford University Press. (p. 100)

Bolger, N., DeLongis, A., Kessler, R. C., & Schilling, E. A. (1989). Effects of daily stress on negative mood. *Journal of Personality and Social Psychology, 57,* 808–818. (p. 390)

Bolwig, T. G., Madsen, T. M. (2007). Electroconvulsive therapy in melancholia: The role of hippocampal neurogenesis. *Acta Psychiatrica Scandinavica, 115,* 130–135. (p. 633)

Bonanno, G. A. (2001). Grief and emotion: Experience, expression, and dissociation. In M. Stroebe, W. Stroebe, R. O. Hansson, & H. Schut (Eds.), *New handbook of bereavement: Consciousness, coping, and care.* Cambridge: Cambridge University Press. (p. 471)

Bonanno, G. A. (2004). Loss, trauma, and human resilience: Have we underestimated the human capacity to thrive after extremely aversive events? *American Psychologist, 59,* 20–28. (pp. 471, 573)

Bonanno, G. A. (2005). Adult resilience to potential trauma. *Current Directions in Psychological Science, 14,* 135–137. (p. 573)

Bonanno, G. A., Galea, S., Bucciarelli, A., & Vlahov, D. (2006). Psychological resilience after disaster. *Psychological Science, 17,* 181–186. (p. 573)

Bonanno, G. A., Galea, S., Bucciarelli, A., & Vlahov, D. (2007). What predicts psychological resilience after disaster? The role of demographics, resources, and life stress. *Journal of Consulting and Clinical Psychology, 75*(5), 671–682. (p. 638)

Bonanno, G. A., & Kaltman, S. (1999). Toward an integrative perspective on bereavement. *Psychological Bulletin, 125,* 760–777. (p. 471)

Bond, C. F, Jr., & DePaulo, B. M. (2006). Accuracy of deception judgments. *Personality and Social Psychology Review, 10,* 214–234. (p. 378)

Bond, C. F., Jr., & DePaulo, B. M. (2008). Individual differences in detecting deception: Accuracy and bias. *Psychological Bulletin, 134,* 477–492. (p. 378)

Bond, C. F., Jr., & the 89 others on The Global Deception Research Team. (2006). A world of lies. *Journal of Cross-Cultural Psychology, 37,* 60–74. (p. 378)

Bond, M. H. (1988). Finding universal dimensions of individual variation in multi-cultural studies of values: The Rokeach and Chinese values surveys. *Journal of Personality and Social Psychology, 55,* 1009–1015. (p. 517)

Bond, R., & Smith, P. B. (1996). Culture and conformity: A meta-analysis of studies using Asch's (1952b, 1956) line judgment task. *Psychological Bulletin, 119,* 111–137. (p. 654)

Bonnie, K. E., Horner, V., Whiten, A., & de Waal, F. B. M. (2007). Spread of arbitrary conventions among chimpanzees: A controlled experiment. *Proceedings of the Royal Society, 274,* 367–372. (p. D-2)

Bono, J. E., & Judge, T. A. (2004). Personality and transformational and transactional leadership: A meta-analysis. *Journal of Applied Psychology, 89,* 901-910. (p. B-12)

Bookheimer, S. H., Strojwas, M. H., Cohen, M. S., Saunders, A. M., Pericak-Vance, M. A., Mazziotta, J. C., & Small, G. W. (2000). Patterns of brain activation in people at risk for Alzheimer's disease. *New England Journal of Medicine, 343,* 450-456. (p. 460)

Bookwala, J., & Boyar, J. (2008). Gender, excessive body weight, and psychological well-being in adulthood. *Psychology of Women Quarterly, 32,* 188-195. (p. 342)

Boos, H. B. M., Aleman, A., Cahn, W., Hulshoff, H., & Kahn, R. S. (2007). Brain volumes in relatives of patients with schizophrenia. *Archives of General Psychiatry, 64,* 297-304. (p. 593)

Booth, F. W., & Neufer, P. D. (2005). Exercise controls gene expression. *American Scientist, 93,* 28-35. (p. C-8)

Boring, E. G. (1930). A new ambiguous figure. *American Journal of Psychology, 42,* 444-445. (p. 161)

Bornstein, M. H., Cote, L. R., Maital, S., Painter, K., Park, S-Y., Pascual, L., Pecheux, M-G., Ruel, J., Venute, P., & Vyt, A. (2004). Cross-linguistic analysis of vocabulary in young children: Spanish, Dutch, French, Hebrew, Italian, Korean, and American English. *Child Development, 75,* 1115-1139. (p. 317)

Bornstein, R. F. (1989). Exposure and affect: Overview and meta-analysis of research, 1968-1987. *Psychological Bulletin, 106,* 265-289. (pp. 427, 678)

Bornstein, R. F. (1999). Source amnesia, misattribution, and the power of unconscious perceptions and memories. *Psychoanalytic Psychology, 16,* 155-178. (p. 678)

Bornstein, R. F. (2001). The impending death of psychoanalysis. *Psychoanalytic Psychology, 18,* 3-20. (p. 490)

Bornstein, R. F., Galley, D. J., Leone, D. R., & Kale, A. R. (1991). The temporal stability of ratings of parents: Test-retest reliability and influence of parental contact. *Journal of Social Behavior and Personality, 6,* 641-649. (p. 278)

Boscarino, J. A. (1997). Diseases among men 20 years after exposure to severe stress: Implications for clinical research and medical care. *Psychosomatic Medicine, 59,* 605-614. (p. 398)

Bösch, H., Steinkamp, F., & Boller, E. (2006a). Examining psychokinesis: The interaction of human intention with random number generators—A meta-analysis. *Psychological Bulletin, 132,* 497-523. (p. 168)

Bösch, H., Steinkamp, F., & Boller, E. (2006b). In the eye of beholder: Reply to Wilson and Shadish (2006) and Radin, Nelson, Dobyns, and Houtkooper, (2006). *Psychological Bulletin, 132,* 533-537. (p. 168)

Bosma, H., Marmot, M. G., Hemingway, H., Nicolson, A. C., Brunner, E., & Stansfeld, S. A. (1997). Low job control and risk of coronary heart disease in Whitehall II (prospective cohort) study. *British Medical Journal, 314,* 558-565. (p. C-2)

Bosma, H., Peter, R., Siegrist, J., & Marmot, M. (1998). Two alternative job stress models and the risk of coronary heart disease. *American Journal of Public Health, 88,* 68-74. (p. C-2)

Bostwick, J. M., & Pankratz, V. S. (2000). Affective disorders and suicide risk: A re-examination. *American Journal of Psychiatry, 157,* 1925-1932. (p. 584)

Bosworth, R. G., & Dobkins, K. R. (1999). Left-hemisphere dominance for motion processing in deaf signers. *Psychological Science, 10,* 256-262. (p. 83)

Bothwell, R. K., Brigham, J. C., & Malpass, R. S. (1989). Cross-racial identification. *Personality and Social Psychology Bulletin, 15,* 19-25. (p. 669)

Bothwell, R. K., Deffenbacher, K. A., & Brigham, J. C. (1987). Correlation of eyewitness accuracy and confidence: Optimality hypothesis revised. *Journal of Applied Psychology, 72,* 691-695. (p. 288)

Botwin, M. D., Buss, D. M., & Shackelford, T. K. (1997). Personality and mate preferences: Five factors in mate selection and marital satisfaction. *Journal of Personality, 65,* 107-136. (p. 499)

Bouchard, T. J., Jr. (1981, December 6). Interview on Nova: Twins [program broadcast by the Public Broadcasting Service]. (p. 98)

Bouchard, T. J., Jr. (1995). Longitudinal studies of personality and intelligence: A behavior genetic and evolutionary psychology perspective. In D. H. Saklofske & M. Zeidner (Eds.), *International handbook of personality and intelligence.* New York: Plenum. (p. 545)

Bouchard, T. J., Jr. (1996a). IQ similarity in twins reared apart: Finding and responses to critics. In R. Sternberg & C. Grigorenko (Eds.), *Intelligence: Heredity and environment.* New York: Cambridge University Press. (p. 544)

Bouchard, T. J., Jr. (1996b). Behavior genetic studies of intelligence, yesterday and today: The long journey from plausibility to proof. *Journal of Biosocial Science, 28,* 527-555. (p. 545)

Bouchard, T. J., Jr., & McGue, M. (1990). Genetic and rearing environmental influences on adult personality: An analysis of adopted twins reared apart. *Journal of Personality, 58,* 263. (p. 98)

Bouton, M. E., Mineka, S., & Barlow, D. H. (2001). A modern learning theory perspective on the etiology of panic disorder. *Psychological Review, 108,* 4-32. (p. 574)

Bowden, E. M., & Beeman, M. J. (1998). Getting the right idea: Semantic activation in the right hemisphere may help solve insight problems. *Psychological Science, 9,* 435-440. (p. 87)

Bower, G. H. (1983). Affect and cognition. *Philosophical Transaction: Royal Society of London, Series B, 302,* 387-402. (p. 277)

Bower, G. H. (1986). Prime time in cognitive psychology. In P. Eelen (Ed.), *Cognitive research and behavior therapy: Beyond the conditioning paradigm.* Amsterdam: North Holland Publishers. (p. 276)

Bower, G. H., Clark, M. C., Lesgold, A. M., & Winzenz, D. (1969). Hierarchical retrieval schemes in recall of categorized word lists. *Journal of Verbal Learning and Verbal Behavior, 8,* 323-343. (p. 265)

Bower, G. H., & Morrow, D. G. (1990). Mental models in narrative comprehension. *Science, 247,* 44-48. (p. 261)

Bower, J. E., Kemeny, M. E., Taylor, S. E., & Fahey, J. L. (1998). Cognitive processing, discovery of meaning, CD4 decline, and AIDS-related mortality among bereaved HIV-seropositive men. *Journal of Consulting and Clinical Psychology, 66,* 979-986. (p. 405)

Bower, J. M., & Parsons, L. M. (2003, August). Rethinking the "lesser brain." *Scientific American,* 50-57. (p. 70)

Bowers, K. S. (1984). Hypnosis. In N. Endler & J. M. Hunt (Eds.), *Personality and behavioral disorders* (2nd ed.). New York: Wiley. (pp. 192, 194)

Bowers, K. S. (1987, July). Personal communication. (p. 193)

Bowers, T. G., & Clum, G. A. (1988). Relative contribution of specific and nonspecific treatment effects: Meta-analysis of placebo-controlled behavior therapy research. *Psychological Bulletin, 103,* 315-323. (p. 622)

Bowlby, J. (1973). *Separation: Anxiety and anger.* New York: Basic Books. (p. 431)

Bowler, M. C., & Woehr, D. J. (2006). A meta-analytic evaluation of the impact of dimension and exercise factors on assessment center ratings. *Journal of Applied Psychology, 91,* 1114-1124. (p. 509)

Bowles, S., & Kasindorf, M. (2001, March 6). Friends tell of picked-on but 'normal' kid. *USA Today,* p. 4A. (p. 362)

Bowling, N. A. (2007). Is the job satisfaction-job performance relationship spurious? A meta-analytic examination. *Journal of Vocational Behavior, 71,* 167-185. (p. B-8)

Bowman, H. (2003, Fall). Interactions between chimpanzees and their human caregivers in captive settings: The effects of gestural communication on reciprocity. *Friends of Washoe, 25(1),* 7-16. (p. D-3)

Boyatzis, C. J., Matillo, G. M., & Nesbitt, K. M. (1995). Effects of the "Mighty Morphin Power Rangers" on children's aggression with peers. *Child Study Journal, 25,* 45-55. (p. 248)

Boyer, J. L., Harrison, S., & Ro, T. (2005). Unconscious processing of orientation and color without primary visual cortex. *Proceedings of the National Academy of Sciences, 102,* 16875-16879 (www.pnas.org). (p. 131)

Boynton, R. M. (1979). *Human color vision.* New York: Holt, Rinehart & Winston. (p. 132)

Braden, J. P. (1994). *Deafness, deprivation, and IQ.* New York: Plenum. (pp. 139, 552)

Bradley, D. R., Dumais, S. T., & Petry, H. M. (1976). Reply to Cavonius. *Nature, 261,* 78. (p. 151)

Bradley, R. B. & 15 others. (2008). Influence of child abuse on adult depression: Moderation by the corticotropin-releasing hormone receptor gene. *Archives of General Psychiatry, 65,* 190-200. (p. 431)

Braiker, B. (2005, October 18). A quiet revolt against the rules on SIDS. *New York Times* (www.nytimes.com). (p. 416)

Brainerd, C. J. (1996). Piaget: A centennial celebration. *Psychological Science, 7,* 191-195. (p. 418)

Brainerd, C. J., & Poole, D. A. (1997). Long-term survival of children's memories: A review. *Learning and Individual Differences, 9,* 125-151. (p. 288)

Brainerd, C. J., & Reyna, V. F. (1998). When things that were never experienced are easier to "remember" than things that were. *Psychological Science, 9,* 484–489. (p. 288)

Brainerd, C. J., & Reyna, V. F. (2002). Fuzzy-trace theory and false memory. *Current Directions in Psychological Science, 11,* 164–169. (p. 288)

Brainerd, C. J., Reyna, V. F., & Brandse, E. (1995). Are children's false memories more persistent than their true memories? *Psychological Science, 6,* 359–364. (p. 288)

Brandon, S., Boakes, J., Glaser, & Green, R. (1998). Recovered memories of childhood sexual abuse: Implications for clinical practice. *British Journal of Psychiatry, 172,* 294–307. (p. 291)

Brang, D., Edwards, L., Ramachandran, V. S., & Coulson, S. (2008). Is the sky 2? Contextual priming in grapheme-color synaesthesia. *Psychological Science, 19,* 421–428. (p. 148)

Bransford, J. D., & Johnson, M. K. (1972). Contextual prerequisites for understanding: Some investigations of comprehension and recall. *Journal of Verbal Learning and Verbal Behavior, 11,* 717–726. (p. 262)

Braun, S. (1996). New experiments underscore warnings on maternal drinking. *Science, 273,* 738–739. (p. 413)

Braun, S. (2001, Spring). Seeking insight by prescription. *Cerebrum,* pp. 10–21. (p. 205)

Braunstein, G. D., Sundwall, D. A., Katz, M., Shifren, J. L., Buster, J. E., Simon, J. A., Bachman, G., Aguirre, O. A., Lucas, J. D. Rodenberg, C., Buch, A., & Watts, N. B. (2005). Safety and efficacy of a testosterone patch for the treatment of hypoactive sexual desire disorder in surgically menopausal women: A randomized, placebo-controlled trial. *Archives of Internal Medicine, 165,* 1582–1589. (p. 350)

Bray, D. W., & Byham, W. C. (1991, Winter). Assessment centers and their derivatives. *Journal of Continuing Higher Education,* pp. 8–11. (p. 509)

Bray, D. W., Byham, W., interviewed by Mayes, B. T. (1997). Insights into the history and future of assessment centers: An interview with Dr. Douglas W. Bray and Dr. William Byham. *Journal of Social Behavior and Personality, 12,* 3–12. (p. 509)

Bray, G. A. (1969). Effect of caloric restriction on energy expenditure in obese patients. *Lancet, 2,* 397–398. (p. 343)

Brayne, C., Spiegelhalter, D. J., Dufouil, C., Chi, L-Y., Dening, T. R., Paykel, E. S., O'Connor, D.W., Ahmed, A., McGee, M. A., & Huppert, F. A. (1999). Estimating the true extent of cognitive decline in the old old. *Journal of the American Geriatrics Society, 47,* 1283–1288. (p. 463)

Breedlove, S. M. (1997). Sex on the brain. *Nature, 389,* 801. (p. 357)

Brehm, S., & Brehm, J. W. (1981). *Psychological reactance: A theory of freedom and control.* New York: Academic Press. (p. 663)

Breland, K., & Breland, M. (1961). The misbehavior of organisms. *American Psychologist, 16,* 661–664. (p. 237)

Breslau, J., Aguilar-Gaxiola, S., Borges, G., Kendler, K. S., Su, M., & Kessler, R. C. (2007). Risk for psychiatric disorder among immigrants and their US-born descendants. *Journal of Nervous and Mental Disease, 195,* 189–195. (p. 599)

Bressan, P., & Dal Martello, M. F. (2002). Talis pater, talis filius: Perceived resemblance and the belief in genetic relatedness. *Psychological Science, 13,* 213–218. (p. 161)

Brewer, C. L. (1990). Personal correspondence. (p. 102)

Brewer, C. L. (1996). Personal communication. (p. 10)

Brewer, M. B., & Chen, Y-R. (2007). Where (who) are collectives in collectivism? Toward conceptual clarification of individualism and collectivism. *Psychological Review, 114,* 133–151. (p. 517)

Brewer, W. F. (1977). Memory for the pragmatic implications of sentences. *Memory & Cognition, 5,* 673–678. (p. 261)

Brewin, C. R., Andrews, B., Rose, S., & Kirk, M. (1999). Acute stress disorder and posttraumatic stress disorder in victims of violent crime. *American Journal of Psychiatry, 156,* 360–366. (p. 572)

Brewin, C. R., Andrews, B., & Valentine, J. D. (2000). Meta-analysis of risk factors for posttraumatic stress disorder in trauma-exposed adults. *Journal of Consulting and Clinical Psychology, 68,* 748–766. (p. 572)

Brewin, C. R., Kleiner, J. S., Vasterling J. J., & Field, A. P. (2007). Memory for emotionally neutral information in posttraumatic stress disorder: A meta-analytic investigation. *Journal of Abnormal Psychology, 116,* 448–463. (p. 270)

Bricker, J. B., Stallings, M. C., Corley, R. P., Wadsworth, S. J., Bryan, A., Timberlake, D. S., Hewitt, J. K., Caspi, A., Hofer, S. M., Rhea, S. A., & DeFries, J. C. (2006). Genetic and environmental influences on age at sexual initiation in the Colorado Adoption Project. *Behavior Genetics, 36,* 820–832. (p. 352)

Brief, A. P., & Weiss, H. M. (2002). Organizational behavior: Affect in the workplace. *Annual Review of Psychology, 53,* 279–307. (p. B-8)

Briers, B., Pandelaere, M., Dewitte, S., & Warlop, L. (2006). Hungry for money: The desire for caloric resources increases the desire for financial resources and vice versa. *Psychological Science, 17,* 939–943. (p. 231)

Briñol, P., Petty, R. E., & Barden, J. (2007). Happiness versus sadness as a determinant of thought confidence in persuasion: A self-validation analysis. *Journal of Personality and Social Psychology, 93,* 711–727. (p. 389)

Brinson, S. L. (1992). The use and opposition of rape myths in prime-time television dramas. *Sex Roles, 27,* 359–375. (p. 674)

Briscoe, D. (1997, February 16). Women lawmakers still not in charge. *Associated Press* (in *Grand Rapids Press,* p. A23). (p. 440)

Brislin, R. W. (1988). Increasing awareness of class, ethnicity, culture, and race by expanding on students' own experiences. In I. Cohen (Ed.), *The G. Stanley Hall Lecture Series.* Washington, DC: American Psychological Association. (p. 661)

Brissette, I., & Cohen, S. (2002). The contribution of individual differences in hostility to the associations between daily interpersonal conflict, affect, and sleep. *Personality and Social Psychology Bulletin, 28,* 1265–1274. (p. 186)

Brissette, I., Scheier, M. F., & Carver, C. S. (2002). The role of optimism in social network development, coping, and psychological adjustment during a life transition. *Journal of Personality and Social Psychology, 82,* 102–111. (p. 588)

British Psychological Society. (1993). Ethical principles for conducting research with human participants. *The Psychologist: Bulletin of the British Psychological Society, 6,* 33–36. (pp. 45, 498)

Brody, J. E. (1999, November 30). Yesterday's precocious puberty is norm today. *New York Times* (www.nytimes.com). (p. 446)

Brody, J. E. (2000, March 21). When post-traumatic stress grips youth. *New York Times* (www.nytimes.com). (p. 572)

Brody, J. E. (2002, November 26). When the eyelids snap shut at 65 miles an hour. *New York Times* (www.nytimes.com). (p. 184)

Brody, J. E. (2003, September). Addiction: A brain ailment, not a moral lapse. *New York Times* (www.nytimes.com). (p. 197)

Brody, J. E. (2003, December 23). Stampede of diabetes as U.S. races to obesity. *New York Times* (www.nytimes.com). (p. 345)

Brody, N. (1992). *Intelligence,* 2nd ed. San Diego: Academic Press. (p. 531)

Brody, N. (2001). Inspection time: Past, present, and future. *Intelligence, 29,* 537–541. (pp. 202, 531)

Broks, P. (2007, April). The mystery of consciousness. *Prospect* (www.prospect-magazine.co.uk). (p. 418)

Broman, S. H. (1989). Infant physical status and later cognitive development. In M. G. Bornstein & N. A. Krasnegor (Eds.), *Stability and continuity in mental development: Behavioral and biological perspectives.* Hillsdale, NJ: Erlbaum. (p. 540)

Bronner, E. (1998, February 25). U.S. high school seniors among worst in math and science. *New York Times* (www.nytimes.com). (p. 549)

Brookes, K. & 61 others. (2006). The analysis of 51 genes in DSM-IV combined type attention deficit hyperactivity disorder: Association signals in DRD4, DAT1 and 16 other genes. *Molecular Psychiatry, 11,* 935–953. (p. 563)

Brooks, D. (2005, April 28). Mourning Mother Russia. *New York Times* (www.nytimes.com). (p. 457)

Brooks, D. J. (2002, October 8). Running down the road to happiness. *Gallup Tuesday Briefing* (www.gallup.com). (p. C-6)

Brooks, R., & Meltzoff, A. N. (2005). The development of gaze following and its relation to language. *Developmental Science, 8,* 535–543. (p. 243)

Brown, A. S. (2003). A review of the déjà vu experience. *Psychological Bulletin, 129,* 394–413. (p. 276)

Brown, A. S. (2004a). *The déjà vu experience.* East Sussex, England: Psychology Press. (p. 276)

Brown, A. S. (2004b). Getting to grips with déja vu. *The Psychologist, 17,* 694–696. (p. 277)

Brown, A. S., Begg, M. D., Gravenstein, S., Schaefer, C. A., Wyatt, R. J., Bresnahan, M., Babulas, V. P., & Susser, E. S. (2004). Serologic evidence of prenatal influenza in the etiology of schizophrenia. *Archives of General Psychiatry, 61,* 774–780. (p. 594)

Brown, A. S., Bracken, E., Zoccoli, S., & Douglas, K. (2004). Generating and remembering passwords. *Applied Cognitive Psychology, 18,* 641–651. (p. 283)

Brown, A. S., Schaefer, C. A., Wyatt, R. J., Goetz, R., Begg, M. D., Gorman, J. M., & Susser, E. S. (2000). Maternal exposure to respiratory infections and adult schizophrenia spectrum disorders: A prospective birth cohort study. *Schizophrenia Bulletin, 26,* 287–295. (p. 593)

Brown, E. L., & Deffenbacher, K. (1979). *Perception and the senses.* New York: Oxford University Press. (p. 138)

Brown, G. K., Ten Have, T., Henriques, G. R., Xie, S. X., Hollander, J. E., & Beck, A. T. (2005). Cognitive therapy for the prevention of suicide attempts. *JAMA: Journal of the American Medical Association, 294,* 563–570. (p. 622)

Brown, J. A. (1958). Some tests of the decay theory of immediate memory. *Quarterly Journal of Experimental Psychology, 10,* 12–21. (p. 267)

Brown, J. D., Steele, J. R., & Walsh-Childers, K. (2002). *Sexual teens, sexual media: Investigating media's influence on adolescent sexuality.* Mahwah, NJ: Erlbaum. (p. 353)

Brown, J. L., & Pollitt, E. (1996, February). Malnutrition, poverty and intellectual development. *Scientific American,* pp. 38–43. (p. 547)

Brown, R. (1965). *Social psychology.* New York: Free Press. (p. 385)

Brown, R. (1986). Linguistic relativity. In S. H. Hulse & B. F. Green, Jr. (Eds.), *One hundred years of psychological research in America.* Baltimore: Johns Hopkins University Press. (p. 320)

Brown, S. L., Brown, R. M., House, J. S., & Smith, D. M. (2008). Coping with spousal loss: Potential buffering effects of self-reported helping behavior. *Personality and Social Psychology Bulletin, 34,* 849–861. (p. 471)

Brown, S. W., Garry, M., Loftus, E., Silver, B., DuBois, K., & DuBreuil, S. (1996). People's beliefs about memory: Why don't we have better memories? Paper presented at the American Psychological Society convention. (p. 284)

Brownell, K. D. (2002). Public policy and the prevention of obesity. In C. G. Fairburn & K. D. Brownell (Eds.), *Eating disorders and obesity: A comprehensive handbook* (2nd ed.). New York: Guilford. (p. 345)

Brownell, K. D., & Nestle, M. (2004, June 7). Are you responsible for your own weight? *Time,* p. 113. (p. 345)

Browning, C. (1992). *Ordinary men: Reserve police battalion 101 and the final solution in Poland.* New York: HarperCollins. (p. 656)

Bruce, D., Dolan, A., & Phillips-Grant, K. (2000). On the transition from childhood amnesia to the recall of personal memories. *Psychological Science, 11,* 360–364. (p. 417)

Bruck, M., & Ceci, S. J. (1999). The suggestibility of children's memory. *Annual Review of Psychology, 50,* 419–439. (p. 289)

Bruck, M., & Ceci, S. J. (2004). Forensic developmental psychology: Unveiling four common misconceptions. *Current Directions in Psychological Science, 15,* 229–232. (p. 289)

Bruder, C. E. G. & 22 others. (2008). Phenotypically concordant and discordant monozygotic twins display different DNA copy-number-variation profiles. *American Journal of Human Genetics, 82,* 763–771. (p. 97)

Bruer, J. T. (1999). *The myth of the first three years: A new understanding of early brain development and lifelong learning.* New York: Free Press. (p. 547)

Brumberg, J. J. (2000). *Fasting girls: The history of anorexia nervosa.* New York: Vintage. (p. 337)

Bryant, A. N. & Astin, H. A. (2008). The correlates of spiritual struggle during the college years. *Journal of Higher Education, 79,* 1–27. (p. 452)

Bryant, R. A. (2001). Posttraumatic stress disorder and traumatic brain injury: Can they co-exist? *Clinical Psychology Review, 21,* 931–948. (p. 291)

Buchanan, T. W. (2007). Retrieval of emotional memories. *Psychological Bulletin, 133,* 761–779. (p. 270)

Buck, L. B., & Axel, R. (1991). A novel multigene family may encode odorant receptors: A molecular basis for odor recognition. *Cell, 65,* 175–187. (p. 149)

Buckingham, M. (2001, August). Quoted by P. LaBarre, "Marcus Buckingham thinks your boss has an attitude problem." *The Magazine* (fastcompany.com/online/49/buckingham.html). (pp. B-8, B-10)

Buckingham, M. (2007). *Go put your strengths to work: 6 powerful steps to achieve outstanding performance.* New York: Free Press. (p. B-3)

Buckingham, M., & Clifton, D. O. (2001). *Now, discover your strengths.* New York: Free Press. (pp. B-3, B-4)

Buckley, C. (2007, January 3). Man is rescued by stranger on subway tracks. *New York Times* (www.nytimes.com). (p. 687)

Buckley, K. E., & Leary, M. R. (2001). Perceived acceptance as a predictor of social, emotional, and academic outcomes. Paper presented at the Society of Personality and Social Psychology annual convention. (p. 361)

Buehler, R., Griffin, D., & Ross, M. (1994). Exploring the "planning fallacy": Why people underestimate their task completion times. *Journal of Personality and Social Psychology, 67,* 366–381. (p. 307)

Bugelski, B. R., Kidd, E., & Segmen, J. (1968). Image as a mediator in one-trial paired-associate learning. *Journal of Experimental Psychology, 76,* 69–73. (p. 264)

Bugental, D. B. (1986). Unmasking the "polite smile": Situational and personal determinants of managed affect in adult-child interaction. *Personality and Social Psychology Bulletin, 12,* 7–16. (p. 378)

Buka, S. L., Goldstein, J. M., Seidman, L. J., Zornberg, G., Donatelli, J-A. A., Denny, L. R., & Tsuang, M. T. (1999). Prenatal complications, genetic vulnerability, and schizophrenia: The New England longitudinal studies of schizophrenia. *Psychiatric Annals, 29,* 151–156. (p. 593)

Buka, S. L., Tsuang, M. T., Torrey, E. F., Klebanoff, M. A., Wagner, R. L., & Yolken, R. H. (2001). Maternal infections and subsequent psychosis among offspring. *Archives of General Psychiatry, 58,* 1032–1037. (p. 594)

Bullough, V. (1990). The Kinsey scale in historical perspective. In D. P. McWhirter, S. A. Sanders, & J. M. Reinisch (Eds.), *Homosexuality/heterosexuality: Concepts of sexual orientation.* New York: Oxford University Press. (p. 354)

Bunde, J., & Suls, J. (2006). A quantitative analysis of the relationship between the Cook-Medley Hostility Scale and traditional coronary artery disease risk factors. *Health Psychology, 25,* 493–500. (p. 402)

Buquet, R. (1988). Le reve et les deficients visuels (Dreams and the visually-impaired). *Psychanalyse-a-l'Universite, 13,* 319–327. (p. 188)

Burcusa, S. L., & Iacono, W. G. (2007). Risk for recurrence in depression. *Clinical Psychology Review, 27,* 959–985. (p. 582)

Bureau of Labor Statistics. (2004, September 14). *American time-user survey summary.* Washington, DC: United States Department of Labor (www.bls.gov). (p. 439)

Bureau of Labor Statistics. (2008). *U.S. Department of Labor, Occupational Outlook Handbook, 2008-09 Edition, Psychologists.* Retrieved on September 4, 2008 from http://www.bls.gov/oco/ocos056.htm. (pp. A-2, A-3)

Bureau of the Census. (2004). *Statistical abstract of the United States 2004.* Washington, DC: U.S. Government Printing Office. (p. 569)

Bureau of the Census. (2007). *Statistical abstract of the United States 2007.* Washington, DC: U.S. Government Printing Office. (p. 466)

Burgess, M., Enzle, M. E., & Schmaltz, R. (2004). Defeating the potentially deleterious effects of externally imposed deadlines: Practitioners' rules-of-thumb. *Personality and Social Psychology Bulletin, 30,* 868–877. (p. B-11)

Buri, J. R., Louiselle, P. A., Misukanis, T. M., & Mueller, R. A. (1988). Effects of parental authoritarianism and authoritativeness on self-esteem. *Personality and Social Psychology Bulletin, 14,* 271–282. (p. 433)

Burish, T. G., & Carey, M. P. (1986). Conditioned aversive responses in cancer chemotherapy patients: Theoretical and developmental analysis. *Journal of Counseling and Clinical Psychology, 54,* 593–600. (p. 226)

Burke, D. M., & Shafto, M. A. (2004). Aging and language production. *Current Directions in Psychological Science, 13,* 21–24. (p. 462)

Burkholder, R. (2005a, January 11). Chinese far wealthier than a decade ago—but are they happier? *Gallup Poll News Service* (www.gallup.com). (p. 394)

Burkholder, R. (2005b, January 18). China's citizens optimistic, yet not entirely satisfied. *Gallup Poll News Service* (www.gallup.com). (p. 394)

Burns, B. C. (2004). The effects of speed on skilled chess performance. *Psychological Science, 15,* 442–447. (p. 311)

Burns, J. F., & Filkins, D. (2006, June 14). Bush makes surprise visit to Iraq to press leadership. *New York Times* (www.nytimes.com). (p. 378)

Burrell, B. (2005). *Postcards from the brain museum: The improbable search for meaning in the matter of famous minds.* New York: Broadway Books. (p. 529)

Burris, C. T., & Branscombe, N. R. (2005). Distorted distance estimation induced by a self-relevant national boundary. *Journal of Experimental Social Psychology, 41,* 305–312. (p. 320)

Burton, C. M., & King, L. A. (2008). Effects of (very) brief writing on health: The two-minute miracle. *British Journal of Health Psychology, 13,* 9–14. (p. C-5)

Bush, G. W. (1999). Quoted by M. Ivins, syndicated column, November 27, 1999. (p. 19)

Bush, G. W. (2001). Quoted in various places, including BBC News (bbc.co.uk), June 16, 2001. (p. 689)

Bushman, B. J. (1993). Human aggression while under the influence of alcohol and other drugs: An integrative research review. *Current Directions in Psychological Science, 2*, 148–152. (p. 672)

Bushman, B. J. (2002). Does venting anger feed or extinguish the flame? Catharsis, rumination, distraction, anger, and aggressive responding. *Personality and Social Psychology Bulletin, 28*, 724–731. (p. 388)

Bushman, B. J., & Anderson, C. A. (2001). Media violence and the American public: Scientific facts versus media misinformation. *American Psychologist, 56*, 477–489. (p. 676)

Bushman, B. J., & Baumeister, R. F. (1998). Threatened egotism, narcissism, self-esteem, and direct and displaced aggression: Does self-love or self-hate lead to violence? *Journal of Personality and Social Psychology, 75*, 219–229. (p. 515)

Bushman, B. J., Baumeister, R. F., & Stack, A. D. (1999). Catharsis, aggression, and persuasive influence: Self-fulfilling or self-defeating prophecies? *Journal of Personality and Social Psychology, 76*, 367–376. (p. 388)

Bushman, B. J., & Bonacci, A. M. (2002). Violence and sex impair memory for television ads. *Journal of Applied Psychology, 87*, 557–564. (pp. 283, 352)

Busnel, M. C., Granier-Deferre, C., & Lecanuet, J. P. (1992, October). Fetal audition. *New York Academy of Sciences, 662*, 118–134. (p. 412)

Buss, A. H. (1989). Personality as traits. *American Psychologist, 44*, 1378–1388. (p. 502)

Buss, D. M. (1991). Evolutionary personality psychology. *Annual Review of Psychology, 42*, 459–491. (p. 101)

Buss, D. M. (1994). The strategies of human mating: People worldwide are attracted to the same qualities in the opposite sex. *American Scientist, 82*, 238–249. (p. 106)

Buss, D. M. (1995). Evolutionary psychology: A new paradigm for psychological science. *Psychological Inquiry, 6*, 1–30. (p. 106)

Buss, D. M. (1996). Sexual conflict: Evolutionary insights into feminism and the "battle of the sexes." In D. M. Buss & N. M. Malamuth (Eds.), *Sex, power, conflict: Evolutionary and feminist perspectives.* New York: Oxford University Press. (p. 106)

Buss, D. M. (2000). *The dangerous passion: Why jealousy is as necessary as love and sex.* New York: Free Press. (p. 106)

Busseri, M. A., Willoughby, T., Chalmers, H., & Bogaert, A. R. (2006). Same-sex attraction and successful adolescent development. *Journal of Youth and Adolescence, 35*, 563–575. (p. 354)

Buster, J. E., Kingsberg, S. A., Aguirre, O., Brown, C., Breaux, J. G., Buch, A., Rodenberg, C. A., Wekselman, K., & Casson, P. (2005). Testosterone patch for low sexual desire in surgically menopausal women: A randomized trial. *Obstetrics and Gynecology, 105*(5), 944–952. (p. 350)

Butcher, L. M., Davis, O. S. P., Craig, I. W., & Plomin, R. (2008). Genome-wide quantitative trait locus association scan of general cognitive ability using pooled DNA and 500K single nucleotide polymorphism microarrays. *Genes, Brain and Behavior, 7*, 435–446. (p. 545)

Butler, A. C., Hokanson, J. E., & Flynn, H. A. (1994). A comparison of self-esteem lability and low trait self-esteem as vulnerability factors for depression. *Journal of Personality and Social Psychology, 66*, 166–177. (p. 587)

Butler, R. A. (1954, February). Curiosity in monkeys. *Scientific American,* pp. 70–75. (p. 329)

Butterfield, F. (1999, July 12). Experts say study confirms prison's new role as mental hospital. *New York Times* (www.nytimes.com). (p. 569)

Butterworth, G. (1992). Origins of self-perception in infancy. *Psychological Inquiry, 3*, 103–111. (p. 433)

Byne, W., & Parsons, B. (1993). Human sexual orientation: The biologic theories reappraised. *Archives of General Psychiatry, 50*, 228–239. (p. 359)

Bynum, R. (2004, November 1). Associated Press article. (p. 143)

Byrne, D. (1971). *The attraction paradigm.* New York: Academic Press. (p. 682)

Byrne, D. (1982). Predicting human sexual behavior. In A. G. Kraut (Ed.), *The G. Stanley Hall Lecture Series (Vol. 2).* Washington, DC: American Psychological Association. (pp. 220, 350)

Byrne, R. W. (1991, May/June). Brute intellect. *The Sciences,* pp. 42–47. (p. D-3)

Cable, D. M., & Gilovich, T. (1998). Looked over or overlooked? Prescreening decisions and postinterview evaluations. *Journal of Personality and Social Psychology, 83*, 501–508. (p. B-5)

Cacioppo, J. T., Hawkley, L. C., Kalil, A., Hughes, M. E., Waite, L., & Thisted, R. A. (2008). Happiness and the invisible threads of social connection: The Chicago Health, Aging, and Social Relations Study. In M. Eid & R. Larsen (Eds.), *The science of subjective well-being.* New York: Guilford. (p. 392)

Cahill, L. (2005, May). His brain, her brain. *Scientific American,* pp. 40–47. (p. 438)

Cahn, B. R., & Polich, J. (2006). Meditation states and traits: EEG, ERP, and neuroimaging studies. *Psychological Bulletin, 132*, 180–211. (p. C-10)

Cale, E. M., Lilienfeld, S. O. (2002). Sex differences in psychopathy and antisocial personality disorder: A review and integration. *Clinical Psychology Review, 22*, 1179–1207. (p. 597)

Call, K. T., Riedel, A. A., Hein, K., McLoyd, V., Petersen, A., & Kipke, M. (2002). Adolescent health and well-being in the twenty-first century: A global perspective. *Journal of Research on Adolescence, 12*, 69–98. (p. 352)

Callaghan, T., Rochat, P., Lillard, A., Claux, M. L., Odden, H., Itakura, S., Tapanya, S., & Singh, S. (2005). Synchrony in the onset of mental-state reasoning. *Psychological Science, 16*, 378–384. (p. 422)

Calle, E. E., Thun, M. J., Petrelli, J. M., Rodriguez, C., & Health, C. W., Jr. (1999). Body-mass index and mortality in a prospective cohort of U.S. adults. *New England Journal of Medicine, 341*, 1097–1105. (p. 341)

Camerer, C. F., Loewenstein, G., & Weber, M. (1989). The curse of knowledge in economic settings: An experimental analysis. *Journal of Political Economy, 97*, 1232–1254. (p. B-15)

Cameron, L., & Rutland, A. (2006). Extended contact through story reading in school: Reducing children's prejudice toward the disabled. *Journal of Social Issues, 62*, 469–488. (p. 690)

Campbell, D. T., & Specht, J. C. (1985). Altruism: Biology, culture, and religion. *Journal of Social and Clinical Psychology, 3*(1), 33–42. (p. 493)

Campos, J. J., Bertenthal, B. I., & Kermoian, R. (1992). Early experience and emotional development: The emergence of wariness and heights. *Psychological Science, 3*, 61–64. (p. 385)

Canli, T. (2008, February/March). The character code. *Scientific American Mind,* pp. 53–57. (p. 575)

Canli, T., Desmond, J. E., Zhao, Z., & Gabrieli, J. D. E. (2002). Sex differences in the neural basis of emotional memories. *Proceedings of the National Academy of Sciences, 99*, 10789–10794. (p. 380)

Cannon, J. (2005). Career planning and opportunities: The bachelor's degree in psychology, *Eye on Psi Chi, 9*, 26–28. (pp. A-1, A-2)

Cannon, W. B. (1929). *Bodily changes in pain, hunger, fear, and rage.* New York: Branford. (pp. 333, 398)

Cannon, W. B., & Washburn, A. (1912). An explanation of hunger. *American Journal of Physiology, 29*, 441–454. (p. 332)

Cantor, N., & Kihlstrom, J. F. (1987). *Personality and social intelligence.* Englewood Cliffs, NJ: Prentice-Hall. (p. 528)

Cantril, H., & Bumstead, C. H. (1960). *Reflections on the human venture.* New York: New York University Press. (p. 663)

Caplan, N., Choy, M. H., & Whitmore, J. K. (1992, February). Indochinese refugee families and academic achievement. *Scientific American,* pp. 36–42. (pp. 444, 553)

Caprara, G. V., Vecchione, M., Barbaranelli, C., & Fraley, R. C. (2007). When likeness goes with liking: The case of political preference. *Political Psychology, 28*, 609–632. (p. 682)

Caputo, D., & Dunning, D. (2005). What you don't know: The role played by errors of omission in imperfect self-assessments. *Journal of Experimental Social Psychology,* 488–505. (p. 508)

Carducci, B. J., Cosby, P. C., & Ward, D. D. (1978). Sexual arousal and interpersonal evaluations. *Journal of Experimental Social Psychology, 14*, 449–457. (p. 683)

Carey, B. (2006, November 11). What's wrong with a child? Psychiatrists often disagree. *New York Times* (www.nytimes.com). (p. 566)

Carey, B. (2007, September 4). Bipolar illness soars as a diagnosis for the young. *New York Times* (www.nytimes.com). (p. 581)

Carey, D. P. (2007). Is bigger really better? The search for brain size and intelligence in the twenty-first century. In S. Della Sala (Ed.), *Tall tales about the* *mind and brain: Separating fact from fiction.* Oxford: Oxford University Press. (p. 530)

Carey, G. (1990). Genes, fears, phobias, and phobic disorders. *Journal of Counseling and Development, 68,* 628–632. (p. 575)

Carli, L. L., & Leonard, J. B. (1989). The effect of hindsight on victim derogation. *Journal of Social and Clinical Psychology, 8,* 331–343. (p. 670)

Carlson, C. L. (2000). ADHD is overdiagnosed. In R. L. Atkinson, R. C. Atkinson, E. E. Smith, D. J. Bem, & S. Nolen-Hoeksema (Eds.), *Hilgard's introduction to psychology, Thirteenth edition.* Fort Worth: Harcourt. (p. 563)

Carlson, M. (1995, August 29). Quoted by S. Blakeslee, In brain's early growth, timetable may be crucial. *New York Times,* pp. C1, C3. (p. 430)

Carlson, M., Charlin, V., & Miller, N. (1988). Positive mood and helping behavior: A test of six hypotheses. *Journal of Personality and Social Psychology, 55,* 211–229. (p. 687)

Carlson, S. (1985). A double-blind test of astrology. *Nature, 318,* 419–425. (p. 498)

Carnahan, T., & McFarland, S. (2007). Revisiting the Stanford Prison Experiment: Could participant self-selection have led to the cruelty? *Personality and Social Psychology Bulletin, 33,* 603–614. (p. 648)

Carnegie Council on Adolescent Development. (1989, June). *Turning points: Preparing American youth for the 21st century.* (The report of the Task Force on Education of Young Adolescents.) New York: Carnegie Corporation. (p. 543)

Carnelley, K. B., Wortman, C. B., Bolger, N., Burke, C. T. (2006). The time course of grief reactions to spousal loss: Evidence from a national probability sample. *Journal of Personality and Social Psychology, 91,* 476–492. (p. 470)

Carpusor, A., & Loges, W. E. (2006). Rental discrimination and ethnicity in names. *Journal of Applied Social Psychology, 36,* 934–952. (p. 665)

Carrière, G. (2003). Parent and child factors associated with youth obesity. *Statistics Canada, Catalogue 82–003,* Supplement to Health Reports, 2003. (p. 344)

Carroll, D., Davey Smith, G., & Bennett, P. (1994, March). Health and socio-economic status. *The Psychologist,* pp. 122–125. (p. C-2)

Carroll, J. (2007, August 16). Most Americans approve of interracial marriages. *Gallup News Service* (www.gallup.com). (p. 665)

Carroll, J. (2008, January 2). Time pressures, stress common for Americans. Gallup Poll (www.gallup.com). (p. 397)

Carroll, J. M., & Russell, J. A. (1996). Do facial expressions signal specific emotions? Judging emotion from the face in context. *Journal of Personality and Social Psychology, 70,* 205–218. (p. 382)

Carroll, J. S., Padilla-Walker, L. M., Nelson, L. J., Olson, C. D., Barry, C. M., & Madsen, S. D. (2008). Generation XXX: Pornography acceptance and use among emerging adults. *Journal of Adolescent Research, 23,* 6–30. (p. 674)

Carroll, P., Sweeny, K., & Shepperd, J. A. (2006). Forsaking optimism. *Review of General Psychology, 10,* 56–73. (p. 507)

Carstensen, L. I., & Mikels, J. A. (2005). At the intersection of emotion and cognition: Aging and the positivity effect. *Current Directions in Psychological Science, 14,* 117–121. (pp. 464, 469)

Carter, R. (1998). *Mapping the mind.* Berkeley: University of California Press. (p. 56)

Cartwright, R. D. (1978). *A primer on sleep and dreaming.* Reading, MA: Addison-Wesley. (p. 180)

Caryl, P. G. (1994). Early event-related potentials correlate with inspection time and intelligence. *Intelligence, 18,* 15–46. (p. 531)

CASA. (2003). *The formative years: Pathways to substance abuse among girls and young women ages 8–22.* New York, NY: National Center on Addiction and Substance Use, Columbia University. (pp. 200, 209)

CASA. (2004). *CASA 2004 teen survey.* National Center on Addiction and Substance Abuse, Columbia University (www.casacolumbia.org). (p. 353)

Casey, B. J., Getz, S., & Galvan, A. (2008). The adolescent brain. *Deveopmental Review, 28,* 62–77. (p. 447)

Cash, T. F., & Henry, P. E. (1995). Women's body images: The results of a national survey in the U.S.A. *Sex Roles, 33,* 19–28. (p. 338)

Cash, T., & Janda, L. H. (1984, December). The eye of the beholder. *Psychology Today,* pp. 46–52. (p. 680)

Caspi, A. (2000). The child is father of the man: Personality continuities from childhood to adulthood. *Journal of Personality and Social Psychology, 78,* 158–172. (p. 428)

Caspi, A., Harrington, H., Milne, B., Amell, J. W., Theodore, R. F., & Moffitt, T. E. (2003). Children's behavioral styles at age 3 are linked to their adult personality traits at age 26. *Journal of Personality, 71,* 496–513. (pp. 473, 586)

Caspi, A., McClay, J., Moffitt, T., Mill, J., Martin, J., Craig, I. W., Taylor, A., & Poulton, R. (2002). Role of genotype in the cycle of violence in maltreated children. *Science, 297,* 851–854. (p. 598)

Caspi, A., Moffitt, T. E., Newman, D. L., & Silva, P. A. (1996). Behavioral observations at age 3 years predict adult psychiatric disorders: Longitudinal evidence from a birth cohort. *Archives of General Psychiatry, 53,* 1033–1039. (p. 597)

Caspi, A., Williams, B., Kim-Cohen, J., Craig, I. W., Milne, B. J., Poulton, R., Schalkwyk, L. C., Taylor, A., Werts, H., & Moffitt, T. E. (2007). Moderation of breastfeeding effects on the IQ by genetic variation in fatty acid metabolism. *Proceedings of the National Academy of Sciences, 104,* 18860–18865. (p. 101)

Cassel, L., & Suedfeld, P. (2006). Salutogenesis and autobiographical disclosure among Holocaust survivors. *The Journal of Positive Psychology, 1,* 212–225. (p. 573)

Cassidy, J., & Shaver, P. R. (1999). *Handbook of attachment.* New York: Guilford. (p. 427)

Castillo, R. J. (1997). *Culture and mental illness: A client-centered approach.* Pacific Grove, CA: Brooks/Cole. (p. 564)

Castonguay, L. G., & Goldfried, M. R. (1994). Psychotherapy integration: An idea whose time has come. *Applied & Preventive Psychology, 3,* 159–172. (p. 606)

Catanese, K. R., & Tice, D. M. (2005). The effect of rejection on anti-social behaviors: Social exclusion produces aggressive behaviors. In K. D. Williams, J. P. Forgas, & W. Von Hippel (Eds.), *The social outcast: Ostracism, social exclusion, rejection, and bullying.* New York: Psychology Press. (p. 673)

Cattell, R. B. (1963). Theory of fluid and crystallized intelligence: A critical experiment. *Journal of Educational Psychology, 54,* 1–22. (p. 464)

Cavalli-Sforza, L., Menozzi, P., & Piazza, A. (1994). *The history and geography of human genes.* Princeton, NJ: Princeton University Press. (p. 553)

Cavigelli, S. A., & McClintock, M. K. (2003). Fear of novelty in infant rats predicts adult corticosterone dynamics and an early death. *Proceedings of the National Academy of Sciences, 100,* 16131–16136. (p. 400)

Cawley, B. D., Keeping, L. M., & Levy, P. E. (1998). Participation in the performance appraisal process and employee reactions: A meta-analytic review of field investigations. *Journal of Applied Psychology, 83,* 615–633. (p. B-12)

CDC. (1992, September 16). *Serious mental illness and disability in the adult household population: United States, 1989.* Advance Data No. 218 from Vital and Health Statistics, National Center for Health Statistics. (p. 600)

CDC. (2003). *Who should get a flu shot (influenza vaccine).* National Center for Infectious Diseases (http://www.cdc.gov/ncidod/diseases/flu/who.htm). (p. 594)

CDC. (2006, June 9). *Youth risk behavior surveillance: United States, 2005.* Morbidity and Mortality Weekly Report, 55, No. SS-5, Centers for Disease Control and Prevention. (pp. 352, 354)

CDC. (2007, February 8). *CDC releases new data on Autism Spectrum Disorders (ASDs) from multiple communities in the United States.* Centers for Disease Control and Prevention (www.cdc.gov). (p. 424)

CDC. (2007, November). *Obesity among adults in the United States—No change since 2003–2004.* NCHS Data Brief, Centers for Disease Control and Prevention (www.cdc.gov/nchs/data/databriefs/db01.pdf). (p. 340)

Ceci, S. J. (1993). Cognitive and social factors in children's testimony. Master Lecture, American Psychological Association convention. (pp. 289, 290)

Ceci, S. J., & Bruck, M. (1993). Child witnesses: Translating research into policy. *Social Policy Report (Society for Research in Child Development), 7(3),* 1–30. (p. 289)

Ceci, S. J., & Bruck, M. (1995). *Jeopardy in the courtroom: A scientific analysis of children's testimony.* Washington, DC: American Psychological Association. (p. 289)

Ceci, S. J., Huffman, M. L. C., Smith, E., & Loftus, E. F. (1994). Repeatedly thinking about a non-event: Source misattributions among preschoolers. *Consciousness and Cognition, 3,* 388–407. (p. 290)

Ceci, S. J., & Williams, W. M. (1997). Schooling, intelligence, and income. *American Psychologist, 52,* 1051–1058. (p. 547)

Centerwall, B. S. (1989). Exposure to television as a risk factor for violence. *American Journal of Epidemiology, 129,* 643-652. (p. 247)

Cepeda, N. J., Pashler, H., Vul, E., Wixted, J. T., & Rohrer, D. (2006). Distributed practice in verbal recall tasks: A review and quantitative synthesis. *Psychological Bulletin, 132,* 354-380. (p. 260)

Cerella, J. (1985). Information processing rates in the elderly. *Psychological Bulletin, 98,* 67-83. (p. 459)

CFI. (2003, July). *International developments. Report.* Amherst, NY: Center for Inquiry International. (p. 169)

Chabris, C. F., & Glickman, M. E. (2006). Sex differences in intellectual performance: Analysis of a large cohort of competitive chess players. *Psychological Science, 17,* 1040-1046. (p. 550)

Chambless, D. L., Baker, M. J., Baucom, D. H., Beutler, L. E., Calhoun, K. S., Crits-Christoph, P., Daiuto, A., DeRubeis, R., Detweiler, J., Haaga, D. A. F., Johnson, S. B., McCurry, S., Mueser, K. T., Pope, K. S., Sanderson, W. C., Shoham, V., Stickle, T., Williams, D. A., & Woody, S. R. (1997). Update on empirically validated therapies, II. *The Clinical Psychologist, 51(1),* 3-16. (p. 624)

Chamove, A. S. (1980). Nongenetic induction of acquired levels of aggression. *Journal of Abnormal Psychology, 89,* 469-488. (p. 247)

Chang, E. C. (2001). Cultural influences on optimism and pessimism: Differences in Western and Eastern construals of the self. In E. C. Chang (Ed.), *Optimism and pessimism.* Washington, DC: APA Books. (p. 507)

Chang, P. P., Ford, D. E., Meoni, L. A., Wang, N-Y., & Klag, M. J. (2002). Anger in young men and subsequent premature cardiovascular disease: The precursors study. *Archives of Internal Medicine, 162,* 901-906. (p. 402)

Chaplin, W. F., Phillips, J. B., Brown, J. D., Clanton, N. R., & Stein, J. L. (2000). Handshaking, gender, personality, and first impressions. *Journal of Personality and Social Psychology, 79,* 110-117. (p. 377)

Charles, S. T., Reynolds, C. A., & Gatz, M. (2001). Age-related differences and change in positive and negative affect over 23 years. *Journal of Personality and Social Psychology, 80,* 136-151. (p. 469)

Charpak, G., & Broch, H. (2004). *Debunked! ESP, telekinesis, and other pseudoscience.* Baltimore, MD: Johns Hopkins University Press. (p. 167)

Chartrand, T. L., & Bargh, J. A. (1999). The chameleon effect: The perception-behavior link and social interaction. *Journal of Personality and Social Psychology, 76,* 893-910. (p. 651)

Chase, W. G., & Simon, H. A. (1973). Perception in chess. *Cognitive Psychology, 4,* 55-81. (p. 264)

Cheek, J. M., & Melchior, L. A. (1990). Shyness, self-esteem, and self-consciousness. In H. Leitenberg (Ed.), *Handbook of social and evaluation anxiety.* New York: Plenum. (p. 517)

Cheit, R. E. (1998). Consider this, skeptics of recovered memory. *Ethics & Behavior, 8,* 141-160. (p. 487)

Chen, E. (2004). Why socioeconomic status affects the health of children: A psychosocial perspective. *Current Directions in Psychological Science, 13,* 112-115. (p. C-2)

Chen, X., Beydoun, M. A., & Wang, Y. (2008). Is sleep duration associated with childhood obesity? A systematic review and meta-analysis. *Obesity, 16,* 265-274. (p. 183)

Cheng, M. (2006, November 16). Europeans OK anti-obesity charter. *Associated Press.* (p. 345)

Cherkas, L. F., Hunkin, J. L., Kato, B. S., Richards, J. B., Gardner, J. P., Surdulescu, G. L., Kimura, M., Lu, X., Spector, T. D., & Aviv, A. (2008). The association between physical activity in leisure time and leukocyte telomere length. *Archives of Internal Medicine, 168,* 154-158. (p. 459)

Chess, S., & Thomas, A. (1987). *Know your child: An authoritative guide for today's parents.* New York: Basic Books. (p. 428)

Child Trends. (2001, August). Facts at a glance. (www.childtrends.org). (p. 352)

Chiles, J. A., Lambert, M. J., & Hatch, A. L. (1999). The impact of psychological interventions on medical cost offset: A meta-analytic review. *Clinical Psychology: Science and Practice, 6,* 204-220. (p. 621)

Chisholm, K. (1998). A three year follow-up of attachment and indiscriminate friendliness in children adopted from Romanian orphanages. *Child Development, 69,* 1092-1106. (p. 430)

Chisolm, T. H., Johnson, C. E., Danhauer, J. L., Portz, L. J. P., Abrams, H. B., Lesner, S., McCarthy, P. A., & Newman, C. W. (2007). A systematic review of health-related quality of life and hearing aids: Final report of the American Academy of Audiology Task Force on the Health- Related Quality of Life Benefits of Amplification in Adults. *Journal of the American Academy of Audiology, 18,* 151-183. (p. 139)

Chivers, M. L. (2005). A brief review and discussion of sex differences in the specificity of sexual arousal. *Sexual and Relationship Therapy, 20,* 377-390. (p. 355)

Chivers, M. L., Seto, M. C., & Blanchard, R. (2007). Gender and sexual orientation differences in sexual response to sexual activities versus gender of actors in sexual films. *Journal of Personality and Social Psychology, 93,* 1108-1121. (p. 355)

Choi, C. Q. (2008, March). Do you need only half your brain? *Scientific American,* p. 104. (p. 82)

Choi, I., & Choi, Y. (2002). Culture and self-concept flexibility. *Personality and Social Psychology Bulletin, 28,* 1508-1517. (p. 517)

Chomsky, N. (1959). Review of B. F. Skinner's Verbal behavior. *Language, 35,* 26-58. (p. 317)

Chomsky, N. (1972). *Language and mind.* New York: Harcourt Brace. (p. 313)

Chomsky, N. (1987). Language in a psychological setting. Sophia Linguistic Working Papers in Linguistics, No. 22, Sophia University, Tokyo. (p. 317)

Christakis, D. S., Zimmerman, F. J., DiGiuseppe, D. L., & McCarty, C. A. (2004). Early television exposure and subsequent attentional problems in children. *Pediatrics, 113,* 708-713. (p. 563)

Christakis, N. A., & Fowler, J. H. (2007). The spread of obesity in a large social network over 32 years. *New England Journal of Medicine, 357,* 370-379. (p. 344)

Christakis, N. A., & Fowler, J. H. (2008, May). The collective dynamics of smoking in a large social network. *New England Journal of Medicine, 358(21),* 2249-2258. (p. 210)

Christensen, A., & Jacobson, N. S. (1994). Who (or what) can do psychotherapy: The status and challenge of nonprofessional therapies. *Psychological Science, 5,* 8-14. (p. 626)

Christophersen, E. R., & Edwards, K. J. (1992). Treatment of elimination disorders: State of the art 1991. *Applied & Preventive Psychology, 1,* 15-22. (p. 611)

Chugani, H. T., & Phelps, M. E. (1986). Maturational changes in cerebral function in infants determined by 18FDG Position Emission Tomography. *Science, 231,* 840-843. (p. 416)

Cialdini, R. B. (1993). *Influence: Science and practice* (3rd ed.). New York: HarperCollins. (p. 647)

Cialdini, R. B., & Richardson, K. D. (1980). Two indirect tactics of image management: Basking and blasting. *Journal of Personality and Social Psychology, 39,* 406-415. (p. 669)

Ciarrochi, J., Forgas, J. P., & Mayer, J. D. (2006). *Emotional intelligence in everyday life,* 2nd edition. New York: Psychology Press. (p. 529)

Cin, S. D., Gibson, B., Zanna, M. P., Shumate, R., & Fong, G. T. (2007). Smoking in movies, implicit associations of smoking with the self, and intentions to smoke. *Psychological Science, 18,* 559-563. (p. 203)

Clack, B., Dixon, J., & Tredoux, C. (2005). Eating together apart: Patterns of segregation in a multi-ethnic cafeteria. *Journal of Community and Applied Social Psychology, 15,* 1-16. (p. 690)

Clancy, S. A. (2005). *Abducted: How people came to believe they were abducted by aliens.* Boston: Harvard University Press. (pp. 179, 286)

Clancy, S. A., Schacter, D. L., McNally, R. J., & Pitman, R. K. (2000). False recognition in women reporting recovered memories of sexual abuse. *Psychological Science, 11,* 26-31. (p. 286)

Clark, A., Seidler, A., & Miller, M. (2001). Inverse association between sense of humor and coronary heart disease. *International Journal of Cardiology, 80,* 87-88. (p. C-3)

Clark, K. B., & Clark, M. P. (1947). Racial identification and preference in Negro children. In T. M. Newcomb & E. L. Hartley (Eds.), *Readings in social psychology.* New York: Holt. (p. 46)

Clark, L. A. (2007). Assessment and diagnosis of personality disorder: Perennial issues and an emerging reconceptualization. *Annual Review of Psychology, 58,* 227-257. (p. 596)

Clark, R., Anderson, N. B., Clark, V. R., & Williams, D. R. (1999). Racism as a stressor for African Americans: A biopsychosocial model. *American Psychologist, 54,* 805-816. (p. 401)

Coan, J. A., Schaefer, H. S., & Davidson, R. J. (2006). Lending a hand: Social regulation of the neural response to threat. *Psychological Science, 17,* 1032–1039. (p. C-4)

Coffey, C. E., Wilkinson, W. E., Weiner, R. D., Parashos, I. A., Djang, W. T., Webb, M. C., Figiel, G. S., & Spritzer, C. E. (1993). Quantitative cerebral anatomy in depression: A controlled magnetic resonance imaging study. *Archives of General Psychiatry, 50,* 7–16. (p. 585)

Cogan, J. C., & Ernsberger, P. (1999). Dieting, weight, and health: Reconceptualizing research and policy. *Journal of Social Issues, 55,* 187–205. (p. 348)

Cohen, D. (1995, June 17). Now we are one, or two, or three. *New Scientist,* pp. 14–15. (p. 578)

Cohen, G. L., Garcia, J., Apfel, N., & Master, A. (2006). Reducing the racial achievement gap: A social-psychological intervention. *Science, 313,* 1307–1310. (p. 555)

Cohen, K. M. (2002). Relationships among childhood sex-atypical behavior, spatial ability, handedness, and sexual orientation in men. *Archives of Sexual Behavior, 31,* 129–143. (p. 359)

Cohen, P. (2007, November 15). Freud is widely taught at universities, except in the psychology department. *New York Times* (www.nytimes.com). (p. 490)

Cohen, S. (1988). Psychosocial models of the role of social support in the etiology of physical disease. *Health Psychology, 7,* 269–297. (p. C-4)

Cohen, S. (2004). Social relationships and health. *American Psychologist, 59,* 676–684. (p. C-4)

Cohen, S., Alper, C. M., Doyle, W. J., Treanor, J. J., & Turner, R. B. (2006). Positive emotional style predicts resistance to illness after experimental exposure to rhinovuros or influenza A virus. *Psychosomatic Medicine, 68,* 809–815. (p. 404)

Cohen, S., Doyle, W. J., Skoner, D. P., Rabin, B. S., & Gwaltney, J. M., Jr. (1997). Social ties and susceptibility to the common cold. *Journal of the American Medical Association, 277,* 1940–1944. (pp. C-2, C-4)

Cohen, S., Doyle, W. J., Turner, R., Alper, C. M., & Skoner, D. P. (2003). Sociability and susceptibility to the common cold. *Psychological Science, 14,* 389–395. (p. 404)

Cohen, S., Kaplan, J. R., Cunnick, J. E., Manuck, S. B., & Rabin, B. S. (1992). Chronic social stress, affiliation, and cellular immune response in nonhuman primates. *Psychological Science, 3,* 301–304. (p. 404)

Cohen, S., Tyrrell, D. A. J., & Smith, A. P. (1991). Psychological stress and susceptibility to the common cold. *New England Journal of Medicine, 325,* 606–612. (p. 404)

Colangelo, N., Assouline, S. G., & Gross, M. U. M. (2004). *A nation deceived: How schools hold back America's brightest students, Volumes I and II. The Templeton National Report on Acceleration.* Iowa City, IA: College of Education, University of Iowa. (p. 543)

Colarelli, S. M., & Dettman, J. R. (2003). Intuitive evolutionary perspectives in marketing. *Psychology and Marketing, 20,* 837–865. (p. 105)

Colarelli, S. M., Spranger, J. L., & Hechanova, M. R. (2006). Women, power, and sex composition in small groups: An evolutionary perspective. *Journal of Organizational Behavior, 27,* 163–184. (p. 436)

Colcombe, S. J., & Kramer, A. F. (2003). Fitness effects on the cognitive function of older adults: A meta-analytic study. *Psychological Science, 14,* 125–130. (p. 459)

Colcombe, S. J., Kramer, A. F., Erickson, K. I., Scalf, P., McAuley, E., Cohen, N. J., Webb, A., Jerome, G. J., Marquex, D. X., & Elavsky, S. (2004). Cardiovascular fitness, cortical plasticity, and aging. *Proceedings of the National Academy of Sciences, 101,* 3316–3321. (p. 459)

Cole, K. C. (1998). *The universe and the teacup: The mathematics of truth and beauty.* New York: Harcourt Brace. (p. 202)

Coleman, P. D., & Flood, D. G. (1986). Dendritic proliferation in the aging brain as a compensatory repair mechanism. In D. F. Swaab, E. Fliers, M. Mirmiram, W. A. Van Gool, & F. Van Haaren (Eds.), *Progress in brain research* (Vol. 20). New York: Elsevier. (p. 459)

Collins, D. W., & Kimura, D. (1997). A large sex difference on a two-dimensional mental rotation task. *Behavioral Neuroscience, 111,* 845–849. (p. 550)

Collins, F. (2006). *The language of God.* New York: Free Press. (p. 109)

Collins, N. L., & Miller, L. C. (1994). Self-disclosure and liking: A meta-analytic review. *Psychological Bulletin, 116,* 457–475. (p. 684)

Collins, R. L., Elliott, M. N., Berry, S. H., Danouse, D. E., Kunkel, D., Hunter, S. B., & Miu, A. (2004). Watching sex on television predicts adolescent initiation of sexual behavior. *Pediatrics, 114,* 280–289. (p. 30)

Collinson, S. L., MacKay, C. E., James, A. C., Quested, D. J., Phillips, T., Roberts, N., & Crow, T. J. (2003). Brain volume, asymmetry and intellectual impairment in relation to sex in early-onset schizophrenia. *British Journal of Psychiatry, 183,* 114–120. (p. 593)

Collishaw, S., Pickles, A., Natarajan, L., & Maughan, B. (2007, June). 20-year trends in depression and anxiety in England. Paper presented at the Thirteenth Scientific Meeting on The Brain and the Developing Child, London, UK. (p. 583)

Colom, R., Jung, R. E., & Haier, R. J. (2006). Distributed brain sites for the *g*-factor of intelligence. *NeuroImage, 31,* 1359–1365. (p. 530)

Colom, R., Lluis-Font, J. M., & Andrés-Pueyo, A. (2005). The generational intelligence gains are caused by decreasing variance in the lower half of the distribution: Supporting evidence for the nutrition hypothesis. *Intelligence, 33,* 83–91. (p. 537)

Colombo, J. (1982). The critical period concept: Research, methodology, and theoretical issues. *Psychological Bulletin, 91,* 260–275. (p. 427)

Comer, R. J. (2004). *Abnormal psychology.* New York: Worth Publishers. (p. 562)

Commission on Children at Risk. (2003). *Hardwired to connect: The new scientific case for authoritative communities.* New York: Institute for American Values. (p. 434)

Comstock, G. (2008). A sociological perspective on television violence and aggression. *American Behavioral Scientist, 51,* 1184–1211. (p. 247)

Conard, M. A. (2006). Aptitude is not enough: How personality and behavior predict academic performance. *Journal of Research in Personality, 40,* 339–346. (p. 499)

Connor-Smith, J. K., & Flachsbart, C. (2007). Relations between personality and coping: A meta-analysis. *Journal of Personality and Social Psychology, 93,* 1080–1107. (p. C-1)

Consumer Reports. (1995, November). Does therapy help? Pp. 734–739. (p. 619)

Conway, M. A., Wang, Q., Hanyu, K., & Haque, S. (2005). A cross-cultural investigation of autobiographical memory. On the universality and cultural variation of the reminiscence bump. *Journal of Cross-Cultural Psychology, 36,* 739–749. (p. 461)

Cook, M., & Mineka, S. (1991). Selective associations in the origins of phobic fears and their implications for behavior therapy. In P. Martin (Ed.), *Handbook of behavior therapy and psychological science: An integrative approach.* New York: Pergamon Press. (p. 386)

Cooke, L. J., Wardle, J., & Gibson, E. L. (2003). Relationship between parental report of food neophobia and everyday food consumption in 2–6-year-old children. *Appetite, 41,* 205–206. (p. 147)

Cooper, K. J. (1999, May 1). This time, copycat wave is broader. *Washington Post* (www.washingtonpost.com). (pp. 249, 651)

Cooper, M. L. (2006). Does drinking promote risky sexual behavior? A complex answer to a simple question. *Current Directions in Psychological Science, 15,* 19–23. (p. 200)

Coopersmith, S. (1967). *The antecedents of self-esteem.* San Francisco: Freeman. (p. 433)

Corballis, M. C. (1989). Laterality and human evolution. *Psychological Review, 96,* 492–505. (p. 88)

Corballis, M. C. (2002). *From hand to mouth: The origins of language.* Princeton: Princeton University Press. (p. D-5)

Coren, S. (1996). *Sleep thieves: An eye-opening exploration into the science and mysteries of sleep.* New York: Free Press. (pp. 182, 184, 186)

Corey, D. P., & 15 others. (2004). TRPA1 is a candidate for the mechanosensitive transduction channel of vertebrate hair cells. *Nature* (advance online publication, October 13, at www.nature.com). (p. 136)

Corina, D. P. (1998). The processing of sign language: Evidence from aphasia. In B. Stemmer & H. A. Whittaker (Eds.), *Handbook of neurolinguistics.* San Diego: Academic Press. (p. 87)

Corina, D. P., Vaid, J., & Bellugi, U. (1992). The linguistic basis of left hemisphere specialization. *Science, 255,* 1258–1260. (p. 87)

Corneille, O., Huart, J., Becquart, E., & Brédart, S. (2004). When memory shifts toward more typical category exemplars: Accentuation effects in the recollection of ethnically ambiguous faces. *Journal of Personality and Social Psychology, 86,* 236–250. (p. 299)

Correll, J., Park, B., Judd, C. M., & Wittenbrink, B. (2002). The police officer's dilemma: Using ethnicity to disambiguate potentially threatening individuals. *Journal of Personality and Social Psychology, 83,* 1314–1329. (p. 666)

Correll, J., Park, B., Judd, C. M., Wittenbrink, B., Sadler, M. S., & Keesee, T. (2007). Across the thin blue line: Police officers and racial bias in the decision to shoot. *Journal of Personality and Social Psychology, 92,* 1006–1023. (p. 666)

Costa, P. T., Jr., & McCrae, R. R. (2006). Trait and factor theories. In J. C. Thomas, D. L. Segal, & M. Hersen (Eds.), *Comprehensive handbook of personality and psychopathology, Vol. 1: Personality and everyday functioning.* Hoboken, NJ: Wiley. (p. 497)

Costa, P. T., Jr., Terracciano, A., & McCrae, R. R. (2001). Gender differences in personality traits across cultures: Robust and surprising findings. *Journal of Personality and Social Psychology, 81,* 322–331. (p. 379)

Costa, P. T., Jr., Zonderman, A. B., McCrae, R. R., Cornoni-Huntley, J., Locke, B. Z., & Barbano, H. E. (1987). Longitudinal analyses of psychological well-being in a national sample: Stability of mean levels. *Journal of Gerontology, 42,* 50–55. (p. 469)

Costello, E. J., Compton, S. N., Keeler, G., & Angold, A. (2003). Relationships between poverty and psychopathology: A natural experiment. *Journal of the American Medical Association, 290,* 2023–2029. (p. 600)

Coughlin, J. F., Mohyde, M., D'Ambrosio, L. A., & Gilbert, J. (2004). *Who drives older driver decisions?* Cambridge, MA: MIT Age Lab. (p. 459)

Couli, J. T., Vidal, F., Nazarian, B., & Macar, F. (2004). Functional anatomy of the attentional modulation of time estimation. *Science, 303,* 1506–1508. (p. B-2)

Courage, M. L., & Howe, M. L. (2002). From infant to child: The dynamics of cognitive change in the second year of life. *Psychological Bulletin, 128,* 250–277. (p. 432)

Courneya, K. S., & Carron, A. V. (1992). The home advantage in sports competitions: A literature review. *Journal of Sport and Exercise Psychology, 14,* 13–27. (p. 658)

Courtney, J. G., Longnecker, M. P., Theorell, T., & de Verdier, M. G. (1993). Stressful life events and the risk of colorectal cancer. *Epidemiology, 4,* 407–414. (p. 405)

Covin, R., Ouimet, A. J., Seeds, P. M., & Dozois, D. J. A. (2008). A meta-analysis of CBT for pathological worry among clients with GAD. *Journal of Anxiety Disorders, 22,* 108–116. (p. 617)

Cowan, G., Lee, C., Levy, D., & Snyder, D. (1988). Dominance and inequality in X-rated videocassettes. *Psychology of Women Quarterly, 12,* 299–311. (p. 674)

Cowan, N. (1988). Evolving conceptions of memory storage, selective attention, and their mutual constraints within the human information-processing system. *Psychological Bulletin, 104,* 163–191. (p. 266)

Cowan, N. (1994). Mechanisms of verbal short-term memory. *Current Directions in Psychological Science, 3,* 185–189. (p. 267)

Cowan, N. (2001). The magical number 4 in short-term memory: A reconsideration of mental storage capacity. *Behavioral and Brain Sciences, 24,* 87–185. (p. 267)

Cowart, B. J. (1981). Development of taste perception in humans: Sensitivity and preference throughout the life span. *Psychological Bulletin, 90,* 43–73. (p. 147)

Cowart, B. J. (2005). Taste, our body's gustatory gatekeeper. *Cerebrum, 7*(2), 7–22. (p. 147)

Cox, J. J., & 18 others. (2006). An *SCN9A* channelopathy causes congenital inability to experience pain. *Nature, 444,* 894–898. (p. 144)

CPP. (2008). *Myers-Briggs Type Indicator® assessment (MBTI®).* CPP, Inc. (www.cpp.com). (p. 494)

Crabbe, J. C. (2002). Genetic contributions to addiction. *Annual Review of Psychology, 53,* 435–462. (p. 208)

Crabtree, S. (2005, January 13). Engagement keeps the doctor away. *Gallup Management Journal* (gmj.gallup.com). (p. B-9)

Craik, F. I. M. (1986). A functional account of age differences in memory. In F. Klix & H. Hagendorf (Eds.), *Human memory and cognitive capabilities.* Amsterdam: Elsevier. (p. 463)

Craik, F. I. M., & Tulving, E. (1975). Depth of processing and the retention of words in episodic memory. *Journal of Experimental Psychology: General, 104,* 268–294. (pp. 261, 262)

Craik, F. I. M., & Watkins, M. J. (1973). The role of rehearsal in short-term memory. *Journal of Verbal Learning and Verbal Behavior, 12,* 599–607. (pp. 260, 261)

Crain-Thoreson, C., & Dale, P. S. (1992). Do early talkers become early readers? Linguistic precocity, preschool language, and emergent literacy. *Developmental Psychology, 28,* 421–429. (p. 540)

Crandall, C. S. (1988). Social contagion of binge eating. *Journal of Personality and Social Psychology, 55,* 588–598. (p. 337)

Crandall, C. S. (1994). Prejudice against fat people: Ideology and self-interest. *Journal of Personality and Social Psychology, 66,* 882–894. (pp. 341, 493)

Crandall, C. S. (1995). Do parents discriminate against their heavyweight daughters? *Personality and Social Psychology Bulletin, 21,* 724–735. (p. 341)

Crawford, M., Chaffin, R., & Fitton, L. (1995). Cognition in social context. *Learning and Individual Differences, Special Issue: Psychological and psychobiological perspectives on sex differences in cognition: 1. Theory and Research, 7,* 341–362. (p. 550)

Crawley, J. N. (2007). Testing hypotheses about autism. *Science, 318,* 56–57. (p. 425)

Crews, F. (Ed.) (1998). *Unauthorized Freud: Doubters confront a legend.* New York: Viking. (p. 490)

Crews, F. T., Mdzinarishvili, A., Kim, D., He, J., & Nixon, K. (2006). Neurogenesis in adolescent brain is potently inhibited by ethanol. *Neuroscience, 137,* 437–445. (p. 199)

Crews, F., He, J., & Hodge, C. (2007). Adolescent cortical development: A critical period of vulnerability for addiction. *Pharmacology, Biochemistry and Behavior, 86,* 189–199. (pp. 199, 447)

Crocker, J., & Park, L. E. (2004). The costly pursuit of self-esteem. *Psychological Bulletin, 130,* 392–414. (p. 515)

Crocker, J., Thompson, L. L., McGraw, K. M., & Ingerman, C. (1987). Downward comparison, prejudice, and evaluation of others: Effects of self-esteem and threat. *Journal of Personality and Social Psychology, 52,* 907–916. (p. 669)

Croft, R. J., Klugman, A., Baldeweg, T., & Gruzelier, J. H. (2001). Electrophysiological evidence of serotonergic impairment in long-term MDMA ("Ecstasy") users. *American Journal of Psychiatry, 158,* 1687–1692. (p. 205)

Crombie, A. C. (1964, May). Early concepts of the senses and the mind. *Scientific American,* pp. 108–116. (p. 126)

Crook, T. H., & West, R. L. (1990). Name recall performance across the adult life-span. *British Journal of Psychology, 81,* 335–340. (p. 461)

Cross, S., & Markus, H. (1991). Possible selves across the life span. *Human Development, 34,* 230–255. (p. 511)

Cross-National Collaborative Group. (1992). The changing rate of major depression. *Journal of the American Medical Association, 268,* 3098–3105. (p. 583)

Crowell, J. A., & Waters, E. (1994). Bowlby's theory grown up: The role of attachment in adult love relationships. *Psychological Inquiry, 5,* 1–22. (p. 427)

Csikszentmihalyi, M. (1990). *Flow: The psychology of optimal experience.* New York: Harper & Row. (p. B-1)

Csikszentmihalyi, M. (1999). If we are so rich, why aren't we happy? *American Psychologist, 54,* 821–827. (p. B-1)

Csikszentmihalyi, M., & Hunter, J. (2003). Happiness in everyday life: The uses of experience sampling. *Journal of Happiness Studies, 4,* 185–199. (p. 452)

Csikszentmihalyi, M., & Larson, R. (1984). *Being adolescent: Conflict and growth in the teenage years.* New York: Basic Books. (p. 470)

Cullen, L. T., & Masters, C. (2008, January 28). We just clicked. *Time,* pp. 84–89. (p. 679)

Cullum, J., & Harton, H. C. (2007). Cultural evolution: Interpersonal influence, issue importance, and the development of shared attitudes in college residence halls. *Personality and Social Psychology Bulletin, 33,* 1327–1339. (p. 653)

Cummins, R. A. (2006, April 4). *Australian Unity Wellbeing Index: Survey 14.1.* Australian Centre on Quality of Life, Deakin University, Melbourne: Report 14.1. (p. 392)

Cunningham, M. R., & others. (2005). "Their ideas of beauty are, on the whole, the same as ours": Consistency and variability in the cross-cultural perception of female physical attractiveness. *Journal of Personality and Social Psychology, 68,* 261–279. (p. 681)

Cunningham, W. A., Johnson, M. K., Raye, C. L., Gatenby, J. C., Gore, J. C., & Banaji, M. R. (2004). Separable neural components in the processing of Black and White faces. *Psychological Science, 15,* 806–813. (p. 666)

Curtis, G. C., Magee, W. J., Eaton, W. W., Wittchen, H-U., & Kessler, R. C. (1998). Specific fears and phobias: Epidemiology and classification. *British Journal of Psychiatry, 173,* 212–217. (p. 571)

Curtis, R. C., & Miller, K. (1986). Believing another likes or dislikes you: Behaviors making the beliefs come true. *Journal of Personality and Social Psychology, 51,* 284–290. (p. 683)

Cushman, F., Young, L., & Hauser, M. (2006). The role of conscious reasoning and intuition in moral judgment: Testing three principles of harm. *Psychological Science, 17,* 1082–1088. (p. 450)

Cutler, B. L., & Penrod, S. D. (1989). Forensically relevant moderators of the relation between eyewitness identification accuracy and confidence. *Journal of Applied Psychology, 74,* 650–652. (p. 288)

Cynkar, A. (2007, June). The changing gender composition of psychology. *Monitor on Psychology,* 46–47. (p. 440)

Czeisler, C. A., Allan, J. S., Strogatz, S. H., Ronda, J. M., Sanchez, R., Rios, C. D., Freitag, W. O., Richardson, G. S., & Kronauer, R. E. (1986). Bright light resets the human circadian pacemaker independent of the timing of the sleep-wake cycle. *Science, 233,* 667–671. (p. 178)

Czeisler, C. A., Duffy, J. F., Shanahan, T. L., Brown, E. N., Mitchell, J. F., Rimmer, D. W., Ronda, J. M., Silva, E. J., Allan, J. S., Emens, J. S., Dijk, D-J., & Kronauer, R. E. (1999). Stability, precision, and near-24-hour period of the human circadian pacemaker. *Science, 284,* 2177–2181. (p. 178)

Czeisler, C. A., Kronauer, R. E., Allan, J. S., & Duffy, J. F. (1989). Bright light induction of strong (type O) resetting of the human circadian pacemaker. *Science, 244,* 1328–1333. (p. 178)

Dabbs, J. M., Jr. (2000). *Heroes, rogues, and lovers: Testosterone and behavior.* New York: McGraw-Hill. (p. 350)

Dabbs, J. M., Jr., Bernieri, F. J., Strong, R. K., Campo, R., & Milun, R. (2001b). Going on stage: Testosterone in greetings and meetings. *Journal of Research in Personality, 35,* 27–40. (p. 672)

Dabbs, J. M., Jr., & Morris, R. (1990). Testosterone, social class, and antisocial behavior in a sample of 4,462 men. *Psychological Science, 1,* 209–211. (p. 672)

Dabbs, J. M., Jr., Ruback, R. B., & Besch, N. F. (1987). Male saliva testosterone following conversations with male and female partners. Paper presented at the American Psychological Association convention. (p. 350)

Daley, T. C., Whaley, S. E., Sigman, M. D., Espinosa, M. P., & Neumann, C. (2003). IQ on the rise: The Flynn effect in rural Kenyan children. *Psychological Science, 14,* 215–219. (p. 537)

Damasio, A. R. (1994). *Descartes error: Emotion, reason, and the human brain.* New York: Grossett/Putnam & Sons. (pp. 376, 529)

Damasio, A. R. (2003). *Looking for Spinoza: Joy, sorrow, and the feeling brain.* New York: Harcourt. (pp. 376, 371)

Damasio, H., Grabowski, T., Frank, R., Galaburda, A. M., & Damasio, A. R. (1994). The return of Phineas Gage: Clues about the brain from the skull of a famous patient. *Science, 264,* 1102–1105. (p. 79)

Damon, W., Menon, J., & Bronk, K. (2003). The development of purpose during adolescence. *Applied Developmental Science, 7,* 119–128. (p. 452)

Danner, D. D., Snowdon, D. A., & Friesen, W. V. (2001). Positive emotions in early life and longevity: Findings from the Nun Study. *Journal of Personality and Social Psychology, 80,* 804–813. (p. C-3)

Danso, H. C., & Esses, V. (2001). Black experimenters and the intellectual test performance of white participants: The tables are turned. *Journal of Experimental Social Psychology, 37,* 158–165. (p. 555)

Dapretto, M., Davies, M. S., Pfeifer, J. H., Scott, A. A., Sigman, M., Bookheimer, S. Y., & Iacoboni, M. (2006). Understanding emotions in others: Mirror neuron dysfunction in children with autism spectrum disorders. *Nature Neuroscience, 9,* 28–30. (p. 425)

Darley, J., & Alter, A. (in press). Behavioral issues of punishment and deterrence. In E. Shafir (Ed.), *The behavioral foundations of policy.* Princeton, NJ: Princeton University Press and the Russell Sage Foundation. (p. 234)

Darley, J. M., & Latané, B. (1968a). Bystander intervention in emergencies: Diffusion of responsibility. *Journal of Personality and Social Psychology, 8,* 377–383. (p. 686)

Darley, J. M., & Latané, B. (1968b, December). When will people help in a crisis? *Psychology Today,* pp. 54–57, 70–71. (pp. 685, 686)

Darrach, B., & Norris, J. (1984, August). An American tragedy. *Life,* pp. 58–74. (p. 597)

Darwin, C. (1859). *On the origin of species by means of natural selection.* London: John Murray. (p. 105)

Daum, I., & Schugens, M. M. (1996). On the cerebellum and classical conditioning. *Psychological Science, 5,* 58–61. (p. 274)

Davey, G. C. L. (1992). Classical conditioning and the acquisition of human fears and phobias: A review and synthesis of the literature. *Advances in Behavior Research and Therapy, 14,* 29–66. (p. 226)

Davey, G. C. L. (1995). Preparedness and phobias: Specific evolved associations or a generalized expectancy bias? *Behavioral and Brain Sciences, 18,* 289–297. (p. 575)

Davidoff, J. (2004). Coloured thinking. *The Psychologist, 17,* 570–572. (p. 320)

Davidson, J. R. T., Connor, K. M., & Swartz, M. (2006). Mental illness in U.S. presidents between 1776 and 1974: A review of biographical sources. *Journal of Nervous and Mental Disease, 194,* 47–51. (p. 600)

Davidson, R. J. (2000). Affective style, psychopathology, and resilience: Brain mechanisms and plasticity. *American Psychologist, 55,* 1196–1209. (p. 371)

Davidson, R. J. (2003). Affective neuroscience and psychophysiology: Toward a synthesis. *Psychophysiology, 40,* 655–665. (p. 371)

Davidson, R. J., Kabat-Zinn, J., Schumacher, J., Rosenkranz, M., Muller, D., Santorelli, S. F., Urbanowski, F., Harrington, A., Bonus, K., & Sheridan, J. F. (2003). Alterations in brain and immune function produced by mindfulness meditation. *Psychosomatic Medicine, 65,* 564–570. (p. C-10)

Davidson, R. J., Pizzagalli, D., Nitschke, J. B., & Putnam, K. (2002). Depression: Perspectives from affective neuroscience. *Annual Review of Psychology, 53,* 545–574. (p. 585)

Davidson, R. J., Putnam, K. M., & Larson, C. L. (2000). Dysfunction in the neural circuitry of emotion regulation—a possible prelude to violence. *Science, 289,* 591–594. (p. 671)

Davies, D. R., Matthews, G., & Wong, C. S. K. (1991). Aging and work. *International Review of Industrial and Organizational Psychology, 6,* 149–211. (p. 466)

Davies, M. F. (1997). Positive test strategies and confirmatory retrieval processes in the evaluation of personality feedback. *Journal of Personality and Social Psychology, 73,* 574–583. (p. 498)

Davies, P. (2007). *Cosmic jackpot: Why our universe is just right for life.* Boston: Houghton-Mifflin. (p. 110)

Davis, B. E., Moon, R. Y., Sachs, H. C., & Ottolini, M. C. (1998). Effects of sleep position on infant motor development. *Pediatrics, 102,* 1135–1140. (p. 416)

Davis, H., IV, Liotti, M., Ngan, E. T., Woodward, T. S., Van Sellenberg, J. X., van Anders, S. M., Smith, A., & Mayberg, H. S. (2008). FMRI BOLD signal changes in elite swimmers while viewing videos of personal failures. *Brain Imaging and Behavior, 2,* 94–104. (p. 585)

Davis, J. O., & Phelps, J. A. (1995a). Twins with schizophrenia: Genes or germs? *Schizophrenia Bulletin, 21,* 13–18. (p. 594)

Davis, J. O., Phelps, J. A., & Bracha, H. S. (1995). Prenatal development of monozygotic twins and concordance for schizophrenia. *Schizophrenia Bulletin, 21,* 357–366. (pp. 97, 594)

Davis, K. C., Norris, J., George, W. H., Martell, J., & Heiman, J. R. (2006). Men's likelihood of sexual aggression: The influence of alcohol, sexual arousal, and violent pornography. *Aggressive Behavior, 32,* 581–589. (p. 200)

Davis, M. (2005). Searching for a drug to extinguish fear. *Cerebrum, 7*(3), 47–58. (p. 630)

Davis, S., Rees, M., Ribot, J., Moufarege, A., Rodenberg, C., & Purdie, D. (2003). Efficacy and safety of testosterone patches for the treatment of low sexual desire in surgically menopausal women. Presented to the American Society for Reproductive Medicine, San Antonio, October 11–15. (p. 350)

Davison, K. P., Pennebaker, J. W., & Dickerson, S. S. (2000). Who talks? The social psychology of illness support groups. *American Psychologist, 55,* 205–217. (p. 617)

Dawes, R. M. (1980). Social dilemmas. *Annual Review of Psychology, 31,* 169–193. (p. 689)

Dawes, R. M. (1994). *House of cards: Psychology and psychotherapy built on myth.* New York: Free Press. (p. 512)

Dawkins, R. (1998). *Unweaving the rainbow.* Boston: Houghton Mifflin. (p. 109)

Dawkins, R. (1999, April 8). Is science killing the soul (a discussion with Richard Dawkins and Steven Pinker). www.edge.org. (p. 175)

Dawkins, R. (2007, July 1). Inferior design. *New York Times* (www.nytimes.com). (p. 103)

de Boysson-Bardies, B., Halle, P., Sagart, L., & Durand, C. (1989). A cross linguistic investigation of vowel formats in babbling. *Journal of Child Language, 16,* 1–17. (p. 315)

de Courten-Myers, G. M. (2002, May 9). Personal correspondence. (p. 415)

de Courten-Myers, G. M. (2005, February 4). Personal correspondence (estimating total brain neurons, extrapolating from her carefully estimated 20 to 23 billion cortical neurons). (pp. 61, 74)

de Cuevas, J. (1990, September-October) "No, she holded them loosely." *Harvard Magazine,* pp. 60–67. (p. 317)

de Hoogh, A. H. B., den Hartog, D. N., Koopman, P. L., Thierry, H., van den Berg, P. T., van der Weide, J. G., & Wilderom, C. P. M. (2004). Charismatic leadership, environmental dynamism, and performance. *European Journal of Work and Organisational Psychology, 13,* 447–471. (p. B-12)

De Houwer, J., Baeyens, F., & Field, A. P. (2005a). Associative learning of likes and dislikes: Some current controversies and possible ways forward. *Cognition and Emotion, 19,* 161–174. (p. 221)

De Houwer, J., Thomas, S., & Baeyens, F. (2001). Associative learning of likes and dislikes: A review of 25 years of research on human evaluative conditioning. *Psychological Bulletin, 127,* 853–869. (p. 220)

De Houwer, J., Vandorpe, S., & Beckers, T. (2005b). On the role of controlled cognitive processes in human associative learning. In A. J. Wills (Ed.), *New directions in human associative learning.* Mahwah, NJ: Erlbaum. (p. 221)

De Koninck, J. (2000). Waking experiences and dreaming. In M. Kryger, T. Roth, & W. Dement (Eds.), *Principles and practice of sleep medicine, 3rd ed.* Philadelphia: Saunders. (p. 188)

de Quervain, D. J-F., Roozendaal, B., & McGaugh, J. L. (1998). Stress and glucocorticoids impair retrieval of long-term spatial memory. *Nature, 394,* 787–790. (p. 271)

De Vogli, R., Chandola, T., & Marmot, M. G. (2007). Negative aspects of close relationships and heart disease. *Archives of Internal Medicine, 167,* 1951–1957. (p. C-4)

de Waal, F. B. M. (1999, December). The end of nature versus nurture. *Scientific American,* pp. 94–99. (p. 439)

de Waal, F. B. M. (2005, September 23). We're all Machiavellians. *Chronicle of Higher Education.* (p. 28)

de Waal, F. B. M., & Johanowicz, D. L. (1993). Modification of reconciliation behavior through social experience: An experiment with two macaque species. *Child Development, 64,* 897–908. (p. 243)

De Wolff, M. S., & van IJzendoorn, M. H. (1997). Sensitivity and attachment: A meta-analysis on parental antecedents of infant attachment. *Child Development, 68,* 571–591. (p. 428)

Deacon, B. J., & Abramowitz, J. S. (2004). Cognitive and behavioral treatments for anxiety disorders: A review of meta-analytic findings. *Journal of Clinical Psychology, 60,* 429–441. (p. 611)

Dean, G. A., Kelly, I. W., Saklofske, D. H., & Furnham, A. (1992). Graphology and human judgment. In B. Beyerstein & D. Beyerstein (Eds.), *The write stuff: Evaluations of graphology.* Buffalo, NY: Prometheus Books. (p. 498)

DeAngelis, T. (2008, February). U.K. gives huge boost to psychologists. *Monitor on Psychology,* p. 51. (p. 623)

Deary, I. J., Batty, G. D., & Gale, C. R. (2008). Bright children become enlightened adults. *Psychological Science, 19,* 1–6. (p. 669)

Deary, I. J., & Caryl, P. G. (1993). Intelligence, EEG and evoked potentials. In P. A. Vernon (Ed.), *Biological approaches to the study of human intelligence.* Norwood, NJ: Ablex. (p. 531)

Deary, I. J., & Der, G. (2005). Reaction time explains IQ's association with death. *Psychological Science, 16,* 64–69. (p. 531)

Deary, I. J., & Matthews, G. (1993). Personality traits are alive and well. *The Psychologist: Bulletin of the British Psychological Society, 6,* 299–311. (p. 501)

Deary, I. J., & Stough, C. (1996). Intelligence and inspection time: Achievements, prospects, and problems. *American Psychologist, 51,* 599–608. (p. 531)

Deary, I. J., Strand, S., Smith, P., & Fernandes, C. (2007). Intelligence and educational achievement. *Intelligence, 35,* 13–21. (p. 538)

Deary, I. J., Thorpe, G., Wilson, V., Starr, J. M., & Whalley, L. J. (2003). Population sex differences in IQ at age 11: The Scottish mental survey 1932. *Intelligence, 31,* 533–541. (pp. 549, 551)

Deary, I. J., Whiteman, M. C., Starr, J. M., Whalley, L. J., & Fox, H. C. (2004). The impact of childhood intelligence on later life: Following up the Scottish mental surveys of 1932 and 1947. *Journal of Personality and Social Psychology, 86,* 130–147. (pp. 540, 541)

DeBruine, L. M. (2002). Facial resemblance enhances trust. *Proceedings of the Royal Society of London, 269,* 1307–1312. (p. 678)

DeBruine, L. M. (2004). Facial resemblance increases the attractiveness of same-sex faces more than other-sex faces. *Proceedings of the Royal Society of London B, 271,* 2085–2090. (p. 678)

DeCasper, A. J., Lecanuet, J-P, Busnel, M-C, Granier-Deferre, C., et al. (1994). Fetal reactions to recurrent maternal speech. *Infant Behavior and Development, 17,* 159–164. (p. 412)

DeCasper, A. J., & Prescott, P. A. (1984). Human newborns' perception of male voices: Preference, discrimination and reinforcing value. *Developmental Psychobiology, 17,* 481–491. (p. 412)

DeCasper, A. J., & Spence, M. J. (1986). Prenatal maternal speech influences newborns' perception of speech sounds. *Infant Behavior and Development, 9,* 133–150. (p. 412)

Deci, E. L., Koestner, R., & Ryan, R. M. (1999, November). A meta-analytic review of experiments examining the effects of extrinsic rewards on intrinsic motivation. *Psychological Bulletin, 125*(6), 627–668. (p. 236)

Deci, E. L., & Ryan, R. M. (1985). *Intrinsic motivation and self-determination in human behavior.* New York: Plenum Press. (p. 237)

Deci, E. L., & Ryan, R. M. (1992). The initiation and regulation of intrinsically motivated learning and achievement. In A. K. Boggiano & T. S. Pittman (Eds.), *Achievement and motivation: A social-developmental perspective.* New York: Cambridge University Press. (p. 237)

Deci, E. L., & Ryan, R. M. (Eds.) (2002). *Handbook of self-determination research.* Rochester, NJ: University of Rochester Press. (pp. 237, 360)

Deeley, Q., Daly, E., Surguladze, S., Tunstall, N., Mezey, G., Beer, D., Ambikapathy, A., Robertson, D., Giampietro, V., Brammer, M. J., Clarke, A., Dowsett, J., Fahy, T., Phillips, M. L., & Murphy, D. G. (2006). Facial emotion processing in criminal psychopathy. *British Journal of Psychiatry, 189,* 533–539. (p. 598)

DeHart, T., Tennen, H., Armeli, S., Todd, M., & Affleck, G. (2008). Drinking to regulate negative romantic relationship interactions: The moderating role of self-esteem. *Journal of Experimental Social Psychology, 44,* 527–538. (p. 200)

Dehne, K. L., & Riedner, G. (2005). *Sexually transmitted infections among adolescents: The need for adequate health services.* Geneva: World Health Organization. (p. 353)

DeLamater, J. D., & Sill, M. (2005). Sexual desire in later life. *Journal of Sex Research, 42,* 138–149. (p. 456)

Delaney, H. D., Miller, W. R., & Bisonó, A. M. (2007). Religiosity and spirituality among psychologists: A survey of clinician members of the American Psychological Association. *Professional Psychology: Research and Practice, 38,* 538–546. (p. 626)

Delaney, P. F., Ericsson, K. A., Weaver, G. E., & Mahadevan, S. (1999). Accounts of the memorist Rajan's exceptional performance: Comparing three theoretical proposals. Paper presented to the American Psychological Society convention. (p. 267)

Delgado, J. M. R. (1969). *Physical control of the mind: Toward a psychocivilized society.* New York: Harper & Row. (p. 75)

DeLoache, J. S. (1987). Rapid change in the symbolic functioning of very young children. *Science, 238,* 1556–1557. (p. 421)

DeLoache, J. S. (1995). Early understanding and use of symbols: The model model. *Current Directions in Psychological Science, 4,* 109–113. (p. 421)

DeLoache, J. S., Uttal, D. H., & Rosengren, K. S. (2004). Scale errors offer evidence for a perception-action dissociation early in life. *Science, 304,* 1027–1029. (p. 418)

Dement, W. C. (1978). *Some must watch while some must sleep.* New York: Norton. (pp. 179, 186)

Dement, W. C. (1997, September). *What all undergraduates should know about how their sleeping lives affect their waking lives.* Stanford University: www.leland.stanford.edu/~dement/sleepless.html. (p. 183)

Dement, W. C. (1999). *The promise of sleep.* New York: Delacorte Press. (pp. 178, 179, E-4, E-6)

Dement, W. C., & Wolpert, E. A. (1958). The relation of eye movements, body mobility, and external stimuli to dream content. *Journal of Experimental Psychology, 55,* 543–553. (p. 188)

Demir, E., & Dickson, B. J. (2005). Fruitless splicing specifies male courtship behavior in Drosophila. *Cell, 121,* 785–794. (p. 357)

Denes-Raj, V., Epstein, S., & Cole, J. (1995). The generality of the ratio-bias phenomenon. *Personality and Social Psychology Bulletin, 21,* 1083–1092. (p. 311)

DeNeve, K. M., & Cooper, H. (1998). The happy personality: A meta-analysis of 137 personality traits and subjective well-being. *Psychological Bulletin, 124,* 197–229. (p. 396)

Dennett, D. C. (1991). *Consciousness explained.* Boston: Little, Brown. (p. 223)

Dennett, D. (1996, September 9). Quoted by Ian Parker, Richard Dawkins' evolution. *The New Yorker,* pp. 41–45. (p. 9)

Denton, K., & Krebs, D. (1990). From the scene to the crime: The effect of alcohol and social context on moral judgment. *Journal of Personality and Social Psychology, 59,* 242–248. (p. 199)

DePaulo, B. M. (1994). Spotting lies: Can humans learn to do better? *Current Directions in Psychological Science 3,* 83–86. (p. 379)

DePaulo, B. M., Blank, A. L., Swaim, G. W., & Hairfield, J. G. (1992). Expressiveness and expressive control. *Personality and Social Psychology Bulletin, 18,* 276–285. (p. 502)

Der, G., Batty, G. D., & Deary, I. J. (2006). Effect of breast feeding on intelligence in children: Prospective study, sibling pairs analysis, and meta-analysis. *British Medical Journal, 333,* 945. (p. 34)

Dermer, M., Cohen, S. J., Jacobsen, E., & Anderson, E. A. (1979). Evaluative judgments of aspects of life as a function of vicarious exposure to hedonic extremes. *Journal of Personality and Social Psychology, 37,* 247–260. (p. 395)

Dermer, M., & Pyszczynski, T. A. (1978). Effects of erotica upon men's loving and liking responses for women they love. *Journal of Personality and Social Psychology, 36,* 1302–1309. (p. 683)

Deroche-Garmonet, V., Belin, D., & Piazza, P. V. (2004). Evidence for addiction-like behavior in the rat. *Science, 305,* 1014–1017. (p. 198)

DeRubeis, R. J., & 10 others. (2005). Cognitive therapy vs. medications in the treatment of moderate to severe depression. *Archives of General Psychiatry, 62,* 409–416. (p. 622)

DeSteno, D., Dasgupta, N., Bartlett, M. Y., & Cajdric, A. (2004). Prejudice from thin air: The effect of emotion on automatic intergroup attitudes. *Psychological Science, 15,* 319–324. (p. 388)

DeSteno, D., Petty, R. E., Wegener, D. T., & Rucker, D. D. (2000). Beyond valence in the perception of likelihood: The role of emotion specificity. *Journal of Personality and Social Psychology, 78,* 397–416. (p. 278)

Dettman, S. J., Pinder, D., Briggs, R. J. S., Dowell, R. C., & Leigh, J. R. (2007). Communication development in children who receive the cochlear implant younger than 12 months: Risk versus benefits. *Ear and Hearing, 28*(2), Supplement 11S-18S. (p. 138)

Deutsch, J. A. (1972, July). Brain reward: ESP and ecstasy. *Psychology Today,* 46–48. (p. 73)

DeValois, R. L., & DeValois, K. K. (1975). Neural coding of color. In E. C. Carterette & M. P. Friedman (Eds.), *Handbook of perception: Vol. V. Seeing.* New York: Academic Press. (p. 133)

Devilly, G. J. (2003). Eye movement desensitization and reprocessing: A chronology of its development and scientific standing. *Scientific Review of Mental Health Practice, 1,* 113–118. (p. 624)

Devilly, G. J., Gist, R., & Cotton, P. (2006). Ready! Fire! Aim! The status of psychological debriefing and therapeutic interventions: In the work place and after disasters. *Review of General Psychology, 10,* 318–345. (p. 573)

Devine, P. G. (1995). Prejudice and outgroup perception. In A. Tesser (Ed.), *Advanced social psychology.* New York: McGraw-Hill. (p. 679)

Devlin, B., Daniels, M., & Roeder, K. (1997). The heritability of IQ. *Nature, 388,* 468–471. (p. 544)

Dew, M. A., Hoch, C. C., Buysse, D. J., Monk, T. H., Begley, A. E., Houck, P. R., Hall, M., Kupfer, D. J., Reynolds, C. F., III (2003). Healthy older adults' sleep predicts all-cause mortality at 4 to 19 years of follow-up. *Psychosomatic Medicine, 65,* 63–73. (p. 184)

DeWall, C. N., Baumeister, R. F., Stillman, T. F., & Gaillot, M. T. (2007). Violence restrained: Effects of self-regulation and its depletion on aggression. *Journal of Experimental Social Psychology, 43,* 62–76. (p. 505)

Diaconis, P., & Mosteller, F. (1989). Methods for studying coincidences. *Journal of the American Statistical Association, 84,* 853–861. (p. 33)

Diamond, J. (2001, February). A tale of two reputations: Why we revere Darwin and give Freud a hard time. *Natural History,* pp. 20–24. (p. 105)

Diamond, L. M. (2007). A dynamical systems approach to the development and expression of female same-sex sexuality. *Perspectives on Psychological Science, 2,* 142–161. (p. 355)

Dick, D. M. (2007). Identification of genes influencing a spectrum of externalizing psychopathology. *Current Directions in Psychological Science, 16,* 331–335. (p. 597)

Dick, D. M. & 14 others. (2007). Association of *CHRM2* with IQ: Converging evidence for a gene influencing intelligence. *Behavior Genetics, 37,* 265–272. (p. 545)

Dickens, W. T., & Flynn, J. R. (2006). Black Americans reduce the racial IQ gap: Evidence from standardization samples. *Psychological Science, 17,* 913–920. (p. 552)

Dickerson, S. S., & Kemeny, M. E. (2004). Acute stressors and cortisol responses: A theoretical integration and synthesis of laboratory research. *Psychological Bulletin, 130,* 355–391. (p. C-2)

Dickinson, H. O., Parkinson, K. M., Ravens-Sieberer, U., Schirripa, G., Thyen, U., Arnaud, C., Beckung, E., Fauconnier, J., McManus, V., Michelsen, S. I., Parkes, J., & Colver, A. F. (2007). Self-reported quality of life of 8–12-year-old children with cerebral palsy: A cross-sectional European study. *Lancet, 369,* 2171–2178. (p. 390)

Dickson, B. J. (2005, June 3). Quoted in E. Rosenthal, For fruit flies, gene shift tilts sex orientation. *New York Times* (www.nytimes.com). (p. 357)

Diener, E. (2006). Guidelines of national indicators of subjective well-being and ill-being. *Journal of Happiness Studies, 7,* 397–404. (p. 393)

Diener, E., & Biswas-Diener, R. (2002). Will money increase subjective well-being? A literature review and guide to needed research. *Social Indicators Research, 57,* 119–169. (p. 392)

Diener, E., & Biswas-Diener, R. (2009). *Rethinking happiness: The science of psychological wealth.* Malden, MA: Wiley Blackwell. (pp. 391, 392)

Diener, E., Emmons, R. A., & Sandvik, E. (1986). The dual nature of happiness: Independence of positive and negative moods. Unpublished manuscript, University of Illinois. (p. 469)

Diener, E., Lucas, R. E., & Scollon, C. N. (2006). Beyond the hedonic treadmill: Revising the adaptation theory of well-being. *American Psychologist, 61,* 305–314. (p. 394)

Diener, E., Nickerson, C., Lucas, R. E., & Sandvik, E. (2002). Dispositional affect and job outcomes. *Social Indicators Research, 59,* 229–259. (p. 389)

Diener, E., & Oishi, S. (2000). Money and happiness: Income and subjective well-being across nations. In E. Diener & E. M. Suh (Eds.), *Subjective well-being across cultures.* Cambridge, MA: MIT Press. (p. 392)

Diener, E., Oishi, S., & Lucas, R. E. (2003). Personality, culture, and subjective well-being: Emotional and cognitive evaluations of life. *Annual Review of Psychology, 54,* 403–425. (p. 396)

Diener, E., & Seligman, M. E. P. (2002). Very happy people. *Psychological Science, 13,* 81–84. (p. 360)

Diener, E., Wolsic, B., & Fujita, F. (1995). Physical attractiveness and subjective well-being. *Journal of Personality and Social Psychology, 69,* 120–129. (p. 680)

Dietz, W. H., Jr., & Gortmaker, S. L. (1985). Do we fatten our children at the television set? Obesity and television viewing in children and adolescents. *Pediatrics, 75,* 807–812. (p. 347)

DiFranza, J. R. (2008, May). Hooked from the first cigarette. *Scientific American,* pp. 82–87. (p. 203)

Dijksterhuis, A., & Aarts, H. (2003). On wildebeests and humans: The preferential detection of negative stimuli. *Psychological Science, 14,* 14–18. (p. 377)

Dijksterhuis, A., Bos, M. W., Nordgren, L. F., & van Baaren, R. B. (2006b). Complex choices better made unconsciously? *Science, 313,* 760–761. (p. 311)

Dijksterhuis, A., & Nordgren, L. F. (2006a). A theory of unconscious thought. *Perspectives on Psychological Science, 1,* 95–109. (p. 311)

DiLalla, D. L., Carey, G., Gottesman, I. I., & Bouchard, T. J., Jr. (1996). Heritability of MMPI personality indicators of psychopathology in twins reared apart. *Journal of Abnormal Psychology, 105,* 491–499. (pp. 98, 583)

Dimberg, U., Thunberg, M., & Elmehed, K. (2000). Unconscious facial reactions to emotional facial expressions. *Psychological Science, 11,* 86–89. (pp. 243, 375, 384)

Dimberg, U., Thunberg, M., & Grunedal, S. (2002). Facial reactions to emotional stimuli: Automatically controlled emotional responses. *Cognition and Emotion, 16,* 449–472. (p. 243)

Dindia, K., & Allen, M. (1992). Sex differences in self-disclosure: A meta-analysis. *Psychological Bulletin, 112,* 106–124. (p. 437)

Dindo, M., Thierry, B., & Whiten, A. (2008). Social diffusion of novel foraging methods in brown capuchin monkeys (*Cebus apella*). *Proceedings of the Royal Society. Series B. Biological Sciences, 275,* 187–193. (p. D-2)

Dinges, N. G., & Hull, P. (1992). Personality, culture, and international studies. In D. Lieberman (Ed.), *Revealing the world: An interdisciplinary reader for international studies.* Dubuque, IA: Kendall-Hunt. (p. 320)

Dingfelder, S. (2007, December). $10 million project aims to integrate law and neuroscience. *Monitor on Psychology,* p. 11. (p. 373)

Dion, K. K., & Dion, K. L. (1993). Individualistic and collectivistic perspectives on gender and the cultural context of love and intimacy. *Journal of Social Issues, 49,* 53–69. (p. 518)

Dion, K. K., & Dion, K. L. (2001). Gender and cultural adaptation in immigrant families. *Journal of Social Issues, 57,* 511–521. (p. 440)

Discover. (1996, May). A fistful of risks. Pp. 82–83. (p. 202)

Dixon, J., Durrheim, K., & Tredoux, C. (2007). Intergroup contact and attitudes toward the principle and practice of racial equality. *Psychological Science, 18,* 867–872. (p. 690)

Dobbs, D. (2006, August/September). Turning off depression. *Scientific American Mind,* pp. 26–31. (p. 635)

Dobel, C., Diesendruck, G., & Bölte, J. (2007). How writing system and age influence spatial representations of actions: A developments, cross-linguistic study. *Psychological Science, 18,* 487–491. (p. 320)

Doherty, E. W., & Doherty, W. J. (1998). Smoke gets in your eyes: Cigarette smoking and divorce in a national sample of American adults. *Families, Systems, and Health, 16,* 393–400. (p. 204)

Dohrenwend, B. P., Levav, I., Shrout, P. E., Schwartz, S., Naveh, G., Link, B. G., Skodol, A. E., & Stueve, A. (1992). Socioeconomic status and psychiatric disorders: The causation-selection issue. *Science, 255,* 946–952. (p. 600)

Dohrenwend, B. P., Pearlin, L., Clayton, P., Hamburg, B., Dohrenwend, B. P., Riley, M., & Rose, R. (1982). Report on stress and life events. In G. R. Elliott & C. Eisdorfer (Eds.), *Stress and human health: Analysis and implications of research* (A study by the Institute of Medicine/National Academy of Academy of Sciences). New York: Springer. (p. 401)

Dohrenwend, B. P., Turner, J. B., Turse, N. A., Adams, B. G., Koenen, K. C., & Marshall, R. (2006). The psychological risks of Vietnam for U.S. veterans: A revisit with new data and methods. *Science, 313,* 979–982. (p. 572)

Doidge, N. (2007). *The brain that changes itself.* New York: Viking. (p. 82)

Dolan, C. M., Kraemer, H., Browner, W., Ensrud, K., & Kelsey, J. L. (2007). Associations between body composition, anthropometry and mortality in women of age 65 and older. *American Journal of Public Health, 97,* 913–918. (p. 341)

Dole, R. (1996, April 20). Quoted by M. Duffy, Look who's talking. *Time,* p. 48. (p. 645)

Dolezal, H. (1982). *Living in a world transformed.* New York: Academic Press. (p. 160)

Domhoff, G. W. (1996). *Finding meaning in dreams: A quantitative approach.* New York: Plenum. (p. 188)

Domhoff, G. W. (2003). *The scientific study of dreams: Neural networks, cognitive development, and content analysis.* Washington, DC: APA Books. (pp. 189, 191)

Domhoff, G. W. (2007). Realistic simulations and bizarreness in dream content: Past findings and suggestions for future research. In D. Barrett & P. McNamara (Eds.), *The new science of dreaming: Content, recall, and personality characteristics.* Westport, CT: Praeger. (p. 188)

Domjan, M. (1992). Adult learning and mate choice: Possibilities and experimental evidence. *American Zoologist, 32,* 48–61. (p. 220)

Domjan, M. (1994). Formulation of a behavior system for sexual conditioning. *Psychonomic Bulletin & Review, 1,* 421–428. (p. 220)

Domjan, M. (2005). Pavlovian conditioning: A functional perspective. *Annual Review of Psychology, 56.* (pp. 220, 224)

Domjan, M., Cusato, B., & Krause, M. (2004). Learning with arbitrary versus ecological conditioned stimuli: Evidence from sexual conditioning. *Psychonomic Bulletin & Review, 11,* 232–246. (p. 224)

Donahoe, J. W., & Vegas, R. (2004). Pavlovian conditioning: The CS-UR relation. *Journal of Experimental Psychology: Animal Behavior, 30,* 17–33. (p. 240)

Donnellan, M. B., Conger, R. D., & Bryant, C. M. (2004). The Big Five and enduring marriages. *Journal of Research in Personality, 38,* 481–504. (p. 499)

Donnellan, M. B., Trzesniewski, K. H., Robins, R. W., Moffitt, T. E., & Caspi, A. (2005). Low self-esteem is related to aggression, antisocial behavior, and delinquency. *Psychological Science, 16,* 328–335. (pp. 504, 516)

Donnerstein, E. (1998). Why do we have those new ratings on television. Invited address to the National Institute on the Teaching of Psychology. (pp. 247, 248)

Donnerstein, E., Linz, D., & Penrod, S. (1987). *The question of pornography.* New York: Free Press. (p. 249)

Dorner, G. (1976). *Hormones and brain differentiation.* Amsterdam: Elsevier Scientific. (p. 358)

Dorner, G. (1988). Neuroendocrine response to estrogen and brain differentiation in heterosexuals, homosexuals, and transsexuals. *Archives of Sexual Behavior, 17,* 57–75. (p. 358)

Doty, R. L. (2001). Olfaction. *Annual Review of Psychology, 52,* 423–452. (p. 150)

Doty, R. L., Shaman, P., Applebaum, S. L., Giberson, R., Siksorski, L., & Rosenberg, L. (1984). Smell identification ability: Changes with age. *Science, 226,* 1441–1443. (p. 458)

Dovidio, J. F., & Gaertner, S. L. (1999). Reducing prejudice: Combating intergroup biases. *Current Directions in Psychological Science, 8,* 101–105. (p. 691)

Dovidio, J. F., ten Vergert, M., Stewart, T. L., Gaertner, S. L., Johnson, J. D., Esses, V. M., Riek, B. M., & Pearson, A. R. (2004). Perspective and prejudice: Antecedents and mediating mechanisms. *Personality and Social Psychology Bulletin, 30,* 1537–154. (p. 691)

Downing, P. E., Jiang, Y., & Shuman, M. (2001). A cortical area selective for visual processing of the human body. *Science, 293,* 2470–2473. (p. 129)

Draguns, J. G. (1990a). Normal and abnormal behavior in cross-cultural perspective: Specifying the nature of their relationship. *Nebraska Symposium on Motivation 1989, 37,* 235–277. (pp. 562, 588)

Draguns, J. G. (1990b). Applications of cross-cultural psychology in the field of mental health. In R. W. Brislin (Ed.), *Applied cross-cultural psychology.* Newbury Park, CA: Sage. (p. 562)

Draguns, J. G. (1997). Abnormal behavior patterns across cultures: Implications for counseling and psychotherapy. *International Journal of Intercultural Relations, 21,* 213–248. (p. 562)

Drake, R. A. (1993). Processing persuasive arguments: II. Discounting of truth and relevance as a function of agreement and manipulated activation asymmetry. *Journal of Research in Personality, 27,* 184–196. (p. 86)

Drake, R. A., & Myers, L. R. (2006). Visual attention, emotion, and action tendency: Feeling active or passive. *Cognition and Emotion, 20,* 608–622. (p. 371)

Druckman, D., & Bjork, R. A. (1991). *In the mind's eye: Enhancing human performance.* National Academy Press: Washington, DC. (p. 494)

Druckman, D., & Bjork, R. A. (Eds.) (1994). *Learning, remembering, believing: Enhancing human performance.* Washington, DC: National Academy Press. (pp. 193, 194)

Duckworth, A. L., & Seligman, M. E. P. (2005). Discipline outdoes talent: Self-discipline predicts academic performance in adolescents. *Psychological Science, 12,* 939–944. (p. B-8)

Duckworth, A. L., & Seligman, M. E. P. (2006). Self-discipline gives girls the edge: Gender in self-discipline, grades, and achievement tests. *Journal of Educational Psychology, 98,* 198–208. (p. B-8)

Duclos, S. E., Laird, J. D., Sexter, M., Stern, L., & Van Lighten, O. (1989). Emotion-specific effects of facial expressions and postures on emotional experience. *Journal of Personality and Social Psychology, 57,* 100–108. (p. 383)

Duenwald, M. (2004, October 26). The dorms may be great, but how's the counseling? *New York Times* (www.nytimes.com). (p. 630)

Duffy, M. (2003, June 9). Weapons of mass disappearance. *Time,* pp. 28–33. (p. 648)

Dugatkin, L. A. (2002, Winter). Watching culture shape even guppy love. *Cerebrum,* pp. 51–66. (p. 242)

Duggan, J. P., & Booth, D. A. (1986). Obesity, overeating, and rapid gastric emptying in rats with ventromedial hypothalamic lesions. *Science, 231,* 609–611. (p. 333)

Dugger, C. W. (2005, January 18). U.N. proposes doubling of aid to cut poverty. *New York Times* (www.nytimes.com). (p. 309)

Dumont, K. A., Widom, C. S., Czaja, S. J. (2007). Predictors of resilience in abused and neglected children grown-up: The role of individual and neighborhood characteristics. *Child Abuse & Neglect, 31,* 255–274. (p. 430)

Duncan, J. (2000, July 21). Quoted by N. Angier, Study finds region of brain may be key problem solver. *New York Times* (www.ny times.com). (p. 530)

Duncan, J., Seitz, R. J., Kolodny, J., Bor, D., Herzog, H., Ahmed, A., Newell, F. N., & Emslie, H. (2000). A neural basis of general intelligence. *Science, 289,* 457–460. (p. 530)

Duncker, K. (1945). On problem solving. *Psychological Monographs, 58* (Whole no. 270). (pp. 303, 304)

Dunn, A. L., Trivedi, M. H., Kampert, J. B., Clark, C. G., & Chambliss, H. O. (2005). Exercise treatment for depression: Efficacy and dose response. *American Journal of Preventive Medicine, 28,* 1–8. (p. C-7)

Dunn, E. W., Aknin, L. B., & Norton, M. I. (2008). Spending money on others promotes happiness. *Science, 319,* 1687–1688. (p. 687)

Dunning, D. (2006). Strangers to ourselves? *The Psychologist, 19,* 600–603. (p. 509)

Dunson, D. B., Colombo, B., & Baird, D. D. (2002). Changes with age in the level and duration of fertility in the menstrual cycle. *Human Reproduction, 17,* 1399–1403. (p. 456)

Durgin, F. H., Evans, L., Dunphy, N., Klostermann, S., & Simmons, K. (2007). Rubber hands feel the touch of light. *Psychological Science, 18,* 152–157. (p. 142)

Dush, C. M. K, Cohan, C. L., & Amato, P. R. (2003). The relationship between cohabitation and marital quality and stability: Change across cohorts? *Journal of Marriage and Family, 65,* 539–549. (p. 467)

Dutton, D. G., & Aron, A. P. (1974). Some evidence for heightened sexual attraction under conditions of high anxiety. *Journal of Personality and Social Psychology, 30,* 510–517. (p. 683)

Dutton, D. G., & Aron, A. P. (1989). Romantic attraction and generalized liking for others who are sources of conflict-based arousal. *Canadian Journal of Behavioural Sciences, 21,* 246–257. (p. 683)

Dweck, C. S. (2006). *Mindset: The new psychology of success.* New York: Random House. (p. 548)

Dweck, C. S. (2007, November 28). The secret to raising smart kids. *Scientific American Mind,* pp. 36–43 (http://www.sciam.com). (p. 548)

Eagly, A. H. (1994). Are people prejudiced against women? Donald Campbell Award invited address, American Psychological Association convention. (p. 667)

Eagly, A. H. (2007). Female leadership advantage and disadvantage: Resolving the contradictions. *Psychology of Women Quarterly, 31,* 1–12. (p. B-12)

Eagly, A. H., Ashmore, R. D., Makhijani, M. G., & Kennedy, L. C. (1991). What is beautiful is good, but . . .: A meta-analytic review of research on the physical attractiveness stereotype. *Psychological Bulletin, 110,* 109–128. (p. 680)

Eagly, A. H., & Carli, L. (2007). *Through the labyrinth: The truth about how women become leaders.* Cambridge, MA: Harvard University Press. (p. 436)

Eagly, A. H., & Crowley, M. (1986). Gender and helping behavior: A meta-analytic review of the social psychological literature. *Psychological Bulletin, 100,* 283–308. (p. 686)

Eagly, A. H., & Wood, W. (1999). The origins of sex differences in human behavior: Evolved dispositions versus social roles. *American Psychologist, 54,* 408–423. (p. 107)

Eastman, C. L., Boulos, Z., Terman, M., Campbell, S. S., Dijk, D-J., & Lewy, A. J. (1995). Light treatment for sleep disorders: Consensus report. VI. Shift work. *Journal of Biological Rhythms, 10,* 157–164. (p. 178)

Eastman, C. L., Young, M. A., Fogg, L. F., Liu, L., & Meaden, P. M. (1998). Bright light treatment of winter depression: A placebo-controlled trial. *Archives of General Psychiatry, 55,* 883–889. (p. 625)

Eastwick, P. W., & Finkel, E. J. (2008a). Speed-dating as a methodological innovation. *The Psychologist, 21,* 402–403. (p. 679)

Eastwick, P. W., & Finkel, E. J. (2008b). Sex differences in mate preferences revisited: Do people know what they initially desire in a romantic partner? *Journal of Personality and Social Psychology, 94,* 245–264. (p. 679)

Ebbesen, E. B., Duncan, B., & Konecni, V. J. (1975). Effects of content of verbal aggression on future verbal aggression: A field experiment. *Journal of Experimental Social Psychology, 11,* 192–204. (p. 388)

Ebbinghaus, H. (1885). Über das Gedachtnis. Leipzig: Duncker & Humblot. Cited in R. Klatzky, (1980), *Human memory: Structures and Processes.* San Francisco: Freeman. (p. 260)

Ebbinghaus, H. (1885/1964). *Memory: A contribution to experimental psychology* (tr. by H. A. Ruger & C. E. Bussenius). New York: Dover. (pp. 280, 281)

Eberhardt, J. L. (2005). Imaging race. *American Psychologist, 60,* 181–190. (p. 666)

Eberhardt, J. L., Davies, P. G., Purdie-Vaughns, V. J., & Johnson, S. L. (2006). Looking deathworthy: Perceived stereotypicality of Black defendants predicts capital-sentencing outcomes. *Psychological Science, 17,* 383–386. (p. 666)

Eberhardt, J. L., Goff, P. A., Purdie, V. J., & Davies, P. G. (2004). Seeing Black: Race, crime, and visual processing. *Journal of Personality and Social Psychology, 87,* 876–893. (p. 666)

Eccles, J. S., Jacobs, J. E., & Harold, R. D. (1990). Gender role stereotypes, expectancy effects, and parents' socialization of gender differences. *Journal of Social Issues, 46,* 183–201. (p. 550)

Eckensberger, L. H. (1994). Moral development and its measurement across cultures. In W. J. Lonner & R. Malpass (Eds.), *Psychology and culture.* Boston: Allyn and Bacon. (p. 449)

Eckert, E. D., Heston, L. L., & Bouchard, T. J., Jr. (1981). MZ twins reared apart: Preliminary findings of psychiatric disturbances and traits. In L. Gedda, P. Paris, & W. D. Nance (Eds.), *Twin research: Vol. 3. Pt. B. Intelligence, personality, and development.* New York: Alan Liss. (p. 575)

Ecklund-Flores, L. (1992). The infant as a model for the teaching of introductory psychology. Paper presented to the American Psychological Association annual convention. (p. 412)

Economist. (2001, December 20). An anthropology of happiness. *The Economist* (www.economist.com/world/asia). (p. 361)

Edelman, S., & Kidman, A. D. (1997). Mind and cancer: Is there a relationship? A review of the evidence. *Australian Psychologist, 32,* 1–7. (p. 405)

Edison, T. A. (1948). *The diary and sundry observations of Thomas Alva Edison,* edited by D. D. Runes. New York: Philosophical Library. Cited by S. Coren (1996). *Sleep Thieves.* New York: Free Press. (p. 182)

Ehrhardt, A. A. (1987). A transactional perspective on the development of gender differences. In J. M. Reinisch, L. A. Rosenblum, & S. A. Sanders (Eds.), *Masculinity/femininity: Basic perspectives.* New York: Oxford University Press. (p. 438)

Eibl-Eibesfeldt, I. (1971). *Love and hate: The natural history of behavior patterns.* New York: Holt, Rinehart & Winston. (p. 381)

Eich, E. (1990). Learning during sleep. In R. B. Bootzin, J. F. Kihlstrom, & D. L. Schacter (Eds.), *Sleep and cognition.* Washington, DC: American Psychological Association. (p. 188)

Einstein, G. O., & McDaniel, M. A. (1990). Normal aging and prospective memory. *Journal of Experimental Psychology: Learning, Memory, and Cognition, 16,* 717–726. (p. 462)

Einstein, G. O., McDaniel, M. A., Richardson, S. L., Guynn, M. J., & Cunfer, A. R. (1995). Aging and prospective memory: Examining the influences of self-initiated retrieval processes. *Journal of Experimental Psychology: Learning, Memory, and Cognition, 21,* 996–1007. (p. 462)

Einstein, G. O., McDaniel, M. A., Smith, R. E., & Shaw, P. (1998). Habitual prospective memory and aging: Remembering intentions and forgetting actions. *Psychological Science, 9,* 284–288. (p. 462)

Eisenberg, N., & Lennon, R. (1983). Sex differences in empathy and related capacities. *Psychological Bulletin, 94,* 100–131. (p. 380)

Eisenberger, N. I., Lieberman, M. D., & Williams, K. D. (2003). Does rejection hurt? An fMRI study of social exclusion. *Science, 302,* 290–292. (p. 362)

Eisenberger, R., & Rhoades, L. (2001). Incremental effects of reward on creativity. *Journal of Personality and Social Psychology, 81,* 728–741. (p. 237)

Eiser, J. R. (1985). Smoking: The social learning of an addiction. *Journal of Social and Clinical Psychology, 3,* 446–457. (p. 203)

Ekman, P. (1994). Strong evidence for universals in facial expressions: A reply to Russell's mistaken critique. *Psychological Bulletin, 115,* 268–287. (p. 381)

Ekman, P. (2003). *Emotions revealed: Recognizing faces and feelings to improve communication and emotional life.* New York: Times Books. (p. 373)

Ekman, P., & Friesen, W. V. (1975). *Unmasking the face.* Englewood Cliffs, NJ: Prentice-Hall. (p. 381)

Ekman, P., Friesen, W. V., O'Sullivan, M., Chan, A., Diacoyanni-Tarlatzis, I., Heider, K., Krause, R., LeCompte, W. A., Pitcairn, T., Ricci-Bitti, P. E., Scherer, K., Tomita, M., & Tzavaras, A. (1987). Universals and cultural differences in the judgments of facial expressions of emotion. *Journal of Personality and Social Psychology, 53,* 712–717. (p. 381)

Elbert, T., Pantev, C., Wienbruch, C., Rockstroh, B., & Taub, E. (1995). Increased cortical representation of the fingers of the left hand in string players. *Science, 270,* 305–307. (p. 442)

Elfenbein, H. A., & Ambady, N. (1999). Does it take one to know one? A meta-analysis of the universality and cultural specificity of emotion recognition. Unpublished manuscript, Harvard University. (p. 381)

Elfenbein, H. A., & Ambady, N. (2002). On the universality and cultural specificity of emotion recognition: A meta-analysis. *Psychological Bulletin, 128,* 203–235. (p. 381)

Elfenbein, H. A., & Ambady, N. (2003a). When familiarity breeds accuracy: Cultural exposure and facial emotion recognition. *Journal of Personality and Social Psychology, 85,* 276–290. (p. 381)

Elfenbein, H. A., & Ambady, N. (2003b). Universals and cultural differences in recognizing emotions. *Current Directions in Psychological Science, 12,* 159–164. (p. 381)

Elkind, D. (1970). The origins of religion in the child. *Review of Religious Research, 12,* 35–42. (p. 448)

Elkind, D. (1978). *The child's reality: Three developmental themes.* Hillsdale, NJ: Erlbaum. (p. 448)

Ellenbogen, J. M., Hu, P. T., Payne, J. D., Titone, D., & Walker, M. P. (2007). Human relational memory requires time and sleep. *Proceedings of the National Academy of Sciences, 104,* 7723–7728. (p. 185)

Elliot, A. J., & McGregor, H. A. (2001). A 2x2 achievement goal framework. *Journal of Personality and Social Psychology, 80,* 501–519. (p. B-11)

Elliot, A. J., & Niesta, D. (2008). Romantic red: Red enhances men's attraction to women. *Journal of Personality and Social Psychology, 95,* 1150–1164. (pp. 224, 225)

Elliot, A. J., & Reis, H. T. (2003). Attachment and exploration in adulthood. *Journal of Personality and Social Psychology, 85,* 317–331. (p. 430)

Ellis, A. (1980). Psychotherapy and atheistic values: A response to A. E. Bergin's "Psychotherapy and religious values." *Journal of Consulting and Clinical Psychology, 48,* 635–639. (p. 628)

Ellis, A., & Becker, I. M. (1982). *A guide to personal happiness.* North Hollywood, CA: Wilshire Book Co. (p. 227)

Ellis, B. J. (2004). Timing of pubertal maturation in girls: An integrated life history approach. *Psychological Bulletin, 130,* 920–958. (p. 454)

Ellis, B. J., Bates, J. E., Dodge, K. A., Fergusson, D. M., John, H. L., Pettit, G. S., & Woodward, L. (2003). Does father absence place daughters at special risk for early sexual activity and teenage pregnancy? *Child Development, 74,* 801–821. (p. 354)

Ellis, L., & Ames, M. A. (1987). Neurohormonal functioning and sexual orientation: A theory of homosexuality-heterosexuality. *Psychological Bulletin, 101,* 233–258. (p. 358)

Elzinga, B. M., Ardon, A. M., Heijnis, M. K., De Ruiter, M. B., Van Dyck, R., & Veltman, D. J. (2007). Neural correlates of enhanced working-memory performance in dissociative disorder: A functional MRI study. *Psychological Medicine, 37,* 235–245. (p. 579)

EMDR. (2008). E-mail correspondence from Robbie Dunton, EMDR Institute. (www.emdr.org). (p. 624)

Emerging Trends. (1997, September). *Teens turn more to parents than friends on whether to attend church.* Princeton, NJ: Princeton Religion Research Center. (p. 453)

Emery, G. (2004). *Psychic predictions 2004.* Committee for the Scientific Investigation of Claims of the Paranormal (www.csicop.org). (p. 167)

Emmons, R. A. (2007). *Thanks! How the new science of gratitude can make you happier.* Boston: Houghton Mifflin. (p. 395)

Emmons, S., Geisler, C., Kaplan, K. J., & Harrow, M. (1997). *Living with schizophrenia.* Muncie, IN: Taylor and Francis (Accelerated Development). (pp. 561, 591)

Emmorey, K., Allen, J. S., Bruss, J., Schenker, N., & Damasio, H. (2003). A morphometric analysis of auditory brain regions in congenitally deaf adults. *Proceedings of the National Academy of Sciences, 100,* 10049–10054. (p. 140)

Empson, J. A. C., & Clarke, P. R. F. (1970). Rapid eye movements and remembering. *Nature, 227,* 287–288. (p. 190)

Emslie, C., Hunt, K., & Macintyre, S. (2001). Perceptions of body image among working men and women. *Journal of Epidemiology and Community Health, 55,* 406–407. (p. 338)

Endler, N. S. (1982). *Holiday of darkness: A psychologist's personal journey out of his depression.* New York: Wiley. (pp. 586, 633)

Engemann, K. M., & Owyang, M. T. (2005, April). So much for that merit raise: The link between wages and appearance. *Regional Economist* (www.stlouisfed.org). (p. 680)

Engen, T. (1987). Remembering odors and their names. *American Scientist, 75,* 497–503. (p. 150)

Engle, R. W. (2002). Working memory capacity as executive attention. *Current Directions in Psychological Science, 11,* 19–23. (p. 258)

Epel, E. S., Blackburn, E. H., Lin, J., Dhabhar, F. S., Adler, N. E., Morrow, J. D., & Cawthon, R. M. (2004). Accelerated telomere shortening in response to life stress. *Proceedings of the National Academy of Sciences, 101,* 17312–17315. (p. 400)

Epley, N., & Dunning, D. (2000). Feeling "holier than thou": Are self-serving assessments produced by errors in self- or social prediction? *Journal of Personality and Social Psychology, 79,* 861–875. (p. 513)

Epley, N., & Huff, C. (1998). Suspicion, affective response, and educational benefit as a result of deception in psychology research. *Personality and Social Psychology Bulletin, 24,* 759–768. (p. 45)

Epley, N., Keysar, B., Van Boven, L., & Gilovich, T. (2004). Perspective taking as egocentric anchoring and adjustment. *Journal of Personality and Social Psychology, 87,* 327–339. (p. 422)

EPOCH. (2000). *Legal reforms: Corporal punishment of children in the family.* (www.stophitting.com/laws/legalReform.php). (p. 234)

Epstein, J., Stern, E., & Silbersweig, D. (1998). Mesolimbic activity associated with psychosis in schizophrenia: Symptom-specific PET studies. In J. F. McGinty (Ed.), *Advancing from the ventral striatum to the extended amygdala: Implications for neuropsychiatry and drug use: In honor of Lennart Heimer. Annals of New York Academy of Sciences, 877,* 562–574. (p. 593)

Epstein, S. (1983a). Aggregation and beyond: Some basic issues on the prediction of behavior. *Journal of Personality, 51,* 360–392. (p. 501)

Epstein, S. (1983b). The stability of behavior across time and situations. In R. Zucker, J. Aronoff, & A. I. Rabin (Eds.), *Personality and the prediction of behavior.* San Diego: Academic Press. (p. 501)

Epstein, S., & Meier, P. (1989). Constructive thinking: A broad coping variable with specific components. *Journal of Personality and Social Psychology, 57,* 332–350. (p. 528)

Erdberg, P. (1990). Rorschach assessment. In G. Goldstein & M. Hersen (Eds.), *Handbook of psychological assessment, 2nd ed.* New York: Pergamon. (p. 486)

Erdelyi, M. H. (1985). *Psychoanalysis: Freud's cognitive psychology.* New York: Freeman. (p. 488)

Erdelyi, M. H. (1988). Repression, reconstruction, and defense: History and integration of the psychoanalytic and experimental frameworks. In J. Singer (Ed.), *Repression: Defense mechanism and cognitive style.* Chicago: University of Chicago Press. (p. 488)

Erdelyi, M. H. (2006). The unified theory of repression. *Behavioral and Brain Sciences, 29,* 499–551. (pp. 487, 488)

Erel, O., & Burman, B. (1995). Interrelatedness of marital relations and parent-child relations: A meta-analytic review. *Psychological Bulletin, 118,* 108–132. (p. 467)

Erel, O., Oberman, Y., & Yirmiya, N. (2000). Maternal versus nonmaternal care and seven domains of children's development. *Psychological Bulletin, 126,* 727–747. (p. 431)

Erickson, M. F., & Aird, E. G. (2005). *The motherhood study: Fresh insights on mothers' attitudes and concerns.* New York: The Motherhood Project, Institute for American Values. (p. 467)

Ericsson, K. A. (2001). Attaining excellence through deliberate practice: Insights from the study of expert performance. In M. Ferrari (Ed.), *The pursuit of excellence in education.* Hillsdale, NJ: Erlbaum. (p. B-8)

Ericsson, K. A. (2002). Attaining excellence through deliberate practice: Insights from the study of expert performance. In C. Desforges & R. Fox (Eds.), *Teaching and learning: The essential readings.* Malden, MA: Blackwell Publishers. (p. 527)

Ericsson, K. A. (2006). The influence of experience and deliberate practice on the development of superior expert performance. In K. A. Ericsson, N. Charness, P. J. Feltovich, & R. R. Hoffman (Eds.), *The Cambridge handbook of expertise and expert performance.* Cambridge: Cambridge University Press. (p. B-8)

Ericsson, K. A. (2007). Deliberate practice and the modifiability of body and mind: Toward a science of the structure and acquisition of expert and elite performance. *International Journal of Sport Psychology, 38,* 4–34. (pp. 527, 548, B-8)

Ericsson, K. A., Roring, R. W., & Nandagopal, K. (2007). Giftedness and evidence for reproducibly superior performance: An account based on the expert performance framework. *High Ability Studies, 18,* 3–56. (p. 527)

Erikson, E. H. (1963). *Childhood and society.* New York: Norton. (p. 450)

Erikson, E. H. (1983, June). A conversation with Erikson (by E. Hall). *Psychology Today,* pp. 22–30. (p. 429)

Ernsberger, P., & Koletsky, R. J. (1999). Biomedical rationale for a wellness approach to obesity: An alternative to a focus on weight loss. *Journal of Social Issues, 55,* 221–260. (p. 346)

Ertmer, D. J., Young, N. M., & Nathani, S. (2007). Profiles of focal development in young cochlear implant recipients. *Journal of Speech, Language, and Hearing Research, 50,* 393–407. (p. 316)

Escobar-Chaves, S. L., Tortolero, S., Markham, C., Low, B., Eitel, P., Thitckstun, P. (2005). Impact of the media on adolescents attitudes and behaviors. *Pediatrics, 116,* 303–326. (p. 353)

ESPAD. (2003). *Summary of the 2003 findings.* European School Survey Project on Alcohol and Other Drugs. (www.espad.org). (p. 209)

Esser, J. K., & Lindoerfer, J. S. (1989). Groupthink and the space shuttle *Challenger* accident: Toward a quantitative case analysis. *Journal of Behavioral Decision Making, 2,* 167–177. (p. 660)

Esterson, A. (2001). The mythologizing of psychoanalytic history: Deception and self-deception in Freud's accounts of the seduction theory episode. *History of Psychiatry, 12,* 329–352. (p. 487)

Esty, A. (2004). The new wealth of nations. *American Scientist, 92,* 513. (p. 393)

Eszterhas, J. (2002, August 9). Hollywood's responsibility for smoking deaths. *New York Times* (www.nytimes.com). (p. 202)

Etkin, A., & Wager, T. D. (2007). Functional neuroimaging of anxiety: A meta-analysis of emotional processing in PTSD, social anxiety disorder, and specific phobia. *American Journal of Psychiatry, 164,* 1476–1488. (p. 576)

Etzioni, A. (1999). The monochrome society. *The Public Interest, 137* (Fall), 42–55. (p. 691)

Euston, D. R., Tatsuno, M., & McNaughton, B. L. (2007). Fast-forward playback of recent memory sequences in prefrontal cortex during sleep. *Science, 318,* 1147–1150. (p. 273)

Evans, C. R., & Dion, K. L. (1991). Group cohesion and performance: A meta-analysis. *Small Group Research, 22,* 175–186. (p. B-12)

Evans, G. W. (2004). The environment of childhood poverty. *American Psychologist, 59,* 77–92. (p. 431)

Evans, G. W., & Kim, P. (2007). Childhood poverty and health: Cumulative risk exposure and stress dysregulation. *Psychological Science, 18,* 953–957. (p. C-2)

Evans, G. W., Palsane, M. N., & Carrere, S. (1987). Type A behavior and occupational stress: A cross-cultural study of blue-collar workers. *Journal of Personality and Social Psychology, 52,* 1002–1007. (p. 402)

Evans, R. I., Dratt, L. M., Raines, B. E., & Rosenberg, S. S. (1988). Social influences on smoking initiation: Importance of distinguishing descriptive versus mediating process variables. *Journal of Applied Social Psychology, 18,* 925–943. (p. 203)

Everson, S. A., Goldberg, D. E., Kaplan, G. A., Cohen, R. D., Pukkala, E., Tuomilehto, J., & Salonen, J. T. (1996). Hopelessness and risk of mortality and incidence of myocardial infarction and cancer. *Psychosomatic Medicine, 58,* 113–121. (p. C-3)

Ewing, R., Schmid, T., Killingsworth, R., Zlot, A., & Raudenbush, S. (2003). Relationship between urban sprawl and physical activity, obesity, and morbidity. *American Journal of Health Promotion, 18,* 47–57. (p. 345)

Exner, J. E. (2003). *The Rorschach: A comprehensive system, 4th edition.* Hoboken, NJ: Wiley. (p. 486)

Eysenck, H. J. (1952). The effects of psychotherapy: An evaluation. *Journal of Consulting Psychology, 16,* 319–324. (p. 620)

Eysenck, H. J. (1990, April 30). An improvement on personality inventory. *Current Contents: Social and Behavioral Sciences, 22*(18), 20. (p. 495)

Eysenck, H. J. (1992). Four ways five factors are *not* basic. *Personality and Individual Differences, 13,* 667–673. (p. 495)

Eysenck, H. J., & Grossarth-Maticek, R. (1991). Creative novation behaviour therapy as a prophylactic treatment for cancer and coronary heart disease: Part II—Effects of treatment. *Behaviour Research and Therapy, 29,* 17–31. (p. C-8)

Eysenck, H. J., Wakefield, J. A., Jr., & Friedman, A. F. (1983). Diagnosis and clinical assessment: The DSM-III. *Annual Review of Psychology, 34,* 167–193. (p. 566)

Eysenck, M. W., MacLeod, C., & Mathews, A. (1987). Cognitive functioning and anxiety. *Psychological Research, 49,* 189–195. (p. 504)

Eysenck, S. B. G., & Eysenck, H. J. (1963). The validity of questionnaire and rating assessments of extraversion and neuroticism, and their factorial stability. *British Journal of Psychology, 54,* 51–62. (p. 495)

Faber, N. (1987, July). Personal glimpse. *Reader's Digest,* p. 34. (p. 301)

Fagan, J. F., & Holland, C. R. (2007). Racial equality in intelligence: Predictions from a theory of intelligence as processing. *Intelligence, 35,* 319–334. (p. 554)

Fagan, J. F., Holland, C. R., & Wheeler, K. (2007). The prediction, from infancy, of adult IQ and achievement. *Intelligence, 35,* 225–231. (p. 540)

Fagan, J. F., III. (1992). Intelligence: A theoretical viewpoint. *Current Directions in Psychological Science, 1,* 82–86. (p. 553)

Fairburn, C. G., Cowen, P. J., & Harrison, P. J. (1999). Twin studies and the etiology of eating disorders. *International Journal of Eating Disorders, 26,* 349–358. (p. 338)

Fantz, R. L. (1961, May). The origin of form perception. *Scientific American,* pp. 66–72. (p. 415)

Farah, M. J., Rabinowitz, C., Quinn, G. E., & Liu, G. T. (2000). Early commitment of neural substrates for face recognition. *Cognitive Neuropsychology, 17,* 117–124. (p. 82)

Farina, A. (1982). The stigma of mental disorders. In A. G. Miller (Ed.), *In the eye of the beholder.* New York: Praeger. (pp. 564, 567)

Farley, M., Baral, I., Kiremire, M., & Sezgin, U. (1998). Prostitution in five countries: Violence and post-traumatic stress disorder. *Feminism and Psychology, 8,* 405–426. (p. 572)

Farley, T., & Cohen, D. (2001, December). Fixing a fat nation. *Washington Monthly* (www.washingtonmonthly.com/features/2001/0112.farley.cohen. html). (p. 345)

Farooqi, I. S., Bullmore, E., Keogh, J., Gillard, J., O'Rahilly, S., & Fletcher, P. C. (2007). Leptin regulates striatal regions and human eating behavior. *Science, 317,* 1355. (p. 334)

Farrington, D. P. (1991). Antisocial personality from childhood to adulthood. *The Psychologist: Bulletin of the British Psychological Society, 4,* 389–394. (p. 597)

Fast, L. A., & Funder, D. C. (2008). Personality as manifest in word use: Correlations with self-report, acquaintance report, and behavior. *Journal of Personality and Social Psychology, 94,* 334–346. (p. 502)

FBI. (2007). *Crime in the United States, 2007. Murder Offenders by Age, Sex, and Race, 2006, Expanded Homicide Data, Table 3.* (www.fbi.gov/ucr/cius2006/offenses/expanded_information/data/shrtable_03.html). (p. 436)

Feder, H. H. (1984). Hormones and sexual behavior. *Annual Review of Psychology, 35,* 165–200. (p. 350)

Feeney, D. M. (1987) Human rights and animal welfare. *American Psychologist, 42,* 593-599. (p. 44)

Feeney, J. A., & Noller, P. (1990). Attachment style as a predictor of adult romantic relationships. *Journal of Personality and Social Psychology, 58,* 281–291. (p. 430)

Feigenson, L., Carey, S., & Spelke, E. (2002). Infants' discrimination of number vs. continuous extent. *Cognitive Psychology, 44,* 33–66. (p. 420)

Feinberg, T. E., & Keenan, J. P. (Eds.) (2005). *The lost self: Pathologies of the brain and identity.* New York: Oxford University Press. (p. 87)

Feingold, A. (1990). Gender differences in effects of physical attractiveness on romantic attraction: A comparison across five research paradigms. *Journal of Personality and Social Psychology, 59,* 981–993. (p. 680)

Feingold, A. (1992). Good-looking people are not what we think. *Psychological Bulletin, 111,* 304–341. (p. 680)

Feingold, A., & Mazzella, R. (1998). Gender differences in body image are increasing. *Psychological Science, 9,* 190–195. (pp. 338, 681)

Fellinger, J., Holzinger, D., Gerich, J., & Goldberg, D. (2007). Mental distress and quality of life in the hard of hearing. *Acta Psychiatrica Scandinavica, 115,* 243–245. (p. 139)

Fellowes, D., Barnes, K., & Wilkinson, S. (2004). Aromatherapy and massage for symptom relief in patients with cancer. *The Cochrane Library, 3,* Oxford, UK: Update Software. (p. C-9)

Feminist Psychologist. (2002, Winter). Justice for Mary Whiton Calkins, p. 11. (p. 5)

Feng, J., Spence, I., & Pratt, J. (2007). Playing an action video game reduces gender differences in spatial cognition. *Psychological Science, 18,* 850–855. (p. 550)

Fenton, W. S., & McGlashan, T. H. (1991). Natural history of schizophrenia subtypes: II. Positive and negative symptoms and long-term course. *Archives of General Psychiatry, 48,* 978–986. (p. 592)

Fenton, W. S., & McGlashan, T. H. (1994). Antecedents, symptom progression, and long-term outcome of the deficit syndrome in schizophrenia. *American Journal of Psychiatry, 151,* 351–356. (p. 592)

Ferguson, E. D. (1989). Adler's motivational theory: An historical perspective on belonging and the fundamental human striving. *Individual Psychology, 45,* 354–361. (p. 360)

Ferguson, E. D. (2001). Adler and Dreikurs: Cognitive-social dynamic innovators. *Journal of Individual Psychology, 57,* 324–341. (p. 360)

Ferguson, E. D. (2003). Social processes, personal goals, and their intertwining: Their importance in Adlerian theory and practice. *Journal of Individual Psychology, 59,* 136–144. (p. 484)

Fergusson, D. M., & Woodward, L. G. (2002). Mental health, educational, and social role outcomes of adolescents with depression. *Archives of General Psychiatry, 59,* 225–231. (p. 582)

Fernandez, E., & Turk, D. C. (1989). The utility of cognitive coping strategies for altering pain perception: A meta-analysis. *Pain, 38,* 123–135. (p. 146)

Fernández-Ballesteros, R., & Caprara, M. (2003). Psychology of aging in Europe. *European Psychologist, 8,* 129–130. (p. 457)

Fernández-Dols, J-M., & Ruiz-Belda, M-A. (1995). Are smiles a sign of happiness? Gold medal winners at the Olympic Games. *Journal of Personality and Social Psychology, 69,* 1113–1119. (p. 382)

Ferri, M., Amato, L., & Davoli, M. (2006). Alcoholics Anonymous and other 12-step programmes for alcohol dependence. *Cochrane Database of Systematic Reviews,* Issue 3. Art. No.: CD005032. (p. 618)

Ferris, C. F. (1996, March). The rage of innocents. *The Sciences,* pp. 22–26. (p. 430)

Feynman, R. (1997). Quoted by E. Hutchings (Ed.), *"Surely you're joking, Mr. Feynman."* New York: Norton. (p. 20)

Fiedler, F. E. (1981). Leadership effectiveness. *American Behavioral Scientist, 24,* 619–632. (p. B-11)

Fiedler, F. E. (1987, September). When to lead, when to stand back. *Psychology Today,* pp. 26–27. (p. B-12)

Fiedler, K., Nickel, S., Muehlfriedel, T., & Unkelbach, C. (2001). Is mood congruency an effect of genuine memory or response bias? *Journal of Experimental Social Psychology, 37,* 201–214. (p. 278)

Field, A. P. (2006). I don't like it because it eats sprouts: Conditioning preferences in children. *Behaviour Research and Therapy, 44,* 439–455. (p. 220)

Field, A. P. (2006). Is conditioning a useful framework for understanding the development and treatment of phobias? *Clinical Psychology Review, 26,* 857–875. (p. 574)

Field, T. (1996). Attachment and separation in young children. *Annual Review of Psychology, 47,* 541–561. (p. 432)

Field, T., Diego, M., & Hernandez-Reif, M. (2007). Massage therapy research. *Developmental Review, 27,* 75–89. (p. 442)

Field, T., Hernandez-Reif, M., Feijo, L, & Freedman, J. (2006). Prenatal, perinatal and neonatal stimulation: A survey of neonatal nurseries. *Infant Behavior & Development, 29,* 24–31. (p. 442)

Fields, R. D. (2004, April). The other half of the brain. *Scientific American,* pp. 54–61. (p. 74)

Fields, R. D. (2005, February). Making memories stick. *Scientific American,* pp. 75–81. (p. 269)

Fields, R. D. (2008, March). White matter. *Scientific American,* pp. 54–61. (p. 53)

Fincham, F. D., & Bradbury, T. N. (1993). Marital satisfaction, depression, and attributions: A longitudinal analysis. *Journal of Personality and Social Psychology, 64,* 442–452. (p. 645)

Fink, G. R., Markowitsch, H. J., Reinkemeier, M., Bruckbauer, T., Kessler, J., & Heiss, W-D. (1996). Cerebral representation of one's own past: Neural networks involved in autobiographical memory. *Journal of Neuroscience, 16,* 4275–4282. (p. 273)

Finkel, E. J., & Eastwick, P. W. (2008). Speed-dating. *Current Directions in Psychological Science, 17,* 193–197. (p. 680)

Finlay, S. W. (2000). Influence of Carl Jung and William James on the origin of alcoholics anonymous. *Review of General Psychology, 4,* 3–12. (p. 618)

Finney, E. M., Fine, I., & Dobkins, K. R. (2001). Visual stimuli activate auditory cortex in the deaf. *Nature Neuroscience, 4,* 1171–1173. (p. 140)

Finzi, E., & Wasserman, E. (2006). Treatment of depression with botulinum toxin A: A case series. *Dermatological Surgery, 32,* 645–650. (p. 383)

Fischer, P., & Greitemeyer, T. (2006). Music and aggression: The impact of sexual-aggressive song lyrics on aggression-related thoughts, emotions, and behavior toward the same and the opposite sex. *Personality and Social Psychology Bulletin, 32,* 1165–1176. (p. 676)

Fischhoff, B. (1982). Debiasing. In D. Kahneman, P. Slovic, & A. Tversky (Eds.), *Judgment under uncertainty: Heuristics and biases.* New York: Cambridge University Press. (p. 307)

Fischhoff, B., Slovic, P., & Lichtenstein, S. (1977). Knowing with certainty: The appropriateness of extreme confidence. *Journal of Experimental Psychology: Human Perception and Performance, 3,* 552–564. (p. 307)

Fishbach, A., Dhar, R., & Zhang, Y. (2006). Subgoals as substitutes or complements: The role of goal accessibility. *Journal of Personality and Social Psychology, 91,* 232–242. (p. B-11)

Fisher, H. E. (1993, March/April). After all, maybe it's biology. *Psychology Today,* pp. 40–45. (p. 466)

Fisher, H. E., Aron, A., Mashek, D., Li, H., & Brown, L. L. (2002). Defining the brain systems of lust, romantic attraction, and attachment. *Archives of Sexual Behavior, 31,* 413–419. (p. 349)

Fisher, H. T. (1984). Little Albert and Little Peter. *Bulletin of the British Psychological Society, 37,* 269. (p. 611)

Fisher, K., Egerton, M., Gershuny, J. I., & Robinson, J. P. (2006). Gender convergence in the American Heritage Time Use Study (AHTUS). *Social Indicators Research, 82,* 1–33. (p. 439)

Fisher, R. P., & Geiselman, R. E. (1992). *Memory-enhancing techniques for investigative interviewing: The cognitive interview.* Springfield, IL: Charles C. Thomas. (p. 289)

Fisher, R. P., Geiselman, R. E., & Raymond, D. S. (1987). Critical analysis of police interview techniques. *Journal of Police Science and Administration, 15,* 177–185. (p. 289)

Fiske, S. T., Harris, L. T., & Cuddy, A. J. C. (2004). Why ordinary people torture enemy prisoners. *Science, 306,* 1482–1483. (p. 649)

Fitzgerald, P. B., & Daskalakis, Z. J. (2008). The use of repetitive transcranial magnetic stimulation and vagal nerve stimulation in the treatment of depression. *Current Opinion in Psychiatry, 21,* 25–29. (p. 634)

Fleming, I., Baum, A., & Weiss, L. (1987). Social density and perceived control as mediator of crowding stress in high-density residential neighborhoods. *Journal of Personality and Social Psychology, 52,* 899–906. (p. C-3)

Fleming, J. H. (2001, Winter/Spring). Introduction to the special issue on linkage analysis. *The Gallup Research Journal,* pp. i–vi. (p. B-10)

Fleming, J. H., & Scott, B. A. (1991). The costs of confession: The Persian Gulf War POW tapes in historical and theoretical perspective. *Contemporary Social Psychology, 15,* 127–138. (p. 381)

Fletcher, G. J. O., Fitness, J., & Blampied, N. M. (1990). The link between attributions and happiness in close relationships: The roles of depression and explanatory style. *Journal of Social and Clinical Psychology, 9,* 243–255. (p. 645)

Fletcher, P. C., Zafiris, O., Frith, C. D., Honey, R. A. E., Corlett, P. R., Zilles, K., & Fink, G. R. (2005). On the benefits of not trying: Brain activity and connectivity reflecting the interactions of explicit and implicit sequence learning. *Cerebral Cortex, 7,* 1002–1015. (p. 488)

Flier, J. S., & Maratos-Flier, E. (2007, September). What fuels fat. *Scientific American,* pp. 72–81. (p. 344)

Flood, M. (2007). Exposure to pornography among youth in Australia. *Journal of Sociology, 43,* 45–60. (p. 674)

Flora, S. R. (2004). *The power of reinforcement.* Albany, NJ: SUNY Press. (p. 238)

Flouri, E., & Buchanan, A. (2004). Early father's and mother's involvement and child's later educational outcomes. *British Journal of Educational Psychology, 74,* 141–153. (p. 429)

Flynn, J. R. (1987). Massive IQ gains in 14 nations: What IQ tests really measure. *Psychological Bulletin, 101,* 171–191. (p. 537)

Flynn, J. R. (2003). Movies about intelligence: The limitations of g. *Current Directions in Psychological Science, 12,* 95–99. (p. 546)

Flynn, J. R. (2007). *What is intelligence?* New York: Cambridge University Press. (pp. 537, 546)

Foa, E. B., & Kozak, M. J. (1986). Emotional processing of fear: Exposure to corrective information. *Psychological Bulletin, 99,* 20–35. (p. 612)

Fodor, J. D. (1999). Let your brain alone. *London Review of Books, 21* (www.lrb.co.uk). (p. 66)

Fogg, N. P., Harrington P. E., & Harrington T. F. (2004). *The college majors' handbook.* Indianapolis, IN: JIST Works, Inc. (pp. A-2, A-4, A-5)

Ford, E. S. (2002). Does exercise reduce inflammation? Physical activity and B-reactive protein among U.S. adults. *Epidemiology, 13,* 561–569. (p. C-7)

Foree, D. D., & LoLordo, V. M. (1973). Attention in the pigeon: Differential effects of food-getting versus shock-avoidance procedures. *Journal of Comparative and Physiological Psychology, 85,* 551–558. (p. 237)

Forer, B. R. (1949). The fallacy of personal validation: A classroom demonstration of gullibility. *Journal of Abnormal and Social Psychology, 44,* 118–123. (p. 498)

Forgas, J. P. (2008). Affect and cognition. *Perspectives on Psychological Science, 3,* 94–101. (p. 376)

Forgas, J. P., Bower, G. H., & Krantz, S. E. (1984). The influence of mood on perceptions of social interactions. *Journal of Experimental Social Psychology, 20,* 497–513. (pp. 278, 588)

Forhan, S. E., Gottlieb, S. L., Sternberg, M. R., Xu, F., Datta, D., Berman, S., & Markowitz, L. (2008). Prevalence of sexually transmitted infections and bacterial vaginosis among female adolescents in the United States: Data from the National Health and Nutrition Examination Survey (NHANES) 2003–2004. Paper presented to the 2008 National STD Prevention Conference, Chicago, Illinois. (p. 353)

Forman, D. R., Aksan, N., & Kochanska, G. (2004). Toddlers' responsive imitation predicts preschool-age conscience. *Psychological Science, 15,* 699–704. (p. 246)

Forste, R. & Tanfer, K. (1996). Sexual exclusivity among dating, cohabiting, and married women. *Journal of Marriage and the Family 58,* 33–47. (p. E-9)

Foss, D. J., & Hakes, D. T. (1978). *Psycholinguistics: An introduction to the psychology of language.* Englewood Cliffs, NJ: Prentice-Hall. (p. 487)

Foster, R. G. (2004). Are we trying to banish biological time? *Cerebrum, 6(2),* 7–26. (p. 177)

Foulkes, D. (1999). *Children's dreaming and the development of consciousness.* Cambridge, MA: Harvard University Press. (p. 191)

Fouts, R. S. (1992). Transmission of a human gestural language in a chimpanzee mother-infant relationship. *Friends of Washoe, 12/13,* pp. 2–8. (p. D-4)

Fouts, R. S. (1997). *Next of kin: What chimpanzees have taught me about who we are.* New York: Morrow. (p. D-4)

Fouts, R. S., & Bodamer, M. (1987). Preliminary report to the National Geographic Society on "Chimpanzee intrapersonal signing." *Friends of Washoe, 7(1),* 4–12. (p. D-4)

Fowler, M. J., Sullivan, M. J., & Ekstrand, B. R. (1973). Sleep and memory. *Science, 179,* 302–304. (p. 283)

Fowler, R. C., Rich, C. L., & Young, D. (1986). San Diego suicide study: II. Substance abuse in young cases. *Archives of General Psychiatry, 43,* 962–965. (p. 584)

Fowles, D. C. (1992). Schizophrenia: Diathesis-stress revisited. *Annual Review of Psychology, 43,* 303–336. (p. 592)

Fox, B. H. (1998). Psychosocial factors in cancer incidence and prognosis. In P. M. Cinciripini & others (Eds.), *Psychological and behavioral factors in cancer risk.* New York: Oxford University Press. (p. 405)

Fox, E., Lester, V., Russo, R., Bowles, R. J., Pichler, A., & Dutton, K. (2000). Facial expression of emotion: Are angry faces detected more efficiently? *Cognition and Emotion, 14,* 61–92. (p. 377)

Fox, J. L. (1984). The brain's dynamic way of keeping in touch. *Science, 225,* 820–821. (p. 83)

Fox, N. A., Hane, A. E., & Pine, D. S. (2007). Plasticity for affective neurocircuitry. *Current Directions in Psychological Science, 16,* 1–5. (p. 428)

Fozard, J. L., & Popkin, S. J. (1978). Optimizing adult development: Ends and means of an applied psychology of aging. *American Psychologist, 33,* 975–989. (p. 458)

Fracassini, C. (2000, August 27). Holidaymakers led by the nose in sales quest. *Scotland on Sunday.* (p. 150)

Fraley, R. C. (2002). Attachment stability from infancy to adulthood: Meta-analysis and dynamic modeling of developmental mechanisms. *Personality and Social Psychology Review, 6,* 123–151. (p. 430)

Frank, J. D. (1982). Therapeutic components shared by all psychotherapies. In J. H. Harvey & M. M. Parks (Eds.), *The Master Lecture Series: Vol. 1. Psychotherapy research and behavior change.* Washington, DC: American Psychological Association. (pp. 625, 626)

Frank, R. (1999). *Luxury fever: Why money fails to satisfy in an era of excess.* New York: Free Press. (p. 663)

Frank, S. J. (1988). Young adults' perceptions of their relationships with their parents: Individual differences in connectedness, competence, and emotional autonomy. *Developmental Psychology, 24,* 729–737. (p. 454)

Frankel, A., Strange, D. R., & Schoonover, R. (1983). CRAP: Consumer rated assessment procedure. In G. H. Scherr & R. Liebmann-Smith (Eds.), *The best of The Journal of Irreproducible Results.* New York: Workman Publishing. (p. 496)

Frankenburg, W., Dodds, J., Archer, P., Shapiro, H., & Bresnick, B. (1992). The Denver II: A major revision and restandardization of the Denver Developmental Screening Test. *Pediatrics, 89,* 91–97. (p. 416)

Franz, E. A., Waldie, K. E., & Smith, M. J. (2000). The effect of callosotomy on novel versus familiar bimanual actions: A neural dissociation between controlled and automatic processes? *Psychological Science, 11,* 82–85. (p. 85)

Frasure-Smith, N., & Lespérance, F. (2005). Depression and coronary heart disease: Complex synergism of mind, body, and environment. *Current Directions in Psychological Science, 14,* 39–43. (p. 403)

Frattaroli, J. (2006). Experimental disclosure and its moderators: A meta-analysis. *Psychological Bulletin, 132,* 823–865. (p. C-5)

Frayling, T. M. & 41 others. (2007, April 12). A common variant in the *FTO* gene is associated with body mass index and predisposes to childhood and adult obesity. *Science, 316,* 889–894. (p. 344)

Frederick, D. A., Peplau, L. A., & Lever, J. (2006). The swimsuit issue: Correlates of body image in a sample of 52,667 heterosexual adults. *Body Image, 3,* 413–419. (p. 338)

Fredrickson, B. L. (2006). The broaden-and-build theory of positive emotions. In M. Csikszentmihalyi & I. S. Csikszentmihalyi (Eds.), *A life worth living: Contributions to positive psychology.* New York: Oxford University Press. (p. 389)

Fredrickson, B. L., & Kahneman, D. (1993). Duration neglect in retrospective evaluations of affective episodes. *Journal of Personality and Social Psychology, 65,* 45–55. (p. 263)

Fredrickson, B. L., Roberts, T-A., Noll, S. M., Quinn, D. M., & Twenge, J. M. (1998). That swimsuit becomes you: Sex differences in self-objectification, restrained eating, and math performance. *Journal of Personality and Social Psychology, 75,* 269–284. (p. 338)

Freedman, D. J., Riesenhuber, M., Poggio, T., & Miller, E. K. (2001). Categorical representation of visual stimuli in the primate prefrontal cortex. *Science, 291,* 312–316. (p. D-1)

Freedman, J. L. (1988). Television violence and aggression: What the evidence shows. In S. Oskamp (Ed.), *Television as a social issue.* Newbury Park, CA: Sage. (p. 247)

Freedman, J. L., & Fraser, S. C. (1966). Compliance without pressure: The foot-in-the-door technique. *Journal of Personality and Social Psychology, 4,* 195–202. (p. 647)

Freedman, J. L., & Perlick, D. (1979). Crowding, contagion, and laughter. *Journal of Experimental Social Psychology, 15,* 295–303. (p. 658)

Freedman, L. R., Rock, D., Roberts, S. A., Cornblatt, B. A., & Erlenmeyer-Kimling, L. (1998). The New York high-risk project: Attention, anhedonia and social outcome. *Schizophrenia Research, 30,* 1–9. (p. 595)

Freeman, W. J. (1991, February). The physiology of perception. *Scientific American,* pp. 78–85. (p. 134)

Frensch, P. A., & Rünger, D. (2003). Implicit learning. Current *Directions in Psychological Science, 12,* 13–18. (p. 488)

Freud, S. (1922/1975). *Group psychology and the analysis of the ego.* New York: Norton. (p. 668)

Freud, S. (1931; reprinted 1961). Female sexuality. In J. Strachey (Trans.), *The standard edition of the complete psychological works of Sigmund Freud.* London: Hogarth Press. (p. 485)

Freud, S. (1935; reprinted 1960). *A general introduction to psychoanalysis.* New York: Washington Square Press. (p. 466)

Frey, M. C., & Detterman, D. K. (2004). Scholastic assessment or g? The relationship between the Scholastic Assessment Test and general cognitive ability. *Psychological Science, 15,* 373–378. (p. 535)

Freyd, J. J., DePrince, A. P., & Gleaves, D. H. (2007). The state of betrayal trauma theory: Reply to McNally—Conceptual issues and future directions. *Memory, 15,* 295–311. (p. 291)

Freyd, J. J., Putnam, F. W., Lyon, T. D., Becker-Blease, K. A., Cheit, R. E., Siegel, N. B., & Pezdek, K. (2005). The science of child sexual abuse. *Science, 308,* 501. (p. 431)

Friedman, M., & Ulmer, D. (1984). *Treating Type A behavior—and your heart.* New York: Knopf. (pp. 402, C-10)

Friedrich, O. (1987, December 7). New age harmonies. *Time,* pp. 62–72. (p. 562)

Friend, T. (2004). *Animal talk: Breaking the codes of animal language.* New York: Free Press. (p. D-6)

Frijda, N. H. (1988). The laws of emotion. *American Psychologist, 43,* 349–358. (p. 394)

Frith, U., & Frith, C. (2001). The biological basis of social interaction. *Current Directions in Psychological Science, 10,* 151–155. (p. 424)

Fromkin, V., & Rodman, R. (1983). *An introduction to language* (3rd ed.). New York: Holt, Rinehart & Winston. (pp. 314, 316)

Fry, A. F., & Hale, S. (1996). Processing speed, working memory, and fluid intelligence: Evidence for a developmental cascade. *Psychological Science, 7,* 237–241. (p. 459)

Fryar, C., Hirsch, R., Porter, K. S., Kottiri, B., Brody, D. J., & Louis, T. (2007, June 28). Drug use and sexual behavior reported by adults: United States, 1999-2002. *Advance Data: From Vital and Health Statistics,* Number 384 (Centers for Disease Control and Prevention). (p. 350)

Fuhriman, A., & Burlingame, G. M. (1994). Group psychotherapy: Research and practice. In A. Fuhriman & G. M. Burlingame (Eds.), *Handbook of group psychotherapy.* New York: Wiley. (p. 617)

Fujiki, N., Yoshida, Y., Ripley, B., Mignot, E., & Nishino, S. (2003). Effects of IV and ICV hypocretin-1 (Orexin A) in hypocretin receptor-2 gene mutated narcoleptic dogs and IV hypocretin-1 replacement therapy in a hypocretin-ligand-deficient narcoleptic dog. *Sleep, 26,* 953–959. (p. 187)

Fuller, M. J., & Downs, A. C. (1990). Spermarche is a salient biological marker in men's development. Poster presented at the American Psychological Society convention. (p. 447)

Fulmer, I. S., Gerhart, B., & Scott, K. S. (2003). Are the 100 best better? An empirical investigation of the relationship between being a "great place to work" and firm performance. *Personnel Psychology, 56,* 965–993. (p. B-8)

Funder, D. C. (2001). Personality. *Annual Review of Psychology, 52,* 197–221. (p. 497)

Funder, D. C., & Block, J. (1989). The role of ego-control, ego-resiliency, and IQ in delay of gratification in adolescence. *Journal of Personality and Social Psychology, 57,* 1041–1050. (p. 450)

Furlow, F. B., & Thornhill, R. (1996, January/February). The orgasm wars. *Psychology Today,* pp. 42–46. (p. 349)

Furnham, A. (1982). Explanations for unemployment in Britain. *European Journal of Social Psychology, 12,* 335–352. (p. 645)

Furnham, A. (2001). Self estimates of intelligence: Culture and gender difference in self and other estimates of both general (g) and multiple intelligences. *Personality and Individual Differences, 31,* 1381–1405. (p. 549)

Furnham, A., & Baguma, P. (1994). Cross-cultural differences in the evaluation of male and female body shapes. *International Journal of Eating Disorders, 15,* 81–89. (p. 340)

Furnham, A., Callahan, I., & Akande, D. (2004). Self-estimates of intelligence: A study in two African countries. *Journal of Psychology, 138,* 265–285. (p. 549)

Furnham, A., Callahan, I., & Rawles, R. (2003). Adults' knowledge of general psychology. *European Psychologist, 8,* 101–116. (p. 21)

Furnham, A., Hosoe, T., & Tang, T. L-P. (2002a). Male hubris and female humility? A cross-cultural study of ratings of self, parental, and sibling multiple intelligence in American, Britain, and Japan. *Intelligence, 30,* 101–115. (p. 549)

Furnham, A., & Mottabu, R. (2004). Sex and culture differences in the estimates of general and multiple intelligence: A study comparing British and Egyptian students. *Individual Differences Research, 3,* 82–96. (p. 549)

Furnham, A., & Rawles, R. (1995). Sex differences in the estimation of intelligence. *Journal of Social Behavior and Personality, 10,* 741–748. (p. 665)

Furnham, A., Reeves, E., & Bughani, S. (2002b). Parents think their sons are brighter than their daughters: Sex differences in parental self-estimations and estimations of their children's multiple intelligences. *Journal of Genetic Psychology, 163,* 24–39. (p. 549)

Furnham, A., & Thomas, C. (2004). Parents' gender and personality and estimates of their own and their children's intelligence. *Personality and Individual Differences, 37,* 887–903. (p. 549)

Furr, R. M., & Funder, D. C. (1998). A multimodal analysis of personal negativity. *Journal of Personality and Social Psychology, 74,* 1580–1591. (p. 588)

Gable, S. L., Gonzaga, G. C., & Strachman, A. (2006). Will you be there for me when things go right? Supportive responses to positive event disclosures. *Journal of Personality and Social Psychology, 91,* 904–917. (p. 468)

Gabrieli, J. D. E., Desmond, J. E., Demb, J. E., Wagner, A. D., Stone, M. V., Vaidya, C. J., & Glover, G. H. (1996). Functional magnetic resonance imaging of semantic memory processes in the frontal lobes. *Psychological Science, 7,* 278–283. (p. 273)

Gaertner, L., & Iuzzini, J. (2005). Rejection and entitativity: A synergistic model of mass violence. In K. D. Williams, J. P. Forgas, & W. von Hippel (Eds.). *The social outcast: Ostracism, social exclusion, rejection, and bullying.* New York: Psychology Press. (p. 673)

Gage, F. H. (2003, September). Repair yourself. *Scientific American,* pp. 46–53. (p. 83)

Gaillot, M. T., & Baumeister, R. F. (2007). Self-regulation and sexual restraint: Dispositionally and temporarily poor self-regulatory abilities contribute to failures at restraining sexual behavior. *Personality and Social Psychology Bulletin, 33,* 173–186. (p. 505)

Gajendran, R. S., & Harrison, D. A. (2007). The good, the bad, and the unknown about telecommunity: Meta-analysis of psychological mediators and individual consequences. *Journal of Applied Psychology, 92,* 1524–1541. (p. 506)

Galambos, N. L. (1992). Parent-adolescent relations. *Current Directions in Psychological Science, 1,* 146–149. (p. 452)

Galambos, N. L., Barker, E. T., & Krahn, H. J. (2006). Depression, self-esteem, and anger in emerging adulthood: Seven-year trajectories. *Developmental Psychology, 42,* 350–365. (p. 454)

Galanter, E. (1962). Contemporary psychophysics. In R. Brown, E. Galanter, E. H. Hess, & G. Mandler (Eds.), *New directions in psychology.* New York: Holt Rinehart & Winston. (p. 120)

Galati, D., Scherer, K. R., & Ricci-Bitti, P. E. (1997). Voluntary facial expression of emotion: Comparing congenitally blind with normally sighted encoders. *Journal of Personality and Social Psychology, 73,* 1363–1379. (p. 381)

Galea, S., Boscarino, J., Resnick, H., & Vlahov, D. (2002). Mental health in New York City after the September 11 terrorist attacks: Results from two population surveys. Chapter 7. *In Mental-Health, United States, 2001,* R. W. Manderscheid, & M. J. Henderson (Eds.). Washington, DC: U.S. Government Printing Office. (pp. 572, 573)

Galea, S., Brewin, C. R., Gruber, M., Jones,R. T., King, D. W., King, L. A., McNally, R. J., Ursano,R. J., Petukhova, M., & Kessler, R. C. (2007). Exposure to hurricane-related stressors and mental illness after Hurricane Katrina. *Archives of General Psychiatry, 64,* 1427–1434. (p. 583)

Galinsky, A. D., Magee, J. C., Inesi, M. E., & Gruenfeld, D. H. (2006). Power and perspectives not taken. *Psychological Science, 17,* 1068–1074. (p. 422)

Gallup. (2002, June 11). Poll insights: The gender gap—post Sept. 11th fear. *The Gallup Organization* (www.gallup.com/poll/pollInsights). (pp. 247, 570)

Gallup Organization. (2003, July 8). American public opinion about Iraq. *Gallup Poll News Service* (www.gallup.com). (p. 648)

Gallup Organization. (2004, August 16). 65% of Americans receive NO praise or recognition in the workplace. E-mail from Tom Rath: bucketbook Self-recognition. *Science, 167,* 86–87. (p. B-11)

Gallup Organization. (2008), February 27). *Worldwide, residents of richer nations more satisfied.* The Gallup Organization. (http://www.gallup.com/poll/104608/Worldwide-Residents-Richer-Nations-More-Satisfied.aspx). (p. 392)

Gallup, G. G., Jr. (1970). Chimpanzees: Self-recognition. *Science, 167,* 86–87. (p. 433)

Gallup, G. G., Jr., & Suarez, S. D. (1986). Self-awareness and the emergence of mind in humans and other primates. In J. Suls & A. G. Greenwald (Eds.), *Psychological perspectives on the self* (Vol. 3.). Hillsdale, NJ: Erlbaum. (p. 433)

Gallup, G. H. (1972). *The Gallup poll: Public opinion 1935–1971 (Vol. 3).* New York: Random House. (p. 689)

Gallup, G. H., Jr. (1994, October). Millions finding care and support in small groups. *Emerging Trends,* pp. 2–5. (p. 618)

Gangestad, S. W., & Simpson, J. A. (2000). The evolution of human mating: Trade-offs and strategic pluralism. *Behavioral and Brain Sciences, 23,* 573–587. (p. 106)

Garber, K. (2007). Autism's cause may reside in abnormalities at the synapse. *Science, 317,* 190–191. (p. 425)

Garcia, J., & Gustavson, A. R. (1997, January). Carl R. Gustavson (1946–1996): Pioneering wildlife psychologist. *APS Observer,* pp. 34–35. (p. 225)

Garcia, J., & Koelling, R. A. (1966). Relation of cue to consequence in avoidance learning. *Psychonomic Science, 4,* 123–124. (p. 224)

Gardner, H. (1983). *Frames of mind: The theory of multiple intelligences.* New York: Basic Books. (p. 525)

Gardner, H. (1998, March 19). An intelligent way to progress. *The Independent* (London), p. E4. (p. 526)

Gardner, H. (1998, November 5). Do parents count? *New York Review of Books* (www.nybooks.com). (p. 444)

Gardner, H. (1999). *Multiple views of multiple intelligence.* New York: Basic Books. (p. 529)

Gardner, H. (1999, February). Who owns intelligence? *Atlantic Monthly,* pp. 67–76. (p. 535)

Gardner, H. (2006). *The development and education of the mind: The selected works of Howard Gardner.* New York: Routledge/Taylor & Francis. (p. 525)

Gardner, J., & Oswald, A. J. (2007). Money and mental well-being: A longitudinal study of medium–sized lottery wins. *Journal of Health Economics, 6,* 49–60. (p. 392)

Gardner, J. W. (1984). *Excellence: Can we be equal and excellent too?* New York: Norton. (p. B-12)

Gardner, M. (2006, January/February). The memory wars, Part One. *Skeptical Inquirer, 30,* 28–31. (p. 291)

Gardner, R. A., & Gardner, B. I. (1969). Teaching sign language to a chimpanzee. *Science, 165,* 664–672. (p. D-3)

Gardner, R. M., & Tockerman, Y. R. (1994). A computer-TV video methodology for investigating the influence of somatotype on perceived personality traits. *Journal of Social Behavior and Personality, 9,* 555–563. (p. 341)

Garfield, C. (1986). *Peak performers: The new heroes of American business.* New York: Morrow. (p. 321)

Garlick, D. (2002). Understanding the nature of the general factor of intelligence: The role of individual differences in neural plasticity as an explanatory mechanism. *Psychological Review, 109,* 116–136. (p. 198)

Gates, G. A., & Miyamoto, R. T. (2003). Cochlear implants. *New England Journal of Medicine, 349,* 421–423. (p. 138)

Geary, D. C. (1995). Sexual selection and sex differences in spatial cognition. *Learning and Individual Differences, 7,* 289–301. (p. 550)

Geary, D. C. (1996). Sexual selection and sex differences in mathematical abilities. *Behavioral and Brain Sciences, 19,* 229–247. (p. 550)

Geary, D. C. (1998). *Male, female: The evolution of human sex differences.* Washington, DC: American Psychological Association. (p. 106)

Geary, D. C., Salthouse, T. A., Chen, G-P., & Fan, L. (1996). Are East Asian versus American differences in arithmetical ability a recent phenomenon? *Developmental Psychology, 32,* 254–262. (p. 553)

Geen, R. G., & Quanty, M. B. (1977). The catharsis of aggression: An evaluation of a hypothesis. In L. Berkowitz (Ed.), *Advances in experimental social psychology* (Vol. 10). New York: Academic Press. (p. 388)

Geen, R. G., & Thomas, S. L. (1986). The immediate effects of media violence on behavior. *Journal of Social Issues, 42(3),* 7–28. (p. 248)

Gehring, W. J., Wimke, J., & Nisenson, L. G. (2000). Action monitoring dysfunction in obsessive-compulsive disorder. *Psychological Science, 11(1),* 1–6. (p. 575)

Geier, A. B., Rozin, P., & Doros, G. (2006). Unit bias: A new heuristic that helps explain the effects of portion size on food intake. *Psychological Science, 17,* 521–525. (p. 336)

Geldard, F. A. (1972). *The human senses* (2nd ed.). New York: Wiley. (p. 132)

Gelman, D. (1989, May 15). Voyages to the unknown. *Newsweek,* pp. 66–69. (p. 382)

Genesee, F., & Gándara, P. (1999). Bilingual education programs: A cross-national perspective. *Journal of Social Issues, 55,* 665–685. (p. 321)

Genevro, J. L. (2003). *Report on bereavement and grief research.* Washington, DC: Center for the Advancement of Health. (p. 471)

Gentile, D. A., Lynch, P. J., Linder, J. R., & Walsh, D. A. (2004). The effects of violent video game habits on adolescent hostility, aggressive behaviors, and school performance. *Journal of Adolescence, 27,* 5–22. (pp. 248, 677)

Gentile, D. A., Saleem, M., & Anderson, C. A. (2007). Public policy and the effects of media violence on children. *Social Issues and Policy Review, 1,* 15–61. (p. 677)

George, L. K., Ellison, C. G., & Larson, D. B. (2002). Explaining the relationships between religious involvement and health. *Psychological Inquiry, 13,* 190–200. (p. C-12)

George, L. K., Larson, D. B., Koenig, H. G., & McCullough, M. E. (2000). Spirituality and health: What we know, what we need to know. *Journal of Social and Clinical Psychology, 19,* 102–116. (p. C-12)

George, M. S. (2003, September). Stimulating the brain. *Scientific American,* pp. 67–73. (p. 634)

George, M. S., & Belmaker, R. H. (Eds.). (2007). *Transcranial magnetic stimulation in clinical psychiatry.* Washington, DC: American Psychiatric Publishing. (pp. 634, 635)

Geraerts, E., Schooler, J. W., Merckelbach, H., Jelicic, M., Hauer, B. J. A., & Ambadar, Z. (2007). The reality of recovered memories: Corroborating continuous and discontinuous memories of childhood sexual abuse. *Psychological Science, 18,* 564–568. (p. 291)

Gerbner, G. (1990). Stories that hurt: Tobacco, alcohol, and other drugs in the mass media. In H. Resnik (Ed.), *Youth and drugs: Society's mixed messages.* Rockville, MD: Office for Substance Abuse Prevention, U.S. Department of Health and Human Services. (p. 209)

Gerbner, G., Morgan, M., & Signorielli, N. (1993). *Television violence profile No. 16: The turning point from research to action.* Annenberg School for Communication, University of Pennsylvania. (p. 676)

Gernsbacher, M. A., Dawson, M., & Goldsmith, H. H. (2005). Three reasons not to believe in an autism epidemic. *Current Directions in Psychological Science, 14,* 55–58. (p. 424)

Gerrard, M., & Luus, C. A. E. (1995). Judgments of vulnerability to pregnancy: The role of risk factors and individual differences. *Personality and Social Psychology Bulletin, 21,* 160–171. (p. 353)

Gershoff, E. T. (2002). Parental corporal punishment and associated child behaviors and experiences: A meta-analytic and theoretical review. *Psychological Bulletin, 128,* 539–579. (p. 234)

Gerstorf, D., Ram, N., Röcke, C., Lindenberger, U., & Smith, J. (2008). Decline in life satisfaction in old age: Longitudinal evidence for links to distance-to-death. *Psychology and Aging, 23,* 154–168. (p. 469)

Geschwind, N. (1979, September). Specializations of the human brain. *Scientific American, 241,* 180–199. (p. 80)

Geschwind, N., & Behan, P. O. (1984). Laterality, hormones, and immunity. In N. Geschwind & A. M. Galaburda (Eds.), *Cerebral dominance: The biological foundations.* Cambridge, MA: Harvard University Press. (p. 88)

Gfeller, J. D., Lynn, S. J., & Pribble, W. E. (1987). Enhancing hypnotic susceptibility: Interpersonal and rapport factors. *Journal of Personality and Social Psychology, 52,* 586–595. (p. 195)

Giancola, P. R., & Corman, M. D. (2007). Alcohol and aggression: A test of the attention-allocation model. *Psychological Science, 18,* 649–655. (p. 672)

Gibbons, F. X. (1986). Social comparison and depression: Company's effect on misery. *Journal of Personality and Social Psychology, 51,* 140–148. (p. 395)

Gibbons, R. D., Brown, C. H., Hur, K., Marcus, S. M., Bhaumik, D. K., & Mann, J. J. (2007). Relationship between antidepressants and suicide attempts: An analysis of the Veterans Health Administration data sets. *American Journal of Psychiatry, 164,* 1044–1049. (p. 632)

Gibbs, J. C., Basinger, K. S., Grime, R. L., & Snarey, J. R. (2007). Moral judgment development across cultures: Revisiting Kohlberg's universality claims. *Developmental Review, 27,* 443–500. (p. 449)

Gibbs, W. W. (1996, June). Mind readings. *Scientific American,* pp. 34–36. (p. 75)

Gibbs, W. W. (2002, August). Saving dying languages. *Scientific American, 287,* 79–85. (p. 314)

Gibbs, W. W. (2005, June). Obesity: An overblown epidemic? *Scientific American,* pp. 70–77. (p. 341)

Gibson, E. J., & Walk, R. D. (1960, April). The "visual cliff." *Scientific American,* pp. 64–71. (p. 153)

Gibson, H. B. (1995, April). Recovered memories. *The Psychologist,* pp. 153–154. (p. 193)

Gigerenzer, G. (2004a). Dread risk, September 11, and fatal traffic accidents. *Psychological Science, 15,* 286–287. (p. 308)

Gigerenzer, G. (2004b). Fast and frugal heuristics: The tools of bounded rationality. In D. Koehler & N. Harvey (Eds.), *Handbook of judgment and decision making.* Oxford, UK: Blackwell. (p. 310)

Gigerenzer, G. (2007). *Gut feelings: The intelligence of the unconscious.* New York: Viking. (p. 310)

Gilbert, D. T. (2006). *Stumbling on happiness.* New York: Knopf. (pp. 285, 298, 374, 468)

Gilbert, D. T., Pelham, B. W., & Krull, D. S. (2003). The psychology of good ideas. *Psychological Inquiry, 14,* 258–260. (p. 21)

Gilbert, D. T., Pinel, E. C., Wilson, T. D., Blumberg, S. J., & Wheatley, T. P. (1998). Immune neglect: A source of durability bias in affective forecasting. *Journal of Personality and Social Psychology, 75,* 617–638. (p. 391)

Gilbertson, M. W., Paulus, L. A., Williston, S. K., Gurvits, T. V., Lasko, N. B., Pitman, R. K., & Orr, S. P. (2006). Neurocognitive function in monozygotic twins discordant for combat exposure: Relationship to posttraumatic stress disorder. *Journal of Abnormal Psychology, 115,* 484–495. (p. 573)

Giles, D. E., Dahl, R. E., & Coble, P. A. (1994). Childbearing, developmental, and familial aspects of sleep. In J. M. Oldham & M. B. Riba (Eds.), *Review of psychiatry* (Vol. 13). Washington, DC: American Psychiatric Press. (p. 180)

Gill, A. J., Oberlander, J., & Austin, E. (2006). Rating e-mail personality at zero acquaintance. *Personality and Individual Differences, 40,* 497–507. (p. 502)

Gillham, J. E., Hamilton, J., Freres, D.R., Patton, K. & Gallop, R. (2006). Preventing depression among early adolescents in the primary care setting: A randomized controlled study of the Penn Resiliency Program. *Journal of Abnormal Child Psychology, 34,* 195–211. (p. 638)

Gilligan, C. (1982). *In a different voice: Psychological theory and women's development.* Cambridge, MA: Harvard University Press. (p. 436)

Gilligan, C., Lyons, N. P., & Hanmer, T. J. (Eds.). (1990). *Making connections: The relational worlds of adolescent girls at Emma Willard School.* Cambridge, MA: Harvard University Press. (p. 436)

Gilovich, T. (1991). *How we know what isn't so: The fallibility of human reason in everyday life.* New York: Free Press. (p. 32)

Gilovich, T. (1996). The spotlight effect: Exaggerated impressions of the self as a social stimulus. Unpublished manuscript, Cornell University. (p. 511)

Gilovich, T., Kruger, J., & Medvec, V. H. (2002). The spotlight effect revisited: Overestimating the manifest variability of our actions and appearance. *Journal of Experimental Social Psychology, 38,* 93–99. (p. 512)

Gilovich, T., & Medvec, V. H. (1995). The experience of regret: What, when, and why. *Psychological Review, 102,* 379–395. (p. 468)

Gilovich, T., & Savitsky, K. (1999). The spotlight effect and the illusion of transparency: Egocentric assessments of how we are seen by others. *Current Directions in Psychological Science, 8,* 165–168. (p. 512)

Gilovich, T., Vallone, R., & Tversky, A. (1985). The hot hand in basketball: On the misperception of random sequences. *Cognitive Psychology, 17,* 295–314. (p. 33)

Giltay, E. J., Geleijnse, J. M., Zitman, F. G., Buijsse, B., & Kromhout, D. (2007). Lifestyle and dietary correlates of dispositional optimism in men: The Zutphen Elderly Study. *Journal of Psychosomatic Research, 63,* 483–490. (p. C-3)

Giltay, E. J., Geleijnse, J. M., Zitman, F. G., Hoekstra, T., & Schouten, E. G. (2004). Dispositional optimism and all-cause and cardiovascular mortality in a prospective cohort of elderly Dutch men and women. *Archives of General Psychiatry, 61,* 1126–1135. (p. C-3)

Gingerich, O. (1999, February 6). Is there a role for natural theology today? *The Real Issue* (www.origins.org/real/n9501/natural.html). (p. 109)

Gingerich, O. (2006). *God's universe.* Cambridge, MA: Belknap Press of Harvard University Press. (p. 1)

Giuliano, T. A., Barnes, L. C., Fiala, S. E., & Davis, D. M. (1998a). An empirical investigation of male answer syndrome. Paper presented at the Southwestern Psychological Association convention. (p. 437)

Giuliano, T. A., Fiala, S. E., Davis, D. M., Barnes, L. C., & Patrick, E. C. (1998b). The reluctance to admit "I don't know": Exploring "male answer syndrome." Paper presented to the American Psychological Society convention. (p. 437)

Gladue, B. A. (1990). Hormones and neuroendocrine factors in atypical human sexual behavior. In J. R. Feierman (Ed.), *Pedophilia: Biosocial dimensions.* New York: Springer-Verlag. (p. 358)

Gladue, B. A. (1994). The biopsychology of sexual orientation. *Current Directions in Psychological Science, 3,* 150–154. (p. 359)

Gladwell, M. (2000, May 9). The new-boy network: What do job interviews really tell us? *New Yorker,* pp. 68–86. (p. B-6)

Gladwell, M. (2005). *Blink: The power of thinking without thinking.* New York: Little Brown. (p. 682)

Glasman, L. R., & Albarracin, D. (2006). Forming attitudes that predict future behavior: A meta-analysis of the attitude-behavior relation. *Psychological Bulletin, 132,* 778–822. (p. 646)

Glass, R. I. (2004). Perceived threats and real killers. *Science, 304,* 927. (p. 309)

Glass, R. M. (2001). Electroconvulsive therapy: Time to bring it out of the shadows. *Journal of the American Medical Association, 285,* 1346–1348. (p. 633)

Gleaves, D. H. (1996). The sociocognitive model of dissociative identity disorder: A reexamination of the evidence. *Psychological Bulletin, 120,* 42–59. (p. 579)

Glenn, N. D. (1975). Psychological well-being in the postparental stage: Some evidence from national surveys. *Journal of Marriage and the Family, 37,* 105–110. (p. 468)

Glick, P., Gottesman, D., & Jolton, J. (1989). The fault is not in the stars: Susceptibility of skeptics and believers in astrology to the Barnum effect. *Personality and Social Psychology Bulletin, 15,* 572–583. (p. 499)

Glick, P., & 15 others. (2004). Bad but bold: Ambivalent attitudes toward men predict gender inequality in 16 nations. *Journal of Personality and Social Psychology, 86,* 713–728. (p. 667)

Gluhoski, V. L., & Wortman, C. B. (1996). The impact of trauma on world views. *Journal of Social and Clinical Psychology, 15,* 417–429. (p. 228)

Godden, D. R., & Baddeley, A. D. (1975). Context-dependent memory in two natural environments: On land and underwater. *British Journal of Psychology, 66,* 325–331. (pp. 276, 277)

Goel, V., & Dolan, R. J. (2001). The functional anatomy of humor: Segregating cognitive and affective components. *Nature Neuroscience, 4,* 237–238. (p. 81)

Goff, D. C. (1993). Reply to Dr. Armstrong. *Journal of Nervous and Mental Disease, 181,* 604–605. (p. 578)

Goff, D. C., & Simms, C. A. (1993). Has multiple personality disorder remained consistent over time? *Journal of Nervous and Mental Disease, 181,* 595–600. (p. 578)

Goff, L. M., & Roediger, H. L., III. (1998). Imagination inflation for action events: Repeated imaginings lead to illusory recollections. *Memory and Cognition, 26,* 20–33. (p. 286)

Golan, O., Baron-Cohen, S., Chapman, E., & Granader, Y. (2007, May). Facilitating emotional understanding and face processing in young children with autism spectrum conditions, using animations of vehicles with faces. Paper presented at the International Meeting for Autism Research (IMFAR), Seattle, WA. (p. 425)

Gold, M., & Yanof, D. S. (1985). Mothers, daughters, and girlfriends. *Journal of Personality and Social Psychology, 49,* 654–659. (p. 453)

Goldapple, K., Segal, Z., Garson, C., Lau, M., Bieling, P., Kennedy, S., & Mayberg, H. (2004). Modulation of cortical-limbic pathways in major depression. *Archives of General Psychiatry, 61,* 34–41. (p. 631)

Goldberg, W. A., Prause, J., Lucas-Thompson, R., & Himsel, A. (2008). Maternal employment and children's achievement in context: A meta-analysis of four decades of research. *Psychological Bulletin, 134,* 77–108. (p. 431)

Golden, R. N., Gaynes, B. N., Ekstrom, R. D., Hamer, R. M., Jacobsen, F. M., Suppes, T., Wisner, K. L., & Nemeroff, C. B. (2005). The efficacy of light therapy in the treatment of mood disorders: A review and meta-analysis of the evidence. *American Journal of Psychiatry, 162,* 656–662. (p. 625)

Goldfried, M. R. (2001). Integrating gay, lesbian, and bisexual issues into mainstream psychology. *American Psychologist, 56,* 977–988. (p. 584)

Goldfried, M. R., & Padawer, W. (1982). Current status and future directions in psychotherapy. In M. R. Goldfried (Ed.), *Converging themes in psychotherapy: Trends in psychodynamic, humanistic, and behavioral practice.* New York: Springer. (p. 625)

Goldfried, M. R., Raue, P. J., & Castonguay, L. G. (1998). The therapeutic focus in significant sessions of master therapists: A comparison of cognitive-behavioral and psychodynamic-interpersonal interventions. *Journal of Consulting and Clinical Psychology, 66,* 803–810. (p. 626)

Golding, J. M. (1996). Sexual assault history and women's reproductive and sexual health. *Psychology of Women Quarterly, 20,* 101–121. (p. 674)

Golding, J. M. (1999). Sexual-assault history and the long-term physical health problems: Evidence from clinical and population epidemiology. *Current Directions in Psychological Science, 8,* 191–194. (p. 573)

Goldin-Meadow, S. (2006). Talking and thinking with our hands. *Current Directions in Psychological Science, 15,* 34–39. (p. D-5)

Goldstein, A. P., Glick, B., & Gibbs, J. C. (1998). *Aggression replacement training: A comprehensive intervention for aggressive youth* (Rev. ed.). Champaign, IL: Research Press. (p. 674)

Goldstein, I., Lue, T. F., Padma-Nathan, H., Rosen, R. C., Steers, W. D., & Wicker, P. A. (1998). Oral sildenafil in the treatment of erectile dysfunction. *New England Journal of Medicine, 338,* 1397–1404. (p. 35)

Goleman, D. (1980, February). 1,528 little geniuses and how they grew. *Psychology Today,* pp. 28–53. (p. B-7)

Goleman, D. (1995). *Emotional intelligence.* New York: Bantam. (p. 371)

Goleman, D. (2006). *Social intelligence.* New York: Bantam Books. (p. 528)

Gómez, R. L., Bootzin, R. R., & Nadel, L. (2006). Naps promote abstraction in language-learning infants. *Psychological Science, 17,* 670–674. (p. 185)

Gonsalkorale, K., & Williams, K. D. (2006). The KKK would not let me play: Ostracism even by a despised outgroup hurts. *European Journal of Social Psychology, 36,* 1–11. (p. 362)

Gonsalves, B., Reber, P. J., Gitelman, D. R., Parrish, T. B., Mesulam, M-M., & Paller, K. A. (2004). Neural evidence that vivid imagining can lead to false remembering. *Psychological Science, 15,* 655–659. (p. 286)

Goodale, M. A., & Milner, D. A. (2004). *Sight unseen: An exploration of conscious and unconscious vision.* Oxford: Oxford University Press. (p. 90)

Goodale, M. A., & Milner, D. A. (2006). One brain—two visual systems. *The Psychologist, 19,* 660–663. (p. 90)

Goodall, J. (1968). The behaviour of free-living chimpanzees in the Gombe Stream Reserve. *Animal Behaviour Monographs, 1,* 161–311. (p. 443)

Goodall, J. (1986). *The chimpanzees of Gombe: Patterns of behavior.* Cambridge, MA: Harvard University Press. (p. 668)

Goodall, J. (1998). Learning from the chimpanzees: A message humans can understand. *Science, 282,* 2184–2185. (p. 28)

Goodchilds, J. (1987). Quoted by Carol Tavris, Old age is not what it used to be. *The New York Times Magazine: Good Health Magazine,* September 27, pp. 24–25, 91–92. (p. 456)

Goode, E. (1999, April 13). If things taste bad, 'phantoms' may be at work. *New York Times* (www.nytimes.com). (p. 144)

Goode, E. (2003, January 28). Even in the age of Prozac, some still prefer the couch. *New York Times* (www.nytimes.com). (p. 608)

Goodhart, D. E. (1986). The effects of positive and negative thinking on performance in an achievement situation. *Journal of Personality and Social Psychology, 51,* 117–124. (p. 507)

Goodman, G. S. (2006). Children's eyewitness memory: A modern history and contemporary commentary. *Journal of Social Issues, 62,* 811–832. (p. 290)

Goodman, G. S., Ghetti, S., Quas, J. A., Edelstein, R. S., Alexander, K. W., Redlich, A. D., Cordon, I. M., & Jones, D. P. H. (2003). A prospective study of memory for child sexual abuse: New findings relevant to the repressed-memory controversy. *Psychological Science, 14,* 113–118. (p. 291)

Goodstein, L., & Glaberson, W. (2000, April 9). The well-marked roads to homicidal rage. *New York Times* (www.nytimes.com). (p. 510)

Goodwin, F. K., & Morrison, A. R. (1999). Scientists in bunkers: How appeasement of animal rights activism has failed. *Cerebrum, 1(2),* 50–62. (p. 44)

Gopnik, A., & Meltzoff, A. N. (1986). Relations between semantic and cognitive development in the one-word stage: The specificity hypothesis. *Child Development, 57,* 1040–1053. (p. 320)

Goranson, R. E. (1978). *The hindsight effect in problem solving.* Unpublished manuscript, cited by G. Wood (1984), Research methodology: A decision-making perspective. In A. M. Rogers & C. J. Scheirer (Eds.), *The G. Stanley Hall Lecture Series* (Vol. 4). Washington, DC. (p. 21)

Gordon, P. (2004). Numerical cognition without words: Evidence from Amazonia. *Science, 306,* 496–499. (p. 320)

Gore, A. (2007, July 1). Moving beyond Kyoto. *New York Times* (www.nytimes.com). (p. 691)

Gore-Felton, C., Koopman, C., Thoresen, C., Arnow, B., Bridges, E., & Spiegel, D. (2000). Psychologists' beliefs and clinical characteristics: Judging the veracity of childhood sexual abuse memories. *Professional Psychology: Research and Practice, 31,* 372–377. (p. 291)

Gorini, A. (2007). Virtual worlds, real healing. *Science, 318,* 1549. (p. 612)

Gortmaker, S. L., Must, A., Perrin, J. M., Sobol, A. M., & Dietz, W. H. (1993). Social and economic consequences of overweight in adolescence and young adulthood. *New England Journal of Medicine, 329,* 1008–1012. (p. 341)

Gosling, S. D., Gladdis, S., & Vazire, S. (2007). Personality impressions based on Facebook profiles. Paper presented to the Society for Personality and Social Psychology meeting. (p. 502)

Gosling, S. D., Ko, S. J., Mannarelli, T., & Morris, M. E. (2002). A room with a cue: Personality judgments based on offices and bedrooms. *Journal of Personality and Social Psychology, 82,* 379–398. (p. 501)

Gosling, S. D., Kwan, V. S. Y., & John, O. P. (2003). A dog's got personality: A cross-species comparative approach to personality judgments in dogs and humans. *Journal of Personality and Social Psychology, 85,* 1161–1169. (p. 496)

Gotlib, I. H., & Hammen, C. L. (1992). *Psychological aspects of depression: Toward a cognitive-interpersonal integration.* New York: Wiley. (p. 588)

Gottesman, I. I. (1991). *Schizophrenia genesis: The origins of madness.* New York: Freeman. (p. 595)

Gottesman, I. I. (2001). Psychopathology through a life span—genetic prism. *American Psychologist, 56,* 867–881. (p. 594)

Gottfredson, L. S. (2002a). Where and why g matters: Not a mystery. *Human Performance, 15,* 25–46. (p. 526)

Gottfredson, L. S. (2002b). g: Highly general and highly practical. In R. J. Sternberg & E. L. Grigorenko (Eds.), *The general factor of intelligence: How general is it?* Mahwah, NJ: Erlbaum. (p. 526)

Gottfredson, L. S. (2003a). Dissecting practical intelligence theory: Its claims and evidence. *Intelligence, 31,* 343–397. (p. 526)

Gottfredson, L. S. (2003b). On Sternberg's "Reply to Gottfredson." *Intelligence, 31,* 415–424. (p. 526)

Gottman, J., with Silver N. (1994). *Why marriages succeed or fail.* New York: Simon & Schuster. (p. 467)

Gougoux, F., Zatorre, R., Lassonde, M., Voss, P., & Lepore, F. (2005). A functional neuroimaging study of sound localization: Visual cortex activity predicts performance in early-blind individuals. *PloS Biology, 3*(2), e27. (p. 140)

Gould, E. (2007). How widespread is adult neurogenesis in mammals? *Nature Neuroscience, 8,* 481–488. (p. 83)

Gould, S. J. (1981). *The mismeasure of man.* New York: Norton. (p. 533)

Gould, S. J. (1997, June 12). Darwinian fundamentalism. *The New York Review of Books, XLIV*(10), 34–37. (p. 107)

Grabe, S., Ward, L. M., & Hyde, J. S. (2008). The role of the media in body image concerns among women: A meta-analysis of experimental and correlational studies. *Psychological Bulletin, 134,* 460–476. (p. 338)

Grady, C. L., & McIntosh, A. R., Horwitz, B., Maisog, J. M., Ungeleider, L. G., Mentis, M. J., Pietrini, P., Schapiro, M. B., & Haxby, J. V. (1995). Age-related reductions in human recognition memory due to impaired encoding. *Science, 269,* 218–221. (p. 280)

Grady, D. (2007, December 26). Finding Alzheimer's before a mind fails. *New York Times* (www.nytimes.com). (p. 460)

Graf, P. (1990). Life-span changes in implicit and explicit memory. *Bulletin of the Psychonomic Society, 28,* 353–358. (p. 462)

Graham, J. E., Christian, L. M., & Kiecolt-Glaser, J. K. (2006). Marriage, health, and immune function. In S. R. H. Beach & others (Eds.), *Relational processes and DSM-V: Neuroscience, assessment, prevention, and treatment.* Washington, DC: American Psychiatric Association. (p. C-5)

Grant, B. F., & Dawson, D. A. (1998). Age of onset of drug use and its association with DSM-IV drug abuse and dependence: Results from the national Longitudinal Alcohol Epidemiologic Survey. *Journal of Substance Abuse, 10,* 163–173. (pp. 210, E-5)

Gray-Little, B., & Burks, N. (1983). Power and satisfaction in marriage: A review and critique. *Psychological Bulletin, 93,* 513–538. (p. 684)

Green, B. (2002). Listening to leaders: Feedback on 360-degree feedback one year later. *Organizational Development Journal, 20,* 8–16. (p. B-7)

Green, C. S., & Bavelier, D. (2003). Action video game modifies visual selective attention. *Nature, 423,* 534–537. (p. 121)

Green, J. D., Sedikides, C., & Gregg, A. P. (2008). Forgotten but not gone: The recall and recognition of self-threatening memories. *Journal of Experimental Social Psychology, 44,* 547–561. (p. 487)

Green, J. T., & Woodruff-Pak, D. S. (2000). Eyeblink classical conditioning: Hippocampal formation is for neutral stimulus associations as cerebellum is for association-response. *Psychological Bulletin, 126,* 138–158. (p. 274)

Greenberg, J. (2008). Understanding the vital human quest for self-esteem. *Perspectives on Psychological Science, 3,* 48–55. (p. 512)

Greenberg, J., Solomon, S., & Pyszczynski, T. (1997). Terror management theory of self-esteem and cultural worldviews: Empirical assessments and conceptual refinements. *Advances in Social Psychology, 29,* 61–142. (p. 489)

Greene, J., Sommerville, R. B., Nystrom, L. E., Darley, J. M., & Cohen, J. D. (2001). An fMRI investigation of emotional engagement in moral judgment. *Science, 293,* 2105. (p. 450)

Greene, R. L. (1987). Effects of maintenance rehearsal on human memory. *Psychological Bulletin, 102,* 403–413. (p. 260)

Greenfeld, L. A. (1998). *Alcohol and crime: An analysis of national data on the prevalence of alcohol involvement in crime.* Washington, DC: Document NCJ-168632, Bureau of Justice Statistics (www.ojp.usdoj.gov/bjs). (p. 672)

Greenwald, A. G. (1992). Subliminal semantic activation and subliminal snake oil. Paper presented to the American Psychological Association Convention, Washington, DC. (pp. 122, 488)

Greenwald, A. G., McGhee, D. E., & Schwartz, J. L. K. (1998). Measuring individual differences in implicit cognition: The implicit association test. *Journal of Personality and Social Psychology, 74,* 1464–1480. (p. 666)

Greenwald, A. G., Oakes, M. A., & Hoffman, H. (2003). Targets of discrimination: Effects of race on responses to weapons holders. *Journal of Experimental Social Psychology, 39,* 399. (p. 666)

Greenwald, A. G., Spangenberg, E. R., Pratkanis, A. R., & Eskenazi, J. (1991). Double-blind tests of subliminal self-help audiotapes. *Psychological Science, 2,* 119–122. (p. 122)

Greenwood, M. R. C. (1989). Sexual dimorphism and obesity. In A. J. Stunkard & A. Baum (Eds.). *Perspectives in behavioral medicine: Eating, sleeping, and sex.* Hillsdale, NJ: Erlbaum. (p. 341)

Greer, G. (1984, April). The uses of chastity and other paths to sexual pleasures. *MS,* pp. 53–60, 96. (p. 351)

Greers, A. E. (2004). Speech, language, and reading skills after early cochlear implantation. *Archives of Otolaryngology—Head & Neck Surgery, 130,* 634–638. (p. 318)

Gregg, L., & Tarrier, N. (2007). Virtual reality in mental health: A review of the literature. *Social Psychiatry and Psychiatric Epidemiology, 42,* 343–354. (p. 612)

Gregory, R. L. (1978). *Eye and brain: The psychology of seeing* (3rd ed.). New York: McGraw-Hill. (p. 159)

Gregory, R. L., & Gombrich, E. H. (Eds.). (1973). *Illusion in nature and art.* New York: Charles Scribner's Sons. (p. 164)

Greif, E. B., & Ulman, K. J. (1982). The psychological impact of menarche on early adolescent females: A review of the literature. *Child Development, 53,* 1413–1430. (p. 447)

Greist, J. H., Jefferson, J. W., & Marks, I. M. (1986). *Anxiety and its treatment: Help is available.* Washington, DC: American Psychiatric Press. (p. 570)

Grello, C. M., Welsh, D. P., & Harper, M. S. (2006). No strings attached: The nature of casual sex in college students. *Journal of Sex Research, 43,* 255–267. (p. 200)

Grèzes, J., & Decety, J. (2001). Function anatomy of execution, mental simulation, observation, and verb generation of actions: A meta-analysis. *Human Brain Mapping, 12,* 1–19. (p. 322)

Griffiths, M. (2001). Sex on the Internet: Observations and implications for Internet sex addiction. *Journal of Sex Research, 38,* 333–342. (p. 198)

Grill-Spector, K., & Kanwisher, N. (2005). Visual recognition: As soon as you know it is there, you know what it is. *Psychological Science, 16,* 152–160. (p. 299)

Grilo, C. M., & Pogue-Geile, M. F. (1991). The nature of environmental influences on weight and obesity: A behavior genetic analysis. *Psychological Bulletin, 110,* 520–537. (p. 344)

Grinker, R. R. (2007). *Unstrange minds: Remapping the world of autism.* New York: Basic Books. (p. 424)

Grobstein, C. (1979, June). External human fertilization. *Scientific American,* pp. 57–67. (p. 412)

Groothuis, T. G. G., & Carere, C. (2005). Avian personalities: Characterization and epigenesis. *Neuroscience and Biobehavioral Reviews, 29,* 137–150. (p. 496)

Gross, A. E., & Crofton, C. (1977). What is good is beautiful. *Sociometry, 40,* 85–90. (p. 682)

Gross, M., Nakamura, L., Pascual-Leone, A., & Fregni, F. (2007). Has repetitive transcranial magnetic stimulation (rTMS) treatment for depression improved? A systematic review and meta-analysis comparing the recent vs. the earlier rTMS studies. *Acta Psychiatrica Scandinavica, 116,* 165–173. (p. 635)

Grossberg, S. (1995). The attentive brain. *American Scientist, 83,* 438–449. (p. 162)

Grossman, M., & Wood, W. (1993). Sex differences in intensity of emotional experience: A social role interpretation. *Journal of Personality and Social Psychology, 65,* 1010–1022. (p. 379)

Gruder, C. L. (1977). Choice of comparison persons in evaluating oneself. In J. M. Suls & R. L. Miller (Eds.), *Social comparison processes.* New York: Hemisphere. (p. 395)

Grunebaum, M. F., Ellis, S. P., Li, S., Oquendo, M. A., Mann, J. J. (2004). Antidepressants and suicide risk in the United States, 1985–1999. *Journal of Clinical Psychiatry, 65,* 1456–1462. (p. 632)

Guerin, B. (1986). Mere presence effects in humans: A review. *Journal of Personality and Social Psychology, 22,* 38–77. (p. 657)

Guerin, B. (2003). Language use as social strategy: A review and an analytic framework for the social sciences. *Review of General Psychology, 7,* 251–298. (p. 313)

Guiso, L, Monte, F., Sapienza, P., & Zingales, L. (2008). Culture, gender, and math. *Science, 320,* 1164–1165. (p. 550)

Gundersen, E. (2001, August 1). MTV is a many splintered thing. *USA Today,* pp. D1, D2. (p. 247)

Güntürkün, O. (2003). Adult persistence of head-turning asymmetry. *Nature, 421,* 711. (p. 88)

Gura, T. (2004). New data on appetite-suppressing peptide challenge critics. *Science, 306,* 1453–1454. (p. 334)

Gustafson, D., Lissner, L., Bengtsson, C., Björkelund, C., & Skoog, I. (2004). A 24-year follow-up of body mass index and cerebral atrophy. *Neurology, 63,* 1876–1881. (p. 341)

Gustafson, D., Rothenberg, E., Blennow, K., Steen, B., & Skoog, I. (2003). An 18-year follow-up of overweight and risk of Alzheimer disease. *Archives of Internal Medicine, 163,* 1524–1528. (pp. 341, 461)

Gustavson, C. R., Garcia, J., Hankins, W. G., & Rusiniak, K. W. (1974). Coyote predation control by aversive conditioning. *Science, 184,* 581–583. (p. 224)

Gustavson, C. R., Kelly, D. J., & Sweeney, M. (1976). Prey-lithium aversions I: Coyotes and wolves. *Behavioral Biology, 17,* 61–72. (p. 224)

Guttentag, M., & Secord, P. F. (1983). *Too many women? The sex ratio question.* Thousand Oaks, CA: Sage. (p. 665)

Guttmacher Institute. (1994). *Sex and America's teenagers.* New York: Alan Guttmacher Institute. (pp. 353, 454)

Guttmacher Institute. (2000). *Fulfilling the promise: Public policy and U.S. family planning clinics.* New York: Alan Guttmacher Institute. (p. 454)

H., Sally. (1979, August). *Videotape recording number T-3, Fortunoff Video Archive of Holocaust Testimonies.* New Haven, CT: Yale University Library. (p. 488)

Haber, R. N. (1970, May). How we remember what we see. *Scientific American,* pp. 104–112. (p. 256)

Haddock, G., & Zanna, M. P. (1994). Preferring "housewives" to "feminists." *Psychology of Women Quarterly, 18,* 25–52. (p. 667)

Haesler, S. (2007, June/July). Programmed for speech. *Scientific American Mind,* pp. 67–71. (p. 316)

Haidt, J. (2000). The positive emotion of elevation. *Prevention and Treatment, 3,* article 3 (journals.apa.org/prevention/volume3). (p. 449)

Haidt, J. (2002). The moral emotions. In R. J. Davidson, K. Scherer, & H. H. Goldsmith (Eds.), *Handbook of Affective Sciences.* New York: Oxford University Press. (p. 449)

Haidt, J. (2006). *The happiness hypothesis: Finding modern truth in ancient wisdom.* New York: Basic Books. (p. 449)

Haidt, J. (2007). The new synthesis in moral psychology. *Science, 316,* 998–1001. (p. 449)

Haidt, J. (2008). Morality. *Perspectives on Psychological Science, 3,* 65–72. (p. 449)

Haier, R. J., Jung, R. E., Yeo, R. A., Head, K., & Alkire, M. T. (2004). Structural brain variation and general intelligence. *NeuroImage, 23,* 425–433. (p. 530)

Hakuta, K., Bialystok, E., & Wiley, E. (2003). Critical evidence: A test of the critical-period hypothesis for second-language acquisition. *Psychological Science, 14,* 31–38. (p. 318)

Halberstadt, J. B., & Niedenthal, P. M. (2001). Effects of emotion concepts on perceptual memory for emotional expressions. *Journal of Personality and Social Psychology, 81,* 587–598. (p. 288)

Halberstadt, J. B., Niedenthal, P. M., & Kushner, J. (1995). Resolution of lexical ambiguity by emotional state. *Psychological Science, 6,* 278–281. (p. 163)

Halberstadt, J., O'Shea, R. P., & Forgas, J. (2006). Outgroup fanship in Australia and New Zealand. *Australian Journal of Psychology, 58,* 159–165. (p. 668)

Haldeman, D. C. (1994). The practice and ethics of sexual orientation conversion therapy. *Journal of Consulting and Clinical Psychology, 62,* 221–227. (p. 355)

Haldeman, D. C. (2002). Gay rights, patient rights: The implications of sexual orientation conversion therapy. *Professional Psychology: Research and Practice, 33,* 260–264. (p. 355)

Haler, R. H., & Sunstein, C. R. (2008). *Nudge: Improving decisions about health, wealth, and happiness.* New Haven, CT: Yale University Press. (p. 312)

Hall, C. S., Dornhoff, W., Blick, K. A., & Weesner, K. E. (1982). The dreams of college men and women in 1950 and 1980: A comparison of dream contents and sex differences. *Sleep, 5,* 188–194. (p. 188)

Hall, C. S., & Lindzey, G. (1978). *Theories of personality* (2nd ed.). New York: Wiley. (p. 489)

Hall, G. (1997). Context aversion, Pavlovian conditioning, and the psychological side effects of chemotherapy. *European Psychologist, 2,* 118–124. (pp. 226, 379)

Hall, G. S. (1904). *Adolescence: Its psychology and its relations to physiology, anthropology, sex, crime, religion and education (Vol. I).* New York: Appleton-Century-Crofts. (p. 445)

Hall, J. A. (1984). *Nonverbal sex differences: Communication accuracy and expressive style.* Baltimore: Johns Hopkins University Press. (p. 379)

Hall, J. A. (1987). On explaining gender differences: The case of nonverbal communication. In P. Shaver & C. Hendrick (Eds.), *Review of Personality and Social Psychology, 7,* 177–200. (p. 436)

Hall, J. A. Y., & Kimura, D. (1994). Dermatoglyphic assymetry and sexual orientation in men. *Behavioral Neuroscience, 108,* 1203–1206. (p. 358)

Hall, J. G. (2003). Twinning. *Lancet, 362,* 735–743. (p. 97)

Hall, S. S. (2004, May). The good egg. *Discover,* pp. 30-39. (p. 412)

Hall, W. (2006). The mental health risks of adolescent cannabis use. *PloS Medicine, 3*(2), e39. (p. 206)

Halpern, D. F. (1991). Cognitive sex differences: Why diversity is a critical research issue. Paper presented to the American Psychological Association convention. (p. 550)

Halpern, D. F. (2000). *Sex-related ability differences: Changing perspectives, changing minds.* Mahwah, NJ: Erlbaum. (pp. 354, 550)

Halpern, D. F. (2005, May 20). *Response to Drs. Pinker and Spelke.* www.edge.org. (p. 551)

Halpern, D. F., Benbow, C. P., Geary, D. C., Gur, R. C., Hyde, J. S., & Gernsbacher, M. A. (2007). The science of sex differences in science and mathematics. *Psychological Science in the Public Interest, 8,* 1–51. (pp. 550, 551)

Halpern, D. F., Benbow, C. P., Geary, D. C., Gur, R. C., Hyde, J. S., & Gernsbacher, M. A. (2007). The science of sex differences in science and mathematics. *Psychological Science in the Public Interest, 8,* 1–51. (pp. 549, 550)

Halpern, D. F., & Coren, S. (1990). Laterality and longevity: Is left-handedness associated with a younger age at death? In S. Coren (Ed.), *Left-handedness: Behavioral implications and anomalies.* Amsterdam: North-Holland. (p. 88)

Hamann, S., Herman, R. A., Nolan, C. L., & Wallen, K. (2004). Men and women differ in amygdala response to visual sexual stimuli. *Nature Neuroscience, 7,* 411–416. (p. 351)

Hamilton, R. H. (2000, November). *Increased prevalence of absolute pitch in blind musicians* (Abstract 739.13). Society for Neuroscience meeting, New Orleans. (p. 140)

Hammack, P. L. (2005). The life course development of human sexual orientation: An integrative paradigm. *Human Development, 48,* 267–290. (p. 354)

Hammer, E. (2003). How lucky you are to be a psychology major. *Eye on Psi Chi,* 4–5. (p. A-11)

Hammersmith, S. K. (1982, August). Sexual preference: An empirical study from the Alfred C. Kinsey Institute for Sex Research. Paper presented at the meeting of the American Psychological Association, Washington, DC. (p. 356)

Hampson, R. (2000, April 10). In the end, people just need more room. *USA Today,* p. 19A. (p. 345)

Hampson, S. E., & Goldberg, L. R. (2006). A first large cohort study of personality trait stability over the years between elementary school and midlife. *Journal of Personality and Social Psychology, 91,* 763–779. (p. 473)

Hancock, K. J., & Rhodes, G. (2008). Contact, configural coding and the other-race effect in face recognition. *British Journal of Psychology, 99,* 45–56. (p. 669)

Hankin, B. L., & Abramson, L. Y. (2001). Development of gender differences in depression: An elaborated cognitive vulnerability-transactional stress theory. *Psychological Bulletin, 127,* 773–796. (p. 587)

Hansen, C. H., & Hansen, R. D. (1988). Finding the face-in-the-crowd: An anger superiority effect. *Journal of Personality and Social Psychology, 54,* 917–924. (p. 377)

Harbaugh, W. T., Mayr, U., & Burghart, D. R. (2007). Neural responses to taxation and voluntary giving reveal motives for charitable donations. *Science, 316,* 1622–1625. (p. 687)

Harber, K. D. (1998). Feedback to minorities: Evidence of a positive bias. *Journal of Personality and Social Psychology, 74,* 622–628. (p. 666)

Hardin, C., & Banaji, M. R. (1993). The influence of language on thought. *Social Cognition, 11,* 277–308. (p. 320)

Hare, R. D. (1975). Psychophysiological studies of psychopathy. In D. C. Fowles (Ed.), *Clinical applications of psychophysiology.* New York: Columbia University Press. (p. 597)

Hariri, A. R., Mattay, V. S., Tessitore, A., Kolachana, B., Fera, F., Goldman, D., Egan, M. F., & Weinberger, D. R. (2002). Serotonin transporter genetic variation and the response of the human amygdala. *Science, 297,* 400–403. (p. 387)

Harker, L. A., & Keltner, D. (2001). Expressions of positive emotion in women's college yearbook pictures and their relationship to personality and life outcomes across adulthood. *Journal of Personality and Social Psychology, 80,* 112–124. (p. 389)

Harkins, S. G., & Szymanski, K. (1989). Social loafing and group evaluation. *Journal of Personality and Social Psychology, 56,* 934–941. (p. 658)

Harlow, H. F., Harlow, M. K., & Suomi, S. J. (1971). From thought to therapy: Lessons from a primate laboratory. *American Scientist, 59,* 538–549. (p. 126)

Harlow, R. E., & Cantor, N. (1996). Still participating after all these years: A study of life task participation in later life. *Journal of Personality and Social Psychology, 71,* 1235–1249. (p. 470)

Harmon-Jones, E., Abramson, L. Y., Sigelman, J., Bohlig, A., Hogan, M. E., & Harmon-Jones, C. (2002). Proneness to hypomania/mania symptoms or depression symptoms and asymmetrical frontal cortical responses to an anger-evoking event. *Journal of Personality and Social Psychology, 82,* 610–618. (p. 371)

Harper, C., & McLanahan, S. (2004). Father absence and youth incarceration. *Journal of Research on Adolescence, 14,* 369–397. (p. 674)

Harris, A., & Lurigio, A. J. (2007). Mental illness and violence: A brief review of research and assessment strategies. *Aggression and Violent Behavior, 12,* 542–551. (p. 568)

Harris, B. (1979). Whatever happened to Little Albert? *American Psychologist, 34,* 151–160. (p. 227)

Harris, J. A. (1999). Review and methodological considerations in research on testosterone and aggression. *Aggression and Violent Behavior, 4,* 273–291. (p. 672)

Harris, J. R. (1998). *The nurture assumption.* New York: Free Press. (pp. 428, 444)

Harris, J. R. (2000). Beyond the nurture assumption: Testing hypotheses about the child's environment. In J. G. Borkowski & S. L. Ramey (Eds.), *Parenting and the child's world: Influences on academic, intellectual, and social-emotional development.* Washington, DC: APA Books. (p. 444)

Harris, J. R. (2006). *No two are alike: Human nature and human individuality.* New York: Norton. (p. 98)

Harris, J. R. (2007, August 8). Do pals matter more than parents? *The Times* (www.timesonline.co.uk). (p. 444)

Harris, R. J. (1994). The impact of sexually explicit media. In J. Brant & D. Zillmann (Eds.), *Media effects: Advances in theory and research.* Hillsdale, NJ: Erlbaum. (p. 675)

Harrison, Y., & Horne, J. A. (2000). The impact of sleep deprivation on decision making: A review. *Journal of Experimental Psychology: Applied, 6,* 236–249. (p. 184)

Harriston, K. A. (1993, December 24). 1 shakes, 1 snoozes: both win $45 million. *Washington Post* release (in *Tacoma News Tribune,* pp. A1, A2). (p. 510)

Hart, D. (1988). The development of personal identity in adolescence: A philosophical dilemma approach. *Merrill-Palmer Quarterly, 34,* 105–114. (p. 452)

Harter, J. K., Schmidt, F. L., & Hayes, T. L. (2002). Business-unit-level relationship between employee satisfaction, employee engagement, and business outcomes: A meta-analysis. *Journal of Applied Psychology, 87,* 268–279. (p. B-9)

Hartmann, E. (1981, April). The strangest sleep disorder. *Psychology Today,* pp. 14, 16, 18. (p. 187)

Harvard Mental Health Letter. (2002, February). EMDR (Eye movement and reprocessing). *Harvard Mental Health Letter, 18,* 4–5. (p. 624)

Harvey, F. (2002, February). Surrounded by sound. *Scientific American,* pp. 94–95. (p. 138)

Haselton, M. G., Mortezaie, M., Pillsworth, E. G., Bleske-Rechek, A., & Frederick, D. A. (2006). Ovulatory shifts in human female ornamentation: Near ovulation, women dress to impress. *Hormones and Behavior, 51,* 40–45. (p. 350)

Hasin, D. S., Goodwin, R. D., Stinson, F. S., & Grant, B. F. (2005). Epidemiology of major depressive disorder: Results from the National Epidemiologic Survey on Alcoholism and Related Conditions. *Archives of General Psychiatry, 62,* 1097–1106. (p. 580)

Haslam, N., & Levy, S. R. (2006). Essentialist beliefs about homosexuality: Structure and implications for prejudice. *Personality and Social Psychology Bulletin, 32,* 471–485. (p. 359)

Haslam, S. A., & Reicher, S. (2007). Beyond the banality of evil: Three dynamics of an interactionist social psychology of tyranny. *Personality and Social Psychology Bulletin, 33,* 615–622. (p. 648)

Hassan, B., & Rahman, Q. (2007). Selective sexual orientation-related differences in object location memory. *Behavioral Neuroscience, 121,* 625–633. (p. 359)

Hatfield, E. (1988). Passionate and companionate love. In R. J. Sternberg & M. L. Barnes (Eds.), *The psychology of love.* New Haven: Yale University Press. (p. 683)

Hatfield, E., & Sprecher, S. (1986). *Mirror, mirror . . . The importance of looks in everyday life.* Albany: State University of New York Press. (p. 680)

Hatfield, J., Faunce, G. J., & Job, R. F. S. (2006). Avoiding confusion surrounding the phrase "correlation does not imply causation." *Teaching of Psychology, 33,* 49–51. (p. 32)

Hathaway, S. R. (1960). *An MMPI Handbook* (Vol. 1, Foreword). Minneapolis: University of Minnesota Press. (Revised edition, 1972). (p. 496)

Hauser, M. (2006). *Moral minds: How nature designed our universal sense of right and wrong.* New York: Ecco. (pp. 317, 450)

Hauser, M. D., Chomsky, N., & Fitch, W. T. (2002). The faculty of language: What is it, who has it, and how did it evolve? *Science, 298,* 1569–1579. (p. 314)

Havas, D. A., Glenberg, A. M., & Rink, M. (2007). Emotion simulation during language comprehension. *Psychonomic Bulletin & Review, 14,* 436–441. (p. 383)

Haxby, J. V. (2001, July 7). Quoted by B. Bower, Faces of perception. *Science News,* pp. 10–12. See also J. V. Haxby, M. I. Gobbini, M. L. Furey, A. Ishai, J. L. Schouten & P. Pietrini, Distributed and overlapping representations of faces and objects in ventral temporal cortex. *Science, 293,* 2425–2430. (p. 129)

Haynes, J-D., & Rees, G. (2005). Predicting the orientation of invisible stimuli from activity in human primary visual cortex. *Nature Neuroscience, 8,* 686–691. (p. 122)

Haynes, J-D., & Rees, G. (2006). Decoding mental states from brain activity in humans. *Nature Reviews Neuroscience, 7,* 523–534. (p. 122)

Hazan, C., & Shaver, P. R. (1994). Attachment as an organizational framework for research on close relationships. *Psychological Inquiry, 5,* 1–22. (p. 431)

Hazelrigg, M. D., Cooper, H. M., & Borduin, C. M. (1987). Evaluating the effectiveness of family therapies: An integrative review and analysis. *Psychological Bulletin, 101,* 428–442. (p. 617)

Head Start. (2005). *Head Start program fact sheet.* (www.acf.hhs.gov.) (p. 548)

Health Canada. (2007). *Canadian addiction survey: Substance use by Canadian youth.* Health Canada Publication 4946 (www.hc-sc.gc.ca). (p. 208)

Heaps, C. M., & Nash, M. (2001). Comparing recollective experience in true and false autobiographical memories. *Journal of Experimental Psychology: Learning, Memory, and Cognition, 27,* 920–930. (p. 292)

Hebb, D. O. (1980). *Essay on mind.* Hillsdale, NJ: Erlbaum. 9–16. (p. 226)

Hebl, M. R., & Mannix, L. M. (2003). The weight of obesity in evaluating others: A mere proximity effect. *Personality and Social Psychology Bulletin, 29,* 28–38. (p. 342)

Hedges, L. V., & Nowell, A. (1995). Sex differences in mental test scores, variability, and numbers of high-scoring individuals. *Science, 269,* 41–45. (p. 549)

Hedström, P., Liu, K-Y., & Nordvik, M. K. (2008). Interaction domains and suicides: A population-based panel study of suicides in the Stockholm metropolitan area, 1991–1999. *Social Forces, 87,* 713–740. (p. 585)

Heider, F. (1958). *The psychology of interpersonal relations.* New York: Wiley. (p. 644)

Heiman, J. R. (1975, April). The physiology of erotica: Women's sexual arousal. *Psychology Today,* 90–94. (p. 351)

Heine, S. J., & Hamamura, T. (2007). In search of East Asian self-enhancement. *Personality and Social Psychology Review, 11,* 4–27. (p. 513)

Heins, M. (2004, December 14). Quoted by B. Kloza, Violent Christmas games. *ScienCentralNews* (www.sciencecentral.com). (p. 677)

Hejmadi, A., Davidson, R. J., & Rozin, P. (2000). Exploring Hindu Indian emotion expressions: Evidence for accurate recognition by Americans and Indians. *Psychological Science, 11,* 183–187. (p. 377)

Helgeson, V. S., Cohen, S., & Fritz, H. L. (1998). Social ties and cancer. In P. M. Cinciripini & others (Eds.), *Psychological and behavioral factors in cancer risk.* New York: Oxford University Press. (p. C-4)

Helgeson, V. S., Reynolds, K. A., & Tomich, P. L. (2006). A meta-analytic review of benefit finding and growth. *Journal of Consulting and Clinical Psychology, 74,* 797–816. (p. 573)

Heller, W. (1990, May/June). Of one mind: Second thoughts about the brain's dual nature. *The Sciences,* pp. 38–44. (p. 87)

Helmreich, W. B. (1992). *Against all odds: Holocaust survivors and the successful lives they made in America.* New York: Simon & Schuster. (pp. 430, 487)

Helmreich, W. B. (1994). Personal correspondence. Department of Sociology, City University of New York. (p. 487)

Helms, J. E., Jernigan, M., & Mascher, J. (2005). The meaning of race in psychology and how to change it: A methodological perspective. *American Psychologist, 60,* 27–36. (p. 553)

Helmuth, L. (2001). Boosting brain activity from the outside in. *Science, 292,* 1284–1286. (p. 634)

Helweg-Larsen, M. (1999). (The lack of) optimistic biases in response to the 1994 Northridge earthquake: The role of personal experience. *Basic and Applied Social Psychology, 21,* 119–129. (p. 507)

Hembree, R. (1988). Correlates, causes, effects, and treatment of test anxiety. *Review of Educational Research, 58,* 47–77. (p. 370)

Hemenover, S. H. (2003). The good, the bad, and the healthy: Impacts of emotional disclosure of trauma on resilient self-concept and psychological distress. *Personality and Social Psychology Bulletin, 29,* 1236–1244. (p. C-5)

Henderlong, J., & Lepper, M. R. (2002). The effects of praise on children's intrinsic motivation: A review and synthesis. *Psychological Bulletin, 128,* 774–795. (p. 237)

Henderson, J. M. (2007). Regarding scenes. *Current Directions in Psychological Science, 16,* 219–222. (p. 123)

Henkel, L. A., Franklin, N., & Johnson, M. K. (2000, March). Cross-modal source monitoring confusions between perceived and imagined events. *Journal of Experimental Psychology: Learning, Memory, & Cognition, 26,* 321–335. (p. 287)

Henley, N. M. (1989). Molehill or mountain? What we know and don't know about sex bias in language. In M. Crawford & M. Gentry (Eds.), *Gender and thought: Psychological perspectives.* New York: Springer-Verlag. (p. 320)

Henninger, P. (1992). Conditional handedness: Handedness changes in multiple personality disordered subject reflect shift in hemispheric dominance. *Consciousness and Cognition, 1,* 265–287. (p. 579)

Henry, J. D., MacLeod, M. S., Phillips, L. H., & Crawford, J. R. (2004). A meta-analytic review of prospective memory and aging. *Psychology and Aging, 19,* 27–39. (p. 462)

Hepper, P. (2005). Unravelling our beginnings. *The Psychologist, 18,* 474–477. (p. 412)

Hepper, P. G., Shahidullah, S., & White, R. (1990). Origins of fetal handedness. *Nature, 347,* 431. (p. 88)

Hepper, P. G., Wells, D. L., & Lynch, C. (2004). Prenatal thumb sucking is related to postnatal handedness. *Neuropsychologia, 43,* 313–315. (p. 88)

Herbert, B. (2001, July 23). Economics 202 at Big Tobacco U. *New York Times* (www.nytimes.com). (p. 202)

Herbert, J. D., Lilienfeld, S. O., Lohr, J. M., Montgomery, R. W., O'Donohue, W. T., Rosen, G. M., & Tolin, D. F. (2000). Science and psudoscience in the development of eye movement desensitization and reprocessing: Implications for clinical psychology. *Clinical Psychology Review, 20,* 945–971. (p. 624)

Herman, C. P., & Polivy, J. (1980). Restrained eating. In A. J. Stunkard (Ed.), *Obesity.* Philadelphia: Saunders. (p. 347)

Herman, C. P., Roth, D. A., & Polivy, J. (2003). Effects of the presence of others on food intake: A normative interpretation. *Psychological Bulletin, 129,* 873–886. (p. 336)

Herman-Giddens, M. E., Wang, L., & Koch, G. (2001). Secondary sexual characteristics in boys: Estimates from the National Health and Nutrition Examination Survey III, 1988–1994. *Archives of Pediatrics and Adolescent Medicine, 155,* 1022–1028. (p. 446)

Hernandez, A. E., & Li, P. (2007). Age of acquisition: Its neural and computational mechanisms. *Psychological Bulletin, 133,* 638–650. (p. 318)

Herrmann, D. (1982). Know thy memory: The use of questionnaires to assess and study memory. *Psychological Bulletin, 92,* 434–452. (p. 293)

Herrmann, E., Call, J., Hernández-Lloreda, M. V., Hare, B., & Tomasello, M. (2007). Humans have evolved specialized skills of social cognition: The cultural intelligence hypothesis. *Science, 317,* 1360–1365. (p. 243)

Herrnstein, R. J., & Loveland, D. H. (1964). Complex visual concept in the pigeon. *Science, 146,* 549–551. (p. 230)

Herrnstein, R. J., & Murray, C. A. (1994). *The bell curve: Intelligence and class structure in American life.* NY: Free Press. (p. 552)

Hershenson, M. (1989). *The moon illusion.* Hillsdale, NJ: Erlbaum. (p. 157)

Hertenstein, M. J., Keltner, D., App, B. Bulleit, B. & Jaskolka, A. (2006). Touch communicates distinct emotions. *Emotion, 6,* 528–533. (p. 427)

Hertenstein, M. J., Verkamp, J. M., Kerestes, A. M., & Holmes, R. M. (2006). The communicative functions of touch in humans, nonhumans primates, and rats: A review and synthesis of the empirical research. *Genetic, Social, and General Psychology Monographs, 132,* 5–94. (p. 141)

Herz, R. S. (2001). Ah sweet skunk! Why we like or dislike what we smell. *Cerebrum, 3*(4), 31–47. (p. 149)

Herz, R. S., Beland, S.L., & Hellerstein, M. (2004). Changing odor hedonic perception through emotional associations in humans. *International Journal of Comparative Psychology, 17,* 315–339. (p. 150)

Hess, E. H. (1956, July). Space perception in the chick. *Scientific American,* pp. 71–80. (p. 160)

Hetherington, M. M., Anderson, A. S., Norton, G. N. M., & Newson, L. (2006). Situational effects on meal intake: A comparison of eating alone and eating with others. *Physiology and Behavior, 88,* 498–505. (p. 336)

Hettema, J. M., Neale, M. C., & Kendler, K. S. (2001). A review and meta-analysis of the genetic epidemiology of anxiety disorders. *American Journal of Psychiatry, 158,* 1568–1578. (p. 575)

Hewlett, B. S. (1991). *Intimate fathers: The nature and context of Aka Pygmy.* Ann Arbor: University of Michigan Press. (p. 429)

Hickok, G., Bellugi, U., & Klima, E. S. (2001, June). Sign language in the brain. *Scientific American*, pp. 58–65. (p. 87)

Hilgard, E. R. (1986). *Divided consciousness: Multiple controls in human thought and action.* New York: Wiley. (p. 195)

Hilgard, E. R. (1992). Dissociation and theories of hypnosis. In E. Fromm & M. R. Nash (Eds.), *Contemporary hypnosis research.* New York: Guilford. (p. 195)

Hill, C. E., & Nakayama, E. Y. (2000). Client-centered therapy: Where has it been and where is it going? A comment on Hathaway. *Journal of Clinical Psychology, 56,* 961–875. (p. 609)

Hill, H., & Johnston, A. (2001). Categorizing sex and identity from the biological motion of faces. *Current Biology, 11,* 880–885. (p. 380)

Hines, M. (2004). *Brain gender.* New York: Oxford University Press. (pp. 438, 439)

Hines, M., & Green, R. (1991). Human hormonal and neural correlates of sex-typed behaviors. *Review of Psychiatry, 10,* 536–555. (p. 439)

Hingson, R. W., Heeren, T., & Winter, M. R. (2006). Age at drinking onset and alcohol dependence. *Archives of Pediatrics & Adolescent Medicine, 160,* 739–746. (p. 210)

Hintzman, D. L. (1978). *The psychology of learning and memory.* San Francisco: Freeman. (p. 264)

Hinz, L. D., & Williamson, D. A. (1987). Bulimia and depression: A review of the affective variant hypothesis. *Psychological Bulletin, 102,* 150–158. (p. 337)

Hirsch, J. (2003). Obesity: Matter over mind? *Cerebrum, 5(1),* 7–18. (pp. 342, 343)

Hirt, E. R., Zillmann, D., Erickson, G. A., & Kennedy, C. (1992). Costs and benefits of allegiance: Changes in fans' self-ascribed competencies after team victory versus defeat. *Journal of Personality and Social Psychology, 63,* 724–738. (p. 589)

HMHL. (2002, August). Smoking and depression. *Harvard Mental Health Letter,* pp. 6–7. (p. 586)

HMHL. (2002, January). Disaster and trauma. *Harvard Mental Health Letter,* pp. 1–5. (p. 400)

HMHL. (2007, February). Electroconvulsive therapy. *Harvard Mental Health Letter,* Harvard Medical School, pp. 1–4. (p. 633)

Hobson, J. A. (1995, September). Quoted by C. H. Colt, The power of dreams. *Life,* pp. 36–49. (p. 189)

Hobson, J. A. (2003). *Dreaming: An introduction to the science of sleep.* New York: Oxford. (p. 190)

Hobson, J. A. (2004). *13 dreams Freud never had: The new mind science.* New York: Pi Press. (p. 190)

Hochberg, L. R., Serruya, M. D., Friehs, G. M., Mukand, J. A., Saleh, M., Caplan, A. H., Branner, A., Chen, D., Penn, R. D. & Donoghue, J. P. (2006). Neuronal ensemble control of prosthetic devices by a human with tetraplegia. *Nature, 442,* 164–171. (p. 77)

Hodgkinson, V. A., & Weitzman, M. S. (1992). *Giving and volunteering in the United States.* Washington, DC: Independent Sector. (p. 687)

Hoebel, B. G., & Teitelbaum, P. (1966). Effects of forcefeeding and starvation on food intake and body weight in a rat with ventromedial hypothalamic lesions. *Journal of Comparative and Physiological Psychology, 61,* 189–193. (p. 333)

Hoeft, F., Watson, C. L., Kesler, S. R., Bettinger, K. E., & Reiss, A. L. (2008). Gender differences in the mesocorticolimbic system during computer game-play. *Journal of Psychiatric Research, 42,* 253–258. (p. 198)

Hoffman, C., & Hurst, N. (1990). Gender stereotypes: Perception or rationalization? *Journal of Personality and Social Psychology, 58,* 197–208. (p. 667)

Hoffman, D. D. (1998). *Visual intelligence: How we create what we see.* New York: Norton. (p. 130)

Hoffman, H. G. (2004, August). Virtual-reality therapy. *Scientific American,* pp. 58–65. (p. 146)

Hogan, J. (1995, November). Get smart, take a test. *Scientific American,* pp. 12, 14. (p. 537)

Hogan, R. (1998). Reinventing personality. *Journal of Social and Clinical Psychology, 17,* 1–10. (p. 501)

Hoge, C. W., & Castro, C. A. (2006). Post-traumatic stress disorder in UK and U.S. forces deployed to Iraq. *Lancet, 368,* 837. (p. 573)

Hoge, C. W., Castro, C. A., Messer, S. C., McGurk, D., Cotting, D. I., & Koffman, R. L. (2004). Combat duty in Iraq and Afghanistan, mental health problems, and barriers to care. *New England Journal of Medicine, 351,* 13–22. (p. 572)

Hoge, C. W., Terhakopian, A., Castro, C. A., Messer, S. C., & Engel, C. C. (2007). Association of posttraumatic stress disorder with somatic symptoms, health care visits, and absenteeism among Iraq War veterans. *American Journal of Psychiatry, 164,* 150–153. (p. 573)

Hogg, M. A. (1996). Intragroup processes, group structure and social identity. In W. P. Robinson (Ed.), *Social groups and identities: Developing the legacy of Henri Tajfel.* Oxford: Butterworth Heinemann. (p. 668)

Hogg, M. A. (2006). Social identity theory. In P. J. Burke (Ed.), *Contemporary social psychological theories.* Stanford, CA: Stanford University Press. (p. 668)

Hohmann, G. W. (1966). Some effects of spinal cord lesions on experienced emotional feelings. *Psychophysiology, 3,* 143–156. (p. 371)

Hokanson, J. E., & Edelman, R. (1966). Effects of three social responses on vascular processes. *Journal of Personality and Social Psychology, 3,* 442–447. (p. 388)

Holahan, C. K., & Sears, R. R. (1995). *The gifted group in later maturity.* Stanford, CA: Stanford University Press. (p. 543)

Holden, C. (1980a). Identical twins reared apart. *Science, 207,* 1323–1325. (p. 98)

Holden, C. (1980b, November). Twins reunited. *Science, 80,* 55–59. (p. 98)

Holden, C. (1993). Wake-up call for sleep research. *Science, 259,* 305. (p. 183)

Holden, C. (2007). Mental illness: The next frontier. *Science, 317,* 23. (p. 595)

Holden, G. W., & Miller, P. C. (1999). Enduring and different: A metaanalysis of the similarity in parents' child rearing. *Psychological Bulletin, 125,* 223–254. (p. 434)

Holliday, R. E., & Albon, A. J. (2004). Minimizing misinformation effects in young children with cognitive interview mnemonics. *Applied Cognitive Psychology, 18,* 263–281. (p. 290)

Hollis, K. L. (1997). Contemporary research on Pavlovian conditioning: A "new" functional analysis. *American Psychologist, 52,* 956–965. (p. 220)

Hollon, S. D., & 10 others. (2005). Prevention of relapse following cognitive therapy vs. medications in moderate to severe depression. *Archives of General Psychiatry, 62,* 417–422. (p. 622)

Hollon, S. D., Thase, M. E., & Markowitz, J. C. (2002). Treatment and prevention of depression. *Psychological Science in the Public Interest, 3,* 39–77. (p. 631)

Holm-Denoma, J., Joiner, T., Vohs, K., & Heatherton, T. (2008). The "freshman fifteen" (the freshman five actually): Predictors and possible explanations. *Health Psychology, 27,* S3–S9. (p. 345)

Holstege, G., Georgiadis, J. R., Paans, A. M. J., Meiners, L. C., van der Graaf, F. H. C. E., & Reinders, A. A. T. S. (2003a). Brain activation during male ejaculation. *Journal of Neuroscience, 23,* 9185–9193. (p. 349)

Holstege, G., Reinders, A. A. T., Paans, A. M. J., Meiners, L. C., Pruim, J., & Georgiadis, J. R. (2003b). *Brain activation during female sexual orgasm.* Program No. 727.7. Washington, DC: Society for Neuroscience. (p. 349)

Holt, L. (2002, August). Reported in "Sounds of speech," p. 26, and in personal correspondence, July 18, 2002. (p. 313)

Holzman, P. S., & Matthysse, S. (1990). The genetics of schizophrenia: A review. *Psychological Science, 1,* 279–286. (p. 123)

Home Office. (2003). *Prevalence of drug use: Key findings from the 2002/2003 British Crime Survey.* London: Research, Development and Statistics Directorate, Home Office. (p. 204)

Homer, B. D., Solomon, T. M., Moeller, R. W., Mascia, A., DeRaleau, L., & Halkitis, P. N. (2008). Methamphetamine abuse and impairment of social functioning: A review of the underlying neurophysiological causes and behavioral implications. *Psychological Bulletin, 134,* 301–310. (p. 201)

Hooper, J., & Teresi, D. (1986). *The three-pound universe.* New York: Macmillan. (p. 73)

Hooykaas, R. (1972). *Religion and the rise of modern science.* Grand Rapids, MI: Eerdmans. (p. 23)

Hopkins, W. D. (2006). Comparative and familial analysis of handedness in great apes. *Psychological Bulletin, 132,* 538–559. (p. 88)

Hopper, L. M., Lambeth, S. P., Schapiro, S. J., & Whiten, A. (2008). Observational learning in chimpanzees and children studied through 'ghost' conditions. *Proceedings of the Royal Society, 275,* 835–840. (p. 243)

Horn, J. L. (1982). The aging of human abilities. In J. Wolman (Ed.), *Handbook of developmental psychology*. Englewood Cliffs, NJ: Prentice-Hall. (p. 464)

Horner, V., Whiten, A., Flynn, E., & de Waal, F. B. M. (2006). Faithful replication of foraging techniques along cultural transmission chains by chimpanzees and children. *Proceedings of the National Academy of Sciences, 103,* 13878-13883. (p. D-2)

Horowitz, T. S., Cade, B. E., Wolfe, J. M., & Czeisler, C. A. (2003). Searching night and day: A dissociation of effects of circadian phase and time awake on visual selective attention and vigilance. *Psychological Science, 14,* 549-557. (p. 184)

Horwood, L. J., & Fergusson, D. M. (1998). Breastfeeding and later cognitive and academic outcomes. *Pediatrics, 101(1).* (p. 30)

House, J. S., Landis, K. R., & Umberson, D. (1988). *Social relationships and health. Science, 241,* 540-545. (p. C-4)

House, R. J., & Singh, J. V. (1987). Organizational behavior: Some new directions for I/O psychology. *Annual Review of Psychology, 38,* 669-718. (p. B-12)

Houts, A. C., Berman, J. S., & Abramson, H. (1994). Effectiveness of psychological and pharmacological treatments for nocturnal enuresis. *Journal of Consulting and Clinical Psychology, 62,* 737-745. (p. 611)

Hovatta, I., Tennant, R. S., Helton, R., Marr, R. A., Singer, O., Redwine, J. M., Ellison, J. A., Schadt, E. E., Verma, I. M., Lockhart, D. J., & Barlow, C. (2005). Glyoxalase 1 and glutathione reductase 1 regulate anxiety in mice. *Nature, 438,* 662-666. (p. 575)

Howard Hughes Medication Institute. (2008). *The quivering bundles that let us hear.* (www.hhmi.org/senses/c120.html.). (p. 135)

Howe, M. L. (1997). Children's memory for traumatic experiences. *Learning and Individual Differences, 9,* 153-174. (p. 290)

Howell, R. T., & Howell, C. J. (2008). The relation of economic status to subjective well-being in developing countries: A meta-analysis. *Psychological Bulletin, 134,* 536-560. (p. 392)

Hoyer, G., & Lund, E. (1993). Suicide among women related to number of children in marriage. *Archives of General Psychiatry, 50,* 134-137. (p. 584)

Hu, F. B., Li, T. Y., Colditz, G. A., Willett, W. C., & Manson, J. E. (2003). Television watching and other sedentary behaviors in relation to risk of obesity and type 2 diabetes mellitus in women. *Journal of the American Medical Association, 289,* 1785-1791. (p. 345)

Hu, X-Z. & 13 others. (2007). Association between a functional serotonin transporter promoter polymorphism and citalopram treatment in adult outpatients with major depression. *Archives of General Psychiatry, 64,* 783-792. (p. 584)

Hu, X-Z., Lipsky, R. H., Zhu, G., Akhtar, L. A., Taubman, J., Greenberg, B. D., Xu, K., Arnold, P. D., Richter, M. A., Kennedy, J. L., Murphy, D. L., & Goldman, D. (2006). Serotonin transporter promoter gain-of-function genotypes are linked to obsessive-compulsive disorder. *American Journal of Human Genetics, 78,* 815-826. (p. 575)

Huart, J., Corneille, O., & Becquart, E. (2005). Face-based categorization, context-based categorization, and distortions in the recollection of gender ambiguous faces. *Journal of Experimental Social Psychology, 41,* 598-608. (p. 299)

Hubbard, E. M., Arman, A. C., Ramachandran, V. S., & Boynton, G. M. (2005). Individual differences among grapheme-color synesthetes: Brain-behavior correlations. *Neuron, 45,* 975-985. (p. 148)

Hubel, D. H. (1979, September). The brain. *Scientific American,* pp. 45-53. (p. 123)

Hubel, D. H., & Wiesel, T. N. (1979, September). Brian mechanisms of vision. *Scientific American,* pp. 150-162. (p. 129)

Hublin, C., Kaprio, J., Partinen, M., & Koskenvuo, M. (1998). Sleeptalking in twins: Epidemiology and psychiatric comorbidity. *Behavior Genetics, 28,* 289-298. (p. 187)

Hublin, C., Kaprio, J., Partinen, M., Heikkila, K., & Koskenvuo, M. (1997). Prevalence and genetics of sleepwalking—A population-based twin study. *Neurology, 48,* 177-181. (p. 187)

Hucker, S. J., & Bain, J. (1990). Androgenic hormones and sexual assault. In W. Marshall, R. Law, & H. Barbaree (Eds.), *The handbook on sexual assault.* New York: Plenum. (p. 350)

Hudson, J. I., Hiripi, E., Pope, H. G., & Kessler, R. C. (2007). The prevalence and correlates of eating disorders in the National Comorbidity Survey Replication. *Biological Psychiatry, 61,* 348-358. (p. 337)

Huey, E. D., Krueger, F., & Grafman, J. (2006). Representations in the human prefrontal cortex. *Current Directions in Psychological Science, 15,* 167-171. (p. 79)

Huffcutt, A. I., Conway, J. M., Roth, P. L., & Stone, N. J. (2001). Identification and meta-analytic assessment of psychological constructs measured in employment interviews. *Journal of Applied Psychology, 86,* 897-913. (p. B-6)

Hugenberg, K., & Bodenhausen, G. V. (2003). Facing prejudice: Implicit prejudice and the perception of facial threat. *Psychological Science, 14,* 640-643. (p. 666)

Hughes, H. C. (1999). *Sensory exotica: A world beyond human experience.* Cambridge, MA: MIT Press. (p. 120)

Hugick, L. (1989, July). Women play the leading role in keeping modern families close. *Gallup Report, No. 286,* p. 27-34. (p. 437)

Huizink, A. C., & Mulder, E. J. (2006). Maternal smoking, drinking or cannabis use during pregnancy and neurobehavioral and cognitive functioning in human offspring. *Neuroscience and Biobehavioral Reviews, 30,* 24-41. (p. 207)

Hulbert, A. (2005, November 20). The prodigy puzzle. *New York Times Magazine* (www.nytimes.com). (p. 543)

Hull, H. R., Morrow, M. L., Dinger, M. K., Han, J. L., & Fields, D. A. (2007, November 20). Characterization of body weight and composition changes during the sophomore year of college. *BMC Women's Health, 7,* 21 (biomedcentral.com). (p. 184)

Hull, J. G., Young, R. D., & Jouriles, E. (1986). Applications of the self-awareness model of alcohol consumption: Predicting patterns of use and abuse. *Journal of Personality and Social Psychology, 51,* 790-796. (p. 200)

Hull, J. M. (1990). *Touching the rock: An experience of blindness.* New York: Vintage Books. (pp. 275, 680)

Hulme, C., & Tordoff, V. (1989). Working memory development: The effects of speech rate, word length, and acoustic similarity on serial recall. *Journal of Experimental Child Psychology, 47,* 72-87. (p. 267)

Hummer, R. A., Rogers, R. G., Nam, C. B., & Ellison, C. G. (1999). Religious involvement and U.S. adult mortality. *Demography, 36,* 273-285. (pp. C-11, C-12)

Humphrey, S. E., Nahrgang, J. D., & Morgeson, F. P. (2007). Integrating motivational, social, and contextual work design features: A meta-analytic summary and theoretical extension of the work design literature. *Journal of Applied Psychology, 92,* 1332-1356. (p. 506)

Humphreys, L. G., & Davey, T. C. (1988). Continuity in intellectual growth from 12 months to 9 years. *Intelligence, 12,* 183-197. (p. 540)

Hunsberger, J. G., Newton, S. S., Bennett, A. H., Duman, C. H., Russell, D. S., Salton, S. R., & Duman, R. S. (2007). Antidepressant actions of the exercise-regulated gene VGF. *Nature Medicine, 13,* 1476-1482. (p. C-8)

Hunsley, J., & Di Giulio, G. (2002). Dodo bird, phoenix, or urban legend? The question of psychotherapy equivalence. *Scientific Review of Mental Health Practice, 1,* 11-22. (p. 622)

Hunt, C., Slade, T., & Andrews, G. (2004). Generalized anxiety disorder and major depressive disorder comorbidity in the *National Survey of Mental Health and Well-Being. Depression and Anxiety, 20,* 23-31. (p. 570)

Hunt, E. (1983). On the nature of intelligence. *Science, 219,* 141-146. (p. 531)

Hunt, E., & Carlson, J. (2007). Considerations relating to the study of group differences in intelligence. *Perspectives on Psychological Science, 2,* 194-213. (pp. 554, 555)

Hunt, J. M. (1982). Toward equalizing the developmental opportunities of infants and preschool children. *Journal of Social Issues, 38(4),* 163-191. (p. 547)

Hunt, M. (1990). *The compassionate beast: What science is discovering about the humane side of humankind.* New York: William Morrow. (p. 14)

Hunt, M. (1993). *The story of psychology.* New York: Doubleday. (pp. 4, 5, 6, 51, 227, 451, 543)

Hunter, J. E. (1997). Needed: A ban on the significance test. *Psychological Science, 8,* 3-7. (p. 41)

Hunter, S., & Sundel, M. (Eds.). (1989). *Midlife myths: Issues, findings, and practice implications.* Newbury Park, CA: Sage. (p. 465)

Hurst, M. (2008, April 22). Who gets any sleep these days? Sleep patterns of Canadians. *Canadian Social Trends*. Statistics Canada Catalogue No. 11–008. (p. 181)

Hussein, S. (2002, July 17 and August 28). Speeches to the Iraqi people as reported by various media. (p. 689)

Huston, A. C., Donnerstein, E., Fairchild, H., Feshbach, N. D., Katz, P. A., & Murray, J. P. (1992). *Big world, small screen: The role of television in American society*. Lincoln, NE: University of Nebraska Press. (p. 247)

Hvistendahl, M. (2008, July 9). No country for young men. *New Republic* (www.tnr.com). (p. 665)

Hyde, J. S. (1983, November). Bem's gender schema theory. Paper presented at GLCA Women's Studies Conference, Rochester, IN. (p. 285)

Hyde, J. S. (2005). The gender similarities hypothesis. *American Psychologist, 60,* 581–592. (p. 435)

Hyde, J. S., Fennema, E., & Lamon, S. J. (1990). Gender differences in mathematics performance: A meta-analysis. *Psychological Bulletin, 107,* 139–155. (p. 549)

Hyde, J. S., Mezulis, A. H., & Abramson, L. Y. (2008). The ABCs of depression: Integrating affective, biological, and cognitive models to explain the emergence of the gender difference in depression. *Psychological Review, 115,* 291–313. (pp. 549, 582)

Hyman, R. (1981). Cold reading: How to convince strangers that you know all about them. In K. Frazier (Ed.), *Paranormal borderlands of science*. Buffalo, NY: Prometheus. (p. 498)

Iacoboni, M. (2008). *Mirroring people: The new science of how we connect with others*. New York: Farrar, Straus & Giroux. (p. 243)

IAP. (2006, June 21). IAP statement on the teaching of evolution. *The Interacademy Panel on International Issues* (www.interacademies.net/iap). (p. 108)

Inman, M. L., & Baron, R. S. (1996). Influence of prototypes on perceptions of prejudice. *Journal of Personality and Social Psychology, 70,* 727–739. (p. 300)

Irwin, M. R., Cole, J. C., & Nicassio, P. M. (2006). Comparative meta-analysis of behavioral interventions for insomnia and their efficacy in middle-aged adults and in older adults 55+ years of age. *Health Psychology, 25,* 3–14. (pp. 185, 186)

Iso, H., Simoda, S., & Matsuyama, T. (2007). Environmental change during postnatal development alters behaviour. *Behavioural Brain Research, 179,* 90–98. (p. 83)

Iversen, L. L. (2000). *The science of marijuana*. New York: Oxford. (p. 207)

Ickes, W., Snyder, M., & Garcia, S. (1997). Personality influences on the choice of situations. In R. Hogan, J. Johnson, & S. Briggs (Eds.). *Handbook of Personality Psychology*. San Diego, CA: Academic Press. (p. 503)

Idson, L. C., & Mischel, W. (2001). The personality of familiar and significant people: The lay perceiver as a social-cognitive theorist. *Journal of Personality and Social Psychology, 80,* 585–596. (p. 645)

Ikonomidou, C., Bittigau, P., Ishimaru, M. J., Wozniak, D. F., Koch, C., Genz, K., Price, M. T., Stefovska, V., Hoerster, F., Tenkova, T., Dikranian, K., & Olney, J. W. (2000). Ethanol-induced apoptotic neurodegeneration and fetal alcohol syndrome. *Science, 287,* 1056–1060. (p. 413)

Ilardi, S. S. (2009). *The depression cure: The 6-step program to defeat depression without drugs*. NY: Da Capo Press. (p. 636) Ilardi, S. S., Karwoski, L., Lehman, K. A., Stites, B. A., & Steidtmann, D. (2007). We were never designed for this: The depression epidemic and the promise of therapeutic lifestyle change. Unpublished manuscript, University of Kansas. (pp. 586, C-8)

Independent Sector. (2002). *Faith and philanthropy: The connection between charitable giving behavior and giving to religion*. Washington, DC: Independent Sector. (p. 687)

Ingham, A. G., Levinger, G., Graves, J., & Peckham, V. (1974). The Ringelmann effect: Studies of group size and group performance. *Journal of Experimental Social Psychology, 10,* 371–384. (p. 658)

Inglehart, R. (1990). *Culture shift in advanced industrial society*. Princeton, NJ: Princeton University Press. (pp. 361, 392, 469, 506, B-2)

Inglehart, R. (2008, June 30). Subjective well-being in 97 countries based on reported happiness and life satisfaction, equally weighted. World Values Survey distributed by University of Michigan News Service: umich.edu/news/happy_08/HappyChart.pdf. (p. 392)

Inglehart, R. (2009). Cultural change and democracy in Latin America, in F. Hagopian (Ed.), *Contemporary Catholicism, religious pluralism and democracy in Latin America*. South Bend: Notre Dame University Press, in press. (p. 506)

Insana, R. (2005, February 21). Coach says honey gets better results than vinegar (interview with Larry Brown). *USA Today*, p. 4B. (p. B-11)

Inzlicht, M., & Ben-Zeev, T. (2000). A threatening intellectual environment: Why females are susceptible to experiencing problem-solving deficits in the presence of males. *Psychological Science, 11,* 365–371. (p. 555)

Inzlicht, M., & Gutsell, J. N. (2007). Running on empty: Neural signals for self-control failure. *Psychological Science, 18,* 933–937. (p. 505)

Ipsos. (2006, February 21). *Sexual behaviour and lack of knowledge threaten health of Canadian teens*. Ipsos Reid (www.ipsos-na.com). (p. 352)

IPU. (2009). *Women in national parliaments: Situation as of 3 May April 2009*. International Parliamentary Union (www.ipu.org). (p. 436)

Iraq Family Health Survey Study Group. (2008). Violence-related mortality in Iraq from 2002 to 2006. *New England Journal of Medicine, 358,* 484–493. (p. 643)

Ironson, G., Solomon, G. F., Balbin, E. G., O'Cleirigh, C., George, A., Kumar, M., Larson, D., & Woods, T. E. (2002). The Ironson-Woods spiritual/religiousness index is associated with long survival, health behaviors, less distress, and low cortisol in people with HIV/AIDS. *Annals of Behavioral Medicine, 24,* 34–48. (p. C-12)

Ishida, A., Mutoh, T., Ueyama, T., Brando, H., Masubuchi, S., Nakahara, D., Tsujimoto, G., & Okamura, H. (2005). Light activates the adrenal gland: Timing of gene expression and glucocorticoid release. *Cell Metabolism, 2,* 297–307. (p. 625)

Ito, T. A., Chiao, K. W., Devine P. G., Lorig, T. S., & Cacioppo, J. T. (2006). The influence of facial feedback on race bias. *Psychological Science, 17,* 256–261. (p. 383)

Ito, T. A., Miller, N., & Pollock, V. E. (1996). Alcohol and aggression: A meta-analysis on the moderating effects of inhibitory cues, triggering events, and self-focused attention. *Psychological Bulletin, 120,* 60–82. (p. 672)

Iverson, J. M., & Goldin-Meadow, S. (1998). Why people gesture when they speak. *Nature, 396,* 228. (p. D-5)

Iverson, J. M., & Goldin-Meadow, S. (2005). Gesture paves the way for language development. *Psychological Science, 16,* 367–371. (p. D-5)

Iyengar, S. S., & Lepper, M. R. (2000). When choice is demotivating: Can one desire too much of a good thing? *Journal of Personality and Social Psychology, 79,* 995–1006. (p. 506)

Izard, C. E. (1977). *Human emotions*. New York: Plenum Press. (pp. 381, 384)

Izard, C. E. (1994). Innate and universal facial expressions: Evidence from developmental and cross-cultural research. *Psychological Bulletin, 114,* 288–299. (p. 381)

Jablensky, A. (1999). Schizophrenia: Epidemiology. *Current Opinion in Psychiatry, 12,* 19–28. (p. 593)

Jackson, J. M., & Williams, K. D. (1988). Social loafing: A review and theoretical analysis. Unpublished manuscript, Fordham University. (p. 658)

Jackson, J. S., Brown, K. T., Brown, T. N., & Marks, B. (2001). Contemporary immigration policy orientations among dominant-group members in western Europe. *Journal of Social Issues, 57,* 431–456. (p. 665)

Jackson, L. A., & Gerard, D. A. (1996). Diurnal types, the "Big Five" personality factors and other personal characteristics. *Journal of Social Behavior and Personality, 11,* 273–283. (p. 499)

Jackson, S. W. (1992). The listening healer in the history of psychological healing. *American Journal Psychiatry, 149,* 1623–1632. (p. 626)

Jacobi, C., Hayward, C., deZwaan, M., Kraemer, H. C., & Agras, W. S. (2004). Coming to terms with risk factors for eating disorders: Application of risk terminology and suggestions for a general taxonomy. *Psychological Bulletin, 130,* 19–65. (p. 337)

Jacobs, B. L. (1987). How hallucinogenic drugs work. *American Scientist, 75,* 386–392. (p. 205)

Jacobs, B. L. (1994). Serotonin, motor activity, and depression-related disorders. *American Scientist, 82,* 456–463. (pp. 586, C-7)

Jacobs, B. L. (2004). Depression: The brain finally gets into the act. *Current Directions in Psychological Science, 13,* 103–106. (p. 631)

Jacobs, B., van Praag, H., & Gage, F. H. (2000). Adult brain neurogenesis and psychiatry: A novel theory of depression. *Molecular Psychiatry, 5,* 262–269. (p. 586)

Jacoby, L. L., Bishara, A. J., Hessels, S., & Toth, J. P. (2005). Aging, subjective experience, and cognitive control: Dramatic false remembering by older adults. *Journal of Experimental Psychology: General, 154,* 131–148. (p. 290)

Jacoby, L. L., & Rhodes, M. G. (2006). False remembering in the aged. *Current Directions in Psychological Science, 15,* 49–53. (p. 290)

Jacques, C., & Rossion, B. (2006). The speed of individual face categorization. *Psychological Science, 17,* 485–492. (p. 115)

Jacques-Tiura, A. J., Abbey, A., Parkhill, M. R., & Zawacki, T. (2007). Why do some men misperceive women's sexual intentions more frequently than others do? An application of the confluence model. *Personality and Social Psychology Bulletin, 33,* 1467–1480. (p. 645)

Jaffe, E. (2004, October). Peace in the Middle East may be impossible: Lee D. Ross on naive realism and conflict resolution. *APS Observer,* pp. 9–11. (p. 165)

James, K. (1986). Priming and social categorizational factors: Impact on awareness of emergency situations. *Personality and Social Psychology Bulletin, 12,* 462–467. (p. 276)

James, W. (1890). *The principles of psychology* (Vol. 2). New York: Holt. (pp. 61, 141, 196, 278, 294, 367, 511, 650)

James, W. (1902; reprinted 1958). *Varieties of religious experience.* New York: Mentor Books. (p. 389)

Jameson, D. (1985). Opponent-colors theory in light of physiological findings. In D. Ottoson & S. Zeki (Eds.), *Central and peripheral mechanisms of color vision.* New York: Macmillan. (p. 158)

Jamison, K. R. (1993). *Touched with fire: Manic-depressive illness and the artistic temperament.* New York: Free Press. (p. 581)

Jamison, K. R. (1995). *An unquiet mind.* New York: Knopf. (pp. 581, 632)

Janis, I. L. (1982). *Groupthink: Psychological studies of policy decisions and fiascoes.* Boston: Houghton Mifflin. (p. 660)

Janis, I. L. (1986). Problems of international crisis management in the nuclear age. *Journal of Social Issues, 42*(2), 201–220. (p. 304)

Janoff-Bulman, R., Timko, C., & Carli, L. L. (1985). Cognitive biases in blaming the victim. *Journal of Experimental Social Psychology, 21,* 161–177. (p. 670)

Javitt, D. C., & Coyle, J. T. (2004, January). Decoding schizophrenia. *Scientific American,* pp. 48–55. (p. 592)

Jeffery, R. W., Drewnowski, A., Epstein, L. H., Stunkard, A. J., Wilson, G. T., Wing, R. R., & Hill, D. R. (2000). Long-term maintenance of weight loss: Current status. *Health Psychology, 19,* No. 1 (Supplement), 5–16. (p. 347)

Jenkins, J. G., & Dallenbach, K. M. (1924). Obliviscence during sleep and waking. *American Journal of Psychology, 35,* 605–612. (pp. 282, 283)

Jenkins, J. M., & Astington, J. W. (1996). Cognitive factors and family structure associated with theory of mind development in young children. *Developmental Psychology, 32,* 70–78. (p. 422)

Jensen, A. R. (1980). *Bias in mental testing.* New York: The Free Press. (p. 538)

Jensen, A. R. (1983, August). The nature of the black-white difference on various psychometric tests: Spearman's hypothesis. Paper presented at the meeting of the American Psychological Association, Anaheim, CA. (p. 555)

Jensen, A. R. (1989). New findings on the intellectually gifted. *New Horizons, 30,* 73–80. (p. 531)

Jensen, A. R. (1998). *The g factor: The science of mental ability.* Westport, CT: Praeger/Greenwood. (p. 555)

Jensen, J. P., & Bergin, A. E. (1988). Mental health values of professional therapists: A national interdisciplinary survey. *Professional Psychology: Research and Practice, 19,* 290–297. (p. 626)

Jensen, P. S., & 20 others. (2007). 3-year follow-up of the NIMH MTA study. *Journal of the American Academy of Child and Adolescent Psychiatry, 46,* 989–1002. (p. 563)

Jepson, C., Krantz, D. H., & Nisbett, R. E. (1983). Inductive reasoning: Competence or skill. *The Behavioral and Brain Sciences, 3,* 494–501. (pp. 42, E-2)

Jessberger, S., Aimone, J. B., & Gage, F. H. (2008). Neurogenesis. In *Learning and memory: A comprehensive reference.* Oxford: Elsevier. (p. 83)

Job, D. E., Whalley, H. C., McIntosh, A. M., Owens, D. G. C., Johnstone, E. C., & Lawrie, S. M. (2006). Grey matter changes can improve the prediction of schizophrenia in subjects at high risk. *BMC Medicine, 4,* 29. (p. 593)

Johansson, P., Hall, L., Sikström, S., & Olsson, A. (2005). Failure to detect mismatches between intention and outcome in a simple decision task. *Science, 310,* 116–119. (p. 119)

John, O. P., & Srivastava, S. (1999). The Big Five trait taxonomy: History, measurement, and theoretical perspectives. In L. A. Pervin & O. P. John (Eds.), *Handbook of personality: Theory and research.* New York: Guilford. (p. 497)

Johnson, C. B., Stockdale, M. S., & Saal, F. E. (1991). Persistence of men's misperceptions of friendly cues across a variety of interpersonal encounters. *Psychology of Women Quarterly, 15,* 463–475. (p. 106)

Johnson, D. F. (1997). Margaret Floy Washburn. *Psychology of Women Newsletter,* pp. 17, 22. (p. 6)

Johnson, D. L., Wiebe, J. S., Gold, S. M., Andreasen, N. C., Hichwa, R. D., Watkins, G. L., & Ponto, L. L. B. (1999). Cerebral blood flow and personality: A Positron Emission Tomography study. *American Journal of Psychiatry, 156,* 252–257. (p. 495)

Johnson, E. J., & Goldstein, D. (2003). Do defaults save lives? *Science, 302,* 1338–1339. (p. 312)

Johnson, J. A. (2007, June 26). Not so situational. Commentary on the SPSP listserv (spsp-discuss The status of subjacency in the acquisition of a second language. *Cognition, 39,* 215–258. (p. 648)

Johnson, J. G., Cohen, P., Kotler, L., Kasen, S., & Brook, J. S. (2002). Psychiatric disorders associated with risk for the development of eating disorders during adolescence and early adulthood. *Journal of Consulting and Clinical Psychology, 70,* 1119–1128. (p. 337)

Johnson, J. S., & Newport, E. L. (1991). Critical period affects on universal properties of language: The status of subjacency in the acquisition of a second language. *Cognition, 39,* 215–258. (pp. 318, 319)

Johnson, K. (2008, January 29). For many of USA's inmates, crime runs in the family. *USA Today,* pp. 1A, 2A. (p. 598)

Johnson, L. C. (2001, July 10). The declining terrorist threat. *New York Times* (www.nytimes.com). (p. 308)

Johnson, M. E., & Hauck, C. (1999). Beliefs and opinions about hypnosis held by the general public: A systematic evaluation. *American Journal of Clinical Hypnosis, 42,* 10–20. (p. 193)

Johnson, M. H. (1992). Imprinting and the development of face recognition: From chick to man. *Current Directions in Psychological Science, 1,* 52–55. (p. 427)

Johnson, M. H., & Morton, J. (1991). *Biology and cognitive development: The case of face recognition.* Oxford: Blackwell Publishing. (p. 415)

Johnson, R. E., Chang, C-H., & Lord, R. G. (2006). Moving from cognition to behavior: What the research says. *Psychological Bulletin, 132,* 381–415. (p. B-11)

Johnson, S. C. & 13 others. (2006). Activation of brain regions vulnerable to Alzheimer's disease: The effect of mild cognitive impairment. *Neurobiology of Aging, 27,* 1604–1612. (p. 460)

Johnson, S. K. (2008). *Medically unexplained illness: Gender and biopsychosocial implications.* Washington, DC: American Psychological Association. (p. 576)

Johnson, W., McGue, M., & Krueger, R. F. (2005). Personality stability in late adulthood: A behavioral genetic analysis. *Journal of Personality, 73,* 523–552. (p. 473)

Johnston, L. D., O'Malley, P. M., Bachman, J. G., & Schulenberg, J. E. (2007). *Monitoring the Future national results on adolescent drug use: Overview of key findings, 2006.* Bethesda, MD: National Institute on Drug Abuse. (p. 209)

Johnston, L. D., O'Malley, P. M., Bachman, J. G., & Schulenberg, J. E. (2009). *Monitoring the Future national results on adolescent drug use: Overview of key findings, 2008* (NIH Publication No. 09-7401). Bethesda, MD: National Institute on Drug Abuse. (pp. 204, 208)

Johnstone, E. C., Ebmeier, K. P., Miller, P., Owens, D. G. C., & Lawrie, S. M. (2005). Predicting schizophrenia: Findings from the Edinburgh High-Risk Study. *British Journal of Psychiatry, 186,* 18–25. (p. 596)

Joiner, T. E., Jr. (1999). The clustering and contagion of suicide. *Current Directions in Psychological Science, 8,* 89–92. (p. 651)

Joiner, T. (2006). *Why people die by suicide.* Boston, MA: Harvard University Press. (p. 585)

Jolly, A. (2007). The social origin of mind. *Science, 317,* 1326. (p. D-1)

Jonas, E., & Fischer, P. (2006). Terror management and religion: Evidence that intrinsic religiousness mitigates worldview defense following mortality salience. *Journal of Personality and Social Psychology, 91,* 553–567. (p. 489)

Jones, A. C., & Gosling, S. D. (2005). Temperament and personality in dogs (*Canis familiaris*): A review and evaluation of past research. *Applied Animal Behaviour Science, 95*, 1–53. (p. 496)

Jones, J. M. (2003, February 12). Fear of terrorism increases amidst latest warning. *Gallup News Service* (www.gallup.com/releases/pr030212.asp). (p. 570)

Jones, J. M. (2007, July 25). Latest Gallup update shows cigarette smoking near historical lows. *Gallup Poll News Service* (poll.gallup.com). (p. 204)

Jones, J. T., Pelham, B. W., Carvallo, M., & Mirenberg, M. C. (2004). How do I love thee? Let me count the Js: Implicit egotism and interpersonal attraction. *Journal of Personality and Social Psychology, 87*, 665–683. (p. 678)

Jones, L. (2000, December). Skeptics New Year quiz. *Skeptical Briefs*, p. 11. (p. 499)

Jones, M. C. (1924). A laboratory study of fear: The case of Peter. *Journal of Genetic Psychology, 31*, 308–315. (p. 611)

Jones, M. V., Paull, G. C., & Erskine, J. (2002). The impact of a team's aggressive reputation on the decisions of association football referees. *Journal of Sports Sciences, 20*, 991–1000. (p. 165)

Jones, S. S. (2007). Imitation in infancy: The development of mimicry. *Psychological Science, 18*, 593–599. (p. 243)

Jones, S. S., Collins, K., & Hong, H-W. (1991). An audience effect on smile production in 10-month-old infants. *Psychological Science, 2*, 45–49. (p. 382)

Jones, W. H., Carpenter, B. N., & Quintana, D. (1985). Personality and interpersonal predictors of loneliness in two cultures. *Journal of Personality and Social Psychology, 48*, 1503–1511. (p. 43)

Jonides, J., Lewis, R. L., Nee, D. E., Lustig, C. A., Berman, M. G., & Moore, K. S. (2008). The mind and brain of short-term memory. *Annual Review of Psychology, 59*, 193–224. (p. 267)

Jorm, A. F., Korten, A. E., & Henderson, A. S. (1987). The prevalence of dementia: A quantitative integration of the literature. *Acta Psychiatrica Scandinavica, 76*, 465–479. (p. 460)

Joseph, J. (2001). Separated twins and the genetics of personality differences: A critique. *American Journal of Psychology, 114*, 1–30. (p. 99)

Judge, T. A., Thoresen, C. J., Bono, J. E., & Patton, G. K. (2001). The job satisfaction/job performance relationship: A qualitative and quantitative review. *Psychological Bulletin, 127*, 376–407. (p. B-8)

Juffer, F., & van Ijzendoorn, M. H. (2007). Adoptees do not lack self-esteem: A meta-analysis of studies on self-esteem of transracial, international, and domestic adoptees. *Psychological Bulletin, 133*, 1067–1083. (p. 433)

Jung, R. E., & Haier, R. J. (2007). The Parieto-Frontal Integration Theory (P-FIT) of intelligence: Converging neuroimaging evidence. *Behavioral and Brain Sciences, 30*, 135–187. (p. 530)

Jung-Beeman, M., Bowden, E. M., Haberman, J., Frymiare, J. L., Arambel-Liu, S., Greenblatt, R., Reber, P. J., & Kounios, J. (2004). Neural activity when people solve verbal problems with insight. *PloS Biology 2*(4), e111. (p. 300)

Kagan, J. (1976). Emergent themes in human development. *American Scientist, 64*, 186–196. (p. 429)

Kagan, J. (1984). *The nature of the child*. New York: Basic Books. (p. 426)

Kagan, J. (1995). On attachment. *Harvard Review of Psychiatry, 3*, 104–106. (p. 428)

Kagan, J. (1998). *Three seductive ideas*. Cambridge, MA: Harvard University Press. (pp. 110, 473)

Kagan, J., Arcus, D., Snidman, N., Feng, W. Y., Hendler, J., & Greene, S. (1994). Reactivity in infants: A cross-national comparison. *Developmental Psychology, 30*, 342–345. (p. 428)

Kagan, J., Lapidus, D. R., & Moore, M. (December, 1978). Infant antecedents of cognitive functioning: A longitudinal study. *Child Development, 49*(4), 1005–1023. (p. 473)

Kagan, J., & Snidman, N. (2004). *The long shadow of temperament*. Cambridge, MA: Belknap Press. (p. 428)

Kagan, J., Snidman, N., & Arcus, D. M. (1992). Initial reactions to unfamiliarity. *Current Directions in Psychological Science, 1*, 171–174. (p. 428)

Kahlor, L., & Morrison, D. (2007). Television viewing and rape myth acceptance among college women. *Sex Roles, 56*, 729–739. (p. 674)

Kahneman, D. (1985, June). Quoted by K. McKean, Decisions, decisions. *Discover*, pp. 22–31. (p. 621)

Kahneman, D. (1999). Assessments of objective happiness: A bottom-up approach. In D. Kahneman, E. Diener, & N. Schwartz (Eds.), *Understanding well-being: Scientific perspectives on enjoyment and suffering.* New York: Russell Sage Foundation. (p. 145)

Kahneman, D. (2005, February 10). Are you happy now? *Gallup Management Journal* interview (www.gmj.gallup.com). (p. 394)

Kahneman, D. (2005, January 13). What were they thinking? Q&A with Daniel Kahneman. *Gallup Management Journal* (gmj.gallup.com). (pp. 305, 390)

Kahneman, D., Fredrickson, B. L., Schreiber, C. A., & Redelmeier, D. A. (1993). When more pain is preferred to less: Adding a better end. *Psychological Science, 4*, 401–405. (p. 145)

Kahneman, D., Krueger, A. B., Schkade, D. A., Schwarz, N., & Stone, A. A. (2004). A survey method for characterizing daily life experience: The day reconstruction method. *Science, 306*, 1776–1780. (pp. 182, 390)

Kahneman, D., & Renshon, J. (2007, January/February). Why hawks win. *Foreign Policy* (www.foreignpolicy.com). (p. 514)

Kahneman, D., & Tversky, A. (1972). Subjective probability: A judgment of representativeness. *Cognitive Psychology, 3*, 430–454. (p. 33)

Kail, R. (1991). Developmental change in speed of processing during childhood and adolescence. *Psychological Bulletin, 109*, 490–501. (p. 459)

Kaiser. (2001). *Inside-out: A report on the experiences of lesbians, gays and bisexuals in America and the public's views on issues and policies related to sexual orientation.* The Henry J. Kaiser Foundation (www.kff.org). (p. 359)

Kaiser Family Foundation. (2003, October 28). *New study finds children age zero to six spend as much time with TV, computers and video games as playing outside.* www.kff.org/entmedia/entmedia102803nr.cfm. (p. 30)

Kamarck, T., & Jennings, J. R. (1991). Biobehavioral factors in sudden cardiac death. *Psychological Bulletin, 109*, 42–75. (p. 402)

Kamena, M. (1998). Repressed/false childhood sexual abuse memories: A survey of therapists. Paper presented to the Sexual Abuse memories Symposium at the American Psychological Association convention. (p. 290)

Kamil, A. C., & Cheng, K. (2001). Way-finding and landmarks: The multiple-bearings hypothesis. *Journal of Experimental Biology, 204*, 103–113. (p. 272)

Kaminski, J., Call, J., & Fischer, J. (2004). Word learning in a domestic dog: Evidence for 'fast mapping.' *Science, 304*, 1682–1683. (p. D-3)

Kanaya, T., Scullin, M. H., & Ceci, S. J. (2003). The Flynn effect and U.S. policies: The impact of rising IQ scores on American society via mental retardation diagnoses. *American Psychologist, 58*, 778–790. (p. 542)

Kanazawa, S. (2004). General intelligence as a domain-specific adaptation. *Psychological Review, 111*, 512–523. (p. 525)

Kanazawa, S. (2006). Mind the gap . . . in intelligence: Re-examining the relationship between intelligence and health. *British Journal of Health Psychology, 11*, 623–642. (p. C-2)

Kandel, D. B., & Raveis, V. H. (1989). Cessation of illicit drug use in young adulthood. *Archives of General Psychiatry, 46*, 109–116. (p. 210)

Kandel, E. R., & Schwartz, J. H. (1982). Molecular biology of learning: Modulation of transmitter release. *Science, 218*, 433–443. (p. 268)

Kane, M. J., Brown, L. H., McVay, J. C., Silvia, P. J., Myin-Germeys, I., & Kwapil, T. R. (2007). For whom the mind wanders, and when: An experience-sampling study of working memory and executive control in daily life. *Psychological Science, 18*, 614–621. (p. 258)

Kaplan, A. (2004). Exploring the gene-environment nexus in anorexia, bulimia. *Psychiatric Times, 21* (www.psychiatrictimes.com/p040801b.html). (p. 338)

Kaplan, H. I., & Saddock, B. J. (Eds.). (1989). *Comprehensive textbook of psychiatry, V.* Baltimore, MD: Williams and Wilkins. (p. 629)

Kaplan, R. M., & Kronick, R. G. (2006). Marital status and longevity in the United States population. *Journal of Epidemiology and Community Health, 60*, 760–765. (p. C-4)

Kaprio, J., Koskenvuo, M., & Rita, H. (1987). Mortality after bereavement: A prospective study of 95,647 widowed persons. *American Journal of Public Health, 77*, 283–287. (p. 401)

Kaptchuk, T. J., Stason, W. B., Davis, R. B., Legedza, A. R. T., Schnyer, R. N., Kerr, C. E., Stone, D. A., Nam, B. H., Kirsch, I., & Goldman, R. H. (2006). Sham device v inert pill: Randomised controlled trial of two placebo treatments. *British Medical Journal, 332*, 391–397. (p. 146)

Karacan, I., Goodenough, D. R., Shapiro, A., & Starker, S. (1966). Erection cycle during sleep in relation to dream anxiety. *Archives of General Psychiatry, 15*, 183–189. (p. 180)

Karau, S. J., & Williams, K. D. (1993). Social loafing: A meta-analytic review and theoretical integration. *Journal of Personality and Social Psychology, 65*, 681–706. (p. 658)

Kark, J. D., Shemi, G., Friedlander, Y., Martin, O., Manor, O., & Blondheim, S. H. (1996). Does religious observance promote health? Mortality in secular vs. religious kibbutzim in Israel. *American Journal of Public Health, 86*, 341–346. (p. C-11)

Karni, A., Meyer, G., Rey-Hipolito, C., Jezzard, P., Adams, M. M., Turner, R., & Ungerleider, L. G. (1998). The acquisition of skilled motor performance: Fast and slow experience-driven changes in primary motor cortex. *Proceedings of the National Academy of Sciences, 95*, 861–868. (p. 443)

Karni, A., & Sagi, D. (1994). Dependence on REM sleep for overnight improvement of perceptual skills. *Science, 265*, 679–682. (p. 190)

Karno, M., Golding, J. M., Sorenson, S. B., & Burnam, A. (1988). The epidemiology of obsessive-compulsive disorder in five US communities. *Archives of General Psychiatry, 45*, 1094–1099. (p. 571)

Karpicke, J. D., & Roediger, H. L. III, (2008). The critical importance of retrieval for learning. *Science, 319*, **966–968.** (p. 260)

Karremans, J. C., Stroebe, W., & Claus, J. (2006). Beyond Vicary's fantasies: The impact of subliminal priming and brand choice. *Journal of Experimental Social Psychology, 42*, 792–798. (p. 122)

Kasen, S., Chen, H., Sneed, J., Crawford, T., & Cohen, P. (2006). Social role and birth cohort influences on gender-linked personality traits in women: A 20-year longitudinal analysis. *Journal of Personality and Social Psychology, 91*, 944–958. (p. 438)

Kashdan, T. B., & Steger, M. F. (2006). Expanding the topography of social anxiety: An experience-sampling assessment of positive emotions, positive events, and emotion suppression. *Psychologial Science, 17*, 120–128. (p. 570)

Kashima, Y., Siegal, M., Tanaka, K., & Kashima, E. S. (1992). Do people believe behaviours are consistent with attitudes? Towards a cultural psychology of attribution processes. *British Journal of Social Psychology, 31*, 111–124. (p. 517)

Kasser, T. (2000). Two version of the American dream: Which goals and values make for a high quality of life? In E. Diener (Ed.), *Advances in quality of life theory and research.* Dordrecth, Netherlands: Kluwer. (p. 393)

Kasser, T. (2002). *The high price of materialism.* Cambridge, MA: MIT Press. (p. 393)

Kaufman, A. S., Reynolds, C. R., & McLean, J. E. (1989). Age and WAIS-R intelligence in a national sample of adults in the 20- to 74-year age range: A cross-sectional analysis with educational level controlled. *Intelligence, 13*, 235–253. (p. 464)

Kaufman, J., & Zigler, E. (1987). Do abused children become abusive parents? *American Journal of Orthopsychiatry, 57*, 186–192. (p. 430)

Kaufman, J. C., & Baer, J. (2002). I bask in dreams of suicide: Mental illness, poetry, and women. *Review of General Psychology, 6*, 271–286. (p. 581)

Kaufman, L., & Kaufman, J. H. (2000). Explaining the moon illusion. *Proceedings of the National Academy of Sciences, 97*, 500–505. (p. 157)

Kavsek, M. (2004). Predicting later IQ from infant visual habituation and dishabituation: A meta-analysis. *Journal of Applied Developmental Psychology, 25*, 369–393. (p. 540)

Kayser, C. (2007, April/May). Listening with your eyes. *Scientific American Mind*, pp. 24–29. (p. 148)

Kazdin, A. E., & Benjet, C. (2003). Spanking children: Evidence and issues. *Current Directions in Psychological Science, 12*, 99–103. (p. 234)

Keesey, R. E., & Corbett, S. W. (1983). Metabolic defense of the body weight set-point. In A. J. Stunkard & E. Stellar (Eds.), *Eating and its disorders.* New York: Raven Press. (p. 335)

Keith, S. W. & 19 others. (2006). Putative contributors to the secular increase in obesity: Exploring the roads less traveled. *International Journal of Obesity, 30*, 1585–1594. (p. 344)

Keller, J. (2007, March 9). As football players get bigger, more of them risk a dangerous sleep disorder. *Chronicle of Higher Education*, pp. A43–44. (p. 187)

Keller, M. B., McCullough, J. P., Klein, D. N., Arnow, B., Dunner, D. L., Gelenberg, A. J., Markowitz, J. C., Nemeroff, C. B., Russell, J. M., Thase, M. E., Trivedi, M. H., & Zajecka J. (2000), A comparison of nefazodone, the cognitive behavioral-analysis system of psychotherapy, and their combination for the treatment of chronic depression. *New England Journal of Medicine, 342*, 1462–1470. (p. 631)

Keller, M. C., Neale, M. C., & Kendler, K. S. (2007). Association of different adverse life events with distinct patterns of depressive symptoms. *American Journal of Psychiatry, 164*, 1521–1529. (p. 583)

Kellerman, J., Lewis, J., & Laird, J. D. (1989). Looking and loving: The effects of mutual gaze on feelings of romantic love. *Journal of Research in Personality, 23*, 145–161. (p. 377)

Kellermann, A. L. (1997). Comment: Gunsmoke—changing public attitudes toward smoking and firearms. *American Journal of Public Health, 87*, 910–913. (p. 671)

Kellermann, A. L., Rivara, F. P., Rushforth, N. B., Banton, H. G., Feay, D. T., Francisco, J. T., Locci, A. B., Prodzinski, J., Hackman, B. B., & Somes, G. (1993). Gun ownership as a risk factor for homicide in the home. *New England Journal of Medicine, 329*, 1084–1091. (p. 671)

Kellermann, A. L., Somes, G. Rivara, F. P., Lee, R. K., & Banton, J. G. (1998). Injuries and deaths due to firearms in the home. *Journal of Trauma, 45*, 263–267. (p. 671)

Kelley, J., & De Graaf, N. D. (1997). National context, parental socialization, and religious belief: Results from 15 nations. *American Sociological Review, 62*, 639–659. (p. 100)

Kelling, S. T., & Halpern, B. P. (1983). Taste flashes: Reaction times, intensity, and quality. *Science, 219*, 412–414. (p. 147)

Kellner, C. H., & 15 others. (2005). Relief of expressed suicidal intent by ECT: A consortium for research in ECT study. *American Journal of Psychiatry, 162*, 977–982. (p. 633)

Kellner, C. H. & 16 others. (2006). Continuation electroconvulsive therapy vs. pharmacotherapy for relapse prevention in major depression: A multisite study from the Consortium for Research in Electroconvulsive Therapy (CORE). *Archives of Gneeral Psychiatry, 63*, 1337–1344. (p. 633)

Kelly, A. E. (2000). Helping construct desirable identities: A self-presentational view of psychotherapy. *Psychological Bulletin, 126*, 475–494. (p. 615)

Kelly, D. J., Quinn, P. C., Slater, A. M., Lee, K., Ge, L., & Pascalis, O. (2007). The other-race effect develops during infancy: Evidence of perceptual narrowing. *Psychological Science, 18*, 1084–1089. (p. 669)

Kelly, I. W. (1997). Modern astrology: A critique. *Psychological Reports, 81*, 1035–1066. (p. 498)

Kelly, I. W. (1998). Why astrology doesn't work. *Psychological Reports, 82*, 527–546. (p. 498)

Kelly, T. A. (1990). The role of values in psychotherapy: A critical review of process and outcome effects. *Clinical Psychology Review, 10*, 171–186. (p. 626)

Kempe, R. S., & Kempe, C. C. (1978). *Child abuse.* Cambridge, MA: Harvard University Press. (p. 430)

Kempermann, G., Kuhn, H. G., & Gage, F. H. (May, 1998). Experience-induced neurogenesis in the senescent dentate gyrus. *Journal of Neuroscience, 18*(9), 3206–3212. (p. 459)

Kendall-Tackett, K. A. (Ed.) (2004). *Health consequences of abuse in the family: A clinical guide for evidence-based practice.* Washington, DC: American Psychological Association. (p. 431)

Kendall-Tackett, K. A., Williams, L. M., & Finkelhor, D. (1993). Impact of sexual abuse on children: A review and synthesis of recent empirical studies. *Psychological Bulletin, 113*, 164–180. (pp. 291, 431)

Kendler, K. S. (1996). Parenting: A genetic-epidemiologic perspective. *The American Journal of Psychiatry, 153*, 11–20. (p. 434)

Kendler, K. S. (1997). Social support: A genetic-epidemiologic analysis. *American Journal of Psychiatry, 154*, 1398–1404. (p. 504)

Kendler, K. S. (1998, January). Major depression and the environment: A psychiatric genetic perspective. *Pharmacopsychiatry, 31*(1), 5–9. (p. 583)

Kendler, K. S., Gardner, C. O., & Prescott, C. A. (2006). Toward a comprehensive developmental model for major depression in men. *American Journal of Psychiatry, 163*, 115–124. (p. 582)

Kendler, K. S., Gatz, M., Gardner, C. O., & Pedersen, N. L. (2006). A Swedish national twin study of lifetime major depression. *American Journal of Psychiatry, 163*, 109–114. (p. 583)

Kendler, K. S., Jacobson, K. C., Myers, J., & Prescott, C. A. (2002a). Sex differences in genetic and environmental risk factors for irrational fears and phobias. *Psychological Medicine, 32*, 209–217. (p. 575)

Kendler, K. S., Karkowski, L. M., & Prescott, C. A. (1999). Fears and phobias: Reliability and heritability. *Psychological Medicine, 29*, 539–553. (p. 575)

Kendler, K. S., Myers, J., & Prescott, C. A. (2002b). The etiology of phobias: An evaluation of the stress-diathesis model. *Archives of General Psychiatry, 59,* 242–248. (p. 575)

Kendler, K. S., Neale, M. C., Kessler, R. C., Heath, A. C., & Eaves, L. J. (1992). Generalized anxiety disorder in women: A population-based twin study. *Archives of General Psychiatry, 49,* 267–272. (p. 575)

Kendler, K. S., Neale, M. C., Thornton, L. M., Aggen, S. H., Gilman, S. E., & Kessler, R. C. (2002). Cannabis use in the last year in a U.S. national sample of twin and sibling pairs. *Psychological Medicine, 32,* 551–554. (p. 208)

Kendler, K. S., Thornton, L. M., & Gardner, C. O. (2001). Genetic risk, number of previous depressive episodes, and stressful life events in predicting onset of major depression. *American Journal of Psychiatry, 158,* 582–586. (p. 582)

Kenrick, D. T., & Funder, D. C. (1988). Profiting from controversy: Lessons from the person-situation debate. *American Psychologist, 43,* 23–34. (p. 501)

Kenrick, D. T., & Gutierres, S. E. (1980). Contrast effects and judgments of physical attractiveness: When beauty becomes a social problem. *Journal of Personality and Social Psychology, 38,* 131–140. (p. 352)

Kenrick, D. T., Gutierres, S. E., & Goldberg, L. L. (1989). Influence of popular erotica on judgments of strangers and mates. *Journal of Experimental Social Psychology, 25,* 159–167. (p. 352)

Kenrick, D. T., Nieuweboer, S., & Bunnk, A. P. (2009). Universal mechanisms and cultural diversity: Replacing the blank slate with a coloring book. In M. Schaller, S. Heine, A. Norenzayan, T. Yamagishi, & T. Kameda (Eds.), *Evolution, culture, and the human mind.* Mahwah, NJ: Erlbaum. (pp. 106, 441)

Kensinger, E. A. (2007). Negative emotion enhances memory accuracy: Behavioral and neuroimaging evidence. *Current Directions in Psychological Science, 16,* 213–218. (p. 270)

Keough, K. A., Zimbardo, P. G., & Boyd, J. N. (1999). Who's smoking, drinking, and using drugs? Time perspective as a predictor of substance use. *Basic and Applied Social Psychology, 2,* 149–164. (p. 481)

Kernis, M. H. (2003). Toward a conceptualization of optimal self-esteem. *Psychological Inquiry, 14,* 1–26. (p. 515)

Kerr, N. L., & Bruun, S. E. (1983). Dispensability of member effort and group motivation losses: Free-rider effects. *Journal of Personality and Social Psychology, 44,* 78–94. (p. 658)

Kessler, M., & Albee, G. (1975). Primary prevention. *Annual Review of Psychology, 26,* 557–591. (p. 638)

Kessler, R. C. (2000). Posttraumatic stress disorder: The burden to the individual and to society. *Journal of Clinical Psychiatry, 61*(suppl. 5), 4–12. (p. 572)

Kessler, R. C. (2001). Epidemiology of women and depression. *Journal of Affective Disorders, 74,* 5–1. (p. 587)

Kessler, R. C., Akiskal, H. S., Ames, M., Birnbaum, H., Greenberg, P., Hirschfeld, R. M. A., Jin, R., Merikangas, K. R., Simon, G. E., & Wang, P. S. (2006). Prevalence and effects of mood disorders on work performance in a nationally representative sample of U.S. workers. *American Journal of Psychiatry, 163,* 1561–1568. (p. 581)

Kessler, R. C., Berglund, P., Demler, O., Jin, R., Merikangos, K. R. & Walters, E. E. (2005). Lifetime prevalence and age-of-onset distributions of DSM-IV disorders in the National Comorbidity Survey Replication. *Archives of General Psychiatry, 62,* 593–602. (pp. 566, 599)

Kessler, R. C., Foster, C., Joseph, J., Ostrow, D., Wortman, C., Phair, J., & Chmiel, J. (1991). Stressful life events and symptom onset in HIV infection. *American Journal of Psychiatry, 148,* 733–738. (p. 406)

Kessler, R. C., Soukup, J., Davis, R. B., Foster, D. F., Wilkey, S. A., Van Rompay, M. I., & Eisenberg, D. M. (2001). The use of complementary and alternative therapies to treat anxiety and depression in the United States. *American Journal of Psychiatry, 158,* 289–294. (p. 623)

Keynes, M. (1980, December 20/27). Handel's illnesses. *The Lancet,* pp. 1354–1355. (p. 581)

Keys, A., Brozek, J., Henschel, A., Mickelsen, O., & Taylor, H. L. (1950). *The biology of human starvation.* Minneapolis: University of Minnesota Press. (p. 332)

Kiecolt-Glaser, J. K., & Glaser, R. (1995). Psychoneuroimmunology and health consequences: Data and shared mechanisms. *Psychosomatic Medicine, 57,* 269–274. (p. 405)

Kiecolt-Glaser, J. K., Loving, T. J., Stowell, J. R., Malarkey, W. B., Lemeshow, S., Dickinson, S. L., & Glaser, R. (2005). Hostile marital interactions, proinflammatory cytokine production, and wound healing. *Archives of General Psychiatry, 62,* 1377–1384. (p. 404)

Kiecolt-Glaser, J. K., & Newton, T. L. (2001). Marriage and health: His and hers. *Psychological Bulletin, 127,* 472–503. (p. C-4)

Kiecolt-Glaser, J. K., Page, G. G., Marucha, P. T., MacCallum, R. C., & Glaser, R. (1998). Psychological influences on surgical recovery: Perspectives from psychoneuroimmunology. *American Psychologist, 53,* 1209–1218. (p. 404)

Kihlstrom, J. F. (1990). The psychological unconscious. In L. A. Pervin (Ed.), *Handbook of personality: Theory and research.* New York: Guilford Press. (pp. 284, 488)

Kihlstrom, J. F. (1994). The social construction of memory. Paper presented at the American Psychological Society convention. (p. 285)

Kihlstrom, J. F. (1997, November 11). Freud as giant pioneer on whose shoulders we should stand. Social Psychology listserv posting (spsp A unified theory of a will-o'-the-wisp. *Behavioral and Brain Sciences, 29,* 523. (p. 490)

Kihlstrom, J. F. (2005). Dissociative disorders. *Annual Review of Clinical Psychology, 1,* 227–253. (p. 579)

Kihlstrom, J. F. (2006). Repression: A unified theory of a will-o'-the-wisp. *Behavioral and Brain Sciences, 29,* 523. (p. 488)

Kihlstrom, J. F., & McConkey, K. M. (1990). William James and hypnosis: A centennial reflection. *Psychological Science, 1,* 174–177. (p. 196)

Killeen, P. R., & Nash, M. R. (2003). The four causes of hypnosis. *Internal Journal of Clinical and Experimental Hypnosis, 51,* 195–231. (p. 196)

Kim, B. S. K., Ng, G. F., & Ahn, A. J. (2005). Effects of client expectation for counseling success, client-counselor worldview match, and client adherence to Asian and European American cultural values on counseling process with Asian Americans. *Journal of Counseling Psychology, 52,* 67–76. (p. 627)

Kim, H., & Markus, H. R. (1999). Deviance or uniqueness, harmony or conformity? A cultural analysis. *Journal of Personality and Social Psychology, 77,* 785–800. (p. 517)

Kim, K. H. S., Relkin, N. R., Lee, K-M., & Hirsch, J. (1997). Distinct cortical areas associated with native and second languages. *Nature, 388,* 171–174. (p. 80)

Kimata, H. (2001). Effect of humor on allergen-induced wheal reactions. *Journal of the American Medical Association, 285,* 737. (p. C-3)

Kimble, G. A. (1956). *Principles of general psychology.* New York: Ronald. (p. 223)

Kimble, G. A. (1981). *Biological and cognitive constraints on learning.* Washington, DC: American Psychological Association. (p. 223)

Kimmel, A. J. (1998). In defense of deception. *American Psychologist, 53,* 803–805. (p. 45)

King, L. A., Hicks, J. A., Krull, J. L., & Del Gaiso, A. K. (2006). Positive affect and the experience of meaning in life. *Journal of Personality and Social Psychology, 90,* 179–196. (p. 389)

King, R. N., & Koehler, D. J. (2000). Illusory correlations in graphological interference. *Journal of Experimental Psychology: Applied, 6,* 336–348. (p. 498)

Kinnier, R. T., & Metha, A. T. (1989). Regrets and priorities at three stages of life. *Counseling and Values, 33,* 182–193. (p. 468)

Kirby, D. (2002). Effective approaches to reducing adolescent unprotected sex, pregnancy, and childbearing. *Journal of Sex Research, 39,* 51–57. (p. 354)

Kirkpatrick, B., Fenton, W. S., Carpenter, Jr., W. T., & Marder, S. R. (2006). The NIMH-MATRICS consensus statement on negative symptoms. *Schizophrenia Bulletin, 32,* 214–219. (p. 592)

Kirkpatrick, L. (1999). Attachment and religious representations and behavior. In J. Cassidy & P. R. Shaver (Eds.), *Handbook of attachment.* New York: Guilford. (p. 427)

Kirmayer, L. J., & Sartorius, N. (2007). Cultural models and somatic syndromes. *Psychosomatic Medicine, 69,* 832–840. (p. 576)

Kirsch, I. (1996). Hypnotic enhancement of cognitive-behavioral weight loss treatments: Another meta-reanalysis. *Journal of Consulting and Clinical Psychology, 64,* 517–519. (p. 194)

Kirsch, I., & Braffman, W. (2001). Imaginative suggestibility and hypnotizability. *Current Directions in Psychological Science, 10,* 57–61. (p. 192)

Kirsch, I., Deacon, B. J., Huedo-Medina, T. B., Scoboria, A., Moore, T. J., & Johnson, B. T. (2008) Initial severity and antidepressant benefits: A meta-analysis of data submitted to the Food and Drug Administration. *Public Library of Science Medicine, 5,* e45. (p. 631)

Kirsch, I., & Lynn, S. J. (1995). The altered state of hypnosis. *American Psychologist, 50,* 846–858. (p. 194)

Kirsch, I., Moore, T. J., Scoboria, A., & Nicholls, S. S. (2002, July 15). New study finds little difference between effects of antidepressants and placebo. *Prevention and Treatment* (journals.apa.org/prevention). (p. 631)

Kirsch, I., & Sapirstein, G. (1998). Listening to Prozac but hearing placebo: A meta-analysis of antidepressant medication. *Prevention and Treatment, 1,* posted June 26 at (journals.apa.org/prevention/volume1). (pp. 35, 631)

Kisley, M. A., Wood, S., & Burrows, C. L. (2007). Looking at the sunny side of life: Age-related change in an event-related potential measure of the negativity bias. *Psychological Science, 18,* 838–843. (p. 469)

Kisor, H. (1990). *What's that pig outdoors.* New York: Hill and Wang. (p. 139)

Kitayama, S., Ishii, K., Imada, T., Takemura, K., & Ramaswamy, J. (2006). Voluntary settlement and the spirit of independence: Evidence from Japan's "northern frontier." *Journal of Personality and Social Psychology, 91,* 369–384. (p. 517)

Kitts, R. L. (2005). Gay adolescents and suicide: Understanding the association. *Adolescence, 40,* 621–628. (p. 355)

Kivimaki, M., Leino-Arjas, P., Luukkonen, R., Rihimaki, H., & Kirjonen, J. (2002). Work stress and risk of cardiovascular mortality: Prospective cohort study of industrial employees. *British Medical Journal, 325,* 857. (p. C-2)

Klayman, J., & Ha, Y-W. (1987). Confirmation, disconfirmation, and information in hypothesis testing. *Psychological Review, 94,* 211–228. (p. 302)

Klein, D. N., & 16 others. (2003). Therapeutic alliance in depression treatment: Controlling for prior change and patient characteristics. *Journal of Consulting and Clinical Psychology, 71,* 997–1006. (p. 626)

Klein, E., Kreinin, I., Chistyakov, A., Koren, D., Mecz, L., Marmur, S., Ben-Shachar, D., & Feinsod, M. (1999). Therapeutic efficacy of right prefrontal slow repetitive transcranial magnetic stimulation in major depression. *Archives of General psychiatry, 56,* 315–320. (p. 634)

Kleinfeld, J. (1998). *The myth that schools shortchange girls: Social science in the service of deception.* Washington, DC: Women's Freedom Network. Available from ERIC, Document ED423210, and via www.uaf.edu/northern/schools/myth.html. (p. 551)

Kleinke, C. L. (1986). Gaze and eye contact: A research review. *Psychological Bulletin, 1000,* 78–100. (p. 377)

Kleinmuntz, B., & Szucko, J. J. (1984). A field study of the fallibility of polygraph lie detection. *Nature, 308,* 449–450. (p. 373)

Kleitman, N. (1960, November). Patterns of dreaming. *Scientific American,* pp. 82–88. (p. 178)

Klemm, W. R. (1990). Historical and introductory perspectives on brainstem-mediated behaviors. In W. R. Klemm & R. P. Vertes (Eds.), *Brainstem mechanisms of behavior.* New York: Wiley. (p. 69)

Kline, D., & Schieber, F. (1985). Vision and aging. In J. E. Birren & K. W. Schaie (Eds.), *Handbook of the psychology of aging.* New York: Van Nostrand Reinhold. (p. 458)

Kline, G. H., Stanley, S. M., Markman, J. H., Olmos-Gallo, P. A., St. Peters, M., Whitton, S. W., & Prado, L. M. (2004). Timing is everything: Pre-engagement cohabitation and increased risk for poor marital outcomes. *Journal of Family Psychology, 18,* 311–318. (p. 467)

Klineberg, O. (1938). Emotional expression in Chinese literature. *Journal of Abnormal and Social Psychology, 33,* 517–520. (p. 380)

Klineberg, O. (1984). Public opinion and nuclear war. *American Psychologist, 39,* 1245–1253. (p. 691)

Klinesmith, J., Kasser, T., & McAndrew, F. T. (2006). Guns, testosterone, and aggression: An experimental test of a mediational hypothesis. *Psychological Science, 17,* 568–576. (p. 672)

Kluft, R. P. (1991). Multiple personality disorder. In A. Tasman & S. M. Goldfinger (Eds.), *Review of Psychiatry, (Vol. 10).* Washington, DC: American Psychiatric Press. (p. 578)

Klump, K. L., & Culbert, K. M. (2007). Molecular genetic studies of eating disorders: Current status and future directions. *Current Directions in Psychological Science, 16,* 37–41. (p. 338)

Knapp, S., & VandeCreek, L. (2000, August). Recovered memories of childhood abuse: Is there an underlying professional consensus? *Professional Psychology: Research and Practice, 31,* 365–371. (p. 291)

Knäuper, B., Kornik, R., Atkinson, K., Guberman, C., & Aydin, C. (2005). Motivation influences the underestimation of cumulative risk. *Personality and Social Psychology Bulletin, 31,* 1511–1523. (p. 353)

Knickmeyer, E. (2001, August 7). In Africa, big is definitely better. *Associated Press (Seattle Times, p. A7).* (p. 338)

Knight, R. T. (2007). Neural networks debunk phrenology. *Science, 316,* 1578–1579. (p. 79)

Knight, W. (2004, August 2). *Animated face helps deaf with phone chat.* NewScientist.com. (p. 148)

Knoblich, G., & Oellinger, M. (2006, October/November). The Eureka moment. *Scientific American Mind,* pp. 38–43. (p. 301)

Knutson, K. L., Spiegel, K., Penev, P., & Van Cauter, E. (2007). The metabolic consequences of sleep deprivation. *Sleep Medicine Reviews, 11,* 163–178. (p. 183)

Ko, C-K., Yen, J-Y., Chen, C-C., Chen, S-H., & Yen, C-F. (2005). Proposed diagnostic criteria of Internet addiction for adolescents. *Journal of Nervous and Mental Disease, 193,* 728–733. (p. 198)

Koch, C., & Greenfield, S. (2007, October). How does consciousness happen? *Scientific American,* pp. 76–83. (p. 90)

Koenig, H. G. (2002, October 9). Personal communication, from Director of Center for the Study of Religion/Spirituality and Health, Duke University. (p. C-11)

Koenig, H. G., & Larson, D. B. (1998). Use of hospital services, religious attendance, and religious affiliation. *Southern Medical Journal, 91,* 925–932. (p. C-12)

Koenig, L. B., McGue, M., Krueger, R. F., & Bouchard, T. J., Jr. (2005). Genetic and environmental influences on religiousness: Findings for retrospective and current religiousness ratings. *Journal of Personality, 73,* 471–488. (p. 100)

Koenigs, M., Young, L., Adolphs, R., Tranel, D., Cushman, F., Hauser, M., & Damasio, A. (2007). Damage to the prefrontal cortex increases utilitarian moral judgements. *Nature, 446,* 908–911. (pp. 79, 450)

Koestner, R., Lekes, N., Powers, T. A., & Chicoine, E. (2002). Attaining personal goals: Self-concordance plus implementation intentions equals success. *Journal of Personality and Social Psychology, 83,* 231–244. (p. B-11)

Kohlberg, L. (1981). *The philosophy of moral development: Essays on moral development* (Vol. I). San Francisco: Harper & Row. (p. 449)

Kohlberg, L. (1984). *The psychology of moral development: Essays on moral development* (Vol. II). San Francisco: Harper & Row. (p. 449)

Kohler, I. (1962, May). Experiments with goggles. *Scientific American,* pp. 62–72. (p. 160)

Köhler, W. (1925: reprinted 1957). *The mentality of apes.* London: Pelican. (p. 300)

Kohn, P. M., & Macdonald, J. E. (1992). The survey of recent life experiences: A decontaminated hassles scale for adults. *Journal of Behavioral Medicine, 15,* 221–236. (p. 401)

Kohout, J., & Wicherski, M. (2004). 2001 *Doctorate employment survey.* Washington, DC: American Psychological Association. (p. A-5)

Kolassa, I-T., & Elbert, T. (2007). Structural and functional neuroplasticity in relation to traumatic stress. *Current Directions in Psychological Science, 16,* 321–325. (p. 576)

Kolata, G. (1986). Youth suicide: New research focuses on a growing social problem. *Science, 233,* 839–841. (p. 584)

Kolata, G. (1987). Metabolic catch-22 of exercise regimens. *Science, 236,* 146–147. (p. 347)

Kolb, B. (1989). Brain development, plasticity, and behavior. *American Psychologist, 44,* 1203–1212. (p. 82)

Kolb, B., & Whishaw, I. Q. (1998). Brain plasticity and behavior. *Annual Review of Psychology, 49,* 43–64. (p. 442)

Kolb, B., & Whishaw, I. Q. (2006). *An introduction to brain and behavior,* 2nd edition. New York: Worth Publishers. (p. 301)

Kolivas, E. D., & Gross, A. M. (2007). Assessing sexual aggression: Addressing the gap between rape victimization and perpetration prevalence rates. *Aggression and Violent Behavior, 12,* 315–328. (p. 106)

Kolker, K. (2002, December 8). *Video violence disturbs some: others scoff at influence.* Grand Rapids Press, pp. A1, A12. (p. 676)

Kolodziej, M. E., & Johnson, B. T. (1996). Interpersonal contact and acceptance of persons with psychiatric disorders: A research synthesis. *Journal of Consulting and Clinical Psychology, 64,* 1387–1396. (p. 568)

Koltko-Rivera, M. E. (2006). Rediscovering the later version of Maslow's hierarchy of needs: Self-transcendence and opportunities for theory, research, and unification. *Review of General Psychology, 10,* 302–317. (p. 330)

Koole, S. L., Greenberg, J., & Pyszczynski, T. (2006). Introducing science to the psychology of the soul. *Current Directions in Psychological Science, 15,* 212–216. (p. 489)

Kopta, S. M., Lueger, R. J., Saunders, S. M., & Howard, K. I. (1999). Individual psychotherapy outcome and process research: Challenges leading to greater turmoil or a positive transition? *Annual Review of Psychology, 30,* 441–469. (p. 621)

Koriat, A., Goldsmith, M., & Pansky, A. (2000). Toward a psychology of memory accuracy. *Annual Review of Psychology, 51,* pp. 481–537. (p. 288)

Kosslyn, S. M. (2005). Reflective thinking and mental imagery: A perspective on the development of posttraumatic stress disorder. *Development and Psychopathology, 17,* 851–863. (p. 573)

Kosslyn, S. M. (2007). *Human intelligence can be increased, and can be increased dramatically.* World Question Center, The Edge (www.edge.org). (p. 547)

Kosslyn, S. M., & Koenig, O. (1992). *Wet mind: The new cognitive neuroscience.* New York: Free Press. (p. 61)

Kosslyn, S. M., Thompson, W. L., Costantini-Ferrando, M. F., Alpert, N. M., & Spiegel, D. (2000). Hypnotic visual illusion alters color processing in the brain. *American Journal of Psychiatry, 157,* 1279–1284. (p. 195)

Kotchick, B. A., Shaffer, A., & Forehand, R. (2001). Adolescent sexual risk behavior: A multi-system perspective. *Clinical Psychology Review, 21,* 493–519. (p. 353)

Kotkin, M., Daviet, C., & Gurin, J. (1996). The Consumer Reports mental health survey. *American Psychologist, 51,* 1080–1082. (p. 619)

Kraft, C. (1978). A psychophysical approach to air safety: Simulator studies of visual illusions in night approaches. In H. L. Pick, H. W. Leibowitz, J. E. Singer, A. Steinschneider, & H. W. Stevenson (Eds.), *Psychology: From research to practice.* New York: Plenum Press. (p. B-14)

Kraft, R. N. (2002). *Memory perceived: Recalling the Holocaust.* Westport, CT: Praeger. (p. 293)

Kramer, A. F., & Erickson, K. I. (2007). Capitalizing on cortical plasticity: Influence of physical activity on cognition and brain function. *Trends in Cognitive Sciences, 11,* 342–348. (p. C-8)

Kranz, F., & Ishai, A. (2006). Face perception is modulated by sexual preference. *Current Biology, 16,* 63–68. (p. 357)

Kraus, N., Malmfors, T., & Slovic, P. (1992). Intuitive toxicology: Expert and lay judgments of chemical risks. *Risk Analysis, 12,* 215–232. (p. 311)

Krauss, R. M. (1998). Why do we gesture when we speak. *Current Directions in Psychology, 7,* 54–60. (p. D-5)

Kraut, R. E., & Johnston, R. E. (1979). Social and emotional messages of smiling: An ethological approach. *Journal of Personality and Social Psychology, 37,* 1539–1553. (p. 382)

KRC Research & Consulting. (2001, August 7). Memory isn't quite what it used to be (survey for General Nutrition Centers). *USA Today,* p. D1. (p. 461)

Krebs, D. L., & Denton, K. (2005). Toward a more pragmatic approach to morality: A critical evaluation of Kohlberg's model. *Psychological Review, 112,* 629–649. (p. 449)

Krebs, D. L., & Van Hesteren, F. (1994). The development of altruism: Toward an integrative model. *Developmental Review, 14,* 103–158. (p. 450)

Kring, A. M., & Gordon, A. H. (1998). Sex differences in emotion: Expression, experience, and physiology. *Journal of Personality and Social Psychology, 74,* 686–703. (p. 380)

Kristensen, P., & Bjerkedal, T. (2007). Explaining the relation between birth order and intelligence. *Science, 316,* 1717. (p. 41)

Kristof, N. D. (2004, July 21). Saying no to killers. *New York Times* (www.nytimes.com). (p. 685)

Kroll, R., Danis, S., Moreau, M., Waldbaum, A., Shifren, J., & Wekselman, K. (2004). Testosterone transdermal patch (TPP) significantly improved sexual function in naturally menopausal women in a large Phase III study. Presented to the American Society of Reproductive Medicine annual meeting, Philadelphia, October. (p. 350)

Krosnick, J. A., Betz, A. L., Jussim, L. J., & Lynn, A. R. (1992). Subliminal conditioning of attitudes. *Personality and Social Psychology Bulletin, 18,* 152–162. (p. 121)

Krueger, A. (2007, November/December). What makes a terrorist. *The American* (www.american.com). (p. 673)

Krueger, J., & Killham, E. (2005, December 8). At work, feeling good matters. *Gallup Management Journal* (www.gmj.gallup.com). (p. B-11)

Krueger, J., & Killham, E. (2006, March 9). Why Dilbert is right. Uncomfortable work environments make for disgruntled employees—just like the cartoon says. *Gallup Management Journal* (www.gmj.gallup.com). (p. 506)

Kruger, J., & Dunning, D. (1999). Unskilled and unaware of it: How difficulties in recognizing one's own incompetence lead to inflated self-assessments. *Journal of Personality and Social Psychology, 77,* 1121–1134. (p. 507)

Kruger J., Epley, N., Parker, J., & Ng, Z-W. (2005). Egocentrism over e-mail: Can we communicate as well as we think? *Journal of Personality and Social Psychology, 89,* 925–936. (pp. 379, 422)

Krupa, D. J., Thompson, J. K., & Thompson, R. F. (1993). Localization of a memory trace in the mammalian brain. *Science, 260,* 989–991. (p. 274)

Krützen, M., Mann, J., Heithaus, M. R., Connor, R. C., Bejder, L., & Sherwin, W. B. (2005). Cultural transmission of tool use in bottlenose dolphins. *Proceedings of the National Academy of Sciences, 102,* 8939–8943. (p. D-2)

Kubey, R., & Csikszentmihalyi, M. (2002, February). Television addiction is no mere metaphor. *Scientific American,* pp. 74–80. (p. 247)

Kübler, A., Winter, S., Ludolph, A. C., Hautzinger, M., & Birbaumer, N. (2005). Severity of depressive symptoms and quality of life in patients with amyotrophic lateral sclerosis. *Neurorehabilitation and Neural Repair, 19(3),* 182–193. (p. 391)

Kubzansky, L. D., Sparrow, D., Vokanas, P., Kawachi, I. (2001). Is the glass half empty or half full? A prospective study of optimism and coronary heart disease in the normative aging study. *Psychosomatic Medicine, 63,* 910–916. (pp. 402, 403)

Kuhl, P. K., & Meltzoff, A. N. (1982). The bimodal perception of speech in infancy. *Science, 218,* 1138–1141. (p. 315)

Kuhn, D. (2006). Do cognitive changes accompany developments in the adolescent brain? *Perspectives on Psychological Science, 1,* 59–67. (p. 447)

Kujala, U. M., Kaprio, J., Sarna, S., & Koskenvuo, M. (1998). Relationship of leisure-time physical activity and mortality: The Finnish twin cohort. *Journal of the American Medical Association, 279,* 440–444. (p. C-8)

Kuncel, N. R., & Hezlett, S. A. (2007). Standardized tests predict graduate students' success. *Science, 315,* 1080–1081. (p. 538)

Kuncel, N. R., Nezlett, S. A., & Ones, D. S. (2004). Academic performance, career potential, creativity, and job performance: Can one construct predict them all? *Journal of Personality and Social Psychology, 86,* 148–161. (p. 526)

Kunkel, D. (2001, February 4). *Sex on TV.* Menlo Park, CA: Henry J. Kaiser Family Foundation (www.kff.org). (p. 353)

Kunkel, D., Cope-Farrar, K., Biely, E., Farinola, W. J. M., & Donnerstein, E. (2001). *Sex on TV (2): A biennial report to the Kaiser Family Foundation.* Menlo Park, CA: Kaiser Family Foundation. (p. 676)

Kuntsche, E., Knibbe, R., Gmel, G., & Engels, R. (2005). Why do young people drink? A review of drinking motives. *Clinical Psychology Review, 25,* 841–861. (p. 209)

Kupper, N., & Denollet, J. (2007). Type D personality as a prognostic factor in heart disease: Assessment and mediating mechanisms. *Journal of Personality Assessment, 89,* 265–276. (p. 402)

Kurtz, P. (1983, Spring). Stars, planets, and people. *The Skeptical Inquirer,* pp. 65–68. (p. 499)

Kushner, M. G., Kim, S. W., Conahue, C., Thuras, P., Adson, D., Kotlyar, M., McCabe, J., Peterson, J., & Foa, E. B. (2007). D-cycloserine augmented exposure therapy for obsessive-compulsive disorder. *Biological Psychiatry, 62,* 835–838. (p. 630)

Kutas, M. (1990). Event-related brain potential (ERP) studies of cognition during sleep: Is it more than a dream? In R. R. Bootzin, J. F. Kihlstrom, & D. Schacter (Eds.), *Sleep and cognition.* Washington, DC: American Psychological Association. (p. 176)

Kutcher, E. J., & Bragger, J. D. (2004). Selection interviews of overweight job applicants: Can structure reduce the bias? *Journal of Applied Social Psychology, 34,* 1993–2022. (p. B-6)

Labouvie-Vief, G., & Schell, D. A. (1982). Learning and memory in later life. In B. B. Wolman (Ed.), *Handbook of developmental psychology.* Englewood Cliffs, NJ: Prentice-Hall. (p. 462)

Lacayo, R. (1995, June 12). Violent reaction. *Time Magazine,* pp. 25–39. (p. 27)

Lacey, H. P., Smith, D. M., & Ubel, P. A. (2006). Hope I die before I get old: Mispredicting happiness across the lifespan. *Journal of Happiness Studies, 7,* 167–182. (p. 468)

Lacey, M. (2004. April 9). A decade after massacres, Rwanda outlaws ethnicity. *New York Times* (www.nytimes.com). (p. 691)

Lachman, M. E. (2004). Development in midlife. *Annual Review of Psychology, 55,* 305–331. (p. 465)

Ladd, E. C. (1998, August/September). The tobacco bill and American public opinion. *The Public Perspective,* pp. 5–19. (p. 210)

Ladd, G. T. (1887). *Elements of physiological psychology.* New York: Scribner's. (p. 175)

LaFleur, D. L., Pittenger, C., Kelmendi, B., Gardner, T., Wasylink, S., Malison, R. T., Sanacora, G., Krystal, J. H., & Coric, V. (2006). N-acetylcysteine augmentation in serotonin reuptake inhibitor refractory obsessive-compulsive disorder. *Psychopharmacology, 184,* 254–256. (p. 575)

Laird, J. D. (1974). Self-attribution of emotion: The effects of expressive behavior on the quality of emotional experience. *Journal of Personality and Social Psychology, 29,* 475–486. (p. 383)

Laird, J. D. (1984). The real role of facial response in the experience of emotion: A reply to Tourangeau and Ellsworth, and others. *Journal of Personality and Social Psychology, 47,* 909–917. (p. 383)

Laird, J. D., Cuniff, M., Sheehan, K., Shulman, D., & Strum, G. (1989). Emotion specific effects of facial expressions on memory for life events. *Journal of Social Behavior and Personality, 4,* 87–98. (p. 383)

Lakin, J. L., & Chartrand, T. L. (2003). Using nonconscious behavioral mimicry to create affiliation and rapport. *Psychological Science, 14,* 334–339. (p. 651)

Lalumière, M. L., Blanchard, R., & Zucker, K. J. (2000). Sexual orientation and handedness in men and women: A meta-analysis. *Psychological Bulletin, 126,* 575–592. (p. 359)

Lam, R. W., Levitt, A. J., Levitan, R. D., Enns, M. W., Morehouse, R., Michalak, E. E., & Tam, E. M. (2006). The Can-SAD study: A randomized controlled trial of the effectiveness of light therapy and fluoxetine in patients with winter seasonal affective disorder. *American Journal of Psychiatry, 163,* 805–812. (p. 625)

Lambert, K. G. (2005). Rising rates of depression in today's society: Consideration of the roles of effort-based rewards and enhanced resilience in day-to-day functioning. *Neuroscience and Biobehavioral Reviews, 30,* 497–510. (p. C-8)

Lambert, K. (2008, August/September). Depressingly easy. *Scientific American Mind,* pp. 31–37. (p. C-8)

Lambert, W. E. (1992). Challenging established views on social issues: The power and limitations of research. *American Psychologist, 47,* 533–542. (p. 321)

Lambert, W. E., Genesee, F., Holobow, N., & Chartrand, L. (1993). Bilingual education for majority English-speaking children. *European Journal of Psychology of Education, 8,* 3–22. (p. 321)

Lamberth, J. (1998, August 6). Driving while black: A statistician proves that prejudice still rules the road. *Washington Post,* p. C1. (p. 665)

Lambird, K. H., & Mann, T. (2006). When do ego threats lead to self-regulation failure? Negative consequences of defensive high self-esteem. *Personality and Social Psychology Bulletin, 32,* 1177–1187. (p. 515)

Lampinen, J. M. (2002). What exactly is déjà vu? *Scientific American* (sci-eam.com/askexpert/biology/biology63). (p. 277)

Landau, M. J., Solomon, S., Greenberg, J., Cohen, F., Pyszczynski, T., Arndt, J., Miller, C. H., Ogilvie, D. M., & Cook, A. (2004). Deliver us from evil: The effects of mortality salience and reminders of 9/11 on support for President George W. Bush. *Personality and Social Psychology Bulletin, 30,* 1136–1150. (p. 669)

Landauer, T. (2001, September). Quoted by R. Herbert, You must remember this. *APS Observer,* p. 11. (p. 293)

Landauer, T. K., & Whiting, J. W. M. (1979). Correlates and consequences of stress in infancy. In R. Munroe, B. Munroe & B. Whiting (Eds.), *Handbook of Cross-Cultural Human Development.* New York: Garland. (p. 398)

Landrum, E. (2001). I'm getting my bachelor's degree in psychology. What can I do with it? *Eye on Psi Chi,* 22–24. (p. A-2)

Landry, M. J. (2002). MDMA: A review of epidemiologic data. *Journal of Psychoactive Drugs, 34,* 163–169. (p. 205)

Langer, E. J. (1983). *The psychology of control.* Beverly Hills, CA: Sage. (p. 506)

Langer, E. J., & Abelson, R. P. (1974). A patient by any other name . . .: Clinician group differences in labeling bias. *Journal of Consulting and Clinical Psychology, 42,* 4–9. (p. 568)

Langer, E. J., & Imber, L. (1980). The role of mindlessness in the perception of deviance. *Journal of Personality and Social Psychology, 39,* 360–367. (p. 568)

Langleben, D. D., Dattilio, F. M., & Gutheil, T. G. (2006). True lies: Delusions and lie-detection technology. *Journal of Psychiatry and Law, 34,* 351–370. (p. 373)

Langleben, D. D., Loughead, J. W., Bilker, W. B., & others. (2005). Telling truth from lie in individual subjects with fast event-related fMRI. *Human Brain Mapping, 26,* 262–273. (p. 373)

Langleben, D. D., Schroeder, L., Maldjian, J. A., Gur, R. C., McDonald, S., Ragland, J. D., O'Brien, C. P., & Childress, A. R. (2002). Brain activity during simulated deception: An event-related functional magnetic resonance study. *NeuroImage, 15,* 727–732. (p. 373)

Langlois, J. H., Kalakanis, L., Rubenstein, A. J., Larson, A., Hallam, M., & Smoot, M. (2000). Maxims or myths of beauty? A meta-analytic and theoretical review. *Psychological Bulletin, 126,* 390–423. (pp. 680, 681)

Langlois, J. H., & Roggman, L. A. (1990). Attractive faces are only average. *Psychological Science, 1,* 115–121. (p. 681)

Langlois, J. H., Roggman, L. A., Casey, R. J., Ritter, J. M., Rieser-Danner, L. A., & Jenkins, V. Y. (1987). Infant preferences for attractive faces: Rudiments of a stereotype? *Developmental Psychology, 23,* 363–369. (p. 680)

Lángström, N., Rahman, Q., Carlström, E., & Lichtenstein, P. (2008). Genetic and environmental effects on same-sex sexual behavior: A population study of twins in Sweden. *Archives of Sexual Behavior.* (p. 357)

Larkin, K., Resko, J. A., Stormshak, F., Stellflug, J. N., & Roselli, C. E. (2002). Neuroanatomical correlates of sex and sexual partner preference in sheep. Society for Neuroscience convention. (p. 357)

Larsen, R. J., & Diener, E. (1987). Affect intensity as an individual difference characteristic: A review. *Journal of Research in Personality, 21,* 1–39. (pp. 376, 428)

Larsen, R. J., Kasimatis, M., & Frey, K. (1992). Facilitating the furrowed brow: An unobtrusive test of the facial feedback hypothesis applied to unpleasant affect. *Cognition and Emotion, 6,* 321–338. (p. 383)

Larson, R. W., & Verma, S. (1999). How children and adolescents spend time across the world: Work, play, and developmental opportunities. *Psychological Bulletin, 125,* 701–736. (p. 553)

Larsson, H., Tuvblad, C., Rijsdijk, F. V., Andershed, H., Grann, M., & Lichetenstein, P. (2007). A common genetic factor explains the association between psychopathic personality and antisocial behavior. *Psychological Medicine, 37,* 15–26. (p. 597)

Larzelere, R. E. (2000). Child outcomes of non-abusive and customary physical punishment by parents: An updated literature review. *Clinical Child and Family Psychology Review, 3,* 199–221. (p. 235)

Larzelere, R. E., & Kuhn, B. R. (2005). Comparing child outcomes of physical punishment and alternative disciplinary tactics: A meta-analysis. *Clinical Child and Family Psychology Review, 8,* 1–37. (p. 235)

Larzelere, R. E., Kuhn, B. R., & Johnson, B. (2004). The intervention selection bias: An underrecognized confound in intervention research. *Psychological Bulletin, 130,* 289–303. (p. 235)

Lashley, K. S. (1950). In search of the engram. In *Symposium of the Society for Experimental Biology* (Vol. 4). New York: Cambridge University Press. (p. 268)

Lassiter, G. D., & Irvine, A. A. (1986). Video-taped confessions: The impact of camera point of view on judgments of coercion. *Journal of Personality and Social Psychology, 16,* 268–276. (p. 645)

Latané, B. (1981). The psychology of social impact. *American Psychologist, 36,* 343–356. (p. 658)

Latané, B., & Dabbs, J. M., Jr. (1975). Sex, group size and helping in three cities. *Sociometry, 38,* 180–194. (p. 686)

Latham, G. P., & Locke, E. A. (2007). New developments in and directions for goal-setting research. *European Psychologist, 12,* 290–300. (p. B-11)

Laudenslager, M. L., & Reite, M. L. (1984). Losses and separations: Immunological consequences and health implications. *Review of Personality and Social Psychology, 5,* 285–312. (p. C-2)

Laumann, E. O., Gagnon, J. H., Michael, R. T., & Michaels, S. (1994). *The social organization of sexuality: Sexual practices in the United States.* Chicago: University of Chicago Press. (p. 354)

Laws, K. R., & Kokkalis, J. (2007). Ecstasy (MDMA) and memory function: A meta-analytic update. *Human Psychopharmacology: Clinical and Experimental, 22,* 381–388. (p. 205)

Lazaruk, W. (2007). Linguistic, academic, and cognitive benefits of French immersion. *Canadian Modern Language Review, 63,* 605–628. (p. 321)

Lazarus, R. S. (1990). Theory-based stress measurement. *Psychological Inquiry, 1,* 3–13. (p. 401)

Lazarus, R. S. (1991). Progress on a cognitive-motivational-relational theory of emotion. *American Psychologist, 46,* 352–367. (p. 376)

Lazarus, R. S. (1998). Fifty years of the research and theory of R. S. Lazarus: An analysis of historical and perennial issues. Mahwah, NJ: Erlbaum. (pp. 376, 397)

Lea, S. E. G. (2000). Towards an ethical use of animals. *The Psychologist, 13,* 556–557. (p. 45)

Leaper, C., & Ayres, M. M. (2007). A meta-analytic review of gender variations in adults' language use: Talkativeness, affiliative speech, and assertive speech. *Personality and Social Psychology Review, 11,* 328–363. (p. 436)

Leary, M. R. (1999). The social and psychological importance of self-esteem. In R. M. Kowalski & M. R. Leary (Eds.), *The social psychology of emotional and behavioral problems.* Washington, DC: APA Books. (p. 512)

Leary, M. R., Haupt, A. L., Strausser, K. S., & Chokel, J. T. (1998). Calibrating the sociometer: The relationship between interpersonal appraisals and state self-esteem. *Journal of Personality and Social Psychology, 74,* 1290–1299. (p. 360)

Leary, W. E. (1998, September 28). Older people enjoy sex, survey says. *New York Times* (www.nytimes.com). (p. 456)

Leask, S. J., & Beaton, A. A. (2007). Handedness in Great Britain. *Laterality, 12,* 559–572. (p. 88)

LeDoux, J. E. (1996). *The emotional brain: The mysterious underpinnings of emotional life.* New York: Simon & Schuster. (p. 273)

LeDoux, J. E. (2002). *The synaptic self.* London: Macmillan. (pp. 375, 442)

LeDoux, J. E., & Armony, J. (1999). Can neurobiology tell us anything about human feelings? In D. Kahneman, E. Diener, & N. Schwartz (Eds.), *Well-being: The foundations of hedonic psychology.* New York: Sage. (p. 376)

Lee, K., Byatt, G., & Rhodes, G. (2000). Caricature effects, distinctiveness, and identification: Testing the face-space framework. *Psychological Science, 11,* 379–385. (p. 162)

Lee, L., Frederick, S., & Ariely, D. (2006). Try it, you'll like it: The influence of expectation, consumption, and revelation on preferences for beer. *Psychological Science, 17,* 1054–1058. (p. 162)

Lefcourt, H. M. (1982). *Locus of control: Current trends in theory and research.* Hillsdale, NJ: Erlbaum. (p. 505)

Legrand, L. N., Iacono, W. G., & McGue, M. (2005). Predicting addiction. *American Scientist, 93,* 140–147. (p. 209)

Lehavot, K., & Lambert, A. J. (2007). Toward a greater understanding of antigay prejudice: On the role of sexual orientation and gender role violation. *Basic and Applied Social Psychology, 29,* 279–292. (p. 682)

Lehman, A. F., Steinwachs, D. M., Dixon, L. B., Goldman, H. H., Osher, F., Postrado, L., Scott, J. E., Thompson, J. W., Fahey, M., Fischer, P., Kasper, J. A., Lyles, A., Skinner, E. A., Buchanan, R., Carpenter, W. T., Jr., Levine, J., McGlynn, E. A., Rosenheck, R., & Zito, J. (1998). Translating research into practice: The schizophrenia patient outcomes research team (PORT) treatment recommendations. *Schizophrenia Bulletin, 24,* 1–10. (p. 629)

Lehman, D. R., Wortman, C. B., & Williams, A. F. (1987). Long-term effects of losing a spouse or child in a motor vehicle crash. *Journal of Personality and Social Psychology, 52,* 218–231. (p. 470)

Leigh, B. C. (1989). In search of the seven dwarves: Issues of measurement and meaning in alcohol expectancy research. *Psychological Bulletin, 105,* 361–373. (p. 200)

Leitenberg, H., & Henning, K. (1995). Sexual fantasy. *Psychological Bulletin, 117,* 469–496. (pp. 350, 352)

Lemonick, M. D. (2002, June 3). Lean and hungrier. *Time,* p. 54. (p. 334)

L'Engle, M. (1973). *A wind in the door.* Bantam Doubleday Dell Books for Young Readers. (p. 20)

Lennox, B. R., Bert, S., Park, G., Jones, P. B., & Morris, P. G. (1999). Spatial and temporal mapping of neural activity associated with auditory hallucinations. *Lancet, 353,* 644. (p. 78)

Lenzenweger, M. F., Dworkin, R. H., & Wethington, E. (1989). Models of positive and negative symptoms in schizophrenia: An empirical evaluation of latent structures. *Journal of Abnormal Psychology, 98,* 62–70. (p. 629)

Lerner, M. J. (1980). *The belief in a just world: A fundamental delusion.* New York: Plenum Press. (p. 670)

Leserman, J., Jackson, E. D., Petitto, J. M., Golden, R. N., Silva, S. G., Perkins, D. O., Cai, J., Folds, J. D., & Evans, D. L. (1999). Progression to AIDS: The effects of stress, depressive symptoms, and social support. *Psychosomatic Medicine, 61,* 397–406. (p. 405)

Lessard, N., Pare, M., Lepore, F., & Lassonde, M. (1998). Early-blind human subjects localize sound sources better than sighted subjects. *Nature, 395,* 278–280. (p. 140)

Lester, W. (2004, May 26). AP polls: Nations value immigrant workers. *Associated Press* release. (p. 665)

Leucht, S., Barnes, T. R. E., Kissling, W., Engel, R. R., Correll, C., & Kane, J. M. (2003). Relapse prevention in schizophrenia with new-generation antipsychotics: A systematic review and exploratory meta-analysis of randomized, controlled trials. *American Journal of Psychiatry, 160,* 1209–1222. (p. 630)

Leung, A. K-Y., Maddux, W. W., Galinsky, A. D., & Chiu, C-Y. (2008). Multicultural experience enhances creativity: The when and how. *American Psychologist, 63,* 169–181. (p. 302)

LeVay, S. (1991). A difference in hypothalamic structure between heterosexual and homosexual men. *Science, 253,* 1034–1037. (p. 357)

LeVay, S. (1994, March). Quoted in D. Nimmons, Sex and the brain. *Discover,* p. 64–71. (p. 357)

Levenson, R. W. (1992). Autonomic nervous system differences among emotions. *Psychological Science, 3,* 23–27. (p. 370)

Lever, J. (2003, November 11). Personal correspondence reporting data responses volunteered to *Elle/MSNBC.com* survey of weight perceptions. (p. 338)

Levesque, M. J., & Kenny, D. A. (1993). Accuracy of behavioral predictions at zero acquaintance: A social relations analysis. *Journal of Personality and Social Psychology, 65,* 1178–1187. (p. 502)

Levin, I. P., & Gaeth, G. J. (1988). How consumers are affected by the framing of attribute information before and after consuming the product. *Journal of Consumer Research, 15,* 374–378. (p. 312)

Levine, R., Sato, S., Hashimoto, T., & Verma, J. (1995). Love and marriage in eleven cultures. *Journal of Cross-Cultural Psychology, 26,* 554–571. (p. 684)

Levin, R., & Nielsen, T. A. (2007). Disturbed dreaming, posttraumatic stress disorder, and affect distress: A review and neurocognitive model. *Psychological Bulletin, 133,* 482–528. (p. 188)

Levine, J. A., Eberhardt, N. L., & Jensen, M. D. (1999). Role of nonexercise activity thermogenesis in resistance to fat gain in humans. *Science, 283,* 212–214. (p. 344)

Levine, J. A., Lanningham-Foster, L. M., McCrady, S. K., Krizan, A. C., Olson, L. R., Kane, P. H., Jensen, M. D., & Clark, M. M. (2005). Interindividual variation in posture allocation: Possible role in human obesity. *Science, 307,* 584–586. (p. 344)

Levine, R. V., & Norenzayan, A. (1999). The pace of life in 31 countries. *Journal of Cross-Cultural Psychology, 30,* 178–205. (pp. 29, 662)

Levy, B., & Langer, E. (1992). Avoidance of the memory loss stereotype: Enhanced memory among the elderly deaf. Paper presented at American Psychological Association convention, Washington, DC. (p. 140)

Levy, P. E. (2003). *Industrial/organizational psychology: Understanding the workplace.* Boston: Houghton Mifflin. (p. B-6)

Lewald, J. (2007). More accurate sound localisation induced by short-term light deprivation. *Neuropsychologia, 45,* 1215–1222. (p. 140)

Lewandowski, G. W., Jr., Aron, A., & Gee, J. (2007). Personality goes a long way: The malleability of opposite-sex physical attractiveness. *Personality Relationships, 14,* 571–585. (p. 682)

Lewicki, P. (1985). Nonconscious biasing effects of single instances on subsequent judgments. *Journal of Personality and Social Psychology, 48,* 563–574. (p. 276)

Lewicki, P., Hill, T., & Czyzewska, M. (1992). Nonconscious acquisition of information. *American Psychologist, 47,* 796–801. (p. 488)

Lewicki, P., Hill, T., & Czyzewska, M. (1997). Hidden covariation detection: A fundamental and ubiquitous phenomenon. *Journal of Experimental Psychology: Learning, Memory, and Cognition, 23,* 221–228. (p. 488)

Lewinsohn, P. M., Hoberman, H., Teri, L., & Hautziner, M. (1985). An integrative theory of depression. In S. Reiss & R. Bootzin (Eds.), *Theoretical issues in behavior therapy.* Orlando, FL: Academic Press. (p. 582)

Lewinsohn, P. M., Petit, J., Joiner, T. E., Jr., & Seeley, J. R. (2003). The symptomatic expression of major depressive disorder in adolescents and young adults. *Journal of Abnormal Psychology, 112,* 244–252. (p. 582)

Lewinsohn, P. M., Rohde, P., & Seeley, J. R. (1998). Major depressive disorder in older adolescents: Prevalence, risk factors, and clinical implications. *Clinical Psychology Review, 18,* 765–794. (p. 582)

Lewinsohn, P. M., & Rosenbaum, M. (1987). Recall of parental behavior by acute depressives, remitted depressives, and nondepressives. *Journal of Personality and Social Psychology, 52,* 611–619. (p. 278)

Lewis, C. S. (1967). *Christian reflections.* Grand Rapids, MI: Eerdmans. (pp. 4, 280)

Lewis, D. O., Pincus, J. H., Bard, B., Richardson, E., Prichep, L. S., Feldman, M., & Yeager, C. (1988). Neuropsychiatric, psychoeducational, and family characteristics of 14 juveniles condemned to death in the United States. *American Journal of Psychiatry, 145,* 584–589. (p. 430)

Lewis, D. O., Pincus, J. H., Feldman, M., Jackson, L., & Bard, B. (1986). Psychiatric, neurological, and psychoeducational characteristics of 15 death row inmates in the United States. *American Journal of Psychiatry, 143,* 838–845. (p. 671)

Lewis, D. O., Yeager, C. A., Swica, Y., Pincus, J. H., & Lewis, M. (1997). Objective documentation of child abuse and dissociation in 12 murderers with dissociative identity disorder. *American Journal of Psychiatry, 154,* 1703–1710. (p. 579)

Lewis, M. (1992). Commentary. *Human Development, 35,* 44–51. (p. 278)

Lewontin, R. (1976). Race and intelligence. In N. J. Block & G. Dworkin (Eds.), *The IQ controversy: Critical readings.* New York: Pantheon. (p. 552)

Lewontin, R. (1982). *Human diversity.* New York: Scientific American Library. (pp. 104, 553)

Li, J., Laursen, T. M., Precht, D. H., Olsen, J., & Mortensen, P. B. (2005). Hospitalization for mental illness among parents after the death of a child. *New England Journal of Medicine, 352,* 1190–1196. (p. 470)

Li, J. C., Dunning, D., & Malpass, R. L. (1996). Cross-racial identification among European-Americans Basketball fandom and the contact hypothesis. Unpublished manuscript, Cornell University. (p. 669)

Li, W., Moallem, I., Paller, K. A., & Gottfried, J. A. (2007). Subliminal smells can guide social preferences. *Psychological Science, 18,* 1044–1049. (p. 122)

Libet, B. (1985). Unconscious cerebral initiative and the role of conscious will in voluntary action. *Behavioral and Brain Sciences, 12,* 181–187. (p. 91)

Libet, B. (2004). *Mind time: The temporal factor in consciousness.* Cambridge, MA: Harvard University Press. (p. 91)

Licata, A., Taylor, S., Berman, M., & Cranston, J. (1993). Effects of cocaine on human aggression. *Pharmacology Biochemistry and Behavior, 45,* 549–552. (p. 205)

Lieberman, J. A. (2006). Comparative effectiveness of antipsychotic drugs. *Archives of General Psychiatry, 63,* 1069–1072. (p. 629)

Lieberman, J. A., & 11 others. (2005). Effectiveness of antipsychotic drugs in patients with chronic schizophrenia. *New England Journal of Medicine, 353,* 1209–1223. (p. 629)

Lieberman, M. D., Eisenberger, N. L., Crockett, M. J., Tom, S. M., Pfeifer, J. H., & Way, B. M. (2007). Putting feelings into words: Affect labeling disrupts amygdala activity in response to affective stimuli. *Psychological Science, 18,* 421–428. (p. C-5)

Lilienfeld, S. O., & Arkowitz, H. (2007, April/May). Autism: An epidemic. *Scientific American Mind,* pp. 82–83. (p. 424)

Lilienfeld, S. O., & Arkowitz, H. (2007, December, 2006/January, 2007). Taking a closer look: Can moving your eyes back and forth help to ease anxiety? *Scientific American Mind,* pp. 80–81. (p. 624)

Lilienfeld, S. O., Lynn, S. J., Kirsch, I., Chaves, J. F., Sarbin, T. R., Ganaway, G. K., & Powell, R. A. (1999). Dissociative identity disorder and the sociocognitive model: Recalling the lessons of the past. *Psychological Bulletin, 125,* 507–523. (p. 579)

Lilienfeld, S. O., Wood, J. M., & Garb, H. N. (2001, May). What's wrong with this picture? *Scientific American,* pp. 81–87. (p. 486)

Lin, L., Faraco, J., Li, R., Kadotani, H., Rogers, W., Lin, X., Qiu, X., de Jong, P. J., Nishino, S., & Mignot E. (1999). The sleep disorder canine narcolepsy is caused by a mutation in the hypocretin (orexin) receptor 2 gene. *Cell, 98,* 365–376. (p. 186)

Linde, K., & 10 others. (2005). Acupuncture for patients with migraine: A randomized controlled trial. *Journal of the American Medical Association, 293,* 2118–2125. (p. C-9)

Linder, D. (1982). Social trap analogs: The tragedy of the commons in the laboratory. In V. J. Derlega & J. Grzelak (Eds.), *Cooperative and helping behavior: Theories and research.* New York: Academic Press. (p. 689)

Lindskold, S. (1978). Trust development, the GRIT proposal, and the effects of conciliatory acts on conflict and cooperation. *Psychological Bulletin, 85,* 772–793. (p. 692)

Lindskold, S., & Han, G. (1988). GRIT as a foundation for integrative bargaining. *Personality and Social Psychology Bulletin, 14,* 335–345. (p. 692)

Linville, P. W., Fischer, G. W., & Fischhoff, B. (1992). AIDS risk perceptions and decision biases. In J. B. Pryor & G. D. Reeder (Eds.), *The social psychology of HIV infection.* Hillsdale, NJ: Erlbaum. (p. 311)

Lippa, R. A. (2002). Gender-related traits of heterosexual and homosexual men and women. *Archives of Sexual Behavior, 31,* 83–98. (p. 356)

Lippa, R. A. (2005a). *Gender, nature, and nurture* (2nd ed.). Mahwah, NJ: Erlbaum. (p. 437)

Lippa, R. A. (2005b). Sexual orientation and personality. *Annual Review of Sex Research, 16,* 119–153. (p. 355)

Lippa, R. A. (2006a). Is high sex drive associated with increased sexual attraction to both sexes? It depends on whether you are male or female. *Psychological Science, 17,* 46–52. (p. 355)

Lippa, R. A. (2006b). The gender reality hypothesis. *American Psychologist, 61,* 639–640. (p. 437)

Lippa, R. A. (2007a). The relation between sex drive and sexual attraction to men and women: A cross-national study of heterosexual, bisexual, and homosexual men and women. *Archives of Sexual Behavior, 36,* 209–222. (pp. 355, 359, 680)

Lippa, R. A. (2007b). The preferred traits of mates in a cross-national study of heterosexual and homosexual men and women: An examination of biological and cultural influences. *Archives of Sexual Behavior, 36,* 193–208. (p. 359)

Lippa, R. A. (2008) Sex differences and sexual orientation differences in personality: Findings from the BBC Internet survey. *Archives of Sexual Behavior, Special Issue: Biological research on sex-dimorphic behavior and sexual orientation, 37*(1), 173–187. (pp. 106, 359, 437)

Lippman, J. (1992, October 25). Global village is characterized by a television in every home. *Los Angeles Times Syndicate* (in *Grand Rapids Press,* p. F9). (p. 247)

Lipps, H. M. (1999). *A new psychology of women: Gender, culture, and ethnicity.* Mountain View, CA: Mayfield Publishing. (p. 665)

Lipsey, M. W., & Wilson, D. B. (1993). The efficacy of psychological, educational, and behavioral treatment: Confirmation from meta-analyses. *American Psychologist, 48,* 1181–1209. (p. 543)

Lipsitt, L. P. (2003). Crib death: A biobehavioral phenomenon? *Current Directions in Psychological Science, 12,* 164–170. (p. 416)

Livesley, W. J., & Jang, K. L. (2008). The behavioral genetics of personality disorder. *Annual Review of Clinical Psychology, 4,* 247–274. (p. 597)

Livingstone, M., & Hubel, D. (1988). Segregation of form, color, movement, and depth: Anatomy, physiology, and perception. *Science, 240,* 740–749. (p. 130)

LoBue, V., & DeLoache, J. S. (2008). Detecting the snake in the grass: Attention to fear-relevant stimuli by adults and young children. *Psychological Science, 19,* 284–289. (p. 575)

Loehlin, J. C., Horn, J. M., Ernst, J. L. (2007). Genetic and environmental influences on adult life outcomes: Evidence from the Texas adoption project. *Behavior Genetics, 37,* 463–476. (p. 100)

Loehlin, J. C., McCrae, R. R., & Costa, P. T., Jr. (1998). Heritabilities of common and measure-specific components of the Big Five personality factors. *Journal of Research in Personality, 32,* 431–453. (p. 499)

Loehlin, J. C., & Nichols, R. C. (1976). *Heredity, environment, and personality.* Austin: University of Texas Press. (p. 97)

Loewenstein, G., & Furstenberg, F. (1991). Is teenage sexual behavior rational? *Journal of Applied Social Psychology, 21,* 957–986. (p. 232)

Loftus, E. F. (1979). The malleability of human memory. *American Scientist, 67,* 313–320. (p. 286)

Loftus, E. F. (1980). *Memory: Surprising new insights into how we remember and why we forget.* Reading, MA: Addison-Wesley. (p. 193)

Loftus, E. F. (1993). The reality of repressed memories. *American Psychologist, 48,* 518–537. (p. 487)

Loftus, E. F. (1995, March/April). Remembering dangerously. *Skeptical Inquirer,* pp. 20–29. (p. 487)

Loftus, E. F. (2001, November). Imagining the past. *The Psychologist, 14,* 584–587. (p. 286)

Loftus, E. F., Coan, J., & Pickrell, J. E. (1996). Manufacturing false memories using bits of reality. In L. Reder (Ed.), *Implicit memory and metacognition.* Mahwah, NJ: Erlbaum. (p. 291)

Loftus, E. F., & Ketcham, K. (1994). *The myth of repressed memory.* New York: St. Martin's Press. (pp. 188, 268, 292)

Loftus, E. F., Levidow, B., & Duensing, S. (1992). Who remembers best? Individual differences in memory for events that occurred in a science museum. *Applied Cognitive Psychology, 6,* 93–107. (p. 286)

Loftus, E. F., & Loftus, G. R. (1980). On the permanence of stored information in the human brain. *American Psychologist, 35,* 409–420. (p. 268)

Loftus, E. F., Milo, E. M., & Paddock, J. R. (1995). The accidental executioner: Why psychotherapy must be informed by science. *The Counseling Psychologist, 23,* 300–309. (p. 291)

Loftus, E. F., & Palmer, J. C. (October, 1974). Reconstruction of automobile destruction: An example of the interaction between language and memory. *Journal of Verbal Learning & Verbal Behavior, 13(5),* 585–589. (p. 285)

Logan, T. K., Walker, R., Cole, J., & Leukefeld, C. (2002). Victimization and substance abuse among women: Contributing factors, interventions, and implications. *Review of General Psychology, 6,* 325–397. (p. 209)

Logue, A. W. (1998a). Laboratory research on self-control: Applications to administration. *Review of General Psychology, 2,* 221–238. (p. 232)

Logue, A. W. (1998b). Self-control. In W. T. O'Donohue, (Ed.), *Learning and behavior therapy.* Boston, MA: Allyn & Bacon. (p. 232)

London, P. (1970). The rescuers: Motivational hypotheses about Christians who saved Jews from the Nazis. In J. Macaulay & L. Berkowitz (Eds.), *Altruism and helping behavior.* New York: Academic Press. (p. 246)

Looy, H. (2001). Sex differences: Evolved, constructed, and designed. *Journal of Psychology and Theology, 29,* 301–313. (p. 107)

Lopes, P. N., Brackett, M. A., Nezlek, J. B., Schutz, A., Sellin, II, & Salovey, P. (2004). Emotional intelligence and social interaction. *Personality and Social Psychology Bulletin, 30,* 1018–1034. (p. 529)

Lopez, D. J. (2002, January/February). Snaring the fowler: Mark Twain debunks phrenology. *Skeptical Inquirer* (www.csicop.org). (p. 52)

Lord, C. G., Lepper, M. R., & Preston, E. (1984). Considering the opposite: A corrective strategy for social judgment. *Journal of Personality and Social Psychology, 47,* 1231–1247. (p. 307)

Lord, C. G., Ross, L., & Lepper, M. (1979). Biased assimilation and attitude polarization: The effects of prior theories on subsequently considered evidence. *Journal of Personality and Social Psychology, 37,* 2098–2109. (p. 307)

Lorenz, K. (1937). The companion in the bird's world. *Auk, 54,* 245–273. (p. 427)

Los Angeles Times. (1998, 14 March). Daughters give birth on same day. P. A15. (p. 33)

Louie, K., & Wilson, M. A. (2001). Temporally structured replay of awake hippocampal ensemble activity during rapid eye movement sleep. *Neuron, 29,* 145–156. (p. 190)

Lourenco, O., & Machado, A. (1996). In defense of Piaget's theory: A reply to 10 common criticisms. *Psychological Review, 103,* 143–164. (p. 423)

Lovaas, O. I. (1987). Behavioral treatment and normal educational and intellectual functioning in young autistic children. *Journal of Consulting and Clinical Psychology, 55,* 3–9. (p. 613)

Love, J. M., & 13 others. (2003). Child care quality matters: How conclusions may vary with context. *Child Development, 74,* 1021–1033.e, J. M., & 13 others. (2003). Child care quality matters: How conclusions may vary with context. *Child Development, 74,* 1021–1033. (p. 431)

Lowry, P. E. (1997). The assessment center process: New directions. *Journal of Social Behavior and Personality, 12,* 53–62. (p. 510)

Lu, Z-L., Williamson, S. J., & Kaufman, L. (1992). Behavioral lifetime of human auditory sensory memory predicted by physiological measures. *Science, 258,* 1668–1670. (p. 266)

Lubinski, D., & Benbow, C. P. (1992). Gender differences in abilities and preferences among the gifted: Implications for the math-science pipeline. *Current Directions in Psychological Science, 1,* 61–66. (p. 549)

Lubinski, D., & Benbow, C. P. (2000). States of excellence. *American Psychologist,* 137–150. (p. 543)

Lubinski, D., & Benbow, C. P. (2006). Study of mathematically precocious youth after 35 years: Uncovering antecedents for the development of math-science expertise. *Perspectives on Psychological Science, 1,* 316–345. (p. 543)

Luborsky, L., Rosenthal, R., Diguer, L., Andrusyna, T. P., Berman, J. S., Levitt, J. T., Seligman, D. A., & Krause, E. D. (2002). The dodo bird verdict is alive and well—mostly. *Clinical Psychology: Science and Practice, 9,* 2–34. (p. 622)

Lucas, A., Morley, R., Cole, T. J., Lister, G., & Leeson-Payne, C. (1992). Breast milk and subsequent intelligence quotient in children born preterm. *Lancet, 339,* 261–264. (p. 34)

Lucas, R. E. (2007a). Adaptation and the set-point model of subjective well-being. *Current Directions in Psychological Science, 16,* 75–79. (p. 391)

Lucas, R. E. (2007b). Long-term disability is associated with lasting changes in subjective well-being: Evidence from two nationally representative longitudinal studies. *Journal of Personality and Social Psychology, 92,* 717–730. (p. 391)

Lucas, R. E. (2008). Personality and subjective well-being. In M. Eid & R. Larsen (Eds.), *The science of subjective well-being.* New York: Guilford. (p. 396)

Lucas, R. E., Clark, A. E., Georgellis, Y., & Diener, E. (2003). Re-examining adaptation and the setpoint model of happiness: Reactions to changes in marital status. *Journal of Personality and Social Psychology, 84,* 527–539. (p. 471)

Lucas, R. E., Clark, A. E., Georgellis, Y., & Diener, E. (2004). Unemployment alters the set point for life satisfaction. *Psychological Science, 15,* 8–13. (p. 396)

Lucas, R. E., & Donnellan, M. B. (2007). How stable is happiness? Using the STARTS model to estimate the stability of life satisfaction. *Journal of Research in Personality, 41,* 1091–1098. (p. 396)

Luciano, M., Posthuma, D., Wright, M. J., de Geus, E. J. C., Smith, G. A., Geffen, G. M., Boomsma, D. I., & Martin, N. G. (2005). Perceptual speed does not cause intelligence, and intelligence does not cause perceptual speed. *Biological Psychology, 70,* 1–8. (p. 531)

Ludwig, A. M. (1995). *The price of greatness: Resolving the creativity and madness controversy.* New York: Guilford Press. (pp. 356, 581)

Luntz, F. (2003, June 10). Quoted by T. Raum, "Bush insists banned weapons will be found." *Associated Press* (story.news.yahoo.com). (p. 648)

Luria, A. M. (1968). In L. Solotaroff (Trans.), *The mind of a mnemonist.* New York: Basic Books. (p. 256)

Lustig, C., & Buckner, R. L. (2004). Preserved neural correlates of priming in old age and dementia. *Neuron, 42,* 865–875. (p. 272)

Lutgendorf, S. K., Russell, D., Ullrich, P., Harris, T. B., & Wallace, R. (2004). Religious participation, Interleukin-6, and mortality in older adults. *Health Psychology, 23,* 465–475. (p. C-12)

Lyall, S. (2005, November 29). What's the buzz? Rowdy teenagers don't want to hear it. *New York Times* (www.nytimes.com). (p. 458)

Lykins, A. D., Meana, M., & Strauss, G. P. (2008). Sex differences in visual attention to erotic and non-erotic stimuli. *Archives of Sexual Behavior, 37,* 219–228. (p. 355)

Lykken, D. T. (1982, September). Fearlessness: Its carefree charm and deadly risks. *Psychology Today,* pp. 20–28. (p. 387)

Lykken, D. T. (1991). Science, lies, and controversy: An epitaph for the polygraph. Invited address upon receipt of the Senior Career Award for Distinguished Contribution to Psychology in the Public Interest, American Psychological Association convention. (p. 372)

Lykken, D. T. (1995). *The antisocial personalities.* Hillsdale, NJ: Erlbaum. (pp. 597, 672)

Lykken, D. T. (1999). *Happiness.* New York: Golden Books. (pp. 463, 544)

Lykken, D. T. (2001). Happiness—stuck with what you've got? *The Psychologist, 14,* 470–473. (p. 99)

Lykken, D. T., & Tellegen, A. (1993) Is human mating adventitious or the result of lawful choice? A twin study of mate selection. *Journal of Personality and Social Psychology, 65,* 56–68. (p. 466)

Lykken, D. T., & Tellegen, A. (1996). Happiness is a stochastic phenomenon. *Psychological Science, 7,* 186–189. (p. 396)

Lyman, D. R. (1996). Early identification of chronic offenders: Who is the fledgling psychopath? *Psychological Bulletin, 120,* 209–234. (p. 598)

Lynch, G. (2002). Memory enhancement: The search for mechanism-based drugs. *Nature Neuroscience, 5* (suppl.), 1035–1038. (p. 269)

Lynch, G., & Staubli, U. (1991). Possible contributions of long-term potentiation to the encoding and organization of memory. *Brain Research Reviews, 16,* 204–206. (p. 269)

Lynn, M. (1988). The effects of alcohol consumption on restaurant tipping. *Personality and Social Psychology Bulletin, 14,* 87–91. (p. 199)

Lynn, R. (1991, Fall/Winter). The evolution of racial differences in intelligence. *The Mankind Quarterly, 32,* 99–145. (p. 552)

Lynn, R. (2001). *Eugenics: A reassessment.* Westport, CT: Praeger/Greenwood. (p. 552)

Lynn, R., & Harvey, J. (2008). The decline of the world's intelligence. *Intelligence, 36,* 112–120. (p. 538)

Lynn, S. J., Rhue, J. W., & Weekes, J. R. (1990). Hypnotic involuntariness: A social cognitive analysis. *Psychological Review, 97,* 169–184. (p. 195)

Lynne, S. D., Graber, J. A., Nichols, T. R., Brooks-Gunn, J., & Botvin, G. J. (2007). Links between pubertal timing, peer influences, and externalizing behaviors among urban students followed through middle school. *Journal of Adolescent Health, 40,* 181.e7–181.e13. (p. 447)

Lyons, L. (2002, June 25). Are spiritual teens healthier? *Gallup Tuesday Briefing,* Gallup Organization (www.gallup.com/poll/tb/religValue/20020625b.asp). (p. C-11)

Lyons, L. (2003, September 23). Oh, boy: Americans still prefer sons. *Gallup Poll Tuesday Briefing* (www.gallup.com). (p. 667)

Lyons, L. (2004, February 3). Growing up lonely: Examining teen alienation. *Gallup Poll Tuesday Briefing* (www.gallup.com). (p. 452)

Lyons, L. (2005, January 4). Teens stay true to parents' political perspectives. *Gallup Poll News Service* (www.gallup.com). (p. 453)

Lytton, H., & Romney, D. M. (1991). Parents' differential socialization of boys and girls: A meta-analysis. *Psychological Bulletin, 109,* 267–296. (p. 440)

Lyubomirsky, S. (2001). Why are some people happier than others? The role of cognitive and motivational processes in well-being. *American Psychologist, 56,* 239–249. (p. 394)

Lyubomirsky, S., King, L., & Diener, E. (2005). The benefits of frequent positive affect: Does happiness lead to success? *Psychological Bulletin, 131,* 803–855. (p. 389)

Lyubomirsky, S., Sousa, L., & Dickerhoof, R. (2006). The costs and benefits of writing, talking, and thinking about life's triumphs and defeats. *Journal of Personality and Social Psychology, 90,* 692–708. (p. C-5)

Ma, L. (1997, September). On the origin of Darwin's ills. *Discover,* p. 27. (p. 571)

Maas, J. B. (1999). *Power sleep. The revolutionary program that prepares your mind and body for peak performance.* New York: HarperCollins. (pp. 183, 184, 186)

Maass, A., D'Ettole, C., & Cadinu, M. (2008). Checkmate? The role of gender stereotypes in the ultimate intellectual sport. *European Journal of Social Psychology, 38,* 231–245. (p. 555)

Maass, A., Karasawa, M., Politi, F., & Suga, S. (2006). Do verbs and adjectives play different roles in different cultures? A cross-linguistic analysis of person representation. *Journal of Personality and Social Psychology, 90,* 734–750. (p. 518)

Maass, A., & Russo, A. (2003). Directional bias in the mental representation of spatial events: Nature or culture? *Psychological Science, 14,* 296–301. (p. 320)

Macaluso, E., Frith, C. D., & Driver, J. (2000). Modulation of human visual cortex by crossmodal spatial attention. *Science, 289,* 1206–1208. (p. 148)

Macan, T. H., & Dipboye, R. L. (1994). The effects of the application on processing of information from the employment interview. *Journal of Applied Social Psychology, 24,* 1291. (p. B-5)

Maccoby, E. E. (1980). *Social development: Psychological growth and the parent-child relationship.* New York: Harcourt Brace Jovanovich. (p. 433)

Maccoby, E. E. (1990). Gender and relationships: A developmental account. *American Psychologist, 45,* 513–520. (p. 437)

Maccoby, E. E. (1995). Divorce and custody: The rights, needs, and obligations of mothers, fathers, and children. *Nebraska Symposium on Motivation, 42,* 135–172. (p. 439)

Maccoby, E. E. (1998). *The paradox of gender.* Cambridge, MA: Harvard University Press. (p. 438)

Maccoby, E. E. (2002). Gender and group process: A developmental perspective. *Current Directions in Psychological Science, 11,* 54–58. (p. 659)

Maccoby, E. E. (2003, July 22). In Susan Gilbert, Turning a mass of data on child care into advice for parents. *New York Times* (www.nytimes.com). (p. 432)

MacDonald, G., & Leary, M. R. (2005). Why does social exclusion hurt? The relationship between social and physical pain. *Psychological Bulletin, 131,* 202–223. (p. 362)

MacDonald, N. (1960). Living with schizophrenia. *Canadian Medical Association Journal, 82,* 218–221. (p. 590)

MacDonald, T. K., & Hynie, M. (2008). Ambivalence and unprotected sex: Failure to predict sexual activity and decreased condom use. *Journal of Applied Social Psychology, 38,* 1092–1107. (p. 353)

MacDonald, T. K., Zanna, M. P., & Fong, G. T. (1995). Decision making in altered states: Effects of alcohol on attitudes toward drinking and driving. *Journal of Personality and Social Psychology, 68,* 973–985. (p. 199)

MacFarlane, A. (1978, February). What a baby knows. *Human Nature,* pp. 74–81. (p. 415)

Macfarlane, J. W. (1964). Perspectives on personality consistency and change from the guidance study. *Vita Humana, 7,* 115–126. (p. 445)

Maciejewski, P. K., Zhang, B., Block, S. D., & Prigerson, H. G. (2007). An empirical examination of the stage theory of grief. *JAMA (Journal of the American Medical Association), 297,* 722–723. (p. 471)

Mack, A., & Rock, I. (2000). *Inattentional blindness.* Cambridge, MA: MIT Press. (p. 118)

MacKinnon, D. W., & Hall, W. B. (1972). Intelligence and creativity. In *Proceedings, XVIIth International Congress of Applied Psychology* (Vol. 2). Brussels: Editest. (p. 301)

MacLachlan, M., Desmond, D., & Horgan, O. (2003). Psychological correlates of illusory body experience. *Journal of Rehabilitation Research and Development, 40,* 59–66. (p. 142)

MacNeilage, P. F., & Davis, B. L. (2000). On the origin of internal structure of word forms. *Science, 288,* 527–531. (p. 315)

Maddieson, I. (1984). *Patterns of sounds.* Cambridge: Cambridge University Press. (p. 313)

Maddox, K. B. (2004). Perspectives on racial phenotypicality bias. *Personality and Social Psychology Review, 8,* 383–401. (p. 666)

Madrian, B. C., & Shea, D. F. (2001). The power of suggestion: Inertia in 401(k) participation and savings behavior. *Quarterly Journal of Economics, 116,* 1149–1187. (p. 312)

Maes, H. H. M., Neale, M. C., & Eaves, L. J. (1997). Genetic and environmental factors in relative body weight and human adiposity. *Behavior Genetics, 27,* 325–351. (p. 344)

Maestripieri, D. (2003). Similarities in affiliation and aggression between cross-fostered rhesus macaque females and their biological mothers. *Developmental Psychobiology, 43,* 321–327. (p. 99)

Maestripieri, D. (2005). Early experience affects the intergenerational transmission of infant abuse in rhesus monkeys. *Proceedings of the National Academy of Sciences, 102,* 9726–9729. (p. 430)

Magnusson, D. (1990). Personality research—challenges for the future. *European Journal of Personality, 4,* 1–17. (p. 597)

Magnusson, P. E. E., Rasmussen, F., Lawlor, D. A., Tynelius, P., & Gunnell, D. (2006). Association of body mass index with suicide mortality: A prospective cohort study of more than one million men. *American Journal of Epidemiology, 163,* 1–8. (p. 584)

Maguire, E. A., Spiers, H. J., Good, C. D., Hartley, T., Frackowiak, R. S. J., & Burgess, N. (2003a). Navigation expertise and the human hippocampus: A structural brain imaging analysis. *Hippocampus, 13,* 250–259. (p. 273)

Maguire, E. A., Valentine, E. R., Wilding, J. M., & Kapur, N. (2003). Routes to remembering: The brains behind superior memory. *Nature Neuroscience, 6,* 90–95. (pp. 264, 273)

Mahowald, M. W., & Ettinger, M. G. (1990). Things that go bump in the night: The parsomias revisted. *Journal of Clinical Neurophysiology, 7,* 119–143. (p. 180)

Maier, S. F., Watkins, L. R., & Fleshner, M. (1994). Psychoneuroimmunology: The interface between behavior, brain, and immunity. *American Psychologist, 49,* 1004–1017. (p. 404)

Malamuth, N. M. (1996). Sexually explicit media, gender differences, and evolutionary theory. *Journal of Communication, 46,* 8–31. (p. 674)

Malamuth, N. M., & Check, J. V. P. (1981). The effects of media exposure on acceptance of violence against women: A field experiment. *Journal of Research in Personality, 15,* 436–446. (p. 351)

Malamuth, N. M., Linz, D., Heavey, C. L., Barnes, G., & Acker, M. (1995). Using the confluence model of sexual aggression to predict men's conflict with women: A 10-year follow-up study. *Journal of Personality and Social Psychology, 69,* 353–369. (p. 675)

Malamuth, N. M., Sockloskie, R. J., Koss, M. P., & Tanaka, J. S. (1991). Characteristics of aggressors against women: Testing a model using a national sample of college students. *Journal of Consulting and Clinical Psychology, 59,* 670–681. (p. 675)

Malan, D. H. (1978) "The case of the secretary with the violent father." In H. Davanloo (Ed.), *Basic principles and techniques in short-term dynamic psychotherapy.* New York: Spectrum. (p. 608)

Malinosky-Rummell, R., & Hansen, D. J. (1993). Long-term consequences of childhood physical abuse. *Psychological Bulletin, 114,* 68–79. (p. 430)

Malkiel, B. G. (1989). Is the stock market efficient? *Science, 243,* 1313–1318. (p. 33)

Malkiel, B. G. (1995, June). Returns from investing in equity mutual funds 1971 to 1991. *Journal of Finance,* pp. 549–572. (p. 33)

Malkiel, B. G. (2004). *A random walk down Wall Street* (8th ed.). New York: Norton. (p. 307)

Malle, B. F. (2006). The actor-observer asymmetry in attribution: A (surprising) meta-analysis. *Psychological Bulletin, 132,* 895–919. (p. 645)

Malle, B. F., Knobe, J. M., & Nelson, S. E. (2007). Actor-observe asymmetries in explanations of behavior: New answers to an old question. *Journal of Personality and Social Psychology, 93,* 491–514. (p. 645)

Malmquist, C. P. (1986). Children who witness parental murder: Posttraumatic aspects. *Journal of the American Academy of Child Psychiatry, 25,* 320–325. (p. 488)

Malnic, B., Hirono, J., Sato, T., & Buck, L. B. (1999). Combinatorial receptor codes for odors. *Cell, 96,* 713–723. (p. 149)

Manber, R., Bootzin, R. R., Acebo, C., & Carskadon, M. A. (1996). The effects of regularizing sleep-wake schedules on daytime sleepiness. *Sleep, 19,* 432–441. (p. 186)

Mandel, D. (1983, March 13). One man's holocaust: Part II. The story of David Mandel's journey through hell as told to David Kagan. *Wonderland Magazine (Grand Rapids Press),* pp. 2–7. (p. 331)

Maner, J. K., DeWall, C. N., Baumeister, R. F., & Schaller, M. (2007). Does social exclusion motivate interpersonal reconnection? Resolving the "porcupine problem." *Journal of Personality and Social Psychology, 92,* 42–55. (p. 362)

Mann, T., Tomiyama, A. J., Westling, E., Lew, A-M., Samuels, B., & Chatman, J. (2007). Medicare's search for effective obesity treatments: Diets are not the answer. *American Psychologist, 62,* 220–233. (p. 346)

Manson, J. E. (2002). Walking compared with vigorous exercise for the prevention of cardiovascular events in women. *New England Journal of Medicine, 347,* 716–725. (p. C-7)

Maquet, P. (2001). The role of sleep in learning and memory. *Science, 294,* 1048–1052. (p. 190)

Maquet, P., Peters, J-M., Aerts, J., Delfiore, G., Degueldre, C., Luxen, A., & Franck, G. (1996). Functional neuroanatomy of human rapid-eye-movement sleep and dreaming. *Nature, 383,* 163–166. (p. 191)

Mar, R. A., & Oatley, K. (2008). The function of fiction is the abstraction and simulation of social experience. *Perspectives on Psychological Science, 3,* 173–192. (p. 244)

Marangell, L. B., Martinez, M., Jurdi, R. A., & Zboyan, H. (2007). Neurostimulation therapies in depression: A review of new modalities. *Acta Psychiatrica Scandinavica, 116,* 174–181. (p. 634)

Marcus, B., Machilek, F., & Schütz, A. (2006). Personality in cyberspace: Personal web sites as media for personality expressions and impressions. *Journal of Personality and Social Psychology, 90,* 1014–1031. (p. 502)

Marcus, G. F., Vijayan, S., Rao, S. B., & Vishton, P. M. (1999). Rule learning by seven-month-old infants. *Science, 283,* 77–80. (p. 317)

Maren, S. (2007). The threatened brain. *Science, 317,* 1043–1044. (p. 576)

Margolis, M. L. (2000). Brahms' lullaby revisited: Did the composer have obstructive sleep apnea? *Chest, 118,* 210–213. (p. 187)

Markowitsch, H. J. (1995). Which brain regions are critically involved in the retrieval of old episodic memory? *Brain Research Reviews, 21,* 117–127. (p. 273)

Markowitz, J. C., Svartberg, M., & Swartz, H. A. (1998). Is IPT time-limited psychodynamic psychotherapy? *Journal of Psychotherapy Practice and Research, 7,* 185–195. (p. 608)

Markus, G. B. (1986). Stability and change in political attitudes: Observe, recall, and "explain." *Political Behavior, 8,* 21–44. (p. 289)

Markus, H. R., & Kitayama, S. (1991). Culture and the self: Implications for cognition, emotion, and motivation. *Psychological Review, 98,* 224–253. (pp. 320, 387, 517)

Markus, H. R., & Nurius, P. (1986). Possible selves. *American Psychologist, 41,* 954–969. (p. 511)

Markus, H. R., Uchida, Y., Omoregie, H., Townsend, S. S. M., & Kitayama, S. (2006). Going for the gold: Models of agency in Japanese and American contexts. *Psychological Science, 17,* 103–112. (p. 518)

Marley, J., & Bulia, S. (2001). Crimes against people with mental illness: Types, perpetrators and influencing factors. *Social Work, 46,* 115–124. (p. 568)

Marmot, M. G., Bosma, H., Hemingway, H., Brunner, E., & Stansfeld, S. (1997). Contribution to job control and other risk factors to social variations in coronary heart disease incidents. *Lancet, 350,* 235–239. (p. C-2)

Marschark, M., Richman, C. L., Yuille, J. C., & Hunt, R. R. (1987). The role of imagery in memory: On shared and distinctive information. *Psychological Bulletin, 102,* 28–41. (p. 263)

Marsh, A. A., Elfenbein, H. A., & Ambady, N. (2003). Nonverbal "accents": Cultural differences in facial expressions of emotion. *Psychological Science, 14,* 373–376. (p. 381)

Marsh, H. W., & Craven, R. G. (2006). Reciprocal effects of self-concept and performance from a multidimensional perspective: Beyond seductive pleasure and unidimensional perspectives. *Perspectives on Psychological Science, 1,* 133–163. (p. 512)

Marsh, H. W., & Parker, J. W. (1984). Determinants of student self-concept: Is it better to be a relatively large fish in a small pond even if you don't learn to swim as well? *Journal of Personality and Social Psychology, 47,* 213–231. (p. 395)

Marshall, M. J. (2002). *Why spanking doesn't work.* Springville, UT: Bonneville Books. (p. 234)

Marshall, R. D., Bryant, R. A., Amsel, L., Suh, E. J., Cook, J. M., & Neria, Y. (2007). The psychology of ongoing threat: Relative risk appraisal, the September 11 attacks, and terrorism-related fears. *American Psychologist, 62,* 304–316. (p. 306)

Marshall, W. L. (1989). Pornography and sex offenders. In D. Zillmann & J. Bryant (Eds.), *Pornography: Research advances and policy considerations*. Hillsdale, NJ: Erlbaum. (p. 675)

Marteau, T. M. (1989). Framing of information: Its influences upon decisions of doctors and patients. *British Journal of Social Psychology, 28*, 89-94. (p. 311)

Marti, M. W., Robier, D. M., & Baron, R. S. (2000). Right before our eyes: The failure to recognize non-prototypical forms of prejudice. *Group Processes and Intergroup Relations, 3*, 403-418. 409-416. (p. 300)

Martin, C. K., Anton, S. D., Walden, H., Arnett, C., Greenway, F. L., & Williamson, D. A. (2007). Slower eating rate reduces the food intake of men, but not women: Implications for behavioural weight control. *Behaviour Research and Therapy, 45*, 2349-2359. (p. 347)

Martin, C. L., & Ruble, D. (2004). Children's search for gender cues. *Current Directions in Psychological Science, 13*, 67-70. (p. 440)

Martin, C. L., Ruble, D. N., & Szkrybalo, J. (2002). Cognitive theories of early gender development. *Psychological Bulletin, 128*, 903-933. (p. 440)

Martin, R. A. (2001). Humor, laughter, and physical health: Methodological issues and research findings. *Psychological Bulletin, 127*, 504-519. (p. C-3)

Martin, R. A. (2002). Is laughter the best medicine? Humor, laughter, and physical health. *Current Directions in Psychological Science, 11*, 216-220. (p. C-3)

Martin, R. J., White, B. D., & Hulsey, M. G. (1991). The regulation of body weight. *American Scientist, 79*, 528-541. (p. 335)

Martin, R. M., Goodall, S. H., Gunnell, D., & Smith, G. D. (2007). Breast feeding in infancy and social mobility: 60-year follow-up of the Boyd Orr cohort. *Archives of Disease in Childhood, 92*, 317-321. (p. 34)

Martin, S. J., Kelly, I. W., & Saklofske, D. H. (1992). Suicide and lunar cycles: A critical review over 28 years. *Psychological Reports, 71*, 787-795. (p. 599)

Martino, S. C., Collins, R. L., Kanouse, D. E., Elliott, M., & Berry, S. H. (2005). Social cognitive processes mediating the relationship between exposure to television's sexual content and adolescents' sexual behavior. *Journal of Personality and Social Psychology, 89*, 914-924. (p. 353)

Martins, Y., Preti, G., Crabtree, C. R., & Wysocki, C. J. (2005). Preference for human body odors is influenced by gender and sexual orientation. *Psychological Science, 16*, 694-701. (p. 357)

Marx, J. (2005). Preventing Alzheimer's: A lifelong commitment? *Science, 309*, 864-866. (p. 461)

Marx, J. (2007). Evidence linking *DISC1* gene to mental illness builds. *Science, 318*, 1062-1063. (p. 595)

Masicampo, E. J., & Baumeister, R. F. (2008). Toward a physiology of dual-process reasoning and judgment: Lemonade, willpower, and the expensive rule-based analysis. *Psychological Science, 19*, 255-260. (p. 505)

Maslow, A. H. (1970). *Motivation and personality (2nd ed.)*. New York: Harper & Row. (pp. 330, 331, 491)

Maslow, A. H. (1971). *The farther reaches of human nature*. New York: Viking Press. (p. 330)

Mason, C., & Kandel, E. R. (1991). Central visual pathways. In E. R. Kandel, J. H. Schwartz, & T. M. Jessell (Eds.), *Principles of neural science* (3rd ed.). New York: Elsevier. (p. 59)

Mason, H. (2003, March 25). Wake up, sleepy teen. *Gallup Poll Tuesday Briefing* (www.gallup.com). (p. 183)

Mason, H. (2003, September 2). Americans, Britons at odds on animal testing. *Gallup Poll News Service* (www.gallup.com). (p. 44)

Mason, H. (2005, February 22). How many teens are on mood medication? *The Gallup Organization* (www.gallup.com). (p. 563)

Mason, H. (2005, January 25). Who dreams, perchance to sleep? *Gallup Poll News Service* (www.gallup.com). (pp. 182, 183)

Mason, R. A., & Just, M. A. (2004). How the brain processes causal inferences in text. *Psychological Science, 15*, 1-7. (p. 87)

Masse, L. C., & Tremblay, R. E. (1997). Behavior of boys in kindergarten and the onset of substance use during adolescence. *Archives of General Psychiatry, 54*, 62-68. (p. 209)

Massimini, M., Ferrarelli, F., Huber, R., Esser, S. K., Singh, H., & Tononi, G. (2005). Breakdown of cortical effective connectivity during sleep. *Science, 309*, 2228-2232. (p. 178)

Mast, M. S., & Hall, J. A. (2006). Women's advantage at remembering others' appearance: A systematic look at the why and when of a gender difference. *Personality and Social Psychology Bulletin, 32*, 353-364. (p. 681)

Masten, A. S. (2001). Ordinary magic: Resilience processes in development. *American Psychologist, 56*, 227-238. (p. 430)

Masters, W. H., & Johnson, V. E. (1966). *Human sexual response*. Boston: Little, Brown. (p. 349)

Mastroianni, G. R. (2002). Milgram and the Holocaust: A reexamination. *Journal of Theoretical and Philosophical Psychology, 22*, 158-173. (p. 656)

Mastroianni, G. R., & Reed, G. (2006). Apples, barrels, and Abu Ghraib. *Sociological Focus, 39*, 239-250. (p. 648)

Masuda, T., Ellsworth, P. C., Mesquita, B., Leu, J., Tanida, S., & Van de Veerdonk, E. (2008). Placing the face in context: Cultural differences in the perception of facial emotion. *Journal of Personality and Social Psychology, 94*, 365-381. (p. 382)

Masuda, T., & Kitayama, S. (2004). Perceiver-induced constraint and attitude attribution in Japan and the US: A case for the cultural dependence of the correspondence bias. *Journal of Experimental Social Psychology, 40*, 409-416. (p. 644)

Mataix-Cols, D., Rosario-Campos, M. C., & Leckman, J. F. (2005). A multidimensional model of obsessive-compulsive disorder. *American Journal of Psychiatry, 162*, 228-238. (p. 575)

Mataix-Cols, D., Wooderson, S., Lawrence, N., Brammer, M. J., Speckens, A., & Phillips, M. L. (2004). Distinct neural correlates of washing, checking, and hoarding symptom dimensions in obsessive-compulsive disorder. *Archives of General Psychiatry, 61*, 564-576. (p. 575)

Mather, M., Canli, T., English, T., Whitfield, S., Wais, P., Ochsner, K., Gabrieli, J. D. E., & Carstensen, L. L. (2004). Amygdala responses to emotionally valenced stimuli in older and younger adults. *Psychological Science, 15*, 259-263. (p. 469)

Matsumoto, D. (1994). *People: Psychology from a cultural perspective*. Pacific Grove, CA: Brooks/Cole. (p. 320)

Matsumoto, D., & Ekman, P. (1989). American-Japanese cultural differences in intensity ratings of facial expressions of emotion. *Motivation and Emotion, 13*, 143-157. (p. 381)

Matsumoto, D., & Willingham, B. (2006). The thrill of victory and the agony of defeat: Spontaneous expressions of medal winners of the 2004 Athens Olympic Games. *Journal of Personality and Social Psychology, 91*, 568-581. (p. 381)

Matsumoto, D., & 60 others. (2008). Mapping expressive differences around the world: The relationship between emotional display rules and individualism versus collectivism. *Journal of Cross-Cultural Psychology, 39*, 55-74. (p. 381)

Matsuzawa, T. (2007). Comparative cognitive development. *Developmental Science, 10*, 97-103. (p. D-1)

Matthews, K. A. (2005). Psychological perspectives on the development of coronary heart disease. *American Psychologist, 60*, 783-796. (p. 403)

Matthews, R. N., Domjan, M., Ramsey, M., & Crews, D. (2007). Learning effects on sperm competition and reproductive fitness. *Psychological Science, 18*, 758-762. (p. 220)

Maurer, D., & Maurer, C. (1988). *The world of the newborn*. New York: Basic Books. (p. 415)

May, C., & Hasher, L. (1998). Synchrony effects in inhibitory control over thought and action. *Journal of Experimental Psychology: Human Perception and Performance, 24*, 363-380. (p. 177)

May, P. A., & Gossage, J.P. (2001). Estimating the prevalence of fetal alcohol syndrome: A summary. *Alcohol Research and Health, 25*, 159-167. (p. 413)

Mayberg, H. S. (2006). Defining neurocircuits in depression: Strategies toward treatment selection based on neuroimaging phenotypes. *Psychiatric Annals, 36*, 259-268. (p. 635)

Mayberg, H. S. (2007). Defining the neural circuitry of depression: Toward a new nosology with therapeutic implications. *Biological Psychiatry, 61*, 729-730. (p. 635)

Mayberg, H. S., Lozano, A. M., Voon, V., McNeely, H. E., Seminowicz, D., Hamani, C., Schwalb, J. M., & Kennedy, S. H. (2005). Deep brain stimulation for treatment-resistant depression. *Neuron, 45*, 651-660. (p. 635)

Mayberry, R. I., Lock, E., & Kazmi, H. (2002). Linguistic ability and early language exposure. *Nature, 417*, 38. (p. 318)

Mayer, J. D. Salovey, P., & Caruso, D. (2002). *The Mayer-Salovey-Caruso emotional intelligence test (MSCEIT)*. Toronto: Multi-Health Systems, Inc. (p. 528)

Mayer, J. D., Salovey, P., & Caruso, D. R. (2008). Emotional intelligence: New ability or eclectic traits? *American Psychologist, 63*, 503-517. (p. 528)

Mays, V. M., Cochran, S. D., & Barnes, N. W. (2007). Race, race-based discrimination, and health outcomes among African Americans. *Annual Review of Psychology, 58,* 201–225. (p. 401)

Mazur, A., & Booth, A. (1998). Testosterone and dominance in men. *Behavioral and Brain Sciences, 21,* 353–363. (p. 672)

Mazure, C., Keita, G., & Blehar, M. (2002). *Summit on women and depression: Proceedings and recommendations.* Washington, DC: American Psychological Association (www.apa.org/pi/wpo/women&depression.pdf). (p. 587)

Mazzoni, G., & Memon, A. (2003). Imagination can create false autobiographical memories. *Psychological Science, 14,* 186–188. (p. 286)

Mazzoni, G., & Vannucci, M. (2007). Hindsight bias, the misinformation effect, and false autobiographical memories. *Social Cognition, 25,* 203–220. (p. 289)

Mazzuca, J. (2002, August 20). Teens shrug off movie sex and violence. *Gallup Tuesday Briefing* (www.gallup.com/poll/tb/educayouth/20020820b.asp). (p. 248)

McAdams, D. P., & Pals, J. L. (2006). A new Big Five: Fundamental principles for an integrative science of personality. *American Psychologist, 61,* 204–217. (p. 479)

McAneny, L. (1996, September). Large majority think government conceals information about UFO's. *Gallup Poll Monthly,* pp. 23–26. (p. 276)

McBeath, M. K., Shaffer, D. M., & Kaiser, M. K. (1995). How baseball outfielders determine where to run to catch fly balls. *Science, 268,* 569–572. (p. 156)

McBurney, D. H. (1996). *How to think like a psychologist: Critical thinking in psychology.* Upper Saddle River, NJ: Prentice-Hall. (p. 79)

McBurney, D. H., & Collings, V. B. (1984). *Introduction to sensation and perception* (2nd ed.). Englewood Cliffs, NJ: Prentice-Hall. (pp. 158, 159)

McBurney, D. H., & Gent, J. F. (1979). On the nature of taste qualities. *Psychological Bulletin, 86,* 151–167. (p. 146)

McCain, N. L., Gray, D. P., Elswick, Jr., R. K., Robins, J. W., Tuck, I., Walter, J. M., Rausch, S. M., & Ketchum, J. M. (2008). A randomized clinical trial of alternative stress management interventions in persons with HIV infection. *Journal of Consulting and Clinical Psychology, 76,* 431–441. (p. 405)

McCann, I. L., & Holmes, D. S. (1984). Influence of aerobic exercise on depression. *Journal of Personality and Social Psychology, 46,* 1142–1147. (pp. C-6, C-7)

McCann, U. D., Eligulashvili, V., & Ricaurte, G. A. (2001). (+-)3,4-Methylenedioxymethamphetamine ('Ecstasy')-induced serotonin neurotoxicity: Clinical studies. *Neuropsychobiology, 12,* 11–16. (p. 205)

McCarthy, A., Lee, K., Itakura, S., & Muir, D. W. (2006). Cultural display rules drive eye gaze during thinking. *Journal of Cross-Cultural Psychology, 37,* 717–722. (p. 382)

McCarthy, P. (1986, July). Scent: The tie that binds? *Psychology Today,* pp. 6, 10. (p. 148)

McCaul, K. D., & Malott, J. M. (1984). Distraction and coping with pain. *Psychological Bulletin, 95,* 516–533. (p. 146)

McCauley, C. R. (2002). Psychological issues in understanding terrorism and the response to terrorism. In C. E. Stout (Ed.), *The psychology of terrorism, Vol. 3.* Westport, CT: Praeger/Greenwood. (p. 660)

McCauley, C. R., & Segal, M. E. (1987). Social psychology of terrorist groups. In C. Hendrick (Ed.), *Group processes and intergroup relations.* Beverly Hills, CA: Sage. (p. 660)

McClearn, G. E., Johansson, B., Berg, S., Pedersen, N. L., Ahern, F., Petrill, S. A., & Plomin, R. (1997). Substantial genetic influence on cognitive abilities in twins 80 or more years old. *Science, 276,* 1560–1563. (p. 545)

McClellan, J. M., Susser, E., & King, M-C. (2007). Schizophrenia: A common disease caused by multiple rare alleles. *British Journal of Psychiatry, 190,* 194–199. (p. 595)

McClendon, B. T., & Prentice-Dunn, S. (2001). Reducing skin cancer risk: An intervention based on protection motivation theory. *Journal of Health Psychology, 6,* 321–328. (p. 646)

McClintock, M. K., & Herdt, G. (December, 1996). Rethinking puberty: The development of sexual attraction. *Current Directions in Psychological Science, 5*(6), 178–183. (p. 446)

McClure, E. B. (2000). A meta-analytic review of sex differences in facial expression processing and their development in infants, children, and adolescents. *Psychological Bulletin, 126,* 424–453. (p. 549)

McConkey, K. M. (1995). Hypnosis, memory, and the ethics of uncertainty. *Australian Psychologist, 30,* 1–10. (p. 193)

McConnell, R. A. (1991). National Academy of Sciences opinion on parapsychology. *Journal of the American Society for Psychical Research, 85,* 333–365. (p. 166)

McCool, G. (1999, October 26). Mirror-gazing Venezuelans top of vanity stakes. *Toronto Star* (via web.lexis-nexis.com). (p. 680)

McCord, J. (1978). A thirty-year follow-up on treatment effects. *American Psychologist, 33,* 284–289. (p. 620)

McCord, J. (1979). Following up on Cambridge-Somerville. *American Psychologist, 34,* 727. (p. 620)

McCormick, C. M., & Witelson, S. F. (1991). A cognitive profile of homosexual men compared to heterosexual men and women. *Psychoneuroendocrinology, 16,* 459–473. (p. 359)

McCrae, R. R., & Costa, P. T., Jr. (1986). Clinical assessment can benefit from recent advances in personality psychology. *American Psychologist, 41,* 1001–1003. (p. 497)

McCrae, R. R., & Costa, P. T., Jr. (1990). *Personality in adulthood.* New York: Guilford. (p. 465)

McCrae, R. R., & Costa, P. T., Jr. (1994). The stability of personality: Observations and evaluations. *Current Directions in Psychological Science, 3,* 173–175. (pp. 473, 500)

McCrae, R. R., Costa, P. T., Jr., de Lirna, M. P., Simoes, A., Ostendorf, F., Angleitner, A., Marusic, I., Bratko, D., Caprara, G. V., Barbaranelli, C., Chae, J-H., & Piedmont, R. L. (1999). Age differences in personality across the adult life span: Parallels in five cultures. *Developmental Psychology, 35,* 466–477. (p. 498)

McCrae, R. R., Costa, P. T., Jr., Ostendorf, F., Angleitner, A., Hrebickova, M., Avia, M. D., Sanz, J., Sanchez-Bernardos, M. L., Kusdil, M. E., Woodfield, R., Saunders, P. R., & Smith, P. B. (2000). Nature over nurture: Temperament, personality, and life span development. *Journal of Personality and Social Psychology, 78,* 173–186. (p. 428)

McCrae, R. R., Terracciano, A., & Khoury, B. (2007). Dolce far niente: The positive psychology of personality stability and invariance. In A. D. Ong & M. H. Van Dulmen (Eds.), *Oxford handbook of methods in positive psychology.* New York: Oxford University Press. (p. 428)

McCrink, K., & Wynn, K. (2004). Large-number addition and subtraction by 9-month-old infants. *Psychological Science, 15,* 776–781. (p. 420)

McCullough, M. E., Hoyt, W. T., Larson, D. B., Koenig, H. G., & Thoresen, C. (2000). Religious involvement and mortality: A meta-analytic review. *Health Psychology, 19,* 211–222. (p. C-11)

McCullough, M. E., & Laurenceau, J-P. (2005). Religiousness and the trajectory of self-rated health across adulthood. *Personality and Social Psychology Bulletin, 31,* 560–573. (p. C-11)

McDaniel, M. A. (2005). Big-brained people are smarter: A meta-analysis of the relationship between in vivo brain volume and intelligence. *Intelligence, 33,* 337–346. (p. 530)

McDermott, T. (2005). *Perfect soldiers: The 9/11 hijackers: Who they were, why they did it.* New York: HarperCollins. (p. 673)

McEvoy, S. P., Stevenson, M. R., McCartt, A. T., Woodward, M., Hawroth, C., Palamara, P., & Ceracelli, R. (2005). Role of mobile phones in motor vehicle crashes resulting in hospital attendance: A case-crossover study. *British Medical Journal, 33,* 428. (p. 118)

McEvoy, S. P., Stevenson, M. R., & Woodward, M. (2007). The contribution of passengers versus mobile phone use to motor vehicle crashes resulting in hospital attendance by the driver. *Accident Analysis and Prevention, 39,* 1170–1176. (p. 118)

McFadden, D. (2002). Masculinization effects in the auditory system. *Archives of Sexual Behavior, 31,* 99–111. (p. 358)

McFarland, C., & Ross, M. (1987). The relation between current impressions and memories of self and dating partners. *Psychological Bulletin, 13,* 228–238. (p. 289)

McGarry-Roberts, P. A., Stelmack, R. M., & Campbell, K. B. (1992). Intelligence, reaction time, and event-related potentials. *Intelligence, 16,* 289–313. (p. 531)

McGaugh, J. L. (1994). Quoted by B. Bower, Stress hormones hike emotional memories. *Science News, 146,* 262. (p. 270)

McGaugh, J. L. (2003). *Memory and emotion: The making of lasting memories.* New York: Columbia University Press. (pp. 255, 270)

McGhee, P. E. (June, 1976). Children's appreciation of humor: A test of the cognitive congruency principle. *Child Development, 47(2),* 420–426. (p. 423)

McGlone, M. S., & Tofighbakhsh, J. (2000). Birds of a feather flock conjointly (?): Rhyme as reason in aphorisms. *Psychological Science, 11,* 424–428. (p. 261)

McGrath, J. J., & Welham, J. L. (1999). Season of birth and schizophrenia: A systematic review and meta-analysis of data from the Southern hemisphere. *Schizophrenia Research, 35,* 237–242. (p. 593)

McGrath, J. J., Welham, J. L., & Pemberton, M. (1995). Month of birth, hemisphere of birth and schizophrenia. *British Journal of Psychiatry, 167,* 783–785. (p. 593)

McGue, M., & Bouchard, T. J., Jr. (1998). Genetic and environmental influences on human behavioral differences. *Annual Review of Neuroscience, 21,* 1–24. (p. 99)

McGue, M., Bouchard, T. J., Jr., Iacono, W. G., & Lykken, D. T. (1993). Behavioral genetics of cognitive ability: A life-span perspective. In R. Plomin & G. E. McClearn (Eds.), *Nature, nurture and psychology.* Washington, DC: American Psychological Association. (p. 545)

McGue, M., & Lykken, D. T. (1992). Genetic influence on risk of divorce. *Psychological Science, 3,* 368–373. (p. 97)

McGuire, M. T., Wing, R. R., Klem, M. L., Lang, W., & Hill, J. O. (1999). What predicts weight regain in a group of successful weight losers? *Journal of Consulting and Clinical Psychology, 67,* 177–185. (p. 347)

McGuire, W. J. (1986). The myth of massive media impact: Savings and salvagings. In G. Comstock (Ed.), *Public communication and behavior.* Orlando, FL: Academic Press. (p. 247)

McGurk, H., & MacDonald, J. (1976). Hearing lips and seeing voices. *Nature, 264,* 746–748. (p. 148)

McHugh, P. R. (1995a). Witches, multiple personalities, and other psychiatric artifacts. *Nature Medicine, 1(2),* 110–114. (p. 578)

McHugh, P. R. (1995b). Resolved: Multiple personality disorder is an individually and socially created artifact. *Journal of the American Academy of Child and Adolescent Psychiatry, 34,* 957–959. (p. 579)

McKellar, J., Stewart, E., & Humphreys, K. (2003). Alcoholics Anonymous involvement and positive alcohol-related outcomes: Cause, consequence, or just a correlate? A prospective 2-year study of 2,319 alcohol-dependent men. *Journal of Consulting and Clinical Psychology, 71,* 302–308. (p. 618)

McKenna, K. Y. A., & Bargh, J. A. (1998). Coming out in the age of the Internet: Identity "demarginalization" through virtual group participation. *Journal of Personality and Social Psychology, 75,* 681–694. (pp. 660, 679)

McKenna, K. Y. A., & Bargh, J. A. (2000). Plan 9 from cyberspace: The implications of the Internet for personality and social psychology. *Personality and Social Psychology Review, 4,* 57–75. (p. 679)

McKenna, K. Y. A., Green, A. S., & Gleason, M. E. J. (2002). What's the big attraction? Relationship formation on the Internet. *Journal of Social Issues, 58,* 9–31. (p. 679)

McKone, E., Kanwisher, N., & Duchaine, B. C. (2007). Can generic expertise explain special processing for faces? *Trends in Cognitive Sciences, 11,* 8–15. (p. 130)

McLaughlin, C. S., Chen, C., Greenberger, E., & Biermeier, C. (1997). Family, peer, and individual correlates of sexual experience among Caucasian and Asian American late adolescents. *Journal of Personality and Social Psychology: Journal of Research on Adolescence, 7,* 33–53. (p. 352)

McMahon, F. J. & 12 others. (2006). Variation in the gene encoding the serotonin 2A receptor is associated with outcome of antidepressant treatment. *American Journal of Human Genetics, 78,* 804–814. (p. 584)

McMurray, B. (2007). Defusing the childhood vocabulary explosion. *Science, 317,* 631. (p. 315)

McMurray, C. (2004, January 13). U.S., Canada, Britain: Who's getting in shape? *Gallup Poll Tuesday Briefing* (www.gallup.com). (p. C-6)

McMurray, J. (2006, August 28). Cause of deadly Comair crash probed. Associated Press release. (p. 308)

McNally, R. J. (1999). EMDR and Mesmerism: A comparative historical analysis. *Journal of Anxiety Disorders, 13,* 225–236. (p. 624)

McNally, R. J. (2003). *Remembering trauma.* Cambridge, MA: Harvard University Press. (pp. 286, 291, 573)

McNally, R. J. (2007). Betrayal trauma theory: A critical appraisal. *Memory, 15,* 280–294. (p. 291)

McNally, R. J., Bryant, R. A., & Ehlers, A. (2003). Does early psychological intervention promote recovery from posttraumatic stress? *Psychological Science in the Public Interest, 4,* 45–79. (p. 573)

McNeil, B. J., Pauker, S. G., & Tversky, A. (1988). On the framing of medical decisions. In D. E. Bell, H. Raiffa, & A. Tversky (Eds.), *Decision making: Descriptive, normative, and prescriptive interactions.* New York: Cambridge. (p. 311)

McPherson, J. M., Smith-Lovin, L., & Brashears, M. E. (2006). Social isolation in America: Changes in core discussion networks over two decades. *American Sociological Review, 71,* 353–375. (p. 588)

Meador, B. D., & Rogers, C. R. (1984). Person-centered therapy. In R. J. Corsini (Ed.), *Current psychotherapies* (3rd ed.). Itasca, IL: Peacock. (p. 610)

Medical Institute for Sexual Health. (1994, April). Condoms ineffective against human papilloma virus. *Sexual Health Update, 2.* (p. 353)

Medland, S. E., Perelle, I., De Monte, V., & Ehrman, L. (2004). Effects of culture, sex, and age on the distribution of handedness: An evaluation of the sensitivity of three measures of handedness. *Laterality: Asymmetries of Body, Brain, and Cognition, 9,* 287–297. (p. 88)

Mednick, S. A., Huttunen, M. O., & Machon, R. A. (1994). Prenatal influenza infections and adult schizophrenia. *Schizophrenia Bulletin, 20,* 263–267. (p. 593)

Mehl, M. R., Gosling, S. D., & Pennebaker, J. W. (2006). Personality in its natural habitat: Manifestations and implicit folk theories of personality in daily life. *Journal of Personality and Social Psychology, 90,* 862–877. (p. 501)

Mehl, M. R., & Pennebaker, J. W. (2003). The sounds of social life: A psychometric analysis of students' daily social environments and natural conversations. *Journal of Personality and Social Psychology, 84,* 857–870. (p. 29)

Mehl, M. R., Vazire, S., Ramirez-Esparza, N., Slatcher, R. B., & Pennebaker, J. W. (2007). Are women really more talkative than men? *Science, 317,* 82. (p. 437)

Mehta, M. R. (2007). Cortico-hippocampal interaction during up-down states and memory consolidation. *Nature Neuroscience, 10,* 13–15. (p. 273)

Meichenbaum, D. (1977). *Cognitive-behavior modification: An integrative approach.* New York: Plenum Press. (p. 616)

Meichenbaum, D. (1985). *Stress inoculation training.* New York: Pergamon. (p. 616)

Meltzoff, A. N. (1988). Infant imitation after a 1-week delay: Long-term memory for novel acts and multiple stimuli. *Developmental Psychology, 24,* 470–476. (p. 243)

Meltzoff, A. N., & Moore, M. K. (1989). Imitation in newborn infants: Exploring the range of gestures imitated and the underlying mechanisms. *Developmental Psychology, 25,* 954–962. (p. 243)

Meltzoff, A. N., & Moore, M. K. (1997). Explaining facial imitation: A theoretical model. *Early Development and Parenting, 6,* 179–192. (p. 243)

Melzack, R. (1990, February). The tragedy of needless pain. *Scientific American,* pp. 27–33. (p. 198)

Melzack, R. (1992, April). Phantom limbs. *Scientific American,* pp. 120–126. (p. 144)

Melzack, R. (1998, February). Quoted in Phantom limbs. *Discover,* p. 20. (p. 144)

Melzack, R. (2005). Evolution of the neuromatrix theory of pain. *Pain Practice, 5,* 85–94. (p. 144)

Melzack, R., & Wall, P. D. (1965). Pain mechanisms: A new theory. *Science, 150,* 971–979. (p. 143)

Melzack, R., & Wall, P. D. (1983). *The challenge of pain.* New York: Basic Books. (p. 143)

Mendle, J., Turkheimer, E., & Emery, R. E. (2007). Detrimental psychological outcomes associated with early pubertal timing in adolescent girls. *Developmental Review, 27,* 151–171. (p. 447)

Mendolia, M., & Kleck, R. E. (1993). Effects of talking about a stressful event on arousal: Does what we talk about make a difference? *Journal of Personality and Social Psychology, 64,* 283–292. (p. C-5)

Merari, A. (2002). Explaining suicidal terrorism: Theories versus empirical evidence. Invited address to the American Psychological Association. (p. 660)

Merker, B. (2007). Consciousness without a cerebral cortex: A challenge for neuroscience and medicine. *Behavioral and Brain Sciences, 30,* 63–134. (p. 89)

Merskey, H. (1992). The manufacture of personalities: The production of multiple personality disorder. *British Journal of Psychiatry, 160,* 327–340. (p. 578)

Merton, R. K. (1938; reprinted 1970). *Science, technology and society in seventeenth-century England.* New York: Fertig. (p. 23)

Merton, R. K., & Kitt, A. S. (1950). Contributions to the theory of reference group behavior. In R. K. Merton & P. F. Lazarsfeld (Eds.), *Continuities in social research: Studies in the scope and method of the American soldier.* Glencoe, IL: Free Press. (p. 394)

Messinis, L., Kyprianidou, A., Malefaki, S., & Papathanasopoulos, P. (2006). Neuropsychological deficits in long-term frequent cannabis users. *Neurology, 66,* 737–739. (p. 207)

Mestel, R. (1997, April 26). Get real, Siggi. *New Scientist* (www.newscientist.com/ns/970426/siggi.html). (p. 188)

Meston, C. M., & Frohlich, P. F. (2000). The neurobiology of sexual function. *Archives of General Psychiatry, 57,* 1012–1030. (p. 350)

Metcalfe, J. (1986). Premonitions of *insight* predict impending error. *Journal of Experimental Psychology: Learning, Memory, and Cognition, 12,* 623–634. (p. 301)

Metcalfe, J. (1998). Cognitive optimism: Self-deception or memory-based processing heuristics. *Personality and Social Psychology Review, 2,* 100–110. (p. 306)

Meyer, I. H. (2003). Prejudice, social stress, and mental health in lesbian, gay, and bisexual populations: Conceptual issues and research evidence. *Psychological Bulletin, 129,* 674–697. (p. 562)

Meyer-Bahlburg, H. F. L. (1995). Psychoneuroendocrinology and sexual pleasure: The aspect of sexual orientation. In P. R. Abramson & S. D. Pinkerton (Eds.), *Sexual nature/sexual culture.* Chicago: University of Chicago Press. (p. 358)

Mezulis, A. M., Abramson, L. Y., Hyde, J. S., & Hankin, B. L. (2004). Is there a universal positivity bias in attributions? A meta-analytic review of individual, developmental, and cultural differences in the self-serving attributional bias. *Psychological Bulletin, 130,* 711–747. (p. 513)

Michaels, J. W., Bloomel, J. M., Brocato, R. M., Linkous, R. A., & Rowe, J. S. (1982). Social facilitation and inhibition in a natural setting. *Replications in Social Psychology, 2,* 21–24. (p. 658)

Middlebrooks, J. C., & Green, D. M. (1991). Sound localization by human listeners. *Annual Review of Psychology, 42,* 135–159. (p. 138)

Mikhail, J. (2007). Universal moral grammar: Theory, evidence and the future. *Trends in Cognitive Sciences, 11,* 143–152. (p. 317)

Mikkelsen, T. S., & 66 others (2005). Initial sequence of the chimpanzee genome and comparison with the human genome. *Nature, 137,* 69–87. (p. 96)

Mikulincer, M., Babkoff, H., Caspy, T., & Sing, H. (1989). The effects of 72 hours of sleep loss on psychological variables. *British Journal of Psychology, 80,* 145–162. (p. 183)

Mikulincer, M., Florian, V., & Hirschberger, G. (2003). The existential function of close relationships: Introducing death into the science of love. *Personality and Social Psychology Review, 7,* 20–40. (p. 489)

Mikulincer, M., & Shaver, P. R. (2001). Attachment theory and intergroup bias: Evidence that priming the secure base schema attenuates negative reactions to our-groups. *Journal of Personality and Social Psychology, 81,* 97–115. (p. 669)

Milan, R. J., Jr., & Kilmann, P. R. (1987). Interpersonal factors in premarital contraception. *Journal of Sex Research, 23,* 289–321. (p. 353)

Miles, D. R., & Carey, G. (1997). Genetic and environmental architecture of human aggression. *Journal of Personality and Social Psychology, 72,* 207–217. (p. 671)

Milgram, S. (1963). Behavioral study of obedience. *Journal of Abnormal & Social Psychology, 67(4),* 371–378. (p. 654)

Milgram, S. (1974). *Obedience to authority.* New York: Harper & Row. (pp. 654, 655, 656)

Millar, J. K. & 19 others. (2005). DISC1 and PDE4B are interacting genetic factors in schizophrenia that regulate cAMP signaling. *Science, 310,* 1187–1191. (p. 595)

Miller, E. J., & Halberstadt, J. (2005). Media consumption, body image and thin ideals in New Zealand men and women. *New Zealand Journal of Psychology, 34,* 189–195. (p. 338)

Miller, E. J., Smith, J. E., & Trembath, D. L. (2000). The "skinny" on body size requests in personal ads. *Sex Roles, 43,* 129–141. (p. 341)

Miller, G. (2004). Axel, Buck share award for deciphering how the nose knows. *Science, 306,* 207. (p. 148)

Miller, G. (2005). The dark side of glia. *Science, 308,* 778–781. (p. 74)

Miller, G. (2008). Tackling alcoholism with drugs. *Science, 320,* 168–170. (p. 209)

Miller, G. A. (1956). The magical number seven, plus or minus two: Some limits on our capacity for processing information. *Psychological Review, 63,* 81–97. (p. 266)

Miller, G. E., & Blackwell, E. (2006). Turning up the heat: Inflammation as a mechanism linking chronic stress, depression, and heart disease. *Current Directions in Psychological Science, 15,* 269–272. (p. 403)

Miller, G. E., & Wrosch, C. (2007). You've gotta know when to fold 'em. *Psychological Science, 18,* 773–777. (p. 401)

Miller, J. G., & Bersoff, D. M. (1995). Development in the context of everyday family relationships: Culture, interpersonal morality and adaptation. In M. Killen and D. Hart (Eds.), *Morality in everyday life: A developmental perspective.* New York: Cambridge University Press. (p. 449)

Miller, L. (2005, January 4). U.S. airlines have 34 deaths in 3 years. *Associated Press.* (p. 308)

Miller, L. K. (1999). The Savant Syndrome: Intellectual impairment and exceptional skill. *Psychological Bulletin, 125,* 31–46. (p. 525)

Miller, M. (2005, March 7). Effects of laughter and mental stress on endothelial function: Potential impact of entertainment. Paper presented to the Scientific Session of the American College of Cardiology, Orlando. (p. C-4)

Miller, N. E. (1983). Understanding the use of animals in behavioral research: Some critical issues. *Annals of the New York Academy of Sciences, 406,* 113–118. (p. 44)

Miller, N. E. (1985, February). Rx: biofeedback. *Psychology Today,* pp. 54–59. (p. 241)

Miller, N. E. (1995). Clinical-experimental interactions in the development of neuroscience: A primer for nonspecialists and lessons for young scientists. *American Psychologist, 50,* 901–911. (p. 333)

Miller, N. E., & Brucker, B. S. (1979). A learned visceral response apparently independent of skeletal ones in patients paralyzed by spinal lesions. In N. Birbaumer & H. D. Kimmel (Eds.), *Biofeedback and self-regulation.* Hillsdale, NJ: Erlbaum. (p. 241)

Miller, P. A., Eisenberg, N., Fabes, R. A., & Shell, R. (1996). Relations of moral reasoning and vicarious emotion to young children's prosocial behavior toward peers and adults. *Developmental Psychology, 32,* 210–219. (p. 450)

Miller, P. C., Lefcourt, H. M., Holmes, J. G., Ware, E. E., & Saleh, W. E. (1986). Marital locus of control and marital problem solving. *Journal of Personality and Social Psychology, 51,* 161–169. (p. 505)

Miller, P. J. O., Aoki, K., Rendell, L. E., & Amano, M. (2008). Stereotypical resting behavior of the sperm whale. *Current Biology, 18,* R21–R23. (p. 177)

Miller, S. D., Blackburn, T., Scholes, G., White, G. L., & Mamalis, N. (1991). Optical differences in multiple personality disorder: A second look. *Journal of Nervous and Mental Disease, 179,* 132–135. (p. 579)

Mills, M., & Melhuish, E. (1974). Recognition of mother's voice in early infancy. *Nature, 252,* 123–124. (p. 415)

Milton, J., & Wiseman, R. (2002). A response to Storm and Ertel (2002). *Journal of Parapsychology, 66,* 183–185. (p. 168)

Mineka, S. (1985). The frightful complexity of the origins of fears. In F. R. Brush & J. B. Overmier (Eds.), *Affect, conditioning and cognition: Essays on the determinants of behavior.* Hillsdale, NJ: Erlbaum. (pp. 385, 574)

Mineka, S. (2002). Animal models of clinical psychology. In N. Smelser & P. Baltes (Eds.), *International encyclopedia of the social and behavioral sciences.* Oxford, England: Elsevier Science. (p. 385)

Mineka, S., & Suomi, S. J. (1978). Social separation in monkeys. *Psychological Bulletin, 85,* 1376–1400. (p. 431)

Mineka, S., & Zinbarg, R. (1996). Conditioning and ethological models of anxiety disorders: Stress-in-dynamic-context anxiety models. In D. Hope (Ed.), *Perspectives on anxiety, panic, and fear.* Nebraska symposium on motivation. Lincoln, NE: University of Nebraska Press. (pp. 573, 575)

Mineka, S., & Zinbarg, R. (2006). A contemporary learning theory perspective on the etiology of anxiety disorders: It's not what you thought it was. *American Psychologist, 61*, 10–26. (p. 574)

Miner-Rubino, K., & Winter, D. G., & Stewart, A. J. (2004). Gender, social class, and the subjective experience of aging: Self-perceived personality change from early adulthood to late midlife. *Personality and Social Psychology Bulletin, 30*, 1599–1610. (p. 468)

Mingroni, M. A. (2004). The secular rise in IQ: Giving heterosis a closer look. *Intelligence, 32*, 65–83. (p. 538)

Mingroni, M. A. (2007). Resolving the IQ paradox: Heterosis as a cause of the Flynn effect and other trends. *Psychological Review, 114*, 806–829. (p. 538)

Minsky, M. (1986). *The society of mind.* New York: Simon & Schuster. (p. 89)

Mirescu, C., & Gould, E. (2006). Stress and adult neurogenesis. *Hippocampus, 16*, 233–238. (p. 400)

Mischel, W. (1968). *Personality and assessment.* New York: Wiley. (p. 501)

Mischel, W. (1981). Current issues and challenges in personality. In L. T. Benjamin, Jr. (Ed.), *The G. Stanley Hall Lecture Series* (Vol. 1). Washington, DC: American Psychological Association. (p. 510)

Mischel, W. (1984). Convergences and challenges in the search for consistency. *American Psychologist, 39*, 351–364. (p. 501)

Mischel, W. (2004). Toward an integrative science of the person. *Annual Review of Psychology, 55*, 1–22. (p. 501)

Mischel, W., Shoda, Y., & Peake, P. K. (1988). The nature of adolescent competencies predicted by preschool delay of gratification. *Journal of Personality and Social Psychology, 54*, 687–696. (p. 450)

Mischel, W., Shoda, Y., & Rodriguez, M. L. (1989). Delay of gratification in children. *Science, 244*, 933–938. (pp. 232, 450)

Miserandino, M. (1991). Memory and the seven dwarfs. *Teaching of Psychology, 18*, 169–171. (p. 274)

Mita, T. H., Dermer, M., & Knight, J. (1977). Reversed facial images and the mere-exposure hypothesis. *Journal of Personality and Social Psychology, 35*, 597–601. (p. 678)

Mitchell, D. B. (2006). Nonconscious priming after 17 years: Invulnerable implicit memory? *Psychological Science, 17*, 925–929. (p. 256)

Mitchell, T. M., Shinkareva, S. V., Carlson, A., Chang, K-M., Malave, V. L., Mason, R. A., & Just, M. A. (2008). Predicting human brain activity associated with the meanings of nouns. *Science, 320*, 1191–1195. (p. 81)

Mitchell, T. R., Thompson, L., Peterson, E., & Cronk, R. (1997). Temporal adjustments in the evaluation of events: The "rosy view." *Journal of Experimental Social Psychology, 33*, 421–448. (p. 263)

Mitte, K. (2005). Meta-analysis of cognitive-behavioral treatments for generalized anxiety disorder: A comparison with pharmacotherapy. *Psychological Bulletin, 131*, 785–795. (p. 617)

Moffitt, T. E. (2005). The new look of behavioral genetics in developmental psychopathology: Gene-environment interplay in antisocial behaviors. *Psychological Bulletin, 131*, 533–554. (p. 598)

Moffitt, T. E., Caspi, A., Harrington, H., & Milne, B. J. (2002). Males on the life-course-persistent and adolescence-limited antisocial pathways: Follow-up at age 26 years. *Development and Psychopathology, 14*, 179–207. (p. 473)

Moffitt, T. E., Caspi, A., Harrington, H., Milne, B. J., Melchior, M., Goldberg, D., & Poulton, R. (2007a). Generalized anxiety disorder and depression: Childhood risk factors in a birth cohort followed to age 32. *Psychological Medicine, 37*, 441–452. (p. 570)

Moffitt, T. E., Caspi, A., & Rutter, M. (2006). Measured gene-environment interactions in psychopathology: Concepts, research strategies, and implications for research, intervention, and public understanding of genetics. *Perspectives on Psychological Science, 1*, 5–27. (p. 586)

Moffitt, T. E., Harrington, H., Caspi, A., Kim-Cohen, J., Goldberg, D., Gregory, A. M., & Poulton, R. (2007b). Depression and generalized anxiety disorder: Cumulative and sequential comorbidity in a birth cohort followed prospectively to age 32 years. *Archives of General Psychiatry, 64*, 651–660. (p. 570)

Moghaddam, F. M. (2005). The staircase to terrorism: A psychological exploration. *American Psychologist, 60*, 161–169. (p. 660)

Moises, H. W., Zoega, T., & Gottesman, I. I. (2002, 3 July). The glial growth factors deficiency and synaptic destabilization hypothesis of schizophrenia. *BMC Psychiatry, 2(8)* (www.biomedcentral.com/1471-244X/2/8). (p. 594)

Monaghan, P. (1992, September 23). Professor of psychology stokes a controversy on the reliability and repression of memory. *Chronicle of Higher Education*, pp. A9–A10. (p. 292)

Mondloch, C. J., Lewis, T. L., Budreau, D. R., Maurer, D., Dannemiller, J. L., Stephens, B. R., & Kleiner-Gathercoal, K. A. (1999). Face perception during early infancy. *Psychological Science, 10*, 419–422. (p. 415)

Money, J. (1987). Sin, sickness, or status? Homosexual gender identity and psychoneuroendocrinology. *American Psychologist, 42*, 384–399. (p. 358)

Money, J. (1988). *Gay, straight, and in-between.* New York: Oxford University Press. (p. 675)

Money, J., Berlin, F. S., Falck, A., & Stein, M. (1983). *Antiandrogenic and counseling treatment of sex offenders.* Baltimore: Department of Psychiatry and Behavioral Sciences, The Johns Hopkins University School of Medicine. (p. 350)

Moody, R. (1976). *Life after life.* Harrisburg, PA: Stackpole Books. (p. 206)

Mook, D. G. (1983). In defense of external invalidity. *American Psychologist, 38*, 379–387. (p. 42)

Moorcroft, W. H. (2003). *Understanding sleep and dreaming.* New York: Kluwer/Plenum. (pp. 178, 185, 191)

Moore, D. W. (2004, December 17). Sweet dreams go with a good night's sleep. *Gallup News Service* (www.gallup.com). (p. 181)

Moore, D. W. (2005, June 16). Three in four Americans believe in paranormal. *Gallup New Service* (www.gallup.com). (p. 166)

Moore, D. W. (2006, February 6). Britons outdrink Canadians, Americans. *Gallup News Service* (poll.gallup.com). (p. 209)

Moore, D. W. (2006, March 10). Close to 6 in 10 Americans want to lose weight. *Gallup News Service* (poll.gallup.com). (p. 346)

Moos, R. H., & Moos, B. S. (2005). Sixteen-year changes and stable remission among treated and untreated individuals with alcohol use disorders. *Drug and Alcohol Dependence, 80*, 337–347. (p. 618)

Moos, R. H., & Moos, B. S. (2006). Participation in treatment and alcoholics anonymous: A 16-year follow-up of initially untreated individuals. *Journal of Clinical Psychology, 62*, 735–750. (p. 618)

Mor, N., & Winquist, J. (2002). Self-focused attention and negative affect: A meta-analysis. *Psychological Bulletin, 128*, 638–662. (p. 587)

Moreland, R. L., & Beach, S. R. (1992). Exposure effects in the classroom: The development of affinity among students. *Journal of Experimental Social Psychology, 28*, 255–276. (p. 678)

Moreland, R. L., & Zajonc, R. B. (1982). Exposure effects in person perception: Familiarity, similarity, and attraction. *Journal of Experimental Social Psychology, 18*, 395–415. (p. 678)

Morell, V. (2008, March). Minds of their own: Animals are smarter than you think. *National Geographic*, pp. 37–61. (p. D-1)

Morelli, G. A., Rogoff, B., Oppenheim, D., & Goldsmith, D. (1992). Cultural variation in infants' sleeping arrangements: Questions of independence. *Developmental Psychology, 26*, 604–613. (p. 434)

Moreno, C., Laje, G., Blanco, C., Jiang, H., Schmidt, A. B., & Olfson, M. (2007). National trends in the outpatient diagnosis and treatment of bipolar disorder in youth. *Archives of General Psychiatry, 64*, 1032–1039. (p. 581)

Morey, R. A., Inan, S., Mitchell, T. V., Perkins, D. O., Lieberman, J. A., & Belger, A. (2005). Imaging frontostriatal function in ultra-high-risk, early, and chronic schizophrenia during executive processing. *Archives of General Psychiatry, 62*, 254–262. (p. 592)

Morgan, A. B., & Lilienfeld, S. O. (2000). A meta-analytic review of the relation between antisocial behavior and neuropsychological measures of executive function. *Clinical Psychology Review, 20*, 113–136. (p. 598)

Morgan, B., & Korschgen, A. (2001). Psychology career exploration made easy. *Eye on Psi Chi, 35–36*, 8. (p. A-2)

Morin, R., & Brossard, M. A. (1997, March 4). Communication breakdown on drugs. *Washington Post*, pp. A1, A6. (p. 453)

Morrison, A. R. (2003). The brain on night shift. *Cerebrum, 5(3)*, 23–36. (p. 180)

Morrison, C. (2007). What does contagious yawning tell us about the mind? Unpublished manuscript, University of Leeds. (p. 651)

Mortensen, E. L., Michaelsen, K. F., Sanders, S. A., & Reinisch, J. M. (2002). The association between duration of breastfeeding and adult intelligence. *Journal of the American Medical Association, 287*, 2365–2371. (p. 34)

Mortensen, P. B. (1999). Effects of family history and place and season of birth on the risk of schizophrenia. *New England Journal of Medicine, 340,* 603–608. (p. 593)

Moscovici, S. (1985). Social influence and conformity. In G. Lindzey & E. Aronson (Eds.), *The handbook of social psychology* (3rd ed). Hillsdale, N.J.: Erlbaum. (p. 663)

Moser, P. W. (1987, May). Are cats smart? Yes, at being cats. *Discover,* pp. 77–88. (p. 128)

Moses, E. B., & Barlow, D. H. (2006). A new unified treatment approach for emotional disorders based on emotion science. *Current Directions in Psychological Science, 15,* 146–150. (p. 616)

Mosher, D. L., & Anderson, R. D. (1986). Macho personality, sexual aggression, and reactions to guided imagery of realistic rape. *Journal of Research in Personality, 20,* 77–94. (p. 200)

Mosher, W. D., Chandra, A., & Jones, J. (2005, September 15). Sexual behavior and selected health measures: Men and women 15–44 years of age, United States, 2002. *Advance Data from Vital and Health Statistics,* No. 362, National Center for Health Statistics, Centers for Disease Control and Prevention, U.S. Department of Health and Human Services. (pp. 362, 354, 355, 472)

Moss, A. J., Allen, K. F., Giovino, G. A., & Mills, S. L. (1992, December 2). Recent trends in adolescent smoking, smoking-update correlates, and expectations about the future. *Advance Data No. 221* (from Vital and Health Statistics of the Centers for Disease Control and Prevention). (p. 203)

Moss, H. A., & Susman, E. J. (1980). Longitudinal study of personality development. In O. G. Brim, Jr., & J. Kagan (Eds.), *Constancy and change in human development.* Cambridge, MA: Harvard University Press. (p. 473)

Motivala, S. J., & Irwin, M. R. (2007). Sleep and immunity: Cytokine pathways linking sleep and health outcomes. *Current Directions in Psychological Science, 16,* 21–25. (p. 184)

Moulton, S. T., & Kosslyn, S. M. (2008). Using neuroimaging to resolve the psi debate. *Journal of Cognitive Neuroscience, 20,* 182–192. (p. 169)

Moyer, K. E. (1983). The physiology of motivation: Aggression as a model. In C. J. Scheier & A. M. Rogers (Eds.), *G. Stanley Hall Lecture Series (Vol. 3).* Washington, DC: American Psychological Association. (p. 671)

Mroczek, D. K. (2001). Age and emotion in adulthood. *Current Directions in Psychological Science, 10,* 87–90. (p. 469)

Mroczek, D. K., & Kolarz, D. M. (1998). The effect of age on positive and negative affect: A developmental perspective on happiness. *Journal of Personality and Social Psychology, 75,* 1333–1349. (p. 465)

Muhlnickel, W. (1998). Reorganization of auditory cortex in tinnitus. *Proceedings of the National Academy of Sciences, 95,* 10340–10343. (p. 78)

Mulcahy, N. J., & Call, J. (2006). Apes save tools for future use. *Science, 312,* 1038–1040. (p. 301)

Muller, J. E., & Verrier, R. L. (1996). Triggering of sudden death—Lessons from an earthquake. *New England Journal of Medicine, 334,* 461. (p. 400)

Mullin, C. R., & Linz, D. (1995). Desensitization and resensitization to violence against women: Effects of exposure to sexually violent films on judgments of domestic violence victims. *Journal of Personality and Social Psychology, 69,* 449–459. (p. 249)

Mulrow, C. D. (1999, March). *Treatment of depression—newer pharmacotherapies, summary. Evidence Report/Technology Assessment, 7.* Agency for Health Care Policy and Research, Rockville, MD. (http://www.ahrq.gov/clinic/deprsumm.htm). (p. 630)

Munro, D. A., McCaul, M. E., Wong, D. F., Oswald, L. M., Zhou, Y., Brasic, J., Kuwabara, H., Kumar, A., Alexander, M., Ye, W., & Wand, G. S. (2006). Sex differences in striatal dopamine release in health adults. *Biological Psychiatry, 59,* 966–974. (p. 201)

Murphy, G. E., & Wetzel, R. D. (1990). The lifetime risk of suicide in alcoholism. *Archives of General Psychiatry, 47,* 383–392. (p. 584)

Murphy, K. R., & Cleveland, J. N. (1995). *Understanding performance appraisal: Social, organizational, and goal-based perspectives.* Thousand Oaks, CA: Sage. (p. B-7)

Murphy, S. T., Monahan, J. L., & Miller, L. C. (1998). Inference under the influence: The impact of alcohol and inhibition conflict on women's sexual decision making. *Personality and Social Psychology Bulletin, 24,* 517–528. (p. 200)

Murphy, S. T., Monahan, J. L., & Zajonc, R. B. (1995). Additivity of nonconscious affect: Combined effects of priming and exposure. *Journal of Personality and Social Psychology, 69,* 589–602. (p. 374)

Murray, B. (1998, May). Psychology is key to airline safety at Boeing. *The APA Monitor,* p. 36. (p. B-14)

Murray, C. (2006). Changes over time in the black-white difference on mental tests: Evidence from the children of the 1979 cohort of the National Longitudinal Survey of Youth. *Intelligence, 34,* 527–540. (p. 552)

Murray, C. (2007). The magnitude and components of change in the black-white IQ difference from 1920 to 1991: A birth cohort analysis of the Woodcock-Johnson standardizations. *Intelligence, 35,* 305–318. (p. 552)

Murray, C. A., & Herrnstein, R. J. (1994, October 31). Race, genes and I.Q.—An apologia. *New Republic,* pp. 27–37. (p. 552)

Murray, C. J., & Lopez, A. D. (Eds.) (1996). *The global burden of disease: A comprehensive assessment of mortality and disability from diseases, injuries, and risk factors in 1990 and projected to 2020.* Cambridge, MA: Harvard University Press. (p. 562)

Murray, H. (1938). *Explorations in personality.* New York: Oxford University Press. (p. B-7)

Murray, H. A., & Wheeler, D. R. (1937). A note on the possible clairvoyance of dreams. *Journal of Psychology, 3,* 309–313. (pp. 27, 167)

Murray, J. P. (2008). Media violence: The effects are both real and strong. *American Behavioral Scientist, 51,* 1212–1230. (p. 247)

Murray, R., Jones, P., O'Callaghan, E., Takei, N., & Sham, P. (1992). Genes, viruses, and neurodevelopmental schizophrenia. *Journal of Psychiatric Research, 26,* 225–235. (p. 593)

Murray, R. M., Morrison, P. D., Henquet, C., & Di Forti, M. (2007). Cannabis, the mind and society: The hash realities. *Nature Reviews: Neuroscience, 8,* 885–895. (p. 206)

Murray, S. L., Bellavia, G. M., Rose, P., & Griffin, D. W. (2003). Once hurt, twice hurtful: How perceived regard regulates daily marital interactions. *Journal of Personality and Social Psychology, 84,* 126–147. (p. 165)

Murray, S. L., Rose, P., Bellavia, G. M., Holmes, J. G., & Kusche, A. G. (2002). When rejection stings: How self-esteem constrains relationship-enhancement processes. *Journal of Personality and Social Psychology, 83,* 556–573. (p. 512)

Musallam, S., Corneil, B. D., Greger, B., Scherberger, H., & Andersen, R. A. (2004). Cognitive control signals for neural prosthetics. *Science, 305,* 258–262. (p. 76)

Musick, M. A., Herzog, A. R., & House, J. S. (1999). Volunteering and mortality among older adults: Findings from a national sample. *Journals of Gerontology, 54B,* 173–180. (p. C-12)

Mustanski, B. S., & Bailey, J. M. (2003). A therapist's guide to the genetics of human sexual orientation. *Sexual and Relationship Therapy, 18,* 1468–1479. (p. 357)

Mustanski, B. S., Bailey, J. M., & Kaspar, S. (2002). Dermatoglyphics, handedness, sex, and sexual orientation. *Archives of Sexual Behavior, 31,* 113–122. (p. 358)

Mydans, S. (2002, May 17). In Pakistan, rape victims are the 'criminals.' *New York Times* (www.nytimes.com). (p. 670)

Myers, D. G. (1993). *The pursuit of happiness.* New York: Avon Books. (pp. 395, 396)

Myers, D. G. (2000). *The American paradox: Spiritual hunger in an age of plenty.* New Haven: Yale University Press. (p. 396)

Myers, D. G. (2001, December). Do we fear the right things? *American Psychological Society Observer,* p. 3. (p. 308)

Myers, D. G. (2002). *Intuition: Its powers and perils.* New Haven, CT: Yale University Press. (pp. 4, 33)

Myers, D. G. (2008). *Social Psychology,* 9th edition. New York: McGraw-Hill. (pp. 513, 514)

Myers, D. G., & Bishop, G. D. (1970). Discussion effects on racial attitudes. *Science, 169,* 78–779. (p. 659)

Myers, D. G., & Diener, E. (1995). Who is happy? *Psychological Science, 6,* 10–19. (p. 396)

Myers, D. G., & Diener, E. (1996, May). The pursuit of happiness. *Scientific American.* (p. 396)

Myers, D. G., & Scanzoni, L. D. (2005). *What God has joined together?* San Francisco: HarperSanFrancisco. (pp. 355, 467)

Myers, I. B. (1987). *Introduction to type: A description of the theory and applications of the Myers-Briggs Type Indicator.* Palo Alto, CA: Consulting Psychologists Press. (p. 494)

Myerson, J., Rank, M. R., Raines, F. Q., & Schnitzler, M. A. (1998). Race and general cognitive ability: The myth of diminishing returns to education. *Psychological Science, 9,* 139–142. (p. 554)

Nagourney, A. (2002, September 25). For remarks on Iraq, Gore gets praise and scorn. *New York Times* (www.nytimes.com). (p. 646)

Nairn, R. G. (2007). Media portrayals of mental illness, or is it madness? A review. *Australian Psychologist, 42,* 138–146. (p. 568)

Napolitan, D. A., & Goethals, G. R. (1979). The attribution of friendliness. *Journal of Experimental Social Psychology, 15,* 105–113. (p. 644)

Naqvi, N. H., Rudrauf, D., Damasio, H., & Bechara, A. (2007). Damage to the insula disrupts addiction to cigarette smoking. *Science, 315,* 531–534. (p. 204)

Nasar, J., Hecht, P., & Wener, R. (2008). Mobile telephones, distracted attention, and pedestrian safety. *Accident Analysis and Prevention, 40,* 69–75. (p. 118)

Nash, M. R. (2001, July). The truth and the hype of hypnosis. *Scientific American,* pp. 47–55. (p. 194)

National Academy of Sciences. (2001). *Exploring the biological contributions to human health: Does sex matter?* Washington, DC: Institute of Medicine, National Academy Press. (pp. 206, 439)

National Academy of Sciences, Institute of Medicine. (1982). *Marijuana and health.* Washington, DC: National Academic Press. (p. 206)

National Center for Complementary and Alternative Medicine. (2006). *What is complementary and alternative medicine.* nccam.nih.gov/health/whatiscam. (p. C-9)

National Center for Health Statistics. (1990). *Health, United States, 1989.* Washington, DC: U.S. Department of Health and Human Services. (p. 459)

National Center for Health Statistics. (2004, December 15). *Marital status and health: United States, 1999-2002* (by Charlotte A. Schoenborn). Advance Data from Vital and Human Statistics, number 351. Centers for Disease Control and Prevention. (p. C-4)

National Council on Aging. (1999). *The consequences of untreated hearing loss in older persons.* Washington, DC: Author. (www.ncoa.org). (p. 139)

National Institute on Drug Abuse. (2004). *NIDA InfoFacts: Marijuana.* www.nida.nih.gov/Infofax/marijuana.html. (p. 206)

National Institute of Mental Health. (1982). *Television and behavior: Ten years of scientific progress and implications for the eighties.* Washington, DC: U. S. Government Printing Office. (p. 248)

National Institute of Mental Health. (2003). *Attention deficit hyperactivity disorder.* Bethesda, MD: National Institute of Mental Health. (p. 563)

National Institute of Mental Health. (2008). *The numbers count: Mental disorders in America.* (nimh.nih.gov). (pp. 566, 599)

National Institutes of Health. (1998). *Clinical guidelines on the identification evaluation and treatment of overweight and obesity in adults.* Executive summary, Obesity Education Initiative, National Heart, Lung, and Blood Institute. (p. 346)

National Research Council. (1990). *Human factors research needs for an aging population.* Washington, DC: National Academy Press. (p. 458)

National Safety Council. (2008). Transportation mode comparisons, from *Injury Facts* (via correspondence with Kevin T. Fearn, Research & Statistical Services Department). (p. 308)

National Sleep Foundation. (2009) *2009 sleep in America poll: Summary of findings.* Washington, DC: National Sleep Foundation (www.sleepfoundation.org). (p. 185)

Naylor, T. H. (1990). Redefining corporate motivation, Swedish style. *Christian Century, 107,* 566–570. (p. B-12)

NCASA. (2007). *Wasting the best and the brightest: Substance abuse at America's colleges and universities.* New York: National Center on Addiction and Drug Abuse, Columbia University. (p. 210)

NCHS. (2007). *Health, United States, 2007.* Hyattsville, MD: National Center for Health Statistics. (p. 340)

NCTV News. (1987, July-August). More research links harmful effects to non-violent porn, p. 12. (p. 674)

Neese, R. M. (1991, November/December). What good is feeling bad? The evolutionary benefits of psychic pain. *The Sciences,* pp. 30–37. (pp. 143, 225)

Neidorf, S., & Morin, R. (2007, May 23). Four-in-ten Americans have close friends or relatives who are gay. Pew Research Center Publications (pewresearch.org). (p. 690)

Neisser, U. (1979). The control of information pickup in selective looking. In A. D. Pick (Ed.), *Perception and its development: A tribute to Eleanor J. Gibson.* Hillsdale, NJ: Erlbaum. (p. 118)

Neisser, U. (1997). The ecological study of memory. *Philosophical Transactions of the Royal Society of London, 352,* 1697–1701. (p. 537)

Neisser, U. (1998). *The rising curve: Long-term gains in IQ and related measures.* Washington, DC: American Psychological Association (p. 537)

Neisser, U., Boodoo, G., Bouchard, T. J., Jr., Boykin, A. W., Brody, N., Ceci, S. J., Halpern, D. F., Loehlin, J. C., Perloff, R., Sternberg, R. J., & Urbina, S. (1996). Intelligence: Knowns and unknowns. *American Psychologist, 51,* 77–101. (pp. 544, 555)

Neisser, U., Winograd, E., & Weldon, M. S. (1991). Remembering the earthquake: "What I experienced" vs. "How I heard the news." Paper presented to the Psychonomic Society convention. (p. 271)

Neitz, J., Geist, T., & Jacobs, G. H. (1989). Color vision in the dog. *Visual Neuroscience, 3,* 119–125. (p. 132)

Nelson, C. A., III, Zeanah, C. H., Fox, N. A., Marshall, P. J., Smyke, A. T., & Guthrie, D. (2007). Cognitive recovery in socially deprived young children: The Bucharest Early Intervention Project. *Science, 318,* 1937–1940. (p. 547)

Nelson, M. D., Saykin, A. J., Flashman, L. A., & Riordan, H. J. (1998). Hippocampal volume reduction in schizophrenia as assessed by magnetic resonance imaging. *Archives of General Psychiatry, 55,* 433–440. (p. 593)

Nelson, N. (1988). A meta-analysis of the life-event/health paradigm: The influence of social support. Philadelphia: Temple University Ph.D. dissertation. (p. C-4)

Nemeth, C. J., & Ormiston, M. (2007). Creative idea generation: Harmony versus stimulation. *European Journal of Social Psychology, 37,* 524–535. (p. 661)

Nesca, M., & Koulack, D. (1994). Recognition memory, sleep and circadian rhythms. *Canadian Journal of Experimental Psychology, 48,* 359–379. (p. 283)

Nestoriuc, Y., Rief, W., & Martin, A. (2008). Meta-analysis of biofeedback for tension-type headache: Efficacy, specificity, and treatment moderators. *Journal of Consulting and Clinical Psychology, 76,* 379–396. (p. C-8)

Neubauer, P. B., & Neubauer, A. 1990). *Nature's thumbprint: The new genetics of personality.* **Reading, MA: Addison-Wesley.** (p. 443)

Neumann, R., & Strack, F. (2000). "Mood contagion": The automatic transfer of mood between persons. *Journal of Personality and Social Psychology, 79,* 211–223. (pp. 384, 651)

Newberg, A., & D'Aquili, E. (2001). *Why God won't go away: Brain science and the biology of belief.* New York: Simon and Schuster. (p. C-10)

Newcomb, M. D., & Harlow, L. L. (1986). Life events and substance use among adolescents: Mediating effects of perceived loss of control and meaninglessness in life. *Journal of Personality and Social Psychology, 51,* 564–577. (p. 209)

Newcombe, N. S., Drummey, A. B., Fox, N. A., Lie, E., & Ottinger-Alberts, W. (2000). Remembering early childhood: How much, how, and why (or why not). *Current Directions in Psychological Science, 9,* 55–58. (p. 417)

Newman, A. J., Bavelier, D., Corina, D., Jezzard, P., & Neville, H. J. (2002). A critical period for right hemisphere recruitment in American Sign Language processing. *Nature Neuroscience, 5,* 76–80. (p. 318)

Newman, L. S., & Baumeister, R. F. (1996). Toward an explanation of the UFO abduction phenomenon: Hypnotic, elaboration, extraterrestrial sadomasochism, and spurious memories. *Psychological Inquiry, 7,* 99–126. (p. 193)

Newman, L. S., & Ruble, D. N. (1988). Stability and change in self-understanding: The early elementary school years. *Early Child Development and Care, 40,* 77–99. (p. 433)

Newman, M. L., Pennebaker, J. W., Berry, D. S., & Richards, J. M. (2003). Lying words: Predicting deception from linguistic style. *Personality and Social Psychology Bulletin, 29,* 665–675. (p. 373)

Newman, R., Ratner, N. B., Jusczyk, A. M., Jusczyk, P. W., & Dow, K. A. (2006). Infants' early ability to segment the conversational speech signal predicts later language development: A retrospective analysis. *Developmental Psychology, 42,* 643–655. (p. 315)

Newport, E. L. (1990). Maturational constraints on language learning. *Cognitive Science, 14,* 11–28. (p. 318)

Newport, F. (2001, February). Americans see women as emotional and affectionate, men as more aggressive. *The Gallup Poll Monthly*, pp. 34–38. (p. 379)

Newport, F. (2002, July 29). Bush job approval update. *Gallup News Service* (www.gallup.com/poll/releases/pr020729.asp). (p. 690)

Newport, F. (2007, June 11). Majority of Republicans doubt theory of evolution. *Gallup Poll* (www.galluppoll.com). (p. 109)

Newport, F., Jones, J. M., Saad, L, & Carroll, J. (2007, April 27). Gallup poll review: 10 key points about public opinion on Iraq. *The Gallup Poll* (www.galluppoll.com). (p. 436)

Newport, F., Moore, D. W., Jones, J. M., & Saad, L. (2003, March 21). Special release: American opinion on the war. *Gallup Poll Tuesday Briefing* (www.gallup.com). (p. 648)

Newton, E. L. (1991). The rocky road from actions to intentions. *Dissertation Abstracts International*, 51(8–B), 4105. (p. B-15)

Nezlek, J. B. (2001). Daily psychological adjustment and the planfulness of day-to-day behavior. *Journal of Social and Clinical Psychology*, 20, 452–475. (p. 505)

Ng, S. H. (1990). Androcentric coding of *man* and *his* in memory by language users. *Journal of Experimental Social Psychology*, 26, 455–464. (p. 320)

Ng, W. W. H., Sorensen, K. L., & Eby, L. T. (2006). Locus of control at work: A meta-analysis. *Journal of Organizational Behavior*, 27, 1057–1087. (p. 505)

Nguyen, D. (2005, September 22). JetBlue passengers watched news of drama. Associated Press release. (p. 399)

NHTSA. (2000). *Traffic safety facts 1999: Older population.* Washington, DC: National Highway Traffic Safety Administration (National Transportation Library: www.ntl.bts.gov). (p. 459)

NHTSA. (2006, April). *The 100-car naturalistic driving study phase II: Results of the 100-car field experiment.* Washington, DC: National Highway Traffic Safety Administration (www.nhtsa.gov). (p. 117)

NICHD Early Child Care Research Network. (2002). Structure/process/outcome: Direct and indirect effects of caregiving quality on young children's development. *Psychological Science*, 13, 199–206. (p. 432)

NICHD Early Child Care Research Network. (2003). Does amount of time spent in child care predict socioemotional adjustment during the transition to kindergarten? *Child Development*, 74, 976–1005. (p. 432)

NICHD. (2006). Child-care effect sizes for the NICHD study of early child care and youth development. *American Psychologist*, 61, 99–116. (p. 432)

Nickell, J. (1996, May/June). A study of fantasy proneness in the thirteen cases of alleged encounters in John Mack's Abduction. *Skeptical Inquirer*, pp. 18–20, 54. (p. 193)

Nickerson, R. S. (1998). Applied experimental psychology. *Applied Psychology: An International Review*, 47, 155–173. (p. B-14)

Nickerson, R. S. (1999). How we know—and sometimes misjudge—what others know: Imputing one's own knowledge to others. *Psychological Bulletin*, 125, 737–759. (p. B-15)

Nickerson, R. S., & Adams, M. J. (1979). Long-term memory for a common object. *Cognitive Psychology*, 11, 287–307. (p. 280)

Nicol, S. E., & Gottesman, I. I. (1983). Clues to the genetics and neurobiology of schizophrenia. *American Scientist*, 71, 398–404. (p. 595)

Nicolaus, L. K., Cassel, J. F., Carlson, R. B., & Gustavson, C. R. (1983). Taste-aversion conditioning of crows to control predation on eggs. *Science*, 220, 212–214. (p. 224)

Nicolelis, M. A. L., & Chapin, J. K. (2002, October). Controlling robots with the mind. *Scientific American*, pp. 46–53. (p. 76)

NIDA. (2002). *Methamphetamine abuse and addiction. Research Report Series.* National Institute on Drug Abuse, NIH Publication Number 02-4210. (p. 201)

NIDA. (2005, May). *Methamphetamine. NIDA Info Facts.* National Institute on Drug Abuse. (p. 201)

Nielsen, K. M., Faergeman, O., Larsen, M. L., & Foldspang, A. (2006). Danish singles have a twofold risk of acute coronary syndrome: Data from a cohort of 138,290 persons. *Journal of Epidemiology and Community Health*, 60, 721–728. (p. C-4)

Nier, J. A. (2004). Why does the "above average effect" exist? Demonstrating idiosyncratic trait definition. *Teaching of Psychology*, 31, 53–54. (p. 513)

Nightingale, F. (1860/1969). *Notes on nursing.* Mineola, NY: Dover. (p. C-5)

NIH. (2001, July 20). *Workshop summary: Scientific evidence on condom effectiveness for sexually transmitted disease (STD) prevention.* Bethesda: National Institute of Allergy and Infectious Diseases, National Institutes of Health. (p. 353)

NIH. (2006, December 4). NIDA researchers complete unprecedented scan of human genome that may help unlock the genetic contribution to tobacco addiction. *NIH News*, National Institutes of Health (www.nih.gov). (p. 209)

NIMH. (2002, April 26). *U.S. suicide rates by age, gender, and racial group.* National Institute of Mental Health (www.nimh.nih.gov/research/suichart.cfm). (p. 584)

NIMH. (2003). *Attention deficit hyperactivity disorder.* Bethesda, MD: National Institute of Mental Health. (p. 563)

Nisbett, R. E. (1987). Lay personality theory: Its nature, origin, and utility. In N. E. Grunberg, R. E. Nisbett, & others, *A distinctive approach to psychological research: The influence of Stanley Schachter.* Hillsdale, NJ: Erlbaum. (p. B-5)

Nisbett, R. E., & Cohen, D. (1996). *Culture of honor: The psychology of violence in the South.* Boulder, CO: Westview Press. (p. 673)

Nisbett, R. E., & Ross, L. (1980). *Human inference: Strategies and shortcomings of social judgment.* Englewood Cliffs, NJ: Prentice-Hall. (p. 304)

Nitschke, J. B., Dixon, G. E., Sarinopoulos, I., Short, S. J., Cohen, J. D., Smith, E. E., Kosslyn, S. M., Rose, R. M., & Davidson, R. J. (2006). Altering expectancy dampens neural response to aversive taste in primary taste cortex. *Nature Neuroscience 9*, 435–442. (p. 147)

Nixon, G. M., Thompson, J. M. D., Han, D. Y., Becroft, D. M., Clark, P. M., Robinson, E., Waldie, K E., Wild, C. J., Black, P. N., & Mitchell, E. A. (2008). Short sleep duration in middle childhood: Risk factors and consequences. *Sleep*, 31, 71–78. (p. 184)

Noel, J. G., Forsyth, D. R., & Kelley, K. N. (1987). Improving the performance of failing students by overcoming their self-serving attributional biases. *Basic and Applied Social Psychology*, 8, 151–162. (p. 507)

Noftle, E. E., & Robins, R. W. (2007). Personality predictors of academic outcomes: Big Five correlates of GPA and SAT scores. *Journal of Personality and Social Psychology*, 93, 116–130. (p. 499)

Noice, H., & Noice, T. (2006). What studies of actors and acting can tell us about memory and cognitive functioning. *Current Directions in Psychological Science*, 15, 14–18. (p. 262)

Nolen-Hoeksema, S. (2001). Gender differences in depression. *Current Directions in Psychological Science*, 10, 173–176. (p. 587)

Nolen-Hoeksema, S. (2003). Women who think too much: How to break free of overthinking and reclaim your life. New York: Holt. (p. 587)

Nolen-Hoeksema, S., & Larson, J. (1999). *Coping with loss.* Mahwah, NJ: Erlbaum. (p. 471)

NORC. (2007). National Opinion Research Center (University of Chicago) General Social Survey data, 1972 through 2004, accessed via sda.berkeley.edu. (p. 361)

Nordgren, L. F., van der Pligt, J., & van Harreveld, F. (2006). Visceral drives in retrospect: Explanations about the inaccessible past. *Psychological Science*, 17, 635–640. (p. 332)

Nordgren, L. F., van der Pligt, J., & van Harreveld, F. (2007). Evaluating Eve: Visceral states influence the evaluation of impulsive behavior. *Journal of Personality and Social Psychology*, 93, 75–84. (p. 332)

Norem, J. K. (2001). The positive power of negative thinking: Using defensive pessimism to harness anxiety and perform at your peak. New York: Basic Books. (p. 507)

Norenzayan, A., & Hansen, I. G. (2006). Belief in supernatural agents in the face of death. *Personality and Social Psychology Bulletin*, 32, 174–187. (p. 489)

Norman, D. A. (2001). The perils of home theater. (www.jnd.org/dn.mss/ProblemsOfHomeTheater.html). (p. B-13)

Normand, M. P., & Dallery, J. (2007, June 20). Mercury rising: Exposing the vaccine-autism myth. *eSkeptic: The email newsletter of the Skeptics Society* (www.skeptic.com/eskep. (p. 424)

Noroozian, M., Lofti, J., Gassemzadeh, H., Emami, H., & Mehrabi, Y. (2003). Academic achievement and learning abilities in left-handers: Guilt or gift? *Cortex*, 38, 779–785. (p. 88)

Norton, K. L., Olds, T. S., Olive, S., & Dank, S. (1996). Ken and Barbie at life size. *Sex Roles*, 34, 287–294. (p. 339)

Norton, P. J., & Price, E. C. (2007). A meta-analytic review of adult cognitive-behavioral treatment outcome across the anxiety disorders. *Journal of Nervous and Mental Disease*, 195, 521–531. (p. 617)

Nowak, R. (1994). Nicotine scrutinized as FDA seeks to regulate cigarettes. *Science, 263,* 1555–1556. (p. 204)

Nowell, A., & Hedges, L. V. (1998). Trends in gender differences in academic achievement from 1960 to 1994: An analysis of differences in mean, variance, and extreme scores. *Sex Roles, 39,* 21–43. (p. 551)

NSF. (2001, October 24). Public bounces back after Sept. 11 attacks, national study shows. *NSF News,* National Science Foundation (www.nsf.gov/od/lpa/news/press/ol/pr0185.htm). (p. 400)

NSF. (2008). *2008 sleep in America poll.* National Sleep Foundation (sleepfoundation.org). (p. 182)

Nurnberger, J. I., Jr., & Bierut, L. J. (2007, April). Seeking the connections: Alcoholism and our genes. *Scientific American,* pp. 46–53. (p. 209)

Nuttin, J. M., Jr. (1987). Affective consequences of mere ownership: The name letter effect in twelve European languages. *European Journal of Social Psychology, 17,* 381–402. (p. 678)

O'Connor, A. (2004, February 6). Study details 30-year increase in calorie consumption. *New York Times* (www.nytimes.com). (p. 345)

O'Connor, P., & Brown, G. W. (1984). Supportive relationships: Fact or fancy? *Journal of Social and Personal Relationships, 1,* 159–175. (p. 626)

O'Donnell, L., Stueve, A., O'Donnell, C., Duran, R., San Doval, A., Wilson, R. F., Haber, D., Perry, E., & Pleck, J. H. (2002). Long-term reduction in sexual initiation and sexual activity among urban middle schoolers in the reach for health service learning program. *Journal of Adolescent Health, 31,* 93–100. (p. 354)

O'Reardon, J. P. & 12 others. (2007). Efficacy and safety of transcranial magnetic stimulation in the acute treatment of major depression: A multisite randomized controlled trial. *Biological Psychiatry, 62,* 1208–1216. (p. 635)

Oaten, M., & Cheng, K. (2006a). Longitudinal gains in self-regulation from regular physical exercise. *British Journal of Health Psychology, 11,* 717–733. (p. 505)

Oaten, M., & Cheng, K. (2006b). Improved self-control: The benefits of a regular program of academic study. *Basic and Applied Social Psychology, 28,* 1–16. (p. 505)

Oberlander, J., & Gill, A. J. (2006). Language with character: A stratified corpus comparison of individual differences in e-mail communication. *Discourse Processes, 42,* 239–270. (p. 502)

Oberman, L. M., Winkielman, P., & Ramachandran. V. S. (2007). Face to face: Blocking facial mimicry can selectively impair recognition of emotional expressions. *Social Neuroscience, 2,* 167–178. (pp. 384, 425)

O'Connor, A. (2004, May 14). Pressure to go along with abuse is strong, but some soldiers find strength to refuse. *New York Times* (www.nytimes.com). (p. 663)

Oddone-Paolucci, E., Genuis, M., & Violato, C. (2000). A meta-analysis of the published research on the effects of pornography. In C. Violato, E. Oddone-Paolucci, & M. Genuis (Eds.), *The changing family and child development.* Aldershot, England: Ashgate. (p. 675)

Oetting, E. R., & Beauvais, F. (1987). Peer cluster theory, socialization characteristics, and adolescent drug use: A path analysis. *Journal of Counseling Psychology, 34,* 205–213. (p. 210)

Oetting, E. R., & Beauvais, F. (1990). Adolescent drug use: Findings of national and local surveys. *Journal of Social and Personal Relationships, 1,* 159–175. (p. 210)

Oettingen, G., & Mayer, D. (2002). The motivating function of thinking about the future: Expectations versus fantasies. *Journal of Personality and Social Psychology, 83,* 1198–1212. (p. 507)

Oettingen, G., & Seligman, M. E. P. (1990). Pessimism and behavioural signs of depression in East versus West Berlin. *European Journal of Social Psychology, 20,* 207–220. (p. 506)

Offer, D., Kaiz, M., Howard, K. I., & Bennett, E. S. (2000). The altering of reported experiences. *Journal of the American Academy of Child and Adolescent Psychiatry, 39,* 735–742. (p. 289)

Offer, D., Ostrov, E., Howard, K. I., & Atkinson, R. (1988). *The teenage world: Adolescents' self-image in ten countries.* New York: Plenum. (p. 452)

Ogden, C. L., Fryar, C. D., Carroll, M. D., & Flegal, K. M. (2004, October 27). Mean body weight, heights, and body mass index, Unites States 1960–2002. *Advance Data from Vital and Health Statistics, No. 347.* (p. 345)

Öhman, A. (1986). Face the beast and fear the face: Animal and social fears as prototypes for evolutionary analyses of emotion. *Psychophysiology, 23,* 123–145. (p. 575)

Öhman, A., Lundqvist, D., & Esteves, F. (2001). The face in the crowd revisited: A threat advantage with schematic stimuli. *Journal of Personality and Social Psychology, 80,* 381–396. (p. 377)

Öhman, A., & Mineka, S. (2003). The malicious serpent: Snakes as a prototypical stimulus for an evolved module of fear. *Current Directions in Psychological Science, 12,* 5–9. (p. 386)

Oishi, S., Diener, E., & Lucas, R. E. (2007). The optimum level of well-being: Can people be too happy? *Perspectives on Psychological Science, 2,* 346–360. (p. 389)

Oishi, S., Diener, E. F., Lucas, R. E., & Suh, E. M. (1999). Cross-cultural variations in predictors of life satisfaction: Perspectives from needs and values. *Personality and Social Psychology Bulletin, 25,* 980–990. (p. 330)

O'Keeffe, C., & Wiseman, R. (2005). Testing alleged mediumship: Methods and results. *British Journal of Psychology, 96,* 165–179. (p. 499)

Okun, M. S., & 12 others. (2004). What's in a 'smile?' Intra-operative observations of contralateral smiles induced by deep brain stimulation. *Neurocase, 10,* 271–279. (p. 371)

Olatunji, B. O., Cisler, J. M., & Tolin, D. F. (2007). Quality of life in the anxiety disorders: A meta-analytic review. *Clinical Psychology Review, 27,* 572–581. (p. 570)

Olds, J. (1958). Self-stimulation of the brain. *Science, 127,* 315–324. (p. 72)

Olds, J. (1975). Mapping the mind onto the brain. In F. G. Worden, J. P. Swazey, & G. Adelman (Eds.), *The neurosciences: Paths of discovery.* Cambridge, MA: MIT Press. (p. 72)

Olds, J., & Milner, P. (1954). Positive reinforcement produced by electrical stimulation of the septal area and other regions of rat brain. *Journal of Comparative and Physiological Psychology, 47,* 419–427. (p. 72)

Olff, M., Langeland, W., Draijer, N., & Gersons, B. P. R. (2007). Gender differences in posttraumatic stress disorder. *Psychological Bulletin, 135,* 183–204. (p. 573)

Olfson, M., Gameroff, M. J., Marcus, S. C., & Jensen, P. S. (2003). National trends in the treatment of attention deficit hyperactivity disorder. *American Journal of Psychiatry, 160,* 1071–1077. (pp. 563, 630)

Olfson, M., Marcus, S. C., Wan, G. J., & Geissler, E. C. (2004). National trends in the outpatient treatment of anxiety disorders. *Journal of Clinical Psychiatry, 65,* 1166–1173. (p. 630)

Olin, S. S., & Mednick, S. A. (1996). Risk factors of psychosis: Identifying vulnerable populations premorbidly. *Schizophrenia Bulletin, 22,* 223–240. (p. 595)

Oliner, S. P., & Oliner, P. M. (1988). *The altruistic personality: Rescuers of Jews in Nazi Europe.* New York: Free Press. (p. 246)

Olshansky, S. J., Carnes, B. A., & Cassel, C. K. (1993, April). The aging of the human species. *Scientific American,* pp. 46–52. (p. 457)

Olshansky, S. J., Passaro, D. J., Hershow, R. C., Layden, J., Carnes, B. A., Brody, J., Hayflick, L., Butler, R. N., Allison, D. B., & Ludwig, D. S. (2005). A potential decline in life expectancy in the United States in the 21st century. *New England Journal of Medicine, 352,* 1138–1145. (p. 341)

Olson, M. A., & Fazio, R. H. (2001). Implicit attitude formation through classical conditioning. *Psychological Science, 12,* 413–417. (p. 221)

Olson, S. (2005). Brain scans raise privacy concerns. *Science, 307,* 1548–1550. (p. 495)

Olsson, A., Nearing, K. I., & Phelps, E. A. (2007). Learning fears by observing others: The neural systems of social fear transmission. *Social Cognitive and Affective Neuroscience, 2,* 3–11. (p. 386)

Olsson, A., & Phelps, E. A. (2004). Learned fear of "unseen" faces after Pavlovian, observational, and instructed fear. *Psychological Science, 15,* 822–828. (p. 574)

Olweus, D., Mattsson, A., Schalling, D., & Low, H. (1988). Circulating testosterone levels and aggression in adolescent males: A causal analysis. *Psychosomatic Medicine, 50,* 261–272. (p. 672)

Oman, D., Kurata, J. H., Strawbridge, W. J., & Cohen, R. D. (2002). Religious attendance and cause of death over 31 years. *International Journal of Psychiatry in Medicine, 32,* 69–89. (p. C-11)

O'Neil, J. (2002, September 3). Vital Signs: Behavior: Parent smoking and teenage sex. *New York Times.* (p. 33)

O'Neill, M. J. (1993). The relationship between privacy, control, and stress responses in office workers. Paper presented to the Human Factors and Ergonomics Society convention. (p. C-2)

Onishi, N. (2008, June 13). Japan, seeking trim waists, measures millions. *New York Times* (www.nytimes.com). (p. 341)

ORB. (2008, January). *Update on Iraqi casualty data.* Opinion Research Business (London) (www.opinion.co.uk). (p. 643)

Oren, D. A., & Terman, M. (1998). Tweaking the human circadian clock with light. *Science, 279,* 333–334. (p. 177)

Orlovskaya, D. D., Uranova, N. A., Zimina, I. S., Kolomeets, N. S., Vikhreva, O. V., Rachmanova, V. I., Black, J. E., Klintsova, A. Y., & Greenough, W. T. (1999). Effect of professional status on the number of synapses per neuron in the prefrontal cortex of normal human and schizophrenic brain. *Society for Neuroscience Abstracts, 329.11, 25,* 818. (p. 530)

Orne, M. T., & Evans, F. J. (1965). Social control in the psychological experiment: Antisocial behavior and hypnosis. *Journal of Personality and Social Psychology, 1,* 189–200. (p. 193)

Osborne, C., Manning, W. D., & Smock, P. J. (2007). Married and cohabiting parents' relationship stability: A focus on race and ethnicity. *Journal of Marriage and Family, 69,* 1345–1366. (p. 467)

Osborne, J. W. (1997). Race and academic disidentification. *Journal of Educational Psychology, 89,* 728–735. (p. 555)

Osborne, L. (1999, October 27). A linguistic big bang. *New York Times Magazine* (www.nytimes.com). (p. 317)

Osgood, C. E. (1962). *An alternative to war or surrender.* Urbana: University of Illinois Press. (p. 692)

Osgood, C. E. (1980). *GRIT: A strategy for survival in mankind's nuclear age?* Paper presented at the Pugwash Conference on New Directions in Disarmament. (p. 692)

OSS Assessment Staff. (1948). *The assessment of men.* New York: Rinehart. (p. 509)

Ost, L. G., & Hugdahl, K. (1981). Acquisition of phobias and anxiety response patterns in clinical patients. *Behaviour Research and Therapy, 16,* 439–447. (p. 574)

Ostfeld, A. M., Kasl, S. V., D'Atri, D. A., & Fitzgerald, E. F. (1987). *Stress, crowding, and blood pressure in prison.* Hillsdale, NJ: Erlbaum. (p. C-3)

Oswald, A. J., & Powdthavee, N. (2006). Does happiness adapt? A longitudinal study of disability with implications for economists and judges. Bonn: Institute for the Study of Labor, Discussion Paper No. 2208. (p. 391)

Oswald, A. J., & Powdthavee, N. (2007). Obesity, unhappiness, and *The Challenge of Affluence:* Theory and evidence. *Economic Journal.* (p. 342)

Ott, B. (2007, June 14). Investors, take note: Engagement boosts earnings. *Gallup Management Journal* (gmj.gallup.com). (p. B-9)

Ott, C. H., Lueger, R. J., Kelber, S. T., & Prigerson, H. G. (2007). Spousal bereavement in older adults: Common, resilient, and chronic grief with defining characteristics. *Journal of Nervous and Mental Disease, 195,* 332–341. (p. 471)

Ouellette, J. A., & Wood, W. (1998). Habit and intention in everyday life: The multiple processes by which past behavior predicts future behavior. *Psychological Bulletin, 124,* 54–74. (pp. 510, B-5)

Overmier, J. B., & Murison, R. (1997). Animal models reveal the "psych" in the psychosomatics of peptic ulcers. *Current Directions in Psychological Science, 6,* 180–184. (p. C-2)

Owen, A. M., Coleman, M. R., Boly, M., Davis, M. H., Laureys, S., & Pickard, J. D. (2006). Detecting awareness in the vegetative state. *Science, 313,* 1402. (p. 89)

Owen, R. (1814). First essay in *New view of society or the formation of character.* Quoted in *The story of New Lamark.* New Lamark Mills, Lamark, Scotland: New Lamark Conservation Trust, 1993. (p. B-9)

Oxfam. (2005, March 26). Three months on: New figures show tsunami may have killed up to four times as many women as men. *Oxfam Press Release* (www.oxfam.org.uk). (p. 439)

Ozer, E. J., Best, S. R., Lipsey, T. L., & Weiss, D. S. (2003). Predictors of posttraumatic stress disorder and symptoms in adults: A meta-analysis. *Psychological Bulletin, 129,* 52–73. (p. 573)

Ozer, E. J., & Weiss, D. S. (2004). Who develops posttraumatic stress disorder. *Current Directions in Psychological Science, 13,* 169–172. (p. 573)

Ozgen, E. (2004). Language, learning, and color perception. *Current Directions in Psychological Science, 13,* 95–98. (p. 320)

Pacifici, R., Zuccaro, P., Farre, M., Pichini, S., Di Carlo, S., Roset, P. N., Ortuno, J., Pujadas, M., Bacosi, A., Menoyo, E., Segura, J., & de la Torre, R. (2001). Effects of repeated doses of MDMA ("Ecstasy") on cell-mediated immune response in humans. *Life Sciences, 69,* 2931–2941. (p. 205)

Paddock, S., Laje, G., Charney, D., Rush, A. J., Wilson, A. F., Sorant, A. J. M., Lipsky, R., Wisniewski, S. R., Manji, H., & McMahon, F. J. (2007). Association of GRIK4 with outcome of antidepressant treatment in the STAR*D cohort. *American Journal of Psychiatry, 164,* 1181–1188. (p. 584)

Padgett, V. R. (1989). Predicting organizational violence: An application of 11 powerful principles of obedience. Paper presented to the American Psychological Association convention. (p. 655)

Page, S. (1977). Effects of the mental illness label in attempts to obtain accommodation. *Canadian Journal of Behavioral Science, 9,* 84–90. (p. 568)

Page, S. E. (2007). *The difference: How the power of diversity creates better groups, firms, schools, and societies.* Princeton: Princeton University Press. (p. 661)

Pagnin, D., de Queiroz, V., Pini, S., & Cassano, G. B. (2004). Efficacy of ECT in depression: A meta-analytic review. *Journal of ECT, 20,* 13–20. (p. 633)

Paivio, A. (1986). *Mental representations: A dual coding approach.* New York: Oxford University Press. (p. 263)

Palace, E. M. (1995). Modification of dysfunctional patterns of sexual response through autonomic arousal and false physiological feedback. *Journal of Consulting and Clinical Psychology, 63,* 604–615. (p. 374)

Palladino, J. J., & Carducci, B. J. (1983). "Things that go bump in the night": Students' knowledge of sleep and dreams. Paper presented at the meeting of the Southeastern Psychological Association. (p. 177)

Pallier, C., Colomé, A., & Sebastián-Gallés, N. (2001). The influence of native-language phonology on lexical access: Exemplar-based versus abstract lexical entries. *Psychological Science, 12,* 445–448. (p. 316)

Palmer, S., Schreiber, C., & Box, C. (1991). Remembering the earthquake: "Flashbulb" memory for experienced vs. reported events. Paper presented to the Psychonomic Society convention. (p. 271)

Pandelaere, M., & Dewitte, S. (2006). Is this a question? Not for long. The statement bias. *Journal of Experimental Social Psychology, 42,* 525–531. (p. 289)

Pandey, J., Sinha, Y., Prakash, A., & Tripathi, R. C. (1982). Right-left political ideologies and attribution of the causes of poverty. *European Journal of Social Psychology, 12,* 327–331. (p. 645)

Panksepp, J. (2007). Neurologizing the psychology of affects: How appraisal-based constructivism and basic emotion theory can coexist. *Perspectives on Psychological Science, 2,* 281–295. (p. 370)

Pantev, C., Oostenveld, R., Engelien, A., Ross, B., Roberts, L. R., & Hoke, M. (1998). Increased auditory cortical representation in musicians. *Nature, 392,* 811–814. (p. 82)

Panzarella, C., Alloy, L. B., & Whitehouse, W. G. (2006). Expanded hopelessness theory of depression: On the mechanisms by which social support protects against depression. *Cognitive Theory and Research, 30,* 307–333. (p. 587)

Park, C. L. (2007). Religiousness/spirituality and health: A meaning systems perspective. *Journal of Behavioral Medicine, 30,* 319–328. (p. C-11)

Park, D. C., Lautenschlager, G., Hedden, T., Davidson, N. S., Smith, A. D., & Smith, P. K. (2002). Models of visuospatial and verbal memory across the adult life span. *Psychology and Aging, 17,* 299–320. (pp. 220, 464)

Park, G., Lubinski, D., & Benbow, C. P. (2007). Contrasting intellectual patterns predict creativity in the arts and sciences. *Psychological Science, 18,* 948–952. (p. 543)

Park, R. L. (1999). Liars never break a sweat. *New York Times,* July 12, 1999 (www.nytimes.com). (p. 372)

Parker, C. P., Baltes, B. B., Young, S. A., Huff, J. W., Altmann, R. A., LaCost, H. A., & Roberts, J. E. (2003). Relationships between psychological climate perceptions and work outcomes: A meta-analytic review. *Journal of Organizational Behavior, 24,* 389–416. (p. B-8)

Parker, E. S., Cahill, L., & McGaugh, J. L. (2006). A case of unusual autobiographical remembering. *Neurocase, 12,* 35–49. (p. 279)

Passell, P. (1993, March 9). Like a new drug, social programs are put to the test. *New York Times,* pp. C1, C10. (p. 36)

Pastalkova, E., Serrano, P., Pinkhasova, D., Wallace, E., Fenton, A. A., & Sacktor, T. C. (2006). Storage of spatial information by the maintenance mechanism of LTP. *Science, 313,* 1141-1144. (p. 269)

Patall, E. A., Cooper, H., & Robinson, J. C. (2008). The effects of choice on intrinsic motivation and related outcomes: A meta-analysis of research findings. *Psychological Bulletin, 134,* 270-300. (p. 237)

Pate, J. E., Pumariega, A. J., Hester, C., & Garner, D. M. (1992). Cross-cultural patterns in eating disorders: A review. *Journal of the American Academy of Child and Adolescent Psychiatry, 31,* 802-809. (p. 337)

Patel, S. R., Malhotra, A., White, D. P., Gottlieb, D. J., & Hu, F. B. (2006). Association between reduced sleep and weight gain in women. *American Journal of Epidemiology, 164,* 947-954. (p. 184)

Patrick, H., Knee, C. R., Canevello, A., Lonsbary, C. (2007). The role of need fulfillment in relationship functioning and well-being: A self-determination theory perspective. *Journal of Personality and Social Psychology, 92,* 434-457. (p. 360)

Patten, S. B., Wang, J. L., Williams, J. V. A., Currie, S., Beck, C. A., Maxwell, C. J., & el-Guebaly, N. (2006). Descriptive epidemiology of major depression in Canada. *Canadian Journal of Psychiatry, 51,* 84-90. (p. 580)

Patterson, D. R. (2004). Treating pain with hypnosis. *Current Directions in Psychological Science, 13,* 252-255. (p. 194)

Patterson, F. (1978, October). Conversations with a gorilla. *National Geographic,* pp. 438-465. (p. D-3)

Patterson, G. R., Chamberlain, P., & Reid, J. B. (1982). A comparative evaluation of parent training procedures. *Behavior Therapy, 13,* 638-650. (pp. 235, 674)

Patterson, G. R., Reid, J. B., & Dishion, T. J. (1992). *Antisocial boys.* Eugene, OR: Castalia. (p. 674)

Patterson, M., Warr, P., & West, M. (2004). Organizational climate and company productivity: The role of employee affect and employee level. *Journal of Occupational and Organizational Psychology, 77,* 193-216. (p. B-8)

Patterson, P. H. (2007). Maternal effects on schizophrenia risk. *Science, 318,* 576-577. (p. 593)

Patterson, R. (1951). *The riddle of Emily Dickinson.* Boston: Houghton Mifflin. (p. 589)

Patton, G. C., Coffey, C., Carlin, J. B., Degenhardt, L., Lynskey, M., & Hall, W. (2002). Cannabis use and mental health of young people: Cohort study. *British Medical Journal, 325,* 1195-1198. (p. 206)

Paulesu, E., Demonet, J-F., Fazio, F., McCrory, E., Chanoine, V., Brunswick, N., Cappa, S. F., Cossu, G., Habib, M., Frith, C. D., & Frith, U. (2001). Dyslexia: Cultural diversity and biological unity. *Science, 291,* 2165-2167. (p. 43)

Paulos, J. A. (1995). *A mathematician reads the newspaper.* New York: Basic Books. (p. 632)

Paulos, J. A. (2006, August 6). Who's counting: It's mean to ignore the median. (www.ABCNews.com). (p. 39)

Paus, T., Zijdenbos, A., Worsley, K., Collins, D. L., Blumenthal, J., Giedd, J. N., Rapoport, J. L., & Evans, A. C. (1999) Structural maturation of neural pathways in children and adolescents: In vivo study. *Science, 283,* 1908-1911. (p. 416)

Pavlidis, G. T. (2005, January 17). Eye movements can diagnose preschoolers at high risk for attention deficit/hyperactivity disorder (ADHD). Press release, Brunel University (www.brunel.ac.uk). (p. 563)

Pavlov, I. (1927). *Conditioned reflexes: An investigation of the physiological activity of the cerebral cortex.* Oxford: Oxford University Press. (p. 222)

Payne, B. K. (2006). Weapon bias: Split-second decisions and unintended stereotyping. *Current Directions in Psychological Science, 15,* 287-291. (p. 666)

Payne, B. K., & Corrigan, E. (2007). Emotional constraints on intentional forgetting. *Journal of Experimental Social Psychology, 43,* 780-786. (p. 284)

Pedersen, N. L., Plomin, R., McClearn, G. E., & Friberg, L. (1988). Neuroticism, extraversion, and related traits in adult twins reared apart and reared together. *Journal of Personality and Social Psychology, 55,* 950-957. (p. 98)

Peeters, A., Barendregt, J. J., Willekens, F., Mackenbach, J. P., & Mamum, A. A. (2003). Obesity in adulthood and its consequences for life expectancy: A life-table analysis. *Annals of Internal Medicine, 138,* 24-32. (p. 341)

Peigneux, P., Laureys, S., Fuchs, S., Collette, F., Perrin, F., Reggers, J., Phillips, C., Degueldre, C., Del Fiore, G., Aerts, J., Luxen, A., & Maquet, P. (2004). Are spatial memories strengthened in the human hippocampus during slow wave sleep? *Neuron, 44,* 535-545. (pp. 185, 273)

Pekkanen, J. (1982, June). Why do we sleep? *Science, 82,* p. 86. (p. 185)

Pelham, B. W. (1993). On the highly positive thoughts of the highly depressed. In R. F. Baumeister (Ed.), *Self-esteem: The puzzle of low self-regard.* New York: Plenum. (p. 512)

Pendick, D. (1994, January/February). The mind of violence. *Brain Work: The Neuroscience Newsletter,* pp. 1-3, 5. (p. 672)

Penhune, V. B., Cismaru, R., Dorsaint-Pierre, R., Petitto, L-A., & Zatorre, R. J. (2003). The morphometry of auditory cortex in the congenitally deaf measured using MRI. *NeuroImage, 20,* 1215-1225. (p. 140)

Pennebaker, J. W. (1990). *Opening up: The healing power of confiding in others.* New York: William Morrow. (pp. 488, C-5)

Pennebaker, J. W. (2002, January 28). Personal communication. (p. 690)

Pennebaker, J. W., Barger, S. D., & Tiebout, J. (1989). Disclosure of traumas and health among Holocaust survivors. *Psychosomatic Medicine, 51,* 577-589. (p. C-5)

Pennebaker, J. W., & O'Heeron, R. C. (1984). Confiding in others and illness rate among spouses of suicide and accidental death victims. *Journal of Abnormal Psychology, 93,* 473-476. (p. C-5)

Pennebaker, J. W., & Stone, L. D. (2003). Words of wisdom: Language use over the life span. *Journal of Personality and Social Psychology, 85,* 291-301. (p. 469)

Penny, H., & Haddock, G. (2007). Anti-fat prejudice among children: The "mere proximity" effect in 5-10 year olds. *Journal of Experimental Social Psychology, 43,* 678-683. (p. 342)

Peplau, L. A., & Fingerhut, A. W. (2007). The close relationships of lesbians and gay men. *Annual Review of Psychology, 58,* 405-424. (pp. 354, 467)

Peppard, P. E., Szklo-Coxe, M., Hia, K. M., & Young, T. (2006). Longitudinal association of sleep-related breathing disorder and depression. *Archives of Internal Medicine, 166,* 1709-1715. (p. 187)

Pepperberg, I. M. (2006). Grey parrot numerical competence: A review. *Animal Cognition, 9,* 377-391. (p. D-2)

Perani, D., & Abutalebi, J. (2005). The neural basis of first and second language processing. *Current Opinion in Neurobiology, 15,* 202-206. (p. 80)

Pereira, A. C., Huddleston, D. E., Brickman, A. M., Sosunov, A. A., Hen, R., McKhann, G. M., Sloan, R., Gage, F. H., Brown, T. R., & Small, S. A. (2007). An *in vivo* correlate of exercise-induced neurogenesis in the adult dentate gyrus. *Proceedings of the National Academic of Sciences, 104,* 5638-5643. (pp. 83, 459)

Pereira, G. M., & Osburn, H. G. (2007). Effects of participation in decision making on performance and employee attitudes: A quality circles meta-analysis. *Journal of Business Psychology, 22,* 145-153. (p. B-12)

Perkins, A., & Fitzgerald, J. A. (1997). Sexual orientation in domestic rams: Some biological and social correlates. In L. Ellis and L. Ebertz (Eds.), *Sexual orientation: Toward biological understanding.* Westport, CT: Praeger Publishers. (p. 356)

Perlmutter, M. (1983). Learning and memory through adulthood. In M. W. Riley, B. B. Hess, & K. Bond (Eds.), *Aging in society: Selected reviews of recent research.* Hillsdale, NJ: Erlbaum. (p. 462)

Perls, T., & Silver, M. H., with Lauerman, J. F. (1999). *Living to 100: Lessons in living to your maximum potential.* Thorndike, ME: Thorndike Press. (p. 404)

Perra, O., Williams, J. H. G., Whiten, A., Fraser, L., Benzie, H., & Perrett, D. I. (2008). Imitation and 'theory of mind' competencies in discrimination of autism from other neurodevelopmental disorders. *Research in Autism Spectrum Disorders, 2,* 456-468. (p. 425)

Perrett, D. I. (2002, October 1). Perception laboratory, Department of Psychology, University of St. Andrews, Scotland (www.perception.st-and.ac.uk). (p. 681)

Perrett, D. I., Harries, M., Misflin, A. J., & Chitty, A. J. (1988). Three stages in the classification of body movements by visual neurons. In H. B. Barlow, C. Blakemore, & M. Weston Smith (Eds.), *Images and understanding.* Cambridge: Cambridge University Press. (p. 129)

Perrett, D. I., Hietanen, J. K., Oram, M. W., & Benson, P. J. (1992). Organization and functions of cells responsive to faces in the temporal cortex.

Philosophical Transactions of the Royal Society of London: Series B, 335, 23–30. (p. 129)

Perrett, D. I., Lee, K. J., Penton-Voak, I., Rowland, D., Yoshikawa, S., Burt, D. M., Henzi, S. P., Castles, D. L., Akamatsu, S. (1998, August). Effects of sexual dimorphism on facial attractiveness. *Nature, 394*, 884–887. (p. 667)

Perrett, D. I., May, K. A., & Yoshikawa, S. (1994). Facial shape and judgments of female attractiveness. *Nature, 368*, 239–242. (p. 129)

Persky, S., & Blascovich, J. (2005). Consequences of playing violent video games in immersive virtual environments, In A. Axelsson & Ralph Schroeder (Eds.). *Work and Play in Shared Virtual Environments.* New York: Springer. (p. 677)

Person, C., Tracy, M., & Galea, S. (2006). Risk factors for depression after a disaster. *Journal of Nervous and Mental Disease, 194*, 659–666. (p. 583)

Pert, C. B. (1986). Quoted in J. Hooper & D. Teresi, *The three-pound universe.* New York: Macmillan. (p. 72)

Pert, C. B., & Snyder, S. H. (1973). Opiate receptor: Demonstration in nervous tissue. *Science, 179*, 1011–1014. (p. 57)

Perugini, E. M., Kirsch, I., Allen, S. T., Coldwell, E., Meredith, J., Montgomery, G. H., & Sheehan, J. (1998). Surreptitious observation of responses to hypnotically suggested hallucinations: A test of the compliance hypothesis. *International Journal of Clinical and Experimental Hypnosis, 46*, 191–203. (p. 195)

Peters, M., Reimers, S., & Manning, J. T. (2006). Hand preference for writing and associations with selected demographic and behavioral variables in 255,100 subjects: The BBC internet study. *Brain and Cognition, 62*, 177–189. (p. 88)

Peters, T. J., & Waterman, R. H., Jr. (1982). *In search of excellence: Lessons from America's best-run companies.* New York: Harper & Row. (p. 239)

Peterson, C., & Barrett, L. C. (1987). Explanatory style and academic performance among university freshmen. *Journal of Personality and Social Psychology, 53*, 603–607. (p. 507)

Peterson, C., Peterson, J., & Skevington, S. (1986). Heated argument and adolescent development. *Journal of Social and Personal Relationships, 3*, 229–240. (p. 448)

Peterson, C., & Seligman, M. E. P. (2004). *Character strengths and virtues: A handbook and classification.* New York: Oxford. (p. 567)

Peterson, C. C., & Siegal, M. (1999). Representing inner worlds: Theory of mind in autistic, deaf, and normal hearing children. *Psychological Science, 10*, 126–129. (p. 422)

Peterson, L. R., & Peterson, M. J. (1959). Short-term retention of individual verbal items. *Journal of Experimental Psychology, 58*, 193–198. (pp. 266, 267)

Petitto, L. A., & Marentette, P. F. (1991). Babbling in the manual mode: Evidence for the ontogeny of language. *Science, 251*, 1493–1496. (p. 315)

Petry, N. M., Barry, D., Pietrzak, R. H., & Wagner, J. A. (2008). Overweight and obesity are associated with psychiatric disorders: Results from the National Epidemiologic Survey on Alcohol and Related Conditions. *Psychosomatic Medicine, 70*, 288–297. (p. 342)

Pettegrew, J. W., Keshavan, M. S., & Minshew, N. J. (1993). 31P nuclear magnetic resonance spectroscopy: Neurodevelopment and schizophrenia. *Schizophrenia Bulletin, 19*, 35–53. (p. 592)

Petticrew, C., Bell, R., & Hunter, D. (2002). Influence of psychological coping on survival and recurrence in people with cancer: Systematic review. *British Medical Journal, 325*, 1066. (p. 405)

Petticrew, M., Fraser, J. M., & Regan, M. F. (1999). Adverse life events and risk of breast cancer: A meta-analysis. *British Journal of Health Psychology, 4*, 1–17. (p. 405)

Pettifor, J. P. (2004). Professional ethics across national boundaries. *European Psychologist, 9*, 264–272. (p. 45)

Pettigrew, T. F. (1998). Reactions toward the new minorities of western Europe. *Annual Review of Sociology, 24*, 77–103. (p. 665)

Pettigrew, T. F. (2006). A two-level approach to anti-immigrant prejudice and discrimination. In R. Mahalingam (Ed.), *Cultural psychology of immigrants.* Mahwah, NJ: Erlbaum. (p. 665)

Pettigrew, T. F., Christ, O., Wagner, U., & Stellmacher, J. (2007). Direct and indirect intergroup contact effects on prejudice: A normative interpretation. *International Journal of Intercultural Relations, 31*, 411–425. (p. 690)

Pettigrew, T. F., & Tropp, L. R. (2006). A meta analytic test of intergroup contact theory. *Journal of Personality and Social Psychology, 90*, 751–783. (p. 690)

Pettus, A. (2008, January-February). A cultural symptom? Repressed memory. *Harvard Magazine* (www.harvardmagazine.com). (p. 488)

Pew. (2003). *Views of a changing world 2003.* The Pew Global Attitudes Project. Washington, DC: Pew Research Center for the People and the Press (http://people-press.org/reports/pdf/185.pdf). (p. 440)

Pew. (2006, September 21). *Publics of Asian powers hold negative views of one another.* Pew Global Attitudes Project Report, Pew Research Center (pewresearch.org). (p. 668)

Pew. (2007, January 24). *Global warming: A divide on causes and solutions.* Pew Research Center for the People and the Press. (p. 305)

Pew Research Center. (2006, November 14). Attitudes toward homosexuality in African countries. (pewresearch.org). (p. 354)

Pew Research Center. (2007, July 18). Modern marriage: "I like hugs. I like kisses. But what I really love is help with the dishes." Pew Research Center (www.pewresearch.org). (p. 684)

Pfammatter, M., Junghan, U. M., Brenner, H. D. (2006). Efficacy of psychological therapy in schizophrenia: Conclusions from meta-analyses. *Schizophrenia Bulletin, 32*, S64–S80. (p. 623)

Phelps, J. A., Davis J. O., & Schartz, K. M. (1997). Nature, nurture, and twin research strategies. *Current Directions in Psychological Science, 6*, 117–120. (pp. 97, 594)

Philip Morris Companies, Inc. (1999, Oct. 13). Referenced in Myron Levin, Philip Morris' new campaign echoes medical experts, *Los Angeles Times.* (p. 202)

Philip Morris. (2003). *Philip Morris USA youth smoking prevention. Teenage attitudes and behavior study, 2002.* In "Raising kids who don't smoke," vol. 1(2). (p. 203)

Phillips, D. P. (1985). Natural experiments on the effects of mass media violence on fatal aggression: Strengths and weaknesses of a new approach. In L. Berkowitz (Ed.), *Advances in experimental social psychology* (Vol. 19). Orlando, FL: Academic Press. (p. 651)

Phillips, D. P., Carstensen, L. L., & Paight, D. J. (1989). Effects of mass media news stories on suicide, with new evidence on the role of story content. In D. R. Pfeffer (Ed.), *Suicide among youth: Perspectives on risk and prevention.* Washington, DC: American Psychiatric Press. (p. 651)

Phillips, J. L. (1969). *Origins of intellect: Piaget's theory.* San Francisco: Freeman. (p. 421)

Phillips, T. (2004, April 3). Quoted by T. Baldwin & G. Rozenberg, Britain 'must scrap multiculturalism.' *The Times*, p. 1. (p. 691)

Phonak. (2007). Hear the world (www.hear-the-world.com). (p. 139)

Piaget, J. (1930). *The child's conception of physical causality.* London: Routledge & Kegan Paul. (p. 418)

Piaget, J. (1932). *The moral judgment of the child.* New York: Harcourt, Brace & World. (p. 449)

Picchioni, M. M., & Murray, R. M. (2007). Schizophrenia. *British Medical Journal, 335*, 91–95. (p. 591)

Pieters, G. L. M., de Bruijn, E. R. A., Maas, Y., Hultijn, W., Vandereycken, W., Peuskens, J., & Sabbe, B. G. (2007). Action monitoring and perfectionism in anorexia nervosa. *Brain and Cognition, 63*, 42–50. (p. 338)

Pike, K. M., & Rodin, J. (1991). Mothers, daughters, and disordered eating. *Journal of Abnormal Psychology, 100*, 198–204. (p. 337)

Piliavin, J. A. (2003). Doing well by doing good: Benefits for the benefactor. In C. L. M. Keyes & J. Haidt (Eds.), *Flourishing: Positive psychology and the life well-lived.* Washington, DC: American Psychological Association. (p. 450)

Pillemer, D. (1998). *Momentous events, vivid memories.* Cambridge: Harvard University Press, 1998. (p. 461)

Pillemer, D. B., Ivcevic, Z., Gooze, R. A., & Collins, K. A. (2007). Self-esteem memories: Feeling good about achievement success, feeling bad about relationship distress. *Personality and Social Psychology Bulletin, 33*, 1292–1305. (p. 362)

Pillemer, D. G. (1995). What is remembered about early childhood events? Invited paper presentation to the American Psychological Society convention. (p. 417)

Pillsworth, E. G., & Haselton, M. G. (2006). Male sexual attractiveness predicts differential ovulatory shifts in female extra-pair attraction and male mate retention. *Evolution and Human Behavior, 27,* 247–258. (p. 350)

Pillsworth, M. G., Haselton, M. G., & Buss, D. M. (2004). Ovulatory shifts in female desire. *Journal of Sex Research, 41,* 55–65. (p. 350)

Pinel, J. P. J. (1993). *Biopsychology* (2nd ed). Boston: Allyn & Bacon. (p. 334)

Pingitore, R., Dugoni, B. L., Tindale, R. S., & Spring, B. (1994). Bias against overweight job applicants in a simulated employment interview. *Journal of Applied Psychology, 79,* 909–917. (pp. 341, 342)

Pinker, S. (1990, September-October). Quoted by J. de Cuevas, "No, she holded them loosely." *Harvard Magazine,* pp. 60–67. (p. 313)

Pinker, S. (1995). The language instinct. *The General Psychologist, 31,* 63–65. (pp. 314, D-4, D-6)

Pinker, S. (1998). Words and rules. *Lingua, 106,* 219–242. (p. 313)

Pinker, S. (1999, June 24). His brain measured up. *New York Times* (www.nytimes.com). (p. 530)

Pinker, S. (2002, September 9). A biological understanding of human nature: A talk with Steven Pinker. *The Edge Third Culture Mail List* (www.edge.org). (pp. 99, 104)

Pinker, S. (2005, April 22). The science of gender and science: A conversation with Elizabeth Spelke. *Harvard University* (www.edge.org). (p. 550)

Pinker, S. (2006, January 1). Groups of people may differ genetically in their average talents and temperaments. *The Edge* (www.edge.org). (p. 555)

Pinker, S. (2007). *The stuff of thought.* New York: Viking. (p. 321)

Pinker, S. (2007, March 19). A history of violence. *New Republic* (available at www.edge.org). (p. 305)

Pinker, S. (2008). *The sexual paradox: Men, women, and the real gender gap.* New York: Scribner. (p. 437)

Pinstrup-Andersen, P. & Cheng, F. (2007). Still hungry. *Scientific American, 297,* 96–103. (p. 345)

Pipe, M-E. (1996). Children's eyewitness memory. *New Zealand Journal of Psychology, 25,* 36–43. (p. 290)

Pipe, M-E., Lamb, M. E., Orbach, Y., & Esplin, P. W. (2004). Recent research on children's testimony about experienced and witnessed events. *Developmental Review, 24,* 440–468. (p. 290)

Piper, A., Jr. (1998, Winter). Multiple personality disorder: Witchcraft survives in the twentieth century. *Skeptical Inquirer,* pp. 44–50. (p. 578)

Pipher, M. (2002). *The middle of everywhere: The world's refugees come to our town.* New York: Harcourt Brace. (pp. 361, 400)

Pitcher, D., Walssh, V., Yovel, G., & Duchaine, B. (2007). TMS evidence for the involvement of the right occipital face area in early face processing. *Current Biology, 17,* 1568–1573. (p. 130)

Pitman, R. K., & Delahanty, D. L. (2005). Conceptually driven pharmacologic approaches to acute trauma. *CNS Spectrums, 10*(2), 99–106. (p. 270)

Pitman, R. K., Sanders, K. M., Zusman, R. M., Healy, A. R., Cheema, F., Lasko, N. B., Cahill, L., & Orr, S. P. (2002). Pilot study of secondary prevention of posttraumatic stress disorder with propranolol. *Biological Psychiatry, 51,* 189–192. (p. 270)

Pittenger, D. J. (1993). The utility of the Myers-Briggs Type Indicator. *Review of Eduational Research, 63,* 467–488. (p. 494)

Plassmann, H., O'Doherty, J., Shiv, B., & Rangel, A. (2008). Marketing actions can modulate neural representations of experienced pleasantness. *Proceedings of the National Academy of Sciences, 105,* 1050–1054. (p. 147)

Pleyers, G., Corneille, O., Luminet, O., & Yzerbyt, V. (2007). Aware and (dis)liking: Item-based analyses reveal that valence acquisition via evaluative conditioning emerges only when there is contingency awareness. *Journal of Experimental Psychology: Learning, Memory, and Cognition, 33,* 130–144. (p. 221)

Pliner, P. (1982). The effects of mere exposure on liking for edible substances. *Appetite: Journal for Intake Research, 3,* 283–290. (p. 336)

Pliner, P., Pelchat, M., & Grabski, M. (1993). Reduction of neophobia in humans by exposure to novel foods. *Appetite, 20,* 111–123. (p. 336)

Plöderl, M., & Fartacek, R. (2005). Suicidality and associated risk factors among lesbian, gay, and bisexual compared to heterosexual Austrian adults. *Suicide and Life-Threatening Behavior, 35,* 661–670. (p. 355)

Plomin, R. (1999). Genetics and general cognitive ability. *Nature, 402* (Suppl), C25–C29. (pp. 524, 544)

Plomin, R. (2001). Genetics and behaviour. *The Psychologist, 14,* 134–139. (p. 544)

Plomin, R. (2003). General cognitive ability. In R. Plomin, J. C. DeFries, I. W. Craig, & P. McGuffin (Eds.), *Behavioral genetics in a postgenomic world.* Washington, DC: APA Books. (p. 544)

Plomin, R., & Bergeman, C. S. (1991). The nature of nurture: Genetic influence on "environmental" measures. *Behavioral and Brain Sciences, 14,* 373–427. (p. 102)

Plomin, R., Corley, R., Caspi, A., Fulker, D. W., & DeFries, J. (1998). Adoption results for self-reported personality: Evidence for nonadditive genetic effects? *Journal of Personality and Social Psychology, 75,* 211–219. (p. 99)

Plomin, R., & Crabbe, J. (2000). DNA. *Psychological Bulletin, 126,* 806–828. (p. 102)

Plomin, R., & Daniels, D. (1987). Why are children in the same family so different from one another? *Behavioral and Brain Sciences, 10,* 1–60. (p. 444)

Plomin, R., & DeFries, J. C. (1998, May). The genetics of cognitive abilities and disabilities. *Scientific American,* pp. 62–69. (p. 546)

Plomin, R., DeFries, J. C., McClearn, G. E., & Rutter, M. (1997). *Behavioral genetics.* New York: Freeman. (pp. 97, 104, 344, 545)

Plomin, R., Fulker, D. W., Corley, R., & DeFries, J. C. (1997). Nature, nurture and cognitive development from 1 to 16 years: A parent-offspring adoption study. *Psychological Science, 8,* 442–447. (p. 594)

Plomin, R., & Kovas, Y. (2005). Generalist genes and learning disabilities. *Psychological Bulletin, 131,* 592–617. (p. 545)

Plomin, R., McClearn, G. E., Pedersen, N. L., Nesselroade, J. R., & Bergeman, C. S. (1988). Genetic influence on childhood family environment perceived retrospectively from the last half of the life span. *Developmental Psychology, 24,* 37–45. (p. 102)

Plomin, R., & McGuffin, P. (2003). Psychopathology in the postgenomic era. *Annual Review of Psychology, 54,* 205–228. (pp. 586, 584)

Plomin, R., Reiss, D., Hetherington, E. M., & Howe, G. W. (January, 1994). Nature and nurture: Genetic contributions to measures of the family environment. *Developmental Psychology, 30*(1), 32–43. (p. 102)

Plotkin, H. (1994). *Darwin machines and the nature of knowledge.* Cambridge, MA: Harvard University Press. (p. 583)

Plotnik, J. M., de Waal, F. B. M., & Reiss, D. (2006). Self-recognition in an Asian elephant. *Proceedings of the National Academy of Sciences, 103,* 17053–17057. (p. 433)

Plous, S. (1993). Psychological mechanisms in the human use of animals. *Journal of Social Issues, 49*(1), 11–52. (p. 44)

Plous, S., & Herzog, H. A. (2000). Poll shows researchers favor lab animal protection. *Science, 290,* 711. (p. 45)

Poldrack, R. A., & Wagner, A. D. (2004). What can neuroimaging tell us about the mind? *Current Directions in Psychological Science, 13,* 177–181. (p. 261)

Polivy, J., & Herman, C. P. (1985). Dieting and binging: A causal analysis. *American Psychologist, 40,* 193–201. (p. 347)

Polivy, J., & Herman, C. P. (1987). Diagnosis and treatment of normal eating. *Journal of Personality and Social Psychology, 55,* 635–644. (p. 347)

Polivy, J., & Herman, C. P. (2002). Causes of eating disorders. *Annual Review of Psychology, 53,* 187–213. (p. 338)

Pollack, A. (2004, April 13). With tiny brain implants, just thinking may make it so. *New York Times* (www.nytimes.com). (p. 77)

Pollack, A. (2006, July 13). Paralyzed man uses thoughts to move a cursor. *New York Times* (www.nytimes.com). (p. 77)

Pollak, S. D., Cicchetti, D., & Klorman, R. (1998). Stress, memory, and emotion: Developmental considerations from the study of child maltreatment. *Developmental Psychopathology, 10,* 811–828. (p. 222)

Pollak, S. D., & Kistler, D. J. (2002). Early experience is associated with the development of categorical representations for facial expressions of emotion. *Proceedings of the National Academy of Sciences, 99,* 9072–9076. (p. 378)

Pollak, S. D., & Tolley-Schell, S. A. (2003). Selective attention to facial emotion in physically abused children. *Journal of Abnormal Psychology, 112,* 323–328. (p. 378)

Pollard, R. (1992). 100 years in psychology and deafness: A centennial retrospective. Invited address to the American Psychological Association convention, Washington, DC. (p. 321)

Pollick, A. S., & de Waal, F. B. M. (2007). Ape gestures and language evolution. *Proceedings of the National Academic of Sciences, 104,* 8184–8189. (p. D-5)

Polusny, M. A., & Follette, V. M. (1995). Long-term correlates of child sexual abuse: Theory and review of the empirical literature. *Applied & Preventive Psychology, 4,* 143–166. (p. 431)

Poole, D. A., & Lindsay, D. S. (1995). Interviewing preschoolers: Effects of nonsuggestive techniques, parental coaching and leading questions on reports of nonexperienced events. *Journal of Experimental Child Psychology, 60,* 129–154. (p. 287)

Poole, D. A., & Lindsay, D. S. (2001). Children's eyewitness reports after exposure to misinformation from parents. *Journal of Experimental Psychology: Applied, 7,* 27–50. (p. 287)

Poole, D. A., & Lindsay, D. S. (2002). Reducing child witnesses' false reports of misinformation from parents. *Journal of Experimental Child Psychology, 81,* 117–140. (p. 287)

Poole, D. A., Lindsay, D. S., Memon, A., & Bull, R. (1995). Psychotherapy and the recovery of memories of childhood sexual abuse: U.S. and British practitioners' opinions, practices, and experiences. *Journal of Consulting and Clinical Psychology, 63,* 426–437. (p. 290)

Poon, L. W. (1987). Myths and truisms: Beyond extant analyses of speed of behavior and age. Address to the Eastern Psychological Association convention. (p. 459)

Pope, H. G., Poliakoff, M. B., Parker, M. P., Boynes, M., & Hudson, J. I. (2007). Is dissociative amnesia a culture-bound syndrome? Findings from a survey of historical literature. *Psychological Medicine, 37,* 225–233. (p. 488)

Popenoe, D. (1993). *The evolution of marriage and the problem of stepfamilies: A biosocial perspective.* Paper presented at the National Symposium on Stepfamilies, Pennsylvania State University. (p. 518)

Popenoe, D., & Whitehead, B. D. (2002). *Should We Live Together?,* 2nd Ed. New Brunswick, NJ: The National Marriage Project, Rutgers University. (p. 467)

Popkin, B. M. (2007, September). The world is fat. *Scientific American,* pp. 88–95. (pp. 344, 345)

Poremba, A., & Gabriel, M. (2001). Amygdalar efferents initiate auditory thalamic discriminative training-induced neuronal activity. *Journal of Neuroscience, 21,* 270–278. (p. 71)

Porter, D., & Neuringer, A. (1984). Music discriminations by pigeons. *Journal of Experimental Psychology: Animal Behavior Processes, 10,* 138–148. (p. 230)

Porter, S., Birt, A. R., Yuille, J. C., & Lehman, D. R. (2000, Nov.). Negotiating false memories: Interviewer and rememberer characteristics relate to memory distortion. *Psychological Science, 11,* 507–510. (p. 286)

Porter, S., & Peace, K. A. (2007). The scars of memory: A prospective, longitudinal investigation fo the consistency of traumatic and positive emotional memories in adulthood. *Psychological Science, 18,* 435–441. (p. 293)

Porter, S., & ten Brinke, L. (2008). Reading between the lies: Identifying concealed and falsified emotions in universal facial expressions. *Psychological Science, 19,* 508–514. (p. 378)

Porter, S., Yuille, J. C., & Lehman, D. R. (1999). The nature of real, implanted, and fabricated memories for childhood events: Implications for the recovered memory debate. *Law and Human Behavior, 23,* 517–537. (p. 292)

Posner, M. I., & Carr, T. H. (1992). Lexical access and the brain: Anatomical constraints on cognitive models of word recognition. *American Journal of Psychology, 105,* 1–26. (p. 80)

Posthuma, D., & de Geus, E. J. C. (2006). Progress in the molecular-genetic study of intelligence. *Current Directions in Psychological Science, 15,* 151–155. (p. 545)

Poulton, R., & Milne, B. J. (2002). Low fear in childhood is associated with sporting prowess in adolescence and young adulthood. *Behaviour Research and Therapy, 40,* 1191–1197. (p. 597)

Powell, J. (1989). *Happiness is an inside job.* Valencia, CA: Tabor. (p. 514)

Powell, K. E., Thompson, P. D., Caspersen, C. J., & Kendrick, J. S. (1987). Physical activity and the incidence of coronary heart disease. *Annual Review of Public Health, 8,* 253–287. (p. C-7)

Powell, L. H., Schahabi, L., & Thoresen, C. E. (2003). Religion and spirituality: Linkages to physical health. *American Psychologist, 58,* 36–52. (p. C-12)

Powell, R. A., & Boer, D. P. (1994). Did Freud mislead patients to confabulate memories of abuse? *Psychological Reports, 74,* 1283–1298. (p. 487)

Powers, M. B., & Emmelkamp, P. M. G. (2008). Virtual reality exposure therapy for anxiety disorders: A meta-analysis. *Journal of Anxiety Disorders, 22,* 561–569. (p. 612)

Prairie Home Companion. (1999). *The Prairie Home Companion's Pretty Good Joke Book* (Vol. 4). St. Paul, MN: Prairie Home Companion. (p. 397)

Pratkanis, A. R., & Greenwald, A. G. (1988). Recent perspectives on unconscious processing: Still no marketing applications. *Psychology and Marketing, 5,* 337–353. (p. 122)

PRB. (2002). *2002 Women of our world.* Population Reference Bureau (www.prb.org). (p. 665)

PRB. (2004). *2004 world population data sheet.* Washington, DC: Population Reference Bureau. (p. 457)

Prentice, D. A., & Miller, D. T. (1993). Pluralistic ignorance and alcohol use on campus: Some consequences of misperceiving the social norm. *Journal of Personality and Social Psychology, 64,* 243–256. (p. 210)

Presley, C. A., Meilman, P. W., & Lyerla, R. (1997). *Alcohol and drugs on American college campuses: Issues of violence and harrassment.* Carbondale, IL: Core Institute, Southern Illinois University. (p. 200)

Pressman, S. D., & Cohen, S. (2005). Does positive affect influence health? *Psychological Bulletin, 131,* 925–971. (p. 389)

Price, G. M., Uauq, R., Breeze, E., Bulpitt, C. J., & Fletcher, A. E. (2006). Weight, shape, and mortality risk in older persons: Elevated waist-hip ratio, not high body mass index, is associated with a greater risk of death. *American Journal of Clinical Nutrition, 84,* 449–460. (p. 341)

Prince Charles. (2000). BBC Reith Lecture. (p. 19)

Princeton Review. (2005) *Guide to college majors, 2005 edition.* Princeton, NJ: Author. (p. A-1)

Principe, G. F., Kanaya, T., Ceci, S. J., & Singh, M. (2006). Believing is seeing: How rumors can engender false memories in preschoolers. *Psychological Science, 17,* 243–248. (p. 289)

Pringle, P. J., Geary, M. P., Rodeck, C. H., Kingdom, J. C., Kayamba-Kay's, S., & Hindmarsh, P. C. (2005). The influence of cigarette smoking on antenatal growth, birth size, and the insulin-like growth factor axis. *Journal of Clinical Endocrinology and Metabolism, 90,* 2556–2562. (p. 413)

Prioleau, L., Murdock, M., & Brody, N. (1983). An analysis of psychotherapy versus placebo studies. *The Behavioral and Brain Sciences, 6,* 275–310. (p. 625)

Prior, H., Schwarz, A., & Güntürkün, O. (2008). Mirror-induced behavior in the magpie (*Pica pica*): Evidence of self-recognition. *PloS Biology, 6,* 1642–1650. (p. 433)

Proffitt, D. R. (2006a). Embodied perception and the economy of action. *Perspectives on Psychological Science, 1,* 110–122. (p. 164)

Proffitt, D.R. (2006b). Distance perception. *Current Directions in Psychological Research, 15,* 131–135. (p. 164)

Project Match Research Group. (1997). Matching alcoholism treatments to client heterogeneity: Project MATCH posttreatment drinking outcomes. *Journal of Studies on Alcohol, 58,* 7–29. (p. 618)

Pronin, E. (2007). Perception and misperception of bias in human judgment. *Trends in Cognitive Sciences, 11,* 37–43. (p. 513)

Pronin, E., Berger, J., & Molouki, S. (2007). Alone in a crowd of sheep: Asymmetric perceptions of conformity and their roots in an introspection illusion. *Journal of Personality and Social Psychology, 92,* 585–595. (p. 654)

Pronin, E., & Ross, L. (2006). Temporal differences in trait self-ascription: When the self is seen as an other. *Journal of Personality and Social Psychology, 90,* 197–209. (p. 645)

Pronin, E., & Wegner, D. M. (2006). Manic thinking: Independent effects of thought speed and thought content on mood. *Psychological Science, 17,* 807–813. (p. 581)

Propper, R. E., Stickgold, R., Keeley, R., & Christman, S. D. (2007). Is television traumatic? Dreams, stress, and media exposure in the aftermath of September 11, 2001. *Psychological Science, 18,* 334–340. (p. 188)

Provine, R. R. (2001). *Laughter: A scientific investigation.* New York: Penguin. (p. 28)

Pryor, J. H., Hurtado, S., Saenz, V. B., Korn, J. S., Santos, J. L., & Korn, W. S. (2006). *The American Freshman: National norms for Fall 2006.* Los Angeles, UCLA Higher Education Research Institute. (p. 587)

Pryor, J. H., Hurtado, S., Sharkness, J., & Korn, W. S. (2007). *The American freshman: National norms for Fall 2007.* Los Angeles, UCLA Higher Education Research Institute. (pp. 361, 437)

Psychologist. (2003, April). Who's the greatest? *The Psychologist, 16,* 17. (p. 423)

Puchalski, C. (2005, March 12). Personal correspondence from Director, George Washington Institute for Spirituality and Health. (p. C-11)

Puhl, R. M., & Latner, J. D. (2007). Stigma, obesity, and the health of the nation's children. *Psychological Bulletin, 133,* 557–580. (p. 342)

Pulkkinen, L. (2004). A longitudinal study on social development as an impetus for school reform toward an integrated school day. *European Psychologist, 9,* 125–141. (p. 432)

Pulkkinen, L. (2006). The Jyväskylä longitudinal study of personality and social development (JYLS). In L. Pulkkinen, J. Kaprio, & R. J. Rose (Eds.), *Socioemotional development and health from adolescence to adulthood.* Cambridge studies on child and adolescent health. New York: Cambridge University Press. (p. 432)

Putnam, F. W. (1991). Recent research on multiple personality disorder. *Psychiatric Clinics of North America, 14,* 489–502. (p. 579)

Putnam, F. W. (1995). Rebuttal of Paul McHugh. *Journal of the American Academy of Child and Adolescent Psychiatry, 34,* 963. (p. 579)

Putnam, R. (2000). *Bowling alone.* New York: Simon and Schuster. (p. 663)

Pyszczynski, T. A., Hamilton, J. C., Greenberg, J., & Becker, S. E. (1991). Self-awareness and psychological dysfunction. In C. R. Snyder & D. O. Forsyth (Eds.), *Handbook of social and clinical psychology: The health perspective.* New York: Pergamon. (p. 587)

Pyszczynski, T. A., Solomon, S., & Greenberg, J. (2002). *In the wake of 9/11: The psychology of terror.* Washington, DC: American Psychological Association. (p. 669)

Qirko, H. N. (2004). "Fictive kin" and suicide terrorism. *Science, 304,* 49–50. (p. 660)

Quasha, S. (1980). *Albert Einstein: An intimate portrait.* New York: Forest. (p. 540)

Quinn, P. C. (2002). Category representation in young infants. *Current Directions in Psychological Science, 11,* 66–70. (p. 414)

Quinn, P. C., Bhatt, R. S., Brush, D., Grimes, A., & Sharpnack, H. (2002). Development of form similarity as a Gestalt grouping principle in infancy. *Psychological Science, 13,* 320–328. (p. 152)

Quinn, P. J., Williams, G. M., Najman, J. M., Andersen, M. J., & Bor, W. (2001). The effect of breastfeeding on child development at 5 years: A cohort study. *Journal of Pediatrics & Child Health, 3,* 465–469. (p. 34)

Rabbitt, P. (2006). Tales of the unexpected: 25 years of cognitive gerontology. *The Psychologist, 19,* 674–676. (p. 462)

Rabinowicz, T., Dean, D. E., Petetot, J. M., & de Courten-Myers, G. M. (1999). Gender differences in the human cerebral cortex: More neurons in males; more processes in females. *Journal of Child Neurology, 14,* 98–107. (p. 415)

Rabinowicz, T., deCourten-Myers, G. M., Petetot, J. M., Xi, G., & de los Reyes, E. (1996). Human cortex development: Estimates of neuronal numbers indicate major loss late during gestation. *Journal of Neuropathology and Experimental Neurology, 55,* 320–328. (p. 415)

Radin, D., Nelson, R., Dobyns, Y., & Houtkooper, J. (2006). Reexamining psychokinesis: Comment on Bösch, Steinkamp, and Boller (2006). *Psychological Bulletin, 132,* 529–532. (p. 168)

Rahman, Q., & Koerting, J. (2008). Sexual orientation-related differences in allocentric spatial memory tasks. *Hippocampus, 18,* 55–63. (p. 359)

Rahman, Q., & Wilson, G. D. (2003). Born gay? The psychobiology of human sexual orientation. *Personality and Individual Differences, 34,* 1337–1382. (pp. 357, 359)

Rahman, Q., Wilson, G. D., & Abrahams, S. (2003). Biosocial factors, sexual orientation and neurocognitive functioning. *Psychoneuroendocrinology, 29,* 867–881. (p. 359)

Raine, A. (1999). Murderous minds: Can we see the mark of Cain? *Cerebrum: The Dana Forum on Brain Science 1(1),* 15–29. (pp. 598, 671)

Raine, A. (2005). The interaction of biological and social measures in the explanation of antisocial and violent behavior. In D. M. Stoff & E. J. Susman (Eds.) *Developmental psychobiology of aggression.* New York: Cambridge University Press. (pp. 598, 671)

Raine, A., Brennan, P., Mednick, B., & Mednick, S. A. (1996). High rates of violence, crime, academic problems, and behavioral problems in males with both early neuromotor deficits and unstable family environments. *Archives of General Psychiatry, 53,* 544–549. (p. 598)

Raine, A., Lencz, T., Bihrle, S., LaCasse, L., & Colletti, P. (2000). Reduced prefrontal gray matter volume and reduced autonomic activity in antisocial personality disorder. *Archives of General Psychiatry, 57,* 119–127. (p. 598)

Rainville, P., Duncan, G. H., Price, D. D., Carrier, B., & Bushnell, M. C. (1997). Pain affect encoded in human anterior cingulate but not somatosensory cortex. *Science, 277,* 968–971. (p. 196)

Raison, C. L., Klein, H. M., & Steckler, M. (1999). The mood and madness reconsidered. *Journal of Affective Disorders, 53,* 99–106. (p. 599)

Rajendran, G., & Mitchell, P. (2007). Cognitive theories of autism. *Developmental Review, 27,* 224–260. (p. 424)

Ralston, A. (2004). Enough rope. Interview for ABC TV, Australia, by Andrew Denton (www.abc.net.au/enoughrope/stories/s1227885.htm). (p. 328)

Ramachandran, V. S., & Blakeslee, S. (1998). *Phantoms in the brain: Probing the mysteries of the human mind.* New York: Morrow. (pp. 61, 144)

Ramachandran, V. S., & Oberman, L. M. (2006, November). Broken mirrors: A theory of autism. *Scientific American,* pp. 63–69. (pp. 243, 425)

Ramirez-Esparza, N., Gosling, S. D., Benet-Martínez, V., Potter, J. P., & Pennebaker, J. W. (2006). Do bilinguals have two personalities? A special case of cultural frame switching. *Journal of Research in Personality, 40,* 99–120. (p. 320)

Rand, C. S. W., & Macgregor, A. M. C. (1990). Morbidly obese patients' perceptions of social discrimination before and after surgery for obesity. *Southern Medical Journal, 83,* 1390–1395. (p. 342)

Rand, C. S. W., & Macgregor, A. M. C. (1991). Successful weight loss following obesity surgery and perceived liability or morbid obesity. *Internal Journal of Obesity, 15,* 577–579. (p. 342)

Randi, J. (1999, February 4). 2000 club mailing list e-mail letter. (p. 169)

Randi, J. (2008). 'Twas Brillig . . . . Last chance to win the million-dollar challenge. *Skeptic, 14(1),* 6. (p. 169)

Rapoport, J. L. (1989, March). The biology of obsessions and compulsions. *Scientific American,* pp. 83–89. (pp. 572, 575)

Räsänen, S., Pakaslahti, A., Syvalahti, E., Jones, P. B., & Isohanni, M. (2000). Sex differences in schizophrenia: A review. *Nordic Journal of Psychiatry, 54,* 37–45. (p. 592)

Rasch, B., Büchel, C., Gais, S., & Born, J. (2007). Odor cues during slow-wave sleep prompt declarative memory consolidation. *Science, 315,* 1426–1429. (p. 185)

Ray, J. (2005, April 12). U.S. teens walk away from anger: Boys and girls manage anger differently. *The Gallup Organization* (www.gallup.com). (p. 387)

Ray, O., & Ksir, C. (1990). *Drugs, society, and human behavior* (5th ed.). St. Louis: Times Mirror/Mosby. (p. 204)

Raynor, H. A., & Epstein, L. H. (2001). Dietary variety, energy regulation, and obesity. *Psychological Bulletin, 127,* 325–341. (p. 335)

Raz, A., Fan, J., & Posner, M. I. (2005). Hypnotic suggestion reduces conflict in the human brain. *PNAS, 102,* 9978–9983. (p. 195)

Reason, J. (1987). The Chernobyl errors. *Bulletin of the British Psychological Society, 40,* 201–206. (p. 660)

Reason, J., & Mycielska, K. (1982). *Absent-minded? The psychology of mental lapses and everyday errors.* Englewood Cliffs, NJ: Prentice-Hall. (p. 162)

Reed, P. (2000). Serial position effects in recognition memory for odors. *Journal of Experimental Psychology: Learning, Memory, and Cognition, 26,* 411–422. (p. 260)

Reed, T. E., & Jensen, A. R. (1992). Conduction velocity in a brain nerve pathway of normal adults correlates with intelligence level. *Intelligence, 16,* 259–272. (p. 531)

Rees, M. (1999). *Just six numbers: The deep forces that shape the universe.* New York: Basic Books. (p. 109)

Reichenberg, A., Gross, R., Weiser, M., Bresnahan, M., Silverman, J., Harlap, S., Rabinoqitz, J., Shulman, C., Malaspina, D., Lubin, G., Knobler, H Y., Davidson, M., & Susser, E. (2007). Advancing paternal age and autism. *Archives of General Psychiatry, 63,* 1026–1032. (p. 425)

Reichenberg, A., & Harvey, P. D. (2007). Neuropsychological impairments in schizophrenia: Integration of performance-based and brain imaging findings. *Psychological Bulletin, 133,* 833–858. (p. 590)

Reichman, J. (1998). *I'm not in the mood: What every woman should know about improving her libido.* New York: Morrow. (p. 350)

Reifman, A., & Cleveland, H. H. (2007). Shared environment: A quantitative review. Paper presented to the Society for Research in Child Development, Boston, MA. (p. 100)

Reijmers, L. G., Perkins, B. L., Matsuo, N., & Mayford, M. (2007). Localization of a stable neural correlate of associative memory. *Science, 317*, 1230–1233. (p. 386)

Reis, H. T., & Aron, A. (2008). Love: What is it, why does it matter, and how does it operate? *Perspectives on Psychological Science, 3*, 80–86. (p. 684)

Reisenzein, R. (1983). The Schachter theory of emotion: Two decades later. *Psychological Bulletin, 94*, 239–264. (p. 374)

Reiser, M. (1982). *Police psychology*. Los Angeles: LEHI. (p. 167)

Reiss, D., & Marino, L. (2001). Mirror self-recognition in the bottlenose dolphin: A case of cognitive convergence. *Proceedings of the National Academy of Sciences, 98*, 5937–5942. (p. 433)

Reitzle, M. (2006). The connections between adulthood transitions and the self-perception of being adult in the changing contexts of East and West Germany. *European Psychologist, 11*, 25–38. (p. 454)

Remley, A. (1988, October). From obedience to independence. *Psychology Today*, pp. 56–59. (p. 434)

Renner, M. J., & Renner, C. H. (1993). Expert and novice intuitive judgments about animal behavior. *Bulletin of the Psychonomic Society, 31*, 551–552. (p. 442)

Renner, M. J., & Rosenzweig, M. R. (1987). *Enriched and impoverished environments: Effects on brain and behavior*. New York: Springer-Verlag. (p. 442)

Renninger, K. A., & Granott, N. (2005). The process of scaffolding in learning and development. *New Ideas in Psychology, 23*(3), 111–114. (p. 425)

Rentfrow, P. J., & Gosling, S. D. (2003). The Do Re Mi's of everyday life: The structure and personality correlates of music preferences. *Journal of Personality and Social Psychology, 84*, 1236–1256. (p. 501)

Rentfrow, P. J., & Gosling, S. D. (2006). Message in a ballad: The role of music preferences in interpersonal perception. *Psychological Science, 17*, 236–242. (p. 501)

Repetti, R. L., Taylor, S. E., & Seeman, T. E. (2002). Risky families: Family social environments and the mental and physical health of offspring. *Psychological Bulletin, 128*, 330–366. (p. 398)

Rescorla, R. A., & Wagner, A. R. (1972). A theory of Pavlovian conditioning: Variations in the effectiveness of reinforcement and nonreinforcement. In A. H. Black & W. F. Perokasy (Eds.), *Classical conditioning II: Current theory*. New York: Appleton-Century-Crofts. (p. 223)

Resnick, M. D., Bearman, P. S., Blum, R. W., Bauman, K. E., Harris, K. M., Jones, J., Tabor, J., Beuhring, T., Sieving, R., Shew, M., Bearinger, L. H., & Udry, J. R. (1997). Protecting adolescents from harm: Findings from the National Longitudinal Study on Adolescent Health. *Journal of the American Medical Association, 278*, 823–832. (pp. 31, 453)

Resnick, R. A., O'Regan, J. K., & Clark, J. J. (1997). To see or not to see: The need for attention to perceive changes in scenes. *Psychological Science, 8*, 368–373. (p. 119)

Resnick, S. M. (1992). Positron emission tomography in psychiatric illness. *Current Directions in Psychological Science, 1*, 92–98. (p. 592)

Responsive Community. (1996, Fall). Age vs. weight. Page 83 (reported from a *Wall Street Journal* survey). (p. 346)

Ressler, R. K., Burgess, A. W., & Douglas, J. E. (1988). *Sexual homicide patterns*. Boston: Lexington Books. (p. 675)

Reuters. (2000, July 5). Many teens regret decision to have sex (National Campaign to Prevent Teen Pregnancy survey). www.washingtonpost.com. (p. 353)

Reyna, V. F., & Farley, F. (2006). Risk and rationality in adolescent decision making: Implications for theory, practice, and public policy. *Psychological Science in the Public Interest, 7*(1), 1–44. (p. 447)

Reynolds, A. J., Temple, J. A., Robertson, D. L., & Manri, E. A. (2001). Long-term effects of an early childhood intervention on educational achievement and juvenile arrest. *Journal of the American Medical Association, 285*, 2339–2346. (p. 548)

Rhodes, G., Sumich, A., & Byatt, G. (1999). Are average facial configurations attractive only because of their symmetry? *Psychological Science, 10*, 52–58. (p. 681)

Rhodes, S. R. (1983). Age-related differences in work attitudes and behavior: A review and conceptual analysis. *Psychological Bulletin, 93*, 328–367. (p. 459)

Rholes, W. S., & Simpson, J. A. (Eds.) (2004). *Adult attachment: Theory, research, and clinical implications*. New York: Guilford. (p. 430)

Rholes, W. S., Simpson, J. A., & Friedman, M. (2006). Avoidant attachment and the experience of parenting. *Personality and Social Psychology Bulletin, 32*, 275–285. (p. 430)

Ribeiro, R., Gervasoni, D., Soares, E. S., Zhou, Y., & Lin S-C., Pantoja, J., Lavine, M., & Nicolelis, M. A. L. (2004). Long-lasting novelty-induced neuronal reverberation during slow-wave sleep in multiple forebrain areas. *PloS Biology, 2*(1), e37 (www.plosbiology.org). (p. 185)

Ricciardelli, L. A., & McCabe, M. P. (2004). A biopsychosocial model of disordered eating and the pursuit of muscularity in adolescent boys. *Psychological Bulletin, 130*, 179–205. (p. 338)

Rice, B. (1985, September). Performance review: The job nobody likes. *Psychology Today*, pp. 30–36. (p. 645)

Rice, M. E., & Grusec, J. E. (1975). Saying and doing: Effects on observer performance. *Journal of Personality and Social Psychology, 32*, 584–593. (p. 246)

Richardson, J. (1993). The curious case of coins: Remembering the appearance of familiar objects. *The Psychologist: Bulletin of the British Psychological Society, 6*, 360–366. (p. 280)

Richardson, J. T. E., & Zucco, G. M. (1989). Cognition and olfaction: A review. *Psychological Bulletin, 105*, 352–360. (p. 149)

Richeson, J. A., & Shelton, J. N. (2007). Negotiating interracial interactions. *Current Directions in Psychological Science, 16*, 316–320. (p. 690)

Rieff, P. (1979). *Freud: The mind of a moralist* (3rd ed.). Chicago: University of Chicago Press. (p. 490)

Rieger, G., Chivers, M. L., & Bailey, J. M. (2005). Sexual arousal patterns of bisexual men. *Psychological Science, 16*, 579–584. (p. 355)

Riis, J., Loewenstein, G., Baron, J., Jepson, C., Fagerlin, A., & Ubel, P. A. (2005). Ignorance of hedonic adaptation to hemodialysis: A study using ecological momentary assessment. *Journal of Experimental Psychology: General, 134*, 3–9. (p. 390)

Rindermann, H. (2007). The g-factor of international cognitive ability comparisons: The homogeneity of results in PISA, TIMSS, PIRLS and IQ-tests across nations. *European Journal of Personality, 21*, 667–7006. (p. 526)

Ring, K. (1980). *Life at death: A scientific investigation of the near-death experience*. New York: Coward, McCann & Geoghegan. (p. 206)

Ripple, C. H., & Zigler, E. F. (2003). Research, policy, and the federal role in prevention initiatives for children. *American Psychologist, 58*, 482–490. (p. 548)

Risch, N., Herrell, R., Lehner, T., Liang, K-Y., Eaves, L., Hoh, J., Griem, A., Kovacs, M., Ott, J., & Merkangas, R. (2009). Interaction between the serotonin transporter gene (5-HTTLPR), stressful life events, and risk of depression. *Journal of the American Medical Association, 301*, 2462–2471. (p. 586)

Riskind, J. H., Beck, A. T., Berchick, R. J., Brown, G., & Steer, R. A. (1987). Reliability of DSM-III diagnoses for major depression and generalized anxiety disorder using the structured clinical interview for DSM-III. *Archives of General Psychiatry, 44*, 817–820. (p. 566)

Rizzolatti, G., Fadiga, L., Fogassi, L., & Gallese, V. (2002). From mirror neurons to imitation: Facts and speculations. In A. N. Meltzoff & W. Prinz (Eds.), *The imitative mind: Development, evolution, and brain bases*. Cambridge: Cambridge University Press. (p. 243)

Rizzolatti, G., Fogassi, L., & Gallese, V. (2006, November). Mirrors in the mind. *Scientific American*, pp. 54–61. (p. 243)

Roberson, D., Davidoff, J., Davies, I. R. L., & Shapiro, L. R. (2004). The development of color categories in two languages: A longitudinal study. *Journal of Experimental Psychology: General, 133*, 554–571. (p. 320)

Roberson, D., Davies, I. R. L., Corbett, G. G., & Vandervyver, M. (2005). Free-sorting of colors across cultures: Are there universal grounds for grouping? *Journal of Cognition and Culture, 5*, 349–386. (p. 320)

Roberts, B. W., Caspi, A., & Moffitt, T. E. (2001). The kids are alright: Growth and stability in personality development from adolescence to adulthood. *Journal of Personality and Social Psychology, 81*, 670–683. (p. 473)

Roberts, B. W., Caspi, A., & Moffitt, T. E. (2003). Work experiences and personality development in young adulthood. *Journal of Personality and Social Psychology, 84*, 582–593. (p. 473)

Roberts, B. W., & DelVecchio, W. F. (2000). The rank-order consistency of personality traits from childhood to old age: A quantitative review of longitudinal studies. *Psychological Bulletin, 126*, 3–25. (p. 500)

Roberts, B. W., Kuncel, N. R., Shiner, R., Caspi, A., & Goldberg, L. R. (2007). The power of personality: The comparative validity of personality traits, socioeconomic status, and cognitive ability for predicting important life outcomes. *Perspectives on Psychological Science, 2*, 313–345. (p. 501)

Roberts, B. W., & Mroczek, D. (2008). Personality trait change in adulthood. *Current Directions in Psychological Science, 17,* 31–35. (p. 473)

Roberts, B. W., Walton, K. E., & Viechtbauer, W. (2006). Patterns of mean-level change in personality traits across the life course: A meta-analysis of longitudinal studies. *Psychological Bulletin, 132,* 1–25. (p. 473)

Roberts, L. (1988). Beyond Noah's ark: What do we need to know? *Science, 242,* 1247. (p. C-3)

Roberts, T-A. (1991). Determinants of gender differences in responsiveness to others' evaluations. *Dissertation Abstracts International, 51*(8–B). (p. 437)

Robins, L. N., Davis, D. H., & Goodwin, D. W. (1974). Drug use by U.S. Army enlisted men in Vietnam: A follow-up on their return home. *American Journal of Epidemiology, 99,* 235–249. (p. 210)

Robins, L., & Regier, D. (Eds.). (1991). *Psychiatric disorders in America.* New York: Free Press. (p. 600)

Robins, R. W., & Trzesniewski, K. H. (2005). Self-esteem development across the lifespan. *Current Directions in Psychological Science, 14*(3), 158–162. (p. 468)

Robins, R. W., Trzesniewski, K. H., Tracy, J. L., Gosling, S. D., & Potter, J. (2002). Global self-esteem across the lifespan. *Psychology and Aging, 17,* 423–434. (p. 452)

Robinson, F. P. (1970). *Effective study.* New York: Harper & Row. (p. 14)

Robinson, J. (2002, October 8). What percentage of the population is gay? *Gallup Tuesday Briefing* (www.gallup.com/poll/tb/religValue/20021008b.asp). (p. 354)

Robinson, J. P., & Martin, S. P. (2007, October). Not so deprived: Sleep in America, 1965–2005. *Public Opinion Pros* (www.publicopinionpros.com). (p. 181)

Robinson, T. E., & Berridge, K. C. (2003). Addiction. *Annual Review of Psychology, 54,* 25–53. (p. 198)

Robinson, T. N. (1999). Reducing children's television viewing to prevent obesity. *Journal of the American Medical Association, 282,* 1561–1567. (p. 347)

Robinson, T. N., Borzekowski, D. L. G., Matheson, D. M., & Kraemer, H. C. (2007). Effects of fast food branding on young children's taste preferences. *Archives of Pediatric and Adolescent Medicine, 161,* 792–797. (p. 162)

Robinson, V. M. (1983). Humor and health. In P. E. McGhee & J. H. Goldstein (Eds.), *Handbook of humor research: Vol. II. Applied studies.* New York: Springer-Verlag. (p. C-3)

Rochat, F. (1993). How did they resist authority? Protecting refugees in Le Chambon during World War II. Paper presented at the American Psychological Association convention. (p. 656)

Rock, I., & Palmer, S. (1990, December). The legacy of Gestalt psychology. *Scientific American,* pp. 84–90. (pp. 151, 152)

Rodin, J. (1986). Aging and health: Effects of the sense of control. *Science, 233,* 1271–1276. (pp. 506, C-2, C-3)

Roediger, H. L., III. (2001, September). Quoted by R. Herbert, Doing a number on memory. *APS Observer,* pp. 1, 7–11. (p. 283)

Roediger, H. L., III, & Geraci, L. (2007). Aging and the misinformation effect: A neuropsychological analysis. *Journal of Experimental Psychology, 33,* 321–334. (p. 290)

Roediger, H. L., III, & Karpicke, J. D. (2006). Test-enhanced learning: Taking memory tests improves long-term retention. *Psychological Science, 17,* 249–255. (p. 260)

Roediger, H. L., III, & McDaniel, M. A. (2007). Illusory recollection in older adults: Testing Mark Twain's conjecture. In M. Garry H. Hayne (Ed.), *Do justice and let the sky fall: Elizabeth F. Loftus and her contributions to science, law, and academic freedom.* Mahwah, NJ: Erlbaum. (p. 290)

Roediger, H. L., III, & McDermott, K. B. (1995). Creating false memories: Remembering words not presented in lists. *Journal of Experimental Psychology: Learning, Memory, and Cognition, 21,* 803–814. (p. 288)

Roediger, H. L., III, Wheeler, M. A., & Rajaram, S. (1993). Remembering, knowing, and reconstructing the past. In D. L. Medin (Ed.), *The psychology of learning and motivation: Advances in research and theory (Vol. 30).* Orlando, FL: Academic Press. (p. 286)

Roehling, M. V. (1999). Weight-based discrimination in employment: Psychological and legal aspects. *Personnel Psychology, 52,* 969–1016. (p. 342)

Roehling, M. V., Roehling, P. V., & Pichler, S. (2007). The relationship between body weight and perceived weight-related employment discrimination: The role of sex and race. *Journal of Vocational Behavior, 71,* 300–318. (p. 342)

Roehling, P. V., Roehling, M. V., & Moen, P. (2001). The relationship between work-life policies and practices and employee loyalty: A life course perspective. *Journal of Family and Economic Issues, 22,* 141–170. (p. B-12)

Roenneberg, T., Kuehnle, T., Pramstaller, P. P., Ricken, J., Havel, M., Guth, A., Merrow, M. (2004). A marker for the end of adolescence. *Current Biology, 14,* R1038–9. (p. 177)

Roese, N. J., & Summerville, A. (2005). What we regret most . . . and why. *Personality and Social Psychology Bulletin, 31,* 1273–1285. (p. 468)

Roesser, R. (1998). What you should know about hearing conservation. *Better Hearing Institute* (www.betterhearing.org). (p. 136)

Rofé, Y. (2008). Does repression exist? Memory, pathogenic, unconscious and clinical evidence. *Review of General Psychology, 12,* 63–85. (p. 488)

Rogaeva, E. & 40 others. (2007). The neuronal sortilin-related receptor SORL1 is genetically associated with Alzehimer disease. *Nature Genetics, 39,* 168–177. (p. 460)

Rogers, C. R. (1958). Reinhold Niebuhr's The self and the dramas of history: A criticism. *Pastoral Psychology, 9,* 15–17. (p. 513)

Rogers, C. R. (1961). *On becoming a person: A therapist's view of psychotherapy.* Boston: Houghton Mifflin. (p. 609)

Rogers, C. R. (1980). *A way of being.* Boston: Houghton Mifflin. (pp. 491, 492, 609)

Rogers, L. J. (2003, Fall). Seeking the right answers about right brain-left brain. *Cerebrum, 5*(4), 55–68. (p. 86)

Rohan, K. J., Roecklein, K. A., Lindsey, K. T., Johnson, L. G., Lippy, R. D., Lacy, T. J., & Barton, F. B. (2007). A randomized controlled trial of cognitive-behavioral therapy, light therapy, and their combination for seasonal affective disorder. *Journal of Consulting and Clinical Psychology, 75,* 489–500. (p. 625)

Rohan, M. J., & Zanna, M. P. (1996). Value transmission in families. In C. Seligman, J. M. Olson, & M. P. Zanna (Eds.), *The psychology of values: The Ontario Symposium* (Vol. 8). Mahwah, NJ: Erlbaum. (p. 100)

Rohner, R. P., & Veneziano, R. A. (2001). The importance of father love: History and contemporary evidence. *Review of General Psychology, 5,* 382–405. (pp. 429, 434)

Rohrer, D., & Pashler, H. (2007). Increasing retention without increasing study time. *Current Directions in Psychological Science, 16,* 183–186. (p. 260)

Roiser, J. P., Cook, L. J., Cooper, J. D., Rubinsztein, D. C., & Sahakian, B. J. (2005). Association of a functional polymorphism in the serotonin transporter gene with abnormal emotional processing in ecstasy users. *American Journal of Psychiatry, 162,* 609–612. (p. 205)

Rokach, A., Orzeck, T., Moya, M., & Exposito, F. (2002). Causes of loneliness in North America and Spain. *European Psychologist, 7,* 70–79. (p. 43)

Roney, J. R., Hanson, K. N., Durante, K. M., & Maestripieri, D. (2006). Reading men's faces: Women's mate attractiveness judgments track men's testosterone and interest in infants. *Proceedings of the Royal Society B, 273,* 2169–2175. (p. 106)

Rosch, E. (1978). Principles of categorization. In E. Rosch & B. L. Lloyd (Eds.), *Cognition and categorization.* Hillsdale, NJ: Erlbaum. (p. 299)

Rose, A. J., & Rudolph, K. D. (2006). A review of sex differences in peer relationship processes: Potential trade-offs for the emotional and behavioral development of girls and boys. *Psychological Bulletin, 132,* 98–131. (p. 436)

Rose, J. S., Chassin, L., Presson, C. C., & Sherman, S. J. (1999). Peer influences on adolescent cigarette smoking: A prospective sibling analysis. *Merrill-Palmer Quarterly, 45,* 62–84., (pp. 203, 444)

Rose, R. J. (2004). Developmental research as impetus for school reform. *European Psychologist, 9,* 142–144. (p. 432)

Rose, R. J., Kaprio, J., Winter, T., Dick, D. M., Viken, R. J., Pulkkinen, L., & Koskenvuo, M. (2002). Femininity and fertility in sisters with twin brothers: Prenatal androgenization? Cross-sex socialization? *Psychological Science, 13,* 263–266. (p. 356)

Rose, R. J., Viken, R. J., Dick, D. M., Bates, J. E., Pulkkinen, L., & Kaprio, J. (2003). It *does* take a village: Nonfamiliar environments and children's behavior. *Psychological Science, 14,* 273–277. (p. 444)

Rose, S. (1999). Precis of Lifelines: Biology, freedom, determinism. *Behavioral and Brain Sciences, 22,* 871–921. (p. 107)

Rose, S., Bisson, J., & Wessely, S. (2003). A systematic review of single-session psychological interventions ('debriefing') following trauma. *Psychotherapy and Psychosomatics, 72,* 176–184. (p. 573)

Roselli, C. E., Larkin, K., Schrunk, J. M., & Stormshak, F. (2004). Sexual partner preference, hypothalamic morphology and aromatase in rams. *Physiology and Behavior, 83,* 233–245. (p. 357)

Roselli, C. E., Resko, J. A., & Stormshak, F. (2002). Hormonal influences on sexual partner preference in rams. *Archives of Sexual Behavior, 31,* 43–49. (p. 357)

Rosenbaum, M. (1986). The repulsion hypothesis: On the nondevelopment of relationships. *Journal of Personality and Social Psychology, 51,* 1156–1166. (p. 682)

Rosenberg, N. A., Pritchard, J. K., Weber, J. L., Cann, H. M., Kidd, K. K., Zhivotosky, L. A., & Feldman, M. W. (2002). Genetic structure of human populations. *Science, 298,* 2381–2385. (p. 104)

Rosenhan, D. L. (1973). On being sane in insane places. *Science, 179,* 250–258. (p. 567)

Rosenthal, R., Hall, J. A., Archer, D., DiMatteo, M. R., & Rogers, P. L. (1979). The PONS test: Measuring sensitivity to nonverbal cues. In S. Weitz (Ed.), *Nonverbal communication* (2nd ed.). New York: Oxford University Press. (pp. 378, 549)

Rosenzweig, M. R. (1984). Experience, memory, and the brain. *American Psychologist, 39,* 365–376. (p. 442)

Roseth, C. J., Johnson, D. W., & Johnson, R. T. (2008). Promoting early adolescents' achievement and peer relationships: The effects of cooperative, competitive, and individualistic goal structures. *Psychological Bulletin, 134,* 223–246. (p. 691)

Ross, J. (2006, December). Sleep on a problem . . . it works like a dream. *The Psychologist, 19,* 738–740. (p. 185)

Ross, M., McFarland, C., & Fletcher, G. J. O. (1981). The effect of attitude on the recall of personal histories. *Journal of Personality and Social Psychology, 40,* 627–634. (p. 284)

Ross, M., Xun, W. Q. E., & Wilson, A. E. (2002). Language and the bicultural self. *Personality and Social Psychology Bulletin, 28,* 1040–1050. (p. 320)

Rossi, A. S., & Rossi, P. H. (1993). *Of human bonding: Parent-child relations across the life course.* Hawthorne, NY: Aldine de Gruyter. (p. 437)

Rossi, P. J. (1968). Adaptation and negative aftereffect to lateral optical displacement in newly hatched chicks. *Science, 160,* 430–432. (p. 160)

Rostosky, S. S., Wilcox, B. L., Wright, M. L. C., & Randall, B. A. (2004). The impact of religiosity on adolescent sexual behavior: A review of the evidence. *Journal of Adolescent Research, 19,* 677–697. (p. 354)

Roth, T., Roehrs, T., Zwyghuizen-Doorenbos, A., Stpeanski, E., & Witting, R. (1988). Sleep and memory. In I. Hindmarch & H. Ott (Eds.), *Benzodiazepine receptor ligans, memory and information processing.* New York: Springer-Verlag. (p. 189)

Rothbart, M., Fulero, S., Jensen, C., Howard, J., & Birrell, P. (1978). From individual to group impressions: Availability heuristics in stereotype formation. *Journal of Experimental Social Psychology, 14,* 237–255. (p. 669)

Rothbart, M. K. (2007). Temperament, development, and personality. *Current Directions in Psychological Science, 16,* 207–212. (p. 428)

Rothbart, M. K., Ahadi, S. A., & Evans, D. E. (2000). Temperament and personality: Origins and outcomes. *Journal of Personality and Social Psychology, 78,* 122–135. (p. 428)

Rothbaum, B. O. (2006). Virtual reality exposure therapy. In B. O. Rothbaum (Ed.), *Pathological anxiety: Emotional processing in etiology and treatment.* New York: Guilford. (p. 612)

Rothbaum, F., & Tsang, B. Y-P. (1998). Lovesongs in the United States and China: On the nature of romantic love. *Journal of Cross-Cultural Psychology, 29,* 306–319. (p. 518)

Rothman, A. J., & Salovey, P. (1997). Shaping perceptions to motivate healthy behavior: The role of message framing. *Psychological Bulletin, 121,* 3–19. (p. 311)

Rothstein, W. G. (1980). The significance of occupations in work careers: An empirical and theoretical review. *Journal of Vocational Behavior, 17,* 328–343. (p. 468)

Rotton, J., & Kelly, I. W. (1985). Much ado about the full moon: A meta-analysis of lunar-lunacy research. *Psychological Bulletin, 97,* 286–306. (p. 599)

Rovee-Collier, C. (1989). The joy of kicking: Memories, motives, and mobiles. In P. R. Solomon, G. R. Goethals, C. M. Kelley, & B. R. Stephens (Eds.), *Memory: Interdisciplinary approaches.* New York: Springer-Verlag. (p. 417)

Rovee-Collier, C. (1993). The capacity for long-term memory in infancy. *Current Directions in Psychological Science, 2,* 130–135. (p. 276)

Rovee-Collier, C. (1997). Dissociations in infant memory: Rethinking the development of implicit and explicit memory. *Psychological Review, 104,* 467–498. (p. 417)

Rovee-Collier, C. (1999). The development of infant memory. *Current Directions in Psychological Science, 8,* 80–85. (p. 417)

Rowe, D. C. (1990). As the twig is bent? The myth of child-rearing influences on personality development. *Journal of Counseling and Development, 68,* 606–611. (p. 99)

Rowe, D. C. (2005). Under the skin: On the impartial treatment of genetic and environmental hypotheses of racial differences. *American Psychologist, 60,* 60–70. (p. 553)

Rowe, D. C., Almeida, D. M., & Jacobson, K. C. (1999). School context and genetic influences on aggression in adolescence. *Psychological Science, 10,* 277–280. (p. 671)

Rowe, D. C., Jacobson, K. C., & Van den Oord, E. J. C. G. (1999). Genetic and environmental influences on vocabulary IQ: Parental education level as moderator. *Child Development, 70(5),* 1151–1162. (p. 546)

Rozin, P., Dow, S., Mosovitch, M., & Rajaram, S. (1998). What causes humans to begin and end a meal? A role for memory for what has been eaten, as evidenced by a study of multiple meal eating in amnesic patients. *Psychological Science, 9,* 392–396. (p. 335)

Rozin, P., Millman, L., & Nemeroff, C. (1986). Operation of the laws of sympathetic magic in disgust and other domains. *Journal of Personality and Social Psychology, 50,* 703–712. (p. 222)

Ruback, R. B., Carr, T. S., & Hopper, C. H. (1986). Perceived control in prison: Its relation to reported crowding, stress, and symptoms. *Journal of Applied Social Psychology, 16,* 375–386. (p. 506)

Rubenstein, J. S., Meyer, D. E., & Evans, J. E. (2001). Executive control of cognitive processes in task switching. *Journal of Experimental Psychology: Human Perception and Performance, 27,* 763–797. (p. 117)

Rubin, D. C., Rahhal, T. A., & Poon, L. W. (1998). Things learned in early adulthood are remembered best. *Memory and Cognition, 26,* 3–19. (p. 461)

Rubin, J. Z., Pruitt, D. G., & Kim, S. H. (1994). *Social conflict: Escalation, stalemate, and settlement.* New York: McGraw-Hill. (p. 691)

Rubin, L. B. (1985). *Just friends: The role of friendship in our lives.* New York: Harper & Row. (p. 437)

Rubin, Z. (1970). Measurement of romantic love. *Journal of Personality and Social Psychology, 16,* 265–273. (p. 377)

Rubio, G., & López-Ibor, J. J. (2007). Generalized anxiety disorder: A 40-year follow-up study. *Acta Psychiatrica Scandinavica, 115,* 372–379. (p. 570)

Rubonis, A. V., & Bickman, L. (1991). Psychological impairment in the wake of disaster: The disaster-psychopathology relationship. *Psychological Bulletin, 109,* 384–399. (p. 400)

Ruchlis, H. (1990). *Clear thinking: A practical introduction.* Buffalo, NY: Prometheus Books. (p. 236)

Rudman, L. A., & Goodwin, S. A. (2004). Gender differences in automatic in-group bias: Why do women like women more than men like men? *Journal of Personality and Social Psychology, 87,* 494–509. (p. 667)

Ruffin, C. L. (1993). Stress and health—little hassles vs. major life events. *Australian Psychologist, 28,* 201–208. (p. 401)

Rule, B. G., & Ferguson, T. J. (1986). The effects of media violence on attitudes, emotions, and cognitions. *Journal of Social Issues, 42(3),* 29–50. (p. 249)

Rumbaugh, D. M. (1977). *Language learning by a chimpanzee: The Lana project.* New York: Academic Press. (p. D-4)

Rumbaugh, D. M., & Savage-Rumbaugh, S. (1994, January/February). Language and apes. *Psychology Teacher Network,* pp. 2–5, 9. (p. D-5)

Rumbaugh, D. M., & Washburn, D. A. (2003). *Intelligence of apes and other rational beings.* New Haven, CT: Yale University Press. (p. D-6)

Rush, A. J. & 12 others from the STAR*D Study team (2006). Bupropion-SR, Sertaline, or Venlafaxine-XR after failure of SSRIs for depression. *New England Journal of Medicine, 354,* **1231–1242.** (p. 631)

Rushton, J. P. (1975). Generosity in children: Immediate and long-term effects of modeling, preaching, and moral judgment. *Journal of Personality and Social Psychology, 31,* 459–466. (p. 246)

Rushton, J. P., & Jensen, A. R. (2005). Thirty years of research on race differences in cognitive ability. *Psychology, Public Policy, and Law, 11,* 235–294. (p. 552)

Rushton, J. P., & Jensen, A. R. (2006). The totality of available evidence shows the race IQ gap still remains. *Psychological Science, 17,* 921–922. (p. 552)

Russell, B. (1930/1985). *The conquest of happiness.* London: Unwin Paperbacks. (p. 395)

Russell, J. A., & Carroll, J. M. (1999a, January). On the bipolarity of positive and negative affect. *Psychological Bulletin, 125,* 3–30. (p. 385)

Russell, J. A., & Carroll, J. M. (1999b). The phoenix of bipolarity: Reply to Watson and Tellegan (1999). *Psychological Bulletin, 125,* 611–614. (p. 385)

Russell, J. A., Lewicka, M., & Niit, T. (1989). A cross-cultural study of a circumplex model of affect. *Journal of Personality and Social Psychology, 57,* 848–856. (p. 385)

Rusting, C. L., & Nolen-Hoeksema, S. (1998). Regulating responses to anger: Effects of rumination and distraction on angry mood. *Journal of Personality and Social Psychology, 74,* 790–803. (p. 389)

Rutter, M., and the English and Romanian Adoptees (ERA) study team. (1998). Developmental catch-up, and deficit, following adoption after severe global early privation. *Journal of Child Psychology and Psychiatry, 39,* 465–476. (p. 430)

Ruys, K. I., & Stapel, D. A. (2008). The secret life of emotions. *Psychological Science, 19,* 385–391. (p. 374)

Ryan, R. (1999, February 2). Quoted by Alfie Kohn, In pursuit of affluence, at a high price. *New York Times* (www.nytimes.com). (pp. 393, 394)

Ryan, R. M., & Deci, E. L. (2004). Avoiding death or engaging life as accounts of meaning and culture: Comment on Pyszczynski et al. (2004). *Psychological Bulletin, 130,* 473–477. (p. 515)

Ryckman, R. M., Robbins, M. A., Kaczor, L. M., & Gold J. A. (1989). Male and female raters' stereotyping of male and female physiques. *Personality and Social Psychology Bulletin, 15,* 244–251. (p. 341)

Ryder, A. G., Yang, J., Zhu, X., Yao, S., Yi, J., Heine, S. J., & Bagby, R. M. (2008). The cultural shaping of depression: Somatic symptoms in China, psychological symptoms in North America? *Journal of Abnormal Psychology, 117,* 300–313. (p. 576)

Saad, L. (2001, December 17). Americans' mood: Has Sept. 11 made a difference? *Gallup Poll News* Service (www.gallup.com/poll/releases/pr011217.asp). (p. 401)

Saad, L. (2002, November 21). Most smokers wish they could quit. *Gallup News Service* (www.gallup.com). (p. 204)

Saad, L. (2006, August 10). Anti-Muslim sentiments fairly commonplace. *Gallup News Service* (poll.gallup.com). (p. 665)

Sabbagh, M. A., Xu, F., Carlson, S. M., Moses, L. J., & Lee, K. (2006). The development of executive functioning and theory of mind: A comparison of Chinese and U.S. preschoolers. *Psychological Science, 17,* 74–81. (p. 422)

Sabini, J. (1986). Stanley Milgram (1933–1984). *American Psychologist, 41,* 1378–1379. (p. 654)

Sachdev, P., & Sachdev, J. (1997). Sixty years of psychosurgery: Its present status and its future. *Australian and New Zealand Journal of Psychiatry, 31,* 457–464. (p. 636)

Sackett, P. R., Borneman, M. J., & Connelly, B. S. (2008). High-stakes testing in higher education and employment: Appraising the evidence for validity and fairness. *American Psychologist, 63,* 215–227. (p. 555)

Sackett, P. R., Hardison, C. M., & Cullen, M. J. (2004). On interpreting stereotype threat as accounting for African American-White differences on cognitive tests. *American Psychologist, 59,* 7–13. (p. 555)

Sackett, P. R., & Lievens, F. (2008). Personnel selection. *Annual Review of Psychology, 59,* 419–450. (p. B-4)

Sacks, O. (1985). *The man who mistook his wife for a hat.* New York: Summit Books. (pp. 142, 271)

Sadato, N., Pascual-Leone, A., Grafman, J., Ibanez, V., Deiber, M-P., Dold, G., & Hallett, M. (1996). Activation of the primary visual cortex by Braille reading in blind subjects. *Nature, 380,* 526–528. (p. 82)

Saffran, J. R., Aslin, R. N., & Newport, E. L. (1996). Statistical learning by 8-month-old infants. *Science, 274,* 1926–1928. (p. 317)

Saffran, J. R., Johnson, E. K., Aslin, R. N., & Newport, E. L. (1999). Statistical learning of tone sequences by human infants and adults. *Cognition, 70,* 27–52. (p. 317)

Sagan, C. (1987, February 1). The fine art of baloney detection. *Parade.* (p. 168)

Sakurai, T., Amemiya, A., Ishii, M., Matsuzaki, I., Chemelli, R. M., Tanaka, H., Williams, S. C., Richardson, J. A., Kozlowski, G. P., Wilson, S., Arch, J. R. S., Buckingham, R. E., Haynes, A. C., Carr, S. A., Annan, R. S., McNulty, D. E., Liu, W-S., Terrett, J. A., Elshourbagy, N. A., Bergsma, D. J., Yanagisawa, M. (1998). Orexins and orexin receptors: A family of hypothalamic neuropeptides and G protein-coupled receptors that regulate feeding behavior. *Cell, 92,* 573–585. (p. 333)

Salib, E., & Cortina-Borja, M. (2006). Effect of month of birth on the risk of suicide. *British Journal of Psychiatry, 188,* 416–422. (p. 584)

Salmela-Aro, K., & Nurmi, J-E. (2007). Self-esteem during university studies predicts career characteristics 10 years later. *Journal of Vocational Behavior, 70,* 463–477. (p. 512)

Salmon, P. (2001). Effects of physical exercise on anxiety, depression, and sensitivity to stress: A unifying theory. *Clinical Psychology Review, 21,* 33–61. (p. C-7)

Salovey, P. (1990, January/February). Interview. *American Scientist,* pp. 25–29. (p. 390)

Salthouse, T. A. (2004). What and when of cognitive aging. *Current Directions in Psychological Science, 13,* 140–144. (p. 464)

Sampson, E. E. (2000). Reinterpreting individualism and collectivism: Their religious roots and monologic versus dialogic person-other relationship. *American Psychologist, 55,* 1425–1432. (p. 517)

Samuels, J., & Nestadt, G. (1997). Epidemiology and genetics of obsessive-compulsive disorder. *International Review of Psychiatry, 9,* 61–71. (p. 572)

Samuels, S., & McCabe, G. (1989). Quoted by P. Diaconis & F. Mosteller, Methods for studying coincidences. *Journal of the American Statistical Association, 84,* 853–861. (p. 33)

Sanders, A. R. & 22 others. (2008). No significant association of 14 candidate genes with schizophrenia in a large European ancestry sample: Implications for psychiatric genetics. *American Journal of Psychiatry, 165,* 497–506. (p. 595)

Sanders, G., Sjodin, M., & de Chastelaine, M. (2002). On the elusive nature of sex differences in cognition hormonal influences contributing to within-sex variation. *Archives of Sexual Behavior, 31,* 145–152. (p. 358)

Sanders, G., & Wright, M. (1997). Sexual orientation differences in cerebral asymmetry and in the performance of sexually dimorphic cognitive and motor tasks. *Archives of Sexual Behavior, 26,* 463–479. (p. 359)

Sandfort, T. G. M., de Graaf, R., Bijl, R., & Schnabel, P. (2001). Same-sex sexual behavior and psychiatric disorders. *Archives of General Psychiatry, 58,* 85–91. (p. 355)

Sandkühler, S., & Bhattacharya, J. (2008). Deconstructing insight: EEG correlates of insightful problem solving. *PloS ONE, 3,* e1459 (www.plosone.org). (p. 300)

Sandler, W., Meir, I., Padden, C., & Aronoff, M. (2005). The emergence of grammar: Systematic structure in a new language. *Proceedings of the National Academy of Sciences, 102,* 2261–2265. (p. 317)

Sanford, A. J., Fray, N., Stewart, A., & Moxey, L. (2002). Perspective in statements of quantity, with implications for consumer psychology. *Psychological Science, 13,* 130–134. (p. 312)

Sanz, C., Blicher, A., Dalke, K., Gratton-Fabri, L., McClure-Richards, T., & Fouts, R. (1998, Winter-Spring). Enrichment object use: Five chimpanzees' use of temporary and semi-permanent enrichment objects. *Friends of Washoe, 19(1,2),* 9–14. (p. D-3)

Sanz, C., Morgan, D., Gulick, S. (2004). New insights into chimpanzees, tools, and termites from the Congo Basin. *American Naturalist, 164,* 567–581. (p. D-1)

Sapadin, L. A. (1988). Friendship and gender: Perspectives of professional men and women. *Journal of Social and Personal Relationships, 5,* 387–403. (p. 437)

Sapolsky, B. S., & Tabarlet, J. O. (1991). Sex in primetime television: 1979 versus 1989. *Journal of Broadcasting and Electronic Media, 35,* 505–516. (pp. 353, 676)

Sapolsky, R. (2003, September). Taming stress. *Scientific American,* pp. 87–95. (pp. 398, 583)

Sapolsky, R. (2005). The influence of social hierarchy on primate health. *Science, 308,* 648–652. (pp. C-2, C-3)

Sapolsky, R. M., & Finch, C. E. (1991, March/April). On growing old. *The Sciences,* pp. 30–38. (p. 457)

Satel, S. (2006, March 1). For some, the war won't end. *New York Times* (www.nytimes.com). (p. 573)

Sato, K. (1987). Distribution of the cost of maintaining common resources. *Journal of Experimental Social Psychology, 23,* 19–31. (p. 689)

Saul, S. (2007, March 15). F.D.A. warns of sleeping pills' strange effects. *New York Times* (www.nytimes.com). (p. 186)

Saulny, S. (2006, June 21). A legacy of the storm: Depression and suicide. *New York Times* (www.nytimes.com). (p. 400)

Savage-Rumbaugh, E. S., Murphy, J., Sevcik, R. A., Brakke, K. E., Williams, S. L., & Rumbaugh, D. M., with commentary by Bates, E. (1993). Language comprehension in ape and child. *Monographs of the Society for Research in Child Development, 58* (no. 233), 1–254. (p. D-5)

Savic, I., Berglund, H., & Lindstrom, P. (2005). Brain response to putative pheromones in homosexual men. *Proceedings of the National Academy of Sciences, 102,* 7356–7361. (p. 357)

Savic, I., & Lindström, P. (2008). PET and MRI show differences in cerebral asymmetry and functional connectivity between homo- and heterosexual subjects. *Proceedings of the National Academy of Sciences, 105,* 9403–9408. (p. 357)

Savitsky, K., Epley, N., & Gilovich, T. (2001). Do others judge us as harshly as we think? Overestimating the impact of our failures, shortcomings, and mishaps. *Journal of Personality and Social Psychology, 81,* 44–56. (p. 512)

Savitsky, K., & Gilovich, T. (2003). The illusion of transparency and the alleviation of speech anxiety. Journal *of Experimental Social Psychology, 39,* 618–625. (p. 512)

Savoy, C., & Beitel, P. (1996). Mental imagery for basketball. *International Journal of Sport Psychology, 27,* 454–462. (p. 322)

Sawyer, M. G., Arney, F. M., Baghurst, P. A., Clark, J. J., Graetz, B. W., Kosky, R. J., Nurcombe, B., Patton, G. C., Prior, M. R., Raphael, B., Rey, J., Whaites, L. C., & Zubrick, S. R. (2000). *The mental health of young people in Australia.* Canberra: Mental Health and Special Programs Branch, Commonwealth Department of Health and Aged Care. (p. 583)

Saxe, R., & Powell, L. J. (2006). It's the thought that counts. *Psychological Science, 17,* 692–699. (p. 422)

Sayre, R. F. (1979). The parents' last lessons. In D. D. Van Tassel (Ed.), *Aging, death, and the completion of being.* Philadelphia: University of Pennsylvania Press. (p. 460)

Scarborough, E., & Furumoto, L. (1987). *Untold lives: The first generation of American women psychologists.* New York: Columbia University Press. (p. 5)

Scarr, S. (1984, May). What's a parent to do? A conversation with E. Hall. *Psychology Today,* pp. 58–63. (p. 547)

Scarr, S. (1986). *Mother care/other care.* New York: Basic Books. (p. 431)

Scarr, S. (1989). Protecting general intelligence: Constructs and consequences for interventions. In R. J. Linn (Ed.), *Intelligence: Measurement, theory, and public policy.* Champaign: University of Illinois Press. (p. 526)

Scarr, S. (1990). Back cover comments on J. Dunn & R. Plomin (1990), *Separate lives: Why siblings are so different.* New York: Basic Books. (p. 102)

Scarr, S. (1993, May/June). Quoted by *Psychology Today,* Nature's thumbprint: So long, superparents, p. 16. (p. 444)

Scarr, S. (1997). Why child care has little impact on most children's development. *Current Directions in Psychological Science, 6,* 143–148. (p. 431)

Schab, F. R. (1991). Odor memory: Taking stock. *Psychological Bulletin, 109,* 242–251. (p. 150)

Schachter, S. (1982). Recidivism and self-cure of smoking and obesity. *American Psychologist, 37,* 436–444. (p. 347)

Schachter, S., & Singer, J. E. (1962). Cognitive, social and physiological determinants of emotional state. *Psychological Review, 69,* 379–399. (pp. 367, 373)

Schacter, D. L. (1992). Understanding implicit memory: A cognitive neuroscience approach. *American Psychologist, 47,* 559–569. (p. 271)

Schacter, D. L. (1996). *Searching for memory: The brain, the mind, and the past.* New York: Basic Books. (pp. 271, 272, 289, 386, 459, 488)

Schacter, D. L. (1999). The seven sins of memory: Insights from psychology and cognitive neuroscience. *American Psychologist, 54,* 182–201. (p. 279)

Schafer, G. (2005). Infants can learn decontextualized words before their first birthday. *Child Development, 76,* 87–96. (p. 316)

Schaie, K. W. (1994). The life course of adult intellectual abilities. *American Psychologist, 49,* 304–313. (p. 463)

Schaie, K. W., & Geiwitz, J. (1982). *Adult development and aging.* Boston: Little, Brown. (p. 463)

Schall, T., & Smith, G. (2000, Fall). Career trajectories in baseball. *Chance,* pp. 35–38. (p. 456)

Schechter, R., & Grether, J. K. (2008). Continuing increases in autism reported to California's developmental services system. *Archives of General Psychiatry, 65,* 19–24. (p. 424)

Scheier, M. F., & Carver, C. S. (1992). Effects of optimism on psychological and physical well-being: Theoretical overview and empirical update. *Cognitive Therapy and Research, 16,* 201–228. (p. C-3)

Schein, E. H. (1956). The Chinese indoctrination program for prisoners of war: A study of attempted brainwashing. *Psychiatry, 19,* 149–172. (p. 647)

Schellenberg, E. G. (2005). Music and cognitive abilities. *Current Directions in Psychological Science, 14,* 317–320. (p. 547)

Schellenberg, E. G. (2006). Long-term positive associations between music lessons and IQ. *Journal of Educational Psychology, 98,* 457–468. (p. 547)

Scherer, K. R., Banse, R., & Wallbott, H. G. (2001). Emotion inferences from vocal expression correlate across languages and cultures. *Journal of Cross-Cultural Psychology, 32,* 76–92. (p. 377)

Schiffenbauer, A., & Schiavo, R. S. (1976). Physical distance and attraction: An intensification effect. *Journal of Experimental Social Psychology, 12,* 274–282. (p. 658)

Schilt, T., de Win, M. M. L, Koeter, M., Jager, G., Korf, D. J., van den Brink, W., & Schmand, B. (2007). Cognition in novice Ecstasy users with minimal exposure to other drugs. *Archives of General Psychiatry, 64,* 728–736. (p. 205)

Schimel, J., Arndt, J., Pyszczynski, T., & Greenberg, J. (2001). Being accepted for who we are: Evidence that social validation of the intrinsic self reduces general defensiveness. *Journal of Personality and Social Psychology, 80,* 35–52. (p. 493)

Schimmack, U., & Lucas, R. (2007). Marriage matters: Spousal similarity in life satisfaction. *Schmollers Jahrbuch, 127,* 1–7. (p. 396)

Schimmack, U., Oishi, S., & Diener, E. (2005). Individualism: A valid and important dimension of cultural differences between nations. *Personality and Social Psychology Review, 9,* 17–31. (p. 517)

Schkade, D., Sunstein, C. R., & Hastie, R. (2006). What happened on deliberation day? University of Chicago Law and Economics, Olin Working Paper No. 298. (p. 660)

Schlaug, G., Jancke, L., Huang, Y., & Steinmetz, H. (1995). In vivo evidence of structural brain asymmetry in musicians. *Science, 267,* 699–701. (p. 68)

Schlesinger, A. M., Jr. (1965). *A thousand days.* Boston: Houghton Mifflin. (p. 660)

Schmidt, F. L. (2002). The role of general cognitive ability and job performance: Why there cannot be a debate. *Human Performance, 15,* 187–210. (p. B-4)

Schmidt, F. L., & Hunter, J. E. (1998). The validity and utility of selection methods in personnel psychology: Practical and theoretical implications of 85 years of research findings. *Psychological Bulletin, 124,* 262–274. (pp. 510, B-4, B-6)

Schmidt, F. L., & Zimmerman, R. D. (2004). A counterintuitive hypothesis about employment interview validity and some supporting evidence. *Journal of Applied Psychology, 89,* 553–561. (p. B-6)

Schmitt, D. P. (2005). Sociosexuality from Argentina to Zimbabwe: A 48-nation study of sex, culture, and strategies of human mating. *Behavioral and Brain Sciences, 28,* 247–311. (p. 106)

Schmitt, D. P. (2007). Sexual strategies across sexual orientations: How personality traits and culture relate to sociosexuality among gays, lesbians, bisexuals, and heterosexuals. *Journal of Psychology and Human Sexuality, 18,* 183–214. (p. 106)

Schmitt, D. P., & Allik, J. (2005). Simultaneous administration of the Rosenberg Self-esteem Scale in 53 nations: Exploring the universal and culture-specific features of global self-esteem. *Journal of Personality and Social Psychology, 89,* 623–642. (p. 513)

Schmitt, D. P., Allik, J., McCrae, R. R., & Benet-Martínez, V., with many others (2007). The geographic distribution of Big Five personality traits: Patterns and profiles of human self-description across 56 nations. *Journal of Cross-Cultural Psychology, 38,* 173–212. (p. 497)

Schmitt, D. P., & Pilcher, J. J. (2004). Evaluating evidence of psychological adaptation: How do we know one when we see one? *Psychological Science, 15,* 643–649. (p. 104)

Schnaper, N. (1980). Comments germane to the paper entitled "The reality of death experiences" by Ernst Rodin. *Journal of Nervous and Mental Disease, 168,* 268–270. (p. 206)

Schneider, R. H., Alexander, C. N., Staggers, F., Rainforth, M., Salerno, J. W., Hartz, A., Arndt, S., Barnes, V. A., & Nidich, S. (2005). Long-term effects of stress reduction on mortality in persons > or = 55 years of age with systemic hypertension. *American Journal of Cardiology, 95,* 1060–1064. (p. C-10)

Schneider, S. L. (2001). In search of realistic optimism: Meaning, knowledge, and warm fuzziness. *American Psychologist, 56,* 250–263. (p. 507)

Schneiderman, N. (1999). Behavioral medicine and the management of HIV/AIDS. *International Journal of Behavioral Medicine, 6,* 3–12. (p. 405)

Schoenborn, C. A., & Adams, P. F. (2008). *Sleep duration as a correlate of smoking, alcohol use, leisure-time physical inactivity, and obesity among adults: United States, 2004–2006.* Centers for Disease Control and Prevention (www.cdc.gov/nchs). (p. 183)

Schoeneman, T. J. (1994). Individualism. In V. S. Ramachandran (Ed.), *Encyclopedia of human behavior.* San Diego: Academic Press. (p. 518)

Schofield, J. W. (1986). Black-White contact in desegregated schools. In M. Hewstone & R. Brown (Eds.), *Contact and conflict in intergroup encounters.* Oxford: Basil Blackwell. (p. 690)

Schonfield, D., & Robertson, B. A. (1966). Memory storage and aging. *Canadian Journal of Psychology, 20,* 228–236. (pp. 461, 462)

Schooler, J. W., Gerhard, D., & Loftus, E. F. (1986). Qualities of the unreal. *Journal of Experimental Psychology: Learning, Memory, and Cognition, 12,* 171–181. (p. 286)

Schorr, E. A., Fox, N.A., van Wassenhove, V., & Knudsen, E.I. (2005). Auditory-visual fusion in speech perception in children with cochlear implants. *Proceedings of the National Academy of Sciences, 102,* 18748–18750. (p. 138)

Schuman, H., & Scott, J. (June, 1989). Generations and collective memories. *American Sociological Review, 54*(3), 359–381. (p. 461)

Schwartz, B. (1984). *Psychology of learning and behavior* (2nd ed.). New York: Norton. (pp. 226, 574)

Schwartz, B. (2000). Self-determination: The tyranny of freedom. *American Psychologist, 55,* 79–88. (p. 506)

Schwartz, B. (2004). *The paradox of choice: Why more is less.* New York: Ecco/HarperCollins. (p. 506)

Schwartz, B. (2007, April 12). Unnatural selections. *New York Times* (www.nytimes.com). (p. 312)

Schwartz, J., & Estrin, J. (2004, November 7). *Living for today, locked in a paralyzed body.* New York Times (www.nytimes.com). (p. 391)

Schwartz, J. M., Stoessel, P. W., Baxter, L. R., Jr., Martin, K. M., & Phelps, M. E. (1996). Systematic changes in cerebral glucose metabolic rate after successful behavior modification treatment of obsessive-compulsive disorder. *Archives of General Psychiatry, 53,* 109–113. (pp. 616, 636)

Schwartz, S. H., & Rubel, T. (2005). Sex differences in value priorities: Cross-cultural and multimethod studies. *Journal of Personality and Social Psychology, 89,* 1010–1028. (p. 436)

Schwarz, A. (2007, April 6). Throwing batters curves before throwing a pitch. *New York Times* (www.nytimes.com). (p. 88)

Schwarz, N., Strack, F., Kommer, D., & Wagner, D. (1987). Soccer, rooms, and the quality of your life: Mood effects on judgments of satisfaction with life in general and with specific domains. *European Journal of Social Psychology, 17,* 69–79. (p. 278)

Sclafani, A. (1995). How food preferences are learned: Laboratory animal models. *Proceedings of the Nutrition Society, 54,* 419–427. (p. 336)

Scott, D. J., Stohler, C. S., Egnatuk, C. M., Wang, H., Koeppe, R. A., & Zubieta, J.-K. (2007). Individual differences in reward responding explain placebo-induced expectations and effects. *Neuron, 55,* 325–336. (p. 146)

Scott, D. J., & others. (2004, November 9). U-M team reports evidence that smoking affects human brain's natural "feel good" chemical system (press release by Kara Gavin). University of Michigan Medical School (www.med.umich.edu). (p. 204)

Sdorow, L. M. (2005). The people behind psychology. In B. Perlman, L. McCann, & W. Buskist (Eds.), *Voices of experience: Memorable talks from the National Institute on the Teaching of Psychology.* Washington, DC: American Psychological Society. (p. 486)

Seal, K. H., Bertenthal, D., Miner, C. R., Sen, S., & Marmar, C. (2007). Bringing the war back home: Mental health disorders among 103,788 U.S. veterans returning from Iraq and Afghanistan seen at Department of Veterans Affairs facilities. *Archives of Internal Medicine, 167,* 467–482. (p. 573)

Seamon, J. G., Philbin, M. M., & Harrison, L. G. (2006). Do you remember proposing marriage to the Pepsi machine? False recollections from a campus walk. *Psychonomic Bulletin and Review, 13,* 752–756. (p. 286)

Sebat, J. & 31 others. (2007). Strong association of de novo copy number mutations with autism. *Science, 316,* 445–449. (p. 424)

Sechrest, L., Stickle, T. R., & Stewart, M. (1998). The role of assessment in clinical psychology. In A. Bellack, M. Hersen (Series eds.) & C. R. Reynolds (Vol. ed.), *Comprehensive clinical psychology: Vol 4: Assessment.* New York: Pergamon. (p. 486)

Seeman, P., Guan, H-C., & Van Tol, H. H. M. (1993). Dopamine D4 receptors elevated in schizophrenia. *Nature, 365,* 441–445. (p. 592)

Segal, N. L. (1999). *Entwined lives: Twins and what they tell us about human behavior.* New York: Dutton. (p. 98)

Segal, N. L. (2000). Virtual twins: New findings on within-family environmental influences on intelligence. *Journal of Educational Psychology, 92,* 442–448. (p. 99)

Segal, N. L., McGuire, S. A., Havlena, J., Gill, P., & Hershberger, S. L. (2007). Intellectual similarity of virtual twin pairs: Developmental trends. *Personality and Individual Differences, 42,* 1209–1219. (p. 545)

Segall, M. H., Dasen, P. R., Berry, J. W., & Poortinga, Y. H. (1990). *Human behavior in global perspective: An introduction to cross-cultural psychology.* New York: Pergamon. (pp. 106, 423, 439)

Segerstrom, S. C. (2007). Stress, energy, and immunity. *Current Directions in Psychological Science, 16,* 326–330. (p. 398)

Segerstrom, S. C., Taylor, S. E., Kemeny, M. E., & Fahey, J. L. (1998). Optimism is associated with mood, coping, and immune change in response to stress. *Journal of Personality and Social Psychology, 74,* 1646–1655. (p. C-3)

Seidler, G. H., & Wagner, F. E. (2006). Comparing the efficacy of EMDR and trauma-focused cognitive-behavioral therapy in the treatment of PTSD: A meta-analytic study. *Psychological Medicine, 36,* 1515–1522. (p. 624)

Seidlitz, L., & Diener, E. (1998). Sex differences in the recall of affective experiences. *Journal of Personality and Social Psychology, 74,* 262–271. (p. 587)

Self, C. E. (1994). *Moral culture and victimization in residence halls.* Dissertation: Thesis (M.A.). Bowling Green University. (p. 210)

Seligman, M. E. P. (1974, May). Submissive death: Giving up on life. *Psychology Today,* pp. 80–85. (pp. 385, C-8)

Seligman, M. E. P. (1975). *Helplessness: On depression, development and death.* San Francisco: Freeman. (p. 223)

Seligman, M. E. P. (1991). *Learned optimism.* New York: Knopf. (pp. 175, 223, 588)

Seligman, M. E. P. (1994). *What you can change and what you can't.* New York: Knopf. (pp. 444, 490, 512)

Seligman, M. E. P. (1995). The effectiveness of psychotherapy: The Consumer Reports study. *American Psychologist, 50,* 965–974. (pp. 588, 619, 622)

Seligman, M. E. P. (2002). *Authentic happiness: Using the new positive psychology to realize your potential for lasting fulfillment.* New York: Free Press. (pp. 508, 512, 616)

Seligman, M. E. P. (2004). Eudaemonia, the good life. A talk with Martin Seligman. www.edge.org. (p. 508)

Seligman, M. E. P., Ernst, R. M., Gillham, J., Reivich, K., & Linkins, M. (2009). Positive education: Positive psychology and classroom interventions. *Oxford Review of Education, 35,* 293ñ311. (p. 616)

Seligman, M. E. P., Steen, T. A., Park, N., & Peterson, C. (2005). Positive psychology progress: Empirical validation of interventions. *American Psychologist, 60,* 410–421. (pp. 395, 508)

Seligman, M. E. P., & Yellen, A. (1987). What is a dream? *Behavior Research and Therapy, 25,* 1–24. (p. 178)

Sellers, H. (2010). *Face first.* New York: Riverhead Books. (p. 115)

Selye, H. (1936). A syndrome produced by diverse nocuous agents. *Nature, 138,* 32. (p. 399)

Selye, H. (1976). *The stress of life.* New York: McGraw-Hill. (p. 399)

Sen, A. (2003). Missing women—revisited. *British Medical Journal, 327,* 1297–1298. (p. 665)

Senate Intelligence Committee. (2004, July 9). *Report of the select committee on intelligence on the U.S. intelligence community's prewar intelligence assessments on Iraq.* Washington, DC: Author. (pp. 303, 660)

Senghas, A., & Coppola, M. (2001). Children creating language: How Nicaraguan Sign Language acquired a spatial grammar. *Psychological Science, 12,* 323–328. (p. 317)

Sengupta, S. (2001, October 10). Sept. 11 attack narrows the racial divide. *New York Times* (www.nytimes.com). (p. 691)

Senju, A., Maeda, M., Kikuchi, Y., Hasegawa, T., Tojo, Y., & Osanai, H. (2007). Absence of contagious yawning in children with autism spectrum disorder. *Biology Letters, 3,* 706–708. (pp. 243, 425)

Serruya, M. D., Hatsopoulos, N. G., Paninski, L., Fellow, M. R., & Donoghue, J. P. (2002). Instant neural control of a movement signal. *Nature, 416,* 141–142. (p. 76)

Service, R. F. (1994). Will a new type of drug make memory-making easier? *Science, 266,* 218–219. (p. 269)

Seto, M. C., & Barbaree, H. E. (1995). The role of alcohol in sexual aggression. *Clinical Psychology Review, 15,* 545–566. (p. 200)

Shadish, W. R., & Baldwin, S. A. (2005). Effects of behavioral marital therapy: A meta-analysis of randomized controlled trials. *Journal of Consulting and Clinical Psychology, 73,* 6–14. (p. 622)

Shadish, W. R., Matt, G. E., Navarro, A. M., & Phillips, G. (2000). The effects of psychological therapies under clinically representative conditions: A meta-analysis. *Psychological Bulletin, 126,* 512–529. (p. 621)

Shadish, W. R., Montgomery, L. M., Wilson, P., Wilson, M. R., Bright, I., & Okwumabua, T. (1993). Effects of family and marital psychotherapies: A meta-analysis. *Journal of Consulting and Clinical Psychology, 61,* 992–1002. (p. 617)

Shaffer, D. M., Krauchunas, S. M., Eddy, M., & McBeath, M. K. (2004). How dogs navigate to catch Frisbees, *Psychological Science, 15,* 437–441. (p. 156)

Shafir, E., & LeBoeuf, R. A. (2002). Rationality. *Annual Review of Psychology, 53,* 491–517. *Times,* p. B1. (p. 309)

Shamir, B., House, R. J., & Arthur, M. B. (1993). The motivational effects of charismatic leadership: A self-concept based theory. *Organizational Science, 4*(4), 577–594. (p. B-12)

Shanahan, L., McHale, S. M., Osgood, D. W., & Crouter, A. C. (2007). Conflict frequency with mothers and fathers from middle childhood to late adolescence: Within- and between-families comparisons. *Developmental Psychology, 43,* 539–550. (p. 452)

Shanley, D. P., Sear, R., Mace, R., & Kirkwood, T. B. L. (2007). Testing evolutionary theories of menopause. *Proceedings of the Royal Society, 274,* 2943–2949. (p. 456)

Shapiro, F. (1989). Efficacy of the eye movement desensitization procedure in the treatment of traumatic memories. *Journal of Traumatic Stress, 2,* 199–223. (p. 624)

Shapiro, F. (1995). *Eye movement desensitization and reprocessing: Basic principles, protocols, and procedures.* New York: Guilford. (p. 624)

Shapiro, F. (1999). Eye movement desensitization and reprocessing (EMDR) and the anxiety disorders: Clinical and research implications of an integrated psychotherapy treatment. *Journal of Anxiety Disorders, 13,* 35–67. (p. 624)

Shapiro, F. (Ed.) (2002). *EMDR as an integrative psychotherapy approach: Experts of diverse orientations explore the paradigm prism.* Washington, DC: APA Books. (p. 624)

Shapiro, F. (2007). EMDR and case conceptualization from an adaptive information processing perspective. In F. Shapiro, F. W. Kaslow, & L. Maxfield (Eds.), *Handbook of EMDR and family therapy processes.* Hoboken, NJ: Wiley. (p. 624)

Shapiro, K. A., Moo, L. R., & Caramazza, A. (2006). Cortical signatures of noun and verb production. *Proceedings of the National Academic of Sciences, 103,* 1644–1649. (p. 80)

Sharma, A. R., McGue, M. K., & Benson, P. L. (1998). The psychological adjustment of United States adopted adolescents and their nonadopted siblings. *Child Development, 69,* 791–802. (p. 100)

Shattuck, P. T. (2006). The contribution of diagnostic substitution to the growing administrative prevalence of autism in US special education. *Pediatrics, 117,* 1028–1037. (p. 424)

Shaver, P. R., & Mikulincer, M. (2007). Adult attachment strategies and the regulation of emotion. In J. J. Gross (Ed.), *Handbook of emotion regulation.* New York: Guilford Press. (p. 430)

Shaver, P. R., Morgan, H. J., & Wu, S. (1996). Is love a basic emotion? *Personal Relationships, 3,* 81–96. (p. 385)

Shaw, H. L. (1989–90). Comprehension of the spoken word and ASL translation by chimpanzees (Pan troglodytes). *Friends of Washoe, 9*(1/2), 8–19. (p. D-5)

Shaw, P., Eckstrand, K., Sharp, W., Blumenthal, J., Lerch, J. P., Greenstein, D., Clasen, L., Evans, A., Giedd, J., & Rapoport, J. L. (2007). Attention-deficit/hyperactivity disorder is characterized by a delay in cortical maturation. *Proceedings of the National Academy of Sciences, 104,* 19649–19654. (p. 563)

Shaw, P., Greenstein, D., Lerch, J., Clasen, L., Lenroot, R., Gogtay, N., Evans, A., Rapoport, J., & Giedd, J. (2006). Intellectual ability and cortical development in children and adolescents. *Nature, 440,* 676–679. (p. 530)

Sheehan, S. (1982). *Is there no place on earth for me?* Boston: Houghton Mifflin. (p. 590)

Sheldon, K. M., & Niemiec, C. P. (2006). It's not just the amount that counts: Balanced need satisfaction also affects well-being. *Journal of Personality and Social Psychology, 91,* 331–341. (p. 360)

Sheldon, K. M., Elliot, A. J., Kim, Y., & Kasser, T. (2001). What is satisfying about satisfying events? Testing 10 candidate psychological needs. *Journal of Personality and Social Psychology, 80,* 325–339. (p. 360)

Sheldon, M. S., Cooper, M. L., Geary, D. C., Hoard, M., & DeSoto, M. C. (2006). Fertility cycle patterns in motives for sexual behavior. *Personality and Social Psychology Bulletin, 32,* 1659–1673. (p. 350)

Shenton, M. E. (1992). Abnormalities of the left temporal lobe and thought disorder in schizophrenia: A quantitative magnetic resonance imaging study. *New England Journal of Medicine, 327,* 604–612. (p. 593)

Shepard, R. N. (1990). *Mind sights.* New York: Freeman. (pp. 46, 163)

Shepherd, C. (1997, April). News of the weird. *Funny Times,* p. 15. (p. 98, 345)

Shepherd, C., Kohut, J. J., & Sweet, R. (1990). *More news of the weird.* New York: Penguin/Plume Books. (p. 598)

Sheppard, L. D., & Vernon, P. A. (2008). Intelligence and speed of information-processing: A review of 50 years of research. *Personality and Individual Differences, 44,* 535–551. (p. 531)

Shergill, S. S., Bays, P. M., Frith, C. D., & Wolpert, D. M. (2003). Two eyes for an eye: The neuroscience of force escalation. *Science, 301,* 187. (p. 689)

Sherif, M. (1966). *In common predicament: Social psychology of intergroup conflict and cooperation.* Boston: Houghton Mifflin. (p. 690)

Sherman, P. W., & Flaxman, S. M. (2001). Protecting ourselves from food. *American Scientist, 89,* 142–151. (p. 336)

Shermer, M. (1999). *How we believe: The search for God in an age of science.* New York: Freeman. (p. 166)

Shermer, M. (1999). If that's true, what else would be true? *Skeptic, 7* (4), 192–193. (p. 437)

Sherry, D., & Vaccarino, A. L. (1989). Hippocampus and memory for food caches in black-capped chickadees. *Behavioral Neuroscience, 103,* 308–318. (p. 272)

Shettleworth, S. J. (1973). Food reinforcement and the organization of behavior in golden hamsters. In R. A. Hinde & J. Stevenson-Hinde (Eds.), *Constraints on learning.* London: Academic Press. (p. 237)

Shettleworth, S. J. (1993). Where is the comparison in comparative cognition? Alternative research programs. *Psychological Science, 4,* 179–184. (p. 267)

Shimizu, M., & Pelham, B. W. (2008). Postponing a date with the grim reaper. *Basic and Applied Social Psychology, 30,* 36–45. (p. 458)

Shinkareva, S. V., Mason, R. A., Malave, V. L., Wang, W., Mitchell, T. M., Just, M. A. (2008, January 2). Using fMRI brain activation to identify cognitive states associated with perceptions of tools and dwellings. *PloS One 3*(1), 31394. (p. 89)

Shotland, R. L. (1984, March 12). Quoted in Maureen Dowd, 20 years after the murder of Kitty Genovese, the question remains: Why? *The New York Times,* p. B1. (p. 685)

Showers, C. (1992). The motivational and emotional consequences of considering positive or negative possibilities for an upcoming event. *Journal of Personality and Social Psychology, 63,* 474–484. (p. 507)

Shulman, P. (2000, June). The girl who loved math. *Discover,* pp. 67–70. (p. 549)

Shuwairi, S. M., Albert, M. K., & Johnson, S. P. (2007). Discrimination of possible and impossible objects in infancy. *Psychological Science, 18,* 303–307. (p. 420)

Sieff, E. M., Dawes, R. M., & Loewenstein, G. (1999). Anticipated versus actual reaction to HIV test results. *The American Journal of Psychology, 112,* 297–313. (p. 390)

Siegel, J. (2000, Winter). Recent developments in narcolepsy research: An explanation for patients and the general public. *Narcolepsy Network Newsletter*, pp. 1–2. (p. 187)

Siegel, J. (2001). The REM sleep-memory consolidation hypothesis. *Science, 294,* 1058–1063. (p. 190)

Siegel, J. M. (1990). Stressful life events and use of physician services among the elderly: The moderating role of pet ownership. *Journal of Personality and Social Psychology, 58,* 1081–1086. (p. C-4)

Siegel, J. M. (2003, November). Why we sleep. *Scientific American*, pp. 92–97. (p. 185)

Siegel, R. K. (1977, October). Hallucinations. *Scientific American*, pp. 132–140. (p. 206)

Siegel, R. K. (1980). The psychology of life after death. *American Psychologist, 35,* 911–931. (p. 206)

Siegel, R. K. (1982, October). Quoted by J. Hooper, Mind tripping. *Omni*, pp. 72–82, 159–160. (p. 205)

Siegel, R. K. (1984, March 15). Personal communication. (p. 205)

Siegel, R. K. (1990). *Intoxication.* New York: Pocket Books. (pp. 198, 204, 207)

Siegel, S. (2005). Drug tolerance, drug addiction, and drug anticipation. *Current Directions in Psychological Science, 14,* 296–300. (pp. 216, 227)

Siegler, R. S., & Ellis, S. (1996). Piaget on childhood. *Psychological Science, 7,* 211–215. (p. 418)

Silbersweig, D. A., Stern, E., Frith, C., Cahill, C., Holmes, A., Grootoonk, S., Seaward, J., McKenna, P., Chua, S. E., Schnorr, L., Jones, T., & Frackowiak, R. S. J. (1995). A functional neuroanatomy of hallucinations in schizophrenia. *Nature, 378,* 176–179. (p. 593)

Silva, A. J., Stevens, C. F., Tonegawa, S., & Wang, Y. (1992). Deficient hippocampal long-term potentiation in alpha-calcium-calmodulin kinase II mutant mice. *Science, 257,* 201–206. (p. 269)

Silva, C. E., & Kirsch, I. (1992). Interpretive sets, expectancy, fantasy proneness, and dissociation as predictors of hypnotic response. *Journal of Personality and Social Psychology, 63,* 847–856. (p. 193)

Silver, M., & Geller, D. (1978). On the irrelevance of evil: The organization and individual action. *Journal of Social Issues, 34,* 125–136. (p. 657)

Silveri, M. M., Rohan, M. L., Pimental, P. J., Gruber, S. A., Rosso, I. M., & Yurgelun-Todd, D. A. (2006). Sex differences in the relationship between white matter microstructure and impulsivity in adolescents. *Magnetic Resonance Imaging, 24,* 833–841. (p. 447)

Silverman, K., Evans, S. M., Strain, E. C., & Griffiths, R. R. (1992). Withdrawal syndrome after the double-blind cessation of caffeine consumption. *New England Journal of Medicine, 327,* 1109–1114. (p. 201)

Silverman, P. S., & Retzlaff, P. D. (1986). Cognitive stage regression through hypnosis: Are earlier cognitive stages retrievable? *International Journal of Clinical and Experimental Hypnosis, 34,* 192–204. (p. 193)

Simek, T. C., & O'Brien, R. M. (1981). *Total golf: A behavioral approach to lowering your score and getting more out of your game.* Huntington, NY: B-MOD Associates. (p. 238)

Simek, T. C., & O'Brien, R. M. (1988). A chaining-mastery, discrimination training program to teach Little Leaguers to hit a baseball. *Human Performance, 1,* 73–84. (p. 238)

Simon, G. E., & Savarino, J. (2007). Suicide attempts among patients starting depression treatment with medications or psychotherapy. *American Journal of Psychiatry, 164,* 1029–1034. (p. 632)

Simon, G. E., Von Korff, M., Saunders, K., Miglioretti, D. L., Crane, P. K., van Belle, G., & Kessler, R. C. (2006). Association between obesity and psychiatric disorders in the U.S. population. *Archives of General Psychiatry, 63,* 824–830. (p. 342)

Simon, H. (1998, November 16). Flash of genius (interview with P. E. Ross). *Forbes*, pp. 98–104. (p. B-8)

Simon, H. (2001, February). Quoted by A. M. Hayashi, "When to trust your gut." *Harvard Business Review*, pp. 59–65. (p. 311)

Simons, D. J. (1996). In sight, out of mind: When object representations fail. *Psychological Science, 7,* 301–305. (p. 119)

Simons, D. J., & Ambinder, M. S. (2005). Change blindness: Theory and consequences. *Current Directions in Psychological Science, 14,* 44–48. (p. 119)

Simons, D. J., & Chabris, C. F. (1999). Gorillas in our midst: Sustained inattentional blindness for dynamic events. *Perception, 28,* 1059–1074. (p. 118)

Simonton, D. K. (1988). Age and outstanding achievement: What do we know after a century of research? *Psychological Bulletin, 104,* 251–267. (p. 464)

Simonton, D. K. (1990). Creativity in the later years: Optimistic prospects for achievement. *The Gerontologist, 30,* 626–631. (p. 464)

Simonton, D. K. (1992). The social context of career success and course for 2,026 scientists and inventors. *Personality and Social Psychology Bulletin, 18,* 452–463. (p. 302)

Simonton, D. K. (2000a). Creativity: Cognitive, personal, developmental, and social aspects. *American Psychologist, 55,* 151–158. (p. 301)

Simonton, D. K. (2000b). Methodological and theoretical orientation and the long-term disciplinary impact of 54 eminent psychologists. *Review of General Psychology, 4,* 13–24. (p. 249)

Sinclair, R. C., Hoffman, C., Mark, M. M., Martin, L. L., & Pickering, T. L. (1994). Construct accessibility and the misattribution of arousal: Schachter and Singer revisited. *Psychological Science, 5,* 15–18. (p. 374)

Singelis, T. M., Bond, M. H., Sharkey, W. F., & Lai, C. S. Y. (1999). Unpackaging culture's influence on self-esteem and embarrassability: The role of self-construals. *Journal of Cross-Cultural Psychology, 30,* 315–341. (p. 517)

Singelis, T. M., & Sharkey, W. F. (1995). Culture, self-construal, and embarrassability. *Cross-Cultural Psychology, 26,* 622–644. (p. 517)

Singer, J. L. (1981). Clinical intervention: New developments in methods and evaluation. In L. T. Benjamin, Jr. (Ed.), *The G. Stanley Hall Lecture Series (Vol. 1).* Washington, DC: American Psychological Association. (p. 622)

Singer, T., Seymour, B., O'Doherty, J., Kaube, H., Dolan, R. J., & Frith, C. (2004). Empathy for pain involves the affective but not sensory components of pain. *Science, 303,* 1157–1162. (pp. 145, 244)

Singh, D. (1993). Adaptive significance of female physical attractiveness: Role of waist-to-hip ratio. *Journal of Personality and Social Psychology, 65,* 293–307. (p. 106)

Singh, D. (1995). Female health, attractiveness, and desirability for relationships: Role of breast asymmetry and waist-to-hip ratio. *Ethology and Sociobiology, 16,* 465–481. (pp. 106, 681)

Singh, D., & Randall, P. K. (2007). Beauty is in the eye of the plastic surgeon: Waist-hip ration (WHR) and women's attractiveness. *Personality and Individual Differences, 43,* 329–340. (p. 106)

Singh, S. (1997). *Fermat's enigma: The epic quest to solve the world's greatest mathematical problem.* New York: Bantam Books. (p. 301)

Singh, S., & Riber, K. A. (1997, November). Fermat's last stand. *Scientific American*, pp. 68–73. (p. 302)

Singleton, D., Tate, A., & Kohout, J. (2003). *2002 Master's, specialist's, and related degrees employment survey.* Washington, DC: American Psychological Association. (p. A-5)

Sivard, R. L. (1996). *World military and social expenditures 1996,* 16th edition. Washington, DC: World Priorities. (p. 457)

Sjöstrum, L. (1980). Fat cells and body weight. In A. J. Stunkard (Ed.), *Obesity.* Philadelphia: Saunders. (p. 343)

Skinner, B. F. (1953). *Science and human behavior.* New York: Macmillan. (p. 232)

Skinner, B. F. (1956). A case history in scientific method. *American Psychologist, 11,* 221–233. (p. 233)

Skinner, B. F. (1957). *Verbal behavior.* Englewood Cliffs, NJ: Prentice-Hall. (p. 316)

Skinner, B. F. (1961, November). Teaching machines. *Scientific American*, pp. 91–102. (p. 232)

Skinner, B. F. (1983, September). Origins of a behaviorist. *Psychology Today*, pp. 22–33. (pp. 238, 587)

Skinner, B. F. (1985). Cognitive science and behaviorism. Unpublished manuscript, Harvard University. (p. 316)

Skinner, B. F. (1986). What is wrong with daily life in the western world? *American Psychologist, 41,* 568–574. (p. 238)

Skinner, B. F. (1988). The school of the future. Address to the American Psychological Association convention. (p. 238)

Skinner, B. F. (1989). Teaching machines. *Science, 243,* 1535. (p. 238)

Skinner, B. F. (1990). Address to the American Psychological Association convention. (p. 235)

Skitka, L. J., Bauman, C. W., & Mullen, E. (2004). Political tolerance and coming to psychological closure following the September 11, 2001, terrorist attacks: An integrative approach. *Personality and Social Psychology Bulletin, 30,* 743–756. (p. 388)

Sklar, L. S., & Anisman, H. (1981). Stress and cancer. *Psychological Bulletin, 89,* 369–406. (p. 405)

Skoog, G., & Skoog, I. (1999). A 40-year follow-up of patients with obsessive-compulsive disorder. *Archives of General Psychiatry, 56,* 121–127. (p. 572)

Skov, R. B., & Sherman, S. J. (1986). Information-gathering processes: Diagnosticity, hypothesis-confirmatory strategies, and perceived hypothesis confirmation. *Journal of Experimental Social Psychology, 22,* 93–121. (p. 302)

Slatcher, R. B. & Pennebaker, J. W. (2006) How do I love thee? Let me count the words: The social effects of expressive writing, *Psychological Science, 17,* 660–664. (p. 684)

Slater, E., & Meyer, A. (1959). Contributions to a pathography of the musicians: Robert Schumann. *Confinia Psychiatra, 2,* 65–94. (p. 581)

Slater, M., Antley, A., Davison, A., Swapp, D., Guger, C., Barker, C., Pistrang, N., & Sanchez-Vives, M. V. (2006). A virtual reprise of the Stanley Milgram obedience experiments. *PloS One, 1*(1): e39. Doi: 10.1371/journal.pone.0000039. (p. 655)

Slavin, R. E., & Braddock, J. H., III, (1993, Summer). Ability grouping: On the wrong track. *The College Board Review,* pp. 11–18. (p. 543)

Sleep Foundation (2006). *The ABC's of back-to-school sleep schedules: The consequences of insufficient sleep.* National Sleep Foundation (press release) (www.sleepfoundation.org). (p. 183)

Sloan, R. P. (2005). *Field analysis of the literature on religion, spirituality, and health.* Columbia University (available at www.metanexus.net/tarp). (p. C-11)

Sloan, R. P., & Bagiella, E. (2002). Claims about religious involvement and health outcomes. *Annals of Behavioral Medicine, 24,* 14–21. (p. C-11)

Sloan, R. P., Bagiella, E., & Powell, T. (1999). Religion, spirituality, and medicine. *Lancet, 353,* 664–667. (p. C-11)

Sloan, R. P., Bagiella, E., VandeCreek, L., & Poulos, P. (2000). Should physicians prescribe religious activities? *New England Journal of Medicine, 342,* 1913–1917. (p. C-11)

Slovic, P. (2007). "If I look at the mass I will never act": Psychic numbing and genocide. *Judgment and Decision Making, 2,* 79–95. (p. 306)

Slovic, P., Finucane, M., Peters, E., & MacGregor, D. G. (2002). The affect heuristic. In T. Gilovich, D. Griffin, & D. Kahneman (Eds.), *Intuitive judgment: Heuristics and biases.* New York: Cambridge University Press. (p. 203)

Small, D. A., Loewenstein, G., & Slovic, P. (2007). Sympathy and callousness: The impact of deliberative thought on donations to identifiable and statistical victims. *Organizational Behavior and Human Decision Processes, 102,* 143–153. (p. 306)

Small, M. F. (1997). Making connections. *American Scientist, 85,* 502–504. (p. 435)

Small, M. F. (2002, July). What you can learn from drunk monkeys. *Discover,* pp. 40–45. (p. 209)

Smedley, A., & Smedley, B. D. (2005). Race as biology is fiction, racism as a social problem is real: Anthropological and historical perspectives on the social construction of race. *American Psychologist, 60,* 16–26. (p. 553)

Smelser, N. J., & Mitchell, F. (Eds.) (2002). *Terrorism: Perspectives from the behavioral and social sciences.* Washington, DC: National Research Council, National Academies Press. (p. 670)

Smith, A. (1983). Personal correspondence. (p. 592)

Smith, C. (2006, January 7). Nearly 100, LSD's father ponders his "problem child." *New York Times* (www.nytimes.com). (pp. 205, 402)

Smith, E., & Delargy, M. (2005). Locked-in syndrome. *British Medical Journal, 330,* 406–409. (p. 391)

Smith, J. E., Waldorf, V. A., & Trembath, D. L. (1990). "Single white male looking for thin, very attractive . . ." *Sex Roles, 23,* 675–685. (p. 341)

Smith, M., Franz, E. A., Joy, S. M., & Whitehead, K. (2005). Superior performance of blind compared with sighted individuals on bimanual estimations of object size. *Psychological Science, 16,* 11–14. (p. 140)

Smith, M. B. (1978). Psychology and values. *Journal of Social Issues, 34,* 181–199. (p. 493)

Smith, M. L., & Glass, G. V. (1977). Meta-analysis of psychotherapy outcome studies. *American Psychologist, 32,* 752–760. (p. 622)

Smith, M. L., Cottrell, G. W., Gosselin, F., & Schyns, P. G. (2005). Transmitting and decoding facial expressions. *Psychological Science, 16,* 184–189. (p. 378)

Smith, M. L., Glass, G. V., & Miller, R. L. (1980). *The benefits of psychotherapy.* Baltimore: Johns Hopkins Press. (pp. 621, 622)

Smith, P. B., & Tayeb, M. (1989). Organizational structure and processes. In M. Bond (Ed.), *The cross-cultural challenge to social psychology.* Newbury Park, CA: Sage. (p. B-12)

Smith, S. M., McIntosh, W. D., & Bazzini, D. G. (1999). Are the beautiful good in Hollywood? An investigation of the beauty-and-goodness stereotype on film. *Basic and Applied Social Psychology, 21,* 69–80. (p. 680)

Smith, T. B., Bartz, J., & Richards, P. S. (2007). Outcomes of religious and spiritual adaptations to psychotherapy: A meta-analytic review. *Psychotherapy Research, 17,* 643–655. (p. 627)

Smith, T. W. (1998, December). American sexual behavior: Trends, sociodemographic differences, and risk behavior. National Opinion Research Center GSS Topical Report No. 25. (pp. 354, 355)

Smith, T. W. (2005). Troubles in America: A study of negative life events across time and sub-groups. GSS Topical Report No 40., National Opinion Research Center, University of Chicago. (p. 619)

Smith, T. W. (2006, October). Personality as risk and resilience in physical health. *Current Directions in Psychological Science, 15,* 227–231. (p. 402)

Smolak, L., & Murnen, S. K. (2002). A meta-analytic examination of the relationship between child sexual abuse and eating disorders. *International Journal of Eating Disorders, 31,* 136–150. (p. 337)

Smoreda, Z., & Licoppe, C. (2000). Gender-specific use of the domestic telephone. *Social Psychology Quarterly, 63,* 238–252. (p. 437)

Snedeker, J., Geren, J., & Shafto, C. L. (2007). Starting over: International adoption as a natural experiment in language development. *Psychological Science, 18,* 79–86. (p. 316)

Snodgrass, S. E., Higgins, J. G., & Todisco, L. (1986). The effects of walking behavior on mood. Paper presented at the American Psychological Association convention. (p. 383)

Snowdon, D. A., Kemper, S. J., Mortimer, J. A., Greiner, L. H., Wekstein, D. R., & Markesbery, W. R. (1996). Linguistic ability in early life and cognitive function and Alzheimer's disease in late life: Finds from the Nun Study. *Journal of the American Medical Association, 275,* 528–532. (p. 541)

Snyder, F., & Scott, J. (1972). The psychophysiology of sleep. In N. S. Greenfield & R. A. Sterbach (Eds.), *Handbook of psychophysiology.* New York: Holt, Rinehart & Winston. (p. 190)

Snyder, M. (1984). When belief creates reality. In L. Berkowitz (Ed.), *Advances in experimental social psychology* (Vol. 18). New York: Academic Press. (p. 568)

Snyder, S. H. (1984). Neurosciences: An integrative discipline. *Science, 225,* 1255–1257. (p. 55)

Snyder, S. H. (1986). *Drugs and the brain.* New York: Scientific American Library. (p. 632)

Social Watch. (2006, March 8). No country in the world treats its women as well as its men. (www.socialwatch.org). (p. 440)

Society for Personality Assessment. (2005). The status of the Rorschach in clinical and forensic practice: An official statement by the Board of Trustees of the Society for Personality Assessment. *Journal of Personality Assessment, 85,* 219–237. (p. 486)

Sokol, D. K., Moore, C. A., Rose, R. J., Williams, C. J., Reed, T., & Christian, J. C. (1995). Intrapair differences in personality and cognitive ability among young monozygotic twins distinguished by chorion type. *Behavior Genetics, 25,* 457–466. (p. 97)

Solomon, D. A., Keitner, G. I., Miller, I. W., Shea, M. T., & Keller, M. B. (1995). Course of illness and maintenance treatments for patients with bipolar disorder. *Journal of Clinical Psychiatry, 56,* 5–13. (p. 632)

Solomon, J. (1996, May 20). Breaking the silence. *Newsweek,* pp. 20–22. (p. 568)

Solomon, M. (1987, December). Standard issue. *Psychology Today,* pp. 30–31. (p. 680)

Sommer, R. (1969). *Personal space.* Englewood Cliffs, NJ: Prentice-Hall. (p. 662)

Søndergård, L., Kvist, K., Andersen, P. K., & Kessing, L. V. (2006). Do antidepressants prevent suicide? *International Clinical Psychopharmacology, 21,* 211–218. (p. 632)

Song, S. (2006, March 27). Mind over medicine. *Time,* p. 47. (p. 194)

Sontag, S. (1978). *Illness as metaphor.* New York: Farrar, Straus, & Giroux. (p. 406)

Soon, C. S., Brass, M., Heinze, H., & Haynes, J. (2008). Unconscious determinants of free decisions in the human brain. *Nature Neuroscience, 11,* 543–545. (p. 91)

Sørensen, H. J., Mortensen, E. L., Reinisch, J. M., & Mednick, S. A. (2005). Breastfeeding and risk of schizophrenia in the Copenhagen Perinatal Cohort. *Acta Psychiatrica Scandinavica, 112,* 26–29. (p. 591)

Sorkhabi, N. (2005). Applicability of Baumrind's parent typology to collective cultures: Analysis of cultural explanations of parent socialization effects. *International Journal of Behavioral Development, 29,* 552–563. (p. 434)

Soussignan, R. (2001). Duchenne smile, emotional experience, and autonomic reactivity: A test of the facial feedback hypothesis. *Emotion, 2,* 52–74. (p. 383)

South, S. C., Krueger, R. F., Johnson, W., Iacono, W. G. (2008). Adolescent personality moderates genetic and environmental influences on relationships with parents. *Journal of Personality and Social Psychology, 94,* 899–912. (p. 434)

Sowell, T. (1991, May/June). Cultural diversity: A world view. *American Enterprise,* pp. 44–55. (p. 692)

Spalding, K. L. & 14 others. (2008). Dynamics of fat cell turnover in humans. *Nature, 453,* 783–787. (p. 343)

Spanos, N. P. (1982). A social psychological approach to hypnotic behavior. In G. Weary & H. L. Mirels (Eds.), *Integrations of clinical and social psychology.* New York: Oxford. (p. 194)

Spanos, N. P. (1986). Hypnosis, nonvolitional responding, and multiple personality: A social psychological perspective. *Progress in Experimental Personality Research, 14,* 1–62. (p. 578)

Spanos, N. P. (1991). Hypnosis, hypnotizability, and hypnotherapy. In C. R. Snyder & D. R. Forsyth (Eds.), *Handbook of social and clinical psychology: The health perspective.* New York: Pergamon Press. (p. 194)

Spanos, N. P. (1994). Multiple identity enactments and multiple personality disorder: A sociocognitive perspective. *Psychological Bulletin, 116,* 143–165. (pp. 195, 578)

Spanos, N. P. (1996). *Multiple identities and false memories: A sociocognitive perspective.* Washington, DC: American Psychological Association Books. (pp. 194, 195)

Spanos, N. P., & Coe, W. C. (1992). A Social-psychological approach to hypnosis. In E. Fromm & M. R. Nash (Eds.), *Contemporary hypnosis research.* New York: Guilford. (p. 195)

Spelke, E. (2005). Sex differences in intrinsic aptitude for mathematics and science? A critical review. *American Psychologist, 60,* 950–958. (p. 550)

Spelke, E. S., & Kinzler, K. D. (2007). Core knowledge. *Developmental Science, 10,* 89–96. (p. 420)

Spencer, J., Quinn, P. C., Johnson, M. H., & Karmiloff-Smith, A. (1997). Heads you win, tails you lose: Evidence for young infants categorizing mammals by head and facial attributes. *Early Development & Parenting, 6,* 113–126. (p. 414)

Spencer, K. M., Nestor, P. G., Perlmutter, R., Niznikiewicz, M. A., Klump, M. C., Frumin, M., Shenton, M. E., & McCarley, R. W. (2004). Neural synchrony indexes disordered perception and cognition in schizophrenia. *Proceedings of the National Academy of Sciences, 101,* 17288–17293. (p. 593)

Spencer, S. J., Steele, C. M., & Quinn, D. M. (1997). Stereotype threat and women's math performance. Unpublished manuscript, Hope College. (p. 555)

Sperling, G. (1960). The information available in brief visual presentations. *Psychological Monographs, 74* (Whole No. 498). (p. 266)

Sperry, R. W. (1964). Problems outstanding in the evolution of brain function. James Arthur Lecture, American Museum of Natural History, New York. Cited by R. Ornstein (1977), *The psychology of consciousness (2nd ed.).* New York: Harcourt Brace Jovanovich. (p. 85)

Sperry, R. W. (1985). Changed concepts of brain and consciousness: Some value implications. *Zygon, 20,* 41–57. (p. 131)

Sperry, R. W. (1992, Summer). Turnabout on consciousness: A mentalist view. *Journal of Mind & Behavior, 13*(3), 259–280. (p. 110)

Speth, J. G. (2008). *Bridge at the edge of the world: Capitalism, the environment, and crossing from crisis to sustainability.* New Haven: Yale University Press. (p. 392)

Spiegel, D. (2007). The mind prepared: Hypnosis in surgery. *Journal of the National Cancer Institute, 99,* 1280–1281. (p. 194)

Spiegel, D. (2008, January 31). Coming apart: Trauma and the fragmentation of the self. Dana Foundation (www.dana.org). (p. 579)

Spiegel, K., Leproult, R., L'Hermite-Balériaux, M., Copinschi, G., Penev, P. D., & Van Cauter, E. (2004). Leptin levels are dependent on sleep duration: Relationships with sympathovagal balance, carbohydrate regulation, cortisol, and thyrotropin. *Journal of Clinical Endocrinology and Metabolism, 89,* 5762–5771. (p. 184)

Spiegel, K., Leproult, R., & Van Cauter, E. (1999). Impact of sleep debt on metabolic and endocrine function. *Lancet, 354,* 1435–1439. (p. 184)

Spielberger, C., & London, P. (1982). Rage boomerangs. *American Health, 1,* 52–56. (p. 402)

Spitzer, R. L., & Skodol, A. E. (2000). *DSM-IV-TR casebook: A learning companion to the Diagnostic and Statistical Manual of Mental Disorders, Fourth Edition, Text Revision.* Washington, DC: American Psychiatric Publications. (p. 576)

Spradley, J. P., & Phillips, M. (1972). Culture and stress: A quantitative analysis. *American Anthropologist, 74,* 518–529. (p. 662)

Sprecher, S. (1989). The importance to males and females of physical attractiveness, earning potential, and expressiveness in initial attraction. *Sex Roles, 21,* 591–607. (p. 680)

Sprecher, S., & Sedikides, C. (1993). Gender differences in perceptions of emotionality: The case of close heterosexual relationships. *Sex Roles, 28,* 511–530. (p. 379)

Spring, B., Pingitore, R., Bourgeois, M., Kessler, K. H., & Bruckner, E. (1992). The effects and non-effects of skipping breakfast: Results of three studies. Paper presented at the American Psychological Association convention. (p. 347)

Squire, L. R. (1992). Memory and the hippocampus: A synthesis from findings with rats, monkeys, and humans. *Psychological Review, 99,* 195–231. (p. 272)

Srivastava, A., Locke, E. A., & Bartol, K. M. (2001). Money and subject well-being: It's not the money, it's the motives. *Journal of Personality and Social Psychology, 80,* 959–971. (p. 393)

Srivastava, S., John, O. P., Gosling, S. D., & Potter, J. (2003). Development of personality in early and middle adulthood: Set like plaster or persistent change? *Journal of Personality & Social Psychology, 84,* 1041–1053. (p. 498)

Srivastava, S., McGonigal, K. M., Richards, J. M., Butler, E. A., & Gross, J. J. (2006). Optimism in close relationships: How seeing things in a positive light makes them so. *Journal of Personality and Social Psychology, 91,* 143–153. (p. 507)

St. Clair, D., Xu, M., Wang, P., Yu, Y., Fang, Y., Zhang, F., Zheng, X., Gu, N., Feng, G., Sham, P., & He, L. (2005). Rates of adult schizophrenia following prenatal exposure to the Chinese famine of 1959–1961. *Journal of the American Medical Association, 294,* 557–562. (p. 593)

Stack, S. (1992). Marriage, family, religion, and suicide. In R. Maris, A. Berman, J. Maltsberger, & R. Yufit (Eds.), *Assessment and prediction of suicide.* New York: Guilford Press. (p. 584)

Stafford, R. S., MacDonald, E. A., & Finkelstein, S. N. (2001). National patterns of medication treatment for depression, 1987 to 2001. *Primary Care Companion Journal of Clinical Psychiatry, 3,* 232–235. (p. 630)

Stager, C. L., & Werker, J. F. (1997). Infants listen for more phonetic detail in speech perception than in word-learning tasks. *Nature, 388,* 381–382. (p. 315)

Stanford University Center for Narcolepsy. (2002). Narcolepsy is a serious medical disorder and a key to understanding other sleep disorders. (www.med.stanford.edu/school/Psychiatry/narcolepsy). (p. 186)

Stanley, J. C. (1997). Varieties of intellectual talent. *Journal of Creative Behavior, 31,* 93–119. (p. 543)

Stanovich, K. (1996). *How to think straight about psychology.* New York: HarperCollins. (p. 480)

Staples, B. (1999a, May 2). When the 'paranoids' turn out to be right. *New York Times* (www.nytimes.com). (p. 65)

Staples, B. (1999b, May 24). Why 'racial profiling' will be tough to fight. *New York Times* (www.nytimes.com). (p. 665)

Stark, R. (2002). Physiology and faith: Addressing the "universal" gender difference in religious commitment. *Journal for the Scientific Study of Religion, 41,* 495–507. (p. 437)

Stark, R. (2003a). *For the glory of God: How monotheism led to reformations, science, witch-hunts, and the end of slavery.* Princeton, NJ: Princeton University Press. (p. 23)

Stark, R. (2003b, October–November). False conflict: Christianity is not only compatible with science—it created it. *American Enterprise,* pp. 27–33. (p. 23)

Starr, J. M., Deary, I. J., Lemmon, H., & Whalley, L. J. (2000). Mental ability age 11 years and health status age 77 years. *Age and Ageing, 29,* 523–528. (p. 541)

Stathopoulou, G., Powers, M. B., Berry, A. C., Smiths, J. A. J., & Otto, M. W. (2006). Exercise interventions for mental health: A quantitative and qualitative review. *Clinical Psychology: Science and Practice, 13,* 179–193. (p. C-7)

Statistical Abstract. (2008). *U. S. Bureau of the Census: Statistical abstract of the United States, 2008.* Washington, DC: U.S. Government Printing Office. (p. 585)

Statistics Canada. (1999). *Statistical report on the health of Canadians.* Prepared by the Federal, Provincial and Territorial Advisory Committee on Population Health for the Meeting of Ministers of Health, Charlottetown, PEI, September 16–17, 1999. (p. 453)

Statistics Canada. (2002). (www.statcan.ca). (p. 661)

Statistics Canada. (2007a). *Languages in Canada: 2001 Census.* (www.statcan.ca). (p. 321)

Statistics Canada. (2007b). *Overweight and obesity, by province and territory, 2003 and 2005.* (www.statcan.ca/english/freepub/16–253–XIE/2006000/t446_en.htm). (p. 340)

Statistics Canada. (2008). *Victims and persons accused of homicide, by age and sex.* (Table 253–003). (p. 436)

Staub, E. (1989). *The roots of evil: The psychological and cultural sources of genocide.* New York: Cambridge University Press. (p. 648)

Staub, E., & Vollhardt, J. (2008). Altruism born of suffering: The roots of caring and helping after experiences of personal and political victimization. *American Journal of Orthopsychiatry, 78,* 267–280. (p. 573)

Steel, P., Schmidt, J., & Schultz, J. (2008). Refining the relationship between personality and subject well-being. *Psychological Bulletin, 134,* 138–161. (p. 396)

Steele, C. (1990, May). A conversation with Claude Steele. *APS Observer,* pp. 11–17. (p. 552)

Steele, C. M. (1995, August 31). Black students live down to expectations. *New York Times.* (p. 555)

Steele, C. M. (1997). A threat in the air: How stereotypes shape intellectual identity and performance. *American Psychologist, 52,* 613–629. (p. 555)

Steele, C. M., & Josephs, R. A. (1990). Alcohol myopia: Its prized and dangerous effects. *American Psychologist, 45,* 921–933. (p. 200)

Steele, C. M., Spencer, S. J., & Aronson, J. (2002). Contending with group image: The psychology of stereotype and social identity threat. *Advances in Experimental Social Psychology, 34,* 379–440. (p. 555)

Steele, J. (2000). Handedness in past human population: Skeletal markers. *Laterality, 5,* 193–220. (p. 88)

Steenhuysen, J. (2002, May 8). Bionic retina gives six patients partial sight. *Reuters News Service.* (See also www.optobionics.com/artificialretina.htm.) (p. 138)

Steinberg, L. (1987, September). Bound to bicker. *Psychology Today,* pp. 36–39. (p. 452)

Steinberg, L. (2007). Risk taking in adolescence: New perspectives from brain and behavioral science. *Current Directions in Psychological Science, 16,* 55–59. (p. 447)

Steinberg, L., & Morris, A. S. (2001). Adolescent development. *Annual Review of Psychology, 52,* 83–110. (pp. 434, 447, 452, 453)

Steinberg, L., & Scott, E. S. (2003). Less guilty by reason of adolescence: Developmental immaturity, diminished responsibility, and the juvenile death penalty. *American Psychologist, 58,* 1009–1018. (p. 448)

Steinberg, N. (1993, February). Astonishing love stories (from an earlier United Press International report). *Games,* p. 47. (p. 678)

Steinhauer, J. (1999, November 29). Number of twins rises: so does parental stress. *New York Times* (www.nytimes.com). (p. 97)

Steinmetz, J. E. (1999). The localization of a simple type of learning and memory: The cerebellum and classical eyeblink conditioning. *Contemporary Psychology, 7,* 72–77. (p. 274)

Stengel, E. (1981). Suicide. In *The new encyclopaedia britannica, macropaedia* (Vol. 17, pp. 777–782). Chicago: Encyclopaedia Britannica. (p. 584)

Stern, M., & Karraker, K. H. (1989). Sex stereotyping of infants: A review of gender labeling studies. *Sex Roles, 20,* 501–522. (p. 164)

Stern, S. L., Dhanda, R., & Hazuda, H. P. (2001). Hopelessness predicts mortality in older Mexican and European Americans. *Psychosomatic Medicine, 63,* 344–351. (p. C-3)

Sternberg, E. M. (2001). *The balance within: The science connecting health and emotions.* New York: Freeman. (p. 403)

Sternberg, E. (2006). A compassionate universe? *Science, 311,* 611–612. (p. 302)

Sternberg, R. J. (1985). *Beyond IQ: A triarchic theory of human intelligence.* New York: Cambridge University Press. (p. 527)

Sternberg, R. J. (1988). Applying cognitive theory to the testing and teaching of intelligence. *Applied Cognitive Psychology, 2,* 231–255. (p. 301)

Sternberg, R. J. (1999). The theory of successful intelligence. *Review of General Psychology, 3,* 292–316. (p. 527)

Sternberg, R. J. (2000). The holey grail of general intellicence, *Science, 21,* 399–401. (p. 528)

Sternberg, R. J. (2003). Our research program validating the triarchic theory of successful intelligence: Reply to Gottfredson. *Intelligence, 31,* 399–413. (pp. 301, 527)

Sternberg, R. J. (2007, July 6). Finding students who are wise, practical, and creative. *The Chronicle Review* (www.chronicle.com). (p. 527)

Sternberg, R. J., & Grajek, S. (1984). The nature of love. *Journal of Personality and Social Psychology, 47,* 312–329. (p. 684)

Sternberg, R. J., & Grigorenko, E. L. (2000). Theme-park psychology: A case study regarding human intelligence and its implications for education. *Educational Psychology Review, 12,* 247–268. (p. 543)

Sternberg, R. J., Grigorenko, E. L., & Kidd, K. K. (2005). Intelligence, race, and genetics. *American Psychologist, 60,* 46–59. (p. 553)

Sternberg, R. J., & Kaufman, J. C. (1998). Human abilities. *Annual Review of Psychology, 49,* 479–502. (p. 524)

Sternberg, R. J., & Lubart, T. I. (1991). An investment theory of creativity and its development. *Human Development,* 1–31. (p. 301)

Sternberg, R. J., & Lubart, T. I. (1992). Buy low and sell high: An investment approach to creativity. *Psychological Science, 1,* 1–5. (p. 301)

Sternberg, R. J., & Wagner, R. K. (1993). The g-ocentric view of intelligence and job performance is wrong. *Current Directions in Psychological Science, 2,* 1–5. (p. 527)

Sternberg, R. J., Wagner, R. K., Williams, W. M., & Horvath, J. A. (1995). Testing common sense. *American Psychologist, 50,* 912–927. (p. 527)

Stetter, F., & Kupper, S. (2002). Autogenic training: A meta-analysis of clinical outcome studies. *Applied Psychophysiology and Biofeedback, 27,* 45–98. (p. C-8)

Stevenson, H. W. (1992, December). Learning from Asian schools. *Scientific American,* pp. 70–76. (p. 553)

Stevenson, H. W., & Lee, S-Y. (1990). Contexts of achievement: A study of American, Chinese, and Japanese children. *Monographs of the Society for Research in Child Development, 55* (Serial No. 221, Nos. 1–2). (p. 543)

Stevenson, R. J., & Tomiczek, C. (2007). Olfactory-induced synesthesias: A review and model. *Psychological Bulletin, 133,* 294–309. (p. 148)

Stewart, B. (2002, April 6). Recall of the wild. *New York Times* (www.nytimes.com). (p. 45)

Stice, E. (2002). Risk and maintenance factors for eating pathology: A meta-analytic review. *Psychological Bulletin, 128,* 825–848. (p. 337)

Stice, E., Shaw, H., & Marti, C. N. (2007). A meta-analytic review of eating disorder prevention programs: Encouraging findings. *Annual Review of Clinical Psychology, 3,* 233–257. (p. 339)

Stice, E., Spangler, D., & Agras, W. S. (2001). Exposure to media-portrayed thin-ideal images adversely affects vulnerable girls: A longitudinal experiment. *Journal of Social and Clinical Psychology, 20,* 270–288. (p. 338)

Stickgold, R. (2000, March 7). Quoted by S. Blakeslee, For better learning, researchers endorse "sleep on it" adage. *New York Times,* p. F2. (p. 190)

Stickgold, R., Hobson, J. A., Fosse, R., & Fosse, M. (2001). Sleep, learning, and dreams: Off-line memory processing. *Science, 294,* 1052–1057. (p. 189)

Stickgold, R., Malia, A., Maquire, D., Roddenberry, D., & O'Connor, M. (2000, October 13). Replaying the game: Hypnagogic images in normals and amnesics. *Science, 290,* 350–353. (pp. 188, 189)

Stinson, D. A., Logel, C, Zanna, M. P., Holmes, J. G., Camerson, J. J., Wood, J. V., & Spencer, S. J. (2008). The cost of lower self-esteem: Testing a self- and social-bonds model of health. *Journal of Personality and Social Psychology, 94,* 412–428. (p. C-6)

Stipek, D. (1992). The child at school. In M. H. Bornstein & M. E. Lamb (Eds.), *Developmental psychology: An advanced textbook.* Hillsdale, NJ: Erlbaum. (p. 433)

Stith, S. M., Rosen, K. H., Middleton, K. A., Busch, A. L., Lunderberg, K., & Carlton, R. P. (2000). The intergenerational transmission of spouse abuse: A meta-analysis. *Journal of Marriage and the Family, 62,* 640–654. (p. 247)

Stockton, M. C., & Murnen, S. K. (1992). Gender and sexual arousal in response to sexual stimuli: A meta-analytic review. Presented at the American Psychological Society convention. (p. 351)

Stone, A. A., & Neale, J. M. (1984). Effects of severe daily events on mood. *Journal of Personality and Social Psychology, 46,* 137–144. (p. 390)

Stone, A. A., Schwartz, J. E., Broderick, J. E., & Shiffman, S. S. (2005). Variability of momentary pain predicts recall of weekly pain: A consequences of the peak (or salience) memory heuristic. *Personality and Social Psychology Bulletin, 31,* 1340–1346. (p. 145)

Stone, G. (2006, February 17). Homeless man discovered to be lawyer with amnesia. *ABC News* (abcnews.go.com). (p. 577)

Stone, R. (2005). In the wake: Looking for keys to posttraumatic stress. *Science, 310,* 1605. (p. 572)

Stoolmiller, M. (1999). Implications of the restricted range of family environments for estimates of heritability and nonshared environment in behavior-genetic adoption studies. *Psychological Bulletin, 125,* 392–409. (p. 100)

Stoppard, J. M., & Gruchy, C. D. G. (1993). Gender, context, and expression of positive emotion. *Personality and Social Psychology Bulletin, 19,* 143–150. (p. 379)

Storbeck, J., Robinson, M. D., & McCourt, M. E. (2006). Semantic processing precedes affect retrieval: The neurological case for cognitive primary in visual processing. *Review of General Psychology, 10,* 41–55. (p. 376)

Storm, L. (2000). Research note: Replicable evidence of psi: A revision of Milton's (1999) meta-analysis of the Ganzfeld data bases. *Journal of Parapsychology, 64,* 411–416. (p. 168)

Storm, L. (2003). Remote viewing by committee: RV using a multiple agent/multiple percipient design. *Journal of Parapsychology, 67,* 325–342. (p. 168)

Storms, M. D. (1973). Videotape and the attribution process: Reversing actors' and observers' points of view. *Journal of Personality and Social Psychology, 27,* 165–175. (p. 645)

Storms, M. D., & Thomas, G. C. (1977). Reactions to physical closeness. *Journal of Personality and Social Psychology, 35,* 412–418. (p. 658)

Strack, F., Martin, L., & Stepper, S. (1988). Inhibiting and facilitating conditions of the human smile: A nonobtrusive test of the facial feedback hypothesis. *Journal of Personality and Social Psychology, 54,* 768–777. (p. 383)

Strack, S., & Coyne, J. C. (1983). Social confirmation of dysphoria: Shared and private reactions to depression. *Journal of Personality and Social Behavior, 44,* 798–806. (p. 588)

Strahan, E. J., Spencer, S. J., & Zanna, M. P. (2002). Subliminal priming and persuasion: Striking while the iron is hot. *Journal of Experimental Social Psychology, 38,* 556–568. (p. 122)

Stranahan, A. M., Khalil, D., & Gould, E. (2006). Social isolation delays the positive effects of running on adult neurogenesis. *Nature Neuroscience, 9,* 526–533. (p. 83)

Strand, S., Deary, I. J., & Smith, P. (2006). Sex differences in cognitive abilities test scores: A UK national picture. *Brisith Journal of Educational Psychology, 76,* 463–480. (pp. 549, 551)

Stratton, G. M. (1896). Some preliminary experiments on vision without inversion of the retinal image. *Psychological Review, 3,* 611–617. (p. 160)

Straub, R. O., Seidenberg, M. S., Bever, T. G., & Terrace, H. S. (1979). Serial learning in the pigeon. *Journal of the Experimental Analysis of Behavior, 32,* 137–148. (p. D-4)

Straus, M. A. (2008). Dominance and symmetry in partner violence by male and female university students in 32 nations. *Children and Youth Services Review, 30,* 252–275. (p. 436)

Straus, M. A., & Gelles, R. J. (1980). *Behind closed doors: Violence in the American family.* New York: Anchor/Doubleday. (p. 234)

Straus, M. A., Sugarman, D. B., & Giles-Sims, J. (1997). Spanking by parents and subsequent antisocial behavior of children. *Archives of Pediatric Adolescent Medicine, 151,* 761–767. (p. 234)

Strawbridge, W. J. (1999). Mortality and religious involvement: A review and critique of the results, the methods, and the measures. Paper presented at a Harvard University conference on religion and health, sponsored by the National Institute for Health Research and the John Templeton Foundation. (p. C-11)

Strawbridge, W. J., Cohen, R. D., & Shema, S. J. (1997). Frequent attendance at religious services and mortality over 28 years. *American Journal of Public Health, 87,* 957–961. (p. C-11)

Strawbridge, W. J., Shema, S. J., Cohen, R. D., & Kaplan, G. A. (2001). Religious attendance increases survival by improving and maintaining good health behaviors, mental health, and social relationships. *Annals of Behavioral Medicine, 23,* 68–74. (p. C-11)

Strayer, D. L., & Drews, F A. (2007). Cell-phone-induced driver distraction. *Current Directions in Psychological Science, 16,* 128–131. (p. 118)

Strayer, D. L., Drews, F. A., & Johnston, W. A. (2003). Cell phone-induced failures of visual attention during simulated driving. *Journal of Experimental Psychology: Applied, 9,* 23–32. (p. 117)

Strayer, D. L., & Johnston, W. A. (2001). Driven to distraction: Dual-task studies of simulated driving and conversing on a cellular telephone. *Psychological Science, 12,* 462–466. (p. 117)

Strenze, T. (2007). Intelligence and socioeconomic success: A meta-analytic review of longitudinal research. *Intelligence, 35,* 401–426. (p. 526)

Strickland, B. (1992, February 20). Gender differences in health and illness. Sigma Xi national lecture delivered at Hope College. (p. 457)

Striegel-Moore, R. H., & Bulik, C. M. (2007). Risk factors for eating disorders. *American Psychologist, 62,* 181–198. (p. 338)

Striegel-Moore, R. H., Silberstein, L. R., & Rodin, J. (1993). The social self in bulimia nervosa: Public self-consciousness, social anxiety, and perceived fraudulence. *Journal of Abnormal Psychology, 102,* 297–303. (p. 338)

Stroebe, M., Stroebe, W., & Schut, H. (2001). Gender differences in adjustment to bereavement: An empirical and theoretical review. *Review of General Psychology, 5,* 62–83. (p. 471)

Stroebe, M., Stroebe, W., Schut, H., Zech, E., & van den Bout, J. (2002). Does disclosure of emotions facilitate recovery from bereavement? Evidence from two prospective studies. *Journal of Consulting and Clinical Psychology, 70,* 169–178. (p. 471)

Stroebe, W., Schut, H., & Stroebe, M. S. (2005). Grief work, disclosure and counseling: Do they help the bereaved? *Clinical Psychology Review, 25,* 395–414. (p. 471)

Strupp, H. H. (1986). Psychotherapy: Research, practice, and public policy (How to avoid dead ends). *American Psychologist, 41,* 120–130. (p. 625)

Stumpf, H., & Jackson, D. N. (1994). Gender-related differences in cognitive abilities: Evidence from a medical school admissions testing program. *Personality and Individual Differences, 17,* 335–344. (p. 549)

Stumpf, H., & Stanley, J. C. (1998). Stability and change in gender-related differences on the college board advanced placement and achievement tests. *Current Directions in Psychology, 7,* 192–196. (p. 550)

Stunkard, A. J., Harris, J. R., Pedersen, N. L., & McClearn, G. E. (1990). A separated twin study of the body mass index. *New England Journal of Medicine, 322,* 1483–1487. (p. 344)

Subiaul, F., Cantlon, J. F., Holloway, R. L., & Terrace, H. S. (2004). Cognitive imitation in rhesus macaques. *Science, 305,* 407–410. (p. 242)

Suddath, R. L., Christison, G. W., Torrey, E. F., Casanova, M. F., & Weinberger, D. R. (1990). Anatomical abnormalities in the brains of monozygotic twins discordant for schizophrenia. *New England Journal of Medicine, 322,* 789–794. (p. 595)

Sue, S. (2006). Research to address racial and ethnic disparities in mental health: Some lessons learned. In S. I. Donaldson, D. E. Berger, & K. Pezdek (Eds.), *Applied psychology: New frontiers and rewarding careers.* Mahwah, NJ: Erlbaum. (p. 627)

Suedfeld, P. (1998). Homo invictus: The indomitable species. *Canadian Psychology, 38,* 164–173. (p. 573)

Suedfeld, P. (2000). Reverberations of the Holocaust fifty years later: Psychology's contributions to understanding persecution and genocide. *Canadian Psychology, 41,* 1–9. (p. 573)

Suedfeld, P., & Mocellin, J. S. P. (1987). The "sensed presence" in unusual environments. *Environment and Behavior, 19,* 33–52. (p. 206)

Sugita, Y. (2004). Experience in early infancy is indispensable for color perception. *Current Biology. 14,* 1267–1271. (p. 158)

Suinn, R. M. (1997). Mental practice in sports psychology: Where have we been, Where do we go? *Clinical Psychology: Science and Practice, 4,* 189–207. (p. 322)

Sullivan, P. F., Neale, M. C., & Kendler, K. S. (2000). Genetic epidemiology of major depression: Review and meta-analysis. *American Journal of Psychiatry, 157,* 1552–1562. (2000). Genetic epidemiology of major depression: Review and meta-analysis. *American Journal of Psychiatry, 157,* 1552–1562. (p. 583)

Suls, J. M., & Tesch, F. (1978). Students' preferences for information about their test performance: A social comparison study. *Journal of Experimental Social Psychology, 8,* 189–197. (p. 395)

Summers, M. (1996, December 9). Mister clean. *People Weekly,* pp. 139–142. (p. 561)

Sundet, J. M., Barlaug, D. G., & Torjussen, T. M. (2004). The end of the Flynn effect? A study of secular trends in mean intelligence test scores of Norwegian conscripts during half a century. *Intelligence, 32,* 349–362. (p. 537)

Sundstrom, E., De Meuse, K. P., & Futrell, D. (1990). Work teams: Applications and effectiveness. *American Psychologist, 45,* 120–133. (p. B-12)

Sunstein, C. R. (2007). On the divergent American reactions to terrorism and climate change. *Columbia Law Review, 107,* 503–557. (p. 306)

Suomi, S. J. (1986). Anxiety-like disorders in young nonhuman primates. In R. Gettleman (Ed.), *Anxiety disorders of childhood.* New York: Guilford Press. (p. 575)

Suomi, S. J. (1987). Genetic and maternal contributions to individual differences in rhesus monkey biobehavioral development. In N. A. Krasnegor & others (Eds.), *Perinatal development: A psychobiological perspective.* Orlando, FL: Academic Press. (p. 483)

Super, C., & Super, D. (2001). *Education and Training. Opportunities in psychology careers,* pp. 68–80. Chicago, IL: VGM Career Books. (p. A-4)

Suppes, P. Quoted by R. H. Ennis. (1982). Children's ability to handle Piaget's propositional logic: A conceptual critique. In S. Modgil & C. Modgil (Eds.), *Jean Piaget: Consensus and controversy.* New York: Praeger. (p. 423)

Surgeon General. (1986). *The Surgeon General's workshop on pornography and public health,* June 22–24. Report prepared by E. P. Mulvey & J. L. Haugaard and released by Office of the Surgeon General on August 4, 1986. (p. 675)

Surgeon General. (1999). *Mental health: A report of the Surgeon General.* Rockville, MD: U.S. Department of Health and Human Services. (pp. 568, 585)

Surgeon General. (2001). *The Surgeon General's Call to Action to Promote Sexual Health and Responsible Sexual Behavior 2001.* Office of the Surgeon General (www.surgeongeneral.gov/library). (p. 352)

Susser, E. (1999). Life course cohort studies of schizophrenia. *Psychiatric Annals, 29,* 161–165. (p. 595)

Susser, E., Neugenbauer, R., Hoek, H. W., Brown, A. S., Lin, S., Labovitz, D., & Gorman, J. M. (1996). Schizophrenia after prenatal famine. *Archives of General Psychiatry, 53(1),* 25–31. (p. 593)

Susser, E. S., Herman, D. B., & Aaron, B. (2002, August). Combating the terror of terrorism. *Scientific American,* pp. 70–77. (p. 572)

Susskind, J. M., Lee, D. H., Cusi, A., Feiman, R., Grabski, W., & Anderson, A. K. (2008). Expressing fear enhances sensory acquisition. *Nature Neuroscience, 11,* 843–850. (p. 385)

Sutcliffe, J. S. (2008). Insights into the pathogenesis of autism. *Science, 321,* 208–209. (p. 424)

Sutherland, A. (2006). *Bitten and scratched: Life and lessons at the premier school for exotic animal trainers.* New York: Viking. (p. 240)

Svebak, S., Romundstad, S., & Holmen, J. (2007). Sense of humor and mortality: A seven-year prospective study of an unselected adult county population and a sub-population diagnosed with cancer. The Hunt study. American Psychomatic Society 65th Annual Meeting, Budapest, Hungary. (p. C-3)

Swann, W. B., Jr., Chang-Schneider, C., & McClarty, K. L. (2007). Do people's self-views matter? Self-concept and self-esteem in everyday life. *American Psychologist, 62,* 84–94. (p. 512)

Sweat, J. A., & Durm, M. W. (1993). Psychics: Do police departments really use them? *Skeptical Inquirer, 17,* 148–158. (p. 167)

Swerdlow, N. R., & Koob, G. F. (1987). Dopamine, schizophrenia, mania, and depression: Toward a unified hypothesis of cortico-stiato-pallido-thalamic function (with commentary). *Behavioral and Brain Sciences, 10,* 197–246. (p. 592)

Swim, J. K. (1994). Perceived versus meta-analytic effect sizes: An assessment of the accuracy of gender stereotypes. *Journal of Personality and Social Psychology, 66,* 21–36. (p. 667)

Symbaluk, D. G., Heth, C. D., Cameron, J., & Pierce, W. D. (1997). Social modeling, monetary incentives, and pain endurance: The role of self-efficacy and pain perception. *Personality and Social Psychology Bulletin, 23,* 258–269. (p. 145)

Symond, M. B., Harris, A. W. F., Gordon, E., & Williams, L. M. (2005). "Gamma synchrony" in first-episode schizophrenia: A disorder of temporal connectivity? *American Journal of Psychiatry, 162,* 459–465. (p. 593)

Symons, C. S., & Johnson, B. T. (1997). The self-reference effect in memory: A meta-analysis. *Psychological Bulletin, 121(3),* 371–394. (p. 263)

TADS (Treatment for Adolescents with Depression Study Team). (2004). Fluoxetine, cognitive-behavioral therapy, and their combination for adolescents with depression: Treatment for adolescents with depression study (TADS) randomized controlled trial. *Journal of the American Medical Association, 292,* 807–820. (p. 631)

Taha, F. A. (1972). A comparative study of how sighted and blind perceive the manifest content of dreams. *National Review of Social Sciences, 9(3),* 28. (p. 188)

Taheri, S. (2004a, 20 December). Does the lack of sleep make you fat? *University of Bristol Research News* (www.bristol.ac.uk). (pp. 184, 344)

Taheri, S. (2004b). The genetics of sleep disorders. *Minerva Medica, 95,* 203–212. (pp. 186, 344)

Taheri, S., Zeitzer, J. M., & Mignot, E. (2002). The role of hypocretins (orexins) in sleep regulation and narcolepsy. *Annual Review of Neuroscience, 25,* 283–313. (p. 186)

Tajfel, H. (Ed.). (1982). *Social identity and intergroup relations.* New York: Cambridge University Press. (p. 668)

Talarico, J. M., & Rubin, D. C. (2003). Confidence, not consistency, characterizes flashbulb memories. *Psychological Science, 14,* 455–461. (p. 271)

Talarico, J. M., & Rubin, D. C. (2007). Flashbulb memories are special after all: in phenomenology, not accuracy. *Applied Cognitive Psychology, 21,* 557–578. (p. 271)

Talbot, M. (2002, June 2). Hysteria hysteria. *New York Times* (www.nytimes.com). (p. 650)

Talwar, S. K., Xu, S., Hawley, E. S., Weiss, S. A., Moxon, K. A., & Chapin, J. K. (2002). Rat navigation guided by remote control. *Nature, 417,* 37–38. (p. 73)

Tamres, L. K., Janicki, D., & Helgeson, V. S. (2002). Sex differences in coping behavior: A meta-analytic review and an examination of relative coping. *Personality and Social Psychology Review, 6,* 2–30. (p. 437)

Tang, S-H., & Hall, V. C. (1995). The overjustification effect: A meta-analysis. *Applied Cognitive Psychology, 9,* 365–404. (p. 236)

Tangney, J. P., Baumeister, R. F., & Boone, A. L. (2004). High self-control predicts good adjustment, less pathology, better grades, and interpersonal success. *Journal of Personality, 72,* 271–324. (p. 505)

Tannen, D. (1990). *You just don't understand: Women and men in conversation.* New York: Morrow. (pp. 43, 437)

Tannenbaum, P. (2002, February). Quoted in R. Kubey & M. Csikszentmihalyi, Television addiction is no mere metaphor. *Scientific American,* pp. 74–80. (p. 124)

Tanner, J. M. (1978). *Fetus into man: Physical growth from conception to maturity.* Cambridge, MA: Harvard University Press. (p. 446)

Tarbert, J. (2004, May 14). Bad apples, bad command, or both? *Dart Center for Journalism and Trauma* (www.dartcenter.org). (p. 649)

Tarmann, A. (2002, May/June). Out of the closet and onto the Census long form. *Population Today, 30,* pp. 1, 6. (p. 355)

Tasbihsazan, R., Nettelbeck, T., & Kirby, N. (2003). Predictive validity of the Fagan test of infant intelligence. *British Journal of Developmental Psychology, 21,* 585–597. (p. 540)

Taub, E. (2004). Harnessing brain plasticity through behavioral techniques to produce new treatments in neurorehabilitation. *American Psychologist, 59,* 692–698. (p. 82)

Taubes, G. (2001). The soft science of dietary fat. *Science, 291,* 2536–2545. (p. 347)

Taubes, G. (2002, July 7). What if it's all been a big fat lie? *New York Times* (www.nytimes.com). (p. 347)

Tavris, C. (1982, November). Anger defused. *Psychology Today,* pp. 25–35. (p. 389)

Tavris, C., & Aronson, E. (2007). *Mistakes were made (but not by me).* Orlando, FL: Harcourt. (pp. 284, 648)

Taylor, P. J., Russ-Eft, D. F., & Chan, D. W. L. (2005). A meta-analytic review of behavior modeling training. *Journal of Applied Psychology, 90,* 692–709. (p. 245)

Taylor, S. E. (1989). *Positive illusions.* New York: Basic Books. (p. 307)

Taylor, S. E. (2002). *The tending instinct: How nurturing is essential to who we are and how we live.* New York: Times Books. (p. 437)

Taylor, S. E. (2006). Tend and befriend: Biobehavioral bases of affiliation under stress. *Current Directions in Psychological Science, 15,* 273–277. (p. 399)

Taylor, S. E., Cousino, L. K., Lewis, B. P., Gruenewald, T. L., Gurung, R. A. R., & Updegraff, J. A. (2000). Biobehavioral responses to stress in females: Tend-and-befriend, not fight-or-flight. *Psychological Review, 107,* 411–430. (p. 399)

Taylor, S. E., Pham, L. B., Rivkin, I. D., & Armor, D. A. (1998). Harnessing the imagination: Mental simulation, self-regulation, and coping. *American Psychologist, 53,* 429–439. (p. 322)

Taylor, S. P., & Chermack, S. T. (1993). Alcohol, drugs and human physical aggression. *Journal of Studies on Alcohol, Supplement No. 11,* 78–88. (p. 672)

Teasdale, T. W., & Owen, D. R. (2005). A long-term rise and recent decline in intelligence test performance: The Flynn Effect in reverse. *Personality and Individual Differences, 39,* 837–843. (p. 537)

Teasdale, T., & Owen, D. (2008). Secular declines in cognitive test scores: A reversal of the Flynn Effect. *Intelligence, 36,* 121–126. (p. 537)

Teerlink, R., & Ozley, L. (2000). *More than a motorcycle: The leadership journey at Harley-Davidson.* Cambridge, MA: Harvard Business School Press. (p. B-13)

Teghtsoonian, R. (1971). On the exponents in Stevens' law and the constant in Ekinan's law. *Psychological Review, 78,* 71–80. (p. 123)

Teicher, M. H. (2002, March). The neurobiology of child abuse. *Scientific American,* pp. 68–75. (p. 430)

Tenopyr, M. L. (1997). Improving the workplace: Industrial/organizational psychology as a career. In R. J. Sternberg (Ed.), *Career paths in psychology: Where your degree can take you.* Washington, DC: American Psychological Association. (p. B-2)

Teran-Santos, J., Jimenez-Gomez, A., & Cordero-Guevara, J. (1999). The association between sleep apnea and the risk of traffic accidents. *New England Journal of Medicine, 340,* 847–851. (p. 187)

Terman, J. S., Terman, M., Lo, E-S., & Cooper, T. B. (2001). Circadian time of morning light administration and therapeutic response in winter depression. *Archives of General Psychiatry, 58,* 69–73. (p. 625)

Terman, L. M. (1916). *The measurement of intelligence.* Boston: Houghton Mifflin. (p. 534)

Terman, M., Terman, J. S., & Ross, D. C. (1998). A controlled trial of timed bright light and negative air ionization for treatment of winter depression. *Archives of General Psychiatry, 55,* 875–882. (p. 625)

Terracciano, A., Costa, Jr., P. T., & McCrae, R. R. (2006). Personality plasticity after age 30. *Personality and Social Psychology Bulletin, 32,* 999–1009. (p. 473)

Terrace, H. S. (1979, November). How Nim Chimpsky changed my mind. *Psychology Today,* pp. 65–76. (p. D-4)

Terre, L., & Stoddart, R. (2000). Cutting edge specialties for graduate study in psychology. *Eye on Psi Chi, 23–26.* (p. A-5)

Tesser, A., Forehand, R., Brody, G., & Long, N. (1989). Conflict: The role of calm and angry parent-child discussion in adolescent development. *Journal of Social and Clinical Psychology, 8,* 317–330. (p. 452)

Tetlock, P. E. (1988). Monitoring the integrative complexity of American and Soviet policy rhetoric: What can be learned? *Journal of Social Issues, 44,* 101–131. (p. 692)

Tetlock, P. E. (1998). Close-call counterfactuals and belief-system defenses: I was not almost wrong but I was almost right. *Journal of Personality and Social Psychology, 75,* 639–652. (p. 22)

Tetlock, P. E. (2005). *Expert political judgement: How good is it? How can we know?* Princeton, NJ: Princeton University Press. (p. 22)

Thannickal, T. C., Moore, R. Y., Nienhuis, R., Ramanathan, L., Gulyani, S., Aldrich, M., Cornford, M., & Siegel, J. M. (2000). Reduced number of hypocretin neurons in human narcolepsy. *Neuron, 27,* 469–474. (p. 186)

Thatcher, R. W., Walker, R. A., & Giudice, S. (1987). Human cerebral hemispheres develop at different rates and ages. *Science, 236,* 1110–1113. (pp. 416, 472)

Thayer, R. E. (1987). Energy, tiredness, and tension effects of a sugar snack versus moderate exercise. *Journal of Personality and Social Psychology, 52,* 119–125. (p. C-7)

Thayer, R. E. (1993). Mood and behavior (smoking and sugar snacking) following moderate exercise: A partial test of self-regulation theory. *Personality and Individual Differences, 14,* 97–104. (p. C-7)

Théoret, H., Halligan, H., Kobayashi, M., Fregni, F., Tager-Flusberg, H., & Pascual-Leone, A. (2005). Impaired motor facilitation during action observation in individuals with autism spectrum disorder. *Current Biology, 15,* R84–R85. (p. 425)

Thernstrom, M. (2006, May 14). My pain, my brain. *New York Times* (www.nytimes.com). (p. 146)

Thiel, A., Hadedank, B., Herholz, K., Kessler, J., Winhuisen, L., Haupt, W. F., & Heiss, W-D. (2006). From the left to the right: How the brain compensates progressive loss of language function. *Brain and Language, 98,* 57–65. (p. 83)

Thiele, T. E., Marsh, D. J., Ste. Marie, L., Bernstein, I. L., & Palmiter, R. D. (1998). Ethanol consumption and resistance are inversely related to neuropeptide Y levels. *Nature, 396,* 366–369. (p. 209)

Thomas, A., & Chess, S. (1977). *Temperament and development.* New York: Brunner/Mazel. (p. 428)

Thomas, A., & Chess, S. (1986). The New York Longitudinal Study: From infancy to early adult life. In R. Plomin & J. Dunn (Eds.), *The study of temperament: Changes, continuities, and challenges.* Hillsdale, NJ: Erlbaum. (p. 473)

Thomas, L. (1974). *The lives of a cell.* New York: Viking Press. (p. 149)

Thomas, L. (1983). *The youngest science: Notes of a medicine watcher.* New York: Viking Press. (p. 57)

Thomas, L. (1992). *The fragile species.* New York: Scribner's. (pp. 110, 318, 620)

Thompson, C. P., Frieman, J., & Cowan, T. (1993). Rajan's memory. Paper presented to the American Psychological Society convention. (p. 267)

Thompson, J. K., Jarvie, G. J., Lahey, B. B., & Cureton, K. J. (1982). Exercise and obesity: Etiology, physiology, and intervention. *Psychological Bulletin, 91,* 55–79. (p. 347)

Thompson, P. M., Cannon, T. D., Narr, K. L., van Erp, T., Poutanen, V-P., Huttunen, M., Lönnqvist, J., Standerskjöld-Nordenstam, C-G., Kaprio, J., Khaledy, M., Dail, R., Zoumalan, C. I., & Toga, A. W. (2001). Genetic influences on brain structure. *Nature Neuroscience, 4,* 1253–1258. (p. 545)

Thompson, P. M., Giedd, J. N., Woods, R. P., MacDonald, D., Evans, A. C., & Toga, A. W. (2000). Growth patterns in the developing brain detected by using continuum mechanical tensor maps. *Nature, 404,* 190–193. (p. 416)

Thompson, R., Emmorey, K., & Gollan, T. H. (2005). "Tip of the fingers" experiences by Deaf signers. *Psychological Science, 16,* 856–860. (p. 282)

Thomson, R., & Murachver, T. (2001). Predicting gender from electronic discourse. *British Journal of Social Psychology, 40,* 193–208 (and personal correspondence from T. Murachver, May 23, 2002). (p. 437)

Thorndike, A. L., & Hagen, E. P. (1977). *Measurement and evaluation in psychology and education.* New York: Macmillan. (p. 536)

Thorndike, E. L. (1898). Animal intelligence: An experimental study of associative processes in animals. *Psychological Review Monograph Supplements, 2,* 4–160. (p. 229)

Thornhill, R., & Gangestad, S. W. (1994). Human fluctuating asymmetry and sexual behavior. *Psychological Science, 5,* 297–302. (p. 681)

Thornton, B., & Moore, S. (1993). Physical attractiveness contrast effect: Implications for self-esteem and evaluations of the social self. *Personality and Social Psychology Bulletin, 19,* 474–480. (p. 680)

Thornton, G. C., III, & Rupp, D. E. (2005). *Assessment centers in human resource management: Strategies for prediction, diagnosis, and development.* Mahwah, NJ: Erlbaum. (p. 509)

Thorpe, W. H. (1974). *Animal nature and human nature.* London: Metheun. (p. D-6)

Tickle, J. J., Hull, J. G., Sargent, J. D., Dalton, M. A., & Heatherton, T. F. (2006). A structural equation model of social influences and exposure to media smoking on adolescent smoking. *Basic and Applied Social Psychology, 28,* 117–129. (p. 203)

Tiedens, L. Z. (2001). Anger and advancement versus sadness and subjugation: The effect of negative emotion expressions on social status conferral. *Journal of Personality and Social Psychology, 80,* 86–94. (p. 389)

Tikkanen, T. (2001). Psychology in Europe: A growing profession with high standards and a bright future. *European Psychologist, 6,* 144–146. (p. 8)

Time. (1997, December 22). Greeting card association data, p. 19. (p. 437)

Timlin, M. T., Pereira, M. A., Story, M., & Neumark-Sztainer, D. (2008). Breakfast eating and weight change in a 5-year prospective analysis of adolescents: Project EAT (Eating Among Teens). *Pediatrics, 121,* e638–e645. (p. 30)

Timmerman, T. A. (2007). "It was a thought pitch": Personal, situational, and target influences on hit-by-pitch events across time. *Journal of Applied Psychology, 92,* 876–884. (p. 673)

Tinbergen, N. (1951). *The study of instinct.* Oxford: Clarendon. (p. 328)

Tirrell, M. E. (1990). Personal communication. (p. 220)

Tollefson, G. D., Fawcett, J., Winokur, G., Beasley, C. M., et al. (1993). Evaluation of suicidality during pharmacologic treatment of mood and nonmood disorders. *Annals of Clinical Psychiatry, 5(4),* 209–224. (p. 632)

Tollefson, G. D., Rampey, A. H., Beasley, C. M., & Enas, G. G. (1994). Absence of a relationship between adverse events and suicidality during pharmacotherapy for depression. *Journal of Clinical Psychopharmacology, 14,* 163–169. (p. 632)

Tolman, E. C., & Honzik, C. H. (1930). Introduction and removal of reward, and maze performance in rats. *University of California Publications in Psychology, 4,* 257–275. (p. 236)

Tolstoy, L. (1904). *My confessions.* Boston: Dana Estes. (p. 11)

Tondo, L., Jamison, K. R., & Baldessarini, R. J. (1997). Effect of lithium maintenance on suicidal behavior in major mood disorders. In D. M. Stoff & J. J. Mann (Eds.), *The neurobiology of suicide: From the bench to the clinic.* New York. (p. 632)

Toni, N., Buchs, P.-A., Nikonenko, I., Bron, C. R., & Muller, D. (1999). LTP promotes formation of multiple spine synapses between a single axon terminal and a dendrite. *Nature, 402,* 421–42. (p. 269)

Torrey, E. F. (1986). *Witchdoctors and psychiatrists.* New York: Harper & Row. (p. 626)

Totterdell, P., Kellett, S., Briner, R. B., & Teuchmann, K. (1998). Evidence of mood linkage in work groups. *Journal of Personality and Social Psychology, 74,* 1504–1515. (p. 651)

Towler, G. (1986). From zero to one hundred: Coaction in a natural setting. *Perceptual and Motor Skills, 62,* 377–378. (p. 657)

Tracey, J. L., & Robins, R. W. (2004). Show your pride: Evidence for a discrete emotion expression. *Psychological Science, 15,* 194–197. (p. 385)

Tramontana, M. G., Hooper, S. R., & Selzer, S. C. (1988). Research on the preschool prediction of later academic achievement: A review. *Developmental Review, 8,* 89–146. (p. 540)

Tranel, D., Bechara, A., & Denburg, N. L. (2002). Asymmetric functional roles of right and left ventromedial prefrontal cortices in social conduct, decision-making and emotional processing. *Cortex, 38,* pp. 589–613. (p. 86)

Trautwein, U., Lüdtke, O., Köller, O., & Baumert, J. (2006). Self-esteem, academic self-concept, and achievement: How the learning environment moderates the dynamics of self-concept. *Journal of Personality and Social Psychology, 90,* 334–349. (p. 512)

Treffert, D. A., & Christensen, D. D. (2005, December). Inside the mind of a savant. *Scientific American,* pp. 108–113. (p. 525)

Treffert, D. A., & Wallace, G. L. (2002). Island of genius—The artistic brilliance and dazzling memory that sometimes accompany autism and other disorders hint at how all brains work. *Scientific American, 286,* 76–86. (p. 525)

Treisman, A. (1987). Properties, parts, and objects. In K. R. Boff, L. Kaufman, & J. P. Thomas (Eds.), *Handbook of perception and human performance.* New York: Wiley. (p. 152)

Trewin, D. (2001). *Australian social trends 2001.* Canberra: Australian Bureau of Statistics. (p. 439)

Triandis, H. C. (1981). Some dimensions of intercultural variation and their implications for interpersonal behavior. Paper presented at the American Psychological Association convention. (p. 662)

Triandis, H. C. (1994). *Culture and social behavior.* New York: McGraw-Hill. (pp. 506, 518, 673, 674)

Triandis, H. C., Bontempo, R., Villareal, M. J., Asai, M., & Lucca, N. (1988). Individualism and collectivism: Cross-cultural perspectives on self-ingroup relationships. *Journal of Personality and Social Psychology, 54,* 323–338. (p. 518)

Trickett, P. K., & McBride-Chang, C. (1995). The developmental impact of different forms of child abuse and neglect. *Developmental Review, 15,* 311–337. (p. 431)

Trillin, C. (2006, March 27). Alice off the page. *The New Yorker,* 44. (p. 492)

Trimble, J. E. (1994). Cultural variations in the use of alcohol and drugs. In W. J. Lonner & R. Malpass (Eds.), *Psychology and culture.* Boston: Allyn & Bacon. (p. 209)

Triplett, N. (1898). The dynamogenic factors in pacemaking and competition. *American Journal of Psychology, 9,* 507–533. (p. 657)

Trolier, T. K., & Hamilton, D. L. (1986). Variables influencing judgments of correlational relations. *Journal of Personality and Social Psychology, 50,* 879–888. (p. 32)

Troller, J. N., Anderson, T. M., Sachdev, P. S., Brodaty, H., & Andrews, G. (2007). Age shall not weary them: Mental health in the middle-aged and the elderly. *Australian and New Zealand Journal of Psychiatry, 41,* 581–589. (p. 469)

Trut, L. N. (1999). Early canid domestication: The farm-fox experiment. *American Scientist, 87,* 160–169. (p. 104)

Tsai, J. L., & Chentsova-Dutton, Y. (2003). Variation among European Americans in emotional facial expression. *Journal of Cross-Cultural Psychology, 34,* 650–657. (p. 382)

Tsai, J. L., Miao, F. F., Seppala, E., Fung, H. H., & Yeung, D. Y. (2007). Influence and adjustment goals: Sources of cultural differences in ideal affect. *Journal of Personality and Social Psychology, 92,* 1102–1117. (p. 382)

Tsang, Y. C. (1938). Hunger motivation in gastrectomized rats. *Journal of Comparative Psychology, 26,* 1–17. (p. 333)

Tsankova, N., Renthal, W., Kumar, A., & Nestler, E. J. (2007). Epigenetic regulation in psychiatric disorders. *Nature Reviews Neuroscience, 8,* 355–367. (p. 102)

Tse, D., Langston, R. F., Kakeyama, M., Bethus, I., Spooner P. A., Wood, E. R., Witter, M. P., & Morris, R. G. M. (2007). Schemas and memory consolidation. *Science, 316,* 76–82. (p. 273)

Tsien, J. Z. (2007, July). The memory code. *Scientific American,* pp. 52–59. (p. 268)

Tuber, D. S., Miller, D. D., Caris, K. A., Halter, R., Linden, F., & Hennessy, M. B. (1999). Dogs in animal shelters: Problems, suggestions, and needed expertise. *Psychological Science, 10,* 379–386. (p. 45)

Tucker, K. A. (2002). I believe you can fly. *Gallup Management Journal* (www.gallupjournal.com/CA/st/20020520.asp). (p. B-11)

Tuerk, P. W. (2005). Research in the high-stakes era: Achievement, resources, and no child left behind. *Psychological Science, 16,* 419–425. (p. 547)

Tully, T. (2003). Reply: The myth of a myth. *Current Biology, 13,* R426. (p. 219)

Tulving, E. (1996, August 18). Quoted in J. Gatehouse, Technology revealing brain's secrets. *Montreal Gazette,* p. A3. (p. 272)

Tumulty, K. (2006, March 27). The politics of fat. *Time,* pp. 40–43. (p. 345)

Turkheimer, E., Haley, A., Waldron, M., D'Onofrio, B., & Gottesman, I. I. (2003). Socioeconomic status modifies heritability of IQ in young children. *Psychological Science, 14,* 623–628. (pp. 546, 547)

Turner, J. C. (1987). *Rediscovering the social group: A self-categorization theory.* New York: Basil Blackwell. (p. 668)

Turner, J. C. (2007) Self-categorization theory. In R. Baumeister & K. Vohs (Eds.), *Encyclopedia of Social Psychology.* Thousand Oaks, CA: Sage. (p. 668)

Turner, N., Barling, J., & Zacharatos, A. (2002). Positive psychology at work. In C. R. Snyder & S. J. Lopez (Eds.), *The handbook of positive psychology.* New York: Oxford University Press. (p. B-12)

Turpin, A. (2005, April 3). The science of psi. *FT Weekend,* pp. W1, W2. (p. 166)

Tutu, D. (1999). *No future without forgiveness.* New York: Doubleday. (p. 360)

Tversky, A. (1985, June). Quoted in K. McKean, Decisions, decisions. *Discover,* pp. 22–31. (p. 305)

Tversky, A., & Kahneman, D. (1974). Judgment under uncertainty: Heuristics and biases. *Science, 185,* 1124–1131. (p. 304)

Tversky, B. (2008, June/July). Glimpses of Chinese psychology: Reflections on the APS trip to China. *Observer,* pp. 13–14 (also at psychologicalscience.org/observer). (p. 8)

Twenge, J. M. (1997). Changes in masculine and feminine traits over time: A meta-analysis. *Sex Roles 36*(5–6), 305–325. (p. 108)

Twenge, J. M. (2006). *Generation me.* New York: Free Press. (p. 515)

Twenge, J. M., & Campbell, W. K. (2001). Age and birth cohort differences in self-esteem: A cross-temporal meta-analysis. *Personality and Social Psychology Review, 5,* 321–344. (p. 452)

Twenge, J. M., Baumeister, R. F., DeWall, C. N., Ciarocco, N. J., & Bartels, J. M. (2007). Social exclusion decreases prosocial behavior. *Journal of Personality and Social Psychology, 92,* 56–66. (p. 362)

Twenge, J. M., Baumeister, R. F., Tice, D. M., & Stucke, T. S. (2001). If you can't join them, beat them: Effects of social exclusion on aggressive behavior. *Journal of Personality and Social Psychology, 81,* 1058–1069. (pp. 362, 673)

Twenge, J. M., Catanese, K. R., & Baumeister, R. F. (2002). Social exclusion causes self-defeating behavior. *Journal of Personality and Social Psychology, 83,* 606–615. (pp. 362, 673)

Twenge, J. M., Catanese, K. R., & Baumeister, R. F. (2003). Social exclusion and the deconstructed state: Time perception, meaninglessness, lethargy, lack of emotion, and self-awareness. *Journal of Personality and Social Psychology, 85,* 409–423. (p. 673)

Twenge, J. M., Gentile, B., DeWall, C. D., Ma, D., & Lacefield, K. (2008). A growing disturbance: Increasing psychopathology in young people 1938-2007 in a meta-analysis of the MMPI. Unpublished manuscript, San Diego State University. (p. 515)

Twenge, J. M., & Nolen-Hoeksema, S. (2002). Age, gender, race, socioeconomic status, and birth cohort differences on the children's depression inventory: A meta-analysis. *Journal of Abnormal Psychology, 111,* 578–588. (p. 452)

Twiss, C., Tabb, S., & Crosby, F. (1989). Affirmative action and aggregate data: The importance of patterns in the perception of discrimination. In F. Blanchard & F. Crosby (Eds.), *Affirmative action: Social psychological perspectives.* New York: Springer-Verlag. (p. 31)

Tyler, K. A. (2002). Social and emotional outcomes of childhood sexual abuse: A review of recent research. *Aggression and Violent Behavior, 7,* 567–589. (p. 431)

U.S. Department of State. (2004, April). *Patterns of global terrorism 2003: Appendix G.* (www.state.gov). (p. 305)

U.S. National Center for Education Statistics. (U. S. Department of Education, NCES). (2007a). *Digest of Education Statistics* (NCES 2008-022), table 261, data from U.S. Department of Education, NCES, 1990-91, 1995-96, and 2005–06 Integrated Postsecondary Education Data System, "Completions Survey" (IPEDS–C:91 and 96), and Fall 2006. (pp. A-1, A-3)

U.S. National Center for Education Statistics. (U. S. Department of Education, NCES). (2007b). *Digest of Education Statistics* (NCES 2008-022), tables 262, 263 and 270, data from U.S. Department of Education, NCES, 1990-91, 1995-96, and 2005–06 Integrated Postsecondary Education Data System, "Completions Survey" (IPEDS–C:91 and 96), and Fall 2006. (pp. A-1, A-3)

Uchino, B. N., Cacioppo, J. T., & Kiecolt-Glaser, J. K. (1996). The relationship between social support and physiological processes: A review with emphasis on underlying mechanisms and implications for health. *Psychological Bulletin, 119,* 488–531. (p. C-5)

Uchino, B. N., Uno, D., & Holt-Lunstad, J. (1999). Social support, physiological processes, and health. *Current Directions in Psychological Science, 8,* 145–148. (p. C-5)

Uddin, L. Q., Kaplan, J. T., Molnar-Szakacs, I., Zaidel, E., & Iacoboni, M. (2005). Self-face recognition activates a frontoparietal "mirror" network in the right hemisphere: An event-related fMRI study. *NeuroImage, 25,* 926–935. (p. 87)

Uddin, L. Q., Molnar-Szakacs, Il., Zaidel, E., & Iacoboni, M. (2006). rTMS to the right inferior parietal lobule disrupts self-other discrimination. *Social Cognitive Affective Neuroscience, 1,* 65–71. (p. 87)

Udry, J. R. (2000). Biological limits of gender construction. *American Sociological Review, 65,* 443–457. (p. 438)

Uga, V., Lemut, M. C., Zampi, C., Zilli, I., & Salzarulo, P. (2006). Music in dreams. *Consciousness and Cognition, 15,* 351–357. (p. 188)

UK ECT Review Group. (2003). Efficacy and safety of electroconvulsive therapy in depressive disorders: A systematic review and meta-analysis. *Lancet, 361,* 799–808. (p. 633)

Ullman, E. (2005, October 19). The boss in the machine. *New York Times* (www.nytimes.com). (p. B-1)

Ulrich, R. E. (1991). Animal rights, animal wrongs and the question of balance. *Psychological Science, 2,* 197–201. (p. 44)

UNAIDS. (2005). *AIDS epidemic update, December 2005.* United Nations (www.unaids.org). (p. 405)

UNAIDS. (2008). *Report on the global AIDS epidemic.* United Nations (www.unaids.org). (p. 405)

UNICEF. (2006). *The state of the world's children 2007.* New York: UNICEF. (p. 440)

Unsworth, N., & Engle, R. W. (2007). The nature of individual differences in working memory capacity: Active maintenance in primary memory and controlled search from secondary memory. *Psychological Review, 114,* 104–132. (p. 258)

Urbany, J. E., Bearden, W. O., & Weilbaker, D. C. (1988). The effect of plausible and exaggerated reference prices on consumer perceptions and price search. *Journal of Consumer Research, 15,* 95–110. (p. 312)

Urry, H. L., Nitschke, J. B., Dolski, I., Jackson, D. C., Dalton, K. M., Mueller, C. J., Rosenkranz, M. A., Ryff, C. D., Singer, B. H., & Davidson, R. J. (2004). Making a life worth living: Neural correlates of well-being. *Psychological Science, 15,* 367–372. (p. 371)

USAID. (2004, January). *The ABCs of HIV prevention.* www.usaid.gov. (p. 405)

Uttal, W. R. (2001). *The new phrenology: The limits of localizing cognitive processes in the brain.* Cambridge, MA: MIT Press. (p. 79)

Vaidya, J. G., Gray, E. K., Haig, J., & Watson, D. (2002). On the temporal stability of personality: Evidence for differential stability and the role of life experiences. *Journal of Personality and Social Psychology, 83,* 1469–1484. (p. 498)

Vaillant, G. E. (1977). *Adaptation to life.* New York: Little, Brown. (p. 289)

Vaillant, G. E. (2002). *Aging well: Surprising guideposts to a happier life from the landmark Harvard study of adult development.* Boston: Little, Brown. (p. C-4)

Valdes, A. M., Andrew, T., Gardner, J. P., Kimura, M., Oelsner, E., Cherkas, L. F., Aviv, A., & Spector, T. D. (2005). Obesity, cigarette smoking, and telomere length in women. *Lancet, 366,* 662–664. (p. 457)

Valenstein, E. S. (1986). *Great and desperate cures: The rise and decline of psychosurgery.* New York: Basic Books. (p. 635)

Vallone, R. P., Griffin, D. W., Lin, S., & Ross, L. (1990). Overconfident prediction of future actions and outcomes by self and others. *Journal of Personality and Social Psychology, 58,* 582–592. (p. 22)

van Boxtel, H. W., Orobio de Castro, B., & Goossens, F. A. (2004). High self-perceived social competence in rejected children is related to frequent fighting. *European Journal of Developmental Psychology, 1,* 205–214. (p. 515)

Van Cauter, E., Holmback, U., Knutson, K., Leproult, R., Miller, A., Nedeltcheva, A., Pannain, S., Penev, P., Tasali, E., & Spiegel, K. (2007). Impact of sleep and sleep loss on neuroendocrine and metabolic function. *Hormone Research, 67,* Supp. 1: 2–9. (p. 184)

van den Boom, D. (1990). Preventive intervention and the quality of mother-infant interaction and infant exploration in irritable infants. In W. Koops, H. J. G. Soppe, J. L. van der Linden, P. C. M. Molenaar, & J. J. F. Schroots (Eds.), *Developmental psychology research in The Netherlands.* The Netherlands: Uitgeverij Eburon. Cited by C. Hazan & P. R. Shaver (1994). Deeper into attachment theory. *Psychological Inquiry, 5,* 68–79. (p. 428)

van den Boom, D. C. (1995). Do first-year intervention effects endure? Follow-up during toddlerhood of a sample of Dutch irritable infants. *Child Development, 66,* 1798–1816. (p. 428)

van den Bos, K., & Spruijt, N. (2002). Appropriateness of decisions as a moderator of the psychology of voice. *European Journal of Social Psychology, 32,* 57–72. (p. B-12)

Van der Maas, H. L. J., Dolan, C. V., Raoul, P. P. P., Grasman, R. P. P. P., Wicherts, J. M., Huizenga, H. M., & Raijmakers, M. E. J. (2006). A dynamical model of general intelligence: The positive manifold of intelligence by mutualism. *Psychological Review, 113,* 842–861. (p. 525)

Van Dyke, C., & Byck, R. (1982, March). Cocaine. *Scientific American,* pp. 128–141. (p. 205)

van Engen, M. L., & Willemsen, T. M. (2004). Sex and leadership styles: A meta-analysis of research published in the 1990s. *Psychological Reports, 94,* 3–18. (p. 436)

van Hemert, D. A., Poortinga, Y. H., & van de Vijver, F. J. R. (2007). Emotion and culture: A meta-analysis. *Cognition and Emotion, 21,* 913–943. (p. 382)

van IJzendoorn, M. H., & Juffer, F. (2005). Adoption is a successful natural intervention enhancing adopted children's IQ and school performance. *Current Directions in Psychological Science, 14,* 326–330. (p. 545)

van IJzendoorn, M. H., & Juffer, F. (2006). The Emanual Miller Memorial Lecture 2006: Adoption as intervention. Meta-analytic evidence for massive catch-up and plasticity in physical, socio-emotional, and cognitive development. *Journal of Child Psychology and Psychiatry, 47,* 1228–1245. (pp. 100, 545)

van IJzendoorn, M. H., & Kroonenberg, P. M. (1988). Cross-cultural patterns of attachment: A meta-analysis of the strange situation. *Child Development, 59,* 147–156. (p. 428)

Van Leeuwen, M. S. (1978). A cross-cultural examination of psychological differentiation in males and females. *International Journal of Psychology, 13,* 87–122. (p. 439)

Van Rooy, D. L., & Viswesvaran, C. (2004). Emotional intelligence: A meta-analytic investigation of predictive validity and nomological net. *Journal of Vocational Behavior, 65,* 71–95. (p. 529)

van Schaik, C. P., Ancrenaz, M., Borgen, G., Galdikas, B., Knott, C. D., Singleton, I., Suzuki, A., Utami, S. S., & Merrill, M. (2003). Orangutan cultures and the evolution of material culture. *Science, 299,* 102–105. (p. D-2)

Van Tassel-Baska, J. (1983). Profiles of precocity: The 1982 Midwest Talent Search finalists. *Gifted Child Quarterly, 27,* 139–145. (p. 540)

Van Yperen, N. W., & Buunk, B. P. (1990). A longitudinal study of equity and satisfaction in intimate relationships. *European Journal of Social Psychology, 20*, 287–309. (p. 684)

Van Zeijl, J., Mesman, J., Van Ijzendoorn, M. H., Bakermans-Kranenburg, M. J., Juffer, F., Stolk, M. N., Koot, H. M., & Alink, L. R. A. (2006). Attachment-based intervention for enhancing sensitive discipline in mothers of 1- to 3-year-old children at risk for externalizing behavior problems: A randomized controlled trial. *Journal of Consulting and Clinical Psychology, 74*, 994–1005. (p. 429)

Vance, E. B., & Wagner, N. N. (1976). Written descriptions of orgasm: A study of sex differences. *Archives of Sexual Behavior, 5*, 87–98. (p. 349)

Vandenberg, S. G., & Kuse, A. R. (1978). Mental rotations: A group test of three-dimensional spatial visualization. *Perceptual and Motor Skills, 47*, 599–604. (p. 550)

Vanman, E. J., Saltz, J. L., Nathan, L. R., & Warren, J. A. (2004). Racial discrimination by low-prejudiced Whites. *Psychological Science, 15*, 711–714. (p. 666)

Vaughn, K. B., & Lanzetta, J. T. (1981). The effect of modification of expressive displays on vicarious emotional arousal. *Journal of Experimental Social Psychology, 17*, 16–30. (p. 384)

Vazire, S., & Gosling, S. D. (2004). e-Perceptions: Personality impressions based on personal websites. *Journal of Personality and Social Psychology, 87*, 123–132. (p. 502)

Vecera, S. P., Vogel, E. K., & Woodman, G. F. (2002). Lower region: A new cue for figure-ground assignment. *Journal of Experimental Psychology: General, 13*, 194–205. (p. 155)

Vega, V., & Malamuth, N. M. (2007). Predicting sexaul aggression: The role of pornography in the context of general and specific risk factors. *Aggressive Behavior, 33*, 104–117. (p. 675)

Vekassy, L. (1977). Dreams of the blind. *Magyar Pszichologiai Szemle, 34*, 478–491. (p. 188)

Velliste, M., Perel, S., Spalding, M. C., Whitford, A. S., & Schwartz, A. B. (2008). Cortical control of a prosthetic arm for self-feeding. *Nature, 453*, 1098–1101. (pp. 76, 77)

Verbeek, M. E. M., Drent, P. J., & Wiepkema, P. R. (1994). Consistent individual differences in early exploratory behaviour of male great tits. *Animal Behaviour, 48*, 1113–1121. (p. 496)

Verhaeghen, P., & Salthouse, T. A. (1997). Meta analyses of age-cognition relations in adulthood: Estimates of linear and nonlinear age effects and structural models. *Psychological Bulletin, 122*, 231–249. (p. 459)

Vernon, P. A. (1983). Speed of information processing and general intelligence. *Intelligence, 7*, 53–70. (p. 531)

Vertes, R., & Siegel, J. (2005). Time for the sleep community to take a critical look at the purported role of sleep in memory processing. *Sleep, 28*, 1228–1229. (p. 190)

Vigil, J. M., Geary, D. C., & Byrd-Craven, J. (2005). A life history assessment of early childhood sexual abuse in women. *Developmental Psychology, 41*, 553–561. (p. 447)

Vigliocco, G., & Hartsuiker, R. J. (2002). The interplay of meaning, sound, and syntax in sentence production. *Psychological Bulletin, 128*, 442–472. (p. 315)

Vining, E. P. G., Freeman, J. M., Pillas, D. J., Uematsu, S., Carson, B. S., Brandt, J., Boatman, D., Pulsifer, M. B., & Zukerberg, A. (1997). Why would you remove half a brain? The outcome of 58 children after hemispherectomy—The Johns Hopkins Experience Experience: 1968 to 1996. *Pediatrics, 100*, 163–171. (p. 82)

Vita, A. J., Terry, R. B., Hubert, H. B., & Fries, J. F. (1998). Aging, health risks, and cumulative disability. *New England Journal of Medicine, 338*, 1035–1041. (p. 204)

Vitello, P. (2006, June 12). A ring tone meant to fall on deaf ears. *New York Times* (www.nytimes.com). (p. 458)

Vitevitch, M. S. (2003). Change deafness: The inability to detect changes between two voices. *Journal of Experimental Psychology: Human Perception and Performance, 29*, 333–342. (p. 119)

Vittengl, J. R., Clark, L. A., Dunn, T. W., & Jarrett, R. B. (2007). Reducing relapse and recurrence in unipolar depression: A comparative meta-analysis of cognitive-behavioral therapy's effects. *Journal of Consulting and Clinical Psychology, 75*, 475–488. (p. 631)

Voas, D. (2008, March/April). Ten million marriages: An astrological detective story. *Skeptical Inquirer*, pp. 52–55. (p. 498)

Vogel, S. (1999). *The skinny on fat: Our obsession with weight control.* New York: W. H. Freeman. (p. 102)

von Békésy, G. (1957, August). The ear. *Scientific American*, pp. 66–78. (p. 137)

von Hippel, W. (2007). Aging, executive functioning, and social control. *Current Directions in Psychological Science, 16*, 240–244. (p. 459)

von Senden, M. (193). *The perception of space and shape in the congenitally blind before and after operation.* Glencoe, IL: Free Press. (p. 159)

Voyer, D., Postma, A., Brake, B., & Imperato-McGinley, J. (2007). Gender differences in object location memory: A meta-analysis. *Psychonomic Bulletin & Review, 14*, 23–38. (p. 549)

Vroom, V. H., & Jago, A. G. (2007). The role of the situation in leadership. *American Psychologist, 62*, 17–24. (p. B-12)

VTTI (Virginia Tech Transportation Institute). (2009, July 27). *New data from VTTI provides insight into cell phone use and driving distraction.* Blacksburg, VA: Author. (p. 118)

Vyazovskiy, V. V., Cirelli, C., Pfister-Genskow, M., Faraguna, U., & Tononi, G. (2008). Molecular and electrophysiological evidence for net synaptic potentiation in wake and depression in sleep. *Nature Neuroscience, 11*, 200–208. (p. 185)

Waber, R. L., Shiv, B., Carmon, & Ariely, D. (2008). Commercial features of placebo and therapeutic efficacy. *Journal of the American Medical Association, 299*, 1016–1017. (p. 35)

Wacker, J., Chavanon, M-L., & Stemmler, G. (2006). Investigating the dopaminergic basis of extraversion in humans: A multilevel approach. *Journal of Personality and Social Psychology, 91*, 177–187. (p. 495)

Wadden, T. A., Vogt, R. A., Foster, G. D., & Anderson, D. A. (1998). Exercise and the maintenance of weight loss: 1-year follow-up of a controlled clinical trial. *Journal of Consulting and Clinical Psychology, 66*, 429–433. (p. 347)

Wade, K. A., Garry, M., Read, J. D., & Lindsay, D. S. (2002). A picture is worth a thousand lies: Using false photographs to create false childhood memories. *Psychonomic Bulletin & Review, 9*, 597–603. (p. 286)

Wade, N. G., Worthington, Jr., E. L., & Vogel, D. L. (2006). Effectiveness of religiously tailored interventions in Christian therapy. *Psychotherapy Research, 17*, 91–105. (p. 627)

Wagar, B. M., & Cohen, D. (2003). Culture, memory, and the self: An analysis of the personal and collective self in long-term memory. *Journal of Experimental Social Psychology, 39*, 458–475. (p. 263)

Wager, T. D. (2005). The neural bases of placebo effects in pain. *Current Directions in Psychological Science, 14*, 175–179. (p. 146)

Wagner, U., Gais, S., Haider, H., Verleger, R., & Born, J. (2004). Sleep inspires insight. *Nature, 427*, 352–355. (p. 185)

Wagstaff, G. (1982). Attitudes to rape: The "just world" strikes again? *Bulletin of the British Psychological Society, 13*, 275–283. (p. 645)

Wahlberg, D. (2001, October 11). *We're more depressed, patriotic, poll finds.* Grand Rapids Press, p. A15. (p. 400)

Wai, J., Lubinski, D., & Benbow, C. P. (2005). Creativity and occupational accomplishments among intellectually precocious youths: An age 13 to age 33 longitudinal study. *Journal of Educational Psychology, 97*, 484–492. (p. 543)

Walker, M. P., & Stickgold, R. (2006). Sleep, memory, and plasticity. *Annual Review of Psychology, 57*, 139–166. (p. 185)

Walker, W. R., Skowronski, J. J., & Thompson, C. P. (2003). Life is pleasant—and memory helps to keep it that way! *Review of General Psychology, 7*, 203–210. (pp. 263, 469)

Wall, P. D. (2000). *Pain: The science of suffering.* New York: Columbia University Press. (p. 144)

Wallace, D. S., Paulson, R. M., Lord, C. G., & Bond, C. F., Jr. (2005). Which behaviors do attitudes predict? Meta-analyzing the effects of social pressure and perceived difficulty. *Review of General Psychology, 9(3)*, 214–227. (p. 646)

Wallach, M. A., & Wallach, L. (1983). *Psychology's sanction for selfishness: The error of egoism in theory and therapy.* New York: Freeman. (p. 493)

Wallach, M. A., & Wallach, L. (1985, February). How psychology sanctions the cult of the self. *Washington Monthly*, pp. 46–56. (p. 493)

Walster (Hatfield), E., Aronson, V., Abrahams, D., & Rottman, L. (1966). Importance of physical attractiveness in dating behavior. *Journal of Personality and Social Psychology, 4,* 508–516. (p. 680)

Wampold, B. E. (2001). *The great psychotherapy debate: Models, methods, and findings.* Mahwah, NJ: Erlbaum. (pp. 625, 626)

Wampold, B. E. (2007). Psychotherapy: The humanistic (and effective) treatment. *American Psychologist, 62,* 857–873. (pp. 622, 625)

Wampold, B. E., Mondin, G. W., Moody, M., & Ahn, H. (1997). The flat earth as a metaphor for the evidence for uniform efficacy of bona fide psychotherapies: Reply to Crits-Christoph (1997) and Howard et al. (1997). *Psychological Bulletin, 122,* 226–230. (p. 622)

Wang, S-H., Baillargeon, R., & Brueckner, L. (2004). Young infants' reasoning about hidden objects: Evidence from violation-of-expectation tasks with test trials only. *Cognition, 93,* 167–198. (p. 420)

Wansink, B., & van Ittersum, K. (2003). Bottoms up! The influence of elongation on pouring and consumption volume. *Journal of Consumer Research, 30,* 455–464. (p. 154)

Wansink, B., & van Ittersum, K. (2005). Shape of glass and amount of alcohol poured: Comparative study of effect of practice and concentration. *British Medical Journal, 331,* 1512–1514. (p. 154)

Wansink, B., van Ittersum, K., & Painter, J. E. (2006). Ice cream illusions: Bowls, spoons, and self-served portion sizes. *American Journal of Preventive Medicine, 31,* 240–243. (p. 336)

Ward, A., & Mann, T. (2000). Don't mind if I do: Disinhibited eating under cognitive load. *Journal of Personality and Social Psychology, 78,* 753–763. (p. 347)

Ward, C. (1994). Culture and altered states of consciousness. In W. J. Lonner & R. Malpass (Eds.), *Psychology and culture.* Boston: Allyn & Bacon. (p. 198)

Ward, J. (2003). State of the art synaesthesia. *The Psychologist, 16,* 196–199. (p. 148)

Ward, K. D., Klesges, R. C., & Halpern, M. T. (1997). Predictors of smoking cessation and state-of-the-art smoking interventions. *Journal of Socies Issues, 53,* 129–145. (p. 204)

Ward, L. M., & Friedman, K. (2006). Using TV as a guide: Associations between television viewing and adolescents' sexual attitudes and behavior. *Journal of Research on Adolescence, 16,* 133–156. (p. 353)

Wardle, J., Cooke, L. J., Gibson, L., Sapochnik, M., Sheiham, A., & Lawson, M. (2003). Increasing children's acceptance of vegetables: A randomized trial of parent-led exposure. *Appetite, 40,* 155–162. (p. 147)

Wargo, E. (2007, December). Understanding the have-knots. *APS Observer,* pp. 18–21. (p. C-8)

Warm, J. S., & Dember, W. N. (1986, April). Awake at the switch. *Psychology Today,* pp. 46–53. (p. 121)

Warr, P., & Payne, R. (1982). Experiences of strain and pleasure among British adults. *Social Science and Medicine, 16,* 1691–1697. (p. C-4)

Wason, P. C. (1960). On the failure to eliminate hypotheses in a conceptual task. *Quarterly Journal of Experimental Psychology, 12,* 129–140. (p. 303)

Wason, P. C. (1981). The importance of cognitive illusions. *The Behavioral and Brain Sciences, 4,* 356. (p. 303)

Wasserman, E. A. (1993). Comparative cognition: Toward a general understanding of cognition in behavior. *Psychological Science, 4,* 156–161. (p. 230)

Wasserman, E. A. (1995). The conceptual abilities of pigeons. *American Scientist, 83,* 246–255. (p. D-1)

Wastell, C. A. (2002). Exposure to trauma: The long-term effects of suppressing emotional reactions. *Journal of Nervous and Mental Disorders, 190,* 839–845. (p. C-5)

Waterhouse, R. (1993, July 19). Income for 62 percent is below average pay. *The Independent,* p. 4. (p. 38)

Waterman, A. S. (1988). Identity status theory and Erikson's theory: Commonalities and differences. *Developmental Review, 8,* 185–208. (p. 452)

Watson, D. (2000). *Mood and temperament.* New York: Guilford Press. (pp. 390, C-7)

Watson, D., Suls, J., & Haig, J. (2002). Global self-esteem in relation to structural models of personality and affectivity. *Journal of Personality and Social Psychology, 83,* 185–197. (p. 512)

Watson, D., Wiese, D., Vaidya, J., & Tellegen, A. (1999). The two general activation systems of affect: Structured findings, evolutionary considerations, and psychobiological evidence. *Journal of Personality and Social Psychology, 76,* 820–838. (p. 385)

Watson, J. B. (1913). Psychology as the behaviorist views it. *Psychological Review, 20,* 158–177. (pp. 175, 218, 227)

Watson, J. B. (1924). The unverbalized in human behavior. *Psychological Review, 31,* 339–347. (p. 227)

Watson, J. B., & Rayner, R. (1920). Conditioned emotional reactions. *Journal of Experimental Psychology, 3,* 1–14. (p. 227)

Watson, R. I., Jr. (1973). Investigation into deindividuation using a cross-cultural survey technique. *Journal of Personality and Social Psychology, 25,* 342–345. (p. 659)

Watson, S. J., Benson, J. A., Jr., & Joy, J. E. (2000). NEWS AND VIEWS—Marijuana and medicine: Assessing the science base: A summary of the 1999 Institute of Medicine report. *Archives of General Psychiatry, 57,* 547–553. (p. 207)

Wayment, H. A., & Peplau, L. A. (1995). Social support and well-being among lesbian and heterosexual women: A structural modeling approach. *Personality and Social Psychology Bulletin, 21,* 1189–1199. (p. 467)

Weaver, J. B., Masland, J. L., & Zillmann, D. (1984). Effect of erotica on young men's aesthetic perception of their female sexual partners. *Perceptual and Motor Skills, 58,* 929–930. (p. 352)

Webb, W. B. (1992). *Sleep: The gentle tyrant.* Bolton, MA: Anker. (pp. 180, 186)

Webb, W. B., & Campbell, S. S. (1983). Relationships in sleep characteristics of identical and fraternal twins. *Archives of General Psychiatry, 40,* 1093–1095. (p. 181)

Wechsler, D. (1972). "Hold" and "Don't Hold" tests. In S. M. Chown (Ed.), *Human aging.* New York: Penguin. (p. 463)

Weed, W. S. (2001, May). Can we go to Mars without going crazy? *Discover,* pp. 31–43. (p. B-15)

Wegner, D. M. (2002). *The illusion of conscious will.* Cambridge, MA: MIT Press. (pp. 91, 175)

Weigel, G. (2005, March-April). Is Europe dying? Notes on a crisis of civilizational morale. *New Atlantic Initiative,* American Enterprise Institute for Public Policy Research (www.aei.org/nai). (p. 457)

Weinberger, D. R. (2001, March 10). A brain too young for good judgment. *New York Times.* (p. 447)

Weingarten, G. (2002, March 10). Below the beltway. *Washington Post,* p. WO3. (p. B-1)

Weinstein, N. D. (1980). Unrealistic optimism about future life events. *Journal of Personality and Social Psychology, 39,* 806–820. (p. 507)

Weinstein, N. D. (1982). Unrealistic optimism about susceptibility to health problems. *Journal of Behavioral Medicine, 5,* 441–460. (p. 507)

Weinstein, N. D. (1996, October 4). 1996 optimistic bias bibliography. Distributed via internet (weinstein@aesop.rutgers.edu). (p. 507)

Weis, S., & Süß, H-M. (2007) Reviving the search for social intelligence: A multitrait-multimethod study of its structure and construct validity. *Personality and Individual Differences, 42,* 3–14. (p. 528)

Weiskrantz, L. (1986). *Blindsight: A case study and implications.* Oxford: Oxford University Press. (p. 131)

Weiss, A., Bates, T. C., & Luciano, M. (2008). Happiness is a personal(ity) thing. *Psychological Science, 19,* 205–210. (p. 396)

Weiss, A., King, J. E., & Enns, R. M. (2002). Subjective well-being is heritable and genetically correlated with dominance in chimpanzees (*Pan troglodytes*). *Journal of Personality and Social Psychology, 83,* 1141–1149. (p. 396)

Weiss, A., King, J. E., & Figueredo, A. J. (2000). The heritability of personality factors in chimpanzees (Pan troglodytes). *Behavior Genetics, 30,* 213–221. (p. 396)

Weiss, A., King, J. E., & Perkins, L. (2006). Personality and subjective well-being in orangutans (*Pongo pygmaeus* and *Pongo abelii*). *Journal of Personality and Social Psychology, 90,* 501–511. (p. 496)

Weiss, J. M. (1977). Psychological and behavioral influences on gastrointestinal lesions in animal models. In J. D. Maser & M. E. P. Seligman (Eds.), *Psychopathology: Experimental models.* San Francisco: Freeman. (p. C-2)

Weissman, M. M. (1999). Interpersonal psychotherapy and the health care scene. In D. S. Janowsky (Ed.), *Psychotherapy indications and outcomes.* Washington, DC: American Psychiatric Press. (p. 608)

Weisz, J. R., Rothbaum, F. M., & Blackburn, T. C. (1984). Standing out and standing in: The psychology of control in America and Japan. *American Psychologist, 39,* 955–969. (p. 516)

Weller, S., & Davis-Beaty, K. (2002). The effectiveness of male condoms in prevention of sexually transmitted diseases (Protocol). *Cochrane Database of Systematic Reviews*, Issue 4, Art. No. CD004090. (p. 353)

Wellings, K., Collumbien, M., Slaymaker, E., Singh, S., Hodges, Z., Patel, D., & Bajos, N. (2006). Sexual behaviour in context: A global perspective. *Lancet, 368*, 1706–1728. (pp. 352, 353)

Wellman, H. M., & Gelman, S. A. (1992). Cognitive development: Foundational theories of core domains. *Annual Review of Psychology, 43*, 337–375. (p. 420)

Wellman, H. M., Cross, D., & Watson, J. (2001). Meta-analysis of theory-of-mind development: The truth about false belief. *Child Development, 72*, 655–684. (p. 422)

Wells, B. L. (1986). Predictors of female nocturnal orgasms: A multivariate analysis. *Journal of Sex Research, 22*, 421–437. (p. 352)

Wells, G. L. (1981). Lay analyses of causal forces on behavior. In J. Harvey (Ed.), *Cognition, social behavior and the environment*. Hillsdale, NJ: Erlbaum. (p. 216)

Wells, G. L., Memon, A., & Penrod, S. D. (2006). Eyewitness evidence: Improving its probative value. *Psychological Science in the Public Interest, 7*, 45–75. (p. 289)

Wells, G. L., & Murray, D. M. (1984). Eyewitness confidence. In G. L. Wells & E. F. Loftus (Eds.), *Eyewitness testimony: Psychological perspectives*. New York: Cambridge University Press. (p. 288)

Wener, R., Frazier, W., & Farbstein, J. (1987, June). Building better jails. *Psychology Today*, pp. 40–49. (p. 506)

Westen, D. (1996). Is Freud really dead? Teaching psychodynamic theory to introductory psychology. Presentation to the Annual Institute on the Teaching of Psychology, St. Petersburg Beach, Florida. (p. 485)

Westen, D. (1998). The scientific legacy of Sigmund Freud: Toward a psychodynamically informed psychological science. *Psychological Bulletin, 124*, 333–371. (p. 487)

Westen, D. (2007). *The political brain: The role of emotion in deciding the fate of the nation*. New York: PublicAffairs. (p. 376)

Westen, D., & Morrison, K. (2001). A multidimensional meta-analysis of treatments for depression, panic, and generalized anxiety disorder: An empirical examination of the status of empirically supported therapies. *Journal of Consulting and Clinical Psychology, 69*, 875–899. (p. 622)

Weuve, J., Kang, J. H., Manson, J. E., Breteler, M. M. B., Ware, J. H., & Grodstein, F. (2004). Physical activity, including walking, and cognitive function in older women. *Journal of the American Medical Association, 292*, 1454–1460. (p. 459)

Whalen, P. J., Kagan, J., Cook, R. G., Davis, F. C., Kim, H., Polis, S., McLaren, D. G., Somerville, L. H., McLean, A. A., Maxwell, J. S., & Johnstone, T. (2004). Human amygdala responsibility to masked fearful eye whites. *Science, 302*, 2061. (pp. 375, 376)

Whalen, P. J., Shin, L. M., McInerney, S. C., Fisher, H., Wright, C. I., & Rauch, S. L. (2001). A functional MRI study of human amygdala responses to facial expressions of fear versus anger. *Emotion, 1*, 70–83. (p. 370)

Whaley, S. E., Sigman, M., Beckwith, L., Cohen, S. E., & Espinosa, M. P. (2002). Infant-caregiver interaction in Kenya and the United States: The importance of multiple caregivers and adequate comparison samples. *Journal of Cross-Cultural Psychology, 33*, 236–247. (p. 432)

Whalley, L. J., & Deary, I. J. (2001). Longitudinal cohort study of childhood IQ and survival up to age 76. *British Medical Journal, 322*, 1–5. (pp. 541, C-2)

Whalley, L. J., Starr, J. M. Athawes, R., Hunter, D., Pattie, A., & Deary, I. J. (2000). Childhood mental ability and dementia. *Neurology, 55*, 1455–1459. (p. 541)

Wheeler, B. W., Gunnell, D., Metcalfe, C., Stephens, P., & Martin, R. M. (2008). The population impact on incidence of suicide and non-fatal self harm of regulatory action against the use of selective serotonin reuptake inhibitors in under 18s in the United Kingdom: ecological study. *British Medical Journal, 336*, 542–545. (p. 632)

Wheelwright, J. (2004, August). Study the clones first. *Discover*, pp. 44–50. (p. 97)

White, G. L., & Kight, T. D. (1984). Misattribution of arousal and attraction: Effects of salience of explanations for arousal. *Journal of Experimental Social Psychology, 20*, 55–64. (p. 683)

White, H. R., Brick, J., & Hansell, S. (1993). A longitudinal investigation of alcohol use and aggression in adolescence. *Journal of Studies on Alcohol*, Supplement No. 11, 62–77. (p. 672)

White, K. M. (1983). Young adults and their parents: Individuation to mutuality. *New Directions for Child Development, 22*, 61–76. (p. 454)

White, L., & Edwards, J. (1990). Emptying the nest and parental well-being: An analysis of national panel data. *American Sociological Review, 55*, 235–242. (p. 468)

White, R. A. (1998). Intuition, heart knowledge, and parapsychology. *Journal of the American Society for Psychical Research, 92*, 158–171. (p. 168)

Whitehead, B. D., & Popenoe, D. (2001). *The state of our unions 2001: The social health of marriage in America*. Rutgers University: The National Marriage Project. (p. 467)

Whiten, A., & Boesch, C. (2001, January). Cultures of chimpanzees. *Scientific American*, pp. 60–67. (p. D-2)

Whiten, A., & Byrne, R. W. (1988). Tactical deception in primates. *Behavioral and Brain Sciences, 11*, 233–244, 267–273. (p. 28)

Whiten, A., & van Schaik, C. P. (2007). The evolution of animal 'cultures' and social intelligence. *Philosophical Trnasactions of the Royal Society, 362*, 603–620. (p. D-2)

Whiten, A., Spiteri, A., Horner, V., Bonnie, K. E., Lambeth, S. P., Schapiro, S. J., & de Waal, F. B. M. (2007). Transmission of multiple traditions within and between chimpanzee groups. *Current Biology, 17*, 1038–1043. (p. 243)

Whiting, B. B., & Edwards, C. P. (1988). *Children of different worlds: The formation of social behavior*. Cambridge, MA: Harvard University Press. (p. 434)

Whitley, B. E., Jr. (1990). The relationships of heterosexuals' attributions for the causes of homosexuality to attitudes toward lesbians and gay men. *Personality and Social Psychology Bulletin, 16*, 369–377. (p. 359)

Whitley, B. E., Jr. (1999). Right-wing authoritarianism, social dominance orientation, and prejudice. *Journal of Personality and Social Psychology, 77*, 126–134. (p. 668)

Whitlock, J. R., Heynen, A. L., Shuler, M. G., & Bear, M. F. (2006). Learning induces long-term potentiation in the hippocampus. *Science, 313*, 1093–1097. (p. 269)

WHO. (2000). *Effectiveness of male latex condoms in protecting against pregnancy and sexually transmitted infections*. World Health Organization (www.who.int). (p. 353)

WHO. (2003). *The male latex condom: Specification and guidelines for condom procurement*. Department of Reproductive Health and Research, Family and Community Health, World Health Organization. (p. 353)

WHO. (2007, accessed December 11). *Obesity and overweight*. http://www.who.int/dietphysicalactivity/publications/facts/obesity/en/. (p. 340)

WHO. (2008). *WHO report on the global tobacco epidemic, 2008*. Geneva: World Health Organization (www.who.int). (p. 202)

Whooley, M. A., & Browner, W. S. (1998). Association between depressive symptoms and mortality in older women. *Archives of Internal Medicine, 158*, 2129–2135. (p. 403)

Whorf, B. L. (1956). Science and linguistics. In J. B. Carroll (Ed.), *Language, thought, and reality: Selected writings of Benjamin Lee Whorf*. Cambridge, MA: MIT Press. (p. 319)

Wichman, H. (1992). *Human factors in the design of spacecraft*. Stony Brook, NY: State University of New York. (p. B-15)

Wickelgren, I. (2005). Autistic brains out of sync? *Science, 308*, 1856–1858. (p. 424)

Wickelgren, W. A. (1977). *Learning and memory*. Englewood Cliffs, NJ: Prentice-Hall. (p. 263)

Widom, C. S. (1989a). Does violence beget violence? A critical examination of the literature. *Psychological Bulletin, 106*, 3–28. (p. 430)

Widom, C. S. (1989b). The cycle of violence. *Science, 244*, 160–166. (p. 430)

Wielkiewicz, R. M., & Stelzner, S. P. (2005). An ecological perspective on leadership theory, research, and practice. *Review of General Psychology, 9*, 326–341. (p. B-12)

Wiens, A. N., & Menustik, C. E. (1983). Treatment outcome and patient characteristics in an aversion therapy program for alcoholism. *American Psychologist, 38*, 1089–1096. (p. 613)

Wierson, M., & Forehand, R. (1994). Parent behavioral training for child noncompliance: Rationale, concepts, and effectiveness. *Current Directions in Psychological Science, 3*, 146–149. (p. 239)

Wierzbicki, M. (1993). Psychological adjustment of adoptees: A meta-analysis. *Journal of Clinical Child Psychology, 22*, 447–454. (p. 100)

Wiesel, T. N. (1982). Postnatal development of the visual cortex and the influence of environment. *Nature, 299*, 583–591. (p. 160)

Wiesner, W. H., & Cronshow, S. P. (1988). A meta-analytic investigation of the impact of interview format and degree of structure on the validity of the employment interview. *Journal of Occupational Psychology, 61*, 275–290. (p. B-6)

Wigdor, A. K., & Garner, W. R. (1982). *Ability testing: Uses, consequences, and controversies.* Washington, DC: National Academy Press. (p. 555)

Wike, R., & Grim, B. J. (2007, October 30). Widespread negativity: Muslims distrust Westerners more than vice versa. *Pew Research Center* (www.pewresearch.org). (p. 665)

Wilcox, A. J., Baird, D. D., Dunson, D. B., McConnaughey, D. R., Kesner, J. S., & Weinberg, C. R. (2004). On the frequency of intercourse around ovulation: Evidence for biological influences. *Human Reproduction, 19*, 1539–1543. (p. 350)

Wilder, D. A. (1981). Perceiving persons as a group: Categorization and intergroup relations. In D. L. Hamilton (Ed.), *Cognitive processes in stereotyping and intergroup behavior.* Hillsdale, NJ: Erlbaum. (p. 668)

Wildman, D. E., Uddin, M., Liu, G., Grossman, L. I., & Goodman, M. (2003). Implications of natural selection in shaping 99.4% nonsynonymous DNA identity between humans and chimpanzees: Enlarging genus Homo. *Proceedings of the National Academy of Sciences, 100*, 7181–7188. (p. 96)

Wilford, J. N. (1999, February 9). New findings help balance the cosmological books. *New York Times* (www.nytimes.com). (p. 109)

Williams, C. L., & Berry, J. W. (1991). Primary prevention of acculturative stress among refugees. *American Psychologist, 46*, 632–641. (p. 400)

Williams, J. E., & Best, D. L. (1990). *Measuring sex stereotypes: A multination study.* Newbury Park, CA: Sage. (p. 436)

Williams, J. E., Paton, C. C., Siegler, I. C., Eigenbrodt, M. L., Nieto, F. J., & Tyroler, H. A. (2000). Anger proneness predicts coronary heart disease risk: Prospective analysis from the artherosclerosis risk in communities (ARIC) study. *Circulation, 101*, 17, 2034–2040. (p. 402)

Williams, J. H. G., Waister, G. D., Gilchrist, A., Perrett, D. I., Murray, A. D., & Whiten, A. (2006). Neural mechanisms of imitation and 'mirror neuron' functioning in autistic spectrum disorder. *Neuropsychogia, 44*, 610–621. (p. 243)

Williams, K. D. (2007). Ostracism. *Annual Review of Psychology, 58*, 425–452. (p. 361, 362)

Williams, K. D., & Zadro, L. (2001). Ostracism: On being ignored, excluded and rejected. In M. Leary (Ed.), *Rejection.* New York: Oxford University Press. (p. 362)

Williams, L. M., Brown, K. J., Palmer, D., Liddell, B. J., Kemp, A. H., Olivieri, G., Peduto, A., & Gordon, E. (2006). The mellow years? Neural basis of improving emotional stability over age. *Journal of Neuroscience, 26*, 6422–6430. (p. 469)

Williams, R. (1993). *Anger kills.* New York: Times Books. (p. 402)

Williams, S. L. (1987). Self-efficacy and mastery-oriented treatment for severe phobias. Paper presented to the American Psychological Association convention. (p. 612)

Willingham, W. W., Lewis, C., Morgan, R., & Ramist, L. (1990). *Predicting college grades: An analysis of institutional trends over two decades.* Princeton: Educational Testing Service. (p. 538)

Willis, J., & Todorov, A. (2006). First impressions: Making up your mind after a 100-ms. exposure to a face. *Psychological Science, 17*, 592–598. (p. 378)

Willmuth, M. E. (1987). Sexuality after spinal cord injury: A critical review. *Clinical Psychology Review, 7*, 389–412. (p. 352)

Wilson, A. E., & Ross, M. (2001). From chump to champ: People's appraisals of their earlier and present selves. *Journal of Personality and Social Psychology, 80*, 572–584. (p. 515)

Wilson, C. M., & Oswald, A. J. (2002). How does marriage affect physical and psychological health? A survey of the longitudinal evidence. Working paper, University of York and Warwick University. (p. C-4)

Wilson, D. B., & Shadish, W. R. (2006). On blowing trumpets to the tulips: To prove or not to prove the null hypothesis—Comment on Bösch, Steinkamp, and Boller (2006). *Psychological Bulletin, 132*, 524–528. (p. 168)

Wilson, J. Q. (1993). *The moral sense.* New York: Free Press. (p. 449)

Wilson, M., & Emmorey, K. (2006). Comparing sign language and speech reveals a universal limit on short-term memory capacity. *Psychological Science, 17*, 682–683. (p. 267)

Wilson, R. C., Gaft, J. G., Dienst, E. R., Wood, L., & Bavry, J. L. (1975). *College professors and their impact on students.* New York: Wiley. (p. 659)

Wilson, R. S. (1979). Analysis of longitudinal twin data: Basic model and applications to physical growth measures. *Acta Geneticae medicae et Gemellologiae, 28*, 93–105. (p. 416)

Wilson, R. S., Arnold, S. E., Schneider, J. A., Tang, Y., & Bennett, D. A. (2007). The relationship between cerebral Alzheimer's disease pathology and odour identification in old age. *Journal of Neurology, Neurosurgery, and Psychiatry, 78*, 30–35. (pp. 460, 465)

Wilson, R. S., & Bennett, D. A. (2003). Cognitive activity and risk of Alzheimer's disease. *Current Directions in Psychological Science, 12*, 87–91. (p. 461)

Wilson, R. S., & Matheny, A. P., Jr. (1986). Behavior-genetics research in infant temperament: The Louisville twin study. In R. Plomin & J. Dunn (Eds.), *The study of temperament: Changes, continuities, and challenges.* Hillsdale, NJ: Erlbaum. (p. 428)

Wilson, T. D. (2002). *Strangers to ourselves: Discovering the adaptive unconscious.* Cambridge, MA: Harvard University Press. (p. 117)

Wilson, T. D. (2006). The power of social psychological interventions. *Science, 313*, 1251–1252. (p. 556)

Wilson, W. A., & Kuhn, C. M. (2005). How addiction hijacks our reward system. *Cerebrum, 7*(2), 53–66. (p. 209)

Windholz, G. (1989, April-June). The discovery of the principles of reinforcement, extinction, generalization, and differentiation of conditional reflexes in Pavlov's laboratories. *Pavlovian Journal of Biological Science, 26*, 64–74. (p. 222)

Windholz, G. (1997). Ivan P. Pavlov: An overview of his life and psychological work. *American Psychologist, 52*, 941–946. (p. 220)

Windle, M., & Windle, R. C. (2009). Adolescent health: Understanding and preventing risk behaviors. In R. J. DiClementa, J. S. Santelli, & R. A. Crosby (Eds.), Adolescent health: Understanding and preventing risk behaviors (pp. 165ñ178). San Francisco, CA: Jossey-Bass. (p. 353)

Winerman, L. (2006, January). Screening surveyed. *Monitor on Psychology*, pp. 28–29. (p. 121)

Wingfield, A., McCoy, S. L., Peelle, J. E., Tun, P.A., & Cox, L. C. (2005). Effects of adult aging and hearing loss on comprehension of rapid speech varying in syntactic complexity. *Journal of the American Academy of Audiology, 17*, 487–497. (p. 139)

Wink, P., & Dillon, M. (2002). Spiritual development across the adult life course: Findings from a longitudinal study. *Journal of Adult Development, 9*, 79–94. (p. 470)

Winner, E. (2000). The origins and ends of giftedness. *American Psychologist, 55*, 159–169. (p. 543)

Wiseman, R. (2002). *Laugh Lab—final results.* University of Hertfordshire (www.laughlab.co.uk). (p. 301)

Wiseman, R., Jeffreys, C., Smith, M., & Nyman, A. (1999). The psychology of the seance. *The Skeptical Inquirer, 23*(2), 30–33. (p. 286)

Witelson, S. F., Kigar, D. L., & Harvey, T. (1999). The exceptional brain of Albert Einstein. *The Lancet, 353*, 2149–2153. (pp. 79, 530)

Witt, J. K., & Proffitt, D. R. (2005). See the ball, hit the ball: Apparent ball size is correlated with batting average. *Psychological Science, 16*, 937–938. (p. 164)

Witvliet, C. V. O., Ludwig, T., & Vander Laan, K. (2001). Granting forgiveness or harboring grudges: Implications for emotions, physiology, and health. *Psychological Science, 12*, 117–123. (p. 389)

Witvliet, C. V. O., & Vrana, S. R. (1995). Psychophysiological responses as indices of affective dimensions. *Psychophysiology, 32*, 436–443. (p. 370)

Wixted, J. T., & Ebbesen, E. B. (1991). On the form of forgetting. *Psychological Science, 2*, 409–415. (p. 281)

Wolak, J., Mitchell, K., & Finkelhor, D. (2007). Unwanted and wanted exposure to online pornography in a national sample of youth Internet users. *Pediatrics, 119*, 247–257. (p. 674)

Wolfe, M. S. (2006, May). Shutting down Alzheimer's. *Scientific American*, pp. 73–79. (p. 460)

Wolfson, A. R., & Carskadon, M. A. (1998). Sleep schedules and daytime functioning in adolescents. *Child Development, 69*, 875–887. (p. 190)

Woll, S. (1986). So many to choose from: Decision strategies in videodating. *Journal of Social and Personal Relationships, 3*, 43–52. (p. 680)

Wolpe, J. (1958). *Psychotherapy by reciprocal inhibition.* Stanford, CA: Stanford University Press. (p. 611)

Wolpe, J., & Plaud, J. J. (1997). Pavlov's contributions to behavior therapy: The obvious and the not so obvious. *American Psychologist, 52,* 966–972. (p. 611)

Wonderlich, S. A., Joiner, Jr., T. E., Keel, P. K., Williamson, D. A., & Crosby, R. D. (2007). Eating disorder diagnoses: Empirical approaches to classification. *American Psychologist, 62,* 167–180. (p. 337)

Wong, M. M., & Csikszentmihalyi, M. (1991). Affiliation motivation and daily experience: Some issues on gender differences. *Journal of Personality and Social Psychology, 60,* 154–164. (p. 437)

Wood, C. J, & Aggleton, J. P. (1989). Handedness in `fast ball' sports: Do left-handers have an innate advantage? *British Journal of Psychology, 80,* 227–240. (p. 88)

Wood, J. M. (2003, May 19). Quoted by R. Mestel, Rorschach tested: Blot out the famous method? Some experts say it has no place in psychiatry. *Los Angeles Times* (www.latimes.com). (p. 486)

Wood, J. M. (2006, Spring). The controversy over Exner's Comprehensive System for the Rorschach: The critics speak. *Independent Practitioner* (works.bepress.com/james_wood/7). (p. 486)

Wood, J. M., Bootzin, R. R., Kihlstrom, J. F., & Schacter, D. L. (1992). Implicit and explicit memory for verbal information presented during sleep. *Psychological Science, 3,* 236–239. (p. 283)

Wood, J. M., Nezworski, M. T., Garb, H. N., & Lilienfeld, S. O. (2006). The controversy over the Exner Comprehensive System and the Society for Personality Assessment's white paper on the Rorschach. *Independent Practitioner, 26.* (p. 486)

Wood, J. N., Glynn, D. D., Phillips, B. C., & Hauser, M. C. (2007). The perception of rational, goal-directed action in nonhuman primates. *Science, 317,* 1402–1405. (p. D-2)

Wood, W. (1987). Meta-analytic review of sex differences in group performance. *Psychological Bulletin, 102,* 53–71. (p. 436)

Wood, W., & Eagly, A. (2002). A cross-cultural analysis of the behavior of women and men: Implications for the origins of sex differences. *Psychological Bulletin, 128,* 699–727. (pp. 107, 108, 436, 438)

Wood, W., & Eagly, A. H. (2007). Social structural origins of sex differences in human mating. In S. W. Gagestad & J. A. Simpson (Eds.), *The evolution of mind: Fundamental questions and controversies.* New York: Guilford Press. (pp. 107, 436, 438)

Wood, W., Lundgren, S., Ouellette, J. A., Busceme, S., & Blackstone, T. (1994). Minority influence: A meta-analytic review of social influence processes. *Psychological Bulletin, 115,* 323–345. (p. 664)

Woodruff-Pak, D. S. (1989). Aging and intelligence: Changing perspectives in the twentieth century. *Journal of Aging Studies, 3,* 91–118. (p. 462)

Woods, N. F., Dery, G. K., & Most, A. (1983). Recollections of menarche, current menstrual attitudes, and premenstrual symptoms. In S. Golub (Ed.), *Menarche: The transition from girl to woman.* Lexington, MA: Lexington Books. (p. 447)

Woodward, B. (2002). *Bush at war.* New York: Simon & Schuster. (p. 19)

Woody, E. Z., & McConkey, K. M. (2003). What we don't know about the brain and hypnosis, but need to: A view from the Buckhorn Inn. *International Journal of Clinical and Experimental Hypnosis, 51,* 309–338. (p. 196)

Woolcock, N. (2004, September 3). Driver thought everyone else was on wrong side. *The Times,* p. 22. (p. 653)

World Health Organization. (2008). *Mental health and substance abuse: Facts and figures.* Geneva: World Health Organization (www.who.int). (p. 197)

Worobey, J., & Blajda, V. M. (1989). Temperament ratings at 2 weeks, 2 months, and 1 year: Differential stability of activity and emotionality. *Developmental Psychology, 25,* 257–263. (p. 428)

Worthington, E. L., Jr. (1989). Religious faith across the life span: Implications for counseling and research. *The Counseling Psychologist, 17,* 555–612. (p. 448)

Worthington, E. L., Jr., Kurusu, T. A., McCullogh, M. E., & Sandage, S. J. (1996). Empirical research on religion and psychotherapeutic processes and outcomes: A 10-year review and research prospectus. *Psychological Bulletin, 119,* 448–487. (pp. 627, 628)

Wortman, C. B., & Silver, R. C. (1989). The myths of coping with loss. *Journal of Consulting and Clinical Psychology, 57,* 349–357. (p. 471)

Wren, C. S. (1999, April 8). Drug survey of children finds middle school a pivotal time. *New York Times* (www.nytimes.com). (p. 210)

Wright, J. (2006, March 16). Boomers in the bedroom: Sexual attitudes and behaviours in the boomer generation. Ipsos Reid survey (www.ipsos-na.com). (p. 456)

Wright, P. H. (1989). Gender differences in adults' same- and cross-gender friendships. In R. G. Adams & R. Blieszner (Eds.), *Older adult friendships: Structure and process.* Newbury Park, CA: Sage. (p. 437)

Wright, W. (1998). *Born that way: Genes, behavior, personality.* New York: Knopf. (p. 98)

Wrzesniewski, A., & Dutton, J. E. (2001). Crafting a job: Revisioning employees as active crafters of their work. *Academy of Management Review, 26,* 179–201. (p. B-1)

Wrzesniewski, A., McCauley, C. R., Rozin, P., & Schwartz, B. (1997). Jobs, careers, and callings: People's relations to their work. *Journal of Research in Personality, 31,* 21–33. (p. B-1)

Wu, W., & Small, S. A. (2006). Imaging the earliest stages of Alzheimer's disease. *Current Alzheimer Research, 3,* 529–539. (p. 460)

Wuethrich, B. (2001, March). Features—GETTING STUPID—Surprising new neurological behavioral research reveals that teenagers who drink too much may permanently damage their brains and seriously compromise their ability to learn. *Discover, 56,* 56–64. (p. 200)

Wulsin, L. R., Vaillant, G. E., & Wells, V. E. (1999). A systematic review of the mortality of depression. *Psychosomatic Medicine, 61,* 6–17. (p. 403)

Wyatt, J. K., & Bootzin, R. R. (1994). Cognitive processing and sleep: Implications for enhancing job performance. *Human Performance, 7,* 119–139. (pp. 188, 283)

Wynn, K. (1992). Addition and subtraction by human infants. *Nature, 358,* 749–759. (pp. 420, 421)

Wynn, K. (2000). Findings of addition and subtraction in infants are robust and consistent: reply to Wakeley, Rivera, and Langer. *Child Development, 71,* 1535–1536. (p. 420)

Wynn, K., Bloom, P., & Chiang, W-C. (2002). Enumeration of collective entities by 5-month-old infants. *Cognition, 83,* B55-B62. (p. 420)

Wynne, C. D. L. (2004). *Do animals think?* Princeton, NJ: Princeton University Press. (p. D-4)

Wynne, C. D. L. (2008). Aping language: A skeptical analysis of the evidence for nonhuman primate language. *Skeptic, 13*(4), 10–13. (p. D-4)

Wysocki, C. J., & Gilbert, A. N. (1989). *National Geographic* Survey: Effects of age are heterogeneous. *Annals of the New York Academy of Sciences, 561,* 12–28. (p. 150)

Xu, Y., & Corkin, S. (2001). H.M. revisits the Tower of Hanoi puzzle. *Neuropsychology, 15,* 69–79. (p. 271)

Yach, D., Struckler, D., & Brownell, K. D. (2006). Epidemiologic and economic consequences of the global epidemics of obesity and diabetes. *Nature Medicine, 12,* 62–66. (p. 340)

Yalom, I. D. (1985). *The theory and practice of group psychotherapy* (3rd ed.). New York: Basic Books. (p. 617)

Yamagata, S. & 11 others. (2006). Is the genetic structure of human personality universal? A cross-cultural twin study from North America, Europe, and Asia. *Journal of Personality and Social Psychology, 90,* 987–998. (p. 499)

Yang, N., & Linz, D. (1990). Movie ratings and the content of adult videos: The sex-violence ratio. *Journal of Communication, 40*(2), 28–42. (p. 674)

Yang, S., Markoczy, L., & Qi, M. (2006). Unrealistic optimism in consumer credit card adoption. *Journal of Economic Psychology, 28,* 170–185. (p. 507)

Yankelovich Partners. (1995, May/June). Growing old. *American Enterprise,* p. 108. (p. 455)

Yarnell, P. R., & Lynch, S. (1970, April 25). Retrograde memory immediately after concussion. *Lancet,* pp. 863–865. (p. 270)

Yarrow, L. J., Goodwin, M. S., Manheimer, H., & Milowe, I. D. (1973). Infancy experience and cognitive and personality development at ten years. In L. J. Stone, H. T. Smith, & L. B. Murphy (Eds.), *The competent infant.* New York: Basic Books. (p. 431)

Yates, A. (1989). Current perspectives on the eating disorders: I. History, psychological and biological aspects. *Journal of the American Academy of Child and Adolescent Psychiatry, 28,* 813–828. (p. 337)

Yates, A. (1990). Current perspectives on the eating disorders: II. Treatment, outcome, and research directions. *Journal of the American Academy of Child and Adolescent Psychiatry, 29,* 1–9. (p. 337)

Yates, W. R. (2000). Testosterone in psychiatry. *Archives of General Psychiatry, 57,* 155–156. (p. 351)

Ybarra, O. (1999). Misanthropic person memory when the need to self-enhance is absent. *Personality and Social Psychology Bulletin, 25,* 261–269. (p. 512)

Yonas, A., & Granrud, C. E. (2006). Infants' perception of depth from cast shadows. *Perception and Psychophysics, 68,* 154–160. (p. 153)

Young, R., Sweeting, H., & West, P. (2006). Prevalence of deliberate self harm and attempted suicide within contemporary Goth youth subculture: Longitudinal cohort study. *British Medical Journal, 332,* 1058–1061. (p. 32)

Youngentob, S. L., Kent, P. F., Scheehe, P. R., Molina, J. C., Spear, N. E., & Youngentob, L. M. (2007). Experience-induced fetal plasticity: The effect of gestational ethanol exposure on the behavioral and neurophysiologic olfactory response to ethanol odor in early postnatal and adult rats. *Behavioral Neuroscience, 121,* 1293–1305. (p. 413)

Yücel, M., Solowij, N., Respondek, C., Whittle, S., Fornito, A., Pantelis, C., & Lubman, D. I. (2008). Regional brain abnormalities associated with long-term cannabis use. *Archives of General Psychiatry, 65,* 694–701. (p. 207)

Yuki, M., Maddux, W. W., & Masuda. T. (2007). Are the windows to the soul the same in the East and West? Cultural differences in using the eyes and mouth as cues to recognize emotions in Japan and the United States. *Journal of Experimental Social Psychology, 43,* 303–311. (p. 382)

Zabin, L. S., Emerson, M. R., & Rowland, D. L. (2005). Child sexual abuse and early menarche: The direction of their relationship and its implications. *Journal of Adolescent Health, 36,* 393–400. (p. 447)

Zaccaro, S. J. (2007). Triat-based perspectives of leadership. *American Psychologist, 62,* 6–16. (p. B-12)

Zadra, A., Pilon, M., & Montplairsir, J. (2008). Polysomnographic diagnosis of sleepwalking: Effects of sleep deprivation. *Annals of Neurology, 63,* 513–519. (p. 187)

Zagorsky, J. L. (2007). Do you have to be smart to be rich? The impact of IQ on wealth, income and financial distress. *Intelligence, 35,* 489–501. (p. 527)

Zajonc, R. B. (1965). Social facilitation. *Science, 149,* 269–274. (p. 657)

Zajonc, R. B. (1980). Feeling and thinking: Preferences need no inferences. *American Psychologist, 35,* 151–175. (p. 374)

Zajonc, R. B. (1984a). On the primacy of affect. *American Psychologist, 39,* 117–123. (p. 374)

Zajonc, R. B. (1984b, July 22). Quoted by D. Goleman, Rethinking IQ tests and their value. *The New York Times,* p. D22. (p. 533)

Zajonc, R. B. (1998). Emotions. In D. Gilbert, S. T. Fiske, & G. Lindzey (Eds.), *Handbook of social psychology, 4th ed.* New York: McGraw-Hill. (p. 679)

Zajonc, R. B. (2001). Mere exposure: A gateway to the subliminal. *Current Directions in Psychological Science, 10,* 224–228. (p. 678)

Zajonc, R. B., & Markus, G. B. (1975). Birth order and intellectual development. *Psychological Review, 82,* 74–88. (p. 41)

Zauberman, G., & Lynch, J. G., Jr. (2005). Resource slack and propensity to discount delayed investments of time versus money. *Journal of Experimental Psychology: General, 134,* 23–37. (p. 307)

Zeelenberg, R., Wagenmakers, E-J., & Rotteveel, M. (2006). The impact of emotion on perception. *Psychological Science, 17,* 287–291. (p. 374)

Zeidner, M. (1990). Perceptions of ethnic group modal intelligence: Reflections of cultural stereotypes or intelligence test scores? *Journal of Cross-Cultural Psychology, 21,* 214–231. (p. 552)

Zeidner, M., Roberts, R. D., & Matthews, G. (2008). The science of emotional intelligence: Current consensus and controversies. *European Psychologist, 13,* 64–78. (p. 529)

Zeineh, M. M., Engel, S. A., Thompson, P. M., & Bookheimer, S. Y. (2003). Dynamics of the hippocampus during encoding and retrieval of face-name pairs. *Science, 299,* 577–580. (p. 272)

Zhang, J. V., Ren, P-G., Avsian-Kretchmer, O, Luo, C-W., Rauch, R., Klein, C., & Hsueh, A. J. W. (2005). Obestatin, a peptide encoded by the ghrelin gene, opposes ghrelin's effect on food intake. *Science, 310,* 996–999. (p. 334)

Zhang, P., Dilley, C., & Mattson, M. P. (2007). DNA damage responses in neural cells: Focus on the telomere. *Neuroscience, 145,* 1439–1448. (p. 457)

Zigler, E. F. (1987). Formal schooling for four-year-olds? No. *American Psychologist, 42,* 254–260. (p. 547)

Zigler, E. F., & Styfco, S. J. (2001). Extended childhood intervention prepared children for school and beyond. *Journal of the American Medical Association, 285,* 2378–2380. (p. 548)

Zilbergeld, B. (1983). The shrinking of America: Myths of psychological change. Boston: Little, Brown. (pp. 619, 623)

Zillmann, D. (1986). Effects of prolonged consumption of pornography. Background paper for *The Surgeon General's workshop on pornography and public health,* June 22–24. Report prepared by E. P. Mulvey & J. L. Haugaard and released by Office of the Surgeon General on August 4, 1986. (p. 374)

Zillmann, D. (1989). Effects of prolonged consumption of pornography. In D. Zillmann & J. Bryant (Eds.), *Pornography: Research advances and policy considerations.* Hillsdale, NJ: Erlbaum. (pp. 351, 352, 675)

Zillmann, D., & Bryant, J. (1984). Effects of massive exposure to pornography. In N. Malamuth & E. Donnerstein (Eds.), *Pornography and sexual aggression.* Orlando, FL: Academic Press. (p. 675)

Zimbardo, P. G. (1970). The human choice: Individuation, reason, and order versus deindividuation, impulse, and chaos. In W. J. Arnold & D. Levine (Eds.), *Nebraska Symposium on Motivation, 1969.* Lincoln, NE: University of Nebraska Press. (p. 659)

Zimbardo, P. G. (1972, April). Pathology of imprisonment. *Transaction/Society,* pp. 4–8. (p. 647)

Zimbardo, P. G. (2001, September 16). Fighting terrorism by understanding man's capacity for evil. Op Ed Essay distributed by spsp-discuss@stolaf.edu. (p. 669)

Zimbardo, P. G. (2004, May 25). Journalist interview re: Abu Ghraib prison abuses: Eleven answers to eleven questions. Unpublished manuscript, Stanford University. (p. 649)

Zimbardo, P. G. (2005, January 18). You can't be a sweet cucumber in a vinegar barrel. *The Edge* (www.edge.org). (p. 649)

Zimbardo, P. (2007, September). Person x situation x system dynamics. *The Observer* (Association for Psychological Science), p. 43. (p. 648)

Zimmermann, T. D., & Meier, B. (2006). The rise and decline of prospective memory performance across the lifespan. *Quarterly Journal of Experimental Psychology, 59,* 2040–2046. (p. 462)

Zogby, J. (2006, March). Survey of teens and adults about the use of personal electronic devices and head phones. *Zogby International.* (p. 136)

Zou, Z., Li, F., & Buck, L. B. (2005). From the cover: Odor maps in the olfactory cortex. *Proceedings of the National Academy of Sciences, 102,* 7724–7729. (p. 149)

Zubieta, J.-K., Bueller, J. A., Jackson, L. R., Scott, D. J., Xu, Y., Koeppe, R. A., Nichols, T. E., & Stohler, C. S. (2005). Placebo effects mediated by endogenous opioid activity on μ-opioid receptors. *Journal of Neuroscience, 25,* 7754–7762. (p. 146)

Zubieta, J-K., Heitzeg, M. M., Smith, Y. R., Bueller, J. A., Xu, K., Xu, Y., Koeppe, R. A., Stohler, C. S., & Goldman, D. (2003). COMT val-158met genotype affects μ-opioid neurotransmitter responses to a pain stressor. *Science, 299,* 1240–1243. (p. 144)

Zucco, G. M. (2003). Anomalies in cognition: Olfactory memory. *European Psychologist, 8,* 77–86. (p. 149)

Zucker, G. S., & Weiner, B. (1993). Conservatism and perceptions of poverty: An attributional analysis. *Journal of Applied Social Psychology, 23,* 925–943. (p. 645)

Zuckerman, M. (1979). *Sensation seeking: Beyond the optimal level of arousal.* Hillsdale, NJ: Erlbaum. (p. 330)

Name Index

Aart H., 377
Abbey, A., 106, 200
Abbott, R. D., 460
Abramowitz, J. S., 611
Abrams, D. B., 200, 507
Abrams, L., 282
Abrams, M., 160
Abramson, L. Y., 587
Abutalebi, J., 80
Ackerman, D., 55, 66
Adams, E. M., 33
Adams, P. F., 183
Adelmann, P. K., 468
Adelson, R., 271, 373
Ader, R., 227
Adler, A., 360, 484, 485, 519
Adolphs, R., 378, 386
Affleck, G., 390
Agassi, A., 95
Agassi, J., 95
Aggleton, J. P., 88
Ai, A. L., C-12
Aiello, J. R., 658
Ainsworth, M. D. S., 428, 476
Airan, R. D., 586
Aird, E. G., 467
Åkerstedt, T., 186
Albarracín, D., 646
Albee, G. W., 638
Albert ("Little"), 7, 227
Albert, B., 353
Albon, A. J., 290
Alcock, J. E., 277
Aldrich, M. S., 186
Aldridge-Morris, R., 578
Aleman, A., 591
Alexander the Great, 395
Alexander, C. N., C-10
Allard, F., 264
Allen, J. B., 359
Allen, K., C-5, C-13
Allen, M., 437
Allen, N. B., 580
Allen, W., 186, 489, 607
Allik, J., 513
Alloy, L. B., 588
Allport, G. W., 27, 494, 511, 667
Alter, A., 234
Altman, L. K., 405
Alwin, D. F., 434

Amabile, T. M., 302, 389, 512
Amato, P. R., 439
Ambady, N., 378, 381, 502
Ambinder, M. S., 119
Amedi, A., 82
Amen, D. G., 671
Ames, A., 157, 158, 372
Ames, D. R., B-12
Ames, M. A., 358
Amsterdam, J. D., 630
Andersen, R. A., 76
Andersen, R. E., 347
Andersen, S. M., 276, 450
Anderson, A. K., 71
Anderson, B. L., 406
Anderson, C. A., 43, 247, 272, 673, 676, 677
Anderson, D. C., 673
Anderson, I. M., 630
Anderson, J. R., 650
Anderson, R. C., 275
Anderson, R. D., 200
Anderson, S., 584
Anderson, S. E., 447
Anderson, S. R., D-4
Anderson, U. S., 463
Andrault, O., 340
Andreasen, N. C., 593
Andrew, M., 624
Angell, M., C-9
Angelsen, N. K., 34
Angier, N., 348
Angoff, W. H., 540
Anisman, H., 405
Annan, K., 691
Antoni, M. H., 406
Antony, M. M., 574
Antrobus, J., 190
Apostolova, L. G., 460
Appleby, D., A-1
Appleton, J., 236
Archer, J., 89
Archer, R., 488
Arendt, H., 450
Arenson, K. W., 549
Aries, E., 436
Aristotle, 2, 8, 16, 51, 215, 298, 359, 452, 677, 680
Arkowitz, H., 424, 623, 624
Armel, K. C., 145

Armony, J., 376
Armstrong, B. J., 569
Arnett, J. J., 445, 454
Arnold, K., A-10
Aron, A. P., 683, 684
Aronson, E., 284, 453, 648
Aronson, J., 555
Artiga, A. I., 335
Asch, S. E., 651, 652, 653, 654, 656, 693
Aserinsky, A., 178
Aserinsky, E., 178
Ashbery, J., 590
Ashley (Lady), 109
Ashtari, M., 563
Askay, S. W., 194
Aspy, C. B., 353
Assanand, S., 335
Astin, A. W., 452
Astin, H. A., 452
Astington, J. W., 422
Atance, C. M., 332
Atkinson, R. C., 257, 258
Atta, M., 657
Austin, E. J., 543
Autrey, W., 687
Averill, J. R., 371, 387, 389
Avery, R. D., 552
Ax, A. F., 370
Axel, R., 149
Axinn, W., E-9
Ayres, M. M., 436
Azar, B., 142

Babad, E., 378
Babyak, M., C-7
Bach, J. S., 110, 230
Bachman, J., 209, 210
Bachman, P. M., 210
Backman, L., 140, 465
Bacon, F., 3, 16, 302, 306
Badcock, P. B. T., 580
Baddeley, A. D., 258, 259, 260, 276, 277
Baer, J., 581
Bagemihl, B., 356
Baguma, P., 340
Bahrick, H. P., 260, 274, 281
Bailenson, J. N., 679
Bailey, J. M., 354, 357, 438
Bailey, R. E., 237
Baillargeon, R., 420
Bain, J., 350
Baird, G., 424
Baker, E. L., 194
Baker, T. B., 231
Bakermans-Kranenburg, M. J., 429
Balcetis, E., 164
Baldwin, S., 622
Ballard, M. E., 677
Balsam, K. F., 355, 466
Baltes, P. B., 464
Banaji, M. R., 320
Bandura, A., 215, 244, 245, 249, 251, 252, 253, 466, 503, 521
Barash, D. P., 89
Barbaree, H. E., 200
Barber, C., 630
Barber, T. X., 195
Barbieri, M., 130
Bard, P., 367, 371,
Bargh, J. A., 91, 488., 651, 660, 679
Bar-Haim, Y., 574
Barinaga, M. B., 82, 149, 386, 457, C-7

Barkley, R. A., 563
Barlow, D. H., 616
Barnes, M. L., 379
Barnett, P. A., 588
Barnier, A. J., 193
Barnum, P. T., 499
Baron, R. A., 239
Baron, R. S., 300, 653
Baron-Cohen, S., 423, 424, 425
Barrett, L. C., 507
Barrett, L. F., 370, 371, 379
Barrow, J., 110
Barry, D., 44, 141, 148, 203, 338, 458, 498
Bartholow, B. C., 677
Bashore, T. R., 459
Baskind, D. E., 613
Bassett, D. R., 345
Bat-Chava, Y., 139
Bauer, P. J., 274, 417
Baum, A., 405
Baumeister, H., 562, 599
Baumeister, R. F., 105, 193, 307, 355, 360, 362, 454, 488, 489, 505, 512, 515, 521, 661, 684
Baumgardner, A. H., 512
Baumrind, D., 235, 433
Bavelier, D., 82, 121, 140, 317
Bayley, N., 540
Beach, S. R., 678
Beaman, A. L., 682
Beardsley, L. M., 564
Beatles (group), 22
Beaton, A. A., 88
Beauchamp, G. K., 335
Beaujean, A. A., 544
Beauvais, F., 210
Beck, A. T., 584, 615, 616, 639
Becker, D. V., 379, 380
Becker, I. M., 227
Becker, S., 631
Beckham, D., 70, 71, 246
Becklen, R., 118
Beckman, M., 447
Beecher, H. W., 321
Beeman, M. J., 87
Beethoven (von), L., 529
Behan, P. O., 88
Beilin, H., 423
Beitel, P., 322
Beitman, B. D., 606
Bell, A. P., 356
Bell, R. Q., 540
Bellows, G., 564
Bellugi, U., 314
Belmaker, R. H., 634, 635
Belot, M., 680
Belsher, G., 582
Belsky, J., 432, 598
Belyaev, D., 103, 104
Bem, D. J., 168, 359
Bem, S. L., 440
Benbow, C. P., 543, 549, 550
Benes, F., 67
Benjet, C., 234
Bennett, D. A., 461
Bennett, R., 675
Bennett, W. I., 347
Ben-Shakhar, G., 372
Benson, H., C-8, C-10
Benson, K., 283
Benson, P. L., 437
Benson, R., 346
Ben-Zeev, T., 555

Subject Index

Myelin in adolescence, 447
Myelin sheath, 53
Myers-Briggs Type Indicator (MBTI), 494

Narcissistic personality disorder, 596
Narcolepsy, 186–187
    accidents and, 186
Narcotics, 201
Naturalistic observation, 28–29
Natural killer (NK) cells, 403
Natural selection, 8–9, 103
    adaptation and, 103–104
    fear and, 575
    mating preferences and, 106
    taste aversions and, 225
Nature-nurture issue, 9–10, 94, 101, 109. *See
    also* Behavior genetics; Biological influences;
    Environmental influences; *specific factors*
    developmental psychology and, 411, 472
The Nature of Prejudice (Allport), 667
Near-death experiences, LSD and, 206
Needs. *See also* Motivation
    hierarchy of, 330–331, 491
Negative explanatory style, 586, 587
Negative reinforcement, 231
    punishment contrasted with, 231
Neo-Freudian theories, 484–485
Neophobia, 336
Nerve deafness, 138
Nervous system, 59–62. *See also* Neural *entries*
    autonomic, 59, 369–370, 495–496
    central, 59, 60–62. *See also* Brain
    parasympathetic, 60, 369
    peripheral, 59–60
    somatic, 59
    sympathetic, 59–60, 369
Neural communication, 52–58
    neurons and, 53–55
    neurotransmitters and, 55–58
Neural networks, 61
    mental rehearsal and, 322
    in newborns, 415
Neural pathways, emotion and, 375
Neural processes, psychoneuroimmunology and,
    403–405
Neural processing
    alcohol and, 199
    dreams and, 190
    in late adulthood, 459
    speed of, intelligence and, 531–532
Neural prosthetics, 76–77
Neuroadaptation, 197
Neurogenesis, 73, 630–631
Neuroimaging, 68
    brain activity and. *See* Brain
Neurons, 53–55
    communication by, 55
    formation of, 73
    mirror, 243–244, 425
Neuropsychologists, A–9
Neuroscience. *See also* Brain; Neural *entries*
    cognitive, 7
Neurotransmitters, 55–58, 62
    aggression and, 672
    depression and, 586
    fear and, 575
    narcolepsy and, 186
    nicotine and, 203–204
    schizophrenia and, 592–593
Neutral events, 218
Newborns, 413–415
New Lanark Mills, B–9
Nicotine, 202–204
Night terrors, 187

NK (natural killer) cells, 403
Nociceptors, 143
Noise, hearing loss and, 135
Nondeclarative memory. *See* Implicit memory
Nondirective therapy, 609
Non-rapid-eye-movement (NREM) sleep, 180, 190
Nonverbal communication. *See* Expressed emotion
Noradrenaline, 63
Norepinephrine, 57, 63
    depression and, 586
Norm(s), 662
    for helping, 687
Normal curve, 40, 536–537
Normative social influence, 653
Novelty-preference procedure, 414
NREM (non-rapid-eye-movement) sleep, 180, 190
Nucleus accumbens, emotions and, 371
Numerical ability in animals, D–2
Nutritional supplements in therapeutic life-style
    change, 637

Obedience, 654–657
Obesity, 340–348
    physiology of, 342–346
    sleep apnea and, 187
    sleep loss and, 183–184
    social effects of, 341–342
    weight loss and, 346–348
Obestatin, hunger and, 334
Object permanence, 419–420
Observation, naturalistic, 28–29
Observational learning, 217, 242–249
    applications of, 245–249
    Bandura's experiments in, 244–245
    of fear, 574
    mirror neurons and, 243–244
    violence-viewing effect and, 248–249
Obsessive-compulsive disorder (OCD), 571–572
Occipital lobes, 74
OCD (obsessive-compulsive disorder), 571–572
Oedipus complex, 482
Olfaction, 148–150
One-word stage, 316
Online matchmaking, 679
On the Origin of Species (Darwin), 8–9, 105
Operant behavior, 228
Operant chambers, 229
Operant conditioning, 217, 228–241
    applications of, 238–240, 241
    in behavior therapy, 613–614
    biological predispositions and, 237
    classical conditioning contrasted with, 228,
        240–241
    cognition and, 235–237
    language development and, 315
    punishment and, 234–235
    reinforcement schedules and, 232–233
    shaping and, 229–230
    Skinner's experiments in, 229–235
    types of reinforcers and, 230–232
Operational definitions, 26
Opiates, 201
Opponent colors, 133
Opponent process theory, 133
Optic nerve, 126–127
Optimism, 507–509
    blindness to one's own incompetence and, 507–509
    excessive, 507
    health and, 507, C–3—C–4
Orexin
    arousal and, 186
    hunger and, 333, 334
Organizational psychology, B–2, B–3, B–7—B–13
    leadership and, B–10—B–13

satisfaction and engagement and, B–10—B–12
Orgasm, 349
Ostracism, 361–362
Other-race effect, 669
Outer ear, 135
Outgroup, 667–668
Outgroup homogeneity, 669
Outsourcing, B–2
Oval window, 135
Overconfidence, 21–22, 306–307
    intuition and, 310
Own-race bias, 669

Pain control, 145–146
    hypnosis for, 194, 195–196
Pain sense, 142–146
    biological influences on, 143–144
    pain control and, 145–146, 194, 195–196
    psychological influences on, 145
    social-cultural influences on, 145
Palm reading, 498–499
Panic attacks, 570
Panic disorder, 570
Paradoxical sleep, 178, 180–181, 190
Parallel processing, 258, 274
    of visual information, 130–132
Paranoid schizophrenia, 591
Parapsychology, 166
Parasympathetic nervous system, 60
    emotions and, 369
Parent(s)
    attachment and. *See* Attachment
    modeling of aggression by, 674
Parent-child relationships. *See also* Attachment
    in adolescence, 452–453
Parenting. *See also* Child-rearing
    attachment and, 427–430
    development and, 443–444
    styles of, 433–434
Parietal lobes, 74
Parrots, thinking in, D–2
Partial reinforcement, 232
Passionate love, 683
Passwords, retrieval of, 283
Pavlov, Ivan, 6
    experiments of, 218–222
Peacemaking. *See* Conflict
Peer relationships
    in adolescence, 210, 453
    in childhood, 444
Perceived control, C–1—C–3
Perception(s). *See also* Perceptual *entries*
    biopsychosocial perspective on, 165
    brain and, 156
    depth, 153–155
    disturbed, in schizophrenia, 590–591
    enemy, 689
    extrasensory, 166–169
    form, 151–152
    intuition and, 310
    of loudness, 137
    mirror-image, 689
    of pitch, 137
    sensation compared with, 115
Perceptual adaptation, 160
Perceptual constancy, 156–159
    color, 158–159
    lightness, 158
    shape and size, 156–158
Perceptual interpretation, 159–165
    perceptual adaptation and, 160
    perceptual set and, 160–165
    sensory deprivation and restored vision and,
        159–160